TWENTY-FIFTH EDITION

KOVELS'

Antiques &
Collectibles
PRICE LIST

TWENTY-FIFTH EDITION

KOVELS'

Antiques &
Collectibles
PRICE LIST

For the 1993 Market

ILLUSTRATED

CROWN PUBLISHERS, INC.   NEW YORK

BOOKS BY RALPH AND TERRY KOVEL

American Country Furniture 1780–1875
Dictionary of Marks—Pottery & Porcelain
A Directory of American Silver, Pewter and Silver Plate
Kovels' Advertising Collectibles Price List
Kovels' American Silver Marks
Kovels' Antiques & Collectibles Price List
Kovels' Antiques & Collectibles Fix-It Source Book
Kovels' Book of Antique Labels
Kovels' Bottles Price List
Kovels' Collector's Guide to American Art Pottery
Kovels' Collector's Source Book
Kovels' Depression Glass & American Dinnerware Price List
Kovels' Guide to Selling Your Antiques & Collectibles
Kovels' Illustrated Price Guide to Royal Doulton
Kovels' Know Your Antiques
Kovels' Know Your Collectibles
Kovels' New Dictionary of Marks—Pottery & Porcelain
Kovels' Organizer for Collectors
Kovels' Price Guide for Collector Plates, Figurines, Paperweights,
and Other Limited Editions

Published by Crown Publishers, Inc., 201 East 50th Street, New York,
New York 10022. Member of the Crown Publishing Group.
Random House, Inc. New York, Toronto, London, Sydney, Auckland
CROWN is a trademark of Crown Publishers, Inc.
Manufactured in the United States of America
Library of Congress Catalog Card Number: 83-643618

ISBN: 0-517-59109-X (pbk.)
10 9 8 7 6 5 4 3 2 1

DEDICATION

To all those who helped in the past 25 years (in chronological order)—the Crown executives who first saw the possibility: Bob Simon, Nat Wartels, Alan Mirken, Bruce Harris, Michelle Sidrane, Betty Prashker; the editors who kept adding improvements: Herb Michelman, Brandt Aymar, Jake Goldberg, Pam Thomas, Ann Cahn, Sharon Squibb; the staff at Crown who worried about production: Adrian Shapiro, Rusty Porter, Milt Wackerow, Ken Sansone, Jim Davis, Bill Peabody. To our staff, including Eleanor Dion, Pauline Jaffee, Mike Melman, Debby Herman, Eleanore Melzak, Beth Crockett, Terry Sirko, Sandy Brady, Nancy Saada, Grace Clyde, Edie Smrekar, Gay Hunter, Harriet Goldner, Kim Kovel, Marcia Goldberg, and Gloria Pearlman. Thanks also to the others whose names are lost in 25 years of files. Many of you helped find prices, proofread, or did the many other boring but necessary jobs required to put a book like this together.

To those who helped us with computers and computer problems through the years: Dick Stitt and NCCB, the very first computer company to tackle the programs and problems of a computer-run price list; The Ecocenters group, Fred Finnerty, John Massie, Tim Moeller, Pat Pirro, Frank Piuno, Mark Rossin, Jay Tomb, Bill Webb, and Tim Wood, who have struggled with the new look and other changes in recent years.

DEAR READER,

The economy is improving, say the newspapers and politicians, and we know it is true. The antiques business is thriving in most parts of the country. Many Midwestern dealers have told us business has never been better. Only the Eastern seaboard shows and shops seem to still feel the pinch.

Newspapers reported on a few major art auctions, but the main interest seems to have switched to the collectibles market. Papers have run stories about people who collected Statue of Liberty memorabilia or platform shoes. Trolls, vintage luggage, cigar labels, cocktail shakers, Czechoslovakian pottery, and, of course, baseball cards all made the national papers. The "experts," who have never been collectors, keep talking about investment possibilities. Records are reported and trends are mapped, but if you want to really understand the "investment" values of antiques, look at "Twenty-five Year Analysis of the Antiques Marketplace," the center color section in this book.

Over the years we have read millions of prices and used thousands of pictures in *Kovels' Antiques & Collectibles Price List*. Prices listed here include a random selection of pieces offered for sale *this* year. We report on everyday antiques such as pressed glass and oak furniture, exotic Tiffany and Lalique, and uncommon skorps and roemers. The smallest item this year is probably a 3/4 inch-by-1-inch cameo pendant of Russian silver and agate, worth $550. The largest, a backbar made of mahogany, marble, and stained glass, 9 1/2 feet by 12 feet, sold for $6,500. We do not list the top of the market but concentrate on the average pieces in any category. We will often add one or two high-priced pieces in a category so you will realize that some of the rarities are quite valuable. For example, Ohr pottery can sell for $300 to $5,775. Most pieces we list are less than $10,000. A few pieces of Tiffany, Rookwood, and Gallé sold for very high prices this year, but these records are not included in the general category listings. This year, exceptionally high prices included in the Bank category occurred because of an unusual auction that was held. The highest price in this book is $16,500 for an eighteenth-century marble bust of Nero. The lowest price is $.50 for a Howdy Cola Bottle cap. We even list the weird and wonderful, and this year you can find prices for a bung plunger, a sweat scraper, a firkin, and a niddy-noddy.

The book is changed slightly each year. Categories are added or omitted to make it easier for you to find your antiques. The book is kept about 900 pages long because it is written to go with you to sales. We try to have a balanced format: not too much glass, pottery, or collectibles, not too many items that sell for over $5,000. The prices are *from* the American market *for* the American market. Few European sales are reported. We take the editorial privilege of not including any prices that seem to result from "auction fever."

The computer-generated index is so complete it amazes us. Use it often. An internal alphabetical index is also included. For example, there is a category for "Celluloid." Most items will be found there, but if there is a toy made of celluloid, it will be listed under "Toy" and also indexed under "Celluloid."

All pictures and prices are new every year, except pictures that are pattern examples shown in "Depression Glass" and "Pressed Glass." Pictured antiques are not museum pieces but items offered for sale.

The hints are set in easy-to-notice special type. Leaf through the book and learn how to wash porcelains, store textiles, guard against theft, and much more. Save old *Kovels'* price books for future reference, tax, and appraisal information.

RECORD PRICES

Record prices get the headlines, even though these sales are a small percentage of the business of antiques. There were fewer records than in previous years, although a few unusual collectibles made headlines. A very rare matchcover issued for a luncheon given for Charles Lindbergh when he returned from Paris in 1927 sold at auction for $4,000. The movie poster for the 1933 *King Kong* was $57,200. A rhinoceros horn cup sold for $104,500. The cup is a valuable carved nineteenth-century Oriental piece, and rhinoceros horn is protected under the endangered species laws. Sports collectibles are going up in price, and the records prove it. An 1865 photograph of the Atlantic Champions of America, winners of the first World Series, auctioned for $28,600. A Mickey Mantle shirt used in 1960s Yankees games brought $111,100, while Babe Ruth's 1926 World Series jersey sold for only $82,500, and Gil Hodges' uniform, $24,200. Joe DiMaggio's 1942 baseball cap brought $18,700. The Most Valuable Player award for Zoilo Versalles in 1965 sold for $11,000; a 1903 World Series ticket was $10,459. A collection of 23 golf clubs that belonged to winners of the British Open between 1860 and 1930 brought the amazing sum of $1,034,550 at an English Auction.

Toys also set several records. A "crossover" board game that appealed to both baseball and toy collectors brought $8,250. It was "The New Parlor Game Baseball" published in Boston in 1869. A tinplate toy hose reel decorated with the word "Charles" sold at a tag sale for $125,000. The Fowler mechanical bank made in 1892 sold for $60,500, while the still bank Grinning/Frowning boy was $16,000.

There was only one record price for furniture this year: $4,230,000 for a French jewelry casket on a stand with Sevres porcelain plaques. Glass set more records: a Wistar bottle, $48,000; a Blagrove's Superior Aerated Mineral Water bottle, $15,180; a clear lacy glass vegetable dish with a chain border, $23,100; and a Carnival glass, signed, Northwood tree-trunk funeral vase jardiniere, $4,000.

Pottery and porcelain records were set for eighteenth- and twentieth-century pieces. The English Liverpool factory was represented at several important auctions. A jug decorated with a scene from the Boston Rope Works was $33,000 and a pitcher showing a ship belonging to Caleb Bates was $39,600. Saturday Evening Girls art pottery set a record of $11,000 for a 1915 plate picturing a sky, cottage, and trees. A special Royal Doulton Bunnykins figure wearing a yellow bow tie and known as the "Desert Storm Uncle Sam" brought $1,512 in England.

Three other records of interest were a pictorial appliqued quilt dated 1867 with 40 squares showing the reconciliation of North and South, $264,000; a half-plate daguerreotype of a Cincinnati street scene, $63,800; and a 1939 *Detective 27* comic book featuring Batman, $55,000.

The prices in this book are reports of the general antiques market, not the record-setting examples. Each year, every price in the book is new. We do *not* estimate or "update" prices. Prices are the actual asking price, although the buyer may have negotiated to a lower figure. No price is an estimate. *We do not ask dealers and writers to estimate prices.* Experience has shown that a collector of one type of antique is prejudiced in favor of that item, and prices are usually high or low, but rarely a true report. If a price range is given, it is because at least two identical items were offered for sale at different times. The computer records prices and prints the high and low figures. Price ranges are found only in categories like "Pressed Glass," where identical items can be identified. Some prices in *Kovels' Antiques & Collectibles Price List* may seem high and some may seem low because of regional variations. But each price is one you might have paid for the object.

If you are selling your collection, do *not* expect to get retail value unless you are a dealer. Wholesale prices for antiques are from 20 to 50 percent less than retail. Remember, the antiques dealer must make a profit or go out of business.

ACKNOWLEDGMENTS

Special thanks should go to those who helped us with pictures and deeds: Alderfer Auction Company, Bill Bertoia, Frank H. Boos Gallery, Butterfield & Butterfield, Caropreso Gallery, Christie's, DeFina Auctions, Marlin Denlinger, William Doyle Galleries, DuMouchelles Art Galleries Co., Dunning's Auction Service, Inc., Robert C. Eldred Co., Inc., Morton M. Goldberg Auction Galleries, Gene Harris Antique Auction Center, High Noon Wild West Auction, Leslie Hindman Auctioneers, James D. Julia,

Inc., Leland's, Bonnie Lewis, Joy Luke Auction Gallery, McMasters Doll Auctions, Neal Auction Co., Inc., Oliver's Auction Gallery, Pettigrew's, David Rago, Riba Auctions, Inc., Skinner Inc., Sotheby's, Specks, Theriault's, Wolf's Gallery, and Woody Auction Company. Special help was given by Lee Markley, Pamela Curran, Mike Pender, and Rachel Davis, all experts in their fields.

To the others in the antiques trade who knowlingly or unknowingly contributed prices to this book, we say "Thank you!" We could not do it without you. Some of you are: Abbey Hill Antiques, Jack Adamson, The Aluminist, America West Archives, American Eagle Antiques, Jon Anderson, Antiques by Wallace, Elizabeth Austin Antiques, The Autograph Gallery, Ruby Long Baker, Bill Ballor, Barbara's Dolls, R. E. Barnett, Pat Barrett Antiques, Noel Barrett Antiques & Auctions Ltd., Lee Barry, Mark Bergin, Bertoia-Brady, Bixby Hill Antiques, Block's Box, Blue Onion Antiques, Bobin's Antiques, Brass Bed Antiques, The Brass Horse Antiques, Allan Brink, Brinkline Antiques, Stuart & Karen Brody, Paul J. Brown, Burns Auction Service, Lavonia Chait, Cincinnati Art Galleries, Cobweb Corner Antiques, Cock-N-Kettle Antiques, Continental Hobby House, Crooked Creek Shop, Crosby's Antiques, Gary Crossen, Curran Miller Auction/Realty, John Darnell, Scott De Wolfe, Jean Deibel Antiques, Jeff & Mary Dickeson, Dorothy Dous, Edgehill Antiques, Al Eiber, Susan Endo, Jack T. Ericson, D. J. Ewald, W. Fagin & Co., Fenner's Antiques, Lew Fisher, Robert J. Flagor, Forgotten Elegance, Lee Foster, Gameroom, Frank Garcia, Garth's Auctions, Inc., The Gatsby Collection, David R. Geiger Antiques, Lynda Givens, Gold Nugget Antiques, Russ & Karen Goldberger, June Greenwald Antiques, Greg & Barbara Hall, R. A. Hamed Oriental Rugs, Hartley's Antique Toys, Basil & Mary Hayes, Stan & Peggy Hecker, The Hickory Club Mart, Barbara Hillman Antiques, Homestead Collectibles, Tom Horvitz, Bob Hritz, Jack & Scottie Imrie, Isaacs Gallery, Marilyn Isham, E. B. Jesse, Robert A. Jordan, Richard A. Karam, Bob Kay Mail Auction, Linda Ketterling, Madia Kline, Klingenberg's Nostalgiana, Ann & Jim Kopp, Walter Kraus Jr., Don Lamberton, Bob Lang, Jane Langol Antiques, Doris Lechler, Leo P. Legare Auctioneer, Sheldon J. Lewis, Lincoln Antiques, Lionwood Antique Gallery, Litchfield Auction Gallery, Howard Lowery, Debbie Lund, Lyons Ltd. Antique Prints, Mad Hatter Antiques, Madcap, Dorothy & David Mallory, Samuel A. Marcum, Martines' Antiques, Kevin McGrath's Auction, Bob Merry, Merry Householder, Metal Kettle Antiques, Midwest Quilt Exchange, Mike's General Store, Barbara Miller, W. R. Miller, MJ's Collectibles, Carolyn Moore, Moser's Collectables, The Mouse Man Ink, Mr. Cereal Box, Pat Multz, National Bottle & Advertising Show Dealers, Joan Nicholson, Northeast Auction, Ida A. Noser, Old Friends Antiques, The Olive Branch, Anita Pagani Antiques, Paper Collectors' Marketplace,

Betty Parker, Pascoe & Co., Patrick's Little Charmers, Marilyn Payne, Peg's Choice Antiques, John Perrault, Pine Tree Antiques, Gary L. Piper, Tom & Betty Polansky, Political Gallery, Postcards International, Powder Puff, Patricia Pratt Antiques, Gary & Judy Promey, Publick House Antiques, G. D. Querry, Jack Raudenbush, Red Brick Farm, Charlie Reynolds, Jack & Berta Reynolds, R. Neil Reynolds, Reynold's Antiques Inc., Leo E. Rishty, Bryan Roberts Antiques, Rosyln Rose Paperweights, Sandwich Auction House, Bill Sawyer, Fred & Mary Schrock, The Shopper, The Sign Sez, Simon-World Arts, Bill Smith, Sophie's Antiques, Barbara Spears, Tony Steffen, Sunshine Peddler, Swann Galleries, Carroll Swope Antiques, James Tabaska, Jan Taggart, Jean W. Taylor, Judy Taylor, Tesseract, Berry Thomsen, Three's Company, Time Will Tell Unlimited, Inc., Tool Ads, The Tool Shop, Toy Scouts, Inc., Don Treadway, Greg Tunks, Mary Twigg, Unique Antiques & Collectibles, Patricia V. Upson, Pat & Pat Van Vactor, Victorian Galleries, Victorian House Antiques, Joieaux Warren, Annette Weintraub Antiques, Larry D. Wells, Western Pennsylvania Antiques, Western Reserve Lamp Works, Whitman-Crafford, Betty G. Williams, John & Ellen Williams, R. F. Willis Gallery, Tom Witte's Antiques, Sharon Wojciechowski, Jane & John Woodring, The Workshop, Inc., Veryl M. Worth, Yesterday's South, and Yesteryear II Antiques.

MORE ANTIQUE PRICE NEWS

Have you kept up with prices? They change! Last year a set of golf clubs sold for more than a million dollars, a Carnival glass whimsey brought $4,000, and a child's game auctioned for $8,250. How did the owners know these collectibles had such a special value? Prices change with discoveries, auction records, even historic events. Every entry and every picture in this book is new and current, thanks to modern computer technology, making this book a handy overall price guide. But you also need current news about collecting.

Books on your shelf get older each month, and prices do change. Important sales produce new record prices. Rarities are discovered. Fakes appear. You will want to keep up with developments from month to month rather than from year to year. *Kovels on Antiques and Collectibles*, a nationally distributed, illustrated newsletter, includes up-to-date information on the world of collectors. This monthly newsletter reports current prices, collecting trends, landmark auction results for all types of antiques and collectibles, and tax, estate, security, and other pertinent news for collectors.

Additional information and a free sample newsletter are available from the authors at P.O. Box 420420, Palm Coast, FL 32142.

HOW TO USE THIS BOOK

There are a few rules for using this book. Each listing is arranged in the following manner: CATEGORY (such as Pressed Glass or Furniture), OBJECT (such as vase), DESCRIPTION (as much information as possible about size, age, color, and pattern). Some types of glass are exceptions to this rule. These are listed CATEGORY, PATTERN, OBJECT, DESCRIPTION. All items are presumed to be in good condition and undamaged, unless otherwise noted.

Several special categories were formed to make the most sensible listing possible. For instance, "Tool" includes special equipment because the casual collector might not know the proper name for an "adze." This year we reorganized the glass entries into these categories: "Glass-Art," "Glass-Contemporary," "Glass-Midcentury," and "Glass-Venetian." Major glass factories are still listed under the factory names and well-known types of glass such as cut, pressed, Carnival, etc., can be found in their own sections. New categories include "Daniel Boone," "Erphila," and "Howard Pierce." The index can help you locate items.

Several idiosyncrasies of style appear because the book is printed by computer. Everything is listed according to the computer alphabetizing system. This means words such as "Mt." are alphabetized as "M-T," not as "M-O-U-N-T." All numerals fall before all letters; thus 2 comes before A. A quick glance will make this clear, as it is consistent throughout the book.

We made several editorial decisions. A bowl is a "bowl" and not a "dish" unless it is a special dish, such as a pickle dish. A butter dish is a "butter." A salt dish is called a "salt" to differentiate it from a saltshaker. It is always "sugar and creamer," never "creamer and sugar." Where one dimension is given, it is the height; or if the object is round, the dimension is the diameter. The height of a picture is listed before the width. Glass is clear unless a color is indicated.

Every entry is listed alphabetically, but the problem of language remains. Some antiques terms, such as "Sheffield" or "snow baby," have two meanings. Be sure to read the paragraph headings to know the meaning used. All category headings are based on the language of the average person at an average show, and we use terms like "mud figures" even if not technically correct.

This book does not include price listings of fine art paintings, books, comic books, stamps, coins, and a few other special categories.

All pictures in *Kovels' Antiques & Collectibles Price List* are listed with the prices asked by the seller. "Illus" (illustrated nearby) is part of the description if a picture is shown.

There have been misinformed comments about how this book is written. We *do* use the computer. It alphabetizes, ranges prices, sets type, and does other time-consuming jobs. Because of the computer, the book can be produced quickly. The last entries are added in June; the book is available in October. This is six months earlier than would be possible any other way. But it is human help that finds prices and checks accuracy. We read everything at least twice, sometimes more. We edit from 100,000 entries to the 50,000 entries found here. We correct spelling, remove incorrect data, write category headings, and decide on new categories. We sometimes make errors. Information in the paragraphs is reviewed and updated each year.

Prices are reported from all parts of the United States and Canada (translated to U.S. dollars at the rate of 84¢ U.S. to $1 Canadian) between June 1991 and June 1992. A few prices are from auctions; most are from shops and shows. Every price is checked for accuracy, but we are not responsible for errors.

It is unprofessional for an appraiser to set a value for an unseen item. Because of this, we cannot answer your letters asking for specific price information. But please write if you have any requests for categories to be included in future editions or any corrections to information in the paragraphs.

When you see us at the shows, stop and say hello. Since our television show has aired in all parts of the country, we find we can no longer be anonymous buyers. It may mean the dealers know us before we ask a price, but it has been wonderful to meet all of you. Don't be surprised if we ask for your suggestions for the next edition of *Kovels' Antiques & Collectibles Price List*. Or you can write us at P.O. Box 22200-K, Beachwood, OH 44122.

RALPH AND TERRY KOVEL
Senior Members, American Society of Appraisers
July 1992

Collecting began for us in the 1950s when as newlyweds we were furnishing our first apartment. In those days there were only a few antiques shows in cities like New York, Chicago, Atlanta, Cleveland, or Los Angeles. These were expensive shows that featured eighteenth-century furniture, silver, and porcelains. Antiques were bought as home furnishings more than as part of a serious collection. The socially correct gift to a well-to-do bride in those days might have been an English Dr. Wall Worcester bowl or a Chinese export dish. Large antique silver serving trays, tureens, and ladles and English, French, or German single cups and saucers made before 1820 were also on the lists. Couples with antique furniture usually had pieces handed down from past generations. Most newlyweds wanted new furniture, often reproductions of older styles. Worn paint, mellowed wood, slightly faded fabrics (unless they came from grandmother) were signs of poverty, not desirable signs of antiquity.

We chose reproduction English furniture for our apartment and added unusual antique lamps and accessories. The search turned serious. We were bitten by the collecting bug. We went to house sales at mansions in older neighborhoods. We brought home an eighteenth-century French bronze for a lamp base, a blue and white Delft plaque that we hung on a wall, and many pieces of eighteenth-century porcelain, including Worcester, New Hall, Chelsea, Meissen, and Sevres. They all were "finds." Most were low priced because there was little demand and because the house sale staff didn't know about antiques. As we kept buying porcelains we discovered that we also knew little about them. What did the marks on the bottom mean? What was the history of the piece? The library was not very helpful. There were few books about antique porcelains. Each book was written for someone who knew if the porcelain was English, German, or French, eighteenth century or modern. Ralph compiled a list to help us at the sales. He wrote the names of makers and dates of manufacture, drew the marks, and then sorted the list by the mark shape, not by country or age. Because the idea was so original, he mentioned it to a friend who owned a bookstore. Three sample pages were sent to Crown Publishers in New York, and a few months later they sent a contract to write a book and an advance check of $500. That was more than a month's salary.

"Who will help you?" asked Terry. "You will," Ralph said. "Whose name is on the book?" "Well," he said, "Mine." Terry said, "If my name isn't there I won't help. So Ralph agreed to put both names on the book, but he said "My name is first." So we began writing as Ralph and Terry Kovel. There were no photocopy machines and no computers in the early 1950s. The book was handwritten on index cards. Each factory was listed with the date, country, and other information. Then a hand-drawn mark was added. All of this was done while we were chasing after our infant son and waiting for the birth of our daughter. She was born the day the first printed and bound copy of the book came from the publisher. That first book, *Dictionary of Marks, Pottery and Porcelain*, is still available at bookstores, although we wrote another book about marks in 1985, *Kovels' New Dictionary of Marks,* to reflect new collector interests. The young collector of the eighties rarely found a Worcester cup at a house sale, instead the "finds" were Fiesta pottery or Clarice Cliff dishes.

Soon after our first book was published we began writing a weekly newspaper column about antiques. It became nationally syndicated a year later. A regular feature on antiques was a new type of feature for a newspaper. Before that, only a few New England papers carried articles about antiques. As the 1960s rolled on, the United States was slowly becoming interested in antiques, history, and collecting things from the past.

It was five years before we wrote another book. Once again we did an entire book without a single text paragraph, just listings of name, city, shop, and mark for American silver and silver plate makers. *The Directory of American Silver, Pewter and Silver Plate* published in 1958 was replaced by an updated version in 1989 renamed *Kovels' American Silver Marks*. In 1963 we finally wrote paragraphs for *American Country Furniture*. *Know Your Antiques*, written in 1967, became a best-seller and was revised and renamed *Kovels' Know Your Antiques* in 1973. It was updated in 1981 and 1990. Our publisher decided to make the books a series in 1973, and the name "Kovel" was placed first in the titles of all our books. The titles say "Kovels' " because there are two of us. Now if only we could explain how to pronounce our name. It rhymes with "Oh well," not "novel" or "shovel."

We decided late one night in 1967 that we had to write a price book. We were probably the only people in America who got hundreds of letters about antiques each month from readers all over the country. We knew the questions asked by collectors, and their first question usually was "What is it worth?" We knew what collectors owned, what they wanted to buy and sell. We should be able to keep track of prices. Crown Publishers agreed it was a good idea for a book, and we started on the project.

The most important part of writing a price book is to get accurate price reports and get them into print as quickly as possible. In the 1960s it took two years to typeset and print a book using conventional methods. At first we planned to type each price on a special card, file it in a special slotted folder, then photograph each page of cards. Technology saved us. Ralph suggested using computers. Remember those huge machines that had arrived in some offices a few years earlier? We could rent a keypunch machine, type keypunch cards with a description and price, sort the cards, and then hire a computer service to print the book. We talked to many experts. They made all sorts of suggestions about how to code each entry to get it sorted. We planned to list hundreds of different types of antiques and felt that it would be impossible to learn all of the codes. Then we asked another expert, the father of our son's classmate. He made a simple comment, "But the alphabet is a code."

And so we developed "Kovelese," the strange listing form that is now used by most antiques price reports. We decided to list by category (pressed glass, Worcester porcelain, doll), followed by the name of the thing (plate, vase, apple peeler), and then the description, including, if possible, material, color, size, and age. We then skipped some spaces and put the price in the last available punches on the 79-space keypunch card. A few problems arose. Should we list bronzes with the word "figurine" or the name of the maker as the next part of the listing? Wouldn't it make more sense to list glass by pattern name first, then object? How do we decide what will be a category?

We spent about a year gathering prices. Each card was typed. Terry read them, and if there was an error, the card was discarded and a new card typed. You could not erase a keypunch card. (Rejected cards made good notepaper or bookmarks and even today we still find them in forgotten files or inside books.) Next came the problem of alphabetizing 40,000 cards. Remember how in the movie comedies those early keypunch-card sorters spit out rejected cards? Well, those machines had not yet been invented. So we hired 15 college students, set up 10 card tables with boxes on each table, and put everyone to work sorting. All the cards beginning with A in the first box, B in the second box, until we got to Z. One student lasted only an hour. It was such dull work he wouldn't continue. The rest stayed. We sorted, then each person took a box and sorted by the first word, then the second word, until we had what seemed to be a completely sorted set of prices.

Eventually the boxes of cards were sent to the computer and printed out. Each line was given a number so that we could delete entries or correct errors in the information now stored in the computer. We took the huge printout, read it for errors, and started correcting. We typed three keypunch cards to add, delete, and correct each mistake. They were kept in order. A month later we went back to the computer only to discover some unsuspected problems. Computers demand perfection, yet human error of 1% has always to be expected. If we made an error, the computer didn't know what to do, and we had to go back into the box of cards, correct the error, and continue. We had over 5,000 correction cards, so there were at least 50 errors. It took more than two weeks for the first correction run. The problems varied. One superstitious computer operator was unnerved by a ghostlike problem that appeared as the computer insisted on printing "Baccarat, paperweight, John F. Kennedy memorial, John F. Kennedy memorial" over and over and over. The error vanished as strangely as it had appeared.

At last came the day of final printing! The computer's type was cleaned, we installed new, all-white computer paper rolls, and the prices were printed with the only type-style available on a computer at the time. The roll was sent to Crown, where it had to be cut and pasted into pages with the specially typed category paragraphs, bound into books, and rushed to the bookstores 90 days later. *The Complete Antiques Price List* had a plain hard cover, no pictures, and no index. But collectors bought the ''over 28,000 accurate up-to-date prices'' for $5.95. If you can find a copy today with the blue and yellow dust jacket picturing a young Ralph and Terry on the back flap, buy it. The going price is over $75. After 25 years it, too, has become a collectible. The book was the *first* commercially published popular bookstore book to have been printed on a computer. Only company price lists and pamphlets had used such technology before us.

It should have been easier the next year, but it seems that each edition had its own problems. We have even nicknamed some editions. The 5th, for instance, is the lavender edition. That year the keypunchers misspelled the word ''lavender'' as ''lavendar.'' And the error appeared over 500 times. Before we wrote the 6th edition we created a spelling list of almost 1,000 antiques-related special words. It is amended regularly and is still in use as part of a computer spell-check program. Ever wonder if the correct spelling is bowback or bow back, Wedgewood or Wedgwood?

''Lockout'' was the 9th edition; it got caught in a bankruptcy. The computer-printing company had been padlocked by the courts because of financial problems. We had to go to court to have our tapes released so the book could be printed somewhere else and be in the bookstores by November. ''Major Disaster'' is the name for the 14th edition. The finished tape was in the computer being printed when lightning struck the building. The first 7,000 entries were lost. We hired ten keypunch operators and worked night shifts on rented machines recreating the lost information. Fortunately everything had been printed for the proofreading run. In all, four different companies have printed the book, and each time that we changed companies we also changed the way we used our keypunch machines, then word processors, then computers.

As computer technology improved, our book improved. The title changed to *The Kovels' Complete Antiques Price List* in 1974. The word ''complete'' was dropped by the 12th edition because a reader wrote to ask if it was really ''complete.'' *The Kovels' Antiques & Collectibles Price List* was the new title in 1982. Pictures were added in the 2nd book. The color insert was added in the 3rd book. A variety of type styles were available by the 5th book. Company logos and marks were included in 1973, the 6th edition. A computer-produced index was possible for the 13th. We changed from keypunch to word processing for the 17th. The computer could not alphabetize both copy and corrections until the 18th. Tips on how to care for your antiques were added in the 17th book. This was one of many improvements that put more information on the same number of pages. We started writing the special report inserts in 1988. Twice we rewrote every introductory paragraph to help the computer improve the sorting or printing. This year we again redesigned the entire book using a new type style, new placement of entries, additional logos, more entries in the index, and all newly rewritten, revised paragraphs.

But if you look carefully at past books you will find that we have rewritten bits and pieces each year. Dates are corrected, sometimes spelling is changed. Even names change. For example, buttermilk glass is now called custard glass. Changes are often suggested by letters or comments from readers. But sometimes readers are wrong and we ignore the requests. One reader, who signed each letter "Flo Blue," wanted us to redefine ivory to include only elephant ivory, although Webster's dictionary, collectors, and the Kovels all agree that there is "vegetable" ivory. Another letter writer, "Ann Teak," insisted our prices for Oriental pottery were far too low because they were exactly what she charged in her shop—and everyone knew what *bargains* she had.

About ten new categories are used each year, and five to ten are dropped, sometimes temporarily. We were first to list bottles, first to list Depression glass, first to include lunch boxes, Mexican silver, and fifties enamels in a general price book. As collector interest changes, the book changes.

We keep trying to find new features that will interest readers. Having been first with computers, logos, tips, color sections, and computer indexing, we plan to find even more improvements. Our staff evaluates how we can best use the space and still keep the price down. We discuss if it would be better to have more prices and fewer pictures, more pictures and fewer prices, longer paragraphs and fewer prices. For now we are sure the 50,000 prices and as many pictures as space allows is best. And for 25 years we have insisted on recording ALL NEW PRICES EACH YEAR. We literally ignore the old book and start fresh each July 1 to produce an accurate report of the market for the next year.

We collected antiques even before we were married and we still collect strange and wonderful things. We have never become dealers because Ralph won't sell anything he owns. If he owns it, he says it's "priceless." He does give things away from time to time, but still he always claims that our house sinks a few inches each year. We have remodeled three different times, filling one garage with bookshelves and adding a new garage each time. There are over 12,000 books in the three-garage library-office.

You will find some of our interests reflected in *Kovels' Antiques & Collectibles Price List* because we too have changed. Our first collection was eighteenth-century porcelain. Our newest is from the 1940s and 1950s. We collect kitchen items, lithographed tins, paper can-labels and other advertising and country-store items, head vases, art pottery, American decorated Satsuma, Gustavsberg pottery, battery operated toys, and Victorian furniture—all listed in this book. We also buy dated printed textiles,

American porcelains, bird-shaped pitchers, flower frogs, clothes hangers, Melmac dishes, and even those new little wind-up toys that ''walk.'' None of these have their own special listings yet. There is also no category for Terry's newest collection, as it has no dollar value yet: banana and other fruit and vegetable stickers.

It is hard to believe that in the past years we have written 60 books as well as 456 newspaper columns, 156 magazine columns, 216 newsletters and 65 of our own TV shows. If we count the prices recorded for all our price books, including the special ones on bottles, Royal Doulton, limited editions, Depression glass, and advertising, we can recite some mind-boggling statistics: We have captioned and checked 21,714 pictures, many photographed by Ralph. We have read over 3 million prices, edited them to 1.9 million, then reread them just to be sure. That means that somewhere in our heads and partially in our computers are 3 or 4 million antiques and collectibles, listed and priced. Even with all this information it is still true that we find something novel and wonderful at almost every antiques show and flea market. And if Terry isn't careful, Ralph will buy it and take it home, hoping that someday we can solve the mystery of where and why it was made. Then, once we learn enough, we can add the information to the next edition of *Kovels' Antiques & Collectibles Price List.*

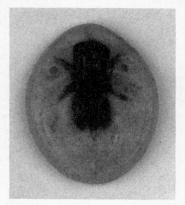

*A. Walter, Pendant, Beetle, Pate-De-Verre,
Signed, 1 1/2 In.*

A. WALTER made pate–de–verre glass under contract at the Daum glassworks from 1908 to 1914. He started his own firm in Nancy, France, in 1919. Pieces made before 1914 are signed *Daum, Nancy* with a cross. After 1919 the signature is *A. Walter Nancy*.

Box, Cover, Berries, Leaves, Grasshopper, Round, Pate–De–Verre, 3 In.	4950.00
Box, Cover, Flaring Cylinder, Geometric, Pate–De–Verre, 6 1/4 In.	3300.00
Box, Mottled Fish On Cover, Silver Plated, 1925, 4 3/4 x 7 1/4 In.	880.00
Box, Pin, Cover, Blossoms & Leaves, Signed, c.1925, 7 1/4 In.	1870.00
Cache Pot, White, Blue, Green & Red Leaves, Cover, Lug Handles	4300.00
Dish, Figural, Lizard, Flowers, Leaf Shape, Greens, H. Berge, 7 In.	7700.00
Dish, Green & Blue Spotted Lizard, Mauve, Signed, 9 In.	1100.00
Figurine, Frog, On Lily Pad Leaves, Green, 6 In.	6500.00
Figurine, Woman On Bench, Grecian Dress & Hair, Signed, 8 In.	2500.00
Figurine, Yellow Seal, Sitting On Rocky Base, Pate–De–Verre	975.00
Inkwell, Berried Branches, Bee, Marked, 4 3/4 In.	825.00
Paperweight, On Grape Leaves, Pate–De–Verre, Signed, 4 1/2 In.	5000.00
Paperweight, Salamanders, Foliage, Pate–De–Verre, 3 1/4 In.	7500.00
Paperweight, Sea Nymph, Pate–De–Verre, Green Surf, 9 3/4 In.	7700.00
Pendant, Beetle, Pate–De–Verre, Signed, 1 1/2 In. ......*Illus*	275.00
Tray, Inside Design Of Gold Mica Flakes, Signed, 10 In.	1275.00
Vase, Pendant Fruiting Grape Vines, Signed, c.1925, 6 5/8 In.	2200.00
Vase, Stylized Flowers At Neck, Pate–De–Verre, 4 1/2 In.	1100.00

ABC plates, or children's alphabet plates, were most popular from 1780 to 1860, but are still being made. The letters on the plate were meant as teaching aids for children learning to read. The plates were made of pottery, porcelain, metal, or glass. Mugs and other items were also made with alphabet decorations.

Cup & Saucer, Pink Luster, Germany	58.00
Cup & Saucer, Rooster & Chick, Germany	85.00
Cup, For A Good Boy, Tin, Yellow Paint	65.00
Mug, Crusoe Reaching Friday, Complete Alphabet, Pottery	150.00
Plate, Black Transfer, Polychrome Enameling, Staffordshire, 6 In.	115.00
Plate, Boy With Guitar, Bird, Multicolored, 7 3/4 In.	120.00 To 145.00
Plate, Brighton Beach Bathing Pavilion, Pottery, 7 1/2 In.	115.00 To 145.00
Plate, Brownie Figures, Alphabet Around Rim, Ring, 8 7/8 In.	175.00
Plate, Children & Liberty, Tin, 5 1/2 In.	75.00
Plate, Clock Center, Glass	30.00
Plate, Cock Robin, Tin	68.00
Plate, Comic Transfer, Man Falling In River, Staffordshire, 8 5/8 In.	85.00

Plate, Crusoe On Raft, Pottery	95.00 To 125.00
Plate, Dog Head Center, Glass, 6 In.	55.00
Plate, Elephant With Howdah, Glass, 6 In.	95.00
Plate, Elephant, Ripley	65.00
Plate, Franklin Proverb, Staffordshire, 5 3/4 In.	150.00
Plate, Frosted Deer Center, Raised Alphabet Rim, Glass, 6 In.	68.00
Plate, Frosted Stork Center, Raised Alphabet Rim, Glass, 6 In.	68.00
Plate, George Washington, Tin	155.00
Plate, Girl & Dogs, Pink Border, Pottery, Germany	80.00
Plate, Girl On Swing, Lithograph, Aluminum	25.00
Plate, Hen & Chicks, Glass, 6 In.	45.00
Plate, Hi Diddle Diddle, Tin, 8 3/4 In.	75.00
Plate, Hickory Dickory Dock, Graniteware	35.00
Plate, Horse, Tin, 1860	50.00
Plate, Jumbo, Tin, 5 1/2 In.	100.00
Plate, Jumbo, Tin, 6 In.	85.00
Plate, Man & Child Carrying Donkey Over Bridge, Pottery, 7 1/4 In.	85.00
Plate, Mary Had A Little Lamb, Figures, Tin, 8 In.	68.00
Plate, People In Front Of Fence, Motto, Staffordshire, 7 1/2 In.	140.00
Plate, Peter Rabbit, Clouds, Animals, ABC Rim, Tin, 8 1/2 In.	70.00
Plate, Rabbits, Green, Haynsley Longton, England	125.00
Plate, Seesaw Margery Daw, Amber, Glass, 8 In.	10.00
Plate, Sioux Indian Chief, Brown, 8 In.	135.00 To 165.00
Plate, This Little Piggy, Glass, 6 1/2 In.	24.50
Plate, Who Killed Cock Robin, Tin, 8 In.	45.00 To 100.00

ABINGDON POTTERY was established in 1934 by Raymond E. Bidwell as the Abingdon Sanitary Manufacturing Company. The company made art pottery and other wares. Sixteen varieties of cookie jars are known. The factory ceased production of art pottery in 1950.

Bookends, Horsehead, Black	45.00
Bowl, Console, Gray & Green, 14 x 9 In.	18.00
Candleholder, Double Scroll, White, Gold Trim, Pair	35.00
Cookie Jar, Choo Choo	50.00
Cookie Jar, Clock	87.00
Cookie Jar, Collegiate Owl	50.00
Cookie Jar, Daisy	25.00
Cookie Jar, Engine	90.00
Cookie Jar, Girl With Braids, Cooky	70.00 To 95.00
Cookie Jar, Humpty Dumpty	100.00 To 225.00
Cookie Jar, Lil' Old Lady, White Glaze	235.00
Cookie Jar, Little Girl	110.00
Cookie Jar, Little Miss Muffet	185.00 To 275.00
Cookie Jar, Money Sack, White	75.00
Cookie Jar, Paddy Pig	85.00
Cookie Jar, Rooster	48.00
Cookie Jar, Three Bears	95.00
Cookie Jar, Train Engine, Green & Orange	80.00 To 135.00
Cookie Jar, Train Engine, Turquoise & Rose, Sticker	135.00
Figurine, Wall Shelf, Cherub Face, Wings, Yellow, 7 x 4 1/2 In.	30.00
Vase, Fan, White, Horizontal Ribs, Scroll, 5 x 7 In.	22.00
Wall Pocket, Double Lily, Turquoise, Pair	45.00

ADAMS china was made by William Adams and Sons of Staffordshire, England. The firm was founded in 1769 and is still working. All types of tablewares and useful wares have been made through the years. Other pieces of Adams will be found listed under Flow Blue.

Cup & Saucer, Ivory, Demitasse	5.00
Plate, Cries Of London, 10 In.	55.00
Plate, Rose, Scalloped, Signed, 9 In.	110.00
Platter, Regent, 16 In.	50.00
Sugar & Creamer, Royal Ivory, Titianware	75.00

Advertising, Ashtray, Moxie, 5 In.

ADVERTISING containers and products sold in the old country store are
now all collectibles. These stores, with the crackers in a barrel and a
potbellied stove, are a symbol of an earlier, less hectic time. Listed here are
many of the advertising items. Other similar pieces may be found under
the product name, such as Planters Peanuts. We have tried to list items in
the logical places, so large store fixtures will be found under the
Architectural category, enameled tin dishes under Graniteware, paper items
in the Paper category, etc. Store fixtures, cases, and other items that have
no advertising as part of the decoration are listed in the store category.

Ad, Jell–O, Parrish, Framed, 1923	45.00
Ashtray, Abbey Rents, Bedpan	20.00
Ashtray, Chicago Daily News, Metal	17.00
Ashtray, Coon Chicken Inn, Pottery	50.00
Ashtray, Firestone Tire, Glass Insert	12.00
Ashtray, G. E., Mr. Magoo, Glass, Light Bulb Border, Large	75.00
Ashtray, General Tire, Tire Shape	8.00
Ashtray, Goodrich Silvertown, Rubber Tire, Glass Insert, 6 In.	25.00
Ashtray, Goodyear Tire, 100th Anniversary	25.00
Ashtray, Mack Truck	50.00
Ashtray, Mission Orange, Bottle In Center	150.00
Ashtray, Moxie, 5 In. ....*Illus*	35.00
Ashtray, Nash, Figural, 1949	35.00
Ashtray, Piper Cub, Aluminum	3.00
Ashtray, RCA, Logo In Enameled Red & Silver, 1930s, 5 In.	35.00
Ashtray, Reddy Kilowatt .... 10.00 To	30.00
Ashtray, Sieberling, Green Glass Insert, Rubber, 4 In.	22.00
Ashtray, Southland Newsreel, Movie Camera, Metal, 1930s	87.00
Ashtray, United Airlines, 1960s	25.00
Bag, Colonial Salt, 3 Lb.	5.00
Bag, Flour, Cincinnati Flour, Cloth	2.25
Banner, AFGA Photos, Orange & White Canvas, 24 x 40 In.	75.00
Banner, Atlantic Motor Oil, Airplane, Oil Cans, 36 x 60 In.	245.00
Banner, Butterball Turkey, Squeaker In Drumstick, 31 x 45 In.	24.00
Banner, Kleanbore Gallery, Cowboy, Puma, 33 x 55 In.	950.00
Banner, Remington, Big Game Hunter, Canvas, 55 1/2 x 50 1/4 In.	77.00
Banner, Sickle Plug Smoking Tobacco, Oil Cloth, 39 x 21 In.	90.00
Banner, Vikings Remedy, Medicine Man, 39 x 21 In.	350.00
Barrel, Hires Root Beer, Oak	400.00
Barrel, Miller Crackers & Biscuits, Terre Haute, Tin, 3 Ft.	170.00
Barrel, Old Kentucky Bourbon, Display, 18 In.	750.00

Barrel, Reid, Murdoch & Co., 50 Lb. 245.00
Basket, Picnic, Kentucky Fried Chicken, Vinyl, 1960s 75.00
Basket, Quaker Oats, Bugs Bunny, 1949 .... 10.00
Bill Hook, Henry Disston & Sons, Cast Steel, 18 In. 45.00
Bin, Blue Ribbon, Austin, Nichols 72.00
Bin, Brother Jonathan 3335.00
Bin, Choice Family Tea, Stenciled Flowers & Bee, 13 1/2 In. 137.00
Bin, Coffee, Wooden, New Jersey 290.00
Bin, Cream City Flour, Sifter, Black, Gold Stenciling, 3 Ft. 250.00
Bin, Cremo Cigars, Picture Of Cigar, Lift Top, Tin, 2 x 4 Ft. 650.00
Bin, Dibbit's Toffees, 2 Parrots On Front, 11 1/2 x 11 In. 330.00
Bin, Flour, Pillsbury, Tin, Dough Boy Picture, 1960s 10.00
Bin, Game Tobacco 450.00
Bin, Hillside Tea, Red, Black & Gold, 13 3/4 x 13 In. 65.00
Bin, Horlick's Malted Milk 48.00
Bin, Hulman's Delicious Roasted Coffee, Old Red Paint 160.00
Bin, Old English Curve Cut Tobacco 450.00
Bin, Old Government Java, Coffee, 1900 .... 120.00
Bin, Pastime Tobacco 200.00
Bin, Sterling Tea, Quebec Landmarks, 11 3/4 x 8 3/4 In. 330.00
Bin, Sure Shot Tobacco .:.. 550.00
Bin, Sweet Cuba Tobacco, Slant Front, Blue 550.00
Bin, Sweet Cuba Tobacco, Slant Front, Butterscotch 550.00
Bin, Sweet Mist Chewing Tobacco, Playing Children, Tin, 11 In. 115.00
Bin, Sweet Mist Tobacco, Cardboard, Tin Top & Bottom 175.00
Bin, Tiger Tobacco, Cardboard, Red 250.00
Bin, Tiger Tobacco, Tin, Orange 300.00
Bin, Wilbur's Feed 700.00
Blanket, TWA, Red & Blue 85.00
Blotter, Antique Whiskey, Many Brands Of Whiskey Boxes, 8 In. 7.00
Blotter, Borden's, Elsie, Elmer, Beulah, Christmas Greetings 8.00
Blotter, Carter's Ink, Graphics, 1920s 12.00
Blotter, Fanny Farmer 10.00
Blotter, House Of Anheuser–Busch, 4 x 9 1/2 In. ....*Illus* 9.50
Blotter, Hoyt's Eau De Cologne, Colorful Floral, 1890s 8.00
Blotter, HyVis Motor Oil, 1930s 10.00
Blotter, Meadow Gold Ice Cream, Large Dish Of Ice Cream, Boy 3.50
Blotter, Mission Orange, Colorful, Canada 8.00
Blotter, Old Forester, Belmont, Bright Pink Ground, 7 x 3 In. 2.00
Blotter, Old Grand–Dad Whiskey, Between 2 Labels, 6 x 3 In. 8.50
Blotter, Pabst Beer, 1933 .... 10.00
Blotter, Philadelphia Story, Movie, Portraits, 1940, Unused 7.00
Blotter, Spencerian Pens, 40 Falcon Silverline Finish, 1900s 5.00
Books may be included in the Paper category
Booklet, Alka–Seltzer, Dr. Miles, Our Presidents, 1930, 32 Pages 6.00
Booklet, Colgate, Beautiful Covers, 1914 .... 18.00
Booklet, Coloring, ABC, Metropolitan Life, 1920s, Unused 6.00

Advertising, Blotter, House of Anheuser-Busch, 4 x 9 1/2 In.

Clockwise from top: Advertising, Bottle Cap, Borden's Pasteurized Milk, 1 In.; Advertising, Bottle Cap, Borden's Hi-Protein Milk, 1 1/2 In.; Advertising, Bottle Cap, Grade D Raw Milk, 1 1/2 In.; Advertising, Bottle Cap, Shady Grove Ice Cream, 1 1/2 In.

Booklet, Dutch Boy Paint, 1926	15.00
Booklet, Human Hair, Benefits Of Cocaine For Scalp, 1892	20.00
Booklet, Jell-O & The Kewpies	36.00
Booklet, Kellogg's Funny Jungleland Moving Pictures, 1932	14.00
Booklet, Watkins Glen, N.Y., Photographs, Color, 1910, 5 x 7 In.	9.00
Bottles are listed in their own category	
Bottle Cap, Borden's Hi-Protein Milk, 1 1/2 In. ....*Illus*	1.00
Bottle Cap, Borden's Pasteurized Milk, 1 In. ....*Illus*	1.00
Bottle Cap, Brownie Chocolate ....*Illus*	.50
Bottle Cap, Christmas Egg Nog, 10 Piece	2.50
Bottle Cap, Grade D Raw Milk, 1 1/2 In. ....*Illus*	1.00
Bottle Cap, Grapefruit Crush ....*Illus*	.50
Bottle Cap, Howdy Cola ....*Illus*	.50
Bottle Cap, Mission Royal Punch ....*Illus*	.50
Bottle Cap, Moxie Ginger Ale	6.00
Bottle Cap, Shady Grove Ice Cream, 1 1/2 In. ....*Illus*	1.00
Bottle Cap, Stroh's Bohemian Beer	3.50
Bottle Cap, Triple AAA Root Beer ....*Illus*	.50
Bottle Openers are listed in their own category	
Bottle Stopper, Bernheim Whiskies, Shield Shape, Long Cork	2.75
Bottle Stopper, Henry M. Rubel Co., Porcelain, Flat, 3/8 In.	5.00
Bowl & Spoon Set, Yellow, Quaker Oats, Box, 1988	15.00
Bowl, Chocks Vitamins, Bugs Bunny, 1971	10.00
Bowl, Skippy, Beetleware, Green, 1933, 5 1/2 In.	10.00 To 17.50
Box, 40% Bran Flakes, Twist-Teezer Puzzle, Flat, 1956	75.00
Box, see also Box category	
Box, Best Pals Candy, Child With Collie Lithograph	25.00
Box, Black Draught	15.00
Box, Butter-Kist Peanut, Children Fishing, 1 Lb.	5.00
Box, Champ Prophylactics, Kicking Football Player, 1950s	75.00
Box, Cheerios, Muppet Movie Trading Cards, 1980	15.00

Top row: Advertising, Bottle Cap, Grapefruit Crush; Advertising Bottle Cap, Mission Royal Punch; bottom row: Advertising, Bottle Cap, Brownie Chocolate; Advertising, Bottle Cap, Howdy Cola; Advertising, Bottle Cap, Triple AAA Root Beer

Box, Corn Chex, Party Mix Recipe Back, 1950s	65.00
Box, Cretor's Popcorn, Cardboard, Blue, Orange, 1929, 2 x 7 In.	12.00
Box, Dina–Mite, Gold & Navy, 1921, Sample, 1 x 3 x 5 In.	85.00
Box, Dr. West Toothpaste, 1930s	3.00
Box, El Toro Cigar	15.00
Box, Flower Seed, D. M. Ferry Co., Label, Oak, 4 x 9 1/2 x 4 In.	55.00
Box, Frosted Flakes, Tony Spoon, 1975	40.00
Box, Fun To Wash Soap, Black Mammy Design, 3 x 5 x 7 In.	55.00
Box, Georgie Porgie Cereal	35.00
Box, Gold Dust Scouring Cleanser, Unopened, 14 Oz.	20.00
Box, Gold Dust Twins, Cardboard	35.00
Box, Gold Dust Washing Powder, Sample	25.00
Box, Hals Home Trade 5 Cent Cigar, Wooden, Lid	2.25
Box, Hill Country Butter, 1940s	3.00
Box, Imperial Tea, Paper Label	10.00
Box, Jell–O, Jack & Jill, 1950s	3.00
Box, Kellogg's Corn Flakes, Magic Mary Doll, Clothes, 1963	65.00
Box, Kellogg's Corn Flakes, Vanessa Williams, 1984	45.00
Box, King Rolled Oats	75.00
Box, Larkin Soap, Wood	20.00
Box, Morton's Plain Salt, Unopened, Dated 1921	18.50
Box, Mother's Crushed Oats, 1940	75.00
Box, Mr. Delish Popcorn, Usher Picture, 1950s	3.00
Box, Nabisco Shredded Wheat, 1942, Flat	65.00
Box, Northern Shirt, 11 x 16 x 4 In.	85.00
Box, Our King Cigar, Wooden	7.00
Box, Peter Paul's Charcoal Gum, Brown, Pink Letters, 11 x 5 In.	45.00
Box, Phillips Jersey Cape Oyster, Pt.	6.00
Box, Post's Super Sugar Crisp, With Terrariums, 1974	35.00
Box, President Suspender, Woman Garden Scene, Green, 13 x 4 In.	10.00
Box, Princely Washed Figs, Paper Label, 1 1/8 x 3 3/4 In.	30.00
Box, Prudential Steamship Corp., P On Flag, Metal, 1 x 4 In.	85.00
Box, Pure Lard, 1940s	3.00
Box, Quaker Puffed Wheat, Space Flight To Moon, No. 8, 1953	100.00
Box, Ralston's Cookie Crisp, Mini Skateboard, Collapsed, 1977	20.00
Box, RCA Television Truck	175.00
Box, Reliable Coffee, Dayton, Oh., Shipping Type, 36 Lb.	52.00
Box, Rice Chex, Red Checked, 1950s	65.00
Box, Rice Krispies, Choco–Cluster Recipe Box, 1965	50.00
Box, Sgt. Preston Quaker Puffed Wheat, Yukon Trail No. 2, 1949	100.00
Box, Superior Water Bottle & Fountain Syringe, Wooden, 10 In.	15.00
Box, T's Morbus Pills, Diarrhea & Dysentery, 1900, 1 1/4 In.	11.50
Box, Webster Typewriter Ribbon, Tin	5.00
Box, Wheaties, Disneyland Light–Up No. 10, Punched Out, 1950s	65.00
Box, Wheaties, Minnesota Twins, Collapsed, 1989	7.00
Broom Holder, Baker's Coconut	175.00
Broom Holder, Gold Medal Flour, 2 Sides, Tin	375.00
Brush, Cumberland Hotel, New York	30.00
Bucket, Country Club Tobacco	75.00
Bucket, Winona–Maid, Red Indian Maiden, Label, Handle, Tin, 5 In.	15.00
Buckle, Belt, Hesston, 1980	15.00
Buckle, Belt, John Deere, 1980	15.00
Buckle, Belt, Rondo Premium Citrus Soda, Brass, Late 1970, 3 In.	20.00
Buckle, Skippy Peanut Butter, Silver Plate, 1921	25.00
Burial Vault, Doswell & Kover, Salesman's Sample, 4 x 8 In.	250.00
Buttonhook, Bond Street Spats	12.50
Buttonhook, Dorothy Dodd Shoes, Iron	3.50
Cabinet, Baker's, White Porcelain Top, Potato Bin, 18 In. Wide	395.00
Cabinet, Collar, Counter Top, Glass & Oak, 12 Collars, 25 In.	350.00
Cabinet, Diamond Dye, Baby In Diamond, Floral Border, 20 In.	300.00
Cabinet, Diamond Dye, Court Jester	500.00 To 725.00
Cabinet, Diamond Dye, Evolution Of Woman Lithograph, Wooden	1150.00
Cabinet, Diamond Dye, Governess	1750.00

Cabinet, Diamond Dye, Mansion 600.00
Cabinet, Diamond Dye, Maypole Balloon Scene, 8 1/2 In. 635.00
Cabinet, Diamond Dye, Washing Lady .... 1350.00 To 1850.00
Cabinet, Display, Oak Ribbon, 4 Sections 475.00
Cabinet, Display, Set Snug Hair Net, Slant Top, Mirror 75.00
Cabinet, Dr. A. C. Daniel's Dog & Cat Remedy 4950.00
Cabinet, Dr. Daniel's Dye, Pricing On Bottom, 27 x 21 In. 2450.00
Cabinet, Dr. Daniel's Veterinary Medicine, Man's Hand 1250.00
Cabinet, Dr. Lesure's Remedy, Horsehead Front 3000.00
Cabinet, Dy–O–La Dye, 17 x 13 In. 225.00
Cabinet, Myers Remedy Co., 3 Shelves, Glass Front, 24 In. 150.00
Cabinet, Pratt's Veterinary Remedies 900.00
Cabinet, Putnam Dye, Horseback Rider, Tin, Large 125.00
Cabinet, Putnam Dye, Metal, Flip Front, 12 In. 400.00
Cabinet, Ray–O–Vac Batteries, Counter Top 65.00
Cabinet, Spool, 31 Drawers, Walnut 725.00
Cabinet, Spool, Belding Bros. & Co., 14 Drawers, Oak, 36 In. 1500.00
Cabinet, Spool, Clark's, 7 Drawer 900.00
Cabinet, Spool, Clark's, O. N. T., Oak, 16 x 18 x 22 In. 950.00
Cabinet, Spool, Clark's, O. N. T., Red Painted, 4 Drawers 270.00
Cabinet, Spool, J & P Coats, 2 Drawers 395.00
Cabinet, Spool, J & P Coats, 6 Drawers 475.00
Cabinet, Spool, J. & P. Coats, 6 Drawers, 26 1/4 In. 440.00
Cabinet, Spool, M. Heminway & Sons, 8 Drawers, Oak 155.00
Cabinet, Spool, Merrick's, Curved Glass, Mirrors, Revolve, Oak 1500.00
Cabinet, Tintex Dye, Woman Dyeing Clothes, Metal 100.00
Cabinet, Tums, Nature's Remedy, Slant Top, Tin 105.00
Calendars may be found in the Paper category
Can, Borden's Cream, Springfield 65.00
Can, Capt. John's Oysters, 12 Oz. 7.00
Can, Daufuski/Oyster, Indian 75.00
Can, Lighthouse Cleanser, Unopened, Round 20.00
Can, Miles Oyster, Lighthouse Picture, 1 Pt. 10.00
Can, North Crystal Oysters, 8 Oz. 5.00
Can, Oyster, Sailboat Picture, 1950–1960, 1 Gal. 15.00
Can, Penzoil Motor Oil, 1 Qt. 46.00
Can, Phillip Morris, Cardboard, Brown, Flat 50s 15.00
Can, Quinby Oyster, Boat Picture 15.00
Can, Sailor Boy Oysters, 8 Oz. 6.00
Can, Seal Brand Oyster, Bail Handle, Sea Lion In Oyster Shell 200.00
Can, Sealshipt Oyster 45.00
Can, Shamrock Oil, Metal, 1 Qt. 15.00
Canisters, see introductory paragraph to Tins in this category
Canteen, Kool–Aid, Smiling Face Logo, 6 In. 19.00
Cards are listed in their own category
Carton, Raleigh Cigarette, 1940s 15.00
Case, Bachelor Cigar, 1915, 10 x 12 x 8 In. 280.00
Case, Milk Bottle, Borden's, Wooden 25.00
Case, Milk Bottle, Jersey Gold, Embossed Wire 15.00
Case, Milk Bottle, Jersey Gold, Wooden 20.00
Case, Miller Milwaukee Beer, Oak, Fitted Slots For Bottles 100.00
Casket, Felt Covered, Salesman Sample 495.00
Casket, Salesman's Sample, 1940s 300.00
Cereal Inserts, Nabisco Shredded Wheat, Board, 1950s, Set Of 20 .... 40.00
Chalkboard, 7–Up, Tin 36.00
Chalkboard, Dr. Pepper, Tin 30.00
Change Receiver, 7–20–4 Cigars 40.00
Change Receiver, see also Tip Tray in this section
Change Receiver, Bartholomay Beer, Girl On Winged Wheel 33.00
Change Receiver, Cottolene Shortening, Blacks In Field 85.00
Charm, Bubble Gum, 1950s, 100 Piece 45.00
Cigar Cutter, Bashful, Trick Lock, 1915 .... 75.00
Cigar Cutter, Cottage Shape, Round Wooden Base 125.00

Cigarette Paper, Half & Half	2.50
Cigarette Roller, Brown & Williamson	7.50
Clicker, Bonnie Laddie Sundial Shoe	40.00
Clicker, Real–Kill Bug Killer	7.00
Clicker, Red Goose Shoes	15.00
Clocks are listed in their own category	
Coaster, Budweiser, 6 Piece	5.00
Coaster, Fort Pitt Beer, Foil & Cardboard	5.00
Coaster, Moffats Ale–3 Star Beer	25.00
Coaster, Simon's Pure Beer, Metal, 6 Piece	18.00
Coffee Grinders are listed in their own category	
Coffee Scoop, Barrington Hall Coffee	6.50
Coffeepot, Blanke's Drip, Ironstone	175.00
Coffeepot, Nestle World	75.00
Collar, Pearl Beer	65.00
Comb, Case, Dant Whiskey, Pocket	1.25
Cookie Cutter, Herkles Flour	7.00
Cookie Cutter, Robin Hood, 5 Piece Set	30.00
Cookie Cutter, Rumford	8.00
Cooler, 7–Up, Electric	350.00
Cooler, 7–Up, White, Red Lettering	15.00
Cooler, Pabst Blue Ribbon, Pressed Paper, 6 Pack	17.50
Cooler, Squirt, Yellow	75.00
Counter, Store Credit, Ford Motor Co., Dated 1918	650.00
Crate, Dr. Hess Fly Chaser, Lid	35.00
Crate, Franklin Sugar	10.00
Crate, Peter's Victor Ammunition, Wooden, Nailed	18.00
Crate, Remington Ammunition, Wooden, Dovetailed	25.00
Crate, Witte, Wooden, Small	30.00
Creamer, Davis Dairy, Creston, Iowa	20.00
Creamer, Neidig's Dairy, Pennsylvania	20.00
Creamer, Pulaski Pure Milk Co., Tennessee	27.00
Crock, Copenhagen Snuff, Ceramic	200.00
Crumb Tray Set, Brass, Steinklein Furniture Co., Ornate, 1800s	20.00
Cuff Links & Earrings Set, Evinrude	15.00
Cuff Links, Prudential Life Insurance	28.00
Cup & Saucer, Johnson's Hot Chocolate, Art Deco	35.00
Cup & Saucer, Nestle's Chocolate	20.00
Cup, Eastern Airlines, Demitasse	2.00
Cup, Measuring, Kodak, Glass, With Wooden Stir Stick, 4 Oz.	8.00
Cup, Measuring, Nash Peanut Butter	75.00
Cup, Measuring, Pillsbury, Red Plastic, Smiling	10.00
Cup, Piedmont Airlines	14.00
Decanter, Borden's Malted Milk, Glass	165.00
Decanter, Fern Hill, Quadruple Plated, Cap, Odd Shape, 9 3/8 In.	50.00
Dice, 7–Up, Always Roll 7, Pair	16.00
Dish, Schraft's Chocolates, Pressed Glass, Clear, 6 x 6 In.	35.00
Dispenser, Alka–Seltzer, Be Wise, Alkalize, Lithograph Sign	275.00
Dispenser, Alka–Seltzer, Chrome, Blue, Wheel On Side, 15 In.	180.00
Dispenser, Alka–Seltzer, Counter Top, Graphics	145.00
Dispenser, Anheuser–Busch, Syrup, 5 Cents	225.00
Dispenser, Bowl, Cherry Smash Syrup, Red Glass, 9 In.	22.00 To 33.00
Dispenser, Bromo–Seltzer	175.00
Dispenser, Coffee, J. Henry Koenig's Co., Cincinnati, 3 Windows	105.00
Dispenser, Crawford's Cherry Fizz	5500.00
Dispenser, Derby Cake Ice Cream Cones, Cabinet Shape	100.00
Dispenser, Grape Julep Syrup	1450.00 To 1700.00
Dispenser, Green River, No Spigot	185.00
Dispenser, Gumball Gas Pump	65.00
Dispenser, Hot Rum, Brass, White Marble, Etched Glass, 23 In.	225.00
Dispenser, Jersey Creme	1400.00
Dispenser, Lash's Orangeade, Green Top, Black, Partial Label	375.00
Dispenser, Lash's, Black Amethyst Base, Yellow Top, Cover	350.00

Dispenser, Lemon Crush, Original Pump 1100.00
Dispenser, Liberty Root Beer, Liner, Large Stein, 5 Cents 250.00
Dispenser, Little Nut Hut, Peanut 75.00
Dispenser, M & M Candy, Box 30.00
Dispenser, Napkin, Royal Crown Cola 225.00
Dispenser, Nesbitt Fruit Products Co., Clear Glass, Spigot 50.00
Dispenser, Orange Crush, Original Pump 900.00
Dispenser, Orange Julep 650.00
Dispenser, Orange Nip, Painted Orange, Tin, 20 1/2 In. 950.00
Dispenser, Syrup, Green River 250.00
Dispenser, Ward's Lemon 950.00
Dispenser, Ward's Lime & Orange Crush, Original Pumps, Pair 2500.00
Dispenser, Ward's Lime Crush, Pump, 13 x 9 x 7 In. 1400.00
Dispenser, Zig Zag Cigarette Paper 24.00
Dispenser, Zipp's Cherri–O, Pump 2090.00
Display Cabinet, Parker 51 Pens, 6 Ft. 1200.00
Display Cabinet, Remington Knives 200.00
Display Case, Adams Gum, Tin, Glass, Chicklets, 1 Cent, 6 1/2 In. 75.00
Display Case, Arrow Collars, Bowed Glass, Decals, 54 In. 895.00
Display Case, Baum's Bologna, You'll Like It, 1930, 2 Doors 195.00
Display Case, Bonnie–B Hair Nets, 6 Sides, Wooden, Mirror Front 187.00
Display Case, Boye Needles, Wood 185.00
Display Case, Condom, Gold Letter Reverse Glass, 10 x 12 In. 125.00
Display Case, Curlox Hair Net, Glass Front, Wood, 19 In. 93.50
Display Case, Dr. Scholl's, 4 Faces, Foot Fetishes, Tin 165.00
Display Case, Eagle Musical Strings, Picks, Reeds 125.00
Display Case, Eveready Batteries & Mazda, Metal, Tester, 1929 .... 200.00
Display Case, Faber Castel 75.00
Display Case, Hohner's Harmonicas, Folds Out, Wooden 88.00
Display Case, Keen Kutter Cutlery, Oak, 2 Sliding Doors, 54 In. 900.00
Display Case, Knives, Case, 8 Knives 325.00
Display Case, Knives, Case, Eagle On Back, Wood, 28 1/2 In. 75.00
Display Case, Presto Auto Products 30.00
Display Case, Ribbons, A. N. Russell & Sons, 4 Sections, Oak 500.00
Display Case, Schmidt's Beer 40.00
Display Case, Seiko, Mickey Mouse, Plastic, 1980s, 16 x 23 In. 100.00
Display Case, Squibb Aspirin, 12 Tins 24.00
Display Case, Waterman's Fountain Pens, Oak, Drawer 550.00
Display Case, Wrigley's Gum, Etched Curved Glass 425.00
Display Case, Zeno Gum 475.00
Display, Adam Hat, Man, Many Hats, Arm Moves, Easel, 21 x 28 In. ... 30.00
Display, Bottle Cap, Old Dutch Beer, Month & Day, Plastic, Large 12.50
Display, Bottle, Ice Cold Moxie, Waist High, Tin Cap 895.00
Display, Bottle, Sterling Beer, Glass, 21 In. 100.00
Display, Butter Kist Bread, Loaf, Butterflies, 1930s, 4 x 14 In. 12.00
Display, Canoe, Ole Town Canoe, Wooden, 4 Ft. 6600.00
Display, Check Bread, Man Holding Sign, Die Cut, Stand Up, 1924 .... 45.00
Display, Elegant Woman, Satchel, Die Cut Painted Tin, 73 In. 9900.00
Display, Gold Star Razor Blade 25.00
Display, Heinz Ketchup, Stand–Up, 1940s 65.00
Display, Herbert Tareyton, Pall Mall Cigarettes, Wood, 10 In. 65.00
Display, Isabella Cigars, 2 For 5 Cents, 8 Arms, Cast Iron 850.00
Display, Keen Kutter Butcher Knife, Stand Up Bull 300.00
Display, Man, Carrying Satchel, Die Cut Painted Tin, 73 In. 5500.00
Display, Norwood Rubber Footwear, 3–D, 10 x 13 In. 28.00
Display, Old Crow Whiskey, Figure, Blinks Hi 250.00
Display, Pearson's Snuff, Cardboard, With Tins 50.00
Display, Philip Morris, Johnny, Ceramic, Cigarette Holder, 9 In. 55.00
Display, Snow King Baking Powder, Cardboard Cutout, 34 In. 275.00
Display, Stewart–Warner Radio, Cardboard, 18 x 25 In. 120.00
Display, Sunshine Biscuits, Counter, Bulbous 60.00
Display, Tetlow's Face Powder, Die Cut Cardboard, 14 x 19 In. 275.00
Display, Tinker Toy, Motorized, 1953 .... 175.00

Left to right: Advertising, Glass, McDonald's, Great
Muppet Caper, 1981, 6 In.; Advertising, Glass, Burger
King, The 1979 Burger Thing, 6 In.; Advertising, Glass,
Burger King, Empire Strikes Back, 1990, 6 In.

Display, Tru Aspirin, Cardboard, Bottles, 11 x 14 In. 55.00
Display, Uncle John's Syrup, Cardboard, 3–D, 12 x 14 x 3 In. 15.00
Display, Wrigley's, Cardboard, Easel, Red Ground, 8 x 14 In. 38.00
Dolls are listed in their own category
Door Handle, 7–Up 50.00
Door Pull, Dandy Bread, Tin 25.00
Door Pull, Double Cola, Aluminum 145.00
Door Pull, Drink Cloverleaf Milk 115.00
Door Push, Bubble Up, Tin 65.00
Door Push, Chesterfield Cigarettes, Porcelain 285.00
Door Push, Dr Pepper, 1950s 120.00
Door Push, Five Roses Flour, Porcelain, Red, White, Black 40.00
Door Push, Fleischmann's Yeast, Porcelain 100.00
Door Push, Grapette 45.00
Door Push, KIK Cola, Tin, Red, White, Black, France, 3 1/2 x 10 In 33.00
Door Push, King Cole Tea, Porcelain, 3 x 30 In. 42.00
Door Push, King Cole, Porcelain, Red, Black, Yellow, 3 x 11 In. 190.00
Door Push, Kist, Aluminum, Gold Finish 50.00
Door Push, Kramer's Beverages 30.00
Door Push, Majors Cement 235.00
Door Push, Master Bread 60.00
Door Push, Perry's Beverages 16.00
Door Push, Pure Spring Ginger Ale, White, Black, Red & Yellow 46.00
Door Push, Red Rose Tea, Tin, Blue, Red, White .... 28.00 To 50.00
Door Push, Rex, Pocket Tin Picture 460.00
Door Push, Robin Hood Flour, Red, White, 3 x 30 In. 32.00
Door Push, Salada Tea, Porcelain, White, Blue & Black, 3 x 30 In 25.00
Door Push, Salada Tea, Porcelain, Yellow, Black, 3 x 30 In. 35.00
Door Push, Schweppes, Gold, Black, Green & White 52.00
Door Push, Sweetheart Flour, Heart Shape 105.00
Dr Pepper, Ice Chest 110.00
Dr Pepper, Pin Tray, Black Child Eating Watermelon, Oval, 3 In. 275.00
Drink Pick, Playboy Bunny, 25 Piece 15.00
Egg Carrier, Star, Rochester, N.Y., Wooden, Dividers, 1 Doz. 45.00
Fans are listed in their own category
Figure, Bainer Beer, Bartender, Tray, 1939, 7 In. 185.00
Figure, Bartles & James Wine Cooler, Cardboard, 6 Ft. 120.00
Figure, Capt. Crunch, Wiggle, Quaker 50.00
Figure, Checkers Cigars, Man In Checkered Pants, 1920s 2900.00
Figure, Dutch Boy Painter, On Rocks, National Lead, 4 1/2 In. 55.00
Figure, Hamm's Beer Bears, Frying Fish, Campfire, 5 1/2 In. 20.00
Figure, Johnny, Philip Morris, Die Cut, 14 In. 68.00
Figure, Nipper, Chalkware, RCA Victor His Master's Voice, 3 In. 18.00
Figure, Nipper, Papier–Mache, Painted Eyes, c.1920, 50 In. 1500.00
Figure, Nipper, Papier–Mache, RCA Victor, 35 In. 460.00
Figure, Nipper, Sitting, Rubber, 13 In. 385.00
Figure, Phosfbring Tonic, Bronze, England, 1900s, 15 In. 395.00

Figure, Red Goose, Chalkware, 12 In. 125.00
Figure, Reddy Kilowatt, Plastic, 5 In. 60.00
Figure, Reimers Pig Forceps, Davenport, Iowa, Glass, 7 In. 75.00
Figure, Scottie Dogs, Fleischmann Distilling, Black & White 150.00
Figure, Spark Plug, Vinyl, Champion, 1960s, 22 In. 65.00
Figure, Waiter, Brown Blatz Beer Bottle Body, Metal 25.00
Flashlight, Schlitz, Amber, Bottle Shape 5.00
Flatware Set, United Airlines 32.00
Flying Saucer, Lucky Charms, Green Plastic, 3 3/4 In. 8.00
Frisbee, Burger King 12.00
Funnel, Wheatlet For Breakfast, Tin 19.00
Glass, Arby, Ice Age, Caveman, 1981 .... 10.00
Glass, Burger King, Empire Strikes Back, 1990, 6 In. ....*Illus* 2.00
Glass, Burger King, Super Heroes, Batman, Wonder Woman, Barkseid 50.00
Glass, Burger King, The 1979 Burger Thing, 6 In. ....*Illus* .75
Glass, Dr Pepper, Fountain, Block Design 38.00
Glass, McDonald's, Great Muppet Caper, 1981, 6 In. ....*Illus* 1.00
Glass, McDonald, Mac Tonight 3.00
Gum Wrapper, Evermore Licorice, Crow Picture, 1947 .... 5.00
Gyro Top, Quaker, Capt. Crunch 25.00
Hammer, Coal, Sunshine Coal Co., Centerville, Iowa 18.00
Hat, McDonald's Restaurants, Cloth, Unused 1.25
Hat, Stetson, Plastic, Gift Certificate, Box, 3 In. 26.00
Hat, Texaco Fire Chief, Child's, 1950s 10.00
Holder, Schaefer Beer, Napkins & Stirrers, Plastic, 1940s 30.00
Holder, Towel, Mechanical, Chula Farmers Mercantile, Iron, 1910 .... 8.50
Hot Water Bottle, Marked Campbell, 1912, Sample, 2 1/2 In. 70.00
Humidor, Dixie Queen, Aunt Jemima, Black Woman 375.00
Humidor, Gene–Vail Cigar Co., Metal Lid, Glass 48.00
Humidor, Imperial Cut Cigar, Glass, Designs 150.00
Humidor, Twin Oaks Tobacco, Casket 65.00
Insignia, Keen Kutter, Iron 24.00
Jar, 3 Star Coffee, Sioux City, Iowa 125.00
Jar, Adam's Pepsin Tutti–Frutti Gum, Label 150.00
Jar, Ardor, Counter, Embossed, Glass Front, Tin Lid 90.00
Jar, Borden's Baby Brand Milk, Glass Insert, Tin Lid 35.00
Jar, Borden's, Mixing, Beater Top, Graduated Qt. 25.00
Jar, Horlick's Malted Milk, Aluminum, Red & Blue, 10 In. 65.00
Jar, Kis–Me–Gum, Glass .... 65.00 To 90.00
Jar, Lance, Glass, Cover 20.00
Jar, Tom's Peanuts, Counter, Blue Enamel Lettering, Red Knob 40.00
Jar, Tom's Toasted Peanuts, 8 1/4 x 7 1/4 In. 45.00
Jar, Tuxedo Tobacco, 1910 Stamp 95.00
Jug, Benton, Myers & Co., Wholesale Druggist, Cleveland, Oh. 50.00
Jug, Gilmour Thomson's Royal Stag Whiskey, Handle, 8 In. 45.00
Jug, Green River Tobacco, Pottery 350.00
Jug, Lionstone Distillery, Sitting Lion, Pub 12.00
Jug, Plymouth Gin, Fish, Pub 20.00
Jug, R. H. Macy & Co., New York, Brown Over White, Qt. 55.00
Jug, Ward Bros. Drug Co., Indianapolis, 3 Gal. 120.00
Jug, Wicklow Distillery, Old Irish Whiskey, Handle, 8 In. 45.00
Jump Rope, Little Sprout, Package .... 8.00 To 12.00
Keg, Beard Cinnamon, Camel Scene, Wooden, 10 Lb. 220.00
Key Fob, Goodyear Blimp, Gold Colored 15.00
Key Tag, Newark Shoe Mfg. Co., Silvered Brass Shoe 8.00
Kit, Cigarette, Bugler, Unused 30.00
Kit, Red Lobster, Lifelike, Movable Parts, Box, 1962, 15 In. 20.00
Kite, Lucky Charms 25.00
Label, Acme Cuban Cigar, Inner, Black & Gold 1.00
Label, Alaska Lager Beer 25.00
Label, American Protectorate Cigar, Inner, Pres. J. Monroe 6.00
Label, Argonaut Beer, San Francisco, 1930s, 4 x 5 In. 3.50
Label, Arthur Donaldson Cigar, Inner, Actor Of 1920s 7.00

Label, Big Wolf Cigar, Inner, Teeth Bared 5.00
Label, Castle Hall Cigar, Inner, Castle In Tropics 1.00
Label, Cranes Imported, Inner, Crane On Building, 2 For 5 Cents 1.00
Label, Dick Custer Cigar, Cowboy & Gun, 6 x 9 In. 6.00
Label, Dixie Boy Grapefruit, 9 x 9 In. 3.00
Label, El Kusto Cigar, Inner, Tropical Setting 2.50
Label, El Predomino, No. 2 Cigars, Romantic Couple, Woods, 4 In. 4.00
Label, Erin's Pride Cigar, Poet Robt. Emnet Of US & Ireland 10.00
Label, Evermore Licorice Gum, Crow Picture 5.00
Label, Flor DeLopez Cigars, Inner, Tobacco Leaves, Gold Coins 3.00
Label, Joe Sammy's Jams, 9 x 9 In. 3.00
Label, John Karl Cigars, Inner, Pillars Flank Medieval Man 3.00
Label, Kentucky Dew Whiskey, Louisville, Ky., 4 1/2 x 5 In. 3.00
Label, King Cotton Cigars, 3 Balls Of Cotton, 4 x 4 In. 3.00
Label, Knickerbocker Club Cigars, Colonial American, 4 In. 5.00
Label, La Victoria Cigars, Inner, Columbus, Men In New World 3.00
Label, Monte Carlo Beer, Southern Brewing Co., Houston, 1933 .... 68.00
Label, Mueller's Perfection Beer 22.00
Label, Normandy Rye Whiskey, Old Kentucky Distillery, 5 In. 2.50
Label, Old Vienna Beer 20.00
Label, Our Best Cigars, World Globe, Coins, 4 x 4 In. .... .50
Label, Pierre's Special Cigars, Inner, Letters, Crest 2.00
Label, Possum Sweet Potatoes, 9 x 9 In. 3.00
Label, Pulver–Hotchu, Tab Gum 15.00
Label, Round Up Cigar, Cowboy & Girl, Campfire, 6 x 9 In. 6.00
Label, Salzburg Cigars, Austrian City, Salzach River, 4 In. 1.00
Label, Sam Clay Whiskey, Julius Kessler & Co., Blue, 5 1/4 In. 3.50
Label, Sheboygan 10 Cents Cigar, 6 1/2 x 9 In. 3.50
Label, Silver Quarter Cigars, Silver Letters, Red, 4 In. 4.00
Label, Stick Of Gum, Pulver Hi–Lo Spearmint 15.00
Label, Storz Bock Beer, 1933–1936 .... 50.00
Label, Sunkist Lemon, Santa, Colorful, 1928, 9 x 12 In. 29.00
Label, Tom Mix Cigar, Pressed Design, 6 x 9 In. 12.00
Label, W. A. Gaines & Co. Whiskey, Green Border, 5 1/2 x 4 In. 5.50
Label, Wilson's Milk, Blue Ground, White Print, 3 1/2 In. .... .50
Label, Woodbury, Genuine Kentucky Whiskey, 4 x 5 In. 2.50
Label, Yosemite Root Beer, 1930s 2.50
Lamp, Budweiser, Clydesdale 30.00
Lazy Susan, Oak, Feder's Pompadour Skirt Protectors, 28 In. 250.00
Light Pull, Fleer's Pepsin Gum 30.00
Lipstick, Princess Pat, On Card, 1930s 5.00
Lunch Boxes are listed in their own category
Magic Show, Disappearing Hamburger Trick, 1985 .... 5.00
Mannequin, Fruit Of The Loom, Wears Housedress, 1930s 900.00
Map, Bob's Big Boy, California 9.00
Marker, Sidewalk, Grapette, Walk Safely, Brass, 4 In. Diam. 9.00
Matchbook, Stangl Pottery, Factory & Map Of Flemington, N. J. 10.00
Medal, Larkin Soap, 1925 .... 35.00
Menu Board, Butternut Bread, Fiberboard, Die Cut Loaf Top 90.00
Menu Board, Kayo Chocolate 65.00
Menu Board, Nature's Remedy, Tin Litho, Self–Framed, 23 In. 110.00
Menu Board, Orange Crush 65.00
Microscope, Wheaties Premium, Package 8.00

Advertising pocket mirrors range in size from 1 1/2 to 5 inches in diameter. Most of these mirrors were given away as advertising promotions.

Mirror, ABC Washer, Pocket 48.00
Mirror, Angelus Marshmallow, Pocket 45.00
Mirror, Aunt Jemima Breakfast Club, Celluloid, Round, Pocket 3.50
Mirror, Bailey's Pure Rye, Tri–Scene, Suggested Uses, Pocket 550.00
Mirror, Brothel, Pocket 75.00
Mirror, Brotherhood Overalls, Victorian Nude, Pocket 50.00

Mirror, Brunswick Records, Pocket 65.00
Mirror, Carmen Powder, Pocket 40.00
Mirror, Ceresota Flour, Pocket 95.00
Mirror, Checker Popcorn Confection, Pocket 57.50
Mirror, Continental Cubes Tobacco, Pocket 160.00
Mirror, Copperclad Stove, Pocket 30.00
Mirror, Crepe De Sante Rumpf, Pocket 27.00
Mirror, Electric Power Co., Philadelphia, Pocket 28.00
Mirror, First National Bank, Gallatin, Tenn., Pocket 70.00
Mirror, Fort Pitt Beer, Metal Frame 45.00
Mirror, Frank Street Hatters, Pocket 37.00
Mirror, Garland Stove, Pocket 22.00
Mirror, Good For 10 Cents, Elmyra, N.Y., Pocket 150.00
Mirror, Good For 10 Cents, Woman, Coldwater, Mich., Pocket 195.00
Mirror, High Times, Magazine Of High Society, 1970s, Pocket 60.00
Mirror, Hire's Root Beer, Woman Holding Mug, Pocket 450.00
Mirror, Horlick's Malted, Woman, Cow, Pocket .... 25.00 To 55.00
Mirror, Kimball Phonographs, Beveled, Pocket 40.00
Mirror, Kist, Get Kist Here, Pocket 55.00
Mirror, Kyonize Varnishes, Pocket 50.00
Mirror, Lava Soap, Soap Container Box, Early 1900s, Pocket 40.00
Mirror, Lischesky Dry Goods Co., Exclusive Ladies Store 40.00
Mirror, Litholin Collar & Wearwel Shoes, Pocket, Pair 110.00
Mirror, Luncheonette, New York City, Celluloid, Pocket 25.00
Mirror, Mascot Tobacco, Pocket 45.00
Mirror, Monument Co., Hawarden, Iowa, Pocket 65.00
Mirror, Morton Salt, Zodiac, Pocket 28.00
Mirror, Mountain States Telephone & Telegraph Co., Pocket 45.00
Mirror, New King Snuff, Celluloid, Early 1900s, 2 3/4 In. 50.00
Mirror, Old Dutch Cleanser, Pocket 25.00
Mirror, Old Reliable Coffee, Pocket 45.00
Mirror, Paperweight, Aetna 40.00
Mirror, Paperweight, Gold Standard Coals 50.00
Mirror, Paperweight, Phillips 66 Silver Anniversary 50.00
Mirror, Queen Shoes, Woman Standing, Pocket 75.00
Mirror, Red Goose Shoes, 1949, Pocket 5.00
Mirror, Red Wing, Pocket 150.00
Mirror, Remington Typewriter, Tin Lithograph, Motto, 3 3/8 In. 65.00
Mirror, Reverse Beach, Night Scene, Boardwalk, Pocket 200.00
Mirror, Savoy Theater, Metal Border, Pocket 35.00
Mirror, Sherwin Williams, Pocket 28.50
Mirror, Star Soap, Ball-In-Mouth Game On Reverse, Pocket 75.00
Mirror, Tailor Made Clothes Co., Chicago, Pocket 30.00
Mirror, Tom Thumb Family, Pocket 250.00
Mirror, Traveler's Insurance, Midnight Train, Pocket 65.00
Mirror, Union Made Cigars, Cigar Makers Union No. 393, Pocket 30.00
Mirror, Victor Talking Machine, Pocket 15.00
Mixer, Stalac, Elsie The Cow 12.00
Mixer, Thompson Homo. Malted Milk, Aluminum, 1 Cup 5.00
Money Clip, Phillips 66 .... 20.00
Money Clip, Rondo Premium Citrus Soda, Brass, 1 1/2 In. 15.00
Mortar & Pestle, Coors Beer, Small 35.00
Movie Viewer, 3 Comic Strips, Quaker Quisp, Miniature 100.00
Mug & Pitcher, Quaker Oats, F & F Label 6.00
Mug, Armour's Vigoral, China, Pink Carnation 17.00
Mug, Budweiser Beer 650.00
Mug, Burger King, Tony Tiger 10.00
Mug, Cambell Tomato Soup 12.50
Mug, Dad's Root Beer, 6 Piece 40.00
Mug, Falstaff Beer, Pressed, Raised Logo, 7 In., 4 Piece 28.00
Mug, Hamm's Bear-United, Aluminum, The Only Way To Fly 35.00
Mug, Hires Root Beer, Boy, Bob, Germany 180.00
Mug, Hires Root Beer, Ceramic, England, 4 In. 235.00

Mug, Hires, Stoneware, 6 In.	40.00
Mug, Hires, Stoneware, 7 In.	40.00
Mug, McDonald's Priority One, Glass, Large	12.00
Mug, Modox Soda, Indian Chief On Handle, 5 In.	33.00
Mug, Monastery Beer, Latrobe, Pa.	145.00
Mug, Musty Ale, Porcelain	32.00
Mug, Pickwick Rare Scotch Whiskey, Christmas, 1983, 1/4 Pt.	12.00
Mug, RCA Nipper & Phonograph, His Masters Voice	5.00
Mug, Royal Oak Stoves, Indian, 1907	75.00
Mug, Schlitz Beer, Woman On World	150.00
Mug, Triple XXX Root Beer, Pottery	12.50
Pack, Cigarettes, Pall Mall, Cork Tip, Gold Watch Certificate	50.00
Pail, American Breakfast Coffee, Green, Red, White, 5 Lb.	39.00
Pail, Armour Lard, Bail Handle, Paper Label, Wooden	195.00
Pail, Armour's Peanut Butter, Color Lithograph, Handle, 3 In.	50.00
Pail, Bowes Peanut Butter, Bowes Co., Ltd., Toronto, 1 Lb.	550.00
Pail, Bright & Early Coffee, Rooster Picture, Worn Paint	185.00
Pail, Buffalo Brand Salted Peanuts, 4 In.	200.00
Pail, Campbell Coffee, 4 Lb.	55.00
Pail, Clark's Peanut Butter, Canadian Outdoor Scenes	1050.00
Pail, Climax Peanut Butter	70.00
Pail, Dairy Maid Coffee, 3 Lb.	45.00
Pail, Dixie Queen Cut Plug	95.00
Pail, Eight Bros. Tobacco	50.00
Pail, Elephant Peanut Butter, Tin Lithograph, 11 In.	45.00
Pail, Fastmail Tobacco	450.00
Pail, Frontenac Peanut Butter, Red, Gold, White, Black, 3 1/2 In.	32.00
Pail, Gorden, Ironside Pure Lard, Fare Card, Bail, 6 In.	20.00
Pail, Hiawatha Tobacco, Wooden, 12 x 13 In.	82.50
Pail, Hill's Coffee, Orange, Black, Blue & White, 5 Lb.	39.00
Pail, Home Rendered Lard, Allentown, Pa., Pig Picture, 50 Lb.	54.00
Pail, Hood's Peanut Butter, Children On See-Saw	498.00
Pail, Jackie Coogan Brand Peanut Butter, Swing Handle	325.00
Pail, John Squire Pure Lard	12.00
Pail, Jolly Time Hulless Pop Corn, 1927	82.00
Pail, Luzianne Coffee, Black Mammy, Tin, 3 Lb.	75.00
Pail, Mammy Coffee, Picture Of Mammy, Lid & Handle	195.00
Pail, Meadowsweet Peanut Butter, 2 Lb.	110.00
Pail, Monarch Teeny Weeny Popcorn, Handle & Lid, 1920s	295.00
Pail, Mosemann Peanut Butter, Circus Animals, 1 Lb.	150.00
Pail, Naphey's Lard, Souvenir Centennial 1876, Small	90.00
Pail, Nash's Coffee, Fathers Of Confederation, 5 Lb.	52.00
Pail, Nigger Hair Tobacco, Tan	285.00
Pail, Nigger Hair Tobacco, Yellow	185.00 To 195.00
Pail, Norse Coffee, Red, Black, 9 x 7 In.	60.00
Pail, Oh Boy Peanut Butter, 2 Lb.	300.00
Pail, Old City Peanut Butter, Boy Fishing, Winter Scene	2530.00
Pail, Parrot Peanut Butter	2530.00
Pail, Peter Rabbit Peanut Butter, Peter & Pals, 3 1/2 In.	473.00
Pail, Red Feather Peanut Butter, Logo Over Feather, 3 1/4 In.	550.00
Pail, Red Seal Peanut Butter, Color Lithograph, Handle, 3 In.	120.00
Pail, Schepps Coconut, 7 1/2 In.	115.00
Pail, School Boy Peanut Butter	165.00
Pail, Shedd's Peanut Butter	12.00
Pail, Sunnyfield Lard, 4 Lb.	28.00
Pail, Supreme Peanut Butter, Children At Beach, 3 3/4 In.	550.00
Pail, Swift's Wizard Of Oz Peanut Butter, 5 Lb.	35.00
Pail, Taylor's Homemade Peanut Butter, Saskatchewan	440.00
Pail, Teddy Bear Peanut Butter, Toy Teddy Bear, 3 1/2 In.	1210.00
Pail, Teenie Weenie Peanut Butter, Monarch, Cartoon Kids	195.00
Pail, Teenie Weenie Popcorn, Cartoon Kids, 1920s	225.00
Pail, Toyland Peanut Butter, Color Lithograph, Handle, 4 In.	88.00
Pail, U.S. Marine Cut Plug, Nautical Images, Tin	220.00

◆◆◆◆◆◆◆◆◆◆◆◆◆◆◆◆◆◆◆◆

Smoke stains can be removed from a stone fireplace with an artgum eraser. Soot on the carpet in front of the fireplace can be removed with salt. Sprinkle dry salt on the soot, wait 30 minutes, then vacuum.

◆◆◆◆◆◆◆◆◆◆◆◆◆◆◆◆◆◆◆◆◆◆

Advertising, Plate, Troll Coal Mining Co.,
Lady's Head, 9 1/2 In.

Pail, Union Leader Tobacco	18.00
Palm Press, Kik Cola, Tin, Red, White, Black, France, 3 x 10 In.	33.00
Palm Press, Orange Crush, Thank You, Call Again, France, 11 In.	95.00
Patch, Dr Pepper, 10–2–4 Hot & Cold	10.00
Pattern, Doll's, Cream Of Wheat, Original Envelope	78.00
Pen Clip, Morton Salt	8.00
Pen Holder, Desk, Eastern Airlines	14.00
Pennant, Beloit Flour	20.00
Picnic Hamper, Heinz Famous Foods, Woven Splint, Cardboard	65.00
Pillow, Pillsbury's Funny Face Drink, Lefty Lemon, 14 In.	60.00
Pin, Chevrolet, Pinback, 1946	12.00
Pin, Heinz Pickles, Plastic, 1 In.	10.00 To 20.00
Pin, Horlicks Malted Milk, Full Lithograph, Celluloid	42.00
Pin, Kellogg's Cornflakes, Pinback, Celluloid, 1 1/2 In.	32.00
Pin, Pig, Squire Foods	100.00
Pin, Red Cap Candy Club, Member's, Euclid Candy Co., 1930s	5.00
Pin, Reddy Kilowatt, On Card	23.00
Pin, Schwinn Bicycle, Lapel	20.00
Pitcher, 4 Roses Black Beer	10.00
Pitcher, Kool–Aid, With 2 Mugs	15.00
Pitcher, Old Harper, Classic, Metal, Handle & Spout, 8 In.	75.00
Pitcher, Water, Canadian Club Whiskey, Black Woman On Front	32.00
Plaque, Brehms Brew, Celluloid, Round, c.1933, 9 In.	65.00
Plate, Anheuser–Busch, Victorian Woman, Flowing Hair, Tin, 1905	275.00
Plate, Hershey, Girl With Calf	20.00
Plate, Krug Brewing Co., 50th Anniversary, 1909, 10 In.	175.00
Plate, McDonald's, 4 Seasons, 4 Piece	20.00
Plate, Quality Bakery, Dunkirk, N.Y., Roses Decal, 8 In.	15.00
Plate, Troll Coal Mining Co., Lady's Head, 9 1/2 In. ....*Illus*	25.00
Platter, Sandwich, Horn & Hardart Baking Co., China, Oval	15.00
Platter, Seaboard Airline, Miami Pattern, 10 1/2 x 7 In.	325.00
Platter, Sparks Liver Pills, Mrs. Cleveland Picture, Porcelain	750.00
Pot Scraper, Mt. Penn Stoveworks, Tin	85.00
Pouch, Horse Shoe Plug Tobacco	35.00
Push Plate, Canada Dry Ginger Ale, Hand & Bottle	55.00
Rack, Baby Ruth Candy, Counter Top, Tin	140.00
Rack, Bag, Sprite Boy	350.00
Rack, Broom, Merkels Blu–Jay, Blue Jay On Each End, Tin	350.00
Rack, Buss Fuse, Tin, 1920s	175.00
Rack, Curtiss Baby Ruth Safety Pop, Wire, Tower Shape, Top Sign	65.00
Rack, Prince Albert Tobacco, Wire	38.00

Rack, Tom's Potato Chips, 3 Columns, 22 1/4 x 12 In. 40.00
Record, Pledge Of Allegiance, Red Skelton, 1969, Burger King 10.00
Ruler, Folding, Cleveland Bag Factory, Celluloid ....*Illus* 3.00
Ruler, Ohio Plate Glass, Dayton, Oh., Folding, 36 In. 1.00
Salt & Pepper shakers are listed in their own category
Scales are listed in their own category
Scarf, Roger Rabbit, McDonald's Logo, Japanese Writing, 1988 .... 30.00
Scraper, Foam, Dexheimer's Beer 25.00
Shaker, Cover, Thompson's Malted Milk, Aluminum 5.00
Sharpening Stone, Bull Brand's Feeds, Cow Lithograph 16.00
Shelves, Display, Vicks, Enameled Tin, Family Picture, 1940 .... 35.00
Shoe Stick, Kirby & Bro., N.Y., Boxwood, Brass, Ivory, 19 In. 140.00
Shoehorn, LMS Shoe Co., Cherokee, Iowa, Iron 1.25
Shoehorn, Schoenecker Princess, Shoe, Lithograph, Colorful 40.00
Shot Glass, A. M. Smith, Merry Christmas, Happy New Year 15.00
Shot Glass, Astor Wine Co., San Francisco & Hornbrook, Etched 34.50
Shot Glass, Bowler's Club Very Old Rye, W. Stastny, Chicago 36.50
Shot Glass, Chester Whiskey, Cahnmann & Co., Rochester, N.Y. 20.00
Shot Glass, Detrick's Whiskey 35.00
Shot Glass, Eastern Airlines 2.00
Shot Glass, Green Bell Whiskey, Reinhold Kroll, Etched, Small 16.50
Shot Glass, H. Guggenheimer & Bros., Gold Rim, Etched 30.00
Shot Glass, Jos. Agress Wines & Liquors, New York, Gold Rim 15.00
Shot Glass, Kentucky Tavern Straight Whiskey, Louisville 15.00
Shot Glass, Paul Jones Highball, Script Inside Wreath 25.00
Shot Glass, Pederson Mercantile Co., St. Paul, Amethyst 20.00
Shot Glass, Stag Hotel, Fluted Base, Etched, Amethyst 25.00
Shot Glass, Zane Liquor Co., Zanesville, Ohio, Barrel Shape 16.50
Sign, 7–Up, Cardboard, 5 x 7 In. 8.00
Sign, 7–Up, Easel Type, Colorful, 1948, 1 x 12 In. 38.00
Sign, 7–Up, Fresh Up, Cardboard, Hanger 25.00
Sign, 7–Up, Sold Here, Rectangular, Tin Lithograph, 18 In. 44.00
Sign, 7–Up, Tin, 12 x 19 In. 85.00
Sign, Acme Beer, Fortune Wheel, Cardboard, Framed, 30 x 24 In. 55.00
Sign, Adam Hats, Benny Goodman, Photograph, Framed, 9 x 11 In. 26.00
Sign, American Airlines, E. Kauffer, Paper, 1948, 30 x 40 In. 175.00
Sign, American Beauty, Adjustable Iron, Paper, 1938, 13 x 20 In. 65.00
Sign, American Oil Motor Club, Flame Logo, Tin, 24 x 27 In. 25.00
Sign, American Stamps, We Give, Redeem, Red, White, Blue, 10 In. 35.00
Sign, Anheuser–Busch, Indians, Raft, Framed, 5 x 15 In. 115.00
Sign, Ansco Film, Save 15 Cents, Red, White, Blue, 10 x 16 In. 50.00
Sign, Apothecary, Zinc Mortar & Pestle, Worn Gilding, 31 In. 450.00
Sign, Arbuckle's Coffee, It Smells Good, Tin Lithograph, 27 In. 175.00
Sign, Arbuckles Coffee, Pure, Wholesome, 27 In. 325.00
Sign, Arm & Hammer Soda, Fish Jumping Out Of Water, Frame, 1902 .... 90.00
Sign, Arrow Oil Corporation, Wooden, Black, Gold, 12 x 120 In. 80.00
Sign, Ask For Quaker State Motor Oil, Tin, Round, 24 In. 78.00

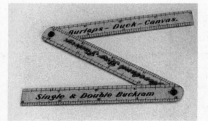

◆◆◆◆◆◆◆◆◆◆◆◆◆◆◆◆◆◆◆◆◆◆

Never wash lacquered wood.
Just wipe it clean with a damp
cloth. Water could seep into
the base wood and cause
damage.

◆◆◆◆◆◆◆◆◆◆◆◆◆◆◆◆◆◆◆◆◆◆

Advertising, Ruler, Folding, Cleveland Bag
Factory, Celluloid

Advertising, Sign, Cletrac Crawler Tractors, 2 Sides,
18 x 22 In.

Advertising, Sign, Squire's Pig,
c.1906, 19 3/4 x 24 1/2 In.

Sign, Ask For Veedol Motor Oils, Porcelain, 28 x 22 In. 150.00
Sign, Athena Underwear, Scheffler, Paper, 1914, 19 x 16 In. 150.00
Sign, Atkins Silver Steel Saws, Reverse Painted, 19 x 10 In. 350.00
Sign, Atlantic Ale & Beer, Waiter With Tray, Porcelain, 38 In. 795.00
Sign, Avalon Cigarettes, Lady Smiling, Paper, 1941, 15 x 10 In. 50.00
Sign, Ayer's Hair Vigor, Glass, 13 x 11 1/4 In. 187.00
Sign, Badger Tire, Tin, Framed, 17 x 34 In. 2400.00
Sign, Baker's Delight Baking Powder, Black Woman, 12 x 14 In, ... 22.00
Sign, Baxter's Cigars, Embossed Tin, 13 1/2 In. 155.00
Sign, Beechnut Peanut Butter, Paper, Framed, 14 x 24 1/2 In. 350.00
Sign, Ben Hur Cigars, Biblical Scene, Wood, 1904, 15 x 21 In. 165.00
Sign, Big Ben Smoking Tobacco, Stallion, Paper, 14 x 20 In. 45.00
Sign, Black Cat Fireworks, Paper, 35 x 24 In. 30.00
Sign, Booster Cigars, Paper, Framed, 21 x 29 In. 1350.00
Sign, Bradley & Metcalf Boots & Shoes, Porcelain, 27 In. 358.00
Sign, Brown Shoe Co., White House Queen, Cardboard, 32 In. 303.00
Sign, Bubble Up Soda, Embossed Tin Lithograph, 27 1/4 In. 88.00
Sign, Buck's Oil, Barrel, Porcelain, Flange, 18 x 28 In. 1100.00
Sign, Buckeye Beer, Tin, 15 x 20 In. 60.00
Sign, Budweiser Draught Beer, Enamel On Steel, 1937, 17 x 7 In. 225.00
Sign, Budweiser, Light–Up, Rotating .... 650.00 To 750.00
Sign, Bull Durham Tobacco, Cardboard, Lithograph, 22 In. 200.00
Sign, Bull Durham Tobacco, My It Am Sweet Tastin', 20 x 30 In. 195.00
Sign, Cadillac Sales & Service, Porcelain, 2 Sides, 42 In. 1350.00
Sign, Cadillac, Carefree Driving Ahead, Paper. 1954, 28 x 42 In. 325.00
Sign, Camels Cigarettes, Aviator, Paper, 1942, 11 x 21 In. 10.00
Sign, Cavalier Cigarettes, Tin, 11 x 19 In. 30.00
Sign, Centlivre Tonic, Cardboard, 12 x 22 In. 60.00
Sign, Champion Spark Plugs, Porcelain, 13 x 30 In. 950.00
Sign, Chesterfield Cigarettes, Embossed Tin, 12 x 18 In. 135.00
Sign, Chesterfield, Pack O'pleasure, Hiker, 1935, 28 x 42 In. 175.00
Sign, Chevrolet Sales & Service, Porcelain, 2 Sides 625.00
Sign, Chevrolet, 42 In. 350.00
Sign, Citroen Automobile, Linen Back, Paper, 47 1/2 x 32 In. 165.00
Sign, Clark Spool Cotton, Tin, 13 3/4 x 19 2/3 In. 170.00
Sign, Cletrac Crawler Tractors, 2 Sides, 18 x 22 In. ....*Illus* 2000.00
Sign, Cockshutt Card Factory, Glass, Wooden Frame, 12 x 23 In. 185.00
Sign, Cole's Peruvian Bark Wild Cherry Bitters, Tin, 16 In. 450.00
Sign, College Club Beverages, Boy, Hot Dog, Cardboard 10 In. 22.50
Sign, Collins Axe, Collinsville, Ct., Cardboard, Embossed, 20 In. 55.00
Sign, Comfy Slippers, Tin Lithograph, Stand–Up 1210.00

Sign, Commonwealth Distiller, Mother–of–Pearl Windows 8250.00
Sign, Conoco Gasoline, Porcelain, Colonial Soldier, 25 In. 2300.00
Sign, Consumer's Beer, Round, 14 In. 50.00
Sign, Cook's Beer, Embossed Fiberboard, 13 1/2 x 11 In. 35.00
Sign, Cresyl Regular, Porcelain, Triangular 175.00
Sign, Curt Distilleries Whiskey, Tin, Framed, 12 x 16 In. 125.00
Sign, Dad's Root Beer, Paper, 1950s, 9 x 11 In. 6.00
Sign, DeLaval Cream Separators, Cows, Tin, 1910, 22 x 33 In. 900.00
Sign, DeLaval, Cow & Calf, Cutout, Tin Lithograph, 3 1/2 & 2 In. 155.00
Sign, DeLaval, Porcelain, 12 x 16 In. 95.00
Sign, Diamond Oil, Ladies Room 100.00
Sign, Dig Em Frog, Figure, Cardboard, Stand–Up, 3 1/2 In. 5.00
Sign, Dixie Gasoline, Power To Pass, Porcelain, 30 In. 145.00
Sign, Dolly Madison Cigars, Tin, 6 x 20 In. 20.00
Sign, Dr B. J. Kendal's Tonic & Blood Purifier, 1890, 5 x 24 In. 22.00
Sign, Dr Pepper Soda, Tin, 20 x 34 In. 10.00
Sign, Dr Pepper, Good For Life, Embossed Tin Lithograph, 24 In. 165.00
Sign, Dr Pepper, Lift For Life, 2 Sides, Cardboard, 25 x 15 In. 22.50
Sign, Dr Pepper, Red, White & Brown, Unused, Canada, 18 x 54 In. 95.00
Sign, Dr Pepper, Tin, 20 x 7 In. 10.00
Sign, Drink Moxie, Fountain Jockey, Paper, c.1920, 19 x 19 In. 210.00
Sign, Drink Mt. Cabin, Embossed Tin, 18 x 12 In. 250.00
Sign, Drive The New DeSoto Automatic, Paper, Folds, 68 x 30 In. 125.00
Sign, Drummond Thick Tobacco, Paper Lithograph, Framed, 16 In. 60.00
Sign, Dupont Gun Powder, Tin Lithograph, Hunters, 31 x 27 In. 7500.00
Sign, E. Scott Payne Co., Hardware, Lithograph, Framed, 18 In. 105.00
Sign, Eagle Motor Oil, 20 Cents A Quart, Porcelain, 8 x 16 In. 450.00
Sign, Eagle, Watch In Beak, Copper, 34–In. Wingspan 1430.00
Sign, Early Times Whiskey, Old Distillery, Plaster, 23 x 29 In. 350.00
Sign, Elizabeth Arden, Powders, Debutante, 1937, 25 x 37 In. 250.00
Sign, Elsie The Borden Cow, Tin Lithograph, 3 x 3 Ft. 250.00
Sign, Esslinger Premium Beer, Light–Up, Reverse Glass, 15 In. 132.00
Sign, Esso Credit Card, Porcelain, 2 Sides 150.00
Sign, Eveready Batteries, Tin Lithograph, Beveled Edges, 11 In. 39.00
Sign, EVM Bicycle & Auto Parts, Paper, 1910, 27 x 19 In. 225.00
Sign, Eye, Reverse On Glass, Optician's, 18 In. 577.50
Sign, Fatima Cigarettes, Lady In Veil, Tin, Oval, 16 x 18 In. 1500.00
Sign, Feed Him Ken–L–Ration, E. A. Stuerken, 1930, 20 x 28 In. 150.00
Sign, Feigenspan, P. G. N., Beer, Ales, Glass, Framed, 7 x 12 In. 29.00
Sign, Fellow Florists Of America, Press Board, Electric, 18 In. 300.00
Sign, Finck's Overalls, Pig, Paper Lithograph, 59 1/4 In. 132.00
Sign, Finck's Overalls, Wear Like A Pig's Nose, 23 1/2 In. 165.00
Sign, Fish Shape, Carved From Log, Lures On Both Sides, 39 In. 875.00
Sign, Fisk Tubes & Tires, Porcelain, 5 Ft. 225.00
Sign, Flor De Franklin 5 Cent Cigar, Canoe, 21 7/8 x 15 In. 495.00
Sign, Ford Batteries, Sales, Porcelain, 2 Sides, 15 x 24 In. 575.00
Sign, Ford Genuine Parts, Porcelain, 2 Sides, 24 In. 303.00
Sign, Garcia Cigar, 5 Cents, Round, 5 In. 10.00
Sign, Gilbey's Wines & Spirits, Porcelain, 2 Sides, 16 x 21 In. 175.00
Sign, Globe Hotel, Rooms 35 Cents & Up, Wood, 41 x 11 1/2 In. 20.00
Sign, Got What It Takes, Camels, Test Pilot, 1946, 22 x 11 In. 75.00
Sign, Granite State Fire Insurance, Reverse On Glass, 25 In. 150.00
Sign, Grant's Cherry Whisky, Tavern Scene, Tin, 15 In. 72.00
Sign, Grape–Nuts, School Girl & St. Bernard, Tin, 20 x 30 In. 925.00
Sign, Grapette Soda, Embossed Tin, Oval, 27 In. 50.00
Sign, Great American Insurance, Reverse Painted, 19 In. 27.50
Sign, Greyhound, White Dog, Porcelain, 2 Sides, 36 In. 495.00
Sign, Grizzly Gasoline, Tin, 3 x 2 Ft. 825.00
Sign, Gulf No–Nox, Gas Pump .... 28.00 To 35.00
Sign, H. D. Foss & Co. Chocolates, Tin, 1905, 28 1/2 x 22 1/2 In. 475.00
Sign, Hand, Whistle Soda Pop, Screwed To Post, Iron, 10 1/2 In. 295.00
Sign, Happy Foot, McGregor Health Socks, Plastic, Easel, 12 In. 30.00
Sign, Harley–Davidson Motorcycle, Framed, 1928, 57 x 40 1/2 In. 3500.00

Sign, Hartford Insurance, Self–Framed, Tin, 24 In. .... 340.00 To 500.00
Sign, Hauswaldts Chocolate, Woman, Chocolate, 1905, 31 x 19 In. 175.00
Sign, Havoline Wax Free Oil, Porcelain, 2 Sides, Flange, 24 In. 750.00
Sign, Hellman Bock Beer, Ram Exiting Keg, Paper, 24 x 18 In. 27.50
Sign, Hershey's Ice Cream, Tin, 2 x 4 Ft. 125.00
Sign, Highland Beer, Bottles, Glass, Tin, 14 x 19 In. 145.00
Sign, Hires, Die Cut Bottle, 5 Ft. 325.00
Sign, Honest Scrap Tobacco, Porcelain, 16 x 22 In. 625.00
Sign, Hot Lemonade, Sunkist Lemons, Paper, 1932, 11 x 21 In. 60.00
Sign, Howe Scale, Woman On Scale, Paper, c.1889, 14 x 28 1/2 In. 330.00
Sign, Hudson & Manhattan, Porcelain, 24 x 24 In. 550.00
Sign, Hunt Club Shoes, Man On Horse, Tin Lithograph, 24 In. 130.00
Sign, Ice Cream Cone, 6 Ft. 4510.00
Sign, Ice Cream Cone, Figural, Jeweled Copper, 33 x 12 In. 880.00
Sign, Indian Motorcycle, Lady Rider, 1913, 27 1/2 x 18 In. 3100.00
Sign, Inecto Hair Dye, Cardboard, 18 Hairdos, 1925, 12 In. 45.00
Sign, Ingersoll Dollar Watch, Figural, Tin, 2 Sides, 34 In. 385.00
Sign, J. P. Davis, Primitive, Black & Green Letters, 8 x 24 In. 190.00
Sign, Jax Beer, 2 Sides, Porcelain, 3 x 5 In. 550.00
Sign, JB Edlington & Co., Ltd., Cast Iron, 22 x 1 3/4 In. 28.00
Sign, Jenkinson's Tobacco, Irregular, Wooden, 32 x 19 In. 450.00
Sign, Jeweler's, Porcelain, 2 Sides, 1890s 465.00
Sign, Johnson Seahorse, Reverse Glass, Electric, 10 x 6 In. 275.00
Sign, Kadee's Cigarettes, 9 Nude Women, Paper, 23 x 17 In. 850.00
Sign, Keen Kutter, Clock, Yellow, Light–Up 425.00
Sign, Keil Tea, Solid Aluminum, 27 In. 125.00
Sign, Kendall's Spavin Cure, Chromolithograph, 16 x 20 In. 110.00
Sign, Kessler Brewery, Tin, Spanish–American Gunboat Picture 1800.00
Sign, Kildow's Old Stock Cigars, Lithograph, 1910, 7 x 14 In. 14.00
Sign, King's Candies, For American Queens, 14 x 18 In. 650.00
Sign, Kodak, Bathing Beauty With Camera, Cardboard, 21 x 62 In. 210.00
Sign, Kodak, We Photograph Anything, Supplies, Tin, 1961 .... 675.00
Sign, L & M Cigarettes, Embossed Tin, 12 x 18 In. 135.00
Sign, Lackawanna Coal Office, Wooden, 1890, 72 x 17 1/2 In. 1850.00
Sign, Lakeside Bouquet Whiskey, Glass, 15 1/2 x 19 1/2 In. 3850.00
Sign, Larkin Soap Co., Factory To Family, Pine, 10 x 28 In. 42.00
Sign, Lawrence's Paint, Figural, Tiger's Head, Porcelain, 23 In. 205.00
Sign, Leisy Beer, Reverse–Painted Glass, 2 x 3 Ft. 600.00
Sign, Life Saver Cough Drops, Colonial Man, Paper Litho, 21 In. 33.00
Sign, Lime Cola, Tin, Mobile, Alabama, 24 x 32 In. 120.00
Sign, Lipton's Cocoa, Woman & Pot, Tin, 13 1/4 x 9 In. 38.50
Sign, Little Orphans Cigars, 50, String Hanger, 1890, 7 x 4 In. 24.00
Sign, Loreley Whiskey, Reverse Painting, 19 1/2 x 22 1/2 In. 5500.00
Sign, Lowenbrau, Lion, Celluloid, 10 x 14 In. 25.00
Sign, Lucky Strike Cigarettes, Tin, 19 1/2 x 1 1/4 In. 25.00
Sign, Lucky Strike, 2 To 1, Red, Yellow, Green, 1939, 11 x 14 In. 75.00
Sign, Lyons Tea, Black, Silver, France, 10 x 7 In. 60.00
Sign, M. Knoble, Dressmaker, Pine, Black, Red, White, 9 x 24 In. 200.00
Sign, Mail Pouch Tobacco, Nuts To You, Cardboard, 21 x 14 In. 15.00
Sign, Mail Pouch, Porcelain, 6 Ft. 190.00
Sign, Marathon Gasoline, 6 1/2 Ft. 375.00
Sign, Marlboro, Cowboy & Horses, Tin, 16 x 22 In. 10.00
Sign, Marvel Cigarettes, Pack Of Cigarettes, 1940s, 16 x 10 In. 20.00
Sign, Marvel Cigarettes, Tin, 6 Colors, 10 x 13 1/2 In. 45.00
Sign, Mavix Chocolate Drink, Tin, c.1930, 27 x 10 In. 75.00
Sign, Meadow Gold Ice Cream, Red & Blue, Neon, 16 In. 165.00
Sign, Meerschaum Tobacco, Mother, Kittens, Cardboard, 5 x 18 In. 85.00
Sign, Meritu Bread, Cowboy On Horse, Tin, 35 x 24 In. 1550.00
Sign, Michelin Tire Pump, Michelin Man Riding Pump, 3 x 2 Ft. 1800.00
Sign, Michelob, Electric, 12 x 16 In. 20.00
Sign, Miller HiLife, Wis. License Plate Design, Box, 23 x 11 In. 20.00
Sign, Mobil Gas, Pegasus, Hanging, 6 Ft. 150.00
Sign, Model Tobacco, Porcelain, 12 x 36 In. 185.00

Sign, Mother's Best Flour, Light–Up, Reverse On Glass, 16 In. 175.00
Sign, National Mazda Auto Lamps, Tin Lithograph, 13 x 24 In. 165.00
Sign, Niagara Shoes, Multicolored, Tin, 1910, 14 x 19 In. 150.00
Sign, Niagara Shoes, Scene Of Falls, c.1910, 19 x 8 1/2 In. 165.00
Sign, Nichol 5 Cent Kola, Multicolor, 1930s, 12 x 36 In. 100.00
Sign, Nichol Kola, 5 Cent Taste Sensation, Tin, 1936, 8 x 24 In. 19.00
Sign, Nickel Kings Cigars, Cardboard, 16 x 18 In. 35.00
Sign, North Carolina Regular Grade, Porcelain, Red, White, Round 200.00
Sign, Novy Norwich Union Fire Ins. Society, 6 x 12 In. 95.00
Sign, Nu–Grape Soda, Yellow, Red, Bottle, Tin, Horizontal, 14 In. 160.00
Sign, Nugget Shoe Polish, Cardboard, Multicolored, 20 x 29 In. 38.00
Sign, O. F. Roddan & Co., Free Standing Brass, 4 x 21 3/4 In. 5.00
Sign, Oldsmobile, Crest, Porcelain, 1 Side, Round, 18 In. 1050.00
Sign, Oldsmobile, Lithograph On Canvas, 1910, 33 x 23 In. 1900.00
Sign, Oldsmobile, Porcelain, 42 In. 350.00
Sign, Optician, Eyeglass Shape 1500.00
Sign, Orange Crush, Bottle Cap Shape, 1950s, 19 In. 55.00
Sign, Orange Crush, Tin, 1940, 22 In. 155.00
Sign, Orphan Boy Smoking Tobacco, Donkey, Paper, 19 x 13 In. 35.00
Sign, Pa. Dutch Birch Beer, Celluloid Over Tin, 1955, 9 x 15 In. 45.00
Sign, Pabst Beer Steins, Plaque Ad Behind, 2 1/2 x 12 x 14 In. 40.00
Sign, Pabst Blue Ribbon, Electric, Engine, Wheels Turn 200.00
Sign, Parker Pen, Carved Wooden Pen, Pencil, Framed, 16 In. 550.00
Sign, Pelican Cigarettes, Pelican, Paper, 31 x 23 In. 357.00
Sign, Pepo Worm Syrup, 25 Cents At Druggists, Tin, 1920, 12 In. 225.00
Sign, Perry's Beverage, Tin, Black Cherry Bottle, 14 x 20 In. 30.00
Sign, Peter Paul Mounds, Native Climber, 1940, 29 x 45 In. 150.00
Sign, Pfieffer's Beer, 1935 Derby Winner, Tin, 11 x 14 In. 175.00
Sign, Philip Morris, Embossed Johnny, Tin, 12 x 14 In. 45.00
Sign, Phillips 66, World's Finest Oil, Shield, 11 x 22 In. 650.00
Sign, Pickwick Ale, 3 Gents, Self–Framed, Tin, 22 1/4 x 28 In. 745.00
·Sign, Picobac Tobacco, Image Of Pocket Tin, 72 1/2 x 36 In. 82.50
Sign, Piedmont Cigarettes, Porcelain, Blue & White, 46 In. 88.00
Sign, Piel Bros. Beer, Elves With Beer Bottles, Tin, 13 In. 465.00
Sign, Plymouth Service, Porcelain, 2 Sides, 16 x 20 In. 1150.00
Sign, Polly Stamps, Enamel Over Metal, 2 Sides, 28 x 20 In. 50.00
Sign, Polly Stamps, Tin, 1940s, 17 x 21 In. 10.00
Sign, Pontiac Service, Indian Silhouette, Porcelain, 41 3/4 In. 125.00
Sign, Poppler's Cigars, Tin, 10 In. 145.00
Sign, Pozzoni's Dove Complexion Powder, 6 1/2 x 10 In. 40.00
Sign, Pride Of World, Warwick Cycle Co., Paper, 21 1/2 x 15 In. 440.00
Sign, Prince Albert, National Joy Smoke, c.1925, 21 x 27 In. 325.00
Sign, Providence Insurance, Washington, Tin, Framed, 24 x 17 In. 210.00
Sign, Pure Oil Tire & Battery, Tin, Round Logo Top, 16 In. 100.00
Sign, Railway Express Agency, Diamond Shape, Porcelain, 1949 .... 950.00
Sign, Raleigh Cigarettes, Couple Dancing, Paper, 18 x 12 In. 65.00
Sign, Rambler Parts–Service, 2 Sides, 42 In. 550.00
Sign, RC Cola, Die Cut Bottle, Tin, 5 Ft. 350.00
Sign, Red Crown Ethyl, Porcelain, 30 In. 400.00
Sign, Red Goose Shoes, Dog In Doghouse, Cardboard, 12 x 17 In. 125.00
Sign, Red Goose Shoes, Neon Light–Up, 8 Ft. 2000.00
Sign, Red Rose Tea, 2 Sides, Tin, Red, White & Black, 30 x 6 In. 115.00
Sign, Red Rose Tea, Red, White & Green, Tin, 1930s, 12 x 16 In. 60.00
Sign, Reddy Kilowatt, Porcelain, 36 x 30 In. 225.00
Sign, Redford's Celebrated Tobacco, Planter, 20 x 25 In. 125.00
Sign, Reinken's Havana Cigars, Pretty Girl, Tin, 13 3/4 In. 45.00
Sign, Reis Union Suits, Trolley, 22 x 12 In. 85.00
Sign, Remington Shotshell, Paper, 1960 .... 10.00
Sign, Royal Bengals Cigars, Trolley, 22 x 12 In. 55.00
Sign, Royal Crown Cola, Tin, 1941 .... 250.00
Sign, Ruppert's Beer, Reverse Glass, Dated 1908, 16 In. 225.00
Sign, Salada Tea, Porcelain, Purple, Yellow, Black, 15 x 3 In. 95.00
Sign, Seagram's Whiskey, Horse & Jockey, 1905, 51 1/2 x 37 In. 880.00

Sign, Seidenberg & Co. Cigars, Reverse Glass, 21 1/2 x 27 In. 1750.00
Sign, Shakespeare, One For Breakfast, Die Cut, 1920, 20 x 30 In. 450.00
Sign, Shaw's Pure Malt, Servant & Woman, Self–Framed, Tin 2200.00
Sign, Shell Motor Oil, Red Shell, Porcelain, 10 x 14 In. 750.00
Sign, Sherwin Williams, Porcelain, Embossed, 19 x 36 In. 400.00
Sign, Sherwin Williams, Porcelain, Flange, 16 x 22 In. 110.00
Sign, Singer Sewing Machine, Tin Lithograph, Calendar, 18 In. 450.00
Sign, Sir Walter Raleigh Pipe Smoking, Pocket, Tin, Pipe 525.00
Sign, Soda, Two Straw, Glass Jewels, Cutout Lettering, 32 In. 1925.00
Sign, Southbend, Fish & Feel Fit, 30 x 50 In. 800.00
Sign, Southern Agriculturist Theft Service, Tin, 7 1/2 x 9 In. 15.00
Sign, Southern Comfort, Reverse On Mirror, Framed, 24 x 21 In. 75.00
Sign, Spalding Bread, Tin, 33 x 69 In. 200.00
Sign, Spratt's Dog Food, Products, Dogs, Paper, 1920, 28 x 10 In. 75.00
Sign, Squire's Pig, c.1906, 19 3/4 x 24 1/2 In. ....*Illus* 2255.00
Sign, Squirt, Tin, Colorful, Early 1940s, 4 x 17 In. 25.00
Sign, St. Julien Tobacco, Fragrant Pipe, Porcelain, 58 1/2 In. 176.00
Sign, Stamper Feeds, Tin, 1940s, 20 x 28 In. 15.00
Sign, Star Tobacco 10 Cents, Embossed, Tin, Framed, 1920s, 10 In. 275.00
Sign, Star Tobacco, Porcelain, Yellow Ground, 24 In. 175.00
Sign, Stetson Hat Man, Easel Back, 9 x 11 In. 16.00
Sign, Sunny Brook, Pure Food Whiskey, Glass, 15 1/2 x 8 In. 65.00
Sign, Sweeper–Vac, 3–In–1 Vacuum, Paper, c.1910, 51 1/2 x 33 In 110.00
Sign, Sweet–Orr Clothing, Porcelain, Yellow Ground, 27 In. 155.00
Sign, Sylvan Grove Whiskey, Reverse Glass, 19 1/2 x 33 1/2 In. 3300.00
Sign, Taylor Freeze, Ice Cream Cone Shape, Light–Up, 2 Ft. 50.00
Sign, Texaco, Black T, Porcelain, Round, 16 In. 295.00
Sign, Texaco, Certified Lubrication, Porcelain, 9 x 39 In. 450.00
Sign, Texaco, Porcelain, No Smoking, 1942 .... 125.00
Sign, Tiolene, Pure Oil Co., Oil Bottle, Raised Logo, 18 In. 65.00
Sign, Trade, Humpback Whale, Iron Hanger, Painted Pine, 31 In. 3850.00
Sign, Triple Smoking Pleasure, Chesterfield, Paper, 21 x 22 In. 185.00
Sign, U.S. Tires, Porcelain, 2 Sides, Round, 24 In. 275.00
Sign, U.S. F. & G., Shield Shape, 2 Children, Cardboard, 1900 .... 1150.00
Sign, UMC Cartridges, Paperboard Lithograph, 11 3/4 In. 132.00
Sign, Union Gasoline Unifuel, Porcelain, 28 In. 100.00
Sign, Van Houten's Cocoa, Louvered, Painted, 10 1/2 In. 132.00
Sign, Victor Records, Enrico Caruso, 16 In. 475.00
Sign, Virginia Dare Beverages, Cardboard, 10 x 7 In. 15.00
Sign, Ward's Orange Lemon Lime Crush, Tin, 1920, 16 In. 225.00
Sign, We Do Our Own Pickling, Reverse On Glass, 13 x 9 In. 165.00
Sign, We Give S & S Green Stamps, Electric 35.00
Sign, Weatherbird Shoes, Paper, 1950, 10 x 17 In. 8.00
Sign, Western Ammunition, Paper Lithograph, Framed, 43 In. 176.00
Sign, Whistle Soda Pop, Sweater Girl, 1950s, 16 x 22 In. 25.00
Sign, Whitely Vertical Cut Mower, Muncie, Horses, 22 x 29 In. 200.00
Sign, Winchester, Guns & Ammunition, Tin, 14 x 18 In. 600.00
Sign, Winchester, Hanging Fowl, Tin Lithograph On Wood, 36 In. 1110.00
Sign, Wm. S. Bickford, Gilded Boot & Shoe, Mica, 32 x 36 In. 6600.00
Sign, Wm. J. Oliver Plows, Steel Lithograph, 18 1/2 In. 110.00
Sign, Wolf's Head Motor Oil, Oil Can Shape, Tin, 2 Sides 40.00
Sign, Won–Up Fruit Juice, Tin Lithograph, Beveled Edges, 13 In. 50.00
Sign, Wonder Bread, Porcelain, 20 x 8 1/2 In. 110.00
Sign, Wrigley's Spearmint Gum, Woman, Bonnet, 1940, 11 x 28 In. 125.00
Sign, Wrigley's, Street Car, Color, 1950s, 11 x 21 In. 46.00
Sign, Wrigley's, Tin Lithograph, Beveled Edges, 13 In. 77.00
Sign, Wynola, Easel Back, Die Cut, 26 x 15 In. 57.00
Sign, XXX Root Beer, Oval, Curved, Porcelain 235.00
Sign, Yankee Girl Chewing Tobacco, Embossed Tin, 13 1/2 In. 60.00
Sign, Yellow Stone Whiskey, Lady, Bottle, Waterfall, 16 x 21 In. 95.00
Slide, Magic Lantern, Dr. Hess Poultry Pan–A–Ce–A 12.50
Slide, Magic Lantern, Easy Washer 12.50
Soap, Doll Shape, Andrew Jergens & Co., Cinci., Box, 4 1/2 In. 95.00

Socks, Burger King, Rhinestone Accents 7.00
Spoon Set, Measuring, Robin Hood Flour, 4 Piece 4.00
Spoon, Baby's, Gerber 7.00
Spoon, Chiclets, Pierced Brass 25.00
Spoon, Medicine, Duffy's Pure Malt Whiskey, Glass 55.00
Spy Kit, Quaker Capt. Crunch 40.00
Sticker, Where's The Beef, 1984, Wendy's 2.00
Stickpin, Atlas Flour, Top Bow, Die Cut Brass Of Flour Bag 10.00
Stickpin, Case, Eagle On Globe 20.00
Stickpin, Dr. Bell's Pine Tar Honey, Cures Colds 12.00
Stickpin, International Harvester Co. 15.00
Stickpin, Keen Kutter, Ax With Handle, Gold 110.00
Stickpin, Libby's Food Products, Brass Die Cut, 1900s 15.00
Stickpin, P & O, Canton, Plow Shape 20.00
Stickpin, Reddy Kilowatt .... 10.00 To 38.00
Sunglasses, Mac Tonight, Adult 9.00
Sunglasses, White Castle, Willis 3.00
Tankard Set, Leisy Brewing Company, Peoria, Ill., 7 Mugs 175.00
Tap Head, Schmidt City Club Beer, 3-Colored Enameled Design 85.00
Tea Set, Gold Over Eggshell, Nautilus Shape, Geo. Bowman, 3 Pc. 55.00
Teapot, Banquet Tea, Ceramic 85.00
Teapot, Fairmount Hotel, San Francisco, Silver Plated 35.00
Teapot, Jackson Square Fine Old Whiskey, Metal, Large 75.00
Telephone, 7-Up, Enterprex, Push Button, 7 In. 50.00
Thermometers are listed in their own category
Thermos, Campbell Soup 10.00
Thermos, Kellogg's Frosted Flakes 30.00
Tie Bar, Reddy Kilowatt 25.00
Tie Clasp, Texaco 8.00

Advertising tin cans or canisters were first used commercially in the
United States in 1819 and were called *tins.* The English language is
sometimes confusing. Today the word *tin* is used by most collectors to
describe many types of containers, including food tins, biscuit boxes, roly
poly tobacco containers, gunpowder cans, talcum powder sprinkle-top cans,
cigarette flat-fifty tins, and more. Beer cans are listed in their own section.
Things made of undecorated tin are listed under Tinware.

Tin, 3 Flowers Dusting Powder, Richard Hudnut, Round 15.00
Tin, A & P Coffee, Special $1. 39 Printed, Early 1950s, 2 Lb. 50.00
Tin, Abbey Tobacco, Gothic Cathedral, Pocket, Blue, 4 x 3 In. 175.00
Tin, Adams Honey Chewing Gum, 6 x 6 x 4 In. 80.00
Tin, Admiration Coffee, Black Lady Serving White Couple, Label 45.00
Tin, Airfloat Talc, 6 Sport Figures 55.00
Tin, American Navy Tobacco, 7 1/2 In. 95.00
Tin, Angelus Shoe Polish 5.00
Tin, April Showers Talc, Girl With Umbrella, 5 3/4 In. 30.00
Tin, Arabia Banquet Coffee, 9 x 5 In. 150.00
Tin, Armand Cold Cream Powder, Round, 9 In. 30.00
Tin, Astor House Coffee, 1 Lb. 55.00
Tin, Aunt Jemima Oil, 5 Gal. 1800.00
Tin, B'ma'cea Salve, June 30, 1906, 1 1/2 In. 25.00
Tin, Bagley's Old Colony Tobacco, Pocket 125.00
Tin, Bambino, Pocket, 4 x 2 In. 1200.00
Tin, Barbour's Salted Peanuts, 10 Lb. 165.00
Tin, Bassett's Egg Shampoo Cream 50.00
Tin, Beefex Cubes, Red, White & Black, 4 x 1 In. 9.00
Tin, Ben Hur Tea, Hero Driving Chariot, Medals, 7 x 7 In. 137.00
Tin, Benson Confection, RMS Queen Mary Cover 5.00
Tin, Betsy Ross Tea, Cardboard, Little Rock, Ark., 10 Cent Size 12.00
Tin, Big Ben Tobacco, Upright, Pocket .... 25.00 To 30.00
Tin, Bigger Hair Tonic, Cardboard, 6 1/2 In. 250.00
Tin, Blue Ribbon Red Cayenne, Red, White & Blue 6.00
Tin, Bond Street Pipe Tobacco, Art Deco, 6 x 4 In. 8.00

Tin, Borden's Malted Milk, c.1920, 25 Lb. 95.00
Tin, Boy–Ur–Ready Marshmallow Topping, Ice Cream Sundae 30.00
Tin, Breakfast Call Coffee, 3 Lb. 68.00
Tin, Brotherhood Tobacco, 6 x 3 x 4 In. 20.00
Tin, Bulldog Tobacco, Pocket, 4 x 2 In. .... 140.00 To 200.00
Tin, Bunnies Salted Peanuts, St. John, New Brunswick, 10 Lb. 440.00
Tin, Burley Boy Tobacco, 5 x 4 x 4 In. .... 265.00 To 290.00
Tin, Burley Boy Tobacco, Upright, Pocket, 4 x 2 In. 1380.00
Tin, Buster Brown Cigars, Comical Image, 6 x 4 In. ....632.00 To 3000.00
Tin, Buttercup Snuff, Round 35.00
Tin, Cadette Talc, Gray 80.00
Tin, Calabash Tobacco, Flat Top, Pocket 495.00
Tin, California Perfume Co., Jack & Jill Jungle Jinks, Metal 30.00
Tin, California Perfume Co., Talcum Powder 40.00
Tin, Calumet Baking Powder, Sample 25.00
Tin, Calumet Baking Soda 3.00
Tin, Campbell's Shag Cut Plug, Pocket 200.00
Tin, Campfire Marshmallow, Red, Round 28.00
Tin, Caravan Condoms 95.00
Tin, Carlton Club Tobacco, Pocket 275.00
Tin, Castle Blend Coffee, Image Of Windsor Castle, 1 Lb. 385.00
Tin, Central Union Tobacco, Face, Quarter Moon, 8 x 6 x 3 In. 325.00
Tin, Central Union Tobacco, Pocket, 4 x 3 In. 85.00
Tin, Chamberlain Cigar, J. M. Fortier, Montreal, 8 x 5 x 1 In. 68.00
Tin, Chamberlain's Stomach Liver Tablets, 2 1/2 x 1 1/4 In. 8.00
Tin, Chase & Sandborn Coffee, Key Lid, 1 Lb. 8.00
Tin, Checkers Tobacco, White Letters, Pocket 395.00
Tin, Chesterfield, White, Flat 50s .... 7.00 To 8.00
Tin, Circus Club Mallows, Cartoon Of Clothed Cat, 7 In. 192.00
Tin, Circus Club Mallows, Cartoon Of Elephant, 7 In. 385.00
Tin, Citadel Tobacco, Citadel & Soldiers All Sides, 6 1/2 In. 880.00
Tin, Clover Farm Pure Spices, Clove, 2 Oz. 10.00
Tin, Club Lido Tobacco, Pocket 100.00
Tin, Club Room Tobacco, Vertical, 4 x 3 In. 750.00
Tin, Clubs Perique Mixture, 3 Portraits In Logo, 6 1/2 In. 38.00
Tin, Colgate Baby Talc, 2 In. .... 110.00 To 125.00
Tin, Colgate Shaving Stick, 2 1/4 In. 10.00
Tin, Colgate's Dactylic Talcum Powder, c.1910 .... 75.00
Tin, Comfort Powder, Chubby Child, 4 In. 165.00
Tin, Comrade Coffee, 2 1/2 Lb. 66.00
Tin, Condor Coffee, Palm Trees, 1 Lb. 385.00
Tin, Cortland 333, Shot 8.00
Tin, Cottage Blend Coffee, House Shape, Lift Top, 7 1/4 x 6 In. 140.00
Tin, Cottolene, Contains No Hog Fat, Gal. 55.00
Tin, Country Club Tobacco, Pocket, 3 x 2 In. 750.00
Tin, Cream Of Tartar, Green Paint, Hinged Lid 25.00
Tin, Crumpsall Cream Crackers, Windup Bus, Figural 3025.00
Tin, Culture Tobacco, Pocket 75.00
Tin, Daily Habit Cigars, Parrot, Round 110.00
Tin, Dalley's Prime Coffee, Pastoral Scene, 1 Lb. 82.00
Tin, Dan Patch, 4 x 6 In. 45.00
Tin, Deer's Mustard Plaster, Lithograph, Yonkers, N.Y., c.1910 .... 90.00
Tin, Del Monte Tobacco, Pocket 400.00
Tin, Dill's Best Tobacco, Short Pocket 28.00
Tin, Dill's Best Tobacco, Square, Flat Pocket 25.00
Tin, Dixie Queen Plug Cut Tobacco, Basketweave 135.00
Tin, Djer–Kiss Talcum, Unopened, Large 30.00
Tin, Doctors Blend Tobacco, Doctor Measuring Dose, 5 x 3 In. 82.50
Tin, Dominion Tire Tobacco, Steamship Line, 4 x 3 In. 95.00
Tin, Dr. J. A. Foster's Wonder Tooth Powder, c.1900 .... 150.00
Tin, Dr. Johnson's Educator Crackers, Yellow 220.00
Tin, Dr. Lesure's Gall Remedy, c.1910, 10 Oz. 75.00
Tin, Dr. LeGears Lice Killer, Colorful Barnyard Scene, Sample 75.00

Tin, Dr. Robinson's Condom 75.00
Tin, Dr. Sayman's Toilet Talcum Powder 143.00
Tin, Dr. Scholl's Foot Powder, Antiseptic & Deodorant, c.1920 .... 80.00
Tin, Dr. Simmon's Liver Medicine 55.00
Tin, Droste Cocoa, Dutch Girl & Boy, 8 Oz. 25.00
Tin, Dupont Gunpowder, Tin, Paper Label .... 20.00 To 65.00
Tin, E–J Workers Coffee, 1 Lb. 82.00
Tin, Eagle Brand Shoe Polish, Yellow, Black 12.00
Tin, Edgeworth Tobacco, Sample 35.00
Tin, Electric Mixture Tobacco, Burlesque Babes, 4 1/2 In. 137.00
Tin, Empress Jelly, Full Lithograph, 5 In. 38.00
Tin, Empress Spice, Painted Side 26.00
Tin, Epicure Tobacco, Pocket 125.00
Tin, Erzinger's Tobacco, Red, Gold, Black, 3 1/2 x 5 x 1 In. 85.00
Tin, Eskimo Smoking Tobacco, Dog, Front Of Igloos, 6 In. 275.00
Tin, Ever Clear Polish, Pictures Eye, Price 10 Cents, 2 1/8 In. 20.00
Tin, Ex–Lax, Silver, White & Black, Sample .... 7.00 To 9.00
Tin, Export Cigarettes, Queen Elizabeth II, 1956, Flat 50s 8.00
Tin, Exquisite Mixture Tobacco, Square Edge 1100.00
Tin, Fairy Peppermint Toffee, 12 In. 40.00
Tin, Farmer's Pride Coffee, Yellow, Hinged Lid, Large 50.00
Tin, Fast Mail Tobacco, Flat, Pocket 800.00
Tin, Fatima Cigars, Round 50s 35.00
Tin, Feathers Tobacco, Pocket 250.00
Tin, Five Brothers Pipe Smoking, Square Box 375.00
Tin, Florient Talc, Contents, 2 In. 35.00
Tin, Forest & Stream Tobacco, Man Fishing, 5 3/4 In. 245.00
Tin, Forest & Stream Tobacco, Men Fishing, Pocket, 4 x 2 In. 605.00
Tin, Forest & Stream Tobacco, Two Fishermen, 3 x 2 In. 295.00
Tin, Fort Garry Coffee, Hudson's Bay Co., 7 x 10 In. 525.00
Tin, Fountain Tobacco, 7 x 4 In. 300.00
Tin, Fox Trot Panatelas, Running Fox 770.00
Tin, Freshpak Mountain Coffee, 1 Lb. 44.00
Tin, Friendship Sliced Plug Tobacco, D. H. McAlpin & Co., Pocket 45.00
Tin, Gail & Ax Tobacco, Kidney Shape 1330.00
Tin, Galleon Cigars, Chest, Hinged Lid, Embossed Ships 20.00
Tin, Garrett & Sons Snuff, Unopened .... 15.00 To 16.00
Tin, Gibson's Cough Lozenge, Paper Label 22.50
Tin, Gibson's Lozenge, Floral, Square, 8 3/4 In. 275.00
Tin, Giencarnock Honey, Red, Black & Yellow, 5 In. 18.00
Tin, Globe Mills, Pepper, Boston, 10 Lb. 55.00
Tin, Globe Tobacco, Flat, Sample 325.00
Tin, Gloub's Belle Coffee, Woman In Flowered Hat, 1 Lb. 1540.00
Tin, Goal Cigars, Football Scene 195.00
Tin, Gobblers Cigars, Round, 6 x 4 In. 800.00
Tin, Gold Dust Tobacco, Canada, Pocket 300.00
Tin, Gold Flake Cigarettes, Red & Gold, Flat 50s 16.00
Tin, Gold Standard Baking Powder, Red, Yellow, Black, 4 In. 12.00
Tin, Golden Pheasant, Condoms .... 55.000 To 75.00
Tin, Golden Rod Coffee, Store Building, 1 Lb. 55.00
Tin, Good Cheer Cigars, Shape Of Beer Stein 85.00
Tin, Granulated 54 Tobacco, Pocket 55.00
Tin, Green Goose Tobacco, 6 x 5 x 3 In. 950.00
Tin, Guide Tobacco, Pocket, 4 x 2 In. 195.00
Tin, Half & Half Tobacco, Pocket 7.00
Tin, Hand Bag Tobacco, Handbag Shape, Tin 45.00
Tin, Hand Made Tobacco, Pocket 260.00
Tin, Harley Davidson Transmission Lubricant, Label, 1961 .... 28.00
Tin, Harry Horne Circus Club Mallow, Bear, Blue Hat, 3 x 7 In. 210.00
Tin, Harry Horne Circus Club Mallow, Cat, Green Hat, 3 x 7 In. 75.00
Tin, Harry Horne Circus Club Mallow, Monkey, Hat, 3 x 7 In. 235.00
Tin, Hercules, Gunpowder, 1940 .... 10.00
Tin, Hi–Plane Tobacco, 2–Motor Airplane, Pocket 125.00

Tin, Hi–Plane Tobacco, 4–Motor Airplane, Pocket .... 250.00 To 265.00
Tin, Hickory Tobacco, Pocket 20.00
Tin, Hillick Coffee, 3 Lb. 30.00
Tin, Hippo Oil, Bucket Of Oil Pouring On Hippo, Pry Open 25.00
Tin, Home Run Cigars, Playing Field & Players, Round 6500.00
Tin, Home Run Stogie Cigars, Baseball Scenes, Batter 1320.00
Tin, Honeymoon Tobacco, 2 On Moon, Pocket, 4 x 2 In. .... 350.00 To 475.00·
Tin, Honeymoon Tobacco, Man Leaning On Moon .... 45.00 To 75.00
Tin, Hope's Denture Powder, c.1910 .... 60.00
Tin, Hormel Ham 5.00
Tin, Hostess Holiday Fruit Cake, Long & Narrow 40.00
Tin, Hudson's Bay Tea, Red Ground, 3 x 3 x 5 1/2 In. 70.00
Tin, Huntley & Palmers, Chinese Lantern 225.00
Tin, Huntley & Palmers, Library, Stack Of Books, Lithograph 175.00
Tin, Huntley & Palmers, Oriental Design 37.00
Tin, Inter–Collegiate Mixture, Student's Solace, 3 1/4 In. 330.00
Tin, Iten Biscuit, Green, Stenciled Label, Large 95.00
Tin, Jam Boy Coffee, 1 Lb. 400.00
Tin, Jamogo Paprika, Gobel Grocery Co., 1 Oz. 10.00
Tin, Jaybra Razorless Shaving Powder, Man Shaving 75.00
Tin, Jess Talcum Powder, Woman Pictured On Both Sides 220.00
Tin, Johnson's Baby Powder, Round, Early 1940s 10.00
Tin, Jolly Time Popcorn, 5 x 3 In. 22.00
Tin, Jule Carr's Tobacco, 4 x 3 In. 105.00
Tin, Jumbo Salted Peanuts, Black Man Eating Corn, 10 Lb. 350.00
Tin, Justrite Tobacco, Vertical, Pocket 75.00
Tin, Kaffee Hag, 1 Lb. 68.00
Tin, KC Baking Powder, 25 Oz. For 25 Cents, Unopened 20.00
Tin, Kentucky Club Tobacco, Pocket 4.00
Tin, Khush–Amadi Talcum Powder, Winged Maid In Pond, 5 In. 220.00
Tin, King Cole Coffee, 3 In., 1/2 Lb. 120.00
Tin, Kkovah Health Salt, Lithograph 29.00
Tin, Knapsack Tobacco, 4 x 3 In. 110.00
Tin, Kodak Tobacco, Factory Image On Lid, 5 In. 110.00
Tin, L'Origan Talc, Coty 12.00
Tin, L. C. Smith Typewriter Ribbon 10.00
Tin, La Paulina Cigar, Senators 4.00
Tin, Lady Helen Coffee, Paper Label, 1 Lb. 27.50
Tin, Lazell's Perfumer Talc, Lithograph, Oriental Girl & Boy 25.00
Tin, Lenox Tobacco, Automobile, Pocket 1800.00
Tin, LeRoy Cigars, Pocket ....68.00 To 135.00
Tin, Lily Of The Valley Coffee, Lilies In Bloom, Logo, 1 Lb. 192.00
Tin, Lipton's Salon Tea, Native Field Worker Scenes, 3 Lb. 75.00
Tin, Lipton's Tea Bags 12.50
Tin, Lipton's Tea, Pictures All Sides, Estates 175.00
Tin, Log Cabin Syrup, Blacksmith 85.00
Tin, Lucky Duck Cigars, Pocket 1100.00
Tin, Lucky Strike Cigarettes, Flat 50s 10.00
Tin, Lucky Strike, 2 1/2 x 3 In. 35.00
Tin, Lucky Strike, Contents, Pocket, 3 x 1 In. 85.00
Tin, Luzianne Coffee, 3 Lb. 35.00
Tin, Madame Butterfly Cigars, 6 x 4 In. 210.00
Tin, Mammy Brand Coffee, Buffalo, N.Y., 1 Lb. 365.00
Tin, Mammy's Favorite Brand Coffee, 10 x 6 In. 260.00
Tin, Manhattan Cocktail Tobacco, Pictures Rooster & Goblet 35.00
Tin, Maryland Club Tobacco, Flip Top, Pocket 225.00
Tin, Mastiff Cut Plug, 7 x 4 x 4 In. 3543.00
Tin, Maxwell House Coffee, 1921, 1 Lb. 45.00
Tin, McCormick Tea Bags, Dated 1938, Large 30.00
Tin, McKesson's Baby Powder, Naked Children, 6 1/4 In. 275.00
Tin, McLaughlin Mocha Java, 1 Lb. 80.00
Tin, Mecca Remedy, Orange, Black, Red, 2 In. 5.00
Tin, Merry Widow, Condom 100.00

Tin, Modene Cleanser, Girl On Telephone Picture, Unopened, 1940 .... 25.00
Tin, Mohican Coffee, Indian In Color, Screw Lid, 1 Lb. 200.00
Tin, Monarch Cocoa, Sample 50.00
Tin, Monarch Peanut Butter, Lion, 55 Lb. 180.00
Tin, Monarch Spice, Black Pepper 6.00
Tin, Monarch Spice, Clove 5.00
Tin, Monarch Tea, 1/4 Lb. 10.00
Tin, Moore's Anti Chafing Talcum Powder, Lithographed Baby 95.00
Tin, Mother's Joy Coffee, 1 Lb. 75.00
Tin, Mother's Mustard Plaster, Yellow Box, c.1910 .... 150.00
Tin, Nail Box, Mrs. McGregor's Family 110.00
Tin, Nash's Coffee, Trumpeters, Father Of Confederation, 5 Lb. 275.00
Tin, Nature's Remedy, Small 12.50
Tin, Nigger Head Stove Polish 300.00
Tin, North Pole Tobacco, Seal On Red, White & Blue, 6 In. 82.00
Tin, Nysis Talcum Powder, Egyptian Portrait, 6 1/4 In. 27.50
Tin, Ohio Boys Cigar, Political Natives, Tin, 6 x 4 1/4 In. 192.00
Tin, Ojibwa Tobacco, Pie Shape, 9 1/2 In. 255.00
Tin, Old Abe Tobacco, Flat, Pocket .... 1450.00 To 1850.00
Tin, Old Abe Tobacco, Pie Shape, 3 x 6 In. 825.00
Tin, Old Chum Tobacco, Scenes All Around, Footed, Round, 5 In. 210.00
Tin, Old Dutch Cleanser, Unopened 20.00
Tin, Old Dutch Typewriter Ribbon, Scene 5.00
Tin, Old Glory Tobacco, Black Man, Child On Back, Pocket 165.00
Tin, Old Homestead Coffee, 1 Lb. 150.00
Tin, Old Seneca Stogies, Dark Green, 6 x 3 In. 195.00
Tin, Old Seneca Stogies, Indian Chief, Light Green, Pocket 250.00
Tin, Old Southern Coffee, Southern Belle, Screw Lid, 1 Lb. 225.00
Tin, Old Squire, Blue, Upright Pocket 600.00
Tin, Optimus Condoms .... 65.00 To 85.00
Tin, Our Husbands Co., Arabian Gall Salve, 1 1/2 x 1 x 2 In. 4.00
Tin, Our Private Plantation Coffee, Paper Label, 1 Lb. 22.00
Tin, Oxo Cubes, Red, White & Black, 4 x 1 In. 5.00
Tin, Packer's Tar Soap 20.00
Tin, Pall Mall Cigarettes, White & Red, Flat 50s 10.00
Tin, Parrot Peanut Butter, Press Lid, 13 Oz. 467.00
Tin, Pastime Tobacco, 8 x 11 In. 95.00
Tin, Patterson's Lucky Strike, Flat Pocket 24.00
Tin, Paxton & Gallagher Butternut Coffee, 1 Lb. 2.75
Tin, Peacock Condom 15.00
Tin, Pearson's Snuff 12.50
Tin, Perfect Pipe Tobacco, Pocket, 4 x 2 In. 395.00
Tin, Perfecto Chocolate Syrup, Tin, 10 In. 175.00
Tin, Peter Pan Peanut Butter, Derby, 1950s 39.00
Tin, Petermans Bedbug Killer, Spout 2.00
Tin, Pheasant Condom 15.00
Tin, Pickwick Club Tobacco, Square Edge 445.00
Tin, Piedmont Airlines Punch, Plane Flying Over Fruit 25.00
Tin, Pilot–Knob Coffee, Pilot Mountain, Bail, 5 Lb. 335.00
Tin, Pioneer Brand Tobacco, Blue, Gold, Box, 5 x 3 In. 90.00
Tin, Pipe Major Tobacco, Pocket, 4 x 2 In. 350.00
Tin, Piper Heidsieck Chewing Tobacco, 10 x 4 x 3 In. 25.00
Tin, Piper Heidsieck Tobacco, 8 x 3 x 3 In. 13.50
Tin, Pixine Veterinary, Horse Friend, Round, 2 1/2 In. 23.00
Tin, Players Cigarettes, Dark Blue, Flat 50s .... 12.00 To 15.00
Tin, Pond Brand Peanut Butter 50.00
Tin, Pony Brand Marshmallow, Horse Logo, 5 x 12 In. 195.00
Tin, Popper Ace Cigars, 7 x 5 In. 300.00
Tin, Prairie Flower Tobacco, Woman Nursing Child, Pocket 125.00
Tin, Presto Stove Polish, Box 7.50
Tin, Presto Stove Polish, Round 1.25
Tin, Prince Albert, Pocket 7.00
Tin, Purest Aspirin Tablets, United Drug, 2 5/8 x 1 7/8 In. 22.00

Advertising, Tin, Russell's Exquisite Mixture
Tobacco

Tin, Quoid, 6 x 3 In. 200.00
Tin, R. Aldrichlung Salve 20.00
Tin, Raleigh Quinine Cold Tablets, Flat 10.00
Tin, Ramses Condoms .... 80.00 To 90.00
Tin, Red Turkey Coffee, 1 Lb. 71.00
Tin, Red Wolf Coffee, 1 Lb. 65.00
Tin, Red Wolf Coffee, Picture Of Wolf On Label, Bail, 6 Lb. 550.00
Tin, Reel Man Talcum Powder, Trout Fisherman, 4 3/4 In. 192.00
Tin, Reo Tobacco, Logo Encircled By Belt, 4 3/4 In. 65.00
Tin, Richelieu Coffee, Red, Orange, Black & White, 1 Lb. 20.00
Tin, Roly Poly, Dutchman, Mayo Tobacco, 7 x 6 In. 465.00
Tin, Roly Poly, Inspector, Dixie Queen 850.00
Tin, Roly Poly, Mammy, Tin 125.00
Tin, Roly Poly, Man From Scotland Yard, Dixie Queen 1155.00
Tin, Roly Poly, Satisfied Customer, Dixie Queen 200.00
Tin, Roly Poly, Satisfied Customer, Mayo Tobacco, 7 x 6 In. 385.00
Tin, Roly Poly, Singing Waiter, Mayo Tobacco, 7 x 6 In. 465.00
Tin, Roly Poly, Storekeeper, Mayo Tobacco, 7 x 6 In. .... 300.00 To 440.00
Tin, Rosenkrantza Vaseline, Round, 2 1/2 In. 12.00
Tin, Royal Navy Cut Plug Smoking Tobacco, Flat, 5 x 4 x 2 In. 25.00
Tin, Royal Purple Poultry Conditioner, 8 x 6 x 6 In. 30.00
Tin, Royal Shield Peanut Butter, Boy Eating Bread, 3 1/2 In. 150.00
Tin, Royal Shield Spice, Red, White, Blue, Gold 8.00
Tin, Royal Triton Oil Can 85.00
Tin, Russell's Exquisite Mixture Tobacco ....*Illus* 1100.00
Tin, Salmon's Tea, Picture Of Fish, 2 1/2 x 2 In. 105.00
Tin, Sawyer's Coffee, Bail Handle, 10 Lb. 45.00
Tin, Scotch Snuff, Unopened, 2 In. 13.00
Tin, Sen–Sen, Throat Ease & Breath Perfume, 1929, 2 1/2 In. 20.00
Tin, Seneca Sage, Red & White 8.00
Tin, Sensation Cigar, Gowned Goddess, 5 1/4 In. 385.00
Tin, Sentinel First Aid, Pilot & Plane Picture, 3 1/2 In. 17.00
Tin, Shadows Condoms 80.00
Tin, Shamrock Oil, Metal, 1 Qt. 15.00
Tin, Sir Haig Cigars, Silhouette Of Soldier, 5 1/2 In. 137.00
Tin, Sir Walter Raleigh Pipe Smoking, Pipe, Pocket 525.00
Tin, Skat Soap, Sample 5.00
Tin, Smith's Rosebud Talcum Powder, 4 1/2 In. 255.00
Tin, Snow White Hair Beautifier, Sample 5.00
Tin, Soderberg's Snuff 15.00
Tin, Spilter's Buttermilk Talcum Powder, Baby On Stork's Back 225.00
Tin, Split Shot 3.00
Tin, Squadron Leader Tobacco, Bi–Plane, 1938, 1 x 3 x 4 In. 35.00
Tin, Stag, Pocket, Small 35.00
Tin, Staple Brand, Peanut Butter, Yellow, 85 Lb. 50.00
Tin, Statue Of Liberty, Biscuit, Octagonal 40.00
Tin, Sterling Fine Cut Tobacco, Large 65.00

Tin, Strong Heart Coffee, Roasted By Charles Hewitt, 1 Lb. 425.00
Tin, Summer Girl Coffee, H. D. Lee Mercantile Co., 1 Lb. 40.00
Tin, Sunset Trail Tobacco, 7 1/2 In. 255.00
Tin, Sunshine Biscuit, Glass Top 60.00
Tin, Sunshine Cracker, Gold Lettering, Black Ground 45.00
Tin, Supreme Dental Powder 12.50
Tin, Surety Aspirin 1.00
Tin, Sweet Caporal, White, Truly Mild, Truly Fresh, Flat 50s 7.00
Tin, Sweet Cuba Tobacco, Square 50.00
Tin, Sweet Mist Tobacco, Cardboard 175.00
Tin, Thornes Toffee, Alice In Wonderland 65.00
Tin, Time Square Tobacco 75.00
Tin, Tonka Tobacco, Soldiers In Field, Urn On Side, 5 In. 460.00
Tin, Triumph Oil, 2 Gal. 30.00
Tin, Trojan Condoms 65.00
Tin, Tuxedo Tobacco, 1 Lb. 40.00
Tin, Tuxedo Tobacco, Dog, Pocket 7.00
Tin, Tuxedo Tobacco, Green & Gold, Pocket 12.00
Tin, Twin Oaks Tobacco, Pocket 24.00
Tin, Uncle Sam Tobacco, Canada, Upright, Pocket 2800.00
Tin, Uneeda Cheese Wafers 7.00
Tin, Union Club Coffee, 1 Lb. 66.00
Tin, Union Leader Tobacco, Gold Eagle Insignia, Red, Black 18.00
Tin, Union Leader Tobacco, Pocket .... 52.00 To 67.00
Tin, Unity Tobacco, Pocket 750.00
Tin, Val Dona Violet Talcum, Picture Woman, c.1910 .... 90.00
Tin, Velvet Smoking Tobacco, Pocket 2.35
Tin, Velvet Tobacco, Pocket, Sample 20.00
Tin, Vinlax, Laxative Tablet, 1 3/4 x 1 1/4 In. 15.00
Tin, Vitrogenized Talc, Contents, 4 5/8 In. 30.00
Tin, Vogue's Royale Talcum Powder, Embossed, c.1912 .... 65.00
Tin, Wampum Coffee, 3 Lb. 125.00
Tin, Watkins Egyptian Bouquet Talc 62.00
Tin, Wedding Breakfast Gas Roasted Coffee, Denver, Co., 3 Lb. 50.00
Tin, Weisert's 54 Tobacco, Upright, Pocket 265.00
Tin, Wellington, Yellow, Pocket 190.00
Tin, Wheat Sheaf Coffee, Gold, White & Brown, 7 x 4 In. 300.00
Tin, White Owl Cigars, Plastic Top 15.00
Tin, Whitman Chocolate, Baseball Players, Green, White 7.00
Tin, Winchester After Shave Talc 110.00
Tin, Worker Tobacco, Green 100.00
Tin, Yale Mixture Tobacco 85.00
Tin, Yankee Boy Tobacco, Brunette 800.00
Tin, Yardley Talc, Cream, Brown 15.00
Tin, Yoo–Hoo Drink, With Yankees Baseball Players 29.00
Tin, Zanzabar Black Pepper 75.00

Advertising tip trays are decorated metal trays less than 5 inches in diameter. They were placed on the table or counter to hold either the bill or the coins that were left as a tip. Change receivers could be made of glass, plastic, or metal. They were kept on the counter near the cash register and held the money passed back and forth by the cashier. Related items may be listed in the Advertising category under Change Receivers.

Tip Tray, A & P, Ruler 5.00
Tip Tray, Admiral Dewey, 5 3/4 In. 95.00
Tip Tray, American Brew, Liberty Beer, Indian Woman, 4 In. 165.00
Tip Tray, Bailey's Pure Rye Whiskey, Phila., Aluminum, 4 1/2 In 17.50
Tip Tray, Ballentine Beer, Wood Grain, 3 Rings, 5 In. 50.00
Tip Tray, Borden's, Mug Set, 4 Different 200.00
Tip Tray, Borden's, Mug, Elsie Running Through Flowers 55.00
Tip Tray, Broadway Brew, Buffalo, Hand Holding Hatchet, 4 In. 85.00
Tip Tray, Bromo–Seltzer, Display Box, 2 Note Pads 225.00
Tip Tray, Choo–Choo Barn 15.00

Tip Tray, Corbys, 4 In.	55.00
Tip Tray, Eisfield Clothing, Burlington, Iowa, Cast Aluminum	20.00
Tip Tray, Fairy Soap, 4 1/4 In. ....*Illus*	65.00
Tip Tray, Fox Beer	10.00
Tip Tray, Fox Head 400 Beer, Fox Logo, 4 x 6 In.	35.00
Tip Tray, Globe Wernicke, Bookcases ....95.00 To 125.00	
Tip Tray, Gram–O–Phone, His Master's Voice, 4 In.	70.00
Tip Tray, Gram–O–Phone, Victor & Berliner, Record Machine	60.00
Tip Tray, Heptol Splits Laxative, Russell Print, 1904	295.00
Tip Tray, Hotel Astor, Rudolstadt, 6 1/4 x 4 1/2 In.	65.00
Tip Tray, Kansas City Brew, Crescent & Star, 4 In.	95.00
Tip Tray, Knickerbocker Beer	10.00
Tip Tray, L. C. Smith Bros., Typewriter	135.00
Tip Tray, Maltosia Brewery, Lady On Swan, 5 In.	125.00
Tip Tray, Maltosia, German American Brewing Co.	65.00
Tip Tray, Mapeline Syrup, Seattle, 4 1/8 In.	22.00
Tip Tray, Mascot Tobacco, Ship On Water At Night, 5 In.	50.00
Tip Tray, Merit Separator Co., 4 7/8 In.	192.00
Tip Tray, Miller, 1950s	18.00
Tip Tray, Monticello Whiskey	95.00
Tip Tray, Moxie, c.1910, 6 In.	295.00
Tip Tray, Moxie, Place Card Center, Green Ground	200.00
Tip Tray, Moxie, Victorian Woman, Pouring Bottle, Maroon	1500.00
Tip Tray, National Beer, Crown & Coats Of Arms, 4 x 6 In.	10.00
Tip Tray, New England Furniture & Carpet Co., 4 1/2 In.	120.00
Tip Tray, Occident Flour, Red	60.00
Tip Tray, Old Reliable Coffee, Dutchman With Pipe	65.00
Tip Tray, Opia Cigars, Beautiful Woman, Spaced Out On Opium	575.00
Tip Tray, Pennsylvania Coat Co., Diving Girl	15.00
Tip Tray, Prudential Insurance, Oval, 2 1/2 x 3 1/2 In.	20.00
Tip Tray, Pure Brand Cigar, Lady	150.00
Tip Tray, Red Raven Splits, It's A Cream	75.00
Tip Tray, RMS Aquatania	95.00
Tip Tray, Rockford Watches, No Picture ....55.00 To 90.00	
Tip Tray, Rockford Watches, Pictures Young Woman, 3 x 5 In.	115.00
Tip Tray, Ruhstaller Brew, Lady With Dove, 5 In.	125.00
Tip Tray, Ruppert's Beer, Hans Flato Picture	55.00
Tip Tray, S & H Green Stamps	45.00
Tip Tray, Schmauss Garden & Cafe, 6 In. ....*Illus*	25.00
Tip Tray, Schober Brewing Co., 1910	355.00
Tip Tray, Seagram, Glass, 8 In.	12.50

Advertising, Tip Tray, Schmauss Garden & Cafe, 6 In.
Advertising, Tip Tray, Fairy Soap, 4 1/4 In.

Advertising, Tray, Virginia
Brewing Co., Woman
Pictured, 10 In.

Advertising, Toy, Bathtub, Changeables, McDonald's   *Advertising, Toy, Train, Wendy's*

Tip Tray, Smith Bros. Typewriter, 3 Horses & Typewriter 250.00
Tip Tray, Smith Wallace Shoes, Pretty Woman, 4 In. 45.00
Tip Tray, Stegmaier Brewing Co., Factory Scene, 4 1/4 In. 95.00
Tip Tray, Tehuagen Mineral Water .... 20.00 To 25.00
Tip Tray, Treasure Line Stoves, Interior Kitchen, 7 1/2 In. 125.00
Tip Tray, Treasure Stove & Ranges, Oval, 7 x 4 In. 82.50
Tip Tray, Tuxedo Club Cigars 125.00
Tip Tray, Welsbah Mantles, Eagle, 4 In. 45.00
Tip Tray, William Tell Flour 65.00
Tip Tray, Wolverine Toy, Multicolored, 4 1/2 x 6 1/2 In. 85.00
Tip Tray, Wrigly's Soap, Cat 175.00
Tip Tray, Zipp's, Soda Fountain Needs 28.00
Tobacco Cutter, LaPalina, Brunhoff, Cincinnati, Iron, Mechanical 225.00
Tobacco Cutter, Mechanical, Get Back Of Peter Schuyler Cigar 75.00
Tobacco Cutter, Reynolds Davis Grocery, Fort Smith, Ark., Iron 65.00
Tobacco Cutter, Save The Tags, Enterprise, Jan. 20, 1885 .... 75.00
Tobacco Cutter, Spearhead, Iron 165.00
Tobacco Cutter, Star 30.00
Toy, Bathtub, Changeables, McDonald's ....*Illus* 1.00
Toy, Boat, PT, Kellogg's Baking Powder, Original Box 150.00
Toy, Dinkey The Dog, Kellogg's, 1935, Uncut 40.00
Toy, Mc Donald's Play Restaurant, Japan 100.00
Toy, Train, Wendy's ....*Illus* 2.00
Tray, Arctic Ice Cream, Bear 145.00
Tray, Aurora Beer, Evangeline, Howard Chandler Christie, c.1910 .... 400.00
Tray, Beer, Beach Co., Coshocton, 12 x 17 In. 30.00
Tray, Bergdoll Brewing Co., Brass 40.00
Tray, Black Hawk Beer 150.00
Tray, Blatz Beer, Vested Man Pouring From Bottle 50.00
Tray, Blatz Old Heidelberg Beer, Tin, 13 x 10 In. ....75.00 To 100.00
Tray, Budweiser Beer, Fox In Fire, Square 245.00
Tray, Bula Beer, Men At Table Eating Lunch, Drinking Beer 1100.00
Tray, Calumet Baking Powder, 7 x 11 In. 10.00
Tray, Card, Cunard, Pewter 10.00
Tray, Christian Fiegenspan Beer, Round, Lithograph, 13 In. 28.00
Tray, Christian Moerlein Brewery, Cincinnati, Ohio 60.00
Tray, Christin's Waters, Dog Spraying Cat, 13 In. 210.00
Tray, Churchill Downs, 100th Anniversary, 1974 .... 65.00
Tray, Climax Stoves, Trademarked Flaming Warrior, 13 In. 60.00
Tray, Congress Beer, Picture Of Label 45.00
Tray, D'Eaux Gazeuses Factory, Quebec, Vehicles, 12 1/4 In. 88.00
Tray, Diogenes Brewing Co., Oval, Brass 250.00
Tray, Display, Apollo Candy Bonbons, 1904 .... 95.00
Tray, Dr Pepper, Cats Drinking Milk, Tin Litho, Round, 21 In. 375.00
Tray, Dr Pepper, Reclining Lion, Oval 500.00
Tray, Du Bois Budweiser Beer, 1930s. 12 In. 95.00
Tray, Du Bois Budweiser Beer, Brewery Buildings, 1930s 85.00

Tray, Duesselborter Beer, Grand Prize Winner, 1904, 12 In. 250.00
Tray, Dutch Club Beer 7.00
Tray, E. M. Neff Dry Goods, Crestline, Ohio, Oval, 16 5/8 In. 55.00
Tray, Fehr Brewery, Toga Clad Couple, 1910 .... 80.00
Tray, Fidelio Brewery, Men At Tavern Table, c.1936, 12 In. 50.00
Tray, Fort Pitt Beer 7.00
Tray, Fox Head 400 Beer 45.00
Tray, Franklin Brewery, Wilkes Barre, Pa., Tavern Scene 125.00
Tray, Frontenac Beer, Factory, Street Scene, 12 In. 88.00
Tray, Gambrinus Beer, c.1900, 13 In. 195.00
Tray, Gerst Beer, Rectangular 165.00
Tray, Goebel Beer, Calendar, 1913 .... 165.00
Tray, Goebel Beer, Dutch Girl, c.1910, 12 In. 75.00
Tray, Golden Drops Beer, Rectangular 195.00
Tray, Hagan Ice Cream, 13 x 13 In. 265.00
Tray, Henry Heman, Philadelphia, Woman Reading Letter 145.00
Tray, Hires Boy, Just What The Doctor Ordered, 1914 .... 385.00
Tray, Imperial Brewing Co., Imperial Seal, KC–MO 750.00
Tray, Iowa Assessment Mutual Insurance, Carnation Girl, 1906 .... 185.00
Tray, Jamestown Ice Cream, 1930 .... 55.00
Tray, Keen Kutter, Woman With Flowers 65.00
Tray, Kist Orange Soda, Woman On Sailboat, 13 1/4 x 10 1/2 In. 65.00
Tray, Leisy Brewery, Scene With Factory 575.00
Tray, McDonald Sap Spout, Implements Of Sugaring, 18 3/4 In. 330.00
Tray, McDonald's Olympics, Tin, 1984, Small 7.00
Tray, Miller High Life Beer, Girl On Moon .... 75.00 To 95.00
Tray, Narragansett Ale, Round, White, Porcelain, 12 In. 88.00
Tray, Nu–Grape, Hand Holding Bottle, 13 x 10 In. 52.00
Tray, Orange Julep, Girl At Beach 225.00
Tray, Paul Luithle's Bakery, Philadelphia, 1911 .... 150.00
Tray, Rainier Beer, Woman & Bear .... 265.00 To 275.00
Tray, Robinson Son's Beer, Scranton, Pa., Factory Scene 135.00
Tray, Senate Beer, 3 Stand–Up Center Bottles, Metal 25.00
Tray, Standard Brewing Co., Indian Execution, 1862, 12 In. 595.00
Tray, Standard Brewing Co., Mankato, Minn., 12 In. .... 595.00 To 625.00
Tray, Standard Brewing, Scranton, Wood Grain, Label 125.00
Tray, Steffen's Ice Cream, Lithograph, Round, 13 In. 44.00
Tray, Sunshine Beer, Wholesome As Sunshine, 13 In. 50.00
Tray, Tennessee Brewing, Brewery Scene 1200.00
Tray, Tip, see Tip Trays in this category
Tray, Union Pacific Tea Co., Children Playing, 8 In. 55.00
Tray, Valley Forge Beer, Washington's Headquarters, 12 In. 40.00
Tray, Vat 69, Logo, Square 15.00
Tray, Velvet Beer, Color Lithograph, Oval, 15 1/4 In. 198.00
Tray, Virginia Brewing Co., Woman Pictured, 10 In. ....Illus 1250.00
Treat Jar, Milkbone Dog House, House Shape 53.00
Trunk, Glycerole Shoe Dressing, Tin, 9 x 13 In. 135.00
Tumbler Set, Beer, Enameled Playing Card Hands, 6 Piece 45.00
Tumbler Set, Wendy's, The Jetsons, 1989, Set Of 6 .... 30.00
Tumbler, Allwiden Beer, Chicago 65.00
Tumbler, Beer, Old German Lager, Barrel Shape, Etched 27.50
Tumbler, Dad's Root Beer 15.00
Tumbler, Ethyl Gasahol 15.00
Tumbler, Fresno Brewing Co., Etched, Early 1900s 91.00
Tumbler, Frosted Flakes, Tony The Tiger, 6 1/2 In. 6.00
Tumbler, Hamm's, Burgie 151.00
Tumbler, Horace Horsecollar, Disney, 1937 .... 135.00
Tumbler, Nestle's Hot Chocolate, Marked Sterling China 28.00
Tumbler, Nestle's, Stoneware, 4 Piece 75.00
Tumbler, Pizza Hut 9.00
Tumbler, Richardson's Liberty, Enameled Syrup Lines, 5 Piece 110.00
Tumbler, Schlitz Shell 10.00
Tumbler, Scooby-Doo, Hanna Barbera, 1976 .... 135.00

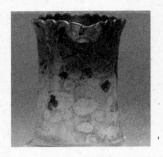

Agata, Vase, Quatraform, Flared, 4 1/2 In.

Tumbler, Squirt, Glow Ball	7.50
Tumbler, Stroh's Beer, Embossed	150.00
Tumbler, Tab	5.00
Wagon, Popcorn & Peanut, Stroh's, Cretor, 1960s	3200.00
Wallet, Wurlitzer Logo, Front & Inside	55.00
Warmer, Campbell's Soup	55.00
Wastebasket, Paper, Mac Tonight, Metal	20.00
Whistle, Cardboard, Keen Kutter, Unusual KK Emblem	200.00
Whistle, Keds, Blue & White, Plastic, 2 1/2 In.	6.00
Whistle, Oscar Meyer Wiener	4.00
Whistle, Red Goose Shoes, Wooden, Slogan	10.00
Wings, Pilot's, Delta Airlines, Pinback	48.00

AGATA glass was made by Joseph Locke of the New England Glass Company of Cambridge, Massachusetts, after 1885. A metallic stain was applied to New England Peachblow and the mottled design characteristic of agata appeared.

Punch Cup, Blue Spots, 2 3/4 x 3 In.	595.00
Punch Cup, Oil Spots, Mottled Handle, 2 3/4 In.	595.00
Toothpick, Cactus, Red	175.00
Tumbler, Blue Spotting, Oily Mottling, 3 3/4 In.	750.00
Tumbler, Deep Rose To Creamy Pink, Gold Oil Mottled, 3 7/8 In.	795.00
Vase, Quatraform, Flared, 4 1/2 In. ....*Illus*	880.00
Water Set, Rose To Pink, 6 Piece	3200.00

AKRO AGATE glass was made in Clarksburg, West Virginia, from 1932 to 1951. Before that time, the firm made children's glass marbles. Most of the glass is marked with a crow flying through the letter *A*.

Ashtray, Blue Marble, Ellipsoid	12.00
Ashtray, Orange Marble, Square	4.00
Ashtray, Red & White, Square, 3 In.	3.00
Ashtray, Turquoise, Square, 3 In.	4.00
Bowl, Ribs & Flutes, Lime Green, 5 1/4 In.	6.00
Bowl, Stacked Disc, Turquoise, 2 3/4 In.	30.00
Bowl, Stacked Disc, Yellow	30.00
Creamer, Chiquita, Green	4.00
Creamer, Stippled Band, Green	14.00
Cup & Saucer, Orange & White, After Dinner	2.00
Cup, Child's, Pumpkin, Open Handle, Octagonal	25.00
Cup, Child's, Raised Daisy, Blue	25.00
Cup, Concentric Ring, Green	3.00
Cup, Concentric Ring, Turquoise	12.00
Cup, Stacked Disc, Opaque Pumpkin	12.00
Cup, Translucent Lavender	30.00
Jar, Apothecary, Black Amethyst	65.00
Jar, Apothecary, Powder Blue, 6 1/2 In.	125.00
Jardiniere, Ribs & Flutes, Scalloped Rim, Blue, 5 In.	35.00

Alabaster, Lamp, 2 Courting Children,

Domed Shade, 31 In.

To clean alabaster, first dust with a soft brush. Then wipe with turpentine or dry–cleaning fluid. Do not use water. Polish with paste furniture wax.

A damaged porcelain clock-face is difficult to repair. It will lower the price of a clock by 20% to 30%.

Pitcher, Water, Green		16.00
Powder Jar, Colonial Lady, Lime Green		195.00
Powder Jar, Colonial Lady, Pink		45.00
Powder Jar, Concentric Ring, Lime Green		15.00
Powder Jar, Mexicali, Orange & White		25.00
Powder Jar, Orange & White Marbelized		30.00
Shaving Mug, Finger Ring, Black Amethyst		50.00
Sugar, Octagonal, Dark Blue		18.00
Tea Set, Child's, Chiquita, Green, Box, 7 Piece		135.00
Tumbler, Octagonal, Yellow		9.00
Vase, Flared Top & Bottom, Black Amethyst, 8 3/4 In.		90.00
Vase, Flared Top & Bottom, Cobalt Blue, 8 3/4 In.		65.00
Vase, Flared Top & Bottom, Lime Green, 8 3/4 In.		45.00

ALABASTER is a very soft form of gypsum, a stone that resembles marble. It was often carved into vases or statues in Victorian times. There are alabaster carvings being made even today. Because the alabaster is very porous, it will dissolve if kept in water, so do not use alabaster vases for flowers.

Bust, Veiled Young Woman, Shaped Base, 19th Century, 21 In.		825.00
Bust, Woman, Wearing Hat, Marble Stand, c.1900, 18 In.		795.00
Candy Dish, Cover, Female Gilt Sphinxes Base, 5 x 10 In.		495.00
Compote, White, Gray, Carved Flowers, Baluster Pedestal, 13 In.		275.00
Figurine, Duck, On Half Round Base, Green, 4 1/2 x 8 In.		192.50
Hat Stand, Head Form, Rose Jade, 15 1/4 In.		302.50
Lamp, 2 Courting Children, Domed Shade, 31 In.	*Illus*	358.00

ALEXANDRITE is a name with many meanings. It is a form of the mineral chrysoberyl that changes from green to red under artificial light. A man–made version of this mineral is sold in Mexico today. It changes from deep purple to aquamarine blue under artificial light. The Alexandrite listed here is glass made in the late nineteenth and twentieth centuries. Thomas Webb & Sons sold their transparent glass shaded from yellow to rose to blue under the name Alexandrite. Stevens and Williams had a cased Alexandrite of yellow, rose, and blue. A. Douglas Nash Corporation made an amethyst–colored Alexandrite. Several American glass companies of the 1920s made a glass that changed color under electric lights and this was also called Alexandrite.

Celery Vase, Inverted Thumbprint, Square Top, 6 In.		515.00
Finger Bowl, Fluted Edge, Blue To Rose To Citron, 5 In.		650.00
Finger Bowl, Fluted, Rose To Amber, 5 x 2 1/2 In.		650.00

Match Holder, Square Top, Diamond–Quilted, 3 In. 650.00
Match Holder, Webb, 3 In. 650.00
Tazza, Pedestal Foot, Diamond–Quilted, 4 1/2 x 1 1/2 In. 695.00
Toothpick, Collared Square Top, Ground Pontil, 3 In. 595.00
Vase, Fluted, Webb, 2 1/2 In. 695.00
Vase, Honeycomb, Corseted Waist, 3 1/4 In. 595.00
Vase, Honeycomb, Shaded Rim, 4 1/4 In. 765.00
Wine, Blue Rim, Rose To Citron, 4 1/2 In. 550.00

ALHAMBRA is a pattern of tableware made in Vienna, Austria, in the
twentieth century. The geometric designs are in applied gold, red, and dark
green. Full sets of dishes can be found in this pattern.

Creamer 50.00
Cup & Saucer 50.00
Plate, 8 In. 35.00
Plate, 10 In. 40.00

ALUMINUM was more expensive than gold or silver until the 1850s.
Chemists learned how to refine bauxite to get aluminum. Jewelry and other
small objects were made of the valuable metal until 1914, when an
inexpensive smelting process was invented. The aluminum collected today
dates from the 1930s through 1950s. Hand-hammered pieces are the most
popular.

Airplane, DC–3, 23–In. Wingspan 500.00
Ashtray, Sailing Ships, Everlast 22.00
Basket, Wild Rose, Everlast 15.00
Berry Basket, Farberware, 9 In. 11.00
Bowl, Buenilum, 6 3/4 In. 3.00
Bowl, Fruit & Compote, China Insert, Farberware, 10 1/2 In. 37.50
Bowl, Hawthorn, Everlast, 9 1/4 In. 11.00
Bowl, Oblong, Wendell August, 14 In. 20.00
Bowl, Waterfowl, Fluted, Federal Silver, 9 x 3 1/2 In. 12.50
Butter, Cover, Buenilum 20.00
Cake Basket, Wild Rose, Square Knot Handle, Continental 10.00
Casserole, Cover, Everlast, 8 In. 25.00
Casserole, Glass Insert & Rest, Cover, Everlast, Individual, Pair 35.00
Coaster, Flamingo, Set Of 6 .... 6.00
Dish, Flower Pattern, T Pedestal, Hand Forged, 6 In. 6.75
Hot Plate, Pine Pattern, Cork Table Protector, Everlast .... .75
Ice Bucket, Bali Bamboo, No Liner, Large Cork, Everlast 25.00
Ice Bucket, Glass Insert, Tongs 15.00
Lazy Susan, Flower Pattern, Everlast 10.00
Napkin Holder, Ribbon Band Forms Feet, Rodney Kent 25.00
Pitcher, Buenilum 25.00
Pitcher, Everlast, 2 Qt. 15.00
Pitcher, Hand Hammered, Everlast 18.00
Pitcher, Tall, Lightweight, Rodney Kent 25.00
Plate, Animal Reserve, Pearlescent, Oscar Bach, 1930, 12 In., 8 Pc. 990.00
Relish, 5 Sections, Chrysanthemum, Continental, 12 In. 22.00
Relish, 5 Sections, Glass Insert, Oak & Acorn, Farberware, 13 In. 25.00
Server, 4 Sections, Glass Insert, Pierced Lip, Forman Family 16.50
Sherbet, Various Colored Bases, Glass Bowl, 7 Piece 42.50
Silent Butler, Fruits Pattern, Cromwell, Rectangular 14.50
Silent Butler, Grapes, Hammercraft 6.00
Sugar & Creamer, Tray, Buenilum 13.00
Tray Set, Tiered, Morning Glories, Forms H, Farberware 15.00
Tray, Garden City Pottery, Cromwell, 18 In. 5.00
Tray, Glass Relish, Cover, Leaf Deco Looped Handles, Cromwell 22.00
Tray, Hammered, Plated, Ornate Handle, Rodney Kent, 16 In. Diam. 20.00
Tray, Palmer Smith, 14 x 20 1/2 In. 10.00
Warmer, Wooden Knob & Handle, Buenilum 35.00

AMBER, see Jewelry category

AMBER GLASS is the name of any glassware with the proper yellow–brown shading. It was a popular color just after the Civil War and many pressed glass pieces were made of amber glass. Depression glass of the 1930s–1950s was also made in shades of amber glass. All types are being reproduced.

Console Set, Short Candleholders, 3 Piece	45.00
Console Set, Tall Candlesticks, 3 Piece	75.00
Dish, Cat On Basketweave Base, 5 1/2 In.	60.00
Dish, Hen On Nest, Basketweave Base	50.00

AMBERETTE pieces are listed in the Pressed Glass section under the pattern name Amberette.

AMBERINA is a two–toned glassware made from 1883 to about 1900. It was patented by Joseph Locke of the New England Glass Company, but was also made by other companies. The glass shades from red to amber. Similar pieces of glass may be found in the Baccarat and Plated Amberina categories. Glass shaded from blue to amber is called *Blue Amberina* or *Bluerina.*

Bowl, 4 1/2 In. Diam.	100.00
Bowl, Diamond–Quilted, Enameled Roses, Silver–Plated Stand, 11 In.	1000.00
Candlestick, 12–Ribbed Base, Plated Fittings, 9 1/2 In., Pair	665.00
Candlestick, Plated Fittings, Twisted Stem, 9 1/2 In., Pair	665.00
Carafe, Water, Hobnail, 8 In.	295.00
Celery Vase, Diamond–Quilted, Square, New England, 6 1/2 In.	325.00
Celery Vase, Inverted Thumbprint, Ruffled Top, 6 1/4 In., Pair	550.00
Celery Vase, Thumbprint, Ribbed Collar, Ruffled Top	265.00
Creamer, Inverted Thumbprint, Squatty, 2 5/8 In.	395.00
Creamer, Square Top, Neck & Shoulder, Reeded Handle, 4 1/4 In.	385.00
Cruet, Inverted Thumbprint, Amber Ball Stopper, 6 1/4 In.	295.00
Cruet, Inverted Thumbprint, Amber Reeded Handle, Faceted Stopper	225.00
Cruet, Inverted Thumbprint, Square Base, Flared Rim, 8 1/4 In.	450.00
Cruet, Inverted Thumbprint, White Flowers, Square Base, 3 3/8 In.	450.00
Cruet, Swirl, Double Loop Handle, Flattened Bulbous, 11 1/4 In.	295.00
Cup, Applied Amber Glass Handle, Rose	40.00
Cup, Punch, Pleated, Amber Applied Handle, White Lining, 2 1/2 In.	1800.00
Dish, Canoe, Daisy & Button, 8 In.	357.50
Finger Bowl, 4 1/2 In.	295.00
Mustard, Mt. Washington, 2 1/2 In.	250.00
Nappy, Daisy & Button, Square	55.00
Pitcher Set, Inverted Thumbprint, 5 Piece	500.00
Pitcher, Bull's–Eye, Amber Reeded Handle	205.00
Pitcher, Diamond–Quilted, 5 1/2 In.	300.00
Pitcher, Diamond–Quilted, Amber Handle, 8 1/2 In.	192.00
Pitcher, Elongated Thumbprint, Amber Handle	200.00
Pitcher, Hobnail, Amber Handle, 6 3/4 In.	815.00
Pitcher, Inverted Thumbprint, Amber Handle, 7 1/2 In.	195.00
Pitcher, Inverted Thumbprint, Amber Handle, Square Top, 7 1/4 In.	275.00
Pitcher, Inverted Thumbprint, Cylindrical Neck, Amber Handle, 8 In	335.00
Pitcher, Inverted Thumbprint, Square Top, Fuchsia, 6 In.	235.00
Pitcher, Optic, Bulbous, Amber Handle, 7 1/4 In.	265.00
Pitcher, Reverse Diamond, Clear Handle, 9 In.	180.00
Pitcher, Swirl, Amber Handle, 7 1/2 In.	225.00
Pitcher, Swirl, Amber Handle, 8 3/4 In.	150.00
Pitcher, Water, Bulbous, Amber Reeded Applied Handle, 7 1/4 In.	265.00
Salt Dip, Melon Ribbed, 2 3/4 In.	50.00
Spooner, Swirl, 4 1/2 In.	110.00
Sugar & Creamer, Inverted Thumbprint, Pairpoint Holder, 3 1/2 In.	995.00
Sugar Shaker, Baby Thumbprint, Flowers, Mt. Washington	875.00
Sugar, Cover, Daisy & Button, 5 1/2 In.	540.00
Toothpick, Daisy & Button	185.00
Toothpick, Inverted Thumbprint, Bulging Base	225.00

American Dinnerware, Teapot, Silhouette,
Crooksville, 7 1/2 In.

Fiesta pottery has been reproduced since 1985 but the new pieces are made in colors different from the old ones.

Toothpick, New England, Ruffled Top, 2 1/4 In.	412.00
Toothpick, Optic Diamond–Quilted, 2 1/2 In.	285.00
Tumble–Up, Inverted Thumbprint	175.00 To 325.00
Tumble–Up, Inverted Thumbprint, Reverse Amberina, 7 In.	110.00
Tumbler, Baby Thumbprint	65.00
Tumbler, Fuchsia	125.00
Tumbler, Inverted Thumbprint, 3 1/2 In., Pair	110.00
Tumbler, Inverted Thumbprint, 3 3/4 In.	50.00
Tumbler, Inverted Thumbprint, Blue	75.00
Tumbler, Inverted Thumbprint, Cranberry	40.00
Vase, Diamond–Quilted, Pinched Tricorn Rim, 5 1/2 In.	522.50
Vase, Floral Design, Amber Wishbone Feet, 12 1/2 In.	165.00
Vase, Flower Form, Diamond–Quilted, Mt. Washington, 6 1/2 In.	385.00
Vase, Jack–In–The–Pulpit, Rigaree, 8 In.	100.00
Vase, Lily, Interior Vertical Ribbing, New England, 12 In.	275.00

American Encaustic Tiling Co., Panel,
Maroon, 3 Piece

To preserve leather–bound books, first dust. Then apply a light application of leather protector (potassium lactate) with a soft cloth. After it dries, apply a little leather dressing (lanolin and neetsfoot oil). This will deacidify the leather and keep it from becoming brittle. In an urban home, repeat this every other year.

To take desirable cards from an old scrapbook or to remove old wallpaper from a box, soak the entire piece in warm water until the paste loosens. Most types of early ink will survive this method, but test ink on handwritten pages before soaking. Test dark wallpapers.

Vase, Lily, Mt. Washington, 9 3/4 In. 275.00
Vase, Lily, Pulled–Up Top, Mt. Washington, 7 In. 357.00
Vase, Optic Panel, Cylinder, 4 In. 195.00
Vase, Swirl, Cylinder, 9 In. 150.00
Whiskey, Fuchsia, Diamond–Quilted, Flint 125.00

AMERICAN ART CLAY Company of Indianapolis, Indiana, made a variety of art pottery wares, especially vases, from about 1930 to after World War II. The company used the mark AMACO, as well as the company name. Do not confuse this company with an earlier art pottery firm from Edgerton, Wisconsin, called the American Art Clay Works.

Bust, Girl With Short Hair, 5 In. 115.00
Figure, Cheetah, Tan, 5 In. 75.00
Vase, Green, Grip Glaze, 9 In. 85.00
Vase, Ivory, Blue & Red, 7 In. 125.00
Vase, Tan, Glossy Glaze, 6 In. 90.00

AMERICAN DINNERWARE is the name used by collectors for ceramic dinnerware made in the United States from the 1930s through the 1950s. Most was made in potteries in southern Ohio, West Virginia, and California. Dishes were sold in gift shops and department stores, or were given away as premiums. Many of these patterns are listed in this book in their own sections, such as Autumn Leaf, Coors, Fiesta, Franciscan, Hall, Harker, Harlequin, Red Wing, Riviera, Russel Wright, Vernon Kilns, and Watt. For more information, see *Kovels' Depression Glass & American Dinnerware Price List.*

Baker, Divided, Currier & Ives, Royal China, 12 In. 12.00
Bowl, Apple Blossom, Crooksville, 5 In. 2.00
Bowl, Calico Fruit, Universal, 6 In. 10.00
Bowl, Cereal, California Ivy, Metlox 8.00
Bowl, Hacienda, Homer Laughlin, 5 In. 5.00
Bowl, Old Curiosity Shop, Green, Royal China, 5 1/2 In. 1.25
Bowl, Poppy Trail, Ivory, Metlox, 5 1/4 In. 3.00
Bowl, Poppy Trail, Turquoise, Metlox, 5 1/4 In. 4.00
Bowl, Tab Handle, Crab Apple, Blue Ridge 4.50
Bowl, Vegetable, Divided, California Provincial 25.00
Bowl, Vegetable, Silhouette, Crooksville 20.00
Bowl, Vistosa, Green, Taylor, Smith & Taylor, 6 In. 3.00
Box, Cigarette, Rose Step, Blue Ridge 110.00
Cake Plate, Handle, Cat–Tail, Universal, 12 1/2 In. 12.00
Cake Plate, Kitchen Kraft, Blue, Homer Laughlin 40.00
Cake Plate, Kitchen Kraft, Red, Homer Laughlin 30.00
Canister Set, Apple, Purinton, 4 Piece 85.00
Canteen, Cat–Tail, Universal Potteries 18.00
Carafe, Poppy Trail, Blue Green, Wooden Handle 25.00
Casserole, Cat–Tail, Cover, Universal Potteries 20.00
Casserole, Cover, Kitchen Kraft, Yellow, Individual .... 60..00
Casserole, Cover, Oven Serve, Homer Laughlin 12.00
Celery, Daisy Leaf, Blue Ridge 30.00
Chop Plate, Apple, Purinton 20.00
Chop Plate, Colonial Homestead, Royal China, 12 In. 7.00
Coffeepot, A. D., Petit Point House, Crooksville 45.00
Coffeepot, California Ivy, Metlox 45.00
Creamer, Casualstone 5.00
Creamer, Flower Ring, Blue Ridge 5.00
Creamer, Mardi Gras, Southern Potteries 6.50
Creamer, Rhythm, Yellow 3.00
Creamer, Rooster, Metlox 10.00
Creamer, Yorktown, Blue, Knowles 4.00
Cup & Saucer, Arlington Apple, Blue Ridge 6.50
Cup & Saucer, Ballerina, Forest Green, Universal 3.00
Cup & Saucer, California Ivy, Metlox 8.00
Cup & Saucer, Casualstone 5.50

Cup & Saucer, Christmas Tree, Blue Ridge 45.00
Cup & Saucer, Harlequin, Homer Laughlin 4.50
Cup & Saucer, Old Curiosity Shop, Green, Royal China 2.00
Cup & Saucer, Poppy Trail, Orange, Metlox 5.00
Cup & Saucer, Rancho, Dark Green, French Saxon 5.00
Cup & Saucer, Sunny, Blue Ridge .... 5.00 To 6.00
Cup & Saucer, Sweet Clover, Demitasse 35.00
Cup, Apple, Purinton 8.00
Cup, Poppy Trail, Metlox 6.00
Cup, Wild Poppy, Metlox 6.00
Cup, Woodfield, Chartreuse, Steubenville 4.00
Dinner Set, Stanhome Ivy, Blue Ridge, 46 Piece 100.00
Dinner Set, Virginia Rose, Homer Laughlin, 29 Piece 90.00
Ginger Jar, Apple, Purinton 27.00
Gravy, Petalware, Yellow, W. S. George 5.00
Grill Plate, Cat–Tail, Universal 12.00
Jug–Pitcher, Cameo Rose, Blue, Harker, Large 35.00
Pitcher, Blossom Grace, Blue Ridge, Large 59.00
Pitcher, Luray, Footed, Large 60.00
Pitcher, Milk, Red Rooster, Metlox, 1 Qt. 15.00
Pitcher, Utility, Calico Fruit, Universal, 6 1/2 In. 32.00
Plate, Apple Blossom, Crooksville, 10 In. 3.50
Plate, Arlington Apple, Blue Ridge, 10 In. .... 2.00 To 6.00
Plate, Ballerina, Burgundy, Universal, 6 In. 2.00
Plate, Black Dancers, Blue Ridge 850.00
Plate, California Provincial, Metlox, 9 In. 5.00
Plate, Christmas Tree, Blue Ridge, 10 In. 50.00
Plate, Colonial Homestead, Royal China, 10 In. 6.00
Plate, Crab Apple, Blue Ridge, 10 In. .... 6.00 To 10.00
Plate, Dinner, Casualstone 4.50
Plate, Fantasia, Blue Ridge, 9 In. 9.00
Plate, Frageria, Blue Ridge, 9 1/2 In. 4.00
Plate, French Peasant, Blue Ridge, 10 In. 35.00
Plate, Fruit, Bamboo, Blue Ridge 2.50
Plate, Handle, Ballerina, Dove Gray, Universal, 10 In. 4.50
Plate, Handle, Yorktown, Maroon, Knowles, 9 In. 5.00
Plate, Old Curiosity Shop, Pink, Royal China, 7 In. 3.00
Plate, Organdy, Homer Laughlin, 9 1/2 In. 5.00
Plate, Petalware, Light Green, W. S. George, 7 In. 2.50
Plate, Poppy Trail, Metlox, 6 In. 4.00
Plate, Quail, Blue Ridge 500.00
Plate, Rancho, Maroon, French Saxon, 9 In. 4.00
Plate, Ring, Blue, Bauer, 15 In. 40.00
Plate, Spider Web, Pink, Blue Ridge, 10 3/8 In. 7.00
Plate, Virginia Rose, Homer Laughlin, 10 1/2 In. 8.00
Plate, Woodfield, Gray, Steubenville, 10 1/2 In. 5.00
Plate, Yorktown, Terra Cotta, Knowles, 9 In. .... 5.00 To 10.00
Platter, Hacienda, Homer Laughlin 15.00
Platter, Petit Point Basket, Salem 7.00
Platter, Red Rooster, Metlox, 13 1/2 In. 20.00
Platter, Ring, Blue, Bauer, 9 In. 18.00
Platter, Spider Web, Pink, Blue Ridge, 13 1/2 x 11 In. 15.00
Platter, Sunny, Blue Ridge, 14 In. 8.00
Platter, Turkey, Acorns, Blue Ridge 175.00
Relish, Ring, Yellow, Bauer 35.00
Salt, Ballerina, Dove Gray, Universal 3.00
Saucer, Ballerina, Blue, Universal 1.00
Saucer, Vistosa, Yellow, Taylor, Smith & Taylor 2.00
Soup, Dish, Bamboo, Blue Ridge, 5 3/4 In. 3.50
Soup, Dish, Cat–Tail, Universal, 7 5/8 In. 8.50
Soup, Dish, Silhouette, Crooksville 7.00
Soup, Dish, Yorktown, Yellow, Knowles 6.50
Sugar & Creamer, Rose Marie, Pedestal, Blue Ridge 65.00

Sugar, Cover, Ballerina, Forest Green, Univeral 3.50
Sugar, Cover, Casualstone 5.00
Sugar, Flower Ring, Blue Ridge 5.00
Sugar, Organdy, Homer Laughlin 8.00
Teapot, Apple, Purinton .... 15.00 To 18.00
Teapot, Country Road, Colonial, Blue Ridge 75.00
Teapot, Ivy, Metlox 40.00
Teapot, Mardi Gras, Southern Potteries, Square 80.00
Teapot, Silhouette, Crooksville, 7 1/2 In. ....*Illus* 5.00
Teapot, Sugar & Creamer, Ivy, Red Flower, Purinton 16.00
Wall Pocket, Poppy Trail, California Provincial 70.00
Water Set, Cat–Tail, Universal, 7 Piece 65.00

AMERICAN ENCAUSTIC Tiling Company was founded in Zanesville, Ohio, in 1875. The company planned to make a variety of tiles to compete with the English tiles that were selling in the United States for use in fireplaces and other architectural designs. The first glazed tiles were made in 1880, embossed tiles in 1881, faience tiles in the 1920s. The firm closed in 1935 and reopened in 1937 as the Shawnee Pottery.

Bookends, Cupid & Rabbit, 1926 .... 150.00
Panel, Maroon, 3 Piece ....*Illus* 85.00
Tile, Floral, Green 25.00
Tile, Margery Daw, Nursery Rhyme Scene 65.00
Tile, McKinley 125.00

AMETHYST GLASS is any of the many glasswares made in the dark purple color of the gemstone called amethyst. Included in this section are many pieces made in the nineteenth and twentieth centuries. Very dark pieces are called *black amethyst* and are listed under that heading.

Cologne, Atomizer, Gold & Applied Flowers 75.00
Cuspidor, Woman's, 3 1/2 In. 50.00
Decanter, Blown, Loop Handle, Mushroom Stopper, 1860s, 11 In. 350.00
Finger Bowl, 3 x 4 1/2 In. 25.00
Plate, Jefferson Davis Bust, Backwards C, 9 In. 45.00
Toothpick, Rings & Beads, Souvenir Of Monroe, Mich. 20.00
Toothpick, Swag With Brackets, Gold 50.00
Vase, Hand Painted Red Flower, Ruffled, Black Type, 12 In. 90.00

AMPHORA pieces are listed in the Teplitz category.

ANDIRONS and related fireplace items are included in the Fireplace category.

ANIMAL TROPHIES, such as stuffed animals or fish, rugs made of animal skins, and other similar collectibles are listed in this section. Collectors should be aware of the endangered species laws that make it illegal to buy and sell some of these items. Any eagle feathers, many types of cats (such as leopard), and many forms of tortoiseshell can be confiscated if discovered by the government.

Antelope Head, 12 x 14–In. Horns 247.50
Blesbok Head, 14 1/2–In. Horns 385.00
Buffalo Head, Female, Mounted 325.00
Buffalo Head, Stuffed 975.00
Buffalo Hide 375.00
Buffalo, Mounted From Shoulder 795.00
Cape Buffalo Head, 40 x 18–In. Horns 660.00
Cape Buffalo Head, Mounted 850.00
Carriage Robe, Bearskin, Red Fox On Reverse, 60 x 70 In. 700.00
Costume, Cheetah Skin, Watusi 1200.00
Deer Head, Mounted On Oak Shield, 31 In. 195.00
Deer, Mounted 100.00
Lap Robe, Bearskin 650.00
Lion, Full, c.1967, 9 Ft. 9 In. 1100.00

Animation Art, Cel, Charlie Brown Christmas, 1965, 9 1/2 x 17 In.

Animation Art, Cel, Lady & The Tramp, Walt Disney, 9 x 12 In.

Lion, Fully Mounted, World's Record Size, 1967	1000.00
Moose Head, Alaska, World's Record Size, 70–In. Antlers	1430.00
Nyala Head, 21–In. Horns	330.00
Platypus, Taxidermist, Mounted In Shadowbox Frame	322.00
Rattlesnake	50.00
Reed Buck Head, 9–In. Horns	165.00
Reed Duiker Head, 4–In. Horns	165.00
Roan Head, 1960, 26 In.	440.00
Robe, Buffalo, 5 1/2 x 6 1/2 Ft.	675.00
Rug, Bearskin, Brown	95.00
Rug, Bearskin, Brown, 8 Ft.	1000.00
Rug, Mountain Lion Skin	450.00
Rug, Zebra Skin	300.00
Rug, Zebra Skin, Lined, 4 Ft. 10 In. x 7 Ft.	770.00
Sable Head, 42–In. Horns	330.00
Situtunga Head, 21–In. Horns	495.00
Springbok Head, 13 3/4–In. Horns	250.00
Squirrel, Gray, Climbing, Wall Bark Plaque, 7 x 14 In.	49.00
Steenbok Head, 4–In. Horns	220.00

ANIMATION ART collectibles include cels that are painted drawings on celluloid needed to make an animated cartoon. Hundreds of cels are made, then photographed in sequence to make a cartoon showing moving figures. Early examples made by the Walt Disney Studios are popular with collectors today. Original sketches used by the artists are also listed here.

Cel, 101 Dalmatians, Anita Walks Perdita Park	900.00
Cel, 101 Dalmatians, Pongo, Hat, Matted, Framed, 1961, 9 In.	1600.00
Cel, 3 Caballeros, 1945, 6 7/8 x 9 In.	385.00
Cel, Alf, Full Background	270.00
Cel, Alice In Wonderland, Alice	1500.00
Cel, All Dogs Go To Heaven, 'gator Holds Charlie In Sari	200.00
Cel, All Dogs Go To Heaven, Itchy & Charlie Out Of Barrel	375.00
Cel, Aristocats, Close–Up Of Tom O'Malley	325.00
Cel, Bambi	350.00
Cel, Batman	290.00
Cel, Berenstain Bears, Family Scene, Papa Reading To Cubs	100.00
Cel, Box Office Bunny, Face, 13 x 17 1/4 In.	8250.00
Cel, Brave Little Tailor, 1938, 9 x 11 3/4 In.	7700.00
Cel, Brave Little Tailor, Knight, 1938, 8 x 11 1/4 In.	880.00
Cel, Bugs Bunny, Full Figure, Signed Friz Freleng	950.00
Cel, California Raisins, Full Figure, Purple Wrinkles	100.00
Cel, Charlie Brown Christmas, 1965, 9 1/2 x 17 In. ....*Illus*	10450.00
Cel, Christmas Carol, Sad Mickey Grasps Tiny Tim's Crutch	2000.00
Cel, Cinderella, Lady Tremaine Looking Elegantly Evil	1000.00
Cel, Dam Disaster At Money Lake, Uncle Scrooge, 16 x 20 In.	1452.00
Cel, Donald Duck, Angry, Clenched Fists, 1940s	880.00
Cel, Donald Duck, Don't Look 200, Shoulders Up, 1985, 7 In.	475.00

Cel, Donald Duck, Hockey Champ, Swings In Cage, 1939 .... 275.00
Cel, Donald Gets Drafted, 7 x 6 1/2 In. 1430.00
Cel, Donald's Golf Game, 1938, 7 1/4 x 9 1/8 In. 770.00
Cel, Dumbo, Circus Tent, 1941, 8 1/2 x 9 1/2 In. 1210.00
Cel, Dumbo, Disney, 1941 .... 3500.00
Cel, Dumbo, Sad, Storyboard Drawing, Timothy On His Trunk 1000.00
Cel, Dumbo, Stork, Delivers Babies, 3 x 5 In. 303.00
Cel, Edgar The Butler, Aristocats, 1970, 7 In. 85.00
Cel, Fantasia, Ben Aligator Twirls Hippo 2000.00
Cel, Flintstones, Barney In Santa Suit, Fred Looks On 150.00
Cel, Flora, Good Fairy, Sleeping Beauty, Label, 1959, 6 In. 175.00
Cel, Fred Flintstone, Jetsons Meet Flintstones 175.00
Cel, Fred Flintstone, TV, With Drawings 85.00
Cel, Grand Canyon, Scope, 1954, 9 1/2 x 12 1/2 In. 3575.00
Cel, How To Play Football, Goofy, Passing Ball, 6 x 6 In. 1150.00
Cel, Huey Duck, Donald's Golf Game, Courvoisier, Large 2400.00
Cel, Jetsons, The Movie, George, Spaceship, Signed 600.00
Cel, Jiminy & Elderly Duck 275.00
Cel, Jiminy Cricket & Donald Duck, Framed, 10 x 7 In. 715.00
Cel, Jiminy Cricket, With Overly Friendly Catfish 247.50
Cel, Jungle Book, King Louie, 1967, 9 x 12 In. 1320.00
Cel, Jungle Book, Mowgli, 1967, 6 In. 675.00
Cel, Lady & The Tramp, 1955, 6 1/4 x 9 1/4 In. 2090.00
Cel, Lady & The Tramp, Framed, 1955, 10 1/2 x 7 1/2 In. 4675.00
Cel, Lady & The Tramp, Romping, Full Figure, Framed 1250.00
Cel, Lady & The Tramp, Walt Disney, 9 x 12 In. ...._Illus_ 1870.00
Cel, Lady & Tramp, Full Figure, Lady Running, Ball In Mouth 1500.00
Cel, Lady & Tramp, Lady 1900.00
Cel, Lady & Tramp, Tramp 1900.00
Cel, Ludwig Von Drake 247.50
Cel, Ludwig Von Drake, 1960s, 6 & 5 1/2 In., 2 Piece 522.00
Cel, Madame Medusa & Mr. Snoops, Rifle, 1977, 8 x 11 In. 350.00
Cel, Maid Marion, Lady Cluck, Laminated, Framed, 1973, 8 In. 450.00
Cel, Merrie Melodies, 9 3/4 x 26 In. 7700.00
Cel, Mickey Mouse, Astronaut Suit, Floating In Space 880.00
Cel, Oliver & Co., Georgette & Bulldog Choose Chocolates 400.00
Cel, Pecos Bill, Widowmaker, Twirling His Guns, 1949 .... 300.00
Cel, Pink Panther, 7 x 9 In. 295.00
Cel, Pink Panther, TV, With Drawings, 1970s 125.00
Cel, Pinocchio, Figaro The Cat 2300.00
Cel, Pinocchio, Seated On Bench, Blue Fairy & Jiminy 3500.00
Cel, Pinocchio, Worthington Foulfellow, 1 Eye Open, 5 In. 500.00
Cel, Popeye, Trys To Shut Door, Famous Studios 650.00
Cel, Raggedy Ann, Raggedy Andy, Back View, Children's Blocks 110.00
Cel, Raggedy Ann, Raggedy Andy, Looking Out Of Window 100.00
Cel, Raggedy Ann, Raggedy Andy, Paddle Boat 120.00
Cel, Raggedy Ann, Raggedy Andy, Pirate & Parrot 100.00
Cel, Reluctant Dragon, Goofy, 1941, 8 7/8 x 11 1/4 In. 1760.00
Cel, Road Runner, Full Figure, Ready To Run 400.00
Cel, Robin Hood, As Blind Beggar 375.00
Cel, Robin Hood, Laminated, Matted, Framed, 1973, 8 3/4 In. 700.00
Cel, Robin Hood, Mangy Lion In Royal Robes, 8 x 10 In. 726.00
Cel, Roger Rabbit, Being Grabbed Round The Throat By Eddie 2100.00
Cel, Sleeping Beauty, Prince Phillip, Framed, 5 x 3 1/2 In. 825.00
Cel, Sleeping Beauty, Prince Riding Samson, Both Full Figure 1000.00
Cel, Smurf 25.00
Cel, Snow White & 7 Dwarfs, 1937 .... 1045.00
Cel, Snow White & 7 Dwarfs, 1937, 5 x 7 1/2 In. 2970.00
Cel, Snow White & 7 Dwarfs, Grumpy, 1937 .... 1870.00
Cel, Snow White, Hands On Hip, 6 x 4 In. 908.00
Cel, Snow White, Wicked Witch 950.00
Cel, Sword In The Stone, Merlin, 1963, 10 1/4 x 10 In. 935.00
Cel, The Pointer, Mickey & Pluto, 1940, 8 1/4 x 16 In. 6050.00

Cel, Tom & Jerry, Lonesome Mouse, Drawing, 1943	200.00
Cel, Top Cat, Publicity	247.00
Cel, Tugboat Mickey, Seasick Pelican, 6 x 11 In.	726.00
Cel, Two–Gun Goofy, Tipping Hat, Framed, 6 x 6 In.	550.00
Cel, Ugly Duckling, 5 Swimming, 1939, 8 7/8 x 11 3/4 In.	880.00
Cel, Uncle Scrooge McDuck, Sport Goofy, Laminated, 1987, 5 In.	265.00
Cel, Who Framed Roger Rabbit, 13 1/4 x 7 3/8 In.	1760.00
Cel, Wind In The Willows, Mr. Toad Himself, Full Figure	300.00
Cel, Winnie The Pooh, Christopher, Eeyore, Pooh, Piglet Paint	600.00
Cel, Winnie The Pooh, Tigger, 1970s, 8 1/2 x 11 1/2 In.	550.00
Cel, Winnie The Pooh, Tigger, Disney Seal, Framed, 7 In.	800.00
Cel, Wizards, Weehawk & His Horse, With Drawing	150.00
Cel, Working For Peanuts, Donald Duck Working With Brush	990.00
Cel, Working For Peanuts, Donald With Elephant Trunk, 1953	495.00
Cel, Yellow Submarine, George Harrison With Butterfly	800.00
Cel, Yellow Submarine, Sgt. Pepper's Band, George, Tuba	125.00
Cel, Yogi, Boo Boo, Snagglepuss, Great Escape, Colored, Signed	500.00
Drawing, 3 Little Pigs, Colored Pencil, Wolf & Pig	1025.00
Drawing, 7 Dwarfs, 1937, 8 x 11 1/4 In.	990.00
Drawing, Cinderella, Pencil, Lips Colored, 1949, 7 3/4 In.	500.00
Drawing, Donald Duck, Full Figure, Pencil, 1930s, 4 In.	200.00
Drawing, Fantasia, Watercolor & Pencil, 1940, 11 x 14 In.	770.00
Drawing, Fifer & Fiddler Pigs, Practical Pig, Pencil, 1939	125.00
Drawing, Gurgi, Black Cauldron, Head, Hand, Pencil, 1985, 5 In.	25.00
Drawing, J. W. Foulfellow, Pinocchio, Pencil, 1940, 5 In.	500.00
Drawing, Mickey Mouse, Full Figure, Pencil, 1930s, 6 In.	350.00
Drawing, Mickey Mouse, Mickey's Rival, Pencil, 1936, 5 In.	450.00
Drawing, Mickey On Ice Skates, 1935, 9 x 10 1/2 In.	550.00
Drawing, Operation Sawdust, Woody Woodpecker, 10 x 33 In.	1320.00
Drawing, Pinocchio, Colored Pencil, 1940, 6 1/4 x 4 7/8 In.	330.00
Drawing, Pluto, Full Figure, Pencil, 1930s, 6 In.	250.00
Drawing, Practical Pig, Full Figure, Pencil, 1939, 4 In.	125.00
Drawing, Prince, Sleeping Beauty, Pencil, Matted, 1959, 7 In.	225.00
Drawing, Snow White & 7 Dwarfs, Framed, 1937	550.00
Drawing, Timothy Mouse, Dumbo, Full Figure, Pencil, 1941, 5 In.	265.00
Drawing, Toliver, More Kittens, Head, Paw, Pencil, 1936, 7 In.	75.00
Drawing, Two Kittens, More Kittens, Pencil, 1936	125.00
Model Sheet Photostat, Figaro, Pinocchio, 1940	125.00
Model Sheet Photostat, Make Mine Music, Peter & Wolf, 1946	75.00
Model Sheet Photostat, Ostrich, Fantasia, 1940	150.00
Model Sheet Photostat, Parrot, Mickey's Parrot, 1938	50.00

ANNA POTTERY was started in Anna, Illinois, in 1859 by Cornwall and Wallace Kirkpatrick. They made many types of utilitarian wares, bricks, drain tiles, and giftware. The most collectible pieces made by the pottery *Anna Pottery* are the pig–shaped bottles and jugs with special inscriptions, applied animals and figures. The pottery closed in 1894.

Pig, Railroad, c.1883, 8 In.	650.00

APPLE PEELERS are listed in the Kitchen section under Peeler, Apple.

ARC–EN–CIEL is the French word for rainbow. A pottery factory named Arc–en–ciel was founded in Zanesville, Ohio, in 1903. The company made art pottery for a short time, then became the Brighton Pottery in 1905.

Vase, Floral Design, Luster, 13 In.	300.00
Vase, Iridescent Luster, Bulbous, 8 In.	250.00

ARCHITECTURAL antiques include a variety of collectibles, usually very large, that have been removed from buildings. Hardware, backbars, doors, paneling, and even old bathtubs are now wanted by collectors. Pieces of the Victorian, Art Nouveau, and Art Deco styles are in greatest demand.

Backbar, Barber Shop, Marble Base, Oak, 9 x 12 Ft.	1600.00
Backbar, Candy Store, Ice Cream Parlor, Large	2000.00

Backbar, Cherry, Carved, Hardware, 8 Ft. 2 In. x 7 Ft. 10 In. 4250.00
Backbar, Raised Panels, Posts, Mirrors, Mahogany, 12 Ft. 3500.00
Backbar, Stained Glass, Marble Top, Mahogany, 9 1/2 x 12 Ft. 6500.00
Backbar, Store, 2–60 Ft. Sections Each Side, Oak 1950.00
Backbar, Walnut, 16 Ft., Front Bar, 27 1/2 Ft. 5000.00
Baluster, Stairway, Louis Sullivan, Cast Iron, c.1895, 30 In. 4950.00
Bathtub, Empire Style, Black & Gold Design, Metal, 58 In. 440.00
Birdbath, Figural, Cherub & Bird On Shell, Lead, 16 In. 1320.00
Birdbath, Figural, Child Holding Shell, Lead, 30 1/2 In. 2640.00
Book, Wallpaper, Karper & Allman, Dated 1931 .... 50.00
Caster, Furniture, Claws Over Glass Balls, 4 Piece 35.00
Cornice, Gold Leaf, Gesso, c.1870, 48 1/2 x 5 In., 4 Piece 880.00
Door Knocker, Flower Basket, 3 3/4 In. 85.00
Door, 4 Panels, Yellow & Brown Graining, Folk Design, 79 In. 175.00
Door, English Pub, Honduras Mahogany, Beveled Glass, Pair 1900.00
Door, Exterior, Carved, Paneled, Leaded Glass Diamond Inset 750.00
Doorknob, Mottled Brown 3.00
Down Spout, Copper, 1840, 18 In., Pair 700.00
Down Spout, Figural Fish, Tin, Wooden Base, China, 21 In., Pair 2800.00
Fence, Victorian, Matching Posts, 2 Gates, Cast Iron, 50 Ft. 3000.00
Fence, Widow's Walk, Iron, 22 Ft. 125.00
Figure, Badger, With Grin, Pottery, Tanoki, Okinawa 820.00
Figure, Man, Holding Lamb, Dog At Feet, Stone, 5 Ft. 9350.00
Figure, Pineapple, Terra–Cotta, 33 In., Pair 825.00
Figure, Stag, Cast Zinc & Copper, Cartier 2800.00
Figure, Woman, In Draped Toga, Cast Iron, 6 Ft. 11000.00
Fireplace, Carved Mahogany, c.1901, 83 x 102 In. ....*Illus* 14300.00
Fireplace, Oak Surround, McKay Co., 1886, 9 x 6 Ft. 2600.00
Fountain, Cherub Holding Dolphin With Nozzle, Lead, 23 In. 1980.00
Fountain, Dolphin, Boy, Fiberglass, W. Sinz, 64 In. ....*Illus* 3180.00
Fountain, Fish, Spews Water, Lead & Zinc, Granite Base 1650.00
Fretwork, Oak, 1880s, Pair 895.00
Gate, Classical, Iron, Pair 352.00
Gate, Iron, Ornate, 78 x 62 In., Pair 3200.00
Gate, Kneeling Angel Center, Cast Iron 975.00
Gate, Masonic Symbol Incorporated Into Design 475.00
Gate, Plants, Silvered, Gilt Bronze, Iron, 61 In., Pair 3850.00
Gate, Spanish Baroque, Iron, 1880s, 75 1/2 x 22 In., Pair 665.00
Gate, Twisted & Floral Design Bars, Iron, c.1920, 77 In., Pair 715.00
Gate, Victorian, Cast Iron, 29 x 21 In., Pair 245.00
Gate, Weeping Willow & Lamb, Cast Iron, 1830s, 30 In. 220.00

Architectural, Fireplace, Carved Mahogany,
c.1901, 83 x 102 In.

Architectural, Fountain, Dolphin, Boy,
Fiberglass, W. Sinz, 64 In.

Gate, Weeping Willow Tree Center	1950.00
Gazebo, White Painted Wire, 4 Supports, France, 1880s	935.00
Hinge, Scrolled & Tooled Ram's Horn, Iron, 11 In., Pair	85.00
Hitching Post, Eagle Head Top, Cast Iron, 39 In.	1760.00
Hitching Post, Seated Dog, 11 3/8 In.	925.00
Hitching Post, Truncated Tree Form, Cast Iron	375.00
Lantern, Garden, Chinese Style, Cast Iron, 16 1/2 In., Pair	357.50
Louver, Fan Shape, Blue & White, Mid–1800s	1125.00
Mantel, Carved Basket Of Fruit Center Panel, France	1000.00
Mantel, Cast Iron Rococo, Tinsel Design, Patent 1860	2650.00
Mantel, Cherry, Bird's–Eye Maple Inserts, Fruit Carved, 1880	2850.00
Mantel, Grain Painted Over Chestnut, Late Victorian	125.00
Mantel, Gray Marble, France, 18th Century	2000.00
Mantel, Oak, Gustav Stickley	900.00
Mantel, Pine, Carved	175.00
Mantel, Putti, Carrara Marble, Wedgwood Plaque, 67 x 47 In.	3850.00
Panel, Winged Figure, Garlands, High Relief, Iron, Pair	495.00
Pedestal, Marble, 44 In.	250.00
Pedestal, Marble, White, Black, 29 3/4 In.	345.00
Planter, 2 Tiers, Wire, 32 In.	330.00
Plinth, White Marble, Carved, 19th–20th Century	853.00
Railing Mounts, Ram's Head, Brass, Pair	605.00
Railing, Acorn & Oak Leaf Design, Iron, 10 x 83 In.	55.00
Sink, Stone, Drain Corner, Carved, E. Bigelow, 1848, 24 x 48 In.	1100.00
Sink, Zinc, J. L. Mott Ironworks	2700.00
Stairs, Wooden, Set Of 4	175.00
Stand, Plant, Single Holder, Wire, 42 In.	715.00
Thumb Latch, Tulip Shape, Iron, M. Alling, 1820s	1800.00
Trumeax, (Pillar)Man & Woman Landscape Painted Upper Panel	1210.00
Urn, Floral Vines, Ram Head Handles, Lead, 31 1/2 In., Pair	8525.00
Urn, Neo–Classical, Plaster, 45 In., Pair	1650.00
Vent, Barn, Triangular, Iron Hinges & Hasp, 42 In.	700.00
Yard Ornament, Windmill, Wooden, 4 1/2 In.	29.00

AREQUIPA POTTERY was produced from 1911 to 1918 by the patients of
the Arequipa Sanitorium in Marin County Hills, California.

Bowl, Incised Leaf Design, Brown & Blue, 4 1/2 In.	800.00
Bowl, Wisteria, Frederick Rhead	4000.00
Vase, Cattails Under Pink Matte, Green & Cream Glaze, 7 In.	1000.00
Vase, Dark Matte Blue, 1912, 5 In.	350.00
Vase, Molded Leaves, 3–Color Luster Glaze	600.00
Vase, Raised Hydrangeas, Leaves, Plum, Marked, 8 In.	1150.00
Vase, Volcanic Glaze, 8 In.	650.00
Vase, Wisteria Blossoms, 5 Colors, Vine Gnarled Reticulated Rim	4400.00

ARGY–ROUSSEAU, see G. Argy-Rousseau category

ARITA is a port in Japan. Porcelain was made there from about 1616.
Many types of decorations were used, including the popular Imari designs,
which are listed under Imari in this book.

Bowl, Red, Blue, Bamboo Sprays, 8 In.	85.00
Box, Figural, Snarling Kirin, Blue & White, Late 18th Century	165.00
Dish, Flowering Trees, 10 In.	150.00
Platter, Spread–Wing Bird, Blue, Red, Green, Scalloped Edge, 24 In.	450.00

ART DECO, or Art Moderne, a style started at the Paris Exposition of
1925, is characterized by linear, geometric designs. All types of furniture
and decorative arts, jewelry, book bindings, and even games were designed
in this style. Additional items may be found in this book in the Furniture
category, various glass categories, etc.

Ashtray & Table Lighter, Marble, Alfred Dunhill	25.00
Ashtray, Black Nude, On Chrome Ball, Metal, Electrolier Co., 24 In.	450.00
Ashtray, Brass, 5 1/2 In.	39.00

Art Deco, Figure, Piano Player, Nickel Finish,
Hagenauer, 8 In.

◆◆◆◆◆◆◆◆◆◆◆◆◆◆◆◆◆◆◆◆◆◆◆

Dust frequently if you live near
the seashore. Salt air causes
problems.

◆◆◆◆◆◆◆◆◆◆◆◆◆◆◆◆◆◆◆◆◆◆◆

Ashtray, Nude, Metal	345.00
Box, Black, Chrome, Dolphin Finial	12.00
Box, Powder, Blue Glass	35.00
Cocktail Shaker, Woman's Leg Shape, Glass, Chrome, 1920s, 16 In.	325.00
Cordial Set, Burgundy & Clear Glass, Etched & Colored Design	375.00
Dresser Set, Porcelain, Hand Painted, Powder Jar & Hair Receiver	30.00
Figure, Jazz Band, Ceramic, Painted, Brayton–Laguna, 7 In., 4 Piece	88.00
Figure, Piano Player, Nickel Finish, Hagenauer, 8 In. ....*Illus*	1100.00
Figurine, Pheasant, Pink, Blue Rhinestones	45.00
Figurine, Woman Dancer, Metal, Marble Base, 9 In.	185.00
Flower Frog, Nude, White Porcelain, 7 In.	35.00
Frame, Leaded, Blue–Green, Bull's-Eye Lens, 18th Century, 2 3/4 In.	17.00
Humidor, Bakelite, Revolving, 1920s	34.00
Incense Burner, Glass In Metal Frame, Etched	300.00
Jug, Hot Water, Green & Black, Pewter Lid, Early 20th Century	75.00
Lamp, 2 Bronze Nudes On 2 Sides Of Round Glass Globe, Geist	125.00
Lamp, Airplane, Cobalt Blue Glass	575.00
Lamp, Enameled Aqua Flowers On Glass, Electric, H. Lazofer, 8 In.	2525.00
Mirror, Red Catalin, Swivel Handle, Chrome Logo Emblem, 3 1/2 In.	25.00
Stand, Smoking, Metal & Celluloid, Lighted Base	45.00
Vase, Stylized Sea Gulls Over Waves, Cream, 9 x 9 In.	300.00
Wall Pocket, Blue Borders Around Roses, Candleholder On Sides	24.00

ART GLASS, see Glass–Art

ART NOUVEAU is a style of design that was at its most popular from
1895 to 1905. Famous designers, including Rene Lalique and Emile Galle,
produced furniture, glass, silver, metalwork, and buildings in the new style.
Ladies with long flowing hair and elongated bodies were among the more
easily recognized design elements. Copies of this style are being made
today. Many modern pieces of jewelry can be found. Additional Art
Nouveau pieces may be found in the Furniture section or in various glass
categories.

Ewer, Hammered Copper, Brass Handle, WMF, 11 In.	95.00
Jar, Dark Greenish Brown Mottled Glaze, Ormolu Trim, 8 7/8 In.	110.00
Mirror, Hand, Floral Design, Silver Plated, 11 In.	65.00
Planter, Brass Repousse, Footed, c.1900, 7 1/2 In.	176.00

ART POTTERY was first made in America in Cincinnati, Ohio, during the
1870s. The pieces were hand thrown and hand decorated. The art pottery
tradition continued until the 1920s when studio potters began making the
more artistic wares. American and English art pottery is listed here. More
recent pottery is listed under the name of the maker or in the Pottery
category.

Ashtray, 4 Depressions, Gustav Stickley, 6 In.	275.00
Bowl, Stylized Turtle Form, Rosa Quezada, 5 x 8 In.	330.00
Charger, Blue, Scheier, 11 In.	990.00

Charger, Sgraffito Design, Sheier, c.1955, 16 3/4 In.	605.00
Dish, Cheese, Shanghai, Losol	225.00
Figurine, Poodle, Gray, Blue, Odorfer, 6 In.	275.00
Figurine, Poodle, Gray, Pink, Odorfer, 15 3/4 In.	950.00
Frog, Robertson	38.00
Inkwell, Double Well, Tray, Wiener Werkstate, 4 1/2 x 9 1/4 In.	192.50
Jar, Raised Maize, Monkey Handle, Mochica, 500 B. C., 9 In.	650.00
Jug, Continual Rim Forms Handle, Linthorpe, Dresser, 8 In.	3840.00
Lamp, Baluster Form, Wooden Base, 23 3/4 In.	278.00
Mug, Stylized Ears Of Corn, Slate Gray Glaze, Abuja, 1960	55.00
Pitcher, Art Nouveau, Pauline Pottery, 12 In.	350.00
Pitcher, Speckled Buff, Globular, Long Flared Neck, St. Ives	100.00
Plate, Fish, Ochre & Brown Glaze, Iron-Brown Interior, Newland	203.00
Plate, Mushroom Glaze, Central Brown Wave Band, B. Leach	590.00
Pot, Hand Turned, Ezra Warne, Dated 1848	2100.00
Sugar & Creamer, Matte Green, Clara Poillon	300.00
Tankard, Brown Glaze, Brushed Yellow, Strap Handle, St. Ives	240.00
Teapot, Ink Blue Glaze, Strap Handle, Chrysanthemum Lid, Leach	480.00
Teapot, Memphis Style, Ettore Sottsass, 11 In.	560.00
Urn, Landscape, Iridescent Gold, Swastika, Skeramos, 12 In.	300.00
Vase, 3 Gazelles, Black, Green, Cream, Primavera, 19 In.	2750.00
Vase, Alternating Gun Metal Stripes, Maija Grotell, 7 1/2 In.	2090.00
Vase, Bottle, Translucent Tenmoku Glaze, Fluted, Bernard Leach	1848.00
Vase, Brown Glaze, Under Speckled Olive, Cylindrical, J. Leach	2032.00
Vase, Byzantine Pattern, Mottled, Charlotte Rhead, 8 1/2 In.	265.00
Vase, Byzantine Pattern, Satin, Charlotte Rhead, 6 7/8 In.	165.00
Vase, Chalice Shape, Beige, Scheier, 12 1/2 In.	3850.00
Vase, Coiled Snake, Turquoise Glaze, Sandoz, 1925, 16 3/4 In.	2310.00
Vase, Crystalline Dripped On Brown, Aqua, Jervis, 3 1/2 In.	380.00
Vase, Green, Orange Glaze, 4 Urns At Top, Vance Avon, 11 In.	125.00
Vase, Incised Bands, Tenmoku Glaze, Cylindrical, B. Leach	4435.00
Vase, Iridescent Mauve, Reptilian Fragmented, Merrimac, 6 In.	665.00
Vase, Iron Brown Glaze Beneath Blue, Waisted, B. Leach	480.00
Vase, Matte Black Glaze, 2 Streaks, Cylindrical Neck, J. Leach	517.00
Vase, Monticello, Handles, Green, 5 In.	175.00
Vase, Pen Tray, Iron Brown Glaze, Under Dark Blue, Slab, B. Leach	739.00
Vase, Pierced Buds, Green, Linthorpe, Dresser, 7 3/4 In.	1387.00
Vase, Rope Work, Speckled Oatmeal Run, Waisted Form, J. Leach	175.00
Vase, Southern Plantation, Blacks Working, Adrian Art, 10 In.	150.00
Vase, Speckled Brown & Green Glaze, Walley, 5 1/2 x 6 In.	248.00
Vase, Tan & Celadon Glaze, University City Pottery, 6 3/8 In.	990.00
Vase, Wild Flowers, Turquoise, Mask & Ring Handles, T. Deck	1860.00

ARTHUR OSBORNE collectibles are found in the Ivorex category.

ARTS & CRAFTS was a design style popular in American decorative arts from 1894 to 1923. In the 1970s collectors began to rediscover Mission furniture, art pottery, metalwork, linens, and light fixtures from this period. The interest has continued. Today everything from this era is collectible, including jewelry, graphics, and silverware. Additional items may be found in the Furniture category, various glass categories, etc.

Book Cover, Tooled Leather, Rabbits, Magazine, 10 x 7 1/2 In.	66.00
Bowl, Matte Yellow Glaze, Scheier, c.1950, 2 1/4 x 6 1/4 In.	110.00
Box, Copper, Silver, Wood Lining, Gorham	1350.00
Box, Slag Paneled Top, Sides, Bottom, Copper Frame, 6 In.	175.00
Humidor, Brass Strapwork On Lid, Copper, Hexagonal, 8 In.	137.50
Skewer Set, Holder, 10 Piece	140.00
Torchiere, 9-Candle, Scrolling Branch Arms, Iron, 72 In., Pr.	522.00
Trophy, Inscribed, Sterling & Bronze, 1929, 12 In., Pair	275.00
Umbrella Stand, Tooled Brass & Copper, 22 3/4 In.	165.00

AURENE glass was made by Frederick Carder of New York about 1904. It is an iridescent gold or blue glass, usually marked *Aurene* or *Steuben*.

AURENE

Bowl, Blue, Mirror Finish Interior, Steuben, 3 x 6 In. 750.00
Bowl, Flared, Pedestal, Signed Steuben, 12 In. 375.00
Bowl, Gold, Calcite, 8 In. 300.00
Bowl, Gold, Calcite, 12 In. 260.00
Candlestick, Blue, Ivrene Base, 6 In., Pair 770.00
Candlestick, Twisted Stem, 10 1/2 In., Pair 1400.00
Dish, Nut, Gold, Stretched & Ruffled, Signed Steuben, 3 1/2 In. 215.00
Lamp Base, Acid–Cut Winged Horses, Black, Gold, Bronze Mounts, 19 In. 5500.00
Lamp Base, Bird Finial, Blue, Urn Form, Gilt Metal Mounts, 26 In. 935.00
Lamp Base, Green, Blue, Acid Cut Flowers, Bronze Swan Mount, 13 In. 660.00
Perfume Bottle, Baluster Form, Flower Stopper, Signed Steuben, 7 In. 495.00
Perfume Bottle, Blue, Glass Dipper, DeVilbiss, 6 1/2 In. 385.00
Salt, Gold, Pedestal, Signed 275.00
Tumbler, Gold Iridescent, Signed, 5 In. 125.00
Vase, Blue, Green, Cut Peacocks, Baluster, Drilled, 12 1/2 In. 2310.00
Vase, Blue, Steuben, 6 In. 900.00
Vase, Bulbous, Cobalt Blue, 1920, Signed Steuben, 11 3/4 In. 2750.00
Vase, Flared Trefoil Rim, Gold, Signed Steuben, 6 1/4 In. 412.50
Vase, Gold Iridescent, Signed, 5 1/4 In. 400.00
Vase, Gold, Gourd Form, Trumpet Neck, Signed Steuben, 6 In. 715.00
Vase, Melon Ribbed, Bulbous Ribs, Paper Label, Steuben, 4 In. 595.00
Vase, Peacock Eye, Green On Gold, 8 In. 4300.00
Vase, Stick, Blue, Steuben, 8 In. 325.00
Vase, Stick, Butterfly Blue, Iridescent, 6 3/4 x 3 In. 495.00
Vase, Tree Trunk, Gold, Blue Tinged Luster, Steuben, 5 In. 110.00
Vase, Tree Trunk, Tripartite, Blue, No. 2744, 6 1/2 In. 550.00
Vase, Trumpet, Iridescent Blue, Green, Purple, Pink, No. 912, 16 1/2 In. 2090.00
Water Set, Corset Shape, Flared, Gold, 6 Piece 2150.00
Wine, Twisted Stem, Signed, 4 3/4 In. 225.00

AUSTRIA is a collecting term which covers pieces made by a wide variety
of factories. They are listed in this book in categories such as Kauffmann,
Royal Dux, or Porcelain.

AUTO parts and accessories are collectors' items today. Gas pump globes
and license plates are part of this specialty. Prices are determined by age,
rarity, and condition. Signs and packaging related to automobiles may also
be found in the Advertising section. Lalique hood ornaments will be listed
in the Lalique category.

Antifreeze, Everflow, Car, With Palm Tree, 1938, 1 Gal. 22.00
Antifreeze, Mobile Freezone, 1950s, Qt. 15.00
Book, Dodge Bros. Dealer's Parts, 1927 .... 75.00
Booklet, Getting Ready To Drive New Kind Of Car, 1941 Nash, 32 Pages 20.00
Catalog, Chevrolet, 1951, 16 Pages, 11 x 8 In. 35.00
Catalog, Chevrolet, Color, 1937 .... 25.00
Clock, Car, New Haven 35.00
Crate, Mobil Oil Gargoyle 55.00
Flag Holder, Columbia, Box, Post World War I 14.00
Flag Set, Columbia, Mounts On Radiator, 5 Piece 28.00
Folder, Chrysler, Silver Anniversary, Convertible, 1949, 20 1/2 x 14 In 60.00
Gas Pump Globe, Ace High, 13 1/2 In. 175.00
Gas Pump Globe, Beacon Kerosene, Porcelain 200.00
Gas Pump Globe, Bell Ethel 325.00
Gas Pump Globe, Blue Crown 400.00
Gas Pump Globe, Dixie Oils & Gasoline, Power To Pass 325.00
Gas Pump Globe, Fleetwing, 13 1/2 In. 225.00
Gas Pump Globe, Flying A 295.00
Gas Pump Globe, Gilbert & Barker T–8 Non–Visible 200.00
Gas Pump Globe, Keystone 130.00
Gas Pump Globe, Magnolia, 2 Sides, Metal Frame 195.00
Gas Pump Globe, Marathon, Best In The Long Run, Man Picture 450.00
Gas Pump Globe, Mobil, 15–In. Metal Frame 225.00
Gas Pump Globe, Paraland 175.00

Gas Pump Globe, Pump, Signal, Yellow & Black 575.00
Gas Pump Globe, Pure Oil 350.00
Gas Pump Globe, Red Crown 175.00
Gas Pump Globe, Shell, Pre-1931 .... 350.00
Gas Pump Globe, Sinclair, Dino 300.00
Gas Pump Globe, Skelly, Glass 275.00
Gas Pump Globe, Southland Ethel, Porcelain 135.00
Gas Pump Globe, Standard Oil, Crown 350.00
Gas Pump Globe, Standard Oil, Red Crown, 1930s 225.00
Gas Pump Globe, Standard Oil, Visible, Crown 2500.00
Gas Pump Globe, Super Shell Ethel 750.00
Gas Pump Globe, Texaco 1100.00
Gas Pump Globe, Texaco, Glass 295.00
Gas Pump Globe, Wayne Conoco 850.00
Gas Pump Globe, White Eagle 1600.00
Goggles, Driving, Wire, Screen 15.00
Greaser, Spring, Charles Falmanzel Co., Buffalo, Nickel Plated, 5 In. 25.00
Grill Ornament, Mustang 45.00
Headlights & Bar, Buick, 1929 .... 125.00
Holder, Drinking Cup, Tin, Double 1.00
Hood Ornament, Mustang 45.00
Hood Ornament, Pontiac, Super Chief, Indian Head .... 65.00 To 75.00
Hood Ornament, Super Chief, Lighted, Instructions, Box 225.00
Hood Ornament, Winged Lady 50.00
Hubcap, LaSalle, 1920s 45.00
Jack, Embossed Pratt 3.25
Key Ring, Signet, Chrysler, 1956, Original Card 12.50
Lamp, Driving, Rayo, 1911 .... 55.00
Lamp, Side, Hupmobile, Steel, Embossed On Top, Pair 50.00
License Plate, Connecticut, 1911, Porcelain 65.00
License Plate, Georgia, 1938 .... 12.75
License Plate, Illinois, Mid–1940s, Official, Made From Soybean Prod. 17.00
License Plate, Indiana, 1913 .... 60.00 To 75.00
License Plate, Iowa, 1946 .... 17.00
License Plate, Massachusetts, 1914, Porcelain .... 155.00 To 200.00
License Plate, Michigan, 1920 .... 35.00
License Plate, Mississippi, 1932, Original Wrapper .... 12.00 To 14.00
License Plate, Missouri, 1935 .... 3.50
License Plate, Texas, 1937 .... 12.50
Light, Front, Kerosene, Model T, Iron 20.00
Light, Side, Kerosene, Model T, Iron 20.00
Light, Tail, Kerosene, Model T, Iron 10.00
Manual, Ford Model A, 1930, 52 Pages, 6 x 9 In. 30.00
Manual, GM Truck Owner's, 1939 .... 15.00
Manual, Oldsmobile, 1938, 298 Pages 10.00
Mirror, Socony Motor Gasoline, Celluloid 30.00
Model, Promotional, Corvette, Anniversary, 1978 .... 65.00
Model, Promotional, Impala Convertible, Metal, 1959, 5 In. 35.00
Model, Promotional, Oldsmobile, Box, 1963 .... 47.50
Model, Promotional, Pontiac, Box, 1956 .... 47.50
Motor Oil, Bull Head, 2 Gal. 150.00
Motor Oil, Many Miles, Stylish Race Car Picture, 2 Gal. 200.00
Motor Oil, Marathon, Graphic Runner In Mid–Stride Picture, 5 Gal. 350.00
Motor Oil, Valvoline, America's First, 1940s, Contents, Qt. 20.00
Motor Oil, Zeppelin, 2 Gal. 195.00
Motor Oilprimus, Early Race Car On Track Picture, 2 Gal. 900.00
Nozzle, Gas Pump, Buckeye, Yellow Brass, Large 25.00
Oilcan, B. S. A. Green, Blue, Red & White, Opened Bottom, Qt. 32.00
Oilcan, Bison, Qt. 20.00
Oilcan, Champlin 10.00
Oilcan, Cross Country Motor Oil, 2 x 8 In. 23.00
Oilcan, Mobile Oil, 4 Oz. 12.00
Oilcan, Shell, 4 Oz. 12.00

Oilcan, Sinclair 10.00
Picture, 1914 Studebaker, Framed, 23 x 14 In. 77.00
Plaque, Bumper, AAA National Award 15.00
Pliers, Model T, Ford Script 10.00
Rack, Map, Sinclair, Logo, 1950s 35.00
Rack, Oil Bottle, Mobil Gargoyle, Holds 8 Diamond–Shaped Bottles 85.00
Rack, Oil Bottle, Tiolene, Holds 16 Bottles, 18 In. 75.00
Screwdriver, Richfield Oil 7.00
Sign, Fire Chief, Pump, 1946 .... 125.00
Sign, Grizzly Gasoline, Watch Your Miles, Tombstone Shape, Tin 625.00
Sign, Mileage Oil & Grease, Tin, Old Wheel & Tire Picture, 1920s 100.00
Sign, Mobil Gas, Pump, Porcelain, 1947 .... 100.00
Sign, Phillips 66 Gas Station, Driveway, Pedestal, Porcelain, 1940s 475.00
Sign, Pump, Atlantic 30.00
Sign, Pump, Fill 'em Fast, Porcelain 165.00
Sign, Pump, Good Gulf, Porcelain, Square 30.00
Sign, Pump, Melrose Gasoline, Porcelain 295.00
Sign, Pump, Mobil Ethel, Shield 70.00
Sign, Pump, Royal 76 Gasoline, Porcelain 85.00
Sign, Pump, Sinclair, Porcelain 55.00
Sign, Pump, That Good Gulf, Porcelain 35.00
Sign, Sinclair, Pump, Porcelain, 1950s 40.00
Sign, Texaco, Round, 1940s 200.00
Spotlight, Clymer, 1921 .... 75.00
Tire Gauge, Balloon Tire 5.00
Tire Gauge, Balloon Tire, Leather Sleeve, Word Buick On 1, 1909, 2 Pc. 75.00
Tire Gauge, Model A Ford, 1927–1930 .... 100.00
Tire Lifter, Hardwood Handle, Brass Head, Pat. Dec. 31, 1907 .... 20.00
Tire, Gauge, Schrader, Nickel Plated, 2 1/2 In. 8.00
Traffic Light, 1950s 375.00
Wrench, Ford, Adjustable, Squared Shank, 9 1/4 In. 10.00
Wrench, Ford, Model A, Ford Script, Double Open End 2.50
Wrench, Monkey, Model T, Ford Script 6.25

AUTUMN LEAF pattern china was made for the Jewel Tea Company beginning in 1933. Hall China Company of East Liverpool, Ohio, Crooksville China Company of Crooksville, Ohio, Harker Potteries of Chester, West Virginia, and Paden City Pottery, Paden City, West Virginia, made dishes with this design. Autumn Leaf has remained popular and was made by Hall China Company until 1978. Some other pieces in the Autumn Leaf pattern are still being made. For more information, see *Kovels' Depression Glass & American Dinnerware Price List.*

Baker, French, Jewel Tea, 3 Pt. 12.00
Bowl Set, Stacking, 8 3/4 In., 7 1/8 In., 6 In. 50.00
Butter, Cover, 1 Lb. 375.00
Butter, Cover, 1/4 Lb. 195.00
Butter, Cover, Hall, 1/4 Lb. 110.00
Cake Pan, Tin 10.00
Cake Plate, Flat, Hall 30.00
Cake Safe, Hall, Pattern On Top 40.00
Candlestick 250.00
Candy Dish, On Base 500.00
Casserole, Cover, Hall 80.00
Coffee Maker, Drip 195.00
Coffeepot, Electric, Hall 160.00
Cookie Jar, Jewel Tea, Tab Handles, Gold 165.00
Cookie Jar, Tab Handles 140.00
Cookie Jar, Tootsie 200.00
Cup & Saucer 10.00
Custard, Hall 4.00
Fruit Bowl, Jewel Tea, 5 1/2 In. 6.00
Gravy Boat, Jewel Tea 13.00
Gravy Boat, Underplate, Jewel Tea 45.00

Pitcher, Rayed, Hall, 2 1/2 Pt.	25.00
Pitcher, Tilt, Hall	60.00
Plate, 10 In.	8.00
Range Set, 3 Piece	40.00
Salad Bowl, Jewel Tea, 9 In.	11.00
Sifter	200.00
Soup, Cream, Jewel Tea	16.00
Soup, Dish, Jewel Tea, 8 1/2 In.	12.00
Tea Set, 3 Piece	250.00
Tea Set, Philadelphia	245.00
Tea Set, Tray, 3 Piece	250.00
Teapot, Long Spout	30.00
Teapot, Strainer	62.50
Tray, Red Design	45.00
Tumbler	17.00

AVON bottles are listed in the Bottle category under Avon

BACCARAT glass was made in France by La Compagnie des Cristalleries de Baccarat, located 150 miles from Paris. The factory was started in 1765. The firm went bankrupt and began operating again about 1822. Cane and millefiori paperweights were made during the 1860 to 1880 period. The firm is still working near Paris making paperweights and glasswares.

BACCARAT

Bottle, Cologne, Amber & Clear Swirl, Pair	160.00
Box, Rose Teinte Swirl, Signed, 8 1/2 In.	345.00
Candelabrum, 3–Light, Prisms, 17 In.	440.00
Candelabrum, 4–Light, Foliate Sockets, Curved Arms, 16 In., Pair	1700.00
Candelabrum, White Enamel & Gold, c.1850, 12 x 24 In., Pair	2700.00
Candlestick, Lobed Sockets, Baluster Support, 12 In., Pair	825.00
Candlestick, Spiral Turned Shaft, Signed, 9 In., Pair	360.00
Decanter, Presentation Box, 10 3/4 In.	105.00
Decanter, Wine, 11 In.	187.00
Dresser Set, White Spirals, Gold Stoppers, Signed, 1925, 3 Piece	550.00
Figurine, Frog, Signed, 2 1/2 In.	75.00
Figurine, Pelican, Signed, 6 1/2 In.	110.00
Figurine, Rabbit, Crystal, 3 In.	75.00
Figurine, Turtle, Signed, 4 In.	65.00
Goblet, Flaring Bowl, Cobalt Overlay, 7 1/2 In., 12 Piece	605.00
Goblet, Water, Perfection, Set Of 6	250.00
Lamp, Fairy, Saucer Base, Sapphire Blue, Marked, 4 x 5 1/2 In.	265.00
Lamp, Hurricane, Prisms, Crystal Shades, 21 1/2 In., Pair	1100.00
Lamp, Oil, Blown Glass, c.1840, 14 In.	110.00
Paperweight, Millefiori	2500.00
Paperweight, Mushroom Top, Honeycomb Center, Leaves, 2 1/4 In.	770.00
Paperweight, Pompon, Stardust Center & White Canes, 2 1/2 In.	440.00
Paperweight, Suphide, Joan Of Arc	60.00
Paperweight, Suphide, John F. Kennedy, Emerald Green Ground	185.00
Paperweight, Suphide, Peter The Great	60.00
Paperweight, White Blossom, Bud, Center Red Star, Arrow, 3 1/4 In.	440.00
Perfume Bottle, Champs Elysees, Turtle, 5 In.	550.00
Perfume Bottle, Ciro's Surrender	140.00
Perfume Bottle, Doque Dior, Guerlain, 3 1/16 In.	400.00
Perfume Bottle, Gabilla Chypre	110.00
Perfume Bottle, Reflections	150.00
Perfume Bottle, Rose Teinte, Embossed Swirl, 5 1/2 In.	70.00
Perfume Bottle, Toujours Fideles	395.00
Tazza, Frosted Greek Key Bowl, 6 1/2 In.	155.00
Toothpick, Diamond Point, Flint	45.00
Tumbler, Rose Teinte, Pinwheel Pattern, Marked, 4 In.	60.00
Vase, Birds, Flowers, Silver–Plated Base, c.1878, 13 7/8 In., Pair	4675.00
Vase, Butterflies, Flowers, Opalescent, 6 In.	245.00
Vase, Tree, Branches, Berries, Bronze Base, c.1880, 8 3/8 In.	660.00

BADGES have been used since before the Civil War. Collectors search for examples of all types, including law enforcement and company identification badges. Well–known prison or law enforcement badges are most desirable. Most are made of nickel or brass. Many recent reproductions have been made.

Air Police	35.00
Byers Transportation	40.00
Cap, Hughes Air West, 10K Gold Filled	75.00
Chauffeur, Illinois, 1940	5.00
Chauffeur, New York, 1916	20.00
Chauffeur, Teamsters & Helpers, 1940	15.00
Deputy Marshal, c.1910	135.00
Dupont Dynamite	75.00
Graf Zeppelin, World Flight, Globe & Zeppelin, Enameled, 1929	50.00
Hat, Colorado Prison	35.00
Junior Forest Ranger	12.00
Los Angeles Police, Shield Shape	250.00
Nevada State Police Captain, Presentation, Gold Front, Diamonds	850.00
Paiute Game Ranger	95.00
Park Ranger, 1930s	135.00
Police, Coroner's, Seattle	95.00
Police, Portland, Oregon, Knobbed Star, c.1900	250.00
Ribbon, 1st Encampment, Nov. 1866, Indianapolis Final Encampment, 1949	18.00
Ribbon, Centennial Anniv. Of Allegheny Co., Pa., Sept. 24, 1888	16.00
Ribbon, Inter. Brotherhood Of Electrical Workers, Chicago Local 134	12.00
Smokey, Junior Forest Ranger	15.00
Wells Fargo Security, Porcelain, Gold Plated, Large	49.00

BANKS of metal have been made since 1868. There are still banks, mechanical banks, and registering banks (those which show the total money deposited on the face of the bank). Many old iron or tin banks have been reproduced since the 1950s in iron or plastic. Pottery, glass, and plastic banks are also listed here. A group of selected high prices from the auction of a major collection are included this year to reflect the prices of the best banks that can be found. Condition and pristine original paint influenced these prices. Average banks sell for much lower prices.

Addams Family Thing, Box	50.00 To 60.00
Airplane, Tin, Wheels Turn	30.00
Alphabet, Tin Lithographed, Oval, 3 In.	145.00
Anvil, With Numerator, Cast Iron & Nickel Plate, 2 3/4 In.	385.00
Arm & Hammer, 1931 Hawkeye Stake	22.00
Atlantic Motor Oil Can, Tin, 3 1/2 In.	10.00
Atlas, Lead, Padlock, 4 3/4 In.	495.00
Auto, Armored Car, Cast Iron, 6 11/16 In.	685.00
Auto, Armored Car, Marx, 1930s	90.00
Bam Bam, From Flintstones	25.00
Barber Pole, Blade	18.00
Barrel, James Saltwater Taffy, Composition, Tin Lid	40.00
Baseball Player, Cast Iron, 6 In.	550.00
Baseball, Los Angeles Dodgers, Ceramic	15.00
Baseball, On 3 Bats, Cast Iron, 5 1/4 In.	155.00
Baseball, Tin, Ohio Art	15.00
Basket Puzzle, Round, 4 In.	495.00
Battleship, Maine, Cast Iron	9.75
Battleship, Oregon, Missing Paint, 5 In.	195.00
Bear, Stealing Honey, Cast Iron, 6 3/8 In.	175.00
Beer Canburgermeister Beer, Label, 3 1/2 In.	10.00
Big Boy, 1973	16.00
Billiken, Painted Cast Iron, 6 1/2 In.	55.00
Billy Bounce, Cast Iron	395.00
Black Face, Cast Iron	225.00
Black Girl, On Alligator, Nodder	125.00

Bank, Dime, Savings, Akron, Ohio,
Celluloid, 2 In.

Bank, Jug, Pottery, F. Ozanne, 7 1/2 In.

Black Mammy, Cast Iron	55.00 To 100.00
Black Mammy, Chalkware, 12 In.	150.00
Black Man, As Policeman, Cast Iron, 6 In.	150.00
Black Woman, 2 Faces, Cast Iron	250.00
Bokar Coffee, A & P, 1949	12.50
Book, Leather Cover, No Key	14.00
Book, Prudential Insurance Co., Leatherette Cover	22.00
Book, Savings For Baby, Stork Holding Baby	35.00
Boscul Coffee, Tin	49.00
Boy Scout, Papier–Mache	38.00
Boy, With Dog, Cast Iron, 5 In.	110.00
Bozo, Ceramic, 1960s	48.00
Budweiser Malt Syrup, Tin, Box	125.00
Buffalo, Cast Iron	80.00
Bugs Bunny, Cast Iron	125.00
Building, Cast Iron, 3 1/2 x 4 In.	150.00
Building, Jarmulowsky, Cast Iron, 7 3/4 In.	1760.00
Building, Multiplying Bank, Optical Illusion Interior, 7 In.	1320.00
Building, Skyscraper, Cast Iron, Gold & Silver, 6 In.	160.00
Building, Woolworth, Cast Iron, 8 In.	75.00
Buster Brown & Tige, Cast Iron	350.00
Butting Ram, Cast Iron, Patent 1895	8700.00
California Raisins	20.00
Calumet Baking Powder	55.00
Camel, In Rocker, Cast Iron, 4 x 5 In.	495.00
Cap'n Crunch, Cereal Bowl Set, Quaker, 1960s	35.00
Captain Kidd, Cast Iron	375.00
Car, Cast Iron, 4 1/2 In.	40.00
Car, Weinermobile, Oscar Meyer, 10 In.	25.00 To 35.00
Carousel, Cast Iron	90.00
Carriage Clock, Time Is Money, Lithographed Paper Face, 5 In.	1320.00
Casey Jones Locomotive, Bronzed Metal	15.00
Cash Register, Cast Iron, Lock Mechanism, 3 x 3 x 4 In.	78.00
Casper, American Bisque	375.00
Casper, The Friendly Ghost, Hard Plastic, 1967, 12 In.	175.00
Cat, Blue Bowtie, Cast Iron	65.00
Cat, Cast Iron, Hubley	175.00
Cat, Cast Iron, Original Paint, 5 In.	22.00
Cat, Seated, Pierced Eyes, Black Speckles, Redware, 5 In.	770.00
Cave Man, With Spear, Composition, Large	5.00
Charlie Tuna	20.00
Checker Cab, Steel Wheels, Cast Iron, 7 7/8 In.	1320.00
Chest Of Drawers, 2 Short, 3 Long Drawers, Glazed, Redware, 7 1/2 In.	330.00
Chevy Banthrico, 1954	60.00
Chick, Cast Iron	25.00
Chicken, Cast Iron	45.00

Clock, Metal, Square, Pat. Dec. 8, 1825	27.50
Clock, My Own Bank, Plastic, Arding Prod., 1940s	15.00
Clock, Owl, Japan, Box	65.00
Clown, Chein	50.00 To 65.00
Clown, Googly Eyes, China	30.00
Colonel Sanders	15.00
Columbia, Building Of Columbia Exhibition Of 1892, 9 1/2 In.	715.00
Cylinder, Horse & Rider On Domed Base, Tin, Green Paint, 5 1/2 In.	220.00
Daisy Mae, Ceramic	75.00
Darth Vader, Silver Plated, 6 In.	195.00
Decker's Iowana, Cast Iron, Worn Gold, 4 3/8 In.	35.00
Dime Register, Chein	20.00
Dime Register, Easy Saver, Buddy L, 1976	15.00
Dime Register, Uncle Sam, 3 Coin	25.00
Dime, Savings, Akron, Ohio, Celluloid, 2 In.	*Illus* 3.00
Dirigible, Cast Iron	225.00
Dog, Boston Terrier, Black & White, Cast Iron, 3 x 3 In.	50.00
Dog, Bulldog, Black, Cast Iron, 1960, 8 x 10 In.	30.00
Dog, Bulldog, Chalkware	25.00
Dog, Cocker Spaniel	25.00
Dog, Huckleberry Hound	15.00
Dog, Hush Puppies, Basset	10.00
Dog, Lying On Victorian Couch, Ceramic, Czechoslovakia, 4 In.	75.00
Dog, Nipper, Metal, 6 1/4 In.	150.00
Dog, On Pillow, Cast Iron	170.00
Dog, On Tub, Cast Iron	55.00
Dog, Puppy, On Cushion, Bee, Cast Iron, 5 3/4 In.	150.00
Dog, Scotty, Hubley	120.00
Dog, Seated On Hind Legs, Beside Tree Trunk, Redware, 5 1/2 In.	1870.00
Dog, Shepherd, Cast Iron	38.00
Dog, Snoopy, On Doghouse, Silver Plate, No Stopper, 1959	25.00
Dog, Snoopy, On Doghouse, UFS, 1970	10.00
Dog, Spaniel, Seated, Redware, c.1860, 13 1/2 In.	1100.00
Dog, St. Bernard, With Pack, Bronze Coating, 5 x 3 1/2 In.	50.00
Donkey, Cast Iron	77.00 To 125.00
Ed Sullivan, Nodder, Mouse Sitting On House, 1950s	55.00
Egyptian Tomb, Cast Iron, 6 1/4 In.	742.00
Eiffel Tower, Cast Iron, 8 3/4 In.	685.00
Eight O'clock Coffee, Tin	12.50
Electrolux Refrigerator, Cast Iron	20.00 To 35.00
Elephant, Bench On Tub, Cast Iron	125.00
Elephant, Cast Iron, 2 3/4 x 4 In.	40.00
Elephant, Cast Iron, 3 x 4 1/2 In.	115.00
Elephant, Grapette, Glass	20.00
Elephant, On Tub, Cast Iron	55.00
Elephant, Seated, Metal	35.00
Elephant, Standing, Cast Iron	70.00
Elmer Fudd, Cast Iron	95.00 To 125.00
Father Christmas, Pewter, Brass Trim, CMF	295.00
Felix, Ceramic	12.00
Fidelity Trust Vault, Cast Iron, 4 7/8 In.	360.00
Ford Model T, 1912, Tractor Supply Company, 1982	25.00
Ford Model T, 1913, Bell Telephone 70th Anniversary, 1981	75.00 To 85.00
Fred Flintstone, Plastic, 1973	22.00
Frog, In Suit, Cast Iron, 3 1/4 In.	275.00
Frog, Round Base	1045.00
Frosty The Snowman, American Bisque	35.00
Gas Pump, Sunoco	40.00
General Pershing, Bronze Electroplate, 7 3/4 In.	93.50
Girl, 2 Faces, Cast Iron, 3 1/2 In.	145.00
Give Me A Penny, Wooden Base, Hubley	60.00
Globe, Cast Iron	2600.00
Globe, Glass, 4 In.	12.50

Globe, Revolving, Universal Stoves & Ranges, Tin 375.00
Globe, Tin, Chein ....8.00 To 10.00
Globe, Tin, Ohio Art 8.00
Gothic Cottage, 3 Chimneys, Peaked Roof, Painted & Stenciled, 6 In. 330.00
Grenadier, English, Creedmore 2500.00
Gulfpride, Motor Oil Can, Tin, 3 In. 10.00
Gunboat, Cast Iron, 8 1/2 In. 550.00
Hamm's Bear, Cast Iron ....35.00 To 45.00
Happy Days, Barrel, Tin, Chein 22.00
Happy Face 22.00
Hen & Her Chicks, Redware, Folk Art, 12 In. 540.00
Hippopotamus, Tin, Box 45.00
Hog, Arkansas Razorback, Cast Iron, Large 24.00
Horse, Cast Iron 20.00
House, 2-Story Victorian, Cast Iron 165.00
House, Dutch Colonial, Maroon Roof, Iron, 1910, 4 In. 83.00
Ice-Cream Freezer, North Pole, Steel Handle, Cast Iron 55.00
Indian Chief Bust, Uiversity Of Michigan, Metal, 6 In. 85.00
Indian Chief, War Bonnet, Cast Iron, 6 In. 350.00
Indian Head, Cast Iron 45.00
Indian Head, Full Headdress, Bronze, 1930s 45.00
Indian Head, National Bank, Cast Iron 150.00
Indian, Cast Iron, 6 In. 95.00
Irishman, Goebel, Lock & Key 50.00
Jack In The Box, Metal, Souvenir Of Reno 15.00
Jazz Man, Trumpet Player, Metal 55.00
Johnny Griffith, 2 Faces, Original Paint 60.00
Jug, Pottery, F. Ozanne, 7 1/2 In. ....*Illus* 25.00
Jukebox, Selecti-O-Matic, Tin Lithograph 75.00
Kangaroo, Baby, CBC Bank, Australia, 6 In. 30.00
Keebler Elf 25.00
Keystone Cop, Cast Iron 8.50
King Kong, Plastic, 16 In. 12.00
Kitten, Cast Iron, 4 3/4 In. 85.00
Liberty Bell, Cast Iron, 4 1/4 In. 30.00
Lighthouse, Cast Iron 50.00
Lion, Cast Iron ....40.00 To 50.00
Little Audrey, Ceramic 95.00
Little Black Sambo, Tin Lithograph, 7 In. 275.00
Little Red Riding Hood, Hull 395.00
Log Cabin, Abe Lincoln 15.00
Log Cabin, Pittsburgh Paints, Glass 20.00
Lucky Joe, Glass, Paper Mouth 22.50
Mack Bulldog, 1926, Dr Pepper 25.00
Mack Bulldog, 1926, Home Federal Savings, 1984 .... 25.00
Magic Chef, Vinyl 25.00
Mailbox, Blue & Red, Cast Iron 45.00
Mailbox, Hanging, Black, Gold Lettering 115.00
Mailbox, Line-Mar, Tin, Box 20.00
Mailbox, Red, White & Blue, Metal, Japan 15.00
Majestic Radio, Cast Iron, 1920s 87.00
Mama Bear Standing, Holding Baby By Neck, Cast Iron, 1970, 5 1/2 In. 75.00
Mammy With Spoon, Painted Cast Iron, Gold, 5 3/4 In. 16.00
Man On Rearing Horse, Cast Iron, 6 In. 660.00
McDonald's, Wastebasket 15.00

Mechanical banks were first made about 1870. Any bank with moving
parts is considered mechanical. The metal banks made before World War I
are the most desirable. Copies and new designs of mechanical banks have
been made in metal or plastic since the 1920s.

Mechanical, Acrobat, Gymnast Kicks Clown, Stands On Head, 5 In. 6270.00
Mechanical, Apple, Worm Grabs Coin, Metal, Plastic 35.00
Mechanical, Artillery, Union, Shepard Hardware, Box 2200.00

Mechanical, Baby Elephant, Charles Bailey 19800.00
Mechanical, Bad Accident, Boy Jumps Out, 10 In. .... 1870.00 To 4620.00
Mechanical, Beehive, Deposit Registered In Window, 5 1/2 In. 440.00
Mechanical, Beehive, Northside Building Loan, Cast Iron, 6 3/4 In. 275.00
Mechanical, Bird On Roof, Coin In Bird's Head, Wire Lever .... 1760.00 To 4400.00
Mechanical, Birdhouse, Lithographed Tin, 5 1/4 In. 55.00
Mechanical, Boy On Trapeze, Barton & Smith .... 1320.00 To 3300.00
Mechanical, Boy On Trapeze, Barton & Smith, Pristine Paint 8800.00
Mechanical, Boy Robbing Bird's Nest, Cast Iron 2800.00
Mechanical, Boy Scout Camp, Raises Flag, J. & E. Stevens Co. 22000.00
Mechanical, Boys Stealing Watermelons, Cast Iron, 6 5/8 In. .... 2400.00 To 4070.00
Mechanical, Bread Winners, J. & E. Stevens 38500.00
Mechanical, Bulldog, Coin On Nose, Opens Mouth, Swallows Coin, 7 In. 3850.00
Mechanical, Butting Buffalo, Coin In Tree Trunk, Kyser & Rex, Mint 27500.00
Mechanical, Butting Ram, Cast Iron, Pat. Oct. 19, 1895, Mint 16500.00
Mechanical, Cabin, Green, J. & E. Stevens, 1875 .... 390.00
Mechanical, Cabin, White-Wash Brush, Man Stands On Head, 3 1/3 In. 550.00
Mechanical, Calamity With Box, J. & E. Stevens Co. 25300.00
Mechanical, Cat & Mouse, Balancing Cat On Top, 11 1/2 In. .... 2530.00 To 5500.00
Mechanical, Chief Big Moon, Frog Springs From Pool, 10 In. .... 1870.00 To 5170.00
Mechanical, Chimpanzee, Lowers Arm & Head As If Recording .... 5280.00 To 6050.00
Mechanical, Christopher Columbus 1150.00
Mechanical, Circus, Crank Turns Platform, Clown Deposits Coin, 8 In. 5170.00
Mechanical, Clown On Globe, Polychrome, Cast Iron, 9 In. .... 1980.00 To 6270.00
Mechanical, Clown, Coins Dropped Cause Eyes To Roll, Cast Iron, 1885 .... 520.00
Mechanical, Clown, Lithographed, Tin, Chein, 5 In. 60.00
Mechanical, Coffin, Windup, Box 45.00
Mechanical, Combat Tank, On Battle Front, Tin, 1960s, 1 x 2 x 7 In. 100.00
Mechanical, Confectionery, Figure Slides To Get Candy, 8 1/2 In. 8800.00
Mechanical, Creedmoor, Man With Gun, Stump, Original Paint .... 385.00 To 585.00
Mechanical, Cupola, Push Doorknob, Cupola Opens, 7 In. .... 8250.00 To 29100.00
Mechanical, Dapper Dan, Dances, Keywind, Lithographed Tin, 10 In. 660.00
Mechanical, Darktown Battery, J. & E. Stevens, Cast Iron .... 1700.00 To 4695.00
Mechanical, Dentist, Blue, J. & E. Stevens Co. 20900.00
Mechanical, Dentist, Book Of Knowledge 300.00
Mechanical, Dinah, Long Sleeves, Cast Iron, 6 1/2 In. .... 405.00 To 700.00
Mechanical, Dog Tray, Coin On Plate, Deposits In Vault, 4 In. 2420.00
Mechanical, Doghouse 605.00
Mechanical, Eagle & Eaglets 165.00
Mechanical, Education & Economy, Question, Drops Into Window, 4 In. 1320.00
Mechanical, Elephant, Man Pops Out, Cast Iron, 5 1/2 In. 495.00
Mechanical, Elephant, Pull Tail, Raises Trunk, Hubley, 5 1/2 In. 550.00
Mechanical, Elephant, Three Clowns, Figures Turn, 5 3/4 In. .... 1430.00 To 4620.00
Mechanical, Excelsior, Door Opens, Cashier Takes Coin, 5 1/2 In. 495.00
Mechanical, Fowler, Red Base, J. & E. Stevens Co. 60500.00
Mechanical, Frog On Rock, Mouth Opens To Receive Coin, 2 3/4 In. 715.00
Mechanical, Frog On Round Base, Mouth Opens, Winks, 4 1/2 In. 1045.00
Mechanical, Germania Exchange, Goat's Tail, Beer, J. & E. Stevens Co. 23100.00
Mechanical, Girl Skipping Rope, Light Blue Dress, J. & E. Stevens Co. 55000.00
Mechanical, Give Billy A Penny, Cast Iron 265.00
Mechanical, Goat, Frog & Old Man, Fraternal Initiating .... 4180.00 To 9900.00
Mechanical, Grenadier, Coin Fired In Tree, John Harper .... 775.00 To 1485.00
Mechanical, Hall's Excelsior, Monkey Gets Coin 660.00
Mechanical, Hall's Lilliput, No Tray 935.00
Mechanical, Haunted House, Tin, Lithographed, 9 x 10 x 9 In. 198.00
Mechanical, Hen & Chick, Hen Clucks & Pecks Head, 10 In. .... 2750.00 To 6860.00
Mechanical, Hold The Fort, Bronze Pattern, 6 1/2 In. .... 2860.00 To 7700.00
Mechanical, Horse Race, Straight Base With Box, J. & E. Stevens Co. 31900.00
Mechanical, Humpty Dumpty, Coin In Hand To Tongue .... 750.00 To 880.00
Mechanical, Indian & Frog, Cast Iron 50.00
Mechanical, Jacobean Figure Shooting At Castle Gate, Iron, 9 1/2 In. 935.00
Mechanical, John Deere, Blacksmith With Sledge Hammer, 1950 .... 150.00 To 175.00
Mechanical, Jolly Nigger, Cast Iron, Black, Red & White .... 125.00 To 195.00

Mechanical, Jolly Nigger, Ears Move, Aluminum, 6 In. 88.00
Mechanical, Jolly Nigger, Shepherd Hardware 165.00
Mechanical, Jolly Nigger, Straw Hat 700.00
Mechanical, Jonah & The Whale, 10 1/2 In. ....880.00 To 3000.00
Mechanical, Leap Frog, Boy Leap Frog Over Other, 5 In. ....7480.00 To 12100.00
Mechanical, Light Of Asia 1500.00
Mechanical, Lighthouse, Nickels In Tower Slot, Registers, 10 1/2 In. 1980.00
Mechanical, Lion & Monkeys, Kyser & Rex Co., Cast Iron .... 450.00 To 950.00
Mechanical, Lion & Two Monkeys, Cast Iron, Patent 1883 ....990.00 To 2200.00
Mechanical, Lion Hunter, Hunter Fires Coin, Lion Rears Up ....8800.00 To 14300.00
Mechanical, Little Jocko Musical Bank, Lithographed Tin .... 4400.00 To 7700.00
Mechanical, Little Red Riding Hood 57200.00
Mechanical, Magic Bank, Cashier, Pat. 1873, Green 2750.00
Mechanical, Magician, Covers Coin With Hat, 8 In. ....4840.00 To 11000.00
Mechanical, Mama Katzenjammer, Eyes Roll, Kenton 26400.00
Mechanical, Mammy & Child, Kyser & Rex, Cast Iron, 8 In. .... 1545.00 To 4400.00
Mechanical, Mason, Coin On Hod, Carrier Leans Forward 3740.00
Mechanical, Merry–Go–Round, Revolves, Bells Ring, Kyser & Rex 19800.00
Mechanical, Mikado, Chimes, Kyser & Rex 55000.00
Mechanical, Milking Cow, Kicks Hindleg, J. & E. Stevens Co. 20900.00
Mechanical, Minstrel, Tips Hat 412.50
Mechanical, Monkey & Coconut, Coconut Opens, Eyes Roll .... 1980.00 To 2970.00
Mechanical, Monkey, Pop–Up, Cast Iron, Original Paint 245.00
Mechanical, Mosque, Tray On Gorilla's Head, Turns Head, 9 1/2 In. 495.00
Mechanical, Mule Entering Barn, Cast Iron .... 430.00 To 770.00
Mechanical, Noah's Ark, Book Of Knowledge 62.00
Mechanical, Octagonal Fort, Coin Fired Into Tower, 10 3/4 In. 6600.00
Mechanical, Organ Grinder & Monkey 175.00
Mechanical, Organ, 6 1/2 In. .... 450.00 To 880.00
Mechanical, Organ, Cat & Dog .... 800.00 To 935.00
Mechanical, Owl, Cast Iron, Original Paint 320.00
Mechanical, Paddy & Pig, Hits Coin With Hoof, 8 In. .... 3850.00 To 4070.00
Mechanical, Patronize Blind Man & His Dog, Cast Iron .... 6050.00 To 8800.00
Mechanical, Peg-Leg Beggar, Coin In Hat, Man Nods Head .... 3520.00 To 5060.00
Mechanical, Pelican, Slot In Head, Mouth Opens, Figure Inside, 8 In. 8800.00
Mechanical, Picture Gallery, Figure Turns & Deposits Coin, 8 1/2 In. 8250.00
Mechanical, Pig In High Chair, Coin On Tray, Lifts To Mouth, 5 1/2 In. 605.00
Mechanical, Pig Tips Hat, Plastic, Box 38.00
Mechanical, Plantation, Key Wind, Dancer Jigs & Strums Banjo 2090.00
Mechanical, Rabbit Standing, Small, Tail Lever, Ears Move, 5 1/2 In. 825.00
Mechanical, Reclining Chinaman, Coin In Pocket, Arm Rises, 8 In. 5060.00
Mechanical, Rocket Ship & Moon, Lithographed Tin, Japan, 7 1/2 In. 42.00
Mechanical, Roller Skating Bank, Kyser & Rex 49500.00
Mechanical, Rooster, Cast Iron, 6 1/4 In. .... 357.00 To 450.00
Mechanical, Santa Claus, On House, Rings Bell, Arms Move 195.00
Mechanical, Santa Claus, Tosses Coin Down Chimney, 6 In. ....800.00 To 3520.00
Mechanical, Scotchman, Tin 675.00
Mechanical, Shoot The Chute, Bronze Pattern, J. & E. Stevens Co. 24200.00
Mechanical, Skeleton, In Casket, Windup, Tin, Yone 65.00
Mechanical, Soldier Shooting Rifle At Southern Comfort .... 50.00 To 60.00
Mechanical, Speaking Dog, Girl Holds Plate, Arm Moves ....995.00 To 1430.00
Mechanical, Squirrel and Tree Stump, Coin In Forepaw .... 1760.00 To 3850.00
Mechanical, Stump Speaker, Coin In Hand Into Carpet Bag .... 1650.00 To 4620.00
Mechanical, Surly Bruin, Opens Mouth, Coin Closes Mouth, 6 1/2 In. 660.00
Mechanical, Tabby, Coin In Cat's Back, Chick Moves, 4 3/4 In. 242.00
Mechanical, Tammany, Cast Iron .... 150.00 To 600.00
Mechanical, Teddy & The Bear, Cast Iron, Book Of Knowledge 45.00
Mechanical, Teddy & The Bear, Cast Iron, Pristine Paint 4400.00
Mechanical, Teddy & The Bear, Cast Iron, Worn Paint 340.00
Mechanical, Teddy Bear, Flat Hat, Pristine Paint 19800.00
Mechanical, Telephone, Nickel, Dime & Quarter, Bell Rings, 6 1/2 In. 1100.00
Mechanical, Thrifty Tom, Key Wind, Dances, Lithographed Tin ....715.00 To 2090.00
Mechanical, Toad On Stump, Cast Iron, Polychrome, 4 In. 285.00

Mechanical, Trick Pony, Coin In Mouth, Drops In Manger .... 1045.00 To 4620.00
Mechanical, Turtle, Neck Extends, Kilgore 27500.00
Mechanical, Uncle Remus, Kyser & Rex ....2530.00 To 11550.00
Mechanical, Uncle Sam, Coin In Carpetbag, Jaw Moves .... 1650.00 To 2420.00
Mechanical, Watchdog Safe, Coin Drops Into Dog's Mouth, 6 1/2 In. 715.00
Mechanical, William Tell 625.00
Mechanical, Zoo, Press Monkey's Face, Animals In Window, 4 1/4 In. 2860.00
Milk Bottle, Glass, 1/2 Pt. 20.00
Mobil Oil 65.00
Money Basket, Hong Kong, Box, 4 In. 20.00
Mr. Mets, Nodder, 1960s 130.00
Mutt & Jeff, Cast Iron .... 150.00 To 170.00
Oilcan, Atlantic Premium 20.00
Oilcan, Gulf Pride 25.00
Oilcan, John Deere 150.00
Oilcan, Shell, Miniature 45.00
Old Beggar Man, 7 1/2 In. 210.00
Old Doc Yak, Cast Iron, 4 1/2 In. .... 230.00 To 467.00
Old Dutch Cleanser, Tin 25.00
Old South Church, Cast Iron .... 4250.00 To 4675.00
Olympia Beer, Beer Can Shape, Small 10.00
Our Kitchen Bank, Cast Iron, 1914 .... 225.00
Owl, Be Wise, Save, Eyes Move, Ceramic 25.00
Owl, Brown, Yellow Accents, Glass Eyes, J. & E. Stevens, Iron, 1880, 4 In. 275.00
Owl, Vindex, Cast Iron 285.00
Pabst Beer, Tin, Commemorating 100 Million Barrels 50.00
Pail, Monarch Paint, 2 In. 75.00
Palace, Cast Iron, 8 In. 1980.00
Pass Around Hat, Cast Iron 75.00
Pebbles Flintstone, In Rocking Chair, Vinyl 25.00
Penny Register, Lithograph, England, 1920 .... 95.00
Phillips 66, Tin, 4 In. 25.00
Pickaninny, Cast Iron, 5 1/8 In. 330.00
Pig In Overalls, Cap, Plastic, Ideal 18.00
Pig, Adolf Hitler, World War II 372.00
Pig, Amber Glass, Large 18.00
Pig, Brown & Blue Sponged, Pottery, 5 7/8 In. 115.00
Pig, Carnival Glass, Marigold .... 10.00 To 18.00
Pig, Cast Iron, 5 x 8 1/2 In. 55.00
Pig, Clover Blossom Meats, Chalkware 225.00
Pig, Decker, Cast Iron 90.00
Pig, Iowana, Cast Iron, 2 1/2 In. 110.00
Pig, Pearl China 60.00
Pig, Pottery, 2-Tone Brown Running Glaze, 4 In. 55.00
Pig, Roseville 85.00
Pig, This Little Pig Goes To First Savings, Plastic 10.00
Pig, WAABI National Convention, Ft. Worth, Falstaff Beer Logo, 1961 .... 10.00
Pirate Sitting On Chest, Cast Iron, 6 In. 65.00
Pirate Trunk, Tin 30.00
Plan-It, Solar System, 1950s 35.00
Plastic Egg, Red Goose Shoes, Gold Tone 6.00
Poll-Parrot, Shoe Shape 20.00
Popeye, Cast Iron 200.00
Poppin' Fresh Doughboy, Ceramic 25.00
Porky Pig, Dakin 18.00
Porky Pig, Die Cast Metal, Warner Brothers, 1940s 125.00
Post Office Box, Metal, Green, 5 3/4 In. 50.00
Premium Metz Beer, Barrel Shape, Ceramic, 7 In. 22.00
Rabbit, On Base, Cast Iron 1250.00
Rabbit, On Cabbage 715.00
Rabbit, Plastic, Wabasso, 10 In. 15.00
Railroad Steam Engine, Silver Plate 125.00
RCA Repairman, Plastic, 1950s, 5 In. 75.00

Red Goose, Shoe, 8 In. 135.00
Register, Buddy L 69.00
Register, Uncle Sam, 3 Coins, Metal, Red 35.00
Reindeer, Cast Iron 22.00
Rocket Ship, Mercury, Silver Gray, No Closure, 8 In. 49.00
Rocking Horse, Gold On Saddle, Red, Cast Iron, 10 1/2 x 8 In. 125.00
Roy Rogers & Trigger, Ceramic, 1950s 295.00
Royal Safe Deposit, Lithographed Portraits Of Girls, 5 1/2 In. 352.00
Saddle Horse, Gold Paint, Cast Iron 445.00
Safe, Bank Of Industry, Kenton, Cast Iron 215.00
Safe, Cast Iron, Kenton, Worn Paint, 3 x 4 In. 42.00
Safe, Coin Deposit 65.00
Sailor With Seabag, Cast Iron 250.00
Santa Claus, Battery Operated, 4 Functions, Box, 1960 .... 90.00
Santa Claus, On Roof, Battery Operated, Japan, 1950 .... 160.00
Santa Claus, Papier–Mache, 9 In. 95.00
Santa Claus, Rubber Face & Shoes, Cast Aluminum, 1950s, 21 In. 15.00
Santa Claus, Silver, Gold Trim 790.00
Santa Claus, Sleeping In Chair 32.00
Security Safe Deposit, Cast Iron, Pat. 1887 .... 85.00
Security Safe, Geometric & Foliate Panels, 6 In. 385.00
Shape & Color Of Orange, Redware, 3 x 3 1/4 In. 175.00
Sharecropper, Original Paint, Cast Iron ....90.00 To 110.00
Sheep, Chalkware, 10 In. 65.00
Shoe House, Cast Iron, 4 1/2 x 5 1/2 In. 45.00
Shoe, Weatherbird Shoes .... 15.00 To 35.00
Sitting Hen, Molded Feathers, Basket Weave Base, Ceramic, 7 In. 350.00
Sitting Hen, Russet, Redware, 7 In. 3520.00
Space Capsule, Bronze Tone, Metal, 6 In. 70.00
Spark Plug, Barney Google 225.00
Speedy, Alka–Seltzer, 4 1/2 In. 600.00
Stove, Amherst Stoves, Buffalo, Cast Iron 49.50
Streetcar, Inscribed Main Street, Cast Iron, 6 In. 330.00
Suitcase, Tin, Marx 60.00
Sunbonnet Girl, Cast Iron 98.00
Sundial, Brass, Key Lock, 8 In. 187.00
Tank, Cast Iron, Small 85.00
Top Hat, Lincoln Type, Ceramic 20.00
Treasure Chest 65.00
Treasury Building 125.00
Tree Trunk, Indian Brave, Redware, 5 1/2 In. 1650.00
Trolley, Bronzed Metal, Banthrico, 1960 .... 15.00
Truck, 1950 Chevy Panel Delivery 17.00
Truck, Armored, White Metal, 5 1/4 In. 35.00
Truck, Bank America, Smith, Miller 250.00
Truck, Mack Bulldog, 1926, Franco American 55.00
Truck, Step Van, Federal Express 22.00
Truck, Texaco No. 1 .... 350.00
Truck, Texaco No. 2 .... 350.00
Truck, Texaco No. 3 .... 250.00
Truck, Texaco No. 5 .... 50.00
Truck, U.S. Postal, Large 35.00
Turkey, Cast Iron 50.00
Uncle Remus, 4 1/2 In. 341.00
Uncle Sam, Porcelain, Worn Paint, 1940, 7 x 5 In. 75.00
Uncle Tom's Cabin, Pat. 1885, 3 1/2 In. 176.00
Uncle Tom, Cast Iron, 5 1/2 In. 302.00
Upright Piano, Black, Iron, 6 x 8 In. 330.00
Urn Form, Branch With 2 Pea Hens, Redware, 9 1/2 In. 715.00
Washington Monument, Metal, 4 3/4 In. 93.50
Watermelon Slice Shape, Pottery, Polychrome, 8 1/2 In. 45.00
Windmill, Tin, Cragstan 85.00
Wise Pig, Fidelity, 3 Dogs, Teller At Window, Cast Iron, 5 In. 352.00

Yellow Cab, Cast Iron 1210.00
Yogi Bear 15.00
Young Nigger, England 250.00

BANKO, Korean ware, and Sumida are terms that are often confusing. We use the names in the way most often used by antiques dealers and collectors. Korean ware is now called *Sumida Gawa* or *Sumida* and is listed in this book under that heading. Banko is a group of rustic Japanese wares made in the nineteenth and twentieth centuries. Some pieces are made of mosaics of colored clay, some are fanciful teapots. Redware and other materials were also used.

Creamer, 3 1/2 In. .... 125.00 To 140.00
Plate, Marble Body, Enameled Cranes In Water, c.1860 .... 475.00
Sugar & Creamer, Cover, Iris On Gray Ware, Brooklyn Souvenir, 1930s 45.00
Teapot, Bear, Reed Handle, Florals 125.00
Teapot, Elephant 150.00
Vase, Cranes, 4 In. .... 135.00 To 155.00

BARBER collectibles range from the popular red and white striped pole that used to be found in front of every shop to the small scissors and tools of the trade. Barber chairs are wanted, especially the older models with elaborate iron trim.

Backbar, Oak, 2 Wooden Barber Chairs, Brass Claw Feet 6000.00
Chair, Koch, Hydraulic, Brass Trim, Wood Pedestal, Oak, c.1890 .... 900.00
Chair, Koch, Oak, Keystone Hotel, Keystone, Nebraska, Patent 1895 .... 750.00
Chair, Koken, Red 1000.00
Chair, Paidair, Green 1150.00
Coat Rack, Cast Iron, c.1890 .... 200.00
Hone, Ira Freeman's Hone & Strop, Ft. Edward, N.Y., Box 18.00
Hone, Noxall, Sears, Box 15.00
Hone, Razor, Stone, Rectangular 3.00
Lamp, Singing, Cobalt Blue, Patent 1883 .... 145.00
Pole, American, 19th Century, 8 Ft. 1155.00
Pole, Cast Iron & White Metal, Painted, 90 In. 175.00
Pole, Hand Crank 975.00
Pole, Koken, Leaded Glass, 1890s .... 350.00 To 1150.00
Pole, Koken, Stained Glass .... 1000.00 To 1250.00
Pole, Milk Glass Globe, Lights, Spring Powered, Wall Mount, 43 In. 450.00
Pole, Red, White & Blue, Tin 115.00
Pole, Sidewalk, Porcelain Finish, 90 In. 2000.00
Pole, Wooden, 6 Ft. 1400.00
Pole, Wooden, Original Paint, 1890s, 76 In. 1295.00
Pole, Wooden, Wall Mount 600.00
Sign, Barber Shop, Double Porcelain, 24 x 12 In. 110.00
Sign, Barber Shop, Look Better, Porcelain, Half Round, 23 In. 125.00
Sign, Master Barber Of America, Tin 70.00
Sign, Shop, Double–Sided, Porcelain, 24 x 12 In. 70.00
Sign, Union Shop, With Eagle, Tin 30.00
Sign, Union, Eagle & Shield 75.00
Strop, Double Duck 18.00
Strop, Empire, West Winstead, Conn., 4–Sided, Wooden Handle, Box 30.00

BAROMETERS are used to forecast the weather. Antique barometers with elaborate wooden cases and brass trim are the most desirable. Mercury column barometers are also popular with collectors. It is difficult to find someone to repair a broken one, so be sure your barometer is in working condition.

Air Guide, With Thermometer & Humidity Indicator, Mahogany 85.00
Banjo, Gallione Galle & Co., New York, 52 1/2 In. ....*Illus*   440.00
Banjo, Rosewood, Ivory Knobs, 19th Century, 38 In. ....*Illus*   385.00
Barigo, Band Around Glass Face, Wood Base, Germany, 5 In. 58.00
Brass Finial, Shell & Flower Inlay, C. Aiano, 38 In. 330.00
Brass Finial, Tagliabue Torre & Co., Mahogany, 38 In. 990.00

Clock, Mahogany Case, Bollenbach Of Barrington, Ill., c.1940 .... 300.00
English, Flame Grain Mahogany Veneer, Brass Trim, 42 3/4 In. 675.00
Louis XVI, Love Birds On Sides, Giltwood, 18th Century, 39 In. 1760.00
Mahogany, Case Has Applied Carvings, English, 36 In. 150.00
Mahogany, Silvered Dials, England, 37 In. 200.00
Musto Bros. Radio & Hardware, New Jersey, Wood 45.00
Parian Figures, Tole Decorated House, 7 1/2 In. 25.00
Regency, Calamander, P. Guarnerio, Huntingdon, 38 In. ....*Illus* 605.00
Stick, Brass Scrolls & Flowers, English, Rosewood, 37 In. 412.00
Stick, Columbiana, Ohio, Walnut 375.00
Stick, Georgian, Brass Face, Broken Arched Pediment, 34 In. 330.00
Stick, Ivory Indicator Plate, Adie & Son, Scotland, Oak, 41 In. 885.00
Stick, Over Silvered Scale, Thermometer, Watkins & Hill, Mahogany 1320.00
Stick, Regency, Brass Face, Ebony Urn, 37 1/2 In. 275.00
Stick, Silver Dial, G. Brogi, Mahogany, 37 In. 880.00
Stick, W. Norton, 19th Century, 36 1/2 In. 385.00
Thermometer, Louis XIV, Tortoiseshell, F. Lesage, 4 Ft. 3 In. 8800.00
Walnut, Porcelain Face, 39 In. 250.00
Wedgwood, Light Blue Jasper, 9 In. 110.00

BASEBALL collectibles are in the Sports section, except for baseball cards, which are listed under Baseball in the Card category.

BASKETS of all types are popular with collectors. Indian, Japanese, African, Shaker, and many other kinds of baskets can be found. Of course, baskets are still being made, so the collector must learn to tell the age and style of the basket to determine the value.

Apple, Oak Splint 45.00
Buttocks, Splint, 1–Egg Size, 3 x 3 1/2 In. 350.00
Buttocks, Splint, Bentwood Handle, 13 x 13 1/2 x 6 3/4 In. 185.00
Buttocks, Splint, Bentwood Handle, 6 In. 75.00
Buttocks, Splint, Boat Shape, Handle, 10 x 12 x 7 In. 55.00
Buttocks, Splint, Brown Varnish, 15 x 15 x 8 1/2 In. 145.00
Buttocks, Splint, Brown Varnish, Bentwood Handle, 13 x 13 In. 300.00
Buttocks, Splint, Eye Of God Design At Handles, 6 x 9 In. 95.00
Cheese, American, 1860 .... 365.00
Double Wrapped Top, Swing Handle, Kicked–Up Bottom, 8 x 16 In. 650.00
Drying, Herb, Splint, 2 1/4 x 15 1/2 In. 135.00
Field, Oak Splint Nailed To Base 55.00
Game, Hanging, Splint, 2 Part, 21 In. 195.00
Hanging, Splint, 13 x 12 In. 100.00

Left to right: Barometer, Banjo, Gallione Galle & Co., New York, 52 1/2 In.; Barometer, Banjo, Rosewood, Ivory Knobs, 19th Century, 38 In.; Barometer, Regency, Calamander, P. Guarnerio, Huntingdon, 38 In.

If you must move a painting in a car trunk, be careful. Put cardboard on each side of the canvas to keep it from being punctured by a tool or holder in the trunk. Close the trunk lid slowly. A quick slam may build up the air pressure and rip the canvas. If going on a long trip through several temperature zones, remember that a very hot, then very cold trunk temperature will damage the painting.

Loom, Splint, 2–Tone Design, 7 1/2 In. 10.00
Lunch, Splint, Orange, Oval Top, Rectangular Base, 2 Wooden Handles 85.00
Nantucket Lightship, Shaped Handle, Dated 1950, 10 1/2 In. 330.00
Nantucket, Lightship, 10 In. Diam. 550.00
Nantucket, Lightship, Henry F. Wyer, 1880 .... 1350.00
Nantucket, Oval, Wooden Base, Splint Staves, Swivel Handle, 8 In. 475.00
Nantucket, Purse Shape, Swing Handle, Carved Whale On Lid 250.00
Nantucket, Splint, Wooden Bottom, Swivel Handle, 11 x 6 In. 300.00
Nantucket, Turned Wood Base, Cane, Splint, Swivel Handle, 4 In. 275.00
Pea Picking, Overlapping Split Wood, Bentwood Handle, 11 x 16 In. 75.00
Potato, Inch Splint Construction, Round, 20 In. Diam. 83.00
Splint, Bentwood Handle, 11 1/2 x 13 x 6 3/4 In. 75.00
Splint, Bentwood Handle, 7 1/2 x 12 1/2 x 4 1/2 In. 75.00
Splint, Bentwood Handle, 8 In. 65.00
Splint, Bentwood Handle, Oblong, 13 x 20 1/2 x 8 1/2 In. 150.00
Splint, Bentwood Handle, Oval, 14 1/2 x 17 x 7 In. 75.00
Splint, Bentwood Handle, Round, 7 In. 185.00
Splint, Bentwood Rim Handle, 12 x 6 1/2 In. 65.00
Splint, Bentwood Rim Handles, 18 1/2 x 12 In. 55.00
Splint, Bentwood Rim Handles, Natural & Blue, 8 3/4 x 12 In. 25.00
Splint, Bentwood Swivel Handle, 4 1/2 In. 175.00
Splint, Carved Bentwood Handle, 7 1/2 x 16 x 26 In. 375.00
Splint, Curliques, Faded, Round, 8 1/2 x 3 1/2 In. 22.50
Splint, Goose Feather, Bentwood Handles, Lid, 16 x 26 In. 95.00
Splint, Laundry, Rim Hand Holes, 15 1/2 In. 55.00
Splint, Melon Rib, Eye Of God Design At Handle, 6 In. 225.00
Splint, Old Green Paint, Bentwood Rim Handles, 11 x 15 x 6 In. 155.00
Splint, Open Weave Bottom, Rim Bentwood Handles, 18 x 9 In. 135.00
Splint, Red & Black Designs, Bentwood Handle, 7 1/2 In. 85.00
Wash, Splint, Bentwood Rim Handles, Marked OHW, 18 x 12 In. 55.00

BATCHELDER products are made from California clay. Ernest Batchelder
established a tile studio in Pasadena, California, in 1909 and expanded
until in 1916 he built a larger factory with a new partner. The Batchelder–   **BATCHELDER**
Wilson Company made all types of architectural tiles, garden pots, and
bookends. The plant closed in 1932. In 1936 Batchelder opened Batchelder   **LOS ANGELES**
Ceramics, also in Pasadena, and made bowls, vases, and earthenware pots.
He retired in 1951 and died in 1957. Pieces are marked *Batchelder
Pasadena* or *Batchelder Los Angeles.*

Tile, Lovebirds & Berries, Gray Glaze, Architectural, 11 3/4 In. 385.00
Tile, Rabbit, 4 In. 95.00
Vase, Omar Khayyan, Stoneware, 5 In. 245.00

BATMAN and Robin are characters from a comic strip by Bob Kane that
started in 1939. In 1966, the characters became part of a popular television
series. There have been radio and movie serials that featured the pair. In
1989 a full–length movie was made.

Batmobile, Eight Figures, 1984 .... 55.00
Batmobile, Matte Black, Instructions, Corgi, Box 500.00
Batmobile, Talking, Palitoy, Box 250.00
Button, Batman & Robin Society, 1966, Large 25.00
Cape, 1965 .... 20.00
Charm Bracelet, Official 60.00
Clock, Alarm, Talking, Box .... 50.00 To 65.00
Clock, Figural, Battery Operated, 1974 .... 150.00
Club Member 20.00
Coloring Book, Whitman, 1967 .... 20.00
Costume, Complete, Box, 1966 .... 425.00
Dish, Ceramic, Batmobile, 1966 .... 150.00
Doll, Cloth, Large 150.00
Doll, Mego, Box, 1973 .... 129.00
Doll, Robin, Mego, 8 In. 50.00
Escape Gun, 1966 .... 35.00

Figure, Batcave, Batman, Robin, Penguin, Joker, Batmobile, Mego 275.00
Game, Card, Koide, 1960s 250.00
Game, Horseshoe, 1966, Pressman 172.00
Game, Pinball, Marx, 1966 ....90.00 To 135.00
Game, Pinball, Tin Lithograph, Marx, 1966 .... 75.00
Gum Card, Batman Strikes!, No. 12, 1966 .... 12.00
Helmet & Cape, Ideal, Box, 1966 .... 150.00
Joker, Squirt Head, Waterworks, England, 4 In. 25.00
Kit, Stardust Velvet Art, Envelope, 1966 .... 70.00
Lamp, Desk, Batman Standing In Front Of Bat Cave, Decals 95.00
License Plate 25.00
Lunch Box, 1966 ....65.00 To 115.00
Magazine, Life, 1966 .... 20.00
Night–Light, 1966 ....15.00 To 20.00
Periscope, 1966 .... 35.00
Puppet, Hand 75.00
Ring, Figural, Rubber, 1966 .... 10.00
Sign, Batman Fruit Drink, 24 x 42 In. 275.00
Silverware, 1940s 15.00
Toy, Dancing, Sound Activated, Battery Operated, Blue, 15 In. 200.00
Tumbler, Bat Girl 20.00
Wallet, Plastic, 1966 .... 49.00

BATTERSEA enamels, which are enamels painted on copper, were made in the Battersea district of London from about 1750 to 1756. Many similar enamels are mistakenly called *Battersea.*

Box, House, Bird, Flowers 175.00
Candlestick, Spiral Fluted Stem, Bobeche, 10 In., Pair 880.00

BAUER pottery is a California–made ware. J.A. Bauer moved his Kentucky pottery to Los Angeles, California, in 1909. The company made art pottery after 1912 and dinnerwares marked *Bauer* after 1929. The factory went out of business in 1962.

Bowl, Indian, Black, 7 1/2 In. 165.00
Butter, Cover, Ring 50.00
Carafe Set, Ringware, Green, 6 Piece 15.00
Carafe, Yellow Handle, 8 x 7 In. 85.00
Casserole, Cover, Ring, Metal Holder, 7 1/2 In. 25.00
Coffeepot, Orange Ring, Red 35.00
Cookie Jar, Speckware 35.00
Cornucopia, Blue, White Inside, 6 x 11 In. 40.00
Pitcher, Ringed, Burgundy 40.00
Plate, Ring, Black, 11 In. 55.00
Plate, Ring, Red, 11 In. 30.00
Teapot, Ring, 4 Cup 20.00
Vase, Fan, Deco Leaf Form, High Gloss Turquoise, 13 x 10 In., Pair 95.00
Vase, Fan, Stylized Leaf Forms, Turquoise, 14 x 10 1/2 In., Pair 90.00
Vase, Gilt & Orange, Signed, 10 1/4 In. 95.00

BAVARIA is a region in Europe where many types of porcelain were made. In the nineteenth century, the mark often included the word *Bavaria.* After 1871, the words *Bavaria, Germany,* were used. Listed here are pieces that include the name *Bavaria* in some form, but major porcelain makers, such as Rosenthal, are listed in their own categories.

Bowl, Rose, Gold Trim Signed Wright 25.00
Butter, Cover, Tiny Roses 65.00
Cake Plate, Large Pink Roses, Open Handles 30.00
Celery, Pink & Gold Floral Design 12.00
Creamer, Cow 35.00
Plate, Flowers, Gold Trim, Iridescent, Signed Lynch 6.00
Plate, Game, Quail 95.00
Plate, Melon Boy, Pierced, Gold Rim, 10 In. 30.00
Plate, Swan, Angels, Handle, Castle, Swan China, 10 In. 70.00

BEADED BAGS are included in the Purse category.

BEATLES collectors search for any items picturing the four members of the famous music group or any of their recordings. Because these items are so new, the condition is very important and top prices are paid only for items in mint condition. The Beatles first appeared on American network television in 1964. The group disbanded in 1971.

Animation Cel, Yellow Submarine, H. Edelman, 11 1/2 x 10 In., Pair	1760.00
Bag, Booty, Vinyl, Pictures 4 Beatles, 1964, 10 1/2 x 15 In.	250.00
Bank, Yellow Submarine, George, Sticker	350.00
Bank, Yellow Submarine, Paul	175.00
Bank, Yellow Submarine, Ringo, Sticker	250.00
Bank, Yellow Submarine, Set Of 4	1200.00
Book, Daily Diary, Photos & Sketches, Color Cover, 1965, 3 x 4 In.	19.00
Book, Pop–Out, Yellow Submarine, 1968	15.00
Book, Pop–Up, 1984–1985	10.00
Book, Song, 1964 & 1966 Tours, Many Photographs	16.00
Book, Song, George Harrison, 1973	10.00
Booklet, The Beatles, 1964, 65 Pages	24.00
Cake Decorations	15.00
Clock, Wall, Battery Operated	30.00
Display, 3–D Cutouts, Beatles & Bass Drum, Framed, 38 x 27 In.	880.00
Doll, Paul, 4 1/2 In.	25.00
Doll, Paul, With Guitar, Remco	65.00
Doll, Ringo, Remco, 5 In.	58.00
Game, Flip Your Wig, Board, Box, 1964	95.00
Holder, Record, 45 RPM, 20 Plastic Sleeves, Square, 7 1/2 In.	32.00
Lunch Box, Blue Metal	195.00
Lunch Box, Yellow Submarine	150.00
Magazine, Teen–World, Beatles Cover & Features, 1964	26.00
Model Kit, Ringo, Beatles, 1964, Revell	79.00
Model Kit, Yellow Submarine, Box	325.00
Nodder, Car Mascots, Box, 6 x 9 1/2 In., 4 Piece	650.00
Phonograph, Album, 2 Virgins, John Lennon, Brown Bag, Unplayed	65.00
Phonograph, Album, Beatles & Frank Ifield, Vee–Jay No. 1085, 1964	150.00
Pin, Paul, 1 In. Diam.	4.00
Plate, Bamboo, Oriental Writing, 1964, 12 In.	150.00
Postcard, Yellow Submarine, Large	25.00
Print, 4 Faces, Irish Linen, Color, 19 x 29 In.	150.00
Program, Autographed, U.S. A. Ltd. Tour, 1964, 12 x 12 In.	1650.00
Puzzle, Official Beatles Fan Club, 1964, Sealed	98.00
Record, Twist & Shout, Tollie Label, 1964	20.00
Ring Chip, Flasher, To Their Individual Name, 1964, Set Of 4	20.00
Rug, Picture, Music Notes, Color, 34 x 21 In.	225.00
Scarf, Irish Linen, Pictures, Color, 19 x 29 In.	150.00
Stationery, Yellow Submarine	25.00
Switch Plate, Yellow Submarine, Sealed	25.00
Toy, Soaky, Paul McCartney	75.00
Toy, Yellow Submarine, Corgi, 1961	150.00
Toy, Yellow Submarine, Corgi, 1968	150.00
Tray, 4 Faces, Signed, Label On Back	45.00
Tumbler, Yea, Yea, Yea, 6 1/2 In.	12.00
Wig, No Cardboard	30.00

BEEHIVE, Austria, or Beehive, Vienna, are terms used in English–speaking countries to refer to the many types of decorated porcelain bearing a mark that looks like a beehive. The mark is actually a shield, viewed upside down. It was first used in 1744 by the Royal Porcelain Manufactory of Vienna. The firm made porcelains, called *Royal Vienna* by collectors, until it closed in 1864. Many other German, Austrian, and Japanese factories have reproduced Royal Vienna wares, complete with the original shield or *beehive* mark. This listing includes the expensive, original Royal Vienna porcelains and many other types of beehive porcelain. The Royal Vienna pieces include that name in the description.

Box, Portrait, Gold Over Cobalt, Marked, 4 In.	295.00
Cake Plate, Pink Flowers, Green Leaves, 13 In.	20.00
Candlestick, Woman & Cupid, Iridescent Maroon, Gold, 5 1/2 In., Pair	595.00
Coffee Set, Classical Woman Scene, Marked, After Dinner, 12 Piece	550.00
Demitasse Set, Classical Scenes, 6 1/2–In. Coffeepot, 10 Pc.	385.00
Fish Set, Center Fish, Sauceboat, 12 Plates, Platter, 22 1/2 In.	775.00
Jardiniere, Figures Of Nude Women, A. Ledru, 22 In.	1650.00
Loving Cup, Cherubs, Woman & Musicians, 3 Handles, Marked	210.00
Plaque, Girl, Pink Dress, Cherub, Sturm, 21 x 16 In. ....*Illus*	13200.00
Plaque, Herrensccho, 1895, 9 x 7 In.	1500.00
Plaque, Konigin Louise, 7 x 5 In.	990.00
Plaque, Ruth, 9 x 6 In.	2475.00
Plate, Allegorical, 3 Fine Arts, Shield Mark, 9 9/16 In.	1540.00
Plate, Blessing Of Potatoes Scene, Bavaria Blank, 9 1/2 In.	125.00
Plate, Constance, Blue, 9 1/4 In.	110.00
Plate, Fox In Forest, River Scene, Blue & Gold Rim, Marked	425.00
Plate, Gleaners, Gold Over Brown Border, Marked, 9 1/2 In.	295.00
Plate, Hand Painted Garden Scene, Women, Courtier, Signed, 8 1/2 In.	595.00
Plate, Portrait, Queen Victoria, 9 1/2 In.	550.00
Plate, Wagner Girl With Fan, Signed, 9 In.	575.00
Sconce, Porcelain & Bronze, 10 x 15 In.	1265.00
Tureen, Sprigged Knop Cover, Stand, Royal Portrait, 1788, 13 1/2 In.	6050.00
Urn, Cover, Painted & Gilt Enameled, Pair	2600.00
Urn, Cover, Scenic, 2 1/4 Ft.	2970.00
Urn, Polychrome Enamel & Gilt, 17 In.	95.00
Urn, Portrait Medallion Of Ruth, Purple & Pink, c.1910, 14 1/2 In.	895.00
Vase, Cover, Portrait, Rosaling, Marked, 13 In.	230.00
Vase, Cover, Three Graces, Hera Mask Handles, Gold, 15 1/2 In.	3500.00
Vase, Diana Huntress, Floral, Gold Trim, 8 In.	895.00
Vase, Hand Painted Scene, Red & Gilt Border, 7 In.	275.00
Vase, Madam LeBrun, Wagner, 8 In.	895.00
Vase, Venus & Cupid, Winged Cherub, Cranberry Ground, 9 1/2 In.	220.00
Vase, Woman, Flowers In Hair, Playing Harp, Blue Luster, 32 1/2 In.	9075.00
Vase, Women, 3 Gold Handles, Gold Rigaree, Marked, 9 1/2 In.	425.00

BEER BOTTLES are listed in the Bottle category under Beer

BEER CANS are a twentieth–century idea. Beer was sold in kegs or returnable bottles until 1934. The first patent for a can was issued to the American Can Company in September of that year; and Gotfried Kruger Brewing Company, Newark, New Jersey, was the first to use the can. The

Royal Vienna, Plaque, Girl, Pink Dress,
   Cherub, Sturm, 21 x 16 In.

•••••••••••••••••••••••••••••

Do not have old monograms removed from silver. It lowers the value. If it bothers you to have an old initial, don't buy the piece. We like to tell people it belonged to a great aunt with that initial.

•••••••••••••••••••••••••••••

cone–top can was first made in 1935, the aluminum pop–top in 1962. Collectors should look for cans in good condition, with no dents or rust. Serious collectors prefer cans that have been opened from the bottom.

007 James Bond, Tab	285.00
7–Eleven Beer, Tab	22.00
9–0–5, Straight Sided	2.00
Amana, Tab Top	6.00
Auchlebach Pilsner, Cone Top	20.00
Ballantine Light Lager Beer	9.00
Bavarian, Tab Top	2.00
BFC Export, Flat Top	15.00
Billy Beer, 6 Pack	45.00
Billy Beer, Tab Top	1.00
Bismarck Export Beer	15.00
Black Hills Gold Premium Light Beer, Berghoff–Huber	1.25
Blanchard's, Tab Top	2.00
Bruck's Jubilee, Cone Top	28.00
Budweiser, Flat Top	5.00
Budweiser, Michelob Top, Misprint	35.00
Budweiser, St. Louis	4.00
Busch, Flat Top	10.00
Canadian Ace	3.00
Canadian Ace Ale	15.00
Champagne Velvet	25.00
Chief Oshkosh Beer	14.00
Colt 45 Dry Malt Liquor, G. H., Aluminum, Tapered	1.25
Coors International Balloon Fiesta, Aluminum, 1990	3.00
Drewry's	8.00
Edelweiss	5.00
Falstaff Draft, Tab Top	20.00
Fehr's, Cone Top	32.50
Frankenmuth, Tab Top	100.00
Garden State Light Beer, Tab	10.00
Genesee, Tax Stamp On Top	8.00
Gettelman Bock, Tab Top	19.00
Griesedieck Bros.	15.00
Hamm's	7.00
Hamm's Draft, Tab, 11 Oz.	15.00
Hamm's, Stamp On Top	4.00
Hapsburg, Michigan Stamp On Top	35.00
Heileman's Special Export	5.00
Highlander	20.00
Hudepohl, Tab Top	3.00
KC's Best	20.00
Koenig Brau	16.00
Krueger Pilsner, Tab	15.00
Lone Star	15.00
Lone Star, Stamp On Top	4.00
Lone Star, Tab	9.00
Miller Ale, Tab	14.00
Montauk Light, Long Island Brewing Co., Utica, Tapered	1.50
Near Beer	5.00
Oertel's 92	20.00
Old Export, Tab Top	2.00
Old Milwaukee Light Biere Beer, Imported, Tapered	3.00
Original $1000, Tab Top	15.00
Pabst Blue Ribbon	6.00
Pathmark	3.00
Pfeiffer	7.00
Rainier Old Stock Ale, Cone Top	65.00
Rams Head, Cone Top, Qt.	95.00
Red Cap Ale, Cleveland, Tab	12.00

If you collect the decorated glasses from fast food restaurants, never wash them in the dishwasher. The heat and detergent will change the coloring and lower the value.

Bell, Colonial Lady, White, Floral,

Porcelain, 4 1/4 In.

Rheingold Scotch Ale	14.00
Schlitz, Dated 1954	4.00
Schmidt Beer, Green Can, Aluminum, Tapered	.85
Ski Country	18.00
Stag, Belleville, Ill., You'll Like, Flat Top	7.00
Stag, Flat Top	8.00
Stroh's Bohemian Style Beer	4.00
Stroh's Light, Aluminum, Tapered Neck, Government Warning	11.25
Tex	22.00
Tiger Beer, Tab	10.00
Utica Club	2.00
Valley Forge	2.00

BELLS have been made of porcelain, china, or metal through the centuries. All types are collected. Favorites include glass bells, figural bells, school bells, and cowbells. Be careful not to buy a bell made from an old glass goblet.

Bell Metal, Iron Yoke & Clapper, G. W. Coffin & Co., Cincinnati, 21 In.	225.00
Church Tower, Cast–Bronze, VanDuzen & Tift, 1894, 28 In.	1550.00
Church Tower, Cast–Bronze, VanDuzen & Tift, Dated 1887, 34 In.	2200.00
Church Tower, Iron–Bronze, Stuckstede Bros., St. Joseph's, 1929, 36 In.	2300.00
Colonial Lady, Pottery, Germany	25.00
Colonial Lady, White, Floral, Porcelain, 4 1/4 In. *Illus*	10.00
Custard Glass, Coney Island	90.00
Custard Glass, Wide Band, Rose, Says Maiden Lane, N.Y.	75.00
Drawbridge, Bronze, Solid Bronze Mounting Bracket, 1930s, 17 In.	2100.00
Jacobean Head, Embossed Warriors, Head Is Handle, Brass, 4 In.	125.00
Night Watchman's, Hand Held, Bradd	35.00
Porcelain, Enameled Birds & Beading, Lavender, Cutout Handle, 6 In.	12.00
R. A. F. Victory, Made From Metal Of German Aircraft, 5 In.	60.00
Schoolmaster, Brass, 9 3/4 x 6 In.	85.00
Schoolmaster, Cypress Lake Senior High School, Brass	125.00
Sleigh Set, Leather Strap, 20 Piece	55.00
Sleigh, Clip–On, Engraved Brass, Leather Strap, 48 Bells	250.00
Sleigh, Leather, Pat. 1878, 15 Piece	85.00
Smoke, Milk Glass, 8 In.	15.00
Teacher's, 10 In.	65.00
Young Warrior, Warrior Handle, Brass, 6 1/4 In.	135.00

BELLEEK china was made in Ireland, other European countries, and the United States. The glaze is creamy yellow and appears wet. The first Belleek was made in 1857. All pieces listed here are Irish Belleek. The mark changed through the years. The first mark, black, dates from 1863 to 1890. The second mark, black, dates from 1891 to 1926 and includes the words *Co. Fermanagh, Ireland.* The third mark, black, dates from 1926 to 1946 and has the words *Deanta in Eirinn.* The fourth mark, same as the third mark but green, dates from 1946 to 1955. The fifth mark, green, dates from 1955 to 1965 and has an R in a circle added in the upper right. The sixth mark, green, dates after 1965 and the words *Co. Fermanagh* have been omitted. The seventh mark, gold, was used after 1980 and omits the words *Deanta in Eirinn.* The word *Belleek* is now used only on the pieces made in Ireland even though earlier pieces from other countries were sometimes marked *Belleek.* These early pieces are listed by manufacturer, such as Ceramic Art Co., Haviland, Lenox, Ott & Brewer, and Willets.

Basket, Nautilus On Coral, 1st Mark, Black, 9 In.	850.00
Biscuit Barrel, Diamond, 1st Mark, Black, 8 In.	1000.00
Biscuit Barrel, New Shell, 2nd Mark, Black, 8 In.	1000.00
Box, Trinket, Shamrock, Oval, 2nd Mark, Black, 5 In.	275.00
Bust, Sorrow, 2nd Mark, Black, 11 In.	2800.00
Butter Tub, Shamrock, Child's, 3rd Mark, Black	45.00
Cornucopia, Cherub, 1st Mark, Black, 7 In.	1600.00
Creamer, Basket Weave, Shamrock, 3rd Mark, Black	60.00
Creamer, Leaves & Berries, 1st Mark, Green	40.00
Creamer, Shamrock, Twig Handle, 2nd Mark, Black, 4 In.	150.00
Creamer, Shell Feet, Green Mark	40.00
Cup & Saucer, Bouquet	135.00
Cup & Saucer, Neptune, Shell Footed, Iridescent Gray Finish	50.00
Cup & Saucer, New Shell, 3rd Mark, Green	55.00
Cup & Saucer, Shamrock, 2nd Mark, Green	65.00
Cup & Saucer, Shamrock, 3rd Mark, Green	60.00
Cup & Saucer, Tridacna, 1st Mark, Green	62.00
Cup & Saucer, Tridacna, 3rd Mark, Black	72.00
Cup & Saucer, Tridacna, Pink Trim, 2nd Mark, Black	50.00
Figurine, Boy With Pierced Basket, 1st Mark, Black, 9 In.	1450.00
Figurine, Dog, Terrier, 3rd Mark, Green	118.00
Figurine, Girl Basket Bearer, 1st Mark, Black, 9 In.	2400.00
Figurine, Leprechaun, 3rd Mark, Green	118.00
Figurine, Nude, 3rd Mark, Green, 14 In.	450.00 To 575.00
Figurine, Owl, Green Mark, 8 1/4 In.	80.00
Figurine, Pig, 1st Mark, Green, Large	125.00
Mug, Basket Weave, Twig Handle, 2nd Mark, Green, 3 3/4 In.	45.00
Mug, Twig Handle, 2nd Mark, Green, 3 3/4 In.	45.00
Pitcher, Aberdeen, 3rd Mark, Black, 6 In.	125.00
Pitcher, Basket Weave & Shamrock, 3rd Mark, Black, 6 1/2 In.	195.00
Pitcher, Ivy, 6 In.	72.00
Plate, Bouquet, 10 1/2 In.	100.00
Plate, Bouquet, 5 3/4 In.	60.00
Plate, Desert, Limpet, Pink Tint, Gilt Trim, 2nd Mark, Black	65.00
Plate, Limpet, 3rd Mark, Black	45.00
Plate, Shamrock, 3rd Mark, Green, 7 In.	20.00
Plate, Tridacna, Pink Trim, 2nd Mark, Black, 6 In.	20.00
Salt & Pepper, Shamrock, 1st Mark, Green	45.00
Salt, New Shell, 2nd Mark, Black, 2 x 3 In.	65.00
Saltshaker, Roses, Pearlized Ground, Palette Mark	75.00
Sauceboat, Shell Feet, Green Mark	50.00
Saucer, Exotic Bird, Tower & Aqueduct Center, 5 3/4 In.	50.00
Sugar & Creamer, Child's, 3rd Mark, Black	120.00
Sugar & Creamer, Ivy, 1st Mark, Green	85.00
Sugar & Creamer, Lily, 1st Mark, Green	60.00 To 85.00
Sugar & Creamer, Lotus, 1st Mark, Green	85.00
Sugar & Creamer, Ribbon, 1st Mark, Green	85.00
Sugar & Creamer, Ribbon, 3rd Mark, Green	45.00
Sugar & Creamer, Ribbon, Open, 1st Mark, Green	45.00
Sugar & Creamer, Shamrock, 1st Mark, Green	65.00
Sugar & Creamer, Shamrock, 3rd Mark, Black	150.00
Sugar & Creamer, Toy Shell, 1st Mark, Green	105.00
Tea Set, Shamrock, Black Mark, 20 Piece	577.00
Teapot, Basket Weave, Overhead Twig Handle, 2nd Mark, Green	145.00

♦♦♦♦♦♦♦♦♦♦♦♦♦♦♦♦♦♦♦♦♦♦

Do not put water in a pottery container with an unglazed interior. The water will be absorbed and eventually stain the container.

♦♦♦♦♦♦♦♦♦♦♦♦♦♦♦♦♦♦♦♦♦♦

Bennington, Cuspidor, Green, Brown &
Cream Glaze

Teapot, Shamrock, 1st Mark, Green	200.00
Teapot, Shamrock, 3rd Mark, Green	195.00
Tray, Tridacna, Pearl, Pink Trim, 2nd Mark, Black, 16 x 14 In.	650.00
Vase, Aberdeen, Applied Flowers, 2nd Mark, Black, 10 In.	495.00
Vase, Corn, All White, 1st Mark, Black, 6 In.	225.00
Vase, Fish, Double, 1st Mark, Black, 12 In.	3100.00
Vase, Sea Horse, Beaded Top Rim, 2nd Mark, Black, 3 In.	365.00
Vase, Shamrock, Panel, 3rd Mark, Green	30.00
Vase, Sunflower, 3rd Mark, Green	125.00
Vase, Thistle, 3rd Mark, Green	395.00
Vase, Tree Trunk, 3 Openings, 2nd Mark, Green, 6 In.	45.00
Vase, Tree Trunk, All White, Brown Vine, 1st Mark, Black, 6 In.	165.00

BENNINGTON ware was the product of two factories working in Bennington, Vermont. Both the Norton Company and the Lyman Fenton Company were out of business by 1896. The wares include brown and yellow mottled pottery, Parian, scroddled ware, stoneware, graniteware, yellowware, and Staffordshire–type vases. The name is also a generic term for mottled brownware of the type made in Bennington.

Bedpan	35.00
Bottle, Coachman	715.00
Bowl, Wash, Flint Enamel, Brown, Blue, Green, 13 1/2 In.	800.00
Creamer, Cow, 1850s, 4 1/2 In.	275.00
Cuspidor, Green, Brown & Cream Glaze ....*Illus*	138.00
Doorstop, Dog	250.00
Flask, Departed Spirits G., 5 1/2 In.	435.00
Flask, Figural, 1850s, 10 1/2 In.	225.00
Flask, Ladies' Companions, Flint	675.00
Pie Plate	115.00
Pitcher, Avenue Of Trees, Green, 8 In.	98.00
Pitcher, Daniel Boone, 9 1/2 In.	85.00
Pitcher, Flint Enamel, Paneled, Brown, Green, 12 3/8 In.	900.00
Pitcher, Peacock On Fence, 9 In.	85.00
Pitcher, Peacock, 9 1/2 In.	300.00
Pitcher, Tulip & Heart, 7 3/8 In.	850.00
Pitcher, Water, Cupid & Psyche, Parian, 9 In.	195.00
Plate, Battle Monument, Blue, 9 3/4 In.	35.00
Soap Dish, Rectangular, 8 In.	65.00
Soap Dish, Round, 6 In.	70.00
Syrup, Day Lily, White Glaze, c.1850, 9 1/4 In.	225.00
Syrup, Spinning Wheel, White Glazed, c.1850, Cover, 7 In.	650.00
Tobacco Container, Lamb	330.00
Tobacco Container, Toby	605.00
Washboard	170.00

BERLIN, a German porcelain factory, was started in 1751 by Wilhelm Kaspar Wegely. In 1763, the factory was taken over by Frederick the Great and became the Royal Berlin Porcelain Manufactory. It is still in operation today. Pieces have been marked in a variety of ways.

Ecuelle, Cover, Classical Figures, Angular Handles, 1800, 6 7/16 In.	1540.00
Plaque, Gypsy Girl, C. S., 10 In.	5500.00
Tureen, Yellow, Swags, c.1820	8000.00
Vase, Putti Riding Dolphin, Mask Handles, 24 In., Pair	3575.00

BESWICK started making earthenware in Staffordshire, England, in 1936. The company is now part of Royal Doulton Tableware, Ltd. Figurines of animals, especially dogs and horses, Beatrix Potter animals, and other wares are still being made.

Figurine, Afghan	45.00
Figurine, Beagle	45.00
Figurine, Chaffinch, Porcelain, 1920	25.00
Figurine, Corgi, Standing	45.00
Figurine, Dalmatian	125.00
Figurine, King Charles Spaniel	45.00
Figurine, Queen Of Hearts	75.00
Figurine, Scottish Terrier	45.00
Figurine, Wire Haired Terrier, Cast Iron	35.00
Plaque, Figures Of As You Like It, That Would I, 12 In.	125.00
Plaque, King, Aide & Girl, Leaf Border, As You Like It, 12 In.	125.00

BETTY BOOP, the cartoon figure, first appeared on the screen in 1931. Her face was modeled after the famous singer Helen Kane and her body after Mae West. In 1935, a comic strip was started. Although the Betty Boop cartoons were ended by 1938, there was a revival of interest in the Betty Boop image in the 1980s and new pieces are being made.

Ashtray	225.00
Candy Container	45.00
Cel, Animation Art, Baby Boop & Pudgy, Gold Pen	650.00
Cookie Jar, Betty Boop Bust, National Silver	60.00
Cookie Jar, Vandon	85.00
Decal, 1950s	12.00
Doll, Bisque	45.00
Doll, Celluloid, Japan, 7 In.	35.00
Doll, Celluloid, Occupied Japan, 3 In.	5.00
Doll, Vinyl, Box	20.00
Figurine, Playing Instruments, 3 1/2 In., 3 Piece	150.00
Hatpin, Goofus Glass Head	28.00
Salt & Pepper	25.00
Ukulele, Pictures Of Betty Boop, Bimbo & Koko, Fleischer	110.00
Wall Pocket, Lusterware	185.00
Watch	45.00
Watercolor & Airbrush On Board, L. Cabarga, Framed, 13 x 12 In.	1100.00

BICYCLES were invented in 1839. The first manufactured bicycle was made in 1861. Special ladies' bicycles were made after 1874. The modern safety bicycle was not produced until 1885. Collectors search for all types of bicycles and tricycles. Bicycle-related items are also listed here.

Attached Wooden Ice Cream Cart, 2 Ft.	325.00
B. F. Goodrich, Motorbike Style, Maroon & Cream, 1930s	300.00
Clamp, Put On Legs Over Pant Legs, Iron, Pair	1.50
Coast King, Boy's	150.00
Colson, Firestone Cruiser, Boy's	200.00
Columbia, Boy's, Locking Springer, 26 In.	50.00
Columbia, Shaft Driven	650.00
Crescent, Girl's, Skirt & Chain Guard, 26 In.	450.00
Cup, Collapsible, Silver Metal, Raised Tandem Riders On Lid	30.00
Cup, Cyclist's, Collapsible, 1890s	38.00

Delivery, Schwinn	550.00
Dirt Bike, Box, Britain	60.00
Elgin, Blackhawk, Restored	3000.00
Elgin, Girl's, Blue & Cream, Pre–War, 26 In.	150.00
Elgin, Oriole, Long Tank, Light, Rack, 1940	400.00
Flocycle, Tool Box Seat	2500.00
Golden Gate, Wooden Rims, 1896	1295.00
Hawthorne Flyer, Boy's, 1930	175.00
Hawthorne, Boy's, All American, 26 In.	325.00
Highwheeler, Front Wheel, 46 In.	4750.00
Highwheeler, Shiny Metal, England, c.1880	8500.00
Indian Motorcycle Co., c.1920	1600.00
Ivers Johnson, Wooden Rim Wheels, 1920	700.00
J. C. Higgins, 1949	1500.00
J. C. Higgins, 1960	150.00 To 300.00
J. C. Higgins, Girl's, Deluxe, Early 1950s	800.00
Monark, Blackout Bike, Boy's, Lightweight, 26 In.	90.00
Monark, Firestone Super Cruiser, Jeweled Tank, Light, Rack	375.00
Monark, Firestone Super Cruiser, Single Spring, Tank, Front Fender	250.00
Murray, Boy's, Springer, 1950s	75.00
Murray, Stratoline, Girl's, Springer, Rocket Ray Headlight	350.00
New Hudson Ltd., X Frame, England	550.00
Olympia, Folding, Light Mounted On Front Fork Bracket	75.00
Peddler's, Chase's Ice Cream	900.00
Raleigh, Woman's, 3–Speed, 1948	100.00
Ranger, Tall Frame, Wood Rims, Flat Top Fenders, 1920s	650.00
Roadmaster, Boy's, Curved Braces, 26 In.	265.00
Roadmaster, Spaceliner	50.00
Royal Flyer, Boy's, Tool Box & Tank, 28 In.	250.00
Schwinn Panther	600.00
Schwinn, 1940	1000.00
Schwinn, Black Phantom, 1956	1695.00
Schwinn, Black Phantom, 1957	4000.00
Schwinn, Collegiate, Woman's, 5–Speed, Leather Seat, Chrome Fenders	125.00
Schwinn, Deluxe Twin Tandem, Looks Like Black Phantom	1200.00
Schwinn, DX, Boy's, 26 In., Pre–War, 26 In.	550.00
Schwinn, Girl's, Hanging Tank, 30 In.	300.00
Schwinn, Green Phantom, Man's, 1952	1200.00
Schwinn, Hornet, Wooden Fenders, 1952	80.00
Schwinn, Motorbike Style Frame, Locking Fork, 1938	275.00
Schwinn, Panther, Green, Restored, 1950	2250.00
Schwinn, Phantom, Red, Chrome	1850.00
Schwinn, Stingray, 3–Speed, 1979	110.00
Schwinn, Town & Country, Tandem, Front & Rear Brakes	175.00
Schwinn, Traveler, 2–Speed, Coaster Brakes, Chrome Fenders & Rims	165.00
Schwinn, Wasp, Locking Fork, Chain Guard, 1959	195.00
Sears, Banana, Screamer, Dual Caliper Rear Brakes, Red	175.00
Sears, Spaceliner, Girl's, 26 In.	125.00
Spider–Man, Boy's	95.00
Tag, Bicycle Tax, Albia, Iowa, Metal, With Clasp, 1939	2.25
Tricycle, Big Wheel, 1 Large Front Wheel	35.00
Tricycle, Convert–O Bike, Aluminum	175.00
Tricycle, Shaped Wooden Frame & Hubs, Metal Fittings, 36 In.	495.00
Velocipede, Horse, Crank At Horse's Head, 3 Wheels, 33 x 29 1/2 In.	650.00
Velocipede, Red Fenders On 2 Large Wheels, Red Velvet Seat, 1920s	1500.00
W. A. Washburn, Jefferson, Ohio	1000.00
Ward Hawthorne, Man's, 1950s	550.00
Ward Hawthorne, Woman's, 1950s	750.00
Western Flyer, 1953	500.00
Western Flyer, Girl's, Needs Rear Fender, 1953	200.00
Western Flyer, Long Trank, Chrome Rack, 1940s	575.00
Westfield, Special Deluxe, Boy's, 26 In.	550.00
Whizzer, Maroon, Chrome, Tank Sticker	3250.00

Zenith, 1950s 155.00

BING AND GRONDAHL is a famous Danish factory making fine
porcelains from 1853 to the present. Underglaze blue decoration was
started in 1886. The annual Christmas plate series was introduced in 1895.
Dinnerwares, stoneware, and figurines are still being made today. The firm
has used the initials B & G and a stylized castle as part of the mark since
1898.

Ashtray, 2 White Mice, Oval 85.00
Figure, Boy, Standing Holding Dog 135.00
Figurine, Accordion Player, 9 In. 125.00
Figurine, Boy Kissing Girl, No. 2162 .... 120.00
Figurine, Boy On Skis, No. 02358, 8 1/4 In. 260.00
Figurine, Boy With Duck, No. 1836 .... 125.00
Figurine, Boy With Teddy Bear, No. 2231 .... 120.00
Figurine, Bulldog, White & Beige, Marked, 4 1/2 x 3 In. 145.00
Figurine, Cat In Basket, No. 01149, 3 1/2 In. 140.00
Figurine, Cat, Gray, No. 2452, 6 1/4 In. 70.00
Figurine, Cat, No. 2256 .... 185.00
Figurine, Cat, Standing, Striped, DJ 01108 .... 265.00
Figurine, Chihuahua, No. 2244 .... 210.00
Figurine, Child Writing, 5 In. 55.00
Figurine, Children, Reading, No. 1567, 3 1/2 In. 165.00
Figurine, Dachshund, Sitting, 1915, BG 11603, 7 1/2 In. 295.00
Figurine, Dog, No. 2027 .... 95.00
Figurine, Fish Market, No. 2233 .... 350.00 To 425.00
Figurine, Fisher Boy, No. 01228, 7 1/2 In. 250.00
Figurine, Gentleman, No. 2312, 7 In. 240.00
Figurine, Girl Hugging Boy, 7 In. 135.00
Figurine, Girl With Doll, No. 1721, 7 3/4 In. .... 135.00 To 150.00
Figurine, Gray Mouse, No. 1801 .... 35.00
Figurine, Gull, No. 1809 .... 38.00
Figurine, Hans Christian Andersen, No. 2037 .... 375.00
Figurine, Harlequin Great Dane, Lying, RC 11452 .... 145.00
Figurine, Karin 60.00
Figurine, Little Match Girl 150.00
Figurine, Love Refused, No. 1614 .... 120.00 To 140.00
Figurine, Lovebird, No. 2210, Blue, 4 In. 105.00
Figurine, Monkey Family, BG 01581 .... 135.00
Figurine, Pardon Me, No. 02372, 7 1/2 In. 110.00
Figurine, Parrot, No. 2019, 5 1/2 In. 155.00
Figurine, Peke Puppy, 2 1/2 In. 195.00
Figurine, Penguin, No. 1822 .... 350.00
Figurine, Puppies, Sitting, RC 10260, 6 In., Pair 150.00
Figurine, Sandman, No. 1055 .... 110.00
Figurine, Sculptor, Dahl Jensen, No. 01244, 8 In. 750.00
Figurine, Sea Gull, No. 1810, 1 1/2 In. 45.00
Figurine, Sealyham, No. 2028 .... 85.00
Figurine, Spilt Milk, No. 2246 .... 130.00 To 165.00
Figurine, Two Friends, No. 1790 .... 135.00
Figurine, White Cat, Stalking, RC 00473, 20 In. 1095.00
Figurine, White Saluki, Lying, No. 11811, 11 In. 450.00
Figurine, Wren, Australian, DJ 01315, 4 In. 125.00
Figurine, Young Girl Kissing Young Boy, 6 3/4 In. 132.00
Plate, Christmas, 1906 .... 85.00
Plate, Christmas, 1909 .... 110.00
Plate, Christmas, 1912 .... 120.00
Plate, Christmas, 1928 .... 75.00
Plate, Christmas, 1971 .... 25.00
Plate, Christmas, 1975 .... 25.00
Plate, Christmas, 1977 .... 25.00
Plate, Christmas, 1978, Box 28.00
Plate, Mother's Day, 1969 .... 225.00 To 360.00

Bisque, Pastille Burner, Castle,
Germany, 7 In.

Bisque, Vase, White Girl, Light Green,
Howard Pierce, 4 In.

BINOCULARS of all types are wanted by collectors. Those made in the eighteenth and nineteenth centuries are favored by serious collectors. The small, attractive binoculars called *opera glasses* are listed in their own section.

Bausch & Lomb, Model, M7, Case	125.00
Lemaire, Leather & Brass, Built–In Compass, Paris	75.00
MIOJ3X, Metal	38.00
Stanhope, Metal, 7/8 In.	30.00

BIRDCAGES are collected for use as homes for pet birds and as decorative objects of folk art. Elaborate wooden cages of the past centuries can still be found. The brass or wicker cages of the 1930s are popular with bird owners.

Automation, Bird, Moving Head, Peak, Tail, France, 19 In.	3000.00
Brass, Hoop, Walking Stand, England	3250.00
Gilt Painted Wrought Iron, Glazed Panels, Stand, 6 Ft. 2 In.	9900.00
Hendryx, Brass, Dome Shape, Glass Feeders	145.00
Hendryx, Brass, Round	100.00
Hendryx, Wirework	38.00
Heywood–Wakefield, Wicker, Turned Leg, Sticker	148.00
On Casket Carrier, Brass, 56 x 20 x 37 In.	1500.00
Parrot, Wrought Iron, Green Paint, On Square Wooden Stand	225.00
Sheraton, Turned Finials, Carved Bird In Cage, Wooden, 1810	1075.00
Victorian House, Iron, Sand Blasted	3630.00
Walnut, 1890s, 2 Ft. x 1 Ft. 15 In.	150.00
Windsor, Bamboo Turnings, Flat Seat	200.00
Wooden, Wire Frame	85.00
Wooden, Wire, 11 x 14 x 21 In.	125.00

BISQUE is an unglazed baked porcelain. Finished bisque has a slightly sandy texture with a dull finish. Some of it may be decorated with various colors. Bisque gained favor during the late Victorian era when thousands of bisque figurines were made. It is still being made. Additional bisque items may be listed under the factory name.

Basket, Cherub	32.00
Bottle, Boot, Leather Strap, Metal Spur, Black, 6 1/2 In.	110.00
Bust, Woman, Hat, Pastel, Marked M & B, France, 11 In.	295.00
Churn, Stump Shape	300.00
Dish, Hen On Nest, White, Yellow Basketweave, 1890, 2 1/4 In.	85.00
Dish, Hen, Maple Base, Red Comb & Wattles, Large	85.00
Figurine, Boy, Holds His Genitals, Painted, Head Hole, Germany, 3 In.	40.00
Figurine, Children As Bride & Groom, Germany, 4 In., Pair	55.00
Figurine, Girl, Sitting, Hand To Face, Painted, Germany, 4 1/2 In.	60.00
Figurine, Group Of Beagles, Pure White, c.1930, 6 In.	88.00
Figurine, Nativity, Molded, 1 Piece	20.00
Heart, Cameo Woman Center, Green & White, Germany	27.00

Pastille Burner, Castle, Germany, 7 In. ....*Illus*   650.00
Plaque, Morning & Night, White, Blue Enereg Mark, 19th Century, Pair 995.00
Vase, White Girl, Light Green, Howard Pierce, 4 In. ....*Illus*   15.00

BLACK AMETHYST glass appears black until it is held to the light, then a dark purple can be seen. It has been made in many factories from 1860 to the present.

Ashtray, Heart Handle 14.00
Box, Mary Gregory Type Woman With Dove, Round, 4 In. 500.00
Dish, Cover, White Enamel Design, 7 3/4 In. 11.00
Jar, Dresser, Metal Lid, Flowers & Lovebirds 35.00
Plate, Mt. Pleasant, Scalloped Rim, 8 In., 6 Piece 65.00
Sherbet, Mt. Pleasant, 5 Piece 50.00
Vase, 12 In. 12.00
Vase, Cherub, Paneled Corners, Square, 3 In. 75.00
Vase, Gold & Enamel Butterfly, Gold Trim, 10 In. 125.00
Vase, Red Flower, Ruffled Rim, Hand Painted, 12 In. 90.00

BLACK memorabilia has become an important area of collecting since the 1970s. The best material dates from past centuries, but many recent items are also of interest. Objects that picture a black person may also be listed in this book under Advertising; Tins; Banks; Bottle Openers; Cookie Jars; Salt & Pepper; Sheet Music; etc.

Ad, Cream Of Wheat 20.00
Apron, Mammy Face 25.00
Ashtray, Coon Chicken Inn .... 35.00 To 38.50
Ashtray, Mammy, Wringer 50.00
Ashtray, Porcelain, Children Lined Up For Outhouse, 4 1/2 In. 28.00
Bag, Clothespin, Mammy 130.00
Bag, Corn Meal, Mammy On Front 10.00
Banner, Aunt Jemima Pancake Jamboree, 12 In. 250.00
Banner, Aunt Jemima, c.1946, 52 x 32 In. 457.00
Bar Set, Black Heads, Heavy Metal, Wooden Stand, 3 Piece 75.00
Bell, Mammy .... 28.00 To 35.00
Book, Black Man's America, Simeon Booker, 1964 ....   10.00
Book, Epaminodas & His Auntie, Hard Cover, Sara Bryant, 1938 ....   12.00
Book, Little Black Sambo, 1905 ....   95.00
Book, Little Black Sambo, Bannerman, McKay Pub., 1931 ....   85.00
Book, Little Black Sambo, Color Illustrations, 1959 ....   30.00
Book, Thompson Street Poker Club, Gambling, Funerals, Hard Cover, 1888 ....   150.00
Book, Topsy, 1800s 125.00
Book, Unprejudiced Singing Teachers, Underground R.R. Songs, 1881 ....   20.00
Booklet, 10 Little Niggers Story, Germany, 1900, 2 1/4 x 3 1/4 In. 35.00
Bowl, Aunt Jemima & Uncle Mose, Yellow, 8 In. 175.00
Bowl, Mammy, Cream Of Wheat, 1950s, 4 Piece 250.00
Box, Candy, Black Picture, Colorful 23.00
Box, Candy, Heide's Black Kids, Man With Banjo, Children Dancing 264.00
Box, High Hat Face Powder, 3 Black Girls Picture, 1940s 6.00
Bumper Tag, Auto, Negro Ocean Playground, Cast Iron 9.85
Card, Advertising, Cottolene, Lady, Cotton Field, Cotton In Apron, 1880 ....   30.00
Card, Going Places, Daindridge Sisters, L. Armstrong, 11 x 14 In. 125.00
Card, Lobby, Fight Never Ends, Joe Louis, Ruby Dee, 27 x 41 In. 200.00
Card, Lobby, Lucky Ghost, Toddy Pictures, 1946, 27 x 41 In. 200.00
Card, Playing, Black Velvet, Black Models Against Black, 1970s, Unused 12.00
Card, Valentine, Black Baby, Top Hat, Held Lollipop, Cardboard 20.00
Clacker, Party, Black Man 10.00
Clock, Alarm, Amos & Andy 285.00
Clock, Alarm, Electric, Aunt Jemima .... 295.00 To 350.00
Clock, Aunt Jemima, Waffle 30.00
Clock, Joe Louis Portrait, Boxing Champion, 1930s 450.00
Cookbook, Southern, Mammy Cover 15.00
Cookie Jar, Cauliflower Mammy 950.00
Cookie Jar, Chef, Pearl China .... 575.00 To 595.00

Cover, Toaster, Mammy, Lace Trimmed Dress & Apron 35.00
Creamer, Mammy, Full Figure 145.00
Cruet, Oil & Vinegar, Black Chef, Mammy, Cork, Ceramic Head, Crazed, Pr. 45.00
Diorama, 6 Dancing Figures, Folk Art 2860.00
Doll, Aunt Jemima, Oilcloth 60.00
Doll, Baby Crissy, Ideal, 24 In. 45.00
Doll, Baby, Bisque Flange Head, Disk Eyes, Cloth Body, Germany, 14 In. 500.00
Doll, Baby, Marked K * R11 In. 1495.00
Doll, Baby, Rubber, Cloth Body, Movable Eyes, Unclothed, Hong Kong 10.00
Doll, Boy, Bisque, Jointed, Overalls, Nicodemus Maggehead, 1966, 11 In. 65.00
Doll, Boy, Celluloid Head, Flocked Hair, Blue Pants, Shirt, 19 1/2 In. 275.00
Doll, Boy, Rag, Checkered Suit, Small 110.00
Doll, Brown Bisque, Brown Eyes, Original Wig, Jointed, Germany, 13 In. 325.00
Doll, Character, Clapping Hands, Wooden Block Torso, Germany, 10 In. 400.00
Doll, Cloth, 5 In. 10.00
Doll, Cloth, Painted, Apron, White & Red Striped Blouse, 13 In. 2.00
Doll, Clown, Rubber, Dressed 150.00
Doll, Composition, Stiff Neck, Cloth Wig, Jointed, No Clothes, 5 In. 65.00
Doll, Dapper Dan, Dancer, Wooden, 1930s 65.00
Doll, Fuzzy Hair, Hasbro, 1872 .... 55.00
Doll, George Washington Carver, Hallmark, 7 In. 20.00
Doll, Girl, Bisque Socket Head, Open Mouth, Simon & Halbig, 20 In. 3300.00
Doll, Girl, Glass Eyes, Nora Welling, 20 In. 400.00
Doll, Golliwog, Felt, Celluloid Disc Eyes, Stitched-On Costume, 14 In. 575.00
Doll, Lester, Ventriloquist 150.00
Doll, Mammy, Embroidered Face, Cloth, 1930s, 18 In. 150.00
Doll, Mammy, Walking, Lindstrom 385.00
Doll, Rag, Embroidered Features, Button Eyes, 1940 .... 65.00
Doll, Rag, Flip Wilson & Geraldine .... 35.00 To 38.00
Doll, Raggedy Ann, Handmade 45.00
Doll, Silk Stockinette, Embroidered Face, 15 In. 40.00
Doll, Toaster, Purple Floral Dress, Bandana 18.00
Doll, Turnabout, Black & White Girl 25.00
Doll, Whisk Broom, Woman, Embroidered Face, Hand Sewn Clothes, 10 In. 30.00
Duster, Mammy 20.00
Fan, Coon Chicken Inn 20.00
Figurine, Black Boy Holding Sweet Potato, 6 In. 467.50
Figurine, Blackamoor, Original Paint, Venetian, 19th Century, Pair 9500.00
Figurine, Boy On Potty, Cast Iron, 4 In. 12.00
Figurine, Boy On Urinal, Occupied Japan, 3 In. 35.00
Figurine, Girl, Holding Watermelon Slice, Rind At Feet, Florida, 4 In. 45.00
Figurine, Louis Armstrong 125.00
Figurine, Negroes In Outhouse, Bisque, Painted, Japan, 1940s, 2 1/2 In. 25.00
Grocery List, We Needs, Pegs 65.00
Key & Potholder, Hanger, Memo Pad, Wooden, Mammy & Friends 25.00
Key Chain With Tape Measure, Aunt Jemima 12.00
Knife Holder, Mammy, Wooden 60.00

If you wear antique jewelry, check the claw settings to be sure the prongs are not worn or loose. It is cheaper to be careful than to replace lost stones.

Black, Pin, Aunt Jemima Breakfast Club, 4 In.

Label, Blacks Singing & Picking Cotton, Cotton 95.00
Lamp, Black Nude, Amber Sphere, Art Deco 65.00
Laundry Bag 25.00
Marionette, Minstrel, Top Hat, American Crayon Co., 1939–1940, 14 In. 45.00
Memo Holder, Mammy, Dated 1954 .... 50.00
Menu, Coon Chicken Inn, 1940s 75.00
Minstrel Album, 2 Blacks On Cover, 66 Pages, 1936, 7 x 10 In. 20.00
Mixer Cover, Mammy, Sock Doll, 1940s 55.00
Needle & Thread, Hanger, Mammy, Figural, Oilcloth 65.00
Noisemaker, Black Man, Straw Hat & Bowtie 15.00
Note Pad, Black Mammy 95.00
Pencil Sharpener, Black Man's Face 65.00
Picture, Flowers Of Ugliness, 6 Caricatured Girls, G. S. Tregear, 1836 .... 150.00
Pie Bird, Mammy, Yellow 70.00
Pin, Aunt Jemima Breakfast Club, 4 In. ....*Illus* 15.00
Pipe, Black Clown Face 40.00
Pitcher, Mammy, Fiedler & Fiedler 55.00
Plaque, Woman, Gold Tooth & Earring, 3–D 45.00
Plate, Coon Chicken Inn, Beige, 10 In. 250.00
Plate, Enameled Men Singing, 6 In. 65.00
Platter, Coon Chicken Inn, Oval, 11 In. 325.00
Postcard, A Darky's Prayer Florida, Man, With Alligators, 1950 .... 25.00
Pot Holder, Mammy, Figural, Wooden, Red Calico Dress, 13 In., 3 Piece 20.00
Pot Scrubber, Chief Holding Pot With Lid Scrubber 125.00
Puppet, Golliwog 250.00
Purse, Little Black Sambo, Shoulder Strap, Cloth 80.00
Salt & Pepper, Boy's Head, Watermelon 25.00
Saltshaker, Black Face, Pearl Drop Earrings, Wooden, 2 3/4 In. 8.00
Saltshaker, Mammy, Red Dress, Brown Spoon, 5 In. 12.00
Sign, Colored Served In Rear, 1950s, 3 x 12 In. 12.50
Sign, For Rent To Colored, Tin, 1950s, 7 x 10 In. 20.00
Sign, No Dogs–Negroes–Mexicans, Tin, 1960s, 5 x 12 In. 25.00
Sign, Sambo Malted Milk, Lithographed, Tin 154.00
Spice Set, Aunt Jemima, F & F Mold, 8 Piece 176.00
Spice Set, Brackets, Copper Shelf, Steamboat Scene, F & F, 1949 .... 550.00
Spice Set, Copper Rack, F & F 525.00
Sprinkler, Lawn, Black Sambo 85.00
Sprinkler, Lawn, Sprinkling Sam, Black Boy Litho On Steel 120.00
Stickpin, Figural, Boy 38.00
String Holder, Mammy 195.00
Sugar & Creamer, Aunt Jemima & Uncle Mose, Green, F & F 300.00
Sugar & Creamer, Aunt Jemima & Uncle Mose, Yellow, F & F 250.00
Swizzle Stick, Zulu–Lulu, On Card 25.00
Thermometer, Baby Peeking Around 20.00
Tin, LaJean Full Dress Hair Pomade, Large 17.00
Tin, Queen Hair Dressing, Black Girl, 1930s 6.00
Toaster Cover 15.00
Towel, Dish, Girl With Turkey, Says Mah Cookin', Embroidered 24.00
Towel, Mammy, Child Eating Watermelon, Linen 40.00
Tumbler, Coon Chicken Inn, 4 1/2 In. 20.00
Tumbler, Coon Chicken Inn, Set Of 6 .... 150.00
Warrant, Negro, Stealing 20 Bushels Corn & 20 Bushels Corn Meal 71.00
Whisk Broom 32.00

BLOWN GLASS was formed by forcing air through a rod into molten
glass. Early glass and some forms of art glass were hand blown. Other
types of glass were molded or pressed.

Ball, Bottle Green, Pontil, 6 In. Diam. 130.00
Bottle, Club Shape, Aqua, 7 3/4 In. 40.00
Bottle, Club Shape, Midwestern, Aqua, 9 In. 95.00
Bottle, Flared Lip, Pale Yellow, 5 3/4 In. 55.00
Bottle, Vertical Ribs, Flattened, Aqua, 7 1/4 In. 105.00
Bowl, Clear, Applied Clambroth Base & Rim, Flared Base, 14 In. 1300.00

Bowl, Expanded Diamond, Applied Foot, Amethyst, 3 1/2 In. 325.00
Decanter, 2 Applied Rings, Bulbous Stopper, 9 In. 65.00
Decanter, Amethyst, 6 Urn Shaped Wines, 8 1/4 In. 300.00
Decanter, Amethyst, Cut To Clear, Stars & Thumbprint 77.00
Decanter, Baroque Pattern, 3–Mold, Large Round Stopper 285.00
Decanter, Hand Painted, Stopper 40.00
Flask, Half–Post, Dairy Pattern, Crystal, 9 In. 55.00
Flycatcher, 19th Century, England, 8 In. 335.00
Mug, Ribbed Base, Polychrome Enameled Flowers, Remember Me 25.00
Pitcher, Water, Enameled, Handles, c.1910, 12 1/2 In. 65.00
Rolling Pin, Dark Amethyst, Knob Handles, c.1820, 27 1/2 In. 350.00
Shade, Hurricane, Engraved Eagles, Leaf Band, 16 3/4 In., Pair 3600.00
Syrup Jug, Peace & Plenty, Clear Flint, Strap Handle 195.00
Vase, Spirals, Circular Base, 24 In. 143.00
Water Set, Enameled Floral Design, Green, 7 Piece 400.00
Witch's Ball, American, 1840 .... 200.00

BLUE GLASS, see Cobalt Blue category

BLUE ONION, see Onion category

BLUE WILLOW pattern has been made in England since 1780. The pattern has been copied by factories in many countries, including Germany, Japan, and the United States. It is still being made. Willow was named for a pattern that pictures a bridge, birds, willow trees, and a Chinese landscape.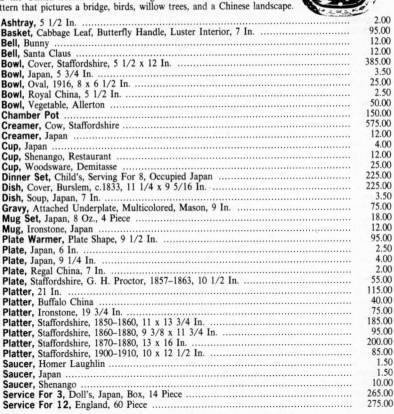

Ashtray, 5 1/2 In. 2.00
Basket, Cabbage Leaf, Butterfly Handle, Luster Interior, 7 In. 95.00
Bell, Bunny 12.00
Bell, Santa Claus 12.00
Bowl, Cover, Staffordshire, 5 1/2 x 12 In. 385.00
Bowl, Japan, 5 3/4 In. 3.50
Bowl, Oval, 1916, 8 x 6 1/2 In. 25.00
Bowl, Royal China, 5 1/2 In. 2.50
Bowl, Vegetable, Allerton 50.00
Chamber Pot 150.00
Creamer, Cow, Staffordshire 575.00
Creamer, Japan 12.00
Cup, Japan 4.00
Cup, Shenango, Restaurant 12.00
Cup, Woodsware, Demitasse 25.00
Dinner Set, Child's, Serving For 8, Occupied Japan 225.00
Dish, Cover, Burslem, c.1833, 11 1/4 x 9 5/16 In. 225.00
Dish, Soup, Japan, 7 In. 3.50
Gravy, Attached Underplate, Multicolored, Mason, 9 In. 75.00
Mug Set, Japan, 8 Oz., 4 Piece 18.00
Mug, Ironstone, Japan 12.00
Plate Warmer, Plate Shape, 9 1/2 In. 95.00
Plate, Japan, 6 In. 2.50
Plate, Japan, 9 1/4 In. 4.00
Plate, Regal China, 7 In. 2.00
Plate, Staffordshire, G. H. Proctor, 1857–1863, 10 1/2 In. 55.00
Platter, 21 In. 115.00
Platter, Buffalo China 40.00
Platter, Ironstone, 19 3/4 In. 75.00
Platter, Staffordshire, 1850–1860, 11 x 13 3/4 In. 185.00
Platter, Staffordshire, 1860–1880, 9 3/8 x 11 3/4 In. 95.00
Platter, Staffordshire, 1870–1880, 13 x 16 In. 200.00
Platter, Staffordshire, 1900–1910, 10 x 12 1/2 In. 85.00
Saucer, Homer Laughlin 1.50
Saucer, Japan 1.50
Saucer, Shenango 10.00
Service For 3, Doll's, Japan, Box, 14 Piece 265.00
Service For 12, England, 60 Piece 275.00

Shaker, Book Shape, 6 Piece	40.00
Shaker, Cup Shape, Handle, 2 1/4 In.	14.00
Sugar & Creamer, Occupied Japan, 1 1/2 In.	20.00
Sugar, Cover, Japan, 4 x 6 In.	15.00
Tea Set, Child's, Box, 1940s, 21 Piece	235.00
Tea Set, Child's, Box, Service For 6	350.00
Tea Set, Doll's, Serving For 2, Occupied Japan	100.00

BOCH FRERES factory was founded in 1841 in La Louviere in eastern Belgium. The wares resemble the work of Villeroy & Boch. The factory is still in business.

Vase, Blue Streak Glaze, Metal Mount, 12 In., Pair	275.00
Vase, Vertical Bands, Cream Ground, Turquoise, Marked, 11 In.	660.00

BOEHM is the collector's name for the porcelains of Edward Marshall Boehm. In 1953 the Osso China Company was reorganized as Edward Marshall Boehm, Inc. The company is still working in England and New Jersey. In the early days of the factory, dishes were made, but the elaborate and lifelike bird figurines are the best known ware. Edward Marshall Boehm, the founder, died in 1961, but the firm has continued to design and produce porcelain. Today, the firm makes both limited and unlimited editions of figurines and plates.

Boehm

MADE IN U.S.A

Bowl, Fluted, Boehm & Tiffany Signed, 4 In.	75.00
Bust, Madonna, White, 6 In. .... 150.00 To	175.00
Charger, Bird Of Peace, 1972	250.00
Figurine, Baby Chickadee, No. 461	135.00
Figurine, Camellia, Helen Boehm, 1978	450.00
Figurine, Canada Geese With Goslings, No. 408, Pair	696.00
Figurine, Cardinal, On Base	1000.00
Figurine, Cat With Kittens, 5 In.	695.00
Figurine, Cocker Spaniel, 5 In.	595.00
Figurine, Common Tern, No. 497	2500.00
Figurine, Cottontail Rabbit, No. 200	1000.00
Figurine, Firebird, 8 1/4 In.	175.00
Figurine, Fledgling Blackburnian Warbler, No. 478RR, 41/2 In.	140.00
Figurine, Fledgling Bluebirds, No. 494, 6 In.	220.00
Figurine, Hooded Merganser, No. 496, Pair	1650.00
Figurine, Indigo Bunting, Signed	725.00
Figurine, Juncos	900.00
Figurine, King Tut Mask	850.00
Figurine, Madonna, Porcelain, 9 In.	295.00
Figurine, Mallards In Flight, No. 406, 11 x 11 1/2 In.	2055.00
Figurine, Mourning Doves, Boehm, 14 3/4 In.	450.00
Figurine, Roadrunner With Horned Toad, No. 493	2200.00
Figurine, Robin, No. 2266	75.00
Figurine, Royal Blessing, 1982	650.00
Figurine, Squirrel, No. 400–94, 4 In.	180.00
Figurine, Thrush, Parrot Tulips, No. 400–29, 1974	1800.00
Figurine, Tree Sparrow, No. 468	350.00
Figurine, Yellow–Throated Warbler, No. 431J, 5 In.	325.00
Letter Opener, Eagle, Made For Bicentennial	75.00
Pitcher, Floral Mold, Unglazed, White, Signed, 7 In.	52.50
Plate, Fox	50.00
Plate, Rabbits	50.00
Plate, Raccoon	65.00
Plate, Songbirds, 1972	40.00

BOHEMIAN GLASS is an ornate overlay or flashed glass made during the Victorian era. It has been reproduced in Bohemia, which is now a part of Czechoslovakia. Glass made from 1875 to 1900 is preferred by collectors.

Box, Cover, Faceted Green Finial, Enameled Floral, 5 1/2 In.	250.00
Candelabra, Cranberry, Cut Glass Prisms, 19 In.	1650.00
Candleholder, Red Overlay, Bobeches, Prisms, Pair	475.00

Compote, Checkerboard Design, Ruby, Rim Ground, 5 7/8 In.	55.00
Compote, Ruby Flashed, Polychrome Floral Enameling, 7 In.	85.00
Decanter, Birds, Monkeys & Foliage, 15 1/2 In.	125.00
Decanter, Buildings, Flowers, Cut To Clear	85.00
Decanter, Cut & Frosted Vintage, 7 3/4 In.	55.00
Decanter, Grape & Vine Design, Ruby, 2 Tumblers, 15 1/2 In.	45.00
Decanter, Pink To Opaque White, Enameled Floral, 9 In.	295.00
Decanter, Ruby Band, Five Matching Tumblers, 6 5/8 In.	125.00
Decanter, Ruby Overlay Etch, Triangular, 10 1/4 In., Pair	250.00
Hand Cooler, Silver Cap, 4 5/8 In.	125.00
Ice Cream Set, Sea Shell, Magenta Floral, 1880s, 12 Piece	325.00
Perfume Bottle, Deer, Garden Scene, Octagonal Stopper, 3 In.	100.00
Pokal, Chartreuse, Enameled Shields, Grapes, 23 1/2 In., Pair	7260.00
Toothpick, Rose	850.00
Vase, 16 Clear Etched Medallions, Ruby, 12 1/4 In.	800.00
Vase, Engraved Flowers, Amber To Clear, c.1920, 11 In.	195.00

BONE DISHES were considered a necessary part of a table setting for the Victorian table. The crescent–shaped dish was kept at the edge of the dinner plate so the bones removed from the fish could be stored away from the uneaten food. Some bone dishes were made in more fanciful shapes and many resemble fish.

Art Deco Pattern, Meakin		9.00
Blue & White Scene, Tonquin, Clarice Cliff	*Illus*	16.00
Fish Shape, Blue		45.00
Flower Design, Ruffled, 1800s, 6 1/2 In., 6 Piece		30.00
Flowers, White Ground, KTK	*Illus*	12.00
Fruit Shape, Plum, Peach & Apple, Gold Flower Border, China, 6 Pc.		40.00
Red Flower, Green Trim, White Ground	*Illus*	12.00

BOOKENDS have probably been used since books became inexpensive. Early libraries kept books in cupboards, not on open shelves. By the 1870s bookends appeared, especially homemade fret–carved wooden examples. Most bookends listed in this book date from the twentieth century.

Abraham Lincoln, Bronze Finish, Cast Lead, 6 1/2 In.	65.00
African Gazelles, Art Deco, Cast Iron	65.00
Anchor, Chase Brass, Bronze Finish	75.00
Angelus, Bronze Finish	35.00
Arabian Knights, Male & Female, Chalkware, Red, Gold & Brown, 8 In.	75.00
Art Deco, Cast Iron	15.00
Buddha, Cast Metal, Bronze Finish, 7 3/4 In.	65.00

◆◆◆◆◆◆◆◆◆◆◆◆◆◆◆◆◆◆◆◆◆◆

Custard glass and milk glass can now be repaired by black light–proof methods. Be very careful when buying antiques.

◆◆◆◆◆◆◆◆◆◆◆◆◆◆◆◆◆◆◆◆◆◆

Bone Dish, Flowers, White Ground, KTK

Bone Dish, Red Flower, Green Trim, White Ground

Bone Dish, Blue & White Scene, Tonquin, Clarice Cliff

Carved Nephrite, Gold Back, Diamonds, Enameled, 3 5/8 In. 4675.00
Child Clinging To Rock, Frog In Rushes, Plaster, Copper, S. Morane 55.00
Copper, Hammered, Sorenson 125.00
Deer, Standing, Bronze, 6 In. 140.00
Dog, Brown Patina, Bronze, E. B. Parsons, 1914, 7 In. 750.00
Dog, Setter, Cast Iron, 1920s, 4 1/2 x 7 1/2 In. 95.00
Dogs, Bronze Finish 58.00
Dr. Seuss Cat In The Hat, Plastic 90.00
Embossed Face Of William Procter, Cast Metal 58.00
Fish, Art Deco, Satin Finish Nickel Plate, 6 In. 100.00
Folding, Mahogany, Ivory Design, 13 In. 95.00
Hammered Copper, Old Mission Koppercraft 165.00
Hartford Fire Insurance Co., Bronze Finish, 1935 .... 55.00 To 95.00
Henry W. Longfellow Bust, Bronze Finish, Cast Iron 40.00
High Top Shoes, Cast Iron 60.00
Horse & Foal, Wooden Base, Cast Iron 65.00
Horse & Saddle, Cast Iron 20.00
Horse Grazing, Cast Iron, Bronze Finish 40.00
Horse, Craftsman 50.00
Horse, Fostoria 45.00
Horsehead, Frosted 150.00
Indian Chief & End Of The Day, Cast Iron 25.00
Indian, Full Headdress, Brass, 8 In. 150.00
Irish Setter, Pressed Glass 165.00
Last Trail, Bronze Finish, 1928 .... 22.00
Lion, Bronze, 3 1/2 In., Pair 110.00
Lions, Cast Iron 35.00
Nudes, Art Nouveau, Cast Iron 75.00
Nudes, Figural, Art Deco, Cast Metal, Bronze Finish, 8 1/2 In. 175.00
Pigeon, Satin Glass 12.00
Poodle, White, Pottery, 6 In. 6.00
Puppy Dog, Bronze, Edith Baretto Parsons, Gorham Foundry 1650.00
Rabbit, Bronze 70.00
Scottie Dog, Figural, Bronze, On Green Marble 75.00
Ship Constitution, Cast Iron 20.00
Ship, Arts & Crafts 200.00
Ship, Painted, Cast Iron, 1928 .... 35.00
Ship, Painted, Dated 1935 .... 30.00
Silhouette Of Daffodil, Bronze, G. Thew, 1928, 6 In. 209.00
Sitting Toad & Mushrooms, With Pen Tray, McClelland Barclay 275.00
Spaniel, Ebonized & Bronze Finish, White Metal, 4 1/4 In. 75.00
Sphinx, Bronze, Alabaster Base, 11 In. 605.00
Stylized Turkeys, Art Deco, Ceramic, Crackled Cream, C. H. France 150.00
Sunbonnet Girl, Cast Iron 125.00
Swan, Onyx 35.00
The Aviator, Cast Iron, 1929 .... 95.00
Tracking West, Covered Wagon, Oxen, Cast Iron, Cincinnati Artistic 50.00
Woman At Well, Cast Iron .... 25.00 To 45.00
Woman, Full Figure, Art Nouveau, Bronze, Harriet Fishmuth 3300.00
Ye Philosopher, Bronze, S. Mordal, 1915 .... 75.00

BOOKMARKS were originally made of parchment, cloth, or leather. Soon
woven silk ribbon, thin cardboard, celluloid, wood, silver, tortoiseshell, and
metals were used. Examples made before 1850 are scarce, but there are
many to be found dating before 1920.

Andes Stove, Paper 20.00
Camp Curry, Yosemite, Metal 8.00
Fraktur, Bird On Branch, Framed, 6 1/8 x 5 In. 900.00
Fraktur, Pinprick Design Of Parrot, Fruit In Talons, 8 1/4 In. 1100.00
Old Gold Cigarettes, Plastic 20.00
Smokey The Bear, 1965 .... 5.00
Sterling Silver, Tiffany 65.00
Tole, American Fire Insurance Co., Mustard Paint, 3 x 12 In. 135.00

BOSTON & SANDWICH CO. pieces may be found in the Lutz and Sandwich Glass categories.

BOTTLE OPENERS are needed to open many bottles. As soon as the commercial bottle was invented, the opener to be used with the new types of closures became a necessity. Many types of bottle openers can be found, most dating from the twentieth century. Collectors prize advertising and comic openers.

4–Eyed Man, Cast Iron	45.00
4–Eyed Woman, Box	110.00
Alligator, Head Down, Cast Iron	65.00 To 85.00
Alligator, Head Up, Cast Iron	200.00
Ambrosia Lager Beer, Dog Head On Handle	45.00
Auto Jack, Cast Iron	35.00
Baby Bear, Aluminum, 3 In.	45.00
Baseball Player, Drink Whistle, Philadelphia	28.00
Bear, At Fence, Aluminum, 4 5/8 In.	65.00
Bird, Chase Brass	35.00
Black Boy & Alligator, Cast Iron	125.00
Black Face, Cast Iron	175.00
Black Man & Alligator, Cast Iron	150.00
Black Man, Bowtie, Figural, Cast Iron, Wall Mount	60.00
Burgomaster, Beer	10.00
Cassville's Lager Beer, Iron, Pocket	2.50
Chef, Cast Iron	125.00
Clown Head, Brass	55.00
Clown Head, Cast Iron	85.00
Clown, Cast Iron	60.00 To 65.00
Cowboy On Sign Post, Cast Iron	150.00
Cowboy With Guitar, Cast Iron	15.00
Cowboy, Cast Iron	125.00
Crab, Iron Art	25.00
Dachshund, Brass	65.00
Devil, Aluminum, 4 In.	45.00
Dog, Pointer, White, Brown & Green, Cast Iron, 4 1/2 In.	45.00
Dog, Setter	55.00
Dolphin, Chrome	20.00
Donkey, Brass, Large	35.00 To 45.00
Donkey, Cast Iron, 4 In.	40.00 To 55.00
Donkey, Chrome	25.00
Drunk At Lamp Post	10.00 To 25.00
Drunk At Lamp Post, Combination Ashtray	30.00 To 38.00
Drunk By Lamp Post, Cast Iron, 4 1/2 In.	25.00
Drunk By Palm Tree, Cast Iron, 4 1/4 In.	35.00
Drunk, High Hat	12.00
Eagle, Aluminum	45.00
Elephant & Donkey, Cast Iron, 3 In.	50.00
Elephant, Brass	40.00
Elephant, Iron	22.00
Elephant, On Ashtray	40.00
Elephant, Pink, Cast Iron	55.00
Elephant, Red, Cast Iron	45.00
Fish, Aluminum	22.00
Fish, Cast Iron	85.00
Fisherman, Cast Iron	95.00
Foundry Man, Cast Iron	125.00
Freddie Frosh, Cast Iron	325.00
Ghost, Aluminum, 4 1/4 In.	45.00
Goat, Cast Iron, White, Green & Yellow, 4 3/8 In.	70.00 To 85.00
Goldilocks, Aluminum, 3 3/4 In.	45.00
Golfer, Cast Iron	55.00
Goose, Cast Iron	75.00

High Hat Sign Post 15.00
Horse's Hind Quarters 55.00
Horse's Leg, Brass 27.00
Horse's Rear, Cast Iron .... 55.00 To 65.00
Jack 35.00
Kangaroo, Brass 15.00
Lady In Kimono, Cast Iron 150.00
Lobster .... 20.00 To 34.00
Mademoiselle 18.00
Mallard Duck, Cast Iron 65.00
Man In Coffin, 1932 .... 350.00
Mandarin Orange, Aluminum, 4 1/4 In. 45.00
Miller High Life Beer, Bottle Shape ....2.00 To 12.00
Minstrel, Holding Chrome Plated Banjo 30.00
Monkey, Black, Cast Iron 238.00
Mr. Dry 55.00
National Press Advertising Iron, Key Chain 2.00
Nude, Brass 28.00
Nude, Globe Brewing 30.00
Nude, Hands Over Head, Brass 20.00
Nude, Pedestal, Brass 48.00
Nude, Standing, Brass 45.00
Ox Cart, Schmid & Sons, Beer 10.00
P. W. A. 5.00
Parrot, Cast Iron, 4 In. ....22.50 To 24.00
Parrot, Cast Iron, 5 In. 75.00
Pelican, Cast Iron, 3 1/2 In. ....38.00 To 55.00
Pelican, Gray & White 65.00
Pheasant 15.00
Pierre, Full Figured Chef, Aluminum, 11 In. 45.00
Pretzel, Cast Iron 45.00
Rooster, Cast Iron ....55.00 To 65.00
Sailor, Cast Iron ....30.00 To 80.00
Schillers Bros. Beer, Iron, Pocket 2.00
Sea Gull, Cast Iron ....30.00 To 85.00
Sea Horse, Cast Iron ....75.00 To 115.00
Skunk, Cast Iron ....119.00 To 145.00
Snifter 40.00
Squirrel, Cast Iron, Small 100.00
Tennis Racquet, Brass 20.00
Toucan, Iron 125.00
Vernorn, 80th Anniversary, 1946 .... 20.00
Western Auto, Man On Celluloid Handle 15.00
White Rock 20.00

BOTTLE collecting has become a major American hobby. There are several
general categories of bottles, such as historic flasks, bitters, household, and
figural. For more bottle prices, see the book *Kovels' Bottles Price List* by
Ralph and Terry Kovel.

Apothecary, Cobalt Blue, Blown, Stopper, 11 3/4 In. 125.00

Avon started in 1886 as the California Perfume Company. It was not until
1929 that the name *Avon* was used. In 1939, it became Avon Products,
Inc. Avon has made many figural bottles filled with cosmetic products.
Ceramic, plastic, and glass bottles were made in limited editions.

Avon, Bay Rum, Keg, Box 10.00
Avon, Black Lady, Club, Box, 1984 .... 7.50
Avon, Decanter, Wine, Cape Cod 15.00
Avon, Dollars 'n' Scents After Shave Lotion, 4 1/2 In. ....*Illus* 30.00
Avon, Fragrance Bell, Box, 1965 .... 10.00
Avon, French Telephone, Box 5.00
Avon, Goblet, George & Martha Washington, Pair 12.00
Avon, Golden Promise Perfume, 1950s 60.00

Bottle, Avon, Dollars 'n' Scents After Shave
Lotion, 4 1/2 In.

Bottle, Figural, Dog, Spots, 3 3/4 In.

Bottle, Barber, Witch-Hazel,
8 In.

Bottle, Coachman, Pottery,
Figural, 11 In.

Bottle, Figural, Viking, Creme
De Menthe, 12 1/2 In.

Avon, Gun, 1977 Derringer	8.50
Avon, Keynote Perfume, 1967	10.00
Avon, NAAC Club, 1972	200.00
Avon, NSDA Convention, 1966	35.00
Avon, Saltshaker, Cape Cod	4.00
Avon, Spring Water, Aqua	325.00
Avon, Stein, Gold Rush	25.00
Avon, Stein, Hunter's, 1972	9.00
Barber, Amberina, Inverted Thumbprint, Narrow Neck, Rolled Lip, 7 In.	195.00
Barber, Cut & Pressed Glass, Original Stopper	65.00
Barber, Dutch Scene, White Bristol	60.00
Barber, Fern Pattern, Cranberry, Rolled Lip, Square	275.00
Barber, Hobnail, Cranberry Opalescent	195.00
Barber, Sapphire, Inverted Thumbprint, Narrow Neck, Rolled Lip, 7 In.	110.00
Barber, Seaweed Pattern, Blue	210.00
Barber, Stars & Stripes, Blue Opalescent	275.00
Barber, Swirl Ribbed, Opalized Turquoise, Polished Pontil, 6 7/8 In.	225.00
Barber, Witch Hazel, Opalescent, 7 3/4 In.	110.00
Barber, Witch–Hazel, 8 In. ....*Illus*	75.00

Beam bottles were made to hold Kentucky Straight Bourbon, made by the
James B. Beam Distilling Company. The Beam series of ceramic bottles
began in 1953.

Beam, B. P. O. E., Centennial	10.00
Beam, Barney's Slot Machine, Casino	15.00

Beam, Bing Crosby, 29th, 1970 .... 25.00
Beam, Camaro, Convertible, Burgundy, 1969 .... 85.00
Beam, Chicago Fire Centennial 15.00
Beam, Convention, No. 1, Denver, 1971 .... 5.00
Beam, Convention, No. 8, Chicago, 1978 .... 10.00
Beam, Decanter, Ducks Unlimited, 1974 .... 6.00
Beam, Decanter, Indianapolis State Series, May 30, 1970 .... 10.00
Beam, Donkey, 1968 .... 22.00
Beam, Duesenberg, 1934 Model, Unopened 130.00
Beam, Elephant & Donkey, 1960, Pair 30.00
Beam, Elephant, 1964 .... 22.00
Beam, Fire Truck, 1930 Model Ford, Unopened 130.00
Beam, Ford Fire Pumper Truck, 1935 .... 54.00
Beam, Stein, Budweiser 13th Beam Convention 151.00
Beam, Texas Jack Rabbit 20.00
Beer, E & J Burke, Olive Green, Embossed Cat On Bottom 20.00
Beer, Pabst, Miniature 10.00
Beer, Patrick Henry 35.00
Beer, Redware, Albany Glaze, 10 1/2 In. 15.00
Beer, Wunder Brewery Co., San Francisco, Split 15.00
Bitters, Atwood's Physical Jaundice, Variant, Cylinder Shape, Label 40.00
Bitters, Augauer, Green, Label 195.00
Bitters, Baker's Orange Grove, Light Amber 125.00
Bitters, Brown's Celebrated Indian Herb, Aqua 6875.00
Bitters, Doyle's Hopp, Amber, 1872 .... 65.00
Bitters, Dr. Farrie's Cherry Wine Bitters, Corset Waisted, 8 In. 185.00
Bitters, Dr. Geo. Pierce's Indian Restorative, Aqua, Pontil 125.00
Bitters, Dr. J. Hostetter's, Amber .... 35.00 To 50.00
Bitters, Drake's 1862 Plantation X, 6 Log, Amber 90.00
Bitters, E. J. Rose's Magador, 8 3/4 In. 65.00
Bitters, Electric, Bucklein, Brown 20.00
Bitters, Greeley's Bourbon Whiskey, Strawberry Puce 200.00
Bitters, Hanlan's Tuna Bitters, Purple, Embossed, Cylinder, 9 1/4 In. ... 50.00
Bitters, Herb Wild Cherry, Cabin, Amber 205.00
Bitters, Mulford's Digestive Malt, Brown 20.00
Blue, Impressed Label, Stoneware, 9 3/4 In. 15.00
Coachman, Pottery, Figural, 11 In. ....*Illus* 650.00
Cobalt Blue Band At Neck, Stoneware, Impressed Label, 9 1/4 In. 150.00
Coca-Cola bottles are listed in the Coca-Cola section
Cold Cream, California Perfume 30.00
Cologne, Black Glass, Lotus, Westmoreland 40.00
Cream, Rosebud, Red Pyro, 3/4 Oz. 6.00
Cure, Grover Graham's Dyspepsia Cure, Newburgh, N.Y. 5.00
Decanter, Crescent Rye, Gold Leaf Letters, Club Shape 24.50
Decanter, Joe Daviess, Gold Leaf Block Letters, Stopper, Club Shape 25.00
Decanter, Kentucky Greenbrier, White Enameled Lettering, Stopper 30.00
Decanter, Old Charter, Incised Gold Leaf Script, Stopper 20.00
Decanter, Old Dearborn, Incised Gold Leaf Script, Cylinder 20.00
Decanter, Royal Velvet Whiskey, White Enameled, Shot-Type Stopper 40.00
Decanter, Sunny Brook, Pure Food Whiskey, Gold Leaf Lettering 45.00
Dr Pepper Syrup, 1940s 35.00
Drug, Bromo-Seltzer, 30 Cents 25.00
Drug, Clear, Ground Stopper, 8 1/2 In. 20.00
Drug, Owl, Round Base, Some Iridescence 10.00
Ezra Brooks, Brahma Bull 10.00
Ezra Brooks, Eagle Dancer, Indian Ceremonial Series 25.00
Ezra Brooks, Kachina, No. 1, Morning Singer 75.00
Ezra Brooks, Owl, Snowy, No. 3 .... 25.00
Ezra Brooks, Trojan Horse 15.00
Ezra Brooks, Whitetail Deer 19.00
Figural, Dog, Spots, 3 3/4 In. ....*Illus* 24.00
Figural, Scotty Dog Head, Roma Gazosa Co., Detroit, Label, 12 Oz. 8.00
Figural, Viking, Creme De Menthe, 12 1/2 In. ....*Illus* 350.00

Figural, Wee Scotch, Japan	25.00
Flask, B. Harrison, One Good Term Deserves Another, 1889–1893	495.00
Flask, B. P. O. E., Elks Tooth Shape, Porcelain, 4 1/2 In.	55.00
Flask, Baltimore Sunburst, Medium Claret, Open Pontil, c.1835, 1 Pt.	875.00
Flask, Cobalt Blue Man's Head, Salt Glaze, 1820s, 7 In.	4400.00
Flask, Incised Heart, C. H. Smith, Sept., 1860, Salt Glaze, 7 1/2 In.	5775.00
Flask, Nickel Silver, Enameled Golfer Center Plaque, Evans	250.00
Flask, Picnic, Regulator, Embossed Clock Face, Clear, 6 x 4 3/4 In.	22.00
Flask, Pumkinseed, Amber, 1 Pt.	30.00
Flask, Regimental, Soldiers, Cannons, Scene & Verse, German, 1903–1905	250.00
Flask, Sunburst	5225.00
Flask, Union, Painted Silver Design, Oval	25.00
Flask, Washington 1 Side, Taylor Other, Aqua, 7 In.	160.00
Flask, Washington, Sheaf Of Grain, Aqua	1430.00
Food, Empress Marmalade, Gold Ground, Ship In Oval, 5 In.	45.00
Food, Franco–American, Cork	13.00
Food, Log Cabin Shape, Mustard, Label, Westmoreland	70.00
Fruit Jar, Champion Syrup Refining Co., Aqua, 1 Qt.	30.00
Fruit Jar, Clarke's Fruit Jar Co., Cleveland, Aqua, c.1885, 1/2 Pt.	175.00
Fruit Jar, Clarks Peerless, Aqua, Glass Lid, 1 Pt.	10.00
Fruit Jar, Doolittle, Script, Clear, 1 Pt.	45.00
Fruit Jar, Eagle, Applied Mouth, Glass Lid, Cast Iron Yoke, 1 Qt.	130.00
Fruit Jar, Easy Vacuum Jar, Wire Bail, Lid, 9 In. *Illus*	30.00
Fruit Jar, Ferndell Jam, Brown Over White, Paper Label, 1 Pt.	55.00
Fruit Jar, Flaccus, Steerhead, Glass Lid, Milk Glass, Pt.	245.00
Fruit Jar, Mason's Shield Union, Aqua, 1 Qt.	260.00
Fruit Jar, Milville Atmospheric, 1/2 Gal.	40.00
Ginger Beer, Double Eagle, Stoneware, Set	15.00
Ginger Beer, J. F. Giering & Brother, Youngstown, Ohio, Crock	65.00
Green River Whiskey, Black Man With Horse, Box, 1933 Prescription	175.00
Ink, Carter's, Cathedral, Deep Cobalt Blue, Qt.	90.00
Ink, Cone Shape, Aqua, Embossed J. J. Butler, Cinci., Ohio, 2 1/4 In.	204.00
Ink, Umbrella, 8 Sides, Olive Green, Open Pontil, Rolled Lip, 2 In.	198.00
Jackman Whiskey, Carnival Glass, 1/2 Pt.	60.00
Jar, Abbey Ice Cigars, Cover	65.00
Jar, Red Rock, Stippled Barrel Shape, 8 Oz.	12.00
Jar, Victoria's Yogurt, Orange Writing, 1/2 Pt.	10.00
Jug, Macy & Jenkins, N.Y., Dark Amber, 9 3/8 In.	17.50
Kerosene, 5 Gal.	25.00
Medicine, Bromo–Seltzer, Light Teal Blue, 4 In.	35.00
Medicine, Citrate Magnesia, Porcelain Stopper, 1 Pt.	5.00

Bottle, Fruit Jar, Easy Vacuum   *Bottle, Milk, Hudson Dairy, 1 Qt.*   *Bottle, S.O.B. Bourbon,*
Jar, Wire Bail, Lid, 9 In.   *Schonebly-O'Neara Co., 11 In.*

Medicine, Dr. King's Pills, Embossed, Label, 2 5/8 In. 8.00
Medicine, Dr. Thatcher's Liver & Blood Syrup, 8 In. 25.00
Medicine, Mrs. Winslow's Soothing Syrup, Aqua 28.00
Medicine, Shaker Fluid, Extract Valerian, Embossed 65.00
Medicine, Thedford's Black Draught Cures Constipation 35.00
Medicine, True Daffy Elixir, Aqua, Green Tone, Rolled Lip, 4 1/4 In. 110.00
Medicine, Turlington's Balsam, Bass Fiddle Shape 15.00
Medicine, Vick's Vapor Rub, Sample 20.00
Medicine, Vicks, Cobalt Blue, Miniature 15.00
Milk, Adams Pasteurized Milk, Rawlins, Wyo., Cowboy On Bronco, 1 Gal. 75.00
Milk, Bart Peterson & Son, Jamestown, N.Y., Farm Picture, Green, 1 Qt. 12.00
Milk, Borden's, Elsie The Cow, 1/2 Pt. 5.00
Milk, Brewer's Dairy, Wabash, Ind., Nursery Rhyme, 1 Qt. 25.00
Milk, Brighton Farm Creamery, Hoboken, N. J., Tooled Lip, 1 Qt. 60.00
Milk, Brookfield, Cobalt Blue, 1 Qt. 42.50
Milk, Brown Dairy, Troy, N.Y., Double Baby Face, 1 Qt. 65.00
Milk, Burrough's Brothers, Walnut Grove, Calif., Cream Top, 1 Qt. 25.00
Milk, Clover Brand Dairy Products, Embossed 3-Leaf Clover, 1 Pt. 9.00
Milk, Darigold, Portland, Oregon, Amber, Square, 1 Qt. 12.50
Milk, Frates Dairy Inc., New N, 2 Sides Red Pyro, Square, Qt. 4.00
Milk, Golden Arrow, Cup Measurements, Plastic Handle, Orange, 1 Gal. 30.00
Milk, Golden Royal Dairy, Amber, 1/2 Gal. 5.00
Milk, Golden State Co., Ltd., Shield, Green, Cream Top, 1 Qt. 18.00
Milk, Hagg Dairy, Tyrone, Penna., Picture Of Little Girl, 1/2 Pt. 10.00
Milk, Hilo Dairymen's Center, Raw & Pasteurized, 1/2 Pt. 75.00
Milk, Home Dairy, Phoenix, Arizona, Shield With Cow, 1/2 Pt. 25.00
Milk, Hudson Dairy, 1 Qt. ....*Illus* 15.00
Milk, Jo-Mar-Farm Guernsey Milk, Embossed, 1/3 Qt. 25.00
Milk, John Swaza Rock Highland Farms, 2 Sides Blue Pyro, 1 Qt. 4.00
Milk, Kee & Chapell Dairy Co., Shield On Shoulder, Amethyst, 1 Pt. 12.00
Milk, Lawton's, Swansea, Mass. On Shoulder, Red Pyro 3.00
Milk, Liberty Milk Co., 1 Pt. 20.00
Milk, Liberty Milk Co., 1/2 Pt. 8.00
Milk, Loma Linda Sanitarium Dairy, California, Orange, Square, 1 Qt. 27.00
Milk, Midwest Dairy, 1/2 Pt. 2.25
Milk, Model Dairy, Remains Property of, Reno, Nevada, Square, 1 Qt. 15.00
Milk, Standard Sairey, Anslyn, Los Angeles, Bowling Pin Shape, 1 Pt. 30.00
Milk, Sunshine Dairy Grade A Milk, Paducah, Kentucky, 1/2 Pt. 10.00
Milk, Sunshine Dairy, St. John, Newfoundland, Red, Round, Imperial Qt. 45.00
Milk, Taylor's Dairy, Amber, 1/2 Pt. 35.00
Milk, Westen Farm's Dairy Co., Amber, 1 Qt. 100.00
Mineral Water, Congress-Empire Spring, Green, 1 Pt. 22.00
Mineral Water, G. W. Merchant, Oak Orchard, Green, Qt. 50.00
Mineral Water, Guilford, Vt., Green 65.00
Mineral Water, John Clarke, Black, 1 Qt. 80.00
Mineral Water, Saratoga Geyser Spring, Aqua, 1 Pt. 22.00
Mineral Water, Twitchell Superior, Emerald Green 25.00
Mineral Water, White Rock, Lid, Brown, 1 Qt. 2.25
Mineral Water, White Rock, Unopened, 1920s 25.00
Miniature, Whiskey, Brown-Forman Co., Louisville, Cylinder, 4 1/4 In. 6.50
Miniature, Whiskey, Harper, Silver Cap, Label Ohio-1928, 4 1/2 In. 16.50
Miniature, Whiskey, Huguley, Boston, Clear, Cylinder, 4 1/4 In. 3.75
Miniature, Whiskey, Seagram's Seven Crown, Clear, Label, Metal Cap 3.50
Miniature, Whiskey, Seagram's VO, Tin Lid 1.25
Miniature, Whiskey, Seagram, 1935, 1/10 Pt. 35.00
Mr. Clean, Plastic, 1950s 29.00
Nurser, Burr, Boston, Medallion, Aqua 40.00
Nurser, Century Of Progress, Rhyme, Baby In Tree, 1933, 8 Oz. 25.00
Nurser, Grip Tite, Box 20.00
Oil, J. Rhode's Co., Kalamazoo, Mich. Embossed 40.00
Oil, Marble, Glass 60.00
Oil, Royal Typewriter, Some Contents, Small 15.00
Oil, Sunoco, Decal 45.00

Bottle, Snuff, Flattened Moon, Maiden On Terrace, Red, c.1850

Bottle, Snuff, Auspicious Symbol, Coral, Turquoise, c.1850

Bottle, Snuff, Flowers, Cobalt & Clear Glass, Baluster

Oil, Vanta Baby, 1930s 20.00
Old Prentice, Red Bell, Clear, Cylinder, 1 Qt. 16.00
Perfume bottles are listed in their own section
Poison, Tincture Of Iodine, Amber, Skull & Crossbones, 3 1/4 In. 30.00
Refrigerator, Green, Pat. Sept. 15, 1931 .... 6.00
S. O. B. Bourbon, Schonebly–O'Neara Co., 11 In. ....*Illus* 75.00
Sachet, Richard Hudnut, Brass Screw Cap, 3 1/2 In. 18.00
Seltzer, Big Chief, Sacramento, Cal., Red, Marked Top 215.00
Seltzer, Jalen, Dancing Girl, Blue 50.00
Seltzer, Mr. Lassen, Susanville, Cal., Red Label 128.00
Seltzer, Nehi, Green 65.00
Seltzer, Royal Palm, Terre Haute, Ind., Brown, Green 130.00
Shoe Polish, Shinola, For Children, Cone Shape, Cork Top 2.35
Siphon, Big Chief, Sacramento, Calif., Red 225.00
Siphon, Mt. Lassen, Susanville, Cal., Red Label 138.00
Siphon, Royal Palm, Terre Haute, Ind., Brown, Green 140.00
Smelling Salts, Dabrook, Aquamarine, Brass Lid 37.50
Smelling Salts, Yardley, 2 1/2 In. 12.00
Snuff, Amethyst, Carved Stand, Oriental, 2 1/4 In. 85.00
Snuff, Auspicious Symbol, Coral, Turquoise, c.1850 ....*Illus* 3025.00
Snuff, Carved Both Sides, Rose Quartz, 2 1/2 In. 95.00
Snuff, Carved Cranes Front & Back, 2 1/2 In. 120.00
Snuff, Carved Jade, Foo Dog & Urn Shape, 2 1/4 In. 385.00
Snuff, Carved Oriental Characters, Serpentine, 2 1/2 In. 95.00
Snuff, Carved Oriental Figures, Pagoda Both Sides, Ivory, 3 In. 85.00
Snuff, Carved White Jade, Oxen Scene, Coral Stopper, Ovoid, 2 1/4 In. ... 1100.00
Snuff, Double Gourd, Ivory, 4 3/4 In. 495.00
Snuff, Dr. Marshall's, Aqua, Contents 25.00
Snuff, Flattened Moon, Maiden On Terrace, Red, c.1850 ....*Illus* 770.00
Snuff, Flowers, Cobalt & Clear Glass, Baluster ....*Illus* 165.00
Snuff, Form Of Beggar Carrying Gourd, Ivory, Ch'ing Dynasty, 7 In. 357.00
Snuff, Frosted, Painted Woman Interior 350.00
Snuff, Hornbill, Figural Scenes, Chain, Stand, China, 8 In. 990.00
Snuff, Interior Painting Of Birds & Flowers, China, 4 1/4 In. 65.00
Snuff, Lapis Lazuli, Wooden Stand, 2 1/2 In. 165.00
Snuff, Maccoboy, Amber, 1898 .... 75.00
Snuff, Porcelain, Man With Camel, Man On Horse, Flat Body, 2 3/4 In. ... 385.00
Snuff, Reverse Painted Glass, Fish In Water, Flat Body, 3 In. 495.00
Snuff, Rock Crystal, Painted Interior, Zhou I, 2 1/4 In. 1210.00
Snuff, Scene Of Scholars, Black Ground, Ivory, Manchu Dynasty, 4 In. ... 330.00
Snuff, Twin Scholar Statuettes, Ivory, Ch'ing Dynasty, 4 In. 140.00
Snuff, Urn Form, Dragon's Head Handles, Foo Dogs, Ivory, 3 1/4 In. 157.00
Soda, California Bottling Works, T. Blauth, Aqua, 6 7/8 In. 25.00
Soda, City Soda Works, Eureka, Bubbles, Aqua, 6 3/4 In. 20.00
Soda, Cliquot Club Ginger Ale, Embossed Script, Label 10.00
Soda, Dillon Montana, Cowboy & Bucking Bronco, ACL 10.00
Soda, Dr. Townsend's Sarsaparilla, Light Blue Green, IP 125.00

Soda, Felix Ginger Ale, Qt. 18.00
Soda, Joy's Sarsaparilla, San Francisco 20.00
Soda, Northrup & Sturgis Co., Portland, Ore., Aqua, 6 1/8 In. 20.00
Soda, Orange Crush, Canada, 7 Oz. 6.00
Soda, Seitz & Bro., Easton, Pa., Dug, Cobalt Blue 25.00
Soda, Teem, Green, 1972, 12 Oz. 10.00
Soda, Up Town, 3 1/2 In. 3.00
Soda, Utica Bottling Establishment, Green, Iron Pontil, Blob Top 150.00
Soda, Wink 9.00
Soda, Yager's Sarsaparilla, Amber 40.00
Syrup, Log Cabin, 1940s 48.50
Toilet Water, Blown 3–Piece Mold, Cobalt Blue, Flared Lip, 6 In. 185.00
Whiskey, Atlantic Pacific Dist. Co., Amethyst, 22 1/2 In. 15.00
Whiskey, Boston League, Back Bar, Gold Leaf Letters, Cylinder 80.00
Whiskey, Duffy Malt Whiskey Co., Rochester, N.Y., Monogram, 3 7/8 In. 12.00
Whiskey, E. Martin & Co., San Francisco, Argonaut, Amber, 11 1/8 In. 25.00
Whiskey, Edgewood Rye, Back Bar, Gold Leaf Lettering, Cylinder 45.00
Whiskey, F. Chevalier Co., Castle, San Francisco, Amber, 11 In. 25.00
Whiskey, General Robert E. Lee, Southern Comfort 200.00
Whiskey, Geo. Wissemann, Sacramento, Monogram, Threads, Amber, 11 In. 20.00
Whiskey, H. Varwig & Son, Portland, Monogram, Amber, 12 1/4 In. 20.00
Whiskey, Hall, Lurhs & Co., Monogram, Sacramento, GLOP Top, 11 7/8 In. 40.00
Whiskey, Hanover Rye, Gilded Bar, With Horse 165.00
Whiskey, Hey & Grauerholz, Davy Crockett Pure Bourbon, 11 7/8 In. 40.00
Whiskey, J. H. Cutter, Bourbon, Crown, Light Amber, 11 3/4 In. 30.00
Whiskey, Jas. E. Pepper, Est. 1780, Gold Leaf Script, Back Bar, Cylinder 45.00
Whiskey, Kellerstras Distilling Co., St. Louis, Mo., 4 3/8 In. 15.00
Whiskey, Kentucky Tavern, Back Bar, White Enameled, Cylinder 85.00
Whiskey, L. Hartman Co., Chicago, Clear, Cylinder, 10 3/4 In. 10.00
Whiskey, Levaggi Co., San Francisco, Monogram, Amber, 11 In. 25.00
Whiskey, M. Cronan & Co., Sacramento, Bubbles, Light Amber, 12 In. 20.00
Whiskey, Morisco, White Enameled Lettering, Pinch Shape 35.00
Whiskey, Newman's, San Francisco, Oakland, Football Shape, 4 1/4 In. 200.00
Whiskey, O. F. C., Large White Enameled Lettering, Pinch Shape 28.50
Whiskey, Old Charter, White Enameled Script, Back Bar, Cylinder 50.00
Whiskey, Old Fortuna Bourbon, White Enameled Lettering, Pinch Shape 30.00
Whiskey, Old Harper, Etched Letters, Salesman Sample 35.00
Whiskey, Old Prentice, White Script, Salesman Sample 55.00
Whiskey, Paul Jones, White Enameled Script, Stopper, Pinch Shape 220.00
Whiskey, Pepper & Co., 4 Mold, Shield Mark, Medium Amber, 11 3/4 In. 150.00
Whiskey, Rum, Confederate Army, Ft. San Marcos, 1860s 66.00
Whiskey, S. O. B. Bourbon, Stoneware, 2 Large Handles, Dark Brown Top 55.00
Whiskey, Schenley Rye, Back Bar, Silver Lettering, Cylinder 70.00
Whiskey, Sun Drug Co., Mortar & Pestle, Sunburst, Amber, 6 In. 115.00
Whiskey, Torrance, Back Bar, Fancy White Enameled Line, Cylinder 105.00
Whiskey, Triple Rye, Bar, Swirled, Stopper 25.00
Whiskey, W. A. Lacey, Figural, Ye Olde Tun Tavern, Unglazed, 1/2 Pt. 24.00
Whiskey, W. J. Van Schuyver & Co., Crown & Shield, Amber, 11 1/4 In. 20.00
Wild Turkey, Charleston Centennial 49.00
Wild Turkey, Habitat, 1988 .... 95.00
Wild Turkey, Mack Bulldog 25.00
Wild Turkey, No. 1, In Flight 75.00
Wild Turkey, No. 4, With Raccoon, Miniature 19.00
Wild Turkey, No. 5, 1976 .... 30.00
Wild Turkey, No. 6, 1977 .... 30.00
Wild Turkey, No. 9, With Bear Cubs 69.00
Wild Turkey, Series 1, No. 1, Male, 1971 .... 165.00 To 300.00
Wine, Los Angeles Wine Co., Spokane, Megaphone Shape, Amber, 1/2 Gal. 100.00

BOXES of all kinds are collected. They were made of thin strips of inlaid wood, metal, tortoiseshell, embroidery, or other material. Additional boxes may be listed in other sections, such as Advertising, Battersea, Ivory, Shaker, Tinware, and various Porcelain categories. Tea Caddies are listed in their own section.

Academy, Decorated, Original Blue Graining, Shells, Landscape, 10 In.	650.00
Amber, Delicate Gold Filigree Overlay, 2 1/4 In.	415.00
Amish, Graining, Dated 1880, Small	175.00
Apple, Pine, Dark Blue Paint, 8 3/4 x 9 1/2 In.	175.00
Augusta Coffee, 5 Cents, 1/4 Lb.	3.00
Ballot, 2 Slots, Dovetailed, Early Nails, Red Stain, 13 x 9 In.	135.00
Band, Amish, Wallpaper Covered, Elizabeth Lapp, 1879	395.00
Band, Floral, Pennsylvania Dutch, Round, 8 In.	90.00
Band, Green & Black Floral Wallpaper Covered, 7 1/2 x 14 In.	490.00
Band, Hand Painted Floral Design, Paper, Brown & Beige	1150.00
Band, Hand Printed Wallpaper, Newspaper Lining, New York State, 1831	398.00
Band, Wallpaper Covered, 1843 Newspaper Lined, Oval, 2 Ft.	110.00
Band, Wallpaper Covered, Bird–Drawn Chariot On Lid, 17 In.	500.00
Band, Wallpaper Covered, Buildings & Trees, Bentwood, 19 In.	400.00
Band, Wallpaper Covered, Deer & Trees, Cardboard, 15 1/2 In.	85.00
Band, Wallpaper Covered, Floral Design, Bentwood, 8 3/4 In.	400.00
Band, Wallpaper Covered, Geometric Floral, Cream Ground, 19 3/4 In.	800.00
Band, Wallpaper Covered, Harbor, Eagle, Bent Cardboard, 17 1/4 In.	225.00
Band, Wallpaper Covered, Heart Shape, 8 x 12 x 22 In.	1185.00
Band, Wallpaper Covered, Lined In Lancaster Newspaper Of 1839	6710.00
Band, Wallpaper Covered, Oval	225.00
Band, Wallpaper Covered, Squirrels On Top, Birds On Side	3600.00
Bentwood, 7 Interior Canisters, Dark Finish, 8 In.	165.00
Bentwood, Floral Design, Brown Ground, 11 1/2 In.	325.00
Bentwood, Gray Repaint, Branded J. M., Round, 8 3/4 In.	175.00
Bentwood, Lid, Dark Green Paint, Striped, Ginger On Label, 7 3/4 In.	515.00
Bentwood, Pine & Beech, Green Repaint, Oval, 5 3/4 In.	200.00
Bentwood, Pine, Dark Green, Floral, Spring Lid, 5 1/4 In.	130.00
Bentwood, Pine, Original Orange Paint, Polychrome Floral Design, 21 In.	750.00
Bentwood, Pine, Polychrome Floral Design, 10 In.	700.00
Bentwood, Red Paint, Oval, 10 In.	275.00
Bentwood, Wallpaper Covered, Classical Figure Designs, 3 3/4 In.	650.00
Bentwood, Wallpaper Covered, Grey Floral Design, Green, 18 1/2 In.	200.00
Bentwood, Worn Red Paint, Floral Design, 3 3/4 In.	135.00
Bible, Carved Oak, Initials WE, England, 18th Century	412.50
Bible, Gold Edges, Red Inside, Metal Clasp, Pine, 10 3/4 x 14 1/2 In.	200.00
Biedermeier, Brass Corners, Fruitwood Interior, Compartments, 19 In.	440.00
Birch, Russian Karehan, Gilded Imperial Eagle On Lid, 4 x 4 In.	115.00
Book Shape, Slide Out Compartment, Walnut, Greenish Paper Cover, 12 In.	200.00
Bordo Dates, Wire Handle, 2 Sections	20.00
Brass Bound, Iron Balance Device, Signed J. H. J., 1791, 10 1/4 x 4 In.	175.00
Brass Cover, Building, Floral, Dated 1870	495.00
Brass, Ornate Gilt, 8 In.	145.00
Bride's, Bentwood, Pine, Blue, Decoupage, Floral, Laced Seams, 16 In.	600.00
Bride's, German Inscription, Oval Bentwood Pine, 19 1/4 In.	850.00
Bride's, Polychrome Floral, Man & Dog Scene On Lid, Pine, 18 3/4 In.	1150.00
Bride's, Polychrome Floral, Red Ground, Laced Seams, Germany, 19 In.	900.00
Brown Vinegar Graining, On Yellow, Needlepoint Hinged Lid, 9 1/2 In.	95.00
Candle, Blue Painted, 19th Century, 14 In.	385.00
Candle, Hanging, Japanning, Tin, 11 3/4 In.	150.00
Candle, Hanging, Scalloped Sides, Arched Top, Square Cut Nails, c.1830	265.00
Candle, Pine, Polychrome Floral Design, Black Panels, 14 1/4 In.	85.00
Candle, Poplar, Green Paint, Sliding Lid, 13 1/4 In.	105.00
Candle, Poplar, Original Brown Graining, 14 In.	150.00
Candle, Punched Compass Star Lid, Tin, Hanging, Cylindrical, 14 In.	125.00
Candle, Sliding Lid, Dovetailed, Cherry, 9 3/4 In.	155.00
Candle, Sliding Lid, Old Red Paint, Poplar, 15 In.	175.00

Candle, Sliding Lid, Pine, Old Green Repaint, 18 In. 75.00
Candle, Walnut, No Lid, American, 1800, 11 x 5 x 18 3/4 In. 485.00
Cardboard, Wallpaper Covered, Oval, Landscape Design, 10 In. 95.00
Carved & Engraved Ivory, Tortoise Shell Veneer, 7 1/2 In. 305.00
Carved, Applied Heart & Geometric Design, Painted, 7 1/2 x 14 1/2 In. 415.00
Chip Carved 1 Piece Wood, Sliding Lid, Maple, 9 1/4 In. 150.00
Chip Carved, Stringing In Base & Lid, Brass Handle, Walnut, 12 1/4 In. 400.00
Chrome Top, White Paint, Polychrome House, Trees, 3 x 4 In. 255.00
Cigarette, Musical, Mechanical 45.00
Cologne, 6 Cut Glass Bottles, Dutch, Tulipwood Parquetry, 7 1/2 x 9 In. 522.50
Cutlery, Horses Carved On Handle 4000.00
Cutlery, Wooden, Cutout Heart Center Top, Scroll Ends 2800.00
Desk, Table Top, Dovetailed, Slant Lid, Lock, Pine, 7 1/8 x 12 1/4 In. 200.00
Desk, Table Top, Poplar, Eagle Design On Lid, Dovetailed Case, 13 In. 250.00
Document, American Flags Inlaid On Lid, 10 In. 350.00
Document, Eagle Carved Top 150.00
Document, Federal, Inlaid Bird's–Eye Maple & Mahogany, 5 x 12 x 6 In. 385.00
Document, Original Leather, Tacks, Handle & Lock, 1833, 12 1/4 In. 135.00
Document, Red Leather, Initials W B In Brass Tacks, 1790s 250.00
Document, Sheraton, Inlaid Drapery Festoon, Brass Handles, 7 1/4 In. 465.00
Dome Top, Brown Rose Mulled Design, Wire Nail, 10 1/2 In. 85.00
Dome Top, Pine, Design, Red & Black Graining, 28 1/2 In. 55.00
Dome Top, Pine, Original Blue Paint, Floral Design, 9 3/4 In. 425.00
Dome Top, Pine, Poplar, Worn Green Paint, Handles, 34 In. 50.00
Dome Top, Pine, Scalloped Bracket Feet, Brown Finish, 10 1/4 In. 115.00
Dome Top, Poplar, Chip Carved Floral & Eagle, 9 In. 775.00
Dome Top, Poplar, Original Red Paint, Black & Yellow Dots, 14 In. 825.00
Dome Top, Poplar, Red Paint, Yellow Stylized Foliage, 21 In. 500.00
Dome Top, Poplar, White Paint, Red Flowers On Lid, 8 3/4 In. 5000.00
Dome Top, Primitive, Covering Of Pen & Ink Spencerian Script, 9 In. 225.00
Dough, Chestnut, Worn Finish, Chip Carved Top Posts, 18 x 43 x 26 In. 450.00
Dough, Lift Top, Red Paint Traces, 1 Board Construction, 18th Century 595.00
Dresser, Clear Glass, Frosted Dog Cutout Top, 6 x 4 1/2 x 2 1/2 In. 40.00
Dresser, Empire, Velvet Lined, 6 Bottles, Key, 1830, 12 x 9 x 6 1/2 In. 335.00
Dresser, Shellwork, 6 x 4 1/2 In. 55.00
Dressing, Man's, Wood Inlays, Felt Liner, Sliding Tray, 11 3/4 In. 165.00
Drop Front, Scroll Designs, 10 Drawers, Italy, 17th Century, 21 1/8 In. 3300.00
Enameled, Butterflies, Marked China, 5 1/4 In. 55.00
Federal, Mahogany, 6 Drawers, Fan Inlay, c.1790, 6 3/4 x 11 In. 8800.00
Ferrier's, Pennsylvania, 1890 .... 65.00
Glove, Rosewood, Silver Mounts, Courtship, Maternity Scenes, 13 3/4 In. 5225.00
Handkerchief, Lady Golfers, Pyrography 12.00
Hanging, Pine, Scalloped Crest, 1 Drawer, 8 1/2 x 12 3/4 In. 125.00
Hanging, Pine, Sloping Top, Drawer, Painted Design, 1750, 14 1/4 In. 8800.00
Hat, Knox Hats, Horseman & Hounds English Country Scene, Oval, 12 In. 22.00
Hat, Leather, Velvet Lining, Strap, For Large Hat 110.00
Hat, Wallpaper Covered, Floral, Hannah Davis, 7 1/2 x 13 In. 445.00
Hat, Woman's, Maroon Cardboard, Large 27.50
Hide Covered, Brass Bale Handle, Worn Gilding, 14 In. 35.00
Hide Covered, Wallpaper Lined, Brass Studs, Bale & Iron Lock, 9 In. 75.00
Jewelry, Brass, Pewter, Silver Plated, Bronze, Secret Interior, Standing 7000.00
Jewelry, Enamel, Blue, Pheasant, Flowering Branch, Landscape, 6 In. 450.00
Jewelry, Silver, Gilt Enameled, Jewel Encrusted, Man On Horseback 3400.00
Jewelry, Silver, Lapis & Jewel Encrusted, Man With Dog 4000.00
Keen Kutter, Paper, For 6 Pocket Knives 15.00
Knife & Fork, Sections, Stenciled, Strap Handle 65.00
Knife, Cover, Inlay, England, Mahogany, 14 1/2 In. 250.00
Knife, Dovetailed Walnut, Center Dividing Handle 230.00
Knife, Dovetailed, Heart Cutout Handle, 9 1/4 x 12 3/4 In, ... 95.00
Knife, Georgian Style, Mahogany, Serpentine Front, 14 In., Pr. 1320.00
Knife, Hardwood, Pine, Yellowed White Paint, 8 3/4 x 12 1/2 In. 150.00
Knife, Inlaid Chevron Herringbone Pattern, Walnut, Ash, 14 In. 125.00
Knife, Mahogany, Ebony Line Inlay, England, 14 In. 350.00

Knife, Sheraton, Satinwood Conch Shell Panel, Mahogany, 16 1/4 In. 495.00
Knife, Silver Plated Escutcheons, Mahogany, England, 12 1/2 In. 350.00
Knife, Silver Plated Handles & Escutcheon, Mahogany Veneer, 13 1/2 In. 450.00
Knife, Walnut, Old Finish, 13 In. 135.00
Lehnware, Red Paint, Woman Portrait, Floral Transfer, Striping, 9 In. 850.00
Letter, Desktop, Brass, Ornate Cast Design, 11 In. 115.00
Letter, Jasperware Medallions In Brass Frames, Calamander, 9 3/4 In. 605.00
Letter, Silver Overlay, Bronze, Arts & Crafts, 5 x 8 In. 125.00
Linen, Sliding Lid, 1850–1860, 36 In x 30 In. 495.00
Liquor, Burl Walnut, Brass Campaign Hardware, 4 Decanters, England 825.00
Mahogany, Carved Flower, Foliage Design, 9 In. 85.00
Mahogany, Dovetailed, Ivory Escutcheon, White Metal Handle, 18 In. 95.00
Mourning Veils, Violet Pattern, Cardboard, 1903, Small 35.00
Mythological Scenes, Tooled, Pewter, 6 3/4 In. 45.00
Packing, Used For Shipping Tea, Papered, China 60.50
Pantry, Baleen, Engraved With House, Fort, Ship, Vine, Oval, 2 x 6 x 5 In. 303.00
Pantry, Blue, Oval, Marked F. M. 2200.00
Pewter & Nacre Inlay, Rosewood Veneer, Hinged Lid, 7 3/4 In. 25.00
Pine, Bevel Edge Dome Top, Green Paint, Applied Cutout Feet, 21 In. 55.00
Pine, Compass Draw, Painted Design Lid, Pine, 20 1/2 In. 300.00
Pine, Dovetailed, Sliding Lid, 9 3/4 In. 85.00
Pine, Oak, Applied Molding, Brass Hardware, Europe, 13 In. 55.00
Pine, Poplar, Black, Yellow Graining, Dovetailed, 23 In. 150.00
Pine, Poplar, Original Iron Lock, Brass Keyhole Cover, 24 In. 1450.00
Pine, Poplar, Original Red Paint, Staple Hinges, 10 In. 475.00
Pine, Smoke Graining, Green Paint, 19 In. 255.00
Pipe, Country, Pine, Black Paint, 1 Dovetailed Drawer, 16 In. 2200.00
Pipe, Hanging, Leather Hinge, Mahogany, 1850s, 17 1/2 In. 100.00
Poplar, Blue Silk Lined, Signed SDL 175.00
Poplar, Dovetailed, Original Red Graining, 12 3/4 In. 75.00
Poplar, Original Reddish Graining, Design, 8 3/4 In. 275.00
Poplar, Original Tan Paint, Gold Stenciled Designs, 9 In. 75.00
Poplar, Original Vinegar Graining, Dovetailed, 14 1/4 In. 500.00
Poplar, Red & Black Graining, Eagle, Shield, Slot In Lid & Base, 6 In. 160.00
Primitive, Pine, Red Paint, 3 Part Interior, Wire Hinges, 13 1/4 In. 60.00
Primitive, Poplar, Worn Dark Finish, Checkerboard Lid, 14 In. 165.00
Pyrography, Hinged, Thistles, Anchors, Dated 1900, 11 1/2 x 4 1/2 In. 45.00
Quarter–Sawed Beech, Rose Mulled Design, Iron Strap Hinges, 12 1/4 In. 400.00
Reclining Nude, Tin Base, Divided Brass Interior, White Metal, 9 In. 60.00
Rosary, St. Anthony Holding Child On Porcelain Lid, Filigreed Brass 175.00
Saffron, Floral Design, Polychrome, Lehnware, 4 5/8 In. 215.00
Saffron, Floral Design, Polychrome, Lehnware, 5 1/8 In. 525.00
Salt, Hanging, Carved, 10 In. 150.00
Scouring, Primitive, 1 Drawer, Lift Lid, Pine, Red Paint, 12 1/2 In. 155.00
Scouring, Walnut, Old Finish, Lid, 12 In. 55.00
Shotshell, Climax, 2 Piece 25.00
Slant Lid, Poplar, Dovetailed, Blue Wallpaper Interior, 14 1/2 In. 275.00
Sliding Lid, Chip–Carved, Moon & Star Design, Red Stain 880.00
Sliding Lid, Pine, Stylized Floral, Black Paint, 8 1/4 In. 3000.00
Snuff, Pocket, Wooden 95.00
Snuff, Wooden, Grandma Dilly Written In Pencil Inside Lid, 1772 .... 185.00
Spice, Poplar, 8 Drawers, Crest, Refinished 9 3/4 x 16 3/4 In. 175.00
Spruce Gum, Carved Framing Design On Front 385.00
Stamp, Relief Pagoda Scene, Enameled, China 45.00
Strong, Embossed Rosettes On Straps, Germany, 17th Century, 24 x 17 In. 2750.00
Tiger's–Eye, Peking Ducks, Curled Wings, Carved Base, 4 x 5 1/2 In., Pr. 550.00
Vanity, Traveling, Rosewood, Thistle Brass Inlay, England, 12 x 9 In. 412.00
Voting, Figuring, Uncle Sam Hat 35.00
Wall, Hanging, Slant–Top Cover, Painted, 1760 .... 8800.00
Wall, Lollipop, Bayberry Paint, Wooden 280.00
Walnut, Dovetailed, 9 x 15 In. 80.00
Walnut, Inscribed Hex, Pennsylvania, 1810 .... 850.00
Woman's, Slide Top, Period Wallpaper Lining, c.1850, 9 1/2 x 5 1/2 In. 165.00

Wooden, Copper Nails, 19th Century, Round, 7 3/4 In. 60.00
Wooden, Dark Finish, Red, 3 3/4 In. 25.00
Wooden, Grained, Divided 425.00
Wooden, Ivory, Nacre Inlay, 6 1/2 In. 35.00
Writing, Inlaid Lid, Veneer, Rosewood, 13 3/4 In. 75.00
Yellow Paint, Striping, Bird On Branch, Hinged Lid, Mar. 1858, 7 3/4 In. 700.00

BOY SCOUT collectibles include any material related to scouting, including patches, manuals, and uniforms. The Boy Scout movement in the United States started in 1910. The first Jamboree was held in 1937. Girl Scout items are listed under their own heading.

Ad, Boy Scout Jamboree, Coca–Cola, Framed, 1938 .... 25.00
Armband, Press, National Jamboree, 1981 .... 100.00
Back Patch, USA Contingent, World Jamboree, 1983 .... 10.00
Back Patch, World Jamboree, 1971, Round 18.00
Belt Buckle, Bronze, Max Silver, World Jamboree, 1971 .... 110.00
Belt Buckle, Pewter, National Jamboree, 1985 .... 8.00
Book, Alexander, Minute Tapioca Book, 1910 .... 90.00
Book, Boy Scouts Down In Dixie, Carter, 1914 .... 11.00
Book, Boy Scouts Motorcycles, Ralph Bictor, 1911 .... 9.00
Book, Capturing A Spy, Sherman, 1913 .... 8.00
Book, Games For Scouts, 1947 .... 10.00
Book, Golden Anniversary Book Of Scouting, 1959 .... 20.00
Book, Scout To Explorer, Signed Paul Siple, 1936 .... 19.00
Book, Scouting 50 Years, Rockwell 35.00
Book, Scouting With Daniel Boone, Rockwell, 1914 .... 15.00
Bracelet, Mother's 24.00
Bugle, Inscribed, Brass 55.00
Calendar, Paper, 1931 .... 38.00
Cap, Overseas, 1950s 2.00
Card, Certificate, In Slip Case, 1930s 10.00
Certificate, Membership, 1929 .... 7.00
Cup, San Diego Council 1981, Ceramic 4.00
Fieldbook, 1948 .... 9.00
Fire Starter Kit, Box 45.00
First Aid Kit, 1940s 15.00
First Aid Kit, Metal, Cloth Cover 25.00
Game, American Boys, Milton Bradley 100.00
Handbook, 1934 .... 12.00
Handbook, 1947 .... 9.00
Handbook, Leather Insignia Jacket, 1st Edition, 1940 .... 25.00
Hat Patch, Green, Brown, Gold, World Jamboree, 1967 .... 30.00
Hat Pin, Eagle Scout, Sterling 125.00
Hat, Canadian Leader, Felt 30.00
Hatchet, Plumb, Boy Scout Logo & Be Prepared, 13 3/4 In. 25.00
Knapsack, 1930 .... 65.00
Knife, Pocket, Bone Handle, Ulster, 4 Blades 65.00
Knife, Pocket, Cub Scout 12.00
Lapel Pin, Onward For God & My Country 6.00
Medal, War Service, Oct., 1917 .... 50.00
Mess Kit, Canvas Cover 14.00
Money Clip, Jamboree, 1957 .... 15.00
Morse Code Signaler, Box 35.00
Mug, Official Round Up, Frankoma, 4 Piece 55.00
Neckerchief, 7th District 15.00
Neckerchief, Boy Scout Jamboree, 1964 .... 35.00
Neckerchief, Green & White, Israel Scout Symbol 5.00
Neckerchief, National Jamboree, 1935, Red 110.00
Neckerchief, National Jamboree, 1953 .... 25.00 To 45.00
Neckerchief, National Jamboree, 1973 .... 5.00
Neckerchief, USA Contingent, World Jamboree, 1983 .... 10.00
Paperweight, Bronze Color, Tenderfoot 5.00
Paperweight, Embossed Figures & Symbols, 1930s, 4 x 2 In. 48.00

Bradley & Hubbard, Lamp, Hanging,
Hobnail, Opalescent

Paperweight, Lucite, National Jamboree, 1977	10.00
Patch, Malaysia, National Jamboree, 1973	5.00
Patch, Silk, Souvenir, World Jamboree, 1933	25.00
Poster, America Builds For Tomorrow, 1930, 28 x 22 In.	75.00
Poster, Toughen Up, Buckle Down, Carry On, 1943, 22 x 15 In.	50.00
Ring, Coin On Top, National Jamboree, 1953	20.00
Ring, Cubs BSA, Sterling	10.00
Shirt, National Jamboree, 1957	35.00
Signal Set, Box, 1950s	65.00
Stickpin, Metal, Silver & Blue, World Jamboree, 1971	10.00
Uniform, 1930s	100.00
Watch, Jamboree, Coca–Cola Advertising, Pocket	30.00
Whistle Ball, Silver	9.00

BRADLEY & HUBBARD is a name found on many metal objects. Walter
Hubbard and his brother–in–law, Nathaniel Lyman Bradley, started
making cast iron clocks, tables, frames, andirons, lamps, chandeliers,
sconces, and sewing birds in 1854 in Meriden, Connecticut. The company
became Bradley & Hubbard Manufacturing Company in 1875. Charles
Parker Company bought the firm in 1940. Their lamps are especially
prized by collectors.

Andirons, Square Finial, Flaring Shaft, Stamped, 21 In.	630.00
Clock, Sambo, Figural	3520.00
Clock, Seated Dog, Figural	3300.00
Clock, Topsy, Figural	7700.00
Doorstop, Cairn Terrier, Cast Iron	135.00
Inkwell, Brass	70.00
Lamp Base, Ivy, 10 In.	125.00
Lamp, 3 Candle Arms, Parrots Bell Shaped Shades, 19 In.	325.00
Lamp, 3 Sockets, Green & White Slag Shade, Marked, 21 In.	412.50
Lamp, Adjustable Standard, Leaded Glass Shade, 56 In.	357.00
Lamp, Banquet, Brass, 19 In.	695.00
Lamp, Banquet, Cherubs On Base, Women Medallions, Brass	600.00
Lamp, Brass, Medallion Trim, Ball Shade, 13 In.	100.00
Lamp, Coralene, Overlay, 12 In.	1050.00
Lamp, Hanging, Hobnail, Opalescent ....*Illus*	1900.00
Lamp, Hanging, Victorian, Cranberry Bull's–Eye Shade	950.00
Lamp, Hurricane, Brass Base, 1930s	325.00
Lamp, Kerosene, Hanging, Torch & Wreath Chimney, 1876	325.00
Lamp, Leaded Glass Shade, 20 In.	165.00
Lamp, Nickel–Plated Brass, Ruby Slag Shade, 20 1/4 In.	145.00

Brass, Candy Dish, Glass Insert,

Chase, 2 x 5 In.

◆◆◆◆◆◆◆◆◆◆◆◆◆◆◆◆◆◆◆◆◆◆

Brass can be polished with this homemade remedy. Make a paste of equal parts salt, flour, and vinegar. Rub the paste on the brass with a soft cloth. Rinse completely. Buff with a clean, dry, soft cloth.

◆◆◆◆◆◆◆◆◆◆◆◆◆◆◆◆◆◆◆◆◆◆

Lamp, Paneled Slag Shade, Metal Overlay, Signed, 16 In.	700.00
Lamp, Piano, Cased Shade, Floor Type, Dated 1878	200.00
Lamp, Student, Oxblood Tam–O–Shanter Shade	425.00
Lamp, Table, Greek Key Design, Signed Baccarat Shade	250.00
Tray, Card, Rabbit With Shamrock	45.00

BRASS has been used for decorative pieces and useful tablewares since ancient times. It is an alloy of copper, zinc, and other metals. Additional brass items may be found under Bell, Candlestick, Tool, or Trivet.

Bed Warmer, Engraved Lid, Turned Wooden Handle, Floral, 44 1/2 In.	250.00
Bed Warmer, Engraved Stylized Floral, Flat Iron Handle, 42 In.	935.00
Bed Warmer, Floral Engraved Lid, Turned Wooden Handle, Copper, 40 In.	150.00
Bed Warmer, Pierced & Engraved Lid, Floral, Wooden Handle, 44 In.	200.00
Bed Warmer, Pierced & Floral Engraved Lid, Turned Handle, 44 1/2 In.	195.00
Bed Warmer, Pierced, Smoke Designed Handle	160.00
Bed Warmer, Turned Handle, American, 19th Century	195.00
Bookends, Horsehead	68.00
Box, Letter, Desk Top, Ornate Cast Detail, 11 In.	115.00
Bucket, Spun, Hiram W. Hayden, Waterbury, Conn., Bale Handle, 7 1/4 In.	55.00
Buckle Pin, Hammered, Apollo Studios, Round, 2 1/4 In.	65.00
Buddha Head, Removable Top Knot, Wooden Base, 22 1/4 In.	350.00
Bust, Woman With A Crown, 10 7/8 In.	185.00
Cake Stand, 19th Century, England	450.00
Candlesnuffer, Ruffled Cup, Chinese	15.00
Candy Dish, Glass Insert, Chase, 2 x 5 In. ....*Illus*	45.00
Card Tray, Art Nouveau, Nude On Side Of Shell, Lo–Mar Works, N.Y.	45.00
Case, Cigarette, Map Of Indiana, Nickel Plated	10.00
Centerpiece, Half Melon–Form, Coiled Handles, J. Hoffmann, 11 1/2 In.	880.00
Cherub, Curved Architectural Ornament, 11 1/2 In.	185.00
Cherub, Red Onyx Base, 4 7/8 In.	195.00
Cigar Cutter, Pocket	37.50
Cigar Cutter, Watch Fob, Figural, Boy Riding Sled	75.00
Cocktail Set, Chase, 10 Piece	95.00
Coffeepot, 3 In.	65.00
Coffeepot, Copper, Hand Wrought, 12 In.	150.00
Compote, Gilded, Stork Finials, 7 3/4 In., Pair	230.00
Cribbage Board, Rectangular, Pierced Top, Sides, 19th Century, 10 In.	445.00
Crucifix, Russian Orthodox, Pre–Revolutionary	100.00
Cuspidor, White Enameled Insert	22.50
Dish, Alms, Adam & Eve, Serpent, Tree, Dutch, 18th Century, 19 3/4 In.	1210.00
Door Knocker, Bear, 4 In.	75.00

Door Knocker, Parrot	45.00
Doorknob, Victorian, Fancy, Solid, Pair	33.00
Doorstop, Indian, 12 1/2 In.	85.00
Doorstop, Rampant Lion, Wooden Base, 13 In.	85.00
Etagere, Polished, Lacquered, 4 Onyx Shelves, 43 1/2 In.	275.00
Ewer, Inverted Conical Form, Hinged Lid, Geometric Handle, 11 In.	77.00
Figurine, Classical Woman Seated On Stool, Marked Jeancout	225.00
Figurine, Female Nude, Astride Rearing Horse, Hagenauer Wien, 9 In.	1540.00
Figurine, Persian Warrior, Rearing Horse, Gold, Silver Gilding, 11 In.	450.00
Figurine, Wolfhound, Hagenauer, Impressed Mark, 14 In.	2200.00
Flowerpot, Large	35.00
Fork, Toasting, Brass, Cast Brass Figural	16.50
Frame, Repousse Florals, Round, 1860s, 7–In. Diam.	25.00
Girandole Set, Bigelo Chapel, Marble, 1848, W. F. Shaw, 3 Piece	1500.00
Grave Marker, Fireman's, Unused	35.00
Hall Tree, 75 1/2 In.	175.00
Incense Burner, Japanese Pagoda, 1930s	25.00
Kettle, Apple Butter	50.00
Kettle, Iron Bail Handle, 5 1/2 In.	45.00
Key Holder, Scroll, Public School, Nebraska	40.00
Knife, Fork & Spoon Set, Child's, Fancy Brass	7.50
Lantern, Auto, Ruby Bull's–Eye, 12 1/2 In.	99.00
Letter Rack, Tower Of London	20.00
Magazine Rack, Nude With Whippet On Leash, 16 x 12 In.	375.00
Mirror, Milliner's, Oval, Brass Adjustable Stand, France, 36 In.	440.00
Mirror, Shaving	110.00
Mitten Warmer, Coat Of Arms, Cambridge University, 9 In.	25.00
Pail, Dated 1865, Large	125.00
Pail, Spun, Ansonia Brass Co., Patent 1866	150.00
Pedestal, Tooled, Marbelized Base, 41 In.	275.00
Pipe Tamp, Figural, Napoleon, Early 19th Century	135.00
Plant Stand, Ornate Art Nouveau Design, 31 1/2 In.	125.00
Planter, Raised Floral Design, Demon Mask & Ring Handles, 8 x 11 In.	247.00
Post Office Box Door, Combination Lock, Hinged, 11 x 6 1/4 In.	12.00
Punch Set, Embossed Flowers & Leaves, With 10 Double Wall Goblets	50.00
Samovar, Russia, 22 In.	195.00
Sconce, Candle, Hands Holding Sockets, 10 In., Pair	900.00
Sconce, Wall, Electric Candles, Ornate, 34 1/2 In., Pair	390.00
Shoehorn, Curved Ram's Horn Curl Handle, 18th Century, 9 In.	250.00
Stirrup, Coronado Brass	85.00
Table, Black Marble Top, Iron, 21 1/4 In.	195.00
Table, Green Marble Top, 21 1/2 In.	350.00
Table, Tilt Top, Handmade, 6 1/4 In.	25.00
Tankard, Strap Handle, 6 1/4 In.	45.00
Tea Cart, Smoked Glass Shelves, 19 x 33 In.	35.00
Teakettle, Iron Floor Stand, Burner, 48 In.	50.00
Teakettle, Swivel Handle, 9 In.	75.00

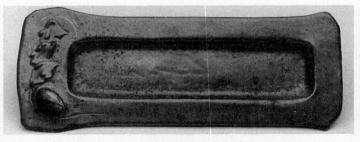

Brass, Tray, Enamel Inset, Rokesly, Cleveland, 13 x 4 1/2 In.

Teakettle, Wooden Handle, Iron Trivet, 4 In.	100.00
Teapot, Pivoted Handle, Jan Eisenloffel, c.1903	220.00
Teapot, Pumpkin Shape, China	300.00
Telescope, Adie, Stand, 19th Century	885.00
Thimble Case, Nutshell, Hinged, Ernest Steiner Originals, 2 x 1 In.	22.00
Tray, Enamel Inset, Rokesly, Cleveland, 13 x 4 1/2 In. ....*Illus*	450.00
Tray, Scrolling Repousse, Interior Figures, Dutch, Round, 25 In.	45.00
Umbrella Stand, Raised Figures, Animal Design, Paw Feet, 26 In.	65.00
Vase, Oviform, Everted Rim, Hammered, Jean Dunand, 1914, 12 In.	2860.00
Vase, Spun, Oriental, 5 5/8 In., Pair	10.00
Wall Pocket, Pair Of Slippers, Early 1900s	25.00
Water Font, Cross, Enameled, Onyx, France, Large	500.00
Weight Set, Nesting, 6 Piece	75.00

BRASTOFF, see Sascha Brastoff category

BREAD PLATE, see various silver categories, porcelain factories, and pressed glass patterns

BRIDE'S BASKETS OR BRIDE'S BOWLS were usually one–of–a–kind novelties made in American and European glass factories. They were especially popular about 1880 when the decorated basket was often given as a wedding gift. Cut glass baskets were popular after 1890. All bride's baskets lost favor about 1905.

BRIDE'S BASKET, Art Glass, Resilvered Holder, Czechoslovakia	145.00
Enameled Floral, Yellow Cased, Silver Plated Frame, 10 In.	260.00
Glass, Yellow, Enameled Flowers, Crown Milano, 8 In.	880.00
Pink Overlay, Piecrust Rim, Gold Bands, Silver Plated Frame	235.00
BRIDE'S BOWL, Amber, Silver Plated Frame	200.00
Amethyst To White, Molded Drape, 6 1/2 In.	60.00
Portrait Center, Enameled, English, 12 In.	465.00
Purple Overlay, Silver Plated Basket, 8 1/2 x 12 1/4 In.	295.00
White Florals, Pleated Rim, Satin Glass, Green, 10 3/4 In.	250.00
White Flowers, Green Leaves, Silver Plated Frame, 10 In.	225.00

BRISTOL glass was made in Bristol, England, after the 1700s. The Bristol glass most often seen today is a Victorian, lightweight opaque glass that is often blue. Some of the glass was decorated with enamels.

Biscuit Jar, Birds & Foliage, Plated Rim, Handle & Lid, 7 1/2 In.	195.00
Biscuit Jar, Life–Size Birds On Branches, Cream Color	280.00
Biscuit Jar, Strawberry Finial, Birds & Foliage, 7 1/2 In.	195.00
Bottle, Blue, White & Gold Design, 7 In.	65.00
Decanter, White Frosted, Gold Floral	135.00
Finger Bowl, Azure Blue, 3 1/4 In.	40.00
Jam Jar, Floral Design, Plated Frame & Lid, White	85.00
Mug, Blown Glass, Handle, Cobalt Blue, 4 1/8 In.	45.00
Mustard, Plated Hinged Top, Leaves, Enameled Daisy, 3 1/8 In.	40.00
Sugar Shaker, Slant Sides, Blue Flowers, Leaves, Pink, 6 1/4 In.	65.00
Toothpick, Buffalo Head	200.00
Tumble–Up, Aqua	75.00
Vase, Blue Trim, Snake, White, 11 1/2 In.	75.00
Vase, Coach & Horses Medallion, Scrolls, 14 In.	140.00
Vase, Crimped Rim, Gold Floral, Pink, White & Blue, 10 In.	75.00
Vase, Enameled Flowers, 11 In.	70.00
Vase, Enameled Lilies, England, 14 1/2 In., Pair	360.00
Vase, Enameled Lily Style Flower, England, Yellow–Green, 14 1/4 In.	360.00
Vase, Enameled, Ruffled, 2 Handles, 12 In.	85.00
Vase, Flowers, Blue, 4 In.	20.00
Vase, Fuchsia Interior, Mauve, 8 1/2 In.	145.00
Vase, Gleaner, 11 In.	90.00
Vase, Raised Pink Floral, Bulbous Base, Cream Color, 13 In.	165.00
Vase, Witch Ball Cover, Cobalt Blue, 12 In.	300.00

BRITANNIA, see Pewter category

Bronze, Bust, A. Drury,
Age of Innocence, 14 1/2 In.

Bronze, Bust, Villanis,
Woman, Draped Shawl, 20 In.

Bronze, Figurine, Yoshimara,
Crouching Tiger, 27 In.

BRONZE is an alloy of copper, tin, and other metals. It is used to make figurines, lamps, and other decorative objects.

Bowl, Carl Sorensen, 12 1/2 In.	125.00
Box, C. Korschann, Adam & Eve On Lid, Foliate & Fruit Banding, 5 In.	550.00
Box, Christofle, Domical Lid, Single Blossom In Gilt, c.1925, 3 In.	880.00
Box, Cigarette, Art Deco Golfer Front, Silver Crest	130.00
Box, Ring, Miniature Portrait On Ivory On Lid, 3 x 2 1/2 In.	247.00
Bust, A. Drury, Age Of Innocence, 14 1/2 In. ....*Illus*	2500.00
Bust, Caracalla, Breast Plate, Parcel Gilt, Marble Base, 17 3/4 In.	5775.00
Bust, Carpeaux, Fisher Boy, Brown Patina, 19 1/2 In.	3025.00
Bust, E. Villanis, Girl, 23 In.	4950.00
Bust, Fare, Marble Base, Dated 1859, Large	1500.00
Bust, Longfellow, White Marble Plinth, 18 1/2 In.	325.00
Bust, Nicholas I, 19th Century, 10 1/2 In.	770.00
Bust, Shakespeare, Rose Marble Plinth, 19 1/4 In.	475.00
Bust, Villanis, Woman, Draped Shawl, 20 In. ....*Illus*	1980.00
Bust, Woman, White Onyx Base, 7 In.	315.00
Candleholder, Floral Pattern, 7 1/2 In.	45.00
Candleholder, Holly & Berry, Signed	150.00
Candlestick, Korschann, Woman, Holding 2 Candleholders, 16 1/8 In.	3350.00
Censer, Foo Dog, Elephant Head Handles, Champleve, 1890, 15 In.	495.00
Chandelier, 9 Lights, Winged Cherub Heads, 42 In.	1600.00
Desk Set, Enameled Medallion, Metal Arts Co., 3 Piece	250.00
Figurine, A. Carrier, Maiden Strewing Flowers, 26 3/4 In.	2500.00
Figurine, Alliott, Maiden, 14 In.	595.00
Figurine, Angel, Trumpet, Laurel Wreath, Sphere At Base, 33 In.	3500.00
Figurine, Anton Hanak, Nude Woman, Rocky Base, c.1916, 31 3/4 In.	1100.00
Figurine, Arson, Four Dogs Burrowing, 8 In.	1650.00
Figurine, August Moreau, Venus Disarming Cupid, 34 1/2 In.	4950.00
Figurine, Austrian, Erotic Seated Nude Woman, Wine Glass, 3 3/8 In.	450.00
Figurine, Balton, Lion, Arrow In Side, 1880s	1750.00
Figurine, Bareau, Call To Arms, Black Marble Base, 21 3/4 In.	4500.00
Figurine, Barrias, Joan–of–Arc, Gilt & Silvered, Ivory, 20 1/4 In.	3300.00
Figurine, Barye, Elk, Small	650.00
Figurine, Barye, Horse, Signed, Small	450.00
Figurine, Barye, Panther Attacking Stag, 13 In.	2750.00

◆◆◆

Don't store alcoholic beverages or perfume in silver. It will cause damage.

◆◆◆

Figurine, Barye, Walking Lion, 9 In. 4800.00
Figurine, Bayre, Walking Lion, Green Patina 2500.00
Figurine, Berman, Peacock, Pair 800.00
Figurine, Bissi, Nude Woman, Art Deco 980.00
Figurine, Boccacio, Devaulx, 1860, 12 In. 770.00
Figurine, C. Valton, Reclining Lioness, 19 1/2 In. 1325.00
Figurine, Camel, Wooden Base, Oriental, 7 1/2 In. 325.00
Figurine, Cartier, Panther On Rock, 15 3/4 In. 2095.00
Figurine, Chaplin, Dog On Hind Legs, 9 1/2 In. 990.00
Figurine, Charles Valton, Picador, Brown Patina, 21 1/2 In. 2750.00
Figurine, Chiparus, Dancer, Ivory Body, c.1925, 16 3/4 In. 5500.00
Figurine, Chiparus, Isadora Duncan, 14 1/2 x 18 In. 6000.00
Figurine, Chiparus, Young Maiden, Ivory Arms & Legs, 9 5/8 In. 4675.00
Figurine, Colinet, Knight, Standing, Ivory Face & Hands, 26 1/4 In. 8525.00
Figurine, Cotton Picker, With Basket, Painted, Cast Metal 577.00
Figurine, Crouching Venus, Bronze & Wood Socle, France, 6 3/8 In. 2750.00
Figurine, Dancer With Cymbals, Nude, c.1925, 19 1/2 In. 1650.00
Figurine, Dancing Man, Monkey, Oriental, 17 3/8 In. 150.00
Figurine, Diego, Standing Cat With Bowl, 11 1/4 In. 1430.00
Figurine, Draped Maiden, Pixie Wings, Pedestal, 18 In. 900.00
Figurine, Draped Maiden, Scroll, Pedestal, 19 In. 275.00
Figurine, Draped Maiden, Strewing Flowers, Cherub, 26 3/4 In. 2500.00
Figurine, Dubucand, Racing Greyhound, 6 In. 550.00
Figurine, E. Maulin, Semi-Nude Female, 40 In. 3300.00
Figurine, Elephant, Ivory Tusk, Wooden Base, 20 In. 375.00
Figurine, Equestrian, 10 1/2 In. 325.00
Figurine, Erte, Woman, Flowing Robe, Sky Blue, 18 In. 3300.00
Figurine, Eugene Lanceray, Bugler, 15 1/4 In. 4200.00
Figurine, F. Picard, St. George & Dragon, 4 Ft. 3 In. 4675.00
Figurine, Falconnet, Pair Of Cherubs 1800.00
Figurine, Fawn, Garden, 35 1/2 In., Pair 9350.00
Figurine, Francois Pompom, Dove, Marked, c.1920, 10 1/4 In. 2420.00
Figurine, Franz Bergman Foundry, Eagle, Rootwood Base, 11 In. 1540.00
Figurine, Fratin, Ape Shaving A Bear, 7 1/4 In. 2750.00
Figurine, Fratin, Bull, 16 In. 1650.00
Figurine, Fratin, Literary Bear, 6 5/8 In. 3300.00
Figurine, G. R. Etling, Turbaned Woman, Holding Marble Ball, 26 In. 1540.00
Figurine, Garden, Nude Bather, Placing Cap On Head, 1890s, 32 In. 6875.00
Figurine, Gerdago, Dancer, Ivory, Geometric Cold Painted, Signed 3916.00
Figurine, Guillemard, Dancer, Ivory Face & Hands, c.1925, 18 In. 5500.00
Figurine, Hagenauer, Elephant, On Hind Legs, Nickel Finish, 5 In. 330.00
Figurine, Hagenauer, Horse's Head, 8 3/4 In. 990.00
Figurine, Hagenauer, Javelin Thrower, Nickel Finish, 11 1/2 In. 935.00
Figurine, Horse, Rearing, Djkarta, Java, 25 x 23 In. 395.00
Figurine, Howes, Peasant Couple On Working Horse, 15 In. 1540.00
Figurine, Huzel, Woman, Grecian Attire, Smelling Flower, 1860, 11 In. 850.00
Figurine, Italy, Bacchanalian Putto, Playing Trumpet, 5 In. 4675.00
Figurine, J. R. Jensen, Buffalos Locking Horns, 12 x 29 In. 5775.00
Figurine, Jack Bryant, Goin' Down The Trail 7800.00
Figurine, Jules Moignierz, Group Of Four Rams, 10 x 15 In. 1540.00
Figurine, Kauba, Indian Child On Mule, 13 In. 2475.00
Figurine, Lorenzl, Dancer, Bat Wing Cape, Ivory Head, 10 1/2 In. 3750.00
Figurine, Louis Emile Cana, Sandpiper, Black Marble Vase, 7 In. 550.00
Figurine, M. L. Beguine, Reclining Nude, 1928, 17 x 12 1/2 In. 1650.00
Figurine, Madonna & Child, Marked D. S. R. 255.00
Figurine, Marshall Fredricks, Neck Shot 8800.00
Figurine, Mathurin Moreau, Maiden, Square Pedestal Base, 11 In. 385.00
Figurine, McKimoy, Ethel Barrymore, Roman Bronze Works, 24 In. 2500.00
Figurine, Mene, Deer, 4 1/2 In. 550.00
Figurine, Mene, Pointer & Setter, Light Brown Patina, 5 1/2 In. 1650.00
Figurine, Metz Castleberry, Authority 1100.00
Figurine, Metz Castleberry, Fury From The Sky 9200.00
Figurine, Metz Castleberry, Great Plains Provider 4200.00

Figurine, Moigniez, Pointer & Partridge, 12 In. 1000.00
Figurine, Moreau, Love Letter, 26 In. 3300.00
Figurine, Musashi, Samurai Warrior, Wooden Stand, 18 In. 900.00
Figurine, Neptune, Red Onyx Base, 22 1/2 In. 850.00
Figurine, P. Tereszczuk, Carmen, Signed, Pedestal, 9 1/2 In. 700.00
Figurine, Paillet, Stallion, 6 In. 880.00
Figurine, Preiss, Girl Standing, Holding Hoop Behind, Marble Base 2772.00
Figurine, Preiss, Sonny Boy, Hands In Pockets, Marble Striated Base 2772.00
Figurine, Psyche, Black Onyx Base, 18 1/2 In. 1525.00
Figurine, Putto, Scythe, Sheaf Of Wheat, 19th Century, 10 1/2 In. 910.00
Figurine, Rearing Horse, Trainer, Two–Tone Bright Gold, 22 In. 500.00
Figurine, Rene–Paul Marquet, Nude Figures, Back To Back, 1925, 15 In. 2530.00
Figurine, Robert Summers, I'm Frank Hammer 6500.00
Figurine, Romain De Tirtoff, Egyptian Queen, 1990, 19 In. 3960.00
Figurine, Rudolf Marcuse, Dancing Flapper, 11 1/2 In. 3250.00
Figurine, Schmidtcassel, Exotic Dancer, Ivory Head, Hands, 9 3/4 In. 3125.00
Figurine, Seated Official, Ming Dynasty, Wooden Stand, 10 3/16 In. 385.00
Figurine, Seikoku, Elephant, Ivory Tusks, 1880s, 14 In. 605.00
Figurine, Sportsman, Binoculars, Riding Crop, Cap, Boots, 2 3/4 In. 175.00
Figurine, Stag, Fire Insurance, Hand Painted, 1935 .... 75.00
Figurine, T. Campaiola, Rape Of Persephone, 48 In. 6050.00
Figurine, T. D Gurande, Hoop Dance With Faun, c.1925, 27 1/4 In. 880.00
Figurine, Titze, Dancing Girl With Tambourine, Marble Plinth, 17 In. 2500.00
Figurine, Trodoux, Cock Pheasant, 5 1/2 In. 660.00
Figurine, Troika, Driver & 2 Riders, Malachite Base, Russia 1300.00
Figurine, Venus De Milo, Embossed Seal, 33 1/4 In. 500.00
Figurine, Victor Szczeblewski, Mousse Siffleur, 17 In. 825.00
Figurine, Vienna, Boy Vendor, Roasting Chestnuts, 6 1/2 In. 285.00
Figurine, Vienna, Bulldog, Enameled, 2 1/2 In. 200.00
Figurine, Villanis, Slave Girl, Draped Gown, Chains, 33 1/2 In. 7150.00
Figurine, Watrin, Maiden, Standing, Ivory Face, Arms & Feet, 15 In. 1325.00
Figurine, Winged Putto, Holding Sea Horse, Stone Pedestal, 57 In. 3410.00
Figurine, Woman, With Hat, 18th–Century Dress, Art Nouveau, 30 In. 1540.00
Figurine, Workman With Ladle, 28 1/2 In. 650.00
Figurine, Wreber, Dog, Laying, Dated 1920, Pair 5500.00
Figurine, Yoshimara, Crouching Tiger, 27 In. ....*Illus* 2090.00
Figurine, Young Woman, Books In Arms, Late To School, 16 In. 4000.00
Group, Barye, Mounted Indian, Stepped Plinth, 27 3/4 In. 3300.00
Group, Carabin, Woman, Perched On Grotesque Man's Head, 15 3/8 In. 3125.00
Group, Cormier, Nymph & Putto, Green Marble Base, France, 22 1/2 In. 5280.00
Group, Else Furst, Male & Female Nude, Brown Patina, 30 1/2 In. 1980.00
Group, Equestrian, Cossack, Sweetheart On Rocky Slope, Russia, 13 In. 2090.00
Group, Grachev, Troika, Man & Woman In Sled, 10 3/8 In. 1210.00
Group, Lanceray, Boy On Mule, With 2 Mules, 8 5/8 In. 2200.00
Group, Lanceray, Equestrian, Arm Outstretched With Sword, 21 In. 5775.00
Group, Lanceray, Equestrian, Mounted Warrior, Long Gun, 9 3/4 In. 1100.00
Group, Lanceray, Falconer, Bird On Shoulder, On Horse, 18 1/4 In. 3850.00
Group, Torokin, 2 Mounted Cossacks, Across The Field, 20 3/4 In. 2200.00
Group, Tourgueneff, Equestrian, Mounted Officer, 24 In. 2650.00
Group, V. Grachev, Old Woman With Cane, Feeding Fish, 6 1/2 In. 1875.00
Jardiniere, Dragon, Footed, Dark, Patina, 9 3/4 In. 320.00
Lamp, Gurschner, Nymph Holding Stem, Glass Panels, 1900, 17 1/2 In. 3300.00
Lamp, Maurice Bouval, 2–Light, Irises Form, Leafy Base, Pair 2956.00
Match Dispenser & Cigar Cutter, 1900 .... 650.00
Mortar, Gothic, Buttresses, Cylindrical Handles, Italy, 10 1/4 In. 5225.00
Pedestal, Square Top, Frieze Of Dolphins, Fluted Body, 46 1/2 In. 1760.00
Sundial, Dolphins Cast On Limestone Pedestal, 4 Ft. 1 In. 6050.00
Umbrella Stand, Dragons In Relief, Japanese, 19th Century, 24 In. 302.50
Urn, Lotus Flowers, Allover Cloud Design, Gargoyle Handles, 12 In. 350.00
Urn, Mounted Classical Heads & Chain Swags, Black Marble, 14 In. 715.00
Vase, Carl Sorensen, 7 3/4 In. 125.00
Vase, Champleve, Mythical Elephant Handles, China, 12 In. 395.00
Vase, Japan, Bird, Peony & Leaves, Silver, Copper & Brass, 16 3/4 In. 350.00

Vessel, Japanese Style, Blown–Out Fruit, France, c.1870 .... 1500.00

BROWNIES were first drawn in 1883 by Palmer Cox. They are characterized by large round eyes, downturned mouths, and skinny legs. Toys, books, dinnerware, and other objects were made with the Brownies as part of the design.

Book, Palmer Cox's Funny Animals, 1903 .... 18.00
Mold, Ice Cream, Pewter, 1900 .... 165.00
Needle Book, Palmer Cox, World's Fair, 1892 .... 35.00 To 50.00
Nodder, Glass Eyes, Papier–Mache, Palmer Cox 225.00
Paperweight, 3 Intaglio Cut Figures, Palmer Cox, 3 In. 135.00
Plate, Brownies Around Rim & Center, Palmer Cox, 8 1/2 In. 65.00
Plate, Playing Gold, Palmer Cox 40.00
Ruler, Palmer Cox, Advertising, 12 In. 35.00
Saltshaker, Dancing With Baby 1 Side, Fan On Other 85.00

BRUSH Pottery was started in 1925. George Brush first worked in 1901 in Zanesville, Ohio. He started his own pottery in 1907, but it burned to the ground and he joined McCoy in 1909. After a series of name changes, the company became The Brush Pottery. It closed in 1982. Collectors favor the figural cookie jars made by this company.

Cookie Jar, 3 Bears .... 100.00 To 125.00
Cookie Jar, Bear, Feet Together, Brown 185.00
Cookie Jar, Cinderella's Pumpkin Coach .... 130.00 To 150.00
Cookie Jar, Clown Bust .... 300.00 To 385.00
Cookie Jar, Clown, Brown Pants 175.00
Cookie Jar, Cookie House 80.00
Cookie Jar, Cow, Brown, Cat Finial 125.00
Cookie Jar, Donkey With Cart .... 185.00 To 250.00
Cookie Jar, Elephant With Ice Cream Cone .... 195.00 To 500.00
Cookie Jar, Formal Pig, Black Coat 195.00
Cookie Jar, Formal Pig, Yellow Coat 250.00
Cookie Jar, Granny 270.00
Cookie Jar, Happy Bunny, Gray .... 280.00 To 380.00
Cookie Jar, Happy Bunny, White 155.00
Cookie Jar, Hen, White 25.00
Cookie Jar, Humpty Dumpty, With Beanie .... 135.00 To 170.00
Cookie Jar, Lantern 95.00
Cookie Jar, Little Red Riding Hood 375.00
Cookie Jar, Old Woman's Shoe ....97.00 To 115.00
Cookie Jar, Owl 135.00
Cookie Jar, Panda Bear .... 135.00 To 210.00
Cookie Jar, Peter Pan 395.00
Cookie Jar, Peter Pumpkin Eater .... 185.00 To 300.00
Cookie Jar, Phonograph, Old Fashioned 50.00
Cookie Jar, Praying Girl 45.00
Cookie Jar, Praying Girl, Yellow 65.00
Cookie Jar, Puppy Police 750.00
Cookie Jar, Rabbit 175.00
Cookie Jar, Squirrel On Log .... 65.00 To 90.00
Cookie Jar, Squirrel, With Top Hat .... 150.00 To 275.00
Cookie Jar, Teddy Bear 90.00
Pitcher, Nurock Peacock, 9 In. 85.00
Planter, Mustard, Horizontal Rib, Rippled Rim, 10 x 4 In. 10.00
Planter, Window Box, Dusty Rose, Flared, 8 1/4 x 4 1/4 In. 9.00
Sign, Dealer, Metal 95.00
Wall Pocket, Dog, Boxer 40.00
Wall Pocket, Owl 125.00
Wall Pocket, Wise Bird, c.1927 .... 95.00

BRUSH McCOY, see McCoy category

BUCK ROGERS was the first American science fiction comic strip. It started in 1929 and continued until 1965. Buck has also appeared in comic books, movies, and, in the 1980s, a television series. Any memorabilia connected with the character Buck Rogers is collectible.

Badge, Chief Explorer	200.00
Badge, Solar Scout	100.00
Book, Pop–Up, 1934	130.00
Book, Pop–Up, Spider Ship, 1935	250.00 To 275.00
Button, Pinback, Celluloid	65.00
Button, Strange World Adventures Club, Pinback, 1939	1230.00
Communications Set, 25th Century, Remco	250.00
Figure, Twiki, Action	30.00
Gun, Rocket, 1934	80.00
Gun, Sonic Ray, Box	150.00 To 175.00
Lunch Box	35.00 To 40.00
Matchbook Cover, Buck Rogers 5 Cent Popsicle	15.00
Pistol, Disintegrator, Marx	125.00
Pop Pistol, Daisy, Pressed Tin, Breaks To Cock, 1930s, 10 In.	165.00
Ring, Saturn	450.00
Strato–Kite, Original Envelope	115.00
Toy, Spaceship, Windup	145.00
Toy, Venus Duo–Destroyer, Tootsietoy, 4 3/4 In.	78.00 To 120.00
Walkie–Talkie	200.00
Watch, Ingram, Pocket	600.00
Watch, Pocket	795.00

BUFFALO POTTERY was made in Buffalo, New York, after 1902. The company was established by the Larkin Company, famous manufacturers of soap. The wares are marked with a picture of a buffalo and the date of manufacture. Deldare ware is the most famous pottery made at the factory. It has khaki–colored or green background with hand painted transfer designs.

BUFFALO POTTERY DELDARE, Bowl, Ye Olden Days, 1908, 6 1/2 In.	395.00
Bowl, Ye Village Street, 1908, 9 In.	500.00
Bowl, Ye Village Tavern, 1909, 9 In.	450.00
Bowl, Ye Village Tavern, Signed, 1924, 9 1/2 In.	425.00
Cake Plate, Emerald, Dr. Syntax, 6 1/2 In.	750.00
Cake Plate, Ye Village Gossips, 1909, 11 1/4 In.	600.00
Candlestick, Signed, 9 In., Pair	450.00
Candlestick, Street Scene, 1909, 9 In., Pair	450.00
Candlestick, Village, Shield Back, 1909, 5 In.	650.00
Chop Plate, An Evening At Ye Lion Inn	500.00 To 595.00
Cup, Chocolate, Village Scene, Signed	400.00
Dish, Fern	700.00
Eggcup, Signed L. Winter	700.00
Fruit Bowl, Ye Village Tavern, 1924, 9 In.	450.00
Humidor, Ye Lion Inn	595.00 To 650.00
Hunt Cup, 8 Figures, Green Ground, 2 1/8 In.	340.00
Mug, Breaking Cover	225.00
Mug, Fallowfield Hunt, Breaking Cover, 3 1/2 In.	400.00
Mug, Ye Lion Inn, 1908, 4 1/4 In.	250.00 To 325.00
Pitcher, Emerald, Dr. Syntax Bound To Tree, 8 In.	1700.00
Pitcher, Fallowfield Hunt, 6 In.	425.00 To 435.00
Pitcher, Fallowfield Hunt, Return, 8 In.	550.00 To 725.00
Pitcher, Robin Hood, Stag On Rear, c.1906, 8 In.	550.00
Pitcher, Spare An Old Broken Soldier	420.00 To 550.00
Pitcher, This Amazed Me, 9 In.	700.00
Pitcher, This Amazed Me, Octagonal, 9 In.	625.00 To 675.00
Plaque, An Evening At Ye Lion Inn, 14 In.	675.00
Plaque, Breakfast At Three Pigeons, 12 In.	595.00
Plaque, Emerald, Friday, Friars Eat Fish, 12 In.	2400.00
Plaque, Emerald, Thursday Friars Fish, 1914, 12 In.	2400.00

Plaque, Fallowfield Hunt, Breakfast, 12 In. 625.00
Plaque, Fallowfield Hunt, Start, 14 In. 695.00
Plate, Breakfast At Three Pigeons, 1908, 12 In. 300.00
Plate, Breaking Cover, Fallowfield Hunt, 10 In. 240.00
Plate, Calendar, 1910 .... 1700.00
Plate, Dr. Syntax Makes A Discovery, 10 In. 600.00
Plate, Dr. Syntax Robbed Of Property, 1911 .... 295.00
Plate, Emerald, Dr. Syntax Sell's Grizzle 1350.00
Plate, Emerald, Dr. Syntax Star Gazing, 1911 .... 1350.00
Plate, Emerald, The Garden Trio, 1911, 16 1/2 In. 1350.00
Plate, Fallowfield Hunt, 1908, 9 1/4 In. 145.00
Plate, Garden Trio, Green, 9 1/4 In. 600.00
Plate, Roosevelt Teddy Bear Scenes, 10 1/4 In. 485.00
Plate, The Gunner, 8 In. 60.00
Plate, Town Crier, 8 In. 135.00
Plate, Ye Village Gossips, 1909, 10 In. 145.00
Plate, Ye Village Street, 1924, 7 1/2 In. 125.00
Platter, Heirlooms, 10 1/2 x 13 1/2 In. 595.00
Salt & Pepper, Emerald, Geometric, Floral 1450.00
Sugar & Creamer, Ye Lion Inn 450.00
Sugar & Creamer, Ye Olden Days 350.00
Tea Set, Village Life In Ye Olden Days, 9 Piece 900.00
Tea Set, Village Life In Ye Olden Days, 11 Piece 650.00
Teapot, Scenes Of Village Life, 5 3/4 In. 445.00
Teapot, Village Life, Olden Days, Signed, 5 3/4 In. 410.00
Teapot, Ye Lion Inn 495.00
Tray, Card, Dr. Syntax Robbed Of Property, 1911 .... 450.00
Tray, Card, Fallowfield Hunt, 1909 .... 375.00 To 550.00
Tray, Dresser, Dancing The Minuet 275.00
Tray, Dresser, Heirlooms 700.00
Tray, Pin, Ye Olden Days, 6 x 3 1/2 In. ....75.00 To 185.00
Tray, Rural Sports, 1911, 12 x 9 1/4 In. 1050.00
Vase, Emerald, Dragonflies, Iris, Lilies, 1911, 8 In. 1950.00
Vase, Emerald, Outdoor Scene, 1911, 13 1/2 In. 1700.00
BUFFALO POTTERY, Box, Powder, Art Nouveau, Cover 950.00
Cup Plate, Wanamaker Store Jubilee Year, 1861-1911 .... 110.00
Inkwell Tray, 2 Children Playing With Bunny, 9 x 6 In. 3950.00
Matchbox Holder, Emerald, Trees, Lake, Mountain, 1911 .... 1700.00
Mug, FOB, Orioles, 1913 .... 50.00
Pitcher, George Washington, 1907 .... 600.00
Pitcher, Gloriana, Teal Green, 1908 .... 495.00
Pitcher, Gunner 450.00
Pitcher, Robin Hood, 1906 .... 370.00 To 495.00
Pitcher, Roosevelt Bears, 1907, 8 In. 950.00
Plaque, Dr. Syntax, Sketching The Lake, 12 In. 1350.00
Plate, Christmas, 1950 .... 50.00
Plate, Christmas, 1951 .... 50.00
Plate, Faneuil Hall, Blue, 10 In. 45.00
Plate, Faneuil Hall, Green Scalloped Rim, 7 1/2 In. 30.00
Plate, Independence Hall, 10 In. 45.00
Plate, Mt. Vernon, Blue & White 35.00
Plate, Niagara Falls, Blue & Green, 10 In. 45.00
Plate, U.S. Capitol, 10 In. 45.00
Plate, White House, 10 In. 45.00
Plate, World's Tallest Smokestack, Great Falls, Mont. 38.00
Teapot, Argyle, Blue & White, With Tea Ball 150.00
Teapot, Attached Metal Infuser, Blue Floral 45.00
Toothpick, Blue Willow 40.00
Vase, Green Geranium On Blue Half Moon 295.00
Wash Set, Cabbage Rose, 7 Piece 575.00

BURMESE GLASS was developed by Frederick Shirley at the Mt. Washington Glass Works in New Bedford, Massachusetts, in 1885. It is a two–toned glass, shading from peach to yellow. Some pieces have a pattern mold design. A few Burmese pieces were decorated with pictures or applied glass flowers of colored Burmese glass. Other factories made similar glass also called *Burmese*. Related items may be listed in the Gunderson category and under Webb Burmese.

Bowl, Design, Silver Plated Holder, 8 In., Pair	4000.00
Bowl, Melon Ribbed, 8–Pointed Star Rim, Mt. Washington, 4 1/2 In.	295.00
Bowl, Tricornered, Turned Up Sides, 6 In.	145.00
Celery Vase, Glossy Finish, Mt. Washington, 11 In., Pair	1200.00
Creamer, Square Mouth, Mums, Yellow Handle, Mt. Washington, 4 3/4 In	650.00
Creamer, Yellow Handle, Yellow & Brown Mums, Mt. Washington	650.00
Cruet, Melon Ribbed Body, Mt. Washington, 6 1/2 In.	1065.00
Cruet, Vinegar, Ribbed, Yellow Applied Handle, Mt. Washington, 6 In.	795.00
Epergne, Silver Plated Tray, 4 Rose Bowls, 3 Bud Vases, 8 In.	495.00
Ewer, Glossy, Mt. Washington, 2 1/2 In.	275.00
Ewer, Mt. Washington, 10 x 8 1/2 In.	335.00
Jam Jar, Hinged Lid, Pansy Design, Mt. Washington	395.00
Jar, Cover, Peach, Yellow Cover & Handles, 6 1/2 In.	440.00
Lamp, Camels, Mt. Washington ....*Illus*	2900.00
Lamp, Fairy, Clarke Insert, Reversible	795.00
Lemonade Set, Egyptian Style, Square Handle, Mt. Washington, 5 Piece	715.00
Mustard, Coral & White Blossoms, Mt. Washington, 3 1/4 In.	385.00
Pitcher, Amber Rigaree Band, 9 In.	700.00
Pitcher, White & Orchid, Frosted Handle, Mt. Washington, 9 In.	575.00
Punch Cup, Yellow Ring Handle, Mt. Washington, 3 4/5 In.	395.00
Rose Bowl, Acid Finish	130.00
Rose Bowl, Floral Transfer, Fruit, White To Pink, 3 In.	285.00
Rose Bowl, Floral, Fruit, White, Pink, Scalloped Top, 3 In.	285.00
Salt & Pepper, Mt. Washington, Pairpoint Holder .... 500.00 To	595.00
Sugar & Creamer, Fish Scale, Gold Enamel Ivy Vine, Signed	485.00
Sugar & Creamer, Natural Applied Handle, Mt. Washington, 3 3/4 In.	750.00
Toothpick, Blue Flowers & Garlands	325.00
Tumbler, Pink To Yellow, Mt. Washington, 3 7/8 In.	225.00
Tumbler, Yellow Roses, Mt. Washington, 3 3/4 In.	565.00
Vase, Berry Pontil, Egg Shape, Shiny, 7 In.	100.00
Vase, Brushed Gold Rim, Coralene, Mt. Washington, 7 1/2 In.	1500.00
Vase, Ivy Leaves, Melon Ribbed, Flared Top, 3 3/4 In.	480.00
Vase, Leaves, Globular, Long Neck, Mt. Washington, 1885, 8 In.	1000.00
Vase, Lily, 3–Petaled, Mt. Washington, 23 In.	985.00
Vase, Lily, Forget–Me–Nots, Stripes, Mt. Washington, 8 In.	1285.00
Vase, Rust Berries, Green Leaves, 8 3/8 In.	850.00
Vase, Song Auld Lang Syne, Grapes & Leaves, Mt. Washington, 8 In.	3450.00
Vase, Trumpet Form, Peach Shading To Yellow, 9 In., Pair	165.00
Vase, Trumpet Form, Ruffled, Yellow, 12 1/2 In., Pair	210.00

Burmese, Lamp. Camels, Mt. Washington

◆ ◆ ◆ ◆ ◆ ◆ ◆ ◆ ◆ ◆ ◆ ◆ ◆ ◆ ◆ ◆ ◆ ◆ ◆ ◆

Do not wash rhinestones with water. It will tarnish the foil background. Use a Q–tip or small, soft brush and glass cleaner. Do not hold the jewelry under running water. Rub dry with a soft cloth.

◆ ◆ ◆ ◆ ◆ ◆ ◆ ◆ ◆ ◆ ◆ ◆ ◆ ◆ ◆ ◆ ◆ ◆ ◆ ◆

Butter Chip, Gray Flowers, Red
Vines, 2 1/2 x 2 1/2 In.

◆ ◆ ◆ ◆ ◆ ◆ ◆ ◆ ◆ ◆ ◆ ◆ ◆ ◆ ◆ ◆ ◆ ◆ ◆ ◆

Dental wax (ask your ortho-
dontist about it) is a good
adhesive to keep figurines on
shelves, or lids on teapots.

◆ ◆ ◆ ◆ ◆ ◆ ◆ ◆ ◆ ◆ ◆ ◆ ◆ ◆ ◆ ◆ ◆ ◆ ◆ ◆

Vase, Tulip, Flared, White, Pink, Scalloped, 4 Inn. 165.00

BUSTER BROWN, the comic strip, first appeared in color in 1902. Buster
and his dog Tige remained a popular comic and soon became even more
famous as the emblem for a shoe company, a textile firm, and others. The
strip was discontinued in 1920, but some of the advertising is still in use.

Ball & Jacks	38.00
Bank, Buster Brown & Tige, Cast Iron	195.00
Bank, Cast Iron, Gold Repaint	140.00
Bench, Graphics Of Tige & Buster, 1930s	1200.00
Book, Comic, 1908	55.00
Book, My Resolutions, Outcault, 1906	60.00
Box, Sock, Boy's, Buster Brown & Tige	90.00
Button, Blue Ribbon Shoes, Pin Back	16.00
Button, Pinback, Celluloid, Color, 1 1/2 In.	32.00
Candy Jar, Cover, Kendall Oil Co., Graphics	65.00
Card, Playing	28.00
Cereal Set, 3 Piece	100.00
Chandelier, Store, Tige, Bakelite	350.00
Clock, Buster Brown Shoes	650.00
Coloring Book	25.00
Cup, Buster Brown & Tige, China	42.50
Fan	85.00
Knife, Pocket	45.00
Mannequin	150.00
Marbles, Bag	25.00
Mask, Advertising, 1915	20.00
Mirror, Full Figure Of Buster & Tige, Pocket	550.00
Mirror, Hand, Brass	30.00
Periscope .... 15.00 To 25.00
Pitcher, 3 1/4 In.	20.00
Postcard, Buster Brown & Tige, 1906	15.00
Poster, Movie, Buster Brown, Tiger Oak Frame, c.1908 ...	650.00
Ring, Face .... 15.00 To 30.00
Shoe Tree, Wrapper, Pair	37.50
Spinning Top	21.00
Whistle, Police Style, Metal	35.00
Wristwatch, Ingersoll, Buster Brown Shoes, 1930s .... 225.00 To 300.00

BUTTER CHIPS, or butter pats, were small individual dishes for butter.
They were in the height of fashion from 1880 to 1910. Earlier as well as
later examples are known.

Flow Blue, Alaska .... 35.00 To 38.00
Flow Blue, Daisy, Maddox	18.00
Flow Blue, Gainsborough	32.00
Flow Blue, Leon	25.00
Flow Blue, Lorne, Grindley	27.00

Flow Blue, Manhattan, Alcock	28.00
Flow Blue, Marechal Niel, Grindley	30.00
Flow Blue, Marie, Grindley	30.00
Flow Blue, Nonpareil	36.00
Flow Blue, Richmond, Meakin	32.00 To 36.00
Gray Flowers, Red Vines, 2 1/2 x 2 1/2 In. ....*Illus*	10.00

BUTTER MOLDS are listed in the Kitchen category under Mold, Butter.

BUTTONS have been known throughout the centuries, and there are millions of styles. Gold, silver, or precious stones were used for the best buttons, but most were made of natural materials, like bone or shell, or from inexpensive metals. Only a few types are listed for comparison.

Building Theme, On Card, 25 Piece	578.00
Conductor's, Trolley Car, Charleston, South Carolina, c.1905, 8 Piece	16.00
Figures, On Card, Satsuma, 6 Piece	1320.00
Hook, Metal, 3 1/2 In.	3.50
Kabuki, Fat Happy Man	75.00
Kachina, Indian, Silver, 4 Piece	30.00
Kaleidoscope, Tray, 63 Piece	413.00
Lapel, Starrett Tools	12.00
Millefiori, Gooderham	35.00
Mottled Brown Bakelite, Buckle, Set Of 6	8.00
Painted Porcelain, Animal Head, Gold Frame, Fitted Case, 11 Piece	825.00
Peacock Eye, On Card, 42 Piece	187.00
Snow White & Dwarfs, 3 1/2 In., 8 Piece	40.00
Victorian, Cupid, Pair	15.00
Victorian, Man & Women, Pair	20.00

BUTTONHOOKS have been a popular collectible in England for many years but only recently have gained the attention of American collectors. The buttonhooks were made to help fasten the many buttons of the old-fashioned high-button shoes and other items of apparel.

Fargo's Ladies Boots	35.00
Sterling Silver Handle	25.00

CALENDARS made to hang on the wall or to be displayed on a desk top have been popular since the last quarter of the nineteenth century. Many were printed with advertising as part of the artwork and were given away as premiums. Calendars with guns, gunpowder, or Coca-Cola advertising are most prized.

1863, Atlantic Savings Bank, Pocket	9.00
1889, Hoyt Perfume	20.00
1890, Horsford's Bread Preparation, Children	59.00
1890, Ivory Soap	125.00
1891, Baltimore American Newspaper, Folds, 28 x 20 In.	65.00
1892, Hood's Sarsaparilla	100.00
1893, Adams Pepsin, Tutti Frutti Gum	35.00
1893, Sing Sing Prison, With Book	50.00
1895, Columbian Fruit Gum	200.00
1895, Youth Companion	12.00
1898, Forget-Me-Not	100.00
1898, Prudential Insurance Co.	75.00
1899, Armour's Army & Navy, Chromolithograph	75.00
1899, Metropolitan Life Ins., 8 Children, Frame, 12 x 20 In.	85.00
1899, Royal Life & Fire Insurance	25.00
1899, Winchester Repeating Arms, Hunting Scene	625.00
1902, Dreamy Eyes, Armstrong, 6 x 10 In.	45.00
1903, Beautiful Children	20.00
1903, Grand Union, Pretty Girl, Roses, 12 1/2 x 28 1/2 In.	150.00
1903, Melotte Cream Separators, Frame, 18 x 23 In.	65.00
1905, Maud Humphrey, 4 Pages	225.00
1907, Deering Harvesting Machines	140.00

1908, Birds, Theo Van Hoytenna, Lithographs, 18 3/4 x 8 In. 1100.00
1908, Buffalo Bill, Top Only, Colorful, Framed, 12 x 14 In. 125.00
1908, Carrier's Greetings, Milwaukee Daily News, 13 In. 12.00
1908, Great Composers 25.00
1908, Listera's Animal Bone Fertilizer, Lithograph 95.00
1908, Orpheum Dramatic Stock Co., Actors, Actresses, 3 Part 85.00
1909, Harrington & Richardson Arms 350.00
1909, Hood's Sarsaparilla 25.00
1910, Prudential 35.00
1910, Schlitz, Lithographed, Beautiful Woman, Roll–Up 295.00
1911, Bristol, Firecracker Mortar, Dupont Fireworks Label 55.00
1911, Hood's Medicines, Original Envelope 38.00
1913, Ceresota Flour, Girl With Flour Bag 85.00
1913, Continental Fire Ins., Co., Remember The Alamo 40.00
1913, Diamond Dye Girl, Woman Picture, Barrick 6 x 12 In. 40.00
1913, Keller Jewelers & Opticians, Forest Scene, 7 x 12 In. 14.00
1913, Waysaglass Needle Pocket 8.00
1914, Continental Fire Insurance 50.00
1915, Portland Atlas Cement, Boy Fishing, 11 x 14 In. 14.00
1918, Firestone Cycle Tires 50.00
1919, Woodrow Wilson 10.00
1920, Chevrolet, Complete Pad, Frame 160.00
1920, Deno Auto Co., S. Kaukauna, Wis., Girl, Pedal Car, 14 In. 50.00
1920, New Year's Eve, Armstrong, 8 x 10 In. 50.00
1921, Green Bay Hardware Co., Mt. Shasta, 15 x 10 In. 14.00
1923, Blotter, Grace Drayton Illustration 24.00
1924, American Book Co., Imp. Inventions In Am. History 8.00
1924, Hercules, Color, Lithograph, 29 In. 94.00
1924, McCormick, Full Pad, France, 12 x 24 In. 47.00
1924, Wrigley's P. K. 15.00
1925, G. W. Herrington's Drug Store, Pretty Lady, 8 x 14 In. 15.00
1925, Joannes Bros. Wholesale Jobbers, Pretty Woman, 23 In. 22.00
1925, Waterfall, Tony Renzil, Shoeshine & Hat Cleaning 50.00
1926, McCormick–Deering, Woman Eating Cherry 65.00
1926, Merry Christmas, Sam Martowitz Groceries, 15 x 9 In. 50.00
1926, Orange Crush, Oak Frame 550.00
1927, Hercules, Color, Lithograph, 29 In. 110.00
1927, Nehi, Color Lithograph, 20 In. 11.00
1928, Shell Oil Co. 85.00
1929, Bob Keppel, Groceries, Meats, Woman Holding Roses 50.00
1929, City Tailor & Barber Shop, Cowboy Picture, 11 3/4 In. 25.00
1929, Farm Equip. Co., Minn. Binders–DeLaval, 10 x 16 In. 40.00
1930, DeLaval Separator Co., Story Of John & Mary 150.00
1930, Gerlach–Barlow Co. Art Deluxe, A. Hiebel, 21 x 46 In. 95.00
1930, Watkins Since 1868, Modern Princess, 7 1/2 x 12 In. 17.00
1932, Birds In Trees, Berstein Clothier, Cory, Pa. 50.00
1932, Foote & David Co., Street, Cars Passing By 15.00
1932, Great Northern Plains Indians, Artist Reiss 30.00
1932, Waterfall & Fountain, T. A. Paver, 16 x 22 In. 50.00
1934, Harvard University, Photogravures, 10 x 13 In., 12 Pc. 75.00
1934, Jewel Tea Co. 45.00
1937, Norman Dairy, Millbury, Ma., 7 1/2 x 10 In. 30.00
1937, Sweet Caporal, Woman's Picture, Round, 10 x 11 In. 39.00
1938, A Tribute To The Dog, Desk, 5 x 6 In. 8.00
1938, Kellogg Lumber Co., Wisc., Weather Forecasts, 19 In. 4.00
1938, Pulaski Flour & Feed Mill, Chas. Adams, 10 x 17 In. 12.00
1939, Early Autumn, Parrish, Large 400.00
1939, Nat'L Mutual Benefit Legal Reserve Life Ins., 20 In. 15.00
1939, Portrait, DeVorss, Color, 12 x 17 In. 25.00
1939, Raleigh's Good Health Products, 9 3/4 x 13 1/4 In. 8.00
1939, Schauble Gen. Mdse., Dreams Come True, 13 x 18 In. 14.00
1940, Dionne Quintuplets, School Days 15.00
1940, Gamble Store Agency, Little Girl, 12 x 18 1/2 In. 24.00

1940, Moonlight Nymph, L. Patten, Bathing Beauty, 20 x 46 In. 30.00
1941, Maid In Baltimore, Earl Moran, 16 x 33 In. 49.00
1941, Pepsi–Cola 175.00
1941, Royal Crown Cola 95.00
1941, West End Brewery, Full Pad 45.00
1942, Hudson's Bay Company, 30 x 18 In. 36.00
1942, Stanhope Smith, Pinup Girl 30.00
1942, Sweet As You Are, Pearl Crush, 10 x 17 1/2 In. 10.00
1943, Hercules Powder, Soldier & Dog, 30 1/2 x 13 In. 110.00
1944, Maas & Steffens 175.00
1945, Double Cola 95.00
1945, Girl On A Swing, Roy Best 22.00
1945, Western Airlines, With Indians 195.00
1946, Art Deco, Pinup 10.00
1947, Audubon 35.00
1947, Royal Crown, Complete 65.00
1947, W. & L. E. Gurley, Telescopic Solar Transit 20.00
1948, Esquire Glamour Gallery, Various Artists, 8 x 24 In. 17.00
1948, Keen Kutter 25.00
1949, Blue Flash Girl, Rolf Armstrong, 16 x 33 In. 19.00
1949, Catch On, Elvgren, 11 x 23 In. 24.00
1949, Texaco, Petromobilia, 13 x 9 In. 30.00
1950, Artist's Sketch Pad, Freeman Elliott, 9 x 14 In. 24.00
1950, I'm Yours, Armstrong, 8 x 11 In. 45.00
1950, MacPherson Pinup, 9 x 12 In., 12 Sheets 19.00
1951, Dr Pepper, 3 Pages, 20 x 12 In. 32.00
1951, Nude Photos, 12 x 13 In. 10.00
1952, Elvgren Pinup, 12 Sheets, 8 x 13 In. 19.00
1954, KIK Cola, Full Pad, 16 x 33 In. .... 39.00 To 42.00
1954, Marilyn Monroe, Miss January, Sketches, T. N. Thompson 60.00
1955, Marilyn Monroe, On Red Velvet, Sales Sample, Story 45.00
1955, Studio Sketches, Pinups, Thompson, 8 x 13 In. 25.00
1956, KIK Cola, Colorful, Full Pad, 26 x 13 In. .... 39.00 To 42.00
1958, Evelyn West, Nude, 10 x 15 In. 30.00
1958, Playboy, In Sleeve 75.00
1960, Jane Mansfield, Bowman Products, 6 Different Pictures 100.00
1961, Union Pacific R.R. 7.00
1964, Joe Blostien & Son Ltd., Unused, 12 x 12 In. 2.00
1964, Joe Blostien & Son Ltd., Unused, 12 x 18 In. 5.00
1964, Playboy 15.00
1966, Playboy 25.00
1967, Seagram's, Outdoor 10.00
1967, Squirt 125.00
1968, Golden Enchantment, Blond Nude Photo, 10 x 16 In. 19.00
1969, Hummel 15.00
1977, Hummel 10.00
1978, Star Wars 35.00
1985, Hummel 7.00
1986, Steiff, In Wrapper 10.00
1990, McDonald's, Japan 20.00

CALENDAR PLATES were very popular in the United States from 1906 to 1929. Since then, plates have been made every year. A calendar and the name of a store, a picture of flowers, a girl, or a scene were featured on the plate.

1908, Crossed Flags, Gold Border, 7 1/2 In. 28.00
1908, Flower Center, 8 1/2 In. 35.00
1908, Pink Rose Border, 8 In. 29.00
1908, Victorian Woman, Flowered Hat, Snyder, Oklahoma 30.00
1908, Woman, Detroit, Michigan 50.00
1909, Green Border, Bird Carrying 1909 Ribbon, 8 In. 35.00
1909, Holly & Berries, Maroon Calendar, Christmas, 7 1/2 In. 15.00
1909, Horse 22.00

1909, James H. Corcoran, Ardock, N. D., 7 1/4 In. 37.50
1909, Lake, Mountains, Green & Gold Border, 8 In. 35.00
1909, Peick's Pharmacy, Edgewood, Iowa 40.00
1909, Rose Center, Advertising 55.00
1909, Water Lilies, Mercerburg, Penna. 45.00
1910, 4 Seasons, Children, Christmas, 9 In. 15.00
1910, Gibson Girl, Dressed In Blue, 8 1/2 In. 40.00
1910, Good Luck, Prospector, Wishbone Arch, 8 In. 30.00
1910, Lighthouse, Boats In Center, 8 In. 35.00
1910, Pope Gosser, Lighthouse 30.00
1910, Sailboats & Dock, Flowers, Gold Edge, 8 In. 40.00
1910, Tiny Pink Roses Border, 9 In. 15.00
1911, Blond Haired Girl, Green Hat, Gold Calendar, 7 In. 30.00
1911, Lavender Border, Yellow & Red Carnations, 7 In. 25.00
1911, Springdale Dairy, Cokeburg, Penna. 35.00
1912, Indian Maiden, 8 1/4 In. 50.00
1912, Lincoln & 2 Other Presidents, Our Martyrs 45.00
1912, Lincoln, Drink Bonnie Rye 55.00
1912, Owl, Augusta, Illinois 35.00
1912, Sunset, Double Calendar, 8 In. 12.00
1912, Woman On Lily Pad, Cherubs Around Edge, 9 1/4 In. 50.00
1913, Airplane, 8 1/4 In. 350.00
1913, Barefoot Boy, Tattered Overalls, 7 In. 38.00
1913, William Soloman, Hartford, Conn., 9 1/2 In. 45.00
1914, Betsy Ross, Norfolk, Virginia .... 25.00 To 45.00
1914, Mt. Vernon 25.00
1916, Man In Canoe, 7 1/4 In. 30.00
1917, Flags, Tan Calendar, Brown School Building, 9 In. 40.00
1918, Birds, Calendar Border, Flag Center, 8 In. 40.00
1920, Flags, 8 1/4 In. 35.00
1920, Great War, Harriston, Virginia 45.00
1920, Mountain Scene, 8 1/4 In. 35.00
1920, Peace Plate, Flags, Doves, 9 In. 35.00
1921, Grapes Center, Bluebird Border, 9 In. 60.00
1921, Grouse, Rusk, Michigan 20.00
1922, Dog Flushing Out Birds, 8 1/4 In. 45.00
1924, Dog Flushing Bird, 9 In. 23.00
1924, Green & Lavender Calendars, Fruit Bottom, 9 In. 55.00
1967, White, Gold Trim, Sheffield 30.00
1970, Frankoma, Box 15.00
1977, Rutherford, N. J. Railroad Station 10.00
1978, Wedgwood 15.00
1984, Johnny Appleseed, State Farm Insurance 85.00

CAMARK POTTERY started in 1924 in Camden, Arkansas. Jack Carnes founded the firm and made many types of glazes and wares. The company was bought by Mary Daniel. Production was halted in 1983.

Basket, No. 138, Green 10.00
Cup & Saucer, Demitasse, 8 Sets 75.00
Ewer, Golden Brown, 6 In. 65.00
Figurine, Cat, Sticker, 12 x 14 In. 55.00
Vase, Green, 4 In. 8.00
Wall Pocket, Pitcher & Bowl, White 18.00

CAMBRIDGE GLASS Company was founded in 1901 in Cambridge, Ohio. The company closed in 1954, reopened briefly, and closed again in 1958. The firm made all types of glass. Their early wares included heavy pressed glass with the mark *Near Cut.* Later wares included Crown Tuscan, etched stemware, and clear and colored glass. The firm used a C in a triangle mark after 1920. Some Cambridge patterns may be included in the Depression Glass section.

Achilles, Champagne, Cut 20.00
Adonis, Champagne 22.00

Adonis, Cocktail	24.00
Adonis, Goblet	24.00
Alpine, Caprice, Bonbon, 2 Handles, Square, 6 In.	28.00
Alpine, Caprice, Bonbon, Footed	22.00
Apple Blossom, Candlestick, Amber, Keyhole, Pair	45.00
Apple Blossom, Candy Dish, Cover, Footed	110.00
Apple Blossom, Candy Dish, Cover, Footed, Pink	125.00
Apple Blossom, Champagne, Yellow	12.00
Apple Blossom, Cup & Saucer	28.00
Apple Blossom, Cup & Saucer, Yellow	20.00
Apple Blossom, Pitcher, Yellow	195.00
Apple Blossom, Sugar & Creamer	42.00
Apple Blossom, Sugar & Creamer, Footed, Yellow	45.00
Apple Blossom, Water Set, 7 Piece	225.00
Apple Blossom, Wine, Yellow	25.00
Ball Shaped, Cordial Set, Amber, 4 Shot Glasses	35.00
Bashful Charlotte, Flower Frog, 6 In.	68.00
Bashful Charlotte, Flower Frog, 8 1/2 In.	70.00
Bashful Charlotte, Flower Frog, Green, 13 1/2 In.	235.00
Blue Jay, Flower Frog	75.00
Calla Lily, Console Set, 3 Piece	110.00
Candlelight, Celery, 12 In.	75.00
Caprice, Ashtray, Amber	10.00
Caprice, Ashtray, Blue	10.00
Caprice, Bonbon, Footed, Blue, 6 In.	30.00
Caprice, Bonbon, Square Handle, Blue, 6 In.	32.00
Caprice, Bowl, 4-Footed, 10 1/2 In.	30.00
Caprice, Bowl, Footed, Oval, 11 In.	30.00
Caprice, Bowl, Footed, Pink, 11 1/2 In.	35.00
Caprice, Bowl, Handles, Blue, 12 In.	65.00
Caprice, Bowl, Oval, 11 In.	25.00
Caprice, Candlestick, 1-Light, Prisms, Blue	110.00
Caprice, Candlestick, 3-Light, Crystal	22.00
Caprice, Candlestick, Triple Cascade, Blue	125.00
Caprice, Cocktail	15.00
Caprice, Compote, Footed, Blue, 7 In.	60.00
Caprice, Creamer, Cone, Blue	18.00
Caprice, Creamer, Pistachio	40.00
Caprice, Cruet, Individual	18.00
Caprice, Cup & Saucer	12.00
Caprice, Cup & Saucer, Blue	45.00
Caprice, Decanter Set, Tray, Pink, 8 Piece	650.00
Caprice, Decanter, Stopper, Farber Ware Holder	165.00
Caprice, Dish, Footed, Blue, 13 1/2 In.	65.00
Caprice, Goblet, Blue, 9 Oz.	45.00
Caprice, Mayonnaise Set, Blue, 2 Piece	60.00
Caprice, Oyster Cocktail	15.00
Caprice, Pitcher, Juice, Blue	225.00
Caprice, Plate, Footed, Blue, 14 In.	95.00
Caprice, Plate, Scalloped Rim, 4-Footed, 14 In.	85.00
Caprice, Relish, 3 Sections, Blue, 8 In.	45.00
Caprice, Sugar & Creamer, Tray, Individual	35.00
Caprice, Tumbler, 5 Oz.	16.00
Caprice, Vase, Amber, 5 1/2 In.	60.00
Caprice, Water Set, Blue, 80 Oz., 7 Piece	325.00
Carmen, Basket, Crystal Handle, 11 In.	85.00
Carnation, Relish, 5 Sections	40.00
Cascade, Candy Dish, Cover, Green	50.00
Cascade, Plate, 6 1/2 In.	8.00
Cascade, Sherbet	10.00
Cascade, Sugar & Creamer	16.00
Cascade, Tumbler, 5 Oz.	10.00
Cascade, Tumbler, 12 Oz.	14.00

Chantilly, Champagne 18.00
Chantilly, Cocktail .... 16.00 To 20.00
Chantilly, Cordial, 1 Oz. .... 30.00 To 32.00
Chantilly, Goblet .... 20.00 To 27.00
Chantilly, Goblet, Pair 22.00
Chantilly, Lamp, Hurricane, Complete 100.00
Chantilly, Pitcher, Martini, Sterling Base, 32 Oz. 295.00
Chantilly, Salt & Pepper, Flat, Sterling Lids 28.00
Chantilly, Sherbet 15.00
Chantilly, Sugar & Creamer 25.00
Cherub, Candlestick, Figural, Green 300.00
Cleo, Plate, Dinner, Green, 9 1/2 In. 20.00
Cleo, Vase, Fan, Green, 6 In. 65.00
Colonial, Creamer, Cobalt Blue 40.00
Colonial, Toothpick 20.00
Crown Tuscan, Bowl, 3–Footed, 10 In. 85.00
Crown Tuscan, Bowl, Flying Nude 195.00
Crown Tuscan, Bowl, Shell, 7 1/4 In. 30.00
Crown Tuscan, Bowl, Shell, 10 In. 50.00
Crown Tuscan, Box, Cigarette, Seashell Cover 60.00
Crown Tuscan, Candlestick, Nude Stem, Lift–Off Prisms, Pink 150.00
Crown Tuscan, Candy Dish, Cover, Floral Design, 8 In. 85.00
Crown Tuscan, Cocktail, Stem, Mandarin Gold Bowl 100.00
Crown Tuscan, Compote, 7 In. 65.00
Crown Tuscan, Compote, Gold Trim, 2 Handles, 6 1/2 In. 25.00
Crown Tuscan, Compote, Pink, Footed, Handles, 2 Sections, 5 1 .... 38.00
Crown Tuscan, Compote, Shell, 8 In. 125.00
Crown Tuscan, Compote, Shell, Flying Nude 350.00
Crown Tuscan, Plate, Gold Shell, 14 In. 45.00
Crown Tuscan, Plate, Shell, 7 In. 25.00
Crown Tuscan, Swan, 3 In. 32.00
Crown Tuscan, Vase, Shell Feet, 8 1/2 In. 75.00
Daffodil, Goblet, Low Stem, 9 Oz. 25.00
Decagon, Basket, 2 Handles, 7 In. 22.00
Decagon, Bonbon, Pink 30.00
Decagon, Cup & Saucer, Emerald 15.00
Decagon, Plate, Emerald, 7 1/2 In. 10.00
Decagon, Sugar & Creamer, Blue 45.00
Decagon, Sugar & Creamer, Tray, Green 44.00
Diane, Ashtray, Cobalt Blue 85.00
Diane, Ashtray, Yellow 65.00
Diane, Bowl, Flowers, Footed, Yellow, 12 In. 45.00
Diane, Candy Dish, Cover, Crystal 85.00
Diane, Cocktail 16.00
Diane, Cocktail, 3 Oz. 20.00
Diane, Compote, 5 3/8 In. 50.00
Diane, Decanter, Amber, 35 Oz. 35.00
Diane, Goblet .... 15.00 To 25.00
Diane, Ice Tube, Pink 325.00
Diane, Plate, 6 In. 8.00
Diane, Relish, 3 Sections, Footed, 12 1/4 In. 35.00
Diane, Sherbet .... 13.00 To 15.00
Diane, Tumbler, Footed, 5 Oz. 20.00
Diane, Tumbler, Footed, 12 Oz. .... 15.00 To 20.00
Diane, Wine 30.00
Draped Lady, Flower Frog, 13 1/2 In. 150.00
Draped Lady, Flower Frog, Dark Amber, 8 1/2 In. 175.00
Draped Lady, Flower Frog, Green, 8 1/2 In. .... 140.00 To 185.00
Draped Lady, Flower Frog, Green, 13 1/2 In. 240.00
Draped Lady, Flower Frog, Pink, 13 1/2 In. 250.00
Draped Lady, Flower Frog, Yellow, 8 1/2 In. 275.00
Eagle, Bookends .... 65.00 To 140.00
Elaine, Candy Dish, Ram's–Head Cover, Gold Encrusted 150.00

Elaine, Dish, 3 Sections	28.00
Elaine, Goblet, Gold Etched	26.00
Elaine, Urn, Cover, 10 In.	175.00
Everglade, Bowl, Tulip	50.00
Everglade, Vase, 6 In.	40.00
Everglade, Vase, Willow Blue, 6 In.	125.00
Flower Frog, Mandolin Lady, Bent Back, Green, 9 1/2 In.	410.00
Flower Frog, Rose Lady, Amber	220.00
Flower Frog, Rose Lady, High Base, Crystal, 9 3/4 In.	220.00
Gadroon, Cup	12.50
Georgian, Sherbet, Topaz	12.00
Georgian, Tumbler, Amethyst, 9 Oz.	15.00
Georgian, Tumbler, Gold Trim, 2 1/2 Oz.	12.00
Gloria, Bonbon, 2 Handles, Green	35.00
Gloria, Candelabrum, Emerald	40.00
Gold Krystol, Cup & Saucer	15.00
Gold Krystol, Plate, 8 3/8 In.	11.00
Heirloom, Bowl, Amber, 9 In.	30.00
Helio, Basket, 5 1/2 In.	55.00
Heron, Flower Frog, 12 In.	95.00
Honeycomb, Compote, Amber, 7 In.	25.00
Jefferson, Sherbet, Emerald, 6 Oz., 6 Piece	40.00 To 70.00
Krystol, Goblet, Gold–Encrusted Gloria Etch	100.00
Krystol, Sherbet, Gold Trim, 6 Oz., 6 Piece	70.00
Laurel Wreath, Bowl, 10 In.	70.00
Laurel Wreath, Candlestick, Pair	55.00
Lorna, Vase, Footed, Yellow, 7 In.	25.00
Lucia, Box, Cigarette	40.00
Lucia, Celery, 5 Sections, 10 In.	35.00
Lynbrook, Cocktail	10.00
Magnolia, Vase, Footed, 11 In.	60.00
Mandarin Gold, Cake Stand, Label, 13 In.	50.00
Martha, Sugar & Creamer	30.00
Montrose, Bell	60.00
Mt. Vernon, Bowl, Fruit, Royal Blue, 4 1/2 In.	15.00
Mt. Vernon, Box, Dresser, Cover, 4 1/2 In.	27.50
Mt. Vernon, Compote, Amber, 7 1/2 In.	35.00
Mt. Vernon, Console, Amber, 40 Oz.	50.00
Mt. Vernon, Cordial, Footed, 1 Oz.	15.00
Mt. Vernon, Decanter, Amber	40.00
Mt. Vernon, Finger Bowl, Underplate, Carmen	150.00
Mt. Vernon, Tumbler, Amber, 3 Oz.	15.00
Mt. Vernon, Tumbler, Carmen, 3 Oz.	20.00
Mt. Vernon, Tumbler, Footed, 10 Oz.	6.00
Mt. Vernon, Tumbler, Green, 3 Oz.	15.00 To 20.00
Mt. Vernon, Tumbler, Iced Tea, Footed, 12 Oz.	8.00
Mt. Vernon, Tumbler, Juice, Footed, 5 Oz.	6.00
Mt. Vernon, Vase, 7 In.	25.00
Mt. Vernon, Wine, 3 Oz.	7.00
Nautilus, Pitcher, Green	65.00
Nude Stem, Brandy Snifter, Carmen, 20 Oz.	43.00
Nude Stem, Brandy, Pistachio	120.00
Nude Stem, Candlestick, Forest Green, 9 In.	300.00
Nude Stem, Claret, Forest Green	80.00
Nude Stem, Cocktail, Amethyst	70.00
Nude Stem, Cocktail, Carmen, Frosted Base	110.00
Nude Stem, Cocktail, Royal Blue	100.00
Nude Stem, Compote, Cobalt	195.00
Nude Stem, Compote, Flared, Cobalt, 9 In.	145.00
Nude Stem, Compote, Hand Painted	195.00
Nude Stem, Compote, Shell, Large	100.00
Nude Stem, Goblet, Royal Blue	120.00
Nude Stem, Ivy Ball, Amethyst	140.00

Nude Stem, Ivy Ball, Carmen 195.00
Portia, Bell, Label 70.00
Portia, Compote, 5 1/2 In. 40.00
Portia, Cordial, 1 Oz. 39.50
Pristine, Candlestick, Ball, 2 3/4 In., Pair 30.00
Pristine, Cornucopia, Blossom Time Etch, 9 In. 100.00
Ram's Head, Candlestick, 9 1/2 In., Pair 300.00
Ram's Head, Candlestick, Moonlight Blue, Pair 100.00
Ram's Head, Console Set, Pink, 12 In. –Bowl, 6 1/2 In. –Stick 250.00
Regency, Goblet 25.00
Ribbon Candy, Sauce, Ruby Stain 32.50
Rondo, Plate, 7 1/2 In. 7.00
Rose Point, Bowl, Gold Encrusted, Footed, 11 1/2 In. 40.00
Rose Point, Candleholder, 2–Light, Etched, 6 In. 100.00
Rose Point, Candleholder, 2–Light, Keyhole 85.00
Rose Point, Candy Dish, 3 Sections 40.00
Rose Point, Candy Dish, Cover 175.00
Rose Point, Champagne .... 20.00 To 30.00
Rose Point, Compote, 5 In. 50.00
Rose Point, Compote, Etched, 5 1/2 In. 65.00
Rose Point, Cordial, Mushroom 75.00
Rose Point, Cup & Saucer .... 30.00 To 42.00
Rose Point, Decanter, Square 450.00
Rose Point, Goblet 35.00
Rose Point, Goblet, Gold Etched 37.00
Rose Point, Goblet, Water 27.50
Rose Point, Marmalade, Cover 120.00
Rose Point, Nut Cup, Footed, Individual 75.00
Rose Point, Plate, 8 1/2 In. 12.00
Rose Point, Plate, Domed Cover, 4 1/2 In. 450.00
Rose Point, Plate, Footed, 12 1/2 In. 60.00
Rose Point, Relish, 3 Sections, Handle, 12 In. .... 55.00 To 65.00
Rose Point, Relish, Amber, 8 In. 27.50
Rose Point, Sherbet, Tall 21.00
Rose Point, Sugar & Creamer 55.00
Rose Point, Tray, Gold Encrusted, 14 In. 60.00
Rose Point, Tumbler, 12 Oz. 55.00
Rose Point, Tumbler, Footed, 7 In., 6 Piece 180.00
Rose Point, Tumbler, Juice 52.00
Rose Point, Tumbler, Water, Footed 25.00
Rose Point, Vase, Globe, 5 In. 55.00
Rose Point, Vase, Gold Encrusted, 10 In. 100.00
Roselyn, Candy Box, Cover 69.50
Stradivari, Cordial, Mocha 40.00
Stradivari, Cordial, Moonlight Etch 45.00
Swan, Amber, 3 In. 95.00
Swan, Carmen, 3 In. 75.00
Swan, Emerald, 3 In. 35.00
Swan, Gold Krystol, 3 In. 40.00
Swan, Mandarin Gold, 3 In. 35.00
Swan, Peachblow, 3 In. 35.00
Swan, Royal Blue, 3 In. 140.00
Tally–Ho, Ice Bucket, Rose Point Etch 195.00
Tally–Ho, Vase, Hat, Cobalt Blue, 10 In. 225.00
Weatherford, Berry Bowl, Ivory 25.00
Wildflower, Basket, Gold Trim, 5 In. 35.00
Wildflower, Bowl, Rectangular, 8 x 9 In. 45.00
Wildflower, Candlestick 20.00
Wildflower, Cordial 50.00
Wildflower, Goblet, Water 20.00
Wildflower, Plate, 14 In. 55.00
Wildflower, Relish, 5 Sections, 12 1/2 x 10 1/2 In. 40.00
Windsor, Ashtray, Attached Cardholder, Blue 65.00

CAMBRIDGE POTTERY was made in Cambridge, Ohio, from about 1895 until World War I. The factory made brown glazed decorated art wares with a variety of marks, including an acorn, the name *Cambridge*, the name *Oakwood*, or the name *Terrhea*.

Vase, Collie Portrait	2000.00
Vase, Jonquil Flower, Brown, Signed, 9 In.	215.00

CAMEO GLASS was made in much the same manner as a cameo in jewelry. Parts of the top layer of glass were cut away to reveal a different colored glass beneath. The most famous cameo glass was made during the nineteenth century. Signed cameo glass pieces are listed under the glasswork's name, such as De Vez or Galle.

Bowl, Bulbous, Red Over Clear, Flowers, Leaves, Pantin, 7 In.	330.00
Carved White Flowers, Citron, Frosted, 3 5/8 x 2 3/4 In.	850.00
Egg, Cover, 3–Footed, Signed, Raspillar, 4 7/8 In.	950.00
Jam Jar, White Flowers, Blue, Notched Lid, England, 5 1/4 In.	1625.00
Perfume Bottle, Lay Down, Flowers, Russian Enamel Cap, England	6500.00
Perfume Bottle, Lay Down, Water Lilies, Dragonfly, England	3250.00
Powder Box, Cut Iris On Lid, Green & Gold Coloring, St. Louis	595.00
Rose Bowl, Diamond–Quilted, Wild Rose Blossoms, Buds, England	1650.00
Rose Bowl, Ivory, England, Miniature	595.00
Toothpick, Orange & Black Layers, Sunset Landscape, Weis	275.00
Vase, 2 Plants With Blossoms, Foliage, England, 2 1/2 In.	850.00
Vase, Baluster, Orange, Black, Landscape, Richard, 19 1/2 In.	1760.00
Vase, Baluster, Orange, Cut Chrysanthemums, Honesdale, 14 In.	1210.00
Vase, Brown & Yellow Scenic, J. Michel Paris, 10 1/4 In.	750.00
Vase, Brown Flowers, Orange Ground, D'Argyl, 9 1/2 In.	2300.00
Vase, Cut Collar, Apricot, White Flowers, England, 9 3/4 In.	2750.00
Vase, Diamond–Quilted, Apricot To Deep Apricot, Lining, 5 In.	3000.00
Vase, Florentine, Floral, 1 Cranberry, Other Sapphire, 8 In., Pr.	550.00
Vase, Mountain Scene View, Signed, La Rochere, 1980, 10 3/4 In.	500.00
Vase, Opaque White, Orange, Cut Blossoms, Pantin, 10 In.	275.00
Vase, Parrot On Tree Limb, Green Ground, Signed Gem, 3 1/4 In.	3250.00
Vase, Red, White Foliage, England, 6 In.	600.00
Vase, Robin's–Egg Blue, Prunus, Pendant Neck, 3 3/8 In.	950.00
Vase, Sailing Ship 1 Side, Lighthouse Other, Michel, 10 1/4 In.	1220.00
Vase, White Flowers On Yellow, English, 6 In.	895.00

CAMPAIGN memorabilia is listed in the Political category.

CAMPBELL KIDS were first used as part of an advertisement for the Campbell Soup Company in 1906. The kids were created by Grace Drayton, a popular illustrator of the day. The kids were used in magazine and newspaper ads until about 1951. They were presented again in 1966; and in 1983, they were redesigned with a slimmer, more contemporary appearance.

Bank, Cast Iron, 3 5/16 In.	285.00
Cookbook, Campbell Kids Chuck Wagon	15.00
Doll, Cloth, Pair	50.00
Doll, Composition	200.00
Doll, Indian, Horsman	450.00
Lunch Box	65.00
Mug, Soup, Plastic, Campbell Kid's Face	2.50
Ornament, Christmas Tree, 1980	15.00
Puppet, Hand, Vinyl, Blond, Chef's Hat, 1950s	80.00
Spoon, Silver Plated, International	15.00
Thermos	85.00

CAMPHOR GLASS is a cloudy white glass that has been blown or pressed. It was made by many factories in the Midwest during the mid–nineteenth century.

Bottle, Art Deco, Stopper, 10 1/2 In.	18.00

Candy Jar, Light Blue, Cover 45.00
Dish, Squirrel, Sitting With Nut In Paws, Scroll, France 75.00
Mug, Tennessee, 3 1/2 In. 45.00
Powder Jar, Rose, Kneeling Nude Base, Art Deco, 7 1/2 x 7 In. 85.00

CANDELABRUM refers to a candleholder with more than one arm to hold
many candles; a candlestick is designed to hold one candle. The
eccentricity of the English language makes the plural of candelabrum into
candelabra.

2–Light, Art Nouveau, Electric, Pair 60.00
2–Light, Iron, Handmade 60.00
2–Light, Putti Supporting Cornucopia, Gilt Bronze, 12 3/4 In. 2750.00
2–Light, Putto Supports, Pierced Base, Gilt Bronze, 17 In., Pr. 880.00
3–Light, Brass, Prisms, Circular Base, Low, Originally Electric 286.00
3–Light, Clear To Vaseline 30.00
3–Light, Figural, Empire Style, Russia, 19 In., Pair 1650.00
3–Light, White, Rudlor, Pair 75.00
3–Light, Winged Female Figure Holding Arms, 29 In. 4620.00
4–Light, Cherubs, Flowers, Gilded Brass, French, 18 1/2 In., Pr. 2500.00
5–Light, George V, Silver 5500.00
5–Light, Victorian, Ornate Silver Plate, VanBergh 150.00
6–Light, Napoleon III, Seated Seminude Female, 34 In. 2475.00
6–Light, Porcelain Body, Landscape, 4 Troupe Feet, 28 In., Pair 2860.00
7–Light, Brass, 18 In., Pair 100.00
10–Light, Winged Figure Holding 2 Cornucopia, Gilt, 40 1/2 In. 9900.00
16–Light, Leaf Tips, Foliate Branches, 5 Ft. 6 In., Pair 8800.00
Brass, 19 1/2 In., Pair 190.00
Cartier, Silver, 4 Piece 2200.00
Whiteware, 2 Porcelain Cups, Gold Trim, Lenox, Green Mark 85.00

CANDLESTICKS were made of brass, pewter, Sandwich glass, sterling
silver, plated silver, and all types of pottery and porcelain. The earliest
candlesticks, dating from the sixteenth century, held the candle on a
pricket (sharp pointed spike). These lost favor because in times of strife the
large church candlesticks with prickets became formidable weapons, so the
socket was mandated. Candlesticks changed in style through the centuries
and designs range from classic to rococo to Art Nouveau to Art Deco.

Brass, 1850, 9 1/2 In., Pair 235.00
Brass, Beehive, Push–Up, 12 In., Pair ....95.00 To 160.00
Brass, Blue & White Latticinio Swirl Cylinder Shade, 5 In. 345.00
Brass, Cherubs, Floral, Blue Enameled, 18 In., Pair 2500.00
Brass, Chippendale, George Grove, c.1770, 8 In., Pair 2310.00
Brass, Cupped Base, Dutch, 8 1/2 In., Pair 2200.00
Brass, Dished Bases, 5 1/4 In., Pair 400.00
Brass, Georgian, Foliate Drip Pan, 9 1/2 In., Pair 605.00
Brass, Jacobean Style, Drip Pan, Baluster, Turned, 18 In., Pair 275.00
Brass, Neoclassical, 7 3/4 In., Pair 150.00
Brass, Octagonal Base, France, 7 1/2 In. 60.00
Brass, On Petal Bases, England, 7 1/4 In., Pair 715.00
Brass, Peg Lamp, Brass Burner, 13 3/4 In. 60.00
Brass, Push–Up, 4 1/2 In. 55.00
Brass, Push–Up, Diamond–Quilted & Beehive, 7 5/8 In., Pair 110.00
Brass, Push–Up, Wedding Band, 8 In. 450.00
Brass, Queen Anne, Engraved, c.1710, 8 In., Pair 9900.00
Brass, Scalloped Base, 3 Hoof Footed, 8 1/2 In. 675.00
Brass, Scalloped Bobeche, Joseph Wood, c.1765, 7 3/4 In., Pair 1980.00
Brass, Serpentine Base, 4 In., Pair 90.00
Brass, Simple Tapered Stems, 9 1/4 In., Pair 50.00
Brass, Snakes, Pair 95.00
Brass, Spiral Twist Stem, 12 1/2 In., Pair 50.00
Brass, Square Base With Feet, Baluster Stem, 9 In. 225.00
Brass, Square Base, 6 In. 165.00
Brass, Tapered Stem, 9 1/4 In., Pair 50.00

Brass, Traces Of Gilding, Red Onyx Base, 23 In., Pair 150.00
Brass, Victorian, 10 3/4 In., Pair 150.00
Brass, Victorian, Push–Up, 9 3/4 In., Pair 130.00
Brass, Victorian, Push–Up, 10 1/4 In., Pair 140.00
Brass, Victorian, Push–Up, 11 In., Pair 150.00
Brass, Victorian, Push–Up, 12 1/4 In., Pair 300.00
Brass, Victorian, Push–Up, 7 7/8 In., Pair 80.00
Brass, Victorian, Push–Up, Beehive & Diamond, 7 1/2 In., Pair 190.00
Brass, Victorian, Push–Up, Marked, 11 3/8 In., Pair 260.00
Brass, Victorian, Push–Up, Square Base, 5 1/4 In. 90.00
Brass, With Snuffer, England, 1860 .... 650.00
Bronze, Figural, Standing Woman, Egyptian Revival, 15 In., Pair 660.00
Bronze, Silver Plated Crest, 12 In., Pair 225.00
Bronze, Tulip, Removable Drip Pan, Jarvie, 18 In., Pair 700.00
Carved & Painted Pricket, Italian Baroque, 2 Ft., Pair 7105.00
Charles X, Urn Nozzle, Palmettes, Floral Swags, 13 1/2 In., Pair 4400.00
Gilded Cast Metal, Red Onyx Base, France, 12 In. 35.00
Gilt Bronze Putto, Figural, Marble Base, Gas, 9 1/4 In. 525.00
Gilt Bronze, Louis Phillippe, Turkish Figure, 16 In., Pair 3575.00
Iron, Sticking Tommy, 11 1/4 In. 105.00
Peacock, Arts & Crafts, Pair 195.00
Pewter, European, 9 1/2 In., Pair 300.00
Pottery, Primitive, Incised Name Evelyn, 3 1/4 In. 20.00
Satin Glass, Green, Pair 55.00
Steel, Spiral Push–Up, Steel, 7 1/4 In. 200.00
Tin, Hog Scraper, 7 1/2 In. 130.00
Tin, Hog Scraper, Push–Up, 6 In. 140.00
Tin, Hog Scraper, Push–Up, 7 In. 300.00
Tin, Hog Scraper, Push–Up, 8 In. 90.00

CANDLEWICK items may be listed in the Imperial and Pressed Glass categories.

CANDY CONTAINERS have been popular since the late Victorian era. Collectors have long favored the glass containers; but now all types, including tin and papier-mache, are collected. Probably the earliest glass container sold commercially was the Liberty Bell made in 1876 for sale at the Centennial Exposition. Thousands of designs were made until the cost became too high in the 1960s. By the late 1970s, reproductions were being made and sold without the candy. Containers listed here are glass unless otherwise described.

Airplane, Passenger 325.00
Airplane, Red Plastic Wing 20.00
Airplane, Spirit Of Goodwill ....85.00 To 165.00
Airplane, Spirit Of St. Louis, Green, Candy 495.00
Alarm Clock, Face Has Gold Gilt Numbers 260.00
Ambulance 65.00
Angel, Felt, Italy, Box 125.00
Auto, Coupe With Long Hood 175.00
Auto, Coupe With Long Hood, Glass Wheels, 2 In. Wide 85.00
Auto, Electric Coupe 85.00
Auto, Limousine, Glass Wheels 125.00
Auto, Limousine, Sliding Tin Roof 22.00
Auto, Streamlined Touring Car 18.00
Auto, Tasseled Windows 175.00
Auto, West Spec. Co., Limousine, Original Wheels 175.00
Auto, Woody Station Wagon, Glass, Contents, 1950s, 2 x 5 In. 20.00
Baby Chick, Clear 80.00
Baby Jumbo 50.00
Baby, Wax Head, Glass Eyes, Cotton Clothes, 10 1/2 In. 375.00
Baby, Wax Head, Paper Bonnet, Sitting In Egg, 4 1/4 In. 195.00
Baby, Wrapped In Paper Blanket, Bonnet, Papier–Mache 175.00
Bank, J. S. Fry & Sons, Tin, 4 1/2 x 4 In. 165.00

Barney Google & Ball .... 285.00 To 350.00
Barrel 60.00
Baseball Player, With Bat, Clear 700.00
Baseball, Frosted Glass 40.00
Battleship .... 16.00 To 18.00
Battleship, Tin Snap 40.00
Bear On Circus Tub 300.00
Billy Club, Amber 105.00
Black Cat For Luck, Painted Glass, 4 1/4 In. 1540.00
Boat, Model Cruiser, Contents 25.00
Boot, Santa Claus Head, Japan 110.00
Box, Valentine, Heart Shape, 5 In. 42.00
Bureau, Painted .... 200.00 To 225.00
Bus 135.00
Bus, Greyhound 250.00
Camera, On Tripod .... 300.00 To 325.00
Candlestick, 2 Handles, Ruby Flashed, Souvenir 350.00
Candy Cane, Mercury Glass 20.00
Cannon, Rapid Fire Gun, Tin, West Bros. 225.00
Cannon, Two Wheel Mount No. 2 .... 360.00
Carpet Sweeper 160.00
Carpet Sweeper, Dolly Sweeper .... 350.00 To 550.00
Cash Register .... 450.00 To 495.00
Cat, Tongue Sticks Out, Bow At Top To Carry 225.00
Chick, Dress & Shoes, Head Moves, Papier–Mache 168.00
Chick, In Front Of Egg, Papier–Mache 45.00
Chick, In Shell Auto, Paint Trace 225.00
Chick, In Suit, Composition, Germany 145.00
Chicken, On Egg In Nest, 3 1/4 In. 25.00
Chicken, On Nest, Contents, Paper Closure 32.00
Chicken, Pull–Off Head, Composition, 3 7/8 In. 105.00
Children, Lithograph, Drawstring Top, Silk, c.1870 .... 150.00
Christmas Tree, Clear 50.00
Cigar, Amber 65.00
Clock, Alarm, Tin, Penny Toy 125.00
Clock, Lynne Clock Bank 500.00
Clock, Mantel, Closure 247.00
Clock, Mantelpaper Face 120.00
Clock, Milk Glass Lighthouse, Sailboat, Souvenir 200.00
Clown 10.00
Derby, Suede–Like, Oval Hat Box, Brown Derby Restaurant 125.00
Dirigible, Los Angeles .... 225.00 To 235.00
Dog 33.00
Dog, Beagle, Nodder Head, Brown, White, Papier–Mache 140.00
Dog, Bulldog .... 60.00 To 95.00
Dog, By Barrel, 8 1/2 In. .... 100.00 To 185.00
Dog, In Window, J. G. Crosetti, 1940s, 5 1/2 In. 8.50
Dog, Mutt, Head Turned, 3 3/4 In. 55.00
Dog, Scotty, Head Up 30.00
Dog, Scotty, Tin Closure, 2 1/2 In. 4.00
Dog, With High Hat, Contents, 1939 .... 15.00
Dog, With Umbrella 27.00
Doll's Nurser 15.00
Dolly's Milk Bottle, Embossed 45.00
Don't Park Here, Marked U.S. A., Two Dots .... 125.00 To 200.00
Donkey Card, Painted Glass 22.00
Duck, Dressed, Papier–Mache, Germany 58.00
Duck, Nodder, Painted Composition, 6 In. 22.00
Duck, Ugly Duckling, Orange Bill 150.00
Duckling 90.00
Egg, Metal 10.00
Elelphant, G. O. P. .... 150.00 To 315.00
Elephant, With Howdah 85.00

Fat Boy, On Drum 250.00
Father Christmas 500.00
Father Christmas, Rabbit Skin Beard, Pushing Sack Of Toys 935.00
Fire Engine, Fire Dept. No. 99 .... 100.00
Fire Engine, Paper Base 65.00
Fire Truck, Ladder Truck 35.00
Firecracker, 5 1/2 In. 45.00
Football 40.00
Gas Pump, 23 Cents Today Both Sides, Painted .... 300.00 To 425.00
George Washington In Boat, Papier-Mache, Germany 145.00
Ghost Head, Flannel Shroud, Papier-Mache, 3 1/2 In. 135.00
Girl, Celluloid Face, Composition Hands & Feet, 5 In. 11.00
Girl, On Stump, Branch, Bisque Head, Painted Eyes, 6 1/2 In. 675.00
Girl, Playing Horn, Bisque Head & Limbs, Germany, 10 In. 750.00
Girl, Wax Head, Glass Eyes, Long Coat, Hat, 7 1/2 In. 250.00
Girl, With 2 Geese 30.00
Goblin Head 325.00
Golf Club 70.00
Guitar, Dresden 140.00
Gun, Cambridge Automatic 225.00
Gun, Colt 35.00
Gun, Indian Head Revolver 50.00
Gun, Revolver, Amber 10.00
Gun, Shoots The Candy, 1950s, 2 1/2 x 3 In. 10.00
Happy Fats On Drum 175.00
Hat, Military, 1 3/8 In. 10.00
Hat, Uncle Sam, Black Brim 35.00
Hat, With Tin Brim, Glass 85.00
Heart Shape, Harrison Fisher, Tin 50.00
Hen On Nest 40.00
Horn, 3 Valve 250.00
Horn, Striped Tube 95.00
Horse & Wagon, Glass 35.00
Horsehead, 6 In. 35.00
Iron, Electric, Original Cord & Plug 50.00
Iron, Tin 35.00
Jack-O'-Lantern, Pop Eyed, Painted 575.00
Jack-O'-Lantern, Slanted Eyes, Painted .... 125.00 To 185.00
Jackie Coogan .... 1200.00 To 1400.00
Kettle, Leather Handle 10.00
Kewpie 28.00
Keystone Kop On Chick, Composition, Germany 185.00
Kiddie Kar 225.00
Lamp, Candlestick Base 475.00
Lamp, George Washington, No Shade 100.00
Lamp, Inside Ribbed Base 165.00
Lamp, Kerosene, Original Box 45.00
Lantern, Barn Type No. 1, Ruby Flashed, Souvenir 90.00
Lantern, Bond Electric Corp., 2 Piece 36.00
Lantern, Railroad, Tin Lid, 6 In. 53.00
Lawn Swing 875.00
Learned Fox, 5 1/4 In. 100.00
Liberty Bell .... 35.00 To 60.00
Liberty Bell, Painted 250.00
Little Red Riding Hood, Tin, Lovell & Covell Co. 195.00
Locomotive, N.Y. C., Brainard's 1923 .... 195.00
Locomotive, Steam 45.00
Mail Box, Clear .... 125.00 To 175.00
Mail Box, Closure, Paint 250.00
Man On Motorcycle, Side Car .... 425.00 To 600.00
Milk Bottle Carrier, 4 Bottles 35.00
Mt. Vernon, Geo. Washington's Home, Currier & Ives Scenes 35.00
Mule, Pulling Barrel, Driver 105.00

Naked Child 75.00
Naked Girl Sucking Thumb, Germany 48.00
Oil Can, Independence Bell Oiler, All Glass 250.00
Opera Glasses, Swirl Ribs, Closure 250.00
Owl, Closure 100.00
Owl, Closure 225.00
Pelican, Papier–Mache 58.00
Pencil, Label, Candy 75.00
Pez, 101 Dalmatians, Feet, On Card 5.00
Pez, Bambi 45.00
Pez, Bambi, On Card 5.00
Pez, Bozo, Die Cut 58.00
Pez, Bugs Bunny 8.00
Pez, Donald Duck 8.00
Pez, Dumbo 45.00
Pez, Dumbo, On Card 5.00
Pez, Elephant, Orange 30.00
Pez, Fireman 45.00
Pez, Goofy 8.00
Pez, Pirate 35.00
Pez, Popeye 65.00
Pez, Santa Claus, Full Figure 85.00
Pez, Smurf 8.00
Pez, Snowman 8.00
Pez, Uncle Scrooge, Feet, On Card 5.00
Pez, Wolf, Feet, On Card 5.00
Phonograph 175.00
Phonograph, Horn, Covered Wood, Papier–Mache, 7 1/2 In. 285.00
Piano, Tin Back Closure 150.00
Piano, Upright 135.00
Piano, Upright, Slotted, Brown Paint 425.00
Pig, Pink, Spring Tail, Wire Hands, 6 1/2 In. 325.00
Pig, West Germany, 9 In. 55.00
Policeman's Nightstick 75.00
Powder Horn 45.00
Pumpkin 90.00
Pumpkin Head Policeman 400.00
Pumpkin Head Witch .... 315.00 To 375.00
Pumpkin Head Witch, Painted 750.00
Pumpkin Head, Multicolored, 8 3/4 In. 165.00
Pumpkin, Papier–Mache 25.00
Puppy, Screw Top 13.00
Rabbit, Basket, Screw Top 75.00
Rabbit, Carrot, Cotton Batting Over Papier–Mache, 7 In. 225.00
Rabbit, Crouching, Painted 165.00
Rabbit, Dressed As Uncle Sam, 23 In. 3520.00
Rabbit, Eating Carrot, 4 1/2 In. 35.00
Rabbit, Glass Eyes, Blue-Gray, Papier–Mache, 10 In. 125.00
Rabbit, Green Jacket, Papier–Mache, Germany, 6 In. 85.00
Rabbit, Holding Egg, Papier–Mache, Germany, 10 In. 95.00
Rabbit, Laid Back Ears 90.00
Rabbit, On All Fours, Silver, Papier–Mache, Germany, 8 In. 85.00
Rabbit, Painted Clown Suit, Glass Eyes, Papier–Mache 245.00
Rabbit, Papier–Mache, Germany 200.00
Rabbit, Paws Together, Clear 90.00
Rabbit, Peter Rabbit, 6 1/2 In. 35.00
Rabbit, Pulling Wooden Cart, Papier–Mache, Germany, 1910s 185.00
Rabbit, Pushing Wheelbarrow, Original Paint, 4 1/8 In. ... 135.00
Rabbit, Running On Log, 4 x 3 1/8 In. .... 150.00 To 350.00
Rabbit, Sitting, Glass Eyes, Papier–Mache, Germany 52.00
Rabbit, Sitting, Neck Closure, Papier–Mache, Germany, 9 In. 95.00
Rabbit, Walking, Papier–Mache, Germany 68.00
Rabbit, Wearing Hat 2300.00

Rabbit, Wheelbarrow, White, Closure 280.00
Radio, Original Closure .... 110.00 To 125.00
Reindeer, Pewter Horns, Glass Eyes 395.00
Rocking Horse, Clown Rider 250.00
Rolling Pin .... 185.00 To 250.00
Rooster, Composition, Germany 30.00
Rooster, Composition, Metal Feet 85.00
Rooster, Crowing 175.00
Rooster, Molded Clothes, Papier–Mache 165.00
Safety First 425.00
Santa Claus, Arm Twists Off For Candy, Composition 95.00
Santa Claus, Banded Coat 150.00
Santa Claus, Banded Coat, Paint Traces 200.00
Santa Claus, Feather Tree, Composition, Felt Coat, Germany 275.00
Santa Claus, Fur Beard, Snow Mound Base, Germany, 10 In. 965.00
Santa Claus, In Sleigh 150.00
Santa Claus, Leaving Chimney, 5 In. .... 70.00 To 85.00
Santa Claus, On Chimney, Cotton Batten, 5 In. 92.00
Santa Claus, On Sled, Red Suit, Fur Beard, Germany, 5 In. 110.00
Santa Claus, On Sled, Reindeer Is Container 1475.00
Santa Claus, Pack Holds Candy, China 22.00
Santa Claus, Snow Mound Base, Germany, 10 In. 395.00
Santa Claus, Tree, Lithographed Face 35.00
Santa's Boot, Candy, Sticker 30.00
Santa, Center Slide, Black Boots, 8 In. 475.00
Santa, Slide Closure, Snow Base, Germany, 10 In. 965.00
Ship, Remember The Maine 125.00
Shoe, Glass, Wale's Goodyear 120.00
Skookum, By Tree Stump .... 180.00 To 300.00
Snowball, With Elf, Spun Cotton, Hanger, 5 In. 100.00
Snowman, Papier–Mache 55.00
Snowman, Pebbly, Bobbing Head, Holds Plastic Lantern, 9 In. 25.00
Soldier, By Tent, Doughboy, Glass 1500.00
Soldier, By Tent, Glass 2800.00
Space Gun, Glass 25.00
Spark Plug, Metal Bottom 50.00
Spark Plug, New Closure 125.00
Spinning Top, Unused 65.00
St. Patrick, Base Closure, Germany, 4 In. 50.00
Stagecoach, Clear 125.00
Suitcase .... 45.00 To 65.00
Suitcase, Slide Closure, 3 5/8 In. 20.00
Tank ....33.00 To 110.00
Tank, 2 Cannons, Old Candy, Clear 30.00
Tank, Man In Turret 55.00
Tank, World War I, Painted Glass 22.00
Taxi, 12 Vents 90.00
Taxi, Tin Slide Closure 30.00
Telephone, Candlestick, Round Center 12.00
Telephone, Dial Type, Victory Glass Co., Closure 115.00
Telephone, Glass Receiver, Painted 65.00
Telephone, Wooden Receiver 30.00
Train, Clear, Red Wheels 35.00
Train, Man In Window 175.00
Trumpet, Milk Glass, Souvenir, Chester, Vermont 75.00
Trunk, Clear Glass 95.00
Trunk, Milk Glass, Gold 37.50
Trunk, Round Top, Milk Glass, Closure 240.00
Turkey, Neck Closure, Metal Feet, Germany, 4 In. 35.00
Turkey, Plug Closure, Papier–Mache, 9 In. 65.00
Turkey, Slide Closure 120.00
Uncle Sam, By Barrel 475.00
Village, Engine Co. No. 23 .... 22.00

Village, English Cottage, Red Chimney 250.00
Village, Princess Theatre 26.00
Village, Schoolhouse, Tin, No Flag, Original Insert 110.00
Wagon, U.S. Express, On Wheels, Lithographed Cardboard 140.00
Washing Machine, Pretty Maid, Glass Tub, Agitator, Crank 170.00
Watch, Original Metal Hanger & Fob 300.00
Wheelbarrow, Original Wheel & Cotter Pin 65.00
Wheelbarrow, Tin 110.00
Windmill, Dutch Wind Mill, Original Blade 75.00
Windmill, Dutch, Closure 225.00
Windmill, Red Tin Blades 75.00
World Globe, Stand, All Glass 90.00
World's Fair, Pressed Glass, 1892 .... 285.00

CANES and walking sticks were used by every well–dressed man in the
nineteenth century, but by World War I the style had changed. Today
canes are used by few but the infirm. Collectors prize old canes made with
special features, like hidden swords, whiskey flasks, or risque pictures seen
through peepholes. Examples with solid gold heads or made from exotic
materials, such as walrus vertebrae, are among the higher priced canes.

Ball Handle, Glass, Orange, Silver Plate, Vienna, 36 1/2 In. ....*Illus*   220.00
Balls–In–Cage Finial, Carved, Folk Art 1700.00
Carved Figures, Jewish Inscriptions 3575.00
Celluloid Whippet Dog's Head Handle, Wooden 25.00
Clear Over Wide Opalescent Ribbon, Red & Blue Stripes, Glass, 36 In. 245.00
Colored Spiral Threads, Blown Glass, 34 1/4 In. 105.00
Crook Handle, Spiral Decoration, Brass, Ebony, 36 1/4 In. ....*Illus*   143.00
Eagle Head Handle, Ivory, Nutwood, Fruitwood, 37 In. ....*Illus*   303.00
Ebony Shaft, Silver Handle, H. J. Fowler, Bristol, Indiana 125.00
Elephant On Ball Handle, Brass, Snakewood, Ebony, 36 1/4 In. .....*Illus*   303.00
G. A. R., Wooden 50.00
Head Of Bearded Man, Tassled Cord, 19th Century, 35 In. 605.00
Ivory Clenched Fist Top 385.00
Opera Handle, Silver Plate, Ebony, 34 In. ....*Illus*   165.00
Panther Head Handle, Brass, Snakewood, 34 1/2 In. ....*Illus*   523.00
Pistol Grip, Black Head, Bead Eyes, Ebony On Teak, Silver Band, 1914 ...... 209.00
Twisted, Blown Glass, Aqua, 49 In. 75.00
Walking Stick, Aqua Glass, Amber Center, Twisted Knob, 37 3/4 In. 75.00
Walking Stick, Ball Handle, Cloisonne, France, 32 1/2 In. ....*Illus*   275.00
Walking Stick, Bamboo, Floral & Bird Carved Bone Handle, 34 In. 135.00
Walking Stick, Bamboo, Floral Carved Ivory Handle 100.00

Left to right: Cane, Panther Head Handle, Brass, Snakewood, 34 1/2 In.; Cane, Eagle Head
Handle, Ivory, Nutwood, Fruitwood, 37 In.; Cane, Crook Handle, Spiral Decoration, Brass,
Ebony, 36 1/4 In.; Cane, Walking Stick, Ball Handle, Cloisonne, France, 32 1/2 In.; Cane,
Elephant On Ball Handle, Brass, Snakewood, Ebony, 36 1/4 In.; Cane, Opera Handle,
Silver Plate, Ebony, 34 In.; Cane, Walking Stick, Knob Handle, Glass, Silver Plate, 32 In.;
Cane, Ball Handle, Glass, Orange, Silver Plate, Vienna, 36 1/2 In.

Walking Stick, Bird's Head Handle, Primitive, Natural Growth, 28 In.	35.00
Walking Stick, Carved Nude Woman Handle, Painted Wood, c.1930, 36 In.	2970.00
Walking Stick, Colored Threads, Blown Glass, 49 1/2 In.	25.00
Walking Stick, Dog's Head, Lever Opens Mouth To Hold Gloves, Austrian	990.00
Walking Stick, Elephant Handle, Plated Ferrule, Ceylon, 37 1/2 In.	198.00
Walking Stick, German Air Force General, Ivory Top	1000.00
Walking Stick, Giraffe's Head Handle, Wooden, Africa, 36 In.	275.00
Walking Stick, Hand & Odd Fellow Insignia, Folk Art, 35 In.	85.00
Walking Stick, Ivory Dragon Head, Ebony Shaft	425.00
Walking Stick, Ivory Grip, Rosewood Shaft, France, 33 1/2 In.	210.00
Walking Stick, Jade Dog Head, Plated Ferrule, Snake Wood, Viennese	550.00
Walking Stick, Knob Handle, Glass, Silver Plate, 32 In. ....Illus	121.00
Walking Stick, Lacquer Opera Handle, Brass Ferrule, Far East, 38 In.	198.00
Walking Stick, Mahogany Threads, Twisted Handle & Tip, 48 1/2 In.	90.00
Walking Stick, Paddle Boat Brass Handle, Southern Comfort, 5 Vials	25.00
Walking Stick, Political, With Slogan, Tin	65.00
Walking Stick, Silver Tiger Head, Snake Wood Shaft, Germany, 37 In.	305.00
Walking Stick, Snakeskin Cover	145.00
Walking Stick, Staghorn Handle, Hunting Scene, Pewter Ferrule, Germany	1210.00
Walking Stick, Staghorn Handle, Vine Distorted Sapling, 1843, 37 In.	125.00
Walking Stick, Swirled Ribs, Aqua, Blown Glass, 39 In.	50.00
Walking Stick, White, Yellow & Mahogany Looping, Blown Glass, 39 In.	150.00
Young Woman Handle, Tilted Right, Chelsea Triangle Mark, 2 13/16 In.	1320.00

CANEWARE is a tan-colored, unglazed stoneware that was first developed by Josiah Wedgwood about 1770. It has been made by many companies since that time and is often used for cooking or serving utensils.

Game Dish, Cover, Birds, Leaves, 8 1/2 In.	500.00
Game Dish, Cover, Grapes, Rabbits, 8 1/2 In.	400.00

CANTON CHINA is blue-and-white ware made near Canton, China, from about 1785 to 1895. It is hand decorated with Chinese scenes.

Bottle, Lip Ground, Blue & White, 7 3/4 In.	85.00
Bowl, Blue & White, 11 1/2 In.	175.00
Candleholder, Recumbent Dog, Gilt Ears & Tail, 5 1/16 In., Pair	3025.00
Candlestick, Blue & White, 9 3/4 In., Pair	1800.00
Chop Plate, Blue & White, 11 3/4 In.	250.00
Creamer, Blue & White, 3 5/8 In.	130.00
Creamer, Blue & White, 4 In.	75.00
Creamer, Helmet Shape, 4 5/8 In.	100.00 To 300.00
Cup & Saucer, Blue & White, After Dinner	50.00
Dish, Blue & White, 9 3/4 In.	300.00
Dish, Cover, Boar's Head Handles, 7 In.	475.00
Dish, Cover, Boar's Head Handles, 12 1/2 In.	500.00
Dish, Cover, Condiment, 4 Sections	1250.00
Dish, Cover, Fruit Finial, Rectangular, 9 5/8 In.	200.00
Dish, Cover, Under Tray, Berry Finial, 6 In.	400.00
Dish, Cover, Under Tray, Boar's Head Handles, 7 3/4 In.	425.00
Dish, Serving, Oval, 1830	350.00
Dish, Shrimp, 10 1/2 In.	775.00
Dish, Vegetable, Cover, 9 1/4 In.	275.00
Dish, Vegetable, Cover, 10 1/4 In.	300.00
Dish, Vegetable, Cover, 10 In.	125.00
Mug, Blue & White, Intertwined Handle, 4 1/2 In.	400.00
Pie Plate, 1830	670.00
Plate, Rain Cloud Border, c.1870, 9 In., 6 Piece	350.00
Platter, Blue & White, 12 1/4 In.	150.00
Platter, Orange Peel Glaze, 13 In.	450.00
Platter, Orange Peel Glaze, 16 In.	375.00
Platter, Orange Peel Glaze, 20 In.	400.00
Platter, Pierced Liner, Canted Corners, Shaped, 1880s, 15 1/4 In.	467.50
Platter, Well & Tree, 19th Century, 17 x 20 In.	885.00
Salt, 19th Century, 4 In., Pair	885.00

Sugar Bowl, Strap Handle, Large	725.00
Tankard	525.00
Tazza, Blue & White, 3 1/4 In.	150.00
Tea Bowl, Blue & White	65.00
Tea Caddy, Orange Peel Glaze, Blue & White, 5 1/4 In.	2000.00
Teapot, Blue & White	425.00
Teapot, Domed Lid, 9 In.	685.00
Teapot, Fruit Finial, 6 In.	105.00
Tureen, Blue & White, Boar's Head Handles, 11 3/4 In.	600.00
Vase, Floral, 2 Handles, 1870s	300.00

CAPO–DI–MONTE porcelain was first made in Naples, Italy, from 1743 to 1759. The factory moved near Madrid, Spain, reopened in 1771, and worked to 1834. Since that time, the Doccia factory of Italy acquired the molds and is using the N and crown mark. Societe Richard Ceramica is a modern-day firm often referred to as Ginori or Capo–di–Monte. This company uses the crown and N mark.

Bowl, Full Relief Putti On Sides, Double Handles, 19 In.	125.00
Box, 3 Cherubs, Woman Sitting At Ocean, 3 In.	180.00
Box, Cover, Children In Garden Scene, 4 x 5 In.	70.00
Box, Decorated, Porcelain, Marked Italy, 10 In.	525.00
Box, Mythological Scenes, Bronze Mounted, 10 x 7 1/2 In.	412.00
Chest, Medieval Style, Pink, White Swirls, Ormolu Trim, 15 In.	1450.00
Figurine, 9 Piece Band, Gold & White, 7 1/2 In., 9 Piece	900.00
Figurine, Cockatoo, 12 In.	255.00
Figurine, Cranes, 17 In.	290.00
Figurine, Gypsy Dancing Girl, 13 In.	300.00
Figurine, Masked Clown, Black, White & Gold, 5 1/2 In., Pair	125.00
Figurine, Musicians, Old Women & Monks, Marked, 6 In., 8 Piece	600.00
Figurine, Old Man, Cranking Music Box, Sheet Music, 9 1/2 In.	345.00
Figurine, Owl, Glass Eyes, Lights Up, Blue Mark	395.00
Figurine, Three Boys Playing Marbles, Marked, 3 3/4 In.	110.00
Figurine, Woman, In Riding Habit, 13 In.	300.00
Figurine, Young Photographer, 9 1/2 In.	175.00
Jardiniere, Frolicking Cherubs, Gilt Rams' Heads, 8 3/8 In.	150.00
Lamp, Small Owl On Log, 5 In.	7975.00
Plaque, Child With Woman, 5 1/2 In.	200.00
Plate, Poppies, Multicolored, 8 In.	8.00
Shield, Battle Scene, Fruits & Flowers Border, Gilt, 23 In.	880.00
Urn, Cherub Finial, Warrior Slaying Man, Swan Handles, 25 In.	950.00
Urn, Cover, Cherubs, Gold Hoop Handles, 20 1/2 In.	550.00
Urn, Cover, Cherubs, Grapes, Bacchus Head Handles, 15 In., Pair	450.00
Urn, Seminude Women & Men, Gold Loop Handles, 13 1/2 In.	350.00
Vase, Children With Garden Tools, 3 1/2 In.	95.00
Vase, Cover, Frolicking Cherubims, Maidens, 12 1/2 In., Pair	165.00

CAPTAIN MARVEL was introduced in February 1940 in Whiz comic books. An orphan named Billy Batson met the wizard Shazam and whenever he said the magic word he was transformed into a superhero. A movie serial was released in 1940. The comic was discontinued in 1954. A second Captain Marvel appeared in 1966, a third in 1967. Only the original was transformed by shouting *Shazam*.

Car, Racing, Tin Lithograph, Windup, 4 In.	65.00
Car, Tin Lithograph, Keywind, Automatic Toy Co., 4 In.	110.00
Tattoo Sheet	15.00
Tie Clasp	35.00
Toy, Flying Captain Marvel, 1944	20.00
Watch	225.00
Wristwatch, Mary Marvel	75.00 To 195.00

CAPTAIN MIDNIGHT began as a radio show in September 1940. The first comic book appeared in July 1941. Captain Midnight was really the aviator Captain Albright, who was to defeat the Nazis. A movie serial was made in 1942 and a comic strip was published for a short time. The comic book Captain Midnight ended his career in 1948. The radio premiums are the prized collector memorabilia today.

Cup, Ovaltine	38.00
Decoder, With Key, 1949	100.00
Manual, 1943	100.00
Manual, 1957	250.00
Manual, Original Mailer, 1948	125.00
Manual, Secret Squadron, 1947	40.00
Map, Treasure Hunt, 1939 Skelly Premium	500.00
Mirror, Flash, Code–O–Graph, 1946	60.00
Mirror, Magic, Code–O–Graph, Red Plastic, 1948	45.00 To 65.00
Mystery Dial Code–O–Graph, 1940–1941	42.00
Newspaper, Flight Patrol Reporter, Volume 1	100.00
Photograph, Autographed	40.00
Photomatic Code–O–Graph, Ovaltine, 1942	50.00
Radio Script, The Snow White Panther	75.00
Ring, Look Around	75.00
Ring, Marine Corps	400.00
Ring, Mystery Eye Detector	165.00
Whistle Decoder, 1947	40.00

CARAMEL SLAG, see Chocolate Glass category

CARDS listed here include advertising cards, greeting cards, baseball cards, playing cards, valentines, and others. Color pictures were rare in the nineteenth century, so companies gave away colorful cards with pictures of children, flowers, products, or related scenes that promoted the company name. These were often collected and stored in albums. Greeting cards are also a nineteenth–century idea that has remained popular. Baseball cards also date from the nineteenth century when they were used by tobacco companies as giveaways. The gum cards were started in 1933, but it was not until after World War II that the bubble gum cards favored today were produced. Today over 1,000 cards are issued each year by the gum companies. Related items may be found in the Postcard category.

Advertising, A Bad Point On A Good Pointer, Currier & Ives, 1879	75.00
Advertising, A Side Wheeler, Bustin' A Trotter, Currier & Ives, 1880	90.00
Advertising, Bromo–Seltzer, Mechanical, 1892	35.00
Advertising, Dawn Of Love, Black Couple Kiss, Currier & Ives	80.00
Advertising, Dubuque Malting Lager Beer	200.00
Advertising, Furrier Co., Black Boys, Fur Tail From Tree, Easel, 6 In.	69.00
Advertising, Gold Camel Tea, Die Cut, 1890s	24.00
Advertising, Gunster Bros., Standard Plumbing Fixtures, 1920s, 21 In.	20.00
Advertising, Heckers' Buckwheat, Hold–To–Light, Man Eating, 1890s	20.00
Advertising, Hires, Little Girls, Battleboro, Vt.	12.00
Advertising, Kellogg's Rice Krispies, Magic Color, Mailer, 1933	20.00
Advertising, Kentucky Branch House, Girl In Fancy Circle, 5 In.	14.50
Advertising, Knox Gelatin, Black Mammy Theme	9.00
Advertising, Monarch Teenie Weenies	10.00
Advertising, Moving Co., Mechanical, Gold Leaf Monkey, A Moving Tale	15.00
Advertising, Pfeister Old Mill Tobacco, 2 5/8 x 1 7/16 In.	770.00
Advertising, Phallas, Harness Horse Racing, Color Litho, 1883	23.00
Advertising, Post Cereal, Circus, Punch Out To Assemble, 1947	15.00
Advertising, Queen's Own, Soldier Aims Rifle, Woman, Currier & Ives	85.00
Advertising, Robert Smith Brewing Co., Domino, 1905, Box	89.00
Advertising, Rocco Bros. & Co., Calif. Wines, Winter Scene, 3 x 5 In.	7.50
Advertising, Singer Sewing Machine, Bird, 1920s, 15 Piece	30.00
Advertising, Stonewall, Pure Drinking Whiskey, Storm Clouds, 4 In.	6.00
Advertising, Try My Rock Spring Fine Whiskies, Jamestown, N.Y., 4 In.	7.50
Advertising, Wrigley's Gum, Radio Premium, Held Lone Wolf Badge, 1932	25.00
Baseball, Al Kaline, Topps, 1954	650.00
Baseball, Al Kaline, Topps, 1960	30.00

Baseball, Babe Ruth, Goudey, 1933 .... 5500.00
Baseball, Babe Ruth, Goudey, 1935 .... 325.00
Baseball, Bob Elliott, Bowman, 1984 .... 40.00
Baseball, Bob Gibson, Topps, 1959 .... 170.00
Baseball, Brooks Robinson, Topps, 1958 .... 27.50
Baseball, Brooks Robinson, Topps, No. 600, 1967 .... 235.00
Baseball, Carl Willis, Topps, 1987 .... .50
Baseball, Carl Yastrzemski, Topps, 1960 .... 175.00 To 375.00
Baseball, Carl Yastrzemski, Topps, 1962 .... 150.00
Baseball, Casey Stengel, Topps, 1959 .... 25.00
Baseball, Catfish Hunter, Topps, 1966 .... 26.00
Baseball, Connie Mack, Topps, 1951 .... 500.00
Baseball, Don Drysdale, Topps, 1958 .... 22.00
Baseball, Don Mattingly, Topps, 1984 .... 32.00
Baseball, Duke Snyder, Topps, 1962 .... 19.00
Baseball, Early Wynn, Topps, 1960 .... 35.00
Baseball, Eddie Mathews, Topps, 1958 .... 11.00
Baseball, Ernie Banks, Bowman, 1955 .... 350.00
Baseball, Ernie Banks, Topps, 1962 .... 32.00
Baseball, George Brett, Topps, 1980 .... 10.00
Baseball, Hank Aaron, Bowman, 1955 .... 195.00
Baseball, Hank Aaron, Topps 770.00
Baseball, Hank Aaron, Topps, 1956 .... 95.00
Baseball, Harmon Killebrew, Topps, 1955 .... 135.00
Baseball, Harmon Killebrew, Topps, 1960 .... 25.00
Baseball, Jim Bunning, Topps, 1965 .... 15.00
Baseball, Jim Palmer, Topps, 1966 .... 225.00
Baseball, Johnny Bench, Topps, 1968 .... 350.00 To 395.00
Baseball, Jose Canseco, Topps, 1987 .... 60.00
Baseball, Louis Aparicio, Topps, 1956 .... 125.00
Baseball, Mickey Mantle, Bowman, 1951 .... 4000.00
Baseball, Mickey Mantle, Topps, 1957, No. 407 .... 775.00
Baseball, Mickey Mantle, Topps, 1961, No. 300 .... 295.00
Baseball, Mike Schmidt, Topps, 1974 .... 40.00
Baseball, Nolan Ryan, Topps, 1968 .... 850.00
Baseball, Phil Rizzuto, Topps, 1951 .... 25.00
Baseball, Reggie Jackson, Topps, 1969 .... 195.00
Baseball, Reggie Jackson, Topps, 1971 .... 55.00
Baseball, Rickey Henderson, Topps, 1980 .... 170.00
Baseball, Roberto Clemente, Topps, 1955 .... 525.00
Baseball, Roberto Clemente, Topps, 1963, No. 540 .... 79.00
Baseball, Robin Yount, Topps, 1975 .... 180.00
Baseball, Rod Carew, Topps, 1967 .... 525.00
Baseball, Roderick John Wallace, Red, 1910–1911, 8 In. ....*Illus* 440.00
Baseball, Roy Campanella, Topps, 1957, No. 400 .... 73.00
Baseball, Sandy Koufax, Topps, 1955 .... 330.00 To 500.00
Baseball, Ted Williams, Topps, 1954 .... 595.00
Baseball, Ted Williams, Topps, 1957 .... 395.00
Baseball, Tommy Lasorda, Topps, 1954 .... 175.00
Baseball, Topps, Complete Set, 1976 .... 375.00
Baseball, Topps, Complete Set, 1977 .... 395.00
Baseball, Ty Cobb, Cracker Jack, 1915 .... 518.00
Baseball, Whitey Ford, Topps, 1960 .... 30.00
Baseball, Willie Mays, Bowman, 1952 .... 825.00
Baseball, Willie Mays, Topps, 1953 .... 2400.00
Calling, Chas. E. Hammond, Wholesale Liquors & Wines, Hagerstown, 4 In. 6.50
Calling, D. Davis Jewelry & Curio Store, Denver, Photograph, 4 x 2 In. 3.00
Calling, Hotel Seward, W. M. Seward Proprietor, Portland, 4 1/2 x 2 In. 5.00
Calling, James A. Thomas, Wine & Liquor Trade Jugs, 4 1/2 In. 10.00
Calling, Old Kentucky Distillery, Louisville, Ky., 4 3/4 x 2 3/4 In. 3.50
Calling, Stoddart Bros., Chemists & Perfumers, Boy Pictured, 3 1/2 In. 5.00
Christmas, Looks Like Bank Check, 1904 .... 3.00
Cigarette, Air Raid Precautions, England, c.1938, 50 Piece 50.00

◆◆◆◆◆◆◆◆◆◆◆◆◆◆◆◆◆◆◆◆◆

To remove the gum stain from a card that has been packaged with the gum for a long time, try using a product called X–Wax.

◆◆◆◆◆◆◆◆◆◆◆◆◆◆◆◆◆◆◆◆◆◆◆◆

Card, Baseball, Roderick John Wallace, Red, 1910-1911, 8 In.

Cigarette, Aviary & Cage Birds, 1930s, 50 Piece	60.00
Cigarette, Eckstein–Halpaufevents, People In History, 250 Piece	252.00
Cigarette, Embossed Leather, Colleges, Universities, 20 Piece	20.00
Cigarette, Gold Saba, Actors, Actresses, Germany, 250 Piece	250.00
Cigarette, Poker Hands, Imperial Tobacco Co., Canada, 1920s, 53 Piece	75.00
Cigarette, School Emblems, England, 1920s, 40 Piece	60.00
Cigarette, Sweet Corporal, Early Stage Stars, 5 Piece	15.00
Cigarette, Turkish Trophies, 6 x 8 In., 25 Piece	65.00
Cigarette, Turkish Trophies, Girls In Native Costumes, 5 Piece	23.00
Easter, Easter Angel, Maud Humphrey, Die Cut, Easel, 8 1/2 In.	95.00
Football, Blanda, Rookie, 1954	400.00
Football, Bo Jackson, Topps, 1987	3.95
Football, Hornung, Rookie, 1957	450.00
Football, Jimmy Brown, No. 62, 1958	495.00
Football, Landry, Rookie, 1951	500.00
Football, Montana, Rookie, 1981	200.00
Football, Namath, Rookie, 1955	1400.00
Football, Starr, Rookie, 1957	450.00
Football, Staubach, Rookie, 1972	100.00
Football, Tarkenton, Rookie, 1962	400.00
Football, Unitas, Rookie, 1957	750.00
Fortune Telling, Agnes G. Bacon, Hand Cut	200.00
Fortune Telling, Hindu, Satish Chandra Ghosh	55.00
Gum, America At War, 1942, Uncut 48 Card Set	225.00
Gum, Dinosaur, Unopened, Pack, 1961	25.00
Hockey, Brett Hull, Gretsky Autograph, 2 Piece	60.00
Hockey, Mario Lemieux, Topps, 1985–1986, No. 9	125.00
Hockey, Phil Esposito, Topps, 1966–1967, No. 73	295.00
Hockey, Terry Sawchuck, Parkhurst, 1952–1953, No. 86	550.00
Hockey, Wayne Gretsky	120.00
Lobby, Flying Tigers, John Wayne, Republic, 1942, 10 x 15 In.	80.00
Lobby, High Noon, Gary Cooper, 1952, 14 x 22 In.	80.00
Lobby, Laurel & Hardy, Our Relations	120.00
Lobby, One More Spring, Jan. Gaynor, Warner Baxter, 1935, 17 In., Pair	110.00
Lobby, Three Weekends, Clara Bow, Hand Tinted, 1930, 17 x 14 In.	125.00
Playing, Air Atlanta	5.00
Playing, Blond With 3 Kittens, Elvgren	20.00
Playing, Canadian Pacific Airlines	7.00
Playing, Drewry's Beer, Mounted Police, 1950, Unopened	8.00
Playing, Eastern Airlines	3.00 To 15.00
Playing, Frigidaire Iceman	30.00

Playing, Gold Flake Cigarette 35.00
Playing, Golf Scene, Dog Caught In Bag Of Clubs, Albert Stackle, Case 25.00
Playing, Green Hornet, Greenway Productions, 1966 .... 35.00
Playing, Green River, Whiskey Without A Headache, Box 45.00
Playing, Hawaiian Punch, America By Campbell Soup, Double Deck, 1970s 5.00
Playing, Mackenson's Stout 35.00
Playing, Marlboro Texan, Poker In The Old West, Brochure 10.00
Playing, Miller High Life Beer, Black, Red, Gold, 1940s, Box 9.00
Playing, Olympia Beer, Calendar Girl 2.50
Playing, Pabst Blue Ribbon Beer, Baldwin Dist. Co., 1960, Unopened 4.00
Playing, Reveries, Maxfield, Complete 200.00
Playing, Robin Hood Flour, Complete 5.00
Playing, United Airlines 8.00
Playing, Veiled Prophet, 1928 .... 65.00
Playing, Western Airlines 8.00
Trolley, Standard Plumbing Fixtures, 1900s, 11 x 21 In. 20.00
Valentine, Airplane, Die Cut Children, Tuck 75.00
Valentine, Auto Racer, 1906 .... 20.00
Valentine, Boy & Girl Under Umbrella, Heart Shape, Colorful, 1920–1930 .... 1.25
Valentine, Guitar, 3–D, Box, Large 75.00
Valentine, Jungle Animals, Boy & Girl, Foldout, Germany, 11 1/2 In. 28.00
Valentine, Lawyer, 1906 .... 20.00
Valentine, Mechanical, Felix The Cat, German 35.00
Valentine, Picaninny, Tuck 12.50
Valentine, Pinocchio, 1939, 5 In. 20.00
Valentine, Pop–Up, Boy & Flower, Blue, White, Germany 20.00
Valentine, Pop–Up, Boy & Girl, Blue, White, Tuck 35.00
Valentine, Roses, Birds, Cherubs, Crepe Paper, Foldout, 1934, 8 In. 30.00
Valentine, Sailor's, Flower Pattern Of Shells, Round, 6 1/2 In. 75.00
Valentine, Smiling Golfer On Course, Stand–Up, Mechanical, c.1915 .... 20.00
Valentine, Snow White, Movable, 1938 .... 42.00
Valentine, Telephone Woman, 1906 .... 20.00
Valentine, Yachtsman, 1906 .... 20.00
Wrestling, Oexjobot, 3 Piece 22.00

CARDER, see Aurene and Steuben categories.

CARLSBAD, Germany, is a mark found on china made by several factories
in Germany. Most of the pieces available today were made after 1891.

Box, Sardine, Victoria 65.00
Ewer, Gold Floral, Brown Leaves, Bamboo Handle, Bulbous, 7 1/2 In. 65.00
Platter, Fish, Victorian Family Fishing, 24 1/2 In. 240.00
Vase, Flowers, 2 Handles, 10 x 6 In. 35.00

CARLTON WARE was made at the Carlton Works of Stoke–on–Trent,
England, about 1890. The firm traded as Wiltshaw & Robinson until 1957.
It was renamed Carlton Ware Ltd. in 1958.

Bowl, Flared, Bleu Royale, 3 Gold Feet, 9 1/2 In. 65.00
Box, Cover, 5 1/2 x 4 In. 50.00
Dish, Blue Enameled, Oval, 8 In. 55.00
Dish, Blue, Gold Edge, Oval, 8 In. 28.00
Dish, Leaf Shape, 6 1/2 In. 25.00
Flower Frog, Iridescent Purple, 5 In. 20.00
Pitcher, Rouge Royale, 6 In. 65.00
Sugar Shaker, Fruit, Yellow Basket, 5 1/4 In. 95.00
Sugar Shaker, Yellow House, Red Roof & Chimney, 5 1/2 In. 110.00
Teapot, Gothic Shape 550.00
Vase, Gold & Enameled Birds & Flowers, Luster Ground, 7 In. 240.00
Vase, Rouge Royale, 8 In. 75.00
Vase, Rouge Royale, Art Deco, 8 In. 45.00

CARNIVAL GLASS was an inexpensive, pressed, iridescent glass made from about 1907 to about 1925. Over 1,000 different patterns are known. Carnival glass is currently being reproduced. Additional pieces may be found in the Northwood section.

Acorn Burrs & Bark pattern is listed here as Acorn Burrs	
Acorn Burrs, Butter, Cover, Purple	175.00
Acorn Burrs, Pitcher, Green	150.00
Acorn Burrs, Punch Set, Green, 7 Piece	1800.00
Acorn, Bowl, Red, 7 In.	160.00
Acorn, Bowl, Red, 8 In.	850.00
Amaryllis pattern is listed here as Tiger Lily	
American Beauty Roses pattern is listed here as Wreath Of Roses	
Apple Blossom Twigs, Bowl, Marigold	75.00
Apple Blossom Twigs, Bowl, Ruffled, Peach	85.00
Apple Blossom Twigs, Plate, Amethyst	29.00
Apple Blossom, Bowl, Marigold, 5 1/2 In.	25.00
Apple Blossom, Plate, Ruffled, Blue	150.00
Apple Tree, Pitcher, White	450.00
Apple Tree, Tumbler, Blue	25.00
Australian Swan, Bowl, Purple, 9 In.	185.00
Bambi, Powder Jar, Cover, Amethyst	25.00
Banded Medallion & Teardrop pattern is listed here as Beaded Bull's Eye	
Basket, Basket, Hexagonal, Green	585.00
Basket, Basket, Hexagonal, Ice Green	575.00
Basket, Basket, Hexagonal, White	150.00
Basket, Basket, Round, Aqua	400.00
Basket, Basket, Round, White	150.00
Battenburg Lace No. 1 pattern is listed here as Hearts & Flowers	
Battenburg Lace No. 2 pattern is listed here as Captive Rose	
Battenburg Lace No. 3 pattern is listed here as Fanciful	
Beaded Bull's Eye, Vase, Purple, 12 In., Pair	75.00
Beaded Cable, Rose Bowl, Amethyst	60.00 To 95.00
Beaded Cable, Rose Bowl, Aqua	265.00 To 320.00
Beaded Cable, Rose Bowl, Green	85.00
Beaded Cable, Rose Bowl, White	600.00
Beaded Medallion & Teardrop pattern is listed here as Beaded Bull's Eye	
Beaded Shell, Mug, Amethyst	85.00 To 95.00
Beaded Shell, Tumbler, Purple	80.00
Beaded Star & Snail pattern is listed here as Constellation	
Big Fish, Candy Dish, Marigold	675.00
Birds & Cherries, Bowl, Ruffled, Blue, 10 In.	315.00
Birds & Cherries, Compote, Amethyst	60.00
Birds & Cherries, Compote, Blue	60.00
Birds on Bough pattern is listed here as Birds & Cherries	
Blackberry A. pattern is listed here as Blackberry	
Blackberry B. pattern is listed here as Blackberry Spray	
Blackberry Spray, Hat, Aqua	75.00
Blackberry Spray, Hat, Marigold	35.00
Blackberry Wreath, Bowl, Green, 5 In.	65.00
Blackberry, Hat, Red	400.00 To 575.00
Brocaded Palms, Console Set, Attached Candlesticks, Green	225.00
Brocaded Palms, Fernery, Cover, 4 Footed, Pink, 8 1/2 In.	165.00
Brocaded Palms, Vase, Melon Ribbed, Ice Green, 8 In.	250.00
Brooklyn Bridge, Bowl, Ruffled, Marigold, 8 In.	325.00
Brooklyn Bridge, Bowl, Ruffled, Marigold, 10 In.	345.00
Bull's Eye & Leaves, Bowl, Green, 8 In.	35.00
Bushel Basket pattern is listed here as Basket	
Butterfly & Berry, Bowl, Footed, Marigold, 10 In.	65.00
Butterfly & Berry, Bowl, Footed, Marigold, 5 In.	25.00
Butterfly & Berry, Bowl, Footed, White, Master, 10 In.	250.00
Butterfly & Berry, Butter, Cover, Marigold	85.00 To 100.00
Butterfly & Berry, Hatpin Holder, Marigold	1900.00

Butterfly & Berry, Table Set, Marigold, 4 Piece 325.00
Butterfly & Berry, Tumbler, Marigold 20.00
Butterfly & Fern, Pitcher, Amethyst 325.00
Butterfly & Fern, Pitcher, Blue 375.00
Butterfly & Fern, Pitcher, Marigold 275.00
Butterfly & Fern, Tumbler, Green 45.00
Butterfly & Grape pattern is listed here as Butterfly & Berry
Butterfly & Plume pattern is listed here as Butterfly & Fern
Butterfly & Tulip, Bowl, Square, Purple 1500.00
Buzz Saw, Cruet, Green, 4 In. 405.00
Cactus Leaf Rays pattern is listed here as Leaf Rays
Captive Rose, Bowl, Green 75.00
Captive Rose, Bowl, Green, 9 In. 65.00
Captive Rose, Bowl, Marigold, 8 In. 85.00
Carolina Dogwood, Plate 500.00
Cattails & Fish pattern is listed here as Fisherman's Mug
Cattails & Water Lily pattern is listed here as Water Lily & Cattails
Chatelaine, Pitcher, Amethyst 2500.00
Cherries & Holly Wreath pattern is listed here as Cherry Circles
Cherry Chain, Bowl, Marigold, 10 In. 65.00
Cherry Chain, Plate, Marigold, 6 In. 60.00
Cherry Circles, Bonbon, Marigold, 7 In. 37.00
Cherry Circles, Bonbon, Green 45.00
Cherry Circles, Bonbon, Marigold 45.00
Cherry Wreathed pattern is listed here as Wreathed Cherry
Cherry, Bowl, Marigold, 7 In. 65.00
Cherry, Bowl, Ruffled, Purple, 8 In. 125.00
Cherry, Powder Jar, Green 2000.00
Christmas Cactus pattern is listed here as Thistle
Christmas Plate pattern is listed here as Poinsettia
Chrysanthemum Wreath pattern is listed here as Ten Mums
Chrysanthemum, Bowl, Footed, Blue, 10 In. 195.00
Chrysanthemum, Bowl, Footed, Marigold, 10 In. 68.00
Chrysanthemum, Bowl, Ruffled, Marigold, 9 In. 65.00
Circle Scroll, Vase, Marigold, 7 3/4 In. 55.00
Coin Dot, Bowl, Cobalt Blue 65.00
Coin Dot, Rose Bowl, Amethyst 60.00
Coin Spot, Compote, Marigold, 8 In. 45.00
Concave Diamonds, Tumbler, Blue 25.00
Constellation, Compote, White 100.00
Constitution pattern is listed here as God & Home
Coral Medallion pattern is listed here as Mayan
Corinth, Plate, Aqua, 8 In. 65.00
Corn Vase, Vase, Green 650.00
Cosmos & Cane, Bowl, Honey Amber, Square, 5 In. 225.00
Cosmos & Cane, Bowl, Ice Cream, Honey Amber, 6 In. 50.00
Cosmos & Cane, Tumbler, Honey Amber ....60.00 To 100.00
Cosmos Variant, Bowl, Marigold, 9 1/2 In. 35.00
Dahlia, Creamer, White 175.00
Dahlia, Pitcher, White, 8 In. 495.00
Daisy & Plume, Candy Dish, Peach 375.00
Daisy & Plume, Rose Bowl, Marigold .... 40.00 To 55.00
Dance Of The Veils, Vase, Marigold 2650.00
Dandelion Variant pattern is listed here as Panelled Dandelion
Dandelion, Mug, Aqua 395.00
Dandelion, Mug, Marigold 425.00
Dandelion, Tumbler, Marigold 50.00
Dandelion, Tumbler, Purple 50.00
Diamond & Daisy, Tumbler, Marigold 45.00
Diamond & Rib, Vase, Marigold, 15 In. 30.00
Diamond Band pattern is listed here as Diamonds
Diamond Lace, Pitcher, Amethyst 250.00
Diamond Lace, Pitcher, Purple 150.00

Diamond Lace, Tumbler, Purple 45.00
Diamond Lace, Water Set, Amethyst, 8 Piece 365.00
Diamond Point & Daisy pattern is listed here as Cosmos & Cane
Diamond Points, Vase, Lavender, 11 In. 85.00
Diamond Points, Vase, White, 11 In. 95.00
Diamonds, Pitcher, Water, Green 225.00
Diamonds, Tumbler, Aqua 85.00
Diamonds, Water Set, Amethyst, 5 Piece 425.00
Diamonds, Water Set, Green, 5 Piece 295.00
Dogwood & Marsh Lily pattern is listed here as Two Flowers
Double Star, Tumbler, Green 40.00
Dragon & Lotus, Bowl, Blue, 9 In. .... 40.00 To 80.00
Dragon & Lotus, Bowl, Marigold, 9 In. .... 75.00 To 95.00
Dragon & Lotus, Plate, Blue, 9 1/2 In. 3400.00
Dragon & Strawberry, Bowl, Marigold 350.00
Drape & Tie pattern is listed here as Rosalind
Drapery, Candy Dish, Blue .... 135.00 To 145.00
Drapery, Candy Dish, White 95.00
Drapery, Rose Bowl, Aqua 285.00
Egyptian Band pattern is listed here as Round–Up
Fan & Arch pattern is listed here as Persian Garden
Fanciful, Bowl, Peach, 8 1/2 In. 95.00
Fanciful, Plate, Ruffled, Peach, 9 In. 250.00
Fantail, Bowl, Footed, Marigold, 9 In. 40.00
Fantasy pattern is listed here as Question Marks
Fashion, Pitcher, Marigold .... 90.00 To 115.00
Fashion, Punch Cup, Marigold 18.00
Fashion, Tumbler, Marigold 15.00
Fern, Compote, Green 75.00
File & Fan, Compote, White Base, Peach 225.00
File, Pitcher, Marigold, 10 In. 250.00
Fine Cut & Roses, Candy Dish, Green 68.00
Fine Cut & Roses, Candy Dish, White 100.00
Fine Cut & Roses, Rose Bowl, Ice Blue 175.00
Fine Cut & Roses, Rose Bowl, Purple 85.00
Fine Rib, Compote, Green, Ruffled 45.00
Fine Rib, Vase, Blue, 17 In. 85.00
Fine Rib, Vase, Marigold, 11 1/2 In., Pair 70.00
Fine Rib, Vase, Red, 10 In. 225.00
Finecut & Star pattern is listed here as Star & File
Fish Net, Lily, For Epergne, Purple Opalescent 125.00
Fisherman's Mug, Mug, Golds, Reds, Blue 175.00
Fleur–De–Lis, Bowl, Collar Base, Purple, 10 In. 295.00
Floral & Diamond Point pattern is listed here as Fine Cut & Roses
Floral & Grape, Pitcher, Water, Blue 200.00
Floral & Grapevine pattern is listed here as Floral & Grape
Floral & Optic, Bowl, Red, 8 3/4 In. 350.00
Floral & Wheat Spray pattern is listed here as Floral & Wheat
Floral & Wheat, Bonbon, Puzzle Interior, Marigold 40.00
Floral & Wheat, Bonbon, Stemmed, Purple 40.00
Flower Pot pattern is listed here as Butterfly & Tulip
Flowering Almonds pattern is listed here as Peacock Tail
Flute, Salt, Marigold, Individual 45.00
Flute, Toothpick, Amethyst 40.00
Flute, Toothpick, Green 50.00
Flute, Toothpick, Purple .... 70.00 To 85.00
Four Flowers, Bowl, Ruffled, Purple, 7 In. 45.00
Four Flowers, Chop Plate, Peach, 11 In. 475.00
Frolicking Bears, Pitcher, Green 8700.00
Fruits & Flowers, Bonbon, Aqua 650.00
Fruits & Flowers, Bonbon, Blue .... 80.00 To 150.00
Fruits & Flowers, Bonbon, Green .... 100.00 To 115.00
Fruits & Flowers, Bonbon, White 420.00

Garden Path, Bowl, Ruffled, White, 6 In.	45.00
Garland, Rose Bowl, Marigold	55.00
God & Home, Tumbler, Blue	180.00 To 185.00
Goddess Of Harvest, Bowl, Marigold, 9 1/2 In.	4300.00
Golden Harvest, Wine Set, Marigold, 7 Piece	275.00
Good Luck, Bowl, Amethyst	250.00
Good Luck, Bowl, Marigold	95.00 To 125.00
Good Luck, Plate, Marigold, 9 In.	200.00
Grape & Cable, Banana Boat, Banded, Marigold	145.00
Grape & Cable, Bonbon, Blue	65.00
Grape & Cable, Bonbon, Blue, Stippled	195.00
Grape & Cable, Bonbon, White	495.00
Grape & Cable, Bowl, Amethyst, 7 1/2 In.	155.00
Grape & Cable, Bowl, Fluted, Purple, 8 1/4 In.	70.00
Grape & Cable, Bowl, Ice Cream, Spatula Feet, Blue, 8 In.	65.00
Grape & Cable, Bowl, Light Amethyst, 7 1/2 In.	63.00
Grape & Cable, Bowl, Red, 7 In.	550.00
Grape & Cable, Bowl, Ruffled, Marigold, 11 In.	75.00
Grape & Cable, Butter, Cover, Amethyst	165.00 To 245.00
Grape & Cable, Butter, Cover, Blue	90.00
Grape & Cable, Compote, Purple	350.00
Grape & Cable, Decanter, Whiskey, Marigold	475.00 To 650.00
Grape & Cable, Hatpin Holder, Amethyst	245.00 To 335.00
Grape & Cable, Hatpin Holder, Green	275.00
Grape & Cable, Hatpin Holder, Marigold	175.00 To 255.00
Grape & Cable, Hatpin Holder, Purple	175.00 To 275.00
Grape & Cable, Humidor, Marigold	265.00
Grape & Cable, Orange Bowl, Blue	300.00 To 320.00
Grape & Cable, Orange Bowl, Marigold	150.00
Grape & Cable, Perfume Bottle, Purple	650.00 To 950.00
Grape & Cable, Pin Tray, Amethyst	295.00
Grape & Cable, Pin Tray, Purple	375.00
Grape & Cable, Pitcher, Amethyst	225.00 To 275.00
Grape & Cable, Plate, Marigold, 7 1/2 In.	145.00
Grape & Cable, Plate, Marigold, 9 In.	85.00
Grape & Cable, Plate, Old Rose Distillery, Green	415.00
Grape & Cable, Powder Jar, Purple	140.00
Grape & Cable, Punch Bowl, Amethyst	500.00
Grape & Cable, Punch Bowl, Blue	2000.00
Grape & Cable, Punch Bowl, Marigold	125.00
Grape & Cable, Punch Set, Blue, 10 Piece	2000.00 To 2300.00
Grape & Cable, Punch Set, Purple, 10 Piece	600.00
Grape & Cable, Punch Set, White, 12 Piece	6000.00
Grape & Cable, Sweetmeat, Amethyst	225.00
Grape & Cable, Tobacco Jar, Cover, Amethyst	400.00
Grape & Cable, Tobacco Jar, Cover, Marigold	235.00
Grape & Cable, Tumbler, Amethyst	40.00
Grape & Cable, Tumbler, Green	25.00 To 45.00
Grape & Cable, Tumbler, Purple, Stippled	60.00
Grape & Cable, Water Set, Green, 6 Piece	250.00
Grape & Cable, Water Set, Marigold, 7 Piece	275.00 To 575.00
Grape & Gothic Arches, Sugar, Cover, Marigold	50.00
Grape & Lattice, Pitcher, Marigold	185.00
Grape & Leaves, Bowl, 3 Footed, Amethyst, 9 In.	88.00
Grape & Lotus, Bonbon, Marigold	45.00
Grape Arbor, Fruit Bowl, Marigold, 11 In.	75.00
Grape Arbor, Pitcher, Marigold	250.00
Grape Arbor, Tankard, Marigold	195.00
Grape Arbor, Tumbler, Blue	100.00 To 200.00
Grape Arbor, Water Set, Marigold, 6 Piece	350.00
Grape Delight pattern is listed here as Vintage	
Grape, Bowl, Nut, Amethyst, 8 In.	65.00
Grape, Candlestick	120.00

Grape, Humidor, Stippled Blue, 7 1/2 In. 795.00
Grapevine Diamonds pattern is listed here as Grapevine Lattice
Grapevine Lattice, Bowl, Ruffled, White, 6 In. 50.00
Grapevine Lattice, Pitcher, Amethyst 495.00
Grapevine Lattice, Plate, Purple, 7 In. 145.00
Grapevine Lattice, Tumbler, Blue 60.00
Grapevine Lattice, Tumbler, Marigold 18.00
Greek Key, Bowl, Amethyst, 9 In. 80.00
Greek Key, Tumbler, Purple 85.00
Harvest Flower, Tumbler, Amethyst 1000.00
Harvest Flower, Tumbler, Marigold ....85.00 To 135.00
Harvest Time pattern is listed here as Golden Harvest
Heart & Vine, Bowl, Green 75.00
Heart & Vine, Plate, Blue, 9 1/2 In. 195.00
Hearts & Flowers, Bowl, Ice Blue .... 285.00 To 435.00
Hearts & Flowers, Bowl, Ruffled, Blue, 8 1/2 In. 300.00
Hearts & Flowers, Compote, Aqua Opalescent .... 395.00 To 600.00
Hearts & Flowers, Compote, White 115.00
Hearts & Flowers, Plate, Amethyst 825.00
Hearts & Vines, Bowl, Marigold, 9 In. 40.00
Heavy Grape, Chop Plate, Amber .... 235.00 To 475.00
Heavy Grape, Chop Plate, Amethyst 395.00
Heavy Grape, Chop Plate, Purple, 11 In. 295.00
Heavy Grape, Plate, Amber, 8 In. 200.00
Heavy Grape, Plate, Green, 8 In. 60.00
Heavy Grape, Plate, Marigold, 7 In. .... 50.00 To 65.00
Heavy Grape, Plate, Purple, 8 In. 200.00
Heavy Iris, Pitcher, Marigold .... 325.00 To 450.00
Heavy Iris, Pitcher, Water, Tankard, Marigold 395.00
Heron & Rushes pattern is listed here as Stork & Rushes
Hobnail pattern is listed in this book as its own category
Hobstar & Feather, Punch Cup, Marigold, 5 Piece 95.00
Hobstar & Torch pattern is listed here as Double Star
Hobstar Band, Pitcher, Pedestal Base, Marigold 150.00
Holly & Berry pattern is listed here as Holly Carnival
Holly Carnival, Bowl, Handle, Fluted, 6 In. 80.00
Holly Paneled, Bonbon, Green 45.00
Holly Spray pattern is listed here as Holly Sprig
Holly Sprig, Bonbon, Pulled-Up Sides, Amethyst, 3 x 3 In. 75.00
Holly, Bowl, Ruffled, Amethyst, 9 1/2 In. 85.00
Holly, Bowl, White, 9 In. 125.00
Holly, Plate, Blue, 9 1/2 In. 350.00
Holly, Plate, Marigold, 9 In. .... 110.00 To 295.00
Imperial Grape, Berry Set, Marigold, 6 Piece 135.00
Imperial Grape, Bottle, Water, Amethyst 225.00
Imperial Grape, Bowl, Green, 8 In. 50.00
Imperial Grape, Decanter, Wine, Marigold 125.00
Imperial Grape, Pitcher, Purple 250.00
Imperial Grape, Tumbler, Marigold 20.00
Imperial Grape, Tumbler, Purple 65.00
Imperial Grape, Water Carafe, Purple 130.00
Imperial Grape, Water Set, Marigold, 7 Piece 250.00
Imperial Grape, Wine Set, Marigold, 7 Piece 225.00
Imperial Grape, Wine, Green .... 35.00 To 40.00
Imperial Pansy, Bowl, Purple, 8 1/4 In. 75.00
Inverted Coin Dot, Tumbler, Marigold 65.00
Inverted Strawberry, Bowl, Green, 6 3/4 In. 125.00
Inverted Strawberry, Powder Jar, Green 125.00
Inverted Strawberry, Tumbler, Amethyst .... 175.00 To 275.00
Inverted Strawberry, Water Set, Amethyst, 7 Piece 1600.00
Iris, Compote, Green, 7 In. 65.00
Iris, Goblet, Buttermilk, Green 55.00
Jack-In-The-Pulpit, Vase, Green, 7 In. 25.00

Jeweled Heart, Berry Set, White, 7 Piece 300.00
Jewels, Bowl, Red, 8 3/4 In. 120.00
Kimberly pattern is listed here as Concave Diamonds
Kittens, Bowl, Marigold 85.00
Kittens, Cup & Saucer, Marigold .... 125.00 To 225.00
Kittens, Dish, Crimped, Marigold 155.00
Kittens, Plate, Frosted, 3 Embossed Kittens, 7 In. 25.00
Kittens, Plate, Marigold 165.00
Kittens, Toothpick, Marigold 225.00
Knotted Beads, Vase, Blue, 16 In. 55.00
Kokomo, Rose Bowl, Marigold 45.00
Labelle Poppy pattern is listed here as Poppy Show
Labelle Rose pattern is listed here as Rose Show
Lattice & Grape, Tumbler, Marigold 20.00
Lattice & Grapevine pattern is listed here as Lattice & Grape
Lattice & Points, Vase, Marigold, 15 1/2 In. 45.00
Leaf & Beads, Rose Bowl, Green .... 60.00 To 85.00
Leaf Chain, Bonbon, Blue 62.00
Leaf Chain, Bonbon, Marigold 45.00
Leaf Medallion pattern is listed here as Leaf Chain
Leaf Rays, Nappy, Purple 55.00
Leaf Rays, Nappy, White 55.00
Leaf Swirl, Compote, Purple 150.00
Leaf Swirl, Compote, Teal, 5 1/2 In. 55.00
Lion, Bowl, Marigold, 7 In. 90.00
Little Stars, Bowl, Amethyst, 7 1/2 In. 120.00
Loganberry, Vase, Amber 450.00
Long Thumbprint, Sugar & Creamer, Marigold 50.00
Lustre Rose, Bowl, Footed, Marigold, 7 1/2 In. 60.00
Lustre Rose, Butter, Cover, Marigold 60.00
Lustre Rose, Fernery, Olive 75.00
Lustre Rose, Pitcher, Marigold 65.00
Magnolia & Poinsettia pattern is listed here as Water Lily
Maine Coast pattern is listed here as Seacoast
Many Stars, Bowl, Green 475.00
Maple Leaf, Pitcher, Amethyst 275.00
Marilyn, Pitcher, Green 950.00
Maryland pattern is listed here as Rustic
Mayan, Bowl, Purple, 9 In. 125.00
Melon & Fan pattern is listed here as Diamond & Rib
Memphis, Berry Set, Marigold, 5 Piece 150.00
Memphis, Bowl, Fluted, Blue, 11 In. 500.00
Memphis, Punch Set, Amethyst, 7 Piece 650.00
Memphis, Punch Set, Marigold, 7 Piece 495.00
Milady, Water Set, Blue, 7 Piece ....*Illus* 800.00
Morning Glory, Vase, Purple, 6 In. 60.00
Morning Glory, Vase, Purple, 13 In. 300.00
Mum, Bowl, Footed, Amethyst, Large 110.00
Nesting Swan pattern is listed here as Swan, Carnival
Oak Leaf pattern is listed here as Leaf Swirl
Oak Leaf & Acorn pattern is listed here as Acorn
Octagon, Goblet, Marigold 30.00
Octagon, Pitcher, Marigold 65.00
Octagon, Tumbler, Purple 75.00
Octagon, Wine Set, Marigold, 7 Piece 250.00
Octagon, Wine, Marigold 22.50
Old Fashion Flag pattern is listed here as Iris
Open Rose, Bowl, Fluted, Stippled, Amber 60.00
Open Rose, Plate, Marigold, 9 In. 125.00
Open Rose, Plate, Stippled, Amber, 9 In. 250.00
Orange Tree & Cable pattern is listed here as Orange Tree Orchard
Orange Tree Orchard, Pitcher, Blue 375.00
Orange Tree Orchard, Tumbler, Cobalt Blue 75.00

Carnival Glass, Milady, Water Set, Blue, 7 Piece

Orange Tree Orchard, Water Set, Blue, 5 Piece	700.00
Orange Tree, Bowl, White, 8 In.	250.00
Orange Tree, Centerpiece Bowl, Marigold, Large	75.00
Orange Tree, Goblet, Amber	60.00
Orange Tree, Hatpin Holder, Blue	275.00 To 395.00
Orange Tree, Hatpin Holder, Marigold	130.00 To 175.00
Orange Tree, Mug, Amber	95.00
Orange Tree, Mug, Blue	95.00
Orange Tree, Mug, Marigold	15.00 To 30.00
Orange Tree, Mug, Vaseline	100.00
Orange Tree, Plate, Bearded Berry Exterior, Blue, 9 In.	550.00
Orange Tree, Plate, Bearded Berry Exterior, White, 9 In.	400.00
Orange Tree, Plate, Blue, 9 1/4 In.	495.00
Orange Tree, Powder Jar, Blue	95.00
Orange Tree, Punch Bowl, Marigold, 2 Piece	150.00
Orange Tree, Punch Bowl, White	450.00
Orange Tree, Punch Cup, Blue	18.00
Orange Tree, Punch Set, Blue, 6 Piece	500.00
Orange Tree, Rose Bowl, Purple	75.00
Orange Tree, Shaving Mug	75.00
Orange Tree, Tumbler, Blue	45.00
Orange Tree, Wine, Marigold	22.50
Oriental Poppy, Tumbler, Amethyst	45.00
Oriental Poppy, Tumbler, Marigold	30.00
Oriental Poppy, Tumbler, Purple	160.00
Paneled Bachelor Buttons pattern is listed here as Milady	
Panelled Dandelion, Pitcher, Marigold	250.00
Panelled Dandelion, Tankard, Blue	490.00
Panelled Dandelion, Tumbler, Blue	65.00
Panelled Dandelion, Tumbler, Purple	50.00
Pansy, Bowl, Ruffled, Purple, 9 In.	65.00
Pansy, Relish, Oval, Marigold	45.00
Pansy, Relish, Purple	50.00
Pansy, Sugar & Creamer, Marigold	65.00
Panther, Bowl, Marigold, 5 In.	48.00 To 60.00
Panther, Bowl, Marigold, 10 In.	160.00
Parlor Panels, Vase, Marigold, 8 In.	40.00
Pastel Panels, Tumbler, Green, 6 Piece	220.00
Peach, Pitcher, White	800.00
Peacock & Grape, Bowl, Amethyst, 7 3/4 In.	175.00
Peacock & Grape, Bowl, Marigold, 7 3/4 In.	45.00

Peacock & Grape, Bowl, Marigold, 8 1/2 In. 90.00
Peacock & Grape, Bowl, Red, 7 3/4 In. .... 250.00 To 550.00
Peacock & Urn, Bowl, Amethyst, 8 3/4 In. 200.00
Peacock & Urn, Bowl, Blue, 9 In. 145.00
Peacock & Urn, Bowl, Ice Cream, Purple, 6 In. 70.00
Peacock & Urn, Bowl, Ice Cream, Stippled, Marigold, 10 In. 650.00
Peacock & Urn, Plate, Blue 1200.00
Peacock & Urn, Plate, Marigold, 9 1/2 In. 275.00
Peacock & Urn, Ruffled, Marigold, 8 1/4 In. 90.00
Peacock At The Fountain, Bowl, Amethyst, 10 In. .... 225.00 To 300.00
Peacock At The Fountain, Orange Bowl, Amethyst .... 365.00 To 395.00
Peacock At The Fountain, Plate, Marigold, 5 3/4 In. 155.00
Peacock At The Fountain, Spooner, Amethyst 80.00
Peacock At The Fountain, Spooner, Blue 265.00
Peacock At The Fountain, Spooner, Green 400.00
Peacock At The Fountain, Sugar, Cover, Blue 265.00
Peacock At The Fountain, Table Set, Marigold, 6 Piece 425.00
Peacock At The Fountain, Tumbler, Marigold .... 40.00 To 50.00
Peacock At The Fountain, Water Set, Marigold, 6 Piece 500.00
Peacock Eye & Grape pattern is listed here as Vineyard
Peacock on Fence pattern is listed here as Peacocks
Peacock Tail, Bowl, Green, 5 1/2 In. 75.00
Peacock Tail, Bowl, Green, 7 In. 90.00
Peacock Tail, Bowl, Three-In-One Rim, Green, 8 1/2 In. 125.00
Peacock Tail, Hat, Central Furniture Co., Green .... 95.00 To 100.00
Peacock Tail, Hat, O'Dell Jewelry, Green 100.00
Peacocks, Plate, Ice Green, 9 In. .... 600.00 To 750.00
Persian Garden, Bowl, Ice Cream, White, 6 In. 85.00
Persian Garden, Bowl, Ice Cream, White, 11 In. .... 285.00 To 310.00
Persian Medallion, Berry Set, Blue, 5 Piece 145.00
Persian Medallion, Bonbon, Handle, Blue 55.00
Persian Medallion, Bonbon, Red 1050.00
Persian Medallion, Bowl, Flared, Marigold, 7 In. 38.00
Persian Medallion, Bowl, Marigold, 7 1/2 In. 40.00
Persian Medallion, Bowl, Ruffled, Blue, 8 In. 185.00
Persian Medallion, Compote, Blue 68.00
Persian Medallion, Hair Receiver, Blue 90.00
Persian Medallion, Plate, Marigold, 6 In. .... 30.00 To 55.00
Petal & Fan, Bowl, Peach, 10 In. 175.00
Petal & Fan, Bowl, White, 11 In. 500.00
Petal & Fan, Plate, Ruffled, Peach, 6 In. 125.00
Peter Rabbit, Bowl, Marigold 450.00
Pine Cone Wreath pattern is listed here as Pine Cone
Pine Cone, Bowl, Blue, 5 3/4 In. 40.00
Pine Cone, Plate, Blue, 6 In. 80.00
Pineapple, Creamer, Marigold 35.00
Pineapple, Rose Bowl, Amber 95.00
Plaid, Bowl, Green, 8 In. 345.00
Plaid, Bowl, Ruffled, Red, 8 In. 3500.00
Poinsettia & Lattice pattern is listed here as Poinsettia
Poinsettia, Bowl, Footed, Amethyst 230.00
Poinsettia, Pitcher, Milk, Marigold 75.00
Poppy Show, Bowl, Amethyst 400.00
Princess Lace pattern is listed here as Octagon
Prism, Bonbon, Handles, Marigold 65.00
Prisms, Bonbon, Marigold 38.00
Queen's Crown pattern is listed here as Royalty
Question Marks, Bonbon, Marigold 27.00
Question Marks, Bonbon, White 50.00
Raspberry, Pitcher, Milk, Purple 125.00
Raspberry, Pitcher, Purple .... 225.00 To 270.00
Raspberry, Tumbler, Purple .... 40.00 To 45.00
Raspberry, Water Set, Purple, 5 Piece 415.00

Rib & Panel, Water Set, Marigold, 7 Piece 295.00
Ripple, Vase, Marigold, 10 In. 30.00
Rising Sun, Pitcher, Marigold .... 775.00 To 825.00
Rising Sun, Tumbler, Marigold 350.00
Robin Red Breast pattern is listed here as Robin
Robin, Water Set, Marigold, 7 Piece 275.00
Rosalind, Bowl, Amethyst, 10 In. 200.00
Rosalind, Bowl, Green, 10 1/2 In. 175.00
Rosalind, Bowl, Ruffled, Green, 10 In. .... 165.00 To 275.00
Rose & Ruffles pattern is listed here as Open Rose
Rose Show, Bowl, Aqua 1275.00
Round–Up, Bowl, White 125.00
Round–Up, Plate, Blue 295.00
Round–Up, Plate, White 218.00
Royalty, Punch Cup, Marigold 10.00
Rustic, Vase, Amethyst, 11 In. 700.00
Rustic, Vase, Marigold, 16 In. 125.00
Sailboat & Windmill pattern is listed here as Sailboats
Sailboats, Bowl, Marigold, 6 In. .... 30.00 To 35.00
Sailboats, Plate, Marigold 400.00
Seacoast, Pin Tray, Green, 5 1/2 x 4 In. 330.00
Shell & Jewel, Creamer, Green 40.00
Singing Birds, Berry Set, Blue, 5 Piece 400.00
Singing Birds, Bowl, Blue, 5 In. 60.00
Singing Birds, Creamer, Amethyst 165.00
Singing Birds, Mug, Aqua Opalescent 695.00
Singing Birds, Mug, Blue 175.00
Singing Birds, Mug, Marigold 60.00
Singing Birds, Tumbler, Green .... 35.00 To 50.00
Ski Star, Banana Boat, Peach 125.00
Ski Star, Bowl, Peach, 10 In. 65.00
Ski Star, Plate, Crimped Edge, Peach, 6 1/2 In. 145.00
Soda Gold, Pitcher, Marigold 125.00
Soda Gold, Salt & Pepper, Marigold 95.00
Soda Gold, Water Set, Marigold, 7 Piece 200.00
Spider Web pattern is listed here as Soda Gold
Stag & Holly, Bowl, Footed, Marigold, 10 In. 95.00
Stag & Holly, Bowl, Footed, Marigold, 11 In. 85.00
Stag & Holly, Bowl, Footed, Peach, 9 In. 1900.00
Stag & Holly, Chop Plate, Marigold 795.00
Star & File, Creamer, Marigold 35.00
Star & File, Tumbler, Marigold 100.00
Star Of David & Bows, Bowl, Blue, 8 1/2 In. 75.00
Star Of David & Bows, Bowl, Gold Star, Purple, 8 1/2 In. 140.00
Star Of David Medallion pattern is listed here as Star Of David & Bows
Star Of David, Bowl, Purple, 8 1/2 In. 95.00
Stippled Clematis pattern is listed here as Little Stars
Stippled Leaf & Beads pattern is listed here as Leaf & Beads
Stippled Posy & Pods pattern is listed here as Four Flowers
Stippled Rays, Bowl, Flared, Marigold, 8 In. 30.00
Stippled Rays, Bowl, Ruffled, Purple, 9 1/2 In. 55.00
Stippled Rays, Compote, Green, 6 1/2 In. 30.00
Stippled Rays, Plate, Marigold, 7 In. 35.00
Stork & Rushes, Berry Set, Marigold, 7 Piece 245.00
Stork & Rushes, Bowl, Amethyst, 4 3/4 In. 150.00
Stork & Rushes, Creamer, Marigold 80.00
Stork & Rushes, Punch Cup, Amethyst .... 17.50 To 19.00
Strawberry Scroll, Tumbler, Marigold 175.00
Strawberry, Bonbon, Marigold 25.00
Strawberry, Bowl, Fluted, 9 In. 80.00
Strawberry, Bowl, Piecrust Rim, Purple, 8 1/2 In. 75.00
Strawberry, Bowl, Ruffled, Purple 85.00
Strawberry, Plate, Green, 9 In. 125.00

Strawberry, Plate, Purple, 9 In. 135.00
Sunflower pattern is listed here as Dandelion
Sunflower–wheat–clover pattern is listed here as Harvest Flower
Swan, Carnival, Bowl, Ruffled, Marigold 165.00
Swirl Hobnail, Rose Bowl, Marigold 275.00
Swirl Hobnail, Rose Bowl, Purple 65.00
Ten Mums, Bowl, Crimped, Green 135.00
Ten Mums, Bowl, Green, 10 In. 75.00
Thin Rib, Vase, Aqua, 10 In. 195.00
Thin Rib, Vase, Green, 11 1/2 In. 75.00
Thistle, Banana Boat, Amethyst .... 345.00 To 450.00
Thistle, Banana Boat, Marigold 225.00
Thistle, Bowl, Advertising, Horlacker, Green 140.00
Three Fruits Medallion Bowl, Footed, Marigold, 10 1/2 In. 125.00
Three Fruits, Bowl, Amethyst, 9 In. 135.00
Three Fruits, Bowl, Olive, 9 In. 95.00
Three Fruits, Bowl, Ruffled, Amethyst, 7 In. 85.00
Three Fruits, Plate, Amethyst 225.00
Three Fruits, Plate, Stippled, Amethyst 425.00
Three Fruits, Plate, Stippled, Purple 425.00
Three Fruits, Tumbler, Marigold, 6 Piece 395.00
Tiger Lily, Water Set, Marigold, 7 Piece .... 195.00 To 295.00
Tree Of Life, Bowl, Marigold 30.00
Tree Trunk, Vase, Funeral, Elephant Foot, Amethyst 900.00
Tree Trunk, Vase, Squatty, Green, 7 1/2 In. 115.00
Tree Trunk, Water Set, Marigold, 8 Piece 125.00
Two Flowers, Berry Bowl, Vaseline, Master .... 195.00 To 245.00
Two Flowers, Bowl, 3–Footed, Cobalt Blue, 11 In. 85.00
Two Flowers, Bowl, 3–Footed, Marigold, 9 In. 85.00
Two Flowers, Bowl, Footed, Blue, 6 In. 30.00
Two Flowers, Bowl, Footed, Marigold, 10 In. 65.00
Two Flowers, Rose Bowl, Blue .... 140.00 To 200.00
Two Flowers, Rose Bowl, Marigold 165.00
Vineyard, Pitcher, Marigold .... 75.00 To 110.00
Vintage Banded, Tumbler, Marigold 75.00
Vintage Leaf, Bowl, Amethyst 74.00
Vintage, Bowl, Flared, Blue, 9 In. 45.00
Vintage, Bowl, Green, 7 In. 95.00
Vintage, Bowl, Marigold, 10 In. 35.00
Vintage, Bowl, Ruffled, Red, 9 In. 1150.00
Vintage, Fernery, Blue .... 50.00 To 68.00
Vintage, Nut Bowl, Blue 80.00
Vintage, Nut Bowl, White 95.00
Vintage, Plate, Scalloped, Marigold, 7 In. 85.00
Vintage, Rose Bowl, 6–Footed, Purple 85.00
Vintage, Rose Bowl, Amethyst 70.00
Vintage, Rose Bowl, Marigold 60.00
Vintage, Rose Bowl, Purple 90.00
Vintage, Wine, Marigold 18.00
Water Lily & Cattails, Bowl, Marigold, 5 1/2 In. 32.00
Water Lily & Cattails, Tumbler, Marigold .... 33.00 To 36.00
Water Lily, Bowl, Footed, Blue, 10 In. 120.00
Windflower, Bowl, Ruffled, Amethyst, 8 In. 75.00
Windmill Medallion pattern is listed here as Windmill
Windmill, Bowl, Marigold, 8 In. 55.00
Windmill, Bowl, Ruffled, Purple, 8 In. 55.00
Windmill, Pitcher, Marigold .... 65.00 To 100.00
Wishbone & Spades, Bowl, Ruffled, Purple, 10 In. 265.00
Wishbone & Spades, Plate, Amethyst, 10 1/2 In. .... 700.00 To 800.00
Wishbone & Spades, Plate, Purple, 10 1/2 In. 600.00
Wishbone, Bowl, Footed, Amethyst, 8 1/2 In. 60.00
Wishbone, Bowl, Green, 10 1/2 In. 130.00
Wisteria & Lattice pattern is listed here as Wisteria

Wisteria, Pitcher, Ice Blue 4000.00
Wreath Of Roses, Cup, Green 37.50
Wreathed Cherry, Bowl, Marigold, 12 1/2 In. 85.00
Zig Zag, Pitcher, Enameled, Blue 200.00
Zig Zag, Pitcher, Enameled, White 395.00

CAROUSEL or merry–go–round figures were first carved in the United
States in 1867 by Gustav Dentzel. Collectors discovered the charm of the
hand–carved figures in the 1970s and they were soon classed as folk art.
Most desirable are the figures other than horses, such as pigs, camels,
lions, or dogs. A jumper is a figure that was made to move up and down
on a pole, a stander was placed in a stationary position.

Cat, France .... 5060.00 To 5100.00
Donkey, Bobbing Head, France 2200.00
Elephant, Bayol, c.1920, 25 In. 1920.00
Horse Head, Cast Iron, Parker 1250.00
Horse, 2nd Row Jumper, Philadelphia Toboggan Co., c.1916 .... 9020.00
Horse, Animal Skin Blanket, Herschell Spillman 3740.00
Horse, Animal Skin Blanket, Parker 3740.00
Horse, Bow On Side, Spillman 6000.00
Horse, Carmel, Bejeweled, c.1915 .... 7700.00
Horse, English Jumper, Spooner 3000.00
Horse, Frederick Heyn, c.1910, 83 In. 5170.00
Horse, Galloper, Savage, 1890 .... 1695.00
Horse, Jumper, American Flag, Parker 4670.00
Horse, Jumper, Armored, Outside Row, Parker, c.1920 .... 1540.00
Horse, Jumper, Armored, Parker .... 5500.00 To 7100.00
Horse, Jumper, Bedecked With Roses, Tucked Head, C. W. Parker, 1920s 7700.00
Horse, Jumper, Carmel 7700.00
Horse, Jumper, Charles Marcus Illions, c.1920 .... 7700.00
Horse, Jumper, Charles Marcus, c.1920 .... 7700.00
Horse, Jumper, Frederick Heyn, c.1910 .... 5200.00
Horse, Jumper, Horsehair Tail, Charles Marcus Illions, c.1910 .... 7700.00
Horse, Jumper, Illions, 1910 .... 8000.00
Horse, Jumper, Inner Row, Herschell–Spillman 9400.00
Horse, Jumper, Jeweled, Carmel, c.1915 .... 7700.00
Horse, Jumper, Levenworth, c.1905 .... 9200.00
Horse, Jumper, Second Row, Philadelphia Toboggan Co. 9000.00
Horse, Jumper, Spooner, England 3000.00
Horse, Jumper, Tucked Head, Parker, 1920 .... 3600.00
Horse, Outside Jumper, Herschell–Spillman, c.1925 .... 3850.00
Horse, Painted, Jewels, PTC 6500.00
Horse, Pegasus Designed, Parker 5500.00
Horse, Pony, Lasso & Six Shooter, C. W. Parker 3575.00
Horse, Prancer, Heyn, c.1900, 55 1/2 In. 2200.00
Horse, Prancing, Dare, Missing Tail 3630.00
Horse, Standing Position, Dentzel 4620.00
Horse, Stripped, Illions 5800.00
Horse, With Rider, Papier-Mache, Carnival 350.00
Horse, Wooden Body, Metal Head, Legs & Tail, Herschell–Spillman 1450.00
Horse, Yellow Body, England, 1890 .... 1950.00
Indian Head, Allan Herschell, Aluminum, 20 In. 135.00
Motorcycle 2250.00
Panel, Mirrored, From Coney Island, Illions 600.00
Pig, Dentzel 7700.00
Rabbit, Bayol .... 3500.00 To 3520.00
Rooster, Coquereau & Marechal, c.1900, 51 In. 3300.00
Rooster, Laminated Wood 1500.00
Rounding Board, Mirrored, 9 Ft. 2640.00
Swan, Swimming Position, Philadelphia Toboggan Co. 1045.00

Carriage, Baby Buggy, Wooden, Umbrella,
Iron Wheels, 46 1/2 In.

Castor Set, 6-Bottle, Silver-Plated, 18 In.

CARRIAGE means several things, so this section lists baby carriages, buggies for adults, horse–drawn sleighs, and even strollers. Doll–sized carriages are listed in the Toy category.

Baby Buggy, Canvas Top With Windows, Cream Color	715.00
Baby Buggy, Open, Folds, 1910	125.00
Baby Buggy, Parasol, Hayward's Brothers–Wakefield Co.	1100.00
Baby Buggy, Victorian, Fringed Surrey, Blue & Cream Paint, c.1860	880.00
Baby Buggy, Victorian, Wicker, 39 x 50 In.	770.00
Baby Buggy, Wooden Spokes, Wicker Both Sides, Portholes, Kroll	255.00
Baby Buggy, Wooden, Umbrella, Iron Wheels, 46 1/2 In. ....*Illus*	1100.00
Buggy Seat, Folding, Carpet Covered, Metal Frame, c.1896	60.00
Buggy, Studebaker, Horse Drawn, Wicker Seat, Side Lamps	1900.00
Cannon, Black Powder, Wagon Wheels, Accessories, Chest	5500.00
Cart, Baby's, Leather On Back, 2 Large Rubber Wheels, Arms	365.00
Cart, Child's, Seat Flips, Can Be Pushed Or Pulled, Wooden	150.00
Push Cart, Iron Canopy Supports, Wheels, Push Bar, Wicker, 2 Seater	2200.00
Riding Chair, White Wicker, Atlantic City Boardwalk, Cushion, 1914	350.00
Sled, Reindeer, Lapland	425.00
Sleigh, Child's, Push, Red Paint, Yellow & Black Stringing	950.00
Sleigh, Push, Paris, Dark Green, 32 x 45 In.	248.00
Sleigh, Refinished, Wrought Iron Hardware, 36 x 21 In.	495.00
Sleigh, Tufted Upholstery, Graves & Eighmy Co., Springboro, Pa.	1200.00
Stroller, Wicker, Retracting Wheels, 1900s	250.00
Surrey, Fringe Top, 2 Seater, 1890s, Full Size	2400.00
Surrey, Kerosene Lamps, 2 Leather Seats, Harness	3000.00
Wagon, Buckboard, Child's, Wood, Wrought Iron, Paint Traces, 39 In.	600.00

CASH REGISTERS were invented in 1884 because an eye on the cash was a necessity in stores of the nineteenth century, too. John and James Ritty invented a large model that resembled a clock and kept a record of the dollars and cents exchanged in the store. John Patterson improved the cash register with a paper roll to record the money. By the early 1900s, elaborate brass registers were made. About World War I, the fancy case was exchanged for the more modern types.

Dayton, Scoop, Scrollwork, Brass, 3 Lb.	115.00
Dodge Register Co., Wooden	795.00
Michigan, Candy Store, Scrollwork	350.00
Michigan, Model 1	500.00

Michigan, Model 2	600.00
National, Chapman House, 1480 488 G	700.00
National, Model 6	750.00
National, Model 31	2700.00
National, Model 47 1/4, 2 Drawers, Wooden	2400.00
National, Model 50, Marquee	1200.00
National, Model 79, Brass, Cranker	500.00
National, Model 130	1000.00
National, Model 135	500.00
National, Model 216, Brass	1400.00
National, Model 313	750.00 To 1495.00
National, Model 313, Candy Shop	550.00
National, Model 313, Candy Store, Brass	825.00
National, Model 313, Ice Cream Parlor, Brass	900.00
National, Model 317	1000.00
National, Model 441	675.00 To 1200.00
National, Model 442XX, Brass	675.00
National, Model 452, Brass	600.00
National, Model 500, Bronze Cabinet, Mahogany Base	4500.00
National, Nickel Plated, Small	160.00 To 650.00
National, Wood Grained Tin	30.00
St. Louis, Brass, Stamped	445.00
Western, Marquee	1200.00

CASTOR SETS holding just salt and pepper castors were used in the seventeenth century. The sugar castor, mustard pot, spice dredger, bottles for vinegar and oil, and other spice holders became popular by the eighteenth century. These sets were usually made of sterling silver. The American Victorian castor set, the type most collected today, was made of silver plated Britannia metal. Colored glass bottles were introduced after the Civil War. The sets were out of fashion by World War I. Be careful when buying sets with colored bottles; many are reproductions. Other castor sets may be listed in various porcelain and glass categories in this book.

4–Bottle, Burmese Glass, Peach To Yellow, Silvered Stand, 8 In.	1540.00
5–Bottle, Clear, Etched, Cover	195.00
6–Bottle, Silver–Plated, 18 In. ....*Illus*	125.00
8–Bottles, Sheffield, 1870, 12 In.	465.00
Florette Pattern, Pink Cased	225.00

CASTORS for pickles are glass jars about six inches in height, held in special metal holders. They became a popular dinner table accessory about 1890. Each jar had a top that was usually silver or silver plate. The frame, also of a silver metal, had a handle that arched above the jar and a hook that held a pair of tongs. By 1900, the pickle castor was out of fashion. Many examples found today have reproduced glass jars in old holders. Additional pickle castors may be found in the various Glass categories.

Pickle, Baby Thumbprint Insert, Cranberry, 11 In.	425.00
Pickle, Baby Thumbprint, Floral Enameling, Frame, Tongs, Cranberry	395.00
Pickle, Baby Thumbprint, White & Green Floral, Saucer Base, Tongs	395.00
Pickle, Bell Shape Ruby Insert, Panel Design, Silver Frame	350.00
Pickle, Chick Finial, Coralene Rose & Coralene Roses Insert, Tongs	495.00
Pickle, Cone Insert, Cranberry, Silver Plated Frame	395.00
Pickle, Cut Glass, Ornate, Silver Plated Frame	280.00
Pickle, Daisy & Button With V Ornament, Crystal, Side Handled Frame	195.00
Pickle, Daisy & Button, Encircling Vine On Frame, Tongs, Vaseline	345.00
Pickle, Daisy & Button, Entwined Vine & Leaves, Vaseline, 9 1/2 In.	375.00
Pickle, Daisy & Button, Silver Plated Frame	225.00
Pickle, Diamond–Quilted Insert, Blue, Frame With Tongs	495.00
Pickle, Enameled Amber Insert, Plated Holder	275.00
Pickle, Florals & Butterflies On Cranberry Insert, Tongs	325.00
Pickle, Hobnail, Silver Frame, Cranberry Opalescent	550.00
Pickle, Inverted Thumbprint Jar, Tongs, 11 1/2 In.	480.00

Pickle, Inverted Thumbprint, Bulbous Jar, Plated Frame, Tongs 265.00
Pickle, Inverted Thumbprint, Caterpillars, Gold Leaves, Fork, Derby 495.00
Pickle, Inverted Thumbprint, Cranberry, Silver Plated Holder 250.00
Pickle, Inverted Thumbprint, Enameled Flowers, Cranberry, 3 1/2 In. 310.00
Pickle, Inverted Thumbprint, Plated Frame, Cover & Tongs, Cranberry 335.00
Pickle, Inverted Thumbprint, Silver Frame 295.00
Pickle, Mother-of-Pearl Insert, Herringbone, Silver Frame 900.00
Pickle, Mother-of-Pearl, Quilted, Apricot 450.00
Pickle, Opalescent Hobnail, Raspberry To White, Frame, Tongs 385.00
Pickle, Optic Panel Insert, Florals, Fork, Derby Frame, Cranberry 295.00
Pickle, Optic Paneled, Wilcox Frame, Tongs 325.00
Pickle, Plated Cucumber Finial, Engraved, Oval 450.00
Pickle, Reverse Baby Thumbprint, Plated Vine Handle, Cranberry 395.00
Pickle, Reverse Swirl Insert, Blue Opalescent, Frame, Tongs 250.00
Pickle, Spanish Lace Insert, Metal Frame, Tongs 345.00
Pickle, Torpedo, Silver Plated Frame & Tongs 135.00
Pickle, Vertical Ribbed Floral Insert, Simpson Hall Frame, 9 In. 315.00
Pickle, Virginia Pattern, Footed, Frame, Tongs 125.00
Pickle, White Floral, Blue, Vertical Ribbed, Footed Saucer, Tongs 275.00
Pickle, Zipper, Silver Plated Frame 135.00

CATALOGS are listed in the Paper category.

CAUGHLEY items may be found in the Salopian category.

CAULDON Limited worked in Staffordshire, Great Britain, and went through many name changes. John Ridgway made porcelain at Cauldon Place, Hanley, until 1855. The firm of John Ridgway, Bates and Co. of Cauldon Place worked from 1856 to 1859. It became Bates, Brown-Westhead, Moore and Co. from 1859 to 1862. Brown-Westhead, Moore and Co. worked from 1862 to 1904. About 1890, this firm started using the words *Cauldon* or *Cauldon ware* as part of the mark. Cauldon Ltd. worked from 1905 to 1920, Cauldon Potteries from 1920 to 1962. Related items may be found in the Indian Tree category.

Cup & Saucer, Flowers, Gold, Blue Trim 25.00
Plate, Landscape, 10 1/2 In. 45.00
Platter, Fish, 23 3/4 In. 495.00

CELS are listed in this book in the Animation Art category.

CELADON is a Chinese porcelain having a velvet-textured green-gray glaze. Japanese, Korean, and other factories also made a celadon-colored glaze.

Bow, Shallow Conical Form, Carved Peony & Foliage, 7 In. 2200.00
Jardiniere, White Central Band, Dragons, Leaves, 7 1/8 x 9 5/16 In. 550.00
Planter, Tree Design, Brown & Blue, 6 3/4 In. 195.00
Urn, 10 1/2 x 8 In. 165.00
Vase, Enamel Flowers, Ormolu Footed Base, 13 1/4 In. 525.00
Vase, Lotus Shape, Oval, Ch'ing Dynasty, 3 In. 110.00

CELLULOID is a trademark for a plastic developed in 1868 by John W. Hyatt. Celluloid Manufacturing Company, the Celluloid Novelty Company, Celluloid Fancy Goods Company, and American Xylonite Company all used Celluloid to make jewelry, games, sewing equipment, false teeth, and piano keys. Eventually, the Hyatt Company became the American Celluloid and Chemical Manufacturing Company—the Celanese Corporation. The name *Celluloid* was often used to identify any similar plastic. Celluloid toys are listed under toys.

Box, Dresser, Blue, White, Orange, Art Deco 75.00
Box, Photo Young Men Rowing On Cover, Harvard 1918, 5 x 3 In. 18.00
Card Holder, Animals, Clowns, 2 In., 4 Piece ....*Illus* 40.00
Clip, Crib, Pair 24.00
Comb, Pale Amber, Green Stones 35.00

Container, Gold Tip Gum	150.00
Dresser Set, Pearlized, Art Deco, Rhinestones, 1920, 16 Piece	300.00
Dresser Set, Raised & Painted Floral & Bird Design, 7 Piece	66.00
Mirror, Hand, Beveled Glass	10.00
Portrait Mirror, Beveled, Hand Painted, 3 x 4 In.	210.00
Rattle, Sailor Boy	80.00
Rattle, Tom Thumb Holding Pit	95.00
Shade, Butterflies, Pair	55.00
Teething Ring, Stork	50.00
Thimble, Cur–Ly–Cue, Beauty Salon, Oakland Ca., 1940	8.00

CERAMIC ART COMPANY of Trenton, New Jersey, was established in 1889 by J. Coxon and W. Lenox and was an early producer of American Belleek porcelain. It became Lenox, Inc. in 1906. Do not confuse this ware with the pottery made by the Ceramic Arts Studio of Madison, Wisconsin.

Cup & Saucer, Engagement Pattern, Rose, CAC Mark	75.00
Mug, Flowers, Leaves	160.00

CERAMIC ARTS STUDIO was founded in Madison, Wisconsin, by Lawrence Rabbett and Ruben Sand. Their most popular products were expensive molded figurines. The pottery closed in 1955. Do not confuse these products with those of the Ceramic Art Co. of Trenton, New Jersey.

Bank, Barber's Head	47.50
Bank, Skunk	110.00
Figurine, Archibald Dragon	115.00
Figurine, Ballerina	25.00
Figurine, Bopeep, Peach & Blue	20.00
Figurine, Calico Dog	16.00
Figurine, Cat, Siamese, Thai Thai	25.00
Figurine, Cats, Small & Large, 4 1/4 In.	40.00
Figurine, Chinese Girl, 6 In.	25.00
Figurine, King's Jester, Lutist & Flutist, 11 In., Pair	225.00
Figurine, Lamb	14.00
Figurine, Lillibelle	35.00
Figurine, Little Boy Blue, Green & Blue Stripes	15.00
Figurine, Native & Elephant	100.00
Plaque, Manchu & Lotus, Pair	125.00
Salt & Pepper, Brown Bear With Baby	45.00
Salt & Pepper, Chihuahua & Doghouse	65.00
Salt & Pepper, Mother & Baby Brown Bear	25.00
Salt & Pepper, Mother & Baby Polar Bear	25.00
Shaker, Horse Head	22.00
Shaker, Kitten	15.00
Shelf Sitter, Boy With Horn	18.00
Shelf Sitter, Chinese Girl	17.00
Shelf Sitter, Dutch Boy & Girl, Blue, Pair	30.00
Shelf Sitter, Michele & Maurice, Pair	45.00

Celluloid, Card Holder, Animals, Clowns, 2 In., 4 Piece

Vase, Art Deco, Duck	35.00

CHALKWARE is really plaster of Paris decorated with watercolors. One type was molded from Staffordshire and other porcelain models and painted and sold as inexpensive decorations in the nineteenth century. Figures of plaster, made from about 1910 to 1940 for use as prizes at carnivals, are also known as chalkware. Kewpie dolls made of chalkware will be found in their own section.

Ashtray, Black Baby, Red Polka Dot Panties, Big Eyes	23.00
Bookends, Colonial Boy & Girl	5.00
Bust, Indian, Baily Co., 1901, 18 In.	675.00
Dog, Collie, 12 In.	8.00
Figurine, Ballerina, Girl, 7 1/2 In.	3.85
Figurine, Cat, Seated, Old Black Paint, 8 1/2 In.	200.00
Figurine, Cat, Seated, Original Polychrome Paint, 9 1/2 In.	1250.00
Figurine, Elsie Cow, Sitting, Crazed, 10 3/4 In.	8.00
Figurine, Girls & Woman, Yardley's Old English Lavender, 14 In.	225.00
Figurine, Indian	10.00
Figurine, Indian On Horse, 1935	20.00
Figurine, Kissing Chickens, 5 1/2 In.	800.00
Figurine, Kissing Doves, 5 1/8 In.	800.00
Figurine, Lovebirds, Original Paint, 11 In., Pair	750.00
Figurine, Pig, Rice	85.00
Figurine, Poodle, Black, Gold, With Silver Glitter Trim	3.00
Figurine, Rabbit, Yellow, 5 In.	1800.00
Figurine, Rin Tin Tin, 7 In.	10.00
Figurine, Rooster, 7 In.	1700.00
Figurine, Scootles Boy & Girl, Jesco, Box, 16 In.	125.00
Figurine, Squirrel, 5 In.	500.00
Head, Black Man, Primitive, Polychrome, 20th Century, 6 In.	220.00
Lamp, 3 Cocker Spaniel Pups	35.00
Lamp, Black Poodle, 20 In.	8.00
Plaque, Chinese Figure, Marked Yamaka, 7 In., Pair	35.00
Plaque, Dutch Figure, Marked Yamaka, 7 In., Pair	35.00
Wall Pocket, Hanging Basket	22.00

CHARLIE CHAPLIN, the famous comic and actor, lived from 1889 to 1977. He made his first movie in 1913. He did the movie *The Tramp* in 1915. The character of the Tramp has remained famous and in the 1980s he appeared in a series of television commercials for computers. Dolls, candy containers, and all sorts of memorabilia picture Charlie Chaplin. Pieces are being made even today.

Bank, Glass, Contained Candy, Original Closure	150.00
Book, Up In The Air, 1917	100.00
Box, Glove, Wood Burnt	45.00
Candy Container, Charlie, Standing Next To Barrel	145.00
Cover, Literary Digest Magazine, 1935	18.00
Hat, Child's, 1915	325.00
Movie Film	30.00
Pencil Holder, Figural, Ceramic, No Umbrella	15.00
Song Sheet, Mandalay, Charlie Chaplin Cover, 1924	30.00

CHARLIE McCARTHY was the ventriloquist's dummy used by Edgar Bergen from the 1930s. He was famous for his work in radio, movies, and television. The act was retired in the 1970s.

Bank, Composition	300.00
Bank, Movable Wooden Jaw, 5 1/2 In.	357.00
Book, Big Little Book, No. 1456	20.00
Car, Charlie & Mortimer Snerd, Tin, Windup, 1939	2900.00
Card, Greeting, Charlie & Actress Andrea Leeds, 1938	28.00
Doll, Dummy, 1930s, 32 In.	150.00
Doll, Ventriloquist, Mouth Moves, Composition, 12 1/2 In.	120.00
Doll, Ventriloquist, Wooden	80.00

Eggcup, Lusterware, 1930s	185.00
Figure, Wood, Composition, String Moves Mouth, 12 In.	175.00
Game, Radio Party, Spinner, 4 Figures, Envelope	50.00
Paper Doll, Set Of 4, Different Costumes, 15 1/2 In.	95.00
Pin, Figural	18.00
Pin, Mechanical	45.00
Puppet, Cardboard, Chase & Sanborn, 8 x 20 In.	62.00
Radio	1850.00
Radio, Majestic, Charlie's Top Hat & Tails, Black Plastic	1800.00
Spoon	10.00 To 12.00
Toy, Benzine Buggy, Windup, Marx	500.00 To 650.00
Toy, Drummer, Windup, Marx, 1930s	825.00
Toy, Walker, Windup, Marx, 1930s	300.00

CHELSEA GRAPE pattern was made before 1840. A small bunch of grapes in a raised design, colored with purple or blue luster, is on the border of the white plate. Most of the pieces are unmarked. The pattern is sometimes called *Aynsley* or *Grandmother.* Chelsea sprig is similar but has a sprig of flowers instead of the bunch of grapes. Chelsea thistle has a raised thistle pattern. Do not confuse these Chelsea patterns with Chelsea Keramic Art Works, which can be found in the Dedham category, or with Chelsea porcelain, which is the next section.

Bowl, 6 In.	9.00
Cup	21.00 To 25.00
Gravy Boat	30.00
Plate, 8 In.	20.00
Sugar Bowl	35.00
Tea Set, Grape Clusters On Finials, 20 Piece	550.00
CHELSEA SPRIG, Bowl, 7 In.	20.00
Plate, 7 In.	18.00
Plate, 10 In.	20.00

CHELSEA PORCELAIN was made in the Chelsea area of London from about 1745 to 1784. Some pieces made from 1770 to 1784 may include the letter *D* for *Derby* in the mark. Ceramic designs were borrowed from the Meissen models of the day. Pieces were made of soft paste. The gold anchor was used as the mark but it has been copied by many other factories. Recent copies of Chelsea have been made from the original molds. Do not confuse Chelsea porcelain with Chelsea Grape, which is the previous category.

Box, Apple, Caterpillar Knop Cover, Red Anchor, 3 15/16 In.	4400.00
Candlestick, Courting Figures With Dogs, Marked, 6 1/2 In., Pair	615.00
Clock, Ship's Bell, Bronze Case & Base Dial, Signed Tiffany, 8 In.	1150.00
Dish, Sunflower, Mauve To Puce To Purple, Red Anchor, 9 1/8 In.	2750.00
Figurine, Girl With Lamb, Boy With Dog, Marked, Pair	5000.00
Jug, Goat & Bee, White, Oak Branch Handle, Triangle, 4 3/16 In.	7975.00
Plate, Botanical, Honeysuckle Sprig, Gold Anchor, 8 7/16 In.	1650.00
Plate, Brown Larch Branch, Buds, Hans Sloane, 1756, 8 3/8 In.	5500.00
Teabowl, Flowering Prunus Tree, Octagonal, Kakiemon, 3 3/8 In.	880.00
Tureen, Cover, Cauliflower, White Flowers, Red Anchor, 4 1/2 In.	2530.00
Tureen, Knop Cover, Asparagus, Red Anchor, 1755, 7 3/8 In.	8800.00

CHINESE EXPORT porcelain comprises all the many kinds of porcelain made in China for export to America and Europe in the eighteenth and nineteenth centuries. Other pieces may be listed in this book under Canton, Celadon, Nanking, and Rose Medallion.

Basket, Stand, Reticulated, Oval, c.1810, 10 In.	1100.00
Berry Dish, Arms Of Charles Talbot, Floral Rim, 6 1/2 In.	885.00
Bidet, Blue & White	2200.00
Bowl, Arms Of Company Of Bakers, c.1755, 11 3/8 In.	4675.00
Bowl, Cover, Peony Branch, Serpent Handles, c.1720, 6 5/8 In.	1200.00
Bowl, Insects, Cluster Of Flowers, Square, c.1780, 9 1/2 In.	935.00
Bowl, John Wilkes Portrait, Crest, c.1775, 10 1/4 In.	995.00

Bowl, Lotus, Quatrefoil Panels, c.1760, 10 1/4 In. 1760.00
Bowl, Pheasants On Pierced Rock, c.1750, 11 1/4 In. 1450.00
Bowl, Polychrome Floral Enameling, 9 In. 325.00
Bowl, Polychrome Floral, 8 In. 50.00
Bowl, Polychrome Nobles, Lobed Rim, Ovoid, 1800s, 11 x 3 In. 210.00
Charger, Arms Of Jacob Pelgrans, Pheasant On Rock, 14 In. 995.00
Charger, Arms Of Van Overveldt, Motto, c.1720, 20 3/8 In. 885.00
Charger, Emmott Arms, Trellis Work Rim, c.1745, 14 7/8 In. 1430.00
Charger, Kakiemon–Style, Brace Of Quail, c.1740, 14 In., Pr. 2750.00
Chocolate Pot, Armorial Crest Of Spanish Count 1980.00
Coffeepot, Europa & Bull, Dutch Silver Base, 1710, 12 In. 6050.00
Coffeepot, Figures On Terrace, Building, c.1785, 8 3/4 In. 660.00
Creamer, 3 Figures, Molded Handle, 4 1/4 In. 150.00
Creamer, Floral Design, Helmet Shape, 5 1/2 In. 175.00
Cup & Saucer, Armorial, Entwined Dragon Border, Pair 220.00
Cup & Saucer, Handleless, Amorial 95.00
Dish, Arms Of Manuel Alvares Pinto, Fluted, 1690, 8 7/16 In. 2350.00
Dish, Cover, Fruit Finial, Floral, Amorial, 4 In. 625.00
Dish, Dragon Border, Overglazed Gold, 7 7/8 In., Pair 660.00
Dish, Enamel, Figural Decoration, 8 3/4 In. Diam. 143.00
Dish, Hot Water, Arms Of Sir William Dalling, c.1785, 11 In. 220.00
Dish, Lotus, Peonies Behind Rocks, c.1760, 10 3/16 In. 1540.00
Dish, Warming, Cover, Blue & White, c.1780 .... 3870.00
Figurine, Bird, Leg Tucked Under Breast, c.1785, 5 1/8 In. 1320.00
Figurine, Shou Lao, Carved Wood, 16 In. 115.00
Flask, Pilgrim, Rose Mandarin, 9 3/4 In., Pair 3575.00
Garden Seat, Chrysanthemum, 19th Century, 18 In. ....*Illus* 550.00
Garden Seat, Hexagonal, Blue, 18 1/4 In. 5500.00
Garden Seat, Rose Medallion, 19th Century, 18 In. ....*Illus* 2200.00
Jar, Cover, Cabbage Leaf & Butterfly, 7 x 8 In. 350.00
Jar, Cover, Enameled Scenes Of Figures, Landscape, 11 In. 550.00
Jar, Famille Rose, Converted To Lamp, Pink & White 600.00
Jar, Ginger, Famille Rose, Ch'ing Dynasty, 8 In. 715.00
Light, Wall, Famille Rose, Scrolled Candle Arm, 14 1/4 In. 3300.00
Mug, Arms Of Martin Impaling Dalling, c.1780, 4 7/8 In. 995.00
Mug, British Maine Design, 1785, 5 3/8 In. 770.00
Mug, Continuous Scenes, River Landscape, c.1785, 5 1/2 In. 660.00
Plate, Amorial Shield, Bird, Crown, Double Border, 9 3/4 In. 225.00
Plate, Amorial, Polychrome Enameling, 9 In. 1050.00
Plate, Arms Of Jacob Pelgrans, Shell & Foliate, 8 1/8 In. 990.00
Plate, Arms Of Rudge, Famille Verte Panels, 9 15/16 In. 2200.00
Plate, Central Floral, Garland Edge, 9 1/4 In., 12 Piece 685.00
Plate, Chinese Woman With Parasol, 1736, 8 5/8 In. 1870.00
Plate, Dutch Couple With Dog, Garden, 1720–1730, 7 5/8 In. 770.00
Plate, Famille Rose, Off–White Ground, 8 3/4 In. 66.00
Plate, Gadrooned Rim, Bow Swags, Florals, 9 1/4 In., 4 Piece 715.00
Plate, Pseudo Tobacco Leaf, c.1785, 6 1/2 In., Pair 900.00

Chinese Export, Garden Seat, Rose
Medallion, 19th Century, 18 In.

Chinese Export, Garden Seat,
Chrysanthemum, 19th Century, 18 In.

Plate, Puce & Gilded Floral Swag, 18th Century, Pair 303.00
Plate, Tobacco Leaf, Sprigs, 1770–1780, 6 5/16 In., 4 Piece 1430.00
Platter, Amorial Shield, Bird, Red & Gilt, 13 In. 350.00
Platter, Arms Of Duke Of Anhalt–Dessau, 1750, 12 15/16 In. 2420.00
Platter, Arms Of Straffan House, c.1770, 11 3/4 In. 1350.00
Platter, Blue & White Floral, 10 In., Pair 190.00
Platter, Blue & White Floral, 12 3/8 In. 150.00
Platter, Blue, Lattice, Borders, Oval, Fitzhugh, 11 3/4 In. 275.00
Platter, Central Pine Cone, Beast Medallions, 14 11/16 In. 445.00
Platter, Eagle Motif, Pink Banded Border, Octagonal, 14 In. 300.00
Platter, Fitzhugh, 1810–1840, 17 3/8 In. ....775.00 To 1150.00
Platter, Floral Enameling, Gilt, 20 3/4 In. 400.00
Platter, Floral, Orange Peel Glaze, 15 1/4 In. 450.00
Platter, Polychrome Floral, Pink Rim, 12 3/4 In. 300.00
Platter, Pseudo Tobacco Leaf, c.1785, 11 1/2 In. 770.00
Platter, Pseudo Tobacco Leaf, c.1785, 12 7/8 In. 2475.00
Platter, Tobacco Leaf, Oval, 1770–1780, 18 15/16 In. 8800.00
Punch Bowl, Courtyard Scenes, Gilded Field, 12 7/8 In. 2860.00
Punch Bowl, Courtyard Scenes, Inside Florals, 10 1/2 In. 665.00
Punch Bowl, Famille Rose, Continuous Scene, c.1765, 15 In. 4125.00
Punch Bowl, Fox Hunting Scenes, Horse & Rider Interior 3600.00
Punch Bowl, Hibiscus Sprays, Gilt Floral, c.1760, 15 1/2 In. 8250.00
Punch Bowl, Panels Of Floral Clusters, c.1785, 14 1/2 In. 1875.00
Punch Bowl, River Scene, Figures, c.1775, 15 7/8 In. 6700.00
Punch Bowl, Rose Mandarin, Courtyard, 1840, 16 In. 2750.00
Punch Pot, Panels Of Dotted Lozenges, 1770, 7 5/8 In. 3300.00
Sauceboat, Leaf–Shaped Stand, Pseudo Tobacco Leaf, c.1785 .... 1450.00
Saucer, 3 Chinamen Hauling Boat, c.1740, 9 1/4 In. 1650.00
Saucer, Arms Of Erskine, c.1795, 8 In., Pair 385.00
Saucer, Spread–Winged Eagle, Clasping Arrows, c.1915, 7 In. 885.00
Soup, Dish, Central Floral, Garland Rim, Blue & White, 12 Pc. 550.00
Soup, Dish, Tobacco Leaf, c.1820, 9 1/4 In., Pair 1980.00
Stand, Teak, Carved, Soapstone Insert, 23 1/2 In. 200.00
Teabowl & Saucer, Arms Of Baker, c.1740, 4 5/8 In., Pair 1550.00
Teabowl & Saucer, Floral Spray Panels, 1765, 12 Sets 1980.00
Teabowl & Saucer, Titled Industria, c.1800, 4 1/2 In. 525.00
Teacup, Looped Handle, Multicolored Florals, Pair 33.00
Teapot, Armorial, Berry Finial, Blue, Gold, Red, 5 5/8 In. 350.00
Teapot, Blue & White, Twisted Rope Handle, c.1800, 4 In. 418.00
Teapot, Cover, Famille Rose, Flowers, Rooks, 4 1/2 In. 1100.00
Teapot, Floral Under Glaze, 5 1/4 In. 215.00
Teapot, Fruit Finial, Floral, Small Gilt Stars, 5 5/8 In. 150.00
Teapot, Fruit Finial, Melon Ribs, Vines, 5 In. 250.00
Teapot, Landscape, Gilt Gold, 5 1/4 In. 200.00
Teapot, Oriental Figures, 5 1/4 In. 125.00
Teapot, Polychrome Floral Design, 5 1/2 In. 250.00
Teapot, Silver Mounted, Late 18th Century, 6 In. 412.00
Tureen, Floral, Dragonflies, Boar's Head Handles, 13 1/4 In. 3350.00
Tureen, Sauce, Leaf Shape, Floral Sprays, Twig Handle, c.1770 .... 2975.00
Tureen, Soup, Stand, Bird On Prunus Tree, c.1770, 13 7/8 In. 3850.00
Tureen, Soup, Stand, Gold Knop, c.1790, 14 In. 2200.00
Tureen, Soup, Strap Handles, Floral Sprays, 14 3/8 In. 2200.00
Tureen, Stand, Arms Of Grant, Boy, Ladies, c.1815, 14 In. 2200.00
Vase, Couple Seated At Table, Hexagonal, c.1775, 15 In., Pair 4400.00
Vase, Cover, Famille Rose, Recumbent Kylin Knop, 11 In., Pair 1760.00
Vase, Famille Rose, Bottle Form, Carved Wood Stand, 25 In. 665.00
Vase, Mandarin Figures, Kylin's Masks, 17 11/16 In. 1540.00
Vase, Mandarin Palette, Couple, Children, c.1785, 11 In., Pair 3025.00
Vase, Polychrome Floral & Gilt, 11 1/2 In., Pair 3300.00
Vase, Qinalong Style, Deer In Landscape, 21 3/8 In. 550.00

CHOCOLATE GLASS, sometimes mistakenly called caramel slag, was made by the Indiana Tumbler and Goblet Company of Greentown, Indiana, from 1900 to 1903. Fenton Art Glass Co. also made chocolate glass from about 1907 to 1915. More recent pieces have been made by Imperial, Heisey, and others.

Berry Set, Leaf Bracket, Spoon, 8 Piece	150.00
Bowl Set, Cactus, Graduated 6 To 8 In., 3 Piece	180.00
Butter, Cover, Cactus	165.00
Butter, Cover, Leaf Bracket	140.00
Candy Jar, Owl, Dolphin Handles, 6 1/2 In.	70.00
Candy Jar, Swirled, Dolphin Handles, 8 1/2 In.	70.00
Chalice, Chrysanthemum Leaf, 6 1/2 In.	750.00
Compote, Cactus, 5 1/2 x 5 1/2 In.	125.00
Compote, Cactus, 8 In.	200.00
Compote, Jelly, Geneva	125.00
Creamer, Cactus	85.00
Creamer, Leaf Bracket	95.00
Creamer, Nautilus, Large	70.00
Cruet, Cactus	80.00 To 155.00
Cruet, Leaf & Bracket	70.00
Cruet, Wild Rose With Bowknot, Greentown	425.00
Dish, Hen On Nest Cover, Greentown	275.00
Dish, Hen With Peeps Cover, Greentown	1600.00
Dish, Small Ducks On Nest, Imperial	45.00
Dish, Sweetmeat, Cover, Cactus	425.00
Dresser Set, Venetian, Tray & Covered Box, 2 Piece	550.00
Figurine, Scotty, Base, Imperial	225.00
Figurine, Scotty, Heisey	200.00
Jar, Cracker, Cactus, Cover, Pair	350.00
Lamp, Leaf Bracket, Miniature	95.00
Lamp, Wild Rose & Festoon, 8 In.	700.00
Lamp, Wild Rose & Festoon, Clear Font, Greentown, 7 In.	550.00
Lamp, Wild Rose & Festoon, Greentown	750.00
Mug, Indoor Drinking Scene, 5 In.	150.00
Mug, Outdoor Drinking Scene, Greentown, 4 1/2 In.	110.00
Nappy, Leaf Bracket	65.00
Nappy, Masonic	125.00
Pitcher, Heron	400.00
Salt & Pepper, Cactus, Bronze Top	50.00
Salt & Pepper, Handled Stand	1250.00
Saltshaker, Cactus	65.00
Sauce, Chrysanthemum Leaf	75.00
Spoon Holder, Leaf Bracket	55.00
Spooner, Cactus, Greentown	45.00
Sugar & Creamer, Leaf Bracket, Greentown	125.00
Sugar, Cactus	100.00
Syrup, Cord Drapery	225.00
Syrup, Shuttle	85.00
Toothpick, Cactus	35.00 To 48.00
Toothpick, Wild Rose, Scrolling	225.00
Tumbler, Leaf Bracket	30.00
Tumbler, Uneeda Milk Biscuit, Pair	125.00
Vase, Scalloped Flange, Greentown, 6 In.	125.00

CHRISTMAS TREES made of feathers and Christmas tree decorations of all types are popular with collectors. The first decorated Christmas tree in America is claimed by many states, including Pennsylvania (1747), Massachusetts (1832), Illinois (1833), Ohio (1838), and Iowa (1845). The first glass ornaments were imported from Germany about 1860. Dresden ornaments were made about 100 years ago of paper and tinsel. Manufacturers in the United States were making ornaments in the early 1870s. Electric lights were first used on a Christmas tree in 1882.

Character light bulbs became popular in the 1920s, bubble lights in the 1940s, twinkle bulbs in the 1950s, plastic bulbs by 1955. In this book a Christmas light is a holder for a candle used on the tree. Other forms of lighting include light bulbs.

Aluminum, Box, 1950s	20.00
Feather, Germany, 45 In.	400.00
Feather, Germany, 5 Ft.	395.00
Feather, Medium Green, Berries, Square Wooden Base	115.00
Feather, White, Berries, Germany, 36 In.	275.00
Fence, 2 Gates, Red & Green, Wood, 25 x 30 In.	85.00
Fence, 22 Posts, 2 Swinging Gates, Iron, 5 Ft. 3 In. x 5 Ft.	225.00
Fence, Red & Green, Folding, Double Gate, Box, 28 x 36 In.	75.00
Fence, Red Frame, Green Pickets, Square, 4 x 18 In.	105.00
Fence, Swinging Gate, 8 Sections, Victorian, Cast Iron	175.00
Fence, Wooden, Red & Green Pickets, Gate, 18-In. Square	105.00
Fence, Wooden, White Pickets, Gate, 45-In. Square	185.00
Holder, Musical, 10 Discs, Walnut, Germany	2800.00
Light Bulb, Angel, Santa, Stars & Bubbles, 7 Piece	30.00
Light Bulb, Betty Boop	25.00
Light Bulb, Bird, In Cage	25.00
Light Bulb, Bird, Yellow Over Clear, Red Beak	15.00
Light Bulb, Blimp	25.00
Light Bulb, Cheerbrite, Elf, Box	8.00
Light Bulb, Dick Tracy	50.00
Light Bulb, Dog In Boot	12.00
Light Bulb, Fairy Tales, Plastic Shade, No String, Box, 8 Pc.	32.00
Light Bulb, Father Christmas, Box, 8 In.	75.00
Light Bulb, Girl Playing Horn	20.00
Light Bulb, Humpty–Dumpty, Painted	35.00
Light Bulb, Ice Cream Cone	25.00
Light Bulb, Japanese Lantern	5.00
Light Bulb, Kewpie	45.00
Light Bulb, Masked Clown	30.00
Light Bulb, Mt. St. Helens, Pink Opalescent, Box	25.00
Light Bulb, Popeye	275.00
Light Bulb, Santa Claus	7.50 To 25.00
Light Bulb, Santa's Face On Bell	25.00
Light Bulb, Santa's Face On Chimney	25.00
Light Bulb, Santa's Head, 2 Sides	20.00
Light Bulb, Santa's Head, Out Of Chimney, Milk Glass	10.00
Light Bulb, Set, Noma, Bubble Light, Box, 1950s	25.00
Light Bulb, Snowball, Italy, 1975	22.00
Light Bulb, Snowman	12.00
Ornament, Angel, Tree Top, Wax Head & Hands	35.00
Ornament, Bear, Jointed, Glass Eyes, Small	40.00
Ornament, Bell, Papier–Mache Santa Claus Face, c.1890	110.00
Ornament, Bird, Celluloid	89.00
Ornament, Bird, On Nest, Wire Wrapped	45.00
Ornament, Bird, White Body, Red Beak, Spun Glass Tail, Clip	18.00
Ornament, Boy Clown	65.00
Ornament, Boy, With Nightcap	75.00
Ornament, Car, Gold Roadster, Blown Glass, 3 In.	60.00
Ornament, Caroler, Papier–Mache & Flocked, Japan	10.00
Ornament, Cat, In Bag, Blown Glass, 4 In.	75.00
Ornament, Clock, With Sundial, Glass	65.00
Ornament, Clown, Blown Glass, 3 1/2 In.	22.00
Ornament, Clown, Blown Glass, 6 In.	30.00
Ornament, Cotton Child, On Sled	58.00
Ornament, Deer, White Celluloid	20.00
Ornament, Dinner Bell, Victorian, Wire Wrapped	72.00
Ornament, Ear Of Corn, Blown Glass, 3 1/2 In.	22.00
Ornament, Elephant, Germany	180.00

Ornament, ET, Box 10.00
Ornament, Flower Basket, Wire Wrapped 45.00
Ornament, Frog, Playing Violin, Green 65.00
Ornament, Fruit, Pink Blush, Spun Cotton, Mica Snow, 2 In. 18.00
Ornament, Girl Skier, Spun Cotton 45.00
Ornament, Girl, On Sled, Spun Cotton 75.00
Ornament, Gold Rings, Towle, 1975 .... 35.00
Ornament, Grape Cluster, Green, Blown Glass, 4 In. 25.00
Ornament, Grapes On Heart, Embossed 25.00
Ornament, Guitar, Candy Container, Dresden 95.00
Ornament, Guitar, Dresden 140.00
Ornament, Horn, Glass 12.00
Ornament, House, Celluloid 87.00
Ornament, Icicles, Glow In Dark .... 12.00 To 15.00
Ornament, Indian Head 210.00
Ornament, Jolly St. Nick, Hallmark, 1986 .... 40.00
Ornament, Kermit, Figural, 1979 .... 15.00
Ornament, Kugel, Glass Ball, Red 135.00
Ornament, Kugel, Grape Cluster, Brass Ring 140.00
Ornament, Kugel, Grape Cluster, Silver, Brass Cap, 4 3/4 In. 150.00
Ornament, Kugel, Red, Silvered 135.00
Ornament, Little Red Riding Hood, Wolf, Cottage 195.00
Ornament, Mandolin, Glass 12.00
Ornament, Miss Piggy, Figural, 1979 .... 15.00
Ornament, My Favorite Santa, Hallmark, 1987 .... 25.00
Ornament, Owl, Blown Glass, 3 In. 25.00
Ornament, Pear, Spun Cotton 35.00
Ornament, Pig, Bisque Head, Corn Husk Body 150.00
Ornament, Pink Boat, Cotton Angels, Wire Wrapped 68.00
Ornament, Pink Poodle, Begging 48.00
Ornament, Pipe, Bent, Blown Glass, 3 In. 20.00
Ornament, Punch & Judy 130.00
Ornament, Puppy, In Bag, Long Ears 78.00
Ornament, Sacred Heart & Jesus, Cross, Stars, 4 In. 195.00
Ornament, Santa Claus, Composition Face, Cotton, 2 1/2 In. 22.00
Ornament, Santa Claus, Hard Plastic, 3 In. 5.00
Ornament, Santa Claus, Hat, Celluloid, 4 In. 35.00
Ornament, Santa Claus, On Ball, Celluloid, Irwin 38.00
Ornament, Snow White & 7 Dwarfs, Glass, Box, 1938 .... 795.00
Ornament, Snowbaby, Spun Cotton, Celluloid Head 45.00
Ornament, Song Bird, Clip On, Black Beak, 3 1/2 In. 20.00
Ornament, Thimble Mouse, No. 1, Hallmark, Box 175.00
Ornament, Thimble Soldier, No. 2, Hallmark, Box 75.00
Ornament, Tree Topper, Santa Claus Face, Celluloid 35.00
Ornament, Wreath Of Memories, Hallmark, 1987 .... 30.00
Ornament, Zeppelin, U.S. Flag, 5 In. 110.00
Stand, Cast Iron, Arcade 45.00
Stand, Cast Iron, Star 35.00
Stand, Musical, Kalliope Discs, 8 Discs, Germany, c.1895 .... 2500.00
Stand, Revolving, Musical, Metal, 1950s 20.00
Stand, Revolving, Silver, 6 In. 40.00
Stand, White Cellophane, Box, 36 In. 95.00
Stander, Bulbs Around Base, Cast Iron 45.00
Streetlight, Kerosene, Metal, Pink Panes, France, 6 In. 38.00

CHRISTMAS collectibles include not only Christmas trees and ornaments listed above, but also Santa Claus figures, special dishes, and even games and wrapping paper. A Belsnickle is a nineteenth-century figure of Father Christmas. A kugel is an early, heavy ornament made of thick blown glass, lined with zinc or lead, and often covered with colored wax.

Bank, Santa Claus, Sylvester, 1960 .... 24.00
Belsnickle, Germany, 8 In. 410.00
Belsnickle, Gold Coat, Red Chenille, Feather Tree, 12 In. 900.00

Belsnickle, Mica Coat, Red Hood, Feather Tree, Germany, 9 In. 325.00
Belsnickle, Papier-Mache, Red Coat, Feather Tree, Germany, 12 In. 580.00
Belsnickle, Santa, Red Flocked, Feather Tree, Fur Beard, 8 In. 295.00
Belsnickle, Yellow Robe, With Feather Tree 357.50
Box, Candy, Kate Greenaway Type Children Playing, Litho, 8 In. 85.00
Box, Santa Claus Cutout, Morse's Candy, Dated 1923 .... 120.00
Candle Pyramid, 3 Tiers, 44 In. 695.00
Candlestick, Holly Leaf, Berries, Iron, 1921, 3 x 5 x 1 In., Pair 115.00
Carousel, Musical, Austria, Wood 85.00
Church, Celluloid, Plays Silent Night, Raylite Electric, 1950s 28.00
Church, White Grainy, Red Windows, Steeple, Electric, 11 In. 65.00
Costume, Santa Claus, Rubber Feet, Hands & Face 125.00
Display, Santa Claus, Cutout, 68 In. 185.00
Doll, Santa Claus, Straw Stuffed, 19 In. 195.00
Doll, Santa Claus, Straw Stuffed, 1940s, 18 In. 110.00
Doll, Santa Claus, Vinyl & Pink Plush, Rushton, 1960s 48.00
Doll, Santa Claus, Vinyl & Red Plush, Rushton, 1970s 38.00
Face, Santa Claus, Papier-Mache, 6 1/2 In. 55.00
Figure, Father Christmas, Holding Feather Tree, 1870-1910, 29 In. 3000.00
Figure, Mr. & Mrs. Santa Claus, Waving Goodbye, On Platform 12.00
Figure, Santa Claus, Bisque Face, Hands, Boots, Japan, 5 In. 40.00
Figure, Santa Claus, Bisque, Flesh Face, 4 In. 40.00
Figure, Santa Claus, Cone Head & Body, Plaster Face, Japan, 4 In. 38.00
Figure, Santa Claus, Hollow Metal, Hand Painted, Old Style, 5 In. 75.00
Figure, Santa Claus, Plastic Face, Paper & Cloth, Japan, 4 1/2 In. 15.00
Figure, Santa Claus, Waving, On Train, Elf On Back, Bisque, 3 In. 35.00
Head, Santa Claus, Papier-Mache, Large 78.00
Kugel, Green Grape Cluster, Brass Hanger 175.00
Mobile, Santa Claus, Bisque 22.00
Mold, Chocolate, 4 Santas, Tin, Germany, 8 In. 55.00
Mold, Santa, Hello Kiddies, Aluminum, 11 3/4 In., 2 Piece 30.00
Nativity Set, 11 Papier-Mache Figures, 24-In. Wooden Crib, Italy 200.00
Nativity Set, Birchback Creche, Twig Roof, Germany, 3 In., 10 Pc. 55.00
Nativity Set, Bisque, Occupied Japan, 3 In., 3 Piece 23.00
Nativity Set, Composition, Occupied Japan, 3 In., 4 Pc. 46.00
Nativity Set, Die Cut, 1959 .... 25.00
Nativity Set, Gesso Paper, Wooden Creche, 2 1/2 In., 12 Piece 30.00
Planter, Santa Claus, Pack Is Planter, Ceramic, 5 1/2 In. 25.00
Plates are listed in the Collector Plate section
Reindeer, Papier-Mache, Brown, Cream, Metal Antlers, Wooden, 4 In. 30.00
Roly Poly, Santa Claus, Germany, 6 3/4 In. 725.00
Rudolph, Red Nosed Reindeer, Pulling Santa In Sleigh 25.00
Saltshaker, Santa Claus, Ceramic, 3 In. 7.00
Santa Claus, Bisque, 4 In. 25.00
Santa Claus, Musical Sled, Fur Beard, Keywind, Wooden, 15 x 18 In. 310.00
Santa Claus, Sleigh, Papier-Mache Reindeer 80.00
Santa Claus, Sleigh, Reindeers, Plays Jingle Bells, Electric 25.00
Sheep, Black Wool, Wood, Pink Collar, Putz, Germany 95.00
Sheep, White Wool, Wooden Legs, Blue Collar, Putz, Germany, 3 In. 35.00
Sheep, Wooly, Paper Label, Germany, Pair 75.00
Sugar & Creamer, Santa & Mrs. Claus, Avon, 1983 .... 13.00
Toy, Santa & Deer, Bell, Windup, Celluloid & Metal 75.00
Toy, Santa Claus, 1 Hand Gifts, Other Ringing Bell, Windup, Alps 95.00
Toy, Santa Claus, Bell Ringer, Wind Up, Tin, Plastic, Cloth, 7 In. 95.00
Toy, Santa Claus, Celluloid, Metal Sleigh, Windup, Box 145.00
Toy, Santa Claus, Gravity Walker, Wood Hands, Feet, c.1930, 54 In. 15.00
Toy, Santa Claus, In Shoe, Pop-Up, 1960s 20.00
Toy, Santa Claus, In Sleigh, Windup, Celluloid, Occupied Japan, Box 145.00
Toy, Santa Claus, On 3-Wheeler, Windup, Celluloid, Suzuki 185.00
Toy, Santa Claus, On Donkey, Windup, Celluloid, Metal Donkey, 6 In. 66.00
Toy, Santa Claus, On Roof, Battery Operated, Japan 155.00
Toy, Santa Claus, On Scooter, Bump & Go, Battery, Japan, 10 In. 175.00
Toy, Santa Claus, On Tricycle, Celluloid Figure, Keywind, Japan 16.00

Toy, Santa Claus, Riding Reindeer, Windup, Tin Body, 6 In.	175.00
Toy, Santa Claus, Ringing Bell, Windup, 1950s, 7 In.	145.00
Toy, Santa Claus, Tennis Racquet, Celluloid, 3 In.	27.00
Wreath, Chenille, Lighted, 1940s	10.00
Wreath, Red Chenille, Lighted Candle Center, 10 1/2 In.	28.00

CHROME items in the Art Deco style became popular in the 1930s. Collectors are most interested in high–style pieces made by the Connecticut firms of Chase Brass and Copper Company and Manning Bowman.

Butter, Cow Finial, Farberware	45.00
Candleholder, Irwin, Pair	35.00
Cocktail Shaker, 4 Cups, Chase Brass	125.00
Cocktail Shaker, Art Deco, 1934	45.00
Cocktail Shaker, Art Deco, Bakelite Handle & Lift Knob, 12 In.	38.00
Cocktail Shaker, Art Deco, Manning Bowman, 8 In.	10.00
Cocktail Shaker, Art Deco, Penguin	150.00
Cocktail Shaker, Art Deco, Red Bakelite Lid Knob & Handle	38.00
Cocktail Shaker, Dumbbell Shape ....*Illus*	200.00
Cocktail Shaker, Spout, Triangular Bakelite Handle ....*Illus*	35.00
Coffee Set, Comet	310.00
Coffee Set, Red Teardrop Bakelite Handles, 1940s	45.00
Coffee Set, Reeded Bakelite Handles, Forman Family, 4 Piece	75.00
Coffeepot, Manning Bowman, Art Deco, Black Bakelite Handles	80.00
Salt & Pepper, Black, Art Deco	6.00
Snack Server, Chase Brass, Electric	15.00
Sugar & Creamer, Black Wooden Handle, Chase, 2 In. ....*Illus*	55.00
Sugar & Creamer, Chase, For Coronet Coffee Set	27.00
Sugar & Creamer, Gold Washed Interior, Manning Bowman	22.00
Vase & Candleholders, Blue Glass	45.00
Vase, Tubes, Chase	22.00

Chrome, Cocktail Shaker,
Dumbbell Shape

Chrome, Cocktail
Shaker, Spout,
Triangular Bakelite
Handle

Chrome, Sugar & Creamer, Black
Wooden Handle, Chase, 2 In.

CIGAR STORE FIGURES of carved wood or cast iron were used as advertisements in front of the Victorian cigar store. The carved figures are now collected as folk art. They range in size from counter type, about three feet, to over eight feet high.

Brave, Walnut	2400.00
Chief, Pine	2500.00
Indian Bust, Signed Arapaho	295.00
Indian, Hand Carved, 6 Ft.	800.00
Indian, On Tobacco Stand	2400.00
Indian, Squaw, Feather Headdress, Wooden, 65 1/2 In.	6600.00
Princess, Headdress, Samuel Robb, c.1880, 53 In.	6600.00
Punch, Holding Bunch Of Cigars, Rotund & Squat, 50 In.	2750.00

CINNABAR is a vermilion or red lacquer. Pieces are made with tens to hundreds of thicknesses of the lacquer that is later carved.

Bookends, Red	245.00
Bottle Snuff, Figures, Mountain Scenes, 2 In.	95.00
Box, Carved, 5 x 3 In.	75.00

CIVIL WAR mementos are important collector's items. Most of the pieces are military items used from 1861 to 1865.

Album, General Sherman & Relatives	500.00
Almanac, Hostetter's, 1864	14.00
Artillery Gunners Pinchers, Locking Handles	34.00
Bond, Confederate, $500, Issued At Montgomery, Ala., 1861, Coupons	85.00
Book, Soldiers Nat'L Cemetery, Gettysburg, Buried Soldiers, 1864	37.50
Box, Carrying Flints, Engraved, Horn, 1770	1100.00
Box, Dressing, Officer's, Mirror On Lift Lid, Cherry, 16 3/4 In.	230.00
Bugle, 29 In.	240.00
Bullet, Lead	1.00
Canteen, Commemorative, B. Wise, Volunteer Infantry, Porcelain	625.00
Canteen, Water, Wooden, 1776–1812	210.00
Chest, U.S. S. Ohio, Inner Drawer, Signed L. B. Cox, 1863	797.50
Drum, Marked C. S., Texas, 9 In.	975.00
Drum, Regimental, 16 1/2 In.	2400.00
Eagle, Hat Ornament, 2 Crossed Rifles, Military Hat, Brass, 5 In.	15.00
Flask, Peace, Batty, Dated 1848	400.00
Handcuffs, Key	90.00
Hat, Cavalry, No. 8, Hardee, Gold Braid	3500.00
Hat, Officer's, Beaver, John Noonan, Wood & Cardboard Box	240.00
Holster, Colt Dragoon	235.00
Invitation, G. A. R., Cloth, 1883	6.00
Iron Wrist Shackles, Confederate, Pair	250.00
Jacket, Label	475.00
Kepi, Union, Label	375.00
Knapsack, Black Canvas, Waterproof	275.00
Lantern, Tent	200.00
Letter Opener, Sword, Gettysburg, 1863, Miniature	49.00
Letter, Soldier's, McDougal Hospital, Fort Schuler, 1864, 3 Pages	30.00
Map, Centennial, Gravy Train Giveaway, 1960s	4.00
Match Safe, 1st Mississippi Cavalry, Gutta–Percha	625.00
Mess Kit, Folding Knife, Fork & Spoon, Metal Grips	95.00
Military Roster, Framed, Dated Aug. 12, 1862	128.00
Mirror, Camp, Foldup, Round	40.00
Musket, Import, Full Length	185.00
Outfit, Union Cavalry Shell Jacket, With Pants	550.00
Pay Voucher, 1865, Signed Lt. Col. Mitchell, Colored Infantry	25.00
Print, Battle Of Pea Ridge, Kurz & Allison, 1976, 18 x 24 In.	20.00
Revolver, Marston	120.00
Saber, With Scabbard, Union, 1864	395.00
Sheet Music, The Soldiers Return March, 1865	12.00
Spurs, Officer's, Brass	145.00

Clarice Cliff, Plate, Copper Luster, 1940s, 9 In.

Spurs, Officer's, Nickel	125.00
Surgeon's Kit, Eye, Mahogany Case, 9 Piece	290.00
Sword & Scabbard, Ames Mfg. Co., Mass., 1864	325.00
Uniform, New York City Militia, 4 Piece	1210.00
Watch Fob, Enameled U.S. Shield, With Love Token	60.00

CKAW, see Dedham category

CLAMBROTH glass, popular in the Victorian era, is a grayish color and is somewhat opaque, like clambroth.

Bowl, Grape & Cable, 8 1/2 In.	90.00
Bowl, Scroll Embossed, Iridescent	35.00
Candlestick, Fluted Stem, Hexagonal Petal Socket, 9 1/4 In.	150.00
Candlestick, Loop Base, Petal Socket, Flint, 7 In., Pair	180.00
Candlestick, Opaque Blue, Hexagonal, 8 3/8 In.	85.00
Candlestick, Petal & Loop, Pair	300.00
Compote, Loop, Pittsburgh, 9 x 7 1/2 In.	165.00
Eggcup, Cover, Bull's–Eye, Sandwich Glass	395.00
Goblet, Button & Arches, Gold Striping	37.50
Mug, Swan, Mauve	85.00
Sugar Shaker, Grape Design, 4 1/2 In.	35.00

CLARICE CLIFF was a designer who worked in several English factories after the 1920s. She died in 1972.

Bone Dish, Tonquin, Blue	12.00
Bowl, Rural Scenes, Mulberry, 8 1/2 In.	25.00
Creamer, Cow	32.50
Creamer, Crocus	75.00
Cup & Saucer, Rural Scenes	17.50
Dish, Bizarre, 3 In.	60.00
Jam Jar, Celtic Harvest, Embossed Wheat, Chrome Handle, 6 In.	55.00
Pitcher, My Garden, Bizarre, 9 In.	350.00
Plaque, Bizarre, Orange, Yellow & Lavender Flowers, 13 In.	595.00
Plate, Charlotte, Blue & White, 6 1/4 In.	17.50
Plate, Copper Luster, 1940s, 9 In. ....*Illus*	35.00
Plate, Ophilia, 6 1/2 In.	25.00
Plate, Trafalgar Square Center, 1944, 11 In.	50.00
Sugar & Creamer, Underplate, Tonquin, 3 Piece	45.00
Sugar Sifter, Bizarre Cone	325.00
Sugar Sifter, Bonjour	255.00 To 265.00
Tazza, Tonquin, 3 Tiers, Marked	40.00
Teapot, Charlotte	85.00
Vase, Embossed Flowers, Gray Ground, Blue Top, 9 In.	90.00

CLEWELL ware was made in limited quantities by Charles Walter Clewell of Canton, Ohio, from 1902 to 1955. Pottery was covered with a thin coating of bronze, then treated to make the bronze turn different colors. Pieces covered with copper, brass, or silver were also made. Mr. Clewell's secret formula for blue patinated bronze was burned when he died in 1965.

Ashtray, Polo Players, 6 x 4 In.	150.00
Vase, Bronze Patina Finish, Cylindrical, Signed, 11 In.	412.00
Vase, Brown To Verdigris Patina, Copper, Pottery, 13 x 6 1/2 In.	825.00
Vase, Dark Green Patina, Baluster Form, Signed, 8 1/4 In.	605.00
Vase, Trumpet, Green Patina On Copper, 8 In.	325.00

CLIFTON POTTERY was founded by William Long in Clifton, New Jersey, in 1905. He worked there until 1908 making a line called *Crystal Patina.* Clifton Pottery made art pottery. Another firm, Chesapeake Pottery, sold majolica marked *Clifton ware.*

Bowl, Indian Design, Partially Closed Form, 8 In.	100.00
Pitcher, Figural, Cockatoo, 15 In.	195.00
Vase, Red Earthenware, Intaglio Geometric Designs, 12 x 9 In.	385.00

CLOCKS of all types have always been popular with collectors. The eighteenth-century tall case, or grandfather's clock, was designed to house a works with a long pendulum. In 1816, Eli Terry patented a new, smaller works for a clock, and the case became smaller. The clock could be kept on a shelf instead of on the floor. By 1840, coiled springs were used and even smaller clocks were made. Battery-powered electric clocks were made in the 1870s.

Aaron Miller, Tall Case, Calendar Dial, Grained, 1750s, 91 In.	6275.00
Abel Hutchins, Tall Case, Brass Works, American	6820.00
Advertising, American Legion, Bakelite	95.00
Advertising, American Legion, Round	45.00
Advertising, B. L. Johnson Confectioners, Knoxville, Tenn., Regulator	950.00
Advertising, Baird, Clapperton Spool Cotton, Figure 8, 1890s	1200.00
Advertising, Benrus Watches, Neon, Needs Repair	350.00
Advertising, Borden's Elsie, Glass, Metal, 1940s	85.00
Advertising, Budweiser Beer, Fish Design, Electric, 18 x 18 In.	20.00
Advertising, Budweiser Beer, Marble Base, 1950s	80.00
Advertising, Budweiser, Rotating, Clock Face 1 Side, Horse On Other	60.00
Advertising, Budweiser, Square, Large	20.00
Advertising, Bull Durham, Regulator, Striker, Miniature	895.00
Advertising, Bulova, Lighted	55.00
Advertising, Calumet, Metal Case, Benrus, 18 1/2 In.	44.00
Advertising, Canada Dry Gingerale, Metal Frame, Curved Glass, Lights	125.00
Advertising, Canada Dry, Plastic Face, Metal, 16 x 16 In.	35.00
Advertising, Cat's Paw Shoes, Light-Up, Reverse On Glass	225.00
Advertising, Cat's Paw, Shoe Repair	175.00
Advertising, Clapperton Spool Cotton, Figure 8 Shape, Baird	1000.00
Advertising, Crawford Watch, Counter Top, Chrome, Neon, Glo-Dial	650.00
Advertising, Double Cola	125.00
Advertising, Dr Pepper, Light-Up	100.00 To 275.00
Advertising, Dr Pepper, Mountain Herbs, For Executives, 1982	375.00
Advertising, Dr Pepper, Reverse Painted Glass, Electric	1150.00
Advertising, Dr Pepper, Telechron, 1940s	140.00
Advertising, Dr Pepper, Wall, Logo On Face, 1940s	125.00
Advertising, Dr Pepper, With Chevron, Light-Up	75.00
Advertising, Dukes Pharmacy, Atlanta, Calendar, Regulator	550.00
Advertising, Embassy Dairy, Light-Up	225.00
Advertising, Four Roses, Electric, 13 x 12 In.	85.00
Advertising, Fram Filter, Double Reverse Glass, 1958	125.00
Advertising, Frostie Root Beer	50.00
Advertising, G. W. Bishop Drugs & Jewelry, Wanewoc, Wisc., Regulator	950.00
Advertising, Gem Razors, Simulated Wood Painted, 1924, 28 3/4 In.	390.00
Advertising, Greyhound Bus Service, Dog Streaking Across Face	325.00

Advertising, Hadon Products, Chicago, Art Deco, Lighted Hour	85.00
Advertising, Heath Dairy Products, Round	70.00
Advertising, Helping Hand	40.00
Advertising, Hornung Beer, Sign	300.00
Advertising, J. Stern & Sons Clothiers, Quincy, Ill., Round	2000.00
Advertising, Jolly Tar Pastime Old Honesty Plank Road, Baird, Round	2000.00
Advertising, Keebler, Cuckoo Type, 5 1/2 In.	50.00
Advertising, Keebler, Novelty, Mechanical Bird, 5 1/2 In.	50.00 To 65.00
Advertising, Keen Kutter, Red, Round	900.00
Advertising, Kelvinator Appliances, Neo, 1930s	325.00
Advertising, Kickapoo Joy Juice, Convex Glass, Electric, 1965	100.00
Advertising, Kist Soda, Light–Up, Classic Logo, 1940	154.00
Advertising, Lionel Trains, Service Station, Neon	850.00
Advertising, Lucky Strike Cigarettes, School, Label, 24 x 16 1/2 In.	475.00
Advertising, M & M, Wall	9.00
Advertising, Majestic Refrigerator	40.00
Advertising, Maremont Mufflers, Light–Up	75.00
Advertising, Marigold Dairy, Bakelite	95.00
Advertising, Mason's Root Beer, Aluminum Frame	95.00
Advertising, Mayo's Tobacco, Baird	1200.00
Advertising, McDonalds, Hamburgler, Wooden, Pendulum	50.00
Advertising, Meadow Gold, It's Mighty Good, Plastic Frame, Round	100.00
Advertising, Merrick's Spool Cotton, School, Octagonal	495.00 To 795.00
Advertising, Mobil Oil	165.00
Advertising, National Union Advertising, NU Radio Tubes	160.00
Advertising, NBC	525.00
Advertising, Nestle's, A Time For Baking, 1979, 50th Anniversary	52.50
Advertising, Nonesuch Mincemeat Pie	850.00
Advertising, NuGrape, Electric, 8 x 7 In.	65.00 To 150.00
Advertising, NuGrape, Pictures Bottle	135.00
Advertising, Orange Squeeze, Counter, Reverse Painted Glass	875.00
Advertising, Oshgosh B'gosh, Neon	250.00
Advertising, Pabst Beer	45.00
Advertising, Packard Automobile, Neon	900.00
Advertising, Pam, Square, Metal Rim	85.00
Advertising, Pard Dog Food, Bobbing Head, Electric, Square, 15 3/4 In.	465.00
Advertising, Pearl Beer, Neon, Center Bottle, Lager Beer Please	395.00
Advertising, Pepsi–Cola, Animated Windup, 1920s, 6 x 6 In.	1200.00
Advertising, Pepsi–Cola, Light–Up, 1950s	125.00
Advertising, Pierces Lignite Floor Varnish, Regulator	950.00
Advertising, Pontiac, Neon, Round, 1955, 17 In.	550.00
Advertising, Pure Spring, Plastic Face, Red, Gold, 12 In.	46.00 To 50.00
Advertising, Purina, Light–Up, Convex, Double Reverse Glass Face	155.00
Advertising, RCA Radiotron, Reverse Enameled, c.1932, 20 In. Diam.	500.00
Advertising, Red Devil, Time To Polish, Wooden Case, 15 1/4 In.	60.00
Advertising, Reed's Gilt Edged Tonic, Yale Clock Co., 17 1/2 In.	575.00
Advertising, Regal Beer, Illuminated	125.00
Advertising, Royal Crown Cola, Light–Up	65.00 To 185.00
Advertising, Royal Crown Cola, Metal Frame, 1939–1941	350.00
Advertising, Shilling Coffee, Neon	850.00
Advertising, Squirt, Green & Yellow Graphics, Rectangular	135.00
Advertising, Starkist Charlie Tuna, 1969	20.00
Advertising, Sweet–Orr Work Clothes, Illusion Wheel, Wall	850.00
Advertising, Tetley Tea, With Circus Elephants	500.00
Advertising, Thompson's Dairy Food, Plastic	10.00
Advertising, Trix, Alarm	85.00
Advertising, Trixy Root Beer, Black	275.00
Advertising, Tuff–Nut, Neon	550.00
Advertising, Vermont's Household Remedies, Regulator	950.00
Advertising, Victor Victrola, Key Wind, Metal Record Face	600.00
Advertising, Willard Batteries, Light–Up, 1920s	225.00
Advertising, Willard Batteries, Red, Black, Electric, Square, 14 In.	120.00
Advertising, Willard, Red, White, Black, Convex Glass Face, 14 In.	120.00

Clock, Ansonia, Shelf, Lady Playing Mandolin, 22 1/2 x 23 In.

◆ ◆ ◆ ◆ ◆ ◆ ◆ ◆ ◆ ◆ ◆ ◆ ◆ ◆ ◆ ◆ ◆ ◆ ◆ ◆

To make a clock run faster, raise the pendulum; to slow it, lower the pendulum.

◆ ◆ ◆ ◆ ◆ ◆ ◆ ◆ ◆ ◆ ◆ ◆ ◆ ◆ ◆ ◆ ◆ ◆ ◆ ◆

Advertising, Winston, Illuminated Sign	5.00
Alarm, Nickel Case, 6-In. Bell On Top, Windup, New York	75.00
Alarm, Snoopy, Baseball Player, UFS, 1958	45.00
Alarm, Snoopy, With Tennis Ball On Front, 1958	40.00
Alarm, Three Pigs & Bad Wolf, Ingersoll, 1934	475.00
Alarm, Windup, Nickel Case, C. H. Scholermann	75.00
American Clock Co., Iron Face, Brass Bezel, Port, Pendulum, 17 In.	220.00
Animated, Big Bird, Alarm	20.00
Animated, Crazy Cat, 1940s	20.00
Animated, Girl, Eyes Roll At The Hour, Iron, 17 In.	1800.00
Animated, Kit Kat, Box	15.00
Animated, Political, FDR, Man Of The Hour, Windup	145.00
Animated, Smurf, Alarm	20.00
Anniversary, Brass, Glass Dome, 11 In.	150.00
Anniversary, Brass, Glass, Marked Le Coultre, 9 1/4 In.	260.00
Ansonia, Apex, Crystal Regulator	2900.00
Ansonia, Calendar, Gingerbread, Carved Oak, 8-Day, Chime, 1880-1900	450.00
Ansonia, Crystal Regulator, Open Escapement, Mercury Pendulum	275.00
Ansonia, Double Statue, Hunter & Fisherman	985.00
Ansonia, Double Statue, Urns	1300.00
Ansonia, Hand Painted, Royal Bonn	350.00
Ansonia, Lenox, Shelf, Black Iron	95.00
Ansonia, Mantel, Bronze Ormolu, Enamel Face, Mercury Pendulum, c.1900	770.00
Ansonia, Mantel, Green Porcelain Case, Wisdom Pattern	200.00
Ansonia, Mantel, La-France, Marble	125.00
Ansonia, Mantel, Oak, Baroque Style, Winged Female Bust Sides, 18 In.	1325.00
Ansonia, Mantel, Royal Bonn Case	742.50
Ansonia, Mantel, Triple Chime, Beveled Glass Door & Side Panels	225.00
Ansonia, Open Escapement, Royal Bonn Case	550.00
Ansonia, Regulator, Calendar, Castle Top	550.00
Ansonia, Regulator, Pine Case, Grain Painted	165.00
Ansonia, Royal Bonn Case, 8-Day	475.00
Ansonia, Shelf, Lady Playing Mandolin, 22 1/2 x 23 In. ....*Illus*	1300.00
Ansonia, Shelf, Layton Case	315.00
Ansonia, Spelter Woman Playing Mandolin, Open Escapement, 22 1/2 In.	1300.00
Ansonia, Wall, Queen Isabella	650.00
Banjo, E. Taber, Federal, Gilt & Mahogany, 41 1/2 In.	6600.00
Banjo, Enamel Face, Brass Finial, Center Mirror, 42 In.	1045.00
Banjo, Federal, 8-Day, Brass Movement, Mahogany, c.1820, 33 In.	660.00
Barnsdale, Victorian, Column-Flanked Case, Enamel Dial, 65 In.	1320.00
Baroque, Oak, Wall, Figural, Lions, 3-Weight, 7-Day, U.S., 36 x 15 In.	400.00
Beehive, Shelf, Etched Glass, c.1840	450.00
Biedermeier, Enamel Dial, Shield-Shaped Case, 1820s, 48 In.	1210.00
Bigelow & Kennard, Tall Case, Pendulum	3740.00
Black Forest, Stag At Top, Cylinder Music Box, Conchon Genova	3575.00
Bracket, Louis XV, 2-Train Movement, White Enamel Dial, 46 1/4 In.	4400.00
Bradley & Hubbard, Blinking Eye, Clock In Stomach Area	1150.00

Breul, Louis Philippe, Repeating, Cartel, c.1840, 16 1/2 In. 3410.00
Brewster & Ingraham, Beehive, Mahogany, Cut Glass Table, 8–Day, 19 In. 440.00
Bronze, Louis XVI Style, Bronze Dial, Roman Numerals, c.1882, 12 In. 550.00
Carriage, Beveled Glass, Germany, 1800s 195.00
Carriage, Chaude Of Paris, Silver Case, Key Wind, c.1896, 2 1/2 In. 2300.00
Carriage, Gold Handle, Feet & Hinge, 9K Gold, Tortoiseshell, English 495.00
Carriage, Music Box, Germany 100.00
Carriage, Musical, Not Because Your Hair Is Curly, German 150.00
Cartel, Louis XV, Enamel Dial, Roman, Arabic Numerals, 19th C., 20 In. 3300.00
Chauncey Jerome, Cottage, Time & Alarm, 30–Hour, 11 x 8 In. 125.00
Chauncey Jerome, Empire, Mahogany, Floral Face, Glass Panel, 26 In. 192.50
Chauncey Jerome, Parlor, Rack & Snail Strike, SCIPO 250.00
Chauncey Jerome, Shelf, Mahogany Veneer, Ogee, Pendulum, 25 3/4 In. 95.00
Colonial Mfg., Empire, Tall Case 800.00
Cuckoo, Black Forest, Eagle On Crest, Birds, Nest Around Dial, 26 In. 412.00
Desk, Patek Phillipe, Art Deco, 18 Jewels, Signed, c.1930 .... 907.00
Dixie, Box 795.00
E. N. Welch, Kitchen, Walnut, Broken Arch Top, Pendulum, Glass 250.00
E. N. Welch, Steeple, Rosewood, Walnut Case, 30–Hour, 14 1/2 In. 120.00
E. N. Welch, Wall, Regulator, Drop Octagon, Mahogany Case, 24 In. 275.00
Elgin, Boudoir, Alarm, Rhinestones 20.00
Eli Terry, Calendar, Victorian 275.00
Eli Terry, Empire, Shelf, Mahogany Veneer, Ebonized, Stencil, 32 In. 345.00
Eli Terry, Pillar & Scroll, Federal, Mahogany, c.1820, 32 In. 995.00
Elisha Hotchkiss, Jr., Shelf, Wooden Works, Weight Driven 525.00
Figural, Classically Draped Woman, Metal, Bronze Finish, 38 1/2 In. 1550.00
Figural, Elephant, Gilt Metal, Porcelain Dial, France 1150.00
Figural, Horse, Brass, Electric, 1950s, Large 45.00
French, Statue, Silk Thread Pendulum, Dore Bronze, 1827 .... 750.00
French, Time & Strike, Mercury Pendulum, Black Marble, 19 x 15 In. 475.00
General Electric, Blue Mirror 60.00
General Electric, Wall, Red, White, c.1950 .... 15.00
George III, Act Of Parliament, c.1790, 60 x 12 x 17 In. ....*Illus* 6380.00
Gilbert, Admiral, Regulator, Oak, 26 In. 295.00
Gilbert, Brass Works, Ebonized & Marbelized Finish, Wood, 12 5/8 In. 85.00
Gilbert, Mantel, Black Wood, Pillars & Pediment, 8–Day, Bell & Gong 100.00
Gilbert, Regulator, Bim Bam, Time & Strike, 8–Day, 24 In. 275.00
Gilbert, Shelf, Gingerbread, 8–Day, Oak 175.00
Gilbert, Trinity 700.00
Glass Column, German 135.00
Gustav Becker, Regulator, 2–Weight, c.1880 .... 1250.00

Clock, George III, Act of Parliament,
c.1790, 60 x 12 x 17 In.

◆◆◆◆◆◆◆◆◆◆◆◆◆◆◆◆◆◆◆◆◆

To set the time, push the minute hand clockwise, never
counterclockwise. If the clock
chimes, be sure to wait until it
stops striking before you ad--
vance the hands again.

◆◆◆◆◆◆◆◆◆◆◆◆◆◆◆◆◆◆◆◆◆

Clock, Regulator, Enameled,
With Portrait Pendulum, France

Gustav Becker, Regulator, 2-Weight, Half Hour & Hour Strike, 50 In.	715.00
Gustav Becker, Regulator, 3-Weight	1250.00
Gustav Becker, Vienna Regulator, Wall, 3-Weight	800.00
Hanging, Walnut, Brass Works, Silvered Dial, Weight, Pendulum, 51 In.	550.00
Harum, Carriage, Original Case	525.00
Herschede, Tall Case, Brass Trim, Gold Face, 9 Tubes, Triple Chime	6500.00
Herschede, Tall Case, Mahogany, Brass Engraved Dial, 1910, 7 Ft. 9 In.	4500.00
Howard Miller, Atom, Brass Face, Rods With Black Spheres, 13 1/2 In.	357.50
Howard Miller, Wall, Aluminum Case, Lucite Enclosed Works, 12 1/2 In.	165.00
In Dome, Walnut Frame, Gilded Cast Metal Figures, 18 1/4 In.	400.00
Ingraham, Calendar, Kitchen, Gila	220.00
Ingraham, Grecian, 8-Day, Time & Strike	385.00
Ingraham, Kitchen, Bristol, Conn., Chimes, 1800s	225.00
Ingraham, Mantel, White Painted Face, Eglomise Flower Panel, 16 In.	255.00
Ingraham, Mantel, Wooden, Metal Columns, 8-Day, Time & Strike	100.00
Ingraham, School, Calendar, Regulator	235.00
Ingraham, School, Drop Octagon, Time Only, Pressed Oak	315.00
Ingraham, Shelf, Curfew, Bell On Top	175.00
Ingraham, Shelf, Kitchen, Admiral Dewey, Oak	350.00
Ingraham, Shelf, Venetian Mosaic Front, Birds, 15 3/4 In.	300.00
Ithaca, Calendar, Double Dial, No. 11	950.00
Ithaca, Calendar, Walnut, Fashion, 8-Day, Pendulum, 1875, 32 In.	1760.00
Ives, Pillar & Scroll, Federal, Mahogany, c.1825	935.00
J. C. Brown, Beehive, Rosewood, 8-Day Time & Strike, 1850, 19 In.	800.00
J. Camdin, Ormolu Cartel, Enameled Dial, Key, Napoleon III, 16 In.	550.00
Jacob Diehl, Tall Case, Mahogany, White Tin Face, Gilt Flowers, 89 In.	5500.00
Jerome & Darrow, Nautical, Black Pillars, Mirrored Door, Gold Stencil	247.50
John Hagey, Tall Case, Mahogany, Broken Arch Pediment	5000.00
Junghans Wuttenberg, Mantel, Mahogany, Camelback, Westminster Chimes	160.00
Junghans, Owl, Blinking Eyes	425.00
Junghans, Parlor, Presentation, 1/4-Hour Chime	350.00
Junghans, Regulator, 2-Weight, Time & Strike, 52 In.	825.00
Junghans, Regulator, Wall, Porcelain Face, Brass Pendulum, Walnut	475.00
Kienzle Clock Co. & Mauthe Clock Co., Carriage, Musical, Germany	150.00
Krober, Parlor, Cupids, Mirrored Pendulum, Ebony	350.00
Lamp, Art Deco, Airplane, Chrome Wings, Wooden Hose, Cockpit Light-Up	175.00
LeCoultre, Alarm	350.00
Liberty & Co., Enameled Dial, Wood Columns, Pewter, 1820s, 12 1/4 In.	3575.00
Liberty & Co., Mantel, Tudric Enameled Pewter, Arched Top, 12 1/4 In.	3575.00
Liberty & Co., Pewter, Round, Enameled Face, Rectangular	4000.00
Long Case, Cherry, Birmingham, c.1790, 87 In.	6600.00
Louis Philippe, Figure Of Caesar, Gilt & Patinated, c.1845, 25 In.	2200.00
Louis XVI, Bronze Figural, Dolphins, Mantel, Pendulum, 16 In.	995.00
Lux, Alarm, Spinning Wheel, Box	165.00
Lux, Animated, Beer Drinkers	200.00
Lux, Black Couple, Alligator Hands, 1935	350.00
Lux, Black Dude, Composition Face, Tie Pendulum, Eyes Move, 8 1/2 In.	385.00
Lux, Black Shoeshine Boy	650.00
Lux, Dixie Boy, Pendulum, 1933	450.00 To 850.00
Lux, Spinning Wheel, Animated	68.00
Mantel, Allegorical Figural Columns, French, 19th Century, 22 In.	2475.00
Mantel, Arts & Crafts, Pottery, 6 1/2 x 6 In.	255.00
Mantel, Black Onyx, Floral Relief, Gilded Brass Face Trim, 15 In.	650.00
Mantel, Brass, Champleve Enamel, Dome Top, 19th Century, France, 16 In.	1900.00
Mantel, Brass, Enameled Face, Arched Foot, Wiener Werkstatte	3524.00
Mantel, Champleve Enameled Bronze, Ovoid, Time & Strike, 10 1/4 In.	1045.00
Mantel, Charles X, Winged Griffins At Side Of Dial, c.1840, 26 In.	7700.00
Mantel, Dance Of Presetalia, Bisque, Elgin Works, Glass Dome, 15 In.	220.00
Mantel, Empire, Ormolu & Patinated Bronze, c.1825, 30 1/2 In.	6600.00
Mantel, Enamel Dial, Brass Surround, Double Fusee Movement, Chinese	715.00
Mantel, Figural, Louis XVI Style, Dolphins, Tritons, Bronze, 16 In.	990.00
Mantel, French Revolutionary, Day Divided Into 10 Segments	6600.00
Mantel, Gilded Brass, Engraved Silver Face, France	900.00

Mantel, Gilded Brass, Figure, Silver Face, Fusee Movement, 15 1/4 In. 900.00
Mantel, Gilded Dial, Open Escapement, Alabaster, c.1890 .... 425.00
Mantel, Gilding, Dark Patina, Black Stone Base, Enameled Face, 20 In. 1650.00
Mantel, Gilt Bronze, Domed Top, Art Nouveau Designs, French, 17 In. 5500.00
Mantel, Hammered Copper, Enameled, Arts & Crafts, Handles, Rectangular 1663.00
Mantel, Japy Freres Movement, Marble & Bronze, c.1865, 13 x 17 In. 895.00
Mantel, Louis Philippe, Seated Scholar At Side, Gilt Bronze, 22 In. 1650.00
Mantel, Louis XV Style, Brass, Enamel Face, Painted, Wood, 11 3/4 In. 330.00
Mantel, Mahogany Veneer, Triple–Decker, Gilt Split Columns, 36 In. 523.00
Mantel, Napoleon III, 2 Putti Around Spherical Dial, Bronze, 16 In. 2420.00
Mantel, Napoleon III, Figure Of Joan Of Arc On Rock, Gilt Brass 660.00
Mantel, Portrait Medallions & Ormolu, Woman, Anchor, France, 13 In. 800.00
Mantel, Rectangular Hardwood Case, Stand, Circular Enamel Dial 715.00
Mantel, Rectangular Hardwood Case, Stand, Double Fusee, Chinese 715.00
Mantel, Seated Artist, Black Marble Base, France 770.00
Mantel, Triple–Decker, Mahogany Veneer, Gilt Eagle, 39 In. 495.00
Marilyn Monroe, Alarm 20.00
Mark Leavenworth, Pillar & Scroll, Reverse Painted Glass, 30 1/2 In. 4100.00
Mark Leavenworth, Shelf, Pillar & Scroll, Painted Dial 1100.00
Mazal, Brass, Swiss 75.00
Mercedes, Windup Brass, 7 In. 45.00
Mirov Requier, Mantel, Porcelain Dial, Village Scene, Brass, 12 In. 770.00
Mission, Oak, Floor, 6 Ft. 1500.00
Movado, Travel, Keyless Lever Movement, Open & Close Case To Wind 220.00
New Haven, Banjo, Time & Strike, Eagle Above Dial, 36 1/4 In. 275.00
New Haven, Clyde, Gingerbread, Oak 120.00
New Haven, Dolphin & Cherubs Supports, Spelter, c.1900, 15 In. 305.00
New Haven, Gallery, 8–Day, Oak Case, Dial, 12 In. 150.00
New Haven, Parlor, 8–Day, Garden Scene, Plated Bronze, c.1885 .... 325.00 To 400.00
New Haven, Regulator, Jeweler & Optician, Oak 250.00
New Haven, School, Miniature 150.00
New Haven, School, Time & Calendar 285.00
New Haven, Shelf, Mahogany, Ogee, Brass Works, Pendulum, 25 3/4 In. 150.00
Parlor, Gilded Bust, Tiny Lower Drawer, Knob Pull, Walnut 475.00
Pocket Watch Shape, Wall, 18 In. 37.50
Putnam Bailey, Mantel, Tiger Maple Face, Reverse Painted Glass 225.00
R. Whiting, Tall Case, Pine, Red & Black Graining, Bonnet, 30 In. 1300.00
Regulator, Enameled, With Portrait Pendulum, France ....*Illus* 3500.00
Regulator, Jeweler's, Cameo Head, Walnut 2400.00
Regulator, Jeweler's, Oak, 92 In. 4000.00
Regulator, Time, Calendar & Date, Railroad, Patent 1876 .... 3850.00
Reuben Tower, Eagle Finial, Lyres & Foliage, Mahogany, 37 1/4 In. 4950.00
Rheinholdt Hanke, Stoneware, Blue & Gray, Germany 125.00
Rick–Rock, Arched Cornice, Enameled Dial, Mahogany, Ireland, 63 In. 660.00
Riley Whiting, Tall Case, Swan's Neck Bonnet, Tiger Maple Columns 1875.00
S. Marti, Patinated Metal, Putti Support Brass Globe, 15 1/2 In. 885.00
School, Waterbury, Oak, Miniature 150.00
School, Windsor, Allover Dark Green Paint, 1800–1815, 27 1/2 In. 550.00
Sessions, Blinkin' Eye, Banjo Player 990.00
Sessions, Chef, Electric, Wall 35.00
Sessions, Dresser, Enameled Floral, Beehive, Frame, 1920s, 5 x 4 In. 69.00
Sessions, Regulator, Pendulum, Country Store 800.00
Sessions, Time & Date Display, Stronghold Plug Tobacco, Oak 350.00
Seth Thomas, Calendar, Double Dial, No. 3 .... 950.00
Seth Thomas, Lincoln 725.00
Seth Thomas, Mantel, 1–Day Weight, Driven Brass Movement, 1860 .... 285.00
Seth Thomas, Mantel, Adamantine, Celluloid Columns, Brass Feet, 1900 .... 200.00
Seth Thomas, Mantel, Chime & Strike, c.1915 .... 310.00
Seth Thomas, Mantel, Mahogany, Camelback 70.00
Seth Thomas, Mantel, Marbelized Wood, Lion's Heads, 8–Day, Time, Strike 80.00
Seth Thomas, Mantel, Senora Chimes 400.00
Seth Thomas, Mantel, Walnut, Double Weight, Reverse Painted Door 300.00
Seth Thomas, Mantel, Wood, Gilt, Brass, Celluloid Onyx Trim, 16 In. 75.00

Clock, Tall Case, Edwardian, Mahogany,   *Clock, Tall Case, George III, Thomas Lister,*
Chimes, c.1905   *34-Hour, c.1780*

Seth Thomas, Model No. 1, 8–Day Weight Driven Time, 1910, 36 In.	885.00
Seth Thomas, Oak, Time & Strike, Alarm	198.00
Seth Thomas, Office, Time Only, 30–Day, Square Oak Case, c.1910	400.00
Seth Thomas, Pillar & Scroll, Shelf, Mahogany, Reverse Painted, 31 In.	1000.00
Seth Thomas, Pillar & Scroll, Shelf, Mahogany, Wooden Works, 32 In.	975.00
Seth Thomas, Porcelain Face, Swags Of Foliage & Roses	425.00
Seth Thomas, Regulator, No. 2	825.00
Seth Thomas, Shelf, Federal, Pillar, Scroll, 31 x 16 1/2 x 4 1/4 In.	3850.00
Seth Thomas, Shelf, Pillar & Scroll, Mahogany, Pendulum, 31 In.	750.00
Seth Thomas, Shelf, White Case, Reverse Painted Glass, 16 1/2 In.	88.00
Seth Thomas, Ship's, Bakelite, World War II Era	50.00
Seth Thomas, Ship's, Outside Bell	550.00
Seth Thomas, Steeple, Mahogany, Gilt, Double Glazed Door, 16 In.	165.00
Seth Thomas, Steeple, Spring Driven, Parcel Gilt Mahogany, 16 1/2 In.	165.00
Seth Thomas, Table, Art Nouveau, Water Nymph, Cattails & Lilies	375.00
Seth Thomas, Time, Strike & Alarm	195.00
Shelf, F. Kroeber, Eastlake Design, Footed, Etched Glass, 24 x 15 In.	445.00
Shelf, Pink Marble Case, Gilded Brass Trim, Beveled Glass, 19 1/4 In.	750.00
Shelf, White Onyx, Ormolu Trim, Beveled Glass, Porcelain Face, 15 In.	495.00
Silas Hoadley, Tall Case, Masonic Dial, 1825–1841	3850.00
Silas Hoadley, Tall Case, Pine, 30–Hour Time & Strike, 91 1/4 In.	1100.00
Skeleton, Brass, Roman Numerals, Single Fusee, England, 12 1/2 In.	665.00
Skeleton, English, Cathedral Style, Figure Of Sir Walter Scott	2420.00
Stromberg, Wall, Large	495.00
Swinging Arm, Alabaster Arch, Girl In Swing, Fagot, French	575.00
Swinging Arm, Huntress	950.00
Tall Case, A. Cheloni, Renaissance Style, Walnut, 1889, 110 In.	9350.00
Tall Case, A. L. Russell, 8–Day, Brass Movement, Birch, 80 In.	1980.00
Tall Case, Abner Rogers, Painted Iron Dial, 8–Day, c.1790, 91 In.	2860.00
Tall Case, C. E. Smithers, George III, Painted Dial, Mahogany, 88 In.	3550.00
Tall Case, Calendar, Metal Face, Second Hand, Cherry, c.1790, 87 In.	6650.00
Tall Case, Case Painted Dark Brown, Polychrome Dial, c.1830, 84 In.	2300.00
Tall Case, Cherry, 8–Day Weight Driven Iron, Brass, 88 In.	2250.00
Tall Case, Cherry, Broken Arch, Old Finish, American	2600.00
Tall Case, Cherry, Chippendale, Bonnet, Weights & Pendulum, 92 In.	5000.00
Tall Case, Cherry, Wooden Works, Hand Painted Dial Dated 1825	1050.00
Tall Case, Colonial Revival, Mahogany, Chimes, Glazed Case, 96 In.	7150.00
Tall Case, Dutch, Moon Phases, Fruitwood Marquetry, Walnut, 7 Ft. 2 In.	8800.00
Tall Case, Edwardian, Mahogany, Chimes, c.1905 ....*Illus*	7425.00
Tall Case, Elyah Yeomans, Brass Dial, Mahogany, c.1775, 76 In.	4950.00
Tall Case, Empire, Cherry, Fluted Posts Crest, Half Columns, 95 In.	1000.00

Tall Case, Federal, Maple, 8–Day Brass Weight, 1806, 92 1/2 In. 7775.00
Tall Case, George III, Fluted Columns, Brass & Steel Dial, Mahogany 2425.00
Tall Case, George III, Painted Landscape Dome Panel, 38 In. 2400.00
Tall Case, George III, Thomas Lister, 34–Hour, c.1780 ....*Illus* 1650.00
Tall Case, J. Elicot, Fruitwood Marquetry, Brass Dial, 100 In. 4450.00
Tall Case, J. Hallett, Calendar, Date & Minute, Mahogany, c.1790, 8 Ft. 6000.00
Tall Case, J. Shepley, Bull's–Eye Glass In Door, Hour Only Hand, 1710 .... 5700.00
Tall Case, Jacob Gorgas, Chippendale, 30–Hour, 1790s 8200.00
Tall Case, Jeffreys & Ham, George III, 1820s, Mahogany, 95 In. 3200.00
Tall Case, John Fite, Iron Face, Reeded Quarter Columns, Mahogany 9999.00
Tall Case, Jon Miller, Shells, Brass Dial, 1740, 6 Ft. 10 1/2 In. 5500.00
Tall Case, Josiah Wood, Brass Spire Finials, Mahogany, c.1797, 94 In. 9350.00
Tall Case, Louis XV Style, Ormolu, Marquetry, 19th C., 92 In. 4950.00
Tall Case, Mahogany Veneer Inlay, Brass Works, Metal Face, 88 1/2 In. 1300.00
Tall Case, Mahogany, Cross Banded Veneers, Waltham, 103 In. 2425.00
Tall Case, Mahogany, Figured Veneer, Inlay, Bracket Feet, 101 In. 1900.00
Tall Case, Oak, Brass Works, Painted Metal Face, 78 1/2 In. 550.00
Tall Case, Painted Dial, Second Ring, Lunar Dial, Mahogany, 99 In. 6600.00
Tall Case, Painted, Connecticut, 1800–1820, 7 Ft. 6 1/2 In. 9500.00
Tall Case, Peter Shutz, Brass Face, Flat Top, Chippendale Feet, 1808 .... 2750.00
Tall Case, Riley Whiting, Grained Case, Wooden Works, c.1825, 7 Ft. 3850.00
Tall Case, Seneca & Thomas Lukens, Moon Phase, Calendar, Cherry 7480.00
Tall Case, Silas Hoadley, Dated Feb. 18, 1829 .... 1210.00
Tall Case, T. Chandler, Painted Dial, Flame Birch, c.1800, 88 1/2 In. 8800.00
Tall Case, W. Bolton, Mahogany Veneer, Moon Phase Dial, 88 1/2 In. 1300.00
Tall Case, W. H. Durfee, Westminster, 8 Bells Chimes, Mahogany, 96 In. 7150.00
Tall Case, Waltham, Mahogany, 3 Brass Finials & Weights, 103 In. 2425.00
Tall Case, Wilson Chickester, Brass Works, Painted Metal Face, Oak 550.00
Telechron, 850, Electric, Silver Plate, Plastic Base, 8 x 5 In. 750.00
Telechron, Desk, Ship's Wheel, Brass Tone 18.00
Telechron, Electric, Brown Bakelite, 7 x 4 In. 45.00
Telechron, Electric, White Bakelite 35.00
Telechron, Pelican, Bright Yellow, Patent 1927 .... 175.00
Terry, Victorian, Calendar 250.00
Thuret, Louis XIV, Repeating, Tortoiseshell, c.1730, 15 In. 9350.00
Tiffany clocks are listed in the Tiffany section
Time, Cleveland Time Clock & Service Co., Oak Case, 4 Ft. 140.00
Traveling, Alarm, Crocodile Leather, England 140.00
Veema, Regulator, 2 Weights, 1880s, 40 In. 895.00
Wag–On–Wall, Brass Gears, Wooden Face, Weights, Pendulum, 12 In. 300.00
Wag–On–Wall, Morbier, Brass Design, Porcelain Face, Alberto Rodriquez 885.00
Wag–On–Wall, Painted Wooden Face, Brass, Gears, 12 1/4 In. 300.00
Wag–On–Wall, Painted Wooden Face, Brass, Weights, Pendulum, 7 In. 550.00
Wall, Made Like A Pocket Watch, Brass, France, 11 1/2 In. 295.00
Wall, Tole Peinte, French, Octagonal, Faux Rosewood Design, 10 1/4 In. 385.00
Waltham, Desk, Art Deco, Beveled Glass, Cobalt Glass Posts, 11 1/2 In. 515.00
Waterbury, Double Dial, Patent 1889 .... 675.00
Waterbury, Steeple, 30–Hour, Time & Strike, 19 1/2 In. 245.00
Waterbury, Wall, Gingerbread, Half Hour & Hour Strike, Alarm, 26 In. 187.00
Waterbury, Weight Driven, Ogee, 1858 .... 135.00
Welch Spring, Calendar, Rosewood, 8–Day Time & Strike, 1885, 30 In. 3850.00
Welch, Mantel, 8–Day, Rosewood, 18 In. 715.00
Welch, Shelf, Gingerbread, Walnut 155.00
Westclox, Tiny Tim, 1927 .... 20.00
Willard, Banjo, Eagle Finial, Reverse Painted Glass 1100.00
Willard, Banjo, Giltwood Acorn Finial, Brass Door, c.1815, 40 1/2 In. 9975.00
Willard, Banjo, Paneled Throat & Base, Wood Side Scrolls 750.00
Willard, Banjo, Stenciled Foliage, Mahogany Case, 40 1/4 In. 3100.00
Winchester, Pine Case, Weights 247.00
Zenith, Convex Verde Marble, Round, 14 In. 465.00

Cloisonne, Teapot, Floral, Black Ground, 2 In.

CLOISONNE enamel was developed during the tenth century. A glass enamel was applied between small ribbons of metal on a metal base. Most cloisonne is Chinese or Japanese. Pieces marked *China* are twentieth-century examples.

Box, Cover, 2 Melon Shape, Metal Vines & Leaves, 10 1/2 x 13 In.	500.00
Box, Cover, Pink & Brown, 3 1/2 x 6 1/2 In.	335.00
Candleholder, White Jade Candle Cup, 10 In., Pair	1500.00
Chamberstick, 6-In. Saucer	148.00
Charger, Gray & White Bird, Flowers, Gold Floral Border, 12 In.	395.00
Ginger Jar, Cover, 4 1/2 In.	175.00
Jar, Cover, Scroll & Floral Design, Brown Ground, 9 In.	120.00
Jar, Polychrome Floral Design, Domed Lid, Black Ground, 13 In.	55.00
Plate, Birds & Flowers, 12 In.	250.00
Plate, Dragon, 11 3/4 In.	125.00
Teapot, Floral, Black Ground, 2 In. ....*Illus*	45.00
Tray, Bronze Bamboo Borders, Florals, Birds, 8 1/2 x 14 1/2 In.	125.00
Vase, Bird On Limb, Black, 11 In.	95.00
Vase, Bottle Form, Yellow Dragons, Blue, Pair	192.50
Vase, Butterflies, 7 1/2 In.	80.00
Vase, Butterflies, Green, 10 In., Pair	1500.00
Vase, Chrysanthemum Design, Blue Ground, Japan, 47 In.	880.00
Vase, Floral, 6 Panels, c.1900, 11 In.	125.00
Vase, Floral, Black Ground, 11 3/4 In.	105.00
Vase, Panels Of Dragons, Phoenix Birds, Dark Blue, c.1900, 12 In.	495.00
Vase, Polychrome Flowers, Pale Blue Ground, 7 1/4 In., Pair	230.00
Vase, Scenic Panel Of Deer & Geese, Floral, 7 1/2 In., Pair	275.00
Water Pot, Peach Design, Bamboo Type Handle, Finial, Spout, 18 In.	1250.00

CLOTHING of all types is listed in this section. Dresses, hats, shoes, underwear and more are found here. Other textiles are to be found in the Coverlet, Quilt, Textile, and World War I and II sections.

Bandana, Red, Cowboys, Horses, Swagger	25.00
Bathing Suit, Man's, Tank Top Style, Wool, 1920s, 1 Piece	55.00
Bathrobe, Floral Print, Beacon	45.00
Bib, Baby's, Hand Quilted, Victorian	24.00
Blouse, Beaded, Squaw Skirt, Aqua, 1960s, Size 14, 2 Piece	15.00
Blouse, Cutwork Collar, Jeweled Buttons, Velvet Skirt, 1930s, 2 Pc.	65.00
Bonnet, Black, Maroon Lining	20.00
Bonnet, Hand Quilted, Silk Fringe, Civil War	50.00
Camisole, Ribbon Inserts, Lace Trim, White	15.00
Cape, Baby's, White Pique	18.00
Cape, Child's, Victorian, Linen	30.00
Cape, Opera, Beaded, Lacy	75.00
Cape, Paisley, Gathered Collar, Full-Length	175.00
Cape, Pendleton Wool, Red Plaid, Worn Lining	40.00
Cape, Persian Paw, 1950s	45.00

Cape, Rain, Marked Ginny	20.00
Cape, Woman's, Black Seal, 1920s	40.00
Cape, Woman's, Black Velour, 1900s	75.00
Coat & Hat, Persian Lamb, 1940s	90.00
Coat, Dress, Calvary, Indian War, Dark Blue Wool, Medal	400.00
Coat, Dress, Kate Greenaway Style, Silk Burgundy, c.1880	75.00
Coat, Evening, Green Velvet, 1930s, Size 14	395.00
Coat, Flapper, Fishtail, Gold Panne Velvet, Smocked Collar & Cuffs	125.00
Coat, Light Green Wool, Black Velvet Trim, Silk Lining	45.00
Coat, Mink, Black Fox Collar, 1950–1960, 3/4–Length, Size 12	165.00
Coat, Mouton, 1940s	50.00
Coat, Raccoon, Large	125.00
Coat, Triangular Embroidery On Collar, Silk Ecru, 1920s	30.00
Coat, Velvet & Chinchilla	550.00
Collar, Black Fox, V Shape, Lined	45.00
Collar, Man's, Detachable, Starched, Box, 6 Piece	10.00
Corset, Victorian, White	40.00
Corset, Warner's, 1920s, Unused	10.00
Dress, Baptismal, Victorian, White	35.00
Dress, Black Georgette, Matching Slip, 1930s	40.00
Dress, Black Satin, Padded Shoulders, 1940	100.00
Dress, Blue Silk & Black Lace, 1910s, 2 Piece	715.00
Dress, Cluny Lace Bodice, Net & Ruffled Sleeves, Lawn	75.00
Dress, Coat Type, Navy, Sophisticated, 1930s	40.00
Dress, Coat, Black Faille, 1950s	50.00
Dress, Cocktail, Black Silk, 1950s	30.00
Dress, Cotton, Floral, Lace Trim	150.00
Dress, Dressing, Kimono Sleeves, Gold Lace Collar, Rosette Closure	395.00
Dress, Evening, Glittering Gold Bow, Fringed Skirt	250.00
Dress, Flapper, Beige Lace, Tiered Skirt, Lined	75.00
Dress, Flapper, Cream Chiffon, Black & Gold Sequins	190.00
Dress, Flapper, Sheer, Beadwork, Green	55.00
Dress, Flapper, Tan & Black Chiffon, Shoulder Fringe	140.00
Dress, Gold Lame, Roses, Letter Of Authenticity, Phyllis Diller	100.00
Dress, Green & Silver Silk, Lace Trim, Stern Bros., N.Y., 2 Piece	605.00
Dress, Lace, 1910s, 2 Piece	192.00
Dress, Lavender Panne Velvet, Gold Metallic, Fur Puff	240.00
Dress, Lingerie, Eyelet Hem, Double Sleeves, 1900	150.00
Dress, Navy Crepe, Taffeta, With Jacket, 1950s	30.00
Dress, Pleated Silk, Yellow, Fortuny	3800.00
Dress, Ruffled Bodice, Leg–O–Mutton Sleeves, Black Polished Cotto	95.00
Dress, Sheath, Black Cut Velvet, 1960s, Size 8	35.00
Dress, Silk Brocade, 2 Bodices, Lace Trimmed Pantaloons	425.00
Dress, Sleeveless, Bias–Cut Green Velvet, 1930s, Long	215.00
Dress, Strapless, Beaded Black Taffeta, Bolero Jacket, Size 10	65.00
Dress, Tea, Lace Inserts, Ecru	65.00
Dress, Victorian, Calf–Length, White	75.00
Dress, Victorian, French Lace, White Batiste, Teenager's	175.00
Dress, Victorian, Lace, Vine & Floral Design, c.1910	205.00
Dress, Victorian, Lawn, Lace Inserts At Bodice	65.00
Dress, Victorian, White, Lace Trim	100.00
Dress, Wedding, Embroidered & Painted Design, Japan, 19th Century	220.00
Dress, Wedding, Handmade, Battenburg Lace, Re–Embroidered	350.00
Dress, Wedding, Joan Collins Of Dynasty	495.00
Dress, Wedding, White Chiffon, Hat, Beaded, Movie Mannequin	375.00
Dress, White, Art Deco Buckle, 1920s	20.00
Gloves, Officer's, Leather, Signed Cap. J. W. Hout C. S. A.	55.00
Gloves, Woman's, Beaded, Gray, Medium Size	16.00
Gloves, Woman's, Black Silk, Full–Length, 1920s	10.00
Handkerchief, Lace Trim Says Bertha	38.00
Handkerchief, Linen, Art Deco Wolfhounds On Box	10.00
Handkerchief, Woman's, Lace Tatted Edge	3.50
Hat, Blue, Lavender Feathers, Schiaparelli Paris Label	85.00

Hat, Boonie, Vietnam, With 5 Patches	85.00
Hat, Conductor's, Seacoast Electric Trolley	45.00
Hat, Fedora, Stetson, Box	30.00
Hat, Man's, Derby, Black, Box	40.00
Hat, Mink Tail, With Veil	40.00
Hat, Orange Velvet, Saks 5th Avenue, Owned By Mae West	125.00
Hat, Pilot, Flying Tiger, Mission Crusher	125.00
Hat, Riding, Woman's, Beaver	100.00
Hat, Schiaparelli, Lavender Feathers, Paris Label	85.00
Hat, Straw, All Lace Overlay, Silk Rosettes, 1880	150.00
Hat, Top, Black Beaver, Original Leather Case	130.00
Hat, Turban, Beige, Custom Made For Mae West	125.00
Hat, Woman's, Black Straw, Bird Of Paradise Feather	100.00
Hat, Woman's, Feather, Round Box	15.00
Hat, Woman's, Pheasant Feathers, 1950s	50.00
Hat, Woman's, Pink & Black Feathers, Round Box	15.00
Helmet, British Bobby, County Badge & Chin Strap	195.00
Helmet, Child's, Riding	19.00
Helmet, Keystone Cop	150.00
Jacket & Hat, Curly Lamb	100.00
Jacket, Edwardian, Lace, Gold, c.1915	225.00
Jacket, Evening, Black Battenburg Lace, c.1880	225.00
Jacket, Mobil Oil, Size 42–44	65.00
Jacket, Pleated Brocade Front, Mother–of–Pearl Buckle, Brown	50.00
Jacket, Tuxedo, Extra Large	65.00
Jacket, Woman's, Black Persian Lamb, Mink Collar, 1950s	55.00
Kimono, Child's, Painted Floral Design, With Obi, Japan	25.00
Mourning Outfit, Black, 5 Piece	200.00
Muff, Black Fox, 1930s	35.00
Night Cap, Peach, Lace Trim	10.00
Night Cap, Pink Satin, Crochet Trim	10.00
Nightgown, Victorian, Lace Trim	95.00
Overalls, Flying Fortress Airplane, World War II	20.00
Pantalets, Entredeux & Lace	27.00
Pants, Flannel, Off–White, Peckinpaugh, Cutshaw & O. Miller, 1915	20.00
Pants, Gold Lame, Liberace's	225.00
Peignoir, Black Lace, Floor–Length	27.50
Petticoat, Baby's, Flannel, Crochet Trim	15.00
Petticoat, Baby's, Linen	20.00
Robe, Geisha, Floral Print Design, Tan, Japan	65.00
Robe, Made Of Various Cigarette Flags, Flannel, 1920s	358.00
Robe, Wedding, Cream Lace, Victorian, Pleated Tulle Collar, Cuffs	800.00
Robe, Wedding, Japanese, Silk On Silk, Dragon, Gold & Red	700.00
Sailor Suit, Boy's, 1912	55.00
Serape, Stripes, Mexican, 60 x 92 In.	40.00
Shawl, Kashmir, Colored Medallions, Florals, Square, 5 Ft. 8 In.	605.00
Shawl, Kashmir, Scrolling Floral, Red Ground, 10 Ft. 6 In. x 5 Ft.	347.50
Shawl, Lace, Black, 1925	65.00
Shawl, Multicolored Fringe, French, 20th Century	1210.00
Shawl, Paisley Design, White Center, France, 123 x 62 In.	357.50
Shawl, Paisley, Black Center, 68 x 72 In.	250.00
Shawl, Paisley, Scrolling Floral, Black Ground, 6 Ft. x 6 Ft.	770.00
Shawl, Paisley, Scrolling Florals, 5 Ft. 5 In. x 10 Ft. 7 In.	467.50
Shawl, Paisley, Stripes, 58 x 112 In.	300.00
Shawl, Paisley, Wool, Woven Design, 69 x 69 In.	50.00
Shawl, Red Paisley, Victorian	125.00
Shawl, Swirling Cones, Patchwork & Needlework, 72 x 68 In.	905.00
Shoes, Baby's, 4 Button, Brown	37.50
Shoes, Baby's, High Top, Green	46.00
Shoes, Girl's, Black Patent Leather, Red Goose	27.00
Shoes, High Button	35.00
Shoes, High Heels, The Vulcan Last Co., Maple, 1927, Pair	28.00
Shoes, Man's, Brown Spectators, 1930s	35.00

Shoes, Wedding, Ivory, Silver, Brocade, Buckle, 1930s, J. McCreery 50.00
Skirt Hoop, Wire Cage, 1880s 38.00
Skirt, Poodle, Full, 1950s 25.00
Slippers, Bedroom, Gunsmoke, Colorful 95.00
Slippers, Wedding, White Satin, Tulle Rose 30.00
Spats, Gray Felt, Bond Street, Box 18.00
Spats, Man's, Gray, Box 13.50
Suit Of Armor, Hand Made, Engraved, Chain Mail On Helmet, 75 In. 850.00
Tea Gown, For Western Market, Wool & Silk, China, 19th Century 1800.00
Tie, Child's, Bugs Bunny, 1940s 38.00
Trousers, Sequins, Off–White, Liberace 235.00
Uniform, Dress, State Officer, New York, Shako, Epaulets, Box 400.00
Uniform, Flying Tiger, CBI Dress, With Wings 250.00
Uniform, Russian Cossack, Boots, Dagger, With Scabbard, Complete 350.00

CLUTHRA glass is a two–layered glass with small air pockets that form white spots. The Steuben Glass Works of Corning, New York, made it after 1903. Kimball Glass Company of Vineland, New Jersey, made Cluthra from about 1925. Victor Durand signed some pieces with his name. Related items are listed in the Steuben category.

Vase, Amethyst, Steuben, 8 1/2 In. 1400.00
Vase, Clouds Of Blue, Green & Teal, 1932, 7 1/2 x 7 In. 525.00
Vase, Green, Steuben, 10 In. 1400.00
Vase, Light Amethyst, Steuben, 8 1/2 In. 1200.00
Vase, White To Black, Steuben, 7 1/2 In. 825.00

COALPORT ware has been made by the Coalport Porcelain Works of England from 1795 to the present time. Early pieces were unmarked. About 1810–1825 the pieces were marked with the name *Coalport* in various forms. Later pieces also had the name *John Rose* in the mark. The crown mark has been used with variations since 1881.

Card Holder, Figural Flower, Bone China 15.00
Cooler, Fruit, Cover, Scroll Finial, Cobalt Ground, 14 In., Pair 2420.00
Cup & Saucer, Floral Reserves, Gold Trim, Box, After Dinner, 6 Sets 450.00
Dessert Set, Botanical, Footed, Saloppian, 1875, 16 Piece 550.00
Dessert Set, Botanical, Yellow Border, John Rose, 1825, 26 Piece 7975.00
Dessert Set, Fruit Clusters, Beige Ground, John Rose & Co., 22 Pc. 8525.00
Dinner Set, King's Pattern, 1810, 60 Piece 6600.00
Figurine, Isadora 65.00
Fruit Cooler, Cover, Church Gresley, Gilt Handles, 1810, 10 3/8 In. 1870.00
Fruit Cooler, Floral Reserves, Cobalt Blue, 14 In., Pr. ....*Illus* 2420.00
Garniture Set, Cobalt Blue, Flowers, Gilt, 2–Handled Vase, 3 Pc. 165.00
Plate, Dessert, King's Pattern, 1810, 7 11/16 In., 11 Piece 1450.00
Plate, Japan Pattern, 1805, 8 3/8 In., 13 Piece 2420.00
Relish, Semi–Scallop 20.00
Tankard, Hand Painted Castle Scene, Gold, Miniature 70.00

Coalport, Fruit Cooler, Floral Reserves,
Cobalt Blue, 14 In., Pr.

Cobalt Blue, Decanter, Blue
Overlay, Mushroom Stopper, 14 In.

COBALT BLUE glass was made using oxide of cobalt. The characteristic bright dark blue identifies it for the collector. Most cobalt glass found today was made after the Civil War.

Decanter, Blue Overlay, Mushroom Stopper, 14 In. ....*Illus*	145.00
Dish, Hen On Nest, Basketweave Base	50.00
Dish, Lounging Cow Cover	210.00
Mug, Humpty–Dumpty	20.00
Rose Bowl, 8–Crimp Top, Daisy Type Flowers, 4 1/2 In.	135.00
Salt & Pepper, Bakelite Handle, Stand, Occupied Japan, 3 Piece	29.00
Salt, Diamond–Quilted, Applied Foot, 3 In.	95.00
Shaker, Fox Hunt Scene	30.00
Tumbler, Child's, Mother Goose	6.00
Vase, Bulbous Body, Ching Dynasty, Stand, 10 In., Pair	665.00

COCA–COLA was first served in 1886 in Atlanta, Georgia. It was advertised through signs, newspaper ads, coupons, bottles, trays, calendars, and even lamps and clocks. Collectors want anything with the word *Coca–Cola,* including a few rare products, like gum wrappers and cigar bands. The famous trademark was patented in 1893, the *Coke* mark in 1945. Many modern items and reproductions are being made.

Ad, Boy Scout Jamboree, Coke, Framed, 1938	25.00
Bank, Coke Machine, Tin	15.00
Bank, Dispenser, Battery Operated, No Glasses, 1950s, 9 x 5 In.	500.00
Blackboard, Store, 1940s	220.00
Blotter, 3 Girls, 1944	10.00
Blotter, Girl In Bathing Suit, 1941	20.00
Book Cover, 1939	38.00
Booklet, Flower Arranging, 1940s	19.00
Booklet, Know Your War Planes, World War II	35.00
Bookmark, Heart Shape, Celluloid, Lithograph, Framed, 2 1/4 In.	132.00
Bottle Opener, 6 In.	5.50
Bottle Opener, Coke, Flat, 1950s	10.00
Bottle Opener, Lion's Head, Drink Goldelle Ginger Ale .... 85.00 To	90.00
Bottle Opener, With Ice Pick, Chesterman & Co. .... 60.00 To	70.00
Bottle, 50th Anniversary, Gold, Pacific Coast Bottling Co.	75.00
Bottle, 6 Stars, Square Sides, 1926	20.00
Bottle, 75th Anniversary, Corinth, Mississippi, 1982	6.00
Bottle, Bear Bryant, 1981	6.00
Bottle, Canton, Ohio, Amber	35.00
Bottle, Coke, Gold	65.00
Bottle, Columbus, Ohio, Amber	35.00
Bottle, Dark Green, Canada, Property Misprint	80.00
Bottle, Lexington, Ky., Amber	35.00
Bottle, Porcelain, 12 In.	85.00
Bottle, Studebaker Club, Painted Label, 1983	20.00
Bottle, Tin, 6 Ft.	475.00
Bottle, Westminster, Mo., Straight Sided, Qt.	110.00
Bowtie, Blues, 1950–1960s	20.00
Calendar Paper, 1935, Frame	295.00
Calendar, 1923, Coke, With Glass, Pad, Matted & Framed	375.00
Calendar, 1931, Boy With Dog, Fishing Pole	60.00
Calendar, 1934, Coke, Pad, Matted & Framed	375.00
Calendar, 1937, Cover Sheet, Wyeth, Boy Fishing	245.00
Calendar, 1945, Cover Sheet, Lady In Scarf	165.00
Calendar, 1947, Girls, Seasonal Costume	95.00
Calendar, 1950, Color Lithograph, Paper, 22 In.	11.00
Calendar, 1953, Armed Forces, Atlanta, Georgia	125.00
Calendar, 1958, French Canadian, 12 x 22 In.	48.00
Calendar, 1976, Montreal Olympics, 12 x 9 In., 4 Pages	8.00
Can, Commemorative, Christmas	3.00
Card Table, Bottle On 4 Corners, 1920s, Samson	125.00
Card, Advertising, Lillian Nordica Coke, 1905	100.00

Card, Playing, 1943, Unopened, Box	70.00
Card, Playing, 1956, Skater	30.00
Card, Playing, 1959	45.00
Card, Playing, Enjoy Coca–Cola It's The Real Thing, Unopened	5.00
Card, Playing, Hund & Eger	65.00
Card, Playing, Pinochle, Hund & Eger	55.00
Carrier, 6–Pack, Christmas, Red, White & Green, 1939	30.00
Carrier, Bottle, Stadium Vendor's	200.00
Carrier, Metal, Wooden Handle, 1940s	28.00
Carrier, Record, 45 RPM, With Index & 12 Sleeves, 1950s, 8 x 9 In.	30.00
Carrier, Wooden, 6–Pack, Yellow & Red	27.50
Case, Wooden, 6 Bottles, Canvas Cover, Coke Picture	125.00
Chalkboard, Tin, Red, Yellow, White, 1950s, 26 x 18 In.	60.00
Clock, Alarm, 15 Years Disney, Box	25.00
Clock, Aluminum Frame, Red, Green & White, 1960s	75.00
Clock, Drink Coca–Cola, Modern Clock Co., Electric, Round, 23 In.	325.00
Clock, Drink Coca–Cola, Price Bros., Table, Electric, 9 x 19 In.	345.00
Clock, Electric, Tin, 1952	88.00
Clock, Green Fishtail	125.00
Clock, Maroon, Red, 1950s, 18 In.	135.00
Clock, Revolving Border, Reverse–Stenciled Glass, 18 In.	525.00
Clock, Silver, Red, 1950s, 18 In.	120.00
Clock, Things Go Better With Coke, Plastic, 1960s	50.00
Clock, Tin Dial, Drink Coca–Cola, Walnut Frame, 1930s	525.00
Clock, Wall, Red & Brown, Round, Electric	125.00
Clock, Wood Frame, 1939	475.00
Clock, Wooden, 1946	635.00
Coaster, Pretty Woman, Tin, Repro	1.25
Coin–Operated Machine, Cavalier, No. 27	1500.00
Coin–Operated Machine, Cavalier, No. 33	800.00
Coin–Operated Machine, Cavalier, No. 72	650.00 To 1900.00
Coin–Operated Machine, Coke, 10 Cents, 1950s	985.00
Coin–Operated Machine, Cooler, Vendo 110	500.00
Coin–Operated Machine, Jacobs 26	2600.00
Coin–Operated Machine, Makes Change, 10 Cents, Vendor, No. 44	6500.00
Coin–Operated Machine, Model No. 110, Restored	900.00
Coin–Operated Machine, Shooting Game, Legs & Skirts	800.00
Coin–Operated Machine, Vendo 27	2400.00
Coin–Operated Machine, Vendo 39, 10 Cents	750.00
Coin–Operated Machine, Vendo 44, 1950s	1850.00
Coin–Operated Machine, Vendo 56	2600.00
Coin–Operated Machine, Vendo 80	650.00
Coin–Operated Machine, Vendo 81	2400.00
Coin–Operated Machine, Vendo V–39, Vertical, 10 Cents	1200.00
Coin–Operated Machine, Vendo, 1944	2200.00
Coin–Operated Machine, Westinghouse 42	1900.00
Cookie Jar, Can Shape, McCoy, 1988–1990, 10 In.	40.00
Cookie Jar, Jug, McCoy	55.00
Cooler, Chest, 1949	525.00
Cooler, Glascock, Counter Top	800.00
Cooler, Office	300.00
Cooler, Red, Tin Lined, Small	160.00
Cooler, Salesman's Sample, 1934	2100.00
Cooler, Vinyl, 1960s	55.00
Cufflinks, Sterling Silver, 1950s	20.00
Dispenser, String, Double–Sided, Newton, Iowa, 1930s, 15 1/2 In.	400.00
Display Case, Corner, Floor, 1890 Tiger Oak, Beveled Glass	900.00
Display, Bottle, Clear, Plastic Cap, 1960s	110.00
Display, Bottle, Dec. 25, 1923	275.00
Display, Bottle, Patent, No Cap	265.00
Display, Good With Food, Cardboard, Hands, Sandwich, 42 x 32 In.	285.00
Display, Santa Claus, Cardboard, 1971	18.00
Display, Window, Airport, Cardboard, 26 Piece	3850.00

Doll, Black Santa Claus, 1960s, 19 In.	85.00
Door Kick, Drink Coca–Cola, Sold Here, Ice Cold, Porcelain, 1939	595.00
Door Pull, Bottle Shape, 1940s	200.00
Door Pull, Bottle Shape, Plastic, Steel, 8 In.	88.00
Door Push, 1950s, Red, Yellow & White Porcelain	125.00
Door Push, Enjoy Coca–Cola Here, Red, White & Yellow, 1950s	85.00
Door Push, Iced Coca–Cola Here, Porcelain, 1950s	125.00
Door Push, Red, Yellow, White, France, Late, 1930s	150.00
Door Push, Red, Yellow, White, Porcelain, Canada	58.00
Door Push, Red, Yellow, White, Porcelain, Canada, 1940s	88.00 To 110.00
Door Push, Thank You–Call Again, Porcelain, 29 3/4 In.	175.00
Fan, Hand Holding Bottle	35.00
Fan, Wood Stick, Cardboard, 1956, 11 x 7 In.	28.00
Fly Swatter, 1950s	12.00
Fountain Dispenser, Child's, Box, 1950s	95.00
Game, Box, 1941	250.00
Game, Checkers, Dragon, Each Individually Marked, Complete	55.00
Game, Dart Board, 1930s, 17 x 17 In.	50.00
Game, Shooting, Legs & Skirts	800.00
Hat Pin, Delivery Man's	6.50
Ice Chest, 1940s	650.00
Ice Pick & Opener	30.00
Jacket, Eisenhower Style, Red	200.00
Kerchief, Kit Carson	50.00
Knife, Pocket	25.00
Knife, Pocket, World's Fair, 1933	135.00
Knife, Truck, Brass	12.00
Lamp, Fairy, Atlanta 1909	350.00
Lantern, Hanging Coke, Plastic, Tin, 1960s	65.00
Lighter, Bottle, Advertising, 1940s	225.00
Lighter, Bottle, Miniature	15.00
Lighter, Drink Coca–Cola, Hahodson, Bluebird, Musical, Pocket	50.00
Lighter, Gold Design, Bottle, 2 1/2 In.	15.00
Lighter, Paperweight	15.00
Matchstriker, Coke, Porcelain, 1938–1939, France, 4 x 4 In.	90.00
Matchstriker, Drink Coca–Cola, Strike Matches Here, Porcelain	325.00
Matchstriker, Red, White, Yellow, Black, Porcelain, Canada, 1938	122.00
Menu Board, Art Deco Style, Embossed Tin Lithograph, 27 In.	175.00
Menu Board, Attached Gold Bottles, Wood, 24 1/4 x 33 In.	250.00
Menu Board, Metal Bottles, Sliding Items, Wooden	250.00
Mirror, Pocket, Coca–Cola Girl, Oval, 1910	300.00
Mirror, Pocket, Coca–Cola Girl, Oval, 1911	145.00
Mirror, Pocket, Elaine, Oval, 1916	275.00
Mirror, Pocket, Woman With Pink Roses On Hat, Oval, 1908	1200.00
Money Clip, Brass, Red Plastic Logo, 1949	22.00
Music Box, Cooler, Drink Coca–Cola, 1950s	1600.00
Nickel, Wooden	.50
Note Pad, Coca–Cola Safety, 1950s	9.00
Note Pad, School, Norman Rockwell Scene, Framed, 1931, 7 x 10 In.	80.00
Paperweight, 1950s, Red	75.00
Paperweight, Calendar, 1986	8.00
Pencil Holder, Ceramic, 1960s	175.00
Pencil Sharpener, Bottle Shape, 1930	35.00
Pencil, Drink Coca–Cola, 1950, Jacket, 12 Piece	36.00
Pencil, Wooden, Unused	1.00
Pin, Delivery Man's Hat	6.50
Plate, Western Bottling Co., Vienna Art, Topless Lady, 1905	450.00
Poster, Hostess, Used For 1936 Tray, Lithograph, 50 x 28 1/2 In.	450.00
Poster, Refresh Yourself, Cardboard, 2 Sides, 14 x 11 In.	50.00
Puzzle, Party Scene, Mounted On Paper, 1950s, Canada, 12 x 18 In.	90.00
Rack, Bottle	120.00
Radio, AM, Blue, Montreal Expo & Coke, Pocket	15.00
Radio, Bottle Shape, AM–FM, 1980s, 8 In.	22.00

Coca-Cola, Sign, Dispenser, 2 Sides, Porcelain   *Coca-Cola, Tray, 1905, Juanita, Oval*

Radio, Cooler, Drink Coca-Cola, Ice Cold, Works 1100.00
Radio, Crystal, Plastic, Earphones, Alligator Clip, 1950s, 3 In. 575.00
Radio–Cassette Player, Plastic, 10 In. 60.00
Screwdriver 1.25
Shade, Lamp, Frosted Glass, Red Letters, 12 1/2 In. 385.00
Sign, 2–Sided Flange, 1940s 350.00
Sign, Arrow, Double Sided, Tin Lithograph, 30 In. 180.00
Sign, Boy, Street Crossing 3000.00
Sign, Button, Porcelain, 36 In. Diam. 200.00
Sign, Button, Porcelain, With Bottle, 36 In. 175.00
Sign, Christmas Bottle, 1930s 550.00
Sign, Coke, Bottle, Tin, 1947 .... 175.00
Sign, Dispenser, 2 Sides, Porcelain ....*Illus* 425.00
Sign, Drink Coca-Cola Ice Cold, 3 x 5 Ft. 265.00
Sign, Drink Coca-Cola, Bottle, Tin, 1950s, 19 x 27 In. 22.00
Sign, Drink Coca-Cola, Bottle, Tin, Framed, 1930, 11 x 34 1/2 In. 242.00
Sign, Drink Coca-Cola, Enjoy That Refreshing Feeling, Tin, 31 In. 60.00
Sign, Drink Coca-Cola, Tin, 1948, 17 x 53 In. 325.00
Sign, Drink Rack, Red, White, 2 Sides, 1940s, 12 x 16 In. 22.00
Sign, Fountain Service, 1930 .... 275.00
Sign, Fountain Service, Die Cut Shield, Porcelain 425.00
Sign, Fountain Service, Drink Coca-Cola, Porcelain, 1950s, 28 In. 150.00
Sign, Fountain Service, Refreshing, Porcelain, 5 x 7 Ft. 450.00
Sign, Green, White, Red, Black, Celluloid, 4 1/2 x 19 In. 17.00
Sign, Ice Cold, Flange, 1950 .... 200.00
Sign, Ice Cold, Sold Here, Tin Lithograph, Round, 19 1/2 In. 135.00
Sign, Light–Up, Plastic Button, Metal Back Frame, 15 In. 170.00
Sign, Policeman, Figural, School Zone, Steel Lithograph, 63 In. 135.00
Sign, Policeman, School Crossing, Wooden ....875.00 To 2500.00
Sign, Policeman, Slow School Zone, Tin, 1953, 5 Ft. 850.00
Sign, Rack, 2 Sides, Red, Yellow, White, 1940s, 18 In. 46.00
Sign, Sign Of Good Taste, Flange, 15 x 18 In. 95.00
Sign, White Button, Bottle, Porcelain, 14 In. 215.00
Sign, Woman In Pink, 1938 .... 625.00
Straw Holder, Coca-Cola, Delicious & Refreshing, 5 Cents, Small 125.00
Straw, Coca-Cola In Red Lengthwise Of Straw, 1940s 2.00
Syrup Dispenser, Cola/Root Beer, c.1936, 16 1/2 x 11 1/2 In. 450.00
Table, Card, Bottle On 4 Corners, Samson, 1920s 125.00
Telephone, Bottle 25.00
Thermometer, 2 Bottles, Embossed Tin Lithograph, 16 In. 155.00
Thermometer, Bottle Shape, 1950s ....85.00 To 95.00

Thermometer, Double Bottle, Tin, 1941 .... 225.00
Thermometer, Drink Coca-Cola In Bottles, Curved Glass, 12 In. 135.00
Thermometer, Gold Bottle, Red Ground, Embossed Tin Litho, 16 In. 50.00
Thermometer, Silhouette Girl, Porcelain, No Bulb, 1939, 18 In. 410.00
Thermometer, Tin, Sprayed Gold, 7 1/2 x 2 1/2 In. 10.00
Thermometer, Woman Drinking, Embossed Tin Lithograph, 16 In. 95.00
Thermometer, Wooden, 1900s, 21 x 5 In. 450.00
Tie Clip, Sterling Silver 25.00
Tin, Coke Syrup, Paper Label, 1939, Gal. 95.00
Tip Tray, 1912, Girl In Hat, Hamilton King .... 225.00 To 350.00
Tip Tray, 1914, Betty .... 72.00 To 425.00
Tip Tray, 1917, Elaine .... 95.00 To 340.00
Tip Tray, 1920, Garden Girl .... 140.00 To 200.00
Tip Tray, 1937, French Canadian 70.00
Tip Tray, 1957, Birdhouse 90.00
Tip Tray, 1957, Rooster 90.00
Tip Tray, 1957, Sandwich 82.00
Tip Tray, 1958, Picnic Cart 34.00
Toy, Truck Set, Buddy L, 5 Piece 40.00
Toy, Truck, Battery Operated, Yellow & White, 1950s 225.00
Toy, Truck, Friction, Tin, Japan, 4 In. 90.00
Toy, Truck, Lincoln, Paint Missing On Flatbed, 16 In. 85.00
Toy, Truck, Lincoln, Red, White, 8 Wood Cases, 1950s, 16 In. 550.00
Toy, Truck, Marx, Decals 1 Side & Back, 1950s 80.00
Toy, Truck, Matchbox .... 33.00 To 85.00
Toy, Truck, Metal, Box 750.00
Toy, Yo-Yo, Plastic, Bottle Cap Shape, Red, White, 1960 .... 10.00
Tray, 1905, Juanita, Oval .... *Illus* 1500.00
Tray, 1914, Betty, Oval .... 215.00 To 325.00.
Tray, 1914, Betty, Rectangular .... 185.00 To 200.00
Tray, 1917, Elaine, Rectangular, 19 In. 99.00
Tray, 1920, Garden Girl, Oval, 13 3/4 x 16 1/2 In. 180.00
Tray, 1922, Autumn Girl, 13 1/4 x 10 1/2 In. 150.00
Tray, 1923, Flapper Girl, Rectangular, 13 In. .... 99.00 To 275.00
Tray, 1924, Smiling Girls, 10 1/2 x 13 In. 93.50
Tray, 1925, Girl At Party 275.00
Tray, 1926, Sports Couple .... 375.00 To 400.00
Tray, 1927, Curb Service 450.00
Tray, 1927, Girl With Bobbed Hair 350.00
Tray, 1931, Farm Boy With Dog, Norman Rockwell .... 375.00 To 600.00
Tray, 1933, Frances Dee, 10 1/2 x 13 1/4 In. .... 165.00 To 325.00
Tray, 1934, Johnny Weissmuller & Maureen O'Sullivan .... 350.00 To 475.00
Tray, 1935, Madge Evans, 10 1/2 x 13 In. 187.00
Tray, 1936, Hostess .... 125.00 To 250.00
Tray, 1937, Running Girl, 10 1/2 x 13 1/4 In. 250.00
Tray, 1937, Running Girl, 10 1/2 x 13 3/4 In. 99.00
Tray, 1938 .... 140.00
Tray, 1938, Girl In The Afternoon 50.00
Tray, 1938, Girl With Yellow Hat 165.00
Tray, 1938, Girl, Yellow Dress 125.00
Tray, 1939, Springboard Girl .... 120.00 To 200.00
Tray, 1939, Springboard Girl, Mexican 85.00
Tray, 1941, Girl Ice Skater .... 88.00 To 150.00
Tray, 1942, Two Girls At Car .... 75.00 To 165.00
Tray, 1948, Girl, Wind In Her Hair, 10 1/2 x 13 1/4 In. .... 30.00 To 65.00
Tray, 1948, Redheaded Girl, France 43.00
Tray, 1948, Woman With Bottle, Rectangular, 13 1/4 In. 33.00
Tray, 1950, Girl With Menu .... 35.00 To 50.00
Tray, 1957, Birdhouse 90.00
Tray, 1957, Sandwich 90.00
Tray, 1957, Umbrella Girl 90.00
Tray, 1958, Picnic Basket 34.00
Tray, 1961, Pansy Garden 30.00

Tray, 1961, TV Tray, Thanksgiving Scene 21.00
Tray, 1976, Indiana University 6.00
Tray, 1976, Montreal Olympics 10.00
Tray, 1978, Captain Cook 6.00
Truck, Decals, Bottles, Pressed Steel, Metalcraft 500.00
Truck, Sprite Boy Decals, 1930s, 21 In. 220.00
Tumbler 3.00
Umbrella, Beach, Stenciled Cloth, 65 In. 145.00
Uniform & Jacket 150.00
Wagon, Bottle Cases, Umbrella, Cast Iron 290.00
Watch Fob, Bulldog 135.00
Watch, Pocket, Boy Scout Jamboree 30.00
Watch, Pocket, Drink Coca-Cola, Delicious, Refreshing 40.00
Watch, Pocket, Windup, 1970s 68.00
Water Set, Yellow Rose, Tex. Sesquicentennial, Whattaburger, 5 Pc. ... 20.00

COFFEE GRINDERS of home size were first made about 1894. They lost
favor by the 1930s. Large floor–standing or counter–model coffee grinders
were used in the nineteenth–century country store. The renewed interest in
fresh–ground coffee has produced many modern electric and hand grinders,
and reproductions of the old styles are being made.

Arcade, Cast Iron, Glass, Wood, Salesman's Sample, 21 In. 88.00
Arcade, Lap Type 85.00
Arcade, No. 3, Crystal, Wall Mount, c.1903 .... 125.00
Arcade, No. 3, Wall 75.00
Charles Parker Co., Blue & Vermilion, Gold Trim, 33 In. 950.00
Corset Shape, Cast Iron, Wooden Knob, Curved Crank Handle 220.00
Country Store, Wood, Brass Top, Studs Design 245.00
Crystal, Wall, Cast Iron & Glass 57.00
Delmar, Wooden 175.00
Deve, Wall, Blue & White, Windmill Scene 145.00
Dovetailed Wood, Italy 15.00
Dovetailed, Handle, Tall 160.00
Elgin National, Cast Iron, 25 In. 400.00
Elgin National, Wheels, 12 In. 395.00
Elgin National, Wheels, 20 In. 495.00
Enterprise, 2 Wheels, Table Top, Red Paint 350.00
Enterprise, Eagle Finial, Original Paint, Stenciled 950.00
Enterprise, Model 2, Decals, Wheels, 8 1/2 In. 650.00
Enterprise, No. 3, Drawer, Cast Iron, 16 x 15 x 11 In. 445.00
Enterprise, No. 3, Original Paint, Wheels, 10 1/2 In. 575.00
Enterprise, No. 5 .... 350.00
Grand Union Tea Co., Wall Mount 50.00
Grand Union, Counter Top, Cast Iron, Original Red Paint 285.00
Imperial, Eagle Trademark, Table Top, 19th Century 85.00
John C. Dell & Son, Philadelphia, Pa., Patent 1880, 2 Wheel 275.00
Kitchen Aide, Electric 50.00
Landers, Frary & Clark, Lap, Corset Shape, Wooden Knob 220.00
Lap, Drawer, Iron Pull, Cup & Handle, c.1880, 5 3/4 In. 85.00
Peugeot Freres 65.00
Red Paint, Gold & Green Design, 1915, Small 475.00
Run Easy, Steel 110.00
S. H. Koffee Krusher, Blue, Clamp On 375.00
Star Mill, No. 7, Counter Top, 2 Wheels, 26 In. 400.00
Wall, Arcade, Embossed Glass Top 135.00
Weiball & Harden, Wall 60.00
Wilmot Castle, Canister Top, Wall, Black Iron 48.00

COIN SPOT is a glass pattern that was named by the collectors for the spots resembling coins which are part of the glass. Colored, clear, and opalescent glass was made with the spots. Many companies used the design in the 1870–1890 period. It is so popular that reproductions are still being made.

Creamer, Mother–of–Pearl Satin Glass, Frosted Handle, 5 1/2 In.	325.00
Cruet, Blue Opalescent	125.00
Cruet, Cranberry	125.00
Cruet, Ring Neck, Blue	150.00
Pitcher, Dimpled, Tricorner Mouth, White Lining, 8 In.	695.00
Pitcher, Square Top, Cranberry Opalescent	150.00
Pitcher, Water, Apple Green Opalescent, 10 In.	125.00
Pitcher, Water, Green	95.00
Pitcher, White Opalescent	125.00
Shaker, Sugar, Blue Opalescent	125.00
Sugar Shaker, Ring Neck, Cranberry Opalescent	145.00
Syrup, Blue Opalescent	85.00 To 100.00
Syrup, Blue Opalescent, 9 Panel Mold	125.00
Syrup, Clear	125.00
Syrup, Liberty Heart Design	145.00
Syrup, Ring Neck	245.00
Tumbler, Blue Opalescent	17.50
Tumbler, Cranberry	45.00

COIN–OPERATED MACHINES of all types are collected. The vending machine is an ancient invention dating back to 200 B.C. when holy water was dispensed in a coin–operated vase. Smokers in seventeenth–century England could buy tobacco from a coin–operated box. It was not until after the Civil War that the technology made modern coin–operated games and vending machines plentiful. Slot machines, arcade games, and dispensers are all collected.

Advance, 2–25 Cent, Condom	125.00
Antique Touring Car Ride	200.00
Apple, 1930	600.00
Aspirin, Blackhawk Specialty Co., 5 Cent	300.00
Automatic Clerk, With Marquee, Mansfield	800.00
Bantam, Pace, 10 Cent	2000.00
Baseball, ABT	425.00
Baseball, With Ping Ball	300.00
Beech–Nut Cough Drops, 10 1/4 In.	215.00
Black Cherry, 50 Cents	1700.00
Challenger ABT Shooting Gallery, 1950s	350.00
Cigarette, Mills, Kounter King, 1 Cent	300.00
Cup, Dixie, 1 Cent	375.00
Dice, Electro–Mechanical, Multiple Play	1195.00
Digger, Buckley, Floor Model	2100.00
Dispenser, Lighter Fluid, Lighthouse	495.00
Drop Picture, Mills, Quarterscope, Floor Model	2300.00
Drop Picture, Mills, Sapho Viewer, Floor Model	3000.00
Fortune Teller, Estrellas Prophesies, Floor	4500.00
Fortune Teller, Grandmas Predictions	4000.00
Fortune Teller, Mills, Palmist, Floor Model	3000.00
Fortune Teller, Mills, Wizard, 1 Cent	450.00
Fortune Teller, Talks, Breathes, Oak Case, 7 Ft.	5800.00
Fruit Cake, 1930	475.00
Gum, Ad Lee E–Z	550.00
Gum, Advance, Wall Bracket, Locks	175.00
Gum, Bluebird	225.00
Gum, Chicklets, Porcelain	525.00
Gum, Columbus, Bi–More	550.00
Gum, Gee–Whiz, Pepsin, 10 Chews 1 Cent, F. H. Fleer Co.	200.00
Gum, J. P. Wrigley, Admiral Dewey, 5 Cent	425.00

Gum, J. P. Wrigley, Little Dream, Skill Game 325.00
Gum, Mill Automatic 6 Column, Stainless Steel 55.00
Gum, Mills, Automatic, Chrome, 1936 .... 75.00
Gum, Pulver's Kola–Pepsin, Animated Figure 4400.00
Gum, Pulver, Black Lettering, Cop Directing Traffic 1200.00
Gum, Pulver, Clown, Blue 1000.00
Gum, Pulver, Too–Choos, Yellow Kid Character 1350.00
Gum, Pulver, Yellow Kid, 1 Cent 300.00
Gum, Stewart & McGuire 45.00
Gum, Universal, Bluebird 235.00
Gumball, Ad–Lee Ez Iron 600.00
Gumball, Atlas, Glass Top, 10 Cent 45.00
Gumball, Atlas, Master Deluxe, 1950s 50.00
Gumball, Atlas, Midget, Decal, 1950 .... 125.00
Gumball, Baby Grand, Golden Oak .... 50.00 To 75.00
Gumball, Caille 1075.00
Gumball, Calvert, Penny Flip Skill Game 600.00
Gumball, Daval, Chicago Club House, 1 Cent 1000.00
Gumball, Daval, Heads & Tails 250.00
Gumball, E–Z, 5 Cent 475.00
Gumball, E–Z, Original Decal Front 600.00
Gumball, Ford, 1919 .... 125.00
Gumball, Ford, 1950 .... 50.00
Gumball, Ford, 1950s 60.00
Gumball, HW, 1930 .... 50.00
Gumball, Northwestern, Forty–Niner, 1 Cent 45.00
Gumball, Simmons 275.00
Gumball, Vendex 125.00
Gumball, Victor Universal 65.00
Gumball, Victor, Topper, 1 Cent 60.00
Gumball, Williams & Michaels, 1 Cent 450.00
Hanson, Grip Machine 200.00
Horoscope & Poker Hand, Victory Vending Co., 1940s 50.00
Horseshoe, Williams Ringer 750.00
Hot Nut, Cebco 325.00
Indy–Style Racer Ride, United States Map, 10 Cent 250.00
Jennings Best Hand, Gambling 600.00
Jennings Best Hand, Rare Coin 600.00
Jumbo Success, Floor Model, 5 Cent 1250.00
Kicker Katcher, Baker 375.00
Koon Hunt, Seaburg 1700.00
Kotex 75.00
Love Capacity Tester 350.00
Love Tester, American Amusement Co., Floor Model 950.00
Manley Popcorn 500.00
Match, Kelly, Metal, 1 Cent 315.00
Matchbox, Griswald, 1 Cent 180.00
Mermaid, Flasher 1000.00
Model T Ride 325.00
Mutoscope, Virgin Of Baghdad, Hand Crank, c.1900 .... 950.00
Nickelodeon, Coinola, Cupid, 1915 .... 8500.00
Old Mill, Candy, Mutoscope 1300.00
Peanut, Atglas, Bantam, 5 Cent, 1940s .... 65.00 To 85.00
Peanut, Blue Regal, Aluminum, 5 Cent 55.00
Peanut, Columbus Model A, 1 Cent 335.00
Peanut, Columbus, Model M, Cast Iron 175.00
Peanut, Happy Jap, Clockwork Mechanism, 1902 .... 1870.00
Peanut, Improved Hilo 2000.00
Peanut, Little Nut Hut 75.00
Peanut, Northwestern, 1 Cent, 1933 .... 100.00 To 125.00
Peanut, Northwestern, 1960s 45.00
Peanut, Northwestern, Deluxe, Penny–Nickel 100.00
Peanut, Northwestern, Frosted Globe 250.00

Peanut, Northwestern, Merchandiser	125.00
Peanut, Northwestern, Model V, 1 Cent	70.00
Peanut, Regal, 1 Cent, Cylinder Globe	100.00
Peanut, Silver King, Cast Iron, 1930s	85.00
Peanut, Silver King, Hot Nut, Red Glass Top	125.00
Peanut, Star, Coin Changer, 1930s	55.00
Peanut, Stewart & McGuire, Empire State	200.00
Peanut, Victor, Model V, 1 Cent	70.00
Pencil Vendor, Scribe, Iron, 5 Cent	245.00
Pencil, Parker	295.00
Penny Drop, Ajax	350.00
Penny Flip	225.00
Perfume Dispenser, Bull's Head, Pull Horn, 1 Cent	9350.00
Perfume, Advance, Coty	75.00
Perfume, Clockwork, Crown, Celluloid Labels, 1892	2400.00
Perfume, Napkin Holder Each Side, Chrome, 1940s	55.00
Perk Up	100.00
Piano, Dog Race Gambling & Betting Device, 8 Roll	8000.00
Pikes Peak	600.00
Pinball, Bally, Bally Hoo, 1 Cent, 1931	250.00
Pinball, Gottlieb, 1950s	250.00
Pinball, Jennings, Wall Street, 1930s	450.00
Play Golf, Arcade, Chestern Pollard Amusement, 1921	5000.00
Popcorn & Peanut Roaster, Holcomb & Hoke, Floor	2500.00
Popcorn, Dumbar	1000.00
Popcorn, Holcomb & Hoke, Gas Fired, Beveled Glass	1600.00
Popcorn, Manley	500.00
Popcorn, Pop & Hot, 1 Bag At A Time	500.00
Postage Stamps, 2 Column, Key, Glass-Sided, 1918	150.00
Prophylactic, 2 Columns, Decals	100.00
Prophylactic, Single, 1930s	90.00
Riding Pig, Leather Saddle, 10 Cent	500.00
Rock-Ola, World Series, 1933	750.00
Rocket Ship Ride	255.00
Salted Peanuts, W. B. Berry & Co., Electrified	385.00
Sandy Horse, Leather Saddle, 10 Cent	500.00
Scramball, Keeney	125.00
Sculptoscope, Whiting	850.00
Shocker, Arcade, Red Metal, 5 Cent	295.00
Shooting Gallery, Wooden Balls, Moving Targets	750.00
Slot, Acme, Roulette, 25 Cent, Console	1150.00
Slot, Bally Mfg. Corp., 3 Bar, 25 Cent	725.00
Slot, Bally, Clovers, Bell	2000.00
Slot, Bally, Double Bell, 5 To 15 Cent	3000.00
Slot, Berger, Owl, 5 Cent, Floor Wheel	6000.00
Slot, Burtmier, Pony	3000.00
Slot, C. & F., Baby Grand, 5 Cent	1450.00
Slot, Caille, Dictator, 5 Cent, 3-Reel	1000.00
Slot, Caille, Good Luck, 1905	1195.00
Slot, Caille, Grand Prize, 10 Cent, 4 Reel	1675.00
Slot, Caille, New Century Puck, 5 Cent, Musical	9500.00
Slot, Caille, Silent Sphinx, 5 Cent, 3-Reel	1200.00
Slot, Caille, Superior, 10 Cent, Nude Front, 3-Reel	1800.00
Slot, Caille, Tiger, 5 Cent, Single Reel, Token Pay	5900.00
Slot, Caille, Victory Bell, 5 Cent, Center Pull	5500.00
Slot, Chester Pollar, Play Golf, 1920s	5500.00
Slot, Chicago Club House, 1 Cent	795.00
Slot, Cigarette, Cent A Pack, On Wheels	175.00
Slot, Evans, Roulette, 25 Cent, Console Floor Model	3250.00
Slot, H. C. Evans, Evans Races, 5 Cent, Console Model	1300.00
Slot, Jennings Club, Chief, 1 Dollar	3500.00
Slot, Jennings, Club Chief, 50 Cent, Light-Up	1900.00
Slot, Jennings, Dixie Bell, Console, 5 Cent	1575.00

Slot, Jennings, Duchess, 5 Cent 1275.00
Slot, Jennings, Dutch Boy, 50 Cent, Side Vendor 2200.00
Slot, Jennings, Four Star Chief 2200.00
Slot, Jennings, Golf Ball Vender, 25 Cent, 1932 .... 7000.00
Slot, Jennings, Greyhound, 50 Cent 1500.00
Slot, Jennings, Pays Off Golf Balls, 1930 .... 8000.00
Slot, Jennings, Rock–Ola, Gooseneck, Oak Sides 1500.00
Slot, Jennings, Rockaway, Penny Drop 1250.00
Slot, Jennings, Silver Moon Console, Clock Style 450.00
Slot, Jennings, Standard Chief, 5 Cent 1350.00
Slot, Keeney, Super Big Ten, Upright 400.00
Slot, Mills, Black Cherry, 10 Cent, c.1947 .... 1725.00
Slot, Mills, Black Cherry, 50 Cent, 3–Reel 1400.00
Slot, Mills, Blue Bell, Stand, 1949 .... 1995.00
Slot, Mills, Bursting Cherry, 10 Cent 1275.00
Slot, Mills, Castle Front, Skill Stops, Side Vendor 2950.00
Slot, Mills, Cherry Front, 25 Cent, 3–Reel 1250.00
Slot, Mills, Dewey, 25 Cent, Floor Wheel 6550.00
Slot, Mills, Diamond Front, Golden Nugget, 10 Cent 1950.00
Slot, Mills, Golf Ball Vender, 25 Cent, 1937 .... 7500.00
Slot, Mills, High Top, 10 Cent 1150.00
Slot, Mills, High Top, 10 Cent, Deuces Wild 1850.00
Slot, Mills, Judge, 5 Cent, Floor Wheel 8750.00
Slot, Mills, Owl, Upright, 5 Cent 6500.00
Slot, Mills, Side Vendor, 1923 .... 3100.00
Slot, Mills, Spinner 1000.00
Slot, Mills, Twin Jackpot, Stand 1995.00
Slot, Mills, Vest Pocket, 1 Cent 375.00
Slot, Pace, Bantam, 1 Cent, 3–Reel 1250.00
Slot, Pace, Baseball, 5 Cent, 1930 .... 3000.00
Slot, Pace, Chrome Front, 1 Dollar 1095.00
Slot, Pace, Comet Deluxe, 25 Cent 1000.00
Slot, Popular Games, Hoot-Mon Golf, 1 Cent, 1920s 5500.00
Slot, R. J. White, Oom–Paul, 5 Cent, Floor Model 2500.00
Slot, Rock–Ola, Luxury, Lite–Up 2200.00
Slot, Star, Jokers Wild, 10 Cent 650.00
Slot, Trade Stimulator, Play Golf, 1 Cent, 1920s 1500.00
Slot, Watling, Baby Lincoln, 25 Cent 2250.00
Slot, Watling, Bird Of Paradise, 5 Cent 3995.00
Slot, Watling, Bird Of Paradise, Rol–A–Top, 10 Cent 3500.00
Slot, Watling, Rol–A–Top, 25 Cent 3995.00
Slot, Watling, Rol–A–Top, Coin Front, 5 Cent 2900.00
Slot, Western, Sweepstakes, 5 Cent, Horse Race, Stand 3250.00
Slot, Williams, Fairway Pinball, 5 Cent, 1953 .... 2000.00
Stamp, 3 Cents, 3 For A Dime, Cast Iron 350.00
Stamp, 3 x 5 In. 195.00
Stamp, 5 & 10 Cents, Uncle Sam, Porcelain 145.00
Stamp, Schermack 100.00
Steamboat Ride, 10 Cent 195.00
Strength Tester, 1 Cent, Are You Strong Or Weak 520.00
Strength Tester, Gottlieb .... 300.00 To 325.00
Strength Tester, Mercury, Floor, 4–Way, Restored 1000.00
Strength, Exhibit Supply, Floor Model 1700.00
Strength, Mills, Electricity Is Life, Floor Model 4700.00
Target Practice, Mills 475.00
Target, Indian Penny Drop, Jennings 725.00
Target, Kill Gun Game, Ball Go Up & Down 320.00
Trade Stimulator, Caille, Bowling, Cigar Award 900.00
Trade Stimulator, Caille, Le Comet, French Model 750.00
Trade Stimulator, Jennings, Indian Target, 1 Cent 425.00
Trade Stimulator, Malley Eclipse, 1 Cent, 18 1/4 In. 1017.00
Trade Stimulator, Mills, Bell Boy 1575.00
Trade Stimulator, ZIP, Cigarette, Gumball, 1 Cent 235.00

Tummy Tabs, 5 Cent	150.00
Vendor, Esco, 2 Cent Card	150.00
Vendor, Eveready, 1937, 1 Cent	60.00
Vendor, Log Cabin	325.00
Vendor, Superior, Cigarette, Gumball	400.00
Vendor, Wilbur Suchard	300.00
Weight, Columbia, 1 Cent	750.00

COLLECTOR PLATES are modern plates produced in limited editions. Some may be found listed under the factory name, such as Bing & Grondahl, Royal Copenhagen, Royal Doulton, and Wedgwood.

Avon, Christmas, 1973	45.00
Avon, Christmas, Box, 1987	15.00
Avon, Christmas, North American Songbird, 1981	15.00
Avon, Mother's Day, Box, 1982	8.00
Disney, Christmas, 1973	300.00
Disney, Christmas, 1974	100.00
Disney, Mother's Day, 1974	30.00
Gorham, Rockwell, Tiny Tim, 1974	40.00
Holly Hobbie, Christmas, 1973, 10 1/2 In.	15.00
Holly Hobbie, Mother's Day, 1978	7.00
Incolay, Ballerina	75.00
Incolay, First Born	75.00
Knowles, Bedtime Story, Box, 1980	18.00
Knowles, Home Run, Box, 1986	24.00
Knowles, Santa By The Fire, 1989	35.00
Knowles, Skating Lesson, Box, 1981	20.00
Knowles, Teacher's Pet, Carol Lawson, Franklin Porcelain	45.00
Monarch Tea Co., Floral, China, Small	29.00
Rockwell, A Young Girl's Dream, 1985	65.00
Rockwell, Bringing Home The Tree, Christmas, 1970	280.00
Rockwell, Carolers, Christmas, 1972	140.00
Rockwell, Lighthouse Keeper's Daughter, 1979	65.00
Rockwell, Toy Maker, 1977	40.00
Rockwell, Under The Mistletoe, Christmas, 1971	140.00
Rorstrand, Christmas, 1968	400.00
Rosenthal, Wiinblad, Christmas, 1972	200.00
Schmid, Christmas, Snoopy, 1976	25.00
Skelton, All American	55.00

COMIC ART, or cartoon art, is a relatively new field of collecting. Original comic strips, magazine covers, and even printed strips are collected. The first daily comic strip was printed in 1907. The paintings on celluloid used for movie cartoons are listed in this book under Animation Art.

Book, Bringing Up Father, 1919	20.00
Book, Bringing Up Father, Series 20	38.00
Book, Coloring, Skeezix, McLaughlin, 1929	30.00
Book, Comic, Bringing Up Father, 1919	65.00
Book, Comic, Moon Mullins, No. 5, 1931	65.00
Book, Comic, Mutt & Jeff, No. 17, 1932	65.00
Creamer, Mutt Of Mutt & Jeff, Porcelain, 1910s, 5 In.	225.00
Display Box, Flintstones, Snow Storms, Linda Products, 1961, 3 Pc.	595.00
Drawing, Dream Of The Rarebit Fiend, India Ink, 19 x 14 In.	1870.00
Drawing, Figaro, Pinocchio, Black, Red Pencil, 5 In., 3 Pictures	550.00
Drawing, High School Teenagers, Fred Tex Avery, 7 1/2 x 5 In.	660.00
Drawing, Mickey Mouse, 7 Ghosts, India Ink, 5 3/4 x 26 1/2 In.	2640.00
Drawing, Mr. Bug, Crayon, Charcoal, Fleischer Std., 6 x 8 In.	715.00
Drawing, Pinocchio, Black, Red Pencil, Disney, Framed, 8 x 5 In.	770.00
Flip Book, 2 Pages, Koko The Clown, Max Fleischer, 5 1/2 & 13 In.	935.00
Section, D. Tracy, Brenda Starr, L'Il Abner, Kansas City Star, 1955	1.00
Strip, Barney Google, King Features Syndicate, 1941	60.00
Strip, Merry Menagerie, Disney, King Features, 1948	150.00
Strip, Skeezix, Uncle Walt, Hey Kids Come Over, Signed King, 1932	450.00

Strip, Tillie The Toiler, Uncut Dolls, 1948 .... 5.00

COMMEMORATIVE items have been made to honor members of royalty and those of great national fame. World's fairs and important historical events are also remembered with commemorative pieces. Related collectibles are listed in the Coronation and World's Fair categories.

Bowl, Queen Victoria Jubilee, Blue, 1887, 10 In. 175.00
Box, Prince Charles Investiture, Prince Of Wales, Wedgwood 50.00
Cup & Saucer, Edward VII, 1902, Royal Doulton 75.00
Medallion, Queen Victoria, Brass, 1897 .... 20.00
Mug, Battleship Maine, China 75.00
Mug, Birth Of Prince William, Box, 1982 .... 21.00
Mug, Charles & Diana's Wedding 22.00
Mug, Queen Elizabeth's Visit To Canada, 1957, 3 In. 35.00
Paperweight, Queen Victoria, Jubilee, Turquoise Glaze, Minton 175.00
Pin, R. M. S. Queen Elizabeth, Box 6.00
Pitcher, Bombay Dry Gin, Queen Victoria, Wade, 7 In. 25.00
Pitcher, Prince & Princess Of Prussia, , 1858, Copper Lustre 185.00
Pitcher, Queen Victoria Jubilee, 1887, 3 1/4 In. 100.00
Plate, Statue Of Liberty, Cobalt Border, Limoges, 1886–1986 .... 68.00
Spoon, Queen Elizabeth Silver Jubilee, Silver Plate 10.00
Spoon, R. M. S. Queen Elizabeth, Signed E. P. N. S., Box 20.00
Stickpin, Maple Leaf, Canada With Heart, King Edward, 2 Piece 10.00
Thimble, Prince William, Firstborn, Bone China, 1982 .... 10.00
Tumbler, Dewey 55.00

COMPACTS hold face powder. A woman did not powder her face in public until after World War I. By 1920, the beauty parlor, permanent waves, and cosmetics had become acceptable. A few companies sold cake face powder in a box with a mirror and a pad or puff. Soon the compact was being designed by jewelers and made of gold, silver, and precious materials. Cosmetic companies began to sell powder in attractive compacts of less valuable metal or plastic. Collectors today search for Art Deco designs, commemorative compacts from world's fairs or political events, and unusual examples. Many were made with companion lipsticks and other fittings.

Ball, Henriette, Dice In Lid, Round 85.00
Beaded, Rows Of Pearls On Lid, Gold & Leather Trim, French 35.00
Bear, Powder Puff, Mirror, Lipstick, 4 In. 715.00
Best & Co., Horse & Pony, Square, 2 3/4 In. 30.00
Black, With Mesh Bottom Pouch, Art Deco 32.00
Book Shape, Fabric 20.00
Brown, Racing Horses, Race Track Names On Lid, Rectangular 32.00
Cara Nome, Rouge, Die Cut Glower Basket, Blue Enamel Ground 25.00
Center Wood Circle, Painted Scottys, Wood Inlay, Gold Metal, 3 In. 35.00
Champagne Glass, Art Deco 2.00
Coin Holder, Braided Silver Strap, Art Deco 145.00
Colored Rhinestones To Form Flowers, Hummingbirds, Beveled Mirror ... 45.00
Coty Purse Make-Up Kit, Woman's Silhouette On Cap, Black & Cream 30.00
Coty, Chrome, 1 3/4 In. 20.00
Coty, Jingle Bells 30.00
Courting Couple On Cover, Rubies, Sapphires & Diamonds, 3 3/8 In. 1450.00
Djer Kiss, Art Deco, Patent October 82.00
Djer Kiss, Winged Fairies In Relief, Chrome, 1926 .... 95.00
Dots & Stripes, Art Deco, Sterling Silver 50.00
Elgin, American Beauty, Mother-of-Pearl, Box 45.00
Elgin, American, Floral 25.00
Elgin, Cigarette Case, American, 4 1/2 In. 65.00
Elgin, Clam Shape, Goldtone 30.00
Elgin, Leaping Gazelles, Gold Tone, Felt Bag, Box 70.00
Elgin, Metallic Colored Flowers, Oblong 22.00
Elgin, Red, With Crown, American 40.00
Elgin, Trapezoid Shape, Etched Flowers, Flannel Case 125.00

Empire State Building, Art Deco 35.00
Enameled Flowers Cover, 3 x 2 1/2 In. 20.00
English Harbor Scene Under Plastic Lid, Goldtone 25.00
Engraved, Sterling, 4 In. Diam. 43.00
Evans, Embossed Leaping Gazelles, Foliage, Sterling, 3 3/4 In. 175.00
Evans, Watch In Lid, Trunk With Straps Shape, Square 100.00
Evans, Watch On Black Enameled Cover, Inside Rouge Powder, Mirror 95.00
Fan Shape, Gold Tone 20.00
Figural, Pocket Watch, Max Factor, 1 3/4 In. 25.00
Flapper, Green Celluloid, Tassel, Rhinestone Trim, Handle 140.00
Flower In Vase, Rhinestones, Enamel Trim, Columbia, 2 5/8 In. 40.00
French Dore Bronze, Century Woman Center, Foil Trim 120.00
George Jensen, Sterling Silver, Signed 350.00
Girey, Chicago World's Fair, Sky Ride Pictured, 1934 .... 40.00
Gold Tone, Black Faille Case, Dorset 15.00
Gold Tone, Dorset 12.00
Gold Tone, In Gold Mesh Envelope 40.00
Houbigant, Diagonal Art Deco Lines, Rouge, Lipstick, Octagonal 45.00
Ivory & Brass, 1940s 25.00
Ivory, 1940s 25.00
K & K, Star In Left Hand Corner, Sterling, Square, 2 3/4 In. 125.00
Kirk Stieff, Raised Scene, Silver, Marked Denmark 45.00
Mary Dunhill, Sterling Silver 75.00
Melissa, Rectangular 25.00
Mother-of-Pearl Cover, 3 x 4 1/2 In. 35.00
Multicolored Rhinestones On Lid 35.00
Oriental Design, Silver & Gold 45.00
Pennsylvania State College, Chain, 1920s 20.00
Petit Point Flowers, Austrian 125.00
Petit Point, 3 Women In Garden, Austrian 135.00
Petit Point, Floral, Beveled Mirror 30.00
Pocket Watch Shape 25.00
Political, America First, On Ring Chain 55.00
Princess Pat, Rouge, Art Deco 12.00
Rex Fifth Avenue, Enamel Under Lucite, 4 x 4 In. 24.00
Rex, Flowers, Round, Large 28.00
Rhinestones, Fancy, 1950s, 3 x 2 1/2 In. 25.00
Richard Hudnut, Art Deco 55.00
Richard Hudnut, Rouge, Three Flowers 12.00
Roulette Wheel, Goldtone, Round, With Puff 70.00
Schildkraut, Green Marbled Bakelite Lid, Gemstones In Circle 35.00
Sea Horses, Ruby Eyes & Collar, Diamond Bubbles, c.1945, 3 x 2 In. 1375.00
Stag Design, Brass 24.00
Stratton, Box 25.00
Stratton, Castle Gate Center, Green Enamel, 3 1/4 In. 30.00
Stratton, Souvenir Of Canada, 1940s 35.00
Stratton, Tourist Attractions, London, 3 In. 30.00
Stratton, Wedgwood Type Scene On Lid, Blue Enamel 25.00
Terrier On Lid, Red 28.00
Volupte, Brass, Purple Stones 25.00
Volupte, Gold Initials, Red Stones, Sterling Silver 65.00
Volupte, Gold Stone, Grass Design On Lid 45.00
Wadworth, Square, Large 30.00
Watch Shape 20.00
White Flowers, Horseshoe Shape, Gold Leather 25.00
World's Fair, 1933 .... 25.00 To 35.00
World's Fair, Box, 1939 .... 40.00
Yardley, Box 20.00
Yardley, Rouge & Powder, White, Blue Arcs 25.00

CONSOLIDATED LAMP AND GLASS COMPANY of Coraopolis,
Pennsylvania, was founded in 1894. The company made lamps, tablewares,
and art glass. Collectors are particularly interested in the wares made after

1925, including black satin glass, Cosmos (listed in its own section in this book), Martele (which resembled Lalique), and colored glasswares. The company closed for the final time in 1967.

Banana Boat, Nuthatch, 2 Colors On Custard Glass	200.00
Lamp, Phoenix, Birds Over Crystal	185.00
Syrup, Cone, Pink	165.00
Vase, Cattail & Dragonfly, Brown & Coral, 6 In.	95.00
Vase, Straw, Chickadee, Opalescent	195.00
Water Set, Satin Glass, Cone, Yellow, 5 Piece	125.00

CONTEMPORARY GLASS is listed in the Glass – Contemporary category.

COOKBOOKS are collected for various reasons. Some are wanted for the recipes, some for investment, and some as examples of advertising. Cookbooks and recipe pamphlets are included in this section.

Alice's Restaurant, Arlo Guthrie Introduction	25.00
American Woman's, Illustrated In Color & Black & White	18.00
Aristos Flour, 1911	6.00
Baker's Chocolate, St. Louis Exposition, 1904	28.00
Better Homes & Gardens, Blender Cook Book, 1971, 96 Pages	5.00
Beverly Hillbillies, Granny's	25.00
Brer Rabbit, Dated 1940s	3.50
Bull Cook & Authentic Recipes & Practices, 1964	8.00
Candy Hits, ZaSu Pitts, 1964	10.00
Capt. Cooky, 1926	10.00
Ceresota, 1930s	15.00
Chicago Daily News, 1930s	9.00
Chicago's Sweet Tooth, Ann Gerber, Autographed, 1985	12.00
Chiquita Banana Recipe, 1956	4.00
Christmas Entertaining, 1985	10.00
Cleveland's Baking Powder, 1917	12.00
Cookies & More Cookies, L. Sumption, 1938	5.00
Cooking For Two, J. Hill, 1938	5.00
Cow Brand Soda, 1916	5.00
Cream Of Wheat, 1890s	5.00
Dr. Oetker German Home Cooking, 175 Pages	25.00
Elsie, 1952	22.00
Engman–Matthews Range Co., 1910	6.00
Enterprise, 1900	25.00
Every Step In Canning, G. Gray, 1920	5.00
Farm Journal, Homemade Bread	5.00
Farm Journal, Homemade Candy	5.00
Fire Insurance, New York City, Fancy, 1860s, Unused	45.00
Fleischmann's Recipes	15.00
For Company	4.00
Four Seasons, Charlotte Adams, Photographs, 8 1/2 x 12 In.	30.00
Gold Medal Flour, 80 Pages, 1909	12.00
Gold Medal Flour, Washburn–Crosby Co., 1917	27.00
Gone With The Wind, Pebe Co.	20.00
Good Housekeeping, Hard Cover, 1930	5.00
Heinz, Book Of Salads, 1925	9.00
Hood's Sarsaparilla, 1889	52.00
Hunt Bros. San Fran. 40 & 9 Fruit Desserts, Can Shape, Early 1890s	19.00
Individual Recipes In Use At Drexel Institute, 1922	7.00
Informal Entertaining Country Style	5.00
Iroquois Indian Recipes, In Envelope, 1978	12.50
Jack Benny's Recipes, 1937	12.00
Jell–O, 1920, 16 Pages	10.00
Jell–O, Polly Put The Kettle On, We'll All Make Jell–O	65.00
Jell–O, Rose O'Neill, 1912	15.00
John Parris Mountain Cooking, Autographed, 1978	10.00
Julia Child, French Chef, 1st Edition, 1968	10.00

K. C. Baking Powder, Soft Cover, 64 Pages, 1916 .... 15.00
K. C. Baking Powder, 1911 .... 20.00
Kate Smith's Favorite Recipes, General Foods, 1940 .... 25.00
Knox Gelatin, 1943 .... 3.50
Knox Gelatin, Black Boy Chef Cover, 1910 .... 20.00
Ladies' Home Companion, 1946 .... 8.00
Libby's Salad Dressing, 1918 .... 9.00
Liebig Extract 30.00
Loran Stove Cookbook, Hard Cover, 1928 .... 15.00
Lowney's Chocolate, 1904 .... 25.00
Mary Dunbar, Jewel Tea, 1933 .... 15.00
Mazola, 1939 .... 8.00
Merrell–Soule, 1920s 15.00
Molly Goldberg's Jewish Cooking, Hard Cover, 1955 .... 12.00
Mrs. Peterson's Simplified Cook, 1924 .... 14.00
Neighbor Lady, No. 1, WNAX 10.00
New American Cookery, D. D. Smith, 1805 .... 400.00
New Yummy, Fluff Marshmallows 2.50
Pennsylvania Dutch, Famous Recipes, 48 Pages, 9 x 6 In. 12.50
Pillsbury Bake Off, 2nd Edition 10.00
Pillsbury Bake Off, 3rd Edition 12.00
Pillsbury Bake Off, 5th Edition 7.00
Pillsbury Bake Off, 6th Edition 9.00
Pillsbury Bake Off, 7th Edition 7.00
Pillsbury Bake Off, 10th Edition 11.00
Pillsbury Bake Off, 11th Edition 9.00
Pillsbury Bake Off, 18th Edition 1.50
Pillsbury's Balanced Recipes, Aluminum Cover, 1933 .... 30.00
Red Wing 45.00
Reliable Recipes, Calumet Baking Powder Co., 75 Pages 15.00
Rockland Fire Department 5.00
Royal Baking Powder 10.00
Rumford Common Sense 7.00
Searchlight Recipe Book, Indexed, 1944 .... 9.00
Silent Hostess, 1912 .... 10.00
Slade's Spices, 1922 .... 10.00
St. Paul's Church 5.00
Sun–Maid Raisins, Colorful, 1921 .... 15.00
Sunkist Busy Day Salads & Desserts, 1920s 5.00
Sunkist, Spiral Bound, 1967 .... 5.00
Thrifty Housewife, 1905 .... 7.00
Walter Baker Best Chocolate & Cocoa Recipes, 1917 .... 15.00
Walter Baker Chocolate, 1893 .... 25.00
Walter Baker Chocolate, 1923 .... 9.00
Walter Baker Chocolate, 1925 .... 15.00
Warners Yeast Co., 1892, 48 Pages 10.00
Watkins 10.00
White House, Hugo Ziemann Gillett 35.00
White House, Mrs. Coolidge, 1923 .... 50.00
Woman's World Magazine Co., 1927 .... 15.00
Yul Brynner, 1983 .... 18.00

COOKIE JARS with brightly painted designs or amusing figural shapes
became popular in the mid–1930s. Many companies made them and
collectors search for cookie jars either by design or by maker's name.
Listed here are examples by the less common makers. Major factories are
listed under their own names in other sections of the book, such as
Abingdon, Brush, Hull, McCoy, Red Wing, and Shawnee. See also the
Black and Disneyana categories.

After School Cookies, American Bisque .... 50.00 To 62.00
After School Cookies, Bell In Lid, American Bisque 40.00
Alien, Pacific Stoneware 45.00
Angel, Treasure Craft 50.00

Animal Cookies, American Bisque 35.00
Animal Cookies, Stoneware, Black 25.00
Apple, Small 30.00
Aunt Jemima, Plastic, 1950s, F & F .... 300.00 To 400.00
Aunt Jemima, Plastic, Quaker 210.00
Baby Elephant, American Bisque .... 65.00 To 70.00
Baby Pig, American Bisque, Small 85.00
Bacon & Eggs Hog, Fitz & Floyd 115.00
Ball, Orange–Red, Ransburg 30.00
Bambi, American Bisque 500.00
Bandito, Yellow, Treasure Craft 45.00
Bantam Rooster, California Originals 48.00
Barrel Of Apples, Metlox 50.00
Bartender, Fredericksburg Art Pottery 65.00
Bartender, Pan American Art 150.00
Baseball Boy, Finger In Mouth, Treasure Craft .... 40.00 To 45.00
Basket Of Fruit, Metlox 50.00
Basket Of Fruit, With Salt & Pepper 80.00
Basket Of Tomatoes, Doranne Of California .... 45.00 To 49.00
Basket, Buns & Biscuits, Inarco 45.00
Basketweave, With Vegetable Lid Finial 30.00
Bear Mama, With Baby, Weiss–Brazil 55.00
Bear, American Bisque .... 65.00 To 70.00
Bear, American Pottery Co. 45.00
Bear, Avon, Spongeware, California Originals 40.00
Bear, Bees In Relief, Doranne Of California .... 50.00 To 66.00
Bear, Blue Coat, Metlox 50.00
Bear, Brown Underglazed, Gilner 30.00
Bear, Chicken In Apron, Blue Spatter, Gustin Potteries 45.00
Bear, Police Chief, Treasure Craft 75.00
Bear, Police Chief, Twin Winton 45.00
Bear, Roller Skates, Metlox 95.00
Bear, Royalware 38.00
Bear, Sombrero Hat, Metlox 60.00
Bear, Sweater & Cookie, Metlox 40.00
Bear, Visor Hat, American Bisque 85.00
Bear, Visor Hat, Green Bow, American Bisque 100.00
Bear, Visor Hat, Treasure Craft 35.00
Bear, White, Gilner 45.00
Bear, With Cookie, American Bisque 65.00
Bear, Yellow & Brown, Terrace Ceramics 45.00
Bell, Blue, With Flowers, Stoneware 25.00
Beulah, Elsie's Baby, Moo–Er In Head, Sticker 315.00
Big Al, Treasure Craft 125.00
Big Bird, Chef, California Originals .... 65.00 To 100.00
Big Bird, Demand Marketing 65.00
Big Bird, Newcor 40.00
Big Macaroon, Reed Handle, Penton 225.00
Black Chef, Pearl China .... 425.00 To 550.00
Black Clown, Pearl China 75.00
Black Little Girl, Sears, Japan 425.00
Black Little Girl, Treasure Craft 90.00
Black Rag Doll, Treasure Craft 80.00
Black Woman With Kitten, Wisecarver 110.00
Blackboard Clown, American Bisque 120.00
Blackboard Saddle, American Bisque .... 130.00 To 185.00
Blue Bonnet Sue 35.00
Blue Bonnet Sue, Taiwan 20.00
Bluebird On Pinecone, Metlox 75.00
Boots, American Bisque .... 105.00 To 175.00
Boys & Girls, Musical Design, Doves Finial 95.00
Brown Bagger, Doranne Of California 35.00
Brown, Flowers & Dots On Side, Marcrest 30.00

Bull & Cow, Turnabout, American Bisque 80.00
Bumper Car, Vandor 125.00
Bunny Hollow, Fitz & Floyd 115.00
Bunny, Glass Eyes, Baker, Hart & Stuart 65.00
Butler, A Company Of Friends, 1982 .... 55.00
Cactus, Treasure Craft .... 40.00 To 44.00
Calf's Head, Metlox 250.00
California Provincial, Metlox 100.00
Camel, Green, Doranne Of California 45.00
Canister, Yellow, With Flowers, Sears, Japan, 1976 .... 15.00
Carousel, American Bisque .... 40.00 To 65.00
Carousel, Treasure Craft 45.00
Casper The Ghost, American Bisque .... 550.00 To 875.00
Cat In Basket 40.00
Cat On Beehive, American Bisque .... 40.00 To 55.00
Cat, Fluffy, Full Color, American Bisque 90.00
Cat, Girl, Glass Eyes, Baker, Hart & Stuart 65.00
Cat, Gold, Regal 400.00
Cat, Stitch In Time, Treasure Craft 40.00
Cat, Teal, American Bisque 65.00
Catherine The Great, Fitz & Floyd 120.00
Cats In Boots, Maurice Of California 24.00
Catwalk, Black & White Cat, Kitten On Back, Treasure Craft 40.00
Cauldron, Wire Handle, Esmond 40.00
Cheerleader, American Bisque 150.00
Chef, Blue, Artistic Potteries 1250.00
Chef, Gold Rim, Pearl China 475.00
Chef, Ivory, No Paint, Artistic Potteries 85.00
Chef, National Silver 250.00
Chef, Pearl China .... 500.00 To 600.00
Chevrolet, '57, Turquoise, Box, Portugal 295.00
Chianti Wine Bottle, Doranne Of California 65.00
Chick 50.00
Chick, American Bisque 45.00
Chick, Blue & White Vest, American Bisque 55.00
Chick, Maroon Vest, American Bisque 65.00
Chick, Yellow, American Bisque 70.00
Chicken Coupe Car, McNutts 75.00
Chicken, Chick On Top, Mottled Brown, Pottery Guild 135.00
Child In Shoe, Twin Winton 42.00
Christmas Angel, Treasure Craft 45.00
Christmas Bear, Sports Car, License Reads "Sno Bear" 98.00
Christmas Tree, California Originals .... 125.00 To 150.00
Churn Boy, American Bisque .... 142.00 To 145.00
Churn, Butterscotch, Pink Flowers, American Bisque 25.00
Cinderella, Napco, Japan 250.00
Circus Wagon, California Originals 55.00
Clear Glass, Tilt Top, Aluminum Lid 25.00
Clown, American Bisque .... 55.00 To 60.00
Clown, California Originals 85.00
Clown, Flasher, American Bisque 175.00
Clown, Lane 192.00
Clown, Metlox .... 25.00 To 75.00
Coffee Grinder, Japan 20.00
Coffeepot, American Bisque .... 30.00 To 35.00
Coffeepot, Cup & Cookies, American Bisque 25.00
Coffeepot, Pinecone Design, American Bisque .... 28.00 To 50.00
Coffeepot, Treasure Craft 30.00
Collegiate Owl, American Bisque .... 55.00 To 60.00
Cookie Barn, Owl Finial, Treasure Craft 40.00
Cookie Barn, Treasure Craft 25.00
Cookie Car, San Francisco Cable Car Type, Twin Winton 125.00
Cookie Club Mushroom, Treasure Craft 45.00

Cookie Cop, Pfaltzgraff 425.00
Cookie Corral 35.00
Cookie Counter Poodle, Gray, Twin Winton 75.00
Cookie Crock, Crocodile, California Originals 55.00
Cookie Factory, Fitz & Floyd 125.00
Cookie Girl, Metlox 70.00
Cookie Monster, California Originals .... 25.00 To 55.00
Cookie Shack, Twin Winton 50.00
Cookie Time Clock, With Mouse, Twin Winton 45.00
Cookie Train, Brown, Pfaltzgraff 120.00
Cookie Trolley, Treasure Craft 50.00
Cookie Truck, American Bisque .... 50.00 To 70.00
Cookies & Milk, American Bisque .... 65.00 To 120.00
Cookies Factory, Removable Fresh Cookies Today Sign, F & F 75.00
Cooky Chef, Pearl China .... 550.00 To 595.00
Corn, Terrace Ceramics .... 80.00 To 90.00
Corvette 50.00
Corvette, Red, Box 295.00
Cottage House, Sierra Vista .... 50.00 To 65.00
Cow & Lamb, Turnabout, American Bisque 165.00
Cow In Overalls, American Bisque 55.00
Cow, Black & White, Twin Winton 115.00
Cow, No Paint, American Bisque 48.00
Cupcake, Doranne Of California 40.00
Dalmatian 65.00
Dinosaur 25.00
Dog In Barrel, Treasure Craft 40.00
Dog In Basket, American Bisque 45.00
Domesticat, Fitz & Floyd 115.00
Duck, Sir Francis Drake, Metlox .... 45.00 To 50.00
Duck, Wearing Yellow Rain Gear, Metlox 60.00
Duck, With Ears Of Corn, Doranne Of California 55.00
Ducks In Flight, Wisecraver 110.00
Dutch Boy, Ludowici Celadon 55.00
Dutch Boy, Metlox 200.00
Dutch Boy, Pottery Guild .... 55.00 To 95.00
Dutch Girl, 1930, Van De Kamps 175.00
Dutch Girl, Pottery Guild 95.00
Dutch Girl, Twin Winton 65.00
Ear Of Corn, Ceramics By Gabrielle 30.00
Ear Of Corn, Stanford Ware .... 60.00 To 85.00
Eeyore, California Originals 285.00
Elephant With Baseball Cap, American Bisque 70.00
Elephant, Brown, Red Hat 25.00
Elephant, Pink & Brown, American Bisque 100.00
Elephant, Roman Ceramics 40.00
Elephant, Sierra Vista 95.00
Elephant, Trumpeting, Gold, Doranne Of California 48.00
Elephant, Yellow, Doranne Of California 25.00
Elf Bakery, Twin Winton 42.00
Elf Head, Yellow Hat 25.00
Elf's Schoolhouse, California Originals .... 30.00 To 50.00
Elsie The Cow, In Barrel, Pottery Guild .... 190.00 To 250.00
Emmett Kelly Jr., Flambro 160.00
Ernie, California Originals 80.00
Famous Amos, Treasure Craft .... 40.00 To 60.00
Farmer Pig, Rabbit Under Arm, Treasure Craft 40.00
Fifi, Maroon, Regal China 600.00
Figaro Cats 285.00
Fire Plug 20.00
Fish, Green, Doranne Of California 50.00
Fish, Metlox 85.00
Football, Treasure Craft 25.00

For Smart Cookies, Head, Cardinal 125.00
Fred & Pebbles Flintstone, Vandor 115.00
Fred Flintstone & Dino, American Bisque 900.00
Fred Flintstone & Pebbles, Vandor 85.00
Fred Flintstone, Vandor 85.00
Freddie Frog, Sears, Japan 40.00
French Chef, Cardinal China 60.00
Friar Tuck, Twin Winton, With Salt & Pepper 95.00
Frog, Reclining, Flower Design 35.00
Frog, With Little Frog On Head, Fitz & Floyd 85.00
Frookie Cookie Boy, R. W. Frookie, Taiwan 35.00
Frosty Penguin, Metlox 65.00
Frosty The Snowman, Treasure Craft .... 45.00 To 50.00
Garbage Can, Doranne Of California .... 40.00 To 42.00
Geronimo Bust, Wisecarver 110.00
Godzilla, Japan 50.00
Goldilocks, Regal China 350.00
Goldilocks, Royal China 130.00
Golf Ball, Treasure Craft 25.00
Goose, Metlox 45.00
Gorilla With Bananas, California Originals 28.00
Gourd, Metlox 25.00
Grandma, American Bisque 55.00
Grandma, Gold Trim, American Bisque 175.00
Grandma, Holding Spoon 38.00
Grandma, Treasure Craft 40.00
Granny, American Bisque 85.00
Granny, Black, Watermelons On Dress, 24K Gold Trim, Gifford 175.00
Granny, Pottery Craft 82.00
Gumball Machine, Japan, 3 Piece 68.00
Gumball Machine, Red, California Originals 70.00
Halloween Witch, Boo On Inside Of Jar, Fitz & Floyd 75.00
Halloween Witch, Fitz & Floyd 115.00
Happy Bull, Twin Winton .... 42.00 To 50.00
Happy Smiling Pig, In Overalls 65.00
Haunted House, Fitz & Floyd .... 100.00 To 125.00
Head, For Smart Cookies, Cardinal China 135.00
Head, Go Ahead Make A Pig Of Yourself, DeForest Of California 75.00
Hen, Chick Finial, Black, White & Red Comb, Morton .... 45.00 To 65.00
Hen, Chick On Back, Fredricksburg .... 30.00 To 40.00
Hermoine Heifer, Fitz & Floyd 115.00
Hershey's Chocolate, Glass, Decal 25.00
Hill Folks, Wisecarver 95.00
Hillbilly Clown, Morton .... 48.00 To 65.00
Hippo, Love Hippy, Doranne Of California 30.00
Hippopotamus, Flowered, Green, Doranne Of California 40.00
Hobo, Treasure Craft 35.00
Hound Dog, Green, Doranne Of California 45.00
Hound Dog, Market Square 25.00
House, Blue, White, Steps, Balcony, Otagiri 42.00
House, Red, Bamboo Handle, American Bisque, 6 In. 25.00
House, Slanted Roof, Brown & Green, Pottery Guild 55.00
House, Twin Winton 48.00
Hubert The Lion Bank, Lefton 45.00
Humpty Dumpty, Maddux 85.00
Humpty Dumpty, Puritan .... 250.00 To 425.00
Humpty Dumpty, Regal China 200.00
Humpty Dumpty, Yellow Wall, Regal China 250.00
Ice Cream Cone, California Originals 20.00
Ice Cream Cone, Cherry On Top, Japan 16.00
Ice Cream Cone, Chocolate Syrup 45.00
Ice Cream Cone, North American Ceramics 30.00
Ice Cream Sundae, With Cherry, Doranne Of California 45.00

Indian Chief, Wisecarver 100.00
Indian Maiden, Wisecarver 100.00
Indian With Lollipop, California Originals 65.00
Jack–In–The–Box, American Bisque .... 75.00 To 80.00
Jonah On The Whale 450.00
Jukebox, Silver, Cookie Songs 95.00
Keebler Elf .... 35.00 To 60.00
Keebler Elf, Plastic, F & F 150.00
Keebler Treehouse, Regal China 85.00
Keystone Cop, California Originals 50.00
Keystone Cop, Twin Winton .... 110.00 To 125.00
Keystone Cop, With Salt & Pepper, Twin Winton 165.00
Kids Watching TV Flasher, American Bisque 150.00
King Lion, Yellow, Lollipop, Japan 30.00
Kitchen Witch, Crazed, Gustin Potteries 65.00
Kittens & Yarn, American Bisque 42.00
Kitty, Polka Dot, American Bisque 85.00
Koala Bear, On Limb, California Originals 145.00
Kraft Marshmallow Bear, Regal China 150.00
Lady Pig 65.00
Lady Turtle, Sitting, With Flowers 35.00
Lamb, American Bisque 50.00
Lamb, Matching Shakers, Twin Winton 55.00
Leopard, Hand Painted, Treasure Craft, 13 In. 45.00
Leopard, Treasure Craft 45.00
Lion On Top Of Cage, California Originals 45.00
Lion, Beetle On Nose 40.00
Lion, Ludowici Celadon, Belmont 50.00
Little Lamb, Twin Winton .... 45.00 To 50.00
Little Red Riding Hood, Pottery Guild .... 80.00 To 135.00
Little Red Riding Hood, Regal China 90.00
Lunch Bag, Beige 18.00
Magic Bunny, American Bisque 55.00
Mailbox, Doranne Of California 45.00
Majorette, Regal China 325.00
Mammy, Blue, Artistic Pottery 1200.00
Mammy, Blue, Brayton Laguna 895.00
Mammy, Churn & Boy, Green Dress, Wisecarver 140.00
Mammy, Cookies In Various Colors, Hand Painted, McCoy 374.00
Mammy, Cookstove, Making Pancakes, Wisecarver .... 140.00 To 180.00
Mammy, Mixing Bowl, Wisecarver .... 135.00 To 180.00
Mammy, Mosaic Tile Co. .... 185.00 To 525.00
Mammy, Mosaic Tile, Yellow & Blue, Pair 975.00
Mammy, National Silver .... 90.00 To 260.00
Mammy, New Orleans .... 95.00 To 210.00
Mammy, Pearl China .... 475.00 To 850.00
Mammy, Plastic, F & F .... 400.00 To 425.00
Mammy, Potbelly Stove, Morning Aggravation, Wisecarver 110.00
Mammy, Yellow, Brayton Laguna 1300.00
Matilda, Brayton 282.00
Memories Of Mama, Mosaic Tile Type 45.00
Milk Can, After School Snacks, American Bisque 52.00
Milk Can, Ear Handles, Peaches & Leaves Design On Knob 20.00
Milk Can, Tan, With Flowers, Stoneware 30.00
Miss Muffet, Gold, Regal China 265.00
Monk, Yellow 35.00
Monkey, Conductor, Maurice Of California .... 38.00 To 47.00
Mother Pig & Baby, Wisecarver 95.00
Mother Rabbit, Fitz & Floyd 105.00
Mother's Cookies 35.00
Mouse, Beige, Gustin Potteries 35.00
Mouse, Holding Rolling Pin, Metlox 60.00
Mouse, With Airplane 18.00

Mrs. Field's Cookie Sack	65.00
Mrs. Santa, White, Wisecarver	105.00
Mushroom House, Metlox	77.00
Mushroom, Sears, 1978, Japan	20.00
Mushrooms With Frog, Sierra Vista	70.00
Nestle Toll House Cookies	85.00
Noah's Ark, California Originals	70.00
Noah's Ark, Treasure Craft	40.00
Old Fashioned Telephone, California Originals	55.00
Old Fashioned Telephone, Cardinal China	65.00 To 70.00
Old Lady In Shoe, Maurice Of California	45.00
Old Woman In A Shoe, Fitz & Floyd	125.00
Old World Santa, Fitz & Floyd	135.00
Oreo Cookies, Market Square	25.00
Oreo Cookies, Market Square, Box	25.00
Oriental Woman, Regal China	325.00 To 365.00
Oscar The Grouch, California Originals	60.00 To 125.00
Owl On Stump, California Originals	25.00
Owl, California Original	25.00
Owl, Fitz & Floyd	85.00
Owl, Golden Amber, Metlox	60.00
Owl, Otagiri	25.00
Owl, Winking, Overalls, California Originals	38.00
Owl, Winking, Treasure Craft	45.00
Ozark Hillbilly, Morton Pottery	50.00 To 65.00
Paddy Pig, Aladdin	18.00
Peasant Woman, Daisies On Dress, Brayton Laguna	425.00
Peasant Woman, Multicolored, Brayton Laguna	125.00
Peek–A–Boo, Van Tellingen, Regal China	675.00 To 1200.00
Pekinese, Bow In Hair, Doranne Of California	40.00
Pelican, California Originals	45.00
Pencil, Budweiser	25.00
Penguin, Black & White, Red & White Cap & Scarf	35.00
Picnic Basket, Tray Top, American Bisque	200.00
Pig Chef	85.00
Pig Chef, Treasure Craft	40.00
Pig Clutching Bunny, Treasure Craft	65.00
Pig In Poke, American Bisque	35.00 To 55.00
Pig, Boy, American Bisque	65.00
Pig, Cookie Bank, DeForest Of California	120.00
Pig, Dancer, Orange	120.00
Pig, Fitz & Floyd	90.00
Pig, Mr. & Mrs., Turnabout, American Pottery Co.	175.00
Pig, Pink, Pfaltzgraff	50.00
Pig, Scarpino, Pacific Stoneware	45.00
Pig, With Flowers, Los Angeles Potteries	40.00
Pink Cadillac, Box, North American Ceramics	275.00
Pixie, Sugar & Creamer, Salt & Pepper, Napco, Japan, 5 Piece	120.00
Poodle Bust, Morton Pottery	45.00
Poodle, American Bisque	65.00
Poodle, Maroon, American Bisque	125.00
Poodle, Powder Blue, American Bisque	150.00
Popeye, American Bisque	950.00
Pot–O–Cookies, Twin Winton	60.00
Potbelly, Stove, Black, American Bisque	20.00
Pretty Ann, Apron, With Pocket, Maurice Of California	90.00
Prunella Pig, Fitz & Floyd	115.00
Puddles, Metlox	28.00
Pumpkin, Clear Glass	20.00
Pumpkin, Skeleton	95.00
Pup In Pot, Cookies Written On Pot, American Bisque	55.00 To 65.00
Pup In Pot, Poinsettia On Head, American Bisque	70.00
Puppy, Blue Pot, American Bisque	50.00

Puppy, Yellow Pot, American Bisque 60.00
Quaker Oats, Regal China ....85.00 To 150.00
Queen Of Tarts 500.00
Queen Of Tarts, Maddux Of California 500.00
R2D2, California Originals 125.00
R2D2, Roman Ceramics .... 110.00 To 180.00
Rabbit In Brown Coat, California Originals 45.00
Rabbit In Hat, American Bisque .... 50.00 To 75.00
Rabbit On Cabbage, Metlox 80.00
Rabbit On Stump, California Originals 40.00
Rabbit, Green, Doranne Of California 60.00
Rabbit, Hand In Pocket, American Bisque 60.00
Rabbit, Maurice Of California .... 50.00 To 55.00
Rabbit, On All Fours, Eating Carrot, Gustin Potteries 40.00
Rabbit, Terrace Ceramics .... 45.00 To 60.00
Rabbit, White, Pink Glass Eyes, Gold Trim, California Originals 300.00
Rabbit, Yellow, Blue Hat, Japan, 9 In. 25.00
Rag Doll, Starnes 150.00
Raggedy Andy, California Originals 60.00
Raggedy Andy, Metlox 75.00
Raggedy Andy, Twin Winton 85.00
Raggedy Ann, Cookie Tin, Ransburg 40.00
Raggedy Ann, Metlox ....75.00 To 105.00
Raggedy Ann, Twin Winton 72.00
Rice Krispies, Snap, Crackle & Pop Head, 5 Piece 140.00
Ring For Cookies, Bell, American Bisque 55.00
Rio Rita, Multicolored, Hand Painted, Fitz & Floyd .... 100.00 To 150.00
Robot, Sigma 80.00
Rocking Horse, Regal China 175.00
Rooster, Gray Underglaze, DeForest Of California 60.00
Rooster, Sierra Vista .... 45.00 To 65.00
Rooster, Solid Tail, All White, American Bisque 40.00
Rooster, Treasure Craft 45.00
Rose, Metlox .... 275.00 To 395.00
Rubbles House, American Bisque 625.00
Sack Of Cookies, American Bisque 55.00
Sack Of Cookies, Cardinal China 50.00
Sadiron, American Bisque .... 65.00 To 90.00
Sailor Elephant, American Bisque .... 65.00 To 85.00
Sailor Elephant, Twin Winton .... 42.00 To 45.00
Sailor Mouse, Twin Winton 45.00
Santa Claus, Black, Metlox .... 175.00 To 300.00
Santa Claus, Black, Sitting, 24K Gold Buckle, Gifford 250.00
Santa Claus, Japan 20.00
Santa Head, Plastic, Carolina Enterprises, 1973 .... 23.00 To 30.00
Santa's Cookie House, Otagiri 125.00
Scarecrow, Royal Sealy, Japan 50.00
School Bus, Doranne Of California 225.00
Schoolhouse, Black Roof, American Bisque 35.00
Seal, Doranne Of California 38.00
Sheriff Bear, Antique Glaze, Treasure Craft 45.00
Sheriff Bear, Twin Winton 42.00
Sheriff, Hole In Hat, California Originals 47.00
Sheriff, Lane 345.00
Shock Of Wheat, House Of Webster 25.00
Shoe House, Mamma Mouse In Door, 2 Mice Outside 35.00
Siesta Time, Treasure Craft 40.00
Slenderella, Pig, Metlox 95.00
Smart For Cookies, Cardinal China 90.00
Smart Owl, Standing On Smart Cookies Book 40.00
Snoopy, Green Holiday Designs 20.00
Soldier, American Bisque .... 75.00 To 95.00
Space Cadet, Brown 100.00

Spaceship, American Bisque	170.00
Sprout, Pillsbury, Taiwan	35.00 To 65.00
Squirrel On Log, Gray, American Pottery Co.	85.00
Squirrel On Pinecone, Metlox	65.00
Squirrel On Stump	60.00
Squirrel On Stump, Vallona Starr	60.00
Squirrel, Twin Winton	45.00
St. Bernard	60.00
Stagecoach, Plastic Windows, Sierra Vista	175.00 To 185.00
Stella Strawberry, Pittman–Dreiter	85.00
Strawberry	8.00
Strawberry Pie A La Mode, Doranne Of California	55.00
Strawberry, Bright Red, Green Lid, SFA	38.00
Strawberry, Sears, Japan	45.00
Teddy Bear, Blue Sweater, Metlox	75.00
Teddy Bear, Treasure Craft	40.00
Telephone, Sierra Vista	55.00
Telephone, Wall	20.00
Thou Shall Not Steal	20.00
Three Kittens, In & On Basket, Wisecarver	95.00
Tigger, Crazed, California Originals	150.00
Tony The Tiger, Plastic, 1968	110.00
Toothache Dog, American Bisque	625.00
Tortoise & Hare, California Originals	25.00 To 45.00
Toucan, Hand Painted, Treasure Craft	45.00
Train, American Bisque	50.00
Train, Twin Winton	45.00
Transformer, Hasbro Bradley Inc.	85.00
Trolley, Dark Brown, Treasure Craft	45.00
Trolley, Otagiri	35.00
Tugboat, Treasure Craft	48.00
Tuggle, Sierra Vista	125.00
Turnabout Bear, Ludowici Celadon	45.00
Turtle, Lady, Sitting, Flowers, California Originals	35.00
Victorian Doll, Mexico	80.00
Victorian House, Treasure Craft	42.00 To 45.00
Wanda Witch, Fitz & Floyd	125.00
Wilma Flintstone, Talking On Phone, American Bisque	375.00
Windmill, Light Green Trim, Fredericksburg Art Pottery	50.00
Winter House, California Cleminsons	75.00
Yarn Doll, American Bisque	70.00 To 90.00
Yogi Bear, 1961, Hanna–Barbera, American Bisque	150.00 To 450.00

COORS ware was made by a pottery in Golden, Colorado, owned by the Coors Beverage Company. Dishes and decorative wares were produced from the turn of the century until the pottery was destroyed by fire in the 1930s. The name *Coors* is marked on the back. For more information, see *Kovels' Depression Glass & American Dinnerware Price List.*

COORS
U.S.A.

Bowl, Rock Mount, 6 1/4 In.	45.00
Casserole, Cover, Rosebud, Blue, 3 1/2 In., Pt.	33.00
Creamer, Rosebud	18.00
Custard Cup, Rosebud	7.50
Pitcher, Mello–Tone	35.00
Pitcher, Milk, Rosebud, Green	35.00
Plate, Mello–Tone, Pink, 9 1/4 In.	4.00
Plate, Rosebud, Aqua, 9 1/4 In.	18.00
Plate, Rosebud, Dark Blue, 10 1/4 In.	22.00
Teapot, Rosebud, 6 Cup	50.00
Vase, Circle, Blue, 7 In.	65.00
Vase, Green Matte, Handles, 8 In.	25.00
Vase, Handles From Rim To Bottom, 7 In.	85.00
Vase, Rope Handles, 8 In.	85.00
Vase, Turquoise, 8 1/2 In.	28.00

Copeland, Figurine, Maidenhood, c.1861,

21 3/4 In.

◆◆◆◆◆◆◆◆◆◆◆◆◆◆◆◆◆◆◆◆◆◆◆◆◆◆◆◆◆◆◆◆◆

Chandeliers can be cleaned in place with a new spray cleaner made for that purpose. Cover the floor with paper or cloth to catch the drips. Then spray the chandelier. It will clean and drip dry.

◆◆◆◆◆◆◆◆◆◆◆◆◆◆◆◆◆◆◆◆◆◆◆◆◆◆◆◆◆◆◆◆◆

Vase, Yellow, 8 In. 40.00

COPELAND SPODE appears on some pieces of nineteenth–century English porcelain. Josiah Spode established a pottery at Stoke–on–Trent, England, in 1770. In 1833, the firm was purchased by William Copeland and Thomas Garrett and the mark was changed. In 1847, Copeland became the sole owner and the mark changed again. W. T. Copeland & Sons continued until a 1976 merger when it became Royal Worcester Spode. Pieces are listed in this book under the name that appears in the mark. Copeland Spode, Copeland, and Royal Worcester have separate listings.

Cup & Saucer, Indian Tree, Farmer	35.00
Cuspidor, Camellia, Pink & White	35.00
Dessert Set, Chelsea Pattern, 36 Piece	303.00
Dinner Set, Cowslip, 12 Place Settings, 78 Piece	650.00
Dinner Set, Tower, Blue, Service For 8, Extra Pieces	750.00
Dresser Set, Butterflies, Dragonflies, 1847 Mark, 4 Piece	275.00
Pitcher & Bowl, Multicolored Spring Flower Bouquets	625.00
Pitcher, Grecian Figures, 5 1/2 In.	70.00
Plate, Fruit & Floral Center Medallion, 10 1/2 In., 12 Pc.	110.00
Platter, Wickerdale, 13 In.	35.00
Relish, Blue & White, Triangular, 9 In.	20.00
Server, Madeira, 3 Tiers	50.00
Toby Jug, 8 In.	170.00

COPELAND pieces listed here are those that have the mark used between 1847 and 1976. See also Copeland Spode and Royal Worcester.

Figurine, Maidenhood, c.1861, 21 3/4 In. ....*Illus*	248.00
Plate, Adams Rose, 9 In.	45.00
Plate, Scenic, Blue & White, 10 In.	30.00
Vase, Beaker Form, Birds In Oval Reserve, Gilt Border, 7 In., Pair	575.00

COPPER LUSTER items are listed in the Luster section.

COPPER has been used to make utilitarian items, such as teakettles and cooking pans, since the days of the early American colonists. Copper became a popular metal with the Arts & Crafts makers of the early 1900s and decorative pieces, like bookends and desk sets, were made. Other pieces of copper may be found in the Bradley & Hubbard, Kitchen, and Roycroft categories.

Ashtray, Cowboy's Hat, Souvenir San Francisco, 5 In.	25.00
Bed Warmer, Turned Wooden Handle, 42 In.	90.00

Bed Warmer, Wooden Handle, 40 In. 110.00
Boiler, Lid 30.00
Bowl, Hammered, Petal Shape, Scalloped, Dirk Van Erp, 7 x 2 1/2 In. 900.00
Bowl, Wola Varon, 10 In. 150.00
Box, Dragon On Lid, Applied Brass Designs, Chinese, 8 x 8 3/4 In. 285.00
Bucket, Peat, Dovetailed, c.1840 .... 150.00
Coffeepot, Coppercraft Guild, 8 1/2 In. 22.00
Hat Rack, Wall, Diamond Shape, Embossed Figures & Ship 50.00
Humidor, Golfer Scenes, Pagoda, Sailboats 85.00
Humidor, Hammered, Revere 25.00
Ice Bucket, Iron Ring Handles, Wall, Germany, 8 3/4 x 9 In. 120.00
Jar, Domed Cover, Hammered, Dirk Van Erp, 13 3/4 In. 2750.00
Jardiniere, Hammered, Arts & Crafts, 10 In. .... 80.00 To 90.00
Kettle, Candy, Iron Handles, 13 In. 180.00
Kettle, Cooking, Iron Handles, Round Bottom, 18 In. 132.00
Mailbox, Hammered, Wall Mount, Arts & Crafts, 12 In. 110.00
Measure Set, Milk, Graduated, Excise Mark, 1 Gill To 1 1/2 Pt., 3 Pc. 85.00
Measure, Haystack, Dovetailed, Marked Pint, 5 In. 75.00
Measure, Haystack, Dovetailed, Marked, England, 10 1/2 In. 125.00
Mitten Warmer, Brass Ferule, Turned Wooden Handle, 9 In. 175.00
Molds are listed in the Kitchen category
Pan, Brass Handle, 8 In. 45.00
Pan, Sauce, Brass Dovetailed, Curved Handle, 18th Century, 6 5/8 In. 120.00
Pan, Sauce, Dovetailed, 5 In., 6 3/4 In. Handle 85.00
Plaque, Medallion Of Woodrow Wilson, Lucy Dorge, 28 x 43 In. 495.00
Plate, Enameled, 6 1/2 In. 125.00
Pot, Cast Iron Handle & Hand Grip, 8 Gal. 150.00
Roaster, Chestnut, Turned Wooden Handle, 4 1/4 In. 10.00
Sugar & Creamer, Flattened Disc Shaped Bodies, Craftsman Studios 70.00
Teakettle, 10 1/4 In. 95.00
Teakettle, Dovetailed, Brass Finial, Labeled Handle, 7 In. 250.00
Teakettle, Gooseneck Spout, Brass Trim, Acorn Finial, 11 In. 145.00
Teakettle, Iron Legs, Side Spout With Flap, 7 In. 200.00
Tray, Flanged Rim, Riveted Scrolled Handles, Hammered, 16 In. 80.00
Vase, Red Patina, Windmill Mark, Dirk Van Erp, 8 In. 2860.00
Water Bottle, Cello, A. S. Campbell Co., Patent 1912 .... 85.00

CORALENE glass was made by firing many small colored beads on the
outside of glassware. It was made in many patterns in the United States
and Europe in the 1880s. Reproductions are made today. Coralene-
decorated Japanese pottery is listed in the Japanese Coralene category.

Ewer, Pink & Green Fruit, Green & Gold Ground, 4 In. 205.00
Pitcher, Gold Seaweed, Amber Handle, Pink Interior, 5 1/4 In. 220.00
Pitcher, White, Bird In Flight, Branch, Webb, Signed Patent, 7 In. 220.00
Rose Bowl, Diamond–Quilted, Mother-of-Pearl, Blue, Yellow, Seaweed 275.00
Rose Bowl, Diamond–Quilted, Mother-of-Pearl, Shell & Seaweed 275.00
Rose Bowl, Yellow Beaded Allover, 6–Crimp Top, 3 1/4 In. 375.00
Tumbler, Flowers, Diamond–Quilted, Mother-of-Pearl, 3 7/8 In. 495.00
Tumbler, Yellow Beaded, White Lining, Blue Overlay, 3 3/4 In. 325.00
Vase, Buds & Leaves, Gold Outlined, Lavender, Kinran, 1909, 10 In. 650.00
Vase, Diamond–Quilted, Mother-of-Pearl, Floral, 7 1/2 In., Webb 138.00
Vase, Diamond–Quilted, Star Center Diamonds, 4 3/4 In. 495.00
Vase, Dusty Rose Top, White To Turquoise Bottom, 11 1/4 In. 665.00
Vase, Iris Beading, Blue, Gold Trim, 6 In. 400.00
Vase, Orange & Yellow Flowers, Bird On Branch, Cranberry, 4 In. 195.00
Vase, Seaweed Over Pink To White, Diamond–Quilted, 10 1/2 In. 1200.00
Vase, Wisteria, 2 Handles, Bulbous, 16 In. 850.00
Vase, Yellow Beaded, Stripes To Shoulder, Pink & Green, 7 3/4 In. 475.00
Vase, Yellow Beading, Off–White Lining, Stripes, 7 In. 475.00
Vase, Yellow Wheat Design On Pink, Diamond–Quilted, 10 1/2 In. 1070.00
Vase, Yellow Wheat, Shaded Pink, Mother-of-Pearl, 10 1/2 In. 1070.00
Vase, Yellow, Mother-of-Pearl, Orange Butterfly, 10 In., Webb 220.00

Corkscrew, Bottle Opener, Wm. J. Lemp
Brewing Co., 4 x 6 In.

◆◆◆◆◆◆◆◆◆◆◆◆◆◆◆◆◆◆◆◆◆

If a bottle stopper is stuck, try using Liquid Wrench, an oil found at the hardware store, to loosen it.

◆◆◆◆◆◆◆◆◆◆◆◆◆◆◆◆◆◆◆◆◆

◆◆◆◆◆◆◆◆◆◆◆◆◆◆◆◆◆◆◆◆◆

Keep your keys on a pull–apart chain so the house keys and car keys can be separated when you leave the car in a parking lot.

◆◆◆◆◆◆◆◆◆◆◆◆◆◆◆◆◆◆◆◆◆

CORDEY China Company was founded by Boleslaw Cybis in 1942 in Trenton, New Jersey. The firm produced gift shop items. In 1969 it was acquired by the Lightron Corp. and operated as the Schiller Cordey Co., manufacturers of lamps. About 1950 Boleslaw Cybis began making Cybis porcelains, which are listed in their own section in this book.

Figurine, Bluebird, On Tree Stump, No. 6004, 9 In.	120.00
Figurine, Colonial Gentleman & Woman, 11 In., Pair	250.00
Figurine, Man Leaning On Stump, Blue, Lavender	235.00
Lamp, Colonial Man & Woman, Lace, Original Shades, 16 1/4 In., Pair	250.00
Vase, Lady's Head, Wall	225.00
Wall Pocket, Head & Bust Of Woman With Large Hat	110.00

CORKSCREWS have been needed since the first bottle was sealed with a cork, probably in the seventeenth century. Today collectors search for the early, unusual patented examples or the figural corkscrews of recent years.

Bottle Opener, Wm. J. Lemp Brewing Co., 4 x 6 In. ....*Illus*	28.00
Butler With Apron, Holding Bottle, Composition, 8 In.	75.00
Carved Irish Setter One End, Sterling Tip At Other	220.00
Ivory Handle, Brush At One End, 6 In.	25.00
M. Heyman Wines & Liquors, New York City, Wooden	5.50
Moerlein, Crown Logo, Cincinnati, U.S.A.	45.00
Monkey, Brass	22.00
Old Barbee Whiskey, Flat Metal Opener, Silver Color	5.50
Old I. W. Harper, Metal, Large Ring, Wooden Holder, 2 1/2 In.	6.50
Saint Louis ABC Bohemian Beer, Black Lettering, Wooden Handle	14.50
Staghorn Handle, 4 x 4 3/4 In.	10.00
Union River Whiskey, Wooden Case	15.00
Wild Boar Tusk, Sterling Capped, 5 1/2 In.	125.00

CORONATION souvenirs have been made since the 1800s. Pottery, glass, tin, silver, and paper objects with a picture of the monarchs and date have been sold at many coronations. The pieces that mention King Edward VIII, the king who was never crowned, are not rare; collectors should be sure to check values before buying. Related pieces are found in the Commemorative category.

Button, King & Queen, England, Celluloid, 1902, 1 1/4 In.	40.00
Cup & Saucer, Queen Elizabeth II, Meakin	27.00
Eggcup, Sterling Spoon, King Edward VII & Queen Alexandria, Box	80.00
Humidor, Queen Elizabeth, Portrait, Flags, 5 1/4 In.	50.00
Jug, Queen Elizabeth, Castle, Throne, Crown Handle, 8 1/2 In.	145.00

Knife, Pocket, Queen Elizabeth II, 1953	35.00
Mug, Edward VIII	55.00
Mug, George V, 1911	45.00
Mug, King & Queen Portraits, 1937	25.00
Pipe, Clay, Edward VII	27.00
Pitcher, Queen Elizabeth II, Embossed Silhouette, 5 In.	40.00
Program, Queen Elizabeth, 1953	20.00
Record, Queen Elizabeth Label, Souvenir, 1953	18.00
Shaving Mug, George VI, Elizabeth, 1937	45.00

COSMOS is a pressed milk glass pattern with colored flowers made from 1894 to 1915 by the Consolidated Lamp and Glass Company. Tablewares and lamps were made in this pattern. A few pieces were also made of clear glass with painted decorations. Other glass patterns are listed under Consolidated Lamp and also in various glass sections.

Butter, Cover, Milk Glass	195.00 To 325.00
Castor, Pickle	395.00
Creamer	135.00
Cruet	95.00
Lamp, Satin Glass, Miniature	125.00
Perfume Bottle, All White	45.00
Pitcher, Water	200.00
Salt & Pepper, Blue Opaque, Tall	110.00
Syrup	235.00 To 375.00
Table Set, 4 Piece	750.00
Tumbler, Pink Band	70.00 To 100.00
Water Set, 7 Piece	600.00

COVERLETS were made of linen or wool during the nineteenth century. Most of the coverlets date from 1800 to 1850. Four types were made: the double weave, jacquard, summer and winter, and overshot. Later coverlets were made of a variety of materials. Quilts are listed in this book in their own section.

Double Weave, Buildings, Flowers, Daniel Pursell, 78 x 72 In.	1200.00
Eagles, Rearing Horses, Fruit Urns, Small Stars, R. B., Dated 1842	750.00
Geometric, Blue & White, Eagle In 1843 Block, 1/2 Size	150.00
Jacquard, 2–Piece, Blue, White Cotton, 80 x 70 In.	275.00
Jacquard, 4 Rose Medallions, D. Cosley, Zenia, 1853, 84 x 94 In.	350.00
Jacquard, 4 Rose Medallions, Star, Navy & White, 71 x 86 In., 2 Pc.	350.00
Jacquard, Almira Woods, Floral, Reversible, 1835, 80 x 84 In.	660.00
Jacquard, Blue & White Floral, Eagles In Border, 80 x 82 In.	115.00
Jacquard, Center 8–Point Star, Surround Of Roses, 83 x 74 In.	300.00
Jacquard, Chickens & Eagles, J. R. Van Houten, 1834, 73 x 85 In.	2300.00
Jacquard, Christian & Heathen Edge, Peacock & Chicks, 77 x 89 In.	750.00
Jacquard, Eagle & Star Borders, John Brosey, 1836, 82 x 96 In.	2050.00
Jacquard, Floral Medallions, Bird Border, J. Corick, 82 x 88 In.	350.00
Jacquard, Floral Medallions, Bird, Tree, House Border, 73 x 93 In.	600.00
Jacquard, Floral Medallions, Navy & Natural, 80 x 92 In., 2 Piece	65.00
Jacquard, Floral Pattern, Navy Blue & Natural White, 68 x 87 In.	165.00
Jacquard, Floral, Bird Border, 74 x 88 In.	175.00
Jacquard, Floral, Blue & White, Dated 1853	425.00
Jacquard, Floral, Borders, P. Warner, Carroll Cty., 1859, 30 x 90 In.	250.00
Jacquard, Floral, House Borders, Elizabeth, 1850, 77 x 100 In.	700.00
Jacquard, Floral, Jacob & Michael Ardner, 1852, 78 x 82 In.	500.00
Jacquard, Floral, Jacob Sherman, 1852, Pink, Gold, Natural, 82 In.	175.00
Jacquard, Floral, John Seibert, Lowhill, 1843, Fringe, 39 x 45 In.	925.00
Jacquard, Floral, M. Hoke, York, Pa., 1844, Navy, Natural, 80 x 80 In.	250.00
Jacquard, Floral, Maroon, Green, Natural, Date 1862, 76 x 90, 2 Pc.	450.00
Jacquard, Floral, Peter Lorenz, 1845, 80 x 68 In., 2 Piece	950.00
Jacquard, Floral, Rooster Borders, John Smith, 1836, 84 x 90 In.	600.00
Jacquard, House & Bird Borders, L. F., Somerset, Oh., 1849, 88 In.	200.00
Jacquard, Leaf, Star & Acorn Pattern, 88 x 73 In.	400.00
Jacquard, Medallions, Floral Borders, Navy, White, 1850, 79 x 91 In.	525.00

Jacquard, Navy Blue, Red, Natural White, 70 x 84 In. 450.00
Jacquard, Peacocks, Urns Of Flowers, Navy, White, 74 x 90 In., 2 Pc. 425.00
Jacquard, Red Wool, Natural Linen, Floral, 1851, 92 x 104 In. 350.00
Jacquard, Shaker House Border, C. Roden, Montgomery County, Ohio 650.00
Jacquard, Single Weave, Floral Medallions, Bird, 73 x 93 In. 600.00
Jacquard, Star Center, Eagles In Corners, 78 x 78 In. 425.00
Jacquard, Star Medallion, Vintage, 81 x 88 In. 475.00
Jacquard, Summer & Winter Floral Design, 62 x 88 In. 90.00
Jacquard, Turkeys, Peacocks, Red, Blue, Natural, 64 x 94 In., 2 Piece 300.00
Jacquard, Urns Of Flowers, Birds, Schoolhouse, 82 x 79 In. 425.00
Jacquard, W. Craig, Greensburg, Ind., Red, White & Blue, 1860 .... 3800.00
Linsey Woolsey, Natural 1 Side, Blue Other, Floral, 100 x 125 In. 275.00
Linsey Woolsey, Red, Blue-Reverse, Circles, 1840, 76 x 76 In. 700.00
Overshot, 2 Piece, Blue, Red, Natural White, 72 x 88 In. 235.00
Overshot, 2 Piece, Blue, Red, Natural White, Woven, 64 x 88 In. 250.00
Overshot, 3 Colors, 70 x 80 In. 185.00
Overshot, Blue & White, 69 x 83 In. 50.00
Overshot, Blue, Red & Natural White, 66 x 94 In. 125.00
Overshot, Blue, Red & White, Fringed, 72 x 88 In. 300.00
Overshot, Geometric Pattern, 80 x 94 In. 300.00
Overshot, Navy Blue & Natural White, 86 x 107 In. 150.00
Overshot, Navy Blue & White Optical Pattern, 74 x 90 In. 150.00
Overshot, Navy Blue, Teal Blue, Red & White, 72 x 79 In. 325.00
Overshot, Navy, Red, Natural, Some Fringe, 61 x 82 In., 2 Piece 175.00
Overshot, Navy, White, 58 x 94 In., 2 Piece 125.00
Overshot, Optical Diamond & Star, 76 x 84 In. 225.00
Overshot, Optical Pattern, Navy Blue, Red, Green, 79 x 89 In. 375.00
Overshot, White On White, 78 x 92 In. 125.00

COWAN POTTERY made art pottery and wares for florists. Guy Cowan made pottery in Rocky River, Ohio, a suburb of Cleveland, from 1913 to 1931. A stylized mark with the word *Cowan* was used on most pieces. A commercial, mass-produced line was marked *Lakeware*. Collectors today search for the Art Deco pieces by Guy Cowan, Viktor Schreckengost, Waylande Gregory, or Thelma Frazier Winter.

Ashtray, Gazelle, Tan, Glossy 135.00
Bowl, Canoe Shape, Pedestal, Orange, 6 x 9 In. 95.00
Bowl, Canoe Shape, Sea Horses, Spotted Blue Glaze, 16 In. 110.00
Bowl, Yellow & Black, 10 In. 75.00
Bucket, Purple Metallic Luster, 6 x 8 In. 250.00
Candelabra, Double, Nude, 10 x 7 In. 450.00
Candleholder, 3-Light, Graduated, Ivory, Pair 110.00
Candleholder, 3-Light, Ivory, 5 1/2 x 10 1/2 In., Pair 65.00
Candleholder, Black, Pleated, 4 In., Pair 165.00
Candleholder, Blue Luster, Handle, 3 1/2 In., Pair 75.00
Candleholder, Dancing Nude, Cream 150.00
Candlestick, Italian Green, 6 In., Pair 35.00
Decanter, Oriental Red & Black, Waylande Gregory Design, 1929 .... 375.00
Figurine, Half Draped Woman, Glossy White, 9 In. 175.00
Figurine, Nude, No. 698 .... 125.00
Flagon, Cider, Mushroom Under Metallic Brown, Potting Rings, H. Davis 315.00
Flower Frog, Deer 175.00
Flower Frog, Nude, 11 1/2 In. 625.00
Flower Frog, Nude, Marked, 6 x 4 In. 75.00
Lamp, Flowers In Relief, Dragon Handles, Blue Luster Base, 14 In. 750.00
Paperweight, Elephant, Blue & Green .... 285.00 To 325.00
Plate, Sgraffito Design, Viktor Schreckengost, 11 1/4 In. 2875.00
Vase, Blue Luster, 6 1/2 In. 65.00
Vase, Fan, Green, 6 1/2 In. 125.00
Vase, Fan, Sea Horse At Base, Lavender, 8 In. 75.00
Vase, Iridescent Copper, Drilled For Lamp, 11 In. 135.00
Vase, Orange Luster, 3 In. 50.00
Vase, Orange Luster, 6 1/2 In. 30.00

Cranberry Glass, Epergne, 3 Lilies

To test ivory to see if it is real, heat the tip of a needle or pin until it is red hot. Put the point on the ivory in an inconspicuous spot. If it goes in more than a tiny pinprick, it is not ivory.

Vase, Pink, Yellow Speckles, 6 1/2 In. 110.00
Vase, Swan, Blue, 10 In. 25.00
Vase, Turquoise, 5 In. 60.00

CRACKER JACK, the molasses-flavored popcorn mixture, was first made in 1896 in Chicago, Illinois. A prize was added to each box in 1912. Collectors search for the old boxes, toys, and advertising materials. Many of the toys are unmarked.

Booklet, Riddle, 1900s .... 60.00 To 75.00
Booklet, Village Baseball Team 42.00
Bookmark, Dogs, Tin 20.00
Bowl, Cereal 5.00
Disc, Fortune Telling, Metal 35.00
Doll, Sailor, 9 In. 35.00
Elephant, Ivory Colored Plastic, 1950s 10.00
Fish, Plastic, Yellow, 1950 .... 7.00
Fortune Teller, Tin 100.00
Fortune Wheel, Tin 25.00
Frog, Jumping 35.00
Game, Midget Auto Race 35.00
Hat, Paper 12.50
Lunch Box .... 35.00 To 40.00
Lunch Box, Thermos 50.00
Mask, 1960s 10.00
Puzzle, Jigsaw, Engelus, Envelope 35.00
Stove, Metal 50.00
Valentine 150.00
Whistle, 2-Note, Metal 12.00
Whistle, 2-Note, Plastic 10.00
Whistle, Embossed Tin, 1930s 10.00

CRACKLE GLASS was originally made by the Venetians, but most of the ware found today dates from the 1800s. The glass was heated, cooled, and refired so that many small lines appeared inside the glass. It was made in many factories in the United States and Europe.

Pitcher, Electric Blue Handle, Clear, 6 In. 42.00
Pitcher, Lemonade, Cover, Vaseline 90.00
Pitcher, Water, Cover, Clear, Bulbous 150.00
Shade, Cranberry Flashed, Chimney, 10 x 7 In. 135.00
Tumbler, Cranberry 45.00

CRANBERRY GLASS is an almost transparent yellow-red glass. It resembles the color of cranberry juice. The glass has been made in Europe and America since the Civil War. It is still being made, and reproductions can fool the unwary. Related glass items may be listed in other categories, such as Northwood, Rubena Verde, etc.

Bowl, Clear Trim At Rim, Berry Pontil, 6 3/4 In. 230.00

Box, Dresser, Mary Gregory Type Girl On Cover, 4 1/2 In.	275.00
Box, Victorian, Enameled, Hinged Cover, 5 1/2 x 3 1/2 In.	295.00
Bride's Bowl, Inverted Thumbprint, Florals, 11 3/4 In.	540.00
Castor, Pickle, Inverted Thumbprint Insert	150.00
Cruet, Enameled Butterflies	165.00
Cruet, Faceted Clear Stopper, Clear Handle, 6 1/2 In.	150.00
Cruet, Wine, Ice Bladder, Overshot, Clear Stopper, 12 In.	325.00
Cup & Saucer, Scrolls, White Figure Of Woman With Harp	175.00
Cup, Gilt Band On Clear, Flashed, 1930s, 2 1/2 In.	12.00
Decanter, Cranberry To Clear Cut, Ferns & Scrolls, 13 In.	600.00
Decanter, Ribbed, Faceted Stopper, Clear Handle	125.00
Decanter, Stopper, Thumbprint	125.00
Decanter, Wine, Enameled Flowers, White Dots, 10 1/2 In.	195.00
Epergne, 3 Lilies ....*Illus*	875.00
Epergne, 7 Lilies, 22 In.	950.00
Fairy Lamp, Frosted Hobnail, Satin Swirl Shade	60.00
Hat, Uncle Sam, Rolled Brim, Opalescent Stars & Stripes	385.00
Hobnail, Pitcher, Milk, 5 1/2 In.	195.00
Humidor, Enamel Design, Gold Trim, Brass Lid, 6 In.	360.00
Jam Dish, Silver Plated Basket, 6 In.	145.00
Jar, Cover, Clear Trim, Flowers & Scrolls, 9 In.	425.00
Jar, Pickle, Silver Plated Stand, Handle, Tongs	375.00
Lamp, Finger, Embossed Design, Clear Handle, 5 1/4 In.	255.00
Lamp, Hobnail, Hanging	225.00
Muffineer, Silver Plated Cover, 12–Sided, 5 3/4 In.	50.00
Pitcher, Enameled Flowers, Ruffled Neck, 7 1/2 In.	245.00
Pitcher, Enameled, Clear Handle, 10 In.	195.00
Pitcher, Gold Flowers, Gold Handle, 4 1/2 In.	135.00
Pitcher, Inverted Thumbprint, Clear Ribbed Handle	115.00
Pitcher, Inverted Thumbprint, Ruffled, Clear Handle	180.00
Pitcher, Milk, Inverted Rib, Clear Handle, 7 In.	95.00
Pitcher, Water, Daisy & Fern, Ball Shape	225.00
Pitcher, White Spatter Clear Handle, 8 1/2 In.	155.00
Plate, Sides Turn Up, Clear Handle & Pedestal, 5 3/4 In.	360.00
Rose Bowl, Egg Shape, Clear Swags, Berries, 4 3/4 In.	260.00
Salt & Pepper, Enameled Flowers	135.00
Salt, Ribbed Lattice	60.00
Sugar Shaker, Leaf Umbrella	325.00
Syrup, Reverse Melon Ribbed, Sterling Neck, Spout & Lid	325.00
Tankard, Inverted Thumbprint, 7 In.	75.00
Tankard, Ribbed Lattice, Opalescent	700.00
Toothpick, Frazier	65.00
Toothpick, Hobnail, Rolled Edge	40.00
Toothpick, Ribbed Lattice	145.00
Tumble–Up, Clear Shell Trim At Neck, 6 In.	195.00
Tumbler, Honeycomb	15.00
Vase, Embossed Ribs, Clear Leaves & Feet, 7 1/2 In.	95.00
Vase, Fleurette, Ground Pontil, 4 3/4 In., Pair	175.00
Vase, Sanded Design Of Roman Key, Gold Trim, 5 3/4 In.	275.00
Vase, Thumbprint, Wide Ruffled, 6 In.	70.00
Vase, Vertical Ribbing, Amber Feet & Rigaree, 5 1/2 In.	195.00
Water Set, Coin Dot, Applied Clear Handle, 7 Piece	355.00
Water Set, Florentine Cameo, White Enamel Foliage, 5 Piece	525.00

CREAMWARE, or queensware, was developed by Josiah Wedgwood about 1765. It is a cream–colored earthenware that has been copied by many factories. Similar wares may be listed under Wedgwood and Pearlware.

Bottle, Canteen Shape, Floral In 4 Colors, 6 1/2 In.	350.00
Bowl, Basket Weave Center, Turquoise, Brown Enameling, 9 3/4 In.	475.00
Compote, Boat Shape, Leaf Designs, Purple Rim, 10 3/4 In.	475.00
Creamer, Enameled Rose Design, 3 1/8 In.	100.00
Creamer, Maroon Transfer, Boats & Figures In Chinese Landscape	55.00
Creamer, Polychrome Floral, Red Band, 5 3/4 In.	195.00

Cup & Saucer, Floral & Foliate Design, Marked, 2 1/2 In.	44.00
Figurine, John Newton, Evangelist, Tree Stump, 1785, 4 5/8 In.	770.00
Mug, Consolidated Ice Co., Polar Bear & Hunter	30.00
Mug, Elk	90.00
Mug, Floral Enameling, Ribbed Handle, 3 7/8 In.	145.00
Mug, Purple Luster Floral, Polychrome Enameling, 4 3/4 In.	50.00
Pitcher, Cider, Farmer's Arms & Bachelor's Wish	265.00
Pitcher, Marriage Of Henry Millicent & Helen Lomas, 1771	605.00
Plate, Flower, Blue Rim, England, 1820	135.00
Tea Caddy, Floral Design In 5 Colors, 4 5/8 In.	325.00
Tea Set, Gaudy Floral, Purple Luster, Polychrome & Enamel, 14 Pc.	775.00
Teapot, Cover, Enameled Chintz Pattern, 1780, England, 5 1/4 In.	1540.00
Teapot, Cover, Enameled Ruins Cartouche, 1765-1770, England, 5 In.	1100.00
Teapot, Enameled Floral, 6 In.	125.00
Teapot, Flower Finial, Woman Pouring Tea, 5 In.	1050.00
Tureen, Molded Finial, Green Feather Edge, 12 1/4 In.	800.00
Waste Bowl, Enameled Portraits, Inscription, 3 7/8 x 2 1/8 In.	180.00

CREDIT CARDS, credit tokens, metal charge plates, and other similar collectibles are now part of the numismatic collecting hobby.

American Express, Charter Member, 10/83, Green	40.00
C-X, Paperboard, May 31, 1955, Tan, Acceptance Colored Logos	70.00
Gold American Express, Executive Money Card, Paperboard	90.00
Hilton Hotels, Paperboard, 1958	45.00
Hotel Corporation Of America, 1956	35.00
Humble, Paperboard, Jan. 31, 1955, White, Orange Border	75.00
Shell, Paperboard, Oct. 31, 1956, 3 1/4 x 1 15/16 In.	65.00
Sinclair, Paperboard, Jul. 31, 1942, Green Dinosaur Back, 4 In.	105.00
Sinclair, Plastic, 3/61, Green Logo Top	28.00
Standard Oil, Paperboard, Dec. 31, 1938, Red, White & Blue	185.00
Texas Company, 3 Coupons, Dated May, June, July, Aug. 1941	165.00
Texas Company, Paperboard, Apr. 30, 1949	80.00
Union 76, 1970s	5.00

CROWN DERBY is the name given to porcelain made in Derby, England, from the 1770s to 1935. Pieces are marked with a crown and the letter *D* or the word *Derby*. The earliest pieces were made by the original Derby factory, while later pieces were made by the King Street Partnerships (1848-1935) or the Derby Crown Porcelain Co. (1876-1890). Derby Crown Porcelain Co. became Royal Crown Derby Co. Ltd. in 1890. It is now part of Royal Doulton Tableware Ltd.

Candelabrum, Figural, Shepherd Musician, 1770, 9 3/16 In., Pair	2200.00
Candlestick, Figural, Allegorical, Shepherd, Shepherdess, 11 In.	2550.00
Coffeepot, Acorn Knop Cover, Floral, Rose, Pear Shape, 9 3/8 In.	1450.00
Cup & Saucer, Dated 1913	50.00
Dish Set, Each Different Fruit Cluster, 7 11/16 In., 4 Piece	5500.00
Figurine, Pheasant, 11 x 11 In.	360.00
Figurine, Pointer, Brown Spots, White, 1795, 6 1/4 In.	825.00
Group, 3 Graces Distressing Cupid, White Biscuit, 1790, 13 In.	2200.00
Plate, Vase, Potpourri, Flower Encrusted, 1835, 6 11/16 In., Pr.	2300.00

CROWN DUCAL is the name used on some pieces of porcelain made by A. G. Richardson and Co., Ltd., England. The name has been used since 1916.

Vase, Stand, Bird Of Paradise, Hand Painted, 2 Piece	235.00
Vase, Stylized Floral Design, 9 In.	35.00

CROWN MILANO glass was made by Frederick Shirley at the Mt. Washington Glass Works about 1890. It had a plain biscuit color with a satin finish. It was decorated with flowers and often had large gold scrolls.

Biscuit Jar, Brown To Pink, Rope Rigaree, 9 1/2 In.	625.00
Biscuit Jar, Butterfly On Lid, Jeweled Starfish	685.00
Biscuit Jar, Butterfly On Lid, Jeweled Starfish, Signed	685.00

Biscuit Jar, Enameled Leaves, Flowers, Gilt, Bail Handle, 6 In. 740.00
Biscuit Jar, Pairpoint Lid & Bail 522.50
Biscuit Jar, Paneled, Hand Painted Florals, Signed, 9 1/2 In. 450.00
Biscuit Jar, White Panels, Wild Roses, Plated Cover, 6 In. 605.00
Bowl, Cover, Enameled Floral, Pig-Tail Handles, 5 3/4 x 9 In. 1250.00
Bowl, Melon Ribbed, 8-Pointed Star Rim, Flowers, 2 In. 265.00
Box, Cover, Dresser, Enameled Scrolls, Signed, 8 In. 785.00
Box, Dresser, Cream, Bulging Sides, Swirls, 4 3/4 x 8 In. 585.00
Box, Dresser, Floral Nosegay Panels On Lid, 8 In. 785.00
Bride's Bowl, Flowers, Pairpoint Stand, 14 In. 800.00
Bride's Bowl, Pairpoint Stand, 14 In. ....*Illus* 800.00
Castor, Pickle, Forget-Me-Not Design, Pairpoint Holder, Tongs 985.00
Cracker Jar, Blossoms, Leaves, Enamel Outlined, Signed, 5 In. 880.00
Cracker Jar, Butterfly On Cover, Starfish, Gourd Shape 900.00
Cruet, Canadian Thistle Blossoms, Outlined In Gold 1450.00
Cup & Saucer, Pastel Roses, Tulips & Blossoms, After Dinner 750.00
Dish, Sweetmeat, Turtle Finial, Gold Spider Mums, Marked, 7 In. 1000.00
Ewer, Gold Laurel Wreath, Portrait, Rope Handle, 10 1/2 In. 750.00
Ewer, Gold Painted Floral Designs, Pastel Accents, 9 1/4 In. 450.00
Lamp, Ball Shaped Poppy Shade, Bulbous Base, 1897, 19 3/4 In. 2950.00
Lamp, Banquet, Maidenhair Fern, Gold Scrolls & Circles, 18 In. 2750.00
Pitcher, Water, Ivy Leaves, Gold Outlined, Mt. Washington, 8 In. 1795.00
Syrup, Hinge Cover, Multicolored Florals, Melon Ribbed 450.00
Vase, Bulbous, Pink & Green Enamel Medallion, White, 6 In. 600.00
Vase, Cover, Ivy Leaves, Outlined In Gold, 10 1/2 In. 2285.00
Vase, Dresden Flowers, Gold Scrolls, Signed, 9 In. 1785.00
Vase, Enameled Geometric Flowers, White, Gilt, 8 In. 715.00
Vase, Hand Painted Flowers Overall, White, Signed, 9 In. 1785.00
Vase, Overall Leaves Background, Gold & Jeweled, 5 1/2 In. 900.00
Vase, Pansies, Gold Highlights, Triangular Base, 8 In. 1875.00
Vase, Pansies, Gold, Triangular Base, Leaf Handle, 8 In. 875.00
Vase, Snow Geese In Flight, Gold At Neck, 14 In. 3500.00
Vase, Thistles, Lusterless, Gilt Enamel Outlines, 12 1/4 In. 1430.00
Vase, Waffle Blank, Allover Leaves, Jewels, 5 1/2 In. 900.00
Vase, White, Gold Scrolls, Handles, Thorn, Curled, Pansies, 9 In. 600.00
Vase, Wild Rose, Gold Against Cream Ground, Signed, 15 In. 1045.00
Vase, Wild Roses & Leaves, Jeweled Stamens, 12 In. 1900.00

CROWN TUSCAN pattern is included in the Cambridge section.

CRUETS of glass or porcelain were made to hold vinegar, oil, and other condiments. They were especially popular during Victorian times and have been made in a variety of styles since the eighteenth century. Additional cruets may be found in the Castor Set category and also in various glass sections.

Chrysanthemum Sprig, Design, Original Stopper, Custard Glass 195.00
Cranberry Glass, Laurel Wreath & Ferns Etched, Initial, Bulbous 195.00

Crown Milano, Bride's Bowl, Pairpoint
Stand, 14 In.

◆◆◆◆◆◆◆◆◆◆◆◆◆◆◆◆◆◆◆◆◆◆

Be sure you have photographs
and descriptions of your collections in case of a robbery.
Keep them in a safe place
away from your house.

◆◆◆◆◆◆◆◆◆◆◆◆◆◆◆◆◆◆◆◆◆◆

Daisy & Button, Amber	95.00
Guttate, Pink Cased	85.00
Jackson, Custard Glass	28.00
Marlboro, Cut Glass, Dorflinger	75.00
Thumbprint, Green	95.00
Tray, Challinor, Green	35.00
Triple–Notched Handle, Tri–Spout, Cut Glass, 6 1/4 x 4 In.	135.00
Vaseline, Pressed Diamond, Stopper	65.00

CT GERMANY was first part of a mark used by a company in Altwasser, Germany, in 1845. The initials stand for C. Tielsch, a partner in the firm. The Hutschenreuther firm took over the company in 1918 and continued to use the *CT*.

C. T.

Bowl, Forget–Me–Nots, 10 In.	75.00
Chocolate Pot, Charlotte Portrait 2 Sides	110.00
Cracker Jar, Melon Rib, Flowers	95.00

CUP PLATES are small glass or china plates that held the cup while a diner of the mid–nineteenth century drank coffee or tea from the saucer. The most famous cup plates were made of glass at the Boston and Sandwich factory located in Sandwich, Massachusetts. There have been many new glass cup plates made in recent years for sale to the gift shops or the limited edition collectors. These are similar to the old plates but can be recognized as new.

Building Center, Lace Border, Brown, 4 1/2 In.	90.00
Building Center, Urn Border, Blue, 12 Sides, Marked, 4 In.	80.00
Butterfly & Flowers, Flint Glass	20.00
Chancellor Livingston, Clear, 3 1/2 In.	25.00
Dewey, Staffordshire	14.00
Garfield Portrait, Glass	135.00
Henry Clay, Flint Glass	25.00
Sampson, Lindley & Co., Cincinnati, 3 3/8 In.	65.00 To 140.00
Yellow, Red Rose, Spatterware, 4 1/8 In.	600.00

CURRIER & IVES made the famous American lithographs marked with their name from 1857 to 1907. The mark used on the print included the street address in New York City, and it is possible to date the year of the original issue from this information. Earlier prints were made by N. Currier and use that name from 1835 to 1847. Many reprints of the Currier or Currier & Ives prints have been made. Some collectors buy the insurance calendars that were based on the old prints. The words *large, small,* or *medium folio* refer to size. Other prints by Currier & Ives may be listed in the Card section under Advertising and in the Sheet Music category.

A Celebrated Stallion Trio, Framed, 19 7/8 x 21 7/8 In.	1425.00
A Fall From Grace, Matted, Framed, 14 3/4 x 19 1/4 In.	325.00
A Home In The Wilderness, Small Folio	308.00
A Trot, With Modern Improvements, Framed, 13 1/2 x 18 In.	350.00
America's Cup, October 7, 1893, Large	3200.00
American Farm Scene, 19 3/4 x 15 1/2 In.	2850.00
American Field Sports, Flushed, 18 3/4 x 26 7/8 In.	3575.00
American Winter Scenes, Evening, 1854, 16 3/4 x 24 1/8 In.	3025.00
Assassination & Death Of Lincoln, 13 x 18 In., Pair	135.00
Beauty Of The Atlantic, Cherry Frame, 18 x 16 In.	35.00
Bodine, Trotting Whirlwind Of West, 19 1/4 x 16 1/4 In.	495.00
Busting The Pool, Framed, 15 1/4 x 19 1/2 In.	425.00
Camping Out, 1856, 19 x 27 3/8 In.	3975.00
Clipper Ship Sweepstakes, 1853, 16 1/2 x 26 7/8 In.	2200.00
Craps–A Busted Game, Matted, Modern Frame, 15 x 19 1/2 In.	350.00
Crystal Palace, World's Fair Of 1851	165.00
Darktown Fire Brigade, 1887, Small	425.00
Darktown Fire Brigade, The Last Shake, 1885	275.00
Darktown Yacht Club, Hard Up For A Breeze, 1885, Small	250.00

Double Team Trot, Framed, 22 7/8 x 31 In. 750.00
Edward & Swiveller, Framed, 25 x 37 In. 525.00
Express Train, 1870, 8 x 12 1/2 In. 1760.00
Favorite Horse, Small Folio 625.00
First Trot Of The Season, 1870, Large 2495.00
France's Alexander, Framed, 13 x 17 3/8 In. · 170.00
Fruit & Flowers, Framed, 16 1/4 x 12 3/8 In. 150.00
Fruits Of The Seasons, Framed, 12 1/2 x 16 1/2 In. 185.00
Futurity Race At Sheepshead Bay, 20 1/4 x 34 1/4 In. 1540.00
General George Washington, 17 x 13 In. 200.00
God Bless Our Home, 12 x 16 In. 195.00
Grand National Democratic Banner, Frame, 17 x 12 3/4 In. 225.00
Grand New Steamboat Pilgrim, Large Folio 2700.00
Grand Pacer Richball, 1890, 11 1/2 x 16 In. 345.00
Grand United Order Of Odd-Fellows Chart, 1881, Small 95.00
Grandpapa's Cane, Child Holding Cane, Doll, Medium 125.00
Great Race At Baltimore, 1877, Small Folio 445.00
Hiawatha's Wedding, Small Folio 55.00
Hiawatha's Wooing, 1860, Large Folio 495.00
Home From The Brook, Large Folio 1540.00
Hopeful, Framed, 25 3/4 x 34 1/2 In. 1250.00
Horse-Man Of The Period, Rebacked, Framed, 12 7/8 x 18 In. 225.00
Hudson, From West Point, F. Palmer, 1862, 16 x 20 In. 1350.00
Hunting On The Susquehanna, Medium Folio 330.00
Initiation Ceremonies Of Darktown Lodge, 1887, Small 100.00
Lady Thorn, Framed, 13 1/8 x 16 3/4 In. 275.00
Life In Country, Large Folio, 1859 .... 350.00
Life Of A Fireman, 1828 .... 9350.00
Life Of A Sportsman, Frame, 12 1/2 x 16 3/8 In. 175.00
Little Ella, 19th Century, 11 x 8 3/8 In. 132.00
Little Sisters, Framed, Small 100.00
Maple Sugaring, Early Spring, 8 1/2 x 8 5/8 In. 1760.00
Mountain Spring, Cozzen's Dock, West Point, 1862, Medium 950.00
New Fashioned Girl, Full Length Woman, Parasol, Small 195.00
Off His Nut, Framed, 18 1/4 x 14 1/4 In. 450.00
Pacing For Grand Purse, Large 2400.00
Phallas, Matted & Framed, 24 x 35 1/8 In. 1200.00
Pigeon Shooting, A. F. Tait, 1862, Large 795.00
Rail Shooting On The Delaware, 1852, 12 3/4 x 19 7/8 In. 3025.00
Red Cloud, Frame, Small Folio 175.00
Royal Mail Steamship Persia, C. Parsons, 1856, Large 1250.00
Sale Of Pet Lamb, Framed, 15 1/4 x 23 1/2 In. 412.50
Schooner Yacht Magic, 1870, 18 1/8 x 27 1/8 In. 2310.00
Small Hopes & Lady Mac, Framed, 26 1/4 x 38 In. 750.00
Spoiling A Sensation, Matted, Modern Frame, 15 3/4 x 19 In. 300.00
St. Julien, Framed, 28 5/8 x 39 In. 1250.00
Stella & Alice Grey, Passing The Stand, Framed, 21 x 31 In. 2150.00
Strawberries, Framed, 12 1/2 x 16 3/4 In. 185.00
Striped Bass, 1872, Small 265.00
Two To Go & Got 'em Both!, Modern Frames, 15 x 19 In., Pair 1100.00
Vase Of Flowers, 1870, Small 115.00
View On Harlem River, 1852, 14 5/8 x 20 1/8 In. 990.00
Washington Family, Black & White 150.00
Wedding Day, Interior, 1846, Small 95.00
White Squadron, U.S. Navy, 1893, 26 x 40 In. 1750.00
Winter Morning, Medium Folio 1250.00

CUSTARD GLASS is a slightly yellow opaque glass. It was first made in the United States after 1886 at the La Belle Glass Works, Bridgeport, Ohio. It is being reproduced. Additional pieces may be found in the Cambridge, Fenton, Heisey, and Northwood categories.

Argonaut Shell, Compote, Jelly 120.00
Argonaut Shell, Creamer .... 125.00 To 190.00

Argonaut Shell, Pitcher, Water	295.00
Argonaut Shell, Sugar, Cover	190.00
Argonaut Shell, Table Set, Green & Gold Trim, 4 Piece	595.00
Argonaut Shell, Toothpick	200.00 To 425.00
Beaded Circle, Berry Bowl, Master	250.00
Beaded Circle, Spooner	150.00
Beaded Circle, Tumbler	125.00
Beaded Swag, Goblet	60.00
Chrysanthemum Sprig, Banana Boat & Sauces, Blue, 5 Piece	450.00
Chrysanthemum Sprig, Berry Set, Blue, 6 Piece	1200.00
Chrysanthemum Sprig, Butter, Cover, Green, Gold Trim	250.00
Chrysanthemum Sprig, Celery Vase	750.00
Chrysanthemum Sprig, Celery Vase, Signed, Blue	1100.00
Chrysanthemum Sprig, Creamer	105.00
Chrysanthemum Sprig, Pitcher	375.00
Chrysanthemum Sprig, Pitcher, Green, Gold Trim	250.00
Chrysanthemum Sprig, Spooner, Blue	245.00
Chrysanthemum Sprig, Spooner, Gold Trim	110.00
Chrysanthemum Sprig, Spooner, Green, Gold Trim	80.00
Chrysanthemum Sprig, Table Set, 4 Piece	450.00
Chrysanthemum Sprig, Toothpick	225.00
Chrysanthemum Sprig, Toothpick, Blue	450.00
Chrysanthemum Sprig, Tumbler	65.00
Chrysanthemum Sprig, Tumbler, Blue	150.00
Chrysanthemum Sprig, Water Set, 7 Piece	735.00
Chrysanthemum Sprig, Water Set, Pitcher 8 1/2 In., 6 Piece	335.00
Delaware, Creamer	35.00
Delaware, Creamer, Breakfast	35.00
Diamond With Peg, Tumbler	50.00 To 85.00
Everglades, Salt & Pepper	445.00
Fan, Water Set, Marked, 5 Piece	275.00
Fine Cut & Roses, Rose Bowl	65.00
Geneva, Banana Boat, Green Stain	145.00
Geneva, Toothpick, Green	25.00
Geneva, Tumbler, Green	55.00
Geneva, Tumbler, Green & Red	50.00
Geneva, Tumbler, Green, Gold Design	80.00
Geneva, Tumbler, Red	45.00 To 55.00
Geneva, Tumbler, Red Florals, Green Foliage, 3 7/8 In.	40.00
Georgia Gem, Butter, Cover, Green & Pink Floral Enameled	175.00
Georgia Gem, Celery Vase	125.00
Georgia Gem, Celery Vase, Gold Trim	120.00
Georgia Gem, Celery Vase, Green, Gold	135.00
Georgia Gem, Spooner, Green & Pink Floral Enameled	65.00
Georgia Gem, Spooner, Green, Gold Trim	60.00
Georgia Gem, Sugar	80.00
Georgia Gem, Sugar, Cover, Green, Gold Trim	80.00
Georgia Gem, Toothpick	45.00 To 60.00
Grape & Cable, Plate, Nutmeg Stain, Northwood	60.00
Grape & Cable, Plate, Ruffled, Nutmeg Stain	60.00
Grape & Gothic Arches, Goblet, Brown Stain	45.00
Grape & Gothic Arches, Sugar, Cover, Blue Stain	195.00
Grape & Thumbprint, Sherbet	50.00
Harvard, Toothpick	45.00
Harvard, Toothpick, Faint Lettering	40.00
Intaglio, Berry Set, 5 Piece	235.00
Intaglio, Butter, Cover	225.00 To 260.00
Intaglio, Butter, Cover, Green	265.00
Intaglio, Compote, Jelly, Green Trim	90.00
Intaglio, Creamer	95.00 To 120.00
Intaglio, Spooner	90.00
Intaglio, Spooner, Green	70.00 To 140.00
Intaglio, Sugar & Creamer	145.00

Intaglio, Sugar, Green 165.00
Intaglio, Tumbler, Blue Design 60.00
Intaglio, Tumbler, Blue, Gold Trim 55.00
Inverted Fan & Feather, Berry Bowl, Pink, Gold Trim 250.00
Inverted Fan & Feather, Berry Set, 7 Piece 600.00
Inverted Fan & Feather, Sauce 78.00
Inverted Fan & Feather, Table Set, 4 Piece 800.00
Ivorina Verde pattern is in this section under Winged Scroll
Jackson, Creamer 95.00
Jackson, Creamer, Gold Trim 73.00
Jackson, Pitcher, Goofus Trim 195.00
Jackson, Saltshaker 85.00
Jefferson Optic, Toothpick, Cooperstown, N. D. 50.00
Jefferson Optic, Toothpick, Rose Decal, Wentworth, S. D. 70.00
Lotus & Grape, Bonbon, Green 65.00
Louis XV, Banana Bowl 85.00
Louis XV, Berry Set, 5 Piece 375.00
Louis XV, Butter, Cover .... 125.00 To 150.00
Louis XV, Creamer, Ivory & Gold 90.00
Louis XV, Salt & Pepper, 3 1/4 In. 220.00
Louis XV, Spooner, Ivory & Gold 85.00
Louis XV, Sugar, Cover, Gold Trim 145.00
Maize is its own category in this book
Maple Leaf, Butter, Cover .... 215.00 To 265.00
Maple Leaf, Butter, Cover, Gold Trim 250.00
Maple Leaf, Creamer .... 135.00 To 140.00
Maple Leaf, Creamer, Maple Leaf 85.00
Maple Leaf, Spooner .... 95.00 To 140.00
Maple Leaf, Spooner, Gold Trim 125.00
Maple Leaf, Table Set, Gold Trim, 3 Piece 485.00
Peacock At Urn, Dish, Ice Cream 75.00
Peacock At Urn, Dish, Ice Cream, Nutmeg Stain, Small 75.00
Ribbed Drape, Spooner .... 85.00 To 125.00
Ribbed Drape, Sugar, Cover .... 175.00 To 195.00
Ribbed Thumbprint, Toothpick, Design 85.00
Ribbed Thumbprint, Tumbler, Villard 45.00
Ring Band, Cruet, Gold Trim, Heisey 295.00
Ring Band, Toothpick 52.50
Ring Band, Toothpick, Cedar Falls, Iowa, Gold, Heisey 70.00
Ring Band, Toothpick, Heisey 45.00
Ring Band, Toothpick, Monmouth 50.00
Smocking, Bell 35.00
Tarentum's Victoria, Butter, Cover 175.00
Tarentum's Victoria, Butter, Cover, Design 225.00
Tarentum's Victoria, Celery Vase, Gold Trim 110.00
Tiny Thumbprint, Toothpick .... 37.50 To 125.00
Tiny Thumbprint, Toothpick, Evansville 45.00
Tiny Thumbprint, Toothpick, Flower Decal, Elmore, Minn. 50.00
Vermont, Butter, Cover, Blue Trim 85.00
Vermont, Creamer 95.00
Vermont, Spooner, Green 75.00
Vermont, Toothpick 135.00
Wild Bouquet, Butter, Cover 585.00
Winged Scroll, Bowl, 8 1/2 In. 145.00
Winged Scroll, Tankard, Gold Trim 230.00
Winged Scroll, Water Set, Gold Trim, 6 Piece 550.00

CUT GLASS has been made since ancient times, but the large majority of the pieces now for sale date from the brilliant period of glass design, 1880 to 1905. These pieces have elaborate geometric designs with a deep miter cut. Modern cut glass with a similar appearance is being made in England, Ireland, and Czechoslovakia. Chips and scratches are often difficult to notice but lower the value dramatically. A signature on the glass adds significantly to the value. Other cut glass pieces are listed under factory names.

Banana Bowl, American Brilliant, Folded Over Sides, 4 1/2 In.	85.00
Banana Bowl, Russian, 3 1/4 In.	180.00
Basket, Allover Hobstar & Fan, 8 In.	125.00
Basket, Candy, Engraved Leaves & Branches, 5 1/2 In.	110.00
Basket, Crosshatched Lozenges, Floral, Bull's–Eye Handle, Large	700.00
Basket, Easter, Royal, Double Bull's–Eye Handle, Hunt, 5 1/2 In.	300.00
Basket, Hobstars & Cane, 10 In.	500.00
Basket, Persian Variation Of Russian, Hoare, 8 x 11 x 7 In.	2450.00
Bell, Hobstars, Button & Fans, Crosscut Diamond Handle	275.00
Bell, Hobstars, Cane, Strawberry Diamond, 5 3/4 x 3 In.	425.00
Bell, Jewel, Clark, 7 x 3 1/2 In.	475.00
Bell, Prism, Pitkin & Brooks, 4 1/2 x 3 In.	245.00
Bottle, Bitters, Pedestal, Faceted Neck Ring, 8 x 3 1/2 In., Pair	380.00
Bottle, Bitters, St. Louis Diamond, Cut Neck, Sterling Stopper	365.00
Bottle, Brandy, Triple Miter Trellis, Dorflinger, 9 In., Pair	700.00
Bottle, Catsup, Prudence, Triple Notched Handle, Blackmer	300.00
Bottle, Cologne, Henry VIII, Clark, 6 1/4 In.	310.00
Bottle, Worcestershire, Hobstars & Cane, Stopper, 8 1/4 x 2 In.	375.00
Bowl, 18 Panels Of 6 Hobstars, Dorflinger, 10 In.	550.00
Bowl, Aberdeen, Jewel Cut Glass Co., 7 In.	240.00
Bowl, Acme, 8 x 3 1/2 In.	425.00
Bowl, Carolyn, Ruffled Rim, Hoare, 9 In.	600.00
Bowl, Croesus, Hoare, Blown, 8 In.	1550.00
Bowl, Eggnog, Cane Bars, Vertical Hobstar Chains, 9 x 10 1/2 In.	1600.00
Bowl, Fan Design On Rim, Diamond Body, 8 1/4 In.	88.00
Bowl, Hampton, Bergen, 9 In.	55.00
Bowl, Harvard, Silver Plate Rim, 8 In.	260.00
Bowl, Heart Pattern, Pitkin & Brooks, 8 In.	137.00
Bowl, Hobstars, Cane, Diamond Point, Handles, 11 In.	300.00
Bowl, Hobstars, Engraving, 9 3/8 In.	225.00
Bowl, Houndstooth Border, Overall Diamond Cut, 10 In.	77.00
Bowl, Lotus, Egginton, 8 In.	250.00
Bowl, Louis XVI Style, Diamond, Ormolu Dolphins, 10 1/2 In.	1320.00
Bowl, Napoleon's Hat, Carolyn, J. Hoare, 4 x 8 3/4 x 13 1/2 In.	1465.00
Bowl, Royal, Hunt, 5 1/2 x 8 In.	285.00
Bowl, Strawberry, Diamond & Fan, Hobstar Base, 5 x 2 1/2 In.	150.00
Bowl, Sunburst, Fan & Geometric, 10 1/2 In.	192.00
Bowl, Sunburst, Flared, Square, 8 1/2 In.	275.00
Bowl, Triple Meter Trellis, Heart Shape, Dorflinger, 9 In.	400.00
Box, Hinged Lid, Chains Of Hobstars, Ovals, C. F. Monroe, 8 In.	1000.00
Bridge Set, Newark Cut Glass Co.	645.00
Butter, Cover, Hobstars, Sawtooth Rim, Flared Top, 7 In.	400.00
Butter, Cover, Pinwheel & Fan	395.00
Cake Tray, Hobstar, Round, 12 In.	625.00
Candleholder, Paperweight, Low, Clark	135.00
Candlestick, Prism & Beading, Lapidary Knobs, 10 In.	400.00
Candlestick, Russian & Swirl, Starred Cup, 10 1/2 In., Pair	1900.00
Candlestick, St Louis Cutting, Diamond Point, 10 In., Pair	450.00
Canoe, Russian, Star–Cut Buttons, 7 3/4 x 3 1/4 In.	360.00
Carafe, Russian, 7 1/2 In., Pair	650.00
Carafe, Water, Hobstars, c.1910	88.00
Carafe, Water, Pinwheel	75.00
Celery Dish, Hobstars & Pinwheels, Oval, c.1910, 12 1/2 x 6 In.	187.00
Celery, Russian	125.00
Chamberstick, Flute & Strawberry, Triple Notched Handle, 4 In.	275.00
Chamberstick, Russian Cut, Handled Snuffer	1300.00
Chandelier, 3–Tier, Faceted Drops, 20th Century, 38 In.	495.00
Cheese Dish, Popcorn & Rosette	595.00
Coffeepot, Flashed Star, Meriden, 11 3/4 x 6 In.	6850.00

Compote, Candy, Pinwheel & Hobstar, Floral Design Base, 9 In.	55.00
Compote, Cover, Gilded Design, Diamond Point Bowl, 11 1/4 In.	50.00
Compote, Cover, Hob Diamond, Cut Finial, Dorflinger, 8 In.	300.00
Compote, Cut Panels & Ellipses, 6 3/4 In.	85.00
Compote, Sunburst, Ornate Stem, Signed Hawkes, 8 In.	165.00
Cuspidor, Triple Miter Trellis & Intaglio	900.00
Decanter, Bakers Gothic, Clark, Neck Notching, 10 x 5 In., Pair	850.00
Decanter, Bands, Diamond, Miters, Flutes, Sinclaire, 13 In., Pair	595.00
Decanter, Cordial, Pinwheel, Pinched Center, Teardrop Stopper	560.00
Decanter, Flutes & Hobstars, Hobstar On Stopper & Base	1125.00
Decanter, Harvard & Intaglio Flowers, Knob Stopper	145.00
Decanter, Irish, 1820, 15 1/2 In.	295.00
Decanter, Overall Geometric Design, Bell Form, 11 In.	110.00
Decanter, Taft, Taylor Brothers	235.00
Dish, Ice Cream, Russian, Hawkes, 6 1/2 In.	130.00
Dish, Nut, Kalana Poppy, Dorflinger	25.00
Dish, Spade In Cards, Hobstars, Cane, Paneled Handle, 5 1/2 In.	50.00
Dresser Set, Perfume, Cut Stoppers, 1920s, 4 Piece	495.00
Flask, Strawberry Diamond, Hobnail & Fan, 4 In.	345.00
Flask, Two 24 Point Hobstars, 5 1/2 In.	465.00
Frame, Butterflies, Daisies Around Oval, 1890, 5 1/4 x 3 1/8 In.	195.00
Glass, Highball, Hoare, 7 Piece	525.00
Goblet, Monarch, Hoare, c.1900	125.00
Goblet, Water, Hobnail Fan, Teardrop, 10 In.	55.00
Hatpin Holder, Prism Cut, 5 In.	425.00
Humidor, Marlboro, Dorflinger, 8 1/2 In.	605.00
Jam Jar, Diamond & Bull's-Eye, Gorham Cover & Handle	130.00
Jar, Cover, Dresser, Pinwheel & Hobstar, Fan Shape, 4 In.	275.00
Jar, Cover, Sterling Silver Lid, Brilliant Period, Meriden	1650.00
Jewel Casket, Hinged Lid, Hobstars, Cane, Prism & Fans, 9 1/2 In.	3300.00
Jug, Oval Flask Form, Chased Silver Gilt Mounts, Handle, 10 In.	2420.00
Knife Rest, Beveled Shaft, Faceted Ball Ends, 3 1/2 In.	35.00
Lamp, Allover Hobstars, Strawberry Diamonds, Fans, 24 1/2 In.	5500.00
Lamp, Kerosene, Diamond & Fans Base	200.00
Loving Cup, Hobstar & Fan, 8 1/2 In.	1800.00
Loving Cup, Monarch Pattern, J. Hoare, 6 x 7 In.	565.00
Mustard, Daisies, Hobstars In Diamonds	130.00
Napkin Ring, Intaglio Flowers & Leaves	65.00
Nappy, Floral & Harvard, 8 In.	55.00
Orange Bowl, Harvard, Brilliant Period, 10 In.	275.00
Paperweight, Russian, Engraved, Book Shape, 3 3/4 x 2 1/4 In.	365.00
Pitcher, Alhambra, Triple Notched Handle, 10 1/2 In.	1600.00
Pitcher, Barrel Shape, Swirled Comet, L. Straus	650.00
Pitcher, Cane & Cross Cut Diamond, Thumbprint Handle, 10 In.	135.00
Pitcher, Champagne, Strawberry Diamond, 11 In.	325.00
Pitcher, Harvard, Hobstar Base, Hoare, 9 In.	650.00
Pitcher, Hobstar & Fan, c.1880, 7 In.	195.00
Pitcher, Hobstars, Diamonds, Buzz Stars, Notched Handle, 11 In.	195.00
Pitcher, Russian, Cut Buttons, 7 In.	425.00
Pitcher, Signed, Sword, Ornate Handle, 9 In.	175.00
Pitcher, Square Top, Hobstars, Miters, Crosshatches, 10 In.	150.00
Pitcher, Sussex, Hobnail Handle, Dorflinger, 12 In.	1200.00
Plate, Grecian, Hawkes, 7 In.	1395.00
Plate, Intaglio Blossoms, 9 In.	170.00
Plate, Leaves & Daisies, 12 1/2 In.	195.00
Plate, Royal, Hunt Cut Glass Co., 7 In.	325.00
Plate, Strawberry Diamond, Crosshatch, Split Vesicas, Stem, 7 In.	150.00
Powder Jar, Hinged Cover, Allover Hobstars, Prism & Fan, 6 In.	650.00
Powder Jar, Large Buzz Stars, Fans, Russian Cut	165.00
Punch Bowl, Arcadia, 12 In.	1210.00
Punch Bowl, Trojan Pattern, Pedestal, Signed Fry	1850.00
Punch Cup, Hobstars, 2 In., 8 Piece	55.00
Punch Cup, Marquise, Triple Notched Handle, Egginton, 6 Piece	120.00

Ramekin Set, Cross–Cut Diamonds & Fans, 2 1/4 x 4 1/2 In. 95.00
Relish, Hobstar & Crosshatching, Canoe Shape, 13 In. 135.00
Relish, Ornate, L. Straus & Sons, 7 1/2 In. 160.00
Relish, Pinwheel, Brilliant Cut 42.50
Rose Bowl, Cane, 8 1/2 In. 550.00
Rose Bowl, Fatima, Pedestal, Straus 2450.00
Rose Bowl, Hobstars, 3 In. 85.00
Rose Bowl, Strawberry & Diamond 145.00
Rose Bowl, Teutonic, Hobstar Base, Signed Hawkes, 5 x 5 3/4 In. 750.00
Salad Set, Gooseberries & Leaves, 2 Piece 2000.00
Salt, Pedestal, Attributed To Hawkes, 1 1/2 x 2 In. 65.00
Spoon Rest, Monarch, Hoare 110.00
Spooner, Strawberry & Fan 175.00
String Holder, Sterling Cover Marked Jacobi & Jenkins 565.00
Sugar & Creamer, Buzz Star 255.00
Sugar & Creamer, Cover, Drape, L. Straus 1000.00
Sugar & Creamer, Egginton 180.00
Sugar & Creamer, Hobstar & Cane, 2 1/2 In. 75.00
Sugar & Creamer, Hobstar & Flowers, Footed, Newark 235.00
Sugar & Creamer, Hobstars & Flowers, Footed 235.00
Sugar & Creamer, Overall Geometric & Fan 93.00
Sugar & Creamer, Rex, Plantation Size 400.00
Sugar Shaker, Meriden Cut, Sterling Lid, Wilcox Mark, 4 1/2 In. 345.00
Sugar Shaker, Notched Prism, Sterling Repousse Lid, 4 1/2 In. 230.00
Sugar Shaker, Strawberry, Diamond & Fan, Sterling Silver Collar 165.00
Sugar, Strawberry 38.00
Syrup, Allover Large Hobstars, Vesicas & Fans 150.00
Syrup, Allover St. Louis Diamond, Gorham Fittings, 4 1/2 In. 210.00
Syrup, Eagle Spout, Scroll Handle, Dorflinger, Sapphire Blue 1800.00
Tankard, Cut Star, Double Thumbprint Handle, Star Base, 8 1/2 In. 110.00
Tankard, Daisy 100.00
Tankard, Hobstars, Sterling Collar & Spout, Honeycomb Handle 145.00
Tray, Allover Crosscut Diamonds & Fans, Hobstar Center, 14 In. 2300.00
Tray, Allover Hobstars & Russian Panels, 11 x 11 In. 660.00
Tray, Cluster Of Hobstars, 13 3/4 In. 2785.00
Tray, Festoon, 12 1/2 In. 3145.00
Tray, Fishtail, Hobstars, Vesicas & Beading, 16 1/2 In. 2000.00
Tray, Ice Cream, Double Vesica, Strawberry Fans Rim, 15 x 11 In. 795.00
Tray, Ice Cream, Hobstars & Fans, 14 x 8 In. 425.00
Tumbler, Geometric Cut, American Brilliant, Hoare 85.00
Tumbler, Panels Of Windmill, House, Church, Lighthouse, Green 55.00
Tumbler, Russian, Cut Buttons, Rayed Bottom, 6 Piece 660.00
Tumbler, Strawberry Diamond With Fan 30.00
Vase, Allover Floral & Leaf, Circles, Loop Feet, 1914, 10 1/2 In. 250.00
Vase, Baluster Form, Flared Rim With Stars, c.1910, 10 In. 121.00
Vase, Chalice, Sunburst, Faceted Knob Stem, Hobstar Base, 14 In. 1295.00
Vase, Crosshatching Alternating With Crossed Vesicas, 12 In. 175.00
Vase, Diamond Point, Rays, 5 In. 35.0
Vase, Etched, Gilded Design, Pressed, 10 1/2 In. 95.00
Vase, Expanding Star, Cut Allover, Square, 6 In. 150.00
Vase, Floral Design, Sawtooth Rim, c.1920, 12 In. 220.00
Vase, Harvard & Floral, 12 In. 95.00
Vase, Harvard, Corset Shape, 12 In. 238.00
Vase, Harvard, Faceted Knob, Scalloped Hobstar Foot, 8 1/4 In. 445.00
Vase, Heart Pattern, Corset Shape, 20 In. 1500.00
Vase, Hobnail & Pyramidal Stars, Pinwheel Base, 8 1/2 x 12 In. 975.00
Vase, Hobstar Border, Notched Prism & Panel At Base, 16 In. 450.00
Vase, Hobstar, Bull's–Eye & Flutes, Clark, 12 In. 325.00
Vase, Hobstars, Fans, Rays & Thumbprint, Green To Clear, 12 In. 2200.00
Vase, Kalana Lily, Dorflinger, 4 1/2 In. 175.00
Vase, Kalana Narcissi, Dorflinger, 14 1/2 In. 295.00
Vase, Parisian, Scalloped Sawtooth Rim, Dorflinger, 14 1/4 In. 650.00
Vase, Russian, Signed, 1883, 11 1/2 In. 900.00

Vase, Strawberry Diamonds, Panels, Roundels, Fans, 14 3/8 In. 145.00
Vase, Trumpet Shape, Long Flutes, Circles, Dorflinger, 5 3/4 In. 195.00
Vase, Trumpet, Floral Design, Highlighted With Gilt, 18 3/4 In. 75.00
Vase, Trumpet, Queens Pattern, 12 In. 625.00
Vase, Trumpet, Rayed Base, Scalloped Sawtooth Rim, 12 In. 325.00
Vase, Vertical Panels Of Bars & Circles, Hobstars, 14 1/2 In. 330.00
Vase, Victorian Lace, Green Cut To Clear, 11 1/2 In. 2600.00
Water Set, Butterfly & Daisy, 6 Piece 345.00
Water Set, Center Diamond, Fans Either Side, Buzz Stars, 7 Piece 495.00
Water Set, Floral Pattern, 7 Piece 350.00
Water Set, Sunburst, 7 Piece 350.00
Wine, Hobstars, Crosscut Diamonds, Cranberry To Clear, Dorflinger 275.00
Wine, Ruby Panels With Gold Tracery, Stemmed, Moser–Type, 7 In. 165.00

CYBIS porcelain is a twentieth–century product. Boleslaw Cybis came to
the United States from Poland in 1939. He started making porcelains in
Long Island, New York, in 1940. He moved to Trenton, New Jersey, in
1942 as one of the founders of Cordey China Co. and started his own
Cybis Porcelains about 1950. The firm is still working. (See also Cordey.)

CYBIS

Figurine, Alexander The Elephant 350.00
Figurine, Baby Brother, Duckling, 4 1/2 In. 85.00
Figurine, Ballerina On Cue, White 375.00
Figurine, Beatrice 950.00
Figurine, Burro 150.00
Figurine, Carmen, 14 3/4 In. 1200.00
Figurine, Circus Bear, 7 In. 125.00
Figurine, Court Jester 1650.00
Figurine, Dahlia, White 750.00
Figurine, Donkey, Gray & White, 7 In. 125.00
Figurine, Duckling 150.00
Figurine, Elizabeth Anne 250.00
Figurine, Girl, Kneeling, With Bird 150.00
Figurine, Harlequin 1650.00
Figurine, Heidi, 7 1/2 In. 150.00
Figurine, Jane Eyre, 12 In. 1250.00
Figurine, Karina, Ballerina, 6 3/4 In. 475.00
Figurine, Little Princess, c.1970 .... 425.00 To 550.00
Figurine, Lotus Blossom 200.00
Figurine, Madonna, Bluebird, Wooden & Marble Base, 10 In. .... 325.00 To 425.00
Figurine, Match Girl 250.00
Figurine, Mouse 180.00
Figurine, Owl, White, 4 1/2 In. 50.00
Figurine, Pegasus, No. 348, 1971 .... 1200.00
Figurine, Puck 1950.00
Figurine, Robin, 10 7/8 In. 600.00
Figurine, Rumples, Clown 300.00
Figurine, Snail, Sir Escargot, 1968 .... 200.00
Figurine, Wood Duck 500.00

CZECHOSLOVAKIA is a popular term with collectors. The name, first
used as a mark after the country was formed in 1918, appears on glass and
porcelain and other decorative items. The name is still used in some
trademarks.

Bottle, Apothecary, Show Globe, Stopper 150.00
Bowl, Yellow & White Spatter, Applied Black Feet, 5 x 2 In. 45.00
Box, Cover, Napoleon & Officers, Black Beehive 355.00
Coffee Set, 24K Gold & Platinum, 16 Piece 300.00
Console, Turquoise, Cream, Pottery 65.00
Decanter Set, Crystal, Bohemian Sticker, 7 Piece 85.00
Figurine, Cat, Sitting, Ferocious, White, 7 1/2 In. 95.00
Figurine, Dog, English Setter, Standing, Erphila, 8 1/2 In. 55.00
Humidor, Figural, Man Smoking Pipe, Hat, 6 1/2 In. 140.00
Lamp, Boudoir, Satin Glass, Silk Shade, Pair 225.00

Perfume Bottle, Blue	30.00
Perfume Bottle, Blue, 5 1/4 In.	185.00
Perfume Bottle, Cut Glass, Allover Cut, Stopper	47.50
Perfume Bottle, Cut Glass, Lay Down, Clear, 7 1/4 In.	180.00
Perfume Bottle, Powder Box, Atomizer, Gold Cut To Clear	175.00
Pitcher Set, Peaches, Grapes, Yellow, Blue, Pottery, 6 Piece	55.00
Pitcher, Bluebell Pattern, 1 1/2 Qt.	13.00
Pitcher, Milk, Barmaid	30.00
Powder Jar, Lady	45.00
Punch Set, Garland & Peacocks, Orange, Bow, Ladle, 6 Cups	375.00
Salt Set, Cut Flowers, Amber, 9 Piece	85.00
Salt, Hanging, Sailboats, Blue, White	75.00
Vase, Blue & Yellow, Cased, 8 In.	50.00
Vase, Green Jade	75.00
Vase, Hand Painted Birds, Cobalt Blue Glass, Large	150.00
Vase, Hand Painted Fox Hunt Scene, Green Glass, 8 1/4 In.	145.00
Vase, Iridescent Lemon Glass, Black Knopped Pedestal, 6 In.	1320.00
Vase, Pear-Shaped Sections, Bound By Iron Frame, 11 In.	295.00
Vase, Red & Black, 9 In., Pair	250.00
Wall Pocket, Blue Bow, Raised Bird, Fan Shape, 5 In, ...	25.00
Wall Pocket, Cardboard, Urn Design, Giveaway, 19 x 6 In.	18.00
Water Set, Glass, 7 Piece	150.00

D'ARGENTAL is a mark used in France by the Compagnie des Cristalleries de St. Louis. The firm made multilayered, acid-cut cameo glass in the late nineteenth and twentieth centuries. D'Argental is the French name for the city of Munzthal, home of the glassworks. Later they made enameled etched glass.

Perfume Bottle, Landscape & Sailboats, Signed, 6 3/4 In.	1250.00
Powder Box, Morning Glories, Wheel Carved, Reds & Browns	1595.00
Vase, Art Deco Design, Orange, Amber & Wine, Signed, 7 In.	1000.00
Vase, Blue, Burgundy, Mulberry Branches, Oviform, Signed, 8 In.	440.00
Vase, Burgundy On Blue, Signed, 6 In.	650.00
Vase, Cottage & Castle Scene, Brown, Orange, Cameo, 7 In.	785.00
Vase, Gray, Berried Branches, Tendrils, Signed, c.1900, 5 1/2 In.	550.00
Vase, Green, Burgundy, Apple Blossoms, Baluster, Signed, 6 In.	770.00
Vase, Jack-In-The-Pulpit Blossoms, Signed, c.1920, 13 3/4 In.	1760.00
Vase, Pine Cone, Amber On Vaseline, 12 1/2 In.	1100.00
Vase, Purple Foxgloves & Foliage, Frost Ground, 9 1/4 In.	1150.00
Vase, Rose Branches, Cameo, Red, Lemon, Burgundy, 11 3/4 In.	2475.00
Vase, Scene, Mahogany Over Gold & Amber Shades, Bulbous, 14 In. ...	2400.00
Vase, Tulips, Leaves, Ferns, Signed, c.1920, 12 5/8 In.	1980.00
Vase, Wheat & Bird Design, Maroon On Vaseline, 17 In.	1600.00

DANIEL BOONE, a pre-revolutionary war folk hero, was a surveyor, trapper, and frontiersman. A television series, which ran from 1964 to 1970, was based on his life and starred Fess Parker. All types of Daniel Boone memorabilia is collected.

Badge	7.00
Cabin, Lincoln Logs	25.00
Holster, Double, Stamped Steel Cover King Of Cowboys, No Guns	42.50
Lunch Box, Fess Parker, 1955 .... 45.00 To 65.00
Lunch Box, Thermos, 1955, Aladdin	79.00
Match Safe, Daniel Boone, GAR 29th Encampment, Brass	350.00
Slate, Fess Parker	20.00
Wristwatch	125.00

DAUM, a glassworks in Nancy, France, was started by Jean Daum in 1875. The company, now called *Cristalleries de Nancy,* is still working. The *Daum Nancy* mark has been used in many variations. The name of the city and the artist are usually both included.

Bottle, Dutch Winter Landscape, Stopper, Signed, 3 In.	1430.00
Bottle, Ink, Berries, Mottled Orange, Square, Signed, 4 3/4 In.	2310.00

Bowl, Applied Maple Leaves, Cameo, Yellow To Pink, 6 1/4 In. 4950.00
Bowl, Cameo, Gray, Purple, Green, Blossoms, 1900, 3 3/4 In. 6600.00
Bowl, Cameo, Inverted Bell Form, Pinks, Amber Shades, 6 In. 4950.00
Bowl, Cameo, Violets, White To Deep Purple, Lobed, 7 1/2 In. 7150.00
Bowl, Flowering Branches, Streaked, Signed, c.1910, 11 1/2 In. 4125.00
Bowl, Lime, Gray, Wheel Carved Thorn Leaf, Cameo, 1910, 4 In. 4950.00
Bowl, Maple Leafage & Buds, Gilt, Signed, c.1910, 8 In. 2200.00
Bowl, Open Work, Clear, 15 3/4 In. 275.00
Bowl, Poppy Blossoms, Gilding At Base, Signed, 5 In. 3850.00
Bowl, Red Flowers & Leaves, Amethyst & Yellow Ground, 7 3/4 In. 1250.00
Bowl, Red Flowers, Green Leaves, Inside Design, Fuchsia, 8 In. 3300.00
Bowl, Transparent Peach, Swirl Handles, Oval, Signed, 4 1/2 In. 110.00
Bowl, Violet Blossoms, Buds, White & Lavender, c.1910, 5 1/2 In. 3025.00
Bowl, Yellow, Etched, Conical, Cross Of Lorraine, 6 In. 880.00
Box, Cover, Mottled, Violet Enamel Design, Signed, 4 x 6 In. 6600.00
Box, Lid, Leaves, Butterfly, Silver Gilt Mount, Signed, 2 1/4 In. 1100.00
Box, Poppy Blossoms On Lid, Enameled Blossoms, Signed, 3 1/2 In. 3520.00
Compote, Cameo, Gray, Yellow, Red, Canoe Shape Lip, 8 1/4 In. 6650.00
Creamer, Berries, Leaves, Mottled Gold, Frosted Ground, 3 1/8 In. 1650.00
Creamer, Enameled Black Scene, Gold Trimmed Top, 2 7/8 In. 995.00
Creamer, Scenic, Pine Trees, Mountain, Green, Signed, 2 3/4 In. 1395.00
Decanter, Cameo, Clear To Emerald, Enameled, Stopper, 9 3/8 In. 8800.00
Decanter, Fleur–De–Lis, Rigaree On Sides, Signed, 12 In. 225.00
Dish, Pate–De–Cristal, Martele Surface, Green To Orange, 4 In. 950.00
Ewer, Thistle Blossoms, Enameled, Gray Glass, c.1900, 3 1/8 In. 2200.00
Ewer, Wine, Hinged Ormolu Lid, Cameo Cut Flowers, 10 1/2 In. 695.00
Figurine, Baby Bird, 2 3/4 x 3 In. 75.00
Goblet, Family Crests, Etched, Enameled, Ribbed Stem, 4 1/4 In. 4950.00
Lamp, 2–Light, Floral Shades, Iron Stem, Signed, c.1910, 19 In. 4400.00
Lamp, Cameo, Maple Leaves, Bullet Form Shade, 1910, 15 In. 9900.00
Lamp, Domical Shade, Foliage, Metal Mounts, c.1925, 17 1/2 In. 7700.00
Lamp, Domical Shade, Iron Support, Signed, c.1920, 19 1/2 In. 2750.00
Liquor Set, Etched Gilt Thistle, Green, Marked, 7 Piece 1100.00
Perfume Bottle, Scenic 2600.00
Pitcher, Leaf Design, 11 In. 750.00
Plate, 4 Seasons, Pate–De–Verre, 4 Piece 495.00
Powder Shaker, Lily–of–The–Valley Blossoms, c.1910, 6 1/2 In. 1485.00
Rose Bowl, Cut Flowers & Leaves, Gold Tracery, 5 1/4 In. 1850.00
Rose Bowl, Summer Scene, Oblong 7000.00
Rose Bowl, Winter Scene 2700.00
Salt, Etched Surface, Land & Seascape, Blue, Signed, 1 1/2 In. 410.00
Salt, Oval, Gondola In Venice Harbor, 2 In. 225.00
Shot Glass, Gold Flowers, Green 495.00
Tumbler, Barrel Shape, Pink, Cream Mottling, 4 3/4 In. 135.00
Vase, 10 Blackbirds, Black Trees, Egg Shape, 2 In. 4250.00
Vase, 10–Sided Rim, Zigzags & Circles, Signed, c.1925, 12 3/8 In. 8250.00
Vase, Anemone Blossoms, Trumpet Neck, Signed, 4 7/8 In. 1650.00
Vase, Art Deco, Frosted & Textured Panels, Marked, 13 In. 1650.00
Vase, Autumnal Landscape Scene, Birch Trees, Signed, 6 1/2 In. 1430.00
Vase, Aventurine, Majorelle Iron Mount, Signed, 11 In. 2640.00
Vase, Bellflowers, Buds & Leaves, Signed, c.1925, 12 In. 4950.00
Vase, Berried Branches, Green Walls, Signed, c.1910, 6 1/4 In. 3850.00
Vase, Boy In Dutch Landscape, Windmills, Signed, 8 In. 7150.00
Vase, Breton Seascape, Boats, Ovoid, Signed, c.1910, 12 In. 2475.00
Vase, Brown Trees, Sailboats, Mottled Ground, Signed, 6 In. 1400.00
Vase, Chevron Design, Azure Blue, Slender Baluster, 15 3/4 In. 1100.00
Vase, Clear, Air Inclusions, Mottled Gray Base, Oviform 5090.00
Vase, Country Scene, Gray Mottled, Signed, 5 5/8 In. 3100.00
Vase, Cut Pendant Fruiting Peach Branches, Signed, 15 In. 2750.00
Vase, Daisies & Leafage, Enameled, Signed, c.1910, 3 3/8 In. 990.00
Vase, Deep Gray, Baluster Form, Marked, 15 1/2 In. 1320.00
Vase, Diamond Shape, Black Over Gray, Blue, Scenic, 4 1/4 In. 715.00
Vase, Diamond Shape, Cameo, Wildflowers, Gilt Enamel, 7 1/4 In. 1100.00

Vase, Emerald Green On Salmon, 10 In.	4000.00
Vase, Enameled Berries With Leaves, Sanded Pedestal, 5 1/8 In.	2600.00
Vase, Enameled Florals Over Gold, Signed, 4 1/2 In.	305.00
Vase, Enameled Flowers, Etched, Baluster, Bulbous Foot, 14 In.	2860.00
Vase, Enameled Snow At Bottom, Green & Brown Trees, 8 In.	2200.00
Vase, Enameled Sprays Of Lilies, Signed, c.1910, 9 7/8 In.	5775.00
Vase, Enameled Sprays Of Trillium, Signed, c.1910, 16 7/8 In.	3850.00
Vase, Enameled Thistles, Cylindrical, Signed, c.1910, 4 1/2 In.	900.00
Vase, Enameled Winter Landscape, Yellow, Orange, Cylindrical	3328.00
Vase, Etched Poppy Blossoms, Double Overlaid, Signed, 11 1/8 In.	8250.00
Vase, Foliage, Double Overlay, Etched, Lavender, Blue, 12 3/4 In.	8800.00
Vase, Forest Of Fir Trees, Signed, 12 1/4 In.	5500.00
Vase, Forest Scene, Summer Colors, Cameo, Signed, 5 1/4 In.	1210.00
Vase, Fruiting Chestnut Branches, Signed, c.1910, 15 3/8 In.	2750.00
Vase, Gilt Enameled Daisies, Raspberry, Cameo, 13 3/4 In.	935.00
Vase, Gold Highlighted Anemones, Amethyst, Flattened, 5 3/4 In.	565.00
Vase, Grapes & Leaves, Spatter Ground, Signed, 13 3/8 In.	2500.00
Vase, Gray, Purple, Mottled Green, Wisteria, Cameo, Handles, 5 In.	9350.00
Vase, Green Jonquils, Blue Martele Ground, Cameo, 8 In.	4300.00
Vase, Hammered Finish, Roses, Pink To White, Signed, 5 3/4 In.	4125.00
Vase, Hydrangea Blossoms, Mauve Lug Handles, Flared, Cameo	4699.00
Vase, Hydrangea, Dragonflies, Enameled, Etched, 25 In.	7700.00
Vase, Internal Design, Flaring Rim, Mottled, Signed, 1910, 11 In.	1650.00
Vase, Jack–In–The–Pulpit, Gray, Lime, Yellow, White, Cameo, 3 In.	3300.00
Vase, Landscape, Ovoid, Cut & Enameled, c.1915, 4 5/8 In.	2750.00
Vase, Landscape, Pumpkin & Tangerine, Cameo, 1910, 8 1/8 In.	2200.00
Vase, Landscape, Trees Reflected In Lake, 13 1/2 In.	4250.00
Vase, Large Poppy On Front, Smaller On Back, 14 1/2 In.	7500.00
Vase, Leafy Trees, River, Streaked, Signed, c.1910, 13 1/4 In.	1650.00
Vase, Lily–of–The–Valley, Cameo, Oviform, Martele Ground, 6 In.	660.00
Vase, Lozenge Shape, Yellow, Clear Cut With Poppies, Gilt, 7 In.	750.00
Vase, Magnolia Blossoms, Buds, Leaves, Signed, 1910, 18 3/8 In.	6600.00
Vase, Mottled Blue, Green, Purple, Triangular, Long Neck, 24 In.	825.00
Vase, Mottled Orange, Majorelle Iron Mount, Signed, 14 3/4 In.	2860.00
Vase, Mottled Yellow, Pillow Shape, Signed, 4 1/2 x 7 In.	725.00
Vase, Mountain Landscape, Gray, Yellow, Cameo, 1915, 18 In.	6600.00
Vase, Orange & Green Layers, Berries, Branches, Signed, 6 1/2 In.	6600.00
Vase, Orange Poppies, Mauve Ground, Signed, 8 3/4 In.	4630.00
Vase, Orchids, Gray Mottled, Lemon, Ochre, Cameo, 1910, 19 3/8 In.	3850.00
Vase, Pale Yellow, Ribs Under Squares, Conical, Footed, 4 1/2 In.	1045.00
Vase, Peacock, Gray, Blue, Purple, Feather Design, 1910, 6 In.	3850.00
Vase, Peacock, Gray, Blue, Purple, Green, Cameo, 1910, 5 3/4 In.	3850.00
Vase, Peacock, Spherical, Gray Mottled, Blue, Purple, Cameo, 6 In.	3850.00
Vase, Pendant Berries, Yellow, Ochre & Salmon, Cameo, 1910, 18 In.	8250.00
Vase, Pendant Branches, Berries, Signed, 8 1/2 In.	4400.00
Vase, Pendant Fuchsia Blossoms, Ovoid, Signed, c.1910, 4 In., Pair	2750.00
Vase, Pillow, Interior Flecks Of Gold, Orange, Daisies, 3 1/8 In.	1600.00
Vase, Pine Trees, Mountains, Yellow Base, 15 1/8 In.	3250.00
Vase, Pink Flecks, Etched Vertical Ribbed, Baluster, 13 In.	1650.00
Vase, Pink Flowers, Plants, Slender Baluster Form, Cameo	6653.00
Vase, Poppies & Leaves, Yellow Ground, Signed, 5 1/4 In.	3850.00
Vase, Poppy Blossoms, Buds, Leaves, Signed, c.1910, 3 5/8 In.	2860.00
Vase, Rainstorm & Blown Trees, Signed, 2 1/4 In.	1540.00
Vase, Red Striations, Black Band, Signed, 9 3/8 In.	5500.00
Vase, River Landscape, Island, Signed, c.1910, 11 7/8 In.	1210.00
Vase, River Landscape, Signed, c.1915, 8 7/8 In.	4950.00
Vase, River, Sailboats, Trees, Ovoid, Signed, c.1910, 4 5/8 In.	1100.00
Vase, Rolled Rim, Leaves, Foil–Backed Acorns, Signed, 5 1/2 In.	4620.00
Vase, Sloping Walls, River Landscape, Signed, 18 3/4 In.	6600.00
Vase, Sprays Of Berried Branches, Clear Sides, c.1910, 4 5/8 In.	880.00
Vase, Sprays Of Bleeding Hearts, Signed, c.1910, 3 3/8 In.	2200.00
Vase, Spring Scene, Signed, 8 1/2 In.	550.00
Vase, Square Petal Blossoms, Gray–Blue, Spherical, 5 5/8 In.	825.00

Vase, Stylized Bellflowers, Berries, Signed, c.1925, 9 In. 1540.00
Vase, Stylized Dragons, Flowers, Baluster, Etched, 12 1/4 In. 4180.00
Vase, Stylized Leafage & Geometrics, Signed, c.1925, 15 5/8 In. 6325.00
Vase, Sweet Pea Blossoms, Leafage, Beaker Form, Signed, 4 3/8 In. 1540.00
Vase, Textured Surface, Gold Thistle Borders, 10 1/2 In. 4125.00
Vase, Trillium Blossoms, Ochre Enamel, Signed, c.1915, 19 3/4 In. 5775.00
Vase, Trumpet Form, Leaves, Green, Gilt Mount, Cameo, 13 3/4 In. 330.00
Vase, Trumpet, Day Lilies, Emerald, Purple, Cameo, 1910, 7 7/8 In. 9900.00
Vase, Trumpet, Leaves & Buds, Poppy Blossoms, Signed, 9 1/2 In. ...,................... 7150.00
Vase, Tulip Blossoms, Etched Walls, Signed, c.1922, 9 1/2 In. 6050.00
Vase, Undulating Anemone Blossoms, Signed, c.1910, 13 5/8 In. 5500.00
Vase, Vaseline, Purple Flowering Cyclamen, Globular, Cameo 5874.00
Vase, Water & Tree Scenes, Signed, 6 In. 1200.00
Vase, Wheel–Cut Gloxinia, Burgundy Overlay, Signed, 6 1/2 In. 2800.00
Vase, White Mottled, Painted Wooded Landscape, Flared, Footed 3524.00
Vase, Wild Grapes, Vines, Cameo, Trumpet, Knobbed Base, 11 1/2 In. 2420.00
Vase, Wild Mushrooms, Landscape, Rim Ears, Signed, 6 1/2 In. 9020.00
Vase, Winter Forest Landscape At Dawn, Signed, 1910, 13 1/8 In. 7700.00
Vase, Winter Scene, 3 In. 1400.00
Vase, Winter Scene, Enameled, Orange & Clear, Swollen Square 3326.00
Vase, Winter Scene, Oval, Signed, 4 3/4 In. 4200.00
Vase, Winter Scene, Signed, 5 In. .... 2495.00 To 2595.00
Vase, Wooded Landscape, Tall Trees, c.1910, 8 3/8 In. 3850.00
Wine, Etched Thistle Blossoms, Gold Rim, 5 1/2 In., 6 Piece 1525.00

DAVENPORT pottery and porcelain were made at the Davenport factory
in Longport, Staffordshire, England, from 1793 to 1887. Earthenwares,
creamwares, porcelains, ironstone, and other ceramics were made. Most of
the pieces are marked with a form of the word *Davenport*.

DAVENPORT
LONGPORT
STAFFORDSHRE

Bowl, Romantic Scene Center, Green, Marked, 12 In. 225.00
Condiment Set, Imari Colors, Silver Plate Holder 135.00
Cooler, Fruit, Twig Handle, Cherry & Pear Sprigs, 12 In., Pair 1325.00
Cup Plate, Bronze Figure Of Woman In Garden 125.00
Plate, Blue Molded Shell Rim, Blue Transfer Of Turkey, 7 1/4 In. 625.00
Plate, Fishing Scene, Blue, 10 In. 40.00
Toby Jug, Woman, Drunken Sal, Blue Dress, 13 In. 1800.00
Vase, Shield Shape, Fruit Cluster, Loop Handles, 6 11/16 In., Pair 885.00

DAVY CROCKETT, the American frontiersman, was born in 1786 and died
in 1836. He became popular in 1954 with the introduction of a television
series about his life. Coonskin caps and buckskins became popular and
hundreds of different Davy Crockett items were made.

Bank, Dime Register, Davy Crockett, Tin ....30.00 To 100.00
Bedspread, Chenille, Davy Fights The Bear 195.00
Belt, Buckle 69.00
Book, Golden Book, 1955 .... 10.00
Box, Toy, Fess Parker As Davy, Vinyl, 1950s 135.00
Button, Indian Scout, Yellow, Red, 1 3/4 In. 7.00
Cap, Raccoon 40.00
Chair, Child's 75.00
Clock, Animated 325.00
Clock, Pendulette, Box .... 150.00 To 250.00
Compass 25.00
Cookie Jar, American Bisque 195.00
Cookie Jar, Beige, Brown Gun, Brush 245.00
Cookie Jar, Beige, White Gun, Brush 170.00
Display, 3 Flashlights, U.S. Electric Mfg. Co., N.Y., Chicago 250.00
Doll, Cloth, Stuffed, Molded Plastic Face, 29 In. 175.00
Flying Arrows, 1955 .... 18.00
Game, Fess Parker Indian Scouting, Board, Walt Disney, Box 95.00
Game, Lariat, 1950s 15.00
Game, Rubber Darts, 2 Hand Held Tin Targets, Box 65.00
Game, Target, All American, Box 95.00

De Morgan, Jar, Iridescent, 11 3/4 In.

Jacket & Cap, Coonskin, Vinyl, Fringed	55.00
Jackknife, 1950s	40.00
Jailer's Keys & Handcuffs	45.00
Lamp, Original Shade	195.00
Lunch Box, Davy Crockett At Alamo, Thermos	195.00 To 250.00
Marionette	185.00
Marionette, With Mug, Box	75.00
Mug, Red	26.00
Mug, Rockingham	25.00
Mug, White	9.00
Neckerchief, Leather Slide	30.00
Neckerchief, Red & White	4.00
Pair Of Socks, Going To Congress, Brown & Pink	25.00
Pencil Case, Fess & Davy On Lid	25.00
Play Set, 24 Pieces	30.00
Play Set, Alamo, Marx	295.00
Puzzles, 3 Different, 1950s	85.00
Rifle, Dart, Wyandotte, Box, 1953	100.00
Rocking Horse, Davy Crockett, Rich	110.00
Shirt, Brown Fringe	18.00
Soap, Davy, Indian & Gun Shape, Box, 3 Piece	85.00
Target Box, Frontier, Metal, Darts With Feathers, 12 x 15 In.	150.00
Toby Jug, Davy As Child, Porcelain, Rifle Handle	75.00
Tool Kit, Tin, Fess Parker, Walt Disney, Box	95.00
Toy, Stagecoach & 2 Horses, Tin, Marx	120.00
Tumbler, Juice	15.00
Wallet, Plastic, Davy Image, 3 1/2 x 4 In.	35.00
Wristwatch, Box	100.00 To 187.00

DE MORGAN art pottery was made in England by William De Morgan from the 1860s to 1907. He is best known for his luster-glazed Moorish-inspired pieces. The pottery used a variety of marks.

Bowl, Red Luster, Eagle Attacking Lizard, Scroll Border, 1890	1100.00
Jar, Iridescent, 11 3/4 In. ....*Illus*	4250.00
Panel, 3 Tile, Hellenistic Sailing Vessel, Bird, 6 1/4 In.	1395.00
Tile, Leafy Branches, Stylized Birds, Red Luster, 9 Squares, 6 In.	1285.00
Vase, Cover, 3 Bands Of Birds & Beasts, Signed, 13 In.	4695.00

DE VEZ was a signature used on cameo glass after 1910. E. S. Monot founded the glass company near Paris in 1851. The company changed names many times. Mt. Joye, another glass by this factory, is listed in its own section.

Lamp, Cows On Hillside, Mountains, Village, Shade, 16 In.	8000.00
Perfume Bottle, Pink & Black, Signed, 9 1/2 In.	400.00
Vase, Cameo, Swans, Lake, Flowering Trees, Bulbous, 12 In.	1650.00
Vase, Girl Standing On Rocky Peak, Goat At Side, 7 3/4 In.	5100.00
Vase, Mountain Lake Landscape, Gray, Blue, Green, 8 In.	1435.00

Vase, Mountain Lake, Forest, Blue On Frosted White, Signed, 6 1/2 In. 1450.00
Vase, Mountain Landscape, Foreground Trees, Signed, c.1925, 15 In. 1320.00
Vase, Scene, Classical Shape, Deep Green, Red Over Amber, 17 1/2 In. 3750.00
Vase, Scenic, Mosque & Palms, 6 3/8 In. 1200.00
Vase, Valley, Mountains Rising In Distance, Signed, c.1920, 8 5/8 In. 995.00
Vase, Winter Landscape, Cabins, Trees, Signed, c.1920, 7 1/4 In. 395.00
Vase, Woodland & Moose, 5 7/8 In. 850.00

DECOYS are carved or turned wooden copies of birds or fish. The decoy
was placed in the water or propped on the shore to lure flying birds to the
pond for hunters. Some decoys are handmade, some are commercial
products. Today there is a group of artists making modern decoys for
display, not for use in a pond.

Black Duck, Elmer Crowell 990.00
Black Duck, Turned Head, Carved Wings & Feathers, 17 1/2 In. 45.00
Black Duck, Working Repaint, Tack Eyes, Marked Oster, 17 In. 75.00
Blackbellied Plover, Crowell, c.1890 .... 6600.00
Bluebill Drake, Capt. Harry R. Jobes, Original Paint, 14 1/2 In. 40.00
Bluebill Drake, Carved Detail, Original Paint, 13 3/4 In. 225.00
Bluebill Drake, Dave Hodgman, Old Paint, Glass Eyes, 14 1/2 In. 55.00
Bluebill Drake, Glass Eyes, Hollow Body, Mason 250.00
Bluebill Drake, Original Paint, Glass Eyes, 12 In. 30.00
Bluebill Drake, Wood, Wire & Canvas, 11 In. 25.00
Bluebill, Bobtail, Glass Eyes, 14 In. 85.00
Bluebill, Drake, One Glass Eye, One Tack Eye, 14 3/4 In. 45.00
Bluebill, Ken Anger, Hallow–Carved, Pair 2090.00
Bluebill, Ward, c.1919 .... 4125.00
Bluewinged Teal Hen, Robert Elliston, Hollow Carved, 1880s 6050.00
Bluewinged Teal, Original Paint, Glass Eyes, 11 In. 175.00
Bufflehead Hen, Mason 595.00
California Pintail, Original 110.00
California Wood Duck, Standing 100.00
Canada Goose, Cork Body, Wooden Head, Glass Eyes, 23 In. 90.00
Canada Goose, Hollow, Long Beach Island, N. J., 21 3/4 In. 255.00
Canada Goose, Levi Rhodes Truex, Hollow–Carved, c.1925 .... 5500.00
Canada Goose, Mark Kears, Hollow Carved 3300.00
Canada Goose, Original Paint, Glass Eyes, 20 3/4 In. 85.00
Canada Goose, Original Paint, Signed, 7 1/2 In. 105.00
Canada Goose, Primitive, Working Repaint, Glass Eyes, 20 In. 100.00
Canada Goose, Taylor Johnson, Hollow Carved 3850.00
Canvasback Drake, Cork, Wood, Original Paint, Glass Eyes, 16 In. 135.00
Canvasback Drake, Currituck Sound 120.00
Canvasback Drake, Dave Hodgman, Repainted, Glass Eyes, 15 In. 65.00
Canvasback Drake, Tack Eyes, 16 3/4 In. 70.00
Canvasback Drake, Turned Head, Glass Eyes, 17 In. 20.00
Canvasback Drake, W. E. Beck, Yellowed Varnish, Glass Eyes, 18 1/2 In. 350.00
Canvasback Drake, Working Repaint, Glass Eyes, 13 In. 55.00
Canvasback Duck, Mason's Decoy Factory, Glass Eyes, 16 In., Pair 230.00
Canvasback Hen, Bobtail, Glass Eyes, Old Paint, 14 3/4 In. 45.00
Canvasback Hen, Glass Eyes, Repaint, 15 3/4 In. 40.00
Curlew, Thomas Gelston 7700.00
Decoy, Bluebill Duck, Hollow Carved, Robert Elliston, 1880s 5280.00
Dove, Masons 440.00
Dowitcher, John Haff 5500.00
Duck, Oscar Peterson, 4 In. 275.00
Durlew, Carved & Painted, Thomas Gilston, 12 1/2 In. 775.00
Egret, Crowell, Maine 9350.00
Fish, Bass, 7 In. 2475.00
Fish, Bat Wing, Heddon 550.00
Fish, Brook Trout, Tin Fins, Lead Weighted, 5 In. 215.00
Fish, Brown Trout, Oscar Peterson 1100.00
Fish, Muskie, Wooden, Tin Fins, Leather Tail, Paint, Line, Weight, 11 In. 175.00
Fish, Northern Pike, Oscar Peterson, Chip–Carved, 9 In. 660.00

Fish, Pike, Wood & Tin, Leather Tail, Polychrome Paint, 10 1/2 In.	185.00
Fish, Pike, Wood, Polychrome Paint, Metal Eyes, Teeth, 19 In.	165.00
Fish, Primitive, Wood, Tin, Bead Eyes, Polychrome, 11 1/4 In.	65.00
Fish, Speckled Fish	70.00
Fish, Sucker, Bud Stewart	908.00
Fish, Wood, Metal, Old Repaint, 14 1/4 In.	85.00
Goldeneye, Original Paint, Glass Eyes, 13 In.	100.00
Goose, Folding, Johnson, Carrying Bag	203.50
Goose, Wildfowler, c.1937	675.00
Loon Drake, Surf Scoter	125.00
Mallard Drake, Factory Carved, Old Paint, Glass Eyes, 16 3/4 In.	105.00
Mallard Drake, Glass Eyes, 18 In.	65.00
Mallard Drake, Glass Eyes, Elliston Decoy, 17 x 6 1/2 In.	145.00
Mallard Drake, Mason, Glass Eyes, Painted, 16 1/4 In.	95.00 To 150.00
Mallard Drake, Relief Carved, Glass Eyes, Benj. Schmidt, 15 1/4 In.	165.00
Mallard Hen, Chesapeake Bay, Maryland, Original Paint, 16 1/4 In.	55.00
Mallard Hen, Mason, 16 1/4 In.	95.00
Mallard Hen, Original Paint, Mason, 16 In.	105.00
Mallard Hen, Stick–Up, Field, Wood & Cork Body, 17 1/2 In.	100.00
Mallard, Bert Graves, 1920s	715.00
Mallard, Henry Holmes	250.00
Mallard, Surf Scoter	125.00
Merganser Hen, Schmiedlin, Turned Head, Glass Eyes, Hollow, 1986, Large	350.00
Quail, Nesting, Crowell, Miniature, Pair	1100.00
Rabbit, Baby, Tack Eyes, Wooden	175.00
Redhead Drake, Ben Schmidt, Glass Eyes, 14 1/2 In.	70.00
Redhead Drake, Glass Eyes, 13 1/4 In.	115.00
Redhead Drake, Original Paint, Glass Eyes, Mason, 14 In.	150.00
Sheldrake, Henry Holmes	150.00
Shore Bird, Cobb Island, Painted, 1920s, 11 5/8 In.	445.00
Speckled Belly Goose, John Tax, Hollow Carved, Stick–Up	7700.00
Swan, Hollow Carved, St. Clair Flats	8800.00
Swan, Painted & Carved, Metal Tack Eyes, 27 In.	412.50
Swan, Signed Capt. Jess Urie, Maryland, Original Paint, 6 3/4 In.	40.00
Widgeon Hen, Stephen Verity, Hollow Carved	4675.00
Yellowlegs, Alligatored Paint, Glass Eyes, 10 1/2 In.	225.00

DEDHAM Pottery was started in 1895. Chelsea Keramic Art Works was established in 1872 in Chelsea, Massachusetts, by members of the Robertson family. The firm used the mark *CKAW*. The factory closed in 1889 and was reorganized as the Chelsea Pottery U.S. in 1891. It became the Dedham Pottery of Dedham, Massachusetts. The factory closed in 1943. It was famous for its crackleware dishes, which picture blue outlines of animals, flowers, and other natural motifs.

Bowl, Rabbit, 6 In., Pair	600.00
Plate, Blue Duck Border, 8 1/2 In.	345.00
Plate, Crabs, 10 In.	935.00

Dedham, Plate, White Dolphins, Cat Faces
Between, Clover, 10 In.

◆◆◆◆◆◆◆◆◆◆◆◆◆◆◆◆◆◆◆◆◆

When stacking dinner plates, put a piece of felt or paper between each plate. Never put more than 24 in one stack.

◆◆◆◆◆◆◆◆◆◆◆◆◆◆◆◆◆◆◆◆◆

Plate, Crackleware, Blue Water Lilies Border, Marked, 8 1/2 In. 195.00
Plate, Dolphin Border, Scalloped Edge, 8 3/4 In., Pair 1540.00
Plate, Ducks, 8 1/2 In. 365.00
Plate, Lobster, 8 In. 880.00
Plate, Rabbits, 6 1/4 In. 80.00
Plate, Rabbits, 8 1/2 In. 325.00
Plate, Turkey, Stamped, Early 20th Century, 10 In. 242.00
Plate, White Dolphins, Cat Faces Between, Clover, 10 In. ....*Illus* 2420.00
Plate, White Rabbits Around Rim, 7 1/2 In. 260.00
Plate, White Rabbits Around Rim, 8 1/2 In. 295.00
Salt & Pepper, Rabbit, 3 1/2 In. 450.00
Salt, Walnut Shape, On Leaf, Pair 1400.00
Stand, Tea, Rabbit, Stamped, Early 20th Century, 6 In. 165.00
Teapot, Rabbit 445.00
Vase, Blooming Iris Bed, Squat, Hugh C. Robertson, Signed, 7 1/4 In. ... 2100.00
Vase, Blue Jar Resting On Branch, Marked, 1931, 8 In. 1100.00
Vase, Japanese Style Fan & Floral Patterns, Marked, 10 1/8 In. 1650.00
Vase, Pillow, 2 Lion Faces, Lion Handles, Flattened Ovoid, 12 1/2 In. .. 470.00
Vase, Pillow, Blue Glaze, Loop Handles, Marked, 13 1/4 In. 165.00
Vase, Red, Turquoise & Green Running Volcanic Glaze, CKAW, 5 In. 3100.00
Vase, Short Neck, Swollen Cylindrical Form, Semi–Gloss, 10 1/2 In. 275.00

DEGENHART is the name used by collectors for the products of the
Crystal Art Glass Company of Cambridge, Ohio. John and Elizabeth
Degenhart started the glassworks in 1947. Quality paperweights and other
glass objects were made. John died in 1964 and his wife took over
management and production ideas. Over 145 colors of glass were made. In
1978, after the death of Mrs. Degenhart, the molds were sold. The D in a
heart trademark was removed, so collectors can easily recognize the true
Degenhart piece.

Ashtray, Hand, Amethyst, Marked 75.00
Dish, Robin, Berry In Beak, Amberina 65.00
Dish, Turkey On Nest, Tan, Brown & White Slag, 5 1/2 In. 75.00
Dish, Turkey, Basketweave Base, Lemon, Custard Glass 75.00
Figurine, Owl, Marked 300.00
Figurine, Pooch, Jade Green 20.00
Figurine, Priscilla, Pink Colonial Woman, Marked 100.00
Plate, Face, Red 25.00

DEGUE is a signature found acid–etched on pieces of French glass made in
the early 1900s. Cameo, mold blown, and smooth glass with contrasting
colored rims are the types most often found.

Lamp, Egyptian Desert Scene, Metal Mount, Signed, 14 1/2 In. 3300.00
Lamp, Trees In Foreground, Scrolling Iron Mounts, c.1925, 27 In. 8250.00
Vase, Allover Floral, Mottled Orange & Red, Signed, 8 1/4 In. 165.00
Vase, Art Deco, Signed, 17 In. 1275.00
Vase, Blossoms Over Undulating Leaves, Signed, c.1925, 23 In. 1545.00
Vase, Blue To Purple, Blossoms, Pink, Signed, 13 In. 995.00
Vase, Dahlia Blossoms, Leaves, Signed, c.1925, 18 1/8 In. 1435.00
Vase, Flaring Rim & Base, Geometric Pattern, Signed, c.1925, 11 In. 1100.00
Vase, Grape Clusters, Leaves, Signed, c.1925, 18 5/8 In. 1100.00
Vase, Olive Green Overlay, Tropical Leaves, Signed, c.1925, 18 3/4 In. .. 935.00
Vase, Poppy Blossoms & Leafage, Gray, Signed, c.1925, 7 In. 550.00
Vase, Triangular Design, Pale Green, Ovoid, Signed, 7 7/8 In. 825.00
Vase, Upright Poppy Blossoms, Leaves, Signed, c.1925, 16 3/4 In. 1650.00
Vase, Upright Poppy Blossoms, Signed, c.1925, 23 1/4 In. 2420.00

DELATTE glass is a French cameo glass made by Andre Delatte. It was
first made in Nancy, France, in 1921. Lighting fixtures and opaque
glassware in imitation of Bohemian opaline were made. There were many
French cameo glass makers, so be sure to look in other appropriate
sections.

Lamp, Woodland Landscape Shade, 3–Armed Standard, c.1925, 14 In. 2750.00

Delft, Tile, Flower, Blue & White, 18th Century, 5 In.

Vase, Green, White Ground, Magenta, Berried Bush, Signed, 7 In.	385.00
Vase, Orange & Blue Cased, Engraved, 8 In.	70.00
Vase, Orange, With Silver Foil, Iron Vertical Ribs, 12 1/8 In.	1100.00
Vase, Rooster, Wheel Cut, Violet, Spatter, 7 1/2 In.	4500.00

DELDARE, see Buffalo Pottery Deldare

DELFT is a tin-glazed pottery that has been made since the seventeenth century. It is decorated with blue on white or with colored decorations. Most of the pieces sold today were made after 1891, and the name *Holland* appears with the Delft factory marks. The word *delft* also appears on pottery from other countries.

Ashtray, With Shoes, Blue	30.00
Bidet, Blue Flowers	195.00
Bowl, Barber's, Bristol, Blue, c.1760, 10 7/16 In.	4400.00
Bowl, Fluted, c.1720, 11 1/2 In.	4950.00
Bowl, Foliate Rim, Chinese Style Design, Blue & White, 14 In.	357.50
Bowl, Piecrust Rim, Bristlington, 1710, 10 1/8 In.	9350.00
Box, Mehl	110.00
Box, Salz	200.00
Canister, Tea, Porcelain, Oval, Germany, 6 1/2 x 5 1/2 In.	35.00
Charger, Blue & White, 13 3/4 In.	250.00
Charger, Blue & White, 14 In.	205.00
Charger, Floral, 13 3/4 In.	350.00
Charger, Floral, Blue & White, 12 1/4 In.	200.00
Charger, Oak Leaf, Lambeth, 1710, 13 7/8 In.	3300.00
Charger, Polychrome, 13 1/2 In.	450.00
Charger, Tulip, 1670, 13 3/8 In.	3300.00
Dish, Cherry Picker Facing Tree, Chamfered, Deep, 1755-1765, 14 In.	1325.00
Dish, Herring, Beaded Roundels Rim, c.1770, 8 3/4 In.	1325.00
Dish, Queen Mary, Between Tulips, 1690-1695, 8 3/4 In.	990.00
Dish, Woman, Picking Cherries Scene, Chamfered, 14 1/16 In., Pair	660.00
Funnel, Blue & White, 1910	75.00
Garniture, Peacock Pattern, Blue, White, 18th Century, 5 Piece	3575.00
Jar, Cover, Blue & White, 14 In.	145.00
Jar, Drug, S. Caryophil, Surrounded By Fruits, c.1700, 8 1/4 In.	770.00
Picture, 9 Tiles, Horse Turning Cogwheel, Craftsman, Frame, 15 In.	990.00
Pitcher, Cow, Mouth Pour	20.00
Plate, Blue & White Floral, 9 1/4 In., Pair	250.00
Plate, Blue & White, Floral Design, 11 7/8 In.	160.00
Plate, Figure In Landscape, Blue & White, 8 7/8 In., Pair	300.00
Plate, Floral, Blue & White, 8 7/8 In.	150.00
Plate, Peacock, Standing On Blue Plateau, Bristol, 1740, 7 15/16 In.	1430.00
Plate, Vase Of Flowers, 8 3/4 In.	400.00
Plate, William III & Queen Mary Portrait, London, 1690, 8 7/16 In.	4125.00
Shoe, Windmill, Florals, 7 In.	95.00
Table, Marked, Miniature, 1 3/4 In.	70.00

Tile, Flower, Blue & White, 18th Century, 5 In. ....*Illus*		18.00
Tile, Sailor		75.00
Tile, Viking Ship, Multicolored, Square, 4 1/2 In.		75.00
Vase, Dutch Woman Carrying Basket, Dragon Handles, 6 In.		245.00
Vase, Floral, Landscape In Reserve, 6 1/2 In.		175.00
Vase, Tulip, Double Gourd, Exotic Birds, DeGrieksche, 11 1/2 In.		6050.00

DENTAL cabinets, chairs, equipment, and other related items are listed here. Other objects may be found in the Medical category.

Cabinet & Desk, Tombour Top, 7 Drawers, Mirrored Top, c.1890	5000.00
Cabinet Pulls, Brass & Crystal, 5 Large & 18 Smaller Size	75.00
Cabinet, 1870, Oak	6000.00
Cabinet, Glass Doors On Top, Metal	650.00
Cabinet, Lined Drawers, Marble Base, 3 Upper Doors, Walnut, 62 In.	2000.00
Cabinet, Oak, Mirror Door & Gallery, Drawers	900.00
Cabinet, Queen Ann Legs, African Mahogany, 1940s	600.00
Cabinet, Victorian, Walnut, Mirror, 2 Marble Shelves	880.00
Case, Tooth Sample, Bakelite, 1930s, Small	40.00
Chair, Copper, Leather, Wood & Brass	5200.00
Extractors, For Various Positions, c.1810, 14 Piece	100.00
Forceps, Samuel S. White, Leather Wrap, 1880s, 8 Piece	200.00
Hone, Wooden Box	10.00
Key, Tooth	135.00
Sterilizer, Toothbrush, Listerine	35.00
Teeth, Model For Filling, Bone	45.00

DENVER is part of the mark on an American art pottery. William Long of Steubenville, Ohio, founded the Lonhuda Pottery Company in 1892. In 1900 he moved to Denver, Colorado, and organized the Denver China and Pottery Company. This pottery, which used the mark *Denver,* worked until 1905 when Long moved to New Jersey and founded the Clifton Pottery. Long also worked for Weller Pottery, Roseville Pottery, and American Encaustic Tiling Company.

DENVER
C T &
P T Co

Vase, Trees, Blue, 8 In.	485.00

DEPRESSION GLASS was an inexpensive glass manufactured in large quantities during the 1920s and early 1930s. It was made in many colors and patterns by dozens of factories in the United States. The name *Depression glass* is a modern one. For more descriptions, history, pictures, and prices of Depression glass, see the book *Kovels' Depression Glass & American Dinnerware Price List.*

Adam, Butter, Cover, Pink	65.00
Adam, Cake Plate, Pink	15.00
Adam, Candy Jar, Cover, Pink	65.00
Adam, Pitcher, Pink	32.00
Adam, Plate, Green, 7 3/4 In.	7.00
Adam, Saltshaker, Pink	16.00
American Sweetheart, Bowl, Pink, 6 In.	6.00
American Sweetheart, Bowl, Pink, 9 In.	15.00
American Sweetheart, Cake Stand, Crystal, 10 In.	22.50
American Sweetheart, Cocktail Shaker, Monax	87.50
American Sweetheart, Cup & Saucer, Monax .... 7.50 To 9.50
American Sweetheart, Plate, Monax, 8 In. .... 7.00 To 8.50
American Sweetheart, Plate, Monax, 9 3/4 In.	16.50
American Sweetheart, Plate, Pink, 6 In., 7 Piece	12.00
American Sweetheart, Plate, Pink, 10 1/4 In.	16.00
American Sweetheart, Platter, Pink, Oval, 13 In.	22.00
American Sweetheart, Salver, Pink, 12 In.	12.00
American Sweetheart, Salver, Red, 12 In.	90.00
American Sweetheart, Sugar & Creamer, Pink	14.50
American Sweetheart, Tumbler, Pink, 4 3/4 In.	175.00
Anniversary, Compote, Pink	5.00
Anniversary, Goblet, Wine, Crystal, 2 1/2 In.	3.50

Depression glass, American
Sweetheart

Depression glass, Bubble

Depression glass, Cameo

Anniversary, Sugar & Creamer, Iridescent 12.50
Anniversary, Vase, Crystal, 6 1/2 In. 5.00
Anniversary, Vase, Pin–Up, Pink 20.00
Apple Blossom pattern is listed here as Dogwood
Aunt Polly, Sherbet, Blue .... 7.00 To 7.50
Aurora, Bowl, Cobalt Blue, 5 3/8 In., 6 Piece 30.00
Aurora, Bowl, Pink, 5 3/8 In. 3.00
Aurora, Plate, Cobalt Blue, 6 3/8 In. 2.50
Avocado, Cake Plate, Handles, Green 35.00
Ballerina pattern is listed here as Cameo
Banded Rib pattern is listed here as Coronation
Banded Rings pattern is listed here as Ring
Baroque, Jelly, Cover, Blue, 7 1/2 In. 80.00
Baroque, Relish, 3 Sections, Yellow .... 22.00 To 25.00
Baroque, Sugar & Creamer, Blue 30.00
Bee Hive, Butter, Cover, Crystal 20.00
Block pattern is listed here as Block Optic
Block Optic, Bowl, Green, 4 1/4 In. 5.00
Block Optic, Bowl, Green, 5 1/4 In. 8.00
Block Optic, Creamer, Cone Shape, Green 7.00
Block Optic, Cup & Saucer, Green 10.00
Block Optic, Cup, Green 3.50
Block Optic, Ice Bucket, Green 22.00
Block Optic, Plate, Green, 6 In. 1.25
Block Optic, Plate, Green, 8 In. .... 3.00 To 5.00
Block Optic, Plate, Green, 9 In. 12.25
Block Optic, Plate, Pink, 6 In. 1.00
Block Optic, Salt & Pepper, Green 25.00
Block Optic, Saucer, Cup Ring, Green 7.00
Block Optic, Saucer, Green 4.00
Block Optic, Sherbet, Green, 3 1/4 In. 3.25
Block Optic, Sherbet, Green, 4 3/4 In. 9.00
Block Optic, Sugar & Creamer, Green 20.00
Block Optic, Sugar, Green 8.50
Block Optic, Tumble–Up, Green 45.00
Bouquet & Lattice pattern is listed here as Normandie
Bowknot, Bowl, Green, 5 1/2 In. 15.00
Bowknot, Plate, Green, 8 1/2 In. 3.75
Bubble, Bowl, Blue, 4 1/2 In. .... 4.50 To 9.00
Bubble, Bowl, Blue, 5 1/4 In. 6.00
Bubble, Candlestick, Crystal 3.00

Bubble, Creamer, Blue 14.00
Bubble, Cup & Saucer, Blue 3.50
Bubble, Cup & Saucer, Crystal 2.00
Bubble, Cup & Saucer, Green 2.50
Bubble, Cup, Blue .... 3.00 To 4.00
Bubble, Grill Plate, Blue 7.00
Bubble, Plate, Blue, 6 3/4 In. 2.00
Bubble, Plate, Blue, 9 3/8 In. .... 4.50 To 5.00
Bubble, Saucer, Blue 1.50
Bubble, Soup, Dish, Blue ....7.00 To 10.00
Bubble, Sugar & Creamer, Blue 17.50
Bullseye pattern is listed here as Bubble
Butterflies & Roses pattern is listed here as Flower Garden with Butterflies
Buttons & Bows pattern is listed here as Holiday
By Cracky, Pitcher, Crystal 13.00
By Cracky, Sherbet, Flared, Crystal 1.50
Cabbage Rose pattern is listed here as Sharon
Cameo, Butter, Cover, Green 225.00
Cameo, Candlestick, Green, Pair ....95.00 To 125.00
Cameo, Candy Dish, Green, 4 In. .... 25.00 To 45.00
Cameo, Cookie Jar, Green .... 22.00 To 37.50
Cameo, Cup, Green 8.00
Cameo, Cup, Yellow .... 6.00 To 6.50
Cameo, Goblet, Green, 6 In. 41.00
Cameo, Grill Plate, Yellow .... 6.00 To 8.00
Cameo, Pitcher, Green, 6 In. 40.00
Cameo, Pitcher, Water, Green 40.00
Cameo, Plate, Green, 8 In. 6.00
Cameo, Plate, Green, 9 1/2 In. 5.50
Cameo, Plate, Pink, 9 1/2 In. 50.00
Cameo, Plate, Yellow, 9 1/2 In. 7.00
Cameo, Relish, 3 Sections, Pink 18.00
Cameo, Salt & Pepper, Green ....60.00 To 110.00
Cameo, Sherbet, Green, 3 1/8 In. 9.00
Cameo, Sherbet, Green, 4 7/8 In. 25.00
Cameo, Sugar & Creamer, Green, 3 1/4 In. 32.50
Cameo, Sugar & Creamer, Green, 4 1/4 In. 38.50
Cameo, Tumbler, Green, 3 3/4 In. 20.00
Candlewick, Bowl, Heart Shape, Handle, Crystal, 9 In. 95.00
Candlewick, Candy Dish, Cover, 3 Sections, Crystal 45.00
Candlewick, Cup & Saucer, Crystal 15.00
Candlewick, Plate, Crystal, 7 In. 10.00
Candlewick, Plate, Crystal, 10 In. 28.00
Candlewick, Sugar & Creamer, Crystal 10.00
Candlewick, Tumbler, Crystal, 7 Oz. 25.00
Candlewick, Vase, Flared, Footed, Crystal, 6 In. 40.00
Caprice pattern is included in the Cambridge Glass category
Cherry Blossom, Bowl, Pink, 5 3/4 In. 20.00
Cherry Blossom, Butter, Cover, Green 65.00
Cherry Blossom, Cake Plate, Pink .... 13.00 To 15.00
Cherry Blossom, Child's Set, Pink, 14 Piece .... 240.00 To 285.00
Cherry Blossom, Creamer, Pink 13.00
Cherry Blossom, Cup & Saucer, Delphite 10.00
Cherry Blossom, Sugar & Creamer, Cover, Pink 36.00
Cherry Blossom, Sugar & Creamer, Pink 20.00
Cherry Blossom, Tumbler, Green, 4 1/4 In. .... 14.00 To 17.50
Circle, Cup, Green 2.00
Circle, Plate, Green, 6 In. 1.00
Cloverleaf, Cup & Saucer, Black 12.00
Cloverleaf, Cup, Green .... 4.50 To 5.50
Cloverleaf, Saltshaker, Green 12.00
Cloverleaf, Saucer, Green 1.75
Cloverleaf, Sugar & Creamer, Black 20.00

Cloverleaf, Sugar, Cover, Green 6.00
Colonial, Bowl, Green, 9 In. 19.00
Colonial, Butter, Cover, Crystal 32.00
Colonial, Grill Plate, Green 18.50
Colonial, Grill Plate, Pink 12.50
Colonial, Tumbler, Pink, 5 1/8 In. 30.00
Columbia, Bowl, Crystal, 5 In. 11.50
Coronation, Berry Bowl, Ruby Red, 8 In. 10.00
Cremax, Salver, Cream, 11 In. 4.75
Cube pattern is listed here as Cubist
Cubist, Creamer, Pink, 3 1/2 In. 3.00
Cubist, Plate, Pink, 8 In. 20.00
Cubist, Saucer, Crystal 1.00
Cubist, Sherbet, Pink 3.50
Cubist, Sugar & Creamer, Cover, Green 25.00
Cubist, Sugar & Creamer, Pink 3.00
Cubist, Tumbler, Pink, 4 In. 25.00
Cubist, Water Set, Green, 7 Piece 135.00
Daisy pattern is listed here as No. 620
Dancing Girl pattern is listed here as Cameo
Diamond Pattern is listed here as Miss America
Diamond Quilted, Sugar, Cover, Blue 10.00
Dogwood, Cup & Saucer, Pink 16.00
Dogwood, Cup, Pink .... 7.00 To 8.50
Dogwood, Grill Plate, Green 16.50
Dogwood, Pitcher, Pink 135.00
Dogwood, Plate, Pink, 6 In. 3.00
Doric & Pansy, Cup & Saucer, Ultramarine 17.00
Doric, Salt & Pepper, Pink 22.50
Doric, Saltshaker, Green 12.00
Double Shield pattern is listed here as Mt. Pleasant
Dutch Rose pattern is listed here as Rosemary
Early American Rock Crystal pattern is listed here as Rock Crystal
English Hobnail, Bowl, Crystal, 6 In. 6.00
English Hobnail, Jam Jar, Chrome Top, Pink 18.00
English Hobnail, Plate, Round, Pink, 8 In. 11.00
English Hobnail, Sherbet, Crystal 4.00
Fine Rib pattern is listed here as Homespun
Fire–King, Batter Bowl, Green 10.00
Fire–King, Casserole, Blue, 10 Oz. 10.00
Fire–King, Cookie Jar, Grape Design, Ivory 20.00
Fire–King, Custard Cup, Blue, 5 Oz. 2.00
Fire–King, Mixing Bowl Set, Blue, 5 Piece 25.00
Fire–King, Mixing Bowl, Blue, 10 1/8 In. 18.00
Fire–King, Mug, Similac Advertising 8.99
Fire–King, Platter, Green 8.00
Flat Diamond pattern is listed here as Diamond Quilted

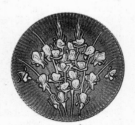

Depression glass,
Cubist

Depression glass,
Florentine No. 2

Depression glass, Iris,
Beaded Edge

Floragold, Bowl, Blue, 5 1/2 In. 3.00
Floragold, Bowl, Ruffled, Crystal, 9 1/2 In. 6.00
Floragold, Bowl, Ruffled, Iridescent, 5 1/2 In. 3.50
Floragold, Bowl, Ruffled, Iridescent, 9 1/2 In. 5.00
Floragold, Bowl, Square, Crystal, 4 1/2 In. 4.50
Floragold, Bowl, Square, Iridescent, 4 1/2 In. 3.50
Floragold, Bowl, Square, Iridescent, 8 1/2 In. 9.50
Floragold, Candy Dish, Footed, Iridescent, 5 1/4 In. 4.00
Floragold, Cup & Saucer, Iridescent .... 11.00 To 12.50
Floragold, Cup, Iridescent .... 3.50 To 5.00
Floragold, Salt & Pepper, Iridescent, Plastic Top 33.00
Floragold, Sugar, Cover, Iridescent 10.50
Floragold, Sugar, Iridescent 4.00
Floragold, Tray, Iridescent, 13 1/2 In. .... 10.00 To 17.50
Floragold, Tumbler, Footed, Pink, 10 Oz. 15.00
Floral, Cup, Crystal, Platinum Trim 20.00
Floral, Salt & Pepper, Footed, Pink 28.00
Floral, Sugar, Cover, Green 21.50
Floral, Tumbler, Footed, Green, 4 In. 16.00
Floral, Vase, 8 Sides, Green 550.00
Florentine No. 1, Bowl, Green, 5 In. 7.00
Florentine No. 1, Cup & Saucer, Pink 10.50
Florentine No. 1, Cup & Saucer, Yellow 11.00
Florentine No. 1, Saltshaker, Green 20.00
Florentine No. 1, Sherbet, Green 8.50
Florentine No. 1, Soup, Cream, Pink 8.00
Florentine No. 1, Sugar, Cover, Green 10.00
Florentine No. 2, Ashtray, Crystal, 5 1/2 In. 15.00
Florentine No. 2, Plate, Crystal, 8 1/2 In. 3.50
Florentine No. 2, Plate, Yellow, 8 1/2 In. .... 5.00 To 7.50
Florentine No. 2, Punch Cup, Green 1.50
Florentine No. 2, Relish, 3 Sections, Crystal 16.00
Florentine No. 2, Salt & Pepper, Yellow 45.00
Florentine No. 2, Sugar, Yellow 7.00
Flower Garden With Butterflies, Ashtray, Blue 150.00
Flower Garden With Butterflies, Bowl, Black, 7 1/4 In. 225.00
Forest Green, Ashtray, Square, Green, 3 In. 1.00
Forest Green, Ashtray, Square, Green, 6 In. 1.50
Forest Green, Bowl, Green, 5 1/4 In. 10.00
Forest Green, Cup, Green, ... 1.50
Forest Green, Punch Set, Green, Box, 14 Piece 20.00
Forest Green, Saucer, Square, Green .... .75
Forest Green, Sugar & Creamer, Green 17.50
Forest Green, Tumbler, Green, 3 1/2 In. 1.00
Forest Green, Vase, Green, 6 3/8 In. 1.50
Fortune, Cup, Pink 3.00
Fortune, Saucer, Pink 2.00
Fortune, Tumbler, Pink, 4 In. .... 5.00 To 6.00
Fruits, Cup & Saucer, Green 6.00
Fruits, Saucer, Green 1.00
Georgian, Berry Bowl, Green 7.00
Georgian, Creamer, Green 10.00
Georgian, Cup & Saucer, Green 11.00
Georgian, Cup, Green 7.50
Georgian, Plate, Green, 6 In. 1.50
Georgian, Plate, Green, 8 In. .... 3.00 To 5.50
Georgian, Powder Jar, Crystal 22.00
Georgian, Sugar, Green .... 6.00 To 13.00
Harp, Cake Plate, Blue .... 20.00 To 22.00
Harp, Cake Plate, Crystal .... 14.00 To 16.50
Harp, Cake Plate, Pink 22.00
Harp, Coaster, Crystal, 10 Piece 3.50
Heritage, Cup & Saucer 6.00

Depression glass,
Madrid

Depression glass,
Mayfair Open Rose

Hex Optic pattern is listed here as Hexagon Optic
Hexagon Optic, Pitcher, Green, 9 In. 35.00
Hobnail, Plate, Pink, 6 In. 1.00
Hobnail, Sherbet, Pink 1.50
Hobnail, Tumbler, Footed, Crystal, 4 In. 18.00
Holiday, Butter, Cover, Pink 18.00
Holiday, Cake Plate, Pink 98.00
Holiday, Console, Pink, 10 In. 100.00
Holiday, Creamer, Pink 5.00
Holiday, Cup, Pink 4.00
Holiday, Pitcher, Pink, 4 3/4 In. 35.00
Holiday, Sandwich Server, Pink 8.50
Holiday, Sugar, Pink 5.00
Holiday, Tumbler, Pink, 4 In. 20.00
Homespun, Sugar, Cover, Pink .... 5.50 To 6.00
Homespun, Tumbler, Footed, Crystal, 4 In. 6.00
Homespun, Tumbler, Pink, 4 In. 4.00
Honeycomb pattern is listed here as Hexagon Optic
Horizontal Ribbed pattern is listed here as Manhattan
Horseshoe pattern is listed here as No. 612
Iris & Herringbone pattern is listed here as Iris
Iris, Bowl, Crystal, 9 1/2 In. .... 8.00 To 8.50
Iris, Bowl, Crystal, 11 1/2 In. 8.50
Iris, Bowl, Iridescent, 11 1/2 In. 6.00
Iris, Candlestick, Crystal, Pair .... 20.00 To 30.00
Iris, Candy Jar, Cover, Crystal 95.00
Iris, Creamer, Crystal .... 8.00 To 10.00
Iris, Cup & Saucer, Crystal 20.00
Iris, Goblet, Water, Crystal, 5 3/4 In. 16.00
Iris, Pitcher, Crystal 30.00
Iris, Sandwich Server, Iridescent, 11 3/4 In. 18.00
Iris, Sauce, Crystal, 5 In. 8.00
Iris, Sherbet, Crystal, 2 1/2 In. 12.00
Iris, Sherbet, Iridescent, 2 1/2 In. 6.50
Iris, Sugar & Creamer, Cover, Crystal 30.00
Iris, Sugar, Cover, Crystal 17.00
Iris, Sugar, Crystal 5.00
Iris, Tumbler, Crystal, 4 In. 100.00
Iris, Tumbler, Iridescent, 6 In. 14.00
Iris, Vase, Crystal, 9 In. 12.00
Iris, Vase, Iridescent, 9 In. .... 10.00 To 22.00
Iris, Water Set, Footed Tumblers, Crystal, 7 Piece 135.00
Jadite, Ashtray 8.00
Jadite, Batter Jug 275.00
Jadite, Bowl Set, Nested 25.00
Jadite, Canister, Tea, Square, Screw On Lid 60.00
Jadite, Condiment Set, Salt & Pepper, 5 Piece 85.00

Jadite, Dispenser, Water, 8 Piece 200.00
Jadite, Measuring Cup, 2 Cup 45.00
Jadite, Measuring Set, 4 Piece 50.00
Jadite, Pitcher, Water, Tilted 45.00
Jadite, Salt & Pepper, Range, Square 14.00
Jadite, Spice Set, Child's, Cover, 4 Piece 190.00
Jadite, Tumbler, Footed 14.00
Jane–Ray, Creamer, Jadite 1.00
Jane–Ray, Cup, Jadite 1.00
Jane–Ray, Plate, Jadite, 7 In. .... .75
Jane–Ray, Plate, Jadite, 9 In. 1.00
Jane–Ray, Plate, Jadite, 10 In. 2.00
Jane–Ray, Saucer, Jadite .... .75
Jane–Ray, Sugar, Cover, Jadite 2.00
June, Pitcher, Azure 525.00
Knife & Fork pattern is listed here as Colonial
Lace Edge, Bowl, Pink, 5 1/2 In. 12.50
Lace Edge, Butter, Pink 55.00
Lace Edge, Cookie Jar, Cover, Pink 45.00
Lace Edge, Ice Bucket, Green 15.00
Lace Edge, Mayonnaise, Blue 105.00
Lace Edge, Relish, 3 Sections, Green 10.00
Lace Edge, Salt & Pepper, Green 35.00
Lace Edge, Tumbler, Footed, Pink, 5 In. 52.50
Lace Edge, Tumbler, Pink, 4 1/2 In. 15.00
Laurel, Berry Bowl, Jade, 5 In. 3.00
Laurel, Bowl, Ivory, 11 In. 25.00
Laurel, Cheese Dish, Cover, Jade 45.00
Laurel, Creamer, Jade 5.00
Lincoln Inn, Finger Bowl, Red 15.00
Line 412 pattern is listed here as Peacock Reverse
Lorain pattern is listed here as No. 615
Lorna pattern is included in the Cambridge Glass category
Louisa pattern is listed here as Floragold
Lovebirds pattern is listed here as Georgian
Madrid, Creamer, Blue 14.00
Madrid, Cup, Amber 5.00
Madrid, Cup, Green 4.50
Madrid, Pitcher, Ice Lip, Amber, 8 1/2 In. 45.00
Madrid, Plate, Amber, 9 In. 7.00
Madrid, Salt & Pepper, Amber 40.00
Madrid, Sugar, Cover, Green 18.00
Madrid, Tumbler, Amber, 5 1/2 In. 12.00
Madrid, Tumbler, Footed, Green, 5 1/2 In. 37.50
Manhattan, Berry Bowl, Crystal, 5 1/2 In. 9.50
Manhattan, Bottle, Water, Crystal 6.50
Manhattan, Bowl, Crystal, 5 1/2 In. 15.00
Manhattan, Butter, Cover, Crystal 19.00
Manhattan, Candy Dish, 3–Footed, Pink 7.50
Manhattan, Compote, Footed, Crystal 13.00
Manhattan, Compote, Pink 12.00
Manhattan, Cookie Jar, Crystal 30.00
Manhattan, Cup & Saucer, Crystal .... 14.00 To 19.00
Manhattan, Pitcher, Pink, 6 3/4 In. 15.00
Manhattan, Plate, Pink, 6 In. 2.50
Manhattan, Relish, 4 Sections, Crystal, 14 In. 12.50
Manhattan, Saucer, Crystal 2.75
Manhattan, Sherbet, Pink 7.50
Manhattan, Sugar & Creamer, Pink 6.50
Manhattan, Sugar, Cover, Pink 5.00
Manhattan, Tumbler, Pink 12.00
Many Windows pattern is listed here as Roulette

Depression glass,

Miss America

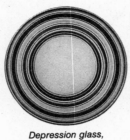

Depression glass,

Moderntone

Depression glass,

Mt. Pleasant

Martha Washington pattern is included in the Cambridge Glass category

Mayfair Open Rose, Bowl, Cover, Blue, 10 In.	85.00
Mayfair Open Rose, Bowl, Oval, Pink, 9 1/2 In.	18.00
Mayfair Open Rose, Cake Plate, Blue	45.00
Mayfair Open Rose, Cake Plate, Pink, 12 In.	21.00
Mayfair Open Rose, Celery, Divided, Blue, 10 In.	27.00
Mayfair Open Rose, Cookie Jar, Blue	150.00
Mayfair Open Rose, Cookie Jar, Pink	37.00
Mayfair Open Rose, Creamer, Pink	15.00
Mayfair Open Rose, Cup, Blue	32.00
Mayfair Open Rose, Decanter, Stopper, Pink	130.00
Mayfair Open Rose, Pitcher, Pink, 6 In.	40.00
Mayfair Open Rose, Plate, Blue, 8 1/2 In.	30.00
Mayfair Open Rose, Plate, Yellow, 9 1/2 In.	220.00
Mayfair Open Rose, Relish, 2 Sections, Blue	65.00
Mayfair Open Rose, Sandwich Server, Green	18.00 To 25.00
Mayfair Open Rose, Saucer, Blue	10.00
Mayfair Open Rose, Soup, Cream, Pink	25.00
Mayfair Open Rose, Sugar, Pink	17.00
Mayflower, Salt & Pepper, Crystal	75.00
Midnight Rose, Relish, 2 Sections, Crystal	25.00
Midnight Rose, Tumbler, Iced Tea, Crystal	24.00
Miss America, Compote, Crystal	7.00 To 10.00
Miss America, Creamer, Footed, Crystal	6.00
Miss America, Cup & Saucer, Crystal	9.00
Miss America, Grill Plate, Pink	23.00
Miss America, Plate, Crystal, 8 1/2 In.	5.00
Miss America, Plate, Crystal, 10 1/4 In.	10.00
Miss America, Plate, Pink, 8 1/2 In.	19.00
Miss America, Platter, Oval, Pink, 2 1/4 In.	10.00
Miss America, Relish, 4 Sections, Crystal	5.00 To 10.00
Miss America, Relish, 4 Sections, Pink	13.25
Miss America, Relish, Divided, Crystal, 11 3/4 In.	15.00
Miss America, Saucer, Pink	5.00
Miss America, Sherbet, Pink	13.00
Moderntone Little Hostess, Service For 6, Pastel, 26 Pc.	300.00
Moderntone Little Hostess, Tea Set, Pastel, 16 Piece	130.00
Moderntone Little Hostess, Teapot, Pastel	130.00
Moderntone, Ashtray, Blue	210.00
Moderntone, Creamer, Cobalt Blue	7.00
Moderntone, Cup & Saucer, Cobalt Blue	11.00
Moderntone, Mixing Bowl, Flared Rim, Amber, 8 3/4 In.	7.50
Moderntone, Mixing Bowl, Flared Rim, Amber, 9 1/2 In.	9.00
Moderntone, Plate, Cobalt Blue, 5 In.	4.00
Moderntone, Plate, Cobalt Blue, 10 1/2 In.	40.00
Moderntone, Salt & Pepper, Cobalt Blue	20.00
Moderntone, Sandwich Server, Cobalt Blue	35.00

Moderntone, Saucer, Cobalt Blue 1.25
Moderntone, Sherbet, Cobalt Blue 7.00
Moderntone, Sugar & Creamer, Cobalt Blue .... 15.00 To 18.50
Moderntone, Sugar, Cobalt Blue 4.00
Moondrops, Bowl, 3–Footed, Ruby, 8 In. 43.00
Moondrops, Butter, Cover, Ruby 385.00
Moondrops, Cup & Saucer, Amber 24.00
Moondrops, Cup & Saucer, Ruby 8.00
Moondrops, Shot Glass, Handle, Ruby 13.00
Moondrops, Sugar & Creamer, Ruby 30.00
Moonstone, Bowl, Cloverleaf, Crystal 7.00
Moonstone, Bowl, Crimped, Crystal, 5 1/2 In. 6.00
Moonstone, Bowl, Crimped, Crystal, 9 1/2 In. 8.00
Moonstone, Candleholder, Crystal 5.00
Moonstone, Candy Dish, Crystal 12.00
Moonstone, Creamer, Crystal 5.00
Moonstone, Cup, Green 4.50
Moonstone, Powder Box, Cover, Round, Crystal, 4 3/4 In. 14.00
Moonstone, Relish, 3 Sections, Crystal .... 6.50 To 7.00
Moonstone, Sherbet, Crystal 6.00
Moonstone, Sugar, Footed, Crystal 5.00
Mt. Vernon pattern is included in the Cambridge Glass category
Mt. Pleasant, Bowl, Footed, Black, 7 In. 37.50
Mt. Pleasant, Creamer, Black 15.00
Mt. Pleasant, Plate, Square, Black, 8 In. 8.00
Mt. Pleasant, Saucer, Black 6.00
Mt. Pleasant, Sherbet, Black 7.50
New Century, Pitcher, Ice Lip, Green, 80 Oz. 27.00
New Century, Plate, Crystal, 6 In. 2.50
New Century, Plate, Crystal, 10 In. 8.00
New Century, Tumbler, Green, 5 1/4 In. 10.00
No. 601 pattern is listed here as Avocado
No. 612, Creamer, Green 15.00
No. 612, Cup & Saucer, Crystal 9.50
No. 612, Sandwich Server, Green, 11 In. 9.50
No. 612, Saucer, Green 4.00
No. 612, Sugar & Creamer, Yellow 28.00
No. 612, Sugar, Green 11.00
No. 615, Sugar & Creamer, Yellow, 4 In. 30.00
No. 620, Grill Plate, Crystal 8.00
No. 620, Plate, Amber, 8 3/8 In. 4.00
No. 620, Plate, Amber, 9 3/8 In. 6.00
No. 620, Platter, Amber 10.00
No. 620, Sherbet, Amber 6.00
No. 620, Sugar & Creamer, Amber 11.00
No. 622 pattern is listed here as Pretzel
Normandie, Berry Bowl, Amber, 5 In. 3.00
Normandie, Berry Bowl, Pink, 5 In. .... 4.00 To 5.00
Normandie, Cup, Pink 7.00
Normandie, Grill Plate, Iridescent 6.00
Normandie, Plate, Pink, 7 3/4 In. 3.00
Normandie, Platter, Iridescent 20.00
Normandie, Saucer, Pink 2.00
Normandie, Sherbet, Pink 4.00
Normandie, Sugar & Creamer, Amber 12.00
Old Cafe, Candy Dish, Cover, Pink 3.50
Old Cafe, Pitcher, Crystal, 80 Oz. 65.00
Old Colony pattern is listed here as Lace Edge
Old Florentine pattern is listed here as Florentine No. 1
Open Lace pattern is listed here as Lace Edge
Open Rose pattern is listed here as Mayfair Open Rose
Optic Design pattern is listed here as Raindrops
Oyster & Pearl, Bowl, Pink, 5 In. 22.00

Depression glass, No. 612

To clean the brasses on your furniture without damaging the wood, try this trick. Cut a semicircle from the edge of a 3 x 5 filing card. Put the card under the brass while you are polishing. It protects the wood.

Patrician, Berry Bowl, Green, 5 In. 8.00
Patrician, Butter, Cover, Amber .... 30.00 To 73.00
Patrician, Butter, Cover, Green 6.00
Patrician, Cup & Saucer, Green 12.00
Patrician, Pitcher, Amber, 8 1/4 In. 100.00
Patrician, Plate, Amber, 9 In. 9.00
Patrician, Plate, Amber, 10 1/2 In. 6.50
Patrician, Plate, Amber, 11 1/2 In. 6.00
Patrician, Plate, Crystal, 9 In. 5.00
Patrician, Plate, Green, 10 1/2 In. 4.00
Patrician, Salt & Pepper, Amber 45.00
Patrician, Saltshaker, Amber 24.00
Patrician, Saucer, Green 5.00
Patrician, Sherbet, Green 5.00
Patrician, Sugar & Creamer, Cover, Amber 17.50
Peacock Reverse, Server, Center Handle, Crystal 40.00
Pear Optic, Cup & Saucer, Green 5.00
Petal Swirl pattern is listed here as Swirl
Petalware, Plate, Cremax, 10 1/2 In. 5.00
Petalware, Plate, Crystal, 8 In. 1.00
Petalware, Plate, Monax, 8 In. 1.50
Petalware, Salver, Monax, 11 In. 9.00
Petalware, Sugar, Cover, Monax 2.50
Poinsettia pattern is listed here as Floral
Poppy No. 1 pattern is listed here as Florentine No. 1
Poppy No. 2 pattern is listed here as Florentine No. 2
Pretty Polly Party Dishes, see also the related pattern Doric & Pansy
Pretty Polly Party Dishes, Set, Ultramarine, 14 Piece 250.00
Pretzel, Plate, Crystal, 11 1/2 In. 5.00
Princess, Butter, Cover, Green 65.00
Princess, Cake Plate, Green 17.00

Depression glass, Normandie

Depression glass, Princess

Depression glass, Royal Lace

Princess, Cup, Topaz .... 4.00 To 7.00
Princess, Grill Plate, Closed Handles, Yellow, 10 3/8 In. 12.00
Princess, Pitcher, Pink, 6 In. .... 30.00 To 65.00
Princess, Plate, Green, 8 In. 6.75
Princess, Plate, Green, 9 1/2 In. .... 17.00 To 17.50
Princess, Plate, Yellow, 9 1/2 In. 18.00
Princess, Sherbet, Footed, Pink 11.00
Princess, Snack Set, Pink, Box, 18 Piece 185.00
Princess, Sugar & Creamer, Yellow 25.00
Princess, Tumbler, Green, 5 1/4 In. 25.00
Prismatic Line pattern is listed here as Queen Mary
Provincial pattern is listed here as Bubble
Queen Mary, Bowl, Pink, 4 1/2 In. 3.75
Queen Mary, Candy Dish, Pink 40.00
Queen Mary, Platter, Pink, 10 In. 18.00
Queen Mary, Sugar, Crystal 3.00
Radiance, Cordial, Red 25.00
Raindrops, Creamer, Green .... 3.50 To 3.75
Raindrops, Tumbler, Crystal, 3 In. 1.00
Ribbon, Sherbet, Green 3.00
Ring, Creamer, Green 3.50
Ring, Cup & Saucer, Green 4.50
Ring, Cup Plate, Green 3.00
Ring, Plate, Crystal, 11 3/4 In. 12.50
Ring, Plate, Green, 8 In. 2.25
Rock Crystal, Bowl, Crystal, 11 1/2 In. 8.50
Rock Crystal, Candelabrum, 2–Light, Crystal, Pr. .... 31.00 To 33.00
Rock Crystal, Plate, Crystal, 8 1/2 In. 7.50
Rock Crystal, Relish, 6 Sections, Crystal, 14 In. 25.00
Rock Crystal, Sherbet, Red 15.00
Rock Crystal, Tumbler, Crystal, 9 Oz. 14.00
Rock Crystal, Wine, Red, 2 Oz. 37.00
Rock Crystal, Wine, Red, 3 Oz. 40.00
Rosalie, Cup, Pink 15.00
Rose Cameo, Sherbet, Green 5.50
Rose Cameo, Tumbler, Footed, Green .... 9.00 To 12.00
Rosemary, Plate, Amber, 9 1/2 In. 5.50
Rosemary, Saucer, Amber 16.00
Rosemary, Tumbler, Amber 14.00
Roulette, Plate, Green, 12 In. 6.00
Royal Lace, Berry Bowl, Blue, 10 In. 58.00
Royal Lace, Berry Bowl, Round, Crystal, 10 In. 25.00
Royal Lace, Bowl, Rolled Edge, Blue, 10 In. 85.00
Royal Lace, Bowl, Straight Edge, 3–Footed, Pink, 10 In. 20.00
Royal Lace, Butter, Cover, Crystal 60.00
Royal Lace, Cookie Jar, Cover, Pink 45.00
Royal Lace, Cookie Jar, Green 47.00
Royal Lace, Creamer, Blue 25.00
Royal Lace, Cup & Saucer, Blue 25.00
Royal Lace, Plate, Blue, 8 1/2 In. 20.00
Royal Lace, Plate, Blue, 9 7/8 In. 45.00
Royal Lace, Plate, Crystal, 10 In. 5.00
Royal Lace, Platter, Oval, Crystal, 13 In. 15.00
Royal Lace, Salt & Pepper, Green 85.00
Royal Lace, Sherbet, Metal Holder, Blue 26.00
Royal Lace, Sugar, Cover, Green 45.00
Royal Lace, Tumbler, Pink, 4 1/8 In. 13.00
Royal Ruby, Ashtray, Red, 4 1/2 In. 1.50
Royal Ruby, Cup & Saucer, Red .... 5.00 To 7.50
Royal Ruby, Cup & Saucer, Square, Red 4.25
Royal Ruby, Cup, Red .... 2.00 To 2.75
Royal Ruby, Pitcher, Prism Base, Red 15.00
Royal Ruby, Plate, Red, 9 1/4 In. 3.50

Depression glass, Sharon   *Depression glass, Swirl*   *Depression glass, Windsor*

Royal Ruby, Plate, Red, 10 In.	7.00
Royal Ruby, Punch Cup, Red	1.25
Royal Ruby, Sugar & Creamer, Cover, Red	25.00
Royal Ruby, Tumbler, 2 In.	1.00
Royal Ruby, Tumbler, 3 In.	3.00
Royal Ruby, Tumbler, Footed, Red, 3 In.	5.00
Royal Ruby, Vase, Ball, Red, 4 In.	2.50
Royal Ruby, Vase, Red, 9 In.	9.00
Royal Ruby, Water Set, Red, 6 Piece	45.00
Sail Boat pattern is listed here as Sportsman Series	
Sandwich, Sherbet, Crystal	20.00
Saxon pattern is listed here as Coronation	
Sharon, Bowl, Amber, 8 1/2 In.	4.00 To 4.50
Sharon, Bowl, Green, 6 In.	14.00
Sharon, Bowl, Oval, Pink, 9 1/2 In.	18.00
Sharon, Butter, Cover, Pink	37.50
Sharon, Cake Plate, Pink	30.00
Sharon, Creamer, Pink	15.00
Sharon, Cup & Saucer, Pink	19.00
Sharon, Cup, Amber	5.00
Sharon, Plate, Amber, 9 1/2 In.	7.50
Sharon, Plate, Pink, 6 In.	5.00
Sharon, Plate, Pink, 9 1/2 In.	10.00
Sharon, Saucer, Amber	2.00
Sharon, Sherbet, Footed, Pink	12.00
Sharon, Soup, Dish, Pink	27.00
Sharon, Sugar, Cover, Green	23.00
Sharon, Sugar, Cover, Pink	25.00 To 30.00
Sharon, Tumbler, Pink, 5 1/4 In.	30.00
Spiral, Sherbet, Green	3.00
Spoke pattern is listed here as Patrician	
Sportsman Series, Pitcher, Water, Ship, Cobalt Blue	70.00
Springtime, Torte Plate, Crystal, 14 In.	35.00
Strawberry, Pitcher, Pink	100.00
Sunflower, Ashtray, Green	7.00
Sunflower, Ashtray, Pink	5.00
Sunflower, Cake Plate, Pink	7.50 To 18.00
Sunflower, Cup, Green	7.00
Sunflower, Plate, Green, 9 In.	9.00
Swirl, Bowl, Blue, 9 In.	17.50
Swirl, Bowl, Ultramarine, 5 1/4 In.	6.00
Swirl, Bowl, Ultramarine, 9 In.	20.00
Swirl, Bowl, Ultramarine, 10 In.	22.00
Swirl, Cup, Blue	6.00
Swirl, Plate, Green, 4 In.	5.00
Swirl, Sugar & Creamer, Ultramarine	27.00
Swirl, Vase, Footed, Ultramarine, 8 1/2 In.	14.00

Tea Room, Bowl, Banana Split, Green 100.00
Tea Room, Sugar & Creamer, Amber 175.00
Tea Room, Sugar & Creamer, Pink 40.00
Tea Room, Vase, Ruffled, Crystal, 9 1/2 In. 9.00
Thistle, Cup, Pink 15.00
Thistle, Saucer, Pink 7.50
Trojan, Creamer, Rose 27.00
Trojan, Plate, Rose, 6 In. 6.00
Twisted Optic, Plate, Green, 6 In. 1.25
Versailles, Chop Plate, Blue, 13 1/2 In. 125.00
Versailles, Pitcher, Blue 475.00
Vertical Ribbed pattern is listed here as Queen Mary
Vesper, Plate, Amber, 8 1/2 In. 9.50
Waffle pattern is listed here as Waterford
Waterford, Salt & Pepper, Crystal .... 5.00 To 5.75
Waterford, Sandwich Server, Crystal .... 3.75 To 5.00
White Ship pattern is listed here as Sportsman Series
Wild Rose pattern is listed here as Dogwood
Windsor Diamond pattern is listed here as Windsor
Windsor, Butter, Cover, Crystal 18.00
Windsor, Butter, Cover, Pink .... 20.00 To 35.00
Windsor, Cake Plate, Footed, Green, 10 3/4 In. 9.00
Windsor, Chop Plate, Pink .... 20.00 To 29.00
Windsor, Creamer, Crystal 2.00
Windsor, Cup & Saucer, Pink 11.00
Windsor, Cup, Crystal 2.00
Windsor, Pitcher, Pink, 6 1/2 In. 25.00
Windsor, Plate, Crystal, 6 In. 1.00
Windsor, Plate, Green, 9 In. 7.00
Windsor, Saucer, Crystal 1.00
Windsor, Sugar, Cover, Pink .... 9.00 To 15.00
Windsor, Tumbler, Footed, Crystal, 7 1/4 In. 7.00

DERBY has been marked on porcelain made in the city of Derby, England, since about 1748. The original Derby factory closed in 1848, but others opened there and continued to produce quality porcelain. The Crown Derby mark began appearing on Derby wares in the 1770s.

Cup & Saucer, Imari 88.00
Figurine, Man & Woman, 18th Century Costumes, 11 In., Pair 110.00
Plate, Imari, 7 1/4 In., Pair 100.00

DeVILBISS Company has made atomizers of all types since 1888 but no longer makes the perfume bottle tops so popular with collectors. These were made from 1920 to 1968. The glass bottle may be by any of many manufacturers even if the atomizer is marked *DeVilbiss.* More atomizer bottles are listed in the perfume bottle section.

Perfume Bottle, Art Deco, Orange, Black Trim 65.00
Perfume Bottle, Atomizer, Cranberry, Gold, 7 1/2 In. 150.00
Perfume Bottle, Atomizer, Silver Crackle 35.00
Perfume Bottle, Bird Finial, Glass Dauber 285.00
Perfume Bottle, Diamond Cut Pattern, Atomizer 35.00
Perfume Bottle, Lavender, Black Trim 65.00
Perfume Bottle, Rose, Gold Overlay, Signed, 6 3/4 In., Pair 77.00

DICK TRACY, the comic strip, started in 1931. Tracy was also the hero of movies from 1937 to 1947 and again in 1990, and starred in a radio series in the 1940s and a television series in the 1950s. Memorabilia from all these activities is collected.

Badge & ID Card, Crime Stoppers 40.00
Badge, Sergeant, 1938, Advertising, Premium 60.00
Book, Capture Of Boris Arson, Pop-Up, 1935 .... 90.00
Book, Popup 325.00
Bracelet, Air Detective, 2 In. 29.00

Car, Police, 6 1/2 In.	75.00
Car, Squad, Friction, Directions, 1949, 11 1/4 In.	295.00
Certificate, Secret Service Membership, 1939	10.00
Coloring Book	35.00
Comic Book, Mystery Mary X, 1959	40.00
Costume, Halloween	85.00
Crime Stopper Set, 1961	32.00
Doll, Bonnie Braids, Box	425.00
Doll, Disney Edition, 15 In.	45.00
Figurine, Gravel Gertie, Plastic, 2 1/2 In.	20.00
Flashlight, Box	25.00
Game, Board, 1961	29.00
Game, Double Target, Gun, Box, 1941	185.00
Gun, Squirt, Submachine, Plastic, Comic Characters, 1948, Box	200.00
Junior, Salt & Pepper, Yellow Overcoat, Black Overcoat, 3 In.	95.00
Knife, Pocket, Warranty Tag & Lanyard	100.00
Lighter, Gun Shape, 2 x 3 In.	35.00
Lunch Box	25.00 To 50.00
Pistol, Clicker, 1940s	45.00
Pistol, Siren, Red & Blue Paint, Decal	295.00
Poster, Dick Tracy Vs. Crime, Serial, Chapter 1	225.00
Punchboard, Bonnie Braids	48.00
Squad Car, Battery Operated, Large Letters, 10 In.	350.00
Squad Car, Battery Operated, Windup, Green, Marx, 11 In.	265.00
Squad Car, Blue, Riot Car, Friction	210.00
Squad Car, Figures, Marx, 1950, 21 In.	250.00
Squad Car, Green, Linemar, Siren, 9 In.	115.00
Stamp Set, Dick & Orphan Annie, 1938, Box	40.00
Wrist Radio, American Doll & Toy, Box	165.00
Wristwatch, New Haven, 1948, Complete	175.00

DICKENS WARE pieces are listed in the Royal Doulton and Weller sections.

DIONNE QUINTUPLETS were born in Canada on May 28, 1934. The publicity about their birth and their special status as wards of the Canadian government made them famous throughout the world. Visitors could watch the girls play; reporters interviewed the girls and the staff. Thousands of special dolls and souvenirs were made picturing the quints at different ages. Emilie died in 1954, Marie in 1970. Yvonne, Annette, and Cecile still live in Canada.

Ad, Carnation Milk, Framed	20.00
Ad, General Motors, Framed	20.00
Ad, Karo Syrup, Framed	20.00
Ad, Quints With Baby Ruth Candy Bars, Framed	10.00
Ad, Yancy Ins., Ontario Govt., 1936, 22 x 30 In.	85.00
Book, We Were Five, Hardcover	25.00
Booklet, Quintuplets Play Mother Goose, 1938	75.00
Cake Plate, Ceramic, Portrait Of Quints	150.00
Calendar, Springtime, Framed, 1942	22.50
Doll, Baby, Composition, Dress, Madame Alexander, 21 In.	350.00
Doll, Baby, Painted Hair, Madame Alexander, 11 In., 5 Pc.	1250.00
Doll, In Continuous High Chair, Alexander Set, 7 In.	995.00
Doll, Marie, Swivel Head, Dress, Madame Alexander, 17 In.	375.00
Doll, Original Clothes, Madame Alexander, 12 In., 5 Pc.	2300.00
Paper Doll, All Aboard For Shut–Eye–Town, 1937, Uncut	65.00
Paper Doll, Uncut	175.00
Perfume Bottle, Floral, Stuart, Wooden Heads, 3 x 5 In.	65.00
Print, Long Dress, Bonnet, Color, Framed, 7 x 8 3/4 In.	25.00
Soap, Box	125.00
Spoon Set, 5 Piece	98.00 To 150.00

DISNEYANA is a collector's term. Walt Disney and his company introduced many comic characters to the world. Collectors search for examples of the work of the Disney Studios and the many commercial products modeled after his characters, including Mickey Mouse, Donald Duck, and recent films, like *Beauty and the Beast* and *The Little Mermaid.*

Airplane, Mickey Mouse In Cockpit, Solid Rubber, Red	75.00 To 85.00
Album, Gum Card, Mickey Mouse, Vol. 2, 1933	90.00
Album, Little Toot, 78 RPM, 1948	15.00
Applique, Mickey Mouse, Figural, For Clothing, 1930s, 6 1/2 In.	65.00
Bag, Flour, Snow White, Master Baker Mills, Vancouver, 5 Lbs, 1930s	15.00
Balloon Pump, Mickey Mouse, Cardboard Tube	7.50
Bank, Donald Duck, Vinyl Head	35.00
Bank, Mickey Mouse, Vinyl Head	35.00
Bank, Minnie Mouse, Hands Move, Occupied Japan	32.00
Bank, Pinocchio, Large	30.00
Bank, Pinocchio, Play Pal	15.00
Bank, Pinocchio, Vinyl Head	35.0
Bank, Snow White, Dime Register	75.00
Bank, Uncle Scrooge In Bed, Pink Cover, Ceramic, Japan, 1961, 6 In.	48.00
Belt Buckle, Snow White, 50th Anniversary	150.00
Bench Seat, Folding, Mickey Mouse Club	135.00
Birthday Card, Original Envelope, 1930s	45.00
Biscuit Tin, Snow White & 7 Dwarfs, Movie Scenes, Belgium, 13 In.	320.00
Blotter, Mickey Mouse, Sunoco, 1940s	22.00
Blotter, Mickey, Donald & Others, Advertising, 3 x 6 In., 1930s	32.00
Book, Adventures Of Mickey Mouse, Book 1, McKay, Hardcover, 1931	38.00
Book, Bambi's Children, Better Little Book, Whitman, 1943	34.00
Book, Bambi, Whitman, 1942, 96 Pages	46.00
Book, Big Little Book, Desert Palace, Mickey Mouse	35.00
Book, Big Little Book, Donald Duck, Hunting For Trouble	10.00
Book, Big Little Book, Donald Duck, In Volcano Valley	20.00 To 27.50
Book, Big Little Book, Dumbo	25.00
Book, Big Little Book, Mickey Mouse, Sails For Treasure Island	45.00
Book, Big Little Book, Mickey Mouse, The Race For Riches	30.00
Book, Big Little Book, Silly Symphonies Stories	30.00
Book, Cinderella's Friends, Golden Book, 1st Printing, 1950	10.00
Book, Cinderella's Friends, Golden Book, 1st Printing, 1956	8.00
Book, Cinderella, Disney, 1950	15.00
Book, Cinderella, Golden Book, 15th Printing, 1964	3.00
Book, Cinderella, Pinocchio, Snow White, Wonder, 1975, Set Of 3	30.00
Book, Coloring, Mickey Mouse, Saalfield, 1931, 10 1/2 x 15 In.	53.00
Book, Coloring, Sword In The Stone, 1963	15.00
Book, Davy Crockett's Keelboat Race, Golden Book, 1st, 1955	12.00
Book, Davy Crockett, King Of Wild Frontier, Golden Book, 3rd, 1955	7.00
Book, Donald Duck & Ghost Morgan's Treasure, Whitman, 1946	84.00
Book, Donald Duck & His Friends, Heath, 1939	22.00
Book, Donald Duck & His Nephews, Heath, 1940	5.00
Book, Donald Duck & Santa Claus, Golden Book, 1st Printing, 1952	7.00
Book, Donald Duck & The Hidden Gold, Simon & Schuster, 1951	66.00
Book, Donald Duck & The Witch, Golden Book, 1st Printing, 1953	6.00
Book, Donald Duck Says Such Luck, Whitman, Flip, 1941	81.00
Book, Donald Duck's Adventure, Golden Book, 1st Printing, 1950	9.00
Book, Donald Duck's Sail Boat, Golden Book, 3rd Printing, 1954	7.00
Book, Donald Duck, 50 Years Of Frustration, Ltd. Ed., Signed, 1984	550.00
Book, Donald Duck, Christmas Carol, Golden Book, 1st, 1960	10.00
Book, Donald Duck, Walt Disney, Birn Bros., England, 1936	134.00
Book, Ferdinand The Bull, Whitman, 1938	10.00 To 18.00
Book, Here They Are, Heath, 1940	32.00
Book, Hiawatha, Golden Book, 1st Printing, 1953	5.00
Book, Johnny Appleseed, Golden Book, 3rd Printing, 1949	10.00
Book, Little Pig's Picnic & Other Stories, Heath, 1939	35.00
Book, Lucky Puppy, 101 Dalmatians, Golden Book, 2nd Printing, 1960	6.00

Book, Mary Poppins, Golden Book, 2nd Printing, 1964 .... 5.00
Book, Mickey Mouse & Donald Duck, Flip 8.00
Book, Mickey Mouse & His Friends, T. Nelson, New York, 1937 .... 17.00
Book, Mickey Mouse & The Pirate Submarine, Whitman, 1939 .... 38.00
Book, Mickey Mouse Alphabet, Whitman, 1936 .... 125.00
Book, Mickey Mouse Cutout Doll, Saalfield, 1933, 10 x 19 1/2 In. 394.00
Book, Mickey Mouse Flies The Christmas Mail, 1956 .... 12.00
Book, Mickey Mouse Illustrated Movie Stories, Dean & Son, 1931 .... 185.00
Book, Mickey Mouse Sails For Treasure Island, Dean & Son, 4 In. 219.00
Book, Mickey Mouse's Picnic, Golden Book, 1st Printing, 1950 .... 15.00
Book, Mickey Mouse's Uphill Fight, Wee Little Book, 1934 .... 48.00
Book, Mickey Mouse, 3 Pop-Ups, 1933 .... 375.00
Book, Mickey Mouse, Cartoons, Story, 1930s, 6 1/2 x 8 1/2 In. 35.00
Book, Mickey Mouse, Pop-Up, 1933 .... 135.00
Book, Mickey Mouse, Pop-Up, Blue Ribbon Books, 1935 .... 232.00
Book, Mickey Mouse, Pop-Up, Raised Mickey Cover, Whitman, 1936 .... 45.00
Book, Nutcracker Suite, Abridged, D. Davis, Australia, 1940 .... 35.00
Book, Paint, Pinocchio, Whitman, 1939, 11 x 15 In. 45.00
Book, Peculiar Penguins, McKay, Hardcover, 1934 .... 75.00
Book, Peter Pan & The Indians, Golden Book, 1st Printing, 1952 .... 12.00
Book, Peter Pan & Wendy, Golden Book, 1st Printing, 1952 .... 9.00
Book, Pinocchio, Golden Book, 2nd Printing, 1948 .... 8.00
Book, Pinocchio, Pinocchio & Fish Cover, Whitman, 1939 .... 50.00
Book, Pop-Up, Minnie Mouse, 1933 .... 185.00
Book, Practical Pig, Disney Autographed, 9 1/2 x 9 In. 1870.00
Book, Recipe, Mickey Mouse, Original Envelope, 1930s 75.00
Book, Robin Hood, Mickey Mouse Club, Golden Book, 1st, 1955 .... 7.00
Book, Santa's Toy Shop, Golden Book, 1st Printing, 1950 .... 8.00
Book, School Days In Disneyville, Heath, 1939 .... 32.00
Book, Snow White & 7 Dwarfs, Linen Like, Whitman, 1938 .... 15.00 To 20.00
Book, Snow White, Collins, London, 1939 .... 25.00
Book, Sword In The Stone, Golden Book, 2nd Printing, 1973 .... 4.00
Book, Tiny Movie Stories, Tiny Golden Books, Set Of 12, 1950 .... 85.00
Book, Tortoise and The Hare, Dust Jacket, Whitman, 1935 .... 75.00
Book, Winnie The Pooh Meets Gopher, Golden Book, 2nd, 1965 .... 6.00
Bookends, Bambi 68.00
Bookends, Snoopy 20.00
Bookmark, Mickey Mouse, Die Cut, 3 x 4 In. 30.00
Bowl, Fantasia, Fairies, Maroon, Vernon Kilns, 1940s, 12 In. 605.00
Bowl, Mickey Mouse, Baby Mickey, Enameled Tin, Europe, 1930s 195.00
Bowl, Mickey Mouse, Beetleware, 1930s 45.00
Bowl, Mickey Mouse, China, Walt Disney, 1930s 85.00
Box, Cereal, Post Toasties, Mickey Mouse, G-Man, Donald, 1936 .... 35.00
Box, Crayons, Donald Duck, Tin, Walt Disney Productions 25.00
Box, Donald Duck Straws, Empty, 1950s 20.00
Box, Mickey Mouse Cookies, National Biscuit Company, 1940s 45.00
Box, Pill, Donald Duck, Dancing, Celluloid, 1 1/2 In. 165.00
Box, Soap, Mickey Mouse, Lightfoot Shultz Co., 1930s 12.00
Bracelet, Charm, Mickey Mouse, 1933 .... 300.00
Bracelet, Charm, Mickey Mouse, 5 Mickeys, W. D. P., 1940s 100.00
Bracelet, Mickey Mouse, Metal, 1933, Box 800.00
Brush, Donald Duck, 1938 .... 50.00
Button, Dress, Mickey Mouse, Die Cut, Original Card 110.00
Buttons, Mickey Mouse, W. D. Ent., On Card, 1930s, 4 Piece 75.00
Cake Pan, Snow White, Colorful, Denmark, 1948, 8 x 8 x 4 In. 250.00
Camera, Mick-O-Matic 35.00
Can, Orange Juice, Donald Duck, No Lid 38.00
Candle, Paper Litho Of Mickey Mouse, England, 1935, 1 3/4 In. 75.00
Candleholders, Mickey Mouse, Birthday, 2 Piece 125.00
Candy Container, Mickey Mouse, Ceramic 150.00
Candy Wrapper, Donald Duck, Milk Chocolate, Comic Candys, N.Y. 45.00
Cane & Hat, Mickey Mouse, 1930s 65.00

Card, Christmas, Mickey As Santa, Pluto, Valentine & Sons, 1930s	50.00
Card, Figural, Mickey Mouse, 1960, 5 x 8 In.	10.00
Card, Lobby, Aladdin & Wonderful Lamp, 11 x 14 In.	385.00
Card, Playing, Jungle Book Solitaire, 1966	42.00
Card, Rialto Theater, Mickey Cartoons, 3 x 4 1/2 In., 1933, 6 Pc.	60.00
Card, Valentine, Mechanical, Pinocchio, Fairy, Heart Shape, 1939	30.00
Card, Valentine, Mechanical, Snow White, Figural, Sweeping, 1938	30.00
Cel, see Animation Art category	
Certificate, War Bonds, 22 Characters, World War II, 1944	125.00
Christmas Lights, Mickey Mouse, Noma, Complete, W. D. Ent., Box	295.00
Clock Radio, Mickey Mouse Club, 1950	125.00
Clock, Alarm, Bambi, Animated, Butterfly On Bambi's Tail, 1972	225.00
Clock, Alarm, Donald Duck, Arms Are Clock Hands, Bradley	35.00
Clock, Alarm, Goofy, Reviels Bayard, France, Box, 1985	150.00 To 165.00
Clock, Alarm, Mickey Mouse, Ingersoll, White, Plastic, 4 x 4 In.	250.00
Clock, Alarm, Mickey Mouse, Metal, 1947	195.00
Clock, Mickey Mouse, Animated, Bradley	45.00
Cookie Jar, Donald Duck's Cookie Express	57.00
Cookie Jar, Donald Duck, Disney Productions	95.00
Cookie Jar, Donald Duck, Hoan	45.00 To 60.00
Cookie Jar, Donald Duck, Pumpkin, California Originals	165.00 To 250.00
Cookie Jar, Dumbo, Greatest Show On Earth, Beige	475.00
Cookie Jar, Dumbo, Turnabout	150.00
Cookie Jar, Dumbo, Turnabout, Poor Paint, WDP	140.00
Cookie Jar, Mickey & Minnie, Cylinder	75.00
Cookie Jar, Mickey & Minnie, Leeds	125.00
Cookie Jar, Mickey & Minnie, Turnabout, WDP	140.00
Cookie Jar, Mickey Mouse & Drum, California Originals	250.00
Cookie Jar, Mickey Mouse Club, Club House, Walt Disney Prod.	125.00
Cookie Jar, Mickey Mouse Head, Chef Hat, All White	200.00
Cookie Jar, Mickey Mouse, Hoan	45.00 To 70.00
Cookie Jar, Mickey Mouse, Tin	45.00
Cookie Jar, Mickey Mouse, White, Treasure Craft	200.00
Cookie Jar, Mickey Mouse, With Cake	115.00
Cookie Jar, Pinocchio, Metlox	160.00 To 250.00
Cookie Jar, Pluto & Dumbo	75.00
Cookie Jar, Thumper, Terrace Ceramics	48.00
Cookie Jar, Tigger	85.00 To 145.00
Cookie Jar, Winnie The Pooh	65.00 To 120.00
Costume, Cinderella	25.00
Costume, Ferdinand The Bull, Horned Mask, Fishbach, 1940, Box	85.00
Costume, Minnie Mouse	75.00
Costume, Zorro, Ben Cooper, Disney, Box	90.00
Creamer, Dumbo, Leeds, 6 In.	35.00
Crystal, Wishing, Jiminy Cricket	5.00
Cuff Links, Mickey Mouse, Red, Yellow & Black, Box, 1934	20.00
Cup, Mickey & Gang On Train, Plastic	5.00
Dinner Set, White China, Tan Lustre Border, Japan, 1934, 14 Piece	125.00
Dish, Feeding, Divided, Mickey, Minnie, Long Billed Donald & Pluto	175.00
Display, Amos Mouse, Wood, Cloth, Metal & Rubber, 31 x 11 x 9 In.	445.00
Display, Mobile, Bedknobs and Broomsticks, Unpunched, 1971, 6 Pc.	30.00
Doll, Bagheera, Jungle Book, 1967, Steiff, 12 In.	120.00
Doll, Cinderella, Wooden, 6 In.	65.00
Doll, Donald Duck, Composition, Knickerbocker, 9 In.	925.00
Doll, Donald Duck, Gund, 10 In.	50.00
Doll, Donald Duck, Jointed Arms, Medium Bill	700.00
Doll, Donald Duck, Long Bill, Knickerbocker	975.00
Doll, Dopey, Composition Head, Cloth Body, 13 In.	150.00
Doll, Dopey, Dwarf, Knickerbocker	75.00
Doll, Faline, Charlotte Clark, 1930, 7 x 2 x 5 1/2 In.	44.00
Doll, Ferdinand The Bull, Composition, Jointed, W. D. E., Large	110.00
Doll, Grumpy, Dwarf, Knickerbocker, 1937	175.00

Doll, Happy, Dwarf, Knickerbocker, 9 In.	165.00
Doll, King Louie, Jungle Book, 1967, Steiff, 12 In.	150.00
Doll, Mickey & Minnie, 1930s, Knickerbocker, 11 In.	1045.00
Doll, Mickey Mouse, Cloth, 1930s, Knickerbocker, 11 In.	475.00
Doll, Mickey Mouse, Dean Rag, England, 6 In.	650.00
Doll, Mickey Mouse, Pie-Eyed, Knickerbocker, 9 In.	1350.00
Doll, Mickey Mouse, Steiff, 7 In.	850.00
Doll, Mickey Mouse, Talking, Knickerbocker	20.00
Doll, Mouseketeer, Red Dress, Hat, Horsman, Box	30.00
Doll, Mouseketeer, Red-Headed Boy, Blond Girl, Horsman, Pair	50.00
Doll, Pinocchio, 1930s, Composition, Knickerbocker, 13 1/2 In.	165.00
Doll, Pinocchio, Wooden, 6 In.	65.00
Doll, Snow White & 7 Dwarfs, Felt Face, Shoes, Chad Valley, Box	2420.00
Doll, Snow White, Porcelain, Grolier, Anniversary, 1987, 18 In.	325.00
Doll, Tinkerbell & Peter Pan, Duchess, Unused, Box, Pair	100.00 To 200.00
Dollhouse, Mickey & Friends, Tin	85.00
Dollhouse, Mickey Mouse, Tin	39.00
Drawing Set, Electric, Suitcase, Dated 1961	115.00
Drum, Snow White & Seven Dwarfs, Chein, Box, 1930s	75.00
Ears, Mickey Mouse Mouseketeer, On Card, 1950s	25.00
Easter Eggs, Transfers, Mickey Mouse, Envelope, 1930s	65.00
Eggcup, Silly Symphony, Paper, W. D. E.	12.00
Fan, 20 Reticulated Die Cut Mickeys On Ribboned Leaves	165.00
Figurine, 3 Little Pigs, Musicians, Bisque	145.00
Figurine, Donald Duck Band, Occupied Japan, 3 In., 5 Piece	60.00
Figurine, Dopey, Bisque, 5 1/2 In.	65.00
Figurine, Jiminy Cricket, Dated 1939	28.00
Figurine, Mickey & Minnie, Bisque, 2 3/4 In., Pair	150.00
Figurine, Mickey Mouse, Drum, Bisque, W. E. Disney, 3 1/4 In.	75.00
Figurine, Mickey Mouse, On Parade, Ceramic, 10 x 6 x 5 In.	220.00
Figurine, Snow White, Bisque, 4 In.	65.00
Figurine, Snow White, Chalkware, 14 In.	65.00
Filmstrip, For Mickey Mouse Viewer, Box Of 13 Different Films	125.00
Game, Cinderella, Board, 1965, Parker Bros.	18.00
Game, Dominoes, Mickey Mouse, Box, 1930s	75.00
Game, Donald Duck, Parker Bros., 1938	145.00
Game, Mickey Mouse Magic Divider	40.00
Game, Mickey Mouse Party Game, Pin The Tail, Original Envelope	85.00
Game, Scatterball, Mickey Mouse, Wood Spinning Top, Box	295.00
Game, Score Around, 1969, Ideal	30.00
Game, Target, Snow White & 7 Dwarfs, 1938, 13 x 19 In.	192.00
Game, Tiddly Winks, Mickey Mouse Club, 1963, Whitman	14.00
Go-Cart, Ludwig Von Drake, Marx, Box, 1961	375.00
Gum Pack, Snow White & 7 Dwarfs, Colorful, 1938	85.00
Hat, Mickey Mouse	5.00
Holder, Earring, Pie-Eyed Mickey Mouse	25.00
Holder, Pencil, Mickey Mouse, Pie-Eyed, Figural, 1930s, Dixon Prod.	250.00
Holder, Toothbrush, 3 Little Pigs, Walt Disney	55.00 To 125.00
Holder, Toothbrush, Doc, Porcelain, Maw, 1930s	265.00
Holder, Toothbrush, Donald Duck, Arm Around Minnie & Mickey	225.00
Holder, Toothbrush, Donald Duck, Long Bill	175.00
Holder, Toothbrush, Mickey & Minnie Mouse, Bisque	105.00 To 325.00
Holder, Toothbrush, Mickey & Minnie Mouse, With Pluto, Bisque	175.00
Holder, Toothbrush, Snow White, 1936, 6 In.	275.00
Holder, Toothbrush, Snow White, 1938, 6 In.	265.00
Jack-In-The-Box, Donald Duck	65.00 To 120.00
Kaleidoscope, Cardboard, Paper, Colorful, 9 In.	30.00
Kaleidoscope, Mickey Mouse	65.00
Lawn Chair, Minnie, Wood, Canvas	350.00
Light Bulb Set, Christmas Tree, Mickey Mouse, Noma, Box	250.00 To 275.00
Light Bulb Set, Christmas, Mickey Mouse, 8 Plastic Covers, Box	70.00
Light Bulb Set, Christmas, Pinocchio, Display Card, Box	35.00
Light, Ceiling Globe, , Disney Characters	70.00

Lunch Box, Disney On Parade 50.00
Lunch Box, Disney's World On Ice, Thermos, 1980 .... 30.00
Lunch Box, Fire Fighters, Thermos ....75.00 To 150.00
Lunch Box, Mickey Mouse Club, Thermos 48.00
Lunch Box, Mickey Mouse, School Bus 25.00
Lunch Box, Pinocchio, Red, 7 x 5 In. 150.00
Lunch Box, School Bus, Domed, Thermos .... 30.00 To 75.00
Lunch Box, Snow White & 7 Dwarfs, Tin, Belgium, 1938 .... 700.00
Lunch Box, Snow White & 7 Dwarfs, U.S. A. 30.00
Lunch Box, Walt Disney Magic Kingdom 25.00
Lunch Box, Walt Disney World 40.00
Magazine, Mickey Mouse, Bad Wolf, Pumpkin Cover, Vol. 3, No. 2, 1937 .... 65.00
Magazine, Mickey Mouse, Donald & Goofy, New Year, Vol. 3, No. 4, 1937 .... 75.00
Magazine, Mickey Mouse, Goofy & Wilber, Vol. 4, No. 7, 1939 .... 125.00
Magazine, T.V. Guide, Walt, Mickey & Others On Cover, 12/14/57 .... 25.00
Marble, Mickey Mouse, Glass, Large 2.35
Marionette, Mickey Mouse, Composition, Pelham Puppets, 23 In. 350.00
Marionette, Pinocchio 35.00
Mask Set, Snow White & 7 Dwarfs, Halloween, Complete 160.00
Mask, Donald Duck, Cheesecloth, A. S. Fishbagh, 1930s, Adult 65.00
Mask, Pinocchio, Paper, Gillette Blue Blades Premium, 1939 .... 9.00
Mug, Ludwig Von Drake 28.00
Music Box, Mickey Mouse & Minnie Mouse In Jalopy 50.00
Night–Light, TV Bulb, Mickey Mouse, Box 95.00
Nodder, Donald Duck, Plastic, 6 In. 65.00
Nodder, Mickey, Bisque 800.00
Ornament, Christmas, 1983, Mickey, Donald, Goofy, Tree, Schmid 6.00
Ornament, Christmas, 1984, Mickey & Minnie Skating, Schmid 6.00
Pail, Donald Duck, Ohio Art, 1938 .... 68.00
Pail, Snow White & 7 Dwarfs, With Shovel, 1938 .... 190.00
Paint Box, Mickey Mouse & Donald Duck, Tin, 1950s, 7 x 4 In. 50.00
Paint Box, Snow White & 7 Dwarfs, Tin Litho, 1930s, 4 x 10 In. 80.00
Paint Set, Mickey Mouse, Box, 1939 .... 85.00
Paint Set, Oil, Disneyland, Box 50.00
Paper, Mickey Mouse Globe Trotter Weekly, Vol. 3, 1937 .... 75.00
Pattern, Transfer, Snow White, McCall, W. D. E. 25.00
Pen, Mickey Mouse, Ballpoint, 1950s 50.00
Pen, Mickey Mouse, Ingersoll, Ballpoint, 1940s 60.00
Pencil Sharpener, Donald Duck, Long Bill, Bakelite, W. D. E. 45.00
Pencil Sharpener, Snow White, Bakelite 75.00
Pencil, Mechanical, Mickey Mouse, 1940s 150.00
Pendant, Chain, Pooh Bear, Gold Electroplate, Box, 1982, 1 In. 275.00
Picture, An Astronomical Predicament, Litho, 22 x 16 In. 605.00
Pillow Cover, Mickey Mouse, 1932 .... 85.00
Pin, Donald Duck, 3 1/2 In. 5.00
Pin, Dopey, Enterprises, Small 30.00
Pin, Goofy, Tokyo, 3 1/2 In. 9.00
Pin, Mickey Mouse & Donald Duck, 1930s 95.00
Pin, Mickey Mouse Club Member, Mickey's Picture, 3 1/2 In. 4.00
Pin, Mickey Mouse, 1937 Official, Store 45.00
Pin, Mickey Mouse, 3 1/2 In. 5.00
Pin, Mickey Mouse, Enameled, Europe, Colorful 125.00
Pitcher, 3 Little Pigs, Big Bad Wolf Handle, 7 In. 195.00
Planter, Bambi, Leeds China .... 30.00 To 45.00
Planter, Dwarf With Shovel, Green Coat, Brown Pants, 4 1/2 In. 28.00
Planter, Pluto, Leeds China 55.00
Planter, Prince, From Cinderella, Shaw Pottery, 1930s 350.00
Planter, Snow White, Leeds China 27.00
Plaster Casting Set, Donald Duck, Rubber Molds, Box 95.00
Plate, 50th Birthday, Donald Duck, Blue, Box 90.00
Plate, Mickey Mouse, Patriot China 125.00
Plate, Pluto, Mickey, Donald, Minnie, Patriot China 125.00
Playsuit, Child's, Mickey Mouse, 2 Piece, 1930s 64.00

Postcard, 3 Mickeys, Riding Sled, Innsbruck, Austria, 1930s 40.00
Poster, Aladdin & The Wonderful Lamp, Ub Iwerks, 41 x 27 In. 990.00
Poster, Alice In Wonderland, Fantasyland, 54 x 36 In. 1100.00
Poster, Fantasia, Psychedelic, Re–Release, 1960s, 27 x 41 In. 70.00
Poster, Haunted Mansion, New Orleans Square, 54 x 36 In. 1100.00
Poster, Matterhorn, Fantasyland, Silk Screen, 54 x 36 In. 550.00
Poster, Snow White & 7 Dwarfs, 1937, 1/2 Sheet 4675.00
Print Shop, Mickey Mouse, Box, 1930s 80.00
Print Shop, Mickey Mouse, Pie–Eyed, Fulton Co., 1935 .... 175.00
Print, Bambi, 1945, 32 x 23 In. 37.00
Projector, Model 488, Mickey Mouse, Box 75.00
Projector, Transogram, 2 Reels, Donald Duck, Box 85.00
Puppet, Dopey 32.00
Puppet, Mickey Mouse, Gund, 1950s 18.00
Puppet, Pinocchio, Composition, Pelham, 1950s, 10 In. 120.00
Puppet, Pluto, Gund, 1950s 18.00
Purse, Leatherette, Mickey Mouse, Pluto On Reverse, 4 In. 45.00
Puzzle Set, Snow White, Box, 1938, Large, 2 Piece 75.00
Puzzle, Jigsaw, Mickey Mouse, Mouse Factory, Jaymar, 1952, Box 20.00
Puzzle, Mickey's Tug Boat, Bantam, Pocket, Box, 1950s 20.00
Puzzle, Mickey, Donald, 3 Pigs, Goofy, Roller Coaster, 1960 .... 8.00
Radio, Mickey Mouse 1850.00
Radio, Mickey Mouse Club 65.00
Radio, Mickey Mouse, Figural, Atlas Battery 10.00
Radio, Mickey Mouse, Wooden Case 125.00
Radio, Pinocchio, Figural, Atlas Battery 10.00
Radio, Snow White 2000.00
Record Album, Pinocchio, Movie Sound Track, 1939, 3 Records 195.00
Record, Mouseketeer, Annette 10.00
Record, Snow White & 7 Dwarfs, Original Sound Track, 1968 .... 25.00
Reel, Viewmaster, Pinocchio, Snow White, Lady & Tramp, 1960s, 3 Pc. 22.00
Refrigerator & Stove, Snow White, Tin, Wolverine 75.00
Ring, Donald Duck, Metal 25.00
Ring, Man's, 20–Year Service, 10K Gold, 1980s 660.00
Ring, Mickey Mouse, Flasher, Plastic, Package 10.00
Rocking Seat, Baby, Mickey Mouse, 1930s, Wood, 34 In. 138.00
Rug, Mickey Mouse & Friends, 45 x 60 In. 185.00
Rug, Pluto, Pulling Rabbit & Skunk, Wagon, 22 x 40 In. .... 25.00 To 75.00
Rug, Walt Disney Characters, Large 3500.00
Salt & Pepper, Donald Duck, Sitting & Standing 30.00
Salt & Pepper, Mickey & Minnie 30.00
Salt & Pepper, Mushroom, Fantasia, 1940s 145.00
Salt & Pepper, Pluto & Dumbo 40.00
Sand Set, Mickey Mouse, Original Card, 1950s 75.00
School Bag, Alice In Wonderland 65.00
Sheet Music, Bibbidi–Bobbidi–Boo, Cinderella, 1949 .... 8.00 To 12.00
Sheet Music, Heigh–Ho, Snow White 20.00
Sheet Music, Snow White, 9 Songs 50.00
Sheet Music, Some Day My Prince Will Come, Snow White 30.00
Sheet Music, Whistle While You Work, Snow White 20.00
Shoe Polish, Mickey Mouse, 1950s, Scuffy 25.00
Shoes, Dumbo's, Head, Clown Hat, Felt Collar, Trimfoot, USA 350.00
Shoes, Dutch, Wooden, Minnie Mouse, Holland Sticker, 1930s 145.00
Silly Symphonies, Pop–Up, 2 Stories, 9 1/2 x 7 1/2 In. 1650.00
Sled, Mickey Mouse & Minnie Mouse, W. D. Enterprises 170.00
Sled, Mickey Mouse, Flexible Flyer 350.00
Slippers, House, Mickey Mouse 150.00
Spoon, Demitasse, Mary Poppins, Figural 12.00
Spoon, Mickey Mouse, Pie–Eyed, Silver Plate, Branford, 5 1/2 In. 20.00
Spoon, Mickey Mouse, Silver Plate, Post Toasties Premium, 1938 .... 14.00
Stove, Mickey Mouse, Electric, 1930s 225.00
Sugar & Creamer, Tin, Beige, Green Inside, Ohio Art, 1939, 2 In. 40.00
Tapestry, Toby Tortoise, Female Bunny, 1930s, 11 x 18 In. 160.00

Tea Set, Disneyland, 1955, 15 Piece 350.00
Tea Set, Disneyland, Chein, Box, 1955, 6 Piece 85.00
Tea Set, Mickey Mouse, Lusterware, 5 Piece 175.00
Tea Set, Snow White, Box 250.00
Teapot, Musical, Mary Poppins 30.00
Telephone, Mickey Mouse, Electric 95.00
Thermometer, Plaque, Donald, Fishing, Ceramic Tile, 1944, 6 In. 35.00
Thermos, Ludwig Von Drake 45.00
Tin, Candy, Snow White & 7 Dwarfs, Cottage Scene, 2 x 2 x 5 In. 320.00
Tin, Disney Characters' Pictures, 1930–1939 .... 725.00
Toy Chest, Alice In Wonderland, Walt Disney Ent., 1936 .... 200.00
Toy Chest, Snow White, Dated 1938, Large 250.00
Toy, Acrobat, Mickey Mouse, Wooden 165.00
Toy, Acrobat, Pluto, Celluloid, Box 350.00
Toy, Blocks, Stacking, Lakeside, 1966 .... 25.00
Toy, Car, Donald Duck & Pluto, Yellow, Red Bumper, Sun Rubber 85.00
Toy, Car, Mickey Mouse Dipsy, Tin Litho, Linemar, 1950s .... 625.00 To 730.00
Toy, Car, Roadster, Disney On Parade 550.00
Toy, Cinderella & Prince, Waltzing, Dancing 175.00
Toy, Donald Duck Choo–Choo, Pull Toy, Fisher–Price, 1940 .... 225.00
Toy, Donald Duck, Baton Twirler, Fisher–Price 145.00
Toy, Donald Duck, Composition, Jointed, Japan, 8 In. .... 375.00 To 675.00
Toy, Donald Duck, High Wire Acrobat, Box 85.00
Toy, Donald Duck, On Tricycle, Tin & Celluloid, Linemar, 4 In. 550.00
Toy, Donald Duck, Pull Toy, Fisher–Price 37.50
Toy, Donald Duck, Skier, Windup, Disney 375.00
Toy, Donald Duck, Sled, Wooden, Painted, Fun–E–Flex, 5 1/2 In. 440.00
Toy, Donald Duck, Tricky Toe, Kicks Football, 1950s 20.00
Toy, Donald Duck, Windup, Japan, Disney, 3 1/2 In. 490.00
Toy, Donald The Drummer, Marx, 1950s, 9 In. 340.00
Toy, Drum, Mickey Mouse, Tin & Paper, England, 6 In. 45.00
Toy, Dumbo, Composition, Flying Elephant, 1930, 8 1/2 In. 850.00
Toy, Ferris Wheel, Mickey Mouse, Lithographed Tin .... 220.00 To 385.00
Toy, Fire Truck, Donald Duck, Windup 65.00
Toy, Fire Truck, Mickey Mouse, Hard Rubber 45.00
Toy, Goofy, Tail Spins, Windup, Head Bobs, Litho, Linemar, 1950s 375.00
Toy, Gymnast, Mickey Mouse, Paper & Wood, Litho, 7 3/4 In. 66.00
Toy, Handcar, Donald Duck & Pluto, Worn Paint, Windup, 11 In. 550.00
Toy, Handcar, Donald Duck, White, Green, Lionel, 1930s .... 550.00 To 880.00
Toy, Handcar, Mickey & Minnie, Red, With Track, Lionel 600.00
Toy, Handcar, Mickey Mouse & Santa Claus, Lionel 2200.00
Toy, Handcar, Mickey Mouse, Lionel 1050.00
Toy, Handcar, Mickey Mouse, Windup, Lionel, c.1934, 7 1/2 In. 302.00
Toy, Ironing Board, Snow White, 7 Dwarfs, Wolverine, 21 x 27 In. 125.00
Toy, Mickey Mouse & Pluto, Windup, Celluloid, 1930s, 6 In. 1540.00
Toy, Mickey Mouse, Jointed, Squeeze Ladder, Does Tricks, 1940s 65.00
Toy, Mickey Mouse, Playing Xylophone, Tin Litho, Windup, 6 In. 855.00
Toy, Mickey Mouse, Pull Toy, Safety Patrol Motorcycle, Siren 350.00
Toy, Mickey Mouse, Skater, Tin, Red Pants, Linemar, 8 1/2 In. 1100.00
Toy, Mickey Mouse, Talking, Pull String, Head Moves, Plastic 15.00
Toy, Mickey Mouse, Wood Jointed, On Card, W. Germany, 1930s 125.00
Toy, Mickey Mouse, Wooden, Jointed, Germany, 11 In. 125.00
Toy, Mickey Tumbling Buggy, Battery Operated 25.00
Toy, Minnie Mouse, Knitting In Rocker, Windup, Linemar .... 400.00 To 500.00
Toy, Minnie Mouse, Knitting In Rocker, Windup, Linemar, Box 1150.00
Toy, Minnie Mouse, Tag, Steiff, 1930s 2600.00
Toy, Pinocchio Plays Xylophone, Battery Operated, Box, Japan 250.00
Toy, Pinocchio, Acrobat, Windup, Marx, 1939 .... 600.00
Toy, Pinocchio, Windup, Tin, Linemar 475.00
Toy, Pluto The Unicyclist, Clockwork, Linemar, 5 1/2 In. 522.00
Toy, Pluto, Drum Major, Windup, Linemar 525.00
Toy, Pluto, Pull Toy, Wood, 1930s 250.00
Toy, Pluto, Windup, Musical 285.00

Toy, Shopping Cart, Minnie Mouse, Battery Operated 125.00
Toy, Submarine, Nautilus, Tin, 20, 000 Leagues, Box 245.00
Toy, Sweeper, Mickey Mouse, Ohio Art, 1930s 350.00
Toy, Train, Circus, Mickey Mouse 1350.00
Toy, Train, Express, Mickey Mouse, Tin, Marx 95.00
Toy, Train, Express, Tin Lithograph, Characters, 13 x 22 In. 295.00
Toy, Train, Handcar, Mickey Mouse & Donald Duck, Standard Gauge 145.00
Toy, Trapeze, Mickey & Minnie Mouse, Windup, Borgfeldt, Box 2500.00
Toy, Truck, Delivery, Pinocchio, Windup, Tin, Marx 1850.00
Toy, Whirligig, Donald Duck, Celluloid 3000.00
Toy, Wristwatch, Mickey Mouse, Marx 15.00
Toy, Xylophone, Donald Duck 250.00
Toy, Xylophone, Mickey Mouse, Fisher–Price 120.00
Train, Circus, Mickey Mouse, Lionel, 1930s 2280.00
Train, Locomotive, Donald Duck, Battery Operated, TN, Box 295.00
Train, Mickey Mouse Choo–Choo, Fisher–Price 75.00
Tray, Sleeping Beauty, Tin, 13 x 16 In. 25.00
Tray, Snow White & Doc, Bowing To Each Other, England 110.00
Tumbler, Funny Bunny, W. D. Ent. 15.00
Tumbler, Horace Horsecollar, Disney, 1937 .... 137.00
Tumbler, Jungle Book, Khan, King Louie, Flunkey, Disney, 1966, 3 Pc. 40.00
Tumbler, Snow White 25.00
Umbrella, Mickey Mouse, 1934 .... 80.00
Wall Pocket, Mickey & Minnie Mouse, Lusterware 225.00
Wall Pocket, Mickey Mouse, Lusterware, Walter E. Disney, Japan 235.00
Wallet, Minnie Mouse, Leather, 3 x 4 1/2 In. 18.00
Watch Fob, Mickey Mouse, England 150.00
Watch, 3 Little Pigs, Big Bad Wolf, Pocket, 1934 .... 500.00
Watch, Mickey Mouse, Lapel, Partial Decal 265.00
Watch, Mickey Mouse, Pocket, 1933 .... 495.00
Watch, Mickey Mouse, Pocket, Bradley 75.00
Wristwatch, Character, Cinderella, U.S. Time 25.00
Wristwatch, Disney World, 15 Years, Lady's, Larus Quartz, 1986 .... 115.00
Wristwatch, Disneyland 35th Anniversary, Kodak 35.00
Wristwatch, Donald Duck, Ingersoll, Original Band, 1947 .... 95.00
Wristwatch, Mickey Mouse, 1939 .... 295.00
Wristwatch, Mickey Mouse, 1950s ....50.00 To 105.00
Wristwatch, Mickey Mouse, Box, 1933 ....595.00 To 795.00
Wristwatch, Mickey Mouse, Box, 1974 .... 45.00
Wristwatch, Mickey Mouse, Electric, Timex, 1970 .... 250.00
Wristwatch, Mickey Mouse, Electric, Timex, Box, 1970 .... 425.00
Wristwatch, Mickey Mouse, Kelton, U.S. Time, Ingersoll, Box, 1946 .... 400.00
Wristwatch, Mickey Mouse, Leather Band, Ingersoll, 1933 .... 335.00
Wristwatch, Mickey Mouse, Quartz, Bradley, 1978 .... 100.00
Wristwatch, Mickey Mouse, U.S. Time, Original Red Strap, 1947 .... 100.00
Wristwatch, Mickey Mouse, Unused, 1947 .... 175.00
Xylophone, Model 135, Box 125.00

DOCTOR, see Dental; Medical

DOLL entries are listed by marks printed or incised on the doll, if possible.
If there are no marks, the doll is listed by the name of the subject or
country.

A. B. G., 136/0, Dutch Girl, Bisque, Sleep Eyes, Lashes, Blond, 13 1/2 In. 400.00
A. B. G., 1123 1/2, Bisque, Turned Head, All Original, c.1880, 28 In. 995.00
A. B. G., 1342, Baby, Breather, Dimples, Long Dress, 12 1/2 In. 450.00
A. B. G., 1361, Ball–Jointed Body, Brown Sleep Eyes, 17 In. 550.00
A. B. G., 1361, Black Sleep Eyes, 10 1/2 In. 275.00
A. B. G., 1361, Brown Sleep Eyes, 11 In. 295.00
A. M., 1, Florodora, Turned Head, Open Mouth, Glass Eyes, DRP, 21 In. 365.00
A. M., 2, Indian, Bisque Character Head, 5 Piece Body, Costume, 16 In. 325.00
A. M., 9, Florodora, Leather Body, Shoes, 17 In. 700.00
A. M., 11/0, Googly, Bisque Head, Pug Nose, Tyrolean Costume, 7 In. 800.00

A. M., 210, Molded Hair, 7 In. 295.00
A. M., 270, Kid Body, Bisque Hands, Brown Sleep Eyes, 24 In. 395.00
A. M., 321, Googly, 7 In. 300.00
A. M., 323, Googly Eyes, Bisque Head, Closed Mouth, Brown Wig, 12 In. 1540.00
A. M., 323, Googly, Blond, Blue Sleep Eyes, 7 1/2 In. 750.00
A. M., 327, Baby, Bisque, Dimples, Chubby Face, 25 In. 1550.00
A. M., 351, Sleep Eyes, Bisque, 22 1/2 In. 825.00
A. M., 370, Bisque, 21 In. 150.00
A. M., 370, Fur Eyebrows, Dressed, 27 In. 450.00
A. M., 370, Kid Body, Bisque Hands, Blond Wig, Dressed, 25 In. 350.00
A. M., 370, Open Mouth, Red Wig, 21 In. 165.00
A. M., 390, Black, Bisque, Composition, Ball–Jointed Body, 16 In. 650.00
A. M., 390, Blue Fixed Eyes, 14 In. 275.00
A. M., 390, Boy, Bisque, Irish Peasant Outfit, 10 In. 165.00
A. M., 390, Boy, Blond, 6 In. 200.00
A. M., 390, Character, Bisque, Dimpled Chin, Jodhpurs, Bolero, Hat 495.00
A. M., 390, Child, Bisque, 34 In. 525.00
A. M., 390, Child, Brown Sleep Eyes, Bisque Socket Head, Clothes, 15 In. 125.00
A. M., 390, Sleep Eyes, Bisque, 5 1/2 In. 95.00
A. M., 971, Character Baby, Original Clothes, Ribbons, Sleep Eyes, 16 In 525.00
A. M., 990, Character, Toddler Body, Checkered Rompers, 16 In. 525.00
A. M., 991, Toddler, Bisque, All Original, 20 In. 675.00
A. M., 996, Toddler, Breather, Sleep Eyes, 14 In. 425.00
A. M., Bisque, Brown Eyes, Open Mouth, Kid Body, 20 In. 325.00
A. M., Bisque, Sleep Eyes, Jointed, 26 In. 330.00
A. M., Character, Bisque, Forelock Curl, Stuck–Out Ears, 1912, 16 In. 650.00
A. M., Dream Baby, 13 In. 395.00
A. M., Dream Baby, Bisque Flange Head, Closed Mouth, Cloth Body, 8 In. 150.00
A. M., Dream Baby, Bisque Flange Head, Cloth Body, Clothes, 15 In. 150.00
A. M., Dream Baby, Bisque, Cloth Body, Dressed, 10 In. 300.00
A. M., Dream Baby, Pillow, Bisque 250.00
A. M., Florodora Boy, Bisque Head, Sleep Eyes, 2 Piece Suit, Hat, 16 In. 175.00
A. M., Florodora, 22 In. 425.00
A. M., Googly, Bisque, Brown Painted Hair, Closed Mouth, 12 In. 2000.00
A. M., Kid Body, Original Dress & Wig, 26 In. 200.00
A. M., Mabel, 18 In. 290.00
A. M., Queen Louise, Ball Jointed, Blond, Dressed, 24 In. 450.00
A. M., Queen Louise, Bisque, Sleep Eyes, Jointed, 16 In. 302.00
Admiral Byrd, Bisque, 5–Piece Composition, Fur Suit, Germany, 8 In. 150.00
Adolf Wislizenus, 110, Character Boy, 24 In. 1750.00
Advertising, Allied Vans, 17 In. 12.00
Advertising, Buddy Lee, Hard Plastic, Lee Overalls, 12 In. 75.00
Advertising, Buddy Lee, Phillips 66, Missing Hat 150.00
Advertising, Buddy Lee, Texaco & Engineer, Pair 485.00
Advertising, Burger King, Cloth, 12 In. 12.00
Advertising, Burger King, Cloth, 24 In. 15.00
Advertising, Burger King, Vinyl, 1980 .... 22.00
Advertising, C & H Sugar, Hawaiian, Huggable, Cloth .... 6.00 To 8.00
Advertising, Campbell's, Wizard Of Oz 10.00
Advertising, Casper, Gelatin, 1950s 75.00
Advertising, Chips Ahoy 6.00
Advertising, Col. Sanders, Bobbing Head, Vinyl, 1960s, 6 3/4 In. 95.00
Advertising, Cream Of Wheat, Cloth 95.00
Advertising, Dr Pepper, 12 In. ....*Illus* 10.00
Advertising, Elsie The Cow, Borden's, Moos, Stuffed 55.00
Advertising, Elsie The Cow, Vinyl & Plush ....12.00 To 30.00
Advertising, Fig Newton, Box 10.00
Advertising, Freddie The Flute, H. R. Puff & N Stuff, Kellogg's 250.00
Advertising, Fry Guy, Cloth, Stuffed, McDonald's 10.00
Advertising, G. E. Radio Man, Composition, Wooden Jointed, 19 In. 475.00
Advertising, Gerber Baby, Flirty Eyes, 1979 .... 25.00
Advertising, Green Giant Sprout, Cloth, 12 In. 5.00
Advertising, Hawaiian Punch 35.00

Advertising, Jack Frost, Cloth, 1950s	95.00
Advertising, Kayo, Oilcloth, 1930s	65.00
Advertising, Kool–Aid Kid	11.00
Advertising, Magic Chef, Vinyl	25.00
Advertising, Marlboro Man	18.00
Advertising, McDonald's, Prof. Gadget	15.00
Advertising, McDonald's, Remco	20.00
Advertising, McDonald's, Takara, Japan, Uniform, Food Accessories	250.00
Advertising, Mr. Salty Pretzel	6.00
Advertising, Munsingwear, Penguin, Hard Vinyl, 7 In.	35.00
Advertising, Ovaltine, 14 In. ....*Illus*	8.00
Advertising, Pepto Bismol Professor, Plush	40.00
Advertising, Pillsbury Doughboy	5.00
Advertising, Ronald McDonald, Cloth	6.00
Advertising, Ronald McDonald, With Whistle, Hasbro, 1978, 24 In.	50.00
Advertising, Sambo's Restaurant, Cloth, Dakin	15.00
Advertising, Speed Queen Beats The Fritz, Rag	20.00
Advertising, Sprite, Lymon, Talking .... 12.00 To 25.00
Advertising, Uneeda, Wishnik, Troll, Green Hair, 6 In.	4.00
Alabama, Baby, Barefoot, 22 In.	2800.00
Alabama, Baby, Cloth, Painted Face, Ella Smith	3600.00
Alexander dolls are listed in this section under Madame Alexander	
Alma, Bisque, Long Blond Hair, Blue Eyes, Germany, 26 In.	575.00
Aluminum, Head & Hands, Metal Eyes, Falk Doll Corp., 19 1/2 In.	395.00
Amberg, Baby, Labeled Dress, 8 In.	250.00
American Character, Betsy McCall, Blond, Plaid School Dress, 8 In.	125.00
American Character, Betsy McCall, Tennis Outfit, Extra Outfit, 14 In.	165.00
American Character, Deanna Durbin, Composition, 25 In.	550.00
American Character, Ella Cinders, Composition, 18 In.	550.00
American Character, Little Joe, Bonanza, With Accessories, 1966, 8 In.	159.00
American Character, Little Ricky, Jr., Curly Hair, Sleep Eyes, 21 In.	150.00
American Character, Petite Sally, Composition, Tin Sleep Eyes, 18 In.	75.00
American Character, Saucy Walker, Flirty Eyes, Hard Plastic, 21 In.	125.00
American Character, Sweet Sue, Bride, Vinyl, All Original, 20 In.	185.00
American Character, Sweet Sue, Hard Plastic, 15 In.	150.00
American Character, Sweet Sue, Taffeta Dress, Blond, 24 In.	250.00
American Character, Tiny Tears	24.00
American Character, Toni, Hard Plastic, Original Dress, 21 In.	195.00
American Character, Toni, Skater, 12 In.	75.00
American Character, Toodles, Vinyl, Painted Hair, Sleep Eyes, 21 In.	85.00
American Schoolboy, Bisque Shoulder Head, Cloth Body, Germany, 12 In.	385.00
Angel, 1956, 11 1/2 In.	50.00
Annalee, Butterfly Elf, 7 In.	110.00
Annalee, Easter Bunny, Boy, Tagged, 1970, 29 In.	225.00
Annalee, Easter Bunny, Girl, Tagged, 1971, 29 In.	225.00
Annalee, Monkey, With Banana, 11 In.	150.00
Annalee, Nun, 8 In.	150.00

Doll, Advertising, Ovaltine, 14 In.
Doll, Advertising, Dr Pepper, 12 In.

✦✦✦✦✦✦✦✦✦✦✦✦✦✦✦✦✦✦✦✦✦

Vinyl dolls should not be put in
a hot attic. Heat may darken
the vinyl.

✦✦✦✦✦✦✦✦✦✦✦✦✦✦✦✦✦✦✦✦✦

Annalee, Skunk, Boy, 12 In. 225.00
Annalee, Yum–Yum Bunny, 13 In. 275.00
Anne Baby, Original Tub 190.00
Annette Himstedt, Ellen, From 1st Barefoot Children, Box, 1987 .... 600.00
Armand Marseille dolls are listed in this section under A. M.
Arranbee, Gretel, Storybook, Composition, 9 In. 115.00
Arranbee, Nancy, Walker, Hard Plastic, 19 In. 145.00
Automaton, Bisque, Closed Mouth, Music, Velvet Box, France, 15 1/2 In. 3750.00
Automaton, Black Man, Plays Fiddle, Woodpecker Keeps Time, 1920s 6500.00
Automaton, Blacksmith, Hammer Strikes, Head Moves, 1920s 4200.00
Automaton, Bru, Playing Mandolin, Bisque Head, Feathered Brows 8470.00
Automaton, Gypsy Dancer, Moving Torso Doing The Samba, Spain 4290.00
Automaton, Magician Lifts Box Cover, Flower Bouquet Pops Out 4070.00
Automaton, Monkey, Fans Himself, Puts Spectacles To Eyes, Key Wind 2500.00
Automaton, Peddler At Oriental Bazaar, France 6250.00
Automaton, Swimmer, France 3500.00
Averill, Bisque, Cloth Body, Original Clothes, c.1920, 22 In. 1500.00
Averill, Bonnie Babe, Bisque Head, Crooked Smile, Germany, 13 In. 1400.00
Averill, Little Lulu, Oilcloth Face, Painted Eyes, Felt Hair, 14 In. 400.00
Averill, Newborn Baby, Original Clothes, Composition 125.00
Averill, Sonny, c.1902, 6 1/2 In. 3000.00
Averill, Sunny Girl, Celluloid Head, Intaglio Eyes, 15 In. 90.00
Baby, Blond Hair, Red Velvet Shoes, Walk With Me, 1950, 25 In. 65.00
Baby, Kicking & Crying, Mechanical, Nursing Gown, Bonnet, France, 17 In. .... · 2250.00
Bahr & Proschild, 300, Child, 21 In. 550.00
Bahr & Proschild, 320–16, Child, Human Hair Wig, Jointed Waist, 28 In. 1500.00
Bahr & Proschild, 585, Baby, Bent Limb, Brown Eyes, 14 In. 595.00
Bahr & Proschild, Baby, Open–Close Mouth, Molded Teeth, 11 In. 750.00
Bahr & Proschild, Open Mouth, 4 Teeth, Pierced Ears, Mohair Wig, 11 In. 1100.00
Barbie dolls are listed in this section under Mattel
Barrois, Bisque, Kid Body, Stiff Neck, Au Nain Bleu Dress, 16 1/2 In. 2900.00
Bebe Olga, Blue Threaded Paperweight Eyes, Pink Silk, 6 Teeth, 12 In. 1200.00
Bebe, Depose, Composition Body, 21 In. 1800.00
Bebe, Walks, Turns Head, Open Mouth, Paperweight Eyes, Dressed, 21 In. 2900.00
Beecher, Black 1800.00
Beloved Belindy, Cloth, Painted Face, 15 In. 241.00
Belton, 807X, Girl, 16 In. 1700.00
Belton, Bisque, All Original Clothes, 4 3/4 In. 950.00
Belton, Gray Threaded Eyes, Blond, Composition Body, Dressed, 15 In. 1700.00
Belton, Wood Log Body, Sheepskin Wig, Dark Glass Eyes, 1880s, 7 In. 425.00
Bergmann dolls are also in this section under S & H and Simon & Halbig
Bergmann, 10, Open Mouth, Blond Wig, 28 In. 302.00
Bergmann, Child, Bisque Head, Blue Eyes, Ball–Jointed, 31 In. 400.00
Bergmann, Jointed Body, Brown Eyes, Antique Clothes, 31 In. 1200.00
Bergmann, Sweet Face, Sleep Eyes, 18 In. 595.00
Bisque, Baby, Blond, Open–Close Mouth, Organdy Dress, 11 In. 2250.00
Bisque, Baby, Jointed Hips, Shoulders, Sculptured Hair, Germany, 4 In. 80.00
Bisque, Boy & Girl, Japanese Costume, Jointed, Pair 52.50
Bisque, Child, Jointed At Shoulders & Hips, Painted Clothes, 6 1/2 In. 75.00
Bisque, Leather Body, Old Cotton Clothes, Brown Human Wig, Germany 250.00
Bisque, Molded Blond Hair, Painted Eyes, Jointed, Germany, 6 In. 140.00
Bisque, Nancy Ann Storybook, Bridesmaid, Bisque, Box, 1941 .... 28.00
Bisque, Open Mouth, Composition Jointed Body, Japan, 22 In. 575.00
Bisque, Oriental Baby, 7 In. ....*Illus* 2500.00
Bisque, Shoulder Head, Painted Blue Eyes, Painted Blond Hair, 12 In. 180.00
Black dolls are included in the Black category
Boy, Pawtucket, Blonde, Brown Eyes, Sateen Body, Sailor Suit, 20 In. 550.00
Bridesmaid, Pink Flowered Gown, Felt Hat, Box, 9 In. 15.00
Bru Jne, Bisque Head, Brown Glass Eyes, Blond Human Hair, 21 In. 3100.00
Bru Jne, Bisque, Swivel Head, Purple & Ivory Silk Dress, 15 In. 6275.00
Bru Jne, No. 4, Brown Eyes, Kid Body, Bisque Face & Hands, 13 In. 1000.00
Bru Jne, No. 8, Bebe Bru, Bisque Head, Wooden, French Body, 19 In. 5500.00
Bru Jne, Senorita, Playing Mandolin 8470.00

Doll, Effanbee, Patsyette,

Doll, Bisque, Oriental   Painted Blue Eyes, Pink   Doll, Jeannie, I Dream of

Baby, 7 In.   Dress, 9 In.   Jeannie, TV Series, Box

Bru Jne, Smiler, Bisque, Articulated Wood Arms, Antique Clothing	4650.00
Bru Jne, Swivel Neck, Mona Lisa Smile, Trunk Of Accessories, 16 In.	6995.00
Bruno Schmidt, Bisque, Blue Eyes, Open Mouth, Jointed Body, 22 In.	775.00
Bugs Bunny, Talking	55.00
Buschow & Beck, Painted Brass Head, Glass Eyes, Leather Arms, 1880	375.00
Bye–Lo, Baby, Bisque, Cloth Body, Celluloid Hands, 10 In.	300.00
Bye–Lo, Baby, Brown Sleep Eyes, Cloth Body, Original Clothes, 10 In.	350.00
Bye–Lo, Bisque Swivel Head & Torso, Painted Hair, c.1923, 5 In.	375.00
Bye–Lo, Blue Sleep Eyes, Life Size, 20 In.	1650.00
Bye–Lo, Twins, 1 Blue Eyed & 1 Brown Eyed, Pair	1500.00
C. O. D., Girl, Bisque, 4 Upper Teeth, Synthetic Wig, Jointed, 23 In.	375.00
Cabbage Patch, Bride & Groom, Box, 1983	400.00
Cabbage Patch, Sabrina Dawn, 1984, Box, 22 In.	150.00
Cameo, Giggles, Box, 12 In.	375.00
Cameo, Kewpie, Composition, Box, 13 In.	350.00
Cameo, Memorial Kewpie, Kallus, Box, 27 In.	150.00
Cameo, Scootles, 12 In.	400.00
Carolle, Baby, With Basket & Outfits, 1970s, 15 In.	300.00
Carolle, Boy, Clement, All Original, 1977, 19 In.	100.00
Carolle, Girl, Casimir, All Original, 1977, 19 In.	100.00
Catterfelder, Character, Germany	7500.00
Celluloid, Baby In Peanut Shell, Japan, 3 1/2 In.	75.00
Celluloid, Boy & Girl, German Outfit, Glass Eyes, 7 In.	100.00
Celluloid, Homemade Body, Composition Hands, Mohair Wig, 18 1/2 In.	250.00
Celluloid, Sleep Eyes, Turtle Mark, 16 In.	25.00
Charlie's Angels, 8 1/2 In., On Card, 3 Piece	35.00
Chase, Baby, Stockinette Head, Cloth Body, Painted Hair, 27 In.	375.00
Chase, Philadelphia Baby	4840.00
Chase, Stockinette, Molded, Painted Blond Hair & Features, 16 In.	300.00
Chef, Campbell Kid, Composition	300.00
Child, Twill Covered Body, Bisque, Skin Wig, Antique Dress, 8 1/2 In.	1300.00
China Head, Brown Eyes, Cloth Body, Original Clothes, 38 In.	850.00
China Head, Flat Top, Civil War Period, 27 In.	750.00
China Head, Flat Top, Original Clothes, 24 In.	425.00
China Head, For Dollhouse, Germany	95.00
China Head, Painted Eyes & Hair, Homemade Cloth Body, Clothes, 29 In.	325.00
China, Low Brow, White Dress, Pantaloon, Germany, 9 In.	85.00
Cloth, Brown–Skinned Boy, Lithographed Clothes, Muslin, c.1890, 15 In.	600.00
Cloth, Child, Painted Oilcloth Face, Victorian, 34 In.	795.00
Cloth, Hen & Chickens, Arnold Printworks, Uncut	75.00
Cloth, Lithographed, Girl In Underwear, Uncut, 8 In.	65.00

Cloth, Printed, Red Stockings, Shoes, Blond Curls, Early 1900s, 24 In. 125.00
Clown, Emmett Kelly 45.00
Clown, Emmett Kelly, Rubber Squeeze Head, 17 In. 125.00
Clown, Roly Poly, Papier-Mache, 8 In. 165.00
Composition, Molded Hair, Sleep Eyes, Cloth Body, 17 In. 42.50
Corncob, Man 6.00
D. F. B., Character, Bisque Socket Head, Painted Eyes, Pouty Mouth, 9 In. 450.00
Danbury, Wedding, Princess Diana, Prince Charles, Flower Girl, Box 500.00
Danel, Paris, Bebe No. 4, Closed Mouth, Bisque, Socket Head, 13 In. 6000.00
Danny O'Day, Ventriloquist, With Record Lessons 65.00
Denamur, Bebe, Bisque, 4 Teeth, Pierced Ears, Human Hair, 25 In. 1600.00
Dennis The Menace, Lace Up, Unused 18.50
Dennis The Menace, Mighty Star Ltd., Box, 13 In. 30.00
Dennis The Menace, Rubber 20.00
DEP, 8, Bisque, 21 In. 900.00
DEP, 10–154, Bisque Head, Shoulder Plate Marked, Kid Body, 22 In. 247.00
DEP, Beaded Earrings, 15 In. 230.00
DEP, Bisque, Brown Glass Eyes, Open Mouth, 4 Porcelain Teeth, 26 In. 1100.00
DEP, Bisque, Upper Teeth, Blond Curls, Jointed, Under Clothes, 17 In. 995.00
DEP, Bisque, Wood & Composition Body, Antique Clothing, 26 In. 5850.00
DEP, Closed Mouth, Blue Paperweight Eyes, 17 In. 2500.00
Dick Clark, 26 In. 195.00
Dolly Dingle, Musical, Catch A Falling Star 160.00
Eegee, Bisque, Paperweight Eyes, Straight Wrist, 18 1/2 In. 8100.00
Eegee, Fashion, Blond, 12 In. 12.00
Effanbee, 1st Club, White Organdy Dress, Vinyl, 1975, 24 In. 475.00
Effanbee, Betsy Wetsy, 1956 .... 30.00
Effanbee, Bubbles, Bisque, Green Eyes, 1920s, 25 In. 350.00
Effanbee, Cinderella 140.00
Effanbee, Claudette Colbert 100.00
Effanbee, Clippo The Clown, Marionette, Composition, Wood, Box 250.00
Effanbee, Dainty Dorothy, Composition, Cloth, Clothes, 14 In. 75.00
Effanbee, Dy–Dee Baby, Composition Head, Rubber, Sleep Eyes, 1930–1940 .... 150.00
Effanbee, Dy–Dee Baby, Plastic Head, Rubber Body, Caracul, 1940, 12 In. 85.00
Effanbee, Emily Ann, Marionette, Box, 1938 .... 245.00
Effanbee, Fleurette, 1978 .... 125.00
Effanbee, Heather 150.00
Effanbee, Honey Walker, Blue Velvet Snowsuit, White Fur, 20 In. 350.00
Effanbee, Jenny 140.00
Effanbee, Lady Angelique 150.00
Effanbee, Lady Nichole 150.00
Effanbee, Lady Stephanie 150.00
Effanbee, Liberace 82.50
Effanbee, Mae West, Gold Tag, Box, 16 In. .... 85.00 To 95.00
Effanbee, Majorette, All Original, Box, 17 In. 595.00
Effanbee, Mickey, Boxer, Boxing Gloves, Trunks, Red Painted Hair, 10 In. 75.00
Effanbee, Patsy 250.00
Effanbee, Patsy Ann 300.00
Effanbee, Patsy Baby, Composition, Brown Fur Wig, Blue Sleep Eyes 100.00
Effanbee, Patsy–Joan, 16 In. 300.00
Effanbee, Patsyette, Painted Blue Eyes, Pink Dress, 9 In. ....*Illus* 150.00
Effanbee, Rosemary, Walks, Talks, Sleep Eyes, Dressed, Marked, 22 In. 175.00
Effanbee, Skippy, W. W. I Soldier, Composition, Khaki Outfit .... 247.00 To 325.00
Effanbee, Suzanne, 14 In. 225.00
Effanbee, Suzette, c.1939, 11 In. ....90.00 To 100.00
Effanbee, Sweet, Patsy Junior 62.00
Effanbee, Sweetie Pie, 18 In. 385.00
Effanbee, Toreador, 1979 .... 25.00
Emma Clear, Jenny Lynn, Blond, Dressed, 1944, 18 In. 250.00
Eugene, Baby, Toddler, Vinyl, Chubby Limbs, 30 In. 45.00
Evel Knievel, On Card 30.00
F. G., Bisque, Ball–Jointed Body, Mohair Wig, Dress, Bonnet, 16 In. 6850.00
F. G., Fashion, Original Clothing, Shoes & Wig, 14 In. 2300.00

F. G., Mannequin, Bisque, Closed Mouth, Antique Silk Dress, 33 In. 8500.00
Farnell, Alpha, All Original, 19 In. 395.00
Fashion Queen, Swimsuit, 3 Wigs, Wig Stand 95.00
Fashion, Walking, Mechanical 6710.00
Felix The Cat, Cloth, Hand–Sewn Whiskers, Teeth, Glass Eyes 176.00
Felix The Cat, Marx, With Red Ball 185.00
Flying Nun 45.00
Fortune–Teller, Painted Hair, Eyes, Tissue Pleats Skirt, France, 11 In. 750.00
FR Nippon, 303, Pouty Baby, Character, 14 In. 1000.00
Francie, Brunette, Swimsuit 95.00
Franz Schmidt, No. 1272/45, Baby, Bisque, 5–Piece Bent Limb, 18 In. 400.00
Franz Schmidt, No. 1295, Toddler Boy, Blue Eyes, 21 In. 1295.00
Franz Schmidt, Toddler, Bisque, Long Curls, Dressed, 9 1/2 In. 350.00
Freddie Krueger, Talking .... 30.00 To 55.00
French, Bisque Head, Open Mouth, Dress, Underclothes, Shoes, 27 In. 1495.00
French, Bisque Head, Paperweight Eyes, Cloth, Kid Arms, 11 In. 1400.00
French, Bisque Head, Wood Jointed, Skin Wig, 15 In. 4500.00
French, Bisque Shoulder Plate, Jointed, Dressed, 15 1/2 In. 2400.00
French, Bisque, Articulated Wood Body, Swivel Neck, 16 In. 6985.00
French, Bordeaux, Peasant, Basket Of Shells, 11 In. 225.00
French, Ferdinand Gaulter, 12 In. 1550.00
French, Kid Body & Hands, Cork Pate, Silk Costume, 14 In. 1875.00
French, Swivel Neck, 2 Costumes, Leather Boots, 22 In. 4750.00
French, Toto, Bisque, Glass Set Eyes, Jointed Body, Silk Dress, 8 In. 395.00
French, Woman, Bisque, Paperweight Eyes, Jointed, Kid Body, 11 In. 1650.00
Frozen Charlie, Blond, 15 In. 385.00
Fulper, Bisque, Blond Hair, Kid Body, Redressed, Bonnet, 20 In. 395.00
Fulper, Character, Bisque Head, Stationary Glass Eyes, c.1918, 19 In. 165.00
G. I. Joe, Army Infantry Soldier, 1964, Hasbro 98.00
G. I. Joe, Action Pilot, Dog Tag, Cap, With 2 Coveralls 30.00
G. I. Joe, Action Sailor, Hasbro, 1964 .... 300.00
G. I. Joe, Australian Jungle Fighter, Blond, Back Pack Has 2 Tanks 200.00
G. I. Joe, Marine, Uniform, Hat 25.00
G. I. Joe, Red Painted Hair, Khaki Shirt, Pants, Black Boots 95.00
G. I. Joe, Russian Infantry, Jacket & Pants 100.00
Gadco, Martina, Box, 28 In. 225.00
Gebruder Heubach dolls are also in this section under Heubach
Gebruder Heubach, Bisque, Blue Eyes, Human Hair Wig, Costume, 25 In. 795.00
Gebruder Heubach, Bisque, Pouty Face, Intaglio Eyes, 17 In. 1200.00
Gebruder Heubach, Character, Painted Lashes, Feathered Brows, 15 In. 850.00
Gebruder Heubach, No. 08, Baby, Bisque Socket Head, Intaglio Eyes, 9 In 150.00
Gebruder Heubach, No. 8191, Baby, Grinning, Side Glance Eyes, 11 In. 750.00
Gebruder Knoch, Brown Bisque Shoulder, Head, Black Painted Hair, 7 In. 400.00
German, Bisque Head, Torso, Legs, Googly Eyes, Our Fairy, c.1915, 11 In. 650.00
German, Bisque Swivel Head, Kid–Lined Bisque Torso, Mohair Wig, 8 In. 1200.00
German, Bisque, Blond Sculpted Hair, Old Muslin Body, c.1870, 16 In. 550.00
German, Bisque, Set Eyes, Upper Teeth, Satin Dress, Shoes, 26 In. 1495.00
German, Child, Bisque Socket Head, Blue Sleep Eyes, Clothes, 24 In. 375.00
German, Googly, 1 Piece Bisque Head & Torso, Mohair Bobbed Wig, 7 In. 1500.00
German, Mystery, Original Bunting, 12 In. 975.00
Gilbert, James Bond 007, Firing Pistol, Scuba Outfit, 1965 .... 225.00
Gilbert, Napoleon Solo, Gun, Id. Card, Badge, 1965 .... 198.00
Girl, Papier–Mache, Blue Paperweight Eyes, 33 In. 450.00
Goebel, Baby, Porcelain, Lace Crib Dress, Bonnet, Doily–Lined Box, 8 In. 350.00
Goebel, Bettina, Musical 120.00
Goebel, Boy, Clockwork, Bisque, Human Hair, Winter Costume, 1915, 10 In. 850.00
Goebel, Brandy 150.00
Goebel, Gray Sleep Eyes, Lashes, Ball–Jointed Body, Dressed, 29 In. 850.00
Golliwog, Red Coat, Striped Pants, Chad Valley Chiltern Hygienic Toys 128.00
Gottschalk & Co., Sculpted Bonnet, Painted Eyes, c.1885, 18 In. 550.00
Groucho Marx, Box 53.00
H & S, 141, Art Doll 8500.00
Half, Wax, Painted Brown Eyes, Human Hair, Jointed Arms, 6 1/2 In. 160.00

Handwerck, 69, Open Mouth, Ball–Jointed Body, Sleep Eyes, 24 In. 550.00
Handwerck, 79/10, Bisque, Open Mouth, Ball–Jointed, 17 1/2 In. 795.00
Handwerck, 109, Girl, Bisque, Sleep Eyes, Pierced Ears, Blond, 19 In. 400.00
Handwerck, Bisque Head, Sleep Eyes, Composition, c.1902, 20 In. 1200.00
Handwerck, Bisque, Ball–Jointed, Black Velvet Skirt, Blouse, 20 In. 1200.00
Handwerck, Bisque, Mohair Wig, Chemise, 23 In. 995.00
Handwerck, Child, Bisque Socket Head, Blue Glass Sleep Eyes, 37 In. 2200.00
Handwerck, Child, Bisque, Open Mouth, 4 Porcelain Teeth, 16 In. 1000.00
Handwerck, Child, Bisque, Wooden Ball–Jointed Body, c.1900, 24 In. 700.00
Handwerck, Sleep Eyes, Jointed, Black Velvet Skirt, 1902, 20 In. 1200.00
Harmon, Oliver Hardy, 8 In. 30.00
Hawaiian, Grass Skirt, Movable Head & Arms, Plastic, 6 In. 15.00
Heebee, Bisque Head, O–Shaped Eyes, White Smock, Germany, c.1920, 7 In. 800.00
Hendren, Baby, Composition Head, Arms, Legs, Sleep Eyes, 1 Tooth, 18 In. 65.00
Hertel Schwab, 151, Bisque, Sleep Eyes, Christening Dress, 23 In. 750.00
Hertel Schwab, 151, Character Baby, Original Clothes, 12 In. 450.00
Hertel Schwab, Googly, Closed Mouth, Wide Cherubic Smile, 16 In. 7000.00
Heubach Koppelsdorf, 163, Googly, Black, Dimples, Rings In Nose, Ears 1595.00
Heubach Koppelsdorf, 250, Ball–Jointed, Brown Sleep Eyes, 30 In. 850.00
Heubach Koppelsdorf, 250–6, Swivel Head, Composition Body, 25 In. 495.00
Heubach Koppelsdorf, 251, Bisque, Sleep Eyes, Dutch Costume, 6 In. 125.00
Heubach Koppelsdorf, 264, Bisque Head, Set Eyes, 14 In. 325.00
Heubach Koppelsdorf, 300, Character Baby, Sleep Eyes, 13 In. 225.00
Heubach Koppelsdorf, 320–3/0, Baby, Bisque Socket Head, 15 In. 275.00
Heubach dolls are also in this section under Gebruder Heubach
Heubach, 261, Kid Body, 21 In. 400.00
Heubach, 7925, Lady, Bisque, Original Wig, 16 In. 4700.00
Heubach, 8550, Baby, Open–Close Mouth, Wicker Basket, Layette, 13 In. 650.00
Heubach, 9573, Googly, Brown Sleep Eyes, Watermelon Mouth, 9 In. 1250.00
Heubach, Baby, Composition Body, Extra Clothes In Trunk, Dressed, 8 In. 265.00
Heubach, Baby, Pouty, Molded Hair, Intaglio Eyes, 12 1/2 In. 675.00
Heubach, Boy, Bisque, Laughing, Squinting Eyes, Kid Body, c.1915, 12 In. 375.00
Heubach, Character, Whistler, 12 In. 845.00
Heubach, Child, Laughing, 16 In. 1300.00
Heubach, Coquette, Kid Body, Old Clothes, 10 In. 675.00
Hilda Baby, Bald Head, Long Baby Dress, 25 In. ..: 6500.00
Holly Hobbie, Vinyl, 11 In. 230.00
Horsman, Baby Dimples, 18 In. 65.00
Horsman, Baby Dimples, Bisque, Green Eyes, Dressed 300.00
Horsman, Baby, Composition Head, Sleep Eyes, Cloth Body, 1940s, 19 In. 135.00
Horsman, Cindy, Platinum Blond, Red Formal, 15 In. 25.00
Horsman, Tessy Talk, Name On Dress, c.1974, 19 In. 45.00
Hummel, Alpine Boy, 12 In. 90.00
Hummel, Boy, Rubber, Original Clothes, 10 In. 50.00
Hummel, Boy, Vinyl, 1981, 11 1/2 In. 75.00
Hummel, Girl, Vinyl, 1981, 11 1/2 In. 75.00
Hurtel & Swab, 151, Baby, Blue Eyes, 13 In. 375.00
Ideal, Baby First Step, All Original, 1965, 18 In. 25.00
Ideal, Baby Pebbles Flintstone 65.00
Ideal, Bam Bam, Rubber, 10 In. 35.00
Ideal, Betsy McCall, 36 In. 200.00
Ideal, Betsy McCall, Box, 36 In. 250.00
Ideal, Bonnie Braids, Box 450.00
Ideal, Boy, Sleep Eyes, Open Mouth, Cloth Body, Dressed, 18 In. .: 45.00
Ideal, Diana Ross, Rooted Hair, Sleep Eyes, Lame Dress, 1970s, 18 In. 95.00
Ideal, Giggles, Box, 1967, 17 In. 50.00
Ideal, Gomez, Hand Puppet, 1960s 125.00
Ideal, Hedda Get Bedda 65.00
Ideal, Kissy Baby, Vinyl, Cloth, 1962 .... 40.00
Ideal, Little Lost Baby, 3 Faces, Pink Snow Suit, 1960s, 21 In. 65.00
Ideal, Magilla Gorilla, 1964 .... 120.00
Ideal, Miss Revlon, Clothes, Box 85.00
Ideal, Mr. Magoo, Vinyl Head, Stuffed Body, 1950s 98.00

Ideal, Pebbles, 16 In.	58.00
Ideal, Pebbles, Rubber, 10 In.	35.00
Ideal, Pinocchio, Wood, 10 1/2 In.	175.00
Ideal, Raggedy Ann & Raggedy Andy, Porcelain, Set	300.00
Ideal, Saucy Walker, 16 In.	50.00
Ideal, Saucy Walker, Flirty Eyes, Tongue & Teeth, Hard Plastic, 23 In.	100.00
Ideal, Scarecrow, From Wizard Of Oz, Cloth, 1939	1512.00
Ideal, Thumbelina, Newborn, Unopened, 1968	38.00
Ideal, Toni, Original Clothes, 14 In.	180.00
Ideal, Toni, Original Clothes, 21 In.	395.00
Ideal, Toni, P–91, Dark Hair, Blue Dress, Leatherette Snap Shoes, 16 In	250.00
Ideal, Toni, P–91, Red Hair, Blue Dress, Vinyl Shoes, 16 In.	125.00
Ideal, Toni, Plastic Head, Bow–Shaped Lips, Box, c.1954, 15 In.	475.00
Indian dolls are listed in the Indian category	
J. D. K. dolls are also listed in this section under Kestner	
J. D. K., 237, Hilda, 17 In.	2650.00
J. D. K., 260, Toddler, Bisque, Sleep Eyes, Old Clothes, 36 In.	3750.00
J. D. K., Baby, Bald Head, Marked 10, 13 In.	500.00
Jackie Robinson, Composition, Dodger's Uniform, 1950s	385.00
Jane West, Box	50.00
Jeannie, I Dream Of Jeannie, TV Series, Box ....*Illus*	400.00
Jim West, Cowboy, Jointed, Molded Clothes, Marx, 1965	65.00
Jimmy Walker, Good Times, Box	60.00
Jumeau, 11, Bebe, Phonographe, Bisque Head, 6 Upper Teeth, 24 In.	5600.00
Jumeau, 252, Character, Pouty	7000.00
Jumeau, 1907, Bisque, Open Mouth, Long Curls, Silk Dress, Hat, 23 In.	1650.00
Jumeau, 1907, Open Mouth, Paperweight Eyes, Redressed, 26 1/2 In.	3450.00
Jumeau, Adult Modeled Body, Bisque Head, Closed Mouth, France, 24 In.	8750.00
Jumeau, Bebe, Bisque Head, Cork Pate, Blue Paperweight Eyes, 11 In.	2750.00
Jumeau, Bebe, Portrait, Blue Eyes, 17 In.	5500.00
Jumeau, Bisque Head, Amber–Brown Glass Paperweight Inset Eyes, 16 In.	3300.00
Jumeau, Bisque Head, Costumed In Bronze, Pale Green Silk, 14 In.	5250.00
Jumeau, Bisque Head, Open Mouth, Blue Glass Sleep Eyes, 14 In.	3200.00
Jumeau, Bisque, Jointed Wrist, Blue Eyes, Dressed, 24 In.	1495.00
Jumeau, Bisque, Open Mouth, Jointed Composition Body, Dressed, 32 In.	3400.00
Jumeau, Bisque, Set Eyes, Upper Teeth, Silk Dress, Shoes, 29 1/2 In.	2950.00
Jumeau, Bisque, Sleep Eyes, Jointed Wrists, Cotton Dress, Purse, 29 In.	3200.00
Jumeau, Bisque, Upper Teeth, Blond Wig, Pink Silk Dress, 29 1/2 In.	550.00
Jumeau, Blue Glass Paperweight Eyes, Wooden–Jointed Body, 32 In.	6250.00
Jumeau, Blue Paperweight Eyes, Open Mouth, 27 In.	2200.00
Jumeau, Closed Mouth, Original Dress, Marked P, 15 In.	3500.00
Jumeau, Laughing, Double Chin, Costume, 28 In.	2000.00
Jumeau, Portrait, Bisque, 8–Ball Body, Old Shoes & Wig, 16 In.	6850.00
Jumeau, Portrait, Blue Glass Paperweight Eyes, Pierced Ears, 22 In.	9000.00
Jumeau, Portrait, Fashion, Bisque Head, Kid Body, Redressed, 22 In.	3800.00
Jumeau, Premier Bebe, 10 In.	7500.00
Jumeau, Socket Head, Drinks From Bottle, Stirs Pot On Stove	4400.00
Jumeau, Swivel Head, Jointed Body, White Dress, 17 In.	3350.00
Jumeau, Walker, Turns Head, Pull Cord To Blow Kiss, Wool Suit, 22 In.	1500.00
Jutta, Baby, Sleep Eyes, Wig, 21 In.	275.00
K * R, 101, Character, Painted Eyes, Jointed, Original Clothes, 18 In.	2600.00
K * R, 101, Marie, Bisque, Blond Human Hair Wig, Antique Dress, 19 In.	5900.00
K * R, 101, Marie, Blue Eyes, 12 In.	3500.00
K * R, 101, Marie, Painted Eyes, Composition, Underclothes, Socks, 12 In.	2500.00
K * R, 101, Pouty Character, Jointed Body, 7 1/2 In.	1100.00
K * R, 114, Marie, Pouty Mouth, Coiled Braids, Crocheted Outfit, 11 In.	3000.00
K * R, 114, Pouty Character, Jointed Body, 9 1/2 In.	1800.00
K * R, 114, Pouty, Bisque, 14 In.	3950.00
K * R, 116A, Character Baby, Bisque, Painted Hair	1700.00
K * R, 117, Mein Leibling, Pouty, Closed Mouth, Tucked Dress, 19 In.	6875.00
K * R, 117, Mein Leibling, Sleep Eyes, Composition Jointed Body, 24 In.	8000.00
K * R, 117N, Bisque, Brown Flirty Sleep Eyes, Human Hair Wig, 28 In.	2800.00
K * R, 121, Baby, Bisque, Chunky Body, Sleep Eyes, 26 In.	2395.00

K * R, 122, Character, Brush Stroke Hair, Original Clothes, 17 In. 1550.00
K * R, 122, Character, Tiny Rows Of Teeth, Sleep Eyes, 16 In. 1250.00
K * R, 126, Baby Boy, Navy Blue Velvet Suit, Flirty Eyes, 24 In. 800.00
K * R, 126, Baby, Bisque Head, Flirty Eyes, 5–Piece Body, 22 In. 650.00
K * R, 126, Character Baby, Bent–Limb Body, Open Mouth, 27 In. 1800.00
K * R, 126, Child, Flirty Eyes, Jointed Composition Body, 20 In. 2300.00
K * R, 126, Toddler, Bisque, 11 In. 775.00
K * R, 126, Toddler, Bisque, Open Mouth, Chemise, c.1912, 10 In. .... 600.00 To 700.00
K * R, 126, Toddler, Blue Flirty Eyes, 22 1/2 In. 1150.00
K * R, 126, Toddler, Blue Flirty Eyes, 5 Piece, Mohair Wig, 21 In. 1250.00
K * R, 126, Toddler, Jointed, 16 In. 600.00
K * R, 127, Toddler, 15 In. 950.00
K * R, 131, Googly Eyes, Bisque Head, 15 In. 8000.00
K * R, 135, Flapper Child, Bisque Head, Elongated Torso, 14 In. 1500.00
K * R, 192, Bisque, Mohair Wig, Wedding Dress & Veil 550.00
K * R, Ball–Jointed Body, Sleep Eyes, Open Mouth, 27 In. 950.00
K * R, Bisque Head, Sleep Eyes, Composition Body, Ball–Jointed, 23 In. 5900.00
K * R, Boy, Bisque, Composition Jointed Body, Red Pants, 17 1/2 In. 895.00
K * R, Child, Bisque, 30 In. 800.00
K * R, Sweet Face, Blond Curls, Bonnet, 15 In. 200.00
Kathe Kruse, Baby, Cloth 7500.00
Kathe Kruse, Boy, Dark Hair, Straw Hat, 14 In. 275.00
Kathe Kruse, Bridget, Box, 1970 .... 75.00
Kathe Kruse, Fannie & Daniel, Blond Twins, 1980s, 14 In. 750.00
Kathe Kruse, Girl, 10 In. 250.00
Kathe Kruse, Girl, 1920s, 15 In. 1000.00
Kathe Kruse, No. 8, Swivel Head 1300.00
Kathe Kruse, Oil–Painted Hair & Face, Cloth, 17 In. 1700.00
Kathe Kruse, School Girl, School Bag, German Book & Slate, 20 In. 1950.00
Kenner, Alien, Plastic, Working Jaws, 1979 .... 142.00
Kestner dolls are also in this section under J. D. K.
Kestner, 1, Barefoot, Undressed, 6 In. 2600.00
Kestner, 10, Bisque Head, Composition Body, Original Clothes, 17 In. 1650.00
Kestner, 11, Swivel Head, Kid–Lined Bisque Shoulder Plate, 19 In. 3250.00
Kestner, 23, Bisque, Open Mouth, Teeth, Mohair Wig, 23 In. 595.00
Kestner, 50, Bisque, Eyes Turned To Side, Pointed Shoes, Socks, 8 In. 250.00
Kestner, 111, Pouty, Composition Body, Sleep Eyes, Barefoot, 8 In. 1150.00
Kestner, 135, Hilda, Dressed, c.1914, 15 In. 3800.00
Kestner, 142, Brown, Antique Clothing, 36 In. 1800.00
Kestner, 143, Character, Bisque, Sleep Eyes, Jointed, Dressed, 18 In. 900.00
Kestner, 146, Excelsior Composition Body, 23 In. 800.00
Kestner, 147, Child, Bisque Head, Sleep Eyes, Kid Body, 22 In. 650.00
Kestner, 150–6, Bisque, Chunky, 11 In. 250.00
Kestner, 152, Baby, Original Wig, 15 In. 650.00
Kestner, 152–10, Character Baby, Bisque, 18 In. 475.00
Kestner, 154, Baby, Bisque, 31 In. 900.00
Kestner, 154, Brown Sleep Eyes, 28 In. 700.00
Kestner, 154, Kid Body, Jointed, 30 In. 1500.00
Kestner, 154, Kid Body, Open Mouth, Sleep Eyes, 13 In. 225.00
Kestner, 154, Leather Body, 22 In. 395.00
Kestner, 154, Leather Body, Bisque, Open Mouth, Dressed, 28 In. 675.00
Kestner, 154, Leather Body, Jointed, 24 In. 485.00
Kestner, 166, Bisque, Kid Body, Ball–Jointed Arms, 22 In. 650.00
Kestner, 166, Bisque, Open Mouth, Red Wig, Jointed Kid Body 110.00
Kestner, 166, Lady, 18 In. 410.00
Kestner, 167, Dressed, 18 In. 475.00
Kestner, 168, Brown Sleep Eyes, Dressed, 21 In. 950.00
Kestner, 171, Daisy, Bisque Body, Auburn Mohair Wig, 21 In. 850.00
Kestner, 171, Daisy, Bisque, Jointed Body, Velvet & Silk Dress, 32 In. 1350.00
Kestner, 171, Daisy, Blue Eyes, Old Clothes, 18 In. 795.00
Kestner, 171, Sleep Eyes, Ball–Jointed Body, 32 In. 895.00
Kestner, 172, Gibson Girl, Cloth Body, Bisque Limbs, Underwear, 11 In. 995.00
Kestner, 196, Young Lady, Bisque, Original Clothing, 22 In. 45.00

Doll, Lenci, Dutch Boy, Blue Felt Smock, 17 In.

Doll, Lenci, Dutch Girl, Stitch-Striped Dress, 17 In.

Kestner, 214, Character, Lace & Ribbon Clothes, Long Curls, 32 In.	1500.00
Kestner, 215, Child, Bisque Socket Head, Brunette Mohair Wig, 25 In.	650.00
Kestner, 245, Hilda, Character Toddler, Batiste Dress, 24 In.	6000.00
Kestner, Baby, Brush Stroke Hair, 14 In.	365.00
Kestner, Boy, Bisque, Stationary Glass Eyes, Painted Hair, Nude, 20 In.	950.00
Kestner, Child, Bisque Socket Head, Sleep Eyes, Open Mouth, 25 In.	650.00
Kestner, Closed Mouth, All Original, 1890	3100.00
Kestner, Googly, All Bisque, Swivel Head, Chubby Toddler Body, 6 In.	1900.00
Kestner, Hilda Baby, Blue Sleep Eyes, 5–Piece Bent Limb, 16 In.	3500.00
Kestner, Molded Boots, 6 In.	1800.00
Kestner, Sammy, 18 1/2 In.	1050.00
Kestner, Turned Shoulder Head, Closed Mouth, Pouty Look, 24 In.	1500.00
Kevin, With Dawn's Dance Party, Stage, Unopened Box	95.00
Kewpie dolls are listed in the Kewpie category	
Kley & Hahn, 250, Walker, Composition Body, Ball–Jointed, 25 1/2 In.	625.00
Kley & Hahn, 525, Intaglio Eyes, Painted Hair, Ball–Jointed, 13 In.	650.00
Kley & Hahn, Bisque, Sleep Eyes, Silk Dress, 24 In.	695.00
Kley & Hahn, Character, Bisque Head, Open Close Mouth, Clothes, 19 In.	3400.00
Kley & Hahn, Sailor Boy, Blond Wig, Composition Body, 31 In.	1950.00
Kley & Hahn, Walker, Bisque, Human Hair Wig, Open Mouth, c.1910, 14 In.	550.00
Kling, Child, Bisque, Accented Nostrils, Open Mouth, Human Hair, 27 In.	1000.00
Knickerbocker, Baby Santa Claus, Plush Body, Vinyl Face	25.00
Knickerbocker, Barney Rubble	55.00
Knickerbocker, Capt. Kirk, Soft, Poseable, 1979, 13 In.	50.00
Knickerbocker, Fred & Barney, Pair	150.00
Knickerbocker, Fred Flintstone, Cloth, 1972, 6 1/2 In.	9.00 To 14.00
Knickerbocker, Fritz, Katzenjammer, Cloth, Glass Eyes, 1925, 15 In.	105.00
Knickerbocker, Raggedy Andy, Blue Hat & Pants, 15 In.	25.00
Knickerbocker, Raggedy Ann, 12 In.	30.00
Knickerbocker, Raggedy Ann, Display Size, 45 In.	235.00
Knickerbocker, Raggedy Ann, Polkadot Dress, 1970s, 20 In.	45.00
Knickerbocker, Spiderman, Cloth, 1978	15.00
Knickerbocker, Wilma Flintstone, Vinyl, Moveable Heads, 1960, 11 In.	50.00
Knickerbocker, Yogi Bear, 1959, 19 In.	35.00
Konig & Wernicke, Baby, Flirty & Sleep Eyes, Old Clothes, 28 In.	1500.00
Laundry Bag, Painted Oilcloth Face, Floral Print Clothes, 1920–1930	45.00
Laurel & Hardy, Ventriloquist	55.00
Lenci, 109, All Original, 22 1/2 In.	1950.00
Lenci, American School Child, Original Clothes, 17 In.	1695.00
Lenci, Boudoir, All Original, 25 In.	1295.00
Lenci, Child, Brown Eyes, Fancy Costume, Tagged, Box, 18 1/2 In.	1850.00

Lenci, Dutch Boy, Blue Felt Smock, 17 In. ....*Illus* 1500.00
Lenci, Dutch Girl, Stitch–Striped Dress, 17 In. ....*Illus* 2500.00
Lenci, Fioletta, 21 In. 275.00
Lenci, Ginnette, Black, 8 In. 35.00
Lenci, Girl, Eyes To One Side, Blue Felt Dress, 13 In. 375.00
Lenci, Girl, Tag, 22 1/2 In. 2200.00
Lenci, Glenda, Holding Jump Rope, Box, 19 In. 275.00
Lenci, Lavinia, Box, 1985 .... 400.00
Lenci, Surprised Eye, Brown Eyes, Floral Hat, 20 In. 2200.00
Lenci, Turkish Boy, Felt Body, Mohair Wig, 17 In. 2800.00
Lenci, Turkish Girl, Felt Body, Mohair Wig, 17 In. 2800.00
Lenci, Vegetable Seller, 17 In. 950.00
Limoges, Child, Bisque Head, Wood Jointed, Human Hair Wig, 19 In. 275.00
Lion, Wizard Of Oz Presents 15.00
Little Lulu, Cloth Mask Face, Red Dress, 1944, 14 In. ....*Illus* 400.00
Lori, Character, Upper Glancing Eyedots, Closed Mouth, Swaine, 24 In. 3000.00
Madame Alexander, Amy, Loop Curls, Cloverleaf Wrist Tag, 14 In. 400.00
Madame Alexander, Betsy Ross, Bent Knee 95.00
Madame Alexander, Binnie Walker, Hand Painted, Original, 15 In. 185.00
Madame Alexander, Brenda Starr, Lace Chemise, 11 1/2 In. 125.00
Madame Alexander, Bride, Hard Plastic, Brown Hair, Veil, Bouquet, 18 In. 450.00
Madame Alexander, Caroline Kennedy, Dressed, 15 In. 200.00
Madame Alexander, Cinderella, Box, 14 In. ....45.00 To 80.00
Madame Alexander, Cissette, 2 Piece Playsuit 150.00
Madame Alexander, Cissette, Net Overskirt, Straw Hat, 1958 .... 325.00
Madame Alexander, Cissy, Blue Dotted Dress, Straw Hat, Tagged 165.00
Madame Alexander, Degas Girl, 1967–1987, Box, 14 In. 60.00
Madame Alexander, Elise, Ballerina, 1979, 17 In. 150.00
Madame Alexander, Elise, Bride, 1983, Box, 17 In. 150.00
Madame Alexander, Elise, Bride, Red Hair, Tagged Dress 250.00
Madame Alexander, First Ladies, Set IV, Box 575.00
Madame Alexander, Friedrich, Sound Of Music, Original, 8 In. ....55.00 To 225.00
Madame Alexander, Groom, Hard Plastic, Fur Wig, Marked Alex, 18 In. 750.00
Madame Alexander, Janie, Smock & Tights 125.00
Madame Alexander, Kathy, Pigtails, Green & Pink Pinafore, 1950, 22 In. 695.00
Madame Alexander, Leslie, Black Bride 250.00
Madame Alexander, Lissy, Pink Organdy Dress, Straw Hat, 12 In. 265.00
Madame Alexander, Little Huggums, Box 30.00
Madame Alexander, Maggie Mixup, 8 In. 375.00
Madame Alexander, Margot Ballerina, Sleep Eyes, Pink Shoes, 17 In. 350.00
Madame Alexander, Mary Bel 100.00
Madame Alexander, McGuffey Ana, 1965, 8 In. 300.00
Madame Alexander, Miss Muffet, 1980 .... 45.00
Madame Alexander, Pamela, Wears Wigs, 12 In. 200.00
Madame Alexander, Princess Elizabeth, Composition, Crown, 15 In. 275.00
Madame Alexander, Princess Elizabeth, Tagged, 18 In. 225.00
Madame Alexander, Quiz–Kin, Boy 300.00
Madame Alexander, Rosy, Italy 55.00
Madame Alexander, Rosy, Poland 55.00
Madame Alexander, Scarlett O'Hara, 14 In. 300.00
Madame Alexander, Scarlett O'Hara, Green Print Dress, 1966, 8 In. 300.00
Madame Alexander, Scarlett O'Hara, Green Sash, Bows, Tag, 8 In. 135.00
Madame Alexander, Scarlett O'Hara, Hard Plastic, Wrist Tag, 12 In. 475.00
Madame Alexander, Scotland, 1976, Box, 8 In. 45.00
Madame Alexander, Snow White, Margaret Face, Tagged, 1952, 14 In. 495.00
Madame Alexander, Sonja Henie, Composition, 14 In. ....250.00 To 300.00
Madame Alexander, Swedish Boy, 10 In. 110.00
Madame Alexander, Tiny Betty, Norwegian, Composition 115.00
Madame Alexander, United States 75.00
Madame Alexander, Victoria, Christening Dress, 1975, 14 In. 55.00
Madame Alexander, Wendy Ann, Blue Flowered Dress, 1936, 7 In. 200.00
Madame Alexander, Wendy Ann, International, Clothes, Italy 78.00
Madame Alexander, Wendy–Kins, Ballerina, Jointed Knees, 7 In. 125.00

Madame Alexander, Wendy-Kins, Matinee, Coat, Long Blond Hair, 8 In. 250.00
Mae West 75.00
Marionette, Daisy Mae, Stringless, National Mask & Puppet, 1940s 175.00
Marionette, Donny & Marie Osmond, Pair 50.00
Marionette, Flub-A-Dub, Box 225.00
Marionette, Jambo The Jiver, Black, Box, 1940s 165.00
Marionette, Joey The Clown, Composition, 1940s, Box 50.00
Marionette, Li'l Abner, Stringless, National Mask & Puppet, 1940s 175.00
Marionette, Mr. Bluster 385.00
Marionette, Princess Summerfallwinterspring 290.00
Martha Chase, Boy, Cloth, Painted Hair, Face, Jointed, 26 In. 990.00
Marx, Miss Seventeen, Box 125.00
Mascotte, Wood & Composition Body, Silk & Lace Outfit, 30 In. 8500.00
Mattel, Barbie, American Girl, Honey Blond, Pale Lips, Bendable Leg 375.00
Mattel, Barbie, Ash Blond, Box, 1970 .... 365.00
Mattel, Barbie, Astronaut, Box, 1985 .... 60.00
Mattel, Barbie, Ballerina, Tutu 25.00
Mattel, Barbie, Blond Ponytail 250.00
Mattel, Barbie, Bride, Porcelain, Box 400.00
Mattel, Barbie, Bubble Cut, 1963 .... 45.00
Mattel, Barbie, Bubble Cut, Blond, 1965 .... 80.00
Mattel, Barbie, Bubble Cut, Blond, Picnic Clothes 60.00
Mattel, Barbie, Bubble Cut, Brunette, Box, 1962 .... 295.00
Mattel, Barbie, Bubble Cut, Red Hair, Bright Pink Coral Lips, Box 195.00
Mattel, Barbie, Cool City Blues 50.00
Mattel, Barbie, Dramatic Living, Platinum, Swimsuit 50.00
Mattel, Barbie, Enchanted Evening, Box, 1987 .... 200.00
Mattel, Barbie, Eskimo, Box 105.00
Mattel, Barbie, Fashion Queen, 3 Wigs, 1963 .... 28.00
Mattel, Barbie, Feelin' Groovy 100.00
Mattel, Barbie, Gay Parisiene, Porcelain, Box .... 165.00 To 220.00
Mattel, Barbie, Hispanic, Box .... 35.00 To 55.00
Mattel, Barbie, Holiday, Red Hair, Box 145.00
Mattel, Barbie, India, Box 105.00
Mattel, Barbie, Miss America, Wrist Tag 90.00
Mattel, Barbie, No. 3, Ponytail, Swimsuit, Glasses, Shoes 275.00
Mattel, Barbie, No. 4, Brunette, Ponytail, Box 65.00
Mattel, Barbie, No. 4, Ponytail, Brunette .... 135.00 To 225.00
Mattel, Barbie, Scottish, Box 165.00
Mattel, Barbie, Sleep Eyes, Wigs 250.00
Mattel, Barbie, Solo In Spotlight, Porcelain, Box 220.00
Mattel, Barbie, Sophisticated Lady, Porcelain, Box 220.00
Mattel, Barbie, Spanish .... 90.00 To 100.00
Mattel, Barbie, Style Magic 20.00
Mattel, Barbie, Sunsational 25.00
Mattel, Barbie, Swedish, Box 65.00
Mattel, Barbie, Swirl Ponytail, Box 250.00
Mattel, Barbie, Teenage Fashion Model, Box 100.00
Mattel, Barbie, Titian Hair, Bendable Legs, Box, 1965 .... 850.00
Mattel, Barbie, Titian Hair, Box, 1961 .... 175.00
Mattel, Barbie, Tropical, 1985 .... 15.00
Mattel, Barbie, Twist 'n Turn, Blond, Pink Sheath Dress, Jacket, 1966 .... 25.00
Mattel, Barbie, U. N. I. C. E. F, Blond 25.00
Mattel, Beany & Cecil, Talking, Pair 195.00
Mattel, Bozo, Hand Puppet, Mattel 95.00
Mattel, Buffy & Mrs. Beasley, Talks, Family Affair TV Show, Box 225.00
Mattel, Casper The Friendly Ghost, Talking 75.00
Mattel, Chatty Baby, Carrying Case, 1962 .... 55.00
Mattel, Chatty Cathy, Original Dress .... 45.00 To 50.00
Mattel, Doug Davis, Bendable, 1968, 6 In. 48.00
Mattel, Dr. Doolittle, Talking 75.00
Mattel, Herman Munster 225.00
Mattel, Julia, Talking Box 150.00

Mattel, Ken, 1960	60.00
Mattel, Ken, 9 Outfits, Box, 1960	140.00
Mattel, Ken, Blond, Box	160.00
Mattel, Ken, Blond, Flocked Hair	25.00
Mattel, Ken, Brunette, Flocked, Box	125.00 To 150.00
Mattel, Ken, King Arthur Outfit, Box	135.00
Mattel, Ken, Mod Hair	40.00
Mattel, Ken, Prince, Box	550.00
Mattel, Ken, Talking, Bendable Legs, Red Swimsuit, Jacket, 1969	25.00
Mattel, Ken, Tropical, 1985	15.00
Mattel, Marie Osmond, Model, Box, 30 In.	130.00
Mattel, Matt Mason, Astronaut, 1965	35.00
Mattel, Matt Mason, Major, Bendable, 1967, 6 In.	45.00
Mattel, Matt Mason, Scuba Driver, 1969	35.00
Mattel, Matty Mattel & Sister Belle, Talking, Pair	95.00
Mattel, Matty Mattel, Talking, Plastic Head, Cloth Body, 18 In.	85.00
Mattel, Midge, Bendable Legs	275.00
Mattel, Midge, Wedding Party, 6 Dolls, Box	125.00
Mattel, Mr. Ed, Talking	65.00
Mattel, Mrs. Beasley, Family Affair, Talking, Box, 22 In.	225.00
Mattel, P. J., Dream Date, 1983	20.00
Mattel, P. J., Sweet Roses, 1983	20.00
Mattel, P. J., Twist, Pink Jersey Mini Dress, Sunglasses, 1969	20.00
Mattel, Skipper, Fun On Wheels, Box	550.00
Mattel, Skipper, Straight Leg, Swimsuit	35.00
Mattel, Skooter, Blond, Bent Knee, Blue Denim Swimsuit	50.00
Mattel, Sweet 16, 3 Outfits, Package	120.00
Mattel, Timey Tell, Not Talking, Box, 1970, 17 In.	50.00
Mattel, Wayne Gretzky, Box	140.00
Mego, Captain Kirk, 1974	50.00
Mego, Mr. Spock, 1974	50.00
Mego, Robin, 1974	35.00
Mego, Sonny & Cher	30.00
Mego, Spiderman, Box, 8 In.	20.00
Milliner's Model, Papier-Mache, Kid Body, Wood Legs, Clothes, 11 In.	250.00
Milliner's Model, Papier-Mache, Shoulder Head, Kid Body, 15 1/2 In.	1300.00
Milliner's, Model, 6 In.	285.00
Minerva, Tin Head, Horsehair Stuffed Body, 22 In.	55.00
Minnie Ivey, Cloth, Stitch-Jointed Limbs, Hand Painted, 15 In.	1100.00
Morimura, Baby, Bisque, Original Clothes, 15 In.	225.00
Morimura, Character Baby, 12 In.	155.00
Munich Art, Boy, Painted Hair, Original Clothing, 14 In.	2650.00
Nancy Ann, Storybook, Baby, Plastic, 3 1/2 In.	40.00
Nancy Ann, Storybook, Little Red Riding Hood	28.00
Nippon, Display, 18 In.	175.00
Nippon, Hilda Baby, Blue Sleep Eyes, 19 In.	895.00
Nora Wellings, Mountie, 14 In.	185.00
Our Fairy, Bisque, Movable Arms, Googly Eyes To Side, Hat, 6 3/4 In.	1600.00
Paper dolls are listed in their own section	
Papier-Mache, Cameo-Shaped Face, Painted Blue Eyes, France, 11 In.	500.00
Papier-Mache, Lady, 1840, Elaborate Hair-Do, Kid Body, Wood Legs, 18 In.	1100.00
Parian, Alice, Bisque Head, Arms & Legs, Cloth Body, Blue Eyes, 15 In.	225.00
Parian, Blond Molded Hair, Cloth Body, Shoes & Clothes, c.1850, 19 In.	375.00
Parian, Blond Wavy Hair, Brush Strokes, Cloth, Bisque Limbs, 13 1/2 In.	300.00
Parian, Cloth Body, Fancy Hairdo, Clothes, 12 1/2 In.	1450.00
Parian, Countess Dagmar, Cloth Body, Kid Hands, Silk Costume, 18 In.	895.00
Parian, Glass Eyes, Pierced Ears, Earrings, Clothes, 21 In.	2450.00
Parian, Grape Snood Lady, All Original, 11 In.	1395.00
Parian, Jewelry, Pierced Ears, Silk Costume, 19 In.	795.00
Parian, Untinted Bisque Shoulder Head, Cloth Body, Kid Arms, 25 In.	275.00
Parker Brothers, Lovey & Dovey Magic, 1921, Pair	20.00
Patty Play Pal, Dark Hair, Blue Sleep Eyes, Red Dress, 36 In.	200.00
Peck Lucy, Poured Wax, Wire Lever Eyes, White Dress & Bonnet, 25 In.	3500.00

Doll, Little Lulu, Cloth Mask Face,
Red Dress, 1944, 14 In.

Doll, Raggedy Ann & Andy, Cloth, c.1915, 16 In., Pair

Pee–Wee Herman, Talking	100.00
Pee–Wee Herman, Ventriloquist, Billy Baloney, Box	25.00
Pee–Wee Herman, Ventriloquist, Box, 1989, 26 In.	80.00
Peggy Nisbett, 325, Royal Highlander, Black Watch, Scotland, Tag, 9 In.	50.00
Peggy Nisbett, Ice Skater	15.00
Peggy Nisbett, Queen's Coronation	75.00
Peggy Nisbett, Silver Anniversary	95.00
Pierotti, Poured Wax, Brown Glass Eyes, Wax Limbs, 20 In.	2850.00
Pincushion dolls are listed in their own section	
Playpal, Brian Jones, Vinyl, 1963, 5 In.	350.00
Porcelain, Brown Eyes, Black Sculpted Hair, Green Dress, 23 In.	1600.00
Porcelain, Lady, Black Sculpted Hair, Center Part, 22 In.	650.00
Porcelain, Pink–Tinted, Closed Mouth, Muslin Body, 18 In.	650.00
Porcelain, Tightly Sculpted Curls, Blue Shaded Eyes, 9 In.	300.00
Poupee, Transformation, 3 Heads, Arms & Legs, For 3 Dolls, England	2600.00
Poured Wax, Child, Blue Eyes, Blond Mohair Hair, Cloth Body, 23 In.	900.00
Pumpkin Head, Cloth Body, Wax Arms, Molded High Top Shoes, 17 In.	350.00
Puppet, Boxo, Talking, Mattel, Hand	95.00
Puppet, Cap'n Crunch Cereal, 2 Piece	30.00
Puppet, Clarabell The Clown, Hand	45.00
Puppet, Devil's Head, Red, Punch & Judy Style, Hand	21.00
Puppet, Dutch Boy Paints, Hand	40.00
Puppet, Gaty Alligator, Steiff, Hand	45.00
Puppet, Green Hornet, Hand	100.00
Puppet, Horse, Pelham, Box	48.00
Puppet, Larry, From 3 Stooges, Hand	50.00
Puppet, Monkey, Steiff, Hand	55.00
Puppet, Mr. Bluster, Hand	45.00
Puppet, Mr. Ed, Mattel, 1962	100.00
Puppet, Polar Bear, Hand	77.00
Puppet, Raggedy Ann & Andy, Knickerbocker, Pair	45.00
Puppet, Scarecrow, Cloth, Japan, 1960s, 10 In.	10.00
Puppet, Teddy Bear, Steiff, Hand	60.00
Puppet, Zorro, Hand	20.00
Putnam, Wax, Sleeping	5500.00
Rabery & Delphieu, Composition Body, Victorian Costume, 17 In.	2400.00
Raggedy Ann & Andy, Cloth, c.1915, 16 In., Pair ....*Illus*	2750.00
Raggedy Ann, Georgene, 36 In.	350.00
Raggedy Ann, Handmade, Embroidered Face, Red Bandana Dress, 26 In.	45.00
Raggedy Ann, Squeeze, Arrow Industries, 10 In.	12.00
Raleigh, Baby, Composition, Painted Eyes, Open Close Mouth, 12 In.	150.00

Ravca, Old Man With Umbrella, 20 In. 375.00
Ravca, Organ Grinder, Jacket 225.00
Remco, Baby Sister Grows Tooth, Black, Box, 1969 .... 50.00
Remco, Herman Munster, Vinyl Head, Synthetic Hair, Plastic, 6 In. 289.00
Remco, Lurch, Addams Family, 1965, Plastic, 5 In. 98.00
Remco, Morticia, Addams Family, 1965, Vinyl Head, Plastic Body, 5 In. 198.00
Remco, Stevie, Charlie, Robbie, My Three Sons, 1958 .... 158.00
Revalo, Open Mouth, Sleep Eyes, Jointed, Antique Clothing, 13 In. 750.00
Reversible, Child–Clown Face, Oilcloth, Painted Face, 21 In. 445.00
Roger Richman, Marilyn Monroe, Red Dress 135.00
Rushkin, Vinyl Rabbit Face, Blue Checked Clothes, Cloth Body, 1940s 30.00
Russia, Pottery Head, Ball–Jointed, Sleep Eyes, All Original, 16 In. 500.00
Russia, Tea Cozy, Peasant Girl, Stockinet Head, Padded Skirt, 10 In. 75.00
S & H dolls are also listed here as Bergmann and Simon & Halbig
S & H, 109, Blond Wig, Blue Sleep Eyes, 14 In. 385.00
S & H, 949, Kid Body, 20 In. 1800.00
S & H, 949, Kid Body, Original Clothing & Shoes 2200.00
S & H, 1079, Boy, Lord Fauntleroy Outfit, 42 In. 3400.00
S & H, 1079, Girl, 30 In. 1200.00
S & H, 1159, Gibson Girl, 16 1/4 In. 1150.00
S & H, 1160, Original Clothes, 6 In. 325.00
S. F. B. J., 13/0, Red Hair, Freckles 400.00
S. F. B. J., 60, Bisque, Stationary Eyes, Upper Teeth, Long Curls, 18 In. 595.00
S. F. B. J., 235, Boy, Molded Hair, Blue Glass Eyes, 2 Upper Teeth, 15 In. 1210.00
S. F. B. J., 235, Molded Hair, Jewel Eyes, Open–Close Mouth, 13 In. 1000.00
S. F. B. J., 236, Bisque, Laughing, 22 In. 1250.00
S. F. B. J., 236, Laughing Girl, 16 In. 1700.00
S. F. B. J., 236, Laughing Girl, Composition Ball–Jointed Body, 23 In. 2395.00
S. F. B. J., 236, Toddler, Bisque, 2 Teeth, Blue Eyes, Nursing Gown, 20 In. 1750.00
S. F. B. J., 251, Toddler, 24 In. 1250.00
S. F. B. J., 252, Pouty Girl, Bisque, Jointed Body, Wool Dress, Hat, 11 In. 4000.00
S. F. B. J., 301, Bisque, Human Hair, Tiara, Jointed, c.1900, 19 In. 880.00
S. F. B. J., 301, Bisque, Open Mouth, Sleep Eyes, Socks, Shoes, 26 1/2 In. 1595.00
S. F. B. J., 301, Clown, 15 In. 800.00
S. F. B. J., 301, Girl, Blond Wig, Braids, Brown Eyes, 20 In. 1000.00
S. F. B. J., 301, Unis, Working Mama–Papa Voice, 21 In. 650.00
S. F. B. J., 639, Blond, 26 In. 675.00
S. F. B. J., Bebe, Bisque Socket Head, 4 Porcelain Teeth, 22 In. 3200.00
S. F. B. J., Bisque, Braided Wig, Lace Apron, Leather Slippers, c.1900 .... 1100.00
S. F. B. J., Bisque, Human Hair Wig, Plaid Slacks, Green Velvet Jacket 660.00
S. F. B. J., Bisque, Jointed Body, Navel, Silk Costume, Gold Trim, c.1900 ...... 770.00
S. F. B. J., Bisque, Open Mouth, Brown Real Hair, Navy Silk Dress, 14 In. 1295.00
S. F. B. J., Bisque, Upper Teeth, Jointed Body, Wrists, Dressed, 21 1/2 In. 1250.00
S. F. B. J., Blue Sleep Eyes, 6 Teeth, Pique Dress & Coat, 31 In. 3000.00
S. F. B. J., Composition Jointed Body, Velvet Jacket & Pants, c.1900 .... 880.00
S. F. B. J., Open Mouth, 2 Beaded Upper Teeth, Human Hair, 13 In. 1500.00
S. F. B. J., Talking, Pull String, 36 In. 1500.00
S. F. B. J., Toddler, Bisque Socket Head, Brunette Human Hair Wig, 13 In. 1500.00
S. F. B. J., Twirp, Toddler, Sleep Eyes, Salmon French Dress, 13 1/2 In. 1500.00
S. F. B. J., Walker, Kiss Thrower, Flirty Eyes, 22 In. 895.00
S. F. B. J., Walker, Kiss Thrower, Flirty Eyes, 24 In. 1500.00
Santon, Terra–Cotta Head, Dressed, 4 1/2 In., Pair 150.00
Sasha, Brunette, Blue & White Checked Dress, Germany, 1970, 16 In. 55.00
Sasha, Prince Gregor, Box, 1974 .... 135.00
Saucy Walker, Composition, Blue Eyes, Black Hair, 22 In. 55.00
Schmitt, Girl, Composition Body, Shortened Limbs, Signed, c.1875, 15 In. 750.00
Schoenau & Hoffmeister, Bisque, Straight Wrist, Tucked Dress, 27 In. 675.00
Schoenau & Hoffmeister, Girl, Sleep Eyes, Upper Teeth, Clothes, 31 In. 600.00
Schoenhut, Baby, Grotesque 2805.00
Schoenhut, Carved Wooden Head, Decalcomania Blue Eyes, 15 In. 750.00
Schoenhut, Character Baby, 15 In. 735.00
Schoenhut, Character Boy, Sleep Eyes, 16 In. 950.00
Schoenhut, Character, Wooden Socket Head, Intaglio Eyes, Blond, 15 In. 325.00

Schoenhut, Foxy Grandpa, Grotesque	2695.00
Schoenhut, Girl, Wooden Head, Pouty Expression, c.1912, 22 In.	750.00
Schoenhut, Jockey, Grotesque	3740.00
Schoenhut, Walker, Baby Face, Redressed, 1911	650.00
Scootle, Bisque, Japan, 6 In.	250.00
SE–Wee, Sun Rubber	34.00
Senorita, Composition, Lace Dress, Fan, Mantilla, Comb, Old Mexico	40.00
Shader, Lynn, Navy Blue & White Outfit	395.00
Shader, Sari, Blue Satin Dress	450.00
Shebee, Bisque Head, Torso, Round Blue O–Shaped Eyes, 7 In.	900.00
Shebee, Bisque, White Modeled Smock, Oversized Pink Slippers, 7 In.	900.00
Shirley Temple dolls are included in the Shirley Temple category	
Siam Soo, Dancing, Complete, Box	350.00
Simon & Halbig dolls are also listed here under Bergmann and S & H	
Simon & Halbig, 126, Baby, Flirty Eyes, Store Clothes, 25 In.	1700.00
Simon & Halbig, 151, Character, Closed Smiling Mouth, 12 1/2 In.	5200.00
Simon & Halbig, 550, Blue Stationary Paperweight Eyes, 22 In.	850.00
Simon & Halbig, 570, Girl, Bisque Head, Upper Teeth, Jointed, 22 In.	550.00
Simon & Halbig, 719, Edison Body, 23 In.	1700.00
Simon & Halbig, 740, Bisque, Kid Gusset–Jointed Body, c.1890, 16 In.	900.00
Simon & Halbig, 759, Bisque, Open Mouth	2000.00
Simon & Halbig, 905, Closed Mouth, Swivel Head, 13 In.	1850.00
Simon & Halbig, 949, Swivel Neck, Leather Body, 16 In.	950.00
Simon & Halbig, 1009, Bisque, Brown Velvet Dress & Jacket, 26 In.	1650.00
Simon & Halbig, 1009, Fashion Lady, Bisque Swivel Head, 23 In.	800.00
Simon & Halbig, 1078, 22 In.	695.00
Simon & Halbig, 1079, Bisque Socket Head, Walking, Clockwork, 13 In.	950.00
Simon & Halbig, 1139, Ball–Jointed Body, Blue Sleep Eyes, 25 In.	850.00
Simon & Halbig, 1159, Gibson Girl, Silk & Velvet Dress, Hat, 20 In.	2200.00
Simon & Halbig, 1249, Bisque, Long Hair, Sleep Eyes, Dressed, 33 In.	2750.00
Simon & Halbig, 1279, Bisque, Brown Sleep Eyes, Original Dress, 10 In.	1400.00
Simon & Halbig, 1329, Oriental Girl, Pierced Ears, Open Mouth, 15 In.	1100.00
Simon & Halbig, 1428, Character Baby, Open Close Mouth, 13 1/2 In.	1295.00
Simon & Halbig, Bisque Head, Fully Jointed, Composition, 13 In.	357.00
Simon & Halbig, Bisque, Auburn Curly Wig, Dress & Shoes, 30 In.	895.00
Simon & Halbig, Bisque, Ball–Jointed Body, Brocade Dress, 28 In.	1500.00
Simon & Halbig, Bisque, Ball–Jointed, Blue Knickers, c.1890, 42 In.	3900.00
Simon & Halbig, Bisque, Upper Teeth, Long Curls, Silk Dress, 30 In.	1495.00
Simon & Halbig, Composition, Blue Sleep Eyes, Long Blond Hair, 27 In.	650.00
Simon & Halbig, Flapper, Woman Body, Green Chiffon Dress, Boa, 13 In.	900.00
Simon & Halbig, Girl, Open Mouth, Blond Mohair, Cotton Dress, 38 In.	2000.00
Simon & Halbig, Santa, Bisque, Mohair Wig, Original Costume, 29 In.	2595.00
Simon & Halbig, Walker, Key Wind, Flirty Eyes, Dressed, 22 In.	750.00
Sluggo, Cloth, Box, 7 In.	25.00
Smokey The Bear, Vinyl, Dakin, 8 In.	10.00 To 35.00
Spock, Star Trek, Original Package, 12 In.	45.00
Stacey, Twist & Turn, Red Short Hair, Swimsuit, 1969	195.00
Steffie, Walk Lively, Original Outfit	75.00
Steiff, Andreas	400.00
Steiff, Annette	375.00
Steiff, Bertha, With Teddy Bear	575.00
Steiff, Dutch Girl, 1913, Cloth, Glass Eyes, 13 In.	825.00
Steiff, Goldilocks & 3 Bears, Box	400.00
Steiff, Hansel & Gretel, 8 1/2 In., Pair	480.00
Steiff, Hubertus	1200.00
Steiff, Lulac, Straw Stuffed	245.00
Steiff, Micki & Mecki, Hedgehog, Original Clothes, 10 In., Pair	350.00
Steiff, Wedding Party, 5 Piece	550.00
Steiner, Bisque Head, Wooden–Jointed Body, Pierced Ears, 23 In.	5750.00
Steiner, Bisque, Curly Blond Wig, Motschmann Body, 14 In.	4900.00
Steiner, Bisque, Open Mouth, Black	5500.00
Steiner, Bisque, Wire–Lever Operated Eyes, Figure C, 22 In.	8500.00
Steiner, Character Baby, 10 In.	295.00

Steiner, Jules, Bebe, Bisque Socket Head, Blond Mohair Wig, 23 In.	5750.00
Steve Trebor, Wonder Woman Series, Box, 12 In.	35.00
Strobel & Wilken, 208, Googly, Sleep Eyes, 7 In.	750.00
Strobel, Darling, Bisque, Human Hair, Redressed, Bonnet, 22 In.	425.00
Swiss, Carved Wood, Painted Eyes, Jointed, Regional Clothes, 14 In.	175.00
Terri Lee, Black, 18 In.	250.00
Terri Lee, Blond Hair, Original Dress, 16 In.	125.00
Terri Lee, Dark Blond Wig, Tagged Dress, 16 In.	225.00
Terri Lee, Linda Baby, Molded Hair, Redressed, 10 In.	125.00
Terri Lee, Silver Skater, Dark Hair, 18 In.	185.00
Tete Jumeau, 1, Paperweight Eyes, Closed Mouth, Mohair Wig, Dressed	5500.00
Tete Jumeau, Ball-Jointed, Human Hair, Sleep Eyes, Clothes, 17 In.	2300.00
Tete Jumeau, Bisque, Applied Ears, Paperweight Eyes, 29 1/2 In.	7900.00
Tete Jumeau, Bisque, Blue Paperweight Eyes, French Body, 16 In.	3900.00
Tete Jumeau, Bisque, Pink Silk & Lace Dress, Bonnet, 16 In.	4600.00
Tete Jumeau, Original Clothes, 20 In.	4400.00
Tete Jumeau, Paperweight Eyes, Human Hair, Old Clothes, 23 1/2 In.	5200.00
Tipsy Tumbler, Box, 1960	55.00
Topo Gigio, Bobbing Head, Box	75.00
Topsy-Turvy, Black Girl & White Girl, Mask Faces, 11 In.	385.00
Topsy-Turvy, Rag, c.1860	265.00
Uncle Wiggily, Pressed & Painted Features, Brown Cotton, 1945, 18 In.	425.00
Ventriloquist, Danny O'Day Type, Dressed, 30 In.	25.00
Vogue, Ginny, Baby, 11 In.	22.00
Vogue, Ginny, Bride & Groom, Mid-1980s, Box, 8 In., Pair	50.00
Vogue, Ginny, Hansel & Gretyl, Mid-1980s, Box, 8 In., Pair	50.00
Vogue, Ginny, Plastic Head, Ruby Lips, Blond Wig, c.1955, 8 In.	375.00
Vogue, Ginny, Prince Charming & Cinderella, Box, 8 In., Pair	95.00
Vogue, Ginny, Sleep Eyes, Original Clothes	27.50
Vogue, Jill, With Tin Trunk, 3 Outfits, 1957	150.00
Vogue, Nurse, Side-Glancing Eyes, Brunette Wig, Dressed, c.1935, 8 In.	300.00
Vogue, Toodles Boy, Composition, Blue Knit Clothes, 8 In.	125.00
Walkure, Flapper, Bisque Head, 4 Upper Teeth, Blond Human Hair, 27 In.	1200.00
Wax, Over Papier-Mache, Shoulder Head, Painted Hair, Cloth Body, 26 In.	625.00
Wax, Woman, Embroidered & Damask Costume, Glass Case, France, 15 In.	225.00
Welsh, Bisque, Composition Body, Blue Eyes, Dressed, 21 In.	325.00
Woman, Wax Over Papier-Mache, Blond Sculpted Hair, 14 In., Pair	850.00
Wood Jointed, Rat Face, Lollipop Hands, Primitive, 2 In.	110.00
WPA, Cloth, Blue Cotton Suit, 1930s, 18 In., Pair	450.00
Wrestler, Bisque, Box Of Clothes, 8 1/2 In.	1500.00

DONALD DUCK items are included in the Disneyana section.

DOORSTOPS have been made in all types of designs. The vast majority of the doorstops sold today are cast iron and were made from about 1890 to 1930. Most of them are shaped like people, animals, flowers, or ships. Reproductions and newly designed examples are sold in gift shops.

Amish Woman, 10 In.	225.00
Amish Woman, Cast Iron, 4 3/4 In.	75.00
Ann Hathaway's Cottage, Cast Iron	175.00 To 450.00
Aunt Jemima, 10 In.	175.00 To 250.00
Aunt Jemima, Full Figure, Cast Iron, Hubley, 12 In.	290.00
Austrian Boy	*Illus* 286.00
Basket Of Flowers	30.00
Basket Of Tulips, Polychrome, Cast Iron, 13 In.	450.00
Bathing Beauties, Cast Iron	425.00
Bobby Blake, Cast Iron	390.00
Bobby Blake, Hubley, Miniature	225.00
Boy, Carrying Flower Basket, Cast Iron	275.00
Camel, Reclining, Cast Iron	140.00
Canoe, Girl	770.00
Car, Antique, Yellow, Cast Iron, Large	15.00
Cat, Black & Bronze, 10 1/2 In.	165.00

Cat, Black Paint, Green Eyes, Cast Iron, 12 1/2 In. 160.00
Cat, Full Figure, White Paint, Pastel Features, Cast Iron, 11 In. 85.00
Cat, Gray & White Paint, Cast Iron, 12 1/2 In. 200.00
Cat, Hunchback, Black, Green Eyes, Cast Iron, 7 x 10 In. 80.00
Cat, Original Paint, Gold Eyes, Iron, 9 1/2 In. 185.00
Cat, Persian, Hubley 160.00
Cat, Seated, Black Paint, Green Eyes, Cast Iron, 12 1/2 In. 125.00
Cat, Seated, Imari Colors, Porcelain, Oriental, 11 In. 110.00
Cat, Silhouette, Black, 9 1/2 In. 235.00
Cats, Twins, Cast Iron 250.00
Cats, Twins, Seated, National Foundry 200.00
Child On Knees, Yawning, Cast Iron 150.00
Child, Yawning 475.00
Christmas Tree, Cast Iron, 11 In. 400.00
Clipper Ship, Brass 65.00
Clipper Ship, Original Paint, Iron, 11 3/4 x 10 1/2 In. 88.00
Coach, London Mail, Hubley 150.00
Coach, Yellow Wheels, Brown Horses, Cast Iron, 8 1/2 x 6 3/4 In. 175.00
Colonial Lawyer, Cast Iron, 7 1/2 In. 180.00
Colonial Woman, Cast Iron ....79.00 To 145.00
Conestoga Wagon, Hubley 135.00
Cottage In Woods, Cast Iron 118.00
Covered Wagon, Oxen, Cast Iron 270.00
Cow, Painted, Cast Iron 265.00
Crash Car, Iron, Hubley 90.00
Dog, Airedale, Full Figure, Black & White, Cast Iron, 8 1/4 In. 130.00
Dog, Boston Terrier, Full Figure, Black & White Paint, 9 In. 95.00
Dog, Boston Terrier, Full Figure, Brown & Black, Iron, 8 1/2 In. 55.00
Dog, Boston Terrier, Original Polychrome Paint, Iron, 10 In. 65.00
Dog, Bulldog, Cast Iron 190.00
Dog, Bulldog, Cast Iron, 8 1/2 In. 135.00
Dog, Cocker Spaniel, Hubley 175.00
Dog, Dachshund, Cast Iron 265.00
Dog, French Bulldog, Seated, Cast Iron 90.00
Dog, German Shepherd, Full Figure, Black & White, Cast Iron, 13 In. 110.00
Dog, Japanese Spaniel, Cast Iron 275.00
Dog, Pointer, Full Figure, Cast Iron, 15 1/2 In. 95.00
Dog, Police, Full Figure, Cast Iron, 9 In. 95.00
Dog, Russian Wolfhound, Spencer 140.00
Dog, Scotty, 2 Sitting, Listen On Base, Cast Iron, 8 1/2 In. 150.00
Dog, Scotty, Double, Cast Iron 60.00
Dog, Scotty, Full Figure, Black, Cast Iron, 10 1/2 In. 100.00
Dog, Setter, Cast Iron, 15 In. 250.00
Dog, Wire–Haired Terrier, Cast Iron, 5 1/2 In. ....85.00 To 135.00
Dog, Wooden, Hand Made 10.00
Duck, Canvasback, Full Figure, Repaint, Cast Iron, 13 In. 65.00
Duck, Cast Iron 185.00
Duck, With Sweater & Cap, Cast Iron 110.00
Ducks, Mallard & Yellow, Cast Iron, 1929 .... 175.00
Dutch Girl, Littco Label 550.00
Elephant, Brass, 12 1/4 In., Pair 55.00
Elephant, Hubley ....150.00 To 195.00
Elephant, Trunk Down, Hubley 95.00
Fisherman, Cape Cod, Cast Iron, 6 In. 85.00
Flower Basket, 3 1/4 In. ....125.00 To 150.00
Folk Art, Cutout Flowers, Painted Wood, 1920s, 10 1/4 In. 16.00
Frog, Hubley ....25.00 To 75.00
Geese, 3 White, Cast Iron, 8 In. 60.00
Geisha, Cast Iron 195.00
Girl, Art Deco, 9 x 7 In. 110.00
Golf Putter, Cast Iron ....245.00 To 275.00
Goose, Long–Necked, Wedge Back, Cast Iron, 13 1/2 In. 250.00
Horse, Jumping Fence 660.00

Horse, Original Paint, Hubley 175.00
Indian Brave, Cast Iron 175.00
Indian Squaw, Cast Iron 175.00
Indian, On Horseback, Cast Iron 110.00
Jackie Coogan, As The Kid, Cast Iron 125.00
Kitten, Cast Iron, Hubley, 8 In. 185.00
Lion, Full Figure, Worn Gold Paint, Cast Iron, 9 In. 215.00
Lion, Rampant, Pitted, 15 In. 80.00
Lion, Sitting, Cast Iron 140.00
Little Red Riding Hood ....*Illus* 182.00
Little Red Riding Hood & Wolf, Cast Iron 306.00
Little Red Riding Hood, Hubley .... 550.00 To 750.00
Major Domo, Black Man In Uniform, Cast Iron 160.00
Major Domo, Hubley 260.00
Mammy, Cloth 37.50
Mammy, Wedge, Cast Iron, 13 1/2 In. 60.00
Man In Livery, Yellow Paint, Cast Iron, 8 3/8 In. 65.00
Mary Contrary, Cast Iron 500.00
Messenger Boy ....*Illus* 440.00
Monkey, Sitting, Tail Curled Around Him, Full Figure, Cast Iron 20.00
Mr. Punch, Cast Iron, 12 In. .... 150.00 To 295.00
Old Salt, Full Figure, Polychrome, Cast Iron, 6 3/4 In. 180.00
Old Woman, Cast Iron 575.00
Olive Picker 340.00
Oxen & Wagon, Cast Iron .... 125.00 To 135.00
Parrot, Perched In Gold Circle, Cast Iron, 7 x 8 In. 160.00
Parrot, Sitting, Cast Iron, 7 1/2 In. .... 145.00 To 195.00
Penguin, Top Hat, Hubley 375.00
Pirate, Cast Iron 115.00
Pirate, On Chest, Cast Iron, 6 In. 165.00
Policeman, Cast Iron, Le Mur Lighting Co. .... 240.00 To 250.00
Popeye, Hubley, Miniature 150.00
Poppy, Hubley 125.00
Pot Of Tulips, Cast Iron, 8 In. .... 135.00 To 140.00
Rabbit, Full Figure, No Paint, Cast Iron, 11 3/4 In. 250.00
Rabbit, Full Figure, White Repaint, Iron, 11 1/2 In. 175.00
Race Horse, Cast Iron, Virginia Metalcrafters, 1949 .... 135.00
Rooster, Painted, Cast Iron 300.00
Sailboat, Cast Iron 45.00
Santa Claus, Cast Iron .... 125.00 To 225.00
Senorita, Cast Iron, 11 1/4 In. 165.00
Sheep, Cast Iron 275.00
Ship, Original Paint, Iron, 9 1/4 x 5 7/8 In. 88.00
Spanish Girl, Cast Iron, 9 1/8 In. .... 225.00 To 325.00
Stag, Standing, Cast Iron 85.00
Stagecoach, Original Paint, Hubley, Paper Label 185.00
Sunbonnet Girl, Cast Iron, Large 575.00

Doorstop, Austrian Boy

Doorstop, Little Red Riding Hood

Doorstop, Messenger Boy

Left and right: Doulton, Vase, Boy, Dog, Horses, Lambeth, H. B. Barlow, 19 In., Pair;
Doulton, Vase, Girl, Goats, Donkeys, Lambeth, H. B. Barlow, 14 1/2 In.

Sunbonnet Sue, Cast Iron	190.00
Totem Pole, Cast Iron, 7 1/2 In.	85.00
Turtle, Cast Iron, Hubley	100.00 To 950.00
Windmill, Cast Iron, 6 3/4 In.	165.00 To 175.00
Windmill, Cast Iron, Greenblatt Studios	325.00
Windmill, Path To Door, Garden On Side, Cast Iron, 1925, 7 1/2 In.	165.00
Windmill, Sea Ground	346.00
Woman, French, Cast Iron, 9 In.	175.00
Woman, Full Bonnet, Black Hair, Pink Gown, 10 In.	175.00
Woman, Grecian Drape, Nibbling Apple, Walks Mastive Dog, Iron	110.00
Woman, Victorian, Full Figure, Cast Iron, 5 In.	75.00
Yankee Soldier, Cast Iron	85.00

DOULTON pottery and porcelain were made by Doulton and Co. of Burslem, England, after 1882. The name *Royal Doulton* appeared on their wares after 1902. Other pottery by Doulton is listed under Royal Doulton.

Ashtray, Colored Bird, Marked, 4 1/4 In.	250.00
Ashtray, Striker On Bottom, Courages Pale Ale, Green & Brown Glaze	85.00
Biscuit Jar, Ferns, Brown Leaves, Silicone Glaze, 7 1/4 In.	280.00
Compote, Burslem, Tapestry Finish, Floral, 5 1/2 x 9 1/2 In.	375.00
Fernery, Dutch Durham, 5 In.	110.00
Mustard, Overlay Of Flowers, Strawberries, 3 1/2 In.	140.00
Pitcher, Incised Cat Frieze, Hannah B. Barlow, c.1895, 9 1/4 In.	2885.00
Pitcher, Incised Dog In Grass, Hannah B. Barlow, c.1890, 6 1/2 In.	1100.00
Pitcher, Incised Goats Running, Hannah B. Barlow, 1876, 9 1/2 In.	1550.00
Pitcher, Kyber, Adams	150.00
Pitcher, Lambeth, Slater	225.00
Pitcher, Pate–Sur–Pate Bird, Florence E. Barlow, c.1882, 7 1/4 In.	475.00
Pitcher, Willow, 6 In.	90.00
Punch Bowl, Tulip Design, Lambeth, 8 x 12 In.	93.00
Tankard, Pewter Lid, Herons, Reeds, Hannah B. Barlow, 1875, 9 1/2 In.	1450.00
Teapot, Goats, Eagle Spout, Hannah B. Barlow, 1880, 5 1/2 In.	1550.00
Tobacco Jar, Cattle, Goats, Plated Fittings, Hannah B. Barlow, 8 In.	990.00
Tobacco Jar, Gold Swirls, Blue & Brown Border, Lambeth, 5 1/2 In.	70.00
Toothpick, Ploughing	80.00
Vase, Boy, Dog, Horses, Lambeth, H. B. Barlow, 19 In., Pair ....*Illus*	2750.00
Vase, Cottage Scene, Hand Painted, Conical, c.1910, 9 In., Pair	490.00
Vase, Cover, Figural & Floral Design, Burslem, 10 1/2 In.	220.00
Vase, Floral, Eliza Simmance, 12 In.	375.00
Vase, Frieze Of Kangaroos, Hannah B. Barlow, 1886, 12 In.	990.00
Vase, Frieze Of Lions, Leaf Rims, Hannah B. Barlow, c.1895, 7 1/2 In.	1750.00
Vase, Girl, Goats, Donkeys, Lambeth, H. B. Barlow, 14 1/2 In. ....*Illus*	3740.00
Vase, Incised Frieze, Pig Scene, Hannah B. Barlow, c.1895, 11 In.	1045.00
Vase, Multicolored Flowers, Gold Outlined, Burslem, 11 1/2 In.	235.00

Dresden, Candelabrum, Woman, Child

◆◆◆◆◆◆◆◆◆◆◆◆◆◆◆◆◆◆◆◆◆◆

Check the metal strips holding any heavy wall–hung shelves. After a few years, the shelf holder may develop *creep* and gradually bend away from the wall.

◆◆◆◆◆◆◆◆◆◆◆◆◆◆◆◆◆◆◆◆◆◆

◆◆◆◆◆◆◆◆◆◆◆◆◆◆◆◆◆◆◆◆◆◆

Sap bleeds from the knots in old wood and stains the paint. This discoloration is one way to determine if paint is old.

◆◆◆◆◆◆◆◆◆◆◆◆◆◆◆◆◆◆◆◆◆◆

DRAGONWARE is a form of moriage pottery. Moriage is a type of decoration on Japanese pottery. Raised white designs are applied to the ware. White dragons are the major raised decorations on the moriage called *dragonware*. The background color is gray and white, orange and lavender, or orange and brown. It is a twentieth–century ware.

Incense Pot	16.00
Plate, 7 1/4 In	35.00
Wall Pocket	35.00

DRESDEN china is any china made in the town of Dresden, Germany. The most famous factory in Dresden is the Meissen factory. Figurines of eighteenth–century ladies and gentlemen, animal groups, or cherubs and other mythological subjects were popular. One special type of figurine was made with skirts of porcelain–dipped lace. Do not make the mistake of thinking that all pieces marked *Dresden* are from the Meissen factory. The Meissen pieces usually have crossed swords marks, and are listed under Meissen. Some recent porcelain from Ireland, called *Irish Dresden,* is not included in this book.

Basket, Blue & Pink Flowers, Baroque Feet, Floral Handle, 7 In.	150.00
Basket, Blue & Pink Flowers, Floral Loop Handle, 7 1/2 In.	125.00
Candelabrum, Woman, Child *Illus*	100.00
Cider Set, Grape & Floral, 7 Piece	300.00
Clock, Courting Couple, Man Playing Bagpipes, c.1880, 9 1/4 In.	850.00
Figurine, 2 Women Chatting, Seated, Lace Dresses, 10 x 12 In.	950.00
Figurine, Amour Tete–A–Tete, 7 x 9 In.	550.00
Figurine, Ballerina, Seated 8 In.	275.00
Figurine, Chess Game, Man In Coat, Woman In Gold Dress, 6 1/2 In.	450.00
Figurine, Couple, Waltzing 7 In.	600.00
Figurine, Dancer, Young Girl, White Lace Dress, 8 In.	225.00
Figurine, Dancing Couple, Marked, 5 x 6 In.	225.00
Figurine, Dancing Woman, 8 In.	350.00
Figurine, Girl On Couch, Polychrome, Gilt With Lace, 6 3/4 In.	85.00
Figurine, Girl, 2–Tier Lace Dress, Hands Outstretched, 3 3/4 In.	75.00
Figurine, Girl, Lace Dress, Boy, Playing Instrument, 7 x 9 In.	550.00
Figurine, Harlequin Serenade, 13 x 12 In.	1150.00
Figurine, Monkey Band, Porcelain, 1900s, 9 Piece	1045.00
Figurine, Ring Around Rosy, 3 Girls, Lace Dresses, 8 1/2 In.	295.00
Figurine, Russian Wolfhound, 6 1/4 x 12 In.	300.00
Figurine, Scots Fusiliers Guards, Polychrome Enameling, 11 1/4 In.	145.00
Figurine, Violin Solo, Woman On Couch, Man Playing Violin, 10 In.	850.00

Figurine, Woman With Wolfhound, 7 x 6 1/2 In.	375.00
Group, Musical, Musicians & Barmaid, Bagpipes & Lute, 11 1/2 In.	1250.00
Group, Woman, Seated, Blackamoor, Kneeling, Flower Basket, 8 1/2 In.	305.00
Jardiniere, Dome Cover, Romantic Scenes, Paneled, Marked, 14 In.	850.00
Lamp, Banquet, Portrait, Applied Porcelain Flowers	320.00
Plaque, Woman, Standing, White Dress, Rectangular, Framed, 9 x 7 In.	1650.00
Plaque, Young Woman, With Flowing Hair, Gilt Frame, Graf, 5 In.	600.00
Teapot, Duck, Hand Painted Feathers, Gray Body, Signed, 6 x 10 In.	345.00
Tray, Fruit, Yellow Ground, Lobed, Rectangular, 16 In.	154.00
Urn, Floral Basket Panels, Turquoise Blue, Gold, c.1870, 10 In., Pair	750.00
Urn, Pierced Cover, Acorn Finial, Flowers, Gilt Ground, 23 In., Pair	775.00
Vase, 2 Women & Cupid, Children In Background, Marked, 12 In.	795.00
Vase, Courting Couple Medallion, Gold Beading, 8 In.	295.00
Vase, Victorian Couple Medallions, Cobalt Blue, Signed, 8 In.	325.00

DUNCAN & MILLER is a term used by collectors when referring to glass made by the George A. Duncan and Sons Company or the Duncan and Miller Glass Company. These companies worked from 1893 to 1955, when the use of the name *Duncan* was discontinued and the firm became part of the United States Glass Company. Early patterns may be listed under Pressed Glass.

American Way, Celery, 3 Sections, Pink	65.00
American Way, Ice Bucket, Handle	55.00
American Way, Punch Bowl, Low Base, 14 In.	200.00
American Way, Vase, Flared, Ruby	125.00
American Way, Vase, Fluted, Ruby, 8 x 8 In.	125.00
Arliss, Mug, Green Handle, Crystal	20.00
Ashtray, Duck, 1940	40.00
Canterbury, Candy Dish, Cover, 3 Sections	18.00
Canterbury, Sherbet	6.00
Caribbean, Eggcup	23.00
Caribbean, Punch Bowl, Underplate, Red Handled Ladle	150.00
Caribbean, Punch Set, Red Handled Cup, Crystal, 27 Piece	450.00
Caribbean, Relish, 4 Sections, Handle, Blue, 12 In.	80.00
Caribbean, Relish, Blue, 12 3/4 In.	40.00
Caribbean, Tray, Fluted	58.00
Caribbean, Vase, Ruffled, Footed, Blue, 9 1/2 In.	98.00
Caribbean, Wine, Ball Stem, 3 1/2 In.	23.00
Cornucopia, 13 In.	35.00
Diamond Ridge, Punch Bowl, 12 In.	45.00
Figurine, Donkey & Peasant	450.00
Figurine, Goose	195.00
Figurine, Goose, Fat, 3	225.00
Figurine, Heron, 6 1/2 In.	95.00
Figurine, Swordfish, Blue	125.00
First Love, Champagne	22.00
First Love, Decanter	150.00
First Love, Goblet	17.00 To 25.00
First Love, Vase, 8 3/4 In.	50.00
Georgian, Mug, Crystal, Amber Handle, 5 In.	16.00
Heron, Sugar & Creamer, Pink	35.00
Hobnail, Bowl, Crimped, 9 In.	16.00
Hobnail, Cocktail, 3 1/2 Oz.	10.00
Hobnail, Plate, 8 1/2 In.	11.00
Hobnail, Powder Box, 4 In.	20.00
Hobnail, Punch Cup	4.50
Hobnail, Tumbler, 10 Oz.	12.00
Hobnail, Tumbler, Iced Tea, 13 Oz.	13.50
Hobnail, Vase, Crimped, 8 In.	15.00
Hobnail, Vase, Violet, Green, 6 1/2 In.	40.00
King Arthur, Toothpick, Gold	40.00
Lovelace, Basket, Scalloped Rim, 1930s, 9 1/2 x 10 In.	125.00
Mardi Gras, Goblet, Sherry	22.00

Mardi Gras, Sugar, Cover, Child's 65.00
Mardi Gras, Toothpick, Spooner Shape 35.00
Pall Mall, Swan, 10 1/2 In. 25.00
Quartered Block, Toothpick 45.00
Remembrance, Tumbler, Iced Tea 18.00
Sandwich, Ashtray, Square 6.00
Sandwich, Basket, Loop Handles, 11 1/2 In. 150.00
Sandwich, Basket, Ruby 95.00
Sandwich, Basket, Shallow, 7 In. 115.00
Sandwich, Bowl, Flared, 12 In. 45.00
Sandwich, Bowl, Flower, Lily Pond, 10 In. 43.00
Sandwich, Cake Plate, Footed, 13 In. 75.00
Sandwich, Cake Stand, 13 In. 85.00
Sandwich, Candlestick, 4 In., Pair 27.00
Sandwich, Cup & Saucer .... 12.50 To 15.00
Sandwich, Epergne, 3 Sections, 12 In. 250.00
Sandwich, Pitcher, 8 In. 115.00
Sandwich, Plate, 8 In. 12.00
Sandwich, Plate, Cupped, Ruby, 13 1/2 In. 90.00
Sandwich, Plate, Deviled Egg, 12 In. 70.00
Sandwich, Relish, 3 Sections, 12 In. .... 30.00 To 34.00
Sandwich, Salt & Pepper, Green 60.00
Sandwich, Sugar & Creamer, 2 1/2 x 3 1/2 In. 12.50
Sandwich, Sugar & Creamer, Tray, Individual 37.00
Sandwich, Tray, Muffin, Ruby 43.00
Sandwich, Vase, Footed, 10 In. 75.00
Sanibel, Muffin Tray, Jasmine Yellow 45.00
Sanibel, Plate, Blue, 8 1/2 In. 25.00
Sanibel, Plate, Yellow, 8 1/2 In. 28.00
Sanibel, Relish, 2 Sections, Blue 28.00
Sanibel, Relish, 2 Sections, Yellow 32.00
Spiral Flutes, Compote, Footed, 9 1/2 In. 14.00
Spiral Flutes, Cup, Seafood, Green 16.00
Spiral Flutes, Soup, Cream, Pink 12.00
Spiral Flutes, Tumbler, Juice, Footed 4.00
Swan, 12–In. Wingspan, 8 1/2 In. 145.00
Swan, Biscayne, Green, 1940s, 7 In. 60.00
Swan, Cobalt Neck, 12 1/2 In. 120.00
Swan, Open, 7 In. 12.00
Swan, Ruby, 7 1/2 In. 23.00
Swan, Ruby, 7 In. 75.00
Swan, Ruby, 10 In. 55.00
Swan, Ruby, 11 1/2 In. 48.00
Swan, Ruby, 12 In. 70.00
Swan, Solid, 5 In. 19.00
Swan, Spread Wing, Pink 125.00
Swan, Sylvan, Blue, 5 1/2 In. 55.00
Sylvan, Candy Dish, Blue, 7 1/2 In. 24.00
Teardrop, Ashtray, Individual 3.00
Teardrop, Butter, Silver Plated Cover 18.50
Teardrop, Pitcher 150.00
Teardrop, Plate, Dinner 50.00
Teardrop, Punch Bowl 175.00
Teardrop, Relish, Handle, 7 1/2 In. 15.00
Teardrop, Torte Plate, 13 1/2in. 28.00
Three–Face, Compote 65.00
Viking, Boat, Clear 195.00
Waterford, Bowl, Green, 5 In. 5.00
Waterford, Goblet, Footed, Green, 6 In. 7.00

DURAND glass was made by Victor Durand from 1879 to 1935 at several factories. Most of the iridescent Durand glass was made by Victor Durand, Jr., from 1912 to 1924 at the Durand Art Glass Works in Vineland, New Jersey.

Ginger Jar, Cover	1980.00
Ginger Jar, King Tut Design, 10 In.	2785.00
Jar, Blue, Cover, Signed	500.00
Lamp, Blue King Tut Design, Metal Mountings, Orange, 13 In.	605.00
Lamp, Torch, Crackle Glass, Gilt Metal Shade, 9 1/2 In.	605.00
Plate, Central Peacock Feather, Cross-Hatch Cutting, 8 1/4 In.	300.00
Plate, Peacock, White & Blue Feathers, 7 1/2 In., Pair	220.00
Shade, Gold Threaded Design, Opal White Ground, 6 In.	110.00
Vase, Ambergris, Intaglio Cut, Signed, 4 In.	370.00
Vase, Blue & White Pulled Feather, Gold, Swelled Cylindrical, 10 In.	715.00
Vase, Classic Vasiform, Iridescent, Signed, 12 In.	275.00
Vase, Gold Hooked Design, Green, Blue & Pink Highlights, 7 In.	605.00
Vase, Gold Iridescent, White Interior, 4 1/4 In.	445.00
Vase, Heart & Clinging Vine, Baluster Form, Signed, 1811, 14 In.	1045.00
Vase, Hearts & Vines, Orange, Green Hearts, Large	1250.00
Vase, King Tut, Iridescent Blue, Green, White, Gold, 6 1/2 In.	550.00
Vase, Random Bubbles, Crystal Rib, Teardrop Shape, 12 In.	1700.00
Vase, Stick, Opalescent Lily Pads, Signed, 16 In.	2540.00

ELFINWARE is a mark found on Dresden-like porcelain that was sold in dime stores and gift shops. Many pieces were decorated with raised flowers. The mark was registered by Breslauer-Underberg, Inc. of New York City in 1947. Pieces marked *Elfinware Made in Germany* had been sold since 1945 by this importer.

Bottle, Pig, Moss Forget-Me-Not, Roses, 3 x 1 1/2 In.	95.00
Box, Cover, Colored Flowers, Grass Ground, 11 3/4 In.	50.00
Carriage, Baby, White & Blue Flowers, Grass, 2 x 2 3/4 In.	55.00
Figurine, Slipper	16.00
Teapot	45.00
Teapot, Shades Of Lavender	35.00
Vase, Wall Pocket	45.00

ELVIS PRESLEY, the well-known singer, lived from 1935 to 1977. He became famous by 1956. Elvis appeared on television, starred in twenty-seven movies, and performed in Las Vegas. Memorabilia from any of the Presley shows, his records, and even memorials made after his death are collected.

Anklet, Dog Tag, 1956, Silver Etched, Package	32.00
Book, Coloring, Large Format	25.00
Bracelet, Charm, 1950s	95.00 To 150.00
Button, Flicker, Portrait To Performing Pose, 1956, 2 1/2 In.	22.00
Calendar, Pocketbook, 1977	2.00
Cape, Brass Studs, Glass Beads, Gold Lining, Cotton, 1972	8250.00
Card, Baseball-Type, Series Of 66	95.00
Card, Christmas, Blue, 5 Views Of Graceland, 1975	30.00
Card, Lobby, Girls, Girls, Girls	20.00
Card, Official Elvis Presley Fan Club, Envelope, 1957	20.00
Cassette Player, Elvis In Concert, Stage, Microphone	100.00
Letter, From Elvis To Anita Wood, Vicksburg, 1958	7700.00
Music Box, Love Me Tender, Elvis Figure, No. 723	125.00
Newspaper, Elvis Presley Dies At 42, L. A. Times, Aug. 17, 1977	27.00
Pajamas, Monogrammed, Black Silk, c.1972	1650.00
Paper Doll, Elvis, Priscilla, 4 Dolls, Outfits, 1st Ed., Uncut	40.00
Pin, Flasher, Older Elvis	18.00
Postcard, Christmas, Elvis In Army Uniform, 1959	10.00
Postcard, Christmas, Hawaiian, 1961	15.00
Print, Elvis, Framed	5.00
Record Set, Special Canadian Issue, Issue 5, Unplayed	75.00

*Enamel, Plaque, Mice, Thelma
Winter, 1950, 15 In.*

*Enamel, Vase, Multicolored,
H. Tishler, 8 1/4 In.*

Record, Love Me Tender, RCA, 78 RPM	75.00
Scarf, Stage, Autographed, White Silk, 34 x 34 In.	605.00
Sheet Music, All Shook Up, 1957	23.00
Sheet Music, G. I. Blues	9.00
Tape Measure	15.00
Tin, Christy's Oyster, Elvis's Picture	370.00
Wallet, Rock N' Roll, Elvis Presley Enterprises, 1956	988.00

ENAMELS listed here are made of glass particles and other materials heated and fused to metal. In the eighteenth and nineteenth centuries, workmen from Russia, France, England, and other countries made small boxes and table pieces of enamel on metal. One form of English enamel is called *Battersea* and is listed under that name. There was a revival of interest in enameling in the thirties and a new style evolved. Graniteware is a separate category and enameled metal kitchen pieces are included in the Kitchen section.

Ashtray, Red, Crackle, Winter, 6 In.	75.00
Beaker, Initials, Eagle, Dated 1896	100.00
Bowl, Beaded Trim, Copper, Nekrassoff, 5 In.	95.00
Box, Sweetmeat, Bilston, Goldfinch Lift–Off Cover, 18th Century	560.00
Cup & Saucer, Turquoise & Blue, White, Copper, Nekrassoff	130.00
Dish, Blue & White, Brass, Rim, Evans	35.00
Flowerpot, Flared, Yellow, Pewter Top Edges, Nekrassoff	165.00
Pitcher, Cider, Grapes, Austria	60.00
Plaque, 3 Angels, Thelma, 10 In.	200.00
Plaque, Mice, Thelma Winter, 1950, 15 In. ....*Illus*	125.00
Plate, Yellow Spatter Inside, Copper, Nekrassoff, 10 In.	165.00
Tray, Floral Center, Black & Gold Edge Design, 26 x 19 1/2 In.	140.00
Tray, Multicolored Peacock, Branches, Green, Gold Edge, Oval, 26 In.	140.00
Vase, 5–Petaled Blossoms, Pyriform, Copper, C. Faure, 1925, 12 In.	4950.00
Vase, Amethyst Glass, Florals, Gold, Unusual Shape, Venetian, 12 In	35.00
Vase, Copper, Checkerboards, Strips, Limoges, c.1925, 10 3/4 In.	4400.00
Vase, Copper, Geometric Design, Limoges, c.1925, 9 3/4 In.	1100.00
Vase, Copper, Overlapping Circles, Limoges, 1925, 6 1/8 In.	1925.00
Vase, Multicolored, H. Tishler, 8 1/4 In. ....*Illus*	95.00
Vase, Overall Multicolored Floral Design, Oriental, 8 1/2 In., Pr.	495.00
Wine, Clear, Striped Bowl, Stemmed, Austria,, 5 1/4 In., 10 Piece	4400.00
Wine, Clear, Stylized Blossoms & Leaf Bowl, M. Flogl, 4 3/4 In., Pr.	2750.00

ERPHILA is a mysterious mark found on 1930s Czechoslovakian pottery and porcelain. It is thought that the mark was used on items imported by Eberling & Reuss, Philadelphia, a giftware firm which is still operating in Pennsylvania. The mark is a combination of the letters *E* and *R* (Eberling & Reuss) and the first letters of the city, Phila(delphia). Many whimsical figural pitchers and creamers, figurines, platters, and other giftwares carry this mark.

Figurine, Hunter, With Bird, Germany, 4 In.	20.00
Pitcher, Bird Shape, Orange, Black, 8 In.	165.00
Pitcher, Dog, Orange, Black	150.00
Pitcher, Duck, Orange, Black	135.00
Teapot, Federal Style Woman, Germany	75.00

ES GERMANY porcelain was made at the factory of Erdmann Schlegelmilch from 1861 to 1925 in Suhl, Germany. The porcelain, marked *ES Germany* or *ES Suhl,* was sold decorated or undecorated. Other pieces were made at a factory in Saxony, Prussia, and are marked *ES Prussia.* Reinhold Schlegelmilch made the famous wares marked *RS Germany.*

Bowl, Florals & Fruit, Black & Orange, 6 In.	75.00
Creamer, Classic Scene, Maroon, Gold Trim	25.00
Plate, Portrait, 6 Flowered Wells, Open Handles, 9 1/2 In.	170.00

ESKIMO artifacts of all types are collected. Carvings of whale or walrus teeth are listed under Scrimshaw. Baskets are in the Basket category. All other types of Eskimo art are listed here.

Basket, Ivory Finial On Lid, Coiled Baleen, 2 x 3 In.	545.00
Basket, Ivory Seal Head On Lid, Disks Woven Into Base, 2 3/4 In.	485.00
Blanket, Button, Red & Gray Trade Cloth, Reds, Blues, 44 x 35 In.	400.00
Cribbage Board, Carved Seal & Fish Figures, 1912, 22 In.	272.00
Cribbage Board, Tusk, Carved Walrus & Reindeer, 13 1/4 In.	245.00
Doll, Beaded Leather Face, Fur Skin Costume, Beaded Boots, 13 In.	500.00
Doll, Carved Ivory Head, Fur Skin Costume, Purple Felt Sash, 6 In.	475.00
Doll, Carved Wooden Head, Fur Skin Costume, Beading, 8 1/2 In.	275.00
Effigy Face, Whale Vertebra	220.00
Figure, Arctic Foxes, Ivory, Petrified Ivory Stand, 11 In.	305.00
Figure, Man Carrying Seal Strapped To Back, Stone, 8 In.	200.00
Moccasins, Floral Beading On Toes, Wolf Fur Trim	200.00
Pendant, Scrimshaw Ivory, Oval, 1 1/2 In.	25.00
Pipe, Ivory, Carved Animals On Stem, Design On Bowl, 11 In.	1925.00
Salt & Pepper, Polar Bear Surmounted By Baby Seal, Ivory, 2 1/2 In.	120.00

ETLING glass is very similar in design to Lalique and Phoenix glass. It was made in France for Etling, a retail shop. It dates from the 1920s and 1930s.

ETLING
FRANCE

Figure, Madonna, 12 In.	1400.00
Figurine, Tropical Fish, Frosted, Clear Base, Signed, 6 3/4 In.	800.00
Vase, Nude Dancing Women, 14 In.	175.00

FABERGE was a firm of jewelers and goldsmiths founded in St. Petersburg, Russia, in 1842, by Gustav Faberge. Peter Carl Faberge, his son, was jeweler to the Russian Imperial Court from about 1870 to 1914. The rare Imperial Easter eggs, jewelry, and decorative items are very expensive today.

Bowl, Silver, Blue Glass, Domed Bud Finial Cover, Rappoport, 6 In.	5775.00
Bowl, Wooden, Silver Rim With Imperial Eagle, Gorianov, 3 1/8 In.	3300.00
Box, Cigar, Enameled Vegetable Forms On Cover, c.1910, 6 1/8 In.	9350.00
Case, Card, Imperial Eagle Set With Diamonds, c.1900, 5 1/2 In.	4950.00
Case, Cigarette, Woman's, 14K Gold, Silver, Diamond Thumbpiece, 3 In.	4950.00
Charka, Carved Nephrite, 14K Gold, Inscription, Perchin, 1 3/4 In.	5500.00
Cuff Links, 2–Color 14k Gold, Enameled, Hollming, 1/2 In., Pair	8250.00
Decanter, Hinged Cover, Cut Glass Body, c.1880, 9 3/8 In.	4950.00
Dish, Cavier, Fish Form, Silver, c.1900, 7 1/2 In.	6050.00

Figurine, Elephant, Obsidian, Standing, Diamond Eyes, 1890, 2 In. 3025.00
Frame, Silver, Lilac, Guilloche, Bow, Nevalainen, Oval, 2 3/8 In. 5500.00
Frame, Silver, Rhondonite Borders, Bow Top, 2 Bun Feet, 1885, 6 In. 8250.00
Kovsh, 14K Gold, White Stripes, Sapphire, Moonstone, 1885, 3 1/8 In. 7425.00
Kovsh, Design To Simulate Jewels, Birds, c.1900, 12 1/4 In. 4950.00
Letter Opener, Nephrite Handle, Silver–Gilt Swags, 1910, 10 In. 7700.00
Letter Opener, Silver Blade, Gold Handle, c.1890, 3 3/8 In. 4400.00
Mirror, Table, Silver, Neo–Rococo Scrolls, Rectangular, 27 1/2 In. 8800.00
Pendant, Enamel Pink Over Guilloche, 14K Gold, 7/8 In. 3575.00
Saltshaker, Fish Form, Open Mouth, c.1910, 5 1/4 In. 6050.00
Spoon, Serving, Silver–Gilt, Shaded Enameled, 1900, 6 3/4 In. 3850.00
Watch, Lapel, Ball Shape, Enameled, Diamonds On Back, 2 In. 9350.00

FAIENCE refers to tin–glazed earthenware, especially the wares made in France, Germany, and Scandinavia. It is also correct to say that faience is the same as majolica or Delft, although usually the term refers only to the tin–glazed pottery of the three regions mentioned.

Box, Knop Cover, Pears, Sceaux, 1755–1760, 6 5/8 In. 8800.00
Bust, Young Woman, 19th Century, 6 1/2 In. 35.00
Dish, of Radishes, Hexagonal, France, 9 13/16 In. 3025.00
Figurine, Lion, Sitting, Blue, White, 1760, 7 3/8 & 7 5/16 In., Pr. 880.00
Jug, Pewter Lid, Allover Florals, Blue & White, Germany, 8 In. 660.00
Pitcher, Gesso, Banded Floral Design, Pale Green, Macintyre, 7 In. 220.00
Plaque, Polychrome Enameling, Gilt, Ormolu Ribbon, 17 In. 300.00
Platter, Caryatid & Dragon Design, Knights Helmet, 13 x 17 In. 220.00
Trivet, Cloisonne Mission Design, California, Round, 5 1/4 In. 330.00
Trivet, Squeeze–Bag Design Of Fruit, California, 5 1/4 In. 248.00
Tureen, Cover, Cabbage, Greens, Sceaux, 1755, 14 5/16 In. 9900.00

FAIRINGS are small souvenir china boxes and figurines that were sold at country fairs during the nineteenth century. Most were made in Germany. Reproductions of fairings are being made, especially of the famous *twelve months of marriage* series.

Figurine, Come Along, These Flowers 165.00
Figurine, First In Bed 80.00
Figurine, Little Girl Coming Out Of Basket, Germany, 4 3/4 In. 125.00
Figurine, Mary Had A Little Lamb 100.00
Figurine, Napoleon & Horse 100.00

FAIRYLAND LUSTER pieces are included in the Wedgwood section.

FAMILLE ROSE, see Chinese Export category

FANS have been used for cooling since the days of the ancients. By the eighteenth century, the fan was an accessory for the lady of fashion and very elaborate and expensive fans were made. Sticks were made of ivory or wood, set with jewels or carved. The fans were made of painted silk or paper. Inexpensive paper fans printed with advertising were giveaways in the late nineteenth and early twentieth centuries. Electric fans were introduced in 1882.

Advertising, Compliments, Hillcrest Dress Shop, Christy, 1923, 10 In. 15.00
Advertising, Croft Ale 30.00
Advertising, Emerson's Drugs, Fountain Giveaway, Girl Playing Tennis 35.00
Advertising, Garrett's Snuff, Paper & Stick, 1929 .... 16.00
Advertising, Garrett's Snuff, The Bribe, Artist Signed 15.00
Advertising, German Bakery, Seattle, Woman With Hat, Cardboard, Color 15.00
Advertising, Gibson Girl, Cigar Advertising On Back, Paper, Pair 10.00
Advertising, Gold Dust Twins, St. Louis World's Fair, 1903 .... 295.00
Advertising, Hillcrest Dress Shop, Omah, Flapper, Cardboard, 1925, 11 In. 8.00
Advertising, J. J. Evans Mfg., San Francisco, Hand Shape, 3 1/2 x 2 In. 2.00
Advertising, Kool Cigarettes 10.00
Advertising, Lucky Strike, Paper, Leaf Shape, Sinatra's Picture, 1940s 38.00
Advertising, Maple Leaf Rubbers Wpg., Victorian Woman, Cardboard 15.00

Advertising, Marshall Field & Co.	35.00
Advertising, Putnam Dye	30.00
Advertising, Putnam Dyes, Cardboard, Colored Litho, Gen. Putnam	20.00
Advertising, Putnam Dyes, Peacock, Cardboard	10.00
Advertising, Red Dot Cigars, Cardboard	65.00
Advertising, Saloon & General Store, Windup	325.00
Advertising, Tums, Cardboard, 1920s	10.00
Baseball, Googly–Eye Players, Spectators, Colorful, 1940s, 5 x 12 In.	5.00
Black Lace, Gold Sparkles, White Leather Silk–Lined Box, France, 1900s	75.00
Black Ostrich Tips, Pierced & Carved Sticks, 12 x 24 In.	225.00
Black Wooden Handle Embossed In Silver Floral Designs, 20 In.	125.00
Blue Ostrich Plumes, Tortoiseshell Handles	55.00
Bride's, Ivory, Carved & Pierced Sticks, Chinese, Gold & Lacquer Case	775.00
Ceiling, Dallas Airplane Fan Co.	650.00
Celluloid, Flower Cutouts, Chain, 30 In.	25.00
Electric, General Electric, Brass	295.00
Electric, General Electric, Chrome, Art Deco	65.00
Electric, Singer Sewing Machine, Box	40.00
Electric, Singer, Oscillating, 9 In.	35.00
Feather Covered, Gilded Frame, Tortoiseshell Type, 14 In.	80.00
Ivory & Silk, Hand Painted Courting Scene, c.1880, 9 1/2 x 18 In.	440.00
Ivory Sticks, Oriental Figures, Monogram, 13 In.	450.00
Ivory, Cherub Scene, Tassel, Signed	175.00
Ivory, Hand Painted Oriental Scene, Signed Tiffany, Box	995.00
Ivory, Oriental Figures, Monogram, Black Lacquer Frame, 15 3/4 In.	450.00
Lace & Mother–of–Pearl, Box, Expands To 19 In.	245.00
Marshall Field & Co., Paper	35.00
Martin Luther King's Portrait, Payne Funeral Directors, Harlem, N.Y.	10.00
Mourning, Black Satin	35.00
Neo–Classical Figures, In Shadow Box, Printed & Ivory, 9 In.	100.00
Ostrich Feathers, French Ivory	65.00
Ostrich Feathers, Tortoise Finger Ring & Ribs	75.00
Ostrich Feathers, Victorian, Tortoise, 18 In.	195.00
Ostrich Feathers, White, Mother–of–Pearl Sticks	100.00
Painted Dance Scene, Tortoiseshell & Cloth, Almeida	160.00
Pictorial Upper Portion, Gold Design, Mother–of–Pearl, Folding	190.00
Romantic Scene, Allover Hand Painted, Ornate Wooden Frame	95.00
Silk Gauze, Hand Painted, Ivory Sticks, Case	175.00
Valentine, Folding, Paper, Girl, With All My Love, My Valentine, 8 In.	21.00
Wallpaper, Palm Leaf Pattern, Aug. 25, 1893, New Vineyard, Maine	22.00
Wedding, Hand Painted Cream Silk, Wooden Sticks, Date & Guests, 1892	300.00
Wooden, Folding, Woman's	4.00

FAST FOOD COLLECTIBLES may be included in several categories, such as Advertising, Coca–Cola, Toy, etc.

FEDERZEICHNUNG is the very strange German name for a pattern of mother-of-pearl satin glass. The pattern had irregularly shaped sections of brown glass covered with a pattern of gold squiggle lines. It was first made in the late nineteenth century.

Vase, Brown, Mother–of–Pearl Air Traps, Pink Lining, 6 In.	2125.00
Vase, Brown, Mother–of–Pearl, White Lining, 7 x 7 1/2 In.	2250.00
Vase, Brown, White Scrolling, Webb, Signed PL, 10 1/4 In.	1000.00

FENTON Art Glass Company, founded in Martins Ferry, Ohio, by Frank L. Fenton, is now located in Williamstown, West Virginia. It is noted for early carnival glass produced between 1907 and 1920. Many other types of glass were also made.

Aqua Crest, Epergne, 1 Lily	65.00
Aqua Crest, Vase, Tri–Top, 8 1/2 In.	45.00
Atlantis, Spittoon, Woman's, Peach Opalescent	55.00
Bicentennial, Mug, Cobalt Blue, 7 In.	35.00
Black Crest, Bonbon, Handles	45.00

Bonbon, Butterfly, Green	58.00
Bubble Optic, Vase, Amber, 11 In.	110.00
Burmese, Nappy, Heart Shape, Handle	70.00
Burmese, Vase, Gloria Finn, 7 1/4 In.	60.00
Burmese, Vase, Jack–In–The–Pulpit, Roses	50.00
Butterfly & Berry, Lamp, Mariner's, 22 In.	350.00
Cactus, Basket, Yellow Opalescent	90.00
Cherry Circles, Bonbon, Marigold	45.00
Coin Dot, Bowl, Double Crimped, French Opalescent, 10 1/2 In.	55.00
Coin Dot, Lamp, Candlestick, French Opalescent, Complete	68.00
Coin Dot, Sugar & Creamer	65.00
Coin Dot, Vase, Cranberry, 4 In.	47.50
Coin Dot, Water Set, Cranberry Opalescent, 1949–1957, 7 Piece	750.00
Coinspot, Lamp, Shade, Yellow, 13 In.	45.00
Console Set, Mandarin Red, 1920s, 3 Piece	125.00
Daisy & Button, Candy Jar, Green	50.00
Daisy & Fern, Water Set, Cranberry, 7 Piece	350.00
Diamond Lace, Epergne, 3 Lilies, Blue Opal, 10 1/2 In.	180.00
Diamond Optic, Basket, Crystal Handle, Ruby Overlay, 6 1/4 In.	48.00
Dolphin, Candlestick, Green, 1928, Pair	40.00
Dot Optic, Ivy Ball, Footed, White & Green	68.00
Dot Optic, Pitcher, 1940	95.00
Dragon & Lotus, Bowl, Purple Iridescent, 9 In.	80.00
Emerald Crest, Flowerpot	55.00
Emerald Crest, Tray, Tidbit, 3 Tier	60.00
Georgian, Sherbet, Footed, Red	5.00
Gold Crest, Candlestick, Cornucopia, 6 In., Pair	45.00
Grape & Cable, Jar, Rosalene	165.00
Grape & Cable, Jar, Tobacco, Rosalene	225.00
Hanging Heart, Cruet, Clear	90.00
Hobnail, Ashtray, Tan	32.00
Hobnail, Bowl, Double Crimp, Footed, 8 In.	14.00
Hobnail, Bowl, Yellow, 10 1/2 In.	50.00
Hobnail, Cake Stand, 12 1/2 In.	35.00
Hobnail, Candy Dish, Cover, White, 9 In.	25.00
Hobnail, Cruet, Blue, 3 Oz.	18.00
Hobnail, Epergne, 3–Lily, 6 1/2 x 8 1/2 In.	75.00
Hobnail, Epergne, Blue	130.00
Hobnail, Jug, Blue, 5 1/2 In.	35.00
Hobnail, Pitcher, Clear Applied Handle, Vaseline, 5 3/4 In.	95.00
Hobnail, Pitcher, Ice Lip, White	65.00
Hobnail, Sugar & Creamer, Blue, Tall	45.00
Hobnail, Tray, Fan, Blue, 10 1/2 In.	50.00
Hobnail, Vase, Blue, Square, 4 1/2 In.	32.00
Hobnail, Vase, Fan, 5 1/2 In.	18.00
Horizontal Threads, Creamer, Child's, Blue	25.00
Horizontal Threads, Spooner, Child's, Blue	25.00
Horizontal Threads, Sugar, Child's, Blue	42.00
Ivory Crest, Vase, 10 In.	55.00
Jamestown, Basket, 8 1/2 In.	35.00
Jamestown, Cake Plate, Footed, Blue	35.00
Jar, Macaroon, Periwinkle Blue, Reed Handle	210.00
Lamp, Cardinals In Winter, Student, 19 1/2 In.	220.00
Lamp, Double Globe, Cranberry, White, 22 In., Pair	250.00
Lamp, Fairy, Burmese, Stickers	110.00
Lincoln Inn, Cup & Saucer, Cobalt Blue	25.00
Lincoln Inn, Finger Bowl, Cobalt Blue	30.00
Lincoln Inn, Tumbler, Footed, Red, 9 Oz.	24.00
Lincoln Inn, Water Set, Amethyst, 7 Piece	160.00
Orange Tree, Bowl, Footed, 1880–1900	225.00
Orange Tree, Bowl, Marigold, Scrolled	175.00
Orange Tree, Mug, 1920s	36.00
Paperweight, Eagle, Bicentennial, Chocolate	45.00

Peach Crest, Basket, 7 In.	35.00
Peach Crest, Basket, Marigold Handle, 7 In.	50.00
Peach Crest, Bowl, 7 In.	40.00
Peach Crest, Ewer, Beaded Melon, 6 1/2 In.	45.00
Peach Crest, Jug, Melon Shape, 8 In.	75.00
Peach Crest, Rose Bowl, Piecrust Top, 3 1/2 In.	40.00
Peach Crest, Vase, 1950s, 8 In.	45.00
Peacock, Vase, 8 In.	65.00
Peacock, Vase, Mandarin Red, 7 1/2 In.	295.00
Peacock, Vase, Opalescent Topaz, 8 In.	38.00
Plymouth, Ice Bucket, Ruby	60.00
Powder Box, Rose Overlay	22.00
Reverse Drape, Bowl, Blue	35.00
Rosalene, Ivy Bowl, Orange Tree	65.00
Rosalene, Vase, Basket Weave, 8 In.	60.00
Rose Bowl, Blown Out, Butterscotch, White Inside, Pair	150.00
Rose Crest, Bowl, Double Crimped, 10 1/2 In.	65.00
Rose Crest, Vase, Double, Crimped, 6 1/2 In.	28.00
Sailboats, Wine	30.00
Silver Crest, Basket, Spanish Lace, 8 In.	38.00 To 46.00
Silver Crest, Bowl, 8 In.	20.00
Silver Crest, Candlestick, 3 In., Pair	25.00
Silver Crest, Compote, Cover, 8 In.	30.00
Silver Crest, Epergne, 3 Piece	85.00
Silver Crest, Ivy Ball	35.00
Silver Crest, Plate, Tidbit, 3 Tiers	35.00
Silver Crest, Tray, Center Handle	15.00
Silver Crest, Vase, Fan, Hand Painted Violets, 6 In.	15.00
Silver Crest, Vase, Fluted, Double, 8 In.	30.00
Snow Crest, Flower Pot, Attached Saucer	65.00
Spiral Optic, Vase, Amber	50.00
Spiral Optic, Vase, Flared, Label, 10 In.	110.00
Spiral Optic, Vase, Hat, Blue Opalescent, 1939	119.00
Spiral Optic, Water Set, Green, 7 Piece	195.00
Syrup, Topaz, 5 1/2 In.	45.00
Vasa Murrhina, 4 In.	35.00
Vintage, Bowl, Caramel, 6 1/2 In.	40.00
Vintage, Fernery, Blue	50.00
Water Lily & Cattails, Butter, Cover	70.00
Water Lily, Box, Candy, Rosalene	65.00
Water Lily, Rose Bowl, Blue	30.00

FIESTA, the colorful dinnerware, was introduced in 1936 by the Homer Laughlin China Co., redesigned in 1969, and withdrawn in 1973. It was reissued again in 1986 in different colors. The simple design was characterized by a band of concentric circles, beginning at the rim. Cups had full-circle handles until 1969, when partial-circle handles were made. Harlequin and Riviera were related wares. For more information and prices of American dinnerware, see the book *Kovels' Depression Glass & American Dinnerware Price List.*

fiesta

Ashtray, Red	30.00
Ashtray, Yellow	27.50
Bowl, Desert, Forest Green, 6 In., Pair	28.00
Bowl, Kitchen Kraft, 10 In.	70.00
Bowl, Mixing, Cover, No. 1, Green	350.00
Bowl, Yellow, 5 1/4 In.	10.00
Candleholder, Bulb, Green, Pair	55.00
Candleholder, Cobalt Blue, Bulb, Pair	45.00
Candleholder, Tripod, Turquoise	130.00
Carafe, Stopper, Cobalt Blue	85.00
Casserole, Green, Kitchen Kraft, 8 1/2 In.	80.00
Casserole, Yellow, Kitchen Kraft, Individual	120.00
Chop Plate, Green, 13 In.	21.75

Chop Plate, Medium Green, 14 In. 47.00
Coffeepot, Cobalt Blue 85.00
Coffeepot, Red 110.00
Coffeepot, Yellow .... 75.00 To 95.00
Compote, Sweets, Turquoise 35.00
Compote, Sweets, Yellow 30.00
Creamer, Stick Handle, Ivory 8.00
Creamer, Stick Handle, Red 27.00
Cup, Gray 22.00
Cup, Yellow 12.00
Eggcup, Old Ivory 28.00
Eggcup, Rose 65.00
Fork, Cobalt Blue, Kitchen Kraft 65.00
Gravy, Red 65.00
Grill Plate, Cobalt Blue, 12 In. 35.00
Grill Plate, Yellow, 10 1/2 In. 25.00
Jar, Green, Cover, Kitchen Kraft 75.00
Jug, Cover, Cobalt Blue, Kitchen Kraft 325.00
Jug, Red, 2 Pt. 50.00
Mug, Medium Green 32.00
Mug, Tom & Jerry, Ivory, Gold Letters, 6 Piece 240.00
Mug, Turquoise .... 17.50 To 30.00
Mustard Jar, Cover, Ivory, Red Rings, Glass Spoon, Experimental 55.00
Mustard Pot, Red 165.00
Mustard, Ivory .... 35.00 To 100.00
Nappy, Turquoise, 8 1/2 In. 22.00
Pitcher, Disc, Dark Green 170.00
Pitcher, Disc, Gray 180.00
Pitcher, Disc, Red 120.00
Pitcher, Disc, Rose 95.00
Pitcher, Ice Lip, Red 95.00
Pitcher, Ice, Green 50.00
Pitcher, Mauve 65.00
Pitcher, Milk, Yellow 15.00
Plate, Amberstone, 10 In. 6.00
Plate, Bread, Green 5.00
Plate, Dinner, Forest Green, 10 In. 20.00
Plate, Green, 9 In. 5.00
Plate, Ivory, Deep, 8 1/2 In. 6.00
Plate, Red, 9 In. 22.00
Plate, Red, Oval, 13 In. 20.00
Platter, Red 32.00
Platter, Red, In Holder, Kitchen Kraft 75.00
Platter, Yellow, Oval, In Holder, Kitchen Kraft, 13 In. 90.00
Platter, Yellow, Small 17.00
Relish, 5 Sections, Ivory Inserts, Green, Gold Trim 98.50
Relish, Yellow Inserts, Green Base 140.00
Salt & Pepper, Orange 12.50
Salt & Pepper, Red 15.00
Salt & Pepper, Red, Kitchen Kraft 95.00
Salt & Pepper, Turquoise 12.00
Salt & Pepper, Yellow 12.00
Sauce Bowl, Green 75.00
Saucer, Dark Green 3.60
Saucer, Red 1.50
Soup Dish, Baby's, Blue 12.50
Soup, Cobalt Blue, Handle 30.00
Soup, Onion, Cover, Yellow 485.00
Spoon, Fork & Cake Server, Yellow, Kitchen Kraft 95.00
Spoon, Red, Kitchen Kraft 65.00
Sugar & Creamer, Cover, With Figure 8 Tray, Chartreuse 275.00
Sugar & Creamer, Red 55.00
Sugar, Blue, Cover 17.50

Syrup, Cobalt Blue, With Top	180.00
Syrup, Red, Original Lid	195.00
Teapot, Ivory, Large	80.00
Teapot, Medium Green	195.00
Teapot, Red, Large	185.00
Tray, Relish, 5 Multicolored Inserts	125.00
Vase, Bud, Green	28.00
Vase, Cobalt Blue, 8 In.	275.00
Vase, Cobalt Blue, 10 In.	585.00
Vase, Italian Green, 8 In.	360.00
Vase, Ivory, 8 In.	360.00
Vase, Ivory, 10 In.	450.00
Vase, Ivory, 12 In.	500.00
Vase, Yellow, 8 In.	295.00

FINCH, see Kay Finch category

FINDLAY ONYX glass was made using three layers of glass. It was manufactured by the Dalzell Gilmore Leighton Company about 1889 in Findlay, Ohio. The platinum, ruby, or black pattern was molded into the glass. The glass came in several colors, but was usually white or ruby.

Celery Vase, Silver Design, 6 3/4 In.	485.00
Spooner, Silver Design, White	395.00
Sugar, Cover, Raspberry	1430.00
Syrup, White	1100.00
Tumbler, Barrel Shape, Platinum Luster Flowers, 3 3/4 In.	375.00
Tumbler, Thick Walls, Silver Flowers	850.00

FIREFIGHTING equipment of all types is wanted, from fire marks to uniforms to toy fire trucks. It is said that every little boy wanted to be a fireman or a train engineer 75 years ago and the collectors today reflect this interest.

Alarm Box, Gamewell	95.00
Alarm Gong, Fire House, Edwards, With Key, 10 In.	100.00
Ax, Fireman's, Parade, Sheath, Strapped 15 In. Handle	150.00
Badge, 10K Gold, Presentation	275.00
Bell, Fire Engine, American LaFrance, Bronze, 12 In.	525.00
Bell, Pumper, S. Bend, Ind., Nickel–Plated Bronze, 1934, 12 In.	600.00
Bucket, Laurel Wreath, Medallion, T. J. Sanborn, 1794, 11 1/2 In.	1000.00
Bucket, Leather, Black Paint, B & A, 11 1/2 In.	300.00
Bucket, Leather, Brass Rim & Rivets, Embossed B., 10 1/2 In.	125.00
Bucket, Leather, Worn Black, M. Bettinger No. 3, 1813, 11 1/2 In.	195.00
Bucket, Oval Reserve, Painted Leather, S. Dinsmoor	605.00
Button, Fire Dept., Brass, 7/8 In., 4 Piece	6.00
Cap, Fireman's, Badge, 1900	65.00
Extinguisher, Phoenix	10.00
Extinguisher, Safety First	27.00

Firefighting, Grenade, Bamum's Hand,
June, 26, 1869, Amber, 6 In.

◆◆◆◆◆◆◆◆◆◆◆◆◆◆◆◆◆◆◆◆

If you have an old wooden table of little value, you might want to try adding color with Rit Dye. The color can never be removed, so don't use this on any good antiques.

◆◆◆◆◆◆◆◆◆◆◆◆◆◆◆◆◆◆◆◆

Fire Mark, Hydrant, Hose	215.00
Grenade, Barnum's Hand, June, 26, 1869, Amber, 6 In. ....*Illus*	975.00
Grenade, Harden Star, Embossed Star, Cobalt Blue, 6 1/2 In.	148.00
Grenade, Harden, Blue Glass .... 100.00 To 150.00	
Hat, Independent Hose Co., JH Within Shield, 7 1/4 In.	8250.00
Hat, Leather, Worn Red & White Paint, 14 3/4 In.	350.00
Hatchet	55.00
Helmet, Red Metal, New York Fire Department, Marked	140.00
Lamp, Hose No. 8, Excelsior	1870.00
Manual, Berkeley, Calif. Jr. Fire Dept., Smokey Bear Cover, 1955	5.00
Nozzle, Fire, Yellow Brass, Small	7.25
Ribbon & Badge, Delegate, Catt. Co. N.Y. VFD, 1947	10.00
Ribbon, Fireman's Convention. S. F. E. Co., Child Pictured, 1895	33.00
Ribbon, Washington Company, Tan, Black Words, 3 In.	40.00
Sign, Fire Chief, Porcelain, 8 x 12 In.	80.00
Siren, Fire Engine, Federal, Q2B	250.00
Tapper, Gamewell, Brass, 6 In.	120.00
Trumpet, Presentation	1760.00

FIREPLACES were used to cook and to heat the American home in past centuries. Many types of tools and equipment were used. Andirons held the logs in place, firebacks reflected the heat into the room, and tongs were used to move either fuel or food. Many types of spits and roasting jacks were made and may be listed in the Kitchen section.

Andirons & Fender, Brass, George III, Neo–Classical Design	3080.00
Andirons, Bellmetal & Iron, Double Urn Finials, Log Guards, 1815	1980.00
Andirons, Bent–Over Ring Finials, Pitted, Penny Feet, 14 In.	100.00
Andirons, Brass & Iron, Ball & Steeple Finial, 17 1/4 In.	2420.00
Andirons, Brass & Iron, Circular Design, Scrolled Feet, 32 In.	450.00
Andirons, Brass & Iron, Federal, Double Lemon–Top Finials, c.1815	1980.00
Andirons, Brass & Steel, Urn Finial, Pierced Legs, 26 In.	220.00
Andirons, Brass Finial, Knife Blade, Penny Feet, 26 In.	220.00
Andirons, Brass, Arched Legs On Ball Feet, 17 1/4 In.	145.00
Andirons, Brass, Ball Feet, Pagoda Finials, 15 In.	200.00
Andirons, Brass, Ball Top, 14 1/4 In.	300.00
Andirons, Brass, Ball Top, 15 1/2 In.	350.00
Andirons, Brass, Bulbous, 1920, England, 20 In.	385.00
Andirons, Brass, Double Lemon Top, 18th Century	2750.00
Andirons, Brass, Double Lemon Tops, 17 In.	200.00
Andirons, Brass, Federal, Spurred Arch Supports, c.1820	450.00
Andirons, Brass, Federal, Spurred Legs, Ball Feet, 18 1/2 In.	155.00
Andirons, Brass, Frog At Front Terminal, 5 1/2 In.	375.00
Andirons, Brass, Goose Head, Mortised Dogs, 18th Century	235.00
Andirons, Brass, Gooseneck, Penny Feet, 20 1/2 In.	115.00
Andirons, Brass, Hunnerman	1540.00
Andirons, Brass, Knife Blade, Goose Neck Finials, 20 In.	675.00
Andirons, Brass, Lemon Top, American	795.00
Andirons, Brass, Louis XVI Style, Floral & Swag, 18 1/2 In.	440.00
Andirons, Brass, Mask Front, Dutch, 17th Century, 31 1/2 In.	1650.00
Andirons, Brass, Mermaids, 25 1/4 In.	700.00
Andirons, Brass, Turned Shafts On Spurred Arched Legs, 14 In.	175.00
Andirons, Brass, Urn Finials, Penny Feet, 22 In.	850.00
Andirons, Bronze, Columnar Form, Floral & Swag Design, 23 In.	550.00
Andirons, Bronze, Sea Serpents, Flame Finials, c.1880, 23 In.	345.00
Andirons, Cast Iron, Indian Warrior Form, Black Paint, 19 1/2 In.	412.00
Andirons, Chippendale, Ball & Claw Feet, Square Plinth, Urn Tops	1450.00
Andirons, Dolphin Form, Bradley & Hubbard, Marked	365.00
Andirons, Fender & Tools, Brass, Iron, U.S., 1835	1320.00
Andirons, George Washington	325.00
Andirons, Hammered Brass, Flaring Column, Cahill, 22 In.	465.00
Andirons, Iron, Foliage Scrolls, 15 1/2 In.	45.00
Andirons, Iron, Formed As Sheaves Of Wheat	247.50
Andirons, Iron, Hammered Copper Roosters	120.00

Andirons, Iron, Spiral Fronds Ending In Duck Heads, 49 3/4 In. 1045.00
Andirons, Mid–Banded Ball Finial, Molineux, Brass, 16 1/2 In. 495.00
Andirons, Pagoda Top, Triple Ball Feet, Brass & Iron, 14 In. 330.00
Andirons, Rocking Trestles 295.00
Andirons, Silvered Bronze, Louis XIV, Acanthus Leaf, 29 In. 1320.00
Andirons, Steeple Top, Brass, 1800, 22 In. 880.00
Andirons, Tool Holder, Screen, Cahill, No. 897, 3 Piece 412.00
Andirons, Tools, Ball Finial, Brass, Penny Feet, 17 In. 1210.00
Andirons, Wrought Iron, Incised Design, Spanish 110.00
Andirons, Wrought Iron, Miniature, 3 1/2 In. 45.00
Bellows, Leather, Green, Stenciled Fruit, Brass Nozzle, 17 1/2 In. 105.00
Bellows, Mechanical, Brass Mounted, Crank Handle, England, 18 In. 155.00
Bellows, Red, Black Graining, Freehand Fruit, Foliage, 16 3/4 In. 230.00
Bellows, Stenciled & Freehand Fruit & Foliage, Turtle Back 225.00
Bellows, Stenciled Design, Gold Fruit, Brass Nozzle, 16 1/2 In. 325.00
Bellows, Turtleback, Black Paint, Gold & Red Stencil Design 325.00
Bellows, Turtleback, Original Paint, Smoked Graining, 18 In. 225.00
Bellows, Turtleback, Worn Green Paint, Floral Stencil, 18 1/4 In. 105.00
Broiler, Uprights In Form Of Stylized Grasses, Iron, 17 1/2 In. 3850.00
Broiler, Whirling, Pierced Handle, Shaped Dividers, Iron, 28 In. 995.00
Broiler, Wrought Iron, 20–In. Handle, 13 x 13 In. 60.00
Bucket, Tool, Cover, 24 In. 140.00
Chenet, Empire, Gilt Bronze, Rectangular, Griffin, 10 1/4 In., Pr. 1100.00
Chenet, Louis XV Style, Scrolling Foliate, Cherub, 13 1/2 In., Pr. 770.00
Clock Jack, Brass, Spring Power, Turn Pots, 19th Century 87.50
Coal Hod, Black, Painted Flowers, Brass Claw Footed 130.00
Coal Scuttle, Glass Panels, Hound & Landscape, Metal, 18 In. 650.00
Coal Scuttle, Metal Liner, Brass Handle, Walnut 275.00
Crane, Folds In Center, Wrought Iron, Y Shape, 52 In. 85.00
Crane, Mounting Hooks, Hand Forged Iron, 18th Century, 20 1/4 In. 140.00
Fender, Bowed Brass Rail Over Wire Work, Brass, 1800, 48 1/2 In. 495.00
Fender, Brass, 36 In. 195.00
Fender, Brass, 54 In. .... 150.00 To 300.00
Fender, Brass, Two Uprights & Removeable Rails, 18 1/2 In. 475.00
Fender, Brass, Wirework, 19th Century, 45 5/8 In. 770.00
Fender, Empire, Recumbent Lions, Cornucopia Of Flowers, 45 In. 8800.00
Fender, Louis XVI Style, Urns & Swags On Pedestal, Bronze, 65 In. 935.00
Fender, Molded D–Form, Bun Feet, Brass, 34 1/2 In. 220.00
Fender, Pierced & Engraved Foliage, Paw Feet, Brass, 53 In. 605.00
Fender, Pierced Foliate & Scroll, Inset Tiles, Brass, 41 In. 330.00
Fender, Pierced Frame, 5 Paw Feet, Brass, English, 43 In. 275.00
Fender, Rolled Brass Rail Over Wire Gallery, Iron, 12 In. 715.00
Fender, Serpentine Edge, 3 Finials, Brass & Wirework, 5 Ft. 3 In. 1540.00
Fender, Serpentine, Brass Rail & 3 Finials, 41 In. 1450.00
Fender, Serpentine, Wire Grid, 3 Brass Finials, 40 In. 625.00
Fender, Swan, Urn & Scroll Rail, 6 Finials, Brass, c.1920, 48 In. 385.00
Fender, Upper Rail, Reticulated Lower Bands, Brass, 60 In. 385.00
Fender, Wire Grill, Brass Rail, Urn Shaped Finials, 26 x 13 In. 200.00
Fire Dogs, Brass, c.1835, Pair 950.00
Fireback, Allegorical Scene, Shaped Top, Cast Iron, 27 In. 385.00
Fireback, Embossed Scene, Iron, Victorian 250.00
Fireback, Macbeth Witches' Scene, Quotation, Cast Iron, 30 In. 200.00
Grate, Gilt–Bronze Panels, Bronze, R. Subes, c.1925, 12 1/2 In. 1760.00
Hook, Crane, Wrought Iron 72.00
Log Box, Embossed Brass, 16 1/2 x 13 3/4 x 20 In. 88.00
Pole Screen, European Castle Scenes, Pair 2310.00
Screen, 4 Panels, Folding, Floral, Indian, Teak, 20 x 74 In. 225.00
Screen, Beaded Frame, Rosettes & Leaves, Wrought Iron, 36 1/2 In. 6600.00
Screen, Bird, Floral, Butterfly, Silvered Metal, Porcelain, 38 In. 487.00
Screen, Brass Frame, Center Copper Shield, 29 x 18 1/2 In. 257.00
Screen, Copper, Arts & Crafts, 13 x 17 In. 200.00
Screen, Lion Mask Medallion, Fan Style, Dore Bronze, 35 x 50 In. 495.00
Screen, Louis Philippe Provincial, Silk Panel, Cherry, 34 1/2 In. 165.00

Screen, Louis XV, Panel Of Aubusson Tapestry, 1770s, 48 x 33 In. 4400.00
Screen, Needlework Screen, Walnut, 50 In. 1705.00
Screen, Opalescent Glass Tiles, Iron Frame, 1885, 35 x 25 1/4 In. 2750.00
Screen, Pole, Boston, Needlework, Frame, 20 x 25 In. 8200.00
Screen, Queen Anne, Needlework, Gold Ground, 1760s, 12 x 10 In. 2090.00
Screen, Raised Figures By Hearth, Brass, 35 x 22 1/4 In. 100.00
Screen, Rosewood, Needlepoint Inset Panel, Etched Glass Frieze 600.00
Screen, Silk Embroidered Flowers, Mahogany Frame, 54 1/2 In. 275.00
Scuttle, Coal, Brass, Raised Floral & Urn Design, 19th Century 65.00
Surround, Cast Iron, Discreet Nouveau, Small 70.00
Tongs, Cast & Wrought Iron, Brass Urn Finial 20.00
Tongs, Cast Iron, Large 6.00
Tongs, Ember, Iron, 14 1/2 In. 125.00
Tongs, Scissor Form, Wrought Iron, 1780s, 19 In. 467.50
Tongs, Scissor Shape, Hand Forged Iron, 18th Century, 11 1/2 In. 150.00
Tongs, Wrought Iron, Brass Handle 10.00
Tongs, Wrought Iron, Primitive, 9 1/4 In. 50.00
Tools & Holder, Standing Knight, Armor, Robe, 15 In. 185.00

FISCHER porcelain was made in Herend, Hungary, by Moritz Fischer. The factory was founded in 1839 and continued working into the twentieth century. The wares are sometimes referred to as *Herend* porcelain.

MF

Bust, Tancsics, White 125.00
Cup & Saucer, Chinee Bouquet, Raspberry, After Dinner 50.00
Figurine, Boy On Goose, 3 In. 50.00
Figurine, Cat, 4 1/2 In. 145.00
Figurine, Folk Dancer, No. 5491, Male, 11 In. 345.00
Figurine, Goose, Enameled, 5 In. 85.00
Figurine, Rabbit, Blue, Gold, 9 In. 275.00
Figurine, Tiger Cubs Playing On White Vase, 7 In. 225.00
Figurine, Turkeys, Rust & Blue, Gold Trim, 8 In., Pair 440.00
Pitcher, Imari Style, Fish, Plants, Animals 250.00
Plate, Hand Painted Florals, Pierced Border, Gilt Edge, c.1900 .... 125.00
Tureen, Underplate, Bird Finial, Gold, Ocher Design, 15 x 11 1/4 In. 770.00

FISHING reels of brass or nickel were made in the United States by 1810. Bamboo fly rods were sold by 1860, often marked with the maker's name. Metal lures, then wooden and metal lures were made in the nineteenth century. Plastic lures were made by the 1930s. All fishing material is collected today and even equipment of the past thirty years is of interest if in good condition with original box.

Bait Box, Wooden, Slatted 55.00
Barometer, Airguide 35.00
Box, Pflueger, Wooden 22.50
Bucket, Bait, Papier–Mache, 8 1/2 In. 18.00
Bucket, Bait, Papier–Mache, 9 1/2 In. 28.00
Bucket, Minnow, Hoosier 35.00
Canoe, E. M. White Guide Special 1200.00
Canoe, Kennebac, Advertising Model 4125.00
Catalog, Iver Johnson Sporting Goods Co., Fishing Tackle, 1920s 22.00
Catalog, Shakespeare's, 1940 .... 10.00
Creel, Maine, 18 In. 165.00
Creel, Wicker, Occupied Japan 55.00
Creel, Wooden 1045.00
Display, Tackle Board, Felt Ground, c.1900, 21 x 23 1/2 In. 110.00
Fly Rod, Chubb Classic, Bamboo, 1920s 475.00
Fly Rod, Montague, Split Bamboo, 2 Tips 30.00
Fly Rod, Shakespeare, Bamboo 25.00
License, Pennsylvania, Nonresident, 1943 .... 20.00
Lure, Automatic Minnow, Lane, c.1913 .... 1875.00
Lure, Bass, South Bend, Oreno Pressed Eyes 15.00
Lure, C. C. B. C. Super Six Assortment 935.00
Lure, Chugger, Jr., Heddon 40.00

Lure, Crazy Crawler, Heddon, Box	35.00
Lure, Creek Chub	10.00
Lure, Dowagiac Killer, Heddon, Box ....*Illus*	1705.00
Lure, Flying Hellgrammite Type 1, Comstock 1883 Patent	2420.00
Lure, Frog, Lou Rhead	1375.00
Lure, Gold Chub, Lou Rhead	330.00
Lure, Grasshopper, Lou Rhead	495.00
Lure, Heddon–Sonar, No. 433	7.00
Lure, Hellgrammite, Lou Rhead	275.00
Lure, Injured Minnow	15.00
Lure, Lane's Automatic Minnow, c.1913	1875.00
Lure, Michigan Lifelike Minnow	660.00
Lure, Mink	10.00
Lure, Minnow, Haskell, 1859	4950.00
Lure, Moonlight Dreadnought, Box	3300.00
Lure, Mouse, Real Fur, Black Shoestring Tail, 2 Hooks, 5 In.	50.00
Lure, Muddler Minnow, Lou Rhead	467.00
Lure, Oriental Wiggler, A. L. Foss, 1918	24.00
Lure, Parker Aeroplane, c.1912	1100.00
Lure, Spin–Diver, Heddon, Box	605.00
Lure, Spoon, Heddon, King Stanley	15.00
Lure, Spoon, May Bug, Pflueger	990.00
Lure, Tiny Torpedo, Heddon	12.00
Lure, Vamp, Heddon, Glass Eyes	25.00
Lure, Welch & Graves, Box	880.00
Reel, B. C. Milam & Son, Casting, No. 5, Jeweled	2200.00
Reel, B. F. Meeks, No. 33, Bluegrass	145.00
Reel, Baby Wide Spool, Left–Hand Wind, Leather Pouch	1650.00
Reel, Bronson Lashless No. 1700–A	15.00
Reel, Bronson Mercury No. 2550, Engraved Fishermen In Boat 2 Sides	15.00
Reel, C. H. Wisner, Trout, c.1900	1540.00
Reel, Edw. Von Hofe Pasque, Salt Water	469.00
Reel, Hardy Bros., Fly, Ivory Handle, Leather Case, 2 3/4 In.	725.00
Reel, J. C. Higgins	20.00
Reel, Julius Vom Hofe, Trout	3850.00
Reel, Keen Kaster, No. S100	105.00
Reel, Mahogany & Brass, 3 In.	55.00
Reel, Meek & Miliam, Casting, No. 4	880.00
Reel, Ocean City, No. 88, Smoothfast	8.00
Reel, Peerless, Size 2, Edward Vom Hofe, Trout, Leather Pouch, 1883	1650.00
Reel, Pflueger, Autopla	50.00
Reel, Pflueger, Casting, Progress, No. 60, Brass	25.00
Reel, Pflueger, No. 1558, Sal–Trout	17.50
Reel, Pflueger, No. 1893	25.00
Reel, Pflueger, No. 1943	20.00
Reel, Pflueger, Progress, Trout, Brass	60.00
Reel, Pflueger, Summit	25.00

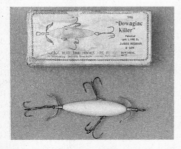

Fishing, Lure, Dowagiac Killer, Heddon, Box

◆◆◆◆◆◆◆◆◆◆◆◆◆◆◆◆◆◆◆

Have your paintings "re–keyed"
if the canvas seems to be
loose. There are small wooden
wedges or "keys" at the back
of the frame that stretch the
canvas. Have a professional
framer do the job.

◆◆◆◆◆◆◆◆◆◆◆◆◆◆◆◆◆◆◆◆

Reel, Pflueger, Supreme .... 15.00 To 30.00
Reel, Philbrook & Paine, Trout, c.1877 .... 7425.00
Reel, Seamaster Mark II, Dual Mode, Salmon 1650.00
Reel, Shakespeare, Classic, No. 1971 .... 35.00
Reel, South Bend Perfectoreno No. 750, Model A 20.00
Reel, Stan Bogdan, Trout, Handmade 1430.00
Reel, Talbot Lotus, Casting 795.00
Reel, Talbot Star, Kansas City 650.00
Reel, Vom Hofe, Trout, 2 3/8 In. 3850.00
Reel, Wm. Mills Fairy Catskill, Trout 825.00
Rod, Fly, E. C. Simmon, Steel 80.00
Rod, Gillum, 6 1/2 Ft. 4400.00
Rod, Gillum, 8 Ft. 3960.00
Rod, Paul Young Perfectionist 2750.00
Rod, Payne, Canadian Canoe, 8 1/2 Ft. 4125.00
Rod, Payne, Model 96, Salmon 6050.00
Rod, Sam Carlson, Trout, 7 Ft. 4125.00
Rod, Shakespeare, Split Bamboo, Case & Aluminum Tube 75.00
Rod, Thomas, Special, 7 1/2 In. 1215.00
Rod, Walt Carpenter Browntone 1320.00
Sinker, Spook 15.00
Spear, Eel 50.00
Spear, Eel, Kent 135.00
Tin, Minnow, A. L. Foss 10.00
Trap, Minnow, Bottle, Wire Handle & Legs, 12 In. 40.00
Trap, Minnow, Hand–Blown Glass 82.50
Trap, Minnow, Orvis, Box 200.00
Trap, Minnow, Tin, Stenciled Green, 2 Ft. 1595.00
Trap, Minnow, Wire Bracket, C. F. Orvis, Manchester, Vermont, Glass 95.00

FLAGS are included in the Textile section.

FLASH GORDON appeared in the Sunday comics in 1934. The daily strip
started in 1940. The hero was also in comic books from 1930 to 1970, in
books from 1936, in movies from 1938, on the radio in the 1930s and
1940s, and on television from 1953 to 1954. All sorts of memorabilia are
collected, but the ray guns and rocket ships are the most popular.

Book, Big Little Book, Jungles Of Mongo 40.00
Book, Big Little Book, The Power Men Of Mongo 30.00
Book, Popup 350.00
Book, Witch Queen Of Mongo .... 15.00 To 16.00
Car, Station Wagon, Wyandotte 45.00
Game, Puzzle, Milton Bradley 110.00
Rocket Fighter, King Features 193.00
Toy, Spaceship, Windup 525.00
Walkie–Talkie, On Illustrated Card, 1940s 125.00

FLORENCE CERAMICS were made in Pasadena, California, from World
War II to 1977. Florence Ward created many colorful figurines, boxes,
candleholders, and other items for the giftshop trade. Each piece was
marked with an ink stamp that included the name *Florence Ceramics Co.*
The company was sold in 1964 and although the name remained the same
the products were very different. Mugs, cups, and trays were made.

Figurine, Amelia 45.00
Figurine, Annette 50.00
Figurine, Ballerina 90.00
Figurine, Boy, Holding Nest 50.00
Figurine, Clarissa 100.00
Figurine, Claudia, Green, 8 In. 90.00
Figurine, Delia ....?..........65.00 To 125.00
Figurine, Dolores, Pink 100.00
Figurine, Elaine, 6 In. .... 30.00 To 65.00
Figurine, Elizabeth, On Settee, Green Gown .... 160.00 To 185.00

Figurine, Ellen, Blue, 6 1/2 In. 70.00
Figurine, Irene 45.00
Figurine, Jeanette 75.00
Figurine, Jennifer 80.00
Figurine, Jim 70.00
Figurine, Joy 30.00
Figurine, Louise, 7 1/2 In. .... 65.00 To 85.00
Figurine, Louise, Pink 100.00
Figurine, Marie Antoinette .... 75.00 To 125.00
Figurine, Matilda, Blue Dress 65.00
Figurine, Melanie .... 65.00 To 95.00
Figurine, Melissa 65.00
Figurine, Oriental Boy & Girl, White, Gold, 8 In., Pair 75.00
Figurine, Oriental Couple 29.00
Figurine, Oriental Man, Black & White, 8 In. 30.00
Figurine, Oriental Woman Dancer, 10 In. 125.00
Figurine, Sarah .... 50.00 To 60.00
Figurine, Scarlett .... 100.00 To 125.00
Figurine, Siamese Cat, 14 1/2 In. 100.00
Figurine, Sue Ellen, Gold Trim 105.00
Figurine, Victor .... 75.00 To 120.00
Figurine, Vivian, Coral 120.00
Figurine, Winkum, 5 1/2 In. 80.00
Figurine, Wood Nymph 90.00
Figurine, Yvonne .... 85.00 To 150.00
Flower Frog, He & She, Pair 100.00
Flower Holder, Wendy 20.00
Planter, Girl, 6 1/2 In. .... 25.00 To 30.00
Planter, Pasadena, Cream, Gold Trim 30.00
Plaque, Woman With Muff 85.00
Plaque, Woman With Parasol 85.00
Snack Set, Driftware, 7 Piece 75.00

FLOW BLUE, or flo blue, was made in England about 1830 to 1900. The
plates were printed with designs using a cobalt blue coloring. The color
flowed from the design to the white plate so that the finished plate has a
smeared blue design. The plates were usually made of ironstone china.

Banana Bowl, La Belle, 13 In. 250.00
Berry Dish, Persian Moss, Utzschneider 30.00
Biscuit Jar, Watteau 450.00
Bone Dish, Belmont, Meakin 45.00
Bone Dish, Gironde 36.00
Bone Dish, Oregon, Johnson Bros., 6 Piece .... 195.00 To 210.00
Bowl, Albany, 10 1/4 In. 85.00
Bowl, Albany, Amoy, 8 1/2 In. 250.00
Bowl, Berkley, Cover, 9 In. 200.00
Bowl, Chapoo, 6 In. 225.00
Bowl, Clover, Oblong, 11 In. 150.00
Bowl, Conway, New Wharf Pottery, 9 1/4 In. .... 85.00 To 95.00
Bowl, Fairy Villas, 10 In. .... 80.00 To 95.00
Bowl, Flenders, Cover, 9 In. 225.00
Bowl, Florida, 8 1/2 In. 60.00
Bowl, Grace, Cover, 9 In. 250.00
Bowl, Janette, 9 In. 75.00
Bowl, Kenworth, Cover, 9 In. 195.00
Bowl, Kin Shan, Oblong, 8 1/2 In. 225.00
Bowl, La Belle, 9 In. 160.00
Bowl, Madras, Doulton, 9 3/4 In. 150.00
Bowl, Melbourne, Cover, Oval, Grindley, 9 In. 125.00
Bowl, Moselle, Square, 9 In. 175.00
Bowl, Neopolitan, 9 In. 45.00
Bowl, Nonpareil, Burgess & Leigh, Oblong, 9 1/2 In. 110.00
Bowl, Oxford, Oval, Johnson Bros., 9 In. 90.00

Bowl, Rose Finial, Carlton, Alcock, 9 In. 350.00
Bowl, Roseville, Cover, 9 In. 300.00
Bowl, Shanghai, Furnival, 9 In. 575.00
Bowl, Soap, Olympia, Cover 165.00
Bowl, Tokyo, 5 In. 13.00
Bowl, Trilby, 9 1/2 In. 100.00
Bowl, Victoria, Wood & Son, 10 In. 120.00
Bowl, Waldorf, 9 3/4 In. 80.00
Bowl, Waldorf, 9 In. 95.00
Bowl, Warwick Pansy, Scalloped Edge, 10 In. 135.00
Bowl, Waste, Kin Shan, Challinor 190.00
Bowl, Watteau, 8 x 10 In. 110.00
Bowl, Watteau, Doulton, 10 x 10 In. 95.00
Bowl, Watteau, Doulton, 8 1/2 In. 95.00
Box, Fairy Villas, Round, 10 In. 110.00
Box, Marble Cover, Toothbrush 250.00
Butter, Candia, Cover 350.00
Butter, Gainsborough, Cover 250.00
Butter, Gironde, Cover, Grindley 180.00
Butter, Neopolitan, Cover 175.00
Butter, Oriental, Cover, Ridgway 60.00
Cake Plate, Gainsborough, 10 In. 125.00
Cake Plate, La Belle, 10 In. 120.00
Cake Stand, Cyprus, Pedestal, Ridgway, Bates 395.00
Casserole, Oriental, Cover, Octagonal, c.1840 .... 450.00
Celery Tray, La Belle, 4 x 13 1/2 In. 110.00
Celery, La Belle, 4 x 13 1/2 In. 210.00
Chamber Pot, Carnation, Minton 210.00
Chamber Pot, Norbury, Doulton 210.00
Charger, La Belle, 11 1/4 In. 180.00
Charger, Peking, Scalloped Rim, Albert Jones, 12 In. 140.00
Coffeepot, Lustre Band 475.00
Creamer, Amoy 375.00
Creamer, Canton, Maddock 295.00
Creamer, Chinese Bells, Wood & Son 60.00
Creamer, Davenport, Wood 50.00
Creamer, Eglington Tournament, Doulton 60.00
Creamer, Gainsborough 125.00
Creamer, Persian Moss 125.00
Creamer, Touraine 195.00
Cup & Saucer, Alexandria 145.00
Cup & Saucer, Amoy, Handleless 75.00
Cup & Saucer, Beauty Rose 60.00
Cup & Saucer, Brooklyn, Johnson .... 65.00 To 68.00
Cup & Saucer, Camellia, Spode, Pink 15.00
Cup & Saucer, Celtic 70.00
Cup & Saucer, Claremont, Handleless 95.00
Cup & Saucer, Clarissa, Johnson Bros., After Dinner 95.00
Cup & Saucer, Clover, Grindley, After Dinner 50.00
Cup & Saucer, Colonial 65.00
Cup & Saucer, Dimmock, Handleless 150.00
Cup & Saucer, Holland, Johnson Bros. 65.00
Cup & Saucer, Hong Kong, Handleless 155.00
Cup & Saucer, Indian, Handleless, Pratt 125.00
Cup & Saucer, Lancaster 85.00
Cup & Saucer, Landscape, Wedgwood, After Dinner 65.00
Cup & Saucer, Navy 50.00
Cup & Saucer, Normandy, After Dinner 55.00
Cup & Saucer, Olympic, Grindley 45.00
Cup & Saucer, Pelew, Handleless 75.00
Cup & Saucer, Poppy, Grindley 65.00
Cup & Saucer, Princeton, Johnson Bros. 70.00
Cup & Saucer, Quebec, Utzschneider, Oversized 65.00

Cup & Saucer, Shanghai, Grindley 65.00
Cup & Saucer, Snowflake, Handleless 165.00
Cup & Saucer, Touraine ....75.00 To 105.00
Cup Plate, Tonquin, Heath 100.00
Cup, Chusan, Clementson, Advertising 125.00
Cup, Poppy, New Wharf Pottery 45.00
Dinner Set, Holland, Meakin, Service To 10 .... 3000.00
Eggcup, Holland ....30.00 To 75.00
Eggcup, Pansies 35.00
Eggcup, Togo, Winkle 58.00
Gravy Boat, Brussels 45.00
Gravy Boat, Celtic 80.00
Gravy Boat, Colonial 75.00
Gravy Boat, Colonial, Tray 145.00
Gravy Boat, Conway 55.00
Gravy Boat, Duchess, Underplate, Grindley 135.00
Gravy Boat, Florida, Johnson Bros. 95.00
Gravy Boat, Holland 95.00
Gravy Boat, Holland, Attached Underplate, Johnson Bros. 150.00
Gravy Boat, Lonsdale 95.00
Gravy Boat, Lotus 85.00
Gravy Boat, Lugano, Underplate 195.00
Gravy Boat, Lugano, Underplate, Ridgway 180.00
Gravy Boat, Neopolitan 75.00
Gravy Boat, Nonpareil 235.00
Gravy Boat, Peking, Wilkinson 125.00
Gravy Boat, Pelew 295.00
Gravy Boat, Portman 110.00
Gravy Boat, Tivoli 125.00
Gravy Boat, Touraine 65.00
Gravy Boat, Touraine, Alcock 135.00
Holder, Shaving Brush, Hawthorne, Dunn Bennett & Co. 75.00
Honey Dish, Formosa, Mayer 60.00
Jardiniere, Lotus, Cockson & Harding, 9 1/2 In. 525.00
Ladle, Sauce, Ideal, Grindley 85.00
Meat Set, Cows, Ridgway, 13 Piece 2700.00
Mug, Abbey, Handleless, Jones, 3 1/2 In. 75.00
Oyster Bowl, Clayton 100.00
Pitcher & Bowl, Coburg, Edwards 1895.00
Pitcher & Bowl, Geneva, Doulton 1000.00
Pitcher & Bowl, Hong Kong 1000.00
Pitcher & Bowl, Jaqueminot, Ridgway 995.00
Pitcher & Bowl, Saskia, Ridgway, c.1891 .... 550.00
Pitcher, 6 Scenes, 6 1/2 In. 135.00
Pitcher, Astoria, 7 In. 215.00
Pitcher, Chusan, Fell 350.00
Pitcher, Diana 295.00
Pitcher, Doreen, 7 1/2 In. 190.00
Pitcher, Gironde, 9 1/2 In. 325.00
Pitcher, La Belle, 6 1/2 In. 325.00
Pitcher, Lincoln Portrait & Quote, Cauldon, 7 In. 450.00
Pitcher, Mandarin, Maddox 395.00
Pitcher, Milk, Morning Glory, J. & R. Godwin, 8 1/2 In. 395.00
Pitcher, Milk, Touraine, Stanley 285.00
Pitcher, Molasses, La Belle, Catch Plate 125.00
Pitcher, Nonpareil, 5 1/4 In. 235.00
Pitcher, Peking, Wood & Sons, 6 1/2 In. 150.00
Pitcher, Sharon 275.00
Plaque, Canal With Boats, Windmill, Dutch, 22 x 15 In. 450.00
Plate, 15 States On Rim, 9 In. 37.50
Plate, Amoy, 9 In. 90.00
Plate, Amoy, Davenport, 9 In. 85.00
Plate, Arabesque, 10 In. 100.00

Plate, Arabic, Grindley, 8 In. 17.50
Plate, Argyle, Grindley, 8 3/4 In. 30.00
Plate, Argyle, Grindley, 10 In. 75.00
Plate, Ashworth, 7 In. 35.00
Plate, Bentick, Meakin, 10 In. 65.00
Plate, Cambridge, 9 In. 75.00
Plate, Canton, Ashworth, 9 In., 6 Piece 390.00
Plate, Carlton, 10 1/2 In. 115.00
Plate, Cashmere, Francis Morley, 10 Sides, 9 In. 145.00
Plate, Celtic, 9 In. 55.00
Plate, Chapoo, Wedgwood, 10 1/2 In. 125.00
Plate, Chinese, 10 1/4 In. 30.00
Plate, Claremont, Johnson Bros., 7 3/4 In. 55.00
Plate, Clytie, Grindley, 9 3/4 In. 70.00
Plate, Colonial, 8 In. .... 50.00 To 60.00
Plate, Commodore McDonnough's Victory, 9 1/8 In. 275.00
Plate, Congo, 9 In. 40.00
Plate, Conway, New Wharf Pottery, 10 In. .... 65.00 To 85.00
Plate, Davenport, Wood & Son, 9 In. 32.50
Plate, Del Monte, 10 1/4 In. 55.00
Plate, Dorothy, 8 1/4 In. 40.00
Plate, Dover, 5 7/8 In. 16.00
Plate, Fairy Villas, Wm. Adams, 7 In. 37.00
Plate, Fall Of Montmorenci Near Quebec, 8 1/2 In. 55.00
Plate, Fern, 9 3/4 In. 135.00
Plate, Gainsborough, 8 In. 65.00
Plate, Gironde, Grindley, 9 1/2 In. 65.00
Plate, Grace, 11 In. 55.00
Plate, Hindustan, 6 1/4 In. 50.00
Plate, Hindustan, 7 In, ... 60.00
Plate, Holland, Johnson Bros., 10 In. 90.00
Plate, Hollywell Cottage, 10 1/8 In. 105.00
Plate, Hollywell Cottage, Riley, 1810s, 10 In. 75.00
Plate, Hong Kong, 9 In. 85.00
Plate, Hunter & Dog, 9 In. 100.00
Plate, Indian Jar, 10 In. 95.00
Plate, Janette, Grindley, 8 3/4 In. 45.00
Plate, Keele, 9 In. 75.00
Plate, Kirkee, 10 1/2 In. 135.00
Plate, Knox, 9 In. 60.00
Plate, Kosciusko's Tomb, 10 1/2 In. 75.00
Plate, Kyber, 10 In. .... 75.00 To 110.00
Plate, La Belle, 9 In. 60.00
Plate, La Hore, 9 In. 100.00
Plate, LaGrange, Marquis Lafayette, 10 1/4 In. 300.00
Plate, Lakewood, 8 In. 60.00
Plate, Landing Of Fathers At Plymouth, 8 1/2 In. 192.00
Plate, Landing Of Gen. Lafayette, 10 In. 300.00
Plate, Lonsdale, Ridgway, 7 7/8 In. 35.00
Plate, Lorne, Grindley, 10 In. 65.00
Plate, Lugano, 7 In. 65.00
Plate, Madras, 8 1/2 In. 35.00
Plate, Madras, 9 1/2 In. 50.00
Plate, Madras, Doulton, 8 1/2 In. 75.00
Plate, Madras, Doulton, 9 1/2 In. .... 60.00 To 85.00
Plate, Marine Hospital, Louisville, Ken., 9 1/4 In. 300.00
Plate, Marquis, 6 In. 28.00
Plate, Morning Glory, J. & R. Godwin, 7 In. 395.00
Plate, Muriel, 10 In. 65.00
Plate, Nahant Hotel Near Boston, 8 1/2 In. 150.00
Plate, Napier, 8 In. 25.00
Plate, Napier, 9 1/2 In. 35.00
Plate, Navy, 6 1/2 In. 25.00

Plate, Nonpareil, 8 3/4 In. 80.00
Plate, Nonpareil, 10 In. 95.00
Plate, Normandy, 10 In. 85.00
Plate, Oregon, Mayer, 9 1/4 In. 85.00
Plate, Oriental, Alcock, 7 In. 45.00
Plate, Oriental, Alcock, 9 1/2 In. 65.00
Plate, Oriental, Ridgway, 6 3/4 In. 35.00
Plate, Paris, New Wharf Pottery, 8 In. 48.00
Plate, Pelew, Challinor, 6 In. 65.00
Plate, Penang, Ridgway, c.1840, 10 1/4 In. 65.00
Plate, Persian Moss, Utzschneider, 7 3/4 In. 40.00
Plate, Richmond, Meakin, 9 In. 50.00
Plate, Roseville, 8 In. 50.00
Plate, Sancho Panza's Debate With Teresa, 9 In. 130.00
Plate, Sciao, 10 1/2 In. 95.00
Plate, Scinde, 9 1/2 In. 95.00
Plate, Scinde, Walker, 7 In. 55.00
Plate, Seville, Wood & Son 48.00
Plate, Shanghai, 7 In. 65.00
Plate, Shanghai, 9 In. 95.00
Plate, Shanghai, Furnival, 8 1/4 In. .... 75.00 To 80.00
Plate, Shell, 6 1/4 In. 45.00
Plate, Singan, T. Goodfellow, c.1840, 8 1/4 In. 55.00
Plate, Sobraon, 8 1/4 In. 85.00
Plate, Spinach, Libertas, 7 In. 55.00
Plate, State Capital Picture, St. Paul, Min., 9 In. 65.00
Plate, State House, Boston, 8 3/4 In. 150.00
Plate, Temple, 9 3/4 In. .... 85.00 To 95.00
Plate, Toddy, English Castle, Adams, 6 In. 105.00
Plate, Toddy, Family Of Sheep, 6 1/2 In. 200.00
Plate, Togo, 10 In. 45.00
Plate, Tonquin, Adams, c.1840, 7 1/2 In. 55.00
Plate, Touraine, 6 1/2 In. 55.00
Plate, Touraine, 7 3/4 In. .... 45.00 To 48.00
Plate, Touraine, 8 3/4 In. .... 45.00 To 75.00
Plate, Valentine, Wilkie's Designs, Clews, 10 In. 35.00
Plate, Victoria, Kauffmann, 8 1/4 In. 115.00
Plate, Waldorf, 9 In. .... 45.00 To 70.00
Plate, Waldorf, 10 In. 95.00
Plate, Washington, 7 3/4 In. 25.00
Plate, Watteau, 6 1/2 In. 25.00
Plate, Watteau, 10 In. 50.00
Plate, Watteau, Doulton, 9 In. 65.00
Plate, Wentworth, 8 1/2 In. 40.00
Plate, Wild Rose, George Jones, 10 1/2 In. 45.00
Plate, Yedo, 9 In. 70.00
Platter, Amoy, 16 In. .... 375.00 To 425.00
Platter, Argyle, Grindley, 12 1/2 x 8 1/2 In. 115.00
Platter, Argyle, Grindley, 15 1/2 x 10 In. .... 125.00 To 235.00
Platter, Argyle, Grindley, 17 x 12 In. 165.00
Platter, Argyle, Oval, 10 1/2 In. 80.00
Platter, Beaufort, Grindley, 14 x 10 In. 150.00
Platter, Beaufort, Grindley, 16 1/4 x 11 1/4 In. 150.00
Platter, Carlton, Alcock, 1850, 16 In. 215.00
Platter, Cashmere, 18 In. 795.00
Platter, Chusan, c.1845, 10 1/2 x 13 1/2 In. 485.00
Platter, Chusan, Podmore, Hall, 26 In. 350.00
Platter, Clarendon, Large 110.00
Platter, Clover, Grindley, 16 1/2 In. 160.00
Platter, Conway, 10 In. .... 95.00 To 125.00
Platter, Dresden, Villeroy & Boch, 14 In. 85.00
Platter, Formosa, Mayer, 10 5/8 x 8 In. 275.00
Platter, Gainsborough, 11 In. 95.00

Platter, Gipsy, Grindley, 18 3/4 x 13 3/4 In. 300.00
Platter, Gironde, Grindley, 15 In. 185.00
Platter, Hong, 15 1/4 x 12 1/4 In. 215.00
Platter, Italian Scenery, 16 7/8 In. 425.00
Platter, Kirkee, 10 1/2 In. 125.00
Platter, Kirkee, Meir, 7 x 10 In. 225.00
Platter, La Belle, 12 x 8 3/4 In. 150.00
Platter, La Belle, Asparagus 50.00
Platter, Lonsdale, Fork, 15 x 13 In. 145.00
Platter, Madras, Doulton, 11 In. 140.00
Platter, Mandarin, 13 1/2 x 10 1/4 In. 350.00
Platter, Marlborough, 14 In. 225.00
Platter, Messina. 18 In. .... 145.00 To 350.00
Platter, Mongolia, 12 In. 120.00
Platter, Ning PO, 14 1/2 In. 29.50
Platter, Normandy, 13 In. 165.00
Platter, Oval, English Castle, 10 In. 255.00
Platter, Peking, 15 In. 175.00
Platter, Peking, Octagonal, 12 x 9 In. 135.00
Platter, Pheasant, 21 x 17 1/2 In. 525.00
Platter, Progress, Grindley, 12 1/2 In. 130.00
Platter, Scinde, 18 In. 550.00
Platter, Scinde, Walker, 12 x 10 In. 180.00
Platter, Shapoo, T & RB, 12 x 15 1/4 In. 370.00
Platter, Tonquin, Dark Blue, 10 1/2 x 13 1/2 In. 485.00
Platter, Touraine, 13 In. .... 135.00 To 185.00
Platter, Touraine, 15 x 10 1/2 In. 195.00
Platter, Touraine, 17 x 11 1/2 In. 245.00
Platter, Touraine, Stanley, 14 1/2 In. 195.00
Platter, Turkey, Doulton, 24 x 19 In. 975.00
Platter, Waldorf, 10 In. 95.00
Platter, Waldorf, 11 In. 95.00
Platter, Watteau, New Wharf, 17 In. 385.00
Platter, Watteau, Wood & Sons, 10 In. 75.00
Platter, Well & Tree, Oriental, Dimmock 650.00
Platter, Whampoa, 17 In. .... 350.00 To 375.00
Platter, Yeddo, Ashworth, 8 1/2 x 11 In. 135.00
Punch Bowl, Candia 1000.00
Relish, Colonial 70.00
Relish, Gironde 85.00
Relish, Oriental, Oval, Ridgway 125.00
Sauce, Amoy, Davenport, 5 In. .... 65.00 To 75.00
Sauce, Chinese, Dimmock 65.00
Sauce, Marie, Grindley 30.00
Sauce, Oregon, Mayer, c.1845, 5 In. 60.00
Sauce, Shell, Challinor 70.00
Sauce, Spinach, Libertas 25.00
Saucer, Chapoo, Wedgwood 50.00
Saucer, Olympia, Grindley 22.00
Saucer, Shapoo, Boote 50.00
Saucer, Touraine 24.00
Shaving Mug, Belmont, Meakin 185.00
Shaving Mug, Olympia 95.00
Soup, Dish, Alexandria, 10 1/2 In. 45.00
Soup, Dish, Argyle, Grindley, 8 3/4 In. 70.00
Soup, Dish, Circassia, 10 1/2 In. .... 100.00 To 115.00
Soup, Dish, Clarence, Grindley, 9 In. 55.00
Soup, Dish, Fairy Villas, 8 3/4 In. 45.00
Soup, Dish, Formosa, Jones, 10 1/4 In. 95.00
Soup, Dish, Gainsborough 55.00
Soup, Dish, Geneva, Royal Doulton 100.00
Soup, Dish, Holland, Johnson Bros., 7 1/2 In. 50.00
Soup, Dish, Japan, V. W. M. Co., 9 1/2 In. 220.00

Soup, Dish, Messina 36.00
Soup, Dish, Milkmaids & Cow, 10 In. 130.00
Soup, Dish, Napier, 9 In. 29.00
Soup, Dish, Neopolitan 35.00
Soup, Dish, Peking, Dimmock, 8 1/2 In. 75.00
Soup, Dish, Scinde 115.00
Soup, Dish, Shanghai, Grindley, 9 In. 45.00
Soup, Dish, Touraine, 7 1/2 In. 80.00
Soup, Dish, Touraine, 9 1/2 In. 70.00
Soup, Dish, Touraine, Handles, 8 1/2 In. 100.00
Sugar & Creamer, Ferrara, Wedgwood 200.00
Sugar & Creamer, Glentine, Cover, Grindley 150.00
Sugar & Creamer, Indian Jar, Jacob & Thomas Furnival 160.00
Sugar & Creamer, Lancaster 110.00
Sugar & Creamer, Marco, Grindley ....85.00 To 135.00
Sugar & Creamer, Seville, Wood & Sons 285.00
Sugar, Baltic 115.00
Sugar, Chapoo, Cover, Wedgwood 375.00
Sugar, Child's, Basket, Cover 150.00
Sugar, Gainsborough 125.00
Sugar, Indian 350.00
Sugar, Kyber, Cover, Adams 225.00
Sugar, Lorne, Cover 125.00
Sugar, Manilla, Cover 495.00
Sugar, Nonpareil, Cover, Burgess & Leigh 175.00
Sugar, Persian Moss, Cover 195.00
Sugar, Touraine, Cover, Stanley 265.00
Sugar, Touraine, Stanley 125.00
Syrup, La Belle 285.00
Tazza, Cheswick, Ridgway 195.00
Tea Set, Peking, Podmore & Walker, c.1850, 3 Piece 795.00
Teapot, Ferrara, Wedgwood 200.00
Teapot, Floral, Striped Banding 600.00
Teapot, Flowers, Pewter Lid, Copper Base, 8 1/2 In. 250.00
Teapot, Gainsborough 395.00
Teapot, Hong Kong, Octagonal 495.00
Teapot, Oregon 285.00
Teapot, Persian Moss 295.00
Tray, Perfume, La Belle, 9 1/2 x 8 1/2 In. 170.00
Tray, Sauce Boat, Chiswick On The Thames, 8 In. 350.00
Tureen, Canton, Sauce, 3 Piece 295.00
Tureen, Chinese, Cover, Allerton, 9 In. 250.00
Tureen, Colonial, Soup, Meakin 395.00
Tureen, Coral, Cover, Johnson Bros., 9 In. 180.00
Tureen, Eastern Vines, Sauce, Cover, Tray 325.00
Tureen, Fleur–De–Lis, Sauce, Cover, Tray 210.00
Tureen, Gainsborough, Cover, Octagonal, Ridgway 325.00
Tureen, Gironde, Cover, Octagonal, Grindley, 10 In. 350.00
Tureen, Hudson, Cover, Footed, Flowers, Beading, Meakin, 1900 .... 240.00
Tureen, Jeannette, Cover, Grindley 175.00
Tureen, Marie, Cover, Grindley 275.00
Tureen, Melba, Cover, Grindley, c.1890 .... 175.00
Tureen, Nancy, Cover, Grinwades, 1911 .... 225.00
Tureen, Nonpareil, Cover, B & L 475.00
Tureen, Normandy, Cover, Johnson Bros. 275.00
Tureen, Oregon, Cover, 8 Feet, Johnson Bros., 6 1/4 x 9 In. 155.00
Tureen, Oriental, Cover, Ridgway 350.00
Tureen, Paisley, Cover, Mercer 300.00
Tureen, Royal Blue, Soup, Burgess & Campbell 450.00
Tureen, Sauce, Jewel, Cover, Tray 220.00
Tureen, Shanghai, Sauce 650.00
Tureen, St. Louis, Cover, Underplate, 14 In. 350.00
Vase, Chinese, Wedgwood, 5 9/10 In. 150.00

Vase, Dorothy, Johnson Bro., 4 1/2 In.	70.00
Waste Bowl, Waldorf	135.00

FLYING PHOENIX, see Phoenix Bird category

FOLK ART is also listed in many sections of this book under the actual name of the object. See categories such as Box, Cigar Store Figure, Weather Vane, Wooden, etc.

Basket, Arched Handle, 3 Hanging Peach Pit Baskets, Wire, 7 In.	125.00
Birdhouse, Carvings Of Small Black Men On Front	265.00
Birdhouse, Log Cabin Shape, Doors, Windows, Chimney, 11 x 14 In.	280.00
Box, Lid With Foliage Design, Poplar, Metallic Paint, 7 In.	35.00
Box, Pine Crate, Primitive Landscapes 4 Sides & Lid, 26 In.	500.00
Box, Pine, Applied Walnut Design, Floral, Sliding Lid, 19 In.	275.00
Box, Sewing, Pine, Poplar, Duck Pincushion, Scissors Form Beak	450.00
Box, Tobacco, Poplar, Smoke With Me, Carved, Brown Finish, 7 1/4 In.	25.00
Busk Board, Sunburst, Geometric, 18th Century, Chip Carved, 12 In.	220.00
Chest, Blanket, Marked WPA, 5 x 2 In.	65.00
Chest, Child's, Made From Crates, Old Paint, Ga.	4000.00
Clown, From Amusement Park, 6 Ft.	4200.00
Comb Rack, Walnut, Wall, Spoon Carving	25.00
Cupboard, Chip Carved, Blue Paint, Red Trim, 3 Drawers, 32 x 57 In.	1100.00
Ferris Wheel, Interchangeable Pendants, Wooden, Large	1250.00
Figure, Bear's Head, Wooden Carved, E. Reed, 9 1/4 In.	295.00
Figure, Bird, Black, Red, Orange Paint, Glass Eyes, Carved, 5 In.	200.00
Figure, Bird, Carved Soft Stone, 20th Century, 6 3/8 In.	25.00
Figure, Bird, Carved Wood, Green, Yellow Base, Wire Legs, 5 In.	105.00
Figure, Bird, Carved, Glass Eyes, Polychrome Paint, 9 1/2 In.	200.00
Figure, Bird, Carved, Polychrome Paint, 6 In.	550.00
Figure, Bird, Clay, Marbelized Red, Black, Yellow Paint, 4 3/4 In.	75.00
Figure, Black Man & Woman, Carved, Polychrome, 5 3/8 In., Pair	350.00
Figure, Black Woman & Child, Carved, Polychrome, 5 In., Pair	310.00
Figure, Black Woman, Rocker, Carved, Polychrome, 3 3/8 In.	85.00
Figure, Cat On Stick, Grayish Finish, 4 x 14 1/2 In.	65.00
Figure, Eagle, Gold Gesso Gilded, 25 In.	300.00
Figure, Eagle, Walnut, 5 3/4 x 24 In.	225.00
Figure, Ox, Carved Wood, Leather Collar, Painted, Brian Smith, 7 In.	50.00
Figure, Parrot, On Perch, Carved Wood, Polychrome Paint, 17 In.	350.00
Figure, Parrot-Like Birds, Carved, Polychrome Paint, 7 In., Pair	450.00
Figure, Peacock, Wire Metal	125.00
Figure, Pig, Carved Wood, Blue & White Paint, 2 1/4 In.	12.50
Figure, Rooster, Carved Wood, Antiqued Polychrome Paint, 12 In.	275.00
Figure, Rooster, Carved, Original Polychrome Paint, 6 In.	950.00
Figure, Squirrel, With Pinecone, Carved, Polychrome Paint, 6 In.	225.00
Figure, Two Doves, Walnut, 10 x 23 1/2 In.	245.00
Figure, Wood Carver, Mallet, Chisel, Polychrome Paint, 25 3/4 In.	525.00
Fish, Wooden Carved, Loren Skaggs, Jamestown, Ky., 7 1/4 In.	40.00
Frame, Pyrography, Indian Design, Squaw, Pipe, Moccasins, With Print	85.00
Fungus, Pink Flowers, 5 1/2 x 9 1/2 In. ....*Illus*	35.00
Hutch, Watch, Oak Veneer On Pine, Inlaid, Reverse Painted, 21 In.	400.00
Lamp, 3 Tiers, Ornately Carved, Indiana, 1910	2200.00
Man & Woman Jigger, Wooden, Painted	198.00
Mask, Theatrical, Fox Fur Hat, Pine, Polychrome, Stuffing	1485.00
Menagerie, Noah's Ark, 16 Pairs Of Animals, c.1890, Noah-2 3/4 In.	1900.00
Mirror, Shaving, Spoon Carved Oak, Wall, Comb Tray	30.00
Mule's Head, Carved Wood, Used As Ring-Toss In Carnival	1370.00
Picture, Bird On Branch, Watercolor, D. Ellinger, Framed, 9 x 8 In.	450.00
Rug, Fish Scale, Center Pot Of Flowers, 22 1/2 x 40 1/2 In.	125.00
Sign, Carnival, Wood, Tin, Green Paint, 2 To 4 Ft., 3 Piece	880.00
Skeleton, With Cigar, Old White Paint, 20th Century, 58 In.	525.00
Stand, Plant, Gold, Black & Red Design, Beaded, 15 3/4 x 31 In.	125.00
Table, Card, Horse Mosaic Of Burned Matches	475.00
Toy, Revolver, Long Hexagonal Barrel, Wooden	10.00

Folk Art, Fungus, Pink Flowers,
5 1/2 x 9 1/2 In.

◆◆◆◆◆◆◆◆◆◆◆◆◆◆◆◆◆◆◆◆◆◆◆

Floodlights facing toward the house are better protection than floodlights facing away from the house. Moving figures and shadows can be seen more easily.

◆◆◆◆◆◆◆◆◆◆◆◆◆◆◆◆◆◆◆◆◆◆◆

Violin, Matchsticks, Inmate In Folsom Prison, Plays, c.1910	6500.00
Wall Pocket, Cardboard, Embroidered Birds & Flowers, 9 x 12 In.	25.00
Whirligig, Farmer Hoeing	350.00
Whirligig, Girl At Pump	90.00
Whirligig, Hessian Soldier, 1860s	4200.00
Whirligig, Man Sawing Wood	45.00
Whirligig, Running Horse, Wooden Vanes, Flat Steel, 24 In.	1175.00
Whirligig, Sailor, Carved, Painted, Early 10th Century, 12 1/2 In.	220.00
Whirligig, Sailor, Nantucket, Wood Stand, 11 1/2 In.	165.00
Whirligig, Soldier, Pine, Pennsylania, 1865	9500.00

FOOT WARMERS solved the problem of cold feet in past generations. Some warmers held charcoal, others held hot water. Pottery, tin, and soapstone were the favored materials to conduct the heat. The warmer was kept under the feet, then the legs and feet were tucked into a blanket, providing welcome warmth in a cold carriage or church.

Brass–Capped Canister, Rosewood, Carpet Cover, 11 3/4 In.	160.00
Buggy, Soapstone, Iron Bail Handle	12.00
Form Of Ram, Redware, 19th Century, 6 7/8 x 13 1/2 In.	357.50
Moira, Stoneware, England	45.00
Pierced Tin, Walnut Post, Wooden Frame, Wire Bail, 6 x 9 In.	190.00
Pierced Tin, Wooden Frame, Oliver Ellsworth, 3rd Chief Justice	195.00
Punched Hearts & Circle Sides, Wire Bail, Red Cherry, 8 In.	280.00
Punched Tin Circle & Corner Design, Tin, 7 1/2 x 8 1/2 In.	195.00
Punched Tin, Cherry Frame, 7 3/4 x 8 3/4 In.	250.00
Punched Tin, Wooden Top, Wire Corners	300.00
Whale Oil, Otis H. Weed & Co., 1865	195.00
Wood & Tin, Hand Punched Hearts, c.1870	235.00
Wood & Tin, RVN 1807 Worked Into Design	850.00
Wood, Punched Tin, 1850s	165.00
Wood, Tin & Glass, Fixed Handle, Rug Lined, 9 1/2 x 8 1/2 In.	975.00

FOOTBALL collectibles may be found in both the Card and the Sports categories.

FOSTORIA glass was made in Fostoria, Ohio, from 1887 to 1891. The factory was moved to Moundsville, West Virginia, and most of the glass seen in shops today is a twentieth–century product. The company was sold in 1983; new items will be easily identifiable, according to the new owner, Lancaster Colony Corporation. Additional Fostoria items may be listed in the Milk Glass category.

American Lady, Goblet, Purple, 10 Oz.	10.00
American, Appetizer Set, 7 Piece	275.00
American, Bowl, 10 In.	17.50
American, Bowl, 3–Footed, Triangular, 11 In.	60.00
American, Bowl, Deep, Oval, 11 In.	40.00
American, Bowl, Divided, 2 Ladles, 6 1/2 In.	39.00

American, Bowl, Low, 5 1/2 In. 12.00
American, Bowl, Rolled Rim, 11 1/2 In. 22.00
American, Bowl, Shrimp 425.00
American, Butter, Cover ....80.00 To 125.00
American, Cake Plate, Pedestal, Square .... 90.00 To 98.00
American, Cake Plate, Round, 10 In. 42.00
American, Cake Stand, Pedestal, Square 60.00
American, Candlestick, Eiffel Tower, Topaz, Pair 495.00
American, Candy Dish, Cover, Pink, 1930 .... 65.00
American, Candy Dish, Tricorner, Handle 11.00
American, Celery, Oblong, 10 In. 12.00
American, Champagne 12.00
American, Cocktail, Swirl Bowl, 5 Oz. 12.00
American, Cup & Saucer 13.50
American, Dish, Divided, Oval, 9 3/4 In. 20.00
American, Dish, Lemon, Cover, Underplate 37.50
American, Goblet, Footed, 8 Oz. 12.00
American, Ice Bucket 40.00
American, Mayonnaise Set, 3 Piece ....22.00 To 45.00
American, Oyster Cocktail, 4 1/2 Oz. 10.00
American, Pitcher, Ice Lip, Straight Sided 75.00
American, Plate, Torte, Ruby, 14 In. 75.00
American, Platter, Oval, 11 In. 30.00
American, Platter, Oval, 12 In. 45.00
American, Punch Bowl, 14 In. 125.00
American, Punch Set, 12 Piece 250.00
American, Rose Bowl, 5 In. 27.00
American, Saucer 10.00
American, Sherbet 6.00
American, Sherbet, Stemmed, Green, 1930, 4 Piece 120.00
American, Straw Holder, Lid ....225.00 To 250.00
American, Syrup, Chrome Top 35.00
American, Tray, Muffin 45.00
American, Tray, Round, 13 1/2 In. 75.00
American, Vase, Footed, Square, 10 In. 40.00
American, Vase, Hat, 4 1/2 In. 32.00
American, Vase, Swung, 20 In. 285.00
American, Wine, 5 Oz. 20.00
Arcady, Cordial 35.00
Avalon, Goblet, 12 Oz. 15.00
Baroque, Candy Dish, Footed, Blue, 9 1/2 In. 70.00
Baroque, Cocktail, 4 Oz. 13.00
Baroque, Compote, Jelly, Cover, 6 1/2 In. 63.00
Baroque, Dish, Mint, Handle, Footed, Topaz, 4 1/4 In. 18.00
Baroque, Goblet, Blue, 9 Oz. 32.00
Baroque, Ice Bucket, Tongs, Silver Overlay 80.00
Baroque, Pitcher, Ice Lip, 7 In. 125.00
Baroque, Plate, 7 In. 9.00
Baroque, Punch Bowl 395.00
Baroque, Punch Set, 11 Piece 265.00
Baroque, Relish, 2 Sections, Square, Blue, 6 In. 35.00
Baroque, Sugar & Creamer, Footed, Blue 48.00
Baroque, Sugar & Creamer, Tray, Blue, Individual 58.00
Baroque, Tray, Oblong, Blue, 8 In. 65.00
Baroque, Tumbler, Iced Tea, Footed, Blue, 6 In. 75.00
Bedford, Toothpick 30.00
Beverly, Celery, Green, 11 In. 23.00
Beverly, Ice Bucket, Amber 25.00
Beverly, Ice Bucket, Topaz 35.00
Beverly, Pitcher, Footed, Green, 7 In. ....120.00 To 210.00
Bouquet, Bowl, Handles, 8 In. 45.00
Bouquet, Butter, Cover, Oblong, Green 50.00
Bouquet, Dish, Pickle, 8 1/2 In. 18.00

Bouquet, Goblet, Water 21.00
Bouquet, Pitcher, 6 1/8 In. 45.00
Buttercup, Bowl, Flared, 12 In. 47.50
Buttercup, Bowl, Handles, 10 In. .... 45.00 To 48.00
Buttercup, Celery 35.00
Buttercup, Goblet 27.50
Camellia, Candy Jar, 7 In. 65.00
Camellia, Sugar & Creamer, Tray, Individual 45.00
Century, Bowl, Vegetable, Round, Handle 30.00
Century, Candleholder, Triple, Pair 60.00
Century, Candy Dish, 3–Footed 12.00
Century, Goblet, Iced Tea 20.00
Century, Mayonnaise, Liner, Square 25.00
Century, Mustard, Cover 45.00
Chintz, Candy Dish, Cover, Stemmed 55.00
Chintz, Cup & Saucer .... 22.00 To 24.00
Chintz, Pickle, 8 In. 22.00
Chintz, Sugar & Creamer, Tray, Individual 67.00
Chintz, Sugar, Cover, Footed 15.00
Coin, Ashtray, 5 1/4 In. 12.50
Coin, Bowl, Amber, 7 1/2 In. 35.00
Coin, Bowl, Frosted, Red, 7 1/2 In. 55.00
Coin, Bowl, Frosted, Red, 8 In. 40.00
Coin, Bowl, Red, Oval, 9 In. 50.00
Coin, Candy Dish, Cover, Amber, 6 1/2 In. 20.00
Coin, Candy Dish, Cover, Green 35.00
Coin, Candy Dish, Cover, Red 45.00
Coin, Candy Jar, Cover, 13 In. 65.00
Coin, Compote, Jelly 15.00
Coin, Compote, Jelly, Amber 20.00
Coin, Creamer, Amber 15.00
Coin, Cruet 50.00
Coin, Lamp, Coach, Electric, Blue, Frosted 250.00
Coin, Pitcher, Green, 1 Qt. 55.00
Coin, Urn, Cover, 10 In. 80.00
Colonial Dame, Cordial 25.00
Colony, Bonbon 15.00
Colony, Cruet 35.00
Colony, Cup & Saucer 10.00
Colony, Mayonnaise, 2 Piece 33.00
Colony, Pitcher 84.00
Colony, Relish, 3 Sections .... 20.00 To 22.00
Colony, Tumbler, Footed, 5 Oz. 12.50
Colony, Tumbler, Juice 12.00
Contour, Goblet, Iced Tea, 14 Oz. 17.00
Coronet, Mayonnaise, 2 Sections 25.00
Coronet, Relish, 3 Sections, 10 In. 18.00
Coronet, Sugar & Creamer 15.00
Coronet, Tray, Muffin 30.00
Corsage, Goblet, 9 Oz. 25.00
Corsage, Relish, 3 Sections, 10 In. 32.00
Corsage, Relish, Handle, 11 In. 35.00
Crosby, Water Set, 7 Piece 175.00
Diadem, Cordial, Topaz 25.00
Diadem, Sherbet, Pink 10.00
Dolly Madison, Cocktail 8.00
Dolly Madison, Sherbet 8.00
Fairfax, Butter, Cover, Green 60.00
Fairfax, Butter, Cover, Orchid 350.00
Fairfax, Butter, Cover, Pink 95.00
Fairfax, Butter, Cover, Rose 125.00
Fairfax, Cruet, Pink 125.00
Fairfax, Cup & Saucer 5.00

Fairfax, Cup & Saucer, 6–Footed, Pink	10.00
Fairfax, Cup & Saucer, Blue	12.50
Fairfax, Cup & Saucer, Topaz, After Dinner	12.90
Fairfax, Cup, Green, After Dinner	10.00
Fairfax, Goblet, Water, Blue	25.00
Fairfax, Mayonnaise Set, Pink, 3 Piece	30.00
Fairfax, Plate, Blue, 6 In.	4.00
Fairfax, Plate, Blue, 8 3/4 In.	12.00
Fairfax, Plate, Cracker, Black, 2 Handles	18.00
Fairfax, Plate, Green, 8 3/4 In.	9.00
Fairfax, Plate, Topaz, 10 1/4 In.	30.00
Fairfax, Plate, Topaz, 7 1/2 In.	10.00
Fairfax, Plate, Topaz, 8 1/2 In.	8.00
Fairfax, Plate, Topaz, 8 3/4 In.	12.00
Fairfax, Plate, Torte, Blue, 14 In.	75.00
Fairfax, Relish, 2 Sections, Blue	22.50
Fairfax, Salt & Pepper, Footed, Topaz	65.00
Fairfax, Sandwich, Server, Center Handle, Pink	20.00
Fairfax, Sugar & Creamer, Footed, Blue	24.00
Fairfax, Sugar & Creamer, Footed, Topaz	22.00
Fairfax, Sugar, Cover, Footed, Pink	10.00
Fairfax, Sugar, Cover, Green	48.00
Fairfax, Sugar, Flat Cover, Footed, Pink	15.00
Figurine, Colt, Standing	40.00
Figurine, Deer, Sitting	45.00
Figurine, Deer, Standing	40.00
Figurine, Fish, Green	70.00
Figurine, Fish, Red	90.00
Figurine, Mermaid	225.00
Grape, Sugar & Creamer, Tray, Pink Milk Glass	50.00
Heather, Bowl, Flared, 5 1/2 In.	30.00
Heather, Bowl, Tricornered, 4 5/8 In.	30.00
Heather, Jam Jar, Cover, 6 In.	65.00 To 75.00
Heather, Jug, Ice Lip, 9 In.	170.00
Heather, Plate, 9 1/2 In.	33.00
Heather, Platter, Oval, 12 In.	80.00
Heather, Relish, 3 Sections	40.00
Heather, Sugar & Creamer	35.00
Heirloom, Bowl & Epergne, White, 16–In. Bowl	75.00
Heirloom, Bowl, Opalescent White, 7 In.	25.00
Heirloom, Bowl, Oval, Pink, 10 In.	45.00
Heirloom, Bowl, Pink To Opalescent, Square	32.00
Heirloom, Candlestick, Blue, 7 1/2 In.	28.00
Hermitage, Plate, 7 1/2 In.	8.00
Hermitage, Tumbler, Juice, Footed	10.00
Holly, Champagne	12.00 To 15.00
Holly, Cocktail	17.50
Holly, Goblet, Water, 10 Oz.	16.00
Holly, Plate, 7 1/2 In.	5.00
Holly, Sherbet, Low, 6 Oz.	12.00
Holly, Sherbet, Tall	10.00
Jamestown, Cocktail, Blue	13.00
Jamestown, Goblet, Iced Tea, Flared, Pink	20.00
Jamestown, Goblet, Pink, 10 Oz.	18.00
Jamestown, Goblet, Red	15.00
Jamestown, Goblet, Water, Pink	15.00
Jamestown, Pitcher, Water, Amber	55.00
Jamestown, Sherbet, Amber	9.00
Jamestown, Tumbler, Footed, Purple, 5 Oz.	14.00
Jamestown, Tumbler, Juice, Blue	20.00
Jamestown, Wine, Red	16.00
Jenny Lind, Box, Glove	250.00
Jenny Lind, Powder Jar	45.00

June, Bouillon, Pink 45.00
June, Bowl, 4 1/2 In. 18.00
June, Bowl, Draped Side, Topaz, 12 In. 45.00
June, Candlestick, 3 In. 18.00
June, Cocktail, Topaz 45.00
June, Cup & Saucer, Blue 42.50
June, Goblet, Water, Blue 47.00
June, Ice Bucket, Topaz 85.00
June, Pitcher, Blue 675.00
June, Plate, Blue, 6 In. 11.00
June, Plate, Blue, 7 1/2 In. .... 12.50 To 22.50
June, Plate, Pink, 9 1/2 In. 45.00
June, Plate, Topaz, 7 1/2 In. 6.00
June, Sherbet, Pink, Tall 32.00
June, Sherbet, Topaz .... 20.00 To 25.00
June, Sugar, Cover, Topaz 20.00
June, Tumbler, Blue, 5 1/4 In. 35.00
June, Tumbler, Footed, 6 In. 27.00
June, Tumbler, Iced Tea, Topaz 30.00
Lido, Oyster Cocktail, 4 Oz. 12.50
Lido, Tumbler 8.00
Mayfair, Baker, Topaz, Oval, 10 In. 22.50
Mayfair, Cup & Saucer, Topaz 9.00
Mayfair, Mayonnaise, Topaz 15.00
Mayfair, Plate, Topaz, 6 In. 4.00
Mayfair, Plate, Topaz, 9 In. 20.00
Mayfair, Syrup, Underplate, Cover, Topaz 87.50
Meadow Rose, Candy Dish, 3 Sections 65.00
Meadow Rose, Goblet, Water 22.00
Meadow Rose, Ice Bucket 95.00
Meadow Rose, Tumbler, Footed, 10 Oz. 22.00
Navarre, Bowl, Divided, Footed, Square, 6 In. 20.00
Navarre, Bowl, Flared, 12 In. 50.00
Navarre, Candlestick, 3-Light, Pair .... 55.00 To 65.00
Navarre, Candlestick, Triple 65.00
Navarre, Compote, 4 1/2 In. 48.00
Navarre, Cordial, 3/4 Oz. 47.00
Navarre, Goblet, Iced Tea, 13 Oz. 19.50
Navarre, Pitcher, Handle, 10 In. 38.00
Navarre, Relish, 3 Sections, 10 In. 29.00
Navarre, Relish, 5 Sections 68.00
Navarre, Sugar & Creamer, Footed .... 39.50 To 48.00
Oriental, Bowl 26.00
Oriental, Goblet, Stemmed, Allover Birds & Foliage 30.00
Priscilla, Toothpick, Green 250.00
Queen Anne, Bowl, Footed, Blue, 7 In. 275.00
Queen Anne, Vase, Green, 12 In. 25.00
Rambler, Plate, 7 1/2 In. 9.00
Rock Crystal, Parfait 11.00
Rogene, Wine, 8 Piece 100.00
Romance, Bowl, Lily Pond 40.00
Romance, Cocktail, 3 1/2 Oz. 18.00
Romance, Cup & Saucer 20.00
Romance, Mayonnaise Set, 3 Piece 27.00
Romance, Pickle, Oval 20.00
Romance, Plate, 7 1/2 In. 12.00
Romance, Plate, 9 1/4 In. 35.00
Romance, Sugar & Creamer 35.00
Romance, Tumbler, Footed, 6 In. 15.00
Rose, Mayonnaise Set, 3 Piece 35.00
Royal, Sandwich, Server, Center Handle, Green, 11 In. 25.00
Royal, Sherbet, Low, Green 16.00
Royal, Tumbler, Footed, Amber, 9 Oz. 20.00

Seascape, Sugar & Creamer 22.50
Shirley, Tumbler, Footed, 12 Oz. 20.00
Sovereign, Toothpick 50.00
Sunray, Ice Bucket 40.00
Sydney, Creamer, c.1905 .... 15.00
Trojan, Claret, Topaz 28.00
Trojan, Cocktail, Topaz 16.00
Trojan, Cruet, Footed, Topaz, 1930, 8 3/4 In. 275.00
Trojan, Cup & Saucer, Topaz 16.00
Trojan, Grill Plate, Topaz, 6 Piece 300.00
Trojan, Plate, Topaz, 6 In. 5.00
Trojan, Salt & Pepper, Pink 125.00
Trojan, Soup, Cream, Pink 24.00
Trojan, Soup, Dish, Topaz 85.00
Trojan, Vase, Pink, 8 In. 150.00
Versailles, Cheese Dish, Footed, Pink 25.00
Versailles, Cup & Saucer, Topaz 22.00
Versailles, Cup, Footed, Topaz 19.00
Versailles, Goblet, Water, Topaz 30.00
Versailles, Ice Bucket 65.00
Versailles, Pitcher, Pink 295.00
Versailles, Pitcher, Rose 275.00
Versailles, Plate, Green, 9 In. 19.50
Versailles, Sandwich, Server, Center Handle, Green 30.00
Versailles, Saucer, Topaz 5.00
Versailles, Sherbet, Topaz. 3 1/2 In. 22.00
Versailles, Sugar & Creamer 27.00
Versailles, Tray, Topaz, 11 In. 25.00
Versailles, Tumbler, Footed, Blue, 5 1/4 In. 30.00
Versailles, Wine, Blue 55.00
Vesper, Candlestick, Amber 12.00
Vesper, Candy Dish, Amber, 3 Piece 65.00
Vesper, Console Set, Amber, 10 1/4–In. Bowl, 3 Piece 90.00
Vesper, Finger Bowl 25.00
Vesper, Goblet, Water, Amber 27.50
Vesper, Plate, Green, 10 1/2 In. .... 12.50 To 18.00
Vesper, Sherbet, Amber, Tall 18.00
Victoria, Toothpick, Frosted 110.00
Willowmere, Goblet, Etched, 10 Oz. 32.00
Willowmere, Plate, 7 In. 12.00
Willowmere, Wine, 3 1/2 Oz. 28.00

FOVAL, see Fry category

FRAMES are included in the Furniture category under frame.

FRANCISCAN is a trademark that appears on pottery. Gladding, McBean
and Company started in 1875. The company grew and acquired other
potteries. They made sewer pipes, floor tiles, dinnerwares, and art pottery
with a variety of trademarks. In 1934, dinnerware and art pottery were
sold under the name Franciscan Ware. They made china and cream-
colored, decorated earthenware. Desert Rose, Apple, El Patio, and
Coronado were best–sellers. The company became Interpace Corporation
and in 1979 was purchased by Josiah Wedgwood & Sons. The plant was
closed in 1984 but a few of the patterns are still being made. For more
information, see *Kovels' Depression Glass & American Dinnerware Price
List.*

Ashtray, Ivy, Individual 10.00
Batter Bowl, Ivy 45.00
Bowl, Coronado, Green, 8 In. 5.00
Bowl, Ivy, 6 In. 11.00
Bowl, Ivy, 7 1/2 In. 25.00
Bread Plate, Ivy 5.00

Butter, Apple	45.00
Candlestick, Apple	20.00
Chop Plate, Coronado, Green, 15 In.	8.00
Cookie Jar, Apple	125.00
Cookie Jar, Desert Rose	150.00
Creamer, Apple	12.00
Creamer, Del Monte	20.00
Creamer, Gold Band	20.00
Creamer, Huntington Rose	20.00
Cup & Saucer, Apple	10.00
Cup & Saucer, Coronado, Green	3.25
Cup & Saucer, Del Monte	20.00
Cup & Saucer, Gold Band, After Dinner	18.00
Cup & Saucer, Huntington Rose	30.00
Cup & Saucer, Ivy	10.00 To 25.00
Eggcup, Autumn Leaf	3.25
Fruit Bowl, Del Monte	14.00
Gravy Boat, Del Monte	60.00
Place Setting, Desert Rose, 6 Piece	49.00
Plate, Apple, 10 1/2 In.	12.00
Plate, Coronado, Coral, 10 1/4 In.	17.00
Plate, Coronado, Green, 9 In.	3.00
Plate, Del Monte, 10 1/2 In.	20.00
Plate, Ivy, 6 1/2 In.	10.00
Plate, Ivy, 8 1/2 In.	12.50
Plate, Ivy, 10 1/2 In.	18.00
Platter, Ivy, 11 3/4 In.	25.00
Platter, Ivy, Oval, 13 In.	25.00
Platter, Renaissance, Gray, 15 3/4 In.	35.00
Platter, Turkey, Apple	175.00
Salt & Pepper, Apple	12.00
Service For 8, Desert Rose, Old Style, Serving Pieces	800.00
Soup, Dish, Ivy, Flat	12.50
Sugar & Creamer, Ivy	40.00
Sugar Bowl, Del Monte	20.00
Sugar, Cover, Huntington Rose	25.00
Teapot, Sugar & Creamer, Coronado, White	35.00
Tumbler, Ivy	14.00

FRANCISWARE is the name of a glassware made by Hobbs, Brockunier and Company of Wheeling, West Virginia, in the 1880s. It is a clear or frosted hobnail or swirl pattern glass with amber-stained rim. Some pieces were made by a pressed glass method, others were mold blown.

Cake Plate, Hobnail, Square	35.00
Toothpick, Frosted, Amber Top	50.00

FRANKART, Inc., New York, New York, mass-produced nude *dancing lady* lamps, ashtrays, and other decorative Art Deco items in the 1920s and 1930s. They were made of white lead composition and spray-painted. *Frankart Inc.* and the patent number and year were stamped on the base.

Ash Ball, Woman, Outstretched Arms, Ball Set In Base, 10 1/2 In.	565.00
Ashtray, Nude On Globe, Stand, 24 In.	350.00
Ashtray, Standing Nude, Green	295.00
Ashtray, Trumpeting Elephant Head, Milk Glass, 7 1/2 In.	300.00
Ashtray, Woman Astride Holding Cigarette Holder, 12 1/2 In.	650.00
Bookends, Boy, Dog	55.00
Bookends, Bust Of Woman, Lips Forming Kiss, Black Paint	95.00
Bookends, Deer, Stylized, 7 In.	195.00
Bookends, Dog, Bronze Finish	75.00
Bookends, Dog, Cocker Spaniel	110.00
Bookends, Horsehead, Bronze Finish	125.00
Bookends, Pony, Rearing, Bronze Finish, 5 1/2 In.	145.00
Bookends, Sailor Boy	75.00 To 95.00

Bookends, Sailor Boy, Dog 45.00
Bookends, Stylized Deer, 7 In. 195.00
Cigarette Holder, Hand Shape 240.00
Figurine, Art Deco Woman Golfer, About To Putt, Bronze Finish 125.00
Figurine, Hand Holding Cigarettes 250.00
Figurine, Nude, Holding Tray, 10 In. 250.00
Lamp, 2 Kneeling Women, Facing, 8 In. Globe 575.00
Lamp, Art Deco, Nude Seated With Shade .... 300.00 To 475.00
Lamp, Desk, 2 Horse's Heads, Signed, c.1920, 12 1/2 x 11 1/2 In. 145.00
Lamp, Green Satin Shade, Ruffles, Gun Metal Finish, Pair 850.00
Lamp, Nude, Kneeling, Arms Extended Hold Globe, Silver Finish 595.00
Lamp, Sailor Boy 275.00

FRANKOMA POTTERY was originally known as The Frank Potteries when John F. Frank opened shop in 1933. The factory is now working in Sapulpa, Oklahoma. Early wares were made from a light cream–colored clay, but in 1956 the company switched to a red burning clay. The firm makes dinnerwares, utilitarian and decorative kitchenwares, figurines, flowerpots, and limited edition and commemorative pieces.

Ashtray, Oklahoma Lions, 15 In. 15.00
Ashtray, White, Marked Sapulpa, Okla. 15.00
Bookends, Nude, Weeping 275.00
Bowl, Jubilee Tulsarama, Gold, 7 In. 20.00
Candleholder, Cloverleaf 5.00
Candleholder, Oral Roberts 5.00
Card, Christmas, 1958 .... 55.00
Cocoa Set, Tan, 7 Piece 95.00
Creamer, Wagon Wheel, Green 6.50
Figurine, Fan Dancer, Black 185.00
Figurine, Fan Dancer, Blue, Brown Highlights 250.00
Figurine, Fan Dancer, White Wash, Over Red Clay 250.00
Figurine, Flower Girl, No. 700, 5 1/2 In. 50.00
Figurine, Garden Girl, Ada Clay, 6 In. 60.00
Figurine, Indian Chief, Brown High Glaze, Ada Clay 65.00
Figurine, Medicine Man 85.00
Figurine, Mountain Girl, Ada Clay 210.00
Figurine, Puma, Seated, No. 114 .... 65.00 To 85.00
Mug, Baseball Player, 1978 .... 12.00
Mug, Cowboy, Red, 1977 .... 4.00
Mug, Cowboy, White, 1977 .... 4.00
Mug, Donkey, Brown, 1975 .... 20.00
Mug, Elephant, 1979 .... 18.00
Mug, Golf, John Frank Memorial, Sand 17.50
Mug, War God, Flame 20.00
Pitcher, Osage Brown 90.00
Pitcher, Prairie Green 35.00
Pitcher, Wagon Wheel, Green 25.00
Planter, Duck, Tan 200.00
Pot, Prairie Green, Silver Floral Overlay, 3 1/2 x 6 In. 500.00
Salt & Pepper, Jubilee Horseshoe, Green 20.00
Sugar, Wagon Wheel, Sand 6.00
Teapot, Wagon Wheel, Green .... 8.50 To 25.00
Trivet, Butterfly 8.00
Trivet, Liberty Bell 5.00
Trivet, Wagon Wheel 35.00
Wall Pocket, Acorn 20.00
Wall Pocket, Woodland Moss, Boots, Brown 12.00

FRATERNAL objects that are related to the many different fraternal organizations in the United States are listed in this category. The Elks, Masons, Odd Fellows, and others are included. Furniture is listed in the Furniture section. Shaving mugs decorated with fraternal crests are included in the Shaving Mug category.

Eastern Star, Necklace, 14K White Gold, Oval Pendant, 18 In.	35.00
Eastern Star, Panel, Crocheted, Eastern Star, Ecru, 16 x 20 In.	15.00
Eastern Star, Pin, 14K Gold, Small	35.00
Eastern Star, Ring, Matron's, Diamond Center, Gold	135.00
Elks, Knife, Brass Handle, Pocket	2.50
Elks, Pitcher, Louisville, 1911, 6 1/2 In.	38.00
Elks, Plate, Limoges	45.00
Elks, Tie Tack, Jeweled, Sterling Silver	28.00
F. O. E., Badge, Brass Link, Convention, Denver, 1905	8.00
Knights Of Columbus, Sword, Etched Design ....85.00 To 110.00	
Knights Of Pythias, Whirligig, Carved Pythias, 11 5/8 In.	467.00
Masonic, Ashtray, 1915	135.00
Masonic, Badge, 14K Gold	125.00
Masonic, Bar & Cuff Links, Large	10.00
Masonic, Book, Bible, 1924	15.00
Masonic, Book, History Of The Masons, Booklet Lodge Bylaws, 1892	11.00
Masonic, Button, Lapel	15.00
Masonic, Candlestick, Symbols Of Sun, Moon & G, Bronze, 23 In., Pr.	1760.00
Masonic, Checkerboard, Symbols, Painted Pine, 19th Century	935.00
Masonic, Chest, Empire, Symbols Inlaid Front Pilasters, 4 Drawers	850.00
Masonic, Club Certificate, Harvard, 1923	8.00
Masonic, Coverlet, Jacquard, New York, July 4, 1829, 81 x 102 In.	880.00
Masonic, Cuff Links, Dated 1898	45.00
Masonic, Cuff Links, Gold Filled, Red Stone	25.00
Masonic, Encyclopedia, 2 Volumes, 1920	50.00
Masonic, Fez, Kaabal	25.00
Masonic, Fez, Mohassen	25.00
Masonic, Goblet, St. Paul, Ruby, 1908	65.00
Masonic, Jacket, Dress, Hat & Sash, 3 Piece	75.00
Masonic, Medal, Master's, 14K Gold	400.00
Masonic, Mug, Kosair, Ceremonial, 1934	75.00
Masonic, Pin, Lapel, Diamond	25.00
Masonic, Pitcher, Blue, 60th Anniversary, Newark, N. J., 1913, 12 In.	95.00
Masonic, Pitcher, Concordia Lodge 67	57.00
Masonic, Plate, Newark, N. J., Officers' Names, Flow Blue, 1853–1903	85.00
Masonic, Ring, 32nd Degree, 14K Gold	95.00
Masonic, Ring, Rose Diamonds, 14K Gold	85.00
Masonic, Spoon, Maccabees Temple, Port Huron, Mich.	38.00
Masonic, Spoon, Masonic Home, Utica, N.Y., Sterling	35.00
Masonic, Spoon, Temple, Chicago, Sterling	38.00
Masonic, Spoon, Temple, Fargo, N. D., Sterling	38.00
Masonic, Sugar, Ascalon Commandery 1898, Colorado, Individual	45.00
Masonic, Sword, Scabbard, Knights Templar	150.00
Masonic, Tie Bar	10.00
Masonic, Watch Fob	17.50
Masonic, Watch Hutch, Carved & Painted, 12 In.	850.00
Odd Fellows, Banner, Embroidered Moon & Stars, Silk, 21 x 33 In.	100.00
Odd Fellows, Certificate, Official, 1916	7.00
Odd Fellows, Chair, Firehouse Windsor, 3 Chain Stencil, Narrow	500.00
Odd Fellows, Staff, Heart In Hand, 1900	2500.00
Odd Fellows, Token, Souvenir, Lexington, Ky., 1916	15.00
Odd Fellows, Trivet, Heart In Hand	165.00
Order Of Moose, Clock, Figural	50.00
Order Of Owls, Sign, Nest 1515, Social Room, 3 Owls	1450.00
Shriner, Bosson No. 87, Karim, Box	25.00
Shriner, Champagne, Louisville, 1909	65.00
Shriner, Champagne, Rochester, 1911	85.00
Shriner, Cup & Saucer, Los Angeles, 1906	70.00
Shriner, Cup, Smile With Nile, Seattle, 1936	65.00
Shriner, Goblet, Los Angeles, May 1907	25.00
Shriner, Measure, Liquor, Double, St. Louis, 1909, Cranberry, Clear	295.00
Shriner, Medal, St. Paul, 1908	12.00
Shriner, Mug, Atlantic City, 1904	65.00

Shriner, Nodder	45.00
Shriner, Plate, Clown Center, 10 1/2 In.	60.00
Shriner, Tie Tack, Jeweled, Gold	28.00
Shriner, Tip Tray, Grain Belt	45.00
Shriner, Wine, 1900	50.00
Shriner, Wine, 1902	50.00

FRY GLASS was made by the H. C. Fry Glass Company of Rochester, Pennsylvania. The company, founded in 1901, first made cut glass and other types of fine glasswares. In 1922, they patented a heat–resistant glass called *Pearl Oven glass.* For two years, 1926–1927, the company made Fry Foval, an opal ware decorated with colored trim. Reproductions of this glass have been made. Depression glass patterns made by Fry may be listed in the Depression Glass section. Some pieces of cut glass may also be included in the Cut Glass category.

FRY FOVAL, Bowl, Fruit, Blue Trim, Footed, 12 In.	550.00
Candlestick, Blue Opalescent, 9 1/2 In., Pair	300.00
Cup & Saucer, Opalescent, Green Handle	48.00
Ice Bucket, Green, Wicker Handle	195.00
Plate, Green Trim, 8 1/2 In.	85.00
Sugar & Creamer, Blue Trim, Handle, 3 1/2 In.	325.00
Vase, Flared Top, Opalescent, Delft Blue Disc Foot, 10 In.	325.00
FRY, Lemonade Set, Golden Glow Crackled Glass, 7 Piece	285.00
Lemonade Set, Oriental Woman, Blossoms, Clear Notched Handle, 6 Piece	412.00
Plate, Sandwich, Fashion, Footed	275.00
Tazza, Venetian, Hobstar Scalloped Foot, Signed, 8 1/2 In.	350.00
Tray, Ice Cream, Nelson	275.00
Tumbler, Footed, Silver Overlay, 7 Piece	140.00
Wine, Etched Roses, 8 Piece	195.00

FULPER is the mark used by the American Pottery Company of Flemington, New Jersey. The art pottery was made from 1910 to 1929. The firm had been making bottles, jugs, and housewares from 1805. Doll heads were made about 1928. The firm became Stangl Pottery in 1929. Fulper art pottery is admired for its attractive glazes and simple shapes.

Bookends, Cat, Anniversary Sticker, Green & Silver	100.00
Bookends, Rameses, Green	650.00
Bookends, Ramses, Verde Green	695.00 To 750.00
Bowl, Allover White Crystals, Mottled Blues & Mustard, 11 In.	550.00
Bowl, Brown & Caramel Flambe Glaze, Marked, c.1910, 13 In.	275.00
Bowl, Effigy, Blue Flambe Glaze, Marked, c.1915, 7 1/2 In.	467.00
Bowl, Effigy, Brown & Gray Flambe, Green Crystalline, 7 x 10 In.	605.00
Bowl, Tan Flambe Over Blue, Handles, 10 x 9 In.	550.00
Bowl, Tiger Eye Flambe Glaze, Flared, With Frog, 8 In.	225.00
Box, Dresser, Art Deco Blond Woman, 6 x 4 In.	245.00
Candlestick, Butterflies, 3 1/2 x 4 3/4 In., Pair	100.00
Candlestick, Famille Rose, Hooded, Gray Edges, 7 1/2 In.	140.00
Chamberstick, Hooded, Bluish Gray, 7 In.	135.00
Figurine, Cat, Brown, Blue & Cream Flambe Glaze, 5 x 9 In.	715.00
Flower Frog, Green	125.00
Flower Frog, Leprechaun	175.00
Flower Frog, Leprechaun, White & Green	45.00
Flower Frog, Nude, Sitting In Grass, Yellow Blooms	120.00
Humidor, Cafe Au Lait & Gunmetal	350.00
Humidor, Green Crystalline, Lid, Silver & Black Cucumber, 7 1/2 In.	385.00
Jar, Ginger, Cover, Green Crystalline, 4 In.	135.00
Jug, Musical, Green Crystalline Stopper, 10 In.	75.00
Jug, Musical, Green, How Dry I Am, Green Drips	185.00
Jug, Musical, Italian & Dark Blue	50.00
Lamp, Cinnamon Brown, Crystalline Glaze, 8 x 7 In.	250.00
Lamp, Musical, Jug Shape, Sea Foam With Crystals	85.00
Lamp, Ovoid Base, Copper Hardware, Blue Crystalline, 15 In.	1450.00
Lamp, Perfume, Ballerina Shape, Yellow, 6 1/2 In.	192

Lamp, Perfume, Lady With Fan, Pink, 9 In.	400.00
Lamp, Perfume, Parrot	750.00
Pitcher, Green & Turquoise Flambe On Rose, 4 In.	90.00
Powder Jar, Woman In Pink Dress On Cover, Mauve, 7 x 5 In.	165.00
Vase, Applied Roses, Hand Thrown, Crystal, 6 1/2 In.	450.00
Vase, Black Mirror Finish, Marked, c.1910, 5 1/2 In.	220.00
Vase, Blue Crystalline, Brown Drip At Top, Handles	250.00
Vase, Blue Crystalline, Handle, 9 In.	350.00
Vase, Blue Crystals Over Powder Blue, Marked, 4 1/2 In.	225.00
Vase, Blue Drip, 7 x 10 In.	350.00
Vase, Blue Flambe On Cream, 7 Sides, 8 1/2 In.	250.00
Vase, Blue Flambe, 4 In.	70.00
Vase, Blue Flambe, Molded Jewels, 7 In.	135.00
Vase, Blue Wisteria, Chinee Flambe Over Matte Cobalt, 11 In.	325.00
Vase, Blue, Olive With Crystals, Handles, 3 In.	125.00
Vase, Bud, Arts & Crafts Design, Green, Brown Crystalline, 8 In.	358.00
Vase, Cascading Crystals, Semigloss Glaze, 7 In.	285.00
Vase, Cat's Eye Glaze, Mustard Matte, 5 In.	110.00
Vase, Dark Blue–Green Flambe Drip, Curled Handles, 11 In.	825.00
Vase, Dripping Olives, Rose, 7 In.	150.00
Vase, Fan, Blue Crystalline, 6 1/2 In., Pair	400.00
Vase, Fan, Butterscotch, 8 In.	225.00
Vase, Fan, Green, 8 In.	175.00
Vase, Green & Turquoise Crystalline, 10 In.	395.00
Vase, Green Crystalline Glaze, 3 Loop Handles, c.1915, 6 3/4 In.	715.00
Vase, Green Crystalline Glaze, Angular Handles, c.1915, 4 3/4 In.	195.00
Vase, Green To Dark Blue Over Rose, 2 Ring Handles, 13 In.	475.00
Vase, Impressed Geometric Design, Rose & Green, Marked, 8 1/4 In.	335.00
Vase, Leopard Skin Glaze, 9 In.	750.00
Vase, Leopard Skin, 9 In.	725.00
Vase, Light To Deep Green Crystalline, 2 Pointed Handles, 8 In.	275.00
Vase, Mirror Black Glaze, Sloping Handles, Marked, 8 In.	160.00
Vase, Molded Leaf Design, Gunmetal Drip Over Caramel Luster, 8 In.	80.00
Vase, Molded Rose Petals, Overall Blue Ground, Marked, 6 1/2 In.	180.00
Vase, Mottled Blue & Green Flambe Glaze, Applied Handles, 8 x 9 In.	550.00
Vase, Mottled Rust Glaze Dripping Over Rim, 3 Handles, 6 1/2 In.	302.50
Vase, Mustard Flambe, Chocolate Brown, 8 In.	135.00
Vase, Semimatte Flambe, Greens, Burgundy & Rose, 4 In.	80.00
Vase, Speckled Matte Brown Glaze, Clip Corners, 4 3/4 In.	193.00
Wall Pocket, Plumed Bird, Double, 7 1/2 x 9 In.	245.00 To 325.00

FURNITURE of all types is listed in this section. Examples dating from the seventeenth century to the 1950s are included. Prices for furniture vary in different parts of the country. Oak furniture is most expensive in the West; large pieces over eight feet high are sold for the most money in the South, where high ceilings are found in the old homes. Condition is very important when determining prices. These are NOT average prices but rather reports of unique sales. If the description includes the word *style*, the piece resembles the old furniture style but was made at a later time. It is not a period piece.

◆◆◆

If you have an instant-on television set, beware! The instant-on works because a current is always running through the set, even when it is off. This means more power is used, the set wears out faster, and most serious for the collector, there is a greater risk of fire. Next time the set needs ʼair, ask the service man to remove the instant-on feature. If you use ʼemote unit to turn off the set, the same dangers exist. While on ʼtion, if your microwave oven has a clock, unplug it, as well as your ʼnt-on TV.

◆◆◆

Furniture, Armchair, Mahogany, Scroll, Late
19th Century, Pair

Furniture, Armchair Set, Marika, Chrome,
Suede, 8 Piece

Aquarium, Figural Pelicans Ends, Bronze, J. Hoffmann, 43 x 27 In. 2750.00
Arm Rest, Prayer, Old North Church, Boston, Early 1800s, 11 In. 165.00
Armchair Set, Arts & Crafts, Phoenix Chair Co., c.1915, 4 .... 350.00
Armchair Set, Marika, Chrome, Suede, 8 Piece ....*Illus* 440.00
Armchair Set, Sussex, Morris, Turned Spindles, String Seat, 4 .... 1475.00
Armchairs may also be listed under Chair in this section.
Armchair, Acanthus & Volute Carved Shell, Mahogany, 1765 .... 6600.00
Armchair, Adjustable Back, Limbert, No. 521, Oak, 37 1/2 In. 6050.00
Armchair, Adjustable, Oak, Casters, Embroidered Upholstery 1665.00
Armchair, Arched Fluted Crest, Upholstered Back, Open Arms 1870.00
Armchair, Bamboo, Caned Seat, Cushion, China, Downswept Arms 885.00
Armchair, Bannister Back, Painted Maple, 1710 .... 1980.00
Armchair, Baroque, Oak Frame, Striped Upholstery, 46 3/4 In. 200.00
Armchair, Bentwood, Cane Seat, High Back 225.00
Armchair, Bow Back, Black Paint, Mahogany Arms, 39 1/2 In., Pair 1985.00
Armchair, Bowknot On Crest, Circular Back, Ebonized Walnut, 1870s 300.00
Armchair, Brass Mounted, Shield Backrest, Mahogany, Russia 3850.00
Armchair, Carved Back Rail, Caned Seat & Back 100.00
Armchair, Carved Crest Rail, Pierced Splat, 19th Century 125.00
Armchair, Carved Frame, Walnut, Figural Arms Holding Game, 1900 .... 2750.00
Armchair, Carved Ivy Vines, Leaves, Upholstered, c.1900, Pair 7150.00
Armchair, Carved Rosettes At Knees, Painted, Parcel Gilt, 1820s 1925.00
Armchair, Carved Walnut Frame, Ireland 2200.00
Armchair, Carver Type, Maple, Pilgrim Era 9500.00
Armchair, Chippendale Style, Barrel Back, Carved Mahogany 425.00
Armchair, Chippendale, Beaker Shaped Splat, Walnut, 1760s 5500.00
Armchair, Dolphin Crest, Mahogany Finish, 37 In. 190.00
Armchair, Ebonized, Gesso, Parcel Gilt, Upholstered Back & Seat 5500.00
Armchair, Empire, Mahogany, Upholstered, Pair 2850.00
Armchair, Finger Carved, Horsehair Upholstery 375.00
Armchair, Foliate Frame, Tufted Velvet Seat, Fruitwood, 1900, Pair 2550.00
Armchair, George III Style, Ivory Paint, Parcel Gilt, 38 In., Pair 1985.00
Armchair, George III, Shaped Back, Beechwood, Upholstered 665.00
Armchair, Hardwood, Boldly Carved Detail, 56 In. 195.00
Armchair, High Back, Upholstered, 48 In. 200.00
Armchair, L. & J. G. Stickley, 6 Vertical Slats, Signed, Oak 220.00
Armchair, Louis XV Style, Upholstered Backrest, 33 1/2 In. 385.00
Armchair, Louis XV, Carved Foliate, Upholstered Back, 36 In., Pair 2100.00
Armchair, Louis XVI Style, Aubusson Upholstery, Pair 4850.00
Armchair, Mahogany, Scroll, Late 19th Century, Pair ....*Illus* 665.00
Armchair, Majorelle, Carved Fiddlehead Ferns, 40 In., Pair 3300.00
Armchair, Marquetry Inlay, Upholstered Seat, 31 3/4 In. 625.00
Armchair, Martha Washington, 18th Century .... 5500.0~

Furniture, Armchair, Turned Oak, Rush
Seat, c.1680

Furniture, Armchair, Walnut, Ladder Back,
Rush Seat, France

Armchair, Mission Oak, Concave Crest Rail, 2 Vertical Slats	385.00
Armchair, Mother–of–Pearl Inlay, Art Deco, Upholstered, 1925, Pair	4125.00
Armchair, Neoclassical, Adam Style, Fruitwood, Caned, Pair	4000.00
Armchair, Ottoman, Reddish Brown Leather, Upholstery	475.00
Armchair, Queen Anne, Mahogany, Flame Stitch Seat, Bear Paw Feet	160.00
Armchair, Queen Anne, New England, 1740s, 39 3/4 In.	1430.00
Armchair, Queen Anne, Shaped Crest Rail, Vasiform Splat, c.1760	1760.00
Armchair, Reclining, G. Russell, Oak, Square, Upholstered, 1928	554.00
Armchair, Reclining, Slant Back, Footrest, Hardwood, China, Pair	825.00
Armchair, Regency, Cane Back & Seat, Shell Knees, Open Arms, Pair	330.00
Armchair, Regency, Mahogany, Red Leather Seat, 32 In.	175.00
Armchair, Regency, X–Form Back, Painted, Down Curving Arms, Pair	1980.00
Armchair, Rosewood Frame, Upholstered Back, France, c.1925, Pair	2750.00
Armchair, Shaker, No. 6, Painted Tape, Black, Mt. Lebanon, 1880–1920	1100.00
Armchair, Sheraton, Mahogany Frame, Brocade Upholstery, 34 In.	85.00
Armchair, Slat Back, Blue Paint, Splint Seat, 1820s, 43 1/2 In.	935.00
Armchair, Turned Oak, Rush Seat, c.1680 ....*Illus*	4950.00
Armchair, Victorian, Balloon Back, Upholstered, Walnut	335.00
Armchair, Wainscot, Ireland, Dated 1656	605.00
Armchair, Walnut, Ladder Back, Rush Seat, France ....*Illus*	220.00
Armchair, Wide Seat, Rococo Revival, Carved Walnut, c.1860	300.00
Armchair, William & Mary, Yoked Crest, Scrolled Armrests, 42 In.	3850.00
Armchair, Wing, Federal, Mahogany Front Legs, Cherry Back Legs	450.00
Armoire, 1 Door, Victorian, Mirror, Francois Seignouret	1980.00
Armoire, 2 Cupboard Doors, Biedermeier, Walnut, c.1840, 80 In.	1100.00
Armoire, 2 Doors, Butterfly Panels, 1760–1780	8900.00
Armoire, 2 Doors, Carved Ornaments, Mahogany, c.1900, 7 Ft. 4 In.	6700.00
Armoire, 2 Doors, Mahogany, England, c.1860, 86 In.	600.00
Armoire, 3 Doors, Majorelle, Walnut, Mahogany, c.1900, 7 Ft. 10 In.	9950.00
Armoire, French Country, Carved Basket Over Doors, 81 In.	2650.00
Armoire, Louis Philippe, Cherry, 2 Carved Panel Doors, 74 In.	1650.00
Armoire, Louis XV, Mahogany, Parquetry Inlay, 8 Ft. 4 In.	2750.00
Armoire, Majorelle, Mirror Door, Marquetry, 1900, 8 Ft. 9 In.	3025.00
Armoire, Mirror Door, 1 Drawer, Rosewood, 1860s, 98 In.	3400.00
Armoire, Mirror Door, Mahogany, Cornice, c.1860, 93 x 58 x 22 In.	1100.00
Armoire, Oak, Hand Carved Detail, 1 Drawer, European, 72 In.	475.00
ire, Red Oak, 2 Serpentine Drawers, Paw Feet, Oval Inserts	225.00
re, Renaissance Revival, Mirror Door, Rosewood, 98 In.	3415.00
orner, Wicker	1275.00
Bureau, Berkey & Gay, Pineapple Posts, Glass Pulls, Mirror	4000.00
orn Finial, Poplar, Red, Side Rails, Rope, 50 x 70 x 37 In.	445.00

Furniture, Bed, Ivory Inlay, Mahogany,

1880s, 64 x 86 In.

Bed, Arched Headboard, Serpentine Footboard, Rosewood, 1870s 2310.00
Bed, Arched Headboard, Shield, Ebonized Walnut, 6 Ft. 2 1/2 In. 3300.00
Bed, Baby's, Curly Maple, Posts, Spindles, Finials, 31 1/4 In. 750.00
Bed, Baby's, Iron, White Paint ....90.00 To 150.00
Bed, Baby's, Victorian, Turned Mahogany, c.1850, 36 x 24 x 41 In. 415.00
Bed, Cannonball, Blanket Rail, Bird's-Eye Maple, Rope, 36 x 76 In. 800.00
Bed, Cannonball, Cherry Color Finish, Rope, Pine, Poplar, 70 In. 450.00
Bed, Cannonball, Curly Maple, Rope, Turned Posts, 48 x 76 x 55 In. 800.00
Bed, Cannonball, Hickory Rails, Rope, Maple & Poplar, 70 1/4 In. 150.00
Bed, Cannonball, Red, Black Graining, Rails, 42 x 52 x 70 In. 460.00
Bed, Cannonball, Shaped Headboard, Maple, 19th Century, 82 In. 412.00
Bed, Canopy, Pencil Post, Cherry, Pine Headboard, 62 1/2 In. 900.00
Bed, Canopy, Pine Headboard, Carved Posts, Birch Rails, 60 1/2 In. 3000.00
Bed, Canopy, Soft Wood, Dark Mahogany, Rope Rails, 72 In. 700.00
Bed, Cherry, 4 Reeded Posts, c.1830 .... 3200.00
Bed, Child's, Four-Poster, Maple, Spool, Spindle Head & Footboards 140.00
Bed, Curly Maple, Poplar, Goblet Finials, Rope, 50 x 69 x 60 In. 500.00
Bed, Curly Maple, Turned Posts & Finials, Rope, 54 x 75 In. 1800.00
Bed, Empire, Scrolled Head & Footboards, Rope, 57 x 75 In. 400.00
Bed, Federal, Canopy, Tall Reeded Posts, Netting, Cherry, 87 In. 1045.00
Bed, Field, Poplar, Pine, Folding Frame, Turned Legs, 36 In. 350.00
Bed, Floral & Basket Inlay, Walnut & Mahogany, Victorian, 80 In. 3575.00
Bed, Floral Inlay, Incised Gilt Design, Kimbel & Cabus, 82 In. 3500.00
Bed, Four-Poster, Barley Twist Design Posts 2650.00
Bed, Four-Poster, Grapevine Carved Posts, Cane Finial Headboard 1400.00
Bed, Four-Poster, Mahogany, Finials On Posts, 1840, 7 Ft. 2 In. 1995.00
Bed, Four-Poster, Pineapple, Acanthus Carving, Brass Capped Feet 2500.00
Bed, Four-Poster, Plaque Of Cupid, Scrollwork, Cherry 2975.00
Bed, Four-Poster, Sheraton, Walnut, c.1825 .... 650.00
Bed, Four-Poster, Walnut, Canopy 1500.00
Bed, Gustav Stickley, Vertical Posts, 5 Wide Slats, c.1907, Double 3350.00
Bed, Half-Tester, Prudent Mallard, Carved Rosewood, c.1850 .... 9350.00
Bed, Half-Tester, Rococo Revival, Faux Rosewood, Mid-19th Century 5225.00
Bed, Herter Bros., Cherry Blossom Inlay, Full Size 8250.00
Bed, High Post, Triangular Headboard, Cherrywood, Pine, c.1790 .... 450.00
Bed, Ivory Inlay, Mahogany, 1880s, 64 x 86 In. ....*Illus* 2420.00
Bed, Leaf Carving, Cornstalk Stuffed Mattress, Rope 247.50
Bed, Low Post, Leidy Type Grain Painted, Berks County 450.00
Bed, Mahogany, Carlo Zen, Art Nouveau, Rounded Headboard, Double 5175.00
Bed, Mahogany, Ormolu Mounted, France, 19th Century, 78 In., Pair 1875.00
Bed, Majorelle, Les Lilas, Walnut & Mahogany, c.1900, 5 Ft. 2 In. 5500.00
Bed, Poplar, Red, Simple Turnings, Head, Footboards, Rope, 35 In. 25.00
Bed, Post, Walnut, Cherry Finish, Steel Rails, 50 x 74 x 83 In. 600.00
Bed, Prairie School, Ash, Double 700.00
Bed, Red Paint, Molded Rails, Rope, 34 x 32 In. 345.00
Bed, Renaissance Revival, Rosewood, Arched Crested Headboard 2315.0
Bed, Rosewood, Pullout Bed Steps, Double Size 35

Bed, Secretary, Bookcase Combination, Folding, Oak, Welsh 2100.00
Bed, Shaker, Wheels, Cherry & Pine, Mount Lebanon, N.Y., 6 Ft. 1 In. 995.00
Bed, Shaped Head & Footboards, Poplar, Rope, 72 1/2 In. 75.00
Bed, Shenandoah Valley, Scroll Headboard, 19th Century 1200.00
Bed, Sleigh, Continental, Fruitwood, 83 In. 385.00
Bed, Sleigh, Flame Mahogany, Full Size 475.00
Bed, Sleigh, Victorian, Carved Rosewood, U.S., 60 In. 2095.00
Bed, Smoke Grained White Paint, Hardwood, Rope, 48 In. 600.00
Bed, Spool Posts, Broken Pediment Headboard, Rope, 3/4 Size 125.00
Bed, Tall Post, Poplar, Dark Varnish, Scrolled Headboard, 70 In. 900.00
Bed, Tester, C. Lee, New Orleans 6325.00
Bed, Tester, Tapered Head Posts, Birch & Pine, 54 x 70 In. 1600.00
Bed, Tester, Walnut, Poplar, 4 Large Turned Columns, 1830 .... 1950.00
Bed, Tiger Maple, 1850, Double 1250.00
Bed, Tiger Maple, Cherry, Rope, Converted 1300.00
Bed, Trundle, Ball Finials, Rope Rails, Wooden Wheels, 52 1/2 In. 300.00
Bed, Trundle, Child's, Hardwood, Short Turned Posts, 39 x 57 In. 165.00
Bed, Trundle, Child's, Turned Posts, Wooden Wheels, Poplar 110.00
Bed, Trundle, Finials, Side Rails, Poplar, Rope, 44 x 61 1/2 In. 150.00
Bed, Trundle, Poplar, Original Rails, Rope, 14 In. 110.00
Bed, Trundle, Scalloped Head & Foot, Rope Rails, Wooden Rollers 300.00
Bed, Trundle, Spool Carved, Cornstalk Stuffed Mattress 467.50
Bedroom Set, Contemporary, Mahogany, Black Onyx, 1950s, 8 Piece 1000.00
Bedroom Set, Dekel, 1930s, 3 Piece 350.00
Bedroom Set, Eastlake, Cherry, Mirror, Washstand, 3 Piece 875.00
Bedroom Set, Floral & Scroll Design, Satinwood, 5 Piece 1210.00
Bedroom Set, Golden Oak, Full High–Back Bed, Dresser, Washstand 1800.00
Bedroom Set, Mitchell & Rammelsburg, Rosewood, Marble, 3 Piece 5445.00
Bedroom Set, Renaissance Revival, Marble Top, Ash, Walnut, 3 Piece 2700.00
Bedroom Set, Russel Wright, American Modern, 2 Double Beds, 5 Pc. 750.00
Bedroom Set, Victorian, Walnut, High Back Bed, Marble Top, 2 Piece 1295.00
Bedroom Set, Victorian, Walnut, Marble Top Dresser, 2 Piece 3100.00
Bedroom Set, Victorian, Walnut, Marble Washstand & Dresser, 3 Pc. 1450.00
Bedroom Set, Walnut, Marble Tops, Tilting Mirrors, 3 Piece 4900.00
Bedroom Set, Yellow, Brown Painted Landscapes, Country, 5 Piece 3800.00
Bench, Arrow–Back, Pine, Arms 675.00
Bench, Bucket, 1 Drawer, Pine, 36 In. 975.00
Bench, Bucket, Backsplash, Plate Rails, Red Paint 7500.00
Bench, Bucket, Bootjack Ends, Shelves, Traces Of Blue, 18 In. Wide 135.00
Bench, Bucket, Dark Finish, Red Paint Traces 425.00
Bench, Bucket, High Back, Mixed Woods, 2 Doors, 3 Top Drawers 650.00
Bench, Carved Frame, Cabriole Legs, Needlepoint Seat, 10 1/2 In. 175.00
Bench, Chippendale, Oak, Dark Finish, England, 75 x 40 1/4 In. 900.00
Bench, Crock, Ohio Chestnut, Square Nail Construction 350.00
Bench, Deacon's, Oak, Curved Seat, Carved Ends Of Arm Rest, 54 In. 450.00
Bench, Dresser, Carved Wooden Frame, Top Upholstered, 23 In. 150.00
Bench, Fireside, High Back, Pine, Red Graining, Country, 48 In. 200.00
Bench, Fluted Legs, Painted & Parcel Gilt, Upholstered, 40 In. 8250.00
Bench, Garden, Double, Cast Iron, Fern Leaves, Fern Arms 6650.00
Bench, Garden, Intertwining Twigs, Iron, Pair 4125.00
Bench, Garden, Minerva Head, Foliage Scrolls, White, Iron, 45 In. 1525.00
Bench, Garden, Rococo, Pierced Back, Scrolled Sides, Iron, 41 In. 3300.00
Bench, Garden, Urn & Swag Back, Cast Iron, 47 In., Pair 1875.00
Bench, Garden, White Paint, Cast Iron, 37 1/2 In. 675.00
Bench, George III Style, Ball & Claw Feet, Mahogany, 36 In. 880.00
Bench, George IV, Mahogany, 17 1/4 x 42 In. 770.00
Bench, Half–Spindle, Original Green Paint, Small 2400.00
    h, Kneeling, Queen Anne, Cabriole Legs, Upholstered, 13 In. 185.00
    1, Limbert, No. 243, 4 Cutout Sides, Splay Slab Legs, 24 In. 3300.00
    Mammy's, Original Gate, Stenciled Design 1650.00
    Mammy's, Original Paint & Stenciling, Boston Co. 825.00
    Mammy's, Vinegar Grained Seat, Painted, 46 In. 3500.00
    Neo–Classical, Bird Splat, Rush Seat, Fruitwood, 71 1/2 In. 2750.00

Bench, Photographer's, Wicker, Wide Arms	285.00
Bench, Pine, 50 1/2 In.	150.00
Bench, Pine, Removed Paint, Cutout Feet, 11 x 24 In.	115.00
Bench, Pine, Worn & Paint Traces, Mortised Legs, 61 In.	85.00
Bench, Poplar, Gray Weathered Patina, Board Top, 18 In.	195.00
Bench, Pub, George III, Curved Paneled High Back, Pine, 59 In.	950.00
Bench, Pub, George III, Curved Paneled High Back, Pine, 64 In.	935.00
Bench, Queen Anne Style, Mahogany, 55 In.	1650.00
Bench, Wash, Shaker, Mortised Legs, Gray Paint, 6 Ft.	400.00
Bench, Water, 3 Drawers, Scrolled Gallery, Pine, Poplar, 54 In.	2200.00
Bench, Water, Cutout Feet, Shaped Sides, Pine, 36 1/2 x 35 In.	525.00
Bench, Water, Oak, Light Green Paint, 29 In.	400.00
Bench, Water, Paneled Doors, 3 Drawers, Pine, Poplar, 50 1/2 In.	1250.00
Bench, Water, Pine, Scalloped Apron, Country, 30 3/4 In.	520.00
Bench, Water, Poplar, Blue Paint, 1 Shelf, Top With Well, 28 In.	350.00
Bench, Water, Shaped Sides, 3 Shelves, Dark Paint, 44 x 36 1/4 In.	200.00
Bench, William & Mary Style, Needlepoint Upholstery, 49 In.	1100.00
Bench, William & Mary Style, Tapestry Covered, Mahogany, 25 In.	315.00
Bench, Window, Italian Neoclassical Style, Walnut, 36 In.	440.00
Bench, Window, Painted Satinwood, Upholstered Seat, Arms, 35 In.	2100.00
Bench, Windsor, Low Back, Shaped Seat, Knuckle Arms, 79 1/2 In.	2600.00
Bench, Yellow Pine, Red Paint, Cutout Feet, 13 In.	150.00
Bin, Country, Corner Posts, Slant Front, Lift Lid, 37 1/2 In.	350.00
Bin, Meal, Pine, 2 Lift Tops, Top Drawer, 2 Base Drawers, Pat. 1880	495.00
Book Stand, Gustav Stickley, No. 93, 1 Door, Oak, c.1910, 40 In.	3300.00
Book Stand, William IV, Oak, Rectangular Galleried Top, 37 In.	935.00
Bookcase, 2 Doors, Carved Walnut, U.S., c.1870, 94 x 60 In.	1450.00
Bookcase, 3 Doors, Center Curved Glass Door, Oak, Large	800.00
Bookcase, 3 Leaded Glass Doors, 53 1/2 x 66 1/2 In.	500.00
Bookcase, 7 Shelves, 2 Sliding Glass Doors, Golden Oak, 102 In.	950.00
Bookcase, Arched Doors, Mother–of–Pearl Inlay, Syria, 66 1/2 In.	3300.00
Bookcase, Baroque, Walnut, 2 Drawers, 2 Doors, 110 In.	1600.00
Bookcase, Bottom Paneled Doors, Walnut & Hardwoods, 72 1/2 In.	250.00
Bookcase, Chippendale, Glazed Cupboard Doors, c.1780, 8 Ft. 2 In.	9075.00
Bookcase, Cupboard Base, Cherry, Mahogany, 84 In., 2 Piece	1000.00
Bookcase, Empire, Law–Type, 3 Top Sections, 6 Base Drawers, 1840	6000.00
Bookcase, Faux Grained, Mahogany, 11 Ft. 8 In.	2090.00
Bookcase, Gilt Metal Mounted, c.1830, 8 Ft. 4 In.	8800.00
Bookcase, Glazed Doors, Painted Trees, Painted Satinwood, 87 In.	5500.00
Bookcase, Globe–Wernicke, Stacking, 3 Sections, Mahogany	275.00
Bookcase, Globe–Wernicke, Stacking, Base Drawer, Oak	340.00
Bookcase, Governor Winthrop Style, Mahogany, 76 In.	300.00
Bookcase, Gustav Stickley, 2 Doors	3000.00
Bookcase, Library, Faux Grained, Mahogany, La., 11 Ft. 8 In. x 9 Ft.	2100.00
Bookcase, Lifetime, Mission Oak, 2 Doors, Original Finish	1750.00
Bookcase, Limbert, No. 350, Winged Corbeled Shelves, Door, 51 In.	4125.00
Bookcase, Limbert, Oak, 3 Doors, Shelved Interior, 4 Ft. 2 1/4 In.	1650.00
Bookcase, Louis Phillipe Style, 6 Shelves, Pine, 100 x 65 In.	5060.00
Bookcase, Mahogany, Adjustable Shelves, 20th Century, 58 In.	110.00
Bookcase, Mahogany, New Orleans, c.1850, 94 1/2 In. ....*Illus*	5280.00
Bookcase, Mahogany, Panel Inlay, Glass Doors	950.00
Bookcase, Neoclassical, 2 Glazed Doors, Mahogany, 57 1/2 In.	175.00
Bookcase, Oak, Lion's Heads Each Side, Scrollwork Top, 5 x 5 Ft.	600.00
Bookcase, Secretary, Traditional, Mahogany, 77 In.	350.00
Bookcase, Stacking, 3 Sections, Drawer At Bottom, Oak	300.00
Bookcase, Stacking, Desk Section, Oak	1395.00
Bookcase, Stickley Bros., No. 4770, 2 Doors, 16 Panes, 36 x 52 In.	2100.00
Bookcase, Victorian, Walnut, 2 Glass Doors	1050.00
Bracket, Louis XV, Serpentine Top Over Foliage, 14 3/4 In., Pair	6600.00
Breakfront, Collinson & Lock, Mahogany, Satinwood, 1885	2772.00
Breakfront, F. L. Wright, Glass Front, Cruciform Base, 76 x 65 In.	2750.00
Breakfront, Mahogany, Open Top Shelves, Green, Gold, 80 1/2 In.	150.00
Buffet, Butternut, Cherry, Cabriole Leg, Rope Inlay, 1800	6150.00

Buffet, Limbert, No. 462 1/2, Oak, 50 x 60 x 23 1/4 In. ....*Illus* 1320.00
Buffet, Oak, Serpentine, 2 Drawers Over 1 Drawer, 2 Doors 485.00
Bureau Bookcase, Bombe Case, Olive Wood, 76 x 41 In. 770.00
Bureau Desk, Burled Walnut, Slant Front, Inlaid Cross Banding 6600.00
Bureau, Dressing, Empire, Stenciled Designs, 62 x 36 1/2 In. 9500.00
Bureau, Eastlake, Walnut, Backsplash, New Teardrop Pulls 150.00
Bureau, Federal, Mahogany Inlay, 43 x 44 1/2 x 21 1/2 In. 4675.00
Bureau, Slant Front, Inlay, Scrolled Pediment, c.1880, 83 In. 2200.00
Cabinet, Apothecary, 36 Drawers, Oak, Glass Door, 13 x 9 x 19 In. 330.00
Cabinet, Apothecary, 60 Drawers, Yellow Pine 275.00
Cabinet, Baker's, Curly Maple, Refinished, 1860–1870, 2 Piece 5875.00
Cabinet, Biedermeier, 2 Drawers, Mahogany, Parcel Gilt, 4 Ft. 9 In. 3300.00
Cabinet, Bombe, Glazed Doors, Graduated Drawers, Pine, 83 In. 1695.00
Cabinet, Button, 6 Drawers, Oak, 20 3/4 x 23 1/2 In. 375.00
Cabinet, Carved Limewood, With Figures, Italy 3630.00
Cabinet, China, 2 Glass Doors, 1 Drawer, Walnut, 74 In. 190.00
Cabinet, China, 4 Cupboard Doors, 4 Drawers, Fruitwood, 82 1/2 In. 250.00
Cabinet, China, Carved Crest, Oak, Bowed, Bull's–Eye Mirror, 1880 .... 2350.00
Cabinet, China, Concave & Convex Glass, Mirrored Back, Oak, 75 In. 2900.00
Cabinet, China, Curved Glass, Claw Feet, Oak, 5 1/2 Ft. 600.00
Cabinet, China, L. & J. G. Stickley, 2 Glass Panels, No, 746, 62 In. 5175.00
Cabinet, China, L. & J. G. Stickley, No. 746, 1912, 62 In. ....*Illus* 5225.00
Cabinet, China, Mahogany, Curved Glass Sides & 2 Doors, Crest 1600.00
Cabinet, China, Mahogany, Middle Glass Door 450.00
Cabinet, China, Oak Veneer, Triple Curved Glass, Claw Feet 2100.00

Furniture, Bookcase, Mahogany, New Orleans, c.1850, 94 1/2 In.

Furniture, Cabinet, China, L. & J. G. Stickley, No. 746, 1912, 62 In.

Furniture, Buffet, Limbert, No. 462 1/2, Oak, 50 x 60 x 23 1/4 In.

◆ ◆

Be sure the big furniture you buy is small enough to go through the door into your room.

◆ ◆

Cabinet, China, Oak, Curved Glass, 5 Ft.	400.00
Cabinet, China, Oak, Curved Glass, Ball & Claw Feet	900.00
Cabinet, China, Oak, Curved Sides, Flat Front, Oval Beveled Mirror	800.00
Cabinet, China, Single Glass Door, Mirror Top, Oak, 66 In.	600.00
Cabinet, China, Step Back, Glass Doors, Drawers, Walnut & Burlwood	1000.00
Cabinet, China, Triple Curved Glass, Mirror Back, Oak Veneer	2100.00
Cabinet, China, Walnut, Step Back, 3 Glass Doors, Burl Trim	1500.00
Cabinet, Corner, Hanging, Aesthetic Movement, Ebonized, Painted	5914.00
Cabinet, Corner, Pegged Construction, 19th Century, 7 Ft.	950.00
Cabinet, Corner, Rosettes & Oak Leaves, Pine, c.1880, 7 Ft. 3 In.	4500.00
Cabinet, Curio, Floral Design, Ormolu Trim, Curved Glass, 56 In.	500.00
Cabinet, Curio, Louis XVI, Curved Glass, Gilt, 54 In.	1150.00
Cabinet, Curio, Mahogany Inlay, Ormolu Trim, Curved Glass, 63 In.	1300.00
Cabinet, Curio, Mahogany, Ebonized, Carved Elephants, 1800s, 67 In.	1980.00
Cabinet, Curio, Oriental, Mahogany, Glass Doors, c.1880, 30 1/4 In.	385.00
Cabinet, Curio, Ormolu Trim, Acrylic Panels In Doors, 71 1/4 In.	300.00
Cabinet, Curio, Painted Scenes, Ormolu Trim, 67 In.	1050.00
Cabinet, Doors, Painted Bouquets, Italy, 1780s, 32 1/4 x 29 In.	3850.00
Cabinet, Dressing, Georgian, Mahogany, Hinged Top, Pull–Up Mirror	660.00
Cabinet, Filing, 4 Drawers, Golden Oak, Handmade, Wood Interior	800.00
Cabinet, Filing, 90 Drawers, Hobart Brothers	350.00
Cabinet, Filing, Eastlake, Oak, Legal Size	300.00
Cabinet, Floral Baskets, Painted Satinwood, 2 Doors, 49 In.	1320.00
Cabinet, Folio, Georgian Style, Mahogany, 6 Drawers	2310.00
Cabinet, Geometric Designs, 2 Over 3 Doors, 17th Century, 66 In.	2200.00
Cabinet, Gothic Style, Oak, 51 1/4 In.	400.00
Cabinet, Hanging, Curved Glass, Stick–and–Ball Design, Walnut	375.00
Cabinet, Hoosier, 2 Doors, Sifter, Green Castle	595.00
Cabinet, Hoosier, 3 Doors, Sifter, Sellers	450.00
Cabinet, Hoosier, Oak, Caramel Glass Panels, Glass Knobs, Jars	745.00
Cabinet, Hoosier, Pine, 2 Doors, Original Hardware, Child's	165.00
Cabinet, Kitchen, Cream Graniteware Top, 2 Top Doors, 3 Drawers	390.00
Cabinet, Leaded Beveled Glass Doors, Over Cupboard Doors, Oak	370.00
Cabinet, Louis XV, Wire Door	4000.00
Cabinet, Majorelle, Carved Branches, Mahogany, 67 1/2 In.	7800.00
Cabinet, Music, Bowfront, Flowers & Instruments Inlay, Mahogany	750.00
Cabinet, Music, Gustav Stickley, No. 70, c.1910, 47 1/2 In.	4950.00
Cabinet, Music, Louis XV, Bombe, Vernis Martin Style	2000.00
Cabinet, Nakashima, Sliding Doors, Rice Paper & Walnut, c.1960	2750.00
Cabinet, Napoleon III, Ebonized & Gilt Bronze, 47 1/2 x 39 In.	1870.00
Cabinet, Oak, 2 Cupboard Doors, 5 Drawers, Heart–Shaped Pulls	1385.00
Cabinet, Oriental, Dark Wood, Opens Into Bar, 48 In.	250.00
Cabinet, Oriental, Dark Wood, Tooled Brass Fittings, 52 In.	200.00
Cabinet, Pagoda Top, Inner Drawers, Gilt, Red Lacquer, 23 In.	995.00
Cabinet, Print, Fall Front, Frank Furness	9900.00
Cabinet, Record, 1 Door, Scrolling Design, Maple, 30 x 31 x 24 In.	110.00
Cabinet, Rosewood Veneer Inlay, 1 Door, Gilt Trim, 44 In.	850.00
Cabinet, Sewing, Pyramid Shape, Pine, 4 Top & 4 Bottom Drawers	1050.00
Cabinet, Spice, 8 Drawers, Pine, Primitive	145.00
Cabinet, W. Werkstatte, 1 Cupboard Door, Black & White Paint, 1910	1860.00
Candlestand, 3 Snake Feet, Round Top, Child's	395.00
Candlestand, Adjustable Arm, Iron, 41 1/4 In.	1050.00
Candlestand, Adjustable Tray, 2 Socket Screw Type	300.00
Candlestand, Cherry, Baluster & Ring Turned Pedestal, 16 3/4 In.	665.00
Candlestand, Chippendale, Mahogany, Tripod, Snake Feet, England	425.00
Candlestand, Chippendale, Tilt Top, Curly Maple, Snake Feet	1100.00
Candlestand, Chippendale, Tilt Top, Mahogany Inlay, c.1785	4950.00
Candlestand, Chippendale, Tilt Top, Mahogany, c.1750, 27 3/4 In.	7700.00
Candlestand, Dish Top, Shod Slipper Feet, Walnut, 1740, 27 1/2 In.	1550.00
Candlestand, Dish Top, Spade Feet, Tiger Maple, c.1800	1500.00
Candlestand, Dish Top, Tripod Base, Pad Feet, Mahogany, 26 1/2 In.	250.00
Candlestand, Federal, Cherry, Oval Top, Turned Pedestal, 16 In.	495.00
Candlestand, Federal, Serpentine Top, Mahogany, c.1780, 28 1/2 In.	4500.00

Candlestand, Federal, Urn–Shaped Pedestal, Mahogany, 1800, 29 In. 1550.00
Candlestand, Hepplewhite, Oval Top, Cherry, 21 1/2 In. 550.00
Candlestand, Regency Style, Pullout Slide, Burl Wood, 25 1/2 In. 275.00
Candlestand, Round Top, Gumwood, 1780 .... 3200.00
Candlestand, Shaker, 2 Drawers, Butternut & Cherry 4125.00
Candlestand, Shaker, Square Top, Spider Legs, Cherrywood, 27 In. 1760.00
Candlestand, Sheraton, Mahogany, Tripod Spider Legs, 28 1/2 In. 350.00
Candlestand, Tilt Top, Cherry & Tiger Maple, c.1820, 27 1/2 In. 468.00
Candlestand, Tilt Top, Federal, Mahogany Inlay, c.1810, 29 In. 990.00
Candlestand, Tilt Top, Flowerpot Inlay In Top, Spider Feet 1250.00
Candlestand, Tilt Top, Hepplewhite, Cherry, 27 1/4 In. 525.00
Candlestand, Tilt Top, Line Inlay, Mahogany, c.1820, 28 3/4 In. 1870.00
Candlestand, Tilt Top, Mahogany, 27 1/4 In. 350.00
Candlestand, Tilt Top, Queen Anne, Pad Feet, Walnut, 27 In. 1100.00
Candlestand, Tilt Top, Snake Feet, Turned Column, Walnut, 28 In. 5400.00
Candlestand, Tilt Top, Snake Feet, Walnut, c.1760, 29 1/2 In. 3575.00
Candlestand, Tilt Top, Spider Legs, New England, 1800 .... 595.00
Candlestand, Tilt Top, Tripod Base, Mahogany, 28 1/2 In. 3080.00
Candlestand, Tilt Top, Turned Column, Snake Feet, Walnut, 28 In. 750.00
Candlestand, Tripod Base, 1 Board Top, Maple, 25 1/2 In. 400.00
Candlestand, Windsor, Nutting, Ash, 25 1/4 In. 187.00
Canterbury, Drawer, 3 Interior Sections, Mahogany, 18 1/2 In. 1210.00
Canterbury, Lyre–Form Supports, Drawer, Mahogany, 17 1/2 x 20 In. 2750.00
Case, Decanter, 6 Bottles, Eagle & Shield Inlay, Mahogany Veneer 2250.00
Case, Gun, Victorian, Brass Mounted Mahogany, 22 x 32 3/4 In. 550.00
Cedar Chest, Lane, Walnut, 1920s 80.00
Cellarette, 2 Handles, On Stand, Brass Bound, Mahogany, 26 In. 1320.00
Cellarette, Domed Lid, 8 Bottle Sections, Brass Handles, Mahogany 1760.00
Cellarette, Stand, Hinged Top Opening, Mahogany, 30 1/2 In. 3850.00
Chair Set, A. L. Robinson, Dark Brown Paint, Stenciled, 5 .... 125.00
Chair Set, Arrow–Back, Curved Crest Rail, Gilt Serpent, 8 .... 6600.00
Chair Set, Arrow–Back, Plank Seat, Painted, 6 .... 1200.00
Chair Set, Back Rails Over Uprights, Painted, Rush Seat, c.1810, 4 .... 1350.00
Chair Set, Balloon Back, Red & Black Graining, Floral, 6 .... 1080.00
Chair Set, Balloon Back, Rosewood, Upholstered, England, 4 .... 450.00
Chair Set, Balloon Back, Yellow Green Paint, 33 1/4 In., 4 .... 180.00
Chair Set, Ballroom, White Frame, Cane Seat, c.1920, 12 .... 1045.00
Chair Set, Bannister Back, 1 With Arms, 6 .... 5550.00
Chair Set, Biedermeier, Arrow–Back, Classical Mounts, 4 .... 4675.00
Chair Set, Biedermeier, Pierced Splat, Walnut, Upholstered Seat, 4 .... 1980.00
Chair Set, Charles Eames, Metal Frame, Rod–Shaped Legs, 6 .... 495.00
Chair Set, Chippendale, Mahogany, Slip Seat, 36 1/4 In., 5 .... 2350.00
Chair Set, Comb–Shaped Rail, 9 Spindles, G. Nakishima, 1955, 6 .... 1540.00
Chair Set, Commemorative, Admiral Sampson, Cane Seat, Oak, 6 .... 800.00
Chair Set, Concave Crest Rail, 8 Spindles, Oak, c.1912, 6 .... 665.00
Chair Set, Concave Crest, Slip Seat, Mahogany, c.1815, 8 .... 3850.00
Chair Set, Country, Plank Seat, Black Paint, 31 1/2 In., 4 .... 140.00
Chair Set, Dining, Carved Birds & Grapes, Oak, 6 .... 1950.00
Chair Set, Dining, George III Style, Marlborough Legs, 8 .... 3520.00
Chair Set, Dining, George III Style, Vasi–Form Pierced Splat, 12 .... 6600.00
Chair Set, Dining, George III, Vasi–Form Pierced Splat, 6 .... 5280.00
Chair Set, Dining, Georgian Style, Shield Back, 14 .... 8000.00
Chair Set, Dining, Gustav Stickley, H–Back, 6 .... 1100.00
Chair Set, Dining, Louis XVI, Painted, 13 .... 5000.00
Chair Set, Dining, Michigan Chair Co., 1 Vertical Slat, c.1912, 4 .... 357.50
Chair Set, Dining, Queen Anne Style, Walnut, 10 .... 7000.00
Chair Set, Dining, Russian Style, Walnut, Upholstered Back, Seat, 8 .... 2200.00
Chair Set, Directoire, Bellflowers Crest, Giltwood, c.1800, 4 .... 3300.00
Chair Set, Eagle On Slats, Painted Foliage, Fruit On Crest, 6 .... 4200.00
Chair Set, Empire, Mahogany, Upholstered Seat, 33 1/3 In., 4 .... 340.00
Chair Set, Empire, Rose Carved Backs, Sabre Leg, Mahogany, 6 .... 2100.00
Chair Set, Federal, Floral & Cherry Design, 1840s, 6 .... 1500.00
Chair Set, Federal, Flower Head Crest, Bellflower Splat, c.1800, 8 .... 6600.00

Chair Set, Federal, Slover & Taylor, Mahogany, c.1805, 8 .... 9350.00
Chair Set, Fruitwood, Gesso & Giltwood, Upholstered, 8 .... 4400.00
Chair Set, Fruitwood, Parcel Gilt, Upholstered, 8 .... 6600.00
Chair Set, Garden, Fern Pattern, Cast Iron, 4 .... 2750.00
Chair Set, Garden, Renaissance Revival Pattern, Cast Iron, 12 .... 6600.00
Chair Set, Georgian, Carved Walnut, 8 .... 8250.00
Chair Set, Georgian, Mahogany, Carved, Floral Upholstered, 12 .... 3630.00
Chair Set, Gustav Stickley, Oak, 6 .... 5000.00
Chair Set, Half Spindle Back, Plank Seat, Brown, Striped, 6 .... 450.00
Chair Set, Half Spindle, Plank Bottom, Black, Floral Stenciled, 4 .... 400.00
Chair Set, Hepplewhite, Mahogany, Satinwood Inlay, 36 In., 6 .... 570.00
Chair Set, Hepplewhite, Pierced Splats, Slip Seat, Mahogany, 4 .... 1000.00
Chair Set, L. & J. G. Stickley, Concave Horizontal Rails, 1912, 6 .... 1870.00
Chair Set, Ladder Back, 3 Slats, Rush Seat, 33 1/2 In., 3 .... 220.00
Chair Set, Ladder Back, Maple, Red Paint, Splint Seat, 39 In., 4 .... 980.00
Chair Set, Louisiana, Cowhide Seat, Pecan Wood, 10 .... 950.00
Chair Set, Mira, Nakashima, 20th Century, 6 .... 2000.00
Chair Set, Neoclassical, Oval Medallion Back, Upholstered, 8 .... 2640.00
Chair Set, Oak, Fruitwood Marquetry Inlay, Holland, 4 .... 3950.00
Chair Set, Queen Anne, Hardwood, Dark Finish, Red Vinyl Seats, 7 .... 455.00
Chair Set, Queen Anne, Mahogany, England, 4 .... 264.00
Chair Set, Queen Anne, Spanish Feet, Vasiform Splat, Rush Seat, 4 .... 4000.00
Chair Set, S. Gragg, Wooden Slat, Elastic, 6 .... 3950.00
Chair Set, Sheraton, Red & Black Paint, Yellow Striping, 6 .... 510.00
Chair Set, Sheraton, Stenciled, Yellow Striping, 2 With Arms, 8 .... 280.00
Chair Set, Spanish Baroque, Folding, Walnut, 42 1/2 In., 6 .... 1320.00
Chair Set, Stenciled By William P. Eaton, Signed, 4 .... 1250.00
Chair Set, Stenciled, Curved Seat, 6 .... 330.00
Chair Set, Thumb Back, Green, Black, & Mustard Paint, 6 .... 3080.00
Chair Set, Tiger Maple, Rolled Crest Rail, Cane Seat, 4 .... 660.00
Chair Set, William & Mary, Caned Seat, 4 .... 1430.00
Chair Set, Windsor, Bamboo, Dark Finish, Cage Back, Medallions, 6 .... 1200.00
Chair Set, Windsor, Bamboo, Spindle Back, 35 1/2 In., 9 .... 2250.00
Chair Set, Windsor, Bow Back, Bamboo Turned Legs, Saddle Seat, 4 .... 1700.00
Chair Set, Windsor, Brown Design, Yellow Paint, Round Seat, 4 .... 3850.00
Chair Set, Windsor; I. Kingsley, Birdcage, 3 .... 165.00
Chair Set, Windsor, Step–Down, Red Paint, 4 .... 5500.00
Chair Set, Yellow & Tan Striping, Painted Crest, Plank Seat, 6 .... 1850.00
Chair, Adirondack–Type Twig, Chip Carved, Painted 850.00
Chair, Arrow–Back, Red & Black Graining, Stencil, Me. History, Pair 700.00
Chair, Bannister Back, Dark Graining, 44 1/2 In. 600.00
Chair, Bannister Back, Dark Varnish, New Rush Seats, Pair 400.00
Chair, Beechwood, Horseshoe Curved Seat Rail, J. & J. Kohn, Pair 1108.00
Chair, Belter, Grapes, Laminated Rosewood, Pair 4400.00
Chair, Belter, Tuthill King, Laminated Rosewood, Woman's 8910.00
Chair, Bentwood, Austria, 1910 .... 35.00
Chair, Bishops, Oak, Ascention Carved, Leather Seat, 17th Century 880.00
Chair, Bowed Crest, Split Baluster Uprights, Mahogany, c.1815, Pr. 5225.00
Chair, Brass Nail Heads, Ash Wood, U.S., c.1881 .... 1935.00
Chair, Carved Crest, Spanish, Rush Seat, 45 In. 85.00
Chair, Carved Knee Shells, Slip Seat, Red Damask Cover, Maple 7000.00
Chair, Carved Pierced Back, Needlepoint Seat, Rosewood 700.00
Chair, Child's, Bow Back, Continuous Arm Rail, 25 In. 550.00
Chair, Child's, Chippendale, Carved Crest Rail, Mahogany, 25 In. 330.00
Chair, Child's, Half Arrow–Back 100.00
Chair, Child's, Ladder Back, Red Repaint 95.00
Chair, Child's, Ladder Back, Splint Seat, 22 1/2 In. 65.00
Chair, Child's, Posture, Ladder Back, Oval Carved Seat, Oak 750.00
Chair, Child's, Step–Down Windsor, Painted Crest 440.00
Chair, Child's, Tiger Maple, Original Rush Seat, 1815–1840 .... 450.00
Chair, Child's, Windsor, Arrow–Back, Worn Red Paint, Black Grained 460.00
Chair, Child's, Windsor, Bow Back, 7 Spindles, Saddle Seat 600.00
Chair, Child's, Windsor, Yellow, Revolving 3190.00

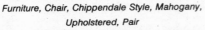

Furniture, Chair, Chippendale Style, Mahogany, Upholstered, Pair

Furniture, Chair, Corner, Italian Renaissance, 19th Century

Chair, Chippendale Style, Mahogany, Upholstered, Pair ....*Illus*	2640.00
Chair, Chippendale, Baluster Form Splat, Walnut, c.1770	1320.00
Chair, Chippendale, Carved Acanthus, Vasiform Splat, Walnut, 1755	6050.00
Chair, Chippendale, Carved Leafage, Peanuts, Walnut, c.1770	6600.00
Chair, Chippendale, Carved Splat, Mahogany, Ball & Claw Feet, 1770	8250.00
Chair, Chippendale, Corner, Slip Seat, 19th Century	375.00
Chair, Chippendale, Country, Maple, Rush Seat, 40 In.	330.00
Chair, Chippendale, Country, Maple, Rush Seat, New England	192.50
Chair, Chippendale, Mahogany, 1785, 39 1/4 In.	1870.00
Chair, Chippendale, Mahogany, Hand Carved Splat & Crest, 37 In.	225.00
Chair, Chippendale, Mahogany, Needlepoint Seats, 38 In., Pair	650.00
Chair, Chippendale, Mahogany, Reupholstered Seat, 37 1/2 In.	300.00
Chair, Chippendale, Mahogany, Shaped Crest Rail, Massachusetts	8250.00
Chair, Chippendale, Mahogany, Slip Seat, 29 3/4 In.	1000.00
Chair, Chippendale, Mahogany, Slip Seat, U.S., 37 3/4 In.	175.00
Chair, Chippendale, Oak, Cabriole Legs, Trifid Feet, 37 In.	300.00
Chair, Chippendale, Pierced Vasiform Splat, Mahogany, c.1775	1870.00
Chair, Chippendale, Refinished Cherry, Slip Seat, Pierced Splat	200.00
Chair, Chippendale, Rush Seat, Birch, 39 In.	350.00
Chair, Chippendale, Serpentine Crest Rail, Vase Splat, 40 In.	4200.00
Chair, Chippendale, Shaped Crest, Carved Shell, Mahogany, c.1760	3300.00
Chair, Chippendale, Trifid Feet, Walnut, Needlepoint Upholstery	3000.00
Chair, Chippendale, Wing, Floral Upholstery, 42 In.	80.00
Chair, Chippendale, Wing, Oriental Design, Upholstered, Pair	400.00
Chair, Chippendale, Wing, Walnut Claw & Ball Feet, Upholstered	350.00
Chair, Church, Carving, Needlepoint Seat	175.00
Chair, Corner, Chippendale, Mahogany, Green Leather Seat, 32 In.	450.00
Chair, Corner, Chippendale, Mahogany, Slip Seat, Boston	2600.00
Chair, Corner, Chippendale, Rush Seat, Maple, Curved Arms	715.00
Chair, Corner, Edwardian, Vasiform Splats, Mahogany Inlay, Pair	1100.00
Chair, Corner, Elm, Rush Seat, 1830	1150.00
Chair, Corner, George II, Walnut, Arched Cresting Rail	1000.00
Chair, Corner, George III, Curved Crest Rail, Mahogany	2200.00
Chair, Corner, Hardwood, Brown Finish, Cherubs, Griffins, 32 In.	350.00
Chair, Corner, Italian Renaissance Style, Mahogany, 36 In.	725.00
Chair, Corner, Italian Renaissance, 19th Century ....*Illus*	660.00
Chair, Corner, Queen Anne, Vasiform Splats, Walnut, c.1755	1980.00
Chair, Corner, Queen Anne, Walnut, Cabriole Front Leg, Upholstered	1200.00
Chair, Curly & Bird's-Eye Maple, Sabre Leg, Rush Seat, Gold, Pr.	310.00
Chair, Deck, Footrest, Arms, Large	195.00
Chair, Desk, Caned Seat & Back, U.S., c.1860	338.00

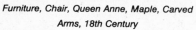

Furniture, Chair, Queen Anne, Maple, Carved Arms, 18th Century

Furniture, Chair, Savanarola-Type, Oak

Chair, Desk, Oak, Face Pressed Into Back	285.00
Chair, Desk, Swivel, Oak, Pressed Back, Bentwood Arms	70.00
Chair, Desk, Tufted Leather, Baker, 20th Century	270.00
Chair, Dining, Molded Ash Plywood, Charles Eames, Pair	770.00
Chair, Dutch Baroque, Walnut, Ivory Inlay, 42 In.	450.00
Chair, Ebonized, Gesso & Parcel Gilt, Sphinx Supports On Arms	3080.00
Chair, Egyptian Torsos Front, Upholstered Back, Wooden Armrests	3300.00
Chair, Empire, Irish, c.1835	1250.00
Chair, Faux Bois & Silver Gilt, Carved Arms, Upholstered Seat	3020.00
Chair, Federal, Bentwood, Shaped Monogrammed Crest Rail	1650.00
Chair, Federal, Birch, New England, Country, 19th Century	770.00
Chair, Federal, Painted, Hoof Feet, Samuel Gragg, c.1810	1650.00
Chair, Federal, Scroll Crest Rail, Reeded Stiles, Mahogany, Pair	3300.00
Chair, Federal, Shield Back, Pierced Splat, Mahogany, c.1800	4675.00
Chair, Federal, Shield Back, Satinwood, Mahogany Inlay, 1805, Pair	4125.00
Chair, Federal, Shield Back, Upholstered Seat Rail, Mahogany, 1810	385.00
Chair, Folding, Victorian, Cameo Back, Crown Lion Head Arms	800.00
Chair, G. Stickley, Cube, Slat Sides	7500.00
Chair, Garden, Fern Back, Ba Be Wire & Iron Works, Cast Iron	525.00
Chair, Garden, Scrolled Back & Legs, Wire	770.00
Chair, George I, Crest Rail Over Shaped Splats, Walnut	525.00
Chair, George I, Square Back, Walnut, Crook Arms, 1730s	1540.00
Chair, George II, Walnut, Petit Point Floral Upholstery, Pair	4400.00
Chair, George III, Silk Lamp Fabric Cover, Pair	8500.00
Chair, Gilt, France, 37 In.	350.00
Chair, Gustav Stickley, 3 Horizontal Slats, Slip Seat, c.1912	110.00
Chair, Gustav Stickley, 5 Slats, Spring Cushion Seat, c.1907	247.00
Chair, Gustav Stickley, No. 374, Mahogany, Spindles, Loose Cushion	1650.00
Chair, Gustav Stickley, No. 391, Spindle Cube, c.1907	8800.00
Chair, Hepplewhite Style, Shield Back, Mahogany, Arms	415.00
Chair, Hepplewhite, Mahogany, Carved Detail, Slip Seat, 39 In.	43.00
Chair, Hitchcock Style, Stencil Design, U.S., 19th Century	100.00
Chair, Hitchcock Type, Red & Black Grained, Rush Seat, Pair	350.00
Chair, Horn, 1920s	1350.00
Chair, Hunzinger, Pipe–Like Spindles	600.00
Chair, Klismos, Painted & Stenciled, 19th Century, 31 1/2 In.	165.00
Chair, Knoll, Barcelona Style, Pair	750.00
Chair, Ladder Back, 2 Slats, High Seat, 37 In.	175.00
Chair, Ladder Back, 3 Arched Slats, Painted Red, 37 1/4 In., Pair	137.50
Chair, Ladder Back, 3 Slats, Turned Finials, Rush Seat, 36 In.	75.00
Chair, Ladder Back, 4 Slats, Carved Mahogany, Arms, c.1780	2750.00

Chair, Ladder Back, 5 Graduated Slats, Hardwood, Scrolled Arms 3000.00
Chair, Ladder Back, Elmwood, England, Arms 275.00
Chair, Ladder Back, Hardwood, Red Paint, Woven Splint Seat, 38 In. 125.00
Chair, Ladder Back, Painted, New England, Arms, c.1790, 42 In. 220.00
Chair, Ladder Back, Rush Seat, Shaped Arms, 43 3/8 In. 2000.00
Chair, Ladder Back, Turned Feet & Posts, Rush Seat, Arms, 46 In. 3700.00
Chair, Ladder Back, Woven Rush Seat, Stamped St. Pauls, Pair 80.00
Chair, Lattice Back, Marable, Foliate Pierced Arms, Pair 1980.00
Chair, Lolling, Chippendale Style, Mahogany Frame, 39 1/2 In. 440.00
Chair, Lolling, Federal, Mahogany, New England, 1840s, 45 In. 4950.00
Chair, Lolling, Lemuel Churchill Label 3850.00
Chair, Lolling, Serpentine Crest, Mahogany, c.1800, 45 In. 4950.00
Chair, Loom, Shaker, Ohio 475.00
Chair, Loom, Wicker, Lloyd, 1925 .... 429.00
Chair, Louis Philippe Style, Oval Set, Fluted Stiles, Gilt, Pair 467.00
Chair, Louis XV Style, Giltwood, Fur Upholstery, 28 In. 715.00
Chair, Louis XV, Cane Backrest, Beechwood, Continuous Arms 1980.00
Chair, Louis XV, Needlepoint Seat, Gold Gilt, c.1850, 38 In. 450.00
Chair, Louis XV, Padded Armrests, White Paint, Pair 2420.00
Chair, Louis XVI Style, Spindle Back, Carved, Gilt, Early 1900s 319.00
Chair, Louis XVI, Gilt, Pink Brocade Upholstery, 35 In. 250.00
Chair, Louis XVI, Ribbon Carved Border On Back, 37 1/2 In., Pair 1100.00
Chair, Lounge, Old Hickory 450.00
Chair, Made Of Snowshoe, Byrd Expedition 1250.00
Chair, Mahogany, Green Vinyl Seats, China, Pair 200.00
Chair, Mahogany, Ribbon Back, Needlepoint Slip Seat, 38 In., Pair 250.00
Chair, Maple, Rush Seat, c.1850, Pair 154.00
Chair, Moravian, Hardwood, Dark Finish, 2 Birds Carved Back 135.00
Chair, Morris, Adjustable Back, Cushion Seat, c.1910 .... 1760.00
Chair, Morris, Gustav Stickley, Bent Arms 5490.00
Chair, Morris, Gustav Stickley, Spindles, Drop Arms 9500.00
Chair, Morris, Lifetime, Bow Arms 1100.00
Chair, Morris, Oak, Lion's Head Figural Arms 160.00
Chair, Music, Abalone Inlay, Lacquered, Cane Seat, Pair 275.00
Chair, Needlepoint Seat, Petit Point Oval, Gold Leaf Over Frame 450.00
Chair, New York, Square Back, Upholstered Seat, 1800, Pair 2500.00
Chair, Nutting, Ladder Back, Black Paint, Rush Seat, Arms 350.00
Chair, Oak, Turned Spindles, Rush Seat, England, 37 1/4 In. 75.00
Chair, Ogival Wings, Mahogany, Upholstered, c.1780 .... 8250.00
Chair, Oriental, Bird Of Prey, Flowers, Carved Dragon Arms, 1900s 1200.00
Chair, Oriental, Carved Irises, Frog, Lily Pad, Scarab Seat, 1900s 1000.00
Chair, Oriental, Foo Lions, Carved Hoofed Dragon Arms, 1900s 1500.00
Chair, Padded Top Rail, Adjustable Support, Mahogany, c.1810 .... 2860.00
Chair, Painted Birds On Crest, Painted, T. M. Morris, 1850s, Pair 975.00
Chair, Papier-Mache, Mother-of-Pearl Inlay, Jennings & Bettridge 485.00
Chair, Parlor, Renaissance Revival, Walnut, U.S., c.1875, Pair 550.00
Chair, Potato Chip, Plywood, Charles Eames, c.1950 .... 330.00
Chair, Queen Anne, Balloon Seat, Vasiform Splat, Walnut, c.1750 .... 3300.00
Chair, Queen Anne, Country, Hardwood, Black, Rush Seat, 41 In. 550.00
Chair, Queen Anne, Country, Yellow Striping, Rush Seat, 39 In. 1000.00
Chair, Queen Anne, Maple, Bulbous Front Stretcher, 38 3/4 In. 250.00
Chair, Queen Anne, Maple, Carved Arms, 18th Century ....*Illus* 4950.00
Chair, Queen Anne, Maple, Turned, Replaced Seat, Mass., 1760, Pair 4500.00
Chair, Queen Anne, Original Stained Surface, Splint Seat, 43 In. 2970.00
Chair, Queen Anne, Rush Seat, Painted Maple, 1740s, Pair 1760.00
Chair, Queen Anne, Walnut, Shepherd's Crook Arms, 38 1/2 In. 550.00
Chair, Queen Anne, Yoke Back, Rush Seat, Pair 1210.00
Chair, Queen Anne, Yoked Crest Rail, Vasiform Splat, Cedar, Pair 5500.00
Chair, Red & Black Graining, Floral Crest & Splat, Gold Striping 75.00
Chair, Regency, Button Tufted Back & Seat, Mahogany 660.00
Chair, Regency, Mahogany, 32 In. 225.00
Chair, Rocker, look under Rocker in this section.
Chair, Rococo Revival, Laminated, Openwork Back, Pair 1760.00

Chair, Rococo Revival, Medallion Back, Damask Upholstery 375.00
Chair, Rococo, Rosewood, Finger Carved Frame, 35 1/4 In., Pair 300.00
Chair, Rolled Arm, Iron Wire 385.00
Chair, Rounded Crest Rail Of 3 Pierced Splats, Elmwood, Pair 467.50
Chair, Saber Legs, Lotus Leaf Arm Terminals, Upholstered, Pair 4070.00
Chair, Sack Back, 7 Spindles, D-Shaped Seat, Green Paint 1600.00
Chair, Sack Back, New England, c.1780 .... 2600.00
Chair, Salmon Paint, Square, Turned Arms 1265.00
Chair, Savanarola-Type, Oak .... *Illus* 303.00
Chair, Scrolled Arms, Thuyawood, Upholstered Arms, 1850s 3300.00
Chair, Shaker, 2 Slats, Harvard 2090.00
Chair, Shaker, Dining, Pine Seat, Birch Back, 25 In. 880.00
Chair, Shaker, Ladder Back, 3 Bowed Splats, Mt. Lebanon, Maple 385.00
Chair, Shaker, Ladder Back, New Hampshire, Red Stain 165.00
Chair, Shaker, Rush Seat, Back Post, Figured Maple, 41 In. 4675.00
Chair, Shaker, Rush Seat, Figured Maple, Canterbury 4675.00
Chair, Shaker, Tilter, Curly & Bird's-Eye Maple, Canterbury 3300.00
Chair, Shaker, Tilter, Steam-Bent Back Posts, 40 1/2 In. 2200.00
Chair, Sheraton, Hitchcock, Red & Black Graining, Rush Seat, Pair 400.00
Chair, Sheraton, Hitchcock, Turtle Back Slats, Caned Seat, Pair 1400.00
Chair, Sheraton, Mahogany Frame, Inlay, 48 In. 175.00
Chair, Sheraton, Mahogany, Ivory, Blue Striped Floral Upholstery 300.00
Chair, Sheraton, Rush Seat, Grain Painted & Bird's-Eye Maple, Pr. 135.00
Chair, Shield Back, Edwardian, Satinwood, c.1900, Pair 275.00
Chair, Shoeshine Stand, 1930s 80.00
Chair, Slipper, Chippendale, Brown Paint, Rush Seat, 38 3/4 In. 220.00
Chair, Slipper, Rush Seat, Painted & Carved Maple, c.1745 .... 3850.00
Chair, Sno Shu Canoe, Webbed Back & Seat 125.00
Chair, Tete-A-Tete, Maple, Carved & Turned 300.00
Chair, Thonet, Bentwood Back, Upholstered Seat, Pair 475.00
Chair, Throne, Prudent Mallard 1870.00
Chair, Tub, Leather Covered, Brass Nailing, Walnut & Parcel Gilt 415.00
Chair, Tub, Regency, Simulated Rosewood, Spoon Back, Thomas Hope 1450.00
Chair, Venetian, Painted Design, Carved Back, Curved Legs 495.00
Chair, Wallace Nutting, Windsor, Bow Back 525.00
Chair, White Wicker, Curved, No Cushion 45.00
Chair, Windsor, 9 Spindle Back, Saddle Seat, 36 In. 250.00
Chair, Windsor, Arrow-Back, Bamboo Turned, Exaggerated Crest 175.00
Chair, Windsor, Bamboo Turnings In Base, Plain Spindles 150.00
Chair, Windsor, Bamboo, Birch Arms, 34 1/2 In., Pair 1000.00
Chair, Windsor, Bamboo, Black Paint, Trace Of Design, 35 1/2 In. 300.00
Chair, Windsor, Bamboo, Brown Over Green Paint 125.00
Chair, Windsor, Bamboo, Country, 33 1/2 In. 80.00
Chair, Windsor, Bamboo, Label, 32 3/4 In. 115.00
Chair, Windsor, Bamboo, Old Red, Traces Of White Striping 700.00
Chair, Windsor, Bamboo, Spindle Back, Step-Down Crest, 35 1/2 In. 150.00
Chair, Windsor, Bamboo, Step-Down Crest, 35 1/4 In. 350.00
Chair, Windsor, Bow Back, 37 1/2 In. 770.00
Chair, Windsor, Bow Back, Alligatored, Bulbous Spindles, Arms 625.00
Chair, Windsor, Bow Back, Bamboo, H Stretcher, Saddle Seat 375.00
Chair, Windsor, Bow Back, Bulbous Turnings, Saddle Seat 1000.00
Chair, Windsor, Bow Back, H Stretcher, Saddle Seat, 36 1/4 In. 1400.00
Chair, Windsor, Bow Back, H Stretcher, Turned Legs, 42 In. 950.00
Chair, Windsor, Bow Back, Knuckle Arms, 37 1/2 In. 400.00
Chair, Windsor, Bow Back, Late 19th Century, 35 1/2 In. 250.00
Chair, Windsor, Bow Back, Maple, U.S., Flaring Arms 880.00
Chair, Windsor, Bow Back, Oval Seat, N. Hall, Traces Of Paint, Arms 700.00
Chair, Windsor, Bow Back, Pierced Splat & Spindles, Elmwood, Arms 275.00
Chair, Windsor, Bow Back, Spindle Back, H Stretcher, Arms 800.00
Chair, Windsor, Bow Back, Splayed Base, Bamboo Turnings 325.00
Chair, Windsor, Bow Back, Splayed Base, Refinished, Knuckle Arms 350.00
Chair, Windsor, Captain's, Yoke Back, Plank Seat, Pine, Pair 100.00
Chair, Windsor, Child's, Black & Green Striping, Yellow, Pair 750.00

Chair, Windsor, Comb Back, Green, Pair 8800.00
Chair, Windsor, Comb Back, Plank Seat, Painted, Arms, c.1785 .... 2475.00
Chair, Windsor, Comb Back, Spindle, Oval Seat, Trace Of Black, Arms 950.00
Chair, Windsor, Continuous Arm, 15 Spindles, c.1780 .... 2200.00
Chair, Windsor, Continuous Arm, Bamboo Turnings, New England, 1810 .... 1375.00
Chair, Windsor, Continuous Arm, New England, c.1790 .... 413.00
Chair, Windsor, Continuous Arm, Worn Black Paint, Saddle Seat 700.00
Chair, Windsor, Fanback, 7 Spindles, Plank Seat, c.1790, Pair 2640.00
Chair, Windsor, Fanback, Black Paint, Saddle Seat, 34 1/2 In. 750.00
Chair, Windsor, Fanback, Black Paint, Splayed Base, H Stretcher 675.00
Chair, Windsor, Fanback, Black Paint, U.S., 36 1/4 In. 1100.00
Chair, Windsor, Fanback, Blunt Arrow Feet 5500.00
Chair, Windsor, Fanback, Low Arms, 34 In. 275.00
Chair, Windsor, Fanback, New England, 19th Century 660.00
Chair, Windsor, Fanback, Oval Shaped Seat, Plugged Potty Seat 1400.00
Chair, Windsor, Fanback, Saddle Seat, Black Painted Arms, 43 In. 1000.00
Chair, Windsor, Fanback, Saddle Seat, Crest Carved Ear, Pair 900.00
Chair, Windsor, High Back, Yew Seat, Arms, 44 In. 150.00
Chair, Windsor, Ladder Back, John Letchworth 4250.00
Chair, Windsor, Natural Refinish, Bulbous Legs, Comb Back Arms 600.00
Chair, Windsor, Pierced Wheel Splat, Saddle Seat, Ash & Pine, Pair 440.00
Chair, Windsor, Sack Back, Green Paint, Adams Express Co. 5775.00
Chair, Windsor, Sack Back, Mass., 1780–1810, 37 In. 935.00
Chair, Windsor, Sack Back, Pine & Ash, c.1800 .... 275.00
Chair, Windsor, Sack Back, Red Wash 1050.00
Chair, Windsor, Sack Back, Scrolled Hand Grips, Hickory 715.00
Chair, Windsor, Spindle Back, Saddle Seat, Black, 38 In. 850.00
Chair, Windsor, Spindle Back, Writing Arm, Stained, c.1800 .... 2750.00
Chair, Windsor, U–Shaped Low Back, 13 Spindles, Arms, c.1765 .... 6325.00
Chair, Wing, Arched Back, Carved Mahogany, Rolled Arms 1045.00
Chair, Wing, Ball & Claw Feet, 40 1/2 In. 175.00
Chair, Wing, Ball & Claw Feet, Stitch Woven Upholstery, 45 In. 275.00
Chair, Wing, Black Leather, Brass Tack Trim, Oak, Scroll Footed 350.00
Chair, Wing, Cabriole Legs, Down Cushion, 2 Needlepoint Pillows 350.00
Chair, Wing, Chippendale Style, North Hickory Furniture Co. 185.00
Chair, Wing, Floral Upholstery, 40 1/2 In. 70.00
Chair, Wing, George III, Needlepoint Upholstery, 1760s, 46 In. 3300.00
Chair, Wing, Georgian Style, Arched Crest, Mahogany, Upholstered 770.00
Chair, Wing, Georgian, Walnut, Cabriole Legs, England, 19th Century 400.00
Chair, Wing, Hickory, Mahogany, Upholstery, Pair 660.00
Chair, Wing, Mahogany, Upholstered Back & Seat 825.00
Chair, Wing, Queen Anne, Mahogany Legs, Gold Brocade Upholstery 350.00
Chair, Wing, Queen Anne, Needlepoint Upholstery, Rosewood, c.1800 .... 3025.00
Chair, Wing, Walnut, Needlepoint Upholstery, 48 3/4 In. 4400.00
Chaise Lounge, French, Blue Flowered Velvet 300.00
Chaise Lounge, High Back, Wicker, Upholstered Seat, 5 Ft. 7 In. 880.00
Chaise Lounge, L. & J. G. Stickley, No. 291, c.1900 .... 935.00
Chaise Lounge, Louis XV Style, Upholstered Back & Seat, 60 In. 330.00
Chaise Lounge, Painted Beechwood, Upholstered, 60 In. 660.00
Chaise Lounge, Wicker, Natural, c.1905 .... 1295.00
Chaise Lounge, Wicker, White 850.00
Chest, 2 Drawers, Mule, Pine, Red, Cutout Feet, 35 In. 2550.00
Chest, 2 Over 4 Drawers, Mahogany Veneer, Light Mahogany 2000.00
Chest, 2 Short Over 3 Long Drawers, Cherry, 48 x 42 In. 250.00
Chest, 3 Drawers, Biedermeier, Painted & Parcel Gilt, 37 1/2 In. 8250.00
Chest, 3 Drawers, Decorated, Pine, Red, Black Graining, 13 1/2 In. 600.00
Chest, 3 Drawers, Dovetailed, Continental, Mahogany, Inlay, 35 In. 2000.00
Chest, 3 Drawers, Dovetailed, Continental, Marquetry, 35 In. 9400.00
Chest, 3 Drawers, Eastlake, Marble Top, Teardrop Pulls 300.00
Chest, 3 Drawers, Mahogany, Grand Rapids, 26 In. 200.00
Chest, 3 Drawers, Oak, Raised Panels, Brasses, England, c.1800 .... 1650.00
Chest, 3 Narrow & 3 Wide Drawers, Maple, c.1795, 52 1/2 In. 3080.00
Chest, 3 Narrow & 3 Wide Drawers, Tiger Maple, 1800, 58 1/4 In. 4400.00

Chest, 4 Drawers, Backsplash, Wooden Pulls, Grained, c.1880, 30 In. 445.00
Chest, 4 Drawers, Brass Pulls, Mahogany, 1820, 12 1/2 x 11 In. 1100.00
Chest, 4 Drawers, Cherry With Inlay, French Feet, 43 1/2 In. 850.00
Chest, 4 Drawers, Cornice, Cherry, 1820, 15 7/8 x 11 1/4 In. 770.00
Chest, 4 Drawers, Curly Maple, Sandwich Glass Knobs 1200.00
Chest, 4 Drawers, Dovetailed, Empire, Country, Walnut, 43 In. 400.00
Chest, 4 Drawers, Federal, Inlaid Mahogany, U.S., c.1805, 44 In. 1540.00
Chest, 4 Drawers, Fluted Quarter Columns, Cherry, 36 x 35 In. 5600.00
Chest, 4 Drawers, Hepplewhite, Bowfront, Bracket Feet, 40 In. 1200.00
Chest, 4 Drawers, Lift Top, Ball Feet, Pine 3300.00
Chest, 4 Drawers, Mahogany, Veneer Facade, Paw Feet, 58 In. 575.00
Chest, 4 Drawers, Oak, Raised Panels, England, c.1800, 36 In. 1750.00
Chest, 4 Drawers, Oak, Rectangular Top, 37 x 38 x 21 In. 1100.00
Chest, 4 Drawers, Quarter Columns, Brasses, Mahogany, c.1770 .... 6875.00
Chest, 4 Drawers, Serpentine Front, Original Brasses, c.1790 .... 6000.00
Chest, 4 Graduated Drawers, New England, Red Paint, 18th Century 1975.00
Chest, 5 Drawers, Oak, Red Marble Top 400.00
Chest, 6 Boards, Painted, Interior With Lidded Till, 46 5/8 In. 2975.00
Chest, 6 Boards, Scratched Design, Pine, Massachusetts, 49 In. 2600.00
Chest, 6 Drawers, Empire, Mahogany, 54 x 37 1/2 x 22 In. 175.00
Chest, 6 Drawers, G. Stickley, Splashboard, No. 902, 1902, 52 1/2 In. 4675.00
Chest, 6 Drawers, George II, Walnut, England, c.1740, 39 1/2 In. 2650.00
Chest, 6 Drawers, Mahogany, Reed Corner Columns, 35 3/4 In. 175.00
Chest, 7 Drawers, G. Dester, Marble Top, Mahogany, 1774, 5 Ft. 3 In. 7975.00
Chest, 7 Drawers, Original Brasses, Maple, Rhode Island, c.1780 .... 9500.00
Chest, 7 Drawers, Sheraton, Mahogany, Bowfront, c.1825, 50 In. 1650.00
Chest, Apothecary, 6 Drawers, Pine, Poplar, Red Finish, 10 In. 175.00
Chest, Apothecary, 12 Varying Sized Drawers, Poplar, 23 1/2 In. 650.00
Chest, Apothecary, 28 Drawers, Square Nails 925.00
Chest, Apothecary, Cock-Beaded Drawers, Sandwich Glass Knobs 2950.00
Chest, Apothecary, Pine Cleaned To Blue Paint, 45 x 71 In. 2600.00
Chest, Bachelor's, George III, 4 Graduated Drawers, Mahogany 1430.00
Chest, Blanket, 1 Drawer, Pine 950.00
Chest, Blanket, 2 Drawers, Camphor Wood, Lift Top, Tray, 41 In. 150.00
Chest, Blanket, 2 Drawers, Cherry, Turned Feet, 23 1/2 In. 400.00
Chest, Blanket, 2 Drawers, Lift Top, Maine 715.00
Chest, Blanket, 2 Drawers, Pine & Maple, Lift Top, 18th Century 1760.00
Chest, Blanket, 2 Drawers, Red & Black Feather Painted 950.00
Chest, Blanket, 2 Drawers, Salmon Grained Wood, 45 x 29 In. 2450.00
Chest, Blanket, 2 Drawers, Thumb-Molded, Lift Top, Red, 43 In. 660.00
Chest, Blanket, 2 Drawers, Walnut, Raised Burl Panels, Refinished 495.00
Chest, Blanket, 2 Short Drawers, Hinged Top, Oak, England, 48 In. 357.00
Chest, Blanket, 3 Drawers, Heart-Shaped Reserves, Pine, 50 1/4 In. 7750.00
Chest, Blanket, 4 Board, Strap Hinges, Curly Maple, 51 1/2 In. 850.00
Chest, Blanket, 6 Board, Pine, Cutout Feet, Scrolled Apron, 30 In. 375.00
Chest, Blanket, 6 Board, Pine, Red, Black Splotches, Till, 38 In. 365.00
Chest, Blanket, 6 Board, Poplar, White Paint, 8 1/4 In. 2175.00
Chest, Blanket, 6 Board, Staple Hinges, Pine, 18 x 50 In. 150.00
Chest, Blanket, Carved Pictorial Scenes, China, 19 1/2 x 35 In. 250.00
Chest, Blanket, Carved, England, c.1620, 24 1/2 x 62 1/2 In. 900.00
Chest, Blanket, Cherry, 43 x 21 x 23 In. .... *Illus* 1600.00
Chest, Blanket, Country, Poplar, Lift Top, 25 x 43 x 19 In. 150.00
Chest, Blanket, Curly Maple, Blue Paint, Tapered Feet, 24 3/4 In. 500.00
Chest, Blanket, Curly Maple, Paneled Construction, 25 3/4 In. 1800.00
Chest, Blanket, Dovetailed Base, Till, Lehman Of New Bedford, Ohio 1050.00
Chest, Blanket, Jacobean, Carved & Paneled Case, Oak, 44 1/2 In. 357.50
Chest, Blanket, Lift Top, Grain Painted, French Bracket Feet, 1824 .... 4400.00
Chest, Blanket, Mahogany, Inlay, Poplar, Cutout Feet, 21 1/2 In. 450.00
Chest, Blanket, Marjorelle, Fruitwood, Marquetry, 27 x 32 x 16 In. 6000.00
Chest, Blanket, Pine & Poplar, Black Trim Feet, 24 1/4 In. 650.00
Chest, Blanket, Pine, Dovetailed, Bracket Feet, 19 1/2 In. 750.00
Chest, Blanket, Pine, Dovetailed, Flame Grain, 36 In. 300.00
Chest, Blanket, Pine, Dovetailed, Iron Strap Hinges, 19 In. 275.00

Chest, Blanket, Pine, New England, 50 1/2 x 38 1/2 x 18 In. 770.00
Chest, Blanket, Pine, Original Graining, Leather Hinges, 18 In. 3350.00
Chest, Blanket, Pine, Red Flame Gaining, Black Trim, 50 x 23 In. 475.00
Chest, Blanket, Pine, Red Paint, c.1750, 37 1/2 x 39 x 18 1/2 In. 1650.00
Chest, Blanket, Pine, Red Paint, Floral Vines, Flowers, 9 1/2 In. 1100.00
Chest, Blanket, Pine, Red, Black Graining, South Salem, 1832, 40 In. 500.00
Chest, Blanket, Pine, Turned Feet, Dovetailed, 18 3/4 In. 650.00
Chest, Blanket, Pine, Yellow Graining, Bear Trap Lock, 21 In. 325.00
Chest, Blanket, Poplar, Blue, Stenciled H. E. B., 17 x 21 In. 1200.00
Chest, Blanket, Poplar, Brownish Yellow Comb Graining, 25 In. 150.00
Chest, Blanket, Poplar, Orange Graining, Dovetailed, 13 In. 900.00
Chest, Blanket, Poplar, Red Paint, Paneled Construction, 26 In. 475.00
Chest, Blanket, Poplar, Red Stain, Bracket Feet, 15 1/4 In. 375.00
Chest, Blanket, Poplar, Worn Red Repaint, Bracket Feet, 49 In. 100.00
Chest, Blanket, Red & Black Graining, New England, 1830s, 44 In. 825.00
Chest, Blanket, Red Finish, Dated 1844, 15 3/5 x 22 1/2 In. 5200.00
Chest, Blanket, Refinished Poplar, Dovetailed, 42 x 20 x 26 In. 300.00
Chest, Blanket, Stenciled Hearts, Flowers, Birds, Ohio, Poplar 2000.00
Chest, Blanket, Tulips, Floral Design, Dovetailed, 17 In. 5200.00
Chest, Blanket, Vinegar Work, 1830 .... 1870.00
Chest, Bombe, Marquetry, Holland, c.1800 .... 4000.00
Chest, Bowfront, 4 Drawers, Glass Pulls, Mahogany, 1830s, 35 In. 330.00
Chest, Bowfront, 4 Drawers, Sheraton, Cherry, Veneer, 39 In. 975.00
Chest, Bowfront, Bird's-Eye Maple, c.1810, 43 In. 1500.00
Chest, Bowfront, Federal, Cherry, 4 Graduated Drawers, 41 1/2 In. 1151.00

◆ ◆ ◆ ◆ ◆ ◆ ◆ ◆ ◆ ◆ ◆ ◆ ◆ ◆ ◆ ◆ ◆ ◆ ◆ ◆

Have an extra key made to fit doors and drawers in old furniture. Stick it to the bottom of the piece with a wad of gum or tape.

◆ ◆ ◆ ◆ ◆ ◆ ◆ ◆ ◆ ◆ ◆ ◆ ◆ ◆ ◆ ◆ ◆ ◆ ◆ ◆

Furniture, Chest, Blanket, Cherry,

43 x 21 x 23 In.

Furniture, Chest, Continental,

Baroque, Walnut, 33 In., Pair

Furniture, Chest,

Chippendale, Tiger Maple, 7

Drawers, c.1790

Furniture, Chest, Bowfront,

Federal, Pennsylvania,

c.1825, 41 In.

Chest, Bowfront, Federal, Pennsylvania, c.1825, 41 In. ....*Illus*   2860.00
Chest, Bowfront, Hepplewhite, 4 Graduated Drawers, Mahogany 1200.00
Chest, Bowfront, Mahogany & Branch Satinwood, c.1805, 38 1/4 In. 6050.00
Chest, Butler's, 5 Drawers, Tiger Maple Interior 990.00
Chest, Campaign, Brass Mounts, Teakwood, 44 x 38 In. 1870.00
Chest, Carved Camphor, Laquered, Scenes 225.00
Chest, Carved Mahogany, Brass Pulls, U.S., 1840, 53 x 45 x 25 In. 495.00
Chest, Chemist's, Portable, Leather Cover, Fitted, Germany 1540.00
Chest, Cherry & Maple, c.1880, 58 1/2 x 18 1/4 x 38 1/4 In. 4400.00
Chest, Cherry, 4 Drawers, Burl Veneer, Turned Feet, 47 1/2 In. 725.00
Chest, Cherry, 4 Drawers, Dovetailed, Country, Paneled Ends, 44 In. 500.00
Chest, Cherry, 4 Drawers, Dovetailed, Turned Feet, 44 3/4 In. 575.00
Chest, Cherry, 4 Graduated Drawers, 30 In. 1250.00
Chest, Cherry, 5 Drawers, Hepplewhite, 41 1/2 In. 550.00
Chest, Cherry, Flame Veneer Facade, Rope Carved Pilasters, 62 In. 850.00
Chest, Cherry, New England, c.1800, 54 In. 1875.00
Chest, Cherry, Paneled Ends, High Turned Front Feet, 45 1/2 In. 675.00
Chest, Chinese Teak, Mortised, Black Design, Lift Top, 34 In. 350.00
Chest, Chippendale, 4 Drawers, Dovetailed, Bracket Feet, 37 In. 2350.00
Chest, Chippendale, 4 Drawers, Dovetailed, Ogee Feet, 38 3/4 In. 2100.00
Chest, Chippendale, 4 Drawers, Oxbow, Maple, 35 3/4 In. 270.00
Chest, Chippendale, 4 Drawers, Quarter Column, Cherry, 33 x 36 In. 6800.00
Chest, Chippendale, 4 Drawers, Rosehead Nails, Wooden Knobs, Pine 2645.00
Chest, Chippendale, 4 Drawers, Thumb Molded Top, Cherry, 35 In. 700.00
Chest, Chippendale, 6 Drawers, Graduated, Maple, Pine, Dark, 52 In. 5200.00
Chest, Chippendale, 6 Drawers, Mahogany, Bracket Feet, 48 3/4 In. 950.00
Chest, Chippendale, 8 Drawers, Dovetailed Case, Walnut, 62 3/4 In. 4850.00
Chest, Chippendale, Cherry, 2 Half Drawers, Fluted Columns 3800.00
Chest, Chippendale, Country, Red & Black Graining, 17 x 29 In. 795.00
Chest, Chippendale, Maple, Cherry Finish, Dovetailed Case, 52 In. 4750.00
Chest, Chippendale, Reverse Serpenting, Birch, 1770–1790, 33 In. 4675.00
Chest, Chippendale, Tiger Maple, 7 Drawers, c.1790 ....*Illus*   4400.00
Chest, Columned Arches, Oak, St. Barbara, Flemish, 60 In. 2475.00
Chest, Continental, Baroque, Walnut, 33 In., Pair ....*Illus*   2860.00
Chest, Curly Maple, Rectangular, Metal Handles, Camphor, 25 In. 277.00
Chest, Dower, 3 Drawers, Pennsylvania, 1790 ....   2970.00
Chest, Dower, Faded Arches & Flowers, Varnish 2700.00
Chest, Dower, Gold Geometric Shapes, Painted Poplar, 1790s, 51 In. 330.00
Chest, Dower, Original Worn Green Paint, 19th Century, 45 In. ./..........................   1550.00
Chest, Dower, Partly Painted, Original Hinges & Lock, c.1762 ....   1700.00
Chest, Dower, Pine, Eagle & Shield Paint Traces, Penna., 51 In. 3000.00
Chest, Dower, Pine, Floral Design, Penna., Sept. 21, 1826, 47 In. 1650.00
Chest, Dower, Rectangular Dome Top, Flaring Case, 1740, 45 1/2 In. 660.00
Chest, Dutch Baroque, 4 Serpentine Drawers, Walnut, 29 x 33 In. 2420.00
Chest, Ebonized Walnut & Oak, 37 3/4 x 40 x 19 In. ....*Illus*   5775.00
Chest, Emigrant's, Dome Top, Dovetailed Case, Oak, 46 1/4 In. 175.00
Chest, Empire, 4 Drawers, Curly Maple, Quarter Columns, 35 3/4 In. 1950.00
Chest, Empire, 4 Drawers, Dovetailed, Birch, Refinished, 48 In. 450.00
Chest, Empire, 4 Drawers, Freestanding Columns, Walnut, 47 In. 600.00
Chest, Empire, 4 Drawers, Walnut, Curly Maple, 52 1/4 In. 600.00
Chest, Empire, 5 Drawers, Cherry, Mahogany, Scrolled Feet, 46 In. 125.00
Chest, Empire, Mahogany, Flame Veneer, High Turned Feet, 57 In. 1050.00
Chest, Federal, 4 Drawers, Line Inlay, Mahogany, 35 1/2 In. 2420.00
Chest, Federal, 5 Drawers, Crossbanded Inlay, Mahogany, 38 In. 3300.00
Chest, Federal, Cherry, Walnut, Curly Maple, 3 Top Drawers, 49 In. 1950.00
Chest, Federal, Hinged Top, Vasiform Legs, Mahogany, 40 x 46 In. 3080.00
Chest, G. Stickley, Harvey Ellis Design, 51 x 32 In. ....*Illus*   3080.00
Chest, George II, Center Drawer, 2 Smaller, Walnut, 40 In. 3100.00
Chest, George III, Mahogany Inlay, 5 Drawers 1450.00
Chest, George III, Mahogany, 4 Cock-Beaded Drawers, 35 1/2 In. 9350.00
Chest, Georgian Style, 4 Graduated Drawers, Mahogany, 38 In. 275.00
Chest, Georgian, Mahogany, Corner Fans Inlay, 36 1/2 In. 4300.00
Chest, Hardwood, Poplar, 6 Drawers, Red Flame Graining, 51 In. 400.00

Furniture, Chest, Ebonized Walnut & Oak,
37 3/4 x 40 x 19 In.

Furniture, Chest, G. Stickley, Harvey Ellis
Design, 51 x 32 In.

Chest, Hepplewhite, 4 Drawers, Flared Feet, Walnut	775.00
Chest, Hepplewhite, Bowfront, Cherry, Flame Veneer Facade, 41 In.	1400.00
Chest, Hepplewhite, French Feet, 4 Dovetailed Drawers, 43 In.	1225.00
Chest, Hepplewhite, Line Inlay On 4 Drawers, Cherry, 46 3/8 In.	1000.00
Chest, Hepplewhite, Mule, Cherry Inlay, Cutout Feet, 39 In.	650.00
Chest, Hepplewhite, Walnut, 5 Drawers, French Feet, Inlay, 41 In.	1550.00
Chest, Hepplewhite, Walnut, French Feet, Stiles, Apron, 39 In.	2500.00
Chest, Herter Bros., Marble Top, Drawer, Rosewood, 50 3/4 In.	7700.00
Chest, Jacobean, 4 Drawers, 1670s, Oak, 38 x 38 1/4 In.	825.00
Chest, Lingerie, Campaign Style, Henredon, 54 1/4 In.	302.00
Chest, Mahogany, Brass Pulls, c.1850, 44 x 45 x 20 In.	445.00
Chest, Mule, Flame Graining, 2 Drawers, Pine & Poplar, 36 1/2 In.	800.00
Chest, Mule, Hinged Top, 2 Dovetailed Drawers, Pine, 40 1/2 In.	1450.00
Chest, Mule, Hinged Top, Paneled Case, 2 Frieze Drawers, 1780s	550.00
Chest, Mule, Pine, Dark Brown, 5 Drawers, 2 False, Lift Top, 42 In.	700.00
Chest, Mule, Queen Anne, Pine, 2 False Drawers, Lift Top, 43 In.	650.00
Chest, Mule, Vinegar Painted Drawers, Striping, Pine, 35 3/4 In.	750.00
Chest, Oxbow, 4 Drawers, Mahogany & Birch, c.1780, 33 1/3 In.	9900.00
Chest, Oxbow, 4 Drawers, Mahogany, Boston, c.1765, 33 3/4 In.	4400.00
Chest, Pine, Dovetailed Case, Lidded Till On Bracket Base, 25 In.	600.00
Chest, Queen Anne, 5 Drawers, Walnut	1430.00
Chest, Queen Anne, Maple, New England, 18th Century, 84 In.	2200.00
Chest, Queen Anne, Paint Traces, Maple, 1760s, 76 1/2 In.	6600.00
Chest, Reverse Serpentine, Cherry Veneer, c.1810, 33 1/8 In.	2750.00
Chest, Shaker, 5 Drawers, Pine, Watervliet, N.Y.	6050.00
Chest, Sheraton, Bird's-Eye Drawer Fronts, Mahogany, c.1800	2750.00
Chest, Sheraton, Bowfront, Cherry, Walnut Inlay, 40 In.	1300.00
Chest, Sheraton, Cherry, Dark Finish, 3 Dovetailed Drawers, 24 In.	925.00
Chest, Sheraton, Curly Walnut, 5 Dovetailed Drawers, 41 In.	900.00
Chest, Sheraton, Mahogany, 4 Dovetailed Drawers, 7 x 13 x 15 In.	600.00
Chest, Sheraton, Tiger Maple, 4 Graduated Drawers, 1830	2600.00
Chest, Silver, Queen Anne, Cherry, Cabriole Legs, 33 3/4 In.	225.00
Chest, Spice, 2 Short, 2 Long Drawers, Cherry, c.1765, 7 3/4 In.	4675.00
Chest, Spice, 10 Drawers, Turned Pulls, Pine, 7 x 14 x 15 In.	475.00
Chest, Sugar, 1 Drawer, Stubby Turned Legs, Cherry	1750.00
Chest, Sugar, 2 Drawers, Walnut, Grant County, Kentucky	3300.00
Chest, Sugar, Sheraton, Tiger Maple & Cherry, c.1810	1475.00
Chest, Transitional Sheraton, Cherry, Inlay, 4 Drawers	1300.00
Chest, Wedding, Floral & Scroll Design, Scandinavia, 18 x 38 In.	770.00
Chest, William & Mary, 2 Drawers Over 3 Drawers, Oyster Walnut	5720.00
Chest, William IV, 2 Cock-Beaded Drawers, 44 In.	660.00

Furniture, Commode, Walnut, French Provincial, 18th Century

Furniture, Commode, Walnut, Fruitwood, Italy, 35 x 62 x 24 In.

Chest, Wood, Brass Fittings, Camphor, 44 In.	210.00
Chest-On-Chest, 3 Over 8 Graduated Drawers, Maple, 83 In.	5100.00
Chest-On-Chest, Block Front, Mahogany, U.S., c.1830, 72 In.	885.00
Chest-On-Chest, Chippendale, 5 Drawers, Poplar, Red Paint	2900.00
Chest-On-Chest, Chippendale, 7 Drawers, Walnut, 1760s, 76 1/2 In.	4400.00
Chest-On-Chest, Chippendale, 9 Drawers, Walnut, 58 3/4 In.	4000.00
Chest-On-Chest, Chippendale, 10 Drawers, Curly Maple, 66 3/4 In.	3500.00
Chest-On-Frame, Queen Anne, Curly Maple, 5 Drawers, 64 1/2 In.	3300.00
Chest-On-Frame, Queen Anne, Figured Maple	8800.00
Chiffonier, Stickley Bros., No. 9022, 4 Small Over 4 Long Drawers	3300.00
Church Pew, Victorian, Walnut	375.00
Coffer, Oak, Carved Inlay, England, 17th Century	6500.00
Coffer, Oak, Dark Finish, Turned Feet, 14 1/2 In.	300.00
Commode, Bird & Floral Marquetry, Fruitwood, 35 1/2 In.	2100.00
Commode, Bowfront, Veined Marble Top, 3 Drawers, Fruitwood, 44 In.	5500.00
Commode, Burled Walnut, 2 Drawers, Serpentine, Borders, France	5500.00
Commode, Burled Walnut, Marble Top, 2 Candlestands, Towel Bar	350.00
Commode, Burled Walnut, Marble Top, 3 Drawers, Candle Shelves	425.00
Commode, Chevron Panels, Fruitwood Parquetry, Walnut, 4 Ft. 2 In.	8800.00
Commode, Demilune, Floral & Shell Design, Satinwood, 34 In.	685.00
Commode, Drop Front, Fruitwood Marquetry, Italy, 34 x 50 In.	6500.00
Commode, Eastlake, 1 Drawer Over 2 Doors, Backsplash	140.00
Commode, French Colonial, 3 Drawers, Walnut & Cherry, 1780	9900.00
Commode, Fruitwood Marquetry, Oval Floral Inlay, 3 Drawers	3300.00
Commode, Grapevine & Leaf Painted Border, Louvered, 30 In.	3750.00
Commode, Louis XV Style, Fruitwood Marquetry, Marble Top, 43 In.	3300.00
Commode, Louis XV, Fruitwood Marquetry, Purplewood, 1780s, 38 In.	8800.00
Commode, Louis XV, Tulipwood, Kingwood & Parquetry, c.1900, 35 In.	1325.00
Commode, Louis XVI, Carved Walnut	3000.00
Commode, Louis XVI, Marble Top, 7 Drawers, Walnut, 46 1/2 In.	775.00
Commode, Louis XVI, Urn & Floral Marquetry & Parquetry, 35 In.	4185.00
Commode, Oak, Lift Top, Splashboard	325.00
Commode, Oak, Mirror, Towel Rack, 3 Drawers, Applied Carving	375.00
Commode, Oak, Serpentine Top Drawer Over 2 Doors, Towel Bar	235.00
Commode, Painted, Carved Splash, 1 Drawer Over Door	50.00
Commode, Serpentine Front, 3 Drawers, Germany, Walnut, 43 1/2 In.	7150.00
Commode, Shaker, Square Lift Top, Open Seat, Butternut, Harvard	665.00
Commode, Walnut, French Provincial, 18th Century ....*Illus*	9900.00
Commode, Walnut, Fruitwood, Italy, 35 x 62 x 24 In. ....*Illus*	15000.00
Console, Louis XV-Style, Shaped Front, Carved Giltwood	4950.00
Console, Marble Top Forming Diamond, Italy, 1780s, 4 Ft. 3 In.	6600.00
Console, Marble Top, Carved Rosewood, c.1860, 21 x 42 x 17 In.	825.00
Console, Marble Top, Serpentine Frieze, Parcel Gilt, 36 In., Pair	3575.00
Console, Rococo, Serpentine, Scrolled Toes, Fruitwood, Italy, 4 Ft.	5500.00
Console, Rococo, Wrought Iron, Parcel Gilt, Marble Top	5750.00
Console, Victorian, Rosewood, Mallard	1485.00
Couch, Fainting, Coral Cut Velvet Cover	325.00

Couch, Fainting, Fruitwood Frame, Yellow Upholstery, 69 In. 1900.00
Cradle, Arched Bonnet, English, Oak, 19th Century, 30 x 33 In. 440.00
Cradle, G. D. Jones, No. 62 S. 4th Street, Philadelphia 3000.00
Cradle, Hood, Red Stained Pine, Early 19th Century, 39 1/2 In. 165.00
Cradle, Hooded Top, Pine, Brown, Fruit Border, 1830, 28 x 38 In. 660.00
Cradle, Keywind, Walnut, Paper Label, Newark, N. J. 2000.00
Cradle, Primitive, Pine, Worn Light Blue Paint, 19 x 37 In. 95.00
Cradle, Turned Posts & Spindles, Cherry Finish, Poplar, 37 In. 200.00
Cradle, Valanced Hood, Rockers, Mahogany, 1830s, 37 3/4 x 41 In. 385.00
Cradle, Wicker, Heywood–Wakefield 650.00
Credenza, Bird's-Eye Maple Interior, Rosewood Inlay, 59 1/2 In. 9350.00
Credenza, Drawer Over Door, Inlay, Walnut, 38 x 28 In. 1650.00
Credenza, Mirror, Carved Florals, Rosewood Veneer, 67 3/4 In. 950.00
Credenza, Neo–Classic Style, Painted Satinwood, A. Kaufmann 1980.00
Credenza, Paneled Case, Drawer Over Door, Walnut, 36 1/2 In. 2860.00
Credenza, Regency, Grill Front, Pair 1760.00
Credenza, Veneer Inlay, Serpentine Marble Top, 37 In. 4500.00
Crib, Sheraton, Peg Construction, Dark Green Paint, 1830–1840 .... 350.00
Cupboard, 1 Piece, Paneled Doors, 1 Drawer, Country, 80 3/4 In. 1700.00
Cupboard, 2 Piece, Pine, Salmon Paint, 2 Drawers, Canadian, 85 In. 1750.00
Cupboard, 4 Beveled Panel Doors, Square Nails, Gray Paint 795.00
Cupboard, Applied Diamonds On Door Panels, Zoar, Oh., 28 In. 600.00
Cupboard, Base Door, Pigeonholes, Pine, 77 1/2 In. 4100.00
Cupboard, Base Doors, 3 Shelves, Plate Bars, Pine, 71 1/2 In. 1200.00
Cupboard, Child's, Gothic, Step Back 1100.00
Cupboard, Child's, Step Back, Primitive, 2 Piece 375.00
Cupboard, Chimney, Grooved Shelves, Pine, 79 1/2 In. 825.00
Cupboard, Chimney, Poplar, Olive Wash Over White, 20 x 76 In. 1000.00
Cupboard, Chimney, Red Paint, New England, 6 1/2 Ft. 695.00
Cupboard, Chippendale, Butternut, 3 Paneled Doors, 42 x 48 In. 800.00
Cupboard, Corner, 1 Piece, Country, Paneled Doors, 75 1/2 In. 4600.00
Cupboard, Corner, 2 Glass & 2 Blind Doors, Drawer 1100.00
Cupboard, Corner, 2 Piece, Poplar, Glass Doors, Drawer, 78 In. 3300.00
Cupboard, Corner, 3 Doors, 1 Drawer, Carved Berries, France, c.1910 .... 6600.00
Cupboard, Corner, 4 Panel Blind Doors, Walnut, 6 Ft. x 50 In. 1000.00
Cupboard, Corner, Butterfly Shelves, Bracket Feet, 2 Piece 2400.00
Cupboard, Corner, Cherry, 1 Piece, Paneled Doors, 75 1/2 In. 4100.00
Cupboard, Corner, Cherry, 8 Panes, Blind Door Base, 1840, 1 Piece 5500.00
Cupboard, Corner, Cherry, 12 Glass Panes, 18th Century 4000.00
Cupboard, Corner, Cherry, 12 Glass Panes, 2 Piece 5500.00
Cupboard, Corner, Cherry, Blind Doors, Handmade, S. Ohio, Small 2200.00
Cupboard, Corner, Cherry, Bracket Feet, 1 Piece, 86 1/2 In. 4000.00
Cupboard, Corner, Cherry, Pegged Construction, 2 Piece 2500.00
Cupboard, Corner, Cherry, Poplar, Paneled Doors, 8 Panes, 83 In. 4100.00
Cupboard, Corner, Cherry, Scalloped Skirt, Pa., 19th Century 7800.00
Cupboard, Corner, Curly Maple, 12 Glass Panes, Cornice, 88 In. 7250.00
Cupboard, Corner, Curly Maple, Arched Glass Doors, Cornice, 57 In. 6500.00
Cupboard, Corner, Curly Maple, Bracket Feet, 9 Glass Panes, 70 In. 2600.00
Cupboard, Corner, Federal, Cherry Glazed Inlay, 86 1/2 In. 3575.00
Cupboard, Corner, Federal, Maple, 2 Paneled Doors, 82 In. 6000.00
Cupboard, Corner, Glass Top Door, Wood Lower Door, Walnut, 75 In. 1500.00
Cupboard, Corner, Hanging, Oak, Curved Front, England, 36 In. 400.00
Cupboard, Corner, Hanging, Pine, Brown Graining, England, 37 In. 1000.00
Cupboard, Corner, Hanging, Tambour Door, Mahogany, Floral, 27 In. 525.00
Cupboard, Corner, Lattice Glazed Door, Cherry & Mahogany, c.1810 .... 5500.00
Cupboard, Corner, Mahogany, Drawer Below Pediment, 1840, 55 In. 190.00
Cupboard, Corner, Painted Pinwheels, Yellow Pine 8910.00
Cupboard, Corner, Pie Shelf, 2 Piece 1300.00
Cupboard, Corner, Pine, Red, Brown, Bracket Feet, 1 Piece, 80 In. 1550.00
Cupboard, Corner, Poplar, Red Stain, 6 Panes, 2 Piece 3200.00
Cupboard, Corner, Raised Panel Doors, H Hinges, Poplar, 78 1/2 In. 750.00
Cupboard, Corner, Turkey Breast, Walnut, Cherry, 1 Piece, 84 In. 7750.00
Cupboard, Corner, Walnut, 2 Doors, 16 Panes, Blind Door 2500.00

Cupboard, Corner, Walnut, 4 Doors, Molded Cornice, 95 3/4 In. 3500.00
Cupboard, Corner, Walnut, 9 Panes, 75 x 32 1/2 In. 1500.00
Cupboard, Corner, Walnut, Blind Door, Raised Panel 4 Doors 1950.00
Cupboard, Corner, Walnut, Original Glass, Late 18th Century 2400.00
Cupboard, Corner, Walnut, Pegged Construction, Deep, 4 1/2 Ft. 495.00
Cupboard, Court, Pilgrim Century, Oak, 58 x 45 x 22 In. 3575.00
Cupboard, Diamond Point Doors, Pine, Canada, 70 x 47 In. 4675.00
Cupboard, Doors In Base, 3 Top Drawers, Pine, 48 1/2 In. 1000.00
Cupboard, Dovetailed Bracket Feet, 3 Drawers, Country, 90 In. 4500.00
Cupboard, Dutch Marquetry, Floral Inlay, 4 Drawers, 88 In. 5000.00
Cupboard, Federal, Step Back, Plate Racks, Walnut, 82 3/4 In. 8250.00
Cupboard, Flat Back, 2 Blind & 2 Punched Tin Doors Over Drawer 155.00
Cupboard, Hanging, 4 Inner Sections, Wooden Eagle On Door, 1850 .... 450.00
Cupboard, Hanging, Cherry, Dovetailed Case, 30 In. 375.00
Cupboard, Hanging, Drawer, Latched Doors, Painted Green, 1870 .... 395.00
Cupboard, Hanging, Empire, 2 Drawers, White & Black Paint 1375.00
Cupboard, Hanging, Mahogany, Simple Inlay, 23 In. 125.00
Cupboard, Hanging, Original Mustard & Brown Paint, Penna., 1860 .... 1150.00
Cupboard, Hanging, Rattail Hinges, Rosehead Nails 3595.00
Cupboard, Hanging, Shaker, 1 Door, 2 Drawers, Red Paint, 15 3/4 In. 5775.00
Cupboard, Hanging, Walnut, Scalloped Tail, Penna., 1800, 29 In. 6500.00
Cupboard, Hardwood, Green Paint, Applied Moldings On Base, 10 In. 200.00
Cupboard, Jelly, Board & Batten Door, 5 Shelves, Pine, 54 1/4 In. 600.00
Cupboard, Jelly, Chestnut, 1 Door, Small 425.00
Cupboard, Jelly, Decorated Country, Pine, Paneled Doors, 45 In. 1000.00
Cupboard, Jelly, Painted, Backsplash, 2 Drawers 350.00
Cupboard, Jelly, Pine, Blue Paint, 2 Drawers, Beaded Rails, 59 In. 2550.00
Cupboard, Jelly, Raised Panel Door, Painted Green 1925.00
Cupboard, Jelly, Spoon Carving, Oak 425.00
Cupboard, Kitchen, Pine, 2 Shelves, Late 19th Century, 73 3/4 In. 357.50
Cupboard, L. & J. G. Stickley, 2 Glazed Doors, 2 Solid Doors 4750.00
Cupboard, Light Blue Paint, 2 Doors, Virginia, 55 1/2 x 41 In. 2800.00
Cupboard, Mahogany, Dark Finish, Dentilated Cornice, 43 In. 275.00
Cupboard, Mahogany, Double Doors, Full Length Drawer, 33 1/4 In. 50.00
Cupboard, Oak, Paneled Doors, 3 Dovetailed Drawers, 84 In. 1300.00
Cupboard, Oak, Pine, Dark Finish, 2 Piece, England, 80 In. 650.00
Cupboard, Oak, Turned Posts, 1 Drawer & Door, 48 1/2 In. 1000.00
Cupboard, Open Pewter, Hardwood, Dark Paint, 1 Piece, 73 1/2 In. 1300.00
Cupboard, Pewter, Step Back, 2 Drawers, 16 Panes, Walnut 2800.00
Cupboard, Pine, Black, Gold Design, 2 Drawers, Open Top, 38 In. 125.00
Cupboard, Pine, Cherry, Brown, Raised Panel Door, Cornice, 51 In. 275.00
Cupboard, Pine, Poplar, Green Paint, Paneled Doors, 9 Panes, 83 In. 2400.00
Cupboard, Pine, Red, Board & Batten Door, Beaded Frame, 36 1/2 In. 550.00
Cupboard, Poplar, Red, Open Top, 1 Dovetailed Drawer, 26 x 37 In. 500.00
Cupboard, Portable, Iron Side Handles, Shelves, Pine, 33 3/4 In. 500.00
Cupboard, Red–Stained Pine, c.1750, 47 x 20 x 11 In. ....*Illus* 7700.00
Cupboard, Rosewood, Burl Veneer, Marquetry Inlay On Door, 49 In. 1400.00
Cupboard, Scalloped Apron, Paneled Doors, Red, Pine, 80 1/4 In. 1100.00
Cupboard, Shaker, 5 Drawers, Mustard Paint Inside & Out, 7 Ft. 5500.00
Cupboard, Slant Back, Green Paint, New England, 81 1/2 In. 3190.00
Cupboard, Sliding Glazed Doors Over Cabinet, Pine, 90 In. 1000.00
Cupboard, Spice, Center Door, 8 Drawers, Ebony & Fruitwood, 20 In. 1100.00
Cupboard, Step Back, 2 Glass Doors, Walnut, Burlwood, 78 1/2 In. 900.00
Cupboard, Step Back, 10 Drawers, Grain Painted, Glass Doors 5100.00
Cupboard, Step Back, Base Doors, 6 Panes, 72 3/4 In. 505.00
Cupboard, Step Back, Carved Doors, Acorns, Walnut, 7 Ft. 8 1/2 In. 5400.00
Cupboard, Step Back, Cherry, Old Finish, 2 Piece 2200.00
Cupboard, Step Back, Glazed Pine, c.1830, 78 1/2 x 44 x 20 In. 1650.00
Cupboard, Step Back, Original Green Paint, Sponged, 2 Piece 250.00
Cupboard, Step Back, Pine, 19th Century, 88 x 48 x 21 In. 1350.00
Cupboard, Step Back, Pine, Dark Refinishing, Paneled Doors, 89 In. 1225.00
Cupboard, Step Back, Rattail Hinges, Blue Paint, Pine, 1830s 4800.00
Cupboard, Step Back, Square Nails, Flat Door, Painted Red, Pine 6820.00

Cupboard, Stepback, Two 4–Pane Glass Doors, Painted, Pine 2500.00
Cupboard, Stickley, Solid Cherry, 71 x 60 In. 3000.00
Cupboard, Stickley, Step Back, Miniature 500.00
Cupboard, Wall, Butternut, Paneled Doors, Brass Hardware, 87 In. 2900.00
Cupboard, Walnut, 2 Doors Above, 16 Panes, Blind Doors On Bottom 2500.00
Cupboard, Walnut, Original Glass, Spoon Notched Shelf, 1850 .... 1450.00
Cupboard, Walnut, Original Red Paint, 1860 .... 560.00
Cupboard, Walnut, Original Red Paint, Mason County, Ill., 1860 .... 560.00
Cupboard, Walnut, Poplar, Original Mustard Paint, 1810, 6 1/2 Ft. 1650.00
Daybed, Biedermeier, Fruitwood, Upholstered Ends & Seat, 75 In. 4180.00
Daybed, Country, Walnut, Square Posts, Mattress, 29 x 60 x 28 In. 150.00
Daybed, Elizabethan Revival, Painted & Upholstered, 74 In. 742.00
Daybed, Grain Painted Rosewood, Scrolled Back & Arms, 78 In. 3960.00
Daybed, Gustav Stickley, No. 216, 5 Vertical Slats, c.1902, 79 In. 2640.00
Daybed, Louis XVI Style, Carved & Painted, France, Late 1800s 2750.00
Daybed, Mahogany, Ogee Frame, Outward Scrolling Arms, 1840, 82 In. 785.00
Daybed, Pierced Splat, Molded Frame, Mahogany, c.1770, 6 Ft. 2 In. 5775.00
Daybed, Rattan, Swept–Back Ends, Spring Seat Support, 79 In. 600.00
Daybed, Rattan, Victorian, Sloping Seat, Painted Legs, 73 In. 440.00
Daybed, Red Paint, Caned Seat and Back, 78 In. 125.00
Daybed, Zebra Skin, Rectangular, Curving Up 1 End, France, 1930s 2400.00
Desk Bookcase, Chippendale, Cherry, 73 1/4 x 36 1/4 x 19 In. 2750.00
Desk Bookcase, Cylinder Front, Mahogany, c.1815, 6 Ft. 2 1/2 In. 5500.00
Desk Bookcase, Fall Front, Cherry Wood, Massachusetts, c.1795 .... 8800.00
Desk Bookcase, Federal, Mahogany Glazed, New England, 82 1/2 In. 2450.00
Desk On Frame, Slant Front, Queen Anne, Walnut, 38 In. 950.00
Desk, 1 Drawer, Hammered Copper Pull, Pail Bros., c.1910, 40 In. 165.00
Desk, 4 Drawers, Slant Front, Fitted Interior, Cherry, 44 1/2 In. 1200.00
Desk, Barrel Front, Burled Trim Inlay, Retracting Top, Walnut 500.00
Desk, Bird & Acanthus Inlay, 1 Drawer, Fruitwood, 30 In. 2450.00
Desk, Bugatti, Mahogany, Walnut Inlay, Vellum, 39 x 23 x 20 In. 7700.00
Desk, Butler's, Flip Top, 4 Drawers, Mahogany, 29 1/2 x 30 1/4 In. 410.00
Desk, Butler's, Satinwood Inlay, Mahogany, c.1790 .... 2860.00
Desk, C Roll Top, A. H. Revell & Co., Chicago, c.1920, 44 In. 2970.00
Desk, C Roll Top, Holds Typewriter, Oak, 40 x 32 In. 1800.00
Desk, C Roll, 2 Typing Shelves, File Drawer, 3 Ft. 8 In. 2500.00
Desk, Captain's, 3 Short Drawers, Side Drawers, Mahogany, c.1840 .... 1320.00
Desk, Captain's, Painting Of Sea Gem Schooner Top, 1856, 5 Ft. 1200.00
Desk, Carlton House, Flame Grain, Mahogany, England, c.1900 .... 6500.00
Desk, Child's, Cylinder Top, Maple 200.00
Desk, Child's, Roll Top, 2 Drawers 195.00

Furniture, Cupboard, Red-Stained Pine,
c.1750, 47 x 20 x 11 In.

◆ ◆ ◆ ◆ ◆ ◆ ◆ ◆ ◆ ◆ ◆ ◆ ◆ ◆ ◆ ◆ ◆ ◆ ◆ ◆

Never push antique furniture across the floor. Pick it up. Old furniture may have weak glue joints and may be damaged.

◆ ◆ ◆ ◆ ◆ ◆ ◆ ◆ ◆ ◆ ◆ ◆ ◆ ◆ ◆ ◆ ◆ ◆ ◆ ◆

◆ ◆ ◆ ◆ ◆ ◆ ◆ ◆ ◆ ◆ ◆ ◆ ◆ ◆ ◆ ◆ ◆ ◆ ◆ ◆

Wooden drawers and cardboard boxes contain acids and resins which can harm textiles. Line containers with clean cotton sheets.

◆ ◆ ◆ ◆ ◆ ◆ ◆ ◆ ◆ ◆ ◆ ◆ ◆ ◆ ◆ ◆ ◆ ◆ ◆ ◆

Furniture, Desk, Federal, Leather Top, Tiger Maple, 36 In.

Furniture, Desk, Slant Front, Chippendale, Tiger Maple, c.1800

Desk, Child's, Roll Top, Oak, Chair	550.00
Desk, Chippendale Style, Slant Front, Curly Maple, 1930s	3100.00
Desk, Chippendale, Drop Front, Maple, Curly Maple Facade, 42 In.	6500.00
Desk, Chippendale, Mahogany Stepped Interior, 18th Century	7040.00
Desk, Chippendale, Mahogany, 4 Dovetailed Drawers, England, 42 In.	2300.00
Desk, Chippendale, Mahogany, Bracket Feet, 4 Drawers, 42 In.	2300.00
Desk, Chippendale, Mahogany, Slant Front, 44 x 42 x 21 In.	5225.00
Desk, Chippendale, Mahogany, Stepped Interior, 18th Century	7040.00
Desk, Chippendale, Slant Front, Double Step-Down Interior, Cherry	4200.00
Desk, Chippendale, Slant Front, Pine, 4 Drawers, 41 3/4 In.	600.00
Desk, Chippendale, Slant Front, Serpentine Front	4750.00
Desk, Continental, Hardwood Inlay, Scroll Bracket, 48 In.	50.00
Desk, Cylinder, Marble Top, 2 Drawers, Fitted Interior, Mahogany	1750.00
Desk, Cylinder, Marble Top, Mirrored Doors, Mahogany, 4 Ft. 10 In.	2475.00
Desk, Davenport, Rosewood, Burl Walnut, Rosewood, Mahogany, England	3100.00
Desk, Drop Front, 4 Drawers, Brass Batwing Pulls, Mahogany, 44 In.	1325.00
Desk, Drop Front, Louis XV Style, Inlaid Marquetry, 56 x 27 In.	4025.00
Desk, Empire, Slant Front, Tiger Maple Interior Drawers, c.1830	1250.00
Desk, Federal, Cherry Inlay, Slant Front, 4 Drawers, 41 3/4 In.	2450.00
Desk, Federal, Leather Top, Tiger Maple, 36 In. ....*Illus*	3960.00
Desk, Flip Top, Stand-Up, Walnut	395.00
Desk, French Provincial, 2 Drawers, Fruitwood Inlay, Walnut	2450.00
Desk, French Style, Fitted Top, Reeded Legs, Painted, 45 In.	775.00
Desk, Front Fall, Art Nouveau, Mahogany, Bird's Eye Maple, 43 In.	2200.00
Desk, Glazed Doors, Fitted, Mahogany, Austria, 1900, 5 Ft. 11 In.	2200.00
Desk, Governor Winthrop, Mahogany, c.1830, 68 x 34 x 17 In.	715.00
Desk, Gustav Stickley, Chalet, Drop Front, No. 505, c.1902, 46 In.	1980.00
Desk, Gustav Stickley, No. 550, Drop Front, c.1902, 47 3/4 In.	5775.00
Desk, Gustav Stickley, No. 720, 2 Drawers, Iron Pulls, 48 x 22 In.	3850.00
Desk, Gustav Stickley, No. 721, Drop Leaf Writing Surface, 29 In.	1045.00
Desk, Gustav Stickley, No. 728, Fall Front	1800.00
Desk, Gustav Stickley, No. 731, Original Hardware	3800.00
Desk, Hepplewhite, Mahogany, Inlay, 3 Drawers, England, 30 1/2 In.	600.00
Desk, Hinged Seat Slides Under Surface, Oilcloth Cover	3300.00
Desk, Kneehole, Brass Rim, 5 Drawers, Fruitwood, 1780s, 47 1/2 In.	7700.00
Desk, Kneehole, Drexel, Pine, 9 Drawers	550.00
Desk, Lap, Civil War, Slant Front, Rosewood	200.00
Desk, Lap, Compartments Under Lift Top, Rosewood, 15 x 10 1/4 In.	150.00
Desk, Lap, Felt Surface, Queen Anne Style Stand, Tiger Maple	1750.00
Desk, Lap, Foldout Writing Surface, Fitted Compartments, 15 In.	150.00
Desk, Lap, Hardwood Box, 19th Century, 6 x 9 1/2 x 16 In.	400.00
Desk, Lap, Landscape, 2 Hinged Sections, Papier-Mache, 14 In.	610.00
Desk, Lap, Maple Interior, Pen Space, Ink Bottle, 12 x 15 In.	800.00
Desk, Lap, On Stand, Victorian, Marquetry, Walnut, 22 x 18 1/4 In.	412.50
Desk, Lap, Rosewood, Leather Writing Surface, Brass Band	385.00
Desk, Lap, Slant Front, Rosewood	200.00
Desk, Limbert, Blind Drawer Pulls, Lift Top, Oak, c.1910, 29 In.	475.00

Desk, Louis XV, Pedestal, Boule & Mother-of-Pearl Inlay	8250.00
Desk, Mahogany Veneer, New England, c.1830, 68 x 34 x 17 In.	715.00
Desk, Partner's, George IV, 2 Banks Of 4 Drawers, Mahogany, 54 In.	5300.00
Desk, Partner's, Greek Key & Floral Top, Iris & Wave Legs, Skirt	4100.00
Desk, Partner's, Leather Top, 3 Drawers, Mahogany, 22 x 60 In.	2420.00
Desk, Partner's, Leather, Center Drawer, Side Drawers, Mahogany	4500.00
Desk, Plantation, Slant Front, 2 Drawers, Pine, 58 x 44 In.	1150.00
Desk, Pyrographic, Inscription On Top, Chair, 1900–1910	1650.00
Desk, Queen Anne, Drop Front, Curly Maple, c.1760, 34 In.	8500.00
Desk, Railroad, Slant Front, 3 Drawers, Oak Leaf Design	890.00
Desk, Regency, Mahogany, Satinwood, Mechanical Action	1320.00
Desk, Roll Top, Adjustable Reading Slope, Rosewood	5170.00
Desk, Roll Top, Cylinder, 2 Glass Doors, 3 Base Drawers, Walnut	1300.00
Desk, Roll Top, Dutch Rococo, Marquetry, Walnut, 43 x 55 In.	605.00
Desk, Roll Top, Interior Drawers, Walnut	1350.00
Desk, Roll Top, Oak, 1920s, 66 In.	1695.00
Desk, S Roll Top, Dark Stained Pine, Double Pedestal, 1890	1200.00
Desk, S Roll Top, Eastlake Style, Cherry, 60 In.	2250.00
Desk, S Roll Top, Oak, Block Panels, Refinished, 50 In.	3000.00
Desk, S Roll Top, Oak, Slots & Drawers, Map Drawer, 65 In.	2400.00
Desk, S Roll Top, Raised Panel, 62 In.	1850.00
Desk, School, Metal Frame, Mixed Wood	125.00
Desk, School, Oak Seat & Top, Black Iron Frame, Piqua, Oh., Small	75.00
Desk, Sewing, Shaker, Pine, Harvard Community	7250.00
Desk, Shaker, Pigeonhole Interior, Birch Legs, Pine, 31 In.	2985.00
Desk, Ship Captain's, Sink Reservoir Top	1300.00
Desk, Slant Front, 10 Pigeonholes Over 5 Drawers, Maple & Birch	4300.00
Desk, Slant Front, 20 Interior Drawers, Walnut, c.1780	4600.00
Desk, Slant Front, 4 Drawers, Fitted Interior, Cherry, 43 In.	2200.00
Desk, Slant Front, 4 Graduated Drawers, Inlay, New Hampshire, 1800	4800.00
Desk, Slant Front, Chippendale, Central Drawer, Maple, 41 1/2 In.	2750.00
Desk, Slant Front, Chippendale, Crossband Top, Mahogany, c.1790	6600.00
Desk, Slant Front, Chippendale, Mahogany, 4 Dovetailed Drawers	7750.00
Desk, Slant Front, Chippendale, Oak, 4 Drawers, 43 1/2 In.	650.00
Desk, Slant Front, Chippendale, Tiger Maple & Maple, 43 1/2 In.	1980.00
Desk, Slant Front, Chippendale, Tiger Maple, c.1800 ....*Illus*	5500.00
Desk, Slant Front, Curly Maple, 3 Graduated Base Drawers	6500.00
Desk, Slant Front, Hepplewhite, Mahogany, Cock-Beaded Drawers	4800.00
Desk, Slant Front, Leather Surface, 5 Drawers, Tiger Maple, 41 In.	3950.00
Desk, Slant Front, Maple, 3 Drawers, Late 19th Century	5500.00
Desk, Slant Front, Marquetry, Holland, 19th Century	6325.00
Desk, Slant Front, Oxbow Front, Mahogany, 41 1/2 In.	6050.00
Desk, Slant Front, Oxbow Front, Mahogany, 45 x 42 In.	3850.00
Desk, Slant Front, Pine, Late 19th Century, 33 In.	175.00
Desk, Slant Front, Serpentine Front, Mahogany, 42 x 38 x 21 In.	250.00
Desk, Slant Front, Tiger Maple Interior, Mahogany	900.00
Desk, Slant Front, Tiger Maple, Hidden Compartments, 18th Century	5100.00
Desk, Slant Front, Walnut Inlay, 4 Overlapping Drawers, 1815	4300.00
Desk, Stand-Up, Lower 2-Door Cabinet, Pine	295.00
Desk, Student, Sheraton, 2 Narrow Drawers Under Small Top, 1850	495.00
Desk, Table Top, 1 Drawer, Lift Top, Pine, 21 1/2 x 13 3/4 In.	700.00
Desk, Table Top, 3 Drawers, Slant Front, Lift Top, Pine, 20 3/4 In.	950.00
Desk, Tambour, Ivory Inlay, Mahogany, Curly Maple, 1810, 50 3/4 In.	3850.00
Desk, Tiger Maple, 4 Drawers, Hidden Top Drawer	1200.00
Desk, Whaling Captain's, Slant Front, Mahogany, 4 Ft.	2450.00
Desk, Wicker, Heywood-Wakefield, 1900	400.00
Desk, Woman's, 2 Parts, Mahogany, Bird's-Eye Maple, Inley, c.1800	1550.00
Desk, Woman's, Ebonized Finish, Ormolu Trim, France, 37 1/2 In.	400.00
Desk, Woman's, Federal, Mahogany Veneer, 1830s, 52 x 39 In.	990.00
Desk, Woman's, Federal, Mahogany, New England, c.1810, 55 In.	950.00
Desk, Woman's, Hepplewhite, Mahogany, Veneer, Removable Top, 47 In.	1300.00
Desk, Woman's, Hinged Surface, Fitted Interior, Rosewood, 39 In.	1550.00
Desk, Woman's, Mahogany, Drop Front, Pigeonholes, 1 Drawer	180.00

Desk, Woman's, Majorelle, Marquetry Fruit, Mahogany, 49 1/2 In. 5500.00
Desk, Woman's, Pigeonholes, Drawers, Painted Satinwood, 40 In. 3750.00
Desk, Woman's, Slant Front, Walnut, 4 Drawers, Victorian 850.00
Desk, Wooton, Pat. Oct. 6, 1874 .... 9500.00
Dining Set, Birchwood, Round, Alvar Aalto, 4 Plywood Chairs 2210.00
Dining Set, Drop Leaf, Black Walnut, Grierson, Inlay, 7 Piece 3500.00
Dining Set, G. Nakashima, Walnut, 2 Leaves, Woven Grass Seat, 7 Pc. 9900.00
Dining Set, Gustav Stickley, Oak, c.1910, 7 Piece ....*Illus* 1880.00
Dining Set, Limbert, 4 Leaves, Oak, Marked, c.1910, 11 Piece 5500.00
Dining Set, Marble Top Server, Walnut, Charles Baudouine, 11 Pc. 3685.00
Dining Set, Oak Leaf Table, Buffet Captain's & 5 Chairs, 1930s 600.00
Dining Set, Oak, 8 Leaves, 60–In., Server, U.S., 13 Piece 4250.00
Dining Set, Walnut, Heritage Furniture, 48–In. Round Table, 6 Pc. 400.00
Dining Set, Wicker, Open Weave, 1900, 5 Piece 1750.00
Dresser & Washstand, Oak, Beveled Mirror, Marble Top, 1900, 2 Pc. 1275.00
Dresser, 3 Drawers, Glove Box, Tilt Mirror, Marble Top, Victorian 275.00
Dresser, 3 Drawers, Wishbone Mirror, Marble Top, Walnut, Victorian 450.00
Dresser, Drop Front, Marble Top, 8 Ft. 750.00
Dresser, Drop Well, Marble Top, Walnut, c.1870, 88 x 47 x 18 In. 605.00
Dresser, Eastlake, Cherry, Mirror 325.00
Dresser, Empire, 4 Dovetailed Drawers, Mirror 350.00
Dresser, Empire, Ogee Mirror, Crotch Mahogany, 63 x 34 1/2 In. 875.00
Dresser, Gentleman's, Oak, Cheval Mirror, With Hatbox 575.00
Dresser, Gustav Stickley, No. 626, 2 Over 3 Drawers, Tenons, 43 In. 4450.00
Dresser, Gustav Stickley, No. 909, 40 x 37 x 19 1/4 In. ....*Illus* 1430.00
Dresser, Marble Top, 3 Drawers, Candle Shelves, Mirror, Fruit Pull 375.00
Dresser, Painted Oak, Wishbone Mirror, Serpentine, 4 Drawers 160.00
Dresser, Victorian, Walnut, Boxes, White Marble Insert, 3 Drawers 100.00
Dresser, Welsh, 3 Shelves Over Hinged Top, Faux Drawers, Oak 3080.00
Dry Sink, 2 Dovetailed Drawers Between 2 Tenoned Doors, Large 1200.00
Dry Sink, 2 Paneled Doors, 2 Drawers, High Back, Red Paint 2150.00

Furniture, Dining Set, Gustav Stickley, Oak, c.1910,
7 Piece

Furniture, Dresser, Gustav Stickley,
No. 909, 40 x 37 x 19 1/4 In.

♦♦♦♦♦♦♦♦♦♦♦♦♦♦♦♦♦♦♦♦♦
To clean a gold leaf frame, rub the gold leaf with a cloth that has been dipped in onion juice.
♦♦♦♦♦♦♦♦♦♦♦♦♦♦♦♦♦♦♦♦♦

Furniture, Frame, Gold Painted Faux Finish,

15 x 17 In.

Dry Sink, 12 Panes, 2 Top Doors, c.1840	2900.00
Dry Sink, 1840–1850, 7 Ft.	3200.00
Dry Sink, Amish, High Back, Cock–Beading, Top Shelf, Design, 1850	475.00
Dry Sink, Country, Poplar, Paneled Doors, 1 Drawer, 32 1/4 In.	750.00
Dry Sink, Gray Paint, Late 19th Century	1050.00
Dry Sink, Paneled Doors & Well, Poplar, 33 1/2 x 38 In.	650.00
Dry Sink, Pullout Breadboard, Lift Top	2600.00
Dry Sink, Zinc Insert, 19th Century	425.00
Dumbwaiter, George III, Mahogany, 2 Tiers, 34 1/2 In.	1210.00
Dumbwaiter, George III, Two Tiers, Mahogany, c.1780, 36 In.	1265.00
Easel, Victorian, Carved Mahogany	525.00
Etagere, 4 Shelves, Federal, Drawer, c.1810, 54 3/4 In.	3850.00
Etagere, 5 Shelves, Drawer, Key, Walnut, 60 x 30 In.	225.00
Etagere, Aesthetic Movement, Giltwood, Hinged Cabinet, 72 In.	1100.00
Etagere, Corner, Carved Rosewood, Open Cupboard, c.1850, 76 In.	665.00
Etagere, Corner, J. & J. W. Meeks, Rosewood & Marble, 69 1/2 In.	5500.00
Etagere, Ivory Cherubs, Etched Glass, Ebonized, 63 1/4 In.	7700.00
Etagere, Pierced & Carved Crest, 3 Drawers, Shelves, China, 81 In.	610.00
Etagere, Sideboard, Rosewood, Marble Top	1550.00
Etagere, Victorian, Cherrywood, Art Nouveau, 2 Beveled Mirrors	1760.00
Etagere, Victorian, Walnut, Mirror, Crest, Marble Shelf, Drawers	1800.00
Fauteuil, 2nd Empire, Gilt Bronze, Mahogany, Pair	7000.00
Footstool, Arts & Crafts, Oak, 7 x 18 1/2 In.	120.00
Footstool, Beveled Poplar Top, Hardwood Legs, 6 1/2 x 13 In.	20.00
Footstool, Carved Base, Needlepoint Upholstery, 16 In.	175.00
Footstool, Cherry, Sponging, Primitive Landscape, 13 1/2 In.	225.00
Footstool, Claw & Ball Feet, Mahogany, Upholstered, 19 1/4 In.	1000.00
Footstool, Continental, Walnut, Square Upholstered Top, 23 In.	440.00
Footstool, Curly Maple, Turned Feet, Carpet Upholstery, 14 In.	175.00
Footstool, Empire, Mahogany, Petit Point Upholstery, U.S., c.1850	45.00
Footstool, George II, Oak, Upholstered Top, 16 x 17 In.	665.00
Footstool, Georgian Style, Carved Knees, Upholstered Seat	145.00
Footstool, Gustav Stickley, Leather Seat, Tacks On Frame, c.1912	715.00
Footstool, Gustav Stickley, No. 725, Leather Upholstery, c.1902	1350.00
Footstool, Hardwood, Country, Three Splayed Legs, 12 3/8 In.	45.00
Footstool, Iron Base, Floral Needlepoint Upholstery, 11 x 14 In.	150.00
Footstool, Lyre Frame, Needlepoint Upholstery, 14 1/4 In.	150.00
Footstool, Maple, Molded Edge Top, Whittled Poplar Legs, 10 In.	45.00
Footstool, Pine Top, Turned Hardwood Legs, Red Finish, 6 x 13 In.	55.00
Footstool, Pine, Chip Carved, Green Paint Over Red, Drawer Base	350.00
Footstool, Pine, Green Paint, Country, 8 In.	180.00
Footstool, Pine, Red, Cutout Feet, 12 1/2 In.	125.00
Footstool, Shaker, Chamfered Plank, Pine & Maple, Alfred, Maine	355.00
Footstool, Stylized Crocodile Legs, Painted & Parcel Gilt, Italy	8800.00
Footstool, Two–Tone Brown, Yellow, White Striping, 6 3/4 x 10 In.	90.00
Footstool, Victorian, Carved Serpentine Apron, Casters, Walnut	165.00
Footstool, Victorian, Shaped Rectangular Top, Ball Feet, 12 In.	250.00

Footstool, Walnut, Square, Cabriole Let, Upholstered, c.1900 .... 935.00
Footstool, Worn Yellow Graining, Oval, 7 3/4 x 10 1/2 In. 75.00
Frame, 3 Oval Painted Plaques, Gilt, Limoges, 27 In., Pair 500.00
Frame, Bird's–Eye Veneer, Gilt Liner, 23 In. 90.00
Frame, Carved Pale Green Jade–Like Stone, Teak, 10 7/8 x 8 In. 140.00
Frame, Cove Moulding, Corner Florals, 37 x 32 In. 200.00
Frame, Curly Maple, 16 1/4 x 13 1/2 In. 130.00
Frame, Gilt Cove Moulding, 1880s, 53 1/2 x 63 1/2 In. 120.00
Frame, Gold Painted Faux Finish, 15 x 17 In. ....*Illus* 75.00
Frame, Inlay, 15 In. 100.00
Frame, Mask & Gargoyle Cornice, Gilt Gesso & Wood, 51 1/2 In. 275.00
Frame, Ornate Gilt, 27 1/4 In. 135.00
Frame, Ornate Gilt, 27 In. 75.00
Frame, Ornate Gilt, 31 1/2 x 36 In. 210.00
Frame, Ornate Gilt, Red Velvet Liner, 40 In. 125.00
Frame, Oval Spandrel, Gilt Florals, 28 3/4 x 23 1/2 In. 45.00
Frame, Pine, Walnut Inlay, Geometric Shapes, 9 x 7 1/4 In. 150.00
Frame, Poplar, Original Graining, Beveled, 19 1/2 In., Pair 950.00
Frame, Shadow Box, Gilt Liner, 16 In. 75.00
Garden Seat, Blue & White, Oriental, 20 In. 85.00
Garden Seat, Elephant, Polychrome Glaze, Pottery, China, Pair 335.00
Garden Seat, Marble, Figural Reserves, China, 17 1/2 In., Pair 445.00
Hall Chair, Limbert, Cutout Heart 450.00
Hall Chair, Limbert, Saddle Seat 675.00
Hall Stand, Beveled Glass Mirror, Jacobean Style, Oak, 80 In. 495.00
Hall Stand, Beveled Mirror, Metal Hooks, Lift Seat, Oak 445.00
Hall Stand, Mirror, Locking Diagonal Doors, Lift Seat, Oak, 78 In. 750.00
Hall Stand, Oak, Oval Mirror, Seat 840.00
Hall Tree, Applied Carvings On Crest & Seat, Oak 1155.00
Hall Tree, Eastlake–Style, Carved Boar's Head, Walnut, 96 In. 850.00
Hall Tree, Gothic, Pierced Scroll & Bird, Triple Arch, 88 1/2 In. 800.00
Hall Tree, Oak, Victorian, Acanthus Column Support, 77 In. 665.00
Hall Tree, Tree Form, Pegs For Hats, Umbrella Holder, Cast Iron 825.00
Hall Tree, Triple Gothic Arch, Metal Base, Painted, 88 1/2 In. 885.00
Hall Tree, Umbrella Stand, Eastlake, Walnut 515.00
Hall Tree, Victorian, Carved Columnar Acanthus Supports, Oak 665.00
Hassock, Frank Lloyd Wright, Hexagonal, Loose Cushion, 29 In., Pr. 1000.00
High Chair, Converts To Stroller, Oak, Pressed Back 250.00
High Chair, George III, Pierced Splat, Woven Reed Seat, Footrest 385.00
High Chair, Ladder Back, Delaware Valley 3200.00
High Chair, Ladder Back, Splint Seat, 3 Slats, Turned Finials, Red 650.00
High Chair, Oak, Cane Seat, 19th Century 125.00
High Chair, Spindle Back, Brown Paint 35.00
High Chair, Wicker, Painted White, Woven Back & Arms, 40 1/2 In. 100.00
High Chair, Wicker, White, Ring Turned Legs, 40 1/2 In. 99.00
High Chair, Windsor, Bamboo, Worn Red Finish, 36 1/2 In. 725.00
High Chair, Windsor, Green Paint, New England, 1850s, 31 In. 137.50
High Chair, Windsor, Red, Black Graining, Yellow Striping, 31 In. 150.00
High Chair, Windsor, Stenciled, Black Striping, Plank Seat 935.00
Highboy, Chippendale, 3 Drawers, 1 Lower Drawer, Oak, 51 1/2 In. 1750.00
Highboy, Chippendale, 4 Over 5 Drawers, Maple, c.1780, 5 Ft. 10 In. 8250.00
Highboy, Chippendale, 4 Small Over 3 Long Drawers, Walnut 4180.00
Highboy, Chippendale, Bonnet Top, Mahogany, 2 Piece, 7 Ft. 1 In. 5225.00
Highboy, Flat Top, 2 Over 3 Drawers, Pine, Maple, Poplar, c.1760 .... 9500.00
Highboy, Inlaid, Old Brasses, England, 18th Century 4500.00
Highboy, Queen Anne, 4 Base Drawers, Curly Maple, 66 1/2 In. 2900.00
Highboy, Queen Anne, Tiger Maple, New Hampshire, 1760–1780 .... 5500.00
Huntboard, Hepplewhite, Poplar, Pine, Blue Paint, 3 Drawers, 50 In. 9500.00
Hutch, Pine, Maple, Molded Pediment, 2 Doors, Dry Sink, 73 In. 220.00
Kas, Cherry, 2 Drawers, Double Doors, 3 Interior Shelves, 81 In. 1200.00
Kas, Distressed Red Paint, Base Drawer, Overhang Top 3200.00
Kas, Hand Painted Cartouches, Florals On 1 Door, 1785, 74 In. 3575.00
Kas, Mahogany, Ebony Trim, 3 Drawers, Double Paneled Doors, 75 In. 1100.00

Furniture, Love Seat, Rosewood, Rose Striped Upholstery

Furniture, Meridienne, Belter, Rosewood, 79 In.

Kas, Oak, Rosewood Veneer, Ebonized Trim, Interior Shelves, 67 In. 550.00
Kas, Pine, Brownish Red Alligatored Finish, 3 Shelves, 65 1/2 In. 1600.00
Kas, Stylized Painted Flowers, 1 Door, Drawer Lock & Strap, 1818 .... 4700.00
Kas, William & Mary, Base Drawer, Gumwood, 1740s, 6 Ft. 8 In. 6875.00
Lectern, Adjustable Top, Plank Sides, Shelves, Oak, c.1910, 44 In. 358.00
Lectern, Eagle, Ball Pedestal, Bronze, 63 In. 2300.00
Lectern, Empire-Era, Yellow & Red Paint Design, 36 x 52 In. 335.00
Library Steps, Brass Handrails, Foil Cutouts, Steel, 83 In. 3850.00
Library Steps, Regency Style, 3 Spiral Steps, Mahogany, 48 In. 165.00
Linen Press, 3 Parts, Dressing Slides, Mahogany, 1790s, 77 In. 3300.00
Linen Press, 4 Drawers, Paneled Doors, Sawed Oak, 1 Piece, 82 In. 1500.00
Linen Press, Open Section For Hanging Clothes, Drawers, Mahogany 1935.00
Linen Press, Paneled Doors, 3 Bottom Sham Drawers, Oak 1870.00
Linen Press, Pullout Shelves, 2 Drawers, Mahogany, 76 In. 4350.00
Living Room Set, Old Hickory, Martinsville, Lamps, Tables, 9 Piece 1350.00
Love Seat, Aubusson Tapestry Upholstery, Walnut, 56 In. 550.00
Love Seat, Curved Sides, Facing Lions' Heads 130.00
Love Seat, Empire, Horsehair 225.00
Love Seat, Full Size Hide-A-Bed, Pastel Upholstery 275.00
Love Seat, J. & J. W. Meeks, Stanton Hall, Rose Velvet 4850.00
Love Seat, J. & J. W. Meeks, Laminated Rosewood 10450.00
Love Seat, Majorelle, Carved Fiddlehead Ferns, 55 In. 5060.00
Love Seat, Oak Frame, Floral Brocade Upholstery 300.00
Love Seat, Oak, Parlor Style, Spoon Carving 60.00
Love Seat, Rosewood, Rose Striped Upholstery ....*Illus* 1650.00
Love Seat, Victorian, Green Velvet Upholstery 250.00
Love Seat, Victorian, Walnut, Grape Carved, Upholstered 1395.00
Love Seat, Victorian, Walnut, Medallion Back, Tufted Upholstery 800.00
Lowboy, Centered Shell Carving, Pad Feet, Walnut, 1790s 9000.00
Lowboy, Chippendale Style, Cabriole Legs, Mahogany, 32 In. 495.00
Lowboy, Chippendale, Long Drawer Over 3 Drawers, Walnut, 34 In. 9900.00
Lowboy, Delaware Valley, 1 Long Over 2 Short Drawers 8800.00
Lowboy, Oak, Cabriole Legs, Shaped Apron, 3 Drawers, England, 1800 .... 4000.00
Lowboy, Queen Anne Style, Side & Central Drawers, Burl Walnut 2650.00
Lowboy, Queen Anne, 5 Drawers, Mahogany, Inlay, 29 3/4 In. 1750.00
Magazine Rack, Lacy Wrought Iron 55.00
Meridienne, Belter, Rosewood, 79 In. ....*Illus* 10175.00
Mirror Stand, Federal, Dressing, Inlay, Bowfront, U.S. 650.00
Mirror, Acanthus & C-Scroll Crest, Giltwood, 47 x 33 In. 2850.00
Mirror, Adams Style, Gilt Frame, 46 In. 175.00
Mirror, Adirondack, Carved Top, 1880, 68 In. 7500.00

Mirror, Beaded & Flowerhead Frame, Giltwood, 5 Ft. 6 In. x 4 Ft. 5775.00
Mirror, Beveled Pine Frame, Original Red Graining, 9 1/4 In. 180.00
Mirror, Beveled, Gilt Brass Frame, Cherubs, 13 In. 285.00
Mirror, Bird Pediment, Gesso & Giltwood, 47 x 27 1/2 In. 2850.00
Mirror, Brass, Repousse Mounts, Fruit & Mask Head, 32 x 28 In. 330.00
Mirror, Brass, Repousse, Rectangle, Rose Border, 23 In. 275.00
Mirror, Bronze & Porcelain, Tulipwood Marquetry, c.1845, 6 Ft. 8250.00
Mirror, Bronze Frame, Beveled Glass, c.1870, 22 1/2 x 18 3/4 In. 175.00
Mirror, Bull's-Eye, Federal, Giltwood, Eagle, c.1900, 43 x 24 In. 440.00
Mirror, Carved & Gilded Frame, GIB 1910, 18 1/2 x 11 1/4 In. 550.00
Mirror, Carved 5-Pointed Stars On Frame, Walnut, 17 x 14 In. 660.00
Mirror, Carved Birds On Black Lacquer Frame, 38 x 28 In. 150.00
Mirror, Carved Gold Gesso Frame, Beads, Florals, 29 x 76 In. 700.00
Mirror, Cast Brass, Wreath Frame, 22 1/2 In. 150.00
Mirror, Cherry Frame, Corner Blocks, 12 1/2 In. 450.00
Mirror, Cheval, Columns, 2-Arm Candleholders, Walnut, 82 x 44 In. 3300.00
Mirror, Chippendale, Curly Maple, Light Natural Finish, 27 In. 45.00
Mirror, Chippendale, Eagle On Crest, Mahogany, 28 x 14 1/2 In. 425.00
Mirror, Chippendale, Giltwood, 19th Century, 46 In. ....*Illus* 4400.00
Mirror, Chippendale, Mahogany Veneer On Pine, 37 x 19 3/4 In. 850.00
Mirror, Chippendale, Mahogany Veneer, Scroll, 45 x 22 In. 900.00
Mirror, Chippendale, Mahogany, 1760-1780, 45 x 22 In. ....*Illus* 3520.00
Mirror, Chippendale, Parcel Gilt Mahogany, 1765, 43 1/2 x 22 In. 7700.00
Mirror, Chippendale, Parcel Gilt Mahogany, c.1770, 39 x 19 In. 2650.00
Mirror, Chippendale, Parcel Gilt Mahogany, c.1780, 44 x 22 In. 1550.00
Mirror, Chippendale, Scroll, Eglomise Angel, 37 In. 150.00
Mirror, Chippendale, Scroll, Mahogany, Eagle, 21 1/2 x 12 1/2 In. 650.00
Mirror, Chippendale, Scroll, Mahogany, Gilt Liner, Eagle, 32 In. 145.00
Mirror, Chippendale, Scroll, Mahogany, Inlay, 35 In. 140.00
Mirror, Chippendale, Scroll, Mahogany, Molded Frame, 17 In. 545.00
Mirror, Chippendale, Scroll, Mahogany, Molded Frame, 30 1/2 In. 650.00
Mirror, Convex, Regency, Eagle Top, Giltwood, 42 x 24 1/2 In. 600.00
Mirror, Courting, Black & Red Japanning, 1725, 14 x 8 3/4 In. 3850.00
Mirror, Courting, Eglomise Crest, 1780s, 16 1/2 x 11 1/4 In. 495.00
Mirror, Courting, Painted Liner, Europe, 18th Century, 16 3/4 In. 357.00
Mirror, Courting, Reverse Painted Glass Strips, 16 1/4 x 11 In. 1600.00
Mirror, Curly Maple Frame, 12 3/4 In. 35.00
Mirror, Curly Maple Frame, 26 1/4 In. 150.00
Mirror, Dark Reddish Brown Paint, Scrolled Crest, Frame, 26 In. 175.00
Mirror, Dressing, Bowfront, Mahogany, Inlay, c.1820, 21 3/4 In. 385.00
Mirror, Dressing, Carved Giltwood, Scrollwork, Flowers, Pedestal 110.00

Furniture, Mirror, Federal, Convex, 19th Century, 34 x 29 In.

Furniture, Mirror, Chippendale, Mahogany, 1760-1780, 45 x 22 In.

Furniture, Mirror, Chippendale, Giltwood, 19th Century, 46 In.

Furniture, Mirror, Federal, Reverse Painted, Giltwood, 48 x 25 In.

Mirror, Dressing, Drawer, Mahogany, c.1850, 14 1/2 x 14 1/2 In. 140.00
Mirror, Eagle Above Arch With Stars, Giltwood, 61 x 24 1/2 In. 2090.00
Mirror, Eagle Finial, Swags, Tassels, Giltwood, c.1800, 41 x 18 In. 2640.00
Mirror, Eagle On Rock, Convex, Giltwood, c.1815, 49 In. 5775.00
Mirror, Eagle, Pierced & Carved Leaves At Top, 37 x 25 In. 825.00
Mirror, Egg & Dart Molding, Giltwood, Oval, 33 1/2 x 25 In. 195.50
Mirror, Eglomise River Landscape, Man In Boat, 29 x 14 1/2 In. 155.00
Mirror, Eglomise Tablet Of Harmony, Giltwood, 46 x 26 1/2 In. 3300.00
Mirror, Eglomise Woman In Arcadia, Giltwood, 39 1/4 x 23 In. 3300.00
Mirror, Empire Frame, Pine, Corner Blocks, 22 1/2 In. 95.00
Mirror, Empire, Bold Turning, Corner Blocks, Framed, 32 x 21 In. 105.00
Mirror, Empire, Gilt Gesso, Wood Frame, 34 In. 120.00
Mirror, Empire, Reverse Painted, Gold, Black Repaint, 36 In., 2 Pc. 400.00
Mirror, Empire, Turned Half Columns, Rosettes, Gold, 33 x 23 In. 150.00
Mirror, Federal Style, Carved Gilt & Mahogany, 50 x 44 In. 825.00
Mirror, Federal, Convex, 19th Century, 34 x 29 In. ....*Illus* 4400.00
Mirror, Federal, Eglomise, Eagle Inlay, Mahogany, 52 In. 1650.00
Mirror, Federal, Eglomise, Gilt, Mahogany, c.1800, 59 1/2 In. 9350.00
Mirror, Federal, Gilt, Painted Panel, 19th Century, 61 x 26 In. 4400.00
Mirror, Federal, Reverse Painted, Giltwood, 48 x 25 In. ....*Illus* 3850.00
Mirror, Federal, Scrolling, Gilt Eagle, Mahogany, 40 x 22 In. 110.00
Mirror, Folding, Cherry Case, Original Glass, 4 x 6 1/2 In. 65.00
Mirror, G. Stickley, No. 66, Oak Frame, 4 Iron Coat Hooks, c.1904 .... 2090.00
Mirror, George III, Rosette Corners, Gilt, 34 1/2 x 13 1/2 In. 550.00
Mirror, Georgian, Mahogany, Gilt, Phoenix Bird, Rectangular, 50 In. 1430.00
Mirror, Gesso & Gilt Liner, Mahogany, 38 3/4 x 20 1/2 In. 1200.00
Mirror, Gilt Brass, Rococo, 17 In. 115.00
Mirror, Gilt Brass, Art Nouveau, Easel Back, 15 In. 75.00
Mirror, Gilt Half Column Frame, Eglomise, 27 1/2 x 13 In. 110.00
Mirror, Gilt, Ebonized Wood, Eagle, Swag Chains, Rectangle, 37 In. 1100.00
Mirror, Giltwood Frame, Cut Floral Design, Sunburst Crest, 54 In. 330.00
Mirror, Giltwood Garland, Urn Crest, Mahogany Veneer, 58 x 22 In. 4000.00
Mirror, Giltwood, Convex, Eagle, 40 In. 325.00
Mirror, Girandole, Candle Arms, Convex Plate, Eagle, c.1820, 43 In. 4400.00
Mirror, Girandole, Giltwood, Black Spread Winged Eagle, 44 In. 3575.00
Mirror, Girandole, Giltwood, Eagle, Stepped Pedestal, Round, 36 In. 1540.00
Mirror, Girandole, Giltwood, England, 40 In. 3200.00
Mirror, Gold Leaf, Stencils, U.S., c.1870, 41 1/2 x 32 x 3 In. 440.00
Mirror, Hand Carved Walnut, France, c.1920, 35 x 20 In. 165.00
Mirror, Hanging, Oval Molded Frame, Shelf, Original Finish, 22 In. 350.00
Mirror, Hepplewhite Style, Urn & Wheat Finial, 59 x 27 1/2 In. 350.00
Mirror, Hepplewhite, Line Inlay, Mahogany, 22 3/4 x 12 1/2 In. 600.00
Mirror, Hepplewhite, Scroll, Mahogany Veneer, 29 x 15 1/2 In. 350.00
Mirror, Inset Portrait Miniatures, Giltwood, 37 1/2 x 32 In. 2970.00
Mirror, James Stokes, Mahogany, 19 3/4 x 4 1/2 In. 2650.00
Mirror, Louis XVI Style, Bowknot Crest, Giltwood, 49 x 29 In. 520.00
Mirror, Louis XVI, Floral Torch & Quiver Crest, 57 x 37 In. 660.00
Mirror, Mahogany Frame, Fruit & Rose Crest, 38 1/2 In. 190.00
Mirror, Mahogany Veneer, Frame, 15 1/2 x 22 In. 75.00
Mirror, Mahogany, Carved Leaf Supports, 1 Drawer, Paw Feet 286.00
Mirror, Mahogany, Partial Gilt, Oval, 25 1/4 x 21 In. 250.00
Mirror, Mahogany, Shadow Box Frame, Ebonized Trim, 53 In. 250.00
Mirror, Mantel, 3 Sections, Carved Gold Gesso Frame, 29 x 76 In. 700.00
Mirror, Mantel, Classical, Gilt, Gesso, U.S., c.1840, 33 x 27 In. 198.00
Mirror, Mantel, Gold Leaf, L. Uter, New Orleans, 1870, 85 x 63 In. 3750.00
Mirror, Mantle, Mahogany, Gilt Trim, 25 3/4 In. 150.00
Mirror, Metal Frame, Scotland, c.1915, 15 x 11 1/4 In. 385.00
Mirror, Mother-of-Pearl, Pediment, Syria, 93 x 49 In. 2970.00
Mirror, Neoclassical Style, Blond Mahogany, 34 1/4 x 24 In. 77.00
Mirror, Neoclassical, 3 Panes, 1800–1820, 58 1/2 In. 7500.00
Mirror, Ogee, Rectangular, 19th Century, U.S., 37 x 25 In. 55.00
Mirror, Oriental, Reverse Painted, Frame, 22 1/2 In. 250.00
Mirror, Ornate Gilt Frame, Oval, 22 3/4 In. 150.00

Mirror, Ornate Rococo Style Frame, 34 1/2 In. 375.00
Mirror, Phoenix Finial, Giltwood, Mahogany, 1770, 53 1/2 x 25 In. 7700.00
Mirror, Pier, Beveled, Walnut, 7 Ft. 6 In. x 53 1/2 In. 1200.00
Mirror, Pier, Eastlake, Hall, Rope-Turned Posts, Carved Crest 385.00
Mirror, Pier, Edwardian, Mahogany, Oval, 4-Footed Base, 75 In. 4400.00
Mirror, Plateau, Beveled, Gilt Metal Frame, Round, 12 3/4 In. 85.00
Mirror, Plateau, Floral & Scroll Border, Silver Plated, 27 In. 415.00
Mirror, Plateau, Leaf & Scroll, Footed, 12 In. 65.00
Mirror, Plateau, Lion Head & Paw At Corners, Beveled, 3 x 12 In. 425.00
Mirror, Plateau, Vintage Border, Silver Plate, 20 1/2 In. 135.00
Mirror, Queen Anne, Arched Frame, Divided Plate, 35 x 17 1/2 In. 3525.00
Mirror, Queen Anne, Carved Outer Frame, 40 In. 2200.00
Mirror, Queen Anne, Molded Frame, Gilt Liner, 31 1/2 In. 225.00
Mirror, Queen Anne, Pine, Red Traces, Scrolled Crest, 17 x 10 In. 250.00
Mirror, Queen Anne, Scroll, Mahogany, 19 1/8 x 9 3/8 In. 450.00
Mirror, Regency, Divided, Scrolls, Birds, Giltwood, 56 x 36 In. 1320.00
Mirror, Regency, Mirrored Borders, Giltwood, 43 x 36 In. 2090.00
Mirror, Reverse Painted Figures, Giltwood Frame, 29 x 30 1/4 In. 1650.00
Mirror, Reverse Painted House, Mahogany Frame, 22 In., 2 Piece 175.00
Mirror, Reverse Painted Houses, Mahogany Frame, 32 3/4 x 18 In. 250.00
Mirror, Rococo, Carved Gilt, Cartouche Shape, Floral Crest, 63 In. 2750.00
Mirror, Rococo, Giltwood, Oriental Bird, Rectangle, Italy, 60 In. 1320.00
Mirror, Scroll Cut Crest, Parcel Gilt, Mahogany, 36 x 19 In. 660.00
Mirror, Scroll, Carved Frame, Mahogany Veneer, 29 x 18 1/4 In. 400.00
Mirror, Scroll, Foliage Top, Bronze, M. Bergue, c.1925, 33 1/2 In. 6600.00
Mirror, Scroll, Gilt Phoenix, Mahogany, 38 1/4 x 20 1/2 In. 1200.00
Mirror, Scroll, Mahogany Veneer, 19th Century, 24 In. 85.00
Mirror, Scroll, Molded Frame, Mahogany Veneer, 39 1/2 x 20 In. 1050.00
Mirror, Scroll, Painted Vines, Parcel Gilt, 30 x 17 1/4 In. 4950.00
Mirror, Scroll, Urn Finial, Mahogany Veneer On Pine, 55 x 23 In. 4000.00
Mirror, Shadow Box Frame, Gilt Liner, 26 1/4 In. 90.00
Mirror, Shaker, Pine Brace, Tiger Maple, Hancock, 27 1/8 In. 3850.00
Mirror, Shaving, 2 Drawers, Mahogany, 18 1/2 x 26 1/2 In. 135.00
Mirror, Shaving, Drawer, Inlay On Frame, Mahogany, 19 1/2 In. 150.00
Mirror, Shaving, Hepplewhite, Mahogany Veneer, Pine Inlay, 16 In. 150.00
Mirror, Shaving, Mahogany, Marble Top, 37 In. 350.00
Mirror, Shaving, Mother-of-Pearl & Bone Inlay, Syria, 23 1/2 In. 357.50
Mirror, Shaving, Shield Shape, Wooden Frame, Turned Base, 15 In. 45.00
Mirror, Shaving, Standing, Brass Claw Feet, Mahogany 305.00
Mirror, Shaving, Swing, Oval, Bracket Frame, Mahogany, 26 In. 467.00
Mirror, Shaving, Victorian, Crotch Mahogany, 1875, England 1850.00
Mirror, Sheraton, Eglomise Of Woman Dancing, Columns, 35 In. 192.00
Mirror, Swan's Neck Crest, Giltwood Urn, Mahogany, c.1795, 56 In. 4400.00
Mirror, Tombstone, Walnut, 1860 .... 295.00
Mirror, Venetian, Blown Glass Frame, Bevelled Plate, 36 x 26 In. 770.00
Mirror, Walnut Frame, 23 1/2 x 16 In. 90.00
Parlor Set, Child's, Walnut, Carved Grapes, Upholstered, 3 Piece 3630.00
Parlor Set, Eastlake, Platform Rocker, 4 Chairs, Sofa, 6 Piece 900.00
Parlor Set, Eastlake, Walnut & Burl, Pink Crushed Velvet, 6 Piece 400.00
Parlor Set, Queen Anne, Down Filled, Carved Rose Pattern, 7 Piece 6500.00
Parlor Set, Renaissance Revival, Rose Velvet, Walnut, 3 Piece 3500.00
Parlor Set, Renaissance Revival, Tufted Back, 5 Piece 3200.00
Parlor Set, Steer Horn, Table, 2 Chairs, 2 Ottomans 2970.00
Pedestal, Alabaster, Circular Form, 39 1/2 In. 275.00
Pedestal, Classical Fluted Column, Ebonized Finish, 38 1/4 In. 350.00
Pedestal, Continental, Giltwood, Squared Column, 45 In. 1100.00
Pedestal, Female Support, Painted & Parcel Gilt, 43 In. 3500.00
Pedestal, Figure Of Whippet, Carved Mahogany, 37 In. 2200.00
Pedestal, Gilt Marquetry Inlay, Figural, Rosewood 4675.00
Pedestal, Louis XV, Regency Gilt, Kingwood, 13 1/4 In., Pair 9900.00
Pedestal, Louis XVI, Gilt, White Marble Top, 29 1/2 In. 500.00
Pedestal, Marble, Gilt Bronze Leaf Tip Ring, 48 In., Pair 4400.00
Pedestal, Napoleon III, Cloisonne Frieze, Marble Top, 20 1/4 In. 2100.00

Pedestal, Napoleon III, Onyx, Marble & Cloisonne, 15 1/2 In. 1650.00
Pie Safe, 2 Doors, 4 Punched Tin Panels, 12 x 18 In. 695.00
Pie Safe, 3 Punched Tin Panels, Pine, Blue Green, 37 x 57 In. 1100.00
Pie Safe, 12 Punched Tin Panels, Floral, Blue Paint, c.1850 .... 1975.00
Pie Safe, Flower & Urn Punched Tin, Green Paint 2650.00
Pie Safe, Pierced Tin Panel On Side, 2 Drawers, Poplar, 57 In. 375.00
Pie Safe, Poplar, Base Drawer 450.00
Pie Safe, Primitive, Poplar, Square Nails, Lap Joint Doors, 1880s 675.00
Pie Safe, Walnut, Painted, Pinwheel Tins 2000.00
Planter, Wicker, Basket Shape, Standing, Unpainted 525.00
Porch Set, Rocker, Swing, Table, Chairs, Rocker, Old Hickory, 5 Pc. 1000.00
Potty Seat, Folding, Wooden 20.00
Rack, French Baker's, Red Paint, Nickel Plated, 1820–1826, 96 In. 7820.00
Rack, Hat, Bentwood, Hanging 65.00
Rack, Magazine, Michigan Chair Co., Oak, Open Shelves, c.1910 .... 495.00
Rack, Plate, 12 Upper & 12 Lower Slots, Walnut 560.00
Rack, Plate, Corbel Supports, 4 Spindles, Oak, 23 3/4 x 42 1/2 In. 225.00
Rack, Plate, Hanging, Pine, Dovetailed Base, Brown, 34 1/4 In. 750.00
Rack, Spoon, Chip Carved, Oak, Spiral Posts, Figural Finial, 21 In. 100.00
Recamier, Belter, Scrolled Frame, c.1855, 6 Ft. 7 In. 6600.00
Recamier, Empire, Dark Paint, Rush Seat Insert, 76 In. 2900.00
Recamier, Vernacular 575.00
Recliner, Mission, Oak, Beast Heads, Royal Chair Co. 500.00
Rocker, Adirondack Type, Dark Brown Finish, 38 In. 65.00
Rocker, Arrow Splats, Cutout Crest Rail, Upholstered Seat 110.00
Rocker, Arts & Crafts, Oak, Scooped Crest Rail, 3 Slats 175.00
Rocker, Arts & Crafts, Wide Crest Rail, 5 Slats, Oak 210.00
Rocker, Bamboo Legs, 7 Curved Spindles, Red & Black Paint, 44 In. 247.50
Rocker, Blue, Yellow Striping, Stenciled Crest, 44 3/4 In. 55.00
Rocker, Carved Back & Women's Heads On Posts, Quartersawn Oak 247.50
Rocker, Carved Winged Sea Horses, Cupids, Dragons, Walnut, Italy 6655.00
Rocker, Carved, Walnut, Tufted Upholstery, Griffin Bust Arms 3850.00
Rocker, Child's, 3 Spindles, Cane Seat 100.00
Rocker, Child's, Black Paint, Gold Stenciled Design, Rush Seat 60.00
Rocker, Child's, Cane Seat, Bent Arm, Little Girl Design 220.00
Rocker, Child's, Dark Alligatored, Blue & White Tape Seat, Arms 225.00
Rocker, Child's, Ladder Back, Tape Seat, Alligatored Brown, Arms 100.00
Rocker, Child's, Ladder Back, Turned Front Posts, Arms & Finials 750.00
Rocker, Child's, Oak, Ladder Back, Cane Seat, Low Arms 115.00
Rocker, Child's, Open Back, Green, Upholstered Seat, 24 1/2 In. 55.00
Rocker, Child's, Pressed & Spindle Back, Replaced Cane Seat 100.00
Rocker, Child's, Roycroft 121.00
Rocker, Child's, Shaker, No. 1, Tape Seat, Mount Lebanon, 29 In. 935.00
Rocker, Child's, Spindle Back, Red & Black Grained, Stenciled 125.00
Rocker, Child's, Turned Finials, Rush Seat, Red Paint, 1780s 225.00
Rocker, Child's, Twig, Bentwood, Natural Varnish, Splat Seat 345.00
Rocker, Child's, Victorian, Fold Up, Original Cloth 80.00
Rocker, Child's, Wicker, Bar Harbor Style, Painted 125.00
Rocker, Child's, Wicker, Brown Paint 65.00
Rocker, Child's, Wicker, White Paint 90.00
Rocker, Curly Maple, 4 Slats, Ladder Back, Splint Seat, Arms 100.00
Rocker, Curly Maple, Serpentine Rush Seat, Armless, 32 1/2 In. 75.00
Rocker, Curved Posts, Step–Down Crest, Scrolled Arms, 38 1/2 In. 550.00
Rocker, Delaware Valley, 5 Back Slats, Bulbous Stretcher 220.00
Rocker, Gustav Stickley, No. 333 1/2, V–Back, 1909 .... 525.00
Rocker, Gustav Stickley, Oak, 3 Horizontal Slats, c.1905 .... 445.00
Rocker, Harden, Concave Crest Rail, 4 Slats, Cushion Seat 440.00
Rocker, High Back, Black, Yellow Striping, Stenciled Crest, 41 In. 100.00
Rocker, Horn, T–Back 1850.00
Rocker, Knoll, Bent Chrome, 20th Century 350.00
Rocker, L. & J. G. Stickley, No. 803, 2 Horizontal Slats, c.1912 ...... 110.00
Rocker, Ladder Back, 4 Slats, Splint Seat, Arms, 41 3/4 In. 110.00
Rocker, Ladder Back, Graining, Floral Traces, Splint Seat, Arms 400.00

Rocker, Ladder Back, Paper Rush Seat, Green Over Old Red, 39 In. 175.00
Rocker, Limbert, No. 518, Adjustable Back, Open Arms, c.1910 .... 1200.00
Rocker, Limbert, Reclining 660.00
Rocker, Mahogany, Face Carving, Plank Bottle 130.00
Rocker, Maple, Oak Stretchers 632.50
Rocker, Mission, Oak, Leather Seat 60.00
Rocker, Nursery, Birch, Cane Seat & Back 65.00
Rocker, Old Hickory 250.00
Rocker, Platform, Victorian, Red Velvet Upholstery 275.00
Rocker, Platform, Wicker, Back Flanked By Scrolls, Curved Arms 1100.00
Rocker, Pressed Back, Arms 100.00
Rocker, Pressed Back, Cane Seat, Early 1900s 110.00
Rocker, Pressed Back, Folding 25.00
Rocker, Pressed Back, Oak, Stick-and-Ball 165.00
Rocker, Red & Black Graining, Gilt Stenciled Crest, Signed 115.00
Rocker, Sewing, Gustav Stickley, No. 359, Leather Seat, Red Decal 825.00
Rocker, Sewing, Ladder Back 25.00
Rocker, Sewing, Limbert, No. 1892, Vertical Slat, Padded Seat 552.00
Rocker, Sewing, Roycroft 297.00
Rocker, Sewing, Splat Back 25.00
Rocker, Shaker, Gold Striping, Splint Seat, New Hampshire 275.00
Rocker, Shaker, Harvard, 5 Slats 9625.00
Rocker, Shaker, No. 3, Armless, Tape Back 457.00
Rocker, Shaker, No. 4, Armless, Tape Seat, Mahogany 385.00
Rocker, Shaker, No. 4, Gold & Brown Tape Seat, Armless, Mt. Lebanon 330.00
Rocker, Shaker, No. 4, Rush Seat, 3 Slats, Maple, Mt. Lebanon 550.00
Rocker, Shaker, No. 7, Arms 1070.00
Rocker, Shaker, No. 7, Taped Seat & Back, Mt. Lebanon 1800.00
Rocker, Shaker, No. 84, Taped Seat, Shawl Rail 357.50
Rocker, Shaker, Red Varnish, Stenciled, Mt. Lebanon, 34 In. 275.00
Rocker, Shaker-Style, Splint Seat, All Original 150.00
Rocker, Spindle Back, Red, Black Graining, Floral Design, 42 In. 70.00
Rocker, Tufted Leather Back & Seat, Steel & Brass, 19th Century 3300.00
Rocker, Twig, Red, White, & Blue Design, 1910 .... 125.00
Rocker, Victorian, Spider Caning, Natural 495.00
Rocker, Wicker, 1920s 125.00
Rocker, Wicker, Heywood-Wakefield, Barrel Type, c.1920 .... 300.00
Rocker, Wicker, Heywood-Wakefield, Natural Finish, 1870 .... 375.00
Rocker, Wicker, Victorian, Arms, c.1870 .... 176.00
Rocker, Windsor, Bamboo, Arms 450.00
Rocker, Windsor, Comb Back, Bamboo Turning, Arms, 38 In. 300.00
Rocker, Windsor, Comb Back, Bamboo, Green Repaint, 41 In. 125.00
Rocker, Windsor, Comb Back, Maple & Ash, c.1820, 42 1/2 In. 468.00
Rocker, Windsor, Country, Bamboo 125.00
Rocker, Zoar, Arrow-Back, Double Slats Above 850.00
Schrank, Baroque, Paneled Doors, Walnut, Germany, 1750s, 80 In. 6100.00
Screen, 2-Panel, Carved Dragon, Mother-of-Pearl, Lacquered 1000.00
Screen, 2-Panel, Flowers By Pavilion, Japan, 66 x 57 In. 1320.00
Screen, 3-Panel, Bead Design, Teak & Brass, 66 1/4 x 67 1/2 In. 220.00
Screen, 3-Panel, Bird's-Eye Maple, Austria, c.1900, 48 1/2 In. 550.00
Screen, 3-Panel, Fox Hunt Design, Painted Canvas 770.00
Screen, 3-Panel, Louis XVI Style, Giltwood, Needlepoint, 68 In. 1755.00
Screen, 3-Panel, Mahogany, Inlaid Ships, Art Nouveau, Italy, 63 In. 4675.00
Screen, 3-Panel, Pyrographic Scenes 6 Sides, c.1910 .... 700.00
Screen, 4 Panel, Silk Screened, Laquered, Piero Fornesetti, 54 In. 7040.00
Screen, 4-Panel, 4 Samurai Along River, Japan, 35 x 71 In. 1750.00
Screen, 4-Panel, Ebonized, Gilt, Botanical Prints, c.1880, 66 In. 885.00
Screen, 4-Panel, Ivory Figures, Lacquered Ground, 71 1/2 In. 115.00
Screen, 4-Panel, Neoclassical Design, Giltwood, 68 1/2 In. 1650.00
Screen, 4-Panel, Neoclassical Figures, Faux Marble, 80 In. 775.00
Screen, 4-Panel, Tapestry, Allegorical Figures, 73 In. 6750.00
Screen, 6-Panel, Birds Amid Flowering Trees, China, 72 In. 660.00
Screen, 6-Panel, Eames, U Shape, Plywood, 5 Ft. 8 In. x 5 Ft. 3300.00

Screen, 6–Panel, Peonies & Rushes On Gilt Ground, 68 x 24 In. 2200.00
Screen, 6–Panel, Semiprecious Stones, Oriental 785.00
Screen, 6–Panel, Village & Household Scenes, Japan, 55 x 22 In. 6600.00
Screen, 6–Panel, Zebras, Mythical Landscape, Olin Dows, 1930, 7 Ft. 7700.00
Screen, 8–Panel, Palace & Garden Scene, China, 96 x 160 In. 1100.00
Screen, Elephant Family, Jungle, J. Ernest Briely, 7 x 8 Ft. 2750.00
Screen, Folding, Hand Painted, Camile Roche, 5 Ft. 450.00
Screen, Pole, Embroidered Panel, Mahogany, c.1810, 57 1/4 In. 1875.00
Screen, Pole, Needlework Pictures, England, 1820, Pair 4000.00
Screen, Scrolling Flowers, Grapes, Adjustable, Iron, c.1925, 32 In. 1625.00
Secretaire Bookcase, Georgian, Mahogany, Case Over Chest, Inlaid 6600.00
Secretaire Bookcase, Hepplewhite, Mahogany, Inlaid, England 5500.00
Secretary Bookcase, Drawer, Mahogany Flame Veneer, Cherry, 81 In. 1000.00
Secretary Bookcase, Finials, Mullioned Doors, Mahogany, 94 In. 4625.00
Secretary Bookcase, Fruitwood Inlay, Mahogany, 79 In. 7700.00
Secretary Bookcase, Gothic Arch, Mullioned Doors, Satinwood 3975.00
Secretary Bookcase, Mahogany, Ormolu, Boston, c.1825, 59 In. 3300.00
Secretary Bookcase, Oak, Claw Feet, 2 Mirrors, Gallery 930.00
Secretary Bookcase, Oak, Glass, Mirror Top 700.00
Secretary Bookcase, Quartersawn Oak, Curved Glass, 2 Mirrors 1225.00
Secretary Bookcase, Side By Side, Slant Front, Mirror 675.00
Secretary Bookcase, Walnut, Curly Maple Interior, c.1860, 54 In. 715.00
Secretary Bookcase, Walnut, England, 18th Century 1870.00
Secretary Bookcase, Walnut, Slant Front, Burl Trim 900.00
Secretary Bookcase, Writing Surface, 3 Drawers, Mahogany, 77 In. 350.00
Secretary, Butler's, George III, Oak 8900.00
Secretary, Cherry, Figured Birch, Dovetailed, N.Y., 1840, 43 In. 1095.00
Secretary, Child's, Maple, Slant Front, Chair, 1900, 62 x 26 In. 985.00
Secretary, Chinoiserie Figures, Black Ground, Lacquered, 87 In. 1320.00
Secretary, Counter Top, Slant Front, Lift Top, Oak, 22 x 14 In. 55.00
Secretary, Cylinder, Victorian, Burl Walnut, c.1870, 85 In. 1650.00
Secretary, Drop Front, 2 Glass Doors Top, Egg & Dart Trim 1500.00
Secretary, Fall Front, Georgian, Chinoiserie, Mirror 6250.00
Secretary, Mahogany, 20th Century, 48 In. 275.00
Secretary, Mirrored Doors Over Fall Front, Marquetry, Holland 3850.00
Secretary, Oak, Amoeba–Shaped Mirror, Curved Glass, Claw Feet 600.00
Secretary, Roll Top, Chip Carved, Dog Finial 995.00
Secretary, Roll Top, Eastlake, Walnut, 1870s 4950.00
Secretary, Slant Front, 2 Doors, Walnut, 1930s 350.00
Secretary, Slant Front, Federal, Cherry, Blind Doors, 18th Century 6000.00
Secretary, Urn–Shaped Finials, Mahogany, 3 Parts, 82 1/2 In. 8250.00
Secretary, Walnut, 1860, 110 x 45 x 23 In. 4250.00
Secretary, Woman's, Federal, Mahogany, Top Doors, 39 x 19 x 61 In. 950.00
Server, Empire, Cherry, Flame Grained Walnut Veneer, Crest, 37 In. 425.00
Server, Gustav Stickley, No. 802, Signed With Red Mark 1650.00
Server, Lift Top, Zinc Lined Compartment, Rosewood, 44 1/2 In. 4950.00
Server, Mahogany, Ebonized, 3 Drawers, Paneled Doors, 36 1/2 In. 1870.00
Server, Regency, Mahogany, Ebonized Doors, 3 Drawers, 21 In. 1870.00
Settee, Art Nouveau, Pierced Back Rail, Carved Arms, c.1900 .... 1320.00
Settee, Butterfly Style, c.1850, 5 Ft. 3 In. 4500.00
Settee, Camelback, Acanthus Carved Apron, Mahogany, 90 In. 1430.00
Settee, Child's, Green, Yellow Pinstriping, Pink Roses, 17 1/2 In. 1430.00
Settee, Child's, Victorian, Carved, Blue Velvet Upholstery 485.00
Settee, Child's, Wicker, Arched Bow Back, 40 In. 145.00
Settee, Chippendale Style, Mahogany, Scrolled, Carved, 40 1/2 In. 1100.00
Settee, Chippendale, Camelback, 50 In. 175.00
Settee, Claw Feet, Mahogany, Eagle's Head Arms, 66 In. 1350.00
Settee, Continental, Marquetry, Double Chair Back, 1800s, 44 In. 1875.00
Settee, Double Chair Back, Medallions, Painted Satinwood, 36 In. 2650.00
Settee, Empire Style, Serpentine Crest, Mahogany, U.S., 68 In. 615.00
Settee, Empire, Carved Mahogany, c.1880, 84 In. 1100.00
Settee, Empire, Rolled Arms, Claw Footed, U.S., 59 In. ....*Illus* 1210.00
Settee, French Provincial, Double Chair Back, Fruitwood, 49 In. 465.00

Settee, George II Style, Needlepoint Upholstery, 54 In.	1650.00
Settee, Hand Stenciled, 8 Legs, Green, 46 In.	1600.00
Settee, Hepplewhite, Camelback, Mahogany, 20th Century, 72 In.	462.00
Settee, Heywood Bros. –Wakefield, Balloon Back, c.1900, 49 In.	900.00
Settee, Josef Hoffmann, Bentwood, Austria	2000.00
Settee, L. & J. G. Stickley, Mission, Oak, Slat Back	3000.00
Settee, Laminated Rosewood, Serpentine Floral Crest Rail	4400.00
Settee, Louis Phillipe Style, Mahogany, Out–Turned Arms, 60 In.	300.00
Settee, Louis XV, Floral Crest, Walnut, Open Arms, 64 In.	1875.00
Settee, Louis XVI Style, Carved Frame, Velvet Upholstery, 56 In.	2150.00
Settee, Louis XVI Style, Rosette & Scroll Crest, Walnut, 60 In.	445.00
Settee, Mahogany, Claw Feet, Tapestry Weave Upholstery, 59 In.	400.00
Settee, Majorelle, Mahogany, Algues Pattern, Upholstered, 54 In.	7750.00
Settee, Meeks, Rosewood, Pierced Crest, Pink Tufted Upholstery	5750.00
Settee, Mermaids On Back Splat, Mahogany, Dolphins On Arms	900.00
Settee, Molded Frame, Serpentine Rails, Velvet Upholstery, 58 In.	665.00
Settee, Pennsylvania Dutch, Wide Seat, Long	750.00
Settee, Queen Anne, Frelish Tapestry Of Birds, Fruit, 77 In.	5000.00
Settee, Queen Anne, Tapesty Cover, Rosewood, 19th Century, 77 In.	5500.00
Settee, Regency, Mahogany, Arched Back, Rolled Arms, 82 In.	1650.00
Settee, Rocker, Arrow–Back, Painted, 32 In.	8250.00
Settee, Rococo Revival, Medallion Back, Carved Walnut, U.S., 1855	615.00
Settee, Rosewood, Serpentine Carved, Ivory Inlay, Austria, 1800s	550.00
Settee, Scrolled Crest, Saber Legs, Scrolled Arms, 78 In.	2640.00
Settee, Serpentine Rail, Ash, Upholstered Back, Russia, 4 Ft. 7 In.	3200.00
Settee, Sheraton, 3 Chair Back, White Canvas Cushion, 1810	3475.00
Settee, Spinkle, G. Nakashima, Walnut, Rectangular Back, Pair	2750.00
Settee, Victorian, c.1870 ....*Illus*	800.00
Settee, Walnut Frame, 3 Section Back, Tufted Upholstery	850.00
Settee, Windsor, 31 Bamboo Turned Spindles, c.1810, 6 Ft. 5 In.	5500.00
Settee, Windsor, Bow Back, Plank Seat, Pine, 54 In.	775.00

Furniture, Settee, Empire, Rolled Arms,
Claw Footed, U.S., 59 In.

• •

If the veneer on old furniture is just loose, make a small slit in the wood with the grain of the wood. Use this as a way to apply the glue under the veneer. If the veneer is bubbled up and loose, place a piece of cardboard on the wood and press with an iron set at medium heat. The heat should soften the glue and you will be able to feel the wood give a little. Press down and weight the spot until the glue has redried.

• •

Furniture, Settee, Victorian, c.1870

Settee, Windsor, Continuous Arm, Philadelphia 2975.00
Settee, Windsor, Oak Arms 1600.00
Settee, Windsor, Painted, Philadelphia, c.1790 .... 2975.00
Settee, Windsor, Sheraton, Old Dark Paint, c.1800, 6 Ft. 3100.00
Settee, Wire, 4 Ft. 5 1/2 In. 885.00
Settle, Arts & Crafts, Low Arm, Slant Back, Oak, 67 In. 880.00
Settle, Galle, Mahogany, Inlay, Openwork Braces, 40 x 15 In. 5675.00
Settle, Gustav Stickley, No. 208, Oak, 29 x 76 x 32 In. ....*Illus* 4400.00
Settle, Gustav Stickley, No. 225, 5 Ft. 8 In. .... 4400.00 To 4750.00
Settle, Half Arrow Spindles, Scrolled Arms, 82 In. 550.00
Settle, Half Spindle Back, Brown Grain Over White, Arms, 81 In. 900.00
Settle, Limbert, Uneven Arm, Oak, 76 In. 1100.00
Settle, Stickley Bros., Flowers Inlay, Leaves, c.1901, 51 3/4 In. 3300.00
Settle, Unsnaps To Become Bed, Panel Back, Red Paint 330.00
Settle, Windsor, Bamboo, Plank Seat, Maple Medallions, 76 In. 550.00
Shaving Stand, Mirror, Cabinet Base, Adjustable, Oak, 5 Ft. 7 In. 440.00
Shelf, 3 Tier Step, Green Paint, Wire, 21 In. 190.00
Shelf, Hanging, 1 Drawer, Towel Rail, Walnut, 8 1/2 x 14 1/2 In. 125.00
Shelf, Hanging, 2 Candle Sockets, Pine Cutouts, Country, 18 In. 325.00
Shelf, Hanging, 2 Shelves, Pine, Scalloped Ends, 23 3/4 In. 225.00
Shelf, Hanging, 3 Shelves, Hardwood, Red Stain, 23 1/4 In. 200.00
Shelf, Hanging, 3 Shelves, Pine, Yellow Paint, 29 In. 125.00
Shelf, Hanging, 4 Shelves, Original Graining, 39 In. 850.00
Shelf, Hanging, 4 Shelves, Poplar, Scalloped Ends & Crest, 30 In. 400.00
Shelf, Hanging, Bracket, Gilt Brass Frame, Marble Top, 26 In. 210.00
Shelf, Hanging, Poplar & Pine, Old Dark Finish, 10 1/2 x 19 In. 25.00
Shelf, Hanging, Poplar, Truncated Sides, Molded Front, 26 In. 1100.00
Shelf, Hanging, Primitive, Pine, Dark Finish, 19 1/4 In. 130.00
Shelf, Hanging, Soft Wood, Red, Molded Edges, Curved Ends, 28 In. 800.00
Shelf, Hanging, Twisted Shell Stem, Gilt, c.1800, 9 x 11 In. 750.00
Shelf, Pine, Dovetailed Drawer, Red Paint, 6 3/8 x 24 x 13 In. 1100.00
Shelf, Plank Ends, 4 Shelves, Exposed Tenons, 36 x 26 1/8 In. 110.00
Shelf, Whatnot, 4 Shelves Over Drawer, 1820, 22 x 15 x 60 In. 3500.00
Sideboard, Art Deco, Ivory Inlay, Burl Walnut, 36 x 82 In. 3190.00
Sideboard, Beveled Mirror, Flower Form Inlay, c.1885, 108 In. 5000.00
Sideboard, Bowfront, Cellarette Drawer, Mahogany, Inlay, 59 In. 5500.00
Sideboard, Carved Teakwood, China 3000.00
Sideboard, Center Doors, 1 Drawer, Mahogany, France, c.1910, 65 In. 6600.00
Sideboard, Charles Rohles, Cabinet Doors, Drawers, Oak, 1900, 5 Ft. 1650.00
Sideboard, Claw Foot, Carved Double Lion Crest, Oak, 85 In. 2100.00
Sideboard, Convex Doors, Concave Drawer, Mahogany, c.1805, 67 In. 5500.00
Sideboard, Demilune Top, Cellaret Drawer, Mahogany, 84 In. 6000.00
Sideboard, Drop Center, Mahogany, Delaware Valley, c.1825, 67 In. 1325.00
Sideboard, Empire, Carved Claw Feet, Flame Mahogany, 61 1/2 In. 700.00
Sideboard, Empire, Mahogany, Anthony Quervelle, c.1820, 92 In. 4500.00
Sideboard, Federal, Mahogany Veneer, 3 Drawers, Inlay, 42 In. 8800.00
Sideboard, Federal, Mahogany, Bottle Drawer, 1790s, 68 3/4 In. 2650.00
Sideboard, George III, Mahogany, Spade Feet, 53 In. ....*Illus* 3520.00
Sideboard, Gustav Stickley, No. 814, Oak, Original Label 2860.00
Sideboard, Hepplewhite, Inlay, Spade Feet, Mahogany 7975.00
Sideboard, Hepplewhite, Line Inlay, Crotch Mahogany Veneer 4950.00
Sideboard, Hepplewhite, Mahogany, Figured Inlay, 34 3/4 In. 1100.00
Sideboard, Hepplewhite, Mahogany, Inlay, 20th Century, 36 1/4 In. 350.00
Sideboard, Hepplewhite, Mahogany, Spade Feet, England, 35 In. 2000.00
Sideboard, Hepplewhite, Satinwood, Inlay, England, 29 3/4 In. 850.00
Sideboard, Hepplewhite, Serpentine, Mahogany, Inlay, 4 Door, 62 In. 3500.00
Sideboard, Hepplewhite, Walnut, Cross Band Inlay, 1920s, 37 In. 105.00
Sideboard, Horizontal Match Stick Molded Panels, Mahogany 1750.00
Sideboard, L. & J. G. Stickley, No. 734, c.1912, 44 1/2 In. 2090.00
Sideboard, Oak, High Mirror Back, 2 Half & 2 Lower Drawers 350.00
Sideboard, Satinwood Inlay, Spade Feet, Mahogany, c.1790, 62 In. 2200.00
Sideboard, Scalloped Apron & Doors, Walnut & Poplar, 55 1/2 In. 575.00
Sideboard, Serpentine Double Doors, Gallery, Mahogany 4400.00

Furniture, Settle, Gustav Stickley, No. 208,
Oak, 29 x 76 x 32 In.

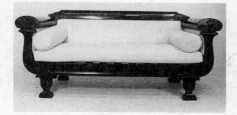

Furniture, Sofa, Biedermeier, Mahogany,
White Upholstery, 60 In.

◆◆◆◆◆◆◆◆◆◆◆◆◆◆◆◆◆◆◆◆

Collectors in a warm, humid climate like Hawaii have special problems. If you collect metal, leather, wool, or textiles, beware. Store pieces in an airtight container or in a place with good air circulation, like a half–filled closet. Keep textiles clean and dry. Best method: after washing, dry in the sun. Use moth balls or cedar closets for textiles. Don't store items in wooden boxes that are kept on the ground; insects may burrow from below. Metal will rust if not kept away from salt air and humidity. Storage in a plastic bag is usually acceptable.

◆◆◆◆◆◆◆◆◆◆◆◆◆◆◆◆◆◆◆◆

Sideboard, Shaped Facade, Mahogany, Inlay, New England, 66 1/4 In. 1650.00
Sideboard, Tiger Maple, 2 Wine Bottle Drawers, Brass Eagle, 1780 .... 7450.00
Sideboard, Victorian, Oak, Mirror, Claw Feet, Crystal Pulls, 5 Ft. 575.00
Sideboard, Walnut & Marquetry, Stepped & Carved, Gillows 2400.00
Sofa, Adams, Brass Castors, Apotheosis Of Franklin Cover, 78 In. 750.00
Sofa, Ash & Poplar, Turned Feet, Spindle Back, Country, 74 In. 175.00
Sofa, Belter, Grapes, Laminated, Rosewood 6325.00
Sofa, Biedermeier, Mahogany, White Upholstery, 60 In. ....*Illus* 1320.00
Sofa, Camelback, Caned Seat & Sides, Tiger Maple, c.1840, 7 Ft. 4600.00
Sofa, Camelback, Chippendale Style, 6 Ft. 385.00
Sofa, Camelback, Mahogany, White Linen Upholstery, 73 5/8 In. 1210.00
Sofa, Carved Frame, Blue & White Upholstery, 1920s, 85 In. 500.00
Sofa, Carved Wooden Frame, Brocade Upholstery, 1930s, 85 In. 230.00
Sofa, Chippendale Style, Hickory, Damask Upholstery, 89 In. 825.00
Sofa, Crest Rail, Down Cushion, Reeded Arms, 72 In. 610.00
Sofa, Empire, Carved Crest, Paw Feet, Flaring Arms 1225.00
Sofa, Federal, Bowed Upholstered Seat, Fluted Arms, c.1805, 6 Ft. 9900.00
Sofa, Federal, Mahogany, New England, c.1810, 33 x 80 x 24 In. 775.00
Sofa, Federal, Mahogany, Turned Reeded Arms & Legs, 74 In. 1765.00
Sofa, Federal, Ribbed Bun Feet, Brass Bead Trim, Upholstered Arms 1250.00
Sofa, Hans Wegner, Open Back, Loose Cushions, Walnut, 7 Ft. 8 In. 995.00
Sofa, Louis XVI, Painted, Molded Backrest, P. Remy, 1750, Pair 3850.00
Sofa, Mahogany & Maple Veneer, c.1815, 36 x 80 x 21 1/2 In. 1985.00
Sofa, Mahogany Veneer, Green Velvet Upholstery, c.1830, 72 In. 2860.00
Sofa, Olive Green Paint, Country, 30 x 73 1/2 x 32 1/4 In. 1875.00
Sofa, Rail Back, Horsehead Grips, Loose Cushions, Oak 170.00
Sofa, Rococo Revival, Rosewood 550.00
Sofa, Sheraton Style, c.1940, 72 In. 715.00
Sofa, Sheraton, Acanthus Arm Posts, Mahogany Frame, 85 3/4 In. 6000.00
Sofa, Sheraton, Curly Maple Frame, Floral Brocade, 72 1/2 In. 3500.00
Sofa, Sheraton, Mahogany Frame, Turned Legs, Country, 72 In. 2400.00

Furniture, Sideboard, George III, Mahogany,
Spade Feet, 53 In.

Furniture, Stand, 1 Drawer, Grain Painted,
New England, 1830

Sofa, Sheraton, Reeded Arms & Post, 73 In.	2200.00
Sofa, Triple Arched Back, Carved Crest Rail, 63 In.	415.00
Sofa, Triple Back, Carved Rosewood Frame	6325.00
Sofa, Walnut, Overall Foliate & Acorn Carved Design, 84 In.	1100.00
Stand, 1 Drawer, 1 Board Top, Cherry, 29 In.	350.00
Stand, 1 Drawer, 1 Board Top, Cherry, Country, 28 1/4 In.	250.00
Stand, 1 Drawer, 1 Board Top, Hepplewhite, Cherry, Inlay, 19 In.	325.00
Stand, 1 Drawer, 2 Board Top, Maple, Country, 28 1/2 In.	400.00
Stand, 1 Drawer, 2 Board Top, Shaker, Refinished	3400.00
Stand, 1 Drawer, Cabriole Legs, Hoof Feet, 19th Century	1300.00
Stand, 1 Drawer, Curly Maple, Applied Edge Beading, 26 3/4 In.	750.00
Stand, 1 Drawer, Curly Maple, Hepplewhite, Cherry, Country, 27 In.	3100.00
Stand, 1 Drawer, Dovetailed, Cherry, Turned Legs, Country, 5 In.	300.00
Stand, 1 Drawer, Drop Leaf, Cherry, Maple, Turned Legs, 27 In.	350.00
Stand, 1 Drawer, Drop Leaf, Tapered Rope Legs, Mahogany	850.00
Stand, 1 Drawer, Federal, Cherry, Turned Legs, Country, 27 1/2 In.	503.00
Stand, 1 Drawer, Federal, Tiger Maple, Turned Legs, Country, 17 In.	495.00
Stand, 1 Drawer, Grain Painted, New England, 1830 ....*Illus*	550.00
Stand, 1 Drawer, Hepplewhite, Birch, Red Stain, Square Legs, 1840	325.00
Stand, 1 Drawer, Hepplewhite, Curly Maple, Red Finish, 17 x 18 In.	1000.00
Stand, 1 Drawer, Hepplewhite, Dovetailed, Cherry, Dark, 28 In.	1000.00
Stand, 1 Drawer, Tiger Maple, Original Sandwich Glass Pulls, 1835	1650.00
Stand, 1 Drawer, Walnut, Curly Maple, Dovetailed, 28 In.	275.00
Stand, 2 Drawers, 1 Board Top, Drop Leaf, Walnut, 29 3/4 In.	450.00
Stand, 2 Drawers, 2 Board Top, Hepplewhite, Cherry, 27 3/4 In.	350.00
Stand, 2 Drawers, Bird's–Eye Maple Drawer Fronts	880.00
Stand, 2 Drawers, Cherry & Tiger Maple, 19th Century ....*Illus*	440.00
Stand, 2 Drawers, Cherry, Bird's–Eye	475.00
Stand, 2 Drawers, Cock–Beaded Top, Brass Pulls, Cherry, 28 1/2 In.	475.00
Stand, 2 Drawers, Dovetailed, Drop Leaf, Curly Maple, Turned Legs	1200.00
Stand, 2 Drawers, Drop Leaf, Poplar, Walnut, Country, 27 In.	225.00
Stand, 2 Drawers, Drop Leaf, Tiger Maple, Sandwich Glass Pulls	1450.00
Stand, 2 Drawers, Empire, Drop Leaf, Pedestal, Mahogany, 28 1/2 In.	160.00
Stand, 2 Drawers, Rope Carved Legs, Mahogany Veneer, 28 In.	575.00
Stand, 2 Drawers, Shaker, Butternut, New Lebanon	7425.00
Stand, 2 Drawers, Sheraton, Cookie Corners, Fluted Legs, 1805	1265.00
Stand, 2 Drawers, Sheraton, Drop Leaf, Dovetailed, Country, 29 In.	375.00
Stand, 2 Drawers, Sheraton, Mahogany, Ring Turned Posts, 28 In.	350.00
Stand, Bedside, Birch, Cherry, Dovetailed Drawers, Country, 13 In.	375.00
Stand, Blind Drawer, Ocher & Umber Graining, c.1830s	2090.00
Stand, Book, Desk Top, Rosewood, 30 Turned Spindles, 19th Century	500.00
Stand, Book, Desk Top, Spindle Gallery, Rosewood, 5 3/4 x 16 In.	995.00
Stand, Book, Galleried Top, Pullout Slides, 2 Shelves, Oak, 44 In.	935.00
Stand, Candle, 3 Turned Spindle Legs, Round Top, 15 x 26 In.	175.00
Stand, Candle, Adjustable Hog Scraper, Weighted Base, 24 1/2 In.	795.00
Stand, Candle, Cherry, Maple, Pine Top, 16 3/4 x 27 3/4 In.	350.00
Stand, Candle, Cherry, Spider Legs, Turned Column, Rectangular Top	425.00

Stand, Candle, Chippendale, Cherry, Tripod, Square Top, Gallery 625.00
Stand, Candle, Chippendale, Maple, 1 Board Top, 26 In. 500.00
Stand, Candle, Poplar, Hardwood, Rectangular Top, Red Traces 275.00
Stand, Candle, Wooden, Iron Socket, Old Red Traces, 31 1/2 In. 285.00
Stand, Carved Teak, Soapstone Insert, China, 35 1/2 In. 200.00
Stand, Chippendale, Mahogany, Pullout Step, 2 Doors, 30 In. 1300.00
Stand, Corner, 4 Tiers, Painted Floral Design, 68 In. 255.00
Stand, Corner, Marble Top, Marquetry Floral Inlay, 1910s, 42 In. 2200.00
Stand, Crock, 3 Tiers, Green, 25 3/4 In. 250.00
Stand, Crock, 5 Curved Tiers, Removable Legs, Green, 52 x 55 In. 200.00
Stand, Crock, Pine, Dark Finish, Scalloped Frame, 34 x 38 In. 295.00
Stand, Curio, Corner, 5 Tiers, Walnut, Scroll Cut Galleries 125.00
Stand, Drop Leaf, Cherry, Dovetailed Drawers, Country, 29 In. 1000.00
Stand, Empire, Curly Maple, Tripod, Scrolled Legs, 1 Board Top 450.00
Stand, Empire, Mahogany, Pedestal, Drop Leaf, 9–In. Leaves, 28 In. 90.00
Stand, Fern, Brass & Onyx 190.00
Stand, Fern, Gray Marble Top, Burled 250.00
Stand, Figured Maple, Chamfered Fronts On Drawers 1700.00
Stand, Flowerpot, 6 Branches, Cast Metal 150.00
Stand, Hepplewhite, Cherry, Tapered Legs, 1 Board Top, 28 In. 195.00
Stand, Hepplewhite, Country, Walnut, 1 Board Top, 25 In. 275.00
Stand, Hepplewhite, Mahogany, Inlay, 31 In. 145.00
Stand, Limbert, No. 214, Trapezoidal Cutouts, 2 Shelves, 34 In. 1200.00
Stand, Louis XV, Floral Marquetry, Ormolu Trim, Marble Top, 31 In. 400.00
Stand, Magazine, 3 Sections, Coil Feet, Wrought Iron, c.1925 .... 1100.00
Stand, Magazine, 5 Shelves, Label, Derby. . . Boston, Oak, c.1915 .... 137.50
Stand, Magazine, Chippendale, 16 x 12 x 19 In. 95.00
Stand, Magazine, Gustav Stickley, 4 Shelves, 44 1/2 In. 2090.00
Stand, Magazine, Push Through Drawer, Rosewood, 27 1/2 In. 1210.00
Stand, Mahogany, Brass Trim, 31 In. 400.00
Stand, Mahogany, Inset Leather Top, 2 Shelves, 26 In. 300.00
Stand, Maple, New England, c.1800, 28 In. 715.00
Stand, Muffin, 3 Tiers, Incised Mahogany, c.1900 .... 198.00
Stand, Muffin, Heywood–Wakefield, Wicker, Natural Finish 199.00
Stand, Music, Adjustable Candleholders, Mahogany, 50 In. 2850.00
Stand, Music, Arts & Crafts, 4 Shelves, 39 In. ....*Illus* 1100.00
Stand, Music, Bird's–Eye Maple & Mahogany, c.1825 .... 2970.00
Stand, Music, Eastlake, Double Easel, Walnut 795.00
Stand, Music, Galle, Marquetry, Inlay, Signed, 1900, 34 1/2 In. 885.00
Stand, Music, Gustav Stickley, No. 670, 4 Shelves, c.1907, 39 In. 1100.00
Stand, Music, Victorian, Mahogany, 41 x 20 In. 187.00
Stand, Napoleon III, Brass Mounted, Rosewood, c.1860, 30 1/2 In. 968.00
Stand, Oval Top, Conforming Shelf, Painted Red, Zoar, Ohio, c.1825 .... 885.00
Stand, Plant, 2 Shelves, Wire, 34 In. 880.00
Stand, Plant, 3 Graduated Shelves, Wire, 49 1/2 In. 1100.00
Stand, Plant, 3 Graduated Shelves, Wire, 7 Ft. 6 In. 2750.00
Stand, Plant, 3 Shelves, Continental, Ormolu, Inlay, 30 1/2 In. 335.00
Stand, Plant, 3 Shelves, Wirework, Demilune, 40 x 43 In. 315.00
Stand, Plant, 6 Pierced Circular Tiered Trays, White, Iron, 39 In. 2975.00
Stand, Plant, Arts & Crafts, Pedestal Shaft, Oak, 36 x 12 In. 110.00
Stand, Plant, Majorelle, Fruitwood, Triangular Top, c.1900, 52 In. 2750.00
Stand, Plant, Victorian, Wire, 6 x 7 Ft. 300.00
Stand, Poplar, Turned Legs, Drawer, Red Paint, J. A. Schultz, 29 In. 150.00
Stand, Quilt, Walnut 175.00
Stand, Rosewood, Rectangular, Carved Frieze, Spade Feet, 34 In. 200.00
Stand, Sewing, 2 Drawers, Drop Leaf, Flame Birch, 28 In. 750.00
Stand, Sewing, Half–Round Bag, Drops, Rosewood 5225.00
Stand, Sewing, Lift Top, Mirrored Back, Fitted, Burled Walnut 800.00
Stand, Sewing, Mirrored Lift Top, Fitted, Burled Walnut, 29 In. 880.00
Stand, Sewing, Shaker, Pine & Butternut, South Family, New Lebanon 7425.00
Stand, Shaving, George III Style, Gallery, Marble Top, 38 In. 198.00
Stand, Shaving, Victorian, Walnut, Swing Mirror, Marble Shelf 1100.00
Stand, Sheraton, Bird's–Eye Veneer Fronts, Poplar, 28 3/4 In. 6800.00

Stand, Sheraton, Cherry, Turned Legs, Walnut Inlay, Country, 29 In.	275.00
Stand, Sink, Brass, 18th Century	725.00
Stand, Smoking, Copper Lined, Walnut	75.00
Stand, Tea, 3 Shelves, Mahogany, 34 In.	100.00
Stand, Teak, Cloisonne Inserts In Top, China, 20 In., Pair	550.00
Stand, Teak, Rouge Marble Top, Oriental, 19th Century, 18 In.	335.00
Stand, Teak, Rouge Marble Top, Oriental, 19th Century, 20 In.	615.00
Stand, Teak, Soapstone Insert, China, 24 In.	230.00
Stand, Telephone, 1 Drawer, Cherry, Poplar, Dovetailed, 36 In.	245.00
Stand, Triangular Base, Paw Feet, Rosewood, England, 19th Century	1350.00
Stand, Umbrella, Arts & Crafts, Oak, 29 1/2 In.	100.00
Stand, Umbrella, Edgar Brandt, Ball Knobs, Spiral Panels, c.1925	3300.00
Stand, Umbrella, Floral Scrolls, China, 19th Century, 24 In.	247.50
Stand, Umbrella, Pictorial, Civil War Leaders, Walnut	445.00
Stand, Urn, George III, Oval Top Over Slide, Mahogany, 26 1/4 In.	495.00
Stand, Urn, Marble Top, Mahogany Drum, Bronze Mounts, 50 In.	2850.00
Stand, Wash Bowl, Tripod, Mahogany, Fluted Urn Column, 14 1/2 In.	550.00
Stand, Wash, Regency, Mahogany, 2 Drawers, Lower Shelf, 32 In.	885.00
Stand, Wig, 2 Middle Section Drawers, Mahogany, 35 In., Pair	2100.00
Stand, Wig, George III, Mahogany, 2 Drawers, 35 In., Pr.	2090.00
Stand, Wig, Queen Anne, Washbowl Holder, Mahogany, Tripod, 31 In.	700.00
Stand, Work, Mahogany, Adjustable Writing Board, c.1825 ....*Illus*	935.00
Stand, Yellow Pine, Poplar, Country, 27 x 18 x 31 In.	600.00
Steps, Sewing, Canterbury, Arched Side Supports, 9 5/8 In.	310.00
Stool, Baroque, Walnut, Bun Feet, Upholstered Seat, 1820s, Pair	6600.00
Stool, Beechwood, Oval Upholstered Seat, 16 1/2 In., Pair	660.00
Stool, Carved Apron, Leaf-Carved Knees, Walnut	2200.00
Stool, Empire, Painted, Carved Bellflowers, 1830s, Pair	5500.00
Stool, George II Style, Oval, Mahogany & Parcel Gilt, 17 x 23 In.	495.00
Stool, George III Style, Printed Velvet Upholstery, Mahogany	1875.00
Stool, Gout, Ratchet Adjustable, Velvet Cushion, Walnut, 20 In.	175.00
Stool, Handmade, Pine, 13 1/2 x 23 3/4 In.	85.00
Stool, Ice Cream, Back	90.00
Stool, Joint, Pine, Old Red Traces, 13 x 18 x 16 In.	200.00
Stool, Piano, Openwork Splat	1100.00
Stool, Piano, Rosette Plaque & Dolphins, Paw Feet, 1820s, 24 In.	2200.00
Stool, Piano, Thonet, Caned Seat, Paper Label	110.00
Stool, Piano, Turned Legs, Glass Ball Feet	95.00
Stool, Piano, Upholstery, Adjustable Seat, Mahogany, 1820s	735.00
Stool, Queen Anne, Carved Knees, Trifid Feet, c.1760	5500.00
Stool, Shoeshine, Attached Footrest, Wire	32.50
Stool, Soda Fountain, Wicker, Porcelain Base	100.00
Stool, Spool Legs, Needlepoint Upholstery, Eagle, 20 x 17 In.	225.00
Stool, Utility, Shaker, Basketweave Splint Seat, New Lebanon	715.00
Stool, Walnut, Scrolled Legs, Upholstered Seat, 26 1/2 In.	2750.00
Stool, Windsor, Bare Top, Worn Paint, 13 x 17 1/4 In.	75.00
Swing, Wicker, Chains, Magazine Racks On Ends, c.1900, 86 In.	450.00

Furniture, Stand, 2 Drawers,
Cherry & Tiger Maple,
19th Century

Furniture, Stand, Music, Arts
& Crafts, 4 Shelves, 39 In.

Furniture, Stand, Work,
Mahogany, Adjustable Writing
Board, c.1825

Table, 1 Drawer, Birch, Butternut, 2 Board Top, Refinished, 30 In. 300.00
Table, 1 Drawer, Drop Leaf, Birch, Country, 29 3/4 x 43 1/2 In. 450.00
Table, 2 Drawers, Mushroom Knobs, Walnut & Cherry, 1820s 2800.00
Table, 2 Drawers, Spool Turned Legs, Walnut, 29 1/2 In. 400.00
Table, 2 Tiers, Parquetry, Late 19th Century, France, 34 In. 410.00
Table, 3 Pine Board Top, Drawer, Country, 19th Century 500.00
Table, 3 Tiers, Cast Iron, White, 29 3/4 In. 250.00
Table, 4 Drawers Each Side, Rosewood & Walnut, 81 In. 9350.00
Table, Accounting, Frank Lloyd Wright, Oak, c.1905, 5 Ft. 9 In. 4300.00
Table, Art Deco, Marble Top, Polished Iron, France, 33 x 43 In. 2300.00
Table, Baker's, Figured Marble Top, France, c.1850 .... 2860.00
Table, Baker's, Marble, Cast Iron, France, c.1840, 41 In. ....*Illus* 2860.00
Table, Baker's, Scrubbed Lift Top, 69 In. 985.00
Table, Balluster Support, Tripod On Casters, Papier–Mache 335.00
Table, Banquet, Federal, Drop Leaf, Spool Legs, Cherry, 48 In. 715.00
Table, Banquet, Hepplewhite, D End, Cherry, Inlay, 82 In. 3500.00
Table, Banquet, Inlay, Drop Leaf, Swing Leg, Cherry, 44 In., Pair 1800.00
Table, Banquet, Louis XVI Style, Burl Walnut, 2 Leaves, 12 1/2 Ft. 775.00
Table, Banquet, Mahogany, 3 Leaves, England, 29 In., Pair 925.00
Table, Banquet, Sheraton, Cherry, Drop Leaf, Extends To 82 In. 4000.00
Table, Banquet, Sheraton, Mahogany, 3 Parts, U.S., c.1825, 103 In. 3450.00
Table, Basket Of Flowers On Stretcher, Rosewood, 46 In. 7150.00
Table, Beadwork Top, Blue, Pink, Floral, Wrought Iron, 19 1/2 In. 165.00
Table, Bedside, Walnut, Curved Back & Sideboards Rim Top 305.00
Table, Biedermeier, Medallion Inlay, Ebonized Fruitwood 1050.00
Table, Blackjack, Claw Foot 2300.00
Table, Breakfast, Drop Leaf, Claw & Ball Feet, Mahogany, 31 In. 6100.00
Table, Breakfast, Drop Leaf, Turned Pedestal, Mahogany, 30 In. 825.00
Table, Breakfast, Mahogany, Tripod Base, 30 3/4 In. 1250.00
Table, Breakfast, Queen Anne, Mahogany, Snake Feet 7700.00
Table, Breakfast, Tilt Top, Paneled Pedestal, Cherry, 54 In. 550.00
Table, Breakfast, Victorian, Tilt Top, Cherry, 54 In. 550.00
Table, Breuer, Black Enamel Top, Chrome Tube Legs, 18 x 19 In. 165.00
Table, Buckley & Bancroft, Marble Top, Grape Carving, 40 In. 4125.00
Table, Butler's, Kittinger, Tray Top, Fold Up Sides, 38 x 28 In. 425.00
Table, Butler's, Oval Hinged Sides, Mahogany, 40 x 31 In. 88.00
Table, Cabriole Legs, Hardwood, Japan, 13 x 46 In. 495.00
Table, Cameo, Carved Woman & Warrior In Top, 22 In. Diam. 700.00
Table, Campaign, Civil War, Folding 600.00
Table, Card, Apron, Exotic Wood Veneer, Inlay, Folding Top, 28 In. 450.00
Table, Card, Brass Stringing, Inlay, Mahogany & Rosewood 5500.00
Table, Card, Carved Mahogany, New England, 19th Century, 30 In. 475.00
Table, Card, Chippendale, Swing Leg, Mahogany, 28 x 33 In., Pair 1800.00
Table, Card, Cookie Corners, Broken Arrow Inlay, Mahogany 3575.00
Table, Card, Curly Maple, Walnut, 4 Folding Chairs, 29 x 29 In. 450.00
Table, Card, Demilune, Inlay 400.00
Table, Card, Ellipse & Half Moon Inlay, Mahogany 6875.00
Table, Card, Federal, Acanthus Carved Legs, Swing Top, Mahogany 3750.00
Table, Card, Federal, Bellflower Inlay, Mahogany, c.1795 .... 2650.00
Table, Card, Federal, Birch Veneer Inlay, Birch 4125.00
Table, Card, Federal, Bowed Top, Flame Birch Veneer, 36 1/2 In. 3100.00
Table, Card, Federal, Cherry, c.1790, 29 x 36 x 17 1/2 In. 1100.00
Table, Card, Federal, Inlay, Elisha Tucker, c.1810 .... 8800.00
Table, Card, Federal, Inlay, Mahogany, c.1790, 28 x 36 In. 2750.00
Table, Card, Federal, Mahogany & Birch Veneer, c.1800 .... 7700.00
Table, Card, Federal, Mahogany, Demilune, Folds, 18th Century 1050.00
Table, Card, Federal, Mahogany, Flame Birch Veneer, 29 1/2 In. 995.00
Table, Card, Federal, Mahogany, Inlay, New England, 29 In. 1450.00
Table, Card, Federal, Maple, Rope Legs, Serpentine Apron, 35 In. 775.00
Table, Card, Federal, Outset Corners, Mahogany, 1790s, 38 In. 2425.00
Table, Card, Geometric, Satinwood Inlay 3300.00
Table, Card, Grained Tiger Maple Top, Bird's–Eye Maple Sides 4950.00
Table, Card, Hepplewhite, Mahogany, Inlay, 29 In. 250.00

Furniture, Table, Baker's, Marble, Cast Iron,
France, c.1840, 41 In.

Furniture, Table, Carved, c.1800, 29 3/4 In.

Furniture, Table, Center,
William & Mary, Maple, Pine,
28 x 37 In.

Furniture, Table, Dressing,
William & Mary, Walnut,
1710-1750

Furniture, Table, Tavern,
Turned Maple,
25 x 40 x 27 3/4 In.

Table, Card, Lyre Pedestal, Brass Feet, Mahogany, 29 3/4 In.	550.00
Table, Card, Mahogany & Bird's-Eye Maple, New Hampshire, 1810	6800.00
Table, Card, Mahogany, Birch Veneer, 29 x 36 x 17 In.	775.00
Table, Card, Mahogany, Maple Veneer, 30 1/4 x 36 x 17 In.	2850.00
Table, Card, Mahogany, New England, c.1825, 29 1/2 x 36 x 17 In.	525.50
Table, Card, Sheraton, Folding Top, Mahogany, 31 In.	175.00
Table, Card, Sheraton, Mahogany, Shaped Top, Bulbous Feet, 1800	6500.00
Table, Card, Sheraton, Serpentine Hinged Top, Mahogany, 28 In.	1100.00
Table, Card, Swing Legs, Marquetry, Holland, 29 x 32 1/4 In.	2550.00
Table, Card, Swing Top, Mahogany, Pedestal Base, 28 1/2 In.	450.00
Table, Card, Triangular Hinged Top, Marquetry, Holland, 40 1/4 In.	1650.00
Table, Carved, c.1800, 29 3/4 In. ....*Illus*	1100.00
Table, Center Bagpipes & Flowers, Marquetry, c.1880, 45 x 33 In.	2750.00
Table, Center, Biedermeier, Long Drawer, Fruitwood, 62 In.	1435.00
Table, Center, Cararra Marble Top, Walnut, 1870s	2975.00

Furniture, Table, Center, Renaissance
Revival, Marble, c.1875

◆◆◆◆◆◆◆◆◆◆◆◆◆◆◆◆◆◆◆◆◆◆◆

Olive oil will remove most alcohol stains from wood.

◆◆◆◆◆◆◆◆◆◆◆◆◆◆◆◆◆◆◆◆◆◆◆

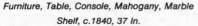

Furniture, Table, Console, Mahogany, Marble   *Furniture, Table, Dressing, Carved*
Shelf, c.1840, 37 In.   *Mahogany, c.1825, 68 x 36 In.*

Table, Center, Mahogany, Majorelle, Gilt Bronze, 29 x 43 In.	2200.00
Table, Center, Mahogany, Tilt Top, Column Shaft, Phila., 1823	2865.00
Table, Center, Renaissance Revival, Marble, c.1875 ....*Illus*	2520.00
Table, Center, Victorian, Mahogany, Marble Top, Cabriole Leg	1100.00
Table, Center, William & Mary, Maple, Pine, 28 x 37 In. ....*Illus*	2475.00
Table, Charles X, Belgian Marble, Claw Feet, Mahogany, 32 1/4 In.	5500.00
Table, Cherry, Scrubbed Top, Original Red Paint, Ohio, 1890	1100.00
Table, Child's, Hickory, Square Top	80.00
Table, Chinese Export, Gilt, Lacquer, Oriental Scene, 28 In.	495.00
Table, Chippendale, Drop Leaf, Mahogany, Cross Stretcher	795.00
Table, Chippendale, Tilt Top, Mahogany, Tripod, 24 In.	650.00
Table, Chippendale, Tilt Top, Snake Feet, Walnut, c.1780, 28 In.	1985.00
Table, Coffee, Bellows Shape, 3 Legs, Pine, 53 1/2 x 35 1/2 In.	45.00
Table, Coffee, Carved Hardwood, Removable Tray Top, 19 1/4 In.	80.00
Table, Coffee, Drop Leaf, Leather Top, Drawer, Mahogany, 35 1/2 In.	82.50
Table, Coffee, Hans Wegner, Teak, 1960s, 4 Ft. 11 In.	665.00
Table, Coffee, Knoll, Plastic Laminate Top, Round, c.1961, 36 In.	275.00
Table, Coffee, Mahogany, Carved Floral, Removable Marble Top	210.00
Table, Coffee, Mahogany, Circular Green Marble Tray, 21 1/2 In.	335.00
Table, Coffee, Painted, Claw Feet, Round, 46 In. Diam.	160.00
Table, Coffee, Polished Pink Stone, Wooden Base, 17 In.	145.00
Table, Conference, Knoll, Steel Legs, Boat Shape, 96 In.	995.00
Table, Conference, Leather Top, 3 Drawers, Mahogany, 1900, 108 In.	1215.00
Table, Console, Carved Lions' Heads, Paw Feet, Marble Top	5000.00
Table, Console, Empire, Marble Top Over Mirror, Mahogany	3500.00
Table, Console, Mahogany, Marble Shelf, c.1840, 37 In. ....*Illus*	825.00
Table, Console, Rococo, Giltwood, Marble, 19th Century, 40 In.	6160.00
Table, Corner, French Provincial, Urn Brace, Marble Top, 2 Legs	400.00
Table, Cricket, Pine, Circular Top, 3 Square Legs, 31 In.	665.00
Table, Dining, 2 Pedestals, Brass Feet, Mahogany, 1820, 7 Ft. 5 In.	7700.00
Table, Dining, Accordion Action, Brass Box Feet, Mahogany, 57 In.	2650.00
Table, Dining, Buffet, Oak, Ornate, Claw Feet, 54 In., Round Top	3500.00
Table, Dining, Carved Mahogany, Winged Lions Base, Round	3520.00
Table, Dining, Carved Squirrels, Dogs, Foxes On Base, Oak	2650.00
Table, Dining, Double Swing Legs, Casters, U.S.	5250.00
Table, Dining, Drop Leaf, Mahogany, c.1770, 47 1/2 In.	3850.00
Table, Dining, Drop Leaf, Trestle Base, Pads, Mahogany, 40 In.	605.00
Table, Dining, Empire, Column Supports, Mahogany, Square, 54 In.	2100.00
Table, Dining, Extension, Brass Feet, Casters, Mahogany, 99 1/4 In.	5500.00
Table, Dining, Gate Leg, D-Shaped Leaves, Walnut, c.1740, 56 In.	4400.00
Table, Dining, Golden Oak, Round, Pedestal, Paw Feet	1000.00
Table, Dining, Gustav Stickley, No. 633, Signed, Oak	1215.00
Table, Dining, Nakashima, Rosewood, Walnut, 20th Century	7000.00
Table, Dining, Queen Anne, Drop Leaf, Cherry, c.1760, 42 In.	2200.00
Table, Dining, Regency, Mahogany, Rosewood Center, England, 28 In.	1985.00
Table, Dining, Trestle, Oak, Heal, 2 Tapering Columns	2956.00
Table, Dressing, Carved Mahogany, c.1825, 68 x 36 In. ....*Illus*	1760.00

Furniture, Table, Drop Leaf, Mahogany,
c.1840, 58 In. Opened

Furniture, Table, Game, Regency, Inlaid
Mahogany, Two 9-In. Leaves

Table, Dressing, Center & Adjustable Side Mirrors 400.00
Table, Dressing, Charles X, Arched Mirror, Marble Top, 5 Ft. 3 In. 5775.00
Table, Dressing, Drawers Over Apron, Mahogany, 1790, 36 x 35 In. 1650.00
Table, Dressing, Gustav Stickley, No. 923, c.1910, 4 Ft. 7 1/4 In. 3025.00
Table, Dressing, Kneehole, 4 Drawers, Mahogany, c.1760, 39 In. 2475.00
Table, Dressing, Mahogany, Rope Twist Legs, 3 Drawers, Brass Pulls 450.00
Table, Dressing, Mirrored Lift Top, 2 Powder Drawers, Walnut 175.00
Table, Dressing, Pine, Green, Black Striping, 1 Drawer, 28 3/4 In. 500.00
Table, Dressing, Queen Anne, Mahogany, 28 x 27 x 17 1/2 In. 9900.00
Table, Dressing, Rope Twist Legs, 3 Drawers, Brass Pulls, Mahogany 450.00
Table, Dressing, Sheraton, Painted Seashells & Florals, Sponged 4100.00
Table, Dressing, William & Mary, Walnut, 1710–1750 ....*Illus* 8800.00
Table, Drop Leaf, 1 Small Drawer, Tiger Maple, 26 1/2 x 21 In. 465.00
Table, Drop Leaf, Ball & Spike Foot, Tiger Maple 950.00
Table, Drop Leaf, Baroque, Bun Feet, Oak, Flemish, 31 x 63 1/2 In. 3300.00
Table, Drop Leaf, Cherry, 1 Drawer, Country, 29 x 34 x 18 In. 385.00
Table, Drop Leaf, Cherry, Shaped Leaves, Turned Legs, 17th Century 1950.00
Table, Drop Leaf, Cherry, U.S., 1840 .... 475.00
Table, Drop Leaf, Chippendale, 1760 .... 6325.00
Table, Drop Leaf, Chippendale, Cherry, c.1780, 27 x 36 In. 550.00
Table, Drop Leaf, Federal, 6 Legs, Mahogany, 28 1/2 x 48 In. 1000.00
Table, Drop Leaf, Federal, Tapered Legs, 26 x 47 In. 975.00
Table, Drop Leaf, Harvest, Pine, Turned Legs, Country, 29 In. 400.00
Table, Drop Leaf, Mahogany, c.1840, 58 In. Opened ....*Illus* 935.00
Table, Drop Leaf, Mahogany, Pedestal Base, 29 3/4 In. 100.00
Table, Drop Leaf, Pembroke, 1800 .... 2500.00
Table, Drop Leaf, Queen Anne Style, Burled Walnut, 25 x 27 In. 265.00
Table, Drop Leaf, Queen Anne Style, Walnut, Cabriole Legs, 50 In. 800.00
Table, Drop Leaf, Regency Style, Rosewood Veneer, 28 In. 700.00
Table, Drop Leaf, Regency, Mahogany, Hairy Paw Feet, 27 In. 1100.00
Table, Drop Leaf, Rosewood, Sunderland, 36 In. ....*Illus* 2200.00
Table, Drop Leaf, Scrolled Skirt, Mahogany, 1770–1790, 47 1/2 In. 4125.00
Table, Drop Leaf, Sheraton Style, Gate Leg, Oval, 29 In. 1100.00
Table, Drop Leaf, Sheraton, Birch, Turned Legs, 28 1/2 In. 800.00
Table, Drop Leaf, Sheraton, Cherry, Pine, 6 Legs, 16 x 50 In. 425.00
Table, Drop Leaf, Sheraton, Curly Maple, Cherry, Drawer, 20 x 38 In 450.00
Table, Drop Leaf, Sheraton, Pine, Hardwood Legs & Leaves, 42 In. 450.00
Table, Drop Leaf, Stop Fluted Legs, Red Paint, Rhode Island 7600.00
Table, Drop Leaf, Tiger Maple, c.1800, 34 3/4 In. 1450.00
Table, Drum, George III, Mahogany, Gilt–Tooled Leather Top, 29 In. 5775.00
Table, Egg & Dart & Vitruvian Scroll Frieze, Walnut, 54 1/2 In. 2000.00
Table, Egg & Dart Border, Marble Top, Painted, Parcel Gilt, 31 In. 2200.00
Table, Eggshell & Gold Leaf Triangles, Black Lacquer, 26 In. 1650.00
Table, Empire, Mahogany, Pedestal Base, Carved Paw Feet, 28 In. 800.00
Table, Empire, Marble Top, Vasiform Support, Mahogany, 38 1/2 In. 3850.00
Table, Extension, Limbert, Mission, Oak 4950.00
Table, Farm, 1 Drawer, Scrubbed Top, 47 In. 625.00

Table, Faux Marble Top, Metal Winged Female Support, 59 In. 2420.00
Table, Federal Pembroke, Mahogany, Shaped Leaves, 10 x 36 In. 900.00
Table, Federal, Mahogany, Inlay, New England, c.1820, 28 In. 775.00
Table, Federal, Ring Turned Legs, Mahogany, 1790s, 93 In. 9350.00
Table, Folding, Pine, Sawbuck Base, 3 Board Top, Primitive 250.00
Table, Foliate Border, Triform Base, Cast Iron, 31 1/2 x 32 In. 1350.00
Table, Foyer, Chippendale, Mahogany, 1 Drawer, 30 In. 155.00
Table, French Provincial, 1 Drawer, 18th Century 1800.00
Table, Fruitwood, 1 Drawer, Early 19th Century, France 2800.00
Table, Galle, 2 Tiers, Marquetry Floral Sprays, 29 In. 3520.00
Table, Galle, 2 Tiers, Rounded Triangle, Marquetry, 30 In. 4950.00
Table, Galle, Art Nouveau, Inlay, Signed, 28 x 24 In. 2200.00
Table, Galle, Marquetry Of Flock Of Penguins, Signed, 29 In. 3100.00
Table, Galle, Marquetry, 2 Tiers, Walnut, Signed, 30 x 22 In. 5500.00
Table, Galle, Rounded Triangular Top, Marquetry, 28 In., Pair 6650.00
Table, Game, Backgammon & Checker Board, Lift Top, Iron Base 995.00
Table, Game, Backgammon & Chess Board, Drop Leaf, Mahogany 4620.00
Table, Game, Backgammon & Chessboard, Calamander Wood, 30 In. 1650.00
Table, Game, Backgammon Board, Brass Lion Paw Feet, Burl Yew 1430.00
Table, Game, Backgammon Board, Triple Fold, Chip Wells, Mahogany 4500.00
Table, Game, Bronze, Marquetry, Cherubs, Scroll Footed, 17 1/2 In. 935.00
Table, Game, Burl Panels, Mahogany, 30 1/2 x 30 In. 385.00
Table, Game, Demilune, Hepplewhite, Mahogany, Tapered Legs, 28 In. 900.00
Table, Game, Federal, Mahogany, Oval Top, U.S., 19th Century 995.00
Table, Game, Fitted Interior, Black Enamel, France, 28 1/2 In. 1750.00
Table, Game, Georgian Style, 1 Drawer, Mahogany, 36 1/2 In. 195.00
Table, Game, Marquetry, Green Felt Covered Top, 29 1/4 In. 575.00
Table, Game, Pine, Spins On Metal Base, Round 125.00
Table, Game, Regency, Inlaid Mahogany, Two 9–In. Leaves ....*Illus* 4620.00
Table, Game, Regency, Mahogany & Satinwood, England, c.1815 .... 9500.00
Table, Game, S. J. Rawson, Mahogany, c.1825, 36 x 31 In. 990.00
Table, Game, Triangular Hinged Top, Marquetry, Dutch, 19th Century 225.00
Table, Garden, Iron, Scalloped Border, Triform, 1880s, 27 x 28 In. 1325.00
Table, Garden, Marble Top, Foliated Supports, Cast Iron, 48 In. 545.00
Table, Garden, Variegated Marble, 19th Century, 9 Ft. 4500.00
Table, Gateleg, Beading, Dark Red Stain, 18th Century, 29 3/4 In. 3850.00
Table, Gateleg, Cherry, Drop Leaf 425.00
Table, Gateleg, William & Mary, Walnut, c.1710, 40 In. ....*Illus* 3960.00
Table, George III, Mahogany, 1790 .... 1950.00
Table, Gray Granite Top, Ormolu Stars, Palmettes, Mahogany, 37 In. 9350.00
Table, Green Paint, Iron, Gray Stone Top, 29 In. 130.00
Table, Gustav Stickley, No. 652, Oak, 30 x 30 x 20 In. 2310.00
Table, Hall, Giltwood, Pietra Dura Tablet, Floral, Marble, F. Betti 9900.00
Table, Hall, Victorian, 3 Drawers, Walnut, 28 In. 445.00
Table, Harvest, Gold Graining, 2–Board Top, Pine, 62 1/2 In. 1000.00
Table, Hepplewhite, 1 Drawer, Pine, Dovetailed Country, 26 1/2 In. 700.00
Table, Hepplewhite, 1 Drawer, Serpentine Top, Mahogany, 29 1/4 In. 700.00

Furniture, Table, Drop Leaf, Rosewood,
Sunderland, 36 In.

Furniture, Table, Gateleg, William & Mary,
Walnut, c.1710, 40 In.

Furniture, Table, Limbert, No. 148, Cross
Base, Round Top, 1908

Furniture, Table, Tilt Top, Mahogany,
c.1760, 39 In. Diam.

Table, Hepplewhite, Cherry, Pinned Apron, 2 Board Top, 29 In.	550.00
Table, Hepplewhite, Design, Pine, Red, Black, Country, 29 1/2 In.	2800.00
Table, Hepplewhite, Pine, Splayed Base, Country, 28 In.	250.00
Table, Hepplewhite, Walnut Base, Pine Top, Country, 28 1/4 In.	250.00
Table, Heywood Bros. –Wakefield, Wicker, c.1900, 31 x 26 In.	905.00
Table, Hunt, Georgian Style, Tapering Legs, Mahogany, 60 In.	775.00
Table, Hutch, 2 Board Round Top, Pine Seat, Hardwood & Pine	3000.00
Table, Hutch, 2 Board Top, Gray Scrubbed Top, Walnut, 65 In.	1450.00
Table, Hutch, 3 Board Top, Pine, 59 1/2 x 40 In.	625.00
Table, Hutch, 4 Board Top, Bootjack Feet, Pine, 28 1/2 x 42 In.	1250.00
Table, Hutch, 4 Board Top, Hinged Top In Base, Pine, 47 3/4 In.	1400.00
Table, Hutch, Breadboard Top, Hinged Seat, Pine, 29 x 31 1/2 In.	1650.00
Table, Hutch, Molded Posts & Rails, England, 3 Part, 70 1/4 In.	1400.00
Table, Hutch, Pine, Poplar, Hinged Seat, Country, 28 1/2 In.	1100.00
Table, Hutch, Red Paint, 72 In.	4290.00
Table, Hutch, Round Top, Hardwood, Pine, Square Legs, 29 In.	3000.00
Table, Hutch, Tilt Top, Square Legs, Birch & Pine, c.1800, 42 In.	995.00
Table, Inlay, Marked Syria, 28 1/2 In.	150.00
Table, Italian Renaissance, Octagonal, Carved Acanthus, 42 In.	3850.00
Table, Kitchen, Art Deco, 1938, 5 Piece	150.00
Table, Kitchen, Yellow Formica, 20th Century	140.00
Table, Kittinger, Carved Frieze, Reeded Legs, Pine, 21 1/2 In., Pr.	250.00
Table, L. & J. G. Stickley, No. 575, Median Shelf, 1912	885.00
Table, Library, 1 Drawer, Rosewood, Serpentine Apron, 31 1/2 In.	2025.00
Table, Library, 2 Drawers, Leather Top, Mahogany, 47 1/2 In.	3100.00
Table, Library, Arts & Crafts, 2 Drawers, Protruding Legs, Oak	470.00
Table, Library, Belter, Hand Carved Rosewood, 35 x 61 In.	2100.00
Table, Library, Chippendale, Walnut, Cabriole Legs, 30 In.	1450.00
Table, Library, Egyptian, Mahogany, Gilt Brass Trim, 29 3/4 In.	4200.00
Table, Library, Frieze Over Drawers, Carved Trestle Support, Oak	890.00
Table, Library, Gustav Stickley, 2 Drawers	1450.00
Table, Library, Gustav Stickley, 13 Spindles, 1905, 36 In.	1200.00
Table, Library, Gustav Stickley, No. 619, Drawers, 1910, 5 Ft. 6 In.	4950.00
Table, Library, Gustav Stickley, No. 6144, Leather Top, 42 x 30 In.	3500.00
Table, Library, Larkin, Drawer, Pressed Design On Skirt	170.00
Table, Library, Pullout Drawer, Mahogany, 30 1/4 In.	275.00
Table, Library, Regency, Drawers, Rosewood Veneer, 48 1/4 In.	3000.00
Table, Library, Rosewood Legs, Walnut, Inlay, 51 In.	1000.00
Table, Library, Wicker, White, Stretcher Shelf, Refinished Top	295.00
Table, Limbert, No. 148, Cross Base, Round Top, 1908 ....*Illus*	1650.00
Table, Long Drop Leaf, 6 Spiral Turned Legs, Cherry	550.00
Table, Louis XV, 1 Drawer, Hoof Feet, Parcel Gilt, 36 1/4 In.	3850.00
Table, Louis XV, Bronze Base, Marble Top, White, Purple, 31 3/4 In.	1900.00
Table, Louis XV, Marble Top, Basket Of Flowers Inlay, Gilt, 36 In.	8250.00
Table, Louis XVI Style, Porcelain Mounted, Painted Wood, 31 In.	6100.00
Table, Louis XVI, Marble Top, Foliate Swags, Giltwood, 39 In.	2300.00
Table, Louis XVI, Oval Marble Top, Kingwood & Tulipwood, 30 In.	3500.00

Table, Mahogany Marquetry, Majorelle, Triangular Top, 3 Legs 1650.00
Table, Mahogany, D–Shaped, 3 Sections, Centennial 1000.00
Table, Majorelle, Clover Leaf Center Shelf, Mahogany, 47 In. 3550.00
Table, Majorelle, Tricorner Form, Marquetry Poppies, 29 1/2 In. 3525.00
Table, Marble Top, Drawer, Ebonized Trim, Mahogany, 38 1/2 In. 6600.00
Table, Marble Top, Legs Formed As Aardvarks, Bronze, 36 1/2 In. 2750.00
Table, Marble Top, Ormolu Trim, Marquetry, 28 1/2 x 25 In. 300.00
Table, Marble Top, Outset Drawer, Tambour Slide, Mahogany, 31 In. 2200.00
Table, Marble Top, Shell & Wave Frieze, Giltwood, 5 Ft. 9 In. 8900.00
Table, Marquetry Inlay, Foliage Scrolls, 29 1/4 In. 800.00
Table, Metal, Leather Insert Top, Chas. Porter, 31 x 13 x 19 In. 3200.00
Table, Mixing, George II, Marble Top, Shell–Carved Knees, Walnut 4850.00
Table, Mixing, George II, Walnut, Rectangular Marble Top, 35 In. 4800.00
Table, Napoleon III, Gilt Bronze, Porcelain Mounted, 24 1/2 In. 7150.00
Table, Neoclassical, Marble Top, Painted Garlands, 28 1/4 In. 2200.00
Table, Nesting, Galle, Magnolia Branches, Marquetry, 28 In., 4 Pc. 9900.00
Table, Nesting, Galle, Mahogany, Inlay, 1900, 3 Piece 5225.00
Table, Nesting, Hepplewhite, Mahogany, Inlay, 23 In., 3 Piece 300.00
Table, Oak, 21 Drawers, Oak, Octagonal Top, Square Legs, G. Russell 370.00
Table, Oak, Claw Feet, 3 Leaves, Round 700.00
Table, Octagonal White Marble Top, Iron, 29 1/4 In. 200.00
Table, Parlor, Empire, Walnut, Square 550.00
Table, Parlor, Turtle Top 1000.00
Table, Patinated Bronze & Smoked Glass, 18 1/4 x 4 Ft. 1100.00
Table, Patio, Black Iron, 22 1/2 x 19 In. 120.00
Table, Pembroke, 1 Long Drawer, Incised Edge, Mahogany, 1810, Pair 8900.00
Table, Pembroke, Chippendale, Ball & Claw Feet, Mahogany 1000.00
Table, Pembroke, Chippendale, Marlborough Legs, 28 1/4 In. 3550.00
Table, Pembroke, Concave Apron, Brass Pulls, Mahogany, 21 3/4 In. 1900.00
Table, Pembroke, Drawer, Shell Inlay, Mahogany, 31 1/2 In. 1350.00
Table, Pembroke, Drop Leaves, Square Butt Joints, Signed, Poplar 600.00
Table, Pembroke, Federal Style, Drop Leaf, Mahogany 100.00
Table, Pembroke, Federal, Pentagonal Leaves, Mahogany, Inlay, 1810 .... 1980.00
Table, Pembroke, George III, 1 Drawer, Sham Drawer, Mahogany, 1800 .... 550.00
Table, Pembroke, Hepplewhite, 1 Drawer, England, 28 1/4 In. 400.00
Table, Pembroke, Hepplewhite, Cherry, 27 1/4 In. 500.00
Table, Pembroke, Hepplewhite, Mahogany, Dovetailed Drawer, 27 In. 875.00
Table, Pembroke, Hepplewhite, Mahogany, Inlay, England, 29 In. 400.00
Table, Pembroke, Line Inlay On Drawer, Cherry, c.1805, 28 1/2 In. 3850.00
Table, Pembroke, Line Inlay, Twin Flaps, Mahogany, 1790, 41 1/2 In. 3550.00
Table, Pembroke, Poplar, Red Paint, 1 Board Top, Country, 28 In. 150.00
Table, Pembroke, Regency, Legs On Castors, Mahogany, 28 In. 1100.00
Table, Pembroke, Regency, Mahogany, Rectangular Top, 30 In. 1100.00
Table, Pembroke, Sheraton Style, Drop Leaf, Mahogany, Oval, 28 In. 990.00
Table, Pembroke, Sheraton, Pine, Varnish, Brown Graining, 2 Leaves 250.00
Table, Pier, Empire Classical, Mahogany, Flame Veneer, 39 In. 1150.00
Table, Pier, Empire, Marble, Ebonized, Giltwood, 42 In. ....*Illus* 3300.00

Furniture, Table, Pier, Empire, Marble,
Ebonized, Giltwood, 42 In.

Furniture, Tray, Papier-Mache, Dog, Painted
Stand, 30 x 24 In.

Table, Pier, Empire, Rosewood, 1 Drawer, Ogee Apron, 31 In. 150.00
Table, Pier, Mahogany, Rectangular Marble Top, Lion Paw Feet 4950.00
Table, Pier, Marble Top, Carved & Gilt Brass, 36 x 51 x 25 In. 3300.00
Table, Pier, Marble Top, Gilt Stenciled Rosewood, c.1825, 33 In. 3850.00
Table, Pier, Stenciled Design, White Marble Columns & Top 6600.00
Table, Pine & Maple, 18th Century, 30 1/4 x 114 x 29 1/4 In. 2650.00
Table, Pine, Oak Graining Over Blue, 2 Board Top, 28 In. 225.00
Table, Poker, Horsehead Medallion Center, Octagonal, Oak 255.00
Table, Poplar, Yellow Smoked Graining, 1 Drawer Top Crest, 37 In. 1700.00
Table, Queen Anne Style, Tray Top, Serving Slides, 29 x 29 In. 445.00
Table, Red Camphor, Dragon Carving, Pierce Carved Between Legs 250.00
Table, Refectory, Baluster Trestle Support, Walnut, 33 x 57 In. 2200.00
Table, Refectory, Baroque, 3 Drawers, Spain, 17th Century, 98 In. 8250.00
Table, Refectory, Carved, Walnut, England, 17th Century, 73 In. 4950.00
Table, Refectory, Italian Renaissance, Walnut, 28 1/2 x 40 In. 825.00
Table, Renaissance Revival, Walnut, Marble Top 650.00
Table, Rohlf, Rectangular Top, 4 Square Legs, 1905, 28 1/2 In. 880.00
Table, Round Beveled Glass Top, Iron, France, 27 1/2 x 55 In. 3100.00
Table, Sawbuck, 2 Board Top, Pine, 28 3/4 x 71 3/4 In. 1500.00
Table, Sawbuck, 2 Board Top, Pine, Brown Finish, 27 1/2 In. 250.00
Table, Sawbuck, 2 Board Top, Traces Of Paint, Pine, 66 In. 450.00
Table, Sawbuck, 3 Board Top, Square Nail Construction, Pine 500.00
Table, Sawbuck, Storage Bin, Pumpkin Paint 625.00
Table, Sawbuck, Tiger Maple Base, Putty Over Red Paint, 1720–1740 ...... 3800.00
Table, Serving, 2 Short Drawers Over 1 Long, Mahogany, 39 1/4 In. 2700.00
Table, Serving, 2 Tiers, Gilt Bronze Mounted, Kingwood, 39 In. 6600.00
Table, Sevres Porcelain Top, Ebonized Wood, 31 x 25 x 19 In. 4950.00
Table, Sewing, 1 Dovetailed Drawer, Country, 27 1/2 In. 250.00
Table, Sewing, 2 Drawers, Bag Drawer, Drop Leaves, Mahogany, c.1825 ...... 1150.00
Table, Sewing, 2 Drawers, Rosewood, Pierced Supports, c.1840 .... 374.00
Table, Sewing, 2 Drawers, Wooden Pulls, Walnut, 29 x 51 In. 220.00
Table, Sewing, 3 Compartments, Rosewood, Tulipwood & Satinwood 1350.00
Table, Sewing, Astragal End, Candle Slides, c.1805 .... 6500.00
Table, Sewing, Beaded Edge, Maple Base, Pine Top, 48 3/4 In. 600.00
Table, Sewing, Boulle Marquetry, Tortoiseshell Ground, 28 In. 600.00
Table, Sewing, Cherry & Rosewood Veneer, Gilt-Stenciled, 30 In. 1650.00
Table, Sewing, Chinese Export, Carved Ivory Interior 495.00
Table, Sewing, Classical Revival, Mahogany, Brass Inlay, 31 1/4 In 775.00
Table, Sewing, Classical, Mahogany, Ebonized Columns, 29 1/2 In. 495.00
Table, Sewing, Crossbanded Veneer & Stringing, Mahogany, 29 In. 400.00
Table, Sewing, Drawers On All Sides, Bag Drawer, Bird's–Eye Maple 4750.00
Table, Sewing, Empire, Mahogany Veneer, Drop Leaf, Leaves, Paw Feet 400.00
Table, Sewing, Empire, Mahogany, Drop Leaf, Rope Legs, 2 Drawers 600.00
Table, Sewing, Federal, Bird's–Eye Maple & Mahogany, c.1810 .... 4500.00
Table, Sewing, Federal, Bird's–Eye Maple, Mahogany, Inlay, 20 In. 9350.00
Table, Sewing, Federal, Cherry, 2 Hinged Leaves, 2 Drawers, 29 In. 995.00
Table, Sewing, Federal, Divided Drawers, Mahogany, c.1810, 31 In. 1980.00
Table, Sewing, Federal, Drawer, Bird's–Eye Maple, Mahogany, c.1810 ...... 9350.00
Table, Sewing, Federal, Drawer, Curly Maple, c.1815, 26 x 19 In. 7150.00
Table, Sewing, Federal, Hinged Leaves, 2 Drawers, Cherry, 29 In. 990.00
Table, Sewing, Federal, Mahogany, Swirl Leg 1000.00
Table, Sewing, Fitted, Abalone Inlay, Painted Papier–Mache, 27 In. 550.00
Table, Sewing, Hardwood, Carved Detail, Marquetry Top, 30 3/4 In. 350.00
Table, Sewing, Hepplewhite, 1 Drawer, Tapered Legs, Pine, 27 1/2 In 205.00
Table, Sewing, Hepplewhite, 3 Board Top, Pine, Blue Paint, 30 In. 350.00
Table, Sewing, Hepplewhite, Full Length Drawer, Pine, 52 3/4 In. 700.00
Table, Sewing, Hepplewhite, Pine, Brown Finish, Drawer, 30 x 36 In. 650.00
Table, Sewing, Hinged Top, Fitted, Writing Flap, Mahogany, 35 In. 4620.00
Table, Sewing, Hinged, Compartmented Interior, Mahogany, c.1800 ...... 4400.00
Table, Sewing, Louis XV Style, Boulle, Hinged Top 335.00
Table, Sewing, Marquetry & Stenciled Lift Top, Ebonized, c.1875 .... 1450.00
Table, Sewing, Oak, Folding Legs 35.00
Table, Sewing, Pine Square Legs, Corner Chamfer, 31 3/4 In. 200.00

Table, Sewing, Queen Anne, Hardwood, Natural Finish, Drawer, 46 In. 750.00
Table, Sewing, Rosewood, Marquetry Inlay, Swing Top, 28 In. 1300.00
Table, Sewing, Shaker, 2–Board Top, Dovetailed Drawer, Brass Pulls 880.00
Table, Sewing, Shaker, Drawer, Pine, Mt. Lebanon, 1830s, 60 1/4 In. 5225.00
Table, Sewing, Wicker Basket Top, Lower Open Wicker Shelf 475.00
Table, Sewing, Yellow Pine, Overlapping Drawer, 39 x 47 In. 535.00
Table, Sheraton, Drop Leaf, Swing Leg, Cherry, Extends To 89 In. 325.00
Table, Sheraton, Pine, Original Red Graining, Country, 29 In. 450.00
Table, Side, Ormolu, Parquetry, Walnut, Kingwood, Fruitwood, 27 In. 695.00
Table, Side, Papier-Mache, Painted Hunt Scene, Victorian, 22 In. 885.00
Table, Skyscraper, Green Lacquer, P. Frankl, c.1925, 5 Ft. 11 In. 1450.00
Table, Spanish Baroque, Rectangular Top, Iron Stretcher, 54 In. 4125.00
Table, Spiral & Leaf Carved Legs, Giltwood, 31 x 46 1/2 In. 3575.00
Table, Stickley Handcraft, Frieze Drawer, Oak, c.1915, 36 In. 3650.00
Table, Tavern, Baluster Legs, Box Stretcher, Oak, 18th Century 535.00
Table, Tavern, Drawer, Single Breadboard Top, Salmon Paint, 29 In. 2000.00
Table, Tavern, Georgian, Center & End Drawer, Oak, 31 x 79 In. 3100.00
Table, Tavern, Hepplewhite, Country, Pine, Square Legs, 27 In. 500.00
Table, Tavern, Hepplewhite, Hardwood, Pine, Splayed Base, 26 1/4 In 450.00
Table, Tavern, Pegged Base, Painted Red 1600.00
Table, Tavern, Pine, Maple, Overhanging Top, Single Drawer, 26 In. 715.00
Table, Tavern, Queen Anne, 1 Drawer, Maple & Pine, 23 1/2 In. 750.00
Table, Tavern, Queen Anne, 2 Board Top, Country, Pine, 25 In. 2300.00
Table, Tavern, Queen Anne, Country, Hardwood, Pine, 24 1/2 In. 2400.00
Table, Tavern, Queen Anne, Country, Pine, Poplar, 22 3/4 In. 1100.00
Table, Tavern, Queen Anne, Cutout Base, Splay Leg 6150.00
Table, Tavern, Queen Anne, Maple, Base Has Red Graining, 26 In. 4900.00
Table, Tavern, Turned Maple, 25 x 40 x 27 3/4 In. ....*Illus* 2750.00
Table, Tea, Chippendale, Carved Flower Edge, Mahogany, c.1880 .... 665.00
Table, Tea, Chippendale, Mahogany, Square Top, 27 x 33 x 33 In. 665.00
Table, Tea, Fruitwood Marquetry, Galle, 3 Tiers, 34 x 28 x 18 In. 3300.00
Table, Tea, Mahogany, 20th Century, 27 In. 135.00
Table, Tea, Maple, Rhode Island 5800.00
Table, Tea, Queen Anne, Dish Top 2700.00
Table, Tea, Queen Anne, Mahogany, Crescent Fold Top, England, 1800s 1435.00
Table, Tea, Queen Anne, Tiger Maple 1325.00
Table, Tea, Queen Anne, Tiger Maple & Maple, 25 1/4 x 30 1/2 In. 3080.00
Table, Tea, Tilt Top, 3 Board Top, Iron Brace, Cherry, 28 1/2 In. 950.00
Table, Tea, Tilt Top, Chippendale, Mahogany, 28 1/2 x 35 In. 4515.00
Table, Tea, Tilt Top, Chippendale, Walnut, Turned Column, 29 In. 725.00
Table, Tea, Tilt Top, Mahogany, 1940s, 26 1/2 In. 250.00
Table, Tea, Tilt Top, Mahogany, 1940s, 29 In. 110.00
Table, Tea, Tilt Top, Mahogany, Tripod Vase, Snake Feet, 28 In. 275.00
Table, Tea, Victorian, Wicker Top, Bar Harbor, 3 Piece 735.00
Table, Tea, Wicker, Unpainted 600.00
Table, Teak, Nacre Inlay, Marble Inserts, Oriental, 32 In., Pair 1300.00
Table, Thonet, Bentwood, Pedestal, 30 x 18 In. 496.00
Table, Tiffany Tile Top, Walnut, Brass, Inley, E. Wormley, 1955 .... 2200.00
Table, Tilt Top, 2 Board Turtle Top, Reeded Column, 27 3/4 In. 275.00
Table, Tilt Top, Abalone Inlay, Painted Papier-Mache, 30 In. 550.00
Table, Tilt Top, Birdcage, Poplar, Red Paint, Oval Top, 29 3/4 In. 350.00
Table, Tilt Top, Colored Wooden Inlay, 7 1/2 In. 190.00
Table, Tilt Top, Gilt Chinoiserie Design, Black Lacquer, 30 In. 650.00
Table, Tilt Top, Louis XVI, Mahogany, N. Petit, 30 1/2 In. 8800.00
Table, Tilt Top, Mahogany, 20th Century, 26 x 22 x 17 In. 155.00
Table, Tilt Top, Mahogany, c.1760, 39 In. Diam. ....*Illus* 5225.00
Table, Tilt Top, Mahogany, Caned Inserts In Top, 29 1/2 In. 110.00
Table, Tilt Top, Mahogany, Inlay In Center Of Dish Top, 27 In. 225.00
Table, Tilt Top, Mahogany, Inlay, 27 3/4 In. 150.00
Table, Tilt Top, Mahogany, Snake Feet With Pads, 27 1/4 In. 450.00
Table, Tilt Top, Mother-of-Pearl, Papier-Mache, Round, 30 In. 1500.00
Table, Tilt Top, Padded Snake Feet, Walnut, U.S., c.1780 .... 5500.00
Table, Tilt Top, Poplar, Tripod Base, Spider Legs, 8 1/2 In. 875.00

Table, Tilt Top, Shoe Feet, c.1820, Round, 45 In. 2200.00
Table, Tilt Top, Star Burst Design, Banded Inlay, c.1920 .... 1525.00
Table, Tilt Top, Walnut Base, U.S., 26 1/2 In. 275.00
Table, Tortoise & Brass Inlay, Ormolu Mounts, France, 30 x 59 In. 3300.00
Table, Tray Top, Mahogany, Shell-Carved Knees, Ireland 8250.00
Table, Tulip Blossoms Inlay, C. A. Gauthier, c.1900, 29 1/2 In. 675.00
Table, Tulip, Knoll Style 200.00
Table, Turtle Top, Marble Top, Walnut, 19th Century, 30 In. 315.00
Table, Turtle Top, Ormolu Trim, Drawer, 1890s, 29 1/2 x 39 1/2 In. 500.00
Table, Urn Pedestals, Walnut & Burl Walnut, Inlay, Extra Leaf 800.00
Table, Veined Gray & White Marble Top, Mahogany, c.1825, 4 Ft. 9900.00
Table, Victorian, Walnut, c.1860, 29 x 24 x 24 In. 176.00
Table, Walnut, G. Nakashima, Irregular Top, 13 x 60 x 24 In. 2750.00
Table, Walnut, Relief Scroll Work, 30 In. 375.00
Table, Windsor, Splayed Legs, 1780, 25 In. 750.00
Table, Writing, Gilt Leather Top, Beechwood, 1780s, 42 1/2 In. 5500.00
Table, Writing, Gothic Revival, 2 Drawers, Trefoil Support, Oak 440.00
Table, Writing, Hinged Top, Fitted Interior, Gateleg, Burl Walnut 2975.00
Table, Writing, Louis XVI, Leather Top, P. Garnier, 44 1/4 In. 9350.00
Tabouret, L. & J. G. Stickley, No. 558, Oak, c.1910, 20 1/4 In. 1210.00
Tabouret, L. & J. G. Stickley, Oak, Octagonal, c.1910, 17 x 15 In. 605.00
Tabouret, Marble Top, Hardwood, China, Late 19th Century, 18 In. 145.00
Tabouret, Marble Top, Hardwood, China, Late 19th Century, 19 In. 245.00
Tabouret, Marble Top, Hardwood, China, Late 19th Century, 25 In. 190.00
Tall Chest, Maple, Inlaid Stringing, Straight Front, America 3740.00
Tea Cart, Liftout Tray, Unpainted Wicker 650.00
Tea Cart, Mahogany 120.00
Tete A Tete, Heywood Bros. –Wakefield, Wicker, c.1900, 48 In. 1815.00
Tie Rack, Mirror, Victorian, Walnut 70.00
Tray, Butler's, Stand, George IV, Mahogany, 35 x 31 In. 715.00
Tray, Butler's, X-Form Stand, Mahogany, 1860s, 32 x 28 In. 495.00
Tray, Galle, Seascape & Sailing Ships Inlay, c.1900, 24 In. 990.00
Tray, Lacquer, Floral Spray, Black Ground, Japan, 23 1/2 In. 385.00
Tray, Majorelle, Sailor In Boat, Bronze Handles, 22 In. 1760.00
Tray, Papier-Mache, Dog, Painted Stand, 30 x 24 In. ....*Illus* . 1650.00
Tray, Papier-Mache, Mother-of-Pearl, Painted Florals, 31 1/2 In. 605.00
Tray, Papier-Mache, Stand, Center Floral Spray, 30 x 22 In. 1320.00
Tray, Victorian, Painted Scene Of Canterbury, Papier-Mache 775.00
Tray, Vienna Silvered Bronze & Rattan, 2 Dogs & Cat 385.00
Urn, Iron, Garden, Man Of Mountain Heads, Griffin Handles, 62 In. 2000.00
Vitrine, Biedermeier, Hexagonal Top, 34 1/2 In. 450.00
Vitrine, Chinese Chippendale, 18 1/2 In. 450.00
Vitrine, Chippendale, Walnut, Plate Glass Tray Top, 28 In. 150.00
Vitrine, French Empire Style, Gilt Bronze & Glass, 65 x 54 In. 2420.00
Vitrine, Louis XV Style, Acanthus Scrolls, Giltwood, 72 In. 1760.00
Vitrine, Louis XV Style, Ormolu, Kingwood Marquetry, 65 In. 1430.00
Vitrine, Louis XV, Tufted Red Velvet Upholstery, Glass Shelves 695.00
Vitrine, Mahogany, Fruitwood, Arched Crest, Conch Shell, 57 In. 550.00
Vitrine, Marble Top, Mahogany, Center & 2 Side Doors, 4 Ft. 1 In. 7700.00
Vitrine, Ornate, Marble Top, France 775.00
Vitrine, Parquetry, Ormolu, Gilt Borders, 20th Century, 83 In. 5500.00
Vitrine, Rosewood, Rectangular Top, Glazed Door, 5 Ft. 6 In. 8500.00
Vitrine, Stand, Gilt Metal & Mahogany, Foliate Feet, 6 Ft. 3 In. 4125.00
Wardrobe, 2 Doors, Walnut, Carved Corners, 1880s, 6 Ft. 10 In., Pair 1980.00
Wardrobe, Alligatored Brown Graining, 1 Drawer, 79 1/4 In. 275.00
Wardrobe, Federal, 5 Parts, Paneled Doors, Mahogany, 1820s, 80 In. 4650.00
Wardrobe, Mahogany, Art Nouveau, 3 Mirrors, Rounded, Carlo Zen 5775.00
Wardrobe, Mahogany, Georgian Style, 19th Century, 77 1/2 In. 2975.00
Wardrobe, Oak Quartersawn, 1890 .... 695.00
Wardrobe, Shaker, Inside Hat & Clothes Pegs, Red Finish 2000.00
Washstand, 1 Drawer, Dovetailed, Chamfered, Walnut & Tiger Maple 325.00
Washstand, 3 Drawers, Fruit Pulls 325.00
Washstand, Cherry, 1 Drawer, Lower Shelf, Towel Rails 450.00

Washstand, Corner, Federal, Mahogany Inlaid, New England, 35 In.	525.50
Washstand, Corner, Hepplewhite, Curly Maple, Small Shelf, 33 In.	3200.00
Washstand, Curly Maple, 2 Dovetailed Drawers, Opalescent Pulls	775.00
Washstand, Double, Mahogany, 2 Drawers, 2 Bowls In Top, 35 In.	750.00
Washstand, Federal, Gallery, Drawer, Mahogany, c.1815, 39 1/2 In.	550.00
Washstand, Gallery, Cherry, Flame Mahogany Veneer, 33 1/2 In.	400.00
Washstand, Gustav Stickley, No. 628, 2 Short Drawers, Doors, 1910	3575.00
Washstand, Louis XV, Mahogany, Marble, Frieze Drawer, 28 3/4 In.	2200.00
Washstand, Mahogany, Burl Veneer, Rosewood Graining, 32 In.	225.00
Washstand, Mahogany, Transfer Shell Inlay Design, 50 In.	180.00
Washstand, Oak, Victorian, Lyre Top, Original Brasses, Small	195.00
Washstand, Pennsylvania Dutch	150.00
Washstand, Sheraton, 1 Drawer, Hardwood, Scalloped Apron, 40 In.	350.00
Washstand, Sheraton, 1 Drawer, Mahogany Veneer Facade, 40 In.	350.00
Washstand, Sheraton, Cherry, Dovetailed Drawer, Country, 33 In.	325.00
Washstand, Sheraton, Cherry, Refinished, Bowl Cutout Top, 18 In.	175.00
Washstand, Wooden Backsplash, Walnut, 34 x 34 In.	450.00
Wastebasket, Stickley Bros.	1760.00
Workstand, Bone Pulls, Dark Red Paint, Grained, c.1815, 28 3/4 In.	467.50

FURSTENBERG Porcelain Works was started in Furstenberg, Germany, in 1747. It is still working. Many of the modern products are made in the old molds.

Figurine, Lady, White Lace Dress, Blue Jacket, Marked, 5 1/2 In.	450.00
Figurine, Monkey, Playing Horn, Tree Stump, 1774–1775, 5 9/16 In.	1870.00

G. ARGY–ROUSSEAU is the impressed mark used on a variety of objects in the Art Deco style. Gabriel Argy–Rousseau, born in 1885, was a French glass artist.

Bowl, Gray Glass, Stylized Birds, Pate–De–Verre, 3 5/8 In.	5225.00
Bowl, Mottled Green & White, Blackberries, Shallow, Footed	1375.00
Bowl, Pate–De–Verre, Mottled Blue & Purple, Green Buds	3145.00
Box, Cover, Pate–De–Verre, Gray & Yellow Glass, 3 1/2 In.	4675.00
Box, Flowerheads On Lid, Brickwork, Signed, 1924, 4 1/4 In.	3300.00
Box, Fuchsia Blossoms, Black & White Center, Marked, 4 In.	5500.00
Coupe, Pate–De–Cristal, Carnation, Wing Handles, 4 1/8 In.	8800.00
Night–Light, Pate–De–Verre, Fuchsia Flowers, 5 1/2 In.	9900.00
Paperweight, Lizard Shape, Black, Pate–De–Verre, 3 1/4 In.	4400.00
Paperweight, Pate–De–Verre, Parrot, Plinth, 1925, 4 7/8 In.	6050.00
Stylized Daisies, Violet & Blue, Signed, 6 In.	7150.00
Vase, 3 Panels Of Blossoms, Gray, 1922, 8 3/4 In.	7150.00
Vase, Crabs, Pate–De–Verre, Seaweed, Ovoid, 1925, 5 1/2 In.	9350.00
Vase, Pate–De–Verre, Amber & Pink Leaves, 3 1/2 In.	6600.00
Vase, Pate–De–Verre, Flowering Cherry Blossoms, 5 3/4 In.	7700.00
Vase, Pate–De–Verre, Flowering Chile Plants, 5 3/4 In.	5280.00
Vase, Pate–De–Verre, Red Anemones, White Centers, 5 3/4 In.	4180.00
Vase, Tragicomique, Grotesque Masks, Signed, 1922, 10 In.	7700.00

GALLE POTTERY was made by Emile Galle, the famous French designer, after 1874. The pieces were marked with the initials *E. Gstoit sed, Em. Galle Faiencerie de Nancy,* or a version of his signature. Galle is best known for his glass, listed in the next section.

Candlestick, Blue, Red, 10 In.	500.00
Compote, Blue, Yellow, Flowers, 9 In.	950.00
Figurine, Cat, Blue Trim, 14 In.	1200.00
Planter, Wall, Rose & Gray Design, Signed, 12 In.	495.00

GALLE was a designer who made glass, pottery, furniture, and other Art Nouveau items. Emile Galle founded his factory in France in 1874. After Galle's death in 1904, the firm continued to make glass and furniture until 1931. The name *Galle* was used as a mark, but it was often hidden in the design of the object. Galle Pottery is listed above and his furniture is listed in the Furniture section.

Bowl, Cut Bleeding Hearts, Lemon, Raspberry, Maroon, Cameo, 7 1/2 In. 2750.00
Bowl, Lobed Rim, Trailing Blossoms, Leaves, Signed, c.1900, 4 5/8 In. 2310.00
Box, Domed Cover, Alsatian Landscape, Gray, Yellow, Brown, 5 3/8 In. 7150.00
Box, Domed Cover, Spiky Thistles, Round, Signed, c.1900, 5 In. 495.00
Box, Marquetry Floral Sprays, Mahogany, On Stand, 29 x 21 1/2 In. 5500.00
Box, Slat Lid, Landscape, Man Rowing Boat, Signed, c.1900, 5 1/8 In. 1875.00
Compote, Cherry Leaf Branches, Gray, Yellow, Cameo, 1900, 8 3/4 In. 3850.00
Cordial Set, Thistles, Cross Of Lorraine, Cameo, Tray, 1900, 6 Piece 4400.00
Cup & Saucer, Colored Enamel, Flowers & Foliage 395.00
Decanter, Green Tinted, Hearts Picture Cards, Footed, Handle, Stopper 5286.00
Goblet, Enameled, Internal Design, Trumpet–Shaped Foot, 6 3/4 In. 7700.00
Jar, Cover, Cameo, Rabbit Scene, Gray Opalescent, Egg Shape, 5 7/8 In. ....: 4125.00
Jardiniere, Enameled Orchids, Gilt, Pale Amber, Steep Sided, Signed 6650.00
Jug, Amber, Wild Flowers, Praying Mantis, Swollen, Pinched Sides 7050.00
Lamp Base, Birds In Flight, Orange Walls, Signed, c.1900, 11 5/8 In. 1765.00
Lamp Base, Magnolia Blossoms, Leaves, Signed, c.1900, 9 5/8 In. 2750.00
Lamp, Boudoir, Cone–Shaped Shade, Flower & Leaves, Signed, 8 In. 9350.00
Lamp, Candle, 2 Eagles 1485.00
Lamp, Candle, 3 Butterflies 1925.00
Lamp, Candle, Birds, 8 In. 3200.00
Lamp, Domed Shade, Grape Clusters, Bronze Mounts, Signed, 9 3/4 In. 5500.00
Lamp, Domed Shade, Wild Flowers, Bronze Mount, Signed, 22 3/4 In. 6875.00
Perfume Bottle, Amber Anemones, White, Cameo, Bronze Urn–Shaped Stand 5485.00
Perfume Bottle, Cut Chrysanthemum, Cameo, 1900, 3 7/8 In. 3575.00
Perfume Bottle, Maroon Trumpet Flowers, Gold Ground, Signed, 6 In. 2000.00
Rose Bowl, Clematis Blossoms, 3 Colors, 5 1/2 In. 1000.00
Sconce, Magnolia Blossoms, Bronze Mount, c.1900, 11 1/2 In. 5500.00
Shot Glass, Carved Maple Seeds, Frosted, Signed, 2 1/2 In. 985.00
Vase, 3 Colors, Wisteria, Leaves, Pink & Frosted Ground, 10 1/4 In. 1100.00
Vase, 4 Shades Of Red, Oblong, Signed, 3 3/4 In. 825.00
Vase, 4–Petaled Blossoms, Stems, Pink To Amethyst, Signed, 6 1/2 In. 1045.00
Vase, Acid Cut Columbines & Leaves, Frosted Ground, Signed, 3 In. 900.00
Vase, Allover Star–Like Flowers, Chartreuse Ground, 13 3/4 In. 4000.00
Vase, Alpine Lake Scene, Sapphire & Purple, Signed, 5 In. 1980.00
Vase, Alsatian Landscape, Conifers, Lake, Signed, c.1900, 7 3/8 In. 3850.00
Vase, Alsatian Mountain Scene, Blue, Purple, Cameo, 7 3/8 In. 3850.00
Vase, Amethyst Foliage, Frosted Ground, Crimped Top, 4 3/4 In. 750.00
Vase, Amethyst, Balloon, Flowers, Signed, 10 3/4 In. 650.00
Vase, Applied Green Cabochon, Foil Floret, Internal Design, 11 In. 8800.00
Vase, Balloon Flowers, Clear Frosted Ground, Cameo, Signed, 11 In. 650.00
Vase, Banjo Form, Mottled, Cut Wild Flowers, Signed, 6 3/4 In. 935.00
Vase, Banjo, 3–Color, Cameo Of Draped Flower Buds, 6 3/4 In. 1210.00
Vase, Banjo, Wisteria Blossoms, Leaves, Frosted Ground, Signed, 6 In. 1050.00
Vase, Blossoms & Leafage, Fire Polished, Signed, c.1900, 4 3/4 In. 775.00
Vase, Blossoms, Pods & Leaves, Layered In Amber, Signed, 4 1/2 In. 525.50
Vase, Brown, Purple, Frosted White, 6 In. 2250.00
Vase, Bud, Clematis, Purple On Frosted White, Signed, 15 In. 3350.00
Vase, Bud, Wild Roses, Frosted Clear & Mauve, Green Overlay, Cameo 775.00
Vase, Cameo, Amber To Frost, Floral, Enameled & Gilt, 10 In. 1650.00
Vase, Campanula Blossoms & Leaves, Signed, 6 In. 3300.00
Vase, Cherry Branches & Fruit, Butterflies, Triangular, Signed, 6 In. 935.00
Vase, Chrysanthemum, Chocolate, Apricot, Gray, Cameo, Conical, 8 5/8 In. 2750.00
Vase, Clematis Blossoms, Buds & Leave, Ovoid, Signed, c.1900, 5 3/4 In. 2200.00
Vase, Clematis, Profusion Of Clematis, Signed, 6 3/4 In. 7700.00
Vase, Cluster Of Queen Anne's Lace, Shades Of Green, Signed, 12 In. 2295.00
Vase, Clusters Of Berries, Spiky Leafage, Signed, c.1900, 7 1/2 In. 1980.00
Vase, Clusters Of Wild Flowers, Leaves, Signed, c.1900, 6 3/4 In. 885.00
Vase, Colorless, Apricot Blossoms, Leafy Stems, Signed, 9 3/4 In. 1200.00
Vase, Crocus, Purple Against Peach Ground, 5 1/4 In. 2950.00
Vase, Cut, Carved & Etched Delphiniums, Yellow Ground, Signed, 13 In. 3875.00
Vase, Cyclamen Blossoms, Cameo, Gray, Raspberry, Rose, 1900, 8 5/8 In. 3850.00
Vase, Delphinium Blossoms, Buds, Gray, Signed, c.1900, 17 1/8 In. 5500.00
Vase, Double Overlay, Irises, Purple, Amber, Slender Baluster Form 1665.00

Vase, Dragon Cartouche, Birds Side, Enameled, 2 Handles, 4 3/8 In. 3300.00
Vase, Everted Rim, Flowering Wood Anemones, Signed, 5 7/8 In. 1430.00
Vase, Ferns, Clover, Foliage, Amber Base, Signed, 11 In. 3750.00
Vase, Ferns, Flattened Ovoid Form, Brown To Green, Signed, 6 3/4 In. 2035.00
Vase, Fisherman, Islands, Cobalt Over Orange & Gold, Cameo, 4 In. 900.00
Vase, Flask Shape, Applied Handles, Gray, Pink, Green, Cameo, 5 1/2 In. 1540.00
Vase, Flowering Cherry Blossom Branches, Signed, 7 1/4 In. 3960.00
Vase, Flowering Prunus, Yellow, Cobalt Streaks, 1910, 14 5/8 In. 9350.00
Vase, Flowers & Leaves, Applied Cabochons, Signed, 19 1/2 In. 8500.00
Vase, French Cock, Prussian Eagle, Yellow, Green, Brown, Signed, 15 In. 1650.00
Vase, Frosted White Ground, Purple, Blue, Landscape, Signed, 10 In. 1765.00
Vase, Gourd Shape, Signed, Cameo, 4 1/2 In. 275.00
Vase, Green Cameo Ferns, 18 In. 1600.00
Vase, Green, Lavender & Peach, White Ground, 16 In. 3900.00
Vase, Hanging, Clematis Blossoms, Signed, c.1900, 14 1/2 In. 8800.00
Vase, Hanging, Rose Hips, Thorny Branches, Signed, c.1900, 9 1/2 In. 2750.00
Vase, Hanging, Young Fruits, Leafy Branches, Signed, c.1900, 11 3/8 In. 1550.00
Vase, Hyacinth Flower, Shades Of Purple, Ovoid, Signed, 7 In. 1100.00
Vase, Hydrangea Blossoms & Foliage, Peach Overlay, Signed, 17 In. 3000.00
Vase, Hydrangea Blossoms & Leaves, Pink To White, Signed, 6 1/2 In. 1650.00
Vase, Inverted Baluster, Fuchsias, Amber To Amber, Signed, 11 In. 4950.00
Vase, Iris, Frosted, Caramel, Purple, Chinese Signed, 10 In. 2860.00
Vase, Jonquils, Green Leaves At Bottom, 10 In. 5500.00
Vase, Lake & Forest Scene, Pinks, Brown, Coral, 5 In. 2600.00
Vase, Landscape Of Trees, Bridge, River, Signed, c.1900, 11 In. 1575.00
Vase, Landscape, Trees, Hills, Dark Green, Signed, 8 In. 1760.00
Vase, Leafage & Fruit Pips, c.1900, 9 3/4 In. 3025.00
Vase, Leaves & Pods, 5 1/2 In. 600.00
Vase, Lilies & Foliage, Carved & Etched On Yellow, 10 In. 3100.00
Vase, Lilies, Olive, Emerald Streaked, Cameo, Baluster, 1900, 23 1/4 In. 4400.00
Vase, Long Stemmed Blossoms, Cylindrical, Spreading Base, Cameo, 7 In. 385.00
Vase, Maple Leaves, Yellow Bird, Amber Overlay, c.1900, 4 In. 785.00
Vase, Marine Plants, Green To Gold, 9 3/4 In. 3500.00
Vase, Maroon Grape Clusters, Coral, Flared, DeLatte Nancy, Cameo 750.00
Vase, Mold Blown, Hanging, Squash Blossoms, Signed, c.1900, 7 3/8 In. 4400.00
Vase, Morning Glories, Pink Ground, 18 1/2 In. 6500.00
Vase, Mottled Yellow, Amethyst Overlay, Violets, Signed, 3 1/2 In. 1450.00
Vase, Mountainous Landscape, Oviform, Signed, 8 In. 3080.00
Vase, Multicolored Poppies & Leaves, Signed, Aqua, 18 1/2 In. 6050.00
Vase, Peach Gui Pods, 23 In. 6500.00
Vase, Pillow, Brown Trees, Lake, Frosty Amber Ground, 8 1/4 In. 2700.00
Vase, Poppies, Green, Orange, Signed, 5 In. 825.00
Vase, Primroses, Leaves, Ovoid, Signed, c.1900, 4 3/4 In. 1450.00
Vase, Prunus Branches, Trumpet Neck, Gray, Sapphire, Pink, 15 In. 4950.00
Vase, Purple Chrysanthemums, Pale Yellow Ground, Ovoid, Overlay 4699.00
Vase, Purple Trailing Clematis, Cameo, Compressed Cylindrical Form 1860.00
Vase, Random Cutting, Abstract Design, Pale Green, Signed, 8 3/4 In. 385.00
Vase, Red & Yellow Leaves, Bulbous, Signed 2750.00
Vase, Red Cherry Design, Yellow Bottom, 2 3/4 In. 850.00
Vase, Red Flowering Plants, Yellow Tinted, Conical, Everted Rim 5875.00
Vase, Red Flowering Rose Branches, Yellow Ground, Inverted Trumpet 7100.00
Vase, River Landscape, Trees, Thick Vessel, Signed, c.1930, 21 3/4 In. 3300.00
Vase, Ruby Red Cut With Cyclamen Blossoms, Signed, c.1900, 4 3/16 In. 880.00
Vase, Scenic, Top Flares Out To Become Scallops, 11 In. 5250.00
Vase, Squash Blossom, Gray, Lemon, Red Sienna, Cameo, 1925, 7 1/4 In. 8250.00
Vase, Step-Type Bends, Flowers & Leaves, Partially Frosted, 12 In. 3200.00
Vase, Sunflowers, Leaves, Glass Centers, Signed, 6 x 8 3/4 In. 5500.00
Vase, Trailing Roses, Cameo, Lemon, Crimson, Ovoid, Everted Rim, 7 In. 8250.00
Vase, Trees By Bank Of River, Signed, c.1900, 13 5/8 In. 7700.00
Vase, Trefoil Top, Large Iris, Buds & Leaves, Signed, 7 In. 3850.00
Vase, Tricornered Top, Fuchsia Flowers On Yellow, 8 In. 2600.00
Vase, Trumpet Vine Flowers, Ovoid Front To Back, Signed, 13 1/2 In. 8500.00
Vase, Undulating Branches Of Bleeding Hearts, Signed, 1900, 8 7/8 In. 7700.00

Vase, Undulating Iris Blossoms, Signed, c.1900, 20 1/4 In. 5775.00
Vase, Unfurling Fern Fronds, Cicada On Shoulder, Signed, 5 7/8 In. 665.00
Vase, Water Lilies, 3 Color, 4 x 4 In. 1500.00
Vase, Water Scene, Double Bud Purple Floral, 13 1/2 In. 675.00
Vase, Wild Flowers, Buds, Leaves, Signed, c.1900, 13 1/4 In. 1200.00
Vase, Wild Orchids, Foliage, Swirled Lines, Signed, 9 1/2 In. 8800.00
Vase, Wild Rose Blossoms, Buds, Signed, c.1900, 17 In. 3850.00
Vase, Wooded Landscape, Leafy Trees, Signed, c.1900, 10 1/8 In. 3850.00
Vase, Yellow & Peach Daisies, Brown Accents, 5 In. 1250.00

GAME PLATES are plates of any make decorated with pictures of birds, animals, or fish. The game plates usually came in sets consisting of twelve dishes and a serving platter. These sets were most popular during the 1880s.

Deer At Stream, Large 25.00
Grouse In Foliage, Reticulated Border, Limoges 45.00
Grouse, 6 Reserves, Reticulated Border, Coronet, 13 In. 95.00
Hanging, Gold Rococo Rim, Quail, Grassy Setting, 13 In. 195.00
Mallard Duck, Coronet, Signed, 10 In. 50.00
Quail, Flowers, Beaded Rim, Gold Trim, Limoges, 13 3/4 In. 225.00
Wild Boars, Gold Scalloped Rim, Coronet, 10 In. 95.00
GAME SET, Fish, Platter, 12 Plates, France 300.00
Fowl Scenes, Green Band, Gilt, Platter, Haviland, 13 Piece 357.50

GAMES of all sorts are collected. Of special interest are any board games or card games. Transogram and other company names are included in the description when known. Other games may be found listed under Card, Toy, or the name of the character or celebrity featured in the game.

6 Million Dollar Man, Board 9.00
Addams Family, Card, Milton Bradley, 1965 .... 12.00 To 50.00
Advance & Retreat, Milton Bradley 50.00
Adventures Of Smiling Jack, Uncut, 1940s, 128 Cards 195.00
Air Raid Warden, Milton Bradley 75.00
Alf, Seated, Board 15.00
Alice In Wonderland, Board, Spears 35.00
All In The Family ....8.00 To 25.00
American Eagle History, Parker Brothers, 1900s 60.00
Animal Lotto 40.00
Apple's Way, Board, 1974 .... 32.00
Archie, Pop Art Game, Whitman, Sealed, 1969 .... 49.00
Arithmetic, Buffalo Toy, Tin 15.00
Autmore, Card, Parker Bros., 1943 .... 40.00
Auto Racing, Metal Cars, Alderman, Fairchild, 1920s 55.00
Banana Republic, Aussie Mfg. 40.00
Barbie–Queen Of The Prom 25.00
Baretta, Board, Robert Blake TV Star, 1976 .... 35.00
Barney Miller, Original Cast From TV, 1977 .... 17.00
Baseball Card, Olson Game Co., Box, c.1922 .... 35.00
Baseball, Electric, All Tin, Box, Large 95.00
Baseball, Official Babe Ruth's, Box, 17 x 25 In. 305.00
Baseball, Roger Maris, Pressman Toy Corp., Box 75.00
Baseball, Spinner Top, Indicated Play, Walter Johnson 180.00
Baseball, Sports Illustrated, 1971 .... 15.00
Bat Masterson, Board, Western Town Replica, Box, 1958 .... 95.00
Batman Vs The Joker, 1965, Hasbro 32.00
Battle Cry, Civil War, Board 20.00
Battle Of The Bulge, 1960s 20.00
Battlestar Gallactica, Milton Bradley, 1976 .... 10.00 To 20.00
Bazooka Bafatelle, Marx 35.00
Beany & Cecil, Jumping Surprise Action 25.00
Ben Casey, Board, 1965 .... 50.00
Ben Casey, Transogram, 1961 .... 20.00 To 25.00
Beverly Hillbillies, Card, 1960s .... 18.50 To 20.00

Bewitched, Card 25.00
Black Beauty, Transogram, 1957 .... 20.00
Black Cat Fortune Telling, 1940s 45.00
Board, Alternating Yellow & Black Squares, American, Square, 14 In. 330.00
Board, Archery, Bull's–Eye, For Rubber Tipped Arrows 55.00
Board, Black & Brown Squares, Back Trays, 2–Sided, 18 1/2 x 31 3/4 In. 175.00
Board, Black & Gold Squares, Green Borders, Square Nail Trim 165.00
Board, Black & Natural, Walnut, Round, 15 In. 130.00
Board, Black Ground, Made From Breadboard, 22 x 25 1/2 In. 400.00
Board, Black On Mirror, Glass Covered, Oak Frame, 1800s, 12 x 12 In. 160.00
Board, Black Squares On Mirror, Oak Frame, 12 x 12 3/4 In. 160.00
Board, Blue & Black Squares, Red, Green & Brown Outlines 275.00
Board, Checkerboard 1 Side, Parcheesi Other, Colorful, 18 x 16 In. 400.00
Board, Checkerboard 1 Side, Parcheesi Other, Gallery, 18 x 18 1/2 In. 425.00
Board, Cribbage, Ivory & Mahogany, Ivory Feet, 9 1/2 x 3 1/4 In. 185.00
Board, Cribbage, Ivory Walrus Tusk 350.00
Board, Cribbage, Pacific Game Co., Box 4.00
Board, Cribbage, Pierced Top & Sides, Turned Legs, Brass, 10 In. 440.00
Board, Cribbage, Priest's Indigestion Powder, Wooden 65.00
Board, Cribbage, Walrus Tusk, Scrimshaw Of Seals & Polar Bears 300.00
Board, Dart, Tim Holt, Metal, Original Box 275.00
Board, Folding, Wooden Carved, 5 Carved Ivory Dice, 6 x 9 1/2 In. 95.00
Board, Gold & Red Squares Outlined In Black, Green Border, 1902 .... 715.00
Board, Graphic, Contrasting Wood Inlay, 29 x 19 In. 650.00
Board, Green & White, Orange Border, 1800s, 18 x 24 1/2 In. .... 160.000 To 215.00
Board, Green, Red & Yellow 225.00
Board, Hinged Case Opens To Surface, Anglo Indian, c.1900, 34 x 34 In. 440.00
Board, Inlaid Squares On Pine, Bird's–Eye Maple & Burled Mahogany 155.00
Board, Inlaid Squares, Brass Corners, Walnut, 16 1/2 x 20 1/2 In. 170.00
Board, Inlaid, Ebony, Satinwood, Cocabola & Mahogany 355.00
Board, Maple & Walnut Inlay On Pine, Glass Cover, 16 1/4 x 20 3/4 In. 170.00
Board, Parcheesi, Corner Leaf Design, Painted, 1890s, 14 x 14 In. 1100.00
Board, Parcheesi, Orange, Green & Black Squares, 18 1/2 x 19 1/2 In. 880.00
Board, Red & Black Squares, U.S., 1880s, 19 3/4 x 39 1/2 In. 467.50
Board, Semiprecious Stones, Marble, Walnut Frame, Italy, 26 x 26 In. 2420.00
Board, Slate, Painted To Look Like Marble, 19th Century 1100.00
Board, Whalebone, Engraved, John Tripp, 16 In. 2310.00
Bobbsey Twins On Farm, Milton Bradley, Box, c.1957 .... 10.00
Bonanza Michigan Rummy, Card, Parker Bros., 1964 .... 49.00
Branded, Milton Bradley, 1966 .... 69.00
Bulls & Bears 12.00
Bullwinkle Supermarket, Whitman, 1976 .... 49.00
Cabbage Patch Kids, Box 15.00
Cadet, McLoughlin Bros. 35.00
Call Me Lucky, Bing Crosby, Parker Bros., 1954 .... 45.00 To 150.00
Camelot, Parker Bros., 1930 .... 50.00
Captain America, Milton Bradley, 1966 .... 52.00 To 105.00
Captain Gallant, Transogram, 1955 .... 98.00
Captain Video, Spaceship Control Panel, Board .... 60.00 To 150.00
Carl Hubbell Baseball, Box 358.00
Carrier Strike, Milton Bradley, 1977 .... 50.00
Carrom, Board With Stand, Game Pieces In 2 Bags, Instructions, 1901 .... 125.00
Casper Bean, Jumping Bean, Milton Bradley, 1960 .... 29.00
Casper The Friendly Ghost, Board 40.00
Casper The Friendly Ghost, Casper Doll Lights Up, Battery Operated 20.00
Cat & Mouse, Board, Parker Bros., 1965 .... 15.00
Charlie Chan Detective, Milton Bradley, Box .... 75.00 To 89.00
Charlie's Angels, Board 12.00
Checker Set, Paladin–Have Gun Will Travel 60.00
Checkerboard, Alligatored Blue & Goldenrod, 16 3/4 x 30 3/4 In. 140.00
Checkerboard, Applied Gallery, Alligatored Red & Black, 10 x 30 In. 200.00
Checkerboard, Green, Black Paint, Yellow Numbers, 18 3/4 x 31 In. 350.00
Checkerboard, Inlaid, 14 x 14 In. 85.00

Checkerboard, Lithographed Tin, Scroll Design, c.1880, 18 x 23 In. 295.00
Checkerboard, Pine, Red & Black Paint, Gilded Molded Edge, 11 x 11 In. 125.00
Checkerboard, Red & Black Squares, Butternut, Pine Frame, Square, 23 In 265.00
Checkerboard, Red Squares Over Butternut, 12 1/2 x 23 1/4 In. 225.00
Checkerboard, Red Squares, Unpainted Pine, 18 x 28 1/2 In. .... 145.00 To 180.00
Checkerboard, Squares In Wood Tray, Folk Art, 1900, 24 x 16 3/4 In. 195.00
Checkerboard, Yellow & Black Paint, Red Trim, 16 1/2 x 24 3/4 In. 500.00
Checkers, Andrews Game Co., Box 3.50
Chenkuk Chec, Board, Instructions & Marbles In Bag, 1937 .... 17.00
Chess, Ivory, Box Opens To Become Board 200.00
Chinese Checkers, All Wood, Chinese Star, Green, Red & Blue Design 40.00
Chinese Checkers, Wooden Frame, Dragons, Pressman & Co., 15 1/2 In. 25.00
Chinese Checkers, Wooden Frame, Dragons, Straits Mfg., 17 In. 28.00
Chinese Checkers, Wooden Frame, Parker Bros., 16 x 16 In. 30.00
Chiromagica, Walnut Case, McLoughlin Bros. 412.00
Christmas Jewel, McLoughlin, 1899, 8 x 17 In. 660.00
Cimarron Strip, Ideal, 1967 .... 79.00
Civil War, The Spy, Lincoln Is Commander In Chief, Card 150.00
Clue, Board, 1963 .... 10.00
Columbo, Milton Bradley, 1973 .... 25.00
Combat, Ideal, Board, 1960 .... 28.00
Concentration, Board, Original Edition 45.00
Coney Island, Technofix, Box 495.00
Consul, Educated Monkey, Multiplies Numbers, Tin, 1916, 5 1/2 x 6 In. 165.00
Coon Hunt, Board, Parker Bros., 1904, 9 x 15 In. 825.00
Cootie, Complete, 1949 .... 25.00
Countdown, Lowe Co., 1967 .... 95.00 To 100.00
Cowboy Roundup, Board, Box, 1952 .... 18.00
Crap Table, From Dunes Hotel, 10 x 12 Ft. 2500.00
Dart Board, Aces, Tin Lithograph, Ohio Art 40.00
Dating Game 10.00
Detective Columbo, Milton Bradley 20.00
District Messenger Boy, McLoughlin Bros. 85.00
Doc Holiday, Transogram, 1960 .... 29.00
Dominoes, Bullet Shape, Double 9 & 6, Box, Directions, Halsam 39.00
Dominoes, Ebony & Ivory, Mahogany Box, Lid, 6 1/2 In. 90.00
Dominoes, Hoods Sarsaparilla 65.00
Dominoes, Ivory, 1800s 145.00
Dominoes, Old Ivory & Ebony Dovetailed Box, 1 Missing 55.00
Dominoes, Red Bell Tobacco 225.00
Down You Go, Board, Belshaw & Righter, 1964 .... 35.00
Dr. Doolittle, Mattel 50.00
Dr. Kildare, Board, Ideal, 1962 .... 15.00 To 29.00
Dr. Kildare, Flash Card, Box 20.00
Dracula, Mystery Game, Hasbro, 1963 .... 139.00
Dragnet, Target, With Gun, Metal, 1955 .... 35.00
Dragnet, Transogram, 1955 .... 59.00
E. T., Board 10.00
E. T., Card, Box 10.00
Eddie Cantor, Tell It To The Judge, Board, 1936 .... 38.00
Ellery Queen, Detective Figural Playing Pieces 20.00
Elsie & Her Family, Selchow & Righter, Box, 1941 .... 65.00 To 85.00
Elsie The Cow Cone Pop Ice Cream, Box, 1958 .... 30.00
Emenee Chocolate Factory, 1966 .... 38.00
Expecting Trouble, Bonanza, Milton Bradley, 1964 .... 425.00
Fantastic Voyage, 1968 .... 18.00
Fantasy Island, Board, 1978 .... 6.00
Fess Parker Trail Blazer, Board, 1964 .... 50.00
Fiddlestix, Cardboard–Tin Tube Container, Instructions 8.00
Finance, Parker Bros., 1935 .... 30.00
Fish Bait, 1965 .... 25.99
Fish Pond, Magnetic, Paperboard Area, 5 Rods, Spear's Games, 12 In. 49.50
Fishing, Magnetic, On Card, 1954 .... 18.00

Flinch, Card, Parker Bros., Dated 1938 ....5.00 To 12.00
Flipper Flips, 1965 .... 29.00
Flying Nun, Milton Bradley, 1968 ....40.00 To 49.00
Football, Cadaco–Ellis, 1946 .... 100.00
Football, Johnny Unitas 15.00
Fortune Teller, Mysticope 50.00
Fox & Hounds, Parker Bros. 25.00
Frank Buck, Board, 1930s 65.00
Game Of Detective, Board, Bliss, 1889 .... 2975.00
Game Of Fox Hunting, Board, Spear, 1930s, 12 x 19 In. 330.00
Game Of Pegpen For Everybody, Whitman, Complete, 1929 .... 19.00
Game Of States, Board, 4 Plastic Trucks, Box, 1930s 35.00
Gee Whiz, Horse Race, Wolverine, Wood Case, 28 In. 125.00
General Hospital, Board 20.00
Get Smart Exploding Time Bomb, Ideal, 1965 .... 79.00
Giant Michigan Rummy, Transogram, 1960s 20.00
Gidget Fortune Teller Game, Board, 1960s 10.00
Gilligan's Island, Board, 4 Pieces, Cards, Diorama, Milton Bradley, 1974 .... 60.00
Goldferino, Box 22.50
Golf, Pivot, Box, 1950s 300.00
Golf, Teed Off, Box, 1966 .... 25.00
Golliwog, 48 Different Cards, Box 235.00
Gomer Pyle, 1963 ....40.00 To 45.00
Gracie Allen Rummy, Box 20.00
Great Grape Ape, Milton Bradley, Box, 1975 .... 30.00
Grizzly Adams, 1978 .... 20.00
Gumball Target, Hit The Target, Win A Gumball, Box, 1960s 30.00
Gumball, Knickerbocker, Box, 1958 .... 30.00
Gunsmoke, Lowe, 1955 .... 89.00
Hand Of Fate, 1901, McLoughlin, Board, 14 x 15 In. 4400.00
Harness & Horse Goods, Metal Balls, Paper Recesses, Pocket 12.00
Hi–Ho Cherryo, Red Cherry Pieces 20.00
Hide–N–Seek, Ideal, Board, 1960s 20.00
Highway Viaduct, Technofix, Box 320.00
Hippety Hop, Corey Game Co., 1940 .... 80.00
Hit The Target, Launch A Spaceship, Box, 1960s 30.00
Hogan's Heroes, Bluff Out, Transogram, 1966 .... 98.00
Home Baseball, Box, 13 x 7 In. ....39.00 To 50.00
Honors, Camp Fire Girls, Card, c.1910 .... 18.00
Hoopla, Ideal, 1966 .... 24.00
Horse Race, Wolverine, Metal, Box, 1924 .... 175.00
Horseshoes, Indoor, Pitch' Em, Wolverine, 1930s 125.00
Horseshoes, Indoor, Steel Reinforced Rubber, Box, 1910 .... 40.00
House Party, Art Linkletter 40.00
Howard Hughes, Board, 1972 .... 32.00
Huckleberry Hound, Box 15.00
Huckleberry Hound, Spin–O–Game, Hannah Barbera, 1959 .... 75.00
Hustler Baseball, Box, 1925 .... 176.00
I Dream Of Jeannie, Milton Bradley, 1965 .... 35.00
I'm George Gobel, 1955 ....60.00 To 65.00
Ilya Kariakin, Card 35.00
Indian Scouting, Walt Disney, Box 95.00
Intercollegiate Football, Hustler Toys, 1925 .... 145.00
Jack and The Bean Stalk, Board, McLoughlin, 1898, 10 x 19 In. 990.00
James Bond, 1964, Milton Bradley 40.00
James Bond, 1965, Spears, England 89.00
Jan Murray, TV Game, Board 22.00
Jeopardy, No. 1, 1964 .... 35.00
Jolly Robbers, Wilder 25.00
Justice League Of America, Wonder Woman, Hasbro, Box 390.00
Kennedys, Board 45.00
Kiss On Tour, American Publishing Co., 1978 .... 22.00
Krull, Board, Parker Bros. 35.00

Lancer Game, Remco, 1968 .... 59.00
Leave It To Beaver, Ambush, Board 30.00
Legend Of Jesse James, Milton Bradley, 1966 .... 42.00
Let's Make A Deal, Board, Ideal, 1974 .... 25.00
Library Of Games, Old Maid, Animal Rummy, Dr. Quack, Slap Jack, 6 Boxes 45.00
Library Of Games, Russell Mfg. Co., 1945 .... 22.00
Lie Detector, Mattel, 1960s 35.00
Light Up The Candles, Orphan Annie, Colmor, Metal & Cardboard 50.00
Lightning Express Railroad, Board, Milton Bradley, 1949 .... 35.00
Lindy Hop–Off, Parker Bros., 1927 .... 400.00
Little Black Sambo, Board 150.00
Little Black Sambo, Target, Metal Lithograph, Stand, Wyandotte 77.00
Little Country Dr. Kit, Transogram, Complete, 1940 .... 50.00
Lone Ranger, Target, Marx, 1939, 10 x 10 In. 125.00
Lost In Space, Board, 1965 ....35.00 To 85.00
Lunar Landing, Box, 1960s 30.00
Mad Magazine, Crazy Instructions, 1979 .... 11.00
Magic Trick, Ball & Vase, Pocket Type, Box, 1930s 12.00
Mah Jong Jr., Box, 1923 .... 25.00
Major League Baseball, Box, 1914 .... 425.00
Man From U. N. C. L. E., Card, Milton Bradley, 1965 ....5.00 To 16.00
Mansion Of Happiness, Board, McLoughlin, 1895, 16 x 19 In. 935.00
Margie's Game Of Whoopie, Milton Bradley, 1961 .... 20.00
Mary Poppins Carousel, Parker Bros., 1964 .... 35.00
McHale's Navy, Pictures Ernest Borgnine, 1962 .... 85.00
McKeever & The Colonel, Bamboozle, Milton Bradley, 1962 .... 39.00
Mighty Mouse, 1978 .... 22.00
Minoru, New Race Game, English Horse Racing, Cloth, Jaques & Sons 195.00
Miss Lively Livin', Mattel, 1970 .... 25.00
Mission Impossible, Figural Playing Pieces, Berwick, 1975 .... 75.00
Monopoly, Board, Parker Bros., 1936 .... 55.00
Monopoly, Darrow 4400.00
Monopoly, Darrow, Board, 1934, 10 x 20 In. 4400.00
Mork & Mindy, Board ....8.00 To 10.00
Morton Downey Jr., Loudmouth, Board 20.00
Movie Wheels, Felix The Cat, Original Package 45.00
Mr. Magoo, Card, Double Deck, GE Electric, 1960s 15.00
Mr. Magoo, Oh Magoo You've Done It Again, Warren, Sealed, 1972 .... 48.00
Mr. Novak, Transogram 45.00
Munsters Drag Race Game, Board, Hasbro, 1965 .... 350.00
Munsters, Card, 1964 ....35.00 To 50.00
My Fair Lady, Board 45.00
My Favorite Martian, Transogram, 1963 .... 98.00
My Mother Sent Me To The Grocery Store, Parker Bros. 145.00
Mystery Date, Board, 1965 .... 25.00
Mystic Skull Voodoo, Ideal 32.00
Name That Tune, Board, 1957 .... 50.00
Nancy Drew Mystery Game, Parker Bros., 1957 .... 30.00
National Game Of The American Eagle, Board, Ives, 1844, 17 x 14 In. 5390.00
New Game Piggies, Board, Selchow & Righter, 1894, 12 x 12 In. 605.00
New Parlor Game–Baseball, Board, M. B. Summer, 1869, 12 x 17 In. 8250.00
Nixon's Nose Ring Toss 27.50
Number Please, Board, 1961 .... 25.00
Old Maid, Card, 1959 .... 10.00
One Of Her Problems, Marble ....100.00 To 150.00
Orbit, Parker Bros., 1959 .... 55.00
Paladin, Have Gun Will Travel, Board, Box, Complete 75.00
Palmistry, McLaughlin 65.00
Parlor Foot–Ball Game 650.00
Parlor Quoits, C. D. Atkins 40.00
Partridge Family, Board 20.00
Patty Duke, Milton Bradley, 1963 ....22.00 To 35.00
Personal Appearance Tour, Mattel, 1980 .... 10.00

Peter Pan, Transogram	25.00
Peter Rabbit's Race Game, Board, Beatrix Potter, Frederick Warne	192.00
Petticoat Junction, 1963	29.00 To 40.00
Phillip Marlow, Transogram, 1960	89.00
Pigskin, Parker Bros., 1935	40.00
Pinball, Home Run King, Glass Cased, Japan, 4 1/2 x 2 1/2 In.	30.00
Pinball, Lucky Clown, Hero Mfg. Co., Box	20.00
Pinball, Table, Space Graphics, Wolverine, 1950s	95.00
Ping-Pong, Wright & Dixon, Set	60.00
Pinky Lee, What's My Line, Board, 1955	90.00
Pinocchio, Parker Bros.	50.00
Pirate & Travelers, 1960	12.00
Pit, Card, 1919	12.00
Pitch-A-Ring, Milton Bradley, 1900s	38.00
Poker Chip Holder, Round, 1920s	20.00
Poker Chip Set, Bakelite, Yellow & Green Case, 208 Piece	85.00
Poker Chip Set, Bone, France, 1900, Box, 200 Piece	75.00
Poker, Chickadee, W. C. Fields	40.00
Polly Put The Kettle On, 1923	35.00
Pollyanna, 1920s	45.00
Practice Target Range, Tin, Plastic, Marx, 11 In.	25.00
Prince Valiant, Board	65.00
Prince Valiant, Transogram, 1955	65.00
Pro Football, 1964	15.00
Punchboard, Barrel Of Winners	25.00
Pussy & The 3 Mice, Board, 1890, 10 x 19 In.	605.00
Puzzle, 4 Picture Puzzles For Children, Milton Bradley, 1935	45.00
Puzzle, A Peep At The Circus, Picture Puzzle, McLoughlin, 1887	500.00
Puzzle, Addams Family, Ghost At Large, Mystery Jigsaw, 1965	178.00
Puzzle, Alice In Wonderland, Circular, 1965	12.00
Puzzle, Alice In Wonderland, Garden Of Live Flowers, 20 Piece	25.00
Puzzle, American Airlines, 1940s	19.00
Puzzle, American Bandstand, Jaymar, Round, 400 Piece	12.00
Puzzle, Animal Antics, Scroll, McLoughlin, 1894	450.00
Puzzle, Battlestar Galactica, Parker Bros., 140 Piece	20.00
Puzzle, Beverly Hillbillies, 1960s	28.00
Puzzle, Bewitched, Endora, Havoc Filled Living Room	45.00
Puzzle, Brady Bunch	10.00
Puzzle, Brain Teaser, Wooden Jig Cut, Teaching Aid, 1900s	39.00
Puzzle, Budweiser Light, Springbok, Sealed	10.00
Puzzle, Captain Kangaroo, Framed Tray, 1960	15.00
Puzzle, Cisco Kid & Pancho, Framed	25.00
Puzzle, Coffin Shaped Box, H-G Toys, 100 Piece	20.00
Puzzle, Dr. Seuss, Esso, Original Envelope	75.00
Puzzle, Felix, Frame Tray, 1959	30.00
Puzzle, Goldfinger, Complete	20.00
Puzzle, Gunga Din, Germany, Wood	25.00
Puzzle, Gunsmoke, 1969	15.00
Puzzle, Harley Davidson Motorcycles & Bicycles, Metal	75.00
Puzzle, Jake & Lena, 1930s	25.00
Puzzle, James Bond 007	8.00 To 10.00
Puzzle, Jigsaw, Dark Shadows	75.00
Puzzle, Jigsaw, Fire Engine, Milton Bradley, 1957, 10 x 14 In., 20 Piece	25.00
Puzzle, Jigsaw, Folger's Coffee, Box, Unopened	75.00
Puzzle, Jigsaw, MASH	20.00
Puzzle, Keen Kutter Logo Shape, Box	950.00
Puzzle, Magic Tricks	35.00
Puzzle, Marilyn Monroe, Black & White, 1974	6.00
Puzzle, Monkees Hey-Hey, Box	35.00
Puzzle, Our Gang, Kids In Old Taxi, 1933	45.00
Puzzle, Rhinoceros, McLoughlin, c.1870	33.00
Puzzle, Sliced Nations, Selchow & Righter, 1875	100.00
Puzzle, Space Patrol, Milton Bradley	65.00

Puzzle, Tarzan Ape, Johnny Weissmuller's 1st Movie, Sleeve, 1932 .... 225.00
Puzzle, The 10 Cents No. 7 Puzzle, Wood Numbered Buttons Slide, Frame 32.00
Puzzle, Thunderball, 11 x 10 In. .... 20.00 To 26.00
Puzzle, Trailways Bus, Framed, 1948, 14 x 21 In. 125.00
Puzzle, Tray, Beverly Hillbillies, Jaymar Spec., Co., 11 1/2 x 13 In. 200.00
Puzzle, Twilight Express Train, Milton Bradley 220.00
Puzzle, Uncle Wiggly, Box, 3 Piece 40.00
Puzzle, Victor Record 90.00
Puzzle, Wood, Farm, Animals, Witch, 2 Sides, Box, Germany 175.00
Quick Draw, 1960, Milton Bradley 32.00
Quints, Card, Token, Chips 190.00
Quiz Kids Own Game, 1940 .... 45.00
Racing Car Set, Race N' Road Speedway, Marx, 1950s 95.00
Radio, All Fair, Megaphone Pieces 90.00
Ramar Of The Jungle, Dexter Wayne, 1950 .... 90.00
Ranger, Target, Tin, Marx, Box, Dated 1939 .... 165.00
Red Goose Shoes, String 15.00
Restless Gun, Milton Bradley, 1959 .... 75.00 To 79.00
Rifleman, Board, 1959 .... 95.00
Rin Tin Tin, Box, 1955 .... 20.00
Rin Tin Tin, Transogram, 1956 .... 39.00
Ring Toss, Goosy Gander, Wooden Goose, Wood Rings 48.00
Ring-A-Peg, Horsman 15.00
Robin Hood Pop-Up, Box, 1955 .... 45.00
Robinson Crusoe, Black Boy, Board, McLoughlin, Box .... 35.00 To 45.00
Rocky, Bullwinkle 6.00
Rol-A-Lite, Battery Operated, Durable Toy & Novelty Corp. 280.00
Roll Astronaut In Orbit, Tootsie Roll 30.00
Roll-O-Card, Card, Box, 17 1/2 In. 45.00
Rook, Card, 1955 .... 10.00
Rootie Kazootie, Card 6.00
Roulette Wheel, Brown Bakelite, 1930s 55.00
Round The World With Nellie Bly, Board, McLoughlin, 1890, 16 x 19 In. 220.00
Route 66, Transogram, 1962 .... 129.00
Ruff & Reddy Spelling 35.00
Salmon & Bittersweet, Board 345.00
Sambo, Hand Painted, Checkerboard On Reverse, 1910s 1100.00
Santa Claus, Whitman 15.00
Satellite, Target, Gun & Rubber Darts, Japan, Box, 1950s 95.00
Scooby Doo, Board 5.00
Secret Agentman, Milton Bradley, 1966 .... 29.00
Secret Of Ninn, Board, Whitman 18.00
Seduction, Create, 1966 .... 38.00
Shadow, Board, Box, 1940 .... 557.00
Silly Sidney, Board, Transogram, 1960 .... 125.00
Skittles, Curly Maple, Board, A. Keesecker, 20th Century, 19 x 46 In. 125.00
Slaptrap, Board, Ideal, 1967 .... 30.00
Smokey Bear, Board, Box, 1950s 200.00
Snagglepuss, Board, Transogram, 1962 .... 75.00
Snake Eyes, Graphics, 1930s .... 195.00 To 200.00
Snuffy Smith Bug Derby, Comic, Box, Small 25.00
Soap Box Derby, 1950s 75.00
Sorry, Parker Bros., 1939 .... 120.00
Space 1999, Milton Bradley, 1975 .... 24.00
Space Patrol, Cardboard Spinner, Japan 48.00
Spin To Win Pool, Pressman, 1967 .... 15.00
Star Trek, Board, 1967 .... 45.00
Starflight, Board, Wilder, 1931, 10 x 15 In. 770.00
Steeple Chase, McLoughlin 200.00
Steve Canyon, Lewell, 1959 .... 85.00
Strategy, Game Of Armies, 1938 .... 60.00
Stymie, Bewitched, Card, Ideal, 1965 .... 32.00
Submarine, Schoenhut, Box 200.00

Sugar Bowl Soda Fountain, Box, 1939 .... 45.00
Sunset Limited, Milton Bradley, 1920 .... 140.00
Super Heroes, Card 10.00
Superboy, Board, Hasbro, 1967 .... 120.00
Supercar, Milton Bradley, 1962 .... 42.00
Swarm Of Bees, Bixby's Royal Polish, Cardboard 40.00
Sweep The Country, Political Election, Democrats & Republican, 1936 .... 35.00
Swinging Peg, Milton Bradley 35.00
Tales Of Wells Fargo, Board, 1959 .... 35.00
Tammy, Ideal, 1963 .... 35.00
Taxi, Selchow & Righter, Car Playing Pieces 20.00
Television, Board, National Novelty, 1953 .... 85.00
The Merry Game Of Old Maid, Board, McLoughlin, 1898, 19 x 10 In. 605.00
They're Off, Board, Parker Bros., 1920 .... 140.00
Tiddlywinks, Clown, Whitman Co., 1958 .... 7.00
Tiddlywinks, McLaughlin 310.00
Tight Squeeze, 1967 .... 38.00
Time Tunnel, Ideal, 1967 ....98.00 To 148.00
Tip The Bellboy, 1929 .... 225.00
Tom & Jerry, Milton Bradley, 1968 .... 20.00
Tom Hamilton's Pigskin Football, 1935 .... 75.00
Toonerville Trolley, Box, 1969 .... 90.00
Touring, Automobile Cards, Box 20.00
Travel, World Cruise, Lowell Thomas, Parker Bros., 1937 .... 285.00
Twilight Zone, Ideal, 1964 .... 219.00
Uncle Wiggly, Board, Milton Bradley, 1920 .... 40.00
Uncle Wiggly, Counters Are Rabbits, Milton Bradley, 1961 .... 68.00
Untouchables, Transogram, 1961 .... 129.00
Visit To The Farm, Board, Bliss, 1893, 7 x 15 In. 550.00
Voo Doo, Board 20.00
Voyage To Bottom Of Sea, 39 Cards, Milton Bradley, Box, 1964 .... 45.00 To 65.00
Voyage To The Bottom Of The Sea, Board, Milton Bradley .... 25.00 To 65.00
Waltons, Board, Milton Bradley, 1974 .... 35.00
Watch On De Rind, Target, All-Fair Inc., 1931 .... 132.00
Waterloo, Board, Parker Bros., 1895, 21 x 14 In. 550.00
Welcome Back Kotter, Board, Ideal, 1976 .... 15.00 To 45.00
Whirl-O-Halloween, Fortune & Stunt 27.00
White Pass & Yukon, Card 150.00
Winnie The Pooh, Board, 1933 .... 45.00
Wizard Of Oz, Board, Cadaco 20.00
World's Educator, Reed Toy Co., 1890 ....70.00 To 125.00
World's Fair, Board, Parker Bros., 1892, 14 x 21 In. 1540.00
Wyatt Earp, Transogram, 1958 .... 89.00
Yacht Race, Board, Parker Bros., 1961 .... 60.00
Yankee Peddler, Cards, McLoughlin, 1850, 5 x 5 In. 1320.00
Yellowstone, Cincinnati Game Co., 1890 .... 50.00
Yogi Bear Ball Toss 50.00
Zorro, Parker Bros., 1966 .... 35.00 To 80.00
Zorro, Target, Box, 1958 .... 125.00

GARDNER Porcelain Works was founded in Verbiki, outside Moscow, by the English-born Francis Gardner in 1766. The Gardner family retained ownership of the factory until 1891 and produced porcelain tablewares, figurines, and faience.   ГАРДНЕРZ

Figurine, Man, Breaking Ice, Sled, Brown Coat, 11 1/2 In. 1045.00
Figurine, Man, Drinking From Kovsh, Seated By Barrel, 5 1/2 In. 665.00
Figurine, Peasant Woman, On Bend, Mixing Bowl On Lap, 6 In. 665.00
Group, Advocate, Arguing Poor Tenants Case, Magistrate, 4 1/2 In. 1100.00
Group, Drunken Man, Wife, Holding Baby, 9 1/4 In. 1875.00

GAUDY DUTCH pottery was made in England for America from about 1810 to 1820. It is a white earthenware with Imari-style decorations of red, blue, green, yellow, and black. Only sixteen patterns of Gaudy Dutch were made: Butterfly, Carnation, Dahlia, Double Rose, Dove, Grape, Leaf, Oyster, Primrose, Single Rose, Strawflower, Sunflower, Urn, War Bonnet, Zinnia, and No Name. Other similar wares are called *Gaudy Ironstone* and *Gaudy Welsh*.

Coffeepot, Butterfly, 9 3/4 In.	325.00
Coffeepot, Carnation, 11 1/2 In.	5225.00
Coffeepot, England, 19th Century, 13 In.	1540.00
Creamer, Dove, 4 7/8 In.	450.00
Creamer, Grape, 4 5/8 In.	160.00
Creamer, Oyster, Soft Paste, c.1820, 4 In.	90.00
Creamer, War Bonnet, 4 3/8 In.	450.00
Cup & Saucer, Butterfly	600.00
Cup & Saucer, Grape	500.00
Cup & Saucer, Handleless, Single Rose	250.00
Cup & Saucer, Oyster	797.50
Cup & Saucer, War Bonnet	825.00
Cup & Saucer, Zinnia	550.00
Cup Plate, War Bonnet	1750.00
Ewer, Grape, 4 1/2 In.	170.00
Mug, Child's, Grape	130.00
Pitcher, Butterfly, 5 1/4 In.	130.00
Pitcher, Grape, 6 5/8 In.	130.00
Pitcher, Oyster	110.00
Plate, Oyster, 10 In.	880.00 To 1320.00
Plate, Single Rose, 8 1/4 In.	110.00
Plate, Toddy, War Bonnet, 4 1/2 In.	1750.00
Plate, Urn, 10 In.	600.00
Plate, War Bonnet, 8 In.	715.00
Plate, War Bonnet, 9 3/4 In.	350.00 To 990.00
Punch Bowl, Butterfly, 11 3/4 In.	260.00
Saucer, Single Rose	100.00
Soup, Dish, Carnation, 8 3/8 In.	425.00
Tea Set, Child's, Oyster, 22 Piece	1700.00
Waste Bowl, Butterfly	140.00
Waste Bowl, Single Rose, 6 3/8 In.	450.00

GAUDY IRONSTONE is the collector's name for the ironstone wares with the bright patterns similar to Gaudy Dutch. It was made in England for the American market. There may be other examples found in the listing for Ironstone or under the name of the ceramic factory.

Bowl, Waste, Strawberry, 5 1/2 x 3 1/2 In.	150.00
Plate, Floral Design, Polychrome Enamel, Blue, 8 In.	150.00
Plate, Polychrome Floral Design, Strawberries, 8 1/2 In.	160.00
Punch Bowl, Floral	1500.00
Saucer, Floral	50.00
Tureen, Ear Of Corn Top Handle, 13 In.	145.00

GAUDY WELSH is an Imari–decorated earthenware with red, blue, green, and gold decorations. Most Gaudy Welsh was made in England for the American market. It was made after 1820.

Bowl, Blue Onion, Staffordshire, 1800s	295.00
Creamer, 5 In.	65.00
Cup & Saucer, Columbine	75.00
Cup & Saucer, Tulip	85.00
Cup Plate, Columbine, 3 7/8 In.	75.00
Pitcher, Snake Handle, 5 1/2 In.	80.00
Plate, Floral Design, 10 In.	130.00
Sugar & Creamer, Floral Designs	130.00
Teapot, Imari Colors	475.00

GEISHA GIRL porcelain was made for export in the late nineteenth century in Japan. It was an inexpensive porcelain often sold in dime stores or used as free premiums. Pieces are sometimes marked with the name of a store. Japanese ladies in kimonos are pictured on the dishes. There are over 125 recorded patterns. Borders of red, blue, green, gold, brown, or several of these colors were used. Modern reproductions are being made.

Biscuit Jar, Cover	65.00
Butter Tub, Insert	40.00
Chocolate Pot, Porch	38.00
Cracker Jar, Red Edge, Pink Flowers, 6 1/4 In.	65.00
Nut Set, Green Trim	55.00
Tea Set, Faces In Cup, 20 Piece	95.00
Tea Set, Red Border, 9 Piece	135.00
Tray, Dresser, Blue Trim	120.00
Vase, Cobalt Blue, Red, 4 In.	625.00

GENE AUTRY was born in 1907. He began his career as the *Singing Cowboy* in 1928. His first movie appearance was in 1934, his last in 1958.

Album, Record, 4 Records	12.50
Billfold, Leather	75.00
Book, Adventure, Hardcover, 1958, 8 x 11 In.	75.00
Book, Better Little, Gene Autry & Bandits Of Silver Tip, 1949	5.00
Book, Big Little Book, Land Grab Mystery	20.00
Book, Big Little Book, Law Of The Range	30.00
Book, Gene Autry & Redwood Pirates, Whitman, Hardbound, 1946	5.00
Book, Gene Autry's Cowboy Songs & Mt. Ballads No. 2, 1934	9.00
Book, Gene Autry's Cowboy Songs & Mt. Ballads, M. M. Cole, 1932	16.00
Book, Song, 1936	15.00
Boots, Cowboy, Rubber, Original Box	125.00
Boots, Rubber, Box	150.00
Button, Pinback, Gene Autry Club	8.00
Cap Gun, Gene Autry, Inlaid Grips	110.00
Cap Gun, Gold Plated	125.00
Cap Gun, Repeating, Cast Iron, Plastic Grips, Signed, Tin, 1930s	165.00
Case, For Guitar, Emenee, Cardboard, Leather–Type Design	95.00
Charm, Photograph	15.00
Flashlight, Cowboy Lariat, Original Box	135.00
Galoshes, Metal Buckles	300.00
Game, Board, 1951	50.00
Game, Dude Ranch, Box	95.00
Guitar, Emenee, Box	150.00
Guitar, Melody Ranch, All Wood, 1950s, 36 In.,	110.00
Gun & Flying A Holster	190.00
Holster Set, 2 Die Cast Guns	250.00
Holster, Flying A Ranch, Lefty	75.00
Holster, Marked Gene Autry, Red & Green Studs	25.00
Lobby Card	30.00
Lunch Box	70.00 To 225.00
Pistol, Cap, Silver Plated, Inlaid Grips	110.00
Record, Christmas, 78 RPM	8.00
Ring, Dell Comics	95.00
Ring, Horseshoe Nail, With Signature, On Card	50.00
Sheet Music, Here Comes Santa Claus, Western Music Co., 1948	6.00
Sheet Music, Red River Valley, Photograph, 1935	10.00 To 25.00
Slate, Magic	55.00
Suspenders, On Card, Pictures Full Body	145.00
Wallet	40.00
Watch, Pocket, 1980s	45.00
Wristwatch	200.00

GIBSON GIRL black–and–blue decorated plates were made in the early 1900s. Twenty-four different 10 1/2-inch plates were made by the Royal Doulton Pottery at Lambeth, England. These pictured scenes from the book *A Widow and Her Friends* by Charles Dana Gibson. Another set of twelve 9–inch plates featuring pictures of the heads of Gibson Girls had all–blue decoration. Many other items also pictured the famous Gibson Girl.

Plate, Failing To Find Rest In The Country, 10 1/2 In.	125.00
Plate, Gibson Girl, Miss Babbles Brings A Copy, Royal Doulton	95.00
Plate, Hostile Criticism, 10 1/2 In.	125.00
Plate, She Becomes A Trained Nurse, 10 1/2 In.	40.00
Plate, She Goes To Fancy Dress Ball As Juliet, 10 1/2 In.	95.00

GIRL SCOUT collectors search for anything pertaining to the Girl Scouts, including uniforms, publications, and old cookie boxes. The Girl Scout movement started in 1912, two years after the Boy Scouts. It began under Juliette Gordon Low of Savannah, Georgia. The first Girl Scout cookies were sold in 1928.

Book, Outdoor Girls At Cedar Ridge, Laura Lee Hope, 1931	8.00
Booklet, 1931	10.00
Catalog, Brownie Scout Equipment, 1951	12.00
Catalog, Girl Scout Equipment, 1950	12.00
First Aid Kit, Metal, Cloth Cover	50.00
Handbook, Brownie Scout, 1951	5.00
Pencil Box, Red Leatherette, Bank, Pen & Pencil, Complete	35.00
Program, Girl Scout Activities, 1938	9.00
Uniform, Hat, Neckerchief, Belt & Badges, With Postcards, 1924	75.00

GLASS–ART. Art glass means any of the many forms of glassware made during the late nineteenth or early twentieth century. These wares were expensive and production was limited. Art glass is not the typical commercial glass that was made in large quantities, and most of the art glass was produced by hand methods. Later twentieth–century glass is listed under Glass–Contemporary, Glass–Midcentury, or Glass–Venetian. Even more art glass may be found in categories such as Burmese, Cameo Glass, Tiffany, Venini, and other factory names.

Basket, Oxblood & Opaline Swirl, Gold Aventurine, Handle, 7 In.	285.00
Basket, Spatter & Gold Aventurine, Pulled Corners, 6 1/2 In.	355.00
Biscuit Jar, Threaded Green & Crystal, Palme–Konig	475.00
Boot, Drinking, Etched & Engraved Florals, 7 1/2 In.	125.00
Bowl, Enameled Art Deco Blossoms, Quenvit, 12 1/2 In.	1100.00
Bowl, Finger, Ruffled Green, Iridescent, Underplate	55.00
Hat, Lime, Flattened To Make 3 Sides, Notch In Brim, 6 1/4 In.	135.00
Humidor–Oil Lamp Combination, 3 Legs, Apollo Studios, 8 1/4 In.	385.00
Lamp, 6–Sided Shade, Concentric Circles, D'Avesn, 16 1/2 In.	1925.00
Lamp, Tree Trunk Base, Leaded Apple Blossom Shade, 19 1/2 In.	550.00
Revolver, Black, 6 In.	12.00
Vase, 4 Diamond Beveled Panels, Crystal & Cranberry, 13 In.	450.00
Vase, Applied Icicles, Amethyst, 4 Footed, Flattened Shape, 9 In.	880.00
Vase, Band Of Fish Scales, 10 In.	330.00
Vase, Birds & Flowers, Heavenly Blue, Pedestal, England, 10 In.	495.00
Vase, Blue Waves, Rose Jar Form, Iridescent, Austria, 6 3/4 In.	550.00
Vase, Butterscotch, Applied Handle, Fluted, 6 In.	60.00
Vase, Cascading Circles, Hunebelle, 13 x 12 In.	600.00
Vase, Clear, Flared, Cylindrical, Leerdam, 7 In.	88.00
Vase, Dragons Made From Butterfly Wings, Stourbridge, 7 In.	320.00
Vase, Enameled Grasses, Enameled Interior, Leune, 1925, 9 3/4 In.	550.00
Vase, Floral, Pale Beige & Green, Raised Gold, 6 In.	40.00
Vase, Flowers, Frosted Neck, Air Bubbles, Bulbous, Schneider, 7 In.	4180.00
Vase, Geometric Circles, Triangles, Leune, c.1925, 7 In.	1320.00
Vase, Graff–Harrach, 13 In.	1150.00
Vase, Hellenic Women Dancing Panels, Georges DeFeure, 5 1/2 In.	357.50
Vase, Internal Bubble–Filled Layers, Benny Motzfeldt, 10 In.	220.00
Vase, Maidens & Shepherd, Handles, Royal Blenheim, 12 In., Pair	250.00
Vase, Molded Stylized Fish, Gray, Spherical, D'Avesn, 10 5/8 In.	1100.00
Vase, Mottled Orange, Oviform, Everted Rim, Schneider, 15 In.	4180.00

Glass-Midcentury, Figurine, Black Striping, White, Nason, 11 In.

Left to right: Glass-Venetian, Vase, Rust, White, Murano, 5 In.; Glass-Midcentury, Vase, White Swirls, Cobalt Blue, 8 3/8 In.

Vase, Orange Poppy, Red, Crimson, Bulbous, Schneider, 16 In. 4620.00
Vase, Purple Iridescent, Gourd Form, Palme–Koenig, 8 3/4 In. 495.00
Vase, Rainbow Swirl, Barrel Shape, 8 x 5 1/2 In. 295.00
Vase, Sapphire, Clear Icicles, Ribbed, 7 1/4 x 3 1/2 In. 650.00
Violet Basket, Green, Braided Handle, 8 In. 100.00

GLASS–CONTEMPORARY includes pieces by glass artists working after 1975. Many of these pieces are free–form, one–of–a–kind sculptures. Paperweights by contemporary artists are listed in the Paperweight section. Earlier studio glass may be found listed under Glass–Midcentury or Glass–Venetian.

Bowl, Burgundy Schmelzglas, Yellow Feather, Labino, 5 In 525.00
Bowl, Copper Swirling Heart Design, Cased, Blue, Baker 135.00
Decanter Set, Blue, Blue Prunts, Labino, 5 Piece 1450.00
Decanter Set, Pale Yellow, Green Prunts, Labino, 6 Piece 1200.00
Figure, Bluegill Fish, Copper, Schmelzglas, Labino 800.00
Figurine, Koala Bear, Amber, Clear Ears, Baker, 3 3/4 In. 125.00
Holder, Teapot Ring, B. & M. St. Clair 40.00
Vase, Copper, Schmelzglas, Loop Overlay, Labino, 7 In. 950.00
Vase, Free–Form, Spots, Convoluted, Chihuly, 1983, 17 In. 6050.00
Vase, Harlequin, Orange, Yellow, White, Clear, Labino, 6 In 750.00
Vase, King Tut, Blue & Purple Iridescent, Lundberg, 5 In 155.00
Vase, Lavender, Cased, Gold Veiling, Labino, 6 1/4 In. 3100.00
Vase, Multicolored Ribbons, Bernstein, 1980, 5 1/2 In. 450.00
Vase, Pale Blue Air Sculpture, Labino, 3 1/2 In. 1150.00
Vase, Pulled Partitions, Stick, Rosy, Manners, 5 1/2 In. 350.00
Vase, Pulled White Loops Turning To Red, Blue, Nygren 275.00

GLASS–MIDCENTURY refers to art glass made from the 1950s to the 1980s. Some glass factories, such as Baccarat or Orrefors, are listed under their own categories. Earlier glass may be listed in the Glass–Art and Glass–Contemporary sections. Italian glass may be found under Venini and Glass–Venetian.

Ashtray, Orange, Black, Gold Abstract, Higgins, 10 In. 66.00
Bowl, Blue, Gold, Clear, Higgins 60.00
Bowl, Gold Striped Design, Pointed Rim, 9 x 4 In. 176.00
Figurine, Black Striping, White, Nason, 11 In. ....*Illus* 1210.00
Tray, Abstract Design, Blues & Gold, Higgins, 10 x 14 In. 210.00
Vase, Allover Silver Deposit Leaves, Blue, Boda, 4 1/2 In. 105.00
Vase, White Swirls, Cobalt Blue, 8 3/8 In. ....*Illus* 1210.00
Vase, Yellow, Cobalt, Green & Yellow Flowers, Baker, 5 In. 110.00

Glass-Venetian, Figurine, Snake Charmer,

Black, Murano, 9 In.

◆ ◆

Be sure a copy of lists of valuables, photographs, and other information can be found in case of an insurance loss. Give a copy to a trusted friend. Do not keep them in the house. If you keep them in your safe deposit box, be sure you have a key off site. The key could be lost in a house fire.

◆ ◆

GLASS–VENETIAN. Venetian glass has been made near Venice, Italy, since the thirteenth century. Thin, colored glass with applied decoration is favored, although many other types have been made. Collectors have recently become interested in the Art Deco and fifties designs. Glass was made on the Venetian island of Murano from 1291. The output dwindled in the late seventeenth century but began to flourish again in the 1850s. Some of the old techniques of glassmaking were revived and firms today make traditional designs and original modern glass. Since 1981, the name *Murano* may only be used on glass made on Murano Island. Other pieces of Italian glass may be found in the Glass–Contemporary, Glass–Midcentury, and Venini sections of this book.

Ashtray, Clown Standing, 7 1/2 In.	125.00
Ashtray, Swirls Of Gold & Rust, Murano	115.00
Bowl, Black Women's Heads On Side, Gold Flecking, 4 1/2 In.	95.00
Bowl, Burgundy & Cream Stripes, In Amber Walls, 3 x 7 In.	358.00
Bowl, Heavy Clear Glass, Red Spiral Interior, Murano, 7 In.	770.00
Bowl, Multicolored Random Canes, Gold Flecks, 4 1/2 In.	75.00
Bowl, Ribbed, White, Orange, Purple Zigzag Design, 3 x 6 In.	770.00
Bowl, Signed Seguso, 9 In.	95.00
Candelabrum, Blue Rigaree On Verre–De–Soie, c.1910, 16 In.	750.00
Chandelier, 2 Tiers, Spiral Turned Arms, Electrified	450.00
Compote, Leaf Shape, Bird Head Finial, Gold, Green, 5 In.	32.00
Cup, Bulbous, 2 Dragon Handles, Gold Flecks, 11 1/2 In.	195.00
Decanter, Clown, Murano, 10 1/2 In.	250.00
Decanter, Millefiori, Silver Specks, Star Canes, 13 In.	357.50
Dish, Lid, White Threaded, Flecked Handle, Seguso, 5 In.	330.00
Dish, Swan, Copper, White, Clear, Murano, 8 In.	55.00
Dresser Set, Green, Black, Copper, Murano, 5 Piece	250.00
Dresser Set, Spirals, Gold Flecked Stoppers, c.1925, 3 Piece	495.00
Figurine, Bird, 10 In.	45.00
Figurine, Bird, Amber, Gold, Red, Cobalt, Murano, 10 In., Pr.	125.00
Figurine, Bird, Internal Green, Blue, Pink, Murano, 8 In.	440.00
Figurine, Clown, Baggy Suit, Red, Blue Hat, Murano, 14 In.	85.00
Figurine, Clown, Colorful, Italy, 9 1/2 In.	75.00
Figurine, Cobbler At Work, Barovier	850.00
Figurine, Duck, Blue, Clear, Gold, Bubbles, Murano, 8 In.	70.00
Figurine, Duck, Cobalt Blue, Gold Flecks, Murano	135.00
Figurine, Nude, Black Lounge Chair, Signed, Murano, 10 In.	2860.00
Figurine, Snake Charmer, Black, Murano, 9 In. ......*Illus*	100.00
Figurine, Woman, Pink Dress & Hat, Gold Trim, 9 In.	225.00
Jardiniere, Yellow, Barovier & Toso, 12 In.	450.00
Lighter & Ashtray, Lavender & Gold Mica, Murano, 2 Piece	45.00
Paperweight, Gold Dust, Murano	45.00
Perfume Bottle, Pink & White Swirl, Gold Flecked Stopper	145.00
Powder Jar, Blue & Gold, Barovier	175.00
Vase, Handkerchief, Murano	125.00

Vase, Internal Chartreuse Lines, Label, 1960, Murano, 8 In. 1760.00
Vase, Internal Design, White Latticinio, 1970s, 24 1/8 In. 1100.00
Vase, Latticinio Handkerchief, Murano, 5 x 5 In. 65.00
Vase, Purple, Bulbous, Long Tapered Neck, 21 In. 176.00
Vase, Red, Pink & Gold Stripes, Barovier, 12 In. 350.00
Vase, Rust, White, Murano, 5 In. ....*Illus* 2310.00
Vase, Swirled Design, White & Caramel Bands, Murano, 7 In. 358.00
Vase, Teardrop, Blue & Green, Flavio Poli, 10 In. 308.00
Vase, Vertical Stripes, Free Form, Barovier, Murano, 9 In. 605.00
Wine, Clear, Blue Crisscross Glass, Stemmed, 10 In., 4 Piece 275.00
Wine, Red, Gold Overlay, Flowers, Murano, 7 3/4 In., 6 Piece 125.00

GLASSES for the eyes, or spectacles, were mentioned in a manuscript in
1289 and have been used ever since. The first eyeglasses with rigid side
pieces were made in London in 1727. Bifocals were invented by Benjamin
Franklin in 1785. Lorgnettes were popular in late Victorian times. Opera
glasses are listed in their own section.

Lorgnette, 14K Gold, c.1900 .... 205.00
Lorgnette, 20 Small Diamonds, Black Stones, Platinum 1100.00
Lorgnette, Art Nouveau, Sterling Silver 295.00
Lorgnette, Pendant, Edwardian, Diamond & Platinum 7700.00
Lorgnette, Sterling Silver, Gorham, 6 In. 295.00
Lorgnette, Tortoiseshell, Victorian, Cartouche, 14K Gold, Case 350.00
Lorgnette, Victorian, Mother–of–Pearl, Velvet Bag 165.00
Pince–Nez, Gold Hairpin, On Chain, Case 39.00
Pince–Nez, Gold Nosepiece, Chain, No Handle 25.00
Pince–Nez, Roll–Up Chain & Pin, Case 39.00
Rhinestone, Prescription 11.00
Spectacles, Gold Rim, 19th Century 40.00
Spectacles, J. Hyde, New Orleans, Sterling, c.1815 .... 575.00
Sun, Child's, Goofy, Red Plastic, 29 Cents On Lens, 1950s 15.00
Sun, Silver Frames, Hard Case, Large 3.50

GOEBEL is the mark used by W. Goebel Porzellanfabrik of Oeslau,
Germany, now Rodental, Germany. Many types of figurines and dishes
have been made. The firm is still working. The pieces marked *Goebel
Hummel* are listed under Hummel in this book.

Cigarette Holder, Felix The Cat, Crown Mark, 1937, 3 Piece 75.00
Cookie Jar, Friar Tuck 400.00
Cookie Jar, Monk, 1956 .... 800.00
Creamer, Monk, 5 In. 35.00
Easter Egg, 1978 .... 15.00
Easter Egg, 1982 .... 12.00
Egg Timer, Double, Monk, Full Bee .... 30.00 To 38.00
Figurine, Bullfinch, Stylized Bee 70.00
Figurine, Colonial Couple, Marked, 10 In. 275.00
Figurine, Irish Setter, CH622 .... 35.00
Figurine, Love Lives On, New Mark 230.00
Figurine, Poodle 35.00
Figurine, Smiling Through, New Mark 192.00
Figurine, St. Francis, Full Bee, 10 In. 45.00
Figurine, What Now?, New Mark 190.00
Figurine, Wise Man, Dark Skin 95.00
Mug, Dog's Head, Great Dane, Black Trim, Marked, 1 1/2 In. 45.00
Mustard, Monk, Full Bee 30.00
Night–Light, Rabbit, Glowing Red Bug Eyes, 8 In. 185.00
Pitcher, Cross–Eyed Monk, Full Bee 50.00
Plaque, Display, Friar Tuck 65.00
Plaque, Display, Porcelain 15.00
Plate, 12 Tribes Of Israel, Ispanky, 1978 .... 200.00
Plate, Hummel, 1971 .... 525.00
Plate, Robin, 1st Edition 20.00
Salt & Pepper, Cardinal Tuck 35.00

Salt & Pepper, Cardinal Tuck, Red 55.00
Salt & Pepper, Cats, White, Green Eyes, 3 1/2 In. 30.00
Salt & Pepper, Dog 30.00
Salt & Pepper, Fish 25.00
Salt & Pepper, Flower The Skunk .... 125.00 To 145.00
Salt & Pepper, Friar Tuck .... 25.00 To 27.00
Sugar & Creamer, Friar Tuck 32.00
Sugar & Creamer, Friar Tuck, Full Bee 60.00
Vase, Figural, 3 Bamboo Shoots, Japanese Girl, 7 In. 55.00
Wall Pocket, Boy & Girl, New Mark 195.00
Wall Pocket, Child's Head, Terra–Cotta, Pair 55.00

GOLDSCHEIDER has made porcelains in three places. The family left
Vienna in 1938 and started factories in England and in Trenton, New
Jersey. The New Jersey factory started in 1940 as Goldscheider–U.S.A. In
1941 it became Goldscheider–Everlast Corporation. From 1947 to 1953 it
was Goldcrest Ceramics Corporation. In 1950 the Vienna plant was
returned to Mr. Goldscheider and the company continues in business. The
Trenton, New Jersey, business, now called *Goldscheider of Vienna,* imports
all of the pieces.

Box, Cigarette, Turquoise, 4 In. 15.00
Figurine, Chinese Love, Orientals, Signed, 11 1/2 In. 150.00
Figurine, Everlast, No. 226, 8 In. 75.00
Figurine, German Shepherd, Reclining, 17 In. 145.00
Figurine, German Shepherd, Seated, 7 1/2 In. 75.00
Figurine, Girl, With Guitar, Flowered Skirt, 1925, 17 1/2 In. 2200.00
Figurine, Lady With Parasol, No. 817, 8 1/2 In. 55.00
Figurine, Nesting Ducks, White, No. 516 .... 68.00
Figurine, Reclining Nude, Terra–Cotta 1250.00
Figurine, Springer Spaniel, Sitting, 4 1/2 x 4 1/2 In. 55.00
Figurine, Temple Dancer, Pair 135.00
Figurine, Woman Leaning Against Fence, Marked, c.1925, 11 In. 2310.00
Figurine, Woman With Parasol, 8 In. 40.00

GOLF, see Sports category

GONDER Ceramic Arts, Inc., was opened by Lawton Gonder in 1941 in
Zanesville, Ohio. Gonder made high–grade pottery decorated with flambe,
drip, gold crackle, and Chinese crackle glazes. The factory closed in 1957.
From 1946 to 1954, Gonder also operated the Elgee Pottery, which made
ceramic lamp bases.

Basket, Aqua, Brown 20.00
Ewer, Gold Crackle 10.00
Luncheon Set, Art Deco 160.00
Pitcher, Tan, Pink, Mottled, 9 In. 10.00
Planter, Swan, 6 In. 15.00

GOOFUS GLASS was made from about 1900 to 1920 by many American
factories. It was originally painted gold, red, green, bronze, pink, purple, or
other bright colors. Many pieces are found today with flaking paint and
this lowers the value.

Bowl, Red Roses On Gold, Footed, 10 1/2 In. 35.00
Bread Tray, Last Supper 50.00
Vase, Peacock, 10 1/2 In. 145.00

GOSS china has been made since 1858. English potter William Henry
Goss first made it at the Falcon Pottery in Stoke–on–Trent. The factory
name was changed to Goss China Company in 1934 when it was taken
over by Cauldon Potteries. Production ceased in 1940. Goss china
resembles Irish Belleek in both body and glaze. The company also made
popular souvenir china, usually marked with local crests and names.

W. H. COSS

Building, Lighthouse Decal 50.00
Bust, Scotsman 30.00

Bust, Shakespeare 30.00
House, Shakespeare's Cottage ....65.00 To 100.00
Jug, St. Albans 30.00

GOUDA, Holland, has been a pottery center since the seventeenth century. Two firms, the Zenith pottery, established in the eighteenth century, and the Zuid–Hollandsche pottery, made the brightly colored wares marked *Gouda* from 1880 to about 1940. Many pieces featured Art Nouveau or Art Deco designs.

Ashtray, Center Match Holder, Floral On Black, 6 1/2 In. 85.00
Dish, Polychrome Foliage Interior, Branched Base, 1921, 7 x 13 In. 440.00
Ewer, Art Nouveau, Bulbous, High Glaze, 4 x 5 In., Pair 350.00
Figurine, Shoe, Light Cream, Art Nouveau, Signed, 6 In. 85.00
Humidor, Cobalt, Signed Goedewaagen, 7 1/2 In. 275.00
Humidor, Dorian, 1926 .... 275.00
Lamp, Blue & Rust Leaves, Black Ground, 12 In. 195.00
Pitcher, Regina, 4 In. 90.00
Pitcher, Signed Zenith 125.00
Pitcher, Tulips, Sticker, c.1930, 5 In. 70.00
Plate, Annual, 1924, Lions 150.00
Tray, Art Nouveau, Glossy, 5 x 8 1/2 In. 175.00
Vase, Art Nouveau Design, Blue & Gold Iris, Zuid, 12 1/2 In. 330.00
Vase, Regina, Handles, Art Nouveau Flowers, 14 In. 295.00
Vase, Zuid Holland, Pair 4675.00

GRANITEWARE is an enameled tinware that has been used in the kitchen from the late nineteenth century to the present. Earlier graniteware was green or turquoise blue, with white spatters. The later ware was gray with white spatters. Reproductions are being made in all colors.

Ashtray, Polar Ware, Bear, Green, 1930s 95.00
Baby's Bath, Gray 70.00
Basin, Gray, 11 In. 15.00
Basin, Panda Printed In Bowl, Floral Outside, White To Blue 65.00
Basin, White, Blue Marble, 16 In. 18.00
Bathtub, Baby's, White, Blue Trim 35.00
Bedpan, Iris, Mottled Blue & White, Hanging Strap 55.00
Berry Bucket, Blue & White Swirl 90.00
Berry Bucket, Cover, Gray 45.00
Boiler, Clothes, White, Brown Letters 165.00
Bowl, Bread Riser, Blue & White Mottled 195.00
Bowl, Dark Blue Marble, Footed, 4 1/2 In. 6.50
Bowl, Milk, Aqua Swirl 45.00
Bowl, Mixing, Blue–Green, White, 9 1/2 x 5 In. 39.00
Bowl, Mixing, Child's, Blue & White, Marked Ker Sweden, 2 Piece 18.00
Bowl, Mixing, Green, Cream Interior, 8 3/4 In. 23.00
Bread Bowl, Gray 30.00
Bread Box, Green, Tall 68.00
Bread Box, Mottled Gray, Round 110.00
Bread Box, Oblong, Red 110.00
Bucket, Berry, Cobalt Blue & White Swirl 200.00
Bucket, Berry, Gray Mottled, Tin Lid & Bail, 4 x 6 In. 70.00
Bucket, Dinner, Gray Mottled, Rectangular, 3 Piece 150.00
Butter Churn, Blue & White Swirl 1650.00
Butter, Blue & White 950.00
Cake Pan, Cover, Blue 95.00
Cake Pan, Gray 8.00
Cake Safe, Green 155.00
Candlestick, Blue 100.00
Candlestick, Red, Black Trim 35.00
Canister Set, Blue, 4 Piece 325.00
Chamber Pot, Gray 20.00
Chamber Pot, Light Blue, Mottled, White Interior, Austria 30.00
Chamber Pot, Light Blue, Pyrolite, White Interior, Germany 30.00

Coffee Boiler, All White, Small 35.00
Coffee Boiler, Blue & White Swirl 85.00
Coffee Boiler, Thistle & Blue Belle, Coil Handle 150.00
Coffee Flask, Gray & White, 4 1/2 x 5 In. 115.00
Coffeepot, Birds & Flowers, Tin Cover, Wooden Handle, White 145.00
Coffeepot, Blue & White Swirl 95.00
Coffeepot, Blue & White, 6 1/2 In. 45.00
Coffeepot, Blue & White, Gooseneck 150.00
Coffeepot, Blue Swirl, Large 125.00
Coffeepot, Blue Swirl, Small 135.00
Coffeepot, Dark Brown, White Speckle, Black Trim 65.00
Coffeepot, Gooseneck Spout, White 28.00
Coffeepot, Gray, Mottled, Large 75.00
Coffeepot, Green & Cream, Drip 45.00
Coffeepot, Percolator, Green, Black Trim, 10 In. 18.00
Coffeepot, Tin Top, Gray, 12 x 27 In. 85.00
Coffeepot, White, Dark Blue Trim, 11 In. 24.00
Coffeepot, White, Red Trim, 9 In. 18.00
Colander, Blue 55.00
Colander, Blue & White, Footed, 10 In. 85.00
Colander, Blue Swirl 25.00
Colander, Bluebell 60.00
Colander, Brown & White Swirl 65.00
Colander, Circle Design, 3 Legs, Blue & White Speckled 32.00
Colander, Cobalt Blue, Green & White 45.00
Colander, Dark Blue, White Specks, 11 1/2 In. .... 10.00 To 22.00
Colander, Gray 15.00
Colander, Gray Swirl, Tin Lid 35.00
Colander, Gray, Footed, Handles, 13 In. 22.50
Cream Can, Blue & White Swirl 325.00
Creamer, Lid, White, Black Rim 8.00
Creamer, Light Blue Swirled 52.50
Cup Cooker, Black & Lavender Interior 225.00
Cup, Blue & White, Demitasse 85.00
Cup, Embossed On Front, Kemp Mfg. Co., White Swirl, 1 Pt. 225.00
Cup, Gray 8.00
Dinner Bucket, Tin Cup Over Domed Top, Wire Bail Handle, Blue 75.00
Dipper, Red & White 19.00
Dish, Cover, Refrigerator, Gray 35.00
Dishpan, Blue & White Swirl, 17 1/2 In. .... 86.00 To 100.00
Dishpan, Snow–On–The–Mountain, 15 1/2 In. 65.00
Double Boiler, Blue & White Swirl 150.00
Double Boiler, Crystolite 300.00
Double Boiler, Gray, Wide Bottom 145.00
Double Boiler, Light Gray, White, Tin Lid 65.00
Double Boiler, Robin's Egg Blue, Mottled, Blue Trim 125.00
Double Boiler, Snow–On–The–Mountain 185.00
Double Boiler, Solid Blue, Black Handles, Large 65.00
Dust Pan, Solid Blue 245.00
Dust Pan, White 95.00
Feeder, Infant, Vollrath Label 35.00
Feeder, Invalid, White, Simplex, 1907 .... 55.00
Fish Cooker, Tin Cover, Light Gray 185.00
Fish Poacher, Cover & Insert, Mottled Gray 150.00
Flask, Coffee, Gray 650.00
Funnel, Blue 25.00
Funnel, Blue & White Mottled 75.00
Funnel, Blue, White Rim 20.00
Funnel, Gray 18.00
Funnel, Gray, 5 1/2 In. 25.00
Funnel, Squatty, Gray, 8 In. 32.00
Funnel, White, Blue Trim .... 8.00 To 20.00
Grater, Blue 45.00

Grater, Gray 450.00
Griddle, Gray 165.00
Hot Plate, 2 Burner, Black & White Mottled 75.00
Kettle, Berlin, Gray, 9 1/2 In. 28.00
Kettle, Blue & White Swirl 37.50
Kettle, Canning, Gray, Bail Handle, Rim Handle, 30 In. 35.00
Kettle, Cover, Gray, Wooden Bail, Large 35.00
Kettle, Preserve, Gray 25.00
Kettle, Preserve, White, Green Trim, Lid, Wooden Bail Handle 110.00
Ladle, Blue & White 35.00
Ladle, Blue Swirled, Black Handle 40.00
Ladle, Cream, Green Trim 8.00
Ladle, Crystolite Swirl 85.00
Ladle, Gray .... 10.00 To 30.00
Ladle, Gray & White 20.00
Ladle, Red & Gray 45.00
Ladle, Red & White 15.00
Ladle, White, Blue Trim, 2 Qt. 75.00
Lobster Pot, Gray, Cover, Large 95.00
Lunch Bucket, 3–Color Blue 85.00
Lunch Bucket, Cover, Wire Handle, Cobalt Blue 25.00
Lunch Bucket, Victor, 3 Piece 85.00
Lunch Pail, Child's, Blue Swirl 175.00
Measure, Dry, Gray, 4 Cup 48.00
Measure, Mottled Black & White, Gill 98.00
Meat Grinder, Green 195.00
Milk Can, Blue & White Swirl, 9 1/4 x 6 In. 400.00
Mold, Cake, Gray, White Swirl, Large 45.00
Mold, Food, Grapes, White 145.00
Mold, Ring, Red, Gray Lining 70.00
Mold, Turk's Head, Gray, 11 In. .... 55.00 To 80.00
Mold, Turk's Head, Gray, 8 Cup 115.00
Muffin Pan, Gray 45.00
Muffin Pan, Gray, 8 Cup 65.00
Muffin Pan, Mottled Blue & White 225.00
Mug, Child's, White, Red Trim 35.00
Mug, Cobalt Trim, Blue Stenciled Flowers, Marked, 4 In. 17.50
Mug, Dark Green, White Dots 6.00
Mug, Mush, 1 Gal. 175.00
Mug, White, Blue Trim, Kockums, Sweden 45.00
Pail, Blue Swirl, Lid 120.00
Pail, Gray, 7 In. 40.00
Pail, Gray, Bail, Small 27.50
Pail, Lunch, Blue, White Lining, Soup Tray 75.00
Pail, Milk, Light Blue, White Swirl 55.00
Pan, Bundt, Gray 15.00
Pan, Cream, Green Trim, 10 1/2 x 12 In. 8.00
Pan, Dark Blue, Mottled, White Domed Cover, Handles, 15 In. 45.00
Pan, Dough, Dark Gray, Light Gray Swirl 80.00
Pan, Gray, Bail Handle, 10 In. 15.00
Pan, Green, Dark Green Trim, 8 1/2 x 11 1/2 In. 8.00
Pan, Jelly Roll, Brown & White Swirl 35.00
Pan, Light Blue & White, Swirl, Flat, 18 In. Diam. 35.00
Pan, Pudding, 11 In. 32.00
Pancake Turner, Gray 25.00
Percolator, Aqua & White Swirl 98.00
Percolator, Gooseneck, Mottled Blue & White, Small 110.00
Picnic Set, Sugar, Creamer, 4 Each Plates, Cups, Bowls, Green 168.00
Pie Pan, Blue Swirl 10.00
Pie Plate, Blue & White Cobweb 37.00
Pie Plate, Brown & White Speckled 15.00
Pie Plate, Cobalt & White Swirl 25.00
Pie Plate, Cobalt Blue & White, Deep 45.00

Pie Plate, Gray 7.50
Pitcher, Cover, Green, Cream Interior 45.00
Pitcher, Gray, 1 Qt. 55.00
Pitcher, Gray, 9 In. 20.00
Pitcher, Milk, Green Swirl 295.00
Pitcher, Water, Blue 65.00
Pitcher, White, Dark Blue Trim, 9 In. 8.00
Plate, Blue & White Interior, 3 1/4 In. 35.00
Plate, White, Dark Blue Rim, 6 In. 3.00
Plate, White, Dark Blue Rim, 8 1/2 In. 3.00
Platter, Blue & White, 4 1/2 In. 35.00
Platter, Gray & White, Large 25.00
Potty, Blue & White Swirl 110.00
Press, Bacon, Green 65.00
Rack, Hanging, Lid, White & Blue Vein 195.00
Rack, Utensil, 3 Spoons, Green 180.00
Rack, Utility Spoon, Green & White, 3 Spoons 190.00
Roaster, Blue & White Speckled, Cover, Round 18.00
Roaster, Blue & White, Insert 360.00
Roaster, Cream City 95.00
Roaster, Gray & White, Cover, Large 65.00
Roaster, Mottled Gray, Large 22.00
Roaster, Savory, Black Bottle, Black & White Marbled Top 40.00
Rolling Pin, Blue & White Striped, England 195.00
Sauce Pan, Gray, White Interior 20.00
Sauce, Gray Handle, Pierced Ear, Large 15.00
Scale, Kitchen, Delft Blue & White 235.00
Scoop, Blue 150.00
Scoop, Grocer's, Gray 135.00
Skillet, Brown Swirl, Cast Iron 285.00
Skillet, Egg, 3 Sections, Cobalt Blue 55.00
Skillet, Egg, 4 Sections, Cobalt Blue 75.00
Skillet, Egg, 6 Sections, Cobalt Blue 95.00
Skimmer, Red 125.00
Soap Dish, With Drainer, White, Wall 22.00
Soup, Dish, Red & White Swirl 35.00
Soup, Dish, Swirl Pattern, Iris 145.00
Spatula, Gray 75.00
Spoon, Gray 22.00
Spoon, Mixing, Brown & White 125.00
Spoon, White Bowl, Blue Hook Handle 6.00
Strainer, Handle, Hanging Hook, Gray, 4 3/4 In. Diam. 85.00
Strainer, Rice, Blue 78.00
Sugar & Creamer, Pewter Trim 625.00
Syrup, Bluebell, Blue & White Mottled 275.00
Tea Strainer, Perforated, Gray 70.00
Tea Strainer, Solid Red 55.00
Teakettle, Child's, Green 35.00
Teakettle, Cobalt Blue 30.00
Teakettle, Cream, Green Trim .... 20.00 To 70.00
Teakettle, Gooseneck, Cobalt & White Swirl 125.00
Teakettle, Gray Mottled 50.00
Teakettle, Olive Green & White 168.00
Teakettle, Slide Top, Wrought Iron Range Co., Gray, 1889 .... 195.00
Teakettle, Solid Cobalt Blue 15.00
Teakettle, White 25.00
Teakettle, White Interior, Cobalt Blue 65.00
Teakettle, White, With Spout 145.00
Teakettle, Yellow Swirl 95.00
Teapot, Brown & White Swirl, Squatty 200.00
Teapot, Clover Design, Austria, Blue 30.00
Teapot, Cobalt Blue Shaded With Lotus, Gold Edge 135.00
Teapot, Cobalt Blue, White Interior 65.00

Teapot, Elite, Austria, Green & White Swirl	80.00
Teapot, Flower Design, White, Pewter Trim, 10 In.	325.00
Teapot, Gooseneck, Red, 4 Cup	100.00
Teapot, Green, Cream Interior	35.00
Teapot, Pewter Lid, Gray	275.00
Teapot, Silver Plate Lid, Wood Handle, Mottled Green	325.00
Teapot, Squatty, 1 Cup, Blue	75.00
Teapot, White, Dark Blue Rim, Individual	8.00
Tray, Steak, Multicolored, Oval, 8 x 12 In., 4 Piece	33.00
Wall Pocket, Stenciled Semmelu, White	65.00
Washboard, Soap Saver, Cobalt Blue	110.00
Washtub, Oval, Blue & White Swirl, 18 In.	150.00

GREENTOWN glass was made by the Indiana Tumbler and Goblet Company of Greentown, Indiana, from 1894 to 1903. In 1899, the factory name was changed to National Glass Company. A variety of pressed, milk, and chocolate glass was made. Additional pieces may be found in other categories, such as Chocolate Glass, Custard Glass, Holly Amber, Milk Glass, and Pressed Glass.

Butter, Cactus, Cover	125.00
Celery Vase, Cactus	175.00
Celery Vase, Shuttle, Crystal	50.00
Compote, Beaded Panel, Crystal	125.00
Cordial, Herringbone Buttress	235.00
Cordial, Shuttle	37.50
Creamer, Dewey, Green	70.00
Cruet, Dewey, Canary	150.00
Dish, Dolphin Cover, Golden Agate	475.00
Dish, Dolphin, Red Agate, Beaded Rim	325.00
Dish, Dome Top Rabbit Cover, Amber	250.00
Dish, Mitted Hand, Novelty	35.00
Figurine, Dolphin, Amber	750.00
Mug, Dewey	375.00
Mug, Serenade, Blue	18.00
Mug, Serenade, Custard Glass	95.00
Mug, Serenade, Green	95.00
Mug, Shuttle, Ruby Stained	35.00
Pitcher, Ruffled Eye, Canary	275.00
Pitcher, Ruffled Eye, Emerald Green	125.00
Pitcher, Water, Heron	160.00
Salt, Wheelbarrow, Opaque Green	275.00
Sugar & Creamer, Cord Drapery, Crystal	45.00
Tray, Dewey, Serpentine, Amber	40.00
Tumbler, Brazen Shield, Blue	55.00
Tumbler, Teardrop & Tassel, Blue, 3 7/8 In.	75.00
Vase, Herringbone Buttress, Green, Gold Trim, 9 1/2 In.	235.00
Water Set, Teardrop & Tassel, Blue, 5 Piece	450.00
Wheelbarrow, Nile Green	195.00 To 225.00
Wine, Berry Spray	30.00

GRUEBY Faience Company of Boston, Massachusetts, was incorporated in 1897 by William H. Grueby. Garden statuary, art pottery, and architectural tiles were made until 1920. The company developed a matte green glaze that was so popular it was copied by many other factories making a less expensive type of pottery. This eventually led to the financial problems of the pottery.

Tile, Blue & Orange, Geometric, 4 x 4 In.	110.00
Tile, Ducks Swimming, Sunrise, Blue, Green, Orange, Artist, Label, 4 In.	385.00
Tile, Galley, Copper Frame, c.1905, Round, 6 1/4 In.	660.00
Tile, Pairs Of Geese, Tan Glazed, Teal Blue Ground, 9 1/2 In.	1210.00
Vase, Alternating Leaf Design, Green Feathered Matt, Artist, 9 In.	1100.00
Vase, Applied Leaves, Green Glaze, Light Green Interior, 2 x 3 In.	605.00
Vase, Broad Leaves, Bud, Trailing Stems, W. Post, 1898, 8 1/4 In.	1200.00

Vase, Crackle Matte Glaze, Gourd Shape, 7 In. 1395.00
Vase, Feathered Yellow Matt Glaze On Leaf Design, 3 x 5 In. 606.00
Vase, Leaf Design, Light Blue Matte Glaze, Pinched Top, 5 x 5 In. 358.00
Vase, Mallet Form, Green, 7 In. 375.00
Vase, Overlapping Blades, Matte Green Glaze, c.1904, 8 3/4 In. 665.00
Vase, Quatrefoil Rim, Molded Leaves & Buds, Green, c.1910, 8 3/8 In. 1650.00
Vase, Tooled Leaves, Scrolled Handles 5000.00
Vase, Yellow, 4 Scrolled Handles, W. Post, 10 In. ....*Illus* 4125.00

GUN is the name used for this category, which includes shotguns, pistols, and other antique firearms. Rifles are listed in their own section. Be very careful when buying or selling guns because there are special laws governing the sale and ownership. A collector's gun should be displayed in a safe manner, probably with the barrel filled or a part missing to be sure it cannot be accidentally fired.

BB, Daisy, Ben Franklin 150.00
BB, Daisy, Buzz Barton, No. 195 .... 125.00
BB, Daisy, Model 25, Pump 85.00
BB, Daisy, Model 40, Red Tryder 75.00
BB, Daisy, Model 105 .... 100.00
BB, Daisy, Model 106 B. A., Repeater, No. 106 B. A. 85.00
BB, Daisy, Model 106, Top Break, Plymouth, Michigan 100.00
BB, Daisy, Model 312, Red Ryder 45.00
BB, Daisy, Model 1938 S. S. B. A. 125.00
BB, Daisy, Model 1938B, Red Ryder 55.00
BB, Daisy, Plymouth, Michigan, Marked 8–13–1899 .... 1400.00
BB, King, Model 2136 .... 75.00
BB, Rifle, Ben Franklin 35.00
Blunderbuss, Brass Barrel, Anderson & Co. 2000.00
Carbine, Hotchkiss, Bold Action 2200.00
Carbine, Sharps 1852, 52 Caliber 825.00
Colt 1860, Springfield Armory, Richard's Conversion, Cylinder Scene 5900.00
Colt Dragoon, 2nd Md., SN9xxx 9800.00
Colt, Peacemaker, Single Action, Ivory Grips, c.1870 .... 3500.00
Flintlock Turn–Off, George Halfide, c.1720, 11 1/2 In. 1100.00
Flintlock, Brown Bess, Inspection Marks, 1780 .... 3200.00
Flintlock, Royal Forresters, English Officer's 850.00
Flintlock, Twist Barrel, Silver Scrolls, Germany, 18 1/2 In. 2750.00
Gambler's Boot, Marlin, 7 Shot, 1878 .... 125.00
Gatling, Barrel 45/70 .... 150.00
Goose, 32–In. Barrel, 1910s 55.00
Handy, Harrington & Richardson, Single Shot 73.00
Luger, German, With Holster, 1918 .... 1250.00
Musket, Flintlock, Original Bayonet & Scabbard, 1816 .... 1540.00
Musket, Percussion, Marked Harper's Ferry, Inspector Marked, 1843 .... 675.00
Musket, Percussion, Springfield, Dated 1811 .... 750.00
Muzzle Loader, Kentucky, Curly Maple, H. Shefler 400.00

Grueby, Vase, Yellow, 4 Scrolled Handles,
W. Post, 10 In.

♦ ♦

A Grueby vase can be cleaned with a nylon scouring pad and a mild abrasive like Soft–scrub. After it dries, rub a little Vaseline or mineral oil on the surface, then wipe it off. This system works for any matt–glazed pottery.

♦ ♦

Pistol, Blunderbuss, Flint, Half Octagonal Barrel, 11 In. 150.00
Pistol, Colt 41 Caliber 550.00
Pistol, Colt 45 Caliber, Army, With Holster, World War I 850.00
Pistol, Derringer, 2–Shot Over–Under, 41 Cal., Ivory Grips, Nickel Plate 350.00
Pistol, Dueling, D. Egg, London, Case, Pair 7425.00
Pistol, Dueling, Joseph Manton & Son, Case, Pair 5500.00
Pistol, Kentucky Flint, Curly Maple, 58 Caliber, Stamped Ashmore 1200.00
Pistol, Mortimer, Percussion Pepperbox, Walnut Grip, Fitted Case 2500.00
Pistol, Pepperbox, Model 1854, Marston & Knox, Barrel 3 1/4 In. 165.00
Pistol, Percussion Truncheon, All Brass, Day's Patent, 1823, 15 3/4 In. 3025.00
Pistol, Remington 1871, Center Fire 795.00
Pistol, Remington, 2 Shot Over & Under, 41 Caliber, Ivory Grips 385.00
Pistol, S. North, Flintlock Model 1813, 69 Caliber 5500.00
Pistol, U.S. Military, Percussion, c.1851 .... 850.00
Remington, Double Derringer 325.00
Revolver, 32 Caliber, Hopkins & Allen, Folding Hammer, Dated 1886 .... 50.00
Revolver, Army, Colt, Spring Action, Case, Centennial 1871, Pair 900.00
Revolver, Colt, 36 Caliber, 24K Gold Inlay, Presentation Case 595.00
Revolver, Colt, Army, Fluted, 1860 .... 1485.00
Revolver, Colt, Model 1851, Navy, Cylinder Scene 695.00
Revolver, Colt, Model 1862, Percussion 1850.00
Revolver, Colt, Model 1871, Centennial, Spring Action 900.00
Revolver, Colt, Model 1961, Percussion, Navy, Ivory Grips 1815.00
Revolver, Colt, Single Action, Ivory Trim 1265.00
Revolver, Lefaucheux, Military, Pin Fire, 12 Mm. .... 250.00 To 275.00
Revolver, Long Hex Barrel, Wooden, Handmade 10.00
Revolver, Perrin, 12 Mm, Walnut Grip, 5 5/8 In. 132.00
Revolver, Smith & Wesson, Frontier, 44 Caliber 300.00
Revolver, Tarus, Model 669, Stainless Steel 250.00
Shotgun, 12 Gauge, Simmons 950.00
Shotgun, Deluxe Model 42, Engraved 4000.00
Shotgun, Harrington & Richardson, 16 Gauge 137.00
Shotgun, L. C. Smith–Baker, 10 Gauge, 1876 .... 2000.00
Shotgun, Spencer, Single Barrel, La Gauge Hammer 32.50
Shotgun, Spencer, Slide Action, 1880s 120.00
Shotgun, Twist Double Barrel, Haymaker, England 350.00
Shotgun, UPRR, Rabbit Ears, 36 1/4 In. 275.00
Shotgun, W. W. Greener, Double Barrel, Leather Case 1320.00
Shotgun, Winchester, Model 12, 12 Gauge, Diamond Carved Walnut Stock 350.00
Trapdoor Cade, U.S. Springfield, Model 1873 .... 190.00

GUNDERSON glass was made at the Gunderson–Pairpoint Glass Works of
New Bedford, Massachusetts, from 1952 to 1957. Gunderson Peachblow is
especially famous.

Compote, Peachblow 430.00
Tumbler, Peachblow 170.00

GUSTAVSBERG ceramics factory was founded in 1827 near Stockholm,
Sweden. It is best known to collectors for its twentieth–century art wares,   **Gustafsberg**
especially a green stoneware with silver inlay called *Argenta*.

Charger, Silver Inlay 523.00
Dish, Fish Shape, 13 In. 90.00
Feeding Set, Porcelain, c.1950, 3 Piece 25.00
Jar, Cover, Argenta, 5 1/2 In. 850.00
Plaque, Wall, Birds, Signed Lisa, 9 x 9 In. 55.00
Tea Set, Gilt & Green Banded, Off–White Ground, 25 Piece 121.00
Toothpick, Argenta 35.00
Tray, Steamship, Swedish American Line, 3 x 6 In. 40.00
Vase, Fish & Bubbles, Argenta, 7 In. 800.00
Vase, Floral, Argenta, 5 In. 275.00
Vase, Harlequin, Black, 7 In. 125.00
Vase, Inlaid Silver Spray Of Flowers, Ferns, Marked, 5 3/4 In. 137.50
Vase, Knight On Horse, Black, Label, 6 In. 125.00

♦ ♦

The English use this old system for cleaning silver. Put the silver in a bowl, cover it with sour milk, and let it stand overnight. Rinse it in cold water the next morning; dry with a soft cloth.

♦ ♦

Hall, Pitcher, Autumn Leaf, 8 In.

Vase, Multicolored, Incised Arts & Crafts Roses, 1910	450.00
Vase, Sprays Of Flowers, Blue–Green Ground, 16 In.	650.00
Vase, Turquoise Glaze, Silver Nude Woman, Signed, 13 1/2 In.	1100.00

HAEGER Potteries, Inc., Dundee, Illinois, started making commercial art wares in 1914. Early pieces were marked with the name *Haeger* written over an *H*. About 1938, the mark *Royal Haeger* was used. The firm is still making florist wares and lamp bases.

Ashtray, Scattered Red Dots, Large	15.00
Ashtray, With 11–In. Cigar Dish, Cover, Royal	25.00
Candleholder, 2–Light, Taupe, Art Deco, Pair	10.00
Candleholder, Twin Stalks, Pink Agate, Pair	25.00
Cookie Jar, Gleep, Crazed	95.00
Decanter, Fat Man, Tuba Player, Dark Brown	35.00
Figurine, Deer, Royal	15.00
Figurine, Gazelles, Blue, Art Deco, Royal, 7 In.	18.00
Lamp, Mermaid, Fish Finial	75.00
Planter, Madonna & Child, 11 In.	15.00
Planter, Mermaid, White, 22K Gold Brushing, 14 x 10 In.	110.00
Plate, Commemorative, Pope's Visit To U.S., 1979	12.00
Sign, Dealer	175.00

HALF–DOLL, see Pincushion Doll category

HALL CHINA Company started in East Liverpool, Ohio, in 1903. The firm made many types of wares. Collectors search for the Hall teapots made from the 1920s to the 1950s. The dinnerwares of the same period, especially Autumn Leaf pattern, are also popular. The Hall China Company is still working. For more information, see *Kovels' Depression Glass & American Dinnerware Price List.* Autumn Leaf pattern dishes are listed in their own category in this book.

HALL'S
SUPERIOR
QUALITY
KITCHENWARE

Ashtray, Stork Club	12.50
Bean Pot, Blue Blossom	125.00 To 135.00
Bean Pot, Rose Parade	35.00
Birdhouse, White	90.00
Bookends, Orchid	450.00
Bowl, Rose Parade	25.00
Casserole, Cover, Red Poppy	55.00
Casserole, Cover, Rose White	45.00
Casserole, Cover, Royal Rose	35.00
Casserole, Red, 8 In., Pair	30.00
Coffeepot, Crocus, Tin, Wall	38.00
Coffeepot, Cube, Ivory	30.00
Coffeepot, Wildfire	35.00
Cookie Jar, Blue & Gold Star	50.00
Cookie Jar, Ivory, Ear Handles, Gold Trim, Dots	25.00
Cookie Jar, Poppy	65.00

Cookie Jar, Poppy, Silver Trim 30.00
Cookie Jar, Zeisel, Dot Design 30.00
Cookie Jar, Zeisel, Pink, Gold Trim 50.00
Cookie Jar, Zeisel, Yellow, Gold Trim 50.00
Cookie Jar, Ziesel, Casual Living 65.00
Cup, Jewel Tea 2.00
Decanter, Figural, I. W. Harper 95.00
Jar, Pretzel, Morning Glory 35.00
Jug, Water, Refrigerator, Blue 20.00
Leftover, Hotpoint, No. 2, Lid, Gray, Square 6.00
Mug, Monk, 6 Piece 120.00
Pie Plate, Tulip, Lifter 25.00
Pitcher, Autumn Leaf, 8 In. ....*Illus* 100.00
Pitcher, Doughnut, Sage Green, Large 25.00
Pitcher, Moderne, Yellow 20.00
Pitcher, Poppy, Streamline 85.00
Pitcher, Schenley's 25.00
Pitcher, Tea, Poppy, Streamline 175.00
Pitcher, Water, Blue 10.00
Plate, Monticello, 6 1/2 In. 3.00
Plate, Monticello, 8 In. 3.50
Punch Set, Tom & Jerry, Cover, Black, Gold, 17 Piece 60.00
Refrigerator Set, General Electric, 5 Piece 75.00
Roaster, Delphinium, Westinghouse Queen, Open 6.00
Salt & Pepper, Angel Fish 10.00
Salt & Pepper, Meadow Flower, Handled 65.00
Salt & Pepper, Red & Black Lettering, Handle 20.00
Salt & Pepper, Red Poppy, Handles .... 15.00 To 16.50
Server, Water, Refrigerator, Blue 45.00
Server, Water, Westinghouse, Refrigerator, Blue 37.50
Sugar & Creamer, Cover, Zeisel 15.00
Sugar, Cover, Poppy 12.00
Teapot, Airflow, Cobalt Blue, Gold, 6 Cup 60.00
Teapot, Airflow, Yellow, Gold Trim, 8 Cup 25.00
Teapot, Aladdin, Black, Gold Infuser 35.00
Teapot, Aladdin, Black, Gold Trim 45.00
Teapot, Aladdin, Cobalt Blue, Gold, Infuser 50.00
Teapot, Aladdin, Yellow 36.00
Teapot, Automobile 350.00
Teapot, Automobile, Red 475.00
Teapot, Bluebell 50.00
Teapot, Canary Parade, Gold 19.00
Teapot, Cream, Gold Polka Dots 25.00
Teapot, French, Black & Gold Daisy, 6 Cup 40.00
Teapot, French, Black, Gold Trim, 6 Cup 24.00
Teapot, Globe, Maroon, Gold Trim 125.00
Teapot, Hollywood, Red 75.00
Teapot, Hook, Blue, Gold Trim 17.00
Teapot, Hook, Cover, Light Blue, Gold, 6 Cup 50.00
Teapot, Los Angeles, Yellow 28.00
Teapot, McCormick, Maroon, Infuser 22.00
Teapot, McCormick, Teal Green, Infuser 24.00
Teapot, Moderne 20.00
Teapot, Parade 28.00
Teapot, Parade, Yellow, Gold Trim 18.00
Teapot, Peach & Gold, Basketweave 30.00
Teapot, Pink Plume, Green 28.00
Teapot, Poppy 95.00
Teapot, Poppy, Streamline 200.00
Teapot, Rutherford, Green Dot 95.00
Teapot, Twin–Tee, Cobalt Blue, Gold 65.00
Teapot, Twin–Tee, Pansy Decal 60.00
Teapot, Windshield, Carrot & Beer Design, Ivory, Gold Trim 58.00

Teapot, Windshield, Maroon, Gold Trim 35.00

HALLOWEEN is an ancient holiday that has been changed in the last 200 years. The jack–o'–lantern, witches on broomsticks, and orange decorations seem to be twentieth–century creations. Collectors started to become serious about collecting Halloween–related items in the late 1970s. The papier–mache decorations, now replaced by plastic, and old costumes are in demand.

Book, Cutout, Whitman, Uncut 15.00
Book, Games For Halloween, Hard Back, Small, 1912 .... 15.00
Candy Box, Devil Top, Composition, Germany 58.00
Candy Box, Pumpkin Man On Top, Germany 148.00
Candy Box, Witch Top, Composition, Germany 68.00
Candy Container, Pumpkin Face, Composition, Germany ....95.00 To 125.00
Candy Container, Witch On Pumpkin, Papier–Mache 98.00
Candy Container, Witch, Molded Hair, Broom, Slide Closure, 5 In. 225.00
Cat, Cardboard, 13 In. ....*Illus*   6.00
Cat, Jack–O'–Lantern, China 120.00
Costume, 8th Man, Ben Cooper, Sealed, 1960s 98.00
Costume, Annie Oakley, Box, 1950s 75.00
Costume, Barbie, Mask, Complete, Box, Size 14 .... 20.00
Costume, Batman, Box, 1966 .... 50.00
Costume, Bewitched, Ben Cooper, 1965 .... 69.00
Costume, Brave Eagle, Box, 1950s 45.00
Costume, Bugs Bunny, 1950s 75.00
Costume, Cecil From Beany & Cecil, Ben Cooper, 1961 .... 89.00
Costume, Charlie Weaver, 1950s 50.00
Costume, Cinderella, Box, 1950s 35.00
Costume, Dick Tracy 50.00
Costume, Doctor Doom, Ben Cooper, 1967 .... 95.00
Costume, Dress, Orange, Black Trim, Black Cat On Skirt, 1920s 75.00
Costume, Evel Knievel, Ben Cooper, 1974 .... 35.00
Costume, Felix The Cat, Box, 1950s 48.00
Costume, Flipper, Collegeville, 1966 .... 42.00
Costume, Fred Flintstone, Ben Cooper, 1973 .... 35.00
Costume, Garrison's Gorillas, Ben Cooper, 1967 .... 69.00
Costume, Golliwog, Full Mask, Blue Pants, Red Jacket 250.00
Costume, Head, Elsie The Cow 125.00
Costume, King Kong, 1965, Ben Cooper 59.00
Costume, Lost In Space, Ben Copper, 1965 .... 198.00
Costume, Master Of Universe 12.00
Costume, Moe, 3 Stooges 145.00
Costume, Morticia, Addams Family, Ben Cooper, 1965 .... 239.00
Costume, Muhammed Ali, Box, 1977 .... 35.00
Costume, Oswald The Rabbit, Box 75.00
Costume, Planet Of The Apes, Box 35.00
Costume, Rat Patrol, Ben Cooper, 1967 .... 59.00

Halloween, Cat, Cardboard, 13 In.

Halloween, Witch, Cardboard, 13 In.

Halloween, Mask, Cardboard, 1940, 7 In.

◆◆◆◆◆◆◆◆◆◆◆◆◆◆◆◆◆◆◆◆

Dust a feather boa with a hairdryer set on cool.

◆◆◆◆◆◆◆◆◆◆◆◆◆◆◆◆◆◆◆◆
◆◆◆◆◆◆◆◆◆◆◆◆◆◆◆◆◆◆◆◆

If possible, hang an oil painting on an inside wall away from direct sunlight. Leave a small gap behind the painting to allow air to circulate.

◆◆◆◆◆◆◆◆◆◆◆◆◆◆◆◆◆◆◆◆

Costume, Sleeping Beauty, Ben Cooper 35.00
Costume, Snoopy, Box, 1966 ...... 18.00
Costume, T. H. E. Cat, Collegeville, 1966 ...... 89.00
Costume, Tarzan, Ben Cooper, 1967 ...... 39.00
Costume, Tom, From Tom & Jerry, Halco, 1952 ...... 32.00
Costume, Underdog, Ben Cooper, 1969 ...... 32.00
Costume, Vampire, Ben Cooper, 1965 ...... 24.00
Costume, Yankee Boy, Pirate Buccaneer, 1950s 100.00
Costume, Zorro, Box, 1960s ...... 45.00 To 65.00
Crepe Paper, Dennison, Original Sleeve 25.00
Display, Black Cat, With Moon, Cats Tongue Out, Dennison 3.00
Figure, Pumpkin Man, Comical, Composition, Germany 78.00
Garland, Orange & Black, Marked Germany 5.00
Horns, Orange & Black, Wood Tips, Germany 5.00
Jack-O'-Lantern, Cat, Arched Back, Orange Cardboard, 7 x 7 In. 90.00
Jack-O'-Lantern, Insert, Germany 110.00
Jack-O'-Lantern, Paper Lining, Tin 695.00
Jack-O'-Lantern, Papier-Mache, Germany 85.00
Jack-O'-Lantern, Pumpkin, Hard Plastic, 1940-50, 5 In. 15.00
Jack-O'-Lantern, Pumpkin, Papier-Mache, Tissue Insert 48.00
Jack-O'-Lantern, Skull, Red Insert, Wire Bail, Papier-Mache, 3 In. 140.00
Lamp, Skull, Kerosene, Chimney, 8 In. 20.00
Lantern, Black Cat, 3 In. 145.00
Lantern, Black Cat, Cardboard 45.00
Lantern, Candle, Tin & Printed Paper, 8 Piece 90.00
Lantern, Cat's Head, Papier-Mache 68.00
Lantern, Devil's Head, Germany 250.00
Lantern, Devil, Cardboard 45.00
Lantern, Double Pumpkin Face, Smile & Sad, Wire Bail, 7 In. 50.00
Lantern, Owl, Glass 42.00
Lantern, Skeleton Head, Glass, Germany 130.00
Mask, Alfred E. Newman, Molded Plastic, 1960s 25.00
Mask, Aunt Jemima, 1905 ...... 465.00
Mask, Cardboard, 1940, 7 In. ......*Illus* 5.00
Mask, Clash Of Titans, 3 Piece 20.00
Mask, Devil, Papier-Mache 65.00
Mask, Donald Duck, Disney, 1930s 65.00
Mask, Gamorean Guard, Star Wars, Box 75.00
Mask, Herman Munster, 1960s 45.00
Mask, Jackie Kennedy, Molded Plastic, 1960s 25.00
Mask, Little Black Sambo, 1950s 50.00
Mask, Tillie The Toiler, Paper 30.00
Mask, Weequay, Star Wars, Box 75.00
Mask, Wicket, Star Wars, Box 50.00
Mold, Chocolate, Witch & Broom, Metal, 6 In. 30.00
Noisemaker, Bats & Witches, Metal, 1940s 15.00
Noisemaker, Cat, Tin 10.00
Noisemaker, Clown Face, Metal, 1920s 40.00
Noisemaker, Clown, Wooden Handle 5.00
Noisemaker, Ghost 10.00
Noisemaker, Litho Tin, Witches, Cats, Orange, Black, Yellow, 4 In. 10.00
Noisemaker, Pumpkin 10.00
Noisemaker, Pumpkin Face, Metal, Early 1900s 35.00
Noisemaker, Witch 10.00
Noisemaker, Witches, Tin Litho, 4 1/2 In. Diam. 12.00
Owl, Glass Eyes, Pressed Cardboard, 12 In. 75.00
Party Favor, Black Cat 25.00
Postcard, A Starry Halloween, Child, Pumpkin, J. Freixas, 1914 ...... 75.00
Scarecrow, Hard Plastic, 1940-50, 5 In. 15.00
Skull, Papier-Mache, White, Red Eyes, 3 In. 195.00
Tambourine, Cat 10.00
Tambourine, Children Bobbing For Apples, 1930s 40.00
Tambourine, Metal, 1920 ...... 65.00

Tambourine, Pumpkin & Dancing Children	40.00
Tambourine, Witch	10.00
Whirligig, Witch	78.00
Witch, Cardboard, 13 In. ....*Illus*	6.00
Witch, Die Cut Cardboard, Germany, Large	30.00
Witch, Hard Plastic, 1940–50, 5 In.	15.00

HAMPSHIRE pottery was made in Keene, New Hampshire, between 1871 and 1923. Hampshire developed a line of colored glazed wares as early as 1883, including a Royal Worcester–type pink, olive green, blue, and mahogany. Pieces are marked with the printed mark or the impressed name *Hampshire Pottery* or *J.S.T. & Co., Keene, N.H.* Many pieces were marked with city names and sold as souvenirs.

Bowl, Raised Water Lilies, Lily Pads, Matte Green, 10 In.	90.00
Candlestick, Chamber, Mottled Blue Gray, Green, Black Glaze, Large	175.00
Chocolate Pot, Holly Decal, Cream, 9 1/2 In.	265.00
Dish, For My Dog, 5th Avenue Back Stamp	165.00
Ewer, Log Chapel, Saranac Inn, Signed, 6 In.	35.00
Lamp, Fairy	185.00
Lamp, Oil, 3 Handles, Matte Green	210.00
Mug, Matte Green	135.00 To 175.00
Mug, Molded Border, Tan & Green Gloss Glaze, 5 1/2 In.	70.00
Pitcher, Matte Green, 9 1/2 In.	225.00 To 350.00
Urn, Matte Green, Architectural Handles, 11 In.	430.00
Vase, 2 Handles, 15 In.	500.00
Vase, 2–Hole, Green, 4 In.	110.00
Vase, Aqua, Signed, 12 1/2 In.	115.00
Vase, Blended Greens & Browns, 5 1/2 In.	275.00
Vase, Blue Matte Glaze, Marked, c.1910, 12 1/4 In.	412.00
Vase, Blue Matte, 8 In.	160.00
Vase, Green, Loop Handles, 6 In.	60.00
Vase, Raised Leaves, Mottled Brown Matte Glaze, c.1910, 3 1/2 In.	247.50
Vase, Wavy Leaf Design, Mottled Blue Glaze, Marked, c.1903, 8 In.	250.00

HANDEL glass was made by Philip Handel working in Meriden, Connecticut, from 1885 and in New York City from 1893 to 1933. The firm made art glass and other types of lamps. Handel shades were made not only of leaded glass in a style reminiscent of Tiffany but also of reverse painted glass. Handel also made vases and other glass objects.

Candlestick, Teroma, Ember Floral Design, Signed, 8 1/2 In.	302.50
Humidor, Art Nouveau–Type, Metal Lid, Signed, Pair	350.00
Humidor, Figural Pipe Finial On Cover, Green & Red, Marked, 4 In.	440.00
Humidor, Owls In Branches, 7 In.	500.00
Humidor, Pipe & Matches On Cover, Hand Painted	250.00
Lamp, Apple Blossom, Red, Green & Beige Shades, Signed	2600.00
Lamp, Arrowroot, Replaced Leaded Glass Shade, 1920s	1195.00
Lamp, Bell Form Frosted & Orange Shade, Metal Harp, 57 In.	467.50
Lamp, Boudoir, Domed Shade, Bluebirds, Metal Base, Signed, 14 In.	2200.00
Lamp, Boudoir, Reverse–Painted Daisies Shade, c.1915, 15 1/4 In.	775.00
Lamp, Boudoir, Reverse–Painted Floral Dome Shade, Signed, 14 In.	665.00
Lamp, Boudoir, Reverse–Painted Landscape Shade, 12 1/2 In.	1100.00
Lamp, Boudoir, Reverse–Painted Moon–Lit Scape, c.1915, 13 3/4 In.	1100.00
Lamp, Boudoir, Roses & Butterfly	3000.00
Lamp, Boudoir, Scenic, Apple Blossoms	2000.00
Lamp, Bronze Overlay Of Palm Trees, Bronze Base, Signed, 25 In.	8800.00
Lamp, Church, Windmill & Ship, Signed, 18 In.	2200.00
Lamp, Conical Shade, Forest, Bronzed Metal Base, Signed, 22 In.	4070.00
Lamp, Curved Green Slag Shade, Metal Frame & Base, Signed, 21 In.	1210.00
Lamp, Desk, Chipped Glass Shade, Bronzed Metal Base, Adjustable Arm	1250.00
Lamp, Ice Crackle, Continuous River Scene, Bronze, 34 x 22 In.	5500.00
Lamp, Interior Wooded Landscape, Rising Sun, Signed, 23 In.	8360.00
Lamp, Leaded Shade, Floral Border, Bronze Base, Signed, 26 In., Pair	4125.00
Lamp, Leaded Shade, Yellow Flowers, Label, 14 In.	385.00

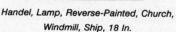

Handel, Lamp, Reverse-Painted, Church,
Windmill, Ship, 18 In.

Handel, Lamp, Reverse-Painted, Sunset
Scene, 15 1/2 In.

Lamp, Painted Shade, Brown Slag Interior, Landscape Rim, 23 In.	770.00
Lamp, Piano, Geometric, Bronzed Metal Arm, Base, Cylindrical Shade	670.00
Lamp, Piano, Paneled Cylindrical Shade, Adjustable Base, 17 In.	825.00
Lamp, Pine, Caramel Slag Panels, 3–Socket Base, Signed, 23 In.	1550.00
Lamp, Poppies, Reverse Painted, Baluster Stem	1800.00
Lamp, Red Roses, Green Leaves, No. 6346, Signed, 14 In.	1650.00
Lamp, Reverse Painted, Nile River Scene Shade, 1915, 26 1/2 In.	5775.00
Lamp, Reverse–Painted Dome Shade, Riverside Landscape, 56 1/2 In.	4400.00
Lamp, Reverse–Painted Glass, Woodland Landscape, Signed, 23 1/4 In.	6100.00
Lamp, Reverse–Painted Sailing Ship, Harbor, Signed, 1920, 23 3/8 In.	9900.00
Lamp, Reverse–Painted Shade, Blossoms Rim, Marked, c.1920, 21 1/2 In.	2860.00
Lamp, Reverse–Painted, 3–Scene Shade, Signed, 18 In.	3300.00
Lamp, Reverse–Painted, Church, Windmill, Ship, 18 In. ....*Illus*	2300.00
Lamp, Reverse–Painted, Sunset Scene, 15 1/2 In. ....*Illus*	3300.00
Lamp, Ribbed Sunset Shade, Signed, 5 1/2 In.	3300.00
Lamp, Table, Dome Shade, 6 Curved Green Slag Panels, Fretwork, 21 In.	1215.00
Lamp, Table, Reverse–Painted, Grove Of Trees, No. 6644	8000.00
Lamp, Teroma Shade, Forest Scene, Signed, 13 In.	1350.00
Lamp, Violets, Swirl Ribbon Border, Florence Lewis	1850.00
Lamp, Woodland Scene, Birds In Flight, Signed, c.1920, 23 In.	6600.00
Lamp, Woodland Scenic Shade, Harp Floor Base, Signed	5500.00
Lantern, Hammered Copper & Slag Glass, Domed Square Top, 10 1/2 In.	1210.00
Shade, Tam–O–Shanter Shape, Chipped Ice Effect, Signed, 10 In.	225.00

HARDWARE, see Architectural category.

HARKER Pottery Company of East Liverpool, Ohio, was founded by
Benjamin Harker in 1840. The company made many types of pottery but
by the Civil War was making quantities of yellowware from native clays.
They also made Rockingham–type brown–glazed pottery and whiteware.
The plant was moved to Chester, West Virginia, in 1931. Dinnerwares
were made and sold nationally. In 1971 the company was sold to Jeanette
Glass Company and all operations ceased in 1972. For more information,
see *Kovels' Depression Glass & American Dinnerware Price List.*

Bean Pot, Cameo Rose, Blue	24.00
Bowl, Cameo Rose, Pink, 9 In.	27.50
Breakfast Set, Cock–O–The–Morn, Cameo Ware, 38 Piece	125.00
Butter, Petit Point, Rectangular, 1 Lb.	50.00
Cake Plate, Cameo Shellware, Blue	8.00
Cake Plate, Petit Point, Rose	7.00
Cake Set, Currier & Ives, 6 Piece	18.00
Cup, Cameo Rose, Blue	4.00
Dish, Cameo Rose, Cover, Pink, 7 In.	27.50
Mug, Child's, Cameo Shellware, Blue	25.00
Pie Plate, Cameo Shellware, Blue	10.00
Pie Plate, Petit Point	12.00
Pitcher, White Rose, Cover	40.00

Plate, Cameo Rose, Blue, 9 In. 27.00
Plate, Cameo Rose, Sandwich, Blue 3.00
Plate, Cameo Shellware, Blue, 9 In. 5.00
Plate, Cameoware, Blue, 8 3/4 In. 9.00
Plate, Rooster, 10 1/4 In. 8.00
Rolling Pin, Mexican & Burro 125.00
Rolling Pin, Morning Glory 95.00
Rolling Pin, Wild Poppies 90.00
Sugar & Creamer, Cameo Rose, Blue 27.00
Sugar & Creamer, Cameo Rose, Cover, Pink 27.50
Tile, Tea, White Rose 10.00

HARLEQUIN dinnerware was produced by the Homer Laughlin Company from 1938 to 1964, and sold without trademark by the F. W. Woolworth Co. It has a concentric ring design like Fiesta, but the rings are separated from the rim by a plain margin. Cup handles are triangular in shape. For more information, see *Kovels' Depression Glass & American Dinnerware Price List.*

Ashtray, Yellow, Basketweave, Pair 25.00
Bowl, Gray, 7 In. 17.50
Candleholder, Rose, Pair 140.00
Casserole, Spruce Green 75.00
Cup & Saucer, Gray 9.00
Cup, Blue, After Dinner 3.50
Cup, Turquoise 3.50
Eggcup, Blue 14.00
Eggcup, Dark Green 15.00
Eggcup, Double, Chartreuse 16.00
Eggcup, Maroon, Single 20.00
Jug, Gray, 22 Oz. 19.00
Lid, Sugar, Turquoise 4.50
Plate, Blue, 7 In. 5.00
Plate, Chartreuse, 6 In. 2.50
Plate, Chartreuse, 7 In. 5.50
Platé, Dark Green, 6 In. 3.50
Plate, Gray, 6 In. 3.50
Relish, Turquoise, Colored Inserts 200.00
Salt & Pepper, Blue 10.00
Saucer, Forest Green 3.00
Teapot, Forest Green, Cover 20.00
Teapot, Red 58.00
Tray, Relish, Complete 200.00

HATPIN HOLDERS were needed when hatpins were fashionable from 1860 to 1920. The large, heavy hat required special long-shanked pins to hold it in place. The hatpin holder resembles a large saltshaker, but it often has no opening at the bottom as a shaker does. Hatpin holders were made of all types of ceramics and metal. Look for other pieces under the names of specific manufacturers.

Berries & Leaves 40.00
Hunchback Man With Staff, 18th Century, 5 1/2 In. 125.00
Kewpie 160.00
Woman's Hand, White, Bisque 60.00

HATPINS were popular from 1860 to 1920. The long pin, often over four inches, was used to hold the hat in place on the hair. The tops of the pins were made of all materials, from solid gold and real gemstones to ceramics and glass. Be careful to buy original hatpins and not recent pieces made by altering old buttons.

Ball Of Rose Cut Garnets, Small Diamond At Top, 7 1/2 In. 325.00
Gold, Sterling Silver 95.00
Lotus Blossom, Silver Filigree, 12 In. 25.00
Man's Head, Turban, Repousse, Sterling .... 35.00 To 65.00

Haviland, Plate, Green Flowers, Pink, 9 1/2 In.

Sapphire & Seed Pearls, 10K Gold	30.00
Violin Design, Sterling Silver	42.00
Winged Dragon, Brass	20.00

HAVILAND china has been made in Limoges, France, since 1842. The factory was started by the Haviland Brothers of New York City. Pieces are marked *H & Co., Haviland & Co.,* or *Theodore Haviland.* It is possible to **HAVILAND & CO.** match existing sets of dishes through dealers who specialize in Haviland china. Other factories worked in the town of Limoges making a similar chinaware. These porcelains are listed in this book under Limoges.

Bowl, Hand Painted Poppies, Oval, 13 1/2 In.	125.00
Chocolate Pot, Pink Flowers, Green, Gold, 8 In.	175.00
Chocolate Set, Gold Banding, c.1900, 10 Piece	82.50
Chocolate Set, Yellow Roses, Brown, Ruby Gem, 1912, 13 Piece	225.00
Cracker Jar, Rouen	150.00
Creamer, Osier Blank	45.00
Cup & Saucer, Bouillon, Princess	20.00
Cup & Saucer, Chocolate, Roses & Ribbons, GDA	15.00
Cup & Saucer, Flowers, Ranson	85.00
Dessert Set, 2 Cake Plates, Booted Bowl, 42 Piece	1430.00
Dinner Set, Trellis, Service For 12	50.00
Fruit Bowl, President Hayes, 8 In.	8000.00
Hair Receiver, Ranson	125.00
Jardiniere, Flowers, Leaves, 12 In. Diam.	175.00
Mustard, Attached Saucer, Gold Trim, Blank II, Kidney Shape	65.00
Pitcher, Souvenir, American Centennial Exposition, c.1876	176.00
Plate, Arts & Crafts Design, Greens & Black, Dated 1910, 7 1/2 In.	100.00
Plate, Green Flowers, Pink, 9 1/2 In. ....*Illus*	10.00
Plate, Oyster, Shell Design	63.00
Platter, Fish, 23 1/4 In.	330.00
Platter, Flowers, Pink, Gold, White, 16 In.	65.00
Platter, Noinville	40.00
Teapot, Bonnivel, Imari Red	175.00
Teapot, Pastel Floral, Gold Trim, Chantilly Blank	65.00
Tray, Oyster Design, Fluted Edge, 21 1/2 x 8 1/4 In.	155.00
Tureen, Cover, Sepia Flowers, Braided Handles, c.1880	125.00

HAWKES cut glass was made by T. G. Hawkes & Company of Corning, New York, founded in 1880. The firm cut glass blanks made at other glassworks until 1962. Many pieces are marked with the trademark, a trefoil ring enclosing a fleur–de–lis and two hawks. Cut glass by other manufacturers is listed under either the factory name or in the general Cut Glass category.

Basket, Candy, Engraved Florals, Sterling Rim & Handle, 3 3/4 In.	85.00
Basket, Etched Grape Design, Blue, Sterling Handle & Rim	250.00
Bottle, Spirits, Silver Cover, Allover Cut Punties, Signed, 9 1/2 In.	225.00
Bowl, Allover Hobstars & Stars, Signed, 3 1/4 x 10 In.	440.00

Bowl, Cluster Of Hobstars Around Hobstar Center, 9 In. 375.00
Bowl, Hobstar & Strawberry Diamond Band, Hobstar Base, Oval, 10 In. 325.00
Bowl, Sterling Rim, 10 In. 1075.00
Box, Glove, Cover, Signed 4900.00
Butter Pat, Cloverleaf Shape, Signed, 6 Piece 240.00
Butter Server, Center Handle, Faceted Knob, Rock Crystal 135.00
Candlestick, Teardrops, Floral Cutting, Green, Signed, 10 In. 150.00
Candlestick, Venetian, Etched, 11 In., Pair 450.00
Carafe, Queen, St. Louis Neck, Signed, 7 1/4 In. 500.00
Carafe, Venetian 250.00
Card Holder, Allover Floral Cut & Etched, Paperweight Stem, 5 In. 125.00
Card Holder, Paperweight Ball Stem, Etched, Crystal, Signed 198.00
Cheese Saver, Hobstar & Cane, Signed 600.00
Cocktail Set, Etched Grape Garland, Italian Green, 7 Piece 325.00
Cocktail Shaker, Grapevine Design, Sterling Top, Green 135.00
Compote, Candy, Cover, Sterling Knob, Floral & Basket Of Flowers 195.00
Compote, Teardrop, 7 In. 125.00
Decanter, Jubilee, Crystal Tusks On Base 750.00
Decanter, Waffle Pattern, Cut Paneled Stopper, Signed, 9 In. 135.00
Decanter, Whiskey, Silver Overlay, Signed 100.00
Dish, Calling Card, Diamond & Strawberry, Pedestal, Signed, 7 In. 165.00
Figurine, Butterfly, Signed 3700.00
Finger Bowl, Wheel Cut 25.00
Goblet Set, Crystal, Square Cut Base, Prism Knobs, 36 Piece 1210.00
Mayonnaise Set, Carnations, Leaves, Gravic, Signed, 3 Piece 200.00
Perfume Bottle, Venetian, Stemmed Stopper .... 225.00 To 350.00
Pitcher, Flutes On Top, Fans, Miters & Hobstars On Bottom, Signed 425.00
Pitcher, Milk, 6 1/2 In. 225.00
Pitcher, Milk, Bull's–Eye Star Clusters 225.00
Pitcher, Russian & Pillar, St. Louis Diamond Cut Handle, 7 In. 2400.00
Plate, Kensington, Signed, 13 In. 715.00
Plate, Later Panel, Signed, 7 In. 90.00
Plate, Millicent, Center Handle, Sterling & Repousse, Signed, 10 In. 250.00
Plate, Star & Stipple, Signed, 7 In. 145.00
Plate, Venetian, 9 In. 300.00
Powder Box, Gravic, Square, 4 In. 275.00
Punch Bowl, Stand, Hobstars With Fans & Swirls, Signed, 15 In. 1950.00
Rose Bowl, Chrysanthemum, Turquoise Cut To Clear 1300.00
Salt & Pepper, Flowers, Leaves, Branches, Signed, 7 1/2 In. 950.00
Shot Glass, Basketweave 80.00
Sugar & Creamer, Crystal, Emerald Green Base & Handles 145.00
Sugar & Creamer, Strawberry, Gravic 375.00
Tray, Lattice & Rosette, 10 In. .... 5000.00 To 5500.00
Tumbler, Whiskey, Fans & Stars, Signed 225.00
Vase, Brunswick, 16 In. 550.00
Vase, China Aster, Pedestal, Signed, 10 In. 440.00
Vase, Crystal, Art Nouveau, 10 In. 125.00
Vase, Devonshire Pattern, 14 1/4 In. 650.00
Vase, Etched Floral, Sterling Rim, Signed, 8 In. 175.00
Vase, Gravic Swirl, 9 3/4 In. 200.00
Vase, Navarre, 10 In. 275.00
Vase, Swag & Ribbon, Blue, Gold Rim, 8 In. 185.00
Vase, Thumbprint Flower, Intaglio Ferns, c.1940, 13 In. 175.00
Vase, Trumpet, Kensington, Hobstar Base, 18 In. 3500.00
Water Set, Strawberry Cut Diamonds, Diamond Panels, Birds, 5 Piece 195.00

HEAD VASES, generally showing a woman from the shoulders up, were
used by florists primarily in the 1950s and 1960s. Made in a variety of
sizes and often decorated with imitation jewelry and other lifelike
accessories, the vases were manufactured in Japan and the U.S.A. Less
elaborate examples were made as early as the 1930s. Religious themes,
babies, and animals are also common subjects.

African, Royal Copley 35.00

Heintz Art, Lamp, Copper, Silver Design,
White Silk Shade, 11 In.

◆◆◆◆◆◆◆◆◆◆◆◆◆◆◆◆◆◆◆◆◆◆◆◆

It is said you can clean silver with a banana peel mashed in a blender.

◆◆◆◆◆◆◆◆◆◆◆◆◆◆◆◆◆◆◆◆◆◆◆◆

◆◆◆◆◆◆◆◆◆◆◆◆◆◆◆◆◆◆◆◆◆◆◆◆

Look behind all hanging pictures once a year to be sure there are no insect nests, dust, or loose wires.

◆◆◆◆◆◆◆◆◆◆◆◆◆◆◆◆◆◆◆◆◆◆◆◆

Art Deco, USA	55.00
Black Girl	45.00
Black Woman, Dorothy Kindell	45.00
Blond, 6 In.	15.00
Blond, Pearls, 6 In.	18.00
Blue Straw Hat, Hand Raised To Mouth	38.00
Child, Holding Bluebird	17.00
Flapper, Art Deco, Small	40.00
Geisha	40.00
Horse, Inarco	15.00
Jackie Kennedy	75.00 To 135.00
Jean	35.00
Lady With Hat, Gloves, Napco, 7 1/2 In.	65.00
Little Cowboy	30.00
Little Girl	35.00
Mr. & Mrs. Chick	30.00
Mr. & Mrs. Skunk	30.00
Oriental Child, Royal Copley	17.00
Oriental With Fan	40.00
Pearl Earrings, Necklace, Napco, 7 In.	40.00
Sandy	35.00
Woman, Napco, C4414b	25.00

HEINTZ ART Metal Shop made jewelry, copper, silver, and brass in Buffalo, New York, from 1906 until 1935, when a new company name was taken and the mark became *Silvercrest*. The most popular items with collectors today are the copper desk sets and vases made with applied silver designs.

Ashtray, Nesting, Sterling On Bronze, 3 Piece	45.00
Ashtray, Sterling On Bronze	95.00
Bookends, Green, Sterling Design	175.00
Box, Cigar, Cedar Lined	375.00
Desk Set, Sterling On Bronze, 8 In., 3 Piece	110.00
Frame, 8 x 10 In.	295.00
Lamp, Copper, Silver Design, White Silk Shade, 11 In. ....*Illus*	75.00
Match Safe, Silver On Bronze	30.00
Tray, Card, Silver Over Bronze	48.00
Vase, Flower Design, Sterling On Bronze, 5 In.	110.00
Vase, Mistletoe, Sterling On Bronze, 1912, 12 In.	85.00
Vase, Nasturtium Blossoms, Leaves On Bronze, 4 1/2 In.	60.00
Vase, Silver Plate Over Bronze, 5 In.	150.00

HEISEY glass was made from 1896 to 1957 in Newark, Ohio, by A. H. Heisey and Co., Inc. The Imperial Glass Company of Bellaire, Ohio, bought some of the molds and the rights to the trademark. Some Heisey patterns have been made by Imperial since 1960. After 1968, they stopped using the *H* trademark. Heisey used romantic names for colors, such as *Sahara*. Do not confuse color and pattern names. The Custard Glass and Ruby Glass categories may also include some Heisey pieces.

Acorn, Plate, Flamingo, 7 In.	8.50
Banded Flute, Butter, Cover	85.00
Banded Flute, Chamberstick, Handle, 4 In.	45.00
Beaded Swag, Berry Set, 7 Piece	135.00
Beaded Swag, Berry Set, Enamel & Gold Trim, White, 7 Piece	225.00
Beaded Swag, Berry Set, Floral, 7 Piece	150.00
Beaded Swag, Cruet, Rose Bud Design	250.00
Beaded Swag, Toothpick, Ruby Glass, Fairfield Street Fair, 10/31/03	23.00
Beaded Swag, Toothpick, White	100.00
Beaded Swag, Tumbler, Hand Painted Rose, Milk Glass, c.1895	65.00
Beaded Swag, Tumbler, Opaque, Floral Design	25.00
Carcassonne, Goblet, Iced Tea, Alexandrite, 12 Oz.	160.00
Cathedral, Vase, Flared, Sahara	135.00
Charter Oak, Cocktail, Flamingo, 3 Oz.	21.00
Charter Oak, Sherbet, Flamingo, 6 Oz.	20.00
Chintz, Goblet, Water, Sahara	30.00
Cobel, Cocktail Shaker	40.00
Colonial, Butter, Cover	85.00
Colonial, Celery Vase	45.00
Colonial, Creamer, Miniature	20.00
Colonial, Eggcup, 6 Oz.	22.00
Colonial, Punch Set, Marked, Bowl 14 In., 13 Piece	220.00
Colonial, Vase, Flared, 7 In.	48.00
Colonial, Wine, 1 1/2 Oz.	20.00
Colonial, Wine, 2 Oz.	16.00
Continental, Toothpick	65.00 To 85.00
Cornucopia, Vase, 9 In., Pair	145.00
Coronation, Mixer, Double Lip, 30 Oz.	85.00
Crystolite, Cake Salver	375.00
Crystolite, Candy Dish, Metal Lid With Glass Flowers, 7 In.	55.00
Crystolite, Compote, 4 1/2 In.	24.50
Crystolite, Goblet, 10 Oz.	27.50
Crystolite, Jam Jar, Cover, Ladle, Marked	50.00
Crystolite, Mustard, Cover	40.00
Crystolite, Nut, Swan, Individual	16.00
Crystolite, Relish, 2 Sections	37.50
Crystolite, Relish, 5 Sections	32.00
Crystolite, Relish, Divided	25.00
Crystolite, Sugar & Creamer	35.00
Crystolite, Sugar & Creamer, Tray, Individual	49.50
Cut Block, Toothpick, Stain	115.00
Diamond Optic, Goblet, Flamingo, 6 Piece	110.00
Diamond Optic, Goblet, Water, Stemmed, Flamingo, 8 Piece	200.00
Dolphin, Match Holder	135.00
Double Rib & Panel, Basket, Flamingo, 6 In.	125.00 To 150.00
Double Rib & Panel, Cruet	45.00
Duck, Bowl, 3 Piece	195.00
Empress, Bonbon, Footed, Orchid Etch	25.00
Empress, Candlestick, 6 In., Pair	75.00
Empress, Candy Dish, Cover, Cobalt Blue, Gold Etch	425.00
Empress, Candy Dish, Cover, Sahara	160.00
Empress, Compote, Sahara, Footed, 6 In.	85.00
Empress, Console Set, Arctic Etch, Bowl, 11 In., 3 Piece	475.00
Empress, Cup & Saucer	115.00
Empress, Jug, Old Colony Etch, Sahara, 3 Pt.	195.00
Empress, Mayonnaise, Sahara	25.00
Empress, Plate, 8 In.	60.00
Empress, Plate, Sahara, 12 In.	40.00
Empress, Punch Bowl, Moongleam	990.00

Empress, Relish, 3 Sections, Sahara, 7 In. 27.00
Empress, Sugar & Creamer, Flamingo 85.00
Empress, Sugar & Creamer, Footed, Sahara 65.00
Empress, Tray, Celery, Flamingo, 13 In. 27.50
Empress, Tray, Pickle, Flamingo, 13 In. 30.00
Fairacre, Champagne, Green 17.50
Fairacre, Champagne, Pink Foot & Stem 25.00
Fairacre, Goblet, Pink Foot & Stem 35.00
Fairacre, Goblet, Water, Pink Foot & Stem 35.00
Fancy Loop, Toothpick 55.00
Fandango, Punch Cup, Gold Trim, Pair 40.00
Figurine, Asiatic Pheasant .... 195.00 To 420.00
Figurine, Balking Pony 165.00
Figurine, Bunny, Head Down 135.00
Figurine, Clydesdale 375.00
Figurine, Colt, Balking 230.00
Figurine, Colt, Kicking 260.00
Figurine, Colt, Standing ....95.00 To 103.00
Figurine, Cygnet 250.00
Figurine, Elephant .... 250.00 To 325.00
Figurine, Filly Horse, Head Backwards 950.00
Figurine, Giraffe, 11 1/2 In. 135.00
Figurine, Giraffe, Head Back 230.00
Figurine, Goose, Wings Halfway Up 75.00
Figurine, Goose, Wings Up .... 85.00 To 95.00
Figurine, Piglet, Sitting 65.00
Figurine, Piglet, Standing 65.00
Figurine, Plug Horse 75.00
Figurine, Pouter Pigeon 850.00
Figurine, Rabbit, Scalloped Free–Form Base, Amber 225.00
Figurine, Ringneck Pheasant .... 120.00 To 165.00
Figurine, Rooster 125.00
Figurine, Scotty ....85.00 To 125.00
Figurine, Show Horse 880.00
Figurine, Sparrow 150.00
Figurine, Wood Duck 830.00
Greek Key, Celery, 8 3/4 In. 40.00
Greek Key, Compote, Jelly, 5 1/2 In. 52.50
Greek Key, Creamer, Ruby & Gold Design 35.00
Greek Key, Dish, Almond, Individual 16.00
Greek Key, Ice Tub, Individual 45.00
Greek Key, Lamp, Kerosene, Pink, Square Base, Large 185.00
Greek Key, Pitcher, Silver Band, 3 Pt. 110.00
Greek Key, Sugar & Creamer, Oval 75.00
Horn Of Plenty, Vase, 7 In. 25.00
Horsehead, Bookends 290.00
Ipswich, Sugar 25.00
Ipswich, Vase, Candle, Sahara 55.00
King Arthur, Wine 30.00
Kohinoor, Goblet, Zircon Bowl, Crystal Stem & Foot, 9 Oz. 125.00
Lariat, Basket, 8 1/2 In. 165.00
Lariat, Candleholder 49.00
Lariat, Candlestick, Skirted Panel, 7 1/2 In. 55.00
Lariat, Candy Dish, Cover 45.00
Lariat, Champagne, Saucer, Blown, 5 1/4 Oz. 15.00
Lariat, Dish, 3–Footed, 8 1/4 In. 45.00
Lariat, Goblet, Blown, 10 Oz. 25.00
Lariat, Goblet, Moonglo Cutting 14.00
Lariat, Mayonnaise 25.00
Lariat, Plate, 6 In. 15.00
Lariat, Plate, 7 In. 20.00
Lariat, Plate, Demijohn–Torte, 10 In. 30.00
Lariat, Platter, Oval, 15 In. 30.00

Lariat, Punch Set, Bowl, Ladle, 12 Cups	100.00
Lariat, Punch Set, No Ladle, 13 Piece	140.00
Lariat, Relish	35.00
Lariat, Relish, Divided	45.00
Lariat, Server, Center Handle, 14 In.	60.00
Lariat, Sherbet, 6 Oz.	15.00
Lariat, Torte Plate, Rolled Edge, 12 In.	48.00
Lariat, Vase, Cornucopia, 9 In., Pair	145.00
Lodestar, Bowl, Dawn, 13 1/2 In.	180.00
Mary 'n Virge, Champagne, Vaseline	350.00
Mary 'n Virge, Goblet, Vaseline	475.00
Medium Flat Panel, Pitcher, 1 Qt.	85.00
Mercury, Candlestick, Pink, Pair	45.00
Mermaid, Rose Bowl, Etch, 8 In.	500.00
Mermaid, Shot Glass, Etch	150.00
Mermaid, Tumbler, Etch, Float, 12 Oz.	95.00
Monte Cristo, Compote, Cut, 7 In.	45.00
Monte Cristo, Wine, Olympiad Etch, 2 1/2 Oz.	60.00
Narrow Flute, Dish, Banana Split	20.00
Narrow Flute, Dish, Nut, Flamingo, With Rim, Individual	12.50
Narrow Flute, Tumbler, Juice, 4 Oz.	12.50
National, Tumbler, Victory Etch, 12 Oz.	20.00
New Era, Candelabra, Crystal Drops, Pair	175.00
New Era, Candleholder, 3 Bulbous Shades	125.00
New Era, Candleholder, Double, Bobeches, Prisms, Pair	150.00
Nude Stem, Ivy Bowl, Amethyst	250.00
Oceanic, Cordial, Orchid Etch, 1 Oz.	125.00
Oceanic, Goblet, Orchid Etch	30.00
Octagon, Bowl, Underplate, Marigold, Gold Border	75.00
Octagon, Ice Tub, Green	60.00
Old Colony, Ashtray, Flamingo	45.00
Old Dominion, Goblet, Moongleam Bowl, 10 Oz.	50.00
Old Dominion, Tumbler, Footed, Alexandrite, 8 Oz.	80.00
Old Sandwich, Bottle, Oil, Moongleam	100.00
Old Sandwich, Candlestick, 6 In.	75.00
Old Sandwich, Oyster Cocktail, 4 Oz.	12.50
Old Sandwich, Oyster Cocktail, Cobalt Blue	95.00
Old Sandwich, Tumbler, Iced Tea, Footed, 12 Oz.	45.00
Old Williamsburg, Candelabra, 2–Light, Pair	300.00
Old Williamsburg, Candelabra, 4–Light, Bobeches, Prisms, 21 In., Pair	1400.00
Old Williamsburg, Candelabrum, 2–Light, Cobalt Base & Bobeches	875.00
Old Williamsburg, Goblet, Water	25.00
Optic Tooth, Pitcher, Moongleam, Footed, Handle, 3 Pt.	160.00
Orchid Etch, Butter, Seahorse Finial	155.00
Orchid Etch, Cocktail Shaker, 12 In.	200.00
Orchid Etch, Compote, Oval, 7 In.	110.00
Orchid Etch, Honey Jar, Footed, 6 1/2 In.	45.00
Orchid, Champagne	30.00
Orchid, Cocktail, 4 Oz.	35.00
Orchid, Goblet, Water	35.00
Orchid, Tumbler, Iced Tea	60.00
Park Avenue, Champagne	50.00
Park Avenue, Claret	45.00
Park Avenue, Cordial	95.00 To 110.00
Park Avenue, Goblet	45.00
Park Avenue, Wine	45.00
Peerless, Claret, 4 1/2 Oz.	11.00
Peerless, Pitcher, Gold Trim, 3 Pt.	97.50
Peerless, Tumbler, Gold Trim, 8 Oz.	11.00
Petal, Sugar & Creamer, Yellow	70.00
Pineapple & Fan, Pitcher, Green, Gold Trim	195.00
Pineapple & Fan, Spoon Holder, Gold Trim	30.00
Pineapple & Fan, Toothpick	45.00

Pineapple & Fan, Toothpick, Green, Gold Trim .... 155.00 To 225.00
Pineapple & Fan, Tumbler, Green, Gold Trim 67.50
Plantation, Claret 24.00
Plantation, Epergne, Candleholder, Footed, 5 In., Pair 150.00
Plantation, Punch Set, Underplate, Embossed Pineapples, 14 Piece 750.00
Plantation, Relish, 3 Sections .... 22.00 To 40.00
Pleat & Panel, Compote, Cover, Flamingo, 6 In. 95.00
Pleat & Panel, Compote, Footed, Flamingo, 8 1/2 In. 95.00
Pleat & Panel, Cup & Saucer, Pink 32.00
Pleat & Panel, Goblet, 7 1/2 Oz. 28.00
Prince Of Wales Plumes, Compote, Jelly, Gold Trim 50.00
Prince Of Wales Plumes, Creamer, Gold Trim .... 22.00 To 35.00
Prince Of Wales Plumes, Punch Set, Marked, 11 Piece 350.00
Priscilla, Jelly, Footed, 2 Handles 30.00
Priscilla, Nappy, 5 In. 12.50
Priscilla, Toothpick 35.00
Prism Block, Ashtray 20.00
Provincial, Candy Jar, Cover, Footed, 8 1/2 In. 95.00
Provincial, Relish, 4 Sections 37.50
Provincial, Relish, 4 Sections, Zircon, 10 In. 170.00
Provincial, Tumbler, Zircon, 9 Oz. 55.00
Punty & Diamond Point, Vase, 10 In. 42.50
Punty Band, Toothpick, Garnet Dream, Beaded Rim, 1902 .... 40.00
Punty Band, Tumbler, Belle Fourche, S. D. 155.00
Puritan, Box, Cigarette, Horsehead On Cover 60.00
Queen Ann, Candleholder, Etched 125.00
Queen Ann, Cruet, Rosalie Etch 60.00
Queen Ann, Stand, Punch Bowl 35.00
Recessed Panel, Basket, Etched 135.00
Rib & Panel, Basket, 6 In. 125.00
Ribbed Octagon, Candlestick, Flamingo, 3 In., Pair 30.00
Ridge & Star, Plate, Moongleam, 8 1/2 In. 21.00
Ridgeleigh, Ashtray, Square 4.50
Ridgeleigh, Bonbon 25.00
Ridgeleigh, Candelabra, Crystal Drops, Pair 175.00
Ridgeleigh, Candlestick, Pair 175.00
Ridgeleigh, Holder, Cigarette, Round 17.50
Ridgeleigh, Mustard, Cover, Paddle 47.00
Ridgeleigh, Vase, Ruffled, 3 1/2 In. 22.50
Ring Band, Butter, Cover, Floral Design .... 165.00 To 250.00
Ring Band, Sugar, Cover, Pink Roses, Gold Trim, 7 In. 135.00
Rooster, Cocktail Shaker .... 85.00 To 450.00
Rooster, Cocktail Shaker, Moonglow Cutting, Pair 250.00
Rooster, Vase 135.00
Rose Etch, Bowl, Floral, Crimped, 12 In. 85.00
Rose Etch, Cordial, 1 Oz. 145.00
Rose, Bowl, Flamingo, 5 1/2 In. 30.00
Rose, Bowl, Fluted 45.00
Rose, Goblet, Stem .... 22.50 To 30.00
Rose, Pitcher 425.00
Rose, Plate, 14 In. 75.00
Rose, Plate, Dessert 20.00
Rose, Plate, Waverly Blank, 14 In. 85.00
Rose, Sherbet 20.00
Saturn, Cruet, Stopper, 2 Oz. 39.50
Saturn, Goblet, 6 Oz. 7.50
Saturn, Goblet, 8 Oz. 10.00
Saturn, Lamp, Green 75.00
Sawtooth Band, Table Set, Child's, 4 Piece 250.00
Spanish, Champagne, Saucer 395.00
Spanish, Champagne, Tangerine 420.00
Spanish, Claret, Barcelona Cut, 4 Oz. 42.00
Spanish, Cocktail, Tangerine 275.00

Spanish, Goblet .... 15.00 To 30.00
Spanish, Goblet, Stem 105.00
Spanish, Goblet, Tangerine .... 395.00 To 420.00
Spanish, Tumbler, Concord Etch, 5 Oz. 15.00
Spanish, Tumbler, Soda, Footed, 12 Oz. 75.00
Stanhope, Bowl, Floral, Oval, 11 In. 46.00
Stanhope, Champagne 35.00
Stanhope, Cocktail .... 22.50 To 35.00
Stanhope, Cocktail, Crystal 18.50
Stanhope, Cup & Saucer, Black Knob 32.00
Stanhope, Cup, Black Knob 24.00
Stanhope, Jam Jar, 6 In. 18.00
Stanhope, Plate, 7 1/4 In. 18.00
Stanhope, Sugar & Creamer, Black Knob 56.00
Stanhope, Sugar, Creamer & Cups, 5 Piece 75.00
Sunburst, Butter, Cover, Marigold Flash 75.00
Sunburst, Punch Set, Bowl, Ladle, 11 Cups 275.00
Sunburst, Spooner, Marigold Flash 45.00
Sunburst, Toothpick 50.00
Sunflower, Bowl, 12 1/2 In. 35.00
Thumbprint & Panel, Bowl, Cobalt Blue, Footed, 11 In. 275.00
Thumbprint & Panel, Candlestick, 2-Light, Cobalt Blue, Pair 375.00
Thumbprint & Panel, Candlestick, Sahara, Pair 140.00
Thumbprint, Custard Cup, Ribbed 95.00
Trident, Candlestick, Orchid Etch, Pair 90.00
Tudor, Candy Dish, Cover 52.50
Twist, Bonbon, Flamingo 30.00
Twist, Bonbon, Moongleam, Handle, 6 In. 29.00
Twist, Bowl, Pink, 9 In. 35.00
Twist, Celery, Green, 9 In. 28.00
Twist, Ice Bucket, Tongs, Moongleam 100.00
Twist, Mustard, Cover 36.00
Twist, Relish, 3 Sections, Marigold 40.00
Twist, Relish, 3 Sections, Yellow, 13 In. 35.00
Twist, Tray, Pickle, Moongleam, 7 In. 27.50
Tyrolean, Goblet, Luncheon 7.50
Victorian, Creamer 20.00
Victorian, Cruet, Oil, Stopper, 3 Oz. 52.50
Victorian, Goblet, 5 1/2 In. 10.00
Victorian, Goblet, Low Foot 21.00
Victorian, Goblet, Stem 15.00
Victorian, Relish, Chrome Lid & Metal Spoon 30.00
Victorian, Sherbet 14.00
Victorian, Tumbler, Old Fashioned 15.00
Victorian, Tumbler, Soda 25.00
Wabash, Goblet, 7 1/2 In. 22.00
Wabash, Sherbet, Flamingo 10.00
Wabash, Tankard, Pied Piper Etch, 3 Pt. 250.00
Wampum, Candlestick, Pair 35.00
Warwick, Vase, Cornucopia, 7 In., Pair 65.00
Warwick, Vase, Horn Of Plenty, 11 In. 55.00
Waverly, Bowl, Crimped, Orchid Etch, 12 In. 68.00
Waverly, Bowl, Gardenia, Orchid Etch, 12 In. 45.00
Waverly, Bowl, Gardenia, Orchid Etch, 13 In. 75.00
Waverly, Cake Stand, Orchid Etch, 13 1/2 In. 275.00
Waverly, Plate, Center Handle, 14 In. 80.00
Waverly, Plate, Salad, Orchid Etch 22.00
Waverly, Plate, Torte, Orchid Etch, 14 In. 65.00
Waverly, Sugar & Creamer, Etched Rose 45.00
Whirlpool, Plate, Amber, 8 In. 18.00
Whirlpool, Sherbet 8.50
Winged Scroll, Bowl, Green, Gold Trim, 9 In. 60.00
Winged Scroll, Pitcher, Silver Band, 3 Pt. 115.00

Winged Scroll, Table Set, 4 Piece	385.00
Winged Scroll, Table Set, Green, Gold Trim, 4 Piece	325.00
Yeoman, Compote, Moongleam	45.00
Yeoman, Eggcup, Marigold	75.00
Yeoman, Preserve, 4 Sections, 2 Handles, Cut	31.50
Yeoman, Sugar & Creamer, Pink	45.00

HEREND, see Fischer category

HEUBACH is the collector's name for Gebruder Heubach, a firm working in Lichten, Germany, from 1840 to 1925. It is best known for bisque dolls and doll heads, their principal products. They also manufactured bisque figurines, including piano babies, beginning in the 1880s, and glazed figurines in the 1900s. Piano babies are listed in their own section. Dolls are included in the Doll category under *Gebruder Heubach* and *Heubach*. Another factory, Ernst Heubach, working in Koppelsdorf, Germany, also made porcelain and dolls. These will also be found in the doll section under Heubach Koppelsdorf.

Figurine, Boy & Girl, Fishing At Beach, Signed, 13 In., Pair	795.00
Figurine, Boy, Holding Duck, Dog At Feet, 17 In.	595.00
Figurine, Boy, With Muff, Boy Throwing Snowball, Gold Overlay	850.00
Figurine, Boy, With Violin, 12 In.	125.00
Figurine, Dancing Girl, Smiling, Aqua Dress, Lace Collar, 11 1/2 In.	510.00
Figurine, Girl, Green Bonnet, Leaning On Hoe, 11 In.	225.00
Figurine, Girl, Wearing Purse, Tree In Background, 17 In.	595.00
Figurine, Hound, Seated, 4 1/2 In.	125.00
Figurine, Little Girls Dancing, Gold Trim, Signed, 12 1/2 In.	325.00
Figurine, Rabbit, Gray & White, Pink Ears & Eyes, Marked, 6 1/2 In.	135.00
Plate, Jasperware, Blown–Out Indian Chief, Headdress, Pipe, 6 In.	95.00
Vase, Embossed Lady, 5 1/2 In.	125.00
Vase, Hand Painted Woman, Rising Sun Mark, 5 3/4 In.	65.00

HIGBEE glass was made by the J. B. Higbee Company of Bridgeville, Pennsylvania, about 1900. Tablewares were made and it is possible to assemble a full set of dishes and goblets in some Higbee patterns. Most of the glass was clear, not colored. Additional pieces may be found in the Pressed Glass section by pattern name.

Bowl, Hawaiian Lei, Marked	25.00
Creamer, Comet Pattern, Footed, Marked	60.00
Nappy, Clear, Handle, Bumblebee Marked	25.00

HISTORIC BLUE, see factory names, such as Adams, Ridgway, and Staffordshire

HOBNAIL is a style of glass with bumps all over. Dozens of hobnail patterns and variants have been made. Clear, colored, and opalescent hobnail have been made and are being reproduced. Other pieces of hobnail may also be listed in the Depression Glass category under Hobnail and in the Fenton and Francisware categories.

Berry Bowl, Ruffled Rim, Opalescent Cranberry	95.00
Bowl, Blue Opalescent, 9 x 3 1/2 In.	65.00
Bowl, Blue Opalescent, Ruffled, 10 In.	57.00
Bowl, Center, Blue Opalescent, 11 1/2 In.	85.00
Bowl, Hobnail, Ruffled, Cranberry Opalescent, 6 In.	60.00
Console Set, White Opalescent, 3 Piece	125.00
Creamer, Amber, Individual	30.00
Cruet, Flint	75.00
Lamp, Crystal Globe, Miniature	30.00
Pitcher, Thumbprint Base, Amber, 8 In.	105.00
Spooner, Blue Opalescent	60.00 To 75.00
Sugar & Creamer, Waste Pot, Blue Opalescent, 3 Piece	36.00
Sugar, Cover, Opalescent	65.00
Sugar, Cover, White Opalescent, Northwood, 1903	65.00
Table Set, Blue, Ruffled, 1870s	195.00

Toothpick, Blue Opalescent .... 10.00 To 45.00
Toothpick, White Opalescent 43.00
Tray, Water, Amber, 11 1/2 In. 55.00
Tumbler, Amber, 7 Rows 20.00
Tumbler, Blue Opalescent 75.00
Tumbler, Hobbs, White Opalescent 25.00

HOCHST, or Hoechst, porcelain was made in Germany from 1746 to 1796. It was marked with a six-spoke wheel. Be careful when buying Hochst; many other firms have used a very similar wheel-shaped mark.

Cup & Saucer, Rooster & 2 Hens, Naturalistic, 1770 .... 880.00
Cup & Saucer, Woman Wearing Puce Hat & Dress, 1755–60 .... 775.00
Figurine, 2 Girls & Rabbit, 6 In. 2350.00
Figurine, Boy & Girl, Dog, 7 In. 2000.00
Plate, Farm Child, Followed By Duck, Farm Ground, 7 In. 115.00

HOLLY AMBER, or golden agate, glass was made by the Indiana Tumbler and Goblet Company of Greentown, Indiana, from January 1, 1903, to June 13, 1903. It is a pressed glass pattern featuring holly leaves in the amber-shaded glass. The glass was made with shadings that range from creamy opalescent to brown-amber.

Berry Bowl, 8 In. 550.00
Bowl 425.00
Butter, Cover, 1903 ....985.00 To 1025.00
Cruet 2405.00
Dish, Sauce, Footed, 3 1/4 x 4 1/2 In. 495.00
Relish 335.00
Salt & Pepper 850.00
Sauce Dish 250.00
Saucer 195.00
Toothpick .... 350.00 To 375.00
Tumbler 5750.00

HOPALONG CASSIDY was named William Lawrence Boyd when he was born in Cambridge, Ohio, in 1895. His first movie appearance was in 1919, but the first Hopalong Cassidy film was not until 1934. Sixty-six films were made. In 1948, William Boyd purchased the television rights to the movies, then later made fifty-two new programs. In the 1950s, Hopalong Cassidy and his horse, named *Topper*, were seen in comics, records, toys, and other products. Boyd died in 1972.

Ad, Chocolate Coated Ice Cream Bar, Colorful, 10 x 21 In. 285.00
Badge, 3–D 18.00
Badge, Teller, Saving Club, Envelope, Instructions 45.00
Bath Mat, Chenille 195.00
Bedspread, Chenille, Beige & Brown 225.00
Binoculars, Metal 65.00
Binoculars, Strap 50.00
Blanket, Bar 20 Ranch 200.00
Book, Publicity & Exploitation, 1950s, 14 In., 15 Pgs. 20.00
Bottle, Hair Tonic 55.00
Bracelet, ID 75.00
Button, With Compass, Plastic 8.00
Camera, Box 125.00
Can, Potato Chip .... 200.00 To 225.00
Card, Playing, Canasta 35.00
Card, Topps, Framed, 1955 .... 15.00
Catalog, Hopalong Cassidy 1950s Merchandise 28.00
Chair, TV 345.00
Chalkboard, Western, Small 45.00
Coaster, Hoppy Spun Honey 3.00
Container, Ice Cream 35.00
Cup, Black 30.00
Display, Butter–Nut Bread, Hoppy's Picture, 1950s, 12 In. 65.00

Display, Figural, Timex Watches, 1950s 1750.00
Figure, Ideal, Box 175.00
Figure, Lead 55.00
Fork 75.00
Game, Board, Hoppy & Topper Center, 1950, 18 1/2 In. 20.00
Game, Lasso, Box 200.00
Guitar, Hoppy, Black Wood, Box 175.00
Gun & Holster School Box 85.00
Gun, Zoomerang, Box .... 185.00 To 200.00
Handkerchief, Set Of 3 .... 50.00
Jacket, Black Denim, Bluebell 245.00
Jewelry, Anson 125.00
Knife, Pocket .... 60.00 To 85.00
Lamp, Bullet 225.00
Lunch Box, Blue Decal 120.00
Mask, Rubber, Box 350.00
Money Clip 35.00
Mug, Milk Glass 18.50
Mug, Red 26.00
Neckerchief, Hoppy Picture, On Galloping Topper 25.00
Necktie, With Slide 45.00
Night–Light, Gun & Holster 245.00
Night–Light, Pistol 195.00
Notebook Filler Paper, Hoppy Pictures 18.00
Pin, Hanging 6–Gun 47.00
Pin, Saving Rodeo Wrangler 25.00
Plate, Black 100.00
Plate, Bowl, Cup, Blue, 3 Piece 150.00
Postcard 4.00
Poster, Hoppy On Topper, Bread Ad, 17 x 22 In. 25.00
Poster, Movie, 24 x 36 In. 60.00
Puzzle, Film 85.00
Pyrograph Set, Box 195.00
Radio, Red, Arvin .... 150.00 To 300.00
Record Album, Hoppy Square Dance Hold Up, 2 Piece 65.00
Ring, Bar 20, Face 35.00
Ring, Hat, Compass .... 45.00 To 200.00
Shooting Gallery 175.00
Sign, Milk, Die Cut, Tin, Hoppy Picture 1650.00
Sweater, Beige, Burgundy, V Neck, Hoppy Front, Topper Back 295.00
Sweatshirt 65.00
Target Board, Tin 55.00
Tie Bar, Box 125.00
Tumbler, Advertising Milk, Hoppy, 5 In. 27.00
Tumbler, Black 75.00
Tumbler, Luncheon 40.00
View Master 5.00
Wallet 55.00
Watch, Pocket, 1980s .... 45.00 To 95.00
Wristwatch, Saddle Box, 1950 .... 375.00 To 425.00

HOWARD PIERCE has been working in southern California since 1936. In 1945, he opened a pottery in Claremont. His contemporary–looking figurines are popular with collectors. Pieces are marked with his name.

Howard Pierce

Figurine, Bear, Brown, 8 In. 85.00
Vase, Deer, Tree In Hollow Center, Green, 12 In. 68.00
Vase, Jasperware, Children, Green, 4 In. 15.00

HOWDY DOODY and Buffalo Bob were the main characters in a children's series televised from 1947 to 1960. Howdy was a redheaded puppet. The series became popular with college students in the late 1970s when Buffalo Bob began to lecture on campuses.

Album, Christmas Party, RCA Victor, 2 Records 16.00

Bandana, Signed Bob Smith	50.00
Bank, Shawnee	325.00
Billfold	32.50
Bottle, Welch's Grape Juice, Dated 1946	100.00
Box, Pudding, Contents, With Trading Card	45.00
Button, It's Howdy Doody Time, 1955	30.00
Button, Red, White, Celluloid, 1 1/2 In.	24.00
Candle Set, Birthday Cake, Plastic, Figural Character, 1950s	35.00
Catalog, Howdy Doody Merchandise, 1955	38.00 To 45.00
Catalog, Howdy Sales, Merchandise From 1947–55, 20 Pages	10.00
Clock, Wall, 40th Anniversary, Box, 26 In.	50.00
Cookie Jar, Purinton	375.00 To 695.00
Cookie Jar, Tin, Cookie Gó Round	135.00
Cookie Jar, Vandor	150.00
Cover, Life, Child's	28.00
Disguise, Howdy As Detective, Unpunched	35.00
Doll, Composition, Sleep Eyes, Cloth Body, 19 In.	100.00
Doll, Mouth Moves, 1970s, Box	65.00
Doll, Mouth Moves, Plastic, NBC Mike In Hand, 5 In.	35.00
Figure, Inflatable, 41 In.	10.00
Fudge Bar Wrapper, 1950	3.00
Game, Adventure, Character Markers, Box, 1950s	30.00
Game, TV, Cragstan	55.00
Game, TV, Milton Bradley	95.00
Glass, Welch's, Yellow, White, 1953	15.00
Handcar, Tin, Windup	175.00
Key Chain, Puzzle	15.00
Marionette, 1950s, 16 In.	60.00
Marionette, Flub–A–Dub, 1950s	265.00
Night–Light, Howdy Sitting	110.00 To 120.00
Night–Light, Leadworks, Ceramic	20.00
Pail, Howdy's Famous Peanut Butter Cookies, Boy, Girl, Seesaw	528.00
Pencil, Howdy's Head	5.00
Pencil, Howdy's Head Top, Red Wood	35.00
Phone Doodle	200.00
Puppet Show, Original Card, 5 Figures	95.00
Puppet, Clarabell, 3 Musketeers & Mars Bars, Animated, 15 In.	55.00
Puppet, Hand, Composition, Cloth, 17 In.	210.00 To 220.00
Ring, Flasher	30.00
Ring, Flasher, Set Of 8	60.00
Ring, Flashlight	95.00 To 175.00
Ring, Flashlight, Battery Operated	175.00
Ring, Red & White Celluloid, 1 1/2 In.	24.00
Salt & Pepper	25.00
Toy, Acrobat, Windup, 1950s	715.00
Toy, Full Figure, Rubber, Cowboy Outfit, 13 In.	120.00
Toy, Game, Bowling, Box	95.00
Toy, Wall Climber	25.00
Toy, Wall Walker, Plastic, On Card, 1950s, 7 In.	80.00 To 85.00
Toy, Wood Press, Box, Conner	185.00
Tumbler	10.00
Wrapper, Popsicle, 1950s	12.00
Wristwatch, Applause	20.00

HULL pottery was made in Crooksville, Ohio, from 1905. Addis E. Hull bought the Acme Pottery Company and started making ceramic wares. In 1917, A. E. Hull Pottery began making art pottery as well as commercial wares. For a short time, 1921 to 1929, the firm also sold pottery imported from Europe. The dinnerwares of the 1940s, including the Little Red Riding Hood line, the high–gloss artwares of the 1950s, and the matte wares of the 1940s, are all popular with collectors. The firm officially closed in March 1986.

Hull
US A.

Ashtray, Ebb Tide	90.00

Ashtray, Ebb Tide, Mermaid 100.00
Ashtray, Serenade, Pink 55.00
Bank, Little Red Riding Hood 395.00
Bank, Pig, Sitting, 6 In. 15.00
Basket, Bow Knot, Pink, 12 In. 1350.00
Basket, Continental, Orange, 12 1/2 In. 35.00
Basket, Glossy Red, Green Interior, Signed, 6 x 9 1/2 In. 55.00
Basket, Hanging, Crab Apple 200.00
Basket, Magnolia, Pink & Blue, 10 1/2 In. .... 150.00 To 200.00
Basket, Mardi Gras, White & Pink, 8 In. 90.00
Basket, Parchment & Pine 75.00
Basket, Royal Woodland, Pink & Gray, 10 1/2 In. 110.00
Basket, Serenade, Pink, 12 In. 200.00
Basket, Sunglow, Pink, 6 1/2 In. 20.00
Basket, Tokay, Green & White, 10 1/2 In. .... 55.00 To 60.00
Basket, Tokay, Moon, 11 In. 50.00
Basket, Tulip, 6 In. 110.00
Basket, Tuscany, 8 In. 30.00
Basket, Tuscany, Green & White, 8 In. 20.00
Basket, Tuscany, Green & White, 10 1/2 In. 40.00
Basket, Wildflower 230.00
Basket, Wildflower, Blue & Pink, 10 In. 295.00
Basket, Wildflower, Blue & Pink, 16 x 10 1/2 In. 120.00
Basket, Woodland, Blue, 8 In. 45.00
Basket, Woodland, Glossy 110.00
Batter Jug, Little Red Riding Hood 55.00
Bookends, Orchid 750.00
Bottle, Elephant, Pink, 8 In. 80.00
Bowl, Blossom Flite, Pink & Black, 10 1/2 In. 50.00
Bowl, Continental, 15 1/2 In. 40.00
Bowl, Ebb Tide, Wine, Gold Trim, 15 3/4 In. ....95.00 To 125.00
Bowl, Mixing, Daisies 26.00
Butter, Cover, Little Red Riding Hood 250.00
Camelia, Vase, 7 In. 45.00
Candleholder, Open Rose, Dove, 6 1/2 In., Pair 150.00
Candleholder, Woodland, 3 1/2 In., Pair 80.00
Candlestick, Parchment & Pine 20.00
Canister, Flour, Little Red Riding Hood 525.00
Canister, Sugar, Old MacDonald 275.00
Console Set, Orchid, 3 Piece 345.00
Console Set, Parchment & Pine, 3 Piece 65.00
Console Set, Woodland, 3 Piece ....95.00 To 110.00
Cookie Jar, Apple .... 25.00 To 28.00
Cookie Jar, Barefoot Boy .... 265.00 To 355.00
Cookie Jar, Bugs Bunny .... 150.00 To 165.00
Cookie Jar, Closed Basket 95.00
Cookie Jar, Gingerbread Boy, Brown 45.00
Cookie Jar, Gingerbread Boy, With Gingerbread Boy Tray 85.00
Cookie Jar, Little Red Riding Hood, Closed Basket .... 200.00 To 225.00
Cookie Jar, Little Red Riding Hood, Open Basket .... 165.00 To 225.00
Cookie Jar, Little Red Riding Hood, White Blank 165.00
Cookie Jar, Winnie The Pooh 95.00
Cornucopia, Blossom Flite Gloss 50.00
Cornucopia, Bow Knot, 7 1/2 In. 50.00
Cornucopia, Bow Knot, Pink To Blue, 8 In., Pair 90.00
Cornucopia, Bow Knot, Pink, 6 1/2 In. 50.00
Cornucopia, Double, Bow Knot 265.00
Cornucopia, Double, Woodland, Gold Trim 195.00
Cornucopia, Double, Woodland, Pre-1950 .... 265.00
Cornucopia, Ebb Tide, Mermaid 60.00
Cornucopia, Pink & Green, 6 1/2 In. 85.00
Cornucopia, Rosella, Ivory, 8 1/2 In. .... 45.00 To 50.00
Cornucopia, Waterlily, Pink Over Green, 6 1/2 In. 45.00

Creamer & Teapot, Water Lily, Gold Covers 135.00
Creamer, Blossom Flite .... 12.50 To 15.00
Creamer, Little Red Riding Hood 55.00
Creamer, Little Red Riding Hood, 5 1/4 In. 85.00
Creamer, Little Red Riding Hood, Head Pour ....65.00 To 185.00
Creamer, Magnolia 9.00
Creamer, Rooster, Old MacDonald 95.00
Creamer, Wildflower, 4 3/4 In. 85.00
Ewer, Bow Knot, Blue & Pink, 5 1/12 In. 90.00
Ewer, Magnolia, Matte, 13 1/2 In. 120.00
Ewer, Open Rose 105.00
Ewer, Parchment & Pine, 14 In. 65.00
Ewer, Tokay, Pink & Green, 12 In. 130.00
Ewer, Tropicana 525.00
Ewer, Tulip, 8 In. 90.00
Ewer, Water Lily, Paper Label, 13 1/2 In. 225.00
Ewer, Woodland, 6 In. 35.00
Ewer, Woodland, Cream & Pink Base, 6 1/2 In. 30.00
Flowerpot, Attached Saucer, Earth Art 38.00
Jardiniere, Bow Knot 105.00
Jardiniere, Butterfly, 6 In. 25.00
Jardiniere, Open Rose 175.00
Lamp, Little Red Riding Hood 1195.00
Lavabo Set, Butterfly, Blue 90.00
Lavabo, Butterfly 60.00
Matchbox, Little Red Riding Hood, Blue Dress 650.00
Matchbox, Little Red Riding Hood, White Dress, Blue Trim 650.00
Mug, Chocolate Soldier, 4 Piece 75.00
Mustard, Little Red Riding Hood, Spoon .... 150.00 To 315.00
Open Rose, Vase, Hand 135.00
Pitcher, Batter, Little Red Riding Hood .... 245.00 To 340.00
Pitcher, Butterfly, 13 1/2 In. .... 90.00 To 95.00
Pitcher, Butterfly, 15 1/2 In. 95.00
Pitcher, Butterfly, Blue & White, 6 In. 35.00
Pitcher, Butterfly, Gold Trim, 8 3/4 In. 125.00
Pitcher, Continental, 12 1/2 In. 50.00
Pitcher, Granada 70.00
Pitcher, Magnolia, 13 1/2 In. 185.00
Pitcher, Milk, Little Red Riding Hood .... 225.00 To 235.00
Pitcher, Sponge, Iowa 575.00
Pitcher, Tokay, Pink, White & Green 145.00
Pitcher, Wildflower, Tan, 8 1/2 In. .... 80.00 To 90.00
Pitcher, Wine, Ebb Tide 115.00
Pitcher, Woodland, Pink, 5 1/2 In. 55.00
Pitcher, Woodland, Yellow & Green, 5 1/2 In. 45.00
Planter, Clown 20.00
Planter, Dancing Girl, Matte Pink & Blue 45.00
Planter, Dancing Lady 40.00
Planter, Dog With Ball Of Yarn 10.00
Planter, Flying Duck 55.00
Planter, Flying Goose 45.00
Planter, Hanging, Iris, 4 In. 45.00
Planter, Kitten 40.00
Planter, Parchment Scroll 40.00
Planter, Pheasant .... 20.00 To 25.00
Planter, Smiling Duck 23.00
Planter, Underplate, Bow Knot 90.00
Plate, Bow Knot, Blue, 10 In. 795.00
Salt & Pepper, Boy & Girl, Old MacDonald 75.00
Salt & Pepper, Little Red Riding Hood, Large 65.00
Salt & Pepper, Little Red Riding Hood, Medium 125.00
Salt & Pepper, Little Red Riding Hood, Small 30.00
Salt & Pepper, Sun Glows 15.00

Sugar, Blossom Flite .... 12.50 To 15.00
Sugar, Cover, Hen, Old MacDonald 120.00
Tea Set, Blossom Flite, 3 Piece .... 65.00 To 75.00
Tea Set, Ebbtide, 3 Piece 110.00
Tea Set, Magnolia, 3 Piece 200.00
Tea Set, Magnolia, Brown & Cream, 3 Piece 135.00
Tea Set, Parchment & Pine, 3 Piece 135.00
Tea Set, Parchment, 3 Piece 100.00
Tea Set, Water Lily, Matte, 3 Piece 120.00
Tea Set, Wildflower, Glossy, 3 Piece 135.00
Tea Set, Woodland, Glossy, 3 Piece .... 78.00 To 100.00
Teapot, Butterfly 95.00
Teapot, Little Red Riding Hood .... 245.00 To 250.00
Teapot, Magnolia 55.00
Teapot, Magnolia, Gloss, Blue 50.00
Teapot, Royal Woodland, Pink 58.00
Vase, Blossom Flite, Drizzled Gold, Pink & Black, 10 1/2 In. 50.00
Vase, Bow Knot, 6 1/2 In. 38.00
Vase, Bow Knot, Pink & Blue, 6 1/2 In. 30.00
Vase, Butterfly, 10 1/2 In. 40.00
Vase, Butterfly, White, 10 x 7 In. 25.00
Vase, Calla Lily, 10 In. 155.00
Vase, Calla Lily, Aqua Over Brown, 7 In. 65.00
Vase, Cornucopia, 8 1/2 In. 45.00
Vase, Dogwood, 6 1/2 In. 45.00
Vase, Dogwood, Pink & Blue, 4 1/4 In. 35.00
Vase, Ebb Tide, 6 In. 28.00
Vase, Ebb Tide, 7 In. 35.00
Vase, Ebb Tide, 9 In. 85.00
Vase, Ebb Tide, Green & Brown, 9 In. 35.00
Vase, Magnolia, 8 1/2 In. 45.00
Vase, Magnolia, 12 1/2 In. 80.00
Vase, Magnolia, Blue & Pink, 6 1/4 In. 30.00
Vase, Magnolia, Gloss, 6 1/2 In. 45.00
Vase, Magnolia, Gloss, 12 1/2 In. 90.00
Vase, Magnolia, Matte, 6 1/4 In. 30.00
Vase, Magnolia, Matte, 15 In. 200.00
Vase, Magnolia, Matte, 6 1/4 In. 35.00
Vase, Magnolia, Matte, Handle, 8 1/2 In. 48.00
Vase, Magnolia, Matte, Pink Over Blue, 8 1/2 In. 52.00
Vase, Magnolia, Pink & Blue, 10 1/2 In. 70.00
Vase, Magnolia, Pink & Blue, 15 In. 250.00
Vase, Magnolia, Yellow & Brown, 6 1/2 In. 35.00
Vase, Open Rose, 8 1/2 In. .... 65.00 To 90.00
Vase, Open Rose, 12 In. 180.00
Vase, Open Rose, Blue Over Pink, 6 1/4 In. 45.00
Vase, Orchid, 9 1/2 In. 50.00
Vase, Parchment & Pine, 16 1/2 In. 75.00
Vase, Parchment & Pine, Green, 5 In. 30.00
Vase, Poppy, 10 1/2 In. 195.00
Vase, Poppy, Pink & Blue, 6 1/2 In. 75.00
Vase, Rosella, Heart Shape, 6 1/2 In. 35.00
Vase, Rosella, Matte Pink & Blue, 5 In. 120.00
Vase, Royal, Fish, Turquoise 50.00
Vase, Tokay, 6 In. 25.00
Vase, Tokay, Pink, White & Green, 12 In. 55.00
Vase, Twin Fish, Green & Pink, 7 In. 45.00
Vase, Water Lily, Gold Trim, 5 1/2 In. 22.00
Vase, Water Lily, Gold Trim, 9 1/2 In. 55.00
Vase, Water Lily, Pink & Green, 6 1/2 In. 40.00
Vase, Wildflower, Cream & Pink, 6 1/2 In. .... 30.00 To 45.00
Vase, Wildflower, Cream & Pink, 8 In. 45.00
Vase, Wildflower, Pink & Blue, 7 1/2 In. 40.00

Vase, Wildflower, Pink & Blue, 9 1/2 In.	65.00
Vase, Wildflower, Pink Over Blue, 8 1/2 In.	60.00
Vase, Windflower, Tan, Label, 8 1/2 In.	65.00
Vase, Woodland, Pre–1950, 12 1/2 In.	175.00 To 195.00
Vase, Woodland, Trial Glaze, 8 1/2 In.	150.00
Vase, Woodland, Yellow & Green, Label, M. Wilson, 6 1/2 In.	55.00
Wall Pocket, Bow Knot, Whiskbroom, Blue	30.00
Wall Pocket, Cup & Saucer	45.00
Wall Pocket, Flying Goose	20.00
Wall Pocket, Iron, Sunglow	40.00 To 60.00
Wall Pocket, Sun Glow, Whiskbroom	40.00
Wall Pocket, Woodland	15.00
Window Box, Serenade, 10 In.	40.00

HUMMEL figurines, based on the drawings of the nun Berta Hummel, are made by the W. Goebel Porzellanfabrik of Oeslau, Germany, now Rodenthal, Germany. They were first made in 1934. The mark has changed through the years. The following are the approximate dates for each of the marks: *Crown* mark, 1935 to 1949; *U.S. Zone, Germany,* 1946 to 1948; *West Germany,* after 1949; *full bee* with variations, 1950 to 1959; *stylized bee,* 1960 to 1972; *three line mark,* 1968 to 1979; *vee over gee,* 1972 to 1979; *new mark, West Germany* 1979 to 1990; and the *Goebel, Germany,* mark introduced in 1991. Other decorative items and plates that feature Hummel drawings have been made by Schmid Brothers, Inc., since 1971.

Ashtray, No. 33, Joyful, Stylized Bee	130.00
Ashtray, No. 34, Singing Lesson, New Mark	90.00
Ashtray, No. 62, Happy Pastime, Stylized Bee	175.00 To 200.00
Ashtray, No. 166, Boy With Bird, Crown Mark	180.00
Bank, No. 118, Little Thrifty, Full Bee	305.00
Bell, Annual, 1978	22.00
Bookends, No. 14A & 14B, Bookworm, Vee Over Gee, Pair	300.00 To 325.00
Bookends, No. 252/A, Apple Tree Boy, Stylized Bee	300.00
Bookends, No. 252/B, Apple Tree Girl, Stylized Bee	300.00
Calendar, 1972	4.00
Calendar, 1975	4.00
Candleholder, No. 24, Lullaby, Crown Mark	375.00
Candleholder, No. 40, Angel With Trumpet, Stylized Bee	50.00
Candleholder, No. 113, Heavenly Song, Full Bee	3500.00
Candleholder, No. 193, Angel Duet, Three Line Mark	185.00
Figurine, Nativity Scene, White Overglaze, 12 Piece	5000.00
Figurine, No. 1, Puppy Love, Stylized Bee	100.00
Figurine, No. 2/II, Little Fiddler, Vee Over Gee	500.00
Figurine, No. 2/III, Little Fiddler, Full Bee	1100.00
Figurine, No. 3/II, Book Worm, Vee Over Gee	300.00
Figurine, No. 7/II, Merry Wanderer, Crown Mark	2000.00
Figurine, No. 9, Begging His Share, Crown Mark	400.00
Figurine, No. 9, Begging His Share, Stylized Bee	200.00
Figurine, No. 10/I, Flower Madonna, Full Bee	240.00 To 485.00
Figurine, No. 10/I, Flower Madonna, Stylized Bee, Color	225.00
Figurine, No. 10/I, Flower Madonna, Stylized Bee, White	129.00
Figurine, No. 11/0, Merry Wanderer, Stylized Bee	125.00
Figurine, No. 12/2/0, Chimney Sweep, Full Bee	110.00
Figurine, No. 12/I, Chimney Sweep, Full Bee	175.00
Figurine, No. 12/I, Chimney Sweep, Stylized Bee	120.00
Figurine, No. 13/2/0, Meditation, Crown Mark	1500.00 To 2300.00
Figurine, No. 15, Hear Ye, Hear Ye, Stylized Bee	350.00
Figurine, No. 15/0, Hear Ye, Hear Ye, Crown Mark	375.00
Figurine, No. 16/2/0, Little Hiker, Stylized Bee	100.00
Figurine, No. 17/0, Congratulations, Full Bee	220.00
Figurine, No. 17/0, Congratulations, Stylized Bee	100.00
Figurine, No. 20, Prayer Before Battle, Crown Mark	305.00
Figurine, No. 20, Prayer Before Battle, Stylized Bee	110.00
Figurine, No. 21/0, Heavenly Angel, Full Bee	110.00

Figurine, No. 23/I, Adoration, Three Line Mark 225.00
Figurine, No. 28/III, Wayside Devotion, Vee Over Gee .... 282.00 To 310.00
Figurine, No. 32/0, Little Gabriel, Crown Mark 220.00
Figurine, No. 32/0, Little Gabriel, Full Bee 150.00
Figurine, No. 43, March Winds, Crown Mark .... 110.00 To 250.00
Figurine, No. 47/0, Goose Girl, Crown Mark 500.00
Figurine, No. 47/3/0, Goose Girl, Full Bee 195.00
Figurine, No. 47/II, Goose Girl, Stylized Bee 210.00
Figurine, No. 49, To Market, Crown Mark 900.00
Figurine, No. 49/3/0, To Market, Full Bee 170.00
Figurine, No. 50/2/0, Volunteers, Stylized Bee 80.00
Figurine, No. 50/2/0, Volunteers, Vee Over Gee .... 108.00 To 120.00
Figurine, No. 51/3/0, Village Boy, Stylized Bee 95.00
Figurine, No. 51/I, Village Boy, New Mark 175.00
Figurine, No. 52/I, Going To Grandma's, Vee Over Gee 350.00
Figurine, No. 53, Joyful, Stylized Bee .... 50.00 To 100.00
Figurine, No. 56/A, Culprits, Full Bee 225.00
Figurine, No. 56/A, Culprits, Three Line Mark 185.00
Figurine, No. 56/B, Out Of Danger, Vee Over Gee 152.00
Figurine, No. 57, Chick Girl, Crown Mark 400.00
Figurine, No. 57/0, Chick Girl, Full Bee 130.00
Figurine, No. 57/0, Chick Girl, Stylized Bee 135.00
Figurine, No. 58/I, Playmates, New Mark 200.00
Figurine, No. 58/I, Playmates, Stylized Bee 100.00
Figurine, No. 59, Skier, Crown Mark 330.00
Figurine, No. 59, Skier, Full Bee 180.00
Figurine, No. 63, Singing Lesson, Stylized Bee 95.00
Figurine, No. 65/I, Farewell, Full Bee 225.00
Figurine, No. 66, Farm Boy, Full Bee 180.00
Figurine, No. 67, Doll Mother, Crown Mark 410.00
Figurine, No. 67, Doll Mother, Stylized Bee 220.00
Figurine, No. 68/0, Lost Sheep, Vee Over Gee 90.00
Figurine, No. 69, Happy Pastime, Stylized Bee 90.00
Figurine, No. 70, Holy Child, Full Bee 175.00
Figurine, No. 71, Stormy Weather, Crown Mark 750.00
Figurine, No. 71, Stormy Weather, Stylized Bee 260.00
Figurine, No. 72, Spring Cheer, Crown Mark 575.00
Figurine, No. 72, Spring Cheer, Vee Over Gee 100.00
Figurine, No. 73, Little Helper, Stylized Bee .... 50.00 To 100.00
Figurine, No. 74, Little Gardener, Crown Mark 235.00
Figurine, No. 74, Little Gardener, Three Line Mark 100.00
Figurine, No. 79, Globe Trotter, Crown Mark 330.00
Figurine, No. 80, Little Scholar, Stylized Bee .... 110.00 To 120.00
Figurine, No. 81/0, School Girl, Stylized Bee .... 80.00 To 120.00
Figurine, No. 81/2/0, School Girl, Stylized Bee .... 60.00 To 125.00
Figurine, No. 82/0, School Boy, Crown Mark 365.00
Figurine, No. 84/0, Worship, Crown Mark 330.00
Figurine, No. 85, Serenade, Full Bee 150.00
Figurine, No. 85/0, Serenade, Stylized Bee 100.00
Figurine, No. 85/II, Serenade, Vee Over Gee 195.00
Figurine, No. 86, Happiness, Full Bee 150.00
Figurine, No. 87, For Father, Full Bee 190.00
Figurine, No. 94, Surprise, Crown Mark 375.00
Figurine, No. 95, Brother, Full Bee 250.00
Figurine, No. 95, Brother, Stylized Bee 100.00
Figurine, No. 95, Brother, Vee Over Gee 90.00
Figurine, No. 97, Trumpet Boy, Three Line Mark 100.00
Figurine, No. 99, Eventide, Crown Mark 495.00
Figurine, No. 110/0, Let's Sing, Three Line Mark .... 45.00 To 100.00
Figurine, No. 111, Wayside Harmony, Full Bee 175.00
Figurine, No. 112/I, Just Reading, Full Bee 230.00
Figurine, No. 118, Little Thrifty, Full Bee 295.00
Figurine, No. 119, Postman, Stylized Bee 160.00

Figurine, No. 124, Hello, Full Bee .... 250.00 To 275.00
Figurine, No. 124/0, Hello, Full Bee 240.00
Figurine, No. 127, Doctor, Full Bee .... 150.00 To 168.00
Figurine, No. 127, Doctor, Stylized Bee .... 100.00 To 125.00
Figurine, No. 128, Baker, Stylized Bee 125.00
Figurine, No. 129, Band Leader, Full Bee .... 195.00 To 250.00
Figurine, No. 129, Band Leader, Stylized Bee .... 100.00 To 125.00
Figurine, No. 130, Duet, Full Bee 300.00
Figurine, No. 132, Star Gazer, Stylized Bee 100.00
Figurine, No. 135, Soloist, Stylized Bee 100.00
Figurine, No. 136/I, Friends, Three Line Mark 120.00
Figurine, No. 136/V, Friends, Vee Over Gee .... 500.00 To 600.00
Figurine, No. 141/V, Apple Tree Girl, Vee Over Gee 500.00
Figurine, No. 142/3/0, Apple Tree Boy, Stylized Bee ....55.00 To 100.00
Figurine, No. 142/V, Apple Tree Boy, Vee Over Gee 500.00
Figurine, No. 143/0, Boots, Full Bee 170.00
Figurine, No. 144, Angelic Song, Crown Mark 275.00
Figurine, No. 153, Auf Wiedersehen, Full Bee 225.00
Figurine, No. 154/0, Waiter, Stylized Bee 125.00
Figurine, No. 169, Bird Duet, Three Line Mark 110.00
Figurine, No. 170, School Boys, Crown Mark 2300.00
Figurine, No. 170/III, School Boys, Vee Over Gee .... 1025.00 To 1300.00
Figurine, No. 174, She Loves Me, She Loves Me Not, Full Bee 170.00
Figurine, No. 174, She Loves Me, She Loves Me Not, Vee Over Gee 96.00
Figurine, No. 175, Mother's Darling, Stylized Bee 90.00
Figurine, No. 176/0, Happy Birthday, Stylized Bee 220.00
Figurine, No. 177/I, School Girls, Three Line Mark 650.00
Figurine, No. 177/III, School Girls, Vee Over Gee .... 1025.00 To 1300.00
Figurine, No. 178, Photographer, Three Line Mark 175.00
Figurine, No. 182, Good Friends, Crown & Full Bee 250.00
Figurine, No. 182, Good Friends, Full Bee 400.00
Figurine, No. 184, Latest News, Full Bee 295.00
Figurine, No. 184/0, Latest News, Vee Over Gee 195.00
Figurine, No. 185, Accordion Boy, Full Bee 210.00
Figurine, No. 185, Accordion Boy, Stylized Bee 110.00
Figurine, No. 186, Sweet Music, Full Bee 250.00
Figurine, No. 186, Sweet Music, Striped Slippers, Crown Mark 1225.00
Figurine, No. 186, Sweet Music, Stylized Bee .... 125.00 To 150.00
Figurine, No. 188, Celestial Musician, Vee Over Gee 140.00
Figurine, No. 194, Watchful Angel, New Mark 220.00
Figurine, No. 195, Barnyard Hero, Full Bee 160.00
Figurine, No. 195/2/0, Barnyard Hero, Full Bee 175.00
Figurine, No. 195/2/0, Barnyard Hero, New Mark 95.00
Figurine, No. 195/2/0, Barnyard Hero, Three Line Mark .... 85.00 To 90.00
Figurine, No. 196, Telling Her Secret, Vee Over Gee 195.00
Figurine, No. 196/0, Telling Her Secret, Full Bee 275.00
Figurine, No. 197, Be Patient, Stylized Bee 70.00
Figurine, No. 198/2/0, Home From Market, Three Line Mark 85.00
Figurine, No. 199, Feeding Time, Stylized Bee 200.00
Figurine, No. 199/0, Feeding Time, Three Line Mark 165.00
Figurine, No. 201/I, Retreat To Safety, Full Bee 275.00
Figurine, No. 201/I, Retreat To Safety, Vee Over Gee 150.00
Figurine, No. 203/2/0, Signs Of Spring, Full Bee 450.00
Figurine, No. 204, Weary Wanderer, Full Bee 195.00
Figurine, No. 214/A, Virgin Mary & Infant Jesus, Full Bee Mark 2000.00
Figurine, No. 214/H, Little Tooter, Three Line Mark 100.00
Figurine, No. 217, Boy With Toothache, Three Line Mark .... 110.00 To 150.00
Figurine, No. 218/2/0, Birthday Serenade, Three Line Mark 125.00
Figurine, No. 220, We Congratulate, Full Bee 175.00
Figurine, No. 220, We Congratulate, New Mark 71.00
Figurine, No. 240, Little Drummer, Three Line Mark 100.00
Figurine, No. 255, Stitch In Time, Three Line Mark 110.00
Figurine, No. 256, Knitting Lesson, Three Line Mark 375.00

Figurine, No. 305, Builder, Three Line Mark 150.00
Figurine, No. 307, Good Hunting, Three Line Mark 160.00
Figurine, No. 309, With Loving Greetings, Blue, New Mark 175.00
Figurine, No. 319, Doll Bath, Vee Over Gee 115.00
Figurine, No. 321, Wash Day, Stylized Bee 185.00
Figurine, No. 321, Wash Day, Three Line Mark 185.00
Figurine, No. 322, Little Pharmacist, Stylized Bee 90.00
Figurine, No. 322, Little Pharmacist, Three Line Mark 245.00
Figurine, No. 322, Little Pharmacist, Vee Over Gee 160.00
Figurine, No. 327, Run–Away, Vee Over Gee 132.00
Figurine, No. 328, Carnival, Three Line Mark .... 130.00 To 150.00
Figurine, No. 328, Carnival, Vee Over Gee 125.00
Figurine, No. 331, Crossroads, Three Line Mark .... 800.00 To 995.00
Figurine, No. 331, Crossroads, Vee Over Gee 200.00
Figurine, No. 333, Blessed Event, New Mark 165.00
Figurine, No. 334, Homeward Bound, Three Line Mark 325.00
Figurine, No. 337, Cinderella, Stylized Bee 60.00
Figurine, No. 340, Letter To Santa, Three Line Mark 400.00
Figurine, No. 340, Letter To Santa, Vee Over Gee 160.00
Figurine, No. 344, Feathered Friends, Vee Over Gee 130.00
Figurine, No. 346, Smart Little Sister, Vee Over Gee 132.00
Figurine, No. 353, Spring Dance, Three Line Mark 450.00
Figurine, No. 361, Favorite Pet, New Mark 120.00
Figurine, No. 363, Big House Cleaning, Vee Over Gee 175.00
Figurine, No. 382, Visiting An Invalid, New Mark 115.00
Figurine, No. 385, Chicken–Licken, Vee Over Gee 140.00
Figurine, No. 387, Valentine Gift, Vee Over Gee 375.00
Figurine, No. 396, Ride Into Christmas, Vee Over Gee 225.00
Figurine, No. 396/2/0, Ride Into Christmas, New Mark 192.00
Figurine, No. 406, Pleasant Journey, New Mark 950.00
Font, No. 26/0, Child Jesus, Full Bee 40.00
Lamp, No. 44A & 44B, Culprits & Out Of Danger, Crown Mark, Pair 1100.00
Lamp, No. 227, She Loves Me, She Loves Me Not, Stylized Bee 250.00
Lamp, No. 235, Happy Days, Stylized Bee 435.00
Plaque, No. 126, Retreat To Safety, New Mark 90.00
Plaque, No. 140, Mail Is Here, New Mark 150.00
Plaque, No. 187, Service 195.00
Plaque, No. 208, Dealer's, French, Full Bee 2900.00
Plaque, No. 460, Authorized German Retailer, New Mark 695.00
Plaque, No. 690, Smiling Through 50.00
Plate, Annual, 1971, Heavenly Angel .... 440.00 To 485.00
Plate, Annual, 1973, Globe Trotter 70.00
Plate, Annual, 1974, Goose Girl ....40.00 To 125.00
Plate, Annual, 1975, Ride Into Christmas ....85.00 To 140.00
Plate, Annual, 1976, Apple Tree Girl 80.00
Plate, Annual, 1977, Apple Tree Boy 43.00
Plate, Annual, 1978, Happy Pastime, Box 40.00
Plate, Annual, 1980, School Girl 125.00
Plate, Annual, 1982, Umbrella Girl 95.00
Plate, Annual, 1988, Little Goat Herder, Box 125.00
Plate, Christmas, 1983, Postman 220.00
Wall Vase, No. 360C, Girl, New Mark 85.00

HUTSCHENREUTHER Porcelain Company of Selb, Germany, was
established in 1814 and is still working. The company makes fine quality
porcelain dinnerwares and figurines. The mark has changed through the
years, but the name and the lion insignia appear in most versions.

LORENZ
HUTSCHEN REUTER

GERMANY

Ashtray, Elfin Flutist Seated On Rim, Square, 5 1/4 In. 125.00
Bowl, Allover Floral, Gold Fruit, Knob Handles, 11 In. 150.00
Bowl, Cardinals, Ivory, Signed, 4 1/2 In. 75.00
Bowl, Fruit, Floral Le Roy, Pedestal, Knob Handles, 11 In. 150.00
Bowl, Swirl Quatrefoil, Gold Center Loop Handle, 10 In. 150.00
Cup & Saucer, Queen's Rose, Syracuse Federal, Demitasse 35.00

Figurine, 2 Cockatoos On Ball, White & Gold, 11 1/2 In. 295.00
Figurine, 2 Macaw Parrots On Tree Stump, Tutter 412.50
Figurine, Boy & Girl Skaters 250.00
Figurine, Cherub Restraining Ram 650.00
Figurine, Cockatoos On Ball, White, Gold, Yellow, 11 1/2 In. 325.00
Figurine, Dancer, Blue Tunic, K. Tutter, 12 1/4 In. 375.00
Figurine, Faust, 7 In. 350.00
Figurine, Flying Blue Jay 95.00
Figurine, Great Dane, Lying, Harlequin, 11 In. 80.00
Figurine, Hunting Dog, Brown Spots, White, Diller, 12 In. 375.00
Figurine, Leopard, With Nude, Signed Tutter 900.00
Figurine, Nude Boy Riding Colt, Marked, 7 3/4 In. 275.00
Figurine, Polar Bear, On Gold Ball, White, 4 In. 145.00
Figurine, Running Dogs, 13 In. 192.00
Figurine, Running Horses 625.00
Figurine, Sealyham Terrier, Comical 120.00
Figurine, Wild Racing Horses, White, 11 1/4 In. 220.00
Plate, Dinner, Gilt Floral Filigree, Cobalt Blue, 20 Piece 2288.00
Plate, Roses Of Redoute, Gold Rim, Box, 6 1/4 In., 8 Piece 250.00
Sugar & Creamer, Cover, Raised Gilt & Blue Design 50.00
Tea Set, Selb, Bavaria, 13 Piece 225.00
Teapot, Selb, Germany 185.00

ICONS, special, revered pictures of Jesus, Mary, or a saint, are usually
Russian or Byzantine. The small icons collected today are made of wood
and tin or precious metals. Many modern copies have been made in the
old style and are being sold to tourists in Russia and Europe.

Anastasis, Resurrection Of Christ, Descent Into Hell, Russia, 12 In. 2640.00
Archangel Michael, Scales At Foot, Greece, 1740s, 18 1/2 x 14 3/4 In. 4125.00
Calendar, Russia, 19th Century, 17 1/4 x 14 1/2 In. 1870.00
Christ Enthroned, Surrounded By 10 Saints, Brass Riza, 14 x 12 In. 330.00
Christ Pantocrator, Gilded Riza, Moscow, 1896, 10 1/2 x 8 7/8 In. 1760.00
Christ Pantocrator, Gold Filigree Oklad, Faberge, 1900, 1 3/4 In. 6600.00
Christ Pantocrator, Silver Rim, Russia, 1859, 21 1/2 x 17 1/4 In. 5500.00
Hodigitria Mother Of God, Greek, 19th Century, 15 3/4 x 11 3/4 In. 1765.00
Holy Trinity, Angels At Table, Russia, 19th Century, 21 x 17 3/4 In. 5120.00
Holy Visage, Shadow Box, Ovchinnikov, 1884, 14 x 12 1/2 In. 5500.00
Intercession Of Holy Virgin, Russia, 18th Century, 32 x 20 3/4 In. 1430.00
Kazan Mother Of God, Robes Of Beadwork, c.1800, 7 1/4 x 6 1/4 In. 2420.00
Kazan Mother Of God, Rococo Scrolls, Russia, 1768, 12 1/2 x 11 In. 8250.00
Mother Of God Feodorovskaya, Moscow, 1864, 12 1/4 x 10 1/2 In. 5500.00
Nativity Of Mother Of God, Russia, 19th Century, 12 1/4 x 10 1/2 In. 1650.00
Nativity, Russia, 11 x 9 In. 275.00
Pokrov, Russia, 19th Century, 14 x 12 1/8 In. 1430.00
Raising Of Cross, Russia, 1880s, 14 1/4 In. 385.00
Resurrection & Descent Into Hell, Russia, 1892, 21 1/4 x 17 3/4 In. 7150.00
Resurrection & Descent Into Hell, Russia, 19th Century, 21 x 17 In. 2860.00
Resurrection & Descent Into Hell, Russia, 19th Century, 21 x 18 In. 2420.00
Resurrection, 12 Feasts, Russia, 25 1/4 x 19 1/4 In. 2200.00
Resurrection, Surrounded By 12 Festivals, 12 x 10 1/2 In. 220.00
Saint Nicholas, Shadow Box, Russia, 1880s, 8 1/2 x 6 1/2 In. 2200.00
Saviour, Russia, Dated 1878, 10 1/2 x 12 In. 1400.00
Smolensk Mother Of God, Russia, c.1885, 2 3/4 In. 1100.00
St. George & Dragon, Polychrome On Wood, 7 1/2 x 5 5/8 In. 225.00
St. George Slaying Dragon, On Horse, Greece, 1815, 16 3/4 x 13 In. 3960.00
St. Matthew, A. Panfilov, Moscow, 1840, 10 1/2 x 9 In. 1985.00
St. Nicholas The Miracle Worker, Silver, Gilded Oklad, Russia, 10 In. 1870.00
St. Nicholas, Halo Set With Ruby & 2 Emeralds, Russia, 9 x 7 3/4 In. 5500.00
St. Nicholas, Russian, 12 1/2 x 10 1/2 In. 715.00
St. Onouphrious The Great, Greece, c.1700, 18 x 14 1/4 In. 2420.00
Transfiguration Of Christ, Russia, 1670s, 34 1/2 x 27 3/4 In. 4675.00
Tryptych, Dormition Of Mother Of God, Saints Alexi & Nicholas, 1900 .... 7700.00
Two Women, Oil Over Gesso, Wood Panel, Mid–1800s, 5 3/4 x 8 5/8 In. 260.00

Valadimir Mother Of God, Emeralds In Halo, 4 1/2 x 8 1/4 In. 5500.00

IMARI patterns are named for the Japanese ware decorated with orange and blue stylized flowers. The design on the Japanese ware became so characteristic that the name *Imari* has come to mean any pattern of this type. It was copied by the European factories of the eighteenth and early nineteenth centuries.

Bottle, Boy Riding Water Buffalo, Rectangular, 10 5/16 In.	880.00
Bowl, Floral Basket Design In Bottom, 9 1/2 In.	245.00
Bowl, Fluted Edge, 9 3/4 x 2 3/4 In.	110.00
Bowl, Gold Figural & Landscape Reserves, 20th Century, 11 In.	605.00
Bowl, Polychrome, 4 1/2 In.	45.00
Bowl, Punch, Scalloped Edge, Underglaze Blue, Floral Medallion, 10 In.	550.00
Bowl, Scalloped Rim, 5 Colors, 6 1/4 In.	170.00
Bowl, Shallow, 8 1/2 In.	16.50
Bowl, Vase Of Flowers Bottom Interior, 9 1/2 In.	290.00
Charger, Central Bouquet, Paneled Border, 19 In.	385.00
Charger, Deep Blue, Orange, Green, Yellow, 12 In.	395.00
Charger, Fan Shape, 16 x 15 In.	290.00
Charger, Fish & Water Design, Stylized Border, 18 In.	465.00
Charger, Floral, Blue & White, Scalloped Rim, 12 In.	395.00
Charger, Garden Scenes, Fish & Blossoms, 19th Century, 18 1/4 In.	905.00
Charger, Panels Of Flowers & Birds, 18 In.	305.00
Charger, Polychrome, 12 1/4 In.	95.00
Chop Plate, Polychrome Enamel With Gilt, 14 3/8 In.	110.00
Condiment Set, Brownfield Mark, Silver–Plated Stand, 3 Pc.	99.00
Cup, Daisy & Horse, c.1820, 3 In.	300.00
Cuspidor, Red & Blue Design	825.00
Dish, Cobalt & Orange, 8 1/2 In.	110.00
Figurine, Sleeping Cat, Signed	412.50
Jar, Blue & White, Wooden Lid, 8 In.	75.00
Jar, Ginger, 2 Phoenixes In Flight, Blossoms, c.1720, 9 1/4 In.	1100.00
Pitcher, Ironstone, England, 5 1/4 In.	88.00
Plate, Brocade Panels, Flowers, Butterflies, Scalloped, 8 1/2 In.	120.00
Plate, Fan, 10 1/2 x 8 1/2 In.	135.00
Plate, Geometric & Floral Design, Late 19th Century, 8 3/4 In.	33.00
Plate, Polychrome, 9 In.	115.00
Plate, Scenes In Rectangles, Brown Border, Impressed Seal, 8 1/2 In.	40.00
Platter, c.1840, 13 In.	1100.00
Platter, England, Marked Mason's, 15 3/8 In.	300.00
Platter, Fish, Elongated, Oval, Ironstone, 20 3/8 In.	235.00
Potpourri Holder, Reticulated Basket, Footed, 8 1/8 x 11 In.	484.00
Shaving Bowl, Floral & Vase Design, Floral & Vine Rim, 10 1/2 In.	825.00
Tureen, Soup, Cover, Peonies, Chrysanthemums, Rocks, c.1770, 13 7/8 In.	2530.00
Urn, Floral Reserves, Baluster, 30 In. ....*Illus*	1650.00
Vase, Foliate & Floral Design, 9 1/4 In., Pair	935.00
Vase, Gildéd Gargoyle Handles, 5 3/4 In.	155.00
Vase, Panels Of Birds In Costume, 1880s, 25 In.	935.00

IMPERIAL GLASS Corporation was founded in Bellaire, Ohio, in 1901. It became a subsidiary of Lenox, Inc., in 1973 and was sold to Arthur R. Lorch in 1981. It was sold again in 1982, went bankrupt that same year, and some of the molds and assets were sold to other companies. The Imperial glass preferred by the collector is stretch glass, art glass, carnival glass, and the top–quality tablewares.

Candlewick, Ashtray, Oblong, 4 1/2 In.	8.00
Candlewick, Bottle, Oil, 4 Oz.	30.00
Candlewick, Bowl, 3–Footed, Gold Design, 8 1/4 In.	295.00
Candlewick, Bowl, Fruit, Footed	12.50
Candlewick, Bowl, Heart, 5 In.	18.00
Candlewick, Cake Plate, Crimped, 2 Handles, 10 In.	25.00
Candlewick, Cake Set, Server & 5 Individual Plates	40.00
Candlewick, Cake Stand, Footed	45.00

Candlewick, Candleholder, Rolled Edge, Pair 20.00
Candlewick, Candleholders, Heart, Pair 100.00
Candlewick, Candy Jar, Cover, Footed 245.00
Candlewick, Compote, 5 1/2 In. 12.00
Candlewick, Compote, Chrome Stem, Blue, 6 In. 45.00
Candlewick, Cup & Saucer 14.00
Candlewick, Ice Tub, Handle, 7 In. 170.00
Candlewick, Lotion Bottle, Powder Box & Tray 155.00
Candlewick, Marmalade Set, 3 Piece 20.00
Candlewick, Mayonnaise Set, 3 Piece .... 20.00 To 38.50
Candlewick, Mayonnaise Set, Lily-of-The-Valley Etch, 3 Piece 58.00
Candlewick, Pitcher, 80 Oz. 110.00
Candlewick, Plate, 2 Handles, 10 In. 15.00
Candlewick, Plate, 6 In. .... 6.00 To 8.50
Candlewick, Plate, 8 In. .... 8.00 To 12.50
Candlewick, Plate, Deviled-Egg Server, 11 1/2 In. 80.00
Candlewick, Plate, Floral Etch, Flat, 12 1/2 In. 45.00
Candlewick, Plate, Salad 9.00
Candlewick, Platter, 13 In. 65.00
Candlewick, Punch Set, Floral, Ladle, Tray & 12 Cups 325.00
Candlewick, Relish, 2 Sections, 6 1/2 In. 20.00
Candlewick, Relish, 2 Sections, Oval 25.00
Candlewick, Relish, 3 Sections, 10 1/2 In. 25.00
Candlewick, Relish, 4 Sections, 8 1/2 In. 38.00
Candlewick, Relish, 5 Sections 45.00
Candlewick, Relish, Divided, Green 65.00
Candlewick, Salt & Pepper, Silver Band 30.00
Candlewick, Sugar & Creamer 19.00
Candlewick, Sugar & Creamer, Tray .... 22.00 To 25.00
Candlewick, Vase, Crimped, 8 In. 25.00
Candy Dish, Frosted Swan, 9 1/2 x 5 1/2 In. 47.50
Cape Cod, Candy Jar, Cover, Bail 95.00
Cape Cod, Champagne 8.00
Cape Cod, Claret, 5 Oz. 9.00
Cape Cod, Cocktail, 3 1/2 Oz. 5.50
Cape Cod, Creamer 7.50
Cape Cod, Cup & Saucer .... 6.00 To 6.50
Cape Cod, Goblet, Water, 5 1/4 In. .... 5.50 To 8.50
Cape Cod, Mustard, Cover 25.00
Cape Cod, Plate, 8 In. .... 3.50 To 4.00
Cape Cod, Punch Cup 3.50

Imari, Urn, Floral Reserves, Baluster, 30 In.

◆◆◆◆◆◆◆◆◆◆◆◆◆◆◆◆◆◆◆◆◆◆◆◆◆◆◆◆◆◆

There are several different types of non-skid mats that are made to be used under a rug to keep the rug in place on a tile or wooden floor.

◆◆◆◆◆◆◆◆◆◆◆◆◆◆◆◆◆◆◆◆◆◆◆◆◆◆◆◆◆◆

◆◆◆◆◆◆◆◆◆◆◆◆◆◆◆◆◆◆◆◆◆◆◆◆◆◆◆◆◆◆

If garage windows are painted, burglars won't be able to tell if cars are home or not. Use translucent paint to get light in the closed garage, if it has an entrance to your house.

◆◆◆◆◆◆◆◆◆◆◆◆◆◆◆◆◆◆◆◆◆◆◆◆◆◆◆◆◆◆

Cape Cod, Punch Set, 15 Piece	180.00
Cape Cod, Punch Set, Bowl, Ladle, Underplate, 8 Cups	155.00
Cape Cod, Relish, 3 Sections	20.00
Cape Cod, Salt & Pepper	8.00
Cape Cod, Sherbet, 6 Oz.	6.50
Cape Cod, Sugar & Creamer	12.00
Cape Cod, Tumbler, 9 Oz.	7.50
Cape Cod, Tumbler, Juice, Footed	5.00
Cape Cod, Wine	8.00 To 9.00
Cathay, Ashtray, Jade	65.00
Cathay, Candlestick, Signed	45.00
Grape, Compote, Marigold	45.00
Grape, Dish, Ruffled, Green, Low	45.00
Grape, Pitcher, Milk, Green	40.00
Hobstar, Vase, Red, 8 In.	38.00
Jewels, Compote, Candy, Cover, Green	37.00
Marigold, Plate, 1905, 9 In.	125.00
Marigold, Punch Set, Octagon, Stand, Ladle & 12 Punch Cups	2400.00
Owl, Jar, Atterbury Type	75.00
Peerless, Bowl, Footed, 9 In.	75.00
Peerless, Condiment Set, Salt & Pepper, Oil Cruet	100.00
Recessed Panel, Basket, Large	100.00
Vase, Free Hand, Gray–Green To Butterscotch, Gray Interior, 10 In.	50.00
Vase, Iridescent Orange, Blue Hearts, Vines, 7 In.	150.00
Vase, Iridescent Orange, Dark Glass Threading, 8 1/2 In.	75.00
Whirlpool, Honey, Cover, Gold Trim	250.00
Whirlpool, Tumbler, Ruby, Tall, 6 Piece	200.00

INDIAN TREE is a china pattern that was popular during the last half of the nineteenth century. It was copied from earlier Indian textile patterns that were very similar. The pattern includes the crooked branch of a tree and a partial landscape with exotic flowers and leaves. Green, blue, pink, and orange were the favored colors used in the design.

Bowl, Coalport	25.00
Creamer, Coalport	15.00
Cup & Saucer, Coral, Coalport	20.00
Cup & Saucer, Scalloped, Coalport	25.00
Sugar & Creamer	25.00
Teapot, England	150.00

INDIAN art from North America has attracted the collector for many years. Each tribe has its own distinctive designs and techniques. Baskets, jewelry, pottery, and leatherwork are of greatest collector interest. Eskimo art is listed in another section in this book.

Armband, Plains, Beaded & Fringed, Beaded Zigzag, 5 1/4 In., Pair	275.00
Bag, Bandoleer, Great Lakes, Geometric & Heart, Fringe, 32 In.	1450.00
Bag, Bandoleer, Woodland, Beaded & Quilled, c.1986, 40 In.	180.00
Bag, Nez Perce, Corn Husk, Gold & Red	495.00
Bag, Nez Perce, Dreamer Style, Contour Beadwork, Late 19th Century	1400.00
Bag, Oto, Beaded Stylized Florals Both Sides, c.1890	1850.00
Bag, Plains, Beaded Design, Leather Tie, 7 In.	385.00
Bag, Plains, Octopus, Blue Broadcloth, Beaded Floral Design	1210.00
Bag, Sioux, Corn Husk, Native Grasses, Dyed Wool, 16 x 22 1/2 In.	750.00
Bag, Tobacco, Sioux, Beaded, Fringed, Cross, Box & Hourglass Design	2420.00
Band, Plains, Loom Beaded, Cheyenne Type Bird, Leather Back, 21 In.	115.00
Basket, Apache, Brown, Wide Weave, 12 x 9 In.	460.00
Basket, Apache, Burden, Polychrome Twine, Devil's Claw, 12 1/2 In.	455.00
Basket, Apache, Human–Figure Design	1700.00
Basket, Apache, Zoomorphic & Geometric Design, 1930s, 13 1/4 In.	187.00
Basket, Baby, Maine, Hood, Splint, 9 1/2 x 17 1/2 x 31 In.	235.00
Basket, Cover, Penobscot, Ribbon With Splint & Rye Grass, 7 In.	75.00
Basket, Cover, Storage, Woven Splint, 7 1/2 In.	95.00
Basket, Hupa, 5 Colors, Rim Ticking, Geometric Design, 1920, 6 1/4 In.	300.00

Basket, Hupa, Finely Woven, Geometric Design, 4 7/8 x 3 1/4 In. 160.00
Basket, Hupa, Twined, Zigzag Design, 5 x 7 In. 770.00
Basket, Maidu, Bowl, Redbud Design, 9 1/2 In. ....*Illus* 787.00
Basket, Miwok, Stepped Geometric Design, c.1920, 9 1/2 In. 600.00
Basket, Navajo, Ceremonial 450.00
Basket, Paiute, Ceremonial, Papers, 1928 .... 700.00
Basket, Papago, Food, Brown Geometric, San Zaier Mission, 1907, 8 In. 85.00
Basket, Papago, Lid, Polychrome, 6 1/4 x 5 In. 35.00
Basket, Penobscot, Splint & Rye Grass, Handle, 6 1/2 In. 55.00
Basket, Pima, Male Figure Design In Weave, c.1915, 6 In. 395.00
Basket, Pima, People & Animals, 15 In. 800.00
Basket, Pomo, Quail Tufts, Cut Shell Beads 4620.00
Basket, Pomo, Zigzag & Geometric Design, Pre–1920, 6 3/4 In. 630.00
Basket, Seneca, Hominy Sifter, Mariam Lee, 1950s, 4 x 10 In. 60.00
Basket, Thompson–Frazier River, Diamond, Lattice Rim, 8 In. 295.00
Basket, Tlingit, Rattle Top, Spruce, Honey–Dyed Grass, 3 7/8 In. 785.00
Basket, Tula, 2 Bands Of Zigzag Design 1045.00
Basket, Woodland, Woven Splint & Sweet Basket, Lid, 9 1/2 In. 35.00
Basket, Woodland, Woven Splint, Curlicue Design, Red, Natural, 6 In. 55.00
Basket, Yokuts, 2 Tiers, Rattlesnake Design, 6 3/4 x 9 1/4 In. 300.00
Basket, Yoqut, Bowl, Black Fern, 7 1/4 In. ....*Illus* 726.00
Basket, Yoqut, Jar, Sawtooth Bands, Yellow Ground, 6 In. ....*Illus* 3460.00
Belt Pouch, Crow, Beaded, Red On Yellow, 4 1/8 x 4 1/2 In. 150.00
Belt, Hopi, Concho 375.00
Belt, Navajo, Silver & Concho, Tooled Leather Strap, 40 1/8 In. 3145.00
Blanket, Ceremonial, Totemic Pattern, Goat Wool & Bark 8800.00
Blanket, Child's, Woven In White, Black & Yellow, Red Ground 2640.00
Blanket, Navajo, Banded Pattern, Dyed Wool, 40 x 29 1/2 In. 485.00
Blanket, Navajo, Checkerboard Pattern, 1930s, 30 x 50 In. 380.00
Blanket, Navajo, Saddle, Homespun Wool, Brown Field, 38 x 29 1/2 In. 785.00
Blanket, Navajo, Saddle, Natural & Aniline Dyed Wool, 25 x 25 In. 90.50
Blanket, Tsimshian, Ceremonial, Killer Whales, Mother–of–Pearl, 1880s 2200.00
Bowl, Acoma Pueblo, 3 Colors, 1950s, 4 x 7 1/2 In. 200.00
Bowl, Apache, Coiled Basketry, Woven Devil's Claw, 4 1/4 x 7 1/2 In. 455.00
Bowl, Hopi, Corn, Polychrome, Pauline Setalla, 7 1/2 In. 45.00
Bowl, Hopi, Painted, 6 1/2 x 4 In. 80.00
Bowl, Laguna Pueblo, Black, White & Red, Buff Clay, 1940s, 4 x 9 In. 350.00
Bowl, Mimbres, Black On White Geometric, 950–1150 A. D. 6325.00
Bowl, Navajo, Pink Design, Rain On Cottonwood Leaves, 5 6/8 In. 150.00
Bowl, Navajo, Rain On Cottonwood Leaves, Red On Buff, 2 x 10 In. 250.00
Bowl, Navajo, Turtle Shell Pattern, Red On Buff, 1 1/2 x 7 1/4 In. 200.00
Bowl, Pima, Pictorial, 10 Figures Descending Into Underworld 1870.00
Bowl, San Ildefonso, Black On Black, Lupita Martinez, 4 1/2 In. 150.00
Bowl, San Ildefonso, Black On Black, Marie, 1926–34, 6 1/2 x 4 In. 425.00
Bowl, Zuni, 4 Raised Frogs, Signed, Large 130.00
Box, Micmac, Cover, Porcupine Quillwork, 8 x 12 In. 2420.00
Box, Navajo, Domed Hinged Lid, Hammered & Stamped Silver, 3 1/4 In. 840.00

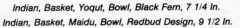

Indian, Basket, Yoqut, Bowl, Black Fern, 7 1/4 In.
Indian, Basket, Maidu, Bowl, Redbud Design, 9 1/2 In.

Indian, Basket, Yoqut, Jar, Sawtooth
Bands, Yellow Ground, 6 In.

Discovered some old silver in
the attic? Wash it with a brush
in warm soapy water before
you polish it. Dirt can scratch
the silver.

Indian, Box, Navajo, Silver, Turquoise,
Domed Cover, 1 3/4 x 3 In.

Box, Navajo, Silver, Turquoise, Domed Cover, 1 3/4 x 3 In. ....*Illus*   840.00
Bracelet, Navajo, 11 Turquoise Stones, Signed KO 120.00
Bracelet, Navajo, Silver Cuff Set, 19 Bezel-Set Turquoise Stones 495.00
Bracelet, Navajo, Silver, Turquoise Stones 130.00
Breastplate, Cherokee, Ceremonial, Slate Gorget, 7 1/2 In. 800.00
Canteen, Hopi, Polychrome Stylized Bird, Loom-Woven Band, 6 1/2 In. 255.00
Carrier, Food, Hewn From Log 350.00
Case, Rifle, Sioux, Beaded Hide 3575.00
Container, Woodland, Deer Hoof 375.00
Costume, Dance, Micmac 4125.00
Dance Shield, Pueblo, Buffalo Hide, Late 19th Century 6500.00
Doll, Hopi, Kachinas, 2 Heads, Ceremonial, Fur Trim 50.00
Doll, Plains, Scalplock Hair, Sinew Sewn Beading, 10 3/4 In. 350.00
Doll, Rag, Quaker Dress, Horsehair Hair, Inked Face, 7 In. 175.00
Doll, Seminole, Patchwork Clothes, Glass Beads, 23 In. 275.00
Dress, Child's, Cheyenne, Navy Trade Cloth, Dentalium Shells, Ribbons 4500.00
Fetish, Plains, Lizard, Sinew, Blue, Yellow, Tin Cone Dangle, 6 1/2 In. 275.00
Gauntlet, Nez Perce, Blue Beading 585.00
Gauntlets, Plateau, Beaded Flowers & Elk, Calico Lined, 14 In., Pair 475.00
Headdress, Iroquois, Chief's 5500.00
Hook, Halibut, Tlinglt, Yew, Yellow Cedar, Raven's Head, 1900, 10 In. 475.00
Jacket, Child's, Crow, Beaded Floral Pattern, Fringed 7000.00
Jacket, Kiowa, Beaded & Embroidered, Spanish Style, 1860s 4700.00
Jar, Acoma Pueblo, Rain Bird Pattern, 3 Colors, 8 x 7 1/2 In. 250.00
Jar, Acoma, Wedding, Red, Black, Bird, Indented Base, 10 In. 675.00
Jar, Basketry, Yokuts, Diamond-Back Rattlesnake, Bands 8800.00
Jar, Hopi, Mottled Orange Body, Hatched & Wing Designs, 4 3/4 In. 550.00
Jar, Hopi, Variegated Orange Body, Paw Designs, 10 In. 485.00
Jar, San Ildefonso, Blackware, Signed Tonita, 1920s 175.00
Jar, Zuni, Flaring Rim, Globular Body, Black Clay, 9 In. 110.00
Jug, Water, Zuni, Flaring Rim, Globular Body, Black Clay, 8 In. 110.00
Kachina, Buffalo Dancer, A. Largo, Wood, Fur, Shells, Leather, 8 1/4 In. 50.00
Kachina, Hopi, Eagle, 1960s 200.00
Kachina, Hopi, Polychrome Wood, 1932, 9 1/4 In. 785.00
Kilt, Dance, Hopi, Ceremonial, Woven 275.00
Ladle, Eastern Woodlands, Stylized Rooster Handle Terminal, 9 In. 357.50
Ladle, Hopi, Black On Red, 5 In. 25.00
Leggings, Cheyenne, Beaded Strips, Loom Woven, Tepee Designs 687.50
Mat, Cherokee, Basketry, River Cane, Rust, Tan, Brown Design 65.00
Mittens, Ojibwa, Beaded, Smoked Tan Hide, 1950s 75.00
Moccasins, Apache, Beaded Polychrome Hide, Parfleche Soles, 9 In. 900.00
Moccasins, Arapaho, Beaded, c.1880 ....   1100.00
Moccasins, Baby's, Beaded Lazy-Stitch Design, Blues, 3 3/4 In. 300.00
Moccasins, Baby's, Plains, Multicolored Beaded Design, 4 1/2 In. 80.00
Moccasins, Cheyenne, Beaded Bird Design On Instep, 10 In. 625.00
Moccasins, Child's, Plains, Beaded Indian Star, 6 1/4 In. 145.00
Moccasins, Delaware, Beaded, 19th Century 1350.00

Moccasins, Nez Perce, Beaded Geometric Design, 11 In.	275.00
Moccasins, Plains, Beaded, Red Wool Cuff, 9 In.	500.00
Moccasins, Seminole, Boot	125.00
Moccasins, Sioux, Beaded, Green Wool Cuff, 9 1/2 In.	350.00
Moccasins, Sioux, Burial, Beaded Sole, Quilled Uppers	5830.00
Moccasins, Sioux, Fully Beaded, Even Soles, 1 Heal Fringe	1650.00
Moccasins, Sioux, Fully Beaded, White Ground, 9 In.	475.00
Moccasins, Sioux, Tin Cone Dangles, c.1880	800.00
Necklace, Fossilized Walrus Ivory, Graduated Round Beads, 24 In.	100.00
Necklace, Navajo, 20 Graduated Turquoise Nuggets, Clam Shell	95.00
Necklace, Navajo, Silver Squash Blossom, 15 Turquoise Nuggets	175.00
Necklace, Navajo, Silver, Squash Blossom, c.1920	1540.00
Necklace, Plains, Suspended Round Feather Pendant, 40 In.	412.00
Necklace, Turquoise & Silver Squash Blossom	195.00
Necklace, Zuni, Fetish, 2 Strand, Hand Carved	98.00
Olla, Acoma Laguna, Red & Brown, Geometric Designs, 9 In.	335.00
Olla, Apache, Figural, c.1890	8500.00
Olla, Pot, Food Storage	5500.00
Olla, San Ildefonso, Banded Geometric, 10 3/4 In. ....*Illus*	1330.00
Olla, San Ildefonso, White Slip, Red & Black Paint, 10 In. ....*Illus*	2660.00
Olla, Santo Domingo, Ivory Slip Over Red Clay, Floral, 10 x 12 In.	2170.00
Olla, Zuni, Painted Scrolled & Hatched Designs, 13 1/4 In.	3265.00
Pin, Zuni, Knife–Wing Man, Silver & Turquoise, 1 3/8 In.	180.00
Pincushion, Beaded Bird, Heart Shape	45.00
Pipe Bag, Sioux, Sinew Stitched, Beaded & Fringed Hide, 22 In.	577.00
Pipe Bowl, Santee Sioux, Catlinite, Horse & Saddle, 1880–1890	2200.00
Pipe, Catlinite, Wooden Stem, Engraved Little Feather, 14 1/2 In.	25.00
Pipe, Plains, Carved Spiral Twists On Stem, Stone Bowl, 29 1/4 In.	2420.00
Pipe, Plains, Carved Turtles On Wood Stem, Stone Bowl, 30 1/2 In.	1570.00
Pipe, Santee Sioux, T Form, Carved Shank Panels, Quilled Stem, 16 In.	2640.00
Pipe, Woodlands, Catlinite Bowl, T Form, Puzzle Form Stem	3740.00
Pot, San Ildefonso, Black On Black, Tonita & Juan, 2 1/4 x 3 3/4 In.	275.00
Pot, Santa Clara, Pot, White On Red, Dolrita, 1 1/2 x 2 3/4 In.	175.00
Pot, Seed, Laguna, Gourd Shape	550.00
Pot, White, Lavender Feathers, Bowls, Arrows, Signed Little Sue, 1953	125.00
Pouch, Crow, Beaded Hide, Bar & Hourglass Designs, 8 x 7 1/2 In.	423.00
Pouch, Plains, Beaded & Fringed, Drawstring Closure, 13 In.	335.00
Pouch, Plains, Beaded, Deerskin, 5 In.	160.00
Pouch, Plains, Octopus, Beaded Edge, Tin Cone Dangles, 10 1/2 In.	450.00
Pouch, Plains, Yellow Ocher, Crow–Style Design, Beaded, Fringed, 4 In.	150.00
Pouch, Sioux, Beaded Geometric, White Ground, Fringe, 4 1/2 In.	225.00
Pouch, Sioux, Geometric Beaded, White Ground, Sinew, Fringe, 11 In.	850.00
Pouch, Woodlands, Polychrome Floral Design, 10 In.	175.00
Quiver, Sioux, Leather, Dyed Porcupine Quills, Bead Work, 27 1/2 In.	3300.00
Rattle, Iroquois, Elm Bark	45.00
Rattle, Seneca, Horn	85.00
Ring, Man's, Zuni, Heavy Silver, Snake, 2 Turquoise Stones	75.00

Indian, Olla, San Ildefonso, Banded Geometric, 10 3/4 In.

Indian, Olla, San Ildefonso, White Slip, Red & Black Paint, 10 In.

Rug, Lukachukai Yeis, 7 Corn Dancers, 34 3/4 x 46 3/4 In.	850.00
Rug, Navajo, 3 Center Diamonds, Wool, c.1920, 6 Ft. 8 In. x 3 Ft. 4 In.	1450.00
Rug, Navajo, 3 Rows Of Diamonds, 6 Ft. x 4 Ft. 2 In.	770.00
Rug, Navajo, Animal & Tree Of Life, 1920s, 60 x 30 In.	9500.00
Rug, Navajo, Center Bow & Arrow, Wool, 7 Ft. 11 In. x 6 Ft. 1 In.	3740.00
Rug, Navajo, Center Lozenge, Banded Sawtooth Border, 61 x 36 In.	545.00
Rug, Navajo, Colorful, 44 x 98 In.	1485.00
Rug, Navajo, Concentric Geometric Designs, c.1920, 90 x 56 In.	575.00
Rug, Navajo, Donkeys, Roosters, Chickens, c.1910, 61 x 45 In.	3850.00
Rug, Navajo, Double Woven, Twilled, Black & Yellow, 30 x 60 In.	300.00
Rug, Navajo, Feather & Stripe Design, 3 Ft. 1 In. x 4 Ft. 2 In.	300.00
Rug, Navajo, Field Of Geometric Designs, 60 x 40 In.	505.00
Rug, Navajo, Field Of Serrated Diamonds, 69 x 53 In.	605.00
Rug, Navajo, Geometric Design, Homespun Wool, 92 x 56 In.	968.00
Rug, Navajo, Geometric Design, Ivory Field, 6 Ft. 6 In. x 4 Ft. 5 In.	412.00
Rug, Navajo, Klagetoh, Hand Carded, Geometric, 1950, 59 x 111 In.	2200.00
Rug, Navajo, Overall Jagged Stripe, 6 Ft. 4 In. x 4 Ft. 4 In.	412.00
Rug, Navajo, Reds & Grays, Black Outlining, 1920s, 38 x 62 In.	275.00
Rug, Navajo, Saltillo Design, Triangular Border, 4 Ft. x 6 Ft. 6 In.	430.00
Rug, Navajo, Saltillo Design, White Ground, 1 Ft. 5 In. x 3 Ft.	150.00
Rug, Navajo, Terraced Blocks, Diamonds, 3 Ft. 1 In. x 6 Ft. 10 In.	350.00
Rug, Navajo, Terraced Diamonds, Outlining, 3 Ft. x 4 Ft. 7 In.	125.00
Rug, Navajo, Third Phase Chief's Pattern, 57 x 93 1/2 In.	2300.00
Rug, Navajo, Triangular Border, Red, White, Gray Ground, 48 x 78 In.	435.00
Rug, Navajo, Yellow, Red, Yellow & White, 35 x 46 1/2 In.	400.00
Saddlebag, Blackfoot, Army Issue, Beaded, Blue Hand On Green	4235.00
Sash, Bandolier, Nez Perce, Beaded, Cowrie Shells, c.1890	2500.00
Serving Set, Navajo, Stamp Design Handles, Silver, 11 1/4 In., 2 Pc.	425.00
Sheath, Knife, Plains, Beaded Bird & Figure, Tin Jinglers, 11 1/2 In.	880.00
Sheath, Knife, Plains, Beaded, Shades Of Blue	360.00
Sheath, Knife, Plains, Red, White & Green Beading	280.00
Sheath, Knife, Sioux, Box & Tepee Design, Wood & Steel Knife	2310.00
Sheath, Knife, Sioux, Fully Beaded, Dangle, 7 In.	225.00
Snowshoes, Large	75.00
Spoon & Fork, Tlingit, Yellow Cedar, Frog, Bear, Alaska, 1917, 10 In.	540.00
Stick, Sioux, Horse, Red Paint & Horsehair, 19 In.	155.00
Tapestry, Navajo Yei, Aniline Dyed Figures, Wool, 31 x 50 In.	475.00
Tray, Apache, Brown, Oval, 14 1/2 x 11 In.	128.00
Tray, Basketry, White Mountain Apache	3080.00
Tray, Navajo, Wedding Basket, Coiled, 13 1/2 In.	332.00
Tray, Navajo, Wedding Basket, Coiled, 15 3/4 In.	453.50
Tunic, Dance, Tlingit, Trade Blanket, Whale Picked Out In Buttons	7500.00
Vase, Hopi, Animals, Frog Handles, Globular, 11 1/2 In.	550.00
Vase, Hopi, Cylindrical, c.1910, 8 In.	425.00
Vase, Hopi, Geometric Panels, Squared Body, 7 In.	88.00
Vase, Navajo, Painted & Glossy Finish, Enamel Design, 1986, 26 In.	665.00
Vase, Santa Domingo, Black On Black Design, 7 In.	75.00
Vase, Santa Domingo, Wedding, 1939, 9 7/8 In.	170.00
Vase, Zuni, Baluster Form, Gray Clay, 12 In.	65.00
Vest, Ojibwa, Beaded, c.1890	2800.00
Vest, Santee Sioux, Hide, Quilled	900.00
Vest, Sioux, Beaded Geometric Design, Fringed, Hide, Sinew Sewn	3355.00
Whip, Horsehair & Leather, Leather Ends, 18 In.	75.00

INKSTANDS were made to be placed on a desk. They held some type of container for ink, and possibly a sander, a pen tray, a pen, a holder for pounce, and even a candle to melt the sealing wax. Inkstands date to the eighteenth century and have been made of silver, copper, ceramics, and glass. Additional inkstands may be found in these and other related categories.

Art Nouveau, Brass, 2 Wells	250.00
Classical Urn, Hinged Lid, Ebonized Wooden Base, 5 1/8 In.	55.00
Double, Inserts, Brush Pen Wiper, U.S. Fidelity Guarantee Co.	165.00

Ebonized Wood, Brass Overlay, Square, 1 Drawer, 9 1/2 In.	140.00
Glass, Double Well, Tarentum, Cover	90.00
Pugilist, 2 Pots, Bronze, Marble Stand, c.1900, 8 1/2 In.	165.00

INKWELLS, of course, held ink. Ready–made ink was first made about 1836 and was sold in bottles. The desk inkwell had a narrow hole so the pen would not slip inside. Inkwells were made of many materials, such as pottery, glass, pewter, and silver. Look in these sections for more listings of inkwells.

Art Nouveau, Bronze, Signed W. M. F.	125.00
Art Nouveau, Hinged Leaf Lid, Lily Pad Base, Bronze	275.00
Bear, Carved Wood	85.00
Black Boy, Brass	250.00
Black Glass, Sliding Top	35.00
Blown Three Mold, Olive Amber, 2 3/4 In.	110.00
Blown Three Mold, Pyramidal, Olive Amber, 2 3/8 In.	85.00 To 95.00
Boar's Head, Continental Silver, UK Marks, 1910	3325.00
Boot, Pressed Glass, Amber, Cover, 1880	85.00
Brass, Hinged Cover, Glass Insert, Square, 4 In., 1920s	50.00
Cat, Cover, Pressed Glass, Daisy & Button, Blue	150.00
Chalet, Ivory, Views Of Germany, Stanhope	125.00
Cherub, Helmet, Mother–of–Pearl, Gilded Brass, 4 1/4 In.	225.00
Cloisonne, Double, Chinese	700.00
Clown, White Costume, Black Collar & Shoes, Robj, c.1925, 5 In.	1430.00
Cone Shape, Copper, Rivets Around Base, Gustav Stickley, 5 1/2 In.	600.00
Cupid Cover, Lions' Heads & Claw Feet, 6 3/4 x 8 In.	270.00
Double Snails, Revolving, 1880s	195.00
Dripless, Esterbrook	38.00
Druid Form, Pewter, Glass Insert, 4 In.	82.50
Elephant, Silvered Bronze, Yellow, 5 1/4 In.	6600.00
Figural, Man & Woman At Piano, Bisque, 1800s, 8 In.	250.00
Foo Dog, Fire Gilt, 2 5/8 In.	45.00
Man Cover, Dolphins, Warriors, Bronze, France, 7 In.	495.00
Mound, Pheasant, Bronze, Austria	275.00
Mushroom Cop Lid, Hobstar Cut Liner, Webster, c.1900, 2 1/2 In.	275.00
Napoleon III, Sleeping Putto, Bronze, Marble Base, 6 In.	660.00
Pewter, Center Insert, 5 Quill Holes, Round, 4 1/4 In.	160.00
Porcelain, Attached Oval Tray, Magenta & Gilt, 8 1/2 In.	50.00
Post Office, Bronze, 2 Wells, 36 x 7 1/2 In.	125.00
Pottery, Signed Henry Grady, 1843	2900.00
Seated Draped Woman, Double Wells, Bouva, Bronze, 11 x 14 1/2 In.	2200.00
Skull, Brass, Porcelain Insert, England, 19th Century	95.00
Snail	125.00
Square Glass Body, Sterling Repousse Cover, c.1890, 4 1/2 In.	357.00
Stoneware, 1 Quill Holder, Mustard Yellow, c.1830, 3 3/4 In.	190.00

INSULATORS of glass or pottery have been made for use on telegraph or telephone poles since 1844. Thousands of different styles of insulators have been made. Most common are those of clear or aqua glass; most desirable are the threadless types made from 1850 to 1870.

6 Ribs, Blue	250.00
Armstrong, 51–2u, Amber	5.00
Baby Battleford	185.00
Boston, Barrel, Aqua	325.00
Brookfield, 31, Keg	32.00
Brookfield, Aqua, Amber Swirls	1200.00
Brookfield, Arc, Ice Blue	15.00
Brookfield, Dark Olive	15.00
Brookfield, Deep Green, Amber Swirled	30.00
Brookfield, New York, Apple Green	10.00
Brookfield, No Leak D, Dark Aqua, Insert	425.00
Brookfield, SDP	48.00
Cable, 4, Dark Aqua	60.00

Cable, Aqua, Pointed Ears	20.00
California Signal, Dark SCA	17.50
California, Purple	2.00
California, Sage	45.00
California, SCA	500.00
Canadian Pacific Ry. Co., Deep Purple, Blot–Out Standard Rear	25.00
Carnival, TS–3, RDP	175.00
Castle, Straw	325.00
Chicago Diamond, Aqua	40.00
Chicago Diamond, Embossed On Skirt, Blue Aqua	50.00
Columbia, 2, Aqua	60.00
Confederate Egg, Aqua To Aqua Green	565.00
Confederate Egg, Dark Green	225.00
Dark Aqua	650.00
Diamond, Ice Yellow–Green	10.00
Diamond, Purple	15.00
Diamond, Royal Purple	20.00
Dominion, 42, Red Amber	25.00
Duquesne Peak Top, Cornflower Blue ,	35.00
E. C. & M., Aqua, Bubbles	65.00
Foster Brothers, Olive Amber	250.00
Gayner, 36–190, Blue	15.00
H. G. Co., Light Apple Green	25.00
H. G. Co., Petticoat, Golden Amber, Beehive	250.00
H. G. Co., Petticoat, Medium Purple	195.00
Hawley, Aqua, Some Milk	12.00
Hemingray, 3, Cable, SDP, Dark Aqua	25.00
Hemingray, 4, Light Green Aqua	15.00
Hemingray, 8, Aqua	20.00
Hemingray, 16, Light Green	10.00
Hemingray, 19, Amber	25.00
Hemingray, 19, Cobalt Blue, Sharp Drips	125.00
Hemingray, 19, Inky Cobalt Blue	90.00
Hemingray, 23, Golden Amber	43.00
Hemingray, 40, Green Aqua, Bubbles & Amber Swirls	10.00
Hemingray, 53, Lime Green	10.00
Hemingray, 61, Aqua	10.00
Hemingray, 95, Aqua	50.00
Hemingray, D 510, Dark Amber	25.00
Hemingray, D 512, Orange Carnival Glass	25.00
Hemingray, E 14B, Opal	20.00
Hemingray, O Provo, Aqua	275.00
Homer Brookes, Rim Embossed, Aqua	95.00
Isorex, 233, Deep Green	40.00
Knowles, 2, Blue Aqua, Slug & Patent Date	6.00
Knowles, Prism Trademark, 1890, Green	75.00
L. A. C., Patent 1895 On Skirt, Aqua	60.00
Locke, 20, Green Aqua	15.00
Locke, Flat Top, Aqua, Embossed	50.00
M. & E. Co., Philadelphia, Aqua	25.00
Manhattan, Yellow Green	35.00
Maydwell, 10, Pinkish Gray	12.00
Maydwell, 62, Light Straw	10.00
McLaughlin, Black Olive	20.00
Mershon, 3–Ridge Type	175.00
Montreal Telegraph, Light–Medium Blue	32.00
Mulford & Biddle, Aqua	135.00
Mulford & Biddle, UPRR, Cobalt Blue	495.00
Nat. Ins. Co., Segmented Threads	140.00
National, Rim Embossed, Segmented Corkscrew, Aqua	85.00
NE. E. Gm. Co., Patent June 17, 1890, Aqua	80.00
New England Tel & Tel, Arc Embossed	135.00
Prism, Blue	135.00

◆◆◆◆◆◆◆◆◆◆◆◆◆◆◆◆◆◆◆◆◆◆

To clean small pieces of iron, try soaking them in white vinegar for 24 to 48 hours.

◆◆◆◆◆◆◆◆◆◆◆◆◆◆◆◆◆◆◆◆◆◆

◆◆◆◆◆◆◆◆◆◆◆◆◆◆◆◆◆◆◆◆◆◆

An old cotton sock is a good polishing cloth. So is an old cloth diaper.

◆◆◆◆◆◆◆◆◆◆◆◆◆◆◆◆◆◆◆◆◆◆

Iron, Cuspidor, Turtle, Shell Opens, Cast Iron

Pyrex, 661, Carnival Glass	45.00
Star, Medium Yellow–Green	27.00
Star, Yellow–Apple Green	10.00
Verlica Belgium BT 15, T–Bar, Aqua	125.00
W. G. M. Co., Purple, Bubbles	15.00
Wade, Blue Aqua	145.00
Wade, Partially Wood–Covered	875.00
Whitall Tatum, No. 1, Amethyst	18.00 To 35.00
Whitall Tatum, SCA	15.00

IRISH BELLEEK, see Belleek category

IRON is a metal that has been used by man since prehistoric times. It is a popular metal for tools and decorative items like doorstops that need as much weight as possible. Items are listed here or under other appropriate headings, such as Bookends, Doorstop, Kitchen, Match Holder, or Tool. The tool that is used for ironing clothes, an iron, is listed in the Kitchen category under Iron and Sadiron.

Aquarium, Pierced–Scroll Base, Plant Stands, Fullis Bros., Mo., 42 In.	1650.00
Boot Scraper, Dachshund, 21 In.	10.00
Boot Scraper, Dachshund, Chain, Leash	145.00
Boot Scraper, Dachshund, Full Figure, Black Paint, 15 In.	295.00
Boot Scraper, Dragon, Cast	100.00
Boot Scraper, Handle, Portable, For Paddock	385.00
Boot Scraper, Ram's–Horn Curls At Post, 18th Century, 8 1/2 x 11 In.	350.00
Boot Scraper, Running Dog	30.00
Boot Scraper, Scrolled Design, 19th Century, 14 1/2 In.	165.00
Boot Scraper, Spiral Coiled Finial, Set In Sandstone Block, 12 In.	300.00
Bootjack, American Bulldog, Folds Into Revolver	160.00 To 195.00
Bootjack, Cricket, Original Marbelized Orange & Black Paint	195.00
Bootjack, Pistol, Folding, Red Paint	85.00
Broiler, Wrought, 13 1/2 In. –Handle, 11 3/4 x 14 In.	27.50
Broom Holder	20.00
Card Holder, Pedestal, Ornate, Signed GF	525.00
Cigar Cutter, Bashful Trick Lock, 1915	50.00
Cigar Snipper, Our Chief, Key Wind	185.00
Cigar Snipper, Stachelberg	135.00
Clipper, Fingernail, LaCross	1.85
Clipper, Fingernail, Widger	2.00
Crown Rack, Pennsylvania, 1830–1840	295.00
Cuspidor, Turtle, Shell Opens, Cast Iron ....*Illus*	330.00
Door Knocker, Cupids, Heavy Cast, Signed	75.00
Door Knocker, Eagle, 8 In.	145.00
Door Knocker, Parrot	40.00
Eagle, 23 1/2 In. –Wingspan, Gold Paint, Wooden Base, 17 1/2 In.	135.00
Eagle, 34 In. –Wingspan, Virginia, 1870	2350.00
Figurine, Fido, Marked Hines, Paint Traces, 1 3/4 In.	35.00

Fork, Heart Ornament In Tines, Wrought, 30 1/2 In. 185.00
Fountain, Garden, Water Spouts From Putti Mask, 38 In. 2200.00
Frame, Picture, Eagle, Several Coats Of Paint 85.00
Garden Set, White Paint, 3 Piece 650.00
Gate, Gothic Style, Wrought, 50 x 35 In. 220.00
Glue Pot, Cast 27.00
Grate, Floor, Fancy, Small 3.25
Grill, Semicircular, Scrolled Foliage, Gold Paint, 18 1/2 In., Pair 260.00
Grill, Wrought, Edgar Brandt, 1925 ....*Illus* 4400.00
Hat Rack, Basket Of Flowers, Painted, 40 1/2 x 33 In. 880.00
Hinge, Ram's Horn, Pitted, 7 1/2 In., Pair 75.00
Hitching Post, Clenched–Hand Shape 200.00
Hitching Post, Horsehead, 14 1/4 In. 85.00
Hitching Post, Jockey, Full Attire, Belair Farm, 45 In., Pair 3300.00
Hitching Post, Jockey, Weathered Layers Of Paint, 44 In. 1050.00
Hitching Post, Stylized Eagle Holding Ring In Beak, 42 1/2 In. 1430.00
Holder–Cutter, Paper 18.00
Horse Weight, Springfield 30.00
Juice Press, Landers 25.00
Mailbox, Griswold, Green Paint 75.00
Mortar & Pestle, 5 5/8 In. 35.00
Padlock, Key & Spikes, Fasten To Door, Wrought, 9 In. 75.00
Pipe Tongs, Primitive, 6 In. 75.00
Planter, Rectangular, c.1860, 9 3/4 x 25 1/4 x 12 1/4 In. 99.00
Plaque, Owl & Quill Pen, Oval, 12 1/2 x 8 1/4 In. 150.00
Rack, Letter, Dated 1886 .... 15.00
Rush Light Holder, Primitive, 36 3/4 In. 425.00
Seat, Farm Implement, C. S. Foos Co., Springfield, Ohio 700.00
Shelf, Gallery Edge, Bracket Supports, Lacy Detail, 10 x 43 In., Pr. 320.00
Skillet, 3 Short Legs, 9 In. 25.00
Sprinkler, Lawn, Alligator, Pair 330.00
Stove Plate, Arches & Tulips, 21 In. 425.00
String Holder 17.50
String Holder, Property U.S. P. O. Dept., Raised Letters 125.00
Sugar Nippers, Pitted, 9 1/4 In. 45.00
Sugar Nippers, Wrought, 9 In. 125.00
Suit Of Armor, Infantryman, Nuremburg, 17th Century, 3/4 Suit, 70 In. 9000.00
Teapot, Sidney, Oh., 6 In. 80.00
Tester, Butter Fat, Centrifugal, Pod Shape, Crank, Vials Inside Door 150.00
Torchere, Triform Standard, Enclosing Leaf Tips, 6 Ft., Pair 3575.00
Urn, Garden, Birds, Flowers, Plinth Base, 1880s, 32 1/2 In., Pair 1980.00

Iron, Grill, Wrought, Edgar Brandt, 1925

Pen collectors look for quality workmanship. A gold pen nib is good. The iridium ball fused to some nibs should be intact. The filling system should work or have only a minor problem like a bad ink sac. Replacement sacs are available. Large pens usually bring higher prices than small pens.

◆◆◆◆◆◆◆◆◆◆◆◆◆◆◆◆◆◆◆◆◆◆

When restoring antiques or houses, take color pictures before and after for records of colors used, exact placement of decorative details, and insurance claims.

◆◆◆◆◆◆◆◆◆◆◆◆◆◆◆◆◆◆◆◆◆◆

Ironstone, Bowl, Blue & White, 3 1/2 In.

Urn, Garden, Elevated Bases, Reticulated Panels, White, 31 In., Pair	160.00
Urn, Garden, Goblet Shape, Anchoring Rod, White Repaint, 19 In., Pair	180.00
Urn, Garden, Man Of Mountain Heads, Winged Griffin Handles, 62 In.	2000.00
Urn, Garden, Minerva Heads On Handles, 23 In.	350.00
Urn, Garden, Neoclassical Form, Black Paint, Wrought, Pair	165.00
Urn, Garden, Portrait Medallion, Scrolling Handles, 41 1/2 In.	4125.00
Urn, Garden, Stand, Kramer Bros., Dayton, Ohio, Cast, 5 Ft., Pair	2900.00
Urn, Garden, Vine & Flower Band Over Leaf Tips, 42 1/2 In.	1980.00
Urn, Garden, White Paint, 33 In., Pair	800.00
Urn, Garden, White Repaint, 19 1/2 In.	245.00
Urn, Garden, White Repaint, 23 1/2 In., Pair	450.00
Weight Ball, For Scale, Set Screw	2.35
Windmill Weight, Bobtail Horse	375.00
Windmill Weight, Bull	650.00 To 695.00
Windmill Weight, Bull, Fairybury, Nebraska, Raised Letters	1200.00
Windmill Weight, Horse, Dempster, Wooden Base	275.00 To 450.00
Windmill Weight, Horse, Short Tail, Box	250.00
Windmill Weight, Rooster On Ball	950.00
Windmill Weight, Rooster, Barnacle–Eye	5600.00
Windmill Weight, Rooster, Hummer, No. 1	295.00
Windmill Weight, Rooster, Hummer, Small	500.00
Windmill Weight, Rooster, Mogul, Hollow Body	3800.00
Windmill Weight, Rooster, Rainbow Tail	900.00 To 2100.00

IRONSTONE china was first made in 1813. It gained its greatest popularity during the mid–nineteenth century. The heavy, durable, off-white pottery was made in white or was decorated with any of hundreds of patterns. Much flow blue pottery was made of ironstone. Some of the decorations were raised. Many pieces of ironstone are unmarked but some English and American factories included the word *Ironstone* in their marks. Additional pieces may be listed in other categories, such as Chelsea Grape, Chelsea Sprig, Flow Blue, Gaudy Ironstone, Moss Rose, Staffordshire, and Tea Leaf Ironstone.

Bowl, Blue & White, 3 1/2 In. ....*Illus*	20.00
Bowl, Cover, Blue Transfer, Polychrome Enameling, Oval, 9 x 10 In.	85.00
Bowl, Gaudy Floral, 11 1/4 x 3 1/2 In.	95.00
Canteen, Cover, Grand Army Of Republic, Vodrey & Brothers, 1885	2200.00
Coffee Server, Red & White	65.00
Coffeepot, Lily, White	195.00
Creamer, Sydenham, Boote	125.00
Dinner Set, Feather Pattern, Mason, Service For 12, c.1830	3500.00
Dinner Set, Table & Flower Pot Pattern, Mason, 1813–1820, 11 Pc.	880.00
Eggcup, Red & White	10.00
Gravy, Underplate, Red & White	25.00
Mold, Fish, White	45.00
Mug, Teaching Tray To Dance, 2 1/2 In.	130.00
Pitcher & Bowl, Corn & Oats	295.00

Pitcher, Milk, Ceres, White 175.00
Pitcher, Ship Acadia, 9 3/4 In. 80.00
Pitcher, Watteau, Mason, 4 1/4 In. 45.00
Plate, Blue Transfer, Commemorating B & O Railroad, 9 In. 45.00
Plate, Vista, Mason, 9 In. 5.00
Platter, Moss Rose, 15 In. 65.00
Platter, Transfer, Russian Buildings, Ashworth, Oval, 17 In. 110.00
Platter, Turkey, Texas Pattern, Brownfield & Son, 20 1/4 In. 25.00
Punch Bowl, Frolicking Cherubs, 3 Dolphin Supports, 8 x 16 In. 605.00
Sugar & Creamer, Hand-Painted Daisy, Green & Clay, c.1891 .... 75.00
Sugar, Cover, Blue Bands & Stripes On White, 4 3/4 In. 75.00
Sugar, Mocha, Sanded Bands, Blue & White Stripes, 5 1/8 In. 75.00
Tea Set, Child's, White, 23 Piece 275.00
Tureen, Raised Leaves, 3 Vine Handles, 13 In. 75.00
Tureen, Soup, Ladle, Blue & White, Cover, 9 1/2 x 15 In. 175.00
Tureen, With Tray & Ladle, Blue Transfer, Red Enameling, 9 In. 175.00

ISPANKY figurines were designed by Laszlo Ispanky, who began his American career as a designer for Cybis Porcelains. In 1966, he established his own studio in Pennington, New Jersey; since 1976, he has worked for Goebel of North America. He works in stone, wood, or metal, as well as porcelain. The first limited edition figurines were issued in 1966.

Abigail 750.00
Figurine, Antony, Roman Suit, Crested Helmet, 11 3/4 In. 750.00
Figurine, Pack Horse 700.00
Lydia 400.00
Susie 450.00

IVOREX plaques were made in England by Arthur Osborne in the beginning of the 1900s. The plaques, made of a material he called *sterine wax*, pictured buildings or room interiors modeled in three dimensions. After Osborne's death, his daughter Blanche ran the company. It was closed in 1965, then purchased by W. H. Bossons Ltd. in 1971. Production of the plaques started again in 1980.

Plaque, Baptistry, Canterbury, Osborne, c.1899 .... 60.00
Plaque, Charles Dickens In His Study, Gadshill 150.00
Plaque, Death Of Nelson, Large 150.00
Plaque, Llanberis Pass 40.00
Plaque, Mr. Pickwick Addressing Members Of Pickwick Club 150.00
Plaque, Oliver Twist, Oval, Osborne 40.00
Plaque, Rheims Cathedral, France 35.00
Plaque, Sydney Harbour Bridge 40.00

IVORY from the tusk of an elephant is thought by many to be the only true ivory. To most collectors, the term *ivory* also includes such natural materials as walrus, hippopotamus, or whale teeth or tusks, and some of the vegetable materials that are of similar texture and density. Other ivory items may be found in the Scrimshaw and Netsuke categories. Collectors should be aware of the recent laws limiting the buying and selling of elephant ivory and scrimshaw.

Board, Cribbage, Polar Bears, Eskimo, Walrus, c.1960, 32 In. 2090.00
Bottle, Opium, Scrimshaw Base, Oriental Characters, 3 1/3 In. 350.00
Box, Cover, Continuous Flora & Foliate, Round, 4 1/2 In. 357.00
Box, Hinged Cover, Continuous Horses, Landscape, Gilt Metal, 4 1/4 In. 880.00
Box, Regency, Scrolled Acanthus, Drawer, 16 x 12 In. 2530.00
Brush Holder, Inlaid Semiprecious Stones, Dragons, c.1930 .... 245.00
Brush, Hair, 1890s 85.00
Brushpot, Carved Boys & Deer In Landscape, Wood Bottom, 6 In. 465.00
Bust, Blackamoor Wearing Feathers, Silver Repousse Wax Seal, 6 In. 264.00
Candle Screen, Animals, Foliage, Signed Hartman, 1862, 18 In. 1900.00
Candle Screen, Carved Stag, Doe & Fawn, 15 1/4 In. 1920.00
Candle Screen, Hunter & Horse, Landscape, Tripod Base, 16 3/4 In. 4125.00
Candle Screen, Stag & Does, Woodland Border, Signed, 1862, 18 In. 1900.00

Ivory, Group, Man, Woman & Child, Family, Signed
Sokoku, 6 In.

Ivory, Figurine, Joan of Arc, Triptych,

Dieppe, 19th Century, 8 In.

Ivory, Figurine, Old Man & Child, Signed SEI, 5 1/2 In.

Card Case, Birds & Flowers	185.00
Chalice, Double, Continuous Putti & Cupid Scenes, 10 In.	4000.00
Chalice, Last Supper Scene, Carved Stem & Base, 8 1/2 In.	850.00
Chess Set, Emperor, Empress, Attendants, c.1930, 2 To 4 In.	695.00
Chess Set, Gaming Surfaced Box, 25 1/2 In.	1650.00
Disc, Scrimshaw Lion's Head, Tinted Natural, Wooden Stand, 1 3/4 In.	80.00
Figurine, 2 Birds, Flowering Branches, 8 In.	750.00
Figurine, 2 Children With Top, Signed, 5 In.	850.00
Figurine, 3–Headed, 6–Armed Indian Deity, Teak Stand, 5 5/8 In.	75.00
Figurine, Actor & Child, Wooden Base, 8 3/4 In.	625.00
Figurine, Babies, 2 Girls, 1 Boy, Continental, 1 Figure 5 In.	935.00
Figurine, Bacchus, Ignaz Elhafen, Gilt Wood Base, 1780s, 8 3/8 In.	6050.00
Figurine, Buddha, Green Stone Base, 2 3/4 In.	60.00
Figurine, Buddha, On Pedestal Of 3 Carved Faces, c.1890, 9 1/2 In.	895.00
Figurine, Cavalier, Standing, Wooden Stand, 19th Century, 13 In.	990.00
Figurine, Christ Child, Nude, Sleeping, Philippine, 18th Century, 7 In.	2750.00
Figurine, Daruma, Holding Hands In Attitude Of Prayer, Box, 7 1/2 In.	495.00
Figurine, Doctor's Model, 7 In.	225.00
Figurine, Emperor & Empress, Seated, c.1900, 5 1/8 In.	520.00
Figurine, Eskimo, Walrus, Inlaid Eyes, Signed Lee Ilot, 2 1/4 In.	125.00
Figurine, Falstaff, Ewer & Cup, Continental, 8 3/4 In.	1210.00
Figurine, Female Hunter, Ivory Stand, Applied Birds, 7 1/2 In.	440.00
Figurine, Foo Dog, Carved Plinths, Open Work Carving, 11 In., Pair	850.00
Figurine, God, 3–Headed, Riding Wild Boar, 11 In.	1000.00
Figurine, Head, Egyptian, 10 1/2 In.	200.00
Figurine, Joan Of Arc, Triptych, Dieppe, 19th Century, 8 In. ....*Illus*	440.00
Figurine, Knight In Armor, Standing, Marked Milan 1520, 9 1/2 In.	935.00
Figurine, Lovers, Standing, Marble Stand, 9 1/4 In.	2200.00
Figurine, Male & Female Equestrian Warriors, 11 3/4 In., Pair	1430.00
Figurine, Man Flower Peddler, Signed	1150.00
Figurine, Man With Monkey On His Back, 3 In.	33.00
Figurine, Man, 2 Boys, Monkey On Hurdy–Gurdy, Japan, c.1900, 5 1/2 In.	395.00
Figurine, Man, Seated, Scroll, 7 1/2 In.	600.00
Figurine, Man, Torso, Open Triptych, Mirabeau & Robespierre, 11 In.	700.00
Figurine, Medicine Lady, Ebonized Carved Base, 1 1/2 x 4 x 2 In.	77.00
Figurine, Medicine Man, With Drum, Mask, Polychrome, 8 1/4 In.	225.00
Figurine, Mother & Child, Stand, 19th Century, 14 In.	770.00
Figurine, Musketeer, Blowing Trumpet, Continental, 9 1/4 In.	1420.00
Figurine, Nude Maiden, Cupid, Ivory Stand, 11 In.	1760.00
Figurine, Old Man & Child, Signed SEI, 5 1/2 In. ....*Illus*	880.00
Figurine, Oriental Man Holding Pipe, Staff, Carved Ebony Base, 8 In.	450.00
Figurine, Oriental Woman, Ebonized Base, 5 1/4 In.	77.00
Figurine, Oriental Woman, Holds Roses & Head On Head Of Child, Pair	2500.00
Figurine, Pegasus Flying Through Clouds, Chinese, 9 x 7 1/2 In.	600.00
Figurine, Philosopher, Signed, 19 1/2 x 10 In.	3200.00
Figurine, Quan Yin, Stand, 12 In.	330.00
Figurine, Roosters On Branches, Gem Overlay, 20th C., 14 3/4 In., Pr.	445.00

Figurine, Royal Female Attendant, c.1930, 7 1/2 In.	450.00
Figurine, Scarab, Black Horn Base, 2 7/8 In.	175.00
Figurine, Seated Man With Scroll, Wooden Stand, 7 1/2 In.	600.00
Figurine, Sumo Wrestler, Polychrome Design, Signed, 10 In.	250.00
Figurine, Tiger, Wooden Base, 8 1/4 In.	450.00
Figurine, Ting, Dragon Handles, Foo Dog Finials, Wooden Stand, 11 In.	450.00
Figurine, Woman With Fruit, 11 3/4 In.	250.00
Figurine, Woman With Parasol, Wooden Base, 3 7/8 In.	125.00
Figurine, Woman With Roses, 12 In.	275.00
Group, 2 Sumo Wrestlers, Referee, Stand, 7 1/2 In.	550.00
Group, Cupid & Psyche, Continental, 9 1/4 In.	1100.00
Group, Man & Woman, Renaissance Style Dress, Continental, 4 3/4 In.	610.00
Group, Man, Woman & Child, Family, Signed Sokoku, 6 In. ....*Illus*	1430.00
Group, Nude Maiden, Seated On Stylized Lion, Ivory Stand, 5 In.	1325.00
Hair Receiver, & Powder Set, Pyralin	12.00
Holder, Cigarette, Enameled	85.00
Letter Opener & Manuscript Page Turner, 16 1/2 In.	200.00
Letter Opener, Mandarin	25.00
Letter Opener, Silver Monogram, 16 In.	200.00
Plaque, Barberini Tabernacle, Tortoise Shell Frame, 11 x 9 1/2 In.	4125.00
Plaque, Battle Scene, Framed, 19th Century, 3 1/4 x 9 1/4 In.	1870.00
Plaque, Classical Women, Putti & Herm, Framed, Germany, 5 1/2 x 7 In.	550.00
Plaque, Medieval Battle Scene, 1820s, 4 x 7 3/4 In.	1650.00
Plaque, Roman Battle Scene, Framed, Germany, 5 1/2 x 13 In.	3300.00
Poker Chips, French, Box, 1900s, 200 Piece	40.00
Safety Razor Case, Gold Plated, 4 1/8 x 2 1/2 In.	1000.00
Shoe Horn, Carved Floral, Foliate & Bird, Early 20th Century, 16 In.	495.00
Snuff Bottle, Brass Mount, Enamel Beads, Ebonized Base, 4 1/2 In., Pr.	176.00
Spoon, Pierced Stags, Landscape Handle, 1880s, 6 In.	110.00
Tankard, Rope Of Sabine, Silver Mounts, 11 In.	5060.00
Triptych, Ball Opening To Scenes Of Columbus Discoveries, 2 In.	175.00
Triptych, Bishop, Biblical Scenes, 12 1/4 In.	1100.00
Triptych, Melon Rib Spheres, Soldiers On Horseback & Afoot, 3 In.	1100.00
Triptych, Noble Woman, Courtship Scenes, 19th Century, 8 3/4 In.	2450.00
Triptych, Noble Woman, King Henry VIII, 19th Century, 9 1/2 In.	2860.00
Triptych, Queen Elizabeth Processional Scene, 6 3/4 In.	665.00
Tusk, Dragons, Pursuing Pearl, Japan, 20 1/4 In., Pair	4800.00
Vase, Made From A Tusk, Geometric Design, 11 In.	125.00

JACK ARMSTRONG, the all-American boy, was the hero of a radio serial from 1933 to 1951. Premiums were offered to the listeners until the mid-1940s. Jack Armstrong's best-known endorsement is for Wheaties.

Airplane Gun, Propeller	60.00
Brooch, Betty Fairfield's, Luminous Gardenia	275.00
Hike-O-Meter	35.00
Lie Detector, Magic Answer Box	375.00
Pedometer	15.00
Pedometer, Silver Rim	35.00
Ring, Siren	48.00 To 65.00
Ring, Whistle, Egyptian	95.00
Telescope, Explorer	18.00
Viewer, Movie, With Film, Original Mailer	50.00

JACK-IN-THE-PULPIT vases, oddly shaped like trumpets, resemble the wild plant called jack-in-the-pulpit. The design originated in the late Victorian years. Vases in the jack-in-the-pulpit shape were made of ceramic or glass and the complete list of page references can be found in the index.

Vase, Amberina, Inverted Thumbprint, 5 3/8 In.	375.00
Vase, Blown, 8 1/2 In.	145.00
Vase, Stripe Interior, White Stripe Exterior, 5 1/4 In.	235.00

JACKFIELD ware was originally a black glazed pottery made in Jackfield, England, from 1750 to 1775. A yellow glazed ware has also been called Jackfield ware. Most of the pieces referred to as *Jackfield* today are black–glazed, red–clay wares made at the Jackfield Pottery in Shropshire, England, in Victorian times.

Bowl, Silver Trim & Finial On Cover	298.00
Teapot, 1790s	175.00
Teapot, Underplate, Hand Painted Flowers	150.00

JADE is the name for two different minerals, nephrite and jadeite. Nephrite is the mineral used for most early Oriental carvings. Jade is a very tough stone that is found in many colors from dark green to pale lavender. Jade carvings are still being made in the old styles, so collectors must be careful not to be fooled by recent pieces. Jade jewelry is found in this book under Jewelry.

Bonsai Tree, Peridot, Gold Plated Branches, Granite Base, 14 x 14 In.	396.00
Brush Washer, Shape Of Curled Lotus Leaves, Snails & Frogs, Green	5500.00
Censor, Domed Pierced Cover, Lion & Loose Ring Handles, Spinach, 8 In.	1430.00
Figurine, Bunch Of Grapes, Green, Pink, Purple, Large	90.00
Figurine, Horses, 1 Standing On Head & Tail Of Other, Base, 4 1/2 In.	225.00
Frame, With Carnelian, Carved, 11 x 13 In.	275.00
Ring, Archer's, Fitted With Lydia Woman's Watch	410.00

JAPANESE CORALENE is a ceramic decorated with small raised beads and dots. It was first made in the nineteenth century. Later wares made to imitate coralene had dots of enamel. There is also another type of coralene that is made with small glass beads on glass containers.

Bowl, Oriental Figures, 8 In.	300.00
Plaque, 2 Indian Faces, Head Feathers, Blown Out	650.00
Vase, Medallions Of Wild Roses, Gold Enamel, 10 1/4 In.	615.00

JAPANESE WOODBLOCK PRINTS are listed in this book in the Print category under Japanese.

JASPERWARE can be made in different ways. Some pieces are made from a solid colored clay with applied raised designs of a contrasting colored clay. Other pieces are made entirely of one color clay with raised decorations that are glazed with a contrasting color. Additional pieces of jasperware may also be listed in the Wedgwood category or under various art potteries.

Barrel, Biscuit, Blue, Gold Classical Figures, Hanley, Dudson	140.00
Cheese Dish, Cover, c.1860, 11 In.	445.00
Hatpin Holder, Egyptian Face, Pink	165.00
Pitcher, Milk, Dark Green, Late 19th Century	275.00
Plaque, Hanging, Dancing Maidens, White Relief, 9 1/2 x 5 In.	235.00
Plaque, Stork With Babies, Blue & White, 5 3/4 In.	27.50
Plaque, White Cameo Goddess & Cherub, Blue, Heubach, 8 x 11 In.	345.00
Plaque, Woman & Winged Cherubs, White & Green, 5 1/2 In.	35.00
Urn, Cover, Dancing Maidens, Blue, Wedgwood, 15 In., Pair	1155.00

JEWELRY, whether made from gold and precious gems or plastic and colored glass, is popular with collectors. Values are determined by the intrinsic value of the stones and metal and by the skill of the craftsmen and designers. Victorian and older jewelry has been collected since the 1950s. More recent interests are Art Deco and Edwardian styles, Mexican and Danish silver jewelry, and beads of all kinds. Copies of almost all styles are being made. Indian jewelry is listed in the Indian category.

Bar Pin, 19 Round Diamonds, Platinum	1045.00
Bar Pin, Clear Stones, Dangling Hearts, Boucher	40.00
Belt, Snake, Whiting Davis	45.00
Bracelet & Earrings, Gold Tone Metal, Jade–Type Section, Givenchy	85.00
Bracelet & Earrings, Ovals Of Mother–of–Pearl, Whiting Davis	150.00

Bracelet & Earrings, Pastel Blue, Yellow Rhinestone, Schiaparelli 225.00
Bracelet & Pin, Red Layered Bakelite, Applied Acorns 225.00
Bracelet, 9 Round Garnets, 14K Gold 300.00
Bracelet, Bakelite Hinged Over Cuff, 1/2 In. 40.00
Bracelet, Bangle, 15K Yellow Gold, 5 Turquoise Cabochons 775.00
Bracelet, Bangle, Engraved, Hinged Safety Catch, 14K Gold, 1 In. 390.00
Bracelet, Bangle, Gold Filled, Gothic, Crown Type Design, 1880–1890 .... 55.00
Bracelet, Bangle, Hinged Closure, Engraved, 14K Yellow Gold 405.00
Bracelet, Bangle, Jade, Set With Vermeil 120.00
Bracelet, Bangle, Nude Ethnic Woman, Fully Carved, Ivory 350.00
Bracelet, Bangle, Peking Glass 25.00
Bracelet, Bangle, Sapphires & Diamonds, 14K Gold 675.00
Bracelet, Bangle, Sterling Silver, Taxco 30.00
Bracelet, Birds, Wide, Georg Jensen 750.00
Bracelet, Bloodstones, 9 Cabocho, 18K Gold, 7 In. 2650.00
Bracelet, Blue Rhinestones, Silver Tone, Emmons 15.00
Bracelet, Center Diamond, 2 Sapphire Baguettes, 14K White Gold 370.00
Bracelet, Charm, 18K Yellow Gold, Heavy Link 395.00
Bracelet, Coiled Snake, Gold, Whiting & Davis 50.00
Bracelet, Coral Stones, Art Deco, Sterling Silver, Jensen 795.00
Bracelet, Coral, 14K Gold 275.00
Bracelet, Cuff, 13 Malachite Panels, Yellow Gold, Cartier 7040.00
Bracelet, Cuff, E. M. Edgar, Sterling Silver, 1950s 95.00
Bracelet, Cuff, Sterling Silver, William Spratling, 2 1/2 In., Pair 440.00
Bracelet, Diamond & Blue Sapphire, White Gold, c.1920 .... 2750.00
Bracelet, Diamond, 32 Round Brilliant Cut, Flexible Mount 8800.00
Bracelet, Diamond, 51 Full Cut, Flexible Link, 14K Gold 1485.00
Bracelet, European Cut Diamonds, Synthetic & Natural Sapphires 8800.00
Bracelet, Filigree, 2 Emeralds, 8 Pt. Diamond, 14K White Gold, 1920s 230.00
Bracelet, Filigree, Center Diamond, 2 Sapphires On Side, 14K Gold 385.00
Bracelet, Garnet, Silver & Gold, Edward Oakes 3960.00
Bracelet, Gold & Coral, Joseph Richardson Sr., c.1750 .... 4675.00
Bracelet, Gold Glass Beads, Pearl & Medallions, Schiaparelli 45.00
Bracelet, Golden Age Of Design 175.00
Bracelet, Green, Pink, Brown Stone, Gold Plated, O. Lisner ....*Illus* 40.00
Bracelet, Hammered Aluminum, Foliage, Wendell August 65.00
Bracelet, Hanging Double 2-In. Fish, Sterling, Enamel, Margot, Mexico 450.00
Bracelet, Herringbone, Lobster Claw Clasp, 14K Gold 225.00
Bracelet, Hinged Snake, Black Gold, Richelieu 75.00
Bracelet, Hinged, Enameled Blue, Green Stripes, Trifari 30.00
Bracelet, ID, Silver, 1940s, Mexico 85.00
Bracelet, Lapis, 8 Sections, Blue, Napier, 7 1/4 In. 75.00
Bracelet, Large Rectangular Links, 14K Gold 135.00
Bracelet, Link, Interlace Links, Taxco, Mexico, 3 1/2 In. 88.00
Bracelet, Medallion With Woman's Profile, Art Nouveau 65.00
Bracelet, Multicolored Segments, Bakelite 100.00
Bracelet, Oval & Round Blue Sapphires, 3 Strands, 18K Gold 9050.00
Bracelet, Pearls, Triple Strand, Haskell 125.00
Bracelet, Rainbow Stones, 6 Oval, Silver Finish, Schiaparelli 250.00
Bracelet, Rectangular Onyx, Oval Cabochon Jades, 14K Yellow Gold 495.00
Bracelet, Rose Cut Garnets, Hinged, 3 Rows, Bohemia 450.00
Bracelet, Sapphires, Small Diamonds, 9 Each, Yellow Gold 665.00
Bracelet, Seed Pod Form, Sterling Silver, Georg Jensen 1430.00
Bracelet, Silver & Coral, 2 Strands, Georg Jensen 525.00
Bracelet, Silver Filigree, Cameos 95.00
Bracelet, Silver, Agate, Rectangular Plaques ....*Illus* 385.00
Bracelet, Snake, Copper, Whiting Davis 35.00
Bracelet, Snake, Ruby Eyes, Opals, 14K Pink Gold 65.00
Bracelet, Snake, Silver Mesh, Whiting Davis .... 35.00 To 40.00
Bracelet, Snake, Silver, Whiting Davis .... 65.00 To 75.00
Bracelet, Solid Link, 14K White Gold, Rectangular Black Onyx Stone 375.00
Bracelet, Sterling Silver & Abalone, Taxco, Mexico, 7 In. 55.00
Bracelet, Tiger Eyes, 5 Sections, Guard Chain, Sorrento, 7 In. 40.00

Clockwise from top: Jewelry, Bracelet, Green, Pink, Brown Stone, Gold Plated, O. Lisner; Jewelry, Earrings, Rhinestones, Silver Plated, Coro; Jewelry, Pin, Leaf, Green Stones, Gold Plated, Coro; Jewelry, Pin, Spray, Blue Stones, Gold Plated, Coro

From top: Jewelry, Pin, Doe & Squirrel, Sterling Silver, Georg Jensen; Jewelry, Pin, Arrow Shape, Silver, Agate, Victorian; Jewelry, Bracelet, Silver, Agate, Rectangular Plaques

Jewelry, Pin, Flower, Moonstone, Ruby, 14K Gold, Tiffany

From top: Jewelry, Earrings, Tortoiseshell, Figure 8, Gold Stars, Victorian; Jewelry, Pin, Memorial, Scroll-Edged Frame, Dated 1846

Bracelet, Triple Strand, Carved Pink Leaves Clasp, Trifari	150.00
Bracelet, Turquoise Bead Clasps, 14K Yellow Gold, Mesh Band	495.00
Bracelet, Victorian, 14K Yellow Gold Mesh & Buckle	485.00
Buckle, Bird Design, 14K Gold, 2 1/2 x 1 1/4 In.	350.00
Buckle, Cut Steel, Art Deco Design, Paris, 1920s, 2 x 1 3/4 In.	8.00
Buckle, Free Form Sterling Silver, Turquoise, London, c.1898	395.00
Buckle, Medusa, Sterling	70.00
Buckle, Shoe, Steel Bead, France, 2 1/2 x 1 3/4 In., Pair	32.00
Buckle, Sterling Silver & Opal, William Hutton, c.1902, 3 1/8 In.	275.00

Cameo, Greco Lady, On Flame Shell, 6 x 4 1/2 In. 950.00
Chain, Rope Twist, 14K Gold, 24 In. 193.00
Chain, Rope, 14K Gold, 24 In. 280.00
Charm, Cross, Maltese, Black & Smoke Stones On Black, 2 1/2 In. 150.00
Charm, Dachshund, 14K Gold 30.00
Chatelaine, 5 Chains, Sterling Silver 625.00
Chatelaine, Aesop Fable Design 1250.00
Chatelaine, Blue Enamel, Fleur-De-Lis, Monogram, Sterling Silver 425.00
Chatelaine, Cotillion Style, Ring 650.00
Cheroot Case, Cupid, Varicolored Gold, Mexico, 1800, 2 1/2 In. 2750.00
Cigarette Case, Geometric, Silver, Niello, G. Sandoz, 1925, 5 In. 1650.00
Cigarette Case, Maroon Bakelite, Sterling Silver Overlay, Dandy 65.00
Cigarette Case, Mother & Daughters Enameled, Silver, Russia, 4 In. 3575.00
Cigarette Case, Woman's, Gold, Enamel Cover, Vienna, 1900, 3 5/8 In. 3500.00
Clasp, Spread-Winged Bird, Joseph Richardson Sr., c.1770, 1 1/8 In. 6875.00
Clip, Fur, Rhinestone, Double Prong 50.00
Clip, Maple Leaf, Red & Clear Rhinestones, Mazer 145.00
Collar, 5 Panels Of Jet Beads, Black Satin 65.00
Comb, Carved Tortoiseshell, Red Jeweled, 4 1/2 x 6 1/2 In. 55.00
Cuff Links, Gold, Diamond, Oyster Enameled, 2 Sides, Russia, 1900 .... 2450.00
Cuff Links, Oval, Monogrammed JBR, 14K Gold 75.00
Dress Clip, Rhinestone, Eisenberg 150.00
Ear Clips, Dangling, Clear Rhinestone, Eisenberg, Large 35.00
Ear Clips, Floriform, Ruby, 18K Yellow Gold, Tiffany 1100.00
Earrings & Bracelet, Blue & Violet Stones, Florenza 50.00
Earrings & Bracelet, Pave Set Stones, Bakelite 135.00
Earrings & Pendant, Borealis, Hollycraft 110.00
Earrings, Aquamarine & Diamond, 14K Gold 330.00
Earrings, Baroque Pearls, Gold, Miriam Haskell 65.00
Earrings, Bead, Turquoise, Miriam Haskell 65.00
Earrings, Black Dangle, Hattie Carnegie 45.00
Earrings, Blue Sapphires, Diamonds, 18K Gold 1875.00
Earrings, Carved Ivory, Rose, 14K Gold Post 20.00
Earrings, Clips, Gold & Diamond, 18K Gold, Van Cleff & Arpels 4125.00
Earrings, Cultured Pearl & Diamond, 14K White Gold 110.00
Earrings, Diamonds In Floral Design 5775.00
Earrings, Drop Cameos, 14K Yellow Gold, Screw Back 55.00
Earrings, Drop, Diamond Flora Design 5775.00
Earrings, Drop, Diamond, 6 Full Cut, 14K Gold 330.00
Earrings, Floriform, Ruby & Diamond, 14K Yellow Gold 1430.00
Earrings, Frog, Joseph Mazer, Card 40.00
Earrings, Geometric Form, Sterling Silver & Turquoise, Taxco 22.00
Earrings, Hoop, 14K Yellow Gold 110.00
Earrings, Lavender Stones, Eisenberg 45.00
Earrings, Pearl, Grape Leaf Design, 14K Yellow Gold 55.00
Earrings, Pearls, Cabochon Coral, Tassels, 2 In. 85.00
Earrings, Peridot, Oval, 14K Gold 75.00
Earrings, Rhinestone, Clip, Eisenberg 160.00
Earrings, Rhinestone, Clip, Kramer, Large 24.00
Earrings, Rhinestones, Silver Plated, Coro ....*Illus* 18.00
Earrings, Rose, 14K Gold Post, Ivory 20.00
Earrings, Ruby & Diamonds, Scroll Design, Trabert & Hoeffer 1210.00
Earrings, Shoe, Filigree, Sterling Silver 40.00
Earrings, Step Cut Diamonds, Platinum Setting 9075.00
Earrings, Sterling Silver & Gold Wash Vermeil, Monet 24.00
Earrings, Tortoiseshell, Figure 8, Gold Stars, Victorian ....*Illus* 605.00
Earrings, Victorian, 4 Ceylon Sapphires, 1 Ruby, 14K Pink Gold 95.00
Hair Comb, Green Rhinestone, 6 x 6 1/2 In. 40.00
Hairpin, Ornate Design, 18K Gold 245.00
Hatpins are listed in this book in the Hatpin category
Jelli Belli, Bug, Crystal Center, Gold On Sterling Silver, Boucher 125.00
Jelli Belli, Grasshopper, Crystal Center, Gold On Sterling, Boucher 125.00
Lavaliere, Aquamarines, Seed Pearls, c.1910 .... 695.00

Lavaliere, Rose Cut Garnets, Set In Heart, 1 1/2 In. 115.00
Lavaliere, Seed Pearls, Dangle Diamond, 14K Pink Gold 98.00
Lavaliere, Seed Pearls, Small Ruby 90.00
Lavaliere, Victorian, Center Red Stone, Seed Pearls, Chain, 10K Gold 165.00
Locket & Necklace, Victorian, Seed Pearl, Gold 3080.00
Locket, Diamond Egg, Green Enamel, Yellow Gold, Van Cleef & Arpels 2210.00
Locket, Embossed Polo Players, Round Diamond, 15K Gold 522.00
Locket, Embossed, 2 Polo Players, Round Diamond, 15K Gold, c.1910 .... 525.00
Locket, Engraved Flowers, Seed Pearls, Colored Stone 70.00
Locket, Memorial, Gold, Black Onyx, Seed Pearls, Victorian 90.00
Locket, Memorial, Seed Pearls, Fluted Gold Chain 345.00
Locket, Pearls, 3 Picture Compartments, 18K Gold, 1 1/8 In. 625.00
Locket, Portrait, Black Enamel, 5 Turquoise Cabochons, 14K Gold 330.00
Locket, Victorian, Embossed, Red Stone, 2 Seed Pearls, Opens 80.00
Money Clip, Cutty Sark, Zippo 12.00
Money Clip, Ford Emblem, Sterling Silver 100.00
Money Clip, Horse Design, Sterling Silver, Taxco 25.00
Money Clip, Robert Hall Stores 35.00
Mourning Pin, Band Of Onyx, 2 Borders, Sterling, 1 1/2 x 1 1/4 In. 345.00
Mourning Pin, Band Of Onyx, 2 Borders, Sterling, 1 x 3/4 In. 275.00
Mourning Pin, Hand Holding A Wreath, Gutta Percha 100.00
Mourning Pin, Onyx & Seed Pearls On Case, Oval, Sterling, 1 3/4 In. 325.00
Necklace & Bracelet, Earrings, Baroque Pearls, Haskell, 24 In. 350.00
Necklace & Bracelet, Gold–Toned Metal, Blue Crystals, Mazer Bros. 50.00
Necklace & Bracelet, Link, 18K Yellow Gold, Antoniazzi 1540.00
Necklace & Bracelet, Simulated Pearl, Trifari, Box 60.00
Necklace & Ear Clips, Silver Tone, Rhinestones Outlined, Trifari 40.00
Necklace & Earrings, Austrian Crystal, 3 Strands, 14 In. 500.00
Necklace & Earrings, Jade Medallions, 12K Gold Filled, 1930s 185.00
Necklace & Earrings, Pearl, 2 Strands, Pendant, Miriam Haskell 450.00
Necklace & Earrings, White Rhinestones, Trifari 35.00
Necklace, Amber Acorns & Leaves, Celluloid Chain, Bakelite .... ˋ 125.00
Necklace, Baroque Pearls, Beige, Pendant 275.00
Necklace, Beaded Design, 18K Yellow Gold Clasp 3300.00
Necklace, Black Onyx, 8 Mm. Beads 50.00
Necklace, Bracelet & Earrings, Leaf Shape, Rhinestones, Pennino 225.00
Necklace, Bracelet & Earrings, Silver, Taxco, Mexico 190.00
Necklace, Butterfly Pendant, Mesh Chain, Haskell, 19 In. 95.00
Necklace, Carnelian, Sterling Silver 65.00
Necklace, Carved Beads, Ivory 50.00
Necklace, Cherries, Bakelite 170.00
Necklace, Cherry Amber, Graduated, Chain, Bead Closing, 1920s, 30 In. 135.00
Necklace, Cherry Amber, Graduated, Faceted, 34 In. 150.00
Necklace, Choker, Green Stones, Trifari 90.00
Necklace, Choker, Pearl, 6 Strands, Vendome 40.00
Necklace, Choker, Pearls, 2 Strands, Haskell 125.00
Necklace, Choker, Pearls, 3 Strands, Haskell 150.00
Necklace, Choker, White & Black Cultured Pearls 660.00
Necklace, Crown Pendant, Gold Chain, Baroque Pearls, Haskell 175.00
Necklace, Cultured Pearls, 6 Strands, Gold Plated Sterling Clasp 140.00
Necklace, Diamond, 103 Full Cut, 1 Marquise, Flexible, 14K Gold 4620.00
Necklace, Egyptian, Clear Lucite, Goldtone Connectors, Trifari 75.00
Necklace, Filigree Pendant, Haskell 90.00
Necklace, Frosted Glass, 2 Strands, Cubes, Hattie Carnegie, 12 In. 150.00
Necklace, Garnet Raspberry Rope 175.00
Necklace, Garnet, Czechoslovakia, 1880s 385.00
Necklace, Glass Balls, Gold, Haskell 50.00
Necklace, Indians Kissing, Castlecliff 325.00
Necklace, Lapis Lazuli Beads, 16 In. 95.00
Necklace, Large Blown Glass Balls, Pearl Finish 40.00
Necklace, Malachite Beads, Graduated, 32 In. 125.00
Necklace, Mauve Celluloid Chain Link, Purple Flower, 1920s 50.00
Necklace, Multicircular Link Design, Tiger's Eye, 18K Gold 3300.00

Necklace, Open Link, 18K Yellow Gold 1650.00
Necklace, Oval Emerald, Trace Links, 10K Gold, Edwardian, 1901–1910 .... 375.00
Necklace, Pave Rhinestones, Gold Tone, Zigzag Design, Roucher 125.00
Necklace, Pearl, Elongated, 2 Strands, Crystal Beads, 24 In. 175.00
Necklace, Pearl, Graduated, White Gold Filigree Clasp, 18 In. 250.00
Necklace, Pearls, Graduated, 83 Round Pearls, 19 In. 220.00
Necklace, Perfume, Estee Lauder 65.00
Necklace, Rhinestone & Crystal, Safety Chain, Weiss 68.00
Necklace, Rose Cut Garnet, Rosettes, Garnet Gold 200.00
Necklace, Shell Cameos, Silver Filigree 95.00
Necklace, Silver Filigree, 3 Small Cameos 150.00
Necklace, Sterling Filigree, 5 Large Hematites, Sorrento 75.00
Necklace, Sterling Silver & Abalone, Taxco, 16 In. 55.00
Pendant, Amethyst, 3 Diamonds, 14K White Gold Mount 115.00
Pendant, Amethyst, Enameled Gold, Rectangular, France, 1 3/4 In. 1045.00
Pendant, Aquamarine, 14K White Gold 1870.00
Pendant, Aztec Design Both Sides, Carlos, 1 3/8 In. 65.00
Pendant, Banded Agate, 14K Gold 1475.00
Pendant, Baroque & Seed Pearls, Haskell 125.00
Pendant, Bowling, Diamond, 14K Gold, Heavy, 1910 .... 235.00
Pendant, Cameo, Floral, 10K Gold 40.00
Pendant, Cameo, Russian Silver & Agate, c.1920, 3/4 x 1 In. 550.00
Pendant, Cross, Raised Floral, Mixed Metal, Shakudo ....*Illus* 522.50
Pendant, Diamond & Black Onyx, Art Deco 1980.00
Pendant, Diamonds, 46 Full Cut & Pear Shaped, Gold Chain, Platinum 4675.00
Pendant, Enamel & Silver, Art Nouveau, Europe, c.1905, 2 1/4 In. 330.00
Pendant, Floriform, Diamond, White Gold, c.1920 .... 4125.00
Pendant, Forest Nymphs, Lalique 225.00
Pendant, Horse, Margot, 1 1/4 In. 65.00
Pendant, Marcasite & Onyx 85.00
Pendant, Marcasite, Ivory, Rubies, Fahrner 595.00
Pendant, Mobe Pearl, Box Link Chain, 14K Gold 235.00
Pendant, Open Heart Design, 40 Full Cut Diamonds, 14K Gold 605.00
Pendant, Pearl, Tourmaline & Emerald, 1880s 210.00
Pendant, Sapphire & Enameled Silver, Bow Shape, Vienna, 4 In. 2200.00
Pendant, Silver Metal, With Pearls, Chain, Joseff, 24 In. 350.00
Pendant, Sunburst, Diamond, Pearl, Sterling Silver, Tiffany 275.00
Pin & Ear Clips, Flower, Blue Green, Enameled Leaves, Weiss 40.00
Pin & Earrings, Baroque Pearls, Pink & Blue Stones, Shiaparelli 165.00
Pin & Earrings, Christmas Tree, Rhinestones, Weiss 35.00
Pin & Earrings, Coral Cameo, Gold, Dated Mid–1850s 1575.00

From top: Jewelry, Pin, Dragonfly,
Platinum, Gold; Jewelry, Watch Chain,
Chrysanthemum Shaped Links,
Shakudo, 58 In.; Jewelry, Pendant,
Cross, Raised Floral, Mixed Metal,
Shakudo

✦✦✦✦✦✦✦✦✦✦✦✦✦✦✦✦✦✦✦✦

A signature on a piece of jewelry adds 30% to the value.

✦✦✦✦✦✦✦✦✦✦✦✦✦✦✦✦✦✦✦✦

✦✦✦✦✦✦✦✦✦✦✦✦✦✦✦✦✦✦✦✦

Your diamond or precious–stone jewelry, antique or modern, should be reappraised every other year.

✦✦✦✦✦✦✦✦✦✦✦✦✦✦✦✦✦✦✦✦

Pin & Earrings, Flower, Amethyst Glass Petals, Hattie Carnegie	85.00
Pin & Earrings, Leaf, Red Stones, Weiss	35.00
Pin & Earrings, Portrait, Enameled, 14K Filigree Mounted	765.00
Pin & Earrings, Silver & Enamel, Margot De Taxco	315.00
Pin & Earrings, Sterling Silver, Coro–Craft, 1940s	100.00
Pin & Earrings, Sterling Silver, Georg Jensen	120.00
Pin, 14K Gold, Rubies, Sapphires, 1940s, Pair ....*Illus*	1100.00
Pin, Angel Skin Coral, Dove In Flight, 2 1/2 In.	165.00
Pin, Arabesque Design, 14K Gold, Enameled, Engraved, 1890, 2 In.	25.00
Pin, Arrow Shape, Silver, Agate, Victorian ....*Illus*	247.50
Pin, Art Deco, Ruby & Diamond, Platinum	2200.00
Pin, Aurora Borealis, Weiss	48.00
Pin, Bar, 7 Sapphires, 12 Diamonds, 14K Gold,	550.00
Pin, Bar, Abalone, 1910	30.00
Pin, Bar, Enameled Pink Rose, Sterling Silver, 2 In.	20.00
Pin, Bar, Filigree, 3 Square Cut Amethyst, 14K Yellow Gold	80.00
Pin, Bar, Love Knot Center, 6 Pearls, 18K Gold	110.00
Pin, Baroque Pearl In Nest, Robert	38.00
Pin, Bee On Leaf, Gold Washed, Pennino	55.00
Pin, Bee, Ruby–Set Eyes, 18K Gold, Tiffany	445.00
Pin, Bellboy, Dangling Keys, Red Plastic	75.00
Pin, Bijoux, Branched, Pave Center, Christian Dior, Box, 1965	115.00
Pin, Bird & Flowers, Yellow, Orange & Green, Coro, 1 3/4 In.	65.00
Pin, Bird In Wreath, Georg Jensen	175.00
Pin, Bird, Faux Moonstone Breast & Pave, Trifari	40.00
Pin, Black Onyx, Center Flower Of Pearls, Victorian, 14K Gold	145.00
Pin, Bow Shape, Sterling Silver, Trifari	130.00
Pin, Bow, Holds Watch, 14K Gold, Enamel, Pearls ....*Illus*	825.00
Pin, Bow, Sterling Silver, Hobe, 3 In.	175.00
Pin, Boy & Girl, Dancing, Dangling Record, Plastic, Sammy Kaye	75.00
Pin, Bracelet, & Earrings, Enameled On Copper, Matisse–Renoir	70.00
Pin, Buddha, Green, Bakelite, 2 In.	85.00
Pin, Bullet, U.S. Army, Hanging Jeep, Bakelite	175.00
Pin, Bumblebee, Diamonds, Gold	1450.00
Pin, Bumblebee, Ruby, Diamond & Sapphire, 18K Yellow Gold	1210.00
Pin, Butterfly, Amethyst, Rubies, Diamonds, 14K Gold ....*Illus*	1540.00
Pin, Butterfly, On Gold Wire, Blue & Green Rhinestone	20.00
Pin, Butterfly, Weiss	115.00
Pin, Caged Bird, Sterling Silver, Lang, 1950	40.00
Pin, Calla Lily, Seed Pearls, Josef	60.00
Pin, Cameo, 10K Yellow Gold Filigree Mounting, Coral	75.00
Pin, Cameo, Grecian Goddess, Staff & Ram's Head, 14K Gold, 2 In.	395.00
Pin, Cameo, Heart Shape, 14K Gold Frame	95.00
Pin, Cameo, Seed Pearls, Sterling Silver Bezel	475.00
Pin, Chariot & Horses, Sterling Silver, Schrage	145.00
Pin, Cherries On Chain, Bakelite	150.00
Pin, Christmas Tree, Boucher	40.00
Pin, Christmas Tree, Eisenberg	45.00
Pin, Cockatoo, Porcelain, Occupied Japan	17.00
Pin, Coral & Seed Pearls, Branch Of Acorns, 2 1/4 In.	245.00
Pin, Cornucopia, Hanging Pearls, Kramer, 3 In.	40.00
Pin, Crescent Moon, Garnet, Bohemia	125.00
Pin, Crescent, Diamond, Sterling Silver, Tiffany	375.00
Pin, Crown, Sterling Silver, Coro	125.00
Pin, Doe & Squirrel, Sterling Silver, Georg Jensen ....*Illus*	330.00
Pin, Dog's Face, Shaggy, Tassel Hair	90.00
Pin, Dog, 18K White Gold, Diamonds, Ruby Eye, 1950 ....*Illus*	3800.00
Pin, Dog, Crystal, Ruby, Diamond, 18K Gold, England, 1870s ....*Illus*	4500.00
Pin, Dog, Hunting, Bird, Crystal, 18K Gold, England, 1880 ....*Illus*	3250.00
Pin, Dolphins, Georg Jensen	200.00
Pin, Double Love Knot, Emerald, 10K Gold	80.00
Pin, Double, Mourning, Black Lava Set In Tortoiseshell Frame	95.00
Pin, Dragonfly, Platinum, Gold ....*Illus*	1320.00

Jewelry, Pin, Dog, Hunting, Bird, Crystal, 18K
Gold, England, 1880

Jewelry, Pin, Dog, 18K White Gold,
Diamonds, Ruby Eye, 1950

Jewelry, Pin, Dog, Crystal, Ruby, Diamond,
18K Gold, England, 1870s

Pin, Dragonfly, Schiaparelli	85.00
Pin, Duette Flowers, Coro	175.00
Pin, Eagle, Butterscotch, Bakelite, 4 In.	125.00
Pin, Elephants, Boucher	65.00
Pin, Enameled Rhinestone, Jomaz, 2 In.	45.00
Pin, Evangeline, Unger	750.00
Pin, Feather, Coroduette	90.00
Pin, Feather, Diamond & Ruby, Yellow & White Gold, 2 1/4 In.	1650.00
Pin, Flapper, Black Woman, Bakelite	125.00
Pin, Floral, Fuchsia Rhinestones, Pennino, 3 1/4 In.	110.00
Pin, Floral, Red Setting, Sterling Silver, Truart, 4 1/2 In.	30.00
Pin, Floral, Sterling Silver, Hobe	160.00
Pin, Flower, Moonstone, Ruby, 14K Gold, Tiffany ....*Illus*	2420.00
Pin, Flower, Orchid Shape, Center Cultured Pearl, 18K Gold	110.00
Pin, Flower, Pave, Hattie Carnegie	65.00
Pin, Flowers, Leaves, Tendrils, 37 Seed Pearls, 14K Gold	75.00
Pin, Four–Leaf Clover, Victorian, 14K Gold	90.00
Pin, Fuchsia Flower, White Stones, Sterling Silver, Pennino, 2 In.	195.00
Pin, Glass, Bridal Rosette, Hunting Dog, Dome Shape, 1880, 1 3/4 In.	39.00
Pin, Globe, Dangling Slate, Pencil & Book, Plastic	50.00
Pin, Gold Sun, Dangling Stars, Joseff	150.00
Pin, Gold, Seed Pearl Tassels	2750.00
Pin, Golf Club, Pearl & Platinum, 1920s, Tiffany	70.00
Pin, Green Rhinestones, Dangling Pearl Drop, Schiaparelli	350.00
Pin, Hair, Gold Cage Work, Teardrop Dangles, 2 x 1 3/4 In.	135.00
Pin, Hair, Oval, 14K Gold	100.00
Pin, Heart Shape, 18K Gold, Georg Jensen	395.00
Pin, Hibiscus, Pink Enamel, Coro, 4 In.	125.00
Pin, Homecoming, University Of Illinois, 1915	65.00
Pin, Horse, Sterling Silver, Coral Craft	95.00
Pin, Jelli Belli, Duck, Sterling Silver	275.00
Pin, Joined Rings, Georg Jensen	200.00
Pin, Lacy, 7 Rubies, 6 Seed Pearls, 14K Gold	145.00
Pin, Lady's Head, Ebony, Lucite, U.S., 4 1/2 In.	65.00
Pin, Lapel, Mine–Cut Aquamarine, 12K Gold	185.00
Pin, Leaf, Green Stones, Gold Plated, Coro ....*Illus*	65.00
Pin, Leaf, Green, Red Rhinestone Accents, Corocraft	75.00
Pin, Lily, Pave & Pearls	55.00
Pin, Lizard, 7 Round Emeralds, 14K Gold .... 200.00 To	225.00
Pin, Lover's Knot, Small Diamond, Enamel, 10K Gold	75.00
Pin, Maltese Cross	95.00
Pin, Memorial, Scroll–Edged Frame, Dated 1846 ....*Illus*	357.00
Pin, Moon–Shape, Rhinestones, Sterling Silver, Trifari	135.00
Pin, Moonstone & Cabochons, Red & Clear Rhinestones, Trifari	200.00
Pin, Moonstone Cabochon, Row Of Diamonds, 14K Gold, Faberge, 3 In.	3300.00
Pin, Moonstone, Gold & Platinum, Tiffany, c.1910 ....*Illus*	1350.00
Pin, Mourning, Bird, Gutta Percha	65.00

Pin, Mourning, Clendenen Family, Enclosed Doll, Gold, Enamel, 2 In.	3850.00
Pin, Mourning, Hand Holding Wreath, Black	100.00
Pin, Openwork Design, Old Mine–Cut Diamonds, Platinum	775.00
Pin, Ornate Bird, Georg Jensen, Sterling	495.00
Pin, Owl, Pave Rhinestones, Jomaz	35.00
Pin, Pansy, Mine–Cut Diamonds, Enamel, 18K Gold ....*Illus*	2100.00
Pin, Peacock On Branch, Enamel, Coro, 1950	80.00
Pin, Peacock, Gems, Pave Diamonds, 18K Gold, Platinum ....*Illus*	5500.00
Pin, Pearl & Rhinestone, Boucher	40.00
Pin, Pelican, Silver, Mexico	380.00
Pin, Peridot, 10K Gold	65.00
Pin, Pheasant On Log, Foliage, Coro, 2 1/4 In.	75.00
Pin, Red Cherries On Log, Bakelite	85.00
Pin, Reindeer, Black, Bakelite	90.00

 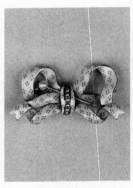 

Jewelry, Pin, 14K Gold, Rubies, Sapphires, 1940s, Pair

Jewelry, Pin, Bow, Holds Watch, 14K Gold, Enamel, Pearls

Jewelry, Pin, Butterfly, Amethyst, Rubies, Diamonds, 14K Gold

Jewelry, Pin, Moonstone, Gold & Platinum, Tiffany, c.1910

Jewelry, Pin, Pansy, Mine-Cut Diamonds, Enamel, 18K Gold

Jewelry, Pin, Peacock, Gems, Pave Diamonds, 18K Gold, Platinum

Jewelry, Watch Pin, Four-Leaf Clover, Diamonds, Enameled

Pin, Rhinestone, Royal Of Pittsburgh 55.00
Pin, Rhinestones, Clip, Eisenberg 150.00
Pin, Rose, Eisenberg 225.00
Pin, Round Brilliant Cut Diamonds, Flexible Platinum Mount 8800.00
Pin, Scarab, Enamel Design, Tiffany, Sterling Silver 605.00
Pin, Scarf, Floral, Gold Tone, Pearls, Haskell 38.00
Pin, Scotty Dog, Marcasite 30.00
Pin, Scrolling Entwined Form, 5 Amethysts, Gold 88.00
Pin, Scrolling, Rubies, Tourmaline, Peridot & Topaz, Yellow Gold 220.00
Pin, Seed Pearl & Horse Hair, Oval, 1840s, 2 x 1 1/2 In. 125.00
Pin, Shell Cameo, 3 Graces, German Silver Bezel 775.00
Pin, Shell Shape, Pearl In Center, Sterling Silver, 1 3/4 In. 45.00
Pin, Shell Shape, Sterling Silver, Pearl In Center, 1 3/4 In. 45.00
Pin, Sleigh, Hattie Carnegie 45.00
Pin, Spray, Blue Stones, Gold Plated, Coro ....*Illus*   80.00
Pin, Starfish, Blue, Weiss 25.00
Pin, Sunburst Design, Etruscan Granulation Braid, Gold, U.S. 280.00
Pin, Sunburst, 1/2 Carat Of Diamonds, Seed Pearls, 14K Gold 1295.00
Pin, Swami Head, Silver, Joseff 150.00
Pin, Swirl, 9 Pearls, 14K Gold 135.00
Pin, Target, Bow & Arrow, Plastic 45.00
Pin, Thief Of Baghdad, Black Face, Korada 250.00
Pin, Tiger Lily, Schreiner, 3 In. 125.00
Pin, Top Hat, Bakelite 65.00
Pin, Tourmaline, Trellis Work, Arts & Crafts, 14K Gold 990.00
Pin, Trembling Butterfly, Black Stones, Weiss, 2 In. 120.00
Pin, Tulips, Georg Jensen 200.00
Pin, Unicorn Head, Silvertone With Rhinestones, Carnegie 65.00
Pin, Victorian Sunburst, 14K Gold, Seed Pearls, Diamond Chip 125.00
Pin, Violin, Sterling Silver, Nettie Rosenstein, Large 275.00
Pin, Virgo With Cupid, Cini, 2 In. 65.00
Pin, Watch Pendant, Pave Pearls, Sterling Silver 45.00
Pin, White Stones, Pearl Center, Nettie Rosenstein, 1 3/8 In. 65.00
Pin, White Stones, White & Black Enamel, Jomaz, 2 1/2 In. 95.00
Pin, Wings, Sterling Silver, Rhinestones, 1940s 35.00
Pin, Woman's Head, Art Nouveau, Sterling Silver, Repousse 125.00
Pin, Wreath & Bird, Georg Jensen 155.00
Pin, Wyvern, Garnet In Mouth, Art Nouveau, Sterling, Gold Wash 150.00
Pin, Yellow Stones, Schiaparelli 135.00
Pin–Pendant, Grotesque Birds, Facing Each Other, Silver, Europe 85.00
Ring Watch, 14K Gold, 1920s 400.00
Ring, 15 Cut Emeralds, 18K Yellow Gold 225.00
Ring, Amber, 14K Pink Gold, Russia 120.00
Ring, Amethyst, 18K Yellow Gold, Oval Shaped Faceted 300.00
Ring, Amethyst, 2 Round & 3 Oval, 14K Yellow Gold 185.00
Ring, Amethyst, 7 Rose Cut, 10K Yellow Gold 95.00
Ring, Amethyst, Openwork, 14K Gold 185.00
Ring, Amethyst, Seed Pearls, Pink Gold 75.00
Ring, Ammolite, 14K Gold 150.00
Ring, Aquamarine, Filigree, 14K White Gold, 1925 .... 800.00
Ring, Baby's, Heart With Diamond, Yellow Gold 25.00
Ring, Black Opal, 10K Yellow Gold, 1940s, Size 10 .... 175.00
Ring, Blue Star Sapphire, 14K Gold 90.00
Ring, Cameo, 18K Gold, 1907 .... 265.00
Ring, Cameo, Agate, Profile Of Achilles, 14K White Gold 88.00
Ring, Cameo, Carnelian Stone, Openwork Setting, 18K Gold 395.00
Ring, Cameo, Coral, Face Of Japanese Woman, 14K Gold 145.00
Ring, Center Diamond, Surround Of Smaller Diamonds, Platinum 410.00
Ring, Center Faience Scarab, 18K Yellow Gold 137.00
Ring, Center Pearl, 18 Brilliant Cut Rubies, 18K Gold 320.00
Ring, Cluster, Garnet, 9K Gold 125.00
Ring, Cocktail, 3 Small Sapphires, Aquamarine, 10K Gold 160.00
Ring, Diamond Cluster, 14K Yellow Gold, 1900–1915, Size 10 1/2 .... 360.00

Ring, Diamond, . 75 Ct., 18K White Gold, Surrounded By 42 Diamonds 2500.00
Ring, Diamond, 3 Center 4 Baguette Sapphires, Platinum 467.00
Ring, Diamond, 33 Marquise Full Cut, Platinum 4400.00
Ring, Diamond, 6 Channel Set Square Cut, Platinum 770.00
Ring, Diamond, Cluster Of 7, Filigree Mounting, 14K White Gold 220.00
Ring, Emerald, 14 Small Diamonds, 10K Gold 300.00
Ring, Emerald, Oval Cut, Surround Of Diamonds, 18K Gold 880.00
Ring, Emerald, Step Cut, 18 Diamonds, 14K Gold 445.00
Ring, Eternity, 21 Rectangular Step Cut Diamonds 6600.00
Ring, Eternity, Diamond, Platinum, 1930s 685.00
Ring, European Diamonds, Filigree 445.00
Ring, Garnet, 8 Pyrope, Leaf, 18K Yellow Gold, 1930–1940, Size 8 1/2 .... 135.00
Ring, Garnet, Seed Pearls, 14K Pink Gold 75.00
Ring, Gold On Sterling, Blue & Green Enamel, Rhinestones, Jomaz 150.00
Ring, Horseshoe, Oval Opal, 9 Diamonds, Victorian, 14K Gold 495.00
Ring, Imperial Topaz, Diamonds, 18K Yellow Gold 360.00
Ring, Lapis, Fahrner 495.00
Ring, Large Cabochon Center, Surrounded By Opals, 14K Gold 350.00
Ring, Man's, Carved Intaglio Moon & Star 110.00
Ring, Man's, Center Diamond, 14K White & Yellow Gold 600.00
Ring, Man's, Diamond, 2. 47 Carat, 14K Yellow Gold 7150.00
Ring, Man's, Gypsy Setting, 2 Sapphires, 14K Rose Gold 75.00
Ring, Mourning, Miniature Of Woman, Black Enamel Border, 1793 .... 400.00
Ring, Nugget Design, Oval Star Sapphire, 1 Brilliant Cut Diamond 550.00
Ring, Opal, 14 Pave Diamonds, Sculptured Band, 14K Gold 245.00
Ring, Pink Tourmaline, 2 Seed Pearls, 14K Pink Gold 65.00
Ring, Quartz & Diamond, Openwork Design, 14K Gold 175.00
Ring, Sapphire, 30 Diamonds, 18K White Gold 650.00
Ring, Smoky Topaz, 10K Gold 120.00
Ring, Snake, Rubies & Opals, 14K Pink Gold 58.00
Ring, Topaz, 10 Diamonds, 14K White Gold 665.00
Ring, Victorian, 2 Rubies, 1 White Sapphire, Carved, Pink Gold 95.00
Ring, Victorian, 3 Rubies In Row, Seed Pearls, 14K Pink Gold 85.00
Ring, Victorian, Gold Cabochon Garnet, Seed Pearls 75.00
Ring, Victorian, Peridot, 2 Seed Pearls, 14K Pink Gold 75.00
Ring, Wedding Band, 12 Diamonds, Platinum, 1915, Size 8 1/2 .... 250.00
Ring, Wedding, 24 Diamonds Carved In Flowers, Platinum 800.00
Ring, Wedding, 40 Diamonds, 14K Yellow Gold 225.00
Ring, Wedding, Gold, 8 Sides, Design, Victorian, Dated 1873 .... 75.00
Stickpin, 3 Cabochon Cut Opals, Frame Of Diamonds, 18K Gold 385.00
Stickpin, 3 Small Prong Set Pearls, 2 Green Enameled Leaves, Gold 25.00
Stickpin, Anchor Buggy 40.00
Stickpin, Avery Bulldogs 35.00
Stickpin, Ball, Molded Leaves, Silver Sterling, Georg Jensen, 1 In. 85.00
Stickpin, Cultured Pearl & Diamond, 14K Gold 120.00
Stickpin, Emerald, 18K White Gold 110.00
Stickpin, Enamel Design, Fresh Water Pearl, Art Nouveau 95.00
Stickpin, Griffin Shape, 2 Rubies, 1 Diamond, 14K Gold 275.00
Stickpin, John Deere Moline Iron Clad Wagons .... 30.00 To 45.00
Stickpin, Panther's Head Shape, Ruby Eyes, 14K Gold 330.00
Stickpin, Sapphire & Diamond, Cartier 3575.00
Stickpin, United States Horseshoe 35.00
Tiara, Victorian, Ivory, c.1840 .... 2400.00
Tie Bar, Chain, With Golf Clubs 25.00
Tie Bar, Sterling Silver, Georg Jensen 125.00
Tie Clasp & Cuff Links, Bulldog, Cini 75.00
Tie Tack, Golfer With Bag, Clubs, 14K Gold 55.00
Watches are listed in their own category
Watch Chain & Fob, Classical Design, 14K Gold 330.00
Watch Chain, 2 Purple Stones, Serpent, Bird, Brass, 9 1/2 In. 85.00
Watch Chain, Chrysanthemum Shaped Links, Shakudo, 58 In. ....*Illus* 1540.00
Watch Chain, Double Circled Horsehair 85.00
Watch Chain, Hair 65.00

Watch Chain, Seed Pearls Slide, 14K Gold 190.00
Watch Chain, Slide, Woman's 75.00
Watch Chain, Victorian, Puffy Heart, Sterling Silver 150.00
Watch Pin, Four–Leaf Clover, Diamonds, Enameled ....*Illus* 1430.00
Wristwatches are listed in their own category

JOHN ROGERS statues were made from 1859 to 1892. The originals were
bronze, but the thousands of copies made by the Rogers factory were of
painted plaster. Eighty different figures were created. Similar painted
plaster figures were produced by some other factories. Rights to the figures
were sold in 1893 and they were manufactured for several more years by
the Rogers Statuette Co. Never repaint a Rogers figure because this lowers
the value to collectors.

Group, Checkers Up At The Farm, Aug. 25, 1875, 17 In. ....385.00 To 450.00
Group, Coming To The Parson, 22 In. 415.00
Group, Horses 420.00
Group, Tap On The Window 500.00
Group, Washington, 30 In. 2200.00

JUDAICA is any memorabilia that refers to the Jews or the Jewish
religion. Interests range from newspaper clippings that mention eighteenth-
and nineteenth-century Jewish Americans to religious objects, such as
menorahs or spice boxes. Age, condition, and the intrinsic value of the
material, as well as the historic and artistic importance, determine the
value.

Beaker, Purim, Silver, Iraqi, Engraved Hebrew, Fish, 3 1/2 In. 770.00
Box, Tzadaka, Renaissance Style, Sterling Silver, 3 3/4 In. 495.00
Buckle, Belt, Day Of Atonement, Jonah & Whale, Continental Silver 1100.00
Candelabrum, Sabbath, Silver, Bezalel Emblem, 6 In. 440.00
Case, Mezuzah, Rampant Lion To Right, Hebrew, Polish Silver 1875.00
Case, Mezuzah, Window For Scroll, Carved Wood, Poland, 4 In. 515.00
Cover, Passover, Israel Views, Silk, Palestine, 16 1/2 x 21 1/2 In. 210.00
Dish, Circumcision, Silver, Repousse Work, Hebrew Engraving, 8 In. 1210.00
Dish, Passover, 9 Vignettes At Rim, Chad Gadyo Scenes, Silver, 1928 .... 4595.00
Dish, Passover, Depicts Slavery In Egypt, Ceramic, American, 10 In. 960.00
Dish, Passover, Pewter, Hebrew Inscriptions, 10 In. 275.00
Dish, Pidyon Haben, Silver, Zodiac Signs, Sacrifice Of Isaac, 13 In. 1650.00
Dish, Sabbath, Synagogue Exterior, Continental Silver, 8 1/4 In. 270.00
Etrog Container, Syrian, Copper & Silver, 5 In. 2200.00
Game, Lotto Of Yiddish Proverbs, Dr. I. Schapira, Box 25.00
Goblet, Kiddush, Grapevines, Filigree Gosses, Bezalel Silver, c.1920 .... 725.00
Goblet, Kiddush, Hebrew Inscription, Flower Heads, 4 3/4 In. 1025.00
Knife, Circumcision, Silver, American, Double Edge, 6 In. 1210.00
Knife, Sabbath, Mother–of–Pearl Inlay, German Silver, 5 3/8 In. 360.00
Lamp, Brass, Scroll, Detachable Oil Jug, Polish, 9 In. 357.00
Lamp, Hannukah, 8 Statues Of Liberty, Bronze, 1986 .... 9075.00
Lamp, Hannukah, Brass, Prague, Moses, Aaron Figures, 8 Oil Pans, 7 In. 880.00
Lamp, Hannukah, Bronze, Italian, Fan Pattern, 8 Oil Pans, 7 In. 2860.00
Lamp, Hannukah, Children's, Tin, Palestinian, 7 In. 121.00
Lamp, Hannukah, Embossed Back Plate, Laurel Flowers, 8 Oil Fonts 510.00
Lamp, Hannukah, Silver, Servant Light, England, 6 1/2 In. 1320.00
Lamp, Hannukah, Wooden, American, Domed, Star Of David, 15 In. 605.00
Lamp, Sabbath, Indian, Brass, Glass, 18 In. 7150.00
Postcard, Jewish New Year Greeting, Woven Silk 65.00
Postcard, View Of Temesvar, Hungary, Synagogue, 3 Fold 40.00
Seder Plate, Hebrew Inscriptions, Pewter, 15 In. 330.00
Spice Box, Bell Within Tower, Polish, Sterling Silver, c.1800 .... 1752.00
Spice Box, Clock Face Inscribed In Hebrew, Germany, Sterling, 1782 .... 6900.00
Spice Box, Fish Form, Red Stone Eyes, Chain, Continental Silver 330.00
Spice Box, Frankfurt–Am–Main, Marked IHS, Sterling, 18th Century 2590.00
Spice Box, German, Sterling Silver, 18th Century 5460.00
Spice Box, Polish, Sterling Silver, 19th Century 1150.00

JUGTOWN Pottery refers to pottery made in North Carolina as far back as the 1750s. In 1915, Juliana and Jacques Busbee set up a training and sales organization for what they named *Jugtown Pottery.* In 1921, they built a shop at Jugtown, North Carolina, and hired Ben Owen as a potter in 1923. The Busbees moved the village store where the pottery was sold to New York City. Juliana Busbee sold the New York store in 1926 and moved into a log cabin near the Jugtown Pottery. The pottery closed in 1958. It reopened and is still working near Seagrove, North Carolina.

Bowl, Dark Blue, Footed, 3 1/4 In.	25.00
Tile, German Shepherd Lying Down, 10 1/2 In.	130.00
Vase, Bulbous, Turquoise, 5 1/2 In.	80.00
Vase, Chinese White Drip Glaze, 3 3/4 In.	135.00
Vase, Chinese, White Flowing Glaze, 4 In.	70.00 To 100.00
Vase, Frogskin	35.00

JUKEBOXES play records. The first coin–operated phonograph was demonstrated in 1889. In 1906 the *Automatic Entertainer* appeared, the first coin–operated phonograph to offer several different selections of music. The first electrically powered jukebox was introduced in 1927. Collectors search for jukeboxes of all ages, especially those with flashing lights and unusual design and graphics.

AMI, Model A	3000.00
Bally, Double Bell, 5 To 25 Cents	3000.00
Holcombe–Hoke, Electramuse, Dancing Girls Marquee	2000.00
Mills, Model 801, 1927	4850.00
Mills, Studio, 1937	2500.00
Mills, Swing King	1500.00
Mills, Swing King, Do–Re–Me	1350.00
Regina, Hexaphone, Edison Player	7500.00
Regina, Model 19	4000.00
Rock–Ola, Model 1422	3800.00
Rock–Ola, Model 1426	8000.00
Rock–Ola, Model 1428	3500.00 To 4250.00
Seeburg, Model 147	4500.00
Seeburg, Model 220	1750.00
Seeburg, Model 100C, 1952	3500.00
Seeburg, Model 1197, 10 Selections	2000.00
Seeburg, Model G	1750.00
Wurlitzer, Model 71, Counter Top, Stand	8500.00
Wurlitzer, Model 780	5500.00
Wurlitzer, Model 1015	3950.00 To 9500.00
Wurlitzer, Model 1050	5850.00
Wurlitzer, Model 1100	7000.00
Wurlitzer, Model 2500	1995.00
Wurlitzer, Model P–10, Stand	1800.00
Wurlitzer, Nickelodeon, Keyboard Style, 1912	7500.00

KATE GREENAWAY, who was a famous illustrator of children's books, drew pictures of children in high–waisted Empire dresses. She lived from 1846 to 1901. Her designs appear on china, glass, and other pieces. Figural napkin rings depicting the Greenaway children may also be found in the Napkin Ring category under Figural.

Castor, Pickle, Girls In Bonnets, Blue Insert, Tongs	450.00
Salt & Pepper, Girl In Pink Hat, Boy In Black Top Hat	65.00
Sugar & Creamer	65.00
Toothpick, Bisque, Germany, 5 1/2 In.	75.00

KAUFFMANN refers to porcelain wares decorated with scenes based on the works of Angelica Kauffmann (1741–1807), a Swiss–born painter who was a decorative artist for Adam Brothers, English furniture manufacturers, between 1766 and 1781. She designed small–scale pictorial subjects in the neoclassic manner and painted portraits as well as historical and classical

Kay Finch, Figurine, Lady & Gentleman,

8 In., Pair

◆◆◆◆◆◆◆◆◆◆◆◆◆◆◆◆◆◆◆◆◆◆

To easily remove wax that has dripped on a candlestick, put the candlestick in the freezer for about an hour. The wax will flake off.

◆◆◆◆◆◆◆◆◆◆◆◆◆◆◆◆◆◆◆◆◆◆

pictures that were later reproduced on chinaware made across Europe. Most porcelains signed *Kauffmann* were made in the late 1800s. She did not do the artwork on the porcelain pieces signed with her name.

Chocolate Pot, Scenic Panels, Female Figures, Signed	80.00
Ewer, Mythological Scene, Flowers, Opaque Body, Signed, 8 1/2 In.	235.00
Plate, Allegorical Scenes, Cherubs, Scalloped Rim, 8 In.	25.00
Vase, Portrait, 8 In.	150.00

KAY FINCH Ceramics were made in Corona Del Mar, California, from 1935 to 1963. The hand-decorated pieces often depicted whimsical animals and people. Pastel colors were used.

Kay Finch
CALIFORNIA

Figurine, Boy, 6 In.	35.00
Figurine, Cat, 11 In.	325.00
Figurine, Cat, Sitting, Flower Face, Pink, Purple & Aqua, 3 1/2 In.	25.00
Figurine, Cats, Sitting, Flower Faces, Blue & Gray, 3 1/2 In.	25.00
Figurine, Dalmatian, Sitting, 17 1/2 In.	135.00
Figurine, Hansel & Gretel, 7 In.	85.00
Figurine, Horse	18.00
Figurine, Lady & Gentleman, 8 In., Pair *Illus*	55.00
Figurine, Owl, 8 1/2 In.	35.00
Figurine, Rabbit	25.00
Figurine, Sleeping Cat, 5 x 7 In.	95.00
Planter, Bear	30.00
Salt & Pepper, Lamb	12.00
Salt & Pepper, Owl	12.00
Teapot, Clown	35.00

KAYSERZINN, see Pewter category

KELVA glassware was made by the C. F. Monroe Company of Meriden, Connecticut, about 1904. It is a pale, pastel-painted glass decorated with flowers, designs, or scenes. Kelva resembles Nakara and Wave Crest, two other glasswares made by the same company.

KELVA

Box, Blue, 4 1/2 In.	395.00
Box, Cover, Blue Daisies, Pink Ground, Footed, Oval, 5 1/2 x 4 In.	540.00
Box, Cover, Wild Roses, Fuchsia Trim, White Dots, Lined, 3 1/2 x 6 In.	690.00
Box, Daisies, Pink Ground, Ormolu Frame, 4 x 5 1/2 In.	650.00
Box, Enamel Orchids On Mottled Green Ground, 8 In.	825.00
Box, Hinged Cover, Violets On Peach Ground, 6 In.	575.00
Box, Hinged Cover, White Orchids, Signed, 2 1/2 x 5 In.	425.00
Box, Hinged Top, Mottled Ground, Pink Hibiscus, Marked, 7 3/4 In.	650.00
Box, Pink Flowers, Blue-Gray Ground, Mirror Lid, 4 1/2 In.	515.00
Box, Wild Roses, Fuchsia Trim, White Dots, 3 1/2 x 6 In.	690.00
Dish, Ring, Green	150.00
Dish, Silver Rim, Blue, 6 In.	285.00
Powder Box, Blown-Out Rose Blossom, Signed	685.00

Toothpick, Hand Painted Pink & White Daisies, White Dotted Rim 225.00
Vase, 18 1/2 In. 1100.00

KENTON HILLS Pottery in Erlanger, Kentucky, made art wares, including
vases and figurines that resembled Rookwood, probably because so many
of the original artists and workmen had worked at the Rookwood plant.
Kenton Hills opened in 1939 and closed during World War II.

Pitcher, Buckeye, Wooden Knob On Handle, Painted 350.00
Vase, Magnolia Blossoms & Buds, 13 In. 1000.00

KEW BLAS is the name used by the Union Glass Company of Somerville,
Massachusetts. The name refers to an iridescent golden glass made from
the 1890s to 1924. The iridescent glass was reminiscent of the Tiffany glass
of the period.

Base, Allover Green Fishscale, Gold, Scallops, Signed, 5 In. 775.00
Creamer, Gold Iridescent, 4 In. 120.00
Creamer, Gold Pulled Feather, Gold Handle, Signed, 3 1/4 In. 550.00
Pitcher, Bulbous, Signed, 4 1/2 In. 1265.00
Pitcher, Hooked Feather, Green & Gold, White, Signed, 4 1/2 In. 770.00
Pitcher, Pulled Feather, Gold Interior, Signed, 4 1/2 In. 770.00
Tumbler, Pinched, Gold Iridescent, 3 1/2 In. 275.00
Vase, Golden Yellow, Iridescent Gold Pulled Feather, Signed, 5 In. 495.00
Vase, Green & Gold Feathering, Gold Cased, 3 In. 2400.00
Vase, Pulled Feather, 8 In. 500.00

KEWPIES, designed by Rose O'Neill, were first pictured in the *Ladies'
Home Journal.* The figures, which are similar to pixies, were a success, and
Kewpie dolls started appearing in 1911. Kewpie pictures and other items
soon followed. Collectors search for all items that picture the little winged
people.

Bank, Chalkware 30.00
Bank, Chalkware, 11 1/2 In. 38.00
Bank, Chalkware, 11 In. 50.00
Bank, Nude Boy, Wire Glasses 50.00
Booklet, Jell-O 22.00
Bulb, Figural, Milk Glass 15.00
Calendar, 1974, 15 Pages 18.00
Candy Container .... 45.00 To 73.00
Candy Container, Kewpie, Next To Barrel 175.00
Child's Set, Cup & Saucer, 7-In. Plate, Rose O'Neill 225.00
Cup & Saucer 110.00
Cup & Saucer, Rose O'Neill 125.00
Doll, All Cloth, Kreuger, 16 In. 135.00
Doll, Bisque, 1 Broken Wing, O'Neill, 4 In. 135.00
Doll, Bisque, Lying On Stomach 275.00
Doll, Cameo, Vinyl, Box, 27 In. 250.00
Doll, Rubber, Glass Eyes, Rose O'Neill, 11 In. 40.00
Doll, Side-Glancing Eyes, Composition 5-Piece Body, Sun Suit, 12 In. 150.00
Doll, Talcum Powder, Signed Rose O'Neill, 7 In. 125.00
Doll, Thinker, O'Neill, 4 1/2 In. 425.00
Doll, Vinyl, Strombecker, Box, Large 65.00
Feeding Dish, 7 Kewpies, Rose O'Neill 100.00
Figurine, Bisque, Signed, 5 1/4 In. 75.00
Figurine, Bisque, Signed, 7 1/2 In. 350.00
Figurine, Bisque, Signed, 9 In. 425.00
Figurine, Bisque, Signed, Paper Label, 6 In. 250.00
Figurine, Bride & Groom, Bisque, Rose O'Neill, 4 1/2 In., Pair 300.00
Figurine, Celluloid, Rose O'Neill, 1914, 2 1/2 In. 20.00
Figurine, Standing On Heart, Arms Move, Chalkware, 18 In. 125.00
Figurine, Thinker, Plaster, 7 In. 15.00
Knife, Kewpie, Pocket 60.00
Light Bulb, Christmas Tree, Kewpie 40.00
Mirror, Pocket, O'Neill 35.00

Plate, Christmas, Rose O'Neill, 1973 .... 20.00
Plate, Time To Be Happy Is Now, 2 Kewpies, Cameo Collections, 8 In. 8.00
Postcard, 1918 .... 15.00
Postcard, Kewpie On Mailbox, 1923 .... 15.00
Poster, Merry Christmas, 30 Kewpies, Christmas Tree, Rose O'Neill 20.00
Saucer 20.00
Toothpick, Berfeld 100.00

KIMBALL, see Cluthra category

KING'S ROSE, see Soft Paste category

KITCHEN utensils of all types, from eggbeaters to bowls, are collected
today. Handmade wooden and metal items, like ladles and apple peelers,
were made in the early nineteenth century. Mass–produced pieces, like iron
apple peelers and graniteware, were made in the nineteenth century. Other
kitchen wares are listed under manufacturers' names or under Advertising,
Iron, Tool, or Wooden.

Apple Corer, Bone, c.1820 .... 35.00
Apple Corer, Fries, Tubular Tin 30.00
Ashtray, Frypan, Griswold 25.00
Basket, Potato, Wireware, Marked 35.00
Beater, Pillow, Ornate 17.00
Beater, Rug, Wicker, Fancy, 1900s 35.00
Beater, Stango, Electric, Green Glass Base, 24 Oz. 22.50
Bin & Sifter, Cream City Flour, Stencils 175.00
Bin, Flour, Poplar, Primitive, 1/2 Size 30.00
Blender, Universal, Mixablend, Model B6405 .... 20.00
Blender, Waring, Model DL202 .... 20.00
Board, Noodle, Raised Backboard To Catch Dough, Table Hook, 30 In. 65.00
Bowl, Wooden, Red, Scrubbed White Interior, 19 1/2 x 6 1/4 In. 475.00
Box, Cracker, House, With Reed Handles, Ceramic 17.00
Box, Pantry, Wire Bail, Wood Handle, Painted Green, c.1830, 12 In. 187.00
Bread Box, Art Deco, White Enameled 50.00
Bread Maker, Universal, Bucket Type, 2 Handles, Directions On Lid 45.00
Bread Rack, Amish, Hanging 180.00
Broiler, Rotary, Wrought Iron, Shaped Handle, 11 3/4 x 19 1/2 In. 225.00
Bucket, Lard, Enterprise, 8 Lb. 27.00
Butter Mold, look under Mold, Butter in the Kitchen category
Butter Paddle, Burl Maple, Soft Finish, Bird Head Handle, 11 In. 245.00
Butter Paddle, Chip Carving, Compass Star In Circle, 12 In. 40.00
Butter Paddle, Lollipop Butter Print Handle, Floral Design, 11 In. 475.00
Butter Paddle, Primitive, Hook Handle, Thick Round Bowl, Patina 45.00
Butter Paddle, Wooden, Face Carved On Handle, 6 1/2 In. 450.00
Butter Paddle, Wooden, Small 18.00
Butter Stamp, 3–Leaf Design, 1–Piece Handle, Scrubbed, 5 3/4 In. 65.00
Butter Stamp, American Eagle 425.00
Butter Stamp, Berry & Leaves, Carved, 4 3/4 In. 185.00
Butter Stamp, Bluejay, Leaves, Knob Handle, Carved Maple, 1810, 3 In. 150.00
Butter Stamp, Cow, 1 Piece Handle, Round, 4 1/8 In. 155.00
Butter Stamp, Cow, Fence & Tree, 3 1/2 x 7 1/2 In. 150.00
Butter Stamp, Cow, Glass & Wood, 19th Century, 5 In. 55.00
Butter Stamp, Cow, Ribbed Border, 4 In. 80.00
Butter Stamp, Cow, Round Cased, Scrubbed, 4 3/4 In. 75.00
Butter Stamp, Cow, Round, With Plunger, Large 230.00
Butter Stamp, Cow, Wooden, 1 1/2 In. 195.00
Butter Stamp, Daisy & Leaf, 3–Rib Border, 3 1/2 In. 65.00
Butter Stamp, Double Pineapple, Rectangular, 2 3/4 x 4 7/8 In. 105.00
Butter Stamp, Double Sheaf Of Wheat, Rectangular Block 230.00
Butter Stamp, Eagle & Star, Round, 1 Piece Handle, 3 3/4 In. 225.00
Butter Stamp, Five Different Designs, Whittled Handle, 4 1/2 In. 50.00
Butter Stamp, Foliage, Rayed Border, Round, 3 1/2 In. 85.00
Butter Stamp, Heart, Chip Carved, Knob Handle, 2 In. 95.00

Butter Stamp, Indian Shawl, Concentric Circles, c.1860, 4 In.	65.00
Butter Stamp, Lollipop, Wood, Handle, Geometric Design, 4 x 3 In.	350.00
Butter Stamp, Pineapple, Knob Handle, 3 5/8 In.	70.00
Butter Stamp, Pineapple, Marked April 7, 1866	130.00
Butter Stamp, Pineapple, Semicircular, 3 1/4 x 7 In.	175.00
Butter Stamp, Pomegranate, Round, 4 3/4 In.	40.00
Butter Stamp, Primitive, Star Flower, Lollipop Handle, 4 In.	35.00
Butter Stamp, Shamrock, 1 Piece Handle, Round, 2 7/8 In.	95.00
Butter Stamp, Sheaf Of Wheat	77.50
Butter Stamp, Shock Of Wheat	150.00
Butter Stamp, Strawberries & Leaves, Patent 1866, 6 1/4 In.	137.50
Butter Stamp, Stylized Eagle, 1–Piece Handle, Round, 4 3/8 In.	100.00
Butter Stamp, Stylized Floral, 1–Piece Turned Handle, 6 1/4 In.	75.00
Butter Stamp, Stylized Floral, Oblong, 4 x 6 1/2 In.	125.00
Butter Stamp, Stylized Flowers, Pomegranate, Almond Shape, 7 In.	150.00
Butter Stamp, Swan On Water	150.00
Butter Stamp, Swan, 5 1/2 In.	225.00
Butter Stamp, Swan, Intricate Detail, Knob Handle, 1 Piece	250.00
Butter Stamp, Swan, Round, With Plunger, Large	110.00
Butter Stamp, Thistles, Leaves, Ring & Swirl Border, 5 In.	350.00
Butter Stamp, Tulip, Pennsylvania German, Whittled Handle	240.00
Butter Stamp, Tulip, Rectangular, 3 3/8 x 5 In.	250.00
Butter Stamp, Tulip, Turned Attached Handle, 5 In.	45.00
Butter Stamp, Wheat, Handle, 2 1/2 In.	70.00
Butter Stamp, Wheat, Round, With Plunger	110.00
Cake Breaker, Red Bakelite Handle	10.00
Cake Decorations, Space Party, 1967	15.00
Cake Server, Marbelized Green Pyroxaline Handle	8.00
Can Opener, Bull's Head, Tail, Cast Iron	125.00
Can Opener, King, Iron	1.25
Canister Set & Salt Box, Oil & Vinegar Cruet, Bisque, 12 Piece	145.00
Canister Set, China, Germany, 7 Piece	195.00
Carpet Stretcher, Victor, Wood, Metal Teeth, Pat. May 7, 1889	15.00
Carrier, Cake & Pie, Wire & Tin	26.00
Carrier, Cake & Pie, Wire Handle, Iron	28.00
Casserole Set, Cover, Striped Gourd Design, Glidden No. 167, 4 Piece	50.00
Casserole, Yellow, Glass Bake, Oval, 1 1/2 Qt.	6.00
Cheese Ladder, Mortise & Pin Construction, Maple, 31 x 11 In.	110.00
Cheese Slicer, Red Bakelite Handle	10.00
Cherry Pitter, Dated 1883, Enterprise, Cast Iron	22.00
Cherry Pitter, Enterprise No. 1	12.50
Cherry Pitter, Enterprise, Cast Iron, 1877	44.00
Cherry Pitter, Green Handle, No. 50	10.00
Chopper, Androck, Orange Bakelite Handle	12.00
Chopper, Food, Double Blade, Green Wooden Handle	3.00
Chopper, Meat & Food, Griswold, No. 3, Box	90.00
Chopper, U Shape, Hickory Bent Handle, Hand Forged, c.1840, 6 In.	45.00
Churn, Ball Jar, 1/2 Gal.	90.00
Churn, Crank Handle, Horizontal, Spain, Pat. 1872, Square Top	150.00
Churn, Cream, Table Model, Tin, 2 Handles, 1840, 4 1/2 x 7 x 8 In.	89.00
Churn, Dazey, 2 Gal.	75.00
Churn, Dazey, Embossed, 1 Qt.	125.00
Churn, Dazey, No. 10, Square, Logo, 1 Qt.	1195.00
Churn, Floor Standing, Tin Dasher, Civil War Era, 42 In.	225.00
Churn, New Blanchard Churn, Patent 1878	205.00
Churn, Stoneware, Blue Flower	60.00
Cleaver, Meat	13.00
Clothes Sprinkler, Chinese Boy, Cleminson	25.00
Clothes Sprinkler, Chinese Boy, Sparkle Plenty	40.00
Coffee Grinders are listed in their own section	
Coffee Mill, Kitchen Aid, 1936	55.00
Coffee Percolator, Art Deco, Manning Bowman	45.00
Coffee Urn, Handle, Electric, 1924	45.00

Coffeepot, Punched, Potted Tulip Design, Hinged Lid, Tin, 11 In. 1540.00
Colander, Wooden 600.00
Cooker, Potato, Rocket Shape, Cast Aluminum 275.00
Cookie Board, Almond Shaped Flower & Fruit, Walnut, 6 x 16 In. 260.00
Cookie Board, Hen On Nest, 3 1/4 x 3 3/4 In. 85.00
Cookie Board, Poplar, Round, 18 1/4 In. 125.00
Cookie Board, Rooster 1 Side, Folk Art Couple Other, Beech, 11 In. 375.00
Cookie Board, Simple Carvings, 6 Sections, 5 1/4 x 8 3/4 In. 75.00
Cookie Board, Springerle, Birds, Animals, 12 Prints, 5 x 8 In. 170.00
Cookie Board, Springerle, Maple, Animals, Birds, 8 Blocks 90.00
Cookie Board, Springerle, Maple, Animals, Birds, 9 Blocks 50.00
Cookie Cutter, Angel, Tin, 8 In. 38.00
Cookie Cutter, Brownie Girl Scout, 1960s 8.00
Cookie Cutter, Chick, Strap Handle, Tin 18.00
Cookie Cutter, Clover, Green Wooden Handle 2.00
Cookie Cutter, Dove, Looking Over Wing, Tin, 1830, 4 1/2 In. 75.00
Cookie Cutter, Father Christmas, Tin, 10 In. 38.00
Cookie Cutter, Fish, Tin, Curved Handle, 5 1/2 In. 35.00
Cookie Cutter, Flag, Red Wooden Handle 3.00
Cookie Cutter, Fleur–De–Lis 10.00
Cookie Cutter, Hand Shape, Heart Center, 3 In. 630.00
Cookie Cutter, Heart, Green Wooden Handle 2.00
Cookie Cutter, Horse, Strap Handle, Tin 22.00
Cookie Cutter, Man Wearing Tails, Tin 425.00
Cookie Cutter, Man With Hat, Tin, Curved Handle, 5 1/2 In. 35.00
Cookie Cutter, Man With Top Hat, Large 1300.00
Cookie Cutter, Rabbit, Davis Baking Powder, Tin 15.00
Cookie Cutter, Santa Claus, Green Wooden Handle 4.50
Cookie Cutter, Santa Claus, Tin, 8 3/4 In. 87.50
Cookie Cutter, Star, Red Wooden Handle 2.00
Cookie Cutter, Stylized Man, Tin, 6 x 13 1/2 In. 450.00
Cookie Cutter, Tin, Scotty Dog, Strap Handle, Dark Patina, 3 x 4 In. 35.00
Cookie Cutter, Turkey, Tin, 4 7/8 In. 235.00
Cookie Cutter, Woman, Big Boobs, Strap Handle, Germany, Tin, 3 x 6 In 87.00
Cookie Print, Bird On Branch, Cast Iron, Oval, 5 In. 75.00
Cookie Roller, Acorns, Vintage, Foliage, Walnut, 12 1/2 In. 500.00
Corn Sheller, Crank Handle, Cob Holder, 1869, 13 x 9 1/2 In. 395.00
Cup, Measuring, Jennyware, Pink, 32 Oz. 120.00
Cutter, Boiled Egg, Scissor Shape, Metal, France, 1850, 3 x 4 In. 5.00
Cutter, Cabbage, Dovetailed Box, Sliding, 2 Blades, 25 1/2 In. 45.00
Cutter, Cabbage, Woolridge & McParlin, Pat. Sept. 6, 1887 .... 45.00
Cutter, Doughnut, Cloverleaf, Iron 75.00
Cutter, Doughnut, Rumford Biscuit 20.00
Cutter, Egg, Movable, Chrome, 1896 .... 6.00
Cutter, Vegetable, Wooden Pusher, Enterprise, No. 49 .... 115.00
Deep Fryer, Griswold 45.00
Dough Board, Wood, 17 x 21 In. 15.00
Dough Scraper, Half–Round Steel Blade, Copper Handle, 4 In. 85.00
Dough Scraper, Wooden 45.00
Dough Tray, 1840 .... 575.00
Dryer, Clothes, Pegged, Large 50.00
Dutch Oven, Cover, Tilt Top, No. 8 .... 110.00
Dutch Oven, Griswold, No. 8, Tite–Top, Lid & Trivet 75.00
Dutch Oven, Griswold, No. 9 .... 55.00
Dutch Oven, Griswold, No. 10 .... 110.00
Dutch Oven, Griswold, With Trivet, Dated 1920, 9 In. 95.00
Dutch Oven, Wagner Ware, No. 9 .... 40.00
Egg Cooker, Fiesta Green, Hankscraft 25.00
Egg Poacher, Copper, Iron Handle, 15 In. 75.00
Egg Poacher, Griswold 35.00
Egg Separator, Rumford .... 12.50 To 30.00
Egg Timer, Vegetable Body, Pumpkin Head 75.00
Eggbeater, A & J, Iron, Red & White Wooden Tee Handle 3.00

Eggbeater, A & J, Spiral Wire Handle, Wood Knob, 1923	12.00
Eggbeater, Archimedian Principle, Wooden Handle	3.50
Eggbeater, Dover, 1891	32.50
Eggbeater, Dover, Cast Iron	28.00
Eggbeater, Dover, Wood Knob, Cast Iron & Tin, 1904	18.00
Eggbeater, Ladd, Spiral Wire Handle, Wood Knob, 1921	14.00
Eggbeater, Taplin, 1908	18.00
Eggbeater, Taplin, Green Wooden Bulb Shaped Handle	3.50
Eggbeater, White, Red Trim	10.00
Flue Cover, Bagpiper Scene	55.00
Flue Cover, Little Red Riding Hood, 7 3/4 In.	45.00
Flue Cover, Man & Wife Praying At End Of Day	35.00
Flue Cover, Man & Woman Embracing	25.00
Flue Cover, Man & Woman In Boat	55.00
Flue Cover, Winter Scene, Hand Painted, 8 1/2 In.	25.00
Flue Cover, Woodman Of World, 4 Colors, Celluloid	65.00
Fly Cover, Screen, Oval	45.00
Fork, Cooking, Rumford, 3 Tines	12.00
Fork, Tooled Handle, Iron, 10 3/8 In.	50.00
Glove Holder, Victorian, Ornate	75.00
Grater, Half Round, Steel Frame, Steel Handle, Brass, 15 In.	230.00
Grater, Hand Punched, Hand Held, 1878	35.00
Grater, Horseradish, Tin, Arched Ends, Drawer, c.1850, 14 In.	295.00
Grater, Mounted On Wooden Frame, Drawer, 14 x 7 In.	295.00
Grater, Nutmeg, Egg Shape, Lift–Off Top, c.1800, 1 1/2 x 1 1/4 In.	325.00
Grater, Nutmeg, Sliding Spring–Loaded Hopper, Tin, 5 1/4 In.	55.00
Griddle, Cast Iron, 3 Short Legs, 11 In.	45.00
Griddle, Hanging, Iron, Early 18th Century	485.00
Griddle, Rotary, Shaped Handle, Wrought Iron, 20 3/4 In.	75.00
Grill, Tote, Griswold, Box	85.00
Grinder, Food, Clamp–On, Wood Pusher, Graniteware, Marked HS 830	45.00
Grinder, Food, Keen Kutter, No. 10	22.00
Grinder, Griswold, No. 11	40.00
Grinder, Herb, Iron & Wood, 19th Century	412.50
Grinder, Meat, Keystone, No. 40, 4 Blades	25.00
Grinder, Mincer, Several Heads, Dated 1902	25.00
Grinder, Poppy Seed, Spun Aluminum Hopper, Beige	37.50
Hamper, Picnic, Wicker, Leather, Asprey Co., Enameled Dishes	150.00
Holder, Ice Cream Cone, Glass	425.00
Holder, Ice Cream Cones	390.00
Huller, Strawberry, Nip–It, Tin, 1906	2.50
Ice Chipper, Gilchrist	12.00
Ice Chipper, Gilchrist, No. 50	8.00
Ice Cream Freezer, White Mountain Jr., Cast Iron, 1920s, 6 In.	425.00
Ice Cream Freezer, Wild Mountain, 1928, 1 Qt.	150.00
Ice Pick, Bakelite Handle	52.50
Icebox, Beveled Mirror, Carved Heads, Claw Feet, Oak	4850.00
Icebox, Victorian, Ornate, Oak	1200.00
Iron, Air Blower, Gas	145.00
Iron, Coleman, Gasoline, Instructions, Box	85.00
Iron, Electric, Barby Jo, Blue Bakelite Handle, 1930s	65.00
Iron, Fluting, Geneva, Cast Iron	65.00 To 75.00
Iron, Fluting, Geneva, Dated 1866	65.00
Iron, Fluting, Penn, Brass Rollers, Iron, Attach To Table, 1875	85.00
Iron, Fluting, The Best, Cast Iron, C. W. Whitefield, 5 1/2 In.	85.00
Iron, Gas, Blue Porcelain	10.00
Iron, Gas, Coleman, Blue Graniteware	48.00
Iron, Gasoline, Chrome, 1936	37.50
Iron, Goffering, Slug	95.00
Iron, Hotpoint, Dated July 1933, NRA Marked Box	22.00
Iron, Silex, Mercedes Benz Form	200.00
Iron, Sunbeam Model A–9	25.00
Iron, Swan Shaped, Trivet, Iron, 2 3/4 In.	65.00

Iron, Travel, Universal Electric, Trivet & Curling Iron 65.00
Iron, Travel, Wiley & Russel Mfg., Greenfield, Mass. 55.00
Iron, Wave Fluter, Geneva, Brass 425.00
Jar Opener, & Bottle Opener, Edlund, Wooden Handle 1.50
Juice Extractor, Enterprise, Hand Crank, Cast Iron 27.00
Juice–O–Mat, Rival, Aluminum 22.00
Juicer, Dazey Churn Mfg. Co., Metal, Crank Wooden Handle 40.00
Juicer, Rival Juice–O–Matic, Hand Operated 18.00
Kettle, Tripod, Cast Iron, Pocasset 137.50
Knife, Chopping, A & J, 4 Blades, Wooden Handle 2.35
Knife, Grapefruit, Geneva, Wooden Handle .... .75
Knife, Keen Kutter, Wooden Box 35.00
Lazy Susan, Insert Of 2 Greens, Wood Base, Sylvan, Pasadena, 1950s 12.00
Lemon Squeezer, Cast Iron, Insert, Ideal 42.00
Lifter, Fruit Jar, Ekco, Scissors Style, Iron 1.25
Malt Mixer, Green Porcelain, Triple Head 175.00
Masher & Pestle, Mortar, Maple Tiger, Freestanding, 2 Ended, 10 In. 250.00
Masher, Potato, Wooden, Pestle End, Shaped & Turned Handle, 11 In. 12.00
Match Safes can be found in their own section
Maul, Burl, Primitive 4.00
Measure, Coffee, Adjustable, Kap Cohen, Clothier, Tin, 3 In. 45.00
Measure, Seville, 3 Spouts, Yellow 195.00
Meat Tenderizer, All Wood 4.00
Memo Clip, Duck Head Shape, Iron, Original Paint, Glass Eyes, 5 In. 85.00
Milk Shake Machine, Arnold, 1920s 75.00
Milk Shake Machine, Hamilton Beach, 3–Way 175.00
Milk Shake Machine, Hamilton Beach, Green 90.00
Milk Shake Machine, Hamilton Beach, Marble Base 115.00
Mixer, Mayonnaise, Universal, Cast Iron, Glass, Wooden Crank Handle 445.00
Mixer, Polar Cub, Electric, Box 40.00
Mixette, Hamilton Beach 50.00
Molds may also be found in the Pewter and Tinware categories
Mold, Bread, Lamb, Large 160.00
Mold, Butter, 8 Squares, Acorn & Stylized Flowers, 5 1/2 x 11 In. 110.00
Mold, Butter, Acorns, Leaves, 2 Lb. 110.00
Mold, Butter, Cow, Glass, Wooden Plunger 35.00
Mold, Butter, Double Shamrocks, Plunger Type 210.00
Mold, Butter, Geometric Design, Cherry, 4 1/2 x 6 7/8 In. 105.00
Mold, Butter, Lollipop Print, Wooden, 3 In. 235.00
Mold, Butter, Maple, Round, Acorn & Leaves, Knob Handle, c.1820 ...... 220.00
Mold, Butter, Pineapple, 1 Lb. 85.00
Mold, Butter, Strawberry, 19th Century 62.50
Mold, Butter, Swan, Wooden, 1 Lb. 195.00
Mold, Cake, Lamb, Griswold .... 100.00 To 125.00
Mold, Cake, Rabbit, Griswold .... 200.00 To 245.00
Mold, Cake, Rabbit, Small 75.00
Mold, Cake, Santa Claus, Griswold 575.00
Mold, Cake, Santa Claus, Griswold, Nickel Plated 450.00
Mold, Cake, Turk's Head, Blue 50.00
Mold, Candle, see Tinware section
Mold, Candy, Cross .... 35.00 To 45.00
Mold, Candy, Fish, Half Of 1 Part Mold, 11 3/4 In. 195.00
Mold, Candy, Pig, Carved Wood, 1/2 Half Of 2–Part Mold, 4 x 7 In. 125.00
Mold, Candy, Rabbit 35.00
Mold, Candy, Rabbits 45.00
Mold, Cheese, Tin, 5 1/2 In. 225.00
Mold, Chocolate, Banana, 7 In. 20.00
Mold, Chocolate, Beetle, 5 In. 22.00
Mold, Chocolate, Boy On Bicycle, Tin, 8 3/4 In. 375.00
Mold, Chocolate, Cigar, 7 1/2 In. 10.00
Mold, Chocolate, Cigar, To Make 11 Pieces, 9 In. 25.00
Mold, Chocolate, Cupid, Lead 65.00
Mold, Chocolate, Hen, Large 250.00

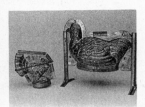

Kitchen, Mold, Food, Turkey,
4 1/2 x 5 1/2 In.

Kitchen, Mold, Food, Chicken,
9 1/2 x 9 1/2 In.

Kitchen, Potato Masher,
Wooden Handle

Kitchen, Toaster,
Marshmallow, Angelus-
Campfire Bar-B-Q, 3 In.

Mold, Chocolate, Rabbit, Basket On Back, 12 In.	72.00
Mold, Chocolate, Rooster, Tin, Large	2300.00
Mold, Chocolate, Santa Claus & Child, Tin, Germany, 7 In.	130.00
Mold, Chocolate, Santa Claus, 6 In.	115.00
Mold, Chocolate, Skeleton, Tin, 5 1/2 In.	60.00
Mold, Chocolate, Tea Cup, 4 In.	15.00
Mold, Cookie, Bird, Each Side, Pine, 4 1/2 x 6 1/4 In.	225.00
Mold, Cookie, Heart, Floral Design, Primitive, 7 In.	275.00
Mold, Cookie, Rooster, Tin, 5 1/2 x 6 1/2 In.	75.00
Mold, Easter Egg, Embossed Rabbit, Anton Reiche, 2 Piece, 3 In.	125.00
Mold, Fish, Hanging Ring, In, 9 1/2 In.	45.00
Mold, Fish, Unfinished Casting, Rough Edge, Iron, 13 1/2 In.	30.00
Mold, Food, Chicken, 9 1/2 x 9 1/2 In. ....Illus	65.00
Mold, Food, Lamb, Cast Iron	110.00
Mold, Food, Turkey, 4 1/2 x 5 1/2 In. ....Illus	40.00
Mold, Ice Cream, see Pewter section	
Mold, Jelly, Rabbit, 8 In.	27.50
Mold, Jelly, Tin, 19th Century, 4 x 5 x 5 In.	75.00
Mold, Lamb Cake, Griswold	95.00
Mold, Lollipop, 3 Hens, 2 x 5 In.	65.00
Mold, Muffin, Griswold, Iron, Miniature	65.00
Mold, Patty, Griswold, Iron, Instructions, Box	18.00
Mold, Patty, Griswold, No. 1, Iron, Box	50.00
Mold, Pudding, Ear Of Corn, Double, Ironstone	47.50
Mold, Pudding, Kreamer, No. 1, Tin	20.00
Mold, Rabbit, Griswold, Iron ....285.00 To 325.00	
Mold, Sugar, Hightop Boot, Wooden, 3 In.	65.00
Noggin, Maple, 1800, 5 1/2 In., 1 Piece	240.00
Oven, Dutch, Iron Spit, Tin, 19 In.	200.00
Oven, Hand Wrought Iron, Sits In Hot Ashes	355.00
Oven, Stove Top, 3 Panel Glass Door, Pressed Design Sides, Tin, 1920	45.00
Oven, Tin, Round Front Door, Flat Back	485.00
Paddle, Lard, Hand Carved Wood, Primitive	6.45
Paddle, Preserving, Wooden, 16 In.	27.00
Pan, Bread, Hinged 4 Loaves	75.00
Pan, Bundt, Griswold	995.00
Pan, Corn Stick, Crispy Corn, Griswold No. 273, Iron	69.00
Pan, Corn Stick, Griswold, No. 173, Iron	30.00
Pan, Griswold, No. 32, Cast Iron, 7 Cups	45.00
Pan, Muffin, Cast Iron, 6 1/4 In.	80.00
Pan, Popover, Griswold No. 10, 11 Cups ....38.00 To 45.00	
Pan, Potato, Poplar, Lathe Type, Last Of 18th Century	245.00
Pan, Swansdown Angel Food, Tin, Large	7.50
Pan, Swansdown, Angel Food, Tin, Large	9.00
Pastry Blender, Blue Wooden Handle	3.00
Peel, Ram's Horn Handle, Iron, 37 1/2 In.	90.00
Peel, Ram's Horn Handle, Iron, 40 1/4 In.	75.00

Peeler, Apple, Cast Iron, Little Star 75.00
Peeler, Apple, Goodell Co., Cast Iron, Patent 1898 .... 55.00
Peeler, Apple, Goodell, Clamp–On, Patent 1898 .... 65.00
Peeler, Apple, Little Star 75.00
Peeler, Apple, Reading Hardware Co. 85.00
Peeler, Apple, Reading, Penna., 1878 .... 50.00
Peeler, Apple, White Mountain, Iron 30.00
Pie Bird, Black Man Playing Banjo 126.00
Pie Bird, Blackbird .... 15.00 To 16.00
Pie Bird, Chef, Black 110.00
Pie Bird, Chef, Black, Holding Rolling Pin 55.00
Pie Bird, Chef, Yellow Clothes 50.00
Pie Bird, Duck 12.00
Pie Bird, Elephant, White, Brown 60.00
Pie Bird, Humpty Dumpty, England 52.00
Pie Bird, Mammy, Pink, White & Blue Clothes 68.00
Pie Crimper, Brass 32.00
Pie Crimper, Brass, Germany 45.00
Pie Crimper, Brass, Late 19th Century 18.50
Pie Crimper, Carved Bone, Cross Hatching, 6 1/4 In. 120.00
Pie Crimper, Cast Aluminum 22.00
Pie Crimper, Cast Iron 40.00
Pie Funnel, Pilgrim Girl, Pottery 12.00
Pitcher & Underplate, Hand Painted China, Brown Flowers, 3 Piece 89.00
Pleater, Tin, Victorian, Instructions, Patent Date, 2 Piece 25.00
Popcorn Machine, Sunbeam 14.00
Pot Scraper, Gooch's Flour 85.00
Pot Scraper, Mt. Penn 50.00
Pot Scraper, Sharples 125.00
Pot Scrubber, Wire–Loop, Early 1900s 24.00
Pot, Rendering, Cradle, Cast Iron, 55 Gal. 275.00
Potato Masher, All Wood 4.00
Potato Masher, Wooden Handle ....*Illus*   5.00 .
Press, Food, Hinged Cast Iron Handle, Silver & Co., 3 x 10 1/2 In. 20.00
Press, Fruit & Lard, Griswold, No. 2, 4 Qt. 85.00
Press, Meat Juice, H. F. Osborne, Patent 1884 .... 145.00
Rack, Blue–J Brooms, Merkle Broom Co., Paris, Illinois 130.00
Rack, Clothes Drying, Folding, 10 x 8 x 11 1/2 In. 85.00
Rack, Lid, Wagnerware 125.00
Rack, Pie, Green Handle, For Getting Pies Out Of Oven 35.00
Rack, Pie, Wall, Folding, Holds 6 Piece, Cast Iron, 1880 .... 225.00
Rack, Utensil, Scalloped Edge, 9 Iron Hooks, 9 1/2 x 42 1/2 In. 250.00
Rack, Utensil, Scrolled, 7 Hooks, Wrought Iron, 14 x 19 1/4 In. 225.00
Raisin Seeder, Enterprise 45.00
Raisin Seeder, Everett, Wooden Frame, Mushroom Handle, Wire Grid 44.00
Reamers are listed in their own section
Roaster, Adjustable Bar, 6 Spikes, Iron, 12 1/2 x 13 In. 195.00
Roaster, Apple, Twisted Handle, Wrought Iron, 34 1/4 In. 1650.00
Roaster, Chestnut, Tin, Extra Wooden Handle 135.00
Roaster, Fowl, 4 Hooks, Revolving Arm, Iron, 11 3/4 In. 150.00
Roaster, Griswold No. 7, With Trivet, Oval 450.00
Roller, Springerle, Pineapples, Crimped Borders, Cherry 85.00
Roller–Cutter, Noodle, Pat. 3/2/20 .... 115.00
Rolling Pin, Baker's, Wooden 24.00
Rolling Pin, Bird's–Eye Maple, c.1810, 16 In. 75.00
Rolling Pin, Blown Glass, Opalescent, 13 3/4 In. 75.00
Rolling Pin, Blue & White Porcelain, A. H. Annaburg 80.00
Rolling Pin, Brass 85.00
Rolling Pin, Cookie Pattern, c.1900, 8 In. 137.00
Rolling Pin, Crystal, Cork End 9.50
Rolling Pin, Curly Maple 45.00
Rolling Pin, Glass, 12 In. 7.00
Rolling Pin, Glass, Glass Marbles, Tin Screw Cap, 1930s, 16 In. 165.00

Rolling Pin, Kelvinator, Porcelain ....85.00 To 100.00
Rolling Pin, Milk Glass, Aluminum Screw–On Handles 85.00
Rolling Pin, Milk Glass, Wooden Handles, Dated 1921 .... 65.00
Rolling Pin, Moline, Illinois, Advertising 345.00
Rolling Pin, Mortised Handle, Beech & Cherry, 16 In. 340.00
Rolling Pin, Noodle 32.00
Rolling Pin, Oak, 17 In., 1 Piece 35.00
Rolling Pin, Olive Green, White Flecks, Blown Glass, 14 1/2 In. 140.00
Rolling Pin, Remember Me, Floral Design, Blown Glass 395.00
Rolling Pin, Stoneware, Blue & White 280.00
Rolling Pin, Tiger Maple 45.00
Rolling Pin, Tin Good Housekeeping Cap, Cobalt Blue Glass 225.00
Rolling Pin, Tin, Oak Handles 345.00
Rolling Pin, Wizard, Milk Glass 45.00
Rolling Pin, Wooden, From 1 Piece 20.00
Rug Beater, Batwin, Pennsylvania, Dated 1927 .... 22.00
Sadiron, Child's, Sensible, No. 6, Detachable Handle 85.00
Sadiron, Colebrookdale Iron Co., Wood Handle 15.00
Salt & Pepper shakers are listed in their own category
Saucepan, Brass Lid, Handle, 4 In. 65.00
Sausage Stuffer, Sandblasted & Painted 85.00
Scoop, Ice Cream Bar 170.00
Scoop, Ice Cream Cone, Size 20, F. S. 170.00
Scoop, Ice Cream Sandwich, Hole In Handle, 12 In. 110.00
Scoop, Ice Cream, A & J, Iron, Wooden Handle, 1/4 Cup 2.00
Scoop, Ice Cream, Arnold, No. 50, 1927 .... 45.00
Scoop, Ice Cream, Banana Split, United Banana Co. 750.00
Scoop, Ice Cream, Clipper, No. 5, Cone Shape 225.00
Scoop, Ice Cream, Clipper, Size 12 Scoop 80.00
Scoop, Ice Cream, Cold Dog, Cylinder ....675.00 To 750.00
Scoop, Ice Cream, Cone Shape, Tin, Turn Key Release Top, Primitive 25.00
Scoop, Ice Cream, Conical, Wood Handle 75.00
Scoop, Ice Cream, Dover Springless, Size 12 .... 95.00
Scoop, Ice Cream, Dover Springless, Size 20 Scoop 90.00
Scoop, Ice Cream, Dover, Brass 68.50
Scoop, Ice Cream, Erie Specialty, B–12 .... 95.00
Scoop, Ice Cream, Erie, C–13, Size 8 .... 250.00
Scoop, Ice Cream, Geer Cone, 1906 .... 235.00
Scoop, Ice Cream, Gem, Trojan 40.00
Scoop, Ice Cream, Gilchrist, No. 3 .... 35.00
Scoop, Ice Cream, Gilchrist, No. 15 .... 68.00
Scoop, Ice Cream, Gilchrist, No. 30 .... 65.00
Scoop, Ice Cream, Gilchrist, No. 31, 11 In. 90.00
Scoop, Ice Cream, Gilchrist, No. 33, Brass 110.00
Scoop, Ice Cream, Gilchrist, No. 41 .... 55.00
Scoop, Ice Cream, Gilchrist, Squeeze Handle, Small Bowl 45.00
Scoop, Ice Cream, Hamilton Beach, No. 30 .... 15.00
Scoop, Ice Cream, Hamilton Beach, No. 67 .... 17.00
Scoop, Ice Cream, Icypi, Wood Handle ....150.00 To 185.00
Scoop, Ice Cream, Indestructo Benedict, No. 12 .... 28.00
Scoop, Ice Cream, Indestructo No. 3, Size 16 Scoop 80.00
Scoop, Ice Cream, Indestructo, No. 4 .... 32.00
Scoop, Ice Cream, Jiffy Dispenser, Sandwich, Adjusts To 3 Sizes 225.00
Scoop, Ice Cream, Kingery, Size 5 .... 150.00
Scoop, Ice Cream, Kingery, Squeeze Handle, 1894 .... 185.00
Scoop, Ice Cream, McLauren Cone Co., D–24 .... 150.00
Scoop, Ice Cream, Nevco 12.00
Scoop, Ice Cream, New Gem 70.00
Scoop, Ice Cream, PC Server 200.00
Scoop, Ice Cream, Penny Scoop, Benedict 200.00
Scoop, Ice Cream, Red Bakelite, Peerless 12.00
Scoop, Ice Cream, Sandwich, Marked Polar–Pak 475.00
Scoop, Shovel Shape, Speckled Carved Bird's–Eye Maple, 1880s 75.00

A 25-Year Analysis of the Antiques Marketplace

Y our collector wish is granted, " said the genie. " You may walk into a 1967 antiques shop and buy one item. If you pick the one that has gone up the most in price during the past 25 years, I will give you another wish." Prices from Kovels' first price book 25 years ago read: "blue and white graniteware coffeepot, $4.00; footstool, marked Shaker, $50; pressed glass Actress goblet, $18; Royal Bayreuth Devil and Card pitcher, green mark, $17.50; silver-plated napkin ring, boy with bat, Greenaway type, $30; Rookwood vase signed Valentien, $40; Charlie McCarthy, Mortimer Snerd windup toy car, $12."

What would you have purchased to put away as an investment to be sold in 1993? What has gone up in value by the greatest percentage? A quick look at prices in this 1993 book shows that the toy would have been the best buy. The graniteware coffeepot is now worth $95; the Shaker footstool, $355; the Actress glass goblet, $60 to $80; the Royal Bayreuth pitcher, $595 to $985; the silver-plated napkin ring, $350; the Rookwood vase, $3,000; and the Charlie McCarthy car, $2,900!

Times, prices, and price books have changed since 1967. The first Kovels' book listed no Fiesta, Depression glass, Disneyana, Black collectibles, Arts and Crafts, Hummel, McCoy, perfume bottles, weather vanes, or scientific instruments. Not even a single wristwatch was included. The 1993 book does not include Bilston enamels, bone china, buttermilk glass, canary glass, girandoles, pigeon blood, sun-colored glass, Swansea pottery, or taffeta glass—all categories in the 1967 book. Today these categories have changed names or are ignored by collectors. Toys were included in a short list with minimal description. There were three pages of Beam bottles, nine pages of milk glass, four pages of pewter, and 36 pages of pressed glass. These categories are shorter today because there is less interest.

Glass from the 1950s is becoming highly popular among collectors. These pieces were made by Kosta of Sweden, Barovier and Toso of Italy, and Orrefors of Sweden (left to right).

Heisey, cut glass, furniture, dolls, Galle, Flow Blue, Rookwood, Tiffany, and tools are about the same length. There were also some embarrassing errors caused by the unfamiliar problems of computer alphabetizing. In recent years we have added sections about motorcycles, contemporary glass, Erphila, Kay Finch, Sascha Brastoff, Howard Pierce, sports collectibles, head vases, Autumn Leaf, architectural objects, and animation art. It's amazing to think that these items would not have been found in the average 1967 antiques shop.

Why have some antiques and collectibles gone up in value faster than the inflated value of the dollar? Why have others lost value over the past 25 years? There are many theories. One is that the population is younger. Those who grew up after World War II have very different memories than those who are older. Television, movies, and even computers have changed our perceptions. A 1967 collector usually bought antiques that were made before 1825. Art historians claimed that before 1825, pieces were handmade; but after 1825, the Industrial Revolution and machine technology lowered the quality and artistic worth of the objects. Collecting everyday items such as advertising or old toys that were less than 100 years old was a hobby for the eccentric, impecunious collector. Many experts thought the

Self-taught artist Silvio Zoratti made this folk-art rabbit in the 1950s. 1990s price: $650.

collections related to industry, assembled by Henry Ford in his museum, were less worthy than the decorative art collections formed by Henry Du Pont or John D. Rockefeller. To many people, antique furniture was considered "used" and of less value than the new. Only inherited pieces were proudly displayed. Collecting was tolerated, not venerated as it is today.

This 19th-century transfer-decorated, hand-painted creamware Liverpool pitcher sold for $39,000.

The psychology of collecting has gradually changed over the past 25 years. Today old things are purchased not only because of their beauty, craftsmanship, and historic interest, but also for nostalgic reasons. Formal antiques, such as 18th-century American pewter, silver, 18th-century English porcelains, and Argand lamps, are not desired by most young collectors. They prefer Danish silver from the 1930s, stoneware jugs from the turn of the century, or chrome lamps by '50s designers. Oriental ceramics of the 19th and 20th centuries, like Satsuma and Imari wares, are collected today but were almost shunned in the 1960s. Nostalgia pieces such as

Mickey Mouse toys, Autumn Leaf dishes, and Depression glass bring back memories of grandmother's house. An "antique" has become anything older than the buyer, and decorative pieces from the 20th century are more and more popular.

Part of the reason collecting has changed is the high price and limited supply of fine 18th-century pieces. Many decorating magazines now feature rooms filled with shelves of affordable tools, bottles, blue and white china of varying ages, or advertising signs and tins. The savvy collector now buys what appeals and not what is proper. Living rooms are decorated with many objects that were originally meant for the kitchen or the store. The aged look of peeling paint, worn spots on chair legs, or even the primitive charm of a table made from tree branches was shunned in the '60s but is sought-after in the '90s. "American country" has become a style so popular that reproductions are now sold in furniture stores.

There are other apparent influences. "Women's work" has begun to be appreciated as a form of art. Quilts, coverlets, samplers, theorem pictures, even lace and hair jewelry have all been reexamined and are now collected. "Folk Art" has become an all-encompassing term that refers to works by untutored craftsmen of any era, up to and including the present time. All of it is collected. Industrial and company histories, especially brand-name products, entice some collectors. Others who might have bought oil paintings from an earlier time

These American dinnerware pieces are an Autumn Leaf pitcher by Hall (right), and a silhouette teapot by Crooksville China Company (left).

now seek newer types of pictures. Photographs, animation cels, and original art for book and magazine illustrations are going up in price. The interest in sports is pushing a demand for all types of sports collectibles, from baseball cards to fishing reels. Celebrity association—links with stars of TV, movies, and music—has become an economic factor in pricing collectibles.

It is difficult, if not impossible, to predict the future. What should we buy today that will be of much greater value in 2018? California pottery? Glass artist sculptures? Italian Memphis furniture? Computer toys? Artist-signed enameled copper dishes from the '40s? Bottle-cap figures? Will Elvis or the Beatles still be important enough to encourage new collectors to buy the old memorabilia? Should we sell our Mission benches or Windsor chairs now because the home of tomorrow will be furnished with overstuffed pieces? Or will real, solid wooden furniture be in the antiques shops at premium prices because, for ecological reasons, trees are rarely cut? Who would have predicted that in 1993 it would be considered poor taste and possibly illegal to buy an elegant new ivory carving?

	1967	1968	1969	1970	1971	1972	1973	1974	1975	1976	1977
1967	0.0304	1.03										
1968	0.0472	1.08	1.05									
1969	0.0611	1.14	1.10	1.06								
1970	0.0549	1.21	1.16	1.13	1.05							
1971	0.0336	1.25	1.23	1.19	1.11	1.03						
1972	0.0341	1.29	1.27	1.23	1.15	1.07	1.03					
1973	0.0880	1.40	1.31	1.27	1.19	1.10	1.07	1.09				
1974	0.1220	1.58	1.43	1.38	1.29	1.20	1.16	1.18	1.12			
1975	0.0701	1.69	1.60	1.55	1.45	1.35	1.31	1.33	1.26	1.07		
1976	0.0481	1.77	1.71	1.66	1.55	1.44	1.40	1.42	1.35	1.15	1.05	
1977	0.0677	1.89	1.80	1.74	1.63	1.51	1.46	1.49	1.41	1.20	1.10	1.07
1978	0.0903	2.06	1.92	1.86	1.74	1.61	1.56	1.59	1.51	1.28	1.17	1.14
1979	0.1331	2.33	2.09	2.02	1.90	1.76	1.70	1.73	1.64	1.40	1.28	1.24
1980	0.1240	2.62	2.37	2.29	2.15	2.00	1.93	1.96	1.86	1.58	1.45	1.41
1981	0.0894	2.85	2.66	2.58	2.41	2.24	2.17	2.21	2.09	1.78	1.63	1.58
1982	0.0387	2.97	2.90	2.81	2.63	2.44	2.36	2.41	2.28	1.94	1.77	1.72
1983	0.0380	3.08	3.01	2.92	2.73	2.54	2.46	2.50	2.37	2.01	1.84	1.79
1984	0.0395	3.20	3.13	3.03	2.84	2.63	2.55	2.59	2.46	2.09	1.91	1.86
1985	0.0377	3.32	3.25	3.15	2.95	2.74	2.65	2.70	2.56	2.17	1.99	1.93
1986	0.0113	3.36	3.37	3.27	3.06	2.84	2.75	2.80	2.65	2.25	2.06	2.01
1987	0.0441	3.51	3.41	3.30	3.09	2.87	2.78	2.83	2.68	2.28	2.09	2.03
1988	0.0442	3.66	3.56	3.45	3.23	3.00	2.90	2.95	2.80	2.38	2.18	2.12
1989	0.0465	3.83	3.72	3.60	3.37	3.13	3.03	3.09	2.92	2.49	2.28	2.21
1990	0.0611	4.07	3.89	3.77	3.53	3.28	3.17	3.23	3.06	2.60	2.38	2.31
1991	0.0306	4.19	4.13	4.00	3.75	3.48	3.37	3.43	3.25	2.76	2.53	2.46

INFLATION VALUE CHART

I bought a plate for $10 and sold it for $20, so I doubled my money." That may or may not be true. If you bought it in 1967 for $10, kept it for 25 years, and sold it for $20 in 1992, you lost money. Inflation has reduced the buying power of 1967 dollars. One dollar in January 1967 bought what $4.19 buys today. To be even, you would have to sell the plate for $41.90. This does not include the interest you would have gained if the $10 had been placed in a bank account or in a Treasury bill. We are also ignoring the cost of insuring and preserving the plate.

The chart above is based on the Consumer Price Index. You can determine the actual value of your antiques in today's dollars by looking up the year of purchase and multiplying the original price by the inflation factor for the year it was sold. For example: You bought a Shawnee pottery pig-shaped cookie jar with a bank top in 1975 for $10.00, the price listed in *Kovels' Antiques & Collectibles Price List*. If you sold it in 1986, you should have charged $2.25 (inflation rate) times $10 (cost) or $22.25. If you kept the cookie jar and sold it this year, you had to charge $2.76 (inflation rate) times $10 (cost) or $27.60. But this is a collectible that has been a good investment. The value listed in 1986 was $90; the value this year is $200. Cookie jars have become very popular collectibles in the past few years, partly

This chart shows the effect of inflation since 1967. It is based on the Consumer Price Index and demonstrates how inflation has changed the actual value of the dollar and of your antiques. The chart assumes you bought on January 1 and sold on December 31 of the years in question. Choose the year you purchased the antique from the horizontal list. Choose the year you sold the antique from the vertical list. Where the two lines meet you will find the inflation factor. Multiply your original cost by this factor to determine the new value.

1978	1979	1980	1981	1982	1983	1984	1985	1986	1987	1988	1989	1990	1991
1.09													
1.19	1.13												
1.35	1.28	1.12											
1.51	1.44	1.26	1.09										
1.65	1.57	1.38	1.19	1.04									
1.71	1.63	1.43	1.23	1.08	1.04								
1.78	1.70	1.48	1.28	1.12	1.08	1.04							
1.85	1.76	1.54	1.33	1.16	1.12	1.08	1.04						
1.92	1.83	1.60	1.38	1.21	1.16	1.12	1.08	1.01					
1.94	1.85	1.62	1.40	1.22	1.18	1.13	1.09	1.02	1.04				
2.03	1.93	1.69	1.46	1.28	1.23	1.18	1.14	1.07	1.09	1.04			
2.11	2.02	1.76	1.52	1.33	1.28	1.24	1.19	1.12	1.14	1.09	1.05		
2.21	2.11	1.85	1.59	1.39	1.34	1.29	1.24	1.17	1.19	1.14	1.10	1.06	
2.35	2.24	1.96	1.69	1.48	1.42	1.37	1.32	1.24	1.26	1.21	1.16	1.13	1.03

because of a well-publicized sale of the Andy Warhol collection in 1988.

Antiques and collectibles go through cycles and there is a best time to buy and a best time to sell. But true collectors rarely think in those terms. There is a right time to buy (when you see it) and a right time to sell (when required by bankruptcy, divorce, death or, occasionally, when enthusiasm wanes).

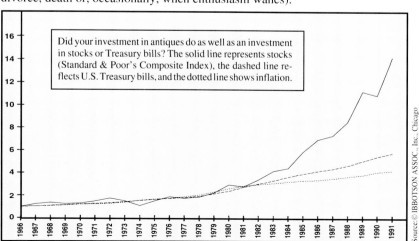

Did your investment in antiques do as well as an investment in stocks or Treasury bills? The solid line represents stocks (Standard & Poor's Composite Index), the dashed line reflects U.S. Treasury bills, and the dotted line shows inflation.

Source: © IBBOTSON ASSOC., Inc., Chicago

This toy was made by Charles Brown around 1875. The hose reel is decorated with the word "Charles." It sold at Christie's in December 1991 for the record-setting price of $231,000.

INVESTING IN ANTIQUES AND COLLECTIBLES

Investing" in antiques was almost a fad in the 1980s. Collecting is a cyclical pastime. A young collector buys for fun or to furnish a home. Incomes, life-styles, and needs change throughout the years. Most antiques have been a good "investment" over time. If you bought in 1967 and sold in 1992, even with inflation you should have made a profit on many items. Toys, art pottery, Mission furniture, and costume jewelry are among the top performers. All collections, however, have two kinds of value—the dollars and the enjoyment. Old chairs, rugs, dishes, and other household furnishings are usually less costly to buy and tend to hold their value better than new pieces. A home filled with special pieces chosen by the collector is unique, and the owner has a sense of pride and accomplishment that is not possible in a decorator-designed house. Collectors can always make room for a special table or picture. They rarely get rid of everything and redecorate. They may get new drapes or paint the walls, but the chairs that they found at a thrift store in the early years of marriage remain favorites.

The collector saves money by not replacing the old household goods and also has the fun of the search, the thrill of the find, and the enjoyment of the beauty, rarity, and "specialness" of the collections. If there is a monetary gain when the collection is finally sold, it is an added bonus and proof of wise collecting.

ADVERTISING (STORE)

Our first book listed store items, boxes, scales, cabinets, counters, or early 19th-century signs. Today the signs would be considered folk art. In 1987 we split the Store section into two parts; the furnishings of the store are still listed under Store, and the Advertising section includes commercial packaging, tobacco tins, can labels, and tin or cardboard signs. Prices for rare tins or signs dating before 1915 have risen to the over-$1,000 range. Prices for ads or packaging for some brand-name products, such as Coca-Cola or Planters Peanuts, are still rising.

Bacon's tomatoes were packed in the can at right, Old Homestead lima beans in the can on the left. The bottle held Lutz Brothers Catsup. These were all late-19th-century products.

TINS

	1ST ED.	5TH ED.	10TH ED.	15TH ED.	20TH ED.	25TH ED.
Chesterfield flat fifty	$1	$4	$4.50	—	$8.50	$7-$8
Nigger hair tobacco pail	—	$65-$85	$75	$105	$145	$185-$285
Sweet Cuba bin	$22.50	$38	$150	$135	$80-$145	$550
Dan Patch can	—	$12	$15	$22.50-$28	$30	$45

ASSORTED ADVERTISING ITEMS

	1ST ED.	5TH ED.	10TH ED.	15TH ED.	20TH ED.	25TH ED.
Diamond Dye cabinet with tin front	$55	$50	$135-$425	$425-$650	$550-$750	$300-$1850
Putnam Dye cabinet with horseback rider on tin	$18	$32	$38.50	$135	$125	$125
Boye needle case	$5	$48	$60	$85	$85	$185
Hires Mettlach mug	$5	$14-$20	$95-$135	—	$65	$40-$180
Ward's Lemon dispenser	$30	—	$165	$345	$275	$950

ART POTTERY

American art pottery was "born" in 1876. Several artists visited the Centennial Exhibition in Philadelphia, where they saw the art pottery from France and determined to make similar pieces. The result was pottery produced by Rookwood, Grueby, and other factories. The art pottery movement continued until the 1920s, when the emphasis shifted and pottery was made by studio potters or by large commercial factories. Rookwood, Weller, and Roseville were the most popular art potteries listed in our first price book. They are still high on the list, but other potteries such as Grueby, Newcomb, and Ohr have gained in recognition and price. When there was enough collector interest, we added new categories to reflect the increasing attention. Fulper was added in 1968; Newcomb, 1970; Grueby, 1971; Teco, 1973; Ohr, 1973; Paul Revere, 1974; Pewabic, 1975; Overbeck, 1980; Marblehead and Volkmar, 1981; Walrath, 1984; Denver and Roblin in 1985.

In the past five years, books, exhibits, and special auctions have added to the collector's interest in art pottery. Any art pottery purchased before 1974—better still, any pieces bought before 1968— have been good investments. The table on the next page shows the range of prices for Rookwood, Weller, and Roseville. Because of the random selection method used to write our price books, many top-priced pieces sold during the year are not included. It is obvious that prices are low for average pieces but very high for the out-of-the-ordinary.

This vase brought the hightest price ever paid for a piece of Rookwood pottery: $198,000 was bid at the Cincinnati Art Galleries in June 1991. The 18 ³/₈-inch vase decorated with electroplated copper fish was made by Shirayamadani.

ART POTTERY

	1ST ED.	5TH ED.	10TH ED.	15TH ED.	20TH ED.	25TH ED.
Rookwood	$5-$85	$8-$325	$13-$550	$20-$3850	$6-$5720	$30-$6500
Weller	$4-$100	$7-$275	$7-$695	$16-$1500	$5-$2200	$15-$3100
Roseville	$5-$13	$4-$98	$7-$145	$14-$225	$8-$2200	$10-$2310

RECORD PRICES—AMERICAN ART POTTERY

Dedham	charger, wolf and owl pattern, 11 ¼ in. (1990)	$6,930
Fulper	vase, "Vasekraft," black flambé over light blue to olive green glaze, 34½ in. (1989)	$12,100
Grueby	vase, melon form, 3 groups of white jonquils on green background, 12 ½ in. (1990)	$30,800
Lonhuda	vase, flattened oviform, scene of monks, brown and orange, footed, 11 ½ in. (1990)	$3,000
Losanti	vase, porcelain, molded whiplash decoration under translucent celadon high glaze, 5 x 4 in. (1989)	$14,300
Marblehead	vase, stylized floral design, brown and black, Hanna Tutt, c. 1910, 7 in. (1990)	$11,100
Merrimac	vase, carved quatrefoils, green semimatte glaze, 7½ x 4¼ in. (1988)	$4,675
Newcomb	vase, bulbous body, 4 large blue alligators on blue-green underglaze, 7½ x 9 in. (1989)	$17,600
North Dakota School of Mines	vase, carved decoration, 3 turkeys in tree, gray on green ground, by Margaret Cable, 8 x 5½ in. (1989)	$2,750
Ohr	vase, black lustre glaze, twisted neck, crimped and folded rim, 13 in. (1990)	$22,000
Overbeck	vase, carved men in landscape, mauve and beige, 7 ½ x 3 in. (1986)	$4,675
Pewabic	vase, green matte, carved leaves, 12½ x 8½ in. (1986)	$4,950
Paul Revere	plate, star-filled sky, cottage, trees by lake, black, blue, green, brown, yellow, 1915, S. Galner, 12 ¼ in. (1992)	$11,000
Rookwood	vase, electroplated copper fish swimming under green glaze, Shirayamadani, 18 ⅜ in. (1991)	$198,000
Tiffany	vase, cylindrical, bulging bottom, embossed poppies, buttermilk matte glaze, 9½ in. (1989)	$4,730
Van Briggle	vase, Lorelei, women in relief, 2-color mint green and cream glaze, dated 1902, 10 in. (1988)	$23,100
Walrath	vase, cylindrical, 3 pink flowers, long stems, green ground (1989)	$2,475
Weller	vase, Hudson marine scenic, 27 ½ in. (1979)	$7,000
Wheatley	vase, cylindrical, bulbous, 4 stalk-like handles, flared and scalloped mouth, matte green, 14 in. (1989)	$2,200

FURNITURE

This elaborate wicker chair dates from the 1890s.

What type of American furniture has been a good investment? What is a good buy now? If you bought the best of American 18th-century furniture in 1967 and sold it in the early 1980s, you made a good investment. If you bought Mission pieces before 1975 or Art Deco furniture by name designers before 1980 or high-style Victorian pieces before 1980, you have a bargain.

A Belter-style armchair sold in 1972 for $650. Today experts are able to identify more pieces of Belter. A carved, laminated rosewood bed set a record in 1990 with a price of $101,750. Mission chairs and sideboards were selling for under $1,000 in the early 1970s, but in 1988 an auction record of $363,000 was set for a Gustav Stickley oak-and-wrought-iron sideboard that he made for his own home. The international market influences Art Deco furniture prices. Buyers from England, France, Germany, and Japan bid for the top pieces.

Perhaps even bigger gains were made by Shaker, Adirondack, and '50s examples. They were not even listed in our early books. Shaker furniture first received national recognition at the World's Fair in 1967. The Japanese saw a relationship between their designs and the simplicity of the Shakers', and international buying began. A Shaker chair that sold for $125 in 1972 was worth $500 in 1982, $1,650 in 1987, and $4,675 today. Painted furniture, once refinished, now brings premium prices. A mustard-colored Shaker tall chest with 12 drawers, made in New Lebanon,

This dining room chest valued at $7,500 was made by Herter of New York City circa 1890 and is marked with the manufacturer's name branded in the wood.

New York, about 1850 sold in 1988 for $99,000; an 1830 pine work-counter with original red paint brought $220,000 in 1990.

Pieces from the '50s are just beginning to sell for higher prices: a 48-inch Noguchi crisscross table by Knowle, $3,190; the four-shelf Eames storage unit, $13,200; the marshmallow love seat by George Nelson, $16,500.

"American Country" became a decorating style in the 1980s. Painted furniture, wicker. Windsor chairs, slat-back chairs, and rope-strung beds became fashionable. Prices went up by 400 percent. Now Western country pieces are the highest priced. Many of the chairs and tables made of rough-hewn logs or with cowboy cutouts sell from $1,000 to $10,000.

Art Nouveau furniture by Emile Gallé, Louis Majorelle, Hector Guimard, and

——RECENT RECORD PRICES—AMERICAN FURNITURE ——

It is difficult to compare prices for much of the furniture made before 1850 because most of the pieces are unique. In 1967, the most expensive piece of American furniture that was sold at an auction was a Philadelphia Federal inlaid mahogany breakfront-secretary-bookcase, c. 1790. It sold for $25,000. In 1989, the record price of $12.1 million was set for a Nicholas Brown mahogany desk and bookcase, made c. 1760 by John Goddard. The following list shows other record prices.

Herter Aesthetic library table, parcel gilt, carved and inlaid ebonized cherry-wood, by Herter Brothers of New York for the Mark Hopkins home in San Francisco, 1877	$280,500
Carved "lotus" center table, top with carved overlapping broad leaves and pods, black finish, John Bradstreet, c. 1905	$27,500
Federal "Turkey-breast" corner cabinet, polychrome painted, early 19th century	$44,000
Chippendale carved mahogany card table, 1760-1770	$1,045,000
Chippendale Cadwalader chair, carved mahogany wing armchair, hairy paw feet and carved skirt, Thomas Affleck, 1770	$2,750,000
Dining room set of 12 chairs, matched Chippendale, carved mahogany, New York, c. 1770	$308,000
Chippendale chest, carved mahogany, serpentine-front bombe, Boston, c.1765	$660,000
Shaker tall chest, poplar, 12 drawers, mustard wash, New Lebanon, New York, 1840-1850	$99,000
Classical inlaid marble-top table, gilt, brass-mounted, H. Lannuier, New York	$704,000
Country tea table, Queen Anne cherrywood, rectangular molded top, Connecticut, c. 1750	$159,000
Frank Lloyd Wright dining set, oak table and 8 high spindle-back chairs, made for Husser house in Chicago in 1899	$1,600,000
Richard Edwards Chippendale carved and painted mirror, rectangular, John Elliot, Philadelphia, c.1755	$242,000
Inlaid, ebonized and brass-mounted rosewood secretary, fall front, cupboard doors, Philadelphia, c. 1815	$302,500
Chippendale mahogany serpentine-back sofa, Philadelphia, 1767-1785	$605,000
Chippendale pier table by Thomas Tuft, gadrooned molding on three sides above a pierced apron, Philadelphia, c. 1775	$4,600,000

others has lost some favor in the United States, but the prices remain stable. European collectors continue paying very high prices for the top examples.

English 18th-century furniture was the American collector's choice 40 years ago. Taste and money then turned buyers to American furniture made before 1800. The English pieces did not regain popularity at auctions until 1985. The best pieces continue to go up in value.

PRESSED GLASS

These patterns are Double Ribbon, Selby, and Good Luck, or Horseshoe.

Pressed or pattern glass was one of the most popular collectibles in America from the 1920s to the 1950s. Price books listed more pressed glass than furniture. Collections were assembled to be used on the table or to be displayed. We still remember a wedding show given by a friend's mother where lunch was served on Vaseline pressed glass plates and goblets. The major books listing and picturing pressed glass patterns were written before 1958 by Ruth Webb Lee, Minnie Watson Kamm, or Alice Hulett Metz. These were the only research sources until improved cross-referenced books on pressed glass were written in the 1980s. Pressed glass was a popular collectible because it was useful, attractive, and inexpensive. As prices rose, interest dwindled, and by the 1970s pressed glass was not attracting many new, younger collectors. A few patterns were still in demand. Serving pieces with frosted figural knobs or stems, Bellflower and banded patterns, U.S. Coin, Liberty Bell, and Actress attracted special collectors. Prices of less distinctive patterns remained at the 1970s range (adjusted for inflation) until about 1985. Depression glass, Heisey, Fenton, and other glasswares that could be collected as sets had gone up in price, and collectors saw the economic sense in again buying pressed glass.

PRESSED GLASS

Prices for a selected list of goblets that were listed in each of these editions.

PATTERN	1st ED.	5th ED.	10th ED.	15th ED.	20th ED.	25th ED.
Buckle	$7.50-$11.50	$15	$14.50-$22	$15-$28.50	$22.50	$23-$40
Diamond Point	$16	$9-$20	$47.50	$45-$65	$48-$52	$35
Frosted Lion	$21.50	$37.50	$45-$55	$48	$55-$65	$60-$65
Honeycomb	$2.50-$6.50	$4-$6	$20	$12-$15	$22.50	$38
New England Pineapple	$17	$20-$25	$45-$52.50	$35-$65	$30	$70

DEPRESSION GLASS

P rices for Depression glass have gone from so unimportant they were not even mentioned in the first book to a range that goes up to thousands of dollars for a few great rarities.

DEPRESSION GLASS

Prices for the Miss America pink grill plate from each of these editions.

1ST ED.	5TH ED.	10TH ED.	15TH ED.	20TH ED.	25TH ED.
—	$3.75	$5-$7.25	$10	$12	$23

ROYAL DOULTON

D oulton and Royal Doulton were of little interest to antiques collectors in 1968. In the first edition, we listed Doulton stoneware and a few pieces made before 1900, most priced under $50. Two figurines were priced, but the HN number and title were not included. There were no character jugs. By the seventh edition, the HN numbers that identify the pieces were included. Prices were going up. Character jugs and toby mugs were fully described with size and mark by the ninth edition. The first major books picturing figurines and character jugs had been published and collectors could learn about identification clues, rarity, and variation. *Kovels' Illustrated Price Guide to Royal Doulton* (1980) included all known figurines and jugs, plus animals, flambé, and other pieces. Prices (inflation adjusted) rose until the 17th edition. Since then, they have remained steady or have even declined slightly.

ROYAL DOULTON

Every piece was not listed in every edition. These are prices
for pieces that appeared in several editions.

FIGURINES	EDITION/PRICE				
Hostess from Williamsburg	2nd, $35	—	19th, $125	20th, $125	25th, $185
Balloon Man	2nd, $30	—	18th, $125	—	25th, $130
Silks and Ribbons	3rd, $25	—	17th, $80	—	24th, $168
CHARACTER JUGS	EDITION/PRICE				
Granny, small	3rd, $18.50	9th, $23.50	17th, $80	20th, $30	25th, $45
John Peel, small	3rd, $18.50	10th, $62	17th, $80	20th, $65	25th, $75
'Arriet, miniature	3rd, $15.50	10th, $90	19th, $60	—	25th, $65-$85
TOBY JUGS	EDITION/PRICE				
Fat Boy	2nd, $19.50	7th, $45	12th, $185	—	25th, $95
Sir Winston Churchill	5th, $55	—	15th, $100	—	25th, $95
Happy John	5th, $22	11th, $29	19th, $98	—	24th, $100

SILVER

S ilver and jewelry have special pricing features. They have a breakup or meltdown value that is independent of the antique or artistic value of the piece. In 1967 silver was $1.55 an ounce; in 1972 it was $1.69; in 1974 it went up to $4.39. Then the price really began to rise, and in 1979 it reached $16. The Hunt brothers tried to corner the silver market and began buying silver futures. They forced the price of silver to more than $44 an ounce. Ultimately their attempt failed, and by June 1980 the price of silver was near $16

19th-century American coin silver pitchers.

an ounce. In 1986 silver was about $5.30 an ounce, in 1992 about $4.10 an ounce.

The estimated value of good, usable, old silver is generally about 2½ times the meltdown or raw-silver value of the piece. Better pieces with artistic value sell for 5 to 10 times meltdown. Exceptional pieces by famous makers sell for higher prices, with no thought as to the weight of the silver. When prices rose in 1979, many people sold their silver to be melted. Many coin silver spoons and dented teapots were sold, and this forever decreased the supply of early American silver. When the price of silver dropped, prices of silver pieces were lower for a year or so; then collectors began buying, and prices are higher now then they were in 1979.

Another factor influenced silver prices. From about 1970 to 1972 there was a sudden surge of interest in England. When the prices fell in England, prices for all types of silver fell until the 1979 boom. Today, top-quality antique English silver (pieces above $10,000 in value) is very high priced. Quality silver in the $1,000 to $10,000 range has remained about the same price.

The 1993 news for silver collectors is that 20th-century makers are selling well. In the past, silver pieces by makers with the prestige of Paul Revere or Paul

ENGLISH SILVER

Prices listed here are for the *most* expensive piece of silver listed for each year.

	1ST ED.	5TH ED.	10TH ED.	15TH ED.	20TH ED.	25TH ED.
game dish	$1386	—	—	—	—	—
tea urn	$1850	—	—	—	—	$4675
candlesticks	—	$4500	—	—	$7700	$4435
tureen	—	$4000	$5500	$5000	—	$8250
epergne	—	—	—	$6000	—	$5000
urn	—	—	—	$5600	—	—
platter	—	—	—	—	$9350	—

Storr have been top priced. Similar pieces by lesser makers have not gone up in value at the same rate. Art Deco, Art Nouveau, and Arts and Crafts silver all started to sell at higher prices in the 1980s. Only a few prominent names such as Georg Jensen or Liberty added extra value. By the end of the '80s there were many museum exhibits and books that identified the silversmiths working in the United States from 1900 to 1975. Such names as Mildred Watkins, Kalo, or Arthur Stone added value, and important pieces sold for thousands of dollars. Mexican silverware and jewelry makers from the 1930s to 1960s, including William Spratling or Margot, are now known. Prices have doubled each of the past three years. The '50s collectors are now looking for silver jewelry by such name designers as Ed Weiner or Henning Koppel, and prices are moving up. A strange group of Oriental-looking silver—pieces made in China for export or pieces made in the United States in the japonisme tradition—have become 10 times more valuable in the past 10 years.

Elaborate sterling and plated Victorian silver took a leap in price when the Wagstaff Collection was sold at auction in January 1989. In 1984 a Gorham "icebowl" and spoon sold for $3,600. At the Wagstaff sale, the same design sold for $44,000. Silver serving spoons and bowls in unusual shapes continued to bring high prices in 1992.

AMERICAN SILVER PLATE

19th-century silver-plated baskets.

Silver-plated Britannia ware was inexpensive and out of favor 25 years ago. The ornate tea sets, tilting water pitchers, napkin rings, and calling-card baskets were plentiful at flea markets but had few buyers. The scrap metal dealers bought them for meltdown and sometimes saved unusual examples for collectors. Only figural spoons were popular. Our first edition listed 123 spoons, about a third of the items listed in silver plate. Figural napkin rings picked up in value after 1971 when a book pictured and identified hundreds of examples. Today a plated figural napkin ring is worth almost three times as much as it was in 1987, 20 times as much as in 1967.

AMERICAN SILVER PLATE					
	1ST ED.	5TH ED.	10TH ED.	15TH ED.	20TH ED.	25TH ED.
napkin ring	$6-$35	$15-$80	$32-$225	$36-$275	$9-$245	$55-$600
tilting water pitcher*	$85	$65	$275	$475	$325	$375

*The highest priced piece of silver plate in the 1st, 5th, 10th, and 15th editions.

In 1991, this Tiffany Trumpet lamp sold for $440,000 at Christie's, New York.

TIFFANY

In the 1950s the leaded Tiffany glass lamp shade was out of fashion. Most collectors never even imagined that this type of glass shade would eventually be used on lamps selling for thousands of dollars. Tiffany glass was rediscovered by a small group of serious collectors in the 1960s when a high-priced lamp sold for under $100. In 1969 we listed 30 lamps ranging in price from $75 to $1,900. Five years later, the 47 listed lamps had prices from $375 to $7,000. A daffodil lamp was $900 in the first book, $4,800 in the fifth. In December 1991 a daffodil lamp sold at auction for $8,800. Lamps listed in *Kovels'* are now the average-priced, not the record-priced, Tiffanys sold during the year. In 1980 a record $360,000 was paid for a spider web table lamp. Nine other Tiffany lamps set records that year. In 1981, prices dropped, and it was ten years before new record prices appeared. The collector who bought before 1964 and sold in 1980 did well.

Gold-colored Tiffany glass vases could be purchased at house or garage sales in the 1960s for under $10. When the book *Louis C. Tiffany, Rebel in Glass* was published, prices rose. Tiffany pottery was not mentioned in *Kovels'* until the seventh edition. Tiffany silverware was included in the eighth. In the 17th we began to list some of the mixed metal pieces in the japonisme designs.

Glass and bronze desk sets always sold well because they were useful, and they were popular as gifts. Prices jumped about 1975, and they have been going up each year. The desk sets continue to sell well and have more than kept up with inflation.

TIFFANY INKWELLS

High and low prices for any Tiffany inkwells listed in these editions.

1ST ED.	5TH ED.	10TH ED.	15TH ED.	19TH ED.	20TH ED.	25TH ED.
$27-$40	$85-$110	$110-$250	$190-$1000	$395-$550	$130-$1500	$350-$8250

ZODIAC DESIGN INKWELL

Prices for the Tiffany Zodiac design inkwell in these editions.

1ST ED.	5TH ED.	10TH ED.	15TH ED.	19TH ED.	20TH ED.	25TH ED.
$40	$41-$65	$110	$295	$550	$350	$495

Scoop, Spade, Hand Carved, 5 In. 75.00
Screen Cover, Food, Round 27.00
Server, Pancake, Pierced Dome Lid, White China, Floral, C. F. H. 95.00
Sifter, Flour, 3 Screens, Androck 15.00
Sifter, Flour, Duplex, Green Handle 22.00
Sifter, Flour, Tin, Green 5.00
Skillet, 3–1, Griswold 25.00
Skillet, Advertising Wertz & Singers, Middletown, Oh., No. 2 .... 21.00
Skillet, Breakfast, Griswold, Yellow Enamel 65.00
Skillet, Colonial, Breakfast, Yellow, Square, 9 In. 160.00
Skillet, Griswold No. 4, Cover 95.00
Skillet, Griswold, No. 3, Large Emblem 25.00
Skillet, Griswold, No. 5, Large Emblem 25.00
Skillet, Griswold, No. 6, Large Emblem 38.00
Skillet, Griswold, No. 6, Small Emblem 25.00
Skillet, Griswold, No. 7, Smoke Ring 20.00
Skillet, Griswold, No. 8, Small Emblem 25.00
Skillet, Griswold, No. 11, Smoke Ring 150.00
Skillet, Griswold, No. 12, Smoke Ring 110.00
Skillet, Hand Wrought Iron, Large 285.00
Skillet, Pancake, Wagner 22.00
Skillet, Victor, No. 7 .... 40.00
Skillet, Wagner, Iron, 12 In. 25.00
Slicer, Vegetable, Wooden, Ripple Tin Blade, 14 In. 15.00
Snow Cone Maker, Snoopy 10.00
Soap Saver, Twisted Wire, Round 15.00
Spice Box, 8 Drawer, Cutout Crest, Hand Made, 16 x 9 1/2 In. 125.00
Spice Cabinet, 8 Drawers, Brass Knobs 158.00
Spice Cabinet, 8 Drawers, Pine 145.00
Spice Cabinet, Tin, Beveled Mirror 750.00
Spice Cabinet, Wall, 20 Drawers, Brown Stain, Pine, 11 1/2 x 21 In. 385.00
Spice Chest, Hanging, 18 Gilt Decorated Drawers 4675.00
Spice Chest, Hinged Lid, 4 Drawers, Pine, 17 x 24 1/2 In. 1700.00
Spice Set, Ceramic, Salt Box, Rooster & Chicken Design, 10 Piece 10.50
Spider Pan, Wrought Iron, Primitive, Handle, High Feet, 7 3/4 In. 105.00
Spoon, Wooden, Fish Shaped Handle, 10 In. 20.00
Strainer, Cheese, Footed, Tin 225.00
Strainer, Wingold Flour, Tin 15.00
Strawberry Huller, Nip–It, 1906 .... 10.00
String Holder, Beehive Shape, Albany Glaze, Stoneware, 6 1/2 In. 130.00
String Holder, Black Boy With Floppy Hat 125.00
String Holder, Black Porter, Fredericksburg 275.00
String Holder, Bulldog 25.00
String Holder, Butler's Head 1200.00
String Holder, Butler, Full Figure 350.00
String Holder, Climinson, Heart Shape 35.00
String Holder, Heinz Pickle 3700.00
String Holder, Mammy Holding Hands Up 245.00
String Holder, Mammy's Face, Ceramic 295.00
String Holder, Man Winking, Ceramic 20.00
String Holder, Pumpkin Face, Ceramic 50.00
String Holder, Red Apple, Chalkware 20.00
String Holder, Red Goose Shoes, Tin 2000.00
String Holder, SSS For The Blood, Cast Iron 35.00
String Holder, Strawberry, Chalkware, Face 30.00
Sugar Devil, Iron, Wood Handle, Patent 1876, 15 In. 150.00
Sugar Nipper, Wrought Iron, 9 1/4 In. 35.00
Sweeper, Karpet King, Wooden 160.00
Teakettle, Gooseneck, Tilter Bar, Iron 550.00
Teapot, Landers, Model E–975, Electric 25.00
Teapot, Metal, Barrel Shape, Long Handle & Spout, Melton, 5 In. 65.00
Tenderizer, Meat, Wildflower, Blue & White 175.00
Tenderizer, Meat, Wood 37.50

Tieback, Curtain, 6–Point Flower, Green, Pewter Center, 3 1/2 In.	35.00
Toast–O–Lator, Toast Slides Conveyor Belt, Art Deco	85.00
Toaster, Automatic, 1950s	25.00
Toaster, Blue Willow	2200.00
Toaster, Cookstove	10.00
Toaster, Door Slides On Track, 1918	25.00
Toaster, General Electric, Model D12, 1st One Made, 8 In.	165.00
Toaster, Hand Wrought Iron, Hold Handle Over Fire	285.00
Toaster, Heart–Shaped Handle, Wrought Iron, 14 1/2 x 18 In.	1025.00
Toaster, Marshmallow, Angelus–Campfire Bar–B–Q, 3 In. ....*Illus*	25.00
Toaster, Marshmallow, Electric, With Tiny Forks, Small	165.00
Toaster, McGraw, Model 1B5, Electric	30.00
Toaster, Meriden, Electric	20.00
Toaster, Pyramid Shape, Tin, 4 Sides	10.00
Toaster, Sandwich, Butler, Bakelite Handle, Chrome Plated	28.00
Toaster, Son Chief, Model 680, Flip–Down	15.00
Toaster, Son–Chief, Unusual, Box	40.00
Toaster, Stove Top, 4 Vented Sides, Pyramid Style	18.00
Toaster, Sun–Chief, Flip–Down, Bakelite Knobs	35.00
Toaster, Swing Handle, New England, Iron, 1780s	200.00
Toaster, Toastmaster, 2nd Pop–Up Model, Mechanical Clock, 1928	70.00
Toaster, Toastmaster, McGraw, Model 1B10, Electric	30.00
Toaster, Universal, 1940s	15.00
Toaster, Universal, Electric	38.00
Toaster, Universal, Model E–79312, Electric	20.00
Toaster, Westinghouse, Flip–Down, Bakelite Knobs, Bell	32.00
Toaster, Whirling, Gentleman With Top Hat Handle, Iron, 20 In.	1650.00
Toaster, Wrought Iron, Twisted Iron & Wooden Handle, 12 1/4 In.	105.00
Tongs, Lifting Fruit Jar, Kerr Glass Co., Mechanical	3.00
Tongs, Potato, Cast Iron	75.00
Tools, Brass Inlay, Engraved, Signed M. B., 4 Piece	500.00
Tray, Snack, TV Show, 1950s, 9 Piece	38.00
Turner, Pancake, A & J, Iron, Green Wooden Handle	1.25
Waffle Iron, All Rite, Indianapolis, Ind.	20.00
Waffle Iron, Child's, Stover Junior, Wood Handles	195.00
Waffle Iron, Griswold American No. 8, Pat. Dec. 1, 1908	75.00
Waffle Iron, Heart & Star, Griswold .... 185.00 To	200.00
Waffle Iron, Heart Shape	90.00
Waffle Iron, Heart, Griswold	20.00
Waffle Iron, Keen Kutter	100.00
Waffle Iron, Stand, Stover	26.50
Washboard, Cast Iron, Cutout Heart Border Trim	450.00
Washboard, Child's, Frontenec	65.00
Washboard, Child's, Glass, Green	200.00
Washboard, Dark Blue Graniteware Insert, Wooden	65.00
Washboard, Four Deuces, Large	22.50
Washboard, Glass Scrubber	25.00
Washboard, Mother Hubbard, Roller	95.00
Washboard, Roller	68.00
Washboard, Roller Type	150.00
Washboard, Sunnyland, Columbus Washboard Co., Stenciled	55.00
Washing Machine, Box Perfection No. 4, Cypress Wood, Stenciled	175.00
Washing Machine, Maytag, Wringer, Square, 2 Rinse Tubs	15.00
Washing Machine, Table Top, Green Graniteware	225.00
Whisk Broom, China Lady Top	95.00
Wrench, Fruit Jar, Cupples Presto, Red Rubber	1.25
Wrench, Fruit Jar, Gunnard, Iron	2.10
Wrench, Towle's Syrup, Tin	35.00
Wringer, Atlantic, Clamp–On Style	60.00

KNIFE collectors usually specialize in a single type. In the 1960s, the United States government passed a law that required knife manufacturers to mark their knives with the country of origin. This seemed to encourage the collectors, and knife collecting became an interest of a large group of people. All types of knives are collected, from top quality twentieth-century examples to old bone- or pearl-handled knives in excellent condition.

All Ivory, 3 Blades, 1 1/4 In.	45.00
Arkansas Toothpick, 10–In. Steel Blade, Double Brass Guard, End Cap	50.00
Boot, Woman's, Victorian	125.00
Bowie, Bridgeport Gun & Implement Co.	295.00
Bowie, Handmade, Ivory Slab Handle	450.00
Castrating, Farmer's, Gillette	3.50
Chamfer, Jigger Type, 3 1/2–In. Blade, Flat Handle	30.00
Chopping, Wooden Handle, Large	47.00
Christy, Union Pacific Tea Co.	9.00
Draw, Cantelo, Folding, Wooden Handles	17.50
Draw, Carpenter's, With Folding Wooden Handles	15.00
Draw, Fulton, Folding, Wooden Handles	18.00
Draw, Shapleigh's Diamond Edge, Folding, Wooden Handles	20.00
Draw, Winchester	95.00
Fish, Kabar, Folding, 5 In.	12.00
Hawbill, Red Bone Handle, Case, 1940	55.00
Horseshoe, Pratt, KS	28.00
Jack, Frontier, Ivorine, 3 In.	12.00
Jack, Lady's Shoe, Ivory Color	25.00
Key Chain, Advertising 1962 Falcon Car	3.50
Kraut, Double Crescent Shaped Blade, Wooden Handle	6.25
Pen, 14K Gold, Monogram	75.00
Phillips 66, 2 In.	20.00
Pocket, 14K Gold & Stainless Steel	65.00
Pocket, Bone, 2 Blades On 1 End, Case, USA, 2 3/4 In.	45.00
Pocket, Colonial, 10 1/2 In.	12.00
Pocket, Double Blade, Black & Cream Marbelized Handle	6.25
Pocket, Kinney Co., Advertising Jewelry, 1942, Miniature	45.00
Pocket, Miller, Scrolled Design, 10K Gold	65.00
Pocket, People's National Band	20.00
Pocket, Polly Parrot	35.00
Pocket, Purina, 2 Blades	5.50
Pocket, Queen, No. 45, Big Chief	22.00
Pocket, Remington, Nickeled Silver, Advertising	200.00
Pocket, Tombstone Casket Co.	20.00
Pocket, U.S. Army, Utility, Unused	12.50
Queen City, 1 Blade, Bone Handle, c.1922, 4 1/2 In.	95.00
Remington, Buttel, No. 1128	475.00
Remington, Rosedale Dairy, Ft. Dodge Creamery Co., Stamped On Blade	270.00
Schrade Cutlery Co., 2 Blades, Bone Handle, 1930s, 4 1/2 In.	120.00
Skinning, Buffalo, George Westerholm	50.00

KNOWLES, TAYLOR & KNOWLES items may be found in the KTK and Lotus Ware categories.

KOCH is the name signed on the front of a series of plates decorated with fruits, vegetables, animals, or birds. The dishes date from the 1910 to 1930 period and were probably decorated in Germany.

KOCH

Plate, Apples Over Water, Signed, 6 In.	55.00
Plate, Apples, Scalloped Rim, 8 In.	35.00
Plate, Grapes Over Water, Signed, 12 In.	145.00

KOREAN WARE, see Sumida

KOSTA, the oldest Swedish glass factory, was founded in 1742. During the 1920s through the 1950s, many pieces of original design were made at the factory. The firm is still working.

KOSTA

Bowl, Bubbles, White & Clear, 4 x 10 In.	75.00

KPM, Vase, Putto, Water Scene, 10 1/4 In.

Bowl, Indigo & Clear, 2 x 6 In.	225.00
Paperweight, Seaweed, Marked, 4 x 4 In.	125.00
Perfume Bottle, Plain, Signed	50.00
Sculpture, Etched Figures, Clear, Mottled, Blue, Green & Amber, 10 In.	1100.00
Vase, Colorless Cylinder, Colored Internal Grasses, 13 1/2 In.	605.00
Vase, Etched Floral, 11 In.	165.00
Vase, Green & Yellow Swirls, Blue Base, Warff, Cylinder, 11 In.	375.00
Vase, Red, Rows Of Bubbles, Teardrop Shale, 12 In.	150.00
Vase, Rounded Triangular Form, Geometric Bubble Design, 5 3/4 In.	65.00
Vase, Rows Of Bubbles, Elongated Teardrop Shape, 12 In.	325.00
Vase, Water Skier Pulled By Dolphin, 1937, 7 In.	700.00

KPM refers to Berlin porcelain, but the same initials were used alone and
in combination with other symbols by several German porcelain makers.
They include the Konigliche Porzellan Manufaktur of Berlin, initials used
in mark, 1823–1847; Meissen, 1723–1724 only; Krister Porzellan
Manufaktur in Waldenburg, after 1831; Kranichfelder Porzellan
Manufaktur in Kranichfeld, after 1903; and the Kister Porzellan
Manufaktur in Scheibe, after 1838.

K.P.M

Bust, Child, Pastel Coloring, Marked, 10 1/2 In.	400.00
Coffeepot & Tray, Roman Key Design, White Flowers, Gold Trim, 9 In.	345.00
Cup, Bouillon, White, Gold Rim, 6 Piece	50.00
Figurine, Stag, 8 In.	350.00
Figurine, Woman Holding Flowers, At Fountain, Hat On Shoulder, 9 In.	625.00
Figurine, Woman, Behind Pedestal, Bouquet Of Flowers, Marked, 9 In.	575.00
Lamp, Fairy, 3–Sided, Owl, Cat & Dog	395.00
Plaque, 2 Young Girls, Oval, Brass Frame, 6 1/2 In.	825.00
Plaque, Bust Young Woman, Gown & Fan, 9 x 6 In.	1650.00
Plaque, Female Nude, On Leopard Skin, Framed, Signed, 6 1/2 x 9 1/2 In.	8250.00
Plaque, Goodnight, 9 x 6 1/4 In.	2200.00
Plaque, Her Favorite, Woman & Parrot, Framed, c.1900, 9 3/4 x 7 In.	1450.00
Plaque, Lake Scene, Houses, People, Boats, Framed, Marked, 4 1/8 x 6 In.	715.00
Plaque, Magdalene, Reading, 8 x 10 In.	3630.00
Plaque, Nude, Asleep On Grassy Hill, Marked, 1880s, 9 1/2 x 6 1/2 In.	4125.00
Plaque, Old Woman, Old Man, Signed, 1857, 7 x 10 In., Pair	6600.00
Plaque, Party Of Arabs, Attacked By 3 Leopards, Marked, 11 x 8 3/4 In.	7150.00
Plaque, Playing Children, Nude, 6 x 8 In.	6600.00
Plaque, Princess Louise, White Gown, Fur Cape, Marked, 13 1/2 x 8 In.	7975.00
Plaque, Rebecca, A. Dittrich, 9 1/2 x 7 In.	2200.00
Plaque, Seminude Woman, 6 x 8 In.	6050.00
Plaque, Small Boys With Picture Book, Framed, 19th Century, 10 x 12 In.	5775.00
Plaque, Trauernde Psyche, After Bernard, 6 x 9 In.	3300.00
Plaque, Two Monks, 10 x 7 1/2 In.	2200.00
Plaque, Woman In Loose Robes Seated By Pool, Oval, Framed, 12 In.	1760.00
Plaque, Young Girl, Long Hair, Scarf Tied, Marked, 9 3/4 x 7 1/2 In.	4125.00
Plaque, Young Girl, Nude, Wind–Blown Drapery, c.1900, 9 1/2 x 6 3/8 In.	6325.00
Plaque, Young Girl, Wavy Golden Hair, Oval, 19th Century, 8 1/2 In.	4400.00

Plaque, Young Jesus, Gilt Frame, 9 x 6 1/4 In. 1300.00
Plaque, Young Violinist & Singer, Framed, Marked, 1900, 12 1/2 x 10 In. 1100.00
Plate, Interior Farm Scene, Pierced & Gilt Vines Rim, Cabinet 110.00
Plate, Princess Royal, 10 1/2 In. 30.00
Shaving Mug, 2 Men Scuffling, Straight Razors, A Close Shave 275.00
Shaving Mug, Gold Band Design 37.50
Vase, Putto, Water Scene, 10 1/4 In. ....*Illus* 1000.00

KTK are the initials of the Knowles, Taylor & Knowles Company of East
Liverpool, Ohio, founded by Isaac W. Knowles in 1853. The company
made many types of utilitarian wares, hotel china, and dinnerwares. They
made the fine bone china known as Lotus Ware from 1891 to 1896. The
company merged with American Ceramic Corporation in 1928. It closed in
1934. Lotus Ware is listed in its own category in this book.

K.T.&K.
CHINA

Bowl, Floral, Twig Handles, 9 In. 1300.00
Cookie Jar, 3 Chefs, 1 With Cake, 1 With Turkey, 1 With Vegetable 275.00
Gravy Boat, Brown Floral Decal 25.00

KU KLUX KLAN items are now collected because of their historic
importance. Literature, robes, and memorabilia are available. The Klan is
still in existence, so new material is found.

Book, Little Blue Book, c.1924 .... 20.00
Card, Membership, 1928 .... 30.00
Flag, 3 x 5 In. 125.00
Holder, Match, Celluloid 75.00
Knife, Pocket, Brass 195.00
Knife, Pocket, Brass Handle 15.00
Knife, Pocket, Loyal Order 4.00
Robe, With Hood, Cotton, With Patch 125.00
Token, Convention, Bristol, Tenn., May 11, 1907 .... 35.00

KUTANI ware is a Japanese porcelain made after the mid–seventeenth
century. Most of the pieces found today are nineteenth–century. Collectors
often use the term *kutani* to refer to just the later, colorful pieces
decorated with red, gold, and black pictures of warriors, animals, and
birds.

Biscuit Jar, Geisha Girl, 1890s 165.00
Bowl, White Ground, Blossoms, Leaves, Elders In Garden, 4 x 9 In. 335.00
Cookie Jar, 7 Shinto Gods, 6 In. 135.00
Cup & Saucer, Lithophane, Gold Trim, After Dinner 95.00
Cup & Saucer, Processional Scene, Phoenix Roundels, 2 1/2 In. 445.00
Figurine, Cat, Ginger Color, Gold, Red & Black, 12 In. 255.00
Tea Set, Hand Painted, Signed, 16 Piece 175.00
Tea Set, Lithopane, Geisha Girl In Bottom Of Cups, 13 Piece 175.00
Vase, Festival Scene, Foliate Borders, 18 In. 2310.00
Vase, Reserves Of Copies Of Ink Paintings, Ovoid, c.1900, 14 1/2 In. 467.50

LACQUER is a type of varnish. Collectors are most interested in the
Chinese and Japanese lacquer wares made from the Japanese varnish tree.
Lacquer wares are made from wood with many coats of lacquer.
Sometimes the piece is carved or decorated with ivory or metal inlay.

Box, Clouds & Wisteria, Nashiji Ground, 7 3/4 x 5 1/4 In. 2100.00
Box, Cover, Gold Flying Bird, Flowers, Japan, 7 1/2 x 5 In. 715.00
Box, Hinged Red Cover & Sides, Black, Maruni, 4 x 4 In. 45.00
Box, Raised Lid, Floral Hiramaki–E Design, 3 1/2 x 2 3/4 In. 165.00
Box, Ring, Woman Spinning, Nobleman, Russia, 2 x 2 3/8 In. 385.00
Case, Pipe, Butterfly Design, 19th Century, 19 In. 2000.00
Inro, Birds & Moon, Koma School, 19th Century, 2 1/2 In. 1100.00
Inro, Cranes & Takarabune, Black Ground, 4 Case, 3 1/4 In. 990.00
Inro, Elephant, Farmer With Hoe, Black Ground, 4 Case, 3 1/2 In. 615.00
Inro, Group Of Swallows Flying Over Waves, Red, 3 1/2 In. 7025.00
Pie Holder, 2 Tiers, Cover, Black, Red, Gold, 11 1/2 x 3 3/4 In. 45.00
Tray, Black, Brown, Rectangular, Eileen Gray, c.1920, 21 1/2 In. 2860.00

LADY HEAD VASE, see Head Vase

LALIQUE glass was made by Rene Lalique in Paris, France, between the 1890s and his death in 1945. The glass was molded, pressed, and engraved in Art Nouveau and Art Deco styles. Pieces were marked with the signature *R. Lalique*. Lalique glass is still being made. Pieces made after 1945 bear the mark *Lalique*.

LALIQUE

Ashtray, Cuba	275.00
Ashtray, Eagle	350.00
Ashtray, Lion, Gargoyle–Form Rim, Signed, 5 3/4 In.	165.00
Ashtray, Mouse In Center, Yellow, Signed, c.1920	395.00
Ashtray, Owl	65.00
Bell, Bird Finial	175.00
Blotter, Deux Sirenes Enlacees, Assises, Mermaids, Satin Glass	2770.00
Bonbon, Raised Leaves, Berries, Frosted Glass, Cover, 4 1/2 In.	695.00
Bookends, Nude Woman, Leaning, 9 In.	625.00 To 950.00
Bowl, Allover Beaded Circles, Blue Opalescent, 10 In.	385.00 To 650.00
Bowl, Beaded Medallions Of Increasing Size, Signed, 10 In.	247.50
Bowl, Branches & Roses In Relief, Square, 9 3/4 x 3 In.	495.00
Bowl, Calypso, Swimming Water Nymphs, Opalescent, 4 3/8 In.	4950.00
Bowl, Calypso, Water Nymphs, Opalescent, Shallow, 14 3/8 In.	4950.00
Bowl, Coquilles, Molded Design On Exterior, Signed, 5 1/4 In.	165.00
Bowl, Dauphins, Fish, Rippling Waters, Signed, 1932, 9 3/8 In.	1320.00
Bowl, Fruit, Overall Roosting Birds, Leaf Fronts, c.1968, 9 1/2 In.	450.00
Bowl, Lily Pads, Yellow Opalescent, 8 1/2 In.	495.00
Bowl, Lovebirds, Amid Branches, Signed, 9 1/4 In.	3000.00 To 4500.00
Bowl, Ondines, 6 Stylized Mermaids, Bubbles, Frosted, 8 1/4 In.	660.00
Bowl, Plumes De Paon, Peacock Feathers, Opalescent, 11 3/4 In.	770.00
Bowl, Poissons, Red, 10 In. Diam. ....*Illus*	12000.00
Bowl, Radiating Fish, Opalescent, Center Bubbles, Signed	2956.00
Bowl, Saint–Denis, Berries, Thorny Branches, Signed, 1926, 8 1/8 In.	1045.00
Bowl, Soaring Maidens, Opaque, Signed, 8 In.	935.00
Bowl, Swirled Hobnails, Opalescent, 7 In.	1800.00
Bowl, Tiers Of Flower Heads, Black Centers, Signed, 1929, 10 In.	880.00
Bowl, Tulip Pattern, Signed, 9 1/4 In.	1000.00
Bowl, Volubilis, Entwined Design Forms Feet, Marked, 8 1/2 In.	880.00
Box, 3 Dahlias, Opalescent Blue, Flowers Under Cover, 8 1/2 x 2 In.	1000.00
Box, Arys, Amber Stained, Molded Eros In Heart Cover, Round	1664.00
Box, Bonbon, Beetles In Relief On Cover, Signed, 6 In.	1950.00
Box, Cover, Coq, Rooster, Frosted Black Glass, Round, 4 1/8 In.	6600.00
Box, Cover, Dans La Nuit, Stars, Blue Ground, Blue Glass, 4 3/4 In.	1650.00
Box, Cover, Deux Sirenes, Sea Nymphs, Opalescent, Blue, 10 1/4 In.	2090.00
Box, Cover, Raised Clusters Of Florets, Frosted Glass, 6 1/4 In.	850.00
Box, Trois Figurines, D'Orsay, 3 Nude Maidens, Frosted, 3 3/4 In.	330.00
Bracelet, 13 Half Cylindrical Pieces, Elasticized, Signed	4180.00
Brooch, Deux Fasians, 2 Pheasants, Clear Glass, Metal, 3 1/2 In.	665.00

Lalique, Bowl, Poissons, Red, 10 In. Diam.

◆ ◆ ◆ ◆ ◆ ◆ ◆ ◆ ◆ ◆ ◆ ◆ ◆ ◆ ◆ ◆ ◆

If one link in your antique gold chain breaks, be very careful. There are probably other worn links that will soon break.

◆ ◆ ◆ ◆ ◆ ◆ ◆ ◆ ◆ ◆ ◆ ◆ ◆ ◆ ◆ ◆ ◆ ◆

Candlestick, Blossom Wreath, Birds, 6 Sided Foot, Marked, 6 In., Pair 600.00
Candlestick, Toyko, Stylized Stem, Hobnail Rows, 8 1/8 In., Pair 3300.00
Champagne Bucket, Nudes, Signed, 9 In. 600.00
Chandelier, Ronces, 4 Geometric Scrolled Figures, Domed, 27 In. 665.00
Charger, Swimming Fish, Signed, 14 1/4 In. 5500.00
Clock, Arched Gray Case, Flowers, Vines, c.1932, 4 1/2 In. 1430.00
Clock, Feuilles, Overlapping Leafy Branches, Arched Form, Clear 1100.00
Clock, Pair Of Love Birds Each Side, Signed, 4 3/8 In. 3850.00
Decanter, Pinched Sides, Man Holding Shovel, c.1960, 12 In. 450.00
Dish, Pin, Black Stamens In Center, Blue Trim, Frosted, Signed, 3 In. 375.00
Dish, Veined Bowl, Flower With Stamens Handle, Signed, 5 1/4 In. 95.00
Dish, Wavy Swirled Design, Acid Stamped, 10 3/4 In. 350.00
Figurine, 2 Dancers, Nude 975.00
Figurine, Clos Sainte-Odile, Woman, Brown Stained, In Clear Dish 740.00
Figurine, Dancer, Nude 500.00
Figurine, Deer 110.00
Figurine, Eagle, Tete D'Aigle 425.00
Figurine, Frog, Poised To Jump, Circular Base, Clear, Satin Finish 7835.00
Figurine, Head Of Christ 500.00
Figurine, Moyenne Voilee, Young Maiden, Draped, Frosted, 5 3/8 In. 1925.00
Figurine, Owl, Frosted On Clear Column, Signed, 3 1/2 In. 110.00
Figurine, Pan, Dancing With Wood Nymph, 1950s, 5 1/2 In. 325.00
Figurine, Thais, Arms Outstretched, Bronze Base, c.1925, 10 3/8 In. 9900.00
Figurine, Thais, Woman, Standing, Drapery, Opalescent, 8 3/8 In. 3575.00
Glass, Liqueur, Frosted Cherub Front & Back, Signed, 2 1/4 In. 110.00
Goblet, Spirals Pattern, Clear, Frosted Stem, Signed 95.00
Holder, Menu, 2 Lovebirds, Frosted & Clear, c.1925 .... 225.00
Holder, Menu, Frosted Glass, Bunch Of Grapes On Vine, 6 x 3 1/2 In. 325.00
Holder, Placecard, Molded Fruit, 12 Piece 1500.00
Holder, Placecard, Nude Figures, Pair 395.00
Hood Ornament, Coq Houdan, Proud Rooster, Frosted, 8 In. 1760.00
Hood Ornament, Falcon, Clear & Frosted 1800.00
Hood Ornament, Falcon, Platform Base, Marked, 6 1/4 In. 935.00
Hood Ornament, Rooster, Ruffed Tail, Disk Base, Marked, 8 1/4 In. 660.00
Ice Bucket, Fougeres, Unfurling Fern Fronds, Green Patine, 9 In. 990.00
Jar, Cover, Coty, Frosted, Maiden Form, Drapery, Gray Patine, 4 In. 1210.00
Jardiniere, Acanthus Leaf Handles, Boat Form, 1927, 18 1/8 In. 1650.00
Lemonade Set, Frosted Oak Leaves, 12 Tumblers, Marked, 9 In. 1210.00
Mirror, Hand, 2 Oiseaux, Blue Green, Raised Handle, Satin, 6 3/8 In. 1500.00
Necklace, Pendant, Deep Green, Dragonflies, Silk Cord, Signed 1800.00
Paperweight, Bison, Lowered Head, Frosted, Rectangular, 5 3/8 In. 550.00
Paperweight, Daim, Young Fawn, Pale Charcoal, Rectangular, 3 1/8 In. 440.00
Paperweight, Deer, 3 1/2 In. 175.00
Paperweight, Double Swans 115.00
Pendant, Nymph Kneeling Amidst Flower Laden Branches, 1 1/4 In. 500.00
Perfume Bottle, 4 Dragonflies At Each Corner, Signed, 5 In. 900.00
Perfume Bottle, 4 Draped Women, Amber Patine Figures, 5 1/4 In. 195.00
Perfume Bottle, Ambre Antique, Coty, Classic Figures Frieze, 6 In. 715.00
Perfume Bottle, Ambre D'Orsay, Black Glass 1200.00
Perfume Bottle, Apple Green, Flattened Ovoid, Stopper, 3 1/4 In. 9350.00
Perfume Bottle, Cat, Seated, Signed, 9 In. 425.00
Perfume Bottle, Cavorting Nudes, Crystal & Brass, Atomizer, 5 In. 352.00
Perfume Bottle, Dahlia .... 200.00 To 250.00
Perfume Bottle, Dans La Nuit, Worth, Stars, Blue, Stopper, 5 3/4 In. 1320.00
Perfume Bottle, Deux Aigles, 2 Eagle's Heads, Gray Stained 1665.00
Perfume Bottle, Elephant, Signed, 6 In. 180.00
Perfume Bottle, Fighting Rooster, Signed, 8 In. 225.00
Perfume Bottle, Fille De Eve 50.00
Perfume Bottle, Flattened Form, Leaf Tips, Signed, Box, 1926, 6 In. 2420.00
Perfume Bottle, Frosted 3 Spiraling Pleated Swirls, Signed, 3 In. 325.00
Perfume Bottle, Frosted Tulips, Marked 1800.00
Perfume Bottle, Le Jade, Bird Of Paradise, Branches, 3 1/4 In. 9350.00
Perfume Bottle, Lovebirds, Signed, 4 1/2 In. 120.00

Perfume Bottle, Martial Et Armand, Moth, Black Patine, 3 1/2 In. 1100.00
Perfume Bottle, Nude Maiden & Fawn, Signed, 4 1/2 In. 100.00
Perfume Bottle, Nudes Dancing, Frosted Stopper 225.00
Perfume Bottle, Nudes On Body & Stopper, Signed, 5 In. 400.00
Perfume Bottle, Nudes, Garlands, Brown Wash, Atomizer, 3 1/2 In. 750.00
Perfume Bottle, Pearls, Blue Wash, Signed, 6 1/2 In. 950.00
Perfume Bottle, Snail, Kneeling Nude Stopper, Signed, 3 3/4 In. 110.00
Perfume Bottle, Sphere, Star Design, Quarter Moon Stopper, 4 In. 357.50
Perfume Burner, Dome Cover, Frosted Mermaids, Marked, 6 3/4 In. 7500.00
Pin Tray, Figural Bird Center 110.00
Plate, 5 Mermaids, Opalescent & Clear, Signed, 15 In. 4950.00
Plate, Annual, 1965 .... 1250.00
Plate, Annual, 1966 To 1973, 8 Piece 200.00
Plate, Dancing Nymphs, Clear & Frosted, 8 1/2 In., 8 Piece 320.00
Plate, Fish Around Circle Of Bubbles, Signed, 11 In. 550.00
Plate, Ondine, Sea–Sprites Frieze, Clear & Satin 1475.00
Plate, Peace, 1976 .... 100.00
Plate, Swirling Fern, 12 In. 395.00
Powder Box, 2 Draped Females, Clear & Frosted, 3 1/2 x 2 1/4 In. 350.00
Powder Box, Cactus, Enameled 195.00
Powder Box, Flowering Branches & Seated Cupid On Cover, Signed 3300.00
Powder Box, Flowering Vines, Seated Putto, Signed, c.1932, 5 1/2 In. 1760.00
Powder Box, Le Lys, Brown Stain 395.00
Powder Box, Metal, 2 Flying Birds, Arched Feathers, Puff, 3 In. Dia. 350.00
Powder Jar, Blossoms On Cover, D'Orsay, Marked, 4 In. 247.50
Punch Bowl, Antilles, Grape, 1960s 1500.00
Ring Holder, Quail In Center, 4 In. 110.00
Scent Bottle, Althea, Stylized Flowerhead, Enameled Center, Clear 1386.00
Scent Bottle, Le Jade, Pale Green, Bird, Branches, Snuff Bottle Form 2960.00
Scent Burner, Artichoke 400.00
Seal, Amber Glass, Eagle's Head, 1932 .... 1200.00
Stick Pin, Serpent, Coiled, Amber Glass, Gold Mount, 2 In. 660.00
Tile, Oiseaux, Bird On Branch, Frosted, Rectangular, 5 3/4 In., Pair 3850.00
Tray, Carnation Blossoms, Frosted Glass, 15 1/2 x 10 In. 750.00
Tray, Raised Blossoms, 2 Sections, Signed, 3 1/2 x 4 1/2 In. 250.00
Tumbler, Classically Clothed Women, Signed, 1911, 3 7/8 In., 4 Piece 880.00
Tumbler, Fruit, 5 In. 395.00
Tumbler, Purple Dots, Clear, Signed 50.00
Tumbler, Raised Beaded Coils, Signed, 3 In., 6 Piece 400.00
Vase, 5 Horizontal Tiers, Flower Heads, Signed, 1930, 6 1/4 In. 770.00
Vase, Acanthes, Yellow Opalescent, Acanthus Leafage, 11 1/4 In. 6050.00
Vase, Antilopes, Leaping Antelopes, Enameled, Ovoid, Clear, 9 1/4 In. 770.00
Vase, Avallon, Birds In Berry Branches, Cylindrical, Clear, Satin 2218.00
Vase, Avallon, Sparrows On Branches, Signed, 1927, 5 3/4 In. 1760.00
Vase, Band Of Nude Male Archers, Birds, Signed, 1921, 10 1/2 In. 3300.00
Vase, Bands Of Flowers, Signed, 7 x 6 In. 2310.00
Vase, Bands Of Geometric Leafage, Signed, 1927, 5 3/16 In. 1210.00
Vase, Blown–Out Blossoms, Raised Branches, Frosted, 6 1/4 In. 525.00
Vase, Bouchardon, Nude Female Seated, Floral Festoons, 4 7/8 In. 6875.00
Vase, Calypso, 5 Mermaids, Signed, 11 3/4 In. 7150.00
Vase, Camaret, 4 Tiers Of Fish Swimming, Frosted, 5 1/2 In. 1540.00
Vase, Ceylan, 4 Pairs Of Parakeets, Marked, 9 1/2 In. .... 3000.00 To 5600.00
Vase, Chevreuse, 5 Tiers, Flower Heads, Frosted, 6 1/4 In. 770.00
Vase, Cone Form, Pedestal Base, Signed, 6 In., Pair 412.00
Vase, Dahlias, Overlapping Blossoms, Enameled Glass, 4 3/4 In. 2475.00
Vase, Dampierre, 6 In. 265.00
Vase, Davos, Allover Bubble Design, Cylindrical, Amber, 11 3/8 In. 3300.00
Vase, Deer In Forest, Honey Amber, Signed, 7 In. 1210.00
Vase, Domremy, Thistles, Thorny Leafage, Red Patina, 8 3/8 In. 1430.00
Vase, Epicea, Overlapping Pine Boughs, Frosted Green, 9 1/8 In. 3850.00
Vase, Esterel, Overlapping Leafage, Opalescent, 6 1/8 In. 990.00
Vase, Ferrieres, Brown Wash, Signed, 7 In. .... 1150.00 To 1300.00
Vase, Fontaines, Irregular Ribbed, Melon Skin, Blue, 5 5/8 In. 880.00

Vase, Frosted Side Leaves, Leaves Rising To Top, Signed, 7 1/2 In. 880.00
Vase, Grenade, Amber, Engraved, 4 1/2 In. 1100.00
Vase, Gui, Mistletoe, Berries, Leaves, Frosted Blue, 6 1/2 In. 3740.00
Vase, Handles Molded Into Clusters Of Flowers, Signed, 7 3/4 In. 3300.00
Vase, Hiboux, 5 1/4 x 5 5/8 In. 495.00
Vase, Lagamar, Geometric Bands, Gray, Black Enameled, 7 1/4 In. 7975.00
Vase, Leaf Design, Frosted & Clear, Signed, 4 1/2 In. 165.00
Vase, Leaves, Opalescent Band Of Rabbits, Intaglio Mold, 6 In. 1800.00
Vase, Lezards Et Bluets, Lizards, Scrolling, Frosted, 13 1/8 In. 6325.00
Vase, Malesherbes, Leafage, Frosted, Ovoid, 9 In. 715.00
Vase, Marisa, 3 Bands Of Undulating Fish, Spherical, Gray, 9 3/8 In. 4400.00
Vase, Martinet, Frosted Birds In Flight, 10 In. 775.00
Vase, Medusa, Coiling Octopus Tentacles, Signed, 1921, 6 1/4 In. 825.00
Vase, Mistletoe, Leaves & Berries, Opalescent, 6 3/4 In. 950.00
Vase, Moissac, Geometric Leafage Bands, Opalescent, 5 3/16 In. 1210.00
Vase, Monnaie Du Pape, Blossoms, Green Patina, Frosted, 9 1/4 In. 2475.00
Vase, Monthery, Relief Festoons, Frosted, 5 1/2 In. 1760.00
Vase, Mures, Blackberries, Thorny Branches, Cylindrical, 7 1/2 In. 5500.00
Vase, Overall Grape Design, Signed, 6 In. 2090.00
Vase, Pattern Of Branches, Opalescent, Rounded Body, 7 In. 950.00
Vase, Peacock's Heads, Blue, Ovoid, Marked, 9 1/16 In. 3300.00
Vase, Poissons, Overlapping Finned Fish, Gray, 1921, 9 In. 1100.00
Vase, Ronces, Entwined Thorny Branches, Blue, 9 1/4 In. 3025.00
Vase, Ronces, Overlapping Thorny Branches, Gray Patina, 9 1/8 In. 1925.00
Vase, Ronsard, Floral Festoons, Female Nude Handles, 8 1/4 In. 3575.00
Vase, Roses, 9 1/2 In. .... 900.00 To 975.00
Vase, Saint-Francois, Birds On Leafy Branches, Frosted, 7 In. 3575.00
Vase, St. Cloud, 4 3/4 In. 260.00
Vase, Tiers Of Jagged-Edged Leaves, Signed, 1931, 3 3/16 In. 1925.00
Vase, Tournesol, Sunflower Blossoms, Marked, 4 3/4 In. 302.50
Vase, Tulipes, Undulating Tulips, Frosted, Ovoid, 8 3/8 In. 2475.00
Vase, Vintage & Nymphs, Frosted To Clear, Signed, 8 5/8 In., Pair 450.00
Vase, Yvelines, Horses Amidst Scrolling Leafage, 7 1/2 In. 2750.00

LAMPS of every type, from the early oil-burning Betty and Phoebe lamps
to the recent electric lamps with glass or beaded shades, interest collectors.
Fuels used in lamps changed through the years; whale oil (1800-1840),
camphene (1828), Argand (1830), lard (1833-1863), turpentine and alcohol
(1840s), gas (1850-1879), kerosene (1860), and electricity (1879) are the
most common. Other lamps are listed by manufacturer or type of material.

Alabaster, 2 Gray Eagles, 23 In. 800.00
Aladdin, 194, Colonial, Clear 110.00
Aladdin, Angle, Double, Ceiling Extension 300.00
Aladdin, B-11, Moonstone, Green 115.00
Aladdin, B-25, Victoria, Filler Cap 450.00
Aladdin, B-26, Simplicity, Decalmania, Burner, 1948-1953 .... 255.00
Aladdin, B-27, Simplicity, Alacite, Plain, 1948-1953 .... 165.00
Aladdin, B-28, Simplicity, Rose, 1948-1953 .... 65.00
Aladdin, B-39, Washington Drape, Clear, Round 80.00
Aladdin, B-50, Washington Drape, Filigree, Green 100.00
Aladdin, B-51, Washington Drape, Filigree, Amber 100.00
Aladdin, B-60, Lincoln Drape, Short, Alacite 450.00
Aladdin, B-62, Lincoln Drape, Short, Ruby 500.00
Aladdin, B-75, Lincoln Drape, Alacite, Ivory, Short, 1940-1947 .... 90.00
Aladdin, B-76, Lincoln Drape, Tall, Cobalt 675.00
Aladdin, B-76A, Simplicity, Alacite, Plain 125.00
Aladdin, B-77, Lincoln Drape, Ruby, Tall, 1940-1949 .... 800.00
Aladdin, B-80, Beehive, Clear 75.00
Aladdin, B-81, Beehive, Green, 1935 .... 75.00
Aladdin, B-82, Beehive, Amber, 1937 .... 90.00
Aladdin, B-83, Beehive, Ruby, 1935 .... 275.00 To 325.00
Aladdin, B-87, Vertique, Rose Moonstone 350.00
Aladdin, B-88, Yellow Vertique, Kerosene, 1937 .... 330.00 To 440.00

Aladdin, B–100, Corinthian, Clear 40.00
Aladdin, B–103, Corinthian, Clear 40.00
Aladdin, B–104, Corinthian, Clear Font, Black Foot, Signed 100.00
Aladdin, B–104, Corinthian, Sawtooth Pattern, Clear, Chimney, 23 In. 80.00
Aladdin, B–107, Cathedral, Clear 85.00
Aladdin, B–112, Cathedral, Moonstone, Burner, 1934 .... 177.50
Aladdin, B–133, Orientale, Silver, 1935 .... 195.00
Aladdin, B–134, Orientale, Bronze, 1935 .... 100.00
Aladdin, B–199, Corinthian, Clear 75.00
Aladdin, Boudoir, Alacite, Electric 400.00
Aladdin, C–166, Bouquet Finial, Moonstone, White 50.00
Aladdin, Caped Lady, 1937 .... 2500.00
Aladdin, Coach & Four Shade, 14 In. 145.00
Aladdin, F–288, Electric 60.00
Aladdin, G–16, Dogwood Shade, Electric, 7 In. 800.00
Aladdin, G–16, Figurine, Frosted, Shade 800.00
Aladdin, G–18, 1 Black, 1 Amber, Electric, 1935, Pair 80.00
Aladdin, G–41, Princess Finial, Amber, 1935 .... 120.00
Aladdin, G–69, Millefleur Finial, Shade, Electric, 1935 .... 105.00
Aladdin, G–92, Blue, 1937, Pair 65.00
Aladdin, G–92, Boudoir, Rose, Paper Labels, Pair 75.00
Aladdin, G–140, Moonstone, White, Electric, ... 37.50
Aladdin, G–144, Isis Finial, Amber, Fluted Shade 115.00
Aladdin, G–187, Alacite, White, Electric, 1939 .... 10.00
Aladdin, G–219, Alacite, Electric, Table, 1940 .... 37.50
Aladdin, G–236, Flowers & Leaf Spray, Alacite, Rose, Electric, Table 17.50
Aladdin, G–267, Alacite, Urn Shape, Electric, Table 70.00
Aladdin, G–281, Ivory, Blue Alacite, Column, Electric, Table, 1947 .... 40.00
Aladdin, Hobnail, Green 140.00
Aladdin, Kerosene, Moonstone, Parchment Shade, Pink 125.00
Aladdin, Lincoln Drape, Shade No. 601 With Cabin Scene 750.00
Aladdin, Model B, Floor 150.00
Aladdin, Moonstone, Pink 185.00
Aladdin, No. 1, Queen Heart, Clear 170.00
Aladdin, No. 2, King Heart, Burner, Kerosene 102.50
Aladdin, No. 2, Queen Heart, Green 220.00
Aladdin, No. 11, Green Milk Glass Shade, Nickel–Plated Brass, 18 In. 55.00
Aladdin, No. 12, Hanging, Brass, Kerosene, 12 1/2 x 26 In. 150.00
Aladdin, No. 12, Lamp, Floor 70.00
Aladdin, No. 100, Venetian, White, Alpha Crystal, 1932 .... 50.00
Aladdin, No. 101, Venetian, Green, A Burner, 1932 .... 50.00 To 85.00
Aladdin, No. 103, Ventian, Rose, Alpha Crystal, 1932 .... 60.00
Aladdin, No. 106, Model B, Green, Kerosene, 1933 .... 100.00
Aladdin, No. 113, Chandelier, Single, Smoke Bell, No. 205 Shade 3100.00
Aladdin, No. 1977, Lincoln Drape, Red, Shade 130.00
Aladdin, Simplicity, Gold Luster 150.00
Aladdin, Simplicity, Green 90.00
Aladdin, Simplicity, Pink 100.00
Aladdin, Simplicity, White 80.00
Alcohol Burner, Bulbous Font, Saucer Base, Mid–1800s, Small 95.00
Art Deco, Metal, Florentine Type, 1930s 395.00
Art Deco, Pattyn Products, Aluminum, Bakelite, Brass, Von Nessen, 19 In. 3300.00
Astral, Brass Font, Clear, Frosted Shade, Prisms, Marble Base, 18 In. 150.00
Astral, Brass Font, Star Etched Ball Shade, Electrified, 18 In., Pair 300.00
Astral, Brass, Marble Base, No Shade, Cornelius & Co., April 1, 1845 .... 176.00
Astral, Brass, Thumbprint & Floral Shade, 36 In., Pair ....*Illus* 935.00
Astral, Cut & Frosted Shade, Electrified, 25 3/8 In. 330.00
Astral, Double Arm, Electrified, Mid–19th Century, 18 In., Pair 710.00
Astral, Etched & Wheel Cut Shade, Faux Marble Shaft, Brass, 25 In. 445.00
Astral, Figural Stem, Black Marble Base, Brass Font, 18 In. 357.00
Astral, Gilded Brass, Marble, Cut Prisms, Frosted Cut, 31 In. 375.00
Astral, J. & I. Cox, Etched, Cut Glass Shade, Lotus, Electrified, 27 In. 935.00
Astral, Lotus Font, Etched & Wheel Cut Shade, Gilt Brass, 19 1/2 In. 357.50

Lamp, Astral, Brass,
Thumbprint & Floral Shade,
36 In., Pair

Lamp, Banquet, Ruby
Cutback, Brass Font,
Frosted Shade

Lamp, Kerosene, Cut Glass,
Frosted Shade, Spelter
Figure, 22 In.

Banker's, Folding, Brass, Patent 1922	35.00
Banquet, Cameo Cut Cranberry & Gold Flowers, Frosted Shade	1600.00
Banquet, Cartouche Of Little Girls, Silver Trim, Miniature	830.00
Banquet, Daisies Shade, Opalescent Vaseline Glass, 21 1/2 In.	850.00
Banquet, Floral Shade, Pewter Base, Stem & Font, 31 In.	595.00
Banquet, Red Satin Glass Ball Shade, Brass	350.00
Banquet, Ruby Cutback, Brass Font, Frosted Shade ....*Illus*	475.00
Betty, Iron, Pitted, Hanger & Pick, 4 1/4 In.	125.00
Betty, Tin, Wick Pick & Hook, Hinged Lid, Wick Tube	350.00
Betty, Trammel, Adjustable Trapezoidal Oil Pan, 1780s, 25 In.	880.00
Betty, Wrought Iron, Stylized Hen Finial, Swivel Lid, 4 In.	115.00
Bicycle, Handle Bar, E. A. Bicycle Accessories, White, Box	20.00
Bouillotte, Double–Light, Toleware, Dark Green, Gilding, 19 In.	3400.00
Bouraine, Fish Scene, Silvered Bronze, Green Onyx Base, 15 x 21 In.	8800.00
Bradley & Hubbard lamps are included in the Bradley & Hubbard category	
Camphene, Twin Tube, Pewter, Side Handle, c.1830, 6 1/2 In.	350.00
Candle, Ship's, Silver Plate, Electrified	120.00
Carbide, Justrite, Tin	45.00
Carriage, Eli Griffiths & Sons, Birmingham, 1914, 15 3/4 In.	75.00
Chandelier, 3–Light, Kerosene, Pat. 1876	600.00
Chandelier, 4 Gas, 4 Electric Lights, Etched Shades, 74 In., Pair	2700.00
Chandelier, 4–Light, Iron, From Crown Shaped Meat Hook, Chain, 21 In.	325.00
Chandelier, 4–Light, Jeweled Frame, Hobnail Shades, Crystal Prisms	950.00
Chandelier, 5–Light, Frosted & Acid Etched Shades, Brass, 60 1/2 In.	520.00
Chandelier, 5–Light, Ornate Crown Ring, Glass Bell Finial, 16 In.	285.00
Chandelier, 6–Light, Clear & Amethyst Swags & Drops, Iron, 23 In.	605.00
Chandelier, 6–Light, Clear & Opaline Shades, Gilt Bronze	5750.00
Chandelier, 6–Light, Gilded Metal, Scrolling Arms, Crystals, 26 In.	220.00
Chandelier, 6–Light, Iron, Partial Gilt, Amethyst Swags, Drops, 23 In.	605.00
Chandelier, 6–Light, Napoleon III, Clear & Tinted Pendants, Brass	990.00
Chandelier, 6–Light, Ormolu, Cut Glass Center Section, 30 In.	7150.00
Chandelier, 6–Light, Winged Lady Sphinx Top, Brass & White Metal	650.00
Chandelier, 8–Light, Spelter, Palm Leaf, Art Deco, Crystal, 36 In.	2200.00
Chandelier, 9–Light, Louis XV Style, Iron, Crystal Pendants, 30 In.	1320.00
Chandelier, 12–Light, Glass Drip Pans, Leaf Nozzles, Prisms, 39 In.	3850.00
Chandelier, 18–Light, Marie Therese Style, Prisms, Prism Chain, 39 In.	1540.00
Chandelier, 18–Light, Resting Birds Support Branches, Bronze, 45 In.	9250.00
Chandelier, 24–Light, 2 Tiers, Glass Tears, Swags, Gilt Bronze, 49 In.	3850.00
Chandelier, Art Nouveau, Butterfly, Patinated Metal, 21 In.	605.00
Chandelier, Cornelius & Baker, Gasolier, c.1860 ....*Illus*	5060.00
Chandelier, Jeweled Frame, 4 Arms, Multicolored Prisms, Electrified	950.00

Chandelier, Kerosene, Brass, Crystal Drops, Opaque Glass Shade	550.00
Copper, Conical Mica Paneled Shade, Dirk Van Erp, 1915, 20 3/4 In.	7700.00
Electric, 5 In. Beaded Fringe Silk Shade, 20 In.	125.00
Electric, 50/50 Advertising, Hanging	30.00
Electric, Art Glass Poppy Shade, Bronze Base, 27 1/4 In.	2800.00
Electric, Art Nouveau, Bronze Finish, 21 In.	475.00
Electric, Art Nouveau, Metal, Bronze Finish, 47 In.	900.00
Electric, Art Pottery, Baluster Form, Orange Body, Wooden Base, 24 In.	275.00
Electric, Black, Oriental Inset Figures, 21 In.	25.00
Electric, Boudoir, Bisque, Pink Funky Look, 1930s	135.00
Electric, Brandt, Cobra Rising From Base, Bronze, Shade, 20 In.	7150.00
Electric, Brandt, Scrolled Iron, Domed Alabaster Shade, 16 3/4 In.	8250.00
Electric, Brass, Floor, 6 Arms, Winged Griffin Base, 8 Ft.	550.00
Electric, Brass, Orange Slag Glass Shade, 14 In.	160.00
Electric, Brass, Yellow Slag Glass Shade, 10 In.	180.00
Electric, Bridge, Wrought Iron, Leaf Design On Legs, 65 1/2 In.	75.00
Electric, Bronze, Column With Dragons & Birds, Japan, 74 In.	522.00
Electric, Bronze, Entwining Vines, Orange To Deep Blue Tulip Shade	325.00
Electric, Bronze, Leaded Glass Shade, Lotus Pads Base, 19 In.	2100.00
Electric, Cameo Cut To Cranberry, White Overlay, Flowers, 36 In.	195.00
Electric, Celadon Porcelain Vases, White Floral Design, 26 In., Pair	110.00
Electric, Charioteer, Model 72, Art Deco, Round Patterned Globe	37.50
Electric, Cherub, Cornucopia, Floral Garlands, Bronze, 32 3/4 In.	450.00
Electric, Cherubs, Satyrs, Lion Heads, Gilded Brass, France, 36 In., Pair	2400.00
Electric, Cheuret, Alabaster, Metal, Lozenge-Shaped Base, 9 In.	4400.00
Electric, Chicago World's Fair, Glass, Square Shade, Decals, 1934	100.00
Electric, Chocolate Glass Paneled Shade, Scenic Metal Grids, 24 In.	715.00
Electric, Classically Draped Maidens, Cast Zinc, 65 In.	6400.00
Electric, Consolidated Glass Co., Torch Type, Paper Label, 10 In.	165.00
Electric, Cylindrical Amber Glass, Wrought Iron, Floor, 70 In.	110.00
Electric, Desk, Emeralite, Labels	250.00
Electric, Desk, Lap, Calamander, Victorian, Arched, Fitted, 7 x 16 In.	495.00
Electric, Desk, Slag Shade, 8 Panels, Adjustable Stem, Marble Base	500.00
Electric, Dirk Van Erp, 2-Light, Conical Shade, c.1916, 20 1/2 In.	5500.00
Electric, Dirk Van Erp, 3-Light, Copper, Mica Shade, c.1910, 20 1/4 In.	5500.00
Electric, Dirk Van Erp, 3-Light, Copper, Mica Shade, c.1912, 24 In.	8800.00
Electric, Dirk Van Erp, Mica Shade, Trumpet Form	8800.00
Electric, Dome Shade, 6 Ribbed & Curved Panels, Windmill Scene, 22 In.	495.00
Electric, Dresser, Carnival Glass Shade, 12 In.	250.00
Electric, Dresser, Cherubs On Teeter-Totter, Polychrome, 17 In., Pair	100.00
Electric, Eichbert, Squatty Dome, 3 Female Masks At Base	5445.00

Lamp, Chandelier, Cornelius & Baker,
Gasolier, c.1860

Lamp, Torchere, Daum Nancy Glass, Iron,
E. Brandt, c.1925

Lamp, Electric, Fruit Basket,   Lamp, Electric, G. Moscagin,   Lamp, Electric, Spelter,
Glass, 32 In.   Marble, 3 Graces, 32 In.   Maiden & Eagle, 29 In.

Electric, Fenton, Ball, Lime Satin, Poppy, Pair 300.00
Electric, Fruit Basket, Glass, 32 In. ....*Illus* 5940.00
Electric, G. Moscagin, Marble, 3 Graces, 32 In. ....*Illus* 3000.00
Electric, Gilded Cast Plaster Knight, Shield, 22 1/2 In. 75.00
Electric, Globe, Hanging, Drugstore, Victorian Style 500.00
Electric, Gordon Russell, Oak, Octagonal Stem, 4 Footed, Floor, 1927 .... 665.00
Electric, Green Depression Glass, Hexagonal Shade, Flowers, Table 95.00
Electric, Guiraud, Riviere, Seated Gold Nude, Marble Column, 15 In. 850.00
Electric, Gustav Stickley, Copper, Strapwork, c.1910, 9 3/4 In. 550.00
Electric, Gustav Stickley, White Bell–Shaped Shade, Oak, 57 1/2 In. 2200.00
Electric, Hall, Vintage Design, Brass, Iron Chain, Austria, 26 1/2 In. 225 0
Electric, Hanging, Mission Oak, Green Glass Panels, Wooden Links .... 45(0
Electric, Jefferson, No. 2362, Reverse Painted, Lake Scene, 15 3/4 In. 1300.00
Electric, Jefferson, Reverse Painted Scene, 16 In. 1600.00
Electric, Jefferson, Reverse Painted Scene, Clouds, Sunrays, 18 In. 2950.00
Electric, Jefferson, Reverse Painted, Hollyhock Shade, Artist, 18 In. 2700.00
Electric, Jockey, Cast Metal, Original Paint, 19 1/2 In. 275.00
Electric, Joe St. Clair, Flowered Paperweight, 28 In. 550.00
Electric, Knobbed Dragon, Diaper Design, Mask Base, Japan, 1910, 30 In. 145.00
Electric, Leaded Glass Shade, Floral, Beige Ground, 14 In. 1300.00
Electric, Lecturer's, Bell In Base, Black Paint, Gold Striping, 10 In. 250.00
Electric, Lotton, Bronze Mermaid, Holding Nautilus Shade 935.00
Electric, Lotton, Kneeling Bronze Nude, Half Hidden By Shade Of Tulip 660.00
Electric, Lotton, Nude Maiden Between 2 Lilies, Art Glass & Bronze 990.00
Electric, Marriage, Brass Base, Blue Opaque 1100.00
Electric, Meissen Type, Floral Design, Dancers, Porcelain Shade, 20 In. 110.00
Electric, Miller, Student, Syphon, Cut, Frosted Glass Font, Vienna Shade 1200.00
Electric, Moe Bridges, Country Road Scene, Signed, 15 In. 2200.00
Electric, Moe Bridges, Interior Flock Of Geese Over Water, 18 In. 4840.00
Electric, Moe Bridges, Landscape Shade, Signed, Table 1430.00
Electric, Moe Bridges, Reverse Painted Waterfront Scene, 21 In. 1430.00
Electric, Moe Bridges, Reverse Painted, Country Road, 15 In. ....*Illus* 2200.00
Electric, Moe Bridges, South Sea Island Scene, 18 In. Diam. 2950.00
Electric, Mt. Washington Shade, Birds & Flowers, Brass Base, 19 1/2 In. 1500.00
Electric, Neoclassical, Painted, Parcel Gilt, Tole Shade, 15 In., Pair 1100.00
Electric, Oak, 6 Legs, Table, 1930s 30.00
Electric, Peacock Feather, Amber 245.00
Electric, Perzel, Chromium Plate, Cylindrical, Circular Concave Base 1850.00
Electric, Phoenix, Hawaiian Scene, Reverse Painted, 18 In. 1100.00
Electric, Pittsburgh, Call Of The Wild, 18 In. 2650.00
Electric, Pittsburgh, Reverse Painted, Lakes Of Killarney, 16 In. 2700.00

Lamp, Electric, Moe Bridges,
Reverse Painted, Country
Road, 15 In.

Lamp, Electric, Slag,
Metal Base

Lamp, Electric, Wilkinson,
Leaded Glass, Grape
Design, 20 In.

Electric, Pittsburgh, Textured Glass Dome, Tropical Trees, 18 In. 715.00
Electric, Pottery Foo Dog, Colored Glaze, 32 In. 150.00
Electric, R. M. Thompson, 2–Light, Wall, Oak, Semicircular Form 444.00
Electric, Rainard, Lake Scene Shade, Candelabra Base, 20–In. Shade 3200.00
Electric, Reverse Painted Shade, Windmill, Gilt Metal Squirrel, 22 In. 495.00
Electric, Roycrofters, No. 913, Gold Ribbed Steuben Shade, 10 1/2 In. 3520.00
Electric, S. Mouille, Triangular Spike Base, Floor, c.1955, 62 In. 4950.00
Electric, Slag, Metal Base ....*Illus* 400.00
Electric, Solar, Gilt–Bronze, Gothic Frosted, Cut Shade, c.1840 .... 1750.00
Electric, Spanish Galleon, TV, Painted Glass Backdrop 39.00
Electric, Spelter, Maiden & Eagle, 29 In. ....*Illus* 350.00
Electric, Statue Of Liberty, Bronzed, 1930s, 16 In. 175.00
Electric, Suess Ornamental Glass Co., Bronze, Glass, Dogwood, 1900s 8800.00
Electric, Tulip, Vine, Leaded Glass Panels, Spelter Base, c.1910, 23 In. 770.00
Electric, TV, Black Panther 20.00
Electric, TV, Nude Woman, Art Deco, Arms Outstretched, New Shade 52.50
Electric, Vanity, Diamond Faceted Clear Glass, Art Deco, Pair 25.00
Electric, Werkstatte, Brass, Baluster, Domed Foot, 20 In. 2937.00
Electric, Wicker, Floor, Large Shallow Shade 895.00
Electric, Wilkinson, Leaded Glass, Grape Design, 20 In. ....*Illus* 2500.00
Electric, Woody Woodpecker, 1974 .... 38.00
Electric, Yarn Swift, All Original 95.00
Fairy, 2 Faces, Child's Head, Clarke Pyramid Shade, 4 1/2 In. 330.00
Fairy, 3 Faces, Clear Font, Frosted, 9 In. 900.00
Fairy, 8–Crimp Top, Colored Jewels, Pink Ruffled Base, 5 3/4 In. 395.00
Fairy, Applied Leaves, Pyramid, Sapphire Blue, 8 1/2 In. 225.00
Fairy, Clear Glass Rigaree Feet, Cranberry Glass 350.00
Fairy, Diamond–Quilted Aqua Shade, Brass Handle, Clarke Insert 225.00
Fairy, Diamond–Quilted Shade, Tuncliffe Flower Holder Base, 6 In. 715.00
Fairy, Diamond–Quilted, Mother–of–Pearl, Clarke Insert, Signed, 7 In. 675.00
Fairy, Diamond–Quilted, Rose Shade, Mother–of–Pearl, Signed Clark 125.00
Fairy, Lighthouse, Frosted 150.00
Fairy, Owl Head, Clarke Base, Enamel On Shade, 4 1/4 In. .... 150.00 To 175.00
Fairy, Pyramid, Mother–of–Pearl Shade, Clear Base, 3 3/4 In. 385.00
Fairy, Pyramid, Webb Burmese Shade, Clear Glass Base, 3 7/8 In. 245.00
Fairy, Ruffled Top & Base, Vaseline, 8 x 7 In. 325.00
Fairy, Swirled Rib Mold, White Spatter On Chartreuse, 5 1/2 In. 580.00
Fairy, Verre Moire, Nailsea Loopings, Clarke Cup, Blue, 6 1/2 x 8 In. 845.00
Fairy, Webb, Yellow, Black, Gold Stand, 5 In. 295.00
Finger, Blue Opalescent, Snowflake, Loop Handle, Flat 375.00
Finger, Bull's–Eye, Clear, Miniature 50.00

Finger, Camphene, Clear, 10 1/2 In.	125.00
Finger, Evening Star, E. R. & Co., 2 1/8 In.	49.50
Finger, Princess Feather, Cobalt Blue, Small	475.00
Fluid, Free–Blown, Ringed Globular Foot, c.1830, 3 1/2 In.	220.00
Fluid, Hexagonal Font, Blue Glass Columnar Base, 4 1/4 In.	412.50
Fluid, Sandwich, Triple Overlay, Pink Cut To White & Clear	3190.00
Gasoline, Coleman, Blue Enamel, Iron	35.00
George Nelson, Hanging, Bubble, Fiberglass Skin, Off–White, 30 In.	225.00
Gilliards, 2–Light, Swag Mounted, Tole Shades, Bronze, 47 In. x 5 Ft.	5775.00
Girandole, 3–Light, Sultan, Gilt Bronze, White Marble Base, 19 In.	135.00
Girandole, Gilded Brass, Amethyst Rock Crystal, Prisms, 17 In., Pair	350.00
Gone With The Wind, 7 Hand Painted Sports Figures, 1895–1900	2000.00
Gone With The Wind, Baby Face, Green Satin Glass	2450.00
Gone With The Wind, Blue & Magenta Flowers, 22 1/2 In.	350.00
Gone With The Wind, Brown Tones Hunting Scene, Electrified, 27 In.	2500.00
Gone With The Wind, Floral Pattern, Red Satin Glass	450.00
Gone With The Wind, Fluid, Beaded Base, Electrified, Miller, 21 In.	495.00
Gone With The Wind, Frosted Iris	135.00
Gone With The Wind, Green Floral Pattern	450.00
Gone With The Wind, Large Pink Flowers, Squatty, Yellow, 20 In.	450.00
Grease, Carlton Brown, Amber Glaze, Pottery, 3 3/4 In.	325.00
Grease, Hanging, Pan With Spout, Twisted Hanger, 9 In.	105.00
Grease, Wick Pick On Chain, Link Hanger, Iron	85.00
Hand, Blown Opalescent Glass, Elongated Loop, c.1850, 3 1/2 In.	110.00
Hand, Coin Spot, Original Brass Burner, Applied Handle, Chimney, 10 In.	465.00
Handel lamps are included in the Handel category	
Hanging, Glass, Cylindrical, Engraved, Frosted Grapes, Vines, 12 In.	1100.00
Hanging, Hall, Cut Overlay, Cobalt Blue, Brass Trim, 20th Century	300.00
Kerosene, Acorn Amber Font, 7 3/4 In.	220.00
Kerosene, Adjustable & Gilded Embossed Brass Font, Floor, 64 1/2 In.	95.00
Kerosene, Angle, Hanging, 2–Light, Angle, Mfg.	375.00
Kerosene, Astral, Figural, Brass Font, 18 In.	358.00
Kerosene, Attebury, Double Glass Layers, Footed, Crystal	135.00
Kerosene, Beaded Drape, Ball Shade, 9 In.	345.00
Kerosene, Bracket Wall Mounted	35.00
Kerosene, Brass Collar, Green Opaque Font, White Opaque Base, 11 In.	65.00
Kerosene, Brass Corinthian Column Base, Panel Cut Ruby Font, 17 In.	115.00
Kerosene, Brass Fittings, Mercury Reflector, Bull's–Eye Pattern	295.00
Kerosene, Brass, Clear Shell Pressed Font, Marble Base, 9 7/8 In.	45.00
Kerosene, Brass, Green Marble Base, Brass Burner, 16 1/2 In., Pair	230.00
Kerosene, Bristol, Cobalt Blue, Font In Vase Base, Enameled, 17 In.	1895.00
Kerosene, Clear Blown Font, Floral Design, Opaque White Base, 12 In.	150.00
Kerosene, Coolidge Drape, Light Green, Pedestal Base	95.00
Kerosene, Cranberry Glass, 8 1/2 In.	412.50
Kerosene, Cut Glass, Diamonds & Fans Base	200.00
Kerosene, Cut Glass, Frosted Shade, Spelter Figure, 22 In. ....*Illus*	165.00
Kerosene, Cut Roman Key, Brass, Spelter Figure, 17 1/4 In.	138.00
Kerosene, Finger, Coin Dot, Cranberry	525.00
Kerosene, Gone With The Wind Style, English Bristol, 26 In., Pair	795.00
Kerosene, Hackle, Burner, Cast Iron, Glass	75.00
Kerosene, Hand, Clear Glass, Finger Grip, Pearl Top, 14 In.	150.00
Kerosene, Lace Maker's, Brass Base, White Lined Shade, 18 1/4 In.	595.00
Kerosene, Lace Maker's, Overshot Cranberry, Brass Base, 16 1/2 In.	395.00
Kerosene, Lomax, Oil Guard, Cast Iron, Glass	75.00
Kerosene, Marriage, Ripley, Opaque Base, Clambroth Holder, Onts, 12 In.	750.00
Kerosene, Paneled Bull's–Eye, Leaded	145.00
Kerosene, Peacock Feather, Clear	85.00
Kerosene, Sunflower Pattern	60.00
Kerosene, Victorian, Brown & White Flowers, Shade	575.00
Lacemaker's, Standing Frosted Figural Base, 11 In.	500.00
Lard, Baker's, Brass, Weighted Base, 13 In.	450.00
Lard, Tin	350.00
Marble, White, Gypsy Girl, Holding Pitcher, At Well, Gugliemo, 25 In.	2500.00

Miner's, Autolite, Brass Carbide 15.00
Miner's, Brass, Wrought Iron Hanger, St. Louis, Mo., Pat. Feb. 27, '77 .... 125.00
Miner's, Cast & Wrought Iron, Brass Shield Finial, 4 1/2 In. 200.00
Miner's, Oil, On Cloth Hat 35.00
Miner's, Safety 40.00
Miner's, Sticking Tommy, Diamonds & Crosses, 18th Century, 2 x 8 In. 395.00
Miner's, Wales, Brass 95.00
Miner's, Winchester 55.00
Oil, Apollo, Amber 95.00
Oil, Art Nouveau, Iris, Satin Glass, Large Flat Base 98.00
Oil, Barred Rib & Swirl, Clear Font, Brass Stem, Marble Base 115.00
Oil, Blue Cut Velvet, Diamond, Footed, Nutmeg Burner, Miniature 1045.00
Oil, Brass, Tube Burner, Round Base, Bulbous Stem & Font, 11 In. 250.00
Oil, Bridgeport, Brass, Chimney, Reflector, Double Ring Handle, 7 In. 165.00
Oil, Bull's-Eye Font, Hexagonal Base, Flint, Pressed Glass, 11 In. 65.00
Oil, Charles X, Marble Stem, Patinated Bronze, 24 In., Pair 6050.00
Oil, Coolidge Drape, Cobalt Blue, 9 In. 225.00
Oil, Cranberry Opalescent Swirl, Glass Base 700.00
Oil, Crown Point, Valkmar 295.00
Oil, Cut Overlay, Opaque White To Green, Brass Base & Trim, 12 In. 275.00
Oil, Cut Overlay, Opaque White To Green, Marble Footed, Brass, 12 In. 175.00
Oil, Enameled & Gilded Metal, Porcelain Inserts, 24 In., Pair 650.00
Oil, Erin Fan, Green 250.00
Oil, Frosted Spider Webb, Miniature 375.00
Oil, Hanging, Crystal Prisms, Painted Rose Design, Brass 467.00
Oil, Hanging, Pull Down, Milk Glass Font, Prisms, Brass Smoke Bell 350.00
Oil, Heart With Thumbprint, Green Opaque, Pansy Design, 8 1/2 In. 325.00
Oil, Inverted Thumbprint, Amber Opalescent, 10 In. 335.00
Oil, Jewel Cluster 125.00
Oil, Little Buttercup, Amethyst 135.00
Oil, Log Cabin, Clear, 3 1/2 In. 506.00
Oil, Loom, Candle Arm On Adjustable Tramel, Iron, Adjusts From 33 In. 150.00
Oil, Marriage, Ripley & Co., 2 Fonts, Match Holder, 13 1/2 In. 695.00
Oil, Mercury Glass Reflector, Wall Mount, Iron Bracket 115.00
Oil, Milk Glass, Blue, Miniature 220.00
Oil, Nellie Bly, Leaf & Floral, White Base, Clear Chimney, 8 7/8 In. 125.00
Oil, Opalescent White Cut To Clear Font, Brass, Marble Base, 9 In. 315.00
Oil, Opaque Blue Font, Brass Stem, Marble Base, 10 1/4 In. 150.00
Oil, Opaque White Cut To Clear Stem, Font, Stepped Marble Base, 13 In. 350.00
Oil, Overlay Glass, Pressed Glass, Gilt Cut To Green, Opaque, 40 In. 467.50
Oil, Parian Cherub Supports, Electrified, 23 In., Pair 275.00
Oil, Piano, Embossed Milk Glass Shade, Brass 325.00
Oil, Piano, Yellow Cased Ball Shade, Brass Font, Electrified, 61 In. 220.00
Oil, Princess Feather 75.00
Oil, Rayo, Opaque Shade 95.00
Oil, Rayo, White Glass Shade, Brass 125.00
Oil, Rayo, With Tripod 55.00
Oil, Riverside Ladies 135.00
Oil, Ruffled Bull's-Eye 95.00
Oil, Saloon, Ceiling 100.00
Oil, Satin Glass, Pink Cased, Puffed Diamond Pattern, Miniature 495.00
Oil, Shield & Star, Vaseline Font 550.00
Oil, Star & Punty, Fluted Column, Brass Collar, Clambroth Base, 11 In. 250.00
Oil, Stepped Marble, Brass Base, Clear Pressed Font, 12 In. 45.00
Oil, Tin, On Stand, Handle, 1840 .... 70.00
Oil, Tin, Saml. Davis, Pat. May 6, 1856, Blue Japanning, Stenciled, 7 In. 165.00
Oil, Tole, Old Yellow Paint, Black Striping, Pewter Collar, 9 3/4 In. 200.00
Oil, Trammel, 1 Candle Cup & Bobeche, Adjustable, Iron, 27 1/4 In. 2530.00
Oil, Triple Overlay, Cranberry Cut To White, Clear, Star & Clover 4500.00
Oil, Yellow Shaded, Diamond, Mother-of-Pearl Satin, Miniature 2035.00
Oil, Zipper Loop 120.00
Pairpoint lamps are in the Pairpoint category
Peg, Brass Candlestick, Lime Green, Enameled Flowers On Shade, 13 In. 325.00

Peg, Button & Drape, Mushroom Shade 1050.00
Peg, Frosted Glass Ball Shade, Pale Yellow, Etched Daisies 300.00
Peg, Palmer Prism, Pair 300.00
Peg, Pink Opalescent, Brass Candlestick, Matching Shade 225.00
Peg, Pink Satin Glass, Swirl, Brass Candlestick, Matching Shade 375.00
Peg, Ruby Flash Cut, Blown Hurricane Globe, 22 In., Pair 522.00
Peg, Whale Oil, 2 Burners, Brass Tube On Handle Side, 1820, 3 x 4 In. 69.00
Peg, Whale Oil, Clear Pressed Glass, Panels & Thumbprint, 4 1/2 In. 135.00
Perfume, Lovebird, U.S. Glass Co., 8 In., Pair 500.00
Pyramid–Shaped Shade, Wicker, Green Stain, 73 In. 1210.00
Rayo, Cherub Faces, 21 In. 85.00
Rushlight, Trammel, Heart Shape Finial, Iron, 1750–1790, 38 1/2 In. 9075.00
Saloon, Ceiling, Brass Font, Tin Shade 135.00
Sconce, 2–Light, Empire Style, Brass & Ebonized, France, 10 In., Pair 110.00
Sconce, 2–Light, Foliate Backplate, Rock Crystal Drops, 22 1/2 In., Pr. 2475.00
Sconce, 2–Light, Glass Backplate, Term Holds Arms, Bronze, 21 In., Pair 6325.00
Sconce, 2–Light, Heart–Shaped Backplate, Tin, 12 1/2 In., Pair 550.00
Sconce, 2–Light, Rococo Style, Coat Of Arms At Top, Silvered, Pair 505.00
Sconce, 3–Light, Candle, Brass, Hand Made, 8 In., Pair 175.00
Sconce, 3–Light, Crystal Sockets, Prisms & Chains, 24 In., Pair 605.00
Sconce, 3–Light, Louis XV Style, Bronze, 15 1/2 In. 75.00
Sconce, 3–Light, Louis XV, Gilt & Patinated Bronze, 21 1/2 In., Pair 7150.00
Sconce, 3–Light, Mirrored, Scalloped Crest, Tin, 1880s, 19 3/4 In. 330.00
Sconce, 4–Light, On Griffin Head, Regency, Gilded Bronze, Pair 7700.00
Sconce, 5–Light, Acanthus Supports, Scrolled Arms, 29 In. 665.00
Sconce, 5–Light, Louis XV Style, Scrolled Branches, Gilt, 31 In., Pair 2750.00
Sconce, Baluster Shape, Drip Pan, Gilt Bronze, 18th Century, 9 In., Pair 1980.00
Sconce, Candle, Crimped Cup, Tin, 9 3/4 In., Pair 950.00
Sconce, Candle, Hardwood, Red & Black Traces, Reflector, Tin, 12 In. 305.00
Sconce, Candle, Tin, Round Mirrored Back, 10 1/2 In., Pair 610.00
Sconce, Carved Military Symbols, Painted & Parcel Gilt, 47 In., Pair 4950.00
Sconce, Cherub Form, Supporting Leafy Top, Composition, 18 In. 250.00
Sconce, Crimped Crests, Tin, Pair 650.00
Sconce, Crimped Drip Pan & Reflector, Tin, 12 1/2 In., Pair 1200.00
Sconce, Gilt Bronze, Acanthus, Scroll, Fluted Glass Shade, c.1900, Pair 245.00
Sconce, Jewels, Bird At Crest, Beveled Mirror, Brass Plated Cast Iron 205.00
Sconce, U.S. Flag Shield, Eagle At Top, Pair 3600.00
Sconce, Victorian, Leaf Form Support, Exterior Wall, Cast Iron 302.50
Signal, Tin, Brown Japanning, Rotating Bull's–Eye Lens, Handle, 5 In. 25.00
Sinumbra, Etched & Wheel Cut Shade, Gilt Brass, 29 In. 935.00
Skater's, Corncob Top Light, Chain, Brass 225.00
Solar, Fluted Shade 650.00
Solar, Ionic Capitol, Ball Shade, Electrified 850.00
Spark Coil, Ruhmkorff, c.1898, 6 In. 1500.00
Sparking, Clear Pressed Glass, Paneled, 1 Spout, 4 1/8 In. 65.00
Sparking, Moon & Star, Flint, 3 In. ....95.00 To 165.00
Student, Brass, Milk Glass Shade, Weighted Base 50.00
Student, Brass, Opaque White Shade, 20 1/4 In. 275.00
Student, Messenger & Sons, Brass Shade, Electrified, 20 1/4 In. 300.00
Student, Nickel Plated Brass Frame, Green Shade, 26 In. 300.00
Student, Ornate Brass, 2 Peachblow Shades, Electrified, 25 3/8 In. 5700.00
Telegraph, Engine Room, Brass, 12–In. Face, 59 In. 1000.00
Tiffany lamps are listed in the Tiffany section
Torchere, 5–Light, Twist Standard, Painted Iron, 79 In. 145.00
Torchere, Baroque Style, Griffins On Standard, 5 Ft. 1 In., Pair 4125.00
Torchere, Blackamoor, 4–Arm Candle Branch, Polychrome, 6 Ft. 1 In. 3575.00
Torchere, Cherub Supporting Urn, Carved & Painted, 4 Ft. 5 In. 660.00
Torchere, Daum Nancy Glass, Iron, E. Brandt, c.1925 ....*Illus* 9350.00
Torchere, George III Style, Mahogany, 38 In., Pair 1200.00
Torchere, Man Standing On Hands Support, Walnut, Italy 995.00
Torchere, Putti Holds Cornucopia, Giltwood, 1850s, 57 In., Pair 3650.00
Torchere, Spanish Baroque, Wrought Iron, Mounted As Lamp, 61 1/2 In. 665.00
Votive, Figural Hindu, Bronze, 18th Century, 3 3/4 In. 100.00

Wall, 1–Light, Louis XIV, Sunflower Backplate, Giltwood, 21 1/2 In. 4675.00
Wall, Iron Ring, Mercury Reflector 395.00
Whale Oil, Amethyst 350.00
Whale Oil, Aquarius, Amber 250.00
Whale Oil, Blown Pressed Font, Pressed Base, Crystal, 10 In. 165.00
Whale Oil, Boston & Worcester, 1850s 900.00
Whale Oil, Cylindrical Font, Tubular Handle, 7 In. 200.00
Whale Oil, Flint Glass, Pair 330.00
Whale Oil, Free–Blown Font, Square Pressed Base, 9 1/4 In. 165.00
Whale Oil, Gilt Brass, Dolphin Handle, New England, c.1830, 7 In., Pair 374.00
Whale Oil, Heart & Crosshatched Design Font, 8 1/2 In. 125.00
Whale Oil, Original Caps & Chains, 7 1/2 In. 155.00
Whale Oil, Pewter, Mid–19th Century, 10 1/4 In., Pair 495.00
Whale Oil, Pressed Loop On Monument Base, Crystal, 11 3/4 In. 220.00
Whale Oil, Star & Punty, Pear Shape, 4 1/2 In. 195.00
Whale Oil, Tin, Saucer Base, Old Black, 6 1/4 In. 55.00
Whale Oil, Wheel Cut Berries & Leaves, Flint 145.00

LANTERNS are a special type of lighting device. They have a light source,
usually a candle, totally hidden inside the walls of the lantern. Light is
seen through holes or glass sections.

Archer & Pancoast 145.00
Barn, Hinged Door, Tin Vent Top, Pine Frame, 12 In. 280.00
Buggy, Dietz, 3 1/2 & 2–In. Lens, 7 1/2 In. 60.00
Candle, Folding, Mica Glazing, Tin, ... 75.00
Candle, Hexagonal, Primitive, 10 In. 325.00
Candle, Pierced Tin, 1800 .... 95.00
Candle, Punched Tin, Paul Revere Type, 14 In. 65.00
Candle, Punched Tin, Paul Revere Type, Conical Top, Ring, 13 1/2 In. 90.00
Candle, Punched Tin, Revere Type, Paint Traces, No Ring, 13 1/2 In. 95.00
Candle, Sliding Cover, Pyramid Top, Bail, 3 Glass Sides, c.1800 .... 185.00
Dentist Dr. Sprague, Lamp Post Style 485.00
Dietz, Little Wizard, Blue Globe, 1918 .... 45.00
Dietz, Little Wizard, Red Globe 75.00
Dietz, Night Watch 65.00
English Gothic Revival, Tin & Pewter Hall, Octagonal, 13 1/2 In. 330.00
Errco, Wire Cage 35.00
Gustav Stickley, Hanging, Brass, Spade Cutouts, Amber Liner, 26 In. 1870.00
Hall, Gothic Revival, Tin, Pewter, Octagonal, England, c.1845, 13 In. 330.00
Hanging, See–Through Owl, Cast Iron 350.00
Isinglass, Folding 25.00
Japanese, Different Colors, Paper, Dated 1901, 9 x 15 In., 10 Piece 75.00
Miner's, Koehler Co., Mass. 125.00
Onion Globe, Pierced Tin, America, 10 In. 165.00
Police, Bull's–Eye 65.00
Punched Tin, Paul Revere Type, Ring Handle, 12 1/4 In. 130.00
Ruby & Frosted Glass Panels, Tin Frame, Smoke Bell, 1880s 330.00
S. H. Co., Liberty Barn, Red Globe 120.00
Shade, Painted Glass, Ice Cream 2750.00
Single Spout Burner, Pressed Paneled Globe, Ring Handle, 9 1/2 In. 175.00
Skater's, Brass 95.00
Skater's, Ribbed Glass Globe, Brass 70.00
Skater's, Tin 35.00
Tin, Blown Bulbous Shade, Gold Repaint Traces, Ring Handle, 9 In. 150.00
Tin, Floral Polychrome Paint & Gilt, Spain, 37 In. 175.00
Traveling, Folding, Japanned, Tin & Isinglass, 1865 .... 125.00
Wall, Gustav Stickley, No. 225, Heart Cutouts, Hook, 1910, 10 In., Pr. 2200.00
Wedding, Porcelain, Reticulated, Candlestand, Oriental, 15 In., Pair 330.00

LE VERRE FRANCAIS is one of the many types of cameo glass made in
France. The glass was made by the C. Schneider factory in Epinay–sur–
Seine from 1920 to 1933. It is a mottled glass, usually decorated with
floral designs, and bears the incised signature *Le Verre Francais.*

Legras, Lamp, Cameo, Maroon Foliate
Painted, Domed Shade, 18 In.

◆◆◆◆◆◆◆◆◆◆◆◆◆◆◆◆◆◆◆◆◆

One antique earring can be used as a stickpin or a charm for a bracelet or necklace.

◆◆◆◆◆◆◆◆◆◆◆◆◆◆◆◆◆◆◆◆◆

Fixture, Ceiling, Inverted Shade, Grapes, 1925, 19 1/2 In.	2750.00
Incense Burner, Bell Flowers, Lavender, Signed, 3 1/2 In.	445.00
Lamp, Matching Silk Shades, Signed, 17 In.	2700.00
Lamp, Mottled Shade, Iron Stem, c.1925, 13 1/4 In.	2200.00
Pitcher, Flower Blossoms, Signed, c.1925, 11 1/2 In.	880.00
Plate, Opaque White, Red, Green, Florals, 13 1/2 In.	330.00
Vase, Palm Trees, Circles, Signed, c.1925, 19 1/8 In.	2850.00
Vase, Art Deco Etched Floral, Signed, 10 3/4 In.	1045.00
Vase, Band Of 3-Leaf Flowers, Signed, c.1925, 8 1/4 In.	1760.00
Vase, Blossoms, Leaves, Signed, c.1925, 16 In.	1100.00
Vase, Blossoms, Leaves, Signed, c.1925, 17 5/8 In.	2100.00
Vase, Blossoms, Trailing Vines, Flared, 9 1/2 In.	880.00
Vase, Blossoms, Yellow, Orange, Red Speckled, Blue, 11 In.	1100.00
Vase, Brown Fruit, Mottled Yellow-Orange, c.1920, 11 In.	1195.00
Vase, Carved Garlands, Pink, Purple, Signed, 14 In.	1430.00
Vase, Carved Leaves, Blossoms, Brown To Orange, 10 In.	1100.00
Vase, Etched Blossoms, Fuchsia, Purple Overlay, 31 In.	2860.00
Vase, Fan-Shaped Blossoms, Signed, c.1925, 12 In.	1320.00
Vase, Flower Blossoms, Short Grasses, 1925, 10 5/8 In.	1540.00
Vase, Geometric Leaves, Signed, c.1925, 23 1/4 In.	1210.00
Vase, Goblet Form, Orange, Burgundy, Black Foot, 18 In.	2200.00
Vase, Gray, Mottled, Signed, c.1925, 17 7/8 In.	3575.00
Vase, Large Beetle, Grip Glaze From Top, 16 In.	2400.00
Vase, Mottled Walls, Flowers, Signed, c.1925, 10 1/8 In.	1430.00
Vase, Orange & Black Florals, Bulbous, 5 In.	357.00
Vase, Palm Trees, Circles, Signed, c.1925, 15 3/8 In.	2750.00
Vase, Pendent Bell Flowers, Signed, c.1925, 18 3/4 In.	1430.00
Vase, Pendent Berries Over Brickwork, c.1925, 9 3/4 In.	2200.00
Vase, Pine Cones, Cushion Form Foot, c.1925, 18 1/2 In.	1210.00
Vase, Poppies, Yellow, Purple, Red, Etched, Signed, 12 In.	660.00
Vase, Repeating Poppies, Elongated, Signed, 16 3/4 In.	1650.00
Vase, Rust, Frosted White Ground, Chocolate Top, 9 In.	1750.00
Vase, Stylized Blossoms, 2 Handles, 8 3/4 In.	660.00
Vase, Sunflowers, Metal Mounts, Signed, 14 1/4 In.	3025.00
Vase, Upright Flowers, Speckled, Signed, c.1925, 18 In.	2970.00

LEATHER is tanned animal hide and it has been used to make decorative and useful objects for centuries. Leather objects must be carefully preserved with proper humidity and oiling or the leather will deteriorate and crack. This damage cannot be repaired.

Belt, Motorcycle Kidney, 1940s		55.00
Boots, Cowboy, Appliqued, Azure, Simon's, 1950s, Size 7	*Illus*	180.00
Boots, Cowboy, Appliqued, Black, Rodeo Boot, 1950s, Size 6D	*Illus*	180.00
Boots, Cowboy, Appliqued, Brown, Rust, 1940s, Size 10	*Illus*	180.00
Boots, Cowboy, Black Ground, Label, 1950s, Size 6D		180.00
Boots, Cowboy, Mustard & Crimson, Azure Ground, 1950s, Size 7		180.00
Bridle & Reins, Horsehair, Handmade		1450.00

Left to right: Leather, Boots, Cowboy, Appliqued, Black, Rodeo Boot, 1950s, Size 6D; Leather, Boots, Cowboy, Appliqued, Azure, Simon's, 1950s, Size 7; Leather, Boots, Cowboy, Appliqued, Brown, Rust, 1940s, Size 10

Bridle, Horse, Braided, 1880	2530.00
Case, Wallet–Cigarette, Crocodile, England	100.00
Cuffs, Cowboy	40.00
Harness, Circus Pony, Feathers, Straps Covered With Bells, Mirrors	495.00
Holster & Belt, Brass Studs, Rawhide Strings, Grommets, Mexico	110.00
Manicure Set, La Cross, Zipper, 1940s	20.00
Saddle Bags, Marked U.S. 14CB27	195.00
Saddle, Child's, Slick Forks, c.1910	85.00
Saddle, Hand Tooled, Silver Mounts, N. Porter, c.1935	1500.00
Saddle, Heiser, 1940s	450.00
Saddle, Mother Hubbard, Porter, 1950s	550.00
Saddle, Olson–Nolte, Sterling Trim	1500.00
Saddle, Western, Carved Foliate Design, c.1940	715.00
Satchel, Letter Carrier's	30.00

LEEDS pottery was made at Leeds, Yorkshire, England, from 1774 to 1878. Most Leeds ware was not marked. Early Leeds pieces had distinctive **LEEDS POTTERY.** twisted handles with a greenish glaze on part of the creamy ware. Later ware often had blue borders on the creamy pottery.

Bowl, Blue & White Gaudy Floral, Pearlware, 13 1/4 x 4 3/8 In.	325.00
Bowl, Scalloped Blue & White Feather Rim, c.1810, 10 x 8 1/2 In.	425.00
Coffeepot, Cobalt Blue & White	545.00
Creamer, Painted Blue Flower, 4 In.	300.00
Loving Cup, 3 3/4 In.	1000.00
Loving Cup, Pearlware, Inscription, 1797, Leaf Handles, 5 1/2 In.	1350.00
Mug, 4 1/2 In.	725.00
Pitcher, Bird, Green Spatter Tree, Leaf Handle, Pearlware, 2 1/4 In.	275.00
Plate, American Spread–Wing Eagle, Blue Rim, 8 1/4 In., Pair	880.00
Tea Caddy, Marked, 6 In.	1125.00
Teapot, 4 In.	275.00
Teapot, Cover, Creamware, Prince William V Portrait, 1787, 4 3/8 In.	550.00

LEFTON is a mark found on many pieces. The Geo. Zoltan Lefton Company has imported porcelains to be sold in America since 1940. The firm is still in business. The company mark has changed through the years; but because marks have been used for long periods of time, they are of little help in dating an object.

Bookends, Basset Hound	25.00
Cookie Jar, Bear, Label, 1984	40.00
Cookie Jar, Cat	98.00
Figurine, 2 Flamingos, On Base, 5 1/2 In.	27.00
Figurine, Abraham Lincoln	35.00
Figurine, Boy & Girl Toddlers, Sitting, 5 1/2 In.	25.00
Figurine, Dog, Poodle, Standing, 6 x 6 1/2 In.	35.00
Figurine, George Washington	35.00
Figurine, Waltzing Lady, Southern Belle	22.00
Figurine, Young Man In Top Hat & Coattails, 7 3/4 In.	5.00

Planter, Woman 40.00
Salt & Pepper, Rooster 30.00
Sugar, Creamer, Salt & Pepper, Cat Head 85.00
Tea Set, Bluebird, Cookie Jar, Salt & Pepper, Sugar & Creamer 160.00
Tea Set, Rose On Green Ground, Hand Painted, Gold Trim, 19 Piece 400.00
Vase, Hand Painted Floral, Footed, 5 In. 18.00

LEGRAS was founded in 1864 by Auguste Legras at St. Denis, France. It is best known for cameo glass and enamel–decorated glass with Art Nouveau designs. Legras merged with Pantin in 1920 and became the Verreries et Cristalleries de St. Denis et de Pantin Reunies.

Bowl, Painted Gold Foliage, Olive, Circular, Inverted Rim, 14 In. 1100.00
Lamp, Cameo, Maroon Foliate Painted, Domed Shade, 18 In. ....*Illus* 2530.00
Vase, Birds, Mottled Brown, White & Colorless, Signed, 15 1/2 In. 770.00
Vase, Cameo, Maroon Leaves, Crystal Ground, France, 11 3/4 In. 515.00
Vase, Enameled Design On Spatter Ground, 21 1/4 In. 475.00
Vase, Enameled Orange & Black Exotic Blossoms, Clear, 12 1/2 In. 825.00
Vase, Enameled Trumpet Blossoms, Leaves, Signed, c.1920, 18 7/8 In. 770.00
Vase, Etched & Cut, Amber, 5 3/4 In. 150.00
Vase, Inverted Trumpet Shape, Signed, 16 In. 575.00
Vase, Maroon Leaves & Flowers Trailing Upwards, Signed, 9 1/4 In. 795.00
Vase, Mountains & Trees, Etched & Enameled, Signed, 11 In. 575.00
Vase, Pastoral Landscape, Black, Green Enamel, c.1915, 5 7/8 In. 1210.00
Vase, River Landscape, Trees, Squared Neck, Signed, c.1920, 9 1/4 In. 1210.00
Vase, Robins, Blue Blossomed Trees, Enameled, Frosted Ground, 14 In. 275.00
Vase, Sailboat, Lake, Autumnal Tones, Signed, 12 In. 660.00
Vase, Trees & Mountain, Blue, Brown, Greens & Oranges, 11 In. 495.00
Vase, Upright Blossoms Between Reserves, Signed, c.1925, 21 In. 2860.00

LENOX is the name of a porcelain maker. Walter Scott Lenox and Jonathan Cox founded the Ceramic Art Company in Trenton, New Jersey, in 1889. In 1906, Lenox left and started his own company called *Lenox.* The company makes a porcelain that is similar to Irish Belleek. The marks used by the firm have changed through the years and collectors prefer the earlier examples. Related pieces may also be listed in the Ceramic Art Co. section.

Ashtray Set, Heart, Club, Diamond & Spade, Cream, 4 Piece 20.00
Ashtray, Gold Mark, 5 In. 12.00
Ashtray–Coaster, Cream, Round, Small 6.00
Bonbon, Ming 125.00
Bowl, Cream, Footed, 6 1/2 In. 25.00
Bust, Woman, Cascading Hair, Hollow Back, White, 8 1/2 In. .... 325.00 To 350.00
Chop Plate, Flirtation, 12 3/4 In. 45.00
Creamer, Figural, Elephant, Soft Colors, Large 20.00
Cup & Saucer, Blue Dot 30.00
Cup & Saucer, Brookdale 25.00
Cup & Saucer, Brown, Demitasse 15.00
Cup & Saucer, Caribbean 30.00
Cup & Saucer, Castle Garden 30.00
Cup & Saucer, Flirtation 30.00
Cup & Saucer, Golden Wreath, After Dinner 22.50
Cup & Saucer, Mandarin Pattern, Lavender, Turquoise & Gold, 1920s 22.50
Cup & Saucer, P & P Railroad 75.00
Cup & Saucer, Rhodora 30.00
Figurine, First Waltz, Woman, 8 1/2 In. .... 95.00 To 110.00
Figurine, Gray Llama 275.00
Figurine, Mistress Mary, Green Mark 475.00
Figurine, Reader 450.00
Figurine, Swan, Gold Mark, 2 In. 25.00
Figurine, Swan, Gold Mark, 5 In. 50.00
Figurine, Tea At The Ritz, Woman, 8 1/2 In. 110.00
Jar, Old Soldiers' Home, Johnson City, Tenn., Egg Shape, 1912 .... 145.00
Perfume Bottle, Art Glass, Hand Blown, Ornate, Ground Stopper 60.00

Letter Opener, Elephant, Brass, 8 In.

Letter Opener, Clown, Brass, 10 In.

Lemon oil is a good polish for brass inside the house. After polishing brass kept outdoors, use a thin coat of paste wax to protect the shine.

Pitcher, William Penn, Indian Handle, Green Mark	125.00
Plate, Bread, Mandarin Pattern, Lavender, Turquoise, Gold, 1920s, 6 In.	12.00
Plate, Dinner, Weatherly	30.00
Plate, Mandarin Pattern, Lavender, Turquoise & Gold, 1920s	20.00
Platter, Flirtation, 13 3/4 In.	50.00
Powder Jar, Hattie Carnegie, 4 1/2 In.	295.00
Rose, Soup, Cream	35.00
Shoe, With Bow, White	185.00
Soup, Cream, Underplate, Rutledge	35.00
Stein, Sterling Lid, Monk Design	325.00
Sugar & Creamer, Silver Overlay, Blue	350.00
Swan, Cream, 2 1/2 In.	20.00
Swan, Ivory, Green Mark, 12 In.	55.00
Tea Set, Silver Overlay, Brown, 3 Piece	750.00
Teapot, Silver Overlay On Cobalt Blue, Signed, 6 In.	195.00
Teapot, Tree, Blue	95.00
Teapot, Washington Wakefield	135.00
Tile, Pheasant	60.00
Toby, William Penn, Pink Handle	150.00
Urn, Swan, Green, 10 In.	110.00
Vase, Bud, Crystal, Etched Lovebirds On Sprig, 4 3/4 In.	85.00
Vase, Cherry Blossoms, Vines, Medallions, Green, Marked, 10 In.	295.00
Vase, Enameled Birds, Blue, Green Mark, 10 In.	168.00
Vase, Gold Trim, Raised Florals, 2 Handles, 4 1/4 In.	65.00
Vase, Raised White Floral, Green, 6 1/2 In.	65.00

LETTER OPENERS have been used since the eighteenth century. Ivory and silver were favored by the well-to-do. In the late nineteenth century, the letter opener was popular as an advertising giveaway and many were made of metal or celluloid. Brass openers with figural handles were also popular.

Amish, Woman In Bonnet, Cast Iron	65.00
Bronze, Chicken Foot Handle	35.00
Buffalo, Pan Am Exposition, Bronze	58.00
Clown, Brass, 10 In. ....*Illus*	50.00
Dirk Van Erp, 1915, 11 In.	225.00
Dupont, Celluloid	20.00 To 35.00
Elephant, Brass, 8 In. ....*Illus*	55.00
Fuller Brush Man, 7 In.	10.00 To 25.00
Indian, With Bow & Arrow, Sterling Silver, 7 3/4 In.	135.00
Miller High Life	5.00
Nabisco Uneeda Biscuit	65.00 To 85.00
Native Head, Silver Neck Band, East African Airlines, Wood	40.00
Nude Man In Barrel, Bronze, Advertising	25.00 To 35.00
Nude, Full-Figured Handle, Brass	98.00
Owl, Brass	28.00
Princeton, Sterling Silver	25.00

Prudential Insurance	23.00
Prudential Life Insurance, Both Sexes	10.00
Repousse, Kirks, Sterling Silver, 5 3/4 In.	40.00
Satan Head, Brass	35.00
Seeley's Trusses, Celluloid	20.00
St. Augustine, Ivory	68.00
Sword Form, Sterling Silver & Mother-of-Pearl, 8 1/2 In.	45.00
Trowel Shape, Plibrico Firebrick Co.	15.00
Victor Evans, Patent Attorney, Brass	12.00
Welsbach Co.	50.00
With Brass Scissors, Holder	295.00
Yarnall's Paints, Celluloid	20.00

LIBBEY Glass Company has made many types of glass since 1888, including the cut glass and tablewares that are collected today. The stemwares of the 1930s and 1940s are once again in style. The Toledo, Ohio, firm was purchased by Owens–Illinois in 1935 and is still working under the name *Libbey* as a division of that company. Additional pieces may be listed under Amberina, Cut Glass, and Maize.

Basket, Russian Cut, 10 In.	1400.00
Bottle, Neck Ring, Cut Collar, Fluted Stopper, Signed, 6 1/2 x 10 In.	785.00
Bowl, Amberina, 3-Footed, 4 x 6 1/2 In.	400.00
Bowl, Amberina, Ribbed, Signed, 7 In.	330.00
Bowl, Amberina, Ruffled, Signed, 7 In.	475.00
Bowl, Cherries, Branches & Leaves, Signed, 8 1/2 In.	600.00
Bowl, Crossed Ovals, Signed, 8 1/2 In.	400.00
Bowl, Hobstars, Cane, 8 In.	175.00
Bowl, Kensington, Thick Blank, Signed, 8 In.	1300.00
Bowl, Neola, Allover Pattern, Lapidary Cut At Neck, Signed	900.00
Bowl, Senora, Triangular, 3 x 10 In.	550.00
Bread Tray, Colonna, 11 In.	325.00
Butter, Cover, O'Zella	395.00
Castor, Pickle, Amberina Swirled Ribs Insert, Loop Handle, Tongs	350.00
Champagne, Rock Crystal Design, Hollow Stem	65.00
Champagne, Squirrel Stem	70.00
Dish, Ice Cream, Stratford, 6 In.	145.00
Flower Center, Express, Signed, 8 x 13 In.	1045.00
Goblet, Eagle Stem	20.00
Goblet, Greyhound, Black Stem	135.00
Goblet, Kangaroo, Black Stem	135.00
Goblet, Polar Bear, Black Stem	135.00
Goblet, Squirrel, Black Stem	135.00
Knife Rest, Harvard, Teardrop Through Entire Piece	350.00
Perfume Bottle, Copper Wheel Cut, Signed	175.00
Pitcher, Poppy, Pattern Cut Into Handle & Base, Signed, 7 1/2 In.	1950.00
Pitcher, Snowflake Pattern, Signed, 12 In.	1180.00
Pitcher, Sonora, Signed	255.00
Plaque, Advertising, Sultana, 11 3/4 In.	4800.00
Plate, Hobstars, Cane & Prism, Signed, 7 In.	175.00
Plate, Ice Cream, Imperial	325.00
Plate, Ice Cream, Wedgmere, Cut Glass, 7 In.	550.00
Plate, Lorraine, Signed, 7 In.	325.00
Punch Bowl, Chrysanthemum, Signed, 14 In.	1100.00
Relish, Laurent	165.00
Rose Bowl, Triangular Rim, Floral Engraving, Signed, 1910, 5 In.	295.00
Salt & Pepper, Columbian Souvenir, Marked, 1893	495.00
Sherbet, Silhouette, Black Rabbit Stem, Signed	135.00
Toothpick, Leaning Egg, Blue Overlay	145.00
Toothpick, Little Lobe	95.00 To 135.00
Tray, Ice Cream, Aztec, Signed, 12 In.	3740.00
Tray, Ice Cream, Star, Oval, Signed, 18 In.	2100.00
Tray, Wisteria, Signed, 10 In.	900.00
Vase, Amberina, Ball-Shaped Bowl, Amber Base, Signed, 11 1/4 In.	1000.00

Vase, Amberina, Flower Form Top, Alexandrite Shading, 7 1/2 In.	1400.00
Vase, Harvard, Cylindrical Shape, 9 1/4 In.	135.00
Vase, Intaglio Cut, Signed, 12 1/4 In.	325.00
Vase, Intaglio Thistles & Leaves, Serrated, Footed, Signed, 12 In.	395.00
Vase, Lily, Amberina, 9 In.	265.00
Vase, Sawtooth Rim, Allover Ferns, Bull's–Eyes, Signed, 5 1/2 In.	225.00
Vase, Triangular Rim, Free Form, Allover Floral, Signed, 5 In.	165.00
Vase, Trumpet, Allover Cut & Engraved, Cherry Blossom, Signed, 12 In.	150.00
Vase, Trumpet, Florals & Cut Flutes, Allover Engraved, Signed, 12 In.	275.00
Vase, Trumpet, Wheel Cut, Signed, 1910, 10 1/2 In.	265.00
Water Set, Brilliant Cut, Signed, c.1896, 5 Piece	450.00
Water Set, Silver Thread Pattern, 11 Piece	350.00
Wine, Moonstone, Signed	115.00

LIGHTERS for cigarettes and cigars are collectible. Cigarettes became popular in the late nineteenth century, and with the cigarette came matches and cigarette lighters. All types of lighters are collected, from solid gold to the first of the recent disposable lighters. Most examples found were made after 1940.

7–Up, Aluminum, 2 x 1 1/2 In.	42.00
Airplane, Art Deco, Hamilton	40.00
Artillery Cannon, 8 In.	50.00
Ashtray, Roosters, Richard Ginori, 1920s	475.00
Bottle, Royal Crown Cola, 1940 .... 11.00 To 30.00
Bowers, Wind Proof, Brass	20.00
Brass, 42 Caliber Shell	20.00
Budweiser Beer, Bottle	50.00
Bullet, Cities Service Gasoline, Oakaloosa, Iowa	3.50
Bullet, Howell Red Band Motors, 1930s	5.00
Camera On Tripod, Occupied Japan	7.00
Camera, Metal, Occupied Japan	30.00
Can, Campbell Soup	30.00
Case, Evans, Art Deco, Silver Plate	18.00
Chevrolet, 1 1/2 In.	12.00
Cigar, Jump Spark, Midland, Counter Top, Oak, 1906	425.00
Cigar, Midland, Jump Spark .... 200.00 To 400.00
Detroit Police Officer's Association	35.00
Dunhill, Classical Design, 18K Yellow Gold	520.00
Dunhill, Nugget Design, Sterling Silver	175.00
Dunhill, Sterling Silver, Patent Numbers	125.00
Eagle, Tilt–Electric, Cobalt, Ceramic	25.00
Elephant & Donkey, Pewter, Set	65.00
Evans, Combined With Cosmetic Section	85.00
Evans, Figural, Pineapple	22.00
Evans, With Case	15.00
Gillette, Musical, Plays Feel Sharp	110.00
Golfer Front, Craftsman	50.00

Lighter, Silver-Plated Top, Cut Crystal, 5 In.

◆◆◆◆◆◆◆◆◆◆◆◆◆◆◆◆◆◆◆◆◆◆◆

Wash silver every time it is used. Before you polish, be sure to wash the silver to remove all dust. Small gritty pieces of dirt will scratch the silver.

◆◆◆◆◆◆◆◆◆◆◆◆◆◆◆◆◆◆◆◆◆◆◆

Golfer, Lucite 25.00
Green Glass Rods, Glass Jewel Feet, France, c.1940, 3 3/8 In. 880.00
Gun, With Stand 30.00
Hand Grenade, Table 15.00
Hot Cha 70.00
Levi's 15.00
Oasis, Box, 1950s 15.00
Phillips' 66, 1930s 60.00
Pistol Shape, Occupied Japan 25.00
Rogers, Golf Figure 35.00
Ronson, Bartender Behind Chrome & Plastic Bar, 7 1/2 x 4 1/2 In. 1200.00
Ronson, Caricature Of Black Bartender, Electric 525.00
Ronson, Pencil, Rhodium Plate 25.00
Ronson, Tray, Chrome, Park Sherman, 1930s 17.00
Royal Crown Cola 35.00
Royal Crown Cola, Bottle, 1940 .... 50.00
Schirano Candy & Tobacco Co., Enameled Storefront 15.00
Silver–Plated Top, Cut Crystal, 5 In. ....*Illus* 55.00
Speedboat, Art Deco 25.00
Squirt, 1957 .... 28.00
Swank, Outboard Motor, Metal 85.00
Table, Phillips' 66 Logo, 1957 Award 15.00
Table, Ronson QA, Worn Finish 12.00
Texaco Gasoline, 1940 .... 50.00 To 65.00
Ticker Tape 60.00
Tivoli Beer, Denver, Col. 14.00
Watch, Brass, Swiss 65.00
Zippo, Black Crackle 6.00
Zippo, Golf Figure 30.00
Zippo, Hoover Vacuum Cleaners, 50th Anniversary, 1950s 60.00
Zippo, Plymouth & DeSoto, Pocket 15.00
Zippo, Table, Advertising 15.00
Zippo, Zodiac 8.00

LIGHTNING ROD BALLS are collected for their variety of shape and color. These glass balls were at the center of the rod that was attached to the roof of a house or barn to avoid lightning damage.

Ball, Blue 15.00
Ball, Milk Glass 18.00
Pendant, Ruby Red 595.00
Shooting Star, Glass Tail 110.00

LIMOGES porcelain has been made in Limoges, France, since the mid-nineteenth century. Fine porcelains were made by many factories, including Haviland, Ahrenfeldt, Guerin, Pouyat, Elite, and others. Modern porcelains are being made at Limoges and the word *Limoges* as part of the mark is not an indication of age. Haviland, Limoges is listed as a separate category in this book.

Berry Set, Floral Design, Gold Trim, 7 Piece 120.00
Bowl, Florals, Rim Scallops, Gold & Green Trim, 10 In. 65.00
Box, Cover, Cherubs In Relief, Blue, c.1890, 4 1/2 In. 175.00
Box, Cover, Seminude Women, Poppies, Daisies, Green Ground, Small 250.00
Box, Patch, Rooster Finial, Artist Signed 295.00
Butter Pat, Gold Rim, Haviland, 16 Piece 185.00
Chocolate Pot, Allover Gold Ribbons, Floral Sprays, Signed, 10 In. 195.00
Chocolate Set, Trailing Roses, Leaves, Gold Trim, Signed, 11 Piece 225.00
Cider Set, Pink & Yellow Fruits, Signed AWM, 7 Piece 285.00
Cracker Jar, Coral, Yellow, White Flowers, Gold & White, 1894, 7 In. 250.00
Cracker Jar, Flowers On Gold & White, Dated 1894, 7 1/2 In. 225.00
Cup & Saucer, Bouillon, Roses, Marked, 5 Piece 165.00
Cup & Saucer, Mustache, Ruffled, Gold Crosshatching, Handle, 1908 .... 95.00
Cup, Violets 38.00
Dinner Set, Greek Key Border, Gold Band, 20 Piece 165.00

Dish, 3 Sections, Flowers, Gold Leaves, Trim & Handle, 11 1/2 In.	195.00
Dish, Cover, Silver & Orange, Black Ground, 1926	65.00
Dresser Set, Blue Flowers, Pastel Blue & White Ground, 6 Piece	325.00
Fish Set, Sauceboat, Stand, Platter, Marked, c.1910, 12 Piece	1430.00
Game Plate, Game Birds, Rococo Border, c.1900, 8 1/2 In., 12 Piece	1200.00
Game Plate, Pheasants, Quail, Green & Gold, Marked, 11 3/4 In., Pair	395.00
Game Set, Birds, Gold Borders, Gold Tracery, 16 In.	250.00
Group, Pottery, 3 Girls, Arms Entwined, Marked, 25 x 13 In.	450.00
Humidor, Melon Ribbed, Pipes On Beige Ground, Tobacco Leaves, 8 In.	125.00
Jardiniere, Yellow Roses, Purple Flowers, Floral Feet, 9 In.	225.00
Lemonade Set, Hand Painted, Freiberg, 19th Century, 11 Piece	132.00
Mug, Napoleon, Blue, 3 In.	40.00
Pitcher, Cider, Grapes, Leaves, Gold Trim, Marked, 5 1/2 In.	145.00
Pitcher, Cider, Round Tray, Red & Orange Apple Design	185.00
Pitcher, Lemonade, Cherries & Leaves, 5 1/4 In.	40.00
Pitcher, Lemonade, Waterlily, Tray, Signed	335.00
Plaque, Game Bird, Gold Scalloped, Beaded Rim, Signed, 11 In.	175.00
Plaque, Landscape, Curved Road, Framed, Marked, c.1915, 9 1/2 x 7 In.	275.00
Plaque, Pond Scene, Stork & Frogs, 12 1/2 In.	120.99
Plaque, Scenic, Mountain Sheep, Rococo Gold Border, 12 In., Pair	795.00
Plaque, Stag & Doe Scene, Gold Rococo Border, Dubois, 13 1/4 In.	835.00
Plate, Black Scarlett, D'Arceau	25.00
Plate, Duck, Signed Max, 9 3/4 In.	150.00
Plate, Fish, Seaweed, Mollusk, Gold Rim, 1885, 8 1/2 In., 12 Piece	350.00
Plate, Flying Pheasant, Gold Rim, Coronet, Fredy, 10 1/2 In.	135.00
Plate, Fox & Rabbit, Gold Trim	475.00
Plate, Monk, Coronet, Signed, 10 In.	95.00
Plate, Old Abby, Fishermen, Boat, Signed Duval, 10 In.	95.00
Plate, Pheasant, Signed Max, 9 3/4 In.	85.00
Plate, Pheasant, Signed Morys, 9 1/2 In.	85.00
Plate, Snow & Foliage, Birds & Fox, Hand Painted, 12 1/2 In.	115.00
Platter Set, Game, Green & Gold, 13 Piece	850.00
Punch Set, Grapes On Vine, Lavender, Pink, Purple, Green, 12 Piece	990.00
Sauceboat, Fish, Baskets & Sailing Ship, Shell Shape, c.1895	95.00
Tea Set, Gold & Black Border Design, White, Gold Handles, 20 Piece	265.00
Tobacco Jar, Roses, Gilded Pipe On Lid, 5 1/2 In.	60.00
Tray, Dresser, Cherubs, Yellow Ground	48.00
Tray, Dresser, Violets, Gold Rim	75.00
Tray, Flowers, Gold Embossed Border, Lanternier, 9 3/4 In.	85.00
Tray, Lovers Making Music, Rounded Rectangular, L. Malerband, 16 In.	990.00
Tray, Pine Cones, Spider Web, 1880s, 16 In.	210.00
Tray, Vanity, Oval, 18 In.	30.00
Tureen, Child's, Cover, Blue Flowers, Gold 7 In.	125.00
Vase, Angels & Roses, Ruffled, Gold Handles, 8 1/2 x 9 1/2 In.	275.00
Vase, Floral, Cream, Green & Gold Neck Handles & Base, 12 1/2 In.	235.00
Vase, Gold Trim, Double Handle, Large	425.00

LINDBERGH was a national hero. In 1927, Charles Lindbergh, the aviator, became the first man to make a nonstop solo flight across the Atlantic Ocean. In 1932, his son was kidnapped and murdered, and Lindbergh was again the center of public interest. He died in 1974. All types of Lindbergh memorabilia are collected.

Pencil Box, Lindy & Spirit Of St. Louis, Metal	37.50
Pin, Spirit Of St. Louis, Brass	7.50
Postcard, Lindy, Spirit Of St. Louis, Gov. Harkness	22.00
Sheet Music, Lindbergh, Eagle Of U.S. A., Lindy & Plane, 1927	30.00
Tapestry, New York To Paris, 54 In.	300.00
Toy, Spirit Of St. Louis, c.1930	1050.00
Watch Fob, New York To Paris, With Compass	48.00

LITHOPHANES are porcelain pictures made by casting clay in layers of various thicknesses. When a piece is held to the light, a picture of light and shadow is seen through it. Most lithophanes date from the 1825–1875 period. A few are still being made. Many lithophanes sold today were originally panels for lampshades.

Cup & Saucer, Pattern	45.00
Lamp, Solar, 2 Shades, c.1845	1150.00
Panel, 4–Color Painted Scene, 5 1/2 x 5 In.	65.00
Panel, Christ Ascending To Heaven, 4 1/2 x 5 1/4 In.	155.00
Panel, Christ In Temple, Questioning Elders, 4 3/8 x 5 1/4 In.	145.00
Panel, Christ Kneeling, Holding Banner, 4 5/8 x 5 1/4 In.	145.00
Panel, Christ On Cross, 4 3/4 x 4 In.	145.00
Panel, Riverside, 9 3/4 In.	115.00
Panel, United States Scenes, White	750.00
Panel, Woman In Doorway, Feeding Pigeons, Kitchen, 4 7/8 x 5 In.	160.00
Plaque, Peasant Mother With Child, Goat, KPM, 5 x 6 In.	225.00
Stein, Battle Scene, Figural Finial, Pewter Cover, Germany	75.00
Stein, Monk With Woman, Black & White, Pewter Mounts, 7 1/4 In.	395.00
Stein, World's Fair, Building Of Liberal Arts, 1904	150.00
Tea Warmer, 3 Harbor Scenes, 1 Scene Damaged	290.00
Tea Warmer, 4 Scenic Panels, Brass Holder, 4 1/2 x 4 1/2 In.	200.00
Victorian Dressed Woman, Looking At Cupid Statue, Round, 5 In.	375.00

LIVERPOOL, England, was the site of several pottery and porcelain factories from 1716 to 1785. Some earthenware was made with transfer decorations. Sadler and Green made print–decorated wares from 1756. Many of the pieces were made for the American market and feature patriotic emblems, such as eagles, flags, and other special–interest motifs.

Figurine, Nun, Seated, Rose Veil, R. Chaffers, 1755–1760, 5 In.	1320.00
Jug, Farmer's Arms	1000.00
Mug, Black Transfer, Classical Ruins, Polychrome Enamel, 6 In.	75.00
Mug, Child's, Flowering Branch, Cylindrical, R. Chaffers, 2 1/2 In.	1350.00
Pitcher, 3 Masted Ship, American Flag, 16 State Names, 8 1/4 In.	3575.00
Pitcher, Arms Of Stearns, Peace, Plenty & Independence, 9 In.	1870.00
Pitcher, Ben Franklin 1 Side, Washington On Other	4600.00
Pitcher, Black Transfer, 3–Masted Ship, American Flag, 8 1/2 In.	3575.00
Pitcher, Black Transfer, Cartoon, Embargo Act In 1806	9350.00
Pitcher, Black Transfer, Monument To Washington, 1800, 9 1/2 In.	2310.00
Pitcher, Eagle & America, Ship Flying American Flag, 9 1/2 In.	2300.00
Pitcher, Farmer's Arms, Sally March 1801 Under Spout	4000.00
Pitcher, Franklin, Washington, Liberty, Justice, Victory, 1818	5060.00
Pitcher, Great Seal	1100.00
Pitcher, Napoleon, Thomas Jefferson & John Bull In Tussle	8500.00
Pitcher, Success To America, Washington, 1804, 10 3/4 In.	1700.00
Plate, Scalloped Rim, Black Transfer, Ship, American Flag, 9 In.	175.00
Vase, Woman, Flower Basket On Head, 1758, 3 15/16 In.	2970.00

LLADRO is a Spanish porcelain. Juan, Jose, and Vicente Lladro opened a ceramics workshop in Almacera in 1951. They soon began making figurines in a distinctive, elongated style. In 1958 the factory moved to Tabernes Blanques, Spain. The company makes stoneware and porcelain vases and figurines in limited and unlimited editions.

Figurine, Angel	60.00
Figurine, Ballerina, 12 In.	350.00
Figurine, Ballerina, 14 1/2 In.	175.00
Figurine, Ballerina, Lying Down, 9 1/4 In.	185.00
Figurine, Ballerina, Seated, 5 1/4 In.	66.00
Figurine, Ballerina, Seated, 6 1/2 In.	185.00
Figurine, Boy, Girl On Seesaw, 9 In.	150.00
Figurine, Choir Girl, 10 3/4 In.	95.00
Figurine, Clown, 14 1/2 In.	77.00
Figurine, Dancer, 11 3/4 In.	85.00

Figurine, Dog, Bloodhound, 10 In.	295.00
Figurine, Eskimo Riders, Box	125.00
Figurine, Flamingo Dancers, 20 In.	275.00
Figurine, Fox, 7 In.	85.00
Figurine, Friends	600.00
Figurine, Geisha, With Flowers, 6 In.	160.00
Figurine, Girl & Boy Holding Puppy, 14 In.	412.00
Figurine, Girl, Sitting On Stump With Flowers, 10 In.	150.00
Figurine, Girl, Sun Hat, 13 3/4 In.	85.00
Figurine, Girl, With Bible, Flower Basket At Feet, 14 In.	200.00
Figurine, Girl, With Dove, 12 In.	170.00
Figurine, Girl, With Parasol, 16 In.	125.00
Figurine, Goose Girl, 10 In.	110.00
Figurine, Grandfather, Seated, Child, Signed, 12 In.	135.00
Figurine, Japanese Cranes	750.00
Figurine, Little Pals, First Issue	1650.00
Figurine, Little Traveler, Second Issue	625.00
Figurine, Man On Horseback, 20 In.	160.00
Figurine, Nativity Set, Mostly Gray, Largest Is 9 In., 9 Piece	1500.00
Figurine, Nativity Set, Multicolored, Largest Is 14 In., 6 Piece	3000.00
Figurine, Woman, Art Deco Style, 13 In.	215.00
Figurine, Woman, Dog, 13 3/4 In.	80.00
Figurine, Woman, Pekingese, 14 3/4 In.	105.00
Figurine, York Terrier	350.00
Figurine, Young Boy, Holding Sailing Ship, 9 In.	70.00
Lamp Base, Man, Sitting Under Tree, Playing Violin, 17 In.	100.00
Plate, Christmas, 1971	100.00
Plate, Christmas, 1973	75.00
Plate, Mother's Day, 1971	75.00

LOCKE ART is a trademark found on glass of the early twentieth century. Joseph Locke worked at many English and American firms. He designed and etched his own glass in Pittsburgh, Pennsylvania, starting in the 1880s. Some pieces were marked *Joe Locke,* but most were marked with the words *Locke Art.* The mark is hidden in the pattern on the glass.

Tumbler, Etched Vertical Lines, Bunches Of Grapes, 4 1/2 In.	275.00
Wine, Grape & Line Design, Signed, 4 1/2 In.	55.00

LOETZ glass was made in many varieties. Johann Loetz bought a glassworks in Austria in 1840. He died in 1848 and his widow ran the company; then in 1879, his grandson took over. Most collectors recognize the iridescent gold glass similar to Tiffany, but many other types were made. The firm closed during World War II.

Loetz Austria

Biscuit Jar, Iridescent Mother-of-Pearl, Raindrop Spatter, 6 1/2 In.	195.00
Bowl, Crystal Green, Rolled Top, Signed, 7 In.	110.00
Bowl, Green & Blue Iridescent, Inverted Scalloped, Circular, 9 In.	110.00
Bowl, Green Iridescent, 11 In.	375.00
Bowl, Green Rain Spots, 10 3/4 In.	595.00
Bowl, Inverted Thumbprint, Ruffled, Pinched, Oil Spots, 10 In.	575.00
Bowl, Lime Rainbow, Ruffled Rim, Polished Pontil, 11 1/2 In.	300.00
Bowl, Purple, Frosted, Gold Iridescent, 9 In.	675.00
Bride's Bowl, Art Deco Feet, Green	195.00
Cracker Jar, Brown Oil Spot, Blown-Out Teardrops, Plated Lid	625.00
Dish, Shell Shape, Diamond Quilted, Melon Ribbed Sections, 3 x 12 In.	450.00
Frame, Mirror, Iridescent, Zigzag Flanked 2 Rectangular Bands, Round	3326.00
Humidor, Oil Spot, Sterling Silver Top	300.00
Inkwell, Art Glass, Angular Quatra-Form Vessel, Hinged Metal Cover	360.00
Inkwell, Art Nouveau, Hinged Metal Cover, Gold Quatraform	357.00
Inkwell, Green Iridescent, Square, 5 In.	495.00
Inkwell, Pyramid Shape, Dark Blue Threaded, 3 1/2 In.	450.00
Lamp, Domed Shade, Upright Serpent Supports, c.1900, 28 1/2 In.	6160.00
Lamp, Floor, Clear & Jeweled Glass Top, Obelisk Shape Stem, Bronze	6325.00
Pitcher, Oil Spot, Pinched Sides, Gilt Metal Neck Band, 12 1/4 In.	625.00

Rose Bowl, Pulled Silver & Gold 675.00
Sugar Shaker, Blue Oil Spot On Ruby Ground, Silver Overlay, 5 In. 2800.00
Vase, Allover Glass Trails Over Blue, 4 1/2 In. 525.00
Vase, Allover Peacock Feathers, Bronze Centers, Green, 4 1/2 In. 3800.00
Vase, Amber Iridescent, Silver Oil Spots, Bulbous, Ovoid, 4 7/8 In. 1320.00
Vase, Amber, Iridescent Silver & Blue Pattern, Everted Rim, Oviform 1386.00
Vase, Applied Silvery Amber Zigzag Tendrils, c.1900, 11 3/4 In. 1980.00
Vase, Art Nouveau Floral & Silver Overlay, 10 In. 1450.00
Vase, Blue Oil Spot, Green Glass, 9 1/4 In. 245.00
Vase, Blue Oil Spot, V–Shaped Top, Snail Shape, 12 In. 4500.00
Vase, Blue Swirl, Turquoise, Gold, Flared Lip, Signed, 6 In. 600.00
Vase, Boat Form Lip, Blue Zigzags & Lappers, Marked, c.1900, 9 In. 1540.00
Vase, Bottle Shape, Horizontal Stripes, Gold Over Yellow, 7 1/2 In. 1850.00
Vase, Bottle Shape, Random Threading, Green, 9 3/4 In. 145.00
Vase, Branches With Seeds, Butterflies, Signed, c.1910, 13 7/8 In. 2310.00
Vase, Bronze Overall Pine Cone & Stem, Twisted, 17 In. 750.00
Vase, Colorless, Metallic Green Layers, Tooled Lip, 5 1/2 In. 1045.00
Vase, Cornucopia Shape, Floral Lip, Footed, Green 475.00
Vase, Dimpled Shoulder, Leaf–Shaped Forms, c.1900, 12 3/4 In. 3300.00
Vase, Fan, Oil Spot, Green, 10 In. 450.00
Vase, Flared Orange Cased, Black Vertical Striping, 7 1/4 In. 660.00
Vase, Fold–Back Lips Shape, Oil Spot, Signed, 5 1/2 In. 850.00
Vase, Gold Flowers, Blue & Gold Iridescent, 9 In. 895.00
Vase, Gold Iridescent Spotted Amber, Signed, 4 1/2 In. 137.50
Vase, Green Iridescent, Fluted, Signed, 8 1/2 In. 225.00
Vase, Green Iridescent, Ribbed, Twisted & Pinched, 9 3/4 In. 195.00
Vase, Green Outside, Rose Inside, Metal Holder, 14 In. 1100.00
Vase, Green Threaded, Rainbow Iridescent, Stag Handle, 6 In. 280.00
Vase, Indented Swirls, Italian Green, 12 1/4 In. 750.00
Vase, Octopus, Amber Glass Over White, Gilt Scrolling Design, Oviform 1386.00
Vase, Oil Spot, Frosted Tree Trunk Base, Cranberry, 12 In. 275.00
Vase, Oil Spot, Whiplash Leafage, Silver Overlay, c.1900, 17 In. 6600.00
Vase, Paperweight, Silver Foliate Mount, 4 1/2 In. 1320.00
Vase, Paperweight, Silver Overlay, Silver Frame, c.1900, 3 3/8 In. 935.00
Vase, Pinched Sides, Oil Spot, Signed, 6 In. 750.00
Vase, Pinched, Green, 7 In. 255.00
Vase, Pitted Surface Texture, Twisted Cylinder, 9 1/2 In. 1450.00
Vase, Portrait Front, Green, Purple, Iridescent, Signed, 7 In. 185.00
Vase, Raindrop, Pinched, 5 1/2 In. 275.00
Vase, Random Oil Spot, Amber, Signed, c.1900, 5 1/4 In. 1760.00
Vase, Ribbed, Dimpled Base, 9 In. 275.00
Vase, Ruffled Rim, Barrel Shape, Green, Signed, 8 1/2 x 6 In. 395.00
Vase, Ruffled Rim, Green Pulled Feather, Signed, 7 1/2 In. 450.00
Vase, Ruffled Rim, Yellow–Green, Silver Overlay, 4 1/2 In. 485.00
Vase, Ruffled, Green Rim, Flowers, Speckled Clear To Purple, 5 x 4 In. 187.00
Vase, Silver Blue Oil Splash Pattern, 3 Scroll Handles, Swollen 1100.00
Vase, Silver Turquoise Oil Spot, Tobacco Ground, 4 Dimples, 7 In. 1750.00
Vase, Stick, Pulled Feather, Platinum, 5 In. 275.00
Vase, Striated, Green & Purple Surface On Ruby, 4 3/4 In. 235.00
Vase, Swirls Of Maroon & Gold, Bronzed Metal Mount, 13 In. 660.00
Vase, Textured Swirl, Twisted Green Walls, 1900, 12 1/8 In. 1210.00
Vase, Tri–Dimpled Body, Blue, Gold, 6 In. 695.00

LONE RANGER, a fictional character, was introduced on the radio in 1932. Over three thousand shows were produced before the series ended in 1954. In 1938, the first Lone Ranger movie was made. Television shows were started in 1949 and are still seen on some stations. The Lone Ranger appears on many products and was even the name of a restaurant chain for several years.

Badge, Chief Scouts 95.00
Badge, Lone Ranger Club, Horseshoe 20.00
Badge, Safety Club 25.00
Bandana, Red, Horse, Guns 45.00

Belt, Glow In The Dark, Box	225.00
Big Little Book, 1968	20.00
Billfold, 1948	75.00
Blotter, Bond Bread	12.00
Book, Big Little Book, Black Shirt Highwayman	20.00
Book, Big Little Book, Great Western Span	27.50
Book, Big Little Book, Lone Ranger & His Horse Silver	40.00
Book, Comic, Giveaway, 1955	8.00
Book, Comic, Lone Ranger In Milk For Big Mike, 1955	12.00
Book, How Lone Ranger Captured Silver, Silvercup Bread, 1936	4.00
Book, Pop–Up, 1981	12.00
Box, Cheerios, With Deputy Kit, 1980	65.00
Box, Film Strip, Lone Ranger Films	8.00
Box, Lone Ranger Film For Cine Vue, Cheerios, 1950s	8.00
Button, Pinback, Celluloid	12.00
Cap Gun, Cast Iron	250.00
Cap Gun, Cast Iron, 1939, 8 1/4 In.	95.00
Card, Silver Cup Bread, 1928, 4 x 6 1/2 In.	9.00
Chalk	35.00
Costume, Tonto, Suedine, Pla–Marker Label, Box	245.00
Cutouts, Merita Bread	175.00
Decal, Blue Ribbon Bread	175.00
Doll, Tonto, Gabriel	50.00
Eggcup, Face Of Clayton Moore, Porcelain, 1950s	45.00
Figurine, Chalkware	50.00
Figurine, Hartland, No Saddle	100.00
Figurine, Rearing Horse	45.00
Film Strip, Lone Ranger Films For Cine Vue, Cheerios, Box	18.00
Flashlight	50.00
Game, Board, 1956	80.00
Game, Hi–Yo	23.00
Game, Parker Bros., Board, 1928	16.00
Game, Target, Lone Ranger, Box	285.00
Guitar, Jefferson, Box, 36 In.	95.00 To 125.00
Gun Set, Plastic, Holster, Leather, Cuffs, Box, 1942, Unused	255.00
Gun Set, Rifle, Holster & Hat Set, Gabriel, Box, 1970s	250.00
Gun Set, Texan Jr., Double Holster	65.00
Gun, Clicker, Silver & White, 1938	50.00 To 89.00
Gun, Cork, Long Barrel	125.00
Gun, Squirt, Figural, Tonto, Pair	40.00
Hat, 1950s	45.00
Hat, Cloth, Hi–Yo Silver	38.00
Hat, Gray Felt	65.00
Lunch Box, 1955	125.00 To 165.00
Paint Book, 1940	75.00
Pattern, Costume, Simplicity	15.00
Pedometer	20.00 To 35.00
Pedometer, Box	100.00
Pen, Bullet, On Card	75.00
Pencil Box, 1930s	110.00
Pencil Box, Lone Ranger & Silver	25.00
Pin, Celluloid	12.00
Pin, Glow, Betty Gardenia	250.00 To 275.00
Pistol, Clicker, Holster, 1938	65.00
Pistol, Long Barrel, Cork	95.00
Play Set, Marx, Box, 1950s	350.00
Pocket Watch, Decal, Lapel Button	400.00
Poster, Legend Of The Lone Ranger, Color, 1981, 26 3/4 x 40 In.	12.00
Radio	2000.00
Ring, Air Force, No Photograph	150.00
Ring, Atom Bomb	75.00 To 100.00
Ring, Filmstrip	135.00
Ring, Flashlight	45.00 To 95.00

Ring, Flashlight, Box 125.00
Ring, Saddle, With Film ....98.00 To 125.00
Ring, Six-Gun, 1947 ....65.00 To 125.00
Ring, Tonto, Capt. Action Series, 1966 .... 12.00
Screen, 3 Panels, Store Display 375.00
Silver Bullet, Secret Compartment, . 45 Cal. 30.00
Slippers, Felt, 1940s .... 85.00 To 95.00
Snow Dome, Lassoing, Calif., Label .... 75.00 To 95.00
Soap, 1939, Box 75.00
Soap, Figural, Tonto, Silver, Set 150.00
Strong Box, Wild West Town, 1957 .... 45.00 To 65.00
Suit, Tonto's, Box, 1950s 85.00
Target Set, 1939 .... 80.00
Tent, Original Box, 1958 .... 195.00
Toy, Frontiertown, Complete & Built .... 700.00 To 900.00
Toy, Range Rider, Marx 200.00
Toy, Windup, Tin, 1938 .... 450.00
Viewer & Film, Comics 50.00
Viewer, Acme, 1940s, Box 125.00
Watch Fob, Metal, 1938 .... 50.00
Wristwatch, Ingraham, Round Chrome Case, Leather Band, 1950 .... 185.00

LONGWY Workshop of Longwy, France, first made ceramic wares in 1798.
The workshop is still in business. Most of the ceramic pieces found today
are glazed with many colors to resemble cloisonne or other enameled
metal. The factory used a variety of marks.

Bowl, Oval, Cobalt With Center Medallion, Pink Roses, 11 In. 250.00
Box, Cover, Red, Blue & Yellow Floral, 4 In. 175.00
Ewer, Gilt Metal Mounted, 13 1/4 In., Pair 180.00
Salt & Pepper 95.00
Tile, Art Deco Lady Portrait, Blues, Cream & Yellow, Primavera, 8 In. ... 286.00
Tile, Art Deco Woman, Flowers, Square, Marked, 8 In. 850.00
Tile, Brass Mounted 175.00
Tile, Woman With Flower, Tree, Primavera, Marked, Square, 8 In. 260.00
Trivet, Woman Picking Cherry Blossoms, 8 In. 500.00
Urn, Floral & Dragon, Yellow Ground, Snake Handles, 26 x 16 In. 2860.00
Vase, Blue Florals, Green, Yellow & Black, Signed, 9 In. 365.00
Vase, Cream Ground, Turquoise Border, Cinnamon, Marked, 13 In. 1100.00
Vase, Floral Enamel, Blues, Yellow, Red, 9 In. 325.00
Vase, Red, Cobalt, Yellow Enameled Flowers, Cylinder, Signed, 9 In. 295.00

LONHUDA Pottery Company of Steubenville, Ohio, was organized in 1892
by William Long, W. H. Hunter, and Alfred Day. Brown underglaze slip-
decorated pottery was made. The firm closed in 1896. The company used
many marks; the earliest included the letters *LPCO*.

Bowl, Flowers, 3-Footed, 7 In. 225.00
Mug, Zinnias, 1st Mark, 6 In. 250.00
Vase, Green Leaves, 8 In. 150.00

LOTUS WARE was made by the Knowles, Taylor & Knowles Company of
East Liverpool, Ohio, from 1890 to 1900. Lotus Ware, a thin porcelain
which resembles beleek, was sometimes decorated outside the factory.
Other types of ceramics that were made by the Knowles, Taylor &
Knowles Company are listed under KTK.

Pitcher, Green Branches & Leaves, White Handle, 8 In. 295.00
Plate, Star Pattern, Bead Work 450.00
Tea Set, Blue, Hand Painted, 3 Piece 800.00
Vase, Prunus Blossom, Footed, 7 In. 950.00

LOW art tiles were made by the J. and J. G. Low Art Tile Works of
Chelsea, Massachusetts, from 1877 to 1902. A variety of art and other tiles
were made. Some of the tiles were made by a process called *natural*, some
were hand modeled, and some were made mechanically.

Greek Woman, Green, 4 In. 75.00
Leaves, Brown, 4 In. 45.00
Roman Warrior 75.00

LOWESTOFT, a factory in Suffolk, England, from 1757 to 1802 made many commemorative gift pieces and small, dated, inscribed pieces of soft paste porcelain. Related items may be found in the Chinese Export category.

Inkwell, 2 Quill Holders 695.00

LOY–NEL–ART, see McCoy category

LUNCH BOXES and lunch pails have been used to carry lunches to school or work since the nineteenth century. Today, most collectors want either early tobacco advertising boxes or children's lunch boxes made since the 1930s. The original Thermos bottle must be inside the children's boxes for the collector to consider the set complete.

LUNCH BOX, Addams Family, 1974 .... 35.00 To 65.00
Alvin & Chipmunks, Vinyl, 1963 .... 329.00 To 375.00
American Flag, Dome Top 25.00
Annie Oakley, 1955 .... 45.00
Archies, 1969 .... 30.00 To 40.00
Astronaut, Dome Top, 1960 .... 100.00 To 189.00
Atom Ant, 1966 .... 75.00
Auto Race, 1967 .... 89.00
Banana Splits, Vinyl, 1970 .... 350.00 To 435.00
Barbie & Francie, 1966–1970 .... 75.00 To 145.00
Barbie, Metal, 1962 .... 195.00
Barbie, Vinyl, 1962–1964 .... 45.00 To 85.00
Bat Masterson, 1958 .... 75.00
Battle Of The Planets, 1979 .... 35.00
Battlestar Galactica, 1978 .... 29.00 To 40.00
Beany & Cecil, Vinyl, 1963 .... 250.00
Bedknobs & Broomsticks, 1972 .... 26.00 To 35.00
Bee Gees, Barry Gibb, Thermos, 1978 .... 30.00
Berenstain Bears 35.00
Beverly Hillbillies, 1963–1965 .... 50.00 To 125.00
Black Hole, 1979 .... 20.00
Black Trunk, Barbie International Fair, Skipper, Francie 75.00
Bonanza .... 50.00 To 150.00
Bozo 145.00
Brady Bunch, 1970 .... 15.00
Brave Eagle, 1957 .... 350.00
Buccaneer, 1957–1958 .... 295.00 To 300.00
Buck Rogers 30.00
Campus Queen, 1967 .... 18.00
Captain Astro, 1966 .... 250.00
Captain Kangaroo, Vinyl, 1964–1966 .... 325.00
Cartoon Zoo, 1962 .... 295.00
Chan Clan, 1973 .... 40.00
Charlie's Angels, 1978 .... 25.00
Chuck Wagon, 1958–1960 .... 145.00
Convoy Alfa, Vinyl, Mexico 115.00
Cowboy, In Africa, Chuck Connors, 1968 .... 80.00 To 120.00
Cracker Jack, 1979 .... 40.00
Daniel Boone 50.00
Debutante, 1958 .... 45.00
Disney On Parade, 1970 .... 50.00
Dixie Kid Tobacco, Black .... 295.00 To 385.00
Dixie Queen Tobacco 150.00
Donny & Marie Brunch Bag, 1977 .... 45.00
Double Decker 25.00
Dr. Dolittle, 1967 .... 45.00

Dr. Seuss, 1970–1971 .... 75.00
Dragon's Lair, Tin, 1984 .... 50.00
Dudley Do–Right, 1962 .... 475.00
Dukes Of Hazzard, Metal .... 20.00 To 22.00
E. T., 1982–1983 .... 25.00 To 28.00
Ed McCauley Space Explorer 300.00
Emergency, 1973–1974 .... 45.00
Emergency, Dome, 1977 .... 100.00
Empire Strikes Back 49.00
Evel Knievel, 1974 .... 35.00 To 65.00
Fall Guy, 1981 .... 13.00
Family Affair, 1969–1970 .... 75.00
Fireball XL–5, King Seeley, 1963 .... 129.00
Flintstones & Dino, 1962–1963 .... 120.00
Flipper, 1966–1968 .... 52.50
Flying Nun, 1968–1969 ....85.00 To 150.00
G. I. Joe, 1967 .... 75.00
G. I. Joe, 1987 .... 35.00
Gene Autry, 1954 .... 75.00
George Washington Cut Plug Tobacco 35.00
Get Smart, 1966 .... 15.00 To 35.00
Globetrotter, 1959 .... 145.00
Go Go, Vinyl, Red, 1966 .... 75.00
Gomer Pyle, 1966 .... 80.00 To 95.00
Green Hornet, 1967 .... 250.00
Green Turtle 265.00
Grizzly Adams, Dome, 1977 .... 50.00 To 95.00
Guns Of Will Sonnett, 1968 .... 50.00
Gunsmoke ....44.00 To 195.00
Gunsmoke, Red 145.00
Handbag Cut Plug Tobacco 75.00
Hansel & Gretel, 1982–1984 .... 25.00
Happiness Candy 95.00
Hardy Boys, 1978–1979 .... 30.00 To 40.00
Hee Haw, Rub On Back Band Rest, 1970 .... 95.00
Hogan's Heroes 80.00
Hogan's Heroes, 1966 .... 139.00 To 275.00
Hometown Airport, 1960 ....800.00 To 1100.00
Hot Wheels, 1969 .... 35.00
How The West Was Won, 1979 .... 35.00
Hulk, 1978 .... 15.00
It's About Time, Dome Top, 1967 .... 450.00
Jet Patrol, 1957–1958 .... 260.00 To 350.00
Jetsons, Dome, Aladdin, 1963 ....500.00 To 1000.00
Jetsons, Hanna Barbera, 1962 .... 950.00
Joe Palooka, 1948 .... 145.00 To 300.00
Johnny Lightning, 1970 .... 45.00
Julia, 1969 .... 45.00
Just Suits Cut Plug Tobacco 35.00
Kansas City A's, Butternut Bread 85.00
Kellogg's Cereals 110.00
Kiss, 1970s .... 49.00 To 65.00
Knight Rider, 1981–1985 .... 25.00
Korg, Tin, 1974 .... 50.00
Kung Fu, 1974 .... 40.00
Land Of The Giants, 1968–1970 .... 75.00 To 85.00
Land Of The Lost, 1975 .... 60.00
Larrabee's Lunch Box, Book Shape, Pressed Tin 43.00
Lassie, 1961–1963 .... 45.00
Laugh–In 85.00
Lawman, 1961 .... 50.00
Loonie Toons, Vinyl, 1959–1961 .... 25.00
Lorillard Tobacco, Basketweave 35.00

Lost In Space, 1967–1968 .... 275.00 To 550.00
Ludwig Von Drake, 1961 .... 100.00
Magic Of Lassie, 1979 .... 29.00
Man From U. N. C. L. E., 1966–1967 .... 90.00
Marvel Super Heroes, 1976–1980 .... 45.00
Monkeys, 1967 .... 250.00
Mr. T., A Team, Paper Inside 50.00
Munsters, 1965–1966 .... 85.00 To 100.00
N. F. L. Football, 1976 .... 10.00
Nancy Drew Mysteries, 1977–1978 .... 24.50
North Pole 340.00
Paladin, Have Gun Will Travel, 1960 .... 60.00 To 65.00
Partridge Family, 1971 .... 22.00 To 40.00
Pathfinder, 1959 .... 90.00 To 200.00
Patterson's Seal Tobacco .... 15.00 To 35.00
Peanuts, Orange 45.00
Peanuts, Red 15.00
Peanuts, Yellow .... 10.00 To 20.00
Pedro Tobacco 100.00
Peter Pan Peanut Butter, Sandwich, F & F 400.00
Peter Rabbit, Harrison Caty 150.00
Pigs In Space, Muppets, 1977 .... 30.00
Pink Panther 25.00
Play Ball, Game On Reverse, 1969–1972 .... 35.00
Plowboy Tobacco 275.00
Polly Pal, Metal, 1974 .... 20.00
Pony Express, 1957 .... 95.00
Pony Express, Frontier Days, 1950s 85.00
Pop Art Bread 225.00
Poppies 12.00
Porky's Lunch Wagon, 1959–1961 .... 250.00
Raggedy Ann & Andy, 1973 .... 45.00
Rat Patrol, 1967 .... 85.00
Red Barn Dome, Open Doors 65.00
Red Indian Cut Plug, Indian Design .... 1150.00 To 1540.00
Red Man Tobacco, Brass Tag 30.00
Red Tartan Plaid 30.00
Return Of The Jedi, 1983 .... 26.00 To 35.00
Road Runner, 1970 .... 32.00 To 65.00
Robin Hood 130.00
Ronald McDonald, Sheriff Of Cactus Canyon, 1983 .... 18.00
Sabrina, 1972 .... 250.00
School Bus, Aladdin, 1960s 20.00
Scooby Doo, Hanna–Barbera, 1973 .... 20.00
Secret Of Nimh, 1982 .... 15.00
Sesame Street, Vinyl, 1980 .... 22.00 To 35.00
Six Million Dollar Man .... 20.00 To 60.00
Snow White, 1938 .... 137.00
Space Cadet, 1952–1953 .... 650.00
Space Shuttle Challenger, Vinyl 175.00
Space Shuttle Orbiter Enterprise 10.00
Star Trek 600.00
Star Trek, The Motion Picture 38.00
Star Wars 15.00
Star Wars, Jedi .... 29.00 To 30.00
Strawberry Shortcake, Vinyl, 1980 .... 22.00 To 25.00
Suitcase, Brown 22.00
Superfriends, 1976–1979 .... 25.00 To 50.00
Tarzan, 1966–1967 .... 100.00
The Fonz, Happy Days, 1978 .... 35.00
Tiger Chewing Tobacco, Blue 225.00
Tiger Chewing Tobacco, Red, Tin .... 15.00 To 35.00
Tom Corbett, Space Cadet .... 300.00 To 650.00

Toronto Blue Jays 20.00
Transformers, 1986 .... 40.00
Trigger, 1956–1957 .... 75.00
Truck, Rainbow Bread 35.00
U.S. Mail 15.00
Union Commander, Cut Plug, Tin, 4 1/4 x 7 In. 475.00
Union Leader, Cut Plug Tobacco 40.00
Voyage To The Bottom Of The Sea, 1967 .... 59.00 To 90.00
Wagon Train, 1964 ....75.00 To 100.00
Waltons, 1973–1975 .... 35.00
West Pony Express, 1982 .... 30.00
Wild Bill Hickok, 1955 .... 75.00
Wild Wild West, 1969 .... 45.00 To 65.00
Will Sonnet 75.00
Woody Woodpecker, 1971 .... 59.00 To 75.00
Yellow Submarine, 1968 .... 325.00
LUNCH PAIL, Dan Patch Tobacco, Wooden Bail Handle, 7 In. 305.00
Mayo's Cut Plug, Collapsible, 7 3/4 x 4 In. 275.00
Nigger Hair Tobacco, Black Woman, Hoops, 6 1/2 In. 270.00
White Castle, Blue, Thermos 8.00
Winner Plug Tobacco, Racing Cars, 7 3/4 x 5 In. ....85.00 To 155.00

LUNEVILLE, a French faience factory, was established about 1730 by Jacques Chambrette. It is best known for its fine biscuit figures and groups and for large faience dogs and lions. The early pieces were unmarked. The firm was acquired by Keller and Guerin and is still working.

Chandelier, Cameo, Burgundy Leaves, Muller Freres, 15 x 13 In. 6050.00
Figure, Recumbent Lion, 19th Century, 13 1/2 x 17 In. 2200.00
Pitcher, Insects, Birds, Butterflies, 8 In. 150.00
Plate, Pears, Obert, 8 3/4 In. 20.00
Vase, Cameo, Brown To Amber To Frost, Landscape, Muller Freres 2100.00

LUSTER glaze was meant to resemble copper, silver, or gold. It has been used since the sixteenth century. Most of the luster found today was made during the nineteenth century. The metallic glazes are applied on pottery. The finished color depends on the combination of the clay color and the glaze. Tea Leaf pieces have their own category.

Canary, Creamer, Embossed Ribs, Blue & Gray Stripes, 3 In. 125.00
Canary, Mug, Black Transfer Landscape, Silver Resist Trim, 3 5/8 In. 250.00
Canary, Mug, Boys, Balancing, Brown Transfer, Leaf Handle, 2 1/4 In. 225.00
Canary, Mug, Child's, Painted Eagle, Welcome Lafayette 2200.00
Canary, Mug, Child, Dog, Remember Me, Purple Luster, Leaf Handle 310.00
Canary, Mug, Children, Playing, Black Transfer, 2 5/8 In. 235.00
Canary, Pitcher, Portrait Of Duke Of Wellington 4000.00
Canary, Plate, Early Steam Engine 1700.00
Canary, Tea Caddy, Marbelized Design 1300.00
Copper & Pink, Pitcher, Enameled Basket Of Flowers, 8 7/8 In. 525.00
Copper, 3 Reserves, Lafayette, Cornwallis & Fruit, 8 3/8 In. 900.00
Copper, Compote, Embossed Garland Of Flowers, 3 1/4 x 4 1/4 In. 65.00
Copper, Creamer, Purple Transfer Of Hope & Faith, 3 5/8 In. 100.00
Copper, Cup & Saucer, Handleless, Tea Leaf, Shaw 45.00
Copper, Pitcher, 2 Transfers Of General Jackson 3000.00
Copper, Pitcher, 3 Reserves, Woman On Recamier, Child, 8 In. 300.00
Copper, Pitcher, Blue Bands, Orange & Pink Luster Floral, 5 3/4 In. 75.00
Copper, Pitcher, Colored Flowers, Octagonal, 8 In. 48.00
Copper, Pitcher, Enameled Flowers, 8 3/8 In. 135.00
Copper, Pitcher, Mask Spout, Embossed 67.00
Copper, Pitcher, Mask Spout, Polychromed Shepherd, 9 3/8 In. 300.00
Copper, Platter, Octagonal 100.00
Copper, Sugar & Creamer, Blue Band, Miniature 65.00
Copper, Tea Set, Gibsons, England, 4 Piece 65.00
Copper, Teapot, Turquoise Band 15.00
Copper, Tumbler, Gold & Tan Floral Design 55.00

Fairyland luster is included in the Wedgwood section

Green, Flower Frog, Tree Trunk, Long–Tailed Bird & Mate, 6 In.	45.00
Pink, Chocolate Set, Gold Design, 7 Piece	150.00
Pink, Creamer, Floral, 3 In.	120.00
Pink, Cup & Saucer, Handleless, Vines, Enameling	70.00
Pink, Oyster Plate, Decorated, 9 1/2 In., 5 Piece	350.00
Pink, Oyster Plate, Gilt Decorated, 8 1/2 In., Pair	120.00
Pink, Plate, Schoolhouse, 5 In.	50.00
Pink, Tea Service, Flowers, Green Glazed Dots, 18 Piece	330.00
Pink, Tea Set, Child's, German, Box, 7 Piece	100.00
Pink, Vintage & Purple Transfers, 4 3/4 In.	275.00
Pitcher, Floral Band, Copper, 4 1/2 In.	45.00
Silver, Jug, Satyr, Enameled Face, England, 1830, 4 1/2 In. ....*Illus*	440.00
Silver, Pitcher, 4 1/2 In.	60.00
Silver, Wall Pocket, Red Parrots, Japan, 6 In., Pair	32.00

Sunderland luster pieces are in the Sunderland category

Tea Leaf luster pieces are listed in the Tea Leaf Ironstone section

LUSTRE ART GLASS Company was founded in Long Island, New York, in 1920 by Conrad Vahlsing and Paul Frank. The company made lampshades and globes that are almost indistinguishable from those made by Quezal. Most of the shades made by the company were unmarked.

Shade, Green Pulled Feather, Random Threading, Signed	190.00
Shade, Marigold	125.00

LUSTRES are mantel decorations, or pedestal vases, with many hanging glass prisms. The name really refers to the prisms, and it is proper to refer to a single glass prism as a lustre. Either spelling, luster or lustre, is correct.

2 Rows Of Prisms, Floral, Cobalt Blue, 12 1/4 In., Pair	1225.00
5–Light, Alabaster, Porcelain Flowers, Onyx Base, 23 In., Pair	410.00
Bohemian Glass, Emerald Green, Trumpet Form, 12 1/2 In., Pair	990.00
Cranberry, 19th Century, 13 In., Pair	550.00
Cranberry, White Overlay, Czechoslovakia, 11 In.	185.00
Cut Glass, Pedestal, Cut Scalloped Top, Faceted Prisms, 14 In., Pair	385.00
Girandole Set, Brass, 3 Piece	600.00
Gold Enamel, Double Rows Of Prisms, Pink On White, 15 1/2 In., Pair	910.00
Hanging Prisms, Engraved Cranberry Shade, Electrified, Pair	250.00
Pink, Enameled Overlay, Double Row Of Prisms, 1880s	200.00
Ruby Glass, Painted Gold Design, Prisms, 19th Century, Pair	950.00
Ruby, Enameled Design, 13 1/2 In., Pair	975.00

LUTZ glass was made by Nicolas Lutz working at the Boston and Sandwich Glass Company from 1869 to 1888. He made delicate and intricate threaded glass of several colors. Other similar wares made by other makers are now known by the generic name *Lutz*.

Cigarette Holder, Document Of Authenticity, Signed	50.00

Luster, Silver, Jug, Satyr, Enameled Face, England, 1830, 4 1/2 In.

Majolica, Bowl, Green, Brown, Pedestal
Foot, 11 1/2 x 17 In.

Vase, Purple Iridescent, Fluted Rim, 8 In. 80.00
Vase, Purple Iridescent, Narrow, 8 In. 60.00

MAASTRICHT, Holland, was the city where Petrus Regout established the De Sphinx pottery in 1836. The firm was noted for its transfer–printed earthenware. Many factories in Maastricht are still making ceramics.

Bowl, Oriental Transfer, Sana Pattern, 6 In. 45.00
Cake Set, Flowers, 6 Piece 35.00
Pitcher, Oriental Transfer, Sana Pattern, 5 In. 45.00
Plate, Dark Blue & Gold Flowers, Spatter Flowers, 6 1/2 In. 65.00
Plate, Stick, Red Cherries, Green Leaves, Spatterware, 8 1/2 In. 56.00

MAIZE glass was made by W. L. Libbey & Son Company of Toledo, Ohio, after 1889. The glass resembled an ear of corn. The leaves were usually green, but some pieces were made with blue or red leaves. The kernels of corn were light yellow, white, or light green.

Bowl, Crystal, Blue Leaves, 9 In. 250.00
Carafe, Water, Custard Leaves 210.00
Celery Vase, Gold Colored Leaves, 6 5/8 In. 165.00
Celery Vase, Green Leaves, White, 6 1/2 In. 175.00
Celery Vase, White 165.00
Celery, Blue Leaves, Clear Corn, Libbey, 6 In. 85.00
Celery, Yellow Leaves, Gold Trim, Cream 400.00
Cruet, Green Leaves 495.00
Pitcher, Clear Body, Amber Rows Of Kernels, 8 3/4 In. 585.00
Pitcher, Golden Husks, White, Strap Handle 495.00
Pitcher, Water, White, Golden Husks, Applied Strap Handle, Libbey 495.00
Pitcher, Yellow Leaves, White Opaque 195.00
Sugar Shaker 350.00
Sugar Shaker, Green 195.00
Toothpick, Leaves 210.00
Tumbler, 4 In. 75.00
Tumbler, Green & Gold Leaves 85.00
Tumbler, Green, Rust Leaves 115.00
Vase, Green On White, 7 In. 65.00

MAJOLICA is a general term for any pottery glazed with an opaque tin enamel that conceals the color of the clay body. It has been made since the fourteenth century. Today's collector is most likely to find Victorian majolica. The heavy, colorful ware is rarely marked. Some famous makers include Wedgwood; Minton; Griffen, Smith and Hill (marked *Etruscan*); and Chesapeake Pottery (marked *Avalon* or *Clifton*).

Ashtray, Bears 48.00
Ashtray, Boy, Sitting On Leaf, Germany 95.00
Basket, Bird's Nest 220.00
Beverage Set, Basketweave & Rope, 7 Piece 145.00
Biscuit Jar, Brass Lid & Bail 175.00

Bowl, Fish, Figural, 13 1/2 In. 250.00
Bowl, Green, Brown, Pedestal Foot, 11 1/2 x 17 In. ....*Illus* 468.00
Bowl, Raised Design, Square, 4 In., Pair 40.00
Bowl, Red & White Flowers, Twisted Serpent Handles, 9 In. 225.00
Bowl, Sunflower, Pedestal, Lear, 9 In. 450.00
Box, Fly, Abdomen & Wings Form Cover, Lily Pad Base, 1872, Pair 3860.00
Box, Game, Liner, Oval 1695.00
Box, Sardine, Basketweave, Fish Handle 595.00
Butter Chip, Strawberry, Brown Luster 30.00
Cake Stand, Maple Leaves, 5 x 9 In. 185.00
Cake Stand, Pineapple 325.00
Cake Stand, Pink Leaves 195.00
Candleholder, Kissing Couple 52.50
Centerpiece, Birds, Ring Shape, 6 Pastel Flower Bowls, France 275.00
Cheese Keeper, Birds & Cattails, Large 1895.00
Cheese Keeper, Embossed Leaf & Flower Design 825.00
Cheese Keeper, Stilton, Cobalt Exterior, Mottled Base 2250.00
Clock, Mantel, Cobalt Blue & Yellow, 19th Century, 13 x 13 In. 440.00
Clock, Mantel, Gilbert Movement, 11 In. 700.00
Compote, Daisy & Salad, Signed, 9 x 5 In. 395.00
Compote, Strawberry, Turquoise, Wedgwood, 9 1/2 In. 395.00
Creamer, Begonia Leaf, Etruscan, 3 1/2 In. 75.00
Creamer, Birds, Turquoise 160.00
Cup & Saucer, Cauliflower, Etruscan 325.00
Cuspidor, Pink 225.00
Decanter, Wine, Allover Floral Design, Rosebud Stopper, 14 In., Pr. 185.00
Dish, Asparagus, Underplate 310.00
Dish, Cover, Artichoke 210.00
Dish, Fan, Blue, 6 In. 55.00
Dish, Leaf Shape, Handle, Etruscan, 12 In. 120.00
Dish, Raised Pine Tree In Center, Leaf Shape 100.00
Epergne, Green, Burgundy Around Small Flowers, 20 x 15 In. 465.00
Ewer, Cobalt Floral, 14 In. 225.00
Fernery, Hanging, Gilt, Chain Stamped N. Winfield, 1851, 9 x 15 In. 480.00
Figurine, Cockatoo 225.00
Figurine, Hen, Grassy Base, 14 1/2 In. 88.00
Figurine, Mallard Duck, Naturalistic Colors, Marked, 17 1/2 In. 660.00
Flower Bowl, Boat Shape, Floral Handles, Mountains, 6 x 12 In. 325.00
Flower Bowl, Molded Pink Lilies, Brown Ground, Boat Shape, 10 In. 180.00
Humidor, Black Bust 395.00
Humidor, Roses, Cobalt Blue 65.00
Inkwell, Girl Sitting On Tree Stump 500.00
Jardiniere, Art Nouveau, Cobalt Blue, 8 1/2 In. 145.00
Jardiniere, Green, Gold, Brown, On Stand, Early 20th C., 46 In. 715.00
Jug, 4 Cherubs, 15 In. .... 1750.00 To 2295.00
Lamp, Kerosene 1000.00
Match Holder, Basketweave 175.00
Match Holder, Black Woman 125.00
Match Holder, Happy Hooligan Family 100.00
Match Striker, Black Boy 375.00
Matchbox, Striker, Black Boy 350.00
Mustard, Attached Saucer, Peony Finial, Peony Pattern 225.00
Oyster Plate, Cobalt Blue Center, England 260.00
Oyster Plate, Moon Shape, 9 1/2 In. 125.00
Pitcher, Acorn, Green & Brown, 6 1/4 In. 95.00
Pitcher, Bamboo & Flower, 5 1/2 In. 85.00
Pitcher, Basket & Floral, Square, 7 In. 225.00
Pitcher, Basketweave, Flowers, Green Interior, 6 In. 125.00
Pitcher, Bird & Fan, Triangular 175.00
Pitcher, Bird & Fan, Wedgwood 750.00
Pitcher, Bird's Nest, 9 1/2 In. 350.00
Pitcher, Bird, Barrel Shape, 10 In. 225.00
Pitcher, Birds In Nest, Leaf Handle, Oak Leaf Accents, 5 1/2 In. 165.00

Pitcher, Cherry Blossom, Etruscan, Large 225.00
Pitcher, Corn, 4 1/2 In. .... 50.00 To 70.00
Pitcher, Corn, Green Leaves, 7 1/4 In. 195.00
Pitcher, Dragon 350.00
Pitcher, Eagle, Large 195.00
Pitcher, Fan Front, Scroll Back, Leather Pottery Wrapped, 8 In. 110.00
Pitcher, Fern, Etruscan, 7 1/2 In. 55.00
Pitcher, Fish, Graduated, 7 1/2 To 12 In., 4 Piece 675.00
Pitcher, Floral, Square Neck, 9 In. 275.00
Pitcher, Gurgling Fish, Salmon Pink Interior, 8 3/4 In. .... 145.00 To 200.00
Pitcher, Heron, 5 In. 140.00
Pitcher, Hummingbird, Basketweave 265.00
Pitcher, Ice Lip, Large Flowers, Leaves, Branches, Blue 345.00
Pitcher, Lavender, Brown Basket Base, Corncobs, Husks, 6 In. 85.00
Pitcher, Milk, Pastel Florals 135.00
Pitcher, Monkey, Marked, 9 In. 850.00
Pitcher, Parrot, 12 1/2 In. 150.00
Pitcher, Pelican, 9 In. 550.00
Pitcher, Pink Floral, Mottled Exterior, Pink Interior, 7 In. 105.00
Pitcher, Pit, The Tastesetter, 10 1/2 In. 90.00
Pitcher, Pond Lily & Bird, Marked, 8 In. 310.00
Pitcher, Ribbon, 5 In. 140.00
Pitcher, Robin On Branch, 7 In. 75.00
Pitcher, Shell, Fielding, 9 1/2 In. 395.00
Pitcher, Water Lilies, 5 3/4 In. 110.00
Pitcher, Yellow & Blue Basketweave, 4 3/4 In. 85.00
Plant Stand, Columnar, Green, Gold Leaf, Berries, 15 In. 192.50
Plaque, Birds, Facing, Flowers, Open Work, 13 In., Pair 610.00
Plate, Apple & Strawberry, Etruscan, 9 In. 100.00
Plate, Asparagus, 9 In. 120.00
Plate, Bamboo, Etruscan, 8 In. 125.00
Plate, Bird On Branch, Basketweave, 9 1/2 In. 38.00
Plate, Birds & Grapes, 6 1/2 In., Pair 30.00
Plate, Blackberries, Blossom & Foliage, 8 In. 95.00
Plate, Chrysanthemum, Wedgwood, 10 In. 140.00
Plate, Grapes & Leaves, 7 3/4 In. 150.00
Plate, Green, Yellow & Pink, 8 1/4 In. 65.00
Plate, Harbor Scene Center, Brown Patterned Border, 9 1/4 In. 15.00
Plate, Oyster, Cobalt Ground, Woman's Head, 8 1/4 In. 275.00
Plate, Shell & Seaweed, 6 In. 165.00
Plate, Shell & Seaweed, Wedgwood, 8 3/4 In. 70.00
Plate, Water Lily, 10 In. 55.00
Plate, Water Lily, Rolled Edge, 8 In. 38.00
Plate, Wedgwood, 1900s, 9 In. 195.00
Platter, Crane, 11 In. 125.00
Platter, Dog & Doghouse, Scalloped Rim, 11 In. 135.00
Platter, Landscape, Griffins & Scrollwork, Round, 24 1/2 In. 445.00
Platter, Shellfish, White Ground, Wedgwood, 23 In. 1275.00
Punch Bowl, Jester Shape, Holly Design, Aqua Interior, 13 1/2 In. 995.00
Server, Asparagus, Attached Underplate, Wedgwood 495.00
Shoe, Shaped Heel, Turned-Up Toe, Scroll & Floral, 2 1/2 x 4 In. 195.00
Stool, Garden, Birds, Flowers, George Jones 2310.00
Sugar Shaker, Basketweave 165.00
Sugar, Cauliflower 185.00
Tea Set, Cauliflower, Etruscan, 3 Piece 695.00
Teapot, Fern & Cattails, Pewter Lid 395.00
Teapot, Hinged Pewter Lid 225.00
Teapot, Shell & Seaweed, 5 In. 585.00
Tray, Eat-Thy-Bread, Mottled Center, 13 In. 170.00
Trivet, Swan 80.00
Urn, Grecian Warriors In Battle, White Ground, Handles, 17 In. 795.00
Urn, Mermaid Handles, Cupid Cover, Germany, c.1875, 19 x 15 In. 1320.00
Vase, Black Girl With Banjo, 15 In. 600.00

Vase, Black Girl, 19 In. 525.00
Vase, Cover, Gilt Outlined Design, Central Medallion, 19 1/2 In. 225.00
Vase, Dark Green, Maroon Rose, Green Leaves, 8 In. 95.00
Vase, Embossed Morning Glories, Stems Are Handles, 6 1/2 In. 75.00
Vase, Fish, Shorter, 9 1/2 In. 200.00
Vase, Lizards & Toads, 16 In. 250.00
Vase, Molded Iris, 12 In. 165.00
Vase, Statue, Peacock, Tail Open, 17 x 14 In. 715.00
Wall Pocket, Large Lavender Flowers 20.00

MAPS of all types have been collected for centuries. The earliest known printed maps were made in 1478. The first printed street map showed London in 1559. The first road maps for use by drivers of automobiles were made in 1901. Collectors buy maps that were pages of old books, as well as the multifolded road maps popular in this century.

Alaska, Geological, Chitna River Valley, 1939, 29 x 50 In. 25.00
Alaska, U.S. Survey Of Point Barrow Region, Color, 1925, 33 x 35 In. 16.00
Arkansas, Public Surveys, Folds, 1856, 18 x 18 In. 13.00
Arkansas, Survey, Cherokee & Choctaw Indian Boundry Lines, 1856 .... 18.00
Atlantic City, Galbreath's Apothecary Advertising, Folder, 1900 .... 30.00
Atlas, Collier's World Atlas & Gazetteer, 1940 .... 6.00
Atlas, Philco Radio Atlas Of World, Color, 1934–35 .... 7.00
Atlas, Rand McNally Unrivaled Atlas Of World, 1913 .... 6.00
Atlas, World War II, 1943 .... 5.00
Bible Atlas, With Maps, Rand McNally, 1899 .... 6.50
California & Nevada, Railroad Lines, Mining Camps, 1886, 13 x 21 In. 30.00
Chicago, Columbian Exposition, 1893, 24 x 36 In. 75.00
Cincinnati, Ohio, Oil Cloth, Dated 1859, Square, 6 Ft. 55.00
Colorado, Leadville Mining District, Saunders, 1901, 31 x 38 In. 350.00
District Of Columbia, City Of Washington, Tenner, 1836, 11 x 14 In. 150.00
East & West Coast Survey, Foldout, 1878, 27 x 32 In., Pair 33.00
East Coast, Maine To Florida & Cuba, US Coast Survey, 1885, 28 x 33 In. 13.00
Geology, Coal, Oil & Gas, Pennsylvania, GPO Publ., 1932, 17 x 28 In., Pair 16.00
Globe, Compass Base, T. Harris & Son, London, Pair 9900.00
Globe, Pocket, New & Correct Globe Of Earth, I. Senex, Case, 2 3/4 In. 1450.00
Globe, Rand McNally, World, Walnut Stand, c.1925, 39 x 22 In. 600.00
Globe, Terrestrial & Celestial, Newton & Barry, 1838, Pair ....*Illus* 10450.00
Globe, Terrestrial, 1816 .... 350.00
Globe, Terrestrial, Gilman Joslin, Brass Meridian, 1855, 18 In. 2420.00
Globe, Terrestrial, Sir Joseph Banks, c.1819, 24 In. 2475.00
Idaho, Counties, Military Forts, Railroads, 1886, 11 x 13 In. 20.00
Indian, Foldout, Linen Back, Color, 1925, 18 x 22 In. 12.00
Kansas & Nebraska, Public Survey Plan, Indian Tribes, 1856, 13 x 23 In. 22.00
La Principaute D'orange 1627, Hand Colored, Matted, Framed, 25 x 29 In. 225.00
Louisiana, Land Districts, Folds, 1856, 18 x 18 In. 10.00
Maine, Hand Colored, Ashier & Adams, 1872, 17 1/2 x 24 In. 17.00
Massachusetts & Rhode Island, S. Augustus Mitchell, 1846 .... 125.00

◆◆◆◆◆◆◆◆◆◆◆◆◆◆◆◆◆◆◆◆◆◆

A mixture of flour and olive oil can sometimes remove a dull film from a lacquered piece. Rub on the paste, then wipe and polish with a soft cloth.

◆◆◆◆◆◆◆◆◆◆◆◆◆◆◆◆◆◆◆◆◆◆

Map, Globe, Terrestrial & Celestial, Newton & Barry, 1838, Pair

Massachusetts, Foldout, Linen, 1903 .... 125.00
Michigan, Gulf Info Map, 1934 .... 4.00
N. H. & Vermont, Jr. Auto Trails, Almy, Bigelow & Washburn Dept., 1923 ...... 5.00
Netherlands, Color, c.1880, 12 1/2 x 14 In. 12.00
New Jersey & Pennsylvania, Hand Colored, Ashler & Adams, 1872, 24 In. 17.00
New York, Standard Oil Co., 1956 .... 3.00
North Dakota, Standard Oil, 1935 .... 8.00
North Dakota, U.S. Survey Of Coal Resources, Color, 1939, 36 x 42 In. 12.00
Northern Hemisphere Exploration, Explorers' Sites, 1886, 11 x 13 In. 10.00
Pennsylvania, Keystone Gas, 1932 .... 12.00
Philadelphia, Pa., Mornung, Litho 595.00
Philippines, Spanish & English, John Jackson, Esq. 1814, 12 x 20 In. 49.00
Route, United Fruit Co., North & South America, 1924 .... 16.00
San Francisco, Prior To Earthquake, Rand McNally, 1901, 19 x 26 In. 60.00
Sheboygan County, Herman Township, Wisconsin, 1889, 14 1/2 x 17 1/2 In. 35.00
Territory Of Arizona, Full Color, Frank Bond, 1903, 20 x 17 In. 60.00
Territory Of Florida, Colored Engraving, Burr, 1835, 14 x 11 In. 240.00
Texas Oil, Yellow, Red, White & Green, 1938, 38 x 38 In. 500.00
United States, 1915 .... 10.00
Upper Canada, Burr, Color Engraving, 1835, 11 x 13 In. 120.00
Virginia, North Carolina & South Carolina, Framed, 1781 .... 90.00
Wall, Long Island, Oil Cloth Back, Folds Like Book, 1852, 39 x 58 In. 175.00
Western U.S. Boundaries, Multiple Boundary Changes, 1886, 11 x 13 In. 10.00
Wisconsin, Highway, 1919 .... 9.00
Wisconsin, Standard Oil, 1936 .... 8.00
World War II, Esso, 1940s 10.00
World, 1865, John & Ward, Color, Center Fold, 18 x 26 In. 25.00
World, Defense Bases On Back, 1942 .... 12.00
World, Linen, Foldout, 1908, 35 x 40 In. 13.00
Wyoming, Counties, Indian Reservations, 1886, 11 x 13 In. 20.00
Yellowstone, Wonders Of Yellowstone, Color, Folded, 1874, 9 1/2 x 28 In. 44.00

MARBLE CARVINGS, such as large or small figurines, groups of people or
animals, and architectural decorations, have been a special art form since
the time of the ancient Greeks. Reproductions, especially of large Victorian
groups, are being made of a mixture using marble dust. These are very
difficult to detect and collectors should be careful. Other carvings are listed
under Alabaster.

Birdbath, Nanna Mathews Bryant, 33 1/2 In. 4450.00
Birdbath, Octagonal Plinth, Scrolling Acanthus, 29 In. 1200.00
Book, Brown & Cream, For Holding Pages Open, 1830, 2 x 3 In. 39.00
Bust, Bacchus, Wreath In Hair, Pelt Around Neck, 23 1/2 In. 8900.00
Bust, Hermes, Winged Helmet, 25 In. 2350.00
Bust, Nero, Italy, 18th Century, 33 In. ....*Illus* 16500.00
Bust, Roman Emperor, Swagged Toga, Tapering Socle, 26 In. 3850.00
Bust, Woman, Carved Lace Color, Floral Spray, 22 In. 715.00
Bust, Woman, Pedestal Base, A. Datie, 21 In. 500.00
Bust, Woman, White, Alabaster Pedestal Base, 68 1/2 In. 750.00
Bust, Young Woman, Bare Breasts, France, 22 1/2 In. 2750.00
Bust, Young Woman, Hat, Lace Drape, 19th Century, 16 In. 600.00
Casolette, Ormolu Trim, 20 1/2 In., Pair 3600.00
Child, Looking Skyward, C. L. Boulogne, 31 1/2 In. 3600.00
Christian Martyr, Nude, Handcuffed, L. Fabbrucci, 43 1/2 In. 3100.00
Clock Case, 2 Figures, 18 1/2 In. ....*Illus* 990.00
Dancer Of Florence, C. Lapini, 55 1/2 In. 6930.00
Dog, Reclining, Garden, 19th Century, 32 In. 6050.00
Font, Leaf–Tip, Foliate Baluster, Ram Heads Base, 28 1/2 In. 2750.00
Girl Standing By Tree, Rossi, Marble Base, 36 In. 2250.00
Goddess, Standing, In Toga, Biagiom M. Florence, 17 In. 335.00
Head, Bodhisattva, Headdress, Wooden Base & Box, 19 In. 4450.00
Headless Nude Female, Flanked By Dolphin, 23 In. 3350.00
Lar, Seated Allegorical Figure, Holding Cornucopia, 11 In. 1550.00
Mercury, Seated, Mid–19th Century, 25 In. 1425.00

Marble Carving, Bust, Nero,   *Marble, Figurine, Winged Putti, Arm Front of Body, Italy, 35 In.*

Italy, 18th C., 33 In.   *Marble, Figurine, Winged Putti, Arms Outstretched, Italy, 35 In.*

Obelisk, Bronze Turtle Support, Italy 250.50
Plaque, Black, Floral, Presented To Eliza, 16 1/4 x 16 In. 30.00
Urn, Floral & Bird Handles, VP Crown, 36 In., Pair 9800.00
Urn, Garden, Gadrooned Base, Fluted Socle, 20 In., Pair 3025.00
Vase, Neoclassical, Baluster Shape, Gray, 18 In., Pair 1100.00
Victorian Woman, Wide Brimmed Hat, E. Fiaschy, 25 In. 990.00
Winged Putti, Arms Outstretched, Italy, 35 In. ....*Illus* 5950.00
Winged Putti, Right Arm Across Body, Italy, 35 In. ....*Illus* 6200.00

MARBLES has been a popular game since the days of the ancient Romans. American children were able to buy marbles by the mid–eighteenth century. Dutch glazed clay marbles were least expensive. Glazed pottery marbles, attributed to the Bennington potteries in Vermont, were of a better quality. Marbles made of pink marble were also available by the 1830s. Glass marbles seem to have been made later. By 1880, Samuel C. Dyke of South Akron, Ohio, was making clay marbles and The National Onyx Marble Company was making marbles of onyx. The Navarre Glass Marble Company of Navarre, Ohio,

Marble Carving, Clock Case, 2 Figures,

18 1/2 In.

◆ ◆

Small cracks in marble can be concealed with a mixture of colored wax and chalk dust. The same mixture can be used to make a new nose or finger for a damaged marble figure.

◆ ◆

◆ ◆

Changes in temperature may cause old ivory to crack.

◆ ◆ ◆ ◆ ◆ ◆ ◆ ◆ ◆ ◆ ◆ ◆ ◆ ◆ ◆ ◆ ◆ ◆ ◆ ◆

made the glass marbles. Ohio remained the center of the marble industry, and the Akron–made Akro Agate brand became nationally known. Sulphides are glass marbles with frosted white figures in the center.

Akro Agate, No. 32, Box Of 10	50.00
Clambroth, 5/8 In., Pair	225.00
Clambroth, Red Strands, 1 3/4 In.	1600.00
Comic Strip, Emma, Bimbo & Smitty, 5/8 In., 3 Piece	260.00
Crystal, 2 White Outer Bands, 3/4 In.	10.00
End Of Day, Joseph's Coat, 5/8 In., Pair	170.00
Indian Swirl, 1 In.	150.00
Latticinio, Core Swirl, White, 2 1/4 In.	145.00
Lutz, 2 Goldstone Bands, 4 Red Bands, Black Glass, 11/16 In.	215.00
Lutz, Blue Banded, 3/4 In.	70.00
Lutz, Indian Swirl, 5/8 In.	425.00 To 770.00
Lutz, Indian Swirl, 5/8 In., Matched Pair	1300.00
Lutz, Onionskin, Multicolored, 3/4 In.	275.00
Onionskin, Alternating Blues, Green, Reds & Oranges, 1 5/8 In.	77.00
Onionskin, Pink, Blue & White Swirl, 2 1/16 In.	425.00
Onionskin, Yellow, Gold, Red & Green Swirl, 2 1/16 In.	525.00
Peltier, Bananas, Box, 5/8 In., 28 Piece	85.00
Peppermint Translucent Swirl, Divided, 1 1/2 In.	120.00
Sulphide, Boar, 1 1/2 In.	75.00
Sulphide, Boar, 1 3/4 In.	160.00
Sulphide, Boy On Rocking Horse, 1 13/16 In.	176.00
Sulphide, Camel, 1 In.	100.00
Sulphide, Dog, 2 1/4 In.	105.00
Sulphide, Elephant, 1 3/4 In.	150.00
Sulphide, Fish In Center	55.00
Sulphide, Grazing Cow, 2 In.	115.00
Sulphide, Lion In Center, 2 1/2 In.	90.00
Sulphide, No. 1, 1 3/4 In.	400.00
Sulphide, Onionskin, Deep Red, Blue, Green, Yellow, 1 3/16 In.	220.00
Sulphide, Onionskin, Green, Yellow, Blue Green, 1 3/16 In.	193.00
Sulphide, Owl, Bird About To Swoop, 2 In.	165.00
Sulphide, Seated Peasant Boy, 1 7/8 In.	320.00
Sulphide, Squirrel, 1 3/4 In.	235.00
Swirl, Multicolored Continuous, 1 1/2 In.	27.50
Swirl, Open Core, 1 1/4 In.	140.00
Swirl, Red, White & Blue Core, 2 In.	235.00
Swirl, White Core, Dark Colored Swirls, 1 3/4 In.	93.00 To 198.00
Swirl, White Core, Multicolored, 2 In.	55.00
Swirl, White Core, Red, 2 In.	71.50
Swirl, Yellow Core, Dark Glass, Looks Like Brown, 1 1/4 In.	44.00

MARBLEHEAD Pottery was founded in 1905 by Dr. J. Hall as a rehabilitative program for the patients of a Marblehead, Massachusetts, sanitarium. Two years later it was separated from the sanitarium and it continued operations until 1936. Many of the pieces were decorated with marine motifs.

Basket, Hanging, Blue, 3 1/2 In.	85.00
Bowl, Brown, 4 1/2 In.	200.00
Bowl, Gray & Blue, 5 In.	265.00
Bowl, Gray Matte Glaze, Large & Thick Form, 5 x 9 In.	175.00
Bowl, Green Leaves, Blue Flowers, 4 Colors, c.1910, 7 In.	715.00
Bowl, Matte Blue, 6 x 2 3/4 In.	110.00
Bowl, Mottled Green, Pink & Gray Glaze, Curved, 2 x 9 In.	120.00
Bowl, Purple Matte Glaze, Marked, 2 x 4 In.	187.00
Bowl, Stylized Grapes & Leaves Band, Glazed, 5 Colors, 9 In.	1870.00
Bowl, Stylized Leaves Band, Over Speckled Mustard, 3 1/2 In.	495.00
Candlestick, Blue, 3 In., Pair	265.00
Chamberstick, Pink Matte, Gray Touches, Unusual Form, 4 x 4 In.	275.00
Jar, Cover, Green Matte Glaze, 3 x 4 1/2 In.	770.00

Marblehead, Vase, Beige
Clay, Sgraffito, Signed   Marblehead, Vase, Grape Medallions, 3 Colors, A. Irwin, 3 1/2 In.
AEB, 4 1/8 In.   Marblehead, Vase, Navy Stylized Trees, Green, H. Tutt, 7 1/4 In.

Lamp, Stylized Trees On Dark Green, Green Glass Globe, 21 In. 5500.00
Rose Bowl, Purple, 5 In. 195.00
Tile, 2 Macaws, On Brown Flower Basket, Cream, Framed, 6 In. 275.00
Tile, Fruit & Leaves In Basket, Blue Matte Ground, Framed, 6 In. 715.00
Tile, Geometric, Green, Brown Border, 6 In. 665.00
Tile, Many Colors, For Test Glaze, Oak Frame, A. E. Baggs, 6 In. 275.00
Tile, Ship, 2 Colors, 4 3/4 In. 250.00
Vase, 4 Macaws On Leafy Branches, Yellow Matte Ground, 7 In. 2500.00
Vase, 5-Color Floral, 6 In. 2300.00
Vase, Band Of Blue Rhododendron Leaves, Marked, 5 3/8 In. 415.00
Vase, Beige Clay, Sgraffito, Signed AEB, 4 1/8 In. ....*Illus* 495.00
Vase, Blue Glaze, Ship Mark, 4 x 5 1/2 In. 245.00
Vase, Blue Matte Glaze, Unusual Form, Bulbous Shoulder, 9 In. 1210.00
Vase, Blue, 4 1/2 In. 165.00
Vase, Blue, Fan Shape, Pleated, Mark & Label, 5 x 8 In. 375.00
Vase, Geometric, Green, Blue Specks, Arts & Crafts, Artist, 9 In. 3575.00
Vase, Grape Medallions, 3 Colors, A. Irwin, 3 1/2 In. ....*Illus* 1100.00
Vase, Gray, 5 1/2 In. 120.00
Vase, Matte Blue Glaze, Flared Rim, Marked, c.1901, 5 1/4 In. 302.50
Vase, Navy Stylized Trees, Green, H. Tutt, 7 1/4 In. ....*Illus* 1100.00
Vase, Pink & Gray Matte Glaze, Bulbous Shoulder, 3 x 4 1/2 In. 138.00
Vase, Pink Matte, 4 x 5 In. 330.00
Vase, Yellow & Dark Brown Specks, Brown Matte, 3 x 6 In. 198.00

MARTIN BROTHERS of Middlesex, England, made martinware, a salt-
glazed stoneware, between 1873 and 1915. Many figural jugs and vases   *Martin Bro.*
were made by the three brothers. Of special interest are the fanciful birds,   *London.*
usually made with removable heads.

Bird, Grotesque, Blue, Brown, Artist, 1893, 3 In. 2550.00
Cup, Figural, Bird, Olive & Brown Salt Glazed, 8 5/8 In. 3190.00
Figure, Bird, Grotesque, Ebonized Wooden Base, 9 3/4 In. 7255.00
Jardiniere, Scrolling Plants, 4-1888, 19 1/2 In. 4695.00
Jug, 4 Incised & Painted Dragons, 3-1889, 9 1/2 In. 854.00
Jug, Grotesque Seal-Like Creature, Mouth Spout, 9 1/2 In. 895.00
Jug, Incised Stork-Like Creature, Green, 2-1898, 9 1/3 In. 1920.00
Jug, Pulled Spout, Handle, Sea Creatures, 12-1888, 9 1/4 In. 2560.00
Jug, Squared Bottle Form, Coil Handle, Salt Glazed, 9 In. 775.00
Spoon Warmer, Grotesque Animal, Salt Glazed, 5 5/8 In. 4675.00
Tile, Foliate Design, Frame, 8 x 8 In. 155.00
Vase, Cellular Design, Grotesque Hound Handles, 7 1/4 In. 895.00
Vase, Incised Fish, Green Ground, Signed, 1904, 6 3/4 In. 660.00
Vase, Irregular Shape, Leaf Designs, Signed, c.1880, 9 In. 1760.00
Vase, Smiling Moon Face, Salt Glazed, Ovoid, 7 7/8 In. 2200.00
Vase, Swimming Fish, Blue, Purple, Green, Ovoid, 8 In. 550.00

MARY GREGORY glass is identified by a characteristic white figure painted on dark glass. It was made from 1870 to 1910. The name refers to any glass decorated with a white silhouette figure and not just to the Sandwich glass originally painted by Miss Mary Gregory. Many reproductions have been made and there are new pieces being sold in gift shops today.

Bottle, Barber, Boy & Foliage, Amethyst	295.00
Bowl, Sand Color, Black Glazed Interior, Shallow, 5 In.	50.00
Box, Hinged Cover, Amber, 1 1/8 x 2 1/8 In.	140.00
Box, Hinged, Woman, Long Dress, Black Amethyst, 3 3/4 x 6 In.	275.00
Box, Jewelry, Cobalt Blue, Hinged Top	95.00
Carafe, Water, Cranberry, White Boy, 11 In.	275.00
Castor, Pickle, Cranberry, Double	650.00
Cruet, Boy In Knickers, Smelling Flower, Sapphire Blue, 8 In.	380.00
Cruet, Girl With Balloon, Cranberry, 7 1/2 In.	350.00
Cruet, White Boy, Optic Pattern, Amber, 9 1/4 In.	250.00
Decanter, Girl Beside Swan In Water, Cranberry, 9 1/4 In.	425.00
Decanter, Tinted Faced Boy, Emerald Green	285.00
Flask, Boy In Garden Picking Flowers, Brass Collar, Purse	250.00
Jar, Cover, Dresser, Girl With Butterfly, c.1880, 6 In.	825.00
Lamp, Girl Fishing, Flowered Shade, Blue & White, 16 1/4 In.	1370.00
Mug, Boy, Girl, Balloons, 4 In., Pair	75.00
Mug, White Boy, 4 3/4 In.	145.00
Pitcher, Boy, Tinted Face, Butterfly Net, Blue, 12 In.	300.00
Pitcher, Girl, Gold Trim At Top, Amber Handle, 10 3/4 In.	375.00
Pitcher, Inverted Thumbprint, Blue	325.00
Pitcher, Syrup, Cobalt Blue, Pewter Lid	255.00
Rose Bowl, Clear, White Girl, Gold & Blue Trim, 3 1/2 In.	75.00
Stein, Pewter Cover, Glass Insert, 3 In.	395.00
Sugar Shaker, White Figures, Silver Top	45.00
Tumble-Up, Boy On Carafe, Girl On Tumbler, Cranberry, 6 In.	550.00
Tumbler, Boy With Flute, 3 3/4 In.	80.00
Tumbler, Juice, Cranberry	85.00
Tumbler, Young Boy, Optic Pattern, Amber, 3 3/4 In.	45.00
Vase, Bottle Shape, Girl & Boy, Facing, 9 In., Pair	375.00
Vase, Boy Blowing Bubbles, Oval, Cranberry, 9 In.	295.00
Vase, Boy Blowing Bubbles, Tree, Shrub, 11 In.	150.00
Vase, Boy Carrying Bowl Of Flowers, Green, 11 1/8 In.	225.00
Vase, Boy Carrying Oars, Paneled, Lime Green, 8 In.	110.00 To 150.00
Vase, Boy In Sailor Suit, Girl Blowing Bubbles, 10 In., Pair	545.00
Vase, Boy With Flower, Paneled, Green, 4 In.	75.00
Vase, Cranberry, Enameled Flowers, Footed, 2 In.	28.00
Vase, Facing Pair, Optic Rib, Cranberry, 9 1/4 In., Pair	495.00
Vase, Facing Pair, Shell Trim, Lime Green, 8 1/2 In., Pair	325.00
Vase, Girl Holding Umbrella, Boy, With Oars, 9 1/8 In., Pair	495.00
Vase, Girl In Hat, Cobalt Blue, Facing, 13 5/8 In., Pair	575.00
Vase, Girl On Tiptoe, Cylindrical, Green, 6 In.	110.00
Vase, Girl Picking Apples, Pointed Rim, Sapphire Blue, 12 In.	255.00
Vase, Girl Standing, Boy Seated, Black Amethyst, 12 1/4 In.	450.00
Vase, Girl Tying Bonnet, Boy Kneeling, Amethyst, 16 1/4 In.	995.00
Vase, Girl With Balloon, Amber, 10 1/4 In.	225.00
Vase, Girl With Basket Of Flowers, Golden Amber, 4 1/2 In.	100.00
Vase, Girl With Flower, Flared Rim, Sapphire Blue, 10 In.	125.00
Vase, Girl, Inverted Thumbprint, Cranberry, 10 In.	395.00
Vase, Sailor, Tapered, Lime Green, 8 In.	105.00
Vase, White Boy, Cranberry, Footed, 9 In.	245.00
Vase, White Girl, Blue, 8 In.	125.00
Vase, Woman Holding Hoop, Perched Birds, Green, 12 1/2 In.	320.00
Vase, Woman In Knickers, Sapphire Blue, 10 1/2 In.	160.00
Vase, Young Boy, Optic Effect, Sapphire Blue, 5 3/4 In.	125.00
Vase, Young Girl, White, Pedestal Foot, Green, 4 1/4 In.	80.00
Warming Stand, Enameled Figure & Landscape, 6 In.	275.00

Left to right: Match Holder, Rounded, Single, Embossed, 5 1/2 x 4 3/4 In.; Match Holder, Double, Embossed, 6 3/4 x 3 1/2 In.; Match Holder, Urn, Double, Swag, 4 x 4 In.; Match Holder, Cylinder, Double, 1859, 5 x 4 1/4 In.; Match Holder, Slippers, Double, Brass, 4 x 3 1/2 In.; Match Holder, Rectangular, Open Sides, Brass, 4 x 2 1/2 In.

MASONIC, see Fraternal category

MASSIER, a French art pottery, was made by brothers Jerome, Delphin, and Clement Massier in Vallauris and Golfe-Juan, France, in the late nineteenth and early twentieth centuries. It has an iridescent metallic luster glaze that resembles the Weller Sicard pottery glaze. Most pieces are marked *J. Massier.*

J.Massier fils

Charger, Lush Landscape, Iridescent, c.1890, 14 In.	825.00
Jardiniere, 2 Eagles, Violet To Green Shading, Conical, 8 3/4 In.	1760.00
Pitcher, Spout Mask, Full Figure Maiden Handle, Signed, 10 1/4 In.	1100.00

MATCH HOLDERS were made to hold the large wooden matches that were used in the nineteenth and twentieth centuries for a variety of purposes. The kitchen stove and the fireplace or furnace had to be lit regularly. One type of match holder was made to hang on the wall, another was designed to be kept on a tabletop. Of special interest today are match holders that have advertisements as part of the design.

Alligator, Bronze	125.00
American Brewing Co., Rochester, Stoneware	250.00
Apollinaris, White, Cobalt Blue, Striker	65.00
Baby In Carriage, Holding Figure Of Santa Claus, 5 In.	125.00
Black Man's Head Is Striker, Milk Glass	135.00
Buffalo, New York, Tin, With Striker	95.00
Ceresota Flour, Tin, 5 1/4 In. ....*Illus*	350.00
Climax Horse Collars, Horse Looking Through Collar Picture	800.00
Coon Chicken Inn, Metal	225.00
Cylinder, Double, 1859, 5 x 4 1/4 In. ....*Illus*	245.00
DeLaval, Box	250.00
DeLaval, Woman With Separator, 5 1/2 x 4 1/2 In. ... 165.00 To 200.00
Devil's Head, Cast Iron	130.00

✦✦✦✦✦✦✦✦✦✦✦✦✦✦✦✦✦✦✦✦✦✦✦✦

The value of a matchcover is lowered by writing or marks, scraps or gouge marks from a carelessly removed staple, or a damaged or missing striker.

✦✦✦✦✦✦✦✦✦✦✦✦✦✦✦✦✦✦✦✦✦✦✦✦

Match Holder, Ceresota Flour, Tin, 5 1/4 In.

Double, Embossed, 6 3/4 x 3 1/2 In. ....*Illus* 70.00
Dr. Morse's Indian Root Pills, Cardboard, Scene, 6 x 10 In. 400.00
Dubonnet Grand Prix, Cone Shape, 1900 .... 35.00 To 45.00
Fly, Figural, Hinged Lid, Cast Iron, 2 x 4 1/2 In. 87.00
Frog, With Telephone, Cast Iron, 1910 .... 215.00
General Electric 10.00
James Quirk Milling Co., 2 Black Children, Cast Iron 1100.00
Kettle Shape, Daisy & Button, Amber Glass, Fits Under Lamp 39.00
Kitchen, Red & White Tin 4.50
Kool Cigarettes, Embossed Penguin, Wall, Tin 25.00
Lion Holding Shield, Striker Base, Sterling, 1 1/2 x 2 In. 125.00
Mammy, Chalkware 65.00
Mammy, Wall, Kitchen 35.00
Masonic Emblem, 2 Pockets, Wall, Tin 25.00
Molson's Gin, Black, Cream, Striker, 4 1/2 x 9 1/2 In. 48.00
Monk, Chalkware, Wall 45.00
Pig, Pink, England 95.00
Puss 'n' Boots, Serving Platter Of Food, 5 1/2 In. 65.00
Rabbit, Pheasant & Horn, Brass, Wall, 1870s, 8 In. 85.00
Rectangular, Open Sides, Brass, 4 x 2 1 /2 In. ....*Illus* 20.00
Romford Mineral Waters, Cone Shape 55.00
Rounded, Single, Embossed, 5 1/2 x 4 3/4 In. ....*Illus* 40.00
Salem Cigarettes, Wood Grained Metal, Wall 27.00
Sharples Cream Separator 350.00
Slippers, Double, Brass, 4 x 3 1/2 In. ....*Illus* 20.00
Strawberry, Tin, White Ground 12.00
Universal Stove .... 100.00 To 105.00
Urn, Double, Swag, 4 x 4 In. ....*Illus* 50.00
Woman, Old Fashioned, Roses, Tin, White & Red Ground 8.00
Wrigley's, Man Juicy Fruit Made Famous .... 85.00 To 125.00
Young Woman, Plumed Hat, White, Bisque, 5 1/2 In. 55.00

MATCH SAFES were designed to be carried in the pocket. Early matches were made with phosphorus and could ignite unexpectedly. The matches were safely stored in the tightly closed container. Match safes were made in sterling silver, plated silver, or other metals. The English call these *vesta boxes.*

Anheuser-Busch, Eagle 95.00
Art Nouveau, Sterling Silver, Monogrammed R 55.00
Book Shape, Gutta-Percha, France 75.00
Brownie's Perfecto Cigar, Germany, Pocket 15.00
Christian Moerlein Brewery 85.00
Climax Cut Plug Tobacco, Tin 47.50
Cloisonne 65.00
Gargoyle Faces, G. Netto, Berlin 195.00
Genesse Bottling Co. 70.00
Horse's Hoof, Nickeled Metal, c.1890, 3 In. 125.00
Man Seated On Chair, Hat Lifts Back 110.00
Maserati, "52" 45.00
Nonsuch Mfg. Co., Black Cat, 5 1/2 x 4 1/4 In. 165.00
Oval Ruby, Surrounded By Diamonds, 14K Yellow Gold 660.00
Pan American Exposition 35.00
Rearing Horse, Sterling Silver 295.00
Red Top Rye Whiskey 50.00
Sterling Silver, Art Nouveau 58.00
U. M. W. A. 18th Convention, 1916 .... 28.00
Violin, Brass 140.00
Violin, Silver Plate 140.00

MATSU-NO-KE was a type of applied decoration for glass patented by Frederick Carder in 1922. There is clear evidence that pieces were made before that date at the Steuben glassworks. Stevens & Williams of England also made an applied decoration by the same name.

Bowl, Green, Handles, Green Rim, Signed, Steuben, 9 1/2 In. 225.00
Celery, Yellow, Stevens & Williams 50.00
Vase, Leaves, White Flowers, Cranberry, 7 In. 650.00
Vase, Purple, 6 In. 325.00

MATT MORGAN, an English artist, was making pottery in Cincinnati, Ohio, by 1883. His pieces were decorated to resemble Moorish wares. Incised designs and colors were applied to raised panels on the pottery. Shiny or matte glazes were used. The company lasted less than two years.

Jug, Birds, Beige, Blue, 5 In. 350.00
Vase, Gold Fired On, 2 Large Applied Handles, Label 2255.00

McCOY pottery was made in Roseville, Ohio. The J. W. McCoy Pottery was founded in 1899. It became the Brush McCoy Pottery Company in 1911. The name changed to the Brush Pottery in 1925. The word *Brush* was usually included in the mark on their pieces. The Nelson McCoy Sanitary and Stoneware Company, a different firm, was founded in Roseville, Ohio, in 1910. The firm made art pottery after 1926. In 1933 it became the Nelson McCoy Pottery. Pieces marked *McCoy* were made by the Nelson McCoy Company. Cookie jars were made from the 1930s until December 1990 when the McCoy factory closed.

Ball, Tan, Angled Finial, 1939 .... 20.00
Bank, Eagle .... 15.00 To 16.00
Bank, Sailor, Seaman's Bank For Savings .... 22.00 To 50.00
Coffeepot, El Rancho 125.00
Cookie Jar, American Eagle, Brown, 1968–1969 .... 30.00
Cookie Jar, Animal Crackers, Clown Finial 45.00
Cookie Jar, Apple, Yellow 22.00
Cookie Jar, Asparagus .... 35.00 To 45.00
Cookie Jar, Baa Baa Black Sheep, Nursery Characters, Cylinder 60.00
Cookie Jar, Bananas 105.00
Cookie Jar, Barn 225.00
Cookie Jar, Barnum's, Animals Crackers .... 225.00 To 285.0
Cookie Jar, Basket Of Potatoes 30.00
Cookie Jar, Bean Pot, Bamboo, Single Handle, 1943 .... 45.00
Cookie Jar, Bear & Beehive, 1983 .... 30.00 To 40.00
Cookie Jar, Bear, Cookie In Vest, 1945 .... 35.00 To 50.00
Cookie Jar, Bear, Feet Together, Brown 135.00
Cookie Jar, Bobby Baker .... 20.00 To 55.00
Cookie Jar, Boy On Football 125.00
Cookie Jar, Burlap Sack 30.00
Cookie Jar, Caboose .... 125.00 To 150.00
Cookie Jar, Chipmunk, 1960–1961 .... 65.00 To 110.00
Cookie Jar, Christmas Tree .... 750.00 To 1200.00
Cookie Jar, Circus Horse, Black .... 125.00 To 150.00
Cookie Jar, Clown In Barrel, Green .... 35.00 To 75.00
Cookie Jar, Clown In Barrel, Pink .... 48.00 To 65.00
Cookie Jar, Clown, Bust, 1945–1947 .... 28.00 To 55.00
Cookie Jar, Coalby Cat 250.00
Cookie Jar, Coffee Grinder, 1961–1968 .... 15.00 To 35.00
Cookie Jar, Coffee Mug, 1963 .... 40.00
Cookie Jar, Cookie Bank 100.00
Cookie Jar, Cookie Bell, Red Orange Lettering, 1963–1966 .... 60.00
Cookie Jar, Cookie Cabin, 1956 .... 75.00
Cookie Jar, Cookie Churn, 1977–1978 .... 25.00
Cookie Jar, Cookie House 95.00
Cookie Jar, Cookie Pot, Pennsylvania Dutch Decal, 1964 .... 45.00
Cookie Jar, Cookie Safe .... 40.00 To 58.00
Cookie Jar, Cookstove, Black 30.00
Cookie Jar, Cookstove, White, 1962 .... 30.00
Cookie Jar, Covered Wagon, 1960–1961 .... 30.00 To 90.00
Cookie Jar, Dalmatians In Rocking Chair .... 245.00 To 350.00
Cookie Jar, Dog On Basketweave 35.00

Cookie Jar, Drum, 1960 .... 55.00
Cookie Jar, Duck On Basketweave, 1956 .... 50.00
Cookie Jar, Dutch Boy, 1945 .... 40.00
Cookie Jar, Dutch Treat Barn, 1968–1973 .... 35.00
Cookie Jar, Engine, Black, 1962 .... 125.00 To 175.00
Cookie Jar, Engine, Yellow, Repainted 150.00
Cookie Jar, Fortune Cookie, 1965–1968 .... 45.00
Cookie Jar, Friendship 7 .... 125.00 To 135.00
Cookie Jar, Frog On Stump .... 135.00 To 150.00
Cookie Jar, Frontier Family, 1964–1971 .... 38.00 To 60.00
Cookie Jar, Fruit In Basket 75.00
Cookie Jar, Garbage Can, 1978–1987 .... 35.00
Cookie Jar, Globe 200.00
Cookie Jar, Grandfather Clock 47.00
Cookie Jar, Granny, White Dress, Gold Glasses .... 55.00 To 100.00
Cookie Jar, Green Pepper 8.00
Cookie Jar, Happy Face, Black Eyes & Mouth, 1972–1979 .... 20.00 To 30.00
Cookie Jar, Hobby Horse .... 70.00 To 125.00
Cookie Jar, Honey Bear, Yellow, Brown, 1953–1955 ...... 60.00 To 75.00
Cookie Jar, Hot Air Balloon .... 28.00 To 35.00
Cookie Jar, Indian .... 225.00 To 275.00
Cookie Jar, Jack-O'-Lantern .... 600.00 To 950.00
Cookie Jar, Jewel Box 130.00
Cookie Jar, Kangaroo, Tan 300.00
Cookie Jar, Keebler Tree House 50.00
Cookie Jar, Kettle, Black, 1961 .... 35.00
Cookie Jar, Kissing Penguins 28.00
Cookie Jar, Kittens In A Basket 850.00
Cookie Jar, Koala Bear 60.00
Cookie Jar, Kookie Kettle, Black, Brass Trim, 1960 .... 25.00
Cookie Jar, Lamb On Basketweave .... 38.00 To 50.00
Cookie Jar, Lollipops .... 15.00 To 35.00
Cookie Jar, Lunch Bucket, 1978 .... 30.00
Cookie Jar, Mac Dog, 1967 .... 50.00
Cookie Jar, Mammy .... 125.00 To 150.00
Cookie Jar, Mammy With Cauliflower, 1939 .... 750.00 To 1250.00
Cookie Jar, Milk Can, Decal With Eagle 25.00
Cookie Jar, Milk Can, Liberty Bell, 1972 .... 35.00
Cookie Jar, Milk Can, Yorkville, 1974 .... 40.00
Cookie Jar, Monkey On Stump, 1970 .... 50.00
Cookie Jar, Mother Goose 125.00
Cookie Jar, Mr. & Mrs. Owl .... 75.00 To 95.00
Cookie Jar, Nabisco .... 45.00 To 75.00
Cookie Jar, Oaken Bucket, Copper Trim, 1961 .... 20.00
Cookie Jar, Owl, Brown, 1978–1979 .... 30.00
Cookie Jar, Peanut, 1976 .... 30.00
Cookie Jar, Peek-A-Boo .... 695.00 To 950.00
Cookie Jar, Pepper, Green 28.00
Cookie Jar, Picnic Basket 40.00
Cookie Jar, Pineapple, 1955–1957 .... 20.00 To 35.00
Cookie Jar, Poppies, On Yellow Cylinder, Black Top 50.00
Cookie Jar, Pot Belly Stove, Black .... 20.00 To 40.00
Cookie Jar, Puppy, Holding Sign 80.00
Cookie Jar, Raggedy Ann .... 55.00 To 75.00
Cookie Jar, Rooster, White With Black Spray 65.00
Cookie Jar, Sack Of Cookies, White, Gold Trim, 1961 .... 70.00 To 98.00
Cookie Jar, School Bus .... 65.00 To 75.00
Cookie Jar, Snoopy On Doghouse, 1970 .... 175.00 To 275.00
Cookie Jar, Snow Bear, 1965 .... 30.00 To 65.00
Cookie Jar, Strawberry, Red, 1972 .... 40.00
Cookie Jar, Stump, With Mushrooms, 1972 .... 45.00
Cookie Jar, Tea Kettle, Bronze 30.00
Cookie Jar, Tepee, Slant Top .... 215.00 To 500.00

Cookie Jar, Tepee, Straight Top 350.00
Cookie Jar, Thinking Puppy, Brown, 1977–1979 .... 20.00 To 30.00
Cookie Jar, Time For Cookies, Mouse, Mouse Finial, 1973 .... 40.00
Cookie Jar, Timmy Tortoise, 1977–1980 .... 35.00 To 45.00
Cookie Jar, Touring Car, 1962–1964 .... 30.00 To 80.00
Cookie Jar, Turkey, Brown 150.00
Cookie Jar, Upside–Down Bear, White, 1978 .... 40.00
Cookie Jar, W. C. Fields .... 128.00 To 165.00
Cookie Jar, Wedding Jar 45.00
Cookie Jar, Woodsey Owl .... 95.00 To 175.00
Cookie Jar, Wren House, With Pink Wrens 122.00
Cookie Jar, Yosemite Sam .... 75.00 To 175.00
Creamer, Pine Cone, Matte Turquoise, Brown 8.50
Decanter, Apollo Missile 28.00
Flowerpot, Green, 6 In. 20.00
Jardiniere, Brown Glaze, 8 In 95.00
Jardiniere, Brownware, 1905, 15 In. 250.00
Lamp, Leaves & Circles, White Matte, 14 In. 125.00
Mug, Brown 105.00
Pitcher, Brown, Beige 325.00
Pitcher, Yellow, 9 1/2 In. 20.00
Planter, Alligator 18.00
Planter, Bird Dog 85.00
Planter, Cache Pot, Double, Bird, Green 15.00
Planter, Novelty, Bird 20.00
Planter, Old Mill, Green, Gray 18.00
Planter, Quail 25.00
Planter, Rooster, Brown 8.00
Planter, Tortoise 5.00
Planter, Triple Lily, White 22.00
Planter, Wishing Well, Blue 16.00
Planter, Wishing Well, Gray & Green 20.00
Sugar & Creamer, Pine Cone 15.00
Sugar, Pine Cone 6.00
Tea Set, 2–Tone Green, Creamer, Sugar, Covered Pot, 3 Piece 40.00
Teapot, Cover, Dark Glossy Brown, Beige Froth 18.00
Teapot, Pine Cone 35.00
Vase, Art Nouveau, Green Foliage, Yellow Grapes, Marked, 6 1/2 In. 125.00
Vase, Flowers, Brown, 1905, 8 In. 125.00
Vase, Orange & Green Foliage, Loy Nel Art, 14 In. 275.00
Vase, Pink Hyacinth 13.00
Vase, Rosewood 35.00
Water Cooler, El Rancho 250.00

McKEE is a name associated with various glass enterprises in the United States since 1836, including J. & F. McKee (1850), Bryce, McKee & Co. (1850 to 1854), McKee and Brothers (1865), and National Glass Co. (1899). In 1903, the McKee Glass Company was formed in Jeannette, Pennsylvania. It became McKee Division of the Thatcher Glass Co. in 1951 and was bought out by the Jeannette Corporation in 1961. Pressed glass, kitchenwares, and tablewares were produced. Jeannette Corporation closed in the early 1980s. Additional pieces may be included in the Custard Glass section.

PRESCUT

Butter, Cover, Croesus, Green, Gold Trim 125.00
Clock, Tambour, Peacock Blue 275.00
Compote, Jelly, Gothic 65.00
Creamer, Comet 40.00
Cup, Measuring, Jade, 24 Oz. 30.00
Dish, Cover, Vaseline, Signed 275.00
Dish, Lamb Cover, Chocolate Glass 1800.00
Dish, Rooster Head Cover, Blue, Milk Glass 110.00
Pitcher, Star Rosette, 5 1/2 In. 65.00
Reamer, Jade 22.00

Medical, Jug, Wm. Radam's Microbe Killer,
1 Gal., 11 In.

Syrup, Sunbeam	35.00
Tumbler, Gladiator	12.00
Vase, Wild Rose With Bowknot, Paper Label, Custard Glass, 10 1/2 In.	250.00
Wine, Ball & Swirl, 1894, 6 Piece	125.00

MECHANICAL BANKS are listed in the Bank category.

MEDICAL office furniture, operating tools, microscopes, thermometers, and other paraphernalia used by doctors are included in this section. Medicine bottles are listed in the Bottle section. There are related collectibles listed under Dental.

Aulmonary Apparatus	325.00
Bag, Doctor's, Leather, With Contents, Early 1900s	50.00
Bleeder, Automatic Spring Loaded, 12 Blade	275.00
Book, German Midwifery Manual, 1813	45.00
Book, Health Fragments–Steps Towards True Life, 1875, 125 Illus.	10.00
Cabinet, Apothecary, 6 Drawer, 3 Locks, Grain Painted, 20 In.	280.00
Cabinet, Apothecary, Glass Door, 34 Drawers, c.1900, 28 x 21 3/4 In.	415.00
Cabinet, Cherry, 2 Doors, Glass Sides, For Medical Instruments, 1880	950.00
Case, Lancet, 6 Compartments, Bright Cut, Sterling, WBS, 2 3/8 In.	145.00
Chest, Apothecary, All Original	3600.00
Chest, Brass Inlay, Ivory Knobs, Vials, Mahogany, Tabletop	950.00
Cup, Spittle, Invalid, White, Gold Bands	45.00
Embalming Bit	100.00
Eye Tester, Copper Trimmed Projector, Early 1900s	125.00
Eyecup, Blue	25.00
Eyecup, Boat Type, Optrex, Cobalt Blue	15.00
Eyecup, Clear	2.00
Eyecup, Green	30.00
Eyecup, John Bull, Cobalt Blue	47.50
Eyecup, John Bull, Crystal, 1917	25.00
Eyecup, John Bull, Green	24.00
Eyecup, John Bull, Green, Patent Aug. 14, 1917	135.00
Eyecup, Marked M In Circle, Blue Glass	15.00
Eyecup, Paneled, Pedestal, Clear, Marked British Made, 2 1/4 In.	18.00
Eyecup, Paneled, Pedestal, Cobalt Blue, Marked M, 2 1/4 In.	24.00
Eyecup, Squat Bowl, Clear	15.00
Feeder, Invalid, White, Germany	10.00
Forceps, Obstetrics, c.1800	250.00
Hot Water Bottle, Jayne Mansfield, Box	115.00
Hot Water Bottle, White China, England, 1890s, 10 1/2 In.	30.00
Instruments, Proctologist's	150.00
Jar, Apothecary, Statue Of Liberty	95.00
Jug, Wm. Radam's Microbe Killer, 1 Gal., 11 In. ......*Illus*	65.00
Kit, First Aid, Bell Telephone, Pocket	15.00
Kit, Ligature, Glass Vials, Johnson & Johnson	65.00
Lens Kit, Optical, Golden Oak Case, With Metal Frames	236.00

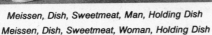

Meissen, Dish, Sweetmeat, Man, Holding Dish

Meissen, Dish, Sweetmeat, Woman, Holding Dish

Meissen, Group, Duke & Duchess of Saxony, 8 1/2 In.

Machine, Blood Pressure, Walnut Case	85.00
Machine, Electric Shock, Quack	47.50
Machine, Violet Ray Generator, Instruments, White Cross	75.00
Mannequin, Illustrating Internal Organs, Paper Covered Tin	2800.00
Mirror, Optician's, 3–Way, Apex Co.	125.00
Mold, Suppository, Brass, 1873	55.00 To 80.00
Mortar & Pestle, Brass	75.00
Mortar & Pestle, Wooden	75.00
Poster, Congenital Syphilis, 14, 000 New Cases, 1945, 15 x 20 In.	90.00
Saddle Bag, Dr. A. J. Ball, Medicine Bottles, 1880s	350.00 To 650.00
Saw, Amputation, 1800	450.00
Saw, Amputation, Brass On Top Of Blade	37.50
Saw, Surgical, Capitol, Brass Frame, Ebony Hand Grips, 12 In.	115.00
Siphon, England, 19th Century	250.00
Snow Globe, Apothecary, Hanging	350.00
Surgeon's Kit, Civil War, Engraved C. C. Pike, Mahogany Case	1385.00
Surgical Instruments, Trimann & Co., Civil War, Box, 17 1/2 In.	3190.00
Syringe, Franklin Veterinary, Brass, Box	7.50
Table, Examining, Adjustable, Storage Drawers, Stirrups, Wooden	600.00
Table, Vitalife Electric Treatment, Control Panel, 3 Knobs	750.00
Tool Set, 1 Folding & 6 Scalpels, Ivory Handles, Mahogany Case	175.00
Vaporizer & Bottle Warmer, Hankscraft, 1940s	50.00
Water Bottle, Rubber, Dated 1900, 8 1/2 In.	95.00

MEERSCHAUM pipes and other pieces of carved meerschaum, a soft
mineral, date from the nineteenth century to the present.

Cigar Holder, 3 Bulldogs, Amber Stem	75.00
Cigar Holder, Amber Tip, Fitted Box	40.00
Cigarette Holder, Reclining Nude, Tropical Surroundings, 9 In.	143.00
Pipe, Carved Seaman, Amber Stem, 10 In.	125.00
Pipe, Case	22.50
Pipe, Dual Horses, Amber Stem, Case, 4 In.	400.00
Pipe, Hunter & Dog, c.1890, 7 1/2 In.	247.00
Pipe, Lion's Head	35.00
Pipe, Man With Turban	45.00
Pipe, Painted Deer On China Bowl, Metal Top, Wood Stem, 24 In.	145.00
Pipe, Silver Hinged Top, Wooden Stem, 27 In.	90.00
Pipe, Turk Head	90.00
Pipe, Woman Standing On Pipe, Removable Dress, Amber Stem, 4 In.	400.00
Plaque, Baptism Of Christ, Oval, Velvet Frame, 10 1/2 x 15 In.	1875.00

MEISSEN is a town in Germany where porcelain has been made since
1710. Any china made in the town can be called Meissen, although the
famous Meissen factory made the finest porcelains of the area. The crossed
swords mark of the great Meissen factory has been copied by many other

firms in Germany and other parts of the world. Pieces of Meissen dinnerware in the Onion pattern are listed in their own category in this book.

Basket, Basketweave Sides, Sprig Handles, 10 In.	300.00
Bowl, Encrusted Gold Design, Reticulated, Oval, 14 1/4 x 10 In.	375.00
Bowl, White Ground, Raised Gold, Marked, 12 x 2 In.	295.00
Box, Cover, Grapes Shape, Puce, Crossed Swords, 5 7/8 In.	3750.00
Box, Cover, Rose Shape, Bud, Crossed Swords, 3 1/8 In.	1750.00
Cake Plate, Leaf Shape, Beaded, Cobalt Blue, Gold Leaves, 11 1/2 In.	325.00
Chandelier, 12–Light, Cherubs, Swags Of Flowers, Gilt, 22 1/2 In.	1650.00
Compote, Enamel & Gilt Design, Fruits & Insects, Marked, 6 3/4 In.	885.00
Compote, Floral Reticulated Top & Base, Gold Outlining, 7 x 9 In.	425.00
Compote, Maiden & Cupid, 19th Century, 16 3/4 In. ....*Illus*	2200.00
Cup & Saucer, Enamel Floral Sprays, Lovers, Marked, 11 Piece	4200.00
Dish, Sweetmeat, Man Stirring Kettle, Twin Shells, Marked, 9 1/2 In.	885.00
Dish, Sweetmeat, Man, Holding Dish ....*Illus*	1000.00
Dish, Sweetmeat, Woman, Holding Dish ....*Illus*	1300.00
Figurine, Bacchus, Porcelain, Purple & Green Wreath, 1755, 5 3/8 In.	665.00
Figurine, Barefoot Girl With Basket, Marked, 6 In.	250.00
Figurine, Boy Feeding Geese, Marked, 19th Century, 5 1/4 In.	665.00
Figurine, Child With Garland, Marked, 3 7/8 In.	90.00
Figurine, Cupid On Pedestal, Wings & Hands Tied Behind Back, 4 In.	550.00
Figurine, Cupid Riding Dolphin, 1750, 4 11/16 In.	2200.00
Figurine, Cupid, Marked, 4 In.	250.00
Figurine, Goddesses Of Poetry & Music, Marked, 6 3/4 In., Pair	995.00
Figurine, Lady, Seated, Basket Of Flowers, Rose In Hand, 5 In., Pr.	152.00
Figurine, Parrot, In Floral Wreath, Porcelain, Brass, 19th Century	7500.00
Figurine, Putto Making Chocolate On Stove, Marked, 4 In.	825.00
Figurine, Putto With Blue Drapery & Owl, Marked, 7 In.	605.00
Figurine, Putto With Fish Trap, 3 7/8 x 5 In.	880.00
Figurine, Shepherdess, Hat, Cape, White Sheep, 1755, 9 3/8 In.	2750.00
Figurine, St. George As Winged Cherub, Slain Dragon, 8 1/2 In.	710.00
Figurine, Standing Fisherman Holds Sail, Marked, 7 1/2 In.	550.00
Figurine, Two Cherubs, Floral Bouquets, Marked, 5 1/2 In.	715.00
Figurine, Venus With Cupid & Doves, 8 In.	1500.00
Figurine, Woman Gardener, With Basket Of Flowers, Crossed Swords	365.00
Gravy Boat, Attached Tray, Marked	195.00
Group, 2 Cherub Astronomers, Marked, 6 x 5 1/4 In.	935.00
Group, 2 Seated Cherub Musicians, 5 x 6 1/2 In.	885.00
Group, Cupids Riding Hen & Rooster, 1750–60, 3 7/8 & 4 In., Pair	2650.00
Group, Duke & Duchess Of Saxony, 8 1/2 In. ....*Illus*	1320.00
Group, Man Aiding Woman, Bridge, Bicentennial Anniversary, 12 In.	825.00
Group, Monkey Orchestra, 12 Costumed Musicians, Marked, 5 1/2 In.	6050.00
Group, Woman Astrologer, Cherub, Enamel, Gilt, Porcelain, 9 5/8 In.	425.00
Jug, Wine, Bear Form, Holding Sash, Removable Head, 10 In.	1290.00
Lamp, Polychrome Enameling, Gilt, 17 In.	115.00
Plate, Astmuster, Prunus Branch, 1735, 8 3/4 & 8 13/16 In., Pair	4125.00
Plate, Bienenmuster, Bow–Knotted Bouquet, 1765, 9 1/2 In.	660.00
Plate, Bride's, White & Gold, Pair	140.00
Plate, Courting Scene, Hand Painted, 19th Century, 9 3/4 In.	300.00
Plate, Gilded Borders, Blue & Green Leaves, 12 Piece	80.00
Plate, Interior Of Fruits, Gilt Border, 8 1/4 In., 4 Piece	1045.00
Plate, Leaf Form, Gilt Decoration, 5 3/4 In., Pair	66.00
Plate, Molded Scroll Design, Hand Painted Flowers, 7 1/4 In.	30.00
Plate, White Scrolls & Flowers, Cobalt Band, Crossed Swords, 12 In.	295.00
Plateau Group, Diana & 4 Allegorical Figures, 6 Parts	4125.00
Slipper, Orange & Gold Florals, Bird On Instep, Signed, 3 1/2 In.	125.00
Soup, Dish, Garden Flowers, Blue Border, Free–Form, 9 1/2 In., 9 Pc.	115.00
Teapot, Blue & White Flowers, Raised Rose On Lid, 1875, Signed	285.00
Tureen, Cover, Lettuce Shape, Porcelain, Crossed Swords, 5 In.	2200.00
Urn, Birds & Flowers, 31 In., Pair ....*Illus*	7000.00
Urn, Cobalt, Floral Reserve, Gilt, Serpent Handles, 11 1/2 In.	600.00

Urn, Cover, Hydrangias, Birds, Vine, Marked, 19th Century, 31 In., Pr. 7700.00
Urn, Polychrome Floral Design, Gilt, Marked, 20 1/2 In. 175.00
Vase, Cherub, Allover Applied Multicolored Flowers 265.00
Vase, Lily, Glazed Creamy Yellow Ribbed, Pink Interior, 15 In. 340.00

MERCURY GLASS, or silvered glass, was first made in the 1850s. It lost favor for a while but became popular again about 1910. It looks like a piece of silver.

Jug, Small 12.00
Rose Bowl, Blue, Czechoslovakia 25.00
Tieback, Flower Design, 3 1/2 In., Pair 35.00
Vase, 12 In. 65.00
Vase, Silver, 4 7/8 In. 7.50
Vase, Stepped, Art Deco, Germany, 7 In. 125.00

METTLACH, Germany, is a city where the Villeroy and Boch factories worked. Steins from the firm are known as Mettlach steins. They date from about 1842. *PUG* means painted under glaze. The steins can be dated from the marks on the bottom, which include a date–number code. Other pieces may be listed in the Villeroy & Boch category.

Beaker, No. 1192 .... 48.00
Beaker, No. 2327, 1/4 Liter, Two Boys Under A Tree 65.00
Cachepot, Villeroy & Boch, Cream Ground, Art Deco Design, 10 In. 99.00
Humidor, No. 1231, Incised Cows, 8 1/2 In. 425.00
Libation Set, No. 1815, 4 Liter, Mosaic & Inlay Type, Florals, 7 Pc. 775.00
Mug, Souvenir, Boothbay Harbor, Maine 75.00
Pitcher, No. 2210, Bowlers, Gargoyle Lip 600.00
Plaque, Boys With Flute & Mandolin, Girl, c.1898, 7 x 10 1/4 In. 635.00
Plaque, German Eagle, Impressed Castle, 27 In. 6600.00
Plaque, Horses, Rider, Signed, 11 3/4 In. 245.00
Plaque, No. 2442, Trojan Warriors On Boat, Signed, 18 In. 1195.00
Plaque, No. 7045, Cameo, Man & Woman In Woods 1760.00
Plate, Jockey, 8 In. 38.00
Plate, Remagen On The Rhine, 12 1/4 In. 325.00
Punch Bowl, Cover, Underplate, No. 2280, King, Gnomes 800.00
Stein, 1/2 Liter, Sharpshooter, Eagle Thumb Press, Schlitt 375.00
Stein, Amerika, Castle Mark 125.00
Stein, No. 171, 1/2 Liter, Man Drinking, Bacchus Lid, 1903 .... 210.00
Stein, No. 1028, 1/2 Liter, Brown & White Tree, German Saying, 1898 .... 195.00
Stein, No. 1091, 1/2 Liter, St. Florian Baptizing Man, Castle Mark 675.00
Stein, No. 1146, 1/2 Liter, Students In Tavern, Warth, Castle Mark 450.00
Stein, No. 1161, 7 Liter, Ladies Of Court, Crown & Eagle Cover 4000.00
Stein, No. 1467, 1/2 Liter, Maidens, Representing 4 Seasons 425.00
Stein, No. 1695, 1/2 Liter, Hunter & Animals 577.50
Stein, No. 2002, 1/2 Liter, Munchen 375.00
Stein, No. 2035, 1/2 Liter, Bacchus, Etched & Inlaid 485.00
Stein, No. 2090, 1/2 Liter, Club, Man, Green Coat, Dice & Cards 625.00

Meissen, Compote, Maiden & Cupid, 19th Century, 16 3/4 In.

Meissen, Urn, Birds & Flowers, 31 In., Pair

Mettlach, Stein, No. 2524, Knight & Castle,
Animal Handle, 20 In.

Mettlach, Urn, Cameo Relief Birds, Buff,
Turquoise, 25 In.

Stein, No. 2100, 1/2 Liter, Knight & Goblin, Pewter Lid		275.00
Stein, No. 2238, 1 Liter, 7th Regimental Guard		875.00
Stein, No. 2524, Knight & Castle, Animal Handle, 20 In. ....*Illus*		990.00
Stein, No. 2714, 1/2 Liter, Man, Woman, 3 Panels, White On Blue		467.50
Stein, No. 2802, 1/4 Liter, Art Nouveau, Blue, White		295.00
Stein, No. 2869, 2 9/10 Liter, Hop Leaves, Munich Maid, Seal		9350.00
Tureen, No. 418, Cover, Undertray, Figural Handles, Signed, 16 In.		600.00
Urn, Cameo Relief Birds, Buff, Turquoise, 25 In. ....*Illus*		2750.00
Urn, No. 1360, Geometric Patterns, Footed		1320.00
Urn, No. 1430/97, Raised Birds & Nests, Pierced Handles, 25 In.		2500.00
Vase, Green Leaves, Brown Birch Handle, Marked, c.1890, 8 1/2 In.		240.00
Vase, No. 1591, 4 Scenes Of Boy In Tree, Shooting Bow, 12 1/2 In.		470.00
Vase, No. 1978, Asiatic & European Women's Head, Handles, 13 In.		750.00
Water Set, No. 1028, Man Carrying Hay, 1/2 Liter Steins, 7 Piece		260.00

MILK GLASS was named for its milky white color. It was first made in England during the 1700s. The height of its popularity in the United States was from 1870 to 1880. It is now correct to refer to some colored glass as blue milk glass, black milk glass, etc. Reproductions of milk glass are being made and sold in many stores. Related pieces may be listed in the Cosmos and Vallerysthal categories.

Bottle, Owl, Cap, 6 1/2 In. ....*Illus*		75.00
Bottle, Statue Of Liberty, Square Base, Pourer Base, 14 3/4 In.		595.00
Bowl, Cereal, Child's, Ranger Joe, Red Graphics		5.00
Bowl, Raised Floral Center, Reticulated Rim, 4 1/2 x 8 1/2 In.		250.00
Butter, Cover, Cube		35.00
Butter, Cover, Lacy Edge		65.00
Butter, Cover, Ribbed With Reticulated, Aqua		65.00
Butter, Cover, Ribbed, Blue		35.00
Butter, Cover, Strawberry, Flint, 1870		95.00
Cake Stand, Old Quilt, Skirt, Westmoreland		45.00

Milk Glass, Bottle, Owl, Cap, 6 1/2 In.

Milk Glass, Shaker, Cord & Tassel, Double, Blue, 3 In.
Milk Glass, Shaker, Shell, Overlapping, Green, 2 In.

Celery, Jewel, Blue 95.00
Celery, Paneled Sprig 110.00
Compote, Atlas, Fluted 60.00
Compote, Atlas, Scalloped Rim 60.00
Cookie Jar, Grape Design, Fire King Anchor Hocking 20.00
Cracker Jar, Pink & Floral Design, Bail Handle 80.00
Creamer, Panel Grape, Westmoreland, 5 In. 12.00
Cruet, Beaded Swag 185.00
Dish, Amethyst Duck's Head Cover, Atterbury 300.00
Dish, Boar's Head Cover, Ferson 1350.00
Dish, Bullfrog, On Basketweave Base, Atterbury 500.00
Dish, Cat Cover, Lacy Edge, Atterbury 300.00
Dish, Cat Cover, Westmoreland 75.00
Dish, Dolphin Cover, Blue, Summit 40.00
Dish, Eagle On Lacy Basket Cover, Westmoreland 125.00
Dish, Entwined Fish Cover 175.00
Dish, Feeding, 3 Kewpies On Rim 55.00
Dish, Fish On Skiff Cover, Ferson 550.00
Dish, Fly On Cover 450.00
Dish, Fox Cover, Lacy Base 165.00
Dish, Frog's Head Cover, Ferson 1025.00
Dish, Hand With Bird Cover, Atterbury 120.00
Dish, Hen On Nest, Westmoreland .... 45.00 To 65.00
Dish, Kitten On Nest Cover, Ribbed Base 48.00
Dish, Lady With Fan 35.00
Dish, Lamb On Picket Fence Cover, Blue, 5 In. 75.00
Dish, Mule Eared Rabbit, Picket Base, Westmoreland, 5 1/2 In. 65.00
Dish, Rabbit Cover, Brown Eyes, 1886, 9 1/2 In. 80.00
Dish, Rooster Cover, Standing, 8 1/2 In. 65.00
Dish, Squirrel Cover, Amber 75.00
Dish, Swan Cover, Gold Edge 460.00
Dish, Swan Cover, Lacy Edge, Atterbury 200.00
Dish, Swan, France 85.00
Dish, Swimming Duck Cover, Blue 55.00
Dish, White Duck's Head Cover, Blue 85.00
Easter Egg, Painted Flowers, Word Easter 65.00
Eggcup, Blackberry 17.50
Eggcup, Chick Base, 2 1/2 In., 6 Piece 35.00
Figurine, Dog, Flaccus Setter, On Wheat Base, Signed 145.00
Figurine, Owl, Amethyst Eyes, Atterbury 35.00
Figurine, Owl, Red Eyes, Atterbury 145.00
Figurine, Pig On Drum, Portieux, Miniature 55.00
Goblet, Fruit, Westmoreland, 6 In., 4 Piece 75.00
Goblet, Paneled Grape 12.00
Jar, Bear Cover, Small 650.00
Jar, Brass Lid, Hazard Chemical Toilette Deluxe, Philadelphia 22.50
Jar, Dresser, Versailles, 3 x 3 1/2 In. 25.00
Jar, Threaded Rim, c.1890, 1 Pt. 150.00
Match Holder, Open Purse Shape 58.00
Mug, Child's, Embossed Cat Dressed As Lady 95.00
Mug, Child's, Gooseberry, Blue 25.00
Mug, Child's, Ranger Joe, Red Graphics 5.00
Pitcher Set, Milk, Hobnail, Aqua, 6 Piece 195.00
Pitcher, Water, Stork & Rushes, Blue 150.00
Pitcher, Wild Iris, Colored Design 65.00
Plate, Bicentennial, White, J. St. Clair, 5 1/2 In. 18.00
Plate, California Mid–Winter Expo., 1894 .... 75.00
Plate, Columbus, Spades, Clubs On Rim, 9 1/2 In. 75.00
Plate, Dart, 7 1/4 In. 30.00
Plate, George Washington 210.00
Plate, Lattice, Enameled Floral 37.50
Plate, Tiny Florals, 7 1/4 In. 30.00
Plate, Twig Border, Painted Scene, 3 Owls, Dated 1901 .... 50.00

Platter, Retriever, Swimming Dog, Relief, 13 1/2 x 9 3/4 In. 95.00
Punch Ladle 32.50
Punch Set, Anchor Hocking, Base, With 9 Cups 75.00
Salt & Pepper, Heart, Pink 75.00
Salt & Pepper, Scroll Two Band 65.00
Salt, Open, Swan, Head Thrown Back, 2 1/2 In. 20.00
Saltshaker, Birch Leaf, Flint 40.00
Saltshaker, Cathedral Panel, Blue 35.00
Saltshaker, Guttate, Green, Pair 85.00
Shade, Gas, 5 In., 12 Piece 400.00
Shaker, Cord & Tassel, Double, Blue, 3 In. ....*Illus* 55.00
Shaker, Shell, Overlapping, Green, 2 In. ....*Illus* 50.00
Spooner, Child's, Wildrose 45.00
Sugar Shaker, Embossed Rabbits 65.00
Sugar Shaker, Paneled Sprig 42.00
Sugar, Child's, Wild Rose 45.00
Sugar, Cover, Paneled Sprig 110.00
Sugar, Cover, Trailing Vine, Blue 200.00
Sugar, Cover, Wild Iris, Gold Paint 25.00
Sugar, Lace Edge 30.00
Sugar, Panel Grape, Westmoreland, 3 1/4 In. 12.00
Syrup, Alba 4.00
Syrup, Fishnet & Poppies 135.00
Syrup, Flat Flower Design, Blue 245.00
Syrup, Pewter Top, Flowers, Leaves, Vines 65.00
Syrup, Stippled Dahlia 65.00
Table Set, Child's, Lamb, Sugar, Creamer, Spooner, 3 Piece 300.00
Table Set, Child's, Thumbelina, Westmoreland, 3 Piece 40.00
Table Set, Lacy Dewdrop, 3 Piece 145.00
Toothpick, 3 Swans 40.00
Toothpick, Acorn 30.00
Toothpick, Baby Owl, Unpainted 40.00
Toothpick, Fleur–De–Lis 40.00
Toothpick, Florette, Green 30.00
Toothpick, Frisco .... 20.00 To 30.00
Toothpick, Lacy Medallion, Decal 25.00
Toothpick, Orinda 32.00
Toothpick, Owl, 1950s 15.00
Toothpick, Squirrel On Stump 22.50
Toothpick, Stork, Painted 28.00
Tumbler, Dr Pepper, Red Design 35.00
Water Set, Grape & Leaf, 5 Piece 200.00

MILLEFIORI means, literally, a thousand flowers. It is a type of glasswork popular in paperweights. Many small pieces of glass resembling flowers are grouped together to form a design.

Inkwell, Mushroom Stopper, Paperweight Base, 5 1/2 In. 415.00
Vase, Paperweight 45.00

MINTON china has been made in the Staffordshire region of England from 1793 to the present. The firm became part of the Royal Doulton Tableware Group in 1968, but the wares continued to be marked *Minton*. Many marks have been used. The one shown dates from about 1873 to 1891, when the word *England* was added.

Biscuit Barrel, Design On Gray–Blue Ground, Woven Handle, Marked 195.00
Demitasse Set, Bird Of Paradise, Signed, 12 Piece 425.00
Figurine, Grecian Dancer, Porcelain, Bronze, 10 In. 225.00
Group, Education Of The Dog, Luigi Guglielmi, 1869–1873, 9 3/4 In. 935.00
Jug, Roses, Hand Painted, Dated 1861, 7 In. 85.00
Plate, Dinner, Penrose 15.00
Plate, Florentine Design, Blue Band, Raised Gold, 10 In., 12 Piece 1500.00
Plate, Salad, Penrose 10.00
Platter, Gold Ancestral, 15 1/4 In. 125.00

Tazza, Roses, Hand Painted, Green, Gold & Brown Border, 9 1/2 In. 100.00
Tea & Coffee Set, Botanical, 1810–1815, Crossed L's & M Mark, 30 Pc. 5775.00
Urn, Cover, Woman, Pate–Sur–Pate On Parian, Frederick Rhead 3325.00
Vase, Drummer Boy, Pate–Sur–Pate On Parian, 5 1/2 In. 495.00
Vase, Mouse Pulling Mouse Holding Egg, Pate–Sur–Pate 1550.00
Vase, Oriental Style, Pierced Scroll, Ivory Ground, Marked, 8 1/2 In. 935.00

MIRRORS are listed in the Furniture category under Mirror.

MOCHA pottery is an English–made product that was sold in America during the early 1800s. It is a heavy pottery with pale coffee–and–cream coloring. Designs of blue, brown, green, orange, black, or white were added to the pottery and given fanciful names, such as *Tree, Snail Trail,* or *Moss.*

Bowl, Blue & Black Earthworm, Stripes, Tooled Rim, 8 1/2 x 4 In. 600.00
Bowl, Blue Seaweed Design On White Band, 8 1/2 In. 265.00
Bowl, Blue Seaweed, 17 In. 450.00
Bowl, Mixing, Blue Seaweed, 4 x 8 3/4 In. 75.00
Bowl, Waste, Blue Stripes, Ochre Band, Black Seaweed, 5 1/4 In. 450.00
Creamer, Black Seaweed, Yellow–Tan Ground, Miniature 250.00
Cup & Saucer, Black Seaweed, Green Ground 900.00
Cup & Saucer, Black Seaweed, Yellow–Tan Ground, Miniature 700.00
Mug, Bands Of Stripes, Interlocking White Circles, Leaf Handle, 6 In. 525.00
Mug, Black Seaweed, Yellow Ground, Marked CRED, 2 5/8 In. 400.00
Mug, Black Stripes, Shades Of Brown 70.00
Mug, Blue Marbelized Band, Stripes, Leaf Handle, 4 3/8 In. 675.00
Mug, Blue, Black Stripes, Seaweed Design, Leaf Handle, 5 In. .... 130.00 To 145.00
Mug, Green Seaweed 195.00
Mug, Impressed Blue, Brown & Green Bands, 19th Century, 6 1/4 In. 770.00
Mug, Stripes, Rope Squiggles, Leaf Handle, 5 5/8 In. 800.00
Mug, Yellow Ochre & Brown Bands, Earthworm, Leaf Handle, 3 1/2 In. 350.00
Pepper Castor, Black Seaweed, Green Ground 725.00
Pitcher, Black Stripes, Cat's–Eye Bands, 6 1/4 In. 400.00
Pitcher, Blue Stripes & Bands, White Wavy Lines, Foliage, 7 1/2 In. 2050.00
Pitcher, Brown & White Earthworm, Molded Band & Leaf Handle, 7 In. 925.00
Pitcher, Earthworm Design, Band & Leaf Handle, 6 3/4 In. 500.00
Pitcher, Milk, Blue–Gray Seaweed, Yellow Ground 880.00
Pitcher, Stripes, Ochre Band, Black Seaweed, Leaf Handle, 7 1/2 In. 1450.00
Pitcher, Stripes, Tan Band, Rope Squiggles, Leaf Handle, 5 3/4 In. 525.00
Salt, Black Stripes, Seaweed, Gray Band, 3 1/4 In. 200.00
Salt, Earthworm Design, Tan Band, Footed, 2 x 3 In. 300.00
Sugar, Cover, Black Seaweed, Yellow–Tan Ground, Miniature 850.00
Tankard, Pewter Lid, Embossed Bands, Black Seaweed, 7 In. 675.00
Tea Caddy, Lid, Geometric Design, Black, Tan, Blue, 4 7/8 In. 525.00
Teapot, Black Seaweed, Yellow–Tan Ground, 3 1/2 In. 925.00
Waste Bowl, Earthworm Design, Blue Band, 5 x 2 3/4 In. 175.00

MONMOUTH Pottery Company started working in Monmouth, Illinois, in 1892. The pottery made a variety of utilitarian wares. It became part of Western Stoneware Company in 1906. The maple leaf mark was used until 1930. If *Co.* appears as part of the mark, the piece was made before 1906.

Crock, Tiny Ears 85.00
Vase, Silver Specks, Horizontally Ribbed, 13 In. 85.00

MONT JOYE, see Mt. Joye

MOORCROFT pottery was first made in Burslem, England, in 1913. William Moorcroft had managed the art pottery department for James MacIntyre & Company of England from 1898 to 1913. The Moorcroft pottery continues today although William Moorcroft died in 1945. The earlier wares are similar to the modern ones, but color and marking will help indicate the age.

Ashtray, Magnolia, Cobalt Blue, Marked, 6 In. 130.00

Ashtray, Oval, 6 1/2 x 3 1/2 In. 35.00
Bowl, Columbine, Blue–Green, Potter To Queen Mary, 9 1/2 In. 610.00
Bowl, Grapes & Leaves, Green Ground, Signed, c.1945, 12 1/2 In. 440.00
Bowl, Hibiscus, Cobalt Blue, Marked, 6 In. 245.00
Bowl, Hibiscus, Flambe, Marked, 5 1/4 In. 450.00
Bowl, Orange Flower, 6 1/4 In. 40.00
Bowl, Orchid, Blue–Green, Marked, 3 In. 85.00
Bowl, Orchid, Blue–Green, Marked, 4 1/2 In. 150.00
Bowl, Orchids, Dark Blue, 5 1/4 In. 150.00
Bowl, Red & Yellow Hibiscus, Blue On White, 10 In. 305.00
Bowl, Spanish, Cornflower, Tulip, Green, Signed, c.1910, 6 1/4 In. 795.00
Box, Cover, Orchid, Cobalt Blue, Script & Royal Mark, 5 In. 300.00
Candy Dish, Cover, Hibiscus, Yellow–Green, Marked, 6 1/2 In. 300.00
Dish, Fruit Pattern, Turned–In Rim 50.00
Ginger Jar, Blue, Green & Deep Pink Design, White, 4 1/4 In. 225.00
Goblet, Pomegranate, Green, Signed, c.1912 .... 1295.00
Lamp, Berries, Leaves, Red, Yellow & Green, Brass Mount, 23 In. 7780.00
Lamp, Orchids, Cobalt Blue Ground, Paper Label, Signed, 14 1/2 In. 1190.00
Lamp, Orchids, Cobalt Blue Ground, Paper Label, Signed, 33 3/4 In. 1295.00
Pitcher, Dura Ware, Floral, Pink Ground, Signed, c.1903, 6 1/2 In. 895.00
Plate, Anemone, Green, Initialed, 8 1/2 In. 165.00
Plate, Claremont Toadstool, Signed, 7 1/4 In. 605.00
Tea Set, Orchid, c.1928, 3 Piece 550.00
Teapot, Orchids, Cobalt Blue, 8 In. 300.00
Tile, Teapot, MacIntyre, c.1904, 6 1/4 In. 425.00
Vase, Anemone, Bulbous, Marked, 4 In. 85.00
Vase, Anemone, Cobalt Blue, Initialed, 7 1/2 In. 295.00
Vase, Aurelian, Blue, Gold, Orange, MacIntyre, c.1897, 6 In. 595.00
Vase, Bermuda Lily, 8 In. 225.00
Vase, Blue & Red Clematis, Yellow–Green Ground, 7 1/2 In. 310.00
Vase, Blue Orchids, Irises, Cobalt Blue Ground, Spherical, 6 In. 495.00
Vase, Bud, Maroon & Yellow Hibiscus, Green 185.00
Vase, Burslem, Orange Luster, c.1913, 9 In. 295.00
Vase, Clematis, Yellow, Initialed, 7 In. 225.00
Vase, Eagle & Owl, 12 In. 495.00
Vase, Floral, Burgundy, Signed, 12 In. 1550.00
Vase, Florian, Poppies, Cream Ground, Signed, c.1903, 9 In. 995.00
Vase, Florian, Tulips, MacIntyre, c.1903, 7 1/4 In. 1015.00
Vase, Hibiscus, Yellow, Slender Neck, Marked, 13 In. 525.00
Vase, Mounted As Lamp, Dawn Landscape, 1926, 12 1/2 In. 1900.00
Vase, Mounted As Lamp, Tulip & Fruit, Cobalt Blue, 1926, 14 In. 400.00
Vase, Pansy, Cobalt Blue, Bulbous, Marked, 1937, 7 In. 850.00
Vase, Pink Flowers, Blue, 3 3/4 In. 195.00
Vase, Pink Flowers, Dark Blue, Signed, 3 1/2 In. 175.00
Vase, Plums, Blue, 6 In. 245.00
Vase, Purple Flowers, Blue, Red, Underglaze Of Green, 7 1/2 In. 286.00
Vase, Red Cornflowers, Brown & Green, 1912–1913, 8 1/2 In. 2280.00
Vase, Red Flower, Green Ground, Signed, 2 x 1 1/2 In. 66.00
Vase, Red Poppies, Forget–Me–Nots, MacIntyre, 6 In. 1320.00
Vase, Rose & Gold Fruit, Signed, 12 1/2 In. 715.00
Vase, Rose & Purple Flowers, Green–Blue Ground, Sticker, 4 In. 150.00
Vase, Russet & Green Peacock Feathers, White Outlined, 5 1/4 In. 1900.00
Vase, White, Yellow Berries, Green Foliage, 7 In. 235.00
Vase, Yellow Leaves & Berries, Green Ground, 3 1/2 In. 275.00

MORIAGE is a special type of raised decoration used on some Japanese pottery. Sometimes pieces of clay were shaped by hand and applied to the item; sometimes the clay was squeezed from a tube in the way we apply cake frosting. One type of moriage is called *Dragonware* and is listed under that name.

Ashtray, Building In Center Reserve 35.00
Bowl, 6 Marbelized Medallions, Flowers, Scalloped, Jeweled, 8 In. 195.00
Candy Dish, Marbelized Medallions, Jeweled, Footed 175.00

Hair Receiver, Purple Floral, Footed, Signed 95.00
Humidor, Jewels In Center Of Spider Webs, Green Ground 500.00
Pitcher, Admiral Togo, 3 In. 195.00
Vase, Allover White Slip Work, Green, 7 1/2 In. 195.00
Vase, Gray-Green Slip Covered Flowers, Turquoise, 10 In. 260.00
Vase, Owl In Tree, Forest Ground, 13 In. 85.00
Vase, Pink Poppies, Green, Handles, 12 In. 400.00

MOSAIC TILE Company of Zanesville, Ohio, was started by Karl Langerbeck and Herman Mueller in 1894. Many types of plain and ornamental tiles were made until 1959. The company closed in 1967. The company also made some ashtrays, bookends, and related giftwares. Most pieces are marked with the entwined *MTC* monogram.

Ashtray, German Shepherd 85.00
Ashtray, Terrier 75.00
Cookie Jar, Mammy, Blue Dress .... 595.00 To 695.00
Cookie Jar, Mammy, Yellow Dress .... 435.00 To 600.00
Paperweight, General Pershing, Blue Ground 35.00
Teddy Roosevelt, Square, 4 1/4 In. 125.00

MOSER glass is made by Ludwig Moser und Sohne, a Bohemian glasshouse founded in 1857. Art Nouveau-type glassware and iridescent glassware were made. The most famous Moser glass is decorated with heavy enameling in gold and bright colors. The firm is still working in Czechoslovakia. Few pieces of Moser glass are marked.

Bonbon, Cranberry Glass, Enameled, Leaf Shape, Clear Handle, 4 In. 65.00
Bowl, Amberina, Quatrefoil, Footed, Enameled Inside & Out, 5 1/2 In. 385.00
Bowl, Blue, White Florals, Flying Bird, Signed, 9 In. 165.00
Bowl, Enameled Oak Leaves, Gold Branches, Buds, Green, 4 1/2 In. 175.00
Bowl, Intaglio, Cranberry, Pedestal, 7 x 9 In. 660.00
Box, Acid Etched Amethyst Glass, 6 In. 605.00
Box, Cover, Amazon Warriors, Ball Feet, Signed, 4 7/8 In. 395.00
Box, Hinged Cover, 4 x 5 1/4 In. 385.00
Box, Jewelry, Enameled, Gilt, Rectangular, 4 1/2 In. 1450.00
Box, Jewelry, Vines, Berries, Leaves, Brass Frame, 5 1/4 x 4 3/4 In. 875.00
Casket, Jewelry, Gold Floral, Ruby, Brass Bound, Handle, 4 x 3 1/2 In. 357.00
Celery, Ribbed Swirl Design, Multicolored Florals, Signed, 7 In. 265.00
Chalice, Cranberry, Clear Pedestal, Gold Rings, Signed, 11 In. 245.00
Champagne, Gilded Band, Blue Panel, Flint, Signed 125.00
Compote, Black Amethyst, Gold Encrusted Pineapple Band 850.00
Compote, Colorless, Enameled Gold Scrolling, Gilt, 9 1/2 In., Pair 385.00
Compote, White Over Cranberry, Signed, 7 In. 175.00
Cordial, Acorns, Cranberry 235.00
Cordial, Oak Leaves, High Relief Acorns, Green, 1 1/2 In. 125.00
Cruet, Enameled Flowers, Faceted Stopper & Handle, Blue, Signed 275.00
Cup & Saucer, Gold Enameled Scrolls, Gold Handle & Rim, Crystal 30.00
Cup & Saucer, Multicolored Enameling, Gold Trim, After Dinner 125.00
Decanter Set, Blue Flashed Faceted Glass, Gilt Filigree, 7 Piece 660.00
Decanter Set, Gold Grape & Leaf, Gold Band, Signed, 8 Piece 495.00
Decanter, Gold Design, Olive Green, Signed, Large 275.00
Decanter, Pink Overlay, Frosted Ground, Stopper, Signed, 15 In. 265.00
Decanter, Star Cut, Amber 225.00
Dish, Dessert, Cranberry Glass, Enameled 100.00
Dish, Sweetmeat, Alexandrite, Pedestal, Signed, 4 In. 160.00
Figurine, Swan, Gold Trim, Signed, 5 x 4 In. 450.00
Jar, Conical Lid, Faceted Sides, Ruby, c.1920, 5 1/2 In. 775.00
Lamp Base, Enameled Gilt Flowers, Cupid, Cherub, Green, 7 1/4 In. 715.00
Mug, Gold Scrolls, Gilded Handle, Yellow & White, 3 1/4 In. 60.00
Perfume Bottle, Melon Ribbed, Enameled Flowers, Red, Sterling Top 150.00
Pitcher, Amber Ribbed, Applied Handle, Florals Front, Signed, 5 In. 135.00
Pitcher, Amberina, Inverted Thumbprint, Beads, 3-D Bird, 6 3/4 In. 2525.00
Pitcher, Cranberry, Scalloped Rim, Signed, 10 In. 235.00
Pitcher, Enameled Grape Leaves & Grapes, Signed, 12 In. 750.00

Pitcher, Enameled Scrolling Flowers, Gilt, 4–Footed, 10 In.	575.00
Pitcher, Grapes & Leaves, Green Ground & Handle, SGD, 12 1/4 In.	750.00
Punch Bowl, Cranberry, Deer Running, Frosted, 10 In.	765.00
Punch Cup, Allover Floral Enameling, Amber, Blue Handle	90.00
Sherbet, Ruby, Gold Design, Signed, 5 In.	35.00
Tazza, Cherries, Leaves On Blue, White & Yellow, 8 1/4 In.	645.00
Tazza, Gold Floral Over Surface, Green Overlay, 6 x 4 1/2 In.	110.00
Toothpick, Cranberry, Gold & Enameled Design, 2 In.	125.00
Tumble–Up, Enameled Daisies, Gold Tracery, Cranberry	575.00
Tumbler, Applied Acorn, Signed	495.00
Tumbler, Blue	100.00
Tumbler, Cranberry Signed, 5 1/4 In., 6 Piece	450.00
Tumbler, Swirl Optic, Amberina	165.00
Urn, Opaque White Cut To Cranberry, Enameled Florals, 13 1/2 In.	715.00
Vase, Amethyst Cut To Clear, Landscape, Trees, Lake, Signed MK, 8 In.	335.00
Vase, Applied Fish, Enameled Plants, Paneled, 11 1/4 In.	275.00
Vase, Applied Glass Acorns, Colored Leaves, Crystal Base, 8 In.	440.00
Vase, Applied Portrait Medallion, Woman, Red, Enamel, Gilt, 15 In., Pair	825.00
Vase, Apricot, Florals, Pedestal, Signed, 8 In.	75.00
Vase, Aquatic Scene, Crackle, Smoke Color, 8 In.	600.00
Vase, Aquatic Scene, Lobed Crackle Glass, 4 1/2 In.	275.00
Vase, Band Stylized Foliage, Amethyst, Low Cylindrical, 5 1/4 In.	665.00
Vase, Beaker Shape, Emerald Green, Acid Cut Flowers, Leaves, 7 1/4 In.	495.00
Vase, Blown–Out Crackled Glass, Large Orchid, Buds, 8 3/4 In.	675.00
Vase, Blue, Blown–Out Fish, Water Snake, Foliage, Signed, 4 In.	215.00
Vase, Cirroseline & Amber, Gold Floral, Signed, 11 In.	775.00
Vase, Clear To Cranberry, Raised Gold, Signed, 10 In.	60.00
Vase, Colorless, Baroque Scrolling, Gilt Enameled, 8 1/4 In., Pair	995.00
Vase, Cover, Allover Gold Leaves, Aqua, Pedestal, Horn Shape, 9 In.	915.00
Vase, Cranberry, Crystal Floral, Stems, 5 In.	315.00
Vase, Cranberry, Gold Overlay, Mauve Florals, Signed, 13 In.	375.00
Vase, Diamond Shape Panels, Roman & Grecian Scenes, 10 1/2 In., Pair	950.00
Vase, Enameled & Gilded Flowers, Salamanders, Purple, 8 In.	650.00
Vase, Enameled Floral Medallions, Gilt Scrolls, 10 1/2 In., Pair	1750.00
Vase, Enameled Gold Floral, Cranberry, 16 In.	425.00
Vase, Enameled Lilies–of–The–Valley, Gold Ground, 12 In.	305.00
Vase, Enameled Moorish Design, Signed, 13 In.	275.00
Vase, Enameled Portrait, Dutch Man, Squared Gilt Handles, 21 1/2 In.	1430.00
Vase, Enameled Spanish Design, Ribbed Amethyst, 1925, 10 1/2 In.	595.00
Vase, Facet Cut Roses, Malachite, Signed, 9 5/8 In.	575.00
Vase, Fern, Vines, Butterflies, Beetles, Cranberry, 9 1/2 In.	750.00
Vase, Frieze Of Amazon Women Warriors, Green, Signed, 6 3/4 In.	245.00
Vase, Frosted Pink, Gold Design, Signed, 11 In.	85.00
Vase, Frosted To Clear White, Raised Daisies, Signed, 6 In.	45.00
Vase, Full Figure Fairy & Florals, Crystal, 9 In.	450.00
Vase, Gilded Flowers, Leaves & Scrolls, 13 1/4 In.	150.00
Vase, Gilt Floral, Metal Bees, Green To Clear	1450.00
Vase, Gold Leaves, Aqua To Blue–Green, Cylindrical, 25 In.	850.00
Vase, Gold Neck Band, Enameled Flowers At Foot, c.1850, 15 In.	825.00
Vase, Gold, Enameled Top, Signed, 8 In.	65.00
Vase, Green Florals, Cobalt Blue, Gold Design, Pin, 10 In.	245.00
Vase, Green Stone Depicts Nude Women, Malachite, 8 3/4 In.	495.00
Vase, Green, Pedestal, Signed, 12 In.	80.00
Vase, Marquetry Design, Signed, 5 In.	400.00
Vase, Nudes, 5 1/4 In.	450.00
Vase, Oriental Lady, Cobalt Blue, Gold Band, 3 In.	150.00
Vase, Pointed Aqua Rim, Applied Plant Stems, Flowers, 12 1/2 In.	700.00
Vase, Red, Hexagonal, 12 1/2 In.	605.00
Vase, Smoky Cranberry, Florals, Signed, 7 1/2 In.	165.00
Vase, Trophy, Crystal To Green, 3 Applied Handles, Signed, 7 In.	275.00
Vase, Tulip Blossom, Buds, Leaves, Square, Signed, c.1900, 13 1/8 In.	1320.00
Vase, Ultramarine, Allover Gold Scrolls, Flowers, Ribbed, 10 1/2 In.	765.00
Vase, Warriors, Facet Cut, Smoke Gray, Gold Band, 11 In.	575.00

Vase, Young Woman Portrait, Green, Gilt, 12 1/2 In.	360.00
Wine, Alexandrite	65.00
Wine, Gold Floral Design, Amethyst Over Clear, 4 In., 10 Piece	665.00
Wine, Green, Twisted Stem, 7 In.	35.00

MOSS ROSE china was made by many firms from 1808 to 1900. It has a typical moss rose pictured as the design. The plant is not as popular now as it was in Victorian gardens, so the fuzz-covered bud is unfamiliar to most collectors. The dishes were usually decorated with pink and green flowers.

Bowl & Pitcher	250.00
Bowl, 10 In.	35.00
Coffeepot	70.00
Creamer	32.00
Cup & Saucer	35.00
Plate, Haviland, 10 In.	25.00
Plate, Sandwich, 9 1/2 In.	15.00
Platter, 15 In.	40.00
Wash Set, Bowl, Pitcher	300.00

MOTHER-OF-PEARL GLASS, or pearl satin glass, was first made in the 1850s in England and in Massachusetts. It was a special type of mold-blown satin glass with air bubbles in the glass, giving it a pearlized color. It has been reproduced. Mother-of-pearl shell objects are listed under Pearl.

Basket, Herringbone, Fan Shape, Blue, 9 1/4 x 8 1/4 In.	625.00
Basket, Herringbone, White, Blue Interior, Handle, 5 3/4 In.	320.00
Bottle, Diamond-Quilted, Faceted Stopper, Pink, 8 In.	460.00
Bowl, Diamond-Quilted, Shaded Deep Pink, Ruffled, 7 3/4 In.	275.00
Bowl, Ruffled Rim, Frosted Thorn Feet, Chartreuse, 9 1/2 In	450.00
Bride's Basket, Coin Spot, Ruffled, Ormolu Base, 14 In.	695.00
Jar, Cover, Quilted, Gilt Enamel, Square, 5 In., Webb	248.00
Pitcher, Diamond-Quilted, Thorn Handle, 8 1/2 In.	595.00
Pitcher, Milk, Rainbow Diamond, 9 In.	1815.00
Rose Bowl, 11 Crimp Top, White Lining, 3 3/4 In.	245.00
Rose Bowl, Diamond-Quilted, Clear Stripes, Signed, 4 In.	1350.00
Tray, Card, Ruffled, Plated Base & Handle, Bird Finial	300.00
Tumbler, Diamond Quilted, Pink, 3 3/4 In.	350.00
Tumbler, Diamond-Quilted, Blue Cornflowers	335.00
Vase, Allover Tiny Multicolored Flowers, Pink, 6 In.	965.00
Vase, Apricot, Wave-Like Air Traps, Narrow Neck, 7 1/2 In.	385.00
Vase, Diamond-Quilted, Rainbow Colors, 3 Petal Top, 6 In.	895.00
Vase, Hobnail, Square Top, Blue, 5 1/2 In.	615.00
Vase, Raindrop Pattern, Flared Lobed Rim, Green, 4 1/2 In.	195.00
Vase, Raindrops, Butterscotch, Stick Neck, 10 In.	195.00
Vase, Rivulet Pattern, White Lining, Blue, 5 1/2 In.	225.00
Vase, Shaded Orange Swirl, 11 In.	295.00
Vase, Yellow Peacock, Pulled Feather, Blue Interior, 5 In.	1500.00

MOTORCYLES of all types are being collected today. Examples can be found that date back to the early years of the twentieth century.

Book, Treasury Of Motorcycles Of The World, Floyd Clymer, 1965	8.50
Buckle, Harley Davidson, 1949	85.00
Humber, England	9000.00
Saddle Bag, Leather	50.00

MOUNT WASHINGTON, see Mt. Washington

MT. JOYE is an enameled cameo glass made in the late nineteenth and the twentieth centuries by Saint-Hilaire Touvier de Varraux and Co. of Pantin, France. This same company made De Vez glass. Pieces were usually decorated with enameling. Most pieces are not marked.

Bowl, Enameled Iris Design, Circular, 6 1/4 In.	192.00

Pitcher, Gilt Design, Silver Plated Handle & Top 1100.00
Vase, 3 White & Burgundy & Gold Flowers, Paneled, 11 In. 350.00
Vase, Amberina, No. 2668, 4 In. 275.00
Vase, Banjo Shape, Enameled, Signed, 13 1/2 In. 775.00
Vase, Crackle Ground, Gold Enameled Chestnuts, Leaves, Signed, 5 In. 225.00
Vase, Enameled Asters, Green Vertical Optic, Gold, 14 x 4 3/4 In. 245.00
Vase, Etched Foliage In Gold, Smoky Glass, 12 3/4 In., Pair 450.00
Vase, Frosted Pink Ground, Purple Mums, 13 In. 150.00
Vase, Gold Leaves & Flowers, Green Textured, Signed, 15 1/4 In. 695.00
Vase, Gold Thistle, Gray Cross Of Lorraine, Clear Ground, 9 1/2 In. 195.00

MT. WASHINGTON Glass Works started in 1837 in South Boston, Massachusetts. In 1870 the company moved to New Bedford, Massachusetts. Many types of art glass were made there until 1894, when the company merged with Pairpoint Manufacturing Co. Amberina, Burmese, Crown Milano, Cut Glass, Peachblow, and Royal Flemish are each listed in their own section.

Biscuit Barrel, Satin Glass, Flowers, Silver Plated Lid 225.00
Biscuit Jar, Cover, Bail, Helms Swirl, Pansies, MW, 6 1/2 In. 295.00
Biscuit Jar, Floral & Gilt Design 400.00
Biscuit Jar, Hand Painted Flowers, Silver Plate Lid 185.00
Biscuit Jar, White Satin, Wild Rose, Pillars, Silver Rim 160.00
Bowl, Silver & Enamel Design, 11 In. 350.00
Castor, Pickle, Pink Flowers Insert, Albertine, 8 1/2 In. 1150.00
Compote, Red Cut To Clear, Frosted Bowl 80.00
Condiment Set, Daisies, Robin's Egg Blue, Holder, 3 Piece 145.00
Creamer, Yellow Mums, Square Mouth, 4 3/4 In. 650.00
Cruet, Amber 350.00
Flower Frog, Mushroom, Dot Berries, Brown Leaves, 5 In. 195.00
Flower Frog, Oak Leaves, Cobalt Blue Berries 295.00
Fruit Bowl, Napoli Glass, Pond Lilies, Pairpoint Base, 10 In. 2200.00
Inkwell, Beveled Edges, Black Glass Well, Signed, 3 1/2 In. 295.00
Lamp, Fairy, Pyramid, Mother-of-Pearl Shade, 3 3/4 In. 385.00
Lamp, Floral Nosegays On White, Acorn Burner, 8 1/4 In. 845.00
Lemonade Set, Polychrome Floral, Amber Handle, 7 Piece 605.00
Mustard, Hinged Lid, Floral Design, Bail Handle, Spoon 180.00
Mustard, Plated Hinged Top, Flowers, Leaves, Handle, 3 1/2 In. 145.00
Pitcher, Fish Swimming Amid Sea Plants, Plants Handle, 5 In. 950.00
Pitcher, Melon Ribbed, Lusterless White, 9 1/2 In. 195.00
Pitcher, Raindrop, Bands Of Orchids, Frosted Handle 495.00
Rose Bowl, Apricot, Yellow, Purple Pansies, Gilt, 4 1/2 In. 190.00
Rose Bowl, Pansies, Pale Blue Ground, 5 1/2 In. 565.00
Salt, Onion 82.00
Saltshaker, Egg, Golden Buttercups, Raised Enamel 225.00
Shade, Cranberry, Acid Etched 185.00
Sugar Shaker, Egg, Forget-Me-Nots, Yellow Centers 285.00
Sugar Shaker, Raindrop Mother-of-Pearl Pattern 875.00
Sugar Shaker, Tomato 265.00
Syrup, Melon Shape, Satin Finish 60.00
Tumbler, Diamond-Quilted, Rose 60.00
Tumbler, Mother-of-Pearl, Herringbone, Blue To White 60.00
Vase, Applied Vines & Flowers, 11 In. 395.00
Vase, Clear, Blue & Gold Overlay, 12 In. 295.00
Vase, Lava, Embedded Chips, Curlicue Handles, 5 5/8 In. 2250.00
Vase, Lily, Lusterless, Ruffled Rim, 9 1/2 In. 75.00
Vase, Verona, Pale Florals, Ruffled Top, Signed, 14 In. 358.00

MUD FIGURES are small Chinese pottery figures made in the twentieth century. The figures usually represent workers, scholars, farmers, or merchants. Other pieces are trees, houses, and similar parts of the landscape. The figures have unglazed faces and hands but glazed clothing.

They were originally made for fish tanks or planters. Mud figures were of little interest and brought low prices until the 1980s. When the prices rose, reproductions appeared.

Fisherman, Hat On Back, Signed	55.00
Man, 8 In.	85.00
Old Man, Cobalt Blue Robe, 5 In.	35.00
Old Man, Long Beard, 6 In.	50.00
Woman, Flowers, 4 In.	55.00

MULBERRY ware was made in the Staffordshire district of England from about 1850 to 1860. The dishes were decorated with a reddish brown transfer design, now called *mulberry*. Many of the patterns are similar to those used for flow blue and other Staffordshire transfer wares.

Bowl, Athens, Adams, Rectangular, 10 x 8 In.	150.00
Bowl, Fluted, Susa, 9 1/4 In.	85.00
Bowl, Vegetable, Cover, Washington Vase, Podmore Walker	250.00
Chamber Pot, Vincennes, Alcock	250.00
Creamer, Jeddo, Adams & Son, 7 1/4 In.	135.00
Creamer, Nankin, Davenport	135.00
Creamer, Panama, Challinor	150.00
Creamer, Rhone Scenery, Podmore	125.00
Creamer, Washington Vase	175.00
Cup & Saucer, Corean	55.00
Cup & Saucer, Jeddo	65.00
Cup & Saucer, Medina	55.00 To 60.00
Cup & Saucer, Pelew	55.00
Cup & Saucer, Pelew, Challinor	55.00
Cup & Saucer, Rose	55.00
Cup & Saucer, Tonquin, Heath	65.00
Cup & Saucer, Washington Vase, Podmore Walker	55.00
Cup Plate, Athens, Adams	50.00
Cup Plate, Corean	60.00
Cup Plate, Pelew, Challinor	45.00
Ewer & Bowl, Flora, Spatter Trim, Walker	625.00
Gravy Boat, Panama, Challinor	125.00
Honey, Jeddo, W. Adams & Son	55.00
Mug, Ning PO	150.00
Pitcher & Bowl, Jeddo, Adams & Son, c.1845	575.00
Pitcher, Flora, T. Walker. 10 1/2 In.	275.00
Pitcher, Milk, Jeddo, Adams & Son, 8 1/4 In.	155.00
Pitcher, Pelew, Challinor, 7 8/10 In.	160.00
Pitcher, Washington Vase, 8 In.	295.00
Plate, Athens, 10 1/2 In, 4 Piece	110.00
Plate, Corean, 9 3/4 In.	60.00
Plate, Corean, Podmore Walker, 9 3/4 In.	48.00
Plate, Cyprus, Davenport, 7 1/2 In.	35.00
Plate, Pelew, Challinor, 9 3/4 In.	45.00
Plate, Peruvian, J. Wedgwood, 7 1/4 In.	25.00
Plate, Sydenham, J. Clementson, 9 1/2 In.	35.00
Plate, Washington Vase, 9 In.	50.00
Plate, Washington Vase, Podmore Walker, 8 1/2 In.	55.00
Platter, Bochara, J. Edwards, 17 1/2 x 13 3/4 In.	300.00
Platter, Chusan, 17 In.	200.00
Platter, Corean, Podmore, 10 3/4 x 8 1/2 In.	120.00
Platter, Cyprus, 15 1/2 In.	195.00
Platter, Rose, 14 In.	160.00
Platter, Washington Vase, 16 In.	200.00
Relish, Vincennes Pattern, Mitten Shape, Alcock	95.00
Server, Alpine Amusements, Davenport, 15 In.	135.00
Soup, Dish, Bochara, J. Edwards, 8 1/2 In.	45.00
Sugar, Nankin	150.00
Sugar, Susa, Meigh	175.00

Teapot, Corea, Clementson	350.00
Teapot, Jeddo, Adams	350.00
Teapot, Neva, Challinor	250.00
Teapot, Pelew	300.00
Teapot, Pelew, 6–Sided	325.00
Teapot, Rhone Scenery, Podmore	350.00
Tureen, Cover, Peruvian Pottery, Wedgwood, c.1830	145.00
Tureen, Soup, Cover, Bryonia	95.00

MULLER FRERES, French for Muller Brothers, made cameo and other glass from the early 1900s to the late 1930s. Their factory was first located in Luneville, then in nearby Croismaire, France. Pieces were usually marked with the company name.

Chandelier, Wrought Iron Hanger, Signed	7700.00
Lamp, Cameo, Dome Shade, Cream & Amber Flecks, Signed, 19 In.	8800.00
Vase, Azalea Blossoms, Buds, Leafage, Signed, c.1920, 7 1/2 In.	2970.00
Vase, Birds In Flight, Striped & Dotted, c.1925, 12 In.	880.00
Vase, Birds, Branches, Snowflakes, Gray, Yellow, 1920, 13 In.	5500.00
Vase, Bowl Shape, Red Fish, Silver Inclusions, 9 In.	950.00
Vase, Chrysanthemum Blossoms, Oviform, Signed, 6 5/8 In.	1800.00
Vase, Clematis Blossoms, Leaves, Signed, c.1920, 6 1/4 In.	1100.00
Vase, Colorless, Internal Silver Speckles, Signed, 9 In.	522.50
Vase, Daisies, Wheel Carved, Gray, Peach, Emerald, 1915, 15 In.	3300.00
Vase, Fluogravure Process, 7 1/2 In.	3025.00
Vase, Hibiscus Blossoms, Ovoid, Signed, c.1900, 6 3/8 In.	2425.00
Vase, Leaves & Blossoms, Royal Blue, Ovoid, 9 3/8 In.	440.00
Vase, Magnolias, Yellow, Cobalt, Opalescent, Cameo, 9 1/2 In.	5500.00
Vase, Maidens Landscape, White, Blue–Green, Cranberry, 11 In.	5775.00
Vase, Mottled Orange, Purple, Signed, 12 1/2 In.	975.00
Vase, Mottled Yellow, Anemone Blossoms, c.1920, 12 1/4 In.	1750.00
Vase, Mottled, 5 1/2 In.	375.00
Vase, Orange & Blue–Black Internal Design, Marked, 7 3/4 In.	335.00
Vase, Peacock Spreading Tail, Black Ground, 8 In.	4500.00
Vase, Pillow, Scenic, Green On Frost, 6 1/4 In.	2200.00
Vase, Poppies, Blossoms, Oviform, Signed, 5 1/2 In.	1210.00
Vase, Poppies, Polished Blossoms, Signed, 6 1/4 In.	1540.00
Vase, Poppy Blossoms, Apricot Opalescent, Cameo, 1920, 12 In.	8800.00
Vase, River Landscape, Gray, Lemon, Red, Cameo, 1920, 13 In.	4400.00
Vase, Rose Sprays, Salmon, Cameo, 1920, Ovoid, 10 1/8 In.	5500.00
Vase, Silver Foil Inside, Pigeons Border, Signed, 1930, 11 In.	2400.00
Vase, Sprays Of Berried Leaves, Signed, c.1920, 12 3/4 In.	1750.00
Vase, Stylized Leaves & Blossoms, Frosted, Gourd, 9 3/4 In.	825.00
Vase, Tranquil Woodland Landscape, Signed, c.1920, 7 1/8 In.	1650.00
Vase, Trumpet, Anemone Blossoms, Yellow, Sapphire, 18 3/8 In.	6100.00

MUNCIE Clay Products Company was established by Charles Benham in Muncie, Indiana, in 1922. The company made pottery for the florist and giftshop trade. The company closed by 1939. Pieces are marked with the name *Muncie* or just with a system of numbers and letters, like *1A*.

Bowl, Console, Green	40.00
Bowl, Glossy Burgundy Glaze, 4 In.	90.00
Lamp, Archers, Art Deco	395.00
Lamp, Art Deco, Phoenix Lovebirds, 27 In.	285.00
Lamp, Dancing Nudes, Pink, Matte, Bulbous, 8 1/2 In.	155.00
Lamp, Lovebirds, 27 In.	165.00
Pitcher & Tumbler, Orange Peel	135.00
Vase, Blue Speckled Glaze, 6 1/2 In.	65.00
Vase, Grasshopper, Maroon To Green, 6 In.	130.00
Vase, Green Drip Over Mauve, Handles, 7 x 6 In.	60.00
Vase, Handles, 8 In.	65.00
Vase, Hourglass Shape, Green, 9 In.	40.00
Vase, Inset Base, Oblong, 7 1/2 In.	65.00
Vase, Obelisk, Pink	25.00

Music, Box, Stella, Mahogany, Jacobs,
c.1897, 75 Discs, 41 1/4 In.

Music, Automation, Dancing Teacher, Pupil,
1870s, France, 21 In.

Vase, Orange, Handles, 10 In. 90.00
Vase, Ruba Rombie 35.00

MURANO, see Glass–Venetian

MUSIC boxes and musical instruments are listed in here. Phonograph
records, jukeboxes, phonographs, and sheet music are listed in other
sections in this book.

Accordion, Tanzabar, Roll Operated 1500.00
Autoharp, Primitive Box 75.00
Automaton, 2 Animated Birds, Gilded Cage, Gold Paint, 20 3/4 In. 1050.00
Automaton, 2 Birds, Moves, Head, Beak & Tail, Coin–Operated, 22 In. 4500.00
Automaton, 3 Birds, Moves Heads, Beaks & Tails, Bontems, 21 In. 5000.00
Automaton, Bird In Case, Moves Head, Beak & Tail, France, 19 In. 3000.00
Automaton, Bird, Chirping, Several Songs, Cage, Brass, Germany, 12 In. 500.00
Automaton, Bird, Several Melodies 605.00
Automaton, Dancing Teacher, Pupil, 1870s, France, 21 In. ....Illus 8800.00
Banjo, Mother–of–Pearl Inlay, C. Bruno & Sons, c.1900 .... 250.00
Banjo, Pearl Trim, 4–String, Tenor, 1920 .... 650.00
Bow, Violin, Ebony Frog, Pearl Eye, Gold Adjuster 715.00
Bow, Violin, Eugene Sartory, Silver Mounted 4200.00
Bow, Violin, Gold Mounted 3000.00
Bow, Violin, Tortoiseshell Frog, Gold Adjuster, Emile Ouchard 8140.00
Bow, Violin, W. E. Hill & Sons, Ivory & Silver Mounted 1200.00
Bow, Violoncello, Charles Claude Husson, Silver Mounted 2800.00
Bow, Violoncello, Silver Mounted 1000.00
Box, 12 Tunes, Bells, Butterflies, Longue Marche, Rosewood Case, 1879 .... 4500.00
Box, 8 Tunes, Inlaid Lid, Switzerland 2000.00
Box, 8 Tunes, With Bells & Butterflies 1800.00
Box, Bank, Ideola, 1950s, 6 In. 200.00
Box, Bird, Chased Scrolls, Masks, Silver Color, Wings Move, Griesbaum 3300.00
Box, Bremond Organocleide, 17–In. Cylinder, 6 Tunes 8200.00
Box, Cylinder, 12 Tunes, 5 Bells, Multi–Hammer Drum, 13 In. 1575.00
Box, Ducommiun Giroux, Key Wind, 4 Tunes, Inlaid Lid 4400.00
Box, Euphonia, 12 Discs 1800.00
Box, F. Nicole, Key Wind, 3 Tunes, Wire Hinges, Program Card On Bottom 3850.00
Box, F. Nicole, Key Wind, 6 Tunes, Program Card 4000.00
Box, Kalliope, 10 Bells, 20 Discs 8500.00
Box, L'Epee, Key Wind, 8 Tunes, Program Card 3500.00
Box, Lecoultre, Key Wind, 4 Tunes, Fine Tooth Comb, Inlaid Lid 3960.00
Box, Lecoultre, Lever Wind, Fruitwood Cabinet, Irish Music 2850.00

Box, Longdorf, Key Wind, 4 Tunes, Refinished Cabinet	3800.00
Box, Mermod Freres, 13–In. Cylinder, 6 Bells, Bee Strikers	3000.00
Box, Mermod, Cylinder, 12 Tunes, Play Card, c.1890	2100.00
Box, Mira, Console, Floor Model, Carved Mahogany, 16 Discs	6800.00
Box, New Century, 18 1/2–In. Single Comb Disc	4000.00
Box, New Century, Single Comb, 15 Discs	4500.00
Box, Nicole Freres, Key Wind, 6 Tunes, c.1861	3000.00
Box, Nicole Freres, Key Wind, 8 Tunes, Inlaid Lid, Program Card	3850.00
Box, Nicole, Key Wind, Piano Forte	4000.00
Box, Nicole, Mandolin, Lever Wind, 8 Tunes, Inlaid Rosary In Lid	6600.00
Box, Nicole, Overture, Key Wind, 4 Tunes, Program Card	9500.00
Box, Otto & Sons Capital Style, Interchangeable Cuff, c.1895, 17 In.	5225.00
Box, Paillard, 8 Tunes, Program Card, 2 Combs, Burl Walnut, 21 1/2 In.	9900.00
Box, Paillard, 18–In. Cylinder	2000.00
Box, Paillard, Longue Marche, Piccola Zither, 8 Tunes, Reduction Gear	4000.00
Box, Photo Album, Celluloid Cover, Scene Of Lovers	175.00
Box, Photo Album, Victorian Woman's Picture, 6 Discs	950.00
Box, Piano, Hinged Top, Fitted With Sewing Implements, Miniature	880.00
Box, Polyphon Disc, 12 Bells, 12 Discs	8000.00
Box, Polyphon, 12 Discs, Germany, c.1895, 16 In.	2700.00
Box, Regina No. 44262, Cherry, 21 Discs	1900.00
Box, Regina No. 59922, Mahogany, 22 Discs	3500.00
Box, Regina, 21 Discs, Cherry Case	1900.00
Box, Regina, 22 Discs, Mahogany Case	3500.00
Box, Regina, Doll Front, Automatic Changer, Tabletop	4000.00
Box, Regina, Double Comb, 15 Discs, Oak Case, 15 In.	3850.00
Box, Regina, Double Comb, Carved Walnut Case, 21 In.	7800.00
Box, Regina, Double Comb, Serpentine, 21 In.	6200.00
Box, Regina, Hexapone, Oak, Floor Model	8000.00
Box, Regina, Single Comb, 15 Discs, Penny Operated, Oak Case	2900.00
Box, Regina, Step–Down Case, Regina Emblem, 15 1/2 In.	3000.00
Box, Regina, Style 50, Serpentine, Mahogany, 20 1/2 In.	6000.00
Box, Regina, Tabletop, 12 Records	2500.00
Box, Stella, 17 1/4–In. Disc, Console, Floor Model	5800.00
Box, Stella, Disk Type, Stand	4950.00
Box, Stella, Double Comb, Mahogany, With Cabinet, 17 1/4 In.	6200.00
Box, Stella, Double Comb, Matching Base, Mahogany	6200.00
Box, Stella, Mahogany, Double Comb, Tabletop, 24 14–In. Discs	4100.00
Box, Stella, Mahogany, Jacobs, c.1897, 75 Discs, 41 1/4 In. ....*Illus*	4950.00
Box, Stella, Stand, 78 Discs, 28 In.	5000.00
Box, Stylus, Victrola, 8 Needles, Metal	27.50
Box, Swiss, 4 Tunes, Operatic Selection, Program Card, 21 In.	4400.00
Box, Swiss, 5 Interchangeable Cylinders, 14 In.	2600.00
Box, Swiss, 10 Tunes, Card, Faux Rosewood Case, c.1900, 20 In.	770.00
Box, Swiss, Cylinder, Enameled Bell Strikers, 17 x 10 x 8 In.	1600.00
Box, Swiss, Floral Border On Lid, 8 American Tunes, 6 x 18 In.	675.00
Box, Swiss, Form Of Grand Piano, Wood Case, 7 In.	250.00
Box, Symphonian, Band Inlay, Floral Decal On Top, 8 x 10 3/4 In.	715.00
Box, Symphonion, 84 Teeth, 2 Combs, 12 Discs, Table Model	6000.00
Box, Symphonion, Model 25A, Corner Columns, Brass Handle, Inlaid Lid	5200.00
Box, Symphonion, Ornate Walnut Case, Brass Handles, 11 1/4 In. Disc	5200.00
Box, Symphonion, Sublime Harmonie, 100 Teeth, 12 Discs, Germany, c.1895	3000.00
Box, Thorens, 5 11–In. Discs	1150.00
Box, Wonder Woman, Figural	20.00
Bugle, Military, Brass, U.S. Regulation	80.00
Clavichord, George III, Inlaid Mahogany, Rectangular Case, Mahogany	990.00
Clavichord, Zuckermann, Ivory & Ebony Keys, 6 Ft.	355.00
Drum, Chinese, Dragon One Side, Fowl Other, Canton, c.1860, 9 1/2 In.	165.00
Fife, Brass Trim, Rosewood	60.00
Flageolet, 1–Keyed, Boxwood & Ivory, J. M. Camp, Late 18th Century	770.00
Flute, Figural, Aztec Style	35.00
Guitar, 0–45, C. F. Margin, 1908	5445.00
Guitar, Arch Top, John D'Angelico, 1938	3080.00

Guitar, Gibson, 6–String 140.00
Guitar, Gibson, Steel 115.00
Guitar, National Duolian, Resonator 1485.00
Harmonica, Century Of Progress, Box, 1933 .... 125.00
Harmonica, Hohner, Comet, Gold, Case 40.00
Harmonica, Hohner, Germany, 1930s, Miniature 25.00
Harmonica, Hohner, Herb Shriner 45.00
Harmonica, Hohner, Herb Shriner, Box 60.00
Harmonica, Hohner, Marine Band 20.00
Harmonica, Hoosier Boy, Herb Shriner, Hohner 75.00
Harmonica, Pohl, Germany, Box 40.00
Harmonica, Roller, 14 Rolls 175.00
Harmonium, Hinged Domed Lid, 30 Bells, Graduated Sizes, Cherry Case 2640.00
Hexaphone, Regina, Model 102 .... 5170.00
Mandolin, Inlay, Neck–37 In. 195.00
Mandolin, Rosewood, Mahogany, Ebony, Inlaid In Spruce, 24 In. 125.00
Mandolin, Victoria 145.00
Markophone 125.00
Megaphone, Eddie Wittstein Orchestra 48.00
Melodeon, Rocking, Caleb H. Packard, Red Painted Case, 1839–1855 .... 450.00
Nickelodeon, Capital, Violin Pipes, All Original 5500.00
Nickelodeon, Coinola, Cupid, 1915 .... 7500.00 To 8500.00
Nickelodeon, National Automatic, Dog Race Mechanism, 12 Roll Changer 8000.00
Nickelodeon, Peerless, Oak, 1 Glass Door Over Another, 1890s 3575.00
Nickelodeon, Seeburg, Ampico, Model L 3900.00
Nickelodeon, Seeburg, Model L, Mahogany Cabinet, Double Doors 6500.00
Nickelodeon, Violin Pipes, N. Tonawanda Instruments, A Rolls 5500.00
Nickelodeon, Wurlitzer, Keyboard Style, 1912 .... 7500.00
Nickelodeon, Wurlitzer, Model 1 .... 2750.00
Nickelodeon, Wurlitzer, Model IX, Bells, 6 Roll Changer 5500.00
Orchestrelle, Style W, Aeolian, Organ Blower, 200 Rolls 7500.00
Orchestrion, Seeburg, Player, Mandolin & Bells 7500.00
Organ, Aeolian, Player, Oak Case, Fretwork 2300.00
Organ, Beckwith, Pump, 1900s 450.00
Organ, Beckwith, Pump, Carved & Applied Oak, Mirror, 6 1/2 Ft. 700.00
Organ, Earhuff, 12 Stops, 61 Keys, Mahogany 1500.00
Organ, Estey, Cottage, Carillon With Keyboard 300.00
Organ, Estey, Eastlake Style, Beveled Center Mirror, 71 In. 1500.00
Organ, Gem, Roller, 13 Rollers 700.00
Organ, Monkey, 26 Keys, 63 Pipes, 4 Ranks, Wooden Trumpet Pipes 4500.00
Organ, Newman Bros., Pump, Original Ivory, Walnut, 1893 .... 4750.00
Organ, Player, Aeolian, Model 1500 .... 5000.00
Organ, Player, Wilcox & White, Console, 46 Key, Golden Oak Cabinet 3750.00
Organ, Portable, World War I Army, Pedal Bellows, Oak, Estey, 36 In. 300.00
Organ, Pump, Eastlake, Lamp Shelves, Oak, 1880s 1000.00
Organ, Pump, Victorian, Mirror Chapel Top, Walnut, Ornate, 1800s 1795.00
Organ, Story & Clark, Pump, Mirror, Tiered Detachable Top Shelves 400.00
Organ, Street, Bacigalupo, 41 Keys, 8 Tune 9500.00
Organ, Street, Molinare .... 5500.00 To 7000.00
Organ, Street, Rubes, 1885 .... 3900.00
Organ, Street, Spain 1600.00
Organ, W. W. Gimbel, Pump, Melodia, Knee Controls 750.00
Organ, Wilcox & White, Pump, Shelves, Beveled Mirror, 1890s 3800.00
Piano, A. B. Chase, Baby Grand, Attached Hammond Organ Keyboard 500.00
Piano, Albrecht, Upright, Rosewood, Ornate, 1890s 2500.00
Piano, Bechstein, Overall Painted Putti, Inlaid Walnut, 6 Ft. 8 In. 9900.00
Piano, Chase, Player, Baby Grand, Flame Mahogany, Restored 3100.00
Piano, Chickering & Sons, Baby Grand, 1941 .... 1430.00
Piano, Chickering, Grand, Square, Rosewood, 1860s 6000.00
Piano, Electrova, Coin–Operated, 5 Leaded Glass Panels 3200.00
Piano, Grinnell Brothers, Baby Grand, Mahogany, Bench, 4 Ft. 6 In. 1760.00
Piano, Gulbransen, Mahogany, Bench 600.00
Piano, Gulbransen, Player, Electrified, Oak 3200.00

Piano, Haines Bros., Upright, Foot & Electric Pump 7000.00
Piano, Haines, Player, Ampico, Upright, Electric 6000.00
Piano, Knabe, Grand, Square 3000.00
Piano, Knabe, Player, Grand, Ampico, Model B, Walnut 5 Ft. 8 In. 7500.00
Piano, Knabe, Player, Telektra, Upright, Bench, 80 Brass Rolls 7500.00
Piano, Marshall & Wendell, Ampico, Model B, Art Case 4900.00
Piano, Marshall & Wendell, Baby Grand, William & Mary Art Case 4500.00
Piano, Marshall & Wendell, Grand 4500.00
Piano, Marshall & Wendell, Marque Ampico, Ivory Keys, Bench, 20 Rolls 2700.00
Piano, Marshall & Wendell, Player, Automated 2500.00
Piano, Merrili, Baby Grand, Black Case, Bench, 4 Ft. 8 In. 350.00
Piano, National, Coin–Operated, Automatic Dog Race 7000.00
Piano, Nickelodeon, Seeburg, Model E, Mandolin Attachment 1500.00
Piano, Nunns & Clark, Empire, Upright, Rosewood, c.1840 .... 3500.00
Piano, Robert & William Nunns, Square, c.1825 .... 4950.00
Piano, Seeburg, Coin–Operated 8500.00
Piano, Seeburg, Theater, Pipes, H–Roll 4500.00
Piano, Segarstrom, Player 275.00
Piano, Starck, Player, All Original, Restored, Electric, 1917 .... 4250.00
Piano, Starck, Player, Manual & Electric, 1917 .... 4250.00
Piano, Steinway, Model B, Ebonized, c.1911, 43 x 83 3/4 In. 2750.00
Piano, Steinway, Parlor Grand, Rosewood, 1860 .... 9500.00
Piano, Steinway, Player, Upright, 1911 .... 9000.00
Piano, Steinway, Upright, Satin Black Finish 5200.00
Piano, Straube, Player, Upright, Tiger Oak Finish 1995.00
Piano, Weber, Themodist, Player, 65 Or 88 Note 4350.00
Piano, Werner, Player 800.00
Piano, Wurlitzer, Mahogany Case, Matching Bench, 39 In. 200.00
Pianoforte, John Broadwood & Sons, London, Mahogany, 5 Ft. 6 In. 2200.00
Pianoforte, Loud Brothers, Philadelphia, c.1835 .... 550.00
Pipe Organ, Albert Stanke, 438 Pipes, Oak Roll Top Console 7500.00
Pipe Organ, Barrel, 1830s 2400.00
Roll, Mills Violano, Virtuoso, Box 95.00
Rolmonica, 14 Rolls, 1920s 110.00
Saxophone, Alto, Buffet Co., Paris, Numbered 350.00
Saxophone, Conn, Curved, Patent 1914 .... 750.00
Saxophone, Martin, Baritone 275.00
Sousaphone, Conn 225.00
Stool, Harpsichord, Regency, Walnut, Early 19th Century 125.00
Symphonion, Libellion, 1895 .... 3900.00
Symphonion, Tabletop Box, Mahogany, Double Comb, 11 Discs, 13 In. 4000.00
Symphonion, With Bells, Mechanical, 1900 .... 4550.00
Ukelele, Martin 125.00
Violin, Guarneri Model, Ludwig Christian Bausch, Bow & Case, c.1820 .... 3000.00
Violin, Guarnerius Copy 450.00
Violin, Leopold Widhalm, Germany 3700.00
Violin, Student's, Case 130.00
Violoncello, Luigu Agostinelli, 1959 .... 8800.00

MUSTACHE CUPS were popular from 1850 to 1900 when the large,
flowing mustache was in style. A ledge of china or silver held the hair out
of the liquid in the cup. This kept the mustache tidy and also kept the
mustache wax from melting. Left–handed mustache cups are rare but are
being reproduced.

A Present, Pink, Germany 20.00
Comb Shaped, Advertising, Early 1900s 35.00
Floral, Woman 35.00
Florals, Gold, Saucer, RS Prussia 225.00
Medallion, Border 40.00

MZ AUSTRIA is the wording on a mark used by Moritz Zdekauer on
porcelains made at his works from about 1900. The firm was established in
the town of Alt–Rohlau, Austria, in 1884 and was nationalized in 1945.

The pieces were decorated with lavish floral patterns and overglaze gold decoration. Full sets of dishes were made as well as vases, toilet sets, and other wares.

Cup & Saucer, Rose With Swags, Rope Twist Edge	12.00
Plate, Fish, Blue Borders, Kostler, Blue Beehive, 10 Piece	350.00
Plate, Roses, Scalloped, Gold, Signed Twieg, 6 In.	30.00
Plate, Tiny Roses Border, Princess, 7 3/4 In.	6.00

NAILSEA glass was made in the Bristol district in England from 1788 to 1873. It was made by many different factories, not just the Nailsea Glass House. Many pieces were made with loopings of either white or colored glass as decoration.

Bottle, Bird, Striped	55.00
Flask, Black & White Looping, Red, Stand, 7 1/2 In. ....*Illus*	480.00
Flask, Flattened Shape, Red & Opaque White, 7 In.	165.00
Flask, Opaque White Cased, Pink Looping, Clear, 8 In.	45.00
Flask, White Opalescent Zigzag Loopings, Cranberry	165.00
Lamp, Fairy, Clear Peg Base, Pairpoint Foot, 7 1/2 In.	275.00
Lamp, Fairy, Matching Ruffled Bowl, Blue	500.00
Lamp, Fairy, White Looping, Clark Insert, Cricklite, 1800s, 7 In.	750.00
Rolling Pin, Colorless Body, White, Pink Looping, Hollow, 16 In.	195.00
Witch Ball, Green, Rose & White Looping, America, 1850s, 2 7/8 In.	467.50

NAKARA is a trade name for a white glassware made about 1900 by the C. F. Monroe Company of Meriden, Connecticut. It was decorated in pastel colors. The glass was very similar to another glass made by the company called *Wave Crest.* The company closed in 1916. Boxes for use on a dressing table are the most commonly found Nakara pieces. The mark is not found on every piece.

NAKARA

Bonbon, Pink Flowers, Blue Ground, 6 3/4 x 6 In.	385.00
Box, Bishop's Hat, Mirror In Lid, Avocado	695.00
Box, Bishop's Hat, Purple, Enamel Dots, Satin Lining	335.00
Box, Collars & Cuffs, 8 In.	975.00
Box, Hinged Cover, Floral On Gray, Square, 4 In.	350.00
Box, Jewelry, Bishop's Hat, Chrysanthemums, Beaded, 5 3/4 In.	600.00
Box, Pink Flowers, White Enamel Dot Trim, Blue, Square, 4 1/4 In.	435.00
Box, Rococo Blown–Out Design, Hand Painted Violets, 9 x 4 In.	1585.00
Dish, Dresser, Ormolu Mount, Pink To Yellow Daisies	245.00
Humidor, Lion, Marked, 8 In.	700.00
Humidor, Owl On Branch, Cigars On Lid, 7 1/2 In.	1750.00
Vase, Metal Rim, Footed, 17 In.	975.00

Nailsea, Flask, Black & White Looping, Red, Stand, 7 1/2 In.

◆◆◆◆◆◆◆◆◆◆◆◆◆◆◆◆◆◆◆

If you are the victim of a theft, be sure to give the police complete information about your antiques. You should have a good description, a photograph, and any known identifying marks. You might want to send information about the stolen antiques to the antiques papers.

◆◆◆◆◆◆◆◆◆◆◆◆◆◆◆◆◆◆◆

NANKING is a type of blue–and–white porcelain made in Canton, China, since the late eighteenth century. It is very similar to Canton, which is listed under its own name in this book. Both Nanking and Canton are part of a larger group now called *Chinese Export* porcelain. Nanking has a spear–and–post border and may have gold decoration.

Cider Jug, 8 5/8 In.	375.00
Cup & Saucer, Pagoda Design, 6 1/2–In. Saucer	192.50
Dish, Cover, Boar's Head Finial, 8 In.	150.00
Mug, Twisted Handle, 4 In.	135.00
Plate, 10 In.	100.00
Platter, 19th Century, 18 In.	660.00
Tureen, Cover, 19th Century, 10 In.	330.00
Tureen, Cover, 19th Century, 11 x 15 In.	1210.00

NAPKIN RINGS were in fashion from 1869 to about 1900. They were made of silver, porcelain, wood, and other materials. They are still being made today. The most popular rings with collectors are the silver–plated figural examples. Small, realistic figures were made to hold the ring. Good and poor reproductions of the more expensive rings are now being made and collectors must be very careful.

Attached Bud Vase, Oriental Fan, Butterfly, Silver Plate		295.00
Cherub, Pulling Salt Dip & Shaker, Simpson Hall	*Illus*	550.00
Figural, 2 Dogs, Red Eyes, Child, Bird On Ring, Osborn		450.00
Figural, Arabian Man, Seated Next To Ring		195.00
Figural, Battleship Maine, Commemorative, Engraved		50.00
Figural, Bear On Haunches, Paws On Ring, Silver Plate		250.00
Figural, Bear Pulling Cart, Wheels Revolve, Silver Plate		295.00
Figural, Berries & Leaves, Water Lily Pad Base		75.00
Figural, Bird, Base Supports Ring, Meriden, Silver Plate		145.00
Figural, Bird, Green, Catalin		30.00
Figural, Bird, Red, Catalin		40.00
Figural, Bird, Yellow, Catalin		20.00
Figural, Boy Sits On Stool, Pulling Boot, Silver Plate		150.00
Figural, Boy With Gun, Silver Plate		250.00
Figural, Boy, Dressed For Work, Rolling Barrel, Silver Plate		150.00
Figural, Boy, Kate Greenaway Type, Oval Base		350.00
Figural, Bulldog, Stands On Side Of Ring, Glaring, Silver Plate		150.00
Figural, Cat On Pillow, Silver Plate		135.00
Figural, Cat Seated By Ring, Silver Plate		375.00
Figural, Cherub Wearing Cap With Feather, Upward Fist		165.00
Figural, Chick, Sits Next To Hammered Ring, Silver Plate		70.00
Figural, Chick, Sits On Wishbone Base, Engraved Kind Wishes		185.00
Figural, Chick, Tufts, Silver Plate		55.00
Figural, Chick, Wishbone, Basket Forming Ring, 4 Ball Feet		170.00
Figural, Chicken Foot, Wishbone On Heart Shaped Foot, Wilcox		155.00
Figural, Child, On Ring, Dog On Leash, Tufts	*Illus*	350.00
Figural, Child, Removing Shoes, Silver Plate, Derby	*Illus*	450.00
Figural, Children, On Teeter–Totter, Simpson Hall	*Illus*	660.00
Figural, Cow, Sheaf Of Wheat Shape, Wilcox, Silver Plate		250.00
Figural, Crossed Hockey Sticks, Wreath At Center, Puck On Top		225.00
Figural, Cupid Sharpening Arrow, Meriden, Silver Plate		195.00
Figural, Dog On Ring, Ball Footed, Rogers, Silver Plate		130.00
Figural, Dog Pulling Sled, Silver Plate		250.00
Figural, Dog, Barking, Bushy Tail, Bird Perched On Ring		210.00
Figural, Dog, Held By Cherub, Tufts, Silver Plate		350.00
Figural, Eagle, Double, Wings Open, Both Sides, Meriden Silver		70.00
Figural, Gazelle, Ring On Back, Meriden	*Illus*	275.00
Figural, Horse Pulling Cart, Wheels Revolve, Silver Plate		325.00
Figural, Horse Theme, Silver Plate, 1855		500.00
Figural, Horse, Reared On Hind Legs, Fore Legs Rest On Ring		225.00
Figural, Horseshoe Leans Against Chased Ring, Silver Plate		75.00
Figural, Lady Watering Flowers, Silver Plate		200.00

Figural, Large Cow, Seated, Hooves On Top Of Ring	200.00
Figural, Lion, Leaning On Decorated Ring, Silver Plate	250.00
Figural, Lion, Lies On Base, Ring On His Back, Meriden & Co.	125.00
Figural, Monkey By Grape Designed Ring	225.00
Figural, Open Salts Each End, Horseshoe Ring, Miller & Co.	235.00
Figural, Oriental Dragons, Each Side	150.00
Figural, Oriental Fans, Each Side, Meriden & Co., Silver Plate	150.00
Figural, Owl, Violin, Ruffled Music Base, Wilcox, Silver Plate	235.00
Figural, Rooster, Cast Iron	15.00
Figural, Scottie Dog, Red, Catalin	45.00
Figural, Sheet Music Base, Violin Leaning On Ring	200.00
Figural, Spanish Lady's Comb, Silver Plate	195.00
Figural, Squirrel, Eating Nut, Chased Ring, Rogers & Bros.	225.00
Figural, Squirrel, Eating Nut, Next To Ring, Silver Plate	135.00

*Napkin Ring, Cherub, Pulling
Salt Dip & Shaker,
Simpson Hall*

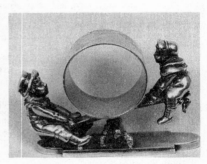

*Napkin Ring, Figural, Children, On Teeter-
Totter, Simpson Hall*

*Napkin Ring, Figural, Child,
On Ring, Dog On Leash, Tufts*

*Napkin Ring, Figural, Child,
Removing Shoes, Silver
Plate, Derby*

*Napkin Ring, Figural, Gazelle, Ring On Back,
Meriden*

Figural, Tennis Racket Base, Ring On Top, Silver Plate 175.00
Figural, Victorian Looped Back Chair Holds Ring 125.00
Figural, Wild Bear, Glares From Side Of Ring, Silver Plate 150.00
Figural, Winged Cherub Pulling Sled, Meriden, Silver Plate 375.00
Figural, Winged Cherub, Heart Base, Mounted, Bird Claw, Wilcox 100.00
Figural, Woman On Toboggan, Rogers, Silver Plate 375.00
Figural, Young Boy In Top Hat & Coattails, Silver Plate 400.00
Red Bakelite, Swirled, 3 In., Pair 24.00
Sterling Silver, Ornate, HCD Monogram 35.00

NASH glass was made in Corona, New York, from about 1928 to 1931. A.
Douglas Nash bought the Corona glassworks from Louis C. Tiffany in
1928 and founded the A. Douglas Nash Corporation with support from his
father, Arthur J. Nash. Arthur had worked at the Webb factory in
England and for the Tiffany Glassworks in Corona.

NASH

Bowl, Blue & Turquoise Vines, Crystal, Signed, 13 In. 425.00
Compote, Chintz, Green Zigzag, Blue Stripes, Scalloped, Pedestal, 2 In. 95.00
Parfait, Blue & Green, Signed, 6 In., Pair 240.00
Vase, Chintz Luster, Silvery Stripes, Signed, 9 1/2 In 500.00
Vase, Chintz, Bulbous Bottom, Green & Blue Stripes, Signed, 11 1/4 In. 325.00
Vase, Chintz, Flared Top, Green & Blue Stripes, Clear Pedestal, 10 In. 300.00
Wine, Cone Shape, Thin Stem, Blue & Green Stripes, Signed, 7 In., Pair 435.00

NAUTICAL antiques are listed in this section. Any of the many objects
that were made or used by the seafaring trade, including ship parts,
models, and tools, are included. Other pieces may be found listed under
Scrimshaw.

Adze, Shipwright's, Hammer Poll, 4 In. Wide Bit 38.00
Adze, Shipwright's, Hammer Poll, England, 3 1/2 To 4 In. Bit 39.00
Ashtray, Cruiser, Clipper Ship, Holland American Lines, Delft 25.00
Ashtray, Cunard Line, Bronze 75.00
Ashtray, Evercast, Hand Forged 25.00
Ashtray, French Line, Akro Agate 24.00
Ashtray, French Line, Steamship, Cobalt Blue, 4 1/2 In. 20.00
Ashtray, U.S. Navy Ship 45.00
Ashtray, U.S. S. Whiteside, Porcelain 15.00
Bell, Liberty Ship, Bronze, Greenleaf, San Fran., Heavy Bracket 550.00
Bell, Ship's, Bell Metal, S. S. T. L., Lenzen, Monrovia 175.00
Bell, Ship's, Brass, Large 150.00
Bevel, Shipwright's, Wooden, 15 In. 15.00
Binnacle, Brass, Hood, Chart Case, Compass, Light, 1930s 950.00
Binnacle, Compass, Wood Base, 1880s 2800.00
Booklet, S. S. Lapland Cruise, Steamship, Southern Hemi., 1923, 4 Pg. 4.00
Booklet, Seattle To Orient, Admiral Oriental Lines, 1923, 28 Pg. 15.00
Booklet, White Star Line Sailing List, Schedule, Fares, 1933 .... 30.00
Bowl, Holland American Line, Silver Plated, Footed, 8 In. 50.00
Bowl, Ship's Mess, HMS Ariadne & Ajax, Pewter, Pair 130.00
Box, Spirits, 12 Sections, Ironbound Lock & Handles, 1800s, 16 In. 180.00
Cabinet, Medical, Mahogany, Compartments, Drawers, 1870, 13 x 18 In. 1265.00
Chest, Sea, Rope Handles, Divided Interior, Blue Paint, Pine, 42 In. 270.00
Chest, Sea, Sailing Ship Painting Inside Of Lid, Blue Paint 2350.00
Chest, Stars Carved On Brackets, Rope Handles, British Flag 852.50
Chronometer, 18K Gold, Gold Anchor Chain Fob, Walnut Box, F. Rotig 2750.00
Clock, Chelsea, Time Only 255.00
Coat, Officer's, Embroidered, Accessories 82.50
Compass Binnacle, Ship's, 12 x 16 In. 250.00
Compass, Kevin & White, Boston, Gimbaled, Spherical, 9 In. 100.00
Compass, Primitive, 5 1/4 In. 20.00
Compass, Ritchie, Mass. 40.00
Creamer, Matson Line, Silver 25.00
Deck Plan, SS Carinthia, 1925 .... 30.00
Desk, Lap, Brass Bound, Mahogany 247.50
Desk, Ship's Captain's, Walnut, Fitted, Interior Oil Paintings 3850.00

Nautical, Model, Warship Lexington, Portia Takakjian, 39 x 51 In.

Nautical, Model, Whaleboat Sunbeam, Mixed Woods, 67 x 23 x 52 In.

Drawing, Storm King Ship, Signed A. James, Sail Maker, 1880, Cardiff 990.00
Figurehead, Bust, Female Angel, Detachable Wings, Oak, 25 1/2 In. 2200.00
Figurehead, Military Jacket & Hat, Wooden, c.1880, 60 In. 2100.00
Figurehead, Roman Centurion, Toga Outfit, 62 In. 330.00
Figurehead, Woman, 1 Arm Held Up, Sailing Ship, Wooden, 54 In. 1200.00
Frame, Cunard R. M. S. Mauretania, Litho On Tin 600.00
Gauge, Slitting, All Whalebone 825.00
Gauge, Submarine, 6 In. 22.00
Gravy Boat, American Yacht Club, Nautical Flag, Jackson China 20.00
Helmet, Deep Sea Diving, 3 View Ports 900.00
Hourglass, 18th Century, 7 1/4 In. 300.00
Iceboat, Wooden, With Sail, Painted, Early 20th Century, 29 In. 126.00
Iron, Hawsing, Shipwright's, 23 In. Iron Handle 65.00
Kit, Sail Maker's, R. Heinishch, Civil War Era, 1859 .... 220.00
Knife, Sailor's, Carved Horn Handle, Brass Inlay, Folding, 15 In. 110.00
Lamp, Brass Burner, Port & Starboard, 10 In., Pair 85.00
Lamp, From U.S. P. T. Boat, Pair 195.00
Lamp, Marine, Perko, Kerosene, 10 x 20 In. 250.00
Lamp, Ship's, Kerosene, Brass, Copper, Clear Bulbous Globe, 15 In. 125.00
Lamp, Steamship, Whistle Mounted On Brass Steam Gauge, 24 In. 800.00
Lantern, Glass Globes, Brass 115.00
Lantern, Kerosene Lamp, Brass, Copper Trim, 25 In. 145.00
Lantern, World War II, Waterproof 20.00
List, Passenger, RMS Queen Mary, From New York, June 5, 1936 .... 12.00
Maul, Trenail, Shipwright's, 9 In. Head, Original Handle 48.00
Menu, Christmas Dinner, S. S. Brazil, 1945 .... 5.00
Menu, Hawaiian Cruise Ship, 1950–1960 .... 18.00
Menu, RMS Queen Mary, Dinner, June 7, 1936 .... 8.00
Model, Sailboat, Wooden, Fabric, Hand Painted, 39 x 48 In. 500.00
Model, Sailboat, Wooden, Metal, Green, White, Varnished Deck, 46 In. 475.00
Model, Ship, Wooden, Gas Powered Engine, Assembled, 32 In. 300.00
Model, Submarine, Tin, Brown Paint, 53 In. 300.00
Model, U.S. Brig Of War Lexington, Wood, 39 x 51 In. 4180.00
Model, USS Bear, Glass Case 1210.00
Model, Warship Lexington, Portia Takakjian, 39 x 51 In. ....*Illus* 4180.00
Model, Whaleboat Sunbeam, Mixed Woods, 67 x 23 x 52 In. ....*Illus* 3850.00
Model, Whaleboat, Painted Wood, Early 20th C., 23 In. ....*Illus* 715.00
Pencil, Mechanical, Cunard Line, Ship Design 8.00
Picture, Steamship, Thomas Powell, Watercolor, Gilt Frame, 12 In. 625.00
Plate, Dinner, New England Steamship Co., Buffalo China, 9 In. 30.00
Porthole, Bronze, Large 65.00

Rule & Compass, Maple, Iron Handle Center, 39 1/4 x 2 5/8 In.	19.00
Rule, Navigation, Ivory	70.00
Shaving Stand, Sea Captain's, Column Shape, Mahogany, 33 In.	3190.00
Ship Model, 1/2 Hull 3 Masted Schooner, American, 1880	3800.00
Ship Model, 1/2 Hull, White, Gold, Laminated Construction, 54 In.	50.00
Ship Model, Ann Marie, Fishing Boat, 1930s, 36 In.	1500.00
Ship Model, British, D. J. Morton, Lucite Case, 30 In. ....*Illus*	248.00
Ship Model, Clipper Ship Flying Cloud, Glass Case, 34 x 24 In.	1430.00
Ship Model, Constitution, 1920s	675.00
Ship Model, English Frigate, Bone, Chinese Export, 19 x 23 In.	9350.00
Ship Model, Lillian Woodruff, Tug, All Metal, 28 In.	2200.00
Stamp Box, S. S. American Ship Lines, 1914	110.00
Teapot, Cube, Queen Mary	32.50
Telescope, Engraved Capt. Sam Thornton, Brass & Wood	100.00
Telescope, Original Signal Flags, William Desilva, Liverpool, 1882	770.00
Ticket, Bob–Lo Boat, Round Trip, 65 Cents	5.00
Tray, Sailor's, Shell & Grass Under Glass, 18 x 11 In.	85.00
Trumpet, Speaking, Brass	75.00
Wheel, Ship's, Brass, Teakwood Handles, Scotland, 30 1/2 In.	250.00
Wheel, Ship's, Riverboat–Type, Pinned Wood, c.1850	500.00

NETSUKES are small ivory, wood, metal, or porcelain pieces used as toggles on the end of the cord that held a Japanese money pouch. The earliest date from the sixteenth century. Many are miniature, carved works of art.

Agate, Nuts, Chestnut, Peanut & Others, 1 5/8 In.	440.00
Bone, Byokuzan Holding Sea Bream, Ebisu, 1 11/16 In.	220.00
Bone, Nude South Sea Figure, 2 1/2 In.	220.00
Bone, Pavilion, 19th Century, 2 In.	330.00
Bone, Wolf & Skull, 1 7/8 In.	412.00
Bronze, Gourd, Fruit, Vine & Leaves, 2 1/8 In.	170.00

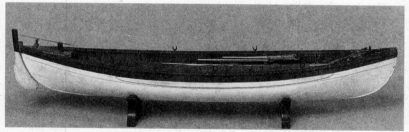

Nautical, Model, Whaleboat, Painted Wood, Early 20th C., 23 In.

Nautical, Ship Model, British, D. J. Morton, Lucite Case, 30 In.

Bronze, Raised Demon Fishing, Bronze Chain, Seated Scholar Clasp	55.00
Ivory, Cat On Fish	120.00
Ivory, Cat, Inlaid Eyes, 2 1/8 In.	410.00
Ivory, Chinese Dog Form, Shounsai, 1 1/4 In.	155.00
Ivory, Chinese Sage On Scholar's Table, Shigemasa, 1 1/2 In.	330.00
Ivory, Eagle Attacking Monkey	125.00
Ivory, Floral, Shell & Sword, Inset 18K Gold Medallion, 1 3/4 In.	440.00
Ivory, Gods Of Good Luck, Yoshiyuki	1600.00
Ivory, Human Skull, Monkey On Top, Signed	120.00
Ivory, Human Skull, Rat On Top, Signed	120.00
Ivory, Kirin, Seated, Scratching, 19th Century, 1 1/2 In.	6600.00
Ivory, Laughing Man, Clamshell Full Of Oni, 2 1/4 In.	385.00
Ivory, Man Carrying Wood, With Pumpkin, Signed	150.00
Ivory, Man Eating Melon, Signed	150.00
Ivory, Monkey, Crouching, Octopus, Inlaid Eyes, 1 1/8 In.	357.00
Ivory, Mouse & Peanut, Kogetsu, 2 1/4 In.	330.00
Ivory, Okame With Tengu Mask, 19th Century	2400.00
Ivory, Ox & Oxherd, Inlaid Eyes, Tomotada, 2 1/4 In.	412.00
Ivory, Pierced Landscape & Chrysanthemum, Byusa, 1 3/8 In.	550.00
Ivory, Revolving Face Changes From Happy To Sad, Signed, 2 1/4 In.	192.00
Ivory, Seated Dog Resting On Crab, Signed, 1 3/4 In.	195.00
Ivory, Seated Goat, Late 19th Century	3200.00
Ivory, Seated Priest With Fan, Signed	150.00
Ivory, Shishi, 19th Century	1200.00
Ivory, Standing Sumo Wrestler, Signed, 1 1/2 In.	220.00
Ivory, Turtle On Lily Pad, Signed	45.00
Wood, Grazing Horse, 19th Century	3500.00
Wood, Monkey & Young, Gyokuko, 19th Century	3500.00
Wood, Mushroom, Hidemasa, 1 1/2 x 1 1/2 In.	550.00
Wood, Pierced Landscape, Ryusa, 1 3/8 In.	440.00
Wood, Skull, Skeleton Draped Over Top, 1 7/16 In.	275.00
Wood, Snake & Turtle, Inlaid Eyes, 2 In.	1100.00
Wood, Water Buffalo, Inlaid Eyes, 2 3/4 In.	770.00

NEW HALL Porcelain Manufactory was started at Newhall, Shelton, Staffordshire, England, in 1782. Simple decorated wares were made. Between 1810 and 1825, the factory made a glassy bone porcelain sometimes marked with the factory name. Do not confuse New Hall porcelain with the pieces made by the New Hall Pottery Company, Ltd., a twentieth–century firm.

Cup & Saucer, Figures, Flowers, Orange	100.00
Teapot, Lion Finial, Floral Design, 5 3/4 In.	275.00

NEW MARTINSVILLE Glass Manufacturing Company was established in 1901 in New Martinsville, West Virginia. It was bought and renamed the Viking Glass Company in 1944 and is still producing fine glasswares.

Ashtray, Swan, Cobalt Blue, 1930s	47.00
Ashtray, Swan, Cobalt Neck, Clear Body, 1930	47.00
Berry Set, Carnation, Clear, 5 5–In. Bowls, 6 Piece	95.00
Bookends, Starfish, Frosted & Clear	75.00
Bowl, Meadow Wreath, 5 1/2 In.	8.00
Bowl, Meadow Wreath, Footed, 11 In.	20.00
Bowl, Ruffled, Peachblow, 10 3/4 In.	70.00
Bowl, Sunburst, Peachblow, Ribbed Body, Ruffled, 5 In.	95.00
Butter, Cut Cover, Clear	175.00
Decanter, Moondrop, Cobalt Blue	45.00
Figurine, Mama Bear	165.00
Figurine, Old Papa Bear	225.00
Figurine, Rooster, Hen & 5 Chicks	150.00
Figurine, Wolfhound, Pair	95.00
Sugar, Cover, Meadow Wreath	7.00
Swan, Red Bowl, Clear Neck, 11 In.	45.00
Toothpick, Studio	45.00

Wine, Moondrops, Red, 4 In. 12.00

NEWCOMB Pottery was founded by Ellsworth and William Woodward at
Sophie Newcomb College, New Orleans, Louisiana, in 1895. The work
continued through the 1940s. Pieces of this art pottery are marked with
the printed letters *NC* and often have the incised initials of the artist as
well. Most pieces have a matte glaze and incised decoration.

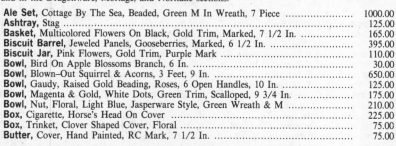

Ink Pot, Ribbed Sides, Jonathan Hunt, c.1931, 2 In. 453.00
Pitcher, High Glaze, White Against Natural & Black Ground 4750.00
Plaque, Oak Trees, Spanish Moss, A. F. Simpson, Frame, 5 1/4 x 8 In. 3850.00
Plate, Moonlight Swamp Landscape, S. Irvine, 1900, 8 1/4 In. 2200.00
Vase, 3 V–Shaped Panels, Corinne Chalaron, 1928, 7 1/2 In. 825.00
Vase, Airbrushed Yellow, White & Aqua, 3 1/2 In. 325.00
Vase, Band Of Flowers, Sadie Irvine, J. Meyer Potter, 3 3/4 In. 467.50
Vase, Band Of Oak Leaves At Shoulder, c.1912, 6 In. 1570.00
Vase, Burgundy, Gray With Blue, Signed LN, c.1901, 3 1/4 In. 675.00
Vase, Corseted, Banded Design Of Bats, Crescent Moons, 10 In. 4000.00
Vase, Cover, Pink Floral, Blue Ground, Flattened Bulbous, 5 x 6 In. 4125.00
Vase, Cypress Trees, Moonlight Landscape, A. F. Simpson, 13 3/4 In. 4125.00
Vase, Double Gourd, Joseph Meyer, Marked, c.1925, 4 1/2 In. 423.00
Vase, Floral Around Shoulder, Blue Ground, S. Irvine, 4 x 8 In. 1100.00
Vase, Incised Purple Grapes, Ivory Ground, S. B. Levy, 8 In. 4000.00
Vase, Landscape, Trees & Spanish Moss, Anna Simpson, 7 In. 5750.00
Vase, Moonlit Landscape, Kenneth Smith, 8 1/2 In. 1430.00
Vase, Narcissus, Simpson, 1920, 9 In. 700.00
Vase, Narcissus, White Flowers, Blue Ground, c.1915, 12 In. 3510.00
Vase, Red & Cream Flowers, Medium Blue Ground, S. Irvine, 9 In. 935.00
Vase, Sculpted Oak Trees, Spanish Moss, Kenneth Smith, 1932, 5 In. 1210.00
Vase, Seed Pods, Adele Ida Duggan, c.1902, 11 1/4 In. 2860.00

NILOAK Pottery (Kaolin spelled backward) was made at the Hyten
Brothers Pottery in Benton, Arkansas, between 1909 and 1946. Although
the factory did make cast and molded wares, collectors are most interested
in the marbelized art pottery line made of colored swirls of clay. It was
called *Mission Ware*.

Candlestick, Marbelized, 3 1/2 In. 175.00
Creamer, Green, 3 1/2 In. 45.00
Cup & Saucer, Impressed Floral, 6 Piece 48.00
Jug, Marbelized, Handle, 5 1/2 In. 750.00
Pitcher, Light Pink, Glazed, 5 In. 75.00
Planter, Squirrel 25.00
Vase, Bud, Marbelized, 7 1/2 In. 85.00
Vase, Marbelized, 4 x 6 In. 145.00
Vase, Marbelized, Brown, Green, Blue, Cream, Wide Neck, 3 7/8 In. 65.00

NIPPON porcelain was made in Japan from 1891 to 1921. *Nippon* is the
Japanese word for *Japan*. A few firms continued to use the word *Nippon*
on ceramics after 1921 as a part of the company name more than as an
identification of the country of origin. More pieces marked Nippon will be
found in the Dragonware, Moriage, and Noritake sections.

Ale Set, Cottage By The Sea, Beaded, Green M In Wreath, 7 Piece 1000.00
Ashtray, Stag 125.00
Basket, Multicolored Flowers On Black, Gold Trim, Marked, 7 1/2 In. 165.00
Biscuit Barrel, Jeweled Panels, Gooseberries, Marked, 6 1/2 In. 395.00
Biscuit Jar, Pink Flowers, Gold Trim, Purple Mark 110.00
Bowl, Bird On Apple Blossoms Branch, 6 In. 30.00
Bowl, Blown–Out Squirrel & Acorns, 3 Feet, 9 In. 650.00
Bowl, Gaudy, Raised Gold Beading, Roses, 6 Open Handles, 10 In. 125.00
Bowl, Magenta & Gold, White Dots, Green Trim, Scalloped, 9 3/4 In. 175.00
Bowl, Nut, Floral, Light Blue, Jasperware Style, Green Wreath & M 210.00
Box, Cigarette, Horse's Head On Cover 225.00
Box, Trinket, Clover Shaped Cover, Floral 75.00
Butter, Cover, Hand Painted, RC Mark, 7 1/2 In. 75.00

Candlestick, Bisque Scene, Beaded, Triangular Shape	50.00
Celery Dish, Pink & Blue Floral	39.00
Charger, Hand Painted, Bamboo Stand, 12 In.	115.00
Chocolate Set, Black Silhouette, 7 Piece	375.00
Chocolate Set, Flowers, Gold On White Ground, 5 Cups & Saucers	335.00
Chocolate Set, Roses, Cobalt Blue, 7 Piece	275.00
Cider Set, Raspberry & Florals, Te–Oh Mark, 7 Piece	200.00
Compote, Cobalt, Gold Rim, 9 In.	45.00
Condiment Server, Flowers, Gold Trim, Hand Painted	15.00
Cookie Jar, Gold Design, Footed, Green Mark	175.00
Cookie Jar, Roses, Gilt, Maple Leaf Mark, 7 1/2 In.	450.00
Cracker Jar, Leaves & Flowers	95.00
Cracker Jar, Pink Flowers On Gold & White, Gold Beading	350.00
Creamer, Blown–Out Child's Face	95.00
Demitasse Set, Flowers, 15 Piece	225.00
Dinner Set, Portland, Service For 8, Marked, 70 Piece	1100.00
Dish, Horsehead Design, Oblong, 6 1/4 x 3 1/4 In.	195.00
Dish, Pink Roses, 3 Sides, Green & Gold Trim, Maple Leaf	69.00
Dresser Set, Floral, Gold, 3 Piece	150.00
Ewer, Cobalt Blue Flowers, Gold, 7 1/2 In.	65.00
Ewer, Flying Dragons, 11 In.	250.00
Ewer, Red & Yellow Roses, Gold Beading, Cobalt Blue, 21 In.	795.00
Fernery, Horse, Men & Women Riders	200.00
Fernery, Teal, Pink Band, Floral	145.00
Flask, Talcum Powder	165.00
Hair Receiver, Greek Key & Roses Panels, 4 Gilded Legs	60.00
Hair Receiver, Roses, Gold Trim, Green Mark	48.00
Hatpin Holder, River, Sampan Scene, Gold Scrolls, Marked	70.00
Hatpin Holder, Violets, Gold Trim	70.00
Humidor, 5 Dogs, Blown Out	750.00
Humidor, Horses & Dogs Scene	625.00
Humidor, Molded Lions, Marked, 7 1/4 In.	750.00
Humidor, Molded Relief Arab On Camel, 7 1/2 In.	750.00
Humidor, Nile Scene, Moriage Trees	435.00
Humidor, Owl, 6 Sides, Footed	220.00
Humidor, Stag & Dogs, Blown Out, Green Mark	675.00
Humidor, Swan, Gray, Small	175.00
Humidor, White Horse, English Rider, Red Coat, Dogs	450.00
Inkwell, Farm Scene, Woman Milking Cow	195.00
Jam Jar, Cover, Underplate, Design, 3 Piece	75.00
Jar, Potpourri, Bluebirds, 2 Covers	95.00
Jug, Whiskey, Dragons & Jewels, Stopper, Signed	295.00
Jug, Whiskey, Scenic, Pagoda, Beaded Top & Base	150.00
Lamp, Pink Roses, Raised Gold, Brass Base, 16 1/2 In.	225.00
Lemonade Set, Art Deco, Grapes, Apple Blossom Mark, 5 Piece	150.00
Lemonade Set, Grape Design, 5 Piece	125.00
Matchbox Holder, Fatima Turkish Cigarettes, Porcelain	28.00
Matchbox Holder, Horsehead	150.00
Matchbox Holder, Indian	150.00
Mug, Clipper Ship Scene	150.00
Mustard Pot, Cover, Spoon, 3 Piece	45.00
Napkin Ring, Cottage Scene	60.00
Nut Set, Floral, Footed, 6 Piece	75.00
Perfume Bottle, Red & Gold	95.00
Pitcher, Brown & Black Geometric Design, Green M, 4 1/2 In.	95.00
Pitcher, Egyptian, Beaded, 3 In.	130.00
Pitcher, Floral, Cobalt Blue	575.00
Pitcher, Milk, Floral, Gold Bead Trim, Maple Leaf	150.00
Plaque, Arab On Camel, Marked, 10 1/2 In.	750.00
Plaque, Blown–Out Face	625.00
Plaque, Elk, 11 In.	700.00
Plaque, Indian, Standing, Dead Bird & Bow, Marked, 10 1/2 In.	695.00
Plaque, Lions, Marked, 10 1/2 In.	650.00

Plaque, Palm Trees & Boat Scene, Beaded Rim, 10 1/4 In. 75.00
Plaque, River & Mountain Scene, Gold Beaded, Signed, 10 In. Diam. 235.00
Plaque, Stag In Woods, Blown Out, 10 1/2 In. 675.00
Plate, Cobalt Scenic, 10 In. 250.00
Plate, Peacock, Flowers, Hand Painted, Deep Colors, Artist, 9 1/2 In. 185.00
Plate, Sampan, 7 In. 75.00
Powder Box, Oriental Rural Scene, Beaded Base & Lid, 7 x 4 In. 225.00
Powder Box, Piano Shape, Florals Outlined With Gold, Octagonal 67.00
Smoking Set, Bisque, Tray, Humidor, Ashtrays, Matchbox, Maple Leaf 225.00
Smoking Set, Sailboats, 3 Piece .... 145.00 To 150.00
Spooner, Flowers, Gold, Laydown 95.00
Stein, Pond Scene, 1 Liter 650.00
Sugar & Creamer, Azalea, 2 1/2 In. 55.00
Sugar & Creamer, Coralene, Yellow, Green 225.00
Sugar & Creamer, Fuchsias, Gold Beading 44.00
Sugar Shaker, Butterfly Design 100.00
Sugar Shaker, Turquoise Beading, Gold 145.00
Sugar, Cover, Hand Painted Floral Panels, Moriage, 3 Feet 95.00
Tea Set, 2 Rabbits On Sled, Child's, 11 Piece 265.00
Tea Set, Cobalt Blue, Gold, 15 Piece 650.00
Tea Strainer, Floral & Gold 195.00
Tea Strainer, Plain 45.00
Tea Strainer, Undercup, Scene Of Lake, Palm Trees, Gold Tracery 90.00
Teapot, Swans Over Marsh, Signed 65.00
Tray, Floral, Gold Trim, Round, 6 In. 15.00
Urn, Cover, Red Floral Medallion, 14 1/2 In. 495.00
Vase, Basket, Floral, 9 1/2 In. 295.00
Vase, Black With Flowers & Birds, 6 In. 75.00
Vase, Bottle, Peony, Butterfly, 2 Handles, Blue, Jasperware, 8 In. 525.00
Vase, Canoe, Indian, 12 1/2 In. 325.00
Vase, Chrysanthemum & Roses, 7 1/2 In. 145.00
Vase, Cobalt, Ostrich, 9 In. 400.00
Vase, Coralene, 2 Cobalt Urn Shape Handles, Light Green, Gold, 9 In. 185.00
Vase, Coralene, Cobalt Blue, Gold, 9 In. 425.00
Vase, Cover, Blue & Red Poppies, Royal Nishiki, 13 1/2 In. 350.00
Vase, Floral Design, 6-Sided, Handles, 9 In. 250.00
Vase, Floral, Maple Leaf Mark, 7 1/2 In. 150.00
Vase, Hand Painted Roses, Pedestal, Gold Trim, Beading, Signed, 9 In. 398.00
Vase, Lake Scene, Beaded, 8 3/4 In. 210.00
Vase, Lake Scene, Gold Handles, 12 1/2 In. 150.00
Vase, Lake, Stream, Gold Tree Scene, Gold Trimmed Handles, 14 1/2 In. 450.00
Vase, Medallions Of Roses, Jeweled, Green, 10 1/2 In. 175.00
Vase, Mount Fuji Scene, 6 Sides, Beaded, Gold, 12 In. 320.00
Vase, Mountain Valley Scene, Pheasants, Handles, Signed, 12 1/2 In. 850.00
Vase, Orange & Gold Poppies, Gold & Green Trim, Marked, 10 In. 450.00
Vase, Outdoor Scene, 12 3/4 In., Pair 300.00
Vase, Pink Roses, Gold Handles, Blue Leaf, 8 In. 120.00
Vase, Poinsettia On Green, Gold Double Ring Handles, 12 In. 395.00
Vase, Scenic Tapestry, Bottle Shape, 8 1/2 In. 425.00
Vase, Swans In Flight, Handles, 10 In. 340.00
Vase, Tapestry, Castle Scene, Drilled For Lamp, Maple Leaf, 9 In. 385.00
Vase, Violets, Moriage Leaves, Handles, Marked, 5 1/2 In. 195.00
Vase, Windmill Water Scene, 2 Handles, 8 1/2 In. 35.00
Vase, Windmill, Lake Scene, Scalloped, Gold Beaded Lip, Signed, 10 In. 245.00
Vase, Woman's Portrait, 10 In. 335.00
Wall Pocket, Parrot, Blown Out 350.00

NODDERS, also called nodding figures or pagods, are porcelain figures
with heads and hands that are attached to wires. Any slight movement
causes the parts to move up and down. They were made in many countries
during the eighteenth, nineteenth, and twentieth centuries. A few Art Deco

designs are also known. Copies are being made. A more recent type of nodder is made of papier–mache or plastic. These often represent sports figures or comic characters.

Atlanta Falcons, Box, 1968	50.00
Bank, Black Boy, Bisque	40.00
Bank, Girl–On–Lounge, Rhinestone Eyes, Double, Pat.	55.00
Bank, Moonshiner Hillbilly, Rhinestone Eyes, Pair	45.00
Ben Casey	125.00
Bird, Wooden, Painted, Small	15.00
Buddha, Bisque	50.00
Canadian Mountie	35.00
Cat, Bisque	65.00
Cat, Black, Red Bow, Porcelain	85.00
Cat, Chalkware, Worn Paint, 6 3/4 In.	200.00
Cat, On Wheels	350.00
Charlie Brown & Lucy, Composition, 1950s, Pair	90.00
Clown, Plastic Head, Red Polka Dot, On Spring, Large	24.00
Comic Rabbit, Glasses, Papier–Mache, 10 In.	175.00
Dog, Brown Spotted, White, Glass Eyes, On Spring, Small	20.00
Donald Duck, Linemar	355.00
Donkey, Celluloid, Occupied Japan	30.00
Dr. Kildare	48.00 To 125.00
Ed Sullivan, Mouse, Sitting On House, 1950s	65.00
Elephant, Celluloid, Occupied Japan	25.00
Football Player, Kansas State, Papier–Mache, Box, 1968	25.00
Golfer	75.00
Hank Aaron, Brewer	40.00
Happy Hooligan, Donkey Cart, Cast Iron, Hubley, 1910, 6 1/2 In.	675.00
Humpty Dumpty, Papier–Mache	95.00
Kissers, Danny Kaye & Girl, Magnetic	95.00
Kissers, Eskimos	55.00 To 60.00
Kissers, Oriental	30.00
Kissers, Oriental, Bisque	20.00
Kissers, Rocking, Double Action	45.00
Lady On Couch, Fan & Legs Move	25.00
Little Black Sambo	40.00
Lord Plushbottom, Bisque, Germany	135.00
Man & Woman, Wooden, Papier–Mache, Mr. & Mrs. Humphreys, 5 1/2 & 7 In.	350.00
Man, Wearing Suit & Hat, Metal, Small	32.50
Muzzled Dog, Celluloid Upper, Leather Covered Lower, 5 1/4 In.	187.00
NFL Cheerleader	10.00
Oriental Man, Gold, Pastel, Bisque, 8 In.	125.00
Oriental Man, Seated, Saber In Hand, 6 In.	85.00
Oriental Woman, Holding Fan, 6 In.	85.00
Orioles, Gold Base	50.00
Pig Couple	40.00
Policeman	35.00
Pumpkin Man, Wooden Platform, German, 7 In.	265.00
Rabbit, Wearing Glasses, Papier–Mache, 10 In.	135.00
Road Runner–Type Bird, Long Neck, Clicker	28.00
Salt & Pepper, Chicken, Center Dip, Pat.	55.00
Santa Claus, Standing, Porcelain	75.00
Scotsman, Bisque, Japan, Prewar	66.00
Shriner, Metal Cigar, Papier–Mache, 7 In.	60.00 To 85.00
Skeleton, Bisque, Japan, Prewar	71.00
Turtle, Germany	15.00
Uncle Bim, Bisque, Germany	135.00
Uncle Walt, Bisque, Germany	135.00
Winnie Winkle, Bisque, Germany	135.00
Woman, Wearing Glasses, Seated, 6 In.	110.00
Worm	20.00

NORITAKE porcelain was made in Japan after 1904 by Nippon Toki Kaisha. The best-known Noritake pieces are marked with the M in a wreath for the Morimura Brothers, a New York City distributing company. This mark was used until 1941. Another famous Noritake china was made for the Larkin Soap Company from 1916 through the 1930s. This dinnerware, decorated with azaleas, was sold or given away as a premium. There may be some helpful price information in the Nippon category, since prices are comparable.

Ashtray, Figural, Cat, 3 x 4 1/2 In.	125.00
Ashtray, Playing Cards	40.00
Bonbon, Azalea	50.00
Bonbon, Azalea, 6 1/4 In.	35.00
Bowl, Cereal, Azalea, 6 In.	12.00
Bowl, Firenze, Oval, 6 In.	18.00
Bowl, Scenic, Cobalt Rim, Gold Trim, Jeweling, Green, 11 In.	65.00
Bowl, Shell, Tree In Meadow, 5 In.	95.00
Bowl, Vegetable, Castella, Oval	15.00
Bowl, Vegetable, Divided, Azalea, 9 1/2 In.	175.00
Bowl, Vegetable, Mirano, 9 1/2 In.	20.00
Butter Chip, Azalea	85.00
Butter Tub, Azalea	45.00
Butter, Mirano	5.00
Cake Plate, Woman, Long Skirt, Black Top, Smelling Rose, 10 1/2 In.	350.00
Candy Dish, Bird Tops Center Divider, 6 1/2 In.	45.00
Candy Jar, Cover, Azalea	400.00
Casserole, Cover, Azalea, Gold Finial	450.00
Celery, Azalea, 10 In.	300.00
Coffeepot, Azalea	425.00
Coffeepot, Azalea, Demitasse	450.00
Compote, Fruit, Panels Of Roses, Flowers, Footed Base, 7 x 10 In.	295.00
Cruet, Azalea	165.00 To 175.00
Cup & Saucer, Azalea	15.00
Cup & Saucer, Bouillon, Azalea	15.00 To 20.00
Cup & Saucer, White & Gold	15.00
Cup & Sucer, Rubigold	22.00
Doll, Dresser, Figural	350.00
Eggcup, Azalea	120.00
Gravy Boat, Attached Underplate, Azalea	65.00
Honey Pot, Lake Scene, Hives, Bees	45.00
Humidor, Pipe Finial	85.00
Jam Jar, Peach & Gold Design, Spoon	65.00
Jar, Tobacco, Lid, Bull Terrier's Head, With Pipe In Mouth	350.00
Mayonnaise Set, Blues, Scene, Bisque, 3 Piece	45.00
Mustard, Azalea	38.50
Napkin Ring, Figural, Man & Woman, Art Deco, Box, Pair	80.00
Place Setting, Alameda, 5 Piece	25.00
Plaque, 3 Dogs, Blown Out, No Trees, 10 1/2 In.	575.00
Plate, Azalea, 6 1/2 In.	7.00
Plate, Azalea, 7 1/2 In.	7.50
Plate, Christmas Bell, 1972, 10 In.	25.00
Plate, Dinner, Azalea, 10 In.	18.00
Plate, Gernand, 9 3/4 In.	10.00
Plate, Mother's Day, 1974, 10 In.	25.00
Plate, Rubigold, 9 3/4 In.	19.00
Plate, Valentine, 1974, 10 In.	15.00
Plate, White & Gold, 7 1/2 In.	10.00
Platter, Azalea, 10 1/4 In.	32.50
Platter, Azalea, 11 1/2 x 8 3/4 In.	50.00
Platter, Azalea, 11 3/4 In.	32.50
Platter, Azalea, 14 x 10 In.	70.00
Platter, Azalea, 16 In.	350.00
Platter, Castella, 13 3/4 In.	15.00

Platter, Turkey, Azalea, 16 In.	325.00
Relish, 4 Sections, Azalea	145.00
Relish, Azalea, 2 Sections	50.00
Relish, Howo Pattern	42.00
Salt & Pepper, Azalea, Individual	25.00
Salt & Pepper, Hen On Nest	40.00
Salt & Pepper, Tree In Meadow, Tall	75.00
Smoking Set, Match Holder, Cigarette Holder, Ashtray, Tray	300.00
Snack Set, Azalea	32.50
Soup, Dish, Azalea, 7 1/8 In.	15.00
Spoon Holder, Spoon, Azalea	65.00
Sugar & Creamer, Castella	18.00
Sugar & Creamer, Cover, Azalea	45.00
Sugar & Creamer, Rubigold	52.00
Sugar Shaker & Creamer, Azalea	135.00
Tea Set, Child's, 9 Piece	150.00
Tea Set, Windmill, 3 Piece	195.00
Teapot, Azalea, Gold Finial	450.00
Tile, Tea, Tree In Meadow	35.00
Tray, Sandwich, Roseara, 8 In.	35.00
Vase, 2 Bluebirds Among Apple Blossoms, Hand Painted, 10 In.	275.00
Vase, Floral Design, Phoenix Bird, Gold Handles, Marked, 11 1/2 In.	180.00
Vase, Horn Of Plenty, Blown-Out Flowers At Base, Luster, 7 In.	85.00
Wall Pocket, Bluebird & Peonies, Yellow	95.00

NORSE Pottery Company started in Edgerton, Wisconsin, in 1903. In 1904 the company moved to Rockford, Illinois. The company made a black pottery, which resembled early bronze relics of the Scandinavian countries. The firm went out of business in 1913.

Bowl, Black, Footed, 9 In.	122.00
Bowl, Rising Sun, Dragon Handles	125.00
Vase, Bud, 9 In.	80.00

NORTH DAKOTA SCHOOL OF MINES was established in 1892 at the University of North Dakota. A ceramic course was included and pieces were made from the clays found in the region. Students at the university made pieces from 1909 to 1949. Although very early pieces were marked *U.N.D.*, most pieces were stamped with the full name of the university.

Ashtray, Rebekah	50.00
Bowl, Grotesque Indian Bird, Ocher, 4 x 7 In.	880.00
Bowl, Sky Blue Glaze, Mattson, 7 In.	85.00
Bowl, Weeping Mushrooms, White & Blue, 8 In.	1850.00
Cookie Jar, Aunt Susan, Black, 1950	4800.00
Figurine, Coyote	150.00
Figurine, Pigeon, Nelson, 1945	90.00
Pitcher, Cable, Mattson	195.00
Pitcher, Floral, 6 In.	225.00
Pitcher, Green & Blue Bands, Flowers, 6 In.	100.00
Plate, Painted American Indian, 1933, 9 In.	225.00
Rose Bowl, Blue Glaze	70.00
Tile, Blue, 1934	35.00
Tray, Pin, Brown	25.00
Vase, Brown Silhouetted Trees, Orange, 9 In.	935.00
Vase, Carved, Brown Matte, Mattson, 3 In.	350.00
Vase, Gray, Mattson, 3 x 4 In.	120.00
Vase, Indian, Signed, 5 1/2 In.	395.00
Vase, King Huck, 8 In.	255.00
Vase, Matte Green, Black Rings, 5 1/2 In.	175.00
Vase, Mattson, 3 x 4 In.	110.00
Vase, Violet & Green, FLH & Huck, 1930, 7 In.	185.00
Vase, Wheat Design, Green, 6 In.	395.00
Vase, Wheat Design, Huck, 4 1/2 x 6 In.	450.00
Vase, Wood-Like, Curls, E. Robinson, 7 In.	286.00

NORTHWOOD Glass Company was founded by Harry Northwood, a glassmaker who worked for Hobbs, Brockunier and Company, La Belle Glass Company, and Buckeye Glass Company before founding his own firm. He opened one factory in Indiana, Pennsylvania, in 1896, and another in Wheeling, West Virginia, in 1902. Northwood closed when Mr. Northwood died in 1923. Many types of glass were made, including carnival, custard, goofus, and pressed. The underlined N mark was used on some pieces.

Berry Set, Green, Gold Trim, 12 Piece	325.00
Berry Set, Jeweled Heart, Clear, 5 Piece	135.00
Beverage Set, Leaf Mold, Vaseline Spatter, Pitcher 8 In., 7 Piece	495.00
Bonbon, Footed, Green & Light Green	50.00
Bowl, Fluted Scroll, Blue Opalescent, 1900, 7 In.	53.00
Bowl, Folded Insides, Stretch Finish, Translucent, Indigo, 6 In.	40.00
Bowl, Lattice Medallion, Green Opalescent, 3 Footed, 8 3/4 In.	70.00
Bowl, Wild Roselight Green, Footed	85.00
Butter, Cover, Intaglio, Green, Gold Trim	58.00
Candleholder, Blue, 1924	59.00
Castor, Pickle, Apple Blossom Swirl	300.00
Castor, Pickle, Pink & White Spatter Insert, Mica Flakes	345.00
Celery Vase, Ribbed Pillar, Pink & White Spatter	85.00
Creamer, Fluted Scrolls, Vaseline	65.00
Creamer, Intaglio, Green, Gold Trim	30.00
Creamer, Memphis, Green, Gold Trim	35.00
Dish, Intaglio, Blue, Pedestal, 4 3/8 In.	29.00
Dish, Poppy, Marigold, Ruffled, 7 In.	95.00
Pitcher, Water, Pink & White Spatter, Silver Flakes, Clear Handle	375.00
Rose Bowl, Pull-Up Mauve Feathers, Crimped, Marked, 4 1/2 In.	895.00
Spoon Holder, Singing Birds, Painted Blue Handle	60.00
Spooner, Aurora, Pink	70.00
Spooner, Jeweled Heart, White, 1910	45.00
Sugar Shaker, Leaf Umbrella, Clear, Satin	295.00
Table Set, Belladonna, Blue, 4 Piece	285.00 To 295.00
Table Set, Blue, Gold & Enamel, 4 Piece	325.00
Table Set, Drapery, Blue, 4 Piece	390.00
Table Set, Flower & Bud, 4 Piece	450.00
Table Set, Regal, 4 Piece	285.00
Toothpick, Flute	40.00
Tumbler, Dandelion, Marigold	50.00
Tumbler, Maiden Blush	21.00
Vase, Drop, 8 1/2 In.	50.00
Vase, Feather Pattern, Yellow & Brown, Scalloped Top, 4 1/4 In.	695.00
Vase, Ruffled, Enameled Bugs & Flowers, White Lining, 10 1/2 In.	650.00
Vase, Tulip, Iridescent, c.1920, 7 1/2 In.	85.00
Water Set, Acorn Burrs, Pitcher & 3 Tumblers	600.00
Water Set, Cherry & Plum, Crystal, Gold Trim, 6 Piece	275.00
Water Set, Cherry Thumbprint, 7 Piece	225.00
Water Set, Golden Rose, Green, Gold Trim, 7 Piece	210.00
Water Set, Intaglio, Green, Gold Trim, 4 Piece	300.00

NU-ART was a trademark registered by the Imperial Glass Company of Bellaire, Ohio, about 1920.

Ashtray, Scotties, Glass Insert	75.00
Lamp, Reclining Nude, Amber Crackle Globe	250.00
Shade, Electric, Iridescent	85.00
Shade, Gas, Iridescent	125.00
Shade, Panel Design, Orange, Signed, 5 1/2 In., 7 Piece	110.00

NUTCRACKERS of many types have been used through the centuries. At first the nutcracker was probably strong teeth or a hammer. But by the nineteenth century, many elaborate and ingenious types were made. Levers, screws, and hammer adaptations were the most popular. Because nutcrackers are still useful, they are still being made, some in the old styles.

Alligator, Brass	20.00
Alligator, Cast Iron	100.00
Deer's Head, Glass Eyes, Black Forest, Germany	185.00
Dog, Brass	110.00 To 125.00
Dog, Cast Iron, Black	45.00
Dog, Counter Top, Althoff, Iron	55.00 To 95.00
Eagle, Brass, 5 1/2 In.	16.00 To 23.00
Eagle, Cast Iron, Counter Top	12.00
Elephant, Red, Cast Iron	125.00
Farmer, Carved Wood	85.00
German Grenadier, Fur Hair, 20 In.	25.00
Perfection, Cast Iron, 1914	25.00
Rooster, Head, Brass	20.00
Squirrel, Cast Iron	30.00 To 50.00
Squirrel, Upright, Cast Iron	25.00
St. Bernard, Bronze	75.00

NYMPHENBURG, see Royal Nymphenburg

OCCUPIED JAPAN was printed on pottery, porcelain, toys, and other goods made during the American occupation of Japan after World War II, from 1945 to 1952. Collectors now search for these pieces. The items were made for export.

Baby Set, Baby, Tub & Chamber Pot, Bisque, China, Box, 3 Piece	30.50
Basket, Lacquerware, Murani	40.00
Basket, Paper Sticker, 8 x 6 x 5 In.	13.00
Bottle, Drunk Man On 19th Hole, 3 In.	65.00
Bottle, Golfer–19th Hole, Blackberry Liqueur, 3 5/8 In.	20.00
Bowl, Cookrite, Fruit Pattern, 10 In.	25.00
Box, Cigarette, Rose Design, 2 Ashtrays, 3 x 4 1/4 In.	22.50
Candlestick, Mexican Woman, Bowl On Head, Bisque, 4 x 5 In.	32.00
Centerpiece, Coach Driver, 2 Horses, Gold Reins, 7 x 6 In.	150.00
Centerpiece, Woman With Flowers, In Carriage, Groom, 9 In.	250.00
Creamer, Cow, Porcelain	35.00
Cup & Saucer, Violets, Demitasse, 8 Piece	80.00
Cup & Saucer, White, Orange, Black, Red & Gold, Ironstone	20.00
Cup, Saki, Orange Interior With Gold Crane, 2 3/8 x 1 In.	10.00
Dinner Set, Stratford, Serving Pieces, 12 Settings, 93 Piece	495.00
Dish, Blue & Red Vines, Scalloped, Hokutosha, 4 1/2 x 3 In.	15.00
Doll, Baby, Holding A Bottle, Jointed, Celluloid, 8 In.	55.00
Figurine, 2 Cherubs, On Base, Bisque, 4 x 5 In.	48.00
Figurine, Accordion Player, Black Mark, 4 1/4 In.	10.00
Figurine, Accordion Player, Red Mark, 5 In.	12.00
Figurine, Angel, With Horn, 2 1/2 In.	6.00
Figurine, Balloon Lady, 6 In.	20.00
Figurine, Balloon Man, 6 In.	20.00
Figurine, Black Musician, 5 1/2 In.	25.00
Figurine, Boy & Girl Dancing, Bisque, 6 In., Pair	65.00
Figurine, Boy With Ice Cream Cone, Red Mark, 4 1/2 In.	12.00
Figurine, Boy, On Bench, 2 1/2 In.	7.00
Figurine, Boy, Playing Violin, 4 1/2 In.	7.00
Figurine, Boys, With Drum, Hummel Type, 6 In.	50.00
Figurine, Cavalier, White & Gold, 5 1/4 In.	8.00
Figurine, Cherub, Holding Bowl, Bisque, 6 In.	48.00
Figurine, Cherub, Mandolin, Bisque, Andrea, 6 3/8 In.	40.00
Figurine, Cherubs, With Lute, Other With Book, 6 In.	75.00
Figurine, Child, Baby Rabbits, Squirrel, Bird, Black Mark	125.00
Figurine, Children, With Sailboat, 5 3/8 In.	50.00
Figurine, Clown With Fiddle, 4 1/4 In.	10.00

Figurine, Clown, Sitting, UGACO, 5 1/2 In.	48.00
Figurine, Colonial Couple, 5 1/4 In.	22.00
Figurine, Colonial Couple, Mirrored, 5 In., Pair	30.00
Figurine, Colonial Man & Woman, 4 In., Pair	15.00
Figurine, Colonial Man, 3 1/2 In.	8.00
Figurine, Colonial Man, Gold Trim	20.00
Figurine, Colonial Man, Holding Bouquet, Bisque, 7 3/8 In.	22.50
Figurine, Colonial Man, Orion China, 10 In.	55.00
Figurine, Colonial Man, Pastels, Bisque, 8 1/4 In.	40.00
Figurine, Colonial Man, Sitting On Chair, 2 1/2 In.	4.00
Figurine, Colonial Woman	13.00
Figurine, Colonial Woman, Holding Umbrella, 9 1/4 In.	55.00
Figurine, Deer, Lying Down, Black Mark, 3 In.	8.00
Figurine, Deer, Standing, Black Mark, 4 In.	10.00
Figurine, Dickens Character, 6 In.	18.50
Figurine, Dog, With Shoe, Celluloid	130.00
Figurine, Donkey, Pulling Ashes, Lusterware	6.50
Figurine, Duck, Waddling, 4 In.	55.00
Figurine, Dutch Girl, Wide–Eyed, With Dog, 3 3/4 In.	5.00
Figurine, Elf Riding Ladybug	20.00
Figurine, Elf, Seated, Green Suit	15.00
Figurine, Flamingo, Sherry Fashions	45.00
Figurine, Football Player	7.00
Figurine, Girl Holding Cake, Dog, 4 1/2 In.	5.00
Figurine, Girl With Chicks, 4 1/4 In.	17.00
Figurine, Girl, Coat, Hands In Pockets, Red Mark, 3 1/4 In.	6.00
Figurine, Girl, Delft Blue, With Tambourine	17.00
Figurine, Girl, Oriental, 3 In.	7.00
Figurine, Girl, Seated, Bisque, Dutch Type, Ucagco, 4 3/4 In.	40.00
Figurine, Girl, Seated, Holding Flower, Blue–Green, 3 In.	5.00
Figurine, Goose Girl, 5 3/8 In.	35.00
Figurine, Lady, Hands Over Ears, Bisque, Paulux, 9 1/4 In.	40.00
Figurine, Lady, Holding Hat, 5 1/2 In.	7.00
Figurine, Little Boy Blue, With Lambs, 4 1/2 In.	5.00
Figurine, Little Shopper, Boy & Girl, Going To Market, 4 In.	33.50
Figurine, Man & Woman, Upturned Hats, Bisque, 8 3/4 In., Pair	135.00
Figurine, Man, Full–Bodied, 3 In.	24.00
Figurine, Man, Guitar, Woman, Boned Bodice, Marked, 10 1/2 In.	375.00
Figurine, Man, With Flowers, Bisque, Andrea, 10 1/4 In.	75.00
Figurine, Mexican Woman, Pastels, Bisque, 7 In.	55.00
Figurine, Musical Colonial Couple, 8 x 8 1/2 x 4 In.	275.00
Figurine, Oriental Boy Drummer, 4 3/4 In.	10.00
Figurine, Oriental Girl, Flowered Skirt, Red Mark, 4 1/2 In.	14.00
Figurine, Oriental Man & Woman, Thin, 7 In., Pair	35.00
Figurine, Oriental Woman, 6 1/2 In.	12.50
Figurine, Oriental Woman, With Fan, Orion, 12 In.	32.00
Figurine, Religious Oriental, 6 In., Pair	35.00
Figurine, Shepherd & Shepherdess, Red Mark, 12 In., Pair	150.00
Figurine, Shepherd & Woman With Lamb, Porcelain	80.00
Figurine, Thai Fan Dancer, 6 In., Pair	35.00
Figurine, Waiting For Rain, Mirrored Couple, 6 In., Pair	40.00
Figurine, Windy Lady, Art Deco, Bisque, 7 In.	27.00
Figurine, Woman Seated With Boy, Maruyama Mark, 7 In.	175.00
Juicer, Clown Shape, Ceramic	25.00
Kazoo, Metal, 2 1/4 In.	7.50
Lamp, Colonial Couple	45.00
Pin, Double–Headed Scotty Dog, 1 3/4 x 1 1/4 In.	15.00
Pin, Scotty Dog Head, 2 x 1 1/2 In.	12.50
Pitcher, Hand Painted Raised Flower, Miniature	10.00
Pitcher, Milk, Beaded Tulip	30.00
Planter, Bird Design, 3 In.	5.00
Planter, Colonial Couple, With Rabbits, Bisque, 7 In.	140.00
Planter, Cupids & Conch Shell Inside Dragon, 9 In.	175.00

Planter, Elephant, 3 In.	6.00
Planter, Elf, 4 x 5 In.	12.50
Planter, Elf, Walking, Orange Suit, 4 1/4 x 3 In.	15.00
Planter, Flamingo, Burger, 7 x 3 In.	29.00
Planter, Seated Boy & Girl, 3 1/2 In.	8.00
Plaque, Chase, Pair	75.00
Plaque, Colonial Figure Leaning Out Window, Bisque, Chase	40.00
Plaque, Colonial Figure On Swing, Bisque, Oval, Pair	35.00
Plaque, Colonial Man & Woman, Relief, SGK, 6 In., Pair	55.00
Plaque, Colonial Woman & Man, Chase Mark, Pair	55.00
Plaque, Couple With Rabbits, Bisque, 5 1/2 x 7 1/2 In.	200.00
Plaque, Dutch Boy & Girl, Marked, Pair	25.00
Plate, Love Birds, Painted, 15 In.	95.00
Plate, Yellow Band, 2 Women & Angel Decal, 8 In.	35.00
Salt & Pepper, Mammy & Chef, 3 1/2 In.	24.00
Salt & Pepper, Panda Bears	15.00 To 25.00
Salt & Pepper, Pink Pig	12.00
Sewing Kit, 6 Spools Of Thread, Thimble, Red Top	10.00
Silent Butler, Bamboo, Lacquerware, Murani, 10 1/2 In.	25.00
Sugar & Creamer, Cover, Morkin Ware	35.00
Sugar, Pear, 3 3/4 In.	8.00
Sugar, Windmill	25.00
Tea Set, Flowers, Wheat Border, Norumi China, 15 Piece	200.00
Tea Set, Flowers, Wheat Border, Yellow, Hira China, 12 Piece	250.00
Tea Set, Hand Painted Spring Violets, Gold Trim, 3 Piece	95.00
Teapot, Windmill	15.00
Teapot, Winking Toby	95.00
Toby Jug, Colonial Woman, Full Figure, 2 3/4 In.	10.00
Toby Jug, Man, Full–Figured, Green Pants, Red Coat, 2 3/4 In.	15.00
Toby Jug, Woman, Full–Figured, Blue Ruffled Skirt, 2 3/4 In.	15.00
Toby Mug, Bearded Man, Marked, 4 In.	30.00
Toothpick, Donkey	10.00
Toothpick, Seated Elf, Blue	17.50
Vase, Art Deco Figure, Lady With Snake Front, Bisque, 6 In.	25.00
Vase, Flower Design, 2 3/4 In.	5.00
Vase, Lady, Bisque, 6 In.	15.00
Wall Pocket, Flowers In Basket	10.00
Wall Pocket, Fruit, Pair	25.00
Wall Pocket, Teapot, Painted Clock Face	25.00
Watering Can, Porcelain, Blue & White, Hokutosha, 3 x 2 In.	15.00

OHR pottery was made in Biloxi, Mississippi, from 1883 to 1918 by George E. Ohr, a true eccentric. The pottery was made of very thin clay that was twisted, folded, and dented into odd, graceful shapes. Some pieces were lifelike models of hats, animal heads, or even a potato. Others were decorated with folded clay *snakes.* Reproductions and reworked pieces are appearing on the market. These have been reglazed, or snakes and other embellishments have been added.

Candlestick, Iridescent Black, Signed, 3 1/2 x 4 In.	375.00
Chamber Pot, Dripping Gun–Metal Gray, Green Glaze, Contents, 2 1/2 In.	330.00
Cornucopia, Red Marbelized Clay, Bisque–Fired, Script Signed, 4 1/2 In.	468.00
Mug, Blue, Glossy Glaze, Incised Name, 6 In.	3400.00
Mug, Puzzle, Brown Glaze, Waisted Body, D Form Handle, c.1891, 3 1/2 In.	725.00
Mug, Puzzle, Brown Glossy Glaze, Signed	775.00
Mug, Puzzle, Brown High Glaze, Pierced Form, Signed, 4 In.	660.00
Mug, Puzzle, Gun Metal & Brown Glaze, Rope Handle, 3 1/2 x 4 3/4 In.	550.00
Mug, Puzzle, Gunmetal, 4 In.	595.00
Mug, Puzzle, Mottled Brown Glaze, Signed	1100.00
Potato	1250.00
Teapot, Knob Cover, Scrolling Handle & Spout, Marked, c.1895, 6 7/8 In.	3650.00
Vase, Black Glazed Body, Flaring Bottom, Signed, c.1891, 3 3/4 In.	365.00
Vase, Charcoal, Doublestruck, Signed, 6 In.	1100.00
Vase, Crimped Rim, Glazed Cobalt Blue, c.1900, 7 1/2 In.	2000.00

Vase, Crimped Rim, Metallic Mottled Green Glaze, Marked, 5 1/4 In. 1200.00
Vase, Deep Cobalt, Overlapped, Spotted Mauve, Fluted, Footed, 11 1/8 In. 5775.00
Vase, Folded Rim, Blue Body, Marked, c.1890, 3 1/2 In. 975.00
Vase, Green Crystalline Glaze, Impressed G. E. Ohr, 5 In. 885.00
Vase, Green Mottled High Glaze, Marked, c.1891, 3 1/4 In. 365.00
Vase, Honey Color Pigeon Feather Glaze, Bottle Shape, 7 In. 440.00
Vase, Indented Ovals, Crimped Rim, Olive Glaze, Marked, 6 1/2 In. 3300.00
Vase, Terra-Cotta, Crimped Rim, Marked 495.00
Vessel, Bisque-Fired, Squat, Spherical, Ovoid Neck, 5 x 4 1/2 In. 578.00

OLD IVORY china was made by Hermann Ohme in Silesia, Germany, at
the end of the nineteenth century. The ivory-colored dishes have flowers, **OLD IVORY**
fruit, or acorns as decoration and are often marked with a crown and the
word *Silesia.* Some pieces are also marked with the words *Old Ivory.* The **84**
pattern numbers appear on the base of each piece.

Berry Set, No. 75, Silesia, 4 Piece 135.00
Berry Set, No. 113, Silesia, 6 Piece 250.00
Biscuit Jar, No. 10 .... 425.00
Bowl, No. 11, Roses, Gold Trim, Silesia, 10 In. 85.00
Bowl, No. 16, 6 1/2 In. 25.00
Bowl, No. 16, 9 1/2 In. 135.00
Bowl, No. 16, 10 In. 125.00
Bowl, No. 16, Oyster 215.00
Bowl, No. 28, Silesia, 4 1/2 In. 120.00
Bowl, No. 28, Silesia, 5 3/4 In. 112.00
Bowl, No. 84, Silesia, 9 1/2 In. .... 85.00 To 95.00
Bowl, Waste, No. 16, Silesia 275.00
Cake Plate, Clairon, 5 Saucers, 6 In. 150.00
Cake Plate, Clairon, Silesia 90.00
Cake Plate, No. 15 .... 135.00
Cake Plate, No. 16 .... 135.00
Cake Plate, No. 75, Silesia .... 135.00 To 140.00
Cake Plate, No. 84 .... 135.00
Cake Set, No. 16, 7 Piece 375.00
Cake Set, No. 84, Silesia, 7 Piece 250.00
Celery, No. 7, Silesia 125.00
Celery, No. 16, 11 1/2 In. .... 95.00 To 125.00
Celery, No. 200, 11 1/2 In. 100.00
Charger, No. 11, Silesia 250.00
Chocolate Pot, No. 16, 10 In. 245.00
Chocolate Pot, No. 84, Silesia 295.00
Chocolate Set, 13 Piece 325.00
Chocolate Set, No. 11, Silesia, 7 Piece 825.00
Chocolate Set, No. 84, Silesia, 13 Piece 750.00
Cracker Jar, No. 11 .... 375.00
Cracker Jar, No. 16, Silesia 350.00
Cracker Jar, No. 84, 6 1/2 In. 245.00
Cracker Jar, No. 200, Silesia 275.00
Creamer, No. 11 .... 100.00
Cup & Saucer, No. 33, Silesia .... 35.00 To 60.00
Cup & Saucer, No. 84, Silesia .... 55.00 To 60.00
Cup & Saucer, No. 200, Silesia 70.00
Dish, Pickle, No. 11, 8 1/2 In. 70.00
Muffineer, No. 11 .... 395.00
Mustard, No. 84, Silesia .... 265.00 To 275.00
Nappy, No. 16, Handle Inside Bowl 75.00
Pepper Shaker, No. 11 .... 35.00
Plate, Dinner, No. 84 .... 195.00
Plate, No. 16, 6 1/2 In. .... 25.00 To 30.00
Plate, No. 16, 7 1/2 In. 35.00
Plate, No. 28, 8 1/2 In. 60.00
Plate, No. 28, Silesia, 10 In. 155.00
Plate, No. 33, 7 1/2 In. 35.00

Plate, No. 84, Silesia, 9 1/2 In. .... 150.00 To 225.00
Plate, No. 200, 8 1/4 In. 55.00
Platter, No. 11, 12 In. 160.00
Relish, No. 84, Silesia 75.00
Salt & Pepper, No. 16 .... 120.00
Spooner, No. 200, 8 1/4 In. 85.00
Sugar, Cover, No. 28, Silesia 95.00
Sugar, No. 58, Gold Butterfly, Surrounded By Roses 35.00
Toothpick, No. 84 .... 275.00
Tray, No. 84, Scalloped Rim, Rectangular, 12 x 7 In. 165.00
Trivet, No. 84, Silesia 245.00
Vase, No. 7, 5 3/4 In. 45.00

OLD PARIS, see Paris

OLD SLEEPY EYE, see Sleepy Eye

ONION PATTERN, originally named *bulb pattern,* is a white ware decorated with cobalt blue or pink. Although it is commonly associated with Meissen, other companies made the pattern in the late nineteenth and the twentieth centuries. A rare type is called *red bud* because there are added red accents on the blue–and–white dishes.

Bowl, Center, Reticulated Basketweave, Vine Handles, Meissen 450.00
Bowl, Meissen, 19th Century, 8 7/8 In. 220.00
Bowl, Reticulated Basketweave, Floral, Meissen, 11 x 3 1/2 In. 150.00
Bowl, Reticulated Basketweave, Scalloped, E. Teichert, 8 3/8 In. 150.00
Box, Brass Feet, Square 200.00
Box, Scalloped, Meissen, 4 x 4 1/2 In. 300.00
Canister 55.00
Compote, Reticulated Basketweave, Floral, Stem, Meissen, 7 In. 275.00
Cruet 65.00
Dish, Fruit, Pierced Rim, Early Mark, 8 In. 75.00
Infant Feeder 37.50
Jar Set, Covers, Nutmeg, Pepper, Allspice & Ginger 80.00
Meat Tenderizer 115.00
Platter, Blue Feather Edge, Octagonal, 15 1/2 In. 75.00
Platter, Fish, Meissen, 23 x 11 In. 395.00
Platter, Oval, Gilt Border, Meissen, 20 3/8 In. 385.00
Rolling Pin, Wood Handles, Meissen 385.00
Salt, Hanging, Blue & White, Czechoslovakia 85.00
Spice Shaker, 7 Piece 55.00

OPALESCENT GLASS is translucent glass that has the tones of the opal gemstone. It originated in England in the 1870s and is often found in pressed glassware made in Victorian times. Opalescent glass was first made in America in 1897 at the Northwood glassworks in Indiana, Pennsylvania. Some dealers use the terms *opaline* and *opalescent* for any of these translucent wares. More opalescent pieces may be listed in Northwood, Pressed Glass, Spanish Lace, and other glass sections.

Banana Stand, Argonaut Shell, Blue 48.00
Basket, Applied Flowers, Vaseline Leaf, Ruffled Rim, 7 1/4 In. 145.00
Berry Bowl, Alaska, Blue 250.00
Berry Bowl, Ribbed Lattice, Cranberry, Master 245.00
Berry Bowl, Seaweed, Blue 45.00
Berry Bowl, Tokyo, Green, Master 65.00
Berry Set, Alaska, Blue, 7 Piece .... 325.00 To 355.00
Berry Set, Beatty Rib, White, 9 Piece 120.00
Berry Set, Diamond Spearhead, Vaseline, 5 Piece 250.00
Berry Set, Inverted Fan & Feather, White, 7 Piece 245.00
Berry Set, Palm Beach, Blue, 5 Piece 225.00
Berry Set, Ribbed Spiral, Blue, 5 Piece 350.00
Berry Set, Scroll With Acanthus, 13 Piece 195.00
Berry Set, Scroll With Acanthus, White, 7 Piece 95.00

Berry Set, Wild Bouquet, Blue, 6 Piece 345.00
Berry Set, Wreath & Shell, Vaseline, Bowl, 8 1/2 In., 7 Piece 225.00
Bottle, Barber, Drape, Corset Shape, Green 245.00
Bottle, Barber, Seaweed Tepee, White 195.00
Bottle, Barber, Seaweed, Flask Shape, White 185.00
Bowl, Abalone, Handles, Blue, Jefferson, 1903, 6 1/2 In. 39.00
Bowl, Argonaut Shell, Turned-Up Sides, Blue 65.00
Bowl, Blossoms & Palms, Green, 8 1/2 In. 35.00
Bowl, Daisy & Scroll, Ruffled, Pink, 9 In. 75.00
Bowl, Dolly Madison, Green, 9 1/4 In. 45.00
Bowl, Herringbone, Ruffled, Blue 80.00
Bowl, Iris With Meander, Green, 9 In. 48.00
Bowl, Jewel & Heart, Green, 10 In. 23.00
Bowl, Lattice, Crimped, 9 In. 85.00
Bowl, Leaf & Beads, Green, 8 In. 35.00
Bowl, Pearl Flowers, Footed, Blue, 9 In. 32.00
Bowl, Reverse Swirl, Ruffled Rim, Blue, 8 1/2 In. 48.00
Bowl, Ruffles & Rings, Green, Jefferson, 1905, 9 1/2 In. 48.00
Bowl, Vintage, Blue, 8 In. 65.00
Bowl, Water Lily With Cattails, Amethyst, Square, 8 1/2 In. 50.00
Bowl, Water Lily With Cattails, Amethyst, Turned Up, Square, 8 In 65.00
Bowl, Water Lily With Cattails, Flat, 9 1/4 In. 35.00
Bride's Bowl, Bull's-Eye, Cranberry, 9 In. 95.00
Bride's Bowl, Bull's-Eye, Ruffled, Cranberry, 9 1/2 In. 265.00
Bride's Bowl, Daisy & Fern, Blue 65.00
Butter, Cover, Argonaut Shell 275.00
Butter, Cover, Drapery, Blue 150.00
Butter, Cover, Everglades, Vaseline 100.00
Butter, Cover, Fan, Blue .... 300.00 To 400.00
Butter, Cover, Flora, Blue 295.00
Butter, Cover, Fluted Scrolls 200.00
Butter, Cover, Idyll, Blue 350.00
Butter, Cover, Intaglio, Gold Trim, Green 120.00
Butter, Cover, Iris With Meander, Blue 250.00
Butter, Cover, Jewel & Flower, Blue .... 175.00 To 225.00
Butter, Cover, Jewel & Flower, Canary, Gold Trim 160.00
Butter, Cover, Reverse Swirl, Vaseline 285.00
Butter, Cover, Sunburst On Shield, Blue 225.00
Celery Tray, Alaska, Blue 125.00
Celery, Alaska, Blue, Enameled 150.00
Celery, Beatty Swirl, Blue 115.00
Celery, Diamond Spearhead, Green 175.00
Chop Plate, 4 Flowers, Peach, 11 In. 525.00
Compote, Coin Spot, Peach, 6 1/2 In. 65.00
Compote, Jelly, Everglades, Blue, Gold Trim .... 75.00 To 85.00
Compote, Prince William, Scalloped, Blue, 5 1/4 x 5 5/8 In. 65.00
Compote, Sandwich, Dolphin Stem 750.00
Condiment Set, Reverse Swirl, Handled Holder, Cranberry, 4 Piece 325.00
Creamer, Alaska, Gold Trim At Top, Blue, 3 1/2 In. 75.00
Creamer, Alaska, Vaseline 60.00
Creamer, Alaska, White 58.00
Creamer, Beatty Rib, Blue 67.00
Creamer, Drapery, Blue 60.00
Creamer, Fluted Scrolls, Blue .... 40.00 To 58.00
Creamer, Fluted Scrolls, Vaseline .... 48.00 To 75.00
Creamer, Fluted Scrolls, White 50.00
Creamer, Intaglio, Blue 65.00
Creamer, Intaglio, Green, Gold Trim 50.00
Creamer, Jackson, Blue 60.00
Creamer, Jewel & Flower, Blue, Gold Trim 85.00
Creamer, Jewel & Flower, Green 38.00
Creamer, Paneled Holly, Green, Gold Trim 35.00
Creamer, Reverse Swirl, Blue 110.00

Creamer, Wild Bouquet, Blue 95.00
Creamer, Wild Bouquet, Green 95.00
Creamer, Wreath & Shell, Blue 130.00
Cruet, Bubble Lattice, Blue 195.00
Cruet, Daisy & Fern, Blue .... 140.00 To 165.00
Cruet, Everglades, Blue 450.00
Cruet, Everglades, Vaseline 425.00
Cruet, Fluted Scrolls, Blue .... 150.00 To 225.00
Cruet, Intaglio, Blue 150.00
Cruet, Jackson, Blue 120.00
Cruet, Jackson, Stopper, Blue 120.00
Cruet, Jeweled Heart, Green 395.00
Cruet, Reverse Swirl 110.00
Cruet, Stars & Stripes, Ruffled Lip 95.00
Cruet, Windows Swirl, Cranberry 335.00
Doughtnut Stand, William & Mary, Vaseline, 8 7/8 In. 110.00
Epergne, 3 Lily, Cranberry, Applied Spiral Clear Design, 22 In. 850.00
Epergne, Ruffled, Jack-In-The-Pulpit Center, Blue, 8 3/4 In. 125.00
Finger Bowl, Hobb's Optic Diamond, Cranberry 45.00
Finger Bowl, Monkey 165.00
Finger Bowl, Optic Almonds, Ruffled, Cranberry, 5 1/2 In. 110.00
Finger Bowl, Seaweed, Cranberry 110.00
Finger Bowl, Stripe, Cranberry 75.00
Lamp, Finger, Snowflake, Blue, Applied Handle, Square 385.00
Lamp, Hand, Inverted Thumbprint, White 365.00
Lamp, Hand, Snowflake, Flat, Green 495.00
Lamp, Oil, Windows, Cranberry, 10 In. 450.00
Lamp, Reverse Swirl, Cranberry, 7 1/2 In. 345.00
Lamp, Snowflake, Cranberry, 11 In. 350.00
Mug, Singing Birds, Blue 135.00
Mustard, Chrysanthemum, Cranberry, Base Swirl 160.00
Mustard, Idyll, White 150.00
Mustard, Reverse Swirl, Bulbous, Cranberry 225.00
Mustard, Reverse Swirl, Chrysanthemum Base, White 45.00
Pitcher, Alaska, Blue 250.00
Pitcher, Buttons & Braids, Blue 120.00
Pitcher, Cranberry, Diamond, Fluted 225.00
Pitcher, Cranberry, Fenton, Squatty, 5 In. 90.00
Pitcher, Daisy & Fern, Ball Shape, Cranberry 295.00
Pitcher, Fern, Cloverleaf Top, Blue 125.00
Pitcher, Flora, Vaseline 350.00
Pitcher, Fluted Scrolls, Blue 195.00
Pitcher, Hobnail, Cranberry, 10 In. 225.00
Pitcher, Idyll, Green 150.00
Pitcher, Intaglio, White 120.00
Pitcher, Milk, Daisy & Fern, Cranberry 125.00
Pitcher, Palm Beach, Vaseline 350.00
Pitcher, Palmette Leaves, Top Ribbed Band, Blue, 6 1/8 In. 55.00
Pitcher, Poinsettia, Blue 275.00
Pitcher, Scroll With Acanthus, Blue 300.00
Pitcher, Seaweed, Blue 225.00
Pitcher, Swag & Brackets, Green 125.00
Pitcher, Swastika, White 225.00
Pitcher, Swirl, Blue 110.00
Pitcher, Swirl, Bulbous, Cranberry 175.00
Pitcher, Swirl, Cranberry 190.00
Pitcher, Thumbprint, Cranberry, 5 In. 40.00
Pitcher, Thumbprint, Vaseline, 8 1/2 In. 125.00
Pitcher, Water, Blue 135.00
Pitcher, Water, Daffodils, Blue 175.00
Pitcher, Water, Fluted Scrolls, Vaseline 155.00
Pitcher, Water, Jackson 180.00
Plate, Palm Beach, Blue, 6 Piece 895.00

Relish, Tokyo, Green, 8 1/2 In. 30.00
Rose Bowl, Beaded Cable, Footed, Aqua, Northwood 315.00
Rose Bowl, Beaded Cable, Sides Up, Blue 45.00
Rose Bowl, Inverted Fan & Feather, Vaseline 95.00
Rose Bowl, Seaweed, Vaseline 145.00
Rose Bowl, Swirl, Vaseline 48.00
Rose Bowl, Wreath & Shell, Blue ..... 50.00 To 55.00
Salt & Pepper, Alaska, White 85.00
Salt & Pepper, Box In Box, Ruby Stain 45.00
Salt & Pepper, Intaglio, Blue 185.00
Salt & Pepper, Jewel & Flower, Blue, Gold Trim 155.00
Salt & Pepper, Periwinkle, Ruby 60.00
Salt & Pepper, Reverse Swirl, Vaseline 65.00
Salt & Pepper, Ribbed Lattice, Cranberry 185.00
Salt & Pepper, Wild Bouquet, Green 195.00
Salt, Bubble Lattice, Cranberry 135.00
Salt, Reverse Swirl, Cranberry 80.00
Saltshaker, Reverse Swirl, Blue 45.00
Saltshaker, Windows Swirl, Blue 45.00
Sauce, Shell, White 20.00
Saucer, Wreath & Shell, Vaseline 37.50
Spooner, Alaska, Blue, 3 1/2 In. 75.00
Spooner, Beaded Ovals & Holly, Blue 80.00
Spooner, Beatty Swirl, White 110.00
Spooner, Big Windows, Blue 65.00
Spooner, Buckeye Lattice, Cranberry 95.00
Spooner, Cabbage Leaf, Green 65.00
Spooner, Circled Scroll, Green 40.00
Spooner, Drapery, Blue 70.00
Spooner, Everglades, Vaseline, Gold Trim ..... 75.00 To 95.00
Spooner, Fern, Ruffled Trim, Blue 55.00
Spooner, Fluted Scrolls 65.00
Spooner, Fluted Scrolls, Blue 60.00
Spooner, Fluted Scrolls, Vaseline 45.00
Spooner, Intaglio, Blue 65.00
Spooner, Jewel & Flower, White 85.00
Spooner, Palm Beach, Vaseline 125.00
Spooner, Swag & Brackets, Vaseline 50.00
Spooner, Windows Swirl, Blue 55.00
Spooner, Wreath & Shell, Blue ..... 80.00 To 125.00
Spooner, Wreath & Shell, Vaseline, 3 1/2 x 4 1/2 In. 85.00
Spooner, Wreathed Cherry, Vaseline 75.00
Sugar & Creamer, Double Dahlia With Lens, Green 50.00
Sugar & Creamer, Hobnail, Blue 36.00
Sugar Shaker, Honeycomb, Blue 195.00
Sugar Shaker, Windows, Blue 165.00
Sugar, Alaska, White 85.00
Sugar, Cover, Alaska, Blue, 5 3/4 In. 135.00
Sugar, Cover, Chrysanthemum Base Swirl, White 110.00
Sugar, Cover, Daisy & Button, Blue 75.00
Sugar, Cover, Drapery, Blue 110.00
Sugar, Cover, Flora, White 67.50
Sugar, Cover, Fluted Scrolls, Blue 172.00
Sugar, Cover, Fluted Scrolls, Vaseline 110.00
Sugar, Cover, Hobnail & Paneled Thumbprint, Blue, 1890 ..... 85.00
Sugar, Cover, Petticoat, Vaseline, Gold Trim 125.00
Sugar, Cover, Sunburst On Shield, Blue Green 65.00
Sugar, Cover, Swag & Brackets, Vaseline 110.00
Sugar, Cover, Wreath & Shell, Vaseline, 4 x 8 In. 110.00
Sugar, Swirl, Amber Rim, Blue 150.00
Sugar, Wreath & Shell, Blue 55.00
Swan, Blue 42.00
Syrup, Coin Spot & Swirl, White 100.00

Syrup, Cranberry, Dot 295.00
Syrup, Swirl & Dot, White 58.00
Syrup, Swirl, Cranberry 290.00
Table Set, Alaska, Vaseline, 4 Piece 465.00
Table Set, Everglades, Gold Trim, 4 Piece .... 265.00 To 365.00
Table Set, Regal, 4 Piece 280.00
Table Set, Swag & Brackets, Green, 4 Piece 350.00
Table Set, Wreath & Shell, 1900, 4 Piece 400.00
Toothpick, Blue, Stripe, Wide, Straight Sided 165.00
Toothpick, Cranberry 225.00
Toothpick, Daisy & Fern, Blue 165.00
Toothpick, Diamond Spearhead, Cobalt Blue 100.00
Toothpick, Diamond Spearhead, Green 60.00
Toothpick, Diamond Spearhead, Scalloped, Vaseline, 2 1/2 In. 55.00
Toothpick, Diamond Spearhead, Vaseline .... 55.00 To 75.00
Toothpick, Florette, Blue 130.00
Toothpick, Iris With Meander, Blue, Gold Trim 115.00
Toothpick, Iris With Meander, White 30.00
Toothpick, Labelle, Vaseline 125.00
Toothpick, Reverse Swirl, Cranberry 245.00
Toothpick, Reverse Swirl, White 35.00
Toothpick, Ring Neck Stripe, Blue 165.00
Toothpick, Wild Bouquet, Blue 375.00
Toothpick, Windows 200.00
Toothpick, Zanzibar 95.00
Tray, Card, Fluted Scroll, Vaseline 42.50
Tumbler, Alaska, Vaseline 60.00
Tumbler, Buttons & Braids, Blue 30.00
Tumbler, Criss–Cross, White .... 50.00 To 75.00
Tumbler, Daffodils, Green 65.00
Tumbler, Everglades, Blue 95.00
Tumbler, Everglades, White 50.00
Tumbler, Fluted Scrolls, Blue 50.00
Tumbler, Hobnail–In–Square, Aetna 30.00
Tumbler, Jeweled Heart, Green 32.00
Tumbler, Jeweled Heart, Green, 3 1/4 In. 30.00
Tumbler, Poinsettia, Blue .... 45.00 To 70.00
Tumbler, Reverse Swirl, Cranberry 95.00
Tumbler, Seaweed, Blue .... 45.00 To 50.00
Tumbler, Snowflake, Blue 60.00
Tumbler, Stars & Stripes, Cranberry 68.00
Tumbler, Swag & Brackets, Blue 50.00
Tumbler, Swag & Brackets, Vaseline 60.00
Vase, Fern Design, Ruffled, Vaseline, 6 In. 65.00
Vase, Jack–In–The–Pulpit, Pink To Vaseline, 11 1/4 In. 135.00
Vase, Reverse Drape, Aqua, 12 In. 20.00
Vase, Scalloped, Leaf Feet, Melon Ribbed, England, Vaseline, 4 In. 55.00
Water Set, Alaska, Vaseline, 7 Piece 850.00
Water Set, Palm Beach, Vaseline, 6 Piece 600.00
Water Set, Poinsettia, Blue, 8 Piece 250.00
Water Set, Wreath & Wheel, Vaseline, 4 Piece 395.00

OPALINE, or opal glass, was made in white, green, and other colors. The glass had a matte surface and a lack of transparency. It was often gilded or painted. It was a popular mid–nineteenth–century European glassware.

Bowl, Enameled Portrait, Griffin's Head & Feet Bronze Stand 395.00
Cracker Jar .... 120.00 To 190.00
Dish, Footed, Gilt Decoration, 3 1/4 In. H. x 8 In. Dia. 132.00
Pitcher, Applied Clear Handle, Pink & White, 8 In. 100.00
Pitcher, White Flowers, Clear Handle, Lavender, 8 In. 150.00
Powder Jar 110.00
Rose Bowl, Under Plate With Ruffled Rim, Pink 125.00
Vase, Bird Amid Flowers & Fruit, Mills, Walker & Co., 10 1/2 In. 435.00

Vase, Indian, Earth Tones 35.00
Vase, Pink Cased, Enameled, 7 1/2 In. 125.00

OPERA GLASSES are needed because the stage is a long way from some
of the seats at a play or an opera. Mother-of-pearl was a popular
decoration.

Le Maire, Mother-of-Pearl Handle 265.00
Le Maire, Paris, Mother-of-Pearl Handle 75.00
Leather Case 65.00
Lorgnette, Mother-of-Pearl, Burgundy & Gold Enamel, Lefils 125.00
Lorgnette, Mother-of-Pearl, Velvet Bag, France 175.00
Mother-of-Pearl & Brass, Tiffany & Co. 195.00
Mother-of-Pearl Inlay, Gold, Tiffany 2800.00
Mother-of-Pearl, Blue Enamel, Long Handle, Lamier 375.00
Mother-of-Pearl, Case 95.00
Mother-of-Pearl, Engraved Annie, Le Maire, Paris, Leather 45.00

ORPHAN ANNIE first appeared in the comics in 1924. The redheaded girl
and her friends have been on the radio and are still on the comic pages. A
Broadway musical show and a movie in the 1980s made Annie popular
again and many toys, dishes, and other memorabilia are being made.

Book, Little Orphan Annie & Punjab The Wizard, 1935 .... 27.00
Book, Song 15.00
Box, Handle, Annie & Sandy In The Rain, Pink, Tin, 61 x 3 In. 40.00
Box, Sunshine Biscuits, 1930s 375.00
Bracelet 30.00
Clothespin Set 60.00
Crayon 30.00
Decoder Badge, Radio Premium, 1937, 1 3/4 In. 28.00
Decoder Badge, Radio, 1938 .... 35.00
Decoder, 1939 .... 45.00
Doll, Remco, Box, 1968 .... 85.00
Doll, Wooden, Jointed, With Sandy 83.00
Figure, Couples & Leon, 1930s 25.00
Game, Treasure Hunt, Little Orphan Annie, Ovaltine, 1933 .... 45.00
Letter, Explaining Membership Rules, 1934 .... 15.00
Light Bulb, Christmas Tree, Orphan Annie 45.00
Lunch Box .... 12.00 To 20.00
Manual, Radio, 1938 .... 50.00
Manual, Secret Society, 1934, Original Envelope 75.00
Mug 35.00
Mug, Ovaltine, Orphan Annie & Sandy 65.00
Nodder, Daddy Warbucks, Bisque, Germany 375.00
Pin, Decoder, Brass, 1936 .... 46.00
Pin, Pep, Kellogg's, 1940s 28.00
Pin, Roa Secret Compartment Decoder, 1936, Advertising 65.00
Pin, Roa Secret Society, Bronze, 1934, Advertising, Premiums 40.00
Pin, Telematic Decoder, 1938 .... 35.00
Radio, 1980 .... 25.00
Ring, Face, 1934, Advertising, Premiums 65.00
Ring, Mystic Eye, Look Around, 1939, Advertising, Premiums 65.00
Ring, Raisin Bran, 1948, Advertising, Premiums 20.00
Ring, Silver Star Secret Message, Advertising, Premiums 65.00
Rulebook, Secret Society, Radio 40.00
Sheet Music, Little Orphan Annie Song, Ovaltine & Radio 8.00
Sheet, Premium Offer 15.00
Snow Dome, Plastic, Paperweight, 1970s 12.00
Stove, Electric, Orphan Annie, Green 70.00
Sun Watch, Instructions, Mailing Envelope 125.00
Toothbrush Holder, Orphan Annie & Sandy, Bisque, Painted 65.00
Toy, Treasure Hunt 38.00
Wristwatch, Rectangular Chrome Case, 1935 .... 100.00

Orrefors, Vase, Fish, Ocean Plants, Edward
Hald, 4 3/4 In.

ORREFORS Glassworks, located in the Swedish province of Smaaland, was
established in 1898. The company is still making glass for use on the table
or as decorations. There is renewed interest in the glass made in the
modern styles of the 1940s and 1950s. Most vases and decorative pieces
are signed with the etched name.

Orrefors

Bowl, Fish In Seaweeds, Cased, Green, Signed, 7 1/2 In.	750.00
Bowl, Radiating Wavy Lines Inside, Aquamarine, 3 7/8 In.	1350.00
Dish, Half–Marbelized Feet, 4 1/2 In.	40.00
Vase, 3 Partially Clad Women Bathers, Signed, 1935, 6 3/4 In.	1350.00
Vase, Blue Fish Net, Palquist, Kraka, 6 In.	95.00
Vase, Boy Watching Bird, 9 1/4 In.	195.00
Vase, Clear, Frieze Of Nude Women, Footed, S. Gate, 1927, 8 3/4 In.	1650.00
Vase, Engraved Pearl Diver, Clear, Marked, 6 7/8 In.	40.00
Vase, Engraved Shark Killer, Clear, V. Lindstrand, 1937, 13 In.	6100.00
Vase, Etched Girl, 5 In.	120.00
Vase, Fish, Ocean Plants, Edward Hald, 4 3/4 In. ....*Illus*	4840.00
Vase, Grail, Goldfish, Edward Hald, 5 1/2 In.	650.00
Vase, Maiden Swinging From Branches, Ovoid, c.1940, 8 In.	715.00
Vase, Nude Male, Horseback, Bottle Green, E. Ohrstrom, 6 3/4 In.	6600.00
Vase, Nude Siren, 2 Birds, Signed, 6 x 11 In.	220.00
Vase, Poseidon, Mermaid, Flattened Cylinder, Landberg, 12 In.	7150.00
Vase, Rose Bowl Shape, Signed, 5 1/2 In.	150.00
Vase, Teardrop, Signed, 11 In.	190.00

OTT & BREWER Company operated the Etruria Pottery at Trenton, New
Jersey, from 1863 to 1893. They started making belleek in 1882. The firm
used a variety of marks that incorporated the initials *O & B*.

Bust, U.S. Grant, c.1876, Broome, 10 In. ....*Illus*	2650.00
Creamer, Gold Paste Florals, Wishbone Handle	135.00
Cup & Saucer, Signed	125.00

Ott & Brewer, Bust, U.S. Grant, c.1876,
Broome, 10 In.

Cup & Saucer, Tridacna, White Exterior, Luster Interior 95.00
Mug, 4 Swallows, Cobalt Blue, Saying, Stein Type, 5 1/2 In. 185.00
Pitcher, Horn Shape 850.00

OVERBECK pottery was made by four Overbeck sisters at a pottery in Cambridge City, Indiana. They started in 1911. They made all types of vases, each one–of–a–kind. Small, hand–modeled figurines are the most popular pieces with today's collectors. The factory continued until 1955 when the last of the four sisters died.

Figurine, Abraham Lincoln 375.00
Figurine, Dagger, Raised Dagger 300.00
Figurine, Elephant, Pink 425.00
Figurine, George Washington 350.00
Figurine, Girl, Arranging Flowers On Stand 375.00
Figurine, Hen, Large 300.00
Figurine, Indian 425.00
Figurine, Man, Blue Jacket, Red Top Hat 75.00
Figurine, Martha Washington 225.00
Figurine, Robin, Wings, Spread, Feeding Chicks In Nest 1100.00
Figurine, Rooster, Large 300.00
Figurine, Woman, Caroler 130.00
Figurine, Woman, Umbrella, Striped Dress 225.00
Vase, Bird Design, Signed E. F. 250.00

OWENS Pottery was made in Zanesville, Ohio, from 1891 to 1928. The first art pottery was made after 1896. Utopian Ware, Cyrano, Navarre, Feroza, and Henri Deux were made. Pieces were usually marked with a form of the name *Owens*. About 1907, the firm began to make tile and discontinued the art pottery wares.

Ewer, Utopian, Pansies, Steele, 6 In. 170.00
Humidor, Matches On Lid, Scene Of Pipes, Cigarette & Bag Of Tobacco 495.00
Jug, Utopian, 1 Pt. 165.00
Tankard, Minerva 125.00
Umbrella Stand, Utopian, Orange Iris, Matte Brown, Signed, 20 In. 525.00
Vase, Corona, Art Nouveau Design, Metal Overlay, 6 In. 650.00
Vase, Cyrano, 4 In. 165.00
Vase, Lotus, Flowers, White, Signed, 10 1/2 In. 195.00
Vase, Utopian, Brown Glaze, Oak Leaves, 3 3/4 In. 110.00
Vase, Utopian, Clover, Signed, 8 In. 160.00
Vase, Utopian, Matte, Converted To Lamp, 13 In. 175.00
Vase, Utopian, Opalescent, 13 In. 595.00
Vase, Utopian, Pansies, Handles, Signed, 5 1/2 In. 145.00
Vase, Wild Roses, Ovoid, 10 1/2 In. 220.00

OYSTER PLATES were popular from the 1880s. Each course at dinner was served in a special dish. The oyster plate had indentations shaped like oysters. Usually six oysters were held on a plate. There is no greater value to a plate with more oysters although that myth continues to haunt antiques dealers. There are other plates for shellfish, including cockle plates and whelk plates. The appropriately shaped indentations are part of the design of these dishes.

6 Wells, Sea Urchins Each Well, c.1855 .... 98.00
Brown Trim, 8 In. 65.00
Napkin Design, Pastel, 8 1/2 In. 65.00
Pillivuyt, Off–White 125.00
Pink & Blue Ground, Fired Gold, Weiman, 8 1/2 In., 8 Piece 195.00

PADEN CITY Glass Manufacturing Company was established in 1916 at Paden City, West Virginia. It is best known for glasswares but also produced a pottery line. The firm closed in 1951.

Bowl, Pea & Rose, Footed, Pink, 9 In. 47.00
Bowl, Pea & Rose, Green, 14 In. 55.00
Compote, Cover, Floral Etch, Ball Stem & Finial, 9 1/2 In. 70.00

Compote, Gazebo, 8 In. 40.00
Cup & Saucer, Crow's Foot, Ruby 12.50
Cup, Penny Line, Green 7.50
Figurine, Pheasant, Blue 110.00
Mayonnaise Set, Pea & Rose, Green 35.00
Powder Jar, Military Hat, Amber, 1942 .... 25.00
Soup, Cream, Crow's Foot, Liner, Ruby 17.00
Soup, Cream, Crow's Foot, Ruby 20.00
Sugar & Creamer, Cupid, Pink 140.00
Tray, Gothic Garden, Yellow, Square, 9 1/2 In. 38.00
Tray, Sandwich, Pea & Rose, Center Handle, Pink, 10 1/2 In. 47.00
Vase, Crow's Foot, Ruby, 10 In. 125.00
Vase, Green, Lela Bird, 12 In. 98.00

PAINTINGS listed in this book are not works by major artists but rather decorative paintings on ivory, board, or glass that would be of interest to the average collector. To learn the value of an oil painting by a listed artist you must contact an expert in that area.

Oil On Academy Board, Lake, Mountain, Fisherman, Gilt Frame, 14 In. 150.00
Oil On Board, 3 Masted Ship, Ergo, Pencil Mark, Framed, 16 x 26 In. 300.00
Oil On Board, Cat Scene, Striped Couch, Framed, 11 x 13 1/2 In. 275.00
Oil On Board, European Tavern Scene, Frame, 14 In. 275.00
Oil On Board, Little Boy Holding A Spoon, U.S., 19th C., 7 x 5 In. 55.00
Oil On Board, Man, Woman, Bag, Basket, Picking Cotton, 11 In., Pair 3200.00
Oil On Board, Woman, Basket On Head, Gilt Frame, 9 1/4 In. 1250.00
Oil On Canvas, 2 Women Wading, Initialed, Dated, Gilt Frame, 31 In. 150.00
Oil On Canvas, Allegorical Scene, Gilt Frame, 37 x 79 In. 2600.00
Oil On Canvas, Artist Painting Own Likeness, Gilt Frame, 33 In. 475.00
Oil On Canvas, Autumn Wooded Landscape, Ornate Gilt Frame, 28 In. 400.00
Oil On Canvas, Borghese Gardens, Rome, Gilt Frame, 16 x 13 In. 300.00
Oil On Canvas, Bouquet Of Lilacs, Gilt Frame, 33 1/2 In. 125.00
Oil On Canvas, Boy Shining Shoes, Framed, 14 1/2 x 12 In. 110.00
Oil On Canvas, Cat With Food Dish, 8 x 10 In. 250.00
Oil On Canvas, Country House, Picket Fence, 20 In. 325.00
Oil On Canvas, Couple In Canoe, Gilt Frame, 15 3/4 In. 300.00
Oil On Canvas, Dutch Scene With Windmills, Gilt Frame, 14 In. 325.00
Oil On Canvas, English Cottage & Garden, Gilt Frame, 17 x 13 In. 175.00
Oil On Canvas, European Castle, Mountain, Gold Frame, 29 1/2 In. 125.00
Oil On Canvas, European Landscape, Cottage, Stream, Frame, 23 In. 425.00
Oil On Canvas, European Military Scene, 2 Armies, Framed, 43 In. 650.00
Oil On Canvas, European Scene, 2 Men, Violin, Guitar, Framed, 42 In. 35.00
Oil On Canvas, Floral Still Life, Shadow Box, Glass Cover, 33 In. 600.00
Oil On Canvas, Gentleman, Diamond Stick Pin, Framed, 33 x 28 In. 1500.00
Oil On Canvas, Gentleman, Lady, Oval, Gilt Frame, 28 1/2 In., Pair 1150.00
Oil On Canvas, Gentleman, Primitive, Gilt Frame, 26 x 21 3/4 In. 425.00
Oil On Canvas, Girl, Cat, Shadow Box Frame, 22 In. 750.00
Oil On Canvas, Gypsy Girl On Ground, Gilt Frame, 17 x 28 In. 500.00
Oil On Canvas, Haying Scene With Oxen, Gilt Frame, 31 In. 425.00
Oil On Canvas, Hunting Dog, Bird, Gilt Frame, 24 1/4 In. 205.00
Oil On Canvas, Impressionistic Landscape, Gilt Frame, 17 x 22 In. 325.00
Oil On Canvas, Lakeside Gazebo, Hudson River School, 1870, 24 In. 400.00
Oil On Canvas, Landscape With Barn & Geese, Gilt Frame, 18 In. 125.00
Oil On Canvas, Landscape With Cottage, Carved Frame, 19 x 29 In. 300.00
Oil On Canvas, Landscape Woods, Lake, Under Glass, Frame, 31 In. 1550.00
Oil On Canvas, Landscape, Church, Mountain, Gilt Frame, 39 x 53 In. 550.00
Oil On Canvas, Landscape, Haystack, Framed, 26 1/4 x 30 In. 350.00
Oil On Canvas, Landscape, House & Barn, Gilt Frame, 19 x 25 In. 70.00
Oil On Canvas, Landscape, Pond, Flying Ducks, Gilt Frame, 30 In. 325.00
Oil On Canvas, Landscape, Rushing Mountain Stream, Frame, 30 In. 600.00
Oil On Canvas, Laying Of Transatlantic Cable, 25 x 30 In. 2600.00
Oil On Canvas, Man & Woman Portrait, Primitive, Frame, 30 In., Pr. 2100.00
Oil On Canvas, Mercury, Dressed By Gods, Gilt Frame, 50 In. 4900.00
Oil On Canvas, Mexican Madonna, Child, Unframed, 29 In. 200.00

Oil On Canvas, Mountain Landscape, Gilt Frame, 24 3/4 x 20 In.	375.00
Oil On Canvas, Mountains & Water, Strip Frame, 25 1/4 In.	50.00
Oil On Canvas, Mountains, Cabin, Signed, Gilt Frame, 24 1/2 In.	75.00
Oil On Canvas, Nude With Tiger Skin, 85 x 48 In.	3300.00
Oil On Canvas, Old Man Shining Shoes, Gilt Frame, 28 1/4 In.	450.00
Oil On Canvas, Pasture With Cows, Signed, Frame, 29 1/4 In.	850.00
Oil On Canvas, Pink Flamingos, Herons, Framed, 23 1/2 In., Pair	200.00
Oil On Canvas, Polynesian Girl, Gilt Frame, Signed, 13 In.	200.00
Oil On Canvas, Portrait Of A Cavalier, 41 In.	150.00
Oil On Canvas, Portrait Of Child, Frame, 27 In.	325.00
Oil On Canvas, Portrait Of Young Woman, Dove, Gilt Frame, 36 In.	550.00
Oil On Canvas, Portrait, Woman, Blonde Hair, Frame, 33 x 28 In.	1000.00
Oil On Canvas, Primitive Portrait, Woman, Lace Bonnet, 34 x 29 In.	1000.00
Oil On Canvas, Primitive Still Life, Frame, 13 In.	125.00
Oil On Canvas, Romantic Landscape, Castle, Gilt Frame, 18 3/4 In.	125.00
Oil On Canvas, Scene Of Sleeping Girl, Dog, Rocky Seacoast, 30 In.	225.00
Oil On Canvas, Sea & Shore Landscape, People, Lean-To, 24 x 36 In.	450.00
Oil On Canvas, Ship, Stormy Sea, Gilt Frame, 46 In.	450.00
Oil On Canvas, Skilling, Greyhound & King Charles Spaniel	3250.00
Oil On Canvas, Snowy Egrets, Water Lilies, Gilt Frame, 42 In.	325.00
Oil On Canvas, South American Scene, Gold Frame, 6 x 7 In., Pair	170.00
Oil On Canvas, Spanish Scene, Horse, Coin, Waif, Gilt Frame, 36 In.	550.00
Oil On Canvas, Still Life With Apples, Gilt Frame, 28 In.	425.00
Oil On Canvas, Still Life, Basket Of Fruit, Gilt Frame, 32 1/2 In.	250.00
Oil On Canvas, Towards Home, English School, 19th C., 30 x 20 In.	468.00
Oil On Canvas, W. H. B., Mountain Landscape, Gilt Frame, 22 x 30 In.	700.00
Oil On Canvas, Winter Landscape, Gilt Frame, 20 In.	250.00
Oil On Canvas, Woman's Portrait, Gold Frame, 1865, 30 x 36 In.	200.00
Oil On Canvas, Woman, Cameo Brooch, Framed, 36 1/4 x 31 1/4 In.	1250.00
Oil On Canvas, Woman, Fur-Trimmed Wrap, Bird's-Eye Frame, 33 In.	925.00
Oil On Canvas, Woman, Red Couch, Ostrich Feather Hat, 42 In.	700.00
Oil On Canvas, Wooded Landscape, Gilt Frame, 16 3/4 In.	145.00
Oil On Canvas, Young Man, Mustache, Gilt Frame, 16 x 12 3/4 In.	100.00
Oil On Canvas, Young Woman, Gilt Frame, 31 3/4 In.	225.00
Oil On Panel, Boy, Lace Collar, Primitive, 17 3/4 x 14 3/4 In.	700.00
Oil On Panel, Old Woman, Lace Bonnet, 1 Board Poplar, 28 x 22 In.	550.00
Oil On Panel, Woman, Elaborate Jewelry, Frame, 34 In.	450.00
Oil On Wooden Panel, Girl Full Portrait, Framed, 22 1/2 x 18 In.	1025.00
On Board, American Homestead, 16 x 24 In.	250.00
On Board, Child, Sitting On Arm Of Rocker, Framed, 21 x 17 3/4 In.	100.00
On Board, French Couple, Ornate Gilt Frame, Oil, 29 1/2 x 19 In.	275.00
On Board, Rooster, Pair Of Doves, Gilt Frame, 15 x 12 In., Pair	270.00
On Board, Wooded Park, Gilt Frame, 21 In.	2100.00
On Copper, English Steamboat, Sails, Bronze Gilt Frame, 11 In.	175.00
On Copper, Sailing Ships, Framed, 11 x 13 In.	200.00
On Ivory, Anson Dickinson, Officer, Gold Case, c.1815, 2 3/4 In.	1760.00
On Ivory, Balloonists In Flight, Tortoiseshell Case, 2 1/2 In.	715.00
On Ivory, Boy, Blue Suit, Ruffled Collar, c.1840, France, Miniature	110.00
On Ivory, Captain Alexander Richards, 1817, Miniature	575.00
On Ivory, Captain James Dawson, John Ramage, c.1783, 1 3/4 In.	3520.00
On Ivory, Catherine, Empress Of Russia, 1 3/4 In.	357.00
On Ivory, Dark-Haired Lady, Watercolor, 3 x 2 1/2 In.	660.00
On Ivory, Gentleman Portrait, Oval, Chased Gold Pendant, 2 1/2 In.	357.00
On Ivory, Gentleman, 3-Masted Schooner, Flag, H. Inman, 1 3/4 In.	1650.00
On Ivory, George & Martha Washington, Ivory Frames, 5 1/2 In., Pr.	350.00
On Ivory, Lady & Gentleman, Thomas Edwards, c.1840, 2 5/8 In., Pr.	990.00
On Ivory, Lady, 1700s Dress, Ivory Frame, Douglas, France, 3 x 2 In.	242.00
On Ivory, Marie Antoinette, 4 1/2 x 3 1/2 In.	220.00
On Ivory, Napoleon & Josephine, Framed, 4 x 5 In.	750.00
On Ivory, Napoleon Bonaparte, 3 1/2 x 2 1/2 In.	330.00
On Ivory, Napoleon, As Young Man, 6 In.	100.00
On Ivory, Napoleon, Remy, 3 3/8 x 2 1/2 In.	135.00
On Ivory, Naval Officer, Anson Dickinson, c.1810, 2 3/4 In.	4125.00

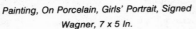

Painting, On Porcelain, Girls' Portrait, Signed   *Painting, Reverse On Glass, Woman, Caged*
Wagner, 7 x 5 In.   *Bird, Chinese, 10 x 7 In.*

On Ivory, Oval Miniature, Taj Mahal, Indian Carved Frame, 5 In.	105.00
On Ivory, Oval Portrait Of A Woman, Ivory Frame, 5 3/4 In.	95.00
On Ivory, Paris, Promenading Figures, 1840, 1 3/4 x 2 1/4 In.	380.00
On Ivory, Portrait Of Little Girl, Gilt Locket Frame, 2 x 1 In.	990.00
On Ivory, Scene Of Diwani Khan, Imperial Palace, Delhi, 4 3/4 In.	135.00
On Ivory, Taj Mahal, Oval	83.00
On Ivory, Terrier Dog, Set In Locket	125.00
On Ivory, Woman Portrait, Gilt Metal Locket, 1836–1889, 2 1/2 In.	605.00
On Ivory, Woman With Bonnet, Oval, Signed, 3 1/2 In.	245.00
On Ivory, Woman, Curly Hair, Classical Gown, 4 1/4 x 5 1/2 In.	245.00
On Ivory, Woman, Pink Dress, Wide Hat, Walnut Frame, Miniature	170.00
On Ivory, Woman, Seated At Pedestal, c.1850, 2 3/4 In.	1100.00
On Ivory, Young Man Portrait, Thomas Barns, May 1846, 1 7/8 In.	300.00
On Panel, European Landscape, Gilt Frame, 18 In.	210.00
On Paper, Amorous Couple, Fireside, Watercolor, Gilt Frame, 52 In.	2600.00
On Paper, Arabian Courtyard Scene, Watercolor, Gilt Frame, 42 In.	800.00
On Paper, Autumn Trees, Gilt Frame, Watercolor, 28 x 24 In.	65.00
On Paper, Basket Of Fruit, Brown, Blue, Green, Watercolor, 18 In.	200.00
On Paper, Black Girl, Holding Dried Flower, Watercolor, 9 x 7 In.	2475.00
On Paper, Boy With Knickers & Cap, Watercolor, Gilt Frame, 29 In.	175.00
On Paper, Boy, Black & White Check Dress, Whip, Framed, 9 x 7 In.	800.00
On Paper, Burning Of Fort Sumter, Gilt Frame, 7 1/2 x 9 1/2 In.	375.00
On Paper, Caribbean Scenes, Watercolor, Mat, Frame, 29 In., Pr.	150.00
On Paper, Clergyman Portrait, Watercolor, Gilt Frame, 7 x 6 In.	125.00
On Paper, Compass Star & Pinwheel, Black Frame, 11 x 13 1/2 In.	550.00
On Paper, European Cathedral Spire, Medieval Street, 23 x 16 In.	150.00
On Paper, Fisher, Shepherd With Sheep, Watercolor, Framed	950.00
On Paper, Fishermen, Boat, Glass-Covered Shadow Box, 25 x 31 In.	1550.00
On Paper, Fishing Boats, Gilt Frame, Watercolor, 16 3/4 In.	750.00
On Paper, Fishing Boats, Low Tide, Watercolor, Gilt Frame, 16 In.	45.00
On Paper, Flowering Tree, 2 Birds, Watercolor, 7 x 9 In.	250.00
On Paper, Folksy Scene, Cat, Frame, 12 1/4 x 14 1/4 In.	165.00
On Paper, Girl, Profile Portrait, Green Frame, 3 5/8 x 3 In.	85.00
On Paper, Harp, Roses, Other Flowers, Red, Blue, Watercolor, 14 In.	75.00
On Paper, Horse, Babe, Watercolor, Tramp Art Frame, 10 x 8 In.	395.00
On Paper, Horse, Pink Cinch Belt, Blue Grass, 10 x 12 1/2 In.	1150.00
On Paper, Idyllic Scene Of Cows, Matted, Framed, 20 1/2 In.	160.00
On Paper, Lake, Fall Foliage, Watercolor, Mat, Frame, 19 1/4 In.	25.00
On Paper, Landscape, Craig Miller's Castle, 7 x 10 In.	75.00
On Paper, Landscape, Framed, 9 3/8 x 11 3/8 In.	80.00
On Paper, Man & Woman, Full Length, Sprig Of Flowers, 10 x 10 In.	1000.00

On Paper, Portrait Study Of Children, Gilded Frame, 19 x 16 In. 100.00
On Paper, River, Swans, Grazing Sheep, Watercolor, Frame, 22 In. 40.00
On Paper, Rooster, Black, Blue, Red, Fly Specks, 5 x 6 In. 325.00
On Paper, Ruined Building By Lake, Watercolor, Mat, Frame, 23 In. 45.00
On Paper, Scene Plowing, Team Of Horses, Watercolor, Frame, 18 In. 55.00
On Paper, Soldier With Drum, Watercolor, Pencil, Ink, Frame, 10 In. 1600.00
On Paper, Study Of Children, Gilded Oak Frame, 19 x 16 1/2 In. 100.00
On Paper, Team Of Horses Plowing, Mat, Frame, 20 In. 135.00
On Paper, Theorem, Fruit, Painted Frame, 10 x 12 In. 450.00
On Paper, Wm Pitt, Monument, Watercolor, Mat, Frame, 22 In. 40.00
On Paper, Woman, Green Dress, Balloon Sleeves, Frame, 10 x 8 In. 700.00
On Porcelain, Child, Bonnet, Gold Frame, c.1820, 2 x 1 3/4 In. 847.00
On Porcelain, Countess Vistulin, Frame, 4 3/4 x 3 1/2 In. 750.00
On Porcelain, Dish, Woman Portrait, Bronze Frame, 8 1/4 In. 290.00
On Porcelain, Girls' Portrait, Signed Wagner, 7 x 5 In. ....*Illus* 4000.00
On Porcelain, Green Ground, Lady, Flowers In Hair, 2 x 3 In. 195.00
On Porcelain, Napoleon, Faux Tortoiseshell Frame, c.1870, 3 In. 575.00
On Porcelain, Swiss Girl, Wood Frame, c.1885, 2 3/4 x 3 1/4 In. 650.00
On Porcelain, Woman Feeding Cat, Signed, Frame, 15 3/4 In. 225.00
On Porcelain, Woman, Blue Hat, Pink Ribbons, Porcelain Frame 235.00
On Porcelain, Young Boy, Short Hair, c.1750, 1 3/8 x 1 1/8 In. 600.00
On Porcelain, Young Woman, Veil, Germany, Frame, 9 3/4 x 7 3/4 In. 750.00
On Silk, British Ship Aleides, Watercolor, Frame, 20 x 24 1/2 In. 800.00
On Velvet, Theorem, Basket Of Fruit, Framed, 12 1/2 x 15 In. 1100.00
On Velvet, Theorem, Basket Of Fruit, Framed, 20 x 20 1/2 In. 495.00
Reverse On Glass, F. Napoleon, White Uniform, Frame, 15 x 11 In. 275.00
Reverse On Glass, Girl, Large Hat, Blue Ground, Frame, 11 x 8 In. 275.00
Reverse On Glass, La Belle Polonaise, 11 3/4 x 9 1/4 In. 300.00
Reverse On Glass, Steeplechase Scene, 1836, 12 1/4 x 14 1/4 In. 550.00
Reverse On Glass, Woman, Caged Bird, Chinese, 10 x 7 In. ....*Illus* 1100.00

PAIRPOINT Manufacturing Company started in 1880 in New Bedford, Massachusetts. It soon joined with the glassworks nearby and made glass, silver-plated pieces, and lamps. Reverse-painted glass shades and molded shades known as *puffies* were part of the production until the 1930s. The company reorganized and changed its name several times but is still working today. Items listed here are glass or glass and metal. Silver-plated pieces are listed under Silver Plate.

Basket, Berry Prunt, Burmese Satin, Rope Handle, 8 In. 90.00
Biscuit Jar, 6 Blown-Out Panels, Green Ground, Silver Plated Lid 395.00
Bowl, Centerpiece, Affixed To Trumpet Vase, 16 1/2 In. 302.50
Bowl, Cut Glass, With Holder 675.00
Box, Collar & Cuff, Silver Domed Lid, Snowballs, Gold Lettering 1250.00
Box, Embossed Florals, Green Ground, 6 1/2 x 4 In. 650.00
Box, Hinged Cover, Scrolls, Wild Roses, Metal Base, 6 3/4 x 4 In. 665.00
Box, Jewel, Pink, Scalloped, Queen Louise On Lid, Lined 550.00
Box, Jewel, Queen Louise Lid, Pink, Floral, 7 1/2 x 6 In. 675.00
Box, Jewel, Queen Louise Portrait On Lid, 3 x 7 1/2 In. 575.00
Candlestick, Engraved Grapes, Green, 10 1/2 In., Pair 375.00
Candlestick, Hollow Stem, Amethyst, 11 In., 4 Piece 330.00
Candy Dish, Crystal & Etched, 7 1/2 In. 200.00
Candy Dish, Heart Shape, Ruby 150.00
Castor Set, 5-Bottle, Swivel Pedestal Holder 425.00
Castor, Pickle, Silver Stand 150.00
Chandelier, Puffy, Butterflies & Yellow Blossoms, Marked, 14 In. 3300.00
Finger Bowl, Underplate, Old Colony 200.00
Gravy Boat, Flower Pattern, Gold 125.00
Humidor, Enameled Satin, Apricot, Gilt Chrysanthemums, 7 In. 440.00
Lamp, Acorns & Oak Leaves, Shade, 21 In. 3500.00
Lamp, Boudoir, Berkeley Shade, Chestnut Tree, Silver Base 3500.00
Lamp, Boudoir, Bronze Tree Trunk Base, 11 In. 3800.00
Lamp, Boudoir, Puffy, Reverse Painted, Signed, 15 In. 1985.00
Lamp, Boudoir, Puffy, Silver Plated Paw Feet, 15 In. 3025.00

Lamp, Boudoir, Reverse Painted Blossoms, Marked, 15 In. 1980.00
Lamp, Boudoir, Reverse Painted, Butterflies & Roses, 14 3/4 In. 3850.00
Lamp, Boudoir, Roses, Floral, Marked 5745.00
Lamp, Candle, Landscape & Painted Chimney, Wood Base, 22 In. 950.00
Lamp, Chestnut Design, W. Macy, 20 In. 3700.00
Lamp, Desk, Fine Arts Line 2100.00
Lamp, Directoire, 3-Light, Floral Shade, Onyx Base, 27 In. 4400.00
Lamp, Directoire, Mountainous Landscape, Onyx Base, 19 In. 1850.00
Lamp, Forest Scene Shade, Bronze, 25 In. 4000.00
Lamp, Four Seasons, 16 In. 3500.00
Lamp, Garden Of Allah, 25 In. 8500.00
Lamp, Metal, Marked, 21 In. 300.00
Lamp, New Bedford Harbor Scene Shade, Handled Base 3410.00
Lamp, Puffy, Poppy Blossoms, Green, 12 x 21 1/2 In. ....*Illus* 9900.00
Lamp, Reverse Painted Arab Scene, Chesterfield Shade, 18 In. 6000.00
Lamp, Reverse Painted Butterflies, Birds, c.1915, 14 1/4 In. 4400.00
Lamp, Reverse Painted Butterflies, Signed, c.1920, 14 1/4 In. 9900.00
Lamp, Reverse Painted Scene, Mill, People, House, Signed, 15 In. 6800.00
Lamp, Reverse Painted Sea Gulls, Copley Shade, c.1915, 35 1/4 In. 3300.00
Lamp, Reverse Painted Shade, 4 Arms, Bronze, c.1915, 23 In. 1875.00
Lamp, Reverse Painted Shade, Acorn, Oak Leaves, 21 In. ....*Illus* 3500.00
Lamp, Reverse Painted Shade, Exotic Birds, Exeter Shade, 22 In. 6050.00
Lamp, Reverse Painted Summer Scene, 18 In. ....*Illus* 7750.00
Lamp, Reverse Painted Woodland, Exeter Shade, c.1920, 21 1/4 In. 2200.00
Lamp, Reverse Painted Woodland, Signed, c.1915, 17 3/4 In. 1980.00
Lamp, Reverse Painted, Bronze Base, 13 1/2 In. Diam. 2750.00
Lamp, Reverse Painted, Pyramids & Mosques, Brass Base 6000.00
Lamp, Reverse Painted, Rose & Buds Melon Shade, 17 1/2 In. 4675.00
Lamp, Reverse Painted, Silvered Metal Base, 22 1/2 In. 6050.00
Lamp, Scenic Shade, Marked W. Macy, 18 In. 3600.00
Lamp, Scenic, Berkeley Shade, Robin Hood Design, 21 In. 2200.00
Lamp, Summer Scene, Signed, 18 In. 7750.00
Lamp, Table, Reverse Painted Castles, Mountains, Signed, 15 In. 2090.00
Lamp, Torchere, Shade Signed 450.00
Lamp, Tree Trunk Base, Flower Clusters On Shade, Signed 7500.00
Mirror, Plateau, 14 In. 95.00
Mirror, Plateau, 4 3/4 In. 50.00
Powder Box, Etched Flowers & Leaf, Blue Glass, 4 In. 145.00
Punch Bowl, Stand & Ladle, Brilliant Period, Signed 1760.00
Talc Shaker, 12 Panels, Florals, Blue Ground 145.00
Toothpick, Dotted Swiss Pattern, Petal Foot, 4 x 5 1/2 In. 575.00
Tumbler, Black Enamel Galleon Under Full Sail, Pre-1932 .... 2235.00
Vase, Amber Blown, Clear Knop & Stem, 11 5/8 In. 115.00
Vase, Controlled Bubbles, Ruby Red, 9 1/2 In. 175.00
Vase, Cut Floral Design, Clear Knop, 12 In. 85.00
Vase, Cylinder, Flared Rim, 12 In. 85.00
Vase, Etched Flowers & Leaves, Signed, 8 In. 125.00

Pairpont, Lamp, Puffy, Poppy
Blossoms, Green,
12 x 21 1/2 In.

Pairpoint, Lamp, Reverse-
Painted Summer Scene, 18 In.

Pairpoint, Lamp, Reverse
Painted Shade, Acorn, Oak
Leaves, 21 In.

Vase, Hand Painted Floral, Gold Button Each Side, Signed, 10 In. 375.00
Vase, Maiden Of Desert, Gold Medallion, Signed, 15 In. 1350.00
Vase, Murillo, Allover Florals & Butterflies, c.1920, 12 In. 135.00
Vase, Twirl Bubble Ball, Ruby, 12 3/4 In. 357.00

PALMER COX, BROWNIES, see Brownies

PAN, Corn Stick, Krusty Korn Kobs, Wagner, Pat. 1920 ....95.00 To 120.00

PAPER DOLLS were probably inspired by the pantins, or jumping jacks, made in eighteenth-century Europe. By the 1880s, sheets of printed paper dolls and clothes were being made. The first paper doll books were made in the 1920s. Collectors prefer uncut sheets or books or boxed sets of paper dolls. Prices are about half as much if the pages have been cut.

Alice Faye, Cut 165.00
Ann Blyth, 1951, Uncut 45.00
Annette, 48 Costumes, Stand-Up Dolls, Whitman, 1960 .... 18.00
Annette, Folder, Cut 25.00
Baby Tender Love, 1971, Uncut 10.00
Barbie & Francie, Box, 1976 .... 25.00
Barbie Sweet 16, Cut 4.00
Betsy McCall, 8 Sheets, 1962-1970, Uncut 45.00
Bette Davis, Cut 95.00
Beverly Hillbillies, 1960s 18.00
Bewitched, Uncut 65.00
Big & Little Sister, 4 Dolls, 1945, Uncut 20.00
Blondie & Her Family, The Hinges, Color, 3-D, Envelope, Uncut 30.00
Brady Bunch, Cut 24.00
Bride & Groom, Merrill, Uncut 20.00
Captain Marvel, 1945, Uncut 50.00
Carmen Miranda, Saalfield, Uncut 150.00
Caroline Kennedy 15.00
Cherrio Cheerleader, Cut 20.00
Cinderella, Merrill, 1957, Uncut 45.00
Cindy & Her Cousin, Uncut 15.00
Cindy Magic Wand, Uncut 20.00
Connie Stevens, Box, 1961, 6 x 11 1/2 In., Uncut 45.00
Cotton Batting Winter Coat, Muff, Die Cut, Tinsel Hanger, 12 In. 150.00
Daisy & Donald Duck 6.00
Day With Dianne, Saalfield, Uncut 25.00
Deanna Durbin, Cut 175.00
Dinah Shore, Folder, Cut 25.00
Dogpatch, Saalfield, 4 Dolls, Clothes, 1941, Cut 35.00
Dolly Dingle & Mamma Dingle, 1924, Uncut 25.00
Dolly Dingle's Big Sister Maxine, 1923, Uncut 25.00
Dolly Dingle's Little Cousin Robin, 1924, Uncut 25.00
Dolly Dingle's Little Friend Peggy & Birthday Cards, Drayton 15.00
Dolly Dingle, Uncut, 1920s .... 10.00 To 15.00
Doris Day, Whitman, Dated 1954, Uncut 65.00
Dr. Miles Nervine, 3 Hats, 3 Dresses 295.00
Elizabeth Taylor, Whitman, 1949, Cut 35.00
Esther Williams, Merrill, 1950, Cut 25.00
Fanny Grey, Box 250.00
Gilda Radner & Saturday Night Live Characters, Whitman, Uncut 12.00
Gilda Radner, Autographed, Uncut 25.00
Gina Gillespie, 1962, Uncut 30.00
Girl Pilots Of The Ferry Command, W. W. II, 6 Dolls, 1943 .... 25.00
Glamour Models, Stephens, Uncut 18.00
Gone With The Wind, 18 Dolls, Costumes From Movie, Uncut 185.00
Gone With The Wind, Cut 100.00
Gulliver's Travels, 1939, Uncut 35.00
Jane Russell, Uncut 90.00
Jaunty Junior, Lilja, Uncut 32.00
June Allyson, Folder, Cut 25.00

Katzenjammer Kids, Hinges, Envelope, 1945	35.00
Lettie Lane, 1908, Uncut, 10 In.	20.00
Liddle Kiddles, Mattel, Uncut	9.00
Little Bopeep, Gertrude Kay, 1923, Uncut	20.00
Little Lulu & Tubby, Saalfield, Uncut	8.00
Little Lulu Kleenex, 1951	11.00
Little Lulu Kleenex, Folds Into Cardboard Display, 1951	18.00
Little Women, 5 Dolls, 9 Outfits, Saalfield, Uncut	20.00
Lydia, Black, 1970s, Uncut	7.00
Margery Mary's Cousin Suzette, 1920, Uncut	25.00
Mary Martin, 2 Dolls, Clothes, Cut	75.00
Mary Poppins, Whitman, Uncut	22.00
Minnie Mouse & Mickey Mouse, Stepping Out, Uncut	10.00
Molly Bee, Uncut	45.00
Mousketeers, 1957, Uncut	45.00
Movie Starlets, Stephens, Uncut	18.00
Nancy & Sluggo, Saalfield, Uncut	9.00
Nanny & Professor, Uncut	25.00
Paper Toys Of Raphael Tuck, B. Whitton Hendricks	75.00
Patti Page, Cut	17.00
Patty's Party, Stephens, Uncut	18.00
Pebbles & Bam–Bam, 1966, Uncut	50.00
Polka Dot Tots, Uncut	20.00
Queen Holden, Cut	95.00
Rock Hudson, Whitman, 1957, Uncut	125.00
Shari Lewis & Her Puppets, Box, 1962, Uncut	85.00
Shirley Temple, 1932, Cut	40.00
Shirley Temple, Clothes, Box, 1976, Uncut	28.00
Sonja Henie, 1930s, Uncut	750.00
Sonja Henie, 2 Dolls, 2 Dresses, Merrill, 1941, Cut	48.00
Southern Belle, 5 Costumes, 1840–1880	10.00
St. Patty's Party, 1950s, Uncut	15.00
Sweetie Pie Twins, 1949, Uncut	16.50
That Girl, Marlo Thomas, 3 Dolls, 20 Outfits, Saalfield, Uncut	25.00
Three Famous Flying Marvels, 1945, Uncut	90.00
Tillie The Toiler, 8 Dolls, Uncut	35.00
Tiny Tots, 4 Dolls, 1958, Cut	10.00
Tyrone Power & Linda Darnell, Cut	155.00
Uncle Sam Little Helpers, Saalfield, 1943, Cut	50.00
Wedding Party, Saalfield, 1951, Uncut	35.00
Ziegfield Girls, Merrill, 16 Stars, 1940, Cut	150.00

PAPER collectibles, including almanacs, catalogs, children's books, stock certificates, and other paper ephemera, are listed here. Paper calendars are listed separately in the Calendar Paper category.

Album, Breakfast Club, Don McNeill, Radio, Hard Cover, 96 Pages	25.00
Almanac, Dr. Miles, 1935	20.00
Almanac, Dr. Pierce, 1928	3.00
Almanac, Raleigh's, 1931	3.00
Bond, Indian Territory Railroad, 1905	35.00
Book, ABC, Little One Series, c.1900	20.00
Book, Accordion Style Fold–Out, Winter Sports, McLaughlin	450.00
Book, Big Little Book, Andy Panda In The City Of Ice	10.00
Book, Big Little Book, Arizona Kid	20.00
Book, Big Little Book, Bringing Up Father, 3rd Series	45.00
Book, Big Little Book, Buck Jones, Two Gun Kid	25.00
Book, Big Little Book, Bugs Bunny	10.00
Book, Big Little Book, Calling W–I–X–Y–Z, Jimmy Kean The Radio Spies	15.00
Book, Big Little Book, Dan Dunn & The Border Smuggler	20.00
Book, Big Little Book, Dan Dunn & The Under World Gorillas	20.00
Book, Big Little Book, Danger Trails In Africa	20.00
Book, Big Little Book, Dead Men's Mine	45.00
Book, Big Little Book, Deadly Treasure	35.00

Book, Big Little Book, Erik Noble & The Forty Niners 10.00
Book, Big Little Book, G–Man, 1936 .... 25.00
Book, Big Little Book, Harold Ten, Swinging At The Sugar Bowl 15.00
Book, Big Little Book, Invisible Scarlett O'Neil Vs. King Of Slums 25.00
Book, Big Little Book, Li'l Abner In New York .... 20.00 To 40.00
Book, Big Little Book, Mandrake The Magician, Flame Pearls 37.00
Book, Big Little Book, Mutt & Jeff 35.00
Book, Big Little Book, Orphan Annie, Big Train Robbery 30.00
Book, Big Little Book, Phantom 50.00
Book, Big Little Book, Range Buster 20.00
Book, Big Little Book, Red Barry, Undercover Man 20.00
Book, Big Little Book, Red Ryder & Western Border Guns 15.00
Book, Big Little Book, Red Ryder, Code Of West 30.00
Book, Big Little Book, Shadow & Ghost Makers 15.00
Book, Big Little Book, Tarzan, Lost Empire 32.00
Book, Big Little Book, Terry & The Pirates, Giants Vengeance 25.00
Book, Big Little Book, Terry Lee, Flight Officer U.S. A. 20.00
Book, Big Little Book, Texan Kid 12.50
Book, Big Little Book, Tillie The Toiler, Wild Man Of Desert Island 25.00
Book, Coloring, Bopeep & Boy Blue, Merrill, 1954, Used 3.50
Book, Coloring, Rin Tin Tin, 1959 .... 22.00
Book, Flip, Girlie Type, 1940s, Small 17.50
Book, Flip, Pop Takes A Nap, J–O Insect Powder 25.00
Book, Little Big Book, Joe Louis, Brown Bomber 45.00
Book, Pop–Up, Cinderella 25.00
Book, Pop–Up, Coloring, Chips 10.00
Book, Pop–Up, Coloring, Laverne & Shirley 10.00
Book, Pop–Up, Doll's House, London, Spiral, 1955 .... 25.00
Book, Pop–Up, Follow Me Animal Book, Animated, 1945 .... 15.00
Book, Pop–Up, Three Little Pigs, 16 Figures, 1930 .... 15.00
Book, Punch Out, Blondie, 1944 .... 13.00
Bookplate, Fraktur, Pen, Ink, Watercolor, Bird, Meyer, 1834, 9 3/8 In. 195.00
Catalog, Alden, 1928, Spring–Summer 70.00
Catalog, Alden, 1931, Fall–Winter 60.00
Catalog, Alden, 1950, Christmas 65.00
Catalog, Brewer Sewing Supplies Co., 1935 .... 25.00
Catalog, Bright Hardware, 1921, Kitchenware, Razors, 500 Pages 85.00
Catalog, Butler Bros., 1922, Santa Claus Edition, 240 Pages 110.00
Catalog, Carpenter Co., 1923, Hardware 30.00
Catalog, Colt Firearms, 1930, 36 Pages 48.00
Catalog, Colt Firearms, 1931, With Price Sheet, 40 Pages 45.00
Catalog, Crepe Paper, 1914, With Parade Floats 15.00
Catalog, Curtiss Aviation School, Early 1900s 75.00
Catalog, FAO Schwarz, 1956, Christmas 75.00
Catalog, FAO Schwarz, 1957, Christmas 45.00
Catalog, FAO Schwarz, 1962, Christmas 100.00
Catalog, FAO Schwarz, 1972, Christmas 50.00
Catalog, Flyer & Silver Wing Bikes, 1931 .... 85.00
Catalog, Hamilton Garment Co., 1923–1924, Fall–Winter 25.00
Catalog, JC Penney, 1963, Spring–Summer 30.00
Catalog, JC Penney, 1964, Fall–Winter 30.00
Catalog, JC Penney, 1969, Christmas 75.00
Catalog, John Wanamaker, 1917 .... 22.50
Catalog, L. L. Bean, 1936, Fall, 60 Pages 65.00
Catalog, L. L. Bean, 1941, Spring, 76 Pages 55.00
Catalog, Lionel, 1947 .... 35.00
Catalog, Marlin Gun, 1965 .... 10.00
Catalog, Meteorological Instruments, 1917, Illustrations, 58 Pages 48.00
Catalog, Montgomery Ward, 1912, No. 81 .... 90.00
Catalog, Montgomery Ward, 1913 .... 80.00
Catalog, Montgomery Ward, 1917 .... 100.00
Catalog, Montgomery Ward, 1923, Fall–Winter 80.00
Catalog, Montgomery Ward, 1924, Spring–Summer 80.00

Catalog, Montgomery Ward, 1929, Aug., Sale 18.00
Catalog, Montgomery Ward, 1932 .... 40.00
Catalog, Montgomery Ward, 1945, Christmas 65.00
Catalog, Montgomery Ward, 1952, Spring–Summer 15.00
Catalog, National Casket Co., 1922, Color Illustrations, 160 Pages 150.00
Catalog, Perfection Oil Stoves, 1937 .... 25.00
Catalog, Sears, 1924, Fall–Winter 80.00
Catalog, Sears, 1930, Spring–Summer 70.00
Catalog, Sears, 1933 .... 40.00
Catalog, Sears, 1934, Wallpaper 18.00
Catalog, Sears, 1935, Christmas 75.00
Catalog, Sears, 1941, Christmas 65.00
Catalog, Sears, 1944, Spring–Summer 15.00
Catalog, Sears, 1954, Christmas, 437 Pages 35.00
Catalog, Spiegel, 1937, Spring–Summer 55.00
Catalog, Spiegel, 1942, Christmas 45.00
Catalog, Spiegel, 1943, Fall–Winter 50.00
Catalog, Spiegel, 1944, Christmas 65.00
Catalog, Spiegel, 1954, Spring–Summer 10.00
Catalog, Spiegel, 1963, Christmas 100.00
Catalog, Stickley Mission Oak, 1914, Art Press, Syracuse, N.Y. 85.00
Catalog, Superior Stoves & Ranges, 1929 .... 25.00
Catalog, Tiffany & Co., 1970 .... 28.00
Catalog, W. Bell, 1982 .... 15.00
Catalog, Williams Telephone, Early Wall Phones 65.00
Check, Die Cut Design Of Fruit, Vegetables, Factory, 1892 .... 3.00
Check, Signed Thomas Walsh, 1903 .... 181.00
Consignment List, Adams & Co. Oceanic Shipping, San Francisco, 1854 .... 125.00
Decal Sheet, Gustav, Leopold, J. George Stickley, 1918 Compass & Clamp 250.00
Directory, Telephone, Richmond, Ind., 1939 .... 5.00
Fraktur, Birds Around Heart, F. Krebs, 1797, 15 1/8 x 12 1/2 In. 550.00
Fraktur, Birds, Tulip Tree, Watercolor, Lined Paper, Framed, 6 x 8 In. 850.00
Fraktur, Birth, 1807, Framed, 14 1/2 x 17 1/4 In. 375.00
Fraktur, Birth, Elisabeth Weik, Pots Of Flowers, 1808, 8 1/3 x 13 In. 250.00
Fraktur, Birth, Friederica Famberd, Wreath Circles Text, 1776 .... 3500.00
Fraktur, Birth, Geburts Und Taufschein, 1803, Frame, 17 1/2 x 14 In. 120.00
Fraktur, Birth, Lebanon County, Framed, 1809, 13 3/4 x 16 3/4 In. 250.00
Fraktur, Birth, Northumberland County, 1792, Framed, 14 x 18 In. 400.00
Fraktur, Birth, Northumberland County, 1816, Framed, 14 1/4 x 17 In. 800.00
Fraktur, Birth, Ruben Poffen Miller, 1815, Framed, 15 x 19 In. 2100.00
Fraktur, Birth, Salome Herby, Framed, 16 1/4 x 11 1/2 In. 1400.00
Fraktur, Birth, Ulrich Gerber, Wayne County, 1874, 7 3/4 x 9 1/2 In. 45.00
Fraktur, Birth, York County, Block Colored, 16 1/4 x 13 1/4 In. 200.00
Fraktur, Budding Tulips, Martin Brechall, 1797, 13 1/8 x 8 In. 528.00
Fraktur, Catherina Bucher, Oct. 22, 1784, & Marriage Record Of 1773 .... 5200.00
Fraktur, Flying Angel, Birth 1797, Death 1872, 17 1/4 x 20 In. 1700.00
Fraktur, Frame, Birth In Lancaster County 1781, 16 1/2 x 19 1/2 In. 250.00
Fraktur, G. G. Perers, Harrisburg, Penna, 1833, 12 1/2 x 15 1/2 In. 190.00
Fraktur, Geburts & Taufschein, Lecha Cty., 1858, 16 3/4 x 13 1/2 In. 150.00
Fraktur, Hannah Konigmacher, Sept. 12, 1758, Cocallico Township 6100.00
Fraktur, Heinrich Mohn, November 20, 1809, Tiger Maple Frame 8800.00
Fraktur, House Blessing, John Ritter, Reading, Frame, 19 1/4 x 15 In. 175.00
Fraktur, Marie Elizabeth Binn, June 9, 1791, Lebanon, Dauphin County 2350.00
Fraktur, Pen & Ink, Watercolor, Pennsylvania German, 18 x 20 3/4 In. 950.00
Fraktur, Pen, Ink, Watercolor, Pennsylvania German, Framed, 10 x 12 In. 1150.00
Fraktur, Pennsylvania German, Bird, Heart, Johannes Lehr, 1830, 9 In. 700.00
Fraktur, Pennsylvania German, Geburts & Taufshein, Frame, 16 x 19 In. 1350.00
Fraktur, Pennsylvania German, Martin Brechall, 1816 Birth, 14 In. 250.00
Indenture, Joshua Hobson Will, 1782, Seal, 2 Blue Stamps, 28 x 32 In. 55.00
License, Hunting, Maryland, 1939 .... 20.00
Menu, Ruppert's Beer, Illustrated By Hans Flato, 1934 .... 20.00
Pamphlet, Anti–Lynching, Scottsboro, Alabama 35.00
Program, 1956 Olympic Games 25.00

Program, Army–Navy Game, 1945 .... 35.00
Program, Barnum & Bailey Circus, Illustrated, 1893, Large 110.00
Program, Follies–Bergere, 1940s 13.00
Program, Rose Bowl, Ohio State & Oregon, 1958 .... 25.00
Program, Sonja Henie Skating 12.00
Program, Sousa & His Band, 1928 .... 75.00
Sign, Fallout Shelter, Dept. Of Defense, Yellow, 1960s, 14 x 20 In. 10.00
Stock Certificate, Bank Of America, 1928 .... 5.00
Stock Certificate, Bank, Denver, Colo., 1889 .... 81.00
Stock Certificate, Indian Mining Co., Indian Portrait, 1910 .... 17.00
Stock Certificate, Lead & Zinc, 1917 .... 10.00
Stock Certificate, Mining, Tombstone Ariz. Territory, Clark, 1886 .... 135.00
Stock Certificate, New Cornella Copper Co., 1921, Mining Vignette 8.00
Stock Certificate, Quincy Mining Co., 1929 .... 5.00
Stock Certificate, Silver Nugget Mining Co., N.Y., 5 x 10 In. 75.00

PAPERWEIGHTS must have first appeared along with paper in ancient Egypt. Today's collectors search for every type, from the very expensive French weights of the nineteenth century to the modern artist weights or advertising pieces. The glass tops of the paperweights sometimes have been nicked or scratched and this type of damage can be removed by polishing. Some serious collectors think this type of repair is an alteration and will not buy a repolished weight; others think it is an acceptable technique of restoration that does not change the value. Baccarat paperweights are listed separately under Baccarat.

9 Floretes Around Cane Center, 19th Century, Miniature 165.00
Admiral Dewey, Hero Of Manila, 1898 .... 150.00
Advertising, A. Martin, Carriage Maker, Metal 35.00
Advertising, A. T. & T. Centennial, Cane Work, Whitefriars 200.00
Advertising, American Powder Co. 160.00
Advertising, American Radiators, Chicago 15.00
Advertising, Baldwin Metal Forges, Reading, Penna. 20.00
Advertising, Bluefield's Bananas, Bunch Of Bananas 35.00
Advertising, Brown & Williams Tobacco, Louisville, Ky. 30.00
Advertising, Merchants Awning Co., Glass, 4 1/4 x 3 In. 20.00
Advertising, New York Telephone Co., Bell Shape, Blue 60.00
Advertising, Orange Crush Bottling Co., Augusta, Ga., 4 x 3 In. 145.00
Advertising, Star Biscuits, Mouse & Biscuit, Figural, Metal 85.00
Advertising, Take Simmons Liver Regulator, Horseshoe, Bronze 85.00
Advertising, Ward's Orange, Lemon & Lime Crush, 1924 .... 200.00
Advertising, Washington Life Insurance 25.00
Advertising, White Cat Cigar 36.00
Advertising, Winchester 100th Anniversary, 1966 .... 15.00
Advertising, Winchester, 1910 .... 42.00
Bird, Full–Bodied, Cast Iron, Black Repaint, 4 3/4 In. 65.00
Birds, Sulphide, Red Woodenware, Green Leaves, Conical Shape 40.00
Bobby Kennedy, Sulphide 65.00
Buxxini, Pulled Flower 150.00
Clichy, Bouquet, Flat, 3 Cane Flowers, 2 1/2 In. 2800.00
Clichy, Garland, 28 Colored Canes 2900.00
Clichy, Garland, Floral Canes 2200.00
Columbus Announcing His Discovery, Sept. 5, 1882 .... 78.00
D'Albret, Albert Schweitzer, Sulphide, Crystal, Cobalt Ground 70.00
Eagle, Iron & Brass, 4 x 5 1/2 In. 50.00
Gentile, Flamingo 25.00
Globe, Applied Glass Snake, Twisted Canes, Opalescent 300.00
Labino, Bottle Glass, Eagle Inside 235.00
Labino, Multicolored Design, Signed 350.00
Lion, Cast Iron, Old Gold Paint, 6 In. 40.00
Lion, Metro Goldwyn Mayer, Bronzed Iron 67.50
Millefiori, Butterfly, Murano 165.00
Millefiori, Random Scattered Canes 145.00
NFBPWC, Brass 75.00

Parian, Bust,

Shakespeare, Robinson &   Parian, Figurine, John A. Andrews, Verse On Back, c.1867, 21 In.

Leadbetter, c.1875, 13 In.   Parian, Figurine, Young Columbus, Mid-19th Century, 15 1/2 In.

Pear, Crackle Glass, Hand Blown, Hollow	45.00
Perthshire, Marmalade Cat	200.00
Perthshire, Thistle, 1974	100.00
Pig, Seated, Iron, 2 1/4 In.	25.00
Pope Pius XII, Sulphide, Star Cut Ruby Ground	150.00
Rooster, Thomas Drills, Gold & Red Paint, 3 1/4 In.	40.00
Simpson, Planet, Large	400.00
Snow Dome, Yellowstone, Bear, Plastic Ashtray Base	25.00
St. Clair, 5 Flowers, Orange	65.00
St. Clair, Bell, Yellow & White, Small	40.00
St. Clair, Bird, Red	30.00
St. Clair, Dome, Black & White, Small	40.00
St. Clair, Strawberry	37.00
St. Louis, Coronation, Queen Elizabeth II, Sulphide	60.00
St. Louis, Dancing Devil, Amethyst, 3 1/4 In.	715.00
St. Louis, Layered Flower, Cone Center, 3 7/8 In.	385.00
St. Louis, Lizard, c.1848	2000.00
St. Louis, Petal Flower, Canes, Candy-Striped Base, 2 1/2 In.	990.00
State Bank Of Chicago, Brass, 1919	15.00
Sulphide, MacArthur	80.00
Sulphide, Paul Revere	80.00
Swan, Cast Lead, 3 In., Pair	70.00
Turkey, Glass, Czechoslovakia	19.00
Warren Harding, Inauguration Date, Bronze	16.00

PAPIER-MACHE is made from paper mixed with glue, chalk, and other ingredients, then molded and baked. It becomes very hard and can be painted. Boxes, trays, and furniture were made of papier-mache. Some of the nineteenth-century pieces were decorated with mother-of-pearl. Furniture made of papier-mache is listed in the Furniture section.

Box, Pewter Inlay, Shoe Shape, Black & Red, 27 In.	180.00
Chicken, Wooden Base, Polychrome Paint, 3 5/8 In.	75.00
Decoy, Hen Turkey, Stick-Up Field, Glass Eyes, 26 1/2 In.	900.00
Dish, Mother-of-Pearl Inlay, Victorian, Label	28.00
Duck, Pip-Squeak, Cloth Covered Silent Bellows, 3 1/4 In.	65.00
Easter Bunny, Basket On Back, Pastel, Pair	60.00
Egg, Easter, Chicks, 8 1/2 In.	45.00
Happy Hooligan, Colorful, 5 In.	65.00
Owl, Gray & Black, Glass Eyes, Large	65.00
Owl, Original Paint, Glass Eyes, 13 3/4 In.	35.00
Tray, Black, Gold, Gilded Brass Handles, English, 25 3/4 In.	975.00

Tray, Faux Bamboo Stand, Floral, Black Lacquer, 19 3/4 In. 1430.00
Turkey, Display, 1920, 7 In. 195.00

PARASOL, see Umbrella

PARIAN is a fine-grained, hard-paste porcelain named for the marble it resembles. It was first made in England in 1846 and gained in favor in the United States about 1860. Figures, tea sets, vases, and other items were made of Parian at many English and American factories.

Bust, Abraham Lincoln, Raised Round Base, English, c.1860, 15 1/2 In. 275.00
Bust, Milton, 8 In. 45.00
Bust, Queen Victoria 65.00
Bust, Schiller, Germany, 9 1/2 In. 175.00
Bust, Shakespeare, R. Monti, Copeland, c.1860, 13 1/4 In. 715.00
Bust, Shakespeare, Robinson & Leadbetter, c.1875, 13 In. ....*Illus* 725.00
Bust, Sir Walter Scott, Copeland, c.1860, 15 In. 495.00
Figurine, Dog, Whippet, Oblong Base, 9 1/2 In. 225.00
Figurine, George Washington, Standing, Heroic Pose, England, 13 In. 580.00
Figurine, John A. Andrews, Verse On Back, c.1867, 21 In. ....*Illus* 1210.00
Figurine, Maidenhood, Copeland, England, c.1861, 21 3/4 In. 247.50
Figurine, Woman With Anchor, 13 1/2 In. 35.00
Figurine, Woman, Holding Dove, Bennington, 9 In. 178.00
Figurine, Young Columbus, Mid-19th Century, 15 1/2 In. ....*Illus* 495.00
Mug, Colonial Man's Head, World's Fair, 1939 .... 18.00
Pitcher, Bust Of Washington, Crossed Flags, Copeland, 8 In. 150.00
Pitcher, Thistle 148.00
Plaque, Portrait Of Gentleman, Gilt Shadow Box Frame, 18 In. 425.00
Teapot, Seal Of America, Liberty Lady, 19th Century, 6 x 9 In. 77.00

PARIS, Vieux Paris, or Old Paris, is porcelain ware that is known to have been made in Paris in the eighteenth or early nineteenth century. These porcelains have no identifying mark but can be recognized by the whiteness of the porcelain and the lines and decorations. Gold decoration is often used.

Bowl, Reticulated, Gilt & Pierced Allover, High Domed Foot 275.00
Bowl, Vegetable, Cover, Gilt Decoration, Set Of 3 .... 176.00
Bowl, Vegetable, Magenta, Gilt Decoration, 10 In., Pair 55.00
Coffeepot, Hand Painted Figural & Landscape Design, 11 In. 88.00
Compote, Reticulated, Gilt, Edw. Honore, c.1810, 7 1/2 In. 176.00
Cup & Saucer, Early 19th Century 80.00
Dessert & Coffee Service, Penna. Retailer's Label, c.1865, 48 Piece 330.00
Dessert Set, Gilt Decorated, 7 Plates, 9 Cups, 13 Saucers, 27 Bowls 99.00
Dinner Set, Pink Band, Gilt Decoration, 50 Piece 550.00
Figurine, Piper, Floral Waistcoat, 19th Century, 15 In. 360.00
Gravy Boat, Eagle Handle, Covered Sauce Dish, Gold, White, Stand 330.00
Perfume Bottle, Arab Chieftain, Consort, Signed, c.1850, 5 1/4 In., Pr. 605.00
Pitcher, Wild Flowers, Pink, Gold Trim 165.00
Platter, Magenta, Gilt Decoration, Handles, 15 1/2 In. 88.00
Relish, Magenta & Gilt Design, Shell Shape, c.1850 .... 85.00
Tea Service, Inverted Pear Form, Floral Panels, 7 Piece 357.50
Tureen, Cover, Gold Band, Acorn & Leaf-Form Handles 154.00
Tureen, Soup, Magenta, Gilt Decoration, Oval, Footed, Large 121.00
Urns, Figural Scenes, Caryatid Handles, 1870s, 12 In., Pair 1100.00
Vase, Amphora Shape, Horseman & Landscape, c.1860, 8 In., Pair 135.00
Vase, Baluster, Circular Foot, Applied Lion Head Handles, 13 In., Pr. 710.00
Vase, Campana Form, Gilt & Floral, Mask-Form Handles, 9 3/4 In. 264.00
Vase, Cavalier, Feathered Hat, Stream On Reverse, 19 1/2 In. 950.00
Vase, Faux Marble Base, c.1815, 14 1/2 In., Pair ....*Illus* 12100.00
Vase, Floral, Heavy Slip, 13 In. 345.00
Vase, Gentleman Courting Maiden, c.1850, 19 In. 845.00
Vase, Hand Painted Figure, 11 In., Pair 325.00
Vase, Pastoral Scenes, Ovoid, 14 In., Pair 330.00
Vase, Shell Rim, Scrolled Handles, Gilt, 19th Century, 13 1/2 In., Pair 1650.00

Paris, Vase, Faux Marble Base, c.1815,

14 1/2 In., Pair

◆◆◆◆◆◆◆◆◆◆◆◆◆◆◆◆◆◆◆◆

Never carry a marble top flat.
It can break under its own
weight. Carry it in a vertical
position.

◆◆◆◆◆◆◆◆◆◆◆◆◆◆◆◆◆◆◆◆

PATE–DE–VERRE is an ancient technique in which glass is made by
blending and refining powdered glass of different colors into molds. The
process was revived by French glassmakers, especially Galle, around the
end of the nineteenth century.

Atomizer, Rose Color Body, Spray Of Green Leaves, 3 3/4 In.	2500.00
Cup, Devil	450.00
Dish, Figural, Owl, Oak Leaves, Gray, Daum, 6 In.	8250.00
Paperweight, Sea Nymph, Green Leaf, Daum, 6 3/4 In.	8800.00
Plate, Nudes, Corbin, 1970, 10 1/2 In.	225.00

PATE–SUR–PATE means paste on paste. The design was made by painting
layers of slip on the ceramic piece until a relief decoration was formed.
The method was developed at the Sevres factory in France about 1850. It
became even more famous at the English Minton factory about 1870. It
has since been used by many potters to make both pottery and porcelain
wares.

Lamp, Oil, Dark Green Ground, Putti, Ferns In Relief, 12 In.	375.00
Pitcher, Mother, Cherub On White Cloud, Blue, 3 3/4 In.	85.00
Plaque, White Scene, Cobalt Blue Ground, Limoges, 6 x 10 In.	1200.00
Powder Jar, Greek God, Chariot, Cobalt, Limoges, 4 1/2 In.	225.00
Urn, Cover, 3 Allegorical Figures, 3 Handles, Minton, 14 In.	3575.00
Vase, Gilt Angel, White & Teal, 9 3/4 In.	275.00
Vase, Mythological Person, Flowing Dress, Gold, Minton, 8 In.	2100.00
Vase, Nude In Veils, Children Overhead, Handles, 8 1/2 In.	375.00
Vase, White Slip Young Nymphs, Ring Handles, 8 1/4 In., Pair	2475.00

PAUL REVERE POTTERY was made at several locations in and around
Boston, Massachusetts, between 1906 and 1942. The pottery was operated
as a settlement house program for teenage girls. Many pieces were signed
S.E.G. for Saturday Evening Girls. The artists concentrated on children's
dishes and tiles. Decorations were outlined in black and filled with color.

Dish, Ducks, 7 In.	25.00
Mug, Motto, Forest Landscape, SEG, 1918, 4 In.	880.00
Paperweight, SEG, 1914	375.00
Pitcher & Bowl, Rabbit & Turtle Rim, SEG, 1918	495.00
Rabbit & Turtle Border, Motto, SEG, 4-26-10, 7 3/4 In.	522.50
Sugar & Creamer	38.00
Tile, Motto, SEG, 6 1/8 x 4 1/8 In.	412.50
Trivet, Tree & Pond	175.00
Tumbler, Blue & Yellow Design, SEG	295.00
Vase, Frog Skin Glaze, 4 Incised Bands, 4 x 5 In.	135.00
Vase, Mottled Aqua On Green, Bulbous, 7 In.	155.00
Vase, Red Drip Over Blue–Green, 6 1/2 In.	275.00
Vase, Yellow Glaze, Cylindrical, c.1924, 8 1/2 In., Pair	220.00
Vase, Yellow, SEG, 6 In.	195.00

PEACHBLOW glass originated about 1883 at Hobbs, Brockunier and Company of Wheeling, West Virginia. It shades from yellow to peach and is lined with white glass. New England peachblow is a one-layer glass shading from red to white. Mt. Washington peachblow shades from pink to blue. Reproductions of all types of peachblow have been made. Some are poor and easy to identify as copies, others are very accurate reproductions and could fool the unwary. Related pieces may be listed under Gunderson and Webb Peachblow.

Bowl, Red To Pink, Ruffled, Gilt Enamel, Prunus, Butterflies, 5 In.	248.00
Bride's Bowl, Derby Claw Foot, Cherub Base, 15 In.	1650.00
Cruet, Bulbous Form, Applied Amber Handle, Cut Stopper, 7 In.	660.00
Darner, New England	225.00
Decanter, Dark Mahogany, Applied Amber Handle, 9 1/2 In.	1250.00
Epergne, 3–Trumpet, Piecrust Base, Cranberry, 21 In.	300.00
Ewer, Lined In White, Amber Handle, 11 In.	475.00
Ewer, Square Base, Twisted Clear Handle, 8 In.	395.00
Lamp, Fairy, Wheeling, Clarke Base, 3 1/2 x 3 In.	550.00
Pear, New England, 5/8–In. Open Stem	60.00
Pitcher, Claret, Amber Rigaree Collar, Wheeling, 10 In.	2250.00
Pitcher, Red Shading To Yellow, Applied Handle, 8 In.	1100.00
Pitcher, Satin Finish, Bulbous, Ovoid, Wheeling, 5 In. ....*Illus*	935.00
Pitcher, Wheeling Drape, Crystal Handle, Square Top, 5 1/2 In.	440.00
Pitcher, Wheeling Drape, Ruffled Top, Amber Handle, 8 In.	880.00
Punch Cup, Reeded Handle, New England, 2 5/8 In.	425.00
Rose Bowl, Crimped, Raspberry To Cream, New England, 2 1/2 In.	295.00
Sherbet, Autumn Leaves, Blue Berries, Mt. Washington, 2 1/2 In.	735.00
Sherbet, Mt. Washington, 2 1/2 In.	735.00
Sugar & Creamer, Ribbed, Raspberry, Pink, New England, 2 3/4 In.	600.00
Sugar Shaker, Acorn, Pink	325.00
Syrup, Acorn	300.00
Toothpick, Acorn	300.00
Tumble Up, Wheeling	1150.00
Tumbler, Etched Circles, 5 In.	205.00
Tumbler, Off–White Lining, Wheeling, 3 3/4 In.	300.00
Tumbler, Pink To White	165.00
Tumbler, Raspberry To Pink, New England, 3 3/4 In.	325.00
Tumbler, Raspberry To Yellow, White Lining, Wheeling, 3 1/2 In.	450.00
Vase, Amberina Cased To Opal White, Wheeling, 8 In.	605.00
Vase, Corset Shape, Pink To Raspberry, New England, 3 1/2 In.	395.00
Vase, Double Gourd, Wheeling, 7 In.	1250.00
Vase, Gold Blossoms & Leaves, Rose To Pink, Webb, 10 In.	450.00
Vase, Indented On 4 Sides, New England, 4 3/4 In.	785.00
Vase, Jack–In–The–Pulpit, Mt. Washington, 7 1/2 In.	2450.00
Vase, Lily, New England, 10 In.	950.00
Vase, Raspberry To Clear, Swirled Satin Finish, Ground Top, 9 In.	95.00
Vase, Stick, Cream Lining, Glossy, Wheeling, 8 1/4 In.	750.00

Peachblow, Pitcher, Satin Finish, Bulbous,
Ovoid, Wheeling, 5 In.

Ivory will darken if kept in the dark. Keep a piano open so the keys will be in natural light. Keep figurines, chess sets, and other ivory in the open.

Vase, Wheeling, No. 5, 6 1/2 In. 750.00

PEARL items listed here are made of the natural mother-of-pearl from shells. Such natural pearl has been used to decorate furniture and small utilitarian objects for centuries. The glassware known as mother-of-pearl is listed by that name. Opera glasses made with natural pearl shell are listed under Opera Glasses.

Button Hook, Chrome Hook	15.00
Carved Game Token, 1830	10.00
Knife, Silver Blade, Pearl Handle, Set Of 12	125.00

PEARLWARE is an earthenware made by Josiah Wedgwood in 1779. It was copied by other potters in England. Pearlware is only slightly different in color from creamware and for many years collectors have confused the terms.

Pearl

Bowl, Overall Brushed Flowers, Shell Edge, 6 3/8 In.	400.00
Coffeepot, Underglaze Blue Swag Design, Miniature	1225.00
Creamer, Enameled Floral, Pearlware, 4 3/4 In.	250.00
Creamer, Queen's Rose	600.00
Plate, Blue Transfer Of Eagle, Hexagonal	475.00
Plate, Chinoiserie Design, Molded Feather Edge, 9 7/8 In.	220.00
Plate, Free-Brushed Flower Center, Blue Feather Edge, 6 5/8 In.	975.00
Plate, Orange & Blue Flowers, Green Scalloped Edge, 5 1/8 In.	650.00
Plate, Orange Flowers, Scalloped Blue Feather Rim, 9 5/8 In.	145.00
Plate, Overall Brushed Flowers, Green Molded Shell Edge	350.00
Platter, Center Eagle, 14 1/2 In.	475.00
Sugar, Cover, Floral Design, 4 1/4 In.	900.00
Sugar, Cover, Swan Finial, Queen's Rose	950.00
Teapot, Blue Adam's Rose, 6 1/8 In.	600.00
Teapot, Blue Underglaze Foliage, Miniature	650.00
Teapot, Queen's Rose, 5 1/2 In.	150.00
Teapot, Queen's Rose, Swan Finial	2600.00
Teapot, Swirled Ribs, Purple Enameling, 6 1/4 In.	105.00

PEKING GLASS is a Chinese cameo glass first made popular in the eighteenth century. The Chinese have continued to make this layered glass in the old manner, and many new pieces are now available that could confuse the average buyer.

Bowl, Carved Floral, Birds, Chinese, Amber, 6 1/4 In.	880.00
Bowl, Floral Design, Blue On White, 6 In.	160.00
Bowl, Florals, Chinese Red On White, 6 In.	185.00
Bowl, Fruit, Green On White, 6 In.	185.00
Bowl, Hydrangeas, Amethyst On White, 6 In.	240.00
Bowl, Line Of Flowering Lotus, Yellow, 1850s, 8 In.	440.00
Bowl, Purple On White, 6 1/2 In.	225.00
Vase, Applied Orange Florals, Bird, 1920, 12 x 5 In.	475.00
Vase, Crane & Lotus Flowers, Red Cut To White, 8 In.	210.00
Vase, Cranes In Vegetation, White Ground, Green Overlay, 8 In.	137.50
Vase, Exotic Fish, Pond, Lilies, White Baluster Form, 12 In.	605.00
Vase, Flying Crane & Trees, Clouds, White, Cobalt Blue, 8 In.	350.00
Vase, Green On White, 7 1/4 In.	190.00

PELOTON glass is a European glass with small threads of colored glass rolled onto the surface of clear or colored glass. It is sometimes called spaghetti, or shredded coconut, glass. Most pieces found today were made in the nineteenth century.

Bowl, Ruffled Rim, Triangular, Lavender, 4 1/4 In.	120.00
Rose Bowl, 6-Crimp Top, Embossed Ribbing, Wishbone Feet, 2 1/2 In.	225.00
Rose Bowl, 6-Crimp Top, Rainbow Coconut Strings, 2 3/8 In.	245.00
Rose Bowl, Alligator Base	200.00
Rose Bowl, Tricorn 6-Crimp Top, Coconut Strings, 2 3/4 In.	225.00
Vase, Coconut Shreds, Lavender Shading To White, 5 1/2 In.	385.00
Vase, Green Satin Threading, 6 In.	150.00

Vase, Ribbed, Ruby With Clear Rigaree, 4 1/2 In.	250.00
Vase, Stick, Blue & White, 7 In.	145.00
Vase, Tricorn Top, Ribbed Ground, Coconut Strings, 3 3/4 In.	350.00
Vase, Tricorner Folded Over Top, Coconut Strings, 4 x 5 In.	350.00
Vase, White Spaghetti On Crystal, Blue Bells, Roses, 6 In.	265.00

PENS replaced hand–cut quills as writing instruments in 1780 when the first steel pen point was made in England. But it was 100 years before the commercial pen was a common item. The fountain pen was invented in the 1830s but was not made in quantity until the 1880s. All types of old pens are collected.

PEN & PENCIL, Admiral	10.00
Baseball Bat, Joe DeMaggio	95.00
Blondie & Dagwood, 1930s	22.00
Hutcheon, Box	85.00
Parker 51, Lustraloy Caps, Black, Chrome Trim, Box	35.00
Parker, 14K Gold Point Pen, Box	175.00
Parker, Duofold, Box	135.00
Parker, Lucky Curve, Duofold	50.00
Parker, Vacuumatic, Case	125.00
Waterman, 100–Year, Case	250.00
Waterman, Leather Vest Case	195.00
PEN, Baseball Bat, Maury Wills	25.00
Conklin, Black & Silver, Dated 1903	150.00
Conklin, Crescent Filler, Patent 1918	35.00
Conklin, Swan, Gold	200.00
Cross, Pepsi Light	25.00
Dip, Wooden Carved Indian Head, Souvenir	18.00
Display Tray, Sheaffer	25.00
Dodge Dealer's, Blue Car Floats In Oil, 1940s	45.00
Esterbrook, Green	17.00
Eversharp, Bell & Howell Thermometer At Base, Box	35.00
Faber, Wooden Handle, Brass	1.25
Ink–O–Graph, Ballpoint, Burgundy	10.00
James Bond 007, Action, Vapor Paper, On Card, 1966, 5 x 11 In.	195.00
Lettering, Barch–Payzant, Freehand, Box, 1921	20.00
Massey–Harris Tractor, Mini Tractor Floats In Oil	35.00
Meisterstuck, Mont Blanc, 1961	175.00
Mother–of–Pearl, Woman's, Edwardian, Case	45.00
Oldsmobile, Mini Car Floats In Oil	15.00
Parker, Black & Mother–of–Pearl Stripes, Gold Filled	60.00
Parker, Duofold, Cigar Shape, Maroon	225.00
Parker, Duofold, Lapis, 3 Bands	85.00
Parker, Lucky Curve, Eye Drop, Dated 1911	80.00
Parker, Lucky Curve, Woman's	65.00
Peerless, Yellow Brass, Cigarette Lighter, Pocket	5.00
Rock Island Lines	20.00
Sheaffer, 14K Gold	15.00
Sheaffer, Gold Nib	15.00
Sheaffer, Lever Filled, Torpedo Style, Gold Tip, Ring, Tortoiseshell	85.00
Sheaffer, Lifetime, Mottled Black & Gold	125.00
Sheaffer, Lifetime, White Dot	65.00
Sheaffer, Lifetime, Wrap Around, 14K Nib	15.00
Sheaffer, Marble Stand	30.00
Sheaffer, Onyx Base, Gold Paint	35.00
Sheaffer, Pilot's	48.00
Sheaffer, Scripto, Big Red, Lever Fill	20.00
Sheaffer, Woman's Ring	55.00
Star, Level Fill, Black Chased Hard Rubber, Gold Trim	25.00
Traveling Dip, Souvenir Brooklyn Bridge, Woolworth Building, Germany	30.00
Wahl, No. 5, Flat Top, Gold Filled Body, 14K Nib, Lever Fill	95.00
Wahl, Skyline, Box	50.00
Wahl–Eversharp, Black & Pearl, Oversized	600.00

Wahl-Eversharp, Gold Seal, Roller Clip, Black & Pearl 285.00
Wahl-Eversharp, Rosewood, Hard Rubber, Clip, 14K Nib 95.00
Waterman, Fountain, Ideal, Sterling Silver, Engraved Flowers, Vines 150.00
Waterman, Ideal, Blue Marble 60.00
Waterman, Ideal, Red & Brown 45.00
Waterman, No. 20, Black Hard Rubber, No. 10 Nib, 14K Gold Band On Cap ....,.... 2500.00
Waterman, No. 52, Hard Rubber, Gold Filled Trim, No. 2 Nib 45.00
Waterman, No. 55 .... 65.00
Waterman, No. 94, Ideal, Brown & Green Marbelized 55.00
Waterman, Sleeve Filler, Hard Rubber, c.1908 .... 145.00
Waterman, Woman's, 18K Gold, Black 75.00
Wearever 10.00

PENCILS were invented, so it is said, in 1565. The eraser was not added
to the pencil until 1858. The automatic pencil was invented in 1863.
Collectors today want advertising pencils or automatic pencils of unusual
design. Boxes and sharpeners for pencils are also collected.

PENCIL SHARPENER, 3 Rotating Blades, Automatic Pencil Sharpener, 1907 .... 165.00
Airplane, Bakelite 25.00
Army Tank Shape 25.00
Charlie McCarthy 15.00
Climax, Drawer, Patent 1900 .... 75.00
Desk, Donald Duck, Rubber & Metal 30.00
Dog In Chair 15.00
Duck, Amber 45.00
Figural, Man, Tin, Germany 50.00
Globe, Metal 12.50
Goofy, Bakelite 8.50
Gun, Metal 35.00
Hippo, Ceramic 8.00
National Cash Register, Figural 15.00
Scotty, Butterscotch 45.00
Sewing Machine Shape, Bronze 15.00
Table Mount, Hand Turn, Chelsea Mfg. Co., Cast Iron 100.00
Typewriter, Metal 35.00
Tyrolean, With Mustache, Suspenders, Crank, W. Germany 39.00
USA Airplane 50.00
USA Army Plane, Red, 2 1/4 In. 55.00
Wizard 35.00
PENCIL, Baseball Bat, Mechanical 36.00
Borden's, Elsie 15.00
Box, Child's, Sports, Eagle Pencil Co. 3.50
Box, Frank Buck, Contents, 1930 .... 35.00
Box, Regular Fellows, Comic 35.00
Box, Skippy, Comic 35.00
Bullet, John Deere 9.00
Case, Deputy Dawg, Hasbro, 1961 .... 55.00
Centerville, Iowa, Bank, Wooden .... .50
Clip, Morton Salt .... 3.00 To 5.00
Compass, Eagle, Iron .... .75
Mechanical, Calendar, Pearlized, 1941 .... 10.00
Mechanical, Eversharp, Green Marbelized, 1936 .... 30.00
Mechanical, Figural Top, Falstaff 18.00
Mechanical, Ingersoll, Rolled Gold, 5 3/8 In. 18.00
Mechanical, Keen Kutter 15.00
Mechanical, Peters Weatherbird Shoes 25.00
Mechanical, Poll-Parrot 25.00
Mechanical, Shaw-Barton, Ivory Marbelized 10.00
Mechanical, Swastika Coal Co. 25.00
Mother-of-Pearl & Gold Filled, Leather Case, Patent 1871 .... 130.00
Mountain Dew .... .50
Mr. Peanut, In Liquid, Mechanical 15.00
Parker, Duofold, Black 35.00

RCA, Mechanical, Battery In Center 55.00
Reddy Kilowatt 7.00
Rummy Soda, Mechanical 18.00
S. H. & L. Co., Engraved, Gold Filled Body 95.00
Sharpener, Baker's Chocolate Girl 95.00
Sheaffer, Lifetime, Woman's, Jade Green Marbelized, Gold Filled 75.00
Wahl, Gold Loop End 30.00
Wahl–Eversharp, Black & Pearl, Oversized 200.00
Wahl–Eversharp, Engraved, Sterling 145.00
Wahl–Eversharp, Mechanical, Gold Filled, With Loop, 3 1/4 In. 15.00
Wahl–Eversharp, Mechanical, Gold Filled, With Loop, Engraved Binnie 18.00

PENNSBURY Pottery worked in Morrisville, Pennsylvania, from 1950 to · *Pennsbury*
1971. Full sets of dinnerware, as well as many decorative items, were   *Pottery*
made. Pieces are marked with the name of the factory.

Ashtray, Amish People 30.00
Ashtray, Doylestown Trust 25.00
Ashtray, Fairless Works, Gray, Box 38.00
Ashtray, Outen The Light .... 30.00 To 35.00
Ashtray, Rooster 23.00
Ashtray, Such Schmootzers 25.00
Ashtray, What Giffs 30.00
Beer & Pretzel Set, Sweet Adeline, 9 Piece 120.00
Bowl, Potato Chip, Sweet Adeline, 12 In. 45.00
Bowl, Pretzel, Quartet, 12 In. 45.00
Bowl, Pretzel, Quartet, 8 x 11 In. 120.00
Butter, Cover, Tulip 35.00
Candy Dish, Heart Shape 25.00
Canister, Sugar, Rooster 125.00
Coaster, Horwitz 30.00
Coaster, Schultz 30.00
Creamer, Amish Women 25.00
Creamer, Hexagonal 15.00
Cruet Set, Amish Head Stoppers, Oil & Vinegar .... 100.00 To 135.00
Cup & Saucer, Black Rooster .... 25.00 To 30.00
Cup & Saucer, Red Rooster 8.00
Cup, Red Rooster 14.00
Figurine, Blue Jay, Pair 575.00
Figurine, Ducklings, Pair 295.00
Figurine, Ducks, Male & Female, 12 In., Pair 500.00
Jug, Sweet Adeline 35.00
Mug, Amish 28.00
Mug, Barber Shop Quartet, 5 In. 30.00
Mug, Beer, Amish Couple 30.00
Mug, Beer, Sweet Adeline 30.00
Mug, Beverage, Red Barn, 4 1/2 In. 75.00
Mug, Gay Ninety, 5 In. 30.00
Mug, Rooster 15.00
Mug, Sweet Adeline 40.00
Pie Plate, Rooster, 9 In. 38.00
Pitcher, 7 In. 35.00
Pitcher, Amish Man, 2 In. 20.00
Pitcher, Amish Woman, 4 In. 30.00
Pitcher, Bird, Redstart 25.00
Pitcher, Eagle, 6 1/4 In. .... 48.00 To 60.00
Pitcher, Red Rooster 35.00
Pitcher, Rooster, 4 In. .... 35.00 To 45.00
Pitcher, Rooster, 6 1/2 In. 40.00
Plaque, B. & O. Railroad, 7 1/2 In. 60.00
Plaque, Outen The Light, 4 In. .... 25.00 To 35.00
Plaque, Rooster, Saying 25.00
Plaque, Western & Atlantic R.R. General 40.00
Plate, Amish, 8 In. 49.00

Plate, Black Rooster, 10 In.	40.00
Plate, Commemorative, Rotary 50th Anniversary	43.00
Plate, Mother's Day, 1971	32.00
Plate, Mother's Day, 1972	20.00 To 32.00
Plate, Red Rooster, 10 In.	34.00
Plate, Yuletide, 1970	27.00
Soup, Dish, Red Rooster, Ruffled Rim	35.00
Sugar, Cover, Red Rooster, 4 In.	26.00
Tray, Horses, Octagonal, 3 x 5 In.	25.00
Wall Pocket, Green & White Floral, Square	36.00

PEPSI–COLA, the drink and the name, was invented in 1898 but was not trademarked until 1903. The logo was changed from an elaborate script to the modern block letters on the 1970 Pepsi label. All types of advertising memorabilia are collected, and reproductions are being made.

Banner, Window, Michael Jackson, Color, 1988, 24 x 32 In.	10.00
Bottle Cap, Crown, 1950–1960	.40
Bottle Cap, Crown, For Swirl Bottle, Mid–1960s	1.00
Bottle Cap, Crown, Yellow, Red Script Logo, 1930s	2.00
Bottle Opener, Figural, Bottle	25.00
Bottle Opener, Star x	5.00
Bottle, ACL, Swirl, 1961, 10 Oz.	8.00
Bottle, Arizona State Univ. Sun Devils, Fiesta Bowl, 1972, 16 Oz.	12.00
Bottle, Burlington, N. C., Red, White & Blue, 1948, 12 Oz.	15.00
Bottle, Charlotte, N. C., Red, White, 1948, 8 Oz.	12.50
Bottle, Commemorative, Fresno, Calif., Map, 1983, Contents, 16 Oz.	14.00
Bottle, Durham, N. C., Clear, Script Embossed, BIMAL, 1910, 7 Oz.	60.00
Bottle, E. State Univ., Johnson City, Tn., 1975, 16 Oz.	14.00
Bottle, Fargo, N. D., Red, White & Blue, 1946, 12 Oz.	17.50
Bottle, Kentucky Bicentennial, 1976, Contents, 16 Oz.	14.00
Bottle, Rose Bowl, U. Of Ill., Big 10 Champs, 1984–1983, 16 Oz.	20.00
Bottle, Sapulpa, Oklahoma, Chieftains Booster Club, 1981, 16 Oz.	12.00
Bottle, South Carolina Historic Contributions, 1976, 12 Oz.	9.00
Bottle, Syrup, Flat River, Mo., 1943, 12 Oz.	21.00
Bottle, Univ. Of Nebraska Cornhuskers, Contents, 1974, 16 Oz.	12.00
Bottle, Wilmington, N. C., Red, White & Blue, 1946, 12 Oz.	17.50
Bottle, World Champions, Cincinnati Reds, 1975	40.00
Calendar, 1941, Complete	200.00
Calendar, 1947, Paintings Of The Year	50.00
Can, Bell's Amusement Park, 1987, 12 Oz.	2.50
Can, Goodwill Games, 1990, 4 Piece	3.00
Can, Strawberry Burst, One Of The Wild Ones, Unopened, 12 Oz.	4.00
Can, Tulsa State Fair, 1986, 12 Oz.	2.50
Card, Playing, With Tin	6.00
Carrier, 6 Pack, Aluminum	20.00
Carrier, Carton, 12 Bottles, 1940s, Unused	45.00
Carrier, Yellow Plastic, 6 Bottles, Black Block Logo, 1960	9.00
Clock, Animated, Windup, 1920s, 6 x 6 In.	1200.00
Clock, Light–Up, Plastic, Metal, Round, 16 In.	160.00
Clock, Plastic, Octagonal Face, Over Logo	15.00
Clock, Say Pepsi Please, Glass, Lights Up, 1960s	375.00
Clock, Steel Can, Lexan Face, Neon, Round, 16 In.	200.00
Coin–Operated Machine, Vendo 27, Skirt	2500.00
Cooler, Picnic	150.00
Cup, Paper, Cone Style, 1930s, Unused	65.00
Display, Michael Jackson, Stand–Up, Life Size, Cardboard	85.00
Door Push, Red, White & Blue, 3 x 30 In.	55.00
Door Push, White, Blue, Red, Black, Beige, 3 x 30 In.	70.00
Fan, Pepsi Pete, 1930s	75.00
Glass, Flare Top, Clear, 6 Piece	130.00
Hanger, War Victory Paper On Back, 1940s, 16 x 6 In.	215.00
Lighter	28.00
Machine, Light–Up	3000.00

Menu Board, Tin Lithograph, Self–Framed, 30 In.	120.00
Pen & Pencil Set, Enameled, Clips, Box	32.00
Pen, Ballpoint, Catch That Pepsi Spirit, White, Blue	1.50
Pencil, Diet Pepsi, Mechanical, Blue	1.50
Pencil, Wooden, Unused	.75
Pin, 100th Rose Bowl Parade, Slice, 1984	6.00
Poster, Indiana Jones & The Last Crusade, 1989, 23 x 35 In.	12.00
Poster, Pepsi Counter, Spy Radio Thriller, 1940s, 8 x 19 In.	30.00
Radio, Bottle Shape, Large	325.00
Record, Voice Of Your Man In Service, World War II	40.00
Salt & Pepper, Blue & Yellow Top, Box, 5 In.	26.00 To 30.00
Santa Claus	75.00
Server, Pepsi Double Dot Dry	7.50
Shelf Talker, Jackson's World Tour, 1984, 11 1/4 x 7 1/4 In.	2.50
Shot Glass, Happy New Year, Blue Script Logo, 1989	6.75
Shot Glass, Merry Christmas–Happy New Year, Blue Script, 1986	7.00
Sign, 2 Sides, Fluorescent, Hanging, 17 x 27 x 4 1/2 In.	190.00
Sign, Block Logo, Metal, Plastic, Wall, Electric, Box, 36 x 48 In.	400.00
Sign, Bottle Cap, Yellow & White, Porcelain	225.00
Sign, Boy, Street Crossing	475.00
Sign, Cardboard, 2 Sides, 13 x 27 In.	42.00
Sign, Green, Embossed Red Border, Tin, c.1910, 8 x 3 In.	275.00
Sign, Hits The Spot, 5 Cents, Porcelain, Double Sided, 56 In.	360.00
Sign, Light Up, Tin, Plastic, Red, White, Yellow, Blue, 12 x 16 In.	210.00
Sign, Pepsi–Cola, Tin, 30 x 26 In.	200.00
Sign, Round, Celluloid & Tin, 1940s, 9 In.	90.00
Sign, The Light Refreshment, Grocery Store, 1956, 11 x 14 In.	9.00
Sign, Tin, Flange, 14 x 16 In.	150.00
Straw Holder, Glass, Chrome Dome Top, Red Script Logo, 12 In.	30.00
Tar Heel State, N. C., 1976, 10 Oz.	9.00
Telephone, Can Shape, Original Package	38.00
Thermometer, Bottle Cap Form	65.00
Thermometer, Girl Sipping On Straw, Paper Face Decal, 1930s	275.00
Thermometer, Logo Top, Light Refreshment On Bottom, 27 1/4 In.	65.00
Thermometer, Say Pepsi Please, Yellow	50.00
Thermometer, Tin, 1950s, 27 x 7 In.	100.00
Tip Tray, Girl In Blue, Roses	450.00
Toy, Truck, Friction, Tin, Red, White & Blue, Japan, 1950s, 4 In.	190.00
Toy, Truck, Yellow, Composition, 2 Cardboard 6 Packs, 18 In.	500.00
Tray, Hits The Spot, Lithograph, Rectangular, 13 3/4 In.	40.00
Tray, Hits The Spot, Red, Blue & White, Shallow, 10 x 14 In.	100.00
Tray, Oval, 1906, 10 x 13 In.	475.00
Tumbler Set, Tray, 75th Anniversary, 1974, Script Logo, Box, 5 Pc.	65.00
Tumbler, Mighty Mouse	307.00
Tumbler, Reggie Jackson	12.00
Tumbler, Shazam, 1976	12.00
Tumbler, Skunk, Warner Bros., 1976, 6 In.	5.00
Visor, Paper, Say Pepsi Please, 1950s	25.00

PERFUME BOTTLES are made of cut glass, pressed glass, art glass, silver, metal, enamel, and even plastic or porcelain. Although the small bottle to hold perfume was first made before the time of ancient Egypt, it is the nineteenth– and twentieth–century examples that interest today's collector. Examples with the atomizer top marked *DeVilbiss* are listed under that name. Glass or porcelain examples will be found under the appropriate name such as Lalique, Czechoslovakia, etc.

Amber, Yellow & Blue Pulled Feather, Stopper, Baker	175.00
Anne Klein Parfum, Sample, 1 In.	5.00
Atomette, Black, Blue Lid & Tassel, Box, Instructions	25.00
Ballerina, Art Deco, Metal Base, China	185.00
Bear, 1920s, 5 In.	412.00
Bear, Green Mohair, Jointed, 5 In.	380.00
Binoculars, Opera Night, Windsor House, 2 Bottles, 3 1/4 In.	75.00

Perfume Bottle, Pink, Floral, Stopper, 9 In.

♦♦♦♦♦♦♦♦♦♦♦♦♦♦♦♦♦♦♦♦♦♦♦

When cleaning old bottles, save all labels and identifying tags.

♦♦♦♦♦♦♦♦♦♦♦♦♦♦♦♦♦♦♦♦♦♦♦

♦♦♦♦♦♦♦♦♦♦♦♦♦♦♦♦♦♦♦♦♦♦♦

Scratches on bronze cannot be polished off without destroying the patina and lowering the value.

♦♦♦♦♦♦♦♦♦♦♦♦♦♦♦♦♦♦♦♦♦♦♦

Black Boy, Germany, Miniature, Pair	18.00
Blown, Christmas Tree, Round, Austria, 2 3/4 In.	25.00
Cachet, Lucien Lelong, 1 3/4 In.	25.00
Cameo Carved, Ruby To Blue, Pewter Stopper	495.00
Carson's, Box	24.00
Charles Of The Ritz, White Dresser Set, Stoppers, 3 Piece	60.00
China, Floral Stopper, Germany, Pair	55.00
Clock, Perfume O'clock, Stuart, Round Face Bottle, 7 3/4 In.	40.00
Cloisonne, Red Roses, Blue, 2 In.	75.00
Colonial Woman, Stopper At Waist, Germany, 5 In.	75.00
Corinthian, Cut Glass, Strauss, Pair	550.00
Coty, Embossed Floral Design, Signed	125.00
Cranberry Cut To Clear, Sterling Repousse Mount, 3 In.	200.00
Crystal, Odd Shape, Sterling Ornate Stopper, 4 1/2 In.	45.00
Cut Glass, Cranberry, Rayed Base, Sterling Hinged Top	245.00
Cut Glass, Enameled, Sterling Stopper, Pedestal	125.00
Cut Glass, Sterling Top, 3 In.	70.00
Cut Rose Glass, Art Nouveau, Sterling, 9 In.	250.00
Czechoslovakia, Yellow Stopper, Dauber, Clear, 3 1/2 In.	185.00
D'Orsay, 3 Bottles, Box	20.00
Dancer, Flowers On Brass Base, 12 In., Pair	600.00
Diamond Quilted Mother-of-Pearl, Satin Topper, Blue, 5 In.	355.00
Duchesse, Colorful Label, Box, 5 In.	20.00
Dutch Girl, Has 2 Bottles On Yoke, Composition, 4 1/2 In.	65.00
Emeraude, Coty, Unopened	17.50
Evening In Paris Cologne & Powder, Cobalt Blue, Box	35.00
Evening In Paris, Bourjois, Eau De Cologne, 5 1/2 In.	45.00
Flask, Evening In Paris, 3 1/4 In.	10.00
Flask, Nickel Plated, Germany, 2 1/2 In.	15.00
Garde Moi, Augler, France	10.00
Gardenia Perfum-A-Lite, Karoff, Brass Shade, 2 3/4 In.	40.00
Golden Autumn, Prince Matchabelli, Crown Shape	15.00
Golliwog	85.00
Golliwog, Label, Small & Large	1000.00
Green & Orange, Clear Layers, Seguso, 6 In.	250.00
Hattie Carnegie, 2 1/2 In.	150.00
Ideal, Houbigant, Heavy Glass, Faceted Stopper, 3 3/4 In.	75.00
Intaglio Cut, 4 1/2 In.	35.00
Jade Green, Black Floral Stopper, Steuben, 5 1/2 In.	375.00
Jockey Club, Jergens, Frosted, Christmas Holly Box, 4 In.	60.00
L'Aimant, Coty, Label, Box	25.00
Lamp, Glass Tube, Wood Base, Cardboard Shade, 5 1/4 In.	35.00
Lentheric Tester, Wood & Metal Base, 4 x 9 3/8 In. 7 Piece	175.00
Leota, Vanity Set, Crystal, Black	85.00
Locket, Sterling Silver, Holds 2 Photographs, Dabber, 2 In.	174.00
Lucien Lelong, 4 Testers, Black Metal Base, 3 x 6 In.	125.00
Magic De Lancome, Lancome, Frosted, Star Design, 5 In.	65.00

Magic, Lancome, Clear, Frosted, Demo., Stopper & Dabber, 3 In. 30.00
Melon Ribbed, Controlled Bubbles, Gold, Venetian Glass 95.00
Melon Ribbed, Green Teardrop Stopper, Steuben, 5 In. 295.00
Nuit De Noel, Caron, 1920s, 4 In. 65.00
Parfum By Charles V 10.00
Parisian Bouque, Tieger, c.1922 .... 15.00
Piano Perfume Ensemble, Bouton, Wood, 2 Bottles, 2 3/4 In. 85.00
Pink & White Flowers, Leaves On Stopper, Blue, 5 3/8 In. 110.00
Pink, Dabber, Occupied Japan 20.00
Pink, Floral, Stopper, 9 In. ....*Illus* 225.00
Pressed Glass, Clear, Large Stopper, 11 In. 125.00
Prima Ballerina, Sweet Honesty, Avon, Frosted, 4 3/4 In. 50.00
Queen Anne, Amber, Signed NM 32.00
Revlon, Display, 8 In. 35.00
Ribbed Tooled Form, Glass Stopper, Steuben, 5 3/4 In. 660.00
Ribbon Pattern, Multicolored Ribbon Base 62.00
Risque Tout, Lentheric, Label, Plastic Box 20.00
Robj, Art Deco, Ladies Of 4 Seasons, Atomizer 475.00
Rudi Gernreich, Pyrex Test Tube, 8 3/4 In. 125.00
Schiaparelli, Embossed S, Pink Cap, 3 1/2 In. 65.00
Skunk, Ceramic, Rhinestones, Head Comes Off, 5 1/2 In. 140.00
Sleeping, Schiaparelli, 5 1/2 In. 150.00
Street Lamp, Ashtray, Metal, Green, 3 Bottles In Lamps, 8 In. 32.00
Styx, Coty, 2 3/8 In. 40.00
Surrender, Ciro, Faceted Stopper, 4 In. 150.00
Teddy Bear, Schuco, 1910, 3 In. 350.00
Threaded Swirl, Amethyst, Steuben, 5 1/4 In. 295.00
Tic Toc Perfume, By Babs, Clear, Filigree Casing, 5 In. 135.00
Verre De Soie, Engraved, Sterling Stopper, Steuben, 5 In. 265.00
Waffle Cut, Diamond Stopper 30.00
Watkins, Colorful Box, 5 1/2 In. 30.00
Wild Roses, White On Amethyst, K. Orme, 7 1/4 In. 350.00
With Pleasure, Caron, Baccarat, 3 7/8 In. 375.00
Woman's Bust, Bisque, Perfume Sprays Out Of Breasts, 3 In. 200.00
Woman's Bust, Eisenberg, Frosted Glass, No. 847, 3 1/2 In. 150.00

PETERS & REED Pottery Company of Zanesville, Ohio, was founded by John D. Peters and Adam Reed in 1897. Chromal, Landsun, Montene, Pereco, and Persian are some of the art lines that were made. The company, which became Zane Pottery in 1920 and Gonder Pottery in 1941, closed in 1957. Peters & Reed pottery was unmarked.

Basket, Hanging, Moss Aztec 85.00
Bowl, Green, Ruffled, 6 1/2 In. 50.00
Bowl, Landsun, Blue, 10 In. 90.00
Bowl, Mistletoe, Copper Dust Glaze, 9 In. 175.00
Bowl, Pereco, 6 In. 15.00
Bowl, Pereco, Twigs, Blue, Signed, 8 In. 125.00
Candleholder, Blue, 7 In. 140.00
Dish, Pink, Vasart, 6 In. 40.00
Ewer, Squat, 4 In. 50.00
Jug, Cavalier, Floral Band, 6 In. 95.00
Mug, Sprigged, 5 1/2 In. 40.00
Umbrella Stand, Marbelized, 17 In. 300.00
Vase, Landsun, Zane, White, Green & Blue, 5 In. 48.00
Vase, Marbelized, 6-Sided, 9 1/4 In. 80.00
Vase, Moss Aztec, 6 In. 48.00
Vase, Moss Aztec, Floral, 12 In. 115.00
Vase, Moss Aztec, Floral, 6 In. 28.00
Vase, Moss Aztec, Grape & Leaves, Outer Glaze, 8 In. 75.00
Vase, Relief Flowers, Brown Glaze, 4 Footed, 13 1/2 In. 235.00
Vase, Shadowware, Green Drip Over Black, 10 In. 80.00
Wall Pocket, Aztec, Grapes In Relief, 8 In. 65.00
Wall Pocket, Egyptian, Green, 9 In. 70.00

Wall Pocket, Florentine, 6 In. 20.00
Wall Pocket, Moss Aztec 75.00
Wall Pocket, Moss Aztec, 10 In. 45.00
Window Box, Ferrell, 9 x 18 In. 175.00

PETRUS REGOUT, see Maastricht

PEWABIC POTTERY was founded by Mary Chase Perry Stratton in 1903 in Detroit, Michigan. The company made many types of art pottery, including pieces with matte green glaze and an iridescent crystalline glaze. The company continued working until the death of Mary Stratton in 1961. It was reactivated by Michigan State University in 1968.

Ashtray, Iridescent 150.00
Bowl, Footed, Matte Glaze, Arts & Crafts, 5 In. 110.00
Box, Cover, Stylized Peacock, Marked, 1920s, 5 x 3 3/4 In. 275.00
Charger, Blue Rabbits, 11 5/8 In. 695.00
Cup & Saucer, Iridescent 125.00
Figurine, Madonna, Red Iridescent Glaze, Impressed Mark, 6 3/4 In. 225.00
Inkwell, Blue 195.00
Lamp, 4 Scrolling Feet, Wrought Iron Finial, Marked, 28 1/2 In., Pr. 4200.00
Plate, Dragonfly, 11 In. 800.00
Plate, Rabbit, 11 In. 800.00
Plate, Rabbit, Early Period 1100.00
Tile, 3 Wise Men, Green & Gold Glaze, 12 x 10 1/2 In. 65.00
Tile, Brown Center, Triangular & Square Tiles 11 1/2 x 11 1/4 In. 120.00
Tile, Crab, 3 In. 75.00
Tile, Gold Crackle Glaze Center, Triangular Blue Tiles, 13 In. 120.00
Tile, Red & Gold Center, Triangular Tiles Background, 13 In. 120.00
Tile, Seahorse, 3 In. 75.00
Tile, Ship At Sea Corner Tile, Green & Gold, Square, 3 In. 55.00
Tile, Turkey, 3 In. 75.00
Tile, University Of Maine 375.00
Vase, Blue Iridescent, 7 In. 1050.00
Vase, Blue Metallic Glaze, Pink & Gold Highlights, Marked, 4 In. 770.00
Vase, Bud, Red, 7 In. 550.00
Vase, Circular Flaring Form, Blue Glaze, 7 x 7 1/2 In. 247.00
Vase, Green Dripped Over Mauve, Bulbous, Flared Rim, Label, 6 In. 935.00
Vase, Iridescent Gray Dripped Glaze Over Royal Blue, 4 1/4 In. 990.00
Vase, Pale Matte Green, Maple Leaf Mark, 5 In. 285.00

PEWTER is a metal alloy of tin and lead. Some of the pewter made after 1840 has a slightly different composition and is called *Britannia metal.* This later type of pewter was worked by machine; the earlier pieces were made by hand. In the 1920s pewter came back into fashion and pieces were often marked *Genuine Pewter.* Eighteenth–, nineteenth–, and twentieth–century examples are listed here.

Basin, Continental, 11 1/4 x 2 5/8 In. 210.00
Basin, Nathaniel Austin, Mass., 8 In. 135.00
Basin, Townsend & Compton, London, 11 In. 300.00
Bowl, Brass Dragon Footed, Large 115.00
Bowl, Kayserzinn, Floral, 4 In. 48.00
Bowl, Kayserzinn, Grapes & Leaves, 11 1/4 In. 175.00
Bowl, Nekrassoff, Tulip Cutwork Around Top, 14 1/2 In. 200.00
Candelabrum, Kayserzinn, Figural, Bat Open Wings, 3–Light, 12 1/8 In. 1925.00
Candlestick, 19th Century, 6 1/2 In., Pair 192.00
Candlestick, 9 7/8 In. 150.00
Candlestick, Baluster Form, Beading, U.S., 1850s, 10 In., Pair 357.50
Candlestick, Flagg & Homan, 7 5/8 In., Pair 420.00
Candlestick, Kayserzinn, Art Nouveau, 12 1/2 In. 160.00
Candlestick, Octagonal Bobeche, England, c.1675, 8 1/2 In. 1700.00
Candlestick, Pushup, 8 In., Pair 150.00
Candlestick, Weighted Bases, Push–Up, 9 1/2 In., Pair 130.00
Chalice, Wedding, Maiden, Gimbaled Cup, Marked, 9 1/2 In. 110.00

Chamberstick, Kayserzinn, Stylized Sunflowers & Leaves	225.00
Charger, 13 3/8 In.	175.00
Charger, Crowned Rose Touch, English, 16 1/2 In.	300.00
Charger, European, 16 1/2 In.	135.00
Charger, Gersham Jones, 14 1/2 In.	800.00
Charger, Stamped MP Initials, William Hulls, London, 18 3/4 In.	385.00
Charger, Success To United States Of America, England, 16 5/8 In.	325.00
Charter, Late 18th Century	130.00
Cocktail Shaker, Engraved Dragon, Chinese, 17 In.	66.00
Coffeepot, 19th Century, 11 1/2 In.	193.00
Coffeepot, 9 3/4 In.	165.00
Coffeepot, Eben Smith, Lighthouse	575.00
Coffeepot, Josiah Danforth, 19th Century, 11 In.	1200.00
Coffeepot, Porter, Lighthouse	425.00
Creamer, Tudric, Hammered, 3 1/2 In.	60.00
Cup, Stirrup, Fox	48.00
Decanter, Wine, Pewter Stopper, Lion Head With Rings, 10 1/4 In.	275.00
Flagon, Boardman & Hart, Domed Lid Handle, Stepped Base, 12 1/2 In.	1320.00
Flagon, Continental, Floral Design, 11 In.	65.00
Flagon, Reed & Barton, 14 1/2 In.	120.00
Flagon, Roswell Gleason	495.00
Humidor, Dunhill, Hog Head Finial	75.00
Humidor, Windsor, Hammered Cover, Bakelite Insert, 4 x 4 In.	95.00
Lamp, James H. Putnam, Sparking, 3 Piece	742.50
Lamp, Replaced Brass Collar, 7 5/8 In.	65.00
Lamp, Whale Oil Burner, 6 3/4 In.	75.00
Loving Cup, Seventh Delphians Champions, Hockey, 1914, 5 3/8 In.	75.00
Mold, Candle, 24 Holes, Pine, 1800	2400.00
Mold, Ice Cream, Dressed Turkey, 5 In.	20.00
Mold, Ice Cream, Engagement Ring	35.00
Mold, Ice Cream, Kewpie, 1913, 6 In.	150.00
Mold, Ice Cream, Mandolin, 1888	45.00
Mold, Ice Cream, Pretzel	32.50
Mold, Ice Cream, Pumpkin	78.00
Mold, Ice Cream, Rabbit	78.00
Mold, Ice Cream, Spade Playing Card, 4 In.	60.00
Mold, Spoon, Hinged Handle, Bronze, 16 1/2 In.	400.00
Pipe Rest, Clipper Ship, Large	25.00
Pitcher, Cider, Sellew, Cincinnati	220.00 To 285.00
Pitcher, Flagg & Holman, 1842	290.00
Pitcher, Kayserzinn, 12 1/2 In.	295.00
Pitcher, Kayserzinn, Art Nouveau, Stylized Flowers, 7 1/2 In.	150.00
Pitcher, Nekrassoff, Melon Ribbed, Round Cutouts At Base	165.00
Pitcher, R. Dunham, Hinged Lid, 8 In.	550.00
Pitcher, Tapered Body, Hinged Lid, Round Finial, c.1860, 10 1/2 In.	185.00
Pitcher, Water, Boardman, Lion Touch, 6 5/8 In.	270.00
Pitcher, Water, R. Gleason, 7 5/8 In.	150.00
Plate, 8 5/8 In.	75.00
Plate, Angel Touch, 9 In.	90.00
Plate, Ashbil Griswold, Griswold, Conn., 7 7/8 In.	130.00
Plate, B. Barns, Philadelphia, Eagle Touch, 7 7/8 In.	190.00
Plate, Blakeslee Barnes, 7 7/8 In.	65.00
Plate, Engraved Harmonie 1822, 8 1/4 In.	55.00
Plate, Jacob Whitmore, Crown Rose, 8 In.	275.00
Plate, James Porter, Baltimore, 8 In.	35.00
Plate, Nathaniel Austin, Charleston, Mass., 8 In.	325.00
Plate, Nathaniel Austin, Eagle, 8 In.	275.00
Plate, Roswell Gleason, 9 1/4 In.	275.00
Plate, S. Kilbourn, 7 3/4 In.	155.00
Plate, Smith & Feltman, Albany, 10 1/4 In.	110.00
Plate, T. Danforth, Philadelphia, Eagle Touch, 7 3/4 In.	275.00
Plate, Thomas Boardman, 7 3/4 In.	325.00
Plate, W. Billings, 8 1/4 In.	45.00

Platter, Imperial Zinn, Pine Branches, Flying Grouse, 20 1/2 In.	260.00
Porringer, Crown Handle, 4 3/8 In.	160.00
Porringer, Crown Handle, 5 In.	175.00
Porringer, Crown Handle, Thomas D. & Sherman Boardman, c.1820, 5 In.	445.00
Porringer, Heart & Crescent Handle, 3 1/4 In.	275.00
Porringer, Samuel E. Hamlin	550.00
Porringer, Samuel Hamlin Sr., Flowered Handle, 5 1/2 In.	400.00
Porringer, Tab Style, Dated 1781	800.00
Pot, Boardman & Co., Eagle Touch, Cover, 11 1/2 In.	375.00
Pot, Dixon & Son, Wooden Handle, 12 In.	90.00
Pot, F. Porter, Westbrook No. 4, 11 3/4 In.	350.00
Pot, Homan & Co., Floral Finial, Copper Bottom, 10 1/4 In.	150.00
Pot, J. H. Palethrop, Philadelphia, Wooden Finial, 10 1/8 In.	250.00
Pot, Rosewell Gleason, Ribbed, Wooden Handle & Finial, 13 In.	300.00
Pot, Sellew & Co., Cincinnati, 11 1/2 In.	325.00
Salt & Pepper, Holder, 2 1/2 In.	20.00
Salt & Pepper, Mayflower Ship, W. B. Mfg.	45.00
Salt & Pepper, Nekrassoff, Scroll Handles, 1 1/2 In.	52.00
Stein, W. Cowlisham, Deficit Club, 8 In.	80.00
Tankard, Cover, Continental, 6 In.	85.00
Tankard, I. H., London, Hinged Lid, 8 In.	150.00
Tankard, James Yates, VR Over 520, 1 Pt.	240.00
Tankard, Measure, T & C, England, 6 In.	115.00
Tankard, Monogram & Crown, 7 3/4 In.	325.00
Tea Set, Tudric, Hammered, 3 Piece	450.00
Teapot, 7 1/2 In.	225.00
Teapot, 7 7/8 In.	140.00
Teapot, Boardman, New York, 7 1/4 In.	400.00
Teapot, Continental	89.00
Teapot, Dixon, 1830s	165.00
Teapot, E. Smith, Beverly, Maine	495.00
Teapot, E. Smith, 9 1/4 In.	300.00
Teapot, F. Porter, 7 1/2 In.	225.00
Teapot, F. Porter, Westbrook, 8 3/4 In.	170.00
Teapot, G. Richardson, 7 3/4 In.	250.00
Teapot, Grenfell, Wooden Handle, Europe, 5 1/2 In.	200.00
Teapot, Handmade, 8 1/2 In.	95.00
Teapot, Lantern Shape, Chinese, 6 1/4 In. ....*Illus*	85.00
Teapot, Leonard Reed & Barton, Paneled, Wooden Handle, Finial, 10 In.	350.00
Teapot, Morey & Ober, 8 3/4 In.	85.00
Teapot, Pear Shaped, Bee Shaped Mark, 7 In.	65.00
Teapot, Simple Design, 19th Century	60.00
Teapot, William Quilman, 1830s	495.00
Teapot, Wooden Handle, Finial, English, 8 3/4 In.	45.00
Tray, Nekrassoff, Elongated Palm Leaf Shape, 17 In.	140.00
Tumbler, Kayserzinn, Oak Leaves, Acorns, 4 1/2 In.	170.00

Pewter, Teapot, Lantern Shape, Chinese,
6 1/4 In.

◆◆◆◆◆◆◆◆◆◆◆◆◆◆◆◆◆◆◆◆◆◆

Metal salt shaker tops can be kept from rusting or oxidizing if they are cleaned or sprayed with a silicone product. Wax will also help.

◆◆◆◆◆◆◆◆◆◆◆◆◆◆◆◆◆◆◆◆◆◆

Phoenix, Lamp, Hawaiian Scene, Reverse
Painted, 18 In.

Phoenix, Plate, 10 In.

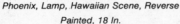

PHOENIX BIRD, or Flying Phoenix, is the name given to a blue–and–white kitchenware popular between 1900 and World War II. A variant is known as Flying Turkey. Most of this dinnerware was made in Japan for sale in the dime stores in America. It is still being made.

Creamer	18.00
Cup	12.00 To 15.00
Cup & Saucer, After Dinner	20.00
Gravy Boat, Attached Underplate	50.00
Plate, 6 In.	6.00
Plate, 8 1/2 In.	22.00
Soup, Dish, Flat	40.00
Teapot, Blue & White, 4 3/4 In.	50.00
Tile, Tea, 6 In.	30.00
Vase, Canada Geese In Flight, Pastel Blue, Label, 9 In.	165.00

PHOENIX GLASS Company was founded in 1880 in Pennsylvania. The firm made commercial products, such as lampshades, bottles, and glassware. Collectors today are interested in the sculptured glassware made by the company from the 1930s until the mid–1950s. The company is still working.

Bowl, Ruba Boncic Pink, 10 In.	325.00
Bowl, Ruba Rombic, Pink, 10 In.	335.00
Box, Cigar	75.00
Box, Sculptured White Flowers, Blue Ground	125.00
Lamp, Cockatoos, Blackbirds, Twigs, Ribbed Base	295.00
Lamp, Dancing Nudes, Blue & White	550.00
Lamp, Floral, Blue, Cream Ground, 24 In.	50.00
Lamp, Hawaiian Scene, Reverse Painted, 18 In. ....*Illus*	1100.00
Lamp, Heart–Shaped Leaves, Violet & Cream Ground	95.00
Lamp, Leaves & Berries, Lime & Cream Ground	95.00
Lamp, Water Lilies & Fern, 8 Panels, Reverse Painted	800.00
Plate, 10 In. ....*Illus*	25.00
Plate, Cake, Light Green, 8 In.	40.00
Vase, Blue Flowers, Green Leaves, 12 In.	90.00
Vase, Blue Foxgloves, Green Leaves, 10 1/4 In.	100.00
Vase, Dancing Nudes, With Pan, 11 In.	395.00
Vase, Dancing Nymph, Pearlized, Gray Ground, 12 In.	575.00
Vase, Dogwood, Custards, Tan, 10 5/8 In.	130.00
Vase, Dragonfly, Opaque, Lavender, 6 In.	160.00
Vase, Flying Geese, Narrow Oval Form, 9 In.	170.00
Vase, Foxglove, Gold On White, 10 In.	145.00
Vase, Grapes, Turquoise & Purple, Brown Twigs, 10 In.	120.00
Vase, Green, Pillow, Label, 9 1/2 In.	225.00
Vase, Parakeets On Flowering Branches, 10 In.	275.00
Vase, Philodendron, 11 1/2 In.	100.00 To 150.00
Vase, Pink Dragonflies, Green Tree Branches, Pillow, 7 1/4 In.	150.00

Vase, White Thistle, Pearlized, Blue Ground, Label, 18 In. 495.00
Vase, Wild Geese, Pillow, Brown, 11 In. 120.00
Vase, Wild Rose, Opaque White Ground, Gold Roses, 9 1/4 In. 95.00

PHONOGRAPH NEEDLE CASES of tin are collected today by music and phonograph enthusiasts and advertising addicts. The tins are very small, about 2 inches across, and often have attractive graphic designs lithographed on the top and sides.

Tin, Berliner 300 Needle, Red, Black, White & Gold 8.00
Tin, Best Needle, Contents, Red, White & Gold 10.00
Tin, Best Talking, Red, Contents 10.00
Tin, Brillantone Needle, Orange, Blue, White & Gold 8.00
Tin, Britain's Best Needle, Red, Black & Gold 6.00
Tin, Columbia Phonograph 35.00
Tin, Columbia, Yellow, Black, White 12.00
Tin, Eatons Concave Dish Needle, Red, Black, Gold 27.00
Tin, His Master's Voice, Red 14.00
Tin, His Master's Voice, Yellow 13.00
Tin, Judge Brand Needle, Green, Black 10.00
Tin, Songster Needle, Green, Gold, Red & Black 5.00
Tin, Songster, Light Yellows, Red 10.00
Tin, Victor Reusable Needle, Red, Gold & White 10.00

PHONOGRAPHS, invented by Thomas Edison in the 1880s, have been made by many firms. This section also includes other items associated with the phonograph. Jukeboxes and records are listed in their own sections.

Baby Jeannette, Child's 425.00
Bingophone, Child's, Outside Horn, Windup, German 400.00
Brunswick, Mahogany, Crank Type, Floor Model 110.00
Brunswick, Model 104, Portable, 1923 .... 75.00
Carola, Nightingale Of Phonographs, Floor Model, 1914 .... 1200.00
Climax, Wood Master Horn 2400.00
Columbia, Cylinder, Large Horn, Working 800.00
Columbia, Grand, Type AG, Brass Horn 1700.00
Columbia, Model AK, Brass Horn 1100.00
Columbia, Table Model, Claw Feet, Mahogany 850.00
Doll, Dancing, Rastus, 5 1/2 In. 275.00
Doll, Dancing, Siam Sue, Box, 11 3/4 In. 800.00
Doll, Madame Hendren, With Cylinder Record 600.00
Edison, Amberola III 2000.00
Edison, Amberola VI, Oak Case 650.00
Edison, Amberola X, 1915 .... 400.00
Edison, Amberola, Cylinder, 25 Rolls 750.00
Edison, Concert, 43-In. Brass Horn 2250.00
Edison, Home Model E, Morning Glory Horn, 2 & 4 Min. Reproducer 700.00
Edison, Home, Model E, Oak Cygnet Horn 2000.00
Edison, Painted Brass Horn, Dated 1904, Restored 525.00
Edison, Standard Model E, Cygnet Horn, B Reproducer 800.00
Edison, Suitcase Model, Mahogany Record Cabinet, 1910s 750.00
Edison, Triumph, Cygnet Horn 1250.00
Edison, Triumph, Tabletop, Metal Horn On Crane, 24 Cylinders 700.00
Englewood, Musical Phone Front 850.00
Gramophone, Monarch, 1902 .... 2300.00
Gramophone, Pathe, 1910 .... 910.00
Harmony Talking Machine 450.00
Heywood–Wakefield, Upright 1850.00
Lindstrom, Electric, Model 777 .... 95.00
Manophone, Oak, Tall Cabinet 165.00
Melodograph, Cast Iron, With Record, Small 155.00
Polly, Paper Horn 100.00
Puritan 310.00
Pygmy, Black Figures, Green 325.00
Reginaphone, Model 139, Mahogany, 20 3/4 In. 8000.00

Sonora, Mahogany, Floor Model	425.00
Victor, Brass Horn, England	1000.00
Victor, Child's, Mother Goose Mural, Dated 1923	450.00
Victor, Model II, Brass Bell Horn	1600.00
Victor, Model III, Outside Horn	1100.00
Victor, Model IV, Mahogany Horn	1200.00
Victor, Model M, Concert Reproducer	1700.00
Victor, Model VI, Mahogany Horn	4500.00
Victor, Monarch	1250.00
Victor, Victrola, Model VI	750.00
Victrola, Floor Model, Oak Case	160.00

PHOTOGRAPHY items are listed here. The first photograph was a view from a window in France taken in 1826. The commercially successful photograph started with the daguerreotype introduced in 1839. Today all sorts of photographs and photographic equipment are collected. Albums were popular in Victorian times. Cartes de visite, popular after 1854, were mounted on 2 1/2–by–4–inch cardboard. Cabinet cards were introduced in 1866. These were mounted on 4 1/4–by–6 1/2–inch cards. Stereo views are listed under Stereo Card.

Album, Man & Woman Front, Key Wind Music Box Back, 6 3/4 In.	45.00
Ambrotype, 4 Civil War Officers	795.00
Ambrotype, Civil War, Copper Frame, Dated 1861	125.00
Ambrotype, European Musician, Brass Instruments, 1/2 Plate	418.00
Ambrotype, Man Holding Reins Of White Horse, 1/6 Plate	100.00
Ambrotype, Soldier With Revolver	250.00
Ambrotype, Well–Dressed Tourist, Watkins Glen, 1/4 Plate	198.00
Cabinet Card, 2 Gamblers, Guns	16.00
Cabinet Card, Civil War, Pictures Matthew B. Brady, 9 Piece	1650.00
Cabinet Card, Francis Wilson, Falk, N.Y., Autographed, 1889	30.00
Cabinet Card, Man Mounting Early Bicycle	25.00
Cabinet Card, Opera, Stage Personalities, 19th Century, 33 Pc.	440.00
Cabinet Card, President Hayes, Home	48.00
Cabinet Card, William McKinley, Launey, N.Y., July 4th, 1896	27.00
Camera, Agfa Shur Shot, Box Type	3.00
Camera, Agfa, Karat, 35 Mm, Folding, 1937	30.00
Camera, Ansco, Goodwin, Box, 1925	15.00
Camera, Argus, C–4, Wide Angle Lens	45.00
Camera, Baby Brownie Special	15.00
Camera, Box, Leather Cover, Dated 1903	3.00
Camera, Brownie, Box, 1830	18.00
Camera, Brownie, No. 2, 1909, Box	45.00
Camera, Brownie, No. 2A, Autographic, Folding	8.00
Camera, Brownie, Target 6–20	15.00
Camera, Eastman Kodak Model B Flexo, Wooden Tripod, Brass	45.00
Camera, Eastman, View, No. 2–D, Takes 5 x 7 In. Photos	300.00
Camera, EHO, Baby Box	145.00
Camera, Gundlach Optical Co., Mahogany, Brass, 1890, 5 x 7 In.	375.00
Camera, Jiffy Kodak II, Box	35.00
Camera, Kampia, Movie, 8 Mm, Film Cartridges, Filters, Russian	700.00
Camera, Kodak, Folding, Art Deco Style Case	85.00
Camera, Kodak, No. 3A, Folding	30.00
Camera, Kodak, No. 6–20	25.00
Camera, Kodak, No. 116, Autographic, Folding	30.00
Camera, Kodak, Pocket, Box, 2 Instruction Books	400.00
Camera, Leica, M3, 35 Mm Range Finder, Light Meter, Leather Bag	770.00
Camera, Mamiya Flex Roll, 80 Mm F2. 8 Lens	205.00
Camera, Minolta, Autocord Roll, 75 Mm F3. 5 Lens	88.00
Camera, Minox, Leather Case, 1950	65.00
Camera, Pocket Kodak, 1896, Small	95.00
Camera, Rolleicord, Leather Case, 1953	95.00
Camera, Rolleicord, VB	75.00
Camera, Roussel Stylophat, France, 4 In.	45.00

Photography, Carte de Visite, Lincoln,
Feb. 24, 1861, Brady Gallery

Photography, Tintype, Lincoln, Gutta Percha
Frame, C. S. German

Camera, Speedex, 1 1/2 x 2 In.	30.00
Camera, Zeiss Ikon, Folding	275.00
Camera, Zeiss Ikon, Leather Case	75.00
Carte De Visite, Album, Civil War, Lincoln, Brass Closure	240.00
Carte De Visite, Civil War Musician	30.00
Carte De Visite, Lincoln, Feb. 24, 1861, Brady Gallery *Illus*	330.00
Carte De Visite, Paddle Wheel Boat, Hand Colored	25.00
Carte De Visite, Young Card Players	20.00
Daguerreotype Case, Man & Company Advertising, Octagonal	125.00
Daguerreotype, Outdoor View, Man On Horse, With Whip, 1/4 Plate	495.00
Daguerreotype, Young Boy With Book	45.00
Display, Kodak Camera, Instamatic	475.00
Lantern, Kodak, Dark Room, Kerosene Burner	20.00
Light Meter, Embossed Case	25.00
Moviegraph, Keystone Model 575, Instruction Booklet	75.00
Mutoscope, Viewer, Tin	300.00
Photograph, Boy & Girl With Bicycle, Doll, 10 x 16 In.	185.00
Photograph, Children, Gymnastic Exhibition, 1930s, 10 x 8 In.	8.00
Photograph, Hotel Warwick, New York, 1920s	28.00
Photograph, Little Wolf Cheyenne, Curtis, 1900, 5 x 7 In.	2800.00
Photograph, Spanish–American Soldier, Holding Rifle, Sepia	28.00
Photograph, String Band From Punxsutawney, 1889	45.00
Photograph, Union Pacific R.R., Building, 23 1/2 x 35 1/2 In.	110.00
Photograph, Wisconsin Assembly, 1876, 106 Men, 8 1/2 x 10 In.	15.00
Projector, Keystone Moviegraph, No. 575, Crank, Instructions	125.00
Projector, Pageant 250s, Kodak, 16 Mm., With Sound	125.00
Projector, Viewmaster Jr., Electric	40.00
Stanhope, Wooden, Views Of Germany	95.00
Tintype, 8 Gettysburg Railway Co. Men, With Badge, 1800s, 7 In.	295.00
Tintype, Boy & Girl Chasing Butterflies, Case	50.00
Tintype, Boy Beside High–Wheel Bicycle	30.00
Tintype, Children With Early Baby Buggy, Holding China Doll	30.00
Tintype, Civil War Sailor, Full Length	95.00
Tintype, Civil War Soldier, With Rifle	250.00
Tintype, Civil War, 2 Cavalry, Drawn Swords, Pistols	285.00
Tintype, Civil War, Soldiers & Tent, 1/4 Plate	220.00
Tintype, Indian, Girls Wearing Beaded Necklace, 1/6 Plate	385.00
Tintype, Lincoln, Gutta Percha Frame, C. S. German *Illus*	2090.00
Tintype, Man & Wife, Young, 10 x 14 In.	25.00
Tintype, Man With 2 Guns Stuck In Sash	30.00

PIANO BABY is a collector's term. About 1880, the well–decorated home had a shawl on the piano. Bisque figures of babies were designed to help hold the shawl in place. They range in size from 6 to 18 inches. Most of the figures were made in Germany. Reproductions are being made. Other piano babies may be listed under manufacturers' names.

Arms Raised, White Gown, Cobalt Blue Trim, KPM, 7 In.	200.00
Boy In Shift, Heubach, 3 3/4 In.	175.00
Boy In Top Hat & Glasses, Heubach, 4 1/2 In.	95.00
Boy Lying On Stomach, Holding Dog	250.00
Girl Lying On Side, Holding Rabbit	250.00
Girl With Cup, Andrea, 13 In.	150.00
Kicking, Heubach	350.00
Lying Down On Elbow, Heubach, 6 In.	145.00
Lying Down, Heubach, Small	39.00
Lying On Back, Heubach	350.00
Lying On Back, Holding Grapes, Heubach	225.00
Seated, Large Hat, Pleated Dress, Heubach	895.00
Seated, Reaching For Toes, 9 In.	225.00
Sitting, Holding Mug, Germany, 12 In.	475.00
Winking, Bisque	25.00

PICKARD China Company was started in 1898 by Wilder Pickard. Hand–painted designs were used on china purchased from other sources. In the 1930s, the company began to make its own china wares in Chicago, Illinois. The company now makes many types of porcelains, including a successful line of limited edition collector plates.

5–Piece Place Setting, Richmond Pattern, 20 Piece		240.00
Bell, Christmas, Cobalt Blue, 14K Gold Nativity Scene, 6 1/2 In.		150.00
Bowl, Currant Design, Scalloped, Octagonal, Signed Reau, 10 In.		200.00
Bowl, Gooseberries, Footed, Signed Tie Roy, 9 1/2 In.		375.00
Bowl, Modern Conventional, Hessler, 4 3/4 In.		285.00
Bowl, Modern Conventional, Hessler, 9 1/4 In.		285.00
Bowl, Poppies, Footed, Lott, 9 1/2 In.	*Illus*	700.00
Bowl, Poppies, Pedestal, Signed Lott, 9 1/2 In.		700.00
Bowl, Poppies, Scalloped, Gold Rim & Handles, Yeschek, 7 3/4 In.		135.00
Bowl, Scalloped, Reau, 10 In.	*Illus*	200.00
Bowl, Turned–In Rim, Nuts, Gold Leaves, Gold Feet, Signed, 7 1/2 In.		250.00
Cake Plate, Basket Of Roses Center, Border Of Roses, Signed, 11 In.		30.00
Candy Dish, Cover, Embossed Design, Gold Rim Overlay, Signed, 9 In.		55.00
Chocolate Set, Art Nouveau Design, Aqua, 15 Piece		210.00
Chocolate Set, Gold Trim, Signed, Osborne, 13 Piece		400.00
Compote, White & Green Dogwood Blossoms, Gold Trim, 5 In.		55.00
Cup & Saucer, Allover Gold, After Dinner, 8 Sets		100.00
Dish, Cutout Gold Handles & Rim, Oval, 9 1/2 x 4 1/2 In.		165.00
Fernery, Lily Design, Signed Leach, 6 In.		150.00
Hair Receiver, Hand Painted Violets, Tone, Marked		50.00
Jam Jar, Underplate, Hand Painted		400.00
Nut Bowl, Hand Painted, Pedestal		258.00
Pitcher, Gold & Floral Design, Signed, 9 In.		325.00
Pitcher, Lemonade, Poppies, Signed F. Plathaman, 6 In.		550.00
Plate, Almonds, Hand Painted, Signed Kenton, 8 1/2 In.		175.00
Plate, Art Deco, Gold Outlined, 1912, 7 3/4 In.		50.00
Plate, Birds, Lockhart, 1971		150.00
Plate, Christmas, 1976		75.00
Plate, Currants, 7 1/2 In.		15.00
Plate, Deserted Garden, 1912, 10 1/2 In.		180.00
Plate, Flowers, 1905, 8 3/4 In.		85.00
Plate, Forest, Mountains, Purple, Gray & Green, Signed		175.00
Plate, Gold, Signed, 8 3/4 In.		85.00
Plate, Golden Melody, Cardinal & Holly Transfer, 5 x 10 In.		75.00
Plate, Landscape, Signed Gasper, 8 1/2 In.		100.00
Plate, Pheasant, Turkey		200.00

Plate, Raised Gilt Floral, 12 In.	65.00
Plate, Red Fox	100.00
Plate, Rose Design, Signed Lora	55.00
Plate, Signed Stahl, 8 1/2 In.	85.00
Plate, Swan	200.00
Plate, Sweet Peas, Gold Trim, Scalloped Rim, 8 1/2 In.	70.00 To 135.00
Plate, Violets, Gilt Border, Signed, 7 1/2 In., 5 Piece	90.00
Plate, Wild Roses, Haviland Blank, E. Aulide	235.00
Plate, Yellow California Poppies, Haviland Blank, Seidel	150.00
Platter, Floral Design, F. V. GDA, 14 1/2 In.	155.00
Powder Box, Flower Basket, Gold Rim	85.00
Punch Bowl, Panels Of Fruit, 2 Handles, Signed Gasper, 13 1/2 In.	2600.00
Relish, Italian Gardens, Gold Trim, Signed	75.00
Relish, Mountain, Lake, Floral, Columns, Signed Gasper, 9 1/4 In.	110.00
Relish, Violets, Oval, Signed, 12 1/2 In.	30.00
Rose Bowl, Day Lily	185.00
Salt & Pepper, Gold, Etched, 3 1/2 In.	20.00
Salt & Pepper, Oriental Poppy, Signed Osborne	20.00
Shaving Mug, Art Nouveau Iris, Gold, Signed Lind, Marked	375.00
Strawberries, Footed, Fuchs, 9 1/2 In.	*Illus* 325.00
Sugar & Creamer, Art Nouveau, Gold Band, Cobalt Blue, Marked	38.00
Sugar & Creamer, Basket Of Medallions, Signed F. Vobot	55.00
Sugar & Creamer, Violets, Limoges Blank, Reury	130.00
Sugar & Creamer, Violets, Signed	375.00
Syrup, Aqua, Gold Band	160.00
Tankard Set, Limoges, Tankard & 4 Mugs, Signed Seidel	2600.00
Tea Set, Art Deco, Orange, Floral On Black & Gold, Hessler, 3 Piece	375.00
Tea Set, Dutch Girl, Windmills, A. Richter, 3 Piece	275.00
Tray, Golden Melody, Cardinal & Holly Transfer, 5 x 10 In.	75.00
Tray, Italian Gardens, Gold Handles & Rim, Gaspar, 16 x 10 1/2 In.	295.00
Tureen, Rust Tulips, Ribbons, Open Gold Handles, 6 In., 3 Piece	150.00

Left to right: Pickard, Bowl, Poppies, Footed, Lott, 9 1/2 In.; Pickard, Bowl, Scalloped, Reau, 10 In.; Pickard, Strawberries, Footed, Fuchs, 9 1/2 In.

Pickard, Vase, Mums, Loba, 14 In.   *Pickard, Vase, Rooster & Hen, 3 Handles, 5 1/2 In.*

Vase, Asters, Gilt Border, 1905, 7 3/4 In. 95.00
Vase, Basket, Fruit Garden, Signed, Slahr, Marked 200.00
Vase, Engraved Basket Of Flowers, Gold Trim, 8 1/2 In. 65.00
Vase, Floral Band Top, Foliage Border Bottom, 7 In. 85.00
Vase, Garden Scene, Double, Signed, 10 In. 495.00
Vase, Gold Floral Design, Sticker, Signed, 14 In. 2300.00
Vase, Landscape, Oval, Signed Osborne, 8 1/2 In. 175.00
Vase, Mums, Loba, 14 In. ....*Illus* 2300.00
Vase, Pearlized, Gold Poppies, Gold Rim, Signed, 8 In. 145.00
Vase, Rooster & Hen, 3 Handles, 5 1/2 In. ....*Illus* 1900.00
Vase, Scene Of Fowl, Flowers & Cherries, 3 Handles, 5 1/2 In. 1900.00
Vase, Scenic Medial Band, Rose Bushes At Riverside, Signed, 12 In. 330.00
Vase, Scenic, Green, Gilt Trim, Signed, 7 1/2 In. 225.00
Vase, Scenic, Palm Trees Beside Water, Signed, 6 1/2 In. 310.00

PICTURE FRAMES are listed in this book in the Furniture section under Frame.

PICTURES, silhouettes, and other small decorative objects framed to hang on the wall are listed here. Some other types of pictures are listed in the Print and Painting categories.

Charcoal On Paper, Girl, With Bird, Cross Corner Frame, 26 x 20 In. 105.00
Crewel Embroidered, Still Life, Framed, 13 1/2 x 14 1/4 In. 660.00
Crewel, House & Lane, Hollyhocks, Framed, 10 x 12 In. 65.00
Diorama, Clipper Ship & Tug Boat, B. A. Evans, 22 x 30 x 27 In. 625.00
Diorama, Clipper Ship, American Flag, Framed, 22 1/4 x 34 1/4 In. 775.00
Diorama, Ship, Wood, Putty, String, Paint, Framed, 11 1/4 x 11 1/2 In. 325.00
Dried Flower, Victorian, Rose Arrangement, Carved Oval Frame 47.50
Embroidery On Red Silk, Oriental, Framed, 18 x 24 In. 9.00
Hair, Bouquet, Black & Gold Shadowbox, 10 x 11 In. 145.00
Hair, Floral, 1950 .... 25.00
Memorial, 2 Floral Sections, 2 Children's Names, 1892, Shadow Box 65.00
Needlepoint, St. Nicholas, Framed, c.1850, 12 x 15 1/2 In. 625.00
Needlework, Floral, Silk, Yellow, Green, Brown, Framed, 9 x 8 In. 1200.00
Panel, Floral, 1 Side, Oval Landscape Other, Painted, 12 x 17 In. 65.00
Paper Doily, Ink Inscription, Mrs. Louisa C. Tatem, Framed, 10 In. 25.00
Pen, Ink, Watercolor, Primitive Bird, Isaac Lehman, 1850, 6 x 10 In. 400.00
Petit Point, Medieval Castle, Leather Flowers, 15 x 19 In. 180.00
Printed Fabric, Multicolored, Egyptian, Framed, 40 x 18 In. 275.00
Reverse On Glass, Mill By River Scene, Ornate Frame 25.00
Reverse On Glass, Washington Fally, Edward Savage, 12 x 15 In. 1800.00
Reverse On Glass, Woman, Silhouette, Ebonized Frame, 2 3/4 In. 55.00
Ribbon, Woven Portrait, Admiral Dewey, 8 1/2 In. 75.00
Silhouette, Boy With Hoop, 4 1/4 x 5 1/2 In. 385.00
Silhouette, Cutout Paper On Velvet, Bache, Framed, 4 x 5 In., Pair 120.00
Silhouette, Duck Hunting Scene, Pin Pricked Details, 6 x 12 In. 248.00
Silhouette, Elderly Lady, 2 3/4 x 3 1/2 In. 155.00
Silhouette, Gentleman, Embossed Brass Frame, 4 1/2 x 3 3/4 In. 105.00
Silhouette, Gentleman, Full Length, Top Hat, Edouart, Framed, 10 In. 750.00
Silhouette, Girl, Blue Dress, White Collar, Frame, 5 x 4 5/8 In. 325.00
Silhouette, James Loader Family, Reverse Painted, 1856, 17 x 13 In. 1200.00
Silhouette, Julia Wood, Elziza Esther Wood, 6 x 5 3/8 In., Pair 250.00
Silhouette, Man With Frock Coat, Full Length, Framed, 7 1/4 x 5 In. 150.00
Silhouette, Man, Full–Length Side View, Gilded Frame, 7 x 6 In. 250.00
Silhouette, Mr. & Mrs. Hiram Woodward, 1800s, 5 In. Diam., Pair 235.00
Silhouette, Reverse Painted, Johnathan Trumbull, 1780, 7 1/4 In. 280.00
Silhouette, Woman, Hollow Cut, Framed, 6 5/8 x 5 1/2 In. 75.00
Silkwork, Woman & Child In Garden, 17 x 15 In. 1600.00
Spencerian Penmanship, Ink, Verse, Framed, 26 x 32 In. 250.00
Spencerian, Napoleon Crossing The Alps, Framed, 23 In. 250.00
Tapestry, Saint Portrait, Woven Silk, Framed, 9 3/4 x 7 1/4 In. 180.00
Theorem, Basket Of Fruit & Flowers, Gilt Frame, 12 1/4 x 13 In. 1600.00
Theorem, Fruit, Flower & Foliage In Basket, Gold Frame, 18 x 21 In. 800.00

Theorem, Fruit, Velvet, Blue, Green, Browns, Gold, Framed, 21 x 27 In. 1400.00
Theorem, On Velvet, Basket Of Fruit, Gilded Frame, 10 x 12 In. 1600.00
Tinsel, Red House, Winter Scene, Handmade 45.00
Tinsel, Theorem Style, Vase Of Flowers, Frame, c.1880, 6 x 8 1/2 In. 235.00

PIERCE, see Howard Pierce

PIGEON FORGE Pottery was started in Pigeon Forge, Tennessee, in 1946. Red clay found near the pottery was used to make the pieces. Molded or thrown pottery with matte glaze and slip decoration was made. The pottery is still working.

Bowl, White, Gray, Turquoise Inside, 4 In. 8.00
Coaster, Blue 7.00
Sugar & Creamer, Dogwoods, Terra–Cotta 10.00
Teapot, Dogwoods, 7 In. 8.00

PILKINGTON Tile and Pottery Company was established in 1892 in England. The company made small pottery wares, like buttons and hatpins, but soon started decorating vases purchased from other potteries. By 1903, the company had discovered an opalescent glaze that became popular on the Lancastrian pottery line. The manufacture of pottery ended in 1937 but decorating continued until 1948.

Vase, Edward Radford, 10 In. 175.00
Vase, Mottled Blue, 12 x 9 In. 125.00
Vase, Orange, Olive Flambe Glaze, 1948, 11 In. 265.00
Vase, Royal Lancastrian, Lions, Trees, Signed, 1910, 13 3/4 In. 1210.00

PINCUSHION DOLLS are not really dolls and often were not even pincushions. Some collectors use the term *half-doll*. The top half of each doll was made of porcelain. The edge of the half-doll was made with several small holes for thread, and the doll was stitched to a fabric body with a voluminous skirt. The finished figure was used to cover a hot pot of tea, powder box, pincushion, whisk broom, or lamp. They were made in sizes from less than an inch to over 9 inches high. Most date from the early 1900s to the 1950s. Collectors often find just the porcelain doll without the fabric skirt.

Arms Away, Brimmed Hat, Pink Skirt Over Wire Frame 165.00
Arms Away, Holding Mirror, Germany 90.00
Bathing Beauty, Reclining, Gold Slippers, 5 In. 195.00
Bisque, Arms Away From Body, Germany 85.00
Blue Hat, Both Arms Extended, 2 1/2 In. 125.00
Boy, Yellow Cap, With Tape Measure, 4 1/2 In. 125.00
Campbell Kids, Celluloid Head 52.00
Crocheted Dress, Germany 35.00
Fan, Germany 43.00
Fixing Hair 25.00
Flapper, On Trinket Box, Legs 125.00
Girl, Pink Dress, Marked Germany, 2 In. 25.00
Gold Shoes, 1920s, 5 1/2 In. 65.00
Gray Colonial Hair, Hands At Chest, Munzer 1926, 5 1/4 In. 90.00
Jointed Arms, Enameled Eyes, With, 5 1/4 In. 450.00
Mammy, Germany 35.00
Nude, Both Arms Extended, 5 In. 145.00
Nude, Pink Beads In Hair, 4 In. 125.00
Pierrette, Black Skullcap, German 95.00
Plumed Headpiece, Extended Arms, Wire Frame, Porcelain 522.00
Princess Lelamballe, 5 In. 225.00
Senorita, Lavish Eye Makeup, 2 1/2 In. 200.00
Senorita, Molded Jewelry, Yellow Castanets, 5 In. 295.00
Twist Top Hair, 1 1/2 In. 35.00
Wax Woman, Bead Eyes 175.00
Wire Hooped Dress, Dress Holds Sewing Utensils, Germany 35.00

PINK SLAG pieces are listed in this book in the Slag category.

PIPES have been popular since tobacco was introduced to Europe by Sir Walter Raleigh. Meerschaum pipes are listed under Meerschaum.

Burl, Elmira Prison, Confederate Flag, Skull, Crossbones, 1864	1250.00
Carved Bone & Wood, Hag In Bonnet	129.00
Carved Bone, Man In Moon	128.00
Carved Wood, Foot With Soccer Ball	48.00
Clay, Man's Head, Gouda	145.00
Cypress, Black Man Riding Alligator	1320.00
Hessian Soldier, Polychromed	1000.00
Meerschaum, Black Woman, Old Case	165.00
Meerschaum, Paris Exposition, 1889, 28 In.	5750.00
Opium, 13 In.	10.00
With Hat, Hand Carved, Italy	40.00

PISGAH FOREST pottery was made in North Carolina from 1926. The pottery was started by Walter R. Stephen in 1914, and after his death in 1941, the pottery continued in operation. The most famous kinds of Pisgah Forest ware are the cameo type with designs made of raised glaze and the turquoise crackle glaze wares.

Cracker Jar	45.00
Creamer, Hillbilly With Dog	395.00
Sugar & Creamer, Blue, 2 1/2 In.	125.00
Sugar & Creamer, Turquoise, Miniature	40.00
Teapot, Green, High Gloss, 6 In.	75.00
Vase, Blue & Purple, 5 In.	55.00
Vase, Blue Crystalline Glaze, 9 In.	825.00
Vase, Crackle Glaze, Purple Over Turquoise, 7 In.	85.00
Vase, Crystalline, White, 6 1/2 In.	235.00
Vase, Forest, Purple Crackle, 5 In.	65.00
Vase, Italian Green, 1939, 6 In.	48.00
Vase, Mottled Green, Bulbous, Dated 1903, 5 3/4 In.	125.00
Vase, Turquoise, 4 In.	55.00
Vase, Turquoise, High Glaze, 4 In.	65.00
Vase, Turquoise, Pink Interior, 2 Handles, Aunt Nancy, 6 In.	250.00

PLANTERS PEANUTS memorabilia is collected. Planters Nut and Chocolate Company was started in Wilkes–Barre, Pennsylvania, in 1906. The Mr. Peanut figure was adopted as a trademark in 1916. National advertising for Planters Peanuts started in 1918. The company was acquired by Standard Brands, Inc., in 1961. Standard Brands merged with Nabisco in 1981. Some of the Mr. Peanut jars and other memorabilia have been reproduced and, of course, new items are being made.

Alarm Clock	75.00
Ashtray, Figural, Gold	55.00 To 75.00
Ashtray, Mr. Peanut, Metal	39.00
Bank, Light Blue	13.00
Bank, Mr. Peanut, Cast Iron, 11 In.	90.00
Bank, Mr. Peanut, Red	15.00
Belt Buckle, Figural	20.00
Blinker, Papier–Mache	7500.00
Book, Complete World Of Mr. Peanut, Recipes, 11 x 8 In.	18.00
Bookmark, Greetings From Mr. Peanut	10.00
Bookmark, Mr. Peanut, Figural	15.00
Bracelet, Charm, 6 Charms	40.00
Button, Mr. Peanut, Pinback, 1930s, 1 1/4 In.	10.00
Card, Trading, Wild Animal, 2 x 2 1/2 In., Pair	10.00
Charm, Mr. Peanut, Plastic, Beige	6.00
Coloring Book, Presidents Of The U.S., 1960	8.00 To 20.00
Cup, Mr. Peanut, Plastic, Red	10.00
Display, Counter, Plastic, Yellow, Blue	40.00

◆ ◆ ◆ ◆ ◆ ◆ ◆ ◆ ◆ ◆ ◆ ◆ ◆ ◆ ◆ ◆ ◆ ◆ ◆ ◆

To clean old paper, try talcum powder. Take a soft brush or powder puff, sprinkle on the powder, leave for an hour, and brush it off.

◆ ◆ ◆ ◆ ◆ ◆ ◆ ◆ ◆ ◆ ◆ ◆ ◆ ◆ ◆ ◆ ◆ ◆ ◆ ◆

Planters Peanuts, Figure, Mr. Peanut, Paper-Mache, 14 1/4 In.

Display, Mr. Peanut, Papier–Mache, Top Hat, Cane	1705.00
Display, Woman, With Box Of Nuts, Die Cut, 1930	175.00
Doll Pattern, Mr. Peanut, Uncut	35.00
Doll, Mr. Peanut, Bendable	12.00
Doll, Mr. Peanut, Cloth	15.00 To 18.00
Figure, Mr. Peanut, Papier–Mache, 14 1/4 In. .....*Illus*	1700.00
Golf Balls, Set Of 3, Spalding	15.00
Ice Bucket, Wood, Round, Mr. Peanut On Lid, 16 x 12 In.	30.00
Jar, Clear, 8 Sides, Design Of Nut On Lid	35.00
Jar, Clip–On Lid, Barrel Shape	75.00
Jar, Clipper Peanut, Lid	40.00
Jar, Cobalt Blue, 8–Sided, Nut Lid	35.00
Jar, Fishbowl, Cover	85.00
Jar, Pink, Large	10.00
Jar, Running Peanut Pennant, Nut Lid	135.00 To 200.00
Jar, Square, Peanut Finial	115.00
Jar, Streamline	55.00
Knife, Yellow, Box	10.00
Lighter, Composition, 2 Piece	89.00
Mr. Peanut, Plastic	12.00
Mug, Drinking, Pewter, 4 3/4 In.	20.00
Mug, Drinking, Plastic, Green	12.00
Mug, Drinking, Plastic, Pink	14.00
Nut Dispenser, Mr. Peanut, Blue Plastic	60.00
Nut Dispenser, Wood Base, Clear Glass Globe, 13 In.	35.00
Nut Set, Mr. Peanut, Logo, Tin, 5 Piece	35.00
Pail, Peanut Butter, 1 Lb.	600.00
Peanut Butter Maker, Box	40.00
Peanut Butter Maker, Mr. Peanut, 1960s, 12 In.	30.00
Peanut Butter Maker, Mr. Peanut, Box, Unused	25.00
Pedal Car, Yellow	165.00 To 175.00
Pencil, Mechanical, Black & Brown	18.00
Pencil, Mechanical, Mr. Peanut, Wrapper	22.00
Pencil, Mechanical, Peanut In Peanut Oil	40.00
Pencil, Mr. Peanut, Mechanical, Peanut Top	15.00
Profit Indicator, Mr. Peanut's Guide To Profits	25.00
Salt & Pepper, Silver–Colored Plastic, 3 In.	15.00
Salt & Pepper, Yellow & Black	20.00
Shoe Polish & Picture Balloon, Mr. Peanut, 1960s, Box	45.00
Spoon, Mr. Peanut, Red, Slotted	9.00
Tin, 10 Lb.	75.00
Toothpicks, Party, Multicolored Plastic, Set Of 13	13.00
Train Set	75.00
Tumbler, Circus	150.00
Whistle, Tan Plastic, 2 1/2 In.	8.00
Whistle, Yellow & Blue	7.00

PLATED AMBERINA was patented June 15, 1886, by Joseph Locke and made by the New England Glass Company. It is similar in color to amberina, but is characterized by a cream colored or chartreuse lining (never white) and small ridges or ribs on the outside.

Pitcher, Amber Handle	3500.00
Punch Cup, Ribbed, Amber Handle	2500.00
Tumbler, 4 In.	2700.00

PLIQUE–A–JOUR is an enameling process. The enamel is laid between thin raised metal lines and heated. The finished piece has transparent enamel held between the thin metal wires. It is different from cloisonne because it is transparent.

Case, Cigarette, Polychrome Peacock, Russian, 3 9/16 In.	1210.00
Salt, Open, Spoon, Russian Silver, 2 3/8 In., Pair	467.00
Spoon, Floral, Twisted Coiled Handle, Sterling, 5 In.	250.00

POLITICAL memorabilia of all types, from buttons to banners, is collected. Items related to presidential candidates are the most popular, but collectors also search for material related to state and local offices. Many reproductions have been made.

Album, President McKinley On Cover, Celluloid	65.00
Ashtray, Richard & Pat Nixon, Address Change, White House, 1961	100.00
Ashtray, U.S. Senate Seal, Leaded Crystal, Engraved, Large	23.00
Badge, Hoover Inaugural, Pennsylvania Delegation	75.00
Badge, Inauguration, Lyndon Baines Johnson, 3 1/2 In.	20.00
Badge, Wilson Inaugural, Princeton Colors, 1913	195.00
Bandana, Bryan & Sewall, Free Coinage, 1896, Square, 18 1/4 In.	50.00
Bandana, Cleveland & Thurman, Eagles & Shields, 18 x 20 In.	165.00
Bandana, Cleveland & Thurman, Red, White & Blue, 21 x 24 In.	150.00
Bandana, Harrison & Reid, Pictures, Square, 20 In.	155.00
Bandana, Harrison, Morton, Protection & Industry, 20 1/2 x 19 In.	225.00
Bandana, I Like Ike	52.00
Bandana, Jugate, Theodore Roosevelt, 24 In.	250.00
Bandana, W. H. Harrison, On Horseback, Battles, 23 1/2 x 25 In.	700.00
Bandana, Wilson, Eagle, Picture, Flags Of World, Silk, 15 x 16 In.	100.00
Bank, Bust, Eisenhower, Metal, 5 In.	25.00
Bank, Bust, F. D. Roosevelt, Bottom Slot, Metal, 5 In.	60.00
Bank, Dukakis & Bensen, 1988, Set	225.00
Bank, Happy Days, Chein & Co., 4 In.	15.00
Banner, Kennedy & Johnson Inaugural, Felt, 1962	45.00
Banner, Welcome Democrats, National Convention, 25 x 42 In.	225.00
Beanie, I Love Ike, Figural Elephant, Plastic	38.00
Beanie, Win With Stevenson, Figural Donkey, Plastic	38.00
Bookends, Kennedy & Johnson, Mottoes, Chalkware	22.50
Bottle, Figural, Bust Of Grover Cleveland, Crystal, 1884	225.00
Bottle, Whiskey, Eisenhower Inauguration, Amber, 1953, Qt.	25.00
Box, Stogie, Henry Clay, 1844	2800.00
Bumper Sticker, Vote For Kennedy, Johnson, 1960	12.00
Bumper Sticker, Wallace In '72	10.00
Button, Al Smith For Governor	16.00
Button, Arts & Letters For McGovern/Shriver, 3/4 In.	4.00
Button, Bryan, From Denver To Washington ....*Illus*	1200.00
Button, Bryan, Large B With 1908 On Side ....*Illus*	725.00
Button, Bush, Quayle, Voinovich Team, Ohio Outline, 1 In.	6.00
Button, Buy American Because Japan Doesn't, 3/4 In.	2.00
Button, Carter & Mondale, Jugate	8.00
Button, Clean Sweep For Democracy, Bryan & Kern, 1 1/8 In.	400.00
Button, Eisenhower, Woman Power, Female Elephant Over V	225.00
Button, Elect The Underachiever, Head Of Quayle & Bart Simpson	1.00
Button, Ford & Dole, Jugate, 2 In.	13.00
Button, Friends Of Franklin Roosevelt, Portrait	20.00
Button, George Wallace For Governor	15.00

Left to right: Political, Button, Bryan, From
Denver To Washington; Political, Button,
Bryan, Large B With 1908 On Side

Button, God Bless America, Center Flag, 3/4 In.	1.00
Button, Goldwater & Miller, Jugate, 1 1/4 In.	8.00
Button, Goldwater & Miller, Jugate, 3 1/2 In.	17.00
Button, Goldwater, Vote In '64, 1 In.	20.00
Button, Harriman Is The Man, Picture, 3/4 In.	6.00
Button, Harry Truman For Judge, Eastern District, 3/4 In.	700.00
Button, Hats Off To The Best, Humphrey & Muskie, 1970s, On Card	2.00
Button, Hoover & Curtis, Pictured, 1/2 In.	95.00
Button, Humphrey For President, 2 In.	3.00
Button, I'm For Jimmy & Fritz, 1 In.	6.00
Button, Iacocca For President, Evansville, Ind., 1984, 3 In.	18.50
Button, Ike & Dick, 1/2 In.	2.50
Button, Indiana Convention Delegate, 1982, 2 In.	7.50
Button, JFK, I Told You So, Blue & White, 1 3/4 In.	15.00
Button, Jimmy Carter For President In '76, Picture, 1 1/2 In.	6.00
Button, John Weeks For President, Ribbon	48.00
Button, Kemp, The Right Choice, Picture, 3/4 In.	1.00
Button, Kennedy To Reagan, Shadowbox Frame	110.00
Button, Kennedy, Johnson, Picture Of Each, 7/8 In.	68.00
Button, Labor For Carter, Mondale, 3/4 In.	4.00
Button, Lafollette For President, Picture, 3/8 In.	45.00
Button, Landon, Knox, GOP, Pinback	8.00
Button, Let's Back Ike, 2 1/2 In.	5.00
Button, Let's Back Ronald Reagan For Governor, 1 In.	15.00
Button, McGovernment By George, 3 In.	26.50
Button, Mondale, Ferraro, Picture Of Each, 1 1/4 In.	4.00
Button, Mondale, Ferraro, Star & Drape, 1 1/8 In.	5.00
Button, Mondale, Ferraro, United Paper Workers, 3/4 In.	20.00
Button, Nebraskans For Kennedy, Picture, 3/4 In.	175.00
Button, New Leadership, Competence '76, Carter, Mondale, 1 1/2 In.	5.00
Button, Nixon For Governor, Photograph Top Half, 5/8 In.	5.00
Button, Nixon For President, 2 In.	3.00
Button, Nixon, Car Dealer	8.00
Button, Nixon, Jugate, 3 1/2 In.	11.00
Button, No Mo'Ron For President, Red, White & Blue, 1 In.	4.00
Button, Peace & Freedom Party, Dove, 3/4 In.	8.00
Button, Progressive, Moose Head, 1/2 In.	15.00
Button, Quayle, U.S. Senator, '80, 2 In.	15.00
Button, Read My Hips, Cartoon Figure Of Bush Running, 3/4 In.	1.00
Button, Reagan & Bush For New Jersey	9.00
Button, Reagan & Bush, Thank You For 4 More, Pictures, 1 1/4 In.	4.00
Button, Reagan For Governor, Green, White & Black	15.00
Button, Reagan, '84, In Cowboy Attire, 1 1/4 In.	4.00
Button, RFK, Kennedy Action Corps, Arrow Pointing Up	16.00
Button, Richard Nixon Inauguration, Original Ribbon, 1969	20.00
Button, Robert Kennedy, Jugate	16.00
Button, Roosevelt, Wallace, Picture Of Each, 1/2 In.	15.00

Button, Spiro Our Hero, Head With Mickey Mouse Ears, 3/4 In. 1.00
Button, Theodore Roosevelt For President, On Horse, 1 1/8 In. 350.00
Button, Truman For Senator, 3/4 In. 125.00
Button, Union Women United For Humphrey, Muskie, 5/8 In. 5.00
Button, Vote Democrat, Johnson & Humphrey Picture, 3 In. 10.00
Button, Vote Socialist Workers In '72, 3/4 In. 4.00
Button, Wallace & LeMay, Jugate, 1 1/2 In. 10.00
Button, Wallace & LeMay, Stand Up For America, AFL–CIO 9.00
Button, Wallace In '76, Head View, 1 1/4 In. 4.00
Button, Wallace, Stand Up For America 4.50
Button, Welcome Ladybird, Train Center, 1 In. 25.00
Button, William Jennings Bryan, Clock Face, Silver Ground 3000.00
Button, Willkie & McNary 4.50
Button, Willkie For President 25.00
Button, Wilson & Marshall & Carlin, Heads Of Each, 1 1/4 In. 500.00
Cane, McKinley 100.00
Card, Hubert & Muriel Humphrey For President, Color, 2 x 4 In. 1.00
Cartoon, Uncle Sam, Pen & Ink, J. Berryman, S. Kemper 110.00
Certificate, Sen. Barry Goldwater, Amateur Radio Club, 9/12/63 .... 325.00
Clicker, Nixon, Click With Dick, Pear Shape, Tin 25.00
Clock, Roosevelt Man Of The Hour 100.00
Clock, Spiro Agnew 30.00
Decanter, Whiskey, Portly Politician, Green, Shot Glass Stopper 45.00
Doll, Barry Goldwater, Dashboard, Remco, Box, 5 1/2 In. 35.00
Doll, L. B. Johnson, Dashboard, Remco, Box, 5 1/2 In. 32.50
Dress, Paper, Nixon Printed On It In Red & Blue 450.00
Ferrotype, Douglas, Johnson 300.00
Ferrotype, Grant 325.00
Flag, Battle, T. Roosevelt, Red, White & Blue, 1912, 22 x 25 In. 145.00
Goblet, Happy Days Are Here Again, Party Scene, 6 1/4 In. 25.00
Inaugural Program, Presidential, 1901 .... 75.00
Jugate, Lincoln, Hamlin 2100.00
Key Chain, Ike, Handley, Indians, 1956 .... 25.00
Land Grant, James Monroe, 8/16/1823 .... 710.00
Lantern, Parade, Harrison, Morton, 8 Panels, Paper 765.00
Letter, William J. Bryan, Handwritten, Political Content, 1896 .... 125.00
License Plate, I Went All De Way With LBJ, Pregnant Girl 154.00
Match Holder, Bust Of Grant, Stars, Flags, Metal, 6 1/4 x 4 In. 195.00
Matches, Pull For Willkie 22.00
Menu, Pres. Roosevelt, En Route Via C & NW, 1934, 7 x 10 In. 50.00
Menu, Trip Of Pres. Truman, Washington To Coulee City, 1950, 8 In. 50.00
Mirror, Wm. McSherry For Congress, Sepia, 1 3/4 In. 10.00
Mug, Adlai Stevenson 15.00
Mug, Happy Days Are Here Again, Green, 5 In. 25.00
Mug, New Deal, Roosevelt, Stoneware 35.00
Mug, Nixon, Agnew, Frankoma 45.00
Mug, Reagan, 1977, 3 In. 15.00
Necktie, John Lindsay, Campaign 12.00
Necktie, Kennedy For President, Mustard Color 18.00
Necktie, Thomas Dewey, Campaign 20.00
Nodder, John F. Kennedy & Jackie, Composition, Pair 235.00
Nodder, Nixon, Figure Of Elephant, Composition, 1960 .... 250.00
Paperweight, Abraham Lincoln, Gillinder & Sons, Centennial 1876 .... 155.00
Paperweight, Churchill & Roosevelt, United For Victory 65.00
Pennant, Dewey For President 40.00
Pennant, F. D. Roosevelt, Inauguration, 1937, White On Blue, 28 In. 35.00
Pennant, Nixon, 1950, 12 x 30 In. 25.00
Pennant, Republican Convention, 1964 .... 15.00
Pepper Shaker, Jackie Kennedy, Picture Of Jackie, Ceramic 12.00
Photograph, Harry S. Truman, Autographed 125.00
Picture, John F. Kennedy, Handmade Wooden Inlay, 1960s, Border 350.00
Pin Dish, President & Mrs. John Fitzgerald Kennedy, 4 3/4 In. 20.00
Plate, Coin, John F. Kennedy, Imperial Glass, Box, 1964 .... 35.00

Plate, F. D. Roosevelt & Churchill, Champions Of Democracy	37.50
Plate, F. D. Roosevelt, Birth & Death Date, 10 In.	22.50
Plate, F. D. Roosevelt, Pink Border, Gold Trim, 11 In.	55.00
Plate, F. D. Roosevelt, Surrounded By Allied Flags, 10 3/4 In.	40.00
Plate, Federation Of Republican Women, Los Angeles County, 9 In.	12.00
Plate, General & Mrs. Eisenhower, Gold Band Border, 10 3/4 In.	17.50
Plate, Harry S. Truman, 10 In.	25.00
Plate, J. F. Kennedy, Information On Life, 10 In.	25.00
Plate, James Garfield, Pictured In Center, Word Memorial, 10 In.	35.00
Plate, Jimmy Carter, Face, Flag, Blue & White, 10 In.	22.00
Plate, Kennedy Family, 1961, 8 In.	10.00
Plate, Lyndon B. Johnson, Gold Trim, 9 In.	25.00
Plate, McKinley, Picture & Birthplace, Brown & White, 9 In.	15.00
Plate, Robert Taft, Gold Rim, Brown & White, 10 1/4 In.	30.00
Plate, Smiling Bill, Taft, Sunny Jim, Sherman, 7 In.	75.00
Plate, Theodore Roosevelt, Bears Digging Panama Canal	135.00
Plate, Theodore Roosevelt, Events Of His Life, 10 In.	50.00
Plate, U.S. Grant, Patriot & Soldier, Glass, Square, 9 1/2 In.	45.00
Plate, William Howard Taft, Gold Trim, 10 1/4 In.	30.00
Plate, William McKinley, Shield, Protection & Plenty, 7 1/4 In.	20.00
Postcard, Mechanical, Taft, Pull My Tail & See Next President	48.00
Postcard, Pres. & Mrs. Carter, V. P. & Mrs. Mondale, Inaugural, 1977	3.00
Postcard, Pres. F. D. Roosevelt, Great Smoky Mts. Dedication	12.00
Postcard, Sen. Ted Kennedy, National Dem. Conv., Speaking, Podium	2.50
Postcard, T. Roosevelt New Year Greeting, Ribbon Attached, 1905	85.00
Poster, Campaign, Eisenhower, Nixon, Pictures, 21 x 16 In.	35.00
Poster, Carry On With Franklin D. Roosevelt, 1936, 9 x 11 In.	100.00
Poster, Goldwater For President, 22 x 14 In.	25.00
Poster, Henry Clay Cigars, 1890	225.00
Poster, LBJ For The USA, 1964, 21 x 13 In.	25.00
Poster, McGovern In '72, Sam Francis, Framed, 38 x 25 In.	165.00
Poster, McGovern, President '72, Color Portrait, 21 x 26 In.	4.00
Poster, McKinley, Hobart, Lithogravure, 1896, 25 x 18 In.	19.00
Poster, Nixon Campaign, Vote Like World Depended, 21 x 13 In.	18.00
Poster, Warren G. Harding, Calvin Coolidge, 1920, 11 x 7 In.	125.00
Poster, William McKinley, Theodore Roosevelt, 1900, 20 x 29 In.	125.00
Raincoat, Kennedy	45.00
Ribbon, Memorial, Zachary Taylor, Masonic	250.00
Ribbon, Roosevelt, Johnson, Straus, Davenport, Bull Moose	85.00
Ribbon, U.S. Grant, Election & Mourning, Silk, 4 1/2 & 7 In.	165.00
Ribbon, Willkie War Veteran, Red, White & Blue	32.00
Sheet Music, Dewey's Victory, Grand Gallop, 1899, 11 x 14 In.	45.00
Sheet Music, Landon & Knox, Have You Ever Counted To A Billion?	15.00
Sheet Music, New Deal Rose With Roosevelt, Picture	38.00
Sheet Music, Our Landon	15.00
Sign, Repeal 18th Amendment, Tin	65.00
Sign, Ronald Reagan, Chesterfield Cigarettes, Framed, 1948	40.00
Sticker, Window, Ike, Dick, Red, White & Blue, 5 x 5 In.	4.00
Sticker, Window, Kennedy, Johnson, Red, White & Blue, 4 x 8 In.	5.00
Stickpin, Harrison, Head At Top	22.00
Stickpin, James Monroe, 5th President, Celluloid, c.1900, 1 In.	12.00
Stickpin, Seymour, Ferrotype	175.00
Stickpin, Teddy Roosevelt, Bear, Gold Paint, 2 1/4 In.	60.00
Teddy & Charge Of Rough Riders, Framed, 26 x 32 In.	275.00
Textile, Benjamin Harrison, Protection, Reciprocity, 18 x 19 In.	95.00
Ticket, Tour, Republican Pre-Convention, 1964, Unused	15.00
Tintype, Abraham Lincoln, 1864	750.00
Tintype, Stephen Douglas	1200.00
Toby Jug, Al Smith, Name In Script	125.00
Toby Jug, Dwight D. Eisenhower	85.00
Toby Jug, Herbert Hoover, Syracuse China, 7 In.	125.00
Top, Protection, Money, Prosperity, Picture, Wood, Metal, 2 1/2 In.	1155.00
Toy, Nixon On Elephant, Caricature Face, Rubber, 4 In.	25.00

Tray, Benjamin Harrison, Levi Morton, 1888 Campaign, Picture 145.00
Tray, F. D. Roosevelt & White House, 10 1/2 x 13 In. 65.00
Tray, Taft, Sherman, G. O. P. Standard Bearers, 1908 .... 150.00
Tumbler, McKinley, Our Martyr President, Flags, Date, 4 In. 25.00
Wastebasket, Spiro Agnew, Tin, Chein & Co., 1970, Unused 25.00
Watch Fob, Herbert Hoover, Horseshoe Shape 50.00
Watch Fob, Taft For President 75.00
Wristwatch, Nixon, I'm Not A Crook 195.00

POMONA glass is a clear glass with a soft amber border decorated with pale blue or rose–colored flowers and leaves. The colors are very, very pale. The background of the glass is covered with a network of fine lines. It was made from 1885 to 1888 by the New England Glass Company. First grind was made from April 1885 to June 1886. It was made by cutting a wax surface on the glass, then dipping it in acid. Second grind was a less expensive method of acid etching that was developed later.

Bowl, Cornflowers, Ruffled Amber Rim, 2nd Grind, 5 In. 150.00
Castor, Pickle, Inverted Thumbprint, Enameled Daisies, 9 In. 395.00
Creamer, 1st Grind, Miniature 150.00
Creamer, Inverted Thumbprint, 1st Grind, 2 1/2 x 5 In. 245.00
Finger Bowl, Amber Stain, 2nd Grind, 5 1/2 In. 50.00
Finger Bowl, Ruffled, Cornflowers, 2nd Grind 90.00
Jug, Cover, Water, Square Top, Amber Cornflowers 295.00
Lamp, Oil, Leaf & Jewel Stem, Clear Font, 1893 .... 45.00
Pitcher, Cornflowers, 2nd Grind, 7 In. 195.00
Pitcher, Curlicues Etched On Optic Diamonds, 1st Grind, 5 1/2 In. 485.00
Punch Cup, Cornflower, 1st Grind, 2 3/4 In. 195.00
Sugar & Creamer, Ruffled Rims, Amber Handles, 1st Grind 585.00
Syrup, Pewter Top, Fish, 6 1/2 In. 465.00
Toothpick, Tricorner 165.00
Toothpick, Tricornered, 2nd Grind 165.00
Tumbler, Blueberry, Gold Leaves, 2nd Grind, 3 3/4 In. 175.00
Tumbler, Cornflower, 2nd Grind, 3 7/8 In. 145.00
Tumbler, Cornflower, Amber Leaves, 2nd Grind, 3 1/2 In. .... 110.00 To 145.00
Tumbler, Inverted Thumbprint, 1st Grind 75.00
Vase, 1st Grind, 5 In. 85.00
Vase, Ruffled Top, Blueberry Design, 2nd Grind, 6 In. 195.00
Water Set, Coin Spot Pitcher, 6 Expanded Diamond Tumblers 220.00

PONTYPOOL, see Tole

POPEYE was introduced to the Thimble Theater comic strip in 1929. The character became a favorite of readers. In 1932, an animated cartoon featuring Popeye was made by Paramount Studios. The cartoon series continued and became even more popular when they were used on television starting in the 1950s. The full–length movie with Robin Williams as Popeye was made in 1980.

Airplane, Popeye The Pilot, Windup, Marx, 8 1/2 In. 850.00
Airplane, Windup, Marx, 8 1/2 In. 875.00
Bank, Bubble Gum, Figural Head 30.00
Bank, Cast Iron 45.00
Bank, Chalkware 32.00
Bank, Dime 85.00
Book, Big Little Book 10.00
Book, Popeye & Queen Olive Oyl .... 17.00 To 20.00
Box, Crayon, Cardboard 12.00
Bubble Set, Pipe, Dish, Soap, Unused, 1935 .... 50.00
Cartoon Kit, Colorform, 1957 .... 35.00
Chalkware, Box, 1953 .... 42.00
Cookie Jar, American Bisque .... 375.00 To 950.00
Costume, Mask, Cap, Jacket, Pants, 1936 .... 55.00
Doll, Jointed, Wooden, 1935 .... 270.00
Doll, Olive Oyl, Vinyl, Bronco, 7 In. 10.00

Doll, Uneeda, 12 In.	45.00
Eggcup, Hand Colored, Ceramic, Japan, 2 1/4 In.	26.00
Express, Windup	638.00
Figure, Popeye, Olive Oyl, Wood Jointed, String, 1930s, 4 3/4 In., Pair	125.00
Game, Ball, Popeye The Juggler, 1929	75.00
Game, Board, Popeye Pipe Toss, 1935	50.00
Game, Pin The Pipe On Popeye, 1937, 14 x 27 In.	48.00 To 75.00
Game, Popeye The Juggler, Ball, 1929	85.00
Game, Ring Toss, Box, 5 x 11 In.	50.00 To 60.00
Game, Target, Roly Poly, Gun, Box, Knickerbocker	165.00 To 225.00
Game, Transogram, 1957	95.00
Holder, Toothbrush, Popeye, Skater, Linemar	750.00
Holster Set & 2 Guns, Hubley, On Card	135.00
Jeep Game, 1937	115.00
Jigger, Windup, Marx, 9 1/2 In.	800.00 To 925.00
Light Bulb, Popeye, Christmas Tree	20.00
Lunch Box, 1964	60.00 To 125.00
Marionette, Olive Oyl, Cloth, Plastic Head & Hands, 1950s, Gund	98.00
Mask, Rubber, 1955	45.00
Music Box, Mayell, Box, 1961	250.00
Night–Light, Celluloid	30.00
Nodder, Olive Oyl, Large	85.00
Paint & Crayon Set, Hasbro, 1960s	28.00
Paint Box, Popeye & Family Picture, 5 x 5 In.	25.00
Pen, Fountain, 1940s	60.00
Pencil Case, With Popeye Ruler	75.00
Pencil Sharpener, Pluto	55.00
Pencil Sharpener, Popeye, Amber Bakelite	55.00 To 60.00
Pencil Sharpener, Tin, Dated 1929	95.00
Pencil, Mechanical, Instructions, Box	65.00
Pipe Toss, Popeye, Rosebud, Box, 1935	35.00 To 55.00
Pipe, Bubble	10.00
Printing Kit, Photo, 1958	65.00
Puppet, Hand, Gund	30.00
Puzzle, Jigsaw, 1963, Jaymar	10.00
Salt & Pepper	40.00
Scrapbook, 1929	45.00
Set, Cut & Sew Pillow, Olive Oyl	8.00
Sparkler, Chein & Co., 1959	200.00
Tank	650.00
Toy, Airport, Marx	1975.00
Toy, Bubble Blowing, Battery Operated, Linemar, Box	1950.00
Toy, Popeye & Olive Oyl Acrobat, Windup, Japan, 9 1/2 In.	1120.00
Toy, Popeye Pushing Wheelbarrow Of Spinach, Windup, Tin	400.00
Toy, Popeye, In Barrel, Windup	675.00
Toy, Popeye, Windup, Tin, Linemar	625.00
Toy, Wimpy, Plastic, Walk A Way, 4 x 4 1/2 In.	110.00
Wristwatch, Characters At Hour Position Around Dial, 1935	250.00
Wristwatch, Full Figure, Arms Keep Time	71.50 To 100.00
Wristwatch, New Haven, 1935	950.00

PORCELAIN factories that are well known are listed in this book under the factory name. This section lists pieces made by the less well known factories.

Basket, Floral Scrolling, Blue Ground, England, 1820, 7 11/16 In.	825.00
Bowl, Basketweave, Cherubs Holding Bowl, 6 1/2 x 12 1/2 In.	675.00
Bowl, Cover, Painted Multicolored Florals, Gilt Border, 8 3/4 In.	45.00
Bowl, Fern, Hamlet & Falstaff Scenes, Altrohlau, 1880, 8 In.	165.00
Bowl, Footed, Polychrome Decoration, Oriental, 8 1/2 In.	88.00
Bowl, Inlaid Sgraffito, Pink Glaze, Lucie Rie, c.1980, 7 In.	5550.00
Bowl, Manganese Glaze, Etruscan Ring, Lucie Rie, 1970, 9 In.	597.00
Bowl, Polychrome Enamel, Oriental, 6 1/2 In.	225.00
Box, Dresser, Wave Crest–Type, Green, White, Gilded Flowers, 5 In.	230.00

Bust, Man, Woman, Gilt, Sitzendorf, 13 In., Pair	605.00
Butter, Teddy Bear & 2 Dolls, Germany	120.00
Candlestick, Cherub, Arm Around Stick, Sitzendorf, 15 In.	350.00
Candlestick, Figural, Youth, Maid, Blue Enameling, 11 In., Pair	110.00
Canister Set, Child's, Floral, Germany, 17 Piece	385.00
Canister Set, Grape Design, Hanging Salt, Wooden Tops, 9 Piece	95.00
Cat, Tan, Black & Green, 3 5/8 In.	115.00
Centerpiece, Putti & Flowers, Von Schierholz, 19 In. ....*Illus*	750.00
Charger, Blue & White, Oriental, 15 In.	110.00
Chop Plate, Polychrome, Enameled Birds, Flowers, Black, 12 In.	50.00
Coffee Set, Allegorical, Oak Chest, Russia, Individual, 5 Piece	3575.00
Container, Lid, Stenciled Allspice, Germany, 4 1/2 x 2 1/2 In.	38.00
Cup & Saucer, Cherubs, Figural Bird On Handle Is Whistle, German	45.00
Decanter, Rip Van Winkle, Cardinal, 1974	22.00
Dish, Leaf Shape, Presidential Service, 9 1/2 In.	575.00
Dish, Leaf, Cottage Scene, Longton Hall, 1755–1757, 8 5/8 In.	970.00
Dish, Oval, Enameled Landscape, Gilt Rim, Footed, 11 1/4 In.	115.00
Dish, Quatrefoil, Leaf Mold, Green To Yellow, Longton Hall, 8 In.	2090.00
Dish, Vegetable, Pink, Gold Floral Swags, Cover, 11 1/2 In., Pair	80.00
Dresser Jar, Doll, Mme. Pompadour, Large	55.00
Dresser Set, Art Nouveau, Royal Austria, 3 Piece	50.00
Egg, Easter, Raised Flowers, Gold Ground, Russia, 1860, 4 In.	1980.00
Egg, Easter, St. Nicholas, Flowers, Imperial Porcelain, 4 1/4 In.	4400.00
Egg, Young Woman Portrait, Reverse Gilded, Russia, 3 3/4 In.	2090.00
Eye Cup, Blue, White, Diamond–Hatched Band, St. Cloud, 1 In.	1450.00
Figurine, Allegorical, Autumn, Girl, Longton Hall, 1755, 4 1/2 In.	3080.00
Figurine, Apple Pickers, Sitzendorf, 21 In.	2150.00
Figurine, Apple Pickers, Sitzendorf, 9 1/2 In.	650.00
Figurine, Beaucaire, Coventry	50.00
Figurine, Bird, Oriental, Brightly Enameled, 8 1/8 In.	105.00
Figurine, Boy Selling Birds, Girl, Flowers, Kister, 1920, 7 In., Pr.	325.00
Figurine, Charmaine, Coventry	50.00
Figurine, Chinese Foo Dog, Ch'ing Dynasty, 26 In., Pair ....*Illus*	2640.00
Figurine, Chinoiserie, Tartar, Hat, White, France, 1735, 10 5/8 In.	3850.00
Figurine, Colonial Couple, Potschapel, 21 In.	1350.00
Figurine, Couple With Russian Wolfhounds, Sitzendorf, 9 x 10 In.	850.00
Figurine, Dancing Boy & Girl, Anzengruber, 9 1/2 x 7 1/2 In.	325.00
Figurine, Dancing Lady, Billowing Skirt, Platinum, Heidi Schoop	75.00
Figurine, Draped Maiden, 2 Water Jugs, Pastel Enameling, 20 In.	250.00
Figurine, Draped Nude, Schaubackunst, 12 In.	375.00
Figurine, Flower Couple, Potschapel, 9 In.	695.00

Porcelain, Centerpiece, Putti & Flowers, Von
Schierholz, 19 In.

Porcelain, Tray, Gold, Black, Fornesetti,
4 x 5 In.

Porcelain, Figurine, Chinese Foo Dog, Ch'ing
Dynasty, 26 In., Pair

Porcelain, Figurine, Parrot, Germany,
17 1/2 In., Pair

Figurine, Flower Couple, Sitzendorf, 7 1/2 In. 550.00
Figurine, Gardener & Wife, Sitzendorf, 9 1/2 In. 450.00
Figurine, Male Dancer, Yellow, Brown, Green, Lenci, 12 In. 1980.00
Figurine, Man Peddler, Beret, Knee Breeches, Bow, 6 5/8 In. 1430.00
Figurine, Monkey Band, 8 Costumed Musicians, Germany, 7 In. 2420.00
Figurine, Oriental Woman, Festive Headdress, Lenci, 17 In. 2420.00
Figurine, Painting Session, Oval Plinth, Sitzendorf, 17 In. 850.00
Figurine, Parrot, Germany, 17 1/2 In., Pair ....*Illus* 4500.00
Figurine, Roman Festival, Sitzendorf, 11 1/2 x 15 In. 1950.00
Figurine, Sculptress, Classically Draped, Enamel, Gilt, 6 1/2 In. 145.00
Figurine, Swan, Flowers, Von Scherholz, c.1950, 8 1/4 In. 125.00
Figurine, Two Wolfhounds, Oval Base, Black, White, 7 1/8 In. 115.00
Figurine, Woman & Child, Seated, Black, Yellow, Mauve, Lenci, 12 In. 1650.00
Figurine, Woman In Chair, Polychrome Enameling, Gilt, 9 1/2 In. 800.00
Figurine, Woman With Fan, Polychrome Enamel With Gilt, 12 In. 220.00
Fruit Cooler, Urn Shape, Gilded Edges, Pineapple Finials 2200.00
Honey Pot, Flower On Lid, Honeybee Handle, Robj, c.1925, 7 1/2 In. 660.00
Inkstand, Rococo, Floral, 2 Women's Heads Wells, Sitzendorf, 9 In. 425.00
Jar, Polychrome Enamel, Gilt, Chinese, 5 1/4 In. 95.00
Jardiniere, Hunting Scenes, Circular, Oriental, 15 x 15 In. 302.50
Jardiniere, Scenic, Blue & Orange, Stand, 9 x 10 x 8 1/2 In., Pair 165.00
Mug, Child's, H. M. S. Pinafore Black Transfer, Verse, 2 3/4 In. 45.00
Mug, Child's, River & House Scene, Twig Handle, Longton Hall, 1755 .... 1540.00
Mug, Gran Pappy, Imperial Porcelain Co., 4 1/2 In. 130.00
Mug, Musical, John Peel, Fielding's, Crown Devon 140.00
Pastille Burner, Gothic Cottage, England, 1820–1825, 4 3/8 In. 1100.00
Pea Pod, Green Shell, Leaves, England, 1830, 2 3/6 In. 660.00
Penholder, Quill, 1870s 55.00
Pitcher, Embossed Drinking Scene, Vintage, Enameling, 6 7/8 In. 90.00
Pitcher, Embossed Leafy Base, Twig Handle, Germany 25.00
Pitcher, Federal Symbols, Pursell, Cartiledge, 11 1/2 In. 8500.00
Planter, Figural Bird Handles, Oriental 800.00
Plaque, Woman & 2 Children, Gadrooned Frame, Germany, 6 In. Diam. 750.00
Plate, Child's, Teddy Bear Scene, Germany 32.50
Plate, Chinaman In Punt, Blue, Bow, 1758–1762, 9 9/16 In., Pair 1430.00
Plate, Felix The Cat, 1930s, 8 In. ....*Illus* 45.00
Plate, Polychrome Enameled Chinoiserie Design, 8 3/4 In. 30.00
Plate, Rustic Landscape Scene, Sepia, Philadelphia, c.1830, Pair 187.00
Platter, Victorian Couple, Gold Tracery, Tirschenreuth, 15 In. 75.00
Platter, Worker, Black & Mustard Banner, Russia, 1920, 15 In. 6600.00
Pot, Brush, Polychrome Landscape, Oriental, 11 1/4 In. 45.00

Powder Jar, Colonial Ladies On Lid	37.00
Punch Bowl, Cabbage & Moth, Chinese, 11 5/8 In.	330.00
Sauceboat, Underplate, Blue, Polychrome Floral Design, 6 3/4 In.	105.00
Saucer, 3 Plants Inside, White, Handles, France, 6 13/16 In., Pair	220.00
Sugar & Creamer, Pansies, Stanley	17.00
Sugar, Cover, Tucker–Type	425.00
Sweetmeat Dish, Scalloped Shells, White, Bow, 1752–1755, 8 1/4 In.	990.00
Sweetmeat, Stand, Famille Rose, Shell, Bow, 1753–1755, 7 5/16 In.	2310.00
Syrup, Pewter Top, T. Boote Hanley, c.1861	125.00
Teapot, Polychrome Enamel Figures, Character Writing, 4 1/4 In.	50.00
Teapot, Thousand Butterfly, Chinese, 9 In.	100.00
Tray, Gold, Black, Fornesetti, 4 x 5 In. *Illus*	35.00
Tray, Round, 3 Children, Hand Painted, Gilt Trim, 8 7/8 In.	95.00
Tureen, Cover, Blue Sprigs, Gold Bandine, 12 3/8 In.	475.00
Tureen, Cover, Giblet, Tucker–Type, Pair	500.00
Tureen, Grapes Shape, Stem Knop Cover, Continental, 7 1/2 In.	2640.00
Urn, Cover, Metal Mounted, Figures, 18th–Century Dress, 17 1/2 In.	330.00
Urn, Ormolu Trim, Floral Enameling & Gilt, France, 21 In.	775.00
Urn, Ormolu Trim, Midnight Blue, Enameling, Gilt, 18 In., Pair	750.00
Vase, Birds On Branch, Peony, Eggshell, Blue Seal Mark, 11 In.	250.00
Vase, Blue & White, Dragon, Oriental, 23 In.	95.00
Vase, Blue & White, Oriental, 23 1/2 In., Pair	170.00
Vase, Courting Scenes, Raised Flowers, Germany, 31 1/2 In., Pair	2200.00
Vase, Ear, Cobalt, Gilt, Polychrome Floral Design, 16 In.	150.00
Vase, Famille Noire, Overall Floral, 36 In.	440.00
Vase, Flared, Fluted Rim, Polychrome, Gilt Handles, Oriental, 7 In.	27.50
Vase, Potpourri, White, Basket, Fruit Filled, St. Cloud, 1740, 5 In.	775.00
Vase, Roses, Cream Ground, Gold Rim, 2 Handles, Crown Devon, 10 In.	250.00
Vase, Tea Jar Shape, Wooden Base, Lamp Mounted, Chinese, 18 In.	2475.00
Vase, White, Grapes On Bowl, Cherubs Holding, Japan, 6 1/2 In.	22.00
Wall Pocket, Village Mountain Scene, China, 19th Century, 10 In.	125.00
Watering Can, Baroque Floral, Double Handles, Fancy Spout, 8 In.	250.00
Wine Cooler, White, Grotesque Animal Head Handle, St. Cloud, 7 In.	4125.00

POSTCARDS were first legally permitted in Austria on October 1, 1869. The United States passed postal regulations allowing the card in 1872. Most of the picture postcards collected today date after 1910. The amount of postage can help to date a card. The rates are: 1872 (1 cent), 1917 (2 cents), 1919 (1 cent), 1925 (2 cents), 1928 (1 cent), 1952 (2 cents), 1959 (3 cents), 1963 (4 cents), 1968 (5 cents), 1973 (8 cents), 1975 (7 cents), 1976 (9 cents), 1978 (10 cents), 1981 (12 cents), 1981 (13 cents), 1985 (14 cents), 1988 (15 cents), 1991 (19 cents).

3 Apache Warriors, Colored, 1906	10.00
7 Blackfoot Indian Men On Horseback, 1890s	10.00
A Season's Catch, Photo, Moore & Stone, Wimmemuca, Nevada, 1911	40.00
Aviator Cap, G. Curtis, Photograph	176.00
Baby Rena, Sitting, Pressback Rocker, Photograph, 1910	1.25

Porcelain, Plate, Felix The Cat, 1930s, 8 In.

◆ ◆ ◆ ◆ ◆ ◆ ◆ ◆ ◆ ◆ ◆ ◆ ◆ ◆ ◆ ◆ ◆ ◆ ◆ ◆

To remove the musty smell from an old trunk, put a bowl of freshly ground coffee inside.

◆ ◆ ◆ ◆ ◆ ◆ ◆ ◆ ◆ ◆ ◆ ◆ ◆ ◆ ◆ ◆ ◆ ◆ ◆ ◆

Baby, Christening Gown, Photograph, Early 1900s	1.00
Bartender In Front Of Elaborate Bar, Photograph, Unused	17.50
Broadmoor Hotel, Parrish	42.00
Burke's Stout Beer, U.S. Govt., 1908	100.00
Carnival, Canal Street, New Orleans, 1907	3.50
Chase & Sanborn Coffee, Red & Black Illustration, 1887	50.00
Christmas, Woman Holds Santa Claus Mask, S. Schmucker	40.00
Comic Golf, Here's Wishing You A Mole In One	15.00
Comic Golf, Keep Your Eye On The Ball!	15.00
Comic Yellow Kid Characters, Valentine Type, R. F. Outcault, 1906	25.00
First Baptist Church, Cochran, Georgia	2.50
First Methodist Church, Cochran, Georgia	2.50
Fiske Tires, 3 Sleepy Boys With Candles & Tires, 1917	40.00
Freddie Miller, Oh., Featherweight Champion, World's Title, 1930	35.00
Globe Cafe, C. Juarez, Mexico, Back Bar Picture, 1927 Postmark	3.00
Golf View Hotel, Black, White, Nairn, Unused, 1920	15.00
Grand Hotel & Golf Links, Grange–Over–Sand	10.00
Happy Hooligan	55.00
Harold Lloyd, 1922	9.00
Interior View, Union Bank & Trust Co., San Francisco, c.1915	6.50
International Livestock, 6 Horses & Wagon, Expo, 1921	25.00
J. W. Sargent & Son Co., Tent Display, 1916 Maxwell Auto, Photo	35.00
Johnston's Chocolate Nut Clusters, City Pharmacy, Leadville, Col.	40.00
Jolly Green Giant, Jingle On Reverse, Oversized	25.00
Katzenjammer Kids, Color Your Own, With Color Palettes, 1907	10.00
Keen Kutter Store, Photograph	165.00
Lawn Grass Catcher, Whitman & Barnes Co., Boston, Red, 1892	65.00
Main Room, Will Rogers's Ranch	7.50
Mammy Chicken Inn	30.00
Marilyn Monroe, 1950s	12.00
Memorial Day, Embossed 13 Stars Flag, Mailed April 1903	8.00
Moxie Girl, Moxie Boy, Moxie Cases	100.00
Nestle's Milk, Crying Baby, Happy Dog, Signed Mauzan	60.00
Niagara Falls & Pan–American Expo, Buffalo, 1907	100.00
Notaseme Hosiery, Woman, Wooded Scene	40.00
Olympics, Stockholm, 1912	10.00
Oregon Trail, Ezra Meeker	1.00
P. G. A. National C. C., Palm Beach Garden, Fla., Color, 1968	12.00
Rising Sun Flour, F. W. Jenkins & Bro., Green, 1877	50.00
San Francisco, In Mailing Folder, 1–Cent Stamp, Miniature, 1934	7.00
Santa Claus Dressed As Uncle Sam, Squeaker, German	65.00
Sarasota Municipal Golf Course, Color Photo, Unused	12.00
Seagram Distillery Company, Louisville, Ky., Factory, Linen, 1940s	1.50
Sears Roebuck Wallpaper Advertising, 1 Cent, 1930s	.75
Seminole Indian, 1901	10.00
Shorey's Ready–To–Wear Clothes, Red, Black & White, Montreal, 1898	50.00
Snake River Bridge & Tetons, Jackson To Yellowstone, 1940	6.00
Spring Hill Distillery–Frankfort, Kentucky, 1909	7.00
St. Andrews Golf Courses, From Air, Photo, Black, White, Valentine	15.00
St. Patrick's Day, Hold To Light, Remember Erin	50.00
Teddy Bear, Figural, Leather	40.00
Teddy Roosevelt, Back Of Train, Whistle Stop, Photograph	231.00
Thanksgiving Greetings, Pilgrim, Turkey, S. Schmucker, 1911	30.00
Trinity Episcopal Church, Cochran, Georgia	2.50
Wanamaker Store, Philadelphia, Linen, 1952	3.50
West Grand Ave., Ponca City, Oklahoma, 1910	4.00
White House Coffee, Jamestown Exposition, Brown & White, 1907	45.00
Yacht Club Whiskey, Kayser & Hegner Co., Blue & White, 1898	65.00

POSTERS have informed the public about news and entertainment events since ancient times. Nineteenth-century advertising or theatrical posters and twentieth-century movie and war posters are of special interest today. The price is determined by the artist, the condition, and the rarity. Other posters may be listed under Political and World War I and II.

7–Up, Cardboard, 1960, 17 x 12 In.	12.00
Air France, Linen Backing, 39 x 24 In.	450.00
Alfa Romeo, Black, Gray, 1960	220.00
Amer Picon, Carlos Courmont, Blue, Yellow Figure, Black, 62 x 46 In.	715.00
American–Hawaiian Steamship Co., Single Stack Steamer, c.1900	975.00
Barnum & Bailey, Coney Island Water Carnival, 1898, 39 x 30 In.	1500.00
Barnum & Bailey, Greatest Show On Earth, Menagerie, 64 x 29 In.	1320.00
Ben Shahn, Lincoln Center, Black, White, 45 x 30 In.	825.00
Bombers, B–52, Natalie Wood, 1957, 41 x 27 In.	95.00
Boys & Girls, You Can Help Uncle Sam Win The War, 1918, 30 x 20 In.	275.00
Build & Fight In Navy Seabees, c.1943, 14 x 20 In.	175.00
Bull–Dogger, Silent Movie, Bill Pickett, 1923, 41 x 81 In.	1870.00
Bus Stop, Marilyn Monroe, 22 x 28 In.	175.00
Buy War Bonds, Uncle Sam, Flag, Soldiers, Airplanes, 40 x 29 1/2 In.	65.00
Carnival Of Picayune, Procession Of Rex, Floats, 1893, 28 x 42 In.	385.00
Carter The Great, World's Weird Wonderful Wizard, 74 x 38 In.	670.00
Cat & The Canary, Terrified Woman, 1905, 20 x 28 In.	110.00
Chang & Fak–Hong's United Magicians, Stone Litho, 23 x 15 In.	165.00
Christiani Bros. Circus, Elephant, Trainer, 1950s, 28 x 49 In.	75.00
Christmas Carol, Reginald Owen, Gene Lockhart, 1938, 27 x 41 In.	175.00
Cleveland War Fund, All For Victory, 31 x 42 In.	175.00
Clifton Comedy Co., Blackface Comic Portrait, 20 x 30 In.	154.00
Clifton Comedy Co., Lucky Irishman, 1910s, 20 x 30 In.	77.00
Clyde Beatty–Cole Bros., Ferocious Tiger, Butler, 1950s, 28 x 21 In.	85.00
Cole Bros., Circus, Clown, 80 x 138 In.	880.00
Cole Bros., Clown's Head, Muslin Back, 108 x 72 In.	1870.00
Cote D'Azur, French Travel Commission, Framed, 40 1/2 x 26 1/2 In.	330.00
Crime Without Passion, Claude Rains, 1934, 27 x 41 In.	350.00
Dancing Lady, Clark Gable, Joan Crawford, 1933	3025.00
Deadly Mantis, 28 x 22 In.	150.00
Dial M For Murder, French, 1954, 63 x 47 In.	200.00
Dr Pepper, Lady Reaches For Drink, 1950s, 15 x 24 In.	25.00
Edward Penfield, Harper's, May 1895, 16 x 13 In.	247.00
Empire Strikes Back, Coca–Cola, 1980, 24 x 33 In.	9.00
F. D. Roosevelt, We Can, We Will, We Must, Savings Bonds, 11 x 22 In.	10.00
Feed A Fighter, Doughboy Drinking Coffee, 20 x 30 In.	95.00
Fiesta In Havana, Senoritas On Balcony, Art Deco, 1937, 14 x 23 In.	300.00
Folies Bergere, La Cavalieri, Can–Can Dancer, c.1895, 32 x 48 In.	1000.00
Furness Caribbean Cruises, Adolph Treidler, Silk Screen, 1950, 50 In	200.00
G. Ripart, Cavailier, On Horse, Laubenheimer, 1920, 47 x 32 In.	70.00
Gentlemen's Agreement, Gregory Peck, 1947	1870.00
Gone With The Wind, Greater Than Ever, 11 x 17 In.	25.00
Gordon The Master Magician, Stone Lithograph, 26 x 18 In.	220.00
Great Chang & Fak–Hong's Magic Show, Stone Litho, 33 x 26 In.	220.00
Gulliver's Travels, Max Fleischer, 41 x 27 In.	1980.00
Harper's Weekly, Red, White, Brown, 16 x 12 In.	121.00
Have You A Red Cross Service Flag, J. Wilcox Smith, 21 x 28 In.	125.00
Hippy Nude Girl With Hookah, 1960s	35.00
Holland America Line, Tugs, Freighters, Frame, c.1920, 22 x 27 In.	250.00
Hudson Lake, Leslie Ragan, 1920, 28 x 36 In.	150.00
I Gave A Man, Will You Give 10% Of Your Pay, 16 1/2 x 22 In.	50.00
If You Want To Fight, Join The Marines, Christy, 1915, 30 x 41 In.	650.00
Invisible Boy, With Robby Robot, 1957, 41 x 27 In.	400.00
King Kong, Movie, 41 x 27 In.	700.00
Law & Order, Ronald Reagan, 1953, 27 x 41 In.	425.00
Le Tour De Mt. Blanc, 1927, 42 x 31 In.	600.00
Let's Go Get 'Em, U.S. Marines, Recruitment, 1942, 28 x 38 In.	275.00

Little Eva's Temptation, Blacks & Shanty, 1933, 29 x 41 In.	325.00
Little Rascals, Fish Hooky, 1952, 41 x 27 In.	137.50
Lone Ranger, Clayton Moore, Full Color, 20 x 24 In.	50.00
Mack Sennett's Vacation Loves, Acme Litho, 41 x 27 In.	330.00
Magnificent Obsession, Irene Dunne, Universal, 1935	300.00
Marilyn Monroe, Black & White, Cardboard, 1960s, 24 x 30 In.	55.00
N. C. Wyeth, Buy War Bonds, Multicolored, 40 x 30 In.	330.00
Notice, Business Of Selling, Spiritous–Intoxicating Liquors, 1902	72.00
Pan–American Exposition, Buffalo, 1901, Multi Color, 48 x 25 In.	2420.00
Postman Always Rings Twice, Color, 1981, 26 3/4 x 40 1/2 In.	12.00
Primrose & Dockstader Minstrels, Black Man, Chickens	410.00
Queen Elizabeth, C. E. Turner, Framed, 1946, 31 x 21 In.	210.00
Red Dot Cigar, 1930, Redhead, Cardboard Cigar, String	25.00
Revenge Of The Jedi, Rolled	245.00
Rin Tin Tin, Lithograph, 1930	500.00
Ringling Bros. & Barnum & Bailey, Horses, 5 Rings, 1929, 28 x 42 In.	195.00
Ringling Bros. & Barnum & Bailey, Smiling Clown, 106 x 80 In.	660.00
Ripley's Believe It Or Not, Snookie The Chimp, 9 Ft. x 6 Ft. 10 In.	55.00
Rockwell, Let's Give Him Enough and On Time, 1942, 28 x 40 In.	495.00
Rolling Stones, Jet & Heavens, 36 x 24 In., 10 Piece	185.00
Season's Best, Brown & Bigelow, Pinups, Folded, 1945, 25 x 17 In.	14.00
She Done Him Wrong, Mae West, Cary Grant, 1933	4400.00
Singin' In The Rain, Gene Kelly, 1952	1870.00
Sullivan's Travels, Preston Sturges, 1941, 27 x 41 In.	6050.00
Tarzan, Against Mau–Mau, 47 x 27 In.	375.00
Tell That To The Marines, Montgomery Flagg, 30 x 40 In.	300.00
The Mark Of Zorro, Tyrone Power, 1940	5225.00
The Virginian, Gary Cooper, 1929	3850.00
Thurton Magic, Vanishing Whippet	425.00
Tophat Cigarettes, Gentleman, Paper, 1920, 22 x 13 In.	110.00
Topsy, Uncle Tom's Cabin, Stone Lithograph, On Linen, c.1900	180.00
Toys In Window, Color, Red Border, 28 x 14 In.	10.00
U.S. Army, Make Haste Safely, America Is The Loser, World War II	90.00
U.S. Postal Service, Jim Thorpe Stamp, Envelope	25.00
Uncle Tom & Eva, Stone Lithograph On Linen, c.1900, 21 x 28 In.	180.00
Uncle's Darling, Blue, Red, 1880s, 25 x 37 In.	715.00
Victory Liberty Loan, 90 x 40 In.	302.00
Votes For Women's Suffrage, Broadside, 1917	69.00
White Star Liner, Queen Mary, Linen Back, 1935, 33 x 25 In.	450.00
Wild & Woolfy, Cartoon, MGM, 41 x 27 In.	286.00
Willsons Circus, Clown With Animals, Full Color, 40 x 30 In.	100.00
Women Awake, Your Country Needs You, Hazel Roberts, 1916, 25 In.	275.00
WPA, Fire Destroys Everything, Family Silhouette, 1934, 11 x 14 In.	150.00
Zombies Of Mora Tau, 1957, 41 x 27 In.	90.00

POTLIDS are just that, lids for pots. Transfer–printed potlids had their heyday from the 1840s to the early 1900s. The English Staffordshire potteries made ceramic containers with decorative lids for bear's grease, shrimp or meat paste, cold cream, and toothpaste. Printed advertising and pictures of historical events, portraits of famous people, or scenic views were designed in black and white or color. Reproductions have been made.

Army and Navy Almond Shaving Cream, Green	65.00
Bazin Genuine Beef Marrow, Blue	450.00
Best Card & Sandringham	170.00
Boston Baked Beans, Pottery, Blue & White	225.00
Circus Scene, Bear Trainer, Pratt	225.00
Dr. Johnson, Square Frame	125.00
Seat Of H. R. H.	170.00
Yardley's Tooth Paste, London, Paris	45.00

POTTERY and porcelain are different. Pottery is opaque; you can't see through it. Porcelain is translucent. If you hold a porcelain dish in front of a strong light you will see the light through the dish. Porcelain is colder to

Pottery, Bowl, Red Design,   Pottery, Creamer, Bird, Orange   Pottery, Puzzle Jug, Flowers,
Winblad, 1950s, 9 In.   & Green, Germany, 4 In.   Bevete, 4 1/4 In.

the touch. Pottery is softer and easier to break and will stain more easily
because it is porous. Porcelain is thinner, lighter, and more durable.
Majolica, faience, and stoneware are all pottery. Additional pieces of
pottery are listed in this book in the Art Pottery category and under the
factory name.

Birdhouse, Aqua Glaze 20.00
Bowl Set, Nested, Morton Pottery, 5 Piece 225.00
Bowl, Clown Face, Blue On White, Dorchester, 5 3/4 In. 110.00
Bowl, Mixing, Stacking Rim, Dark Green, Orange Spots, 6 1/4 In. 150.00
Bowl, Ormolu Trim, Marked, France, Oval, 12 1/2 In. 125.00
Bowl, Red Design, Winblad, 1950s, 9 In. ....*Illus* 95.00
Bust, Attenuated Head, Square Base, Sponged, G. Baudische, 7 1/4 In. ... 4400.00
Candlestick, Duchess Ware, Handle, Wannopee, 12 x 8 In. 175.00
Coffeepot, Cottage, Metal Insert, Fraunfelter, 2 Cup 25.00
Console Set, Turquoise, Pedestal Base, Hyalyn, 3 Piece 90.00
Console, Pink, Gray, With Bird Figure, Los Angeles Potteries, 2 Pc. 24.00
Creamer, Bird, Orange & Green, Germany, 4 In. ....*Illus* 35.00
Cup & Saucer, Mythological Scenes, Venus & Mars, Frankenthal, 1770 ...... 880.00
Cup, Bottoms–Up, Nude, Black 32.00
Dish, Combware, Brown Glazed, Striations, 1790–1820, 13 1/2 In. 880.00
Dish, Combware, Painted Interior, Serrated Sides, 1760–1800, 20 In. 880.00
Dish, Combware, Serrated Sides, Rectangular, 10 x 16 1/2 In. 885.00
Dish, Grape Pattern, Cobalt Blue, Royal Stanley 65.00
Dish, Hen On Nest, Colorful, Lancaster & Sundland 65.00
Figurine, Boxer, Pup, Bowing, Morten Studios 48.00
Figurine, Boxer, Sitting, Morten Studios 65.00
Figurine, Boy, With Peep Show, Frankenthal, 1760, 4 1/8 In. 1100.00
Figurine, Bugs Bunny, Walking, Ears Up, Carrot, Shaw, Label, 9 In. 150.00
Figurine, Cockatiel, Double, Maddox 32.00
Figurine, Frog Orchestra, Voight Brothers 2310.00
Figurine, German Shepherd, Standing, Morten Studios 35.00
Figurine, German Shepherd, Wien Keramos R. Knight Ceramics 95.00
Figurine, Lion, Oval Base, Gray Brown, White Traces, Ohio, 15 In. 100.00
Figurine, Mandy, Flower Girl, Black, Brayton Laguna 65.00
Figurine, Orchid Girl, Armani 950.00
Figurine, Peasant Girl, Heidi Schoop, 12 In. 25.00
Figurine, Pomeranian, Standing, Morten Studios 35.00
Figurine, Spanish Lady, Water Jug, Weil Ware, 12 1/2 In. ....*Illus* 35.00
Flower Pot, Saucer, Finger Crimped Rims, 8 1/4 In. 45.00
Humidor, Pipe On Lid, Austria, 5 In. 50.00

Pottery, Figurine, Spanish Lady, Water Jug,
Weil Ware, 12 1/2 In.

Pottery, Napkin Holder, Lady, Salt & Pepper,
Pink, 10 In., 3 Piece

Jar, Dark Brown Glaze, Double Applied Handles, 15 1/4 In.	85.00
Jar, Greenish Brown Glaze, Black Stripes, Applied Handles, 15 In.	140.00
Jar, Powder, Cover, White, France, 1860, 2 1/2 x 1 3/4 In.	35.00
Jar, Southern, Red Clay, Applied Handles, 14 In.	25.00
Jardiniere, Pale & Medium Green, Blue & Brown, 13 1/2 In.	315.00
Jug, Greenish Glaze, Sloping Shoulders, Applied Handle, 8 In.	150.00
Jug, Greenish Mottled Glaze, Tooled Lip, Applied Handle, 8 5/8 In.	400.00
Jug, Grotesque, Green Ash Glaze, Contemporary, Craig, Vale, 16 In.	165.00
Jug, Harvest, Slipware, Red, Amber Glaze, Royal Arms, 12 3/16 In.	6600.00
Jug, R. M. Hughes & Co., Monogram Fruit Vinegar, Miniature	65.00
Mug, Indian Head, Figural, Cash Family Pottery, 1948	50.00
Mug, Tony Weller, Avonware, England	35.00
Napkin Holder, Lady, Salt & Pepper, Pink, 10 In., 3 Piece ....*Illus*	45.00
Pie Plate, Combware, Serrated Rim, Yellow Interior, c.1800, 8 In.	605.00
Pie Plate, Combware, Serrated, Yellow, Brown Striations, 1800, 11 In.	440.00
Pin Tray, Thistle Design, Waylande Gregory, 5 1/2 x 3 1/2 In.	125.00
Pitcher, A. R. Cole, Sanford, N. C.	12.50
Pitcher, Applied Handle & Spout, Basalt	185.00
Pitcher, Buff Clay, Brown Glaze, Dark Flecks, Strap Handle, 5 In.	85.00
Pitcher, Cover, Clear Glaze, Yellow, Brown, Side Spout, 7 1/2 In.	215.00
Pitcher, Heron, George Jones	1540.00
Pitcher, Matte Teal Blue, Marked II KK Zark, 8 In.	450.00
Pitcher, Plaid, Blair	10.00
Planter, 3 Children Carrying Boat, Hertwig, 8 x 11 In.	250.00
Planter, 3 Frogs Are Holding Handles, Mouths Open, Yellow, Japan	59.00
Planter, Bird, Green, Florida, Royal Hickman	25.00
Planter, Boat Shape, Blue, Black Stripes, Glidden, 10 In.	70.00
Planter, Figural, Sally, Brayton	25.00
Plaque, Arab Girl, Buildings, Musterschutz, 14 In.	350.00
Plate, Divided, Persian Ware, Blue & White, Germany	28.00
Platter, Bluebird, Carrolton, 13 In.	45.00
Puzzle Jug, Flowers, Bevete, 4 1/4 In. ....*Illus*	50.00
Rice Bowl, Blue & White, Free Standing Spoon, China, 1890, 6 Piece	45.00
Sugar, Cover, Widow Finial, Ribs, Cherubs, Basalt, Impressed Mayer	165.00
Teapot, Iroquois Intaglio, Art Deco, Ben Seibel	35.00
Toothpick, Owl In Tree	55.00
Vase, 3 Musician Frogs, White, Japan	39.00
Vase, Baby, Brayton Laguna	22.00
Vase, Catalina Island, Blue, Oval, 6 In.	17.00
Vase, Futuristic Cat, Yellow Glaze, Louis Wain, 10 7/8 In.	2530.00
Vase, Stump, F. B. Norton, 12 In.	220.00

POWDER FLASKS AND POWDER HORNS were made to hold the
gunpowder used in antique firearms. The early examples were made of
horn or wood; later ones were of copper or brass.

POWDER FLASK, Running Rabbit, Brass 75.00

POWDER HORN, 3-Masted & 2-Masted Gun Ships, Whaling Scene, John Rook, 1836 .... 4250.00
    Crowned Lion Of George III, England, 1780, 10 1/2 In. 880.00
    Dated 1830 .... 85.00
    Deer-Pine Embossed, Zinc, 1890 .... 45.00
    Engraved Map, New York, British Coat Of Arms, 1758, 14 In. 825.00
    Indians, Eagle & Various Animals, Brass Spout, 1847, 13 In. 330.00
    Owner Ezekiel Bradley, Written Line Of Descent, 14 In. 1100.00
    Primitive Mermaid, Church, Freel's N. J. Volunteers 1783, 17 In. 220.00
    Queen Anne Style, Tapered Screw Cop, Flat Butt Plug, 5 3/8 In. 85.00
    Screw Top, George Washington, President, 1795, 5 x 3 In. 450.00
    Scrimshaw Wilderness Scenes, James Lakin Pepperel, 1812 .... 2875.00
    Turned Butt Plug, 11 1/4 In. 225.00
    Turned Butt Plug, York County, Penna. 75.00

PRATT ware means two different things. It was an early Staffordshire pottery, cream-colored with colored decorations, made by Felix Pratt during the late eighteenth century. There was also Pratt ware made with transfer designs during the mid-nineteenth century in Fenton, England. Reproductions of the transfer-printed Pratt are being made.

PRATT
FENTON

    Figurine, 4 Seasons, Maidens & Youths, 1810, 8 1/2 To 8 7/8 In., 4 Pc. 3575.00
    Figurine, Elijah, Widow Of Zarephath, 18th Century, 9 1/2 In., Pair 665.00
    Figurine, Lion, Standing, Brown Curly Main, Ocher, 1815-1820, 7 1/4 In. 2200.00
    Jar, Enthusiast 225.00
    Jar, Shakespeare House 295.00
    Jug, Embossed Drinking Scenes, 8 In. 150.00
    Plaque, Embossed Lions, Oval, 8 3/4 x 10 3/4 In. 1050.00
    Plaque, The Miser, Counting Coins, Circular, 8 1/2 In. 1210.00
    Plate, Commemorative, King George IV, 1822, 8 1/2 In. 522.50
    Plate, Persuasion, 7 3/8 In. 48.00
    Plate, Scenic Panels, 8 1/2 In., Pair 70.00

PRESSED GLASS was first made in the United States in the 1820s after the invention of glass pressing machines. Hundreds of patterns of pressed glass were made in complete table settings. Although the Boston and Sandwich Works was the most famous of the pressed glass factories, there were about sixteen other factories making pressed glass from 1830 to 1850, and still more from 1850 to 1900, when pressed glass reached its greatest popularity. It is now being widely reproduced. The pattern names used in this listing are based on the information in the book *Pressed Glass in America* by John and Elizabeth Welker. There may be pieces of pressed glass listed in this book in other sections, such as Lamp, Ruby, Sandwich, and Souvenir.

    1000-Eye pattern is listed here as Thousand Eye
    101 pattern is listed here as One-Hundred-One
    Aberdeen, Goblet 22.50
    Acanthus pattern is listed here as Ribbed Palm
    Acme pattern is listed here as Butterfly With Spray
    Acorn Medallion pattern with beading is listed here as Beaded Acorn Medallion
    Acorn, Sauce, 5 In. 16.00
    Acorn, Sugar Shaker, Peach 150.00
    Actress, Cake Stand 145.00
    Actress, Cake Stand, Frosted Stem & Base 165.00
    Actress, Cheese Dish, Cover 235.00
    Actress, Compote, 8 In. 100.00
    Actress, Compote, Cover, High Standard, 7 In. 175.00
    Actress, Creamer 50.00
    Actress, Creamer, Frosted 125.00
    Actress, Goblet .... 60.00 To 80.00
    Actress, Jam Jar .... 85.00 To 95.00
    Actress, Pitcher, Water 385.00
    Actress, Platter, 7 x 11 In. 92.50
    Actress, Relish 40.00

Pressed glass, Actress   Pressed glass, Austrian   Pressed glass, Artichoke, frosted   Pressed glass, Beaded Grape Medallion

Actress, Spooner	75.00
Actress, Sugar & Creamer	140.00
Actress, Sugar, Cover	80.00
Admiral Dewey pattern is listed here as Spanish American	
Alabama, Compote, Cover, 8 In.	125.00
Alabama, Sugar, Child's	25.00
Alabama, Table Set, 4 Piece	200.00
Alaska, Berry Bowl, Green, Enamel, Square, Master	110.00
Alaska, Creamer, Green	30.00
Alaska, Cruet, Blue	195.00
Alaska, Cruet, Vaseline, Clear Stopper	175.00
Alaska, Pitcher, Clear, Gold Enameling	115.00
Alaska, Pitcher, Flowers, Vaseline	425.00
Alaska, Salt, Shaker, Vaseline	75.00
Alaska, Sugar & Creamer, Yellow	120.00 To 175.00
Alaska, Sugar, Cover	60.00 To 100.00
Alaska, Sugar, Cover, Vaseline	145.00
Alaska, Tumbler	65.00
Albany, Butter, Cover	50.00
Albany, Cracker Jar	60.00
Albany, Cruet	36.00
Albany, Spooner	45.00
Albany, Wine	15.00 To 35.00
Amazon, Spooner, Child's	25.00
Amazon, Tumbler	35.00
Amazon, Tumbler, Etched	37.50
Amazon, Wine	20.00
Amberette, Relish	95.00
Amberette, Salt & Pepper	185.00
America, Creamer, Engraved	30.00
Amulet, Goblet, Gold Trim	15.00
Anthemion, Pitcher, Water	37.50
Anthemion, Plate, 10 In.	25.00
Anvil, Toothpick	50.00
Apollo, Butter, Cover, Etched	58.00
Apollo, Cake Stand, Etched, 9 In.	47.50
Apollo, Lamp, Kerosene, Blue, 8 3/4 In.	265.00
Apollo, Relish	14.50
Apollo, Toothpick	28.00
Arabesque, Creamer	75.00
Arabesque, Goblet	45.00
Arched Fleur–De–Lis, Toothpick, Ruby Flashed	250.00
Arched Grape, Goblet	35.00
Arched Leaf, Compote, Flint, 8 In.	35.00
Arched Leaf, Plate, 10 In.	35.00
Arched Ovals, Cake Stand, 9 In.	30.00
Arched Ovals, Compote, 10 In.	40.00

Arched Ovals, Toothpick 16.00
Arched Ovals, Tumbler 12.00
Arched Ovals, Wine 15.00
Arched Ovals, Wine, Souvenir, Bessie, Green 10.00
Argonaut Shell, Sugar & Creamer, Cover, Blue 70.00
Argus, Eggcup, Flint 80.00
Argus, Goblet, Flint 60.00
Arrowhead in Oval pattern is listed here as Style
Arrowhead, Pitcher, Water 55.00
Art Novo, Table Set, Ruby Stained, 4 Piece 425.00
Art, Bowl, 9 3/4 In. 38.00
Art, Cake Stand, 10 1/2 In. 65.00
Art, Celery Vase, 6 In. 47.50
Art, Compote, , High Standard, 6 In. 65.00
Art, Goblet 55.00
Art, Sugar, Cover 38.50
Artichoke, Butter, Cover, Frosted 50.00
Artichoke, Goblet, Frosted 60.00
Artichoke, Spooner, Frosted 25.00
Artichoke, Sugar, Cover, Frosted 50.00
Artichoke, Syrup 75.00
Artichoke, Syrup, Footed, Spring Lid 145.00
Artichoke, Tumbler, Frosted 48.00
Ashburton With Sawtooth, Mug, Whiskey, Flint 55.00
Ashburton, Claret, Flint 75.00
Ashburton, Cordial, Flint .... 48.00 To 55.00
Ashburton, Creamer, Applied Handle, 6 3/4 In. 135.00
Ashburton, Creamer, Flint, 5 7/8 In. 125.00
Ashburton, Decanter, Bar Lip, Flint 85.00
Ashburton, Goblet, Flint, 6 In. 55.00
Ashburton, Sugar, Flint, 7 In. 30.00
Atlanta, Banana Boat 50.00
Atlanta, Bowl, 5 1/2 In. 30.00
Atlanta, Creamer 42.50
Atlanta, Cruet 75.00
Atlanta, Punch Cup 20.00
Atlanta, Relish 25.00
Atlanta, Spooner 30.00
Atlanta, Sugar & Creamer 70.00
Atlanta, Sugar, Cover, Etched 125.00
Atlanta, Syrup 75.00
Atlanta, Toothpick 20.00
Atlanta, Toothpick, Square Lion's Head, Frosted 60.00
Atlas, Berry Set, 7 Piece 65.00
Atlas, Berry Set, Bowl, 5 Piece 50.00
Atlas, Bowl, 9 In. 20.00
Atlas, Champagne 35.00
Atlas, Sauce, 4 In. 15.00
Atlas, Toothpick 18.50
Austrian, Creamer 18.00
Austrian, Goblet 55.00
Austrian, Nappy, Cover, Handle 45.00
Austrian, Toothpick 45.00
Austrian, Wine 42.50
Aztec, Wine Set, 6 Piece 75.00
Baby Face, Knife Rest 100.00
Baby Thumbprint pattern is listed here as Dakota
Balder pattern is listed here as Pennsylvania
Balky Mule pattern is listed here as Currier & Ives
Ball & Swirl, Goblet 18.50
Baltimore Pear, Butter, Cover 40.00
Baltimore Pear, Plate, 8 1/2 In. 20.00
Baltimore Pear, Sugar & Creamer 18.50

Baltimore Pear, Sugar, Cover 20.00
Baltimore Pear, Table Set, 1898, 4 Piece 150.00
Baltimore Pear, Tray, Handle, 6 In. 25.00
Bamboo, Table Set, 4 Piece 250.00
Banded Buckle, Eggcup 18.50
Banded Buckle, Goblet 25.00
Banded Knife & Fork, Cordial, 6 Piece 50.00
Banded Portland, Celery, Boat Shape, Pink Flashed 75.00
Banded Portland, Cup 12.50
Banded Portland, Goblet, Pink Flashed 47.00
Banded Portland, Pitcher 95.00
Banded Portland, Toothpick, Pink Flashed 55.00
Banded Raindrop, Wine 34.00
Bar & Diamond pattern is listed here as Kokomo
Barberry, Celery 30.00
Barberry, Celery Vase 65.00
Barberry, Compote, High Standard, 8 3/4 In. 140.00
Barberry, Wine 28.00
Barley & Oats pattern is listed here as Wheat & Barley
Barley & Wheat pattern is listed here as Wheat & Barley
Barley, Celery 55.00
Barred Forget–Me–Not, Goblet, Wide Band 22.00
Barred Forget–Me–Not, Sugar & Creamer, Cover 65.00
Barred Ovals, Berry Set, Ruby Stained, 7 Piece 245.00
Barred Ovals, Pitcher, c.1870, 1/2 Gal. 140.00
Barreled Block pattern is listed here as Red Block
Basket Weave, Cruet Set, Blue 285.00
Bead Swag, Water Set, Opaque, Floral Design, 7 Piece 445.00
Beaded Acorn Medallion, Goblet 37.50
Beaded Bull's–Eye & Drape pattern is listed here as Alabama
Beaded Cable, Table Set, Green, 4 Piece 350.00
Beaded Circle, Compote, Jelly 70.00
Beaded Circle, Compote, Jelly, Green, Gold & Enamel Trim 38.00
Beaded Column, Compote, Cover, 5 In. 35.00
Beaded Dart Band, Goblet 15.00
Beaded Dewdrop pattern is listed here as Wisconsin
Beaded Fan, Rose Bowl, Blue 32.00
Beaded Grape Medallion, Celery 48.00
Beaded Grape Medallion, Champagne, Flint 95.00
Beaded Grape Medallion, Creamer 65.00
Beaded Grape Medallion, Eggcup 30.00
Beaded Grape Medallion, Goblet 38.00
Beaded Grape Medallion, Salt, Individual 22.50
Beaded Grape Medallion, Salt, Master, Oval 85.00
Beaded Grape Medallion, Spooner 30.00
Beaded Grape, Bowl, Square, 7 In. 15.00
Beaded Grape, Cake Stand, Green .... 70.00 To 95.00
Beaded Grape, Cruet, Green 95.00
Beaded Grape, Dish, Olive, Tab Handle, Green 25.00
Beaded Grape, Goblet 45.00
Beaded Grape, Pitcher, Green 125.00
Beaded Grape, Relish, Green, Gold Trim 13.00
Beaded Grape, Toothpick 55.00
Beaded Grape, Wine 18.00
Beaded Loop, Cake Stand, 8 In. 48.00
Beaded Loop, Cake Stand, 9 In. 55.00
Beaded Loop, Compote, Cover, 7 In. 95.00
Beaded Loop, Mug 38.00
Beaded Loop, Pitcher, Milk 55.00
Beaded Loop, Pitcher, Water 68.00
Beaded Loop, Salt & Pepper 55.00
Beaded Loop, Spooner, Green 95.00
Beaded Loop, Tumbler 48.00

Beaded **Medallion,** Cruet 45.00
Beaded **Medallion,** Tumbler, Green 40.00
Beaded **Mirror,** Goblet, Flint 14.00
Beaded **Mirror,** Pitcher, Buttermilk 45.00
Beaded **Ovals In Sand,** Cruet, Blue 100.00
Beaded **Ovals In Sand,** Salt & Pepper, Blue 95.00
Beaded **Scroll,** Cruet, Green 205.00
Beaded **Scroll,** Table Set, Green, Gold Trim, 3 Piece 95.00
Beaded **Swirl & Disc,** Berry Bowl, 8 1/2 In. 50.00
Beaded **Swirl & Disc,** Berry Set, 5 Piece 75.00
Beaded **Swirl,** Berry Bowl, Master 15.00
Beaded **Swirl,** Cruet 30.00
Beaded **Swirl,** Sauce, Green, Gold Trim 22.50
Beaded **Swirl,** Table Set, Green, 4 Piece 360.00
Beaded **Tulip,** Goblet .... 30.00 To 35.00
Beaded **Tulip,** Tray, Wine, 9 In. 25.00
Beaded **Tulip,** Wine 25.00
Bearded Head pattern is listed here as Viking
Bearded Man pattern is listed here as Queen Anne
Beatty **Waffle,** Sugar, Cover, Blue 75.00
Beautiful **Lady,** Vase, 6 1/2 In. 9.50
Beggar's **Hand,** Toothpick 17.50
Bellflower **Double Vine,** Plate, 10 1/2 In. 45.00
Bellflower **Double Vine,** Wine 325.00
Bellflower, Bowl, Scalloped Rim, 7 1/2 In. 110.00
Bellflower, Compote, Scalloped Rim, 8 In. 60.00
Bellflower, Creamer 135.00
Bellflower, Goblet, Flint 35.00
Bellflower, Goblet, Knob Stem 55.00
Bellflower, Spooner 30.00
Bent Buckle pattern is listed here as New Hampshire
Bethlehem **Star,** Cruet 35.00
Bethlehem **Star,** Wine 25.00
Beveled Diamond & Star pattern is listed here as Albany
Beveled **Star,** Spooner 30.00
Beveled **Star,** Tumbler 18.00
Bible, Bread Plate, Etched 75.00
Big Block pattern is listed here as Henrietta
Big **Button,** Pitcher, Amber Stained 125.00
Birch **Leaf,** Eggcup, Flint 37.50
Birch **Leaf,** Toothpick 75.00
Bird **& Strawberry,** Berry Set, 10-In. Flared Master, 6 Piece 525.00
Bird **& Strawberry,** Bowl, Oval, 5 x 10 In. 45.00
Bird **& Strawberry,** Tumbler 58.00
Birds **At Fountain,** Goblet 45.00
Bismarc **Star,** Wine 22.50
Blackberry, Celery 60.00

Pressed glass, Bird &   *Pressed glass, Buckle*   *Pressed glass, Button*   *Pressed glass,*
Strawberry   *Arches*   *Cardinal Bird*

Blackberry, Goblet	55.00
Blackberry, Spooner	18.00
Blaze, Goblet, Flint	50.00
Bleeding Heart, Butter, Cover	50.00
Bleeding Heart, Cake Stand, 9 In.	72.50 To 80.00
Bleeding Heart, Cake Stand, 11 In.	65.00 To 145.00
Bleeding Heart, Compote, Cover, High Standard, 8 In.	195.00
Bleeding Heart, Creamer, Flat	18.00
Bleeding Heart, Creamer, Footed	45.00 To 62.50
Bleeding Heart, Goblet	30.00
Bleeding Heart, Pitcher, Buttermilk	45.00
Bleeding Heart, Punch Cup, Child's	25.00
Bleeding Heart, Spooner	25.00
Bleeding Heart, Sugar, Cover	70.00 To 125.00
Bleeding Heart, Wine, Knob Stem	150.00
Block & Double Bar, Celery	20.00
Block & Fan pattern is listed here as Romeo	
Block & Fine Cut pattern is listed here as Fine Cut & Block	
Block & Honeycomb, Celery	25.00
Block & Lattice pattern is listed here as Big Button	
Block & Palm, Berry Set, 7 Piece	30.00
Block & Star pattern is listed here as Valencia Waffle	
Block, Spooner, Ruby Stained	37.50
Block, Tumbler, Amber Stained	37.50
Bluebird pattern is listed here as Bird & Strawberry	
Bohemian Grape, Juice Set, 6 Piece	225.00
Bohemian Grape, Juice Set, Green, Gold Trim, 6 Piece	175.00
Bohemian, Berry Bowl, Rose Flashed, Gold Trim, Master	145.00
Bohemian, Creamer, Frosted, Rose Flashed, Green Flowers	40.00
Bohemian, Creamer, Green, Individual	18.50
Bohemian, Juice Set, Green, Gold Trim, 6 Piece	225.00
Bohemian, Tumbler, Rose Flashed, Gold Trim	45.00
Bordered Ellipse, Goblet	20.00
Bosworth, Goblet	25.00
Bouquet, Sugar, Cover	18.00
Bowtie, Goblet	50.00 To 62.50
Bowtie, Jam Jar	50.00
Bowtie, Pitcher	140.00
Bowtie, Spooner	60.00
Box-In-Box, Bowl, 8 1/2 In.	48.00
Box-In-Box, Creamer	70.00
Box-In-Box, Creamer, Ruby Stained	70.00
Box-In-Box, Salt & Pepper, Ruby Stained	95.00
Box-In-Box, Toothpick	55.00
Box-In-Box, Tumbler, Etched	23.00
Boxed Star, Tumbler	15.00 To 18.00
Bradford Blackberry, Goblet, Flint	80.00
Bradford Grape pattern is listed here as Bradford Blackberry	
Brazen Shield, Spooner	25.00
Bridal Rosettes, Wine	14.00
Brilliant, Goblet	95.00
Brilliant, Goblet, Flint, McKee	60.00
Britannic, Tray, Condiment, Amber Stained	42.00
Britannic, Wine, Ruby Stained	63.00
Broken Column, Cake Stand, 9 In.	85.00
Broken Column, Cake Stand, 10 In.	95.00
Broken Column, Celery Dish	32.50
Broken Column, Celery Vase	55.00
Broken Column, Compote, 7 In.	55.00
Broken Column, Compote, Cover, 10 1/2 In.	60.00
Broken Column, Creamer	38.00
Broken Column, Goblet	55.00
Broken Column, Plate, 8 In.	50.00

Broughton pattern is listed here as Pattee Cross
Bryce pattern is listed here as Ribbon Candy
Buck & Doe, Goblet 95.00
Bucket pattern is listed here as Oaken Bucket
Buckle & Star, Compote, Cover, Maltese Cross Finial 125.00
Buckle, Compote, 8 In. 17.50
Buckle, Eggcup, Flint 20.00
Buckle, Goblet .... 23.00 To 40.00
Buckle, Spooner 30.00
Budded Ivy, Creamer 57.50
Bulging Loops, Berry Bowl, Master, Blue 88.00
Bulging Loops, Creamer, Pink 78.00
Bulging Loops, Pitcher, Milk, Pink 125.00
Bulging Loops, Pitcher, Pink 350.00
Bulging Loops, Spooner, Pink 100.00
Bulging Loops, Toothpick, Green 35.00
Bull's-Eye & Bar, Eggcup, Flint 125.00
Bull's-Eye & Daisy, Butter, Cover, Gold Trim 150.00
Bull's-Eye & Daisy, Butter, Cover, Green Stained Eyes 110.00
Bull's-Eye & Daisy, Sugar, Open 30.00
Bull's-Eye & Daisy, Wine, Ruby Stained 22.50
Bull's-Eye & Fan, Spooner, Blue, Gold Trim 42.00
Bull's-Eye & Fan, Toothpick 22.50
Bull's-Eye & Spearhead, Basket 85.00
Bull's-Eye & Spearhead, Pitcher, Water 38.00
Bull's-Eye & Wishbone, Goblet, Flint 75.00
Bull's-Eye Band, Celery Vase 55.00
Bull's-Eye Band, Compote, Jelly 40.00
Bull's-Eye Band, Spooner 25.00
Bull's-Eye Variant, Goblet 28.00
Bull's-Eye Variant, Wine 15.00
Bull's-Eye With Diamond Point, Celery 175.00
Bull's-Eye, Cruet 80.00
Bull's-Eye, Jar, Pomade, Flint 135.00
Bull's-Eye, Pitcher, Blue, Gold Trim 40.00
Bullet Emblem, Creamer 205.00
Butterfly With Spray, Mug, 3 In. 25.00
Butterfly, Plate, 5 In. 12.00
Button Arches, Creamer, Ruby Stained 60.00
Button Arches, Mug, Ruby Stained, Oxford Fair, 1909 .... 38.00
Button Arches, Salt & Pepper 35.00
Button Arches, Toothpick, Ruby Stained, 2 1/4 In. 30.00
Button Arches, Water Set, Frosted Band, Ruby Stained, 7 Piece 295.00
Button Band, Compote, Cover, 9 x 12 In. 145.00
Button Panel, Creamer & Spooner, Child's 65.00
Button Panel, Saltshaker, Ruby Stained 45.00
Buttressed Sunburst, Spooner 22.00
Buzz Star, Punch Cup, Child's 5.00
Buzz Star, Punch Set, Child's, 3 Piece 30.00
Buzz Star, Punch Set, Child's, 5 Piece 45.00
Buzz Star, Punch Set, Child's, 7 Piece 65.00
Buzz Star, Toothpick .... 12.00 To 22.00
Cabbage Leaf, Celery 90.00
Cable With Ring, Sugar, Cover, Flint 75.00
Cable, Spooner 72.00
Cable, Spooner, Opaque 75.00
California pattern is listed here as Beaded Grape
Camel Caravan, Goblet .... 65.00 To 125.00
Camel Caravan, Pitcher .... 175.00 To 195.00
Cameo pattern is listed here as Profile & Sprig
Canadian, Creamer 50.00
Canadian, Goblet .... 45.00 To 50.00
Canadian, Plate, 8 In. 55.00

Canadian, Plate, 10 In. 50.00
Candlewick as a pressed glass pattern is properly named *Banded Raindrop*. There is also a pattern called *Candlewick*, which has been made by Imperial Glass Corporation since 1936. It is listed in this book in the Imperial section.
Candy Ribbon pattern is listed here as Ribbon Candy
Cane & Rosette, Celery 35.00
Cane & Rosette, Pitcher 55.00
Cane, Cruet 30.00
Cane, Fruit Bowl, Amber, 9 In. 28.00
Cane, Goblet, Green 35.00
Cane, Pitcher, Water, Blue 58.00
Cape Cod, Goblet 42.50
Cape Cod, Plate, 10 In. 50.00
Cardinal pattern is listed here as Cardinal Bird
Cardinal Bird, Goblet .... 25.00 To 32.00
Cardinal Bird, Spooner 25.00
Carmen pattern is listed here as Paneled Diamond & Finecut
Carnation, Pitcher, Ruby Stained, Gold Trim 265.00
Carolina, Compote, Cover, 8 1/2 x 13 1/2 In. 125.00
Cat & Dog, Cup & Saucer, Blue, Child's 85.00
Cathedral, Goblet, Ruby Stained 65.00
Cathedral, Spooner 25.00
Cathedral, Tumbler 25.00
Celtic Cross, Compote, Cover, Square, 6 1/2 x 11 1/2 In. 85.00
Centennial, see also the related patterns Liberty Bell and Washington Centennial
Centennial, Tumbler, Ale, 1876 .... 45.00
Ceres pattern is listed here as Profile & Sprig
Chain & Shield, Pitcher 42.00
Chain & Shield, Spooner 15.00
Chain With Diamonds pattern is listed here as Washington Centennial
Chain With Star, Creamer 20.00
Chain With Star, Goblet 30.00
Chain With Star, Pitcher 50.00
Chain With Star, Sauce 12.50
Chain With Star, Spooner 15.00
Chain With Star, Water Set, 7 Piece .... 135.00 To 150.00
Chain With Star, Wine 25.00
Champion, Cake Stand, 9 In. 18.50
Champion, Cruet, Amber Stained 125.00
Champion, Toothpick, Green 95.00
Chandelier, Compote, 6 In. 65.00
Chandelier, Goblet 38.00
Chandelier, Pitcher 125.00
Chandelier, Sauce 14.50
Chandelier, Tumbler 40.00
Checkerboard, Celery, Gold Trim 35.00
Checkerboard, Wine 18.50
Cherry Thumbprint, Berry Set, 7 Piece 135.00
Cherry Thumbprint, Celery Vase 100.00
Cherry Thumbprint, Creamer 45.00
Cherry Thumbprint, Spooner 50.00
Cherry Thumbprint, Sugar Bowl 75.00
Chicken, Salt & Pepper 65.00
Chrysanthemum Leaf, Syrup, Hinged Lid 65.00
Chrysanthemum Leaf, Toothpick 45.00
Chrysanthemum Sprig, Spooner, Blue 210.00
Chrysanthemum, Toothpick, Blue 195.00
Church Windows pattern is listed here as Tulip Petals
Circle, Saltshaker, Frosted 22.50
Civil War, Mug 245.00
Classic Medallion, Spooner 15.00
Classic, Bowl, Log Feet, 8 1/4 In. 95.00
Classic, Bowl, Log Feet, Hexagonal, 7 3/8 In. 135.00

Pressed glass, Classic   Pressed glass, Cube   Pressed glass, Clear   Pressed glass, Deer
                                                      Diagonal Band   & Dog

Classic, Butter, Cover .... 175.00 To 225.00
Classic, Celery, Log Feet .... 115.00 To 155.00
Classic, Compote, Cover, 6 1/2 In. 225.00
Classic, Creamer, Log Feet 175.00
Classic, Pitcher, Collared Base 310.00
Classic, Pitcher, Log Feet 425.00
Classic, Spooner, Log Feet .... 110.00 To 135.00
Classic, Sugar, Cover, Log Feet .... 65.00 To 95.00
Clear & Diamond Panels, Creamer, Child's 20.00
Clear & Diamond Panels, Spooner, Child's 20.00
Clear Block, Pitcher 50.00
Clear Block, Punch Cup, Handle, 4 Piece 32.00
Clear Diagonal Band, Goblet 15.00
Clear Diagonal, Jam Jar 35.00
Clematis, Butter, Cover, Rose Point Band 95.00
Clover, Toothpick 32.50
Co–Op, Pitcher, Ruby Stained, 5 In. 40.00
Coin Spot pattern is listed in this book in its own category
Colonial Panel, Cruet 15.00
Colonial, Spooner, Enameled Flowers 20.00
Colorado, Banana Boat, Green, Gold Trim 35.00
Colorado, Bowl, Green, Etched Ellie, 1908, Small 25.00
Colorado, Bowl, Green, Footed, 5 In. 10.00
Colorado, Bowl, Green, Gold Trim, 10 In. 68.00
Colorado, Butter, Cover 60.00
Colorado, Butter, Cover, Green 100.00
Colorado, Nappy, Tri–Corner, Blue 40.00
Colorado, Sugar & Creamer, Green, Individual 45.00
Colorado, Sugar, Cover, Green 50.00
Colorado, Sugar, Cover, Green, Gold Trim 65.00
Colorado, Sugar, Green, Gold Trim, 3 In. 45.00
Colorado, Sugar, Green, Individual 17.00
Colorado, Table Set, Green, Gold Trim, 4 Piece .... 325.00 To 350.00
Colorado, Toothpick, Cobalt Blue, Gold Trim .... 35.00 To 55.00
Colorado, Toothpick, Green, 1907 .... 7.50
Colorado, Toothpick, Green, Gold Trim, 1911 .... 27.50
Colorado, Toothpick, Souvenir, Ruby Stained 55.00
Colorado, Tumbler, Green, Gold Trim 32.50
Colorado, Tumbler, Salt Lake City, Purple Stained 30.00
Colossus, Goblet 38.00
Columbia, Pitcher, Gold Trim 150.00
Columbia, Pitcher, Water, Gold Trim 45.00
Columbian Coin, Spooner, Gold Trim 95.00
Columbus, Mug 125.00
Comet, Compote, Flint, 6 1/2 x 8 In. 125.00
Comet, Goblet, Flint 120.00
Compact pattern is listed here as Snail

Cone, Salt & Pepper, Pink 60.00
Cone, Sugar Shaker, Squatty, Pink 150.00
Connecticut Flute, Goblet, Flint 24.50
Connecticut, Toothpick, Floral Design 75.00
Continental, Bread Plate 145.00
Cord & Tassel, Compote, Cover, Low Standard 75.00
Cord & Tassel, Goblet .... 40.00 To 45.00
Cord & Tassel, Saltshaker, Pink 45.00
Cord & Tassel, Wine .... 32.00 To 38.00
Cord Drapery, Pitcher, Water, Green 225.00
Cordova, Toothpick 12.00
Cordova, Toothpick, Ruby Stained 40.00
Cornell, Creamer, Gold Trim 18.00
Cornell, Cup & Saucer, Green, Gold Trim 25.00
Cornell, Sugar, Gold Trim 12.00
Cornell, Syrup 27.50
Corner Medallion, Creamer 35.00
Cosmos pattern is listed in this book as its own category
Cottage, Cake Stand, 9 In. .... 42.00 To 45.00
Cottage, Cake Stand, 10 In. 37.50
Cottage, Celery 35.00
Cottage, Creamer, Amber 45.00
Cottage, Cruet 65.00
Cottage, Pitcher 35.00
Cottage, Plate, 6 In. 27.50
Crane pattern is listed here as Stork
Crescent & Fan, Cruet 30.00
Crescent, Butter, Cover, Ruby Stained 65.00
Crescent, Pitcher, Ruby Stained 110.00
Croesus, Breakfast Set, Green, Gold Trim, 3 Piece 298.00
Croesus, Breakfast Set, Green, Gold Trim, 4 Piece 425.00
Croesus, Butter, Cover, Green 140.00
Croesus, Butter, Cover, Green, Gold Trim .... 125.00 To 135.00
Croesus, Creamer, Amethyst, Gold Trim 145.00
Croesus, Dish, Pickle 25.00
Croesus, Pitcher 275.00
Croesus, Pitcher, Green, Gold Trim 245.00
Croesus, Salt & Pepper, Green 120.00
Croesus, Saltshaker 125.00
Croesus, Saltshaker, Green, Gold Trim 85.00
Croesus, Spooner, Green .... 50.00 To 55.00
Croesus, Spooner, Green, Gold Trim .... 60.00 To 75.00
Croesus, Sugar, Cover, Green, Gold Trim 110.00
Croesus, Table Set, Green, 3 Piece 325.00
Croesus, Toothpick, Gold, Green 125.00
Croesus, Toothpick, Green, Gold Rim 60.00
Croesus, Tumbler, Amethyst 60.00
Croesus, Tumbler, Green 35.00
Croesus, Water Set, Green, 7 Piece 500.00
Crowfoot, Goblet .... 25.00 To 37.50
Crowfoot, Lamp, Finger, Pedestal, Amber 155.00
Crowfoot, Spooner 25.00
Crown Jewels is a name used for two different patterns listed here as Chandelier or
Queen's Necklace
Crystal Queen, Pitcher, Water 68.00
Crystal Wedding, Cake Stand 55.00
Crystal Wedding, Compote, Cover, 11 In. 62.50
Crystal Wedding, Spooner 30.00
Crystal Wedding, Table Set, 4 Piece 175.00
Crystal Wedding, Tankard 160.00
Crystal Wedding, Tumbler 55.00
Cube With Fan pattern is listed here as Pineapple & Fan
Cube, Butter, Cover 35.00

Cupid & Psyche pattern is listed here as Psyche & Cupid
Cupid & Venus, Bowl, Footed, 8 1/2 In. 45.00
Cupid & Venus, Bread Plate, Vaseline 145.00
Cupid & Venus, Bread Tray, Vaseline 145.00
Cupid & Venus, Celery 35.00
Cupid & Venus, Compote, Cover, 9 In. 55.00
Cupid & Venus, Compote, Cover, 10 In. 70.00
Cupid & Venus, Creamer 65.00
Cupid & Venus, Jam Jar 125.00
Cupid & Venus, Pitcher, Milk .... 45.00 To 75.00
Cupid & Venus, Pitcher, Water ....75.00 To 125.00
Cupid & Venus, Plate, Handles, 10 1/2 In. .... 33.50 To 42.50
Cupid & Venus, Sauce, Footed, 3 1/2 In. 13.00
Currant, Celery 45.00
Currant, Compote, Cover, 8 In. 140.00
Currant, Compote, Open, 8 In. 25.00
Currier & Ives, Bowl, Ark Shape, 10 In. 33.00
Currier & Ives, Bread Plate, Balky Mule 70.00
Currier & Ives, Goblet .... 20.00 To 32.00
Currier & Ives, Goblet, Amber 95.00
Currier & Ives, Pitcher 60.00
Currier & Ives, Pitcher, Milk 35.00
Currier & Ives, Salt & Pepper, Blue 115.00
Currier & Ives, Syrup, Amber .... 75.00 To 130.00
Currier & Ives, Tumbler 30.00
Currier & Ives, Wine 25.00
Curtain Tieback, Goblet 35.00
Curtain, Salt & Pepper 65.00
Cut Log, Cake Stand .... 45.00 To 75.00
Cut Log, Celery .... 45.00 To 50.00
Cut Log, Compote, Cover, 7 In. 95.00
Cut Log, Goblet 45.00
Cut Log, Saltshaker .... 45.00 To 65.00
Cut Log, Wine .... 18.00 To 20.00
Czarina, Toothpick 32.50
Daisies in Oval Panels pattern is listed here as Bull's-Eye & Fan
Daisy & Button With Crossbar, Bowl, 8 In. 20.00
Daisy & Button With Crossbar, Compote, 8 1/2 In. 70.00
Daisy & Button With Crossbar, Creamer, Blue 50.00
Daisy & Button With Crossbar, Cruet, Amber 225.00
Daisy & Button With Crossbar, Pitcher, Milk .... 45.00 To 95.00
Daisy & Button With Crossbar, Pitcher, Water 100.00
Daisy & Button With Crossbar, Pitcher, Water, Vaseline 75.00
Daisy & Button With Crossbar, Spooner 30.00
Daisy & Button With Crossbar, Spooner, Amber 28.00
Daisy & Button With Narcissus, Pitcher 48.00
Daisy & Button With Narcissus, Punch Cup 9.00
Daisy & Button With Narcissus, Sugar, Cover 30.00
Daisy & Button With Narcissus, Tumbler 17.00
Daisy & Button With Thumbprint Panels, Celery 25.00
Daisy & Button With Thumbprint Panels, Compote, Amber, 6 In. 32.00
Daisy & Button With Thumbprint, Bowl, Square, Amber, 8 In. 28.00
Daisy & Button With Thumbprint, Pitcher, Amber 85.00
Daisy & Button With V-Ornament, Mug, Blue 35.00
Daisy & Button With V-Ornament, Toothpick, Amber 17.00
Daisy & Button With V-Ornament, Toothpick, Amber 25.00
Daisy & Button, see also the related pattern Paneled Daisy & Button
Daisy & Button, Bath Tub, Sietz 145.00
Daisy & Button, Berry Bowl, Square, 4 1/2 In. 20.00
Daisy & Button, Creamer, Blue 40.00
Daisy & Button, Cruet, Amber Stopper, Blue 45.00
Daisy & Button, Goblet, Blue 8.00
Daisy & Button, Match Holder, Wall, Blue 35.00

Daisy & Button, Tray, Water, Curved Triangle, Vaseline 60.00
Daisy & Button, Tumbler, Amber 25.00
Daisy & Plume, Candy Dish, Green Opalescent 50.00
Daisy Band, Cup & Saucer 20.00
Dakota, Butter, Cover, Piecrust Rim 70.00
Dakota, Cake Stand, 10 In. 65.00
Dakota, Cake Stand, Etched, 10 In. .... 40.00 To 60.00
Dakota, Cake Stand, Fern & Berry Etch, 9 1/2 In. 95.00
Dakota, Celery, Fern & Berry Etch .... 48.00 To 55.00
Dakota, Compote, Etched, 6 In. 35.00
Dakota, Creamer 60.00
Dakota, Creamer, Fern & Berry Etch 55.00
Dakota, Cruet Set, Etched, Pair 435.00
Dakota, Goblet, Etched 30.00
Dakota, Pitcher, Milk, 1 Qt. 85.00
Dakota, Pitcher, Water, Fish Etch 295.00
Dakota, Tankard, Milk 65.00
Dakota, Tankard, Water, Bluebird, Fern & Butterfly Etch 225.00
Dakota, Tray, Wine, Round, 10 1/2 In. 100.00
Dakota, Wine, Etched .... 35.00 To 45.00
Deer & Dog, Celery Vase, Etched, Gillinder & Sons 95.00
Deer & Dog, Celery, Etched 75.00
Deer & Dog, Goblet 80.00
Deer & Dog, Goblet, U-Shape 80.00
Deer & Dog, Pitcher, Etched 155.00
Deer & Dog, Sauce, Footed 15.00
Deer & Dog, Sugar, Cover .... 125.00 To 135.00
Deer & Oak Tree, Pitcher 250.00
Deer & Pine Tree, Bread Plate 95.00
Deer & Pine Tree, Bread Plate, Amber 80.00
Deer & Pine Tree, Bread Plate, Green 110.00
Deer & Pine Tree, Bread Tray 135.00
Deer & Pine Tree, Compote, Cover, 8 In. 225.00
Deer & Pine Tree, Goblet 55.00
Deer & Pine Tree, Mug, Amber, 3 1/4 In. 40.00
Deer & Pine Tree, Mug, Child's 37.50
Deer & Pine Tree, Pitcher, Water 125.00
Deer & Pine Tree, Platter, Blue 140.00
Deer & Pine Tree, Spooner 45.00
Deer & Pine Tree, Sugar, Cover 67.50
Deer & Pine Tree, Tray, Water 125.00
Deer & Pinetree, Celery 95.00
Delaware, Banana Boat, Green, Gold Trim .... 75.00 To 80.00
Delaware, Banana Boat, Rose, Gold Trim 95.00
Delaware, Banana Bowl, Green, Gold 65.00
Delaware, Berry Set, Rose, Gold Trim, 7 Piece 300.00
Delaware, Bowl, Flared, Green, 9 In. 47.50

*Pressed glass,
Delaware*

*Pressed glass,
Diagonal Band & Fan*

*Pressed glass,
Diamond Point*

*Pressed glass, Egg in
Sand*

Delaware, Bowl, Green, Gold Trim, 6 1/4 In. 28.00
Delaware, Bowl, Green, Gold Trim, 9 In. 60.00
Delaware, Creamer 40.00
Delaware, Custard Cup 45.00
Delaware, Custard Cup, Rose, Gold Trim .... 24.00 To 35.00
Delaware, Pitcher, Water, Bulbous, Rose 85.00
Delaware, Powder Jar, Jeweled Lid 335.00
Delaware, Spooner 50.00
Delaware, Sugar & Creamer, Rose 55.00
Delaware, Sugar, Cover, Rose, Gold Trim 65.00
Delaware, Table Set, Rose, 3 Piece 330.00
Delaware, Tankard, Green, Gold Trim ....90.00 To 100.00
Delaware, Toothpick, Green, Gold Trim 90.00
Delaware, Toothpick, Ruby Stained 80.00
Delaware, Tray, Pin, Rose Stained, Gold Trim 25.00
Delaware, Tumbler, Cranberry Flashed 37.50
Delaware, Tumbler, Rose, Gold Trim 35.00
Delaware, Water Set, Green, 7 Piece 550.00
Delaware, Water Set, Rose, 7 Piece 250.00
Dewdrop With Sheaf Of Wheat, Bread Plate .... 35.00 To 50.00
Dewdrop With Star, Goblet 24.50
Dewey, see also the related pattern Spanish American
Dewey, Butter, Cover 125.00
Dewey, Butter, Cover, Amber 72.50
Dewey, Butter, Cover, Green .... 65.00 To 70.00
Dewey, Cruet, Amber .... 65.00 To 80.00
Dewey, Cruet, Vaseline 195.00
Dewey, Pitcher 72.00
Dewey, Saltshaker, Amber 62.50
Diagonal Band & Fan, Goblet .... 25.00 To 30.00
Diagonal Band & Fan, Sugar, Cover 25.00
Diagonal Band & Flower, Mug, Child's, Daisy, 4 In. 28.00
Diagonal Band, Jam Jar, Cover 55.00
Diamond & Sunburst Zippers, Sauce, Ruby Stained 12.50
Diamond Band, Wine, Amber 35.00
Diamond Cut With Leaf, Mug 35.00
Diamond Medallion pattern is listed here as Grand
Diamond Point Loop, Toothpick 42.50
Diamond Point With Panels, Goblet, Flint, 1850s 85.00
Diamond Point With Panels, Sugar, Cover, Pagoda Type Lid 80.00
Diamond Point, Candlestick, 8 1/2 In., Pair 82.00
Diamond Point, Cruet 30.00
Diamond Point, Eggcup, Cover 100.00
Diamond Point, Goblet, Flint 35.00
Diamond Point, Sugar, Cover, Flint 75.00
Diamond Quilted, Bowl, Amethyst, 8 1/4 In. 25.00
Diamond Quilted, Goblet, Amber 50.00
Diamond Quilted, Goblet, Vaseline 35.00
Diamond Quilted, Mustard, Cover, 4 In. 20.00
Diamond Ridge, Creamer, Child's 63.00
Diamond Spearhead, Toothpick, Green 50.00
Diamond Sunburst, Compote, Jelly 15.00
Diamond Sunburst, Goblet 25.00
Diamond Thumbprint, Decanter, Bar Lip, Qt. 110.00
Diamond With Double Fans, Pitcher, Water 50.00
Dice & Block, Cruet, Blue 75.00
Divided Squares, Butter, Cover 30.00
Dog With Rabbit In Mouth, Tumbler 95.00
Dolphin, Spooner 175.00
Doric pattern is listed here as Feather
Double Arch, Compote 20.00
Double Arch, Toothpick, Ruby Stained 195.00
Double Beaded Band, Goblet, Seattle, Wash. 30.00

Pressed glass, Excelsior with
Maltese Cross

Pressed glass, Frosted Eagle

Pressed glass, Grape &
Festoon

Pressed glass, Harp

Pressed glass,
Hildalgo

Pressed glass,
Horseshoe

Pressed glass,
Inverted Fern

Double Beetle Band, Wine, Amber 35.00
Double Circle, Cruet, Green 125.00
Double Daisy pattern is listed here as Rosette Band
Double Doughnut, Creamer 20.00
Double Fan, Celery 25.00
Double Loop pattern is listed here as Ribbon Candy
Double Ribbon, Relish 12.50
Double Ribbon, Sugar, Cover 37.50
Double Scroll, Syrup 65.00
Double Snail, Water Set, Ruby Flashed, 6 Piece 795.00
Double Spear, Goblet 35.00
Double Vine pattern is listed here as Bellflower Double Vine
Double Wedding Ring pattern is listed here as Wedding Ring
Doyle's #500, Butter, Cover, Amber, Child's 65.00
Doyle's #500, Butter, Cover, Blue, Child's 70.00
Doyle's #500, Spooner, Blue, Child's 60.00
Drum, Creamer, Child's .... 35.00 To 50.00
Ear Of Corn, Cup & Saucer, Child's 35.00
Earl pattern is listed here as Spirea Band
Early Thistle, Goblet 35.00
Egg In Sand, Goblet 24.00
Egg In Sand, Goblet, Blue 72.00
Egyptian, Bread Plate 50.00
Egyptian, Butter, Cover 55.00
Egyptian, Celery ....90.00 To 125.00
Egyptian, Compote, Cover, Sphinx On Base, 12 In. 100.00
Egyptian, Creamer 40.00
Egyptian, Dish, Pickle 20.00
Egyptian, Goblet ....42.50 To 47.00
Egyptian, Pitcher 235.00
Egyptian, Relish 35.00

Egyptian, Spooner 50.00
Egyptian, Table Set, 4 Piece 225.00
Elephant Toes, Sugar & Butter, Covers, Green Toes 145.00
Elephant Toes, Toothpick, Green Toes 55.00
Elephant Toes, Tumbler 20.00
Elephant, Goblet, Etch 85.00
Emerald Green Herringbone, Berry Set, 1905, 7 Piece 68.00
Emerald Green Herringbone, Cruet 165.00
Emerald Green Herringbone, Pitcher, Milk 85.00
Emerald Green Herringbone, Pitcher, Water 65.00
Empress, Cruet, Green, Gold Trim 325.00
Empress, Sugar & Creamer, Green 270.00
Empress, Table Set, Green, Gold Trim, 1892, 4 Piece 650.00
Empress, Toothpick, Gold Trim 95.00
English Hobnail Cross pattern is listed here as Amberette
Esther, Cruet 35.00
Esther, Goblet 95.00
Esther, Pitcher, Amber Stained .... 175.00 To 200.00
Esther, Toothpick 20.00
Esther, Tumbler, Amber Stained 55.00
Esther, Tumbler, Green, Gold Trim 65.00
Etched Dakota pattern is listed here as Dakota
Euclid, Cake Stand, Miniature 37.50
Euclid, Cruet, Stopper 18.00
Eureka, Sugar, Flint 35.00
Excelsior Variant, Eggcup, Flint 37.50
Excelsior With Maltese Cross, Tumbler, Bar 42.50
Eyewinker, Butter, Cover 95.00
Eyewinker, Cake Stand 50.00
Eyewinker, Celery 55.00
Eyewinker, Compote, 9 In. 75.00
Eyewinker, Goblet 25.00
Eyewinker, Pitcher 85.00
Eyewinker, Sauce, 4 In. 28.00
Eyewinker, Sugar & Creamer, Cover 60.00
Falcon Strawberry, Toothpick 42.50
Falmouth Strawberry, Goblet 45.00
Fan & Flute, Sauce, Ruby Stained, 4 In. 32.50
Fan with Diamond pattern is listed here as Shell
Fan, Butter, Cover 330.00
Fancy Cut, Creamer, Child's .... 20.00 To 30.00
Fancy Cut, Punch Cup, Child's 25.00
Fancy Cut, Spooner 30.00
Fancy Cut, Water Set, Child's, 9 Piece 75.00
Feather Duster, Pitcher, Water 45.00
Feather Duster, Plate, 7 1/2 In. 24.50
Feather Duster, Tumbler, Green 37.50
Feather, Butter, Cover 55.00
Feather, Butter, Cover, Green 195.00
Feather, Cake Stand, 11 In. 72.00
Feather, Compote, Jelly 13.50
Feather, Cruet 32.00
Feather, Goblet, Clear 60.00
Feather, Pitcher, Water 65.00
Feather, Relish, Oval 10.00
Feather, Spooner 40.00
Feather, Sugar, Cover 75.00
Feather, Table Set, 4 Piece 135.00
Feather, Wine 42.50
Fern Garland, Champagne, 4 3/4 In. 16.50
Fern Garland, Cordial 18.50
Fern With Lily-of-The-Valley, Celery 40.00
Fernland, Table Set, Child's, 4 Piece .... 95.00 To 110.00

Festoon & Grape pattern is listed here as Grape & Festoon
Festoon, Berry Set, 7 Piece 75.00
Festoon, Cake Stand, 9 In. 80.00
Festoon, Creamer 35.00
Festoon, Mug, Handle 55.00
Festoon, Pitcher, Water 80.00
Festoon, Plate, 7 1/2 In. 30.00
Festoon, Plate, 8 1/4 In. 45.00
Festoon, Spooner 25.00
Festoon, Sugar, Cover 55.00
Fine Cut & Block, Creamer, Amber .... 40.00 To 45.00
Fine Cut & Block, Pitcher, Water, Blue Blocks 125.00
Fine Cut & Block, Salt Dip 12.00
Fine Cut & Block, Saltshaker, Amber 90.00
Fine Cut & Block, Spooner 45.00
Fine Cut & Feather pattern is listed here as Feather
Fine Cut & Panel, Goblet, Blue 20.00
Fine Cut & Panel, Goblet, Vaseline 45.00
Fine Cut & Panel, Wine, Amber 25.00
Fine Cut & Roses, Plate, Blue, 7 In. 35.00
Fine Rib, Sugar, Flint 55.00
Fish Scale, Cake Stand 19.50
Fish Scale, Compote, Cover, 7 In. 75.00
Fish Scale, Compote, Cover, 10 In. 38.50
Fish Scale, Compote, Jelly, Cover, 4 1/2 In. 39.50
Fish Scale, Compote, Jelly, Open 10.00
Fish Scale, Goblet 25.00
Fish Scale, Plate, 8 In. 15.00
Fish Scale, Plate, 9 In. .... 17.00 To 20.00
Fish Scale, Relish .... 15.00 To 22.50
Flamingo Habitat, Compote, Cover, 8 In. 67.50
Flamingo Habitat, Creamer .... 35.00 To 40.00
Flamingo Habitat, Goblet .... 25.00 To 35.00
Flamingo Habitat, Wine 30.00
Flat Diamond & Panel, Decanter 95.00
Flat Diamond & Panel, Eggcup, Cover 245.00
Flat Diamond & Panel, Wine, Flint .... 65.00 To 100.00
Flattened Finecut, Saltshaker, Amber 32.50
Fleur–De–Lis & Drape, Tumbler 20.00
Fleur–De–Lis & Tassel, Plate, 6 In. 5.50
Fleur–De–Lis & Tassel, Saltshaker 40.00
Fleur–De–Lis, Spooner 20.00
Flora, Spooner, Vaseline 95.00
Flora, Sugar & Spooner, Cover, Vaseline 325.00
Floral Diamond, Butter, Cover, Gold Trim 90.00
Florette, Celery Vase, Pink 145.00
Florette, Cracker Jar, Puffy Lid 250.00
Florette, Pitcher 250.00
Florette, Table Set, Pink, 4 Piece 298.00
Florette, Toothpick, Green 65.00
Florette, Toothpick, Pink 145.00
Florette, Tumbler 75.00
Florette, Water Set, Pink, 7 Piece 450.00
Florida Palm, Compote 20.00
Florida pattern pieces are listed here as Sunken Primrose if made Of clear class and
as Emerald Green Herringbone if made Of green glass
Florodora pattern is listed here as Bohemian
Flower Flange pattern is listed here as Dewey
Flower Medallion, Bowl, 8 1/2 In. 12.50
Flower Paneled Cane pattern is listed here as Cane & Rosette
Flower Pot, Creamer .... 27.50 To 35.00
Flower Pot, Saltshaker 32.50
Flower With Cane, Toothpick 65.00

Flower With Cane, Tumbler, Amethyst, Gold Trim 25.00
Flowered Scroll, Sugar 28.00
Flute, Tumbler, Child's, 6 Panels 8.00
Fluted Scrolls, Bowl, 4–Footed, 7 In. 16.50
Fluted Scrolls, Cruet, Enameled Flowers 115.00
Flying Birds, Goblet ....95.00 To 125.00
Flying Birds, Mug 75.00
Flying Robin pattern is listed here as Hummingbird
Flying Stork, Goblet 85.00
Forget–Me–Not In Scroll, Goblet 35.00
Four Petal, Creamer, Applied Handle, Flint 55.00
Frazier, Salt & Pepper, Cranberry Flashed, Enameled Design 125.00
Frosted Circle, Compote, 9 In. 50.00
Frosted Circle, Creamer 37.50
Frosted Circle, Spooner 30.00
Frosted Crane pattern is listed here as Frosted Stork
Frosted Eagle, Butter, Cover 190.00
Frosted Eagle, Sugar, Cover .... 135.00 To 195.00
Frosted Leaf, Eggcup, Flint 100.00
Frosted Leaf, Goblet, Flint 110.00
Frosted Leaf, Salt, Flint 50.00
Frosted Leaf, Salt, Flint, Master 125.00
Frosted Stork, Bowl, Oval, 9 x 6 In. 45.00
Frosted Stork, Compote, 8 In. 60.00
Frosted Stork, Jam Jar 350.00
Frosted Stork, Plate, Egg & Dart Border, 9 In. 80.00
Frosted Stork, Platter, Iowa City Border, Flower Handle 120.00
Frosted Stork, Spooner 45.00
Frosted Waffle pattern is listed here as Hidalgo
Frosted patterns may also be listed under the name of the main pattern
Fulton, Tumbler 15.00
Galloway, Butter, Cover 55.00
Galloway, Celery 25.00
Galloway, Compote 27.50
Galloway, Cracker Jar 125.00
Galloway, Creamer, Gold Trim 14.00
Galloway, Goblet .... 65.00 To 95.00
Galloway, Mug 37.50
Galloway, Salt & Pepper 33.00
Galloway, Syrup .... 65.00 To 75.00
Galloway, Toothpick 25.00
Galloway, Water Set, 7 Piece 195.00
Galloway, Water Set, Child's, Rose Blush, 6 Piece 135.00
Garden Fruits, Goblet 35.00
Garden Fruits, Sugar, Cover 40.00
Garden Of Eden, see also the related pattern Lotus & Serpent
Garden Of Eden, Pitcher .... 85.00 To 90.00
Garden Of Eden, Pitcher, Serpent .... 70.00 To 95.00
Garfield Drape, Compote, Cover, 6 In. 75.00
Garfield Drape, Pitcher, Milk .... 75.00 To 95.00
Garfield Memorial, Bread Plate, Star Border, 6 In. 47.50
Garfield Memorial, Mug, Martyr 67.50
George Peabody, Sauce 47.50
Georgia Gem, Creamer, Green, Gold Trim 40.00
Georgia Gem, Spooner, Green, Gold Trim 60.00
Giant Bull's–Eye, Decanter, 3 Pt. 90.00
Giant Prism With Thumbprint Band, Celery 125.00
Gibson Girl, Creamer .... 75.00 To 95.00
Gibson Girl, Tumbler 65.00
Girl With Fan, Goblet .... 75.00 To 95.00
Gladstone, Sauce 42.50
Gloria, Pitcher, Ruby Stained, Gold Trim 225.00
Gonterman Swirl, Sugar 70.00

Gonterman Swirl, Toothpick, Frosted Amber Rim 250.00
Gonterman, Spooner 125.00
Good Luck pattern is listed here as Horseshoe
Gooseberry, Goblet .... 25.00 To 35.00
Gothic, Celery Vase 67.00
Gothic, Eggcup 50.00
Gothic, Goblet 75.00
Grand, Compote, Cover, 8 In. 80.00
Grand, Goblet, Ring Stem 32.50
Grant, U.S., Bread Plate, Let Us Have Peace, 10 1/2 In. 65.00
Grape & Festoon, Spooner 20.00
Grape Band, Compote 20.00
Grape Band, Goblet 17.50
Grape With Overlapping Foliage, Creamer 25.00
Grape, see also the related patterns Beaded Grape, Beaded Grape Medallion, Magnet
& Grape, Paneled Grape, and Paneled Grape Band
Grape, Spooner 18.00
Grapevine With Ovals, Creamer, Child's 80.00
Grapevine With Ovals, Mug, Child's 20.00
Grapevine With Ovals, Spooner, Child's 80.00
Grapevine With Ovals, Sugar, Child's 80.00
Grasshopper, Celery 110.00
Grasshopper, Celery, Insect .... 60.00 To 75.00
Grasshopper, Spooner .... 45.00 To 75.00
Grasshopper, Spooner, Insect 40.00
Greek Key, Plate, 5 1/4 In. 18.50
Greenfield Swirl, Goblet, Vaseline 35.00
Gridley, Pitcher .... 120.00 To 125.00
Hairpin With Rayed Base, Eggcup 35.00
Hairpin With Rayed Base, Goblet, Flint 45.00
Hairpin With Thumbprint, Goblet 55.00
Hairpin, Goblet 40.00
Hairpin, Wine 62.00
Halley's Comet, Tankard, Etched 95.00
Hamilton With Clear Leaf pattern is listed here as Hamilton with Leaf
Hamilton With Leaf, Butter, Cover, Flint 65.00
Hamilton With Leaf, Eggcup, Flint 65.00
Hamilton, Compote, 8 In. .... 55.00 To 70.00
Hamilton, Compote, High Standard 150.00
Hamilton, Goblet 45.00
Hamilton, Spooner 25.00
Hand & Bar, Butter, Cover 75.00
Hand & Bar, Sugar, Cover 75.00
Hand & Fish Scale, Salt & Pepper, Frosted 75.00
Hand, Cake Stand, Etched, 12 1/4 In. 175.00
Hand, Celery Vase .... 42.50 To 65.00
Hand, Claret 85.00
Hand, Compote, Cover, 7 In. 95.00
Hand, Goblet 50.00
Hand, Pitcher 95.00
Hand, Relish 22.50
Hand, Salt & Pepper, Binocular Type 47.50
Harp, Goblet 1600.00
Harp, Salt, Footed 80.00
Harvard Yard, Jug 45.00
Harvard Yard, Toothpick .... 47.50 To 85.00
Hawaiian Lei, Bread Plate, Bee, 10 1/2 In. 12.00
Hawaiian Lei, Celery, 2 Handles 42.00
Hawaiian Lei, Pitcher, Milk, 6 1/2 In. 50.00
Hawaiian Lei, Spooner, Child's 20.00
Hawaiian Lei, Vase, Flared, 6 3/4 In. 25.00
Heart Band, Mug, Ruby Stained 40.00
Heart Plume, Spooner, Pink Flashed 65.00

Heart Stem, Compote, Cover, 7 In. 85.00
Heart With Thumbprint, Cruet 48.50
Heart With Thumbprint, Goblet 55.00
Heart With Thumbprint, Plate, 12 In. 55.00
Heart With Thumbprint, Punch Cup 22.50
Heart With Thumbprint, Punch Cup, Green 145.00
Heart With Thumbprint, Sugar, Green, Individual 45.00
Heart With Thumbprint, Sugar, Individual 35.00
Heart With Thumbprint, Syrup, Small 95.00
Heart With Thumbprint, Vase, 6 In. 32.00
Heart With Thumbprint, Vase, 10 In. 65.00
Heart, Toothpick, Blue 135.00
Heavy Gothic, Celery Vase, Ruby Stained 85.00
Heavy Paneled Fine Cut pattern is listed here as Paneled Diamond Cross
Henrietta, Celery Vase 18.00
Hercules Pillar, Eggcup, Double 65.00
Hero, Spooner, Ruby Rosette 15.00
Hero, Sugar, Ruby Rosette 15.00
Herringbone, Goblet 45.00
Herringbone, Toothpick, Ruby Flashed 65.00
Hexagon Block, Punch Cup, Amber Stained, Etched Flowers 50.00
Hexagon Block, Syrup, Ruby Stained 225.00
Hexagon Block, Table Set, Ruby Stained, Etched, 4 Piece 325.00
Hickman, Pitcher, Blue 95.00
Hidalgo, Celery Vase, Frosted 47.50
Hidalgo, Goblet 25.00
Hidalgo, Sugar, Cover, 8 1/2 In. 55.00
Hinoto pattern is listed here as Diamond Point with Panels
Hobnail pattern is in this book as its own category
Hobnail With Thumbprint Base, Creamer, Amber, Individual 35.00
Hobnail With Thumbprint Base, Pitcher, Ruby Stained, 7 In. 52.00
Holland, Compote, Cover, 7 In. 48.00
Holly Band, Celery 50.00
Honeycomb, Eggcup, Success Raises The Dough 40.00
Honeycomb, Goblet, Flint 38.00
Honeycomb, Mug, Child's, Flint, 3 1/4 In. 30.00
Honeycomb, Mustard Pot, Pewter Top, Etched 75.00
Honeycomb, Rose Bowl, Deep Opalescent 245.00
Honeycomb, Tumbler, Daisy & Button Bottom, Amber 20.00
Hooks & Eyes, Goblet 15.00
Horizontal Oval Frames, Saltshaker, Flint 34.00
Horizontal Threads, Butter, Cover 70.00
Horizontal Threads, Creamer 25.00
Horizontal Threads, Spooner 30.00
Horizontal Threads, Spooner, Child's 18.00
Horn Of Plenty, Celery 175.00
Horn Of Plenty, Compote, Flint, 7 In. 110.00
Horn Of Plenty, Cordial, Flint 150.00
Horn Of Plenty, Eggcup, Flint .... 35.00 To 65.00
Horn Of Plenty, Goblet, Flint .... 60.00 To 75.00
Horn Of Plenty, Sugar, Cover, Flint 125.00
Horsehead Medallion, Celery 40.00
Horseshoe Daisy, Sauce, Ruby Stained, 6 Piece 147.50
Horseshoe, Bowl, 9 1/4 In. 27.50
Horseshoe, Cake Stand, 7 In. 35.00
Horseshoe, Cake Stand, 8 In. 60.00
Horseshoe, Cake Stand, 10 In. 95.00
Horseshoe, Celery Dip, Horseshoe Shape 125.00
Horseshoe, Compote, Cover, 8 In. .... 145.00 To 150.00
Horseshoe, Creamer .... 22.00 To 47.50
Horseshoe, Goblet 65.00
Horseshoe, Goblet, Plain Stem 17.50
Horseshoe, Pitcher, Water .... 125.00 To 145.00

Horseshoe, Plate, 7 In.	75.00
Horseshoe, Relish	17.00 To 22.50
Horseshoe, Sauce, Flat	12.50
Horseshoe, Spooner	18.00 To 40.00
Huber, Champagne, Flint	45.00
Huber, Goblet	30.00
Huckle pattern is listed here as Feather Duster	
Hummingbird, Breadplate	55.00
Ibex, Goblet	95.00
Icicle With Loops, Goblet	55.00
Icicle With Loops, Pitcher, Buttermilk, Flint	45.00
Icicle, Plate, Flint, 6 3/8 In.	10.00
Ida pattern is listed here as Sheraton	
Idaho, Table Set, 4 Piece	175.00
Idyll, Toothpick, Gold Trim	40.00
Idyll, Tumbler, Blue, Gold Trim	65.00
Illinois, Creamer	40.00
Illinois, Creamer, Individual	25.00
Illinois, Cruet, Square Stopper	110.00
Illinois, Pitcher, Water, Silver–Plated Top	85.00
Illinois, Vase, Square, 8 In.	40.00
Indiana Swirl pattern is listed here as Feather	
Intaglio, Cruet, White	35.00
Intaglio, Water Set, Green, Gold Trim, 4 Piece	250.00
Interlocked Hearts, Wine	18.50
Inverted Fan & Feather, Berry Set, Green, 7 Piece	210.00
Inverted Fan & Feather, Butter, Cover, Green, Gold Trim	150.00
Inverted Fan & Feather, Candy Dish, Vaseline	95.00
Inverted Fan & Feather, Cruet	30.00
Inverted Fan & Feather, Tumbler, Green, Gold Trim	42.50
Inverted Fan & Feather, Water Set, Green, Gold Trim, 7 Piece	300.00
Inverted Fern, Goblet	45.00
Inverted Fern, Honey, Individual, 3 1/2 In.	3.00
Inverted Fern, Spooner, Ribbed Foot	75.00
Inverted Strawberry, Compote, Jelly	42.50
Inverted Strawberry, Wine	55.00
Inverted Thistle, Spooner	40.00
Inverted Thistle, Tumbler, Ruby Stained	35.00
Inverted Thumbprint & Star, Goblet	30.00
Inverted Thumbprint, Cruet, Amber	75.00
Iowa, Saltshaker, Gold Trim	28.00
Iris With Meander, Butter, Cover, Green, Gold Trim	145.00
Iris With Meander, Sugar & Creamer, Cover, Blue, Gold Trim	100.00
Iris With Meander, Sugar, Cover, Green, Gold Trim	38.50 To 50.00
Iris With Meander, Toothpick, Blue, Opalescent Rim	60.00
Iris With Meander, Toothpick, White Opalescent Rim	40.00
Ivy In Snow, Cake Stand, Square, 10 In.	65.00
Ivy In Snow, Celery	25.00
Ivy Leaves, Cup & Saucer, Child's	30.00 To 32.00
Jacob's Ladder, Celery Vase	45.00
Jacob's Ladder, Goblet	50.00
Jacob's Ladder, Salt, Master	8.00
Japanese, Celery	48.00 To 70.00
Jenny Lind, Compote	170.00
Jewel & Dewdrop, Compote, Cover, 7 In.	125.00
Jewel & Dewdrop, Compote, Scalloped, 7 x 8 In.	57.50
Jewel & Dewdrop, Goblet	72.50
Jewel & Dewdrop, Tumbler	55.00
Jewel & Flower, Sugar	100.00
Jewel Band, Celery Vase	30.00
Jeweled Heart, Bowl, Blue, Gold Trim, 9 In.	70.00
Jeweled Heart, Tumbler, Blue	12.00

Jeweled Moon & Star pattern is listed here as Moon & Star Variant or Moon & Star

Job's Tears pattern is listed here as Art

Jubilee pattern is listed here as Hickman

Jumbo, Goblet 600.00
Kaleidoscope, Celery, Etched 28.00
Kamoni pattern is listed here as Pennsylvania
Kansas pattern is listed here as Jewel & Dewdrop
Kentucky, Sauce, Footed, 4 1/4 In. 16.00
Kentucky, Wine 45.00
King's 500, Tumbler, Blue, Gold Trim 85.00
King's Crown, see also the related pattern Ruby Thumbprint
King's Crown, Cake Stand, 9 In. 85.00
King's Crown, Compote, Cover, 7 In. 95.00
King's Crown, Compote, Etched, 8 1/2 In. 145.00
King's Crown, Compote, Etched, 9 In. 145.00
King's Crown, Compote, Open, Small 30.00
King's Crown, Goblet, Amethyst Stained, Gold Trim 25.00
King's Crown, Spooner 35.00
King's Crown, Tumbler 30.00
Klondike pattern is listed here as Amberette
Knobby Bull's-Eye, Goblet 22.50
Kokomo, Decanter, Wine, 9 1/2 In. 45.00
Kokomo, Wine 15.00
Krom, Goblet, Flint 55.00
Lacy Daisy, Berry Bowl, Child's, 4 Piece 35.00
Lacy Scroll, Saltshaker, Yellow Cased 92.50
Lacy Spiral pattern is listed here as Colossus
Ladder With Diamond, Cruet 16.50
Lamb, Creamer, Child's .... 75.00 To 85.00
Lamb, Spooner, Child's 80.00
Lamb, Sugar, Cover, Child's 80.00
Late Block, Spooner 20.00
Late Butterfly, Bowl, 9 In. 24.50
Late Paneled Grape, Goblet .... 17.50 To 30.00
Late Paneled Grape, Water Set, Gold Design, 7 Piece 295.00
Late Thistle pattern is listed here as Inverted Thistle
Lattice & Oval Panels pattern is listed here as Flat Diamond & Panel
Leaf & Dart, Sugar 25.00
Leaf & Flower, Berry Set, Amber Stained, 13 Piece 325.00
Leaf & Flower, Butter, Cover, Amber Shield, Frosted 295.00
Leaf & Flower, Celery, Amber Stained, Frosted 125.00
Leaf & Flower, Sugar & Creamer 95.00
Leaf & Flower, Water Set, Amber Stained, Frosted, 7 Piece 750.00
Leaf & Rib, Pitcher, Water, Amber 58.00
Leaf Medallion, Creamer, Green 85.00
Leaf Medallion, Spooner, Amethyst, Gold Trim 75.00
Leaf Medallion, Sugar, Cover, Amethyst, Gold Trim 175.00
Leaf Medallion, Sugar, Cover, Gold Trim 50.00
Leaf Rosette, Butter, Cover, Frosted 125.00
Leaf Umbrella, Toothpick, Blue 275.00
Leverne pattern is listed here as Star in Honeycomb
Liberty Bell, Bread Plate, Signers, 10 In. .... 75.00 To 90.00
Liberty Bell, Butter, Cover 125.00
Liberty Bell, Creamer 87.00
Liberty Bell, Goblet 45.00
Liberty Bell, Mug, 2 In. .... 95.00 To 125.00
Liberty Bell, Spooner .... 35.00 To 65.00
Lightning, Goblet 42.50
Lily-of-The-Valley, Butter, Cover 95.00
Lily-of-The-Valley, Cake Stand 52.00
Lily-of-The-Valley, Compote, 7 In. 47.50
Lily-of-The-Valley, Compote, Cover, 8 In. 125.00

Pressed glass, Jumbo

Pressed glass, Liberty Bell

Pressed glass, Magnet &
Grape with Stippled Leaf

Lily-of-The-Valley, Creamer, 3-Footed	65.00
Lily-of-The-Valley, Cruet, Footed	225.00
Lily-of-The-Valley, Goblet	25.00
Lily-of-The-Valley, Salt, 3-Footed, Master	85.00
Lily-of-The-Valley, Spooner, 3-Footed	75.00
Lincoln Drape With Tassel, Goblet, Flint	145.00
Lincoln Drape, Compote, Flint, 7 1/2 In.	87.50
Lincoln Drape, Goblet, Flint	135.00
Lion In The Jungle, Goblet, Etched	85.00
Lion's Leg pattern is listed here as Alaska	
Lion, Butter, Cover, Child's	115.00
Lion, Butter, Cover, Frosted, Etched	140.00
Lion, Compote, Cover, Frosted, Lion's Head Finial	145.00
Lion, Compote, Frosted, 8 x 7 1/2 In.	70.00
Lion, Creamer, Child's	125.00
Lion, Creamer, Frosted	55.00 To 60.00
Lion, Cup & Saucer, Child's	45.00
Lion, Goblet	50.00
Lion, Goblet, Frosted	60.00 To 65.00
Lion, Paperweight, Frosted	100.00
Lion, Pitcher, Frosted	275.00
Lion, Salt & Pepper, Rope Base	75.00
Lion, Spooner, Frosted	50.00 To 60.00
Lion, Sugar, Cover, Child's	95.00
Lion, Sugar, Cover, Frosted	75.00
Locket On Chain, Butter, Cover	65.00
Log & Star, Cruet, Amber	45.00 To 60.00
Log Cabin, Creamer	52.00 To 95.00
Log Cabin, Spooner	145.00
Loop & Block, Creamer	75.00
Loop & Block, Sugar, Cover	85.00

Pressed glass, Paneled
Forget-Me-Not

Pressed glass,
Open Rose

Pressed glass, Pennsylvania

Pressed glass, Pleat & Panel

Pressed glass, Primrose

Loop & Block, Sugar, Cover, Ruby Stained	85.00
Loop & Dart With Round Ornaments, Champagne, Flint	85.00
Loop & Dart With Round Ornaments, Eggcup	25.00
Loop & Dart With Round Ornaments, Goblet	27.50
Loop & Dart, Butter, Cover, Portland, Flint	78.00
Loop & Dart, Champagne, Barrel Shape	85.00
Loop & Dart, Creamer	42.50
Loop & Dart, Eggcup	25.00
Loop & Dart, Pitcher, Buttermilk	45.00
Loop & Dart, Spooner	35.00
Loop & Noose, Spooner	26.00
Loop with Stippled Panels pattern is listed here as Texas	
Loop, see also the related pattern Seneca Loop	
Loop, Compote, 8 x 8 In.	75.00
Loop, Pitcher, Applied Handle, Flint, 8 3/4 In.	175.00
Loops & Drops pattern is listed here as New Jersey	
Loops & Fans, Pitcher, Water	45.00
Lord's Prayer, Tumbler	25.00
Lotus & Serpent, Butter, Cover, Log Finial, Scalloped Base	48.00
Lotus & Serpent, Pitcher	85.00
Louise, Spooner	20.00
Magnet & Grape, Goblet	40.00
Magnet & Grape, Goblet, Flint	75.00
Magnet & Grape, Tumbler	60.00
Maiden Blush, see pink flashed Banded Portland pieces	
Majestic, Carafe, Water, Ruby Stained	195.00
Majestic, Rose Bowl	12.50
Majestic, Toothpick	32.50
Maple Leaf, Bowl, Cover, Vaseline, 9 In.	85.00
Mardi Gras, Bottle, Water	65.00
Mardi Gras, Champagne	30.00
Mardi Gras, Compote, 9 3/4 In.	75.00
Mardi Gras, Cordial	30.00
Mardi Gras, Nappy, Triangular	15.00
Mardi Gras, Pickle Jar	50.00
Mardi Gras, Tankard	75.00
Mardi Gras, Vase, 9 1/2 In.	75.00
Mario, Celery	20.00
Marquisette, Sugar, Cover	33.00
Marsh Fern, Cake Stand	47.50
Marsh Fern, Compote, Cover, Etched, 7 In.	75.00
Marsh Fern, Creamer	37.50
Marsh Fern, Plate, Pink, 10 In.	32.50
Marsh Fern, Saltshaker, Pink	21.00
Maryland, Cake Stand, 8 In.	45.00
Maryland, Cake Stand, 9 In.	65.00
Maryland, Celery Vase	30.00

Maryland, Goblet .... 37.50 To 40.00
Mascotte, Cake Basket 45.00
Mascotte, Cake Stand, 10 1/2 In. 55.00
Mascotte, Compote, Cover, 8 In. 65.00
McKinley, Bread Plate 50.00
McKinley, Mug, Cover .... 65.00 To 85.00
Medallion Sprig, Cruet, Cobalt Blue To Clear 150.00
Medallion Sprig, Cruet, Green To Clear 265.00
Medallion Sunburst, Cruet, Stopper, Large 40.00
Medallion, Creamer 25.00
Medallion, Creamer, Amber 42.50
Medallion, Goblet, Amber 32.50
Melrose, Saltshaker 20.00
Melrose, Wine 15.00
Memphis, Creamer, Gold Trim 35.00
Memphis, Creamer, Green, Gold Trim 45.00
Memphis, Punch Set, Gold Trim, 8 Piece 185.00
Memphis, Sugar, Green, Gold Trim 60.00
Memphis, Table Set, Green, Gold Trim, 4 Piece 450.00
Memphis, Tumbler, Gold Trim 20.00
Memphis, Tumbler, Green, Gold Trim 30.00
Menagerie, Butter, Cover, Turtle 850.00
Menagerie, Spooner, Fish, Amber 110.00
Menagerie, Spooner, Fish, Blue 125.00
Mephistopheles, Tumbler, Ale .... 45.00 To 55.00
Michigan, Creamer, Pink Stained 25.00
Michigan, Goblet, Gold Enameled Trim 43.00
Michigan, Pitcher, 8 In. 45.00
Michigan, Vase, Gold Enameled Trim, 6 3/4 In. 25.00
Michigan, Vase, Pink Stained, Enameled Trim, 6 In. 40.00
Minerva, Cake Stand, 8 In. 95.00
Minerva, Cake Stand, 11 In. 150.00
Minerva, Creamer 45.00
Minerva, Goblet 110.00
Minerva, Pitcher 200.00
Minerva, Plate, Handles, 10 In. 65.00
Minerva, Plate, J. C. Gates Center, 8 In. 67.50
Minerva, Spooner 42.00
Minerva, Sugar, Cover 75.00
Minnesota, Cracker Jar 95.00
Minnesota, Goblet, Gold Trim 24.00
Minnesota, Toothpick, 3 Handles .... 18.50 To 38.00
Minnesota, Wine 25.00
Missouri, Cake Stand 27.50
Mitered Bars, Goblet 28.00
Mitered Diamond Points pattern is listed here as Mitered Bars
Mitered Diamonds, Wine, Amber 28.00
Mitered Prisms, Cake Stand 25.00
Mitered Prisms, Goblet 22.00
Monkey Climber, Mug, Child's 55.00
Monkey, Mug 95.00
Monkey, Spooner 125.00
Moon & Star Variant, Cake Stand, Frosted, 10 In. 115.00
Moon & Star, Bowl, 8 1/2 In. 45.00
Moon & Star, Cake Stand 75.00
Moon & Star, Celery 24.00
Moon & Star, Eggcup 25.00
Moon & Star, Goblet 32.50
Moon & Star, Lamp 195.00
Moon & Star, Spooner 35.00
Moon & Star, Sugar & Creamer, Cover 50.00
Moon & Star, Sugar Shaker, Pewter Top 55.00
Moon & Stork pattern is listed here as Ostrich Looking At The Moon

Nail, Goblet, Etched 65.00
Nail, Goblet, W. P. Halley, 1893 World's Fair 75.00
Nail, Pitcher, Water, Ruby Stained, Etched 195.00
Nail, Syrup 40.00
Nailhead, Butter, Cover 46.00
Nailhead, Celery 75.00
Nailhead, Pitcher, Water 35.00
Nailhead, Wine 18.50
Nautilus pattern is listed here as Argonaut Shell
Near Cut, Creamer 8.00
Nebraska pattern is listed here as Bismarc Star
Nestlings, Goblet .... 60.00 To 85.00
Nestor, Butter, Cover, Amethyst 125.00
Nestor, Sugar, Cover, Amethyst 75.00
Netted Oak, Cruet, Child's 125.00
Nevada, Toothpick, Crystal, Gold 65.00
Nevada, Toothpick, Frosted 37.50
New England Pineapple, Eggcup, Flint 65.00
New England Pineapple, Goblet, Flint 70.00
New Hampshire, Creamer 8.00
New Hampshire, Cruet 60.00
New Hampshire, Goblet 32.00
New Hampshire, Relish 20.00
New Hampshire, Saltshaker, Pink Stained 37.50
New Jersey, Bread Plate 25.00
New Jersey, Butter, Cover, Gold Trim 72.50
New Jersey, Compote, Gold Trim, 6 x 8 In. 35.00
New Jersey, Creamer 35.00
New Jersey, Goblet 35.00
New Jersey, Toothpick 45.00
New Jersey, Vase, 6 In. 48.00
New Jersey, Water Set, 6 Piece 95.00
Nicotiana, Goblet .... 12.00 To 15.00
Nursery Tales, Berry Set, Child's, 7 Piece 150.00
Nursery Tales, Butter, Cover .... 55.00 To 75.00
Nursery Tales, Cake Plate, Ring Around The Rosie, 10 In. 295.00
Nursery Tales, Creamer 60.00
Nursery Tales, Cup & Saucer, Jack In The Beanstalk 195.00
Nursery Tales, Pitcher, Water 105.00
Nursery Tales, Plate & Bowl, Child's, Amber 95.00
Nursery Tales, Punch Bowl, Milk Glass 125.00
Nursery Tales, Punch Cup 20.00
Nursery Tales, Punch Set, 7 Piece 200.00
Nursery Tales, Spooner .... 42.00 To 60.00
Nursery Tales, Sugar, Cover 75.00
Nursery Tales, Table Set, Child's, 4 Piece .... 210.00 To 450.00
Nursery Tales, Table Set, Christmas 1909, Box, 4 Piece 360.00
Nursery Tales, Vase, Jack & Jill, 6 In. 225.00
O'Hara's Diamond, Cruet, Ruby Stained .... 175.00 To 225.00
Oaken Bucket, Pitcher 70.00
Oaken Bucket, Spooner, Blue 55.00
Oaken Bucket, Sugar & Creamer 125.00
Oaken Bucket, Toothpick, Amber 25.00
Oasis, Pitcher, Etched .... 185.00 To 195.00
Ohio, Goblet 30.00
Old Abe pattern is listed here as Frosted Eagle
One–Hundred–One, Bread Plate, Agricultural Center 75.00
One–Hundred–One, Bread Plate, Motto 30.00
One–Hundred–One, Butter, Cover 70.00
One–Hundred–One, Celery .... 35.00 To 38.00
One–Hundred–One, Creamer 28.00
One–Hundred–One, Goblet 32.00
One–Hundred–One, Pitcher 120.00

One–Hundred–One, Plate, 7 In.	18.00
One–Hundred–One, Relish, Oval, 8 1/2 In.	15.00
One–Hundred–One, Toothpick, Opaque Green	75.00
One–Hundred–One, Toothpick, Opaque White	45.00
One–Hundred–One, Toothpick, Pink	65.00
One–Hundred–One, Water Set, 7 Piece	295.00
One–O–One pattern is listed here as One–Hundred–One	
One–Thousand Eye pattern is listed here as Thousand Eye	
Open Rose, Plate, 9 In.	25.00
Opposing Drops, Celery	25.00
Opposing Pyramids, Goblet	25.00
Optica, Table Set, Painted, 4 Piece	160.00
Oregon, see also the related patterns Beaded Loop and Skilton	
Oregon, Butter, Cover	62.50
Oregon, Goblet	55.00
Oregon, Salt & Pepper	45.00
Oregon, Toothpick	87.50
Orion pattern is listed here as Cathedral	
Ostrich Looking At The Moon, Goblet	125.00
Oval Panels, Goblet, Blue	25.00
Oval Star, Butter, Cover, Child's	25.00 To 30.00
Oval Star, Sugar, Cover, Child's	25.00 To 30.00
Oval Star, Table Set, Child's, 4 Piece	90.00
Oval Star, Tumbler, Child's	13.00
Oval Star, Water Set, Child's, 6 Piece	65.00
Owl pattern is listed here as Bull's–Eye with Diamond Point	
Owl & Possum, Goblet	105.00
Owl & Pussycat, Cheese Dish, Dome Cover	130.00
Owl in Fan pattern is listed here as Parrot	
Paddlewheel, Cruet	20.00
Paddlewheel, Cruet, Stopper	45.00
Palm Beach, Table Set, Red & Green, Gold Trim, 4 Piece	380.00
Palmette, Cup Plate	45.00
Pampas Flower, Creamer	15.00
Panama, Wine	15.00
Paneled 44, Berry Set, Gold Stained, 5 Piece	85.00
Paneled 44, Berry Set, Gold Stained, 7 Piece	225.00
Paneled 44, Butter, Gold Trim	50.00
Paneled 44, Cruet	58.00
Paneled 44, Pitcher, Pedestal, Platinum Stained	125.00
Paneled 44, Pitcher, Rose, Gold Stained	105.00
Paneled 44, Saucer, Footed, Rose Stained, 4 1/2 In.	40.00
Paneled 44, Tankard, Platinum Stained	105.00 To 155.00
Paneled Beads, Compote, Cover, 11 x 6 1/2 In.	75.00
Paneled Cane, Mug, Child's	15.00
Paneled Cane, Vase, 8 In.	13.50
Paneled Cherry, Goblet	35.00
Paneled Cherry, Toothpick	18.00
Paneled Daisy & Button, Berry Bowl, Master, Oval, Amber	30.00
Paneled Daisy & Button, Bowl, Footed, Amber, 7 1/4 In.	40.00
Paneled Daisy & Button, Celery Vase	30.00
Paneled Daisy & Button, Compote, Cover, 11 1/2 In.	105.00
Paneled Diamond & Finecut, Cake Stand, 9 In.	48.00
Paneled Diamond & Finecut, Creamer	32.00
Paneled Diamond Cross, Goblet	34.00
Paneled Finecut, Saltshaker, Amber	37.50
Paneled Finecut, Wine, Blue	32.50
Paneled Forget–Me–Not, Celery	35.00 To 40.00
Paneled Forget–Me–Not, Compote	25.00
Paneled Forget–Me–Not, Goblet	35.00
Paneled Forget–Me–Not, Pitcher, Milk	60.00
Paneled Grape Band, Eggcup, Flint	35.00
Paneled Grape, Creamer, Vine	30.00

Paneled Grape, Tumbler 15.00
Paneled Heather, Goblet .... 27.50 To 35.00
Paneled Herringbone, Celery 20.00
Paneled Honeycomb, Pitcher, Pewter Lid 45.00
Paneled Jewels, Wine, Amber 28.00
Paneled Nightshade, Goblet 15.00
Paneled Ovals, Eggcup 30.00
Paneled Sprig, Castor, Pickle 275.00
Paneled Star & Button, Wine 14.50
Paneled Thistle, Compote, Jelly 45.00
Paneled Thistle, Cruet 25.00
Paneled Thistle, Vase, 13 1/2 In. 35.00
Paneled Thistle, Wine 22.50
Paneled Wheat, Pitcher 50.00
Paris, Vase, 6 1/2 In. 9.50
Parrot, Goblet 50.00
Pathfinder, Wine 15.00
Pattee Cross, Creamer, Amethyst Stained, Gold Trim 45.00
Pattee Cross, Tumbler, Child's 12.00
Pavonia, Bowl, Rectangular, 8 1/2 In. 20.00
Pavonia, Bowl, Waste, Etched .... 45.00 To 58.00
Pavonia, Butter, Cover, Pedestal 85.00
Pavonia, Butter, Cover, Pedestal, Etched 85.00
Pavonia, Cake Stand 58.00
Pavonia, Celery .... 20.00 To 35.00
Pavonia, Compote, Cover, Etched, 7 In. 125.00
Pavonia, Goblet 35.00
Pavonia, Mug, Ruby Stained, 4 In. 22.00
Pavonia, Sauce, Flat, Etched, 4 In. 15.00
Pavonia, Spooner, Ruby Stained 38.00
Pavonia, Tankard 85.00
Pavonia, Tankard, Etched .... 70.00 To 80.00
Pavonia, Tumbler, Etched 28.00
Peach, Spooner, Green 60.00
Peacock Feathers, Butter, Cover 35.00
Peacock Feathers, Creamer, Child's 125.00
Peacock Feathers, Cruet 40.00
Peacock Feathers, Cup Plate, 5 1/2 In. 10.00
Peacock Feathers, Mug, 3 1/2 In. 40.00
Peacock Feathers, Tumbler 20.00
Peacock's Eye pattern is listed here as Peacock Feathers
Peek-A-Boo, Toothpick, Amber 42.50
Pennsylvania, see also the related pattern Hand
Pennsylvania, Bowl, 9 In. 18.50
Pennsylvania, Butter, Cover, Child's 65.00
Pennsylvania, Cruet 25.00
Pennsylvania, Goblet .... 20.00 To 22.50
Pennsylvania, Spooner & Creamer, Child's, Green .... 125.00 To 145.00
Pennsylvania, Sugar, Child's, Green 115.00
Pennsylvania, Sugar, Cover, Child's, Green 75.00
Pennsylvania, Table Set, 4 Piece 225.00
Pennsylvania, Table Set, Gold Trim, 4 Piece 220.00
Pennsylvania, Table Set, Green, 4 Piece 450.00
Pennsylvania, Toothpick, Green, Gold Trim 150.00
Pennsylvania, Wine 25.00
Petticoat Fluting, Celery 28.00
Petticoat, Table Set, Vaseline, Gold Trim, 4 Piece 395.00
Petticoat, Toothpick, Hat, Vaseline 65.00
Pheasant, Dish, Cover, Frosted 165.00
Philadelphia Centennial, Goblet 30.00
Picket Fence, Goblet 45.00
Picket, Creamer .... 30.00 To 40.00
Picket, Pitcher, Water 65.00

Picket, Sugar, Cover 45.00
Pillar & Bull's-Eye pattern is listed here as Thistle
Pillar, Syrup, Hinged Pewter Lid, 8 3/4 In. 550.00
Pillow Encircled, Sugar, Cover, Ruby Stained, Etched 125.00
Pinafore pattern is listed here as Actress
Pineapple & Fan, Cruet 35.00
Pineapple & Fan, Cruet, Green 235.00
Pineapple & Fan, Toothpick 18.00
Pineapple, Compote 20.00
Pineapple, Goblet .... 80.00 To 95.00
Pineapple, Spooner 25.00
Plain Smocking pattern is listed here as Smocking
Pleasant To Labor–Love, Bread Plate, 11 In. 45.00
Pleat & Panel, Bread Plate 25.00
Pleat & Panel, Cake Stand, 8 In. 42.00
Pleat & Panel, Cake Stand, 9 In. 55.00
Pleat & Panel, Celery 38.00
Pleat & Panel, Goblet 30.00
Pleat & Panel, Plate, 7 In. 15.00
Pleat & Panel, Relish, Cover 65.00
Pleating, Berry Bowl, Small 12.00
Pleating, Creamer 30.00
Pleating, Pitcher, Ruby Stained 75.00
Plume & Block, Celery .... 20.00 To 35.00
Plume, Goblet 32.50
Pointed Panel Daisy & Button pattern is listed here as Paneled Daisy & Button
Polar Bear, Goblet 100.00
Polar Bear, Goblet, Frosted .... 100.00 To 140.00
Polar Bear, Tray, Frosted 265.00
Popcorn, Goblet, Flat Ear Of Corn 25.00
Popcorn, Goblet, Raised Ear Of Corn 50.00
Portland with Diamond Point Band pattern is listed here as Banded Portland
Portland, Pitcher, Child's, Gold Trim .... 35.00 To 40.00
Portland, Sugar & Creamer 55.00
Portland, Water Set, 6 Piece 130.00
Posies & Pods, Creamer, Green 35.00
Posies & Pods, Creamer, Green, Gold Trim 30.00
Posies & Pods, Sugar, Cover, Green, Gold Trim 75.00
Potted Plant pattern is listed here as Flower Pot
Powder & Shot, Goblet, Flint .... 40.00 To 80.00
Powder & Shot, Spooner 35.00
Prayer Rug pattern is listed here as Horseshoe
Pressed Diamond, Creamer, Amber 38.00
Pressed Diamond, Cruet, Blue 48.00
Pressed Diamond, Cruet, Blue, Clear Stopper 65.00
Pressed Leaf With Chain, Goblet 25.00
Pressed Leaf, Goblet 26.00

*Pressed glass, Princess
Feather*

*Pressed glass,
Profile & Sprig*

Pressed glass, Rose in Snow

Pressed Leaf, Salt, Flint 20.00
Pressed Leaf, Spooner 17.50
Primrose, Plate, Blue, 7 In. 12.50
Princess Feather, Goblet .... 20.00 To 42.00
Princess Feather, Salt & Pepper 70.00
Princess Feather, Spooner 45.00
Priscilla, Basket, 8 In. 75.00
Priscilla, Compote, Round, 8 In. 85.00
Priscilla, Compote, Square, 7 1/2 In. 55.00
Priscilla, Toothpick 27.50
Prism, Goblet, Flint 35.00
Prize, Creamer, Green, Gold Trim 45.00
Profile & Sprig, Table Set, 4 Piece 130.00
Psyche & Cupid, Celery 45.00
Psyche & Cupid, Creamer 40.00
Puffed Bands, Goblet, Amethyst 20.00
Puffed Bands, Goblet, Blue 16.50
Puritan, Butter, Cover, Ruby Etched 110.00
Quaker Lady, Cake Stand 75.00
Quaker Lady, Celery 45.00
Queen Anne, Butter, Cover 75.00
Queen Anne, Celery 40.00
Queen Anne, Creamer .... 45.00 To 50.00
Queen Anne, Pitcher 60.00
Queen Anne, Spooner 40.00
Queen Anne, Sugar, Large 40.00
Queen's Necklace, Toothpick 60.00
Queen, see also the related pattern Paneled Daisy & Button
Queen, Goblet, Amber 45.00
Queen, Pitcher, Amber 70.00
Queen, Wine 22.00
Quilted Phlox, Salt & Pepper 25.00
Quilted Phlox, Saltshaker, Opaque White, Blue Flowers 45.00
Ray, Creamer 20.00
Rayed Flower, Pitcher, Water 75.00
Rayed Flower, Wine 15.00
Reaper, McCormick Reaper, Bread Plate 90.00
Red Block, Celery Vase 135.00
Red Block, Goblet 30.00
Red Block, Table Set, 4 Piece 125.00
Red Block, Water Set, 8 Piece 350.00
Regal Block, Celery 25.00
Regal Block, Wine, Gold Trim 18.50
Regent pattern is listed here as Leaf Medallion
Remember The Maine, Compote, Cover 75.00
Reticulated Cord, Pitcher, Amber, 9 In. 90.00
Reverse Torpedo pattern is listed here as Bull's–Eye Band
Rex, Lemonade Set, Child's, 7 Piece 115.00
Ribbed Grape, Goblet 55.00
Ribbed Grape, Plate, 6 In. 45.00
Ribbed Ivy, Decanter, Child's 85.00
Ribbed Ivy, Goblet 55.00
Ribbed Ivy, Spooner 25.00
Ribbed Palm, Pitcher, Flint .... 250.00 To 295.00
Ribbed Palm, Spooner, Footed, Flint 50.00
Ribbon Candy, Cake Stand, Child's 55.00
Ribbon Candy, Goblet 95.00
Ribbon Candy, Spooner .... 20.00 To 25.00
Ribbon Candy, Wine 17.00
Ribbon, Butter, Cover, Frosted 80.00
Ribbon, Celery Vase, Frosted, Etched 35.00
Ribbon, Compote, Dolphin Stem 250.00
Ribbon, Compote, Dolphin Stem, Frosted, 8 In. 295.00

Pressed glass, Ruby Thumbprint

Pressed glass, Shell

Ribbon, Goblet, Frosted	60.00
Ribbon, Jam Jar, Frosted	75.00
Ribbon, Pitcher, Water, Frosted	120.00
Ribbon, Tray, Cut Corners, Frosted, 13 In.	50.00
Ring & Block, Tumbler, Ruby Stained	35.00
Rising Sun, Goblet, Green Stained	20.00
Rising Sun, Sugar, 3 Handles, Rose Stained	35.00
Rising Sun, Toothpick	35.00
Rochelle pattern is listed here as Princess Feather	
Roman Key, Goblet, Ribbed	35.00
Roman Rosette, Compote, Jelly	20.00
Roman Rosette, Plate, 7 In.	34.00
Romeo, Celery	20.00
Romeo, Saltshaker	25.00
Romeo, Wine	62.00
Rose In Snow, Butter, Cover, Round	60.00
Rose In Snow, Butter, Cover, Square	45.00
Rose In Snow, Cake Stand	95.00
Rose In Snow, Creamer	30.00
Rose In Snow, Goblet, Amber	40.00
Rose In Snow, Mug	38.00
Rose In Snow, Mug, Blue	110.00
Rose In Snow, Mug, In Remembrance	45.00
Rose Sprig, Cake Stand, 10 In.	67.50
Rose Sprig, Celery	28.00
Rose Sprig, Goblet, Amber	42.00
Rose Sprig, Punch Bowl	58.00
Rosette & Palms, Compote, 9 In.	60.00
Rosette & Palms, Goblet	30.00
Rosette & Palms, Sugar, Cover	45.00
Rosette & Palms, Wine	13.00
Rosette Band, Butter, Cover, Ruby Flashed	85.00
Rosette Band, Goblet, Etched	32.50
Rosette Medallion pattern is listed here as Feather Duster	
Rosette With Pinwheels, Creamer	20.00
Rosette With Pinwheels, Sugar, Cover	25.00
Royal Ivy, Castor, Pickle, Vaseline, Silver Frame, Tongs	295.00
Royal Ivy, Cruet, Rubina	260.00 To 295.00
Royal Ivy, Rose Bowl	80.00
Royal Ivy, Sugar Shaker	138.00
Royal Ivy, Tumbler, Rubina	72.50
Royal Ivy, Water Set, Rainbow Craquelle, 7 Piece	955.00
Royal Lady, Butter, Cover	85.00
Royal Lady, Celery Vase	45.00
Royal Lady, Sugar, Cover	65.00
Royal Oak, Berry Set, 7 Piece	310.00
Royal Oak, Sugar Shaker, Clear & Frosted, Northwood	65.00

Royal Oak, Sugar Shaker, Cover 75.00
Ruby Rosette pattern is listed here as Hero
Ruby Thumbprint, see also the related pattern King's Crown
Ruby Thumbprint, Creamer, Etched 75.00
Ruby Thumbprint, Saltshaker 35.00
Ruby Thumbprint, Wine 28.00
S–Repeat, Condiment Set, Blue, 5 Piece 245.00
S–Repeat, Condiment Set, Green, 5 Piece 195.00
S–Repeat, Syrup 80.00
S–Repeat, Toothpick, Green 25.00
S–Repeat, Tumbler, Blue 65.00
S–Repeat, Tumbler, Blue, Gold Trim 35.00
S–Repeat, Wine, Blue 22.00
Sandwich Star & Buckle, Syrup 225.00
Sandwich Star, Salt 65.00
Sawtooth Band pattern is listed here as Amazon
Sawtooth, Butter, Cover 50.00
Sawtooth, Butter, Cover, Flint 85.00
Sawtooth, Cake Stand, 10 3/4 In. 70.00
Sawtooth, Compote 35.00
Sawtooth, Decanter, Acorn Stopper, Flint, 1/2 Pt. 110.00
Sawtooth, Salt, Cover, Flint 35.00
Sawtooth, Sugar, Cover 22.00
Sawtooth, Wine, Knob Stem 12.50
Saxon, Celery .... 25.00 To 35.00
Scalloped Lines, Spooner 25.00
Scalloped Swirl, Toothpick, Ruby Stained, Souvenir 35.00
Scalloped Tape pattern is listed here as Jewel Band
Scarab, Goblet, Flint 140.00
Scroll With Cane Band, Bowl, Amber 43.00
Scroll With Cane Band, Toothpick .... 15.00 To 35.00
Scroll With Cane Band, Tray, Condiment, Amber Stained 42.00
Scroll With Flowers, Bread Plate 25.00
Scroll With Flowers, Salt, Handles, Footed 28.50
Seashell, Celery 38.00
Sedan pattern is listed here as Paneled Star & Button
Seneca Loop, Compote, Flint, 7 3/8 x 9 1/4 In. 50.00
Seneca Loop, Goblet 32.00
Sequoia, Compote, Cover 45.00
Sheaf & Block, Pitcher, Milk, Ruby Flashed 28.00
Sheaf & Block, Pitcher, Ruby Stained, 7 1/2 In. 70.00
Sheaf & Diamond, Compote, 7 1/2 In. 50.00
Sheaf Of Wheat pattern is listed here as Wheat Sheaf
Shell & Jewel, Pitcher .... 30.00 To 50.00
Shell & Jewel, Pitcher, Green 50.00
Shell & Jewel, Spooner 30.00
Shell & Jewel, Tumbler 12.50
Shell & Jewel, Tumbler, Amber 30.00
Shell & Jewel, Tumbler, Green 40.00
Shell & Tassel, Bread Plate, 8 x 12 In. 57.50
Shell & Tassel, Butter Pat .... 15.00 To 18.00
Shell & Tassel, Butter, Cover, Dog Finial .... 105.00 To 125.00
Shell & Tassel, Cake Stand 224.00
Shell & Tassel, Celery Vase, 8 In. 95.00
Shell & Tassel, Oyster Plate 245.00
Shell & Tassel, Pickle Jar 140.00
Shell & Tassel, Pitcher, Water 225.00
Shell & Tassel, Spooner 35.00
Shell & Tassel, Vase, Etched 125.00
Shell, Goblet 12.00
Shell, Sugar 30.00
Sheraton, Celery 18.00
Shields, Creamer 225.00

Short Teasel pattern is listed here as Teasel
Shoshone pattern is listed here as Victor
Shovel, Creamer 12.00
Shrine, Mug 65.00
Shrine, Pitcher .... 60.00 To 95.00
Six Panel Finecut, Bowl, 8 In. 27.50
Skilton, Compote, Ruby Stained, 7 In. 67.50
Smocking, Sugar, Cover, Flint 85.00
Snail, Bowl, Oval, 8 In. 30.00
Snail, Butter, Cover 85.00
Snail, Celery 40.00
Snail, Cruet .... 110.00 To 125.00
Snail, Pitcher, Water 100.00
Snail, Relish, Oval, 9 In. 32.00
Snail, Rose Bowl, Small 24.00
Snail, Salt Dip 15.00
Snail, Salt, Ruby 50.00
Snail, Sauce, 4 In. 15.00
Snail, Spooner 35.00
Snail, Sugar Shaker 110.00
Snail, Sugar, Cover, Individual 75.00
Snail, Syrup, Brass Lid 110.00
Snail, Vase, 11 In. 85.00
Snake Drape, Goblet 18.00
Snow Drop, Ice Cream Set, Shell–Shaped Sauces, Tray, 6 Piece 175.00
Spanish American, Pitcher 75.00
Spanish American, Water Set, 7 Piece 225.00
Spanish Coin pattern is listed here as Columbian Coin
Spearpoint Band, Toothpick, Gold Trim 40.00
Spirea Band, Cake Stand, Blue 75.00
Spirea Band, Sugar, Cover, Berry Etch 25.00
Spirea Band, Wine 15.00
Spirea Band, Wine, Blue 25.00
Sprig, Cake Stand, 10 In. 42.00
Sprig, Compote, Cover, 8 In. 95.00
Square Fuchsia, Compote, Cover, Handle, Pink, 5 In. 50.00
Square Fuchsia, Mug 35.00
Square Fuchsia, Pitcher, Apple Green 55.00
Square Fuchsia, Pitcher, Blue 120.00
Square Fuchsia, Pitcher, Water 40.00
Square Fuchsia, Plate, Apple Green, 9 In. 42.50
Square Fuchsia, Plate, Handle, Vaseline, 9 In. 45.00
Square Fuchsia, Platter, Grape Handles 45.00
Square Panes, Butter, Cover, Etched 67.50
Square Panes, Celery, Etched 30.00
Square Panes, Compote, Cover, 8 In. 85.00
Square Panes, Goblet, Etched 40.00
Square Panes, Pitcher, Water, Etched 78.00
Star & Bar, Goblet, Amber, Deer Etch .... 25.00 To 28.00
Star & Punty pattern is listed here as Moon & Star
Star Band pattern is listed here as Bosworth
Star In Bull's–Eye, Salt & Pepper 35.00
Star In Bull's–Eye, Toothpick, Double 25.00
Star In Bull's–Eye, Toothpick, Single 12.50
Star In Honeycomb, Pitcher, Water .... 50.00 To 65.00
Stars & Bars, Cake Stand, 10 In. 80.00
Stars & Bars, Pitcher, Water 100.00
Stars & Stripes, Goblet 48.00
Stars & Stripes, Punch Cup .... 18.00 To 45.00
States pattern is listed here as The States
Stippled Dahlia pattern is listed here as Square Fuchsia
Stippled Dewdrop & Raindrop, Creamer, Child's 63.00
Stippled Double Loop, Wine 47.50

Stippled Forget–Me–Not, Cup & Saucer 30.00
Stippled Forget–Me–Not, Goblet 45.00
Stippled Forget–Me–Not, Tray, Water, Wildlife 75.00
Stippled Fuchsia, Goblet .... 35.00 To 37.50
Stippled Grape & Festoon, Compote, Cover, High Pedestal 110.00
Stippled Grape & Festoon, Compote, Cover, Low Pedestal 42.50
Stippled Grape & Festoon, Spooner 30.00
Stippled Grape & Festoon, Sugar, Cover 70.00
Stippled Ivy, Spooner 20.00
Stippled Medallion, Goblet, Flint 30.00
Stippled Sandbur, Toothpick 40.00
Stippled Star Variant pattern is listed here as Stippled Sandbur
Stippled Star, Celery 35.00
Stippled Vine & Beads pattern is listed here as Vine & Beads
Stork Looking at the Moon pattern is listed here as Ostrich Looking At The Moon
Stork, Tumbler 85.00
Strawberry & Currant, Goblet .... 13.00 To 30.00
Strawberry With Roman Key Band, Tumbler 25.00
Strawberry, Goblet 35.00
Strawberry, Spooner .... 25.00 To 35.00
Strawberry, Toothpick, Footed 65.00
Strigil, Bowl, Flared, 9 In. 24.50
Strigil, Plate, 8 In. 22.50
Strigil, Plate, 11 In. 26.50
Strigil, Spooner 15.00
Strigil, Tumbler 32.50
Style, Sugar, Cover, Child's 35.00
Style, Toothpick 37.50
Sunbeam, Toothpick, Blue, Gold Trim 125.00
Sunburst & Bar, Finger Bowl 45.00
Sunk Daisy, Toothpick 32.50
Sunk Honeycomb, Compote, Cover, Ruby Stained, 11 x 7 In. 165.00
Sunk Honeycomb, Cruet, Ruby Stained 145.00
Sunk Honeycomb, Cruet, Ruby Stained, 5 In. 110.00
Sunk Honeycomb, Toothpick, Vine Etch, 2 1/4 In. 45.00
Sunk Honeycomb, Wine, Etched, Ruby Stained 45.00
Sunken Buttons, Sauce, Amber 7.00
Sunken Buttons, Tray, 8 x 11 In. 25.00
Sunken Buttons, Tumbler, Amber 26.00
Sunken Primrose, Goblet 17.50
Sunrise pattern is listed here as Rising Sun
Swag With Brackets, Berry Bowl, Blue, 8 In. 47.50
Swag With Brackets, Creamer, Blue 44.00
Swag With Brackets, Toothpick, Amethyst 45.00
Swan, Jam Jar, Cover 110.00
Swan, Mug, Blue 45.00
Sweetheart, Table Set, Child's, 4 Piece 65.00
Swirl, Bowl, 7 1/2 In. 35.00
Swirl, Bowl, 8 1/2 In. 20.00
Swirl, Cake Stand 35.00
Swirl, Creamer 30.00
Swirl, Custard Cup 52.00
Swirl, Dresser Tray, Fan Shape 30.00
Swirl, Goblet .... 20.00 To 40.00
Swirl, Plate, 8 In. 20.00
Swirl, Plate, 10 In. 20.00
Swirl, Salt, Amber 20.00
Swirl, Salt, Blue 20.00
Swirl, Sugar, Cover 35.00
Swirl, Tumbler 20.00
Tacoma, Celery, Ruby Stained 35.00
Tacoma, Table Set, Ruby Stained, 4 Piece 365.00
Tandem Bicycle, Celery Vase 45.00

Pressed glass, Shell   Pressed glass, Square   Pressed glass, Thistle   Pressed glass,
& Tassel   Fushsia   Wedding Ring

Pressed glass, Three
Face   Pressed glass, Tree of Life   Pressed glass, Westward Ho

Tandem Diamonds & Thumbprint, Goblet	15.00
Tape Measure pattern is listed here as Shields	
Tappan, Sugar, Cover, Child's, Aqua	25.00
Tarentum's Atlanta, Saltshaker, Ruby Stained	65.00
Teardrop & Tassel, Butter, Cover	65.00
Teardrop & Tassel, Pitcher, Water	65.00
Teardrop & Tassel, Pitcher, Water, Blue	85.00
Teardrop & Tassel, Water Set, Blue, 7 Piece	495.00
Teasel, Spooner	25.00
Tennessee, Celery Vase	27.00
Tennessee, Toothpick	90.00
Tepee, Creamer	8.00
Tepee, Sauce	5.00
Texas Bull's–Eye pattern is listed here as Bull's–Eye Variant	
Texas, Celery	75.00
Texas, Compote, Jelly	110.00
Texas, Cruet, Stopper	90.00
Texas, Goblet	110.00
Texas, Relish, 8 1/2 In.	12.00
Texas, Sauce, Footed, 4 1/2 In.	35.00
Texas, Toothpick	32.00
The States, Butter, Cover	65.00
The States, Celery, Oval	20.00
The States, Compote, Pedestal, 7 In.	35.00
The States, Creamer	23.00
The States, Creamer, Individual	20.00
The States, Dish, Jelly	27.00
The States, Salt & Pepper	40.00
The States, Sugar	23.00 To 25.00
The States, Toothpick, Flat	45.00
The States, Tumbler, Green	55.00

Theodore Roosevelt, Bread Plate, Teddy Bear Edge, 10 In. 195.00
Thistle, Creamer 110.00
Thousand Eye, Bread Plate, Amber, 10 In. 32.50
Thousand Eye, Compote, Amber .... 35.00 To 38.00
Thousand Eye, Compote, Green 50.00
Thousand Eye, Cruet 25.00
Thousand Eye, Goblet, Blue 50.00
Thousand Eye, Spooner, 3–Knob Stem, Amber 52.00
Thousand Eye, Toothpick, Amber 18.00
Thousand Eye, Tray, Water, Amber 65.00
Threaded, Sugar Shaker 135.00
Three Face, Butter, Cover, Etched 195.00
Three Face, Compote, 6 1/2 x 4 1/2 In. 100.00
Three Face, Creamer, Face Under Spout 30.00
Three Face, Goblet, Etched 150.00
Three Face, Lamp, Oil, Frosted Stem, Clear Font 55.00
Three Face, Sauce, Footed, 4 In. 25.00
Three Face, Sugar .... 125.00 To 140.00
Three Face, Sugar Shaker 165.00
Three Face, Toothpick 45.00
Three Panel, Berry Bowl, Master, Amber .... 25.00 To 35.00
Three Panel, Creamer, Blue 40.00
Three Panel, Spooner, Green 45.00
Three Presidents, Bread Plate, Frosted 70.00
Three Sisters pattern is listed here as Three Face
Thumbprint & Hobnail, Salt, Cover, Footed 95.00
Thumbprint, Bowl, Scalloped Rim, Flint, 9 3/4 In. 40.00
Thumbprint, Compote, Cover, Flint, 7 1/4 x 11 In., Pair 350.00
Thumbprint, Decanter, Flint, 10 3/4 In. 105.00
Thumbprint, Vase, Flint, 10 1/4 In. 115.00
Tokyo, Toothpick, Blue 30.00
Toltec, Toothpick 45.00
Toltec, Tumbler 25.00
Tong, Celery, Flint 95.00
Torpedo, Berry Bowl, 9 1/4 In. 33.00
Torpedo, Bowl, 8 In. 32.50
Torpedo, Celery 40.00
Torpedo, Cruet 45.00
Torpedo, Cup & Saucer 65.00
Torpedo, Pitcher, Milk 50.00
Torpedo, Pitcher, Milk, Ruby Stained 110.00
Torpedo, Salt & Pepper 95.00
Torpedo, Syrup 60.00
Torpedo, Wine 90.00
Tree Of Life With Hand, Butter, Cover ....75.00 To 110.00
Tree Of Life, Cruet, Jug Shape 95.00
Tree Of Life, Ice Cream Set, Tray & 6 Leaf–Shape Sauces 100.00
Tree Of Life, Table Set, Silver–Plated Holder, 3 Piece 180.00
Tree Of Life, Toothpick, Green 48.00
Tree Of Life, Tumbler, Lemonade 135.00
Triple Triangle, Mug, Ruby Stained 25.00
Triple Triangle, Sugar, Cover, Ruby Stained 75.00
Trophy, Toothpick 35.00
Tulip & Honeycomb, Creamer, Child's 20.00
Tulip & Honeycomb, Punch Cup, Child's 8.00
Tulip & Honeycomb, Punch Set, Child's, 5 Piece 65.00
Tulip & Honeycomb, Spooner, Child's 20.00
Tulip & Honeycomb, Sugar & Creamer, Child's 22.00
Tulip & Honeycomb, Table Set, Child's, 4 Piece 120.00
Tulip Petals, Pitcher, Rose Flashed, Gold Trim 95.00
Tulip With Sawtooth, Compote, Tulip Rim, Flint, 9 1/8 In. 135.00
Tulip With Sawtooth, Salt, Master 35.00
Tulip With Sawtooth, Sugar, Cover, Flint 35.00

Tulip With Sawtooth, Wine	20.00
Twist, Butter, Cover, Child's	25.00
Two Band, Butter, Cover	45.00
Two Band, Table Set, Child's, 4 Piece	185.00
Two Camels, Goblet	85.00
Two Panel, Creamer, Green	35.00 To 45.00
U.S. Coin, Berry Bowl, Half Dollars, 8 In.	320.00
U.S. Coin, Cake Stand, Dollars	425.00
U.S. Coin, Compote, Cover, Quarters & Dollars, 7 In.	495.00
U.S. Coin, Relish, Quarters & Half Dollars, 7 1/2 In.	110.00
U.S. Coin, Sauce, Flat, Quarters	120.00
U.S. Coin, Sugar, Cover, Half Dollars	450.00
U.S. Peacock, Vase, 12 In.	37.50
U.S. Peacock, Wine	18.50
Valencia Waffle, Butter, Cover, Green	60.00
Valencia Waffle, Goblet, Amber	35.00
Venetian, Butter, Cover, Cranberry	88.00
Venetian, Creamer, Cranberry	70.00
Venetian, Saltshaker, Cranberry	45.00
Vermont, Creamer, Green, Gold Trim	55.00
Vermont, Spooner, Green, Gold Trim	75.00
Vermont, Toothpick, Amber	35.00
Victor, Butter, Cover, Gold Trim	62.50
Victor, Cake Stand, Green	60.00
Victor, Plate, Green, 7 1/4 In.	27.50
Victor, Table Set, Ruby Stained, 3 Piece	265.00
Victor, Toothpick	14.00
Viking, Bowl, Cover, 8 In.	95.00
Viking, Butter, Cover	75.00
Viking, Celery	40.00 To 45.00
Viking, Compote, Cover, 9 In.	120.00
Viking, Creamer	25.00 To 50.00
Viking, Eggcup	65.00
Viking, Salt, Master	42.50
Viking, Sugar, Cover	50.00 To 75.00
Vine & Beads, Table Set, Child's, 4 Piece	300.00
Waffle & Thumbprint, Decanter, Flint, 1 Pt.	100.00
Waffle & Thumbprint, Sugar, Cover, Flint	195.00
Waffle, Celery, Flint, Pair	150.00
Waffle, Creamer, Applied Handle, Flint	95.00
Waffle, Plate, Flint, 6 In.	45.00
Waffle, Salt, Master, Flint	53.00
Waffle, Sugar, Cover, Flint	125.00 To 162.00
Waffle, Tumbler, Flint	13.00
Washboard, Sugar, Cover	25.00
Washington Centennial, Bread Plate	75.00
Washington Centennial, Cake Stand	75.00
Washington Centennial, Goblet	60.00
Washington Centennial, Salt, Master	60.00
Washington Centennial, Sugar, Cover	70.00
Washington Centennial, Wine, Blue	42.00
Way's Currant, Goblet	20.00
Wedding Bells, Spooner, Pink Stained	27.50
Wedding Bells, Toothpick	40.00
Wedding Ring, Spooner	30.00
Wedding Ring, Spooner, Flint	65.00
Wedding Ring, Syrup	165.00
Wedding Ring, Wine, Flint	95.00
Wee Branches, Creamer, Child's	80.00
Wee Branches, Mug, Child's, 2 In.	30.00
Wee Branches, Spooner, Child's	80.00
Wee Branches, Sugar, Cover, Child's	80.00
Westward Ho, Bread Plate, William H. Harrison, 8 In.	195.00

Westward Ho, Celery Vase 110.00
Westward Ho, Compote, Cover, High Pedestal, 6 In. 325.00
Westward Ho, Compote, Cover, High Pedestal, 7 In. 395.00
Westward Ho, Compote, Cover, High Pedestal, 9 In. 325.00
Westward Ho, Compote, Open, Low Pedestal, 5 In. 95.00
Westward Ho, Compote, Open, Oval 225.00
Westward Ho, Creamer ....95.00 To 145.00
Westward Ho, Goblet .... 50.00 To 85.00
Westward Ho, Jam Jar .... 195.00 To 295.00
Westward Ho, Pitcher 395.00
Westward Ho, Spooner .... 85.00 To 100.00
Westward Ho, Sugar, Cover 235.00
Wheat & Barley, Bread Plate, Amber 30.00
Wheat & Barley, Compote, Jelly, Blue 40.00
Wheat & Barley, Goblet, Amber .... 30.00 To 45.00
Wheat & Barley, Goblet, Blue .... 25.00 To 75.00
Wheat & Barley, Mug, Pressed Handle 45.00
Wheat & Barley, Salt & Pepper 35.00
Wheat & Barley, Sugar, Cover 30.00
Wheat Sheaf, Berry Bowl, Master, Child's 45.00
Wheat Sheaf, Berry Set, Child's, 6 Piece 50.00
Wheat Sheaf, Berry Set, Child's, 7 Piece .... 80.00 To 85.00
Wheat Sheaf, Goblet 25.00
Wheat Sheaf, Punch Set, Child's, 7 Piece .... 70.00 To 75.00
Wheel & Comma, Pitcher, Water 32.00
Wheeling Block, Toothpick 65.00
Whirligig pattern is listed here as Buzz Star
Wild Bouquet, Berry Bowl, Blue, 8 In. 145.00
Wild Bouquet, Table Set, 4 Piece 275.00
Wild Rose With Bowknot, Pitcher 95.00
Wild Rose With Bowknot, Pitcher, Frosted, Gold Trim 50.00
Wild Rose With Bowknot, Sugar & Creamer, Frosted 125.00
Wild Rose With Bowknot, Toothpick 125.00
Wild Rose With Bowknot, Tumbler 35.00
Wild Rose, Punch Set, Child's, Green, 5 Piece 200.00
Wildflower, Bowl, Amber, Square, 8 In. 22.50
Wildflower, Celery, Blue 75.00
Wildflower, Pitcher, Amber 70.00
Wildflower, Syrup, Green 150.00
Willow Oak, Cake Plate, 11 In. 22.00
Willow Oak, Cake Plate, Blue, 11 In. 48.00
Willow Oak, Cake Stand .... 30.00 To 35.00
Willow Oak, Compote, Cover, 6 In. 75.00
Willow Oak, Compote, Open, High Pedestal 55.00
Willow Oak, Creamer, Amber 50.00
Willow Oak, Goblet 35.00
Willow Oak, Goblet, Amber 45.00
Willow Oak, Goblet, Blue 55.00
Willow Oak, Pitcher, Amber 85.00
Willow Oak, Spooner 30.00
Willow Oak, Spooner, Amber 45.00
Willow Oak, Table Set, Amber, 4 Piece 350.00
Windflower, Goblet 75.00
Windflower, Spooner 18.00
Windmill, Mug, Child's 40.00
Wisconsin, Cup & Saucer 55.00
Wisconsin, Vase, 6 In. 58.00
Wooden Pail pattern is listed here as Oaken Bucket
Worcester, Goblet, Flared 55.00
Wreathed Cherry, Creamer, Blue 65.00
Wyoming, Cake Stand, 9 In. .... 50.00 To 58.00
Wyoming, Creamer, Cover 58.00
Wyoming, Pitcher 125.00

X-Ray, Berry Bowl, Master, Sawtooth Rim, Green 68.00
X-Ray, Berry Set, Green, Gold Trim, 7 Piece 110.00
X-Ray, Butter, Cover, Amethyst, Gold Trim 165.00
X-Ray, Butter, Cover, Green 95.00
X-Ray, Butter, Cover, Green, Gold Trim .... 75.00 To 90.00
X-Ray, Celery Vase, Green 50.00
X-Ray, Compote, Green, 6 1/4 x 5 In. 110.00
X-Ray, Creamer, Green, Gold Trim .... 40.00 To 50.00
X-Ray, Cruet, Green, Gold Trim 90.00
X-Ray, Spooner, Green, Gold Trim 45.00
X-Ray, Table Set, Green, Gold Trim, 4 Piece 195.00
X-Ray, Toothpick, Green, Gold Trim .... 45.00 To 65.00
X-Ray, Tumbler, Green, Gold Trim 30.00
Yale pattern is listed here as Crowfoot
Yoked Loop, Tumbler, Whiskey, Handle, Flint 80.00
Zanesville, Cruet, Frosted, Enameled Floral 125.00
Zig-Zag, Goblet 28.00
Zipper Slash, Butter, Cover, Etched, Amber Stained 67.50
Zipper Slash, Goblet, Clear Leaf, Amber Stained 75.00
Zipper Slash, Wine, Ruby Stained 37.50
Zipper, Salt, Polished Base 12.00

PRINT, in this listing, means any of many printed images produced on paper by one of the more common methods, such as lithography. The prints listed here are of interest primarily to the antiques collector, not the fine arts collector. Many of these prints were originally part of books. Other prints will be found in the Advertising, Currier & Ives, and Poster sections.

Armstrong, Beautiful Lady 40.00
Armstrong, Bride, 1923, 7 x 23 In. 75.00
Armstrong, Forever Yours, 1945, 16 x 16 In. 60.00
Armstrong, June, Full-Figure Nudes, Framed, 1923, 20 x 28 In. 225.00

Audubon bird prints were originally issued as part of books printed from 1826 to 1854. They were issued in two sizes, 26 1/2 inches by 39 1/2 inches and 11 inches by 7 inches. The quadrupeds were issued in 28-by-22-inch prints. Later editions of the Audubon books were done in many sizes, and reprints of the books in the original size were also made. The bird pictures have become so popular they have been copied in myriad sizes by both old and new printing methods. This list includes originals and later copies because Audubon prints of all ages are sold in antiques shops.

J.W.Audubon

Audubon, Blue-Winged Teal, 1836, 14 5/8 x 20 3/8 In. 5225.00
Audubon, Carolina Pigeon, 1831, 38 3/4 x 26 In. 4675.00
Audubon, Carolina Turtledove, 1833, 25 7/8 x 20 5/8 In. 9350.00
Audubon, Cuvier's Regulus, 1836, 19 1/2 x 11 7/8 In. 715.00
Audubon, Long-Tailed Duck, 1836, 21 1/8 x 30 3/8 In. 1320.00
Audubon, Mockingbird, 1837, 33 1/8 x 23 5/8 In. 3850.00
Audubon, Pigeon Hawk, 1836, 25 3/4 x 20 1/2 In. 1320.00
Audubon, Red-Throated Diver, 20 1/2 x 27 1/2 In. 275.00
Audubon, Scaup Duck, 12 1/2 x 19 1/2 In. 264.00
Audubon, Wood Ibis, 1834, 34 1/2 x 23 7/8 In. 6600.00
Church, Heart Of Andes, c.1880, 13 5/8 x 25 In. 660.00
Comic Woman, Pantaloons, Standing, Ridiculed By Townsfolk, Germany 90.00
Curran, The Water Gate, Columbian Expo, 1894, 11 3/4 x 16 In. 15.00
Curtis, Camellia, London, 1790, 9 x 5 1/4 In. 227.50
Curtis, Crocus, London, 1795, 9 x 5 3/8 In. 167.50
Curtis, Cyclamen, London, 1790, 9 x 5 1/4 In. 147.50
Curtis, Morning Glory, London, 1790, 9 x 5 1/4 In. 187.50
D. F. Smith, Brooklyn, N.Y., 1853, 23 7/8 x 40 3/4 In. 2750.00
Deering, Indian Maiden, From Calendar Top, Framed, 22 1/4 x 16 In. 100.00
Edwards, Calla Lily, London, 1805, 9 x 5 1/4 In. 187.50
Edwards, Narcissus, London, 1806, 8 7/8 x 5 3/8 In. 227.50
Edwards, Tulip, London, 1805, 9 1/8 x 5 5/8 In. 387.50

Fischer, Here's Happiness To You, Bride, Original Frame, 14 x 19 In. 75.00
Fox, Atkinson, Mountain Scene, Framed 40.00
Fox, Blue Lake, Framed, 15 x 21 In. 45.00
Fox, Garden Of Contentment, 9 x 18 In. 55.00
Fox, Garden Path, Framed, 10 x 14 In. 37.50
Fox, Hunter's Paradise 95.00
Fox, Poplar Trees, 10 x 16 In. 85.00
Fox, Sailing Scene, Framed, 16 x 18 In. 45.00
Fox, Stately Sentinels, 18 x 30 In. 55.00
George Edwards, Engraving, Bird, AD 1758, Framed, 18 x 15 In., Pair 250.00
Gerhard Miller, Abandoned Boat, Matted, Framed 125.00
Gould & Richter, Oldemia Fusca, Birds, Framed, 20 3/4 x 26 1/4 In. 150.00
Gould, Hummingbirds, Framed, Large 75.00
Gutmann, A Little Bit Of Heaven, Framed 35.00
Gutmann, Baby, Reclining Nude, Contentment, Metal Frame 22.00
Gutmann, Friendly Enemies, 11 x 14 In. 50.00
Gutmann, Hearing 95.00
Gutmann, Homebuilders 110.00
Gutmann, In Port Of Dreams, 11 x 14 In. 75.00
Gutmann, Message Of Roses, 11 x 14 In. 175.00
Gutmann, On Dreamland's Border, Framed, 13 3/4 In. 85.00
Gutmann, Seeing, Black & White, No. 211, 11 x 14 In. 50.00
Gutmann, To Love & Cherish 150.00
Guttmann, The Butterfly 115.00
Harrison Fisher, Girl With Duelists, Walnut Frame, Pair 58.00
Havell, Panoramic View Of New York, 1840, 11 7/8 x 35 1/4 In. 9350.00
Humphrey, Little Folks Wide Awake 125.00
I. T. Bowans, Black Hawk, Saukie Brave, Colored 300.00
Icart, Bird Of Prey, Framed, 18 3/4 x 13 1/8 In. 1870.00
Icart, Bubbles, 1930, 12 x 17 In. 9680.00
Icart, Chestnut Vendor, 1928, 18 7/8 x 14 In. 1100.00
Icart, Cigarette Memories 3410.00
Icart, Cinderella, Framed, 1927, 15 1/2 x 19 3/8 In. 1870.00
Icart, Coursing II, Drypoint & Etching, 16 x 25 3/4 In. .... 2090.00 To 3300.00
Icart, Coursing II, Framed, 1929, 16 x 25 3/4 In. 5500.00
Icart, Don Juan, Framed, Dated 1928, 16 x 24 In. 1600.00
Icart, Dressing, 1926, 14 x 18 In. 1100.00
Icart, Ecstasy, 1935, Blindstamped, Framed 4065.00
Icart, Faust, Blindstamped 1108.00
Icart, Fishbowl, 1925, 17 x 11 In. 1650.00
Icart, Gatsby, Drypoint & Etching, Colored, Oval, 1929 .... 3132.00
Icart, Girl & Puppy, Blue Parrot, Oval, Framed, 1928, 9 x 11 In. 900.00
Icart, Human Grenade, Drypoint & Etching, Colored, 1917 .... 2937.00
Icart, Japanese Garden 495.00
Icart, Kiss Of The Motherland, Framed, c.1917, 19 1/2 x 11 3/4 In. 2200.00
Icart, Lacquered Screen, 1922, Blindstamped 2772.00
Icart, Lady Of The Camellias, Signed, 17 x 21 In. 2200.00
Icart, Lemon Tree 1870.00
Icart, Lilies, Drypoint & Etching, Colored, 1934 .... 5874.00
Icart, Love's Blossom, Signed, 1937, 17 1/2 x 25 1/2 In. 5170.00
Icart, Madame Butterfly, Signed, 1927 .... 1250.00
Icart, Meditation, 1928, 11 x 16 In. 2750.00
Icart, Memories, 1931, 15 x 18 In. 2200.00
Icart, Minuet, Drypoint & Etching, Colored, 1929 .... 2741.00
Icart, Orchids, Drypoint & Etching, Colored, 1937 .... 7832.00
Icart, Petits Papillons, Framed, 1926, 14 1/2 x 18 3/4 In. 1925.00
Icart, Pink Lady, 1935, Blindstamped 1848.00
Icart, Puppets, Drypoint 2500.00
Icart, Puppies, 1925, 16 x 20 In. 1980.00
Icart, Sleeping Beauty, Framed, 1927, 15 1/2 x 19 1/4 In. .... 2200.00 To 2750.00
Icart, Speed, 1927, 14 x 24 In. 4620.00
Icart, Sweet Pickings, Drypoint & Etching, Colored, 1930 .... 1958.00
Icart, The Poem, 1928, 18 x 22 In. 2200.00

Print, Japanese, Yoshitora, Balloons, Triptych, Dated 1867

◆◆◆◆◆◆◆◆◆◆◆◆◆◆◆◆◆◆◆◆◆◆

The best place to store paintings is in a closet with no exterior walls. The temperature and humidity levels will be the best in your house.

◆◆◆◆◆◆◆◆◆◆◆◆◆◆◆◆◆◆◆◆◆◆

Print, Locomotive, Lawrence's Machine Shop, 1853, Large Folio

Icart, The Swing, 1928, 18 x 13 In.	6600.00
Icart, Tosca, 1928, 20 x 13 In.	2090.00
Icart, Vitesse, Maiden, 3 Dogs, Drypoint & Etching, Colored, 1927	7832.00
Icart, Waltz Echoes, 1938, Blindstamped	3880.00
Icart, Wisteria, Drypoint & Etching, Colored, 1940	5482.00
Icart, Woman In Bonnet, Framed	2000.00
Icart, Wounded Dove	2500.00

Japanese woodblock prints are listed as follows: Print, Japanese, name of artist, title or description, type, and size. Dealers use the following terms: Tate–e is a vertical composition. Yoko–e is a horizontal composition. The words Aiban (13 by 9 inches), Chuban (10 by 7 1/2 inches), Hosoban (12 by 6 inches), Oban (15 by 10 inches), and Koban (7 by 4 inches) denote size. Modern versions of some of these prints have been made.

Japanese, Bunro, Man & Woman Holding 2 Falcons, c.1805	660.00
Japanese, Comic Scene, Diptych, 2 Figures, Framed, 21 x 26 In.	375.00
Japanese, Eisen, Courtesans Along Tokaido, c.1845, 14 3/4 x 10 In.	250.00
Japanese, Gakutei, Figures In Boat, Diptych, Framed, c.1775, 13 3/4 In.	200.00
Japanese, Hasui, River Scene, Framed	220.00
Japanese, Hiroshige, Iraqi Shrine Oji, 1857	605.00
Japanese, Hiroshige, Landscape & Coastal Scene, c.1860	220.00
Japanese, Hiroshige, Landscape, Campers, Mt. Kiwana By Moonlight	44.00
Japanese, Hiroshige, Maple Trees At Mama, 1857, 14 x 9 1/2 In.	5500.00
Japanese, Hiroshige, Rainstorm, 1855, 14 1/8 x 9 1/2 In.	6000.00
Japanese, Hokusai, 100 Poems Told By Nurse, 1839, 9 1/2 x 13 3/4 In.	8000.00
Japanese, Hokusai, Snow On Sumida River, 1832, 9 1/2 x 14 1/4 In.	8000.00
Japanese, Kawase Hasui, Palace Surrounded By Moat	275.00
Japanese, Kiyoshi Saito, Jacko–In–Kyoto, 20 1/2 x 14 3/4 In.	1320.00
Japanese, Kiyoshi Saito, Profile Of Woman, Colored, Signed	465.00
Japanese, Kiyoshi Saito, Rain, Paris, Signed, Dated 1962	1625.00
Japanese, Kiyoshi Saito, Shinsen–Do–Kyoto, 20 1/2 x 14 1/2 In.	1210.00
Japanese, Kiyoshi Saito, Woman With Firewood, Colored, Signed	660.00
Japanese, Koson, Raven, c.1910, 17 1/4 x 10 1/2 In.	600.00
Japanese, Koson, Sparrows, c.1910, 17 1/4 x 10 1/2 In.	225.00
Japanese, Kunisata, Woman In Butterfly Costume, 12 1/4 x 8 1/2 In.	110.00
Japanese, Royal Progression, Triptych, Framed, 16 1/2 x 31 In.	250.00
Japanese, Shiro, Lights At Dusk, c.1950, 10 7/8 x 16 In.	150.00
Japanese, Tokuriki, Hibiscus, 1980, 11 3/4 x 10 3/4 In.	150.00
Japanese, Toyokuni, Woman Making Up Before Mirror, c.1856, 14 x 9 In.	165.00
Japanese, Yedo Meisho, Woman Reading, Curly Maple Framed, 19 1/2 In.	305.00
Japanese, Yoshitora, Balloons, Triptych, Dated 1867 ....*Illus*	1760.00

Japanese, Yoshitoshi, Moon Of Shinobugaoka, 1889, 14 x 9 1/2 In. 1500.00
Japanese, Yoshitoshi, Moonlight On Ruin, 1886, 14 1/4 x 9 3/4 In. 1500.00
Japanese, Yoshitoshi, Sadanobu Threatening Demon, 1889, 1889 .... 2400.00
Kow, Madame Bastandsury, Framed, 16 x 12 In. 850.00
Kurz & Allison, Battle Between Monitor & Merrimac, Large Folio 350.00
Kurz & Allison, Battle Five Forks, Virginia, Large Folio 195.00
Kurz & Allison, Battle Of Atlanta, Gen. McPherson Killed, Large Folio 290.00
Kurz & Allison, Battle Of Bull Run, Large Folio 385.00
Kurz & Allison, Battle Of Cedar Creek, Large Folio 265.00
Kurz & Allison, Battle Of Champion Hills, Large Folio 240.00
Kurz & Allison, Battle Of Chancellorsville, Large Folio 265.00
Kurz & Allison, Battle Of Chattanooga, Large Folio 265.00
Kurz & Allison, Battle Of Chickamauga, Large Folio 195.00
Kurz & Allison, Battle Of Franklin, Tenn., Large Folio 265.00
Kurz & Allison, Battle Of Kenesaw Mountain, Large Folio 265.00
Kurz & Allison, Battle Of Williamsburg, Virginia, Large Folio 265.00
Locomotive, Lawrence's Machine Shop, 1853, Large Folio ....*Illus* 2035.00
McKenny & Hall, Ca Ta He Cassee, Black Hoof, Shawnee 198.00
McKenny & Hall, Jackopa, Chippewa 325.00
McKenny & Hall, Little Crown, Sioux 170.00
McKenny & Hall, Major Ridge, Cherokee 198.00
McKenny & Hall, Meeta Koesega, Pure Tobacco, Chippewa 180.00
McKenny & Hall, Pashepaha, The Stabber, Sioux 190.00
McKenny & Hall, Red Jacket, Seneca 495.00
McKenny & Hall, Selecta, Creek Chief 315.00
McKenny & Hall, Timpoochee Barnard, Uchii 315.00
McKenny & Hall, Tshusick, Ojibwa Squaw 325.00
McKenny & Hall, Wa Kaun Ha Ka, Winnebago 325.00
McKenny & Hall, Wanata The Charger, Sioux 695.00

Nutting prints are now popular with collectors. Wallace Nutting is known
for his pictures, furniture, and books. Nutting *prints* are actually hand
colored photographs issued from 1900 to 1941. There are over 10,000
different titles.

Nutting, A Bit Of Sewing, Lady Sewing, Fireplate, 10 x 12 In. 110.00
Nutting, A Breezy Call, 1910 .... 175.00
Nutting, A Peep At The Hills 100.00
Nutting, A Sip Of Tea, 10 3/4 x 13 3/4 In. 165.00
Nutting, A Warm Spring Day 185.00
Nutting, All In A Garden Fair 100.00
Nutting, Birch Brook, 1916, 13 x 7 In. 75.00
Nutting, Birch Trees 25.00
Nutting, Coming Of Rosa 80.00
Nutting, Decked As A Bridge 210.00
Nutting, Disappearing Walk 70.00
Nutting, Fair Weather Today 115.00
Nutting, Fairways 60.00
Nutting, Farm Scene With Rail Fence 45.00
Nutting, Grace 85.00
Nutting, Honeymoon Stroll 22.00
Nutting, Hope Of The Year 65.00
Nutting, Indoor Bedroom Scene, Woman, Fireplace, 7 3/4 x 5 3/4 In. 85.00
Nutting, Larkspur, 10 x 7 1/2 In. ....85.00 To 155.00
Nutting, Last Leaves, 13 x 16 In. 100.00
Nutting, Life Of The Golden Age, Sheep Scene 275.00
Nutting, On The Slope, Sheep 245.00
Nutting, Pastoral Brook 130.00
Nutting, River Scene 60.00
Nutting, Roadside Beauty 50.00
Nutting, Sheep 100.00
Nutting, Spring In The Dell 75.00
Nutting, Stone Fence In Field 65.00
Nutting, Story Of Chivalry 120.00

Nutting, Stream	55.00
Nutting, Sunset	100.00
Nutting, Swimming Pool	180.00
Nutting, Sylvan Dell	30.00
Nutting, Tea At Webb House, 16 x 11 In.	248.00

Parrish prints are wanted by collectors. Maxfield Frederick Parrish was an illustrator who lived from 1870 to 1966. He is best known as a designer of magazine covers, posters, calendars, and advertisements.

Maxfield Parrish

Parrish, Cadmus	175.00
Parrish, Canyon, 20 x 26 1/2 In.	45.00
Parrish, Contentment	175.00
Parrish, Daybreak, 10 1/2 x 18 In.	45.00
Parrish, Daybreak, 18 x 30 In.	95.00
Parrish, Daybreak, Framed, 1935, 23 1/2 x 19 In.	335.00
Parrish, Dinky Bird	165.00
Parrish, Dreaming Of October, 1928, Small	200.00
Parrish, Dreaming, 18 x 30 In.	700.00
Parrish, Dreamlight, 17 3/4 x 28 In.	65.00
Parrish, Ecstasy, 17 3/4 x 24 3/4 In.	75.00
Parrish, Enchantment, 20 x 25 1/2 In.	45.00
Parrish, Garden Of Allah, 9 x 18 In.	45.00
Parrish, Hilltop, Framed, 12 x 20 In. .... 300.00 To	315.00
Parrish, Lute Player, Medium	300.00
Parrish, Old King Cole, 6 1/2 x 25 In. .... 695.00 To	725.00
Parrish, Pierrot's Serenade, Collier's Magazine, 1908, 10 3/4 x 16 In	45.00
Parrish, Royal Gorge, 16 1/2 x 20 In.	350.00
Parrish, Rubaiyat .... 300.00 To	390.00
Parrish, Sea Nymphs	150.00
Parrish, Stars, Large	800.00
Parrish, Stars, Small	450.00
Parrish, Wild Geese, 20 1/2 x 28 In.	45.00
Paul DeLongpre, Pansies, Signed, Framed, 1896, 13 1/2 x 17 1/2 In.	125.00
Paul DeLongpre, Rose	30.00
Prang & Mayer, Bird's–Eye View Of Harvard, 18 5/8 x 25 3/4 In.	1320.00
Prang & Mayer, New Bedford, Mass., 1858, 16 1/8 x 32 1/4 In.	2475.00
Prang, Battle Of Antietam, Large Folio	75.00
Prang, Battle Of Kenesaw Mountain, Large Folio	75.00
Prang, Battle Of Manila, Large Folio	125.00
Prang, Battle Of Port Hudson, Large Folio	150.00
Prang, Sheridan's Final Charge At Winchester, Large Folio	150.00
Resting Setters, Etching, Signed Leon Danchin, 1938	110.00
Reynard, Happyland, 9 x 12 In.	30.00
Roberts, Karnac, London, Matted, Color, 1848	825.00
Sarony & Major, Jersey City, Staten Island, c.1850, 12 1/2 x 38 In.	4675.00
Smith, Goldilocks, Framed, 1912	17.00
Sowerby, Rose, Matted, 1787, 18 x 15 In.	387.50
Tait, A Chance For Both Barrels, Hunter Fires At 2 Birds	1695.00
Yard Long, 3 Little Girls, With Song Sheets	100.00
Yard Long, Baby Chicks	75.00
Yard Long, Children	225.00
Yard Long, Lavender & Light Purple Pansies, New Frame	50.00
Yard Long, Playful Puppies	20.00

PURSES have been recognizable since the eighteenth century, when leather and needlework purses were preferred. Beaded purses became popular in the nineteenth century, went out of style, but are again in use. Mesh purses date from the 1880s and are still being made. How to carry a handkerchief and lipstick is a problem today for every woman, including the Queen of England.

Alligator, Alligator Head & Body, Shoulder Strap, Cuba	60.00
Alligator, Envelope, Brown, Leather Lining, Adjustable Strap, 13 In.	58.00
Alligator, Red, Cuba	40.00

Alligator, Shoulder Strap	20.00
Alumesh, Whiting & Davis	40.00
Beaded, Art Deco, Blue Milk Glass, Enameled Frame, France	175.00
Beaded, Black Velvet	15.00
Beaded, Black Velvet, Horse Hair, Chenille Tassels, Drawstring	185.00
Beaded, Black, Multicolored Flowers	125.00
Beaded, Blue & Gold Silver Steel, France	75.00
Beaded, Blue Milk Glass Beads, Art Deco, France	175.00
Beaded, Blue Steel, Drawstring, Tassels	55.00
Beaded, Blue, Tortoiseshell Top & Chain, 1921	75.00
Beaded, Change, Metal Cherub Top, 1920s	45.00
Beaded, Cherub Frame, Chain Handle	75.00
Beaded, Coin, Multicolored Mushroom Design	20.00
Beaded, Enameled Frame, Blue Milk Glass Beads, Art Deco	175.00
Beaded, Flowers, White Ground, Crocheted Drawstring Closure	125.00
Beaded, Foldover, Persian Carpet	225.00
Beaded, Green, Stylized Floral Design	38.00
Beaded, Jet, Art Deco	55.00
Beaded, Multicolored Vase Of Flowers, Chain Handle, 8 1/2 x 7 In.	65.00
Beaded, Red	12.50
Beaded, Red, Butterfly Shape, Red Lining, Filigree Closure, 3 x 8 In.	225.00
Beaded, Scenic	350.00
Beaded, Steel, Bakelite Handle	65.00
Billfold, Silver Mesh, Whiting & Davis	45.00
Black Cloth, Marcasite Frame	30.00
Brass & Copper, Blue Velvet Liner	28.00
Brocade, Art Deco, Engraved Gold–Filled Frame	75.00
Brocade, Rhinestone Closure	20.00
Carnival Beaded Design, Flap, Clutch, Brown Satin, 5 x 10 In.	48.00
Carnival Beads, Over Brown Cloth, Late 1800s	150.00
Chatelaine, Victorian, Silver Plate	125.00
Coin, Wool Flame Stitch, Initials P. M., 1771, 5 3/4 x 8 In.	1760.00
Crocodile, Black, England	225.00
Crocodile, Brown, England	225.00
Faille, Black, 1950s	15.00
Gilt Embossed Pockets, Jacob Townsend, Oyster Bay, 1743, Leather	660.00
Goat Leather, Mottled Yellow Catalin Clasp	35.00
Gold Mesh, Whiting & Davis, Coin, 2 1/2 In.	20.00
Leather, Art Nouveau, Hand Tooled, Meeker	70.00
Leather, Art Nouveau, Reedcraft	25.00
Leather, Fitted, Perfume Bottle, Fan, Opera Glasses, Comb, Mirror, 6 In.	250.00
Leather, Foxy Grandpa, Child's	35.00
Leather, Green, Josef	250.00
Leather, Italy, 1950s	28.00
Lucite, Box, Art Deco	35.00
Lucite, Clutch, Clear, Rhinestones	20.00
Lucite, Lunch–Pail Style, White, 1950s	22.00
Marcasite, Frame	35.00
Mesh, 18K Gold, Cartier, 1920s	3000.00
Mesh, Black, Silver, Zig–Zag Enamel, Fringe, Whiting & Davis, 6 In.	250.00
Mesh, Chatelaine, Floral Chased Frame, Silver Beads, Chain Handle	210.00
Mesh, Compact Top	175.00
Mesh, Dolphins, Sterling Silver	135.00
Mesh, Enamel, Mandalian	75.00
Mesh, Enamel, Openwork Frame, Cobalt Stone In Clasp, Mandalian	115.00
Mesh, German Silver	78.00
Mesh, Gold, Double Blue Sapphire Closure, Whiting & Davis	98.50
Mesh, Gold, Made In United States	2100.00
Mesh, Gold, Rhinestones, Germany	25.00
Mesh, Jeweled, 14K Gold Mesh Strap, Inside Mirror, 14K Yellow Gold	440.00
Mesh, Pewter, Enamel Design At Bottom, Whiting & Davis	95.00
Mesh, Roses, Enameled, Whiting & Davis	75.00
Mesh, Silk Screened, Whiting & Davis	75.00

Mesh, Silver, Fringe, Germany, 4 x 5 1/2 In.	60.00
Mesh, Whiting & Davis, 2 1/2 x 4 In.	50.00
Mesh, Whiting & Davis, 7 x 12 In.	120.00
Nantucket, Ivory Whale On Wood, Swing Handle, 7 1/2 In.	715.00
Nantucket, Outline Of Island, J. Formoso Reyes, 4 1/2 In.	671.00
Needlepoint, Austrian	25.00
Needlepoint, Flame Stitch, N. Richard Of Roxbury, Satin Lining, 1769	4400.00
Patent Leather, Blue, Chrome Frame, Box Shape	15.00
Plastic Tortoiseshell, Box	22.50
Plastic, Flat Clear Ends, Striped Amber, Charles S. Kahn, 7 3/4 In.	95.00
Plastic, Geometric Shape, Gold Lame	30.00
Plastic, Gold Metal Basket Bottom, Lucite Top, Dorset & Rex	50.00
Plastic, Pointed Ends, Rattlesnake Skin Color, Roban, 3 1/2 x 9 In.	125.00
Plastic, Rounded Ends, Gold Glitter On Black, Patricia Of Miami	125.00
Plastic, Suitcase Style, Gold Glitter, Made In Miami, 5 x 7 In.	95.00
Silk, Beaded Fringe, Drawstring	18.00
Silver Metal Discs, Tortoiseshell Handles, Whiting & Davis, 12 In.	95.00
Snakeskin, Brass Trim, Snake Strap, 1940s	95.00
Snakeskin, Clutch, Hard Case, 9 x 4 1/2 In.	50.00
Snakeskin, Green, Envelope Style, Handle, 6 x 9 In.	45.00
Sterling Silver, Diamond & Sapphire Chips, Small	265.00
Straw, Bag, Occupied Japan	7.00
Tapestry, Hungary	40.00
Velvet, Blue, Cosmetics, Compact, & Cigarette Section	25.00
Vinyl, Dodgers, Souvenir Of 1959	27.00
Wooden, Musical Score On Front	12.50

QUEZAL glass was made from 1901 to 1920 by Martin Bach, Sr., in Brooklyn, New York. Other glassware by other firms, such as Loetz, Steuben, and Tiffany, resembles this gold–colored iridescent glass. After Martin Bach's death in 1920, his son continued the manufacture of a similar glass under the name *Lustre Art Glass.*

Quezal

Bowl, Iridescent Gold Interior & Exterior, 3 Layers, 9 x 6 In.	950.00
Lamp, 2–Light, Floriform, Shades, Signed	950.00
Lamp, Desk, Amber Shade, Gooseneck Standard, 12 3/4 In.	550.00
Lamp, Hanging, 5 Floriform Shades, Feather Pattern, Signed, Pair	2750.00
Nut Cup, Gold Iridescent, 4 x 2 1/2 In.	85.00
Salt, Ribbed, Gold Iridescent, Signed	195.00
Shade, Gold Zipper Pattern, Signed, 3 Piece	450.00
Shade, Gold, Feather Pattern	100.00
Shade, Green Cased Over White, Damascene, Signed, c.1915, 12 1/4 In.	1870.00
Shade, Inverted Onion Form, Feather Pattern, c.1915, 8 1/4 In.	770.00
Shade, On Gooseneck Desk Lamp, Green, 5 1/2 In.	495.00
Shade, Pulled Feather, Calcite & Gold, Signed	185.00
Shade, White Feathers, Gold Glass, Signed, Pair	350.00
Vase, Blue Iridescent, 7 In.	495.00
Vase, Bud, Trilobite Rim, Feathering, Signed, 1905–1920, 5 3/4 In.	880.00
Vase, Emerald Green, Baluster Shape, Flared Rim, Signed, 6 1/2 In.	750.00
Vase, Floriform, Green & Gold Feathering, Signed, c.1920, 6 In.	770.00
Vase, Jack–In–The–Pulpit, 10 3/4 In.	950.00
Vase, Jack–In–The–Pulpit, Rows Of Hearts Under Rim, 9 1/4 In.	2750.00
Vase, Swirling King Tut–Type Design, Signed, 7 In.	770.00
Vase, Trefoil Rim, Gold Iridescent, Domed Foot, Signed, 5 In.	400.00

QUILTS have been made since the seventeenth century. Early textiles were very precious and every scrap was saved to be reused. A quilt is a combination of fabrics joined to a filler and a backing by small stitched designs known as quilting. An appliqued quilt has pieces stitched to the top of a large piece of background fabric. A patchwork, or pieced, quilt is made of many small pieces stitched together. Embroidery can be added to either type.

Amish, Patchwork, Bar, Diamond & Cable Quilting, 72 x 72 In.	825.00
Amish, Patchwork, Nine Patch Variant, Faded Blue Shades, 71 x 82 In.	500.00

Amish, Patchwork, Pastel Pink, Blue & Green, Child's, 45 x 61 In.	275.00
Amish, Patchwork, Stars & Foliage, Scroll Border, 74 x 87 In.	550.00
Amish, Patchwork, Sunshine & Shade, Cotton & Rayon, 80 x 86 In.	253.00
Amish, Patchwork, Tulips, Floral, Black, Zigzag Border, 70 x 70 In.	435.00
Appliqued, 30 Blocks, G. Washington, Shields, 1910, 76 x 86 In.	935.00
Appliqued, 9 Stylized Floral Medallions, Initial E. H., 92 x 92 In.	975.00
Appliqued, Album, Cities, Ann Coppock, 1846, 94 x 105 In.	400.00
Appliqued, Album, Signed Squares, Wedding Gift, 1847, 88 x 90 In.	350.00
Appliqued, Arrowheads, Squares, Red, White, Blue, c.1890, Cotton, Double	295.00
Appliqued, Broken Pinwheel, Orange Sash, Blues, Red, 72 x 86 In.	295.00
Appliqued, Broken Star, 1930, Blue, Red, Yellow, Green, Blue, 76 x 80 In.	350.00
Appliqued, Butterfly, Yellow On White, 1930s, 70 x 88 In.	150.00
Appliqued, Cactus Basket, Yellow, Blue, Pink, White, 1935, 64 x 82 In.	250.00
Appliqued, Calico, 12 Stylized Floral Medallions, 55 x 77 In.	425.00
Appliqued, Calico, 16 Stylized Tulip Medallions, 83 x 83 In.	600.00
Appliqued, Calico, 18 Stylized Stars & Suns, 72 x 82 In.	155.00
Appliqued, Carolina Lily, Green Calico, Solid Goldenrod, 78 x 78 In.	395.00
Appliqued, Carolina Lily, Yellow & Green Calico, 72 x 79 In.	275.00
Appliqued, Center Flower Medallion, Mary Swartz, 1853, 80 x 78 In.	5500.00
Appliqued, Chintz, Shells, Birds, Floral & Insects, 122 x 109 In.	770.00
Appliqued, Dogwood, Yellow, Pink, Leaves, Pink Ribbon, 80 x 92 In.	395.00
Appliqued, Double Irish Chain, Green & Beige, 1900, Full Size	325.00
Appliqued, Double Wedding Ring, White Ground, 1930s, 80 x 82 In.	225.00
Appliqued, Dutch Doll, Turquoise Sashing, 52 x 72 In.	125.00
Appliqued, Embroidered Silk, L. A. S., 1885, 72 x 73 In.	770.00
Appliqued, Floral Medallions, Vining Border, 73 x 78 In.	225.00
Appliqued, Floral, Concentrically Ringed Oval, 79 x 84 In.	7975.00
Appliqued, Floral, Goldenrod On White Ground, 75 x 82 1/2 In.	975.00
Appliqued, Flower Garden, Prints, White Ground, 1930, 72 x 84 In.	250.00
Appliqued, Flower Garden, White Ground, Green, Red, 1930s, 70 x 72 In.	150.00
Appliqued, Friendship Chat, Maine, 19th Century, 72 x 96 In.	270.00
Appliqued, Friendship, 72 x 82 In.	200.00
Appliqued, Grandma's Flower Garden, 1930, Pink, White, 70 x 80 In.	300.00
Appliqued, Green Flowerpots, Ear Handles, Calico, 92 x 92 In.	3575.00
Appliqued, London Steps, Wine, Cobalt Blue, Black, Red, 1880, 74 x 88 In	350.00
Appliqued, Lone Star, Red, Blue, Yellow, Diamonds, 1936, 78 x 82 In.	250.00
Appliqued, Maple Leaf Medallions, Solid Border, 78 x 78 In.	500.00
Appliqued, Mariner's Compasses, Scalloped Border, 82 x 82 In.	600.00
Appliqued, Mill Wheel, Purple, Gingham, Calico, 1910, 76 x 86 In.	195.00
Appliqued, New York Beauty Pattern, c.1870, 84 x 74 In.	605.00
Appliqued, Pansies, Scalloped Edge, 100 x 62 In.	357.50
Appliqued, Pennsylvania Volunteers No. 62, c.1865, 88 x 92 In.	3300.00
Appliqued, Poinsettia, Gold Silk Embroidery, 76 x 80 In.	990.00
Appliqued, Pomegranate, Pomegranate & Vine At Corners, 76 x 76 In.	1430.00
Appliqued, Poppy, Tan, Peach, Brown, Green Leaves, 78 x 82 In.	250.00
Appliqued, President's Wreath, Floral Wreath Feathers, 100 x 100 In.	1045.00
Appliqued, Red & Green Calico Floral, Vine Border, 83 x 80 In.	550.00
Appliqued, Red & White Variation, 19th Century, 92 x 92 In.	1540.00
Appliqued, Stylized Floral Medallions, Green, Red Calico, 80 x 80 In.	400.00
Appliqued, Stylized Floral Medallions, Medallion Center, 84 x 84 In.	1050.00
Appliqued, Stylized Tulip Medallions, Prints, Solids, 66 x 80 In.	325.00
Appliqued, Stylized Tulip Medallions, Red, Goldenrod, Ecru, 64 x 79 In	275.00
Appliqued, Sunbonnet Babies, Chintz Print Lining, 74 x 85 In.	95.00
Appliqued, Sunflower, Anne Bradley, Findlay, Ohio, c.1930, 82 x 72 In.	358.00
Appliqued, Trees With Red Berries, Birds, Leaves, 81 1/2 x 98 In.	1300.00
Appliqued, Tulip, 94 x 74 In.	137.00
Appliqued, Tulip, Meandering Border, Adelphia, Oh., 76 x 89 In.	400.00
Appliqued, Tulip, Stem, 2 Leaves, Yellow Tulips, Blue, 1930, 68 In.	250.00
Appliqued, Turkey Track, Multicolored Print, White, 1930, 80 x 82 In.	225.00
Appliqued, Wild Rose, Teal, Green, Pencil Pattern, 90 x 90 In.	600.00
Appliqued, Windmill Blade, Reds, Blues, Peach Sash, 1930s, 70 x 76 In.	295.00
Central Wreath Medallion, White-On-White, 102 x 105 In.	2200.00
Crazy, Patchwork, Pink, Green, Blue, Yellow, Triangular, 82 x 84 In.	275.00

Crazy, Patchwork, Silk On Velvet, 64 x 76 In. 905.00
Crazy, Patchwork, Silk Ties, 1940s, 70 x 70 In. 95.00
Crazy, Patchwork, Silk, Velvet Patches, Baseball Players, 68 x 74 In. 770.00
Crazy, Patchwork, Tobacco Silks, Velvet Patches, 68 x 74 In. 770.00
Hawaiian Pattern, Anne Bradley, Findlay, Ohio, c.1910, 76 x 72 In. 770.00
Patchwork & Trapunto, Carolina Lily, c.1850, 83 x 95 In. 1100.00
Patchwork, 16 Pots Of Flowers, Green Calico & Red, 74 x 74 In. 350.00
Patchwork, 4 Spinning Wheels, Oak–Leaf Center, 90 x 96 In. 4100.00
Patchwork, 4–Leaf Clover, Greens, Mustard Border, 1800s, 72 x 82 In. ·............... 275.00
Patchwork, 4–Point Star Flowers, Prints & Checks, 70 x 80 In. 225.00
Patchwork, 9 Navy & Salmon Medallions, White Ground, 80 x 82 In. 495.00
Patchwork, 9 Stars, Red, Green & Goldenrod, White Ground, 81 x 81 In. 650.00
Patchwork, Alternating Bars Of Yellow, Blue, Squares, 69 x 83 In. 400.00
Patchwork, Animals, Birds, Dragons, Eliza Crane Smith, 1884 .... 825.00
Patchwork, Basket, Diamond & Circle Quilting, 1880s, Square, 84 In. 176.00
Patchwork, Baskets, Multicolored Prints, White, Navy, 80 x 88 In. 300.00
Patchwork, Bear's Paw, 100 x 105 In. 350.00
Patchwork, Bear's Paw, Blue & Ecru Calico, 70 x 78 In. 350.00
Patchwork, Bow Tie, Multicolored, 68 x 50 In. 68.00
Patchwork, Bow Tie, Wine, Blue, 1900, 64 x 82 In. 325.00
Patchwork, Cactus Baskets, Pink & Green Calico, 70 x 78 In. 125.00
Patchwork, Calico, 2 Shades Pink, 2 Shades Green, 74 x 78 In. 90.00
Patchwork, Carpenter's Wheel, Cube Field, 1800s, 85 1/2 x 85 In. 1650.00
Patchwork, Carpenter's Wheel, Yellow, Pink, 68 x 78 In. 300.00
Patchwork, Christmas Cactus, Red & White, Wreaths, 90 x 88 In. 2200.00
Patchwork, Circle, Blue & White, 70 x 80 In. 450.00
Patchwork, Cornered Nine Patch, Pink Ground, Blues, 1930s, 66 x 72 In. 100.00
Patchwork, Daisy Wheels, Outlined In Black, Calico, 60 x 72 In. 60.00
Patchwork, Delectable Mountain, White Field, 1850s, 100 x 108 In. 2200.00
Patchwork, Double H, Blue, Wine, Brown Print Sashing, 1880, 68 x 70 In. 275.00
Patchwork, Double Wedding, 1930s, 72 x 84 In. 900.00
Patchwork, Drunkard's Path, Aqua, 90 x 100 In. 350.00
Patchwork, Drunkard's Path, Blue Polkadot Print & White, 72 x 82 In. 550.00
Patchwork, Drunkard's Path, Blue, Brown, Mustard Yellow, 86 x 96 In. 175.00
Patchwork, Drunkard's Path, Red & Green Calico, 73 x 87 In. 150.00
Patchwork, Drunkard's Path, Red & White, 79 x 69 In. 500.00
Patchwork, Drunkard's Path, Red, White, 66 x 82 In. 145.00
Patchwork, Feathered Star, White Field, 1860s, 79 3/4 x 82 1/2 In. 3300.00
Patchwork, Floral Medallions, Orange & Green Calico, 86 x 86 In. 80.00
Patchwork, Flower Garden, 70 x 76 In. 325.00
Patchwork, Flower Garden, Multicolored Prints, 1930, 72 x 84 In. 425.00
Patchwork, Flower Garden, Multicolored Prints, 78 x 78 In. 200.00
Patchwork, Four Patch, Blue, 74 x 82 In. 200.00
Patchwork, Four Patch, Floral & Printed Calico, 100 x 112 In. 1320.00
Patchwork, Grandmother's Fan, 75 x 88 In. 200.00
Patchwork, Grandmother's Flower Garden, Scalloped, 1920s, 74 x 76 In. 385.00
Patchwork, Irish Chain Variant, Multicolored Prints, 79 x 80 In. 90.00
Patchwork, Irish Chain, Blue On Mustard–Gold Ground, 91 x 91 In. 300.00
Patchwork, Irish Chain, Blue Print, White Ground, 81 x 81 In. 450.00
Patchwork, Irish Chain, Navy & Pink Calico, 88 x 93 In. 500.00
Patchwork, Irish Chain, Red, Green Calico, Feather Border, 87 x 88 In. 250.00
Patchwork, Irish Chain, Solid Red, Green, Calico, 87 x 88 In. 250.00
Patchwork, Log Cabin Multicolored Medallions, 74 x 88 In. 2400.00
Patchwork, Log Cabin, 75 x 53 In. 93.00
Patchwork, Log Cabin, Blue, 100 x 103 In. 350.00
Patchwork, Log Cabin, Blue, Brown, Red Center Squares, 66 x 78 In. 175.00
Patchwork, Log Cabin, Calico Patches, 88 x 80 In. 330.00
Patchwork, Log Cabin, Multicolored Prints, 80 x 80 In. 350.00
Patchwork, Lone Star, 72 x 78 In. 200.00
Patchwork, Lone Star, Golden, Olive, Red Ground, Striped, 77 x 83 In. 220.00
Patchwork, Lone Star, Yellow, Gold & Tangerine, 78 x 78 In. 180.00
Patchwork, Maple Leaf, 78 x 94 In. ....200.00 To 250.00
Patchwork, Mariner's Compass Medallions, 96 x 108 In. 1250.00

Patchwork, Marriage, Ellen Child, 1847, 92 x 78 In. 125.00
Patchwork, Merry Kite, Blue Ground, 1930s, 80 x 82 In. 325.00
Patchwork, Mexican Rose, Running Shell Quilting, 80 x 86 In. 385.00
Patchwork, Monkey Wrench, Beige Floral, Homespun Back, 69 x 75 In. 125.00
Patchwork, Navy Blue, White, Border Stripe, 73 x 85 In. 600.00
Patchwork, Nine Patch Variant, Pastel, Crib, 24 x 26 1/2 In. 150.00
Patchwork, Nine Patch, Doll's, c.1900, 14 x 14 In. 65.00
Patchwork, Nine Patch, Multicolored Print, 67 x 86 In. 375.00
Patchwork, Nine Patch, Multicolored Prints, White Ground, 66 x 82 In. 125.00
Patchwork, Nine Patch, Wool, Earthy Colors, 60 x 80 In. 125.00
Patchwork, Paper Dolls, Polkadot Patches, White Cotton, 100 x 80 In. 1980.00
Patchwork, Pilot's Wheel, Blue, Cone & Triangle Border, 72 x 84 In. 325.00
Patchwork, Pinwheel Star, 1930s, 72 x 84 In. 900.00
Patchwork, Plantation, 60 x 70 In. 550.00
Patchwork, Postage Stamp, Solid Calico Patches, 1875, 79 x 79 In. 4400.00
Patchwork, Red Floral Roller, Printed Border, 81 x 90 1/4 In. 330.00
Patchwork, Red, White, Compass Stars, White Stars, 83 x 83 In. 650.00
Patchwork, Rob Peter To Pay Paul, Pink & White, Twin Size 295.00
Patchwork, Rocky Road To Kansas, Lavender, Yellow, 1930s, 60 x 74 In. 100.00
Patchwork, Sailboat, Polka Dot Patches, JMD, 1880s, 67 x 80 In. 2475.00
Patchwork, Schoolhouse, Filled Doorknobs, Red & White, 64 x 85 In. 6050.00
Patchwork, Star Of Bethlehem, Cotton, Crib, 41 x 40 In. 330.00
Patchwork, Star Of Bethlehem, Feather & Diamond, 102 x 102 In. 880.00
Patchwork, Star, Pink & White Calico, 28 1/2 x 31 1/2 In. 375.00
Patchwork, Star, Red, White Cotton Patches, 84 x 90 In. 385.00
Patchwork, Star, Yellow, White, 1930, 68 x 84 In. 300.00
Patchwork, Stars, Horizontal & Vertical Bands, 1860, 78 x 87 In. 1760.00
Patchwork, Stepping Stones, 95 x 105 In. 350.00
Patchwork, Sugar Loaf, Mustard Print Ground, Blue Border, 68 x 80 In. 295.00
Patchwork, Sunbonnet Girl, Embroidered, 73 x 48 In. 78.00
Patchwork, Sunshine & Shadow, Multicolored Prints, 76 x 76 In. 240.00
Patchwork, Trapunto Baskets, Edge Stripes, 86 x 100 In. 500.00
Patchwork, Tree Of Paradise, 68 x 86 In. 850.00
Patchwork, Triple Irish Chain, Reds, Blacks, 1940s, 88 x 96 In. 200.00
Patchwork, Turkey Track, Red, Green, White, 76 x 78 In. 300.00
Patchwork, Turkey Track, Wine, Black, Blue, White, 1880, 70 x 86 In. 495.00

QUIMPER pottery has a long history. Tin-glazed, hand-painted pottery
has been made in Quimper, France, since the late seventeenth century. The
earliest firm, founded in 1685 by Jean Baptiste Bousquet, was known as
HB Quimper. Another firm, founded in 1772 by Francois Eloury, was
known as Porquier. The third firm, founded by Guillaume Dumaine in
1778, was known as HR or Henriot Quimper. All three firms made similar
pottery decorated with designs of Breton peasants and sea and flower
motifs. The Eloury (Porquier) and Dumaine (Henriot) firms merged in
1913. Bousquet (HB) merged with the others in 1968. The group was sold
to a United States family in 1984. The American holding company is
Quimper Faience Inc., located in Stonington, Connecticut. The French firm
has been called Societe Nouvelle des Faienceries de Quimper HB Henriot
since March 1984.

HR.
Quimper

Bowl, Peasant Figures, Blue Sponge Bands, 5 3/4 In. 55.00
Bowl, Peasant Figures, Blue Sponge Bands, 6 1/4 In. 60.00
Bowl, Peasant Figures, Blue Sponge Bands, 7 1/4 x 5 3/4 In. 70.00
Butter, Cover, Shell Shape, Small 235.00
Candlestick, Woman's Figure, Flowers, Marked, 5 1/2 In. 230.00
Charger, Geometric Design 165.00
Cup & Saucer, Art Deco 48.00
Dish, Basket, Peasant Design, Signed, 4 x 3 In. 95.00
Dish, Sweetmeat, Woman Peasant, Trefoil Shape, Green Handle, 6 In. 250.00
Eggcup, Pedestal, Attached Saucer 175.00
Figurine, Peasant Woman With Wheat, Signed, 8 In. 140.00
Font, Peasant Kneeling Before Cross, 9 1/2 In. 225.00
Inkstand, Double Wells, 6 1/4 x 13 1/2 In. 795.00

Match Holder, Wall, Marked	220.00
Pitcher, Breton Man	445.00
Pitcher, Female Peasant, Signed, 5 1/2 In.	275.00
Pitcher, Male Peasant, Yellow, Signed, 5 1/2 In.	175.00
Pitcher, Peasants, 1890	195.00
Plate, 6 In.	28.00
Plate, Breton Figures	95.00
Salt, Dutch Shoe, Signed, Pair	45.00
Syrup, Starflower, Blue & White, Marked	175.00
Teapot, Signed	185.00
Vase, Breton Peasants, Bulbous	195.00

RADFORD pottery was made by Alfred Radford in Broadway, Virginia, Tiffin and Zanesville, Ohio, and Clarksburg, West Virginia, from 1891 until 1912. Jasperware, Ruko, Thera, Radura, and Velvety Art Ware were made. The jasperware resembles the famous Wedgwood ware of the same name.

RADURA.

Vase, Eagle, Classical Figures, 17 In.	285.00
Vase, Radura, 4 Elephant Trunk Buttresses, 11 In.	350.00

RADIO broadcast receiving sets were first sold in New York City in 1910. They were used to pick up the experimental broadcasts of the day. The first commercial radios were made by Westinghouse Company for listeners of the experimental shows on KDKA Pittsburgh in 1920. Collectors today are interested in all early radios, especially those made of Bakelite plastic or decorated with blue mirrors.

7–Up, Earphones Look Like Bottle Caps, Unused	45.00
Airline, 1925	185.00
Antique Scale Shape, Japan, 1960s, Box	75.00
Arvin, Green Plastic	27.00
Atlas Car Battery	40.00
Atwater Kent, 32 Volts, Antenna, Grained	75.00
Atwater Kent, Breadboard, Type TA, Model 10	1050.00
Atwater Kent, Lift Top, Floor Model	130.00
Atwater Kent, Model 55–60, Instruction Book	45.00
Atwater Kent, Type F, Model 4330	700.00
Avon Skin–So–Soft	38.00
Beer Can, 12 In.	45.00
Beetle, Figural, Atlas Battery	10.00
Bendix, Catalin	475.00
Bendix, Model 115, Green & Black	850.00
Car, Pontiac, 1930s	45.00
Catalin, Addison Model 5, Red & Yellow	1000.00
Champion Spark Plug, AM	85.00
Cinnamon Toast Crunch Cereal, 3–Ring Notebook Shape, Cover Controls	20.00
Colonial Globe	1400.00
Coors, Figural, Beer Can	25.00
Crosley, Model 10–138, Maroon	50.00
Crosley, Model 54	250.00
Crosley, Model 100 U, White	265.00
Crosley, Model 628B, Brown Plastic	25.00
Crystal Set, Howe	110.00
DeForest, Interpanel	2500.00
Dr Pepper, Cooler, Wooden	975.00 To 1075.00
Dumont, Chinese Lacquer, Novelty	250.00
Dumont, Model RA346, Red & Gold	175.00
Echophone	255.00
Emerson, Aristocrat, Brown Swirled	650.00
Emerson, Catalin	600.00
Emerson, Figural, Violin, Wooden, 1930s	110.00
Emerson, Model 510, Wooden Cabinet, Black Catalin Front	65.00
Emerson, Model 520, Brown & Tan Swirled Catalin Bakelite	495.00
Emerson, Model 520, Brown Swirled Catalin, White Front	150.00

Emerson, Model AX–235, Black & Orange 3000.00
Emerson, Model AX–235, Black & Yellow .... 385.00 To 450.00
Emerson, Red & Cream 190.00
Fada, Blue Moon, Model 1000, 1946 .... 3850.00
Fada, Bullet, Green 850.00
Fada, Bullet, Model 1000, Green, Lime Green Trim, Marbelized 1300.00
Fada, Bullet, Model 1000, Marbelized Blue Body, Yellow Knobs, Handle 2800.00
Fada, Bullet, Model 1000, Yellow Bakelite 585.00
Fada, Bullet, Model 1000, Yellow Body, Red Knobs, Handle, Bezel 1000.00
Fada, Temple, Blue 2750.00
Fada, Temple, Yellow & Red 750.00
Flintstones, Box, 1972 .... 55.00
General Electric, Floor Model 85.00
General Electric, Green Plastic, 1950 .... 20.00
General Electric, Model 505d 10.00
General Electric, Model GD–520, Marbelized White 395.00
General Electric, Model T23b 10.00
General Electric, Red Plastic, Color Flecks, 5 x 8 In. 49.00
Gold Stripe Canadian Whiskey 40.00
Grand Piano, Tube, Wooden 350.00
Guild, Spice Chest 100.00
Hallicrafter, Model S– 38, Steel Case .... 50.00 To 95.00
Hallicrafter, Model S–120 SW 40.00
Kollerola, Hotel, Table Model, Coin–Operated, Wooden Case 250.00
Kolster, Model 6–D 185.00
Mail Pouch, Package Front, Seal On Top 2800.00
Majestic, Bank 75.00
Majestic, Melody Cruiser, Sailing Ship, Wooden Hull, Chrome Sails 500.00
Microphone Shape .... 125.00 To 145.00
Minerva, Wooden Cabinet 75.00
Monroe, Model D–7, 2 Piece 250.00
Motorola, Catalin, S Grill, Yellow, Green 3150.00
Motorola, Handy Talkie, Red, White & Blue 25.00
Motorola, Pee Wee, Red 325.00
Motorola, Plastic 20.00
Neugrodyne, No Speaker 200.00
New York World's Fair 1750.00
Northern Electric, White Over Bakelite, 6 x 11 In. 90.00
Old Globe 35.00
Owl, Brass Wings 95.00
Pepperidge Farm Stuffing, Unused 45.00
Pet Milk 40.00
Philco, Art Deco Design, Maroon 50.00
Philco, Beehive, c.1930 .... 175.00
Philco, Cathedral, Model R91 .... 30.00
Philco, Model 19 .... 150.00
Philco, Model 70, With Grandfather Clock 350.00
Philco, Model 610, Tombstone, BC & SW 175.00
Philco, Transitone 25.00
Pinocchio, Philgee Int. Works 25.00
Polaroid, Figural, 600 Film 23.00
Punchy, Atlas Battery 10.00
Radio Development & Research Corp., Porcelain Keg, 6 Whiskeys, 6 In. 250.00
Radiocron, Clock Radio 195.00
Radiola II .... 315.00 To 370.00
Raggedy Ann & Andy, Bobbs Merrill, 1973 .... 35.00
Raisin 30.00
RCA, Brown Plastic 35.00
RCA, Oriental, Table Model 120.00
Rogers, Glass Face, Bubble Glass, Red, Yellow, Green, 16 In. 76.00
Schlitz Beer 25.00
Sesame Street 35.00
Sesame Street, Muppets 35.00

Silvertone, Model 132–021, Bakelite	20.00
Silvertone, Wooden Case, Table Model	50.00
Sinclair, Transistor, Box	50.00
Smurf, Wall, 1982	20.00
Snoopy Doghouse	55.00
Snoopy, 1974	30.00
Snow White	2000.00
Sparton, 3 Knobs	3000.00
Sparton, Blue Mirror	600.00
Sparton, Bluebird, Table Model	2250.00
Stroh's Beer	25.00
Stromberg Carlson, Model 1101H	40.00
Sunoco, Transistor, Box	75.00
Sylvania, Thermometer, Tube	225.00
Tom Thumb, Model TT–600	40.00
Tradio, Coin–Operated, Box & Lock, Metal	250.00
Truck, Studebaker, 1948	25.00
Trutone	150.00
Western Electric, 7–A Amp	175.00
Westinghouse, Baby Blue, Portable, 1940s, Small	195.00
Westinghouse, Dual Speaker, Plastic, Dark Red	18.00
Westinghouse, Model H122, Plastic In Wooden Phonograph Cabinet, 1946	100.00
Westinghouse, Model H126, Figural, Refrigerator	95.00 To 165.00
Winston Cigarette	30.00
Zenith, Model 5S237, Chairside	30.00
Zenith, Model 9526A, Clamshell Console, 3 Bands	325.00 To 350.00
Zenith, Model R721, AM–FM, Plastic, Table Model, 1942	10.00
Zenith, Trans–Oceanic, Portable, Black Leatherette Finish	75.00
Zenith, Transistor	30.00
Zenith, Transoceanic	400.00

RAILROAD enthusiasts collect any train memorabilia. Everything is wanted, from oilcans to whole train cars. The Chessie system has a store that sells many reproductions of their old dinnerware and uniforms.

Ashtray, C & O, George Washington, China, Rectangular	100.00 To 125.00
Ashtray, Chesapeake & Ohio, Chessie Cat, 4 In.	50.00
Ashtray, Chessie In Center	65.00
Ashtray, Pullman, Floor Model, 26 In.	125.00
Ashtray, Santa Fe, Turquoise Room, Glass, Aztec Design, Box, 4 In.	15.00
Ashtray, Southern Railway	12.50
Ashtray, Union RR	12.00
Badge, Hat, Engineer's, Southern Pacific	25.00
Bell, From Narrow Gauge Engine, Bronze, Nev. Silver Mines, 13 In.	700.00
Bell, Locomotive, Cast Iron Hanger, 18 In.	1100.00
Bell, Locomotive, With Yoke & Cradle, Bronze, 12–In. Diam.	695.00
Bench, Depot, E. Chicago & Lake Huron RR, Cast Iron Ends, 1870s	500.00
Bottle, Missouri Pacific, Sunnymeade Farm, Clear, Buzz Saw Design	10.00
Bouillon, B & O Centenary	95.00
Box, Conductor's, Penn. RR	200.00
Brochure, Lewis–Clark Centennial Expo., Great Northern RY, 1905	38.00
Butter Pat, Baltimore & Ohio, Centenary	45.00
Button, Old Colony, 5 Piece	75.00
Calendar, Chesapeake & Ohio Lines, 1942, 16 x 24 In.	42.00
Calendar, New York Central, Leslie Ragan, 1940, 16 x 21 In.	300.00
Calendar, Santa Fe RR, E. I. Couse, 1937, 14 x 13 In.	75.00
Can, Kerosene, C & O RR, 2 Gal.	50.00 To 60.00
Can, Kerosene, C & O RY	60.00
Card, Playing, New York, New Haven & Hartford, Wrapper, Box	65.00
Card, Playing, Nickel–Plate Road, Double Deck, Case	20.00
Card, Playing, Union Pacific Railroad, Leather Case	15.00
Cart, Baggage	75.00
Clipboard, ACL	65.00
Cover, Hot Food, Baltimore & Ohio, 6 In.	100.00

Creamer, Southern Pacific	8.00
Cup & Saucer, B & O RR, Blue & White	40.00
Cup & Saucer, B & O, Lamberton, After Dinner	48.00
Cup & Saucer, Chesapeake & Ohio, Gazebo Silhouette, After Dinner	60.00
Cuspidor, Pullman Co., Brass, 8 In.	90.00
Cuspidor, Pullman Co., Nickel Plated, Round, 7 In., 2 Piece	50.00
Dish Towel, Burlington Route, White Cotton, 15 x 25 In.	12.50
Dish Towel, Illinois Central, White Cotton, Safety Is Our Dish	12.50
Dish, Canadian National RR, Square, Small	20.00
Display, Train, Norfolk & Western, Cardboard	10.00
Door Knob, L & N RR, Iron	40.00
Fire Extinguisher, Brass, Bracket, N & W RR	100.00
Footstool, Porter's, Atchison, Topeka & Santa Fe	160.00
Footstool, Porter's, Denver & Rio Grande RR	160.00
Fork, Dining Car, Missouri Pacific Lines, Silver	15.00
Globe, Lantern, LVRR, Clear, Embossed, 5 3/8 In.	75.00
Gravy, New York Central, 1831	23.00
Hammer, Blacksmith's, Wood Handle, C R I & R Railroad	12.00
Handcuffs, B & O	85.00
Hat, Conductor's, Missouri Pacific	85.00
Hat, Trainman, Burlington Route	90.00
Headrest Cover, Illinois Central, Brown Cotton, 15 x 16 In.	15.00
Inkwell, N & W, Glass	75.00
Inkwell, Pennsylvania Railroad, Pair	95.00
Lamp, Cab, Electric	75.00
Lamp, Cab, Oil	75.00
Lamp, Caboose, Armspear, Bell Bottom, L & N RR	185.00
Lamp, Caboose, Brass Base, Pair	175.00
Lamp, Caboose, CNRY	50.00
Lamp, Caboose, Model 23 Spring Loaded, 1940s	195.00
Lamp, Caboose, Wall, Tank Type	100.00
Lamp, Dietz, No. 2, Blizzard	100.00
Lamp, Dietz, Traffic Guard	30.00
Lamp, Econolite, Revolves When Lighted, Image Of John Bull, 1956	195.00
Lamp, Inspector's, CPR	90.00
Lamp, Safety Always, GNRY, Adams & Westlake, 5 3/8 In.	175.00
Lamp, Signal, Safety Always, NPRR, Clear, 5 3/8 In.	200.00
Lamp, Station, B & M, Brass	225.00
Lamp, Switch, Adlake, Pennsylvania Railroad, Small	160.00
Lamp, Wall, Bunk Car, Dressel, Rack & Pot	55.00
Lantern, 3 C's, Cleve., Cincinnati, Chicago, & St. Louis, Clear Globe	37.50
Lantern, Adams & Westlake, Green Globe, GNRY, 5 3/8 In.	200.00
Lantern, Adlake, Cannonball, Pair	100.00
Lantern, Adlake, Kerosene, Ring Base, Clear Cast Globe	55.00
Lantern, B & A RR, Dietz, No. 6, Red Globe	85.00
Lantern, B & M RR, Red Globe, Adlake Rel., 5 3/8 In.	100.00
Lantern, B & O RR, Loco Casey, Red Cast Capital Globe	350.00
Lantern, Buckley, Brass Top, Bell Bottom	100.00
Lantern, C M & S P Railroad, Red Globe	125.00
Lantern, CCC & St. Louis, Kerosene, Kietz-Vesta, USA On Red Globe	68.00
Lantern, Cincinnati, Hamilton & Dayton, Clear Globe, Patent 1895	100.00
Lantern, Clear Globe, Raised Wabash Letters	125.00
Lantern, Conductor's Retirement, Presentation, Brass, 1862	500.00
Lantern, Conductor's, No. 3, Brass, Kerosene, Dietz	285.00
Lantern, Crank Trunk Railway, Armspear, Bell Bottom, Clear Globe	175.00
Lantern, Crossing Gate Signal, 2 Red Bull's-Eyes, 2 Amber	125.00
Lantern, Crossing Gate Signal, Dressel, 2 Green Bull's-Eyes	115.00
Lantern, Dietz, Monarch, Red Globe	55.00
Lantern, Dietz, No. 3, Brass	285.00
Lantern, Dietz, No. 39, Curly Bell Bottom	160.00
Lantern, Dietz, No. 100	65.00
Lantern, Dietz, Vesta, Blue Globe	60.00
Lantern, Grand Rapids & Indiana, Clear Etched Globe	300.00

Lantern, Hand, Pennsylvania Railroad, High Globe	65.00
Lantern, IRY Co., Clear Globe, Adlake Rel., 5 3/8 In.	100.00
Lantern, M & St. L Squat Etched Globe	60.00
Lantern, N & W RY, Adlake, No. 250, Blue Etched Globe	95.00
Lantern, New York Lake Erie & Western, Clear Globe	225.00
Lantern, NPRR, Safety Always, Clear, 5 3/8 In.	150.00
Lantern, NUS & W, Dressel, Short Globe, Clear	100.00
Lantern, NYCRR Marked, Clear Glass Globe	79.00
Lantern, P & R RY, Armspear, Wire Bottom, Clear Globe, 1910	60.00
Lantern, Pullman, Conductor's	680.00
Lantern, Pyle, Cannonball, Pair	100.00
Lantern, Safety Always, NPRR, Clear, 5 3/8 In.	200.00
Lantern, Switch, Kerosene, 1920s	225.00
Lantern, Switchman's, Dietz, Red Globe	35.00
Lantern, USY & TCO, Clear Globe, Adlake Rel., 5 3/8 In.	100.00
Lantern, Wabash, Bell Bottom, Clear Cast Flag Globe	325.00
Lantern, Whale Oil, Boston & Worcester, Fixed Globe	850.00
Lantern, Wheeling & Lake Erie, Kerosene, Dietz–Vesta, Clear Globe	68.00
Lock, BR&P, Steel, Marked Key	55.00
Lock, DRGW, Key, Iron	35.00
Lunch Pail, Atchison, Topeka & Santa Fe, Round, 13 In.	160.00
Map, S. D., Chicago, Milwaukee & St. Paul RY, In Folder, 1906	20.00
Matchbook, Matches Are Figural Black Chefs, Reading RR	45.00
Medal, Table, N & W Railroad, Box, 1852–1952	85.00
Mirror, C & O, Peake, Chessie's Old Man	40.00
Monkey Wrench, C & M Western RR, Iron, 18 In.	30.00
Napkin, Dinner, Soo Line, Interwoven Dollar Line Logo, 18 x 18 In.	15.00
Oil Can, B & O Railroad	45.00
Oil Can, ICRR	10.00
Padlock, B & O Signal, Brass, Steel Shackler, 1 1/2 x 2 1/2 In.	20.00
Padlock, Rock Island Lines Signal, Brass, 2 x 3 1/2 In.	40.00
Padlock, UPRR Signal, Use No Oil, Brass, 1 1/2 x 2 1/2 In.	35.00
Paperweight, Soo Line, 75th Anniversary, Domed Magnifying Glass	47.50
Pass, Southern Railroad, For Colored Employees, 1917	8.00
Pattern, To Make Foundry Molds For Wheels	220.00
Pillow, Headrest, N & W RR	18.00
Pin, Collar, Burlington Route, Enameled Logo, Square, 6/8 In.	20.00
Pin, Missouri Pacific Booster Club, Lapel, Round, 5/8 In.	15.00
Plate, 100th Anniversary, Erie RR, 1951	40.00
Plate, B & O Railroad, Dark Blue Transfer, Wood, 10 1/8 In.	200.00
Plate, Baltimore & Ohio, Centenary, 6 3/4 In.	60.00
Plate, Dinner, Missouri Pacific Railroad, Steam Engine	225.00
Plate, MK & T, Alamo, Buffalo, 10 1/2 In.	550.00
Plate, Pullman, Indian Tree, 4 Sections, 12 1/4 In.	225.00
Plate, Purple Laurel, PRR, 9 3/4 In.	50.00
Plate, Service, C & O G W	850.00
Plate, Sesquicentennial	75.00
Platter, B & O, Capitol, 13 1/2 In.	175.00
Platter, Baltimore & Ohio, Gold Capitol Dome, 11 x 8 In.	75.00
Platter, Maine Central Railroad, China, Small	300.00
Postcard, G. N. Depot, Train Arriving, Picket Photo Co.	55.00
Postcard, GRI & P, Depot, Train Taking On Passengers, Photo	45.00
Postcard, Train Time, GB & O, Station, Riverside, 1912	55.00
Print, Engine, Hudson River, N.Y. Central, Framed	125.00
Ribbon, Illinois Central Logo, Signed Waterloo–Topeka, 1903	22.50
Rule Book, Norfolk & Western, 1941	8.00
Ruler, M & St. L	20.00
Sheet Music, Northern Route March, Burlington & N. RY, 1876	13.00
Sign, Railway, Porcelain, Chinese Writing Warning, England, 1900	2000.00
Sign, Sante Fe RR, Scout, Chicago To Los Angeles, 42 x 20 In.	9350.00
Signal Light, Cab, Brass & Steel	100.00
Spoon, NYC	25.00
Step, Passenger, 1920s	75.00

Stove, Caboose, Lehigh & New England, Hamilton, Ohio, Patent 1905 .... 800.00
Stove, Potbelly, Caboose, Cast I Am Good, Tell Others, 27 In. 200.00
Switch Key, Brass, Tapered Barrel, Marked St. L & S. F. RR 90.00
Switch Light, Adlake RR 35.00
Tablecloth, Burlington Route, White Cotton, Logo, 36 x 36 In. 25.00
Teaspoon, NPRR 25.00
Thermos, Pullman 90.00
Tie Pin, NP & F & CC, Nickel Plate 10.00
Timetable, Baltimore & Ohio, 98 Pages, 1929 .... 12.00
Timetable, Seaboard, Rates & Map, 38 Pages, 1906 .... 12.00
Timetable, Union Pacific RR, 1937, 48 Pages, 8 x 9 In. 16.00
Token, Binghamton Railway 6.00
Torch, Erie, Cast Iron 75.00
Torch, Hanlan, Brass, Steel 75.00
Towel, Hand, Pullman Co., White Cotton, Gold Stripe, 1942 .... 20.00
Tumbler, Ill. Central 1964 Special New Orleans Derby Train, 5 In. 20.00
Tumbler, Juice, C & O 14.00
Tumbler, Water, D & HRR, Etched 45.00
Wall Lamp, Candle, Brass 65.00
Washstand, Pullman, Fold Up, Stainless Steel, Box 275.00
Watch Fob, Rock Island Railroad, 1852–1922, Miss. River Bridge 45.00
Water Bag, Section Gang, D & RGW, Canvas, Rope Handle, 12 x 14 In. 30.00
Wax Sealer, American RY Express, Cottonwood, Minn. 60.00
Wax Sealer, American RY Express, Ruso, N. D. 50.00
Whistle, Baltimore & Ohio, Brass 50.00
Whistle, Luckenheimer, Brass 100.00
Whistle, Powell, Single Chime, 8 1/4 In. 100.00
Whistle, Steam, Buckeye, 3–Chime, Brass, 12 1/2 In. 200.00
Whistle, Steam, Crosby, Single Chime, 7 In. 125.00

RAZORS were used in ancient Egypt and subsequently wherever shaving
was in fashion. The metal razor used in America until about 1870 was
made in Sheffield, England. After 1870, machine–made hollow–ground
razors were made in Germany or America. Plastic or bone handles were
popular. The razor was often sold in a set of seven, one for each day of
the week. The set was often kept by the barber who shaved the well–to–do
man each day in the shop.

Blade, Blue Star, Double Edge, On Display Card, 10 Boxes 22.00
Box, Straight, Salmon Paint, Slide Lid, Tab Handle, 2 1/2 x 7 1/2 In. 175.00
Combined With Comb, Durham Demonstrator, Composition Handle, 1907 .... 18.00
Corn, Pearl Handle, 3 3/4 In. 75.00
Darwin, Safety, Built In Strop, Chrome Container 95.00
Darwin, Safety, With Strop 75.00
Display Box, Gem Jr., 6 Razors, Box, 1947 .... 75.00
Dubl–Duck 18.00
Duplex, Safety 10.00
G. Wostenholm & Son, Sheffield, Inscribed Blade, Celluloid Handle 75.00
G. E. Jones, Shake Sharp, Instructions, Case 100.00
Gem, Micromatic, Bakelite Case 12.00
Gemco Jessop, Red & Black Marbelized Handle, Box 32.00
Geneva Cutlery, Seneca Chief Pictured, Celluloid Handle, Pair 58.00
Gillette, Safety, Brass Case 10.00
Gillette, Sterling Silver, Silver Box 60.00
Hone, Pure Gold, Stone 1.00
Imp, Straight, Red Handle, Case 20.00
Junior Razor Shaving Kit, Keen Kutter, Case 90.00
Keen Kutter, Safety 15.00
Keen Kutter, Safety, Box 25.00
Kriss Kross, With Strop, Box, 1927 .... 65.00
Nude Lady Handle, Straight, Celluloid, Solingen 37.00
Pakistan, Straight 11.00
Robeson's Shuredge, Marbelized Tan & Cream Handle, Box 30.00
Royal Keen Kutter, Box 75.00

Sharpener, Barberiana	20.00
Sharpener, Metal Harp–Shaped Frame, 1 Glass Marble, Early 1900s	10.00
Straight, Engraved S. S. St. Louis	115.00
Straight, Marbelized Brown Celluloid Handle, Eclipse On Blade	55.00
Strop, Box	18.00
Strop, Valet	6.00
Tark, Vibrating	17.50
Union, Bone & Mother–of–Pearl, Straight, Box	55.00
Valet Autostrop, Box	30.00
Vibro Electric Safety, 1930s	40.00
W. R. Case, Marbelized Tan & Brown Handle, Box	28.00
Wade & Burcher, Sheffield, Celebrated Hollow Ground On Blade	45.00
Wm. Elliot, Nymph On Handle, Box	75.00
Woman's, Kewtie, Safety, Pink Celluloid Case	15.00 To 20.00
Wostenholm's Best Hollow Ground, Straight	6.00

REAMERS, or juice squeezers, have been known since 1767, although most of those collected today date from the twentieth century. Figural reamers are among the most prized.

Blue Flowers, Japan, Small, 2 Piece	28.00
Clambroth, Green, Tab Handle, Hocking	100.00
Clown, Pink Hat	85.00
Ertl, Clear	8.00
Fry, Pink	145.00
Green, Loop Handle	12.00
Jeanette, Green, Tab Handle, 5 In.	25.00
Lemon, 1 Piece	35.00
Lemon, Carved Ribs, Turned Handle, Cherry, 5 3/4 In.	130.00
Monkey Face, Japan	95.00
Sunkist, Chalaine, Blue	195.00
Sunkist, Chocolate Glass	150.00
Sunkist, Crown Tuscan	365.00
Sunkist, Embossed Oranges & Lemons	29.00
Sunkist, Green, Depression Glass, Handle & Lip, 4 x 6 x 9 In.	10.00
Sunkist, White	18.00
White, Loop Handle	10.00

RECORDS have changed size and shape through the years. The cylinder–shaped phonograph record for use with the early Edison models was made about 1889. Disc records were first made by 1894, the double–sided disc by 1904. High–fidelity records were first issued in 1944, the first vinyl disc in 1946, the first stereo record in 1946. The 78 RPM became the standard in 1926 but was discontinued in 1957. In 1932, the first 33 1/3 RPM was made but was not sold commercially until 1948. In 1949, the 45 RPM was introduced. Compact discs became available in the U.S. in 1982 and many companies began phasing out the production of phonograph records.

20 Golden Greats, Buddy Holly, RCA	7.00
30 Greatest Hits, Platters, TVP	5.00
Album, Beatrice Lilly, 1 Piece	85.00
At The Astor Roof, Sammy Kaye, Joyce, 1944	7.00
Basin Street Blues, Clyde McCoy, Vogue Picture Records	55.00
Black Beauty, Duke Ellington, Victor No. 21580	25.00
California Blues, Blue Bayou, Roy Orbison, 45 RPM	5.00
Compliments Of Ted Williams, Sears, 45 RPM	25.00
Dangerous, Michael Jackson, 2 Records	20.00
Double Gold, Neil Diamond, 2 Records	12.00
Engelbert Humperdinck, After The Lovin', 45 RPM	3.00
Friends, Elton John, Movie Soundtrack, Paramount Label	8.00
Genius Of Ray Charles, Ray Charles, 1960 Mono	14.00
Girl Come Running, Four Seasons, 45 RPM, Philips	5.00
Greatest Hits, Monkees	15.00
I Love Lucy, With Lyrics, Desi Arnaz, 78 RPM, Early 1950s	40.00
I Say A Little Prayer For You, Aretha Franklin, 45 RPM, ATL	6.00

I'm On Fire, Bruce Springsteen	15.00
If You Could Read My Mind, Gordon Lightfoot, 45 RPM, WL RPO	4.00
Knight Time, Gladys Knights & The Pips, Soul	7.00
Legendary Masters Series, Rick Nelson, 2 Records	10.00
Lionel Hampton, Golden Vibes, Columbia	25.00
Live On Broadway, Lena Horne, Quest, 2 Records	7.00
Lost Horizon, Bacharach Score	8.00
Mancini Presents 31 Academy Award Songs, RCA	18.00
Merry, Merry Christmas, Lennon Sisters, 45 RPM, Brunswick	5.00
Music From Peter Gunn, Mancini, RCA, 1956	12.00
Peggy Lee, Fever, 45 RPM	3.00
Peter, Paul & Mary, Warner Bros.	10.00
Pied Piper, Album, Narrated By Ingrid Bergman, 78 RPM, 1946	150.00
Santa Claus Is Coming To Town, Bruce Springsteen, 45 RPM	15.00
Showboat, The Movie, 45 RPM, Set, Pictured Box	25.00
The Garland Touch, Judy Garland, Capitol	18.00
The Hollies, The Air That I Breathe, 45 RPM	2.50
Together Again, Benny Goodman, Quartet, Bluebird	7.00
Way Down Yonder In New Orleans, Clyde McCoy, Vogue Picture	45.00
Yesterday's Song, Neil Diamond, 45 RPM	3.00

RED WING Pottery of Red Wing, Minnesota, was a firm started in 1878. The company first made utilitarian pottery. In the 1920s art pottery was made. Many dinner sets and vases were made before the company closed in 1967. Rumrill pottery was made for George Rumrill by the Red Wing Pottery and other firms. It was sold in the 1930s. For more information, see *Kovels' Depression Glass & American Dinnerware Price List.*

Ashtray, Fish, Yellow	25.00
Ashtray, Green State, Eisenhower Shape, Small	95.00
Ashtray, Hiawatha Bridge Dedication, Green, 1960	65.00
Ashtray, Minnesota Twins, World Series, 1965	80.00 To 90.00
Bank, Bear, Hamm's	275.00 To 550.00
Bean Pot, Saffron	75.00
Beater Jar, Stanhope, Iowa	87.50
Beater Jar, Titonka, Iowa	95.00
Bottle, Hot Water	265.00
Bowl, Cap, Sponged, Smooth Sides, 7B	85.00
Bowl, Cereal, Hamm	90.00
Bowl, Grape, 10 In.	10.00
Bowl, Gray Line, Advertising, 8 In.	95.00
Bowl, Saffron Ware, Fluted Panel Sides, Rust & Blue, 9 1/2 In.	130.00
Bowl, Salad, Hamm, Large	170.00
Bowl, Spongeware, 5 In.	260.00
Bowl, Spongeware, Manitowoc, Wis., Advertising, 7 In.	85.00
Bowl, Vegetable, Bobwhite	14.00
Bowl, Vegetable, Bobwhite, Divided	20.00
Butter, Cover, Bail, Blue Banded, 3 Lb.	199.00
Butter, Cover, Bail, Blue Banded, 5 Lb.	225.00
Butter, Cover, Gray Line, Advertising, Dated 1935, 5 Lb.	320.00
Butter, Cover, Village Green	18.00
Butter, Stoneware, Minnesota, Low, 1 Lb.	50.00
Candy Dish, Pear	.25
Card, Trade, Red Wing Milling Bixota Flour	6.00
Casserole, Bobwhite, Large	25.00
Casserole, Cover, Gray Line, 8 1/2 In.	400.00
Casserole, Yellow Rose	10.00
Chicken Waterer, Tibodeau's, No Lid, 3 Gal.	175.00
Chop Plate, Yellow Rose	10.00
Churn, Birch Leaf, No Lid, 3 Gal.	15.00
Churn, Cover, Blue Leaf, Flower, 3 Gal.	185.00
Churn, Cover, Double Leaf, 2 Gal.	185.00
Churn, Elephant Ear, Union Stamp, Minnesota S. W., 3 Gal.	550.00
Churn, Salt Glaze, Blue Flowers, 3 Gal.	550.00

Clock, Mammy	195.00
Cookie Jar, Baker, Beige	60.00
Cookie Jar, Baker, Blue	75.00 To 90.00
Cookie Jar, Baker, Green	250.00
Cookie Jar, Baker, Yellow	50.00 To 110.00
Cookie Jar, Bunch Of Bananas, Pink	65.00
Cookie Jar, Bunch Of Grapes	110.00
Cookie Jar, Chef, Tan	45.00 To 55.00
Cookie Jar, Drummer Boy	325.00
Cookie Jar, Dutch Girl	50.00 To 80.00
Cookie Jar, Dutch Girl, Beige	60.00
Cookie Jar, Dutch Girl, Yellow	35.00 To 65.00
Cookie Jar, Dutch People, Gray	65.00
Cookie Jar, Jack Frost	355.00
Cookie Jar, Katrina, Green	90.00
Cookie Jar, King Of Tarts, Blue	325.00 To 330.00
Cookie Jar, Little Red Riding Hood, Closed Basket	300.00
Cookie Jar, Monk, Beige	80.00
Cookie Jar, Monk, Blue	65.00 To 70.00
Cookie Jar, Monk, Yellow	50.00
Cooler, Water, Stand, Bobwhite, 2 Gal.	375.00
Creamer, Lotus	2.00
Crock, 1 Wing, Blue, 10 Gal.	27.50
Crock, Beehive, Birch Leaf, 4 Gal.	325.00
Crock, Blue, P Below	85.00
Crock, Butter, Land O'Lakes, 3 Lb.	150.00
Crock, Large Wing, Blue, Salt Glaze, 1 Gal.	375.00 To 450.00
Crock, Lid & Wire Bail, Stoneware, 6 Gal.	310.00
Crock, No. 3 Union Stoneware Co.	55.00
Crock, Pickling, Blue Leaves, 30 Gal.	88.00
Crock, Salt Glaze, 3 Gal.	65.00
Crock, Salt Glaze, Blue Bands, 6 Gal.	320.00
Crock, Salt Glaze, Butterfly, 20 Gal.	340.00
Crock, Small Wing, Blue, 1 Gal.	325.00
Crock, White Leaves, Stoneware, 2 Gal.	45.00
Cruet Set, Bobwhite, With Stand	220.00
Cup & Saucer, Bobwhite	7.00 To 12.00
Cup, Bobwhite	5.00
Cup, Random Harvest	5.00
Dinner Set, Merrileaf, True China, 50 Piece	125.00
Dish, Chafing, Round–Up	375.00
Feeder, Ko–Rec	100.00
Figurine, Canoe, Large	135.00
Figurine, Dachshund, Green	25.00
Figurine, Pig, Brown, Red Wing	425.00
Funnel, Acid Proof	450.00
Jar, Fruit, Dome Top, Shield,, 1 Qt.	1075.00
Jar, Fruit, Mason, Qt.	180.00
Jar, Pantry, 3 Gal.	650.00
Jar, Preserving, Straight Sides, 1 Qt.	150.00
Jar, Safety Valve, 1/2 Gal.	95.00
Jar, Stone Mason, 1 Gal.	375.00
Jug Set, Beehive, 3, 4 & 5 Gal., 3 Piece	900.00
Jug Set, Excelsior Springs Advertising, 2, 4, 8 & 16 Oz., 4 Piece	425.00
Jug, Beehive, Birch Leaf, 4 Gal.	325.00
Jug, Beehive, Blue Band, Incised 3	225.00
Jug, Beehive, Leaf, 5 Gal.	165.00
Jug, Beehive, Victoria Sanatorium, 5 Gal.	950.00
Jug, Beehive, Wing, 4 Gal.	575.00
Jug, Brown Top, Wing, 1/2 Gal.	145.00
Jug, General Store, 1/2 Pt.	150.00 To 190.00
Jug, Joe Matteuci Liquor, 1 Gal.	195.00
Jug, Minnesota–Michigan	140.00

Jug, Moose, Miniature	375.00
Jug, North Star, Salt Glaze, 1/2 Gal.	220.00
Jug, Overland Rye, Stoneware, 1/2 Gal.	295.00
Jug, Shoulder, Salt Glazed, 4 Gal.	185.00
Jug, Steinmeyer Co., Milwaukee, Wis., Advertising, 1/2 Gal.	110.00
Jug, White, 1/2 Gal.	45.00
Marmalade, Cover, Bobwhite	25.00
Mug, Village Green	4.00
Pitcher & Bowl, Lily	375.00
Pitcher, Batter, Saffron	90.00
Pitcher, Bobwhite, 60 Oz.	35.00
Pitcher, Gray Line, Commemorative, 1989	160.00
Pitcher, Gray Line, Searles, Minn.	200.00
Pitcher, Russian, 1/2 Gal.	135.00
Pitcher, Water, Tampico, Green	50.00
Pitcher, Water, Yellow Rose	30.00
Planter, Art Deco, 2 Women	45.00
Planter, Lion, Brown	75.00
Plate, Bobwhite, 11 1/2 In.	9.00
Plate, Chrysanthemum, 10 1/2 In.	15.00
Plate, Hors D'Oeuvre, Bird Shape	30.00
Plate, Orleans, 10 1/2 In.	8.00
Plate, Random Harvest, 10 1/2 In.	7.00
Plate, Tampico, 11 1/2 In.	8.00
Platter, Smart Set, 20 In.	20.00
Reamer, Grapefruit, Signed	150.00
Reamer, Gray Line	950.00
Rolling Pin, Wildflower, Blue & White	155.00
Salt & Pepper, Bird Shape	25.00
Salt & Pepper, Bobwhite	12.00 To 20.00
Salt & Pepper, Hamm	110.00
Server, Beverage, Bobwhite	65.00
Server, Beverage, Bobwhite, Stopper	85.00
Soup, Cover, Orleans, Individual	13.50
Stand, Christmas Tree, Printed Instructions	365.00
Sugar & Creamer, Yellow Rose	10.00
Sugar, Cover, Orleans	10.00
Sugar, Tampico	7.00
Table Service, Driftwood, 60 Pieces	145.00
Teapot, Bobwhite	37.50
Teapot, Orleans, Cover	37.50
Trivet, Capistrano	30.00
Trivet, Centennial	60.00
Tumbler, Bobwhite	6.00
Tumbler, Brushware, Lady With Harp, 5 In.	75.00
Umbrella Stand, Red & Blue Spongeware	1250.00
Vase, Birch Bark, 8 In.	50.00
Vase, Cactus Design, 2 Handles	22.50
Vase, Figural, Fish, 12 In.	25.00
Vase, High Top Shoe, Black	135.00
Vase, Shallow, Art Pottery	22.50
Wall Pocket, Asymmetrical, Matte Black, 12 In.	85.00
Water Cooler, Bobwhite	325.00
Water Cooler, Cover, Tampico, With Base	340.00
Water Cooler, Success Filter	240.00

REDWARE is a hard, red stoneware that originated in the late 1600s and continues to be made. The term is also used to describe any common clay pottery that is reddish in color.

Bank, Egg Shape	275.00
Bank, Hen & Chicks, Cylindrical, 12 In.	540.00
Bank, Knob Finial, Mottled Glaze, 6 In.	145.00
Bank, Man's Face Form	154.00

Bean Pot, Dark Brown Sponging, Side Spout	250.00
Bean Pot, Glazed, Sponged Brown, Ribbed Strap Handle, Ovoid, 7 In.	250.00
Bottle, Glazed Inside, Dated 1806, 5 In.	225.00
Bottle, William Harrison, 1840	2800.00
Bowl, 2 Eared Handles, Large	595.00
Bowl, Cup Shaped, Ribbed Strap Handle, Dark Amber Glaze, 4 1/4 In.	185.00
Bowl, Domed Cover, Molded Handles, 13 1/2 x 11 1/2 In.	275.00
Bowl, Milk, Bands Of Wavy Lines, Brown & Green Glaze, 13 1/2 In.	1200.00
Bowl, Milk, Brown Daubs In Glazed Interior, 11 1/2 In.	150.00
Bowl, Milk, Green Wavy Line, Yellow Slip Stripes, 11 1/4 In.	400.00
Bowl, Milk, Wavy Lines, Stripes & Bands, 13 1/4 In.	250.00
Bowl, Sieve Holes, Coggled Rim, B. A. 1752, 13 1/2 In.	1250.00
Bowl, Stripes, Wavy Lines & Dots, Rope Twist Handles, 13 1/4 In.	1850.00
Bowl, Yellow Glaze, Vines Incised Brown, Meddinger, Pa.	1450.00
Bread Tray, Trailed Intertwined Lines, Oblong, 14 1/4 In.	2310.00
Bust, Oriental Man, Marked, 9 1/2 In.	110.00
Butter Stamp, 4 Tulips & Ferns, Round, 4 In.	250.00
Candlestick, Brown Glaze, 2 3/4 In.	30.00
Charger, Calligraphic Designs, Reddish–Brown Ground, 15 In.	3575.00
Charger, Coggled Rim, Yellow Slip, 14 1/4 In.	45.00
Charger, Green Polliwogs, 1826, 11 3/4 In.	750.00
Charger, Wavy Lines, Crossed Tulips, 14 In.	300.00
Charger, Yellow Slip, Waves Of Brown, 1790–1800	5500.00
Coffeepot, Tooled Design, Tall Dome Top, England, 11 1/4 In.	350.00
Cradle, Inlaid Slip Design, Tooling, Date 1733, 8 In.	1400.00
Creamer, Side Spout, Ribbed Strap Handle, 4 1/2 In.	35.00
Creamer, Yellow Glaze, Incised P Signature, 6 1/4 In.	275.00
Crock, Bulbous Lip, No. 2, Tooled Lines, Mottled Orange Glaze, Galena	25.00
Crock, No. 3, Tooled Lines, Greenish Orange Glaze, Galena, 12 3/4 In.	65.00
Cup, 3 Holes For Quills, Interior Glaze, 2 3/4 In.	575.00
Cup, Greenish Glaze, Ribbed Strap Handles, 3 5/8 In.	125.00
Dish, 6 Parallel Wavy Lines, 7 3/8 In.	175.00
Dish, Black Patina On Exterior, Interior Orange Color, 2 In.	100.00
Dish, Brown Sponged Glaze, 6 1/4 In.	200.00
Dish, Brown Sponged Glaze, 7 In.	200.00
Dish, Brown Sponged Glaze, Flecks, 7 In.	225.00
Dish, Coggeled Rim, 3 Line Yellow Slip, 7 In.	140.00
Dish, Coggeled Rim, Yellow Slip Free–Form Design, 5 In.	325.00
Dish, Divider, White Slip Design, 10 3/4 x 13 3/4 In.	25.00
Dish, Sgraffito Design, Medinger Potteries, 8 In.	1430.00
Dish, Stylized Leaf Forms, Yellow On Reddish Brown, 4 1/2 In.	2750.00
Dish, White Slip, Sgraffito Pinwheels, Green, Brown Sponging, 8 In.	1300.00
Dish, Yellow Slip Free–Form Design, 4 3/4 In.	215.00
Figurine, Lamb, White Slip, Shenandoah, 12 In.	1350.00
Flask, Brown Albany Glaze, 7 1/2 In.	130.00
Flowerpot, Attached Saucer, Hanging, Applied Stars, Galena, 9 In.	55.00
Flowerpot, Attached Saucer, John Bell, Waynesboro, 6 In.	300.00
Flowerpot, Brown Glaze, W. Smith, Womelsdorf	220.00
Jar, Amber Glaze, Impressed 4, Galena, 12 3/4 In.	45.00
Jar, Brown Splotches, Cover, 8 1/4 In.	155.00
Jar, Brownish Green Glaze, Brown Flecks, Impressed Label, 9 1/2 In.	495.00
Jar, Brushed Tulip, John Bell, Waynesboro, 3 Gal.	900.00
Jar, Canning, Cover, Green, Orange Spots, Galena, 10 In.	110.00
Jar, Canning, Greenish Amber Glaze, Green Spots, Galena	65.00
Jar, Clear Glaze, Straight & Wavy Lines, Brown Swags, Flared, 7 In.	225.00
Jar, Cover, Brown & White Swirled Slip, Tooled Band, 8 1/2 x 6 In.	215.00
Jar, Dark Amber Glaze, Black Splotches, 5 3/8 In.	95.00
Jar, Dark Brown Mottled Glaze, 12 1/2 In.	45.00
Jar, Glazed, 19th Century, 7 1/2 In.	467.50
Jar, Green Glaze, 2 Handles, 1 Gal.	425.00
Jar, Green Splotches, Inscription, Mary Ford, 1812, 12 3/4 In.	3850.00
Jar, Greenish Orange Glaze, Brown Flecks, No. 3, Galena, 12 1/2 In.	30.00
Jar, Greenish Orange Spotted Glaze, 3 1/2 In.	175.00

Jar, Incised Coggle Wheel Design, Eared Handles, 10 In. 1320.00
Jar, Incised, Mandeville Pottery, 9 1/2 In. 7150.00
Jar, Mottled Green Brown Glaze, Wavy Line, Winchester, Va., 7 In. 300.00
Jar, No. 5, Greenish Glaze, Orange Spots, Galena, 12 3/4 x 13 1/2 In. 70.00
Jar, S. H. Sonner, Strasburg, Va., L, Green Glaze, 7 5/8 In. 45.00
Jar, Sloping Shoulders, Brown Sponging, Galena, 8 3/4 In. 85.00
Jar, Tooled Lines At Shoulder, Clear Glaze, Splotches, 9 3/4 In. 200.00
Jar, Tooled Lip, Strap Handle, Green Glaze, Galena, 10 In. 25.00
Jar, Tooled Ribbed Shoulder, Applied Handles, 9 3/8 In. 60.00
Jar, Yellow Slip, Reddish Flecks, 8 1/4 In. 205.00
Jug, Amber Glaze, Spots, Handles Glued, 7 In. 75.00
Jug, Brown Flecks Of Running Glaze, Strap Handle, 6 5/8 In. 150.00
Jug, Bulbous Top, Strap Handle, Orange Spots, Galena, 10 1/4 In. 50.00
Jug, Coggle Wheel Design At Neck, Slip Design, 4 1/2 In. 1430.00
Jug, Dark Brown Glaze, 6 In. 35.00
Jug, Dark Mottled Glaze, Strap Handle, 11 3/8 In. 525.00
Jug, Green Glaze, 11 3/4 In. 95.00
Jug, Green Glaze, Red Highlights, Strap Handle, Tooled Lines, 7 In. 75.00
Jug, Helmet Type Cover With Handle, Man's Face, Yellow Slip 6500.00
Jug, Mottled Glaze Over Colored Slip, Strap Handle, Galena, 10 In. 25.00
Jug, Pouring Spout Lip, Yellow Glaze, Yellow Slip Design, 8 In. 115.00
Jug, Strap Handle, Dark Running Glaze, Paper Label, 7 1/4 In. 350.00
Jug, Tapered Bulbous Body, Strap Handle, Amber, 6 1/2 In. 35.00
Jug, Tooled Lines, Ribbed Strap Handle, Brown, Orange, 4 3/8 In. 225.00
Jug, White Slip, Green & Brown Running Glaze, Europe, 10 In. 75.00
Lamp, Grease, Greenish Glaze, Handle, 3 3/4 In. 525.00
Loaf Dish, St. Nicholas, Bishop Of Mira, Yellow Slip 4125.00
Loaf Pan, Coggled Edge, 3 Line Slip Design, 12 x 16 3/4 In. 1400.00
Loaf Pan, Yellow Design, Wavy Line, Crossing Lines, 11 1/4 x 10 In. 225.00
Milk Pan, Interior Glaze, 16 x 4 In. 95.00
Mold, Cake, Brown Design, John Bell, c.1850, 4 In. 3100.00
Mold, Fish, Amber & Brown Glaze, 11 3/4 In. 100.00
Mold, Food, Fish Shape, Embossed Detail, 11 1/2 In. 125.00
Mold, Food, Scalloped Rim, Dark Amber Glaze, 4 1/2 In. 75.00
Mold, Food, Turk's Head, 2–Tone Green Glaze, 3 1/8 x 7 In. 65.00
Mold, Food, Turk's Head, Deep Yellow Glaze, 9 In. 65.00
Mold, Food, Turk's Head, Running Brown Glaze, 8 1/2 In. 95.00
Mold, Jelly, John Bell, Waynesboro, 1 3/4 x 5 7/8 In. 5500.00
Mold, Pudding, 7 1/2 x 7 In. 50.00
Mug, Brown Splotched Glaze, Handle, 3 7/8 x 5 In. 25.00
Mug, Rust Glaze, 5 In. 32.00
Mustache Cup, Brownish Glaze, George Bollinger, 4 5/8 In. 115.00
Pie Plate, Coggled Rim, 3 Line Crow's Foot Design, 8 In. 200.00
Pie Plate, Coggled Rim, 3 Line Slip Design, 10 3/4 In. 550.00
Pie Plate, Coggled Rim, 3 Line Yellow Slip Crow's Foot, 7 3/4 In. 225.00
Pie Plate, Coggled Rim, 3 Line Yellow Slip Design, 10 In. .... 325.00 To 700.00
Pie Plate, Coggled Rim, Brown Slip Design, 7 5/8 In. 90.00
Pie Plate, Coggled Rim, Yellow Slip Crow's Foot Design, 9 In. 400.00
Pie Plate, Coggled Rim, Yellow Slip Puddle Center, 7 1/4 In. 125.00
Pie Plate, Rust Glaze, 1800, 10 In. 175.00
Pie Plate, Slip Design, Initials WH, 11 3/4 In. 1100.00
Pie Plate, Wavy Lines, Yellow Slip, 9 In. 350.00
Pie Plate, Yellow Slip Crossed Lines, 11 1/2 In. 125.00
Pitcher, Black Spotted Glaze, Strap Handle, 6 3/8 In. 600.00
Pitcher, Cover, Tooled Band & Rim Spout, Strap Handle, 6 In. 2500.00
Pitcher, Dark Brown & Green Glaze, Bell & Son, Strasburg, 10 In. 665.00
Pitcher, Embossed Bands, Tooled Rim, Brown Drip Glaze, 10 3/4 In. 500.00
Pitcher, Mottled Amber & Brown Glaze, 4 1/4 In. 125.00
Pitcher, Ribbed Strap Handle, Yellowish Slip, Brown Flecks, 8 In. 200.00
Pitcher, Slip Design, Squat, Late 19th Century, 3 1/2 In. 165.00
Pitcher, Strap Handles, Orange & White Slip, 7 In. 3025.00
Pitcher, Yellow & Brown Splotches, Rib Handle, 7 1/2 In. 325.00
Plaque, Rooster, Polychrome, 6 3/4 In. 195.00

Plate, Coggled Rim, 3 Line Crow's Foot Design, 7 3/4 In.	200.00
Plate, Coggled Rim, Yellow Slip Design, 6 1/4 In.	400.00
Plate, Crimped Rim, 3 Yellow Wavy Lines, 16 In.	1870.00
Plate, Crimped Rim, Yellow & Brown–Black Dabs, Oval, 14 1/4 In.	4950.00
Plate, Lafayette Written In Slip	1700.00
Plate, Serrated Border, Design On Red Ground, c.1830, 11 In.	665.00
Plate, Serrated Border, Slip Design Center, c.1830, 12 In.	775.00
Plate, Slip Design, Notched Rim, 13 In.	275.00
Plate, St. Justin The Apologist, Yellow Slip, 14 1/2 In.	800.00
Plate, Yellow & Brown–Black Dabs, Oval, 14 1/2 In.	4950.00
Plate, Yellow & Green Slip Trailing, 15 In.	3575.00
Plate, Yellow, Green & Brown Dabs, Oval, 14 1/2 In.	1870.00
Platter, Yellow, Green & Brown Slip, Oval, 1825, 14 1/2 In.	1870.00
Pot, Cover, Spout, Dark Brown Glaze, 4 3/4 In.	175.00
Pot, Pouring Spout Lip, Ribbed Strap Handle	175.00
Strainer, Cheese, 12 In.	165.00
Sugar, Dark Glaze, White & Red Slip, 4 3/4 In.	45.00
Tray, Loaf, Yellow Slip, St. Nicholas, Bishop Of Mira, 14 In.	4125.00
Urn, Grecian Style, Black Enamel Wash, 1 Loop Handle, 14 3/4 In.	550.00
Vase, Dragon In Clouds, 10 1/2 x 8 In.	80.00
Vase, Greenish Brown Glaze, Orange Spots, 6 1/4 In.	25.00
Vase, Leaf–Shaped Sgraffito, Yellow Slip, 5 In.	235.00

REGOUT, see Maastricht

RICHARD was the mark used on acid–etched cameo glass vases, bowls, night–lights, and lamps made in Lorraine, France, during the 1920s. The pieces were very similar to the other French cameo glasswares made by Daum, Galle, and others.

Box, Cover, Fuchsia Florals On Turquoise, Amethyst Finial	1250.00
Cup Plate, Florals, Cream Cut To Gold, Signed, 3 In.	85.00
Goblet, Boat Scene, Blue, 8 In.	895.00
Vase, Brown Flowers, 3 Black Handles, 4 1/2 In.	450.00
Vase, Classical Scene, Coffee Brown Over Frost, 16 In.	2250.00
Vase, Scenic, Village, 15 In.	3200.00

RIDGWAY pottery has been made in the Staffordshire district in England since 1808 by a series of companies with the name Ridgway. The transfer–design dinner sets are the most widely known product. They are still being made. Other pieces of Ridgway are listed under Flow Blue.

Biscuit Jar, Coaching Days, Brown, Rattan Handle, 6 1/2 In.	235.00
Bowl, Willow, 9 1/2 In.	48.00
Casserole, Cover, Willow	110.00
Cuspidor, Dogs & Cats, Painted, Pottery ....*Illus*	192.00
Dessert Plate, Gilt Roundel, Scalloped, Floral, 1810, 9 In., 12 Piece	880.00
Dish, Coaching Days, Charles Recognized, Oval, 13 1/2 In.	65.00
Ladle, Willow	68.00

Ridgway, Cuspidor, Dogs & Cats, Painted, Pottery

◆◆◆◆◆◆◆◆◆◆◆◆◆◆◆◆◆◆◆◆◆◆

Never spray liquid glass cleaner directly on the glass in a picture frame. The dripping liquid may fall behind the glass and may stain the picture. Spray the cleaning cloth, then rub the glass with the damp cloth.

◆◆◆◆◆◆◆◆◆◆◆◆◆◆◆◆◆◆◆◆◆◆

Mug, Royal Vista	32.00
Plaque, Coaching Days, In A Snowdrift, 12 In.	135.00
Plaque, Coaching Days, Taking Up The Mails, 12 In.	135.00
Plate, Willow, 7 In.	8.00
Plate, Willow, 8 In.	10.00
Platter, Willow, 9 1/2 In.	40.00
Platter, Willow, 13 1/2 In.	110.00
Sugar, Cover, Willow	45.00
Tea Caddy, Coaching Days, Square, 5 3/4 x 4 1/2 In.	155.00

RIFLE is a firearm that has a rifled bore and that is intended to be fired from the shoulder. Other firearms are listed under Gun.

Air Pump, Benjamin Franklin Model 312, Brass Barrels	65.00
Air, Quackenbush	300.00
Boy's, 14 Silver Inlays, Patch Box, Octagonal Barrel, 34 1/2 In.	2800.00
Burnside, Carbine, 54 Caliber, Percussion, Inspector's Mark	775.00
Buzz Barton, No. 103	40.00
Carbine, Model 1865, 52 Caliber, Spencer Repeating Rifle Co.	1000.00
Curly Maple, Silver Eagle Inlay, Full Stock	4500.00
Derringer, With Patch Box, Lock Dated 1823	750.00
Flintlock, 50 Caliber, Octagonal Barrel, Case	665.00
Flintlock, Kentucky, Part Round Barrel, Thomas Boone, 1797	3000.00
Flintlock, Royal Foresters English Officer's, Revolutionary War	850.00
Flintlock, Tower Lock, Pennsylvania State Militia, 1823	875.00
Hall–North, Percussion Carbine, Breech Loading	875.00
Harper's Ferry U.S. Flint Musket, 69 Caliber, Dated 1837	1400.00
Kentucky, Double Set Triggers, Engraved Patch Box, 43 In.	2900.00
Kentucky, Flintlock, Full Stock, Thomas Boone 1796	3000.00
Kentucky, Full Curly Maple Stock, 14 Silver Inlays, Boy's, 34 1/2 In.	2800.00
Kentucky, Muzzle–Loading, 38 Caliber, Silver Inlay	467.50
Kentucky, Percussion, Curly Maple Stock, Powder Horn, Pouch, 52 In.	770.00
Kentucky, Tiger Maple Stock, Henry Parker, Brass Fittings, 53 1/2 In.	1100.00
Marlin Model 1881, Deluxe Factory Engraved	6600.00
Maynard, Percussion Carbine, 50 Caliber	400.00
Military, Mauser, Model 98, Lyman Peep Sight, 8 Mm	75.00
Navy Arms, 58 Caliber Zouve, Brass Patch Box	195.00
Percussion, Bear, 46 Caliber	170.00
Percussion, Mahogany Stock, Patchbox, Martin & Smith, 41 1/5 In.	550.00
Percussion, Spanish	100.00
Pocket, Wesson	145.00
Scheutzen	1260.00
Sharps, Carbine, Model 1859	800.00
Shotgun, Ithaca Model 3–E, 16 Gauge, Double Barrel	1425.00
Shotgun, Percussion Double–Barrel, Belgium	1100.00
Shotgun, Winchester–Parker, Double, 28 Gauge, Fitted Leather Case	2600.00
Springfield, Trapdoor, Model 1878, Bayonet, 36 In.	330.00
Springfield, USM M 1903–A1	165.00
Swiss Army Training	33.00
Trap Door, Springfield, 1864	475.00
W. J. Jeffrey Mauser, 404 Caliber, English Walnut	1750.00
Winchester '73, 44 Caliber, Original Finish	825.00
Winchester 1886, Saddle Ring Carbine, Walnut, 24–In. Barrel	1450.00
Winchester 70, Standard Bolt–Action, 375 H & H Magnum	1850.00
Winchester 94, Takedown, 38–55 Caliber, Original Blue & Case Colors	1600.00
Winchester, Model 06, Pump Action	632.50
Winchester, Model 1886, Sporting	2475.00

RIVIERA dinnerware was made by the Homer Laughlin Co. of Newell, West Virginia, from 1938 to 1950. The pattern was similar in coloring and in mood to Fiesta and Harlequin. The Riviera plates and cup handles were square. For more information, see *Kovels' Depression Glass & American Dinnerware Price List.*

COLONIAL

Bowl, Ivory, 5 In.	5.00

Bowl, Red, 5 In. 8.00
Butter, Red, 1/4 Lb. ....75.00 To 175.00
Butter, Yellow, 1/4 Lb. ....95.00 To 155.00
Casserole, Cover, Ivory 80.00
Creamer, Ivory 6.00
Creamer, Red 8.00
Creamer, Yellow 6.00
Cup, Blue 8.00
Cup, Green 8.00
Gravy, Ivory 12.00
Jug, Disk, Mauve Blue 135.00
Jug, Open, Yellow 65.00
Pitcher, Juice, Yellow 75.00
Plate, Green, 6 In. 2.50
Plate, Mauve Blue, 7 In. 2.50
Plate, Yellow, 6 1/2 In. 6.00
Saltshaker, Maroon 20.00
Saltshaker, Red 8.00
Saltshaker, Spruce 20.00
Saltshaker, Tango 20.00
Saucer, Green 1.50
Soup, Dish, Red 11.00
Sugar & Creamer, Cover, Light Green 20.00
Sugar, Cover, Green 10.00
Sugar, Green 4.00
Syrup, Cover, Red 195.00
Teapot, Cover, Yellow 65.00
Teapot, Green 55.00
Tumbler, Green, Handle 55.00
Tumbler, Handle, Red 38.00

ROBLIN Art Pottery was founded in 1898 by Alexander W. Robertson and
Linna Irelan in San Francisco, California. The pottery closed in 1906. The
firm made faience with green, tan, dull blue, or gray glazes. Decorations
were usually animal shapes. Some red clay pieces were made.

Vase, Carved Rings, Buff, 2 1/2 In. 250.00

ROCKINGHAM, in the United States, is a pottery with a brown glaze that
resembles tortoiseshell. It was made from 1840 to 1900 by many American
potteries. Mottled brown Rockingham wares were first made in England at
the Rockingham factory. Other types of ceramics were also made by the
English firm. Related pieces may be listed in the Bennington category.

Bank, Man Clutching Pitcher, Inscription On Back, 4 1/2 In. 170.00
Bottle, Gin, Mermaid Form 185.00
Bottle, Gin, Potato Form 185.00
Bowl, 2 3/4 x 9 1/2 In. 30.00
Bowl, Marked National, 5 1/4 In. 57.00
Creamer, Cow, 5 1/2 In. ....50.00 To 300.00
Creamer, Cow, Brown Glaze, Oval Base, 5 1/2 x 7 In. 440.00
Creamer, Cow, Brown, Yellow, 3 x 5 x 7 In. 440.00
Dish, Oval, 11 1/2 In. 35.00
Dish, Soap, Molded Leaf, 6 In. 45.00
Dish, Soap, Oval, 4 3/4 In. 55.00
Dish, Vegetable, Spotted Glaze, Octagonal, 11 1/2 In. 175.00
Figurine, Dog, Seated, Oblong Base. 9 1/2 In. 85.00
Figurine, Seated Dog, Open Front Legs, 10 In. 125.00
Flask, Molded Floral Design, Band, 8 In. 35.00
Inkwell, Shoe Shape, 4 1/8 In. 55.00
Jar, Canning, Keg Shape, 5 1/2 In. 20.00
Jug, Figural, Man's Head, 2 Tone Green & Brown Glaze, 8 In. 35.00
Jug, Figural, Wellington, 7 1/2 In. 265.00
Kettle, Croup, 1847–1858, 6 1/2 In. 375.00
Mold, Food, Fish, Oval, 7 1/2 In. 155.00

Mold, Food, Turk's Head, 9 1/2 In.	25.00
Mold, Turk's Head, Spiraled Flutes, 9 1/4 In.	45.00
Mug, 3 3/4 In.	105.00
Pan, Muffin, 19th Century, 14 3/4 x 10 In.	220.00
Pie Plate, 8 1/2 In.	30.00
Pie Plate, 10 1/4 In.	65.00
Pie Plate, 11 1/4 In.	135.00
Pitcher, 9 3/4 In.	62.00
Pitcher, Batter, 7 In.	110.00
Pitcher, Bust Of Washington	165.00
Pitcher, Cover, Oval Design Of Hanging Fish, 9 1/4 In.	135.00
Pitcher, Embossed Arched Panels & Foliage, 8 1/4 In.	195.00
Pitcher, Embossed Berries, 8 3/4 In.	65.00
Pitcher, Hanging Game, 9 1/8 In.	65.00
Pitcher, Hanging Game, Hound Handle, 7 3/8 In.	350.00
Pitcher, Hanging Game, Hound Handle, 8 7/8 In.	300.00
Pitcher, Hound Handle, Hunting Scene, Mask Spout, 10 1/2 In.	165.00
Pitcher, Molded Foliage, 7 3/4 In.	50.00
Pitcher, Molded Foliage, Scrolls & Ivy, 9 1/4 In.	150.00
Pitcher, Molded Panels, 10 1/4 In.	45.00
Pitcher, Molded Peacock, 8 1/4 In.	65.00
Pitcher, Molded Tulips, 9 In.	55.00
Pitcher, Strap Handle, Squat, 4 1/4 In.	45.00
Platter, Oval, 13 3/4 In.	95.00
Shaving Mug, 19th Century, 4 1/4 In.	302.50
Sugar, Cover, Dark Spots, 7 1/2 In.	170.00
Tea Set, Floral & Fruit Reserves, Pink Ground, 36 Piece	1540.00
Teapot, 2 Women At Tea Table, Eagle & American Flag, Individual	175.00
Teapot, Molded Rebekah At The Well, 9 In.	25.00
Toby, Barmaid, 7 3/4 In.	65.00

ROGERS, see John Rogers

ROOKWOOD pottery was made in Cincinnati, Ohio, from 1880 to 1960. All of this art pottery is marked, most with the famous flame mark. The R is reversed and placed back to back with the letter P. Flames surround the letters. After 1900, a Roman numeral was added to the mark to indicate the year. The name and some of the molds were purchased in 1984. A few new pieces were made, but these were glazed in colors not used by the original company.

Ashtray, Blue Fish, 1922	90.00
Ashtray, Free–Form, 1957	30.00
Ashtray, Green, 1924	85.00
Ashtray, Horsehead, King, 1946	325.00
Ashtray, Pelican, White & Green, 1932	70.00 To 125.00
Ashtray, Rook, Tan, 1949	135.00
Ashtray, Satyr Figure, Gunmetal	175.00
Bird Bath, 3 Panels, Foliate Design, Incurved, 30 1/2 x 23 In.	550.00
Bookends, Basset Hound, White Matte	350.00
Bookends, Bouquet Of Flowers, Multicolor	375.00
Bookends, Elephant, Ivory Semimatte, 1919	295.00
Bookends, Floral Bouquet	425.00
Bookends, Kneeling Egyptian Maidens, Feather Covered Arms	385.00
Bookends, Multicolored High Glaze	450.00
Bookends, Penguins, 2–Tone Blue Matte, 1927	285.00
Bookends, Penguins, Blue Matte, 1927	275.00
Bookends, Rook, Cobalt Blue, 1928	245.00
Bookends, Women	250.00
Bowl, Brown, Yellow, Outlined Pansies, 1885, 4 In.	600.00
Bowl, Geometric, High Glaze, 1916, 8 In.	468.00
Bowl, Margaret McDonald, 8 In.	425.00
Bowl, Matte Green, 1925, 10 1/2 x 3 In.	255.00
Box, Dresser, Cover, Harriette R. Strafer, 1894, 5 1/4 In.	220.00

Candleholder, 1923	70.00
Candleholder, Triple Seahorse, Pink To Green, Matte, 1912	215.00
Candlestick, Blue, 1926, 2 In.	70.00
Candlestick, Figural Magnolia Cups, 1927, Pair	135.00
Candlestick, Lotus, Pink, Shape 1067, 1924	95.00
Creamer, Berries, Tricorn Top, Sara Sax, 4 In.	495.00
Cup & Saucer, Tea, Rolled Rim, 5 Sides, 1890	1500.00
Ewer, Floral, Blue, 1880s, 5 In.	750.00
Ewer, Persimmons, Standard Glaze, Amelia Sprague, 1891, 10 In.	775.00
Ewer, Standard Glaze, Tulips & Irises, Ed Hurley, 1900, 10 1/2 In.	800.00
Ewer, Underglazed Petaled Roses, Matthew Daly, c.1896, 9 3/4 In.	415.00
Ewer, White Floral & Spider, A. Humphreys, 1882, 5 In.	725.00
Figurine, Bird On Branch, D1940, Mottled Blue On Brown, 6 x 7 In.	225.00
Figurine, Cockatoo, Tan, 9 1/2 In.	175.00
Figurine, Puppy, Ivory, Louise Abel, No. 1998	150.00
Flower Frog, Boat & Boy, 1910	310.00
Flower Frog, Nude, Ivory, 1920	145.00
Flower Frog, Pan Playing Pipes, Glossy Brown, 1922, 7 In.	195.00
Flower Frog, Pineapple Finial, Mauve, 1921	135.00
Font, Holy Water, St. Francis, Clotilda Zanetta	150.00
Gravy Bowl, Blue Flowers, Standard Glaze, Charles Dibowski, 1894	475.00
Humidor, Dark Red, 1910	225.00
Inkwell, On Large Leaf, 1920, 3 Piece	250.00
Jar, Cover, Floral Garland Around Top, Pink Glaze, 1922, 4 In.	335.00
Jug, Black Trees, Birds, White Clouds, Hattie Horton, 1883, 5 In.	725.00
Jug, Spiders & Webs, Anchor Mark, 1883, 4 3/4 In.	600.00
Jug, Standard Glaze, Stopper, 1902, 8 In.	495.00
Jug, Yellow Daisies, Wishbone Handle, Laura Fry, 1896, 11 In.	525.00
Lamp, Boxelder Branches, Margaret McDonald, 1940, 21 In.	4000.00
Lamp, Pink & Cream Floral, 1946, 8 In.	650.00
Loving Cup, Chief White Man, Kiowa, Edith Felten, 3 Handles	2300.00
Loving Cup, Incised Red Flower, Matte Green, Albert Pons	695.00
Mug, Caramel Glaze, Advertising, 1900, 5 In.	120.00
Mug, Earl Gillanders On Side, 6 Piece	245.00
Mug, Underglaze Of Lion's Head, Ed Hurley, 1900, 4 3/4 In.	885.00
Paperweight, Elephant, Matte Olive, Label, Dated 3-5-30	195.00 To 300.00
Paperweight, Fox, Matte	250.00
Paperweight, Goat	200.00
Paperweight, Lamb, Ivory, 1939	145.00
Paperweight, Nude, White Matte Glaze, No. 2868, Abel, Dated 1929	225.00
Paperweight, Purple & Gray Duck	70.00
Paperweight, Rooster, 4 Colors, 1945, 5 In.	225.00
Paperweight, Rooster, Multicolored, 1946	275.00
Paperweight, White Rook	135.00
Planter, Village Scene, Style Of Jens Jensen, 1951, Rectangular	910.00
Plaque, In The Woods, Vellum, Framed, Ed Diers, 1912	1900.00
Plaque, L. Epply, 3 3/4 x 7 1/2 In.	1650.00
Plaque, Mountain Scene, Ed Diers, 7 1/2 x 8 1/2 In.	5400.00
Plaque, Scenic, Vellum Glaze, Ed Diers, 1922	3300.00
Plaque, Venetian Fishing Boats, Vellum, C. Schmidt, 1926, 11 7/8 In.	5225.00
Plaque, Woodland Landscape, Vellum, E. Diers, Framed, 11 7/8 In.	4500.00
Pot, Black Iris Glazed, Classical Figure, Harriet Wilcox	6500.00
Sign, Dealer, Blue, 1900	350.00
Sign, Dealer, Cream Color, 14 In.	115.00
Sign, Dealer, Green, 1990	135.00
Sign, Dealer, Matte Blue, 1940	695.00
Sign, Dealer, Triangular, Blue	175.00
Sugar & Creamer, Floral, Pinches Sides, 1890	500.00
Sugar & Creamer, Standard Glaze, Butterfly Handles, Toohey, 1889	895.00
Tankard, 2 Satyrs Holding Boy 1 Side & Man On Other Side, Bisque	1100.00
Tankard, Allover White Pansies, Green Drip Design, 1897, 10 In.	1375.00
Tea Set, Matte Pink, 1917, 3 Piece	395.00 To 495.00
Teapot & Sugar, Bisque Finish, Wicker Handles, 1884	358.00

Rookwood, Vase, Dark Blue
Trees, E. T. Hurley, 1916,   *Rookwood, Vase, Mountain,*   *Rookwood, Vase, Water Lily,*
10 1/4 In.   *Trees, Lavender, Pink, 8 In.*   *Blue Ground, 1924, 17 In.*

Tile, Faience, Purple Grapes, Green Leaves, Blue Ground	185.00
Tile, Multicolored Floral, Octagonal	375.00
Tile, Pinecone, 6 In.	35.00
Tile, Rook On Branch, Round, 6 1/4 In.	175.00
Tile, Sea Gulls, Round	250.00
Tile, Wax Matte, 8 In.	525.00
Trivet, Birds	300.00
Trivet, Parrot & Flowers, 7 Colors	175.00
Trivet, Ship, Water, Blue Sky, Chicago 1910, Framed, 6 In.	385.00
Trivet, Southern Belle, 1922, 6 x 6 In.	250.00
Vase, 4 White Fish, Dark Blue Ground, Jens Jensen, 1934, 5 1/4 In.	1950.00
Vase, 5 Carp Underwater, Circling Base, 1910, 8 In.	700.00
Vase, Abstract Design, M. McDonald, 1930, 6 x 4 1/2 In.	350.00
Vase, Amphora, 4 Handles Are Stems Of Pond Lilies, 17 In.	875.00
Vase, Art Deco Design, Green & Brown, 6 1/2 In.	135.00
Vase, Art Deco, Matte, Sallie Coyne, 1918, 8 1/2 In.	750.00
Vase, Band Of Cherry Blossoms, Vellum, Squat, 3 1/2 x 6 In.	750.00
Vase, Band Of Oak Leaves & Acorns, Lenore Asbury, 1911, 8 In.	605.00
Vase, Bird On Branch, Mottled Blue On Brown, 6 1/2 x 7 In.	275.00
Vase, Black & Blue High Glaze, 1929	140.00
Vase, Black Florals, Turquoise Slip, E. Barrett, 1930, 6 1/2 In.	600.00
Vase, Black Opalescent, Floral, Sara Sax, 6 1/2 In.	1500.00
Vase, Blue Forget–Me–Nots, Purple To Lavender, 1916, 6 1/2 In.	595.00
Vase, Blue Matte, Floral, Jens Jensen, 1946, 8 In.	475.00
Vase, Blue To Red, L. N. L., 1923, 7 1/2 In.	995.00
Vase, Blue, Arts & Crafts Design, 1915	150.00
Vase, Bluebirds On Branches, E. T. Hurley, 5 1/4 In.	2000.00
Vase, Brown Feathered Matte Glaze Top, Arts & Crafts, 1914, 11 In.	475.00
Vase, Bud, Nude, Ivory, 1922, 12 In.	245.00
Vase, Butterflies, 1920, 6 In.	68.00
Vase, Carved, Green Matte, 5 In.	495.00
Vase, Cattail, Brown, 1945, 5 1/4 In.	85.00
Vase, Cherries & Leaf Design, Clara C. Lindeman, 6 In.	440.00
Vase, Country Landscape, Farmhouses, 1926, 11 7/8 In.	1760.00
Vase, Daisies, Sara Sax, Dated 1909, 7 In.	255.00
Vase, Dark Blue Trees, E. T. Hurley, 1916, 10 1/4 In. ....*Illus*	1980.00
Vase, Dark Gray, Branches, Apple Blossoms, 1908, 10 In.	925.00
Vase, Doves & Flowering Vines, High Glaze, Kay Ley, 1945	1980.00
Vase, Dragonfly, Artist Initialed, Date 1924, 5 3/4 In.	357.50
Vase, Dusky Scene Of Waves, Sea Gulls, Hurley, 1906, 8 1/8 In.	5775.00
Vase, Elongated Flaring Neck, Geometric Border, 1927, 20 In.	660.00

Vase, Fish & Flowers, J. Jensen, 1920s, 8 x 8 In. 2200.00
Vase, Flared Top, Floral Bouquet, K. Shirayamadani, 1925, 5 In. 1700.00
Vase, Floral, Brown Glaze, 1900, 6 In. 300.00
Vase, Floral, Brown Glaze, Artus Van Briggle, 1891, 11 In. 1075.00
Vase, Floral, Gray To Cream, Vellum, L. N. L., 7 In. 1150.00
Vase, Floral, Lavender, Blue, Vellum, 8 1/2 x 9 1/2 In. 1500.00
Vase, Floral, Pale Wax Blue Matte, 1922, 7 3/4 In. 625.00
Vase, Flowers & Vines, Gray, 1923, 8 In. 175.00
Vase, Flowers, Green Matte, 1928, 10 In. 200.00
Vase, Flying Storks, Billowing Clouds, A. R. Valentien 880.00
Vase, Gold Chevron Bands, Leaves & Flowers, M. Daly, 1887, 8 In. 715.00
Vase, Green Matte Glaze, Blue Drip, 1906, 12 In. 358.00
Vase, Greenish Stalks, Flowers In Each, Loretta Holtkamp, 8 In. 150.00
Vase, Handles, Floral, Lenore Asbury, 1896, 9 1/2 In. 250.00
Vase, Impressionistic Landscape, Beige Ground, c.1905, 6 In. 453.50
Vase, Incised Line & Petal, Cylindrical Neck, 1915, 12 1/2 In. 385.00
Vase, Incised Oak Leaves, S. Toohey, 1904, 5 In. 350.00
Vase, Iris Glaze, 1902, 8 In. 1200.00
Vase, Iris Glaze, Gray & Blue Flowers At Shoulder, 1901, 6 In. 1200.00
Vase, Iris Glaze, Petunia, Katherine Van Horne, 1907 .... 1320.00
Vase, Iris, 1897, 6 1/2 In. 495.00
Vase, Iris, 1928, 8 In. 795.00
Vase, Iris, Yellow Flowers, Tan To White, 1902, 9 In. 625.00
Vase, Jeweled, White Jonquils, Oxblood & Purple, H. E. Wilcox, 7 In. 605.00
Vase, Leaves & Berries, Pink, 1950 .... 68.00
Vase, Leaves & Berries, Shirayamadani, 1890, 10 3/4 In. 2500.00
Vase, Lincoln, Floral, 13 In. 1900.00
Vase, Marigolds & Leaves, Cobalt Blue Ground, Vellum, 6 1/4 In. 665.00
Vase, Matte Blue, Air–Brushed Glaze, Shape 2977, 1926, 8 In. 175.00
Vase, Matte Blue, Elizabeth Barrett, 1928 .... 2860.00
Vase, Matte Turquoise, AMV, 1901, 6 In. 3000.00
Vase, Mountain, Trees, Lavender, Pink, 8 In. ....*Illus* 1100.00
Vase, Multicolored Daisies, Lenore Asbury, 1928, 6 In. 1250.00
Vase, Mustard, 1925, 5 3/4 In. 95.00
Vase, Mythical Oriental Scene, K. Shirayamadani, 10 In. 3000.00
Vase, Nudes In Relief, Celadon Green, 1935, 9 1/2 In. 700.00
Vase, Orange Tulips, Olga Geneva Reed, Pink To Green, 1903, 10 In. 1550.00
Vase, Oriental Screen Design, Blue, 6 Sides, 6–Footed, 1919, 5 In. 150.00
Vase, Paneled Floral, Green, 1966, 9 1/8 In. 295.00
Vase, Peaches & Leaves, Leona Van Briggle, 1903, 7 In. 800.00
Vase, Peacock Feather, Cobalt Blue, 1928, 6 In. 165.00
Vase, Peacock Feather, Embossed Feathers, 1904, 12 In. 3995.00
Vase, Pink & Green From Top To Halfway Down, 1920, 10 1/4 In. 275.00
Vase, Pink Morning Glory, Pink Ground, Rothenbusch, 8 In. 575.00
Vase, Poppy, Burgundy, 1922, 11 In. 425.00
Vase, Rose Colored, 1916, 6 1/2 In. 125.00
Vase, Salmon Swimming Up Stream, Tiger's–Eye Glaze, c.1900, 7 In. 800.00
Vase, Scenic Vellum, Sallie Coyne, 1922, 5 3/4 In. 715.00
Vase, Sea Green, Marked L. A., 1910, 8 In. 550.00
Vase, Semimatte Turquoise, 1917, 9 In. 250.00
Vase, Shamrocks, Matte Green, 1935, 3 1/2 In. 85.00
Vase, Spade Leaves, Brown, 1926, 4 In. 120.00
Vase, Standard Glaze, Clara Lindeman, 1898, 7 In. 775.00
Vase, Streaked Aquamarine Blue, 5 1/2 In. 65.00
Vase, Stylized Tulips Lid, Vellum, Sallie Coyne, 1921, 8 In. 775.00
Vase, Swirl Shoulder Design, Speckled Ground, c.1915, 4 x 6 In. 330.00
Vase, Tan Over Ivory, 3 Handles, 1931, 3 In. 75.00
Vase, Tapering Ovoid Form, Stems Of Tulips, Gorham Marks, 10 In. 1870.00
Vase, Tiger Lilies, High Glaze, Lenore Asbury, 1929, 10 In. 3750.00
Vase, Todd, 5 1/2 In. 395.00
Vase, Tree & River Landscape, 1921, 14 In. 1870.00
Vase, Treed Landscape, Lake At Sunset, 1920, 11 In. 1760.00
Vase, Trial Glaze, Sprague, 1913, 9 In. 300.00

Vase, Tulip Shape, Royal Blue, 1934, 7 1/2 In. 245.00
Vase, Tulips, Pink, 1929, 5 In. 110.00
Vase, Turquoise, 1918, 8 1/2 In. 225.00
Vase, Vellum, Steinle, 6 1/4 In. 595.00
Vase, Water Lily, Blue Ground, 1924, 17 In. ....*Illus* 1210.00
Vase, Wax Matte, Bleeding Hearts, Blue Leaves, 1921, 12 1/2 In. 800.00
Vase, Wild Grapes, Standard Glaze, 2 Handles, Anna Valentien, 1889 .... 1430.00
Vase, Winter Landscape, Vellum, Shirayamadani, 1912, 8 In. 3000.00
Vase, Yellow Floral, Sea Green Glaze, Laura Lindeman, 1903, 7 In. 1265.00
Vase, Yellow, 3 1/2 In. 130.00
Wall Pocket, Blue Crow, Grapes, Foliage, 1916, 13 1/2 In. 715.00

ROSALINE, see Steuben category

ROSE BOWLS were popular during the 1880s. Rose petals were kept in
the open bowl to add fragrance to a room, a popular idea in a time of
limited personal hygiene. The glass bowls were made with crimped tops,
which kept the petals inside. Many types of Victorian art glass were made
into rose bowls.

Blue Satin Glass ....50.00 To 100.00
Fan & Pineapple, Clear, 3 1/2 In. 12.00
Green, Enameled, 4 In. 45.00
Pink Satin Glass 100.00
Pink Satin Glass, Small White Flowers 70.00
Swirl, Opalescent, Large 60.00
Vaseline Opalescent, Fancy Fantails 50.00
Vaseline Opalescent, Inverted Fan & Feather 75.00
Victorian, Allover Enameled Flowers, Sheffield Holder, 1850 .... 90.00
Yellow Satin Glass 95.00

ROSE CANTON china is similar to Rose Medallion, except no people are
pictured in the decoration. It was made in China during the nineteenth
and twentieth centuries in greens, pinks, and other colors.

Bowl, Cover, Acorn Finial, Allover Design Inside, 9 x 8 In. 595.00
Bowl, Cover, Orange Peel Glaze, 10 1/2 In. 200.00
Bowl, Flowers & Butterflies, 19th Century, 10 7/8 In. 250.00
Bowl, Vegetable, Cover, Birds & Flowers, 9 x 8 In. 595.00
Candleholder, Elephant, Blue Saddle, 6 1/8 In. 2420.00
Candleholder, Recumbent Dog, 6 5/8 In. 1320.00
Jar, Temple, Cover 2850.00
Lantern, Blossoms, Scrolls, Flowers, 19th Century, 22 In., Pair 8800.00
Plate, 7 1/2 In. 47.50
Plate, Black Butterfly & Flowers, 8 1/2 In. 75.00
Plate, Scalloped, 7 In. 50.00
Platter, Thousand Butterfly Border, 14 3/4 In. 440.00
Vase, Cover, Birds & Insect Panels, Mounted As Lamp, 13 1/2 In. 467.50

ROSE MEDALLION china was made in China during the nineteenth and
twentieth centuries. It is a distinctive design picturing people, flowers,
birds, and butterflies. Pieces are colored in greens, pinks, and other colors.
It is similar to Rose Canton.

Bowl, Mandarin Figure Alternating Panels, 6 1/2 x 16 In. 1320.00
Bowl, Mandarin, Gold In Hair, Orange Peel, 8 1/2 x 8 1/2 In. 595.00
Bowl, Underplate, Reticulated Sides, Rim, 11 1/4 In. 425.00
Box, 6 Figures On Lid, Black Butterflies On Gold, 7 1/2 In. 695.00
Butter Pat 50.00
Candlestick, 9 1/2 In., Pair 1045.00
Dish, Orange Peel Glaze, 11 1/2 In. 150.00
Dish, Shrimp, Butterfly Reserve Cipher, Gilt, 10 1/2 In., Pr. 825.00
Flask, Pilgrim, Lizard Handle, 1840, 9 3/4 In., Pair 3575.00
Ginger Jar, 12 In. 75.00
Jardiniere, 12 x 14 1/2 In. 770.00
Pitcher, Gilt, 16 In. 1045.00

Planter, Underplate, Circular, Bulbous, 9 1/2 In.	900.00
Plate, 6–Sided, 7 In.	65.00
Plate, Gold In Hair, 5 1/2 In.	75.00
Plate, Gold Trim, 19th Century, 8 In., 3 Piece	330.00
Plate, Scalloped & Fluted, 10 In.	125.00
Platter, Fruit, Floral & Figural Panels, c.1860, 15 In.	990.00
Platter, People, Butterflies Panels, 11 1/4 x 9 3/4 In.	350.00
Punch Bowl, Courtyard Scenes, c.1840, 15 7/8 In.	2750.00
Punch Bowl, Panels Of Mandarin Figures, 13 1/2 In.	715.00
Seat, Garden, 19th Century, 19 In.	770.00
Tea Bowl, Cover, 3 1/2 In.	55.00
Teapot, Cup, Wicker Basket	150.00
Urn, 28 In.	1210.00
Vase, Lion Head Ring Handles, 9 1/4 In., Pair	460.00
Vase, Mandarin Figures, Squirrel Handles, 34 In., Pair	1650.00
Wash Basin, Gilt, 16 1/2 In.	1045.00

ROSE O'NEILL, see Kewpie category

ROSE TAPESTRY porcelain was made by the Royal Bayreuth factory of Tettau, Germany, during the late nineteenth century. The surface of the porcelain was pressed against a coarse fabric while it was still damp, and the impressions remained on the finished porcelain. It looks and feels like a textured cloth. Very skillful reproductions are being made that even include a variation of the Royal Bayreuth mark, so be careful when buying.

Basket, Braided Handle, Blue Mark, 5 In.	425.00
Basket, Courting Couple, Blue Mark, 5 x 5 1/2 In.	350.00
Basket, Gold Rope Handle & Trim, Mums, 5 1/4 x 7 1/2 In.	450.00
Box, Cover, Trinket, Pheasant In Woods, 2 1/4 x 4 In.	165.00
Box, Jewel, Cover	375.00
Candy Dish, Game Bird In Marsh, Double Strand Handle, 5 In.	200.00
Creamer, Blue Mark, 3 1/2 In.	255.00
Cup & Saucer, Chocolate, Blue Mark, 3 3/4 x 4 1/2 In.	198.00
Cup & Saucer, Tavern Scene	195.00
Dresser Set, Hair Receiver, Powder Box, Hatpin Holder, Tray	1400.00
Fernery, Cows Grazing, 2 Handles	275.00
Flowerpot, Blue Mark, 3 3/4 In.	185.00
Hair Receiver, Scenic, Goat, Marked	175.00
Match Holder, Green Leaves, Gold Trim, Blue Mark	395.00
Nut Set, Ruffled, Gold Footed, Blue Mark, 7 Piece	1050.00
Pitcher, 5 In.	330.00
Pitcher, Blue Mark, 4 3/4 In.	255.00
Pitcher, Milk, Musician Scene	195.00
Pitcher, Pink Roses, 5 1/4 In.	420.00
Pitcher, Roses, Leaves, Ferns, Blue Mark, 24 Oz.	395.00
Planter, Low Handles	200.00
Plaque, Pink Roses, 9 1/2 In.	325.00
Plate, Hunter & Dog, 8 In.	125.00
Plate, Scalloped, Embossed Shells, Gold Trim, 7 1/4 In.	195.00
Powder Box, Mountain, Castle, Train, Blue Mark	225.00
Salt & Pepper, Blue Mark	395.00
Sugar & Creamer, Blue Mark	550.00
Sugar, Cover, Blue Mark	235.00
Teapot, Gold Handle & Cover	250.00
Toothpick, Gold Handles, Ruffled Rim Outlined In Gold	395.00
Toothpick, Handle, 3 1/4 In.	225.00
Toothpick, Polar Bear	850.00
Tray, Courting Couple, Blue Mark, 10 x 7 1/2 In.	325.00
Tray, Dresser, 3 Color Roses, Blue Mark	285.00
Tumbler, Scenic	150.00
Vase, Bud, Polar Bear, Stick Neck, 4 1/4 In.	495.00
Vase, Castle Scene, Winter & Spring, 10 In.	325.00

Vase, Courting Scene, 4 In.	350.00
Vase, Lady In Hat, 7 x 4 In.	375.00
Vase, Pheasant Scene, Bulbous, Narrow Neck, Blue Mark, 4 In.	395.00
Vase, Pheasant, Handles, 6 In.	255.00
Vase, Polar Bear, Blue Mark, 5 5/8 In.	750.00
Vase, Scenic, Gazebo, Animal Scene, 3 3/4 In.	195.00

ROSEMEADE Pottery of Wahpeton, North Dakota, worked from 1940 to 1961. The pottery was operated by Laura A. Taylor and her husband, R.I. Hughes. The company was also known as the Wahpeton Pottery Company. Art pottery and commercial wares were made.

Ashtray, Angus	50.00
Ashtray, Kansas	20.00
Ashtray, North Dakota Advertising	55.00
Bank, Bear	55.00
Figurine, Bunny	80.00
Figurine, Cocks, Fighting	90.00
Figurine, Indian God Of Peace	175.00
Figurine, Pheasant	32.50 To 185.00
Figurine, Roadrunner, Pair	28.00
Figurine, Turkey	100.00
Flower Frog, Stork	22.50
Planter, Dove	200.00
Planter, Peacock, 8 In.	110.00
Planter, Pony, Pink	75.00
Planter, Sticker	22.00
Rose Bowl	18.00
Salt & Pepper, Bears	30.00 To 35.00
Salt & Pepper, Black Bears	35.00 To 45.00
Salt & Pepper, Bloodhounds	25.00
Salt & Pepper, Buffalo	75.00
Salt & Pepper, California Quail	35.00
Salt & Pepper, Chow Dog Heads, Brown	35.00
Salt & Pepper, Cowboy Hats	35.00
Salt & Pepper, Cucumbers	35.00
Salt & Pepper, Dog Heads	18.00
Salt & Pepper, Donkeys	35.00
Salt & Pepper, Flamingos	60.00 To 75.00
Salt & Pepper, Goats	145.00
Salt & Pepper, Greyhound Dogs	20.00
Salt & Pepper, Greyhound Dogs' Heads	35.00
Salt & Pepper, Horseheads	40.00 To 50.00
Salt & Pepper, Leaping Deer	45.00
Salt & Pepper, Mallard Ducks	60.00
Salt & Pepper, Mice	35.00
Salt & Pepper, Mountain Goats	77.50
Salt & Pepper, Ox Heads	45.00
Salt & Pepper, Parrots	65.00
Salt & Pepper, Paul Bunyan & Babe	65.00
Salt & Pepper, Pheasant	22.00 To 30.00
Salt & Pepper, Pheasants, Cock & Hen, Paper Label	45.00
Salt & Pepper, Pigs	55.00
Salt & Pepper, Quail	18.00
Salt & Pepper, Rabbits	65.00
Salt & Pepper, Roadrunners	70.00
Salt & Pepper, Running Rabbits	67.50
Salt & Pepper, Skunks	35.00
Salt & Pepper, Sunfish	150.00
Salt & Pepper, Tulips, Blue	32.50
Salt & Pepper, Turkeys	60.00
Shoe, Aqua	20.00
Spoon Rest, Huron, South Dakota	35.00
Teapot, Brown	25.00

Vase, Fawn, Pastel Rose & Blue, 8 In.	65.00
Wall Pocket, Deer	35.00

ROSENTHAL porcelain was made at the factory established in Selb, Bavaria, in 1880. The factory is still making fine-quality tablewares and figurines. A series of Christmas plates was made from 1910. Other limited edition plates have been made since 1971.

MARKE

Rosenthal

Bowl, Duke & Duchess Of Devonshire Portrait, Marked, 10 In., Pair	600.00
Candelabra, Foliate Design, Sterling Over Porcelain, 11 In., Pair	1550.00
Creamer, Isolde	15.00
Dish, Frankfurt Opera House, 3 In.	25.00
Dresser Set, Cream & Pink Flowers, Tray, 5 Piece	295.00
Figurine, Angel, Pink Gown, Signed, 1950s, 5 1/4 In.	145.00
Figurine, Angelfish, White, c.1963, 16 x 10 In.	950.00
Figurine, Black Man Playing Banjo, 8 In.	245.00
Figurine, Blackamoor Minstrel, 7 1/2 In.	200.00
Figurine, Colt, No. 1528, Ears Forward, Tan & Gray	125.00
Figurine, Dachshund, Sitting, Prof. Karner	275.00
Figurine, Dog, No. 7247, Sitting, Long-Eared, Marked, 6 In.	275.00
Figurine, Dog, No. 7509, Sitting, G. Kusper, 4 In.	195.00
Figurine, Duck, W. Zugel, 7 1/2 In.	275.00
Figurine, Kneeling Nude, Klimsch, 14 In.	765.00
Figurine, Nude, Seated, M. H. Fritz	375.00
Figurine, Princess & Frog, 8 1/2 In.	250.00
Figurine, Rabbit, Laughing, White, 6 In.	95.00
Figurine, Sealyham, No. 7721	95.00
Figurine, Seminude Female, Blue Robe, 1923, 8 1/2 In.	395.00
Figurine, Squirrel, Sitting, No. 7290, 6 In.	185.00
Figurine, Standing Nude, Davmiller, 15 In.	635.00
Figurine, Woman, 10 In.	225.00
Lamp, Boudoir, Man & Woman, c.1900, 6 1/4 In.	55.00
Pendant, Woman Silhouette, Hoop Skirt, Porcelain, 1920s, 2 3/8 In.	450.00
Plate, Serving, Central Floral Sprays, 10 In., 12 Piece	660.00
Tea Set, Premier, Teapot, Creamer, Sugar, 3 Piece	148.00
Teapot, Isolde	40.00
Teapot, Sugar & Creamer, Premier	150.00
Vase, Enameled Winter Scene, Germany, 9 5/8 In.	25.00

ROSEVILLE Pottery Company was organized in Roseville, Ohio, in 1890. Another plant was opened in Zanesville, Ohio, in 1898. Many types of pottery were made until 1954. Early wares include Sgraffito, Olympic, and Rozane. Later lines were often made with molded decorations, especially flowers and fruit. Pieces are marked *Roseville*.

Roseville
U.S.A.

Ashtray, Bushberry	95.00
Ashtray, Capri, Red	42.00
Ashtray, Hyde Park, Copper Car	15.00 To 18.00
Ashtray, Magnolia, Blue	45.00
Ashtray, Meteor	15.00
Ashtray, Pine Cone	80.00
Ashtray, Silhouette, Terra-Cotta	45.00
Ashtray, Wincraft, Blue	30.00
Basket, Apple Blossom, Green, 10 In.	145.00
Basket, Apple Blossom, Pink, 12 In.	85.00 To 250.00
Basket, Bittersweet, Green, 10 In.	135.00
Basket, Bushberry, Blue, 10 In.	75.00
Basket, Bushberry, Green & Orange, 12 In.	155.00
Basket, Clematis, Blue, 10 In.	135.00
Basket, Clematis, Green & White, 1944, 10 x 11 In.	150.00
Basket, Clematis, Green, Pink, 8 In.	72.00
Basket, Columbine, Blue, 10 In.	170.00
Basket, Columbine, Pink, 10 In.	170.00
Basket, Cosmos, Green, 10 In.	235.00
Basket, Dogwood, 6 In.	63.00

Basket, Foxglove, Pink, 12 In. 170.00
Basket, Freesia, Brown, 8 In. ....95.00 To 110.00
Basket, Freesia, Flat Loop Handle, Flowers, 7 1/2 x 8 1/2 In. 70.00
Basket, Gardenia 125.00
Basket, Hanging, Apple Blossom, Blue 175.00
Basket, Hanging, Bittersweet, Green 65.00
Basket, Hanging, Bushberry 240.00
Basket, Hanging, Clematis 135.00
Basket, Hanging, Futura, Brown, 6 In. 450.00
Basket, Hanging, Gardenia, Gray ....95.00 To 145.00
Basket, Hanging, Ming Tree, Blue 140.00
Basket, Hanging, Mostique, 5 x 7 In. 145.00
Basket, Hanging, Peony, Chains, Liner 135.00
Basket, Hanging, Peony, Gold 145.00
Basket, Hanging, Peony, Green & Tan 95.00
Basket, Hanging, Pine Cone, Brown 275.00
Basket, Hanging, Pine Cone, Green, 8 In. 275.00
Basket, Hanging, Poppies, Gray 235.00
Basket, Hanging, Silhouette, Blue 110.00
Basket, Hanging, Silhouette, Rust, Chains 95.00
Basket, Hanging, Snowberry, Pink 125.00
Basket, Hanging, Velmoss Scroll, 10 In. 225.00
Basket, Hanging, Vista 325.00
Basket, Hanging, Wincraft, Orange, 12 In. 95.00
Basket, Hanging, Zephyr Lily, Blue 125.00
Basket, Imperial 68.00
Basket, Ixia, Green, 10 In. 170.00
Basket, Magnolia, Blue, 10 In. 155.00
Basket, Magnolia, Pink & White Flowers, Loop Handle, 12 1/2 In. 160.00
Basket, Ming Tree, White, 8 In. 85.00
Basket, Ming Tree, White, 12 In. 245.00
Basket, Ming Tree, White, 14 In. 250.00
Basket, Monticello, Brown, 6 In. 275.00
Basket, Monticello, Tan, 6 1/2 In. 425.00
Basket, Morning Glory, White, 4 In. 150.00
Basket, Peony, Green, 12 In. 160.00
Basket, Pine Cone, Boat Shape, 10 In. 395.00
Basket, Rozane, Pink, 1917, 6 In. 115.00
Basket, Rozane, Pink, 1917, 8 In. 65.00
Basket, Rozane, White, 6 In. 125.00
Basket, Snowberry, Green 110.00
Basket, Water Lily, Blue, 10 In. 120.00
Basket, Water Lily, Blue, 8 In. 135.00
Basket, White Rose, Blue, 12 In. 285.00
Basket, White Rose, Gray, 7 1/2 In. 110.00
Basket, Wincraft, 12 In. 195.00
Basket, Wincraft, Tan, 15 In. 75.00
Basket, Zephyr Lily, Brown, 8 In. 80.00
Basket, Zephyr Lily, Green & Tan, 10 In. 75.00
Boat, Mock Orange 65.00
Bookends, Burmese, Black ....100.00 To 165.00
Bookends, Dawn 42.00
Bookends, Freesia ....50.00 To 225.00
Bookends, Magnolia, Blue 85.00
Bookends, Magnolia, Green ....115.00 To 135.00
Bookends, Ming, Blue 125.00
Bookends, Peony, Gold 175.00
Bookends, Pine Cone, Blue ....140.00 To 350.00
Bookends, Pine Cone, Brown ....195.00 To 245.00
Bookends, Snowberry, Blue 225.00
Bookends, Snowberry, Green 100.00
Bookends, Snowberry, Pink 40.00
Bookends, Waterlily, Brown 155.00

Bookends, Wincraft, Blue 92.00
Bookends, Wincraft, Lime Green 125.00
Bookends, Wisteria, Brown 155.00
Bookends, Zephyr Lily, Dark Green .... 110.00 To 195.00
Bowl, Apple Blossom, Green, 10 In. 65.00
Bowl, Baneda, Green, 11 In. .... 325.00 To 350.00
Bowl, Baneda, Pink, 8 In. 285.00
Bowl, Beads, Red, 7 1/2 In. 275.00
Bowl, Blackberry, 4 In. 175.00
Bowl, Bleeding Heart, Pink, 11 1/2 In. 185.00
Bowl, Carnelian I, Green, 11 In. 35.00
Bowl, Carnelian I, Pink & Gray, 9 In. 50.00
Bowl, Carnelian II, Bowl, Rose, Turquoise & Black, 9 x 12 1/2 In. 85.00
Bowl, Cherry Blossom, Blue, 11 In. 350.00
Bowl, Cherry Blossom, Brown, 5 In. 165.00
Bowl, Columbine, 6 In. 48.00
Bowl, Columbine, Blue, 10 In. 55.00
Bowl, Corinthian, 9 1/4 In. 55.00
Bowl, Dahlrose, Oval, 10 In. .... 65.00 To 115.00
Bowl, Donatello, 8 1/2 In. 85.00
Bowl, Ferella, Attached Frog, 10 In. 295.00
Bowl, Ferella, Brown, 8 In. 375.00
Bowl, Foxglove, Blue, 14 In. 30.00
Bowl, Foxglove, Pink, 10 In. 75.00
Bowl, Freesia, 4 In. 75.00
Bowl, Fuchsia, Blue, ... 115.00
Bowl, Gardenia, Gray, 14 In. 85.00
Bowl, Imperial, Double Handle 115.00
Bowl, Iris, 10 In. 65.00
Bowl, Jonquil, 3 1/2 x 9 In. 155.00
Bowl, Jonquil, 5 1/2 In. .... 65.00 To 85.00
Bowl, Jonquil, 6 In. 120.00
Bowl, Ming Tree, Green, 9 In. 75.00
Bowl, Morning Glory, Green, 10 In. 395.00
Bowl, Mostique, 7 In. 38.00
Bowl, Mostique, Glossy, Handles, 9 In. 85.00
Bowl, Mostique, Gray, 3 In. 30.00
Bowl, Peony, 3 In. 45.00
Bowl, Peony, 13 In. 100.00
Bowl, Pine Cone, Twig Handle, 4 In. 55.00
Bowl, Primrose, Brown, 8 In. 100.00
Bowl, Rosecraft, Black, 8 In. 15.00
Bowl, Rosecraft, Hexagonal, Green, 2 x 4 1/2 In. 125.00
Bowl, Rosecraft, Paneled, Green, Stamped, 4 In. 75.00
Bowl, Savona, Light Orange, Black Label, 6 In. 90.00
Bowl, Silhouette, Nude, Rust, 6 x 9 In. 245.00
Bowl, Snowberry, 5 In. 60.00
Bowl, Snowberry, Blue, 6 In. 45.00
Bowl, Snowberry, Blue, 11 In. 75.00
Bowl, Snowberry, Pink, 5 In. 60.00
Bowl, Snowberry, Pink, 8 In. 110.00
Bowl, Snowberry, Pink, 10 In. 98.00
Bowl, Sunflower, 12 1/2 In. 300.00
Bowl, Topeo, Red, 6 In. 90.00
Bowl, Tuscany, Pink, 4 In. 35.00
Bowl, Velmoss, Blue, 7 In. 45.00
Bowl, Victorian Art, Gray, 10 In. 375.00
Bowl, Vintage, 6 In. 40.00
Bowl, Water Lily, Tan To Brown Ground, Green Leaves, 6 x 10 In. 60.00
Bowl, White Rose, Pink, 6 In. 45.00
Bowl, White Rose, Pink, 8 In. 65.00
Bowl, Wisteria, 4 In. 85.00
Bowl, Wisteria, Brown, 12 In. 175.00

Candlestick, 2 Twig Handles, 4 3/4 In. 65.00
Candlestick, Apple Blossom, Blue 75.00
Candlestick, Brown, 5 In. 40.00
Candlestick, Cherry Blossom, Brown, 4 In. 250.00
Candlestick, Clematis, Pair 30.00
Candlestick, Dahlrose 95.00
Candlestick, Donatello, 2–Light 80.00
Candlestick, Florentine, Brown, 10 1/2 In., Pair 210.00
Candlestick, Florentine, Pair 30.00
Candlestick, Foxglove, Blue, 4 1/2 In., Pair 45.00
Candlestick, Foxglove, Green 55.00
Candlestick, Fuchsia, Blue, 5 In., Pair 65.00
Candlestick, Gardenia, Brown, 5 In., Pair 75.00
Candlestick, Ixia, Green, 3 In., Pair 70.00
Candlestick, Lily, 5 In., Pair 65.00
Candlestick, Luffa, Green, 4 In. 145.00
Candlestick, Magnolia, Blue, 4 In., Pair .... 50.00 To 75.00
Candlestick, Morning Glory, Green, 5 In. 200.00
Candlestick, Moss, Green, Orange, 2 In. 80.00
Candlestick, Pine Cone, 3–Light, Green 100.00
Candlestick, Pine Cone, 5 Triple, Green 175.00
Candlestick, Pine Cone, Brown, 2 3/4 In., Pair 150.00
Candlestick, Pine Cone, Brown, 4 In., Pair 150.00
Candlestick, Rosecraft, Blue, Black Label, 15 In., Pair 225.00
Candlestick, Scroll, Velmoss, 10 In., Pair 165.00
Candlestick, Snowberry, Pink 65.00
Candlestick, Tuscany, Pink, Pair 75.00
Candlestick, Water Lily, Blue 70.00
Candlestick, Windsor, Blue, Green, 4 1/2 In., Pair 160.00
Candlestick, Windsor, Brown, 4 1/2 In. 250.00
Candlestick, Zephyr Lily, Brown, 2 In., Pair 45.00
Candy Dish, Double, Pine Cone, Blue, 6 1/2 x 13 In. 275.00
Chamber Pot, Dutch, 12 x 13 In. 350.00
Chamberstick, Donatello 65.00
Chamberstick, Egypto, Handle, 5 In. 225.00
Chocolate Set, Wincraft, Blue 250.00
Cider Set, Indian, Tankard, 6 Mugs 950.00
Clock, Louwelsa, Mantel, 12 In. 895.00
Compote, Florentine, 5 In. 38.00
Console Set, Baneda, Pink, 3 Piece 750.00
Console Set, Cornelian, Blue, c.1919, 10–In. Bowl, 3 Piece 135.00
Console Set, Poppy, Gray, 3 Piece 175.00
Console Set, Rosecraft, Signed, 3 Piece 95.00
Console, Clematis, Brown, 11 In. 120.00
Console, Freesia, 9 In. 130.00
Console, Imperial II 300.00
Console, Velmoss 89.00
Console, White Rose, Pink, 9 In. 145.00
Cookie Jar, Clematis .... 110.00 To 195.00
Cookie Jar, Freesia 335.00
Cookie Jar, Magnolia 195.00
Cookie Jar, Magnolia, Blue 250.00
Cookie Jar, Magnolia, Green, 8 In. 350.00
Cookie Jar, Water Lily, Brown .... 250.00 To 300.00
Cookie Jar, Water Lily, Rose 195.00
Cornucopia, Bittersweet, Green, 8 In. 125.00
Cornucopia, Bushberry, Brown, 6 In. 35.00
Cornucopia, Ivory II, 10 In., Pair 40.00
Cornucopia, Magnolia, Green, 6 In. 52.00
Cornucopia, Peony, Gold, 6 In. 60.00
Cornucopia, Water Lily, Brown, 6 In. 55.00
Creamer, Child's, Bunny, Side Pour 115.00
Creamer, Child's, Sunbonnet Girl, 3 1/2 In. 135.00

Creamer, Medallion	35.00
Cup & Saucer, Juvenile, Rabbit	100.00
Cup, Custard, Creamware, Landscape, 1 3/4 x 3 1/2 In.	85.00
Dealer Sign, Apple Blossom, Pink, 4 x 7 In.	1000.00
Dealer's Sign, Blue Script	1800.00
Dealer's Sign, Moderne	1500.00
Dish, Juvenile, Chick, 6 In.	75.00
Dish, Juvenile, Puppies, Rolled Edge	60.00
Dish, Juvenile, Rabbit	135.00
Dish, Juvenile, Sunbonnet Girl, Rolled Rim, 8 1/2 In.	125.00
Dresser Set, Forget-Me-Not, 3 Piece	105.00
Eggcup, Juvenile	150.00
Ewer, Bleeding Heart, Pink, 10 In.	225.00
Ewer, Bushberry, Blue, 15 In.	375.00
Ewer, Bushberry, Brown, 6 In.	58.00
Ewer, Bushberry, Russet, 10 In.	175.00
Ewer, Clematis, 17 In.	72.00
Ewer, Magnolia, Blue, 6 In.	40.00
Ewer, Magnolia, Green, 10 In.	175.00
Ewer, Ming Tree, Blue, 10 In.	95.00
Ewer, Pine Cone, Green, 18 In.	600.00
Ewer, Rozane, Daisies	100.00
Ewer, Wincraft, Blue, 8 In.	85.00
Flower Box, Vista, 1920s	465.00
Flower Frog, Clemna, Green	75.00
Flower Frog, Tuscany, Gray, 5 In.	80.00
Flower Frog, Tuscany, Pink, 3 In.	10.00
Flowerpot, Bittersweet, 5 In.	75.00 To 90.00
Flowerpot, Donatello, Ivory	55.00
Flowerpot, Jonquil, Fixed Frog, 6 In.	165.00
Flowerpot, Mostique	195.00
Flowerpot, Pine Cone, Green, 5 In.	125.00
Flowerpot, Pine Cone, Saucer	175.00
Flowerpot, Snowberry, Brown, Underplate	68.00
Jar, Luffa, Green, 5 In.	90.00
Jardiniere, Apple Blossom, Blue, 8 In.	850.00
Jardiniere, Apple Blossom, Green, 6 In.	50.00
Jardiniere, Apple Blossom, Green, Pedestal, 8 In.	135.00
Jardiniere, Apple Blossom, Pedestal, 24 1/2 In.	695.00
Jardiniere, Bittersweet, Green, Pedestal, 25 In.	650.00
Jardiniere, Bittersweet, Rose, Gray, 6 In.	140.00
Jardiniere, Blackberry, 7 x 10 In.	260.00
Jardiniere, Bleeding Heart, Pink, 6 In.	65.00
Jardiniere, Bushberry, Brown, Pedestal, 30 In.	1200.00
Jardiniere, Corinthian, 6 In.	125.00
Jardiniere, Dahlrose, 4 In.	50.00 To 60.00
Jardiniere, Dahlrose, 6 In.	125.00
Jardiniere, Dahlrose, 9 1/2 In.	350.00
Jardiniere, Dahlrose, 10 In.	290.00
Jardiniere, Donatello, 4 In.	45.00
Jardiniere, Donatello, Pedestal, 29 In.	750.00
Jardiniere, Donatello, Pedestal, 34 In.	2295.00
Jardiniere, Florentine, Ivory, 11 In.	250.00
Jardiniere, Freesia, Brown, Pedestal, 24 1/2 In.	650.00
Jardiniere, Fuchsia, Brown, 6 1/2 In.	165.00
Jardiniere, Iris, Blue, 8 In.	145.00
Jardiniere, Jonquil, 9 x 12 In.	350.00
Jardiniere, Mostique, Gray, 8 1/2 In.	75.00
Jardiniere, Mostique, Tan, 9 In.	125.00
Jardiniere, Peony, Green, 5 In.	60.00
Jardiniere, Pine Cone, Blue, 6 1/2 In.	228.00
Jardiniere, Primrose, Pink, 4 In.	75.00
Jardiniere, Rozane, 1917, 5 1/2 In.	85.00

Jardiniere, Rozane, Pedestal, 28 In. 600.00
Jardiniere, Snowberry, Blue, Pedestal, 25 In. 695.00
Jardiniere, Snowberry, Pedestal, 24 1/2 In. 625.00
Jardiniere, White Rose, Blue, Pedestal, 25 In. 600.00
Jardiniere, White Rose, Pink, Pedestal, 28 In. 800.00
Jardiniere, Wisteria, Brown, 5 In. 235.00
Jardiniere, Zephyr Lily, Blue, Pedestal, 28 In. 650.00
Lamp, Blue, High Gloss, No Shade 425.00
Lamp, Cherry Blossom, No Shade 750.00
Lamp, Leaves From Center To Top, Metal Base, Marked, 12 1/2 In. 275.00
Lamp, Luffa, Yellow Flowers, Green & Blue Glaze, 10 In. 220.00
Mug, Bushberry, Russet, 3 1/2 In., 3 Piece 135.00
Mug, Eagle 100.00
Mug, Elk, Creamware .... 50.00 To 60.00
Mug, Osman Temple, 1914 .... 125.00
Pansy Bowl, Panel, Green 50.00
Pedestal, Peony, Gold, 20 1/2 In. 350.00
Pitcher, Acanthus, Gray 95.00
Pitcher, Bridge & Grape 120.00
Pitcher, Bushberry, Ice Lip, Green 225.00
Pitcher, Buttermilk, Windmill, Blue & White 350.00
Pitcher, Cider, Magnolia, Blue, 7 In. .... 225.00 To 250.00
Pitcher, Cow, 7 1/2 In. 200.00
Pitcher, Della Robbia 2310.00
Pitcher, Dutch Children 150.00
Pitcher, Fuchsia, Blue 100.00
Pitcher, Magnolia, Green, Ice Lip 150.00
Pitcher, Owl 350.00
Pitcher, Pine Cone, Brown, 9 In. 325.00
Pitcher, Pine Cone, Green, 9 In. 300.00
Pitcher, Pine Cone, Ice Lip, Brown 395.00
Pitcher, Raymor, Art Deco, Gray 40.00
Pitcher, Rozane, White, 7 In. 225.00
Pitcher, Teddy Bear 1800.00
Pitcher, Utility, Yellow, Green Band, 7 In. 25.00
Planter, Artwood, Gray, 8 1/2 In. 55.00
Planter, Bittersweet 45.00
Planter, Bittersweet, Gray & Rose, 10 In. .... 43.00 To 48.00
Planter, Bittersweet, Hanging 95.00
Planter, Clematis, 2 Handles, 11 In. 60.00
Planter, Gardenia, Gray, 10 In. 75.00
Planter, Medallion 35.00
Planter, Ming Tree 32.00
Planter, Mostique 200.00
Planter, Pine Cone, Blue, 6 In. 85.00
Planter, Pine Cone, Blue, 8 In. 185.00
Planter, Pine Cone, Green, 7 In. 85.00
Planter, Wincraft, Blue, 12 In. 55.00
Pot, Strawberry, Earlam, 8 In. .... 185.00 To 375.00
Potty, Child's, Chicks Pattern 225.00
Rose Bowl, Poppy, Pink, 5 In. 65.00
Shelf, Wall, Pine Cone, Brown .... 225.00 To 600.00
Shelf, Wall, Velmoss, Green 95.00
Sign, Dealer, Blue Script, Pottery 775.00
Smoke Set, Creamware, Green Design On Cream, 4 Piece 195.00
Strawberry Pot, Jonquil, Attached Saucer 175.00
Sugar & Creamer, Bushberry, Brown 70.00
Sugar & Creamer, Clematis 95.00
Sugar & Creamer, Snowberry 55.00
Tankard Set, Dutch, Creamware, 6 Mugs 400.00
Tankard Set, Loyal Order Of Moose, 6 Piece 450.00
Tankard, Louwelsa, 4 1/2 In. 135.00
Tea Set, Apple Blossom, 3 Piece .... 165.00 To 275.00

Tea Set, Bittersweet, 3 Piece 265.00
Tea Set, Bushberry, Rust, 3 Piece 175.00
Tea Set, Clematis, Brown, 3 Piece 175.00
Tea Set, Peony, Green, 3 Piece 195.00
Tea Set, Peony, Yellow, 3 Piece 200.00
Tea Set, Snowberry, 3 Piece 295.00
Teapot, Apple Blossom 135.00
Teapot, Clematis, Green 100.00
Teapot, Della Robbia, Viking Ships, Birds, Green, Squatty 1950.00
Teapot, Raymor, Swinging 65.00
Teapot, Zephyr Lily, Green 145.00
Tray, Dresser, Medallion 85.00
Tray, Mayfair, Brown & Tan, 10 In. 60.00
Tumbler, Pine Cone, Brown, Pair 295.00
Umbrella Stand, Dogwood I, 20 1/2 In. 250.00
Umbrella Stand, Dogwood II, c.1924 .... 450.00
Umbrella Stand, Pine Cone, Brown ....900.00 To 1500.00
Urn, Baneda, Green, 6 In. 365.00
Urn, Baneda, Green, 8 In. 500.00
Urn, Cherry Blossom, Brown, 4 1/4 In. 220.00
Urn, Cremona, Green, 5 In. 60.00
Urn, Jonquil, 4 In. 60.00
Urn, Jonquil, Handles, Gold Paper Label, 6 In. 65.00
Urn, Rosecraft, Brown, Stamped, 7 x 4 In. 85.00
Urn, Tourmaline, 6 In. 95.00
Urn, White Rose, Blue, 8 In. 55.00
Urn, Wisteria, Vase Shape, Blue, 8 In. 425.00
Vase, Apple Blossom, Pink, 7 In. 68.00
Vase, Apple Blossom, Pink, 9 In. 155.00
Vase, Apple, Blue, 10 In. 90.00
Vase, Art Deco, Matte Yellow, 4 In. 55.00
Vase, Artwood, Green, 9 In. 65.00
Vase, Azurine, Orchid, 10 In. 70.00
Vase, Baneda, Green, 4 In. ....250.00 To 275.00
Vase, Baneda, Green, 6 1/2 In. 325.00
Vase, Baneda, Green, 8 In. 575.00
Vase, Baneda, Green, 9 In. 475.00
Vase, Baneda, Pink, 6 In. 250.00
Vase, Baneda, Pink, Volcano Shape, 4 1/2 In. 245.00
Vase, Bittersweet, 10 In. 60.00
Vase, Bittersweet, Handles, 8 In. 55.00
Vase, Blackberry, 2 Handles, 5 In. ....225.00 To 285.00
Vase, Blackberry, 4 In. ....235.00 To 250.00
Vase, Blackberry, 5 In. 245.00
Vase, Blackberry, 6 In. ....225.00 To 275.00
Vase, Bleeding Heart, 4 In. 40.00
Vase, Bleeding Heart, Blue, 7 In. 115.00
Vase, Bud, Double, Florentine, Brown, 9 In. 40.00
Vase, Bud, Magnolia, Blue, 7 In. 70.00
Vase, Bud, Triple, Pine Cone, Blue, 8 1/2 In. 325.00
Vase, Bushberry Blue, 14 In. 325.00
Vase, Bushberry, Blue, 6 In. 65.00
Vase, Bushberry, Blue, 8 In. 85.00
Vase, Bushberry, Green, 4 In. 25.00
Vase, Carnelian II, Cobalt Blue, Experimental Glaze 450.00
Vase, Cherry Blossom, Brown, 8 In. 250.00
Vase, Cherry Blossom, Pink, 16 In. 1800.00
Vase, Chrysanthemums, Pastel, Signed A. V. Lewis, 11 1/2 In. 295.00
Vase, Clemana, Brown, 6 1/2 In. 235.00
Vase, Clematis, Blue, 10 In. 95.00
Vase, Clematis, Brown, 6 In. 65.00
Vase, Columbine, Blue, 2 Handles, 26 In. 135.00
Vase, Columbine, Blue, 8 In. 55.00

Vase, Cremona, 2 Handles, 8 In. 65.00
Vase, Cremona, Blue, 7 In. 185.00
Vase, Cremona, Green, 10 1/2 In. 195.00
Vase, Dahlrose, 6 In. 65.00
Vase, Della Robbia, Design On 3 Sides, Signed E. C., 9 1/2 In. 1000.00
Vase, Dogwood II, 8 In. 75.00
Vase, Donatello, 10 In. ....82.00 To 215.00
Vase, Donatello, 6 1/2 In. 50.00
Vase, Donatello, 8 In. 95.00
Vase, Donatello, 9 3/4 In. 70.00
Vase, Earlam, Green, 5 In. 110.00
Vase, Earlam, Green, 7 In. 200.00
Vase, Egypto, 12 In. 325.00
Vase, Falline, Blue, 7 In. ....485.00 To 530.00
Vase, Falline, Brown, 6 In. 325.00
Vase, Fan, Nude Panel, Brown, 6 In. 275.00
Vase, Fan, Pine Cone, Brown, 6 In. 135.00
Vase, Ferella, Pink, 10 1/2 In. 595.00
Vase, Ferella, Red, 6 In. 345.00
Vase, Florentine, Brown, Beige, 6 1/2 In. 65.00
Vase, Foxglove, 9 In. 95.00
Vase, Foxglove, Blue, 15 In. 400.00
Vase, Freesia, 9 In. 85.00
Vase, Freesia, Brown, 7 In. 65.00
Vase, Freesia, Brown, 8 In. 75.00
Vase, Freesia, Orange & Brown, 18 In. ....365.00 To 385.00
Vase, Fuchsia, Blue, 2 Handles, 5 In. 32.50
Vase, Fuchsia, Blue, 2 Handles, 8 1/4 In. 150.00
Vase, Fuchsia, Brown, 10 In. 275.00
Vase, Fuchsia, Brown, 18 In. 650.00
Vase, Fuchsia, Brown, 8 In. 110.00
Vase, Fuchsia, Green, 7 1/2 In. 80.00
Vase, Fuchsia, Green, 10 1/2 In. 225.00
Vase, Fuchsia, Green, 12 In. 240.00
Vase, Futura, 13 In. 200.00
Vase, Futura, 2-Tone Blues, 9 In. 495.00
Vase, Futura, Blue, 4 In. 265.00
Vase, Futura, Blue, 8 In. 225.00
Vase, Futura, Blue-Green, 6 In. 325.00
Vase, Futura, Brown, 12 In. .... 485.00 -
Vase, Futura, Green, 1928, 8 In. 355.00
Vase, Futura, Mauve, 8 In. 150.00
Vase, Futura, Victory, 8 In. 325.00
Vase, Gardenia, Aqua, 10 In. 68.00
Vase, Gardenia, Green, Bulbous, 12 In. 120.00
Vase, Imperial I, Bulbous, 1916, 10 In. 65.00
Vase, Imperial II, Blue, 6 In. 120.00
Vase, Imperial II, Mottled Green & Lavender Glaze, 4 1/2 In. 195.00
Vase, Imperial II, Mottled Raspberry, 4 1/2 x 6 In. 195.00
Vase, Iris, Blue, 6 In. 75.00
Vase, Iris, Pink, 12 In. 220.00
Vase, Ixia, Green, 10 In. 95.00
Vase, Ixia, Yellow, 8 In. 63.00
Vase, Jonquil, 12 In. 230.00
Vase, Jonquil, 2 Handles, 3 In. 40.00
Vase, Jonquil, 6 1/2 In. ....200.00 To 225.00
Vase, Jonquil, 7 In. 175.00
Vase, Laurel, Gold & Black, 6 In. 125.00
Vase, Laurel, Green, 6 In. ....80.00 To 175.00
Vase, Laurel, Rust, 9 In. 225.00
Vase, Lombardy, Brown Glaze, 6 In. 100.00
Vase, Lotus, Brown, Beige, 10 1/2 In. 175.00
Vase, Luffa, Brown, 6 1/2 In. 75.00

Vase, Luffa, Green, 6 1/4 In. 55.00
Vase, Magnolia, Blue, 18 In. 475.00
Vase, Magnolia, Green, 10 In. 135.00
Vase, Ming Tree, Green, 12 1/2 In. 140.00
Vase, Ming Tree, White, 10 In. 95.00
Vase, Mock Orange, 19 1/2 In. 400.00
Vase, Monticello, Brown, 4 In. 135.00
Vase, Monticello, Brown, 8 In. 140.00
Vase, Monticello, Tan, 4 1/2 In. 175.00
Vase, Morning Glory, Green, 4 In. 240.00
Vase, Morning Glory, Green, 6 In. 300.00
Vase, Morning Glory, Handles At Base, 8 1/2 In. 325.00
Vase, Morning Glory, Pink & Blue Flowers, White, 15 1/2 In. 275.00
Vase, Morning Glory, White, Green, Lavender, 3 x 6 In. 325.00
Vase, Moss, Blue, Double Handles, 13 In. 225.00
Vase, Moss, Caramel With Green Ground, 7 In. 65.00
Vase, Mostique, Gray, 6 In. 40.00
Vase, Nude Panel, Brown, 10 In. 425.00
Vase, Orian, Blue, 12 1/2 In. 195.00
Vase, Panda, Green, 6 In. 225.00
Vase, Panel, Brown, 6 In. 45.00
Vase, Panel, Brown, 8 In. 150.00
Vase, Pauleo, Iridescent, Drilled For Lamp, 20 In. 200.00
Vase, Peony, Yellow, 2 Handles, 8 In. 95.00
Vase, Peony, Yellow, 7 In. 40.00
Vase, Pillow, Pine Cone, 8 1/2 In. 190.00
Vase, Pillow, Rozane, Royal Seal, 5 In. 175.00
Vase, Pine Cone, 6 In. 90.00
Vase, Pine Cone, Blue, 7 In. 140.00
Vase, Pine Cone, Brown, 14 1/2 In. 540.00
Vase, Pine Cone, Brown, 6 In. .... 55.00 To 65.00
Vase, Pine Cone, Green, 10 In. .... 185.00 To 225.00
Vase, Pine Cone, Green, 12 In. 340.00
Vase, Poppy, Green, 11 In. 145.00
Vase, Poppy, Pink, 10 In. 250.00
Vase, Primrose, 7 1/2 In. 135.00
Vase, Rosecraft, Black, Handles, Paper Label, 8 x 9 In. 175.00
Vase, Rosecraft, Deep Blue, Bulbous, 1916, 13 1/2 In. 195.00
Vase, Rozane, 1905, 18 In. 500.00
Vase, Rozane, Brown Standard Glaze, Chilcote, 13 In. 565.00
Vase, Rozane, Brown, 8 In. 45.00
Vase, Rozane, Gold & Red Fuji Mums, Signed, 13 In. 695.00
Vase, Rozane, Pink, 8 In. 45.00
Vase, Rozane, Twisted, Floral, Square, V. Adams, 10 In. 265.00
Vase, Rozane, Yellow, 12 In. 250.00
Vase, Russco, Metallic Gold Over Ivory, Green Interior, 8 1/2 In. 125.00
Vase, Savona, 1920s, 11 In. 38.00
Vase, Silhouette, Blue, 6 In. 45.00
Vase, Silhouette, Nude, Brown, 10 In. 375.00
Vase, Silhouette, White, 6 In. 48.00
Vase, Snowberry, Blue, 7 In. 60.00
Vase, Snowberry, Pink, 8 1/2 In. 65.00
Vase, Snowberry, Pink, 9 In. 65.00
Vase, Sunflower, 4 In. 200.00
Vase, Sunflower, 6 In. 165.00
Vase, Sunflower, 8 In. 350.00
Vase, Sunflower, Bulbous, 10 In. 535.00
Vase, Teasel, Blue, 6 In. 63.00
Vase, Thornapple, Blue, 15 In. 325.00
Vase, Thornapple, Pink, 10 1/2 In. 235.00
Vase, Thornapple, Pink, 6 In. 60.00
Vase, Topeo, Blue, 6 In. 195.00
Vase, Topeo, Blue, 7 In. 175.00

Vase, Topeo, Red, 7 In. .... 125.00 To 170.00
Vase, Topeo, Red, 8 In. 300.00
Vase, Tourmaline, Aqua, 7 In. 63.00
Vase, Tourmaline, Blue, 5 1/2 In. 70.00
Vase, Tourmaline, Blue, 8 1/2 In. 135.00
Vase, Tourmaline, Blue, 9 In. 70.00
Vase, Tourmaline, Turquoise, 7 In. 50.00
Vase, Tuscany, Green Leaves At Bottom, Pink, 4 In. 75.00
Vase, Tuscany, Pink, 7 1/2 In. 68.00
Vase, Tuscany, Pink, 9 In. 125.00
Vase, Vista, 10 In. .... 175.00 To 300.00
Vase, Volcanic Rose & Green Glaze, c.1930, 14 In. 330.00
Vase, Water Lily, Blue, 7 In. 45.00
Vase, Water Lily, Blue, 15 In. 190.00
Vase, Water Lily, Brown, 9 In. 135.00
Vase, White Rose, Blue, 15 1/2 In. 335.00
Vase, White Rose, Blue, 4 In. 25.00
Vase, White Rose, Pink, 12 In. 250.00
Vase, White Rose, Pink, 15 In. 300.00
Vase, Wincraft, Blue, 8 1/2 In. 50.00
Vase, Wincraft, Blue, 12 In. 65.00
Vase, Wincraft, Blue, 5 In. 65.00
Vase, Wisteria, Blue, 4 In. .... 200.00 To 250.00
Vase, Wisteria, Blue, 5 In. 325.00
Vase, Wisteria, Brown, 4 In. .... 155.00 To 245.00
Vase, Wisteria, Brown, 9 In. 150.00
Vase, Wisteria, Brown, 10 In. 450.00
Vase, Woodland, 9 In. 695.00
Vase, Zephyr Lily, Blue, 10 In. 150.00
Vase, Zephyr Lily, Blue, Handle, 6 1/2 In. 85.00
Vase, Zephyr Lily, Brown, Green, 12 In. 195.00
Vase, Zephyr Lily, Green, 18 In. 390.00
Wall Pocket, Apple Blossom, Blue, 8 1/2 In. 200.00
Wall Pocket, Carnelian I, Green 100.00
Wall Pocket, Cherry Blossom 400.00
Wall Pocket, Clematis, Blue, 8 In. 110.00
Wall Pocket, Corinthian, 9 In. 165.00
Wall Pocket, Corinthian, 12 In. 148.00
Wall Pocket, Florane, Rust, 9 In. .... 70.00 To 95.00
Wall Pocket, Freesia, Brown, 8 In. 95.00
Wall Pocket, Freesia, Green, 8 1/2 In. 95.00
Wall Pocket, Imperial I, 10 In. 75.00
Wall Pocket, Magnolia, Blue, Green 145.00
Wall Pocket, Magnolia, Brown 135.00
Wall Pocket, Pine Cone, Bucket, Green 295.00
Wall Pocket, Primrose, Pink 265.00
Wall Pocket, Rosecraft, Blue, 10 In. 110.00
Wall Pocket, Rosecraft, Hexagonal, Brown 295.00
Wall Pocket, Snowberry, Green 95.00
Wall Pocket, Snowberry, Rose 135.00
Wall Pocket, Sunflower, 5 In. 245.00
Wall Pocket, Sunflower, 10 In. .... 525.00 To 535.00
Wall Pocket, Tuscany, Pink 65.00
Wall Pocket, Vista, 12 In. 500.00
Wall Pocket, Zephyr Lily, Brown .... 85.00 To 110.00
Wall Pocket, Zephyr Lily, Tan 180.00
Wall Shelf, Iris, Brown, 8 In. 275.00
Wall Shelf, Pine Cone, Brown 285.00
Window Box, Cosmos, Green 85.00
Window Box, Gardenia, 3 x 8 1/2 In. 45.00
Window Box, Gardenia, Brown, 8 In. 50.00
Window Box, Ming Tree, 11 1/2 In. 105.00
Window Box, Orian, Aqua, 15 In. 80.00

Window Box, Pine Cone, Blue	350.00
Window Box, Pine Cone, Brown	145.00
Window Box, Velmoss, 16 In.	65.00
Window Box, Zephyr Lily, Brown, 8 In.	45.00

ROWLAND & MARSELLUS Company is part of a mark that appears on historical Staffordshire dating from the late nineteenth and early twentieth centuries. Rowland & Marsellus is believed to be the mark used by the British Anchor Pottery Co. of Longton, England, for some pieces made for export to a New York firm. Many American views were made. Of special interest to collectors are the blue and white plates with rolled edges.

Plate, Denver, Colorado, Capitol Building, 10 In.	65.00
Plate, Landing Of Hudson, Cobalt Blue, 10 In.	45.00
Plate, Souvenir, Buffalo, N.Y., Sweeney Co., Rolled Rim	60.00
Plate, Theodore Roosevelt, 10 In.	60.00
Plate, Valley Forge, 1777–1778, 10 In.	65.00

ROY ROGERS was born in 1911 in Cincinnati, Ohio. In the 1930s, he made a living as a singer; in 1935, his group started work at a Los Angeles radio station. He appeared in his first movie in 1937. From 1952 to 1957, he made 101 television shows. Roy Rogers memorabilia is collected, including items from the Roy Rogers restaurants.

Badge, Deputy, Copper	12.00
Bank, Roy On Rearing Trigger, Porcelain, Signed	250.00
Bedspread, Cotton, Embroidered Figures, Roy, Nellie Belle, Ranch	195.00
Binoculars, Roy & Trigger, 3 Power, Box	150.00
Book, Coloring, No. 1186	15.00
Book, Dale Evans & The Coyote, Little Golden Book	10.00
Book, Outlaws Of Sundance Valley, Big Little Book	20.00
Book, Punch Out, Roy, Dale Evans, Set Up Your Own Cowtown, Large	120.00
Book, Roy Rogers & The Gopher Creek Gunman, Autographed	45.00
Bow & Arrow Set, Box	125.00
Bowl, Roy & Trigger, 7 In.	40.00
Cap Gun, Black Grips, 9 1/2 In.	100.00
Cap Gun, Lever Release Break Front, Chrome Finish, 10 In., Pair	300.00
Card, Pop–Out, Post Cereal, 6 Piece	10.00
Chaps, Leather, Juvenile Size	125.00
Clay Set, Modeling, Toycraft Products, Box	55.00
Clock, Alarm, Animated	165.00 To 250.00
Coat, Denim Rider	225.00
Coin Set, Good Luck	45.00
Comic Book, Coral Tin Stand	50.00
Crayon Set, With Stencils, Unused	195.00
Creamer, Roy With Trigger Rearing, 3 In.	45.00
Cup	15.00 To 20.00
Curtains	150.00
Figurine, Chuck Wagon, 2 Horses, Accessories	95.00
Figurine, Plastic, Roy, Dale, Trigger, Bullet, Marx, 1950s, 4 Piece	42.00
Guitar, 1940	115.00
Guitar, Plastic, Black, Silvered, Reliable Toys, Canada, 20 In.	19.00
Gun & Holster	165.00
Gun, Double, Holster	275.00 To 325.00
Harmonica	25.00
Hat, Western, Quick Shooter Secret Gun Snaps Out Of Hat, Box	150.00
Jewelry Set, Boy's, Cuff Links	20.00
Jewelry Set, On Card, 1950s, 3 Piece	10.00
Kerchief Slide	18.50
Kerchief Slide, Holster Shape	59.00
Kerchief Slide, R–R Brand, Silver Plated	30.00
Lamp	130.00
Lamp, Dale Evans On Rearing Horse, Buttercup, Signed	250.00
Lamp, Roy Rogers On Rearing Horse, Trigger	120.00
Lamp, With Trigger	225.00

Lantern, Ranch, Box .... 200.00 To 250.00
Lucky Horseshoe Set, Dale Evans, On Card, 1950s 5.00
Lunch Box, 8 Scenes, Green Band 85.00
Lunch Box, Chow Wagon, Tin ....95.00 To 100.00
Lunch Box, Dale Evans & Roy, Thermos 100.00
Lunch Box, Dome, Thermos 165.00
Lunch Box, Saddle Bag, Vinyl 145.00
Lunch Box, Trigger 150.00
Magic Playaround Set 250.00
Mirror & Thermometer, Dale Evans 35.00
Mug, Roy & Trigger, 3 In. 25.00
Neck Tie 20.00
Paint Set, Sugar Crisp Premium, 1954 .... 25.00
Paper Doll, Roy Rogers & Dale Evans, 1957, Uncut 95.00
Play Set, Rodeo Ranch, Marx 135.00
Play Set, Western Town, Marx 250.00
Poster, Rodeo, Madison Square Garden 125.00
Print, Happy Trails, Roy Rogers & Trigger, 8 x 11 In. 2.50
Punch–Outs, Ranch, Post Cereal, Unpunched 85.00
Rifle, Silver Slicker 135.00
Ring, Branding Iron 125.00
Ring, Microscope, Advertising, Premiums, 1949 .... 45.00
Saddle, Child's, 1950s 575.00
Scarf 13.00
Sheet Music, Bible Tells Me So, Roy & Dale Evans, 1940 .... 4.00
Shirt, Frontier 50.00
Slippers, Indian, Moccasin Type, Box 225.00
Sweatshirt, Roy & Trigger, 1950s 59.00
Tablet, Paper, 8 x 10 In. 22.00
Telephone, Ranch 45.00
Tent, Graphics, Young Roy On Trigger 145.00
Thermos, Roy, Dale Evans, 1953 .... 58.00
Thermos, Roy, Dale Evans, Double R Ranch, 1955 .... 65.00
Tile, Roy On Trigger, Square, 4 1/4 In. 165.00
Toy, Bar M Ranch House, Marx 30.00
Toy, Chuck Wagon 125.00
Truck, Cattle Trailer, Roy, Trigger & Trigger Jr., Marx 195.00
Viewmaster, Roy Rogers & Cisco Kid, 1950s 25.00
Wallet, Tooled Picture Of Roy & Trigger, 1950s 45.00
Wristwatch, Dale Evans, Trigger & Horseshoe Picture 70.00
Wristwatch, Flicking Gun 325.00
Wristwatch, On Trigger 100.00
Yo–Yo, Roy & Trigger On Side 15.00

ROYAL BAYREUTH is the name of a factory that was founded in Tettau, Bavaria, in 1794. It has continued to modern times. The marks have changed through the years. A stylized crest, the name *Royal Bayreuth,* and the word *Bavaria* appear in slightly different forms from 1870 to about 1919. Later dishes may include the words *U.S. Zone,* the year of the issue, or the word *Germany* instead of *Bavaria.* Related pieces may be found listed in the Rose Tapestry, Sand Babies, Snow Babies, and Sunbonnet Babies categories.

Ashtray, Eagle 500.00
Ashtray, Elk, Blue Mark 195.00
Basket, Flowers, Gold Trim, Blue Mark, 5 1/4 x 4 3/8 In. 95.00
Basket, Swans On Lake, Blue Mark, 5 3/4 In. 95.00
Bell, Corinthian 95.00
Bell, Jack & Jill 250.00
Bowl & Plate, Dutch Boy & Girl, Blue Mark 65.00
Bowl & Plate, Little Jack Horner, Blue Mark 300.00
Bowl, Grape, Pearlized Lavender, Deponiert 350.00
Bowl, Lobster, Blue Mark, 8 In. 275.00
Bowl, Peacock, Jeweled Rolled Rim 675.00

Bowl, Portrait, Woman With Horse, 10 In.	310.00
Bowl, Ring Around The Rosie, Blue Mark, 9 In.	250.00
Bowl, Roses, Blown–Out Scalloped Rim, Blue Mark, 10 In.	195.00
Candleholder, Corinthian, Black, Roman Figures, Blue Mark	155.00
Candleholder, Jack & Jill	165.00
Candleholder, Little Jack Horner, Shield	325.00
Candleholder, Red Clown, Blue Mark	700.00
Candleholder, Rose Handle, Pearlized	110.00
Candy Dish, Lobster	95.00
Celery, Lobster	175.00
Chocolate Pot, Gibson Girl, Blue Mark, 9 In.	275.00
Chocolate Pot, Poppy, Apricot Color	1200.00
Compote, Brittainy Maid, 3 Footed	98.00
Cracker Jar, Tomato, Blue Mark	375.00
Creamer, Alligator	295.00 To 325.00
Creamer, Apple, Blue Mark	160.00
Creamer, Arab Scene, Green Mark	85.00
Creamer, Art Nouveau Woman	550.00
Creamer, Bull, Dark To Light Gray, Blue Mark	165.00
Creamer, Butterfly	275.00
Creamer, Butterfly, Closed Wings, Blue Mark	295.00
Creamer, Cat, Black	150.00 To 165.00
Creamer, Cat, Gray, Blue Mark, 5 In.	225.00
Creamer, Chimpanzee	475.00
Creamer, Chrysanthemum, Blue Mark	245.00
Creamer, Clown, Red	325.00
Creamer, Coachman, Blue Mark	160.00 To 185.00
Creamer, Cow, Gray, Blue Mark	245.00
Creamer, Crow	125.00 To 155.00
Creamer, Dachshund	155.00 To 175.00
Creamer, Duck	89.00 To 195.00
Creamer, Eagle, Blue Mark	250.00 To 295.00
Creamer, Elk, Blue Mark	90.00 To 110.00
Creamer, Fish Head	195.00
Creamer, Frog	125.00 To 155.00
Creamer, Frog Handle	150.00
Creamer, Girl With Pitcher, Marked	395.00
Creamer, Grape	125.00 To 195.00
Creamer, Jack & Jill	60.00
Creamer, Lamplighter, Blue Mark	195.00 To 275.00
Creamer, Little Boy Blue, Full Rhyme, Double Handle, Marked	195.00
Creamer, Lobster, Blue Mark	90.00 To 110.00
Creamer, Man In The Mountain	75.00
Creamer, Maple Leaf	495.00
Creamer, Melon	275.00
Creamer, Monkey, Green, Blue Mark	345.00
Creamer, Moose	80.00
Creamer, Oak Leaf, Blue Mark	150.00
Creamer, Old Man In The Mountain	140.00
Creamer, Owl	495.00
Creamer, Pansy, Blue Mark	195.00
Creamer, Parakeet	195.00
Creamer, Pear	325.00
Creamer, Pelican	225.00 To 295.00
Creamer, Penguin	495.00
Creamer, Pig, Blue Mark	495.00
Creamer, Poodle, Black	185.00
Creamer, Poodle, Gray	150.00
Creamer, Poppy, Blue Mark	85.00 To 165.00
Creamer, Portrait Of Woman, Hand Shielding Eyes, 3 1/4 In.	325.00
Creamer, Robin	95.00 To 165.00
Creamer, Rooster, Black	265.00
Creamer, Seal	210.00

Creamer, Shell, Green Mark .... 65.00 To 85.00
Creamer, Snake 950.00
Creamer, St. Bernard, Blue Mark .... 155.00 To 185.00
Creamer, Strawberry 145.00
Creamer, Sunflower .... 550.00 To 575.00
Creamer, Turkey & Hunter 125.00
Creamer, Turtle .... 425.00 To 450.00
Creamer, Water Buffalo, Black, Blue Mark ....95.00 To 195.00
Cup & Saucer, Chocolate, Poppy, Pink 200.00
Cup & Saucer, Devil & Dice, Demitasse 125.00
Cup & Saucer, Jack & Beanstalk, Blue Mark 155.00
Cup & Saucer, Little Jack Horner, Demitasse 60.00
Cup & Saucer, Poppy, Blue Mark 125.00
Cup & Saucer, Rose 525.00
Dish, Child's, Girl With Dog, Blue Mark, 7 3/4 In. 265.00
Dish, Child's, Jack & Jill 150.00
Dish, Child's, Little Bopeep, Blue Mark 25.00
Dish, Child's, Little Miss Muffet, 8 In. 225.00
Dish, Children In Snow, Square, 4 In. 65.00
Easter Egg, 1974 .... 15.00
Ewer, Cattle, Signed, Miniature 70.00
Fernery, Blown Out, Boy With Horses, Footed, Handle, Large 225.00
Fernery, Little Jack Horner, Liner Pot 110.00
Figurine, Shoe, Woman's, Oxford, Matte Ivory 135.00
Flowerpot, 3 Color Roses, With Drainer, Blue Mark 165.00
Flowerpot, Cockerels, Liner, 3 1/2 x 3 In. 75.00
Gravy Boat, Poppy 135.00
Gravy Boat, Underplate, Tomato 175.00
Hair Receiver, Hunting Scene 115.00
Hatpin Holder, Cornucopia, Hanging 265.00
Hatpin Holder, Deer & Fawn Scene, Blue Mark 235.00
Hatpin Holder, Grazing Sheep, Blue Mark 125.00
Hatpin Holder, Man On Horse, Woman In Cart, Blue Mark 250.00
Hatpin Holder, Owl 395.00
Hatpin Holder, Penguin, 5 In. 600.00
Hatpin Holder, Poppy, Pink & Gold Trim, Pearlized 325.00
Humidor, Elk 995.00
Humidor, Fishing Scene 265.00
Humidor, Lobster 625.00
Jardiniere, Corinthian, 8 In. 95.00
Match Holder, Cavalier Design 190.00
Match Holder, Elk 225.00
Match Holder, Pastel Pink & Green, , Hanging, Blue Mark 225.00
Match Holder, Poppy, Red, Hanging 225.00
Match Holder, Shell, Hanging 125.00
Match Holder, Tavern Scene, Striker 200.00
Mug, Arabs On Horses, Blue Mark 95.00
Mug, Arabs On Horses, Mosque, 8 In. 325.00
Mug, Beer, Devil & Cards 450.00
Mug, Beer, Elk 395.00
Mustard, Lemon 275.00
Mustard, Lobster 95.00
Mustard, Shell 75.00
Mustard, Shell, Spoon 145.00
Mustard, Snowballs 135.00
Nut Dish, Almond, Deponiert, 6 Piece 270.00
Pitcher, Apple, 7 1/2 In. 1250.00
Pitcher, Clown, Red, Marked, 6 1/2 In. 925.00
Pitcher, Coachman, 7 In. 850.00
Pitcher, Coachman, Blue Mark, 4 3/4 In. 275.00
Pitcher, Devil & Cards, 5 In. 345.00
Pitcher, Devil & Cards, 7 1/2 In. .... 595.00 To 985.00
Pitcher, Duck, 6 1/2 In. 1295.00

Pitcher, Eagle, 5 In. 320.00
Pitcher, Elk, Blue Mark, 7 In. 325.00
Pitcher, Fish Head, 5 1/2 In. 195.00
Pitcher, Hunting Dogs, Moose, River On Border, 6 In. 85.00
Pitcher, Lady Bug, 5 In. 1995.00
Pitcher, Lobster, 7 In. 160.00
Pitcher, Lobster, Blue Mark, 7 In. 360.00
Pitcher, Pelican, 6 1/2 In. 450.00
Pitcher, Penguin, 5 In. 450.00
Pitcher, Perch, 7 1/4 In. 1395.00
Pitcher, Rooster, 7 In. 1495.00
Pitcher, Santa Claus, 6 1/4 In. 2995.00
Pitcher, Seal, 7 In. 1495.00
Pitcher, Snake, 6 1/4 In. 2995.00
Pitcher, St. Bernard, 4 In. 165.00
Pitcher, Sunflower, 4 1/2 In. 895.00
Pitcher, Tomato, 6 1/4 In. 395.00
Plate, Boy With Donkey, 13 In. 325.00
Plate, Christmas, 1972 .... 60.00
Plate, Christmas, 1974 .... 20.00
Plate, Elderly Man Fishing In Boat, 7 1/2 In. 40.00
Plate, Forest & Mountain Scene, Signed, 12 In. 110.00
Plate, Leaf, Curled Stem, Yellow Flower, Blue Mark, 5 1/2 In. 65.00
Plate, Man With Dog, Shooting Gun, 7 1/2 In. 40.00
Plate, Mother's Day, 1973 .... 25.00
Plate, Mother's Day, 1974 .... 75.00
Plate, Nursery Rhyme, Jack & Jill, 6 In. 80.00
Plate, Nursery Rhyme, Little Bopeep, 6 1/2 In. 90.00
Plate, Nursery Rhyme, Little Boy Blue, 6 In. 80.00
Plate, Nursery Rhyme, Little Miss Muffet, Blue Mark, 6 In. 135.00
Plate, Oak Leaf, 5 1/2 In. 20.00
Posy Pot, Girl Gleaner, Chickens 65.00
Pot, Stork Design, Demitasse 255.00
Salt & Pepper, Elk 155.00
Salt & Pepper, Lobster 95.00
Salt & Pepper, Tomato, Blue Mark .... 125.00 To 135.00
Saltshaker, Lobster, Blue Mark 65.00
Saucer, Pink Rose, Demitasse 95.00
Shoe, Man's, Oxford, Brown .... 75.00 To 95.00
Shoe, Woman's, High Button, Brown, Pair 275.00
Stein, Beer, Elk, Blue Mark 395.00
String Holder, Rooster 300.00
Sugar & Creamer, Corinthian, Blue Mark .... 75.00 To 100.00
Sugar & Creamer, Cover, Shell 150.00
Sugar & Creamer, Lemon 400.00
Sugar & Creamer, Little Bopeep, 2 Handles, Marked 145.00
Sugar & Creamer, Pansy 595.00
Sugar & Creamer, Pink Rose 510.00
Sugar & Creamer, Poppy 185.00
Sugar & Creamer, Rooster 495.00
Sugar & Creamer, Roses, Gold Trim, Blue Mark 75.00
Sugar & Creamer, Tomato, Blue Mark .... 175.00 To 185.00
Sugar, Cover, Grape, Purple, Black Mark .... 85.00 To 130.00
Tea Set, Grape, Green, 3 Piece 385.00
Tea Set, Tomato, Blue Mark, 3 Piece 235.00
Teapot, Tomato, Blue Mark 105.00
Tomato, Cover, 3 1/2 In. 49.00
Toothpick, 2 Men Fishing, Rowboat, 3 Handles, Blue Mark 135.00
Toothpick, Coachman 265.00
Toothpick, Devil & Cards 235.00
Toothpick, Dutch Boy & Girl, 3 Handles, Signed, 2 3/4 In. 300.00
Toothpick, Dutch Children, Barrel Shape, Blue Mark 225.00
Toothpick, Elk, Blue Mark 125.00

Toothpick, Floral, 3 Handles	220.00
Toothpick, Lamplighter, Blue Mark	450.00
Toothpick, Little Miss Muffet, 3 Handles	460.00
Toothpick, Man & Hunting Dog, 3 Handles	260.00
Toothpick, Man On Horse, Woman In Car, 3 Handles, Marked	145.00
Toothpick, Man With 2 Horses, Footed	20.00
Toothpick, Musician Scene, Ball Shape, 4 Ball Feet, Marked	95.00
Toothpick, Musicians, Sterling Rim, 2 Handles, Blue Mark	125.00
Toothpick, Pink & White Floral, Blue Mark	125.00
Toothpick, Shell, Blue Mark	58.00
Tray, Dresser, Man With Horse, 11 1/2 In.	250.00 To 325.00
Tray, Dresser, Woman Feeding Geese	260.00
Vase, Cavaliers, 4 3/4 In.	58.00
Vase, Cow, Orange, Marked, 7 In.	150.00
Vase, Deer Scene, Hand Painted, Gold Rim	96.00
Vase, Green Cavaliers Base, Mandolin Top, Blue Mark, 6 In.	95.00
Vase, Old Ivory, Footed, Bulbous	235.00
Vase, Portrait In Medallion, Leaf Design In Gold, 5 1/4 In.	170.00
Vase, Running Dutch Boy & Dog, Blue Mark, 3 In.	45.00
Vase, Stag & Doe Design, 7 1/2 In.	325.00
Vase, Strawberry, Wall	750.00
Wall Pocket, Devil & Cards	185.00
Wall Pocket, Grape, Pearlized	225.00

ROYAL BONN is the nineteenth– and twentieth–century trade name for the Bonn China Manufactory. It was established in 1755 in Bonn, Germany. A general line of porcelain was made. Many marks were used, most including the name *Bonn,* the initials *FM,* and a crown.

Clock, Flowers, Ansonia	145.00
Clock, Open Escapement, Pink, Ansonia	550.00
Ewer, Hand Painted Flowers, Leaves, Serpent Handles, 12 1/2 In.	395.00
Ewer, Tapestry, Brass Spout, 19 In.	495.00
Urn, Scenic, Signed Sticher, 40 In.	4000.00
Vase, Central Vignette Of Ships, 25 In.	550.00
Vase, Children Scene, 6 In., Pair	100.00
Vase, Cover, Tapestry, Rose, Butterfly & Bluebird, 16 In.	375.00
Vase, Enameled Thistles, Signed, 12 In.	110.00
Vase, Floral Mold, Roses & Gilt, Signed, 15 In.	80.00
Vase, Floral, Flower Inset In Pierced Handles, 10 1/2 In.	225.00
Vase, Flowers, 2 Handles, 12 1/2 In.	100.00
Vase, Green Top, Gold Foliage, Roses, Marked, 5 1/2 In.	125.00
Vase, Hand Painted Floral, 9 In.	375.00
Vase, Lavender Flowers, Gold Outlines, 1825	70.00
Vase, Old Dutch, 7 In.	115.00
Vase, Oval Reserves, Bust Portrait, Gold Frieze, Signed, 8 In.	100.00
Vase, Portrait, Woman, Blond Hair, Marked, 10 1/2 In.	495.00
Vase, Portrait, Woman, Brown & Gold Ground, Marked, 10 1/2 In.	550.00
Vase, Seminude In Forest Scene, Signed, 11 1/2 In.	650.00
Vase, Tapestry, 2 Handles, 14 1/2 In.	650.00
Vase, Woman With Flowing Hair, 9 In.	650.00
Vase, Woman's Portrait, Gold Handles & Trim, Marked, 10 3/4 In.	450.00

ROYAL COPENHAGEN porcelain and pottery have been made in Denmark since 1772. The Christmas plate series started in 1908. The figurines with pale blue and gray glazes have remained popular in this century and are still being made. Many other old and new style porcelains are made today.

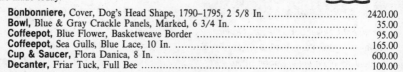

Bonbonniere, Cover, Dog's Head Shape, 1790–1795, 2 5/8 In.	2420.00
Bowl, Blue & Gray Crackle Panels, Marked, 6 3/4 In.	35.00
Coffeepot, Blue Flower, Basketweave Border	95.00
Coffeepot, Sea Gulls, Blue Lace, 10 In.	165.00
Cup & Saucer, Flora Danica, 8 In.	600.00
Decanter, Friar Tuck, Full Bee	100.00

Dish, Lobster	110.00
Dish, Serving, Flora Danica	100.00
Figurine, Boy Cutting Stick, No. 905, 7 1/2 In.	275.00
Figurine, Boy With Calf, No. 772, 6 1/2 In.	415.00
Figurine, Boy With Calves, No. 1858	325.00
Figurine, Boy With Sailboat, No. 01234, 5 1/2 In.	395.00
Figurine, Brown Bear With 4 Cubs	525.00
Figurine, Canoe Girl, No. 1243	950.00
Figurine, Churchgoing Woman, No. 892, 9 1/2 In.	345.00
Figurine, Dancing Girl, No. 2444, 8 1/2 In.	340.00
Figurine, Deadly Boxer, No. 01069, 5 1/2 In.	250.00
Figurine, Faun & Crow, No. 02113, 6 1/2 In.	450.00
Figurine, Faun With Parrot, No. 752	300.00
Figurine, Goose Girl, No. 527, 9 1/2 In.	235.00
Figurine, Goose Girl, No. 528, 7 1/4 In.	145.00
Figurine, Greenland Boy, No. 12419	695.00
Figurine, Greenland Girl, No. 12415, 5 1/2 In.	2500.00
Figurine, Ground Hog, With Dish, 1940, 3 1/2 In. ....*Illus*	100.00
Figurine, Kangaroo, No. 05154, 6 In.	400.00
Figurine, Knitting Girl, No. 1314, 6 In.	250.00
Figurine, Owl, No. 2999, 6 1/2 In.	200.00
Figurine, Pan & Parrot, No. 752	200.00
Figurine, Pug, No. 3169	90.00
Figurine, Rabbit, 1950, 4 In. ....*Illus*	85.00
Figurine, Scotch Terrier, Standing, No. 11066	240.00
Figurine, Terrier, No. 3020, 6 1/2 x 5 1/2 In.	150.00
Figurine, Turkey, No. 04784, White, 3 In.	110.00
Ice Dome, Underplate, Flora Danica	6250.00
Plate, Christmas, 1962 .... 145.00 To	170.00
Plate, Christmas, 1978	25.00
Plate, Flora Danica, 7 3/4 In.	425.00
Plate, Flora Danica, 9 In.	650.00
Plate, Flora Danica, Scalloped Rim, 8 In., 12 Piece	2975.00
Platter, Flora Danica, Large	1750.00
Soup, Dish, Flora Danica, Marked, 9 15/16 In., 12 Piece	1650.00
Sugar, Flora Danica	900.00
Teapot, Blue, White, Flowers, Palmetto Leaves, 10 In.	60.00
Tureen, Cover, Underplate, Flora Danica	1750.00
Vase, Fluted, Gold Design, White Ground, 10 1/2 In.	55.00
Vase, Mermaid On Rock, Langelinie, 6 3/4 In.	225.00
Vase, Royal Blue & Plum, Bottle Shape, 11 In.	85.00

ROYAL COPLEY china was made by the Spaulding China Company of Sebring, Ohio, from 1939 to 1960. The figural planters and the small figurines, especially those with Art Deco designs, are of great collector interest.

Bank, Pig, Large	32.00

Left to right: Royal Copenhagen, Figurine, Ground Hog, With Dish, 1940, 3 1/2 In.; Royal Copenhagen, Figurine, Rabbit, 1950, 4 In.

◆◆◆◆◆◆◆◆◆◆◆◆◆◆◆◆◆◆◆◆◆

Brass that has been laquered should be cleaned only with warm sudsy water, then rinsed and dried. Polish will harm the lacquer.

◆◆◆◆◆◆◆◆◆◆◆◆◆◆◆◆◆◆◆◆◆

Candy Dish, Hummingbird	20.00
Figurine, Bear Cub, On Stump	17.00
Figurine, Duck, Signed	52.00
Figurine, Elf, Log, Gold Trim	25.00
Figurine, Puppy, With Basket	15.00
Planter, Bear Cub, On Stump	20.00
Planter, Birdhouse With Bird	42.50
Planter, Doe, Fawn, Sticker	12.00
Planter, Gazelle, 9 In.	15.00
Planter, Kitten With Boot	15.00
Planter, Mandolin Bear	30.00
Planter, Pink Angel	18.00
Planter, Pup In Basket	40.00
Smoke Set, Figural, Mallard, 3 Piece	45.00
Wall Pocket, Colonial, Pair	45.00

ROYAL CROWN DERBY Company, Ltd., was established in England in 1890. There is a complex family tree that includes the Derby, Crown Derby, and Royal Crown Derby porcelains. The Royal Crown Derby mark includes the name and a crown. The words *Made in England* were used after 1921. The company is now a part of Royal Doulton Tableware Ltd.

Cup & Saucer, Mandarin Blue	30.00
Cup & Saucer, Old Imari	145.00
Dessert Set, Imari, 58 Piece	3300.00
Dessert Set, Red Birds, Cobalt, Gold & Green, 23 Piece	192.00
Dish, Cheese, Shell Shape Cover, Marked, 12 In.	357.00
Ewer, Floral, Gilt Design, Cobalt Blue, Signed, 7 1/2 In.	195.00
Figurine, Pigeon, 6 1/2 In.	55.00
Napkin Ring, Floral, Set Of 6	45.00
Tea Set, Kedleston, 1920s, 3 Piece	275.00
Teapot, Imari, Miniature	475.00
Vase, Cobalt Blue, Gold Flowers & Fruit, 6 1/2 In.	450.00
Vase, Imari, 9 In.	950.00
Vase, Imari, Handles, c.1887, 6 In.	200.00

ROYAL DOULTON is the name used on Doulton and Company pottery made from 1902 to the present. Doulton and Company of England was founded in 1853. Pieces made before 1902 are listed in this book under Doulton. Royal Doulton collectors search for the out-of-production figurines, character jugs, and series wares.

Animal, Brown Bear, Chatcull Range, HN 2659	250.00
Animal, Cat, Seated, 5 1/4 In.	135.00
Animal, Dog, Airedale, HN 1023	135.00
Animal, Dog, Airedale, K–5	90.00
Animal, Dog, Bloodhound, Sitting, Flambe, 6 In.	450.00
Animal, Dog, Bone In Mouth, HN 1159	85.00
Animal, Dog, Bull Terrier, HN 1132	750.00
Animal, Dog, Bulldog, Brindle, HN 1042	695.00
Animal, Dog, Bulldog, Brindle, HN 1043	495.00
Animal, Dog, Bulldog, Brindle, HN 1044	140.00
Animal, Dog, Bulldog, Brown & White, HN 1047	90.00
Animal, Dog, Bulldog, White, HN 1072	900.00
Animal, Dog, Bulldog, White, HN 1074	100.00
Animal, Dog, Cairn, Charming Eyes, HN 1033	500.00
Animal, Dog, Cairn, Charming Eyes, HN 1034	245.00
Animal, Dog, Cocker Spaniel & Pheasant, HN 1001	225.00
Animal, Dog, Cocker Spaniel, Golden, HN 1187	125.00
Animal, Dog, Cocker Spaniel, Liver & White, HN 1036	165.00
Animal, Dog, Cocker Spaniel, Liver & White, HN 1037	125.00
Animal, Dog, Collie, Ashstead Applause, HN 1059	80.00
Animal, Dog, Collie, Ashstead Applause, HN 1057	650.00
Animal, Dog, Dachshund, HN 1140	270.00
Animal, Dog, English Setter, Maesydd Mustard, HN 1049	650.00

Animal, Dog, Great Dane, HN 2601 .... 900.00
Animal, Dog, Greyhound, Brown, HN 1065 .... 1200.00
Animal, Dog, Greyhound, Sitting, Flambe, 5 In. 750.00
Animal, Dog, Pekinese, Biddee Of Ifield, HN 1012 .... 98.00
Animal, Dog, Pekinese, Sitting, K 6 .... 50.00
Animal, Dog, Scottish Terrier, Albourne Arthur, HN 1008 .... 700.00
Animal, Dog, Scottish Terrier, Standing, Flambe, 7 In. 650.00
Animal, Dog, Spaniel, Black & White, HN 1108 .... 30.00
Animal, Dog, With Plate, HN 1158 .... 85.00
Animal, Duckling, Flambe, 3 1/2 In. 245.00
Animal, Elephant, Flambe, Large 155.00
Animal, Mountain Sheep, Chatcull Range, HN 2661 .... 275.00
Animal, Rhinoceros, Flambe 750.00
Animal, Tiger, Flambe, Charging Position, 6 x 14 In. 1050.00
Animal, Tiger, On Rock, HN 2639 .... 3000.00
Ash Pot, Auld Mac 125.00
Ash Pot, Old Charlie 90.00
Ash Pot, Parson Brown .... 90.00 To 95.00
Ash Pot, Sairey Gamp 100.00
Ashtray, Mr. Pickwick, Dickens Ware 27.50
Ashtray, Mr. Squeers, Dickens Ware 27.50
Ashtray, Parson Brown .... 88.00 To 90.00
Bowl, Battle Of The Nile, Inside & Out, Signed, 8 In. 225.00
Bread Plate, Melrose 6.00
Candlestick, Canadian Scenes, Bow Valley 70.00
Candlestick, Lake Louise 70.00
Candlestick, Mr. Micawber, Dickens Ware, Pair 80.00

Royal Doulton character jugs depict the head and shoulders of the subject.
They are made in four sizes: large, 5 1/4 to 7 inches; small, 3 1/4 to 4
inches; miniature, 2 1/4 to 2 1/2 inches; and tiny, 1 1/4 inches. Toby jugs
portray a seated, full figure.

Character Jug, 'Ard Of 'Earing, Large 820.00
Character Jug, 'Arriet, Miniature .... 65.00 To 85.00
Character Jug, 'Arriet, Small .... 110.00 To 125.00
Character Jug, 'Arry, A Mark, Miniature 75.00
Character Jug, 'Arry, Large 200.00
Character Jug, 'Arry, Miniature .... 85.00 To 140.00
Character Jug, 'Arry, Tiny 180.00
Character Jug, Athos, Large 140.00
Character Jug, Athos, Miniature 50.00
Character Jug, Athos, Small 30.00
Character Jug, Auld Mac, Small .... 30.00 To 50.00
Character Jug, Auld Mac, Tiny .... 150.00 To 185.00
Character Jug, Bacchus, Large 80.00
Character Jug, Bacchus, Small 30.00
Character Jug, Beefeater, Large .... 57.00 To 130.00
Character Jug, Beefeater, Miniature 45.00
Character Jug, Blacksmith, Small 55.00
Character Jug, Bootmaker, A Mark, Miniature 50.00
Character Jug, Bootmaker, Large 60.00
Character Jug, Cap'n Cuttle, Small 70.00
Character Jug, Captain Ahab, Miniature 40.00
Character Jug, Captain Hook, Large ....*Illus* 425.00
Character Jug, Captain Hook, Small ....*Illus* 340.00
Character Jug, Cardinal, Large .... 125.00 To 150.00
Character Jug, Cardinal, Miniature 65.00
Character Jug, Cardinal, Tiny .... 160.00 To 185.00
Character Jug, Cavalier, Large .... 100.00 To 145.00
Character Jug, Cavalier, Small .... 50.00 To 60.00
Character Jug, Clown, White Hair, Large ....*Illus* 850.00
Character Jug, D'Artagnan, Large 70.00
Character Jug, Dick Turpin, Miniature 48.00

Royal Doulton, Character Jug,   Royal Doulton, Character Jug,   Royal Doulton, Character Jug,

Captain Hook, Large   Clown, White Hair, Large   Farmer John, A Mark, Small

Royal Doulton, Character Jug,   Royal Doulton, Character Jug,

Captain Hook, Small   Farmer John, A Mark, Large

Character Jug, Dick Turpin, Small	50.00
Character Jug, Don Quixote, Large	100.00
Character Jug, Don Quixote, Small	40.00
Character Jug, Drake, A Mark, Large	90.00
Character Jug, Drake, Large	120.00 To 155.00
Character Jug, Falconer, Small	30.00
Character Jug, Falstaff, Large	57.00
Character Jug, Falstaff, Small	30.00
Character Jug, Farmer John, A Mark, Large ....*Illus*	110.00
Character Jug, Farmer John, A Mark, Small ....*Illus*	75.00
Character Jug, Farmer John, Large	160.00
Character Jug, Farmer John, Small	75.00
Character Jug, Fat Boy, A Mark, Small	40.00
Character Jug, Fat Boy, Miniature	70.00
Character Jug, Fat Boy, Tiny	90.00 To 95.00
Character Jug, Fireman, Large ....*Illus*	65.00
Character Jug, Fortune Teller, Large	500.00
Character Jug, Fortune Teller, Miniature	300.00
Character Jug, Fortune Teller, Small	350.00
Character Jug, Gardener, Large	140.00
Character Jug, Gardener, Miniature	50.00
Character Jug, Gladiator, Small	400.00
Character Jug, Gondolier, Large	595.00
Character Jug, Gondolier, Miniature	285.00 To 360.00
Character Jug, Gone Away, A Mark, Miniature	60.00
Character Jug, Gone Away, Large	90.00
Character Jug, Gone Away, Small	50.00
Character Jug, Granny, Small	45.00
Character Jug, Guardsman, Large	80.00
Character Jug, Gulliver, Small	270.00 To 340.00
Character Jug, Gunsmith, Large	80.00
Character Jug, Henry Morgan, Miniature	40.00
Character Jug, Jarge, A Mark, Large	350.00
Character Jug, Jarge, Small	180.00 To 225.00
Character Jug, Jester, Small	95.00
Character Jug, Jockey, Large	275.00
Character Jug, John Barleycorn, A Mark, Large	140.00
Character Jug, John Barleycorn, Large	160.00
Character Jug, John Barleycorn, Small	60.00
Character Jug, John Peel, A Mark, Large ....*Illus*	175.00
Character Jug, John Peel, Small	40.00 To 75.00

Character Jug, John Peel, Tiny .... 175.00 To 190.00
Character Jug, Lord Nelson, Large 260.00
Character Jug, Lumberjack, Small 55.00
Character Jug, Mad Hatter, Miniature 55.00
Character Jug, Mark Twain, Large 65.00
Character Jug, Mephistopheles, With Verse, Large 1750.00
Character Jug, Mikado, Small .... 270.00 To 300.00
Character Jug, Mine Host, Miniature 40.00
Character Jug, Mine Host, Small 50.00
Character Jug, Monty, Large 70.00
Character Jug, Mr. Pickwick, Large 130.00
Character Jug, Mr. Pickwick, Tiny 160.00
Character Jug, Neptune, Miniature 25.00
Character Jug, Old Charley, Large 57.00
Character Jug, Old Charley, Miniature 78.00
Character Jug, Old Charley, Tiny .... 80.00 To 90.00
Character Jug, Old King Cole, A Mark, Small .... 65.00 To 125.00
Character Jug, Old King Cole, Large .... 245.00 To 275.00
Character Jug, Paddy, Large 125.00
Character Jug, Paddy, Small .... 35.00 To 60.00
Character Jug, Paddy, Tiny .... 70.00 To 80.00
Character Jug, Parson Brown, Large .... 125.00 To 155.00
Character Jug, Parson Brown, Small 40.00
Character Jug, Pickwick, Tiny 225.00
Character Jug, Pied Piper, Small 45.00
Character Jug, Poacher, Large 50.00
Character Jug, Porthos, Small 30.00
Character Jug, Punch & Judy, A Mark, Small 400.00
Character Jug, Punch & Judy, Miniature 350.00
Character Jug, Regency Beau, Miniature 650.00
Character Jug, Rip Van Winkle, Large 90.00
Character Jug, Rip Van Winkle, Small 30.00
Character Jug, Robinson Crusoe, Miniature 40.00
Character Jug, Sairey Gamp, Large 60.00
Character Jug, Sairey Gamp, Miniature 27.00
Character Jug, Sairey Gamp, Small .... 50.00 To 110.00
Character Jug, Sam Weller, A Mark, Large 140.00
Character Jug, Sam Weller, Small 80.00
Character Jug, Sam Weller, Tiny .... 75.00 To 80.00
Character Jug, Samuel Johnson, Large 250.00
Character Jug, Samuel Johnson, Small 132.00
Character Jug, Sancho Panza, Large 95.00
Character Jug, Sancho Panza, Miniature 45.00
Character Jug, Scaramouche, Large 450.00
Character Jug, Scaramouche, Small 345.00
Character Jug, Simon The Cellarer, Small .... 45.00 To 60.00
Character Jug, Smuggler, Large .... 57.00 To 75.00
Character Jug, Smuggler, Small .... 45.00 To 55.00
Character Jug, Toby Philpots, Miniature 38.00
Character Jug, Toby Philpots, Small 35.00
Character Jug, Tony Weller, A Mark, Miniature 50.00
Character Jug, Tony Weller, Small 40.00
Character Jug, Touchstone, Large .... 160.00 To 225.00
Character Jug, Town Crier, Large .... 170.00 To 185.00
Character Jug, Town Crier, Miniature .... 87.00 To 110.00
Character Jug, Town Crier, Small 90.00
Character Jug, Trapper, Large .... 70.00 To 95.00
Character Jug, Trapper, Small 55.00
Character Jug, Ugly Duchess, Large .... *Illus* 400.00
Character Jug, Ugly Duchess, Small .... *Illus* 300.00
Character Jug, Uncle Tom Cobbleigh, Large 375.00
Character Jug, Veteran Motorist, A Mark, Large 120.00
Character Jug, Vicar Of Bray, A Mark, Large .... *Illus* 160.00

Royal Doulton, Cuspidor, Tree Scene,

Glazed Pottery

Character Jug, W. C. Fields, Large	90.00
Character Jug, Walrus & Carpenter, A Mark, Miniature	60.00
Character Jug, Yachtsman, Large	80.00
Charger, Fagin, Dickens Ware, 13 1/2 In.	150.00
Charger, Jackdaw Of Rheims, 13 In.	175.00
Charger, Under The Greenwood Tree, 13 In.	175.00
Chop Plate, Long John Silver, Marked, 13 3/8 In.	195.00
Chop Plate, Tony Weller With Whip, Marked, 13 1/2 In.	165.00
Chop Plate, Under The Greenwood Tree, 13 1/2 In.	300.00
Clock, Monk	725.00
Compote, Cream, Silver & Gold Flowers, 5 x 9 In.	3875.00
Creamer, Gondoliers	70.00
Creamer, Hunt Scene, Brown & Tan, 8 In.	120.00
Cup & Saucer, Dickens Ware	55.00
Cup Plate, Dickens Ware, Blue & White Floral, Burslem, 6 Pc.	300.00
Cuspidor, Isaac Walton Ware, Marked, 7 In.	302.50
Cuspidor, Tree Scene, Glazed Pottery ....*Illus*	375.00
Dinner Set, Glamis Thistle, Artist, 62 Piece	496.00
Dish, Child's, Bunnykin	40.00
Figurine, Abdullah, HN 2104	325.00
Figurine, Afternoon Tea, HN 1747	325.00
Figurine, Alexandra, HN 2398	185.00
Figurine, All Aboard, HN 2940	150.00
Figurine, Angela, HN 2389	100.00
Figurine, Antoinette, HN 2326	112.00
Figurine, Autumn Breezes, HN 1913	120.00
Figurine, Autumn Breezes, HN 1934	100.00 To 200.00
Figurine, Autumn Breezes, HN 2147	350.00
Figurine, Autumn, HN 2087	425.00
Figurine, Babie, HN 1679	88.00
Figurine, Baby Bunting, HN 2108	250.00
Figurine, Ballerina, HN 2116	195.00
Figurine, Balloon Man, HN 1954	130.00
Figurine, Basket Weaver, HN 2245	300.00 To 495.00
Figurine, Bedtime Story, HN 2059	120.00 To 250.00
Figurine, Belle, HN 754	725.00
Figurine, Bess, HN 2002	270.00 To 295.00
Figurine, Betsy, HN 2111	325.00
Figurine, Biddy Penny Farthing, HN 1843	245.00
Figurine, Blithe Morning, HN 2021	125.00 To 135.00
Figurine, Bluebeard, HN 2105	325.00 To 340.00
Figurine, Bonnie Lassie, HN 1626	500.00
Figurine, Bride, HN 2166	165.00 To 200.00
Figurine, Bridesmaid, HN 2148	395.00
Figurine, Bridget, HN 2070	275.00
Figurine, Broken Lance, HN 2041	375.00 To 495.00
Figurine, Bunny, HN 2214	135.00

Figurine, Buttercup, HN 2309 .... 148.00
Figurine, Captain Cook, HN 2889 .... 395.00
Figurine, Captain, HN 2260 .... 325.00
Figurine, Carolyn, HN 2112 .... 195.00 To 235.00
Figurine, Carpet Seller, HN 1464 .... 110.00 To 245.00
Figurine, Celia, HN 1727 .... 1450.00
Figurine, Cellist, HN 2226 .... 325.00 To 395.00
Figurine, Centurion, HN 2726 .... 225.00
Figurine, Charlotte, HN 2421 .... 180.00
Figurine, Chief, HN 2892 .... 150.00
Figurine, Chloe, HN 1476 .... 300.00
Figurine, Choice, HN 1960 .... 995.00
Figurine, Christine, HN 1840 .... 550.00
Figurine, Christmas Morn, HN 1992 .... 140.00
Figurine, Cissie, HN 1809 .... 112.00 To 150.00
Figurine, Clown, HN 2890 .... 225.00 To 250.00
Figurine, Cobbler, HN 1283 .... 425.00
Figurine, Cobbler, HN 1706 .... 170.00 To 200.00
Figurine, Cookie, HN 2218 .... 100.00
Figurine, Coralie, HN 2307 .... 75.00
Figurine, Country Lass, HN 1991A 200.00
Figurine, Daffy Down Dilly, HN 1712 .... 175.00 To 275.00
Figurine, Dancing Years, HN 2235 .... 350.00
Figurine, Dandy, HN 753 .... 1250.00
Figurine, Darling, HN 1319 .... 150.00 To 165.00
Figurine, Darling, HN 1985 .... 140.00
Figurine, Delphine, HN 2136 .... 265.00
Figurine, Detective, HN 2359 .... 250.00
Figurine, Diana, HN 1986 .... 112.00
Figurine, Dinky Do, HN 1678 .... 45.00 To 75.00
Figurine, Dinky Do, HN 2120 .... 90.00
Figurine, Dorcas, HN 1558 .... 185.00 To 300.00
Figurine, Easter Day, HN 2039 .... 225.00 To 295.00
Figurine, Elaine, HN 2791 .... 200.00 To 225.00
Figurine, Eleanore, HN 1754 .... 1250.00
Figurine, Elegance, HN 2264 .... 100.00
Figurine, Ermine Coat, HN 1981 .... 275.00
Figurine, Fair Lady, HN 2193 .... 125.00
Figurine, Farmer's Boy, HN 2520 .... 800.00 To 895.00
Figurine, Farmer's Wife, HN 2069 .... 400.00
Figurine, Fat Boy, HN 2096 .... 225.00
Figurine, Favourite, HN 2249 .... 125.00 To 185.00
Figurine, Fiddler, HN 2171 .... 600.00
Figurine, Fleur, HN 2368 .... 200.00 To 225.00
Figurine, Flounced Skirt, HN 77 .... 1250.00
Figurine, Flower Seller's Children, HN 1342 .... 325.00 To 440.00
Figurine, Folly, HN 1335 .... 1375.00
Figurine, Fortune Teller, HN 2159 .... 400.00 To 425.00
Figurine, Forty Winks, HN 1974 .... 150.00 To 200.00
Figurine, Fragrance, HN 2334 .... 105.00
Figurine, French Peasant, HN 2075 .... 435.00 To 595.00
Figurine, Gaffer, HN 2053 .... 395.00 To 425.00
Figurine, Gay Morning, HN 2135 .... 175.00 To 275.00
Figurine, Genevieve, HN 1962 .... 180.00
Figurine, Gollywog, HN 1979 .... 260.00 To 300.00
Figurine, Good Catch, HN 2258 .... 195.00
Figurine, Good King Wenceslas, HN 2118 .... 250.00 To 325.00
Figurine, Goody Two Shoes, HN 2037 .... 70.00 To 90.00
Figurine, Gossips, HN 2025 .... 240.00 To 250.00
Figurine, Grace, HN 2318 .... 87.00
Figurine, Grandma, HN 2052 .... 240.00 To 295.00
Figurine, Granny's Heritage, HN 2031 .... 300.00 To 375.00
Figurine, Gretchen, HN 1397 .... 795.00

Royal Doulton, Character Jug, John
Peel, A Mark, Large

Royal Doulton, Character
Jug, Ugly Duchess, Small

Royal Doulton, Character
Jug, Fireman, Large

Royal Doulton, Character Jug, Vicar
of Bray, A Mark, Large

Royal Doulton, Character
Jug, Ugly Duchess, Large

Figurine, Harlequin, HN 2186	200.00
Figurine, Heather, HN 2956	145.00
Figurine, Her Ladyship, HN 1977	175.00 To 250.00
Figurine, Herminia, HN 1646	715.00
Figurine, Hilary, HN 2335	95.00 To 130.00
Figurine, Home Again, HN 2167	135.00
Figurine, Honey, HN 1909	350.00 To 395.00
Figurine, Hostess Of Williamsburg, HN 2209	185.00
Figurine, Huntsman, HN 1226	1995.00
Figurine, Ibrahim, HN 2095	600.00
Figurine, Jack Point, HN 2080	2900.00
Figurine, Jack, HN 2060	112.00
Figurine, Janet, HN 1916	125.00
Figurine, Janice, HN 2022	395.00 To 450.00
Figurine, Janice, HN 2165	375.00 To 395.00
Figurine, Janine, HN 2461	100.00
Figurine, Jean, HN 2032	220.00
Figurine, Jersey Milkmaid, HN 2057	160.00 To 250.00
Figurine, Jester, HN 1295	1395.00
Figurine, Jovial Monk, HN 2144	90.00
Figurine, Julia, HN 2705	115.00
Figurine, June, HN 2027	305.00
Figurine, Karen, HN 2388	220.00
Figurine, Kate Hardcastle, HN 1719	595.00
Figurine, Lady Anne Revill, HN 2006	750.00
Figurine, Lady April, HN 1958	240.00
Figurine, Lady Charmian, HN 1948	160.00
Figurine, Lady Clare, HN 1465	575.00
Figurine, Lady Pamela, HN 2718	135.00
Figurine, Lambing Time, HN 1890	95.00 To 155.00
Figurine, Leopard On Rock, HN 2638	3000.00
Figurine, Lilac Time, HN 2137	220.00
Figurine, Lily, HN 1798	80.00 To 110.00
Figurine, Lydia, HN 1908	135.00
Figurine, Lynne, HN 2329	100.00
Figurine, Magic Dragon, HN 2977	120.00
Figurine, Margot, HN 1628	450.00
Figurine, Market Day, HN 1991	165.00 To 255.00
Figurine, Mary Had A Little Lamb, HN 2048	95.00 To 115.00
Figurine, Mask Seller, HN 2103	210.00
Figurine, Masquerade, HN 2251	260.00

Figurine, Master, HN 2325 .... 165.00
Figurine, Matilda, HN 2011 .... 450.00
Figurine, Maureen, HN 1770 .... 195.00 To 275.00
Figurine, Maytime, HN 2113 .... 300.00
Figurine, Melanie, HN 2271 .... 95.00
Figurine, Memories, HN 2030 .... 325.00 To 450.00
Figurine, Mermaid, HN 97 .... 450.00
Figurine, Midinette, HN 2090 .... 225.00 To 345.00
Figurine, Midsummer Moon, HN 1899 .... 550.00
Figurine, Midsummer Noon, HN 2033 .... 595.00
Figurine, Minuet, HN 2019 .... 200.00
Figurine, Miss Demure, HN 1402 .... 180.00
Figurine, Miss Muffet, HN 1936 .... 140.00
Figurine, Miss Muffet, HN 1937 .... 200.00
Figurine, Moor, HN 2082 .... 2500.00
Figurine, Mrs. Fitzherbert, HN 2007 .... 485.00
Figurine, My Love, HN 2339 .... 65.00
Figurine, Nicola, HN 2839 .... 150.00
Figurine, Ninette, HN 2379 .... 115.00 To 165.00
Figurine, Old Balloon Seller, HN 1315 .... 140.00 To 150.00
Figurine, Old King Cole, HN 2217 .... 525.00
Figurine, Old Lavender Seller, HN 1492 .... 395.00
Figurine, Omar Khayyam, HN 2247 .... 130.00
Figurine, Orange Lady, HN 1759 .... 165.00 To 200.00
Figurine, Orange Lady, HN 1953 .... 165.00 To 235.00
Figurine, Pantalettes, HN 1362 .... 375.00
Figurine, Pearly Boy, HN 2035 .... 160.00
Figurine, Peggy, HN 2038 .... 100.00
Figurine, Penelope, HN 1901 .... 190.00 To 295.00
Figurine, Perfect Pair, HN 581 .... 650.00
Figurine, Pied Piper, HN 2102 .... 175.00
Figurine, Pierrette, HN 644 .... 695.00
Figurine, Pirouette, HN 2216 .... 150.00
Figurine, Poacher, HN 2043 .... 200.00
Figurine, Primroses, HN 1617 .... 575.00
Figurine, Priscilla, HN 1337 .... 900.00
Figurine, Prized Possessions, HN 2942 .... 450.00 To 600.00
Figurine, Professor, HN 2281 .... 160.00
Figurine, Prue, HN 1996 .... 190.00
Figurine, Rag Doll, HN 2142 .... 80.00 To 90.00
Figurine, Reverie, HN 2306 .... 250.00
Figurine, Romany Sue, HN 1757 .... 700.00
Figurine, Roseanna, HN 1926 .... 160.00 To 190.00
Figurine, Rosebud, HN 1983 .... 395.00
Figurine, Rosemary, HN 2091 .... 350.00
Figurine, Rosina, HN 1364 .... 750.00
Figurine, Rowena, HN 2077 .... 700.00
Figurine, Ruth, HN 2799 .... 170.00
Figurine, Sabbath Morn, HN 1982 .... 160.00 To 180.00
Figurine, Sairey Gamp, HN 2100 .... 300.00
Figurine, Scottish Highland Dancer, HN 2436 .... 1300.00
Figurine, Sea Sprite, HN 1261 .... 650.00
Figurine, Shepherd, HN 1975 .... 135.00 To 140.00
Figurine, Shore Leave, HN 2254 .... 137.00 To 200.00
Figurine, Simone, HN 2378 .... 150.00
Figurine, Sir Walter Raleigh, HN 2015 .... 475.00
Figurine, Skater, HN 2117 .... 260.00
Figurine, Soiree, HN 2312 .... 105.00 To 117.00
Figurine, Southern Belle, HN 2229 .... 220.00 To 248.00
Figurine, Spring Flowers, HN 1807 .... 225.00
Figurine, Spring, HN 2085 .... 425.00
Figurine, St. George, HN 2051 .... 250.00
Figurine, Summer's Day, HN 2181 .... 300.00

Figurine, Summer, HN 2086 .... 450.00
Figurine, Sunday Best, HN 2206 .... 250.00
Figurine, Susan, HN 2056 .... 200.00 To 325.00
Figurine, Suzette, HN 2026 .... 160.00
Figurine, Sweet & Twenty, HN 1298 .... 160.00 To 220.00
Figurine, Sweet Maid, HN 2092 .... 425.00
Figurine, Symphony, HN 2287 .... 270.00
Figurine, Taking Things Easy, HN 2677 .... 250.00
Figurine, Tess, HN 2865 .... 110.00
Figurine, Thanks Doc, HN 2731 .... 235.00 To 295.00
Figurine, Thanksgiving, HN 2446 .... 200.00
Figurine, Tom, HN 2864 .... 130.00
Figurine, Tootles, HN 1680 .... 95.00
Figurine, Top O' The Hill, HN 1834 .... 100.00
Figurine, Top O' The Hill, HN 1849 .... 85.00
Figurine, Toymaker, HN 2250 .... 325.00 To 400.00
Figurine, Uncle Ned, HN 2094 .... 275.00
Figurine, Valerie, HN 2107 .... 150.00
Figurine, Vanity, HN 2475 .... 90.00
Figurine, Veronica, HN 1517 .... 315.00
Figurine, Viking, HN 2375 .... 250.00
Figurine, Vivienne, HN 2073 .... 165.00 To 225.00
Figurine, Votes For Women, HN 2816 .... 220.00
Figurine, Wendy, HN 2109 .... 75.00
Figurine, Willy–Won't He, HN 2150 .... 325.00
Figurine, Winter, HN 2088 .... 380.00
Figurine, Wistful, HN 2396 .... 475.00
Figurine, Young Love, HN 2735 .... 650.00
Figurine, Young Master, HN 2872 .... 192.00 To 200.00
Figurine, Young Miss Nightingale, HN 2010 .... 675.00
Jam Jar, Coaching Days, Metal Lid & Spoon, 4 1/4 In. 170.00
Jar, Ginger, Flambe, Multicolored Floral, 8 In. 125.00
Jug, Blue Willow, Earth Ground, Sterling Rim, 5 In. 320.00
Jug, Don Quixote 540.00
Jug, Kingsware, Quarrelsome Drinker, Motto 575.00
Lamp, Uriah Heep 3000.00
Lighter, Bacchus 222.00
Lighter, Buz Fuz 335.00
Lighter, Falstaff 100.00
Napkin Ring, Pickwick 460.00
Napkin Ring, Sairey Gamp 185.00
Napkin Ring, Sam Weller 185.00
Pitcher, Coaching Days, 7 1/4 In. 230.00
Pitcher, Dutch Scene, 3 Men On Front, Girl With Child Back 110.00
Pitcher, Gondolier, 7 1/2 In. 165.00
Pitcher, Milk, Gondoliers 95.00
Pitcher, Norfolk 65.00
Pitcher, Old Curiosity Shop, 6 In. 120.00
Pitcher, Oliver Twist 135.00
Plate, 2 Pointer Dogs, 10 1/4 In. 150.00
Plate, Admiral 58.00
Plate, Artful Dodger, Dickens Ware, 6 In. 150.00
Plate, Coaching Days, 6 3/4 In. 65.00
Plate, Coaching Days, 7 3/4 In. 70.00
Plate, English Setter, 10 1/4 In. 150.00
Plate, Golf, Caddy Blowing Ball, 10 In. 325.00
Plate, Jackdaw, Rheims, 10 1/2 In. 110.00
Plate, Melrose, 9 In. 10.00
Plate, Parsons 50.00
Plate, Rustic England, 10 In. 32.00
Plate, Shakespeare, Merchant Of Venice, 10 1/2 In. 75.00
Plate, Tony Weller, Dickens Ware, Signed, Square, 7 1/2 In. 125.00
Platter, Melrose, 14 In. 30.00

Saucer, Kirkwood	10.00
Sugar, Gondoliers	70.00
Sugar, Old Charley	650.00
Tankard, Christmas Carol, 1972	50.00
Tankard, Don Quixote	575.00
Tea Set, Reynard The Fox, 16 Piece	650.00
Teapot, Bopeep	149.00
Teapot, Gondoliers	145.00
Teapot, Norfolk	65.00
Teapot, Old Salt	160.00
Teapot, Pillar Rose	45.00
Toby Jug, Cap'n Cuttle, 4 1/4 In.	30.00
Toby Jug, Charrington	750.00
Toby Jug, Falstaff, Large	75.00
Toby Jug, Fat Boy, 4 1/2 In.	95.00
Toby Jug, Goaler	90.00
Toby Jug, Sherlock Holmes, 8 3/4 In.	60.00
Toothpick, Drinking Scenes, Lambeth	75.00
Toothpick, Sunset Scene, 2 Handles	95.00
Tray, Flambe, Scenic, Noke, 9 x 7 In.	275.00
Umbrella Stand, Diamond Shaped Panels, c.1910, 23 1/2 In.	495.00
Vase, Babes In Woods, 2 Girls Under Tree, 4 1/2 In.	275.00
Vase, Babes In Woods, Children With Umbrella, 7 1/2 In.	535.00
Vase, Dragon Draped Around, Glazed, Chang Ware, 8 1/8 In.	7150.00
Vase, Red & Black, 10 In.	320.00
Vase, Red Flambe, Veined, No. 1618, 10 In.	450.00
Vase, Veined Flambe, 10 In.	300.00
Wall Mask, Greta Garbo, HN 1593	850.00
Wall Mask, Lion Of The East, HN 1784	1650.00
Wall Mask, Marlene Dietrich, HN 1591	950.00
Wall Mask, Sweet Ann, HN 1602	850.00

ROYAL DUX is the more common name for the Duxer Porzellanmanufaktur which was founded by E. Eichler in Dux, Bohemia, in 1860. By the turn of the century, the firm specialized in porcelain statuary and busts of Art Nouveau-style maidens, large porcelain figures, and ornate vases with three-dimensional figures climbing on the sides. The firm is still in business.

Bowl, Applied Figure Of Maiden, Flowers, Green Leaves, 13 1/2 In.	440.00
Bust, Caesar, Gold Shirt, Toga On Shoulder, Marked, 9 In.	350.00
Bust, Young Woman, Flowing Blond Hair, 1900, 20 3/4 In.	2475.00
Centerpiece, 2 Applied Maidens, Gilt, Ovoid, Pedestal, 18 In.	550.00
Fernery, Woman, Poppy Handles, Marked	425.00
Figurine Vase, Man, Lady, Earth Tones, Tree, Marked, 14 In., Pair	825.00
Figurine, Boy & Girl, Carrying Jug & Glass, 8 1/2 In., Pair	95.00
Figurine, Boy On Donkey, 12 In.	450.00
Figurine, Boy With Dog, 14 In.	325.00
Figurine, Cockatoo	40.00
Figurine, Colonial Couple, Marked, 11 1/2 In., Pair	1150.00
Figurine, Dancing Couple, Cobalt Coat, Dress, Filigree Base, 9 In.	350.00
Figurine, Elephant, Trunk Up, Signed, 8 1/4 x 11 1/4 In.	125.00
Figurine, German Shepherd, Seated	165.00
Figurine, Girl With Goose, Boy With Dog, 15 In.	750.00
Figurine, Girl With Wheat, Boy, Fisherman's Net, 1925, 21 In., Pair	895.00
Figurine, Hunting Dog, 8 1/2 x 11 In., Pair	295.00
Figurine, Lady Godiva, On Horse, Marked, 15 In.	465.00
Figurine, Lady, Relaxing, Cobalt, White, Marked, 15 In.	850.00
Figurine, Military Officer, Formal Dress, Majolica, 16 In.	295.00
Figurine, Mother, Seated, With Child, Signed JAH, 21 In.	770.00
Figurine, Nude, Seated, Butterfly On Knee, 8 In.	145.00
Figurine, Polar Bear, 10 1/2 In.	95.00
Figurine, Rebecca At Well, Gold Dress, Pink Apron, Marked, 17 In.	950.00
Figurine, Royal Couple, Woman, Gold Dress, Man In Toga, 9 In., Pair	350.00

◆◆◆◆◆◆◆◆◆◆◆◆◆◆◆◆◆◆◆◆◆

Clean a leather sofa by dusting regularly. When necessary, wipe with a damp cloth dipped in detergent–free soapy water. If someone spills food on the leather, wipe it off immediately, but wipe the entire sofa to avoid a spot.

◆◆◆◆◆◆◆◆◆◆◆◆◆◆◆◆◆◆◆◆◆

Royal Dux, Vase, Figural, Man & Woman,
Palm Tree, 36 In., Pair

Figurine, Senorita, Hands On Hips, 14 In.	800.00
Group, Brown Hunting Dogs, Irish Setter, Marked, c.1930, 16 In.	495.00
Group, Two Lovers, Classical Dress, 19 In.	465.00
Group, Woman In Sedan Chair, 2 Attendants, Signed, 15 1/4 In.	425.00
Group, Woman, Classic Dress, Man, Holding Scroll, 12 1/2 In.	1120.00
Lamp, Shepherd & Shepherdess, Wooden Base, Silk Shade, 36 In., Pr.	2700.00
Vase, Art Nouveau Portrait, Ivory Medallions, Signed, 19 1/2 In.	425.00
Vase, Boy, Girl, Beige Ground, Earth Tones, Purple Mark, 10 In., Pr.	685.00
Vase, Figural, Man & Woman, Palm Tree, 36 In., Pair ....*Illus*	715.00
Vase, Girl With Jug Side, Other With Lily, Floral Top, 12 In., Pr.	1250.00
Vase, Maiden With Goats, Ivory, Gold & Lavender Floral, 16 In.	450.00
Vase, Poppies, Blue, 5 In.	60.00

ROYAL FLEMISH glass was made during the late 1880s in New Bedford, Massachusetts, by the Mt. Washington Glass Works. It is a colored satin glass decorated with dark colors and raised gold designs. The glass was patented in 1894. It was supposed to resemble stained glass windows.

Bowl, Enameled Flying Ducks, Gilt Stars, Frosted, 7 In.	1700.00
Castor, Pickle, Blue Frosted, Pairpoint Holder	750.00
Rose Bowl, Pansies, Gilded & Embossed, Signed, 3 3/4 In.	750.00
Sugar, Apple Blossoms In Gilt Enameled Design, 6 1/4 In.	415.00
Urn, Cover, Cupid & Griffin, Gilt Webbing, 16 In.	5500.00
Vase, Allover Pansies, Gold Tracery, 7 1/2 In.	1950.00
Vase, Dragon, Gilt, Green Enamel, Mt. Washington, 7 1/2 In.	2865.00
Vase, Pansies, Gold Outlined, Leaf Handles, 5 3/4 In.	1700.00
Vase, Windowpane & Coin Design, 3 Handles, 9 In.	850.00

ROYAL HAEGER, see Haeger category

ROYAL IVY pieces are listed in the Pressed Glass section by that pattern name.

ROYAL NYMPHENBURG is the modern name for the Nymphenburg porcelain factory which was established at Neudeck–ob–der–Au, Germany, in 1753 and moved to Nymphenburg in 1761. The company is still in existence. Marks used by the firm include a checkered shield topped by a crown, a crowned *CT* with the year, and a contemporary shield mark on reproductions of eighteenth–century porcelain.

Figurine, Courtier, c.1900, 9 1/2 In.	330.00
Figurine, Owl, On Book, 5 In.	150.00
Figurine, Putto As Cybele, Holding Book, 4 In.	3300.00
Figurine, Scottish Terrier	450.00
Vase, Scenic, 1937, 9 In., Pair	600.00

ROYAL OAK pieces are listed in the Pressed Glass section by that pattern name.

Royal Worcester, Cup & Saucer, Pinecones, Demitasse

Royal Worcester, Figurine, Bather, Surprised, c.1868, 26 In.

ROYAL RUDOLSTADT, see Rudolstadt

ROYAL VIENNA, see Beehive category

ROYAL WORCESTER is a name used by collectors. Worcester porcelains were made in Worcester, England, from about 1751. The firm went through many different periods and name changes. It became the Worcester Royal Porcelain Company, Ltd., in 1862. Today collectors call the porcelains made after 1862 *Royal Worcester*. In 1976, the firm merged with W. T. Copeland to become Royal Worcester Spode. Some early products of the factory are listed under Worcester.

Basket, Basketweave, Gold Trim, 1911, 3 x 4 1/2 In.	125.00
Biscuit Jar, Allover Hop Flowers & Leaves, Gold Trim	350.00
Biscuit Jar, Cobalt Blue Leaves, On White Bamboo, 7 In.	355.00
Bowl, Floral Design, Ivory Ground, Square, 4 In.	467.50
Bowl, Florals Inside & Outside, Gold Handles, c.1867, 9 In.	235.00
Bread Plate, Gold Chantilly	8.00
Butter, Cover, Pinecone Finial, Floral On Lid & Base	525.00
Candle Snuffer, Monk, 1896, 4 1/2 In.	185.00
Console Set, Children, Hadley, 3 Piece	3200.00
Cup & Saucer, Bridal Lace	15.00
Cup & Saucer, Gold Chantilly	18.00
Cup & Saucer, Pinecones, Demitasse *Illus*	35.00
Cup & Saucer, Pink & Yellow Roses, Gold Trim, 1906	95.00
Cup & Saucer, Regency, 8 Sets	120.00
Demitasse Set, Cobalt Blue, Gold Design	580.00
Demitasse Set, Silver Lid & Rim, Gold Bands, 1912, 3 Piece	250.00
Ewer, Floral & Butterfly, Artist Signed	215.00
Ewer, Floral, Gold Handle & Trim, c.1894, 5 In.	195.00
Ewer, Flowers & Butterflies, Dragon Handle, 11 1/2 In.	595.00
Figurine, Bather, Surprised, 1875, 15 3/4 In.	605.00
Figurine, Bather, Surprised, c.1868, 26 In. *Illus*	385.00
Figurine, Boy, Dandelion, No. 3084	150.00
Figurine, Budgerigar On Stump	340.00
Figurine, Caroline, 1960	145.00
Figurine, Child, With Flowers, No. 3075	110.00
Figurine, Corgi, No. 3243, 3 In.	375.00
Figurine, December	275.00
Figurine, Dutch Girl	75.00
Figurine, Eagle, Holds Reticulated Bowl In Wings, 7 In.	325.00
Figurine, English Sheepdog	450.00
Figurine, Fortune Teller	350.00
Figurine, Friday's Child	93.00
Figurine, Hunter & Huntress, 1893, 14 In., Pair	2200.00
Figurine, Lisette, No. 3442	850.00
Figurine, Mischief, No. 2914	150.00

Figurine, Parakeet Boy	175.00
Figurine, Parakeet, No. 2663	110.00
Figurine, Polly Put The Kettle On, 6 In.	110.00
Figurine, Water Carriers, 1890, 18 In., Pair	2200.00
Jardiniere, Carnations, Ruffled, Signed, 9 1/2 x 11 In.	395.00
Jug, Gold–Trimmed Flowers, Dragon Handle, Marked, 9 1/4 In.	495.00
Jug, Ice, Multicolored Flowers, c.1890, 8 3/4 In.	295.00
Jug, Multicolored Flowers, Flat Back, c.1890, 5 1/2 In.	235.00
Jug, Owl On Branch Scene, Serpent Handle, 1885, 11 1/4 In.	930.00
Pitcher, Florals, Leaves, Gold Outlined, c.1887, 12 In.	350.00
Pitcher, Flowers, Ivory Ground, 12 In.	825.00
Pitcher, Multicolored Floral, Fruit, Green Mark, 4 1/2 In.	45.00
Pitcher, Zigzag Block Mold, 1884, 13 In.	350.00
Plate, Bournemouth, 7 In.	7.00
Plate, Dinner, Gold Chantilly	10.00
Plate, Salad, Bridal Lace	8.00
Plate, Shell, Floral, Gold Gilt, 8 3/8 In.	45.00
Platter, Bridal Lace, 12 In.	15.00
Sconce, Cornucopia, Gilt, Yellow Ground, Wall, 10 In., Pair	630.00
Syrup, Pewter Lid, Shadow Floral Ground, Marked, c.1881	195.00
Urn, Cover, Female Caryatids, Blue Jeweled Beaded, 12 In.	1980.00
Vase, Bud, Reticulated Handles, c.1893, 6 1/2 In.	225.00
Vase, Dragonfly & Roses, Slip Decorated, 3 x 4 In.	195.00
Vase, Florals, Handles, Cream Ground, c.1903, 6 1/8 In.	175.00
Vase, Multicolored Florals, Wide Base, Signed, 10 In.	325.00
Vase, Nautilus Shell, Gold Trim, Marked, 8 1/2 In.	450.00
Vase, Roman Gold & Green Trim, Marked, 1888, 8 1/2 In.	450.00

ROYCROFT products were made by the Roycrofter community of East Aurora, New York, in the late nineteenth and early twentieth centuries. The community was founded by Elbert Hubbard, famous philosopher, writer, and artist. The workshops owned by the community made furniture, metalware, leatherwork, embroidery, and jewelry. A printshop produced many signs, books, and the magazines that promoted the sayings of Elbert Hubbard. Furniture by the Roycroft community is listed in the furniture section.

Bench, Ali Baba, Slab Seat, Plank Ends, Oak, c.1910, 42 In.	1650.00
Bookends, Arch, Hammered Copper, Brass	220.00
Bookends, Art Nouveau, Leaf Design	155.00
Bookends, Bird Design, Hammered Brass	135.00
Bookends, Ship	140.00
Bowl, Fluted Rim, Original Patina, 9 3/4 In.	200.00
Bowl, Green & Brown On Cream, Rectangular, 5 x 4 In.	65.00
Box, Goodie, Metal Hardware, Mahogany, c.1910, 10 x 22 1/2 In.	275.00
Candlestick, 11 3/4 x 12 In., Pair ....*Illus*	1760.00
Desk Set, Inkwell, Pen Tray, Calendar, Letter Opener, Blotter, 5 Pc.	275.00
Humidor, Mottled Brown, 5 In.	150.00
Inkwell, Copper	175.00
Inkwell, Hammered Copper, Glass Insert	175.00
Lamp, Hammered Copper, Amber Iridescent Domed Shade, 16 In.	1650.00
Mat, Leather, Pair	429.00
Tray, Copper, Octagonal, 10 In.	70.00
Vase, American Beauty, Long Neck, Bulbous, 19 In. ....*Illus*	1540.00
Vase, Copper, 2 Rows Square Openings Around Top, Marked, 7 In.	3575.00
Vase, Copper, Applied Nickel Silver Band, 6 1/2 In.	800.00
Vase, Flared Rim, Long Neck, Squat Base, Signed, c.1910, 15 1/2 In.	300.00
Vase, Hammered Copper, Signed, 8 1/2 In.	275.00
Vase, Nickel Silver, Appliqued, Rectangular, 7 In. ....*Illus*	6050.00
Vase, Pierced Silver Appliqued, Karl Kipp, 6 x 3 In. ....*Illus*	440.00
Vase, Trapezoidal, Cut–Out Top, Applied Orb	5500.00

ROZANE, see Roseville category

ROZENBURG worked at The Hague, Holland, from 1890 to 1914. The most important pieces were earthenware made in the early twentieth century with pale–colored Art Nouveau designs.

Charger, Painted Flowers, Concentric Ridges, 1904, 15 In.	1350.00
Jar, Loops In Lid Form Handle, Roses, Butterflies, c.1900, 16 In.	2500.00
Plate, Wall, Hand–Painted Thistles, 1898, 10 3/4 In.	775.00
Vase, Art Nouveau, 9 1/2 In.	950.00
Vase, Floral & Dragon, Shoulder Handles, Marked, 1898, 9 1/2 In.	1430.00
Vase, Freesia & Foliage, Marked, c.1900, 6 In.	2320.00
Vase, Polychrome Flowers & Foliage, 1901, 13 1/2 In.	1430.00

RRP is the mark used by the firm of Robinson–Ransbottom. It is not a mark of the more famous Roseville Pottery. The Ransbottom brothers started a pottery in 1900 in Ironspot, Ohio. In 1920, they merged with the Robinson Clay Product Company of Akron, Ohio, to become Robinson–Ransbottom. The factory is still working.

Cookie Jar, Canister, Flowers	20.00
Cookie Jar, Chef	50.00 To 65.00
Cookie Jar, Chicken	60.00
Cookie Jar, Dutch Girl	175.00
Cookie Jar, Hootie Owl	35.00 To 75.00
Cookie Jar, Oscar, Green Hat	125.00
Cookie Jar, Sheriff Pig	60.00
Cookie Jar, Snowman	575.00
Cookie Jar, Whale	550.00

RS GERMANY is part of the wording in marks used by the Tillowitz, Germany, factory of Reinhold Schlegelmilch from about 1869 until about 1956. The porcelain was sold decorated and undecorated. The Schlegelmilch families made porcelains marked in many ways. See also ES Germany, RS Poland, RS Prussia, RS Silesia, RS Suhl, and RS Tillowitz.

Basket, Bonbon, Chinese Pheasants, Cream Ground 7 In.	185.00 To 245.00
Bowl, Floral Design, Green, White, Footed	60.00
Cake Plate, Peach & Yellow Roses, Gold Trim, 11 In.	55.00
Cake Plate, White Flowers, Foliage, Gold Rim, 11 In.	75.00
Candlestick, Green & White Lilies, 5 In., Pair	60.00
Celery Set, 2–Handled Dish, 6 Salt Dips, 7 Piece	40.00
Celery, Blue Flowers, Oval, 13 In.	70.00

Left to right: Roycroft, Candlestick, 11 3/4 x 12 In., Pair; Roycroft, Vase, Nickel Silver,

Appliqued, Rectangular, 7 In.; Roycroft, Vase, American Beauty, Long Neck,

Bulbous, 19 In.; Roycroft, Vase, Pierced Silver Appliqued, Karl Kipp, 6 x 3 In.

Celery, Floral, Basket–Type Handle Across Length, 12 x 8 In. 125.00
Celery, Hand Painted Flowers 45.00
Cup & Saucer, Black Swans, Gold Steeple Mark, Large 1200.00
Cup & Saucer, Pink Florals, Gold Trim 22.00
Dish, Cheese & Cracker, 2 Tiers, Pink Orchid, Signed, 8 1/2 In. 125.00
Hatpin Holder, Floral, Tan Ground 60.00
Pitcher, Hand Painted Florals, c.1900, 14 In. 155.00
Plate, Bird Of Paradise, 6 1/4 In., Pair 500.00
Plate, Cream Roses, White To Dark Gray Ground 5.00
Teapot, Steeple Finial, Cabbage Roses, Gold Trim, 8 1/2 In. 125.00
Toothpick, Hand Painted Flowers, Gold Handles & Trim, 2 1/2 In. 75.00

RS POLAND (German) is a mark used by the Reinhold Schlegelmilch factory at Tillowitz from about 1946 to 1949, although the factory continued production until 1956. This is one of many of the RS marks used. See also ES Germany, RS Germany, RS Prussia, RS Silesia, RS Suhl, and RS Tillowitz.

Candlestick, Peach Roses, Pair 225.00
Dresser Set, Tray, Powder Box & Ring Tree, Peach Roses, 3 Piece 325.00
Planter, Pink Flowers Band, Gold Highlights, Pedestal, 6 3/4 In. 235.00
Server, Center Handle, Lavender & Pink Roses, Gold Rim, 11 In. 515.00
Urn, Bird Of Paradise, Brown, Green & Gray Shaded, 11 In. 2250.00
Vase, Cottage Scene, Woman, Sheep, Ornate Handles, 10 In. 650.00
Vase, Crowned Cranes Design, Salesman's Sample, 3 1/2 In. 800.00
Vase, Mill Scene, Ornate Handles, 10 In. 640.00

RS PRUSSIA appears in several marks used on porcelain before 1915. Reinhold Schlegelmilch started his porcelain works in Tillowitz, Germany, in 1869. See also ES Germany, RS Germany, RS Poland, RS Silesia, RS Suhl, and RS Tillowitz.

Berry Set, Acorn Mold, Red Mark, 10 In., 7 Piece .... 470.00 To 495.00
Berry Set, Pink Poppies, Green Ground, 8–In. Bowl, 5 Piece 375.00
Berry Set, Pink, White Roses, 6 Piece 165.00
Berry Set, Poppy, Red Mark 225.00
Biscuit Barrel, Cover, Reflections Over Water, 5 1/2 x 9 In. 295.00
Bowl, Acorn, Bowl–Within–Bowl, Gold Trim, 10 3/8 In. 375.00
Bowl, Blown Out, Flowers, Gold & Green Rim, Red Mark, 10 1/2 In. 150.00
Bowl, Blown Out, Gold, Red Mark, 10 1/2 In. 200.00
Bowl, Bowl In Bowl Mold, Winter Scene, Red Mark 1150.00
Bowl, Cattail & Water Lily Mold, Lebrun Girl ....*Illus* 700.00
Bowl, Center Pink Roses, White Rim, Gold, 10 1/4 In. 410.00
Bowl, Colonial Woman With Fan, 10 3/4 In. 1295.00
Bowl, Daisies & Roses, Jeweled, White & Green Ground, 11 In. 225.00
Bowl, Daisy Mold, Pink Poppies, 10 1/4 In. 215.00
Bowl, Diana The Huntress, 6 Lebrun Medallions, 10 1/2 In. 1800.00
Bowl, Dice Players, Ribbon & Jewel 2100.00
Bowl, Drapery Mold, Pink & Red Roses, Pink, 10 In. 210.00
Bowl, Easter Lilies & Maidenhair Fern, 10 In. 375.00
Bowl, Embossed Leaf Mold, Floral, Pink, 10 1/2 In. 110.00
Bowl, Floral Center, Red Cabbage, Red Mark, 9 In. 850.00
Bowl, Floral Mold, Lebrun Hairpin Girl, 10 1/2 In. 1050.00
Bowl, Flower Design, Touches Of Gold, Red Mark, 10 In. 125.00
Bowl, Flowers Reflected In Water, Green, Red Mark, 10 3/4 In. 135.00
Bowl, Fruit, Pink Roses, Pearl Luster Finish, Red Mark, 10 In. 125.00
Bowl, Fruit, Scalloped Rim & Foot, Cabbage Roses, Marked, 10 In. 285.00
Bowl, Iris Mold, Red Roses, Iridescent Rim, 11 In. 190.00
Bowl, Iris Mold, Winter Season, Satin Finish, 10 In. 1275.00
Bowl, Madame Recamier, Iridescent Finish, 10 In. 1000.00
Bowl, Magnolias, Pink, 10 1/2 In. 410.00
Bowl, Melon Eaters, Jeweled, 10 1/2 In. ....*Illus* 1725.00
Bowl, Old Man & The Mountain, Red Mark, 11 In. 950.00
Bowl, Pink Poppies, Yellow & Green Ground, 10 1/2 In. 350.00
Bowl, Pink Roses, Green Ground, 3–Footed, 6 1/2 In. 70.00

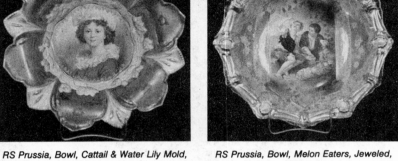

RS Prussia, Bowl, Cattail & Water Lily Mold,
Lebrun Girl

RS Prussia, Bowl, Melon Eaters, Jeweled,
10 1/2 In.

Bowl, Poppies Center, Blue, Green & Brown Floral, 10 1/4 In.	865.00
Bowl, Roses & Snowballs, Green Ground, 10 1/2 In.	210.00
Bowl, Roses, 10 In.	140.00
Bowl, Sawtooth Mold, Cottage Scene, Brown, Red Mark, 10 In.	450.00
Bowl, Summer Season, 6 Portraits Around	1500.00
Bowl, Swan	375.00
Bowl, Turkeys, Evergreens, 11 In.	950.00
Box, Hairpin, Hidden Image, Star Mark	195.00
Cake Plate, Carnation Mold	135.00
Cake Plate, Carnation Mold, Floral, 10 1/2 In.	135.00
Cake Plate, Dice Thrower, Red Mark	1250.00
Cake Plate, Drapery Mold, Pearlized, 10 In.	190.00
Cake Plate, Mill Scene, 10 In.	130.00
Cake Plate, Pheasant & Fir Trees, Red Mark, 9 3/4 In.	900.00
Cake Plate, Pink Floral, Green & Yellow Ground, 9 1/2 In.	120.00
Cake Plate, Pink Floral, White, 9 1/2 In.	60.00
Cake Plate, Roses, 11 1/2 In.	200.00
Cake Plate, Sawtooth Mold, Cottage Scene, Red Mark, 10 1/4 In.	675.00
Cake Plate, Sawtooth Mold, Cottage, Brown, Open Handle, 10 In.	810.00
Cake Plate, Sawtooth Mold, Mill Scene, Red Mark, 10 1/4 In.	625.00
Cake Plate, Snow Bird, 11 In.	1200.00
Cake Plate, Swag & Tassel Mold, Swallows, Chickens, Duck, 10 In.	1010.00
Cake Plate, White Roses, Red Poppy, Iridescent Glaze, 11 In.	135.00
Candleholder & Hairpin Box, Combination, Floral, Blue Ground	700.00
Celery Tray, Pink Roses, Signed, 12 1/4 In.	80.00
Celery, Iris Mold, Large Roses, Signed, 12 1/4 In.	140.00
Celery, Iris, 12 In.	140.00
Celery, Lily Mold, Roses On Lavender, White Ground, 12 1/2 In.	125.00
Celery, Medallion Mold, Poppies, Woman, Red Mark, 14 In.	995.00
Celery, Melon Boy, Red Mark	575.00
Celery, Pink Roses, Stipple Mold, Green, 12 In.	150.00
Celery, Purple Azaleas	135.00
Celery, Roses & Daisies, Stippled Mold, 12 1/2 In.	100.00
Celery, Roses, Green, 12 In.	70.00
Chocolate Pot, Easter Lily, White Ground	500.00
Chocolate Pot, Green Panels, Pink Roses, Red Mark, 8 1/2 In.	335.00
Chocolate Pot, Leaf Mold, Purple & Green Lilacs	350.00
Chocolate Pot, Madame Lebrun, Green	1600.00
Chocolate Pot, Pink Roses, Gold, Red Mark	325.00
Chocolate Pot, Princess Potocka, Tiffany Border	1500.00
Chocolate Pot, Snowballs & Roses, Footed	525.00

Chocolate Pot, Swans On Lake, Red Mark 100.00
Chocolate Pot, Teapot, Sugar & Creamer, Pink Flowers, Red Mark 675.00
Chocolate Set, Melon Eaters, With 4 Cups & Saucers 3100.00
Chocolate Set, Satin Rose 125.00
Coffeepot, Bouquets & Sprays Of Roses, Red Mark, 11 In. 495.00
Coffeepot, Roses, Daisies Reflected In Water, Red Mark 375.00
Cookie Jar, Green Ivy, Yellow & Brown Flowers, Red Mark 175.00
Cracker Jar, Daisy With Garland, Red Mark 250.00
Cracker Jar, Feather Mold 340.00
Cracker Jar, Spring Season, Bronze Tiffany Border 2100.00
Creamer, Cottage, Brown & Yellow, Red Mark 145.00
Creamer, Quiet Cove, Red Mark 185.00
Cup & Saucer, Drape Mold, Blue & Pink Roses, White, 4–Footed 40.00
Cup & Saucer, Drape Mold, Duck & Trees, 4–Footed 425.00
Cup & Saucer, Old Man & The Mountain, Pedestal 425.00
Dish, Icicle Mold, Barnyard Scene, Multicolored, 12 In. 550.00
Ewer, Victorian Girls, Pedestal, 18 3/4 In., Pair 2300.00
Hair Receiver, Ivy Leaves, Gold Florets, Marked 175.00
Hatpin Holder, Castle Scene, Blues & Greens 250.00
Humidor, Roses & Snowballs 325.00
Mayonnaise Set, Pink To Red Roses On Cream, Red Mark, 3 Piece 400.00
Mustache Cup, Flowers In Basket, 4–Footed 70.00
Mustache Cup, Left Hand, Pink Roses 85.00
Mustard, Basket Of Flowers, Stipple Mold 50.00
Mustard, Cover, Finial, Cobalt Blue 220.00
Mustard, Fleur–De–Lis Mold, Carnations, Red Mark 145.00
Mustard, Morning Glory Mold, Daisies, Violets 95.00
Mustard, Stippled Floral, Spoon, Red Mark 160.00
Pitcher, Chocolate, Floral 425.00
Pitcher, Milk, Blown–Out White, Purple Pansies, Marked, 6 In. 175.00
Pitcher, Red Mark, 4 In. 110.00
Pitcher, Swans, Red Mark 550.00
Pitcher, Syrup, Cobalt Blue, Underplate 150.00
Plaque, Blown–Out Acorn Mold, Woman With Dog, 10 x 14 In. 1850.00
Plaque, Mill Scene, Green Ground, Colored Border, 11 1/4 In. 715.00
Plate, 3 Swans & Castle, 6 In. 95.00
Plate, Bellflowers, Swags, Tapestry, Gold Beads, 10 3/8 In. 455.00
Plate, Canal Scene, 8 In. 360.00
Plate, Dice Players & Melon Eaters, Rope Rim, 8 3/4 In., Pair 1200.00
Plate, Dice Players, Rope Edge Mold, Green, 8 3/4 In. 800.00
Plate, Floral Center, Various Flowers On Rim, Marked, 8 1/2 In. 225.00
Plate, Icicle Mold, 4 Swans On Blue Water, Pods, Red Mark, 11 In. 625.00
Plate, Icicle Mold, Snow Birds, Open Handles, 10 In. 350.00
Plate, Melon Eater, Keyhole, Red Mark, 6 In. 495.00
Plate, Melon Eaters, 10 1/2 In. 1400.00
Plate, Melon Eaters, Jeweled, 8 1/2 In. 825.00
Plate, Melon Eaters, Rope Edge Mold, Green, 8 3/4 In. 800.00
Plate, Monk, Embossed Ruffled Rim, 10 In. 175.00
Plate, Pink & Yellow Roses, Satin, 6 In. 40.00
Plate, Point & Clover Mold, Red Mark, 8 3/4 In. 95.00
Plate, Poppies, Swags Reflected In Water, Red Mark, 10 3/8 In. 475.00
Plate, Queen Louise, Steeple Mark, 14 In. 925.00
Plate, Roses, Double Handle, 9 In. 245.00
Plate, Sawtooth Mold, Woman Watering Flowers, 11 In. 550.00
Plate, Scalloped Medallions, Center Roses, Red Mark, 8 1/2 In. 215.00
Plate, Spring Season, Keyhole, Red & Gold Trim, 10 In. 1300.00
Plate, Summer Season, Keyhole, White & Gold Trim, 9 In. 1600.00
Plate, Village Scene, Brown, Red Mark, 6 1/4 In. 275.00
Plate, Winter Season, Keyhole, White & Gold Trim, 9 In. 1300.00
Relish, Clover Mold, Pink Mums, Green Ground, 10 In. 75.00
Relish, Iris Mold, Summer Season 450.00
Relish, Medallions Of Pink Roses, Blue Border, 7 1/2 In. 75.00
Relish, Pink Roses, 10 In. 115.00

Relish, Pink, White & Orange Roses, Green Ground, 10 In.	80.00
Shaving Mug, Florals, Red Mark	225.00
Sugar & Creamer, Blue Floral, White, Pedestal	300.00
Sugar & Creamer, Castle & Mill Scene, Red Mark	400.00
Sugar & Creamer, Floral, Pedestal	130.00
Sugar & Creamer, Mold 501, Multicolored Roses	145.00
Sugar & Creamer, Pink Floral, Swirl, White Ground	120.00
Sugar & Creamer, Pink Roses, Satin	150.00
Sugar & Creamer, Poppies & Snowballs, Blue	190.00
Sugar & Creamer, Red & Pink Roses, Beige & Green Ground	70.00
Sugar Shaker, Calla Lily, Red Mark	180.00
Sugar Shaker, Colonial Couple, Red Mark	335.00
Sugar Shaker, Pink Roses, Garlands Of Gold, 4 3/4 In.	260.00
Syrup, Pink & Yellow Roses, Footed, Red Mark	185.00
Tankard, Iris Mold, Foliage Ground, Red Mark, 10 1/2 In.	600.00
Tankard, Iris Mold, Summer Season, Red Mark, 10 In.	1650.00
Tankard, Madame Recamier, 11 1/2 In.	1500.00
Tankard, Mill Scene, Leaf Base, 11 In.	1800.00
Tankard, Pink Poppies, Satin, 13 1/2 In.	675.00
Tankard, Tiger, 11 1/2 In.	4100.00
Tankard, Winter Season, 11 1/2 In.	2200.00
Tankard, Winter Season, Red Mark, 13 1/2 In.	3750.00
Tea Set, Cottage Scene, Red Mark, 3 Piece	900.00
Tea Set, Pink & White Poppies, Yellow Ground, Red Mark, 3 Piece	650.00
Tea Set, Pink Roses, Pearlized, 3 Piece	300.00
Teapot & Sugar, Child's, Scenic, Cover, 2 Piece	400.00
Teapot, Carnation Mold, Yellow & Pink Roses, Green Ground	450.00
Teapot, Colored Flowers On Blue, Gold Trim, Beads	195.00
Teapot, Poppies, Satin	150.00
Toothpick, Blue Floral, Ruffled, 3 Handles	95.00
Toothpick, Floral Design, 6 Small Feet	165.00
Toothpick, Iris Mold, Water Lilies	110.00
Toothpick, Shepherd	245.00
Tray, 3 Scenes, Turkey, Bluebird & Swan, 13 1/2 In.	1025.00
Tray, Countess Potocka Portrait	1600.00
Tray, Dresser, Carnation Mold, Gold Trim, Red Mark	280.00
Tray, Dresser, Carnation Mold, Spring Season	1700.00
Tray, Dresser, Draped Rim, Roses, Pearls & Red Jewels, Red Mark	300.00
Tray, Dresser, Fleur-De-Lis Mold	800.00
Tray, Dresser, Icicle Mold, Swan Scene, 11 x 7 In.	525.00
Tray, Dresser, Iris Mold, Floral, 11 1/2 In.	145.00
Tray, Dresser, Pink Roses & Daisies, Stipple Mold, 11 In.	160.00
Tray, Dresser, Roses, Gold Edge	280.00
Tray, Pink & White Roses, Handles, Gold Trim, 12 1/2 x 9 In.	175.00
Tray, Reflecting Poppies & Daisies, Red Mark, 11 3/4 x 7 In.	300.00
Tray, Rococo, 12 x 8 In.	365.00
Urn, Cover, Mill Scene, Castle Scene, 11 3/4 In., Pair	3475.00
Vase, 4 Portraits, Gold Handles & Trim, 8 3/4 In.	525.00
Vase, Art Nouveau, Orchids On Back, Flat Neck, 10 In.	295.00
Vase, Girl With Dove, 3 Handles, Gold Trim, Beading, 5 In.	350.00
Vase, Lebrun, Tinted Green & Gold, 10 1/2 In.	695.00
Vase, Madame Racamier, Greens, Golds, 9 1/2 In.	595.00
Vase, Melon Eaters, Cobalt Blue, 2 Handles, 8 In.	1500.00
Vase, Melon Eaters, Jeweled, 6 In.	1075.00
Vase, Melon Eaters, Mountain Background, 6 In.	695.00
Vase, Oriental Girl Portrait, Handles, 7 x 8 1/2 In.	375.00
Vase, Swans & Evergreens, Open Handle, 11 1/2 In.	650.00
Vase, Turkey, Mold 909, Salesman's Sample, 3 1/2 In.	280.00 To 365.00

RS SILESIA appears on porcelain made at the Reinhold Schlegelmilch factory in Tillowitz, Germany, during the 1930s. The Schlegelmilch families made porcelains marked in many ways. See also ES Germany, RS Germany, RS Poland, RS Prussia, RS Suhl, and RS Tillowitz.

Cake Plate, Basket Of Flowers, Gold Trim, Red Mark, 11 In.	275.00
Chocolate Set, Footed Cups, Red Mark, 5 Piece	550.00
Cup & Saucer, Pink Roses, Blue Ground, Pedestal	55.00
Vase, Landscape, Mill, Water Wheel, Double Handles, 3 1/2 In.	275.00

RS SUHL is a mark used by the Erdmann Schlegelmilch factory in Suhl, Germany, before 1917. The Schlegelmilch families made porcelains in many places. See also ES Germany, RS Germany, RS Poland, RS Prussia, RS Silesia, and RS Tillowitz.

Bowl, Pale Pink Roses, Gold Trim, Satin, White, 10 In.	210.00
Cake Plate, Floral Mold, Pink, 10 1/2 In.	100.00
Cracker Jar, Pink & White Poppies, Green Ground	300.00
Plate, Lions, Crimped & Scalloped Border, Red Mark, 8 1/2 In.	3000.00
Tray, Center Roses In Basket, Pierced Handles, 7 x 11 In.	110.00
Vase, Melon Eaters, 9 In.	815.00

RS TILLOWITZ was marked on porcelain by the Reinhold Schlegelmilch factory at Tillowitz in the 1930s and 1940s. Table services and ornamental pieces were made. See also ES Germany, RS Germany, RS Poland, RS Prussia, RS Silesia, and RS Suhl.

Bowl, Brown Mill Scene, Red Mark, 10 In.	325.00
Bowl, Floral, High Relief Iris Mold, Purple Iridescent, 11 In.	1000.00
Teapot, Long Spout, Floral, Pedestal, Satin Finish, 7 In.	310.00
Tray, Dresser, White Dogwood, Marked, Oval, 11 3/4 In.	50.00

RUBENA VERDE is a Victorian glassware that was shaded from red to green. It was first made by Hobbs, Brockunier and Company of Wheeling, West Virginia, about 1890.

Epergne, 1–Light, Applied Rigaree, Opalescent, 16 In.	335.00
Pitcher, Water, Ruffled	350.00
Vase, Latticinio Stripes, Rigaree, 10 1/2 In.	250.00

RUBENA is a glassware that shades from red to clear. It was first made by George Duncan and Sons of Pittsburgh, Pennsylvania, about 1885. This coloring was used on many types of glassware. The pressed glass patterns of Royal Ivy and Royal Oak are listed under Pressed Glass.

Celery Vase, Inverted Thumbprint, Enameled Birds & Flowers, 8 In.	375.00
Epergne, Ruffled, Lily Center, Metal Base Bolts To Bowl, 12 3/8 In.	325.00
Pitcher, Hobnail, Satin Pointed	245.00
Pitcher, Water, Hobnail, Opalescent, 1 Tumbler	215.00
Powder Box, Removable Lid, Clear Cut Glass Finial	95.00
Water Set, Tankard & 6 Tumblers, Floral Design, Gold Trim	890.00

RUBY GLASS is the dark red color of the precious gemstone known as a *ruby.* It was a popular Victorian color that never went completely out of style. The glass was shaped by many different processes to make many different types of ruby glass. There was a revival of interest in the 1940s when modern–shaped ruby table glassware became fashionable. Sometimes the red color is added to clear glass by a process called flashing or staining. Flashed glass is clear glass dipped in a colored glass, then pressed or cut. Stained glass has color painted on a clear glass. Then it is refired so the stain fuses with the glass. Pieces of glass colored in this way are indicated by the word *stained* in the description. Related items may be found in other sections, such as Cranberry Glass, Pressed Glass, and Souvenir.

Bowl, Iridescent, Monet & Stumph, 5 In.	140.00
Cocktail Shaker Set, Sterling Overlay, 5 Piece	145.00
Creamer, Block	80.00
Cruet, Clear Handle & Stopper	95.00
Decanter Set, Cut Glass, Clear Stopper, 5 Piece	125.00
Dish, Hen Cover, Wright, 7 In.	50.00
Figurine, Strawberry, Viking	30.00
Mug, Thumbprint, Souvenir, Jackson	28.00

Pitcher, Silver Overlay	150.00
Tumbler, Silver Band	30.00
Vase, Painted Birds, Blown	20.00

RUDOLSTADT was a faience factory in the Thuringia region of Germany from 1720 to about 1791. In 1854, Ernst Bohne began working in the area. From about 1887 to 1918, the New York and Rudolstadt Pottery made decorated porcelain marked with the RW and crown familiar to collectors. This porcelain was imported by Lewis Straus and Sons of New York, which later became Nathan Straus and Sons. The word *Royal* was included in their import mark. Collectors often call it *Royal Rudolstadt.* Most pieces found today were made in the late nineteenth or early twentieth century. Additional pieces may be listed in the Kewpie section.

Bowl, Center & Side Roses, Molded, Gold Rim, Royal	50.00
Bowl, Hand Painted Roses, Royal	22.50
Cake Plate, Hummingbird, Flowers, 12 In.	20.00
Figurine, Athena Leaning Against Column, Royal, 11 1/2 In.	220.00
Figurine, Hunchback, Marked, c.1880, 5 1/2 In.	125.00
Group, Seated Lady & Maid, Boudoir Setting, 14 7/8 x 13 3/8 In.	935.00
Smoke Set, Dog After Cat On Fence, Flowers, 6 x 6 1/2 In.	165.00
Tea Set, Pearlized Yellow Finish, Service For 6	150.00
Vase, Flared Gold Rim, Semi-Nude Maiden Handles, 14 In.	450.00

RUGS have been used in the American home since the seventeenth century. The Oriental rug of that time was often used on a table, not on the floor. Rag rugs, hooked rugs, and braided rugs were made by housewives from scraps of material.

Afshar, Flowering Plants Design, Red, Blue, Gold, 5 Ft. 4 In. x 4 Ft.	600.00
Amish, Woven Felt, 28 x 65 In.	165.00
Anatolian Yastik, Octagonal Medallion, Rust, 3 Ft. x 2 Ft. ....*Illus*	330.00
Anatolian, 2 Ft. 1 In. x 5 Ft. 4 In.	35.00
Anatolian, Hooked Hexagonal Medallion, 7 Ft. 2 In. x 4 Ft. 6 In.	495.00
Art Deco, Overlapping Rectangles, Germany, 1925, 12 Ft. x 8 Ft. 9 In.	2750.00
Aubusson, Chain Stitched, Floral & Geometric Design, 6 x 9 Ft.	410.00
Aubusson, Louis XVI, Musical Instruments, 9 Ft. 4 In. x 8 Ft. 4 In.	7150.00
Avar, Many Necked House Design, Red Field, 4 Ft. 5 In. x 3 Ft.	495.00
Bahktiari, Geometric & Acanthus Design, 9 x 12 Ft.	2200.00
Bahktiari, Vases Of Flowers, Vine Border, 6 Ft. 6 In. x 4 Ft. 6 In.	1435.00
Bakshaish, Lobed Medallion Inset, Camel Field, 3 Ft. 7 In. x 3 Ft. 5 In.	6600.00
Belouch, Hooked Diamonds, c.1875, 8 Ft. x 4 Ft. 3 In.	6050.00
Belouch, Ivory Blossoms, 7 Ft. 5 In. x 3 Ft. 7 In.	3850.00
Belouch, Vertical Stripes, Vines, 5 Ft. 2 In. x 3 Ft. 4 In.	660.00
Bergama, Angular Vinery, 5 Ft. 8 In. x 5 Ft. 4 In.	6050.00
Bergama, Hexagonal Medallion With Pendants, 2 Ft. 6 In. x 1 Ft. 10 In.	1325.00
Bijar, 2 Ft. 8 In. x 4 Ft.	450.00
Bijar, Overall Floral, Floral Border, 14 Ft. x 8 Ft. 2 In.	2750.00
Bijar, Overall Rosettes, Leaves, Vines, 1930s, 9 Ft. 2 In. x 6 Ft. 6 In.	660.00
Bijar, Rose Palmettes, Starflower Border, c.1900, 5 Ft. 8 In. x 3 Ft.	3080.00
Bokhara, Geometric Design, Maroon Ground, 2 Ft. 1 In. x 6 Ft. 3 In.	170.00
Bokhara, Octagonal Gul Motifs, Red Ground, 7 Ft. 6 In. x 9 Ft. 4 In.	2750.00
Bokhara, Oriental, 2 Ft. 10 In. x 4 Ft. 3 In.	105.00
Bokhara, Pakistan, 2 Ft. 9 In. x 6 Ft. 8 In.	200.00
Bokhara, Rebound Edges, 3 Ft. x 3 Ft. 5 In.	425.00
Bokhara, Runner, Oriental, 2 Ft. x 6 Ft.	165.00
Bokhara, Wool & Silk, 9 Ft. 6 In. x 11 Ft. 9 In.	1600.00
Braided, Crazy Quilt Design, Wool Yarns, 127 1/2 x 68 In.	880.00
Cabistan, 3 Ft. 9 In. x 6 Ft. 5 In.	850.00
Cabistan, Chinese Clouds, 3 Ft. 11 In. x 5 Ft. 4 In.	2400.00
Cabistan, Oriental, 4 Ft. 2 In. x 6 Ft.	2250.00
Cabistan, Prayer With Animals, Oriental, 3 Ft. 3 In. x 5 Ft.	3050.00
Cabistan, Rebound, 3 Ft. 1 In. x 4 Ft. 10 In.	450.00
Cashan, 4 Ft. 6 In. x 6 Ft. 9 In.	6325.00
Caucasian, Geometric, 9 Borders, 37 x 56 In.	700.00

Caucasian, Geometric, Tightly Woven, 6 x 9 Ft. 3700.00
Caucasian, Konagkend, Kufesque Border, c.1900, 6 Ft. 10 In. x 3 Ft. 8 In. 5280.00
Caucasian, Oriental, White, Blue Border, 1890, 5 x 3 Ft. 2500.00
Caucasian, People, Animal Borders, Salmon, 5 Ft. 2 In. x 8 Ft. 11 In. 500.00
Chichi, Hooked Polygons, Midnight Blue Field, 5 Ft. 10 In. x 4 Ft. 2200.00
Chichi, Overall Starflowers, c.1900, 5 Ft. 9 In. x 4 Ft. 1 In. 7425.00
Chinese, Art Deco, Radiating Arches, c.1930, 11 Ft. 8 In. x 8 Ft. 10 In. 7150.00
Chinese, Blossoming Shrubs, Pagodas, 11 Ft. 4 In. x 8 Ft. 10 In. 1100.00
Chinese, Blue Border, Floral Design, 12 Ft. 2 In. x 13 Ft. 2 In. 400.00
Chinese, Blue Field, Phoenix, Floral Sprays, 11 Ft. x 9 Ft. 6 In. 5390.00
Chinese, Chinese Design Balls Overall, c.1900, 4 Ft. 7 In. x 2 Ft. 4 In. 1650.00
Chinese, Embroidered Silk, Figures, Flowers, Butterflies, 69 x 20 In. 305.00
Chinese, Floral Design, Wine Red Ground, Peking, 4 Ft. x 6 Ft. 9 In. 275.00
Chinese, Floral Spray, Vases Of Flowers Edge, 8 Ft. 6 In. x 6 Ft. 2 In. 2750.00
Chinese, Lake & Village Scene, Mid–20th Century, 9 Ft. 9 In. ....*Illus* 2200.00
Chinese, Navy Blue Ground, Mythical Phoenix, 11 x 6 In. 5390.00
Chinese, Pictorial, Landscape Of Hills, Lake, 9 Ft. 6 In. x 9 Ft. 8 In. 2200.00
Chinese, Vase Of Flowers, Floral Sprays, 1950s, 15 Ft. x 9 Ft. 10 In. 6600.00
Continental, Geometric, Wool, Gray Ground, 10 Ft. 4 In. x 10 Ft. 1100.00
Daghestan, Floral Buds, Diamonds, 5 Ft. 3 In. x 3 Ft. 8 In. 2640.00
Daghestan, Flowering Plants, Vine Border, 3 Ft. 8 In. x 2 Ft. 8 In. 2310.00
Daghestan, Overall Flowering Plants, 3 Ft. 8 In. x 2 Ft. 2 In. 1210.00
Donegal, Scrolling Florals, C. Voysey, c.1900, 20 Ft. 6 In. x 10 Ft. 9900.00
Erglas, Rosette, Foliate Design, Cream Border, 2 Ft. 8 In. x 6 Ft. 6 In. 525.00
Ersari, Serrated Diamond Design Border, 9 Ft. x 9 Ft. 7 In. 7150.00
Felt, Embroidered Floral, Red, Black Fishscale Border, 19 x 45 In. 75.00
Fereghan, 4 Diamond Medallions, 4 Ft. 6 In. x 9 Ft. 7 In. 800.00
Fereghan, Rebound, 4 Ft. 1 In. x 6 Ft. 2 In. 3550.00
Fereghan, Sarouk, Medallion, Blue Ground, 9 x 12 Ft. ....*Illus* 10000.00
Flax, Cotton, Red & Blue Stripes, Red Fringe, 25 1/2 x 140 In. 150.00
Floral Design, Blue Border, Gray Ground, Chinese, 11 Ft. 7 In. x 12 Ft. 700.00
Floral Design, Wine Red Ground, Chinese, 9 x 12 Ft. 1250.00
Floral Pattern, Ivory, Salmon, Blue Ground, 3 Ft. 11 In. x 5 Ft. 6 In. 85.00
Geometric Floral, 4 Ft. 5 In. x 6 Ft. 250.00
Geometric Floral, Central Medallion, 6 Ft. 3 In. x 9 Ft. 6 In. 125.00
Geometric, 8 Ft. 10 In. x 11 Ft. 8 In. 2100.00
Hamadan, Floral Geometric, 3 Ft. 3 In. x 8 Ft. 800.00
Hamadan, Floral, Blue, Peach, Orange, Gold, Cream Border, c.1930, 5 x 7 Ft. 1760.00
Hamadan, Floral, Red, Blue, Tan, Persia, c.1930, 4 Ft. 10 In. x 2 Ft. 6 In. 143.00
Herati, Iran, 4 Ft. 1 In. x 6 Ft. 6 In. 3100.00
Heriz, c.1930, 10 Ft. 7 In. x 7 Ft. 1 In. 5250.00
Heriz, Rosette Medallion, Rust Field, 11 Ft. 6 In. x 8 Ft. 3 In. 1210.00
Heriz, Rust Field, Navy Medallion & Border, India, 6 Ft. x 8 Ft. 7 In. 1100.00
Heriz, Terra–Cotta Red Field, 12 Ft. 6 In. x 8 Ft. 4 In. 2530.00
Hooked, 2 Horned Goats, Flora Vine Border, c.1930, 35 1/2 x 65 1/4 In. 2200.00
Hooked, Adam & Eve, In Garden Of Eden, 1920s 2250.00
Hooked, Berries & Flowers, 30 x 52 In. 40.00
Hooked, Bouquet Of Flowers, Cream Ground, Cotton & Wool, 75 x 85 In. 308.00
Hooked, Braided, Eagle & Totem Pole Design, 60 x 27 In. 4000.00
Hooked, Children In Schoolyard, Signed, 4 Ft. 4 In. x 2 Ft. 6 In. 2090.00
Hooked, Cow & Girl, Brown, Gold & Blue, c.1850, 16 x 32 In. 1550.00
Hooked, Dog, Brown Spots On Chest, Gray Ground, Stripes, 24 x 36 In. 370.00
Hooked, Dog, Floral Frame, 14 x 37 1/2 In. 275.00
Hooked, Fine & Floral Borders, Brown, 11 Ft. 6 In. x 8 Ft. 8 In. 55.00
Hooked, Folk Art Design, Colored Cat, Oval, 30 x 41 1/2 In. 600.00
Hooked, Folk Art Design, Fox & Stork, 18 1/2 x 35 In. 195.00
Hooked, Fort With U.S. Flag, One Star, Round, 29 1/2 In. 190.00
Hooked, Fruit, Flowers, Vegetables, Cottages, c.1940, 9 x 12 Ft. 4125.00
Hooked, Horse, Border, 1900, 30 x 44 1/2 In. 880.00
Hooked, Overall Floral & Leaf Design, 5 Ft. 10 In. x 3 Ft. 3 In. 525.00
Hooked, Pictorial, Dog, Flower Heads, Tulips, Kitten, 27 x 34 In. 990.00
Hooked, Pictorial, Reclining Dog, Foliate Scroll Borders, American 165.00
Hooked, Pictorial, Sailing Ship, Zodiac Signs, Blue, Yellow, Beige, 86 In. 275.00

Rug, Anatolian Yastik,
Octagonal Medallion, Rust,
3 Ft. x 2 Ft.

Rug, Chinese, Lake & Village
Scene, Mid-20th Century,
9 Ft. 9 In.

Rug, Fereghan, Sarouk,
Medallion, Blue Ground,
9 x 12 Ft.

Hooked, Pictorial, Sands Of Time, U.S., 35 x 48 In. 2750.00
Hooked, Prayer Type, Turtle Border, Purple, Maroon, Blue, 40 x 46 In. 385.00
Hooked, Rag, 2 Brown Puppies, Grass, Yellow Picket Fence, 20 x 36 In. 225.00
Hooked, Rag, Dog, Striped Ground, Rebacked, 31 x 53 In. 135.00
Hooked, Rag, Floral Design, Blue, Red, Green, Beige Ground, 23 x 38 In. 250.00
Hooked, Rag, Geometric Design, Maroon Ground, 24 x 38 In. 70.00
Hooked, Rag, Green In Olive Squares, Braided Binding, 39 x 61 In. 145.00
Hooked, Rag, Lion In Faded Colors, On Stretcher, 27 1/2 x 56 In. 85.00
Hooked, Rag, Stripes, Alternating Squares, 40 1/2 x 58 In. 350.00
Hooked, Rag, Two Scotties, One Brown, One White, Red Collars, 30 x 39 In. 400.00
Hooked, Shell Pattern, Center Band Of Ovals, 78 x 35 1/2 In. 275.00
Hooked, Spinning Wheel, Chair, Broom, Floorboards, 23 3/4 x 39 1/2 In. 150.00
Hooked, Stylized Floral, 2 Bluejays, Foliage, 33 x 65 In. 500.00
Hooked, Stylized Floral, 30 x 45 In. 445.00
Hooked, Whaling Scene, 39 x 27 In. 450.00
Hooked, Wool, Maple Sugaring Scene, Framed, 36 1/2 x 48 In. 475.00
Indo-Pakistani, Orange Tan Ground, 3 Ft. 6 In. x 5 Ft. 6 In. 50.00
Iranian, Floral, 3 Ft. 6 In. x 5 Ft. 1 In. 180.00
Isphahan, Central Medallion, Ivory, Wool, Silk, 3 Ft. 6 In. x 5 Ft. 7 In. 2200.00
Isphahan, Cranberry Vinery, Post-1945, 6 Ft. 10 In. x 4 Ft. 8 In. 3300.00
Isphahan, Floral Vinery, Post-1945, 6 Ft. x 3 Ft. 10 In. 3575.00
Jomud, Hexagonal Lattice, 2 Ft. 6 In. x 1 Ft. 4 In. 660.00
Jugendstil, Brick Red Hexagonal Panel, Brush-Strokes Border 7832.00
Karabagh, Sunburst Medallions, 1880s, 8 Ft. 5 In. x 4 Ft. 10 In. 1100.00
Karistan, 11 Ft. 4 In. x 14 Ft. 2 In. 575.00
Kashan, Red, Multicolored Floral, Turkey, 11 Ft. 6 In. x 8 Ft. 8 In. 2530.00
Kashan, Rosettes & Curved Leaves, Blue Field, 6 Ft. 9 In. x 4 Ft. 6 In. 2530.00
Kasim, Lobed Ivory, Medallion, 4 Ft. 8 In. x 3 Ft. 5 In. 3850.00
Kasvin, Gabled Medallion, Floral Sprays, 1820s, 3 Ft. 8 In. x 8 Ft. 3 In. 440.00
Kazak, 3 Lesghi Stars In Field, 20th Century, 6 Ft. 2 In. x 4 Ft. 7 In. 880.00
Kazak, Five Center Geometric Medallions, 52 x 81 In. 8800.00

Kazak, Hexagonal Medallion, Blue, Ivory, 7 Ft. 6 In. x 4 Ft. 9 In. 1540.00
Kazak, Hooked Diamond Medallions, Red Field, 7 Ft. 3 In. x 4 Ft. 9 In. 2310.00
Kazak, Ivory Center, Rust, Blues, Cream Border, 5 Ft. 8 In. x 6 Ft. 2 In. 1540.00
Kazak, Karachopt Design, 7 Ft. 8 In. x 6 Ft. 9 In. 3410.00
Kazak, Polychrome Floral Forms, c.1900, 6 Ft. 4 In. x 4 Ft. 4 In. 7975.00
Kazak, Prayer, 2 Royal Blue, Teal Medallions, Red Field, 54 x 46 In. 495.00
Kazak, Signed & Dated, 3 Ft. 10 In. x 7 Ft. 10 In. 4600.00
Kazak, Star Flowers, Hexagons, 3 Ft. 11 In. x 2 Ft. 8 In. 3080.00
Kazak, Two Hooked Diamond Medallions, Blue, 3 Ft. 2 In. x 2 Ft. 4 In. 468.00
Kirman, Central Medallion, Corner Designs, 12 Ft. 3 In. x 9 Ft. 2 In. 825.00
Kirman, Ivory Field, Floral, Red, Blue, Green, Persia, 11 Ft. x 16 Ft. 4 In. 880.00
Kirman, Ivory Ground, Oriental, 11 Ft. 2 In. x 11 Ft. 11 In. 1700.00
Kirman, Ivory, Red & Navy Medallion, Persia, 11 Ft. 3 In. x 14 Ft. 7 In. 2640.00
Kirman, Overall Tree & Flower Design, 20 Ft. 9 In. x 13 Ft. 7 In. 7700.00
Kirman, Pictorial, c.1900, 4 Ft. 3 In. x 7 Ft. 7150.00
Kirman, Rose Colored, Floral Design, Ivory Ground, 8 Ft. x 9 Ft. 9 In. 1600.00
Kirman, Rose, Ivory & Green Field, 10 x 14 Ft. 1695.00
Kuba, 4 Flower Heads, Red, Rose, Vine Border, 5 Ft. 4 In. x 3 Ft. 8 In. 1045.00
Kuba, Running Dog Border, Ivory Ground, 40 1/2 x 66 In. 6875.00
Kuba, Stylized Dragon Design, 17 Ft. 9 In. x 8 Ft. 5225.00
Lenkoran, 2 Calyx Medallions, Brown Field, 8 Ft. 9 In. x 5 Ft. 8 In. 825.00
Lesghi, 2 Star Medallions, Royal Blue Field, 4 Ft. 2 In. x 3 Ft. 2 In. 1760.00
Lilihan, Center Medallion, Overall Floral, 3 Ft. 8 In. x 5 Ft. 198.00
Lilihan, Medallion, Wine, Cobalt, Brown, 6 Ft. 4 In. x 5 Ft. 5 In. 880.00
Mahal, Acanthus Design, Red Border, 6 Ft. 10 In. x 10 Ft. 7 In. 1210.00
Mahal, Central Medallion, Overall Acanthus, 10 Ft. x 12 Ft. 2 In. 2640.00
Mahal, Triangular Medallion, Floral, Foliate, 14 Ft. 8 In. x 11 Ft. 3 In. 3300.00
Malair, Ivory Field, Blue & Red, Red Border, 3 Ft. 7 In. x 5 Ft. 9 In. 725.00
Meshed, Flower Heads, Vines, Burgundy, 13 Ft. 6 In. x 10 Ft. 6 In. 4620.00
Mexican, Mythical Beasts, 5 Ft. x 3 Ft. 6 In. 88.00
Navy Field, Mythical Phoenix, Floral Spray, Chinese, 11 Ft. 6 In. x 9 Ft. 5390.00
Needlepoint, Continental, Overall Floral, 11 Ft. 9 In. x 17 Ft. 8 In. 6820.00
Needlepoint, Overall Floral, Ivory Field, 8 Ft. 10 1/2 In. x 4 Ft. 6 In. 440.00
Needlepoint, Overall Florals, Brown, Portuguese, 11 Ft. x 12 Ft. 2 In. 770.00
Needlepoint, Overall Flowering Shrubs, European, 15 x 12 Ft. 770.00
Needlepoint, Palmettes, Leaves, European, 8 Ft. 4 In. x 5 Ft. 9 In. 770.00
Oriental, Tree Of Life, Floral Border, Silk, 6 Ft. 1 In. x 4 Ft. 770.00
Oushak, Plum Field, Ivory, Blue Central Medallion, 14 x 20 Ft. 2200.00
Penny, Wool Felt, Blue Denim Ground, Green Felt Border, 27 1/2 x 61 In. 205.00
Perepedil, Ram's Horn Design, Bird Medallions, 4 Ft. 5 In. x 3 Ft. 5 In. 1980.00
Perepedil, Salmon Field, c.1850, 45 x 51 1/2 In. 1210.00
Persian, Grid Of Floral Sprays, Leaf Border, 6 Ft. 8 In. x 4 Ft. 5 In. 2200.00
Persian, Latched Diamond Medallions, 6 Ft. 6 In. x 4 Ft. 9 In. 1650.00
Persian, Lattice Within Vinery Border, 11 Ft. 8 In x 6 Ft. 2640.00
Persian, Pole, Turtle Border, Blue, Rust, Green, 7 Ft. 10 In. x 4 Ft. 5 In. 770.00
Prayer, Silky Textured Wool, 1 Ft. 11 In. x 3 Ft. 1 In. 95.00
Qasha'l, Horizontal Bands Stepped Diamonds, 8 Ft. 8 In. x 5 Ft. 3 In. 1980.00
Qashquai, Concentric Medallions, 10 Ft. 2 In. x 5 Ft. 2530.00
Salor, Bokhara, Prayer, 4 Ft. 1 In. x 4 Ft. 10 In. 750.00
Sarouk, Dark Blue, Red & Beige, 4 x 6 Ft. 3740.00
Sarouk, Dark Floral Design, Replaced Fringe, 3 Ft. 1 In. x 6 Ft. 4 In. 850.00
Sarouk, Deep Red, 11 Ft. x 6 Ft. 10 In. 5250.00
Sarouk, Floral Medallion, c.1900, 4 Ft. 11 In. x 3 Ft. 5 In. 3850.00
Sarouk, Multicolored Geometric & Floral, 4 Ft. 11 In. x 6 Ft. 3 In. 440.00
Sarouk, Rose Bouquets, 5 Ft. 3 In. x 3 Ft. 6 In. 4840.00
Sarouk, Vinery Formed Medallion, c.1900, 12 Ft. 4 In. x 8 Ft. 10 In. 8800.00
Serapi, 4 Ft. 3 In. x 5 Ft. 5 In. 2900.00
Serapi, Persia, 3 x 5 Ft. 1300.00
Serebend, 3 Ft. 1 In. x 9 Ft. 7 In. 650.00
Serebend, Overall Boteh Design, Navy, 5 x 11 Ft. 1210.00
Serebend, Rows Of Boteh, Red Field, 4 Ft. 9 In. x 3 Ft. 3 In. 412.50
Seychour, Floral Medallions, c.1885, 6 Ft. 3 In. x 3 Ft. 9 In. 3630.00
Seychour, Floral Vinery, c.1880, 5 Ft. 3 In x 3 Ft. 8 In. 3850.00

Seychour, Ivory Ground, Cruciform Medallions, 5 Ft. 5 In. x 3 Ft. 11 In.	1650.00
Shirvan, Diamond & Cruciform Medallions, 5 Ft. 4 In. x 3 Ft. 2 In.	1760.00
Shirvan, Geometric Medallions, Floral Border, 10 Ft. 6 In. x 3 Ft. 8 In.	1100.00
Shirvan, Staggered Polygon Rows, Blue & Camel, Gold Field, 5 x 4 Ft.	1320.00
Sivas, Herati, Blue Violet, Rust Border, Turkey, 6 Ft. 8 In. x 9 Ft. 2 In.	770.00
Soumac, Indigo Medallions, 6 Ft. 1 In. x 5 Ft. 4 In.	4950.00
Sultanabad, Herati Design, Turtle Border, 10 Ft. 4 In. x 7 Ft.	3135.00
Sultanabad, Overall Flower Heads, 6 Ft. 4 In. x 4 Ft. 4 In.	2310.00
Tabriz, Central Navy Medallion, 10 Ft. 11 In. x 16 Ft.	4840.00
Tabriz, Contemporary, Handmade, Wool, 3 Ft. 2 In. x 5 Ft. 4 In.	215.00
Tabriz, Hexagonal Medallion, 6 Ft. 6 In. x 4 Ft. 5 In.	1045.00
Tabriz, Overall Palmette Design, c.1900, 13 Ft. x 9 Ft. 4 In.	9350.00
Tabriz, Overall Vase Design, Silk, 6 Ft. 2 In. x 4 Ft.	9350.00
Tabriz, Tree Of Life, Blue Ground, 1 Ft. 11 In. x 2 Ft. 9 In.	300.00
Tekke, Bokhara, Bag Face, 1 Ft. 10 In. x 4 Ft. 1 In.	300.00
Tekke, Guls Flanked By Minor Guls, 6 Ft. 7 In. x 8 Ft. 8 In.	2200.00
Tribal, Cream, Blue & Tan Florals, Animal Border, 12 Ft. x 14 Ft. 4 In.	715.00
Ushak, Oriental, 12 Ft. x 17 Ft. 8 In.	1000.00
Wool, Leafage & Flowers, Art Deco, 1930, 11 Ft. 8 In. x 9 Ft.	4675.00
Yomud, Bokhara, Bag, 1 Ft. 6 In. x 2 Ft. 11 In.	925.00
Yomud, Oval Designs, Pole Tree, 5 Ft. 4 In. x 4 Ft. 4 In.	2310.00

RUMRILL Pottery was designed by George Rumrill of Little Rock, Arkansas. From 1933 to 1938, it was produced by the Red Wing Pottery of Red Wing, Minnesota. In 1938, production was transferred to the Shawnee Pottery in Zanesville, Ohio. Production ceased in the 1940s.

Nappy, Calla Lily, Handle	12.00
Pitcher, No. 547	28.00
Vase, 8 In.	20.00
Vase, Coiled, Turquoise, White Interior, Handles, 7 In.	17.50

RUSKIN is a British art pottery of the twentieth century. The Ruskin Pottery was started by William Howson Taylor and his name was used as the mark until about 1899. The factory, at West Smethwick, Birmingham, England, stopped making new pieces in 1933 but continued to glaze and sell the remaining wares until 1935. The art pottery is noted for its exceptional glazes.

Jardiniere, White Speckling On Cream Ground, Marked, 1925, 7 In.	770.00
Vase, Blue, Red, Cream Dip Glaze, 10 In.	500.00
Vase, Orange, Red, Blue, 8 In.	195.00

RUSSEL WRIGHT designed dinnerwares in modern shapes for many companies. Iroquois China Company, Harker China Company, Steubenville Pottery, and Justin Tharaud and Sons made dishes marked *Russel Wright.* The Steubenville wares, first made in 1938, are the most common today. Wright was also a designer of domestic and industrial wares, including furniture, aluminum, radios, interiors, and glassware. Dinnerwares and other pieces by Wright are listed here. For more information, see *Kovels' Depression Glass & American Dinnerware Price List.*

Bowl, Cereal, Theme Informal, Dune	500.00
Bowl, Divided, Iroquois, Cover, Lettuce, 10 In.	18.00 To 25.00
Bowl, Salad, American Modern, Glacier Blue	135.00
Bowl, Vegetable, American Modern, Divided, Seafoam	50.00
Carafe, Iroquois	40.00
Carafe, Iroquois, Blue	75.00
Carafe, Iroquois, Dark Green	55.00
Casserole, Cover, Divided, Iroquois, Gray, 10 In.	35.00 To 40.00
Casserole, Theme Informal, Dune	1200.00
Celery, American Modern, Canteloupe	35.00 To 75.00
Celery, American Modern, Glacier Blue	35.00
Cocktail, Theme Formal	350.00
Coffeepot, American Modern, Gray, After Dinner	75.00
Cordial, Theme Formal, 3 In.	450.00

Creamer, American Modern, Canteloupe	18.00
Creamer, American Modern, Chartreuse	8.00
Cup & Saucer, American Modern, Glacier Blue	15.00
Cup & Saucer, Theme Informal, Dune	400.00
Gravy Boat, Underplate, Coral & Gray	35.00
Humidor, Sandwich, Aluminum	50.00
Jar, Refrigerator, American Modern, Seafoam	100.00 To 125.00
Pitcher, American Modern, Gray	40.00
Plate, American Modern, Seafoam, 10 In.	10.00
Plate, American Modern, Seafoam, 6 1/4 In.	4.00
Plate, American Modern, Seafoam, 8 In.	8.00
Plate, Iroquois, Lemon, 10 In.	9.00
Plate, Theme Informal, Dune, 10 1/2 In.	400.00
Plate, Theme Informal, Dune, 6 In.	250.00
Plate, White Clover, 7 In.	8.00
Plate, White Clover, 9 1/2 In.	12.00
Platter, Iroquois, Oval, Lemon, 12 3/4 In.	22.00
Platter, Theme Formal, Dune, 16 In.	650.00
Relish, American Modern, Lettuce	110.00
Salt & Pepper, American Modern, Seafoam	8.00
Salt & Pepper, Iroquois, Lettuce	12.00
Saucer, American Modern, Chartreuse, After Dinner	3.00
Saucer, Iroquois, Ice Blue	2.00
Saucer, Iroquois, Lemon	3.00
Soup, Dish, Iroquois, Lemon	18.00
Sugar, American Modern, Chartreuse	10.00
Sugar, Iroquois, Ice Blue	10.00
Teapot, American Modern, Seafoam	65.00
Tumbler, Eclipse, Box, 8 Piece	100.00
Tumbler, Iced Tea, Smoke, Imperial	25.00

SABINO glass was made in the 1920s and 1930s in Paris, France. Founded by Marius–Ernest Sabino (1878–1961), the firm was noted for Art Deco lamps, vases, figurines, and animals in clear, colored, and opalescent glass. Production stopped during World War II but resumed in the 1960s with the manufacture of nude figurines and small opalescent glass animals. The new pieces are a slightly different color and can be recognized.

Sabino
France

Figurine, Butterfly, Stylized, Opalescent, 1930, 5 3/4 In.	990.00
Group, Woman & Birds, Kneeling Nude, Signed, c.1925, 6 1/8 In.	550.00
Plate, 3 Nude Maidens, Spiraling Motion, Signed, c.1930, 11 3/4 In.	660.00
Sconce, Opalescent, Stylized Women Ends, Chromed Metal, 14 x 40 In.	4450.00
Vase, 8 Maidens In Flowing Gowns, Dance Poses, Signed, 1930, 14 In.	2750.00
Vase, Allover Molded Fish, Paper Label, Signed, 5 1/4 In.	600.00
Vase, Nude Maiden In Dance Pose, Pale Green, Signed, c.1930, 10 In.	2750.00

SALOPIAN ware was made by the Caughley factory of England during the eighteenth century. The early pieces were blue and white with some colored decorations. Another ware referred to as *Salopian* is a late twentieth–century tableware decorated with color transfers.

Salopian

Bowl, Brown Transfer, Scene Of Lamb & Sheep, Orange Rim, 5 1/4 In.	90.00
Cake Plate, Deer Transfer, 7 5/8 In.	900.00
Coffeepot, Brown Transfer, Orange Rim, 10 1/2 In.	200.00
Creamer, 4 1/2 In.	85.00
Cup & Saucer, Brown Transfer, Blue Rim	40.00
Cup & Saucer, Deer Pattern	130.00
Dish, Meat Draining, Marked Mare, c.1775	1200.00
Plate, Cottage & Shepherds, 7 1/8 In.	525.00
Sugar, Cover, Brown Scenic View Transfer	100.00
Teapot, Brown Transfer	190.00

SALT AND PEPPER SHAKERS in matched sets were first used in the nineteenth century. Collectors are primarily interested in figural examples made after World War I. *Huggers* are pairs of shakers which appear to embrace each other. Many salt and pepper shakers are listed in other categories and can be located through the index at the back of this book.

Ace Of Hearts & Stack Of Coins	25.00
Alligators, Brown, 3 1/2 In.	1.50
Apple & Pear, 3 In.	2.75
Apples, Lying On Side, 2 1/2 In.	1.50
Aunt Jemima & Uncle Mose, Plastic	35.00
Ball Shape, Gray, 2 1/2 In.	1.50
Baseball Players, Holder, Luster	12.50
Bears, Huggers, Van Tellingen, Pink	25.00
Bears, Huggers, Van Tellingen, Yellow	14.00 To 16.00
Bears, Mamma & Baby, Ceramic Arts Studio	40.00
Beer Bottles, Budweiser	8.00
Beer Bottles, Fort Pitt	3.00
Beer Bottles, Fort Pitt & Piels, Box	12.00
Beswick Couple, Dickens Type	35.00
Birds, Colorful, 3 1/2 In.	3.50
Black Boy & Alligator, 2 1/2 x 4 In.	22.00
Black Boy Holding Heart, Girl In Pinafore, 4 In.	160.00
Black Boy Holding Heart, Girl In Pinafore, 5 In.	145.00
Black Boy On Whale	55.00
Black Boy Wears Beret, Girl Wears Bandana, 4 1/2 In.	85.00
Black Boy With Watermelon Slice	55.00
Blatz, Beer Bottle, Metal Cap	10.00
Bowling Pin & Ball	9.00
Bride & Groom, Turnabout	50.00
Butter Churn & Cream Can	25.00
Camel, Shakers In Hump, Plastic	5.00
Car & Stop Sign	25.00
Carrot & Bean, Vegetable People, 4 In.	6.00
Catalin Jewelry, Red	35.00
Chef, Hat Says Tappan, 4 In.	20.00
Chicken, Ceramic	3.00
Coffeepot & Grinder	25.00
Corn, Custard	70.00
Coyote, Treasure Craft	15.00
Dog & Cat, Ken–L–Ration	16.00
Dustpan & Broom	25.00
Dutch Maid, Ceramic Art Co.	12.90
Elf & Bottle, Peerless Brewery, Amber, Celluloid, 5 In.	65.00
Elsie & Elmer	50.00
Eskimo & Igloo, 2 In.	1.50
Esso, Plastic, Red, Blue & White, Decal, 3 In.	9.00
Falstaff, Beer Bottle	25.00
Fish & Fishing Basket	25.00
Flintstones	30.00
Fruit Basket, 4 1/2 In.	1.50
G. E. Refrigerator, Milk Glass	25.00
Gas Pump, Conoco	38.00
Ghost	15.00
Girl With Hatboxes	12.00
Glueck's Pilsner Ale	40.00
Goldilocks, Regal China	95.00 To 165.00
Hour Glass, Pewter, 2 1/2 In.	1.50
Humpty Dumpty, Regal China	85.00
Kewpie Bride & Groom, Huggers, Papier–Mache	50.00
Kittens, Sitting	9.00
Lamb, Huggers, Van Tellingen, Maroon	25.00
Lamp, Kerosene, Brown & White Design	1.50

Lamp, Table, Flower Design, 2 In. 2.00
Lancer's 35.00
Leaf & Spear 80.00
Lenny Lennox 50.00
Lobsters, Standing, Orange, 3 1/4 In. 2.50
Love Bug, Huggers, Van Tellingen .... 25.00 To 44.00
Low Scroll, Pink Cased 40.00
Mammy & Chef, Black, White Apron, Red Spoon, 4 1/2 In. 25.00
Mammy & Chef, Green Dress, White Apron, 3 1/4 In. 14.00
Mammy & Chef, Roly Poly, Chalkware 25.00
Mammy & Chef, White Clothing, Green Trim, 4 In. 22.00
Mammy, Luzianne Coffee, Red, Yellow, Blue, White, 5 In. 175.00
Mermaid & Sailor, Huggers, Van Tellingen 65.00
Milk Can, Brown, White House Design, 3 1/4 In. 1.50
Montana Map & Pistol 12.00
Mouse In Cheese, Ceramic Arts Studio 30.00
Mr. & Mrs. Claus, Holder, Luster 12.50
Mr. & Mrs. Fish, Regal China .... 90.00 To 110.00
Old MacDonald, Regal China 45.00
Owls, Holder, Luster 12.50
Paint Can & Brush 25.00
Parrots, Holder, Luster 12.50
Peasant Couple, Brayton Laguna, 5 1/2 In. .... 35.00 To 40.00
Peek-A-Boo, Huggers, Van Tellingen .... 62.00 To 90.00
Pig Chef, Ceramic 80.00
Pigs, Formal Dress 25.00
Pillsbury Dough Boy 15.00
Pipe & Slippers 25.00
Pleated Skirt, Pink 50.00
Poodle In Basket 9.00
Poppie & Poppin' Fresh 16.00
Purse & Pocket Watch 25.00
Puss 'n Boots 18.00
Rabbits, Yellow, Van Tellingen 25.00
Range, Pomco Perfect Foods, White, 5 In. 14.00
Ranger Bears, TW 16.00
RCA Nipper & Phonograph, Ceramic, 5 In. 45.00
RCA Nipper & Phonograph, Plastic, Box 18.00
S & P, Figural Letters, White, 2 1/2 In. 1.50
Santa Claus & Bag, 3 1/2 In., Box 3.00
Schlitz, Beer Bottle, Metal Cap 10.00
Seagram's 20.00
Sealtest 20.00
Ship, Smokestacks Are Shakers 3.00
Singing Strawberry & Cucumber Head, Ladies 23.00
Smokey The Bear 25.00
Snoopy & Woodstock 22.00
Snuffy Smith & Barney Google, Dated 1942, Box 60.00
Steam Iron & Ironing Board 30.00
Strawberries & Peaches, Enesco 12.00
Sunbonnets, White, Black Design, 4 1/4 In. 6.00
Swag & Bracket, Amethyst 45.00
Tappan 15.00
Teakettles, Wire Handles 4.00
Westinghouse Washer & Dryer .... 15.00 To 18.00
Willie & Millie, Penguins, Kool Cigarettes ....5.50 To 18.00
Willy & Oswald, 1958 .... 98.00

SALT GLAZE has a grayish white surface with a texture like an orange
peel. It is a method of decoration that has been used since the eighteenth
century. Salt-glazed pieces are still being made.

Bank, Fleur-De-Lis Design, David Morgan, c.1800, 4 1/2 In. 2100.00
Bank, Mary Warren Inscribed At Slot, 1866, 6 1/2 In. 4675.00

Churn, Cobalt Blue Bee–Sting Design, 5 Gal. 145.00
Cooler, Barrel Form, Incised Banding, Word Wine, 13 In. 2200.00
Cooler, Baskets Of Flowers, No. 10, Double Handle, 1847, 20 In. 5500.00
Crock, Blue, 19th Century, 11 1/2 x 11 In. 155.00
Crock, M. Mead, Mogadore, Ohio, 19th Century, 12 1/4 In. 275.00
Figurine, Greyhound 30.00
Jar, Bird, Warne & Letts, Coggle Wheel Rim Design, 1806 .... 2090.00
Jar, Cobalt Blue Tornado Design, 2 Gal. 200.00
Jug, Cobalt Blue, Head Of Devil, Ovoid, c.1830, 16 In. 3300.00
Jug, Incised Figure Of Mermaid, Cobalt Blue, 17 3/4 In. 3575.00
Jug, Incised Sloop, 2 Men, Banner, Heavy Waves, 15 1/4 In. 6600.00
Jug, L & BG Chase, Somerset, Ovoid 250.00
Pitcher, Cobalt Floral Design, New England, 1830, 3 3/4 In. 2530.00
Pitcher, Wheat & Flowers, Pewter Top, 9 In. 190.00
Pitcher, Windmill Scene, Blue 95.00
Spittoon, Blue Design ....95.00 To 125.00
Sugar, England, 1810 .... 450.00
Teapot, Castleford, England, 1810 .... 675.00

SAMPLERS were made in America from the early 1700s. The best
examples were made from 1790 to 1840. Long, narrow samplers are
usually older than square ones. Early samplers just had stitching or
alphabets. The later examples had numerals, borders, and pictorial
decorations. Those with mottoes are mid–Victorian. A revival of interest in
the 1930s produced simpler samplers, usually with mottoes.

ABCDE

Adage, Animals, Sarah Dawkin, Age 11, 19th Century, 12 x 12 1/2 In. 440.00
Albany Female Academy, Margaret Trotter Lush, 17 1/2 x 19 1/2 In. 1100.00
Alphabet & Bible Verse, Age 10, 1863, 8 x 12 In. 110.00
Alphabet & Numbers, Age 9, 1883, 9 x 9 In. 150.00
Alphabet, Angel, Adam, Eve, Other Figures, Homespun, 14 x 15 1/2 In. 350.00
Alphabet, Emma Arnold, September 18, 1873, 12 x 9 In. 225.00
Alphabet, Family Register, Homespun, Gilt Frame, 22 x 24 In. 325.00
Alphabet, Floral Designs, Homespun, 11 3/4 x 16 In. 245.00
Alphabet, Flowers, Mary Beatties, Births 1824 To 1845, 17 3/4 In. 550.00
Alphabet, Homespun, Janet Robertson Aged 10 Years, Frame, 19 In. 425.00
Alphabet, Homespun, Numbers, Flowers, Trees, Green, Brown, Frame 425.00
Alphabet, Homespun, Numbers, Pale Blue Pinstripe, 19 x 18 In. 225.00
Alphabet, Homespun, Numbers, Stylized Flowers, Frame, 13 x 31 In. 375.00
Alphabet, House, Hannah Headher, Frame, Year 1801, 22 x 14 In. 180.00
Alphabet, Martha Gilmore, 1741–1814 .... 825.00
Alphabet, Nancy Stones, Age 9, Frame, 8 3/4 x 8 3/4 In. 100.00
Alphabet, Numbers, 38 Figures, Signed & Dated 1866, 16 x 20 In. 550.00
Alphabet, Numerals, Stylized Birds, Flowers, Homespun, 15 x 12 In. 270.00
Alphabet, Stylized Floral Design, Homespun, Frame, 15 x 17 In. 250.00
Alphabet, Verse, Eliza Griswold, August 1826, 22 1/2 x 18 5/8 In. 575.00
Butterflies, Swans, Flowers, Harriet Thorpe, 12 x 13 In. 495.00
Christ On Cross, Marie Besseleers, 1804, 12 x 17 In. 357.00
Cross–Stitch, Animals, Flowers, 19th Century, 24 3/4 x 25 1/2 In. 775.00
Flame–Stitched Tree, Christania Heard, March 8, 1808, 17 x 17 In. 3575.00
Floral & Animal, Hannah Drake, Age 10, 1838, 12 1/2 x 12 1/2 In. 550.00
Floral Basket, Altar, Mary Fenton, 13 Years, 23 1/4 x 15 1/4 In. 290.00
Floral Border, Sarah M. Noyes, Born Jan. 15, 1817, 17 3/8 x 22 In. 800.00
Flowers, Birds, H. M. Sugden, Aged 12 Years, Frame, 16 3/4 x 20 In. 325.00
Genealogical, Sarah Ann Turner, Family Record Back To 1777 .... 550.00
God Is Love, Rosetta Hornsby, Age 12, Pot Of Flowers, 14 x 15 In. 295.00
Homespun, Blue & White, Woven, 1 Piece, Hand Hemmed, 39 x 65 In. 65.00
Homespun, Flowering Border, Parrot, Dog, Swans, Red, Rose, 26 x 24 In. 1250.00
Homespun, Linen, Sarah Brown, Born Dec. 31, 1783, Frame, 14 x 14 In. 475.00
Homespun, Vining Border, Stylized Flowers, Birds, 16 x 15 In. 375.00
Horse, Trees, Hannah Schellinger, Aged 10, 1809, 10 x 11 1/2 In. 550.00
Linen, Sarah Dove, 1811, 9 3/4 x 10 In. 325.00
Linen, Vining Border, Bowl Of Flowers, Verse, Gilt Frame, 25 In. 450.00
Lord's Prayer, Sara Ann Denson, 1819, 24 x 24 In. 1015.00

Sandwich Glass, Lamp, Fluid, Pink Cut To White, c.1865

Sandwich Glass, Lamp, Whale Oil, Acanthus, Blue, White, 11 In., Pair

Numbers, Ann Rutherford, Aged 11, 1851, Frame, 15 1/2 x 20 1/2 In.	395.00
Prayer, Elizabeth Jennings, December 19, 1840, 16 x 13 In.	880.00
Schoolhouse, Angels, Lydia Paulden, 1835, 17 1/2 x 16 1/2 In.	470.00
Silk Threads, Black, Green, Blue, Tan, Mary L. Montaqu, 19 x 14 In.	165.00
Stylized Flowers, Susan Shell, April 1835, 11 x 9 In.	405.00
Verse, Jane Maude Stavely, Aged 11, 1879, Frame, 18 1/2 x 22 In.	425.00
Verse, Sarah Ann Cooper, Sherborne, Dorset, 1850, 18 3/8 x 14 In.	500.00
Vining Border, Lou Vosneck Work, 1844, 29 x 24 In.	1100.00

SAMSON and Company, a French firm specializing in the reproduction of collectible wares of many countries and periods, was founded in Paris in the early nineteenth century. Chelsea, Meissen, Famille Verte, and Chinese Export porcelain are some of the wares that have been reproduced by the company. The firm uses a variety of marks on the reproductions. It is still in operation.

Cup & Saucer, Chinese Export Type	450.00
Tea Caddy	125.00
Vase, Cover, Chinese Export Type, 10 In.	300.00

SAND BABIES were used as decorations on a line of children's dishes made by the Royal Bayreuth China Company. The children are playing at the seaside. Collectors use the names *Sand Babies* and *Beach Babies* interchangeably.

Bell, Wooden Clapper, Royal Bayreuth	325.00 To 350.00
Inkwell, Skipping Rope	325.00

SANDWICH GLASS is any of the myriad types of glass made by the Boston and Sandwich Glass Works in Sandwich, Massachusetts, between 1825 and 1888. It is often very difficult to be sure whether a piece was really made at the Sandwich factory because so many types were made there and similar pieces were made at other glass factories. Additional pieces may be listed under Pressed Glass and in related categories.

Bowl, Petal & Loop, c.1850, 4 3/8 In.	50.00
Candlestick, Clambroth, Blue Top, Pair	650.00
Candlestick, Loop & Petal, Clambroth Base, 7 In., Pair	1200.00
Lamp, Fluid, Pink Cut To White, c.1865 ....*Illus*	3190.00
Lamp, Whale Oil, Acanthus, Blue, White, 11 In., Pair ...*Illus*	1100.00
Perfume Bottle, Vines, Octagonal, Stipple Stopper, Amber	325.00
Sugar, Striations Of Amber On Lid, Gothic Arch, Opaque Blue	3500.00
Vase, Overshot Cranberry, Clear, Tripod Legs, 8 In.	240.00

SARREGUEMINES is the name of a French town that is used as part of a china mark. Utzschneider and Company, a porcelain factory, made ceramics in Sarreguemines, Lorraine, France, from about 1775. Transfer-printed wares and majolica were made in the nineteenth century. The nineteenth-century pieces, most often found today, usually have colorful transfer-printed decorations showing peasants in local costumes.

Centerpiece, Majolica, Sea Nymphs, 1875, 14 3/4 In. ....*Illus* 880.00
Fruit Basket, Ribbon Entwined, Twisted Wire, 8 1/2 In. 125.00
Pitcher, Character, 8 1/2 In. 175.00
Plate, Black Transfer, 9 In. ....*Illus* 35.00
Urn, Campana Form, Cloisonne–Like Enamels, 26 In. 715.00

SASCHA BRASTOFF made decorative accessories, ceramics, enamels on
copper, and plastics of his own design. He headed a factory, Sascha
Brastoff of California, Inc., in West Los Angeles, from 1953 until about
1973.

Sascha Brstoff

Bowl, Burst Pussy Willows, 10 In. 25.00
Bowl, Divided, Pink & Silver, 8 In. 45.00
Bowl, Enameled Green, Gold Marbelized, Footed, 5 1/2 In. 50.00
Bust, Woman's Head, White, Signed, 13 In. 195.00
Dinner Set, Service For 4, Pink & Silver, 19 Piece 200.00
Dish, Egg, Cover, 10 1/2 In. 50.00
Dish, Stylized Horse, 10 In. 30.00
Plate, Enameled, 6 In. 10.00
Tea Set, Pink & Silver, Signed, 3 Piece 165.00
Teapot, Pink & Silver 85.00
Tray, Gold Grapes, Aqua, 8 In. 35.00

SATIN GLASS is a late nineteenth–century art glass. It has a dull finish
that is caused by hydrofluoric acid vapor treatment. Satin glass was made
in many colors and sometimes has applied decorations. Satin glass is also
listed by factory name, such as Webb, or in the Mother–of–Pearl category
in this book.

Basket, Quilted Swag, Yellow, White Interior, 11 In. 110.00
Biscuit Jar, Fleurette Lid, Fleurette Pattern, Pink, 6 1/4 In. 225.00
Biscuit Jar, Pink Flowers 600.00
Biscuit Jar, Pink To White, Flowers, Silver Plated Lid, 9 In. 525.00
Biscuit Jar, Quilted, Enameled, Pink Shading, Flowers, 8 In. 140.00
Bowl, Brown, Floral Enameled, Gilt Stems, Footed, 9 1/2 In. 140.00
Bowl, Flower Frog, Black 12.50
Bowl, Ribbon, Pink Ribbed, Mother–of–Pearl, Crimped, 4 1/2 In. 295.00
Bowl, Turned Up Back, Enameled Daisies, Gold Branches, 10 In. 275.00
Box, Patch, Hand Painted Strawberries Around, Fancy Hinged Top 85.00
Bride's Bowl, Ruffled, White Underside, Gold Foliage, Blue 350.00
Castor, Pickle, Pumpkin Mold, Silver Plated Holder 240.00
Console Set, Blue, 3 Piece 175.00
Creamer, Butterscotch Raindrop, Square Mouth, Lined, 5 In. 225.00

Sarreguemines, Centerpiece, Majolica, Sea Nymphs, 1875, 14 3/4 In.

Sarreguemines, Plate, Black Transfer, 9 In.

Satsuma, Jar, Shogan, Geishas, Signed, 18 In.   *Satsuma, Vase, 1880, 12 In.*

Cruet, Guttate	175.00
Ewer, Birds & Flowers, Frosted Handle, 12 3/4 In.	245.00
Ewer, Blue, Pink Floral, White Lining, 9 3/4 In., Pair	225.00
Ewer, Purple Raspberries, Pink Overlay, Mellon, 12 1/4 In.	225.00
Finger Bowl, Underplate, Drape, Mother-of-Pearl, Plate 7-In.	515.00
Lamp, Peg, Diamond-Quilted, Mother-of-Pearl, Pink, 13 In.	650.00
Lamp, Pink, 4 In.	87.00
Rose Bowl, Diamond-Quilted, Cut Velvet, 4-Crimp Top, 3 In.	165.00
Rose Bowl, Rainbow Diamond, Mother-of-Pearl, 3 x 4 1/4 In.	1395.00
Salt & Pepper, Bulging Petal, Blue	50.00
Vase, Applied Reeded Camphor Handle Ornaments, Oval, 10 In.	360.00
Vase, Enameled Bluebird, Camphor Handle Ornaments, 10 In.	357.00
Vase, Flower & Acorn, Mother-of-Pearl, Green, 5 x 4 1/4 In.	425.00
Vase, Flower & Acorn, Mother-of-Pearl, Tricorner Top, 6 In.	895.00
Vase, Swirl, Reeded Handle, Ruffled Top, 11 1/2 In.	355.00

SATSUMA is a Japanese pottery with a distinctive creamy beige crackled glaze. Most of the pieces were decorated with blue, red, green, orange, or gold. Almost all Satsuma found today was made after 1860. During World War I, Americans could not buy undecorated European porcelains. Women who liked to make hand painted porcelains at home began to decorate plain Satsuma. These pieces are known today as *American Satsuma*.

Bowl, Deities On Rim, Wisteria Blossoms Interior, 14 3/4 In.	2200.00
Bowl, Kwannon Scene Surrounded By Arhats, 6 1/4 In.	175.00
Charger, 5 Warriors, Gold	1100.00
Dish, Figural Interior Scene, 19th Century, 7 In.	137.00
Flask, Moon, Battling Samurai Scene, Signed, 6 1/2 In.	1980.00
Jar, Figural Reserves, 7 In.	880.00
Jar, Shogan, Geishas, Signed, 18 In. ....*Illus*	1980.00
Jardiniere, Figural Scenes & Diaper Designs, 11 x 12 1/2 In.	192.00
Jardiniere, Trailed Enamel, Seated Dignitaries, 13 3/4 x 16 In.	325.00
Lamp, Rakan, Buddha, Shimazo Mons & Dragon Gilt Scenes, 12 1/2 In.	500.00
Luncheon Set, War Lords, Kikusui, 15 Piece	50.00
Plate, Brocaded Pattern, Gold Floral Bands, Kizan, 9 5/8 In.	357.00
Plate, Geisha & Warlord Design, Gold, 7 In.	170.00
Tea Caddy, Mountain Scenes, Red Moon	50.00
Tea Set, Gold Design, Enamels Of Kwannon, Cloud Pattern, 9 Piece	550.00
Umbrella Stand, Applied Dragon, Nobleman & Attendants, 24 5/8 In.	330.00
Vase, 1880, 12 In. ....*Illus*	880.00
Vase, 2 Figural Panels, Floral, Geometric, Gold, 1880, 10 7/8 In.	225.00
Vase, 2 Panels With Masters & Attendants, Floral, 1880, 10 7/8 In.	250.00

Vase, Dragon Handles, 22 In. 155.00
Vase, Faces, Gilded, 4 3/4 In. 50.00
Vase, Figural & Diaper Design, 1880s, 8 5/8 In. 275.00
Vase, Haloed Arhats & Kwannon, Marked, c.1910, 12 1/2 In., Pair 450.00
Vase, Moriage Figures & Floral, Stand, Ovoid, 44 In. 550.00
Vase, Nishikide Diapered Top, Elephant Handles, c.1920, 16 In. 150.00
Vase, Ormolu, France, 24 1/2 In. 400.00
Vase, Panel Of Children 1 Side, Geisha & Man Other, 7 1/4 In. 145.00
Vase, Paneled Baluster Form, Thousand Faces, Signed, 12 In. 550.00
Vase, Raised Enamel Dragons & Scholars, 7 1/2 In., Pair 1150.00
Vase, Raised Leaves, Florals, Brown Ground, 12 In. 85.00
Vase, Serpent & Arhats Encircling Body, Signed, 6 In. 375.00

SATURDAY EVENING GIRLS, see Paul Revere Pottery Category.

SCALES have been made to weigh everything from babies to gold.
Collectors search for all types. Most popular are small gold dust scales and
special grocery scales.

Baby, Stork On Dial 20.00
Balance, 2 Small Drawers, Brass, Walnut Cabinet, 19 x 16 In. 275.00
Balance, Brass, Oak, 28 In. 65.00
Balance, Butter, Wooden, Turned Pans, Replaced Twine Ropes 65.00
Balance, Gold Coin, Steel Beam, Ring Top, Brass Pans, 18th Century ... 95.00
Balance, Gold, Portable, Box 70.00
Bathroom, Charlie The Tuna, 1960s 45.00
Candy, Pelouze, 2 Lb. Scoop, Pat. 1915 .... 90.00
Chatillon's Improved, Spring Balance, Brass, Iron Hook, 3 Lbs. 23.00
Chatillon, Hand, Brace Face 12.00
Chatillon, Milk, Brass Dial, Round 55.00
Columbia, Brass Face, Cast Iron, 8 1/2 x 6 In. 25.00
Computing Scale Co., Grocery, Light–Up Display 522.50
Dayton, Gold With Black & Red Stenciling, Scoop, 1916 .... 120.00
Detecto, Hanging 20.00
Eastman Kodak Co., Rochester, N.Y., 6 Graduated Weights, 9 In. 55.00
Forschner's, Improved Circular Spring Balance, Brass Template 65.00
Frary's, Spring, Brass Face 12.00
Grain, Brass 185.00
Hanson, Kitchen 17.50
Henry Westwood, Peddler's, Traveling, Small 18.00
I. Edwards, N.Y., Lobe Support, Acorn–Tipped Finial, Iron, 26 1/2 In. 1100.00
IBM Canada, Candy, Bronze Scoop & Trim 200.00
Imperial Computing, Candy 45.00
Jacobs Bros., Candy, Pedestal, 3 Weights 98.00
Ohaus, Balance 60.00
Opium, Teakwood Holder 85.00
Peerless Aristocrat, Lollipop, Porcelain & Cast Iron, c.1916 .... 800.00
Pelouze, Avoirdupois, Photo Laboratory, Brass Weights, Complete 50.00
Pharmacy, Oak & Marble 175.00
Platform, On Wheels, 1860, 1000 Lb. 300.00
Rock–Ola, Lo–Boy, 1 Cent, Green 175.00
RX Penny 275.00
Spring Balance, Hanging, Star, Embossed Brass 6.50
Steelyard, 15 In. 25.00
Steelyard, 3 Hooks & Counter Weight, Iron, 10 To 50 Lbs, 21 1/2 In. ... 22.00
Toledo, Candy 325.00
Universal, Balance, Walnut Platform, Brass Pedestal & Arms, 21 In. 95.00

SCHAFER & VATER, makers of small ceramic items, are best known for
their amusing figurals. The factory was located in Volkstedt–Rudolstadt,
Germany, from 1890 to 1962. Some pieces are marked with the crown and
R mark, but many are unmarked.

Bottle, Jeweled, Metallic, 8 In. 150.00

Box, Cover, Woman, Poke Bonnet, Jasperware, Marked, 3 1/2 In. 85.00
Box, Figural, Lobster Forms Lid, Marked, 4 5/8 In. 85.00
Box, Medallion Design On Cover, Gold Trim, 2 x 2 5/8 In. 65.00
Box, Woman & Rose On Lid, Jasperware, Round, 3 In. 88.00
Creamer, Cow Wearing Dress, 5 1/2 In. 195.00
Creamer, Oriental Girl 175.00
Ewer, Glossy, Handle, 5 In. 55.00
Hair Receiver & Powder Jar, 2 Piece 95.00
Hatpin Holder, Woman's Head Top, Sphinx On Sides, Pink 185.00
Jar, Cover, Pink Biscuit, Signed, 3 1/4 In. 45.00
Match Holder, Dutch Boy, 5 3/8 In. 125.00
Mug, Blown-Out Elk, Head Each Side, Marked, 3 1/4 In. 75.00
Pitcher, Figural, Girl Carrying Pitcher, Marked, 4 In. 125.00
Pitcher, Grecian, Bisque, Tan, 6 1/4 In. 95.00
Shaving Mug, Blown-Out Moose, Tan, Beige Ground, 3 1/2 In. 95.00
Sugar Shaker, Art Nouveau, Lady's Head, Flowing Hair 85.00
Sugar, Cover, Figure Of Woman, Cupid, Jasperware, Marked 95.00
Vase, Woman & Birds, Jasperware, Handle, Blue, 7 7/8 In. 85.00

SCHNEIDER Glassworks was founded in 1903 at Epinay-sur-Seine, France, by Charles and Ernest Schneider. Art glass was made between 1903 and 1930. The company still produces clear crystal glass. *Schneider*

Lamp Base, Cameo, Orange, Pink Floral, Marked, 12 In. 650.00
Lamp, Floral Cut Top, Tortoiseshell Cut Base, Marked, 12 In. 750.00
Night-Light, Onion Form, Leaf Feet, Signed, c.1925, 5 3/4 In. 1760.00
Vase, Basket Of Fruit, Geometric Band, Signed, c.1925, 7 In. 880.00
Vase, Brown & Orange Mixed, Bubbles, Square Top, 9 In. 765.00
Vase, Colorless Body, Art Deco Blossoms, Signed, 12 1/2 In. 1072.00
Vase, Dark Purple, Clear, Etched, Signed, 16 In. 1320.00
Vase, Gray Mottled, Grape Clusters, Wrought Iron Base, 9 7/8 In. 3300.00
Vase, Mottled Blue, Signed, 10 x 14 In. 1500.00
Vase, Mottled Orange-Yellow, Red Streaks, Signed, 12 1/2 In. 1295.00
Vase, Orange Base, Frosted Clear Top, Iron Stem, Signed, 6 In. 775.00
Vase, Orange, Iron Armature & Foot, Marked, 9 In. 990.00
Vase, Orange, Random Bubbles, Purple Footed, 1920, 14 1/8 In. 3850.00
Vase, Purple & White Mottled, Blue Spatters, Art Glass, 10 In. 795.00
Vase, Red Domical Foot, Mottled, Spherical, c.1925, 8 1/2 In. 665.00
Vase, Spiral Design, Dark Gray, Trumpet, Circular Foot, 12 In. 1100.00
Vase, Tomato Red, Purple Pulled Lip, 1925, 2 1/2 In., Pair 4125.00
Vase, Triangles, Blown Into Iron Frame, Signed, 1925, 16 1/8 In. 2100.00
Vase, Trumpet, Clear, Pink & Lime Streak, Iron Mount, 14 3/16 In. 2475.00
Vase, White To Lemon To Chinese Red, Teardrop, 15 7/8 In., Pair 5775.00
Vase, Wiggly Trailings Inside, Dots, Signed, c.1930, 7 1/4 In. 1320.00
Vase, Yellow, Orange, Lavender Splotches, Signed, 15 3/4 In. 990.00
SCHNIEDER, Vase, Cameo, Black-Eyed Susans, Gray, Lavender, Deep Plum, 7 In. 3575.00

SCIENTIFIC INSTRUMENTS of all kinds are included in this category. Other categories, such as Barometer, Binoculars, Dental, Nautical, Medical, and Thermometer, may also price scientific apparatus.

Adder, C. H. Webber, Dated 1868 .... 500.00
Adding Machine, Burroughs, Flatbed, Restored, 1920s 250.00
Calculator, Odhner, Portable, Hand Held, Case, 1930s 140.00
Checkwriter, Todd 30.00
Chronometer, Hamilton, Gyro Mount 1250.00
Chronometer, Kelvin & White, Silvered Dial, 7 In. 1320.00
Compass, Kelvin White Co., U.S. Navy, Oak Box 125.00
Compass, Loupe 30.00
Compass, Nesso, Pocket-Watch Type 35.00
Compass, Sundial, Celluloid, Brass 35.00
Compass, Surveyor's, Wrightman Sculp, Case, 14 In. 770.00
Compass, Troughton & Sims, London, Table Box, 1915 .... 95.00
Field Glasses, With Case, France, 1920 .... 295.00
Hygrothermograph, Bendix Friez, Model 594 .... 300.00

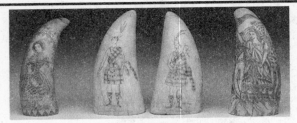

Left: Scrimshaw, Tooth, Whale, Woman & Child, 19th
Century, 4 1/2 In.; center two: Scrimshaw, Tooth, Whale,
Scotsman, Ships On Reverse, 4 5/8 In., Pr.; right:
Scrimshaw, Tooth, Whale, Liberty, American Flags, 4 1/2 In.

Marking Machine, Jr. Monarch, Pat. June 14, 1904	48.00
Microscope, Field, Wooden Case, Germany	95.00
Microscope, Octopus Co., Traveling, Case, England	143.00
Money Changer, Bank, Staats, Chicago, Pat. Feb. 25, 1890	250.00
Orrery	850.00
Planetarium, Trippensee, Dated 1908	1050.00
Propeller, Plane, Laminated Wood, Brass, 6 Ft. 4 In.	295.00
Sextant, Heath & Co., 155 Degree Scale, Eye Pieces	522.50
Sextant, Samuel Emery, Ebony, 11 1/2 In.	605.00
Sundial, Equinoctial Dial, 19th Century, Pocket	495.00
Telescope, Adie, With Stand, Brass, 38 In.	885.00
Telescope, Brass, 4 Tubes, Leather Cover, France	115.00
Telescope, C. Hutchinson, Brass & Mahogany, c.1860	5225.00
Telescope, Elliot Bros., Stand, Brass Barrel, 62 In.	1350.00
Telescope, Nurnberg, Wood, 1800s	2350.00
Telescope, S & B Solomons, Canvas & Tin, 52 In.	695.00
Telescope, T. Harris, Table Mount, Brass, Cased	1100.00
Tellurion, Uses Kerosene Lamp, Germany, 1870	2500.00
Theodolite, Kern, Horizontal & Vertical Lines, 1910	3110.00
Transit, Samuel Thaxton, Brass & Steel, 13 3/4 In.	335.00
Transit, Surveyor's, Stackpole & Brothers, 1741	495.00
Wind Indicator, Fully Clothed Black Figures	3250.00

SCRIMSHAW is bone or ivory or whale's teeth carved by sailors and
others for entertainment during the sailing–ship days. Some scrimshaw was
carved as early as 1800. There are modern scrimshanders making pieces
today on bone, ivory, or plastic. Other pieces may be found in the Ivory
and Nautical sections.

Horn, Map, Scenes Of City Names Of New York & Eastern Canada	3500.00
Ivory, Top, Drum Shape, Black Numbers 1 Through 8, 2 1/2 In.	165.00
Pie Wheel, Jagging, Curved Handle, 6 In.	300.00
Spoon, Carved Horn, Alaska, 19th Century, 10 In.	335.00
Tooth, Whale, Cougar, 5 In.	325.00
Tooth, Whale, Liberty, American Flags, 4 1/2 In. ....*Illus*	770.00
Tooth, Whale, Sailing Ship, 6 x 3 In.	460.00
Tooth, Whale, Scotsman, Ships On Reverse, 4 5/8 In., Pr. ....*Illus*	525.00
Tooth, Whale, Woman & Child, 19th Century, 4 1/2 In. ....*Illus*	495.00
Whalebone Shaft, Cane, Tortoiseshell & Ebony Inlay	2750.00

SEBASTIAN MINIATURES were first made by Prescott W. Baston in 1938
in Marblehead, Massachusetts. More than 400 different designs have been
made and collectors search for the out–of–production models. The mark
may say *Copr. P. W. Baston U.S.A.,* or *P. W. Baston, U.S.A.,* or *Prescott
W. Baston.* Sometimes a paper label was used.

Colonial Bell Ringer	18.00
Colonial Kitchen	40.00
Colonial Watchman	18.00

Coronado 50.00
Doctor, Neisler .... 135.00 To 150.00
Farmer's Wife, 1947 .... 150.00
Franklin D. Roosevelt 18.00
Giraffe, Everyone Reaches For Jell–O 425.00
Harvey Girl 200.00
Jim 35.00
John & Priscilla Alden, Box 125.00
Madonna Of The Goldfinch, Blue Label 65.00
Old Covered Bridge, 1954 .... 50.00
Old Salt, 1950 .... 150.00
Pilgrims, 1947 .... 35.00
Pocahontas 65.00
Shoemaker, First County National Bank 200.00
Sidewalk Days, Girl & Boy, Green Label, Pair 50.00
Sistine Madonna, 4 In. 75.00
Stork, Jell–O .... 125.00 To 375.00
Swan Boat, 1950 .... 55.00
Toy Maker 100.00
Uncle Sam, With Barrel, 1937 .... 25.00 To 45.00

SEG, see Paul Revere Pottery category

SEVRES porcelain has been made in Sevres, France, since 1769. Many
copies of the famous ware have been made. The name originally referred to
the works of the Royal Porcelain factory. The name now includes any of
the wares made in the town of Sevres, France. The entwined lines with a
center letter used as the mark is one of the most forged marks in antiques.
Be very careful to identify Sevres by quality, not just by mark.

Box, Enameled Scene Of 3 Cherubs On Lid, Marked, 7 3/4 In. 105.00
Coffee Can & Saucer, Turkish Couple, Gilt Bands, 1777 .... 2300.00
Cup & Saucer, Floral Garland, Gilt Trim, 1760 .... 1700.00
Dish, Flower Cluster & Fruit, Dated 1787, 11 3/8 In., Pair 1550.00
Figurine, Dancing Couple, Floral Dress, Green Trousers, 11 x 12 In. 1650.00
Figurine, Goat Kid, A. Bonobeau 375.00
Lamp, Portrait Of Woman Central Oval, Courting Scene, 15 1/2 In. 2475.00
Pitcher, Cherries, 8 In. 75.00
Plaque, Nude Juno, Floral Rim, Signed, 1897, 18 3/8 In. 4675.00
Plate, Duchess De Bourgogne, 1846, 9 1/2 In. 150.00
Plate, Gold Napoleonic Crest, Gold Rim, 6 Piece 363.00
Plate, Lovers In Forest, Gilt Border, Green Ground, R. Pajot, 10 In. 300.00
Plate, Madame De Cavalliere, 1846, 9 1/2 In. 150.00
Plate, Madame De Pompadour, 9 1/2 In. 275.00
Plate, Pink Roses Center, Gilt Bands, Dated 1793, 9 9/16 In. 3025.00
Plate, Scroll Border, Interlaced L's, 9 11/16 In., 12 Piece 4675.00
Tazza, Floral Medallions, Pink, Gold Tracery, 1859 .... 495.00
Tray, Landscape, Floral & Diaper Design Border, Oval, 11 In. 3575.00
Tray, Louis XIV, Chateau St. Cloud, 1846, 11 In. 315.00
Tureen, Stand, Flowers & Fruit, Shell Handles, 1766, 20 3/8 In. 2750.00
Urn, Allegorical Figure, Landscape Reverse, Bronze Base, 39 1/2 In. 4400.00
Urn, Blue Cover, Neck & Stem, Dore Base & Collar, 21 1/2 In., Pair 6750.00
Urn, Cover, Continuous Figural & Landscape, Signed, 19 3/4 In., Pair 4950.00
Urn, Portrait, Cobalt Blue, 25 In., Pair 1300.00
Urn, Portrait, Gold On White, 1821, 9 3/4 In. 695.00
Vase, Butterflies, Marguerites, Silvered Metal, Lime, 1900, 10 In. 2750.00
Vase, Cover, Front Figures, Landscape Reverse, Bronze Base, 30 In. 5500.00
Vase, Dark & Pale Blue Curving Lines, White Glaze, Oviform, Footed 2775.00
Vase, Ormolu Mounts, 22 In., Pair 5650.00
Vase, Th. Fragonard, 1866, 30 In. 9000.00

SEWER TILE figures were made by workers at the sewer tile and pipe
factories in the Ohio area during the late nineteenth and early twentieth
centuries. Figurines, small vases, and cemetery vases were favored. Often

the finished vase was a piece of the original pipe with added decorations and markings. All types of sewer tile work are now considered folk art by collectors.

Bank, Bust Of Man, Incised Green's Bank, 10 In.	900.00
Bank, Pig, 8 3/4 In.	25.00
Birdhouse, Pagoda Roof, Hand Tooling	175.00
Cabin	410.00
Dog, Flat Head, Hand Tooling, 10 1/2 In.	450.00
Dog, Scotty, 3 3/4 In.	25.00
Dog, Seated, Solid Mold, Tooled, Overpaint Traces, 8 1/4 In.	110.00
Dog, Small, 4 In.	150.00
Flowerpot, Attached Saucer, Hand Tooled, 8 1/2 In.	95.00
Frog, 6 1/4 In.	90.00
Lion, Mellinger, 1889, 9 5/8 In.	325.00
Owl, Incised Initials E. J. E., 14 1/4 In.	950.00
Planter, Stump, 6 In.	25.00
Sample, Signed Union Sewer Pipe Co.	625.00

SEWING equipment of all types is collected, from sewing birds that held the cloth to old wooden spools.

Basket, Straw, Tassels, Beads, Coins, Jade, 9 In.	18.00
Basket, Sweetgrass, Contents, 3 1/2 x 6 1/2 I.	23.00
Bird, 2 Pincushions, Silver Plate	105.00
Bird, Clamp–On, Red Pincushion, Open Heart–Shaped Thumbscrew, 1853	165.00
Bird, Dolphin Shape	235.00
Bird, Pincushion In Center, Mid–1800s	385.00
Box, Gold & Silver Stenciled Design, Round, 13 1/2 In	100.00
Box, Hinged Lid, Pedestal, Inlaid Mixed Woods	250.00
Box, Ivory Inlay	425.50
Box, Lehnware, Pine, Brown Paint, Striping, Decoupage, 1875, 11 In.	350.00
Box, Nakara, Hinged Lid, Hand Painted Flowers	275.00
Box, Pincushion Top, 3 Drawers, Wooden	2950.00
Box, Supplies, Darning Silk, J. P. Coats Mending Floss, Buttons, Lace	15.00
Box, Victorian, Celluloid Cover	68.00
Box, Wicker, Bone & Mother–of–Pearl Tools, c.1900	155.00
Buttonholer, Hand–Held, Singer, Cast Iron	35.00
Cabinet, Spool, see Advertising section under Cabinet, Spool	
Case, Gold Over Sterling, Set In Ivory, France, 6 Piece	1195.00
Case, Scissors, Gold, Enameled Tulips, Blue, Chain, Flemish, 3 1/4 In.	1750.00
Case, Thimble, Nutshell, Brass, Ernest Steiner Orig., 2 x 1 1/2 In.	22.00
Case, Thimble, Vegetable Ivory, Acorn Shape, Burled Walnut, 2 In.	135.00
Crochet Needle, No. 1–14, Needle Screw In Handle, Boye, No. 10 Missing	30.00
Darner, Glove, Sterling Silver, Foster & Bailey	90.00
Darner, Sock, Wooden	2.50
Darner, Sock, Wooden, Mushroom Shape	15.00
Darning Egg, Wooden, Handle	6.50

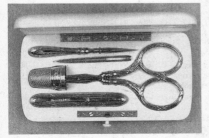

Sewing, Kit, 18K Gold, Ivory, Tiffany, 1900s

◆ ◆ ◆ ◆ ◆ ◆ ◆ ◆ ◆ ◆ ◆ ◆ ◆ ◆ ◆ ◆ ◆ ◆ ◆

Stuff hats with acid–free tissue for storage. Try to make the stuffing deep enough so the hat brim does not touch the shelf.

◆ ◆ ◆ ◆ ◆ ◆ ◆ ◆ ◆ ◆ ◆ ◆ ◆ ◆ ◆ ◆ ◆ ◆ ◆

Emory, Strawberry Shape, Sterling Tip, Unger Bros. 125.00
Hem Gauge, Sterling Silver 135.00
Hem Marker, Adjustable, Iron, Dated 1911 .... 5.00
Kit, 18K Gold, Ivory, Tiffany, 1900s ....*Illus* 2090.00
Kit, Bullet Shape, Mt. Royale 18.00
Kit, General Electric Vacuum Cleaner 28.00
Kit, Locket, Thimble, Brass 18.00
Kit, Luzianne Mammy 50.00
Kit, Machine Shape, Brass, Pincushion, Thimble, Tape Measure, 4 In. 45.00
Kit, Papier–Mache Turtle, c.1880 .... 395.00
Knitting Needles, Pair 4.00
Machine, Black Stenciled, Germany 85.00
Machine, Child's, Reliable 200.00
Machine, Hand Powered, Gold Stenciling, Germany 150.00
Machine, Howe, Treadle, 1870s 195.00
Machine, Lap Held, Flowers Painted On Base, Cast Iron 75.00
Machine, McLelland & Bennett, Wood Lithograph 350.00
Machine, Oak Cabinet 80.00
Machine, Singer For Girls, Box, 1910 .... 95.00
Machine, Singer, Child's, Heavy Metal 175.00
Machine, Singer, Featherweight, Instructions, Case 175.00
Machine, Singer, Featherweight, Model 221 .... 175.00 To 250.00
Machine, Stenciled, M Brand, Germany, Salesman's Sample 295.00
Machine, White, Treadle, 6 Drawers, Ornate Cabinet 75.00
Machine, White, Treadle, Drawers Full Of Notions 55.00
Machine, Wilson, Treadle, 1870s 195.00
Needle Book, Black Mammy, Luzianne, Coffee–Can Shape 25.00
Needle Book, Deaf, Mute, Suitcase Shape 10.00
Needle Case, Blue Beaded 45.00
Needle Case, Crystal Baking Powder 10.00
Needle Case, Darning, Wooden, Large, Pair 2.25
Needle Case, Ivory, Brass, Stamped Reddich, England 210.00
Needle Case, Lap Desk, Avery & Son 275.00
Needle Case, Letter–Post 295.00
Needle Case, Owl Shape, Wall, Maroon Felt, 1910, 3 1/2 x 6 In. 65.00
Needle Case, Space Sewing, 1950s 18.00
Needle Case, Vegetable Ivory, 3 Piece 55.00
Needle Case, Wooden 4.00
Pin Holder, Prudential Company, Mother Holding Child 10.00
Pincushion dolls are listed in their own category
Pincushion, Apple, 2 1/2 In. 78.00
Pincushion, Beaded & Scalloped 22.50
Pincushion, Beaded, Cat & Dog, Exhibition Toronto Inscription 95.00
Pincushion, Beaded, Crossed Flags, Tassels 38.00
Pincushion, Camel, Metal 32.00
Pincushion, Cat Sitting On Persian Rug, Austria 40.00
Pincushion, Dachshund, Porcelain 35.00
Pincushion, Heart Shape, Red Satin, Pins With Colored Heads, 6 In. 45.00
Pincushion, Man's Shoe, Metal 12.00
Pincushion, Pig In Boot 42.00
Pincushion, Rabbit & Stump, Metal 105.00
Pincushion, Reindeer Hoof, Fur & Velvet, 1908 .... 25.00
Pincushion, Revolving, Tape Measure In Base, Thimble 30.00
Pincushion, Sterling Silver, Gorham 45.00
Pincushion, Success Horse–Drawn Manure Spreader 60.00
Pincushion, Vegetable Ivory 55.00
Pincushion, Velvet Top, Metal Lid, Occupied Japan 5.00
Pincushion, Woman & Man Golfers, Christmas, 1905 .... 55.00
Pincushion, Woman's Shoe, Metal 15.00
Punch, Adjustable 12.00
Ruler, Hem & Seam, Metal, Adjustable 2.25
Scissors, Buttonhole 18.00
Scissors, Embroidery, Steel 15.00

Scissors, Embroidery, Stork	35.00
Scissors, Stork, Silver	25.00
Sharpener, Needle, Cat	48.00
Shuttle, Tatting, Celluloid	7.50
Skirt Form, Metal, Opens Like Umbrella, Iron Base, 1800s	125.00
Spool cabinets are in the Advertising section under Cabinet, Spool	
Spool Holder, 5th Avenue Drug Co.	100.00
Spool Holder, 6 Spindles, 2 Tiers, Pincushion Top, 7 1/2 In.	110.00
Spool Holder, Victorian, Revolving, Tin, 2 1/2 In.	45.00
Swift, On Box, 1 Drawer, Mother-of-Pearl Inlay, Whalebone, 17 1/2 In.	1350.00
Table, Folding, 3 Drawers	90.00
Tape Measure, Alarm Clock	99.00
Tape Measure, American Uniform Co.	15.00
Tape Measure, Apple	40.00
Tape Measure, Apple, Red, Leaf Pull, Hard Plastic	18.00
Tape Measure, Aunt Jemima	15.00
Tape Measure, British & American Flags, Bundles For Britain, Brass	9.00
Tape Measure, Celluloid, St. Louis, 1904	30.00
Tape Measure, Champion Tools, Tire Shape	12.00
Tape Measure, Coach Shape, Brass, England	450.00
Tape Measure, Covered Wagon, Celluloid	58.00
Tape Measure, Crown, Pincushion	25.00
Tape Measure, Dog, Corduroy	12.00
Tape Measure, English Terrier On Ball, Celluloid	85.00
Tape Measure, Feeney's Grocery Store	18.00
Tape Measure, Fish Shape, Metal	98.00
Tape Measure, Fish, Celluloid	25.00
Tape Measure, General Electric Vacuum Cleaner	35.00
Tape Measure, John Deere	22.00
Tape Measure, Lady's Man	15.00
Tape Measure, Lydia Pinkham, Pictures Lydia, Celluloid	38.00
Tape Measure, Mirror On Pedestal	45.00
Tape Measure, Nancy Lynn Hosiery, Celluloid, 1951	12.00
Tape Measure, Owl Front, Brasse, Germany, Chrome	55.00
Tape Measure, Pennsylvania Salt Mfg., Celluloid	65.00
Tape Measure, Pennsylvania Station, Round	55.00
Tape Measure, Pig	30.00
Tape Measure, Pig, Denver, Colorado, Celluloid	65.00
Tape Measure, Pig, N.Y. City, Celluloid	30.00
Tape Measure, Pig, Winding Tail	88.00
Tape Measure, Pink Egg With Fly	75.00
Tape Measure, Pull-Out, Mellin's Food	12.00
Tape Measure, Rooster, China	65.00
Tape Measure, Scotty, Black	25.00
Tape Measure, Texaco, 1949	12.00
Tape Measure, This Little Pig, Celluloid	45.00
Tape Measure, Turtle, Says Pull My Head & Not My Leg	125.00
Thimble, Grants Hygienic Crackers, Silver, Green, 1905, Aluminum	10.00
Thread Holder, Carved Shamrock, Dogwood, Irish, 2 1/4 In.	85.00
Thread Holder, Victorian Woman, Celluloid	30.00
Thread Waxer, Chatelaine, Sterling	98.00
Thread Winder, Fish	56.00
Threader, Needle, Tastee-Cake, Germany	8.00
Winder, Yarn, Weasel, Marked A. G.	100.00

SHAKER items are characterized by simplicity, functionalism, and orderliness. There were many Shaker communities in America from the eighteenth century to the present day. The religious order made furniture, small wooden pieces, and packaged medicines, herbs, and jellies to sell to *outsiders.* Other useful objects were made for use by members of the community. Shaker furniture is listed in this book in the Furniture category.

Bag, Grain, Cotton, Enfield, 20 x 42 In.	150.00

Basket, Rectangular, Handles, By J. A. May, 1890 .... 775.00
Basket, Sewing, Cover, Woven Square Convex, 1850s, 3 1/2 x 5 5/8 In. 995.00
Basket, Sewing, Painted Floral On Cover, Heart Shape, 4 In. 105.00
Basket, Sewing, Poplar Splint, Lined, Sabbathday Lake, 4 3/4 In. 180.00
Basket, Slate, Alternating Ash & Maple Slats, 14 x 16 In. 375.00
Basket, Splint, Carved Handle, Tapering Sides, 8 1/2 x 12 In. 295.00
Beater, Bentwood, Salmon Paint, Turned Handle, 20 1/2 In. 95.00
Bonnet, Straw, Silk Liner 1350.00
Bowl, Molded Rim, Turned & Painted Ash, New Lebanon, 1825, 28 1/4 In. 3300.00
Box, 3-Finger, Brick Red Paint, Sabbathday Lake, Oval, 12 In. 2200.00
Box, 3-Finger, Fitted Interior, Oval, Red Paint, 7 In. 5500.00
Box, 4-Finger, Storage, Pine, Hardwood, Scrubbed, 11 In. 250.00
Box, Bentwood, Old Varnish, Copper Tacks, 12 In. 190.00
Box, Corbett's Medicated Lozenges, Canterbury, 2 x 2 3/4 In. 75.00
Box, Cutlery, Divided Into 3 Sections 775.00
Box, Garden Seeds, Cover, Mount Lebanon, N.Y. 1215.00
Box, Mahogany Veneer, Pine, Inlay, Paper Lined Interior, 11 1/4 In. 55.00
Box, Opposing Fingers, Oval, 5 In. 185.00
Box, Pantry, Fingered, Light Green Paint 2600.00
Box, Pincushion Cover, Maple & Pine, Harvard 450.00
Box, Sewing, Copper Tacks, Oval, Bentwood, 7 1/4 In. 250.00
Box, Sewing, Hardwood, Red Varnish, 1 Drawer, Thread Section, 7 In. 75.00
Box, Sewing, Inlaid Crested Lid, Mirror, Walnut, 9 1/2 x 5 3/4 In. 180.00
Box, Thread, 8 Shaker Spools Of Silk Thread 398.00
Box, Utility, Single-Finger Lid, Double-Finger Case, 3 1/4 In. 2200.00
Broom, Cobweb, Lebanon, 1920s, 8 Ft. 360.00
Bucket, Bail Handle, Diamond Mounts, Red Paint 190.00
Bucket, Diamond-Shape Metal Supports, Metal Bail 65.00
Bucket, Sap, 2 Wooden Buttonhole Bands 65.00
Candle Dryer, Clothespin Post, Cherry, Watervliet 450.00
Carrier, 4 Fingers, Swing Handle, Oval, Dark Patina, 15 In. 2400.00
Carrier, Hand, Sabbathday Lake 275.00
Carrier, Herb, Fixed Interior Handle, 13 x 9 1/2 In. 1210.00
Carrier, Herb, Sister Alice Howland, Canterbury, N. H., Yellow Wash 880.00
Carrier, Sabbathday Lake, Lined, Needle Book, Bees Wax, Pincushion 475.00
Carrier, Sewing, Bail Handle, Satin Lined, Round 138.00
Doll, Canterbury, c.1917 .... 475.00
Dress, Purple, Labeled M. A. W. 880.00
Dust Mop, Blue Wool, Enfield, N. H., 65 In. 335.00
Dust Pan 170.00
Flour Dipper, Wood 150.00
Flour Scoop, Turned Side Handle, Wooden, 4 x 7 In. 260.00
Hood, Woman's, Blue Wool 335.00
Iron, Coat Sleeve, Canterbury, N. H. 22.50
Pepper Pot, Pierced, Thistle Design, Wooden, 6 In. 260.00
Pincushion, Red Strawberry 275.00
Pincushion, Thread Holder, 5 3/4 In. 130.00
Place Mat, Thomas Fisher, Enfield, Oval, Signed, 4 Piece 390.00
Postcard, Canterbury Sisters Making Poplar Ware, c.1955 .... 25.00
Postcard, Elder Daniel Offord, Brother Levi Shaw, Mt. Lebanon 85.00
Postcard, Group Of North Family Shakers, Mt. Lebanon 125.00
Postcard, Sister Sarah Collins, Taping Chair 100.00
Rack, Peg, Signed Shaker Society, SDL 85.00
Rug, Hooked, Knitted Background, Round 1210.00
Rug, Rag, Consecutive Rectangle Pattern, 38 x 22 In. 298.00
Scoop, Apple, Carved From One Piece Of Wood, 14 In. 290.00
Seed Packet, Cucumber, West Pittsfield, Mass., 2 7/8 x 4 In. 85.00
Seed Packet, Purple Top Rutabaga, Enfield, 3 1/4 x 2 3/4 In. 75.00
Seed Packet, White Marrowfat Bush Beans, New Lebanon, 3 1/2 x 6 In. 90.00
Sewing Basket, Accessories, Signed 325.00
Sieve, Horsehair, 4 In. 93.00
Stereo Card, Canterbury Sisters Making Maple Sugar Candy 135.00
Stereo Card, Congregation Of Strangers After Leaving Church, 1878 .... 110.00

Shaving Mug, Purple Flower, Gold Trim,

Germany, 3 1/2 In.

To remove glass rings from wooden table tops, rub the spot with a mixture of mayonnaise and toothpaste. Wipe, then polish.

Stereo Card, Elder Frederick Evans	125.00
Swift, Original Yellow Varnish, 23 1/2 In.	100.00
Yarn Winder, Clock Reel, Canterbury, N. H.	335.00

SHAVING MUGS were popular from 1860 to 1900. Many types were made, including occupational mugs featuring pictures of men's jobs. There were scuttle mugs, silver-plated mugs, glass-lined mugs, and others.

Fraternal, F. L. T. In Loops, G. A. Minzey, Gold & White, Limoges	100.00
Fraternal, Masonic, Limoges	75.00
Masonic, Royal Arch Keystone, Gold Symbol	95.00
Milk Glass, Badger Brush, Silver Plated Holder	55.00
Occupational, 2 Flags, Shield, C. W. Smith In Gold, France	185.00
Occupational, 2 Men Rip Sawinglumber, Steam Tractor	4500.00
Occupational, Bar Scene, Limoges	375.00
Occupational, Baseball, Bat & Flags, Lew Jones In Gold, 1880s	885.00
Occupational, Billiards Player, 2 Men, Stick Rack, Gas Light	550.00
Occupational, Blacksmith	300.00
Occupational, Brewery Wagon Driver, Name In Gold	525.00
Occupational, Butcher & Brush	95.00
Occupational, Butcher, Bull's Head	185.00
Occupational, Carpenter, Man Sawing Lumber, John Wahlin	1050.00
Occupational, Carpenter, Man Working On Table, Monogram	400.00
Occupational, Clerk Selling Yard Goods	925.00
Occupational, Drayman, Name Of Company On Side	395.00
Occupational, Farmer Plowing A Field, Limoges	550.00
Occupational, Fire Wagon, c.1880	225.00
Occupational, Fireman, Horse-Drawn Hook & Ladder, 5 Men	1550.00
Occupational, Football Player	3100.00
Occupational, Head In Horseshoe, Surrounded By Flowers	275.00
Occupational, Horse-Drawn Buggy, Faded Name	300.00
Occupational, House Painter, Can Of Paint, Brushes, Gold Wreath	395.00
Occupational, Hunter & Dog, Name In Gold	275.00
Occupational, Ice Delivery Wagon, R. L. Newman	2500.00
Occupational, Locomotive & Tender, Faded Name	175.00
Occupational, Lumberjack, 2 Men Sawing Lumber	4500.00
Occupational, Lumberyard Owner, Building, Stacked Wood	395.00
Occupational, Mail Carrier	1100.00
Occupational, Masonry	80.00
Occupational, Oil Driller, Man Next To Derrick, Name In Gold	575.00
Occupational, Peanut Vendor, David C. Gairing	5000.00
Occupational, Pharmacist, Porcelain	225.00
Occupational, Photographer, Otto Doehn, 30th Anniversary	1550.00
Occupational, Physician At Patient's Bedside	8800.00
Occupational, Pipe Fitter	375.00
Occupational, R. C. A. Victor Talking Machine, Logo	1000.00
Occupational, Racetrack Scene	650.00
Occupational, Shoemaker, Laced Low Boot, Gold Name	225.00 To 425.00

Occupational, Steam Engine 155.00
Occupational, Store Clerk, Selling Yard Goods 825.00
Occupational, Store Clerk, Waiting On 2 Women 1700.00
Occupational, Tailor, Man At Table, Sewing 475.00
Occupational, Tailor, Man Cutting Bolt Of Cloth, Name In Gold 195.00
Occupational, Tailor, Pressing Trousers 1500.00
Occupational, Telegrapher 550.00
Occupational, Trolley Wire Installer 4500.00
Occupational, Undertakers, White Calla Lilies, Name, Limoges 375.00
Occupational, Yacht Builder, Boat In Boat House 5400.00
Odd Fellow 110.00
Purple Flower, Gold Trim, Germany, 3 1/2 In. ....*Illus* 80.00
Stutz Bearcat Race Car, Theo. Woodhull 6250.00
Use Tonique DeLuxe The Liquid Head Rest 77.00
Wildroot, Double Cup 165.00

SHAWNEE POTTERY was started in Zanesville, Ohio, in 1937. The
company made vases, novelty ware, flowerpots, planters, lamps, and cookie
jars. Three dinnerware lines were made: Corn, Lobster Ware, and Valencia
(a solid color line). White Corn pattern utility pieces were made in 1945.
Corn King was made from 1946 to 1954; Corn Queen, with darker green
leaves and lighter colored corn, from 1954 to 1961. Shawnee produced
pottery for George Rumrill during the late 1930s. The company closed in
1961.

Bowl, Mixing, Corn King, 6 1/2 In. 20.00
Butter, Cover, Corn King, No. 42 .... 32.00 To 45.00
Casserole, Cover, Lobster Tab Handles, Gray, Label 45.00
Coaster, Pastels, Set Of 4 .... 20.00
Cookie Jar, Clown & Seal 200.00
Cookie Jar, Cookie, Decals & Tulip, Gold Trim .... 150.00 To 225.00
Cookie Jar, Corn King .... 125.00 To 150.00
Cookie Jar, Cottage House .... 600.00 To 875.00
Cookie Jar, Drummer Boy .... 125.00 To 200.00
Cookie Jar, Dutch Boy, Blue Pants 45.00
Cookie Jar, Dutch Boy, Happy, Patches, Blue & Gold .... 158.00 To 200.00
Cookie Jar, Dutch Boy, Striped Pants 135.00
Cookie Jar, Dutch Girl, Blue Base .... 65.00 To 68.00
Cookie Jar, Dutch Girl, Cooky, Gold Trim .... 100.00 To 150.00
Cookie Jar, Dutch Girl, Tulip 69.00
Cookie Jar, Elephant, Lucky .... 75.00 To 85.00
Cookie Jar, Muggsy 85.00
Cookie Jar, Muggsy, Gold Trim .... 175.00 To 240.00
Cookie Jar, Octagon, Blue 35.00
Cookie Jar, Owl, Gold Trim 225.00
Cookie Jar, Owl, Winking .... 75.00 To 95.00
Cookie Jar, Puss 'n Boots .... 75.00 To 140.00
Cookie Jar, Puss 'n Boots, Gold Trim, Decals 350.00
Cookie Jar, Sailor Boy .... 35.00 To 65.00
Cookie Jar, Smiley Pig, Blue Collar, Gold Trim, Decals 225.00
Cookie Jar, Smiley Pig, Green Scarf, Gold Trim, Decals 110.00
Cookie Jar, Smiley Pig, Green Scarf, Shamrocks .... 165.00 To 185.00
Cookie Jar, Smiley Pig, Pink Scarf, Flowers 200.00
Cookie Jar, Smiley Pig, Yellow Collar, Gold Trim 200.00
Cookie Jar, Winnie Pig, Blue Collar & Flowers 125.00
Creamer, Corn King 20.00
Creamer, Elephant, No Decals .... 16.00 To 35.00
Creamer, Smiley Pig, No Decals .... 25.00 To 40.00
Jar, Utility, Corn King, Knob Cover, No. 78 .... 30.00
Mug, Corn King, No. 69 .... 26.00 To 42.00
Pitcher, Bo Peep, No. 47 .... 65.00 To 110.00
Pitcher, Chanticleer, Rooster .... 40.00 To 75.00
Pitcher, Little Boy Blue, No. 46 .... 65.00
Pitcher, Smiley Pig, Flowers On Chest .... 50.00 To 70.00

Pitcher, Sunflower 55.00
Planter, 4 Birds On Perch, No. 502 .... 40.00
Planter, Black Gazelle With Baby, No. 841 .... 80.00
Planter, Boy At Fence 7.00
Planter, Boy At Stump, Low Stump, No. 533 .... 10.00
Planter, Boy With Chicken, No. 645 .... 20.00
Planter, Boy With Wheelbarrow, No. 750 .... 18.00
Planter, Bull, Black, Pink .... 20.00 To 45.00
Planter, Cherub, Gold, No. 536 .... 18.00
Planter, Cherub, No. 536 .... 7.00
Planter, Children, Shoe, Blue, No. 525 .... 14.00
Planter, Clock, No. 1262 .... 14.00
Planter, Coal Bucket 8.00
Planter, Covered Wagon, No. 733 .... 18.00
Planter, Deer .... 15.00 To 22.00
Planter, Dutch Children At Well, No. 710 .... 18.00
Planter, Elf On Shoe, No. 765 .... 15.00 To 20.00
Planter, Flying Goose, No. 820 .... 18.00
Planter, Girl At Basket, No. 534 .... 10.00
Planter, Girl With Flowers, Gold Trim, No. 616 .... 20.00
Planter, Girl With Mandolin 22.00
Planter, Hound 8.00
Planter, Open Car, No. 506 .... 16.00
Planter, Oriental With Parasol, No. 601 .... 8.00
Planter, Piano, Green, No. 528 .... 22.00
Planter, Piano, Yellow, Gold Trim, No. 528 .... 35.00
Planter, Poodle Riding Bicycle, No. 712 .... 20.00
Planter, Ram, No. 515 .... 16.00
Planter, Rickshaw, No. 539 .... 6.00
Planter, Rooster, No. 503 .... 24.00
Planter, Shell, No. 154 .... 10.00
Planter, Squirrel, No. 664 .... 10.00
Planter, Stagecoach, No. 514, Small 12.00
Planter, Toy Horse, No. 660 .... 18.00
Planter, Train Set, 4 Piece 125.00
Planter, Wheelbarrow With Flower 12.00
Salt & Pepper, Chanticleer, Large 30.00
Salt & Pepper, Chanticleer, Small 15.00
Salt & Pepper, Corn King, Large .... 19.50 To 40.00
Salt & Pepper, Corn King, Small .... 11.00 To 18.00
Salt & Pepper, Dutch Boy & Girl .... 38.00 To 60.00
Salt & Pepper, Flowerpot 9.00
Salt & Pepper, Fruits, Large 25.00
Salt & Pepper, Fruits, Small 15.00
Salt & Pepper, Milk Cans 14.00
Salt & Pepper, Muggsy, Small .... 22.00 To 24.00
Salt & Pepper, Owl .... 15.00 To 20.00
Salt & Pepper, Owl, Gold Trim 25.00
Salt & Pepper, Owl, Green Eyes 35.00
Salt & Pepper, Puss 'n Boots .... 16.00 To 25.00
Salt & Pepper, Sailor Boy & Bo Peep 15.00
Salt & Pepper, Smiley Pig, 3 1/4 In. 25.00
Salt & Pepper, Smiley Pig, Blue Scarf, 5 In. .... 45.00 To 55.00
Salt & Pepper, Smiley Pig, Green Scarf, 5 In. 55.00
Salt & Pepper, Swiss Children, 5 In. 32.00
Salt & Pepper, White Corn, Small 20.00
Salt & Pepper, Winnie Pig & Smiley Pig, 5 In. 50.00
Sugar, Cover, White Corn 40.00
Teapot, Corn King .... 45.00 To 110.00
Teapot, Corn Queen, Individual 85.00
Teapot, Elephant, Glazed 400.00
Teapot, Granny Ann, Orange & Blue, Gold Trim, Decals 135.00
Teapot, Granny Ann, Purple & Green, Gold Trim, Decals 135.00

Teapot, Tom Tom The Piper's Son .... 35.00 To 75.00
Teapot, Tulip 35.00
Teapot, White Corn 55.00
Vase, Dove, Green, No. 829 .... 20.00
Vase, Philodendron, Yellow 26.00
Wall Pocket, Bo Peep 24.00
Wall Pocket, Bowknot 12.00
Wall Pocket, Head, Little Girl Holding Doll 25.00
Wall Pocket, Little Jack Horner 12.00

SHEARWATER pottery is a family business started by Mr. and Mrs. G.
W. Anderson, Sr., and their three sons. The local Ocean Springs,
Mississippi, clays were used to make the wares in the 1930s. The company
is still in business.

Figurine, Pirate 65.00
Pot, Cobalt To Blue To White, Marked, 4 x 5 1/2 In. 400.00
Vase, Green, 4 In. 25.00
Vase, Mottled Matted Greens, 9 1/2 In. 115.00

SHEET MUSIC from the past centuries is now collected. The favorites are
examples with covers featuring artistic or historic pictures. Early sheet
music covers were lithographed, but by the 1900s photographic
reproductions were used. The early music was larger than more recent
sheets and you must watch out for examples that were trimmed to fit in a
twentieth–century piano bench.

42nd Street 20.00
America I Love You, Alice Faye, John Payne Cover 12.00
America To–Day, Woodrow Wilson & Statue Of Liberty, 1917 .... 10.00
As Time Goes By, Bogart & Bergman 10.00
At The Levee On Revival Day, 1912 .... 25.00
Babes In Arms, Judy Garland 20.00
Barney Google Fox Trot, Color Cartoon By DeBeck, 1923 .... 5.00
Battle Of Nations, E. T. Paull 15.00
Beautiful Isle Of Somewhere, Sung At McKinley's Funeral, 1901 .... 18.00
Cairn's Quick Step, Currier & Ives, 4 Pages 135.00
Cincinnati Red Stockings, Snyder, Black & Sturn, N.Y., 1869 .... 1100.00
Cincinnati Reds Baseball, Team Picture, 1919 .... 1550.00
Colorado Moon, Baby Rose Marie, N. B. C., 1933 .... 8.00
Come On Papa, Eddie Cantor 20.00
Commander–In–Chief, Gen. Pershing, Flag, Joan Of Arc, 1918, Small ... 30.00
Commodore Dewey's Victory March, Dewey Picture, 1898 .... 5.00
Connecticut Yankee 20.00
Detroit Accordion Club March, 1926 .... 10.00
Do Your Honey Do, Comical Song, Framed, 1890 .... 60.00
Full Moon & Empty Arms, Frank Sinatra, 1946 .... 9.00
Galway Bay, Bing Crosby 5.00
Gone With The Wind, Movie, Advertising For Movie On Cover 19.00
Grace Darling, Currier & Ives, 1838, 4 Pages 250.00
Hail To President, F. D. Roosevelt, 1933 .... 17.50
Honeymooners, 1954 .... 22.00
Horse Feathers, Marx Bros. 24.00
Hurray For Our Baseball Team, Cleveland's League Park, 1909 .... 330.00
Hurricane March, E. T. Paull, 1906 .... 30.00
I Never Had A Mammy, Black & White Girls, 1923 .... 10.00
I'll Be Home For Christmas, Bing Crosby 15.00
It Might As Well Be Spring, Jeanne Crain, Dick Haymes, 1945 .... 6.00
Laugh Clown Laugh, Lon Chaney Cover 15.00
Liberace Song Book, 1979, 226 Page 11.00
Lily–Belle, Frank Sinatra, 1945 .... 4.00
Love Me Tender 55.00
Miss Lulu From Louisville, Betty Grable Cover 15.00
Moonlight Cocktail, Glenn Miller, 1941–1942 .... 8.00
Mounted Police 2 Step, Illustrated, 1909 .... 30.00

Oh Helen, Fatty Arbuckle Cover	12.00
On The Atcheson, Topeka & Santa Fe, Judy Garland, 1934	6.00
Operatic Quadrilles, Opera House, Currier & Ives, 9 Pages	125.00
Pickaninny Serenade	11.00
Poor Little Rich Girl, Shirley Temple	12.00
River Of No Return, Marilyn Monroe	22.00
San Fernando Valley, Bing Crosby	8.00
Shortnin' Bread	25.00
Silver Bells, Bob Hope	4.00
Skookum, Advertising Skookum Apples, Indian Logo	15.00
Some Sunday Morning, Erroll Flynn & Alexis Smith	10.00
Song For Me, Bromo–Seltzer, No Cocaine, 1890	12.00
Sooner Or Later, Song Of The South, Driscoll & Patten Picture	18.00
Stephen Foster Song Book, With History, 1939	8.00
Take Me Back To My Boots & Saddle, Gene Autry	8.00
That's Where I Came In, Kate Smith	5.00
The Bee, Jack Benny, Fred Allen Cover	30.00
The Parting, Currier & Ives, 4 Pages	150.00
Theme From Pepsodent Hour, Amos & Andy	15.00
Three Little Words, Amos & Andy	10.00
Tijuana Brass Song Book, Herb Alpert, 1960, 64 Pages	6.50
Two Sleepy People, Shirley Ross, Bob Hope Cover	20.00
Untamed, Joan Crawford, MGM, 1929	25.00
Very Precious Love, Gene Kelly, Natalie Wood Cover	14.00
We're Sunday Drivers	20.00
When A Nigger Makes 100, 99 Goes On His Back	88.00
When I Grow Too Old To Dream, Ramon Navarro, 1935	16.00
White Christmas, Bing Crosby	15.00
Wild Horses, Perry Como, 1953	4.00
Would You, Clark Gable, Jeannette MacDonald Cover	17.00

SHEFFIELD items are listed in the Silver–English and Silver Plate sections.

SHELLEY first appeared on English ceramics about 1912. The Foley China Works started in England in 1860. Joseph Ball Shelley joined the company in 1862 and became a partner in 1872. Percy Shelley joined the firm in 1881. The company went through a series of name changes and in 1910 the then Foley China Company became Shelley China. In 1929 it became Shelley Potteries. The company was acquired in 1966 by Allied English Potteries, then merged with the Doulton group in 1971. The name *Shelley* was put into use again in 1980.

Ashtray, Dainty Blue, 5 In.	25.00
Ashtray, Dainty Pink	35.00
Bowl, Vegetable, Cover, Georgian, H. Pardo, 8 In.	95.00
Bowl, Vegetable, Dainty Blue, Oval, 9 1/2 In.	100.00
Butter, Cover, Rock Blue	100.00
Cake Plate, Rosebud, Fluted	50.00
Chocolate Pot, Phlox	135.00
Chocolate Pot, Versailles, Court Shape	125.00
Chop Plate, Dainty Blue, 13 In.	150.00
Coffeepot, Bridal Rose	130.00
Coffeepot, Rosebud	260.00
Coffeepot, Rosebud, After Dinner	140.00
Creamer, Dainty Blue, 5 In.	60.00
Creamer, Rock Blue	25.00
Creamer, Rock Garden	20.00
Cup & Saucer, Begonia	35.00
Cup & Saucer, Blue Rock, Demitasse	30.00
Cup & Saucer, Cake Plate, Wild Anemone	65.00
Cup & Saucer, Daffodil Time	45.00
Cup & Saucer, Dainty Blue	50.00 To 65.00
Cup & Saucer, Flowers, Miniature	105.00
Cup & Saucer, Orchid, Fluted	40.00

Cup & Saucer, Pansies, Roses 28.00
Cup & Saucer, Pink Tulip Outside, Roses Inside, Large 50.00
Cup & Saucer, Ribbed Shape, 1st Mark 65.00
Cup & Saucer, Rock Blue, Fluted 35.00
Cup & Saucer, Rosebud 35.00
Cup & Saucer, Windflowers 40.00
Dish, Daffodil Time, 4 1/2 In. 35.00
Dish, Fluted, Hydrangeas, 4 1/2 In. 35.00
Dish, Muffin, Cover, Dainty Blue 200.00
Dish, Regency, Gold Handle, 4 1/2 x 6 In. 30.00
Eggcup, Campanula 45.00
Eggcup, Dainty Blue, 3 5/8 In. 45.00
Eggcup, Rock Blue, Double 35.00
Mug, Nursery 55.00
Mustard, Underplate, Cover, Dainty Blue 65.00
Mustard, Underplate, Rose & Red Daisy 85.00
Place Setting, Begonia, 4 Piece 85.00
Place Setting, Blue Rock, 4 Piece 85.00
Place Setting, Dainty Brown, 4 Piece 125.00
Place Setting, Dainty Green, 4 Piece 125.00
Place Setting, Rambler Rose, 4 Piece 85.00
Place Setting, Rosebud, 4 Piece 85.00
Place Setting, Wild Flowers, 4 Piece 85.00
Plate, Blue Iris, Queen Anne Shape, 6 1/4 In. 25.00
Plate, Blue Rock, 6 In. 18.00
Plate, Commemorating London Colony, Fluted, 8 1/2 In. 24.00
Plate, Commemorating Trafalgar Square, Fluted, 8 1/2 In. 24.00
Plate, Dainty Blue, 6 In. 25.00
Plate, Dainty Blue, 7 In. 25.00
Plate, Dainty Blue, 8 1/4 In. 35.00
Plate, Dainty Blue, 10 3/4 In. 45.00
Plate, Dainty Blue, 11 In. 65.00
Plate, Rock Blue, 6 1/2 In. 18.00
Plate, Rose Spray, 8 In. 42.00
Plate, Rosebud, Fluted, 6 In. 20.00
Platter, Dainty Blue, 14 3/4 In. 200.00
Platter, Georgian, Round, 13 In. 55.00
Saucer, Dainty Blue .... 10.00 To 15.00
Saucer, Primrose 10.00
Sugar & Creamer, Allover Florals, Yellow Ground 45.00
Sugar & Creamer, Begonia, Footed 42.00
Sugar & Creamer, Blue Rock, Individual 55.00
Sugar & Creamer, Dainty Blue 95.00
Sugar & Creamer, Rose & Red Daisy 45.00
Sugar, Cover, Dainty Blue 35.00
Sugar, Cover, Rock Blue 25.00
Teapot, Dainty Blue, 6 3/4 x 10 In. 250.00
Teapot, George V, 1911 .... 125.00

SHIRLEY TEMPLE, the famous movie star, was born in 1928. She made
her first movie in 1932. Thousands of items picturing Shirley have been
and still are being made. Shirley Temple dolls were first made in 1934 by
Ideal Toy Company. Millions of Shirley Temple cobalt blue glass dishes
were made by Hazel Atlas Glass Company and U.S. Glass Company from
1934 to 1942. They were given away as premiums for Wheaties and
Bisquick. A bowl, mug, and pitcher were made as a breakfast set. Some
pieces were decorated with the picture of a very young Shirley, others used
a picture of Shirley in her 1936 *Captain January* costume. Although
collectors refer to a cobalt creamer, it is actually the 4 1/2–inch–high milk
pitcher from the breakfast set. Many of these items are being reproduced
today.

Badge, Police, Bronze 125.00
Book, Coloring, Shirley Temple Crosses The Country, 1939 .... 89.00

Book, Little Colonel	22.00
Book, Music, Sing With Shirley Temple	40.00
Book, Rebecca Of Sunnybrook Farm	35.00
Book, Spirit Of Dragonwood, Hard Cover, 1945	10.00
Book, Stowaway	45.00
Book, Wee Willie Winkie, 1937	30.00
Bowl, Cobalt Blue	25.00
Box, Quaker Puffed Wheat, Glued On Plain Box, 1937	95.00
Box, Slipper, Photographically Done, 1930s	155.00
Box, Wheaties, No. 1, Back	28.00
Card, Playing, Little Colonel, Box	140.00
Doll, Blond Mohair Wig, Dressed, Ideal, 18 In. ....*Illus*	275.00
Doll, Child, 5 Piece Body, Button, Ideal, 22 In. ....*Illus*	375.00
Doll, Composition, All Original, 1939, 18 In.	475.00
Doll, Composition, Blue Sailor Jumpsuit, 1930s, 22 In.	450.00
Doll, Composition, Crazed Eyes, Original Dress, Ideal, 22 In.	400.00
Doll, Composition, Hawaiian, Yarn Hair, 18 In.	750.00
Doll, Composition, Sleep Eyes, 5 Piece Body, Ideal, 18 In.	275.00
Doll, Composition, Sleep Eyes, Original Outfit, 17 In.	467.00
Doll, Heidi Outfit, 1957, 12 In.	160.00
Doll, Ideal, 19 In.	165.00
Doll, Ideal, Extra Clothes, 19 In.	195.00
Doll, Ideal, Original Clothes, Outfits, Box, 13 In.	1450.00
Doll, No. 13	420.00
Doll, Outfit, Rebecca Of Sunnybrook Farm, Box	30.00
Doll, Pink, Baby Takes A Bow Dress, 1934	675.00
Doll, Sleep Eyes, 5 Piece Body, Ideal, 13 In.	250.00
Fan, RC Cola, I'll Be Seeing You	40.00
Figurine, Chalkware	25.00
Film, Famous Funnies Box, 16 Mm	15.00
Magazine, Movie Mirror, Shirley On Cover, May 1940	45.00
Magazine, Photoplay, Shirley On Cover, March 1936	45.00
Mirror, Pocket, 1937, 2 1/4 In.	10.00
Mug, Cobalt Blue	40.00
Pamphlet, Shirley Temple Doll Contest, 1930s	95.00
Paper Doll, 1958, Uncut	35.00
Paper Doll, 1959, 18 In., Uncut	95.00
Paper Doll, 1976, Uncut	28.00
Paper Doll, Book, Saalfield No. 2112, Uncut	37.00
Pen, Gold Ribbon Runs Through Green Case	165.00
Pencil, Mechanical, Name Imprinted	75.00
Photograph, Shirley Temple Hats	75.00
Picture, Art Deco Frame, Color, Signed	25.00
Pitcher, Cobalt Blue	28.00 To 45.00
Plate, Cobalt Blue	40.00
Purse, Child's, Leather	75.00
Sheet Music, From Stowaway, 1936	25.00

Shirley Temple, Doll, Blond Mohair Wig,
Dressed, Ideal, 18 In.

Shirley Temple, Doll, Child, 5 Piece Body,
Button, Ideal, 22 In.

Sheet Music, Good Ship Lollipop, Photo Cover, 1934 .... 13.00 To 27.00
Sheet Music, Poor Little Rich Girl 25.00
Sheet Music, The Bluebird 22.00
Sugar, Cobalt Blue 38.00

SHRINER, see Fraternal category

SILVER DEPOSIT glass was made during the late nineteenth and early twentieth centuries. Solid sterling silver was applied to the glass by a chemical method so that a cutout design of silver metal appeared against a clear or colored glass. It is sometimes called silver overlay.

Pitcher, Floral, 4 3/4 In. 145.00
Plate, 25th Anniversary, 13 In. 40.00
Water Set, Art Nouveau, 6 Piece 375.00

SILVER FLATWARE includes many of the current and out-of-production silver and silver-plated flatware patterns made in the past eighty years. Other silver is listed under Silver-American, Silver-English, etc. Most silver flatware sets that are missing a few pieces can be completed through the help of one of the many silver matching services listed in *Kovels' Guide to Selling Your Antiques & Collectibles.*

SILVER FLATWARE PLATED, Aldine, Bouillon Spoon, Rogers & Hamilton 9.00
Ambassador, Cocktail Fork, Rogers 6.00
Ambassador, Gravy Ladle, Rogers 20.00
Ambassador, Jelly Server, Rogers 5.00
Arbutus, Pastry Fork, Rogers 45.00
Assyrian Head, Gravy Ladle, 1886 .... 40.00
Assyrian Head, Soup Ladle 80.00
Avalon, Salad Serving Fork, Community 35.00
Berkshire, Berry Spoon, Rogers 20.00
Berkshire, Berry Spoon, Rogers & Hamilton 30.00
Berkshire, Sauce Ladle, Rogers & Hamilton 16.00
Bird Of Paradise, Ice Cream Spoon, Community 25.00
Bird Of Paradise, Sugar Tongs, Community 40.00
Charter Oak, Salad Fork, Rogers 30.00
Charter Oaks, Dinner Fork, Rogers 18.00
Charter Oaks, Dinner Knife, Rogers, 8 3/4 In. 18.00
Cordova, Dinner Fork, Rogers 12.00
Coronation, Butter Spreader, Oneida 3.00
Coronation, Jelly Spoon, Community 15.00
Coronation, Pastry Server, Pierced, Community 30.00
Coronation, Salad Fork, Community 8.00
Coronation, Tablespoon, Oneida 2.50
Coronation, Teaspoon, Oneida 4.00
Deauville, Service For 5, Community, 26 Piece 69.00
Densmore, Service For 8, 50 Piece 150.00
Empire, Teaspoon, Rogers 12.00
Eternally Yours, Butter Knife, Rogers 8.00
Eternally Yours, Sugar Shell, Rogers 4.00
Evening Star, Berry Spoon, Community 25.00
Fair Oaks, Cocktail Fork, Rogers & Son 7.00
Fiddleback, Soup Ladle, Bailey Banks & Biddle 25.00
Georgia, Gravy Ladle, Community 10.00
Georgia, Tomato Server, Community 10.00
Grosvenor, Bouillon Spoon, Community 7.50
Grosvenor, Chipped Beef Fork, Community 30.00
Grosvenor, Sugar Tongs, Community 40.00
Imperial B, Service For 8, Rogers, Box, 1939, 48 Piec 75.00
Kenisco, Soup Ladle, Williams 20.00
La Vigne, Teaspoon, 1917, Rogers 9.00
Lorne, Tongs, Claw Ends, Rogers & Hamilton 18.00
Moselle, Oyster Ladle 195.00
Moselle, Pastry Fork 50.00

Silver Flatware Sterling, Acorn, Service

For 12, Jenson, 100 Pc.

Always dry silver immediately after using it. The chemicals in the water may stain.

Mystic, Fruit Knife, Serrated Edge, Lancaster	10.00
Mystic, Soup Ladle, Rogers	40.00
Nenuphar, Cocktail Fork, American Silver, 6 Piece	75.00
Old Colony, Service For 5, Rogers, 31 Piece	98.00
Orange Blossom, Cold Meat Fork, 1910, Rogers	10.00
Orange Blossom, Fruit Spoon, Rogers	9.00
Orange Blossom, Salad Fork, Rogers	10.00
Orange Blossom, Tomato Server, Rogers	25.00
Oxford, Butter Spreader, Rogers	8.00
Oxford, Cold Meat Fork, Rogers	22.00
Oxford, Dinner Fork, Rogers	12.00
Oxford, Tablespoon, Rogers	9.00
Patrician, Ice Cream Fork, Community	15.00
Patrician, Sugar Tongs, Community	38.00
Persian, Ladle, Rogers, 13 In.	50.00
Prestige, Service For 8, Rogers, Box, 50 Piece, 1931	48.00
Queen Bess II, Service For 8, 68 Piece	350.00
Raphael, Soup Spoon, Oval, Rogers & Hamilton	16.00
Rosemont, Salad Serving Fork	18.50
Siren, Soup Ladle, Monogram, 1891, Rogers	75.00
Vintage, Baby Spoon & Food Pusher, Rogers	70.00
Vintage, Dinner Fork, Rogers	23.00
Vintage, Tablespoon, Rogers	16.00
White Orchid, Soup Ladle, Hollow Handle, Community	75.00
White Orchid, Tablespoon, Community	10.00
White Orchid, Teaspoon, Community	3.00
York, Soup Ladle, Rogers	30.00
SILVER FLATWARE STERLING, Abbottsford, Ladle, International	350.00
Acorn, Service For 12, Jenson, 100 Pc. ....*Illus*	7700.00
Acorn, Sugar Tongs, Jensen	155.00
Adolphus, Pea Server, Mt. Vernon	175.00
Aegean Weave, Luncheon Set, Wallace, 4 Piece	75.00
Albermarle, Tea Caddy Spoon, Gorham	85.00
Albermarle, Tomato Server, Gorham	265.00
Alexandra, Steak Carving Set, Lunt, 2 Piece	45.00
American Beauty Rose, Bouillon Spoon, Sheibler	45.00
American Beauty Rose, Ice Cream Fork, Sheibler	45.00
American Classic, Carving Set, Easterling	95.00
American Classic, Cocktail Fork, Easterling	14.00
American Classic, Dinner Fork, Easterling	19.00
American Classic, Soup Spoon, Round, Easterling	18.00
American Victorian, Luncheon Fork, Lunt	18.00
American Victorian, Teaspoon, Lunt	13.00
Andante, Dinner Setting, Gorham, 4 Piece	84.00
Angelique, Luncheon Setting, International, 4 Pc.	54.00
Apollo, Ice Cream Fork, Alvin, 10 Piece	250.00
Arlington, Cocktail Fork, Towle	17.00

Aspen, Ladle, Gorham, 6 7/8 In. 33.00
Athene, Cheese Scoop, Whiting 55.00
Avalon, Asparagus Fork, International 250.00
Avalon, Chocolate Muddler, International 95.00
Ballet, Sugar Spoon, Weidlich 17.00
Baltimore Rose, Bread & Butter Plate, Schofield 150.00
Baronial, Citrus Spoon, Gorham 20.00
Baronial, Cracker Scoop, Gorham 250.00
Baronial, Dinner Setting, Alvin, 4 Piece 100.00
Baroque Set, Wallace, 179 Piece 6200.00
Bead, Cream Ladle, Whiting 25.00
Belvedere, Luncheon Setting, Lunt, 4 Pc. .... 60.00 To 85.00
Belvedere, Tablespoon, Lunt 17.00
Botticelli, Butter Knife, Oneida 25.00
Botticelli, Place Setting, Oneida, 4 Piece 75.00
Bridal Lace, Luncheon Fork, Lunt 18.00
Bridal Lace, Teaspoon, Lunt 13.00
Bridal Rose, Cucumber Server, Alvin 175.00
Bridal Rose, Gravy Ladle, Alvin 135.00
Bridal Rose, Sugar Shell, Alvin 35.00
Bridal Rose, Teaspoon, Alvin 14.00
Burgundy, Cream Soup Spoon, Reed & Barton 27.00
Burgundy, Demitasse Spoon, Reed & Barton 15.00
Burgundy, Sugar Spoon, Reed & Barton 35.00
Buttercup, Cold Meat Fork, Gorham 70.00
Buttercup, Cream Soup Spoon, Gorham 24.00
Buttercup, Luncheon Setting, Gorham, 4 Piece 85.00
Buttercup, Olive Spoon, Gorham 45.00
Buttercup, Salad Fork, Gorham 28.00
Buttercup, Sardine Fork, Gorham, 5 In. 38.00
Buttercup, Tomato Server, Pierced, Gorham 115.00
Cactus, Salt, Enameled Bowls, Jensen, 4 Piece 660.00
Calvert, Butter Pick, Kirk, 5 1/2 In. 28.00
Cambridge, Jelly Knife, Gorham 95.00
Cambridge, Mayonnaise Ladle, Gorham 45.00
Camelia, Dinner Setting, Gorham, 4 Piece 50.00
Camelia, Luncheon Setting, Gorham, 4 Pc. .... 45.00 To 50.00
Candlelight, Serving Fork, Towle 21.00
Candlelight, Sugar Spoon, Towle 15.00
Canterbury, Bouillon Ladle, Towle 175.00
Canterbury, Cheese Scoop, Towle 65.00
Canterbury, Mustard Ladle, Towle 55.00
Canterbury, Strawberry Fork, Towle, 4 Piece 125.00
Carillon, Place Setting, Lunt, 4 Piece 75.00
Caroline, Olive Spoon, Pierced, Lunt 16.00
Chantilly, Bouillon Spoon, Gorham 28.00
Chantilly, Butter Pick, Gorham 65.00
Chantilly, Carving Set, Gorham 155.00
Chantilly, Infant Feeding Spoon, Lunt 25.00
Chantilly, Luncheon Fork, Gorham 30.00
Chantilly, Pastry Fork, 4 Tines, Gorham 28.00
Chantilly, Sardine Fork, Gorham 75.00
Chantilly, Soup Spoon, Gorham, 6 Piece 120.00
Chapel Bells, Luncheon Knife, Alvin .... 12.00 To 20.00
Charles II, Pea Server, Alvin 225.00
Charmaine, Luncheon Set, International, 4 Piece 54.00
Chased Romantic, Luncheon Setting, Alvin, 4 Piece 45.00
Chased Romantique, Cream Soup Spoon, Alvin 14.00
Chased Romantique, Salad Fork, Alvin 17.00
Chased Romantique, Teaspoon, Alvin 12.00
Chateau Rose, Cream Soup Spoon, Alvin 14.00
Chateau Rose, Ladle, Alvin, 6 In. 50.00
Chateau, Service For 8, Lunt, 1918 .... 400.00

Chestnut, Tea Strainer, Kerr	160.00
Chrysanthemum, Asparagus Server, Durgin	475.00
Chrysanthemum, Gravy Ladle, Durgin	175.00
Chrysanthemum, Jelly Spoon, Durgin	85.00
Chrysanthemum, Pie Server, Durgin	350.00
Chrysanthemum, Pie Server, Shiebler	225.00
Classic Rose, Dinner Fork, Reed & Barton	17.00
Classic Rose, Teaspoon, Reed & Barton	13.00
Cloeta, Jelly Trowel, International	175.00
Cluny, Cheese Scoop, Gorham	175.00
Cluny, Ice Cream Knife, Gorham	375.00
Cluny, Soup Ladle, Gorham	475.00
Colonial Antique, Sugar Spoon, Watson	15.00
Columbia Gold, Place Setting, Lunt, 3 Piece	75.00
Columbia, Place Setting, Lunt, 4 Piece	75.00
Contour, Tablespoon, Towle	50.00
Corinthian, Cake Knife, Gorham, 9 3/4 In.	150.00
Cottage, Teaspoon, Gorham, 12 Piece	75.00
Courtship, Cold Meat Fork, International	48.00
Craftsman, Luncheon Setting, Towle, 4 Piece	45.00
Cromwell, Asparagus Tongs, Gorham, 9 In.	495.00
Cypress, Salad Set, Jensen	495.00
Damask Rose, Luncheon Setting, Oneida, 4 Piece	55.00
Dauphin, Luncheon Fork, Durgin	32.00
Dawn Star, Cold Meat Fork, Wallace	30.00
Debussy, Teaspoon, Towle	25.00
Dresden Scroll, Luncheon Setting, Lunt, 4 Piece	60.00
Dresden, Gravy Ladle, Whiting	80.00
Dresden, Punch Ladle, Whiting	395.00
Eighteenth Century, Fork, Reed & Barton	22.00
El Grandee, Luncheon Setting, Towle, 4 Piece	95.00
English Gadroon, Berry Spoon, Gorham, 8 7/8 In.	125.00
English Gadroon, Tomato Server, Pierced, Gorham	55.00
English King, Claret Ladle, Hampton, 16 3/4 In.	350.00
English King, Stuffing Spoon, Hampton	725.00
English Shell, Tablespoon, Lunt	15.00
Essex, Tablespoon, Durgin	33.00
Etruscan, Ladle, Gorham, 5 7/8 In.	35.00
Etruscan, Luncheon Knife, Gorham	19.00
Etruscan, Luncheon Setting, Gorham, 4 Piece	62.00
Fairfax, Butter Spreader, Durgin	12.00
Fairfax, Carving Set, Durgin	95.00
Fairfax, Ice Cream Fork, Durgin	35.00
Fairfax, Ladle, Gorham, 6 1/4 In.	45.00
Fairfax, Lettuce Fork, Durgin	75.00
Fairfax, Salt & Pepper, Durgin, 4 In.	115.00
Fairfax, Sugar Shell, Durgin	15.00
Fiddle Thread, Salad Fork, Gorham	18.00
Fiorito, Ice Tongs, Shiebler	325.00
Floral, Oyster Ladle, Gorham, 13 In.	500.00
Florentine, Asparagus Tongs, Alvin	395.00
Florentine, Sugar Tongs, Gorham, 5 In.	65.00
Fragrance, Salad Fork, Reed & Barton	16.00
French Provincial, Luncheon Set, Towle, 4 Piece	70.00
French Scroll, Tablespoon, Alvin	50.00
Frontenac, Asparagus Fork, International	375.00
Frontenac, Carving Knife, International	115.00
Frontenac, Olive Spoon, International	85.00
Frontenac, Petit-Four Tongs, International	250.00
Gadroonette, Ladle, Manchester, 5 7/8 In.	36.00
George & Martha, Sugar Spoon, Westmoreland	15.00
Georgian Maid, Carving Set, International	95.00
Georgian Rose, Service For 12, Reed & Barton	1400.00

Georgian, Croquette Server, Towle	395.00
Georgian, Stuffing Spoon, Towle	750.00
Golden Sovereign, Place Setting, Gorham, 4 Piece	110.00
Golden Winslow, Luncheon Setting, Kirk, 4 Piece	120.00
Gossamer, Place Setting, Gorham, 4 Piece	95.00
Granado, Butter Knife, Lunt	15.00
Granado, Teaspoon, Lunt	14.00
Grand Colonial, Carving Set, Wallace	35.00
Grand Colonial, Dinner Knife, Wallace	32.00
Grand Colonial, Fork, Wallace, 8 In.	22.00
Grand Colonial, Gravy Ladle, Wallace	42.00
Grand Colonial, Lemon Fork, Wallace	14.00
Grand Colonial, Salad Fork, Wallace	25.00
Grand Renaissance, Teaspoon, Reed & Barton	25.00
Grand Victorian, Teaspoon, Wallace	25.00
Grande Baroque, Punch Ladle, Wallace	400.00
Grande Baroque, Sugar & Creamer, Wallace	1250.00
Greenbrier, Carving Set, Gorham	95.00
Greenbrier, Dinner Fork, Gorham	25.00
Hepplewhite, Ice Tongs, International	295.00
Heraldic, Mustard Ladle, Whiting	75.00
Heraldic, Sardine Fork, Whiting	195.00
Holly, Cream Ladle, Gold Washed Bowl, Hampton	395.00
Horizon, Carving Set, Easterling	95.00
Hunt Club, Dinner Setting, Gorham, 4 Piece	70.00
Imperial Chrysanthemum, Cheese Fork, Gorham	65.00
Imperial Chrysanthemum, Fish Server Fork, Gorham	165.00
Imperial Chrysanthemum, Ice Cream Knife, Gorham	295.00
Imperial Chrysanthemum, Jelly Knife, Woman's	495.00
Imperial Queen, Asparagus Fork, Whiting	275.00
Imperial Queen, Berry Spoon, Whiting, 7 1/2 In.	70.00
Imperial Queen, Teaspoon, Whiting	12.00
Intaglio, Teaspoon, Reed & Barton, 5 1/4 In.	25.00
Iris, Carving Set, Durgin, 2 Piece	295.00
Iris, Ice Cream Spoon, Durgin	65.00
Iris, Ladle, Durgin, 8 In.	295.00
Iris, Vegetable Spoon, Durgin	350.00
Irving, Luncheon Fork, Wallace	19.00
Irving, Pie Server, Wallace	29.00
Ivy, Pie Server, Hampton	295.00
Japanese, Teaspoon, Whiting	12.99
John Adams, Sugar Shell, Watson	10.00
Jonquil, Strawberry Fork, Durgin, 4 Piece	180.00
King Albert, Coffee Spoon, Whiting	11.00
King Albert, Knife, Whiting	18.50
King Edward, Bouillon Spoon, Whiting, 12 Piece	115.00
King Edward, Carving Set, Gorham	125.00
King Edward, Cream Soup Spoon, Whiting, 7 In.	32.00
King Edward, Gravy Ladle, Whiting	125.00
King Edward, Salad Set, Whiting, 9 3/4 In.	300.00
La Rochelle, Cream Soup Spoon, Schofield	25.00
La Rochelle, Salad Fork, Schofield	25.00
La Salle, Teaspoon, Dominick & Haff	10.00
La Scala, Dinner Setting, Gorham, 4 Piece	110.00
La Scala, Ladle, Gorham, 7 In.	65.00
La Scala, Luncheon Setting, Gorham, 4 Piece	90.00
La Scale, Dinner Fork, Gorham	35.00
Labors Of Cupid, Dessert Spoon, Dominick & Haff	95.00
Lace Point, Luncheon Knife, Lunt	18.00
Lace Point, Teaspoon, Lunt	13.00
Lady Washington, Stuffing Spoon, Gorham	425.00
Lancaster, Cracker Spoon, Gorham	195.00
Lancaster, Cucumber Server, Gorham	95.00

Lancaster, Dessert Spoon, Gorham	35.00
Lancaster, Ice Cream Slice, Gorham	245.00
Lancaster, Ladle, Gorham, 5 3/8 In.	28.00
Lancaster, Ladle, Gorham, 6 7/8 In.	65.00
Lancaster, Lobster Pick, Gorham	45.00
Lasting Grace, Tablespoon, Lunt	65.00
Les Six Fleurs, Cake Server, Reed & Barton	425.00
Lily Of The Valley, Asparagus Tongs, Whiting	225.00
Lily Of The Valley, Cake Breaker, Whiting	150.00
Lily Of The Valley, Egg Spoon, Ruffled, Whiting	45.00
Lily Of The Valley, Roast Holder, Whiting	225.00
Lily Of The Valley, Roast Set, Whiting	435.00
Lily Of The Valley, Salad Serving Set, Whiting	325.00
Lily, Butter Pick, Whiting	150.00
Lily, Crumber, Whiting	550.00
Lily, Lettuce Fork, Whiting	175.00
Lily, Sugar Tongs, Whiting	75.00
Louis XIV, Entree Spoon, Towle	65.00
Louis XIV, Tablespoon, Towle	25.00
Louis XV, Asparagus Fork, Whiting	265.00
Louis XV, Cocktail Fork, Durgin	19.00
Louis XV, Cracker Scoop, Whiting	175.00
Louis XV, Cream Soup Spoon, Whiting	35.00
Louis XV, Gravy Ladle, Whiting	155.00
Louis XV, Ice Cream Slice, Whiting	225.00
Louis XV, Lemonade Muddler, Whiting	150.00
Louis XV, Oyster Server, Wood & Hughes	195.00
Louis XV, Serving Fork, Whiting, 8 7/8 In.	150.00
Louis XV, Soup Ladle, Whiting	225.00 To 275.00
Louis XV, Tablespoon, Whiting	25.00
Louvre, Berry Spoon, Ornate, Wallace	75.00
Lucerne, Tablespoon, Wallace	38.00
Luxembourg, Fish Fork, Gorham	40.00
Lyric, Bread & Butter Knife, Gorham, 4 Piece	50.00
Lyric, Ladle, Gorham, 7 In.	65.00
Madrigal, Gravy Ladle, Lunt	25.00
Madrigal, Luncheon Setting, Lunt, 4 Piece	52.00
Madrigal, Pickle Fork, Lunt	13.00
Madrigal, Sugar Spoon, Lunt	14.00 To 33.00
Majestic, Luncheon Fork, Reed & Barton	25.00
Majestic, Sardine Fork, Alvin	40.00
Majestic, Soup Spoon, Oval, Reed & Barton	24.00
Majestic, Tablespoon, Reed & Barton	30.00
Manchester, Sauce Ladle, Manchester	15.00
Margaret Rose, Cream Soup Spoon, National	13.00
Margaret Rose, Teaspoon, National	12.00
Marie Antoinette, Salad Set, Gorham, 8 3/4 In.	250.00
Martinique, Place Setting, Oneida, 4 Piece	65.00
Mary Chilton, Strawberry Fork, Towle	24.00
Mary Chilton, Teaspoon, Towle	7.00
Maryland, Fish Server, Kirk	46.00
Mask, Mustard Ladle, Whiting	65.00
Mayflower, Tomato Server, Kirk	175.00
Mazarin, Ice Cream Knife, Dominick & Haff	350.00
Mazarin, Nut Spoon, Dominick & Haff	45.00
Mazarin, Pea Server, Dominick & Haff	195.00
Mazarin, Soup Ladle, Gold Gilt, Dominick & Haff	225.00
Medallion, Egg Spoon, Gorham	65.00
Melrose, Cocktail Fork, Gorham, 8 Piece	128.00
Melrose, Ice Teaspoon, Gorham, Set Of 8	200.00
Melrose, Ladle, Alvin, 6 In.	33.00
Mignonette, Olive Fork, Lunt	15.00
Modern Victorian, Luncheon Setting, Lunt, 4 Pc.	75.00

Modern Victorian, Olive Spoon, Lunt	35.00
Modern Victorian, Tomato Server, Lunt	125.00
Mount Vernon, Tablespoon, Lunt, 5 3/4 In.	12.00
Mythologique, Ice Cream Knife, Gorham	395.00
Mythologique, Tomato Server, Gorham	295.00
Narcissus, Croquette Server, Durgin	325.00
Narcissus, Gravy Ladle, Durgin	125.00
New Art, Asparagus Fork, Durgin	650.00
New Art, Berry Spoon, Durgin	350.00
New King, Egg Spoon, Dominick & Haff, 5 Piece	175.00
New Stanton Hall, Dinner Setting, Oneida, 4 Pc.	80.00
New Stanton Hall, Luncheon Setting, Oneida, 4 Pc.	75.00
Number 10, Sugar Sifter, Alvin	85.00
Old Colonial, Cream Ladle, Towle	65.00
Old Colonial, Dinner Fork, Towle	45.00
Old Colonial, Sugar Shell, Towle	40.00
Old French, Luncheon Setting, Gorham, 4 Piece	80.00
Old London, Ladle, Gorham, 5 1/4 In.	30.00
Old Master, Citrus Spoon, Towle	24.00
Olive, Condiment Ladle, Speer & Cooper	35.00
Olympian, Asparagus Fork, Hampton	695.00
Olympian, Tomato Server, Hampton	395.00
Orange Blossom, Butter Knife, Alvin	55.00
Orange Blossom, Lettuce Fork, Alvin	175.00
Orange Blossom, Sauce Ladle, Alvin	95.00
Orient, Teaspoon, Alvin	10.00
Orientalia, Salad Set, Gorham	350.00
Palm, Salad Set, Whiting	160.00
Paul Revere, Asparagus Server, Footed, Towle	300.00
Peep O'Day, Butter Knife, Unger	35.00
Persian, Punch Ladle, Rogers, 13 In.	55.00
Personna, Place Setting, Stieff, 5 Piece	100.00
Plymouth Colony, Luncheon Set, Wallace, 4 Piece	45.00
Plymouth, Asparagus Fork, Gorham	450.00
Plymouth, Beef Fork, Gorham	45.00
Plymouth, Butter Knife, Gorham	20.00
Plymouth, Butter Spreader, Solid Handle, Gorham	12.50
Plymouth, Cold Meat Fork, Gorham	45.00
Plymouth, Crumber, Gorham	250.00
Plymouth, Gravy Ladle, Gold Wash, Gorham	20.00
Plymouth, Lettuce Fork, Gorham	55.00
Plymouth, Strawberry Fork, Gorham	35.00
Prelude, Luncheon Fork, International	17.00
Prelude, Teaspoon, International	12.00
Prince Eugene, Dinner Setting, Alvin, 4 Piece	110.00
Puritan, Cocktail Fork, Watson, 12 Piece	180.00
Queen Elizabeth, Sauce Ladle, Dominick & Haff	18.00
Radiant, Soup Ladle, Whiting, 14 In.	450.00
Raleigh, Ladle, Alvin, 5 3/4 In.	30.00
Raleigh, Tomato Server, Alvin	110.00
Raphael, Teaspoon, Alvin	90.00
Renaissance Scroll, Teaspoon, Reed & Barton	25.00
Renaissance, Cold Meat Fork, Alvin	95.00
Renaissance, Pie Server, Dominick & Haff	225.00
Repousse, Luncheon Setting, Kirk, 4 Piece	90.00
Repousse, Nutcracker, Kirk	115.00
Repousse, Sauce Ladle, Kirk, 1925	38.00
Repousse, Serving Spoon, Kirk, Raised Fruit Bowl	35.00
Revere, Horseradish Spoon, International	75.00
Rococo, Bouillon Spoon, Rogers, 4 1/4 In., 6 Piece	85.00
Rococo, Soup Spoon, Oval, Dominick & Haff	20.00
Rose Point, Luncheon Setting, Wallace, 4 Piece	72.00
Rose, Lettuce Fork, Stieff	80.00

Rose, Salver, Footed, Round, Stieff, 1917, 6 In. 345.00
Rose, Sugar Tongs, Stieff, 1892, 4 1/4 In. 50.00
Rosepoint, Set, Wallace, 59 Piece 1100.00
Royal Danish, Carving Set, International, 2 Piece 70.00
Royal Danish, Fish Serving Fork, Stieff, 9 In. 125.00
Royal Danish, Meat Fork, 3 Tines, International 95.00
Rubayait, Place Setting, Reed & Barton, 4 Piece 85.00
San Lorenzo, Cheese Knife, Hampton 150.00
San Lorenzo, Crumber, Hampton 275.00
Saratoga, Tongs, Hampton, 10 1/2 In. 695.00
Saxon Stag, Berry Spoon, Gorham ....425.00 To 450.00
Saxon Stag, Gravy Ladle, Gorham 450.00
Scroll, Dinner Setting, Jensen, 5 Piece 795.00
Soliloquy, Butter Knife, Wallace 12.00
Soliloquy, Salad Fork, Wallace 15.00
Sorrento, Asparagus Tongs, Alvin 375.00
Southern Grandeur, Carving Set, Easterling 95.00
Sovereign, Cold Meat Fork, International 65.00
Spanish Lace, Pickle Fork, Wallace 14.00
Spanish Lace, Sugar Spoon, Wallace 15.00
St. Cloud, Butter Knife, Gorham 85.00
St. James, Stuffing Spoon, Hampton 450.00
Star, Butter Knife, Reed & Barton 15.00
Starfire, Service For 8, Servers, Lunt 495.00
Strasbourg, Butter Spreader, Gorham, 6 Piece 95.00
Strasbourg, Crumb Knife, Gorham 150.00
Strasbourg, Luncheon Setting, Gorham, 4 Piece 95.00
Strasbourg, Stuffing Spoon, Gorham 495.00
Tablespoon, S. Bailey, Engraved HCL On Back, Pair 300.00
Talisman Rose, Cream Soup Spoon, Oval, Whiting 19.00
Talisman Rose, Lemon Fork, Whiting 15.00
Talisman Rose, Teaspoon, Whiting 12.00
Teddy Bear, Porringer, Lunt 65.00
Trojan, Fish Fork, Reed & Barton, 7 1/8 In. 45.00
Versailles, Bouillon Ladle, Gorham 50.00
Versailles, Cream Sauce Ladle, Gorham 75.00
Versailles, Gravy Ladle, Gorham, Small 105.00
Versailles, Salad Set, Gorham 450.00
Violet, Dessert Spoon, Whiting 55.00
Violet, Fish Slice, Whiting, c.1905 .... 240.00
Violet, Luncheon Setting, Wallace, 4 Piece 100.00
Violet, Salad Serving Spoon, Whiting, 9 1/8 In. 150.00
Virginia, Sugar Spoon, Lunt 16.00
Whitehall, Tablespoon, International 65.00
Will O' Wisp, Dinner Fork, Oneida 21.00
Will O' Wisp, Sugar Spoon, Oneida 16.00
Willow, Place Setting, Gorham, 4 Piece 85.00
Wood Lily, Luncheon Setting, Frank Smith, 4 Piece 100.00

SILVER PLATE is not solid silver. It is a ware made of a metal, such as
nickel or copper, that is covered with a thin coating of silver. The letters
EPNS are often found on American and English silver–plated wares.
Sheffield silver is a type of silver plate.   Ⓔ Ⓟ ⓝ Ⓝ Ⓢ

Basket Stand, Bristol Insert, Crimped Edges, 11 1/4 In. 120.00
Basket, Applied Flowers, Twist Handle, S. H. & M. Co., 11 In. 395.00
Berry Bowl, Oval Shell & Tassel, Tufts Frame 250.00
Bowl, Centerpiece, Pedestal, Gorham, 19th Century, 9 1/2 In. 137.00
Bowl, Centerpiece, Side Buttresses, M. Desny, 11 In. 1650.00
Bowl, NSSA Eastern Open, Wallace, Square, 1963 .... 50.00
Bowl, Nut, Full Figure Squirrel On Top, 12 In. 450.00
Bowl, Nut, Squirrel On Top, Elaborate 225.00
Bowl, Nut, Squirrel Sitting On Branch On Rim, 7 1/2 In. 65.00
Box, Jeweled Hinged Cover, Wood Liner, T & T Mark 35.00

Butter Keeper, Telescope, Simpson, Hall & Miller, 1875, 13 In. 286.00
Butter, Cover, Standing Cow Finial, Meriden 135.00
Butter, Cover, Teardrop, Heritage 20.00
Cake Basket, Engraved Birds On Base, Floral Interior, 9 In. 175.00
Candelabrum, 3–Light, Figural, Art Nouveau Woman, 22 In., Pair 6600.00
Candleholder, Pairpoint, Signed, 11 In. 50.00
Candlesnuffer, Scissor Action, England, 7 In. 55.00
Candlestick, 6 7/8 In., Pair 170.00
Candlestick, 10 In., Pair 150.00
Candlestick, Corinthian Column, Italy, 8 1/2 In., 4 Piece 410.00
Candlestick, Leaves & Angels Border, Sheffield, 12 In., 4 Pc. 2310.00
Candlestick, Peg Lamp Attachment, Sheffield, 1830, Pair 1095.00
Centerpiece, Ovoid, Scroll & Leaves, Mirrored Glass, 6 1/2 In. 385.00
Cocktail Shaker, Washington Air Derby Assoc., 1935 .... 50.00
Coffee & Tea Set, Regency Style, W. & S. Blackington, 6 Piece 275.00
Coffee & Tea Set, Regent, Reed & Barton, 6 Piece 200.00
Coffee Urn, Urn Finial, Looped Handles, Shield, 20 1/2 In. 198.00
Coffeepot, Open Scroll Handle, Egg Shape, Reed & Barton, 12 In 50.00
Crumb Set, Hammered, Homan Manufacturing 28.00
Decanter Set, 3 Whiskey Barrels On 4–Wheel Cart, 10 1/2 In. 1210.00
Dish, Chafing, Black Wooden Handles, Dated 1893 .... 95.00
Dish, Serving, Fish Finial, Shell Shape, 13 1/2 x 16 In. 120.00
Dish, Serving, Oval, Engraved Foliage, Ivory Lid Handle, 14 In. 425.00
Dome, Turkey, Greek Key, Cartouche Reserves, Sheffield 550.00
Epergne, 3–Light, Cut Glass Inserts, Sheffield, 16 In. 1925.00
Epergne, Clear Cut Glass Inserts, 15 1/2 In. 425.00
Fruit Basket, Embossed Interior, Derby Silver Co., 8 1/2 In. 200.00
Glove Stretcher, Gorham 45.00
Knife Rest, Boys Jumping Over Fence Each End 80.00
Knife Rest, Large Squirrels, Rod Between 20.00
Knife Rest, Leaping Squirrel One End Only 45.00
Lamp, Hurricane, Clear Glass Globe, 15 1/2 In., Pair 250.00
Lazy Susan, Old English, 5 Wells, Center Cover, Poole, 19 In. 225.00
Mirror, Beveled, Reclining Woman, Wurtembergerische, 1895 .... 1900.00
Mug, Engraved Garlands, Pansies, Wilcox, 3 1/2 In. 50.00
Napkin rings are listed in their own section
Pitcher, Stand, Greek Designs, Simpson, Hall & Miller, 18 In. 220.00
Pitcher, Tilting, Goblet On Stand, Pairpoint, 20 In. 375.00
Porringer, 4 1/2 In. 125.00
Punch Bowl, Bearded Man Handles, Meriden, 13 1/2 x 19 In. 800.00
Salver, Scalloped & Gadrooned Border, American, 18 1/4 In. 88.00
Silent Butler, Paw Footed, Rogers 25.00
Spoon, souvenir, see Souvenir category
Spooner, Bird On Cover, 8 In. 210.00
Spooner, Bird On Top Of Lid 195.00
Sugar & Spooner, Bird Finial, 12 Hooks .... 100.00 To 115.00
Sugar & Spooner, Flying Bird Finial, Sheffield 150.00
Syrup, Woman Finial & Handle, Meriden, 1868 .... 90.00
Syrup, Woman Finial Handle & Lid, Dated 1868 .... 90.00
Tankard, Horse Jumping Fence On Lid, Rogers .... 235.00 To 285.00
Tankard, Wee Burn, 18 Doubles Winner, Glass Bottom, 5 1/2 In. 50.00
Tea Set, Baroque, 5 Piece 750.00
Tea Set, Figural Legs & Fox Finials, Wilcox, 6 Piece 975.00
Tea Set, Regency Style, Sheffield, 3 Piece 220.00
Tea Urn, Bulbous, Handles, Repousse, Late 19th C., 21 In. 450.00
Toast Rack, 4 Spike Feet, Vertical Handle, A. James Dixon 3300.00
Toast Rack, Wirework Frame, 4 Bead Feet, 1881, 4 7/8 In. 1100.00
Tray, Bail Handle, Footed, Square, 10 1/4 In. 80.00
Tray, Floral Openwork Around, Flat, Round, Pairpoint, 9 5/8 In. 195.00
Tray, Georgian Style, Shell & Leaf Design, 31 In. 825.00
Turkey Dome, Acanthus, Berry Loop Handle, James Dixon, 19 In. 550.00
Vase, Laurel & Crest, Serpents On Base, English, 22 In., Pair 3740.00
Vase, Trumpet, Pierced Rim, Floral, Wallace, c.1900, 18 In. 225.00

Wall Planters, Inserts, 14 In., Pair	300.00
Wine Cooler, Scrolls, Lion Mask Ring Handles, W. M. F., 10 In.	550.00
Wine Trolley, Rogers	110.00

SILVER, SHEFFIELD, see Silver Plate; Silver–English

SILVER–AMERICAN. American silver is listed here. Most of the sterling silver listed in this book is subdivided by country. There are also other pieces of silver and silver plate listed under special categories, such as Napkin Ring, Silver Plate, Silver Flatware, Silver–Sterling, and Tiffany Silver.

SILVER–AMERICAN, Baby Rattle, Gilt, Coral Handle, Whistle Tip, Brass Bells	660.00
Basket, Pierced Ribbon & Leaf Panels, Unger Bros., 12 In.	335.00
Beaker, Molded Rim & Base, Tapered Body, A. Rasch, c.1815	467.00
Beaker, Presentation, Butler Bement, 1826, 3 5/8 In.	660.00
Beaker, Reeded Border, E. J. Baldwin & Co., 1850, 2 3/8 In.	550.00
Bonbon, Heart Shape, Grande Baroque, Gorham, 6 x 5 In.	125.00
Bonbon, Medallion Profiles, Shiebler, c.1885, 9 1/2 In.	1650.00
Bowl, Center, Floral Designs, Mauser Mfg. Co.	3100.00
Bowl, Center, Poppy, Art Nouveau, Simpson, Hall & Miller	125.00
Bowl, Centerpiece, Poppies, George D. Davidson, 14 In.	3300.00
Bowl, Chantilly, Gorham, 8 In.	90.00
Bowl, Child's, Scenes From Nursery Rhymes, William Kerr	230.00
Bowl, Flutes At Intervals, Lebolt & Co., c.1920, 15 In.	1540.00
Bowl, Foliate Form, Monogram, Wallace, c.1920, 10 1/2 In.	165.00
Bowl, Foliate Hand–Hammered Rim, Gorham, 1925	330.00
Bowl, Footed, Smooth Presentation, 1915, Jarvie, 8 1/2 In.	615.00
Bowl, Francis I, Reed & Barton, c.1948	250.00
Bowl, Fruit, Floral Design, Gorham, 3 7/8 x 10 In.	1045.00
Bowl, Fruit, Ruffled, Floral Design, Shreve & Co.	1760.00
Bowl, Greek Key Rim, Gorham, c.1860, 7 x 7 1/2 In.	1850.00
Bowl, Hammered Surface, Kalo Shop, 3 1/8 x 5 1/8 In.	295.00
Bowl, Oval, Rose, Stieff, 1923, 8 1/8 In.	295.00
Bowl, Petal Form, Round, Kalo Shop, Squatty	990.00
Bowl, Pierced Overall With Foliage, Roger Williams	1215.00
Bowl, Prelude, International, 3 x 6 1/2 In.	70.00
Bowl, Raised Molded Rim, Footed, Gorham, 9 In.	175.00
Bowl, Relief Irises, Hand Chased, R. H. Halford & Sons	1900.00
Bowl, Revere Style, R. Blackington, 8 1/4 In.	595.00
Bowl, Scrolling Vine, Molded Foot, Davis & Galt, 9 In.	360.00
Bowl, Tulip At Intervals, Footed, Stone Assoc., 11 7/8 In.	1100.00
Bowl, Wave Border, Footed Base, Arthur J. Stone, 11 1/4 In.	1430.00
Box, Cigarette, Chinoiserie, Bridge Scene, 1935, 12 1/2 In.	1100.00
Box, Cigarette, Engraved Signature Of Giver, Gorham, 1958	110.00
Box, Cover, Gold Wash, HT, Sheffield, 1 1/2 In.	100.00
Box, Dresser, Repousse Floral, Swag & Leaf, Gorham, 1893	550.00
Box, Pepper, Pierced Cover, J. Tanner, 3 3/4 In. ....*Illus*	2420.00

Silver-American, Caster, Domed Cover,
Z. Brigden, 1760, 5 1/4 In.
Silver-American, Box, Pepper,
Pierced Cover, J. Tanner, 3 3/4 In.
Silver-American, Cocktail Shaker, Golf
Bag, International, c.1930

Box, Pill, Round, Gold Washed, Hinged, Stone, 1 1/2 In.	525.00
Brandy Spoon, Gorham	75.00
Bread Tray, Cherubs, Sheibler	375.00
Buckle, Rolled Rods, J. Hutton, Philadelphia, 2 3/4 In., Pr.	1500.00
Butter Pail, Cow Finial, Liner, R. & W. Wilson, c.1850, 5 In.	2750.00
Butter, Cover, Floral Finial, C. Bard, 1825, 5 1/2 In.	2250.00
Butter, Cover, Grape Rim, C. Bard, 1825, 7 1/2 In.	2250.00
Buttonhook, Shiebler	175.00
Cake Basket, Pierced Rim & Sides, Black, Starr & Frost	825.00
Cake Plate, Cherubs, Griffins, Dolphins, R. Williams, 11 In.	1100.00
Cake Plate, Floral Rim, Kirk, c.1920, 10 3/4 In.	495.00
Candlestick, Chased Floral, Dominick & Haff, 10 In., Pair	550.00
Candlestick, Fluted Column, Gorham, c.1909, 7 1/2 In.	170.00
Candlestick, Graff, Washbourne & Dunn, 11 1/2 In., 4 Piece	3850.00
Candy Dish, Repousse, Kirk	125.00
Case, Card, Church On Front, Swan On Back	175.00
Case, Card, U.S. Capitol Building	185.00
Caster, Chased Grapevines, Paw Feet, F. Smith, Pair	165.00
Caster, Domed Cover, Z. Brigden, 1760, 5 1/4 In. ....*Illus*	2640.00
Caster, Inverted Pear Shape, Myer Myers, c.1765, 6 In.	8800.00
Caster, Sloping Panels, c.1760, 6 5/8 In.	770.00
Coaster, Wine Bottle, Graff, Washbourne & Dunn, 7 1/4 In.	185.00
Cocktail Shaker, Flagon Form, Tuttle, c.1942	330.00
Cocktail Shaker, Golf Bag, International, c.1930 ....*Illus*	1200.00
Coffee & Tea Set, Bigelow Bros., Coin Silver, 1845, 6 Piece	5200.00
Coffee & Tea Set, Black, Starr & Frost, c.1880, 7 Piece	6050.00
Coffee & Tea Set, Engraved Design, Gorham, 1868, 7 Piece	2530.00
Coffee & Tea Set, Tray, Winthrop, Reed & Barton, 6 Piece	900.00
Coffee Set, Demitasse, Gorham, 1895, 3 Piece	495.00
Coffee Set, Egg-and-Dart Rim, Gerardus Boyce, c.1815, 3 Pc.	1650.00
Coffee Set, Inverted Pear, Gale, Wood & Hughes, 1833, 3 Pc.	5500.00
Coffeepot, Acanthus Leaves, George Sharp, 1840, 12 In.	3500.00
Coffeepot, Art Nouveau, Whiting, 1910, Demitasse	440.00
Coffeepot, C. Wiltberger, Engraved W, 10 7/8 In.	9000.00
Coffeepot, Hinged Lid, Carved Handle, 1895, Gorham, 7 In.	165.00
Coffeepot, Inverted Pear Shape, Wm. Adams, 1831, 9 In.	3250.00
Coffeepot, Oak Branch Finial, Jones, Ball & Co., 1852	445.00
Coffeepot, Overall Roses, Ram Handles, A. E. Warner, c.1880	825.00
Coffeepot, Persian Style, Gorham, 1888, 11 1/2 In.	1980.00
Comb & Brush, Lunt	30.00
Compote, Fox At Base Of Grapevine, P. L. Krider, c.1870	7700.00
Compote, Mythical Bird On Stem, Ball, Black & Co., 1876	660.00
Compote, Partial Gilt Interior, E. Moore, 1860, 9 1/2 In.	3500.00
Compote, Repousse, Kirk, 1903, 7 x 13 1/2 In.	375.00
Creamer & Tongs, Edmund Milne, Philadelphia, 1800	3200.00
Creamer, Federal, Ribbed Rim, McConnell, Virginia, 6 In.	1100.00
Creamer, George Fox, Charles Fox, 1850s	575.00
Creamer, Scrolled Handle, Jacob Hurd, c.1750, 3 7/8 In.	990.00
Cup, Bead Rim Top & Bottom, Colton & Collins, 1825, 3 In.	395.00
Cup, Gale & Hayden, 1849	125.00
Cup, Hyde & Goodrich, New Orleans, c.1850 ....*Illus*	2970.00
Cup, Sorbet, Whiting, 10 Piece	165.00
Demitasse Set, Holders & Saucers, Lenox Liners, 12 Sets	575.00
Dish, Cover, Terrapin, Shell Finials, Gorham, 1901, 5 1/8 In.	2750.00
Dish, Entree, Gadroon Edge, Jones, Ball & Poor, 1850, 12 In.	1430.00
Dish, Scrolled Rim, Dominick & Haff, 1891, 12 In. ....*Illus*	2970.00
Dish, Serving, Pierced Rim, Mildred Watkins, 5 1/8 In.	1325.00
Dresser Set, Art Nouveau, Foster & Bailey, 5 Piece	247.50
Dresser Set, Webster Co., 7 Piece	110.00
Ewer, Baluster Form, Foliate, Acanthus Design, 15 1/2 In.	1500.00
Ewer, Band Of Acanthus, Davis, Palmer & Co., 1846, 8 1/2 In.	335.00
Ewer, Bulbous, Pedestal, S. White & Co., c.1830, 13 In.	3000.00
Ewer, Floral Garlands, Wm. Gale Son & Co., c.1860, 12 In.	3200.00

Silver-American, Cup, Hyde & Goodrich, *Silver-American, Dish, Scrolled Rim,*

New Orleans, c.1850 *Dominick & Haff, 1891, 12 In.*

Flagon, Leaves On Cover, Geoff & Shepherd, c.1845, 8 In.	1760.00
Fork, Fiddle Thread, E. Jaccard, Pair	40.00
Fork, Oval Thread, Platt & Bros., New York, 1816	225.00
Fruit Bowl, Ruffled Rim, Floral, Shreve & Co., 10 7/8 In.	1750.00
Fruit Knife, Folding, Beaded Handle	30.00
Goblet, Birds In Grapevines, Jones Ball & Poor, c.1850	385.00
Goblet, Communion, R. & W. Wilson, c.1828, 4 3/4 In.	850.00
Goblet, Inverted Bell, Wallace & Sons, 6 1/2 In., 8 Piece	800.00
Goblet, Presentation, Coin Silver, Philadelphia, Dated 1855	295.00
Goblet, Stepped Pedestal, Rope Rim, S. Hoyt & Co., c.1842	650.00
Gravy Ladle, Aesthetic Movement, Whiting Mfg. Co., c.1875	65.00
Gravy Ladle, Faralon, Schultz & Fischer, c.1860	125.00
Gravy Ladle, Jenny Lind, G. Spence, c.1850	125.00
Gravy Ladle, Josephine, A. Coles, New York City, c.1850	95.00
Humidor, Art Nouveau Cover, Cut Glass, Gorham	605.00
Ice Tongs, Pierced Design, Watson, 7 3/8 In.	66.00
Iced Tea Spoon, Hand Hammered, Allan Adler, 6 Piece	385.00
Inkstand, 2 Cut Glass Bottles, Graff Washbourne & Dunn	770.00
Inkwell, Chased Floral Scrolls, Glass Liner, Gorham, 1892	395.00
Julep Cup, G. Sharp, Jr., 3 5/8 In.	650.00
Julep Cup, Hayden & Whilden, c.1855, 3 7/8 In.	400.00
Julep Cup, J. Werne, Monogram MMH	350.00
Julep Cup, John B. Akin, 3 5/8 In.	400.00
Julep Cup, Shield Cartouche, S. Kirk, 3 3/4 In., Pair	240.00
Kettle, Ice Water, Tilting, Stand, Reed & Barton	770.00
Kettle, Stand, Scrolls, Flower Heads, N.Y., c.1840, 15 In.	1980.00
Knife Rest, Dog, Boxer, Tufts	165.00
Knife, Butter, Grecian, Wm. G. Whilden, c.1855, Master	195.00
Knife, Wedding Cake, Repousse, Kirk	55.00
Ladle, Bright Cut Design, N. Harding, 19th Century	165.00
Ladle, Fiddle Thread, Baldwin Gardiner, 1814, Large	750.00
Ladle, Punch, Royal Oak, Gorham	220.00
Ladle, Sauce, A. Reeder, c.1820	95.00
Ladle, Sauce, Fiddle, P. Miller, c.1820	85.00
Ladle, Sauce, W. A. Platt, c.1817, 6 1/8 In.	255.00
Ladle, Soup, Coin, Olive Pattern, Jones Ball & Co., 12 In.	295.00
Ladle, Soup, Faralone, Schultz & Fischer	350.00
Ladle, Sussex, Cut Glass Handle, Dorflinger, 15 1/2 In.	725.00
Lemonade Set, Frank Smith, 14 Piece	1595.00
Lighter, Resting Camel Form, Chained Extinguisher, 1905	3100.00
Loving Cup, Mitchell & Tyler, Mid–19th Century	665.00
Loving Cup, Western Pennsylvania Golf Assoc. 1902, 6 In.	200.00
Marrow Spoon, Fiddle Thread, Hayden Brothers, 1852, 10 In.	1500.00
Money Clip, 1925 Liberty Silver Quarter, Dated 1925	65.00
Muffineer, Bailey, Banks & Biddle, Footed	375.00
Mug, Double Scroll Handle, Joseph Rice, c.1780, 5 In.	2640.00
Mug, Double Scroll Handle, Leaf Grip, A. Carlile, 5 1/4 In.	3300.00

Mug, Double Scroll Handle, Samuel Bartlett, 1770s 2100.00
Mug, Scroll Handle, John Edwards, c.1720, 4 3/8 In. 5500.00
Nut Dish, George Fox, Charles Fox, 6 Piece 180.00
Nut Dish, Repousse & Floral, Kirk & Son, 6 Piece 165.00
Pepper Box, 2 Bands At Base, Daniel Parker, c.1740, 4 In. 2200.00
Pepper Caster, Daniel Parker, 1768 .... 3850.00
Perfume On Chain, Medallion, Shiebler 350.00
Pitcher, Acanthus Spirals, Bigelow Kennard, 7 In. 770.00
Pitcher, Applied Top Border, Schofield, 8 3/4 In. 550.00
Pitcher, Art Nouveau, Raised Lilies, Towle, 9 1/4 In. 880.00
Pitcher, Chased Scroll & Floral, Gorham, c.1952, 8 1/2 In. 440.00
Pitcher, Chased Vintage, Bigelow Kennard, 13 In. ....*Illus* 1320.00
Pitcher, Classical Revival, Gorham, 1879, 9 3/8 In. 1100.00
Pitcher, Cover, Bud Finial, Fluted, J. Jones, c.1830, 9 In. 880.00
Pitcher, Floral Handle, Leaf Spout, Lincoln & Foss, 10 In. 770.00
Pitcher, Leaves, Leaf–Capped Handle, Farnam & Ward, 10 In. 2200.00
Pitcher, Submerged Diving Mallard, Whiting, 1880, 9 1/8 In. 9900.00
Pitcher, Swirling Poppies, Shreve & Co., 14 1/4 In. 1870.00
Pitcher, Trailing Foliate Vines, Gorham, c.1859, 11 5/8 In. 1870.00
Pitcher, Vintage Design, Dominick & Haff, 13 3/4 In. 1320.00
Pitcher, Water, Whiting, 13 1/2 In. 825.00
Plate, Art Nouveau, Frank Herschede, 7 In. 200.00
Plate, Rim Of Leaves, Ball, Black & Co., 9 5/8 In., 12 Piece 5500.00
Plate, Service, Samuel Kirk & Son, 1925, 10 7/8 In., 12 Pc. 4125.00
Plate, T. Hausmann & Sons, c.1911, 7 1/2 In., 5 Piece 485.00
Platter, Fish Form, Scales, Fins, Gorham, 1884, 17 1/2 In. 5500.00
Porringer, Convex Sides, J. Howell & Co., 1802, 5 3/4 In. 5000.00
Porringer, Pierced Keyhole Handle, Samuel Casey, 1750s, Pr. 4400.00
Porringer, Vine, Leaf Finial, Wm. Forbes, c.1856, 4 1/2 In. 2500.00
Punch Bowl, Floral Sprays, Black, Starr & Frost, c.1890 .... 3025.00
Punch Bowl, Grape Vine Garlands, G. Shiebler, 14 1/4 In. 4950.00
Punch Bowl, Trophy, Gorham, Oct. 15, 1902, 18 3/4 In. 4400.00
Punch Ladle, Michael Gibney, 1845, 14 1/2 In. 495.00
Rattle, Ball Shape, Embossed Design, Beaded Rims, 6 In. 425.00
Rattle, Funnel–Shaped Handle, Whistle Tip, 5 In. 550.00
Salt Cellar & Spoon, C. Bard & Son, c.1840, Pair 850.00
Salt Cellar, Beaded Rims, Vansant & Co., c.1850, 2 1/2 In. 250.00
Salt Spoon, Bright Cut Floral, A. Stowell & Co., Pair 45.00
Salt Spoon, Downturned Ends, R. Wilson, c.1805, Pair 175.00
Salt Spoon, Fiddle, J. H. Clark, Portsmouth, N. H., 1812 .... 55.00
Salt Spoon, Fiddle, Tipped Down, William Carrington, c.1850 .... 145.00
Salt Spoon, Gothic, Shreve & Co., Pair 65.00
Salt Spoon, Shell, J. B. Jones, Boston, c.1820, Pair 195.00
Salt Spoon, Upturned Fiddle, Meadows & Co., c.1840, Pair 45.00
Salt, Hoof Feet, Alexander Petrie, c.1740, 2 1/2 In. 2420.00
Salt, Hoof Feet, Samuel Minott, c.1770, 2 3/8 In., Pair 2640.00
Salt, Lobes Form 5 Sections, C. Pratt, 2 1/2 In., Pair 192.50
Salt, Loops, Swags, Rope Rim, Wm. Gale & Son, 1856, 2 1/2 In. 220.00
Salt, Oval Trencher, Abraham Dubois, 1777, 2 In. 1450.00
Salver, Engraved Design, Jones, Ball & Poor, 12 3/8 In. 330.00
Salver, Piecrust Edge, Raised Feet, Gorham, 10 In., Pair 275.00
Sauce Ladle, Lownes, c.1790, Pair 375.00
Sauce Ladle, R. H. Bailey, Woodstock, Vt., c.1840 .... 75.00
Sauceboat, Double Scroll Handle, Myer Myers, c.1760 .... 6600.00
Sconce, Wall, Gothic Arch Top, Hammered, c.1900, 9 1/2 In. 775.00
Serving Set, Fish, Bailey & Kitchen, Box, 1840 .... 523.00
Serving Spoon, Sulgrave, Mt. Vernon, c.1911, 12 In. 55.00
Soap Box, Traveling, Hinged Lid, Scroll & Floral, Gorham 192.00
Spoon, Basket Of Flowers, Hastings, Coin, 8 3/4 In. 55.00
Spoon, Custard, Beaded & Pierced Fiddle Handle, Towle 302.00
Spoon, Gold Washed Bowl, Gorham, Demitasse 35.00
Spoon, Sauce, Fiddle Handle, Erickson, 5 In., Pair 55.00
Spoon, Shell On Handle, John W. Forks, 8 3/4 In., 3 Piece 135.00

Strainer, Lemon, Jacob Hurd, c.1750, 10 3/4 In. 3575.00
Strainer, Lemon, William Burt, c.1745, 10 /2 In. 4950.00
Sugar & Creamer, Cover, Federal Style, Gorham 357.50
Sugar & Creamer, Cover, Watson & Brown, Boston, 1820 .... 3000.00
Sugar & Creamer, Gadrooned Borders, Stevens & Lakeman 250.00
Sugar Nips, Joseph Richardson, c.1750, 5 In. 2535.00
Sugar Shell, Angelo, Wood & Hughes 45.00
Sugar Shell, Jenny Lind, G. Spence, c.1850 .... 45.00
Sugar Tongs, Bright Cut Engraved, B & W, Coin 40.00
Sugar, Acorn Finial, Bead Rims, Hayden & Gregg, 1843 .... 1850.00
Sugar, Band Of Acorns, Shepherd & Boyd, 8 1/2 In. 1250.00
Sugar, Cover, Acorn Finial, 9 In. 450.00
Sugar, Cover, Fluted Urn Form, G. Boyce, 1850s, 9 1/2 In. 335.00
Sugar, Cover, Urn Shape, C. Wiltberger, Engraved W, 9 In. 4750.00
Sugar, Cover, Urn Shape, Moore & Ferguson, 7 3/8 In. 450.00
Tablespoon, A. Dumesnil, c.1820 .... 150.00
Tablespoon, B. Mayo, c.1860 .... 30.00
Tablespoon, Benjamin Halstead & Myer Myers, c.1776 .... 990.00
Tablespoon, Coffin Lid Handle, I. Reeves, 9 1/4 In. 35.00
Tablespoon, Coffin Lid Handle, Warford, Albany, 10 In. 130.00
Tablespoon, Fiddle Thread, Lows, Ball & Co., 6 Piece 295.00
Tablespoon, Fiddle Thread, Monogram, Coin, J. Cook, 6 Piece 210.00
Tablespoon, Fiddle Tipped Down, J. Ewan, 1823, Pair 600.00
Tablespoon, Fiddle, J. Draper, Wilmington, Del., 1816 .... 195.00
Tablespoon, G. Spence, Newark 55.00
Tablespoon, Hanover, William Jones, 1695 .... 2100.00
Tablespoon, J. Gibbs, c.1760 .... 325.00
Tablespoon, Shellback Bowl, Paul Revere Jr., c.1770 .... 2400.00
Tablespoon, Trailing Flowers, Paul Revere Jr., c.1780 .... 2300.00
Tablespoon, Upturned Terminals, Myer Myers, c.1760 .... 2200.00
Tablespoon, W. McGrew, Cincinnati, Pair 60.00
Tankard, Domed Hinged Cover, Joseph Richardson Sr., c.1750 .... 8900.00
Tankard, Flat–Domed Hinged Cover, John Coddington, c.1710 .... 3575.00
Tea & Coffee Set, Grojean & Woodward, c.1852, 5 Piece 5100.00
Tea & Coffee Set, Swan Neck Spout, J. E. Caldwell, 3 Piece 4500.00
Tea & Coffee Set, Woodward & Lothrop, 4 Piece 1395.00
Tea Caddy, Bulbous, Dominick & Haff, Monogram, 4 In. 45.00
Tea Set, Edward Rockwell, 1830s, 3 Piece 8000.00
Tea Set, Flaring Vertical Bands, Reed & Barton, 4 Piece 6050.00
Tea Set, Grand Baroque, Plated Tray, Wallace, 4 Piece 1500.00
Tea Set, Hampton Court, Reed & Barton, 5 Piece 4800.00
Tea Set, John Sayre, c.1825, 3 Piece 995.00
Tea Set, Nicholas J. Bogert, c.1825, 3 Piece 1045.00
Tea Set, Talisman Rose, Whiting, Plated Tray, 6 Piece 2700.00
Tea Set, Urn Shape, J. Sayre, c.1815, 3 Piece 1870.00
Tea Set, Urn Shape, William Thompson, c.1815, 3 Piece 1325.00
Tea Strainer, Kirk 110.00

Silver-American, Pitcher, Chased Vintage,
Bigelow Kennard, 13 In.

Silver-American, Teapot, Pear Shape, Ebony,
18th Century, 7 In.

Tea Strainer, Whiting, Gilt, Pierced Geometric Form, 4 In. 495.00
Tea Urn, Beaded Ball Finial, Gorham, c.1865, 15 3/4 In. 3575.00
Teapot, Bell Finial, Ephraim Brasher, c.1790, 7 1/4 In. 4450.00
Teapot, Pear Shape, Ebony, 18th Century, 7 In. ....*Illus* 1980.00
Teaspoon, B. Woodcock, Wilmington, Dela., c.1790 .... 60.00
Teaspoon, Bright Cut, Bruce & Till, 5 Piece 100.00
Teaspoon, Bruno & Virgins, Columbus, Georgia, Pair 50.00
Teaspoon, Coffin End, T. Keeler, c.1790 .... 115.00
Teaspoon, E. & D. Kinsey, 5 3/4 In. 15.00
Teaspoon, Fiddle With Rattail, J. Doll, 1820, Pair 65.00
Teaspoon, Fiddle, Barrington & Davenport, 1806, Pair 195.00
Teaspoon, French Thread, Farrington & Hunnewell, 6 Piece 120.00
Teaspoon, Harris & Stanwood, c.1835, 6 7/8 In., 6 Piece 90.00
Teaspoon, Initials, Coin, R. W. Preston, 6 In., 6 Piece 36.00
Teaspoon, J. Caldwell, Engraved A. B., 5 1/2 In., 4 Piece 40.00
Teaspoon, Jaccard, St. Louis, 6 Piece 210.00
Teaspoon, L. Holland, Baltimore 30.00
Teaspoon, Mayflower, Lewis Chamberlain, c.1824 .... 125.00
Teaspoon, Picture Back, E. Lownes, 1785, 4 Piece 800.00
Teaspoon, S. Masi, Washington 30.00
Teaspoon, S. D. Smith 20.00
Teaspoon, Stephen Baker 135.00
Teaspoon, T. Spear 25.00
Teaspoon, T. D. Currier 40.00
Teaspoon, T. P. Emerson, Lafayette, Indiana, 6 Piece 195.00
Teaspoon, V. W. Skiff, 6 Piece 125.00
Tongs, Asparagus, Baltimore Silversmiths Mfg., 1903 .... 165.00
Tongs, Bright Cut, McFee & Reeder, c.1795 .... 175.00
Tongs, George III, Engraved Design, John Langlands, Jr. 82.50
Tongs, Scrolling Acanthus, Leaf Grips, Kirk 82.00
Tongs, Sheaf Of Wheat, Whitney, c.1825 .... 175.00
Tongs, Sugar, Bright Cut, John Benjamin, 4 3/8 In. 247.00
Toothpick, Victorian, St. Louis Silver Co. 150.00
Tray, Bate's Family Arms, Newel Harding & Co. 4400.00
Tray, Cinderella, Gorham, 1926, 12 In. 300.00
Tray, Floral & Foliate Repousse Border, Kirk, 13 In. 550.00
Tray, Louis XIV, Towle, 11 In. 165.00
Tray, Oak Leaves, Acorns, Newel Harding, c.1855, 21 In. 4400.00
Tray, Oval, Lobed Rim, Reed & Barton, 17 In. 275.00
Tray, Oval, Monogram, Shreve, Crump & Low, 27 In. 1100.00
Tray, Perfume, Overall Scrolling, Matthews Co., 9 In. 250.00
Tray, Reticulated Border, Dominick & Haff, 9 1/2 In. 75.00
Tray, Salam, Dominick & Haff, 9 1/2 In. 137.00
Tray, Scalloped Form, Floral, International, 9 3/4 x 14 In. 145.00
Tray, Scalloped Rim, Oval, Kalo Shop, 10 3/4 In. 412.50
Tray, Shallow Well, Stylized Paw Foot, C. Pratt, 6 In. 330.00
Tray, Shell & Scroll Rim & Feet, Howard, 10 1/2 In., Pair 880.00
Tray, Square Rounded Form, Erickson, 10 3/4 x 10 3/4 In. 192.00
Tray, Swirling Poppy Plants, Gorham, 1901, 14 1/4 In. 2200.00
Tray, Trailing Leaves, Flowers, Gorham, c.1905, 18 In. 3300.00
Trivet, Crystal Overlay, Scrolling Foliate, Webster, 8 In. 55.00
Trophy, Point Judith Country Club, J. E. Caldwell, 1897 .... 390.00
Tureen, Deer Finial, Ring Handles, Gorham, 1878, 11 1/2 In. 4400.00
Tureen, Oval Cover, Leaf Design Handles, Gorham, 13 In. 2200.00
Tureen, Soup, Cover, Ovolos & Darts, Gorham, 1870, 14 1/2 In. 2750.00
Tureen, Soup, Fruit Pendants, Bird's Head Handles, Gorham 3300.00
Urn, Hot Water, R. & W. Wilson 3200.00
Vase, Acanthus Handles, Peter Krider, c.1850, 7 In. 550.00
Vase, Japanese Style, Wood & Hughes, c.1875, 6 In., Pair 1450.00
Vinaigrette, Etched Dot Design, Joseph Willmore, 1810 .... 325.00
Vinaigrette, Overall Engraved Design, S. Pemberton, 1819 .... 400.00
Whisk Broom, Floral & Leaf Design Handle, Gorham, 1893 .... 220.00
Wine, Hammered Surface, Whiting, 1923, 5 In., 12 Piece 525.00

Wine, Pear Shape, Anthony Rasch & Co., 4 3/4 In., Pair 2500.00
SILVER–ARABIAN, Salad Set, Fork & Spoon, Horn Handles 82.50
SILVER–AUSTRIAN, Vase, Bud, Beaded Rim, Pierced, Wiener Werkstatte, 8 3/8 In. ... 4200.00
SILVER–BELGIAN, Snuffbox, Erotic Figure On Cover, c.1825, 3 1/4 In. 625.00
SILVER–BULGARIAN, Dish, Cover, Twig Handles, Floral Design, 5 3/4 In., Pair 2750.00
SILVER–CHINESE, Cocktail Shaker, 4 Stemmed Cups, Scrolling, Dragon, 19 Oz. 650.00
    Mug, Bamboo Handle, Bamboo Design, Khecheong, 1840, 5 In. 1045.00
    Tray, Dragon Border, Bamboo Interior, Wang Hing, 14 In. 1650.00
    Tray, Hand Hammered, 14 x 22 In. 2000.00
SILVER–CONTINENTAL, Biscuit Box, Stand, Molded Form, 20th Century, 8 In. 525.00
    Bowl, Grape Bunch, Basketweave Border, 16 x 14 3/4 In. 1450.00
    Box, Tobacco, Portraits, Frederick II, Ferdinand, 6 In. 522.50
    Coffeepot, Camel's Head Spout, Allover Design, 1900 .... 705.00
    Desk Seal, Zigzag Border, Peter Jay, 1722, 3 1/8 In. 2970.00
    Pitcher, Figure Finial, Old Testament Scenes, 8 1/4 In. 1100.00
    Pitcher, Water, 7 In. 225.00
    Sugar Box, Bombe Form, Bright Cut Design, 19th Century 467.50
SILVER–DANISH, Bowl, Art Deco Stepped Design, Georg Jensen, 1945, 7 In. 825.00
    Bowl, Gadrooned, Grapes & Vines, Georg Jensen, 10 1/4 In. 5225.00
    Bowl, Grape Cluster Handles & At Base, Georg Jensen, 1933 .... 6600.00
    Bowl, Openwork Stem, Leaves & Grapes, Georg Jensen, 7 7/8 In. 2100.00
    Bowl, Trailing Grape Vines, Georg Jensen, 6 1/8 In., Pair 8800.00
    Candlestick, Grapevine, Georg Jensen, Marked, 8 1/4 In., Pair 7700.00
    Carving Set, Acanthus, Georg Jensen 395.00
    Case, Cigarette, Georg Jensen 895.00
    Centerpiece, Openwork Border Over Foot, Georg Jensen, 10 In. 4125.00
    Cheese Slicer, Acanthus, Georg Jensen 125.00
    Cocktail Set, Grapevine Finial, Twisted Rope, 13 Pc. 4400.00
    Coffee Set, Blossom, Blossom Finials, Georg Jensen, 3 Piece 8250.00
    Coffee Set, Blossom, Georg Jensen, 4 Piece 6000.00
    Coffee Set, Tray, Ebony Finial, George Jensen, 3 Piece 2640.00
    Compote, Grapevine, Georg Jensen, 7 3/8 In. 1650.00
    Dish, Fruit, Shallow, 2 Stylized Floral Handles, Georg Jensen 4435.00
    Fork, 4 Prongs, Owl–Shaped Handle, 9 1/2 In. 475.00
    Inkwell, Hinged Lid, Attached Tray, Georg Jensen, 9 1/2 In. 2200.00
    Knife & Fork, Pattern, Georg Jensen, 8 Piece 395.00
    Ladle, Leaf, Bead & Pod, Georg Jensen, 1945, 8 In. 305.00
    Letter Opener, Georg Jensen 225.00
    Lighter, Amber Glass Finial, Georg Jensen, 6 7/8 In. 3080.00
    Pepper Shaker, Acorn, Georg Jensen, Individual, 12 Piece 1450.00
    Pitcher, Spot Hammered, Handle, Georg Jensen, 1945, 11 3/8 In. 3520.00
    Platter, Acorn, Georg Jensen, 1915, 14 1/4 In. 3300.00
    Salt Dish, Georg Jensen, 2 In. 125.00
    Sauceboat, Grapevine, Georg Jensen, 1925–1927, 9 1/2 In. 2200.00
    Sauceboat, Grapevine, Georg Jensen, No. 296, 9 1/4 In. 4950.00
    Spoon, Baby, Acorn, Georg Jensen, 4 In. 100.00
    Spoon, Candy Dish, Georg Jensen 225.00
    Spoon, Cheese, Acorn, Georg Jensen 125.00
    Spoon, Christening, c.1786 .... 350.00
    Spoon, Compote, Georg Jensen 95.00
    Spoon, Marrow, Leaf Bead & Pod, Georg Jensen 395.00
    Spoon, Serving, Buds In Relief, Georg Jensen, 8 1/4 In. 93.00
    Spoon, Serving, Georg Jensen, Copenhagen, 8 1/4 In. 95.00
    Tazza, Shallow Bowl, Trailing Vines, Grapes, Georg Jensen 2100.00
    Tea & Coffee Set, Blossom, Georg Jensen, No. 2D, 4 Pc. 7700.00
    Tea & Coffee Set, Hammered, Ivory Handles, G. Jensen, 4 Piece 2850.00
    Tray, Ivory Handles, Georg Jensen, c.1940, Oval, 20 3/4 In. 6600.00
    Tray, Scroll Handles, Engraved On Reverse, 1925, 15 1/2 In. 5280.00
SILVER–DUTCH, Bowl, Floral, Foliate Scroll, Floral Handles, 1750s, 7 3/4 In. 275.00
    Box, Cover, Coffered Chest Form, Repousse 302.00
    Box, Tobacco, Hinged Lid, Incised Design, 5 In. 302.00
    Case, Cheroot, Scenes In Relief, c.1850, 2 3/8 In. 350.00
    Case, Traveling, Cigar Shape, Opens To Form Candlestick, 1814 .... 175.00

Cup, Floral Repousse, 3 In. 82.00
Sailing Vessels, Marked, c.1900, 3 1/2 In. 250.00
Server, Fish, Fiddle Thread, Openwork, N. Thune, 11 1/8 In. 375.00
Teapot, Child's, Repousse, Stand With Burner, 7 1/2 In. 1800.00

SILVER–ENGLISH. English silver is marked with a series of four or five small hallmarks. The standing lion mark is the most commonly seen sterling quality mark. The other marks indicate the city of origin, the maker, and the year of manufacture. These dates can be verified in many good books on silver.

SILVER–ENGLISH, Basket, Handle, Pierced, Robinson, Edkins & Aston, 1846 .... 2950.00
Basket, Sweetmeat, Pierced Floral, Hester Bateman, 1809 .... 1540.00
Beaker, Molded Rim & Base, Engraved Monogram, c.1815 .... 467.00
Belt, Woman's, Art Nouveau, c.1898 .... 895.00
Bowl, Engraved Crest, William Fountain, 1804 .... 770.00
Bowl, Hammered, 4 Handles, Liberty, Conical, Flanged Rim 1848.00
Bowl, Hammered, Rose Briar Frieze, Artificers Guild, 1912 .... 3696.00
Box, Stepped Circular Foot, Cylindrical, H. G. Murphy 924.00
Bread Basket, Pierced, Sheffield, 9 1/2 In. 220.00
Cake Basket, Foliate Flutes, Joseph & John Angel, 1840 .... 1210.00
Cake Server, Foliage Scrolls, 11 1/2 In. 155.00
Candleholder, Hurricane Shade, T. & D. Leader, 1811, 6 In. 285.00
Candlestick, Bands Of Acorns, Sheffield, 1890, 5 In., Pair 467.50
Candlestick, Hammered, Entwined Strapwork, Liberty, Pair 4435.00
Candlestick, James Deakin, c.1912, 9 In. 160.00
Cann, Scroll Handle, Thomas Wright, 1763, 5 1/2 In. 3200.00
Casket, Hinged Cover, Stylized Cartouches, A. William Hutton 1665.00
Castor, 6 Cut Glass Bottles, Robert Hennell, 1778 .... 2500.00
Castor, 8 Bottles, Shell Design, Charles Fox, 1837, 9 In. 1250.00
Castor, Fluted Baluster Body, Queen Anne, Charles Adam, 1705 ...... 885.00
Castor, Rolled Rim Pedestal, Samuel Wood, 1744, 4 In. 850.00
Chocolate Jug, Ebony Handle, Birmingham, 5 In. 90.00
Chocolate Pot, Knop Finial, S–Scrolled Handle, 1709, 10 In. 4850.00
Cigarette Case, Gilt Interior, Leighton, 1937, 7 x 3 1/2 In. 350.00
Coffee Set, Enameled, Bone Handle, Wm. Hutton & Sons, 3 Pc. 2950.00
Coffeepot, George II, Acanthus Spout, Branches, 9 1/2 In. 605.00
Cream Jug, John Crouch 577.00
Creamer, Classical, Chased, Andrew Fogelberg, 1796, 4 3/4 In. 650.00
Creamer, George III, Floral & Chinoiserie Design 120.00
Creamer, Inverted Pear Form, Thos. Swift, 1772, 4 1/2 In. 110.00
Creamer, Samuel Moulton, 5 In. 742.00
Cup, Engraved Inscription, P. & W. Bateman, 1809, 7 In. 275.00
Cup, George III, S–Scrolled Handles, Thomas Wilson, 1770 .... 210.00
Cup, Inscription, Hester Bateman, 1785 .... 130.00
Dish, Shell, Harrison Brothers & Howson, 1910–1911 .... 40.00
Epergne, Cut Crystal, Joseph & Albert Savory, 1853, 18 In. 5000.00
Epergne, Edward VII, 6 Arms, TL & EM, 16 In. ....*Illus* 3190.00
Ewer, Wine, John S. Hunt, 8 1/2 In., Pair 6100.00
Fish Set, Pistol Handle, Sheffield, Service For 6 .... 195.00
Fork, Dinner, Fiddle, John Lias, Henry Lias, 1865 .... 145.00
Fork, Fiddle & Shell, George Adams, 1850, Pair 250.00
Fork, Fiddle Tip, J. Stone, 1851, 8 In., Pair 265.00
Fork, Venetian, Martin Hall & Co., 1878, 8 1/4 In. 95.00
Goblet, Chased, Henry Cowper, 1795 3/8 In. 1500.00
Grape Shears, Grapes & Vines, Eley & Fearn, 1821, 7 In. 725.00
Grater, Nutmeg, Form Of Walnut, 1 1/4 In. 220.00
Inkstand, George IV, Wells, Tray, J. Angell, 1829, 8 1/2 In. 1540.00
Kettle, Hot Water, Stand, Marked 2475.00
Knife Rest, Spoke Form, C. E. Eley, 1820, 2 1/2 In., Pair 165.00
Knife, Patterned Handle, George Unite, 1856 .... 65.00
Ladle, Engraved Initials On Handle, 12 3/4 In. 115.00
Ladle, Shell, Jas. Williams, 1860 .... 625.00
Ladle, Soup, Fiddle Thread, George Angell, 1846, 14 In. 495.00

Silver-English, Epergne, Edward VII, 6 Arms,

TL & EM, 16 In.

◆ ◆ ◆ ◆ ◆ ◆ ◆ ◆ ◆ ◆ ◆ ◆ ◆ ◆ ◆ ◆ ◆ ◆ ◆

If you break the handle on an old silver coffee pot, have it resoldered. That repair detracts little from the resale value, but a new handle lowers the value by 50%.

◆ ◆ ◆ ◆ ◆ ◆ ◆ ◆ ◆ ◆ ◆ ◆ ◆ ◆ ◆ ◆ ◆ ◆ ◆

Ladle, Soup, Old English, Thomas Wallis, 1804, 13 In.	450.00
Letter Rack, Arched Base, Pad Feet, A. Heath & Middleton	1200.00
Loving Cup, South Pond Cabins, Junior Tennis, 1937, 5 In.	85.00
Manicure Set, Case, Birmingham, 2 Crystal Jars, 7 Piece	225.00
Mirror, Plateau, J. E. W. & J. Barnard, 13 In.	660.00
Mug, Baby's, Baby Bunting	30.00
Necessaire, Engraved Floral, With Utensils, 1725, 3 7/8 In.	880.00
Needle Case, Fish, Emerald–Set Eyes, Late 19th Century	55.00
Pap Bowl, Peter, Ann & William Bateman, c.1801	495.00
Plate, Coat Of Arms, Paul Storr, 6 7/8 In., 6 Piece	9000.00
Powder Box, Cow On Cover	225.00
Rattle & Whistle, 3 Bells, Coral, George Unite, c.1869	275.00
Rattle, Baby, Bells, Funnel–Shaped Handle, Whistle Tip	550.00
Salt, Beaded Border, Henry Househill, 1820, 3 1/2 In., Pair	465.00
Salt, George III, Globular, Hoof Feet, 1703, Pair	110.00
Salt, Pedestal Base, Edward Wood, 1743, 2 In., Pair	665.00
Salver, George III, Beaded Border, Engraved Center, 8 In.	445.00
Salver, Pierced Gallery, Hester Bateman, 1780, 7 In.	605.00
Salver, Shell Rim, Hoof Feet, Ebenezer Coker, 1762, 10 In.	467.50
Scoop, Cheese, Fiddle, Peter & Wm. Bateman, 1806	375.00
Scoop, Marrow, Edward Bennett, 1733, 9 1/8 In.	350.00
Skewer, G. Smith & W. Fern, 1788, 7 In.	165.00
Snuffbox, George Unite, Birmingham	302.00
Spoon, Charles I, Apostle, Fig–Shaped Bowl, 7 1/2 In., Pair	1775.00
Spoon, Dessert, Old English, Richard Chawner, 1806, 7 In., Pr.	225.00
Spoon, Dessert, Thread, George Adams, 1841, 6 Piece	330.00
Spoon, Dressing, Rattail, A. Coghill, c.1750, 12 In.	450.00
Spoon, James I, Apostle, Saints On Stem, 7 1/2 In., Pair	3400.00
Spoon, Mustard, Gold Wash Bowl, London Hallmark, 1934	55.00
Spoon, Salt, Georgian, Hester Bateman, 1782, 3 5/8 In., Pair	170.00
Spoon, Serving, Old English, Henry Skidman, 1807, Pr.	225.00
Spoon, Stuffing, Old English, John Beldon, 1804, 12 In.	485.00
Spoon, Stuffing, Onslow, Thomas & William Chawner, 11 In.	330.00
Spoon, Tea Caddy, Engraved, S. Pemberton, 1808	325.00
Spoon, Tea Caddy, Kings, Thomas Pemberton, 1833, 5 In.	265.00
Sugar Tongs, Plain, William Summer, 1802, 6 In.	195.00
Sweet Creamer, Peter & Ann Bateman	660.00
Tablespoon, Old English, Wm. Bateman, 1836, 9 In.	285.00
Tea & Coffee Set, Gadroon & Shell Border, 1935, 4 Piece	1795.00
Tea Set, George V, London, 1927, 7 1/2–In. Pot, 3 Piece	660.00
Tea Set, Sprays, Leaf Scrolls, C. T. Fox & G. Fox, 1839, 4 Piece	3100.00
Tea Urn, George III, Louisa & Samuel Courtauld, 23 In.	4675.00
Teapot, George III, Heraldic Crests, W. Plummer, 1788	1215.00
Teapot, Hinged Dome, Fluting, Francis Crump, 1765, 12 In.	5800.00
Teapot, Ivory Finial, Anthemion Bands, B. Smith II, 1812	1045.00
Teapot, Stand, Wrigglework, Motto, Henry Chawner, 1793, 7 In.	1550.00
Teaspoon, Fiddle Thread, George Angell, 1864, 5 1/2 In.	50.00

Teaspoon, Fiddle, James Beebe, 1836, 5 1/2 In., 4 Piece 260.00
Toast Rack, Floral & Shell Corners, J. C. Folkard, 1820 .... 335.00
Toast Rack, Joseph Craddock & William Reid 615.00
Tongs, Bright Cut, Hester Bateman, c.1780 .... 250.00
Tongs, Bright Cut, Thomas Wallace & Jonathan Hayne, 1810 .... 185.00
Tray, 4 Ball & Claw Feet, R. Rudd, 1777, 16 x 11 In. 5500.00
Tray, Coat Of Arms, Leaf Scrolls, P. Rundell, 1820, 24 In. 7480.00
Tray, George III, John Eames, 1797 .... 2500.00
Tray, George III, Robert Jones & John Schofield, 1777, 8 In. 445.00
Tray, Shell & Scroll Border, Hugh Mills, 1750, 7 1/2 In. 440.00
Tureen, George III, Cover, Thomas Robin, 1811 .... 8250.00
Tureen, Sauce, Urn Finial, James Young, 1792, 9 In. 4950.00
Vase, King Facing Left Mark, 1784, 6 In. 185.00
Vinaigrette, Enameling, Flask Shape, 1840s, 1 3/4 In. 115.00
SILVER–FRENCH, Basket, Red Enamel Strawberries, Cartier 1760.00
Bell Push, Enameled 1200.00
Bell, Table, Engine–Turned Decoration, 19th Century 132.00
Bowl, Cover, Knop Finial, Bracket Handles, 8 In. 355.00
Box, Cigarette, 2 Hinged Covers, Rope Twist Handle, Cartier 4625.00
Box, Cover, Lapis Lazuli, Round, Cardeilhac, c.1935, 5 1/2 In. 6600.00
Box, Patch, Mask & Floral Repousse, 3 3/4 In. 120.00
Kettle, Hot Water, Stand, Pear Form, 19th Century, 14 1/2 In. 995.00
Pitcher, Baluster Form, Rococo Scrolls, M. Fray, 12 1/2 In. 1980.00
Sauceboat, Helmet Form, Mythical Beast Handle, 1880s, Pair 4950.00
Tea & Coffee Set, Marked H & Cie, c.1930, 4 Piece 1650.00
Tray, Octagonal, Handles, Wooden Inserts, 1940, 21 1/2 In. 3025.00
Wine Taster, Chased Vines, EP In Lozenge, 4 In. 385.00
SILVER–GERMAN, Breast Star, Hessian Order Of Ludwig 1000.00
Breast Star, Saxon Order Of The Rue Crown 800.00
Bun Warmer, 3 Part Globular Form, Bacchus Figure, 9 1/2 In. 2450.00
Candelabrum, 2–Light, Ram's Head Candle Arms, 13 In., Pair 2200.00
Candelabrum, 3–Light, Art Deco, Scrolled Arms, 12 1/4 In., Pr. 3850.00
Candlestick, Engraved, F. Korock, c.1845, 13 3/4 In., Pair 1350.00
Candlestick, Palmetted Molding, 1765, 6 1/2 In., Pair 300.00
Case, Cigarette, Portrait Of Woman On Porcelain Cover, 1902 .... 195.00
Casket, Jewelry, Applied Oak Leaf Branches, Acorns, 3 5/8 In. 715.00
Centerpiece, Coach & Six, 22 In. 1760.00
Cup, Cover, Lion Finial, Coin Inset Lid & Body, 11 In. 715.00
Fruit Basket, Figural & Floral Design, Marked, 19th Century 2200.00
Goblet, Cover, Renaissance Style, 11 In. 247.50
Jewel Casket, Rectangular, Paw Feet, 3 3/16 x 5 x 3 5/8 In. 715.00
Ornament, Pheasant Form, Hinged Wings, 14 1/2 & 12 1/2 In. 3575.00
Salt, Shell–Shaped Bowl, Dolphin Support, 6 In., 4 Piece 355.00
Stirrup Cup, Stags' Heads, Gilt Interior, 5 1/2 In., Pair 1435.00
Tankard, Caryatid Loop Handle, Procession, 1920s, 5 In. 775.00
Tankard, Cover, Scroll Handle, Foliage, 1880s, 10 1/4 In. 1650.00
Tea Set, Art Deco Style, 20th Century, 5 Piece 6900.00
Teapot, Acanthus Border, Serpent Spout, Altona, 6 In. 660.00
Vase, Pierced & Chased Putti, Scrolls, Bottle Form, 17 In. 2200.00
SILVER–INDIAN, Box, Cigar, Cover, Lion With Saber, Peacock Ends, 10 1/2 In. 1650.00
SILVER–IRISH, Spoon, Drain, John Shields, 1768 .... 302.00
Spoon, Serving, George III, John Pittar, 1780, 12 1/4 In. 220.00
Spoon, Stuffing, Shell Terminal, David Peter, 1762, 11 1/2 In. 165.00
Sugar Tongs, Plain, J. Buckton, 1821 .... 295.00
Sugar, Gadroon Border, William Doyle, 1813, 7 3/4 In. 950.00
Tea Set, Fluted Pear Shape, Flowers, Edward Power, 1825, 3 Pc. 1100.00
SILVER–ITALIAN, Tea & Coffee Set, Rococo Foliage, Peruzzi, 5 Piece 1765.00
SILVER–JAPANESE, Case, Cigarette, Scene Of Mt. Fuji, Signed Ikko, Box, 5 In. 120.00
Cocktail Shaker, Applied Dragon, Hammered, M. Yokahama 302.00
Cocktail Shaker, Hammered, 9 In. 175.00
Plate, Samurai Shokai, c.1900, 9 5/8 In., 6 Piece 1760.00
Punch Bowl, Repousse, Meiji Period 6050.00
Tea Set, Chased Dragons, 6 Piece 2420.00

SILVER–MEXICAN, Bowl, Bird Handles, Repousse Flowers, Sanborns, 5 1/2 In. 295.00
Bowl, Eagle, Scalloped Top & Base, 7 In. 375.00
Bowl, Lotus Blossom Shape, 20th Century, 2 3/4 x 6 1/4 In. 110.00
Bowl, Spiral Flutes, Foliage Feet, 3 5/8 In. 60.00
Box, Lift–Off Lid, Egg Shape, DH With Shield, 2 3/8 In. 75.00
Coffeepot, Urn–Type Body, Inverted Acorn Finial, 9 1/2 In. 195.00
Flatware Set, Stylized Scroll, Ebony Insert, Taxco, 62 Piece 6325.00
Knife, Dragon Handle, Handmade 35.00
Sauceboat, Scrolled Rim, 12 1/4 In. 250.00
Sugar & Creamer, Cover, Tray, Taxco, 3 Piece 350.00
Tray, Chased Flower Heads, Vine, Handles, Lilyan, 28 In. 523.00
Tray, Fluted & S–Scroll Border, Handles, Oval, 26 In. 415.00
Tray, Oval, Sanborns, 17 x 12 In. 217.00
Tray, Scalloped Gadrooned Border, Round, 13 In. 625.00
Tray, Sterling, Taxco, 21 x 15 In. 450.00
Whiskey Glass, William Spratling, Pair 150.00
SILVER–PERUVIAN, Candlestick, Octagonal Knopped Form, Pair 110.00
Figurine, Fighting Cock, Vermeil Tail, 14 In., Pair 3975.00
Rooster, Fighting Stance, 6 3/4 In., Pair 467.50

SILVER–RUSSIAN. Russian silver is marked with the Cyrillic, or Russian, alphabet. The numbers 84, 88, or 91 indicate the silver content. Russian silver may be higher or lower than sterling standard. Other marks indicate maker, assayer, or city of manufacture. Many pieces of silver made in Russia are decorated with enamel. Faberge pieces are listed in their own section.

SILVER–RUSSIAN, Beaker, Enameled Stylized Foliage, Khlebnikov, 6 In. 1430.00
Bowl, Pierced Rim, High Handle, c.1908, 6 In. 360.00
Box, Cigar, Trompe l'oeil, c.1910, 6 In. 2475.00
Box, Jewel, Hinged Cover, Foliage Engraved, Werner, 6 1/4 In. 1765.00
Cake Basket, Trompe l'oeil, Basketweave, Postnikov, 12 In. 1870.00
Candelabrum, 4–Light, Scrolling Branches, c.1900, 22 1/2 In. 1980.00
Candlestick, Chased Foliage, S. Szkarlat, 1870, 12 In., Pair 715.00
Candlestick, Foliage, Square Base, Karlin, 13 3/4 In., Pair 885.00
Case, Cigar, Nielo 295.00
Cup, Bird, Tiger Eye & Garnet, 2 x 3 In. 1100.00
Cup, Blue To Green Flowers, Enameled & Vermeil, 3 1/4 In. 1100.00
Cup, Coronation, Czar Nicholas II, 1896 .... 395.00
Cup, Cover, Palmette Rim, Reeded Body, N. Dubrovin, 4 In. 225.00
Cup, Marine Life, Plants, P. Ovchinnikov, 1885, 3 In., 4 Piece 1325.00
Egg, Enameled Floral & Swan, Gilt Borders, 4 1/2 In. 1760.00
Egg, Floral Design, Enameled, Blue & Turquoise, 4 1/2 In. 2200.00
Egg, Floral, Enameled, Gold Washed Interior, 5 1/2 In. 2750.00
Egg, Floriform Design, Enameled, Vermeil, 4 1/4 In. 1980.00
Figurine, Seated Bulldog, Inlaid Eyes, Marked 770.00
Frame, Enameled & Vermeil, 1892, 5 1/2 x 4 1/2 In. 550.00
Kovsh, Enameled Foliage, Stippled, M. Semyonova, 5 3/4 In. 3190.00

Silver-Russian, Stirrup Cup, Fox Head,
S. Arndt, c.1850
Silver-Russian, Stirrup Cup, Hound Head,
c.1859

To remove lacquer from a piece of silver, immerse the piece in very hot water for a few hours. This should loosen the lacquer. The process may have to be repeated to get all of the lacquer. There are several commercial lacquer removers.

Kovsh, Imperial Eagle, Green, Enameled, Agafonov, 9 3/4 In. 7700.00
Kovsh, Lapis Lazuli, Agafon Faberge, 19th Century, 6 1/2 In. 3850.00
Kovsh, Shaded Enameled Flower Scrolling, 9 1/2 In. 4400.00
Samovar, Barrel Shape, Ivory Handles & Tap, Heinoin, 15 In. 5775.00
Spoon, Blue & Ruby, Enameled, Vermeil, 7 3/4 In., Pair 880.00
Spoon, Caviar, Enameled, Box, 6 Piece 1800.00
Spoon, Serving, Polychrome Enamel, 7 15/16 In. 440.00
Stirrup Cup, Fox Head, S. Arndt, 1850, 4 3/4 In. 4125.00
Stirrup Cup, Fox Head, S. Arndt, c.1850 ....*Illus* 4125.00
Stirrup Cup, Hound's Head, c.1859 ....*Illus* 4400.00
Sugar Sifter, Enamel Trim, Anton Kuzmichev 750.00
Tankard, Repousse, Scrolling, Chased Ground, Sazikov, 10 In. 2750.00
Teapot, Enameled Foliage Bands, Lubavin, Globular, 4 1/4 In. 1325.00
Tray, Applied Dragonfly, P. Ovchinnikov, 1885, 13 In. 2100.00
SILVER–SCOTTISH, Bowl, William IV, Hunt Scene, L. Urouhart, 1835, 9 In. 2550.00
Cup, Cover, Urn Finial, High Handles, M & F, 12 1/2 In. 550.00

SILVER–STERLING. Sterling silver is made with 925 parts silver out of
1,000 parts of metal. The word *sterling* is a quality guarantee used in the
United States after about 1860. The word was used much earlier in
England and Ireland. Pieces listed here are not identified by country. Other
pieces of sterling quality silver are listed under Silver–American, Silver–
English, etc.

SILVER–STERLING, Basket, Filled, Enamel Strawberries, White Flowers, Cartier 1750.00
Berry Spoon, Rococo Foliage Detail, 9 In. 40.00
Bib Clip, Figural, Clothespins, Pair 32.00
Bowl, Cast Floral Designs On Rim, Footed, 4 7/8 In. 400.00
Bowl, Chased Roses, Fluted Interior, Woodside, 11 In. 522.50
Bowl, Circular Form, 3 Scroll Feet, Arms, 5 3/4 In. 990.00
Bowl, Engraved Rim, 2 In. 195.00
Bowl, Foliate Barbed Rim, Crest, 10 In. 330.00
Bowl, Footed, Paneled, Scalloped Rim, 3 3/4 In. 145.00
Bowl, Fruit, Overlay, Fruits, Leaves, Elliptical, 11 1/2 In. 150.00
Bowl, Fruit, Round Form, Chased Poppy Rim, 11 In. 600.00
Bowl, Reticulated Rim, Gadroon, 2 1/4 In. 150.00
Brush & Mirror Set, Embossed 145.00
Brush, Baby's, Engraved 30.00
Butter, Cover, Cow Finial, Pierced Insert, 1860, 10 1/2 In. 715.00
Buttonhook, Sitting Teddy Bear 85.00
Case, Card, Engraved Crest, Blue Enamel Lines 170.00
Case, Card, Envelope Form, Postage, Address, 3 1/8 In. 385.00
Case, Cigarette, Engraved Butterflies & Flowers 250.00
Case, Cigarette, Pierced Body, W. G. De Matteo, 1958 .... 55.00
Caster, Chrysanthemum, Monogrammed, 5 1/2 In. 1100.00
Coffee & Tea Set, Chantilly, Kettle On Stand, 1900, 6 Piece 4400.00
Coffee & Tea Set, Samovar, Tray, R. Denfert, 1920s, 5 Piece 3800.00
Comb, Raised Border, Victorian, Marked 195.00
Compote, Boat Shape, Engraved K, 5 In. 85.00
Compote, Reeded Rim, Hammered Finish, Karl Leinonen, 5 In. 225.00
Compote, Reticulated, Engraved Rim, 3 1/2 In. 70.00
Dish, Feeding, Baby's, Tom, Tom The Piper's Son 55.00
Dish, Fluted Rim, 6 1/8 In. 35.00
Dish, Sweetmeat, 7 3/4 In., Pair 270.00
Dish, Vegetable, Cover, Monogram, Oval, 12 1/2 In. 900.00
Dispenser, Cigarette, Rand & Crane, Dated Feb. 11, 1915 .... 250.00
Dresser Set, Mirror, Brush, Comb, Dated 1921 .... 150.00
Figurine, Gamecock, Marked 925, 4 1/4 In., Pair 585.00
Frame, Double Heart, 3 In. 125.00
Gravy Boat, Neoclassical, Fluting, 3 3/4 In. 75.00
Knife Set, Fish, Cluny, Bright Work Blades, 8 Piece 1000.00
Ladle, Punch, Fancy Bowl, Monogrammed D 195.00
Loud Hailer, Trumpet Form, Gilt Mouthpiece, 1856, 22 In. 2650.00
Mustard, Hinged Cover, Cranberry Glass Insert, Spoon 215.00

Pitcher, Madam D'Almay, 5 1/2 Pt. 688.00
Place Card Holders, Monogrammed MCM, Original Box, 12 Pc. 325.00
Plate, Engraved Design, Handle, 10 3/4 In. 65.00
Platter, Gadrooned Border, Oval, U.S. 2000.00
Porringer, Cabochon On Wirework Handles, 1901, 11 1/2 In. 5500.00
Porringer, Monogram, 4 In. 65.00
Porringer, Swept Wirework Leaf Handle, 1907, 6 In. 1320.00
Punch Ladle, Grande Baroque 275.00
Rattle, Doll's, Whistle Tip, 5 Hanging Silver Bells 550.00
Salt & Pepper, Barrel Shape 75.00
Salt & Pepper, Beaded Lid & Base 20.00
Salt, Viking Ship 45.00
Seal, Initial S, Porcelain Handle, Hallmark 30.00
Smoke Set, Box, 6 Matchbox Covers, 6 Ashtrays, Cartier 350.00
Spoon, Baby's, Cock Robin Verse 50.00
Spoon, Feeding, Child's, Mother Goose 65.00
Spoon, Feeding, Child's, Prelude 45.00
Spoon, Souvenir, see Souvenir category
Tea Set, Plymouth, Hot Water Kettle, Ebony Finials, 7 Piece 3200.00
Tea Strainer, Carved Ivory Handle, 4 1/2 In. 495.00
Tea Urn, Ovoid Body, Ebonized Wood Handles, 15 3/4 In. 3575.00
Vase, Diving Dolphin Handles, Minerva, c.1890, 25 In. 6600.00
Vase, Trumpet Form, Chrysanthemums, Wavy Mouth, 24 In. 4125.00
Vase, Trumpet, 12 In. 80.00
Vase, Trumpet, Engraved and Reticulated Bowl, 22 In. 750.00
Vase, Trumpet, Lion, Unicorn, Initials, 25 In. 100.00
SILVER–SWEDISH, Punch Ladle, Fruitwood Handle, L. Lundstrom, 15 In. 385.00

SINCLAIRE cut glass was made by H. P. Sinclaire and Company of
Corning, New York, between 1905 and 1929. He cut glass made at other
factories until 1920. Pieces were made of crystal as well as amber, blue,
green, or ruby glass. Only a small percentage of Sinclaire glass is marked
with the S in a wreath.

Bowl, Cross Miter & Hobstar, Signed, 2 3/4 x 9 1/4 In. 165.00
Bowl, Intaglio Fish, Swirling Waters, Signed, 9 1/2 In. 550.00
Candlestick, Etched Floral Base, Prisms, Marked, 9 In., Pair 150.00
Candlestick, Etched Floral, Green, Signed, 3 In., Pair 175.00
Candlestick, Twisted Stem, Amber, Numbered, 12 In., Pair 192.00
Clock, Beehive, Silver Threads Medallion & Diamond, Signed 5000.00
Clock, Mantel, Adam No. 2, Medallion & Diamond, 10 x 9 In. 2410.00
Jug, Basketball Shape, Bengal, Silver Lock Top, 13 In. 5000.00
Sugar & Creamer, Etched Floral Design 160.00
Tray, Sandwich, Silver Thread, 4 Flower Medallions, Signed, 10 In. 850.00
Vase, Stars & Pillars, Hobstar Bottom, Signed, 12 In., Pair 5400.00

SLAG GLASS resembles a marble cake. It can be streaked with different
colors. There were many types made from about 1880. Pink slag was an
American Victorian product of unknown origin. Purple and blue slag were
made in American and English factories. Red slag is a very late Victorian
and twentieth–century glass. Other colors are known but are of less
importance to the collector. New versions of chocolate glass and colored
slag glass are being made.

Caramel slag is listed in the Chocolate Glass category
Green & Pink, Shade, Tulip Shape, 6 Piece 300.00
Green, Lighter, Cigarette, Art Deco 68.00
Green, Match Holder 85.00
Pink, Berry Bowl, Inverted Fan & Feather 235.00
Pink, Berry Set, Inverted Fan & Feather, 7 Piece 1345.00
Pink, Compote, Jelly, Inverted Fan & Feather 685.00
Pink, Saucer, Inverted Fan & Feather 235.00
Pink, Toothpick, Inverted Fan & Feather 775.00
Pink, Tumbler, Inverted Fan & Feather .... 280.00 To 350.00
Purple, Basket, Flower Design, 10 In. 70.00

Purple, Candlestick, Bulbous Base, 2 In. 45.00
Purple, Compote, Jelly, Ribbed 65.00
Purple, Dish, Cow Cover, Basketweave Base, 5 1/2 In. 50.00
Purple, Dish, Ducks On Nest Cover, Imperial 45.00
Purple, Dish, Hen, Dancing Sailor Base 85.00
Purple, Figurine, Shoe, Victorian, Diamond-Shaped Base, 1880, 6 1/2 In. 225.00
Purple, Lamb, Basketweave Base, 5 1/2 In. 50.00
Purple, Match Holder 40.00
Purple, Mug, Child's, Rabbit 35.00
Purple, Mustard Jar, Bull's Head 65.00
Purple, Nappy, Challinor, Majestic Crown, Pair 120.00
Purple, Platter, Tam O' Shanter 135.00
Purple, Toothpick, Inverted Fan & Feather 65.00
Purple, Toothpick, Ring Handle 47.50
Red, Pitcher, Imperial 45.00
Red, Toothpick, Cornucopia 25.00

SLEEPY EYE collectors look for anything bearing the image of the
nineteenth-century Indian chief with the drooping eyelid. The Sleepy Eye
Milling Co., Sleepy Eye, Minnesota, used his portrait in advertising from
1883 to 1921. It offered many premiums, including stoneware and pottery
steins, crocks, bowls, mugs, and pitchers, all decorated with the famous
profile of the Indian. The popular pottery was made by Western Stoneware
and other companies long after the flour mill went out of business in 1921.
Reproductions of the pitchers are being made today. The original pitchers
came in only five sizes: 4 inches, 5 1/4 inches, 6 1/2 inches, 8 inches, and
9 inches. The Sleepy Eye image was also used by companies unrelated to
the flour mill.

Blotter, Framed 20.00
Butter Carton .... 10.00 To 32.50
Butter Crock .... 425.00 To 650.00
Cigar Box .... 650.00 To 1000.00
Cookbook, Loaf Of Bread .... 75.00 To 140.00
Creamer 150.00
Fan .... 100.00 To 195.00
Flour Sack .... 49.00 To 100.00
Label, Barrel, Chief 150.00
Label, Barrel, Cream 190.00
Label, Eggcrate 25.00
Matchholder, Chalkware 525.00
Mug, 4 3/4 In. 145.00
Mug, Blue On Gray, 4 3/4 In. .... 210.00 To 350.00
Mug, Brown, 1952 .... 150.00 To 250.00
Mug, Commemorative, 1976 .... 130.00
Mug, Commemorative, 1977 .... 100.00
Mug, With Verse, Red Wing 1500.00
Paperweight, Bronze 210.00
Pin, Membership, Blue & White 15.00
Pitcher, 5 1/4 In. 195.00
Pitcher, No. 1, Blue On Gray 180.00
Pitcher, No. 1, Blue On White .... 85.00 To 200.00
Pitcher, No. 2, Blue On Gray 230.00
Pitcher, No. 2, Blue On White .... 125.00 To 300.00
Pitcher, No. 3, Blue On Gray .... 110.00 To 450.00
Pitcher, No. 3, Blue On White .... 110.00 To 375.00
Pitcher, No. 4, Blue On Gray 290.00
Pitcher, No. 4, Blue On White .... 100.00 To 290.00
Pitcher, No. 4, Green 800.00
Pitcher, No. 5, Blue On Gray .... 225.00 To 310.00
Pitcher, No. 5, Blue On White .... 220.00 To 225.00
Plaque, 1972 .... 10.00
Plate, Commemorative, 1978 .... 22.50
Plate, Commemorative, 1984 .... 15.00

Plate, Commemorative, 1987	20.00
Postcard Set, 9 Piece	760.00
Salt Crock	240.00 To 425.00
Spoon, Demitasse	65.00 To 120.00
Stein, Blue On Gray	400.00
Stein, Blue On White	360.00
Stein, Blue On White, Kohler & Heinrichs Advertising	685.00
Stein, Board Of Directors	85.00 To 165.00
Stein, Brown On White	375.00
Stein, Brown On Yellow	800.00
Stein, Green On White	1500.00
Sugar, Blue On White	420.00 To 550.00
Vase, Blue On Gray, 8 1/2 In.	155.00
Vase, Brown	600.00
Vase, Brown On Yellow	750.00 To 850.00
Vase, Green	3100.00

SLIPWARE is named for *slip,* a thin mixture of clay and water, about the consistency of sour cream, which is applied to pottery for decoration. It is a very old method of making pottery and is still in use.

Mug, Design, Hand Made, Western Germany, 4 1/2 In.	15.00

SLOT MACHINES are included in the Coin–Operated Machine category.

SMITH BROTHERS glass was made after 1878. Alfred and Harry Smith had worked for the Mt. Washington Glass Company in New Bedford, Massachusetts, for seven years before going into their own shop. They made many pieces with enamel decoration.

Smith Bros. Co.

Bowl, Autumn Leaves, Acorn, Silver Plated Rim, 8 1/2 In.	375.00
Bowl, Daisies, Melon Rib, Plated Rim, Signed, 10 1/2 In.	475.00
Bowl, Flowers, Marked, World's Fair, 1893, 5 In.	295.00
Bowl, Maidenhair Fern, Melon Ribbed, Signed, 9 In.	325.00
Bowl, Oak Leaves, Acorns, Gold Outline, Marked, 8 3/4 In.	550.00
Bowl, Yellow Daisies, Blue Ground, Melon Ribbed, 4 1/4 In.	265.00
Cracker Jar, Pansies, Ribbed	400.00 To 475.00
Cracker Jar, Shasta Daisies & Leaves, Tan Ground, Signed	845.00
Creamer, Daisies	300.00
Lamp, Oil, Student, Brass, Shade	475.00
Powder Box, Cover, Gold Iris Blossoms, Melon Ribbed, 4 In.	335.00
Rose Bowl, Daisies, Signed, 4 In.	295.00
Rose Bowl, Pansies, Cream Ground, Marked, 4 1/4 In.	310.00
Salt, Gold Florals, Beaded Rim, Melon Ribbed, Signed	110.00
Sugar & Creamer, Bulbous Segments, Gilt Beading, 4 In.	360.00
Syrup, Rampant Lion, Cream Ground, Gold Tracery Blossoms	495.00
Vase, Bowl Type, Florals, Creamy Beige, 4 x 3 In.	350.00
Vase, Enameled Daisies, Swirl Mold, Marked, 7 In.	565.00
Vase, Lavender Wisteria, Gold Tracery, Double Pilgrim, 7 In.	1220.00
Vase, Violets, Beaded Rim, Marked, 4 1/2 In.	395.00

SNOW BABIES, made from bisque and spattered with glitter sand, were first manufactured in 1864 by Hertwig and Company of Thuringia. Other German and Japanese companies copied the Hertwig designs. Originally, Snow Babies were made of candy and used as Christmas decorations. There are also Snow Babies tablewares made by Royal Bayreuth. Copies of the small Snow Babies figurines are being made today and can easily confuse the collector.

Cheese Dish, Cover, Hunting, Blue Mark	58.00
Figurine, 2 On Cardboard Toboggan	100.00
Figurine, Blue Boy & Girl Pushing Large Snowball, 5 In.	650.00
Figurine, Holding Stick, 1 1/2 In.	80.00
Figurine, Outstretched Arms, 2 1/2 In.	125.00
Figurine, Sitting On Sled, 2 1/2 In.	100.00
Figurine, Snowball, Germany, 2 In.	75.00

Soapstone, Match Holder,

Buds & Vines, 2 1/2 x 4 In.

◆◆◆◆◆◆◆◆◆◆◆◆◆◆◆◆◆◆◆◆◆◆

When framing a charcoal or
pastel drawing, avoid plastic;
use real glass. The plastic will
pick up static electricity and
actually pull the charcoal or
pastel dust off the paper.

◆◆◆◆◆◆◆◆◆◆◆◆◆◆◆◆◆◆◆◆◆◆

Mug, Child's, Sledding, Blue Mark 80.00
Plate, 1 Sliding, Other Standing, Royal Bayreuth, 8 In. 125.00

SNUFF BOTTLES are listed in the Bottle section.

SNUFFBOXES held snuff. Taking snuff was popular long before cigarettes
became available. The gentleman or lady would take a small pinch of the
ground tobacco or snuff in the fingers, then sniff it and sneeze. Snuffboxes
were made of many materials, including gold, silver, enameled metal, and
wood. Most snuffboxes date from the late eighteenth or early nineteenth
centuries.

Bird On Cover, Applied Goldfish, Snails & Quail, 2 x 2 1/2 In. 135.00
Bloodstone, Gold Mounted, Shellwork & Floral Cover, 1765, 3 In. 5500.00
Brass & Scrimshaw, Geometrics & Stars 1265.00
Bright Cut Design, Scrolling Foliate, France, c.1850, 3 1/8 In. 125.00
Burl & Tortoiseshell, Tooled Lid, Round, 3 1/2 In. 125.00
Cardboard Gilt Paper, Reverse Glass Transfer, Garden, 5 1/2 In. 75.00
Carved Agate Cameo Cover, Silver Gilt, England, 3 1/4 In. 2640.00
Gold & Enamel, Cover, John Angell, 1825, 3 In. 5225.00
Gold & Enamel, Flower Sprays, Switzerland, 1830, 3 In. 7425.00
Gold, Enamel & Jewels, Red Over Guilloche Ground, 3 3/8 In. 3575.00
Gold, Enamel, Cut Corners, Reserve, Switzerland, 1800, 4 In. 4950.00
Gold, Scroll Vine Borders, Plaque Cover, Paris, 1803-1909, 2 In. 1650.00
Inlaid Mother-of-Pearl Design On Cover, 2 1/2 In. 65.00
Iron Cross Cover, Gun Metal Finish, World War I, Square, 2 In. 47.00
Mahogany, Hand Painted Castle, 19th Century, 2 1/2 x 4 1/2 In. 245.00
Marbelized Paper, Reverse Glass Transfer, Landscape, Mirror Lid 45.00
Milk Glass, Blue Landscape Design, Round, 1 3/8 x 2 In. 95.00
Papier-Mache, Maidens & Cupid Scene, Pornographic Base, 3 1/2 In. 135.00
Papier-Mache, Shoe, Black Lacquer, Floral Pearl, Wire Inlay, 5 In. 95.00
Reeded Lid & Base, Allover Gold Wash, MK, Vienna, c.1880, 3 3/8 In. 200.00
Scottish Horn, Brass Fittings, 3 In. 200.00
Shell, Gold Washed Boy, Sterling Closure 200.00
Silver & Niello, Courting Couples, Russia, 1780, 4 1/8 In. 4450.00
Silver-Gilt, Shaded Enameled, Domed Cover, Russia, 2 7/8 In. 1200.00
Sterling, Allover Gold Washed, Overall Design, J. Wilmore, 1825 .... 395.00
Tortoiseshell & Sterling Silver 195.00
Tortoiseshell, Alibert, Plays 2 Tunes 2700.00

SOAPSTONE is a mineral that was used for foot warmers or griddles
because of its heat-retaining properties. Soapstone was carved into figurines
and bowls in many countries in the nineteenth and twentieth centuries.
Most of the soapstone seen today is from China or Japan. It is still being
carved in the old styles.

Figurine, Beauty With Tray, Oriental Girl, Arms Raised, 13 In. 95.00
Figurine, Bird In Flowering Tree, 6 3/4 In. 45.00
Figurine, Foo Dog, 8 In., Pair 110.00

Match Holder, Buds & Vines, 2 1/2 x 4 In. ....*Illus* 50.00
Teapot, Chicken Finial, Rooster, Tail Forms Handle, Head Is Spout 45.00
Vase, Carved Rose & Cream, 9 In. 90.00

SOFT PASTE is a name for a type of pottery. Although it looks very much like porcelain, it is a chemically different material. Most of the soft paste wares were made in the early nineteenth century. Other pieces may be listed under Gaudy Dutch or Leeds.

Basket, Fruit, Underplate, Staffordshire, 1820s, 12 x 8 1/2 In. 1200.00
Creamer, King's Rose, Vine Border, 4 In. 85.00
Cup & Saucer, Handleless, Floral Enameling 45.00
Cup & Saucer, Handleless, King's Rose, Pink Border 140.00
Pitcher, Scenic, Strawberry Luster, 7 1/2 In. 175.00
Pot, Gaudy Floral, 4 Colors, 10 5/8 In. 125.00
Teapot, Gaudy Floral, 5 Colors, 8 1/2 In. 200.00
Teapot, King's Rose, Vine Border, 6 1/4 In. 85.00
Vase, Finger, Floral, 4 Colors, 7 1/2 In. 275.00

SOUVENIRS of a trip—what could be more fun? Our ancestors enjoyed the same thing and souvenirs were made for almost every location. Most of the souvenir pottery and porcelain pieces of the nineteenth century were made in England or Germany, even if the picture showed a North American scene. In the twentieth century, the souvenir china business seems to have gone to the manufacturers in Japan, Taiwan, Hong Kong, England, and America. Another popular souvenir item is the souvenir spoon, made of sterling or silver plate. These are usually made in the country pictured on the spoon. Related pieces may be found in the Coronation and World's Fair categories.

Ashtray, Figural, Rex, Mardi Gras, Metal, 1908 ...... 65.00
Ashtray, Horse Racing, Driver, Metal, Cornwall Wood Prod., 11 In. 165.00
Bowl, Green, Catalina Island, 15 In. 75.00
Bread Plate, U.S.S. Maine, Blue Ship, Steubenville 21.00
Buckle, American Motorcycle Association Tour, 1959 ...... 35.00
Button, Horseman, Kansas State Fair, 1943 ...... 37.50
Button, With Ribbon, Colorado State Fair, 1930s 37.50
Creamer, Knickered Golfer Putting, Whitfield Club, 2 In. 50.00
Cup, Rome City, Ruby Stained 11.00
Figurine, Statue Of Liberty, Cast Metal, 8 In. 35.00
Figurine, Statue Of Liberty, Centennial, Benedictine, 10 In. 40.00
Handbill, Our Boys, Chestnut St. Theater, Silk, 1876 ...... 75.00
Loving Cup, Hamburg, Minn., Green Glass, 3 3/4 In. 25.00
Mug, Battle Creek, Mich., Ruby Stained 7.00
Mug, Knights Of Labor, Glass 35.00
Nappy, Glens Falls, N.Y. 40.00
Piano, Liberace's, Radisson Hotel, Minn., Autograph, 1948, Miniature 50.00
Pillow Cover, Olympics, 1932, Los Angeles 65.00
Pin, Sonja Henie, Hollywood Ice Revue, Chicago Stadium, Plastic 125.00
Pin, Welcome Back To Earth Glenn, Col. Glenn Picture, 1 3/4 In. 8.00
Pitcher, Scene Of Flagstaff Park, Roses, Krystol, 7 1/2 In. 38.50
Plate, Carriage Builders National Assoc., Metal, 1906, 10 In. 75.00
Plate, Lewis & Clark Expo, 1905 ...... 38.00
Ribbon, Silk Flag, Women's Relief Corps, 1890s 30.00
Ring Band, Toothpick, Custard Glass, Terre Haute, Ind., Heisey 50.00
Spoon, Gold, Detroit City Seal In Bowl, Coat Of Arms On Handle 135.00
Spoon, Knotts Berry Farm, Demitasse 12.00
Spoon, Sterling Silver, Aerial Bridge, Duluth, Minn., Emblem Bowl 27.00
Spoon, Sterling Silver, Alamo, Texas 20.00
Spoon, Sterling Silver, Alaska, Totem Pole 40.00
Spoon, Sterling Silver, Andrew Jackson, Bust, Hermitage In Bowl 95.00
Spoon, Sterling Silver, Aspen, Skier On Handle 22.00
Spoon, Sterling Silver, Atlantic City, Emblem In Bowl 40.00
Spoon, Sterling Silver, Bloomfield, La., H. S. Engraved In Bowl 27.00
Spoon, Sterling Silver, California Mission, San Diego 20.00

Spoon, Sterling Silver, California, Cutout Flower Handle	28.00
Spoon, Sterling Silver, Canada, Niagara Falls Bowl	22.00
Spoon, Sterling Silver, Carnegie Library, Pitts., Enameled Bowl	181.00
Spoon, Sterling Silver, Centralia, Washington, Miner's Handle	30.00
Spoon, Sterling Silver, Chicago, Cutout Handle	35.00
Spoon, Sterling Silver, Chicago, Engraved Flower Handle	27.00
Spoon, Sterling Silver, Chicago, Masonic Cityscape Handle	65.00
Spoon, Sterling Silver, Chillicothe, Mo., Engraved In Bowl	27.00
Spoon, Sterling Silver, Clear Lake, South Dakota	20.00
Spoon, Sterling Silver, Colorado, Cupid Handle	45.00
Spoon, Sterling Silver, Colorado, Cutout Flower Handle	28.00
Spoon, Sterling Silver, Colorado, Rifle, Gold Engraved	28.00
Spoon, Sterling Silver, Columbia Anniversary, Ship, 1492-1892	60.00
Spoon, Sterling Silver, Columbus, Ind., Gold Engraved In Bowl	27.00
Spoon, Sterling Silver, Congregational Church, Courtland, Kansas	20.00
Spoon, Sterling Silver, Congregational Church, Iowa Falls	30.00
Spoon, Sterling Silver, Connor Hotel, Joplin, Missouri	25.00
Spoon, Sterling Silver, Cowboy & Indian, Engraved Bowl	75.00
Spoon, Sterling Silver, Deadwood, S. D., Stagecoach, Twisted Stem	70.00
Spoon, Sterling Silver, Denver & Mule In Gold Bowl	22.00
Spoon, Sterling Silver, Elgin Watch Factory, Elgin, Ill.	50.00
Spoon, Sterling Silver, Eureka, Kansas	25.00
Spoon, Sterling Silver, Fort Ticonderoga, N.Y., Ethan Allen	35.00
Spoon, Sterling Silver, George Washington's Death, 1899	30.00
Spoon, Sterling Silver, George Washington, Whitman Memorial Bldg.	25.00
Spoon, Sterling Silver, Goldfield, Nevada, Miner, Engraved Bowl	160.00
Spoon, Sterling Silver, Golfer, New Milford, Penna.	80.00
Spoon, Sterling Silver, Grand Rapids Courthouse, 1900	22.00
Spoon, Sterling Silver, Green Bay, Gold Engraved Bowl	27.00
Spoon, Sterling Silver, Hannover, Germany, Enameled Bowl	76.00
Spoon, Sterling Silver, Henry Hudson Ship, Half Moon, Emblem Bowl	55.00
Spoon, Sterling Silver, Illinois State Prison, Cutout Corn Handle	110.00
Spoon, Sterling Silver, Kansas City, Stockyards	40.00
Spoon, Sterling Silver, La Jolla, Cutout Cave On Handle	28.00
Spoon, Sterling Silver, Lachine Rapids	25.00
Spoon, Sterling Silver, Lake George, N.Y., Inscribed In Bowl	45.00
Spoon, Sterling Silver, Lead, S. D., Miner On Pile Of Nuggets	30.00
Spoon, Sterling Silver, Longfellow's Home, Portland, Me.	35.00
Spoon, Sterling Silver, Los Angeles, Stork	40.00
Spoon, Sterling Silver, Minnehaha Falls	65.00
Spoon, Sterling Silver, Missouri State Capital	20.00
Spoon, Sterling Silver, Monmouth, Ill., Gold In Handle, Pat. 1898	27.00
Spoon, Sterling Silver, Mormon Temple, Engraved Bowl	5.00
Spoon, Sterling Silver, Mt. Hood, Oregon	35.00
Spoon, Sterling Silver, Munchen Maid, Plain Bowl	30.00
Spoon, Sterling Silver, Nebraska, Custer Courthouse	35.00
Spoon, Sterling Silver, New Mexico, Cutout Pueblo Women On Handle	47.00
Spoon, Sterling Silver, New York Skyline	65.00
Spoon, Sterling Silver, Niagara Falls, N.Y.	22.00
Spoon, Sterling Silver, Oklahoma, Eagle, Indians	35.00
Spoon, Sterling Silver, Omaha, Cutout Indian On Handle	28.00
Spoon, Sterling Silver, Paul Revere, Statehouse Emblem Bowl	47.00
Spoon, Sterling Silver, Pomona, California, High School	20.00
Spoon, Sterling Silver, Portland, Indian Head, Coin On Handle	45.00
Spoon, Sterling Silver, Portland, Longfellow, Engraved Bowl	75.00
Spoon, Sterling Silver, Public School, Oregon, Ill., Engraved Bowl	12.00
Spoon, Sterling Silver, Recuerdo De Mexico State, Emblem In Bowl	10.00
Spoon, Sterling Silver, San Diego, 1769 Mission, Cutout	28.00
Spoon, Sterling Silver, Saratoga, Engraved Bowl	13.00
Spoon, Sterling Silver, Saugatuck, Michigan	20.00
Spoon, Sterling Silver, Seattle, Totem Pole On Handle	30.00
Spoon, Sterling Silver, Seattle, Wash., Washington Handle, Enameled	59.00
Spoon, Sterling Silver, Simpson College Chapel, Iowa, Emblem Bowl	27.00

Spoon, Sterling Silver, Soldiers & Sailors Monument, Cleve., Oh. 35.00
Spoon, Sterling Silver, South Dakota, Buffalo, Indian With Shield 40.00
Spoon, Sterling Silver, Stanford University, Girl Graduate Handle 85.00
Spoon, Sterling Silver, Statue Of Liberty 86.00
Spoon, Sterling Silver, Teddy Roosevelt, Man & Horse 55.00
Spoon, Sterling Silver, Terre Haute, Indiana, St. Mary's 20.00
Spoon, Sterling Silver, Van Vleet Mansfield Drug Co., Memphis 25.00
Spoon, Sterling Silver, Wagner Theater, Bayreuth 28.00
Spoon, Sterling Silver, Walla Walla, Wash., Indian, Engraved Bowl 55.00
Spoon, Sterling Silver, Washington, D.C., Emblem In Bowl 28.00
Spoon, Sterling Silver, Washington, Emblem Bowl 125.00
Spoon, Sterling Silver, Washington, Mt. Vernon, Gold Wash 25.00
Spoon, Sterling Silver, West Virginia Hospital For Insane 32.00
Spoon, Sterling Silver, Wichita, Kansas, Post Office 20.00
Spoon, Sterling Silver, Witch Hunt, Bonbon, Pierced Bowl 300.00
Spoon, Sterling Silver, Wyoming, Bronco Bowl 35.00
Swizzle Stick, Roosevelt Hotel, New Orleans, Cobalt Blue Glass 15.00
Tape Measure, Rockefeller Center 25.00
Token, Kansas State Sales Tax, Zinc .... .50
Toothpick, Amboy, Minnesota, Marigold Carnival Glass 45.00
Toothpick, Cedar Point, Stained Glass, 1907 .... 3.00
Toothpick, Ring Band, Old Orchard, Me., Custard Glass, Gold, Heisey 65.00
Tray, Greatest Show On Earth, Circus Scene, Tin, Paramount, 1952 .... 69.00
Tumbler, Custard, Northwest Bottling, Iowa Falls, Heisey 50.00
Tumbler, Indy 500, Lists '47 To '51 Winners, 4 1/2 In., 7 Piece 50.00
Tumbler, Yellowstone, Old English Script, 4 1/4 In. 18.50
Vase, Courthouse, Columbia City, Ind., Custard Glass 32.50
Vase, Old Hancock House, Hanover, Pa., Germany 20.00
Whiskey Glass, Fairmont Confectionery, Horizontally Etched 11.50
Whiskey Glass, Niagara Falls, On Frosted Pennant, Etched, Large 15.00

SPANGLE GLASS is multicolored glass made from odds and ends of
colored glass rods. It includes metallic flakes of mica covered with gold,
silver, nickel, or copper. Spangle glass is usually cased with a thin layer of
clear glass over the multicolored layer. Similar glass is listed in the Vasa
Murrhina section.

Bowl, Mica Flakes, White Interior, Stand, 7 x 16 In. 450.00
Castor, Pickle, Apricot 325.00
Ewer, Silver On White, Crimped Handle, 9 1/2 In. 155.00
Pitcher, Optic Ribbing, Pebbled Texture, Amber Handle, 8 In. 345.00

SPANISH LACE is a type of Victorian glass that has a white lace design.
Blue, yellow, cranberry, or clear glass was made with this distinctive white
pattern. It was made in England and the United States after 1885. Copies
are being made.

Castor, Pickle, Apple Blossom Mold, Cranberry, 9 1/2 In. 425.00
Celery Vase, Vaseline 95.00
Finger Bowl, Cranberry 75.00
Lamp, Silver Filigree, Miniature 125.00
Lemonade Set, Ruffled Rim, Clear & White, 4 Piece 195.00
Pitcher, Cranberry Opalescent 1000.00
Pitcher, Water, Blue 225.00
Spooner, Blue Opalescent, Ruffled 110.00
Syrup, Opalescent Blue 310.00
Vase, Cranberry 165.00

SPATTER GLASS is a multicolored glass made from many small pieces of
different colored glass. It is sometimes called *End–Of–Day* glass. It is still
being made.

Basket, Pointed Edge, Gold & Pink, Thorn Handle, 7 3/4 In. 145.00
Cracker Jar, Cranberry, Dark Amber & White Predominant 110.00
Pitcher, Embossed Basketweave & Rib, Pink & White, 9 3/4 In. 145.00
Pitcher, Inverted Thumbprint, Maroon & White 125.00

Rolling Pin, Original Cork 70.00
Vase, Jack–In–The–Pulpit, Maroon & White, 11 In. 95.00

SPATTERWARE is the creamware or soft paste dinnerware decorated with colored spatter designs. The earliest pieces were made in the late eighteenth century, but most of the spatterware found today was made from about 1800 to 1850, or it is a form of kitchen crockery with added spatter designs made in the late nineteenth– and twentieth–century. The early spatterware was made in the Staffordshire district of England for sale in America. The later kitchen type is an American product.

Bowl, Blue & White, 6 In. 95.00
Bowl, Peafowl, Blue, 5 1/2 In. 55.00
Coffeepot, Blue Peafowl 900.00
Creamer, Blue 450.00
Creamer, Blue Paneled, Rose, 5 1/2 In. 275.00
Creamer, Brown Paneled, Blue Flower, 5 3/4 In. 200.00
Creamer, Columbine, Rosebud, Thistle, Green, 3 1/2 In. 150.00
Creamer, Leaf Embossed Handle Ends, Red & Green, 3 1/2 In. 325.00
Creamer, Paneled, Red Rose, Blue, 5 3/4 In. 270.00
Creamer, Rainbow, Blue & Green, Crazed, 4 1/2 In. 625.00
Creamer, Violet–Type Flower, Green, Border Stripe, 4 1/4 In. 70.00
Cup & Saucer, Blue Sponge 60.00
Cup & Saucer, Blue, Red & Green, Adams 300.00
Cup & Saucer, Handleless, Black Pattern, Green, Red 150.00
Cup & Saucer, Handleless, Clover Flower 135.00
Cup & Saucer, Handleless, Flower, Miniature 75.00
Cup & Saucer, Handleless, Fort, Black Green, Red 175.00
Cup & Saucer, Handleless, Fort, Blue, Miniature 550.00
Cup & Saucer, Handleless, Memorial Tulip, Blue 175.00
Cup & Saucer, Handleless, Peafowl, Blue 245.00
Cup & Saucer, Handleless, Red & Blue Rainbow, Miniature 375.00
Cup & Saucer, Handleless, Red, Blue & Green Stripes 475.00
Cup & Saucer, Handleless, Rooster, Purple 650.00
Cup & Saucer, Handleless, Rose, Blue & Purple Rainbow 200.00
Cup & Saucer, Handleless, Stick, Blue, Red Rim 90.00
Cup & Saucer, Handleless, Thistle, Yellow, Miniature 950.00
Cup & Saucer, King's Rose 235.00
Cup & Saucer, Peafowl, Blue 185.00
Cup & Saucer, Peafowl, Green .... 200.00 To 250.00
Cup & Saucer, Plate, Floral, Yellow, Stick, 3 Piece 85.00
Cup & Saucer, Purple 375.00
Cup & Saucer, Tulip, Red & Green Rainbow 750.00
Cup & Saucer, Wigwam, Blue 550.00
Cup Plate, King's Rose 100.00
Cup Plate, Rainbow With Bull's–Eye, Blue & Green, 3 1/2 In. 675.00
Cup, Handleless, Black & Green Tree 125.00
Mug, Blue & Green, 2 3/4 In. 250.00
Mug, Peafowl, Black Transfer, John Wesley, Born–Died, 2 3/8 In. 2150.00
Pitcher, Blue & White Sponge, Blue Stripes, 8 In. 275.00
Pitcher, Leaf Mold, Cranberry 395.00
Pitcher, Raised House & Landscape, Gray, 19th Century, 8 In. 95.00
Pitcher, Tree Design, Purple, 8 7/8 In. 550.00
Plate, 6–Pointed Star, Blue, 9 3/8 In. 550.00
Plate, Gaudy Floral, Stick, Belgium, 11 In. 110.00
Plate, Peafowl, Blue, 8 1/2 In. 800.00
Plate, Peafowl, Blue, 9 3/8 In. 2550.00
Plate, Peafowl, Blue, 10 3/4 In. 950.00
Plate, Peafowl, Red, Blue, Green, Black, 9 3/8 In. 200.00
Plate, Pomegranate, Red, Blue, Green & Black, 6 5/8 In. 550.00
Plate, Pomegranate, Red, Blue, Green, Black, 8 1/2 In. 105.00
Plate, Rabbit, Yellow, Red, Blue & Green, 12 1/2 In. ....*Illus* 1250.00
Plate, Rainbow, Blue & Green, 8 1/4 In. 300.00
Plate, Red & Blue, 6 3/8 In. 325.00

Plate, Red & Green, 8 1/2 In.	95.00
Plate, Rose & Bud, Red, 8 3/8 In.	275.00
Plate, Schoolhouse, Blue Border, 9 5/8 In.	3800.00
Plate, Tulip, Red & Blue, Cotton & Barlow, 9 7/8 In.	275.00
Plate, Tulip, Red, Green, Blue, Black, 9 3/8 In.	450.00
Platter, Violet–Type Flower, Blue, 14 3/8 In.	150.00
Salt, Rainbow, Yellow & Dark Green, Master	2200.00
Sauce, Peafowl, Red, Green, Yellow & Black, 4 1/2 In.	75.00
Saucer, Peafowl, Blue, 6 In.	95.00
Saucer, Peafowl, Red	105.00
Saucer, Tulips, Red	110.00
Soup Dish, Blue Sponged Rim, Red Tulip, Green, Black, 11 In.	150.00
Sugar Shaker, Cranberry & White	95.00
Sugar, Cover, Blue Peafowl, Yellow, Red, Black, 4 1/2 In.	750.00
Sugar, Cover, Columbine, Rosebud, Thistle, Green, 4 1/8 In.	100.00
Sugar, Cover, Rainbow, Blue & Purple	350.00
Sugar, Cover, Tulips, 4 3/4 In.	175.00
Sugar, Cover, Violet–Type Flower, Red Border Stripe	90.00
Sugar, Green	85.00
Sugar, Peafowl, Blue, Green, Red & Black, 4 7/8 In.	150.00
Sugar, Rainbow, Blue & Purple, 4 3/4 In.	225.00
Tea Bowl & Saucer, Thistle, Red & Yellow Rainbow	4200.00
Tea Set, Child's, Blue, 7 Piece	175.00
Teapot, Blue & White, 5 1/2 In.	205.00
Teapot, Cluster Of Red & Green Buds, Blue, 5 1/4 In.	250.00
Teapot, Domed Cover, Violet–Type Flower, Border, 8 3/8 In.	300.00
Teapot, Rainbow, Red & Blue, 4 In.	175.00
Teapot, Tulip, Green Panels, 7 5/8 In.	950.00
Teapot, Yellow Rooster, Red, Blue & Black, 5 3/4 In.	350.00
Waste Bowl, Fort, Blue, 4 3/4 x 3 1/4 In.	235.00

SPELTER is a synonym for a zinc alloy. Figurines, candlesticks, and other pieces were made of spelter and given a bronze or painted finish. The metal has been used since about the 1860s to make statues, tablewares, and lamps that resemble bronze. Spelter is soft and breaks easily. To test for spelter, scratch the base of the piece. Bronze is solid; spelter will show a silvery scratch.

Clock, Cherubs Flank Dial, Floral & Scroll Feet, 26 In.	605.00
Ewer, Conical Body, Head Figural Handles, 1880s, 18 1/4 In., Pair	55.00
Figurine, 1 Man & His Lion, Green Patinated, Marble, M. LeVerrier	3328.00
Figurine, Black Child Holding Brass Wire Basket, 5 1/4 In.	90.00
Figurine, Man At Battle, Birds At Feet, France, 23 In.	500.00
Figurine, Nude Woman With Peacock, 65 In.	330.00
Figurine, Sower, 16 In.	160.00
Figurine, Vendanges, Man With Grapes, Par Chas. Levy, 1914, 16 In.	75.00
Garniture Set, Woman & Cupid, On Clock, Cupids On Vases, 19 1/2 In.	650.00
Lamp, Nude, Surrounded By Leaves, Bulbs Are Flower's Centers	495.00

Spatterware, Plate, Rabbit, Yellow, Red, Blue & Green, 12 1/2 In.

Umbrella Stand, Raised Oriental Figures, Flying Birds, 23 1/2 In. 110.00
Vase, Cherubs On Top, Footed, Bronze 270.00

SPINNING WHEELS in the corner have been symbols of earlier times for the past 100 years. Although spinning wheels date back to medieval days, the ones found today are rarely more than 200 years old. Because the style of the spinning wheel changed very little, it is often impossible to place an exact date on a wheel.

Ash & Maple, U.S., 1810–1830 .... 400.00
Cherry, 24–In. Diam. Wheel, Early 1800s 290.00
Flax Holder, Wooden, 9 1/2 In. 125.00
Flax, Castle, Small 300.00
Hand Crank, Table Clamp, Striping, Cast Iron, 19 1/4 In. 85.00
Hardwoods, Brown Patina, 38 In. 250.00
Hardwoods, Double Bobbins & Spinners, Vertical, 46 In. 245.00
Hardwoods, Turned & Chip Carved, 39–In. Plus Distaff 150.00
Maple, Hex Sign, Chip Carved, Beaded, Oak Legs 220.00
Mennonite Colony In Ontario, Salmon Paint 305.00
Oak, 19th Century, U.S., 67 In. 220.00
Shaker, Canterbury, New Hampshire, c.1840, 59 x 72 In. 220.00
Table Top Type 210.00
Upright Style, Varnished, Primitive 210.00
Various Hardwoods, Dark Finish, 34 In. 100.00
Various Hardwoods, Dark Finish, 39 1/2 In. 200.00
Wool Holder, Standard Size, Primitive 325.00
Worn Green Paint 425.00

SPODE pottery, porcelain, and bone china were made by the Stoke-on-Trent factory of England founded by Josiah Spode about 1770. The firm became Copeland and Garrett from 1833 to 1847, then W. T. Copeland or W. T. Copeland and Sons until 1976. It then became Royal Worcester Spode Ltd. The word *Spode* appears on many pieces made by the factories. Most collectors include all the wares under the more familiar name of Spode. Porcelains are listed in this book by the name that appears on the piece. Related pieces are listed under Copeland and Copeland Spode.

Stone-China

Bone Dish, Leaf Design, White Design, 8 Piece 90.00
Bowl, Dessert, Cowslip 5.00
Casserole, Apple Finial, Round 90.00
Charger, Gainsborough, 15 In. 65.00
Inkstand, 3 Wells, Oriental, 4 Lion's Paw Feet, 7 13/16 In., 4 Piece 1100.00
Plate, Cobalt & Gilt Design, Painted Fruit, c.1870, 9 In., 10 Piece 605.00
Plate, Gainsborough, 9 In. 20.00
Plate, Peacock, Octagonal, New Stone Mark, 7 7/8 To 8 In., 10 Piece 770.00
Platter, Gainsborough, 14 In. 40.00
Platter, Gainsborough, 16 1/2 In. 60.00
Stand, Fruit, Oriental Flowers, Garden, Marked, 1810–1815, 11 3/4 In. 2420.00
Tea Set, Mayfair, 3 Piece 320.00
Teapot, Florence 100.00
Toothpick, Pink & White Flowers 38.00
Vase, Domed Cover, Oriental, 3 Lion's Paw Feet, 1815–1820, 5 7/8 In. 880.00

SPONGEWARE is very similar to spatterware in appearance. The designs were applied to the ceramics by daubing the color on with a sponge or cloth. Many collectors do not differentiate between spongeware and spatterware and use the names interchangeably. Modern pottery is being made to resemble the old spongeware, but careful examination will show it is new.

Bank, Monkey 200.00
Bank, Pig 225.00
Bean Pot, Bail Handle 285.00
Beater Jar, 4 Blue Stripes 16.00
Bowl, 9 1/4 In. 180.00
Bowl, Band, Blue & White, 12 1/2 In. 145.00

Bowl, Blue & Brown, 6 1/4 In.	40.00
Bowl, Blue & White, 7 In.	145.00
Bowl, Blue & White, Ribbed, Scalloped Band	165.00
Bowl, Cream, Blue, Bail, Black Wooden Grip, 4–Footed, 8 x 4 In.	185.00
Bowl, Dilley Bros., Bennett, Iowa, 7 3/4 In.	175.00
Bowl, Mixing, Dark Blue, White Ground, 3 1/2 x 9 1/2 In.	65.00
Cooler, Water, Cover, Blue & White, Wide Blue Band, 5 Gal.	125.00
Creamer, Ormsby Farmers Grain Co., Brown, 4 1/2 In.	165.00
Crock, Butter, Cover, Blue & White, Large	35.00
Cup Plate, Peafowl, Red	195.00
Cuspidor, 12 1/4 In.	150.00
Jug, Grandmother's Maple Syrup	160.00
Pitcher & Bowl, Blue & White, 6 1/2 In.	195.00
Pitcher & Bowl, Pitcher 11 1/2 In., Bowl 14 1/2 In.	725.00
Pitcher, Banded, 7 1/8 In.	425.00
Pitcher, Barrel Shape, 7 1/2 In.	75.00
Pitcher, Cylindrical, 8 7/8 In.	250.00
Pitcher, Honor Bilt Flour, Magnum, Oklahoma, Brown & Cream	97.50
Pitcher, Red, Green & Blue Panels, 9 1/2 In.	225.00
Salt & Pepper, Brown, Cream, Green, Large	45.00

SPORTS equipment, sporting goods, brochures, and related items are listed here. Other sections of interest are Bicycle, Card, Fishing, Gun, Rifle, Sword, and Toy.

Baseball, Ashtray, World Series, Pittsburgh, New York, 1960, 3 1/2 In.	28.00
Baseball, Autograph, Abner Doubleday	350.00
Baseball, Ball, Autographed, All Star, 1987	150.00
Baseball, Ball, Autographed, Bo Jackson	50.00
Baseball, Ball, Autographed, Darryl Strawberry	32.95
Baseball, Ball, Autographed, Detroit Tigers, 1937	120.00
Baseball, Ball, Autographed, Hank Aaron	35.00
Baseball, Ball, Autographed, Johnny Bench	40.00
Baseball, Ball, Autographed, Jose Canseco	45.00
Baseball, Ball, Autographed, Lou Boudreau	15.00
Baseball, Ball, Autographed, N.Y. Yankees, 1980	150.00
Baseball, Ball, Autographed, New York Yankees, 1934	1870.00
Baseball, Ball, Autographed, Nolan Ryan	50.00
Baseball, Ball, Autographed, Nolan Ryan, 5th No–Hit Game	7150.00
Baseball, Ball, Autographed, Pete Rose	50.00
Baseball, Ball, Autographed, Sincerely, Babe Ruth	2750.00
Baseball, Ball, Autographed, Will Clark	45.00
Baseball, Ball, Autographed, Yankees, Mantle, Berra, Rizzuto, 1955	225.00
Baseball, Ball, Cincinnati & Yankees, World Series, 1961	65.00
Baseball, Bat, Advertising Peters Weatherbird Shoes, Wooden, Large	25.00
Baseball, Bat, Autographed, Bo Jackson	150.00
Baseball, Bat, Autographed, Don Mattingly	350.00
Baseball, Bat, Autographed, Mickey Mantle, September 18, 1965	8250.00
Baseball, Bat, Autographed, Wade Boggs	65.00
Baseball, Bat, Louisville Slugger, Signed Babe Ruth	495.00
Baseball, Bat, Simmons Hardware Co., Swatter Model	310.00
Baseball, Bat, Simmons, Junior League	260.00
Baseball, Bat, Simmons, King Of The Diamond	220.00
Baseball, Bat, Ty Cobb, 1909	35.00
Baseball, Bat, Winchester	300.00
Baseball, Bat, Winchester Major League	225.00
Baseball, Cap, Mickey Mantle, 1968	6600.00
Baseball, Cap, Roy Campanella	3300.00
Baseball, Clock, Figure Holding Bat, Gilt Pot Metal, 1920s, 4 x 4 In.	308.00
Baseball, Constitution & By–Laws Of National Assoc., 1860	5000.00
Baseball, Fan, Advertising, 1906	65.00
Baseball, Figurine, Carl Yastrzemski, 1989, 4 In.	90.00
Baseball, Figurine, Hank Aaron, Milwaukee Braves	225.00
Baseball, Flag, Roof, Wrigley Field, Cubs Logo, 1969, 3 x 5 Ft.	125.00

Baseball, Flip Book, Signals, Paul Richards Signaling, Gillette 30.00
Baseball, Glove, Fielder's, Simmons Hardware Co., Box 525.00
Baseball, Glove, Winchester 100.00
Baseball, Jersey, Autographed, Pete Rose, Reds, 1975 .... 3000.00
Baseball, Jersey, Johnny Bench, Reds, 1976 .... 2000.00
Baseball, Jersey, Reggie Jackson, World Champions, Home, No. 44 .... 2800.00
Baseball, Jersey, Reggie Jackson, World Series, 1977 .... 3100.00
Baseball, Jersey, Tom Seaver, Reds 2500.00
Baseball, Mitt, Carl Yastrzemski 35.00
Baseball, Mitt, Catcher's, 1920s ....*Illus* 110.00
Baseball, Pennant, Cincinnati Reds, Team Photograph, 1962 .... 50.00
Baseball, Pennant, Cleveland Indians World Series, 1948 .... 175.00
Baseball, Pennant, Cleveland Indians, Felt, 1946–1947 ....*Illus* 99.00
Baseball, Pennant, Cleveland Indians, Felt, 1950s 25.00
Baseball, Pennant, New York Yankees, Felt, 1950s 25.00
Baseball, Pennant, Yankees, American League Champs, 1961 .... 85.00
Baseball, Photograph, Joe DiMaggio, N.Y. Yankees, 8 x 10 In. 100.00
Baseball, Photograph, Lou Boudreau, Red Sox, 8 x 10 In. 7.00
Baseball, Photograph, Ted Williams, Red Sox, Color, 8 x 10 In. 35.00
Baseball, Photograph, Willie Mays, Autographed 20.00
Baseball, Photograph, Yogi Berra, N.Y. Yankees, Color, 8 x 10 In. 20.00
Baseball, Pin, Babe Ruth, Scorekeeper Back, Shreddies Cereal, 2 In. 85.00
Baseball, Pin, Tom Haller, 1 1/2 In. 50.00
Baseball, Player Set, Post Cereal, 1950s, 21 Piece 145.00
Baseball, Poster, Red Sox, Champions 1912 .... 1210.00
Baseball, Poster, White Sox, Pabst Premium, 1930 .... 85.00
Baseball, Program, Dodgers & Yankees, World Series, 1963 .... 75.00
Baseball, Program, Yankees World Series, 1932 .... 3750.00
Baseball, Punch Board, 1930s 18.00
Baseball, Scorebook, Brooklyn Players' League, 1890 .... 6000.00
Baseball, Scorebook, Cleveland Indians, Erin Brew Beer 5.00
Baseball, Sign, Brooklyn Dodgers, Schaefer Beer, 3-D, 1955 .... 1500.00
Baseball, Sun Visor, Yankees, 1937 .... 8.00
Baseball, Ticket, 1946 World Series, Pair 15.00
Baseball, Trophy, East Brookfield Club, Massachusetts 1100.00
Baseball, Uniform, Detroit Tigers, Willie Horton, Size 48, Gray, 1973 .... 475.00
Baseball, Uniform, L. A. Dodgers, Mike Marshall, Size 42, Gray, 1975 .... 275.00
Baseball, Uniform, Minnesota Twins, Jim Holt, Size 42, Gray, 1972 .... 275.00
Baseball, Uniform, Princeton Univ., Used By Dick Bell, 1930 .... 595.00
Baseball, Uniform, Princeton University, 1930s 595.00
Baseball, Wristwatch, Babe Ruth, Exact Time 275.00
Baseball, Yearbook, Red Sox, Yaz–Tiant Cover, 1976 .... 2.00
Basketball, Ball, Autographed, Lakers World Champions, 1986–1987 .... 450.00
Basketball, Ball, Autographed, Michael Jordan 160.00
Basketball, Jersey, Alford, Mavericks, 1988 .... 275.00
Basketball, Jersey, Autographed, Michael Jordan, Bulls 160.00
Basketball, Jersey, Jordan, Bulls, 1986 .... 2600.00

Sports, Baseball, Mitt, Catcher's, 1920s

Sports, Baseball, Pennant, Cleveland Indians, Felt, 1946–1947

Basketball, Jersey, Leavell, Rockets, Mid-1980s 90.00
Basketball, Jersey, McHale, Celtics, Mid-1980s 775.00
Basketball, Jersey, Walker, Nets, 1982 .... 135.00
Basketball, Photograph, Larry Bird, Autographed 17.00
Billiard, Table, Brunswick, Oak, 1892 .... 3100.00
Billiard, Table, Union League Expert, Brunswick 3300.00
Boxing, Bag, Kansas City Joe Walker, Hand Painted, Large 325.00
Boxing, Bell, Used In Ring 50.00
Boxing, Clock, Joe Louis World Champion, Figural, Early 1950s 475.00
Boxing, Gloves, Autographed, Jack Dempsey, 1940s, 2 3/4 In., Pair 50.00
Boxing, Photograph, Joe Frazier, Color, 8 x 10 In. 20.00
Boxing, Photograph, Muhammad Ali, Color, 8 x 10 In. 25.00
Boxing, Robe, Autographed, Joe Frazier, Training Camp, c.1972 .... 3960.00
Football, Ashtray, Jim Brown, 1939 .... 7.00
Football, Jersey, Autographed, Jim Brown, Browns 5500.00
Football, Jersey, Autographed, Roger Staubach, Cowboys 2750.00
Football, Jersey, Dan Marino, Dolphins 2200.00
Football, Jersey, Paul Warfield, Browns 2500.00
Football, Photograph, Mike Ditka, Dallas Cowboys, Color, 8 x 10 In. 15.00
Football, Photograph, Roger Staubach, Dallas Cowboys, 8 x 10 In. 20.00
Football, Pin, San Francisco 49ers, World Champions, 2 1/4 In. 5.00
Football, Program, Army Vs. Navy, 1943 .... 45.00
Football, Scorecard, Harvard Vs. Princeton, 1916 .... 40.00
Golf, Ashtray, Knickered Golfer, Brass, England 110.00
Golf, Card, Betty Fairfield, Wheaties, 1935 .... 30.00
Golf, Club, Acushnet, John Reuter 5.00
Golf, Club, Brassie, Tom Harmon, Jr., 43 In. Shaft, 1920 .... 50.00
Golf, Club, Driver, Winchester, Wood Shaft 175.00
Golf, Club, General Electric, Textolite Head, 1931-1935 .... 50.00
Golf, Club, Lee Trevino 18.00
Golf, Club, Left Hand, Winchester 140.00
Golf, Club, Mashie, Kroydon, Black Grip, 1920-1930 .... 65.00
Golf, Club, Mashie, Niblick, Woman's 15.00
Golf, Club, Mashie, Winchester Sporting Goods, J. Hutchison No. 4 .... 125.00
Golf, Club, Mashie, Wood Handle, Kroydon, P-8, Wood Handle 45.00
Golf, Club, Mills Fairway, Wood 150.00
Golf, Club, Morristown Iron, Spalding, 1900s 40.00
Golf, Club, Putter, Gorman No. 262 .... 50.00
Golf, Club, Putter, Great Lakes Golf Corp., 7-In. Hosel, 1920-1930 .... 250.00
Golf, Club, Putter, Jr., Spalding, 1912, 28 1/2 In. 65.00
Golf, Club, Putter, Long Nose, J. Holland, Feather Ball Period 9000.00
Golf, Club, Putter, Spalding, Midget Dimple, 1911 .... 30.00
Golf, Club, Putter, Tom Watson Autograph 130.00
Golf, Club, Putter, Wilson, Sarazen 50, Dimple Pattern, 1930-1950 .... 20.00
Golf, Club, Sam Snead 18.00
Golf, Club, Set, J. J. Madden, Stainless Steel, 8 Irons With Putter 400.00
Golf, Club, Winchester, Wooden Shaft 95.00
Golf, Coaster Set, Bing Crosby National Pro Am, Brass Medallion, Box 50.00
Golf, Figurine, Golfer, Argyle Socks, Knickers, Steel, c.1920, 21 In. 650.00
Golf, Flask, Knickered Golfer, Evans, Black, Enameled, 2 x 1 In. 275.00
Golf, Glove, Autographed, Billy Casper .... 65.00 To 75.00
Golf, Golf, Clubs, Child's, Aluminum, Linen Bag, 1940s 75.00
Golf, Lamp, Art Deco, Golfing Figure, Chrome 135.00
Golf, Photograph, Lee Trevino, 8 x 10 In. 15.00
Golf, Photograph, Nancy Lopez, Color, 8 x 10 In. 15.00
Golf, Photograph, Sam Snead, Color, 8 x 10 In. 15.00
Hockey, Jersey, Wayne Gretsky, All Star Game, 1991 .... 7150.00
Hockey, Stick, Autographed, Wayne Gretzky 195.00
Hockey, Sweater, Bruins, Wool, Size 28 .... 35.00
Horse Racing, Glass, Kentucky Derby, 1949 .... 125.00
Horse Racing, Glass, Kentucky Derby, 1952 .... 110.00
Horse Racing, Glass, Kentucky Derby, 1957 .... 80.00 To 81.00
Horse Racing, Glass, Kentucky Derby, 1959 .... 35.00 To 39.00

Horse Racing, Glass, Kentucky Derby, 1960 .... 33.00
Horse Racing, Glass, Kentucky Derby, 1962 .... 45.00
Horse Racing, Glass, Kentucky Derby, 1964 .... 35.00
Horse Racing, Glass, Kentucky Derby, 1965 .... 35.00
Horse Racing, Glass, Kentucky Derby, 1967 .... 32.00
Horse Racing, Glass, Kentucky Derby, 1969 .... 29.00
Horse Racing, Glass, Kentucky Derby, 1970, 5 1/2 In. 15.00
Horse Racing, Glass, Kentucky Derby, 1971 .... 18.00 To 25.00
Horse Racing, Glass, Kentucky Derby, 1973 .... 22.00 To 25.00
Horse Racing, Glass, Kentucky Derby, 1974 .... 8.00
Horse Racing, Glass, Kentucky Derby, 1975 .... 5.00 To 9.00
Horse Racing, Glass, Kentucky Derby, 1976 .... 5.00 To 14.00
Horse Racing, Glass, Kentucky Derby, 1978 .... 4.00
Horse Racing, Glass, Kentucky Derby, 1980 .... 15.00
Horse Racing, Glass, Kentucky Derby, 1981 .... 3.50 To 8.00
Horse Racing, Glass, Kentucky Derby, 1984 .... 6.00 To 8.00
Horse Racing, Glass, Kentucky Derby, 1990 .... 3.00
Horse Racing, Program, Kentucky Derby, 1957 .... 25.00
Hunting, Duck Call, Blue Bill, Directions 55.00
Hunting, Duck Call, Faulks 12.00
Hunting, Duck Call, Long, F. A. Alien 55.00
Hunting, Duck Call, Tongue Pincher, Rosewood & Chrome 95.00
Hunting, Goose Call, Herter 20.00
Hunting, License, California, Duckstamp, 1957 .... 8.00
Hunting, License, Missouri, Duck Stamp, 1928 .... 8.00
Skating, Sharpener, Ice Skates, Bergman, Pat. 1920, Instructions 34.00
Skating, Skates, Ice, Acorn Tipped, Scroll Prow, Wirths & Bros., 1880s ... 250.00
Skating, Skates, Ice, Canal, Turned Up Blades, Norway 825.00
Skating, Skates, Ice, Clamp–On, Union Hardware 38.00
Skating, Skates, Ice, E. C. Simmons Hardware 24.00
Skating, Skates, Ice, Simmons Klipper Klub, Box 80.00
Skating, Skates, Ice, Winchester 34.00
Skating, Skates, Ice, Wooden, Peters, Box, 1928 .... 25.00
Skating, Skates, Roller, Mousketeer, Walt Disney, Box 65.00
Skating, Skates, Roller, Winchester .... 34.00 To 35.00
Snow Shoes, Bear Paw, Bentwood, Leather Straps 125.00
Tennis, Racket, A. G. Spalding, Case, 1920s 75.00

STAFFORDSHIRE, England, has been a district making pottery and
porcelain since the 1700s. Hundreds of kilns are still working in the area.
Thousands of types of pottery and porcelain have been made in the many
factories that worked and still work in the area. Some of the most famous
factories have been listed separately, such as Adams, Davenport, Ridgway,
Rowland & Marsellus, Royal Doulton, Royal Worcester, Spode,
Wedgwood, and others. Some Staffordshire pieces are listed under sections
like Fairing, Flow Blue, Mulberry, Shaving Mug, etc.

Bowl, Lafayette At Tomb Of Franklin, Blue Transfer, 12 In. 850.00
Bowl, Pitcher Set, Black Transfer, Arabian Peddler, 11 In. 325.00
Box, Cover, Child Pushing Child On Sled 65.00
Box, Trinket, Rectangular, Cover, White, Gold Trim, 2 x 4 In. 125.00
Bust, John Wesley Bush, Black Robe, Red Pedestal, 11 In. 275.00
Candlestick, Figural, Peasant, Near Tree Stump, 9 13/16 In. 1980.00
Character Jug, Chelsea Pensioner, 8 3/4 In. 40.00
Chimney Piece, Scottish Couple, Polychrome, 8 1/4 In. 215.00
Chimney Piece, Scottish Lad & Lassie With Clock, 25 In. 245.00
Coffeepot, Blue Transfer, Bird, Thatched Cottage, 12 In. 415.00
Coffeepot, Cover, Enameled Design, Glazed Stoneware 2850.00
Coffeepot, Cover, Salt Glaze, Chinese Woman, 5 9/16 In. 1100.00
Coffeepot, Tonquin, Red, Meakin 50.00
Creamer, Cow, Willow 575.00
Creamer, Dark Blue Transfer, Flowers & Bird, Wood, 6 In. 230.00
Creamer, Floral Design, Polychrome Enamel, Gaudy, 5 3/4 In. 175.00
Creamer, Green Transfer, Feather Pattern, 4 3/4 In. 50.00

Creamer, Guernsey Cow, Oval Glass Base, Gold Trim On Horns 275.00
Creamer, Washington Vase, Purple Transfer, P. W. & Co., 1850 .... 110.00
Cup & Saucer, Handleless, Gaudy Swag Design 155.00
Cup & Saucer, Handless, Floral Design, Red, Blue, Green, Black 25.00
Cup & Saucer, Jenny Lind, Brown 15.00
Cup Plate, Dark Blue Transfer, 3 7/8 In. 100.00
Cup Plate, Dark Blue Transfer, Boat, Sails Half Down, 5 In. 170.00
Cup Plate, Dark Blue Transfer, Boat, Wood 170.00
Cup Plate, Red Transfer, Ruins, 4 In. 35.00
Cup Plate, Rhine Pattern, Brown Transfer, 1875, John Meir 25.00
Cup, Posset, Percy Pattern, Handle, Morley 60.00
Cup, Stirrup, Fox, Polychrome Enameling, 5 In. 235.00
Cup, Trellis Diaperwork, Rose, Enameled, 1760, 2 13/16 In. 3300.00
Dish, Cheese Keeper, Green & White, c.1865, 10 x 10 1/2 In. 400.00
Dish, Cover, Serving, Castle Scene, Blue, 12 In. 467.50
Dish, Creamware, Leaf Shape, 1765–1770, 11 1/16 In. 1100.00
Dish, Hen On Basket Cover, 5 3/4 x 7 In. 225.00
Dish, Hen On Basket Cover, Grass Under Hen, 7 1/2 x 8 In. 325.00
Dish, Hen On Basket Cover, Red Comb, Green Grass, 6 3/4 In. 245.00
Dish, Hen On Nest Cover, 6 x 8 In. 395.00
Dish, Leaf Shape, Green Glaze, 1765–1775, 10 1/16 In. 1215.00
Dish, Vegetable, Dark Blue, America, Independence, 11 In. 825.00
Dish, Vegetable, Light Blue, Octagonal, 9 3/4 In. 195.00
Figurine, Black Dog, Glass Eyes, Large, Pair 650.00
Figurine, Caballero, On Horseback, 1880s, 12 In. 135.00
Figurine, Cat, Blue Collar, Gold Bow, Gray & White, 7 In. 750.00
Figurine, Cat, Green Glass Eyes, 12 1/2 In. 275.00
Figurine, Cat, Seated, Salt Glaze, 1750–1760, 4 7/8 In. 1550.00
Figurine, Child, With Ball, Dog By Side, 4 In. 55.00
Figurine, Cow & Calf, Oval Base 100.00
Figurine, Deer, Pearlware, 1820–1825, 7 1/8 & 8 7/16 In., Pair 1760.00
Figurine, Dog With Pup 325.00
Figurine, Dog, Carrying Gold Basket, Porcelain, Miniature 75.00
Figurine, Dog, Glass Eyes, Chain, Neck Collar, 13 1/2 In., Pair 275.00
Figurine, Dog, Poodle, Sanded, 4 3/4 In. 70.00
Figurine, Dog, Poodle, Sanded, 6 1/4 In. 90.00
Figurine, Dog, Recumbent, Salt Glaze, 1750, 2 1/16 In. 1100.00
Figurine, Dog, Seated, Black, White, 6 3/4 In., Pair 250.00
Figurine, Dog, Seated, Black, White, 6 In. 65.00
Figurine, Dog, Seated, Green, White Enamel, Luster, 9 In., Pair 400.00
Figurine, Dog, Seated, Sanded Coat, White, 8 In. 130.00
Figurine, Dog, Seated, White Enamel, Gilt, 12 3/4 In., Pair 250.00
Figurine, Dog, Spaniel, Sanded, 6 1/2 In. 95.00
Figurine, Dog, Standing, Sanded Coat, Flowers At Feet, 4 In. 75.00
Figurine, Eros, Fanning Flames Of Love, Marked, 8 1/2 In. 275.00
Figurine, Franklin, Mistitled Washington, c.1850, 14 3/4 In. 660.00
Figurine, Girl, Flower Basket, Polychrome, Miniature 105.00
Figurine, King Charles Spaniel, Recumbent, 1860–1880, 13 In. 3300.00
Figurine, King Charles Spaniel, Rust & White, c.1850, 4 In. 110.00
Figurine, King Charles Spaniels, White, 1890–1895, 10 In., Pr. 525.00
Figurine, Lion & Lamb, Polychrome, 3 1/4 In. 135.00
Figurine, Lion, Earthenware, Tan, Black Base, 1825, 12 In. 1750.00
Figurine, Lion, Shaggy Mane, Green Glazed, 1780–1790, 3 In. 665.00
Figurine, Little Red Riding Hood 275.00
Figurine, Man & Wife With Rabbit, 6 1/2 In. 335.00
Figurine, Man With Dog, Polychrome Enamel, 11 1/4 In. 200.00
Figurine, Poodle, 7 In. 175.00
Figurine, Poodle, White, Gold, Orange Roses, 15 In., Pair 500.00
Figurine, Pug Dog, Standing, Salt Glaze, 1760, 3 In. 1210.00
Figurine, Reclining Dalmation, 4 In. 325.00
Figurine, Sheep, Rough Surface, Fairing, 2 x 2 1/2 In. 130.00
Figurine, Spaniel Dog, Sitting, Burnt Orange–Red, 4 1/4 In. 175.00
Figurine, Sultan & Sultana, Gilded, 7 x 6 13/16 In., Pair 1450.00

Staffordshire, Jug, Satyr,
Silver Luster, Yellow,
c.1810, 5 1/2 In.

Staffordshire, Jug, Satyr, Black
Feathered Field, c.1815, 4 In.

Staffordshire, Plate, Blue
Transfer, Geneva, 6 In.

Gravy Bowl, Jenny Lind	25.00
Group, Allegorical, Liberty & Matrimony, Wood Family, 11 In.	1750.00
Group, Bull–Baiting, O. Sherratt, 1830–1835, 13 13/16 In.	3025.00
Group, Ewe & Lamb, Recumbent, Rock Base, Salt Glaze, 5 1/8 In.	445.00
Group, Lion & Lamb, 1845–1855, 3 3/4 x 4 3/4 In.	550.00
Group, Shepherdess & Dog, Salt Glaze, 1750, 4 3/4 In.	2090.00
Holder, Pen, Dog, Whippet	125.00
Holder, Quill, Bird With 1 Nesting Young, 2 3/4 In.	120.00
Holder, Quill, Reclining Dalmatian Dog, Cobalt, 4 3/4 In.	425.00
Holder, Quill, Reclining Dogs	125.00
Inkwell, Bird On Nest	250.00
Inkwell, Dog, Whippet, Blue & White	325.00
Jug, Cream, Green Leafy Branch, Pear Shape, 3 1/16 In.	660.00
Jug, Man Holding Goblet, Diaperwork, Salt Glaze, 1760, 7 In.	9625.00
Jug, Satyr, Black Feathered Field, c.1815, 4 In. ....*Illus*	110.00
Jug, Satyr, Silver Luster, Yellow, c.1810, 5 1/2 In. ....*Illus*	605.00
Jug, Tax Collector, Gold Vest, Blue Jacket, 10 In.	395.00
Loving Cup, Salt Glaze, Scratch Blue Initials H H, 5 3/8 In.	3980.00
Mug, Child's, Seasons, Month Of May, Green Transfer, 2 1/4 In.	145.00
Mug, Iron Bridge, Pink Transfer, 19th Century	110.00
Mug, Little Boy Proposing, 2 1/4 In.	55.00
Piggin, Salt Glaze, Bucket Shape, Peony, 1755–1760, 1 7/16 In.	3575.00
Pitcher & Bowl, Roses On White & Blue Ground, Clementson	345.00
Pitcher, 3 Different Portraits Of Lafayette, Inscription	3000.00
Pitcher, Brownstone	295.00
Pitcher, Commemorating Lafayette's Visit In 1824	1700.00
Pitcher, Figural, Bearded Man With Crown, Marked, 7 5/8 In.	100.00
Pitcher, George Peabody, Rope Twist Handle, c.1870, 7 3/4 In.	110.00
Pitcher, Milk, Charlotte, Meakin	35.00
Pitcher, Pawtucket Falls & Old Jones School House, 7 In.	75.00
Pitcher, Priory, Octagonal, 7 In.	95.00
Pitcher, Purple Transfer, European Scenery, 9 In.	125.00
Plate, America & Independence, Dark Blue, 10 1/2 In.	300.00
Plate, Black Transfer, Make Hay While Sun Shines, 8 In.	85.00
Plate, Black Transfer, Scroll, 9 In.	35.00
Plate, Blue Transfer, Geneva, 6 In. ....*Illus*	25.00
Plate, Blue, Landing Of The Fathers At Plymouth, Mark, 8 In.	195.00
Plate, Blue, Philadelphia, Cities Series, c.1820, 5 In.	375.00
Plate, Brown Transfer, City Hall New York, 10 1/2 In.	130.00
Plate, Brown Transfer, Knight On Horse, Daisy Rim, 6 5/8 In.	25.00
Plate, Child's, History Of Joseph & His Brethren, 6 1/2 In.	75.00
Plate, Daisy Rim, Black Transfer, Windsor Castle, 7 In.	22.50
Plate, Floral In Red, Black, Blue & Green, Gaudy, 7 1/8 In.	12.50
Plate, Floral, Red, Green & Yellow, Gaudy, 6 7/8 In., Pair	90.00
Plate, Gunton Hall, Norfolk, 7 1/2 In.	85.00
Plate, Milking, Octagonal, 6 3/4 In.	45.00
Plate, Mormon Temple, Blue & White, 10 In.	45.00

Plate, Purple Transfer, Bologna, 7 3/8 In. 25.00
Plate, R. Hall's Select Views Pains Hill, Surrey, Blue, 10 In. 65.00
Plate, Red Transfer, European Scenery, 9 3/8 In. 25.00
Plate, Robinson Crusoe's First Crop, Octagonal, 6 3/4 In. 45.00
Plate, Rose, Gaudy, 9 1/4 In. 45.00
Plate, Sunflower, Gaudy, 6 3/4 In. 40.00
Platter, American Cities & Scenery, Albany, 13 1/2 In. 250.00
Platter, Brown Transfer, Palestine, 13 1/4 In. 115.00
Platter, Country Landscape Center, Floral Border, 21 In. 465.00
Platter, Floral Sprigs, Phoenix Works, 15 1/4 x 19 1/2 In. 335.00
Platter, Folay, A. F. & Co., 14 In. 125.00
Platter, Jenny Lind, 14 In. 20.00
Platter, Marquise, Brown Transfer, 16 In. 30.00
Platter, Salt Glaze, Foliate Edged Cartouches, 16 3/8 In. 1540.00
Platter, Walsingham Priory, Norfolk, Blue, 18 3/4 In. 350.00
Puzzle Jug, Blue, White, Peach Floral, Pierced Top, 4 1/4 In. 85.00
Sauce Boat, Enameled Cows 1 Side, Sheep Other, 1765, 7 In. 1550.00
Sauce Boat, Roses & Flowers, Salt Glaze, 1760–1765, 6 In. 885.00
Soup, Dish, Black Transfer, Pomerama, 10 3/8 In. 55.00
Soup, Dish, Lady Of The Lake, Blue, 9 7/8 In. 85.00
Spoon Tray, Quatrefoil Shape, Stylized Branch, 6 1/16 In. 3850.00
Spoon Tray, Quatrefoil, Birds, Branches, 1750–1760, 6 1/2 In. 1540.00
Stickpin Holder, Bearded Viking, Pierced Shield, 3 In. 225.00
Stirrup Cup, Hound's & Fox's Head, Base, 4 1/2 & 4 7/8 In. 880.00
Sugar Bowl, Floral Design, Embossed Shell Handles, 4 7/8 In. 70.00
Sugar, Cover, Child's, Green & Blue Floral Band, 3 3/4 In. 75.00
Sugar, Cover, Child's, Lady With Apron 35.00
Sugar, Cover, Gaudy Floral, 4 In. 95.00
Sugar, Cover, Horse Drawn Sleigh, Blue Transfer, 6 3/4 In. 175.00
Sugar, Floral Design, Red, Green, Blue, Black, 8 In. 110.00
Sugar, Gaudy Floral Design, Orange, Green, Mahogany, 6 1/4 In. 125.00
Sugar, Red Transfer Of Shepherd, 5 7/8 In. 125.00
Sugar, Washington Holding Scroll, Blue, Signed 500.00
Tea Caddy, Chinaman & Exotic Bird, Salt Glaze, 1760, 4 In. 1760.00
Tea Caddy, Cover, Enameled Floral, 1760, 4 7/16 In. 935.00
Tea Set, Child's, Alaska, Whittaker & Co., 23 Piece 345.00
Tea Set, Child's, Cable Pattern, Gold Luster, 15 Piece 335.00
Tea Set, Child's, Sprig Design, 9 Piece 400.00
Teapot, Child's, Lady With Apron, Brown 45.00
Teapot, Child's, Little Mae, Pink & White 40.00
Teapot, Cover, Crabstock Spout & Handle, 1750, 3 1/2 In. 1100.00
Teapot, Cover, King Of Prussia, Salt Glazed, 1757–1760, 4 In. 1875.00
Teapot, Cover, Quatrefoil, Oak Leaves & Acorns, 5 1/16 In. 6100.00
Teapot, Enameled Design, Salt Glaze 2850.00
Teapot, Floral In Red, Black, Blue & Green, Gaudy, 5 In. 115.00
Teapot, Knop Cover, Insect, Cranes, Loop Handle, 1755, 4 In. 5500.00
Teapot, Lake Scene, Light Blue Transfer, Shell Border 575.00
Teapot, Mad Hatter 40.00
Teapot, Pelew Pattern, Octagonal 250.00
Teapot, Punchinello 40.00
Tile, Shaded Pecten Shell, Checkered Ground, 1750–1760, 5 In. 4675.00
Toby Jugs are listed in their own section
Tureen, Cover, Dixcove On The Gold Coast Africa, 10 1/2 In. 82.50
Tureen, Gray, Black Transfer, Naples Shield, c.1850 .... 110.00
Tureen, Sauce, Cover, Green Transfer, Royal Cottage 110.00
Urn, Creamware, Lamp Mounted, Putti, 1780–1790, 9 7/8 In., Pair 1550.00
Vase, Salt Glaze, Scratch Blue, Baluster, 1760, 3 3/8 In. 660.00
Vase, Salt Glaze, Sprigs, Cartouche, Bottle Form, 4 9/16 In. 1210.00
Vase, Seated Dogs, Polychrome Enamel, 12 3/4 In., Pair 650.00
Vase, Seated Doves, 12 3/4 In., Pair 650.00
Vase, Spill, Sheep & Deer Group, 1820–1815, 6 3/16 & 5 16 In. 770.00
Vegetable, Open, English Fishing Scene, 7 3/4 In. 250.00
Waste Bowl, Bird, Stylized Rock, Salt Glaze, 1760, 6 5/8 In. 2475.00

Whippet, Seated, Blue Pillow Base, 4 3/4 In. 185.00

STANGL Pottery traces its history back to the Fulper Pottery of New Jersey. In 1910, Johann Martin Stangl started working at Fulper. He bought into the firm in 1913, became president in 1926, and in 1929 changed the company name to Stangl Pottery. The pottery made dinnerwares and a line of limited–edition bird figurines. The company went out of business in 1978.

Ashtray, Bird Dog & Flying Quail Center, 7 1/2 In. 18.00
Ashtray, Blueberry 15.00
Ashtray, Canada Goose, Oval, 10 In. 45.00
Ashtray, Duck, Sportsmen 25.00
Bean Pot, Tulip, 6 Qt. 55.00
Bird, Bird Of Paradise, No. 3408 ....72.00 To 135.00
Bird, Blue Headed Vireo, No. 3448 ....75.00 To 95.00
Bird, Bluebird, No. 3276 ....77.00 To 80.00
Bird, Bluebirds, No. 3276D, 7 1/2 In. 140.00
Bird, Bobolink, No. 3595 ....65.00 To 155.00
Bird, Brewers Blackbird, No. 3591 .... 95.00
Bird, Broadbill Hummingbird, No. 3629 .... 105.00
Bird, Canary, No. 3747, 6 In. ....95.00 To 175.00
Bird, Cardinal, No. 3444, Pink ....60.00 To 95.00
Bird, Cerulean Warbler, No. 3456 ....55.00 To 80.00
Bird, Chickadee, No. 3581 .... 185.00
Bird, Cliff Swallow, No. 3752 .... 125.00
Bird, Cock Pheasant, No. 3492 .... 260.00
Bird, Cockatoo, No. 3405 ....65.00 To 75.00
Bird, Cockatoo, No. 3580 .... 135.00
Bird, Evening Grosbeak, No. 3813 .... 115.00
Bird, Flying Duck, Gray, No. 3443 .... 285.00
Bird, Flying Duck, Green, No. 3443 ....265.00 To 325.00
Bird, Golden Cream Kinglets, No. 3848 .... 50.00
Bird, Gray Cardinal, No. 3596, Gray ....65.00 To 85.00
Bird, Hen Pheasant, No. 3491 ....155.00 To 260.00
Bird, Key West Quail Dove, No. 3454 ....245.00 To 350.00
Bird, Kingfisher, No. 3406 .... 95.00
Bird, Lovebirds, No. 3402D 110.00
Bird, Nuthatch, No. 3593 ....35.00 To 60.00
Bird, Oriole, No. 3402 ....40.00 To 65.00
Bird, Orioles, No. 3402D 125.00
Bird, Painted Bunting, No. 3452 ....100.00 To 155.00
Bird, Parakeet, No. 3582D 225.00
Bird, Parula Warbler, No. 3583 .... 50.00
Bird, Passenger Pigeon, No. 3450 .... 750.00
Bird, Red Faced Warbler, No. 3594 .... 110.00
Bird, Redstarts, No. 3490D 230.00
Bird, Reiffers Hummingbird, No. 3628 .... 125.00
Bird, Rufous Hummingbird, No. 3585 ....80.00 To 125.00
Bird, Titmouse, No. 3592 ....45.00 To 50.00
Bird, Wilson Warbler, No. 3597 .... 40.00
Bird, Woodpecker, No. 3751 .... 120.00
Bird, Wren, No. 3401 .... 75.00
Bird, Wrens, No. 3401D 135.00
Bird, Yellow Warbler, No. 3447 .... 65.00
Bird, Yellow Warbler, No. 3850 .... 60.00
Bowl, Brown Stippling, Handles, 6 In. 95.00
Bowl, Serving, Fruits 17.50
Bowl, Thistle, 8 In. 22.00
Box, Cigarette, Blue Flower, Divided 20.00
Casserole, Cover, Fruits 30.00
Casserole, Cover, Thistle, 9 1/2 In. 32.50
Chop Plate, Festival 22.00
Chop Plate, Lyric 18.00

Chop Plate, Magnolia, 12 1/2 In.	22.00
Coffeepot, Thistle	45.00
Cup, Blueberry	6.00
Cup, Country Garden	2.75
Cup, Mother Hubbard, Kiddieware	30.00
Dinner Set, Starflower, 90 Piece	450.00
Dish, Divided, Cat Design	60.00
Dish, Divided, Kiddieware	80.00
Dish, Leaf, 14 1/2 In.	15.00
Figurine, Penguin	295.00
Gravy Boat, Golden Harvest	14.00
Lamp, Base, Yellow, Turquoise, Rose & Green, Paper Label Also Fulper	325.00
Luncheon Set, Chickory	55.00
Mug, Preacher With Hat Used As Ashtray	275.00
Mug, Rooster, 2 Cup	26.00
Mug, Town & Country, Brown	20.00 To 22.00
Pitcher, Franklin D. Roosevelt, Caricature, 7 1/2 In.	135.00
Pitcher, Orchard Song, 10 In.	5.00
Pitcher, Terra Rose	12.00 To 15.00
Place, Country Garden, 6 In.	5.00
Plate, Canada Goose, 5 In.	22.00
Plate, Pheasant, 5 In.	22.00
Plate, Thistle, 6 In.	5.00
Plate, Thistle, 10 In.	11.00
Platter, Fruits, Round	20.00
Salt & Pepper, Thistle	7.00
Server, Orchard Song, Center Handle	9.00
Sign, Dealer's, Antique Gold, 3 x 6 1/2 In.	135.00
Sugar & Creamer, Bittersweet	18.00
Sugar & Creamer, Town & Country, Brown, White	30.00
Sugar, Garland	6.00
Wall Pocket, Terra Rose	35.00

STEINS have been used by beer and ale drinkers for over 500 years. They have been made of ivory, porcelain, stoneware, faience, silver, pewter, wood, or glass in sizes up to nine gallons. Although some were made by Mettlach, Meissen, Capo–di–Monte, and other famous factories, most were made by less important German potteries. The words *Geschutz* or *Musterschutz* on a stein are the German words for *patented* or *registered design,* not company names. Steins are still being made in the old styles. Lithophane steins may be found in the Lithophane category.

Anheuser–Busch, Centennial–Bicentennial	950.00
Blown Glass, Deep Cobalt Blue, Enameled Foral Design, c.1860, 1 Liter	170.00
Blown Glass, Engraved, Enameled Arion Fruhschoppen Klubb, 1 Liter	350.00
Budweiser, Bud Label	12.00
Budweiser, Budman, 1975	290.00
Budweiser, Christmas, 1989	10.00
Budweiser, Clydesdale Stables	19.00
Budweiser, Corporate, 1975	220.00
Budweiser, German Olympia, 1975	240.00
Character, Monk, Dwarf Patting His Behind Thumb Lift, 1/2 Liter	275.00
Character, Nun, Pottery, Inlaid Lid, 1/2 Liter	220.00
Character, Rabbit, Schierholz, Porcelain, Porcelain Lid, 1/2 Liter	345.00
Character, Rich Woman, Mother–In–Law, Bag Of Money, Pottery, 1/2 Liter	700.00
Character, Sad Radish, Porcelain, Schierholz, Inlaid Lid, 1/2 Liter	185.00
Dragon, Moriage, Green Mark, 5 1/2 In.	200.00
Enameled Flowers & Leaves, Pewter Lid & Thumb Lift, Glass	125.00
Enameled Glass, Pewter Cover, Farm Scene, German Verse, 6 In.	88.00
Etched, 3 Large Men Drinking, Wheat & Hops Lid, Pottery, 3 Liter	465.00
Figural Head Lid, Pewter Knob & Handle, Schultz & Dooley, c.1955, Pr.	265.00
Fish, Merkelback & Wick	335.00
Flemish, Stoneware, 17 In.	95.00
Football Shape, Textured Lacing, Stoneware, Germany, 6 1/2 In.	64.50

Four Seasons, Inlaid, German Pottery, 8 In., Pair	192.00
Goblin & Banner, Pewter Lid & Thumb Lift, Stoneware, 1909	275.00
House Of Heilman	120.00
Hunting Scene, Deer & Boars, Large Fox Handle, Pottery, 2 1/2 Liter	180.00
Leaves & Flowers, Silver Plate Lid & Thumb Lift, Glass, 1889	275.00
Lederhosen, Raised Relief, Stoneware, 1/2 Liter, 7 1/2 In.	62.75
Lovers, Dancing, Man With Accordion, Pewter Lid, Pottery, 1 Liter	175.00
Man, Woman Plays Instrument, Dwarfs, Pewter Lid, Pottery, 1 Liter	200.00
Mettlach steins are listed in the Mettlach category.	
Monk, Figural, Pewter Thumbpiece, Pottery, 1/2 Liter, 7 In.	250.00
Monk, Pewter Lid & Thumb Lift, Stoneware, Germany	40.00
Mozart's Portrait, Centennial In Salzburg On Death, 1891	225.00
Multicolored Design, Pewter Lid, S–Scroll Handle, Salt Glaze, Germany	110.00
Munich Maid, Brown, Porcelain, 1/3 Liter	245.00
Mushroom Lady, Figural, Porcelain Lid, Musterschutz, 1/2 Liter, 6 In.	1800.00
Neuweiler's Pronghorn Antelope Beer	150.00
Norman Rockwell, Box, 1948	40.00
Olive Amber Glass, Pewter Hinged Lid, Amber Handle, 7 3/4 In.	275.00
Pewter, Tankard Shape, Pewter Lid, Engraved F. G. E. 1797, 1 Liter	275.00
Pressed Glass, Engraved Pewter Lid, Michelob Brewery, 1/2 Liter	205.00
Pressed Glass, Fluted Pattern, Glass Lid, Enameled Edelweiss, 1 Liter	75.00
Rainier Brewery, Seattle, Wash., c.1900	95.00
Regimental, Field Artillery, Darmstadt 1898, 2–Sided Scene, 1/2 Liter	440.00
Regimental, Twenty–Third Infantry, Pewter Lid, Soldier, Lion, 11 In.	330.00
Santa Claus, Gerz, 1/2 Liter, 7 1/2 In.	60.00
Scenic, Woman & 2 Men, Stoneware, Pewter Lid & Thumb Lift, Germany	300.00
Schlitz, 125th Anniversary	150.00
Sun Burst, Moon, Stars, Stoneware, Verse, Merkelbach & Wick, 1/2 Liter	120.00
Wedding, Blown Glass, Cobalt Blue, Flowers, Deer Thumb Lift, 1 Liter	1040.00
Werrbach, Salt Glaze, 1910s	135.00
Wood, Silver Plated Ornamental Animal Design, Silver Lid, 1/2 Liter	110.00

STEREO CARDS that were made for stereopticon viewers became popular after 1840. Two almost identical pictures were mounted on a stiff cardboard backing so that, when viewed through a stereoscope, a three-dimensional picture could be seen. Value is determined by maker and by subject. These cards were made in quantity through the 1930s.

Europe, Set	25.00
Graf Zeppelin In Hangar, Lakehurst, New Jersey	40.00
Holyland, Set	20.00
International Exposition, 1876, James Cremer, 12 Piece	66.00
Renault Tanks Going To Front, World War I, Keystone View	20.00
San Francisco Earthquake, Johnstown Flood, Others, 30 Piece	110.00
Sears–Roebuck, Box, c.1900, 50 Piece	45.00 To 60.00
World War I, Display Case, 71 Piece	250.00
World War I, Set	95.00
World's Columbian Exposition, Kiburn, 9 Piece	52.00

STEREOSCOPES, or stereopticons, were used for viewing stereo cards. The hand viewer was invented by Oliver Wendell Holmes, although more complicated table models were used before his was produced in 1859.

Hand Held	30.00

STERLING SILVER, see Silver–Sterling category

STEUBEN glass was made at the Steuben Glass Works of Corning, New York. The factory, founded by Frederick Carder and T. C. Hawkes, Sr., was purchased by the Corning Glass Company. They continued to make glass called *Steuben.* Many types of art glass were made at Steuben. The firm is still making exceptional quality glass but it is clear, modern–style glass. Additional pieces may be found in the Aurene and Cluthra sections.

Ashtray, Sloping Bowl, David Hills, 1950, 7 1/8 In.	77.00
Bonbon, Alabaster Foot & Knob, Lavender Jade, 6 1/2 In.	550.00

Bowl, 3 1/4 In. 175.00
Bowl, Calcite, Gold Aurene Lining, 5 1/2 In. 205.00
Bowl, Florentia, Internal Blossoms, Signed, 3 1/2 x 12 1/2 In. 2750.00
Bowl, Grotesque, Free–Form, Ivory, 7 In. 275.00
Bowl, Ivrene, Iridescent Blue Interior, 5 3/4 In. 325.00
Bowl, Rosaline, Alabaster 100.00
Bowl, Verre De Soie Bands, Oriental Poppy, Signed, 5 1/4 x 7 In. 1875.00
Candlestick, Donald Pollard Design, 1956, 3 In. ....90.00 To 110.00
Candlestick, Ivrene, Gold Border, 8 1/2 In., Pair 1200.00
Candlestick, Selenium Red, Pair 495.00
Candy Dish, Ram's Head Finial, Benton, 1943, 6 1/2 In., Pr. .... 400.00 To 440.00
Champagne, Alabaster Twisted Stem, Jade, 5 1/2 In. 125.00
Cocktail Set, Threaded, Decanter & 6 Cups, Signed 525.00
Compote, Folded Rim, Pedestal Foot, Amber, Signed, 10 1/4 In. 110.00
Compote, Gold Calcite, 8 In. 325.00
Compote, Peach Pedestal, Clear Intaglio Cut, Signed, 4 3/4 In. 90.00
Compote, Ribbed, Blue Foot & Top, Clear Stem, Signed, 8 In. 135.00
Compote, Rosaline, Twisted Alabaster Stem & Base, 8 1/4 In. 295.00
Compote, Seafoam Blue 150.00
Compote, Swirl Ribbed Stem, Green Rim, Green Punts, Signed, 6 1/4 In 325.00
Cordial, Selenium, Signed, 4 In. 110.00
Dish, Inward Scrolling Handles On 1 Side, 7 1/2 In. 155.00
Dish, Olive, Signed, 5 1/4 In. 100.00
Figurine, Apple Of Eden, 18K Gold Serpent, Leaves, Signed, 5 3/4 In. 1750.00
Figurine, Buddha, On Stepped Glass Base, Green, Signed, 8 1/2 In. 550.00
Figurine, Cat, No. 8274, Green Peridot Eyes 500.00
Figurine, Elephant, Ivory, 5 1/2 In. 950.00
Figurine, Hippopotamus, Signed, 7 In. 250.00
Figurine, Nude, Kneeling, Black Jade, Signed 975.00
Figurine, Owl, 5 x 5 In. 350.00
Figurine, Penguin, Signed, 3 1/2 In. 200.00
Figurine, Songbird, Signed, 5 In. 250.00
Finger Bowl, Hemispherical, Cobalt Blue, Marked, c.1905, 12 Piece 1450.00
Finger Bowl, Rose Base, Engraved Van Dyke 95.00
Finger Bowl, Underplate, Jade 95.00
Flower Holder, Buddha, Alabaster 525.00
Goblet, Cat Design, Ivrene Stem, Jade, 7 In. 200.00
Goblet, Cintra Twist Stem 145.00
Goblet, Green Cut To Clear, Thistles, Square Cut Foot, Signed 250.00
Goblet, Paneled Ribs, Random Threading On Bowl, Signed, 8 1/2 In. 125.00
Jar, Cover, Indian, 1943, 5 3/4 In. 605.00
Lamp, Alabaster Cintra, Celery Green, 32 In. 1850.00
Lamp, Art Nouveau, 4 Aurene Shades, Iron Standard, 31 In. 1980.00
Lamp, Cintra Acid, Mums & Stems, Black Jade, 18 In. 1500.00
Lamp, Oriental Poppy, Green Platform Base, Silk Shade, 18 In. 1100.00
Lamp, Perfume, Pierced Lid, Aurene & Gilt Bronze, c.1920, 9 In. 990.00
Lamp, Rose Quartz, Cintra, 12 1/2 In. 1350.00
Lemonade Set, Green, Alabaster, Handled Mugs, Signed, 9 Piece 1350.00
Luminor, Florentia, Colorless Sphere, Florentia Design, Box, 7 In. 825.00
Paperweight, Controlled Bubbles, c.1928, 4 1/2 In. .... 295.00 To 350.00
Paperweight, Teardrops & White Swirl, Clear 295.00
Parfait, Stemmed, Rosaline & Alabaster, 6 1/2 In. 125.00
Pitcher, John Dreves, 1939, 9 In. 192.00
Pitcher, Water, Mandarin, Yellow, Bulbous, Everted Spout, 6 1/2 In. 775.00
Plate Set, Clear, With Blue, Pink & Amber Edge, 8 1/2 In., 9 Piece 315.00
Plate Set, Green, 10 Piece 990.00
Plate, Rosaline, 6 In. 49.00
Plate, Sterling Rim, Blue, 8 1/2 In., 6 Piece 360.00
Punch Cup, Bristol Yellow 195.00
Salt, Flared & Scalloped Rim, Signed 295.00
Salt, Pedestal, Ribbed, Blue, Signed, 1 1/2 x 2 1/2 In. 150.00
Salt, Pedestal, Signed, Green 150.00
Shade, Pink Feathers, Signed 525.00

Steuben, Vase, Green & Gold Aurene,

Alabaster, Leaf, 1900, 7 In.

Sherbet, Underplate, Calcite & Gold	150.00
Sherbet, Verre De Soie, 8 Piece	56.00
Sugar & Creamer, Irene Benton, 1947	192.00
Tazza, Diamond Optic, Ruffled Rim, Black Threading, 5 In.	375.00
Torchere, Tripod Base, Ram's Head, Poppy Shade, 68 In.	2860.00
Tumble-Up, Verre De Soie, Engraved, 6 1/2 In.	575.00
Urn, Cut Back In Rosaline Over Alabaster, Floral & Vine, 9 In.	335.00
Vase, 3 Lilies, Ivrene, 12 In.	1150.00 To 1400.00
Vase, 3 Thorny Jade Prongs, Jade, 6 1/8 In.	275.00
Vase, 4 Dimples, Scalloped Stretched Collar Rim, Signed, 3 1/2 In.	395.00
Vase, 5-Leaf Clover Form, Signed, 6 In.	120.00
Vase, Acanthus, Green Over Yellow Jade, 12 In.	1700.00
Vase, Bulbous Body, Cylindrical Neck, Blue Iridescent, 12 In.	2750.00
Vase, Bulbous Urn Top, Vines, Flowers & Hearts, Signed, 12 In.	4125.00
Vase, Cornucopia Shape, Ivrene, 6 In.	150.00
Vase, Cornucopia, Ruffled Rim, Platform Base, Signed, 6 1/4 In., Pair	110.00
Vase, Dark Blue, Jade, Ribbed, 7 In.	1400.00
Vase, Deep Amethyst Cut To Alabaster, Mum Pattern, 15 1/2 In.	3700.00
Vase, Diamond Optic, Green Threading, Signed, 12 In.	275.00
Vase, Diamond Pattern, Threads Of Pomona Green, Marked, 7 1/2 In.	192.50
Vase, Fan, Light Green, Pre-1932	165.00
Vase, Fan, Light Green, Signed, 9 1/2 In.	93.00
Vase, Figure Suspended From Parachute, Clouds, c.1932, 12 In.	770.00
Vase, Florentia, Trumpet, Green, 13 In.	6500.00
Vase, Floriform, Trumpet Neck, Ruffled Rim, Signed, 1904, 10 1/4 In.	935.00
Vase, Gold Aurene On Calcite, 10 In.	660.00
Vase, Green & Gold Aurene, Alabaster, Leaf, 1900, 7 In. *Illus*	6160.00
Vase, Grotesque, Amethyst, 9 1/4 In.	395.00
Vase, Grotesque, Cranberry, 3 In.	100.00
Vase, Grotesque, Ivory, 5 In.	310.00
Vase, Jade & Alabaster, Swirled Upper, 8 In.	195.00
Vase, Jade Green, Signed, 7 1/4 In.	450.00
Vase, Jade On Alabaster, 10 In.	250.00
Vase, Light To Dark Green, Inverted Baluster, 11 In., Pr.	2200.00
Vase, Lotus, 14 In.	750.00
Vase, Matsu Pattern, Jade Green, Textured White, 4 x 7 3/4 In.	850.00
Vase, Matsu Pattern, Spherical Shape, Rose Over Alabaster, 8 In.	1450.00
Vase, Oriental Design Carved To Frosted Layer, Signed, 7 In.	385.00
Vase, Plum Jade, 11 x 8 1/2 In.	3500.00
Vase, Rosaline, 20 In.	350.00
Vase, Trailing Berried Leaves, Intarsia Glass, c.1929, 8 1/4 In.	4400.00
Vase, Tulip Form, Calcite, Gold Iridescent Interior, 6 In.	325.00

STEVENGRAPHS are woven pictures made like fancy ribbons. They were manufactured by Thomas Stevens of Coventry, England, and became popular in 1862. Most are marked *Woven in silk by Thomas Stevens* or were mounted on a cardboard that tells the story of the Stevengraph. Other similar ribbon pictures have been made in England and Germany.

Bookmark, At Old Jerome	175.00
Bookmark, Birth Of Our Nation's Flag	175.00
Bookmark, Buffalo Bill	250.00
Bookmark, Death Of Nelson, Framed, 11 1/2 x 8 1/2 In.	350.00
Bookmark, Declaration Of Independence	150.00
Bookmark, For Life Or Death	200.00
Bookmark, George Washington Centennial, 1876	110.00
Bookmark, Good Old Days	48.00
Bookmark, Loves Remembrance, Silk	75.00
Bookmark, Married At St. George's Chapel	200.00
Bookmark, Old Armchair	200.00
Bookmark, Philadelphia Centennial	200.00
Bookmark, Shaker Cloak Factory	246.50
For Life Or Death, Framed, Small	200.00
For Life Or Death, Heroism On Land, 1879	300.00
Tennis, First Set	225.00

STEVENS & WILLIAMS of Stourbridge, England, made many types of glass, including layered, etched, cameo, and art glass, between the 1830s and 1930s. Some pieces are signed *S & W.* Many pieces are decorated with flowers, leaves, and other designs based on nature.

Basket, Applied Flowers, Amber Thorn Handle, Blue	275.00
Biscuit Jar, Metal Lid & Handle, Ribbed Exterior, 8 In.	450.00
Bowl, Berry Pontil, Amber & Clear, 9 In.	200.00
Bowl, Blue Swirls & Stripes, Piecrust Rim, 8 1/2 In.	650.00
Bowl, Quilted, Satin, 4–Footed, Signed Patent, 8 In.	275.00
Bowl, Ruffled, Swirled & Striped, 8 1/2 In.	650.00
Box, Cover, Finial, Cream Casing, Pink, 4 1/2 x 5 In.	355.00
Box, Cover, Intaglio Cut, Cream & Pink Cased, 5 In.	355.00
Cheese Dish, Cover, Gilt Ball Finial, Rainbow, 5 1/2 In.	550.00
Cruet, Arabesque, Crackled, Bubble Stopper, Blue	145.00
Cuspidor, Woman's	975.00
Jam Jar, Arabesque, White Crackled Design, 4 3/4 In.	135.00
Lamp, Applied Fruit, 22 In.	2100.00
Lamp, Applied Fruit, Pink Opaline, 22 In.	4100.00
Lamp, Fairy, Stripes, Turned–Down Bottom Rim, 5 1/4 In.	815.00
Mustard, Plated Hinged Top, Flowers, Vines, 3 1/4 In.	225.00
Rose Bowl, Applied Strawberry, Blue Opalescent, 3 In.	515.00
Rose Bowl, Box–Pleated Top, Blue Swirl, 3 3/4 In.	195.00
Salt, Berry Punt, Threaded Crystal With White Swirl	245.00
Sugar & Creamer, Rainbow, Silver Plate Frame	235.00
Tray, Glass Strawberries, Blossoms, 10 x 4 1/2 In.	735.00
Tumbler, Applied Fruit, Amber Branches, Green Leaves	245.00
Tumbler, Enameled Leaves & Flowers	165.00
Vase, 4 Clear Opalescent Leaves, 12 In.	395.00
Vase, Amber Ruffled Rim, Applied Leaves, 7 1/2 In.	225.00
Vase, Applied Cherries, Amber Handles, 10 1/4 In.	895.00
Vase, Applied Pears & Leaves, Amber, 10 In.	295.00
Vase, Applied Ruffled Leaves, Green, Amber, 7 In.	145.00
Vase, Bulbous, Cylindrical Neck, Cased Rainbow, 11 In.	225.00
Vase, Canterbury Bells, Butterflies, 12 1/4 In.	4400.00
Vase, Cased Rainbow, Gold Rim, Bulbous, 10 1/2 In., Pair	225.00
Vase, Colored Leaves, Ruffled Top, 7 1/2 In.	225.00
Vase, Enamel Floral Neck, Pear Shape, Marked, 13 In.	285.00
Vase, Enameled Purple & Yellow Irises, Footed, 15 In.	195.00
Vase, Gourd Shape, Maize, Pink, Applied Handles, 9 In.	220.00
Vase, Leaves & Grass Cut To White, Dots At Neck, 5 In.	295.00

Vase, Mother-of-Pearl, Swirl, Creamy Lining, 5 1/8 In. 895.00
Vase, Optic, Salamander Handles, Signed, 12 In. 725.00
Vase, Rainbow Swirl, 7 1/4 In. 390.00
Vase, Red Berries, Amber Foliage, 6 In. 110.00
Vase, Ruffled Leaf Overlay, Cream, 6 x 5 In. 165.00
Vase, Ruffled Rim, 3 Ruffled Amber Leaves, 5 3/4 In. 165.00
Vase, Stylized Floras, Rigaree Panels, 7 1/4 In. 605.00
Vase, White Ferns, Pink Outside, 5 1/4 In. 275.00
Vase, White, Applied Leaf & Cone, 7 In. 50.00
Vase, White, Pink, Amber Leaves, Bell, Signed, 11 In. 325.00

STIEGEL type glass is listed here. It is almost impossible to be sure a piece was actually made by Stiegel, so the knowing collector refers to this glass as *Stiegel type.* Henry William Stiegel, a colorful immigrant to the colonies, started his first factory in Pennsylvania in 1763. He remained in business until 1774. Glassware was made in a style popular in Europe at that time and was similar to the glass of many other makers. It was made of clear or colored glass and was decorated with enamel colors, mold blown designs, or etching.

Bottle, Enamel Girl, 6 In. 65.00
Flask, Etched, Pewter Stopper, 1907 .... 45.00
Goblet, Flowers, Animals 1500.00

STOCKTON Terra Cotta Company was started in Stockton, California, in 1891. The art pottery called *Rekston* was made there after 1897. The factory burned in 1902 and never reopened.

Vase, Rekston, Flowers, 8 In. 450.00
Vase, Yellow, 8 In. 200.00

STONEWARE is a coarse, glazed, and fired potter's ceramic that is used to make crocks, jugs, bowls, etc. It is often decorated with cobalt blue decorations. Stoneware is still being made.

Batter Jar, Cobalt Blue At Ears, Spout, Label, 7 7/8 In. 155.00
Batter Jar, Long Tailed Bird On Branch & 4, Wire Bale, 9 1/4 In. 575.00
Batter Jar, Stenciled Snowflake, Tulip Below Spout, Cowden, Gal. 3000.00
Batter Jar, Tulip 1 Side, Foliage Other, Even Jones, 4, 8 7/8 In. 1200.00
Batter Jug, Cobalt Floral, Cork Stoppers, 9 In. 100.00
Batter Pail, Cowden & Wilcox, Blue Flower Petals, 1 Gal. 1450.00
Bean Pot, Heinz, Restaurant, Electric 125.00
Beater Jar, Advertising, Blue & White 65.00
Beater Jar, Grand Meadow, Minnesota .... 75.00 To 85.00
Berry Bowl, Flying Birds, Blue & White 79.50
Bookends, Indian, Full Headdress 65.00
Bowl, Applied Handles, Albany Slip Interior, Floral Design, 6 In. 300.00
Bowl, Apricots & Honeycomb, 9 1/4 In. 115.00
Bowl, Daisy, Blue & White, Bail, Large 125.00
Bowl, Incised Flower Head, St. Ives, Bernard Leach, 4 3/4 In. 750.00
Bowl, Milk, Brushed Cobalt Blue Floral, 4 3/4 x 8 1/2 In. 300.00
Bowl, Oatmeal Glaze, Manganese Rim, Lucie Rie, c.1972, 5 1/2 In. 600.00
Bowl, Spatter, Geneva, Iowa 100.00
Bowl, Wedding Ring, Blue & White, 8 In. 90.00
Butter, Wood Handle, Butterfly, Blue & White 95.00
Canister, Sugar, Cover, Blue & White 95.00
Canteen, Utica Commandery, Miniature 375.00
Chicken Waterer, Brown 125.00
Churn, A. O. Whitmore, Havana, N.Y., Cobalt Bird, 6 Gal. 1500.00
Churn, Blue Flower, 4 In. 2750.00
Churn, Dasher, Stylized Floral, No. 4, 16 1/2 In. 275.00
Churn, Double Bird Design, J. Burger, Jr., 6 Gal. 2100.00
Churn, E. W Farrington, N.Y., Bird, Design On Handles, 19 1/2 In. 650.00
Churn, General's Bust, Evan R. Jones, 6 Gal. ....*Illus* 12650.00
Churn, Haxton Ottman & Co., Port Edward, Floral Design, 16 In. 275.00
Churn, J. Hamilton, 4 Gal. 300.00

Churn, Marvel Butter Merger, Reed & Tyerman Co., 1/2 Gal. 70.00
Churn, N. A. White, Cobalt Blue Bird & Leaves, 6 Gal. 2420.00
Churn, Reed & Tyerman Co., Chicago, Illinois, 1 Gal. 195.00
Churn, Western, Salt & Bristol Glazed, 4 Gal. 120.00
Cookie Jar, Red, With Flowers 15.00
Cooler, Blue Band, 3 Gal. 155.00
Cooler, Blue Band, 4 Gal. 280.00
Cooler, Blue Band, 6 Gal. 200.00
Cooler, Cupid, Blue & White, 5 Gal. 595.00
Cooler, Foliage Designs, Wood Plug & Spigot, A. B. Lake, 23 1/4 In. 7600.00
Cooler, Monmouth, Blue & White, 6 Gal. 500.00
Cooler, Union Stoneware, Birch Leaf, 4 Gal. 235.00
Cooler, White & Blue Bands, 3 Gal. 35.00
Cooler, White Hall 160.00
Crock, 2 Lovebirds, Cobalt Blue, J. Norton & Co., 6 Gal. 1075.50
Crock, 8–Pointed Star, Face, T. Harrington, 3 Gal. ....*Illus* 4125.00
Crock, A. W. Eddy & Son, Macomb, Ill., Salt & Bristol Glazed, 5 Gal. 80.00
Crock, Bird In Flight, James Riley, 2 Gal. 1155.00
Crock, Bird On Leaves, S. L. Pewtress & Co., 3 Gal. 600.00
Crock, Bird, R. H. Macy & Co., 5 Gal. 750.00
Crock, Blue Design, New Brighton, Penna., 6 Gal. 80.00
Crock, Blue Hand Painted Slashes, No. 2, Dark Gray, 2 Gal. 180.00
Crock, Brewer & Holm, Bird Looking Back, 4 Gal. 525.00
Crock, Brewer & Holm, Havana, Blue Floral, 3 Gal. 130.00
Crock, Brushed Cobalt Blue Flower Design, 5 In. 150.00
Crock, Butter, Boston General Dept. Store, Blue & White 550.00
Crock, Butter, Cover, Apricot, Blue & White .... 125.00 To 150.00
Crock, Butter, Cover, Cow, Blue & White, Bail 195.00
Crock, Butter, Cover, Daisy & Lattice, S–Repeat Band Top 125.00
Crock, Butter, Cover, Flemish Grape Leaves, Blue & White 150.00
Crock, Butter, Cover, New Geneva, Concave Sides 2900.00
Crock, Butter, Rose Trellis, Blue & White 38.00
Crock, Butter, Whites, Utica, Deer–Hunting Scene, Blue, White 245.00
Crock, Butter, Wooden Cover, Apricot, Blue & White 95.00
Crock, Butter, Wooden Cover, Daisy, Blue & White 95.00
Crock, Charles McDonald, Fulper Brothers, 1889, 9 x 10 In. 4125.00
Crock, Cheese, Cobalt Blue Molded Design, Bail 300.00
Crock, Chicken, J. Norton & Co., 5 Gal. .... *Illus* 2475.00
Crock, Cobalt Blue Design, Applied Handles, 12 3/4 In. 1980.00
Crock, Cobalt Blue Design, Bird Perched On Stump, 9 In. 4950.00
Crock, Cobalt Blue Design, Deer, Applied Handles, 9 3/8 In. 7700.00
Crock, Cobalt Blue Design, Nichols & Boynton, 5 Gal. 1200.00
Crock, Cobalt Blue Design, Norton & Son, 19th Century, 3 Gal. 110.00
Crock, Cobalt Blue Feather Quillwork, No. 1, 7 1/2 In. 110.00
Crock, Cobalt Blue Rooster, 3 Gal. 980.00
Crock, Crow, Farrar & Co., 1 Gal 5115.00
Crock, Dark Blue Birds On Stump, J. Norton 3300.00
Crock, Double Bird, New York Stoneware Co., 5 Gal. 950.00
Crock, E. & L. P. Norton, 3, Cobalt Blue Leaf Design, 10 1/2 In. 275.00
Crock, Ewald Brothers Dairy, Blue, 2 Lb. 65.00
Crock, F. B. Norton & Co., Bird On Leaves, 3 Gal. 600.00
Crock, Fish Design 6350.00
Crock, Floral, N. A. White & Son, 3 Gal. 385.00
Crock, Fruit, Minnesota, 1 Gal. 90.00
Crock, George W. Helme, 3 Gal. 95.00
Crock, Gray, Blue Decorations, 4 Gal. 80.00
Crock, Hamilton, Eagle Design, 2 Earred Handles, 20 In. 3200.00
Crock, Haxstun & Co., Fort Edward, 4, Stylized Floral, 11 1/2 In. 350.00
Crock, Heinz Apple Butter, Cover, Bail Handle, Dated 1883 .... 395.00
Crock, Homebrew, Wennersten, Chicago, 5 Gal. 295.00
Crock, Impressed Label, Floral Design, Cobalt Blue, 9 In. 100.00
Crock, Impressed Label, Floral Design, Cobalt Blue, 12 1/2 In. 85.00
Crock, Impressed Label, Long–Tailed Bird, Cobalt Blue, 11 In. 95.00

Crock, J. Burger, Rochester, N.Y., Cobalt Bird, 5 Gal. 950.00
Crock, Lipton Tea, 5 In. ....:.......... 275.00
Crock, Lipton Tea, 6 In. 325.00
Crock, Long-Tailed Bird, Branch, Cobalt Blue Slip, 9 1/2 In. 195.00
Crock, Long-Tailed Parrot On Branch, J. Norton, 8 1/4 In. 675.00
Crock, Monmouth, 2 Men In A Crock Scene, 8 Gal. 130.00
Crock, Mrs. Jane Henderson, Springfield, Applied Handles, 8 In. 325.00
Crock, Pecking Chicken, 5 Gal. 495.00
Crock, Pecking Chicken, Cobalt Blue Slip, 9 1/2 In. 385.00
Crock, Quill Work 5, M. W. Sackett, 124 Water St., 12 3/4 In. 350.00
Crock, Raised Cobalt Bird Design, White's, 4 Gal. 375.00
Crock, Repperts, Stenciled Design, 2 Gal. 95.00
Crock, Salt, Butterfly, Blue & White 135.00
Crock, Salt, Cow Handle Lid 50.00
Crock, Single Bird, Black & Van Arsdale, 3 Gal. 220.00
Crock, Single Bird, Lamson & Swayzees, 2 Gal. 247.00
Crock, Stetzenmeyer, 4 Gal. 1025.00
Crock, Straight Sides, R. T. Williams, Blue & Gray, 6 Gal. 325.00
Crock, Stylized Design, 2 Birds, Cobalt Blue Slip, 8 3/4 In. 1500.00
Crock, Stylized Foliage Design, Brushed Cobalt Blue, 11 3/4 In. 85.00
Crock, White, Blue Band, 5 Lb. 25.00
Crock, Whitehall Pottery Works, A. D. Ruckel & Son, Tiny, 2 In. 700.00
Crock, Wright Gardiner, Branch Of Grapes & Foliage, 2 Gal. 225.00
Cruet, Mottled Brown, Glazed, 8 In. 12.50
Cuspidor, Dark Blue, Raised Grape Design 20.00
Flagon, Cobalt Blue Design, 10 1/4 In. 25.00
Flagon, Cobalt Blue Design, 14 3/4 In. 45.00
Flowerpot, Attached Saucer, Embossed Floral, 5 3/4 In. 25.00
Foot Warmer, Blue & White, Logan Pottery, 12 x 6 In. 175.00
Foot Warmer, Henderson, Embossed Cobalt Blue, Cap, With Chain 48.00
Footbath, Salt Glazed, Blue, White, C. Seafield, 1879, 14 x 7 In. 395.00
Inkwell, Gray Salt Glaze, 3 5/8 In. 55.00
Jar, Applied Handles, Cobalt Blue Floral Design, 11 5/8 In. 600.00
Jar, Applied Handles, Cobalt Blue Floral Design, 13 In. 250.00
Jar, Applied Handles, Cobalt Blue Foliage Design, 8 In. 145.00
Jar, Applied Side Handles, Cobalt Blue Floral Design, 11 In. 450.00
Jar, B. C. Milburn, Alex, Floral Tree, 2 Gal. 1050.00
Jar, Blue Daubs, Applied 2 Handles, Impressed, 10 1/2 In. 55.00
Jar, Canning Stone Fruit, Bail Handle, 1 Qt. 425.00
Jar, Canning, Blue Straight & Wavy Lines, 8 1/4 In. 325.00
Jar, Canning, Cobalt, Hamilton & Jones, Greensboro, Pa., 10 In. 95.00
Jar, Canning, Stenciled Label, A. Conrad, New Geneva, 9 1/2 In. 250.00
Jar, Canning, Stenciled Label, J. C. Pickett & Bro., 10 1/4 In. 400.00
Jar, Canning, W. B. Lowry, Roseville, 1 Qt. 40.00
Jar, Cobalt Blue Brushed Floral Band, 8 1/4 In. 400.00
Jar, Cobalt Blue Design, 9 1/4 In. 75.00
Jar, Cobalt Blue Floral, J. Swank & Co., 4, Ovoid, 15 1/4 In. 175.00
Jar, Cobalt Blue Floral, Ovoid, Impressed 4, 14 1/2 In. 400.00
Jar, Cobalt Blue Slip, Flower One Side, 1851 & 2 Other, 13 In. 275.00
Jar, Cobalt Blue Stenciled, Freehand Label, 11 1/2 In. 360.00
Jar, Cobalt Blue Stenciled, Freehand Label, 12 1/4 In. 125.00
Jar, Cobalt Blue Stripes & Commas, 6 1/4 In. 400.00
Jar, Cobalt Blue Stripes, 6 3/4 In. 300.00
Jar, Cobalt Blue Stripes, Foliage, Ovoid, 8 1/4 In. 80.00
Jar, Cobalt Blue Stripes, Wavy Lines, 8 In. 200.00
Jar, Cobalt Blue, Design, Marked, 15 In. 95.00
Jar, Cobalt Blue, Impressed Label, 9 In. 150.00
Jar, Cover, Cobalt Blue Floral, Jordon 3, Ovoid, 13 1/4 In. 115.00
Jar, Cowden & Wilcox, Man In Moon, Ear Handles, 2 Gal. 2800.00
Jar, Floral, Little-St. N.Y., Pottery Works 2, 11 1/2 In. 150.00
Jar, Geometric Design, A. P. Donaghho, 3, 14 1/2 In. 375.00
Jar, Hannah & Co. Snuff, Impressed 4, Blue, 15 1/4 In. 300.00
Jar, Impressed Label, Foliage Design, Cobalt Blue Guill, 11 In. 525.00

Stoneware, Churn, General's
Bust, Evan R. Jones, 6 Gal.

Stoneware, Crock, 8-Pointed
Star, Face, T. Harrington,
3 Gal.

Stoneware, Crock, Chicken,
J. Norton & Co., 5 Gal.

Stoneware, Jug, Anchor, West Troy
Pottery, 5 Gal.

Stoneware, Jug, Tree On Dotted Ground,
Haxstun Ottman, 3 Gal.

Jar, J. E. Enelx, New Geneva, Pa., Applied Handles, 16 1/4 In.	650.00
Jar, L. Minier 4, Cobalt Blue Flower, Applied Handles, 13 1/2 In.	225.00
Jar, Label, Kampfer & Muhleman, Clarington, Ohio 4, 14 3/4 In.	200.00
Jar, New York Stoneware Co. 1, Stylized Blue Floral, 11 1/2 In.	75.00
Jar, Ovoid, Applied Handles, Cobalt Blue Floral Design, 15 In.	200.00
Jar, Ovoid, Brushed Cobalt Blue, Straight, Wavy Lines, 6 1/2 In.	150.00
Jar, Pickle, Brown On White, Dated April 1907	45.00
Jar, Polkadot Bird On Branch, Roberts, Binghamton, 7 1/4 In.	300.00
Jar, Preserving, Cobalt Blue Brushed Stripes, 8 In.	165.00
Jar, Preserving, Cobalt Blue Floral, Applied Handles, 7 1/2 In.	240.00
Jar, R. T. Williams Mfg., New Geneva, Pa., Applied Handles, 14 In.	205.00
Jar, Random Cobalt Blue Marks, 7 5/8 In.	200.00
Jar, Red Clay, Brownish Gray Salt Glaze, Cobalt Blue, 5 3/4 In.	305.00
Jar, Red, Gray Salt Glaze, A. Black, Confluence, Pa., Ovoid, 14 In.	1100.00
Jar, Salt Glazed, Ottoman Bros., Cobalt Blue Design, 1 Gal.	75.00
Jar, Stenciled, Hamilton & Jones, Greensboro, Pa. 5, Ovoid, 16 In.	225.00
Jar, Williams & Reppert, 2, Cobalt Blue Stenciled, 11 3/4 In.	205.00
Jug, 2 Blue Lines, Altschul, 14 In.	125.00
Jug, 2-Tone Brown Glaze, Hahn, 13 3/4 In.	85.00
Jug, Anchor, West Troy Pottery, 5 Gal. ....*Illus*	4950.00
Jug, Backwards Looking Polkadot Bird, Cobalt Blue, 13 1/2 In.	375.00
Jug, Bird On Branch, Cobalt Blue Quillwork, 11 1/4 In.	350.00
Jug, Blue Flowers, Cowden & Wilcox, 2 Gal.	445.00
Jug, C. Hart, Ogdensburgh, Penna., 2 Gal.	250.00
Jug, C. Crolius Mfg., Manhattan Mills, N.Y., Handle, 11 3/8 In.	700.00
Jug, Chicken Waterer, Inverted, Western, 1 Gal.	95.00
Jug, Cobalt Bird Design, Norton, 1 Gal.	650.00
Jug, Cobalt Blue Bird Design, Semi-Ovoid, 2 Gal.	180.00
Jug, Cobalt Blue Design, Strap Handle, Sloped Body, 14 In.	4950.00
Jug, Cobalt Blue Floral Design, Handles, 9 In.	175.00
Jug, Cobalt Blue Flowers, Tan, 3 Gal.	80.00

Jug, Cobalt Blue Foliage & Incised 2, Handle, 14 In. 85.00
Jug, Cobalt Blue Foliage Vine, R. W. Russell, Pa. & 2, 12 1/4 In. 350.00
Jug, Cobalt Blue Quillwork Label, M. J. Madden, 12 In. 150.00
Jug, Cobalt Blue Stenciled Label, 13 3/4 In. 80.00
Jug, Cobalt Blue Stenciled Label, 13 In. 100.00
Jug, Cobalt Blue Stenciled Label, Hamilton & Jones, 14 3/4 In. 275.00
Jug, Cobalt Blue, Impressed Label, 13 3/4 In. 200.00
Jug, Cobalt Blue, Impressed Label, 16 1/2 In. 100.99
Jug, Cobalt Fired To Dark Gray Blue, Floral Design, Ovoid, 12 In. 175.00
Jug, D.C. Fry & Co., Colfax Mineral Water, Brown Over White 250.00
Jug, Dark Glaze, Applied Strap Handle, Ovoid, Incised 2, 13 In. 25.00
Jug, Dog–Like Animal, Grayish Blue Slip, 11 In. 925.00
Jug, Double Ear Handles, Stylized Flower Design, 17 1/4 In. 625.00
Jug, Double Sunflowers, Polkadots, Cobalt Blue, 17 1/4 In. 600.00
Jug, F. T. Wright, 1 Gal. 48.00
Jug, Floral Design, Cobalt Blue Slip, Impressed Label, 5 1/2 In. 400.00
Jug, Floral Design, Cobalt Blue, Pebble Glaze, 18 In. 495.00
Jug, Front In Form Of A Face, Bulging Eyes, Handle On Back, 6 In. 3850.00
Jug, Geddes, Syracuse, N.Y., No. 2, Design 1000.00
Jug, Gilson & Co., Reading, Pa., Cobalt Blue At Handle, 11 In. 150.00
Jug, Gray Glaze, Red Clay, Amber Highlights, Strap Handle, 13 In. 150.00
Jug, Grotesque Double Face, Salt Glaze, 1840s, 7 1/4 In. 8800.00
Jug, Hamilton & Jones, 12 Gal. 1100.00
Jug, Harrington & Burger, Flower, 3 Gal. 1100.00
Jug, Harrington & Burger, No. 3, Flower 350.00
Jug, Harvest, Gray Salt Glaze, Blue Highlights, 8 1/2 In. 140.00
Jug, Impressed Design, Fish & Berries, Grayish Brown Glaze, 9 In. 410.00
Jug, Impressed Label, Brushed Cobalt Blue Floral Design, 16 In. 350.00
Jug, Impressed Label, Cobalt Blue, 11 1/2 In. 225.00
Jug, Impressed Label, Long Tail–Birded, Branch, Cobalt Blue, 16 In 600.00
Jug, Incised & Ochre Design, Strap Handle, 16 1/2 In. 2475.00
Jug, Incised Bird On Branch, Basket, Star, Blue, 3 5/8 In. 3300.00
Jug, Incised Foliage, Brown Slip On Lip, Tooled Neck, 14 1/2 In. 223.00
Jug, L. W. Fenton, Ft. Lounsberg, Vt., Foliage Design, 11 1/2 In. 175.00
Jug, Little Brown Jug, Old 1869 Rye Whisky, Cylinder, 1 Qt. 45.00
Jug, Long–Tailed Polkadot Bird, White's & 2, 13 3/4 In. 550.00
Jug, Motto, Ado, Fred Molly, St. Louis, 1 Qt. 65.00
Jug, Motto, Deitrich Distillery, 1 Qt. 65.00
Jug, Nock & Snyder, Louisville, Ky., Black Letters, 1 Gal. 75.00
Jug, Ovoid, Brushed Design, Cobalt Blue, 10 3/4 In. 95.00
Jug, P. H. Donahue & Co., Wines & Liquors, Lowell, Mass., 2 Gal. 65.00
Jug, Pecking Chicken, Cobalt Blue Slip, Impressed Label, 11 In. 1550.00
Jug, Pouring Spout, Stylized Floral Design, Cobalt Blue, 13 In. 220.00
Jug, Pure Cider Vinegar, C. E. Lowe, Allegheny, Pa., Brown, 1/4 Pt. 55.00
Jug, Ribbed Strap Handle, Blue Paint, 7 1/4 In. 70.00
Jug, Running Rabbit, Trees, J. C. Waelde, Quillwork 2, 13 3/4 In. 1550.00
Jug, Salt Glazed, Nathan Porter, West Troy, N.Y., 2 Gal. 125.00
Jug, Scovil, Pelee Island Wine Co., Impressed Label, 9 1/4 In. 45.00
Jug, Seated Polkadot Lion, Troy, N.Y. 4, 17 1/4 In. 450.00
Jug, Starburst, 2 Gal. 900.00
Jug, Stenciled & Freehand Label, James Hamilton, 14 1/4 In. 525.00
Jug, Stetzenmeyer, Rochester, N.Y. No. 2, Picture 850.00
Jug, Stylized Floral Design, Cobalt Blue Slip, 15 3/4 In. 525.00
Jug, Stylized Floral, E. & A. K. Ballard, 2, Blue Slip, 14 In. 195.00
Jug, Stylized Fruit, Stem In Cobalt Blue, 12 1/4 In. 125.00
Jug, Stylized Tulip & 2, Cortland, 13 5/8 In. 400.00
Jug, Thompson & Co., Gardiner, Cobalt Blue At Handle, 11 1/2 In. 105.00
Jug, Tree Branch, Brown–Black Glaze, Strap Handle, 6 In. 65.00
Jug, Tree On Dotted Ground, Haxstun Ottman, 3 Gal. ....*Illus* 1265.00
Jug, W. Rooker, Easton, Pa., Florals, Strap Handle, 3 Gal. 225.00
Jug, Western Stoneware, 1 Gal. 25.00
Jug, Whiskey, M. J. Miller's Sons, Dark Top, 3 Gal. 200.00
Jug, Wise & Bros., Mound Valley, Kansas, 3 1/4 In. 55.00

Match Holder, Cobalt Blue Base Band, Striker, 2 5/8 In. 20.00
Meat Tenderizer, Wild Rose, Blue & White 175.00
Meat Tenderizer, Wood Handle, Yellow, Patent 1877 .... 60.00
Meat Tenderizer, Wooden Handle, 9 In. 70.00
Mixing Bowl, Cream, Blue Band 25.00
Mixing Bowl, Green, 10 x 5 1/2 In. 12.00
Mortar & Pestle, Drugstore, 1800s, 9 In. 135.00
Mug, Barrel, Blue, 8 Oz. 25.00
Mug, Cairo Water Purifier, Frog Interior 1000.00
Mug, Flying Bird, Blue & White ....95.00 To 125.00
Pie Plate, Blue & White, Blue Wall, Brick Edge 165.00
Pitcher & Bowl, Feather & Swirl, Blue & White 165.00
Pitcher, Albany Slip, Zigzag Band, John Fowler, 1867, 7 3/4 In. 65.00
Pitcher, Applied Tavern Scenes, 5 5/8 In. 65.00
Pitcher, Arc & Leaf, Blue & White, 10 In. ....65.00 To 75.00
Pitcher, Batter, Cobalt Blue Stylized Foliage, Bail, Handle, 9 In. 500.00
Pitcher, Brushed Cobalt Blue Floral Design, 10 1/4 In. 175.00
Pitcher, Brushed Cobalt Blue Leaf Design, Blue At Handle, 13 In. 350.00
Pitcher, Butterfly, 9 In. 105.00
Pitcher, Castle, Blue & White, 10 In. 165.00
Pitcher, Cattail & Rushes, Blue & White, 10 In. 150.00
Pitcher, Cherry Cluster, 9 In. 200.00
Pitcher, Cobalt Blue Floral Design, 10 3/4 In. 700.00
Pitcher, Cobalt Blue Floral, R. C. R. Phila., 7 5/8 In. 1300.00
Pitcher, Cow, Blue & White, 8 In. 150.00
Pitcher, Cow, Green & White, 8 In. 175.00
Pitcher, Cow, Yellow & Green, 9 In. 225.00
Pitcher, Doe & Fawn, Blue & White, 10 In. 250.00
Pitcher, Dutch Boy & Girl Kissing, Windmill, Blue & White, 8 In. 225.00
Pitcher, Dutch Boy & Girl, Blue & Gray, 7 In. 80.00
Pitcher, Dutch Boy & Girl, Kissing 130.00
Pitcher, Eagle With Shield, Blue & White 275.00
Pitcher, Edelweiss, 11 In. 165.00
Pitcher, Embossed Doe & Fawn, Rust & Cream 120.00
Pitcher, Fish Scale & Rose, Blue & White, 8 In. 95.00
Pitcher, Fish Scale & Rose, Blue & White, 12 In. ....125.00 To 135.00
Pitcher, Flying Bird, Blue & White, 8 In. ....550.00 To 725.00
Pitcher, Girl & Dog, Blue & White, 8 In. 650.00
Pitcher, Good Luck, Blue, 10 In. 155.00
Pitcher, Hunting Scene, Outlined In Blue, Blue & White 350.00
Pitcher, Indian In War Bonnet, Blue & White, 10 In. 195.00
Pitcher, Kissing Pilgrims, 9 In. 225.00
Pitcher, Leaping Deer, 8 In. ....195.00 To 250.00
Pitcher, Light Brown Albany Slip, 8 1/4 In. 75.00
Pitcher, Lovebirds, Brown Glaze, 9 In. 98.00
Pitcher, Lyons, Cobalt Blue Leaf Sprigs, 10 1/2 In. 302.50
Pitcher, Poinsettia, 10 In. ....125.00 To 225.00
Pitcher, Raised Bands & Rivets, Blue & White, 10 In. 125.00
Pitcher, Rose On Trellis, Blue & White, 6 3/4 In. 120.00
Pitcher, Rose On Trellis, Gray & Blue, 6 3/4 In. 98.00
Pitcher, Stag & Pine Tree, 9 In. 475.00
Pitcher, Stag & Pine, Tree, 9 In. 400.00
Pitcher, Swastika, Blue & White 185.00
Pitcher, Wild Rose, 9 In. 265.00
Pitcher, Wildflower, Blue & White, 10 In. 210.00
Pitcher, Windmill & Bush, Blue & White, 8 In. 195.00
Pitcher, Windmill, Blue, 9 In. 135.00
Pitcher, Windy City, Blue & White, 9 In. 425.00
Rolling Pin, Blue & White Swirl 850.00
Rose Bowl, Blue Gray, Molded, Whites, Utica, N.Y., Raised Horsehead 120.00
Salt Box, Apricot, Blue & White 150.00
Salt Box, Butterfly, Blue & White ....115.00 To 130.00
Salt Box, Cover, Blackberry, Blue & White 95.00

Salt Box, Hanging, Daisies On Snowflakes, Blue, White 80.00
Salt Box, Hanging, Waffle, Blue & White 125.00
Salt Box, Maple Leaf, Blue & White 95.00
Salt Box, Windmill, Blue & White, Germany 65.00
Salt Box, Wooden Lid, Lovebirds, Blue & White 195.00
Saucer, For Flowerpot, Blue & White, 6 1/2 In. 22.50
Soap Dish, Flower Cluster, Blue & White 115.00
Soap Dish, Rose Decal, Blue & White 65.00
Soap Dish, Rose, Blue & White 115.00
Strainer, Shiny Albany Slip Glaze 100.00
Teapot, Brown Glaze, Bulbous 45.00
Teapot, Rebecca 45.00
Toothpick, Swan .... 35.00 To 65.00
Tray, Bread, Redware & Slip Design, Speckled, Striped Bird, 13 In. 1760.00
Vase, Incised Leaf & Floral, Bailey, c.1875, 9 1/2 In. 440.00
Vase, Metallic Glaze, Indian Hills Pottery, 6 In. 40.00
Vase, Mushroom, Celadon Glaze, Robert Arneson, c.1955, 16 1/8 In. 2530.00
Vase, Speckled Celadon Glaze, St. Ives, Bernard Leach, 3 1/2 In. 470.00
Vase, Textured Matte Pooling To Foot, Lucie Rie, c.1958, 9 1/2 In 770.00
Vase, Turquoise, Broadmore Pottery Co., 7 In. 60.00
Wash Set, Fish Scale & Roses, Blue & White 375.00

STORE fixtures, cases, cutters, and other items that have no advertising as
part of the decoration are listed here. Most items found in an old store are
listed in the Advertising section in this book.

Auto Dupligraph, Paper Roll, Furniture Store, Zanesville, Oh., 1883 .... 95.00
Bin, Bolt, 98 Drawers, Hexagonal, Pine 1795.00
Bin, Flour, Large Tapered Legs, Diamond Design Front, Unusual 375.00
Cabinet, Bulk Spices, Decorated Tins, Beveled Mirror 750.00
Cabinet, Hardware, Pine, Poplar, 8 Graduated Drawers, N.Y., 1890 .... 425.00
Cabinet, Oak, Made For National Cash Register Base, 7 Small Drawers 200.00
Cabinet, Ribbon, Walnut 500.00
Cabinet, Walnut, 76 Drawers, White Porcelain Knobs, 1860–1890 .... 850.00
Candy Jar, Zatek Chocolate Billits 350.00
Case, Cigar, Counter Top, Oak, 12 x 52 In. 200.00
Case, Display, Paw Feet, Circular, Gilt Wood & Gesso, Pair 4950.00
Cheese Cutter, Cast Iron 75.00
Chest, Apothecary, 28 Drawers 2000.00
Counter, General Store, Oak, 10 Ft. 300.00
Counter, Grain, Sherer Brand, 7 Ft. 1500.00
Counter, Seed, 12 Drawers, Oak 1850.00
Counter, Seed, 12 Windows 1200.00
Counter, Seed, Mixed Wood, 2 Doors, Beside 10 Drawers 1000.00
Cup Dispenser, Dixie, Wall Bracket & Cups, 1 Cent 350.00
Cupboard, Sellers, Oak, Stenciled Design On Door, 21 x 71 In. 90.00
Dispenser, Cigarette, Elephant, Iron 125.00
Dispenser, Fountain Syrup, 4 Pumps, Porcelain, Stainless Steel 225.00
Display Cabinet, Revolving, Cast Iron Frame, Westphal Co. 550.00
Display Case, Pine, Glass Front, Rear Sliding Doors, 84 x 40 x 30 In. 225.00
Display, Case, Candy Store, For Penny Candy 350.00
Display, Dancing Pig, Bowtie, For Meat Market, Plywood, 7 1/2 Ft. 525.00
Display, Screwdriver, Oversized 190.00
Display, Stand, Hat, Wooden, Set Of 4 .... 37.50
Display, Stork, Celluloid, For Children's Store, 16 In. 55.00
Display, Window, Santa Claus, Composition Face, Boots, 10 In. 310.00
Figure, Alice In Wonderland, Mechanical 550.00
Figure, Mad Hatter, Mechanical 550.00
Figure, Tweedledee & Tweedledum, Mechanical, Pair 550.00
Holder, Bag, Attached String Holder 1600.00
Holder, Ice Cream Cone, Metal Lid & Pull, Glass, 3 Stacks 385.00
Machine, Pop & Hot Popcorn, 1 Bag At A Time 500.00
Machine, Popcorn, Dumbar 1000.00
Machine, Popcorn, Manley 500.00

Mannequin, Half Round, Waved Hair, Adjustable Arms, Wood Base, 70 In. 1760.00
Measuring Device, For Cloth, Mechanical 55.00
Mirror, Free Standing, Mahogany, Ice Cream Parlor, 1910, Large 600.00
Rack, Pants, Pullman, Chrome, Rochester 20.00
Showcase, Jewelry, Brass Claw Feet, Walnut, 10 Ft. 1500.00
Straw Dispenser, Glass, Wide Ribbed, Metal Top & Insert 78.00
Straw Holder, Paneled, Green, Insert 425.00
Straw Holder, Soda Fountain, Glass, Cover 55.00
Straw Holder, Wooden, Pat. 1943 .... 50.00
String Holder, With Cone Holder & String, Cast Iron, Dated 1899 .... 38.00
Theater Seat, Cherrywood, 100 Piece 4000.00
Tobacco Cutter, Boy On Sled, Pocket 95.00
Tobacco Cutter, Counter Top, Brass, Sliding Cutter 85.00
Tobacco Cutter, Enterprise, Cast Iron, 1885 .... 65.00
Tobacco Cutter, Figural, Temperance Bitter Bottle 125.00
Tobacco Cutter, Figure, Depress Arm, Cutter In Mouth, Iron, 6 In. 577.00
Tobacco Cutter, Griswold, Iron, Dated 1883 .... 125.00
Tobacco Cutter, Guillotine, Handmade, Iron 145.00
Tobacco Cutter, Keywind, Harvard 275.00
Tobacco Cutter, Man, Movable Arm 55.00
Tobacco Cutter, Mechanical, Clockwork, Pure Cuban, Nickeled, 7 In. 265.00
Tobacco Cutter, Scissor Type 17.50
Tobacco Cutter, Spearhead, Iron 120.00

STOVES have been used in America for heating since the eighteenth century and for cooking since the nineteenth century. Most types of wood, coal, gas, kerosene, and even some electric stoves are collected.

Black Enameled Tin, Turquoise Door Oven, High Legs, Early Electric 165.00
Child's, Jewel, Iron 350.00
Cook, Conowingo, 6 Plate 150.00
Cook, Glenwood, Gray & White Granite, Gas, 2 Drawers, Oven 425.00
Cook, Keen Kutter, Blue Enameled 650.00
Cook, Quick Meal, Blue Granite, Nickel Plated Trim, 1920s 850.00
Cook, Universal, Gray & White Granite, Electric 425.00
Cook, Wayne, Visible Gas Pump, Positive Stop 850.00
Cook, Windsor, Blue & White, Chrome Trim, 1930s 1200.00
Crawford, Cast Iron 275.00
Eclipse, Fancy Cast Iron, Salesman's Sample 910.00
Florence Stove Co., White Porcelain, Legs, Gas, Late 1920-1930 .... 1500.00
Heating, Brass Doors & Fittings, Foliate Design, Porcelain, France 1760.00
Heating, Gas, Graniteware, Gray, Green Legs, 6 x 13 In. 20.00
Home Comfort, Blue Porcelain, With Reservoir 495.00
Keen Kutter, Salesman's Sample 800.00
Laurel Potbelly, No. 153, Florence Hot Blast–Air Tight, Mica Windows 1500.00
Majestic Junior, Painted Metal, Warming Oven, Hinged Doors, 31 In. 660.00
Parlor, Albany, No. 3 .... 260.00
Parlor, American Beauty 200.00
Parlor, Colonial, Pillars, Nickel Bumpers, Urn Finial 1500.00
Potbelly, Sears, Coal Type 175.00
Traveling, Embossed March 28, 1877 .... 98.00

STRAWBERRY, see Soft Paste category

STRETCH GLASS is named for the strange stretch marks in the glass. It was made by many glass companies in the United States from about 1900 to the 1920s. It is iridescent. Most American stretch glass is molded; most European pieces are blown and may have a pontil mark.

Bowl, Fenton, Blue, 6 In. 25.00
Console Set, Blue, 3 Piece 125.00
Console Set, Candleholder, 11 1/2 In. Bowl, Twist Stem, 3 Pc. 85.00
Pitcher, Lemonade, Cobalt 150.00
Plate, Server, Center Handle, 11 In. 20.00
Plate, Yellow Orange, 6 In. 16.00

SULPHIDES are cameos of unglazed white porcelain encased in transparent glass. The technique was patented in 1819 in France and has been used ever since for paperweights, decanters, tumblers, marbles, and other type of glassware. Paperweights and marbles are listed in their own sections.

Bottle, Cut, Military Man	400.00
Tumbler, Molded, Green, Flower	750.00

SUMIDA, or Sumida Gawa, is a Japanese pottery. The pieces collected by that name today were made about 1895 to 1970. There has been much confusion about the name of this ware, and it is often called *Korean Pottery.* Most pieces have a very heavy orange–red, blue, or green glaze, with raised three–dimensional figures as decorations.

Bowl, 6 Figures, 7 In.	345.00
Lamp, Raised Figures Of Children	200.00
Mug, Figure Of Boy & Bird, 5 In.	50.00
Vase, Flying Cranes, Black & White Medallions, 15 In.	400.00

SUNBONNET BABIES were first introduced in 1902 in the *Sunbonnet Babies Primer.* The stories were by Eulalie Osgood Grover, illustrated by Bertha Corbett. The children's faces were completely hidden by the sunbonnets. The children had been pictured in black and white before this time, but the color pictures in the book were immediately successful. The Royal Bayreuth China Company made a full line of children's dishes decorated with the Sunbonnet Babies. Some Sunbonnet Babies plates have been reproduced, but are clearly marked.

Bell, Fishing	410.00
Bell, Fishing, Royal Bayreuth	410.00
Bell, Friday, Sweeping, Royal Bayreuth	50.00
Cake Plate, Washing, Blue Mark, 8 1/4 In.	225.00
Candleholder, Fishing, Shield Back	350.00
Creamer, Cleaning, Pinch Spout, Blue Mark	275.00
Creamer, Ironing Day, Marked	195.00
Creamer, Sweeping, Royal Bayreuth	145.00
Creamer, Washing, Bulbous	95.00
Cup & Saucer, Mending & Ironing	145.00
Cup & Saucer, Washing, Royal Bayreuth	225.00
Dish, Feeding, Roll Top, Blue Mark, Large	335.00
Dish, Ironing, Cloverleaf Shape, Blue Mark	195.00
Hair Receiver, Washing, Tall Legs, Royal Bayreuth	450.00
Mustard, Attached Underplate, Spoon, Blue Mark	395.00
Nappy, Sweeping, Club Shape, Royal Bayreuth	150.00
Pitcher, Ironing, Gold Trim & Handle, Royal Bayreuth	525.00
Pitcher, Milk, Cleaning, Blue Mark, 5 In.	295.00
Plaque, Signed, Round, 11 1/2 In.	22.00
Plate, Ironing, Royal Bayreuth, Blue Mark, 6 In.	175.00
Plate, Washing, 7 1/2 In.	135.00
Relish, Sweeping, Royal Bayreuth	225.00
Rose Bowl, Marked	295.00
Sauce, Sewing, Royal Bayreuth	140.00
Sauce, Washing, Royal Bayreuth, Blue Mark	125.00
Sugar & Creamer, Fishing On Sugar, Cleaning On Creamer	395.00
Teapot, Sewing, Blue Mark	475.00
Vase, Cleaning, Blue Mark	295.00

SUNDERLAND luster is a name given to a special type of pink luster made by Leeds, Newcastle, and other English firms during the nineteenth century. The luster glaze is metallic and glossy and appears to have bubbles in it. Other pieces of luster are listed in the Luster section.

Bowl, Green Transfer, Sailor's Farewell, Masonic Design, 11 In.	135.00
Cup & Saucer, Handleless, Strawberry Luster	100.00
Jug, Sailor's Tear, Noble Bark, Iron Bridge, Pink, 1810, 7 1/4 In.	825.00

Pitcher, Black Transfer, Garibaldi, Foresters, Luster, 8 3/4 In.	125.00
Plaque, Wall, William Gladstone Center, Spatter Edge, 8 1/2 In.	75.00
Plate, Dickens' Days, Copper Luster, 7 In.	95.00
Salt, Cloud Pattern, Footed, Pink Luster, Master	40.00
Shaving Mug, Saucer, Mariner's Compass	195.00

SUPERMAN was created by two seventeen–year–olds in 1938. The first issue of *Action* comics had the strip. Superman remains popular and became the hero of a radio show in 1940, cartoons in the 1940s, a television series, and several major movies.

Bank, Dime Register, 2 1/2 x 2 1/2 In.	185.00
Bank, Figural, Plastic, 1965, Transogram	49.00
Belt Buckle, 1975	6.00
Book, Coloring, 1939	200.00
Box, Post Honeycombs, With Superman Action Poster, 1979	75.00
Button, Action Comics, Pin Back	75.00
Button, America Club	50.00
Button, Kirk Alyn Autographed	15.00
Cake Decoration Set, Marked DC Comics, 6 Piece	2.50
Cookie Jar, California Originals	250.00 To 295.00
Doll, Rubber, 5 1/2 In.	3.75
Figure, Wooden, 1940s	1224.00
Film Strip, Superman, Cheerios, 4 Different	16.00
Fork & Spoon Set, Stainless Steel, Imperial Knife Co., 1966	42.00
Game, Board, Speed, 1940, Milton Bradley	239.00
Game, Calling Superman, A Game Of News Reporting, 1954, Transogram	198.00
Game, Flying Bingo, 1966	40.00
Game, Superman II, Milton Bradley	40.00
Gumball Machine, 1960s	25.00
Horseshoe Set, Box, 1940s	95.00
Horseshoe Set, Sports Club Card	125.00
Lunch Box, 1978	12.00
Lunch Box, Thermos, 1967	125.00 To 150.00
Model Kit, Superboy, Unassembled, 1965, Aurora	149.00
Movie Viewer, Box	45.00
Movie Viewer, Film, On Card, 1955	350.00
Movie, Serial, Superman Vs. The Atom Man, 1950	169.00
Necktie	145.00
Paddle Ball Set, Red Plastic Paddle, 1966, Complete	15.00
Paddler, Kiddie, Box, 1950s	90.00
Pin, Pep, Kellogg's, 1940s	28.00
Pistol, Krypton Ray	250.00
Pistol, Water Gun, On Card, 1967	125.00
Pistol, Water, Shape Of Superman Flying	15.00
Poster, Superman II, Color, 1981, 26 3/4 x 40 1/2 In.	12.00
Puppet, Hand, Superman	100.00
Ring, Black Plane	175.00
Ring, Crusader	200.00
Sliding Puzzle, 1960s, Roalex	75.00
Spoon, 1960	17.00
Tank, Battery Operated	250.00 To 895.00
Tumbler, Pepsi–Cola, Moon Series, 1976	15.00
Wristwatch, 1976	60.00
Yo–Yo, Clark Kent, Duncan, 1970	45.00

SWANKYSWIGS are small drinking glasses. In 1933, the Kraft Food Company began to market cheese spreads in these decorated, reusable glass tumblers. They were discontinued from 1941 to 1946, then made again from 1947 to 1958. Then plain glasses were used for most of the cheese, although a few special decorated Swankyswigs have been made since that time. A complete list of prices can be found in *Kovels' Price Guide to Depression Glass & American Dinnerware.*

Band No. 2	1.75

Black Band, Red 1.50
Bustlin' Betsy, Brown 1.75
Bustlin' Betsy, Orange 1.50
Cornflower, No. 1, Blue 2.00
Cornflower, No. 2, Red 1.75
Cornflower, No. 2, Yellow .... 1.50 To 1.75
Daisy, Red 1.50
Forget–Me–Not, Dark Blue 1.75
Forget–Me–Not, Light Blue 1.50
Forget–Me–Not, Red 1.75
Jonquil 1.50
Kiddie, Black 1.75
Kiddie, Green 2.00
Kiddie, Orange 3.00
Sailboat, Green 10.00
Tulip, No. 1, Black 3.00
Tulip, No. 1, Red .... 1.50 To 2.50
Tulip, No. 3, Dark Blue 2.75
Tulip, No. 3, Red 1.75
Tulip, No. 3, Yellow .... 1.50 To 2.75
Violet 1.50

SWORDS of all types that are of interest to collectors are listed here. The
military dress sword with elaborate handle is probably the most wanted. Be
sure to display swords in a safe way, out of reach of children.

Bayonet, British, Triangular, With Scabbard, 1870s 28.00
Bayonet, Faschinenmesser, German Dress, Frog, Dated 1939 .... 60.00
Bayonet, World War II, Enfield, British 40.00
Cavalry, Large Brass Guard, Marked Berlin 65.00
Chinese River Pirate's, 1800s 350.00
Civil War, Officer's, Brass Knuckle Guard, Engraved Eagle, J. B. Hinton 495.00
Confederate, Charleston, S. C., Leather Covered Scabbard, 19 In. 825.00
Confederate, Naval Officer's, Courtney & Tenant 5170.00
Cutlass, Civil War, U.S. Navy, Ames Mfg. Co., c.1890 .... 395.00
Cutlass, U.S. Navy, Large Brass Cup Guard, Copper Rivets Sheath, 1860 .... 210.00
Dagger, Nazi SA, Scabbard, Marked Christian Werk 210.00
Foot Artillery, Model 1833, N. P. Ames, Cabotville, Dated 1847 .... 1200.00
French Officer's, Dress, Engraved Steel Blade, Leather Scabbard 1320.00
German Artillery, Lion's Head, Inlaid Ruby Eyes, c.1910 .... 345.00
Katana, Japan, Dated 1789, 35 In. 440.00
Naval Officer's, Presentation, Owner's Name, Leather Case, 1852 .... 650.00
Nazi, Army Officer's, Lion Head, Eagle, Swastika, Solingen 395.00
Revolutionary War, Lion's Head Pommel 1870.00
Saber, Lion's Head Pommel, Brass Hilt, American, Peterson, No. 13, 1775 .... 2200.00
Samurai, World War II Naval Fittings, Sharkskin Scabbard, c.1325 .... 1700.00

SYRACUSE is a trademark used by the Onondaga Pottery of Syracuse,
New York. The company was established in 1871. It is still working. The
name became the Syracuse China Company in 1966. It is known for fine
dinnerware and restaurant china.

Ashtray, Dog, 4 In. 12.00
Compote, Flower Bands, Women, 9 In. 20.00
Cup & Saucer, Rosalie 20.00
Dinner Set, Jefferson Pattern, Old Ivory, Gold Leaves, 40 Piece 300.00
Plate, Coventry, 10 In. 15.00
Plate, Rosalie, 9 3/4 In. 18.00
Plate, Tugo Restaurant Logo, 10 In. 18.00

TAPESTRY, PORCELAIN, see Rose Tapestry category

TEA CADDY is the name for a small box made to hold tea leaves. In the eighteenth century, tea was very expensive and it was stored under lock and key. The first tea caddies were made with locks. By the nineteenth century, tea was more plentiful and the tea caddy was larger. Often there were two sections, one for green tea, one for black tea.

Black Lacquer, Landscape Cover, 2 Sections, England, 7 x 4 In.	425.00
Brass, Handwrought Cover & Finial, c.1850, 9 1/2 In.	130.00
Chased Florals, Ovoid, S. Kirk, 1903, 3 7/8 In.	357.50
Embossed Dragons, Tin Over Copper	50.00
English, 3 Interior Compartments, Secret Drawer, 9 In.	375.00
George II, Thomas Blake, Exeter, Sterling Silver, 1741	8800.00
George III, Sterling, Wrigglework, Motto, Henry Chawner, 5 1/2 In.	1430.00
George IV, Hinged Top, 2 Sections, Rosewood, 7 x 12 In.	412.00
George IV, Tortoiseshell, Mid-19th Century, 6 x 7 In. ......*Illus*	880.00
Georgian, , Tortoiseshell, Bow Front, Silver Escutcheons, Pewter	1540.00
Mahogany, 2 Interior Lidded Compartments, 9 1/4 In.	245.00
Mahogany, Hepplewhite, English, c.1780, 9 1/2 x 6 1/2 In.	770.00
Mahogany, Inlaid Flowers & Garlands, Oval	1100.00
Melon Shape, Wood	2860.00
Mistress Hermitage Her Canister, Hexagonal, 1775	6250.00
Paneled Body, Lion Masks At Sides, Sheffield, 5 In.	330.00
Regency, Brass Foliate Inlay, Rosewood, 6 1/4 x 13 In.	357.50
Regency, Stepped Hinged Top, Burl Yew, 6 1/2 In.	715.00
Rosewood, Paper Lined, 2 Sections, Mid–1800s, 5 x 8 3/4 In.	195.00
Serpentine Front, 2 Compartments, Tortoiseshell, 4 3/4 x 7 In.	545.00
Sheraton, Tortoiseshell, Octagonal	1760.00
Sterling Silver, Scenic Medallion Of Woman With Mandolin, 6 In.	250.00
Tole, Black Paint, Yellow Band, Design, 8 1/8 In.	325.00
Tole, Dark Brown Japanning, Floral Design, 4 1/4 In.	50.00
Tole, Red Paint, Comma Design, Loose Collar, 4 1/4 In.	325.00
Tole, Red Paint, Stylized Sunburst Flower, 4 1/8 In.	625.00
Underplate, Silver Plate, Flower Finial, Acanthus, 7 1/2 In.	220.00
Yellow Slip, Potted Tulip, Brown Glaze, Redware, 1846	5200.00

TEA LEAF IRONSTONE dishes are named for their decorations. There was a superstition that it was lucky if a whole tea leaf unfolded at the bottom of your cup. This idea was translated into the pattern of dishes known as *tea leaf.* By 1850, at least twelve English factories were making this pattern, and by the 1870s, it was a popular pattern in many countries. The tea leaf was always a luster glaze on early wares, although now some pieces are made with a brown tea leaf.

Bowl, Nesting, Piecrust Rim, Square, Meakin, 3 Piece	95.00
Bowl, Pagoda, Handles, Octagonal, Wedgwood, 7 x 11 In.	165.00
Bowl, Square, 8 In.	40.00
Butter Chip, Ribbed At Corners, Meakin	12.00
Butter Chip, Wedgwood, Square	12.00

Tea Caddy, George IV, Tortoiseshell,
Mid-19th Century, 6 x 7 In.

◆◆◆◆◆◆◆◆◆◆◆◆◆◆◆◆◆

To clean tortoiseshell, rub it with a mixture of jeweler's rouge and olive oil.

◆◆◆◆◆◆◆◆◆◆◆◆◆◆◆◆◆

◆◆◆◆◆◆◆◆◆◆◆◆◆◆◆◆◆

Catsup is a good emergency copper cleaner.

◆◆◆◆◆◆◆◆◆◆◆◆◆◆◆◆◆

Tea Leaf Ironstone, Dish,
Royal, 2 1/2 x 2 1/2 In.

Butter, Cover, Drain, Square Ribbed Corners, Meakin	95.00
Butter, Cover, Square, Mellor, Taylor & Co.	137.50
Cake Plate, Child's, Cloverleaf, Gold Luster	15.00
Chamber Pot, Bamboo Finial On Lid	65.00
Chamber Pot, Cover, Wedgwood	200.00
Coffee Set, Copper Luster, Wedgwood, 3 Piece	300.00
Coffeepot, 10 In.	150.00
Compote, Scalloped Top, Meakin, 9 5/8 In.	350.00
Creamer, Child's, Cloverleaf, Gold Luster	35.00
Creamer, Fishhook, Meakin, 5 1/2 In.	137.50
Creamer, Meakin	65.00 To 135.00
Cup & Saucer, Copper Luster	45.00
Cup & Saucer, Meakin	65.00
Cup Plate, Meakin, 3 1/2 In.	55.00
Cup Plate, Wilkinson, 3 1/4 In.	50.00
Cup, Posset, Lily Of The Valley	325.00
Dish, Royal, 2 1/2 x 2 1/2 In. ....*Illus*	25.00
Eggcup, Double	80.00
Ewer, New York Shape	220.00
Gravy Boat, Fishhook, Meakin, 2 3/4 x 8 In.	65.00
Mug, Child's, 2 1/2 In.	195.00
Mug, Meakin, 3 1/2 In.	69.00
Oyster Bowl, Footed, 6 1/4 In.	75.00
Pitcher & Bowl, Bamboo, Grindley	225.00
Pitcher & Bowl, Meakin	275.00
Pitcher & Bowl, Shaw	245.00 To 375.00
Pitcher, Bamboo Handle, Meaking, 8 3/4 In.	20.00
Pitcher, Bamboo, Meakin, 7 In.	170.00
Pitcher, Milk, Bamboo, Meakin, 7 1/2 In.	225.00
Plate, 8 In.	15.00
Plate, 9 In.	18.00
Plate, Mellor, Taylor & Co., 9 In.	20.00
Plate, Shaw, 8 In.	15.00
Plate, Wedgwood, 7 3/4 In.	13.50
Plate, Wilkinson, 9 1/4 In.	20.00
Platter	35.00
Platter, Embossed Leaves, Meakin, 13 1/2 x 9 1/2 In.	65.00
Platter, Mellor, Taylor & Co., 10 x 13 3/4 In.	95.00
Platter, Oval, Wilkinson, 11 In.	40.00
Platter, Rectangular, Mellor, Taylor & Co., 12 x 9 In.	45.00
Platter, Wedgwood, 10 1/4 x 14 In.	55.00
Relish Tray, Meakin	35.00
Soup, Dish, Mellor, Taylor & Co., 9 1/4 In.	18.00
Soup, Dish, Wedgwood, 9 In.	20.00
Sugar, Cover, Bamboo, Grindley	75.00
Sugar, Cover, Child's, Gothic	175.00
Sugar, Cover, Fishhook, 6 1/2 In.	137.50

Sugar, Cover, Fishhook, Meakin, 7 In.	135.00
Sugar, Cover, Lily Of The Valley, Shaw, 6 1/2 In.	145.00
Teapot, Cloverleaf, Gold Luster, Bridgwood	65.00
Teapot, Fishhook, Meakin	225.00
Teapot, Portland Shape, Reverse Teaberry	525.00
Toothbrush Holder, Meakin	95.00
Toothbrush Holder, Mellor, Taylor & Co.	165.00
Tureen, Sauce, Gothic Handles, Burgess, Square	65.00
Tureen, Vegetable, Cover	90.00

TECO is the mark used on the art pottery line made by the American Terra Cotta and Ceramic Company of Terra Cotta and Chicago, Illinois. The company was an offshoot of the firm founded by William D. Gates in 1881. The Teco line was first made in 1885 but was not sold commercially until 1902. It continued in production until 1922. Over 500 designs were made in a variety of colors, shapes, and glazes. The company closed in 1930.

Chamberstick, Green Matte Glaze, 6 1/2 In. ....*Illus*	385.00
Jardiniere, Concentric Rings, Florets In Relief, c.1910, 10 3/4 In.	495.00
Smoke Set, 3 Piece	375.00
Smoke Set, 4 Piece	1200.00
Vase, Brown, 4 In.	325.00
Vase, Brown, Dimpled Sphere, 4 In.	550.00
Vase, Charcoal Green Matte Glaze, No. 223, 15 In.	3575.00
Vase, Charcoal Green Matte Glaze, No. 297, N. Forester, 5 1/4 In.	500.00
Vase, Crystalline Glaze, 5 1/2 In.	495.00
Vase, Domed Cover, Blossoms, Gray, Teal Glaze, Pinon, 27 1/2 In.	1210.00
Vase, Double Handles, 10 x 10 In.	260.00
Vase, Floor, Green Glaze, 4 Buttress Handles Over Recessed Neck	8800.00
Vase, Green Glaze, 4 Buttress Designs, Signed, 10 In.	1100.00
Vase, Green Glaze, Long Pinched Neck, Marked, 16 3/8 In.	522.00
Vase, Green Matte Glaze, Charcoal Top & Base, No. 147, W. D. Gates, 7 In.	253.00
Vase, Green Matte Glaze, Floral Form, 4 Handles, Signed, 13 x 11 In.	6930.00
Vase, Green Matte, Holly Leaves & Berries, F. Albert, 2 x 8 In.	286.00
Vase, Green Matte, Marked	1265.00
Vase, Green Matte, Overlapping	7150.00
Vase, Green, 3 Closed Handles, 7 In.	750.00
Vase, Green, 4 Buttress Handles Down Side, 6 In.	1600.00
Vase, Green, Buttress Handles, 6 In.	1900.00
Vase, Green, Handle, 8 x 5 In.	750.00
Vase, Green, Pompeiian, Long Neck, 8 In.	675.00
Vase, Green, Small Mouth, 4 In.	345.00
Vase, Ivory Matte Glaze, Art Nouveau Form, No. 420, Moreau, 13 In.	1870.00
Vase, Matte Green, Incised, 7 1/2 x 7 In.	750.00
Vase, Mottled Moss Green, Glaze Over Metallic Burgundy, 11 1/4 In.	475.00
Vase, Reticulated Leaves, Fluted Flaring Shaft, Marked, 11 3/4 In.	6600.00
Wall Pocket, Geometric, Green Matte Glaze, 6 1/2 In. ....*Illus*	585.00

Teco, Chamberstick, Green Matte
Glaze, 6 1/2 In.

Teco, Wall Pocket, Geometric, Green Matte
Glaze, 6 1/2 In.

TEDDY BEARS were named for a President of the United States. The first teddy bear was a cuddly toy said to be inspired by a hunting trip made by Teddy Roosevelt in 1902. Morris and Rose Michtom started selling their stuffed bears as *teddy bears* and the name stayed. The Michtoms founded the Ideal Novelty and Toy Company. The German version of the teddy bear was made about the same time by the Steiff Company. There are many types of teddy bears and all are collected. The old ones are being reproduced.

Adrian, Long Mohair, Jointed, 3 Floss Claws Each Paw, 22 In.	175.00
Adrian, Mohair, Jointed, Brown Glass Eyes, Felt Pads, 13 In.	100.00
Albert, North American Running, 21 In.	100.00
American, Yellow Mohair, Jointed, 1920, 19 In.	138.00
Blue Mohair, Germany, 18 In.	300.00
Blue Tipped Mohair, 11 In.	500.00
Christmas, Red Mohair, Sitting, Squeaker, 6 1/2 In.	52.00
Cinnamon, Long Limbs, Hump, Jointed, 23 In.	175.00
Curly Mohair, Jointed, Blue Eyes, England, 1930s, 16 In.	295.00
Fur, Long Nose & Arms, Big Feet, Shoebutton Eyes, 13 In.	375.00
Gold Bristly Mohair, Jointed, Straw, Early 1930s, 22 In.	395.00
Gold Bristly Mohair, Wire Jointed, Glass Eyes, Squeaker, 13 In.	275.00
Gold Mohair, Articulated Limbs, Button Eyes, 20 1/2 In.	225.00
Gold Mohair, Bell Toy, 12 In.	285.00
Gold Mohair, Shoebutton Eyes, Long Arms & Large Feet, 23 In.	250.00
Herman, Frosted Mohair, 20 In.	220.00
Herman, Frosted Mohair, 27 In.	325.00
Herman, White, On Red Wheels	75.00
Ideal, Smokey The Bear, Belt, Badge, 18 In.	35.00
Klein Archie, Brown Mohair, Jointed, Open Mouth, 1945, 17 In.	715.00
Knickerbocker, Gold, 1930s, 18 In.	150.00
Knickerbocker, Humpty–Dumpty, 3 In.	23.00
Long White Mohair, Shaved Pointed Spout, Velvet Pads, 13 In.	165.00
Mohair, Jointed, Brown Glass Eyes, Felt Pads, 20 In.	225.00
Mohair, Shoebutton Eyes, 1920s, 8 In.	100.00
Mohair, Shoebutton Eyes, Old Clothes, Pre–1912, 12 In.	300.00
Mohair, Yellow, White, Jointed, Glass Eyes, Straw, 1926, 11 In.	220.00
Musical, Long Mohair, Open–Close Mouth, Sailor Suit, 11 In.	200.00
Petz, Germany, U.S. Zone, Miniature	275.00
Pink Tipped Long Mohair Fur, 15 In.	1900.00
Schuco, 2–Faced, Comic, Other Tongue Sticking Out, 1940, 4 In.	825.00
Schuco, No Ears, 21 In.	475.00
Schuco, Yellow Mohair, 14 In.	210.00
Schuco, Yellow Mohair, Steel Eyes, On Scooter, Friction, 6 In.	1760.00
Schuco, Yes–No Head, 17 In.	525.00
Smokey Bear, 18 In.	32.00
Stearnsy Bear, Arnie, 22 In.	150.00
Stearnsy Bear, George Burns, 20 In.	150.00
Steiff, Blond Mohair, Button Eyes, Embroidered Nose, 1906, 16 In.	770.00
Steiff, Champagne Mohair, Growler, 1966, 14 In.	375.00
Steiff, Cozey, 9 In.	300.00
Steiff, Creamy Beige, Long Pointed Nose, Printed Buttons, 14 In.	1550.00
Steiff, Dark Brown Mohair, Replaced Ears, 5 1/2 In.	75.00
Steiff, Gold Mohair, Long Feet, Button, 5 1/2 In.	250.00
Steiff, Leather Boxing Gloves & Trunks, Mohair, Hump, 8 In.	475.00
Steiff, Long Arms, White Fur, Gump, 15 In.	900.00
Steiff, Mohair, Hump, Growler, Yarn Nose, Jointed, Button, 21 In.	650.00
Steiff, Mohair, Jointed, Button Eyes, 1906, 19 In.	1540.00
Steiff, Papa Bear, 1st Limited Edition, Box, 1980, 17 In.	495.00
Steiff, Papa Bear, Lst Limited Edition, Box, 1980, 17 In.	695.00
Steiff, Straw Stuffed, Glass Eyes, Jointed, c.1950, 3 1/2 In.	300.00
Steiff, Tea Party Set	350.00
Steiff, White, 25 In.	4500.00
White Mohair, Jointed, Glass Eyes, 1932, Growler, 17 In.	275.00

Xavier Roberts, Appalachian Artwork, Artist Signed, 24 In. 150.00

TELEPHONES are wanted by collectors if the phones are old enough or unusual enough. The first telephone may have been made in Havana, Cuba, in 1849, but it was not patented. The first publicly demonstrated phone was used in Frankfurt, Germany, in 1860. The phone made by Alexander Graham Bell was shown at the Centennial Exhibition in Philadelphia in 1876, but it was not until 1877 that the first private phones were installed. Collectors today want all types of old phones, phone parts, and advertising. Even recent figural phones are popular.

Book, Chicago, 1931	12.00
Candlestick, Ringer Box, 1913	135.00
Candlestick, Western Electric, Brass	125.00
Candlestick, Western Electric, Nickel Over Brass	125.00
Chicago Telephone Supply	750.00
Desk, Mother–In–Law Receiver, For Second Listener, France, 1928	950.00
Desk, Stromberg–Carlson	25.00
Desk, Stromberg–Carlson, Pink, 1950s	40.00
Figural, Bozo The Clown, Laughs When Rings	95.00
Figural, Crest Toothpaste	47.50
Figural, Winston Cigarette Carton, Box	70.00
Pay Phone, Booth, Mahogany, Light & Fan, Working, 82 In.	1250.00
Pay, 3–Slot, Bell, Black, 1950s	150.00
Wall, Cracraft, Oak	225.00
Wall, Crank, Oak, c.1908, 23 In.	175.00
Wall, Crank, Oak, c.1908, 26 In.	150.00
Wall, Double Box, Oak	250.00
Wall, Northern Electric, Oak	450.00
Wall, Stromberg–Carlson, Oak, Cranker, 36 In.	275.00
Wall, Western Electric, Kellogg	335.00
Wall, Western Electric, Oak, Ringer Box, Black Brass Bells, 1879	40.00
Wall, Western Electric, Railroad	150.00

TELEVISION sets are twentieth–century collectibles. Although the first television transmission took place in England in 1925, collectors find few sets which pre–date 1946. The first sets had only five channels, but by 1949 the additional VHF channels were included. The first color television set became available in 1951.

Admiral, Model 17TI	100.00
Philco, Blond, Floor Model, 1955	2800.00
Philco, Safari	275.00
Predicta	535.00
Predicta, Table Model	400.00

TEPLITZ refers to art pottery manufactured by a number of companies in the Teplitz–Turn area of Bohemia during the late nineteenth and early twentieth centuries. The Amphora Porcelain Works and the Alexandra Works were two of these companies.

Ashtray, Art Nouveau, 2 Cameo Portraits, Amphora, 6 1/2 In.	40.00
Basket, White Flowers, Turquoise, Marked, 11 In.	325.00
Bowl, Double Twisted Gold Handles, Leaves, Chestnuts, Signed, 15 In.	625.00
Bowl, Figural, Boy, 2 Hunting Dogs In Forest, c.1925, 11 1/2 In.	450.00
Bowl, Lily Pond Pads & Stems Border, Purple Lake, Marked, 8 In.	495.00
Bowl, Stylized Floral, 6 x 2 In.	95.00
Ewer, Egyptian Heads & Animals, Blue Satin Ground, 5 1/2 In.	145.00
Ewer, Embossed Ovals, Robed Figures, Mottled Gray, 8 In.	95.00
Ewer, Scattered Embossed Florals, Blue Ground, 7 3/4 In.	90.00
Jug, Profile Of Wise Man, Amphora, 5 1/2 In.	350.00
Nappy, Man's Encircled Face, 2 Handles	125.00
Pitcher, Applied Leaves & Fruit, Amphora, 6 1/2 In.	195.00
Pitcher, Green Leaves, Cream Ground, Flower Form Opening, 14 In.	325.00
Pitcher, Pebbly Surface, Gilded Medallion, Rings, Amphora, 9 1/2 In.	300.00
Sugar & Creamer, 24K Gold Overlay Inside & Outside	75.00

Teapot, Roses, Amphora, 4 1/2 In. 50.00
Vase, 2 Parrots On Branch, Matte Brown, Overglazed, Marked, 7 In. 99.00
Vase, 3 Men Pictured, Blue Shades, Loving Cup, 3 Handles, 7 1/4 In. 350.00
Vase, Applied Wolfhound, Bronze Color, Art Nouveau, Amphora, 11 In. 695.00
Vase, Butterfly, 1892–1905, 10 In. 1650.00
Vase, Chariot & Egyptian Design, Cross Handle, Amphora, 14 In. 400.00
Vase, Cherries, Gold Flowers, Ruffled Rim, Artist Signed, 5 In. 75.00
Vase, Cherub, 1905–1910, 10 In. 770.00
Vase, Crab Attacking Serpent, 1905–1910, 22 In. 2090.00
Vase, Embossed Flowers, Leaves At Base, Marked, 10 1/2 In., Pair 195.00
Vase, Embossed Green Leaves, Art Nouveau, Double Handle, 14 In. 450.00
Vase, Enameled Flowers, Art Nouveau, Signed, 7 1/2 In. 275.00
Vase, Farm Scene, 8 x 8 In. 95.00
Vase, Flowers, Woman's Face, Art Nouveau, Marked, 6 3/4 In. 450.00
Vase, Flowing Art Nouveau Design, Jeweled, Tan Ground, 5 1/2 In. 170.00
Vase, Jeweled, Perforated, 3 Handles, Amphora, 6 1/2 In. 395.00
Vase, Multicolored Floral Bands At Neck, Vertical Lines, 10 In. 120.00
Vase, Overlapped Flying Birds, Blue–Green Field, Amphora 170.00
Vase, Owl, Amphora, 10 In., Pair 270.00
Vase, Owl, Amphora, 11 1/2 In. 160.00
Vase, Portrait, Art Nouveau, Amphora, Signed, 5 1/2 In. 550.00
Vase, Portrait, Woman, Long Hair, Holding Flowers, 5 3/4 In. 395.00
Vase, Shadow Florals, Band Of Deco Flowers, Marked, 9 In. 195.00
Vase, Woman's Head In Relief, Twig Handles, Signed, 12 1/4 In. 495.00
Wall Pocket, Reptile, Amphora 245.00

TERRA–COTTA is a special type of pottery. It ranges from pale orange to
dark reddish–brown in color. The color comes from the clay, which is
fired but not always glazed in the finished piece.

Bust, Dauphin, 19th Century, 12 In. 165.00
Figure, Lion, Sitting, Front Paw Up, 1920, Pair 2650.00
Figurine, Madonna & Suckling Child, Florentine, 20 In. 6600.00
Humidor, Black Boy Bust, 6 In. 125.00
Lamp, Black Glaze, Blue Stripes, Gilded Greek Design, 14 In. 25.00
Plate, Molded Classical Scene, Marked, 10 1/4 In. 25.00
Teapot, Oriental Design, England, 6 1/2 In. 150.00
Urn, Lawn, Pair 475.00
Vase, Fox Hunt Scene, Green, Marked, 4 In. 85.00

TEXTILES listed here include many types of printed fabrics and table and
household linens. clothing. Some other textiles will be found under
Clothing, Coverlet, Rug, Quilt, etc.

Altar Frontal, Embroidered Silk, Framed, 17th Century, 75 x 39 In. 2500.00
Apron, Western Queen Flour 30.00
Banner, Side Show, Sword Swallower, Siegler, 8 x 10 Ft. 1295.00
Bedspread, Bonanza, Original Package 45.00
Bedspread, Crocheted, Full Size 85.00
Bedspread, Embroidered Linen, Scalloped, Queen Size 225.00
Bedspread, Matching Pillow Cover, Crocheted, Ecru, Double Size 150.00
Bedspread, Popcorn, Crocheted, 83 x 80 In. 125.00
Bedspread, Popcorn, Crocheted, 84 x 108 In. 135.00
Bedspread, Trapunto Style, Marseille, Twin Size 95.00
Blanket, Chenille Embroidery, Wool, Ivory & Blue, 66 x 90 In. 475.00
Blanket, Homespun, Natural Cotton & Wool, Center Seam, 72 x 90 In. 25.00
Blanket, Homespun, Wood, Natural, Blue End Stripe, 56 x 90 In. 65.00
Blanket, Homespun, Wool, Cotton, Gray & Natural Stripes, 68 x 75 In. 65.00
Blanket, Sleigh, Florals, Mohair, Stroock 110.00
Bolster Cover, Homespun, Navy, White, Hand Sewn, 23 x 56 In. 40.00
Bunting, Bolt, Unused, 41 Yards 465.00
Chair Set, Crocheted, Birds, Flowers, 3 Piece 18.00
Comforter, Patchwork, Crazy, Knotted, Embroidered, 1893, 70 x 82 In. 550.00
Coverlet, Crib, Crocheted, Flowers, Animals, Cream, 40 x 66 In. 195.00
Coverlet, Embroidered Silk, Chinoiserie, 18th Century, 7 x 5 Ft. 4400.00

Divan Cover, Anatolian, Vines, c.1875, 6 Ft. x 2 Ft. 6 In. 3300.00
Duvet Cover, Linen, Button, Fancy Turn Back, Germany, 20 In., Pair 100.00
Flag, American, 13 Stars On Blue Field, Woven Stripes 895.00
Flag, American, 13 Stars, Wool, 1870s 925.00
Flag, American, 35 Stars, 12 Ft. 300.00
Flag, American, 40 Stars, Wool, 1930s, 5 x 9 Ft. 85.00
Flag, American, 44 Stars, Linen, Stitchery, 16 1/2 x 13 1/2 In. 150.00
Flag, American, 45 Stars, Large .... 15.00 To 35.00
Flag, American, 48 Stars 10.00
Mat, Prayer, Hindu, Nepal, c.1900 .... 95.00
Mattress Cover, Cotton, Blue, White, Hand Sewn, Buttons, 65 x 79 In. 200.00
Mattress Cover, Homespun, Blue & White, Hand Sewn, 53 x 76 In. 125.00
Mattress Cover, Homespun, Navy & White Cotton Plaid, 60 x 72 In. 150.00
Panel, Central Peacock, Fringed, China, c.1900, 82 x 92 In. 390.00
Panel, Curtain, Ecru, Hand Made Lace Inserts, 78 x 18 In. 22.00
Panel, Embroidered, Dragon, Pearl, Wave & Cloud, 37 3/4 x 22 1/2 In. 65.00
Panel, Embroidered, House, 4 Panels Of Flowers, 54 x 26 1/2 In. 1100.00
Panel, Embroidered, Wise Man Under Tree, Gilt Threads, 27 x 24 In. 1210.00
Panel, Needlepoint, Lovebirds, Red Ground, Pine Frame, 17 x 17 In. 85.00
Panel, Printed Floral, Linen, 2 Piece 275.00
Panel, Tapestry, Birds Among Acanthus & Rosettes, 20 1/2 x 43 In. 145.00
Piano Bench, Cover, Crewel Embroidered 15.00
Pillow Cover, Tobacco Silks, 15 x 21 In. 165.00
Pillow Sham, Red Embroidered Roses, Bees, Flowers, 26 x 28 In. 43.00
Place Mat & Napkin, Cutwork, Ecru 250.00
Robe, Lap, Dog & 2 Deer's Heads, Glass Eyes, 2 Rifles & Campfire 123.00
Runner, Homespun, Blue & White, C. F. Initials, 40 x 152 In. 75.00
Runner, Table, Battenburg Lace, 2 Flowers Each End, 12 x 37 In. 125.00
Scarf, Crocheted, Ecru, Maltese Cross, 190 1-In. Squares, 12 x 24 In. 12.00
Scarf, Linen, Art Nouveau Design, Silk Embroidery, Pre-1950, 20 In. 35.00
Scarf, Mantel, Heavy Crash, Re-Embroidered, 23 x 72 In. 35.00
Scarf, Piano, Floral Embroidered, Silk 295.00
Scarf, Piano, Silk, Rose Design, Occupied Japan, 17 x 50 In. 6.00
Stair Tread, Hooked, Flowers & Leaves, 10 1/2 x 18 In., 13 Piece 495.00
Table Cover, Oilcloth, Stenciled Scenes, Framed, 51 1/2 x 41 In. 357.00
Tablecloth, 3 Woven Decorative Bands, Ends Hand Sewn, 43 x 81 In. 15.00
Tablecloth, Battenburg Lace & Drawn Work, White, Round, 50 In. 140.00
Tablecloth, Battenburg Lace, 64 In. Diam. 250.00
Tablecloth, Battenburg Lace, 68 In. Diam. 245.00
Tablecloth, Birds, Swans, Flower Urns, Signed Quaker, 71 x 90 In. 95.00
Tablecloth, Blue & White Plaid, Off-Center Seam, 60 x 76 In. 165.00
Tablecloth, Crocheted, 1923, 76 x 60 In. 125.00
Tablecloth, Crocheted, Ecru, 50 x 54 In. 75.00
Tablecloth, Crocheted, Sisters At Carmel, 1920s, 68 x 78 In. 45.00
Tablecloth, Crocheted, White, 60 x 52 In. 75.00
Tablecloth, Cutwork, 103 x 166 In. 1045.00
Tablecloth, Damask, White, Monogram, 72 x 108 In. 28.00
Tablecloth, Embroidered Crewel Floral, 80 x 104 In. 95.00
Tablecloth, Embroidered Openwork, White Linen, 12 Napkins, 80 In. 95.00
Tablecloth, Hand Crocheted, 60 x 60 In. 20.00
Tablecloth, Homespun, Blue & White Plaid, 58 x 72 In. 90.00
Tablecloth, Homespun, Diamond Design, Center Seam, 58 x 72 In. 25.00
Tablecloth, Homespun, Gold & White Plaid, 54 x 76 In. 125.00
Tablecloth, Pointe Venice, 12 Linen & Lace Napkins, 138 In. 600.00
Tablecloth, Quaker Lace, Heavy, 3 Yd. 65.00
Tablecloth, White On Pattern, Linen Homespun, 38 x 71 In. 35.00
Tablecloth, White On White, Embroidered Date, 1862, 60 x 74 In. 25.00
Tablecloth, Woven Silk, White, Fringed, 1901 Buffalo Exposition 35.00
Tapestry, 3 Wise Men, Camels, 25 x 40 In. 80.00
Tapestry, Allegory Of Peaceable Kingdom, 6 Ft. 8 In. x 7 Ft. 9 In. 3300.00
Tapestry, Arab Bazaar Scene, Belgium, 24 x 30 In. 50.00
Tapestry, Aubusson, Couple In Landscape, 3 x 4 1/2 Ft. 9950.00
Tapestry, Figures, Flowers & Butterflies, China, 69 1/2 x 20 In. 305.00

Tapestry, France, 1880, 36 x 56 In. 2100.00
Tapestry, Garden Scene, Victorian Figures, Belgium, 20 x 55 In. 65.00
Tapestry, Gobelins, Landscape, House, 7 Ft. 11 In. x 6 Ft. 3 In. 4200.00
Tapestry, Medieval Figure In Garden, Flemish, 1800, 68 x 46 In. 500.00
Tapestry, Peasant Girl With Lover, Framed, 28 x 46 In. 850.00
Tapestry, Screen, 4 Panels, 18th Century, 73 x 23 In. ....*Illus* 6750.00
Tapestry, Screen, Four Panels, Hunt Scenes, Verdure, 13 x 84 In. 3960.00
Tapestry, St. Mark's Square, Venice, 26 x 59 In. 35.00
Tapestry, Venice, Canals, Boats, Garden, Men With Dogs, 46 x 68 In. 165.00
Tapestry, Verdure Style, Mountains, 6 1/2 Ft. x 8 Ft. 9 In. 995.00
Tapestry, Woodsmen, Hound, Forest, Brussels, 4 Ft. 5 In. x 3 Ft. 3 In. 1100.00
Tapestry, Woven Floral, Silk & Metallic Thread, 48 x 68 In. 225.00
Tea Cozy, White On White Embroidery 40.00
Towel, Homespun, Woven Overshot Bands, 16 1/2 x 51 In. 25.00
Towel, Show, Amish, Hand Embroidered, Lydia Stoltzfus, 1890s, 3 Piece 225.00
Towel, Show, Cross–Stitch, Flowers, Elithabeth Eperly, 1849, 63 In. 700.00
Towel, Show, Cross–Stitch, Flowers, Mare W. Able, 1833, 57 1/2 In. 400.00
Towel, Show, Needlepoint & Cross–Stitch, Mary Sauder, 1851, 56 In. 300.00
Towel, Show, Woven Design, Urn Of Flowers, Linen, 57 In. 45.00

THERMOMETER is a name that comes from the Greek word for heat. The
thermometer was invented in 1731 to measure temperature of either water
or air. All kinds of thermometers are collected, but those with advertising
messages are the most popular.

7–Up, Glass Front, Red Square, 12 In. 40.00
7–Up, Porcelain, 15 x 6 In. .... 40.00 To 67.00
Aetna Insurance Co., Tin & Glass, Round, 6 In. 55.00
Ajax Antifreeze, Tin Lithograph, Wooden Frame, 36 In. 165.00
Art Deco Mirror, Advertising 30.00
B–L Lemon Lime 28.00
Baltimore Tank & Tower Co., Wooden 110.00
Barges, Bottle Picture 75.00
Black Boy, Multi Products, 1949 .... 55.00
Bottle, Green, 19 In. 75.00
Bowes Spark Plug, Race Car 275.00
Brechet & Richter Co., Minneapolis, Minn., Wooden, 14 In. 32.00
Buy 5 Roses Flour, Porcelain, Red & White, 8 x 39 In. 125.00
Calumet Steel Drive Posts, Wooden 30.00
Caster Drilling, Cleveland, N.Y., Stenciled, Wooden, 24 In. 38.50
Chesterfield Cigarettes, Tin, Wall 5.00
Clark Candy Bar, Wooden, 1920, 19 In. 125.00
Cobbs Creek Whiskey, Red, White, Blue, Steel, 1936, 38 In. 125.00
Cott Ginger Ale, Tin, 1940s 40.00
Curlee Clothes, Curlee Pants, Porcelain, 27 In. 265.00
Dairy, Floating Glass 1.85
Diamond Crystal Salt, Today's Weather, Sign Shape 65.00
Double Cola, You'll Like It Better, Blue 15.00

Textile, Tapestry, Screen, 4 Panels, 18th
Century, 73 x 23 In.

◆◆◆◆◆◆◆◆◆◆◆◆◆◆◆◆◆◆◆◆◆◆◆

Hanging textiles should be
given a rest from time to time.
The weight of the hanging
causes strain on the threads. If
the textile is taken down and
stored for a few months, the
threads regain some strength.

◆◆◆◆◆◆◆◆◆◆◆◆◆◆◆◆◆◆◆◆◆◆◆

Dr Pepper, Tin, With Chevron, 1960s 75.00
Dr. Chase, Blue, White, Man At Top, 8 x 39 In. 400.00
Ex–Lax, Porcelain, 8 x 36 In. 130.00
Fatima Cigarettes, Barometer, Blue, Porcelain, 27 In. 275.00
Fatima Cigarettes, Porcelain 325.00
Figural, Fish, Chalkware 6.00
Folgers Coffee, Porcelain 385.00
Frostie Root Beer, Frostie Man, Glass, 12 In. .... 40.00 To 75.00
Frostie Root Beer, Plastic, 14 x 18 In. 12.00
Funeral Home, Evansville, Ind., Dial Type, Round 12.50
Grapette, Thirsty Or Not, Embossed Tin Lithograph, 16 1/2 In. 45.00
Gunthers Beer 275.00
Hill's Bros. Coffee, Porcelain, Figure Holding Cup, 22 In. 275.00
Hire's Root Beer, Bottle Shape .... 27.50 To 65.00
Honest Scrap Tobacco, Porcelain 900.00
Hotel Jefferson, St. Louis, Painted, Stenciled, Wooden, 24 In. 44.00
Kasco Dog Food 75.00
Kleen–Maid Bread, Wooden 30.00
Komfo Bedding, Lehigh–Bernstein Co., Porcelain, Round 45.00
Kool 28.00
La Creole Hair Restorer, Wooden 175.00
Lash's Bitters, Homer's Ginger Brandy, Stenciled Wood, 21 In. 120.00
Mail Pouch Tobacco, Porcelain, 8 x 40 In. 250.00
Mail Pouch Tobacco, Tin 170.00
Mail Pouch, Treat Yourself To The Best, Porcelain, 39 In. 50.00
Mathieu Syrup For Coughs & Colds, Wooden, 24 x 4 In. 195.00
Mohawk Liquor, Tin 25.00
Montreal Malt Rye, Wooden, c.1910, 25 In. 95.00
Morton Salt 10.00
Moxie, Red Tin 350.00
Nash, Wooden, Large 300.00
National Sawdust Co., Wooden 35.00
Nature's Remedy, Porcelain, 5 x 27 In. .... 125.00 To 200.00
Nesbitt's Orange Drink, Yellow & Orange, Tin 115.00
Nesbitt's Soft Drink, Professor, Tin, 5 x 27 In. 130.00
Nesbitt's, Round, Pam Clock Type 80.00
New Jersey Ready Mixed Paints, Blue & White, Porcelain 110.00
NR Laxative–Tums, Porcelain, 27 In. 135.00
Old Capitol Rye, Old Governor Bourbon, Wooden, 4 x 14 In. 35.00
Old Chum Tobacco, Porcelain, 38 1/2 x 8 In. 195.00
Orange Crush, 6 x 19 In. 170.00
Orange Crush, Glass Face, Orange, White, Green, 12 In. 57.00
Orange Crush, Stenciled Fiberboard, 16 In. 28.00
Ornate Gilded Cast Brass Frame, Easel Back, 10 3/4 In. 95.00
Peters Shoes, Porcelain 195.00
Pollack Wheeling Stogies, Blue & Yellow, Tin 110.00
Prestone Antifreeze, Porcelain, Grey, Red, Blue, 8 x 36 In. 45.00
Prestone, Porcelain, Gray, Red, Blue, White, 8 x 36 In. 45.00
Ramon's Brownie Pills, Ramon's Pink Pills, Tin, 21 In. 155.00
Ramsay's Paint & Varnishes, Porcelain Over Steel 55.00
Raybestos Brake Lining, Stenciled, Steel, 30 3/4 In. 77.00
RC Cola, Mirror 55.00
RC Cola, Tin, Red, White, Blue, 10 x 26 In. 37.00
Red Seal Battery, Porcelain, 27 In. 130.00
Rislone Oil, Picture Of Can, Metal, 10 x 24 In. 55.00
Royal Crown Cola, Arrow, Metal, 10 x 28 In. 15.00
Royal Crown Cola, Mirror, 1930s 65.00
Sealtest, Round 75.00
St. Lawrence's Flour, Porcelain, Red, Green, White, 8 x 30 In. 78.00
Standard Home Heating Oils 27.50
Standard Oil Co., Tin, 3 x 12 In. 25.00
Stephenson's Union Suits, Porcelain 395.00
Sun Crest, Multicolored, 1950s, 16 x 7 In. 58.00

♦♦♦♦♦♦♦♦♦♦♦♦♦♦♦♦♦♦♦♦♦

Never use mending tape or transparent tape on a book. It will eventually permanently damage the paper. Even Post-its will eventually leave a spot.

♦♦♦♦♦♦♦♦♦♦♦♦♦♦♦♦♦♦♦♦♦

Tiffany Glass, Bowl, Favrile, Signed, 4 5/8 In.

Taylor, Victorian, Solid Brass, Hanging, Patent 1887	225.00
Taylor, Wooden, Painted, 6 x 24 In.	60.00
Thirsty? Just Whistle, Metal	42.00
Tums	37.50
Victor Radio, 39 In.	290.00
Wheatland Kennels, Reg., Puppies & Crown Stock For Sale, Wood	60.00
Wheatlet Eaten, All Kinds Of Weather, Barometer, Tin	85.00 To 95.00
Winchester, Shotgun Shell Shape	20.00
Wishing Well, Yellow, Blue, Red, Tin, Late 1950s, 10 x 40 In.	135.00

TIFFANY GLASS was made by Louis Comfort Tiffany, the American glass designer who worked from about 1879 to 1933. His work included iridescent glass, Art Nouveau styles of design, and original contemporary styles. He was also noted for stained glass windows, unusual lamps, bronze work, pottery, and silver. Other types of Tiffany are listed under Tiffany Pottery, Tiffany Silver, or at the end of this section under Tiffany. The famous Tiffany lamps are under Tiffany, Lamp. Reproductions of some types of Tiffany are being made. Tiffany jewelry is listed in the jewelry and wristwatch sections.

Louis C. Tiffany

TIFFANY GLASS, Bonbon, Gold Dore, Scalloped Rim, Signed, 4 1/2 In.	150.00
Bowl, Favrile, Flower, 2-Tiered Flower Frog Center, 7 In.	1100.00
Bowl, Favrile, Flower, Peacock Blue Iridescent, Holder, 12 In.	3500.00
Bowl, Favrile, Gold Iridescent, Ruffled, Signed, 7 In.	650.00
Bowl, Favrile, Gold, 6 1/2 In.	425.00
Bowl, Favrile, Signed, 4 5/8 In. …………………………………*Illus*	465.00
Bowl, Gold Favrile, Intaglio Prunes Blossoms Inside, 7 In.	975.00
Bowl, Gold Iridescent, Flared & Ruffled Rim, 2 1/2 x 8 In.	600.00
Bowl, Gold Iridescent, Ribbed, Signed, 6 In.	350.00
Bowl, Gold Iridescent, Ruffled, Short Center Well, 9 In.	650.00
Bowl, Intaglio Leaf Vine, Gold, 7 1/2 In.	1100.00
Bowl, Opalescent Feather, Green Stretch Interior, 6 In.	830.00
Bowl, Queen, Favrile, 1-Ribbed Swirl, Signed, 8 In.	945.00
Bowl, Underplate, Favrile, Electric Blue, Bowl 5-In., 2 Piece	700.00
Candlestick, Gold Iridescent, Oval Top, 4 In., Pair	2800.00
Compote, Copper Wheel Engraved, Leaves, Gold, Signed, 6 In.	950.00
Compote, Curved Stem, Engraved Leaves & Vines, Signed, 6 In.	695.00
Compote, Favrile, Gold Iridescent, Ruffled Edge, Footed, 5 In.	595.00
Compote, Favrile, Pedestal, Signed, 4 3/4 In.	900.00
Compote, Favrile, Ruffled Edge, Footed, 3 In.	595.00
Compote, Optic Ribs On Underside, Green, Signed, 4 1/2 In.	550.00
Compote, Stretch Glass, Laurel Leaves, Signed, 3 3/4 x 5 In.	500.00
Cordial, Aquamarine Top & Bottom, Hollow Blue Stem, 4 In.	175.00
Cordial, Favrile, Gold Luster, Signed, 4 1/2 In.	240.00
Cordial, Gold Iridescent, Swirl, Slender Stem, 4 In., Pair	625.00
Cordial, Intaglio Grapes & Leaves, Stem, 5 1/2 In., 3 Piece	975.00
Cup & Saucer, Gold, Octagonal, Demitasse, 6 Piece	350.00
Decanter, Opalescent Iridescent, Red, Violet, Blue, 10 In.	1500.00

Dish, Serving, Favrile, Pedestal Base, Iridescent, 10 In. 750.00
Dish, Serving, Gold Iridescent, Ruffled Edge, Footed, 6 In. 750.00
Finger Bowl, Underplate, Favrile, Queen, Ruffled, 1904, 6 Sets 5500.00
Goblet, Favrile, White Latticinio Design, Aqua, 8 1/2 In., Pr. 1500.00
Goblets, Iridescent Pale Pink, Gold, Blue, 3 1/2 In., 4 Piece 335.00
Jar, Favrile, Gold Iridescent, Sterling Lid & Handle, 4 In. 750.00
Parfait, Favrile, Paneled Bell Form, Green, 6 In., 10 Piece 1210.00
Pitcher, Blue, Signed, Paper Label, 4 In. 850.00
Pitcher, Curved Body, Spout, Purple, Handle, Paper Label, 4 In. 850.00
Pitcher, Gold, Applied Blue Handle, 3 In. 625.00
Punch Cup, Opalescent & Green Wavy Design, Ribbed Handle 350.00
Salt, Favrile, Gold Iridescent, Blue Flared Rim, 1 1/4 In. 225.00
Salt, Favrile, Gold Iridescent, Raised Twist, Signed, 1 In. 375.00
Salt, Favrile, Gold Iridescent, Ribbed, Pedestal, 1 1/2 In. 275.00
Salt, Favrile, Side Handles, Silver Blue Rim, Signed, 1 In. 275.00
Salt, Ruffled Edge, Rainbow Of Colors, Flat Bottom, Signed 200.00
Sherbet, Favrile, Curved Stem, Signed, 3 1/2 In. 275.00
Tile, 4–Petal Rosette In Circle, Iridescent Blue, 2 In. 400.00
Tile, Dragon, Green & Red Slag Glass, Swirl Design, 4 In. 200.00
Tile, Favrile, Turtleback, Amber, 5 3/4 x 5 1/4 In., 4 Piece 550.00
Tile, Raised Diamond Design, Translucent Glass, 1 1/2 In. 50.00
Tile, Turtleback, Diamond Shape, Opaque Center, 5 1/2 In. 150.00
Toothpick, Favrile Threaded, Signed, 1 3/4 In. 300.00
Toothpick, Favrile, Gold & Blue Highlights, Signed, 2 1/4 In. 350.00
Toothpick, Gold Iridescent, Ruffled Top, 4 Footed, Signed 525.00
Toothpick, Knotty Mold, Gold Iridescent, Blues, Signed 250.00
Vase, Bamboo Leaves & Stalks, Black, Signed, c.1901, 9 7/8 In. 3575.00
Vase, Black Vasiform, 5 Blue Pulled Feathers, 3 3/4 In. 1760.00
Vase, Bud, Favrile, Bronze, Slight Flare–Out Top, 5 1/2 In. 750.00
Vase, Bud, Favrile, Hexagon Top, Blue & Red Tones, 5 3/4 In. 475.00
Vase, Carved, 5 Leaf Forms, 14 In. 3300.00
Vase, Custard, Gold Swirls, 6 In. 3000.00
Vase, Cypriote, Blue, Purple Iridescent, 5 1/4 In. 850.00
Vase, Favrile, Amber Streaked With Gold Swirls, c.1908, 9 In. 330.00
Vase, Favrile, Amber, Bulbous Base, c.1917, 19 3/4 In. 2090.00
Vase, Favrile, Blue, Flared Flattened Top, Oval Body, 6 In. 2800.00
Vase, Favrile, Blue, Round Body, Raised Ribs To Base, 5 In. 1200.00
Vase, Favrile, Dark Green, Peacock, Baluster, 20 1/2 In. 6050.00
Vase, Favrile, Everted Scalloped Rim, Baluster Shape, 10 In. 1100.00
Vase, Favrile, Floriform, Cobalt Blue, 1915, 13 3/8 In. 1350.00
Vase, Favrile, Gold Iridescent, Ribbed, Dimpled, Signed, 4 In. 650.00
Vase, Favrile, Gold Iridescent, Ribbed, Pinched Neck, 3 In. 650.00
Vase, Favrile, Gold Iridescent, Ruffled Edge, Signed, 4 In. 650.00
Vase, Favrile, Gold, Pink, Green Leaves & Vines, 20 In. 5500.00
Vase, Favrile, Gold, Rainbow, Baluster, Everted Rim, 18 In. 9350.00
Vase, Favrile, Gold, Rose, Ribbed Baluster, 18 1/2 In. 2860.00
Vase, Favrile, Gold, White Design, 8 1/2 In. 850.00
Vase, Favrile, Gourd Form, Vertical Ribs, c.1907, 4 In. 660.00
Vase, Favrile, Grecian Urn, Amber, Signed, Label, 3 7/8 In. 525.00
Vase, Favrile, Green Feather Pulls, White Ground, 14 3/4 In. 3520.00
Vase, Favrile, Intaglio Heart–Shaped Leaves, 1916, 12 In. 2300.00
Vase, Favrile, Pale Yellow, Double Tier Leaf Design, 5 In. 1400.00
Vase, Favrile, Peacock Blue, Leaves, Bronze Arranger, 4 In. 2500.00
Vase, Favrile, Peacock, Green, White Scrolls, 16 1/2 In. 8800.00
Vase, Favrile, Turquoise Ground, Leaves & Vines, 14 1/4 In. 5280.00
Vase, Flared, Filigree Holder, Signed, 10 In. 1000.00
Vase, Floriform, Paneled, Signed, c.1919, 6 7/8 In. 1100.00
Vase, Floriform, Ruffled, Cylindrical Stem, c.1905, 9 5/8 In. 880.00
Vase, Flower Form, Short Stem, Gold Iridescent, 7 In. 675.00
Vase, Gold Iridescent, Double Handle, Ovoid, Signed, 4 In. 665.00
Vase, Gold Iridescent, Open Spread Top, Ruffled Edge, 4 In. 650.00
Vase, Iridescent Tapering Body, Flaring Rim, Signed, 5 In. 423.00
Vase, Italian Gold, Pierced Handles, 2 x 2 In. 850.00

Vase, Jack–In–The–Pulpit, Gold Stem, Signed, 19 3/4 In. 8800.00
Vase, Jack–In–The–Pulpit, Signed, 18 In. 5750.00
Vase, Lava, Black Metallic, Gold Iridescent, Signed, 7 In. 5280.00
Vase, Melon Ribbed, Deep Green, Gourd Shape 1100.00
Vase, Moravian, Ruffled Top Rim, Gold, 6 In. 1650.00
Vase, Pink–Gold Highlights, Free–Form, Signed, 3 3/4 In. 440.00
Vase, Random Swirling Trailings, White, Signed, c.1899, 8 In. 1650.00
Vase, Round Body, Peacock Blue, Silver Overcast, Signed, 4 In. 800.00
Vase, Silver Hooked Feathers, Clear Cased, Signed, 4 1/2 In. 3200.00
Vase, Stand–Out Ribs, Blue–Purple, Signed, 5 1/2 In. 850.00
Vase, Trumpet, Favrile, Ribbed, Signed, 13 1/2 In. 1400.00
Vase, Trumpet, Gold, Knobbed Base, Flared, Signed, 10 1/2 In. 935.00
Vase, Trumpet, Green & Gold Feather, Gold Dore, Signed, 15 In. 1695.00
Vase, Trumpet, Pastel Blue, 12 In. 1900.00
Vase, Trumpet, Peacock Blue, Purple Highlights, Signed 1485.00
Vase, Trumpet, Ribbed Ball Stem, Signed, 1900, 14 1/4 In. 400.00
Vase, Trumpet, Ribbed, Signed, 13 1/2 In. 2100.00
Vase, Twisted Body, Pedestal Base, 6 1/2 In. 400.00
Wine, Inverted Bell Form, Amber, 1899–1928, 3 7/8 In., 6 Piece 2200.00
TIFFANY POTTERY, Jar, Cover, Glazed, Ivory, Green–Brown Raised Leaves, 9 In. 3000.00
Lamp, Melon Ribbed, Mesh Shade, Large 4125.00
Vase, Birds, Circles, Vines, Glazed, Blue, Purple, 5 1/2 In. 3000.00
Vase, Center Hanging Pods, Leaves At Top, Signed, 6 1/2 In. 2000.00
Vase, Deep Green Lines, Green Glaze, Flared Top, 6 In. 950.00
Vase, Glazed, Green Leaves Raised, 8 In. 2000.00
Vase, Green Glaze, Narrow Neck, Flare–Out Top, 6 In. 950.00
Vase, Leaves At Collar, Green Interior, Signed, 4 1/2 In. 750.00
Vase, Overlapping Upright Iris Leaves, Signed, 8 In. 2500.00
Vase, Raised Blossoms, Vines, Green Interior, 13 1/4 In. 1500.00
Vase, Trumpet Vines, Green Glaze, Marked, c.1906, 12 3/4 In. 550.00
Vase, Tulips At Top, Bronze Rim, Signed, 7 In. 1850.00
TIFFANY SILVER, Bonbon, Forget–Me–Not 110.00
Bookmark, Double Heart 45.00
Bowl, Boat Shape, 4 5/8 In. 1000.00
Bowl, Centerpiece, 12–Lobed Rim, Spiral Shell Bosses, 1890s 5200.00
Bowl, Circular Petal Form, 7 In. 385.00
Bowl, Clover, 1902, 9 In. 412.50
Bowl, Fruit, Shaped & Molded Rim, c.1937 .... 660.00
Bowl, Hammered, Bombe Form, c.1915, 10 1/4 In. 3400.00
Bowl, Openwork Near Top, B Center, 9 In. 395.00
Bowl, Paul Revere, 7 1/2 In. 410.00
Bowl, Presentation, Egg and Dart Molding, c.1860 .... 550.00
Box, Cigarette, Monogram 350.00
Box, Wood Liner, 1907, 9 1/2 In. 880.00
Candlestick, 11 1/2 In., Pair 1750.00
Candlestick, Detachable Nozzles, c.1915, 16 3/4 In., Pair 7750.00
Caster, Chrysanthemum, Marked, c.1891, 5 1/2 In. 1100.00
Chatelaine, Foliate & Mask Design, 5 Chains, Marked, 11 In. 995.00
Coffeepot, Birds Nesting, Perching, 1870, 10 1/2 In. 3190.00
Compact, With Lipstick, Enameled, Gold Trim 145.00
Compote, Multitude Of Flowers, 1890s, 5 1/4 In., Pair 2750.00
Dinner Set, Audubon, 108 Piece 7750.00
Dish, Basketweave, 20th Century, 5 3/4 In., Pair 4125.00
Dish, Cover, Entree, Flowers & Ferns, c.1899, 9 3/4 In., Pair 6600.00
Dish, Hors D'Oeuvres, Leaping Dogs, 1889, 5 3/8 In., Pair 2090.00
Ewer, Repousse Floral Design, Cast Handle, 11 7/8 In. 1200.00
Fish Set, Wave Edge 550.00
Food Pusher, Child's 60.00
Fork & Spoon, Serving, Richelieu 600.00
Fork, Asparagus, Winthrop 475.00
Fork, Cold Meat, Grapevine, 9 In. 350.00
Fork, Cold Meat, Winthrop 110.00
Fork, Ice Cream, Palm, Gold Wash Bowl, 12 Piece 467.50

Fork, Ice Cream, Winthrop	45.00
Fork, King's Pattern, 6 3/4 In.	100.00
Fork, Luncheon, Faneuil	48.00
Fork, Luncheon, Wave Edge	55.00
Fork, Salad, Richelieu	75.00
Fork, Salad, Winthrop	35.00
Fork, Sardine, Chrysanthemum	295.00
Fork, Serving, Audubon	145.00
Fork, Serving, Polhemus, 5–Tine, c.1860, 9 3/4 In.	365.00
Fork, Shrimp, 8 Piece	295.00
Frame, Picture, Pierced Art Nouveau, Table Standing	825.00
Glove Stretcher, Pair	275.00
Jelly Server, Linenfold	125.00
Kettle, Lampstand, Swing Handle, c.1915, 13 3/4 In.	2090.00
Knife, Cake, Chrysanthemum	195.00
Knife, Dinner, Palm	65.00
Knife, Luncheon, Flemish	36.00
Ladle, Beekman, 12 1/2 In.	308.00
Ladle, Gravy, Beekman	120.00
Ladle, Gravy, Persian	295.00
Ladle, Persian, Scalloped Bowl, 10 1/2 In.	600.00
Ladle, Punch, Double Lip, Colonial, Gold Wash	650.00
Ladle, Punch, Olympian	1200.00
Ladle, Soup, Winthrop	525.00
Meat Server, Repousse, Plated, 3 Piece	275.00
Pastry Server, Serrated, St. Dunstan	175.00
Pie Server, Wave Edge, Serrated, Marked, 11 In.	425.00
Pitcher, Chased Vertical Lobes On Lower Body, c.1880, 7 In.	2300.00
Pitcher, Flowers & Ferns, Matted Ground, c.1880, 8 1/2 In.	3200.00
Pitcher, Japanese Style, Hammered, c.1880, 9 In.	5500.00
Pitcher, Presentation, Footed, Marked, Dated 1855	3575.00
Plate, Engraved Design, 3 In.	45.00
Punch Bowl, Grapevine & Satyr Mask, c.1895, 12 3/4 In.	4950.00
Slice, Fish, Vine	450.00
Spoon, Berry, Strawberries In Relief On Handle	357.50
Spoon, Bonbon, Blackberry Vine	260.00
Spoon, Dessert, Wave Edge	45.00
Spoon, Preserve, Richelieu	90.00
Spoon, Serving, Entwined Dolphins, 1883, 9 3/4 In.	1760.00
Spoon, Serving, German Renaissance Design	467.50
Spoon, Serving, Queen Anne, 9 5/8 In.	165.00
Spoon, Sip, Mint Leaf Design Bowl, Box, 6 Piece	143.00
Spoon, Stuffing, English King	650.00
Spreader, Butter, Audubon, 6 Piece	245.00
Sugar Shell, Persian, Gold Wash	110.00
Sugar Sifter, Olympian	250.00 To 325.00
Sugar Sifter, Vine	225.00
Tablespoon, Chrysanthemum, 7 3/4 In., 4 Piece	660.00
Tazza, 8 Panels, Chased Flowers, Pierced Square Stem, 8 In.	3520.00
Tazza, Applied Parrots On Border, 1870–1875, 14 In.	2750.00
Tea Caddy, Engraved Anthemia Bands, c.1870, 5 7/8 In.	2090.00
Tea Strainer, Chrysanthemum, c.1891, 6 5/8 In.	1320.00
Teaspoon, Wave Edge	28.00
Tongs, Asparagus, Arabesque, Monogram, c.1855, 10 5/8 In.	440.00
Tongs, Asparagus, Broom Corn	475.00
Tongs, Asparagus, Chrysanthemum	825.00
Tongs, Asparagus, Marquise, 1902	385.00
Tongs, Ice, Olympian	550.00
Tongs, Ice, San Lorenzo	295.00
Tongs, Sandwich, Vine	550.00
Tongs, Sugar, Faneuil	55.00
Tray, Reticulated, Round, 12 In.	895.00
Tureen, Soup, Cover, Heart–Shaped Finial, c.1875, 14 1/8 In.	4675.00

Tureen, Soup, Undertray, Fluted & Gadrooned, 16 x 10 In. 550.00
Vase, Amphora Form, Shell & Leaf Footed, 1902, 23 1/8 In. 3850.00
Vase, Applied Dragonfly, Water Beetle, 11 1/2 In. 8250.00
Vase, Flowers & Leaves, Water Leaves Border, 1902, 6 1/4 In. 2200.00
Vase, Japanese Style, Birds & Actors, c.1875, 9 3/8 In. 7975.00
Vase, Shells, Flowers Border, Kissing Putti, 1891, 19 1/2 In. 7425.00
Vase, Trumpet, Flowering Branches, 1891–1902, 14 5/8 In., Pr. 8250.00
Watch Holder, French Enamel 295.00
Watch Holder, Marble Base 195.00
Youth Set, Fork, Knife, Cereal Spoon, Persian 150.00

TIFFANY objects made from a mixture of materials, such as bronze and
glass boxes, are listed here. Tiffany lamps are included in this section.

TIFFANY, Ashtray & Lighter, Gold Club Attached To Rim 192.50
Ashtray & Match Safe, Zodiac, Signed, 4 1/2 x 4 1/2 In. 150.00
Ashtray, Match Safe, Bronze, Pink & Red Enamel Design, 4 In. 250.00
Ashtray, Zodiac, Bronze, Gold Dore, 4 x 3 In. 135.00
Basket, Bronze, Enameled Design, Blue, Green, Yellow, Handle, 6 In. 250.00
Basket, Bronze, Enameled Design, Shaped Handle, Pedestal, 8 In. 1500.00
Basket, Gold Dore, Bronze, Enameled, Shaped Handle, 9 1/2 In. 1500.00
Blotter Ends, Adam, Signed, 12 1/4 x 2 1/4 In., Pair 175.00
Blotter Ends, Pine Needle, Etched Bronze, Signed, 19 x 2 In., Pair 350.00
Blotter, Hand, Adam, Signed, 5 x 3 In. 150.00
Bonbon, Favrile, Gold Threading, Applied Drops, Signed, 4 1/4 In. 275.00
Bonbon, Gold Iridescent, Short Pedestal, Signed, 4 3/4 .... 650.00
Book Rack, Bronze, Grapevine, Green Slag Glass, 23 In. 1500.00
Bookends, Adam, Bronze & Enamel, Scroll Design, 4 x 6 In. 850.00
Bookends, Bronze, Colored Enamel, Gilding, 5 1/2 In., Pair 410.00
Bookends, Bronze, Line & Curved Design, Signed, 6 x 5 In. 750.00
Bookends, Bronze, Relief Buddha On Platform, Ribbed Border, 6 In. 650.00
Bookends, Ninth Century, Bronze & Jeweled, 6 In., Pair 900.00
Bookends, Ninth Century, Etched Bronze, Blue & Green Jewels 900.00
Bookends, Oriental, Bronze & Jeweled, 5 1/2 x 5 In., Pair 1200.00
Bookends, Oriental, Bronze, Jeweled, Signed, 5 1/2 In. 1200.00
Bookends, Symbols Of Chau Dynasty, Gold Dore, Bronze 750.00
Bookrack, Abalone, Bronze, Signed, 6 In. 1200.00
Bookrack, Grapevine, Etched Bronze, Green Slag Glass, Signed, 14 In. 1500.00
Box, Bronze, 2 Round Handles, 4 Dividers Inside, 4 1/2 In. 225.00
Box, Bronze, Abalone, Hinged Lid, 5 x 3 x 1 In. 575.00
Box, Card, Bookmark, Gold Dore, Hinged Cover, Signed, 4 1/4 x 3 In. 800.00
Box, Card, Pine Needle, Green Slag Glass, Hinged Lid, 3 x 4 x 1 In. 500.00
Box, Card, Pine Needle, Hinged Cover, Green Slag Glass, 4 1/2 In. 800.00
Box, Cigar, Bronze, Floral Design 3300.00
Box, Cigar, Byzantine, Bronze, 12 Favrile Inserts, 6 1/2 x 6 In. 1760.00
Box, Cigar, Celtic Design On Cover & Sides, Mahogany Lined, c.1920 .... 1760.00
Box, Favrile, Gold Dore Bronze Top, Yellow Opalescent, Round 975.00
Box, Filigree, Monogram Emblem, Signed, 8 3/8 In. 850.00
Box, Glove, Grapevine, Hinged Beaded Edge Cover, Favrile, Bronze 1760.00
Box, Jewel, Grapevine, Bronze, Green Glass, Beaded, Velvet Liners 1200.00
Box, Jewel, Grapevine, Bronze, Original Gold Finish, 3 In. 1500.00
Box, Jewel, Pine Needle, Amber Glass, Signed, 9 1/4 x 6 1/2 In. 825.00
Box, Stamp, Bronze, Gold Dore, Abalone Disc Cover, Line Design 475.00
Box, Stamp, Grapevine, Bronze, Amber Slag Glass, Ball Feet, Tray 400.00
Box, Stamp, Zodiac, Symbols On Hinged Cover, Signed, 3 3/4 In. 300.00
Box, Zodiac, Bronze, Symbols On Top, Hinged Cover, 5 x 3 x 1 In. 350.00
Calendar Frame, Pine Needle, Bronze, Slag Glass, 4 1/2 x 3 1/2 In. 275.00
Calendar Frame, Pine Needle, Green Slag Glass, 6 1/2 x 4 1/4 In. 575.00
Candelabrum, 3 Candle Cups Each Arm, Bronze, Marked, 21 1/2 In. 2475.00
Candelabrum, 6 Arms, 3 Candle Cups On Each Arm, 1900–1918, 22 In. 1450.00
Candelabrum, 6 Arms, Handle, Bobeches & Snuffer, 1900, 20 1/2 In. 4675.00
Candelabrum, Bronze, Favrile Glass Insets 1650.00
Candlestand, Whiplash Curves, Gold Dore, Signed 750.00
Candlestick, Bronze, 2 Arms, Curved Double Arms, 6 In., Pair 2000.00

Candlestick, Bronze, 3 Arms, Scrolling Arms, Favrile, 12 In.	2650.00
Candlestick, Bronze, 3–Prong Supports, 1899–1928, 11 3/8 In.	625.00
Candlestick, Bronze, Blue Iridescent Holder, Horseshoe Base, 9 In.	2250.00
Candlestick, Bronze, Glass, Round Bottom Platform, 21 In., Pair	2250.00
Candlestick, Bronze, Green Glass Candleholder, Tripod Base, 13 In.	2250.00
Candlestick, Bronze, Silver Blue Trailing, Favrile, 9 1/2 In.	1650.00
Candlestick, Everted Rim, Reeded Bronze Base, Green Glass, 18 In.	2200.00
Candlestick, Favrile, Bronze, Wild Carrot, 17 5/8 In.	825.00
Candlestick, Favrile, Gold Iridescent, Oval Shaped Top, 4 In., Pair	2100.00
Candlestick, Favrile, Wisteria, Square, Signed, 1916, 3 3/4 In., Pair	1500.00
Candlestick, Gilt Bronze, Bamboo, Split & Flaring, 10 1/4 In.	770.00
Candlestick, Gold Favrile, Rope Twist Body, Shaft, Gorham Shade	775.00
Candlestick, Queen Anne's Lace Bronze Base, Green Glass, 21 In.	1650.00
Candlestick, Rice Pattern, Pastel, Signed	1085.00
Candlestick, Slender Stick Body, Gold Dore Finish, 10 In., Pair	2500.00
Canister, Bronze, Round, Curved Lid, Signed, 3 1/2 In.	225.00
Castor Set, 3–Wheel Cut Bottles, Silver Frame, 3 Piece	525.00
Chamberstick, 2 Arms, Fleur–De–Lis Base, Snuffer, Signed, 9 In.	2000.00
Chandelier, Acorn, Leaded Dome Shade, Bronze Beaded Rim, 20 1/2 In.	7150.00
Chandelier, Bronze, 6 Arms, Blossom Form Shades, Prisms, 29 In.	3100.00
Chandelier, Swirling Leaf	8250.00
Charger, Bronze, Enameled, 12 In. Diam.	350.00
Chest, Bronze Jewel, Arches & Patterned Squares, 8 x 4 x 3 In.	2000.00
Clock, Carriage, Grapevine, Bronze & Glass	1700.00
Clock, Champleve Enamel & Brass, Moorish Spires, c.1900, 10 1/2 In.	885.00
Clock, Gilt Bronze, Blue Enameled, Marked, 5 5/8 In.	1550.00
Clock, Mantel, Woman & 2 Putti, Ormolu Bronze	4950.00
Clock, Spider Web Design, Slag Glass, Signed	1000.00
Coffeepot, Spot–Hammered, Palmette Bands, 9 7/8 In.	3550.00
Compote, Bronze, Line Design, 3–Footed, 3–In. Base, 7–In. Diam.	225.00
Compote, Bronze, Sunburst Design, Footed, 3 1/4 In.	225.00
Desk Set, Chinese, Marked, 7 Piece	1980.00
Desk Set, Graduate, Bronze Dore, 7 Piece .... 1100.00 To	1570.00
Desk Set, Pine Needle, 13 Piece	6050.00
Desk Set, Zodiac, Bronze Dore, Marked, 5 Piece	715.00
Desk Set, Zodiac, Bronze, 11 Piece	2800.00
Frame, Abalone, Bronze, Original Gold Dore Finish, 7 x 10 In.	2800.00
Frame, Grapevine, Bronze & Glass, Easel Style, 12 x 14 In.	3200.00
Frame, Grapevine, Bronze, Green Slag Glass, Beading, 8 x 9 1/2 In.	2000.00
Frame, Heraldic, Bronze, Red Enamel Border, Silver Edges, 9 x 12 In.	3500.00
Frame, Picture, Grapevine, Favrile, Bronze, 14 In.	5280.00
Frame, Pine Needle, Bronze & Glass, Easel Style, 9 x 7 In.	1800.00
Frame, Pine Needle, Bronze, Amber Glass, Oval Opening, 12 x 14 In.	3200.00
Frame, Venetian Style, 14k Gold Plate, Row Of Minks, 11 3/4 In.	2800.00
Hatpin Holder, Dore Bronze, 3 1/2 In.	575.00
Humidor, Grapevine, Bronze & Glass, Green Slag, Cover	3200.00
Humidor, Pine Needle, Bronze Gold Dore Liner, Bronze, Signed	2000.00
Inkwell, Abalone, Hinged Cover, Bronze, Signed	650.00
Inkwell, Adam, Bronze, Glass Insert, Oval, Signed, 2 1/2 In.	350.00
Inkwell, Art Nouveau, Bronze, Swirl Design, Attached Tray, 12 In.	1800.00
Inkwell, Art Nouveau, Bronze, Swirls, Glass Insert, Curved Tray	1200.00
Inkwell, Bronze, Bell Shape, Round Dome Cover, 4 1/2 In.	2000.00
Inkwell, Bronze, Butterflies, Gold Favrile Insert, Marked, 5 In.	3750.00
Inkwell, Byzantine, Bronze & Jewel, 4 1/2 x 2 3/4 In.	2500.00
Inkwell, Chinese, Bronze, Dark Patina Finish, 2 1/4 In.	450.00
Inkwell, Chinese, Overall Design, Bronze, Signed, 4 1/2 x 4 In.	800.00
Inkwell, Grapevine, Bronze & Glass, Green Slag Glass, 7 In.	1500.00
Inkwell, Hinged Dome, Gold–Mounted Lapis Lazuli, c.1900, 4 1/2 In.	8250.00
Inkwell, Nautical, Bronze, Hinged Seashell Cover, Glass Insert	1200.00
Inkwell, Pine Needle, Bronze, Green Slag Glass, Hinged Lid, 7 In. D.	1500.00
Inkwell, Spider Web Design, Slag Filigree, Signed	3450.00
Inkwell, Zodiac, Insert, 6 In.	495.00
Inkwell, Zodiac, Tray, Hinged Lid, Bronze, Marked, 4 In.	2450.00

Jar & Pen Brush, Pine Needle, Bronze, Green Slag Glass, 2 1/4 In. 250.00
Lamp, Acorn Shade, Favrile, Pairpoint Base, 1899–1928, 20 3/4 In. 3650.00
Lamp, Acorn Shade, Green, Yellow, 3 Arm Bronze Base, 21 In. 5450.00
Lamp, Acorn, Favrile, Domed Shade, Bronze Base, 21 3/4 In, ... 4675.00
Lamp, Acorn, Leaded Glass, Bronze, Greek Urn Base, 24 In. 7700.00
Lamp, Acorn, Leaded Glass, Bronze, Signed, 20 In. 9350.00
Lamp, Adam, Octagonal Shade, Bronze, Glass, 17 In. 6000.00
Lamp, Bell Shape, Favrile, Bronze, 13 1/4 In. 2200.00
Lamp, Bridge, Bronze Harp Base, Favrile Leaf & Cut Glass Shade 6100.00
Lamp, Bridge, Glass, Bronze, Harp Style Top, Adjustable, 57 In. 6500.00
Lamp, Bridge, Linen Fold, Green Glass, Bronze Frame, 4 Ft. 7 In. 7700.00
Lamp, Bronze & Glass Bridge, Slender Stick Body, 57 In. 6500.00
Lamp, Bronze, Adjustable, 4 Curved Feet, Pine Needle Shade, 15 In. 1500.00
Lamp, Bronze, Favrile Glass Shade, Ivory Color, 13 In. 2000.00
Lamp, Candle, Aurene, Electrified, 16 In. 1250.00
Lamp, Candle, Bronze & Iridescent Jeweled, 17 In., Pair 4200.00
Lamp, Candle, Egyptian Woman Holding Shade Over Head, 10 In. 400.00
Lamp, Candle, Favrile, Peacock Blue, Ribbed Body, Flange Top, 14 In. 6000.00
Lamp, Candle, Favrile, Spiral Twisted, Ruffled Shade, Signed, 12 In. 2300.00
Lamp, Candle, Favrile, White, Gold Shade & Base, Signed, 13 In., Pr. 4000.00
Lamp, Candle, Ribbed, Gold Shade, Gorham Insert, Signed, 13 1/2 In. 885.00
Lamp, Candle, Ruffled Shade, Twisted Hollow Stem, Signed, 15 1/4 In. 770.00
Lamp, Candle, Spiral Swirled, Gorham Fitting, Signed, 17 1/2 In. 935.00
Lamp, Candle, Tulip Shade, Gold Iridescent, Bronze Base, 17 1/2 In. 2000.00
Lamp, Candle, Twisted Ribbed Body, Ruffled Shade, Signed, 13 In. 1800.00
Lamp, Chinese, Bronze Octagonal Shade, Signed, 17 In. 6000.00
Lamp, Counter Balance, Gooseneck Arm, Glass & Bronze, 15 In. 4650.00
Lamp, Counterweight, Bronze Base, Double Curved Arms, 15 In. 6500.00
Lamp, Domed Green Shade, Swirling Rainbow Iridescence, 24 In. 5500.00
Lamp, Favrile Glass, Gilt–Bronze, Waisted Domical Shade, 17 1/2 In. 4537.00
Lamp, Favrile Glass, Green Damascene Shade, 22 In. 5500.00
Lamp, Favrile Shade, Damascene Design, Signed, 50 To 60 In. 8500.00
Lamp, Fleur–De–Lis, Mottle & Striated Glass, Bronze Base, 21 In. 7500.00
Lamp, Floor, Silvered Mesh Metal Shade, Geometric Dot Design 4500.00
Lamp, Geometric Leaded Shade, Golden Bottom, Bronze, Singed, 20 In. 6500.00
Lamp, Geometric, Favrile, Green Tiles, Gilt–Bronze, 19 1/4 In. 3650.00
Lamp, Geometric, Favrile, Squares & Rectangles, Bronze, 26 In. 9350.00
Lamp, Geometric, Green, Gold, 1913, 18 In. 5500.00
Lamp, Gold Design, Leaf & Vine, Signed, 6 1/2 In. 950.00
Lamp, Greek Key, Table, 15 In. 9900.00
Lamp, Hall, Lozenge Form, Amber Prisms, Beaded Chain, 20 Ft. 1350.00
Lamp, Ivy Leaf, Gold, Green, White, Bronze Cap & Base, Signed, 22 In. 7500.00
Lamp, Leaded Shade, Geometric, Bronze Base, 20 In. 6500.00
Lamp, Lily, 6–Light, Adjustable Bronze Fittings, Signed, 20 1/2 In. 8250.00
Lamp, Nautilus Shade, Opalescent Green, Bronze Base, 14 In. 4250.00
Lamp, Nautilus, Ball Feet, 2 Arms Hold Shade, Bronze, 13 1/2 In. 7500.00
Lamp, Piano, Lily, 3 Arms 2800.00
Lamp, Pine Needle, Bronze Shade & Base, Green Glass Liner, 13 In. 2000.00
Lamp, Pine Needle, Green Slag Glass, 8 1/2 In. 3500.00
Lamp, Pomegranate, Yellow, Green, Greek Urn Base, 22 In. 8800.00
Lamp, Student, Abalone Discs, Bronze Shade, Amber Slag Liner, 9 In. 3200.00
Lamp, Student, Adjustable, Favrile Glass & Bronze, 19 7/8 In. 3750.00
Lamp, Student, Counterweight, Damascene, Bronze Base, Signed 6000.00
Lamp, Torchere, 4–Light, Woman Holding Amphora, c.1880, 49 In. 5500.00
Lamp, Urn Style Base, Bronze & Glass, 15 1/2 In. 1800.00
Lamp, Zodiac, Bronze Base, Curved Arms Form Harp, 13 In. 3000.00
Lamp, Zodiac, Leaded Mica Shade, Bronze, Signed, 18 In. 2500.00
Lamp, Zodiac, Upright Bronze Base, Geometric, 18 In. 2500.00
Lantern, Hanging, Leaded Glass, Acorn Finial, Marked, 34 In. 7700.00
Lantern, Turtleback, 4–Sided, Bottom Door, Chain, Signed, 13 In. 5500.00
Letter Opener, Abalone, Iridescent Discs, Gold Dore, Signed, 10 In. 275.00
Letter Opener, Grapevine, Amber Slag Glass In Handle, Signed, 9 In. 275.00
Letter Opener, Ninth Century, Gold Dore, Signed, 10 1/4 In. 250.00

Letter Opener, Pine Needle, Gold Dore, Amber Glass, Signed, 9 In.	275.00
Letter Opener, Zodiac, Symbols On Handle, 10 1/2 In.	200.00 To 225.00
Letter Rack, Abalone, Bronze, 2 Compartments, Set In Leaf Design	900.00
Letter Rack, Adam, Bronze, Tiny Ribs, 2 Compartments, 6 In.	450.00
Letter Rack, Bronze, Jeweled, 2 Compartments, Blue, Green, 6 In.	850.00
Letter Rack, Grapevine, 2 Sections, Green Slag Glass, Signed, 10 In.	950.00
Letter Rack, Pine Needle, Green Slag Glass, Metal, Signed, 10 In.	950.00
Letter Rack, Pine Needle, Metal & Glass, 2 Compartments, 6 1/2 In.	950.00
Lighter, Cigar, Byzantine, Orange Glass Jewels, Beaded Band, 3 In.	880.00
Magnifying Glass, American Indian, 8 3/4 In.	500.00
Magnifying Glass, Bookmark, Gold Dore, Signed, 8 3/4 In.	550.00
Magnifying Glass, Bookmark, Symbols On Handle, Signed, 8 3/4 In.	500.00
Magnifying Glass, Ninth Century, Pattern On Handle, Signed, 9 In.	700.00
Magnifying Glass, Pine Needle, Open Bronze, Amber Slag Glass	700.00
Magnifying Glass, Zodiac, Gold Dore Bronze, Signed, 8 3/4 In.	550.00
Mirror, Hand, Bronze & Glass, Bronze Curved Handle, 11 3/4 In.	1800.00
Mirror, Hand, Grapevine, Filigree Bronze Frame, 11 1/8 In.	1550.00
Note Pad, Zodiac, Bronze, Signed	150.00
Paperweight, Bulldog, Sitting, Bronze, Dark Patina, 2 x 2 x 1 In.	475.00
Paperweight, Commemorative, Bronze Formed Into Letters, 3 1/2 In.	250.00
Paperweight, Commemorative, Fancy Letters, Top Knob Handle, 3 In.	250.00
Paperweight, Dog, Pointer, Bronze, Marked Shando, Signed, 3 1/4 In.	850.00
Paperweight, George Washington, Favrile, Logo, 4 x 5 In.	275.00
Paperweight, Giraffe, Bronze, Stand, Signed, 2 3/4 In	295.00
Paperweight, Lioness, Bronze, Gold Dore Finial, 5 x 1 x 1 1/2 In.	700.00
Paperweight, Owl, Bronze, 3 x 1 1/4 In.	850.00 To 1045.00
Paperweight, Turtleback, Bronze Edging, 5 x 6 1/4 In.	400.00
Paperweight, Turtleback, Bronze Frame, Signed, 5 3/4 x 4 3/4 In.	935.00
Pen Holder, Bronze & Glass, Easel Style, 3 Curved Arms, 3 In.	500.00
Pen Tray, Adam, Curved Side Handles, 3 Sections, 9 x 3 In.	200.00
Pen Tray, Pine Needle, Bronze Ball Feet, Signed, 9 3/4 x 3 In.	250.00
Pencil, Mechanical	350.00
Pendant, Dragonfly, Jewel Eyes, Bronze Overlay, Chain, 10 In.	1450.00
Planter, Geometric, Bronze, Gold Dore Finish, 8 1/2 x 2 In.	650.00
Planter, Gilt Bronze, Mother-of-Pearl Rondels, Liner, 8 1/2 In.	1430.00
Planter, Pine Needle, Amber Panels, Liner, Gilt Bronze, 10 3/4 In.	990.00
Plaque, Mosaic Lotus Blossoms, Favrile Glass & Bronze, 1899, 11 In.	6875.00
Plate, Gold Dore, 12 In.	99.00
Platter, Bronze, Pink Enamel Flowers, Green & Yellow Leaves, 8 In.	250.00
Platter, Gold Dore, Raised Outer Border, Bronze, Signed, 14 In.	195.00
Scale, Letter, Zodiac, Green & Brown	275.00
Scale, Postage, Grapevine, Bronze, Green Slag Glass, 6 1/2 In.	3500.00
Scale, Postage, Pine Needle, Amber Slag Glass	650.00
Shade, Acorn, Opalescent Green, Heart-Shaped Leaves, 16 In.	3850.00
Shade, Damascene, Irregular Trailings, 1899-1920, 14 In.	1980.00
Shoehorn, Spot-Hammered, Spatula Handle, c.1880, 7 1/2 In.	1650.00
Smoking Stand, Stem Holds Ashtray, Match Box, Cigar Holder,	770.00
Thermometer, Bronze & Jeweled, 19th Century, 8 1/4 In.	1250.00
Tray, Abalone, Bronze, 12 In.	325.00
Tray, Bronze, Incised Pattern, Round, 10 In.	230.00
Tray, Card, Peacock Feather, Monogrammed, Gold Dore, Signed, 6 1/2 In	125.00
Tray, Geometric Rim Design, Gold Dore Finish, Bronze, Signed, 8 In.	250.00
Tray, Leaves & Berries Edge, Gold Dore, Bronze, Signed, 6 3/4 In.	195.00
Tray, Pen, Pine Needle, Green Glass Under Bronze, Signed, 9 1/2 In.	250.00
Tray, Scrolled Grip Handles, Oval, 20th Century, 28 3/4 In.	4125.00
Tray, Serving, Bronze, Round, Twisted Rope Design, 8 1/4 In.	150.00
Tray, Serving, Geometric, Bronze, Round, 8 In.	250.00
Vase, Bud, Favrile, Gold Iridescent, Bronze Holder, 5 1/2 In.	750.00

TIFFIN Glass Company of Tiffin, Ohio, was a subsidiary of the United States Glass Co. of Pittsburgh, Pennsylvania, in 1892. The U.S. Glass Co. went bankrupt in 1963, and the Tiffin plant employees purchased the building and the inventory. They continued running it from 1963 to 1966, when it was sold to Continental Can Company. In 1969, it was sold to Interpace, and in 1980, it was closed. The black satin glass, made from 1923 to 1926, and the stemware of the last twenty years are the best-known products.

Bowl, Twilight, 5 In.	15.00
Bowl, Watermelon, Satin Glass, 10 In.	45.00
Candlestick, Watermelon, Satin Glass, 8 In., Pair	50.00
Champagne, Flanders, Pink	25.00
Champagne, Persian Pheasant	25.00
Cocktail, Cherokee Rose, 5 1/2 In.	20.00
Cocktail, June Night, 4 Oz.	10.00
Cocktail, Seafood, Desert Red	22.00
Cordial, Persian Pheasant	40.00
Cordial, Wisteria	45.00
Goblet, Desert Red	28.00
Goblet, Iced Tea, Festival, 12 Oz.	12.50
Goblet, Juno, Green	20.00
Goblet, La Fleur, Topaz, 8 In.	32.00
Goblet, Water, Cadena, Yellow	35.00
Goblet, Water, Flanders, Pink	35.00
Goblet, Water, La Fleur, Topaz	32.00
Goblet, Wisteria	25.00
Iced Tea, Flanders, Pink, Footed	35.00
Lamp, Torchere, Sterling Silver Overlay Design, Pair	110.00
Perfume Bottle, Clear, Long Black Stopper	45.00
Plate, Cherokee Rose, 14 1/2 In.	50.00
Relish, Cherokee Rose, 3 Sections, 12 1/2 In.	65.00
Rose Bowl, Poppies, Black Amethyst	60.00
Sugar & Creamer, Nymph With Flute, Green Handle	125.00
Tumbler, Juice, Flanders, Crystal, Footed	30.00
Tumbler, Juice, Wisteria	25.00
Vase, Cherokee Rose, Bud, 10 1/2 In.	45.00
Vase, Cherokee Rose, Bud, Sterling Base, 10 1/4 In.	50.00
Vase, Cornucopia, Blue, 8 1/4 In.	75.00
Vase, Frosted Amberina, Poppies, 9 In.	70.00

TILES have been used in most countries of the world as a sturdy building material for floors, roofs, fireplace surrounds, and surface toppings. Many of the American tiles are listed in this book under the factory name.

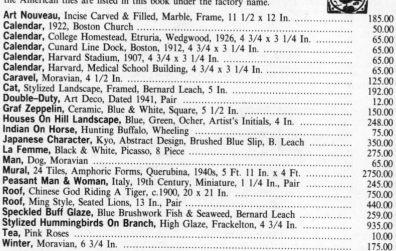

Art Nouveau, Incise Carved & Filled, Marble, Frame, 11 1/2 x 12 In.	185.00
Calendar, 1922, Boston Church	50.00
Calendar, College Homestead, Etruria, Wedgwood, 1926, 4 3/4 x 3 1/4 In.	65.00
Calendar, Cunard Line Dock, Boston, 1912, 4 3/4 x 3 1/4 In.	65.00
Calendar, Harvard Stadium, 1907, 4 3/4 x 3 1/4 In.	65.00
Calendar, Harvard, Medical School Building, 4 3/4 x 3 1/4 In.	65.00
Caravel, Moravian, 4 1/2 In.	125.00
Cat, Stylized Landscape, Framed, Bernard Leach, 5 In.	192.00
Double–Duty, Art Deco, Dated 1941, Pair	12.00
Graf Zeppelin, Ceramic, Blue & White, Square, 5 1/2 In.	150.00
Houses On Hill Landscape, Blue, Green, Ocher, Artist's Initials, 4 In.	248.00
Indian On Horse, Hunting Buffalo, Wheeling	75.00
Japanese Character, Kyo, Abstract Design, Brushed Blue Slip, B. Leach	350.00
La Femme, Black & White, Picasso, 8 Piece	275.00
Man, Dog, Moravian	65.00
Mural, 24 Tiles, Amphoric Forms, Querubina, 1940s, 5 Ft. 11 In. x 4 Ft.	2750.00
Peasant Man & Woman, Italy, 19th Century, Miniature, 1 1/4 In., Pair	245.00
Roof, Chinese God Riding A Tiger, c.1900, 20 x 21 In.	750.00
Roof, Ming Style, Seated Lions, 13 In., Pair	440.00
Speckled Buff Glaze, Blue Brushwork Fish & Seaweed, Bernard Leach	259.00
Stylized Hummingbirds On Branch, High Glaze, Frackelton, 4 3/4 In.	935.00
Tea, Pink Roses	10.00
Winter, Moravian, 6 3/4 In.	175.00

TINWARE containers for household use have been made in America since the seventeenth century. The first tin utensils were brought from Europe, but by 1798, tin plate was imported and local tinsmiths made the wares. Painted tin is called *tole* and is listed separately. Some tin kitchen items may be found listed under Kitchen. The lithographed tin containers used to hold food and tobacco are listed in the Advertising category under Tin.

Box, Candle, Hinged Lid, Tabs For Hanging, 14 In.	175.00
Bread Maker, Embossed Directions On Cover, Bucket Type	30.00
Can, Watering, Lithographed Children Scenes, 4 1/2 In.	105.00
Card Tray, Coffin End, Painted Crescent Moon, Octagonal, 1820, 9 In.	110.00
Chamberstick, Handmade, Crimped Pan, Rectangular Base, 5 In.	105.00
Chamberstick, Push–Up, Gray Marbelized Plating On Steel, 6 In.	145.00
Coffee Boiler, Gold Floral, Copper Bottom, Conical Lid, Black	98.00
Coffee Urn, Triangular Tray, Painted Red, 19th Century, 16 1/2 In.	250.00
Coffeepot, Stylized Floral Punched Design, 11 In.	1300.00
Feeder, Handle At Right Angles To Spout	400.00
Foot Warmer, Punched Hearts, Circles, Mortised Wooden Frame, 18 In.	250.00
Foot Warmer, Wood	395.00
Mold, Candle, 1 Tube	340.00
Mold, Candle, 3 Tube, Round Top	275.00
Mold, Candle, 4 Tube, Double Ear Handles, 11 In.	75.00
Mold, Candle, 8 Tube, Unusual Serpentine Handle, 10 3/4 In.	70.00
Mold, Candle, 9 Tube	190.00
Mold, Candle, 12 Tube, 10 1/2 In.	150.00
Mold, Candle, 12 Tube, 11 In.	140.00
Mold, Candle, 12 Tube, Pine Frame, 16 x 16 x 16 1/4 In.	825.00
Mold, Candle, 12 Tube, Pine Frame, 20 3/4 x 20 In.	900.00
Mold, Candle, 12 Tube, Ring Handle, Round, 12 1/2 In.	300.00
Mold, Candle, 12 Tube, Widely Spaced	175.00
Mold, Candle, 12 Tube, Widely Spaced Tubes, Ear Handle, 11 1/2 In.	250.00
Mold, Candle, 17 1/4 In.	245.00
Mold, Candle, 24 Tube, 9 1/2 In.	200.00
Mold, Candle, 24 Tube, 12 x 12 In.	200.00
Mold, Candle, 36 Tube, Double, 23 1/2 x 11 3/4 In.	400.00
Mold, Candle, 36 Tube, Wooden Frame, Old Red Paint, Late 1700–1800s	2100.00
Mold, Candle, 42 Tube, Wood Frame	800.00
Mold, Candle, 72 Tube, 11 1/4 In.	400.00
Mold, Candle, Red, J. Walker, 19th Century, 11 x 13 x 7 In. *Illus*	935.00
Mold, Candle, Wooden Handle, 18 In.	275.00
Mold, Lady Finger, 19th Century	25.00
Mug, Bonanza	10.00
Pail, Lard, Cover, 5 Gal.	8.00
Plate, ABC, 19th Century, 6 In.	65.00
Saltshaker, Large	27.50
Shaker, Mohawk Indian Side, 1877 Calender On Lid	125.00
Skimmer, Cream	10.00

Tinware, Mold, Candle, Red, J. Walker, 19th Century, 11 x 13 x 7 In.

◆ ◆ ◆ ◆ ◆ ◆ ◆ ◆ ◆ ◆ ◆ ◆ ◆ ◆ ◆

Rusty tin may be helped. Rinse the metal, scrub, dry, then coat with a thin layer of Vaseline.

◆ ◆ ◆ ◆ ◆ ◆ ◆ ◆ ◆ ◆ ◆ ◆ ◆ ◆ ◆ ◆

Teapot, Cast Pewter Handle, 5 3/4 In. 30.00

TOBACCO CUTTERS may be listed in both the Advertising and the Store sections.

TOBACCO JAR collectors search for those made in odd shapes and colors. Because tobacco needs special conditions of humidity and air, it has been stored in special containers since the eighteenth century.

Brownstone, Staffordshire 275.00
Chinese Man's Head, Black Moustache & Hat, 5 3/4 In. 118.00
Chinese Man's Head, Porcelain, 5 1/4 In. 95.00
Comical Duck, Orange Beak, Green Hat, 5 1/2 In. 115.00
Japanese Woman's Head, 4 3/4 In. 88.00

TOBY JUG is the name of a very special form of pitcher. It is shaped like the full figure of a man or woman. A pitcher that shows just the top half of a person is not correctly called a toby. More examples of toby jugs can be found under Royal Doulton and other factory names.

George V, Wilkinson, 1919 .... 750.00
Jailer, Occupied Japan, 7 1/2 In. 75.00
Peddler, Occupied Japan, 5 In. 60.00
Philpot, Woods & Son 35.00

TOLE is painted tin. It is sometimes called *japanned ware, pontypool,* or *toleware.* Most nineteenth–century tole is painted with an orange–red or black background and multicolored decorations. Many recent versions of toleware are made and sold. Related items may be listed in the Tin category.

Box, Deed, Dome Top, Red Paint, Miniature, 3 In. 35.00
Box, Deed, Dome Top, Red Paint, Stenciled Floral, Yellow Striping, 8 In. 150.00
Box, Deed, Dome Top, Stenciled Floral Design, 8 1/2 In. 75.00
Box, Deed, Dome Top, Worn Black Paint, Redecoration, 10 In. 200.00
Box, Deed, Embossed Lid, Stenciled Floral Design, 8 1/2 In. 100.00
Box, Deed, Green Paint, Red Striping, Stenciled Gold Lid, 6 1/2 In. 200.00
Box, Document, Blue, Tray, Gold Stencil Of Boston Pharmacy 75.00
Box, Polychrome Design, 3 1/4 x 2 1/4 In. 14.00
Box, Spice, 6 Removable Compartments, 19th Century 95.00
Bread Tray, Brown Crystallized Center, Floral Design, 8 x 12 5/8 In. 900.00
Bucket, Coal, Floral, Scrolling Handles, Lion's Head Feet, 22 1/2 In. 82.00
Caddy, Red Paint, Gold Stenciled Label Says Coffee, 2 5/8 In. 150.00
Canister Set, Seashells, Gilt Filigree, Red, Lamp Mounted, 19 In., Pair 1210.00
Canister, Design, 1840 .... 1540.00
Canister, Lamp Mounted, Black, Gilt, Foliage, No Shade, 33 In., Pair 330.00
Canister, Multicolored Floral, Brown Japanning, 6 In. 300.00
Chandelier, 20 Candle Arms, U.S., 28 In. 450.00
Clock, Peinte, Wall, Faux Rosewood Design, Guillaume, 15 In. 385.00
Coffee Urn, Empire, Bust On Top, Swags, 20 In. 3575.00
Coffeepot, Brown Japanning, Floral, 8 1/2 In. 300.00
Coffeepot, Brown Japanning, Floral, Gooseneck Spout, 10 1/2 In. 700.00
Coffeepot, Red Paint, 2 3/4 In. 120.00
Coffeepot, Red, White, Green & Yellow Floral, Black Ground 1900.00
Coffeepot, Red, Yellow & Green Floral, Gooseneck Spout 3400.00
Creamer, Brown Japanning, Floral, 4 In. 475.00
Garnitures, Paneled Flower Pots, Painted, 12 In., Pair 195.50
Lamp, 2–Light, Scroll Supports, Weighted Base, Green, 19 In. 3450.00
Lamp, Chinoiserie Design, Lace Shade, France, 17 In., Pair 600.00
Lamp, Kerosene, Post, C. T. Ham Mfg. Co., 26 In. 75.00
Match Holder, Hanging, Black Japanning, Design In Red, 7 1/2 In. 295.00
Match Safe, Design, New England, c.1840 .... 295.00
Mug, Black Japanning, Floral, 4 3/8 In. 625.00
Mug, Brown Japanning, Floral, 5 3/4 In. .... 450.00 To 700.00
Mug, Red Paint, Worn Stencil Says My Girl, 2 In. 35.00
Pitcher, Cover, Red, 4 1/2 In. 700.00

Pitcher, Hinged Lid, Gilt Stenciled Floral Design, 4 1/2 In. 175.00
Pot, Black Japanning, Floral Design, Yellow, Red, 8 1/2 In. 1900.00
Shaker, Flower, Green, Red, White, 2 3/4 In. 95.00
Sugar Shaker, Simple Flower, Brown 95.00
Sugar, Brown Japanning, Floral Design, 4 In. 110.00
Sugar, Cover, Black Japanning, Floral, 3 3/4 In. 375.00
Sugar, Worn Black Paint, Red & Yellow, 3 3/4 In. 90.00
Tea Caddy, Black Japanning, White Band, Floral Design, 4 1/8 In. 175.00
Tea Caddy, Brown Japanning, Floral, 4 In. 450.00
Tea Caddy, Dome Top, Divided, Portrait Medallion, Young Man, 4 1/8 .... 275.00
Tea Caddy, Red Paint, Floral, 5 1/4 In. 2300.00
Teapot, Dark Brown Japanning, Polychrome Floral, 8 3/4 In. 275.00
Teapot, Floral & Bird, Red Ground, England, 14 In. 305.00
Tray, Black Paint, Stenciled & Freehand Floral Design, 11 3/4 In. 100.00
Tray, Brown Crystallized Center, White Band, Octagonal, 9 x 12 In. 450.00
Tray, Brown Crystallized Paint, Stylized Floral, Octagonal, 12 1/2 In. 200.00
Tray, Brown Japanning, Floral, Octagonal, 8 5/8 In. 825.00
Tray, Brown Japanning, White Band, Octagonal, 8 5/8 In. 600.00
Tray, Floral Design, Scalloped Rim, 12 In. 250.00
Tray, Florals, Faux Bamboo Stand, 19th Century, 26 x 19 1/2 In. 137.00
Tray, Gilt Floral Design, Green Ground, 29 x 24 In. 1200.00
Tray, Gilt Floral, Butterfly Border, 30 x 22 In. 525.00
Tray, Golden Tones On Black, Civil War Era, 36 x 30 1/2 In. 300.00
Tray, Painted Classical Figures In Landscape, c.1840, 22 x 26 In. 550.00
Tray, Reticulated Gallery Rim, Center Fruit & Foliage, 19 1/4 In. 200.00
Tray, Woman With Parasol Scene, Primitive, Black Ground, 20 x 28 In. 170.00

TOM MIX was born in 1880 and died in 1940. He was the hero of over
100 silent movies from 1910 to 1929, and 25 sound films from 1929 to
1935. There was a Ralston Tom Mix radio show from 1933 to 1950, but
the original Tom Mix was not in the show. Tom Mix comics were
published from 1942 to 1953.

Arrowhead, Glow In Dark 65.00
Arrowhead, Lucite 65.00
Badge, Gold 90.00
Badge, Ranch Boss 375.00
Book, Tony & His Pals, Whitman, Jacket 85.00
Boots, Cowboy, Box, 1930s .... 325.00 To 350.00
Bracelet, Identification 25.00
Decoder .... 50.00 To 65.00
Flashlight, Bird Call 100.00
Gum Wrapper, Chicle, Coupon For Deputy Ring 125.00
Knife, Pocket, Tom & Tony .... 60.00 To 65.00
Movie Film 30.00
Neckerchief, Checkerboard 150.00
Poster, Circus & Wild West, Tom On Tony, Lithograph, 42 x 28 In. 330.00
Program, Life Of Tom Mix, Fleto Circus 85.00
Rifle, Single Shot, . 22 Cal., Williams Peep Sight, 1936 .... 325.00
Ring, Brand 95.00
Ring, Firearm's Bull's-Eye 160.00
Ring, Look Around 85.00
Ring, Look In Picture, Premium 40.00
Ring, Magnet 125.00
Ring, Magnet, Instructions & Mailer 200.00
Ring, Mystery Picture 75.00
Ring, Signature 200.00
Ring, Siren 65.00
Ring, Sliding Whistle .... 60.00 To 95.00
Ring, Straight Shooter .... 50.00 To 100.00
Ring, Target 150.00
Ring, Tiger Eye .... 175.00 To 250.00
Rocking Horse 350.00
Shooting Gallery, Cardboard, Parker Bros., 1935, 7 x 12 In. 265.00

Signal Arrow & Gun 85.00
Spinner .... 35.00 To 55.00
Spinner, Ralston Straight Shooters Good Luck, 1933 .... 60.00
Target, Blow Gun, Paper, 1940 .... 65.00
Telegraph Signal Set, Original Box 85.00
Telescope, Birdcall 135.00
Tin, Makeup 25.00
Watch Fob, Gold Ore, 1940 .... 40.00
Watch Fob, Pocket 150.00
Wristwatch, Anniversary, Ralston, 1980s 300.00

TOOLS of all sorts are listed here, but most are related to industry. Other
tools may be found listed under Iron, Kitchen, Tinware, and Wooden.

Adze, Cooper's, 8 1/2 x 9 In. 150.00
Adze, Small Bowl, 6–In. Coltsfoot Handle 98.00
Ax, Broad, Goosewing, Inlaid Steel Bit, 18th Century 132.00
Ax, Camp, Leather Sheath, Maine Hickory Handle, 5 1/4–In. Head 60.00
Ax, Indian, Speckled Granite, Polished Blade, Michigan 90.00
Ax, Safety, Marble, Dog & Hare Handle 275.00
Ax, Single Bit, Firestone 30.00
Ax, W. O. W. Lodge, Original Paint, All Wooden, 34 1/2 In. 55.00
Balling Iron, Veterinary, J. Nelson & Sons, Steel, Brass, Rosewood 110.00
Battery Tester, W. C. Fields Red Nose, Nose Lights Up, 1974, 5 x 11 In. 8.00
Bed Wrench, Key, Combination, L Shape, 6 x 6 In. 14.00
Bee Smoker, Woodman 10.00
Bench, Chair Caner's, Turned Legs, Hand–Forged Iron Clamps 77.00
Bench, Cobbler's, Oak, 32 1/2 In. 75.00
Bench, Stave, Cooper's, Spring Pole, 6 Ft. 4 In. 30.00
Bench, Wool Carding 280.00
Bevel, Rosewood, Brass, Nonadjustable, 5 1/2 x 8 In. 12.00
Bevel, Stanley No. 18, Nickel Plated Bearing, Pat. 7/14/08, 8 In. 12.00
Bootjack, Red & Green Lines, Initial T, Wooden, c.1870, 16 In. 195.00
Bottle Corker, Cherry, Mushroom Knob Handle, 1870, 14 1/2 In. 49.00
Bow Drill, Stone Cutter's, All Iron 110.00
Box, Cabinet Maker's, 6 Interior Walnut Compartments, Oak, 1860s 500.00
Box, Fordson Tractor 10.00
Box, Locksmith's, Auto Keys, Code Book, Antique Keys 50.00
Brace, Brass Framed, Colquhoun & Cadman, Lever Pad 450.00
Brace, Brass Framed, Ebony Trade Brace 375.00
Brace, Brass Framed, Ebony, Alfred Ridge 450.00
Brace, Cherry, 7 Bit Pads & Brackets, American, 16 In., With 5 In. Throw 275.00
Brace, Cherry, American, Primitive 235.00
Brace, Sheffield Style, Stewart, Edinburgh, Unplated, Brass Chuck 125.00
Brace, T. Tillotson, Sheffield, Beech, Quarter–Plated, Self–Acting, 1846 .... 315.00
Brace, Ultimatum, Ebony, Ivory Ring 495.00
Branding Iron, Initials JC, Iron, Long Handle 14.00
Breast Drill, Goodell–Pratt Toolsmiths, 2 Speed, Patent 1915 .... 500.00
Bucket, Feed, Military, Collapsible Canvas 24.00
Bung Hole Auger, Barrel Maker's, Wooden Tee Handle 10.00
Bung Plunger, Iron & Brass 40.00
Button Machine, Fastens Buttons On Shoes, Tag 375.00
Caliper Rule, Carpenter's, Stanley, No. 39, Ivory & German Silver 80.00
Calipers Set, Leg Shaped, Known As Dancing Master's, Or He–She, Pair 578.00
Calipers, Blacksmith's, Double, Hinged At Different Points, 21 In. 75.00
Calipers, Bowl, Smith, Brass Washers Each Side, Blued Steel, Legs 10.00
Calipers, Double, Wheelwright's, Hand Forged Iron, 19 In. 150.00
Calipers, Wm. Gent., Double, Blued Steel, 6 In. Legs 15.00
Cap Bomb, Dupont, Keg Shape 110.00
Capper, Bottle, Sampson, Nickel Plated Cast Iron, 1921 .... 25.00
Chest, Machinist's, 6 Drawers, Oak, 17 x 10 1/2 In. 165.00
Chest, Tools, Shipwright's 750.00
Chisel Set, Stanley No. 66, Tang Style, Plastic Handles, 6 Piece 80.00
Chisel, 1/2–In. Butt, Keen Kutter 12.00

Chisel, Lock Mortise, 1/2 In. 35.00
Chisel, Mortise, Shipwright's Style, Hooped Ash Handles, Pair 24.00
Chisel, Paring, L. & I. J. White, Buffalo, N.Y., 1837, Hardwood Handle 14.00
Chisel, Pattern Maker's, Buck & Ryan, Ash Handle, 7 In. 25.00
Chisel, Pattern Maker's, John Bull, Ash Handle, 8 In. 18.00
Chisel, Pattern Maker's, Long Paring, 1/2 In. 20.00
Chisel, Pattern Maker's, Wm. Marples, Boxwood Handle, 7 In. 18.00
Chisel, Shipwright's, Wm. Greaves & Sons, Socket Handle, 13 3/4 In. 40.00
Chisel, Stanley, No. 20, Everlasting, Hickory Handle, 7 In. 18.00
Clamp, Furniture, Threaded Rod Inside Frame, Screw-Type 82.50
Clipper, Starrett, No. 456, Gear Tooth, Instructions, Case 200.00
Cobbler's Bench, Shaker, Blue Paint, Canterbury, N. H., 54 1/2 In. 4125.00
Compass, Cooper's, Iron, Chamfered, 10 In. 28.00
Compass, Surveyor's, HM Pool, Box, 6-In. Dial 467.50
Compass, Surveyor's, Philadelphia, Case 850.00
Cooper's, Grooving Heads Of Wine Casks 450.00
Corn Planter, Wood & Metal, c.1870, 7 x 9 x 13 In. 385.00
Corn Sheller, Cobs Go Through Beak Of Iron Eagle 165.00
Crate Opener, Tomahawk No. 99, Bridgeport Manufacturing, 12 1/2 In. 12.00
Croze, Cooper's, Cherry 65.00
Cupboard, Machinist's, Octagonal Revolving Cupboard Inside 650.00
Cutter, Blubber, Long Handle, Signed 110.00
Demagnetizer, Watch, South Bend 15.00
Divider, Angle, Stanley, No. 30, Box 40.00
Drill, Hand, Millers Falls, Level, 2 Speed, Adjustable 27.50
Drill, Sugar, Break Up Blocks Of Sugar, Cast Iron, Wooden Handle 15.00
Fence, Eclipse 25.00
Fence, Joiner, Iron, Nickel Plated, 8 x 5 In. 36.00
Flashlight, Winchester, Copper 60.00
Flashlight, Winchester, No. 9810 ...... 25.00
Flax Ratchet, Primitive, Wooden, 8 Metal Teeth, 3 1/2 x 5 In. 10.00
Flax Winder, Chip Carving, Sheraton Turnings 150.00
Fleem, 2 Blades, Unwin & Rogers 35.00
Fleem, Veterinary, Marked Batm, 3 Blades, Brass Covered, 3 5/8 In. 75.00
Fork, Hay, Wooden 75.00
Gauge, Lumber, Lufkin Rule Co., Brass Finger, 4 In. 80.00
Gauge, Marking, Stanley, No. 65, Boxwood 25.00
Gauge, Mortise, Ebony, Oval Head, Brass Face 55.00
Gimlet, Shell, Turned Beech Handle, Stamped No. 0, 7 In. 8.00
Glove Stretcher, Full Thumb, Wooden, Pair 195.00
Gouge, Carving, Marked I Cam, 18th Century, 3/16 x 7 1/4 In. 20.00
Gouge, Pattern Maker's, J. Howarth, Boxwood Handle 45.00
Grain Counter, Sherer, 7 Ft. 1500.00
Grain Flail, Wooden, Leather Thongs, 2 Part 25.00
Hacksaw, Dated 1885 ...... 30.00
Hammer, Billboard Posters, Vaughan & Bushnell, Extension Handle 30.00
Hammer, Brick Layer's, Stanley, No. 431A, Unused, Label On Handle 12.00
Hammer, Cigar Box Opener, R-B, 5 Cent, Metal 20.00
Hammer, Claw, Delicately Shaped, 3-In. Head, 9 1/2-In. Handle 20.00
Hammer, Claw, Smith, Bell Face, Iron, 12-In. Replaced Handle 20.00
Hammer, Claw, Winchester 27.50
Hammer, Combination, Thayer's Pat., June 24, 1862, Screwdriver Handle 115.00
Hammer, Farrier's, 11 1/2-In. Tiger Maple Handle 10.00
Hammer, Machinist's, Built-In Magnifying Glass 150.00
Hammer, Miner's, Wallace Coal Co., St. Louis 16.00
Hammer, Slatter's, Ringed Leather Handle, 18-In. Handle 36.00
Hammer, Tack, Upholsterer's, Clawed Pein, 12-In. Handle 21.00
Handcuffs, Peerless, 1915 ...... 24.00
Hat Stretcher, Polished Wood 32.50
Hatchet Bench, Dovetailed Cover, 18 In. 110.00
Hatchet, Flax, Hand Drawn & Tapered Nails, Dated 1778 ...... 77.00
Hatchet, Keen Kutter 85.00
Hatchet, Plumb, Anchor Trademark, 12 3/4-In. Handle 15.00

Hay Fork, Wooden, 5 Tine 50.00
Haystack Measure, Copper, Hand Made, J. Sykes, Cin., Ohio, 8 1/4 In. 225.00
Holder, Cigarette, Mechanical, Bird Picks Up With Beak 28.00
Ice Tongs, Cast Iron 15.00
Iron, Cauterizing, Veterinary, Blacksmith Made, 12 1/2 In. 14.00
Iron, Gophering, Heart Shaped Base 300.00
Iron, Hat Maker's, Toklliker, Curved, Shapes Brims 135.00
Jack, Conestoga Wagon, Hand Forged Iron Parts, Dated 1835 .... 66.00
Jack, Wagon, Wood & Iron, 1855, 18 3/4 In. 125.00
Jackplane, Dovetailed, Norris, 17 1/2 In. 850.00
Jig, Doweling, Stanley, No. 59 .... 15.00
Jigsaw, Foot Powered 270.00
Knife, Chamfer, Cooper's, Jigger Type, 3 1/2–In. Blade, Flat Handle 30.00
Knife, Putty, Keen Kutter 21.00
Last, Cobbler's, Mounted On Wooden Base, Cast Iron 185.00
Lathe, Jeweler's, 51 Collets, 3 Jaw Chuck, Universal Chuck 650.00
Lathe, Jeweler's, Elson, Motor & Speed Control 175.00
Lawn Sprinkler, Tractor Form, Cast Iron 1500.00
Level, A. Mathison & Son, Scotland, Brass Top, 11 In. 65.00
Level, C. F. Richardson, Japanning, 12 In. 60.00
Level, David, No. 7 .... 40.00
Level, Goodell–Pratt, Brass Bound, Rosewood, 24 In. 125.00
Level, L. L. Davis, 24 In. 3800.00
Level, Stanley, Cast Iron, Glass 25.00
Level, Stanley, No. 98, Brass Bound Rosewood, 12 In. 225.00
Level, Stratton Brothers, Brass Bound, Plumb In End, 10 In. .... 165.00 To 375.00
Level, Universal, All Angle, Brass, Steel 35.00
Map Pencil, Automatic 1 End, Miles & Kilometer Dial Other, Selsi 30.00
Measure, Foot, Dr. Scholl's, Wooden 18.00
Measuring, Green River Wheel, Cooper & Wheelwright, Movable Pointer 65.00
Mill, Vertical, Rockwell, With Vise & Collets, 3 Phase With Converter 1875.00
Miter Box, Stanley No. 148, With Backsaw, 26 x 4 In. 75.00
Miter Square, Stanley, Mahogany Body 15.00
Mold, Brick, New Ulm, Minn., 1 Original Brick, 5 Piece 145.00
Mold, Bullet, Winchester 40–50 .... 80.00
Mold, For Casting Pewter Spoons, Bronze, 2 Part, 8 In. 275.00
Mortising Machine, Cincinnati, 1857 .... 250.00
Nail Feeder, Fed 1 By 1 Down Channel Into Tin Hopper, Automatic 30.00
Needlework, Bone Knitting Needle, Guards, Hoof Shape, Pair 145.00
Niddy–Noddy, Hand Held, Mortised & Pinned, 18 In. 75.00
Niddy–Noddy, Worn Dark Finish, 21 1/2 In. 25.00
Nipper, Cigar, Horseshoe Shape, Spring Loaded, Chain 65.00
Padlock, Keen Kutter, Brass, K. K. Logo Shape 100.00
Padlock, Simmons Keen Kutter, Brass, Key 90.00
Pattern, Pattern Maker's, Mahogany, Power Head, 8 x 6 In. ....'............... 12.00
Peel, Baker's, Long Handle 90.00
Piano Tuner's Kit, Complete With Ivory 4–Fold Ruler & Tools 165.00
Pipe Wrench, Stillson, Wood Handle, 6 In. 20.00
Pipe, Tamper, Animal Leg, Hoof, Carved Bone 58.00
Pipe, Tamper, Lady's Leg, Wearing Black Shoe, Carved Ivory, 18th C. 228.00
Plane, Arm Plow, Skate Nose, Brass Tips & Wing Nuts 70.00
Plane, Bead, Beech 10.00
Plane, Block, Stanley, No. 20, 2–Tone, Red Lever Cap 20.00
Plane, Brass Bullnose, Rosewood Wedge, Mathieson 150.00
Plane, Bullnose, M. Slater, Cast Steel, Mahogany Wedge, 3 3/4 In. 65.00
Plane, Cabinet Maker's, Stanley, No. 9, c.1910 .... 1000.00
Plane, Carriage Maker's, Stanley, No. 10 1/4 .... 425.00
Plane, Circular, Stanley, No. 113 .... 80.00 To 90.00
Plane, Combination, Silcock & Lowe, Beech, Metal 1350.00
Plane, Compass, Adjustable, Beech, Coffin Shape, 7 In. 60.00
Plane, Cornering, Low Angle, Gunmetal 310.00
Plane, Craftsman, Combination, 22 Cutters In Canvas Roll 115.00
Plane, Crown Molding, 5 1/2 In. 440.00

Plane, Crown Molding, Single Iron, JMS, 6 In.	350.00
Plane, Dado, Beech, Wooden Depth Stop, Maker's Marks	13.00
Plane, Dado, Ohio Tool Co., No. 48, 1 In.	40.00
Plane, Dovetailed, Mathieson, 14 1/2 In.	325.00
Plane, Duplex Rabbet, Stanley No. 78, Pat. 6/7/10	18.00
Plane, Floor, Stanley, No. 74, Original Handle & Brackets	650.00
Plane, H. Wetherel In Norton, 1-In. Ogee In Yellow Birch	1925.00
Plane, Jack Rabbet, Owasco Tool Co., N.Y., No. 54, 15 In.	60.00
Plane, Jack, Bedrock, Stanley, No. 605C, April, 19'10	60.00
Plane, Jack, Stanley, No. 105, October 5, 1875	130.00
Plane, Jack, Winchester, No. 3010, Japanning	70.00
Plane, Jointer, Bedrock, Stanley, No. 607, April, 2, '95 Behind Frog	95.00
Plane, Miter, Dovetailed, Spiers, Lever Cap Style, 8 1/2 In.	760.00
Plane, Miter, William Marples, Steel, Mahogany Infill, 9 1/2 In.	250.00
Plane, Moulding, H. Weatherall, Beech, 18th Century, 9 3/4 In.	160.00
Plane, Moulding, I. Sleeper, 18th Century, 9 3/4 In.	225.00
Plane, Moulding, Manners, Beech, 18th Century, 9 3/8 In.	115.00
Plane, Moulding, R. Bloxham, Beech, 18th Century, 9 5/8 In.	85.00
Plane, Ogee Cornice Molding	325.00
Plane, Panel Raising, I. Kendall, Beech, 1765–1814, 9 In.	145.00
Plane, Panel, Norris, No. 1, Dovetailed Steel, Cutter By Mawhood	360.00
Plane, Panel, Spier's, No. 1, Steel, Rosewood, 13 1/2 In.	275.00
Plane, Plow, Adjustable Scissor-Type Fence, Floral Decals, Morris	2400.00
Plane, Plow, Adjustable, Key Operated Threaded Shaft	450.00
Plane, Plow, Boxwood Screw Arms, Ivory Tips, Rosewood, A. Howland & Co.	1000.00
Plane, Plow, Brass Trim, Gladwin & Appleton, Boxwood	750.00
Plane, Plow, Closed Handle, Winsted Plane Co., Rosewood, 1850s	425.00
Plane, Plow, J. W. Peace, Rosewood Skate Nose Handle, 12 3/4 In.	2100.00
Plane, Plow, Sandusky, No. 119	75.00
Plane, Plow, Stanley Miller, Filletster Bed, Long & Short Fence	330.00
Plane, Prelateral, No. 6, Bailey's Patent 1855	65.00
Plane, Rabbet, Nat Gamble	962.00
Plane, Rabbet, Spier's, No. 3, Steel, Rosewood Infill, 7 1/2 x 5/8 In.	95.00
Plane, Rabbet, Stanley, No. 75, Bullnose	15.00
Plane, Rounding, R. Rowell, No. 12, Beech, 1771–1800, 9 3/8 In.	55.00
Plane, Router, Oak, Coffin Shape, Primitive, W. Richardson, 7 In.	48.00
Plane, Sandusky Tool Co., Wooden, 1 1/8 In.	52.00
Plane, Shoulder, Norris, No. 22, Dovetailed	225.00
Plane, Side Rabbet, Stanley, No. 79, c.1967	40.00
Plane, Smooth, Copeland & Co., Beech, Coffin Shape, Pat. May 27, 1856	195.00
Plane, Smooth, Liberty Bell, Stanley No. 122, Unmarked Wood	28.00
Plane, Smooth, Stanley, No. 1	535.00
Plane, Smooth, Stanley, No. 3, Box	65.00
Plane, Spelk, Basket Maker's, Dated 1799, 26 In.	110.00
Plane, Stanley, No. 45	45.00
Plane, Stanley, No. 62	235.00
Plane, Stanley, No. 190	45.00
Plane, Steel Block, Stanley No. 118, Iron	15.00
Plane, Steel Jack, Stanley, No. S5	75.00
Plane, Sun, Cooper's, Left Hand, Beech, 14 In.	35.00
Plane, Tongue & Groove, Union, No. 42	45.00
Plane, Wood, Bailey, No. 6	30.00
Plane, Wood, Bailey, No. 7	45.00
Plane, Wood, Stanley, No. 4	25.00
Planter, Corn, Acme, Red, Black Stenciled	10.00
Plierench, Eiffle Flash, 1916	45.00
Pliers, Blacksmith's, Hand Forged, Iron	10.50
Plow, Garden, Primitive, Wooden Beam	72.00
Plumb Bob, Brass, Large	30.00
Plumb Bob, Steel, Turned Brass Top, 5 Oz.	12.00
Plumb Box, Internal Reel	195.00
Probe, Grain, Checks For Moisture In Corn, Beans, Brass, Large	100.00
Rack, Candle Drying, 8 Removable Disks, Hooks, Hardwood & Pine, 40 In.	575.00

Rake, Cranberry, Spring–Loaded Wire Screen 120.00
Rake, Cranberry, Tin 25.00
Reel, Geared Counting Mechanism, Red Paint, 36 In. 90.00
Reel, Table Top, Crank, Mortised Shoe Frame, Hardwood, 19 In. 55.00
Rope Maker, Iron, Pat. 1901 .... 60.00
Rounder, B. D. Company, J. Lord, Beech, 9 1/2 x 3 In. 35.00
Router, J. Roche, Rosewood Handle, 9 In. 65.00
Router, Paten, Edward Preston, 5 x 2 1/4 In., Hardwood Knobs 40.00
Router, Rabbeting, Coach Maker's, Stanley, Bronze, Iron, 13 In. 38.00
Router, Stanley, No. 71 1/2, Pat. October 29, '01, 3 Irons 36.00
Rule & Caliper, Buttonhole, Belcher Bros., Boxwood & Brass 200.00
Rule, CS Co., No. 68, Folding 15.00
Rule, Lufkin, No. 2, Hickory Board, 36 In. 36.00
Rule, Lufkin, No. 34V, 1 Piece, 24 In. 20.00
Rule, Lufkin, No. 372 .... 25.00
Rule, Stanley, No. 68, Folding 12.00
Rule, Stanley, No. 87, Ivory 285.00
Rule, Stanley, No. 94, 4–Fold 100.00
Rule, Stanley, No. 425 .... 18.00
Rule, Upson, No. 32 1/2 .... 15.00
Ruler, Carpenter's, Stanley, No. 6, Folding, Ivory 500.00
Ruler, Carriage Maker's, Lufkin, No. 4883, Brass Fittings, Boxwood, 4 Ft. 50.00
Ruler, Combination, Rabone, No. 1190 .... 100.00
Ruler, Lufkin, Folding, Brass & Wood 12.50
Ruler, Metric & Imperial, Ivory, Adie, 15 Pall Mall, London, 4 Fold 265.00
Ruler, Surveyor's, Rabone, England, Boxwood, 6 Fold, 6 In. 25.00
Ruler, Type Counter For Newspaper, Brass 28.00
Ruler, With Caliper, German Silver Mounts, J. Barore, 4 Fold, 12 In. 330.00
Sabot Set, Clog Maker's, Knife, Spoon Bits & Long Bottom Knife 88.00
Saw, Butcher's, Henry Disston, Cast Steel, 18 1/2 In. Blade, 25 In. 75.00
Saw, Butcher's, Winchester, Pitted Frame, 22 1/2 In. Blade, 31 In. 45.00
Saw, Crosscut, E. C. Stearns, No. 103 .... 20.00
Saw, Hand, Keen Kutter, No. 88, Cherry Handle, 23 In. 25.00
Saw, Ice, Iron, Small 9.50
Saw, Keyhole, Folding, Pat. Date Feb. 19, 1899 .... 45.00
Saw, Keyhole, Keen Kutter, Dated 1877 .... 60.00
Saw, Meat, Butcher's, Wooden Handle 3.50
Saw, Metal Cutting, Keen Kutter, No. 106, Cherry Handle, 18 In. Blade 25.00
Saw, Pit, Wood Box At End, Keystone, 5 Ft. 175.00
Saw, Plumber's, Geo. H. Bishop & Co., Adjustable Cherry Handle, 23 In. 50.00
Saw, Stair–Builder's, E. C. Atkins 30.00
Scoop, Cranberry, Maple, 1880 .... 195.00
Scraper, Cabinet, Stanley, No. 80M, Blue Finish 19.00
Scraper, Plane, Stanley, No. 80 .... 18.00
Scraper, Plane, Stanley, No. 85 .... 535.00
Screwdriver, Beech Octagon Handle, Brass Ferrule, 24 In. 36.00
Screwdriver, Stanley, SW Mark 50.00
Screwdriver–Flashlight, Stanley, No. 1021, Brass, 5 1/4 In. 165.00
Scribe, Carpenter's, Iron, Wooden Handle 2.50
Scythe, Hand, Beech Handle, Nickel Plated, 10 1/2 x 7 1/2 In. 55.00
Sharpener, Lawn Mower Blade, Dunlap, Sears Roebuck, Box 2.25
Sharpener, Scissors, Keen Kutter 650.00
Shopsmith, All Accessories, 1950 .... 600.00
Shovel, Grain, Hand Hewn & Carved, D Handle, 1910, 36 In. 85.00
Shuttle, Tatting, Green Marbelized Bakelite 24.00
Silversmith's, Assorted, 16 Piece 260.00
Skate Rollers, Winchester, Box 50.00
Slick, Carpenter's, D. R. Barton, Rochester, 2 x 25 1/2 In. 30.00
Slick, Carpenter's, Socket Style, L. & I. J. White, 30 3/4 In. 65.00
Slide Rule, Keuffel & Esser, Case 25.00
Smoothing Board, Horse Handle, Red, Green & Black, 25 In. 300.00
Smoothing Board, Horse–Shaped Handle, Birch, c.1800, 30 1/2 In. 695.00
Spokeshave, Coach Maker's, Brass, 9 1/2 In. 35.00

Spokeshave, Rabbet, Stanley No. 68, Type Y Mark On Iron, Varnished 30.00
Spokeshave, Stanley, No. 55, Hollow Face, V Mark On Iron 35.00
Spokeshave, Stanley, No. 60, 2 Cutters, New Style, 5 Mark On Irons 35.00
Square, Carpenter's, Southington Hardware Co., Wooden Handle 4.00
Square, Folding, Higgison, Birmingham Warranted, Boxwood, 27 x 18 In. 28.00
Square, Goodell & Pratt, 18 In. 30.00
Square, Rochester Athenaeum & Mechanics Inst., Boxwood, Brass Brace 28.00
Stand, Coffin, Sawhorse Type, Folding, Black Paint, 21 3/4 In., Pair 95.00
Stencil, Brass, 3 Different, 12 In., 3 Piece 35.00
Stretcher, Glove, Bone, Sterling Fleur–De–Lis Handle 85.00
Stretcher, Hat, Turner Danbury 25.00
Sweat Scraper, Groom Horse's Withers, Hickory, 15 In. 35.00
Swift, Squirrel Cage, Adjustable Top Reel, Hard & Soft Woods, 47 In. 105.00
Swift, Table Clamp, Wooden, Natural Patina 110.00
Swift, Umbrella, Accordion Folding Slats, Table Clamp, 24 In. 125.00
Swift, Wooden, Table Clamp, Wooden Staves, 23 In. 75.00
Tape Measure, Stanley, No. 8, Mylar, 8 Ft. 9.00
Ticket Punch, McGill Co. 4.00
Trammel, Roof Thatcher's, Wood 55.00
Vacuum Cleaner, Pneumatic Cleaner, Hand Pump, Regina, 1907 .... 225.00
Vise, Gunsmith's, Stephens, Quick Adjustable, 2 In. 15.00
Vise, Miter, Marsh 50.00
Vise, Pole 90.00
Voltmeter, Westinghouse, Instructions, Box 22.00
Wagon Jack, Pine, Oak, 26 1/2 x 15–In. Base 36.00
Wallpaper Roller, 18th Century, 4 1/2 In. x 22 In. 15.00
Water Carrier Yoke, Woman's, 2 Metal Hooks For Pails 40.00
Weaner, Calf, Daisy, Cast Iron, 1932 .... 35.00
Wheel Boys, To Turn Large Wool Wheels, Mushroom Ends, 1800s, 6 In. 15.00
Wheel Gauge, Cooper's, Cast Iron, Wileys Russel Mfg. Co., 12 3/4 In. 35.00
Wheelbarrow, Oak, Red Paint, Metal Spoke Wheels 155.00
Wheelbarrow, Red Paint, Hex Signed, Pennsylvania 350.00
Wheelbarrow, White Painted Over Green, Metal Spoke Wheels 75.00
Whetstone, Ford Tractor, Celluloid 45.00
Winder, Yarn Table, 19th Century 65.00
Workbench, Cabinetmaker's, Wooden Vises Each End, Tray, Stop Holes 357.50
Workbench, Caver's, Oak & Maple, 17 Drawers, Ring Pulls, 39 x 96 In. 550.00
Workbench, Maple, Student Size 300.00
Wrench, Billmount Master, Wooden Box 85.00
Wrench, Buggy, Smith 20.00
Wrench, Cam & Lever, Lake Superior Wrench Co., Sault Ste. Marie, 9 In. 25.00
Wrench, Crescent, Diamond Calk Horseshoe Co., Double Ended, 8 In. 25.00
Wrench, Indian Motorcycle 25.00
Wrench, Motorcycle, Hendee Indian 125.00
Wrench, Planet Jr., No. 3 .... 16.00
Wrench, Polly, Gellman Mfg. Co., No. 91, Rock Island, Ill., 9 In. 10.00
Yarn Winder, Clockwork, Handcrafted, Wooden 145.00
Yarn Winder, Hand Held, 1900s 45.00

TOOTHPICK HOLDERS are sometimes called *toothpicks* by collectors. The variously shaped containers used to hold small wooden toothpicks are made of glass, china, or metal. Most of the toothpick holders are Victorian. Additional items may be found in other categories, such as Bisque, Silver Plate, Slag, etc.

Alexis 25.00
Allover Hobnail, Blue Opalescent 65.00
Amberina, Optic Diamond, Straight Sided Cylinder 145.00
Anvil, Daisy & Button, Amber 15.00
Banded Flute, Handle 55.00
Blazing Cornucopia, Lavender Dots, Paisley 45.00
Blue Opalescent, Fenton 10.00
Blue Opalescent, Tokyo 250.00
Boat, Pedestal, Electric Blue 75.00

Brazilian, Green	75.00
Britannia, With Bird	35.00
Button Star	30.00
Carnival Glass, Souvenir Amboy, Minnesota	37.50
China, Czechoslovakia, Square	50.00
China, Petticoat Shape, Allover Gold & White Floral, 2 Handles	20.00
Clear Glass, Gold, Souvenir Minnesota	50.00
Cluthra, Monart	100.00
Colonial Prism	25.00
Continental, Handle	80.00
Croesus, Amethyst, Gold	30.00
Czarina, U.S. Glass	25.00
Diamond & Button, Figural, Light Blue	35.00
Diamonds, Urn, Signed Waterford	35.00
Dog, Boston Baked Beans	65.00
Elephant, Baby Mine Bottom, Frosted, Gold	28.00
Elephant, C. D. Kenny Co.	30.00
Empress, Green, Gold	210.00
Eureka National, Stain	45.00
Fandanga	60.00
Frosted Coin	65.00
Golfer, Silver Plate	175.00
Heart Band, Clear, Ruby Stain, Niagara Falls, N.Y.	28.00
Horseshoe & Clover, Milk Glass	60.00
Iris & Meander, Opalescent Electric Blue	115.00
Kitten, Silver Plate	50.00
Lamar, Violets & Leaves	25.00
Lay Down, Diamonds & Rib	10.00
Man With Hat, Historical	225.00
Manhattan, Crystal	25.00
Milk Glass, Bees On Basket, No Handle	45.00
Nestor, Green	150.00
Nude Girl In Shell, Glen Falls, New York, 3 1/2 In.	48.00
Nursery Rhyme, Little Red Riding Hood	100.00
Oregon	125.00
Paddlewheel & Star, Crystal, Pedestal	35.00
Paneled Cane, Handle	30.00
Paneled Palm, Rose Flash	80.00
Peerless, Handle	28.00
Pillows, Worn Gold, Handle	90.00
Porcupine, Silver Plate, Meriden	125.00
Portland, Worn Gold	20.00
Pottery, Signed Ute Mountain	10.00
Priscilla, Handle	20.00
Puritan, Handle	70.00
Rib & Bead, Burst Bubble Type	45.00
Rib & Bead, Clear, Gold	30.00
Ribbed Thumbprint, Braddock, Pa.	20.00
Royal Ivy, Frosted Cranberry To Clear	40.00
Saddle, Amber	17.00
Sam'l Meyers, Franklin, Pa., Crystal	25.00
Sunbeam, Green, Gold Top	50.00
Sunk Honeycomb, Souvenir Mary C. Coffin, 1898	32.00
Swan, Stoneware, Blue & White	20.00
Swan, Stoneware, White	20.00
Tastee Freeze Grill, Celluloid, Case, Pocket	1.25
Thumbnail, Clear, Gold	25.00
Trophy, Souvenir, Weeks Mills, Me., Green, Gold	10.00
Waldorf Astoria, Silver Overlay	50.00
Wild Rose, Bow Knots	100.00
Windemere's Fan, Yellow, Aqua Fan	38.00
Winged Scroll, Green	25.00
Zipper Slash, Souvenir, T. E. Clark, Yellow Stain, 1903	40.00

Tortoiseshell Glass, Cruet, Clear Handle &

Stopper, 6 In.

To restore the sheen to a tortoiseshell box, rub it with a cloth dipped in lemon juice and salt. Rinse with cold water, dry. Sometimes rubbing yogurt on the shell will help.

TORQUAY is the name given to ceramics by several potteries working near Torquay, England, from 1870 until 1962. Until about 1900, the potteries used local red clay to make classical–style art pottery vases and figurines. Then they turned to making souvenir wares. Items were dipped in colored slip and decorated with painted slip and sgraffito designs. They often had mottoes or proverbs, and scenes of cottages, ships, birds, or flowers. The *Scandy* design was a symmetrical arrangement of brush strokes and spots done in colored slips. Potteries included Watcombe Pottery (1870–1962); Torquay Terra–Cotta Company (1875–1905); Aller Vale (1881–1924); Torquay Pottery (1908–1940); and Longpark (1883–1957).

TORQUAY

Bowl, Scandy Interior, Motto, Some Hae Meat, 7 3/4 In.	145.00
Candlestick, Motto Ware, Ship Design, Longpark, 4 1/2 In.	65.00
Carafe, Water, Ruby	195.00
Condiment Set, Pattern, Deep Rose Stripes, 4 Piece	265.00
Cream Pot, Motto Ware, Black Cockerel Pedestal, Wavy Rim	110.00
Creamer, Motto Ware	35.00
Cup, Child's, Motto Ware	35.00
Dish, 3 Sections, Motto Ware, Windmill	60.00
Jug, Sailboat, 5 1/4 In.	48.00
Mustard, Cover, Long Park	47.00
Pin Tray, Fresh From The Dairy, Motto Ware	50.00
Pitcher, Cottage, 2 3/16 In.	32.00
Pitcher, Cover, Cottage, 5 3/4 In.	85.00
Pitcher, Falmouth, 9 1/2 In.	50.00
Pitcher, Motto Ware, Scandy 4–Line, Allervale, 5 In.	65.00
Plate, Cottage, Motto Ware, 10 In.	55.00
Plate, Motto Ware, Cottage Design, Watcombe, 7 1/4 In.	50.00
Porringer, Cottage, Motto Ware	55.00
Salt & Pepper, Motto Ware	28.00
Salt, Cottage, Motto Ware, Pedestal	75.00
Teapot, Motto Ware, Drink It While It's Hot, Blue & Brown, 5 In.	25.00
Tray, Pen, Motto Ware, Black Cockerel	85.00
Vase, Devonshire Lavender, 5 1/2 In.	47.00
Vase, Scenic, Parrot, Blue High Glaze, 8 In.	165.00

TORTOISESHELL GLASS was made during the 1800s and after by the Sandwich Glass Works of Massachusetts and some firms in Germany. Tortoiseshell glass is, of course, named for its resemblance to real shell from a tortoise. It has been reproduced.

Cruet, Clear Handle & Stopper, 6 In.	*Illus*	85.00
Pitcher & Bowl, Free–Form Brown Design, 9 1/2 In.		120.00
Vase, 3 1/2 In.		45.00
Vase, 8 In.		95.00
Vase, Leg At Side, 8 In.		85.00

TORTOISESHELL is the shell of the tortoise. It has been used as inlay and to make small decorative objects since the seventeenth century. Some species of tortoise are now on the endangered species list, and objects made from these shells cannot be sold legally.

Comb, Engraved Gold Frame, Natural Gray Pearls	450.00
Comb, Mantilla, Cutout, Pair	17.50
Comb, Spanish Style, Rose Leaves, Scrollwork	85.00
Holder, Calling Card	35.00 To 37.50

TOY collectors have special clubs, magazines, and shows. Toys are designed to entice children, and today they have attracted new interest among adults who are still children at heart. All types of toys are collected. Tin toys, iron toys, battery operated toys, and many others are collected by specialists. Dolls, Games, Teddy Bears, and Bicycles are listed in their own categories. Other toys may be found under company or celebrity names.

Accordion, Emenee, 1955	27.00
Acrobat Wonder, Windup, Celluloid, Japan, Box, 1930s	250.00
Acrobat, Single, Dark Blue Clothes, Ives	2310.00
Acrobat, Single, Light Blue Clothes, Ives	2090.00
Acrobat, Swinging Trick, Windup, Celluloid, Japan, 1930s	115.00
Acrobat, Toto, Marx, Box	300.00
Acrobat, Windup, Celluloid, LN, 1930s	145.00
Acrobat, Windup, Tin, Wyandotte	140.00
Activity Box, Zorro	35.00
Adding Machine, Wolverine	15.00
Airplane Kit, Lockheed Vega, Balsa Wood, 1932, 30–In. Span	48.00
Airplane Pack, 2 Cars, Masudaya, Box, 16–In. Wingspan	915.00
Airplane Set, Spirit Of St. Louis, c.1928	600.00
Airplane, 1 Engine, Scheible	990.00
Airplane, 3 Engines, Scheible	253.00
Airplane, American Airlines Passenger Jet, Tin, Plastic, 13–In. Wingspan	42.00
Airplane, Battery Operated, Rubber Wheels, 20–In. Wingspan	245.00
Airplane, Big Bang Bombing, Cast Iron, Box	577.50
Airplane, Big Parade, Windup, Tin, Marx, Box, 1927	1400.00
Airplane, Black Knight, Friction, Japan	150.00
Airplane, Boeing 707, Battery Operated, Linemar	185.00
Airplane, Boeing 727, Battery Operated, 4 Actions, Tin	90.00
Airplane, Bomber, Tipco	1540.00
Airplane, Circus, Windup, Runs Forward, Flips Over, Japan, 4 In.	45.00
Airplane, City Of Los Angeles, Kenton, Cast Iron	250.00
Airplane, Dive Bomber, Dinky Toy	65.00
Airplane, Douglas F45–1, Friction, Tin Lithograph, Japan, 8–In. Wingspan	90.00
Airplane, Fighter Pilot, Bump 'n Go, Friction, Tin, 5 1/2 In.	135.00
Airplane, Fighter, Signed Joey, England, 14 In.	475.00
Airplane, Fighter, Steel, Marx, 12 In.	65.00
Airplane, Flying Fox, Jet–Propelled, Battery Operated, Remco, 18 In.	265.00
Airplane, Gas Powered, A. C. Gilbert, 21 5/8–In. Wingspan	85.00
Airplane, Jet Bomber, Motor Runs, Battery Operated, Marx, 1960s	85.00
Airplane, Kingsbury, Painted Steel, Windup, 15 In.	605.00
Airplane, Lockheed FA982 Starfire, Yonazawa, Japan, 18–In. Wingspan	110.00
Airplane, Monoplane, Big Boy, No. 337, Kenry Katz & Co.	300.00
Airplane, Monoplane, Girard	150.00
Airplane, Monoplane, Mettoy, Blue & White, 18 1/2–In. Wingspan	180.00
Airplane, Pan Am, 4 Prop, Schuco	350.00
Airplane, Pan Am, Jet, Tin Lithograph, Friction, Japan, 7 1/2 In.	27.50

◆ ◆

Scratches can be rubbed off the mirror glass by using a piece of felt and polishing rouge from a paint store.

◆ ◆

Airplane, Pan Am, Metal, 20–In. Wingspan 185.00
Airplane, Patrol, Japanese, Friction, Tin, 1950s, 14 In. 145.00
Airplane, Right Place, Tin Body, Metal Wheels, Decals, 29 In. 900.00
Airplane, Royal Blue Glass, Stainless Steel, Art Deco, 8 In. 568.00
Airplane, Sky Ranger, Small Airplane Circles Tower, Tin, Windup, 25 In. 325.00
Airplane, Snoopy In Cockpit, Die Cast Metal, Box 59.95
Airplane, Sonic Jet, Friction, Marx 60.00
Airplane, Spirit Of America, Tin, Windup, Chein, 1930s, 6 x 6 1/2 In. 225.00
Airplane, Spirit Of St. Louis, Airplane–Go–Round, Electric, Reeves 1250.00
Airplane, Spirit Of St. Louis, Metalcraft 250.00
Airplane, Spirit Of St. Louis, Metalcraft, Box 400.00
Airplane, Stratocruiser, Propels In Circles, Windup, Japan, 21 In. 1700.00
Airplane, Stratocruiser, Wyandotte 50.00
Airplane, Tower, Carousel, Windup, 3 Airplanes, Germany, 16 In. 55.00
Airplane, Tri–Motor, Orange & Yellow, Metalcraft 300.00
Airplane, U.S. Army, Sparkling, Marx 325.00
Airplane, U.S. Mail, Gray, Green & Yellow Paint, Wooden 225.00
Airplane, U.S. Mail, Windup, Marx 145.00
Airport, Tin Lithograph, Windup, 2 Planes, W. Germany, Box 375.00
Airship, EPL–1, Blimp, Gold, Lehmann, 1907, 7 1/2 In. .... 650.00 To 850.00
Alabama Coon Jigger, Lehmann, Germany, 1914, 8 In. 412.00
Alabama Coon Jigger, Windup, Tin Litho, Partial Box, Lehmann 417.00
Alabama Coon Jigger, Windup, Tin, Strauss, 10 In. 425.00
Alien Target Chase Set 95.00
Alligator, Schoenhut 425.00
Alphabet Board, Foxy 68.00
Alpine Dancers, Man & Woman, Wooden, Papier–Mache, 3 1/2 In., Pair 30.00
Ambulance Limousine, Bing, c.1912 .... 7040.00
Ambulance, Bulldog, Rear Doors Open, Rubber Tires, Marusan, 12 In. 95.00
Ambulance, Medical Corp, Marx 125.00
Ambulance, Metalcraft, Pressed Steel, 1930s 175.00
Ambulance, Siren, Friction, Japan, 6 In. 60.00
Ambulance, Wyandotte .... 100.00 To 110.00
Amos 'n' Andy Fresh Air Taxi 770.00
Armoire, Doll's, Bamboo Trim, Door Mirror, France, 15 3/4 In. 225.00
Arnold Monkey On Tricycle, Windup 160.00
Atomic Cape Canaveral Missile Base, 1960s, Marx, 24 x 14 In. 139.00
Automatic Rope Skipper 4070.00
B. O. Plenty & Sparkle, Windup, Walks Forward, Hat Tips, Marx, 8 In. 295.00
Babe, Toddling, Windup, Occupied Japan, Box 100.00
Baby, Crawling, Ives, Red Dress, Cast Iron 975.00
Baby, Crawling, Windup, Celluloid & Tin, Japan 30.00
Bagpipes, Bullwinkle's Play–A–Tune, Larami, 6 x 9 In. 30.00
Balancing Canary, For Edge Of Drinking Glass, Celluloid, 1914, 3 In. 10.00
Balky Mule, Windup, Marx, 1950s .... 100.00 To 135.00
Banjo, Hand Crank, Tin 15.00
Barn, With Animals, Tin, Germany 85.00

Toy, Wilson Walkie, Soldier, 1930, 4 In.

Toy, Wilson Walkie, Mammy, Flowered Dress, 1930, 4 In.

Toy, Wilson Walkie, Mammy, 1930, 4 In.

Toy, Boy, On Stilts, Windup,

Tin, 8 3/4 In.

Toy, Wilson Walkie, Nurse, 1930, 4 In.

Bartender, Battery Operated, Box .... 32.00 To 38.00
Bartender, Windup, Rosco, Box, 7 In. 90.00
Baseball Molding & Coloring Set, Dated 1948, Box 95.00
Battleship, Clockwork, Marklin 1400.00
Battleship, New York, Pull Toy, Black Trim, Cast Iron, 20 In. 1700.00
Battleship, Riding, Painted, Wooden, S. A. Smith, Late 19th Century 2800.00
Bead Set, Loom, Beads, Thread, Instructions, Walco Indian Beadcraft, 1935 .... 26.00
Bears are also listed in the Teddy Bear category
Bear, Bruno, Walking, Battery Operated, Alps, Japan 50.00
Bear, Drinking, Battery Operated, Alps, Box, 1960 .... 100.00
Bear, Hustling Teddy, Tin, Box 395.00
Bear, Loop The Hoop, Wire, Tin & Cloth, Keywind, Japan, Box, 8 In. 143.00
Bear, Loving, Battery Operated, Maxwell House Coffee, Box 175.00
Bear, Mama Feeding Baby, Battery Operated 100.00
Bear, On Wheels, Mouth Opens In Snarl, Leather Muzzle, c.1896 .... 950.00
Bear, On Wheels, Steiff, 1914 .... 895.00
Bear, On Wooden Wheels, Steiff, 1940s, 13 In. 345.00
Bear, Polar, Blue Leather Collar, Bell, Blue Eyes, Steiff 195.00
Bear, Polar, Peach Pads, On All Fours, Steiff, 1950s, 7 In. 90.00
Bear, Polar, Pull, Hits Bell, Seal Balances Ball, Tin, 10 In. 193.00
Bear, Reading Baby Book, Flipping Pages, Windup 150.00
Bear, Sawing Log, Windup, Japan, 5 In. 45.00
Bear, Sitting On Log, With Cup, Battery Operated, Black & White Plush 11.00
Bear, Sleeping, Battery Operated, Linemar 150.00
Bed, Doll's, Brass, 21 x 28 x 18 In. 192.00
Bed, Doll's, Brass, Tick Mattress 80.00
Bed, Doll's, Canopy, Metal, Lace Covers, Victorian 125.00
Bed, Doll's, Canopy, Walnut Color, Rope, Antique Fabric Bedding, 19 In. 400.00
Bed, Doll's, Elegant 90.00
Bed, Doll's, Four-Poster, Sheraton Style, Mahogany, 16 1/2 x 12 x 17 In. 165.00
Bed, Doll's, Four-Poster, Walnut, Original Mattress & Quilt, 16 1/2 In. 200.00
Bed, Doll's, Mahogany, Mattress Frame, Arched Headboard, 1800s, 15 In. 175.00
Bed, Doll's, Metal, Half Moon Shaped Headboard 55.00
Bed, Doll's, Rope, Cannonball, Turned Post, 10 1/2 x 16 x 25 In. 495.00
Bed, Doll's, Rope, Mattress, Pillow & Liner, Hardwood, 10 x 16 In. 55.00
Bed, Doll's, Turned Finials, Arched Headboard, Mattress, Mahogany, 1800s 125.00
Beetle, Clockwork, Hand Painted, Multi-Action, Tin, Germany 395.00
Beetle, Windup, Tin, Lehmann, 1895 .... 450.00
Bell, Monkey On Tricycle, Cast Iron, J. & E. Stevens 3740.00
Bell, Pull, Disc Revolves Showing Clown Face, Bell Rings, Tin, 9 1/2 In. 95.00
Bell, Wild Mule Jack, Cast Iron, 1895 .... 1095.00
Bellhop, Windup, Celluloid, Occupied Japan, 4 1/2 In. 90.00
Belt & Buckle, Buffalo Bill Jr., Original Mailer 275.00
Belt Buckle, Agent Zero, Mattel, 1959 .... 50.00
Belt, Zorro, Z Buckle, On Card 75.00
Bench, Doll's, Rail Seat & Back, 15 1/2 x 19 In. 110.00
Bicycles are listed in their own section
Binoculars, Secret Sam Exploding Topper, 1965 .... 26.00
Binoculars, Secret Sam Exploding, Topper, 1965 .... 24.00
Binoculars, Space Patrol 225.00
Binoculars, Tom Corbett 90.00
Birds With Worm, Windup, Tin, Gebruder Einfalt, 1928, 9 In. 385.00
Bison, Tags, Steiff, 10 In. 250.00
Blocks, Alphabet & Christmas, McLoughlin 275.00
Blocks, Hills Spelling Blocks, Wooden, Sliding Lid, 6 x 6 In., 16 Piece 150.00
Blocks, Mother Goose, McLoughlin, Box, 1894, 20 Piece, 13 1/2 In. 415.00
Blocks, Nesting, 1880s, 9 Piece 650.00
Blocks, Nesting, Wooden, Paper Lithograph Cover, 11 Piece 1000.00
Blocks, Picture Blocks, McLoughlin 578.00
Blocks, Puzzle, Zoo Animals 125.00
Blocks, Railroad ABC, McLoughlin, Box, c.1903, 9 Piece ....*Illus* 743.00
Blocks, Richter's Anchor, Ceramic, 3 Colors, Original Box, 9 1/2 In. 77.00
Blocks, Spelling, Wooden, Painted, Box, Sliding Lid, Hill's, 6 In. 175.00

Toy, Blocks, Railroad ABC, McLoughlin, Box, c.1903, 9 Piece

Toy, Dollhouse, 2 Rooms, Porch, Bliss

Blocks, Wooden, Grooved To Interlock, 1 1/2 In., 11 Piece	25.00
Blocks, Wooden, Paper Lithograph Cover, 7/8 x 2 3/8 x 3 1/2 In., 12 Pc.	300.00
Blushing Willie, Battery Operated, Japan, 1960	80.00
Boar, Steiff, Straw Stuffed, Mohair, Glass Eyes, Tusks, 1964, 8 x 11 In.	200.00
Boat, Cargo Liner, Cragstan	125.00
Boat, Coast Guard, Runs Forward, Flag Waves, Battery Operated, Japan	195.00
Boat, Cruiser, Diana, Clockwork, Tin, Sutcliff, Box	150.00
Boat, Delfino, Schuco, 12 1/2 In.	395.00
Boat, Dragon, Dragon's Eyes Light, Battery Operated, Japan, 18 1/2 In.	695.00
Boat, Evinrude, Starflite 450, Tin & Die Cast, 1958, 6 In.	260.00
Boat, Evinrude, Starflite V-4, Die Cast, Japan, 1959, 5 1/2 In.	275.00
Boat, Flash Blast Attack, String Motion, Tootsietoy	90.00
Boat, Gun, Kasuga, Clockwork, Painted Steel, Bing	1760.00
Boat, Navy Destroyer, Keywind, Gebruder Bing, Box	2860.00
Boat, Navy Dreadnaught, Keywind, Gebruder Bing, Box	1320.00
Boat, Ocean Liner, Arnold, 13 In.	145.00
Boat, Paddle, Side Wheel, Tin, Red & Green Paint, Alcohol Driven, Box	3520.00
Boat, Queen Mary, Pull Toy, Wooden, Souvenir	350.00
Boat, River Queen Paddle Wheeler, Plastic, Marx, 9 In.	25.00
Boat, Sailboat, Green, White, Wood, Metal, A. Rich Toy, 24 In.	10.00
Boat, Scott Atwater Bail-A-Matic, Tin & Die Cast, K & O, 6 In.	200.00
Boat, Side Wheeler, Cast Iron, Worn Polychrome, 5 5/8 In.	200.00
Boat, Speed, Harbor Patrol, Tin Lithograph, Friction, Box	135.00
Boat, Speed, Steam Driven, Japan, 1950s, 5 In.	25.00
Boat, Speed, With Skier, Friction, 1950, Japan	100.00
Boat, Steam, Horizontal Boiler, Weeden, 16 In.	425.00
Boat, Torpedo, Sparkling, Ideal, Box	75.00
Boat, U.S. Liner, Tin, Marx, Box, 14 In.	250.00
Boat, Water Pumping, Siren, Crank Operated, Wheels For Floor Play, 1955	85.00
Boat, Windup, Lindstrom, 7 In.	65.00
Boat, Windup, Tin, Chein, 8 In.	30.00
Boat, With Trailer, Ford, Haji, Red Tin Car, Tin Lithograph Boat, 15 In.	345.00
Boat, Yacht, Phillip's 66 Power, Plastic, Box	72.50
Bowler, Andy Mill, 8 Metal Balls, 19 1/2 In.	132.00
Boxers, Black, Wooden, Mechanical, Box	125.00
Boy Skier, Jumper, Sun Valley, Paper Lithograph, Wolverine, 27 In.	110.00
Boy Skier, Windup, Tin, Chein	175.00
Boy, Black, Eating Watermelon, Dog, Windup, Tin	750.00
Boy, Bubble Blowing, Windup, Moves Head & Arm, Japan, 7 3/4 In.	120.00
Boy, On Bicycle, Windup, Korea	7.00
Boy, On Sled, Windup, Tin, 6 3/4 In.	105.00

Boy, On Stilts, Windup, Tin, 8 3/4 In. ....*Illus* 880.00
Boy, On Tricycle, Tin Lithograph, Windup, Bell, 9 In. 187.00
Bridge, Hellgate, No. 300, Lionel 880.00
Broom, Bewitched, Detailed Head Of Samantha, Remco, 1965 .... 79.00
Bubble Pipe, Yogi Bear, 1963 .... 20.00
Buddy Bullfrog, Fisher–Price, Box, 1959 .... 125.00
Buffalo, Schoenhut 375.00
Bugle, Rin Tin Tin, Box 125.00
Build A Road Set, Matchbox, 1967 .... 85.00
Building, Military, Tin, Marx 45.00
Bulldozer, Giant, Tonga, Box 105.00
Bullwinkle, Stick On, Gold Metal, Rubber Suction Cup, Moving Eyes, 1969 .... 75.00
Bunkhouse, Marx, Tin 39.00
Bus, Blue, Cast Iron, Arcade, 8 In. 425.00
Bus, Continental Trailways, Friction, Japan, 1950s 65.00
Bus, Double–Decker, Windup, Tin, Great Britain, Box, 1930s 145.00
Bus, Fairyland, 8 Passengers Move As Bus Moves, Battery Operated 175.00
Bus, Greyhound, Americruiser, Box 75.00
Bus, Greyhound, Scenicruiser, Japan, 6 1/4 In. 75.00
Bus, Greyhound, Stop & Go Action, Tin Lithograph, Battery Operated 200.00
Bus, Greyhound, Tootsietoy, 1930s 20.00
Bus, Greyhound, Utaka, Tin 35.00
Bus, Horse Drawn, Plastic Case, London, 1950 .... 120.00
Bus, Jackie Gleason, Tin 395.00
Bus, Kenton, 5 1/2 In. 195.00
Bus, Liberty Bus Co., No. 62, Marx 75.00
Bus, Radio Controlled, Radicon, 1950s 385.00
Bus, Robot, Tin Lithograph, Windup, Woodhaven, 1950s, 14 In. 250.00
Bus, Robot, Windup, Marx, 1950s 175.00
Bus, School, Yellow, Gabriel Decals, Tin, 1975 .... 10.00
Bus, Ship & Express Mystery, Wolverine, Box 195.00
Bus, Sightseeing, Tin, Battery Operated, Japan, 1960s, 14 In. 125.00
Busy Box, Snoopy, 1966 .... 45.00
Busy Bridge, On Trestles, Tin, Marx, 1930s 195.00
Busy Housekeeper, Bear, Lighted Vacuum Cleaner, Battery Operated, Alps 225.00
Cabinet, Doll's, Painted 17.50
Camel, 1 Hump, Schoenhut 400.00
Camel, 2 Humps, Schoenhut 375.00
Camel, Bactrian, Glass Eyes, 2 Humps, Schoenhut, Small 55.00
Camel, Fallows, Pull Toy, Tin, Iron Wheels, 7 1/4 In. 198.00
Camel, On Wheels, Flannel & Wool, Glass Eyes, Sheet Metal Wheels, 8 In. 302.00
Camel, Spinning Tail & Moving Head, Key Wind, Germany 110.00
Camel, Walking, Windup, Tin, 1900 .... 150.00
Camera, Picture Story, Fisher–Price ....5.00 To 12.00
Cane, Bat Masterson, Black, Wooden, Silver Plastic Nob, Embossed Name 42.00
Cane, Secret Sam Shooting, Plastic, Lion's Head Top, Topper, 1965 .... 89.00
Cannon Ring, Gabby Hayes, With Plunger 125.00
Cannon, 2 Wheels, Cast Iron, 4 In. 35.00
Cannon, Big Bang, 17 In. 65.00
Cannon, Firecracker, Kilgore 20.00
Cannon, Tootsietoy 40.00
Cap Gun, Army, Hubley 45.00
Cap Gun, Atomic Disintegrator, Repeater, Box, Hubley, 1940s 375.00
Cap Gun, Ben Cartwright, 12 Shot, Metal, Box 35.00
Cap Gun, Big Bill, 5 1/2 In. 50.00
Cap Gun, Big Horn, Revolving Cylinder, Kilgore, 1950s, 7 In. 55.00
Cap Gun, Black Sambo, 1890 .... 385.00
Cap Gun, Buck–A–Roo Kilgore, Cast Iron, Box 185.00
Cap Gun, Buffalo Bill, Cast Iron, 1930s ....65.00 To 95.00
Cap Gun, Captain 20.00
Cap Gun, Colt 38, Hubley, Box 500.00
Cap Gun, Colt 45, Hubley ....125.00 To 189.00
Cap Gun, Colt Detective Special, Hubley 15.00

Cap Gun, Cowboy, Matched Pair, 3 1/2 In. 65.00
Cap Gun, Cowboy, Revolving Cylinder, Hubley .... 45.00 To 75.00
Cap Gun, Cowpoke, Card, Hubley 40.00
Cap Gun, Deputy, Kilgore, Silver Finish, Revolving Cylinder, 1950s 75.00
Cap Gun, Derringer, Hawkeye, Repeater, Store Caps In Handle, 1940s 35.00
Cap Gun, Dragnet, On Car, 1955 .... 32.50
Cap Gun, Fanner 50, Smoking, Chrome, Cylinder, Mattel .... 195.00 To 250.00
Cap Gun, Frontier Smoker, Zamak, 9 1/2 In. 125.00
Cap Gun, Gene Autry, Cast Iron .... 110.00 .
Cap Gun, Invincible, Kilgore, Cast Iron, 1930s 95.00
Cap Gun, Kit Carson, Kilgore ....95.00 To 100.00
Cap Gun, Lightning Express 425.00
Cap Gun, Lion Head, Cast Iron, 1890 .... 235.00
Cap Gun, Long Barrel, Hubley 85.00
Cap Gun, Marshall, Stag Grip 10.00
Cap Gun, Maverick, Revolving Cylinder, Bronze Finish, 1959, 10 1/2 In. 125.00
Cap Gun, McCloud 35.00
Cap Gun, Mustang 500 .... 155.00
Cap Gun, Nichols Stallion, Chrome Die Cast, Bullets 45.00
Cap Gun, Nigger Head, Pat. 1887, Ives, Working, 5 In. 880.00
Cap Gun, Pal, Hubley 20.00
Cap Gun, Pet, 6 In. 15.00
Cap Gun, Pirate, Double Barrel 67.50
Cap Gun, Police 38, Cast Iron, Hubley, 1930s 95.00
Cap Gun, Punch & Judy 6050.00
Cap Gun, Range Rider 55.00
Cap Gun, Ranger 75.00
Cap Gun, Red Ranger, Plastic Handle, 9 In. 27.00
Cap Gun, Remington 36, Hubley 75.00
Cap Gun, Restless, Secret Compartment In Handle 95.00
Cap Gun, Ric–O–Shay Jr., Card, Hubley 100.00
Cap Gun, Ric–O–Shay, 45 Caps, Holster & Wooden Bullets, Hubley 225.00
Cap Gun, Rodeo, Hubley .... 20.00 To 40.00
Cap Gun, Safety Trooper, Cast Iron 65.00
Cap Gun, Scout, Bronze Color 100.00
Cap Gun, Secret Ring, 24 Rings 225.00
Cap Gun, Silent Sam, Die Cast, Cap Strip, Miniature 3.00
Cap Gun, Spitfire, Box 30.00
Cap Gun, Texan Jr., Cast Iron, Bakelite Steer Head Trim, Hubley 70.00
Cap Gun, Texan Jr., Hubley, Box .... 100.00 To 250.00
Cap Gun, Texan, Rearing Horse, Hard Shell Box, 1941 .... 350.00
Cap Gun, Trooper, Chrome Finish, Hubley .... 20.00 To 35.00
Cap Gun, Wagon Train 65.00
Cap Gun, Wyatt Earp, Holster 65.00
Car, Ambulance, Kenton, Cast Iron, 1910 .... 1650.00
Car, Ambulance, Lincoln, 1959 Model, Bandai, Box 325.00
Car, Aston–Martin, Green, Dinky Toy 80.00
Car, Aston–Martin, James Bond 007, Battery Operated, 1960s ..... 350.00 To 705.00
Car, Austin, Atlantic Blue, Dinky Toy ....70.00 To 125.00
Car, Austin, Keywind, Tin Lithograph, Lehmann, 4 In. 220.00
Car, Back To The Future, Battery Operated 100.00
Car, Batmobile, Radio Controlled, Matsushiro, 10 In. 145.00
Car, Battery Operated, Aoshin 75.00
Car, Bentley, 1929, Yesteryear No. 5, Green, Box 40.00
Car, Beverly Hillbillies, Box 325.00
Car, BMW, Isetta, Battery Operated 175.00
Car, Buick, Convertible, 1953 Model, Red, Metal, 11 In. 30.00
Car, Buick, Red, Remote Controlled, Cragstan, 8 1/2 In. 185.00
Car, Bump, Pop–Up Clown, Friction, Tin, Japan, Box 275.00
Car, Bumper, Windup, Carnival, 9 1/2 In. 350.00
Car, Cadillac, 1959 Model, Tin Lithographed, Battery Operated, Japan 295.00
Car, Cadillac, 1960 Model, Friction, Japan, 11 In. 450.00
Car, Cadillac, 1967 Model, Friction, Ichiko, 28 In. 975.00

Car, Cadillac, Black, Chrome, Marusan, 1951, 13 In. 1400.00
Car, Cadillac, El Dorado, Box, Dinky Toys 150.00
Car, Cadillac, Gray, Khaki Green, Chrome, Marusan, 1951, 13 In. 900.00
Car, Cadillac, King Size Convertible, Battery Operated, Iways, Box 180.00
Car, Cadillac, Musical, Rolls Forward, Battery Operated, Japan, 9 In. 475.00
Car, Cadillac, Red, Friction, Japan, 9 In. 50.00
Car, Cadillac, Stop & Go, Battery Operated, Tin, Box, 1950s 40.00
Car, Camper, Barbie Country, Box, 1972 .... 80.00
Car, Camper, Tonka 40.00
Car, Chevrolet Coupe, 1928 Model, 8 In. 2495.00
Car, Chevrolet, Red, White, Japan, 1950, 12 In. 300.00
Car, Chick-Mobile, Peter Rabbit, Composition, Keywind, Lionel, 10 In. 413.00
Car, Chitty Chitty Bang Bang, Metal, Corgi, 1968 .... 112.00
Car, Chitty Chitty Bang Bang, Plastic, Post, 1968 .... 29.00
Car, Chrysler, Airflow, Brown Paint, Cor-Cor, 16 In. 1400.00
Car, Chrysler, Airflow, Kingsbury 395.00
Car, Chrysler, Airflow, Nickel Plated, Rubber Tires, Hubley, 6 1/4 In. 165.00
Car, Chrysler, Airflow, Pressed Steel, Painted, Wyandotte, 6 In. 33.00
Car, Chrysler, Imperial, 1958 Model, Friction, Cream, White, Bandai, 8 In. 185.00
Car, Convertible, Bobble Head Driver, Tin Lithograph, Marx, 1950s 175.00
Car, Convertible, DLX-721 Crusader 101, Battery, Deluxe Reading, 30 In. 425.00
Car, Coo-Coo, Marx 475.00
Car, Cord, 1930s, Wyandotte 525.00
Car, Corgi, 007, James Bond, Moon Buggy, Painted 70.00
Car, Corgi, 007, James Bond, Toyota 2000, Rear Missiles, Box 185.00
Car, Corgi, No. 153, Bluebird Blue .... 39.00 To 42.00
Car, Corvette, 1954 Model, Ideal 65.00
Car, Corvette, Matchbox 5.00
Car, Cougar, 1978, Matchbox 5.00
Car, Coupe, Cast Iron, Black, Gold Trim, Arcade, 5 In. 175.00
Car, Crazy Clown, Crazy Car, Windup, Box 95.00
Car, Crazy Rodeo Joe, Windup, Marx, 9 In. 180.00
Car, Dodge Charger, Racing Set, 1966 .... 100.00
Car, Duesenberg Coupe, Friction, 17 1/2 In. 850.00
Car, Figure, Kojak, Die Cast, Box 55.00
Car, Fire Chief, Hoge 325.00
Car, Fire Chief, Siren, Plastic, Windup, Battery Operated, Marx, 13 In. 100.00
Car, Flapper's Flivver, Marx, 7 In. 400.00
Car, Flip Over, Flintstone 45.00
Car, Flivver, Fred Flintstone 400.00
Car, Ford Cortina, Matchbox 10.00
Car, Ford Coupe, Blue, No. 6253 Classic, Hot Wheels, 1969 .... 25.00
Car, Ford, 1950 Model, Tin Lithograph, Friction, Brown, ET, Japan, 10 In. 86.00
Car, Ford, Thunderbird Convertible, Tekno 200.00
Car, Gang Busters, Windup, Marx, 1930s 575.00
Car, GM Jalopy, Funny Circling Beatup Movement, Battery Operated, Box 20.00
Car, Herbie, White, Volkswagen, No. 53, Blinking Back Lights, Box 95.00
Car, Horseless Carriage, Tiller Steered, Keywind, Kenton, 1903 .... 2200.00
Car, Hot Rod, T Ford, Battery Operated, Alps, Japan, 1950 .... 195.00
Car, Huckleberry Hound, Tin Friction, Box 195.00
Car, International Agent, Friction, Driver, Marx, Box, 1966, 4 In. 125.00
Car, Jaguar, 21 In. 35.00
Car, Jaguar, Green, Dinky Toy 60.00
Car, Jaguar, No. 700, Friction, Box 50.00
Car, Jeep, United Airlines, Driver's Arm Raises, Friction, Tin, 7 In. 35.00
Car, Key Wind, Tin, Early 1900s, 15 In. 595.00
Car, Limousine, Yellow & Black Striping, Carrette 9000.00
Car, Lincoln, Zephyr, Parker Erie, 3 1/2 In. 95.00
Car, Matchbox, No. 5, Yesteryear, 1929 Bentley, Green, Box 40.00
Car, Matchbox, No. 8, Yellow, Box 32.00
Car, Matchbox, No. 22, Red & White, Box 34.00
Car, Matchbox, No. 41, Green, Box 32.00
Car, Matchbox, No. 54, Green, Box 27.00

Car, Mercedes Benz, 180, Tekno 175.00
Car, Mercedes Benz, 230SL, Matchbox, 1965 .... 9.00
Car, Mercedes Benz, 300, Marklin, Box 90.00
Car, Mercedes Benz, Friction, Ichiko, 1970s, 24 In. 275.00
Car, Mercedes Benz, Racing, Windup, Schuco, 1940s 125.00
Car, Mercedes Benz, Stunt, Runs Forward, Tumbles Over, Repeats, 7 1/2 In. 145.00
Car, Mercedes Benz, Tin, Friction, Box, Japan 85.00
Car, Mercer, 1913 Model, Windup, Germany, 8 In. 145.00
Car, Model T, Battery Operated, Green & Gold Stenciling, Tin 110.00
Car, Modern Bakery, Courtland, Windup, 7 In. 72.00
Car, Molly Moos, Pull Toy, Fisher-Price, 1956 .... 135.00
Car, Mustang Champion Stunt, Flip Over, Box 95.00
Car, Mustang, Green, Marx, 1965, 6 In. 40.00
Car, Mystery, Coupe, Mechanical, Wolverine, 13 In. 225.00
Car, Nottie The Driver, Bakelite Girl, Tin Crazy Car, Marx, Box 195.00
Car, Old Jalopy, Marx 200.00
Car, Old Jalopy, Marx, Box 350.00
Car, Oldsmobile, Friction, Japan, 1960s, 7 In. 75.00
Car, Oldsmobile, Sedan, Auburn Rubber, 1939 Model, White Tires, 6 In. 65.00
Car, Open Roadster, Wooden & Metal, Painted, Electric, Ohlmacher, Box 880.00
Car, Packard Clipper, Dinky Toy, Box 250.00
Car, Packard Roadster, 1918 Model, Rumble Seat, 18 In. 900.00
Car, Packard Syncromatic, Manual Or Automatic, Schuco, 10 1/2 In. 1430.00
Car, Packard Convertible, Tin, Friction, Alps, 16 In. 6200.00
Car, Penny, Green, 3 In. ....90.00 To 100.00
Car, Police, 1959 Cadillac, Battery Operated 550.00
Car, Police, Battery Operated, Linemar, Box 90.00
Car, Police, Highway Patrol, Friction, Box 75.00
Car, Police, Siren, Flashing Light, Remote Controlled, Linemar 140.00
Car, Police, Siren, Tin, Lupor, Box 95.00
Car, Police, Tin Lithograph, 8 1/2 In. 35.00
Car, Police, Wagon, Cast Iron & Steel, 1920 .... 300.00
Car, Racing Set, Star Wars, 1977, Box 195.00
Car, Racing Set, Star Wars, Box 150.00
Car, Racing, Bearcat, Structo, 12 1/2 In. 850.00
Car, Racing, Buffalo Toy Co., 1920s 300.00
Car, Racing, Cast Iron Hood & Driver, Hubley, 8 In. 135.00
Car, Racing, Champion, Red Painted, Cast Iron, 8 1/2 In. 298.00
Car, Racing, Driver, Metal Wheels, Cast Iron, A. C. Williams, 6 In. 175.00
Car, Racing, Driver, Navigator, White Rubber Tires, Cast Iron 165.00
Car, Racing, Grand Prix, With Driver, Box 95.00
Car, Racing, Hubley, Green, 5 1/2 In. 195.00
Car, Racing, International Stock, Box 95.00
Car, Racing, Kellogg's, Plastic, Spring Loaded, Red, Yellow, Box, 5 1/2 In. 39.00
Car, Racing, Kingsbury, Buddy L, Windup, Box 575.00
Car, Racing, Maverick, Bandai, Box 95.00
Car, Racing, Rex Mays, Windup, Scale Model, Box 165.00
Car, Racing, Silver Dash, Spring Drive, Buffalo Toys, 1925 .... 435.00
Car, Rambler Wagon, No. 193, Yellow, White, Dinky Toy, Box, 8 1/2 In. 12.00
Car, Remote Controlled, Marx 30.00
Car, Roadster, Arcade, Red 1980.00
Car, Roadster, Cast Iron, Bing 550.00
Car, Roadster, Uncle Walt, Tootsietoy, 1932 .... 575.00
Car, Robot, Tin Lithograph, Plastic & Rubber, Japan, 7 1/2 In. 187.00
Car, Run-A-Bout, Cast Iron, Kenton, 1930s, 5 1/2 In. 180.00
Car, Saloon, Windup, Red & Black, Chad Valley, 1947, 9 1/2 In. 335.00
Car, Sedan, 2 Windows, Arcade 600.00
Car, Sedan, Cast Iron, Kilgore, 3 In. 95.00
Car, Sightseeing Auto, Kenton 5500.00
Car, Soapbox Derby, Wooden, Red & White, Yellow Lettering, Won In 1951 ..... 1200.00
Car, Sparkling Rocket, Japan 75.00
Car, Spider Man, Friction, Lithograph Characters, Marx, 1967, 4 In. 95.00
Car, Station Wagon, Ford, 1959 Model, Red, White, Japan, Box, 10 In. 140.00

Car, Station Wagon, Woody, 1940 Model, Rubber Tires, Metal Masters, 9 In. 45.00
Car, Stock, 4 Horses, Men On Top, Cast Iron, Ideal, 1900s 1000.00
Car, Stock, Friction, Tin Lithograph, Japan, 1960s, 16 In. 95.00
Car, Studebaker, 1951 Model, 8 In. 95.00
Car, Terra, Windup, Lehmann, 10 In. 875.00
Car, Tin Lizzie, Ford, Backfires 100.00
Car, Tin Lizzie, Windup, Black, 4 Door, Driver, Marx, 1929, 7 In. 220.00
Car, Touring Sedan, Kingsbury 1140.00
Car, Touring, Alphonse & Gaston, Kenton 7480.00
Car, Touring, Friction, Tin, Driver & Child, Worn Paint, 7 3/4 In. 225.00
Car, Touring, Friction, Wooden, Tin, Cast Iron, Polychrome Paint, 8 In. 350.00
Car, Triumph TR2, Yellow, Tekno 70.00
Car, Triumph, Light Brown 50.00
Car, U.S. Army, Tin Lithograph, Marx, Box, 26 In. 500.00
Car, Volkswagen, Forward & Reverse, Battery Operated, Bandai, 8 1/2 In. 180.00
Car, Volkswagen, Tin, See Through Back Motor 65.00
Car, Volkswagen, Tootsietoy, 1960, 6 In. 6.00
Car, Volvo PV544, Tekno, Box 175.00
Car, Windup, Tin Lithograph, Carette 5500.00
Car, With Motorcycle Chasing, Friction, Japan, 1950 .... 150.00
Car, Wolverine Supply Bumper, Red Tin, Windup, Marx 300.00
Carousel, Airplane Tower, 3 Airplanes, Windup, West Germany, 16 In. 55.00
Carousel, Clockwork Motor, Tin Lithograph, Painted 210.00
Carousel, Clockwork, Boats, Riders, Painted Tin, Germany, 1909, 17 In. 3850.00
Carousel, Kiddy-Go-Round, Windup, Wyandotte 120.00
Carousel, Mechanical, Penny 830.00
Carousel, Passengers In Swings, Equestriennes, Painted Tin 2100.00
Carousel, Sailaway, Unique Art 195.00
Carousel, Steam Driven, Germany 8500.00
Carousel, Tin Propeller-Driven Boats, Muller & Kadeder 3850.00
Carousel, Wolverine, 1930s 450.00
Carpet Sweeper, Bissell, Wooden & Wire, Black & Gold Lettering, 35 In. 33.00
Carpet Sweeper, Little Queen, Bissell, 1940s 45.00
Carriage, Bunny, Windup, Celluloid, Japan, Box 275.00
Carriage, Doll's, Amish Style, Yellow, Red Stenciling On Wheels 825.00
Carriage, Doll's, Black Wire Wheels, Original Paint 175.00
Carriage, Doll's, Iron, Late 19th Century 55.00
Carriage, Doll's, Juanita Lettered In Gold On Front 1350.00
Carriage, Doll's, Large Wheels, Fringed Top 425.00
Carriage, Doll's, Rubber Wheels, Metal, Wyandotte 75.00
Carriage, Doll's, Stenciled, Joel Ellis 600.00
Carriage, Doll's, White Wicker, Round Side Windows 160.00
Carriage, Doll's, Wicker, Brocade Upholstery, 34 In. 385.00
Carriage, Doll's, Wicker, Car Shape, Hood With Side Windows, Small 300.00
Carriage, Doll's, Wooden, 3 Wheels, Oilcloth Hood, Red Paint, 22 In. 400.00
Carriage, Doll's, Wooden, Blue Paint, Oilcloth Canopy, Stenciled, 27 In. 500.00
Carriage, Doll's, Wooden, Chip Carved, Worn Red & Green Paint, 23 In. 190.00
Carriage, Doll's, Wooden, Wooden Wheels, 32 In. 247.00
Carriage, Wicker, Aluminum Bumpers & Fenders, Rubber Wheels, Schlegel 600.00
Cart, Baggage, Windup, Lithograph, Unique Art, 13 In. 190.00
Cart, Bunny Rabbit, Fisher-Price 175.00
Cart, Doll's, Red Paint Traces, Bardstown, Ky., 1870 .... 245.00
Cart, Horse & Driver, Cast Iron, Wilkins, Late 1800s, 10 1/4 In. 895.00
Cart, Horse Drawn, Tin Lithograph, Red Wheels, Yellow Cart, 8 1/2 In. 110.00
Case, Barbie Doll, 1961 .... 22.00
Cash Register, American Flyer 42.00
Cash Register, Metal, Black, Maple Leaf, 1930s, 4 3/4 x 4 3/4 In. 65.00
Cash Register, Tom Thumb, Red .... 12.50 To 30.00
Cat, Chasing Ball, Windup, Japan, 1950 .... 85.00
Cat, Dog, Pull Toy, Cast Iron 250.00
Cat, Felix The Cat, Black, Orange Mice, Red Wheels, Tin, Pull, 1930s, 7 In. 755.00
Cat, Felix The Cat, Wooden Jointed, Leather Ears, 1920-1930, 4 In. 190.00
Cat, Gray & White, Tag & Button, Steiff, 13 In. 65.00

Cat, Knitting, Windup	38.00
Cat, Roll Over, Marx	85.00
Cat, Walking, Battery Operated, Marx, Box	62.00
Cat, With Ball Of Yarn, Windup, Tin, Occupied Japan	15.00
Chair, Doll's, Ice Cream, Metal Caning	37.50
Chair, Doll's, Ladder Back, Splint Seat, 13 1/2 In.	185.00
Chair, Doll's, Original Red Paint, Yellow Striping, 8 1/4 In.	95.00
Chalkboard, Chair, Red Metal Jobo Chair, Sebel Products	95.00
Chalkboard, Spaceman, 1950s	55.00
Chariot, Lost In Space, Aurora	65.00
Charleston Trio, Middle Man With Banjo, Jigger, Windup, Box	1200.00
Charlie Weaver, Battery Operated, Rosko, Japan	100.00
Cheery Cook, Celluloid, Windup, Occupied Japan, Box	46.00 To 100.00
Chemistry Set, Gilbert, 1957	75.00
Chest, Doll's, 4 Drawers, Bamboo Trim, France, 9 x 14 In.	245.00
Chest, Doll's, 5 Drawers, Brass Pulls, Square Nails, Pine, 14 In.	350.00
Chick & Butterfly, Butterfly Moves, Chick Waddles, Windup, 4 In.	65.00
Chick, Carousel With Chimes, Spinning Canopy, Plastic, Windup	65.00
Chicken Snatcher, Dog Bites Thief, Windup, Tin Lithograph, Marx, 1926	3000.00
Chimes, Musical, Push Toy, Tin, Wooden Wheels, Fisher–Price, 1951	35.00
Chimp, Musical Jolly, Battery Operated, Japan	50.00
China Cabinet, Doll's, Wooden, Glass Doors, 14 x 7 In.	68.00
Chinaman, Walker, Ives	5500.00
Chompy, The Beetle, Windup, Marx, 6 In.	150.00
Cigarette Pack, Lark, Windup, Walking Feet	25.00
Circus Cage, Horse Drawn, Wild Animals, Kyser & Tex	9900.00
Circus Cage, On Wheels, 2 Horses, Tin Lithograph, Harrison, 11 In.	725.00
Circus Wagon, Overland, Cast Iron Bear, Kenton, 14 In.	350.00
Circus, Acrobat, Toto, Weights In Head For Action, Japan, Box	895.00
Circus, Bullwinkle, Balancing Bullwinkle On Elephant	45.00
Circus, Calliope, Elephant, 4 Wagons, Teddy Clown Driver, Steiff	2250.00
Circus, Humpty Dumpty, Wooden Figures, Schoenhut, Box, c.1920	450.00
Circus, J. F. Doolan, 130 Piece	2750.00
Circus, Set, Big Performing Circus, No. 250, Fisher–Price, Box	800.00
Circus, Super Circus, Tin, Marx	150.00
Circus, Tricycle, Windup, Celluloid Boy, Tin Tricycle, Occupied Japan	110.00
Circus, Wagon, Musicians, Cast Iron, Kenton, 15 In.	450.00
Circus, Wagon, Performers, No. 900, Fisher–Price	120.00 To 155.00
Circus, Wagon, Teddy Clown Driver, Steiff	2200.00
Circus, Wagon, Wooden, Cardboard Lithograph, Tony Sarge, 18 In.	275.00
City, Wizard Of Oz, 1975	40.00
Clarinet, Woody Herman, Tin, Box	28.00
Clicker, Shooting Cowboy, Animated, 1940	60.00
Clock, Teaching, Fisher–Price	18.00
Clown Face, Pull Toy, Revolving Disc, Bell Rings On Top, 9 1/2 In.	95.00
Clown, Bows Violin, Windup, Schuco, 4 1/2 In.	210.00
Clown, Dancing, Windup, Tin Lithograph, Chein, 6 In.	255.00
Clown, Dog Team, Tin Lithograph, Germany, 8 In.	990.00
Clown, Drumming, Lighted Nose, Battery Operated, Box	225.00
Clown, Drumming, Windup, Tin, Felt Costume, Germany, 4 1/4 In.	55.00
Clown, Gravity Toy, Tin Lithograph, Tower, 10 In.	66.00
Clown, Horse & Cart, Lehmann, 1903	180.00
Clown, Jolly Tune, Jack–In–The–Box, Musical, Mattel	25.00
Clown, Juggler, Tin, Windup, Plate On Head, 1910, 9 1/2 In.	467.00
Clown, Playing Trombone, Windup, Tin, Cloth Clothes, 9 1/2 In.	170.00
Clown, Pull Toy, Disc Revolves, Picture Of Face, Bell Rings, Tin	95.00
Clown, Red, Green, Wags Head, Tin, Windup, German, 1910, 6 In.	1045.00
Clown, Smokes, Germany, 1914, 2 1/2 In.	22.50
Clown, Walking, Drumming, Tin Lithograph, Cloth, Windup, Japan, 11 In.	110.00
Clown, With Mouse, Windup, Vibrates Tossing Mouse In Air, Key, Schuco	235.00
Clown, With Umbrella, Windup, Tin Lithograph, Chein, 8 In.	35.00
Clowns, Catapult Onto Trapeze, Wooden, Metal, Polychrome, 23 1/2 In.	75.00
Coach, Passenger, 1927 Model, Buddy L, 28 3/4 In.	1210.00

Computer, Thin-A-Tron 75.00
Coon Jigger, Tombo, Box 750.00
Couple, Dancing, Accordion Squeaks, Paper Lithograph, Germany, 8 In. 85.00
Couple, Dancing, Celluloid, Key Wind, Occupied Japan, 4 3/4 In. ....66.00 To 115.00
Cow, Battery Operated, Raises Head & Walks, Black & White 95.00
Cow, Pull Toy, Fisher-Price 20.00
Cow, Pull Toy, Wooden Base & Wheels, Papier-Mache Body, 7 In. 195.00
Cowboy Set, Mounted, Britains, Box 525.00
Cowboy, Rider, Windup, Marx, Box 235.00
Cowboy, Riding White Horse, Hartland 50.00
Cradle, Doll's, Stenciled, Baby Mine 95.00
Crayons, Priscilla, Tankard Toycraft, 1937 .... 35.00
Crib, Doll's, Doll-E-Crib, Wooden Rollers, Blue Metal, Amsco, 25 1/2 In. 48.00
Crossing Signal, American Flyer 50.00
Cup, Drinking, Bonanza, Tin 20.00
Cupboard, Doll's, Glazed Upper Doors, 2 Drawers, 35 1/2 In. 275.00
Cupboard, Doll's, Step Back 295.00
Cycle, Cap'n Crunch, Plastic, Quaker, 1960s 59.00
Cycle, New Century, Lehmann, 1904, 5 1/2 In. 495.00
Dancing Man, Kool-Aid, Box 55.00
Desk, Lap, Slant Top, 7 Learning Tablets, Hunt Scenes, 1885 .... 195.00
Dinosaur, Brosus Brontosaurus, Steiff, 12 In. 700.00
Dinosaur, Riding, Cloth Covered, Battery Operated, Marx, 2 Ft. 385.00
Dinosaur, Sinclair, Unopened, 1960s 12.00
Dirigible, Marx 350.00
Dirigible, Shenandoah, Tin & Plastic, Windup, Lehmann, Box, 9 In. 825.00
Dirigible, Silver Paint, Cast Iron, 1925, 6 In. 193.00
Dog With Shoe, Windup, Celluloid, Japan ....35.00 To 60.00
Dog, Airedale, Steiff 70.00
Dog, Barky Dog, Friction, Japan, Box, 1950 .... 60.00
Dog, Bulldog, Musical, Battery Operated 550.00
Dog, Buttons, Puppy With Brain, Mechanical, Tin, Marx 95.00
Dog, Cat & Squirrel, Skip Rope, Windup, Tin, TPS, 1950s 76.00
Dog, Cloth, Black, Curly Ears, Glass Eyes, Straw & Wire, Victorian, 7 In. 85.00
Dog, Dachshund, Waldi, On Wooden Wheels, Steiff 275.00
Dog, Itchy, Windup, Celluloid 125.00
Dog, Jolly Pianist, Piano, Tin, Battery Operated, 1950s, 10 In. 225.00
Dog, Lamb's Wool Mane, Black Glass Eyes, White Cloth, 12 In. 50.00
Dog, Lassie, In Box, Plastic, Tenite, 6 1/4 In. 145.00
Dog, Plush Puppy, Battery Operated, Hong Kong 30.00
Dog, Poodle, Begging, Windup, Box, Occupied Japan 75.00
Dog, Poodle, Jointed, Steiff, 9 In. 75.00
Dog, Poodle, Musician, Frock Coat, Plays Drum, Tin, Windup, 7 In. 1045.00
Dog, Poodle, Windup, 6 Actions, Box 35.00
Dog, Puppy & Show, Windup, Celluloid, LN, Box 250.00
Dog, Puppy, Blue Wheels, Lithograph, Pull Toy, H. D. Allen 75.00
Dog, Rin Tin Tin, Stuffed, Tag To Join Rin Tin Tin Club 100.00
Dog, Roll Over Rover, Battery Operated, CU, Taiwan, 1975, Box 30.00
Dog, Roll Over, Marx 60.00
Dog, Rover The Poodle, Battery Operated, Walks, Barks, Box, Japan 40.00
Dog, Snoopy Sniffer, Fisher-Price 44.00
Dog, Sparky, Battery Operated, Voice Activated, 1940, 4 x 6 In. 35.00
Dog, Terrier, Turning Head, Eyes Open & Close, Squeaker, Arrow Toys 22.00
Dog, Wooden Jointed, Black, Red & Yellow, Ted Toy Co., 1920s, 12 In. 175.00
Dogpatch Band, Windup, Unique Art ....590.00 To 750.00
Dolls are listed in their own section
Dollhouse, 2 Rooms, Porch, Bliss ....*Illus* 3300.00
Dollhouse, 3 Story, Morning Paper On Front Lawn 325.00
Dollhouse, Baby Stroller, Renwal 12.00
Dollhouse, Barbie's Dream House, 1962 .... 120.00
Dollhouse, Bliss, 21 1/2 x 19 1/2 In. 3950.00
Dollhouse, Bliss, Adirondack, 2 Story, 4 Rooms, Wooden, 1904, 17 In. 1230.00
Dollhouse, Bliss, Victorian, Wooden, Porch, Paper Lithograph, 23 In. 3300.00

Dollhouse, Cabinet, Wheels, Glass Windows, Victorian, 1900, 45 x 31 In. 1100.00
Dollhouse, Colonial Revival 475.00
Dollhouse, Furniture, Bathroom Set, Green, Tootsietoy, 6 Piece 77.00
Dollhouse, Furniture, Bathroom Set, Kilgore, 6 Piece 55.00
Dollhouse, Furniture, Bathroom, Tin, Germany, 1920s 170.00
Dollhouse, Furniture, Bedroom Set, Sleigh Bed, Chest, Chairs, Green, Tin 660.00
Dollhouse, Furniture, Bedroom, Tootsietoy, Box, c.1927 .... 140.00
Dollhouse, Furniture, Bench, Mammy, Wooden, 14 In. 132.00
Dollhouse, Furniture, Breakfront, Renwal 10.00
Dollhouse, Furniture, Bunk Bed, Rocker, Chifforobe, Kohner 35.00
Dollhouse, Furniture, Bureau, 3 Drawers, Attached Mirror 45.00
Dollhouse, Furniture, Chair, Renwal 5.00
Dollhouse, Furniture, Clock, Wall, Pendulum, Wooden, Germany, 1920s, 4 In. 10.00
Dollhouse, Furniture, Couch, Coffee Table, Highboy, Vanity, Plastic 8.00
Dollhouse, Furniture, Crib, With Wheels, Cast Iron 16.50
Dollhouse, Furniture, Divan, Wooden, Upholstered, 19 In. 220.00
Dollhouse, Furniture, Dog, Cat, Built–Rite, 1940s, 27 Piece, 11 In. 66.00
Dollhouse, Furniture, Dresser, Stroller, Feeding Table, Swing, Suzy Cute 85.00
Dollhouse, Furniture, Fireplace, Renwal 10.00
Dollhouse, Furniture, Grand Piano, Renwal 10.00
Dollhouse, Furniture, High Chair, Cast Iron 14.50
Dollhouse, Furniture, Hoosier Cabinet, Cast Iron, Arcade 325.00
Dollhouse, Furniture, Kitchen Set, Metal, Sunny Suzie, 3 Piece 40.00
Dollhouse, Furniture, Kitchen Set, White, Tootsietoy, Box 357.00
Dollhouse, Furniture, Kitchen Set, Yellow, Tootsietoy, 6 Piece 55.00
Dollhouse, Furniture, Kitchen, Pink, 3 Piece 95.00
Dollhouse, Furniture, Living Room Set, Tootsietoy, 5 Piece 66.00
Dollhouse, Furniture, Parlor Set, Blue & White, Iron, 6 Piece 22.00
Dollhouse, Furniture, Parlor Set, China, 1930s, 6 Piece 275.00
Dollhouse, Furniture, Potty Chair, Cast Iron 14.50
Dollhouse, Furniture, Refrigerator, Stove, Cabinet, Sink, Wolverine 100.00
Dollhouse, Furniture, Sewing Machine, Renwal 12.00
Dollhouse, Furniture, Stove, Cast Iron, Daisy 42.00
Dollhouse, Furniture, Swing, Child's, Renwal 12.00
Dollhouse, Furniture, Victorian, 4 Rooms, Cabinet, Wheels, 45 x 31 In. 1100.00
Dollhouse, Handmade, Polychrome, Glass Windows, Removable Roof, 23 In. 400.00
Dollhouse, Log Cabin, Missouri, 1920s 375.00
Dollhouse, Marx, Ranch, Furniture, Box 55.00
Dollhouse, Marx, Take–A–Long, Box 75.00
Dollhouse, Marx, Tin, 33 x 17 In. 32.00
Dollhouse, McLoughlin, Folding, Box 85.00
Dollhouse, Mystery Dollhouse, Victorian Style, 6 Rooms 9900.00
Dollhouse, Oak, Collapsible, 1865 .... 8800.00
Dollhouse, Rustic, Cottage Type, Oversized, 1920s 950.00
Dollhouse, Schoenhut, 1 Room, Bungalow, Hinged Wall, 1928, 9 x 12 In. 220.00
Dollhouse, Schoenhut, 1 Story, Brick, 3–Dimensional Paper, 15 In. 755.00
Dollhouse, Schoenhut, Wooden, Painted, Stucco, Electrified, 48 In. 225.00
Dollhouse, Strombecker, Dream, 4 Rooms, Shrubbery, Dog, 1940, 13 In. 55.00
Dollhouse, Wolverine, Metal, Large 30.00
Donkey, Mohair, Jointed, Shoebutton Eyes, Painted Accents, 15 In. 150.00
Donkey, Painted Eyes, Schoenhut 65.00
Donkey, Stubborn, Clown & Cart, Lehmann 375.00
Donkey, Windup, Plastic & Tin, Mohair, Leatherized Paper, 4 3/4 In. 40.00
Donkey, Wooden, Kicks When String Pulled, Green & Brown, S. C., 32 In. 235.00
Dopey, Windup, Tin, Marx, 1938 .... 650.00
Double Acrobats, Gymnasts, Ives 2200.00
Dow Bathroom Scrubbing Bubble, Vinyl 20.00
Drawing Set, Electric, Laugh–In, 1968 .... 59.00
Drawing Set, G. I. Joe, Electric 45.00
Dray, Automotive, Painted Pressed Steel, Iron Tires, Wooden Barrels 220.00
Dresser, Doll's, Mirror, Oak, 25 1/2 x 13 3/4 In. 230.00
Dresser, Doll's, Pine, With Mirror 200.00
Drum Major, No. 27, Windup, Tin, Wolverine, 13 3/4 In. 70.00

Drum, Circus Animals, Tin Lithograph, Canada, 12 In. Diam. 23.00
Drum, Metal, Ohio Art 12.00
Drum, Spanish American War, 6 Naval Vessels, Pressed Wood 425.00
Drummer Boy, Play While You Swing & Sway, Windup, Marx, 1930s 595.00
Drummer Boy, Plays While Riding Dancing Horse, England, Pre-WWII 245.00
Drummer Boy, Tin, Windup, Marx .... 150.00 To 300.00
Duck, Dilly, I Can Really Walk & Quack, Windup, Japan, Box, 4 3/4 In. 50.00
Duck, Furry & Feathers, Glass Eyes, Windup 50.00
Duck, Plush, Straw-Filled, Felt Beak & Feet, Black Eyes, Steiff, 9 In. 400.00
Duck, Walking, Windup, Japan, Box 95.00
Duck, Windup, Chein, 1930, 4 In. .... 30.00 To 35.00
Duck, Windup, Tin, Occupied Japan, Box 35.00
Duck, Worried Mother, Battery Operated, Box 88.00
Duckling, Plush, Button Eyes, Steiff, 1950s, 6 In. 40.00
Ducks, Swimming, With Ball, Battery Operated, Japan 100.00
Eggbeater, Betty Taplin 15.00
Elector-Radar Scope Set, Motor, 68 Parts, Instructions, Metal Box 30.00
Elephant, Baby, Gray Felt, Cast Iron Frame, Wheels, Steiff, 31 In. 1775.00
Elephant, Baby, On Wheels, Steiff 1760.00
Elephant, Circus, Lifts Dumbbells, Twists Tail, Windup, Tin, 5 In. 135.00
Elephant, Jumbo, Bubble Blowing, Battery Operated, Box 100.00
Elephant, Jumbo, Snuggy, Steiff 495.00
Elephant, Jumbo, Windup 220.00
Elephant, Leather Tusks & Ears, Glass Eyes, Schoenhut, 6 1/4 In. 50.00
Elephant, Musical, 1948 Republican Convention, Fisher-Price 115.00
Elephant, Pull, Papier-Mache, On Wheels, Germany, 9 In. 137.00
Elephant, Windup, Red & Yellow Stenciling, Tin, 6 In. 132.00
Elephant, Windup, Tin, Cloth Cover, Celluloid, Occupied Japan, 5 3/4 In. 45.00
Elsie, No. 131, Milk Wagon, Fisher-Price 17.00
Engine, Chemical Pump, Red, Rubber Tires, Hose, Keystone, 27 In. 715.00
Erector Set, Gilbert, Musical Ferris Wheel, Metal Case 200.00
Erector Set, Gilbert, No. 3, Extra Motors, Manuals, 1920 .... 195.00
Erector Set, Gilbert, No. 6 1/2, Box .... 45.00 To 65.00
Erector Set, Gilbert, No. 7 1/2, Cardboard Chest 120.00
Erector Set, Gilbert, No. 10084, Amusement Park, 1950s 45.00
Erector Set, Gilbert, Rocket Launcher 93.00
Fainting Couch, Doll's, Victorian 485.00
Falk Steam Plant, Hand Painted, Lithograph, 1920-1930s, 14 x 10 In. 600.00
Farmer In The Dell, Crank, Mattel, 1950 .... 250.00 To 350.00
Felix The Cat, Pull Toy, Tin Lithograph, 1930, 7 1/2 In. ....*Illus* 755.00
Ferdinand The Bull, Windup, Marx, Box .... 135.00 To 350.00
Ferris Wheel, 6 Compartments, Windup, Bell, Chein, 1930, 16 In. .... 325.00 To 350.00
Ferris Wheel, Hercules, Tin Lithograph, Motor, Chein, 16 In. .... 110.00 To 250.00
Ferris Wheel, Painted Metal Figures, Wheel & Base, 11 In. 465.00
Fido Doghouse, Tin, Ohio Art 39.00
Fighting Men, Thingmaker, 1960s 60.00
Fingerprint Set, G-Men, Colorful Box, 1937 .... 125.00
Finnigan The Baggage Porter, Unique Art, Box 675.00
Fire Department, Wooden, Keystone 150.00
Fire Pumper, 2 Teams, Iron, White Horse, Red Wheels, Kenton, 1911, 18 In. 220.00
Fire Rig, 3 Horse, Water Tower, Wilkins 1980.00
Fire Truck, 4 Doors, Tonka 55.00
Fire Truck, Aerial Ladder, Buddy L, 1935 .... 1200.00
Fire Truck, Aerial Ladder, Cast Iron, Buddy L 925.00
Fire Truck, Aerial, Friction, Telescoping Tower, Box, 1950s, 12 In. 150.00
Fire Truck, Buddy L, 1930s 1000.00
Fire Truck, Chief, Hoge 550.00
Fire Truck, Extension Ladder, Firestone Tires, Doepke, 1940s, 28 In. 150.00
Fire Truck, Hook & Ladder, 2 Horses, Driver, Cast Iron, c.1900, 30 In. 205.00
Fire Truck, Hook & Ladder, Arcade, 18 In. 150.00
Fire Truck, Hook & Ladder, Cast Iron & Pressed Steel, Wilkins, 28 In. 247.00
Fire Truck, Hook & Ladder, Wyandotte, Box 240.00
Fire Truck, Hubley, 5 In. 20.00

Fire Truck, Ladder, Cast Iron, Arcade 425.00
Fire Truck, Ladder, LF Mack, Smith Miller 650.00
Fire Truck, Ladder, No. 3, Buddy L .... 140.00 To 190.00
Fire Truck, Ladder, Red, Yellow Removable Yellow Ladders 350.00
Fire Truck, No. 4652, Tootsietoy 85.00
Fire Truck, Original Ladders, American National, 29 In. 1200.00
Fire Truck, Original Paint, Sheet Metal, Structo, 24 In. 75.00
Fire Truck, Pumper, Copper Boiler, Bell, Steel & Tin, Marklin 6000.00
Fire Truck, Pumper, Kingsbury 1550.00
Fire Truck, Pumper, No. 2010, Doepke 350.00
Fire Truck, Pumper, No. 2014, Doepke 500.00
Fire Truck, Pumper, Structo 75.00
Fire Truck, Pumper, Tonka 95.00
Fire Truck, Rubber, Auburn, 7 1/2 In. 15.00
Fire Truck, Snorkel, Plastic, Japan, Box, 14 1/2 In. 50.00
Fire Truck, Tonka, 17 1/2 In. 75.00
Fire Truck, Trailer, Friction, Tin, Fireman, Japan, 1950s, 12 1/2 In. 135.00
Fire Truck, Trailer, Rolls Forward, Rubber Tires, Tin, Box, 12 3/4 In. 150.00
Fire Truck, Water Tower, Tootsietoy, Pre–War 75.00
Fire Wagon, Ladder, Horse Drawn, Cast Iron 325.00
Fireman, Ladder Climbing, Tin Lithograph, Windup, Marx, 22 In. 27.50
Flashlight, Spaceboy, 1950s 45.00
Flintstone On Dinosaur, Battery Operated, Marx, Box, 2 Ft. .... 425.00 To 840.00
Flintstone Shaker Maker, Box 95.00
Flub–A–Dub Ring Toss, Agran, 1950s 65.00
Flying Bird, Painted Tin Body, Paper Wings, Windup, Lehmann, Box, 7 In. 412.00
Flying Saucer, Tin Lithograph, Japan, 1950s, 7 x 5 1/2 In. 275.00
Fork Lift, Dinky Toy 25.00
Fort Apache Set, Original Metal Case, Marx .... 25.00 To 28.00
Fort Cheyenne, Soldiers, Indians, Horses, Ideal 115.00
Fox, Steiff, 11 In. 225.00
Foxy Grandpa, Sitting On Nodder Donkey, Pull Toy, Composition, 1900 .... 450.00
Frankenstein Monster, Battery Operated, Roscoe, Box 250.00
Freddie Krueger, From Elm Street, Talking, Box 47.00
Friendly Bartender, Battery Operated, Amico, Box, 1970 .... 50.00
Frog With Butterfly On Mushroom, Mechanical, Penny 990.00
Frog, Hopping, Windup, Linemar, Box 35.00
Froggy The Gremlin, Squeeze Toy, Hard Rubber, 5 In. 85.00
Frontier Play Set, Daniel Boone, 1950s, Marx 98.00
G. I. Joe & His Jouncing Jeep, Windup, Tin 185.00
G. I. Joe & K–9 Pups, Tin, Windup .... 175.00 To 250.00
G. I. Joe, Jouncing Jeep, Windup, Unique Art, 1941 .... 210.00
G. I. Joe, Space Capsule, Record, Box 175.00
G. I. Joe, Windup, Tin Lithograph, Marx, 1940 .... 250.00
Games are listed in their own section
Garage, Automatic Car Wash, Windup, Tin Lithograph, Marx, Box, 9 In. 100.00
Garage, Fire Department, Chief & Car, Courtland 45.00
Garage, Keystone, 1930s 75.00
Gentleman, Top Hat Covers Head, 3 Ethnic Faces, Windup, Unique Art 4000.00
Giraffe, Steiff, 8 Ft. 1250.00
Girl, Riding Goose, Key Wind, Celluloid Figure, 5 In. 8.00
Glider, Swan, Single Seat 160.00
Globe, Tin Lithograph, Ohio Art 30.00
Gloves, Cheyenne 15.00
Gloves, Huckleberry Hound, 1959 .... 30.00
Go–Cart, Babes In Toyland, Linemar 150.00
Go–Cart, Lite–O–Wheel, Battery Operated, Box 250.00
Go–Cart, Windup, Schuco, 6 In. 600.00
Goat, Leather Horns, Ears & Beard, Painted Eyes, Schoenhut, 7 1/2 In. 275.00
Goat, Navy, Steiff, 6 In. 395.00
Goat, Pull Toy, Goatskin, Germany, 9 x 10 In. 550.00
Golf Set, Indoor, Woman Golfer, 1 Club, Greens, Schoenhut, Box 715.00
Golfer, Trigger Activator, Wooden, Metal Arms & Club, Schoenhut, 35 In. 797.00

Good Time Charley, Smokes, Drinks, Battery Operated, 1960 .... 110.00 To 195.00
Goose, Golden, Pecking, Windup, Hops, Marx, 1924, 9 1/2 In. 280.00
Goose, Hopping, Mechanical, Tin, Windup, 5 x 9 In. 150.00
Goose, Nodding Head, Pull Toy, Tin, 3 1/2 In. 350.00
Goose, Riding, Red Goose Shoes, Head & Neck Swivel, Wooden 1450.00
Goose, Waddles Forward, Wings Flap, Windup, Germany, 5 In. 135.00
Gorilla, Carved Ears, 2–Piece Head, Schoenhut 1540.00
Graf Zeppelin, Cast Iron, 8 1/2 In. 80.00
Graf Zeppelin, Cast Iron, 8 In. 35.00
Grandfather's House, Handmade, White, Green & Red Paint, Porch, 30 In. 450.00
Grandpa Car, Battery Operated, Japan, 1950 .... 60.00
Grasshopper, Wooden, Green, Pull Toy, 10 In. ....*Illus* 27.00
Great Garloo, Marx, Box, 1960s 550.00
Greyhound Bus, Express, Friction, Tin Lithograph, 1960s, 12 In. 150.00
Griddle, Oval, 4 In. 18.00
Grocery Store, Bestmaid, Tin, Box 850.00
Grocery Store, Tin Lithograph, Products, Box 290.00
Guitar, Buck Jones, Wooden, 36 In. 225.00
Guitar, Monkees, Plastic, Pictures All Four Members 39.00
Guitar, Palomino Pony 30.00
Guitar, Traveling Wilburys, Electric, 34 x 11 In. 350.00
Guitar, Wyatt Earp, Jefferson 145.00
Gumball Machine, Fred Flintstone 25.00
Gun & Holster Set, Belt, Have Gun Will Travel, Large 35.00
Gun & Holster Set, Deputy Dawg 40.00
Gun & Holster Set, Double, Bonanza, Diamond Brand, 1960 .... 450.00
Gun & Holster Set, Double, Texan, Halco, Windowed Box 350.00
Gun & Holster Set, Double, Wyatt Earp, Box .... 150.00 To 395.00
Gun & Holster Set, Gunsmoke, Leather 45.00
Gun & Holster Set, I Spy, Plastic Pellets, Ray–Line, 1965 .... 150.00 To 198.00
Gun & Holster Set, Major Adams, Wagon Train 100.00
Gun & Holster Set, Texas Ranger, Box 50.00
Gun & Holster, Daisy, Box 125.00
Gun, Astroray, Sparks, Sound, Japan, 9 3/4 In. 75.00
Gun, BB, Winchester, Germany 120.00
Gun, Chief, Blank Shooter, Cast Iron, 1915 .... 70.00
Gun, Colt 45, Hubley 135.00
Gun, Cosmic Smoke, Space Patrol 150.00
Gun, Daisy Targeteer, Spinner Target, 4 Tubes Of Shot, Box 50.00
Gun, Fanner 50, Mattel, Pamphlet, Box 90.00
Gun, Flying Saucer, Box, 1950s 65.00
Gun, Kilgore No. 5 .... 5.00
Gun, Krypto–Ray, Set No. 94, Daisy, Box .... 750.00 To 900.00
Gun, Lone Rider, Steel 25.00
Gun, Luger, Knickerbocker 8.00
Gun, Machine, Great Eagle, Battery Operated, Japan, 1950 .... 125.00
Gun, Moonraker, James Bond, Box .... 45.00 To 65.00

Toy, Felix The Cat, Pull Toy, Tin Lithograph, 1930, 7 1/2 In.

Toy, Grasshopper, Wooden, Green, Pull Toy, 10 In.

Gun, Popgun, Double Barrel, Wyandotte, Box 38.00
Gun, Popgun, Weasel, Picture Of Weasel Both Sides, 1906 .... 45.00
Gun, Smoke, Space Patrol, Cosmic 275.00
Gun, Space Patrol, Red Cosmic Smoke 275.00
Gun, Space, Chein 30.00
Gun, Sparkling, G–Man Automatic, Marx, Box 135.00
Gun, Squirt, 1928 .... 25.00
Gun, Squirt, 1950s 7.50
Gun, Squirt, Daisy, No. 8 .... 50.00
Gun, Squirt, Planet Of The Apes, Ape Head, Plastic, Head Of Caesar, 1967 .... 29.00
Gun, Squirt, Royal Liquid, 1920s 65.00
Gun, Squirt, Rubber Squeeze, Cast Iron Barrel, Occupied Japan 40.00
Gun, Squirt, Wyandotte 17.00
Gun, Star Trek Tracer, Grand, 1967 .... 49.00
Gun, Windup, Marx, 6 In. 16.00
Gunboat, Lifeboats, Turrets, Clockwork, Painted Tin, Germany, 1904, 14 In. 3575.00
Gyroscope, Dandy, 1918 .... 7.50
Gyroscope, Metal, Box 12.00
Gyroscope, Painted Tin, Dandy, Box, 3 1/2 In. 22.00
Ham & Sam, Minstrel Team, Windup, Tin, Strauss .... 374.00 To 880.00
Handbag, With Strap, Beany & Cecil 70.00
Hangar, Airplane, Buddy L 200.00
Hangar, Airplane, Tin, Marx 125.00
Happy Bunny, Tin Lithograph, Marx, 1957, 5 1/2 In. 100.00
Happy Chick, Tin Lithograph, Marx, 1957, 5 1/2 In. 100.00
Happy Hooligan, Cop, Windup, Tin, Chein, 1930 .... 375.00
Happy Hooligan, Rubber Neck, Iron Donkey Cart, Hubley, 1910, 6 1/2 In. 635.00
Happy Munching Bunny, Windup, White, Fuzzy, Bucket Of Vegetables, 7 In. 75.00
Happy Naughty Chimp, Battery Operated, Daishin, Japan, 1960 ......75.00 To 125.00
Happy Violinist, Mechanical, Windup, Box 300.00
Harmonica, Tom Sawyer's, Box 22.00
Harold Lloyd, Funny Face, Windup, Marx, 11 In. .... 370.00 To 400.00
Hedgehog, Joggi, Raised Button, Tag, Steiff, 1950s 90.00
Helicopter, Hubley 45.00
Helicopter, Pull Toy, Paco Mfg. Co. 55.00
Helicopter, Smoking, Battery Operated, Alps, Box 175.00
Helicopter, Windup, Tin Lithograph, Box, 1950s, 3 x 6 In. 25.00
Helijet, Dad's Root Beer, 1950s 15.00
Hen, Cackling, Fisher–Price 35.00
Hen, Clucking, Lays Eggs, Crank, Tin Lithograph, Baldwin, 1950 .... 60.00 To 75.00
Hickory Dickory Dock, Mouse Ran Up The Clock, Fisher–Price 12.00
High Chair, Doll's, Tin Lithograph 125.00
Highway Henry, Tin Lithograph, Clockwork 6325.00
Highway, 4 Lanes, Raised Tunnel, Tollhouse, Cards, 1949 .... 225.00
Highway, Tunnel, Car, Bus, Electric Vibration Motion, Marx, Box, 1949 .... 225.00
Historiscope, Scenes On Rollers, Wooden Box, Milton Bradley, 10 1/4 In. 550.00
Hobby Kit, U.S. Navy Frogman, Precision, Box 150.00
Hobbyhorse, Cisco Kid 85.00
Hobbyhorse, Cottontail, Gabby Hayes, 1950s 250.00
Hobbyhorse, Dapple Gray, Lithograph 300.00
Hobbyhorse, Romper Room, 1950s 38.00
Hobbyhorse, Spring Action, Locking Wheels, 1930s 850.00
Hobbyhorse, Swing Action, White & Light Gray, Red Base 275.00
Hobo, Riding Bicycle, Tin Lithograph, American Flyer 145.00
Hobo, Skating, Windup 242.00
Hod Carrier, Boy, With Sand, Automatic, Tin, Chein, Box 145.00
Hoky–Poky Hand Car, 2 Clowns, Windup, Wyandotte 225.00
Hometown Movie Theater, Trip To North Pole, Marx, 1920s 150.00
Hopping Doggy, Mechanical, Windup, Tin, Japan, 1950s, Box 48.00
Horse & Carriage, Mechanical, Penny 110.00
Horse & Cart, Cast Iron, Original Paint, 19th Century 325.00
Horse & Groom, Pull Toy, Painted Tin, Althof Bergmann 2640.00
Horse & Wagon, Borden's, Wooden 400.00

Horse & Wagon, Pull Toy, Rider, Papier–Mache Over Wood, 29 In. 350.00
Horse Drawn, Wagon, Lowenbrau Beer, 4 Horses, 2 Alpine Drivers, 54 In. 225.00
Horse, Bucking Bronco, Celluloid, Windup, Japan, Pre–War, 5 In. 75.00
Horse, Bucking, Windup, Leather Tail, Celluloid Cowboy, Box, Japan 225.00
Horse, Gliding, Wooden, Dapple Gray, Glass Eyes, 28 In. 495.00
Horse, Platform, Tin, 7 x 7 In. 128.00
Horse, Pull Toy, Wooden Base, Tin Wheels, Painted, 8 In. 145.00
Horse, Pull Toy, Wooden Platform, Black, 7 In. 128.00
Horse, Pull Toy, Wooden, Black Mohair Cover, Original Harness, 13 In. 95.00
Horse, Pull Toy, Wooden, Hide Cover, Glass Eyes, Harness & Saddle, 29 In. 325.00
Horse, Pull Toy, Wooden, Hide Cover, Original Harness, Saddle, 12 In. 250.00
Horse, Pulling 4–Wheeled Wagon, Iron 550.00
Horse, Racing Trotter, Surrey & Driver, Mechanical, Box 120.00
Horse, Rocker, Harness, Steiff, 1963 .... 1500.00
Horse, Rocking, Brown Mohair, Burlap Type Covering, Platform, 25 In. 335.00
Horse, Rocking, Dapple Painted, 39 x 72 In. 2090.00
Horse, Rocking, High–Back Seat, Red Stenciled, Fruit Design, c.1870 .... 1200.00
Horse, Rocking, Horsehair, 1900s 950.00
Horse, Rocking, Horsehair, Glass Eyes, Oak Rockers 275.00
Horse, Rocking, Red Base, Springs, Leather Ears, Black Painted Tail 330.00
Horse, Rocking, Red Paint, Yellow Piping 165.00
Horse, Rocking, Red Saddle, Leather Ears, Cocked Head, Horsehair Mane 550.00
Horse, Rocking, Sleigh Bells, Stationary Base, 30 x 36 1/2 In. 200.00
Horse, Rocking, Stenciled Base, Original Wheels 440.00
Horse, Rocking, White, Dapple Covered, Leather Saddle, Platform, 27 In. 350.00
Horse, Rocking, White, Dapple Patterned Cloth, 24 In. 350.00
Horse, Rocking, Wooden, 45 x 37 In. 1700.00
Horse, Sulky & Driver, Cast Iron, Kenton, 7 1/2 In. 95.00
Horse, Sulky & Driver, Metal, Windup, Composition, Germany, 6 In. 110.00
Horse, With Wagon, Paper Over Wood, Henlith, Cincinnati, Oh. 235.00
Horse, Wooden, Spring, Red & Green Paint 575.00
Horses, Covered Wagon, Driver, Pioneer Spirit, Tin, Alps 65.00
Horses, Pacing, Shoofly Friction, Cast Iron, D. P. Clark Co., Pair 935.00
Hospital Set, Ben Casey M. D., Transogram, 1962 .... 98.00
House Kit, Happitime, House, Barn, Fence, Animals, Cardboard 85.00
House, Mexican Stall, Wooden, Painted Pottery, Baskets, Rugs, 21 In. 110.00
Hula Girl, Celluloid, Tin Legs & Feet, Occupied Japan 135.00
Hunter & Target Set, Marx, Box, 1960s 50.00
Hyena, Glass Eyes, Schoenhut 2750.00
Ice Skaters, On Frozen Country Lake, Electric 60.00
Incredible Edibles, Mattel, 1960s 75.00
Indian Joe, Plays Drum, Battery Operated 75.00
Indian Set, Lead, Box, Occupied Japan, 5 Piece 65.00
Indian, Windup, Holding Spear, On Horseback, Celluloid, Japan, 1930s 295.00
Inner Tube Swimming, Mighty Mouse, Vinyl, Terrytoon, Ideal, 1956 .... 89.00
Ironing Board, Folding, Metal, Pink 12.00
Ironing Board, Little Bopeep, Metal, Wolverine 15.00
Jack–In–The–Box, Casper The Ghost, Box 275.00
Jack–In–The–Box, Snoopy, Metal, Mattel .... 15.00 To 25.00
Jackie The Hornpipe Dancer, Tin Lithograph, Windup, Strauss, 9 In. 50.00
Jazzbo Jim Twin, Jigger, Windup, Unique Art .... 395.00 To 420.00
Jazzbo Jim, Dancer On The Roof, Tin Lithograph, Unique Art 220.00
Jeep, Ack Ack, Friction, Driver, Tin, Box 50.00
Jeep, Blue, Marx, 9 1/2 In. 100.00
Jeep, Dune Buggy, Tonka, Box, 1950s 65.00
Jeep, Green, Matchbox 75.00
Jeep, Jolly Joe Jumpin', Windup, Marx 125.00
Jeep, Jumping, Army, Marx 175.00
Jeep, Military Police, Tin, Arnold 45.00
Jeep, Ranger, Side–Slip Turn, Firing Machine Gun & Light, Japan, 11 In. 215.00
Jeep, TWA, Friction, 9 In. 50.00
Jeep, U.S. Navy, Friction, Tin, Japan 50.00
Jeep, Willy's, Trailer, Marx, 22 In. 100.00

Jeep, Willys, Metal, 11 In. 65.00
Jewelry Kit, Seashell, Walco Bead Co., 1945 .... 40.00
Jewelry Set, Penelope Pitstop, Card, Larami Corp., 1971, 7 1/2 x 12 In. 20.00
Joe Penner, Walker With Duck, Windup 385.00
Jolly Pals, Bulldog Pulls Monkey Cart, Tin Lithograph, Windup, 8 In. 865.00
Josie, The Walking Cow, Battery Operated, Rosko, Box 121.00
Jukebox, Bing Crosby Jr., Celluloid .... 150.00 To 400.00
Jumping Jack, Acrobat, Wooden, White Paint, Handle, 7 In. 10.00
Jumping Jack, Pull Toy, 8 In. 28.00
Kaleidoscope, Cap'n Crunch, 1964, Quaker 49.00
Kaleidoscope, Children Picture, 1974 .... 6.00
Kaleidoscope, Indian Trade Beads Pattern, 6 3/4 In. 220.00
Kandy Kitchen, Candy Maker, Hasbro, 1966 .... 35.00
Kangaroo, Straw Stuffing, Head & Arms Pivot, Stieff, 21 In. 165.00
Kazoo, Metal, 2 1/2 In. 5.00
Kettle, Bail Handle, 1 In. 15.00
Keystone Cop, Squeezer, From Happy Hooligan 85.00
Kitchen, Tole, Hanging Utensils, Stenciled Design, 19 x 11 1/2 In. 475.00
Kitten, Floppy, Tag & Button, Steiff 65.00
Knitting Machine, Automatic, Knit–O–Matic, 1966, Kenner 25.00
Laboratory Set, Microscope, Tin Lithograph, Gilbert, Box 150.00
Ladybug, On Wheels, Steiff 195.00
Lamb, White, Tag, Steiff, Box, 1950, 9 In. 285.00
Laundry Set, Wooden & Tin, Excelsior 250.00
Legos, No. 706 .... 20.00
Leopard, Mohair Plush, Green Glass Eyes, Steiff, 9 In. 40.00
Leopard, Painted Eyes, Schoenhut 825.00
Li'l Abner Dogpatch Band, Windup, Lithograph 480.00
Lincoln Logs, No. 2–LF, Box 45.00
Lincoln Logs, Original Cylinder, Complete, 1940s 20.00
Lincoln Logs, Oxen & Wagon, Box 75.00
Lion Cub, Reclining, Button, Steiff, 1950s, 8 In. 65.00
Lion, Key Wind, Schuco 85.00
Lion, On Wheels, Steiff 800.00
Lion, Windup, Mohair Covered, Tin, 5 In. 45.00
Lizard, Mechanical Action Mouth, Franz Bergman 3250.00
Locomotive, Diesel, Battery Operated, F Y T, Taiwan, 1975, Box 40.00
Locomotive, Diesel, Western Pacific, Friction, Tin, Japan, 14 1/2 In. 75.00
Looney Car, Kentucky Fried Chicken, Set Of 4 .... 32.00
Maggie & Jiggs, Spring Windup 550.00
Magic Carpet, Clockwork, Aeronautical, c.1920 .... 1300.00
Magic Kit Transogram, 1960s 38.00
Magic Lantern, 10 Slides, Instructions, Germany 185.00
Magic Slate, Atom Ant, Watkins Strathmore, 1967 .... 42.00
Magic Slate, Dr. Kildare, Doodle, Ideal, 1962, 8 x 14 In. 39.00
Magic Slate, Felix The Cat, Lowe, 1953 .... 69.00
Magic Slate, Flipper, Erasable, Lowe, 1963 .... 39.00
Magic Slate, Hector Heathcote, Lowe, 1963 .... 59.00
Magic Slate, Jetsons, Whitman, 1962 .... 59.00
Magic Tricks Set, My Favorite Martian, Gilbert 100.00
Magnastiks, Ohio Art, Box 30.00
Mail Coach, Hide–Covered Horse, Driver, Germany, 1930s 100.00
Main Street, Windup, Marx, 24 In. 225.00
Mammy, Walking, Windup, Lindstrom 365.00
Man, At Grinding Wheel, Tin, c.1915 .... 50.00
Man, Black, Dancing On Roof, Motorized, Tin Cabin, 1920 .... 385.00
Martian Totem Head, Space Patrol, Complete, Original Envelope 135.00
Mask, Cisco Kid, Face, Paper 30.00
Mask, Darth Vader, Don Post 95.00
Mask, Outer Limits, Latex 75.00
Mask, Pez, Paper 150.00
McGregor, Stands, Smokes, Sits, Battery Operated 70.00
Meat Grinder, Box 8.00

Melody Player, 5 Music Rolls, Chein, Box 100.00
Merry Makers, Windup, Tin, Marx 650.00
Merry–Go–Round, 3 Dirigibles, 2 Airplanes, Lever Action, Tin, 10 In. 550.00
Merry–Go–Round, Airplanes, Windup 150.00
Merry–Go–Round, Musical, Crank Type, Metal Lithograph, Ohio Art, 1940 .... 45.50
Merry–Go–Round, Tin Lithograph, Lever Action, Germany, 9 3/4 In. 300.00
Merry–Go–Round, Windup, Chein, 1930 .... 450.00 To 750.00
Mess Kit, G. I. Joe, Box, 1964 .... 10.00
Microscope Set, Gilbert, No. 13042, 1958 .... 110.00
Microscope Set, Gilbert, Polarized Junior, 1938 .... 85.00
Microscope, Space Patrol .... 125.00 To 135.00
Milk Wagon, Toyland, Tin Lithograph, Windup, Marx, 9 In. 120.00
Mirror, On Stand, Doll's, Swivel Oval, In Frame, 10 In. 275.00
Miss Friday The Typist, Battery Operated 225.00
Missile Launcher, Double Nike, Fires Plastic Missiles, Buddy L, 10 In. 45.00
Mixer, Cement, Foden, Matchbox, 1956 .... 20.00
Mod Monster, Battery Operated, Arms Move, Pants Fall Down, Japan 350.00
Model Kit, Airplane Construction, Spirit Of St. Louis, Metalcraft, Box 80.00
Model Kit, Airplane, Baby V Shark 45.00
Model Kit, Airplane, Fokker D7 WWI, Aurora, 1958 .... 20.00
Model Kit, Airplane, Rite–Pitch, Props, Decals, Wooden, 12 In. 4.00
Model Kit, Airplane, Tigercat, Grumman 25.00
Model Kit, Airplane, World War II Bomber, Box 20.00
Model Kit, Alfred E. Neuman, Mad's, Plastic, Aurora, 1965, 7 x 13 In. 395.00
Model Kit, Black Knight, Aurora, Complete 19.00
Model Kit, Boxcar, HO Gauge Train, Ideal 35.00
Model Kit, Build A Road, Matchbox, 1967, Box 85.00
Model Kit, Dark Shadows, Barnabas, MPC, 1968 .... 98.00
Model Kit, Dracula's Dragster, Aurora, Unassembled, Sealed, 1964 .... 498.00
Model Kit, Land Of The Giant Snake Attack, Aurora, 1968 .... 579.00
Model Kit, Little Doctor, Box, 1950s 35.00
Model Kit, London Horse–Drawn Bus 75.00
Model Kit, Maxwell Roadster, Box 35.00
Model Kit, Mercedes, 1928 Model, Box 50.00
Model Kit, Model A Station Wagon, Hubley, Unassembled, Box 150.00
Model Kit, Mummy, Plastic, Aurora 285.00
Model Kit, Paddy Wagon, Flintstones 350.00
Model Kit, Parkard Landault, 1912 Model, Box 30.00
Model Kit, Phantom & Voodoo Witch Doctor, Revell, Box 100.00
Model Kit, Pirate Blunderbuss Gun Factory, Revell, 1950s 149.00
Model Kit, Planet Of The Apes, Box 15.00
Model Kit, Rat Patrol, Plastic, Aurora, Box, 1967 .... 200.00
Model Kit, Rolls–Royce Silver Ghost, Box 35.00
Model Kit, Stingray, Midori 195.00
Model Kit, Stutz Roadster, Box 25.00
Model Kit, Torture Wheel, Ripley's Believe It Or Not Series, 1965 .... 129.00
Model Kit, Winter Scene, Cast Metal, Germany, 1930, Miniature, 31 Piece 240.00
Mold, Cat In Boot 45.00
Mold, Fox Holding Goose 45.00
Mold, Palm Tree 45.00
Mold, Steamboat 45.00
Monkey & Mouse, Dancing, Windup, Schuco 400.00
Monkey, Acrobatic, On Motorcycles, Windup, 1930s, Box 375.00
Monkey, Bellhop, Steiff, 16 In. 425.00
Monkey, Bubble Blowing, Battery Operated, Alps, Japan, 1950 .... 195.00
Monkey, Butter Churning, Clockwork, Ives 4400.00
Monkey, Clancy, Great Roller Skating, Box 150.00
Monkey, Climbing, Jocko, Tin Lithograph, Linemar, Box, 6 1/2 In. 22.00
Monkey, Climbing, Zippo, Marx 65.00
Monkey, Climbs Up & Down Tree, Coconuts, Mechanical, Tin, Emporium, 1930s 225.00
Monkey, Crapshooting, Cragston, Box, 9 1/2 In. .... 75.00 To 120.00
Monkey, Cymbal Playing, Hops & Plays, Japan, 1940s, 6 In. 35.00
Monkey, Drinking, Lighting Glass Eyes, Tin, Battery Operated, Japan 125.00

Monkey, Drummer, Windup, Schuco, Box	250.00
Monkey, Hopping, Mohair, 1912	85.00
Monkey, Hula Hoop, Key Wind, Tin Lithograph, Plastic, Japan, 9 1/2 In.	11.00
Monkey, Jacko Drinking, Windup, Marx	75.00
Monkey, On Seesaws, Tin, Windup	200.00
Monkey, On Tricycle, Tin Lithograph, Clockwork, Arnold	595.00
Monkey, Roller Skating, Frankie, Battery Operated, Box	95.00
Monkey, Sambo, Windup, Moves Arms, Head, Musical Sound, Japan, 9 1/2 In.	210.00
Monkey, Somersaulting, Windup, Tin	175.00
Monkey, Tumbling, Balancing On Tin Chair, Long Coat, Windup, 1920s	175.00
Monkey, Yes/No, Brown Mohair, Schuco, 1930s, 10 In.	225.00
Monkey, Yes/No, Schuco, 12 In.	650.00
Monkey, Zippo, Marx, 1930	130.00 To 150.00
Monorail Rocket Express, Battery Operated, Box	375.00
Moon Car, Space 1999, Friction, 1976	30.00
Moon Mullins Handcar, 6 In.	750.00 To 780.00
Moon Rocket Launcher, Ideal, Box, 1950s	50.00
Mortimer Snerd, Playing Drum, Windup, Marx	1100.00
Motorcycle, Bump 'n Go, Battery Operated, Box	75.00
Motorcycle, Echo, Lehmann	2400.00
Motorcycle, Electric Headlights, Marx, Box	50.00
Motorcycle, Harley-Davidson, Hubley, c.1933	4180.00
Motorcycle, Harley-Davidson, Iron Wheels, Green, 5 In.	350.00
Motorcycle, Harley-Davidson, Policeman Driver, Cast Iron	450.00
Motorcycle, Harley-Davidson, Sidecar, Cast Iron, Hubley	500.00
Motorcycle, Harley-Davidson, Tin Lithograph	245.00
Motorcycle, Patrol, Red, Hubley	225.00
Motorcycle, Police, Turn Signals, Sound, Battery Operated, Bandai, 11 In.	350.00
Motorcycle, Policeman, Cast Iron, Marx, 8 1/2 In.	250.00
Motorcycle, Policeman, Friction, Hadson	85.00
Motorcycle, Policeman, Sidecar, Marx, 1940s, 8 1/2 In.	375.00
Motorcycle, Policeman, Windup, Metal, Rubber Tires, Ny-Lint, 7 In.	165.00
Motorcycle, Red, Gold Trim, Rubber Tires, Hubley, 1934, 7 In.	385.00
Motorcycle, Rookie Cop, Cast Iron, Marx, 1930s	225.00
Motorcycle, Rubber, Pink, Auburn, 4 In.	25.00
Motorcycle, Sidecar & Driver, Hubley	150.00
Motorcycle, Sidecar, Cast Iron, Marked 12, 1889	110.00
Motorcycle, Sidecar, Marx	325.00
Motorcycle, Sidecar, Sales Tag, Marusan, 8 1/2 In.	2300.00
Motorcycle, Spider Man's, Corgi, Box	60.00
Motorcycle, Tricky, Tin, Windup, Marx, Box, 1930s, 4 1/2 In.	300.00
Motorcycle, Windup, Camouflage, Sparks, Tin, Japan	275.00
Motorcycle, Windup, Technolix, Box, 7 In.	395.00
Motorcycle, Windup, Tin, 1951	210.00
Mouse, Somersaulting, Velvet Cloth On Wire, Key Wind, Schuco, 3 3/4 In.	66.00
Mr. Bunny, Spectacles, Papier-Mache, Yellow Pants, 6 In.	65.00
Mr. Dan Coffee Drinking Man, Windup, Japan, 1950	150.00
Mr. Fox, Magician, Disappearing Rabbit, Battery Operated	135.00 To 325.00
Mr. Gori Gorilla, Tumbling, Battery Operated, Alps, Japan, 1960	50.00
Music Box, Smurf	15.00
Myriopticon Optical, Milton Bradley	1100.00
Mystery Box, Popsicle Pete, Prize, Ice Cream Stick, Toys, Clicker	50.00
Naughty Boy, Battery Operated, Lehmann, Germany, 1904, 5 In.	935.00
Neapolitan Balloon Blower, Gino, Battery Operated, Box, Rosho	130.00
Negro Head, Pull String, Bug Eyes Spin, Tin, 1910	25.00
Nursing Set, Doll's, Box, Occupied Japan, 7 Piece	28.00
Nutty Mad Indian, Battery Operated, Marx, Box, 14 In.	125.00
Nuttynibs, Battery Operated, Tin, Marx, c.1955	110.00
Organ, Church, Hand Crank, Tin, Chein	120.00 To 150.00
Ostrich, Schoenhut	750.00
Our Gang, On Card, Mego, 1975, Set Of 6	260.00
Outer Space Apeman, Battery Operated, Walks, Swings Arms, Box	95.00
Owl, Tag & Button, Steiff, 2 In.	35.00

Ox & Cart, Cast Iron, Yellow, Red, 5 In. 76.00
Paddy & The Pig, Lehmann, Germany, 1903, 5 3/4 In. 825.00
Pail & Tea Set, Little Red Riding Hood, Ohio Art, 1960 .... 115.00
Pail, Children, Tin, 1920, 2 3/4 In. 32.00
Pail, Cover, Sand, Flags, Tin 50.00
Pail, Cowboy Roping Steer, 5 In. 25.00
Pail, Humpty Dumpty, Ohio Art 35.00
Pail, Peter Rabbit, Shovel, Chein, Large 10.00
Pail, Raggedy Ann & Andy, Chein, 1973 .... 18.00
Pail, Scenes, Gold, Green, MacDonald Mfg. Co. Ltd., Toronto, 4 In. 300.00
Paint Set, Call To The Colors, Transogram 30.00
Paint Set, Pinky Lee, Box, 1955 .... 70.00
Paint Set, Scrappy & Girlfriend, Crayons, Sheets, 1930s, 17 x 12 x 2 In. 45.00
Paint Set, Zorro, Oil, Unused 125.00
Panda, Drummer, Windup, Tin, Box 20.00
Panda, Drumming, Clockwork, China, Box, 4 1/2 In. 45.00
Panda, In Rocking Chair, Battery Operated 155.00
Panda, Jointed, Schuco, Miniature 175.00
Panda, Yes–No Head, 8 In. 310.00
Parrot, Articulated Legs, Steiff, 6 In. 138.00
Pastry Set, Transogram, Box 40.00
Peacock, Windup, Tin, Germany 800.00
Pedal Car, Airflow, Red, Black & White Stripes, Skippy Mfg. Co. 3500.00
Pedal Car, Airplane, Airmail, Steelcraft 2000.00
Pedal Car, Airplane, Falcon, Full Instrumentation, Toledo 2500.00
Pedal Car, Airplane, Gypsy Moth, Radial Engine 1600.00
Pedal Car, Airplane, Spirit Of St. Louis, Gendron 2250.00
Pedal Car, Auburn Roadster, Supercharged, Steelcraft 4250.00
Pedal Car, Austin J40, Pneumatic Tires, 1955 .... 3220.00
Pedal Car, Austin, Pathfinders, c.1948 .... 3650.00
Pedal Car, Austin, Twin–Cam, Racing Car 7000.00
Pedal Car, Blue Line Motorcoach 1800.00
Pedal Car, Cadillac Convertible, No. 585, Dark Red, A. N. Co., 1914, 47 In. 5000.00
Pedal Car, Chrysler, Maroon, Convertible, Silver Accents, Murray, 36 In. 367.00
Pedal Car, Chrysler, Steelcraft, 1941 .... 995.00
Pedal Car, Corvette, 1960 Model 50.00
Pedal Car, Dodge, Black Fenders, Apple Red, Steelcraft, 1937 .... 1600.00
Pedal Car, Dud Wagon, 1955 .... 80.00
Pedal Car, Duesenberg, Tandem 4600.00
Pedal Car, Fire Truck, 1949 .... 250.00 To 395.00
Pedal Car, Fire Truck, Air Flow, Red & White Paint, Steelcraft 3400.00
Pedal Car, Fire Truck, American 7000.00
Pedal Car, Fire Truck, Fire Fighter Unit No. 808 .... 165.00
Pedal Car, Fire Truck, Ladder, 45 In. 875.00
Pedal Car, Firetruck 150.00
Pedal Car, Ford, Model A, Roadster Pickup 7000.00
Pedal Car, Horse & Buggy, Arney Specialty Co., 1909, 28 x 60 In. 3025.00
Pedal Car, Horse, Steel, England .... 260.00 To 390.00
Pedal Car, Kiddie Car, Eagle 3630.00
Pedal Car, Kiddie Car, Wooden, Stencils, 1915, 39 x 18 In. 3630.00
Pedal Car, Lincoln, 1937 .... 2200.00
Pedal Car, MG 7080.00
Pedal Car, Mustang 250.00
Pedal Car, No. 8, Orange & Yellow 1100.00
Pedal Car, Oswald, 1930s 3700.00
Pedal Car, Pacer, Yellow, c.1965 .... 198.00
Pedal Car, Packard, Painted Steel, Upholstered Seats, 53 In. 1870.00
Pedal Car, Police, 1952 .... 700.00
Pedal Car, Racing Car, Orange & Yellow, Painted Exhaust 1100.00
Pedal Car, Streamliner Car, Steelcraft 2825.00
Pedal Car, Stutz, 1947 Model, 47 In. 4500.00
Pedal Car, Tow Truck, 1949 .... 475.00
Pedal Car, Tractor, Case, 1956 .... 235.00

Pedal Car, Tractor, Chain Driven	55.00
Pedal Car, Tractor, International Harvester, With Trailer	180.00
Pedal Car, Tractor, Western Flyer	80.00
Pedal Car, Vauxhall, Coach Built, Wooden & Sheet Metal	7700.00
Pedal Car, Wooden, Spoke Wheels, Iron Rims, Green Paint, 59 In.	450.00
Pedal Horse, Mobo, Tin, Victorian	600.00
Pedometer, Sgt. Preston	40.00
Peep Show, Wooden Case, 6 Part Tableaus, Cards, 14 In.	660.00
Penguin, Skier, Windup, Japan, 1950	65.00
Periscope, Secret Agent, 1950s	45.00
Phaeton, Open, Hess, c.1915	3740.00
Phonograph, Genola	300.00
Piano, Painted Cherubs, Mahogany Finish, Schoenhut	50.00
Piano, Player, Loden, 16 Rolls, Chein, Box	500.00
Piano, Player, Plastic, 8 Rolls, Chein	300.00
Piano, Schoenhut, 16 x 21 In.	85.00
Piano, Schroeder's, Peanuts Comic Strip	50.00
Piano, Upright, 15 Ivory Keys, Schoenhut	65.00
Pierrot, Tumbling, Somersaults, Windup, Occupied Japan	320.00
Piggy Cook, Cooks & Seasons Eggs Over Stove, Battery Operated, Box	175.00
Pile Driver, Panama, Tin Lithograph, Wire, Wolverine, 17 In.	120.00
Pinocchio, Cymbal Player, Windup, Tin, Japan, Box, 1950s. 12 In.	250.00
Pip–Squeak, Baby In Cradle, Hand Painted, Wooden, Leather Bellows	110.00
Pip–Squeak, Boy, Pie–Eyed, J. L. Prescott	20.00
Pip–Squeak, Cat, Papier–Mache	125.00
Pip–Squeak, Cat, Victorian	95.00
Pip–Squeak, Chicken & Chicks	660.00
Pip–Squeak, Clown's Head, Atop Accordion	195.00
Pip–Squeak, Duck	247.50
Pip–Squeak, Lamb In Cage	225.00
Pip–Squeak, Parrot	275.00
Pip–Squeak, Rooster, Spring Legs	75.00
Pirate Ship, Battery Operated, 1960, Japan	125.00
Pith Helmet, Soap Box Derby, 1950s	38.00
Play Golf, Windup, Strauss, Box	825.00 To 1250.00
Play Set, Battle Of The Blue & Gray, Marx, 1960, 26 x 14 In.	995.00
Play Set, Ben Hur, Marx	995.00
Play Set, Cape Canaveral, No. 4526, Marx	135.00
Play Set, Fort Apache, Marx, 1959, 14 x 26 In.	98.00
Play Set, Fort Apache, No. 3680, Metal Log Cabin, Stockade, 24 x 15 In.	100.00
Play Set, Green Giant Farm–N–Factory	75.00
Play Set, Lost In Space, Mattel, 1966	1250.00
Play Set, Robin Hood, Marx, Box	295.00
Play Set, Shop King, Marx, Box	95.00
Play Set, Super Circus, Marx, 1950s	325.00
Play Set, The Blue & The Gray, Marx	195.00
Play Set, Tom Corbett Space Academy, Marx	295.00
Play Set, Wizard Of Oz, Box	75.00
Playdoh, Captain Kangaroo, 4 Pack	45.00
Playground Set, Dollhouse, Cast Iron, Kilgore, 3 Piece	65.00
Playsax, QRS, 6 Rolls, Directions, Box	150.00
Pogo Stick, Spiderman, Box	75.00
Police Set, Dragnet, On Card, 1950s	45.00
Pony, Riding, Leather Hooves, Wheels, Steiff, 1950s	325.00
Porky Pig, Sun Rubber	25.00
Porter, Train, Black, Barclay, 3 In.	45.00
Potty, Blue & White Graniteware	20.00
Pound A Peg Table, 1940s	30.00
Printing Press, Star, Box	40.00
Printing Press, Superior, Box	39.00
Printing Set, Western Tire Store Giveaway, 1950s	10.00
Projector, Brown Metal, Kodatoy, Box	125.00
Projector, Electric, Tan Metal, Sawyer	30.00

Projector, Give–A–Show, Kenner .... 30.00 To 55.00
Pumper, Fire, Twin Horse Drawn, Cast Iron, James Fallows 5280.00
Rabbit, Boy, Seesaw Action & Rotates, Windup, Japan, 7 In. 235.00
Rabbit, Drumming, Remote Control .... 65.00 To 70.00
Rabbit, Mohair, Sitting On Haunches, Brown, Germany, 1926, 32 In. 330.00
Rabbit, On Wheels, Clemens 85.00
Rabbit, Pulling Egg Carriage, Yellow Chick, Celluloid, 4 In. 45.00
Rabbit, Pushing Cart, Chein 47.00
Rabbit, Trix Cereal, Squeeze, Split 12.00
Rabbit, Windup, Chein, 1930s 150.00
Race Track, Indy 500, Marx, Box 90.00
Radio, Music Box, Fisher–Price, Pocket 3.50
Radio, Trick, Mouse Jumps Out, Tune, Tin Lithograph, 1950s, 3 x 5 In. 25.00
Railbus, Working Headlights, Plastic Body, Zinc Frames, Box, Marklin 22.00
Railroad System, No. 114 Station & Tracks, Ives, Miniature 800.00
Rake & Plow, Marx 25.00
Range Rider, On Black Horse, Swinging Rope, Windup 110.00
Rattle, 5 Small Bells Attached To Silver Holder, Pearl Handle 100.00
Rattle, Bells, Heart, Whistle, Twisted Stem, Sterling Silver 155.00
Rattle, Clown, Blue, Celluloid, 1920s, 7 3/4 In. 20.00
Rattle, Father Christmas, Teether, Mother–of–Pearl Ring 275.00
Rattle, Whistle Handle, Tin 25.00
Ray Gun Ring, Quaker Quisp 150.00
Redcap, Black, Bags, Barclay, 3 In. 50.00
Refrigerator, Alaska, Glass Cubes 85.00
Refrigerator, Multi–Brown, Lithograph Food, Wolverine 50.00
Refrigerator, Polar 27.50
Reindeer, Felt Antlers, Steiff 60.00
Rex Mars Planet Patrol, Tin Building, Plastic Figures, Marx, 1950s 415.00
Rifle, Agent Zero M, Radio, Mattel, 24 In. 150.00
Rifle, Land Of The Giants, Shot 'n Stick, Shots Missiles, Remco, 32 In. 300.00
Rifle, Red Ryder, Plastic Stock, Daisy, 34 In. 25.00
Rifle, Wanted Dead Or Alive 25.00
Ring, Cap'n Crunch Cannon, 1963, Quaker 39.00
Ring, Captain Video, Seal 350.00
Ring, Green Hornet, Logo, 1966 .... 20.00
Ring, Kellogg's Baseball Game 35.00
Ring, Kellogg's Crackle, Moveable Face 200.00
Ring, King Kong, Figural, 3–D, 1962 .... 4.00
Ring, Sky King, Magni–Glo Writing, 1949 .... 65.00
Ring, Sky King, Mystery Picture 35.00
Ring, Sky King, Radar 200.00
Ring, Sky King, Teleblinker 125.00
Ring, Space Patrol, Hydrogen Ray Gun ....90.00 To 100.00
Ring, Terry & The Pirates, Gold Detector, 1943 .... 60.00
Ring, Zorro, Black Plastic 22.00
Road Grader, Tonka 75.00
Road Race, Mechanical, 3 Cars, Ohio Art, Box, Large 195.00
Road Race, Windup, 2 Cars, Figure 8 Track, Havana, U.S. Zone, Box 76.00
Road Roller, Hubley, 15 In. 3800.00
Robot Bus, No. 300, Windup, Woodhaven, 1950s, 14 In. 250.00
Robot, Astronaut, Tin, Black, Battery Operated, S. H., Japan, Box, 12 In. 250.00
Robot, Atomic Man, Lithograph, Box 950.00
Robot, Attacking Martian, Battery Operated, Tin, Plastic, Japan, 10 In. 77.00
Robot, Blue Zoomer, Windup 625.00
Robot, Colonel Haphazard, Walks, Battery Operated, Marx, 11 1/2 In. 950.00
Robot, High Wheel, Black, Box 485.00
Robot, In Mercedes, Rolls Forward, Sparking Turret, Sound, Japan, 8 In. 425.00
Robot, Jupiter, Box 6000.00
Robot, King Ding, Plastic, Red, Yellow & Blue, Complete, 14 In. 42.00
Robot, Lost In Space, Box 150.00
Robot, Man From Mars, Windup, Walks Forward, Shooting Gun, Irwin, 11 In. 900.00
Robot, Marvelous Mike, On Bulldozer, Swadar, 1950s 225.00

Robot, Mighty, Keywind, Noguchi Shoten, 5 1/2 In. 77.00
Robot, Missile, Mechanical, Plastic, Japan, Box, 5 1/2 In. 16.50
Robot, Monster, Battery Operated, Helmet Opens, Dragon Head, Box 95.00
Robot, Monster, Battery Operated, Plastic, Japan, Box, 9 In. 5.50
Robot, Monster, Mechanical, Tin, Japan, Box, 9 1/2 In. 242.00
Robot, Mr. Machine, Whistles This Old Man, Walks 45.00
Robot, Mr. Mercury, Battery Operated, Walks, Blinks Eyes, Japan, 10 In. 110.00
Robot, On Tractor, Runs Forward & Reverse, Spinning Fan, Showa, 10 In. 440.00
Robot, Planet, Remote Controlled, Tin, 9 In. 523.00
Robot, Radical, Battery Operated, Cragston 1500.00
Robot, Radicon, Box 7500.00
Robot, Ranger, Plastic, Battery Operated, Japan, Box 595.00
Robot, Red Fighter Bandit, Battery Operated, Plastic, Japan, 10 In. 13.00
Robot, Robert, Gray & Red Plastic, Talks, Remote Gun, Ideal, 1950s, 14 In. 659.00
Robot, Roboy, Silver Warrior, Battery Operated, Hong Kong 60.00
Robot, Rom The Space Knight, Battery Operated, Parker Bros., 13 In. 22.00
Robot, Silver Sparky, Windup 250.00
Robot, Silver Warrior, Battery Operated, CDI, Hong Kong, Box, 1978 .... 60.00
Robot, Singing, Missile Shooting, Battery, Plastic, Japan, 11 In. 50.00
Robot, Space Fighter, Battery Operated, Japan, Box 100.00
Robot, Space Rocket Solar–X, Battery Operated, Tin, Japan, 15 In. 55.00
Robot, Space Tank, Skuper, Friction, Tin, Japan, Box, 9 In. 578.00
Robot, Spaceman, Windup, Tin, Plastic, Alps, Box, 7 1/2 In. 230.00
Robot, Sparking Mike, Windup, Tin, 1950s, 8 In. 825.00
Robot, Sparkling, Box 375.00
Robot, Sparky, Windup, Gray, Red, Japan, Box, 8 In. 230.00
Robot, Super Astronaut, Silver, Japan, Box, 12 In. 280.00
Robot, Train, 1955 .... 4500.00
Robot, Tulip Head, 1960 .... 1550.00
Robot, Windup, Silver, Japan, 7 1/2 In. 215.00
Robot, X–2, 1952 .... 600.00
Robot, YM–3, Plastic, Says Warning In Japanese & English, Box, 16 In. 85.00
Robotoy, Chain Driven, Electric, Red, Green, Headlights, Buddy L, 1932 .... 1650.00
Rocker, Raggedy Ann, 1972 .... 65.00
Rocket Ship, Mechanical, Hungary, Box 85.00
Rocket Ship, Monorail, Linemar, Box 250.00
Rocket Ship, Tin Lithograph, Original Labels, Set Of 3 .... 135.00
Rocket, Docking, Battery Operated, Tin, Plastic, Daiya, Japan, 16 In. 165.00
Rocket, Fighter, Windup, Marx 375.00
Rocket, Rolls Forward, Sparks & Noise, Japan, 12 3/4 In. 385.00
Rocket, Runway, Space Patrol, Battery Operated 350.00
Rocket, Space Lithograph Allover, Windup, Japan, 5 x 5 In. 295.00
Rocket, V–1, Friction, Japan, 1950s, 12 In. 695.00
Rocket, V–2, Friction, Japan, 1950s, 7 1/2 In. 235.00
Rocket, XX–2, Red Plastic Rotating Tail, Sparkling, Friction, Tin, 1960s 225.00
Roller Coaster, 1 Car, Windup, Chein, 1950 .... 195.00 To 250.00
Roller Skating Chef, Windup, Japan, Box 475.00
Rolling Pin, Wooden, 7 In. 7.50
Roly Poly, Clown, Schoenhut, 15 In. .... 445.00 To 470.00
Roly Poly, Clown, Schoenhut, Yellow, 11 In. 725.00
Roly Poly, Clown, Tin Lithograph, Chein, 6 In. 220.00
Roly Poly, Dutch Girl, Papier–Mache, 5 3/4 In. 33.00
Roly Poly, Keystone Kop, Papier–Mache, 5 1/2 In. 66.00
Roly Poly, Man, Clown Face, Yellow Hat, Germany 245.00
Roly Poly, Rabbit, Pressed Paper, Glass Eyes, 8 In. 44.00
Roly Poly, Santa Claus 325.00
Roly Poly, Witch, Red Plastic, Celluloid, 4 In. 270.00
Rooster, Cock–A–Doodle–Do, Battery Operated, Japan 150.00
Sailor, Windup, Tin, Cloth Clothes, Lehmann, 1903, Box 1480.00
Sally The Seal, Battery Operated, Alps, Box, 1981 .... 45.00 To 50.00
Sam The Gardener, Windup, Marx, 1940 .... 250.00
Satellite Launcher, Ideal, Box, 1950s 60.00
Saxophone, Silver, Emenee Toys, Case, 1953 .... 35.00

Schoolboy, Windup, Tin, Germany	995.00
Scissors, Puppy, Electric, Linemar	45.00
Scooter, 3 Wheels, Clips On Child's Shoe, Small	50.00
Scooter, Footrests For Guiding, Original Stencil, c.1900	650.00
Scooter, Pee Wee Herman, Box	125.00
Scooter, Red, 1950s	22.50
Scope, Sooper Snooper, 4–Way, Marx, 1960s	55.00
Sea Lion, Painted Eyes, Performing Ball, Schoenhut	550.00
Sea Sled, G. I. Joe, Box, 1966	85.00
Seal & Polar Bear, Pull Toy, Bear Rings Bell, Seal Bounces Ball, 10 In.	220.00
Seal, Trick, Windup, Celluloid, Occupied Japan	75.00
Secret Print Putty, Man From U. N. C. L. E., 1965	24.00
Sewing Kit, Little Miss Seamstress, Sewing Machine, Doll, Patterns, Case	35.00
Sewing Machine, Holly Hobbie	5.00 To 7.50
Sewing Machine, Iron Table Top, Black, Hand Crank Wheel, 6 1/2 In.	325.00
Sewing Machine, Junior Gateway, Red	45.00
Sewing Machine, Kay & EE, Instructions	50.00
Sewing Machine, Little Betty, England	35.00 To 75.00
Sewing Machine, Little Mother, Red Metal, 8 x 7 1/2 In.	58.00
Sewing Machine, Necchi, 6 5/8 x 5 1/4 In.	45.00
Sewing Machine, Singer, Cast Iron Top, Hand Operated Wheel, 6 In.	300.00
Sewing Machine, Singer, Hand Crank, Traveling Case	45.00
Sewing Machine, Singer, Touch & Sew, Battery Or Electric, Case	55.00
Sewing Machine, Stenciled, Germany	80.00
Sewing Machine, Stitch Master	45.00
Sewing Machine, Stitchwell, Box	65.00
Sheep, Pull Toy, Papier–Mache, Lamb's Wool Cover, Platform, 6 In.	500.00
Sheep, Wooden, Papier Mache, White Flannel Coat, Germany, 3 1/2 In.	75.00
Sheriff, 2 Guns, Battery Operated, Cragstan	165.00
Shooting Gallery, No. 9, Baby Rack, Brinkman Engineering Co.	500.00
Shooting Gallery, Paper Lithograph, Wooden, Schoenhut	550.00
Shooting Gallery, Rubber Ball, Wooden Framework, Schoenhut, 17 In.	550.00
Shooting Gallery, Windup, Ohio Art, Box	50.00 To 100.00
Shooting Gallery, Windup, Tin, Wyandotte	45.00
Showdown Sam, Battery Operated, Box	35.00
Shuttling Dog Train, Battery Operated, Cragstan, Japan, 1950	150.00
Sign Set, Matchbox, No. 4, Box, 8 Piece	25.00
Signal System, Mobile Radio Loudspeaker, Remco, Box	135.00
Simpsons, Homer, Maggie, Bart, Marge, Lisa, Burger King	25.00
Sketch Board, Bugs Bunny Looney Tunes Cartoon O'graph, Box	65.00
Ski Ride, Skiing Lithograph, Rider, Chein	350.00
Skillet, Cast Iron, 4 In.	17.50
Skip Rope Animals, Mechanical, Japan, Windup, Box	142.00
Skull, Windup	12.00
Sled, Auto Wheel Coaster, Wooden, George W. Wetherbee & Co.	305.00
Sled, Blue Paint, Gold Striping & Red Runners, 15 In.	1320.00
Sled, Child's, Wood, Original Varnish, Red, Black, Striping, 40 1/4 In.	425.00
Sled, Clipper, Wooden, Painted & Stenciled, 14 1/2 In.	412.00
Sled, Doll's, Blue Stenciled	495.00
Sled, Doll's, Push	175.00
Sled, Enclosed, Plush Lining, Tasseled Curtains, Canada	990.00
Sled, Flexy Racer, Wheels, Flexible Flyer, 1940s	400.00
Sled, Gooseneck, Red Ground, Landscape Scene	895.00
Sled, Ochre Paint, Floral Sprig, Polychrome, Late 19th Century, 36 In.	825.00
Sled, Oil Painted Lake & Trees, Original Paint, 1880	875.00
Sled, Pace Arctic Clipper, Painted Reindeer & Snow Scene	1200.00
Sled, Painted Floral Pattern, Wooden & Metal, 35 In.	250.00
Sled, Painted Platform, Iron Runners, 19th Century, 33 In.	247.00
Sled, Push, Carved Pinwheel On Side, Red Paint	302.50
Sled, Snowbird, Iron Faced Rails, Austria, 19th Century, 47 In.	100.00
Sled, Torpedo, Wooden, Iron Runners	68.00
Sled, Whitney Point, N.Y., Monogrammed	2640.00
Smoking Grandpa, Japan, Box	150.00

Toy, Stove, Buck's Jr., Cast Iron, Cooking
Utensils

Toy, Wastebasket, Cowboy, Metal, 11 In.

So–Hi Walking Figure & Rickshaw, Plastic, 1965, Post	89.00
Soaky, Quick Draw McGraw	45.00
Soldier, Argyll & Sutherland Highlanders, Britains, 3/4 To 2 1/2 In.	100.00
Soldier, Black Watch Pipers, Cherilea, Set Of 8	65.00
Soldier, Canadian Mounted Police, Britains, No. 1349, 5 Piece	165.00
Soldier, Canadian Mounties, Lead, Red & Blue Uniforms, England, 12 Piece	77.00
Soldier, Coldstream Guards Band, Britains, 1950s, 37 Piece	295.00
Soldier, Confederate, Britains, 7 Piece	82.50
Soldier, Coronation Display, Britains, Box, 19 Piece	275.00
Soldier, Egyptian Infantry, Multicolored Uniforms, Britains, 2 1/2 In.	154.00
Soldier, Horse Guard, Britains, 5 Piece	150.00
Soldier, Infantry, Britains, No. 432, 8 Piece	88.00
Soldier, Marble Shooter, Wooden, Metal Fittings, Folk Art, 12 In.	75.00
Soldier, Marine Corps Band, Dress Uniform, Britains, 21 Piece	2640.00
Soldier, Marlboro Black Watch Pipe & Drum Parade, Boxes, 18 Piece	225.00
Soldier, Motorcycle Corps, Britains, No. 1791, 4 Piece	225.00
Soldier, Mountain Artillery, Britains, No. 28, Box, 14 Piece	440.00
Soldier, Mounted, Brown & Black Horses, Britains, 3 In., 7 Piece	88.00
Soldier, Range Finder & Operator, Britains, No. 1639	29.00
Soldier, Royal Marine Band, Britains, No. 1291, Box, 12 Piece	550.00
Soldier, Royal Marine Parade Band, Britains, No. 9140, Box	225.00
Soldier, Scottish Highlanders, Britains, 7 Piece	175.00
Soldier, Stretcher Party, Britains, No. 1719, 3 Piece	48.00
Soldiers, Beachhead Landing Play Set, World War II, Ideal, 1960s	395.00
Son Of Garloo, Windup, Metal, Marx	295.00
Space Bubble, Matt Mason, Box	45.00
Space Capsule, G. I. Joe, Official, Box	400.00
Space Patrol Set, Rex Mars, Marx, Box	295.00
Spaceman, Man From Mars, Windup, Irwin, Box	1200.00
Spaceman, Tin, Windup, Plastic, Linemar, 6 In.	175.00
Speed Wagon, Windup, Strauss	198.00
Sprinkling Can, Tin Lithograph Of Porky Pig, Ohio Art	17.50
Spur Set, Western, On Card	22.00
Stagecoach, Britains, Box	300.00
Stagecoach, Removable Roof, Painted, Wooden	3500.00
Stamping Set, Laurel & Hardy, 6 Stampers, Larry Harmon, 6 x 9 In.	25.00
Stamping Set, Sky King	20.00
Station, Gasoline, Tin Lithograph, Penny Toy, 4 In.	220.00
Steam Engine, Big Giant, Wheeden, Box	275.00
Steam Engine, Falk, Germany	350.00
Steam Engine, Mandola	150.00
Steam Engine, Weeden Eureka, Cast Iron, Smokestack, 1910, 6 x 7 In.	247.00
Steam Roller, Wooden Roller, Cast Iron, 6 1/2 In.	300.00
Steam Shovel, Caterpillar Treads, Structo	95.00
Steam Shovel, No. 395, Wyandotte	125.00
Steam Shovel, On Tracks, Buddy L, 22 In.	4500.00
Steam Shovel, Rubber Threads, Structo	195.00

Stove, A–Burner, Brass Oven, Doors & Feet, 10 1/2 x 7 3/4 In. 250.00
Stove, Arcade, Buff & Green, Signed 125.00
Stove, Buck's Jr., Cast Iron, Cooking Utensils ....*Illus* 3410.00
Stove, Cook, Eagle, Cast Iron 895.00
Stove, Cook, Queen, Cast Iron 40.00
Stove, Crescent, Cast Iron, 8 In. 60.00
Stove, Crescent, Cast Iron, 12 In. ....70.00 To 100.00
Stove, Crown, Nickel Plated Cast Iron, Removable Burner, 11 1/2 In. 70.00
Stove, Eagle, Embossed Nickel Plated Cast Iron, 2 Doors, Scuttle, 13 In. 50.00
Stove, Gothic, Cast Iron, Wette, 15 x 18 In. 995.00
Stove, Holly Hobbie, Electric 45.00
Stove, Karr, Warming Oven, Blue Graniteware, 21 x 13 In. 5500.00
Stove, Kitchen, Tin, Marx, 16 x 15 In. 27.00
Stove, Little Cook 1050.00
Stove, Little Lady, Electric, Green & White 275.00
Stove, Majestic, 31 In. 4000.00
Stove, Mt. Penn 750.00
Stove, Nickle Plated, Doors Open, Cast Iron, Pastime 360.00
Stove, Queen, Cast Iron, Utensils 50.00
Stove, Quick Meal, Pots, Canisters, Cast Iron 900.00
Stove, STAR On Front, Baking Pans 95.00
Stove, Tasty Bake, Electric, Metal Utensils 40.00
Stroller, Baby, Lithograph Figure In Stroller, Penny Toy, 2 3/4 In. 145.00
Stroller, Doll's, Blondie & Dagwood, 1949 .... 125.00
Stroller, Doll's, Wicker, Heywood Wakefield 260.00
Stroller, Doll's, Wicker, Wooden, Metal Frame & Wheels, 29 In. 400.00
Stroller, Doll, Stenciled Joel Ellis 350.00
Strutting Sam, Battery Operated 192.00
Submarine, Automatic, Seawolf, Dives & Surfaces 125.00
Submarine, Nautilus, Propeller Driven, Crank Friction, Japan, 12 1/2 In. 60.00
Submarine, Sea Wolf Atomic, Keywind, Sutcliffe, Box, 10 1/2 In. 195.00
Suffragette, Clockwork, Ives 8250.00
Suitcase, Ginny, Vogue's, 1950s 35.00
Super Jet, Fisher–Price 210.00
Sure Shot Marble Shooter, Original Box 85.00
Sweeper, Musical, Susy Goose 6.00
Swimmer, Windup, Celluloid & Tin, Japan, 1930s, 5 In. 125.00
Swing Band Set, Cast Iron, Original Paint, Hubley, 6 Piece 1045.00
Swing, Doll's, Victorian 105.00
Swing, Horse, Original Paint & Tack, Whitney Reed 895.00
Switch 'n Go Dump Trailer, Mattel, Box, 1966 .... 22.00
Sword, Zorro, 1950–1960 .... 22.00
Table, ABC, Noah's Ark 295.00
Talking Teeth, Windup, Box, 1949 .... 15.00
Tank, 1940s Model, Arcade 800.00
Tank, Army Corps, Tin Lithograph, Marx, 1960s 145.00
Tank, Army, No. 12, Sparking, 1940s, 9 1/2 In. 260.00
Tank, Army, Ride–On, Ideal 28.00
Tank, Battery Operated, Plastic, Daisy, Box 125.00
Tank, Bulldog, Battery Operated, Plastic, Remco, Box, 15 x 10 1/2 In. 100.00
Tank, Crank Turret, 10 Wooden Wheels, Structo 150.00
Tank, Gama, Clockwork, 6 In. 145.00
Tank, Key Wind, Figure Pops Out, Marx, 10 In. 93.00
Tank, Space Explorer, Friction, Tin, 7 In. 65.00
Tank, Tiger Joe, Remco, 1959, 23 x 14 In. 98.00
Tank, Tin Lithograph, Sparker, Mechanical, Windup, Marx, 10 In. 198.00
Tank, TR–2 Robo, Arms Move, Lights & Sound, Japan, 5 1/2 In. .... 215.00 To 275.00
Tank, Turnover, Windup, Marx ....40.00 To 110.00
Tank, World War I, Doughboy & Flag Move Up & Down, Marx 495.00
Tank, World War I, Soldier Pops Up, Beige, Green, Windup, Marx, 10 In. 83.00
Tank, World War I, Weight Driven, Shoots, Germany, 10 In. 192.00
Tap Tap The Gardener, Lehmann 475.00
Target Set, Charlie's Angels, Placo, 1978 .... 75.00

Target Set, Gunsmoke, Stand–Up	150.00
Target Set, Planet Patrol, Marx, 1950s	119.00
Target Set, Quick Draw McGraw, Baba Looey, Moving, Battery Operated, Box	180.00
Target Set, Untouchables, Arcade	175.00
Taxi, Amos 'n' Andy, Fresh Air Taxi	825.00 To 1700.00
Taxi, Arcade, Cast Iron, Yellow, 8 In.	695.00
Taxi, Bing	1980.00
Taxi, Checker, Windup, Courtland, 1940s	120.00
Taxi, Checker, Yellow & Orange Lithograph, 13 In.	170.00
Taxi, Driver, Rear Doors Open, Windup, Tin, Orber	75.00
Taxi, Model, 5 Windows, Desk Top, G. M. C., 1950s	85.00
Taxi, Yellow, Arcade, 5 In.	600.00
Taxi, Yellow, Battery Operated, Door Opens, Meter Turns, Box	145.00
Tea Set, Bopeep, Tableware Included, Tin, 1944	125.00
Tea Set, Bunnies, Lions, Giraffes, Duchess, Box, 1950s	65.00
Tea Set, Child's, Platonite, Fired On Colors, 10 Piece	18.00
Tea Set, Child's, White, Cobalt & Gold Trim, 7 Piece	395.00
Tea Set, Children Playing With Animals, Seesaw, Germany, 18 Piece	250.00
Tea Set, Circus Design, Tin, Ohio Art, 30 Piece	70.00
Tea Set, Doll's, Graniteware, Solid Blue, 16 Piece	325.00
Tea Set, Doll's, Occupied Japan, 10 Piece	35.00
Tea Set, Girl With Kitten, Tin, 7 Piece	20.00
Tea Set, Ideal, Box, 23 Piece	100.00
Tea Set, Laurel, Ivory, Red Trim	300.00
Tea Set, Mistress Mary, Tin, Ohio Art, 20 Piece	48.00
Tea Set, Punch & Judy, Allerton	250.00
Tea Set, Tin, Service For 3, 1930s	30.00
Teakettle, Aluminum, No. 8018	95.00
Teddy Bears are also listed in the Teddy Bear section	
Teddy Bear, Balloon Blowing, Eyes Light, Battery Operated, 1960s, 11 In.	225.00
Teddy The Drummer, Battery Operated, Alps, Box, 1970	75.00
Teddy Zilo, Fisher–Price	45.00
Teddy, Rhythmical Bear, Battery Operated, Alps, Japan	95.00
Teepee, Indian, Leather, 1950, 7 In.	18.00
Teeter–Totter, Tin Lithograph Figure, Reversible Action, 12 1/2 In.	66.00
Telephone, Black & Silver, Tin, Conn. Mfg., 7 1/2 In.	39.00
Telephone, Candlestick, Gong Bell Mfg. Co.	60.00
Telephone, Chatter, Pull Toy, Fisher–Price	15.00
Telephone, Girl, Talking, 1950, Hubley, 14 In.	75.00
Telephone, Mattel–O–Phone, Barbie & Kiddles, 1965	40.00
Telephone, Talking, Mary Poppins, Hasbro, Box	95.00
Terminal, Truck, Marx	150.00
Thresher, McCormick Deering, Gray & Red Trim, Nickel Feeder, Cast Iron	795.00
Tiger, Painted Eyes, 1 Piece Head & Neck, Schoenhut	770.00
Tiger, Walks, Growls, Windup, Marx	100.00
Toaster, Teen Popper, Tin	20.00
Toboggan, Green, Red & Yellow Stenciled, With Ed W. Raetz Name	325.00
Tool Chest, Boy's Favorite, No. 2700, Tools, Dovetailed Wooden Box	300.00
Tool Chest, Boy's Union Tool Chest, 8 Tools, Tray, Oak, 18 1/2 x 9 In.	245.00
Tool Chest, Outfitted, Wooden, Boy's Union Tools	40.00
Toonerville Trolly, Windup, Fontaine Fox, Germany, 6 3/4 In.	475.00 To 900.00
Top, Children, Donkeys, Ohio Art	11.00
Top, Figural, Couple Dancing, Skirt Turns, Cast Iron, 3 1/2 In.	253.00
Top, Figural, Gentleman, Bulbous Base, Polychrome, Wooden, France, 5 In.	132.00
Top, Figural, Humming, 2 Clowns, Spin On Gyro, 7 1/2 In.	688.00
Top, Figural, Humming, Polychrome, Wooden, Woman, Hoop Skirt, 4 3/4 In.	253.00
Top, Figural, Porcelain, Tin, Cloth, Toupee, Breveted, France, 3 In.	330.00
Top, Gyro Cycle, Painted Tin, Jockey, Horse, Fairylite Foreign, 3 1/2 In.	198.00
Top, Gyro, Painted Tin, 4 In.	71.00
Top, Gyro, Red & White Painted Steel, Wooden Handle, 3 3/4 In.	27.50
Top, Humming, Painted Tin, Red Wooden Handle, 13 In.	27.50
Top, Humming, Polychrome, Wooden, Ball Shape, Oriental Village, 10 In.	60.00
Top, Humming, With Launcher, Polychrome, Wooden, Ball Shape, Floral, 7 In.	275.00

Top, Spinning, Musical, Box, 8 1/2 In.	55.00
Top, Whistling, Snow White, Chein	65.00
Torpedo Boar, Taku, Tin Lithograph, 1913, Lehmann, 9 1/2 In.	412.00
Tote Bag, Twiggy Fashion, Yellow Plastic, Photo Of Twiggy, 1967, Mattel	98.00
Tractor, & Cart, Farm, Allis Chalmers, Arcade	185.00
Tractor, & Disc Harrow, Tootsietoy, Box	200.00
Tractor, & Magic Barn, Windup, Door Opens, Tractor Goes In, Marx, Box	225.00
Tractor, Allis Chalmers, Model AC-9, 1950	90.00
Tractor, Caterpillar, Matchbox	55.00
Tractor, Climbing, Sparkling, Driver, Windup, Marx	165.00
Tractor, Crawler, Windup, Steel, 1920s, 11 In.	85.00
Tractor, Farm, Mower, Tin Driver, Windup, Marx	165.00
Tractor, Farm, Windup, Structo	350.00
Tractor, Ford 4000 HO, Remote Controlled, Box	350.00
Tractor, Ford 8000, Blue, Hard Rubber Wheels, Metal	35.00
Tractor, International, Cast Iron	120.00
Tractor, John Deere, Battery Operated, Cast Iron	75.00
Tractor, McCormick Deering, Solid Red Wheels, Gray, Gold Trim, Arcade	495.00
Tractor, No. 661, Recovery, Green, Dinky No. 661, Box	155.00
Tractor, Reversing, Tin, Windup, Marx, 12 In.	125.00
Tractor, Scoop Shovel, Tootsietoy, Box	150.00
Tractor, Tin, Driver, Marked N.Y. 200-5 Ave., Marx	75.00
Tractor, Windup, Courtland	30.00
Tractor, With Magic Barn, Tin Lithograph & Plastic, Marx, 1950s	135.00
Tractor, With Plow, Hubley	45.00
Trailer, Farm, Buddy L, 12 1/2 In.	23.00
Train Engine, Camel, 1970, Kellogg's	50.00
Train Kit, Reno 4-4-0 Locomotive, 0 Scale, Rivarossi, Box	90.00
Train Set, American Flyer, Standard Gauge, 1925	595.00
Train Set, Berkshire, Locomotive, Tender, 3 Freight Cars, Lobaugh, Box	308.00
Train Set, Cast Iron, Engine, 3 Passenger Cars, Paint Traces, 23 In.	195.00
Train Set, KBN, Tin Lithograph, Windup, Tracks, 11 In.	155.00
Train Set, Lionel, 75th Anniversary	325.00
Train Set, Lionel, Blue Comet, Locomotive, Tender, 5 Coaches, Box	522.00
Train Set, Lionel, Engine, Freight Cars, Station, RR Signs, 1951	155.00
Train Set, Lionel, No. 248, Red, Box	350.00
Train Set, Lionel, No. 1776	400.00
Train Set, Lionel, No. 1815	275.00
Train Set, Lionel, No. 2020, Pennsylvania Turbine, 6 Cars, Boxes	250.00
Train Set, Lionel, No. 7500	300.00
Train Set, Lionel, No. 8473	250.00
Train Set, Lionel, Presidential, Engine, 3 Cars, Standard Gauge, Box	2500.00
Train Set, Lionel, Pullman, Vista Dome, Silver, Red Letters, Box	357.00
Train Set, Lionel, Spirit Of '76, Locomotive, 13 Box Cars, Caboose	440.00
Train Set, Lionel, Texas Special, 6 Cars, Track, Transformer	140.00
Train Set, Marx, No. 10000, Union Pacific	215.00
Train Set, Marx, No. 10005, Union Pacific	135.00
Train Set, Marx, Santa Fe Streamline, Box	480.00
Train Set, Marx, Smoking Locomotive, 1954	85.00
Train Set, Marx, Track, Engine, 4 Cars, Tin Lithograph	75.00
Train Set, Monorail, Tin Lithograph, Windup, Box, Japan, 5 Piece	55.00
Train Set, Ranger, Windup, Tin Lithograph Base, 1940s, Box, 3 Piece	45.00
Train Set, Tasty Foods Ltd., Canister, Tin, 3 Piece	480.00
Train Set, Tin Lithograph, Windup, 4 Sections, Germany, 11 In.	154.00
Train Set, Union Pacific, Passenger, Engine, Caboose, 5 Cars & Track	130.00
Train Station, Lionelville, 10 1/4 x 7 x 8 In.	350.00
Train Station, Talking, Moma, 1950s	95.00
Train, American Flyer, No. 1107, Passenger Car, Erie, 5 1/2 In.	75.00
Train, American Flyer, No. 20605	200.00
Train, American Flyer, Oil Drum Loader, Box	55.00
Train, Angel, Friction, Box	125.00
Train, Bing, Boxcar, Open, Tin	52.00
Train, Bing, Engine, Windup, Tin, Box	185.00

Train, Bing, Freight Platform, Tin Lithograph	22.00
Train, Bing, Handcar, Windup, Tin Lithograph	305.00
Train, Buddy L, Sit & Ride, Pressed Steel	85.00
Train, Cast Iron, Original Paint, 5 In.	80.00
Train, Coal Car, 4 In.	45.00
Train, Courtland	30.00
Train, Doll Co., Steam Engine, Nickel Plated Moving Parts, 13 1/2 In.	468.00
Train, Engine, Red Metal, With Cow Catcher, 6 In.	100.00
Train, Engine, V–8, Visible, 1960s, Box	85.00
Train, Engine, Wooden, 1 Car, Handmade, Green Paint	220.00
Train, Fisher–Price, Huffy Puffy, Box, 1955	250.00
Train, Harner, Tin, Windup	95.00
Train, Hill Climber, Tin, Dayton, Oh.	350.00
Train, Honeymoon Cottage, Tin, Windup, 1950s	85.00
Train, Hornby 2270, Locomotive, Tin Lithograph, Black, Keywind, England	77.00
Train, Ives, Engine, Clockwork, 6 In.	125.00
Train, Ives, Freight Station, Tin Lithograph, Painted	165.00
Train, Ives, Locomotive, Clockwork, Tin, P & W, 1800s, 9 In.	1100.00
Train, Ives, No. 11, Locomotive	2200.00
Train, Ives, Red Locomotive, Black Diamond, 0 Gauge, 4 Piece	5225.00
Train, Ives, Ticket Office, Tin Lithograph & Paint	110.00
Train, Lionel, Caboose, 0 Gauge	155.00
Train, Lionel, Caboose, Standard Gauge 117, N.Y. Central, Red & Black	68.00
Train, Lionel, Caboose, Standard Gauge, 1930	75.00
Train, Lionel, Dump Car, Aluminum, 0 Gauge	550.00
Train, Lionel, Engine, No. 408E, 0 Gauge	400.00
Train, Lionel, Freight Station, Box	85.00
Train, Lionel, Handcar, Santa Claus, Tree, Box	1760.00
Train, Lionel, Locomotive, Chessie Diesel	155.00
Train, Lionel, Locomotive, Diesel, Rock Island, 0 Gauge, Box	630.00
Train, Lionel, Locomotive, Tender, Tanker, Gondola & Caboose, Track	187.00
Train, Lionel, Lumber Shed, Box	143.00
Train, Lionel, Newsstand, Animated, Box	135.00
Train, Lionel, No. 3, Electric Rapid Transit, 1906–1909	7975.00
Train, Lionel, No. 7, Locomotive, Copper & Nickel	1100.00
Train, Lionel, No. 30, Water Tank, Box	85.00
Train, Lionel, No. 60, Trolley, Box	175.00
Train, Lionel, No. 117, Caboose, Red Black	70.00
Train, Lionel, No. 145, Gateman, Automatic, Box	40.00
Train, Lionel, No. 332, Railway Mail Car, Green, Red, Original Paint	100.00
Train, Lionel, No. 455, Oil Derrick, Box	225.00
Train, Lionel, No. 1105, Handcar, Santa Claus Figure	1870.00
Train, Lionel, No. 2243, Diesel, Santa Fe	297.00
Train, Lionel, No. 3656, Cattle Car, Box	95.00
Train, Lionel, No. 8020, Locomotive, Sante Fe	170.00
Train, Lionel, No. 8406, Locomotive & Tender, Box	1000.00
Train, Lionel, O Gauge, General Electric, Box, 1957	850.00
Train, Lionel, Observation & Pullman, N.Y. Central, Standard Gauge, Pair	170.00
Train, Lionel, Operating Switch Tower	115.00
Train, Lionel, Peter Rabbit Chick–Mobile, Key Wind, 10 In.	413.00
Train, Lionel, Switcher, Seaboard, 0 Gauge	198.00
Train, Lionel, Trailer Platform, Piggyback, Box	242.00
Train, Locomotive, 3 Passenger Cars, Black & Gold, 24 In.	77.00
Train, Locomotive, Red, Black, Yellow Stripe, Iron, Wooden, Friction	220.00
Train, Marklin, Express Locomotive, Steam Type, Plastic & Metal, Box	44.00
Train, Marklin, Freight Locomotive, Electric Type, Metal Body, Box	110.00
Train, Marklin, Freight Locomotive, Steam Type, Black Smoke Box, Green	66.00
Train, Marklin, Freight, HO Scale, German Federal RR, Metal Body, Box	110.00
Train, Marklin, HO, Engine, 3 Cars & Truck, Box, 1950s	225.00
Train, Marklin, Locomotive, Diesel, German Federal RR, Metal	27.00
Train, Marklin, Locomotive, Express, Steam, Plastic, Black, Red Wheels	44.00
Train, Marklin, Locomotive, Industrial, Plastic Body, Zinc Frames, Box	15.00
Train, Marklin, Locomotive, Tender, 4 Cars, Transformer, Track, Box	43.00

Train, Marklin, Rail Zeppelin, Propeller Spins, Non–Skid Tires 66.00
Train, Marse, Engine, Coal, Tanker, Boxcar, Flat, Caboose, 1947, 6 Piece 110.00
Train, Marx, Blue Mercury, 1940 .... 950.00
Train, Marx, Freight Terminal 125.00
Train, Marx, Honeymoon Express, Windup, Tin, 1947 .... 200.00 To 475.00
Train, Marx, Pullman, Blue 50.00
Train, Max Gray, Locomotive & Tender, 0 Scale 352.00
Train, Mechanicraft, Tin, Windup, 2 Cars, Track 125.00
Train, MP Davis, Locomotive & Tender, 00 Scale 44.00
Train, N.Y. C., 3 Passenger, Black & Gold, Red, White, Iron, 24 In. 77.00
Train, Nason, Locomotive, 00 Scale, Painted 22.00
Train, Parmele & Sturges, Locomotive, 0 Scale, Decals 418.00
Train, Pierre Bourassa, Locomotive & Tender, 00 Scale, 4–6–2 .... 65.00
Train, Santa Fe, Friction 25.00
Train, Scalecraft, Locomotive & Tender, 0 Scale, Decals 195.00
Train, Scalecraft, Locomotive & Tender, 00 Scale, Decals 480.00
Train, Schorr, Locomotive & Tender, 00 Scale, Decal 77.00
Train, Siders Bros., Diesel, 0 Scale 45.00
Train, Silver Meteor, Windup, Box 75.00
Train, Silver Mountain Express, Engine, Battery Operated 185.00
Train, Technofix, Coal, Tin, Windup, Box 115.00
Train, Tender, Riding Car & Engine, Steam Powered, 66 In. 1320.00
Train, Tunnel, Papier–Mache, Wooden, Germany, Box, 6 x 5 In. 17.50
Train, Tyco, Petticoat Junction, 1960 .... 65.00
Train, Unique Art, Baggage Car, Windup, Full Lithograph, 13 In. 190.00
Train, Unique Art, Engine, Tin Lithograph 200.00
Train, Unique Art, Hill Billy Express, Windup, 1930 .... 300.00
Train, Wilkins, Locomotive & Tender, Cast Iron, 1880s, 13 In. 550.00
Travel Case, Barbie, 1961 .... 25.00
Travelling Salesman, Windup, Tin Lithograph Suitcase, Japan, Box, 1930s 325.00
Tricky Trolley, Mattel 35.00
Tricycle, Delivery, Speed Boy, Windup, Marx, 1930s 475.00
Trolley, & Trailer, 0 Gauge, Carette, 1911 .... 1250.00
Trolley, Battery Operated, Moving Driver, Headlight, Clanging, Tin 165.00
Trolley, Electric Rapid Transit, Lionel, No. 3 .... 2200.00
Trolley, Green & Gold Paint, Cast Iron, 13 In. 135.00
Trolley, Mohawk, Tin 65.00
Trolley, No. 200, Marx 195.00
Trolley, Prospect, Horse Drawn, Georg Brown 700.00
Trolley, Tin, Lever Action, Friction, Japan 55.00
Trolley, Union Pacific, Erie Electric, Tin Lithograph, Japan, 13 1/4 In. 325.00
Trolley, Windup, Tin Lithograph, Germany, 1930s, 8 In. 495.00
Trolley, Windup, Tracks, Metal, 1950s 55.00
Trolley, Women Passengers, Tin, Lead Weighted, c.1890 .... 880.00
Truck, & Trailer, Circus, Painted Steel, Cage, Animals, 18 1/2 In. 247.00
Truck, & Trailer, Motor Express, Hubley 100.00
Truck, 3 In 1, Wooden Wagon, Dual Back Wheels, Green Sides, Boy Craft 285.00
Truck, 5 Ton, Hubley, 14 1/2 In. 1495.00
Truck, Aerial Ladder, Buddy L, 1926, 30 In. 1030.00
Truck, Aerial Ladder, Buddy L, 39 In. 900.00
Truck, Airmail, Buy Defense Bonds, Buddy L 325.00
Truck, Allied Van Lines, Tonka, 1955 .... 155.00
Truck, Anti–Aircraft, Battery & Friction, Linemar, 1950, 12 In. 150.00
Truck, Anti–Aircraft, Skysweeper, Searchlight Projects Images, Ideal 50.00
Truck, Army, Canvas Top, All Metal Products Co., 20 In. 75.00
Truck, Army, Marx, 1960s 150.00
Truck, Artillery, Kingsbury 225.00
Truck, B. B. C., No. 968, Green, Gray, Dinky Toy 42.00
Truck, Bell Telephone, Remote Controlled, Rubber Tires, Box 175.00
Truck, Bell Telephone, Tonka 10.00
Truck, Bell Telephone, With Accessories, Hubley 800.00
Truck, Borden, Fisher–Price 325.00
Truck, Car Carrier, 4 Cars, Hubley 250.00

Truck, Car Carrier, Cars, Cast Iron 1540.00
Truck, Car Carrier, Deluxe Transport, Marx, 1940s, 21 In. 135.00
Truck, Car Carrier, Ertl, 22 In. 65.00
Truck, Car Carrier, International, Tootsietoy, 1940s 85.00
Truck, Car Carrier, Marx 65.00
Truck, Car Carrier, Round Nose, 9 In. 38.00
Truck, Car Carrier, Structo, 1960s, 22 In. 40.00
Truck, Carnation Milk, Tonka, 1954 .... 195.00
Truck, Cement Mixer, Cast Iron, Kenton Jaeger, 9 In. 2500.00
Truck, Cement, Pull, Fisher–Price 20.00
Truck, Chipperfield's Circus, International, Corgi, 6 x 6 In. 95.00
Truck, Coal, Original Paint, Buddy L, 1920s, 26 In. 1300.00
Truck, Coal, Pressed Tin Lithograph, Lever Dump, Marx, 13 In. 132.00
Truck, Coal, Red & Black, American National Co. 3750.00
Truck, Coal, Windup, Tin, Marx 675.00
Truck, Coast To Coast, Tootsietoy, Box 135.00
Truck, Concrete Mixer, Buddy L 700.00
Truck, Concrete Mixer, Siren, Spinning Barrel, Friction 75.00
Truck, Crane, Structo 45.00
Truck, Delivery, Easter Bunny, Marx 85.00
Truck, Delivery, Pull Toy, Casper The Friendly Ghost, Wooden, Box, 1967 .... 65.00
Truck, Delivery, Silver, Buddy L 1300.00
Truck, Delivery, Steel Motor, Blue, Structo, 1920s, 22 3/4 In. 440.00
Truck, Delivery, Wonder Bread, Banner Toy Co. 175.00
Truck, Desert Patrol Jeep, Working Bazooka 350.00
Truck, Dragline, Tonka 120.00
Truck, Dump, 4–Way, Marx 165.00
Truck, Dump, Allstate, Hydraulic, Marx, 27 In. 100.00
Truck, Dump, Black, Red Bed, American National Co. 1500.00
Truck, Dump, Chevrolet, 1956, 19 In. 75.00
Truck, Dump, Deluxe Rider, Buddy L 350.00
Truck, Dump, Hydraulic, Buddy L 75.00
Truck, Dump, Hydraulic, Metal, Tonka, 1980s 48.00
Truck, Dump, International Harvester, Cast Iron 825.00
Truck, Dump, Lumar Contractors, Marx 85.00
Truck, Dump, Mack, Arcade 900.00
Truck, Dump, No. 6, Tonka, Box 125.00
Truck, Dump, Original Green Paint, Buddy L, 1920s, Box, 26 In. 650.00
Truck, Dump, Pressed Steel, Turner 150.00
Truck, Dump, Ride–Em, Paper Label, Keystone 395.00
Truck, Dump, Riding, Metal, Buddy L, 21 In. 235.00
Truck, Dump, Sand & Gravel, Marx 25.00
Truck, Dump, White, Pressed Steel, Kelmet, 26 In. 1800.00
Truck, Dump, With Scoop, Friction, Japan, 12 In. 65.00
Truck, Dunlop, No. 25, Blue, Matchbox, Box 38.00
Truck, Earthmover, Tournahopper, Nylint 125.00
Truck, Excavating, Structo 50.00
Truck, Fire Chief Engine, Pressed Steel, Texaco, Buddy L, Box, 25 In. 220.00
Truck, Flatbed Semi, Tonka 125.00
Truck, Flatbed, Metal, 1950s, 6 1/2 In. 20.00
Truck, Futuristic, Sun Rubber, 5 1/2 In. 25.00
Truck, Gasoline Mack, Tin Tank, Cast Iron, Arcade, 13 In. 1300.00
Truck, Gasoline, CalTex, Tekno, Box 225.00
Truck, Gasoline, Friction, Tin, Box, Japan 48.00
Truck, Gasoline, Hess 25.00
Truck, Gasoline, Mack, Arcade, 13 In. 1300.00
Truck, General, Digger, Hubley, 8 In. 875.00
Truck, Good Humor Ice Cream, Friction, Japan 230.00
Truck, Grain, Lever Dump, Rubber Tires, Pressed Steel, Sturditoys, 25 In. 1540.00
Truck, Hauler, Green, Structo 40.00
Truck, Heinz Pickle, Decals, Metalcraft, 28 In. .... 225.00 To 450.00
Truck, Hill Climber, Pressed Steel, Yellow, Red, Black, 14 In. 370.00
Truck, Hydraulic Dumper, Structo 85.00

Truck, Hydraulic Highway Maintenance, Buddy L 50.00
Truck, Ice Cream, Black Open Door, Metal Body, 10 x 4 1/2 In. 55.00
Truck, Ice, Cast Iron, Rubber Wheels, Arcade, 6 3/4 In. 360.00
Truck, Ice, Marx, 1940s, 11 In. 165.00
Truck, Incredible Hulk, Mazada, Corgi, 1979 .... 50.00
Truck, International, Painted Cast Iron, Yellow, Arcade, 9 1/2 In. 275.00
Truck, Kroger Food Express, Pressed Steel, Metalcraft 235.00
Truck, Livestock Carrier, Open, Box 95.00
Truck, Livestock, Marcrest Lines, Metal Lithograph, Marx, 17 In. 49.50
Truck, Livestock, Red, Tonka, 1952 .... 125.00
Truck, Livestock, Structo 70.00
Truck, Logger, Tootsietoy, Box 135.00
Truck, Logger, With Logs, Tonka, 1957 .... 250.00
Truck, Lumber, Pressed Tin Lithograph, Chein, 8 1/2 In. 110.00
Truck, Mack, Stenciled Gasoline, Cast Iron, Arcade, 13 In. 1300.00
Truck, Mail, Keystone, 26 In. 650.00
Truck, Milk & Cream, 6 Wooden Bottles, Tin, Barclay 75.00
Truck, Milk, Detroit Creamery, Pressed Steel, 21 1/2 In. 82.50
Truck, Open Stake, Rosko, Box, Large 120.00
Truck, P. I. E., Back Doors Open, Close With Latch, Japan, 12 1/2 In. 165.00
Truck, Pickup, Chevrolet, Tin, Japan, Box, 8 In. 50.00
Truck, Pickup, Model T, Spoke Wheels, Tootsietoy 85.00
Truck, Pickup, Nissan, Bandai 350.00
Truck, Pickup, Studebaker, Bell Telephone, Box 135.00
Truck, Pickup, Studebaker, Remote Controlled, Rubber Tires 165.00
Truck, Pile Driver, Buddy L, 17 In. 60.00
Truck, Power Crane, Scoop Bucket, Japan, 1950s, 11 1/2 In. 125.00
Truck, Power Shovel, Friction, Tin, Linemar, Box 175.00
Truck, Pure Oil Co., Metal 850.00
Truck, Refrigeration, Wyandotte, 8 In. 85.00
Truck, Riding, Wyandotte, 1930s 225.00
Truck, Road Grader, Kenton, 7 1/2 In. 225.00
Truck, Road Grader, Tonka, 12 In. 45.00
Truck, Roller, Huber, Cast Iron, 8 In. 650.00
Truck, Safeway, Japan, 1970s, 13 In. 125.00
Truck, Sand & Gravel, Marx 75.00
Truck, Sand & Gravel, Pressed Steel, Buddy L, 25 In. 1450.00
Truck, Sand Loader, Tin, Chein, Box 135.00
Truck, Sand, Black, Red Chassis, Steel, Buddy L, 1900s, 25 In. 440.00
Truck, Sanitation, Marx, 13 In. 295.00
Truck, Semi, Boat Transport, 28 In. 200.00
Truck, Semi, Coast To Coast, Wyandotte 125.00
Truck, Semi, Grain Hauler, Structo 40.00
Truck, Semi, Livestock, Structo 95.00
Truck, Semi, McDonald's, Canada, Maple Leaf Logo 35.00
Truck, Semi, Metal Cab, Plastic Trailer, Are You Hungry, 6 In. 5.00
Truck, Shell Oil, 6 Barrels, Metalcraft ....550.00 To 1250.00
Truck, Sit & Ride, Pressed Steel, Buddy L 85.00
Truck, Sprinkler Tank, Keystone 975.00
Truck, Sprite Boy, 1950s 375.00
Truck, Stake, Ford, Japan, 1960, 15 In. 120.00
Truck, Stake, International Cab, Auburn Rubber, 1939, 5 In. 40.00
Truck, Stake, Lazy Day Farms, Marx, 1950s, 18 In. 65.00
Truck, Stake, Pressed Steel, Wyandotte, 1930s 120.00
Truck, Sunoco, Buddy L 75.00
Truck, Sunshine Dairy, Cast Iron, 1940s 75.00
Truck, Tanker, Esso, Red, Matchbox 100.00
Truck, Tanker, Shell Gasoline, Tin, Box, 14 In. 65.00
Truck, Tankline Street Sprinkler, Black & Green, Buddy L 2400.00
Truck, Texaco Tanker, Buddy L 175.00
Truck, Tip–Top Bread Toy Town, Bread Loaves, Punch–Out, 1955 .... 24.00
Truck, Tow, Riding, Buddy L 145.00
Truck, Tow, Winch, Spare Tire, Rubber Tires, Canada, 1950s, 13 In. 75.00

Truck, Trailer, Mack, No. 100, Tootsietoy, 1947 .... 95.00
Truck, Transport Rapides, Tin, France, c.1930 .... 154.00
Truck, Transport, Semitrailer, 4 Cars, Structo 85.00
Truck, Transport, Tootsietoy 30.00
Truck, Trash, Buddy L 50.00
Truck, U.S. Mail, Marx, 14 In. 175.00
Truck, Utility, Wood Load, Tonka, 1952 .... 175.00
Truck, Van, Jewel Tea, Wyandotte 235.00
Truck, White Oil, Kelmet, 26 In. 2800.00
Truck, Winnebago, Tonka, 22 In. 40.00
Truck, With Crane, Tin, Plastic, Gama, Box, 15 In. 85.00
Truck, Wrecker, Black, Red, Crane, Buddy L 1800.00
Truck, Wrecker, Cast Iron, Arcade, 3 In. 85.00
Truck, Wrecker, Ford, 1960 Model, Friction, Tin Lithograph, Japan, 15 In. 225.00
Truck, Wrecker, Goodrich 245.00
Truck, Wrecker, Red, White Wheels, Green Winch, Arcade 185.00
Truck, Wrecker, Tin Lithograph, Wyandotte, 8 1/2 In. 95.00
Truck, Wrecker, Tonka, 1949 .... 200.00
Truck, Wrigley's Spearmint, Metal 425.00
Trunk, Camelback, Tray, Leather Handles 110.00
Trunk, Dome Top, Paper Lithograph Cover, 8 x 12 In. 100.00
Trunk, Dome Top, Pine, Small 225.00
Trunk, Humpback, Tray 120.00
Trunk, Marbelized Paper, 13 x 8 In. 58.00
Trunk, Steamer, Roll Top, Tin Lithograph, 1900s, 3 x 4 1/2 x 3 In. 50.00
Trunk, Tray, Plaid Paper, Wooden, Paper Lining 125.00
Trunk, Wardrobe, Metal 35.00
Trunk, Wooden, Metal Trim, 18 In. 100.00
Tugboat, Tin, Battery Operated, Whistles & Chugs, Neptune, Japan, 14 In. 140.00
Tugboat, Windup, Tin, Ives 325.00
Turkey, Windup, Rolls Along, Changes Direction, Germany, 4 1/2 In. 88.00
Turtle, Native On Back, Windup, 1950, Chein .... 150.00 To 250.00
Typewriter, Cub Reporter, Lithograph, 1940s 40.00
Typewriter, Dial, Marx Jr. .... 20.00 To 35.00
Typewriter, Gold, Berwin, Box, 1960 .... 60.00
Typewriter, Simplex, Model R, Box 55.00
Typewriter, Tin, Directions, Box 65.00
Typewriter, Tom Thumb, Green .... 20.00 To 40.00
Van, Police Patrol, Tin, Structo 550.00
Van, RCA Service, Linemar 35.00
Velocipede, Blue Paint, Red Striping, Iron Wheels, Horsehead At Front 1250.00
Viewmaster, 3 Reels, 1971 .... 21.00
Viewmaster, Black Sambo & Others, Box, 1948 .... 15.00
Viewmaster, Flintstones, Pebbles & Bamm–Bamm, 3 Reels, 1964 .... 23.00
Viewmaster, Viewer, Cowboy Heroes, Elizabeth Coronation, 45 Reels, Box 55.00
Village, Tin, Colorful Lithograph, 3 1/4 In., 7 Piece 75.00
Wacky Races Bi–Plane With Muttley, Kellogg's, 1969 .... 49.00
Waffle Iron, Dover 95.00
Wagon, Aeroflite, Coaster, Car Shape, Headlights, Globe–Biltwell 650.00
Wagon, Auto Wheel Coaster, Wooden, Wooden Spoked Wheels, Old Red Paint 475.00
Wagon, Calliope, Steiff, Box 600.00
Wagon, Coaster, Lindy Flyer, Rubber Tires, Full Size 125.00
Wagon, Express, Tin Rimmed Wheels, Wooden, Red & Black Paint, 12 In. 375.00
Wagon, Milk, Fisher–Price 20.00
Wagon, Milk, Oak Dale Farm, Tin, 1884–1931, Morton Converse Co. 308.00
Wagon, Milk, Tin Horse, White, Red, Yellow Roof, 1920, 11 In. 385.00
Wagon, National Biscuit Co., Tin Lithograph, Hinged Rear Door, 20 In. 357.00
Wagon, Police Patrol, Stencil, Blue Paint, Wooden Wheels 2700.00
Wagon, Radio Flyer 145.00
Wagon, Road Test Coaster 250.00
Wagon, Rocket Coaster, Keen Kutter, Metal 225.00
Wagon, Skeezix, Wooden, Wire Wheels 495.00
Wagon, Stake, Green Paint, Tennessee 450.00

Wagon, World War I, Tin, Olive Drab, Driver 120.00
Wagon, Yale, Chair Type, 2 Small & 2 Large Back Wheels, Original Paint 1450.00
Walkie Talkie, Crest Toothpaste, Star Trek, Box 35.00
Wash Set, Tub, Hand Wringer, Glass Washboard, Wooden Clothes Rack 195.00
Washing Machine, Doll's, Electric 95.00
Washing Machine, Doll's, Metal & Glass 95.00
Washing Machine, Doll's, Wringer, Chein 275.00
Washing Machine, Dolly Duds, Naxon, White Metal, Glass Tub, Agitator 140.00
Washing Machine, Electric, Outside Motor, Teddy Bear On Front 25.00
Washing Machine, Lil–Mills, Battery Operated 17.00
Washing Machine, Modern Miss, Red & White Paint, C. G. Wood Co. 33.00
Washing Machine, Polly Wringer, Box 195.00
Washing Machine, Wringer, Wolverine 75.00
Washstand, Doll's, Bamboo Trim, Mirror, 9 1/4 x 23 1/2 In. 395.00
Washstand, Doll's, Tin, Gray Paint, Bowl & Pitcher, Dish & Pot, 7 In. 300.00
Wastebasket, Cowboy, Metal, 11 In. ....*Illus* 110.00
Water Bottle, Pig 16.00
Watering Can, Dutch Girl 40.00
Watering Can, Elephant, Orange Plastic, Ohio Art 20.00
Watering Can, Ohio Art 13.00
Watering Can, Tin Lithograph, Ohio Art, 1940s 15.00
Wheelbarrow, Wooden, Paris Mfg. Co. 125.00
Whirligig Set, Aero–Circus Aeroplane, Newton, Box, 1931 .... 395.00
Whistle, Composition, Buster Brown Type 25.00
Whistle, Dragnet 8.00
Whistle, Elmer Fudd 8.00
Whistle, Sgt. Preston, Signature 50.00
Wicker Set, Doll's, 2 Armless Chairs, Settee, Table, 4 Piece 40.00
Wilson Walkie, Mammy, 1930, 4 In. ....*Illus* 35.00
Wilson Walkie, Mammy, Flowered Dress, 1930, 4 In. ....*Illus* 35.00
Wilson Walkie, Nurse, 1930, 4 In. ....*Illus* 25.00
Wilson Walkie, Soldier, 1930, 4 In. ....*Illus* 25.00
Winter Scene, Metal, Miniature, 31 Piece 75.00
Wolf, Glass Eyes, Wooden, Schoenhut 3850.00
Wrist Radio, Green Hornet, Box 475.00
Xylophone Player, Windup, Celluloid & Tin, 1950s, Japan 250.00
Xylophone, 8 Notes, Schoenhut .... 40.00 To 50.00
Xylophone, Cupid, Schoenhut 55.00
Xylophone, Ding Dong School, National Broadcasting Co. 20.00
Yo–Yo, Burger Chef, 1971 .... 5.00
Yo–Yo, Figural, Fred Flintstone 15.00
Yo–Yo, General Electric, Wooden 25.00
Yo–Yo, Kist 10.00
Yo–Yo, Spaulding Luxury Bread, Tin 40.00
Yo–Yo, Whistling, Tin 2.40
Yo–Yo, Yogi Bear, Figural, 1970s 15.00
Zeppelin, Little Giant, Pressed Steel, Silver Gray, N.Y., 27 In. ...., 575.00
Zeppelin, Papier–Mache, Wooden Wheels, Los Angeles, 14 In. 1200.00
Zeppelin, Strauss, Box, 10 In. 535.00
Zilotone, Tin Lithograph, Metal, 4 Music Discs, Windup, Wolverine, 7 In. 495.00

TRAMP ART is a form of folk art made since the Civil War. It is usually made from chip–carved cigar boxes. Examples range from small boxes and picture frames to full–sized pieces of furniture.

Bed, Doll's 95.00
Box, Geometric Design, Metal Eagle Finial, Bottom Drawer, 8 In. 80.00
Box, Jewelry, 3 Tiers 95.00
Box, Jewelry, Blue Velvet Interior, Mirror, Drawer, 14 In. 195.00
Box, Jewelry, Chest Of Drawers Shape, Gold Paint, 11 1/4 In. 100.00
Box, Jewelry, Maroon Velvet Inserts, Interior Mirror, 12 In. 125.00
Box, Mirror Inside Cover, Red Velvet Lined, 7 x 13 In. 165.00
Box, Music, Embossed Brass Tacks, Brass Ring Handle 285.00
Box, On Stand, Annie May, Late 19th Century, 30 x 20 1/2 x 16 In. 825.00

Box, Red & Green Painted Design, Hinged Lid, Till, 10 x 11 In. 440.00
Box, Storage, Notch–Carved Pyramids 250.00
Box, Wall, Hanging, Dark Varnish Finish 245.00
Bureau, Doll's, Attached Mirror, 7 x 5 x 13 In. 195.00
Chest, Incised Leaves & Eagles Designs, Cedar Lined, Handles 235.00
Clock, Painted, Brookfield, Mass., Adelard Courville, 21 In. 935.00
Frame, 11 x 13 1/2 In. 45.00
Frame, 15 x 20 In. 95.00
Frame, 38 x 27 In. 495.00
Frame, Grain Painted, Applied Heart Design, 8 x 10 In. 247.00
Lamp, Floor, 6 Ft. 4100.00
Mirror, Pocket At Base, 11 x 18 In. 350.00
Ornament, Wall, Geometric, Heart Enclosed By Glass Liner, 13 In. 55.00
Sign, Parade, Needlework, Says Feed My Lambs, 8 Ft. 5 In. 825.00
Stand, Geometric Design, Hexagonal, Small 37.50
Stand, Late 19th Century, 24 1/2 In. 55.00
Wall Pocket, 16 Layers Of Wood, Large 5200.00

TRAPS for animals may be handmade. One of the most unusual is the mousetrap made so that when the mouse entered the trap, it was hit on the head with a mallet. Other traps were commercially manufactured and often are marked with the name of the manufacturer. Many traps were designed to be as humane as possible, and they would trap the live animal so it could be released in the woods.

Animal, Oneida Victor, 17 In. 95.00
Bear, Hand Forged, Double Spring, Chain, 55 In. 1800.00
Bear, Mackenzie District Fur Co., Double Spring, Chain, 34 In. 1500.00
Bear, Mackenzie District Fur Co., Teeth, H. B. Co., 1886 .... 235.00
Fly, Embossed Glass, Large 130.00
Fly, Glass 35.00
Fly, Wooden, Screen Wire Around, Round, 1920–1930 .... 8.50
Mouse, 4 Hole 25.00
Mouse, Delusion .... 30.00 To 35.00
Mouse, Hung Above Hole, Spring–Leaded Tines To Impale Mouse 50.00
Mouse, Ketch–All, Automatic Windup, Metal 25.00
Mouse, Runaway Trap Co., Tin 15.00
Mouse, Victor, 4–Hole Choker, Animal Trap Co., Bakelite 30.00
Sta Kawt, Iron, With Chain 5.00

TREEN, see Wooden category

TRENCH ART is a form of folk art made by soldiers. Metal casings from bullets and mortar shells were cut and decorated to form useful objects, such as vases.

Ashtray, Lighter, 20 Mm. Cartridge, World War II 55.00
Bowl, Dough 185.00
Lamp, From Cartridge Case, World War II, 2 1/2 Ft. 175.00
Maple Leaves, Artillery Shell 35.00
Planter, Hanging, Shell 40.00
Shelf, Veefun, Polished, 13 In. 50.00
Vase, Brass Shell, World War I 35.00

TRIVETS are now used to hold hot dishes. Most trivets of the late nineteenth and early twentieth centuries were made to hold hot irons. Iron or brass reproductions are being made of many of the old styles.

Brass, Iron Frame & Feet, Turned Wooden Handle, 13 1/4 In. 185.00
Cast Iron, Fancy, For Wooden Cookstove 3.00
Cutout Hearts Quatrefoils & Mandolas, Cast Iron, 9 x 12 1/2 In. 150.00
Daisy, Leaves & Stem, Iron, 4 1/2 x 3 1/2 In. 95.00
Diamond Shape, T In Center, Cast Iron, 7 x 4 In. 40.00
Enterprise, Philadelphia, Iron 10.00
Firefighting, Slogan, Brass 85.00
Good Luck, Iron, Patented 1885 .... 15.00

Good Luck, Pat. 1885	15.00
Horseshoe Shape, Center Date, 1884	65.00
Jenny Lind, Cast Iron	85.00
Kettle Shelf, Reticulated Brass Top, Iron Base, 8 x 9 x 10 In.	115.00
N. R. Streeter & Co., Groton, N.Y., Iron	10.00
Ober, Chagrin Falls, Ohio, Iron	10.00
Old Ironsides, Cast Iron	20.00
Ornate, Rotates	295.00
Penny Feet, Rivets, Tin & Iron, 13 1/2 x 13 1/4 In.	265.00
Pierced, Treen Handle, Iron Legs, England, 14 In.	100.00
Pleuger & Renger, St. Louis, Iron	10.00
Smiling Cat, Good Luck, Brass, 19th Century	65.00
Vine Pattern, Cast Iron, Triangular, 9 In.	35.00
W. H. Howell Co., Geneva, Ill., Iron	10.00

TRUNKS of many types were made. The nineteenth–century sea chest was often handmade of unpainted wood. Brass–fitted camphorwood chests were brought back from the Orient. Leather–covered trunks were popular from the late eighteenth to mid–nineteenth centuries. By 1895, trunks were covered with canvas or decorated sheet metal. Embossed metal coverings were used from 1870 to 1910. By 1925, trunks were covered with vulcanized fiber or undecorated metal.

Brass Tack Trim, Iron Lock, Leather Covered, Wallpaper Lined, 14 In.	145.00
Brass Tacks, Brass Lock & Handle, Dome Top, Leather Bound, 10 In.	230.00
Camelback, Brass Lock, Scenic Picture Inside Top, Oak	90.00
Child's, Dovetailed, Pine	150.00
Chinese Export, Painted, c.1825	1925.00
Deer Hide, Lined With Broadside Of Show Starring Horse Othello	50.00
Dome Top, Design, Tray & Compartments	75.00
Dome Top, Hide Covered, Tin Trim, Brass Tacks, Brass J. W. R., 24 In.	150.00
Dome Top, Pennsylvania Birds Painted On Front, Red Paint	3000.00
Dome Top, Watercolor Ship Scene In Lid, Some Cowhide, 18 x 39 In.	1320.00
Flat Top, Dovetailed, Wood	420.00
Humpback, Iron Bands, Bail Handles, Hand Made Nails, 25 x 42 In.	330.00
Immigrant's, Dome Top, Iron Bound, Floral Design, 31 In.	190.00
Kneeling Woman Playing Drum, Cactus Border, Oak, 17 1/2 x 37 1/2 In.	495.00
Leather Bound, Initialed GAD, Chicago, French, 22 x 28 x 20 In.	465.00
Leather Covered, Brass Studs & Ring Handles, Black, 12 1/4 In.	225.00
Leather, Brass, Camphorwood, China, 19th Century, 11 x 25 x 12 In.	467.00
Leather, Dome Top, Brass Tacks, Lock & Handle, 10 1/4 In.	110.00

TUTHILL Cut Glass Company of Middletown, New York, worked from 1902 to 1923. Of special interest are the finely cut pieces of stemware and tableware.

Bowl, Athena, Signed, 9 In.	750.00
Bowl, Rex Pattern, Signed, 8 1/4 In.	1210.00
Bowl, Vintage & Brilliant Combination, 3 Sections, Signed	550.00
Bride's Bowl, Intaglio Carnations, Plated Holder, Signed, 8 1/2 In.	2100.00
Compote, Primrose & Geometric, 7 1/2 In.	300.00
Lemonade Set, Engraved Vintage Pattern, Pedestaled Mugs, 5 Piece	495.00
Sugar & Creamer, Intaglio Dahlia Cutting, Notched Rims, Signed	225.00
Tray, Brilliant & Intaglio, Frisbee Shape, Signed, 10 In.	700.00
Tray, Four Fruits, Scalloped Border, Intaglio Cut, Signed, 12 In.	1100.00
Tray, Vintage & Brilliant Combination, Signed, 9 1/2 x 7 In.	350.00
Tray, Vintage & Hobstars, Signed, 7 1/4 x 5 1/2 In.	575.00
Tray, Vintage, Intaglio & Chain Of Hobstars Rim, Signed, 10 In.	550.00
Vase, Bud, Intaglio Cut Pedestal, Signed, 12 In., Pair	110.00
Vase, Corset, Primrose & Geometric, 10 In.	400.00
Vase, Intaglio Floral & Hobstar, Signed, 10 In.	192.00
Vase, Vintage, Urn Shape, Handles, Signed, 11 In.	475.00

TYPEWRITER collectors divide typewriters into two main classifications: the index machine, which has a pointer and a dial for letter selection, and the keyboard machine, most commonly seen today. The first successful typewriter was made by Sholes and Glidden in 1874.

Berwin Jr., Executive Type	25.00
Corona, No. 3, Case	45.00
Corona, No. 4, Case	45.00
Fox	100.00
Hall	770.00
Hammond Multiplex, Wooden Case	78.00
Hammond, Oak Case	175.00
L. C. Smith, Super Speed	25.00
L. C. Smith, No. 3, Decals	45.00
Merritt	797.00
Oliver, No. 5	60.00 To 80.00
Oliver, No. 9, Standard Visible Writer	65.00
Remington, 1906	75.00
Remington, Streamliner Type	25.00
Simplex, Box	55.00
Smith–Corona, 1910	25.00
Tin, American Brand	5.00
Tin, Burroughs	6.00
Tin, Ivory Brand	7.00
Tin, Kreko	6.00
Tin, Sil Kee Lox	8.00
Tin, Type Art	7.00
Tin, Underwood, Green	7.00
Tin, Wonder Brand	6.00
Western Union	5.00

UHL pottery was made in Evansville, Indiana, in 1854. The pottery moved to Huntingburg, Indiana, in 1908. Stoneware and glazed pottery were made until the mid–1940s.

Casserole, Cover, Blue, 7 1/2 In.	22.00
Cookie Jar, Globe, Blue, Pottery	80.00
Dish, Dog	60.00 To 100.00
Figurine, Elephant, Miniature	70.00
Jug, 3 Gal.	50.00
Jug, 5 Gal.	55.00
Jug, Canteen Form, Blue	55.00
Mug, Barrel Shape, Pink, Miniature	60.00
Mug, Tan, 6 Piece	50.00
Mug, Tan, Pair	35.00
Pitcher, White	40.00
Vase, Blue, 10 In.	35.00

UMBRELLA collectors like rain or shine. The first known umbrella was owned by King Louis XIII of France in 1637. The earliest umbrellas were sunshades, not designed to be used in the rain. The umbrella was embellished and redesigned many times. In 1852, the fluted steel rib style was developed and it has remained the most useful style.

Black Silk, Child's	70.00
Black Silk, Ruffled, Victorian	50.00
Parasol, Black Silk Brocade, Chenille Fringe, Floral Lining	125.00
Parasol, Black Silk, Hanging Lace, Red Lining, Cloth Case	125.00
Parasol, Carved Ivory Handle, Folding, Civil War	85.00
Parasol, Child's, Black Silk, Folding Handle	65.00
Parasol, Doll's, Figural Wooden Frog Handle, Pink, Turn Of Century	48.00
Parasol, Ivory Handle, Various Monkeys, Japan, 32 1/2 In.	220.00
Parasol, Lace Trim, Carved Bear Handle, Ecru	65.00
Parasol, Pleated Allover, Ebony Handle	95.00

UNION PORCELAIN WORKS was established at Greenpoint, New York, in 1848 by Charles Cartlidge. The company went through a series of ownership changes and finally closed in the early 1900s. The company made a fine quality white porcelain that was often decorated in clear, bright colors.

Figurine, Eagle	2550.00
Oyster Plate, 8 1/2 In.	225.00
Pitcher, Chinese Gambler, 9 5/8 In.	4200.00

UNIVERSITY OF NORTH DAKOTA, see North Dakota School of Mines

VAL ST. LAMBERT Cristalleries of Belgium was founded by Messieurs Kemlin and Lelievre in 1825. The company is still in operation. All types of table glassware and decorative glassware were made. Pieces were often decorated with cut designs.

Biscuit Jar, Red & Green Grapes & Leaves, Signed, 5 1/4 In.	1400.00
Bowl, Red Flash Overlay, Signed, 10 In.	350.00
Plate, Blue On Crystal, 9 In.	175.00
Vase, Engraved Fish & Net Design, Crystal, 14 In.	195.00
Vase, Green & Crystal, Signed, 9 In.	100.00
Vase, Green Overlay, Diamond Variant Cut, 9 3/4 In.	495.00
Vase, Scenic, Sailboat, Trees, Flat Oval, Signed, 6 1/4 In.	1100.00

VALLERYSTHAL Glassworks was founded in 1836 in Lorraine, France. In 1854, the firm became Klenglin et Cie. It made table and decorative glass, opaline, cameo, and art glass. A line of covered, pressed glass animal dishes was made in the nineteenth century. The firm is still working.

Bottle, Dresser, Gold Star Design, Blue, Marked, Pair	75.00
Dish, Robin Cover	105.00
Dish, Setter Dog Cover, 6 In.	185.00
Dish, Squirrel On Acorn Cover, Signed, 7 In.	105.00
Figurine, Cat, White	48.00
Figurine, Dog, Blue, White	75.00
Figurine, Dog, Collie, Floral Base, Signed	265.00
Figurine, Rooster, Blue, White Head	50.00
Sugar, Beehive	95.00
Sugar, Raised Grape & Leaf Design On Lid, Green	50.00

VAN BRIGGLE pottery was made by Artus Van Briggle in Colorado Springs, Colorado, after 1901. Van Briggle had been a decorator at the Rookwood Pottery of Cincinnati, Ohio. He died in 1904. His wares usually had modeled relief decorations and a soft, dull glaze. The pottery is still working and still making some of the original designs.

Ashtray, Hopi Maiden Doing Laundry, Signed, 5 3/4 In.	65.00
Ashtray, Persian Rose, 2 Cigarette Rests, 4 In.	25.00
Bookends, Dogs, Turquoise, Monogram	145.00
Bookends, Peacock, Maroon, 5 In.	200.00
Bookends, Polar Bear, Persian Rose Glaze, 5 x 5 1/2 In.	275.00
Bookends, Puppy, Maroon	140.00
Bookends, Ram	185.00
Bookends, Walking Bear, Turquoise Glaze, Paper Label, 4 In.	175.00
Boot, Persian Rose, Santa Claus Style, 2 1/2 x 2 1/4 In.	26.00
Bottle, Gray, 1906	250.00
Bowl, 2-Tone Blue Matte Finish, 9 1/2 In.	55.00
Bowl, 3 Frog, Persian Rose, Dragonfly Bowl, 8 1/2 In.	85.00
Bowl, Blue, Relief Pod Type Design, 1919, 5 x 6 1/2 In.	275.00
Bowl, Dragonfly, Blue Over Turquoise, 1919, 12 In.	200.00
Bowl, Leaf, Blue Over Turquoise, 4 1/2 x 7 In.	250.00
Bowl, Leaves & Acorns, Mountain Craig Brown, 5 1/2 In.	60.00
Bowl, Ming Turquoise, Dark Blue, 1919, 4 In.	65.00
Bowl, Papyrus, 8 3/4 In.	125.00

Bowl, Persian Rose, Stylized Leaves, 6 5/8 In.	50.00
Bowl, Siren Of The Sea, Shell Frog, Turquoise	150.00
Bowl, Stylized Leaves, Blue, 6 3/8 In.	60.00
Bowl, Stylized Leaves, Robin's-Egg Blue Glaze, 3 1/2 x 7 In.	335.00
Candlestick, Burgundy, Hexagonal, 1920s, 10 In., Pair	125.00
Chamberstick, Leaf Forms Hood Over Socket, Green, 5 1/2 In.	110.00
Compote, Oval Flower Frog, Mulberry Glaze	37.50
Console Bowl, Double Candlesticks, Persian Rose	125.00
Console Set, Persian Rose, Colorado Springs, 10 In., 3 Piece	105.00
Console, Blue Dragonfly, Dated 1919, 3 1/2 x 11 1/2 In.	295.00
Dish, Burgundy, Flat, 9 In.	45.00
Figurine, Cat, Brown Glaze, 15 In.	95.00
Figurine, Rabbit, Brown, 3 In.	40.00
Figurine, Rearing Horse, Brown, Mustard, Anne Van Briggle, 9 In.	125.00
Flower Frog, Duck, 1960	125.00
Lamp Base, Oriental Woman, 13 1/2 In.	85.00
Lamp Base, Squirrel, Turquoise, 6 7/8 In.	65.00
Lamp, Day Dreamer	265.00
Lamp, Persian Rose, Butterfly Shade, 15 x 9 In.	250.00
Mug, Blue, 1902	250.00
Night-Light, Owl	75.00
Paperweight, Elephant, 3 1/4 In.	55.00 To 125.00
Planter, Tulip Design, Blue Matte, Frog, Boat Shape	65.00
Plaque, Wall, Big Buffalo, Little Star, Pair	190.00
Plate, Bisque, 1907, 8 1/2 In.	325.00
Plate, Poppy, Blue Feathering, Maroon, 1907	550.00
Rose Bowl, Acorns, Ming Blue, 3 1/4 In.	40.00
Urn, Dark Burgundy, 3 1/2 In.	75.00
Vase, 3 Flamingos, Turquoise, Signed, c.1935, 21 1/2 In., Pair	3850.00
Vase, Acorns & Leaves, Ming Turquoise, 6 x 3 1/2 In.	50.00
Vase, Aqua, 1906, 4 In.	425.00
Vase, Black, Art Deco, Signed, 8 In.	75.00
Vase, Blossom, Turquoise, 4 In.	25.00
Vase, Blue & Green, Dated 1915, 5 1/2 In.	395.00
Vase, Blue Glaze, Channels On Length Of Body, 1909, 6 1/4 In.	400.00
Vase, Brown Glaze, 1905, 6 1/2 In.	500.00
Vase, Brown, Green, 8 1/2 In.	100.00
Vase, Bud, Heart-Shaped Leaves, Gray Green, 1904, 4 1/2 In.	775.00
Vase, Columbine, 11 1/4 In.	385.00
Vase, Conch Shell, 12 In.	45.00
Vase, Corset, Persian Rose, 14 In.	90.00
Vase, Crescent, Ming Blue, 6 In.	35.00
Vase, Daffodils, Maroon, 10 In.	250.00
Vase, Daffodils, Purple, 10 In.	325.00
Vase, Dark Red Yucca Flowers, Tall Tapering, 15 1/2 In.	2550.00
Vase, Deep Maroon Matte, Shape No. 349, 5 In.	358.00
Vase, Deep Rosy Matte Glaze, Shape No. 268, 1904, 4 x 7 In.	495.00
Vase, Floral, Mountain Craig Brown, 9 1/2 In.	325.00
Vase, Floral, Plum Colored, 1914, 7 In.	195.00
Vase, Green, 1905, 7 In.	685.00
Vase, Iris, Blue & Aqua Swirl, 11 In.	165.00
Vase, Lorelei, Mermaid, Cascading Hair, White Glaze, 10 1/2 In.	155.00
Vase, Lotus, Maroon, 1920, 8 In.	75.00
Vase, Made Of 4 Leaves, Turquoise, 1940s, 5 In.	65.00
Vase, Maroon & Dark Blue, Chocolate Clay, 13 1/2 In.	400.00
Vase, Molded Flowers, Blue Glaze, 2 Lower Handles	3100.00
Vase, Mustard Over Tan, 7 1/2 In.	1200.00
Vase, Papyrus, 7 In.	58.00
Vase, Peacock Feathers, Matte Green Blue Glaze, 11 1/4 In.	1875.00
Vase, Persian Rose, 1920s, 8 In.	160.00
Vase, Persian Rose, Bulbous, 7 1/4 In.	95.00
Vase, Persian Rose, Corset Shape, 14 In.	90.00
Vase, Persian Rose, Greek Urn Shape, 1930s, 5 1/4 In.	60.00

Vase, Persian Rose, Steel Blue, 1920, 12 In. 550.00
Vase, Pink & Green Matte, 1913, 7 In. 660.00
Vase, Poppy Pods Design, Red Matte Glaze, 1905, 9 In. 523.00
Vase, Poppy Pods, Persian Rose, Blue, 7 1/2 In. 185.00
Vase, Raised Butterfly, 4 In. 75.00
Vase, Rose, Cloverleaf Top, Twisted Base, 7 1/2 In. 45.00
Vase, Row Of Upright Arrowroot Leaves, Signed, 1906, 9 1/2 In. 2475.00
Vase, Stylized Daffodils, Ochre Glaze, Cylindrical, 13 1/2 In. 1435.00
Vase, Swirling Poppies, Under Olive Matte Glaze, 1902, 4 In. 715.00
Vase, Yucca, 13 In. 175.00

VASA MURRHINA is the name of a glassware made by the Vasa Murrhina
Art Glass Company of Sandwich, Massachusetts, about 1884. The
glassware was transparent and was embedded with small pieces of colored
glass and metallic flakes. The mica flakes were coated with silver, gold,
copper, or nickel. Some of the pieces were cased. The same type of glass
was made in England. Collectors often confuse Vasa Murrhina glass with
aventurine, spatter, or spangle glass. There is uncertainty about what
actually was made by the Vasa Murrhina factory. Related pieces may be
listed under Spangle Glass.

Basket, Gold Interior, Twisted Handle, 7 1/2 In. 175.00
Basket, Lobed Bowl, Pink To Glossy White, 9 In. 165.00
Basket, Ruffled Top, Clear Thorn Handle, 7 In. .... 145.00 To 175.00
Basket, Thorn Handle, Pink, 6 1/2 In. 135.00
Cordial Set, Green, White, Crystal & Gold, 4 Piece 195.00
Finger Bowl, Green To Red, Ruffled, Numbered 75.00
Finger Bowl, Red To Blue, Ruffled, 6 In. 175.00
Pitcher, Silver Flakes Over Earth & Red Tones 195.00
Pitcher, Silver Mica, Multicolored 165.00
Sugar & Creamer, Blue & White Spatter 118.00
Tumbler, Inverted Thumbprint, Pink & Cream, 3 7/8 In. 40.00
Vase, 4–Petal Top, Rose Mica, Wishbone Feet, 6 1/4 In 95.00
Vase, Blue Mist, 14 In. 90.00
Vase, Crystal Shell Trim, Ruffled, Pink, 9 1/4 In. 145.00
Vase, Fan, Rose Mist, 7 In. 55.00
Vase, Jack–In–The–Pulpit, Fluted Rim, 7 1/8 In. 80.00
Vase, Pink, White Lining, Silver Mica, 8 1/8 In., Pair 95.00
Vase, Silver Mica, 6 1/4 In. 135.00

VASELINE GLASS is a greenish–yellow glassware resembling petroleum
jelly. Some vaseline glass is still being made in old and new styles. Pressed
glass of the 1870s was often made of vaseline–colored glass. Additional
vaseline glass may also be listed under Pressed Glass in this book.

Basket, 4 In. 35.00
Bowl, Fluted Scroll, Opalescent, Scalloped, Footed 25.00
Box, Cover, Round, 7 1/2 In. 50.00
Candleholder, Fostoria, 1924, 8 In., Pair 42.00
Candlestick, Opaque, 12 In., Pair 40.00
Compote, Teaberry Gum, Pedestal 125.00
Cruet, Faceted Stopper 195.00
Cruet, Pressed Diamond 65.00
Dish, Pickle, Loves Request Is Pickle, Bottom Portrait 65.00
Perfume Bottle, Ovals On Sides, Vaseline, 4 1/2 In. 110.00
Pitcher, Syrup 95.00
Toothpick, Diamond Spearhead, Opal Edge, Northwood 85.00
Vase, Auto, Daisy, Bracket 80.00
Vase, Clear, 8 In. 8.00
Vase, Enamel Bird, Opalescent Ribbed, 5 3/4 In. 95.00

VENINI glass was first designed by Paolo Venini, who established his
factory in Murano, Italy, in 1925. He is best known for pieces of modern
design, including the famous *handkerchief* vase. The company is still

venini
murano
ITALIA

working. Other pieces of Italian glass may be found in the Glass–
Contemporary, Glass–Midcentury, and Glass–Venetian sections of this
book.

Bottle, Dark Green Fused To White On Lower Half, Signed, 12 3/4 In.	412.50
Bowl, Aqua & White Striped, Signed, 5 In.	300.00
Bowl, Irregular Blue, Green, Red & Clear Rectangles, Flared, Signed	6285.00
Bowl, Pink, Murano, Signed, Small	200.00
Lamp, 2 Cylindrical Blue Glass Sections, White Stripes, Electric	2218.00
Lamp, Ceiling, White Globe, Irregular Wide Center Band, 19 In.	3203.00
Sconce, 7–Flower Branch, White, Gold Foil, Air Bubbles, Pair	3326.00
Vase, Amethyst, Gold & White Stripes, 9 In.	350.00
Vase, Blue & Green Spirals, Marked, Label, c.1968, 14 In.	1100.00
Vase, Bottle, Green Cylinder, Belted By Red Ribbon, Marked, 10 In.	1045.00
Vase, Canes In Red, Blue, Green & Clear, Signed, c.1955, 9 In.	3410.00
Vase, Domed Cover, Pale Violet, N. Martinuzzi, 1930, 19 In.	6050.00
Vase, Double Pierced, Flattened Oval, Stamped, 11 1/2 In.	880.00
Vase, Handkerchief	180.00
Vase, Handkerchief, Blue Outside, Light Blue Cased, Signed, 7 x 7 In.	650.00
Vase, Handkerchief, Colorless Crystal Surface, Signed, 9 1/4 In.	605.00
Vase, Handkerchief, Colorless, Vertical Latticinio Panels, 5 3/4 In.	275.00
Vase, Handkerchief, Pink & White Latticinio, Signed, 3 3/4 In.	275.00
Vase, Handkerchief, Striped Lavender, Pink & White, 13 x 8 1/2 In.	750.00
Vase, Hourglass Shape, Blue & Green, 12 In.	750.00
Vase, Oval, Vasiform, Colorless Cased To Opaque White, Marked, 24 In.	550.00
Vase, Patchwork Squares On Sides, Flared, Marked, c.1955, 8 5/8 In.	7700.00

VERLYS glass was made in France after 1931. It was made in the United
States from 1935 to 1951. The glass is either blown or molded. The
American glass is signed with a diamond–point–scratched name, but the
French pieces are marked with a molded signature. The designs resemble
those used by Lalique.

Blown, Sculptured Roses, Frosted, 5 1/4 In.	50.00
Bowl, Butterflies, Frosted & Clear, 14 In.	115.00
Bowl, Poppy, Etched Crystal, Signed, 14 In.	195.00
Bowl, Thistle, Blue, 9 In.	185.00
Bowl, Thistle, Signed, 8 1/2 In.	65.00
Charger, Gulls & Geese, Clear & Frosted, Signed, 13 1/2 In.	140.00
Powder Box, Bubble Design, Art Deco, Signed	130.00
Vase, Autumn & Spring Figures, Signed, 8 1/4 In.	295.00
Vase, Boat Shape, Frosted Birds At Base, Signed, 4 1/2 x 6 1/2 In.	80.00
Vase, Lovebirds, Clear, 5 In.	135.00
Vase, Mermaid & Dolphin, Signed, 19 In.	1295.00

VERNON KILNS was the name used after 1958 by Vernon Potteries, Ltd.
The company, which started in Vernon, California, in 1931, made
dinnerware and figurines until it closed in 1958. Collectors search for the
brightly colored dinnerware and the pieces designed by Rockwell Kent,
Walt Disney, and Don Blanding. For more information, see *Kovels'
Depression Glass & American Dinnerware Price List.*

Ashtray, Kentucky, 5 3/4 In.	25.00
Bowl Set, Mixing, Shadows, 4 Piece	65.00
Bowl, City Hall & Fire Dept. Abilene, Kans., Wheelock	20.00
Bowl, Coral Reef, Don Blanding	65.00
Bowl, Organdy, 9 In.	10.00
Bread Plate, Homespun	4.00
Butter, Cover, Homespun	20.00
Coaster, Texas, 4 1/2 In.	20.00
Creamer, Homespun	6.00
Cup & Saucer, Homespun	10.00
Plate, Abraham Lincoln, 10 1/2 In.	25.00
Plate, California	6.00
Plate, Dinner, Tam O'Shanter	1.50

Plate, Douglas MacArthur, Maroon, 10 1/4 In.	10.00
Plate, Frontier Days, Paul Davidson, 14 In.	60.00
Plate, Girard College	10.00
Plate, Grand Canyon, Fred Harvey	40.00
Plate, Homespun, 6 In.	2.50
Plate, Lei Lani, 14 In.	55.00
Plate, Marshall Texas Historic Sights	7.00
Plate, Organdy, 9 1/2 In.	4.00
Plate, Organdy, 10 1/2 In.	6.00
Plate, Our America, Blacks Picking Cotton, 7 1/2 In.	65.00
Plate, President, 1942	20.00
Plate, Salad, Homespun	5.00
Plate, Stage Robbers	27.50
Plate, Statue Of Liberty, E. Lazarus Poem On Back, 10 In.	45.00
Plate, Vernon Rotary Club, 1943	25.00
Plate, Will Rogers	10.00
Platter, Tam O'Shanter, 14 In.	12.00
Platter, Tidbit, Our America, 14 In.	135.00
Salt & Pepper, Frontier Days	38.50
Saucer, Tam O'Shanter	1.25
Sugar & Creamer, Raffia	10.00
Syrup, Homespun	25.00
Teapot, Brown–Eyed Susan	28.00
Tureen, Cover, Hibiscus, Underplate	325.00
Vase, White Spheres, May & Vieve Hamilton, 5 In.	95.00 To 125.00

VERRE DE SOIE glass was first made by Frederick Carder at the Steuben Glass Works from about 1905 to 1930. It is an iridescent glass of soft white or very, very pale green. The name means *glass of silk,* and it does resemble silk. Other factories have made verre de soie, and some of the English examples were made of different colors. Verre de soie is an art glass and is not related to the iridescent, pressed, white carnival glass mistakenly called by its name. Related pieces may be found in the Steuben category.

Goblet, Blue Rigaree On Stems, Threaded Foot, 4 Piece	595.00
Sherbet Set, Stemmed Dish, Undertray, 6 1/4 In., 8 Sets	522.50
Vase, 6 In.	35.00
Vase, Etched & Cut Floral Swags, Silver Mounted, 10 In.	385.00
Vase, Ruffled Rim, Steuben, 8 1/2 In.	275.00

VIENNA ART plates are round metal serving trays produced at the turn of the century. The designs, copied from Royal Vienna porcelain plates, usually featured a portrait of a woman encircled by a wide, ornate border. Many were used as advertising or promotional items and were produced in Coshocton, Ohio, by J. F. Meeks Tuscarora Advertising Co. and H. D. Beach's Standard Advertising Co.

Plate, Jamestown, 1607–1907	50.00
Plate, Marguerite, Western Coke	300.00
Plate, Woman Holding A Candle, Jos. Silverman & Co., 10 In.	275.00
Plate, Woman With Urn	50.00
Plate, Women, Topless	400.00

VIENNA, see Beehive category

VILLEROY & BOCH Pottery of Mettlach was founded in 1841. The firm made many types of wares, including the famous Mettlach steins. Collectors can be confused because although Villeroy and Boch made most of its pieces in the city of Mettlach, Germany, they also had factories in other locations. The dating code impressed on the bottom of most pieces makes it possible to determine the age of the piece. Additional items may be found in the Mettlach category.

Dish, Child's, Silhouette Of Boy Fishing	80.00
Figurine, Chinese Man, Seated, Rabbit On Shoulder, 4 In.	6600.00

Volkmar, Plaque, Landscape Scene, Green

Gray, 14 In.; Volkmar, Plaque, Windmill

Scene, Green Gray, 14 In.

Plate, Aerial View Of Coblenz, 13 3/4 In. 200.00
Plate, Tennis Player Center, 7 In. 160.00
Tobacco Jar, No. 116 .... 90.00
Tray, Allover Fruits, 6 3/4 x 18 In. 37.50

VOLKMAR pottery was made by Charles Volkmar of New York from 1879
to about 1911. He was associated with several firms, including the
Volkmar Ceramic Company, Volkmar and Cory, and Charles Volkmar and
Son. Volkmar had been a painter, and his designs often look like oil
paintings drawn on pottery.

VOLKMAR
Corona N.Y

Plaque, Landscape Scene, Green Gray, 14 In. ....*Illus*   1870.00
Plaque, Windmill Scene, Green Gray, 14 In. ....*Illus*   1430.00
Plate, Trees, House, Blue and White, 14 In. 175.00
Vase, Blue Green, Matte Glaze, c.1880, 8 In. 308.00
Vase, Feathered Deep Blue & Green Glaze, Bulbous, 10 3/4 In. 413.00
Vase, Green Matte, 4 In. 225.00

VOLKSTEDT was a soft-paste porcelain factory started in 1760 by Georg
Heinrich Macheleid at Volkstedt, Thuringia. Volkstedt-Rudolstadt was a
porcelain factory started at Volkstedt-Rudolstadt by Beyer and Bock in
1890. Most pieces seen in shops today are from the later factory.

Figurine, Beauty, Girl In Floral Dress, 6 In. 125.00
Figurine, Chess Duel, Man & Woman, Chess Pieces, 6 x 9 In. 850.00
Figurine, Musical, 2 Women & Man, Playing Instruments, 9 In. 995.00
Figurine, Portrait Painter, Woman & Artist, 7 1/2 x 9 In. 650.00
Figurine, Woman With Fan, White Robe & Hat, 11 In. 85.00
Group, Wedding March, Bride & Groom, Girls, Page Boy, 9 x 13 In. 1250.00
Jar, Cover, Asparagus, 1780-1790, 8 9/16 In., Pair 8800.00
Plaque, Maiden, Flower In Hand, Flower Over Head, 5 1/2 x 13 In. 325.00

WAHPETON POTTERY, see Rosemeade category

WALLACE NUTTING photographs are listed under Print, Nutting. His reproduction furniture is
listed under Furniture.

WALRATH was a potter who worked in New York City, Rochester, New
York, and at the Newcomb Pottery in New Orleans, Louisiana. Frederick
Walrath died in 1920. Pieces listed here are from his Rochester period.

Walrath
Pottery

Bowl, Nude Kneeling, 6 In. 225.00
Vase, Green, Blue, 8 In. 800.00
Vase, Raised Flower Stems, 4 In. 800.00

WALT DISNEY, see Disneyana

WALTER, see A. Walter

WARWICK china was made in Wheeling, West Virginia, in a pottery working from 1887 to 1951. Many pieces were made with hand painted or decal decorations. The most familiar Warwick has a shaded brown background. The name *Warwick* is part of the mark and sometimes the mysterious word *IOGA* is also included.

Chocolate Set, Transfer Monk, 7 Piece	44.00
Cuspidor, Florals, IOGA, 6 1/2 In.	70.00
Ewer, Hibiscus, 8 In.	125.00
Lemonade Set, Monks, IOGA Mark, 10 1/2–In. Pitcher, 6 Mugs	450.00
Mug, F. O. E., IOGA	45.00
Mug, Laughing Monk, IOGA, 4 1/2 In.	75.00
Pitcher, Brown Tones, Large Flower, 7 1/2 In.	70.00
Pitcher, Lemonade, Fruit, Brown, IOGA, 6 1/2 In.	85.00
Pitcher, Poppies, IOGA, 10 1/2 In.	110.00
Plate, Coach Scene, Gold Band, Yellow Ground, 10 In.	95.00
Plate, Coach Scene, Yellow Band, 10 In.	95.00
Platter, Ironstone, 12 In.	27.00
Tankard, F. O. E., IOGA, 10 1/2 In.	130.00
Tobacco Jar, Indian On Front, Tobacco On Back	185.00
Tray, Dresser, Fluted, Blue & Yellow Flowers, Marked, 10 x 6 In.	30.00
Vase, Beechnuts, Brown Matte, IOGA, 13 1/2 In.	150.00
Vase, Bud, Helmet & Swords, IOGA, 8 3/4 In.	125.00
Vase, Flowers, Cylinder, IOGA Mark, 10 1/2 In.	120.00
Vase, Flowers, IOGA, 10 1/2 In.	120.00
Vase, Gypsy Girl, Long Hair, Gold Coin Necklace, Twig Handles	155.00
Vase, Hibiscus Design, Double Handle, Geran, 11 1/2 In.	115.00
Vase, Portrait Of Woman, Bulbous, IOGA, 9 In.	250.00
Vase, Red Roses, Greenish Blue, 10 1/2 In.	90.00
Vase, Verbena, Brown, Floral, 7 In.	200.00
Vase, Woman, Curly Hair, Draped Shoulder, Twig Handle, 10 1/2 In.	145.00

WATCH FOBS were worn on watch chains. They were popular during Victorian times and after. Many styles, especially advertising designs, are still made today.

Abraham Fur Co., Black	80.00
Alaska–Yukon Pacific Exposition, Seattle, 1909	32.50
Allis–Chalmers, Crawler Tractor	50.00
Allis–Chalmers, Grader	28.00
Alumina Soapalite, Celluloid Lion's Head Center	65.00
American Assn. Of Traveling Passenger Agents, 1916	5.00
American Legion, 50th Anniversary, 1919–1969	22.50
American Snow Plows & Wings	25.00
Anheuser–Busch, Eagle	75.00
Argonaut Insurance Co.	22.00
Avery Tractor Co., Bulldog	85.00 To 125.00
Baker Steam Tractor	75.00
Bay City Shovels	50.00
Birdshell Thresher, Bronze	50.00
Bucking Bronco Rider	75.00
Bueeker True Tone, Band Instruments	28.50
Butler M. C. Scales, Pumps, Water Supplies, Kansas City	30.00
Caterpillar, With Strap	28.00
Cedar Rapids Crushers, Enameled Shield	30.00
Chicago Business Men's Association, Ins.	15.00
Chicago Technical College, Silvered Brass, Logo	5.00
Child's, Lone Wolf	40.00
Cincinnati Horseshoe Company	85.00
Columbian Exposition, 1893	25.00
Dead Shot Powder, Celluloid Center	250.00
DeLaval, Enameled	75.00 To 100.00
Dempster, Windmill	45.00
Disston Tools, Enamel	75.00

Dr Pepper, Billiken	125.00
Dr Pepper, Louisiana Purchase Exposition	150.00
Duenning Construction Co., Slinger, Wi., Enameled	10.00
E. C. Simmons, Keen Kutter	65.00
E. C. Atkins Silver Steel Saws, Saw Picture	38.00
El Paso Saddlery, 1889	140.00
Finck & Co., Railroad Overalls, B. L. E. Logo, Celluloid Center	85.00
Ford Tractor, 1965	30.00
Fred Mueller Saddle Co., Denver, Working Man's Saddle	155.00
Galion Iron Works, 3 Machines Pictured	28.00
Gardner Denver Jackhammer	22.00
Gold, Iowa State Tennis Association, 1920	45.00
Golden Nugget, Las Vegas	27.50
Grand Island Horse & Mule Co., Nebraska, 1917	80.00
Green River Whiskey	45.00 To 75.00
Gypsy Tour, 1921	200.00
H. W. Starr, Oakland, California, Saddle	125.00
Hamely Roundup Saddle, Pendleton, Oregon	125.00
Heinz 57 Varieties, Good Luck	35.00
Hickock, Cutout M	10.00
Hohner, Little Lady Harmonica	30.00
Hunter, Trader, Trapper, Columbus, Oh.	75.00
Hunter–Trader–Trapper	225.00
Illinois Central RR, Green Diamond	35.00
Illinois Watch Co., Lincoln's Profile	75.00
Indianapolis Saddlery Co.	80.00
Industrial Exposition	30.00
International Harvester	45.00
International Harvester, Euclid	10.00
Jamestown Exposition, Connecticut House	45.00
John Deere, 1837–1937	55.00
John Deere, Key Shape	30.00
John's Leather Shop, Denver, Co.	125.00
Kansas Livestock, Co., Horse & Shoe	45.00
Kearney, Nebraska, Buffalo	42.50
Kellogg's	75.00
Levi Strauss Overalls, Mirror, Celluloid	175.00
Lima Shovels, Draglines	22.00
Manitowoc Speed Shovel, Nickel, Enameled	28.00
Mayflower, Calfskin, Germany	12.50
McCormick, Deering	35.00
McFarland Carriage Co., Kansas City, Mo.	95.00
Modern Woodmen Of America	45.00
National Park Gun Club, Sterling, 1908	145.00
National Sportsman, Deer Head, Rod & Gun, Bronze	47.50
National Sportsman, Nickel Plated	38.00
New England Industrial Exposition, 1911	28.00
Odd Fellows, 1910	38.00
Pan Automobile	150.00
Paul Revere Life Insurance Co.	25.00
Peck Brothers Livestock Commission Co., Ogden, Utah, Pig Shape	90.00
Race Horses	37.50
Red Goose Shoes, Red & Yellow Enamel, Brass	75.00
Remember The Maine, Afloat & Sinking	40.00
Remington, 100th Anniversary	195.00
Richards Wilcox Hardware Spec., Aurora	28.00
Rock Island Plow	95.00
Roi–Tan, 1930s Chevrolet, From Kate Smith Radio Program	35.00
Salvet Worm Destroyer	60.00
Samuel Rosenthal & Bros., Boy Holding Trousers, N.Y. C., 1890s	30.00
Savage Rifles, Facing Left	195.00 To 225.00
Savage Rifles, Facing Right	250.00
Savage Rifles, Panama Pacific Exposition, San Francisco, 1915	250.00

Schaeffer Leather Shop, Saddle Shape 125.00
Seal Of Atlantic City, Scantily Clad Women, Dated 1884 .... 35.00
Silverman & Sons Fur Co. 150.00
Sioux City Stockyards, Indian Head 90.00
Sportsman's Digest Magazine 40.00
Spur Farmland, Spur, Texas 75.00
Stan Brand Shoes Are Better 40.00
State Of Massachusetts Seal 14.00
Texas, Arrowhead, Saddle, Souvenir 35.00
Tonopah, Nevada, Brass, 1880 .... 135.00
Traveler's Protective Ass'n., Illinois State Shape, Compass 25.00
Trojan Powder, War Service Munitions Mfg. 150.00
U.S. Masters Brewers, 1911 .... 48.00
Union Horse Nail Co., Chicago 80.00
Unit Crane Shovels 25.00
Unit Crane, Berlin, Wisconsin 20.00
United States Horseshoe Co., Erie .... 40.00 To 75.00
West Cast Steel Motor, Truck Wheel 60.00
West Pennsylvania Volunteer Firemen's Assoc. 2.50
Western Pa. Firemen's Association, 1929 .... 15.00
Wilson Aldridge Livestock Commission Co. 90.00
Women's Heads, Silver, Unger Bros. 295.00
Worcester Salt 30.00
Woven Horsehair 175.00
Zeb Pike, Silver, 1906 .... 45.00

WATCH pockets held the pocket watch that was important in Victorian
times because it was not until World War I that the wristwatch was used.
All types of watches are collected: silver, gold, or plated. Watches are
arranged by company name or by style. Pocket watches are listed here;
wristwatches are a separate category.

A. S. Tobias, 18K Gold, Key Wind, Buildings Engraved 3000.00
Agazziz, Woman's, 18K, Hunting Case 515.00
Alpina, Chronograph, Silver Case 185.00
American Waltham, Silveroid Case, 7 Jewel 25.00
Aristocrat, Railroad Special, Box 55.00
B. W. Raymond, 14K White Gold Filled, 5 Position, 21 Jewel, Size 16 .... 425.00
B. W. Raymond, 14K White Gold Filled, 6 Position, 23 Jewel, Size 16 .... 490.00
B. W. Raymond, 5 Position, 19 Jewel, Size 16 .... 130.00
B. W. Raymond, 8 Position, 21 Jewel, Size 16 .... 170.00
B. W. Raymond, Monitor, 19 Jewel, Size 18 .... 65.00
Ball, Jewel Scrolled Hunting Case, 20 Year Railroad, Size 16 .... 210.00
Ball, Standard Railroad, 10 Year, 17 Jewel, Size 16 .... 100.00
Baum & Mercier, Platinum, 104 Sapphire Chips Around Rim, Loop 2000.00
Bucherer, Silver, Marcasite, Domed Hinged Lid, Swiss, 1930 .... 195.00
Burlington, Gold Case, VMA Monogram, Gold Chain, Seed Pearl 90.00
Charles Taylor & Son, Carved 18K Gold Case, Fusee, Key Wind 2400.00
Columbus, 17 Jewel, Size 18, Silveroid Case 85.00
Dunham, Repeater, 14K Gold 1125.00
Dunlop Tire & Rubber Co., Dealer's, Sterling Silver Case & Chain 225.00
E. N. W. Co., Yellow Gold Filled, 7 Jewel, Size 16, 1884 .... 60.00
Elgin National, 14K Gold, Open Face 135.00
Elgin, Desk Type, 14K White Gold Filled, 17 Jewel, Size 12 .... 65.00
Elgin, Father Time, 5 Position, 21 Jewel, Size 16 .... 500.00
Elgin, Gold Case, Enameled Face 70.00
Elgin, Gold Filled, Open Face, 15 Jewel, Size 12 .... 80.00
Elgin, Hunting Case, 5-Color Gold Steam Engine, 15 Jewel, Size 16 .... 225.00
Elgin, Hunting Case, Coin Silver, 7 Jewel, Size 18 .... 80.00
Elgin, Hunting Case, Etched Birds, 7 Jewel 70.00
Elgin, Hunting Case, Floral Design, 7 Jewel, Size 16 .... 170.00
Elgin, Hunting Case, Key Wind, Silver, Size 18, 1880 .... 225.00
Elgin, Hunting Case, Roman Numerals, Second Hand, 15 Jewel, Box 220.00
Elgin, Model 2, Size 0 .... 75.00

Elgin, No. 60819, 18K Gold Hunting Case, Silver Plated Chain	600.00
Elgin, Open Face, Key Wind, Silver Case	275.00
Elgin, Railroad, 17 Jewel, Crystal Front & Back, Hand For Time Zones	150.00
Elgin, Rolled Gold Plate, 10K	55.00
Elgin, Woman's, Hunting Case, 17 Jewel	125.00
Ernest Borel, Ring, Cocktail, Revolving Dial	25.00
F. Sagnelocle, Jeweled, Second Hand, Key Wind, Enamel Face, 18K Gold	195.00
For First Automobiles, Leather Strap For Hanging On Dashboard	195.00
G. W. Welsh, Woman's, Jeweled Nickel Movement, Pocket, 3–Color Gold	495.00
Gallet, Woman's, 15 Jewel, 20 Year Case, Cloth Band	65.00
Gold Dial, Arabic Symbols, Key Wind, 18K Gold	1500.00
Grantham, Calendar, Seconds Dial, Silver Case, Chain, London, 1762	550.00
Gruen, 36 Small Diamonds, 14K White Gold	435.00
H. H. Taylor, Hunting Case, 17 Jewel, Size 18	80.00
Hamilton, 17 Jewel, Open Face, Silveroid Case	100.00
Hamilton, 21 Jewel, Hunter Case, 14K Gold	300.00
Hamilton, 940, Motor Barrel, 5 Position, 21 Jewel, Size 18	90.00
Hamilton, 992b, 6 Position, 21 Jewel, Size 16	225.00
Hamilton, 996, Motor Barrel, 5 Position, 19 Jewel	210.00
Hamilton, Engraved, 17 Jewel, 14K Gold Filled, 1930s	65.00
Hamilton, Hunting Case, 16 Jewel, Sterling Silver	675.00
Hamilton, Model 931, Hunting Case, Diamond & Rubies, 14K Gold	2750.00
Hamilton, Model 992B, 21 Jewel, 10K Gold Filled	290.00
Hamilton, Railroad	175.00
Hamilton, Stop Watch, 23–Position Base, 19 Jewel	125.00
Hampden, 603, 17 Jewel, Size 16	40.00
Hampden, Dueber Grand, 17 Jewel, Silveroid Case	90.00
Hampden, Molly Stark, Open Face, Neck Chain, Gold Plated, 1896	150.00
Hampden, T. A. Norton, Multicolor 17K Gold Filled, Stag Back, Size 18	160.00
Hever, Chronograph, Moon Phase, Date, Box	995.00
Howard, Engraved Case, Series VII, 14K Gold	1200.00
Howard, Railroad Chronometer, Swing–Out Case, Series 11, Size 16	375.00
Howard, Railroad, 23 Jewel, Hunting Case, 14K Gold	1495.00
Hunting Case, Key Wind, 18K Yellow Gold, Arabesque Design	195.00
Illinois Springfield, Transition Swing–Out, 7 Jewel, Size 18	65.00
Illinois, A. Lincoln, 10K Rolled Gold, 5 Position, 21 Jewel, Size 16	130.00
Illinois, Auto Craft, 17 Jewel, Size 12	45.00
Illinois, Bun Special, 10K Gold Filled Case, 23 Jewel, Size 16	425.00
Illinois, Bun Special, 6 Position Isochronism, 21 Jewel, Size 18	120.00
Illinois, Burlington, 14K White Gold Stellar Case, 19 Jewel, Size 16	140.00
Illinois, Hunting Case, Deer Scene On Case, 14K Gold, 1887	550.00
Illinois, Piccadilly, White Gold Filled	895.00
Illinois, Springfield Rockland Montauk E. X. C., 19 Jewel, Size 16	100.00
Illinois, Woman's, Gold Hunting Case, 1887	550.00
Illinois, Yellow Gold Filled Case, 10K, 21 Jewel, Size 12	75.00
Ingersoll, New York To Paris	300.00
Ingersoll, Three Pigs & Bad Wolf, Box	1250.00
J. Boss, 10K Gold Filled, 5 Position, 21 Jewel, Size 16	300.00
J. Boss, Hunting, 20 Year Railroad Case, 16 Jewel, Size 16	160.00
John Wilter, Open Face, Key Wind, Dust Cover, Silver, London	110.00
Jules Jurgensen, 14K Yellow Gold	150.00
Jules Jurgensen, Woman's, 20 Diamonds, 17 Jewel, 14K White Gold	650.00
KBG, Russia	495.00
Keystone, 21 Jewel, Size 12	50.00
Keystone, Hunting Case, Gold Filled, Cardinals, 17 Jewel, Size 18	65.00
LeCoultre, Memodate Alarm, Yellow Gold Filled, Automatic	375.00
Lord Elgin, 10K Yellow Gold Filled, 19 Jewel, Size 12	70.00
Milan, Repeater, Half Chronometer, Porcelain Face	1350.00
Movado, Woman's Purse Style	1200.00
New Haven, Popeye, 1934	950.00
Omega, Woman's, 14K White Gold	125.00
Open Face, 18K Gold, Key Wind, Gilt Movement, Genre Scene	825.00
Open Face, Diamond Palace, San Francisco, 1878	75.00

P. Buhre, Hunter, Eagle, Imperial Presentation, Gold, 1 7/8 In. 3300.00
Patek Philippe, Open Face, Hand Wind, 18 Jewels, 18K Gold 1870.00
Patek Phillipe, Serial 119192, Open Face Case, 18K Gold 1375.00
Regina, New York Standard, Scroll Work, 7 Jewel, Size 6 .... 35.00
Robert Roskell, Key Wind, Open Face, Fitted Box, Key, 18K Gold 825.00
Rockford, Key Wind, Silver Hunting Case, 1885 .... 250.00
Rolex, President, Bark Band, 18K White Gold 5000.00
Shell Oil Dealer's 200.00
South Bend, Swing–Out Movement, 21 Jewel, 25–Year Case 375.00
Swiss, 1/4 Hour Repeater, Chronograph Hunting Case, 14K Gold 3000.00
Tiffany, Serial 112109, Open Face Case, 18K Gold 3850.00
Vacheron & Constantin, 17 Jewel, Double Door Back, 14K Gold Case 500.00
Waltham, Apple Trary & Co., 17 Jewel, Size 18 .... 40.00
Waltham, Crescent St. Bristol, Hunting Case, 17 Jewel 80.00
Waltham, Dated 1892, 23 Jewel 450.00
Waltham, Engraved Train On Rear, 21 Jewel 275.00
Waltham, Gold Filled, Open Face, 7 Jewel 75.00
Waltham, Hunting Case, 14K Gold, White Enamel Face, Second Hand 440.00
Waltham, Key Wind, Open Face, Silver Case, 1860 .... 300.00
Waltham, Maximus, Colonial Series, 23 Jewel 300.00
Waltham, Model 1980, 15 Jewel, 14K Gold Case 220.00
Waltham, Premier, 25 Jewels, 14K Yellow Gold 195.00
Waltham, Railroad, Vanguard, 23 Jewel, Gold Filled 275.00
Waltham, Ruby & Pearls, Hunting Case, 14K Gold, Gold Rope Slide Chain 325.00
Waltham, Woman's, Gold Hunting Case 250.00
Waltham, Woman's, Open Face, Arabic Numerals 110.00
William Frantz, Woman's, Open Face, White Dial, 14K Gold 55.00
Woman's, Chain, 14K Yellow Gold Tricolor, Black Onyx, Seed Pearl 500.00
Woman's, Chain, 14K Yellow Gold, Engraved Back, Blue Enamel 350.00
Woman's, Hunter, 14K Yellow Gold, Arabic Numerals 495.00
Woman's, Movado, Purse, 18K Gold, 1935 .... 1000.00
Woman's, Pin & Pendant, 14K Yellow Gold, Woman's Portrait, Red Ground 825.00
Zeppelin, Chain, Warranty, 1929 .... 65.00

WATERFORD type glass resembles the famous glass made from 1783 to
1851 in the Waterford Glass Works in Ireland. It is a clear glass that was
often decorated by cutting. Modern glass is being made again in
Waterford, Ireland, and is marketed under the name *Waterford.*

Candlestick, Everted Bobeches, Diamond Banding, 12 In. 145.00
Champagne, Colleen, Signed, c.1930, 11 Piece 250.00
Chandelier, 9–Light, Prisms, Swags, Electrified, 38 x 29 In. 5500.00
Decanter, Allover Diamond Design, 13 In. 145.00
Decanter, Baltray Pattern 150.00
Decanter, Inverted Arches & Thumbprints, Fluted Neck, 10 1/4 In. 150.00
Decanter, Lismore 175.00
Goblet, Colleen, Signed, c.1930, 14 Piece 305.00
Ornament, Christmas, 1987, Box 15.00
Plate, Christmas, 1990 .... 50.00
Salt & Pepper, Pedestal, Signed, 6 In. 138.00
Wine, Colleen, Signed, c.1930, 9 Piece 220.00
Wine, Lismore 25.00

WATT family members bought the Globe pottery of Crooksville, Ohio, in
1922. They made pottery mixing bowls and dishes of the type made by
Globe. In 1935 they changed the production and made the pieces with the
freehand decorations that are popular with collectors today. Apple,
Starflower, Rooster, Red & Blue Tulip, and Autumn Foliage are the best-
known patterns. Apple, the most popular pattern, can be dated from the
leaves. Originally, the apples had three leaves; after 1958 two leaves were
used. The plant closed in 1965. For more information, see *Kovels'
Depression Glass & American Dinnerware Price List.*

Bowl Set, Starflower, 4 Piece 122.00
Bowl, Apple, 3 1/2 In. 70.00

Bowl, Apple, 4 In.	26.00
Bowl, Apple, No. 7, 8 In.	50.00
Bowl, Apple, No. 39, Spaghetti	115.00
Bowl, Apple, No. 65	45.00
Bowl, Apple, No. 74	75.00
Bowl, Mixing, Rooster	40.00
Bowl, Pansy, No. 5, Pair	24.00
Bowl, Pansy, Spaghetti	60.00
Bowl, Poinsettia, With Advertising	25.00
Bowl, Starflower, 6 1/2 In.	22.00
Bowl, Yellow Swirl	34.00
Canister Set	45.00
Casserole, Apple, No. 96, Metal Rack, Double	90.00
Casserole, Bleeding Heart	53.00
Casserole, Cover, Apple, No. 601	65.00
Casserole, Cover, Brown Bands, Advertising	55.00
Casserole, Cover, No. 18–N, Green Flower	39.50
Chop Plate, Cherries, No. 49	120.00
Cookie Jar, Apple, No. 76	80.00 To 120.00
Cookie Jar, No. 100, Basket Weave, Green & White	150.00
Cookie Jar, No. 617–W	120.00
Creamer, Advertising, Madison, South Dakota	40.00
Creamer, Autumn Foliage	48.00
Creamer, Radcliffe, Iowa	35.00
Creamer, Rooster, No. 62	85.00
Creamer, Starflower	75.00
Creamer, Tulip, No. 62	59.50 To 75.00
Cruet, Autumn Foliage, Pair	325.00
Cup, Pansy	65.00
Grease Jar, Apple Curd, Advertising	225.00
Lazy Susan	200.00
Mug, Apple, Advertising	155.00
Mug, Starflower	95.00
Mug, Starflower, No. 501	75.00
Pepper Shaker, Rooster	18.00
Pie Plate, Apple, Advertising	95.00
Pitcher, Apple, No. 15, Soderville, Minnesota	45.00
Pitcher, Apple, No. 15, Worthington, South Dakota	45.00
Pitcher, Apple, No. 17	120.00
Pitcher, Apple, No. 62	30.00 To 85.00
Pitcher, Apple, No. 64	60.00
Pitcher, Autumn Foliage, No. 16	25.00
Pitcher, Bleeding Heart	225.00
Pitcher, Brown Bands, No. 115, Hourglass Shape	60.00
Pitcher, Cherries, No. 15	65.00
Pitcher, Dogwood	135.00
Pitcher, Leaf, No. 98, Advertising	125.00
Pitcher, Morning Glory, No. 97	90.00
Pitcher, Poinsettia, No. 15, Advertising	47.00
Pitcher, Poinsettia, No. 17	98.00
Pitcher, Rooster, No. 2, Square	225.00
Pitcher, Rooster, No. 16	70.00
Pitcher, Rooster, No. 62, 4 1/2 In.	50.00
Pitcher, Starflower, No. 15	25.00 To 30.00
Pitcher, Starflower, No. 16	65.00
Pitcher, Starflower, No. 17	50.00
Pitcher, Tulip, Blue & Red, No. 15	45.99
Pitcher, Tulip, No. 16	75.00 To 85.00
Plate, Apple, No. 49, Advertising, 9 3/4 In.	500.00
Plate, Apple, No. 49, Advertising, 12 In.	200.00
Platter, Starflower, 15 In.	135.00
Salad Set, Kale Apple, 5 Piece	200.00
Salad Set, Pansy, No. 39 Bowl, With 4 8–In. Bowls, 5 Piece	52.50

Salt & Pepper, Starflower	80.00
Saltshaker, Tyler Feed Store, Purina Chows, Guymon, Oklahoma	110.00
Sugar, Apple, Pease, Minnesota	85.00
Sugar, Autumn Foliage, No. 98, Advertising	90.00
Sugar, Morning Glory	140.00
Teapot, Apple, No. 505	985.00
Tumbler, Poinsettia	25.00

WAVE CREST glass is a white glassware manufactured by the Pairpoint
Manufacturing Company of New Bedford, Massachusetts, and some **WAVE CREST**
French factories. It was decorated by the C. F. Monroe Company of
Meriden, Connecticut. The glass was painted in pastel colors and decorated **WARE**
with flowers. The name *Wave Crest* was used after 1898.

Biscuit Jar, Pink & Blue Crescents, Gold Outlined, Clouds	325.00
Biscuit Jar, Scrolling, Floral Design, Marked, 11 In.	325.00
Biscuit Jar, White, Rococo Florals, Marked	175.00
Bonbon, Swirl Design, Floral, Metal Lid, Bail, Marked, 6 In.	295.00
Box, Bridge Scene On Lid, Bridge Scene, Marked, 3 1/2 In.	325.00
Box, Collar & Cuff, Gilded Rim & Clasp, Asters, 6 x 9 In.	1550.00
Box, Collar & Cuff, Rococo Gold Highlights	850.00
Box, Cover, Ship Scene, 8 In.	1750.00
Box, Cover, Swirls, Blue & White Daisies, Silk Lined, 4 1/2 In.	130.00
Box, Dresser, Shell, Dark Pink Painted Roses, Baroque, Round	225.00
Box, Egg Crate, Roses, Square, 7 In.	595.00
Box, Floral, Blue, White, Ormolu Rim & Handles, Rococo, 3 1/2 In.	150.00
Box, Glove, Dark Green Ground, 5 1/2 x 10 x 4 1/2 In.	1750.00
Box, Glove, Footed, Dark Green, White Flowers, Gold Trim, 10 In.	1750.00
Box, Handkerchief, Embossing, Pink, White, Marked, 9 x 6 In.	1250.00
Box, Hinged Cover, Courting Scene, 5 1/2 In.	1500.00
Box, Hinged Cover, Floral Design, Blue Borders, Marked, 4 x 5 In.	550.00
Box, Hinged Cover, Helmschmied Swirl & Floral, 7 In.	450.00
Box, Jewelry, Fern Design, Paper Label & Price Sticker	495.00
Box, Letter, Flower, Gold Metal Rim, 4 x 6 In.	275.00
Box, Locking Cover, Lattice & Scroll, Marked, 7 In.	375.00
Box, Opaque White, Blue Tint, Florals On Lid, Marked, 4 1/2 In.	210.00
Box, Oval, Blue, 5 1/2 In.	285.00
Box, Pink Daisies, Lavender Outlined, Baroque Shell Mold, 7 In.	765.00
Box, Pink Roses, Footed, 8 In.	475.00
Box, Pink Roses, Scrollwork, Footed, Square, 6 x 4 3/4 In.	635.00
Box, Puffy Egg Crate Cover, Blue Flowers, 5 1/4 x 2 3/4 In.	425.00
Box, Rococo, Brass Collar, Oval, Light Blue, Marked, 5 1/2 In.	425.00
Box, Swirl, Hand Painted Purple Flowers, 7 In.	595.00
Box, Violets, Baroque Shell, Marked C. F. M. Co., 7 1/2 In.	500.00
Cracker Jar, Raised Embossing Forms Frame, Blossoms	350.00
Creamer, Floral Design, Helmschmied Swirl	65.00
Creamer, Helmschmied Swirl, Roses	70.00
Ewer, Ormolu Collar & Foot, Flowers, Blues, 12 In.	275.00
Fernery, Bishop Hat Shape, Pink, Fern Design, 9 In.	450.00
Fernery, Fern On Pink, Brass Insert	450.00
Fernery, Floral On Pink, Brass Insert, Marked	450.00
Fernery, Insert, Ferns, Bishop Hat Shape, 9 In.	495.00
Fernery, Liner, Blue Flowers, Puffy, Marked	400.00
Holder, Jewelry, Ormolu Rim, Pedestal Base	135.00
Humidor, Cigar, Pink Wild Roses, Lock Mechanism, 6 In.	640.00
Humidor, Silver Cover, Panels Of Flowers, 7 1/4 In.	350.00
Humidor, Yellow Flowers Panels, Pink Ground, 7 1/4 In.	350.00
Jar, Cigar, Allover Embossed Florals, Bulbous, Hinged Lid, Large	525.00
Lamp, Electrified, 24 In.	100.00
Powder Box, Hinged Cover, Swirl, Yellow Florals, 4 In.	325.00
Salt & Pepper, Blue Florals, Square	135.00
Salt & Pepper, Brown & Blue Leaves	115.00
Salt & Pepper, Hunting Dogs	145.00
Salt & Pepper, Leaf Spear	75.00

Salt & Pepper, Meriden Holder 120.00
Salt & Pepper, Rooster Head, Clear 250.00
Salt & Pepper, Square, Blown Out 135.00
Salt & Pepper, Tulips 65.00
Sugar & Creamer, Silver Covers, Pink Rosebuds, White Swirls 635.00
Sugar Sifter 195.00
Toothpick, Embossed Petals Rim, Hand Painted Floral 145.00
Toothpick, Flower Design 60.00
Tray, Jewelry, Dotted Flowers, Ormolu Collar & Base, Marked 195.00
Tray, Jewelry, Handle, Swirl, Marked, 5 1/4 In. 250.00
Tray, Running Bunnies On Front & Back, Marked, 3 1/2 In. 225.00
Tray, Trinket, Bishop's Hat Mold, Pansies, Marked, 4 1/4 In. 225.00
Vase, Beaded Border, Light Blue, 9 1/4 In. 210.00
Vase, Enameled Florals, Dotting, Egg Shape, 7 In. 225.00

Weather Vane, Car,
Copper, Cast Iron, Gilded,
13 x 20 1/4 In.

Weather Vane, Cow, Cast Zinc,
Molded Copper, 24 x 36 In.

Weather Vane, Cow,
Copper & Zinc, Cushing &
White, 27 1/2 In.

Weather Vane, Grasshopper,
Copper, Repousse,
20 x 33 In.

Weather Vane, Horse &
Jockey, Molded Copper, Zinc,
Fiske, 35 In.

Weather Vane, Horse,
Sunburst, Copper, Iron,
20 1/4 x 31 1/2 In.

Weather Vane, Logger, 3 Logs, Sheet Metal,
Paint Traces, 35 In.

Weather Vane, Rooster, Copper, Repousse
Feathers, 26 In.

Vase, Metal Top & Bottom, Marked, 8 1/2 In. 400.00
Vase, Pink Chrysanthemums, White Dotting, 10 In. 395.00

WEATHER VANES were used in seventeenth–century Boston. The direction of the wind was an indication of coming weather, important to the seafaring and farming communities. By the mid–nineteenth century, commercial weather vanes were made of metal. Today's collectors often consider weather vanes to be examples of folk art, even though they may not have been handmade.

Airplane, Wood, Metal, Gray, Red, Black, Modern Base, 35 In. 425.00
American Eagle, Copper & Zinc, 27–In. Wingspan 5200.00
American Eagle, Gilt Zinc & Copper, Spread Wings, 18 1/2 In. 413.00
American Flag, Star Finial, Sheet Metal 3500.00
Arrow, Hearts In Dark Blue Glass Tail 100.00
Arrow, Pierced Geometric Design, Sheet Copper, 58 In. 825.00
Beaver, Rod & Directionals, Copper, Modern 110.00
Bull, Gilded Copper, Zinc Head, 23 x 38 In. 2310.00
Bull, Standing, Molded & Gilded, c.1875, 23 7/8 In. 2090.00
Car, Copper, Cast Iron, Gilded, 13 x 20 1/4 In. ....*Illus* 1650.00
Chicken, Pine, Folk Art, Original Traces Of Orange, Red Paint 1900.00
Cock, Directionals, Gilt, 16 In. 440.00
Cock, Molded Copper, 19th Century, 24 In. 468.00
Codfish, Carved & Painted Wood, 4 Ft. 4500.00
Codfish, Hand Carved Wood, Laid Over Copper, 54 In. 4800.00
Colonel Patchen, Molded Gilt Copper, Zinc, 21 x 30 In. 1210.00
Cow, Cast Zinc, Molded Copper, 24 x 36 In. ....*Illus* 7975.00
Cow, Copper & Zinc, Cushing & White, 27 1/2 In. ....*Illus* 2640.00
Cow, Copper, c.1880 .... 6500.00
Cow, Full–Bodied, Zinc, Wooden Base, 24 x 27 1/2 In. 800.00
Cow, Gilded Copper, 19th Century, 22 x 32 In. 4450.00
Cow, Standing, Upswept Horns, Molded Copper, c.1875, 27 5/8 In. 4200.00
Dove, Sheet Metal, Flower In Beak, Blue, 35 In. 1320.00
Eagle Perched On Sphere, Copper, Iron Directionals, 40 In. 525.00
Eagle, Arrow, Gilded Copper 440.00
Eagle, Flying On Ball, Arrow, Copper, Worn Gilt, 18 1/2 In. 450.00
Eagle, Full–Bodied, Copper, 29 In. 100.00
Eagle, Gilt & Green, 13 In. 400.00
Eagle, Spread Wings, Arrow, Copper Gilt, 15 1/2 In. 495.00
Fish, Flat Cut Tin 143.00
Gabriel, White Painted Iron 9500.00
Goose, Silhouette, Sheet Metal, 19th Century, 44 x 25 1/2 In. 1650.00
Grasshopper, Copper, Repousse, 20 x 33 In. ....*Illus* 6600.00
Griffin Silhouette, Sheet Copper, Tulip Finial, 43 In. 2750.00
Horse & Jockey, Molded Copper, Zinc, Fiske, 35 In. ....*Illus* 2860.00
Horse Trotting, Copper & Zinc, American, 15 x 29 1/2 In. 2200.00
Horse, Rider, Sheet Steel, Lead Weighted Head, 30 1/2 In. 400.00
Horse, Running, Black Hawk, 19th Century 2310.00
Horse, Running, Full Body, 13 1/2 In. 125.00
Horse, Running, Full Body, Molded Copper, c.1875, 30 1/4 In. 7700.00
Horse, Running, Hand–Forged Directions 745.00
Horse, Running, Molded Copper, Cast Zinc Head, Ethan Allen 2200.00
Horse, Silhouette, Painted, Sheet Metal, 16 1/2 x 21 In. 2090.00
Horse, Sunburst, Copper, Iron, 20 1/4 x 31 1/2 In. ....*Illus* 1320.00
Hunter & Stag, Sheet Iron, c.1930, 34 x 26 1/2 In. 4950.00
Indian Chief On Horseback, Sheet Iron, 21 x 35 In. 1320.00
Indian Kneeling, Sheet Iron 1050.00
Locomotive, Silhouette, Cast Iron, 35 x 70 In. 3850.00
Logger, 3 Logs, Sheet Metal, Paint Traces, 35 In. ....*Illus* 1100.00
Man Riding Horse 3300.00
Quill, Directionals, Sheet Iron 2090.00
Rooster Silhouette, Sheet Iron, Green & White, 20 1/2 In. 2150.00
Rooster, Arrow, Hollow, Cast Iron, Copper, Tin, 20 1/2 In. 115.00
Rooster, Copper, Repousse Feathers, 26 In. ....*Illus* 3300.00

Rooster, Crowing, Gold Leaf, 1880 .... 3080.00
Rooster, Sheet Copper, Mounted On Iron Rod, 31 1/2 x 19 In. 1320.00
Rooster, Silhouette, Serrated Comb, Sheet Metal, 34 1/4 In. 1980.00
Rooster, Swell–Bodied, Metal Stand, 26 1/2 x 30 In. 3850.00
Rooster, Zinc, Hollow Molded, Hanger, 13 3/4 In. 130.00
Running Deer, Gilded Copper, 65 1/2 x 34 In. 7425.00
Running Horse, Copper Body, Zinc Head, Full–Bodied, 40 In. 2365.00
Running Horse, Copper, Hollow Body, Green Patina, 28 In. 1750.00
Running Horse, Full Directionals, Brown Patina, 40 In. 1870.00
Running Horse, Hollow Body, Copper 1750.00
Running Horse, J. Harris & Co., Gilded Copper, 30 In. 3025.00
Running Horse, Rochester Iron Works, Iron, 26 x 36 In. 6050.00
Sailboat, Full–Dimensional, Copper 495.00
Sloop, 3 Masts, Sail, Sheet Copper, 1870s, 32 x 46 In. 3300.00
Smuggler, Verdigris Surface, Copper, New England, 24 x 41 In. 2650.00
Stag, Molded Copper, Verdigris Surface, 19th Century, 25 In. 4675.00
Steam Shovel, Welded Plate Steel, Red Paint, c.1930, 32 In. 350.00

WEBB BURMESE is a colored Victorian glass made by Thomas Webb & Sons of Stourbridge, England, from 1886. They also made Webb Peachblow and many other types of art and cameo glass during the Victorian era. The factory is still producing glass.

Webb

Bottle, Scent, Lay Down, Mistletoe, Sterling Screw Top, 5 In. 945.00
Bowl, 6–Sided Top, Red Berries, Leaves, 3 1/4 In. 325.00
Bowl, Floral Design, Applied Glass Rim, Marked, 3 3/4 In. 1110.00
Bowl, Silver Plated Holder, 2 1/2 x 5 In. 685.00
Dish, Honey, Silver Plated Frame, 7 1/4 In. 295.00
Fairy Lamp, Apron On Mirror, 4 Lamps, Ruffled Holder, Signed 3250.00
Fairy Lamp, Pink To Yellow, Clarke Base, 4 In. 175.00
Fairy Lamp, Pleated, Peach, Cream, Clear Candle Cup, 5 1/2 In. 1075.00
Fairy Lamp, Reversible Base, Clear Cup, Salmon, Yellow, 5 In. 650.00
Fairy Lamp, Ruffled Base, 6 In. 835.00
Finger Bowl, Raised Rib Stripes, Fluted Rim, 4 3/4 In. 295.00
Pitcher, 6–Sided Top, Green Pine Cones & Needles, 3 1/8 In. 595.00
Rose Bowl, 8–Crimp Top, 5 Petal Lavender Flowers, 3 1/4 In. 375.00
Rose Bowl, 8–Crimp Top, 5–Petal Flowers, 2 7/8 In. 395.00
Rose Bowl, 8–Crimp Top, Lavender Flowers, 2 3/8 In. 295.00
Rose Bowl, 8–Crimp Top, Lavender Flowers, Foliage, 2 1/2 In. 295.00
Rose Bowl, 8–Crimp Top, Red Flowers, Green Leaves, Miniature 295.00
Shade, Prunus Blossom, 6 1/2 x 6 In., Pair 1950.00
Toothpick, 6–Sided Top, Leaves, Red Berries, 2 5/8 In. 275.00
Vase, 6–Sided Top, 5–Petal Flowers, Foliage, 3 3/4 x 3 1/4 In. 325.00
Vase, 6–Sided Top, 5–Petal Lavender Flowers, 3 1/4 In. 295.00
Vase, Black Chain Bands, Forget–Me–Nots, 3 3/4 In. 275.00
Vase, Bulbous, Ruffled Top, Striping, 4 In. 225.00
Vase, Dimpled Sides, Blue Flowers, Brown Leaves, 7 5/8 In. 495.00
Vase, Floral Design, Silver Plated Frame, 8 1/4 In. 515.00
Vase, Flower Petal Top, Squatty, 3 x 3 1/8 In. 200.00
Vase, Folded Over Star–Shape Top, Signed, 3 3/8 In. 225.00
Vase, Ruffled, Acorns, Green Oak Leaves, 3 3/4 In. 325.00
Vase, Ruffled, Pink To Yellow, 5–Petal Flowers, 3 1/2 In. 300.00
Vase, Ruffled, Pink To Yellow, Ruffled Pedestal, 4 3/8 In. 200.00
Vase, Star–Shaped Top, Red Berries, Marked, 3 1/4 In. 335.00
Vase, Trumpet, Glossy Finish, 6 In. 195.00

WEBB PEACHBLOW is a colored Victorian glass made by Thomas Webb & Sons of Stourbridge, England, from 1885. The factory is still in business.

Fairy Lamp, Multicolored Leaves, Clarke Cup, 4 3/4 In. 505.00
Rose Bowl, 8 Crimps, Rose Red To Pink Amber, 3 In. 225.00
Vase, Floral & Dragonfly, White Lining, 7 1/2 In. 395.00
Vase, Gold Floral & Dragonfly, Cream Lining, 7 In. 550.00
Vase, Gold Floral & Dragonfly, Handles, 7 1/2 In. 395.00
Vase, Gold Prunus Blossoms, Cream Lining, 7 3/4 In. 650.00

Vase, White Flowers & Berries, Marked, 5 1/2 In. 395.00

Webb glasswares which are not the Burmese or Peachblow listed above are included here.

Bowl, Berry Prunt, Turquoise, Light Blue Interior, 5 1/2 In. 235.00
Bowl, Brown To Cream, Gold Prunus, Butterfly, Tricorner, 2 1/2 In. 300.00
Bowl, Gold Prunus Blossoms, 6–Crimp, Turquoise Lining, 6 1/2 In. 795.00
Bowl, Tightly Ruffled, Enameled, Green, 11 In. 265.00
Bride's Basket, Pulled Up Ruffled Sides, Pleated, Silver Plated 450.00
Bride's Basket, Yellow Cased, Enameled, Silver Plated Frame, 10 In. 260.00
Bride's Bowl, Opaque White To Pink, Florals & Fruit, Ribbed 195.00
Compote, Fuchsia, Florals, Bird, Signed 165.00
Creamer, Diamond–Quilted, Blue, 5 In. 350.00
Creamer, Diamond–Quilted, Blue, Frosted Handle, Signed, 5 In. 350.00
Decanter, Butterfly On Frosted Citron, Twig Handle, Chain, 1882, 9 In. 4800.00
Ewer, Enameled Fern Leaves, Bulbous, Cylindrical Neck, 10 In. 55.00
Ewer, Satin Glass, Blue, Large 475.00
Jar, Cover, Cylindrical, Red Over White, Berries, Metal Rim, 2 1/2 In. 465.00
Jar, Potpourri, Lid, Gold Fringed Top, Flowers, Brass Bottom, 5 1/2 In. 615.00
Lamp Base, Cameo, Yellow, White, Leafy Stalk, 9 3/4 In. 450.00
Lamp, Oil, Joseph Webb Shade, c.1912 .... 850.00
Perfume Bottle, Green Enamel, Gilt Prunus Branches, Silver Top, 3 In. 110.00
Pitcher, Clambroth Cased, Fading To Diamond Optic, 8 1/2 In. 205.00
Pitcher, Honeycomb, Blue & White Cased, Threaded Handle, 7 1/2 In. 295.00
Pitcher, Morrish Crackle, Satin Handle 645.00
Pitcher, White, Pink To Apricot, 16 Vertical Ribs, Green Vines, 4 In. 210.00
Plaque, Cameo, Yellow, White, Blooming Plant, 5 1/4 In. 495.00
Rose Bowl, Butterfly, White & Yellow, 4 In. 575.00
Rose Bowl, Swirled Satin, Quilted, Crimped Rim, Signed Patent, 5 In. 495.00
Seal, Ovoid Handle, Turquoise Over White, Flowers, Leaves, 4 1/2 In. 880.00
Vase, Allover Floral, Yellow, Bulbous, 7 In. 2000.00
Vase, Amethyst Berries & Leaves, Thorny Branches, Marked, 6 1/4 In. 467.50
Vase, Apricot Satin To Pink, Floral, Off–White Lining, 11 7/8 In., Pair 395.00
Vase, Beige, Ribbed, Opaque, 7 In. 60.00
Vase, Blossoms, Buds, Leafy Branch, Butterfly, Insects, Marked, 6 In. 1760.00
Vase, Bronze Glass, Gold, Green & Blue, 7 In. 325.00
Vase, Budding Branches, Butterfly, Red Body, 2 1/2 In. 1045.00
Vase, Cameo, Basketweave Top, 8 1/2 In. ....*Illus* 5225.00
Vase, Cameo, Clematis Flowers, Amber, Yellow, White, 5 In. 775.00
Vase, Cameo, Ovoid, White, Raspberry, Stylized Scrolls, 7 In. 1540.00
Vase, Cameo, Rubrum Lilies, Circular Foot, Emerald Over Clear, 8 In. 335.00
Vase, Cameo, Wildflowers, Moth, Yellow, White, 5 1/4 In. 550.00
Vase, Caramel, Gilt Enameled Prunus Flowers & Moth, 7 3/4 In. 165.00
Vase, Cobalt Blue Tulips, Stippled Crystal Ground, 9 1/4 In. 515.00
Vase, Corset Shape, Different Floral Each Side, Blue, 6 In. 2000.00
Vase, Cut Velvet, Bird Design, 12 In. 395.00
Vase, Dragons, Leaves, Elephant Neck Handles, Signed, 8 7/8 In. 3100.00
Vase, Enamel, Cornucopia Shape, Wild Flowers, 12 In. 445.00
Vase, Enamel, Japonisme Style, Applied Feet, Drip Forms, 12 In. 335.00
Vase, Enamel, Rainbow, Flowering Branches, 14 1/2 In. 600.00
Vase, Enameled Gilt & Silver Gilt Phoenix Bird, Raspberry, 9 3/4 In. 675.00
Vase, Enameled Gilt Prunus Flowers, Cranberry To Pink, 9 1/2 In. 165.00
Vase, Enameled, Bird, Flowering Branch, Flattened Base, 12 In. 140.00
Vase, Flared Top, Iris, Amber Iridescent, Signed, 8 In. 165.00
Vase, Frosted Blue, White Enamel Flowers, Signed, 9 In. 195.00
Vase, Gilt Enamel, Scrolling Leaf Forms, Wine Red, Baluster, 9 1/4 In. 190.00
Vase, Gold Floral & Rim, Signed, 11 In. 335.00
Vase, Gold Floral, Glossy Pink, Clear Wafer Foot, 7 1/2 In. 325.00
Vase, Gold Florals, Signed, Propeller Mark, 11 In. 335.00
Vase, Gold Prunus & Butterfly, Cobalt Blue, Marked, 4 5/8 In. 195.00
Vase, Ivory Cameo, Grape Design, Signed, 7 In. 1200.00
Vase, Japanese Style, Enameled Branches, Insects, 8 In. 275.00
Vase, Leaves & Berries, 6 In. 2000.00

Webb, Vase, Cameo, Basketweave

Top, 8 1/2 In.

◆◆◆◆◆◆◆◆◆◆◆◆◆◆◆◆◆◆◆◆◆

Lacquered wood can be damaged by a sudden change in humidity. Keep lacquer away from heat sources, preferably in a room with high humidity.

◆◆◆◆◆◆◆◆◆◆◆◆◆◆◆◆◆◆◆◆◆

Vase, Lily, Ambrina, Honeycomb Pattern, 12 In.	235.00
Vase, Melon Shape, Twisted Handles, Hand Painted Floral, Signed, 10 In.	295.00
Vase, Mother–of–Pearl, Quilted, Pink, Blue, Expanding Ovals, 15 In.	248.00
Vase, Narcissus, White On Citron, 5 In.	950.00
Vase, Pale To Deep Pink, 4 Blown–Out Seashells, Signed, 5 In.	135.00
Vase, Passion Flowers, White Over Purple, Frosted Turquoise, 8 1/2 In.	3900.00
Vase, Pink, Orange, White, Gray, Blue, Gold Stripes, Signed, 13 In.	175.00
Vase, Pink, White Ground, Gold & Black Rim, Hourglass Stem, Signed, 9 In	235.00
Vase, Poppies, Butterflies, Citron Ground, Bulbous, Cameo, 11 In.	2600.00
Vase, Seaweed & Fern Coralene, Blue, 8 In.	975.00
Vase, Seaweed Design, Yellow, Blue, 5 In.	195.00
Vase, Simulated Ivory, Berries & Leaves, Signed, 5 1/4 In.	950.00
Vase, Simulated Ivory, Pine Cones, Sterling Rim, Signed, 5 1/4 In.	950.00
Vase, White, Pink Florals, Brown Leaves, Signed, 6 In.	185.00
Vase, Wild Geraniums & Grasses, Amber To Rose, 6 1/2 In.	1045.00
Vase, Yellow Over Red & White, Morning Glories, 1 3/4 In.	1100.00

WEDGWOOD, one of the world's most successful potteries, was founded by Josiah Wedgwood, who was considered a cripple by his brother and was forbidden to work at the family business. The pottery was established in England in 1759. A large variety of wares has been made, including the well-known jasperware, basalt, creamware, and even a limited amount of WEDGWOOD porcelain. There are two kinds of jasperware. One is made from two colors of clay, the other is made from one color of clay with a color dip to create the contrast in design. The firm is still in business. Other Wedgwood pieces may be listed under Flow Blue or in other porcelain sections.

Ashtray, Ashford, Gray	6.00
Biscuit Jar, Classical Ladies, Cupids, Salmon & White, 7 In.	395.00
Biscuit Jar, Jasperware, Cupids All Sides, Marked, Salmon, 7 In.	395.00
Biscuit Jar, Jasperware, Olive, 19th Century, 9 In.	247.00
Biscuit Jar, Jasperware, Yellow & White, Acorn Finial, 6 In.	495.00
Biscuit Jar, Silver Plated Lid, Lavender, Marked TUG & 4	895.00
Biscuit Jar, Yellow, Black & White	775.00
Bowl & Pitcher, Ironstone	140.00
Bowl, Black Basalt, Neoclassical White Design, 7 5/8 In.	88.00
Bowl, Butterfly Luster, 9 In.	425.00
Bowl, Dragon Luster, Blue Exterior, Marked, c.1925, 8 3/4 In.	470.00
Bowl, Dragon Luster, Orange Exterior, c.1925, 9 In.	330.00
Bowl, Fairyland Luster, 4 x 10 In.	2900.00
Bowl, Fairyland Luster, Moorish Exterior, 8 1/2 In.	3175.00
Bowl, Hummingbird Luster, Blue Exterior, Marked, c.1925, 8 In.	522.50
Bowl, Vegetable, Rosalinde, Oval	100.00
Box, Bicentennial, Washington Portrait Cameo On Cover, 1 1/2 In.	225.00
Bread Plate, Asia, Black	7.00
Bust, Milton, Parian, E. W. Lyon, 14 3/4 In.	795.00
Butter Tub, Jasperware, Blue, Silver Plated Lid, Base, c.1860, 4 In.	225.00
Butter Tub, White & Tan, Green, Plated Plate & Lid, 4 1/4 In.	495.00

Candlestick, Figures, Flowers, 5 In. 135.00
Candlestick, Jasperware, Blue, Marked, 6 1/4 In., Pair 275.00
Charger, Gold Sunburst Center, Cobalt Blue Footed, Green Trim 950.00
Coffee Can & Saucer, Trophy, Lilac, Green & White 1275.00
Coffee Can, Jasperware, White, Green Dice, Blue Squares, 4 1/8 In. 1650.00
Coffeepot, Ball Finial, Figures, c.1870 .... 450.00
Coffeepot, Cover, Jasperware, Green, White Figures, 8 3/4 In. 1870.00
Creamer, Cherbourg 20.00
Creamer, Drabware, Marked, c.1840 .... 140.00
Creamer, Figures, 2 Bands, c.1860, 6 1/2 In. 325.00
Creamer, Jasperware, Crimson 485.00
Creamer, Seaweed 150.00
Cup & Saucer, Apple Blossom 35.00
Cup & Saucer, Ashford, Gray 18.00
Cup & Saucer, Ashford, Yellow 18.00
Cup & Saucer, Bouillon, Vining Foliage 25.00
Cup & Saucer, Cherbourg 18.00
Cup & Saucer, Chinese Tigers 25.00
Cup & Saucer, Creamware, Marked, c.1870 .... 20.00
Cup & Saucer, Handleless, Basalt, Marked 60.00
Cup & Saucer, Jasperware, Tricolor, Medallions 595.00
Cup & Saucer, Rosalinde 42.00
Demitasse Set, Florentine, Pot, 6 Cups & Saucers 285.00
Dessert & Tea Set, Botanical Flowers, 1815, Marked, 32 Piece 3630.00
Dish, Clamshell Shape, Gilt Decoration, c.1790 .... 198.00
Dresser Set, Blue On White, c.1900, 6 Piece 495.00
Ewer, Classical Figures, c.1860, 8 1/2 In. 185.00
Figurine, Bull, Signs Of Zodiac, Marked, c.1945, 15 3/4 In. 855.00
Figurine, Elephant, Trunk Lowered, Basalt, c.1916, 3 1/2 In. 302.50
Figurine, Nymph At Well, Holding Shell, Basalt, c.1840, 11 In. 1045.00
Figurine, Rhinoceros, Flambe, Raised Trunk & Horn, 9 x 17 In. 1250.00
Figurine, Squirrel, Holding Nut, Basalt, Marked, c.1915, 5 1/2 In. 225.00
Flowerpot, Stand, Terra–Cotta, Brown Slip, 7 1/2 & 9 3/8 In., 2 Pc. ... 2750.00
Ginger Jar, Blue Dragon Luster, Enameled Inside Cover, 9 1/4 In. 650.00
Inkwell, Black Basalt, Egyptian Style, 18th Century, 2 5/8 In. 600.00
Jar, Cover, Flower Garlands Held By Ram's Heads, 4 3/4 In. 350.00
Jardiniere, Black Basalt, Neoclassical Figures, Ball Feet, 8 In. 300.00
Jardiniere, Figures, Garlands, Rams' Heads, Green, 9 x 10 1/4 In. 425.00
Jardiniere, Jasperware, Blue, White Classical Figures, 6 1/2 In. 225.00
Jardiniere, Jasperware, Olive Green, Marked, c.1920, 8 3/4 In. 412.50
Jardiniere, Magnolia Pattern, Large 2310.00
Jug, Milk, Encaustic Design, Floral Spout, Basalt, 2 5/8 In. 880.00
Lamp, Queensware, Blue On White, 16 In., Pair 275.00
Match Holder, Butterfly Luster, 3 Handles 375.00
Mug, Sunflower 165.00
Pie Dish, Game, Caneware, 12 x 6 In. 575.00
Pitcher, Bulbous, Basalt, 5 1/4 In. 55.00
Pitcher, D'ye Ken John Peel, Hunt Scene, Hound Handle, 1829, 8 In. ... 150.00
Pitcher, Grapes & Leaves, Cream Color, 8 In. 55.00
Pitcher, Hinged Plated Top, Sage Green & White, Marked, 8 In. 225.00
Pitcher, Jasperware, Classical Figures, Crimson, 4 1/4 In. 795.00
Pitcher, Jasperware, Green, Silver Plated Lid, 6 In. 125.00
Pitcher, Milk, Classical Figures, c.1860, 5 3/4 In. 300.00
Pitcher, Milk, Doric Face On Lid, Figures, 6 1/4 In. 325.00
Pitcher, Milk, Leaf Border, Cherubs, Gray & White, 6 1/2 In. 375.00
Pitcher, Tricolor, 3 1/2 In. 595.00
Planter, Jasperware, Dark Blue, 19th Century, 7 x 8 In. 195.00
Plaque, Bacchus Playing Blind Man's Bluff, Green, c.1860, 20 In. 2650.00
Plaque, Body Of Hector Dragged By Chariot Of Achilles, 16 In. 1210.00
Plaque, Dancing Hours, Jasperware, Green, Blue & White, 18 1/2 In. ... 1320.00
Plaque, Roman Scene, Black Basalt, Etruria, Leather Box, 1789 .... 295.00
Plate, Apple Blossom, 10 1/2 In. 35.00
Plate, Ashford, Gray, 10 1/2 In. 10.00

Plate, Ashford, Yellow, 10 1/2 In.	15.00
Plate, Asia, Black, 6 In.	10.00
Plate, Blue Transfer, Owl's Head, Maine, 9 1/4 In., Pair	90.00
Plate, Cherbourg, 10 1/2 In.	15.00
Plate, Christmas, 1970	15.00
Plate, Columbia University, Different Scenes, 1930s, 12 Piece	450.00
Plate, Creamware, Brown, White, 10 In. _Illus_	75.00
Plate, Creamware, Shell Shape, Marked	40.00
Plate, Gold Dragon, Mottled Blue, Marked, 8 7/8 In.	125.00
Plate, Landing Of Pilgrims, Blue Floral, 1909, 9 In.	35.00
Plate, Rosalinde, 10 1/2 In.	36.00
Plate, Seashell, Etruria	45.00
Plate, University Of Michigan, Dated, 1928, 10 In.	40.00
Platter, Cherbourg, 11 1/2 In.	30.00
Platter, St. Austell, Oval, 15 In.	145.00
Powder Jar, Dragon Luster, Marked, 9 1/4 x 11 In.	995.00
Rose Jar, Cover, Gold Passion Flower, Gold Band, Signed, 11 In.	850.00
Sugar & Creamer, Dark Blue & White	225.00
Sugar, Cover, Jasperware, Crimson	495.00
Syrup, Jasperware, Parakeet, Dark Blue, 8 In.	82.50
Syrup, Pewter Lid, White Figures, Dark Blue	95.00
Syrup, Pineapple	265.00
Tankard, Harry Barnard, Dark Blue	400.00
Tankard, Jasperware, Green, Marked, 4 In.	100.00
Tea Caddy, Cover, Classical Figures, c.1870, 5 In.	350.00
Tea Caddy, Yellow, Black & White	450.00
Tea Set, Jasperware, Blue, Sterling Rimmed, 3 Piece	440.00
Tea Set, Primrose & Terra Cotta, 3 Piece	225.00
Teapot, Canada, Basalt, Marked	100.00
Teapot, Dark Blue Floral Borders, Gray & White	400.00
Teapot, Florentine Gold	150.00
Teapot, Jasperware, Light Blue, Medallion, c.1780	595.00
Teapot, Widow Finial, c.1874, 7 In.	600.00
Tile, Calendar, 1900	45.00
Tile, Little Red Riding Hood	100.00
Toby Jug, Benjamin Franklin, 5 1/2 In.	60.00
Toothpick, Jasperware, 3 Handles	42.00
Tureen, Florentine, Turquoise	495.00
Tureen, Trentham, Rams' Head Handles, 1922	75.00
Urn, Acorn Finial, Black Basalt, Figural Reserves, 10 1/2 In.	885.00
Urn, Cover, White Figures, Jasperware, Lavender, 9 1/4 In.	1190.00
Vase, Basalt, Encaustic Design, Classical, 1800, 9 In.	1980.00
Vase, Bedouin Fighter On Horse, 14 In.	95.00
Vase, Concentric Rings, Brown Matte Glaze, Marked, 9 In.	825.00
Vase, Dragon & Cricket, Blue Luster, 5 1/4 In.	305.00
Vase, Dragon Luster, 8 In.	750.00
Vase, Fairyland Luster, Firbogs V, Square, 1919–1921, 7 5/8 In.	1980.00

Wedgwood, Plate, Creamware, Brown,
White, 10 In.

◆◆◆◆◆◆◆◆◆◆◆◆◆◆◆◆◆◆◆◆

Never wash a bronze. Never
use metal polish on a bronze.
Dust frequently.

◆◆◆◆◆◆◆◆◆◆◆◆◆◆◆◆◆◆◆◆

Vase, Fairyland Luster, Tree Serpent, D. Makeig–Jones, 12 In., Pair 8250.00
Vase, Jasperware, Crimson, 5 In. 495.00
Vase, Light Blue & White, 2 Handles, 12 In. 975.00
Vase, Lion Head Both Sides, Classical Figures, 7 In. 250.00
Vase, Orchid, Black Basalt, 19th Century, 12 In. 220.00

WELLER pottery was first made in 1873 in Fultonham, Ohio. The firm
moved to Zanesville, Ohio, in 1882. Art wares were introduced in 1893.
Hundreds of lines of pottery were produced, including Louwelsa, Eocean,
Dickens, and Sicardo, before the pottery closed in 1948.

Basket, Copra, Daisies, 14 In. 320.00
Basket, Flemish, 7 x 9 1/2 In. 75.00
Basket, Hanging, Drapery, Blue 125.00
Basket, Hanging, Forest, 5 In. 235.00
Basket, Hanging, Forest, Chains, 10 In. 225.00
Basket, Louwelsa, 5 1/2 In. 65.00
Basket, Scenic, Waterfall 52.50
Basket, Silvertone, Twig Handle, 8 1/2 In. 165.00
Bowl, Atlas, Blue Star, 6 x 9 In. 85.00
Bowl, Blue Drapery, 3 In. 55.00
Bowl, Bulb, Claywood, 8 In. 55.00
Bowl, Etna, Blue To Gray, 5 1/2 x 6 1/2 In. 135.00
Bowl, Hudson, 9 In. 300.00
Bowl, Roma, Yellow, 3 In. 40.00
Bowl, Savona, Blue, 12 In. 100.00
Bowl, Squirrel On Rim, 9 In. 125.00
Bowl, Woodcraft, 3 In. 75.00
Bowl, Woodcraft, 8 1/4 In. 125.00
Bucket, Woodrose, 3 1/2 In. 75.00
Bust, Woman's Head, Etched, Matte, 8 In. 375.00
Candleholder, Glendale, Pair 165.00
Candleholder, Lavonia, Purple, 4 In. 15.00
Candleholder, Wannopee, 12 1/2 In. 200.00
Candlestick, Claremont, Floral, 8 In., Pair 175.00
Candy Dish, Squirrel 80.00
Chamberstick, Louwelsa, Floral, 5 1/2 In. 145.00
Clock, Louwelsa, 12 x 12 In. 895.00
Compote, Black Band, 5 In. 45.00
Console Set, Ardsley, 3 Piece 135.00
Console Set, Glendale, 3 Piece 500.00
Console Set, Golden Glow, 3 Piece 165.00
Console Set, Silvertone, Bowl, Frog, Candlesticks 345.00
Cookie Jar, Watermelon 600.00
Cornucopia, Lido, Turquoise, Footed, 7 1/4 In., Pair 50.00
Doorstop, Roma 350.00
Ewer, Flask, Dickens Ware 295.00
Ewer, Floretta, 12 1/2 In. 260.00
Ewer, Louwelsa, Berry Design, Artist, 9 1/2 In. 225.00
Ewer, Oak Leaf, 8 In. 40.00
Ewer, Roma, Yellow, 6 In. 70.00
Figurine, Bulldog, Brown High Gloss Glaze, 11 1/2 x 14 In. 695.00
Figurine, Bulldog, Brown, 10 x 15 In. 1400.00
Figurine, Elephant 2500.00
Figurine, Frog, Coppertone, On Lily Pad, Arms Around Blossom, 4 In. 155.00
Figurine, Frog, On Lily Pad, Coppertone 155.00
Figurine, Monkey, On A Peanut, White 95.00
Figurine, Pelican, Evergreen 75.00
Figurine, Pop–Eyed Dog, 10 In. 1500.00
Figurine, Pop–Eyed Dog, White, Black Spots, 4 In. 425.00
Figurine, Squirrel, To Hang On Tree, 13 In. 850.00
Flower Frog, Brighton, Double Canaries 200.00
Flower Frog, Crab, Muskota 150.00
Flower Frog, Double Salamander 95.00

Flower Frog, Frog In Water, Lily Blossom, Peach & Gray 95.00
Flower Frog, Girl With Watering Can, Muskota 375.00
Flower Frog, Lizard On Lily Pad, Muskota 110.00
Flower Frog, Lorbeck, 7 In. 95.00
Flower Frog, Mushroom 35.00
Flower Frog, Pagoda, Muskota, 6 In. 100.00
Flower Frog, Standing Cherub, Draped Nude, Muskota 295.00
Flower Frog, Swan, Muskota ....90.00 To 115.00
Flower Frog, Woodcraft 75.00
Flower Frog, Woodcraft, Kneeling Cherub 295.00
Ginger Jar, Greora 175.00
Hudson, Vase, Trumpet, Cosmos, Dorothy England, 9 In. 295.00
Humidor, Roma 150.00
Jardiniere & Pedestal, Baldwin, 34 In. 450.00
Jardiniere & Pedestal, Louwelsa, Miniature 550.00
Jardiniere, Blue Ware, 9 In. 275.00
Jardiniere, Children Walking Hand In Hand, Forest, 8 1/2 In. 495.00
Jardiniere, Cornish, Tan, 7 In. 95.00
Jardiniere, Cream, 5 1/2 In. 65.00
Jardiniere, Dickens Ware, Leaf, Marked, 9 x 9 In. 350.00
Jardiniere, Etna, 5 In. 95.00
Jardiniere, Fairfield, Ivory Glaze, 6 In. 65.00
Jardiniere, Flemish, 8 1/2 x 10 In. 195.00
Jardiniere, Forest, 4 1/2 In. 125.00
Jardiniere, Forest, 8 1/2 In. 150.00
Jardiniere, Forest, 8 Girls Walking Through Forest, 7 x 8 In. 795.00
Jardiniere, Louwelsa, 10 In. 230.00
Jardiniere, Louwelsa, 12 x 14 In. 250.00
Jardiniere, Louwelsa, Underglaze Painted Tulips, 10 1/2 In. 210.00
Jardiniere, Marvo, 8 In. 85.00
Jardiniere, Parian, Gray, 4 1/2 In. 40.00
Jardiniere, Roma, Blue Floral Medallions, White, Octagonal, 8 In. 70.00
Jardiniere, San Juan Bells, Brown Gloss 450.00
Jardiniere, Silvertone, 10 In. 350.0C
Jardiniere, Woodrose, 7 In. 60.00
Jug, Dickens Ware, 5 In. 125.00
Jug, Louwelsa, Wheat Design, 5 In. 175.00
Lamp Base, LaSa, 13 1/2 In. 650.00
Lamp Base, Louwelsa, 10 x 7 1/2 In. 275.00
Lamp, Aurelian, 3 Handles, Oil, Signed 550.00
Lamp, Floral Design, Signed, 18 1/2 In. 575.00
Lamp, Louwelsa, 13 In. 295.00
Mug, Dickens Ware II, Blue Hawk Indian, 6 3/4 In. 525.00
Mug, Dickens Ware, Cavalier 275.00
Mug, Dickens Ware, Monk Drinking Ale 295.00
Mug, Dickens Ware, Stag & Deer, Green 400.00
Mug, Dickens Ware, Stag, 5 In. 265.00
Mug, Eocean, Grapes, 6 In. 125.00
Pitcher, 6 Mugs, Crackle Glazed, Purple Grapes On Vine, 14 In. 450.00
Pitcher, Forest, 18 In. 395.00
Pitcher, Grotesque Fish, 5 In. 325.00
Pitcher, Ideal, Rose 75.00
Pitcher, Kingfisher 400.00
Pitcher, Louwelsa, Grapes & Leaves, 11 In. 375.00
Pitcher, Louwelsa, Plums & Leaves, Brown, 7 1/2 In. 100.00
Pitcher, Souevo 350.00
Pitcher, Zona, Apples On Branch, 7 In. 135.00
Pitcher, Zona, Kingfisher 350.00
Planter, Chrysanthemum Design, 9 1/2 x 11 1/4 In. 125.00
Planter, Dupont, White, Square, 5 In. 95.00
Planter, Lido, Triangular 30.00
Planter, Marvo, Green, 10 In. 80.00
Planter, Sea Horses, Sabrinian 295.00

Plaque, World's Fair, St. Louis 1904, 5 In. 175.00
Plate, Glendale, 9 In. 285.00
Pot, Hanging, Claywood, 10 1/2 In. 75.00
Sand Jar, Ivory 140.00
Strawberry Pot, Greenbriar, 9 1/2 In. 135.00
Strawberry Pot, Greora, 9 In. 65.00
Sugar & Creamer, Basketweave 10.00
Tankard, Aurelian, Grapes Cluster Both Sides, F. Ferrell, 13 In. 1575.00
Tankard, Blackberries, Brown Glaze, McGrath, 13 In. 475.00
Tankard, Dickens Ware, Fish Mouth Spout, Inverted Dolphins, 14 In. 1475.00
Tankard, Dickens Ware, Signed 600.00
Tankard, Incised Grapes & Leaves, Signed, 16 1/2 In. 110.00
Tankard, Mr. Pickwick, Dickens Ware, 5 3/4 In. 530.00
Teapot, Mammy ....850.00 To 1250.00
Tile, Coppertone 75.00
Tile, Jungle Landscape, Elephants, M. Timberlake, Framed, 8 1/2 In. 3100.00
Tobacco Jar, Chinaman's Head, Dickens Ware 850.00
Umbrella Stand, Ardsley 495.00
Umbrella Stand, Aurelian, Twisted, 22 In. 1450.00
Umbrella Stand, Man Of The North, Green, 20 In. .... 150.00 To 175.00
Umbrella Stand, Trees, Purple Fruit, Striated Glaze, 21 1/2 In. 470.00
Urn, Marvo, Gold, 10 In. 125.00
Urn, Scene, Green, 10 In. 80.00
Vase, 2 Handles, 8 In. 15.00
Vase, Alton, 9 In. 60.00
Vase, Art Nouveau, Full Figure Of Woman, 17 In. 995.00
Vase, Arts & Crafts Form, Dark Matte Green, 6 1/2 x 5 In. 200.00
Vase, Atlantic, White, 9 In. 90.00
Vase, Aurelian, Charles Fouts, 8 In. 400.00
Vase, Aurelian, Ovoid, Signed, 8 In. 175.00
Vase, Banquet, 6 In. 65.00
Vase, Barcelona, 6 1/2 In. 115.00
Vase, Bird In Nest With 4 Eggs, 5 In. 215.00
Vase, Blue & White, Sgraffito Carved Monk, Hammered, 16 In. 575.00
Vase, Blue Ware, 10 In. 260.00
Vase, Blue Ware, 11 In. 185.00
Vase, Bonito, 4 In. 55.00
Vase, Bonito, 5 In. 60.00
Vase, Bronzeware, 10 1/2 In. 150.00
Vase, Bronzeware, 18 In. 1200.00
Vase, Brown Gunmetal, Ribbed, 8 In. 80.00
Vase, Bud, Double, Ardsley, 10 In. 110.00
Vase, Bud, Floral, Foliate Design, Cylindrical, Crackle Glaze, 11 In. 35.00
Vase, Bud, Glendale, 7 In. 235.00
Vase, Bud, Hobart Woman, Glossy White, 10 In. 135.00
Vase, Bud, Lustre Orange, 7 In. 25.00
Vase, Burntwood, 3 Wise Men, 10 In. 225.00
Vase, Camelot, Bulbous, White On Green Ground, c.1914, 7 3/4 In. 305.00
Vase, Cherry Blossoms, 7 In. 140.00
Vase, Claywood, Grapes, 10 1/4 In. 85.00
Vase, Cloudburst, Yellow Luster, 10 In. 80.00
Vase, Coppertone, Handle, 12 In. 225.00
Vase, Dickens Ware II, Monk, Bulbous, 10 In. 525.00
Vase, Dickens Ware, Golfer, Handles, 6 1/2 In. 200.00
Vase, Dickens Ware, Monk, Bulbous, 10 In. 525.00
Vase, Dickens Ware, Northwestern Landscape, A. Daugherty, 11 1/2 In. 440.00
Vase, Dickens Ware, Stag, 11 In. 375.00
Vase, Dickens Ware, Women Strolling, Landscape, c.1900, 17 1/2 In. 2750.00
Vase, Elberta, Green, 5 In. 45.00
Vase, Eocean, 10 1/2 In. 275.00
Vase, Eocean, Berries, Handles, 6 In. 550.00
Vase, Eocean, Floral, Roses, Signed, 10 In. 750.00
Vase, Eocean, Poppy, 12 In. 200.00

◆ ◆

Splint baskets should have an
occasional light shower. Shake
off the excess water. Dry the
basket in a shady spot.

◆ ◆

Weller, Vase, Sicard, Stylized Design, 7 In.

Weller, Vase LaSa, Mountain Scene, 6 1/4 In.

Vase, Etna, Floral, 5 In.	95.00
Vase, Etna, Squatty Hydrangeas, Braided Handles, 7 1/2 In.	150.00
Vase, Evergreen, 12 In.	50.00
Vase, Fan, Coppertone, 8 In.	240.00
Vase, Fan, Voile, 8 1/2 In.	95.00
Vase, Flemish, Brown, 6 1/2 In.	95.00
Vase, Floral, Pillsbury, 10 1/2 In.	495.00
Vase, Florenzo, 7 In.	50.00
Vase, Floretta, Grape Cluster, Incised B, 8 In.	65.00
Vase, Floretta, Gray, Pink Flowers, 19 In.	530.00
Vase, Flowers, Blue, McLaughlin, 8 In.	450.00
Vase, Flowers, Standard Glaze, Signed, 7 In.	245.00
Vase, Forest, 4 1/2 In.	90.00
Vase, Fudzi, Mums, 11 In.	400.00
Vase, Glendale, 3 1/2 In.	180.00
Vase, Glendale, 6 In.	195.00
Vase, Glendale, Bird On Nest, 5 In.	185.00
Vase, Glendale, Bird On Nest, 8 In.	130.00
Vase, Greenbriar, 5 In.	30.00
Vase, Greora, Cylindrical, Marked, 9 In.	65.00
Vase, Greora, Orange & Green, 10 In.	150.00
Vase, Grotesque Fish, 2 Handles, 5 In.	325.00
Vase, Hudson Perfecto, Iris, Signed, 10 In.	275.00
Vase, Hudson, Bird On Tree Branch, Hexagonal, 12 In.	695.00
Vase, Hudson, Blue Design, 9 In.	250.00
Vase, Hudson, Bulbous, Strap Handles, 14 In.	1200.00
Vase, Hudson, Clusters Of Lilacs On Blue–Gray Ground, 12 In.	500.00
Vase, Hudson, Delicate Flowers, Pale Pink To Dark Green Top, 10 In.	395.00
Vase, Hudson, Dogwood Floral, McLaughlin, 7 In.	245.00
Vase, Hudson, Dogwood, Blue, Signed Walch, 6 1/2 In.	250.00
Vase, Hudson, Dogwood, Shaded Ground, Signed LBM, 7 In.	285.00
Vase, Hudson, Floral, Timberlake, 7 3/4 In.	345.00
Vase, Hudson, Iris, Leaves, 11 In.	850.00
Vase, Hudson, Kennedy, 12 In.	450.00
Vase, Hudson, Multicolored Berries, McLaughlin, 7 In.	335.00
Vase, Hudson, Pastel Flowers, 9 In.	225.00
Vase, Hudson, Pink & White Dogwood All Sides, Gray To Blue, 9 In.	425.00
Vase, Hudson, Pink Flowers, Blue, Signed Davis, 7 In.	395.00
Vase, Hudson, Poppies, Signed Timberlake, 7 3/4 In.	450.00
Vase, Hudson, Purple Clematis On Gray To White Ground, 9 In.	250.00
Vase, Hudson, Roses, Artist Signed, 7 In.	275.00
Vase, Hudson, Signed Hood, 11 In.	350.00
Vase, Hudson, Yellow Roses On Multicolored Ground, Signed, 8 In.	375.00
Vase, Hudson, Yellow Roses, Dark Blue Ground, Signed, 8 In.	450.00
Vase, Kenova, Cylindrical, 9 In.	90.00
Vase, Kenova, Lizard, Gray, 6 1/2 In.	235.00
Vase, Klyro, White, 7 In.	20.00

Vase, Knifewood, 7 In. .... 265.00 To 275.00
Vase, Knifewood, Daisy & Butterflies, 7 In. 210.00
Vase, Knifewood, Squirrels, 11 In. 375.00
Vase, LaSa, 7 1/2 In. 295.00
Vase, LaSa, 9 In. 500.00
Vase, LaSa, Mountain Scene, 6 1/4 In. ....*Illus* 330.00
Vase, LaSa, Trees & Mountains, Signed, 5 1/4 In. 300.00
Vase, LeMar, 7 1/2 In. 195.00
Vase, Lorenzo, Frog Cover, 7 1/2 In. 130.00
Vase, Louwelsa, Dogwood, 6 1/2 In. 225.00
Vase, Louwelsa, Glossy Brown & Rust, Green Leaves, Marked, 7 In. 175.00
Vase, Louwelsa, Minnie Mitchell, 9 In. 110.00
Vase, Louwelsa, Pansies, Brown, Signed, 4 1/2 In. 250.00
Vase, Louwelsa, Violets, Leaves, Shades Of Green, 6 3/8 In. 140.00
Vase, Luxor, 10 1/2 In. 295.00
Vase, Manhattan, 6 1/2 In. 75.00
Vase, Marbelized, Green, Gray, Pink, 10 In. 40.00
Vase, Mi–Flo, Tulips, 10 In. 150.00
Vase, Mirror Black, 13 1/2 In. 20.00
Vase, Oak Leaves & Acorns, 16 In. 125.00
Vase, Ocean, Leaves & Berries, Levi Burgess, 14 In. 605.00
Vase, Orris, Leaves & Flowers, 11 3/4 x 6 3/4 In. 700.00
Vase, Panella, Handle, Pedestal, 5 In. .... 90.00 To 95.00
Vase, Pansies, Footed, 3 Handles, Brown, 6 In. 25.00
Vase, Paragon, 7 In. 195.00
Vase, Parian, Gray, 7 1/2 In. 135.00
Vase, Perfecto, Pine Cones, Pillsbury, 7 In. 60.00
Vase, Perfecto, Water Lily, 16 In. 325.00
Vase, Pillow, Art Nouveau, 11 In. 1100.00
Vase, Pillow, Chase, 9 In. 500.00
Vase, Pillow, Louwelsa, Mums, Marked, 4 In. 295.00
Vase, Pillow, Penguin, 5 In. 250.00
Vase, Pink Roses, Pillsbury, 7 In. 350.00
Vase, Raised Leaves & Flowers, 1930, 7 3/4 In. 235.00
Vase, Roma, Yellow, 11 In. .... 110.00 To 135.00
Vase, Roses, Shaded Blue To Green To Pink, Timberlake, 14 In. 625.00
Vase, Sabrinian, 9 1/2 In. 140.00
Vase, Sicard, 6 In. 450.00
Vase, Sicard, Iridescent Blossom Glaze, 4 In. 302.50
Vase, Sicard, Purple & Green Floral, 8 In. 600.00
Vase, Sicard, Stylized Design, 7 In. ....*Illus* 660.00
Vase, Silvertone, 8 In. 95.00
Vase, Silvertone, Bulbous, 7 3/4 In. 130.00
Vase, Silvertone, Iris, 6 In. 110.00
Vase, Silvertone, Irises, 5 1/2 In. 125.00
Vase, Silvertone, Swirl, 6 1/2 In. 175.00
Vase, Softone, Yellow, 7 In. 28.00
Vase, Stellar, White Stars, Blue Ground, Signed, 9 In. 500.00
Vase, Sydonia, Blue, 9 In. 95.00
Vase, Timberlake, 9 In. 275.00
Vase, Tivoli, 6 In. 45.00
Vase, Tree Stump, Matte Green, 9 In. 50.00
Vase, Tulip Shape, Tulip Design, 12 In. 45.00
Vase, Umbrella, Bushberry, Brown, 20 In. 525.00
Vase, Voile, Green, 6 1/2 In. 70.00
Vase, Warwick, 8 In. 60.00
Vase, Warwick, 10 In. 120.00
Vase, White Daisies, Signed, 8 In. 225.00
Vase, White Rose, Green, 8 In. 40.00
Vase, Wild Rose, Handle, 8 In. 35.00
Vase, Wild Rose, Tan, Handles, 16 In. 110.00
Vase, Women's Faces, Ivory, 6 In. 65.00
Vase, Woodcraft, 9 In. 90.00

Whieldon, Teapot, Cauliflower,

Late 18th C., 6 In.

You can clean your silver with a paste of baking soda and water. Rub it on, rinse, wipe.

Vase, Woodcraft, Green Over Brown, 9 1/2 In.	45.00
Vase, Woodcraft, Owl & Squirrel On Side, 17 In.	995.00
Vase, Woodcraft, Owl & Squirrel, 18 In.	1050.00
Vase, Woodrose, 7 In.	80.00
Wall Pocket, Art Nouveau Female, Outstretched Arms, Signed, 8 In.	220.00
Wall Pocket, Glendale, 9 In.	250.00 To 275.00
Wall Pocket, Oak Leaf	75.00
Wall Pocket, Owl, 10 In.	195.00
Wall Pocket, Roma, 10 In.	100.00
Wall Pocket, Woodcraft, Azalea	96.00
Wall Pocket, Woodrose, Aqua, 10 In.	45.00 To 95.00
Wild Rose, Basket, Peach, 6 In.	31.00
Window Box, Woodrose	85.00

WEMYSS ware was made by Robert Heron in Kirkaldy, Scotland, from 1850 to 1929. It is a colorful peasant type pottery.

Bowl, Love Me Love My Dog, 7 In.	675.00
Figurine, Pig, Clovers, 6 1/2 In.	750.00
Figurine, Pig, Seated, Pink, Black, 17 1/2 In.	2500.00

WHEATLEY Pottery was established in 1880. Thomas J. Wheatley had worked in Cincinnati, Ohio, with the founders of the art pottery movement, including M. Louise McLaughlin of the Rookwood Pottery. Wheatley Pottery was purchased by the Cambridge Tile Manufacturing Company in 1927.

Bowl, Open Petaled Flowers, Matte Green Glaze, c.1900, 7 1/2 In.	885.00
Vase, Daisies, 1880, 8 In.	385.00
Vase, White Blossoms, Green Ground, Bulbous, 1881, 6 x 5 1/2 In.	110.00

WHIELDON was an English potter who worked alone and with Josiah Wedgwood in eighteenth–century England. Whieldon made many pieces in natural shapes, like cauliflowers or cabbages.

Creamer, Tortoiseshell Glaze, Scalloped Lid, 3 5/8 In.	450.00
Figurine, Cat, Brown Tortoiseshell Glaze, 4 In.	650.00
Plate, Black Tortoiseshell Glaze, Octagonal, 9 1/8 In.	775.00
Plate, Black With Green Tortoiseshell Glaze, Octagonal, 9 In.	450.00
Plate, Tortoiseshell Glaze, Scalloped Rim, 9 1/8 In.	475.00
Sugar, Black Mottled Glaze, Molded Finial, 3 1/2 In.	350.00
Teapot, Cauliflower Design, Individual, 4 In.	475.00
Teapot, Cauliflower, Late 18th C., 6 In. ....*Illus*	900.00
Teapot, Pineapple Ware, Cover	2750.00

WILLETS Manufacturing Company of Trenton, New Jersey, worked from 1879. The company made belleek in the late 1880s and 1890s in shapes similar to those used by the Irish Belleek factory. They stopped working about 1912. A variety of marks was used, all including the name Willets.

Bowl, Roses, Ruffled Rim, 9 1/2 In.	295.00

Window, Stained, Leaded, Woman, Gazing

Out Window, 72 x 64 In.

Bowl, Scalloped Gold Rim, Roses, Leaves, Thorned Stems, 4 1/2 In. 325.00

WILLOW, see Blue Willow category

WINDOW glass that was stained and beveled was popular for houses during the late nineteenth and early twentieth centuries. The old windows became popular with collectors in the 1970s; today, old and new examples are seen.

Chevron Designs On Clear Ground, Frank Lloyd Wright, c.1903, 33 In.	6000.00
Foliate Design, Frank Lloyd Wright, c.1900, 41 x 21 3/4 In.	4950.00
Leaded Textured Glass, Frank Lloyd Wright, c.1900, 63 1/2 In.	3300.00
Leaded, Geometric, Orange & White, F. L. Wright, 22 5/8 x 11 In.	2200.00
Stained, 2 Boys Playing Marbles, 26 x 34 In.	357.00
Stained, Center Portrait Of Pelican Feeding Chicks, 36 In.	400.00
Stained, Central Peony, Oak Frame, Arts & Crafts, 44 x 14 In.	825.00
Stained, Floral & Geometric Design, Arts & Crafts, 55 In.	335.00
Stained, Floral, 62 x 55 In.	2000.00
Stained, Jesus Christ, Double Backed Frame, 1890, 3 x 7 Ft.	2500.00
Stained, Leaded, Woman, Gazing Out Window, 72 x 64 In. ....*Illus*	2640.00
Stained, Pelican, Feeding Babies, Nest, La. State Logo, Round, 36 In.	400.00

WOOD CARVINGS and wooden pieces are listed separately in this book. There are also wooden pieces found in other sections, such as Kitchen.

3 Raised Fish, Primitive, Black Paint, On Natural Wood, 18 In.	25.00
Bellboy, Silent Butler, Silhouette, Painted, No Tray, 34 In.	130.00
Bird, Folk Art, Red & Black Paint Over White, 3 1/2 In.	30.00
Blackamoor, Polychrome Paint With Gilt, 63 In.	3900.00
Blue Jay, Relief Carving, Paint, Burl Base, 8 1/4 In.	450.00
Buffalo Head, Display, Buffalo Brewery, 1901, 24 x 24 In.	5500.00
Bull's Head, Advertising Sign, Real Horns	2200.00
Bull, Standing, Solid Walnut, 14 x 8 1/2 In.	145.00
Butler, Standing, Formal Attire, 1920, 42 In.	1250.00
Cherub, Mermaid, Polychrome Paint, Shield Has Eagle, 21 In.	275.00
Dog, Glass Eyes, Worn Brown Finish, 5 1/2 In.	30.00
Eagle & Shield, Polychrome & Gold Over Red, 44-In. Wingspan	650.00
Eagle, 29-In. Wingspan	1800.00
Eagle, Black, Brown & Gold, 13 1/2-In. Wingspan	455.00
Eagle, Crossed Flags & Shield, 27 3/4 x 36 3/4 In.	1900.00
Fish, Glass Eyes, 18 In.	310.00
Flapper, Bathing Costume, Silhouette, Painted, No Tray, 33 In.	275.00
Frog, Shellac, White Pine, 1930s	120.00
Horse Head, Carousel, Weathered, D. W. Dare, 1890	1200.00
Horse, Rearing, Colors, 30 x 30 In.	435.00
Humidor, Cover, Squirrels, Partridges, Running Around, Large	660.00
Leopard, Carved, Painted Spots, 6 1/2 In.	45.00
Madonna & Child, Seated, Gilt & Painted, Spain, 20 1/2 In.	9350.00
Owl, Stylized Relief Carving, Glass Eyes, 10 3/4 In.	250.00

Persian Lion, Stylized, Made From Clipper Ship Block Of Wood	33.00
Plaque, Lincoln, Primitive, Polychrome, Velicoff, 9 In.	25.00
Rooster, Pine, Polychrome Paint, Schimmel Type, 3 7/8 In.	175.00
Saint Florian, Full Armor, Village, Germany, 35 7/8 In.	4675.00
Saint Joseph, Christ Child In Arm, Spain, 17th Century, 22 In.	885.00
St. Francis, Gazing At Heaven, Austria, 18th Century, 36 In.	1450.00

WOODEN wares were used in all parts of the home. Wood was used for many containers and tools. Small wooden pieces are called *treenware* in England, but the term *woodenware* is more common in the United States. Additional pieces may be found in the Advertising, Kitchen, and Tool sections.

Barrel, Liberty Root Beer, Oak & Stainless Steel	600.00
Bed Key, Maple, For Rope Bed, 16 1/2 x 18 1/2 In.	45.00
Bowl, 19th Century, 10 In. Diam.	120.00
Bowl, Bird's-Eye Maple, 13 1/2 In.	125.00
Bowl, Brown & Putty Grained, 17 In.	2640.00
Bowl, Burl Figure, Primitive, 6 In.	375.00
Bowl, Burl, Black Paint Interior, Varnished Exterior, 11 In.	275.00
Bowl, Burl, Deep, Scrubbed Finish, 7 3/8 x 4 In.	375.00
Bowl, Irregular Oval Shape, Short End Handles, 7 5/8 x 9 1/4 In.	450.00
Bowl, Oblong, Protruding End Handles, 4 1/4 In.	125.00
Bowl, Primitive, 13 1/2 x 24 1/2 x 4 In.	115.00
Bowl, Refinished, Simple Footed, 5 x 2 1/4 In.	400.00
Bowl, Treenware, 10 1/2 x 22 x 2 1/4 In.	95.00
Box, Cheese, 5 Lb.	5.00
Box, Conestoga Wagon	350.00
Box, Salt, 1940s	7.00
Brush, Pincushion, Long Bodied Dog Shape, Brush Under Body, 1870	285.00
Bucket, 1 Piece Of Wood, Label, Our Favorite, Brass Band, 3 5/8 In.	50.00
Bucket, Sponged With Reds, Yellows, Blues & Greens, Ohio	3600.00
Bucket, Stave Constructed, Green, Iron Bands, Bale Handle, 3 5/8 In.	105.00
Bucket, Stave Constructed, Iron Bands, Heart Cutout Handles, 10 In.	35.00
Bucket, Sugar, Lid, Wooden Stave, F. Lane & Son, 9 3/4 In.	85.00
Bucket, Sugar, Stave Constructed, Green Repaint, 9 In.	175.00
Bucket, Sugar, Stave Constructed, Stenciled Hoover—Co., 9 1/2 In.	160.00
Bucket, Sugar, Stave Constructed, Varnish Finish, 9 3/4 In.	60.00
Bucket, Sugar, Wooden, Old Gray Repaint, Wire Handle, 6 1/2 In.	165.00
Bucket, Sugar, Wooden, Old Green Repaint, Wire Handle, 8 In.	185.00
Carrier, Pine, 12 x 7 x 7 In.	75.00
Cookie Board, Stag, Refinished, 5 x 7 1/4 In.	65.00
Cricket, Chip Carved Ends, Gray Paint, N. Corthell	135.00
Cup, Footed, Lehnware, Polychrome Floral, Blue Ground, 3 1/8 In.	925.00
Cup, Footed, Lehnware, Polychrome Floral, Light Green, 2 7/8 In.	625.00
Dovecote, Virginia, 1860s	2200.00
Dummy Board, Maid, Painted, 18th Century	1000.00
Eggcup, Yellow Ground, Lehnware, 2 5/8 In.	3400.00
Firkin, Lid, 6 In.	225.00
Firkin, Lid, Refinished, 1830–1860, 8 In.	185.00
Ironing Board, Clamps To Table, Pat. 2–17–03	35.00
Jar, Barrel, Treen, Polychrome, Made In USSR, 5 7/8 In.	45.00
Jar, Original Varnish Finish, Wood & Wire Bale Handle, 7 3/4 In.	275.00
Jar, Pease, Footed, Original Varnish, 3 3/8 In.	115.00
Jar, Pease, Wire Bale, Varnished, Wooden Handle, 3 In.	75.00
Jar, Treen, Old Varnish, Embossed Brass Button Lid, 4 1/2 In.	25.00
Mold, Cigar	35.00
Mortar & Pestle, Roller Pestle, Crescent Mortar, 13 1/2 In.	325.00
Pipe Rack, Monk's, Pyrography	26.00
Plate, Cherry, 18th Century, 11 1/4 In.	350.00
Rack, Drying, 3 Mortised & Pinned Bars, Shoe Feet, Pine, 41 1/2 In.	60.00
Rack, Drying, Greenish Gray Paint, Shoe Feet, 3 Bars, Pine, 49 In.	175.00
Rack, Drying, Vertical Pole, Tripod Base, 5 Accordion Arms, 57 In.	25.00
Scoop, Graduated, 6 1/4 To 15 1/2 In., 8 Piece	1600.00

◆◆◆◆◆◆◆◆◆◆◆◆◆◆◆◆◆◆◆◆◆◆◆◆◆◆◆

Wooden items should be kept off the sunny window sill. Direct sunlight will harm wood finishes.

◆◆◆◆◆◆◆◆◆◆◆◆◆◆◆◆◆◆◆◆◆◆◆◆◆◆◆

◆◆◆◆◆◆◆◆◆◆◆◆◆◆◆◆◆◆◆◆◆◆◆◆◆◆◆

Store parasols and umbrellas closed.

◆◆◆◆◆◆◆◆◆◆◆◆◆◆◆◆◆◆◆◆◆◆◆◆◆◆◆

Wooden, Torchere, Venice, Late 19th C., 87 In.

Spoon, Burl, 4 5/8 In.	220.00
Stand, Coffin, Turned Legs, Worn Red & Black Paint, 30 In., Set Of 4	200.00
Tankard, Staved Handle, 19th Century, 10 In.	225.00
Ten Pins, Oak, Maple Balls, 1880s	90.00
Tinder Box, Steel Ram's Horn Scroll, Striker, Flint, 2 x 1 7 In.	455.00
Tobacco Press	35.00
Torchere, Venice, Late 19th Century, 87 In. ....*Illus*	3080.00
Towel Rack, Pine, Graining, Shoe Feet, Curved Top Rails, 18 x 36 In.	115.00
Tub, Stave Constructed, Grained, Wire Rim Handles, 13 x 6 1/2 In.	135.00
Urn, Knife, Acorn Finial, Sliding Lid, Satinwood, 24 1/2 In., Pair	7150.00
Vase, Frog & Snail, Copper Insert, Oriental, 12 In.	165.00
Wall Pocket, Hanging, Pine, Nut Brown Color, 4 Sections, 18 In.	145.00
Wall Pocket, Refinished Pine, Shaped Crest, Front Rail, 6 x 10 In.	45.00
Washtub, Mother Hubbard, Corrugated Rolls	85.00
Water Cask, Prospector's, Ely, Nevada	75.00

WORCESTER porcelains were made in Worcester, England, from 1751. The firm went through many name changes and eventually, in 1862, became The Royal Worcester Porcelain Company Ltd. Collectors often refer to *Dr. Wall, Barr, Flight,* and other names that indicate time periods or artists at the factory. It became part of Royal Worcester Spode Ltd. in 1976. Related pieces may be found in the Royal Worcester category.

Basket, Chestnut, Quatrefoil, Reticulated Cover, Stand, 10 3/8 In.	3400.00
Basket, Reticulated, Blue Scale, Flowers, Cartouches, 1770, 9 In.	995.00
Basket, Reticulated, Floral, Yellow Ground, 1770, 9 7/8 In.	1550.00
Bowl, Fence Pattern, Blue Crescent Mark, 6 1/4 In.	192.00
Candlestick, Japan Pattern, Hexagonal Foot, BFB, 4 7/8 In., Pair	2310.00
Cream Jug, Cover, Fence Pattern, 4 1/4 In.	250.00
Cup & Saucer, Exotic Bird, Leaves, Gilt Scrollwork, 1770–1775	445.00
Dessert Set, Japan Pattern, Gilt Flame Knops, BFB, 27 Piece	6100.00
Dish, 2 Overlapping Leaves, Blue Scale, 1770, 10 1/4 In., Pair	1550.00
Dish, Basket Mold, Floral, Yellow Ground, 1765, 11 13/16 In.	5775.00
Dish, Bishop Sumner, Famille–Verte, Scalloped, 9 5/8 In., Pair	6100.00
Dish, Blind Earl, Rose Leaf Sprays, Scalloped Rim, 7 1/2 In.	467.00
Dish, Blue Scale, Floral, Scalloped, 1770, Deep, 9 1/16 In., Pair	1210.00
Dish, Blue Scale, Kidney Shape, Floral, 1770–1775, 10 7/16 In.	935.00
Dish, Blue Scale, Scalloped, Lozenge Shape, 1770, 10 5/8 In.	550.00
Dish, Chantilly Sprig, Square, 9 In.	575.00
Dish, Hot Water, Botanical, Nabob–Carnatic, 11 5/8 In., Pair	1875.00
Dish, Ram's Head Yeo Crest, Chamberlain, Square, 8 5/16 In., Pair	1875.00
Inkstand, Cover, Sepia Romulus & Remus, 1800, 4 11/16 In.	880.00
Inkwell, Turquoise, Lion's Paw Feet, Barr, Flight & Barr, 4 In.	935.00
Mug, Marquis Of Granby, Black Transfer, Hancock, 1760, 4 7/8 In.	1320.00
Mug, May Day 1 Side, 3 Milkmaids Other, Hancock, 5 3/4 In.	1100.00
Plate, Dessert, Blue, Fruit & Flower Cluster, H. Martin, 18 Piece	2100.00
Plate, Dessert, Different Rose Center, Green, FBB, 8 3/4 In., 5 Pc.	1200.00
Plate, Floral, Reticulated Rim, 3 Shell Feet, Grainger, 10 1/2 In.	755.00

Sauceboat, Cob Lettuce Leaves, Curled Handle, c.1760, 8 1/2 In.	475.00
Sweetmeat Dish, Blind Earl, Twig Handle, Hancock, 6 1/4 In.	2650.00
Teapot, Printed Rose, Globular, Bent Loop Handle, 4 1/4 In.	165.00
Tureen, Cover, Stand, Cartouches, Bud Sprig Knop, Handles, 9 In.	1775.00
Tureen, Cover, Stand, Gilt Scrollwork, Knopped, 9 1/16 In.	1450.00
Vase, Floral, Pate–Sur–Pate On Parian, 6 3/4 In.	385.00
Vase, Japan Pattern, Ring Handles, B Mark, 6 1/8 & 6 3/16 In., Pr.	3400.00
Vase, Lamp Mounted, Rococo Scroll Handles, Floral, 11 1/2 In., Pr.	1100.00
Vase, Milk Scene 1 Side, Rural Lovers Other, Hancock, 6 3/4 In.	825.00

WORLD WAR I and World War II souvenirs are collected today. Be careful not to store anything that includes live ammunition. Your local police will tell you how to dispose of the explosives. See also Gun, Sword, and Trench Art.

WORLD WAR I, Beaker, Peace, City Of Manchester, Crackled, 1919	35.00
Flag Set, Signal, U.S. Army	20.00
Insignia, Uniform, Soldier's, Yellow Brass, USA	2.45
Mess Kit, Cast Iron, 1916	50.00
Mess Kit, U.S. Army	3.50
Pillow Cover, Silk, U.S. Army, Camp Carson, Colorado	10.00
Pillow, Velvet, Soldier & Child Scene	24.00
Postcard, Soldiers, Crossed Flags, Linen	1.25
Poster, 5th Royal Highlanders, Canada, Framed, 27 x 41 In.	95.00
Poster, All Together, Enlist In Navy, Sailor, 1917, 31 x 43 In.	435.00
Poster, Ambulance Corps, L. L. Wilbur, 41 x 30 In.	285.00
Poster, Back Him Up, Victory Bonds, Framed, 24 x 36 In.	150.00
Poster, Be A Sea Soldier, Marines, Underwood, 20 x 40 In.	180.00
Poster, Call To Duty, Join The Army, Bugler, Flag, 40 x 30 In.	225.00
Poster, Canadian, Your Chums Are Fighting, Aren't You, 38 In.	259.00
Poster, Enemy Sighted–Attack, Navy, Aircraft, 42 x 28 In.	100.00
Poster, Enlist In The Navy, Raemakers, 1917, 30 x 40 In.	150.00
Poster, Enlist Now & Go With Your Friends, Edrop, 28 x 40 In.	225.00
Poster, Fight Or Buy Bonds, H. C. Christy, 30 x 40 In.	125.00
Poster, For Home & Country, Soldier, Orr, 1918, 20 x 30 In.	55.00
Poster, For Our Aviators, Soaring Eagle, C. B. Falls	510.00
Poster, Idle Dollar Helps Kaiser, 4th Liberty, 11 x 21 In.	76.00
Poster, Join The Canadian Grenadier, Framed, 27 x 41 In.	125.00
Poster, Keep'em Smiling, Doughboy, Big Smile, Blue, Red, White	65.00
Poster, Men Wanted For The Army, Whelan, 1916, 30 x 40 In.	300.00
Poster, Men Wanted, U.S. Marines, Marine, Gun, 1916, 40 x 30 In.	200.00
Poster, Now! Victory Bonds, Canadian Soldier, Sampson, 33 In.	150.00
Poster, Patriotic Lady, Framed, 39 x 53 In.	475.00
Poster, Soldier, Salvation Army Girl, 1918, 24 x 38 In.	60.00
Poster, Spirit Of '18, Uncle Sam As Farmer, 30 x 20 In.	85.00
Poster, Stand By The Boys, Mine Coal, Coal Miner, Doughboy	175.00
Poster, Sure! We'll Finish The Job, Beneker, 1918, 26 x 38 In.	55.00
Poster, U.S. Marines–Soldiers Of Sea, Leyendecker, 29 x 40 In.	175.00
Poster, U.S. Navy, Help Your Country, Reuterdahl, 27 x 41 In.	275.00
Poster, United War Work Campaign	25.00
Poster, Victory Liberty Loan	60.00
Poster, YWCA–Women Of France, Munitions Factory, 28 x 39 In.	29.00
Sheet Music, America To–Day, War Babies, Etc. 1916–1918, 25 Pc.	69.00
Sheet Music, Good–Bye Alexander, Parade, Black Troopers	15.00
Surgeon's Kit, Army, Small Operating Case, Fred Haslam & Co.	250.00
Wall Pocket, Soldier's Verse & Cloth Flag	9.50
Watch Fob, German, Brass	50.00
WORLD WAR II, Badge, Field Cap, SS	65.00
Bag, Paper, Save On House Heat, Make Things Hotter For Hitler	25.00
Bank, Adolf Hitler Pig	372.00
Battleship, Japanese, Porcelain, Souvenir	48.00
Bayonet, Japan	45.00
Belt & Buckle, Nazi, Red Cross	120.00
Book, Puptent Poets, Stars & Stripes Mediterranean, 1945	12.00

Buckle, Belt, Nazi, Eagle With Swastika, Large	15.00
Button, Hitler & People Speak	8.00
Cap, Field, Afrikacorps	220.00
Cap, Field, Nazi Army	75.00
Cap, Garrison	25.00
Cap, Visor, Nazi Pilot's	300.00
Card, Mother's Day, From 355th Infantry Reg., In Germany	8.00
Card, Playing, We're Not Forgetting, Standard Oil Servicemen	15.00
Chisel, Nazi Insignia, Steel, Made In Chicago	42.00
Compass, Nazi March	40.00
Dagger, Italian, Fascist Officer's	450.00
Dagger, Nazi SA, Christian Werk, With Scabbard	210.00
Door Plaque, Brass, Nazi	50.00
Figure, Anti–Mussolini, Chalkware, Grotesque	48.00
Flag, Nazi, Municipal, 5 x 9 Ft.	75.00
Flag, State Service, Nazi, Eagle In Corner, 5 x 7 Ft.	180.00
Gloves, Field, Camouflage, Nazi	100.00
Gloves, Heated, From Flying Suit, F–2	65.00
Goggles, Flyers, Yellow Lenses, Japan, Box	20.00
Goggles, Nazi, Rommel Style, Package	2.00
Helmet, Constellation Airplane, Japanese	250.00
Helmet, Japan, Liner	135.00
Holder, Ration Token, Red & Blue, Tokens, 2 In.	15.00
Insignia, Women's Corp, Original Card	39.00
Jacket, Capt. W. J. Cline, Flying Tigers Emblem, Leather	475.00
Join The Wacs, Epreherz, 22 x 28 In.	100.00
Knife, Sheath, Nazi Technical Emergency Corp.	950.00
Leaflet, I Surrender, For Japanese Soldier	58.00
Little Girl Crying & Big Swastika, 1943, Large	95.00
Map, War Orientation Unit, Navy, Pacific Combat, 26 In.	15.00
Newspaper, F. D. R. Dies, Southeast Missourian, Apr. 12, 1945	37.00
Newspaper, Pearl Harbor Attack, S. F. Chronicle, Dec. 8, 1941	55.00
Nodder, Hitler, Bent Over, Stick Pins In Seat Of Pants, 1941	45.00
Paperweight, Nazi, Cast Iron	65.00
Phonograph, Album, Marches, Songs & Speeches, Nazi Germany	95.00
Photograph, Army, Patton's 4th Armored, 16 x 20 In., 26 Piece	390.00
Photograph, King George & Pres. Truman, Plymouth, Framed, 8 In.	18.00
Pilot's Wings, Glider's, U.S. Air Force, Sterling Silver	305.00
Pin, Berlin Olympic, Nazi, 1936	65.00
Pin, Ordnance Efficiency, Air Force, Blue Star In Flag, Silver	10.00
Pincushion, Hitler, Dated 1941	45.00
Pistol, Nazi Police, Walther PPK, 7. 65 Caliber, 3 In. Barrel	1050.00
Postcard, British Recruitment, Who's Absent? Is It You?	60.00
Postcard, Hitler's Dream, Earth–Moon Is Germany, Bachier, 1939	45.00
Postcard, We Shall Defend Every Village, W. Churchill, Russia	35.00
Poster, Army Air Force Safety, 1943, 16 x 20 In.	95.00
Poster, Attack, Attack, Attack, Buy War Bonds, 1942, 22 x 28 In.	17.00
Poster, Back The Attack, Buy War Bonds, Parachute, 10 x 28 In.	40.00
Poster, Build & Fight For Victory, Join Seabees, Falter	150.00
Poster, Buy War Bonds, Uncle Sam, 40 x 29 1/2 In.	65.00
Poster, Buy War Bonds, Wyeth, 14 x 22 In.	150.00
Poster, Defend Your Country, Enlist Now U.S. Army, Woodburn	150.00
Poster, Deliver Us From Evil, Anti–Hitler, 14 x 11 In.	48.00
Poster, For Liberty & Peace On Earth, Give War Bonds, 1944	85.00
Poster, Guard Our Shores, U.S. Army, Artillery, 25 x 38 In.	125.00
Poster, Hitler–Tojo–Mussolini, Folded	65.00
Poster, I'm Counting On You, Uncle Sam, Points Finger	100.00
Poster, If You Must Talk, Tell It To Marines, 27 x 19 In.	100.00
Poster, Keep 'em Flying Is Our Battle Cry, Smith & Downe	150.00
Poster, Keep Your Red Cross At His Side, Whitman, 14 x 20 In.	85.00
Poster, Landing Craft, Fighter Planes, GIs, 1944, 40 x 28 In.	250.00
Poster, Open Trap Make Happy Jap, Ear To Keyhole, 40 x 30 In.	150.00
Poster, Silence Means Security, Enlisted Schmoo, 14 x 20 In.	200.00

Poster, This Is My Fight Too! War Bonds, 1942, 28 x 22 In. 30.00
Poster, United Nations Fight For Freedom, 1942, 40 x 28 In. 65.00
Poster, Want Action? Join U.S. Marines, Flagg, 28 x 41 In. 300.00
Poster, Your Scrap, Rubber, Metal, Rags, 1942, 40 x 28 In. 275.00
Puzzle, Jigsaw, Buy War Bonds & Stamps, Box, 2 Piece 5.00
Ribbon, Serviceman's, U.S. Military 2.00
Sake Bottle, Crossed Flags, Japanese Military 85.00
Sake Cup, Japanese, Military 27.00
Shaving Kit, Toiletries 75.00
Shell Case, Machine Gun, Brass, Dated 1943, Large 2.00
Sign, Iron Cross, Swastika Center, Porcelain, 1939, 28 x 13 In. 200.00
Swagger Stick, Nazi, Swastika On Knob, Brass 500.00
Target, U.S. Bombing, Nazi Insignia 150.00
Telescope, Tank 75.00
Toy, Fist Punches Hitler In Eye, Push Toy, Wooden, 37 In. 245.00
Tumbler, Buy U.S. War Bonds, Stamps, V For Victory 12.00
Uniform, Navy, With Hat 85.00
Wings, Navigator, U.S. Navy 235.00

WORLD'S FAIR souvenirs from all of the fairs are collected. The first fair was the Great Exhibition of 1851 in London. Other important exhibitions and fairs include Philadelphia, 1876 (Centennial); Chicago, 1893 (World's Columbian); Buffalo, 1901 (Pan-American); St. Louis, 1904 (Louisiana Purchase); San Francisco, 1915 (Panama-Pacific); Philadelphia, 1926 (Sesquicentennial); Chicago, 1933 (Century of Progress); Cleveland, 1936 (Great Lakes); San Francisco, 1939 (Golden Gate International); New York, 1939 (World of Tomorrow); Seattle, 1962; New York, 1964; Montreal, 1967; New Orleans, 1984; Tsukuba, Japan, 1985; Vancouver, B.C., 1986; Brisbane, Australia, 1988; and Seville, Spain, 1992; and Genoa, Italy, 1992. Memorabilia of fairs include directories, pictures, fabrics, ceramics, etc.

Ashtray, 1962, Seattle, White, Logo, Space Needle, 5 1/2 In. 8.00
Ashtray, 1964, New York, Main Mall 10.00
Ashtray, 1964, New York, Republic Of China, Box 25.00
Badge, 1893, Chicago, Attendant's, Nickel 100.00
Badge, 1893, Chicago, Shell, 24 Mm., Gilt Brass 75.00
Banner, 1939, New York, Satin, Trylon, Perisphere, Fringe, 31 In. 250.00
Book, 1893, Chicago, Guide, Map, Color, S. S. Sleeper Co., 40 Pages 16.00
Book, 1893, Chicago, Martin's World's Fair Album, Hardbound 19.00
Book, 1933, Chicago, Husum Publishing, 9 x 11 In., 150 Pages 65.00
Book, 1933, Chicago, Official Guidebook Of The Fair, 176 Pages 19.00
Book, 1933, Chicago, Official Pictures, Unused Mailer 5.00
Book, 1939, New York, Fair Views, 48 Pages, 9 x 12 In. 15.00
Book, 1939, New York, World Of Tomorrow 75.00
Book, 1962, Seattle, Official Souvenir 10.00
Book, 1964, New York, Souvenir 9.00
Bookends, 1939, New York, Alabaster, Trylon & Perisphere 95.00
Booklet, 1893, Chicago, Singer Sewing Machine, 8 Pages 15.00
Booklet, 1904, St. Louis, Photographic 32.50
Booklet, 1939, San Francisco, Railroad, Golden Gate Pullman 15.00
Boot, 1904, St. Louis, Cascades, Fancy, 4 1/2 In. 65.00
Bottle, 1939, San Francisco, Milk Glass, 9 In. 20.00
Bottle, Beer, 1893, Chicago, Rheingold, Wire Ceramic Stopper 90.00
Box, Cigarette, 1933, Chicago, Jehol Temple Picture 14.00
Bracelet, Charm, 1939, San Francisco 25.00
Button, Lapel, 1939, New York, On Card, Large 15.00
Button, Uniform, 1964, New York, Pepsi-Cola Pavilion, 4 Piece 30.00
Card, Playing, 1939, New York, Original Box 50.00
Coaster Set, 1939, San Francisco, 5 Colors 20.00
Compact, 1933, Chicago, A Century Of Progress, Elgin 45.00
Cup, 1901, Buffalo, Ruby Stained 12.00
Cup, 1933, Chicago, Stewarts Coffee 80.00
Cup, 1939, San Francisco, Crystal Palace 25.00

◆◆◆◆◆◆◆◆◆◆◆◆◆◆◆◆◆◆◆◆

Soiled white quilts or fabrics in
good condition can be helped.
Soak the textile in the washing
machine in a solution of warm
water and a cup or more of
powdered dishwasher detergent for an hour. Then put on
gentle wash cycle for a few
minutes.

◆◆◆◆◆◆◆◆◆◆◆◆◆◆◆◆◆◆◆◆

World's Fair, Plate, 1939, New York, 6 In.

Dish, 1933, Chicago, Scenes, Copper, 4 3/4 In.	20.00
Dress, 1962, Seattle, Scenes Of City, 2 Piece	50.00
Egg, 1904, St. Louis, Tin, Ferris Wheel Lithograph	35.00
Game, Card, 1939, New York, Complete	25.00
Guide, 1904, St. Louis, Louisiana Purchase, Official	75.00
Handkerchief, 1893, Chicago	50.00
Handkerchief, 1904, St. Louis, Printed Opening Day Ceremony	295.00
Ice Pick, 1939, San Francisco	10.00
Kerchief, 1939, San Francisco, 20 x 20 In.	30.00
Key Chain, 1933, Chicago, Leonard Refrigerator	12.00
Lamp, 1939, San Francisco, Saturn, Planet & Stars, Blue Ground	275.00
Letter Opener, Chicago, 1933	6.00
License Plate, 1939, San Francisco	25.00
Light Bulb, 1939, San Francisco, Reddy Kilowatt	600.00
Lithograph, 1939, San Francisco, Gardens On Parade, 8 x 10 In.	75.00
Map, 1893, Chicago, Bird's-Eye View Of Chicago, 13 x 30 In.	37.00
Map, 1939, New York, TWA Skysleeper Pictures	15.00
Match Safe, 1904, St. Louis, Woman's Head, Brass	165.00
Mirror, 1904, St. Louis, Palace Of Machinery, Pocket	55.00
Mouse, 1893, Chicago, Holding Stein	225.00
Mug, 1893, Chicago, Washington & Columbus	150.00
Mug, 1933, Chicago, Woman On Handle	45.00
Mug, 1982, Knoxville, Color	8.00
Pen, 1962, Seattle, Ballpoint, Space Needle Shape	5.00
Pencil Sharpener, 1939, New York, Trylon & Perisphere, Box	85.00
Pencil, 1939, New York, Large	30.00
Pencil, Mechanical, 1933, Chicago, Box, Large	35.00
Pendant, 1933, Chicago, Art Deco, Cutout Emblem & Logo	12.00
Pillow Sham, 1933, Chicago	15.00
Plate, 1904, St. Louis, Lattice Border	18.50
Plate, 1939, New York, 6 In. *Illus*	25.00
Plate, 1940, San Fran., Logo, Poppies, Homer Laughlin, 10 In.	40.00
Plate, 1962, Seattle, 10 1/2 In.	10.00 To 30.00
Plate, 1964, New York, Picture Center, Gold Trim, Miniature	12.00
Postcard, 1904, St. Louis, Greetings–Indianapolis Brewing Co.	85.00
Postcard, 1904, St. Louis, Red, White & Blue Border	85.00
Postcard, 1904, St. Louis, Tissera's Ceylon Teas	40.00
Postcard, 1939, San Francisco, 12 Miniature In Mailing Holder	14.00
Poster, 1933, Chicago, Federal Building, Art Deco, 27 x 40 In.	675.00
Poster, 1939, New York, For Peace & Freedom, 13 x 20 In.	200.00
Poster, 1939, New York, For Your Summer Vacation, 20 x 30 In.	225.00
Poster, 1962, Seattle, Space Needle, Monorail, Blue & Red	20.00
Powder Box, 1939, New York, Musical, Trylon & Perisphere	40.00
Puzzle, 1964, New York, Test Of Tomorrow, Large	25.00
Puzzle, Jigsaw, 1933, Chicago, Century Of Progress	65.00
Ribbon, 1893, Chicago, Machinery Hall, Orange & White Silk	150.00
Salt & Pepper, 1939, New York	20.00 To 35.00

Salt & Pepper, 1964, New York, Steel Unisphere 16.00
Saltshaker, 1939, San Francisco, Frosted, Metal Base, 4 In. 10.00
Saltshaker, 1962, Seattle, Pink Scene Of Logo 9.00
Shot Glass, 1893, Chicago 70.00
Silk, 1915, San Francisco, Emancipation Proclamation 140.00
Spoon Set, 1939, New York, Redwood Box, Wm. Rogers, 12 Piece 140.00
Spoon, 1893, Chicago, Columbus, Engraved Bowl 16.00
Spoon, 1893, Chicago, Machinery Hall In Bowl, Sterling Silver 60.00
Spoon, 1893, Chicago, Plain Bowl, Durgin 85.00
Spoon, 1901, Buffalo, Indian On Handle, Sterling Silver 20.00
Spoon, 1915, San Francisco, Jeweled Tower, Sterling Silver 45.00
Spoon, 1933, Chicago, Century Of Progress, Gold Tone 18.00
Spoon, 1933, Chicago, Science Court 10.00
Spoon, 1962, Seattle, Space Needle, Sterling, 6 In. 20.00
Swizzle Stick, 1939, New York, Du Pavilon Belge, Glass 12.00
Table, Card, 1939, New York 150.00
Thermometer, 1933, Chicago, Key Shape, Wood 8.00
Thimble, 1904, St. Louis, Buffalo, Cowboys, Horses, Sterling 90.00
Ticket, 1962, Seattle, Pair 4.00
Tin, Coffee, 1893, Chicago, Chase & Sandborn Java Mocha, 6 In. 125.00
Tip Tray, 1904, St. Louis, Embossed Birds, Building, 5 In. 20.00
Tip Tray, 1962, Seattle, Gold Space Needle, White 5.00
Tip Tray, 1964, New York 12.00
Toothpick, 1893, Chicago, Kings Royal, Rev. Andrew Gray 18.00
Toothpick, 1893, Chicago, Scalloped Swirl, Red, Mary 45.00
Toothpick, 1933, Chicago, Blocked Thumbprint 20.00
Totem Pole, 1962, Seattle, Wooden, Space Needle, Painted, 15 In. 15.00
Toy, Bus, 1933, Chicago, Cast Iron, Arcade, 10 In. .... 125.00 To 195.00
Toy, Stratosphere Balloon, 1939, New York, Unopened Package 100.00
Toy, Wagon, 1933, Chicago 95.00
Tray, Coffee, 1939, San Francisco, Medaglia D'Oro 60.00
Tumbler, 1904, St. Louis, Palace Of Electricity, Cast Metal 125.00
Tumbler, 1962, Seattle, 6 1/2 In. 7.00
Tumbler, 1964, New York, Unisphere 10.00
Tumbler, Juice, 1962, Seattle, Space Needle, Green 18.00
Umbrella, 1933, Chicago .... 32.00 To 35.00
Watch Fob, 1904, St. Louis, Picture Of Harvesting Machine 35.00

WRISTWATCHES came into use during World War I. Wristwatches are
listed here by manufacturer or as advertising or character watches. Pocket
watches are listed in the Watch category.

Accutron, Day, Date, 14K Gold Filled, Metal Band 100.00
Accutron, Man's, Gold Filled 135.00
Advertising, Gulf Oil 25.00
Alton, Swiss Movement, Square Face, Separate Minute Dial 95.00
Audemars Piguet, 20 Dollar American Gold Coin Face, 20K Gold 4180.00
Audemars Piguet, Silvered Dial, 18K Gold Case, 1950s 6900.00
Benrus, 14K Gold 165.00
Berlin Wall Guard Duty, Russia 175.00
Bulova Accutron, Man's, Space View Skeleton, Gold Bezel, Band 250.00
Bulova, 2 Garnets, 10K Gold Filled Band 200.00
Bulova, Accutron, 14K Yellow Gold Oval Case, Calender 440.00
Bulova, Accutron, Astronaut, Time Zone, 14K Gold 650.00
Bulova, Accutron, Mark IV, Time Zone, Stainless 200.00
Bulova, Art Deco, Rectangular, Sterling, Multicolored Dial 249.00
Bulova, Automatic, Steel Case 40.00
Bulova, Man's, Rectangular, 1950s 125.00
Bulova, Woman's, 14K Gold, Diamonds 75.00
Bulova, Woman's, Diamonds, 23 Jewel, 14K Gold 135.00
C. P. Shipley, Mother-of-Pearl, Steer Strap 375.00
Cartier, Pasha, Date Window, Waterproof Case, 1987 .... 7500.00
Cartier, Woman's, Burgundy Face, Tank Style, Windup, Box 375.00
Character, Alice In Wonderland, U.S. Time 25.00

Character, Babe Ruth 325.00
Character, Barbie, Ponytail, Pink Numbers, Mattel, Bradley, 1964 .... 145.00
Character, Barbie, With Pocket Watch, 1960s 175.00
Character, Bugs Bunny 235.00
Character, Hollie Hobby, Bradley, 1972 .... 45.00
Character, Hoppity Hooper, 17 Jewels, Second Hand, Chrome Case 275.00
Character, Lester Maddox, Box 150.00
Character, Lucy, From Peanut's Comics 25.00
Character, Mary Poppins 65.00
Character, Roger Rabbit, Swiss Quartz, Movement, 1987, Box 75.00
Character, Snoopy, Floating Tennis Ball, 1958 .... 50.00
Character, Tom Corbett, Space Cadet, 1951 .... 175.00 To 220.00
Character, Zorro, 1950s .... 60.00 To 100.00
Chronograph, Pilot, Russia 200.00
Commemorative, Gorbachev & Bush Iceland Meeting 195.00
Commemorative, KGB, Victory, 1945 .... 350.00
Corum, 18K Yellow Gold, 17 Jewel, Oval, Peacock Feather Dial 550.00
Elgin, Direct Reader, Windup, 14K Gold Filled, Leather Band 200.00
Elgin, Woman's, 14K Gold 60.00
Girard Pergaraux, Woman's, 14K Gold 95.00
Gruen, Convertible, 17 Jewels, 10K Gold Filled Case, 1930s 2200.00
Gruen, Curvex, Pink Gold Filled 200.00
Gruen, Oblong, 10K Gold 45.00
Gruen, Woman's, 10K White Gold 60.00
Hamilton, Clevelander, No. 19 Jewel, 14K Gold Filled Case 190.00
Hamilton, Lady's, 14K White Gold, 12 Full Cut Diamonds 275.00
Hamilton, Military, Black Dial, Chrome Case, Cloth Band 65.00
Jaeger, Stainless Steel 22.00
Jurgensen, 17 Jewel, 14K Gold, Gold Strap 625.00
Lady Hamilton, 2 Diamond Chips, 14k Gold 47.50
LeCoultre, Alarm, Gold Filled 350.00
LeCoultre, Futurmatic, Gold Filled 350.00
Longines, 18 Diamonds, 14K White Gold Watch & Band 175.00
Lord Elgin, Bessemer & L. E. Railroad 65.00
Man's, Quartz, Rectangular, Sapphire, Box 595.00
Mido, Woman's, 14K Yellow Gold 250.00
Movado, Woman's, 14K Gold, 1950s 550.00
Movado, Woman's, Sapphire Crown, Gold Dial, Mesh Bracelet 275.00
Movado, World Time Zone, Rotating Bezel, 17 Jewels, 1940s 5500.00
Omega, 24 Jewel, Automatic, Blue Dial, Leather Band 150.00
Omega, Automatic Movement, Silver Dial, Mesh Bracelet, 18K Gold 715.00
Omega, Diamond Band, 14K White Gold 675.00
Patek Phillipe, Handwind, 18 Jewel, Diamonds, Platinum 4500.00
Penard, Gervais, 17 Jewels 95.00
Piguet, 18 Jewels, 18K Gold 1495.00
Pilot's, World War I 50.00
Rockford, Jane Russell 200.00
Rolex, Army, Sterling Silver 995.00
Rolex, Cage Cover, Black Numerals, 15 Jewels, Silver Case, 1920s 4500.00
Rolex, Oyster, Perpetual Chronometer, Sterling Case 450.00
Rolex, Oyster, Perpetual Gold Bezel, 2-Tone Steel, 1950s 4200.00
Rolex, President Model, Blue Enamel Dial, Diamonds Set Bezel 5775.00
Rolex, Prince, Railway Dial, Sterling Case, 1930s 8300.00
Sussex, Gold Filled Band, 1940s Style 95.00
Swatch, Black Friday 200.00
Swatch, Goldfinger 200.00
Swatch, Keith Haring Personnages, Yellow & Red 1995.00
Swatch, Silver Star 200.00
Tiffany, Woman's, Bracelet Style, 18K Gold 3300.00
Vendome, 17 Jewel, Roman Numerals, Tiger Heads Link Bracelet 120.00
Waltham, 14K Gold Case, Black Face, Second Hand, 17 Jewel 302.00
Wittnauer, Red Crystal, 10K Gold Stepped Case 185.00
Wittnauer, Windup, Square, Diamond, 10K Gold Filled 65.00

YELLOWWARE is a heavy earthenware made of a yellowish clay. It varies in color from light yellow to orange–yellow. Many nineteenth– and twentieth–century kitchen bowls and jugs were made of yellowware. It was made in England and in the United States. Another form of pottery that is sometimes classed as yellowware is listed in the Mocha category.

Bowl, 5 In.	21.00
Bowl, 14 In.	65.00 To 85.00
Bowl, Blue Sponging, Gilt Trim, 8 1/4 x 2 3/4 In.	145.00
Bowl, Blue Stripes, 10 In.	35.00
Bowl, Bread, 16 In.	200.00
Bowl, Brown & Blue Bands, 12 In.	30.00
Bowl, Brown Bands, 4 x 8 In.	35.00
Bowl, Child Watering Flowers, 10 x 5 In.	35.00
Bowl, Colander Shape, Star Design, 5 In.	175.00
Bowl, Mixing, 11 1/2 In.	40.00
Bowl, Mixing, Brown Stripes, 13 1/2 In.	48.00
Bowl, Mixing, Girl Watering Flowers, House	85.00
Bowl, Mixing, Mocha, c.1850, 4 x 9 In.	240.00
Bowl, Pink & Blue Band, 8 x 3 In.	20.00
Bowl, Pitcher, Stripes Of Black, Tan, Blue, Marked, 9 1/4 In.	225.00
Bowl, Plum Embossed, 5 1/8 x 2 3/8 In.	45.00
Bowl, Spout, Wooden Handle, Wire Bale, Blue Sponging, 7 In.	125.00
Butter Crock, Brown & White Stripes, 4 x 7 1/4 In.	135.00
Butter Tub, Molded Staves, Blue Glaze, 4 x 4 3/4 In.	285.00
Chamber Pot, Mocha, Blue Seaweed, Miniature, 2 1/4 In.	110.00
Cookie Jar, Rope Handle	45.00
Cookie Jar, USA	40.00
Creamer, Blue Bands, 3 1/4 In.	85.00
Creamer, Molded Floral Design, Classical Figures, 9 5/8 In.	165.00
Creamer, Molded Tavern Scenes & Vintage, 4 1/4 In.	15.00
Crock, Butter, Cover, Brown & White Stripes, 7 1/4 x 4 In.	125.00
Crock, Kraft Old English Cheese, Cover, Paper Label, 3 Lb.	95.00
Dish, Baking, Applied Vintage, Cauliflower Handle, Oval, 12 In.	175.00
Dish, Hunting Tableau, 5 1/2 In.	70.00
Dog, Seated, Basket, Greenish Glaze, 5 In.	225.00
Figurine, Spaniel, 19th Century, 12 1/2 In.	330.00
Jar, Lid, Sanded Bands, Blue Stripes, 5 1/2 x 3 3/4 In.	155.00
Jug, Centennial Face Of Jenny Lind, 1876	375.00 To 398.00
Mold, Corn, 8 1/2 In.	55.00
Mold, Ear Of Corn, 9 5/8 In.	135.00
Mold, Rabbit	85.00
Mold, Sheaf Of Wheat	50.00
Mold, Turk's Head, Brown Sponging, 9 In.	105.00
Mug, New Deal	45.00
Mug, White Band, Black Seaweed Design, 2 7/8 In.	210.00
Pie Plate, Coggled Edge, 7 3/4 In.	105.00
Pitcher & Bowl, Rockingham Glaze, Miniature	2200.00
Pitcher, Advertising Label, Brown & Green Sponging, 4 1/2 In.	55.00
Pitcher, Blue Spotted Glaze, 6 1/4 In.	40.00
Pitcher, Cow Scene, Green Glaze, H–Line	135.00
Pitcher, Gothic Arch Design, Brown Sponging, 4 3/4 In.	35.00
Pitcher, Raised Grape Design, Green Glaze	155.00
Plate, Gothic Rim, Impressed Hall & Sons, 9 1/8 In.	55.00
Rolling Pin	185.00 To 395.00
Spoon Rest, Berea, Kentucky	45.00
Sugar, Molded Floral Design, Classical Figures, 4 5/8 In.	135.00
Tenderizer, Meat	145.00

ZANE Pottery was founded in 1921 by Adam Reed and Harry McClelland in South Zanesville, Ohio, at the old Peters and Reed Building. Zane pottery is very similar to Peters and Reed pottery, but it is usually marked. The factory was sold in 1941 to Lawton Gonder.

Vase, Brown, Blue, Black, 6 In. 85.00
Vase, Moss Aztec, 5 In. 37.50

ZANESVILLE Art Pottery was founded in 1900 by David Schmidt in
Zanesville, Ohio. The firm made faience umbrella stands, jardinieres, and
pedestals. The company closed in 1962. Many pieces are marked with just
the words *La Moro.*

LA MORO

Jardiniere, Landscape, Matte Glaze, Art Pottery, 1908, 8 1/2 In. 165.00
Vase, La Moro, Draped Woman, 14 In. 1800.00

ZSOLNAY pottery was made in Hungary after 1862 and was characterized
by Persian, Art Nouveau, or Hungarian motifs. A series of new Zsolnay
figurines with green–gold luster finish is available in many shops today.
Early Zsolnay was not marked, but by 1878, the tower trademark was
used.

ZSOLNAY PÉCS

Ewer, Crowing Cock, Beak Spout, Iridescent, Blue–Purple, 14 3/8 In. 2200.00
Figurine, Greyhound, Seated 225.00
Figurine, Nude, Reclining 350.00
Jardiniere, Hexagonal Pierced Rim, Lizards On Side, c.1900, 13 In. 1875.00
Jardiniere, Oval Body, Flowers, Protruding Pierced Roundels, 16 In. 415.00
Pitcher, Iridescent, Red, Purple Handle, Twisted Vine, 6 3/4 In. 2090.00
Plate, Center Flowers, Gold Trim, Reticulated Border, 12 In. 225.00
Vase, Drowning Sailors Lured By Siren, Tawny Ground, 24 In. 4125.00
Vase, Picasso Type Women, 6 1/2 In. 375.00
Vase, Stylized Blossoms, Iridescent, Purple To Ochre, 10 1/4 In. 2200.00

This index is computer-generated, making it as complete as possible. References in uppercase type are to main category listings. Those in lowercase letters refer to additional pages in which the piece can be found. There is also an internal cross-referencing system used in the main part of the book, so that, for instance, if you look for a Kewpie doll in the doll category section you will be told it is in the Kewpie section. There is additional information about where to find prices of pieces similar to yours at the end of many paragraphs.

Other Indispensable Books from the Kovels

Kovels' Bottles Price List, Ninth Edition, 1992
The complete guide to collecting old and new bottles in hundreds of categories. Contains lists of bottle collectors' clubs, as well as recommended reading and an extensive bibliography.
240 pages/$13.00 paperback/0-517-58944-3

Kovels' Depression Glass & American Dinnerware Price List, Fourth Edition, 1991
Provides current prices of more than 6,000 pieces listed by pattern, along with dates, descriptions, marks, and illustrations. Also contains charts of factories with all the known patterns and their name variations.
256 pages/$13.00 paperback/0-517-58444-1

Kovels' Antiques & Collectibles Fix-it Source Book
Lists the names and addresses of the people and organizations that know how to repair fine antiques and minor treasures, plus advice on how to care for them yourself.
192 pages/$9.95 paperback/0-517-57333-4

(continued on next page)

Kovels' Guide to Selling Your Antiques & Collectibles, Updated Edition, 1991
Whether you inherit a house filled with old furniture or find a few old comic books, learn how to get the best price for your treasures. Covers more than 75 categories of collectibles.
240 pages/$9.95 paperback/0-517-58008-X

Kovels' Know Your Antiques, Third Edition, Revised, 1991
The best guide in print today for beginning collectors. Shows how to evaluate, purchase, and care for virtually every type of antique.
368 pages/$15.00 paperback/0-517-57806-9

Kovels' Know Your Collectibles, Updated 1992
Focuses on silver, glass, furniture, and other objects made since 1890 that, while not old enough to be considered antiques, are nonetheless rapidly becoming valuable to collectors.
416 pages/$15.00 paperback/0-517-58840-4

Dictionary of Marks—Pottery and Porcelain
The best-selling guide to 5,000 marks on American and European pottery and porcelain made from 1580 to 1880.
288 pages/$14.95 hardcover/0-517-00141-1

Kovels' New Dictionary of Marks—Pottery and Porcelain, 1850–Present
A reference illustrated with more than 3,500 black-and-white marks for 19th- and 20th-century American, European, and Oriental pottery and porcelain most likely to be encountered today.
304 pages/$17.95 hardcover/0-517-55914-5

Kovels' American Silver Marks: 1650 to the Present
Written for collectors and professional dealers alike—includes listings for more than 10,000 silversmiths, with cross-indexing for monograms and pictorial marks.
432 pages/$40.00 hardcover/0-517-56882-9

American Country Furniture 1780–1875
All the information you need to be an expert—with more than 700 photos, plus an illustrated glossary of accessories and terms.
256 pages/$14.95 paperback/0-517-54668-X

K O V E L S

SEND ORDERS & INQUIRIES TO: **Crown Publishers, Inc.,**
c/o Random House, 400 Hahn Road
Westminster, MD 21157
ATT: ORDER DEPT.

SALES & TITLE INFORMATION
1-800-733-3000

NAME _____

ADDRESS _____

CITY & STATE _____   ZIP _____

PLEASE SEND ME THE FOLLOWING BOOKS:

ITEM NO.	QTY.	TITLE		PRICE	TOTAL
59109X	_____	Kovels' Antiques & Collectibles Price List 25th Edition	PAPER	$13.00	_____
54668X	_____	American Country Furniture 1780–1875	PAPER	$14.95	_____
001411	_____	Dictionary of Marks—Pottery and Porcelain	HARDCOVER	$14.95	_____
559145	_____	Kovels' New Dictionary of Marks	HARDCOVER	$17.95	_____
568829	_____	Kovels' American Silver Marks	HARDCOVER	$40.00	_____
589443	_____	Kovels' Bottles Price List 9th Edition	PAPER	$13.00	_____
584441	_____	Kovels' Depression Glass & American Dinnerware Price List 4th Edition	PAPER	$13.00	_____
578069	_____	Kovels' Know Your Antiques Revised and Updated	PAPER	$15.00	_____
588404	_____	Kovels' Know Your Collectibles Updated	PAPER	$15.00	_____
58008X	_____	Kovels' Guide to Selling Your Antiques & Collectibles Updated Edition	PAPER	$ 9.95	_____
573334	_____	Kovels' Antiques & Collectibles Fix-It Source Book	PAPER	$ 9.95	_____

_____ TOTAL ITEMS   TOTAL RETAIL VALUE _____

CHECK OR MONEY ORDER ENCLOSED MADE PAYABLE TO
CROWN PUBLISHERS, INC.
or telephone 1-800-733-3000
(No cash or stamps, please)

Charge: ☐ MasterCard ☐ Visa ☐ American Express
Account Number (include all digits)   Expires MO.   YR.

_____

Signature _____

Thank you for your order.

Shipping & Handling
Charge $2.00 for one book;
50¢ for each additional book.
Please add applicable
sales tax.   _____

TOTAL AMOUNT DUE _____

PRICES SUBJECT TO CHANGE
WITHOUT NOTICE. If a more
recent edition of a price list has
been published at the same price, it
will be sent instead of the old edition.

J. S & T New Hampshire